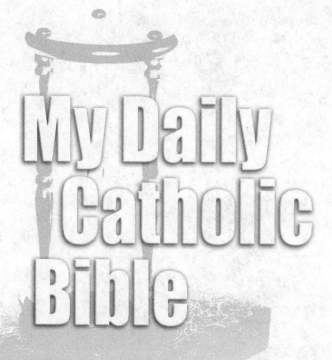

My Daily Catholic Bible

20-MINUTE DAILY READINGS

My Daily Catholic Bible

20-MINUTE DAILY READINGS

Our Sunday Visitor Publishing Division
Our Sunday Visitor, Inc.
Huntington, Indiana 46750

New American Bible, Revised Edition

Translated From the Original Languages
With Critical Use of All the Ancient Sources

Authorized by the Board of Trustees of the
Confraternity of Christian Doctrine
And Approved by the Administrative Committee
of the United States Conference of Catholic Bishops

NEW TESTAMENT
Nihil Obstat

> Stephen J. Hartdegen, O.F.M., L.S.S.
> Censor Deputatus

Imprimatur

> + James A. Hickey, S.T.D., J.C.D.
> Archbishop of Washington
> August 27, 1986

PSALMS
Imprimatur

> Most Rev. Daniel E. Pilarczyk
> President, National Conference of Catholic Bishops
> October 10, 1991

OLD TESTAMENT
In accord with canon 825 §1 of the Code of Canon Law, the United States Conference of Catholic Bishops hereby approves for publication the New American Bible, Revised Old Testament, a translation of the Sacred Scriptures authorized by the Confraternity of Christian Doctrine, Inc.

The translation was approved by the Administrative Committee of the United States Conference of Catholic Bishops in November 2008 and September 2010. It is permitted by the undersigned for private use and study.

Given in the city of Washington, the District of Columbia, on the Feast of Saint Jerome, Priest and Doctor of the Church, the 30th day of September, in the year of our Lord 2010.

> Francis Cardinal George, O.M.I.
> Archbishop of Chicago
> President, USCCB

The Introduction is by Paul Thigpen, who also compiled the quotations from the saints that begin the daily readings.

Copyright © 2004, 2011 by Our Sunday Visitor Publishing Division, Our Sunday Visitor, Inc. Published 2011.

23 22 21 20 19   8 9 10 11 12

Our Sunday Visitor Publishing Division
Our Sunday Visitor, Inc.
200 Noll Plaza
Huntington, IN 46750

ISBN: 978-1-59276-144-9 (Inventory No. T1189)
eISBN: 978-1-61278-322-2
LCCN: 2010942130

Cover design by Amanda Falk
Interior design by Sherri L. Hoffman

PRINTED IN USA

The aforementioned information regarding theon, bibliographies, and copyrights is only for the scripture text of the New American Bible, Revised Edition (NAB) used in this work. Every reasonable effort has been made to determine copyright holders of excerpted materials and to secure permissions as needed. If any copyrighted material have been inadvertently used in this work without proper credit being given in one form or another please notify Our Sunday Visitor in writing so that future printings of this work may be corrected accordingly.

The Introduction is by Paul Thigpen who also compiled the quotations from the saints that begin the daily readings.

Editor's Introduction

An Invitation to the Scriptures

"Ignorance of Scripture," observed St. Jerome, "is ignorance of Christ." Jesus Christ himself is the Word of God made flesh (see John 1:14), and in reading the Scriptures we can encounter Him in all His power, wisdom, and glory.

My Daily Catholic Bible is intended to help you get better acquainted with Our Lord by reading the entire Bible through in one year. To make that challenge less daunting, the text is broken down into small, "bite-sized" readings, one for each day from the Old Testament and one from the New. You don't have to start on January 1; just begin reading on any day of the calendar, and twelve months later you'll have made your way through all seventy-three books of the biblical canon.

This edition of the Bible is not intended to provide commentary or other study helps; you can find those aids in abundance in other places. It simply gives you a workable plan for reading the Scriptures all the way through, a few chapters at a time. Nevertheless, we offer here one special feature that may help you in your reflection: a quote for each day from a Catholic saint (including those not yet fully canonized, but designated by the Church as "Venerable" or "Blessed").

Wherever possible, the quote comes from one of the saints whose memorial is observed that day (also noted). If it is a feast of the Church, the quote is related to that special occasion. Otherwise, the quote is related to some topic in the reading, or to the value of the Scripture reading itself.

Like the Bible, the writings of the saints are so extensive that they may seem daunting at first to those who approach them for wisdom. So, from this rich, inexhaustible treasury, we offer a single gem each day for your spiritual profit. Some quotes will crystallize and confirm what you may already know, such as the words from St. Jerome already cited. Others may surprise or puzzle you: for example, St. Brigid's wish for "a great lake of ale for the King of kings" (February 1). Either way, all of these saintly thoughts bear careful consideration, given the lives of great holiness in which they are rooted.

At the same time, we encourage you to ask the saint who is quoted to pray for you as you read the scriptural texts. The saints loved the Scriptures and took them to heart, so they no doubt desire to help you deepen your understanding of them and apply their truths to your everyday life.

If on some days the readings seem a bit dry, don't give up. Some parts of the Scriptures are more immediately helpful than others, and eventually, the big picture will emerge. Keep reading: You'll be laying up God's Word in your heart (see Psalm 119:11), to be brought to mind again some day when its application will be more evident.

The biblical text used here is from the *New American Bible, Revised Edition*. The scheme for dividing the text into daily readings is similar to the "One-Year Reading Plan" in Carmen Rojas' work *How to Read the Bible Every Day* (Ann Arbor, Michigan: Servant, 1988; pages 196–207). The quotes from the saints come from a variety of sources, though you can find most of them — and countless more — in my *Dictionary of Quotes from the Saints* (Ann Arbor, Michigan: Servant, 2001).

A note about the numbering of verses in some sections of the Books of Sirach, 1 Chronicles, and Wisdom, and of some chapters in the Book of Esther. Both of these books have unique numbering systems, and explanations for this can be found in Catholic Bible commentaries. To avoid confusion, simply ignore the jumbled or unusual numbering and read the texts designated for the day, which are in the correct order. Regarding the omission of Matthew 23:14, the notes in the *New American Bible, Revised Edition* explain:

Some manuscripts add a verse here or after Mt 23:12 "Woe to you, scribes and Pharisees, you hypocrites. You devour the houses of widows and, as a pretext, recite lengthy prayers. Because of this, you will receive a very severe condemnation." Cf. Mk 12:40; Lk 20:47. This "woe" is almost identical with Mk 12:40 and seems to be an interpolation derived from that text.

Jesus Christ waits to meet you again and again in the pages of this sacred book. His saints are eager to help you find your way to Him there. If you seek Him in Scripture and prayer every day, and if you persevere in your search for a year, I guarantee that you will encounter Him in ways you never dreamed of before, and you will never be the same again.

PAUL THIGPEN
Editor

January 1

A gentle maiden, having lodged God in her womb, asks as its price: peace for the world, salvation for those who are lost, and life for the dead.

— St. Peter Chrysologus

☐ GENESIS 1-2

The Story of Creation. 1:1 In the beginning, when God created the heavens and the earth— ²and the earth was without form or shape, with darkness over the abyss and a mighty wind sweeping over the waters—

³Then God said: Let there be light, and there was light. ⁴God saw that the light was good. God then separated the light from the darkness. ⁵God called the light "day," and the darkness he called "night." Evening came, and morning followed—the first day.

⁶Then God said: Let there be a dome in the middle of the waters, to separate one body of water from the other. ⁷God made the dome, and it separated the water below the dome from the water above the dome. And so it happened. ⁸God called the dome "sky." Evening came, and morning followed—the second day.

⁹Then God said: Let the water under the sky be gathered into a single basin, so that the dry land may appear. And so it happened: the water under the sky was gathered into its basin, and the dry land appeared. ¹⁰God called the dry land "earth," and the basin of water he called "sea." God saw that it was good. ¹¹Then God said: Let the earth bring forth vegetation: every kind of plant that bears seed and every kind of fruit tree on earth that bears fruit with its seed in it. And so it happened: ¹²the earth brought forth vegetation: every kind of plant that bears seed and every kind of fruit tree that bears fruit with its seed in it. God saw that it was good. ¹³Evening came, and morning followed—the third day.

¹⁴Then God said: Let there be lights in the dome of the sky, to separate day from night. Let them mark the seasons, the days and the years, ¹⁵and serve as lights in the dome of the sky, to illuminate the earth. And so it happened: ¹⁶God made the two great lights, the greater one to govern the day, and the lesser one to govern the night, and the stars. ¹⁷God set them in the dome of the sky, to illuminate the earth, ¹⁸to govern the day and the night, and to separate the light from the darkness. God saw that it was good. ¹⁹Evening came, and morning followed—the fourth day.

²⁰Then God said: Let the water teem with an abundance of living creatures, and on the earth let birds fly beneath the dome of the sky. ²¹God created the great sea monsters and all kinds of crawling living creatures with which the water teems, and all kinds of winged birds. God saw that it was good, ²²and God blessed them, saying: Be fertile, multiply, and fill the water of the seas; and let the birds multiply on the earth. ²³Evening came, and morning followed—the fifth day.

²⁴Then God said: Let the earth bring forth every kind of living creature: tame animals, crawling things, and every kind of wild animal. And so it happened: ²⁵God made every kind of wild animal, every kind of tame animal, and every kind of thing that crawls on the ground. God saw that it was good. ²⁶Then God said: Let us make

human beings in our image, after our likeness. Let them have dominion over the fish of the sea, the birds of the air, the tame animals, all the wild animals, and all the creatures that crawl on the earth.

²⁷God created mankind in his image;
　　in the image of God he created
　　　　them;
　　male and female he created them.

²⁸God blessed them and God said to them: Be fertile and multiply; fill the earth and subdue it. Have dominion over the fish of the sea, the birds of the air, and all the living things that crawl on the earth. ²⁹God also said: See, I give you every seed-bearing plant on all the earth and every tree that has seed-bearing fruit on it to be your food; ³⁰and to all the wild animals, all the birds of the air, and all the living creatures that crawl on the earth, I give all the green plants for food. And so it happened. ³¹God looked at everything he had made, and found it very good. Evening came, and morning followed—the sixth day.

2:1 Thus the heavens and the earth and all their array were completed. ²On the seventh day God completed the work he had been doing; he rested on the seventh day from all the work he had undertaken. ³God blessed the seventh day and made it holy, because on it he rested from all the work he had done in creation.

The Garden of Eden. ⁴This is the story of the heavens and the earth at their creation. When the LORD God made the earth and the heavens— ⁵there was no field shrub on earth and no grass of the field had sprouted, for the LORD God had sent no rain upon the earth and there was no man to till the ground, ⁶but a stream was welling up out of the earth and watering all the surface of the ground— ⁷then the LORD God formed the man out of the dust of the ground and blew into his nostrils the breath of life, and the man became a living being.

⁸The LORD God planted a garden in Eden, in the east, and placed there the man whom he had formed. ⁹Out of the ground the LORD God made grow every tree that was delightful to look at and good for food, with the tree of life in the middle of the garden and the tree of the knowledge of good and evil.

¹⁰A river rises in Eden to water the garden; beyond there it divides and becomes four branches. ¹¹The name of the first is the Pishon; it is the one that winds through the whole land of Havilah, where there is gold. ¹²The gold of that land is good; bdellium and lapis lazuli are also there. ¹³The name of the second river is the Gihon; it is the one that winds all through the land of Cush. ¹⁴The name of the third river is the Tigris; it is the one that flows east of Asshur. The fourth river is the Euphrates.

¹⁵The LORD God then took the man and settled him in the garden of Eden, to cultivate and care for it. ¹⁶The LORD God gave the man this order: You are free to eat from any of the trees of the garden ¹⁷except the tree of knowledge of good and evil. From that tree you shall not eat; when you eat from it you shall die.

¹⁸The LORD God said: It is not good for the man to be alone. I will make a helper suited to him. ¹⁹So the LORD God formed out of the ground all the wild animals and all the birds of the air, and he brought them to the man to see what he would call them; whatever the man called each living creature was then its name. ²⁰The man gave names to all the tame animals, all the birds of the air, and all the wild animals; but none proved to be a helper suited to the man.

²¹So the LORD God cast a deep sleep on the man, and while he was asleep, he took out one of his ribs and closed up its place with flesh. ²²The LORD God then built the rib that he had taken from the man into a woman. When he brought her to the man, ²³the man said:

"This one, at last, is bone of my bones
    and flesh of my flesh;
This one shall be called 'woman,'
    for out of man this one has been
        taken."

□ MARK 1:1-13

1:1 The beginning of the gospel of Jesus Christ [the Son of God].

The Preaching of John the Baptist. [2]As it is written in Isaiah the prophet:

"Behold, I am sending my messenger
    ahead of you;
he will prepare your way.
[3]A voice of one crying out in the
    desert:
'Prepare the way of the Lord,
    make straight his paths.'"

[4]John [the] Baptist appeared in the desert proclaiming a baptism of repentance for the forgiveness of sins. [5]People of the whole Judean countryside and all the inhabitants of Jerusalem were going out to him and were being baptized by him in the Jordan River as they acknowledged their sins. [6]John was clothed in camel's hair, with a leather belt around his waist. He fed on locusts and wild honey. [7]And this is what he proclaimed: "One mightier than I is coming after me. I am not worthy to stoop and loosen the thongs of his sandals. [8]I have baptized you with water; he will baptize you with the holy Spirit."

The Baptism of Jesus. [9]It happened in those days that Jesus came from Nazareth of Galilee and was baptized in the Jordan by John. [10]On coming up out of the water he saw the heavens being torn open and the Spirit, like a dove, descending upon him. [11]And a voice came from the heavens, "You are my beloved Son; with you I am well pleased."

The Temptation of Jesus. [12]At once the Spirit drove him out into the desert, [13]and he remained in the desert for forty days, tempted by Satan. He was among wild beasts, and the angels ministered to him.

[24]That is why a man leaves his father and mother and clings to his wife, and the two of them become one body. [25]The man and his wife were both naked, yet they felt no shame.

January 2

Sts. Basil the Great and Gregory Nazianzus

We must neither doubt nor hesitate with respect to the words of the Lord; rather, we must be fully persuaded that every word of God is true and possible, even if our nature should rebel against the idea — for in this lies the test of faith.

— ST. BASIL THE GREAT

□ GENESIS 3-4

Expulsion from Eden. 3:1 Now the snake was the most cunning of all the wild animals that the LORD God had made. He asked the woman, "Did God really say, 'You shall not eat from any of the trees in the garden'?" [2]The woman answered the snake: "We may eat of the fruit of the trees in the garden; [3]it is only about the fruit of the tree in the middle of the garden that God said, 'You shall not eat it or even touch it, or else you will die.'" ⁴But the snake said to the woman: "You certainly will not die! ⁵God knows well that when you eat of it your eyes will be opened and you will be like gods, who know good and evil." ⁶The woman saw that the tree was good for food and pleasing to the eyes, and the tree was desirable for gaining wisdom. So she took some of its fruit and ate it; and she also gave some to her husband, who was with her, and he ate it. ⁷Then the eyes of both of them were opened, and they knew that they were naked; so they sewed fig leaves together and made loincloths for themselves.

⁸When they heard the sound of the Lord God walking about in the garden at the breezy time of the day, the man and his wife hid themselves from the Lord God among the trees of the garden. ⁹The Lord God then called to the man and asked him: Where are you? ¹⁰He answered, "I heard you in the garden; but I was afraid, because I was naked, so I hid." ¹¹Then God asked: Who told you that you were naked? Have you eaten from the tree of which I had forbidden you to eat? ¹²The man replied, "The woman whom you put here with me—she gave me fruit from the tree, so I ate it." ¹³The Lord God then asked the woman: What is this you have done? The woman answered, "The snake tricked me, so I ate it."

¹⁴Then the Lord God said to the snake:

Because you have done this,
    cursed are you
    among all the animals, tame or wild;
On your belly you shall crawl,
    and dust you shall eat
    all the days of your life.
¹⁵I will put enmity between you and
        the woman,
    and between your offspring and hers;
They will strike at your head,
    while you strike at their heel.

¹⁶To the woman he said:

I will intensify your toil in
        childbearing;
    in pain you shall bring forth
        children.
Yet your urge shall be for your husband,
    and he shall rule over you.

¹⁷To the man he said: Because you listened to your wife and ate from the tree about which I commanded you, You shall not eat from it,

Cursed is the ground because of you!
    In toil you shall eat its yield
    all the days of your life.
¹⁸Thorns and thistles it shall bear for
        you,
    and you shall eat the grass of the
        field.
¹⁹By the sweat of your brow
    you shall eat bread,
Until you return to the ground,
    from which you were taken;
For you are dust,
    and to dust you shall return.

²⁰The man gave his wife the name "Eve," because she was the mother of all the living. ²¹The Lord God made for the man and his wife garments of skin, with which he clothed them. ²²Then the Lord God said: See! The man has become like one of us, knowing good and evil! Now, what if he also reaches out his hand to take fruit from the tree of life, and eats of it and lives forever? ²³The Lord God therefore banished him from the garden of Eden, to till the ground from which he had been taken. ²⁴He expelled the man, stationing the cherubim and the fiery revolving sword east of the garden of Eden, to guard the way to the tree of life.

Cain and Abel. 4:1 The man had intercourse with his wife Eve, and she conceived and gave birth to Cain, saying, "I have produced a male child with the help of the

LORD." [2]Next she gave birth to his brother Abel. Abel became a herder of flocks, and Cain a tiller of the ground. [3]In the course of time Cain brought an offering to the LORD from the fruit of the ground, [4]while Abel, for his part, brought the fatty portion of the firstlings of his flock. The LORD looked with favor on Abel and his offering, [5]but on Cain and his offering he did not look with favor. So Cain was very angry and dejected. [6]Then the LORD said to Cain: Why are you angry? Why are you dejected? [7]If you act rightly, you will be accepted; but if not, sin lies in wait at the door: its urge is for you, yet you can rule over it.

[8]Cain said to his brother Abel, "Let us go out in the field." When they were in the field, Cain attacked his brother Abel and killed him. [9]Then the LORD asked Cain, Where is your brother Abel? He answered, "I do not know. Am I my brother's keeper?" [10]God then said: What have you done? Your brother's blood cries out to me from the ground! [11]Now you are banned from the ground that opened its mouth to receive your brother's blood from your hand. [12]If you till the ground, it shall no longer give you its produce. You shall become a constant wanderer on the earth. [13]Cain said to the LORD: "My punishment is too great to bear. [14]Look, you have now banished me from the ground. I must avoid you and be a constant wanderer on the earth. Anyone may kill me at sight." [15]Not so! the LORD said to him. If anyone kills Cain, Cain shall be avenged seven times. So the LORD put a mark on Cain, so that no one would kill him

at sight. [16]Cain then left the LORD's presence and settled in the land of Nod, east of Eden.

Descendants of Cain and Seth. [17]Cain had intercourse with his wife, and she conceived and bore Enoch. Cain also became the founder of a city, which he named after his son Enoch. [18]To Enoch was born Irad, and Irad became the father of Mehujael; Mehujael became the father of Methusael, and Methusael became the father of Lamech. [19]Lamech took two wives; the name of the first was Adah, and the name of the second Zillah. [20]Adah gave birth to Jabal, who became the ancestor of those who dwell in tents and keep livestock. [21]His brother's name was Jubal, who became the ancestor of all who play the lyre and the reed pipe. [22]Zillah, on her part, gave birth to Tubalcain, the ancestor of all who forge instruments of bronze and iron. The sister of Tubalcain was Naamah. [23]Lamech said to his wives:

"Adah and Zillah, hear my voice;
    wives of Lamech, listen to my
        utterance:
I have killed a man for wounding me,
    a young man for bruising me.
[24]If Cain is avenged seven times,
    then Lamech seventy-seven times."

[25]Adam again had intercourse with his wife, and she gave birth to a son whom she called Seth. "God has granted me another offspring in place of Abel," she said, "because Cain killed him." [26]To Seth, in turn, a son was born, and he named him Enosh.

At that time people began to invoke the LORD by name.

☐ MARK 1:14-28

The Beginning of the Galilean Ministry.
1:14 After John had been arrested, Jesus came to Galilee proclaiming the gospel of God: [15]"This is the time of fulfillment. The kingdom of God is at hand. Repent, and believe in the gospel."

The Call of the First Disciples. [16]As he passed by the Sea of Galilee, he saw Simon and his brother Andrew casting their nets into the sea; they were fishermen. [17]Jesus said to them, "Come after me, and I will make you fishers of men." [18]Then they abandoned their nets and followed him. [19]He walked along a little farther and saw James, the son of Zebedee, and his brother John. They too were in a boat mending their nets. [20]Then he called them. So they left their father Zebedee in the boat along with the hired men and followed him.

The Cure of a Demoniac. [21]Then they came to Capernaum, and on the sabbath he entered the synagogue and taught. [22]The people were astonished at his teaching, for he taught them as one having authority and not as the scribes. [23]In their synagogue was a man with an unclean spirit; [24]he cried out, "What have you to do with us, Jesus of Nazareth? Have you come to destroy us? I know who you are—the Holy One of God!" [25]Jesus rebuked him and said, "Quiet! Come out of him!" [26]The unclean spirit convulsed him and with a loud cry came out of him. [27]All were amazed and asked one another, "What is this? A new teaching with authority. He commands even the unclean spirits and they obey him." [28]His fame spread everywhere throughout the whole region of Galilee.

January 3

The Most Holy Name of Jesus

Nothing restrains anger, curbs pride, heals the wounds of malice, bridles self-indulgence, quenches lustful passions, checks greed, and puts unclean thoughts to flight as does the name of Jesus.

— St. Bernard of Clairvaux

☐ GENESIS 5-6

Generations: Adam to Noah. 5:1 This is the record of the descendants of Adam. When God created human beings, he made them in the likeness of God; [2]he created them male and female. When they were created, he blessed them and named them humankind.

[3]Adam was one hundred and thirty years old when he begot a son in his likeness, after his image; and he named him Seth. [4]Adam lived eight hundred years after he begot Seth, and he had other sons and daughters. [5]The whole lifetime of Adam was nine hundred and thirty years; then he died.

[6]When Seth was one hundred and five years old, he begot Enosh. [7]Seth lived eight hundred and seven years after he begot Enosh, and he had other sons and daughters. [8]The whole lifetime of Seth was nine hundred and twelve years; then he died.

[9]When Enosh was ninety years old, he begot Kenan. [10]Enosh lived eight hundred and fifteen years after he begot Kenan, and he had other sons and daughters. [11]The whole lifetime of Enosh was nine hundred and five years; then he died.

[12]When Kenan was seventy years old, he begot Mahalalel. [13]Kenan lived eight hundred and forty years after he begot Mahalalel, and he had other sons and daughters. [14]The whole lifetime of Kenan was nine hundred and ten years; then he died.

[15]When Mahalalel was sixty-five years old, he begot Jared. [16]Mahalalel lived eight hundred and thirty years after he begot Jared, and he had other sons and daughters. [17]The whole lifetime of Mahalalel was eight hundred and ninety-five years; then he died.

[18]When Jared was one hundred and sixty-two years old, he begot Enoch. [19]Jared

lived eight hundred years after he begot Enoch, and he had other sons and daughters. [20]The whole lifetime of Jared was nine hundred and sixty-two years; then he died.

[21]When Enoch was sixty-five years old, he begot Methuselah. [22]Enoch walked with God after he begot Methuselah for three hundred years, and he had other sons and daughters. [23]The whole lifetime of Enoch was three hundred and sixty-five years. [24]Enoch walked with God, and he was no longer here, for God took him.

[25]When Methuselah was one hundred and eighty-seven years old, he begot Lamech. [26]Methuselah lived seven hundred and eighty-two years after he begot Lamech, and he had other sons and daughters. [27]The whole lifetime of Methuselah was nine hundred and sixty-nine years; then he died.

[28]When Lamech was one hundred and eighty-two years old, he begot a son [29]and named him Noah, saying, "This one shall bring us relief from our work and the toil of our hands, out of the very ground that the Lord has put under a curse." [30]Lamech lived five hundred and ninety-five years after he begot Noah, and he had other sons and daughters. [31]The whole lifetime of Lamech was seven hundred and seventy-seven years; then he died.

[32]When Noah was five hundred years old, he begot Shem, Ham, and Japheth.

Origin of the Nephilim. 6:1 When human beings began to grow numerous on the earth and daughters were born to them, [2]the sons of God saw how beautiful the daughters of human beings were, and so they took for their wives whomever they pleased. [3]Then the Lord said: My spirit shall not remain in human beings forever, because they are only flesh. Their days shall comprise one hundred and twenty years. [4]The Nephilim appeared on earth in those days, as well as later, after the sons of God had intercourse with the daughters of human beings, who bore them sons. They were the heroes of old, the men of renown.

Warning of the Flood. [5]When the Lord saw how great the wickedness of human beings was on earth, and how every desire that their heart conceived was always nothing but evil, [6]the Lord regretted making human beings on the earth, and his heart was grieved.

[7]So the Lord said: I will wipe out from the earth the human beings I have created, and not only the human beings, but also the animals and the crawling things and the birds of the air, for I regret that I made them. [8]But Noah found favor with the Lord.

[9]These are the descendants of Noah. Noah was a righteous man and blameless in his generation; Noah walked with God. [10]Noah begot three sons: Shem, Ham, and Japheth.

[11]But the earth was corrupt in the view of God and full of lawlessness. [12]When God saw how corrupt the earth had become, since all mortals had corrupted their ways on earth, [13]God said to Noah: I see that the end of all mortals has come, for the earth is full of lawlessness because of them. So I am going to destroy them with the earth.

Preparation for the Flood. [14]Make yourself an ark of gopherwood, equip the ark with various compartments, and cover it inside and out with pitch. [15]This is how you shall build it: the length of the ark will be three hundred cubits, its width fifty cubits, and its height thirty cubits. [16]Make an opening for daylight and finish the ark a cubit above it. Put the ark's entrance on its side; you will make it with bottom, second and third decks. [17]I, on my part, am about to bring the flood waters on the earth, to destroy all creatures under the sky in which there is the breath of life; everything on earth shall perish. [18]I will establish my covenant with you. You shall go into the ark, you and your sons, your wife and your sons' wives with you. [19]Of all living creatures you shall bring two of every kind into the ark, one male and one female, to keep them alive along with you. [20]Of every kind of bird, of every kind of animal, and of every kind of thing that crawls on the ground, two of each will come to you, that you may keep them alive. [21]Moreover, you are to provide yourself with all the food that is to be eaten, and store it away, that it may serve as provisions for you and for them. [22]Noah complied; he did just as God had commanded him.

☐ MARK 1:29-39

The Cure of Simon's Mother-in-Law. 1:29 On leaving the synagogue he entered the house of Simon and Andrew with James and John. [30]Simon's mother-in-law lay sick with a fever. They immediately told him about her. [31]He approached, grasped her hand, and helped her up. Then the fever left her and she waited on them.

Other Healings. [32]When it was evening, after sunset, they brought to him all who were ill or possessed by demons. [33]The whole town was gathered at the door. [34]He cured many who were sick with various diseases, and he drove out many demons, not permitting them to speak because they knew him.

Jesus Leaves Capernaum. [35]Rising very early before dawn, he left and went off to a deserted place, where he prayed. [36]Simon and those who were with him pursued him [37]and on finding him said, "Everyone is looking for you." [38]He told them, "Let us go on to the nearby villages that I may preach there also. For this purpose have I come." [39]So he went into their synagogues, preaching and driving out demons throughout the whole of Galilee.

January 4

St. Elizabeth Ann Seton

The little daily lesson: to keep soberly and quietly in His presence, trying to turn every little action on His will, and to praise and love through cloud and sunshine — this is all my care and study.
— St. Elizabeth Ann Seton

☐ GENESIS 7-8

7:1 Then the LORD said to Noah: Go into the ark, you and all your household, for you alone in this generation have I found to be righteous before me. [2]Of every clean animal, take with you seven pairs, a male and its mate; and of the unclean animals, one pair, a male and its mate; [3]likewise, of every bird of the air, seven pairs, a male and a female, to keep their progeny alive over all the earth. [4]For seven days from now I will bring rain down on the earth for forty days and forty nights, and so I will wipe out from the face of the earth every being that I have made. [5]Noah complied, just as the LORD had commanded.

The Great Flood. [6]Noah was six hundred years old when the flood came upon the earth. [7]Together with his sons, his wife, and his sons' wives, Noah went into the ark because of the waters of the flood.

[8]Of the clean animals and the unclean, of the birds, and of everything that crawls on the ground, [9]two by two, male and female came to Noah into the ark, just as God had commanded him. [10]When the seven days were over, the waters of the flood came upon the earth.

[11]In the six hundredth year of Noah's life, in the second month, on the seventeenth day of the month: on that day

All the fountains of the great abyss
    burst forth,
and the floodgates of the sky were
    opened.

[12]For forty days and forty nights heavy rain poured down on the earth.

[13]On the very same day, Noah and his sons Shem, Ham, and Japheth, and Noah's wife, and the three wives of Noah's sons had entered the ark, [14]together with every kind of wild animal, every kind of tame animal, every kind of crawling thing that crawls on the earth, and every kind of bird. [15]Pairs of all creatures in which there was the breath of life came to Noah into the ark. [16]Those that entered were male and female; of all creatures they came, as God had commanded Noah. Then the LORD shut him in.

[17]The flood continued upon the earth for forty days. As the waters increased, they lifted the ark, so that it rose above the earth. [18]The waters swelled and increased greatly on the earth, but the ark floated on the surface of the waters. [19]Higher and higher on the earth the waters swelled, until all the highest mountains under the heavens were submerged. [20]The waters swelled fifteen cubits higher than the submerged mountains. [21]All creatures that moved on earth perished: birds, tame animals, wild animals, and all that teemed on the earth, as well as all humankind. [22]Everything on dry land with the breath of life in its nostrils died. [23]The LORD wiped out every being on earth: human beings and animals, the crawling things and the birds of the air; all

were wiped out from the earth. Only Noah and those with him in the ark were left.

[24]And when the waters had swelled on the earth for one hundred and fifty days,

8:1 God remembered Noah and all the animals, wild and tame, that were with him in the ark. So God made a wind sweep over the earth, and the waters began to subside. [2]The fountains of the abyss and the floodgates of the sky were closed, and the downpour from the sky was held back. [3]Gradually the waters receded from the earth. At the end of one hundred and fifty days, the waters had so diminished [4]that, in the seventh month, on the seventeenth day of the month, the ark came to rest on the mountains of Ararat. [5]The waters continued to diminish until the tenth month, and on the first day of the tenth month the tops of the mountains appeared.

[6]At the end of forty days Noah opened the hatch of the ark that he had made, [7]and he released a raven. It flew back and forth until the waters dried off from the earth. [8]Then he released a dove, to see if the waters had lessened on the earth. [9]But the dove could find no place to perch, and it returned to him in the ark, for there was water over all the earth. Putting out his hand, he caught the dove and drew it back to him inside the ark. [10]He waited yet seven days more and again released the dove from the ark. [11]In the evening the dove came back to him, and there in its bill was a plucked-off olive leaf! So Noah knew that the waters had diminished on the earth. [12]He waited yet another seven days and then released the dove; but this time it did not come back.

[13]In the six hundred and first year, in the first month, on the first day of the month, the water began to dry up on the earth. Noah then removed the covering of the ark and saw that the surface of the ground had dried. [14]In the second month, on the twenty-seventh day of the month, the earth was dry.

¹⁵Then God said to Noah: ¹⁶Go out of the ark, together with your wife and your sons and your sons' wives. ¹⁷Bring out with you every living thing that is with you—all creatures, be they birds or animals or crawling things that crawl on the earth—and let them abound on the earth, and be fertile and multiply on it. ¹⁸So Noah came out, together with his sons and his wife and his sons' wives; ¹⁹and all the animals, all the birds, and all the crawling creatures that crawl on the earth went out of the ark by families. ²⁰Then Noah built an altar to the LORD, and choosing from every clean animal and every clean bird, he offered burnt offerings on the altar. ²¹When the LORD smelled the sweet odor, the LORD said to himself: Never again will I curse the ground because of human beings, since the desires of the human heart are evil from youth; nor will I ever again strike down every living being, as I have done.

²²All the days of the earth,
    seedtime and harvest,
    cold and heat,
Summer and winter,
    and day and night
    shall not cease.

☐ MARK 1:40-45

The Cleansing of a Leper. 1:40 A leper came to him [and kneeling down] begged him and said, "If you wish, you can make me clean." ⁴¹Moved with pity, he stretched out his hand, touched him, and said to him, "I do will it. Be made clean." ⁴²The leprosy left him immediately, and he was made clean. ⁴³Then, warning him sternly, he dismissed him at once. ⁴⁴Then he said to him, "See that you tell no one anything, but go, show yourself to the priest and offer for your cleansing what Moses prescribed; that will be proof for them." ⁴⁵The man went away and began to publicize the whole matter. He spread the report abroad so that it was impossible for Jesus to enter a town openly. He remained outside in deserted places, and people kept coming to him from everywhere.

January 5

St. John Neumann

Speak to me, O my God, let me know Your will, for behold, I am ready to fulfill Your every command. The difficult, the irksome, I will patiently endure for love of You.

— ST. JOHN NEUMANN

☐ GENESIS 9-10

Covenant with Noah. 9:1 God blessed Noah and his sons and said to them: Be fertile and multiply and fill the earth. ²Fear and dread of you shall come upon all the animals of the earth and all the birds of the air, upon all the creatures that move about on the ground and all the fishes of the sea; into your power they are delivered. ³Any living creature that moves about shall be yours to eat; I give them all to you as I did the green plants. ⁴Only meat with its lifeblood still in it you shall not eat. ⁵Indeed for your own lifeblood I will demand an accounting: from every animal I will demand it, and from a human being, each one for the blood of another, I will demand an accounting for human life.

⁶Anyone who sheds the blood of a
　human being,
　by a human being shall that one's
　　blood be shed;
For in the image of God
　have human beings been made.

⁷Be fertile, then, and multiply; abound on earth and subdue it.

⁸God said to Noah and to his sons with him: ⁹See, I am now establishing my covenant with you and your descendants after you ¹⁰and with every living creature that was with you: the birds, the tame animals, and all the wild animals that were with you—all that came out of the ark. ¹¹I will establish my covenant with you, that never again shall all creatures be destroyed by the waters of a flood; there shall not be another flood to devastate the earth. ¹²God said: This is the sign of the covenant that I am making between me and you and every living creature with you for all ages to come: ¹³I set my bow in the clouds to serve as a sign of the covenant between me and the earth. ¹⁴When I bring clouds over the earth, and the bow appears in the clouds, ¹⁵I will remember my covenant between me and you and every living creature—every mortal being—so that the waters will never again become a flood to destroy every mortal being. ¹⁶When the bow appears in the clouds, I will see it and remember the everlasting covenant between God and every living creature—every mortal being that is on earth. ¹⁷God told Noah: This is the sign of the covenant I have established between me and every mortal being that is on earth.

Noah and His Sons. ¹⁸The sons of Noah who came out of the ark were Shem, Ham and Japheth. Ham was the father of Canaan. ¹⁹These three were the sons of Noah, and from them the whole earth was populated.

²⁰Noah, a man of the soil, was the first to plant a vineyard. ²¹He drank some of the wine, became drunk, and lay naked inside his tent. ²²Ham, the father of Canaan, saw his father's nakedness, and he told his two brothers outside. ²³Shem and Japheth, however, took a robe, and holding it on their shoulders, they walked backward and covered their father's nakedness; since their faces were turned the other way, they did not see their father's nakedness. ²⁴When Noah woke up from his wine and learned what his youngest son had done to him, ²⁵he said:

"Cursed be Caanan!
　The lowest of slaves
　shall he be to his brothers."

²⁶He also said:

"Blessed be the LORD, the God of
　Shem!
　Let Canaan be his slave.
²⁷May God expand Japheth,
　and may he dwell among the tents
　　of Shem;
　and let Canaan be his slave."

²⁸Noah lived three hundred and fifty years after the flood. ²⁹The whole lifetime of Noah was nine hundred and fifty years; then he died.

Table of the Nations. 10:1 These are the descendants of Noah's sons, Shem, Ham and Japheth, to whom children were born after the flood.

²The descendants of Japheth: Gomer, Magog, Madai, Javan, Tubal, Meshech and Tiras. ³The descendants of Gomer: Ashkenaz, Diphath and Togarmah. ⁴The descendants of Javan: Elishah, Tarshish,

the Kittim and the Rodanim. ⁵From these branched out the maritime nations.

These are the descendants of Japheth by their lands, each with its own language, according to their clans, by their nations.

⁶The descendants of Ham: Cush, Mizraim, Put and Canaan. ⁷The descendants of Cush: Seba, Havilah, Sabtah, Raamah and Sabteca. The descendants of Raamah: Sheba and Dedan.

⁸Cush became the father of Nimrod, who was the first to become a mighty warrior on earth. ⁹He was a mighty hunter in the eyes of the LORD; hence the saying, "Like Nimrod, a mighty hunter in the eyes of the LORD." ¹⁰His kingdom originated in Babylon, Erech and Accad, all of them in the land of Shinar. ¹¹From that land he went forth to Assyria, where he built Nineveh, Rehoboth-Ir and Calah, ¹²as well as Resen, between Nineveh and Calah, the latter being the principal city.

¹³Mizraim became the father of the Ludim, the Anamim, the Lehabim, the Naphtuhim, ¹⁴the Pathrusim, the Casluhim, and the Caphtorim from whom the Philistines came.

¹⁵Canaan became the father of Sidon, his firstborn, and of Heth; ¹⁶also of the Jebusites, the Amorites, the Girgashites, ¹⁷the Hivites, the Arkites, the Sinites, ¹⁸the Arvadites, the Zemarites, and the Hamathites. Afterward, the clans of the Canaanites spread out, ¹⁹so that the Canaanite borders extended from Sidon all the way to Gerar, near Gaza, and all the way to Sodom, Gomorrah, Admah and Zeboiim, near Lasha.

²⁰These are the descendants of Ham, according to their clans, according to their languages, by their lands, by their nations.

²¹To Shem also, Japheth's oldest brother and the ancestor of all the children of Eber, children were born. ²²The descendants of Shem: Elam, Asshur, Arpachshad, Lud and Aram. ²³The descendants of Aram: Uz, Hul, Gether and Mash.

²⁴Arpachshad became the father of Shelah, and Shelah became the father of Eber. ²⁵To Eber two sons were born: the name of the first was Peleg, for in his time the world was divided; and the name of his brother was Joktan.

²⁶Joktan became the father of Almodad, Sheleph, Hazarmaveth, Jerah, ²⁷Hadoram, Uzal, Diklah, ²⁸Obal, Abimael, Sheba, ²⁹Ophir, Havilah and Jobab. All these were descendants of Joktan. ³⁰Their settlements extended all the way from Mesha to Sephar, the eastern hill country.

³¹These are the descendants of Shem, according to their clans, according to their languages, by their lands, by their nations.

³²These are the clans of Noah's sons, according to their origins and by their nations. From these the nations of the earth branched out after the flood.

☐ MARK 2:1-12

The Healing of a Paralytic. 2:1 When Jesus returned to Capernaum after some days, it became known that he was at home. ²Many gathered together so that there was no longer room for them, not even around the door, and he preached the word to them. ³They came bringing to him a paralytic carried by four men. ⁴Unable to get near Jesus because of the crowd, they opened up the roof above him. After they had broken through, they let down the mat on which the paralytic was lying. ⁵When Jesus saw their faith, he said to the paralytic, "Child, your sins are forgiven." ⁶Now some of the scribes were sitting there asking themselves, ⁷"Why does this man speak that way? He is blaspheming. Who but God alone can forgive sins?" ⁸Jesus immediately knew in his mind what they were thinking to themselves, so he said,

"Why are you thinking such things in your hearts? ⁹Which is easier, to say to the paralytic, 'Your sins are forgiven,' or to say, 'Rise, pick up your mat and walk'? ¹⁰But that you may know that the Son of Man has authority to forgive sins on earth"—

¹¹he said to the paralytic, "I say to you, rise, pick up your mat, and go home." ¹²He rose, picked up his mat at once, and went away in the sight of everyone. They were all astounded and glorified God, saying, "We have never seen anything like this."

January 6

St. Rafaela Maria Porras

Have a good appetite. God does not want His spouses to look as though He fed them on lizards.

— ST. RAFAELA MARIA PORRAS

☐ GENESIS 11-12

Tower of Babel. 11:1 The whole world had the same language and the same words. ²When they were migrating from the east, they came to a valley in the land of Shinar and settled there. ³They said to one another, "Come, let us mold bricks and harden them with fire." They used bricks for stone, and bitumen for mortar. ⁴Then they said, "Come, let us build ourselves a city and a tower with its top in the sky, and so make a name for ourselves; otherwise we shall be scattered all over the earth."

⁵The LORD came down to see the city and the tower that the people had built. ⁶Then the LORD said: If now, while they are one people and all have the same language, they have started to do this, nothing they presume to do will be out of their reach. ⁷Come, let us go down and there confuse their language, so that no one will understand the speech of another. ⁸So the LORD scattered them from there over all the earth, and they stopped building the city. ⁹That is why it was called Babel, because there the LORD confused the speech of all the world. From there the LORD scattered them over all the earth.

Descendants from Shem to Abraham. ¹⁰These are the descendants of Shem. When Shem was one hundred years old, he begot Arpachshad, two years after the flood. ¹¹Shem lived five hundred years after he begot Arpachshad, and he had other sons and daughters. ¹²When Arpachshad was thirty-five years old, he begot Shelah. ¹³Arpachshad lived four hundred and three years after he begot Shelah, and he had other sons and daughters.

¹⁴When Shelah was thirty years old, he begot Eber. ¹⁵Shelah lived four hundred and three years after he begot Eber, and he had other sons and daughters.

¹⁶When Eber was thirty-four years old, he begot Peleg. ¹⁷Eber lived four hundred and thirty years after he begot Peleg, and he had other sons and daughters.

¹⁸When Peleg was thirty years old, he begot Reu. ¹⁹Peleg lived two hundred and nine years after he begot Reu, and he had other sons and daughters.

²⁰When Reu was thirty-two years old, he begot Serug. ²¹Reu lived two hundred and seven years after he begot Serug, and he had other sons and daughters.

²²When Serug was thirty years old, he begot Nahor. ²³Serug lived two hundred years after he begot Nahor, and he had other sons and daughters.

²⁴When Nahor was twenty-nine years old, he begot Terah. ²⁵Nahor lived one hundred and nineteen years after he begot Terah, and he had other sons and daughters.

²⁶When Terah was seventy years old, he begot Abram, Nahor and Haran.

Terah. ²⁷These are the descendants of Terah. Terah begot Abram, Nahor, and Haran, and Haran begot Lot. ²⁸Haran died before Terah his father, in his native land, in Ur of the Chaldeans. ²⁹Abram and Nahor took wives; the name of Abram's wife was Sarai, and the name of Nahor's wife was Milcah, daughter of Haran, the father of Milcah and Iscah. ³⁰Sarai was barren; she had no child.

³¹Terah took his son Abram, his grandson Lot, son of Haran, and his daughter-in-law Sarai, the wife of his son Abram, and brought them out of Ur of the Chaldeans, to go to the land of Canaan. But when they reached Haran, they settled there. ³²The lifetime of Terah was two hundred and five years; then Terah died in Haran.

Abram's Call and Migration. 12:1 The LORD said to Abram: Go forth from your land, your relatives, and from your father's house to a land that I will show you. ²I will make of you a great nation, and I will bless you; I will make your name great, so that you will be a blessing. ³I will bless those who bless you and curse those who curse you. All the families of the earth will find blessing in you.

⁴Abram went as the LORD directed him, and Lot went with him. Abram was seventy-five years old when he left Haran. ⁵Abram took his wife Sarai, his brother's son Lot, all the possessions that they had accumulated, and the persons they had acquired in Haran, and they set out for the land of Canaan. When they came to the land of Canaan, ⁶Abram passed through the land as far as the sacred place at Shechem, by the oak of Moreh. The Canaanites were then in the land.

⁷The LORD appeared to Abram and said: To your descendants I will give this land. So Abram built an altar there to the LORD who had appeared to him. ⁸From there he moved on to the hill country east of Bethel, pitching his tent with Bethel to the west and Ai to the east. He built an altar there to the LORD and invoked the LORD by name. ⁹Then Abram journeyed on by stages to the Negeb.

Abram and Sarai in Egypt. ¹⁰There was famine in the land; so Abram went down to Egypt to sojourn there, since the famine in the land was severe. ¹¹When he was about to enter Egypt, he said to his wife Sarai: "I know that you are a beautiful woman. ¹²When the Egyptians see you, they will say, 'She is his wife'; then they will kill me, but let you live. ¹³Please say, therefore, that you are my sister, so that I may fare well on your account and my life may be spared for your sake." ¹⁴When Abram arrived in Egypt, the Egyptians saw that the woman was very beautiful. ¹⁵When Pharaoh's officials saw her they praised her to Pharaoh, and the woman was taken into Pharaoh's house. ¹⁶Abram fared well on her account, and he acquired sheep, oxen, male and female servants, male and female donkeys, and camels.

¹⁷But the LORD struck Pharaoh and his household with severe plagues because of Sarai, Abram's wife. ¹⁸Then Pharaoh summoned Abram and said to him: "How could you do this to me! Why did you not tell me she was your wife? ¹⁹Why did you say, 'She is my sister,' so that I took her for my wife? Now, here is your wife. Take her and leave!"

²⁰Then Pharaoh gave his men orders concerning Abram, and they sent him away, with his wife and all that belonged to him.

☐ MARK 2:13-17

The Call of Levi. 2:13 Once again he went out along the sea. All the crowd came to him and he taught them. [14]As he passed by, he saw Levi, son of Alphaeus, sitting at the customs post. He said to him, "Follow me." And he got up and followed him. [15]While he was at table in his house, many tax collectors and sinners sat with Jesus and his disciples; for there were many who followed him. [16]Some scribes who were Pharisees saw that he was eating with sinners and tax collectors and said to his disciples, "Why does he eat with tax collectors and sinners?" [17]Jesus heard this and said to them [that], "Those who are well do not need a physician, but the sick do. I did not come to call the righteous but sinners."

January 7

St. Raymond of Peñafort

How do we distinguish the fasting of our God and King from the fasting of that tyrant the devil? Clearly by its moderation. Everything that is extreme is destructive.

— St. Syncletica

☐ GENESIS 13-15

Abram and Lot Part. 13:1 From Egypt Abram went up to the Negeb with his wife and all that belonged to him, and Lot went with him. [2]Now Abram was very rich in livestock, silver, and gold. [3]From the Negeb he traveled by stages toward Bethel, to the place between Bethel and Ai where his tent had formerly stood, [4]the site where he had first built the altar; and there Abram invoked the LORD by name.

[5]Lot, who went with Abram, also had flocks and herds and tents, [6]so that the land could not support them if they stayed together; their possessions were so great that they could not live together. [7]There were quarrels between the herders of Abram's livestock and the herders of Lot's livestock. At this time the Canaanites and the Perizzites were living in the land.

[8]So Abram said to Lot: "Let there be no strife between you and me, or between your herders and my herders, for we are kindred. [9]Is not the whole land available? Please separate from me. If you prefer the left, I will go to the right; if you prefer the right, I will go to the left." [10]Lot looked about and saw how abundantly watered the whole Jordan Plain was as far as Zoar, like the LORD's own garden, or like Egypt. This was before the LORD had destroyed Sodom and Gomorrah. [11]Lot, therefore, chose for himself the whole Jordan Plain and set out eastward. Thus they separated from each other. [12]Abram settled in the land of Canaan, while Lot settled among the cities of the Plain, pitching his tents near Sodom. [13]Now the inhabitants of Sodom were wicked, great sinners against the LORD.

[14]After Lot had parted from him, the LORD said to Abram: Look about you, and from where you are, gaze to the north and south, east and west; [15]all the land that you see I will give to you and your descendants forever. [16]I will make your descendants

like the dust of the earth; if anyone could count the dust of the earth, your descendants too might be counted. [17]Get up and walk through the land, across its length and breadth, for I give it to you. [18]Abram moved his tents and went on to settle near the oak of Mamre, which is at Hebron. There he built an altar to the LORD.

The Four Kings. 14:1 When Amraphel king of Shinar, Arioch king of Ellasar, Chedorlaomer king of Elam, and Tidal king of Goiim [2]made war on Bera king of Sodom, Birsha king of Gomorrah, Shinab king of Admah, Shemeber king of Zeboiim, and the king of Bela (that is, Zoar), [3]all the latter kings joined forces in the Valley of Siddim (that is, the Salt Sea). [4]For twelve years they had served Chedorlaomer, but in the thirteenth year they rebelled. [5]In the fourteenth year Chedorlaomer and the kings allied with him came and defeated the Rephaim in Ashteroth-karnaim, the Zuzim in Ham, the Emim in Shaveh-kiriathaim, [6]and the Horites in the hill country of Seir, as far as El-paran, close by the wilderness. [7]They then turned back and came to En-mishpat (that is, Kadesh), and they subdued the whole country of both the Amalekites and the Amorites who lived in Hazazon-tamar. [8]Thereupon the king of Sodom, the king of Gomorrah, the king of Admah, the king of Zeboiim, and the king of Bela (that is, Zoar) marched out, and in the Valley of Siddim they went into battle against them: [9]against Chedorlaomer king of Elam, Tidal king of Goiim, Amraphel king of Shinar, and Arioch king of Ellasar—four kings against five. [10]Now the Valley of Siddim was full of bitumen pits; and as the king of Sodom and the king of Gomorrah fled, they fell into these, while the rest fled to the mountains. [11]The victors seized all the possessions and food supplies of Sodom and Gomorrah and then went their way. [12]They took with them Abram's nephew Lot, who had been living in Sodom, as well as his possessions, and departed.

[13]A survivor came and brought the news to Abram the Hebrew, who was camping at the oak of Mamre the Amorite, a kinsman of Eshcol and Aner; these were allies of Abram. [14]When Abram heard that his kinsman had been captured, he mustered three hundred and eighteen of his retainers, born in his house, and went in pursuit as far as Dan. [15]He and his servants deployed against them at night, defeated them, and pursued them as far as Hobah, which is north of Damascus. [16]He recovered all the possessions. He also recovered his kinsman Lot and his possessions, along with the women and the other people.

[17]When Abram returned from his defeat of Chedorlaomer and the kings who were allied with him, the king of Sodom went out to greet him in the Valley of Shaveh (that is, the King's Valley).

[18]Melchizedek, king of Salem, brought out bread and wine. He was a priest of God Most High. [19]He blessed Abram with these words:

"Blessed be Abram by God Most High,
the creator of heaven and earth;
[20]And blessed be God Most High,
who delivered your foes into your
hand."

Then Abram gave him a tenth of everything. [21]The king of Sodom said to Abram, "Give me the captives; the goods you may keep." [22]But Abram replied to the king of Sodom: "I have sworn to the LORD, God Most High, the creator of heaven and earth, [23]that I would not take so much as a thread or a sandal strap from anything that is yours, so that you cannot say, 'I made Abram rich.' [24]Nothing for me except what my servants have consumed and the share that is due to the men who went with me—Aner, Eshcol and Mamre; let them take their share."

The Covenant with Abram. 15:1 Some time afterward, the word of the LORD came to Abram in a vision: Do not fear, Abram! I am your shield; I will make your reward very great.

²But Abram said, "Lord GOD, what can you give me, if I die childless and have only a servant of my household, Eliezer of Damascus?" ³Abram continued, "Look, you have given me no offspring, so a servant of my household will be my heir." ⁴Then the word of the LORD came to him: No, that one will not be your heir; your own offspring will be your heir. ⁵He took him outside and said: Look up at the sky and count the stars, if you can. Just so, he added, will your descendants be. ⁶Abram put his faith in the LORD, who attributed it to him as an act of righteousness.

⁷He then said to him: I am the LORD who brought you from Ur of the Chaldeans to give you this land as a possession. ⁸"Lord GOD," he asked, "how will I know that I will possess it?" ⁹He answered him: Bring me a three-year-old heifer, a three-year-old female goat, a three-year-old ram, a turtledove, and a young pigeon. ¹⁰He brought him all these, split them in two, and placed each half opposite the other; but the birds he did not cut up. ¹¹Birds of prey swooped down on the carcasses, but Abram scared them away. ¹²As the sun was about to set, a deep sleep fell upon Abram, and a great, dark dread descended upon him.

¹³Then the LORD said to Abram: Know for certain that your descendants will reside as aliens in a land not their own, where they shall be enslaved and oppressed for four hundred years. ¹⁴But I will bring judgment on the nation they must serve, and after this they will go out with great wealth. ¹⁵You, however, will go to your ancestors in peace; you will be buried at a ripe old age. ¹⁶In the fourth generation your descendants will return here, for the wickedness of the Amorites is not yet complete.

¹⁷When the sun had set and it was dark, there appeared a smoking fire pot and a flaming torch, which passed between those pieces. ¹⁸On that day the LORD made a covenant with Abram, saying: To your descendants I give this land, from the Wadi of Egypt to the Great River, the Euphrates, ¹⁹the land of the Kenites, the Kenizzites, the Kadmonites, ²⁰the Hittites, the Perizzites, the Rephaim, ²¹the Amorites, the Canaanites, the Girgashites, and the Jebusites.

☐ MARK 2:18-28

The Questions about Fasting. 2:18 The disciples of John and of the Pharisees were accustomed to fast. People came to him and objected, "Why do the disciples of John and the disciples of the Pharisees fast, but your disciples do not fast?" ¹⁹Jesus answered them, "Can the wedding guests fast while the bridegroom is with them? As long as they have the bridegroom with them they cannot fast. ²⁰But the days will come when the bridegroom is taken away from them, and then they will fast on that day. ²¹No one sews a piece of unshrunken cloth on an old cloak. If he does, its fullness pulls away, the new from the old, and the tear gets worse. ²²Likewise, no one pours new wine into old wineskins. Otherwise, the wine will burst the skins, and both the wine and the skins are ruined. Rather, new wine is poured into fresh wineskins."

The Disciples and the Sabbath. ²³As he was passing through a field of grain on the sabbath, his disciples began to make a path while picking the heads of grain. ²⁴At this the Pharisees said to him, "Look, why are they doing what is unlawful on the sabbath?" ²⁵He said to them, "Have you never read what David did when he was in need and he and his companions were hungry? ²⁶How he went into the house of God when Abiathar was high priest and ate the bread of offering that only the priests could lawfully eat, and shared it with his companions?" ²⁷Then he said to them, "The sabbath was made for man, not man for the sabbath. ²⁸That is why the Son of Man is lord even of the sabbath."

January 8

However great may be the temptation, if we know how to use the weapon of prayer well we shall come off conquerors at last, for prayer is more powerful than all the devils.

— St. Bernard of Clairvaux

☐ GENESIS 16-18

Birth of Ishmael. 16:1 Abram's wife Sarai had borne him no children. Now she had an Egyptian maidservant named Hagar. ²Sarai said to Abram: "The Lord has kept me from bearing children. Have intercourse with my maid; perhaps I will have sons through her." Abram obeyed Sarai. ³Thus, after Abram had lived ten years in the land of Canaan, his wife Sarai took her maid, Hagar the Egyptian, and gave her to her husband Abram to be his wife. ⁴He had intercourse with her, and she became pregnant. As soon as Hagar knew she was pregnant, her mistress lost stature in her eyes. ⁵So Sarai said to Abram: "This outrage against me is your fault. I myself gave my maid to your embrace; but ever since she knew she was pregnant, I have lost stature in her eyes. May the Lord decide between you and me!" ⁶Abram told Sarai: "Your maid is in your power. Do to her what you regard as right." Sarai then mistreated her so much that Hagar ran away from her.

⁷The Lord's angel found her by a spring in the wilderness, the spring on the road to Shur, ⁸and he asked, "Hagar, maid of Sarai, where have you come from and where are you going?" She answered, "I am running away from my mistress, Sarai." ⁹But the Lord's angel told her: "Go back to your mistress and submit to her authority. ¹⁰I will make your descendants so numerous," added the Lord's angel, "that they will be too many to count." ¹¹Then the Lord's angel said to her:

"You are now pregnant and shall bear
    a son;
    you shall name him Ishmael,
For the Lord has heeded your
    affliction.
¹²He shall be a wild ass of a man,
    his hand against everyone,
    and everyone's hand against him;
Alongside all his kindred
    shall he encamp."

¹³To the Lord who spoke to her she gave a name, saying, "You are God who sees me"; she meant, "Have I really seen God and remained alive after he saw me?" ¹⁴That is why the well is called Beer-lahai-roi. It is between Kadesh and Bered.

¹⁵Hagar bore Abram a son, and Abram named the son whom Hagar bore him Ishmael. ¹⁶Abram was eighty-six years old when Hagar bore him Ishmael.

Covenant of Circumcision. 17:1 When Abram was ninety-nine years old, the LORD appeared to Abram and said: I am God the Almighty. Walk in my presence and be blameless. [2]Between you and me I will establish my covenant, and I will multiply you exceedingly.

[3]Abram fell face down and God said to him: [4]For my part, here is my covenant with you: you are to become the father of a multitude of nations. [5]No longer will you be called Abram; your name will be Abraham, for I am making you the father of a multitude of nations. [6]I will make you exceedingly fertile; I will make nations of you; kings will stem from you. [7]I will maintain my covenant between me and you and your descendants after you throughout the ages as an everlasting covenant, to be your God and the God of your descendants after you. [8]I will give to you and to your descendants after you the land in which you are now residing as aliens, the whole land of Canaan, as a permanent possession; and I will be their God. [9]God said to Abraham: For your part, you and your descendants after you must keep my covenant throughout the ages. [10]This is the covenant between me and you and your descendants after you that you must keep: every male among you shall be circumcised. [11]Circumcise the flesh of your foreskin. That will be the sign of the covenant between me and you. [12]Throughout the ages, every male among you, when he is eight days old, shall be circumcised, including houseborn slaves and those acquired with money from any foreigner who is not of your descendants. [13]Yes, both the houseborn slaves and those acquired with money must be circumcised. Thus my covenant will be in your flesh as an everlasting covenant. [14]If a male is uncircumcised, that is, if the flesh of his foreskin has not been cut away, such a one will be cut off from his people; he has broken my covenant.

[15]God further said to Abraham: As for Sarai your wife, do not call her Sarai; her name will be Sarah. [16]I will bless her, and I will give you a son by her. Her also will I bless; she will give rise to nations, and rulers of peoples will issue from her. [17]Abraham fell face down and laughed as he said to himself, "Can a child be born to a man who is a hundred years old? Can Sarah give birth at ninety?" [18]So Abraham said to God, "If only Ishmael could live in your favor!" [19]God replied: Even so, your wife Sarah is to bear you a son, and you shall call him Isaac. It is with him that I will maintain my covenant as an everlasting covenant and with his descendants after him. [20]Now as for Ishmael, I will heed you: I hereby bless him. I will make him fertile and will multiply him exceedingly. He will become the father of twelve chieftains, and I will make of him a great nation. [21]But my covenant I will maintain with Isaac, whom Sarah shall bear to you by this time next year. [22]When he had finished speaking with Abraham, God departed from him.

[23]Then Abraham took his son Ishmael and all his slaves, whether born in his house or acquired with his money—every male among the members of Abraham's household—and he circumcised the flesh of their foreskins on that same day, as God had told him to do. [24]Abraham was ninety-nine years old when the flesh of his foreskin was circumcised, [25]and his son Ishmael was thirteen years old when the flesh of his foreskin was circumcised. [26]Thus, on that same day Abraham and his son Ishmael were circumcised; [27]and all the males of his household, including the slaves born in his house or acquired with his money from foreigners, were circumcised with him.

Abraham's Visitors. 18:1 The LORD appeared to Abraham by the oak of Mamre, as he sat in the entrance of his tent, while the day was growing hot. [2]Looking up, he saw three men standing near him. When he saw them, he ran from the entrance of the tent to greet them; and bowing to the ground, [3]he said: "Sir, if it please you, do not go on past your servant. ⁴Let some water be brought, that you may bathe your feet, and then rest under the tree. ⁵Now that you have come to your servant, let me bring you a little food, that you may refresh yourselves; and afterward you may go on your way." "Very well," they replied, "do as you have said."

⁶Abraham hurried into the tent to Sarah and said, "Quick, three measures of bran flour! Knead it and make bread." ⁷He ran to the herd, picked out a tender, choice calf, and gave it to a servant, who quickly prepared it. ⁸Then he got some curds and milk, as well as the calf that had been prepared, and set these before them, waiting on them under the tree while they ate.

⁹"Where is your wife Sarah?" they asked him. "There in the tent," he replied. ¹⁰One of them said, "I will return to you about this time next year, and Sarah will then have a son." Sarah was listening at the entrance of the tent, just behind him. ¹¹Now Abraham and Sarah were old, advanced in years, and Sarah had stopped having her menstrual periods. ¹²So Sarah laughed to herself and said, "Now that I am worn out and my husband is old, am I still to have sexual pleasure?" ¹³But the LORD said to Abraham: "Why did Sarah laugh and say, 'Will I really bear a child, old as I am?' ¹⁴Is anything too marvelous for the LORD to do? At the appointed time, about this time next year, I will return to you, and Sarah will have a son." ¹⁵Sarah lied, saying, "I did not laugh," because she was afraid. But he said, "Yes, you did."

Abraham Intercedes for Sodom. ¹⁶With Abraham walking with them to see them on their way, the men set out from there and looked down toward Sodom. ¹⁷The LORD considered: Shall I hide from Abraham what I am about to do, ¹⁸now that he is to become a great and mighty nation, and all the nations of the earth are to find blessing in him? ¹⁹Indeed, I have singled him out that he may direct his children and his household in the future to keep the way of the LORD by doing what is right and just, so that the LORD may

put into effect for Abraham the promises he made about him. ²⁰So the LORD said: The outcry against Sodom and Gomorrah is so great, and their sin so grave, ²¹that I must go down to see whether or not their actions are as bad as the cry against them that comes to me. I mean to find out.

²²As the men turned and walked on toward Sodom, Abraham remained standing before the LORD. ²³Then Abraham drew near and said: "Will you really sweep away the righteous with the wicked? ²⁴Suppose there were fifty righteous people in the city; would you really sweep away and not spare the place for the sake of the fifty righteous people within it? ²⁵Far be it from you to do such a thing, to kill the righteous with the wicked, so that the righteous and the wicked are treated alike! Far be it from you! Should not the judge of all the world do what is just?" ²⁶The LORD replied: If I find fifty righteous people in the city of Sodom, I will spare the whole place for their sake. ²⁷Abraham spoke up again: "See how I am presuming to speak to my Lord, though I am only dust and ashes! ²⁸What if there are five less than fifty righteous people? Will you destroy the whole city because of those five?" I will not destroy it, he answered, if I find forty-five there. ²⁹But Abraham persisted, saying, "What if only forty are found there?" He replied: I will refrain from doing it for the sake of the forty. ³⁰Then he said, "Do not let my Lord be angry if I go on. What if only thirty are found there?" He replied: I will refrain from doing it if I can find thirty there. ³¹Abraham went on, "Since I have thus presumed to speak to my Lord, what if there are no more than twenty?" I will not destroy it, he answered, for the sake of the twenty. ³²But he persisted: "Please, do not let my Lord be angry if I speak up this last time. What if ten are found there?" For the sake of the ten, he replied, I will not destroy it.

³³The LORD departed as soon as he had finished speaking with Abraham, and Abraham returned home.

☐ MARK 3:1-12

A Man with a Withered Hand. 3:1 Again he entered the synagogue. There was a man there who had a withered hand. ²They watched him closely to see if he would cure him on the sabbath so that they might accuse him. ³He said to the man with the withered hand, "Come up here before us." ⁴Then he said to them, "Is it lawful to do good on the sabbath rather than to do evil, to save life rather than to destroy it?" But they remained silent. ⁵Looking around at them with anger and grieved at their hardness of heart, he said to the man, "Stretch out your hand." He stretched it out and his hand was restored. ⁶The Pharisees went out and immediately took counsel with the Herodians against him to put him to death.

The Mercy of Jesus. ⁷Jesus withdrew toward the sea with his disciples. A large number of people [followed] from Galilee and from Judea. ⁸Hearing what he was doing, a large number of people came to him also from Jerusalem, from Idumea, from beyond the Jordan, and from the neighborhood of Tyre and Sidon. ⁹He told his disciples to have a boat ready for him because of the crowd, so that they would not crush him. ¹⁰He had cured many and, as a result, those who had diseases were pressing upon him to touch him. ¹¹And whenever unclean spirits saw him they would fall down before him and shout, "You are the Son of God." ¹²He warned them sternly not to make him known.

January 9

Blessed Tommaso Reggio

I want to become a saint, cost what it may, living my life in accordance with the two cornerstones of Christianity: prayer and discipline.

— BLESSED TOMMASO REGGIO

☐ GENESIS 19-20

Destruction of Sodom and Gomorrah. 19:1 The two angels reached Sodom in the evening, as Lot was sitting at the gate of Sodom. When Lot saw them, he got up to greet them; and bowing down with his face to the ground, ²he said, "Please, my lords, come aside into your servant's house for the night, and bathe your feet; you can get up early to continue your journey." But they replied, "No, we will pass the night in the town square." ³He urged them so strongly, however, that they turned aside to his place and entered his house. He prepared a banquet for them, baking unleavened bread, and they dined.

⁴Before they went to bed, the townsmen of Sodom, both young and old—all the people to the last man—surrounded the house. ⁵They called to Lot and said to him, "Where are the men who came to your house tonight? Bring them out to us that we may have sexual relations with them." ⁶Lot went out to meet them at the entrance. When he had shut the door behind him, ⁷he said, "I beg you, my brothers, do not do this wicked thing! ⁸I have two daughters who have never had sexual relations with men. Let me bring them out to you, and you may do to them as you please. But do not do anything to

these men, for they have come under the shelter of my roof." ⁹They replied, "Stand back! This man," they said, "came here as a resident alien, and now he dares to give orders! We will treat you worse than them!" With that, they pressed hard against Lot, moving in closer to break down the door. ¹⁰But his guests put out their hands, pulled Lot inside with them, and closed the door; ¹¹they struck the men at the entrance of the house, small and great, with such a blinding light that they were utterly unable to find the doorway.

¹²Then the guests said to Lot: "Who else belongs to you here? Sons-in-law, your sons, your daughters, all who belong to you in the city—take them away from this place! ¹³We are about to destroy this place, for the outcry reaching the LORD against those here is so great that the LORD has sent us to destroy it." ¹⁴So Lot went out and spoke to his sons-in-law, who had contracted marriage with his daughters. "Come on, leave this place," he told them; "the LORD is about to destroy the city." But his sons-in-law thought he was joking.

¹⁵As dawn was breaking, the angels urged Lot on, saying, "Come on! Take your wife with you and your two daughters who are here, or you will be swept away in the punishment of the city." ¹⁶When he hesitated, the men, because of the LORD's compassion for him, seized his hand and the hands of his wife and his two daughters and led them to safety outside the city. ¹⁷As soon as they had brought them outside, they said: "Flee for your life! Do not look back or stop anywhere on the Plain. Flee to the hills at once, or you will be swept away." ¹⁸"Oh, no, my lords!" Lot replied to them. ¹⁹"You have already shown favor to your servant, doing me the great kindness of saving my life. But I cannot flee to the hills, or the disaster will overtake and kill me. ²⁰Look, this town ahead is near enough to escape to. It is only a small place. Let me flee there—is it not a small place?—to save

my life." ²¹"Well, then," he replied, "I grant you this favor too. I will not overthrow the town you have mentioned. ²²Hurry, escape there! I cannot do anything until you arrive there." That is why the town is called Zoar. ²³The sun had risen over the earth when Lot arrived in Zoar, ²⁴and the LORD rained down sulfur upon Sodom and Gomorrah, fire from the LORD out of heaven. ²⁵He overthrew those cities and the whole Plain, together with the inhabitants of the cities and the produce of the soil. ²⁶But Lot's wife looked back, and she was turned into a pillar of salt.

²⁷The next morning Abraham hurried to the place where he had stood before the LORD. ²⁸As he looked down toward Sodom and Gomorrah and the whole region of the Plain, he saw smoke over the land rising like the smoke from a kiln.

²⁹When God destroyed the cities of the Plain, he remembered Abraham and sent Lot away from the upheaval that occurred when God overthrew the cities where Lot had been living.

Moabites and Ammonites. ³⁰Since Lot was afraid to stay in Zoar, he and his two daughters went up from Zoar and settled in the hill country, where he lived with his two daughters in a cave. ³¹The firstborn said to the younger: "Our father is getting old, and there is not a man in the land to have intercourse with us as is the custom everywhere. ³²Come, let us ply our father with wine and then lie with him, that we may ensure posterity by our father." ³³So that night they plied their father with wine, and the firstborn went in and lay with her father; but he was not aware of her lying down or getting up. ³⁴The next day the firstborn said to the younger: "Last night I lay with my father. Let us ply him with wine again tonight, and then you go in and lie with him, that we may ensure posterity by our father." ³⁵So that night, too, they plied their father with wine, and then the younger one went in and lay with him; but he was not aware of her lying down or getting up. ³⁶Thus the two daughters of Lot became pregnant by their father. ³⁷The firstborn gave birth to a son whom she named Moab, saying, "From my father." He is the ancestor of the Moabites of today. ³⁸The younger one, too, gave birth to a son, and she named him Ammon, saying, "The son of my kin." He is the ancestor of the Ammonites of today.

Abraham at Gerar. 20:1 From there Abraham journeyed on to the region of the Negeb, where he settled between Kadesh and Shur. While he resided in Gerar as an alien, ²Abraham said of his wife Sarah, "She is my sister." So Abimelech, king of Gerar, sent and took Sarah. ³But God came to Abimelech in a dream one night and said to him: You are about to die because of the woman you have taken, for she has a husband. ⁴Abimelech, who had not approached her, said: "O Lord, would you kill an innocent man? ⁵Was he not the one who told me, 'She is my sister'? She herself also stated, 'He is my brother.' I acted with pure heart and with clean hands." ⁶God answered him in the dream: Yes, I know you did it with a pure heart. In fact, it was I who kept you from sinning against me; that is why I did not let you touch her. ⁷So now, return the man's wife so that he may intercede for you, since he is a prophet, that you may live. If you do not return her, you can be sure that you and all who are yours will die.

⁸Early the next morning Abimelech called all his servants and informed them of everything that had happened, and the men were filled with fear. ⁹Then Abimelech summoned Abraham and said to him: "What have you done to us! What wrong did I do to you that you would have brought such great guilt on me and my kingdom? You have treated me in an intolerable way. ¹⁰What did you have in mind," Abimelech asked him, "that you would do such a thing?" ¹¹Abraham answered, "I thought there would be no fear of God in this place, and so they would kill me on account of my wife. ¹²Besides, she really is my sister, but only my father's daughter, not my mother's; and so she became my wife. ¹³When God sent me wandering from my father's house, I asked her: 'Would you do me this favor? In whatever place we come to, say: He is my brother.'"

¹⁴Then Abimelech took flocks and herds and male and female slaves and gave them to Abraham; and he restored his wife Sarah to him. ¹⁵Then Abimelech said, "Here, my land is at your disposal; settle wherever you please." ¹⁶To Sarah he said: "I hereby give your brother a thousand shekels of silver. This will preserve your honor before all who are with you and will exonerate you before everyone." ¹⁷Abraham then interceded with God, and God restored health to Abimelech, to his wife, and his maidservants, so that they bore children; ¹⁸for the LORD had closed every womb in Abimelech's household on account of Abraham's wife Sarah.

☐ MARK 3:13-35

The Mission of the Twelve. 3:13 He went up the mountain and summoned those whom he wanted and they came to him. ¹⁴He appointed twelve [whom he also named apostles] that they might be with him and he might send them forth to preach ¹⁵and to have authority to drive out demons: ¹⁶[he appointed the twelve:] Simon, whom he named Peter; ¹⁷James, son of Zebedee, and John the brother of James, whom he named Boanerges, that is, sons of thunder; ¹⁸Andrew, Philip, Bartholomew,

Matthew, Thomas, James the son of Alphaeus; Thaddeus, Simon the Cananean, [19]and Judas Iscariot who betrayed him.

Blasphemy of the Scribes. [20]He came home. Again [the] crowd gathered, making it impossible for them even to eat. [21]When his relatives heard of this they set out to seize him, for they said, "He is out of his mind." [22]The scribes who had come from Jerusalem said, "He is possessed by Beelzebul," and "By the prince of demons he drives out demons."

Jesus and Beelzebul. [23]Summoning them, he began to speak to them in parables, "How can Satan drive out Satan? [24]If a kingdom is divided against itself, that kingdom cannot stand. [25]And if a house is divided against itself, that house will not be able to stand. [26]And if Satan has risen up against himself and is divided, he cannot stand; that is the end of him. [27]But no one can enter a strong man's house to plunder his property unless he first ties up the strong man. Then he can plunder his house. [28]Amen, I say to you, all sins and all blasphemies that people utter will be forgiven them. [29]But whoever blasphemes against the holy Spirit will never have forgiveness, but is guilty of an everlasting sin." [30]For they had said, "He has an unclean spirit."

Jesus and His Family. [31]His mother and his brothers arrived. Standing outside they sent word to him and called him. [32]A crowd seated around him told him, "Your mother and your brothers [and your sisters] are outside asking for you." [33]But he said to them in reply, "Who are my mother and [my] brothers?" [34]And looking around at those seated in the circle he said, "Here are my mother and my brothers. [35][For] whoever does the will of God is my brother and sister and mother."

January 10

To search and understand the Scriptures rightly, we need a good life and a pure soul. Christian virtue must guide the mind to grasp, as far as human nature can, the truth concerning God the Word.

— St. Athanasius of Alexandria

☐ GENESIS 21-23

Birth of Isaac. 21:1 The LORD took note of Sarah as he had said he would; the LORD did for her as he had promised. [2]Sarah became pregnant and bore Abraham a son in his old age, at the set time that God had stated. [3]Abraham gave the name Isaac to this son of his whom Sarah bore him. [4]When his son Isaac was eight days old, Abraham circumcised him, as God had commanded. [5]Abraham was a hundred years old when his son Isaac was born to him. [6]Sarah then said, "God has given me cause to laugh, and all who hear of it will laugh with me. [7]Who would ever have told Abraham," she added, "that Sarah would nurse children! Yet I have borne him a son in his old age." [8]The child grew and was weaned, and Abraham held a great banquet on the day of the child's weaning.

[9]Sarah noticed the son whom Hagar the Egyptian had borne to Abraham playing with her son Isaac; [10]so she demanded of Abraham: "Drive out that slave and her son! No son of that slave is going to

share the inheritance with my son Isaac!" [11]Abraham was greatly distressed because it concerned a son of his. [12]But God said to Abraham: Do not be distressed about the boy or about your slave woman. Obey Sarah, no matter what she asks of you; for it is through Isaac that descendants will bear your name. [13]As for the son of the slave woman, I will make a nation of him also, since he too is your offspring.

[14]Early the next morning Abraham got some bread and a skin of water and gave them to Hagar. Then, placing the child on her back, he sent her away. As she roamed aimlessly in the wilderness of Beer-sheba, [15]the water in the skin was used up. So she put the child down under one of the bushes, [16]and then went and sat down opposite him, about a bowshot away; for she said to herself, "I cannot watch the child die." As she sat opposite him, she wept aloud. [17]God heard the boy's voice, and God's angel called to Hagar from heaven: "What is the matter, Hagar? Do not fear; God has heard the boy's voice in this plight of his. [18]Get up, lift up the boy and hold him by the hand; for I will make of him a great nation." [19]Then God opened her eyes, and she saw a well of water. She went and filled the skin with water, and then let the boy drink.

[20]God was with the boy as he grew up. He lived in the wilderness and became an expert bowman. [21]He lived in the wilderness of Paran. His mother got a wife for him from the land of Egypt.

The Covenant at Beer-sheba. [22]At that time Abimelech, accompanied by Phicol, the commander of his army, said to Abraham: "God is with you in everything you do. [23]So now, swear to me by God at this place that you will not deal falsely with me or with my progeny and posterity, but will act as loyally toward me and the land in which you reside as I have acted toward you." [24]Abraham replied, "I so swear."

[25]Abraham, however, reproached Abimelech about a well that Abimelech's servants had seized by force. [26]"I have no idea who did that," Abimelech replied. "In fact, you never told me about it, nor did I ever hear of it until now."

[27]Then Abraham took sheep and cattle and gave them to Abimelech and the two made a covenant. [28]Abraham also set apart seven ewe lambs of the flock, [29]and Abimelech asked him, "What is the purpose of these seven ewe lambs that you have set apart?" [30]Abraham answered, "The seven ewe lambs you shall accept from me that you may be my witness that I dug this well." [31]This is why the place is called Beer-sheba; the two of them took an oath there. [32]When they had thus made the covenant in Beer-sheba, Abimelech, along with Phicol, the commander of his army, left to return to the land of the Philistines.

[33]Abraham planted a tamarisk at Beer-sheba, and there he invoked by name the LORD, God the Eternal. [34]Abraham resided in the land of the Philistines for a long time.

The Testing of Abraham. 22:1 Some time afterward, God put Abraham to the test and said to him: Abraham! "Here I am!" he replied. [2]Then God said: Take your son Isaac, your only one, whom you love, and go to the land of Moriah. There offer him up as a burnt offering on one of the heights that I will point out to you. [3]Early the next morning Abraham saddled his donkey, took with him two of his servants and his son Isaac, and after cutting the wood for the burnt offering, set out for the place of which God had told him.

[4]On the third day Abraham caught sight of the place from a distance. [5]Abraham said to his servants: "Stay here with the donkey, while the boy and I go on over there. We will worship and then come back to you." [6]So Abraham took the wood for the burnt offering and laid it on his son Isaac, while he himself carried the fire and the knife. As the two walked on together, [7]Isaac spoke to his father Abraham. "Father!" he said.

"Here I am," he replied. Isaac continued, "Here are the fire and the wood, but where is the sheep for the burnt offering?" [8]"My son," Abraham answered, "God will provide the sheep for the burnt offering." Then the two walked on together.

[9]When they came to the place of which God had told him, Abraham built an altar there and arranged the wood on it. Next he bound his son Isaac, and put him on top of the wood on the altar. [10]Then Abraham reached out and took the knife to slaughter his son. [11]But the angel of the LORD called to him from heaven, "Abraham, Abraham!" "Here I am," he answered. [12]"Do not lay your hand on the boy," said the angel. "Do not do the least thing to him. For now I know that you fear God, since you did not withhold from me your son, your only one." [13]Abraham looked up and saw a single ram caught by its horns in the thicket. So Abraham went and took the ram and offered it up as a burnt offering in place of his son. [14]Abraham named that place Yahweh-yireh; hence people today say, "On the mountain the LORD will provide."

[15]A second time the angel of the LORD called to Abraham from heaven [16]and said: "I swear by my very self—oracle of the LORD—that because you acted as you did in not withholding from me your son, your only one, [17]I will bless you and make your descendants as countless as the stars of the sky and the sands of the seashore; your descendants will take possession of the gates of their enemies, [18]and in your descendants all the nations of the earth will find blessing, because you obeyed my command."

[19]Abraham then returned to his servants, and they set out together for Beersheba, where Abraham lived.

Nahor's Descendants. [20]Some time afterward, the news came to Abraham: "Milcah too has borne sons to your brother Nahor: [21]Uz, his firstborn, his brother Buz, Kemuel the father of Aram, [22]Chesed, Hazo, Pildash, Jidlaph, and Bethuel."

[23]Bethuel became the father of Rebekah. These eight Milcah bore to Nahor, Abraham's brother. [24]His concubine, whose name was Reumah, also bore children: Tebah, Gaham, Tahash, and Maacah.

Purchase of a Burial Plot. 23:1 The span of Sarah's life was one hundred and twenty-seven years. [2]She died in Kiriatharba—now Hebron—in the land of Canaan, and Abraham proceeded to mourn and weep for her. [3]Then he left the side of his deceased wife and addressed the Hittites: [4]"Although I am a resident alien among you, sell me from your holdings a burial place, that I may bury my deceased wife." [5]The Hittites answered Abraham: "Please, [6]sir, listen to us! You are a mighty leader among us. Bury your dead in the choicest of our burial sites. None of us would deny you his burial ground for the burial of your dead." [7]Abraham, however, proceeded to bow low before the people of the land, the Hittites, [8]and said to them: "If you will allow me room for burial of my dead, listen to me! Intercede for me with Ephron, son of Zohar, [9]so that he will sell me the cave of Machpelah that he owns; it is at the edge of his field. Let him sell it to me in your presence at its full price for a burial place."

[10]Now Ephron was sitting with the Hittites. So Ephron the Hittite replied to Abraham in the hearing of the Hittites, all who entered the gate of his city: [11]"Please, sir, listen to me! I give you both the field and the cave in it; in the presence of my people I give it to you. Bury your dead!" [12]But Abraham, after bowing low before the people of the land, [13]addressed Ephron in the hearing of these men: "If only you would please listen to me! I will pay you the price of the field. Accept it from me, that I may bury my dead there." [14]Ephron replied to Abraham, "Please, [15]sir, listen to me! A piece of land worth four hundred shekels of silver—what is that between you

and me? Bury your dead!" [16]Abraham accepted Ephron's terms; he weighed out to him the silver that Ephron had stipulated in the hearing of the Hittites, four hundred shekels of silver at the current market value.

[17]Thus Ephron's field in Machpelah, facing Mamre, together with its cave and all the trees anywhere within its limits, was conveyed [18]to Abraham by purchase in the presence of the Hittites, all who entered the gate of Ephron's city. [19]After this, Abraham buried his wife Sarah in the cave of the field of Machpelah, facing Mamre—now Hebron—in the land of Canaan. [20]Thus the field with its cave was transferred from the Hittites to Abraham as a burial place.

☐ MARK 4:1-25

The Parable of the Sower. 4:1 On another occasion he began to teach by the sea. A very large crowd gathered around him so that he got into a boat on the sea and sat down. And the whole crowd was beside the sea on land. [2]And he taught them at length in parables, and in the course of his instruction he said to them, [3]"Hear this! A sower went out to sow. [4]And as he sowed, some seed fell on the path, and the birds came and ate it up. [5]Other seed fell on rocky ground where it had little soil. It sprang up at once because the soil was not deep. [6]And when the sun rose, it was scorched and it withered for lack of roots. [7]Some seed fell among thorns, and the thorns grew up and choked it and it produced no grain. [8]And some seed fell on rich soil and produced fruit. It came up and grew and yielded thirty, sixty, and a hundredfold." [9]He added, "Whoever has ears to hear ought to hear."

The Purpose of the Parables. [10]And when he was alone, those present along with the Twelve questioned him about the parables. [11]He answered them, "The mystery of the kingdom of God has been granted to you. But to those outside everything comes in parables, [12]so that

'they may look and see but not perceive,
and hear and listen but not
understand,
in order that they may not be
converted and be forgiven.'"

[13]Jesus said to them, "Do you not understand this parable? Then how will you understand any of the parables? [14]The sower sows the word. [15]These are the ones on the path where the word is sown. As soon as they hear, Satan comes at once and takes away the word sown in them. [16]And these are the ones sown on rocky ground who, when they hear the word, receive it at once with joy. [17]But they have no root; they last only for a time. Then when tribulation or persecution comes because of the word, they quickly fall away. [18]Those sown among thorns are another sort. They are the people who hear the word, [19]but worldly anxiety, the lure of riches, and the craving for other things intrude and choke the word, and it bears no fruit. [20]But those sown on rich soil are the ones who hear the word and accept it and bear fruit thirty and sixty and a hundredfold."

Parable of the Lamp. [21]He said to them, "Is a lamp brought in to be placed under a bushel basket or under a bed, and not to be placed on a lampstand? [22]For there is nothing hidden except to be made visible; nothing is secret except to come to light. [23]Anyone who has ears to hear ought to hear." [24]He also told them, "Take care what you hear. The measure with which you measure will be measured out to you, and still more will be given to you. [25]To the one who has, more will be given; from the one who has not, even what he has will be taken away."

January 11

Just as you seek a virtuous, fair, and good spouse, it is fitting that you should be the same.

— St. Bernardine of Siena

☐ GENESIS 24-26

Isaac and Rebekah. 24:1 Abraham was old, having seen many days, and the Lord had blessed him in every way. ²Abraham said to the senior servant of his household, who had charge of all his possessions: "Put your hand under my thigh, ³and I will make you swear by the Lord, the God of heaven and the God of earth, that you will not take a wife for my son from the daughters of the Canaanites among whom I live, ⁴but that you will go to my own land and to my relatives to get a wife for my son Isaac." ⁵The servant asked him: "What if the woman is unwilling to follow me to this land? Should I then take your son back to the land from which you came?" ⁶Abraham told him, "Never take my son back there for any reason! The Lord, the God of heaven, who took me from my father's house and the land of my relatives, and who confirmed by oath the promise he made to me, 'I will give this land to your descendants'—he will send his angel before you, and you will get a wife for my son there. ⁸If the woman is unwilling to follow you, you will be released from this oath to me. But never take my son back there!" ⁹So the servant put his hand under the thigh of his master Abraham and swore to him concerning this matter.

¹⁰The servant then took ten of his master's camels, and bearing all kinds of gifts from his master, he made his way to the city of Nahor in Aram Naharaim. ¹¹Near evening, at the time when women go out to draw water, he made the camels kneel by the well outside the city. ¹²Then he said: "Lord, God of my master Abraham, let it turn out favorably for me today and thus deal graciously with my master Abraham. ¹³While I stand here at the spring and the daughters of the townspeople are coming out to draw water, ¹⁴if I say to a young woman, 'Please lower your jug, that I may drink,' and she answers, 'Drink, and I will water your camels, too,' then she is the one whom you have decided upon for your servant Isaac. In this way I will know that you have dealt graciously with my master."

¹⁵He had scarcely finished speaking when Rebekah—who was born to Bethuel, son of Milcah, the wife of Abraham's brother Nahor—came out with a jug on her shoulder. ¹⁶The young woman was very beautiful, a virgin, untouched by man. She went down to the spring and filled her jug. As she came up, ¹⁷the servant ran toward her and said, "Please give me a sip of water from your jug." ¹⁸"Drink, sir," she replied, and quickly lowering the jug into her hand, she gave him a drink. ¹⁹When she had finished giving him a drink, she said, "I will draw water for your camels, too, until they have finished drinking." ²⁰With that, she quickly emptied her jug into the drinking trough and ran back to the well to draw more water, until she had drawn enough for all the camels. ²¹The man watched her the whole time, silently waiting to learn whether or not the Lord had made his journey successful. ²²When the camels had finished drinking, the man took out a gold nose-ring weighing half a shekel, and two gold bracelets weighing ten shekels for her wrists. ²³Then he asked her: "Whose daughter are you? Tell me, please. And is

there a place in your father's house for us to spend the night?" [24]She answered: "I am the daughter of Bethuel the son of Milcah, whom she bore to Nahor. [25]We have plenty of straw and fodder," she added, "and also a place to spend the night." [26]The man then knelt and bowed down to the LORD, [27]saying: "Blessed be the LORD, the God of my master Abraham, who has not let his kindness and fidelity toward my master fail. As for me, the LORD has led me straight to the house of my master's brother."

[28]Then the young woman ran off and told her mother's household what had happened. [29]Now Rebekah had a brother named Laban. Laban rushed outside to the man at the spring. [30]When he saw the nose-ring and the bracelets on his sister's arms and when he heard Rebekah repeating what the man had said to her, he went to him while he was standing by the camels at the spring. [31]He said: "Come, blessed of the LORD! Why are you standing outside when I have made the house ready, as well as a place for the camels?" [32]The man then went inside; and while the camels were being unloaded and provided with straw and fodder, water was brought to bathe his feet and the feet of the men who were with him. [33]But when food was set before him, he said, "I will not eat until I have told my story." "Go ahead," they replied.

[34]"I am Abraham's servant," he began. [35]"The LORD has blessed my master so abundantly that he has become wealthy; he has given him flocks and herds, silver and gold, male and female slaves, and camels and donkeys. [36]My master's wife Sarah bore a son to my master in her old age, and he has given him everything he owns. [37]My master put me under oath, saying: 'You shall not take a wife for my son from the daughters of the Canaanites in whose land I live; [38]instead, you must go to my father's house, to my own family, to get a wife for my son.' [39]When I asked my master, 'What if the woman will not follow me?' [40]he re-

plied: 'The LORD, in whose presence I have always walked, will send his angel with you and make your journey successful, and so you will get a wife for my son from my own family and my father's house. [41]Then you will be freed from my curse. If you go to my family and they refuse you, then, too, you will be free from my curse.'

[42]"When I came to the spring today, I said: 'LORD, God of my master Abraham, please make successful the journey I am on. [43]While I stand here at the spring, if I say to a young woman who comes out to draw water, 'Please give me a little water from your jug,' [44]and she answers, 'Drink, and I will draw water for your camels, too—then she is the woman whom the LORD has decided upon for my master's son.'

[45]"I had scarcely finished saying this to myself when Rebekah came out with a jug on her shoulder. After she went down to the spring and drew water, I said to her, 'Please let me have a drink.' [46]She quickly lowered the jug she was carrying and said, 'Drink, and I will water your camels, too.' So I drank, and she watered the camels also. [47]When I asked her, 'Whose daughter are you?' she answered, 'The daughter of Bethuel, son of Nahor, borne to Nahor by Milcah.' So I put the ring on her nose and the bracelets on her wrists. [48]Then I knelt and bowed down to the LORD, blessing the LORD, the God of my master Abraham, who had led me on the right road to obtain the daughter of my master's kinsman for his son. [49]Now, if you will act with kindness and fidelity toward my master, let me know; but if not, let me know that too. I can then proceed accordingly."

[50]Laban and Bethuel said in reply: "This thing comes from the LORD; we can say nothing to you either for or against it. [51]Here is Rebekah, right in front of you; take her and go, that she may become the wife of your master's son, as the LORD has said." [52]When Abraham's servant heard their answer, he bowed to the ground

before the LORD. [53]Then he brought out objects of silver and gold and clothing and presented them to Rebekah; he also gave costly presents to her brother and mother. [54]After he and the men with him had eaten and drunk, they spent the night there.

When they got up the next morning, he said, "Allow me to return to my master." [55]Her brother and mother replied, "Let the young woman stay with us a short while, say ten days; after that she may go." [56]But he said to them, "Do not detain me, now that the LORD has made my journey successful; let me go back to my master." [57]They answered, "Let us call the young woman and see what she herself has to say about it." [58]So they called Rebekah and asked her, "Will you go with this man?" She answered, "I will." [59]At this they sent off their sister Rebekah and her nurse with Abraham's servant and his men. [60]They blessed Rebekah and said:

"Sister, may you grow
 into thousands of myriads;
And may your descendants gain
 possession
of the gates of their enemies!"

[61]Then Rebekah and her attendants started out; they mounted the camels and followed the man. So the servant took Rebekah and went on his way.

[62]Meanwhile Isaac had gone from Beer-lahai-roi and was living in the region of the Negeb. [63]One day toward evening he went out to walk in the field, and caught sight of camels approaching. [64]Rebekah, too, caught sight of Isaac, and got down from her camel. [65]She asked the servant, "Who is the man over there, walking through the fields toward us?" "That is my master," replied the servant. Then she took her veil and covered herself.

[66]The servant recounted to Isaac all the things he had done. [67]Then Isaac brought Rebekah into the tent of his mother Sarah. He took Rebekah as his wife. Isaac loved her and found solace after the death of his mother.

Abraham's Sons by Keturah. 25:1 Abraham took another wife, whose name was Keturah. [2]She bore him Zimran, Jokshan, Medan, Midian, Ishbak, and Shuah. [3]Jokshan became the father of Sheba and Dedan. The descendants of Dedan were the Asshurim, the Letushim, and the Leummim. [4]The descendants of Midian were Ephah, Epher, Hanoch, Abida, and Eldaah. All of these were descendants of Keturah.

[5]Abraham gave everything that he owned to his son Isaac. [6]To the sons of his concubines, however, he gave gifts while he was still living, as he sent them away eastward, to the land of Kedem, away from his son Isaac.

Death of Abraham. [7]The whole span of Abraham's life was one hundred and seventy-five years. [8]Then he breathed his last, dying at a ripe old age, grown old after a full life; and he was gathered to his people. [9]His sons Isaac and Ishmael buried him in the cave of Machpelah, in the field of Ephron, son of Zohar the Hittite, which faces Mamre, [10]the field that Abraham had bought from the Hittites; there he was buried next to his wife Sarah. [11]After the death of Abraham, God blessed his son Isaac, who lived near Beer-lahai-roi.

Descendants of Ishmael. [12]These are the descendants of Abraham's son Ishmael, whom Hagar the Egyptian, Sarah's slave, bore to Abraham. [13]These are the names of Ishmael's sons, listed in the order of their birth: Ishmael's firstborn Nebaioth, Kedar, Adbeel, Mibsam, [14]Mishma, Dumah, Massa, [15]Hadad, Tema, Jetur, Naphish, and Kedemah. [16]These are the sons of Ishmael, their names by their villages and encampments; twelve chieftains of as many tribal groups.

[17]The span of Ishmael's life was one hundred and thirty-seven years. After he had breathed his last and died, he was gathered

to his people. [18]The Ishmaelites ranged from Havilah, by Shur, which is on the border of Egypt, all the way to Asshur; and they pitched camp alongside their various kindred.

Birth of Esau and Jacob. [19]These are the descendants of Isaac, son of Abraham; Abraham begot Isaac. [20]Isaac was forty years old when he married Rebekah, the daughter of Bethuel the Aramean of Paddan-aram and the sister of Laban the Aramean. [21]Isaac entreated the LORD on behalf of his wife, since she was sterile. The LORD heard his entreaty, and his wife Rebekah became pregnant. [22]But the children jostled each other in the womb so much that she exclaimed, "If it is like this, why go on living!" She went to consult the LORD, [23]and the LORD answered her:

Two nations are in your womb,
two peoples are separating while still
within you;
But one will be stronger than the other,
and the older will serve the younger.

[24]When the time of her delivery came, there were twins in her womb. [25]The first to emerge was reddish, and his whole body was like a hairy mantle; so they named him Esau. [26]Next his brother came out, gripping Esau's heel; so he was named Jacob. Isaac was sixty years old when they were born.

[27]When the boys grew up, Esau became a skillful hunter, a man of the open country; whereas Jacob was a simple man, who stayed among the tents. [28]Isaac preferred Esau, because he was fond of game; but Rebekah preferred Jacob. [29]Once, when Jacob was cooking a stew, Esau came in from the open country, famished. [30]He said to Jacob, "Let me gulp down some of that red stuff; I am famished." That is why he was called Edom. [31]But Jacob replied, "First sell me your right as firstborn." [32]"Look," said Esau, "I am on the point of dying. What good is the right as firstborn to me?" [33]But Jacob said, "Swear to me first!" So he sold Jacob his right as firstborn under oath. [34]Jacob then gave him some bread and the lentil stew; and Esau ate, drank, got up, and went his way. So Esau treated his right as firstborn with disdain.

Isaac and Abimelech. 26:1 There was a famine in the land, distinct from the earlier one that had occurred in the days of Abraham, and Isaac went down to Abimelech, king of the Philistines in Gerar. [2]The LORD appeared to him and said: Do not go down to Egypt, but camp in this land wherever I tell you. [3]Sojourn in this land, and I will be with you and bless you; for to you and your descendants I will give all these lands, in fulfillment of the oath that I swore to your father Abraham. [4]I will make your descendants as numerous as the stars in the sky, and I will give them all these lands, and in your descendants all the nations of the earth will find blessing— [5]this because Abraham obeyed me, keeping my mandate, my commandments, my ordinances, and my instructions.

[6]So Isaac settled in Gerar. [7]When the men of the place asked questions about his wife, he answered, "She is my sister." He was afraid that, if he called her his wife, the men of the place would kill him on account of Rebekah, since she was beautiful. [8]But when they had been there for a long time, Abimelech, king of the Philistines, looked out of a window and saw Isaac fondling his wife Rebekah. [9]He called for Isaac and said: "She must certainly be your wife! How could you have said, 'She is my sister'?" Isaac replied, "I thought I might lose my life on her account." [10]"How could you have done this to us!" exclaimed Abimelech. "It would have taken very little for one of the people to lie with your wife, and so you would have brought guilt upon us!" [11]Abimelech then commanded all the people: "Anyone who maltreats this man or his wife shall be put to death."

¹²Isaac sowed a crop in that region and reaped a hundredfold the same year. Since the LORD blessed him, ¹³he became richer and richer all the time, until he was very wealthy. ¹⁴He acquired flocks and herds, and a great work force, and so the Philistines became envious of him. ¹⁵The Philistines had stopped up and filled with dirt all the wells that his father's servants had dug back in the days of his father Abraham. ¹⁶So Abimelech said to Isaac, "Go away from us; you have become far too numerous for us." ¹⁷Isaac left there and camped in the Wadi Gerar where he stayed. ¹⁸Isaac reopened the wells which his father's servants had dug back in the days of his father Abraham and which the Philistines had stopped up after Abraham's death; he gave them names like those that his father had given them. ¹⁹But when Isaac's servants dug in the wadi and reached spring water in their well, ²⁰the shepherds of Gerar argued with Isaac's shepherds, saying, "The water belongs to us!" So he named the well Esek, because they had quarreled there. ²¹Then they dug another well, and they argued over that one too; so he named it Sitnah. ²²So he moved on from there and dug still another well, but over this one they did not argue. He named it Rehoboth, and said, "Because the LORD has now given us ample room, we shall flourish in the land."

²³From there Isaac went up to Beer-sheba. ²⁴The same night the LORD appeared to him and said: I am the God of Abraham, your father. Do not fear, for I am with you.

I will bless you and multiply your descendants for the sake of Abraham, my servant. ²⁵So Isaac built an altar there and invoked the LORD by name. After he had pitched his tent there, Isaac's servants began to dig a well nearby.

²⁶Then Abimelech came to him from Gerar, with Ahuzzath, his councilor, and Phicol, the general of his army. ²⁷Isaac asked them, "Why have you come to me, since you hate me and have driven me away from you?" ²⁸They answered: "We clearly see that the LORD has been with you, so we thought: let there be a sworn agreement between our two sides—between you and us. Let us make a covenant with you: ²⁹you shall do no harm to us, just as we have not maltreated you, but have always acted kindly toward you and have let you depart in peace. So now, may you be blessed by the LORD!" ³⁰Isaac then made a feast for them, and they ate and drank. ³¹Early the next morning they exchanged oaths. Then Isaac sent them on their way, and they departed from him in peace.

³²That same day Isaac's servants came and informed him about the well they had been digging; they told him, "We have reached water!" ³³He called it Shibah; hence the name of the city is Beer-sheba to this day. ³⁴When Esau was forty years old, he married Judith, daughter of Beeri the Hittite, and Basemath, daughter of Elon the Hivite. ³⁵But they became a source of bitterness to Isaac and Rebekah.

☐ MARK 4:26-34

Seed Grows of Itself. 4:26 He said, "This is how it is with the kingdom of God; it is as if a man were to scatter seed on the land ²⁷and would sleep and rise night and day and the seed would sprout and grow, he knows not how. ²⁸Of its own accord the land yields fruit, first the blade, then the ear, then the full grain in the ear. ²⁹And when the grain is ripe, he wields the sickle at once, for the harvest has come."

The Mustard Seed. ³⁰He said, "To what shall we compare the kingdom of God, or what parable can we use for it? ³¹It is like a mustard seed that, when it is sown in the ground, is the smallest of all the seeds on the earth. ³²But once it is sown, it springs up and becomes the largest of plants and puts forth large branches, so that the birds of the sky can dwell in its shade." ³³With

many such parables he spoke the word to them as they were able to understand it. ³⁴Without parables he did not speak to them, but to his own disciples he explained everything in private.

January 12

St. Margaret Bourgeoys

Our Lady's love is like a stream that has its source in the Eternal Fountains, quenches the thirst of all, can never be drained, and ever flows back to its Source.

— St. Margaret Bourgeoys

☐ GENESIS 27-28

Jacob's Deception. 27:1 When Isaac was so old that his eyesight had failed him, he called his older son Esau and said to him, "My son!" "Here I am!" he replied. ²Isaac then said, "Now I have grown old. I do not know when I might die. ³So now take your hunting gear—your quiver and bow—and go out into the open country to hunt some game for me. ⁴Then prepare for me a dish in the way I like, and bring it to me to eat, so that I may bless you before I die."

⁵Rebekah had been listening while Isaac was speaking to his son Esau. So when Esau went out into the open country to hunt some game for his father, ⁶Rebekah said to her son Jacob, "Listen! I heard your father tell your brother Esau, ⁷'Bring me some game and prepare a dish for me to eat, that I may bless you with the LORD's approval before I die.' ⁸Now, my son, obey me in what I am about to order you. ⁹Go to the flock and get me two choice young goats so that with these I might prepare a dish for your father in the way he likes. ¹⁰Then bring it to your father to eat, that he may bless you before he dies." ¹¹But Jacob said to his mother Rebekah, "But my brother Esau is a hairy man and I am

smooth-skinned! ¹²Suppose my father feels me? He will think I am making fun of him, and I will bring on myself a curse instead of a blessing." ¹³His mother, however, replied: "Let any curse against you, my son, fall on me! Just obey me. Go and get me the young goats."

¹⁴So Jacob went and got them and brought them to his mother, and she prepared a dish in the way his father liked. ¹⁵Rebekah then took the best clothes of her older son Esau that she had in the house, and gave them to her younger son Jacob to wear; ¹⁶and with the goatskins she covered up his hands and the hairless part of his neck. ¹⁷Then she gave her son Jacob the dish and the bread she had prepared.

¹⁸Going to his father, Jacob said, "Father!" "Yes?" replied Isaac. "Which of my sons are you?" ¹⁹Jacob answered his father: "I am Esau, your firstborn. I did as you told me. Please sit up and eat some of my game, so that you may bless me." ²⁰But Isaac said to his son, "How did you get it so quickly, my son?" He answered, "The LORD, your God, directed me." ²¹Isaac then said to Jacob, "Come closer, my son, that I may feel you, to learn whether you really are my son

Esau or not." [22]So Jacob moved up closer to his father. When Isaac felt him, he said, "Although the voice is Jacob's, the hands are Esau's." [23](He failed to identify him because his hands were hairy, like those of his brother Esau; so he blessed him.) [24]Again Isaac said, "Are you really my son Esau?" And Jacob said, "I am." [25]Then Isaac said, "Serve me, my son, and let me eat of the game so that I may bless you." Jacob served it to him, and Isaac ate; he brought him wine, and he drank. [26]Finally his father Isaac said to him, "Come closer, my son, and kiss me." [27]As Jacob went up to kiss him, Isaac smelled the fragrance of his clothes. With that, he blessed him, saying,

> "Ah, the fragrance of my son
> is like the fragrance of a field
> that the LORD has blessed!
> [28]May God give to you
> of the dew of the heavens
> And of the fertility of the earth
> abundance of grain and wine.
> [29]May peoples serve you,
> and nations bow down to you;
> Be master of your brothers,
> and may your mother's sons bow
> down to you.
> Cursed be those who curse you,
> and blessed be those who bless you."

[30]Jacob had scarcely left his father after Isaac had finished blessing him, when his brother Esau came back from his hunt. [31]Then he too prepared a dish, and bringing it to his father, he said, "Let my father sit up and eat some of his son's game, that you may then give me your blessing." [32]His father Isaac asked him, "Who are you?" He said, "I am your son, your firstborn son, Esau." [33]Isaac trembled greatly. "Who was it, then," he asked, "that hunted game and brought it to me? I ate it all just before you came, and I blessed him. Now he is blessed!" [34]As he heard his father's words, Esau burst into loud, bitter sobbing and said, "Father, bless me too!" [35]When Isaac said, "Your

brother came here by a ruse and carried off your blessing," [36]Esau exclaimed, "He is well named Jacob, is he not! He has supplanted me twice! First he took away my right as firstborn, and now he has taken away my blessing." Then he said, "Have you not saved a blessing for me?" [37]Isaac replied to Esau: "I have already appointed him your master, and I have assigned to him all his kindred as his servants; besides, I have sustained him with grain and wine. What then can I do for you, my son?" [38]But Esau said to his father, "Have you only one blessing, father? Bless me too, father!" and Esau wept aloud. [39]His father Isaac said in response:

> "See, far from the fertile earth
> will be your dwelling;
> far from the dew of the heavens
> above!
> [40]By your sword you will live,
> and your brother you will serve;
> But when you become restless,
> you will throw off his yoke from
> your neck."

[41]Esau bore a grudge against Jacob because of the blessing his father had given him. Esau said to himself, "Let the time of mourning for my father come, so that I may kill my brother Jacob." [42]When Rebekah got news of what her older son Esau had in mind, she summoned her younger son Jacob and said to him: "Listen! Your brother Esau intends to get his revenge by killing you. [43]So now, my son, obey me: flee at once to my brother Laban in Haran, [44]and stay with him a while until your brother's fury subsides— [45]until your brother's anger against you subsides and he forgets what you did to him. Then I will send for you and bring you back. Why should I lose both of you in a single day?"

Jacob Sent to Laban. [46]Rebekah said to Isaac: "I am disgusted with life because of the Hittite women. If Jacob also should marry a Hittite woman, a native of the land, like these women, why should I live?"

28:1 Isaac therefore summoned Jacob and blessed him, charging him: "You shall not marry a Canaanite woman! ²Go now to Paddan-aram, to the home of your mother's father Bethuel, and there choose a wife for yourself from among the daughters of Laban, your mother's brother. ³May God Almighty bless you and make you fertile, multiply you that you may become an assembly of peoples. ⁴May God extend to you and your descendants the blessing of Abraham, so that you may gain possession of the land where you are residing, which he assigned to Abraham." ⁵Then Isaac sent Jacob on his way; he went to Paddan-aram, to Laban, son of Bethuel the Aramean, and brother of Rebekah, the mother of Jacob and Esau.

⁶Esau noted that Isaac had blessed Jacob when he sent him to Paddan-aram to get himself a wife there, and that, as he gave him his blessing, he charged him, "You shall not marry a Canaanite woman," ⁷and that Jacob had obeyed his father and mother and gone to Paddan-aram. ⁸Esau realized how displeasing the Canaanite women were to his father Isaac, ⁹so Esau went to Ishmael, and in addition to the wives he had, married Mahalath, the daughter of Abraham's son Ishmael and sister of Nebaioth.

Jacob's Dream at Bethel. ¹⁰Jacob departed from Beer-sheba and proceeded toward Haran. ¹¹When he came upon a certain place, he stopped there for the night, since the sun had already set. Taking one of the stones at the place, he put it under his head and lay down in that place.

□ MARK 4:35-41

The Calming of a Storm at Sea. 4:35 On that day, as evening drew on, he said to them, "Let us cross to the other side." ³⁶Leaving the crowd, they took him with them in the boat just as he was. And other boats were with him. ³⁷A violent squall

¹²Then he had a dream: a stairway rested on the ground, with its top reaching to the heavens; and God's angels were going up and down on it. ¹³And there was the LORD standing beside him and saying: I am the LORD, the God of Abraham your father and the God of Isaac; the land on which you are lying I will give to you and your descendants. ¹⁴Your descendants will be like the dust of the earth, and through them you will spread to the west and the east, to the north and the south. In you and your descendants all the families of the earth will find blessing. ¹⁵I am with you and will protect you wherever you go, and bring you back to this land. I will never leave you until I have done what I promised you.

¹⁶When Jacob awoke from his sleep, he said, "Truly, the LORD is in this place and I did not know it!" ¹⁷He was afraid and said: "How awesome this place is! This is nothing else but the house of God, the gateway to heaven!" ¹⁸Early the next morning Jacob took the stone that he had put under his head, set it up as a sacred pillar, and poured oil on top of it. ¹⁹He named that place Bethel, whereas the former name of the town had been Luz.

²⁰Jacob then made this vow: "If God will be with me and protect me on this journey I am making and give me food to eat and clothes to wear, ²¹and I come back safely to my father's house, the LORD will be my God. ²²This stone that I have set up as a sacred pillar will be the house of God. Of everything you give me, I will return a tenth part to you without fail."

came up and waves were breaking over the boat, so that it was already filling up. ³⁸Jesus was in the stern, asleep on a cushion. They woke him and said to him, "Teacher, do you not care that we are perishing?" ³⁹He woke up, rebuked the wind, and said to the sea, "Quiet! Be still!" The wind ceased and there was great calm. [40]Then he asked them, "Why are you terrified? Do you not yet have faith?" [41]They were filled with great awe and said to one another, "Who then is this whom even wind and sea obey?"

January 13

St. Hilary of Poitiers

It is the peculiar property of the Church that when she is buffeted, she is triumphant; when she is assaulted with argument, she proves herself in the right; when she is deserted by her supporters, she holds the field.

— St. Hilary of Poitiers

☐ GENESIS 29-30

Arrival in Haran. 29:1 After Jacob resumed his journey, he came to the land of the Kedemites. [2]Looking about, he saw a well in the open country, with three flocks of sheep huddled near it, for flocks were watered from that well. A large stone covered the mouth of the well. [3]When all the shepherds were assembled there they would roll the stone away from the mouth of the well and water the sheep. Then they would put the stone back again in its place over the mouth of the well.

[4]Jacob said to them, "My brothers, where are you from?" "We are from Haran," they replied. [5]Then he asked them, "Do you know Laban, son of Nahor?" "We do," they answered. [6]He inquired further, "Is he well?" "He is," they answered; "and here comes his daughter Rachel with the sheep." [7]Then he said: "There is still much daylight left; it is hardly the time to bring the animals home. Water the sheep, and then continue pasturing them." [8]They replied, "We cannot until all the shepherds are here to roll the stone away from the mouth of the well; then can we water the flocks."

[9]While he was still talking with them, Rachel arrived with her father's sheep, for she was the one who tended them. [10]As soon as Jacob saw Rachel, the daughter of his mother's brother Laban, and the sheep of Laban, he went up, rolled the stone away from the mouth of the well, and watered Laban's sheep. [11]Then Jacob kissed Rachel and wept aloud. [12]Jacob told Rachel that he was her father's relative, Rebekah's son. So she ran to tell her father. [13]When Laban heard the news about Jacob, his sister's son, he ran to meet him. After embracing and kissing him, he brought him to his house. Jacob then repeated to Laban all these things, [14]and Laban said to him, "You are indeed my bone and my flesh."

Marriage to Leah and Rachel. After Jacob had stayed with him a full month, [15]Laban said to him: "Should you serve me for nothing just because you are a relative of mine? Tell me what your wages should be." [16]Now Laban had two daughters; the older was called Leah, the younger Rachel. [17]Leah had dull eyes, but Rachel was shapely and beautiful. [18]Because Jacob loved Rachel, he answered, "I will serve you seven years for your younger daughter Rachel." [19]Laban replied, "It is better to give her to you than to another man. Stay with me." ²⁰So Jacob served seven years for Rachel, yet they seemed to him like a few days because of his love for her.

²¹Then Jacob said to Laban, "Give me my wife, that I may consummate my marriage with her, for my term is now completed." ²²So Laban invited all the local inhabitants and gave a banquet. ²³At nightfall he took his daughter Leah and brought her to Jacob, and he consummated the marriage with her. ²⁴Laban assigned his maidservant Zilpah to his daughter Leah as her maidservant. ²⁵In the morning, there was Leah! So Jacob said to Laban: "How could you do this to me! Was it not for Rachel that I served you? Why did you deceive me?" ²⁶Laban replied, "It is not the custom in our country to give the younger daughter before the firstborn. ²⁷Finish the bridal week for this one, and then the other will also be given to you in return for another seven years of service with me."

²⁸Jacob did so. He finished the bridal week for the one, and then Laban gave him his daughter Rachel as a wife. ²⁹Laban assigned his maidservant Bilhah to his daughter Rachel as her maidservant. ³⁰Jacob then consummated his marriage with Rachel also, and he loved her more than Leah. Thus he served Laban another seven years.

Jacob's Children. ³¹When the LORD saw that Leah was unloved, he made her fruitful, while Rachel was barren. ³²Leah conceived and bore a son, and she named him Reuben; for she said, "It means, 'The LORD saw my misery; surely now my husband will love me.'" ³³She conceived again and bore a son, and said, "It means, 'The LORD heard that I was unloved,' and therefore he has given me this one also"; so she named him Simeon. ³⁴Again she conceived and bore a son, and she said, "Now at last my husband will become attached to me, since I have now borne him three sons"; that is why she named him Levi. ³⁵Once more she conceived and bore a son, and she said, "This time I will give thanks to the

LORD"; therefore she named him Judah. Then she stopped bearing children.

30:1 When Rachel saw that she had not borne children to Jacob, she became envious of her sister. She said to Jacob, "Give me children or I shall die!" ²Jacob became angry with Rachel and said, "Can I take the place of God, who has denied you the fruit of the womb?" ³She replied, "Here is my maidservant Bilhah. Have intercourse with her, and let her give birth on my knees, so that I too may have children through her." ⁴So she gave him her maidservant Bilhah as wife, and Jacob had intercourse with her. ⁵When Bilhah conceived and bore a son for Jacob, ⁶Rachel said, "God has vindicated me; indeed he has heeded my plea and given me a son." Therefore she named him Dan. ⁷Rachel's maidservant Bilhah conceived again and bore a second son for Jacob, ⁸and Rachel said, "I have wrestled strenuously with my sister, and I have prevailed." So she named him Naphtali.

⁹When Leah saw that she had ceased to bear children, she took her maidservant Zilpah and gave her to Jacob as wife. ¹⁰So Leah's maidservant Zilpah bore a son for Jacob. ¹¹Leah then said, "What good luck!" So she named him Gad. ¹²Then Leah's maidservant Zilpah bore a second son to Jacob; ¹³and Leah said, "What good fortune, because women will call me fortunate!" So she named him Asher.

¹⁴One day, during the wheat harvest, Reuben went out and came upon some mandrakes in the field which he brought home to his mother Leah. Rachel said to Leah, "Please give me some of your son's mandrakes." ¹⁵Leah replied, "Was it not enough for you to take away my husband, that you must now take my son's mandrakes too?" Rachel answered, "In that case Jacob may lie with you tonight in exchange for your son's mandrakes." ¹⁶That evening, when Jacob came in from the field, Leah went out to meet him. She said, "You must

have intercourse with me, because I have hired you with my son's mandrakes." So that night he lay with her, [17]and God listened to Leah; she conceived and bore a fifth son to Jacob. [18]Leah then said, "God has given me my wages for giving my maidservant to my husband"; so she named him Issachar. [19]Leah conceived again and bore a sixth son to Jacob; [20]and Leah said, "God has brought me a precious gift. This time my husband will honor me, because I have borne him six sons"; so she named him Zebulun. [21]Afterwards she gave birth to a daughter, and she named her Dinah.

[22]Then God remembered Rachel. God listened to her and made her fruitful. [23]She conceived and bore a son, and she said, "God has removed my disgrace." [24]She named him Joseph, saying, "May the LORD add another son for me!"

Jacob Outwits Laban. [25]After Rachel gave birth to Joseph, Jacob said to Laban: "Allow me to go to my own region and land. [26]Give me my wives and my children for whom I served you and let me go, for you know the service that I rendered you." [27]Laban answered him: "If you will please! I have learned through divination that the LORD has blessed me because of you." [28]He continued, "State the wages I owe you, and I will pay them." [29]Jacob replied: "You know what work I did for you and how well your livestock fared under my care; [30]the little you had before I came has grown into an abundance, since the LORD has blessed you in my company. Now, when can I do something for my own household as well?" [31]Laban asked, "What should I give you?" Jacob answered: "You do not have to give me anything. If you do this thing for me, I will again pasture and tend your sheep. [32]Let me go through your whole flock today and remove from it every dark animal among the lambs and every spotted or speckled one among the goats. These will be my wages. [33]In the future, whenever you check on my wages, my honesty will testify for me: any animal that is not speckled or spotted among the goats, or dark among the lambs, got into my possession by theft!" [34]Laban said, "Very well. Let it be as you say."

[35]That same day Laban removed the streaked and spotted he-goats and all the speckled and spotted she-goats, all those with some white on them, as well as every dark lamb, and he put them in the care of his sons. [36]Then he put a three days' journey between himself and Jacob, while Jacob was pasturing the rest of Laban's flock.

[37]Jacob, however, got some fresh shoots of poplar, almond and plane trees, and he peeled white stripes in them by laying bare the white core of the shoots. [38]The shoots that he had peeled he then set upright in the watering troughs where the animals came to drink, so that they would be in front of them. When the animals were in heat as they came to drink, [39]the goats mated by the shoots, and so they gave birth to streaked, speckled and spotted young. [40]The sheep, on the other hand, Jacob kept apart, and he made these animals face the streaked or completely dark animals of Laban. Thus he produced flocks of his own, which he did not put with Laban's flock. [41]Whenever the hardier animals were in heat, Jacob would set the shoots in the troughs in full view of these animals, so that they mated by the shoots; [42]but with the weaker animals he would not put the shoots there. So the feeble animals would go to Laban, but the hardy ones to Jacob. [43]So the man grew exceedingly prosperous, and he owned large flocks, male and female servants, camels, and donkeys.

☐ MARK 5:1-20

The Healing of the Gerasene Demoniac.
5:1 They came to the other side of the sea, to the territory of the Gerasenes. [2]When he got out of the boat, at once a man from the tombs who had an unclean spirit met him. [3]The man had been dwelling among the tombs, and no one could restrain him any longer, even with a chain. [4]In fact, he had frequently been bound with shackles and chains, but the chains had been pulled apart by him and the shackles smashed, and no one was strong enough to subdue him. [5]Night and day among the tombs and on the hillsides he was always crying out and bruising himself with stones. [6]Catching sight of Jesus from a distance, he ran up and prostrated himself before him, [7]crying out in a loud voice, "What have you to do with me, Jesus, Son of the Most High God? I adjure you by God, do not torment me!" [8](He had been saying to him, "Unclean spirit, come out of the man!") [9]He asked him, "What is your name?" He replied, "Legion is my name. There are many of us." [10]And he pleaded earnestly with him not to drive them away from that territory. [11]Now a large herd of swine was feeding there on the hillside. [12]And they pleaded with him, "Send us into the swine. Let us enter them." [13]And he let them, and the unclean spirits came out and entered the swine. The herd of about two thousand rushed down a steep bank into the sea, where they were drowned. [14]The swineherds ran away and reported the incident in the town and throughout the countryside. And people came out to see what had happened. [15]As they approached Jesus, they caught sight of the man who had been possessed by Legion, sitting there clothed and in his right mind. And they were seized with fear. [16]Those who witnessed the incident explained to them what had happened to the possessed man and to the swine. [17]Then they began to beg him to leave their district. [18]As he was getting into the boat, the man who had been possessed pleaded to remain with him. [19]But he would not permit him but told him instead, "Go home to your family and announce to them all that the Lord in his pity has done for you." [20]Then the man went off and began to proclaim in the Decapolis what Jesus had done for him; and all were amazed.

January 14

Don't you know that only those who are thoughtless and crazy consider the faithful departed to be dead?

— St. John Eudes

☐ GENESIS 31-32

Flight from Laban. 31:1 Jacob heard that Laban's sons were saying, "Jacob has taken everything that belonged to our father, and he has produced all this wealth from our father's property." [2]Jacob perceived, too, that Laban's attitude toward him was not what it had previously been. [3]Then the LORD said to Jacob: Return to the land of your ancestors, where you were born, and I will be with you.

[4]So Jacob sent for Rachel and Leah to meet him in the field where his flock was.

[5]There he said to them: "I have noticed that your father's attitude toward me is not as it was in the past; but the God of my father has been with me. [6]You know well that with all my strength I served your father; [7]yet your father cheated me and changed my wages ten times. God, however, did not let him do me any harm. [8]Whenever your father said, 'The speckled animals will be your wages,' the entire flock would bear speckled young; whenever he said, 'The streaked animals will be your wages,' the entire flock would bear streaked young. [9]So God took away your father's livestock and gave it to me. [10]Once, during the flock's mating season, I had a dream in which I saw he-goats mating that were streaked, speckled and mottled. [11]In the dream God's angel said to me, 'Jacob!' and I replied, 'Here I am!' [12]Then he said: 'Look up and see. All the he-goats that are mating are streaked, speckled and mottled, for I have seen all the things that Laban has been doing to you. [13]I am the God of Bethel, where you anointed a sacred pillar and made a vow to me. Get up now! Leave this land and return to the land of your birth.'"

[14]Rachel and Leah answered him: "Do we still have an heir's portion in our father's house? [15]Are we not regarded by him as outsiders? He not only sold us; he has even used up the money that he got for us! [16]All the wealth that God took away from our father really belongs to us and our children. So do whatever God has told you." [17]Jacob proceeded to put his children and wives on camels, [18]and he drove off all his livestock and all the property he had acquired in Paddan-aram, to go to his father Isaac in the land of Canaan.

[19]Now Laban was away shearing his sheep, and Rachel had stolen her father's household images. [20]Jacob had hoodwinked Laban the Aramean by not telling him that he was going to flee. [21]Thus he fled with all that he had. Once he was across the Euphrates, he headed for the hill country of Gilead.

[22]On the third day, word came to Laban that Jacob had fled. [23]Taking his kinsmen with him, he pursued him for seven days until he caught up with him in the hill country of Gilead. [24]But that night God appeared to Laban the Aramean in a dream and said to him: Take care not to say anything to Jacob.

Jacob and Laban in Gilead. [25]When Laban overtook Jacob, Jacob's tents were pitched in the hill country; Laban also pitched his tents in the hill country of Gilead. [26]Laban said to Jacob, "How could you hoodwink me and carry off my daughters like prisoners of war? [27]Why did you dupe me by stealing away secretly? You did not tell me! I would have sent you off with joyful singing to the sound of tambourines and harps. [28]You did not even allow me a parting kiss to my daughters and grandchildren! Now what you have done makes no sense. [29]I have it in my power to harm all of you; but last night the God of your father said to me, 'Take care not to say anything to Jacob!' [30]Granted that you had to leave because you were longing for your father's house, why did you steal my gods?" [31]Jacob replied to Laban, "I was frightened at the thought that you might take your daughters away from me by force. [32]As for your gods, the one you find them with shall not remain alive! If, with our kinsmen looking on, you identify anything here as belonging to you, take it." Jacob had no idea that Rachel had stolen the household images.

[33]Laban then went in and searched Jacob's tent and Leah's tent, as well as the tents of the two maidservants; but he did not find them. Leaving Leah's tent, he went into Rachel's. [34]Meanwhile Rachel had taken the household images, put them inside the camel's saddlebag, and seated herself upon them. When Laban had rummaged through her whole tent without finding them, [35]she said to her father, "Do not let my lord be angry that I cannot rise in your presence; I am having my period."

So, despite his search, he did not find the household images.

[36]Jacob, now angered, confronted Laban and demanded, "What crime or offense have I committed that you should hound me? [37]Now that you have rummaged through all my things, what have you found from your household belongings? Produce it here before your kinsmen and mine, and let them decide between the two of us.

[38]"In the twenty years that I was under you, no ewe or she-goat of yours ever miscarried, and I have never eaten rams of your flock. [39]I never brought you an animal torn by wild beasts; I made good the loss myself. You held me responsible for anything stolen by day or night. [40]Often the scorching heat devoured me by day, and the frost by night, while sleep fled from my eyes! [41]Of the twenty years that I have now spent in your household, I served you fourteen years for your two daughters and six years for your flock, while you changed my wages ten times. [42]If the God of my father, the God of Abraham and the Fear of Isaac, had not been on my side, you would now have sent me away empty-handed. But God saw my plight and the fruits of my toil, and last night he reproached you."

[43]Laban replied to Jacob: "The daughters are mine, their children are mine, and the flocks are mine; everything you see belongs to me. What can I do now for my own daughters and for the children they have borne? [44]Come, now, let us make a covenant, you and I; and it will be a treaty between you and me."

[45]Then Jacob took a stone and set it up as a sacred pillar. [46]Jacob said to his kinsmen, "Gather stones." So they got stones and made a mound; and they ate there at the mound. [47]Laban called it Jegar-sahadutha, but Jacob called it Galeed. [48]Laban said, "This mound will be a witness from now on between you and me." That is why it was named Galeed— [49]and also Mizpah, for he said: "May the LORD keep watch between you and me when we are out of each other's sight. [50]If you mistreat my daughters, or take other wives besides my daughters, know that even though no one else is there, God will be a witness between you and me."

[51]Laban said further to Jacob: "Here is this mound, and here is the sacred pillar that I have set up between you and me. [52]This mound will be a witness, and this sacred pillar will be a witness, that, with hostile intent, I may not pass beyond this mound into your territory, nor may you pass beyond it into mine. [53]May the God of Abraham and the God of Nahor, the God of their father, judge between us!" Jacob took the oath by the Fear of his father Isaac. [54]He then offered a sacrifice on the mountain and invited his kinsmen to share in the meal. When they had eaten, they passed the night on the mountain.

32:1 Early the next morning, Laban kissed his grandchildren and his daughters and blessed them; then he set out on his journey back home. [2]Meanwhile Jacob continued on his own way, and God's angels encountered him. [3]When Jacob saw them he said, "This is God's encampment." So he named that place Mahanaim.

Envoys to Esau. [4]Jacob sent messengers ahead to his brother Esau in the land of Seir, the country of Edom, [5]ordering them: "Thus you shall say to my lord Esau: 'Thus says your servant Jacob: I have been residing with Laban and have been delayed until now. [6]I own oxen, donkeys and sheep, as well as male and female servants. I have sent my lord this message in the hope of gaining your favor.'" [7]When the messengers returned to Jacob, they said, "We found your brother Esau. He is now coming to meet you, and four hundred men are with him."

[8]Jacob was very much frightened. In his anxiety, he divided the people who were with him, as well as his flocks, herds and camels, into two camps. [9]"If Esau should come and attack one camp," he reasoned,

"the remaining camp may still escape." [10]Then Jacob prayed: "God of my father Abraham and God of my father Isaac! You, LORD, who said to me, 'Go back to your land and your relatives, and I will be good to you.' [11]I am unworthy of all the acts of kindness and faithfulness that you have performed for your servant: although I crossed the Jordan here with nothing but my staff, I have now grown into two camps. [12]Save me from the hand of my brother, from the hand of Esau! Otherwise I fear that he will come and strike me down and the mothers with the children. [13]You yourself said, 'I will be very good to you, and I will make your descendants like the sands of the sea, which are too numerous to count.'"

[14]After passing the night there, Jacob selected from what he had with him a present for his brother Esau: [15]two hundred she-goats and twenty he-goats; two hundred ewes and twenty rams; [16]thirty female camels and their young; forty cows and ten bulls; twenty female donkeys and ten male donkeys. [17]He put these animals in the care of his servants, in separate herds, and he told the servants, "Go on ahead of me, but keep some space between the herds." [18]He ordered the servant in the lead, "When my brother Esau meets you and asks, 'To whom do you belong? Where are you going? To whom do these animals ahead of you belong?' [19]tell him, 'To your servant Jacob, but they have been sent as a gift to my lord Esau. Jacob himself is right behind us.'" [20]He also ordered the second servant and the third and all the others who followed behind the herds: "Thus and so you shall say to Esau, when you reach him; [21]and also tell him, 'Your servant Jacob is right behind us.'" For Jacob reasoned, "If I first appease him with a gift that precedes me, then later, when I face him, perhaps he will forgive me." [22]So the gifts went on ahead of him, while he stayed that night in the camp.

Jacob's New Name. [23]That night, however, Jacob arose, took his two wives, with the two maidservants and his eleven children, and crossed the ford of the Jabbok. [24]After he got them and brought them across the wadi and brought over what belonged to him, [25]Jacob was left there alone. Then a man wrestled with him until the break of dawn. [26]When the man saw that he could not prevail over him, he struck Jacob's hip at its socket, so that Jacob's socket was dislocated as he wrestled with him. [27]The man then said, "Let me go, for it is daybreak." But Jacob said, "I will not let you go until you bless me." [28]"What is your name?" the man asked. He answered, "Jacob." [29]Then the man said, "You shall no longer be named Jacob, but Israel, because you have contended with divine and human beings and have prevailed." [30]Jacob then asked him, "Please tell me your name." He answered, "Why do you ask for my name?" With that, he blessed him. [31]Jacob named the place Peniel, "because I have seen God face to face," he said, "yet my life has been spared."

[32]At sunrise, as he left Penuel, Jacob limped along because of his hip. [33]That is why, to this day, the Israelites do not eat the sciatic muscle that is on the hip socket, because he had struck Jacob's hip socket at the sciatic muscle.

☐ MARK 5:21-43

Jairus's Daughter and the Woman with a Hemorrhage. 5:21 When Jesus had crossed again [in the boat] to the other side, a large crowd gathered around him, and he stayed close to the sea. [22]One of the synagogue officials, named Jairus, came forward. Seeing him he fell at his feet [23]and pleaded earnestly with him, saying, "My daughter is at the point of death. Please, come lay your hands on her that she may get well and live." [24]He went off with him, and a large crowd followed him and pressed upon him. [25]There was a woman afflicted with hemorrhages for twelve years. [26]She had suffered greatly at the hands of many doctors and had spent all that she had. Yet she was not helped but only grew worse. [27]She had heard about Jesus and came up behind him in the crowd and touched his cloak. [28]She said, "If I but touch his clothes, I shall be cured." [29]Immediately her flow of blood dried up. She felt in her body that she was healed of her affliction. [30]Jesus, aware at once that power had gone out from him, turned around in the crowd and asked, "Who has touched my clothes?" [31]But his disciples said to him, "You see how the crowd is pressing upon you, and yet you ask, 'Who touched me?'" [32]And he looked around to see who had done it. [33]The woman, realizing what had happened to her, approached in fear and trembling. She fell down before Jesus and told him the whole truth. [34]He said to her, "Daughter, your faith has saved you. Go in peace and be cured of your affliction."

[35]While he was still speaking, people from the synagogue official's house arrived and said, "Your daughter has died; why trouble the teacher any longer?" [36]Disregarding the message that was reported, Jesus said to the synagogue official, "Do not be afraid; just have faith." [37]He did not allow anyone to accompany him inside except Peter, James, and John, the brother of James. [38]When they arrived at the house of the synagogue official, he caught sight of a commotion, people weeping and wailing loudly. [39]So he went in and said to them, "Why this commotion and weeping? The child is not dead but asleep." [40]And they ridiculed him. Then he put them all out. He took along the child's father and mother and those who were with him and entered the room where the child was. [41]He took the child by the hand and said to her, "*Talitha koum*," which means, "Little girl, I say to you, arise!" [42]The girl, a child of twelve, arose immediately and walked around. [At that] they were utterly astounded. [43]He gave strict orders that no one should know this and said that she should be given something to eat.

January 15

St. Macarius of Egypt

God gives His Holy Spirit to all, whether celibate or married, in the monastery or in the world, according to how earnest they are in their intention to serve Him.

— St. Macarius of Egypt

☐ GENESIS 33–36

Jacob and Esau Meet. 33:1 Jacob looked up and saw Esau coming, and with him four hundred men. So he divided his children among Leah, Rachel, and the two maidservants, [2]putting the maidservants and their children first, Leah and her children next, and Rachel and Joseph last. [3]He himself went on ahead of them, bowing to the ground seven times, until he reached his brother. [4]Esau ran to meet him, embraced him, and flinging himself on his neck, kissed him as he wept.

⁵Then Esau looked up and saw the women and children and asked, "Who are these with you?" Jacob answered, "They are the children with whom God has graciously favored your servant." ⁶Then the maidservants and their children came forward and bowed low; ⁷next, Leah and her children came forward and bowed low; lastly, Joseph and Rachel came forward and bowed low. ⁸Then Esau asked, "What did you intend with all those herds that I encountered?" Jacob answered, "It was to gain my lord's favor." ⁹Esau replied, "I have plenty; my brother, you should keep what is yours." ¹⁰"No, I beg you!" said Jacob. "If you will do me the favor, accept this gift from me, since to see your face is for me like seeing the face of God—and you have received me so kindly. ¹¹Accept the gift I have brought you. For God has been generous toward me, and I have an abundance." Since he urged him strongly, Esau accepted.

¹²Then Esau said, "Let us break camp and be on our way; I will travel in front of you." ¹³But Jacob replied: "As my lord knows, the children are too young. And the flocks and herds that are nursing are a concern to me; if overdriven for even a single day, the whole flock will die. ¹⁴Let my lord, then, go before his servant, while I proceed more slowly at the pace of the livestock before me and at the pace of my children, until I join my lord in Seir." ¹⁵Esau replied, "Let me at least put at your disposal some of the people who are with me." But Jacob said, "Why is this that I am treated so kindly, my lord?" ¹⁶So on that day Esau went on his way back to Seir, ¹⁷and Jacob broke camp for Succoth. There Jacob built a home for himself and made booths for his livestock. That is why the place was named Succoth.

¹⁸Jacob arrived safely at the city of Shechem, which is in the land of Canaan, when he came from Paddan-aram. He encamped in sight of the city. ¹⁹The plot of ground on which he had pitched his tent he bought for a hundred pieces of money from the descendants of Hamor, the father of Shechem. ²⁰He set up an altar there and invoked "El, the God of Israel."

The Rape of Dinah. 34:1 Dinah, the daughter whom Leah had borne to Jacob, went out to visit some of the women of the land. ²When Shechem, son of Hamor the Hivite, the leader of the region, saw her, he seized her and lay with her by force. ³He was strongly attracted to Dinah, daughter of Jacob, and was in love with the young woman. So he spoke affectionately to her. ⁴Shechem said to his father Hamor, "Get me this young woman for a wife."

⁵Meanwhile, Jacob heard that Shechem had defiled his daughter Dinah; but since his sons were out in the field with his livestock, Jacob kept quiet until they came home. ⁶Now Hamor, the father of Shechem, went out to discuss the matter with Jacob, ⁷just as Jacob's sons were coming in from the field. When they heard the news, the men were indignant and extremely angry. Shechem had committed an outrage in Israel by lying with Jacob's daughter; such a thing is not done. ⁸Hamor appealed to them, saying: "My son Shechem has his heart set on your daughter. Please give her to him as a wife. ⁹Intermarry with us; give your daughters to us, and take our daughters for yourselves. ¹⁰Thus you can live among us. The land is open before you. Settle and move about freely in it and acquire holdings here." ¹¹Then Shechem appealed to Dinah's father and brothers: "Do me this favor, and whatever you ask from me, I will give. ¹²No matter how high you set the bridal price and gift, I will give you whatever you ask from me; only give me the young woman as a wife."

Revenge of Jacob's Sons. ¹³Jacob's sons replied to Shechem and his father Hamor with guile, speaking as they did because he had defiled their sister Dinah. ¹⁴They said to them, "We are not able to do this thing: to give our sister to an uncircumcised man. For that would be a disgrace for us. [15]Only on this condition will we agree to that: that you become like us by having every male among you circumcised. [16]Then we will give you our daughters and take your daughters in marriage; we will settle among you and become one people. [17]But if you do not listen to us and be circumcised, we will take our daughter and go."

[18]Their proposal pleased Hamor and his son Shechem. [19]The young man lost no time in acting on the proposal, since he wanted Jacob's daughter. Now he was more highly regarded than anyone else in his father's house. [20]So Hamor and his son Shechem went to the gate of their city and said to the men of their city: [21]"These men are friendly toward us. Let them settle in the land and move about in it freely; there is ample room in the land for them. We can take their daughters in marriage and give our daughters to them. [22]But only on this condition will the men agree to live with us and form one people with us: that every male among us be circumcised as they themselves are. [23]Would not their livestock, their property, and all their animals then be ours? Let us just agree with them, so that they will settle among us."

[24]All who went out of the gate of the city listened to Hamor and his son Shechem, and all the males, all those who went out of the gate of the city, were circumcised. [25]On the third day, while they were still in pain, two of Jacob's sons, Simeon and Levi, brothers of Dinah, each took his sword, advanced against the unsuspecting city and massacred all the males. [26]After they had killed Hamor and his son Shechem with the sword, they took Dinah from Shechem's house and left. [27]Then the other sons of Jacob followed up the slaughter and sacked the city because their sister had been defiled. [28]They took their sheep, cattle and donkeys, whatever was in the city and in the surrounding country. [29]They carried off all their wealth, their children, and their women, and looted whatever was in the houses.

[30]Jacob said to Simeon and Levi: "You have brought trouble upon me by making me repugnant to the inhabitants of the land, the Canaanites and the Perizzites. I have so few men that, if these people unite against me and attack me, I and my household will be wiped out." [31]But they retorted, "Should our sister be treated like a prostitute?"

Bethel Revisited. 35:1 God said to Jacob: Go up now to Bethel. Settle there and build an altar there to the God who appeared to you when you were fleeing from your brother Esau. [2]So Jacob told his household and all who were with him: "Get rid of the foreign gods among you; then purify yourselves and change your clothes. [3]Let us now go up to Bethel so that I might build an altar there to the God who answered me in the day of my distress and who has been with me wherever I have gone." [4]They gave Jacob all the foreign gods in their possession and also the rings they had in their ears and Jacob buried them under the oak that is near Shechem. [5]Then, as they set out, a great terror fell upon the surrounding towns, so that no one pursued the sons of Jacob.

[6]Thus Jacob and all the people who were with him arrived in Luz (now Bethel) in the land of Canaan. [7]There he built an altar and called the place El-Bethel, for it was there that God had revealed himself to him when he was fleeing from his brother.

[8]Deborah, Rebekah's nurse, died. She was buried under the oak below Bethel, and so it was named Allon-bacuth.

[9]On Jacob's arrival from Paddan-aram, God appeared to him again and blessed him. [10]God said to him:

Your name is Jacob.
You will no longer be named Jacob,
   but Israel will be your name.

So he was named Israel. ¹¹Then God said to him: I am God Almighty; be fruitful and multiply. A nation, indeed an assembly of nations, will stem from you, and kings will issue from your loins. ¹²The land I gave to Abraham and Isaac I will give to you; and to your descendants after you I will give the land.

¹³Then God departed from him. ¹⁴In the place where God had spoken with him, Jacob set up a sacred pillar, a stone pillar, and upon it he made a libation and poured out oil. ¹⁵Jacob named the place where God spoke to him Bethel.

Jacob's Family. ¹⁶Then they departed from Bethel; but while they still had some distance to go to Ephrath, Rachel went into labor and suffered great distress. ¹⁷When her labor was most intense, the midwife said to her, "Do not fear, for now you have another son." ¹⁸With her last breath—for she was at the point of death—she named him Ben-oni; but his father named him Benjamin. ¹⁹Thus Rachel died; and she was buried on the road to Ephrath (now Bethlehem). ²⁰Jacob set up a sacred pillar on her grave, and the same pillar marks Rachel's grave to this day.

²¹Israel moved on and pitched his tent beyond Migdal-eder. ²²While Israel was encamped in that region, Reuben went and lay with Bilhah, his father's concubine. When Israel heard of it, he was greatly offended.

The sons of Jacob were now twelve. ²³The sons of Leah: Reuben, Jacob's firstborn, Simeon, Levi, Judah, Issachar, and Zebulun; ²⁴the sons of Rachel: Joseph and Benjamin; ²⁵the sons of Rachel's maidservant Bilhah: Dan and Naphtali; ²⁶the sons of Leah's maidservant Zilpah: Gad and Asher. These are the sons of Jacob who were born to him in Paddan-aram.

²⁷Jacob went home to his father Isaac at Mamre, in Kiriath-arba (now Hebron), where Abraham and Isaac had resided. ²⁸The length of Isaac's life was one hundred and eighty years; ²⁹then he breathed his last. He died as an old man and was gathered to his people. After a full life, his sons Esau and Jacob buried him.

Edomite Lists. 36:1 These are the descendants of Esau (that is, Edom). ²Esau took his wives from among the Canaanite women: Adah, daughter of Elon the Hittite; Oholibamah, the daughter of Anah the son of Zibeon the Hivite; ³and Basemath, daughter of Ishmael and sister of Nebaioth. ⁴Adah bore Eliphaz to Esau; Basemath bore Reuel; ⁵and Oholibamah bore Jeush, Jalam and Korah. These are the sons of Esau who were born to him in the land of Canaan.

⁶Esau took his wives, his sons, his daughters, and all the members of his household, as well as his livestock, all his cattle, and all the property he had acquired in the land of Canaan, and went to the land of Seir, away from his brother Jacob. ⁷Their possessions had become too great for them to dwell together, and the land in which they were residing could not support them because of their livestock. ⁸So Esau settled in the highlands of Seir. (Esau is Edom.) ⁹These are the descendants of Esau, ancestor of the Edomites, in the highlands of Seir.

¹⁰These are the names of the sons of Esau: Eliphaz, son of Adah, wife of Esau, and Reuel, son of Basemath, wife of Esau. ¹¹The sons of Eliphaz were Teman, Omar, Zepho, Gatam, and Kenaz. ¹²Timna was a concubine of Eliphaz, the son of Esau, and she bore Amalek to Eliphaz. Those were the sons of Adah, the wife of Esau. ¹³These were the sons of Reuel: Nahath, Zerah, Shammah, and Mizzah. Those were the sons of Basemath, the wife of Esau. ¹⁴These were the sons of Esau's wife Oholibamah—the daughter of Anah, son of Zibeon—whom she bore to Esau: Jeush, Jalam, and Korah.

¹⁵These are the clans of the sons of Esau. The sons of Eliphaz, Esau's firstborn: the clans of Teman, Omar, Zepho, Kenaz, ¹⁶Korah, Gatam, and Amalek. These are the clans of Eliphaz in the land of Edom; they are the

sons of Adah. [17]These are the sons of Reuel, son of Esau: the clans of Nahath, Zerah, Shammah, and Mizzah. These are the clans of Reuel in the land of Edom; they are the sons of Basemath, wife of Esau. [18]These were the sons of Oholibamah, wife of Esau: the clans of Jeush, Jalam, and Korah. These are the clans of Esau's wife Oholibamah, daughter of Anah. [19]These are the sons of Esau— that is, Edom—according to their clans.

[20]These are the sons of Seir the Horite, the inhabitants of the land: Lotan, Shobal, Zibeon, Anah, [21]Dishon, Ezer, and Dishan; those are the clans of the Horites, sons of Seir in the land of Edom. [22]The sons of Lotan were Hori and Hemam, and Lotan's sister was Timna. [23]These are the sons of Shobal: Alvan, Mahanath, Ebal, Shepho, and Onam. [24]These are the sons of Zibeon: Aiah and Anah. He is the Anah who found water in the desert while he was pasturing the donkeys of his father Zibeon. [25]These are the children of Anah: Dishon and Oholibamah, daughter of Anah. [26]These are the sons of Dishon: Hemdan, Eshban, Ithran, and Cheran. [27]These are the sons of Ezer: Bilhan, Zaavan, and Akan. [28]These are the sons of Dishan: Uz and Aran. [29]These are the clans of the Horites: the clans of Lotan, Shobal, Zibeon, Anah, [30]Dishon, Ezer, and Dishan; those are the clans of the Horites, clan by clan, in the land of Seir.

[31]These are the kings who reigned in the land of Edom before any king reigned over the Israelites. [32]Bela, son of Beor, became king in Edom; the name of his city was Dinhabah. [33]When Bela died, Jobab, son of Zerah, from Bozrah, succeeded him as king. [34]When Jobab died, Husham, from the land of the Temanites, succeeded him as king. [35]When Husham died, Hadad, son of Bedad, succeeded him as king. He is the one who defeated Midian in the country of Moab; the name of his city was Avith. [36]When Hadad died, Samlah, from Masrekah, succeeded him as king. [37]When Samlah died, Shaul, from Rehoboth-on-the-River, succeeded him as king. [38]When Shaul died, Baal-hanan, son of Achbor, succeeded him as king. [39]When Baal-hanan, son of Achbor, died, Hadad succeeded him as king; the name of his city was Pau. His wife's name was Mehetabel, the daughter of Matred, son of Mezahab.

[40]These are the names of the clans of Esau identified according to their families and localities: the clans of Timna, Alvah, Jetheth, [41]Oholibamah, Elah, Pinon, [42]Kenaz, Teman, Mibzar, [43]Magdiel, and Iram. Those are the clans of the Edomites, according to their settlements in their territorial holdings—that is, of Esau, the ancestor of the Edomites.

☐ MARK 6:1-13

The Rejection at Nazareth. 6:1 He departed from there and came to his native place, accompanied by his disciples. [2]When the sabbath came he began to teach in the synagogue, and many who heard him were astonished. They said, "Where did this man get all this? What kind of wisdom has been given him? What mighty deeds are wrought by his hands! [3]Is he not the carpenter, the son of Mary, and the brother of James and Joses and Judas and Simon? And are not his sisters here with us?" And they took offense at him. [4]Jesus said to them, "A prophet is not without honor except in his native place and among his own kin and in his own house." [5]So he was not able to perform any mighty deed there, apart from curing a few sick people by laying his hands on them. [6]He was amazed at their lack of faith.

The Mission of the Twelve. He went around to the villages in the vicinity teaching.

7He summoned the Twelve and began to send them out two by two and gave them authority over unclean spirits. 8He instructed them to take nothing for the journey but a walking stick—no food, no sack, no money in their belts. 9They were, however, to wear sandals but not a second tunic. 10He said to them, "Wherever you enter a house, stay there until you leave from there. 11Whatever place does not welcome you or listen to you, leave there and shake the dust off your feet in testimony against them." 12So they went off and preached repentance. 13They drove out many demons, and they anointed with oil many who were sick and cured them.

January 16

Our Lord did not say, "You will not be troubled, you will not be tempted, you will not be distressed." He said, "You will not be overcome."

— BLESSED JULIAN OF NORWICH

☐ GENESIS 37-39

Joseph Sold into Egypt. 37:1 Jacob settled in the land where his father had sojourned, the land of Canaan. 2This is the story of the family of Jacob. When Joseph was seventeen years old, he was tending the flocks with his brothers; he was an assistant to the sons of his father's wives Bilhah and Zilpah, and Joseph brought their father bad reports about them. 3Israel loved Joseph best of all his sons, for he was the child of his old age; and he had made him a long ornamented tunic. 4When his brothers saw that their father loved him best of all his brothers, they hated him so much that they could not say a kind word to him.

5Once Joseph had a dream, and when he told his brothers, they hated him even more. 6He said to them, "Listen to this dream I had. 7There we were, binding sheaves in the field, when suddenly my sheaf rose to an upright position, and your sheaves formed a ring around my sheaf and bowed down to it." 8His brothers said to him, "Are you really going to make yourself king over us? Will you rule over us?" So they hated him all the more because of his dreams and his reports.

9Then he had another dream, and told it to his brothers. "Look, I had another dream," he said; "this time, the sun and the moon and eleven stars were bowing down to me." 10When he told it to his father and his brothers, his father reproved him and asked, "What is the meaning of this dream of yours? Can it be that I and your mother and your brothers are to come and bow to the ground before you?" 11So his brothers were furious at him but his father kept the matter in mind.

12One day, when his brothers had gone to pasture their father's flocks at Shechem, 13Israel said to Joseph, "Are your brothers not tending our flocks at Shechem? Come and I will send you to them." "I am ready," Joseph answered. 14"Go then," he replied; "see if all is well with your brothers and the flocks, and bring back word." So he sent him off from the valley of Hebron. When Joseph reached Shechem, 15a man came upon him as he was wandering about in the fields. "What are you looking for?" the man asked him. 16"I am looking for my brothers," he answered. "Please tell me where they are tending the flocks." [17]The man told him, "They have moved on from here; in fact, I heard them say, 'Let us go on to Dothan.'" So Joseph went after his brothers and found them in Dothan. [18]They saw him from a distance, and before he reached them, they plotted to kill him. [19]They said to one another: "Here comes that dreamer! [20]Come now, let us kill him and throw him into one of the cisterns here; we could say that a wild beast devoured him. We will see then what comes of his dreams."

[21]But when Reuben heard this, he tried to save him from their hands, saying: "We must not take his life." [22]Then Reuben said, "Do not shed blood! Throw him into this cistern in the wilderness; but do not lay a hand on him." His purpose was to save him from their hands and restore him to his father.

[23]So when Joseph came up to his brothers, they stripped him of his tunic, the long ornamented tunic he had on; [24]then they took him and threw him into the cistern. The cistern was empty; there was no water in it.

[25]Then they sat down to eat. Looking up, they saw a caravan of Ishmaelites coming from Gilead, their camels laden with gum, balm, and resin to be taken down to Egypt. [26]Judah said to his brothers: "What is to be gained by killing our brother and concealing his blood? [27]Come, let us sell him to these Ishmaelites, instead of doing away with him ourselves. After all, he is our brother, our own flesh." His brothers agreed. [28]Midianite traders passed by, and they pulled Joseph up out of the cistern. They sold Joseph for twenty pieces of silver to the Ishmaelites, who took him to Egypt.

[29]When Reuben went back to the cistern and saw that Joseph was not in it, he tore his garments, [30]and returning to his brothers, he exclaimed: "The boy is gone! And I—where can I turn?" [31]They took Joseph's tunic, and after slaughtering a goat, dipped the tunic in its blood. [32]Then they sent someone to bring the long ornamented tunic to their father, with the message: "We found this. See whether it is your son's tunic or not." [33]He recognized it and exclaimed: "My son's tunic! A wild beast has devoured him! Joseph has been torn to pieces!" [34]Then Jacob tore his garments, put sackcloth on his loins, and mourned his son many days. [35]Though his sons and daughters tried to console him, he refused all consolation, saying, "No, I will go down mourning to my son in Sheol." Thus did his father weep for him.

[36]The Midianites, meanwhile, sold Joseph in Egypt to Potiphar, an official of Pharaoh and his chief steward.

Judah and Tamar. 38:1 About that time Judah went down, away from his brothers, and pitched his tent near a certain Adullamite named Hirah. [2]There Judah saw the daughter of a Canaanite named Shua; he married her, and had intercourse with her. [3]She conceived and bore a son, whom she named Er. [4]Again she conceived and bore a son, whom she named Onan. [5]Then she bore still another son, whom she named Shelah. She was in Chezib when she bore him.

[6]Judah got a wife named Tamar for his firstborn, Er. [7]But Er, Judah's firstborn, greatly offended the LORD; so the LORD took his life. [8]Then Judah said to Onan, "Have intercourse with your brother's wife, in fulfillment of your duty as brother-in-law, and thus preserve your brother's line." [9]Onan, however, knew that the offspring would not be his; so whenever he had intercourse with his brother's wife, he wasted his seed on the ground, to avoid giving offspring to his brother. [10]What he did greatly offended the LORD, and the LORD took his life too. [11]Then Judah said to his daughter-in-law Tamar, "Remain a widow in your father's house until my son Shelah grows up"—for he feared that Shelah also might die like his brothers. So Tamar went to live in her father's house.

¹²Time passed, and the daughter of Shua, Judah's wife, died. After Judah completed the period of mourning, he went up to Timnah, to those who were shearing his sheep, in company with his friend Hirah the Adullamite. ¹³Then Tamar was told, "Your father-in-law is on his way up to Timnah to shear his sheep." ¹⁴So she took off her widow's garments, covered herself with a shawl, and having wrapped herself sat down at the entrance to Enaim, which is on the way to Timnah; for she was aware that, although Shelah was now grown up, she had not been given to him in marriage. ¹⁵When Judah saw her, he thought she was a harlot, since she had covered her face. ¹⁶So he went over to her at the roadside and said, "Come, let me have intercourse with you," for he did not realize that she was his daughter-in-law. She replied, "What will you pay me for letting you have intercourse with me?" ¹⁷He answered, "I will send you a young goat from the flock." "Very well," she said, "provided you leave me a pledge until you send it." ¹⁸Judah asked, "What pledge should I leave you?" She answered, "Your seal and cord, and the staff in your hand." So he gave them to her and had intercourse with her, and she conceived by him. ¹⁹After she got up and went away, she took off her shawl and put on her widow's garments again.

²⁰Judah sent the young goat by his friend the Adullamite to recover the pledge from the woman; but he did not find her. ²¹So he asked the men of that place, "Where is the prostitute, the one by the roadside in Enaim?" But they answered, "No prostitute has been here." ²²He went back to Judah and told him, "I did not find her; and besides, the men of the place said, 'No prostitute has been here.'" ²³"Let her keep the things," Judah replied; "otherwise we will become a laughingstock. After all, I did send her this young goat, but you did not find her."

²⁴About three months later, Judah was told, "Your daughter-in-law Tamar has acted like a harlot and now she is pregnant from her harlotry." Judah said, "Bring her out; let her be burned." ²⁵But as she was being brought out, she sent word to her father-in-law, "It is by the man to whom these things belong that I am pregnant." Then she said, "See whose seal and cord and staff these are." ²⁶Judah recognized them and said, "She is in the right rather than I, since I did not give her to my son Shelah." He had no further sexual relations with her.

²⁷When the time of her delivery came, there were twins in her womb. ²⁸While she was giving birth, one put out his hand; and the midwife took and tied a crimson thread on his hand, noting, "This one came out first." ²⁹But as he withdrew his hand, his brother came out; and she said, "What a breach you have made for yourself!" So he was called Perez. ³⁰Afterward his brother, who had the crimson thread on his hand, came out; he was called Zerah.

Joseph's Temptation. 39:1 When Joseph was taken down to Egypt, an Egyptian, Potiphar, an official of Pharaoh and his chief steward, bought him from the Ishmaelites who had brought him there. ²The LORD was with Joseph and he enjoyed great success and was assigned to the household of his Egyptian master. ³When his master saw that the LORD was with him and brought him success in whatever he did, ⁴he favored Joseph and made him his personal attendant; he put him in charge of his household and entrusted to him all his possessions. ⁵From the moment that he put him in charge of his household and all his possessions, the LORD blessed the Egyptian's house for Joseph's sake; the LORD's blessing was on everything he owned, both inside the house and out. ⁶Having left everything he owned in Joseph's charge, he gave no thought, with Joseph there, to anything but the food he ate.

Now Joseph was well-built and handsome. ⁷After a time, his master's wife looked at him with longing and said, "Lie with me." [8]But he refused and said to his master's wife, "Look, as long as I am here, my master does not give a thought to anything in the house, but has entrusted to me all he owns. [9]He has no more authority in this house than I do. He has withheld from me nothing but you, since you are his wife. How, then, could I do this great wrong and sin against God?" [10]Although she spoke to him day after day, he would not agree to lie with her, or even be near her.

[11]One such day, when Joseph came into the house to do his work, and none of the household servants were then in the house, [12]she laid hold of him by his cloak, saying, "Lie with me!" But leaving the cloak in her hand, he escaped and ran outside. [13]When she saw that he had left his cloak in her hand as he escaped outside, [14]she cried out to her household servants and told them, "Look! My husband has brought us a Hebrew man to mock us! He came in here to lie with me, but I cried out loudly. [15]When he heard me scream, he left his cloak beside me and escaped and ran outside."

[16]She kept the cloak with her until his master came home. [17]Then she told him the same story: "The Hebrew slave whom you brought us came to me to amuse himself at my expense. [18]But when I screamed, he left his cloak beside me and escaped outside." [19]When the master heard his wife's story in which she reported, "Thus and so your servant did to me," he became enraged. [20]Joseph's master seized him and put him into the jail where the king's prisoners were confined. And there he sat, in jail.

[21]But the LORD was with Joseph, and showed him kindness by making the chief jailer well-disposed toward him. [22]The chief jailer put Joseph in charge of all the prisoners in the jail. Everything that had to be done there, he was the one to do it. [23]The chief jailer did not have to look after anything that was in Joseph's charge, since the LORD was with him and was bringing success to whatever he was doing.

☐ MARK 6:14-29

Herod's Opinion of Jesus. 6:14 King Herod heard about it, for his fame had become widespread, and people were saying, "John the Baptist has been raised from the dead; that is why mighty powers are at work in him." [15]Others were saying, "He is Elijah"; still others, "He is a prophet like any of the prophets." [16]But when Herod learned of it, he said, "It is John whom I beheaded. He has been raised up."

The Death of John the Baptist. [17]Herod was the one who had John arrested and bound in prison on account of Herodias, the wife of his brother Philip, whom he had married. [18]John had said to Herod, "It is not lawful for you to have your brother's wife." [19]Herodias harbored a grudge against him and wanted to kill him but was unable to do so. [20]Herod feared John, knowing him to be a righteous and holy man, and kept him in custody. When he heard him speak he was very much perplexed, yet he liked to listen to him. [21]She had an opportunity one day when Herod, on his birthday, gave a banquet for his courtiers, his military officers, and the leading men of Galilee. [22]Herodias's own daughter came in and performed a dance that delighted Herod and his guests. The king said to the girl, "Ask of me whatever you wish and I will grant it to you." [23]He even swore [many things] to her, "I will grant you whatever you ask of me, even to half of my kingdom." [24]She went out and said to her mother, "What shall I ask for?" She replied, "The head of John the Baptist." [25]The girl hurried back to the king's presence and made her request, "I want you to give me at once on a platter the head of John the Baptist." [26]The king was deeply distressed, but because of his oaths and the guests he did not wish to break his word to her. [27]So he promptly dispatched an executioner with orders to bring back his head. He went off and beheaded him in the prison. [28]He brought in the head on a platter and gave it to the girl. The girl in turn gave it to her mother. [29]When his disciples heard about it, they came and took his body and laid it in a tomb.

January 17

St. Anthony the Great

If we do good to our neighbor, we do good to God; if we cause our neighbor to stumble, we sin against Christ.

— St. Anthony the Great

☐ **GENESIS 40-42**

The Dreams Interpreted. 40:1 Some time afterward, the royal cupbearer and baker offended their lord, the king of Egypt. [2]Pharaoh was angry with his two officials, the chief cupbearer and the chief baker, [3]and he put them in custody in the house of the chief steward, the same jail where Joseph was confined. [4]The chief steward assigned Joseph to them, and he became their attendant.

After they had been in custody for some time, [5]the cupbearer and the baker of the king of Egypt who were confined in the jail both had dreams on the same night, each his own dream and each dream with its own meaning. [6]When Joseph came to them in the morning, he saw that they looked disturbed. [7]So he asked Pharaoh's officials who were with him in custody in his master's house, "Why do you look so troubled today?" [8]They answered him, "We have had dreams, but there is no one to interpret them." Joseph said to them, "Do interpretations not come from God? Please tell me the dreams."

[9]Then the chief cupbearer told Joseph his dream. "In my dream," he said, "I saw a vine in front of me, [10]and on the vine were three branches. It had barely budded when its blossoms came out, and its clusters ripened into grapes. [11]Pharaoh's cup was in my hand; so I took the grapes, pressed them out into his cup, and put it in Pharaoh's hand." [12]Joseph said to him: "This is its interpretation. The three branches are three days; [13]within three days Pharaoh will single you out and restore you to your post. You will be handing Pharaoh his cup as you formerly did when you were his cupbearer. [14]Only think of me when all is well with you, and please do me the great favor of mentioning me to Pharaoh, to get me out of this place. [15]The truth is that I was kidnapped from the land of the Hebrews, and I have not done anything here that they should have put me into a dungeon."

[16]When the chief baker saw that Joseph had given a favorable interpretation, he said to him: "I too had a dream. In it I had three bread baskets on my head; [17]in the top one were all kinds of bakery products for Pharaoh, but the birds were eating them out of the basket on my head." [18]Joseph said to him in reply: "This is its interpretation. The three baskets are three days; [19]within three days Pharaoh will single you out and will

impale you on a stake, and the birds will be eating your flesh."

²⁰And so on the third day, which was Pharaoh's birthday, when he gave a banquet to all his servants, he singled out the chief cupbearer and chief baker in the midst of his servants. ²¹He restored the chief cupbearer to his office, so that he again handed the cup to Pharaoh; ²²but the chief baker he impaled—just as Joseph had told them in his interpretation. ²³Yet the chief cupbearer did not think of Joseph; he forgot him.

Pharaoh's Dream. **41:1** After a lapse of two years, Pharaoh had a dream. He was standing by the Nile, ²when up out of the Nile came seven cows, fine-looking and fat; they grazed in the reed grass. ³Behind them seven other cows, poor-looking and gaunt, came up out of the Nile; and standing on the bank of the Nile beside the others, ⁴the poor-looking, gaunt cows devoured the seven fine-looking, fat cows. Then Pharaoh woke up.

⁵He fell asleep again and had another dream. He saw seven ears of grain, fat and healthy, growing on a single stalk. ⁶Behind them sprouted seven ears of grain, thin and scorched by the east wind; ⁷and the thin ears swallowed up the seven fat, healthy ears. Then Pharaoh woke up—it was a dream!

⁸Next morning his mind was agitated. So Pharaoh had all the magicians and sages of Egypt summoned and recounted his dream to them; but there was no one to interpret it for him. ⁹Then the chief cupbearer said to Pharaoh: "Now I remember my negligence! ¹⁰Once, when Pharaoh was angry with his servants, he put me and the chief baker in custody in the house of the chief steward. ¹¹Later, we both had dreams on the same night, and each of our dreams had its own meaning. ¹²There was a Hebrew youth with us, a slave of the chief steward; and when we told him our dreams, he interpreted them for us and ex-plained for each of us the meaning of his dream. ¹³Things turned out just as he had told us: I was restored to my post, but the other man was impaled."

¹⁴Pharaoh therefore had Joseph summoned, and they hurriedly brought him from the dungeon. After he shaved and changed his clothes, he came to Pharaoh. ¹⁵Pharaoh then said to Joseph: "I had a dream but there was no one to interpret it. But I hear it said of you, 'If he hears a dream he can interpret it.'" ¹⁶"It is not I," Joseph replied to Pharaoh, "but God who will respond for the well-being of Pharaoh."

¹⁷Then Pharaoh said to Joseph: "In my dream, I was standing on the bank of the Nile, ¹⁸when up from the Nile came seven cows, fat and well-formed; they grazed in the reed grass. ¹⁹Behind them came seven other cows, scrawny, most ill-formed and gaunt. Never have I seen such bad specimens as these in all the land of Egypt! ²⁰The gaunt, bad cows devoured the first seven fat cows. ²¹But when they had consumed them, no one could tell that they had done so, be-cause they looked as bad as before. Then I woke up. ²²In another dream I saw seven ears of grain, full and healthy, growing on a single stalk. ²³Behind them sprouted seven ears of grain, shriveled and thin and scorched by the east wind; ²⁴and the seven thin ears swallowed up the seven healthy ears. I have spoken to the magicians, but there is no one to explain it to me."

²⁵Joseph said to Pharaoh: "Pharaoh's dreams have the same meaning. God has made known to Pharaoh what he is about to do. ²⁶The seven healthy cows are seven years, and the seven healthy ears are seven years— the same in each dream. ²⁷The seven thin, bad cows that came up after them are seven years, as are the seven thin ears scorched by the east wind; they are seven years of fam-ine. ²⁸Things are just as I told Pharaoh: God has revealed to Pharaoh what he is about to do. ²⁹Seven years of great abundance are now coming throughout the land of Egypt;

[30]but seven years of famine will rise up after them, when all the abundance will be forgotten in the land of Egypt. When the famine has exhausted the land, [31]no trace of the abundance will be found in the land because of the famine that follows it, for it will be very severe. [32]That Pharaoh had the same dream twice means that the matter has been confirmed by God and that God will soon bring it about.

[33]"Therefore, let Pharaoh seek out a discerning and wise man and put him in charge of the land of Egypt. [34]Let Pharaoh act and appoint overseers for the land to organize it during the seven years of abundance. [35]They should collect all the food of these coming good years, gathering the grain under Pharaoh's authority, for food in the cities, and they should guard it. [36]This food will serve as a reserve for the country against the seven years of famine that will occur in the land of Egypt, so that the land may not perish in the famine."

[37]This advice pleased Pharaoh and all his servants. [38]"Could we find another like him," Pharaoh asked his servants, "a man so endowed with the spirit of God?" [39]So Pharaoh said to Joseph: "Since God has made all this known to you, there is no one as discerning and wise as you are. [40]You shall be in charge of my household, and all my people will obey your command. Only in respect to the throne will I outrank you." [41]Then Pharaoh said to Joseph, "Look, I put you in charge of the whole land of Egypt." [42]With that, Pharaoh took off his signet ring and put it on Joseph's finger. He dressed him in robes of fine linen and put a gold chain around his neck. [43]He then had him ride in his second chariot, and they shouted "Abrek!" before him.

Thus was Joseph installed over the whole land of Egypt. [44]"I am Pharaoh," he told Joseph, "but without your approval no one shall lift hand or foot in all the land of Egypt." [45]Pharaoh also bestowed the name of Zaphenath-paneah on Joseph, and he gave him in marriage Asenath, the daughter of Potiphera, priest of Heliopolis. And Joseph went out over the land of Egypt. [46]Joseph was thirty years old when he entered the service of Pharaoh, king of Egypt.

After Joseph left Pharaoh, he went throughout the land of Egypt. [47]During the seven years of plenty, when the land produced abundant crops, [48]he collected all the food of these years of plenty that the land of Egypt was enjoying and stored it in the cities, placing in each city the crops of the fields around it. [49]Joseph collected grain like the sands of the sea, so much that at last he stopped measuring it, for it was beyond measure.

[50]Before the famine years set in, Joseph became the father of two sons, borne to him by Asenath, daughter of Potiphera, priest of Heliopolis. [51]Joseph named his firstborn Manasseh, meaning, "God has made me forget entirely my troubles and my father's house"; [52]and the second he named Ephraim, meaning, "God has made me fruitful in the land of my affliction."

[53]When the seven years of abundance enjoyed by the land of Egypt came to an end, [54]the seven years of famine set in, just as Joseph had said. Although there was famine in all the other countries, food was available throughout the land of Egypt. [55]When all the land of Egypt became hungry and the people cried to Pharaoh for food, Pharaoh said to all the Egyptians: "Go to Joseph and do whatever he tells you." [56]When the famine had spread throughout the land, Joseph opened all the cities that had grain and rationed it to the Egyptians, since the famine had gripped the land of Egypt. [57]Indeed, the whole world came to Egypt to Joseph to buy grain, for famine had gripped the whole world.

The Brothers' First Journey to Egypt. 42:1 When Jacob learned that grain rations were for sale in Egypt, he said to his sons: "Why do you keep looking at one another?"

²He went on, "I hear that grain is for sale in Egypt. Go down there and buy some for us, that we may stay alive and not die." ³So ten of Joseph's brothers went down to buy grain from Egypt. ⁴But Jacob did not send Joseph's brother Benjamin with his brothers, for he thought some disaster might befall him. ⁵And so the sons of Israel were among those who came to buy grain, since there was famine in the land of Canaan.

⁶Joseph, as governor of the country, was the one who sold grain to all the people of the land. When Joseph's brothers came, they bowed down to him with their faces to the ground. ⁷He recognized them as soon as he saw them. But he concealed his own identity from them and spoke harshly to them. "Where do you come from?" he asked them. They answered, "From the land of Canaan, to buy food."

⁸When Joseph recognized his brothers, although they did not recognize him, ⁹he was reminded of the dreams he had about them. He said to them: "You are spies. You have come to see the weak points of the land." ¹⁰"No, my lord," they replied. "On the contrary, your servants have come to buy food. ¹¹All of us are sons of the same man. We are honest men; your servants have never been spies." ¹²But he answered them: "Not so! It is the weak points of the land that you have come to see." ¹³"We your servants," they said, "are twelve brothers, sons of a certain man in Canaan; but the youngest one is at present with our father, and the other one is no more." ¹⁴"It is just as I said," Joseph persisted; "you are spies. ¹⁵This is how you shall be tested: I swear by the life of Pharaoh that you shall not leave here unless your youngest brother comes here. ¹⁶So send one of your number to get your brother, while the rest of you stay here under arrest. Thus will your words be tested for their truth; if they are untrue, as Pharaoh lives, you are spies!" ¹⁷With that, he locked them up in the guardhouse for three days.

¹⁸On the third day Joseph said to them: "Do this, and you shall live; for I am a God-fearing man. ¹⁹If you are honest men, let one of your brothers be confined in this prison, while the rest of you go and take home grain for your starving families. ²⁰But you must bring me your youngest brother. Your words will thus be verified, and you will not die." To this they agreed. ²¹To one another, however, they said: "Truly we are being punished because of our brother. We saw the anguish of his heart when he pleaded with us, yet we would not listen. That is why this anguish has now come upon us." ²²Then Reuben responded, "Did I not tell you, 'Do no wrong to the boy'? But you would not listen! Now comes the reckoning for his blood." ²³They did not know, of course, that Joseph understood what they said, since he spoke with them through an interpreter. ²⁴But turning away from them, he wept. When he was able to speak to them again, he took Simeon from among them and bound him before their eyes. ²⁵Then Joseph gave orders to have their containers filled with grain, their money replaced in each one's sack, and provisions given them for their journey. After this had been done for them, ²⁶they loaded their donkeys with the grain and departed.

²⁷At the night encampment, when one of them opened his bag to give his donkey some fodder, he saw his money there in the mouth of his bag. ²⁸He cried out to his brothers, "My money has been returned! Here it is in my bag!" At that their hearts sank. Trembling, they asked one another, "What is this that God has done to us?"

²⁹When they got back to their father Jacob in the land of Canaan, they told him all that had happened to them. ³⁰"The man who is lord of the land," they said, "spoke to us harshly and put us in custody on the grounds that we were spying on the land. ³¹But we said to him: 'We are honest men; we have never been spies. ³²We are twelve brothers, sons of the same father; but one is

no more, and the youngest one is now with our father in the land of Canaan.' ³³Then the man who is lord of the land said to us: 'This is how I will know if you are honest men: leave one of your brothers with me, then take grain for your starving families and go. ³⁴When you bring me your youngest brother, and I know that you are not spies but honest men, I will restore your brother to you, and you may move about freely in the land.'"

³⁵When they were emptying their sacks, there in each one's sack was his moneybag! At the sight of their moneybags, they and their father were afraid. ³⁶Their father Jacob said to them: "Must you make me childless? Joseph is no more, Simeon is no more, and now you would take Benjamin away! All these things have happened to me!" ³⁷Then Reuben told his father: "You may kill my own two sons if I do not return him to you! Put him in my care, and I will bring him back to you." ³⁸But Jacob replied: "My son shall not go down with you. Now that his brother is dead, he is the only one left. If some disaster should befall him on the journey you must make, you would send my white head down to Sheol in grief."

☐ MARK 6:30-56

The Return of the Twelve. 6:30 The apostles gathered together with Jesus and reported all they had done and taught. ³¹He said to them, "Come away by yourselves to a deserted place and rest a while." People were coming and going in great numbers, and they had no opportunity even to eat. ³²So they went off in the boat by themselves to a deserted place. ³³People saw them leaving and many came to know about it. They hastened there on foot from all the towns and arrived at the place before them.

The Feeding of the Five Thousand. ³⁴When he disembarked and saw the vast crowd, his heart was moved with pity for them, for they were like sheep without a shepherd; and he began to teach them many things. ³⁵By now it was already late and his disciples approached him and said, "This is a deserted place and it is already very late. ³⁶Dismiss them so that they can go to the surrounding farms and villages and buy themselves something to eat." ³⁷He said to them in reply, "Give them some food yourselves." But they said to him, "Are we to buy two hundred days' wages worth of food and give it to them to eat?" ³⁸He asked them, "How many loaves do you have? Go and see." And when they had found out they said, "Five loaves and two fish." ³⁹So he gave orders to have them sit down in groups on the green grass. ⁴⁰The people took their places in rows by hundreds and by fifties. ⁴¹Then, taking the five loaves and the two fish and looking up to heaven, he said the blessing, broke the loaves, and gave them to [his] disciples to set before the people; he also divided the two fish among them all. ⁴²They all ate and were satisfied. ⁴³And they picked up twelve wicker baskets full of fragments and what was left of the fish. ⁴⁴Those who ate [of the loaves] were five thousand men.

The Walking on the Water. ⁴⁵Then he made his disciples get into the boat and precede him to the other side toward Bethsaida, while he dismissed the crowd. ⁴⁶And when he had taken leave of them, he went off to the mountain to pray. ⁴⁷When it was evening, the boat was far out on the sea and he was alone on shore. ⁴⁸Then he saw that they were tossed about while rowing, for the wind was against them. About the fourth watch of the night, he came toward them walking on the sea. He meant to pass by them. ⁴⁹But when they saw him walking on the sea, they thought it was a ghost and cried out. ⁵⁰They had all seen him and were terrified. But at once he spoke with them, "Take courage, it is I, do not be afraid!" [51]He got into the boat with them and the wind died down. They were [completely] astounded. [52]They had not understood the incident of the loaves. On the contrary, their hearts were hardened.

The Healings at Gennesaret. [53]After making the crossing, they came to land at Gennesaret and tied up there. [54]As they were leaving the boat, people immediately recognized him. [55]They scurried about the surrounding country and began to bring in the sick on mats to wherever they heard he was. [56]Whatever villages or towns or countryside he entered, they laid the sick in the marketplaces and begged him that they might touch only the tassel on his cloak; and as many as touched it were healed.

January 18

St. Jaime Hilario

The day you learn to surrender yourself totally to God, you will discover a new world. You will enjoy a peace and a calm unknown, surpassing even the happiest days of your life.

— ST. JAIME HILARIO

☐ GENESIS 43-46

The Second Journey to Egypt. 43:1 Now the famine in the land grew severe. [2]So when they had used up all the grain they had brought from Egypt, their father said to them, "Go back and buy us a little more food." [3]But Judah replied: "The man strictly warned us, 'You shall not see me unless your brother is with you.' [4]If you are willing to let our brother go with us, we will go down to buy food for you. [5]But if you are not willing, we will not go down, because the man told us, 'You shall not see me unless your brother is with you.'" [6]Israel demanded, "Why did you bring this trouble on me by telling the man that you had another brother?" [7]They answered: "The man kept asking about us and our family: 'Is your father still living? Do you have another brother?' We answered him accordingly. How could we know that he would say, 'Bring your brother down here'?"

[8]Then Judah urged his father Israel: "Let the boy go with me, that we may be off and on our way if you and we and our children are to keep from starving to death. [9]I myself will serve as a guarantee for him. You can hold me responsible for him. If I fail to bring him back and set him before you, I will bear the blame before you forever. [10]Had we not delayed, we could have been there and back twice by now!"

[11]Israel their father then told them: "If it must be so, then do this: Put some of the land's best products in your baggage and take them down to the man as gifts: some balm and honey, gum and resin, and pistachios and almonds. [12]Also take double the money along, for you must return the amount that was put back in the mouths of your bags; it may have been a mistake. [13]Take your brother, too, and be off on your way back to the man. [14]May God Almighty

grant you mercy in the presence of the man, so that he may let your other brother go, as well as Benjamin. As for me, if I am to suffer bereavement, I shall suffer it."

¹⁵So the men took those gifts and double the money and Benjamin. They made their way down to Egypt and presented themselves before Joseph. ¹⁶When Joseph saw them and Benjamin, he told his steward, "Take the men into the house, and have an animal slaughtered and prepared, for they are to dine with me at noon." ¹⁷Doing as Joseph had ordered, the steward conducted the men to Joseph's house. ¹⁸But they became apprehensive when they were led to his house. "It must be," they thought, "on account of the money put back in our bags the first time, that we are taken inside—in order to attack us and take our donkeys and seize us as slaves." ¹⁹So they went up to Joseph's steward and talked to him at the entrance of the house. ²⁰"If you please, sir," they said, "we came down here once before to buy food. ²¹But when we arrived at a night's encampment and opened our bags, there was each man's money in the mouth of his bag—our money in the full amount! We have now brought it back. ²²We have brought other money to buy food. We do not know who put our money in our bags." ²³He replied, "Calm down! Do not fear! Your God and the God of your father must have put treasure in your bags for you. As for your money, I received it." With that, he led Simeon out to them.

²⁴The steward then brought the men inside Joseph's house. He gave them water to wash their feet, and gave fodder to their donkeys. ²⁵Then they set out their gifts to await Joseph's arrival at noon, for they had heard that they were to dine there. ²⁶When Joseph came home, they presented him with the gifts they had brought inside, while they bowed down before him to the ground. ²⁷After inquiring how they were, he asked them, "And how is your aged father, of whom you spoke? Is he still alive?"

²⁸"Your servant our father is still alive and doing well," they said, as they knelt and bowed down. ²⁹Then Joseph looked up and saw Benjamin, his brother, the son of his mother. He asked, "Is this your youngest brother, of whom you told me?" Then he said to him, "May God be gracious to you, my son!" ³⁰With that, Joseph hurried out, for he was so overcome with affection for his brother that he was on the verge of tears. So he went into a private room and wept there.

³¹After washing his face, he reappeared and, now having collected himself, gave the order, "Serve the meal." ³²It was served separately to him, to the brothers, and to the Egyptians who partook of his board. Egyptians may not eat with Hebrews; that is abhorrent to them. ³³When they were seated before him according to their age, from the oldest to the youngest, they looked at one another in amazement; ³⁴and as portions were brought to them from Joseph's table, Benjamin's portion was five times as large as anyone else's. So they drank freely and made merry with him.

Final Test. 44:1 Then Joseph commanded his steward: "Fill the men's bags with as much food as they can carry, and put each man's money in the mouth of his bag. ²In the mouth of the youngest one's bag put also my silver goblet, together with the money for his grain." The steward did as Joseph said. ³At daybreak the men and their donkeys were sent off. ⁴They had not gone far out of the city when Joseph said to his steward: "Go at once after the men! When you overtake them, say to them, 'Why did you repay good with evil? Why did you steal my silver goblet? ⁵Is it not the very one from which my master drinks and which he uses for divination? What you have done is wrong.'"

⁶When the steward overtook them and repeated these words to them, ⁷they said to him: "Why does my lord say such things?

Far be it from your servants to do such a thing! [8]We even brought back to you from the land of Canaan the money that we found in the mouths of our bags. How could we steal silver or gold from your master's house? [9]If any of your servants is found to have the goblet, he shall die, and as for the rest of us, we shall become my lord's slaves." [10]But he replied, "Now what you propose is fair enough, but only the one who is found to have it shall become my slave, and the rest of you can go free." [11]Then each of them quickly lowered his bag to the ground and opened it; [12]and when a search was made, starting with the oldest and ending with the youngest, the goblet turned up in Benjamin's bag. [13]At this, they tore their garments. Then, when each man had loaded his donkey again, they returned to the city.

[14]When Judah and his brothers entered Joseph's house, he was still there; so they flung themselves on the ground before him. [15]"How could you do such a thing?" Joseph asked them. "Did you not know that such a man as I could discern by divination what happened?" [16]Judah replied: "What can we say to my lord? How can we plead or how try to prove our innocence? God has uncovered your servants' guilt. Here we are, then, the slaves of my lord—the rest of us no less than the one in whose possession the goblet was found." [17]Joseph said, "Far be it from me to act thus! Only the one in whose possession the goblet was found shall become my slave; the rest of you may go back unharmed to your father."

[18]Judah then stepped up to him and said: "I beg you, my lord, let your servant appeal to my lord, and do not become angry with your servant, for you are the equal of Pharaoh. [19]My lord asked his servants, 'Have you a father, or another brother?' [20]So we said to my lord, 'We have an aged father, and a younger brother, the child of his old age. This one's full brother is dead, and since he is the only one by his mother who is left, his father is devoted to him.' [21]Then you told your servants, 'Bring him down to me that I might see him.' [22]We replied to my lord, 'The boy cannot leave his father; his father would die if he left him.' [23]But you told your servants, 'Unless your youngest brother comes down with you, you shall not see me again.' [24]When we returned to your servant my father, we reported to him the words of my lord.

[25]"Later, our father said, 'Go back and buy some food for us.' [26]So we reminded him, 'We cannot go down there; only if our youngest brother is with us can we go, for we may not see the man if our youngest brother is not with us.' [27]Then your servant my father said to us, 'As you know, my wife bore me two sons. [28]One of them, however, has gone away from me, and I said, "He must have been torn to pieces by wild beasts!" I have not seen him since. [29]If you take this one away from me too, and a disaster befalls him, you will send my white head down to Sheol in grief.'

[30]"So now, if the boy is not with us when I go back to your servant my father, whose very life is bound up with his, he will die as soon as he sees that the boy is missing; [31]and your servants will thus send the white head of your servant our father down to Sheol in grief. [32]Besides, I, your servant, have guaranteed the boy's safety for my father by saying, 'If I fail to bring him back to you, father, I will bear the blame before you forever.' [33]So now let me, your servant, remain in place of the boy as the slave of my lord, and let the boy go back with his brothers. [34]How could I go back to my father if the boy were not with me? I could not bear to see the anguish that would overcome my father."

The Truth Revealed. 45:1 Joseph could no longer restrain himself in the presence of all his attendants, so he cried out, "Have everyone withdraw from me!" So no one attended him when he made himself known to his brothers. ²But his sobs were so loud that the Egyptians heard him, and so the news reached Pharaoh's house. ³"I am Joseph," he said to his brothers. "Is my father still alive?" But his brothers could give him no answer, so dumbfounded were they at him.

⁴"Come closer to me," Joseph told his brothers. When they had done so, he said: "I am your brother Joseph, whom you sold into Egypt. ⁵But now do not be distressed, and do not be angry with yourselves for having sold me here. It was really for the sake of saving lives that God sent me here ahead of you. ⁶The famine has been in the land for two years now, and for five more years cultivation will yield no harvest. ⁷God, therefore, sent me on ahead of you to ensure for you a remnant on earth and to save your lives in an extraordinary deliverance. ⁸So it was not really you but God who had me come here; and he has made me a father to Pharaoh, lord of all his household, and ruler over the whole land of Egypt.

⁹"Hurry back, then, to my father and tell him: 'Thus says your son Joseph: God has made me lord of all Egypt; come down to me without delay. ¹⁰You can settle in the region of Goshen, where you will be near me—you and your children and children's children, your flocks and herds, and everything that you own. ¹¹I will provide for you there in the five years of famine that lie ahead, so that you and your household and all that are yours will not suffer want.' ¹²Surely, you can see for yourselves, and Benjamin can see for himself, that it is I who am speaking to you. ¹³Tell my father all about my high position in Egypt and all that you have seen. But hurry and bring my father down here." ¹⁴Then he threw his arms around his brother Benjamin and wept on his shoulder. ¹⁵Joseph then kissed all his brothers and wept over them; and only then were his brothers able to talk with him.

¹⁶The news reached Pharaoh's house: "Joseph's brothers have come." Pharaoh and his officials were pleased. ¹⁷So Pharaoh told Joseph: "Say to your brothers: 'This is what you shall do: Load up your animals and go without delay to the land of Canaan. ¹⁸There get your father and your households, and then come to me; I will assign you the best land in Egypt, where you will live off the fat of the land.' ¹⁹Instruct them further: 'Do this. Take wagons from the land of Egypt for your children and your wives and bring your father back here. ²⁰Do not be concerned about your belongings, for the best in the whole land of Egypt shall be yours.'"

²¹The sons of Israel acted accordingly. Joseph gave them the wagons, as Pharaoh had ordered, and he supplied them with provisions for the journey. ²²He also gave to each of them a set of clothes, but to Benjamin he gave three hundred shekels of silver and five sets of clothes. ²³Moreover, what he sent to his father was ten donkeys loaded with the finest products of Egypt and another ten loaded with grain and bread and provisions for his father's journey. ²⁴As he sent his brothers on their way, he told them, "Do not quarrel on the way."

²⁵So they went up from Egypt and came to the land of Canaan, to their father Jacob. ²⁶When they told him, "Joseph is still alive—in fact, it is he who is governing all the land of Egypt," he was unmoved, for he did not believe them. ²⁷But when they recounted to him all that Joseph had told them, and when he saw the wagons that Joseph had sent to transport him, the spirit of their father Jacob came to life. ²⁸"Enough," said Israel. "My son Joseph is still alive! I must go and see him before I die."

Migration to Egypt. 46:1 Israel set out with all that was his. When he arrived at Beersheba, he offered sacrifices to the God of his father Isaac. ²There God, speaking to Israel in a vision by night, called: Jacob! Jacob!

He answered, "Here I am." ³Then he said: I am God, the God of your father. Do not be afraid to go down to Egypt, for there I will make you a great nation. ⁴I will go down to Egypt with you and I will also bring you back here, after Joseph has closed your eyes.

⁵So Jacob departed from Beer-sheba, and the sons of Israel put their father and their wives and children on the wagons that Pharaoh had sent to transport him. ⁶They took with them their livestock and the possessions they had acquired in the land of Canaan. So Jacob and all his descendants came to Egypt. ⁷His sons and his grandsons, his daughters and his granddaughters—all his descendants—he took with him to Egypt.

⁸These are the names of the Israelites, Jacob and his children, who came to Egypt.

Reuben, Jacob's firstborn, ⁹and the sons of Reuben: Hanoch, Pallu, Hezron, and Carmi. ¹⁰The sons of Simeon: Jemuel, Jamin, Ohad, Jachin, Zohar, and Shaul, son of a Canaanite woman. ¹¹The sons of Levi: Gershon, Kohath, and Merari. ¹²The sons of Judah: Er, Onan, Shelah, Perez, and Zerah—but Er and Onan had died in the land of Canaan; and the sons of Perez were Hezron and Hamul. ¹³The sons of Issachar: Tola, Puah, Jashub, and Shimron. ¹⁴The sons of Zebulun: Sered, Elon, and Jahleel. ¹⁵These were the sons whom Leah bore to Jacob in Paddan-aram, along with his daughter Dinah—thirty-three persons in all, sons and daughters.

¹⁶The sons of Gad: Zephon, Haggi, Shuni, Ezbon, Eri, Arod, and Areli. ¹⁷The sons of Asher: Imnah, Ishvah, Ishvi, and Beriah, with their sister Serah; and the sons of Beriah: Heber and Malchiel. ¹⁸These are the children of Zilpah, whom Laban had given to his daughter Leah; these she bore to Jacob—sixteen persons in all.

¹⁹The sons of Jacob's wife Rachel: Joseph and Benjamin. ²⁰In the land of Egypt Joseph became the father of Manasseh and Ephraim, whom Asenath, daughter of Potiphera, priest of Heliopolis, bore to him. ²¹The sons of Benjamin: Bela, Becher, Ashbel, Gera, Naaman, Ahiram, Shupham, Hupham, and Ard. ²²These are the sons whom Rachel bore to Jacob—fourteen persons in all.

²³The sons of Dan: Hushim. ²⁴The sons of Naphtali: Jahzeel, Guni, Jezer, and Shillem. ²⁵These are the sons of Bilhah, whom Laban had given to his daughter Rachel; these she bore to Jacob—seven persons in all.

²⁶Jacob's people who came to Egypt—his direct descendants, not counting the wives of Jacob's sons—numbered sixty-six persons in all. ²⁷Together with Joseph's sons who were born to him in Egypt—two persons—all the people comprising the household of Jacob who had come to Egypt amounted to seventy persons in all.

²⁸Israel had sent Judah ahead to Joseph, so that he might meet him in Goshen. On his arrival in the region of Goshen, ²⁹Joseph prepared his chariot and went up to meet his father Israel in Goshen. As soon as Israel made his appearance, Joseph threw his arms around him and wept a long time on his shoulder. ³⁰And Israel said to Joseph, "At last I can die, now that I have seen for myself that you are still alive."

³¹Joseph then said to his brothers and his father's household: "I will go up and inform Pharaoh, telling him: 'My brothers and my father's household, whose home is in the land of Canaan, have come to me. ³²The men are shepherds, having been owners of livestock; and they have brought with them their flocks and herds, as well as everything else they own.' ³³So when Pharaoh summons you and asks what your occupation is, ³⁴you must answer, 'We your servants, like our ancestors, have been owners of livestock from our youth until now,' in order that you may stay in the region of Goshen, since all shepherds are abhorrent to the Egyptians."

☐ MARK 7:1-23

The Tradition of the Elders. 7:1 Now when the Pharisees with some scribes who had come from Jerusalem gathered around him, [2]they observed that some of his disciples ate their meals with unclean, that is, unwashed, hands. [3](For the Pharisees and, in fact, all Jews, do not eat without carefully washing their hands, keeping the tradition of the elders. [4]And on coming from the marketplace they do not eat without purifying themselves. And there are many other things that they have traditionally observed, the purification of cups and jugs and kettles [and beds].) [5]So the Pharisees and scribes questioned him, "Why do your disciples not follow the tradition of the elders but instead eat a meal with unclean hands?" [6]He responded, "Well did Isaiah prophesy about you hypocrites, as it is written:

'This people honors me with their lips,
　　but their hearts are far from me;
[7]In vain do they worship me,
　　teaching as doctrines human
　　　　precepts.'

[8]You disregard God's commandment but cling to human tradition." [9]He went on to say, "How well you have set aside the commandment of God in order to uphold your tradition! [10]For Moses said, 'Honor your father and your mother,' and 'Whoever curses father or mother shall die.' [11]Yet you say, 'If a person says to father or mother, "Any support you might have had from me is *qorban*"' (meaning, dedicated to God), [12]you allow him to do nothing more for his father or mother. [13]You nullify the word of God in favor of your tradition that you have handed on. And you do many such things." [14]He summoned the crowd again and said to them, "Hear me, all of you, and understand. [15]Nothing that enters one from outside can defile that person; but the things that come out from within are what defile." [16]

[17]When he got home away from the crowd his disciples questioned him about the parable. [18]He said to them, "Are even you likewise without understanding? Do you not realize that everything that goes into a person from outside cannot defile, [19]since it enters not the heart but the stomach and passes out into the latrine?" (Thus he declared all foods clean.) [20]"But what comes out of a person, that is what defiles. [21]From within people, from their hearts, come evil thoughts, unchastity, theft, murder, [22]adultery, greed, malice, deceit, licentiousness, envy, blasphemy, arrogance, folly. [23]All these evils come from within and they defile."

January 19

The Incarnation is the most stupendous event which ever can take place on earth; and after it and henceforth, I do not see how we can scruple at any miracle on the mere ground of its being unlikely to happen.

— BLESSED JOHN HENRY NEWMAN

☐ GENESIS 47-50

Settlement in Goshen. 47:1 Joseph went and told Pharaoh, "My father and my brothers have come from the land of Canaan, with their flocks and herds and everything else they own; and they are now in the region of Goshen." ²He then presented to Pharaoh five of his brothers whom he had selected from their full number. ³When Pharaoh asked them, "What is your occupation?" they answered, "We, your servants, like our ancestors, are shepherds. ⁴We have come," they continued, "in order to sojourn in this land, for there is no pasture for your servants' flocks, because the famine has been severe in the land of Canaan. So now please let your servants settle in the region of Goshen." ⁵Pharaoh said to Joseph, "Now that your father and your brothers have come to you, ⁶the land of Egypt is at your disposal; settle your father and brothers in the pick of the land. Let them settle in the region of Goshen. And if you know of capable men among them, put them in charge of my livestock." ⁷Then Joseph brought his father Jacob and presented him to Pharaoh. And Jacob blessed Pharaoh. ⁸Then Pharaoh asked Jacob, "How many years have you lived?" ⁹Jacob replied: "The years I have lived as a wayfarer amount to a hundred and thirty. Few and hard have been these years of my life, and they do not compare with the years that my ancestors lived as wayfarers." ¹⁰Then Jacob blessed Pharaoh and withdrew from his presence.

¹¹Joseph settled his father and brothers and gave them a holding in Egypt on the pick of the land, in the region of Rameses, as Pharaoh had ordered. ¹²And Joseph provided food for his father and brothers and his father's whole household, down to the youngest.

Joseph's Land Policy. ¹³Since there was no food in all the land because of the extreme severity of the famine, and the lands of Egypt and Canaan were languishing from hunger, ¹⁴Joseph gathered in, as payment for the grain that they were buying, all the money that was to be found in Egypt and Canaan, and he put it in Pharaoh's house. ¹⁵When all the money in Egypt and Canaan was spent, all the Egyptians came to Joseph, pleading, "Give us food! Why should we perish in front of you? For our money is gone." ¹⁶"Give me your livestock if your money is gone," replied Joseph. "I will give you food in return for your livestock." ¹⁷So they brought their livestock to Joseph, and he gave them food in exchange for their horses, their flocks of sheep and herds of cattle, and their donkeys. Thus he supplied them with food in exchange for all their livestock in that year. ¹⁸That year ended, and they came to him in the next one and said: "We cannot hide from my lord that, with our money spent and our livestock made over to my lord, there is nothing left to put at my lord's disposal except our bodies and our land. ¹⁹Why should we and our land perish before your very eyes? Take us and our land in exchange for food, and we will become Pharaoh's slaves and our land his property; only give us seed, that we may survive and not perish, and that our land may not turn into a waste."

²⁰So Joseph acquired all the land of Egypt for Pharaoh. Each of the Egyptians sold his field, since the famine weighed heavily upon them. Thus the land passed over to Pharaoh, ²¹and the people were reduced to slavery, from one end of Egypt's territory to the other. ²²Only the priests' lands Joseph did not acquire. Since the priests had a fixed allowance from Pharaoh and lived off the allowance Pharaoh had granted them, they did not have to sell their land.

²³Joseph told the people: "Now that I have acquired you and your land for Pharaoh, here is your seed for sowing the land. ²⁴But when the harvest is in, you must give a fifth of it to Pharaoh, while you keep four-fifths as seed for your fields and as food for yourselves and your households and as food for your children." ²⁵"You have saved our lives!" they answered. "We have found favor with my lord; now we will be Pharaoh's slaves." ²⁶Thus Joseph made it a statute for the land of Egypt, which is still in force, that a fifth of its produce should go to Pharaoh. Only the land of the priests did not pass over to Pharaoh.

Israel Blesses Ephraim and Manasseh.
²⁷Thus Israel settled in the land of Egypt, in the region of Goshen. There they acquired holdings, were fertile, and multiplied greatly. ²⁸Jacob lived in the land of Egypt for seventeen years; the span of his life came to a hundred and forty-seven years. ²⁹When the time approached for Israel to die, he called his son Joseph and said to him: "If it pleases you, put your hand under my thigh as a sign of your enduring fidelity to me; do not bury me in Egypt. ³⁰When I lie down with my ancestors, take me out of Egypt and bury me in their burial place." "I will do as you say," he replied. ³¹But his father demanded, "Swear it to me!" So Joseph swore to him. Then Israel bowed at the head of the bed.

48:1 Some time afterward, Joseph was informed, "Your father is failing." So he took along with him his two sons, Manasseh and Ephraim. ²When Jacob was told, "Your son Joseph has come to you," Israel rallied his strength and sat up in bed.

³Jacob then said to Joseph: "God Almighty appeared to me at Luz in the land of Canaan, and blessing me, ⁴he said, 'I will make you fertile and multiply you and make you into an assembly of peoples, and I will give this land to your descendants after you as a permanent possession.' ⁵So now your two sons who were born to you in the land of Egypt before I joined you here, shall be mine; Ephraim and Manasseh shall be mine as much as Reuben and Simeon are mine. ⁶Progeny born to you after them shall remain yours; but their heritage shall be recorded in the names of their brothers. ⁷I do this because, when I was returning from Paddan, your mother Rachel died, to my sorrow, during the journey in Canaan, while we were still a short distance from Ephrath; and I buried her there on the way to Ephrath [now Bethlehem]."

⁸When Israel saw Joseph's sons, he asked, "Who are these?" ⁹"They are my sons," Joseph answered his father, "whom God has given me here." "Bring them to me," said his father, "that I may bless them." ¹⁰Now Israel's eyes were dim from age; he could not see well. When Joseph brought his sons close to him, he kissed and embraced them. ¹¹Then Israel said to Joseph, "I never expected to see your face again, and now God has allowed me to see your descendants as well!"

¹²Joseph removed them from his father's knees and bowed down before him with his face to the ground. ¹³Then Joseph took the two, Ephraim with his right hand, to Israel's left, and Manasseh with his left hand, to Israel's right, and brought them up to him. ¹⁴But Israel, crossing his hands, put out his right hand and laid it on the head of Ephraim, although he was the younger, and his left hand on the head of Manasseh,

although he was the firstborn. [15]Then he blessed them with these words:

"May the God in whose presence
my fathers Abraham and Isaac
walked,
The God who has been my shepherd
from my birth to this day,
[16]The angel who has delivered me from
all harm,
bless these boys
That in them my name be recalled,
and the names of my fathers,
Abraham and Isaac,
And they may become teeming
multitudes
upon the earth!"

[17]When Joseph saw that his father had laid his right hand on Ephraim's head, this seemed wrong to him; so he took hold of his father's hand, to remove it from Ephraim's head to Manasseh's, [18]saying, "That is not right, father; the other one is the firstborn; lay your right hand on his head!" [19]But his father refused. "I know it, son," he said, "I know. That one too shall become a people, and he too shall be great. Nevertheless, his younger brother shall surpass him, and his descendants shall become a multitude of nations." [20]So he blessed them that day and said, "By you shall the people of Israel pronounce blessings, saying, 'God make you like Ephraim and Manasseh.'" Thus he placed Ephraim before Manasseh.

[21]Then Israel said to Joseph: "I am about to die. But God will be with you and will restore you to the land of your ancestors. [22]As for me, I give to you, as to the one above his brothers, Shechem, which I captured from the Amorites with my sword and bow."

Jacob's Testament. 49:1 Jacob called his sons and said: "Gather around, that I may tell you what is to happen to you in days to come.

[2]"Assemble and listen, sons of Jacob,
listen to Israel, your father.

[3]"You, Reuben, my firstborn,
my strength and the first fruit of my
vigor,
excelling in rank and excelling in
power!
[4]Turbulent as water, you shall no
longer excel,
for you climbed into your father's
bed
and defiled my couch to my sorrow.

[5]"Simeon and Levi, brothers indeed,
weapons of violence are their knives.
[6]Let not my person enter their council,
or my honor be joined with their
company;
For in their fury they killed men,
at their whim they maimed oxen.
[7]Cursed be their fury so fierce,
and their rage so cruel!
I will scatter them in Jacob,
disperse them throughout Israel.

[8]"You, Judah, shall your brothers praise
—your hand on the neck of your
enemies;
the sons of your father shall bow
down to you.
[9]Judah is a lion's cub,
you have grown up on prey,
my son.
He crouches, lies down like a lion,
like a lioness—who would dare
rouse him?
[10]The scepter shall never depart from
Judah,
or the mace from between his feet,
Until tribute comes to him,
and he receives the people's
obedience.
[11]He tethers his donkey to the vine,
his donkey's foal to the choicest
stem.
In wine he washes his garments,
his robe in the blood of grapes.

[12]His eyes are darker than wine,
and his teeth are whiter than milk.

[13]"Zebulun shall dwell by the
seashore;
he will be a haven for ships,
and his flank shall rest on Sidon.

[14]"Issachar is a rawboned donkey,
crouching between the saddlebags.
[15]When he saw how good a settled
life was,
and how pleasant the land,
He bent his shoulder to the burden
and became a toiling serf.

[16]"Dan shall achieve justice for his
people
as one of the tribes of Israel.
[17]Let Dan be a serpent by the
roadside,
a horned viper by the path,
That bites the horse's heel,
so that the rider tumbles
backward.

[18]"I long for your deliverance,
O LORD!

[19]"Gad shall be raided by raiders,
but he shall raid at their heels.

[20]"Asher's produce is rich,
and he shall furnish delicacies for
kings.

[21]"Naphtali is a hind let loose,
which brings forth lovely fawns.

[22]"Joseph is a wild colt,
a wild colt by a spring,
wild colts on a hillside.
[23]Harrying him and shooting,
the archers opposed him;
[24]But his bow remained taut,
and his arms were nimble,
By the power of the Mighty One of
Jacob,
because of the Shepherd, the Rock
of Israel,

[25]The God of your father, who helps
you,
God Almighty, who blesses you,
With the blessings of the heavens
above,
the blessings of the abyss that
crouches below,
The blessings of breasts and womb,
[26]the blessings of fresh grain and
blossoms,
the blessings of the everlasting
mountains,
the delights of the eternal hills.
May they rest on the head of Joseph,
on the brow of the prince among
his brothers.

[27]"Benjamin is a ravenous wolf;
mornings he devours the prey,
and evenings he distributes the
spoils."

Farewell and Death. [28]All these are the twelve tribes of Israel, and this is what their father said about them, as he blessed them. To each he gave a suitable blessing. [29]Then he gave them this charge: "Since I am about to be gathered to my people, bury me with my ancestors in the cave that lies in the field of Ephron the Hittite, [30]the cave in the field of Machpelah, facing on Mamre, in the land of Canaan, the field that Abraham bought from Ephron the Hittite for a burial ground. [31]There Abraham and his wife Sarah are buried, and so are Isaac and his wife Rebekah, and there, too, I buried Leah— [32]the field and the cave in it that had been purchased from the Hittites."

[33]When Jacob had finished giving these instructions to his sons, he drew his feet into the bed, breathed his last, and was gathered to his people.

Jacob's Funeral. 50:1 Joseph flung himself upon his father and wept over him as he kissed him. [2]Then Joseph ordered the physicians in his service to embalm his father. When the physicians embalmed Israel,

[3]they spent forty days at it, for that is the full period of embalming; and the Egyptians mourned him for seventy days. [4]When the period of mourning was over, Joseph spoke to Pharaoh's household. "If you please, appeal to Pharaoh, saying: [5]My father made me swear: 'I am dying. Bury me in my grave that I have prepared for myself in the land of Canaan.' So now let me go up to bury my father. Then I will come back." [6]Pharaoh replied, "Go and bury your father, as he made you promise on oath."

[7]So Joseph went up to bury his father; and with him went all of Pharaoh's officials who were senior members of his household and all the other elders of the land of Egypt, [8]as well as Joseph's whole household, his brothers, and his father's household; only their children and their flocks and herds were left in the region of Goshen. [9]Chariots, too, and horsemen went up with him; it was a very imposing retinue.

[10]When they arrived at Goren-ha-atad, which is beyond the Jordan, they held there a very great and solemn memorial service; and Joseph observed seven days of mourning for his father. [11]When the Canaanites who inhabited the land saw the mourning at Goren-ha-atad, they said, "This is a solemn funeral on the part of the Egyptians!" That is why the place was named Abel-mizraim. It is beyond the Jordan.

[12]Thus Jacob's sons did for him as he had instructed them. [13]They carried him to the land of Canaan and buried him in the cave in the field of Machpelah, facing on Mamre, the field that Abraham had bought for a burial ground from Ephron the Hittite. [14]After Joseph had buried his father he returned to Egypt, together with his brothers and all who had gone up with him for the burial of his father.

Plea for Forgiveness. [15]Now that their father was dead, Joseph's brothers became fearful and thought, "Suppose Joseph has been nursing a grudge against us and now most certainly will pay us back in full for all the wrong we did him!" [16]So they sent to Joseph and said: "Before your father died, he gave us these instructions: [17]'Thus you shall say to Joseph: Please forgive the criminal wrongdoing of your brothers, who treated you harmfully.' So now please forgive the crime that we, the servants of the God of your father, committed." When they said this to him, Joseph broke into tears. [18]Then his brothers also proceeded to fling themselves down before him and said, "We are your slaves!" [19]But Joseph replied to them: "Do not fear. Can I take the place of God? [20]Even though you meant harm to me, God meant it for good, to achieve this present end, the survival of many people. [21]So now, do not fear. I will provide for you and for your children." By thus speaking kindly to them, he reassured them.

[22]Joseph remained in Egypt, together with his father's household. He lived a hundred and ten years. [23]He saw Ephraim's children to the third generation, and the children of Manasseh's son Machir were also born on Joseph's knees.

Death of Joseph. [24]Joseph said to his brothers: "I am about to die. God will surely take care of you and lead you up from this land to the land that he promised on oath to Abraham, Isaac and Jacob." [25]Then, putting the sons of Israel under oath, he continued, "When God thus takes care of you, you must bring my bones up from this place." [26]Joseph died at the age of a hundred and ten. He was embalmed and laid to rest in a coffin in Egypt.

☐ MARK 7:24-37

The Syrophoenician Woman's Faith.
7:24 From that place he went off to the district of Tyre. He entered a house and wanted no one to know about it, but he could not escape notice. ²⁵Soon a woman whose daughter had an unclean spirit heard about him. She came and fell at his feet. ²⁶The woman was a Greek, a Syrophoenician by birth, and she begged him to drive the demon out of her daughter. ²⁷He said to her, "Let the children be fed first. For it is not right to take the food of the children and throw it to the dogs." ²⁸She replied and said to him, "Lord, even the dogs under the table eat the children's scraps." ²⁹Then he said to her, "For saying this, you may go. The demon has gone out of your daughter." ³⁰When the woman went home, she found the child lying in bed and the demon gone.

The Healing of a Deaf Man. ³¹Again he left the district of Tyre and went by way of Sidon to the Sea of Galilee, into the district of the Decapolis. ³²And people brought to him a deaf man who had a speech impediment and begged him to lay his hand on him. ³³He took him off by himself away from the crowd. He put his finger into the man's ears and, spitting, touched his tongue; ³⁴then he looked up to heaven and groaned, and said to him, "*Ephphatha!*" (that is, "Be opened!") ³⁵And [immediately] the man's ears were opened, his speech impediment was removed, and he spoke plainly. ³⁶He ordered them not to tell anyone. But the more he ordered them not to, the more they proclaimed it. ³⁷They were exceedingly astonished and they said, "He has done all things well. He makes the deaf hear and [the] mute speak."

January 20

St. Fabian; St. Sebastian

God is always almighty; He can at all times work miracles, and He would work them now as in the days of old were it not that faith is lacking!

— St. John Vianney

☐ EXODUS 1-2

Jacob's Descendants in Egypt. 1:1 These are the names of the sons of Israel who, accompanied by their households, entered into Egypt with Jacob: ²Reuben, Simeon, Levi and Judah; ³Issachar, Zebulun and Benjamin; ⁴Dan and Naphtali; Gad and Asher. ⁵The total number of Jacob's direct descendants was seventy. Joseph was already in Egypt.

⁶Now Joseph and all his brothers and that whole generation died. ⁷But the Israelites were fruitful and prolific. They multiplied and became so very numerous that the land was filled with them.

The Oppression. ⁸Then a new king, who knew nothing of Joseph, rose to power in Egypt. ⁹He said to his people, "See! The Israelite people have multiplied and become more numerous than we are! ¹⁰Come, let us deal shrewdly with them to stop their increase; otherwise, in time of war they too may join our enemies to fight against us, and so leave the land."

[11]Accordingly, they set supervisors over the Israelites to oppress them with forced labor. Thus they had to build for Pharaoh the garrison cities of Pithom and Raamses. [12]Yet the more they were oppressed, the more they multiplied and spread, so that the Egyptians began to loathe the Israelites. [13]So the Egyptians reduced the Israelites to cruel slavery, [14]making life bitter for them with hard labor, at mortar and brick and all kinds of field work—cruelly oppressed in all their labor.

Command to the Midwives. [15]The king of Egypt told the Hebrew midwives, one of whom was called Shiphrah and the other Puah, [16]"When you act as midwives for the Hebrew women, look on the birthstool: if it is a boy, kill him; but if it is a girl, she may live." [17]The midwives, however, feared God; they did not do as the king of Egypt had ordered them, but let the boys live. [18]So the king of Egypt summoned the midwives and asked them, "Why have you done this, allowing the boys to live?" [19]The midwives answered Pharaoh, "The Hebrew women are not like the Egyptian women. They are robust and give birth before the midwife arrives." [20]Therefore God dealt well with the midwives; and the people multiplied and grew very numerous. [21]And because the midwives feared God, God built up families for them. [22]Pharaoh then commanded all his people, "Throw into the Nile every boy that is born, but you may let all the girls live."

Birth and Adoption of Moses. 2:1 Now a man of the house of Levi married a Levite woman, [2]and the woman conceived and bore a son. Seeing what a fine child he was, she hid him for three months. [3]But when she could no longer hide him, she took a papyrus basket, daubed it with bitumen and pitch, and putting the child in

it, placed it among the reeds on the bank of the Nile. [4]His sister stationed herself at a distance to find out what would happen to him.

[5]Then Pharaoh's daughter came down to bathe at the Nile, while her attendants walked along the bank of the Nile. Noticing the basket among the reeds, she sent her handmaid to fetch it. [6]On opening it, she looked, and there was a baby boy crying! She was moved with pity for him and said, "It is one of the Hebrews' children." [7]Then his sister asked Pharaoh's daughter, "Shall I go and summon a Hebrew woman to nurse the child for you?" [8]Pharaoh's daughter answered her, "Go." So the young woman went and called the child's own mother. [9]Pharaoh's daughter said to her, "Take this child and nurse him for me, and I will pay your wages." So the woman took the child and nursed him. [10]When the child grew, she brought him to Pharaoh's daughter, and he became her son. She named him Moses; for she said, "I drew him out of the water."

Moses' Flight to Midian. [11]On one occasion, after Moses had grown up, when he had gone out to his kinsmen and witnessed their forced labor, he saw an Egyptian striking a Hebrew, one of his own kinsmen. [12]Looking about and seeing no one, he struck down the Egyptian and hid him in the sand. [13]The next day he went out again, and now two Hebrews were fighting! So he asked the culprit, "Why are you striking your companion?" [14]But he replied, "Who has appointed you ruler and judge over us? Are you thinking of killing me as you killed the Egyptian?" Then Moses became afraid and thought, "The affair must certainly be known." [15]When Pharaoh heard of the affair, he sought to kill Moses. But Moses fled from Pharaoh and went to the land of Midian. There he sat down by a well.

[16]Now the priest of Midian had seven daughters, and they came to draw water and fill the troughs to water their father's

flock. [17]But shepherds came and drove them away. So Moses rose up in their defense and watered their flock. [18]When they returned to their father Reuel, he said to them, "How is it you have returned so soon today?" [19]They answered, "An Egyptian delivered us from the shepherds. He even drew water for us and watered the flock!" [20]"Where is he?" he asked his daughters. "Why did you leave the man there? Invite him to have something to eat." [21]Moses agreed to stay with him, and the man gave

☐ MARK 8:1-26

The Feeding of Four Thousand. 8:1 In those days when there again was a great crowd without anything to eat, he summoned the disciples and said, [2]"My heart is moved with pity for the crowd, because they have been with me now for three days and have nothing to eat. [3]If I send them away hungry to their homes, they will collapse on the way, and some of them have come a great distance." [4]His disciples answered him, "Where can anyone get enough bread to satisfy them here in this deserted place?" [5]Still he asked them, "How many loaves do you have?" "Seven," they replied. [6]He ordered the crowd to sit down on the ground. Then, taking the seven loaves he gave thanks, broke them, and gave them to his disciples to distribute, and they distributed them to the crowd. [7]They also had a few fish. He said the blessing over them and ordered them distributed also. [8]They ate and were satisfied. They picked up the fragments left over—seven baskets. [9]There were about four thousand people.

He dismissed them [10]and got into the boat with his disciples and came to the region of Dalmanutha.

The Demand for a Sign. [11]The Pharisees came forward and began to argue with him, seeking from him a sign from heaven to test him. [12]He sighed from the depth of

Moses his daughter Zipporah in marriage. [22]She conceived and bore a son, whom he named Gershom; for he said, "I am a stranger residing in a foreign land."

The Burning Bush. [23]A long time passed, during which the king of Egypt died. The Israelites groaned under their bondage and cried out, and from their bondage their cry for help went up to God. [24]God heard their moaning and God was mindful of his covenant with Abraham, Isaac and Jacob. [25]God saw the Israelites, and God knew. . . .

his spirit and said, "Why does this generation seek a sign? Amen, I say to you, no sign will be given to this generation." [13]Then he left them, got into the boat again, and went off to the other shore.

The Leaven of the Pharisees. [14]They had forgotten to bring bread, and they had only one loaf with them in the boat. [15]He enjoined them, "Watch out, guard against the leaven of the Pharisees and the leaven of Herod." [16]They concluded among themselves that it was because they had no bread. [17]When he became aware of this he said to them, "Why do you conclude that it is because you have no bread? Do you not yet understand or comprehend? Are your hearts hardened? [18]Do you have eyes and not see, ears and not hear? And do you not remember, [19]when I broke the five loaves for the five thousand, how many wicker baskets full of fragments you picked up?" They answered him, "Twelve." [20]"When I broke the seven loaves for the four thousand, how many full baskets of fragments did you pick up?" They answered [him], "Seven." [21]He said to them, "Do you still not understand?"

The Blind Man of Bethsaida. [22]When they arrived at Bethsaida, they brought to him a blind man and begged him to touch him. [23]He took the blind man by the hand

and led him outside the village. Putting spittle on his eyes he laid his hands on him and asked, "Do you see anything?" ²⁴Looking up he replied, "I see people looking like trees and walking." ²⁵Then he laid hands on his eyes a second time and he saw clearly; his sight was restored and he could see everything distinctly. ²⁶Then he sent him home and said, "Do not even go into the village."

January 21

St. Agnes

Christ has made my soul beautiful with the jewels of grace and virtue. I belong to Him whom the angels serve.

— St. Agnes

☐ EXODUS 3-4

3:1 Meanwhile Moses was tending the flock of his father-in-law Jethro, the priest of Midian. Leading the flock beyond the wilderness, he came to the mountain of God, Horeb. ²There the angel of the LORD appeared to him as fire flaming out of a bush. When he looked, although the bush was on fire, it was not being consumed. ³So Moses decided, "I must turn aside to look at this remarkable sight. Why does the bush not burn up?" ⁴When the LORD saw that he had turned aside to look, God called out to him from the bush: Moses! Moses! He answered, "Here I am." ⁵God said: Do not come near! Remove your sandals from your feet, for the place where you stand is holy ground. ⁶I am the God of your father, he continued, the God of Abraham, the God of Isaac, and the God of Jacob. Moses hid his face, for he was afraid to look at God.

The Call and Commission of Moses. ⁷But the LORD said: I have witnessed the affliction of my people in Egypt and have heard their cry against their taskmasters, so I know well what they are suffering. ⁸Therefore I have come down to rescue them from the power of the Egyptians and lead them up from that land into a good and spacious land, a land flowing with milk and honey, the country of the Canaanites, the Hittites, the Amorites, the Perizzites, the Girgashites, the Hivites and the Jebusites. ⁹Now indeed the outcry of the Israelites has reached me, and I have seen how the Egyptians are oppressing them. ¹⁰Now, go! I am sending you to Pharaoh to bring my people, the Israelites, out of Egypt.

¹¹But Moses said to God, "Who am I that I should go to Pharaoh and bring the Israelites out of Egypt?" ¹²God answered: I will be with you; and this will be your sign that I have sent you. When you have brought the people out of Egypt, you will serve God at this mountain. ¹³"But," said Moses to God, "if I go to the Israelites and say to them, 'The God of your ancestors has sent me to you,' and they ask me, 'What is his name?' what do I tell them?" ¹⁴God replied to Moses: I am who I am. Then he added: This is what you will tell the Israelites: I AM has sent me to you.

¹⁵God spoke further to Moses: This is what you will say to the Israelites: The LORD, the God of your ancestors, the God of Abraham, the God of Isaac, and the God of Jacob, has sent me to you.

This is my name forever;

this is my title for all generations.

[16]Go and gather the elders of the Israelites, and tell them, The LORD, the God of your ancestors, the God of Abraham, Isaac, and Jacob, has appeared to me and said: I have observed you and what is being done to you in Egypt; [17]so I have decided to lead you up out of your affliction in Egypt into the land of the Canaanites, the Hittites, the Amorites, the Perizzites, the Girgashites, the Hivites and the Jebusites, a land flowing with milk and honey. [18]They will listen to you. Then you and the elders of Israel will go to the king of Egypt and say to him: The LORD, the God of the Hebrews, has come to meet us. So now, let us go a three days' journey in the wilderness to offer sacrifice to the LORD, our God. [19]Yet I know that the king of Egypt will not allow you to go unless his hand is forced. [20]So I will stretch out my hand and strike Egypt with all the wondrous deeds I will do in its midst. After that he will let you go. [21]I will even make the Egyptians so well-disposed toward this people that, when you go, you will not go empty-handed. [22]Every woman will ask her neighbor and the resident alien in her house for silver and gold articles and for clothing, and you will put them on your sons and daughters. So you will plunder the Egyptians.

4:1 "But," objected Moses, "suppose they do not believe me or listen to me? For they may say, 'The LORD did not appear to you.'" [2]The LORD said to him: What is in your hand? "A staff," he answered. [3]God said: Throw it on the ground. So he threw it on the ground and it became a snake, and Moses backed away from it. [4]Then the LORD said to Moses: Now stretch out your hand and take hold of its tail. So he stretched out his hand and took hold of it, and it became a staff in his hand. [5]That is so they will believe that the LORD, the God

of their ancestors, the God of Abraham, the God of Isaac, and the God of Jacob, did appear to you.

[6]Again the LORD said to him: Put your hand into the fold of your garment. So he put his hand into the fold of his garment, and when he drew it out, there was his hand covered with scales, like snowflakes. [7]Then God said: Put your hand back into the fold of your garment. So he put his hand back into the fold of his garment, and when he drew it out, there it was again like his own flesh. [8]If they do not believe you or pay attention to the message of the first sign, they should believe the message of the second sign. [9]And if they do not believe even these two signs and do not listen to you, take some water from the Nile and pour it on the dry land. The water you take from the Nile will become blood on the dry land.

Aaron's Office as Assistant. [10]Moses, however, said to the LORD, "If you please, my Lord, I have never been eloquent, neither in the past nor now that you have spoken to your servant; but I am slow of speech and tongue." [11]The LORD said to him: Who gives one person speech? Who makes another mute or deaf, seeing or blind? Is it not I, the LORD? [12]Now go, I will assist you in speaking and teach you what you are to say. [13]But he said, "If you please, my Lord, send someone else!" [14]Then the LORD became angry with Moses and said: I know there is your brother, Aaron the Levite, who is a good speaker; even now he is on his way to meet you. When he sees you, he will truly be glad. [15]You will speak to him and put the words in his mouth. I will assist both you and him in speaking and teach you both what you are to do. [16]He will speak to the people for you: he will be your spokesman, and you will be as God to him. [17]Take this staff in your hand; with it you are to perform the signs.

Moses' Return to Egypt. [18]After this Moses returned to Jethro his father-in-law and said to him, "Let me return to my kindred in

Egypt, to see whether they are still living." Jethro replied to Moses, "Go in peace." ¹⁹Then the LORD said to Moses in Midian: Return to Egypt, for all those who sought your life are dead. ²⁰So Moses took his wife and his sons, mounted them on the donkey, and started back to the land of Egypt. Moses took the staff of God with him. ²¹The LORD said to Moses: On your return to Egypt, see that you perform before Pharaoh all the wonders I have put in your power. But I will harden his heart and he will not let the people go. ²²So you will say to Pharaoh, Thus says the LORD: Israel is my son, my firstborn. ²³I said to you: Let my son go, that he may serve me. Since you refused to let him go, I will kill your son, your firstborn.

²⁴On the journey, at a place where they spent the night, the LORD came upon Moses and sought to put him to death. ²⁵But Zipporah took a piece of flint and cut off her son's foreskin and, touching his feet, she said, "Surely you are a spouse of blood to me." ²⁶So God let Moses alone. At that time she said, "A spouse of blood," in regard to the circumcision.

²⁷The LORD said to Aaron: Go into the wilderness to meet Moses. So he went; when meeting him at the mountain of God, he kissed him. ²⁸Moses told Aaron everything the LORD had sent him to say, and all the signs he had commanded him to do. ²⁹Then Moses and Aaron went and gathered all the elders of the Israelites. ³⁰Aaron told them everything the LORD had said to Moses, and he performed the signs before the people. ³¹The people believed, and when they heard that the LORD had observed the Israelites and had seen their affliction, they knelt and bowed down.

☐ MARK 8:27–9:1

Peter's Confession about Jesus. 8:27 Now Jesus and his disciples set out for the villages of Caesarea Philippi. Along the way he asked his disciples, "Who do people say that I am?" ²⁸They said in reply, "John the Baptist, others Elijah, still others one of the prophets." ²⁹And he asked them, "But who do you say that I am?" Peter said to him in reply, "You are the Messiah." ³⁰Then he warned them not to tell anyone about him.

The First Prediction of the Passion. ³¹He began to teach them that the Son of Man must suffer greatly and be rejected by the elders, the chief priests, and the scribes, and be killed, and rise after three days. ³²He spoke this openly. Then Peter took him aside and began to rebuke him. ³³At this he turned around and, looking at his disciples, rebuked Peter and said, "Get behind me, Satan. You are thinking not as God does, but as human beings do."

The Conditions of Discipleship. ³⁴He summoned the crowd with his disciples and said to them, "Whoever wishes to come after me must deny himself, take up his cross, and follow me. ³⁵For whoever wishes to save his life will lose it, but whoever loses his life for my sake and that of the gospel will save it. ³⁶What profit is there for one to gain the whole world and forfeit his life? ³⁷What could one give in exchange for his life? ³⁸Whoever is ashamed of me and of my words in this faithless and sinful generation, the Son of Man will be ashamed of when he comes in his Father's glory with the holy angels."

9:1 He also said to them, "Amen, I say to you, there are some standing here who will not taste death until they see that the kingdom of God has come in power."

January 22

Remember that the Christian life is one of action, not of speech and daydreams. Let there be few words and many deeds, and let them be done well.

— St. Vincent Pallotti

☐ EXODUS 5-6:27

Pharaoh's Hardness of Heart. 5:1 Afterwards, Moses and Aaron went to Pharaoh and said, "Thus says the Lord, the God of Israel: Let my people go, that they may hold a feast for me in the wilderness." [2]Pharaoh answered, "Who is the Lord, that I should obey him and let Israel go? I do not know the Lord, and I will not let Israel go." [3]They replied, "The God of the Hebrews has come to meet us. Let us go a three days' journey in the wilderness, that we may offer sacrifice to the Lord, our God, so that he does not strike us with the plague or the sword." [4]The king of Egypt answered them, "Why, Moses and Aaron, do you make the people neglect their work? Off to your labors!" [5]Pharaoh continued, "Look how they are already more numerous than the people of the land, and yet you would give them rest from their labors!"

[6]That very day Pharaoh gave the taskmasters of the people and their foremen this order: [7]"You shall no longer supply the people with straw for their brickmaking as before. Let them go and gather their own straw! [8]Yet you shall levy upon them the same quota of bricks as they made previously. Do not reduce it. They are lazy; that is why they are crying, 'Let us go to offer sacrifice to our God.' [9]Increase the work for the men, so that they attend to it and not to deceitful words."

[10]So the taskmasters of the people and their foremen went out and told the people, "Thus says Pharaoh, 'I will not provide you with straw. [11]Go and get your own straw from wherever you can find it. But there will not be the slightest reduction in your work.'" [12]The people, then, scattered throughout the land of Egypt to gather stubble for straw, [13]while the taskmasters kept driving them on, saying, "Finish your work, the same daily amount as when the straw was supplied to you." [14]The Israelite foremen, whom the taskmasters of Pharaoh had placed over them, were beaten, and were asked, "Why have you not completed your prescribed amount of bricks yesterday and today, as before?"

Complaint of the Foremen. [15]Then the Israelite foremen came and cried out to Pharaoh: "Why do you treat your servants in this manner? [16]No straw is supplied to your servants, and still we are told, 'Make bricks!' Look how your servants are beaten! It is you who are at fault." [17]He answered, "Lazy! You are lazy! That is why you keep saying, 'Let us go and offer sacrifice to the Lord.' [18]Now off to work! No straw will be supplied to you, but you must supply your quota of bricks."

[19]The Israelite foremen realized they were in trouble, having been told, "Do not reduce your daily amount of bricks!" [20]So when they left Pharaoh they assailed Moses and Aaron, who were waiting to meet them, [21]and said to them, "The Lord look upon you and judge! You have made us offensive to Pharaoh and his servants, putting a sword into their hands to kill us."

Renewal of God's Promise. [22]Then Moses again had recourse to the Lord and said, "Lord, why have you treated this people badly? And why did you send me?

[23]From the time I went to Pharaoh to speak in your name, he has treated this people badly, and you have done nothing to rescue your people."

6:1 The LORD answered Moses: Now you will see what I will do to Pharaoh. For by a strong hand, he will let them go; by a strong hand, he will drive them from his land. **Confirmation of the Promise to the Ancestors.** [2]Then God spoke to Moses, and said to him: I am the LORD. [3]As God the Almighty I appeared to Abraham, Isaac, and Jacob, but by my name, LORD, I did not make myself known to them. [4]I also established my covenant with them, to give them the land of Canaan, the land in which they were residing as aliens. [5]Now that I have heard the groaning of the Israelites, whom the Egyptians have reduced to slavery, I am mindful of my covenant. [6]Therefore, say to the Israelites: I am the LORD. I will free you from the burdens of the Egyptians and will deliver you from their slavery. I will redeem you by my outstretched arm and with mighty acts of judgment. [7]I will take you as my own people, and I will be your God; and you will know that I, the LORD, am your God who has freed you from the burdens of the Egyptians [8]and I will bring you into the land which I swore to give to Abraham, Isaac, and Jacob. I will give it to you as your own possession—I, the LORD! [9]But when Moses told this to the Israelites, they would not listen to him because of their dejection and hard slavery.

[10]Then the LORD spoke to Moses: [11]Go, tell Pharaoh, king of Egypt, to let the Israelites leave his land. [12]However, Moses protested to the LORD, "If the Israelites did not listen to me, how is it possible that Pharaoh will listen to me, poor speaker that I am!" [13]But the LORD spoke to Moses and Aaron regarding the Israelites and Pharaoh, king of Egypt, and charged them to bring the Israelites out of the land of Egypt.

Genealogy of Moses and Aaron. [14]These are the heads of their ancestral houses. The sons of Reuben, the firstborn of Israel: Hanoch, Pallu, Hezron and Carmi; these are the clans of Reuben. [15]The sons of Simeon: Jemuel, Jamin, Ohad, Jachin, Zohar and Shaul, the son of a Canaanite woman; these are the clans of Simeon. [16]These are the names of the sons of Levi, in their genealogical order: Gershon, Kohath and Merari. Levi lived one hundred and thirty-seven years.

[17]The sons of Gershon, by their clans: Libni and Shimei. [18]The sons of Kohath: Amram, Izhar, Hebron and Uzziel. Kohath lived one hundred and thirty-three years. [19]The sons of Merari: Mahli and Mushi. These are the clans of Levi in their genealogical order.

[20]Amram married his aunt Jochebed, who bore him Aaron, Moses, and Miriam. Amram lived one hundred and thirty-seven years. [21]The sons of Izhar: Korah, Nepheg and Zichri. [22]The sons of Uzziel: Mishael, Elzaphan and Sithri. [23]Aaron married Elisheba, Amminadab's daughter, the sister of Nahshon; she bore him Nadab, Abihu, Eleazar and Ithamar. [24]The sons of Korah: Assir, Elkanah and Abiasaph. These are the clans of the Korahites. [25]Eleazar, Aaron's son, married one of Putiel's daughters, who bore him Phinehas. These are the heads of the ancestral houses of the Levites by their clans. [26]These are the Aaron and the Moses to whom the LORD said, "Bring the Israelites out from the land of Egypt, company by company." [27]They are the ones who spoke to Pharaoh, king of Egypt, to bring the Israelites out of Egypt—the same Moses and Aaron.

☐ MARK 9:2-13

The Transfiguration of Jesus. 9:2 After six days Jesus took Peter, James, and John and led them up a high mountain apart by themselves. And he was transfigured before them, ³and his clothes became dazzling white, such as no fuller on earth could bleach them. ⁴Then Elijah appeared to them along with Moses, and they were conversing with Jesus. ⁵Then Peter said to Jesus in reply, "Rabbi, it is good that we are here! Let us make three tents: one for you, one for Moses, and one for Elijah." ⁶He hardly knew what to say, they were so terrified. ⁷Then a cloud came, casting a shadow over them; then from the cloud came a voice, "This is my beloved Son. Listen to him." ⁸Suddenly, looking around, they no longer saw anyone but Jesus alone with them.

The Coming of Elijah. ⁹As they were coming down from the mountain, he charged them not to relate what they had seen to anyone, except when the Son of Man had risen from the dead. ¹⁰So they kept the matter to themselves, questioning what rising from the dead meant. ¹¹Then they asked him, "Why do the scribes say that Elijah must come first?" ¹²He told them, "Elijah will indeed come first and restore all things, yet how is it written regarding the Son of Man that he must suffer greatly and be treated with contempt? ¹³But I tell you that Elijah has come and they did to him whatever they pleased, as it is written of him."

January 23

St. John the Almoner

If we are able to enter the church day and night and implore God to hear our prayers, how careful we should be to hear and grant the petitions of our neighbor in need.

— ST. JOHN THE ALMONER

☐ EXODUS 6:28-8:28

6:28 When the LORD spoke to Moses in the land of Egypt ²⁹the LORD said to Moses: I am the LORD. Say to Pharaoh, king of Egypt, all that I tell you. ³⁰But Moses protested to the LORD, "Since I am a poor speaker, how is it possible that Pharaoh will listen to me?"

7:1 The LORD answered Moses: See! I have made you a god to Pharaoh, and Aaron your brother will be your prophet. ²You will speak all that I command you. In turn, your brother Aaron will tell Pharaoh to let the Israelites go out of his land. ³Yet I will make Pharaoh so headstrong that, despite the many signs and wonders that I work in the land of Egypt, ⁴Pharaoh will not listen to you. Therefore I will lay my hand on Egypt and with mighty acts of judgment I will bring my armies, my people the Israelites, out of the land of Egypt. ⁵All Egyptians will know that I am the LORD, when I stretch out my hand against Egypt and bring the Israelites out of their midst.

⁶This, then, is what Moses and Aaron did. They did exactly as the LORD had com-

manded them. [7]Moses was eighty years old, and Aaron eighty-three, when they spoke to Pharaoh.

The Staff Turned into a Serpent. [8]The LORD spoke to Moses and Aaron: [9]When Pharaoh demands of you, "Produce a sign or wonder," you will say to Aaron: "Take your staff and throw it down before Pharaoh, and it will turn into a serpent." [10]Then Moses and Aaron went to Pharaoh and did just as the LORD had commanded. Aaron threw his staff down before Pharaoh and his servants, and it turned into a serpent. [11]Pharaoh, in turn, summoned the wise men and the sorcerers, and they also, the magicians of Egypt, did the same thing by their magic arts. [12]Each one threw down his staff, and they turned into serpents. But Aaron's staff swallowed their staffs. [13]Pharaoh, however, hardened his heart and would not listen to them, just as the LORD had foretold.

First Plague: Water Turned into Blood. [14]Then the LORD said to Moses: Pharaoh is obstinate in refusing to let the people go. [15]In the morning, just when he sets out for the water, go to Pharaoh and present yourself by the bank of the Nile, holding in your hand the staff that turned into a snake. [16]Say to him: The LORD, the God of the Hebrews, sent me to you with the message: Let my people go to serve me in the wilderness. But as yet you have not listened. [17]Thus says the LORD: This is how you will know that I am the LORD. With the staff here in my hand, I will strike the water in the Nile and it will be changed into blood. [18]The fish in the Nile will die, and the Nile itself will stink so that the Egyptians will be unable to drink water from the Nile.

[19]The LORD then spoke to Moses: Speak to Aaron: Take your staff and stretch out your hand over the waters of Egypt—its streams, its canals, its ponds, and all its supplies of water—that they may become blood. There will be blood throughout the land of Egypt, even in the wooden pails and stone jars.

[20]This, then, is what Moses and Aaron did, exactly as the LORD had commanded. Aaron raised his staff and struck the waters in the Nile in full view of Pharaoh and his servants, and all the water in the Nile was changed into blood. [21]The fish in the Nile died, and the Nile itself stank so that the Egyptians could not drink water from it. There was blood throughout the land of Egypt. [22]But the Egyptian magicians did the same by their magic arts. So Pharaoh hardened his heart and would not listen to them, just as the LORD had said. [23]Pharaoh turned away and went into his house, with no concern even for this. [24]All the Egyptians had to dig round about the Nile for drinking water, since they could not drink any water from the Nile.

Second Plague: the Frogs. [25]Seven days passed after the LORD had struck the Nile. [26]Then the LORD said to Moses: Go to Pharaoh and tell him: Thus says the LORD: Let my people go to serve me. [27]If you refuse to let them go, then I will send a plague of frogs over all your territory. [28]The Nile will teem with frogs. They will come up and enter into your palace and into your bedroom and onto your bed, into the houses of your servants, too, and among your people, even into your ovens and your kneading bowls. [29]The frogs will come up over you and your people and all your servants.

8:1 The LORD then spoke to Moses: Speak to Aaron: Stretch out your hand with your staff over the streams, the canals, and the ponds, and make frogs overrun the land of Egypt. [2]So Aaron stretched out his hand over the waters of Egypt, and the frogs came up and covered the land of Egypt. [3]But the magicians did the same by their magic arts and made frogs overrun the land of Egypt.

[4]Then Pharaoh summoned Moses and Aaron and said, "Pray to the LORD to

remove the frogs from me and my people, and I will let the people go to sacrifice to the LORD." [5]Moses answered Pharaoh, "Please designate for me the time when I am to pray for you and your servants and your people, to get rid of the frogs from you and your houses. They will be left only in the Nile." [6]"Tomorrow," he said. Then Moses replied, "It will be as you have said, so that you may know that there is none like the LORD, our God. [7]The frogs will leave you and your houses, your servants and your people; they will be left only in the Nile."

[8]After Moses and Aaron left Pharaoh's presence, Moses cried out to the LORD on account of the frogs that he had inflicted on Pharaoh; [9]and the LORD did as Moses had asked. The frogs died off in the houses, the courtyards, and the fields. [10]Heaps of them were piled up, and the land stank. [11]But when Pharaoh saw there was a respite, he became obstinate and would not listen to them, just as the LORD had said.

Third Plague: the Gnats. [12]Thereupon the LORD spoke to Moses: Speak to Aaron: Stretch out your staff and strike the dust of the earth, and it will turn into gnats throughout the land of Egypt. [13]They did so. Aaron stretched out his hand with his staff and struck the dust of the earth, and gnats came upon human being and beast alike. All the dust of the earth turned into gnats throughout the land of Egypt. [14]Though the magicians did the same thing to produce gnats by their magic arts, they could not do so. The gnats were on human being and beast alike, [15]and the magicians said to Pharaoh, "This is the finger of God." Yet Pharaoh hardened his heart and would not listen to them, just as the LORD had said.

Fourth Plague: the Flies. [16]Then the LORD spoke to Moses: Early tomorrow morning present yourself to Pharaoh when he sets out toward the water, and say to him: Thus says the LORD: Let my people go to serve me. [17]For if you do not let my people go, I will send swarms of flies upon you and your servants and your people and your houses. The houses of the Egyptians and the very ground on which they stand will be filled with swarms of flies. [18]But on that day I will make an exception of the land of Goshen, where my people are, and no swarms of flies will be there, so that you may know that I the LORD am in the midst of the land. [19]I will make a distinction between my people and your people. This sign will take place tomorrow. [20]This the LORD did. Thick swarms of flies entered the house of Pharaoh and the houses of his servants; throughout Egypt the land was devastated on account of the swarms of flies.

[21]Then Pharaoh summoned Moses and Aaron and said, "Go sacrifice to your God within the land." [22]But Moses replied, "It is not right to do so, for what we sacrifice to the LORD, our God, is abhorrent to the Egyptians. If we sacrifice what is abhorrent to the Egyptians before their very eyes, will they not stone us? [23]We must go a three days' journey in the wilderness and sacrifice to the LORD, our God, as he commands us." [24]Pharaoh said, "I will let you go to sacrifice to the LORD, your God, in the wilderness, provided that you do not go too far away. Pray for me." [25]Moses answered, "As soon as I leave you I will pray to the LORD that the swarms of flies may depart tomorrow from Pharaoh, his servants, and his people. Pharaoh, however, must not act deceitfully again and refuse to let the people go to sacrifice to the LORD." [26]When Moses left Pharaoh, he prayed to the LORD; [27]and the LORD did as Moses had asked, removing the swarms of flies from Pharaoh, his servants, and his people. Not one remained. [28]But once more Pharaoh became obstinate and would not let the people go.

☐ MARK 9:14-29

The Healing of a Boy with a Demon. 9:14 When they came to the disciples, they saw a large crowd around them and scribes arguing with them. [15]Immediately on seeing him, the whole crowd was utterly amazed. They ran up to him and greeted him. [16]He asked them, "What are you arguing about with them?" [17]Someone from the crowd answered him, "Teacher, I have brought to you my son possessed by a mute spirit. [18]Wherever it seizes him, it throws him down; he foams at the mouth, grinds his teeth, and becomes rigid. I asked your disciples to drive it out, but they were unable to do so." [19]He said to them in reply, "O faithless generation, how long will I be with you? How long will I endure you? Bring him to me." [20]They brought the boy to him. And when he saw him, the spirit immediately threw the boy into convulsions. As he fell to the ground, he began to roll around and foam at the mouth. [21]Then he questioned his father, "How long has this been happening to him?" He replied, "Since childhood. [22]It has often thrown him into fire and into water to kill him. But if you can do anything, have compassion on us and help us." [23]Jesus said to him, "'If you can!' Everything is possible to one who has faith." [24]Then the boy's father cried out, "I do believe, help my unbelief!" [25]Jesus, on seeing a crowd rapidly gathering, rebuked the unclean spirit and said to it, "Mute and deaf spirit, I command you: come out of him and never enter him again!" [26]Shouting and throwing the boy into convulsions, it came out. He became like a corpse, which caused many to say, "He is dead!" [27]But Jesus took him by the hand, raised him, and he stood up. [28]When he entered the house, his disciples asked him in private, "Why could we not drive it out?" [29]He said to them, "This kind can only come out through prayer."

January 24

St. Francis de Sales

Every moment comes to us pregnant with a command from God, only to pass on and plunge into eternity, there to remain forever what we have made of it.

— St. Francis de Sales

☐ EXODUS 9-10

Fifth Plague: the Pestilence. 9:1 Then the LORD said to Moses: Go to Pharaoh and tell him: Thus says the LORD, the God of the Hebrews: Let my people go to serve me. [2]For if you refuse to let them go and persist in holding them, [3]the hand of the LORD will strike your livestock in the field—your horses, donkeys, camels, herds and flocks—with a very severe pestilence. [4]But the LORD will distinguish between the livestock of Israel and that of Egypt, so that nothing belonging to the Israelites will die. [5]And the LORD set a definite time, saying: Tomorrow the LORD will do this in the land. [6]And on the next day the LORD did it. All the livestock of the Egyptians died, but not one animal belonging to the Israelites died. [7]But although Pharaoh found upon inquiry that not even so much as one of the livestock of the Israelites had died, he remained obstinate and would not let the people go.

Sixth Plague: the Boils. [8]So the LORD said to Moses and Aaron: Each of you take handfuls of soot from a kiln, and in the presence of Pharaoh let Moses scatter it toward the sky. [9]It will turn into fine dust over the whole land of Egypt and cause festering boils on human being and beast alike throughout the land of Egypt.

[10]So they took the soot from a kiln and appeared before Pharaoh. When Moses scattered it toward the sky, it caused festering boils on human being and beast alike. [11]Because of the boils the magicians could not stand in Moses' presence, for there were boils on the magicians as well as on the rest of the Egyptians. [12]But the LORD hardened Pharaoh's heart, and he would not listen to them, just as the LORD had said to Moses.

Seventh Plague: the Hail. [13]Then the LORD spoke to Moses: Early tomorrow morning present yourself to Pharaoh and say to him: Thus says the LORD, the God of the Hebrews: Let my people go to serve me, [14]for this time I will unleash all my blows upon you and your servants and your people, so that you may know that there is none like me anywhere on earth. [15]For by now I should have stretched out my hand and struck you and your people with such pestilence that you would have vanished from the earth. [16]But this is why I have let you survive: to show you my power and to make my name resound throughout the earth! [17]Will you continue to exalt yourself over my people and not let them go? [18]At this time tomorrow, therefore, I am going to rain down such fierce hail as there has never been in Egypt from the day it was founded up to the present. [19]Therefore, order your livestock and whatever else you have in the open fields to be brought to a place of safety. Whatever human being or animal is found in the fields and is not brought to shelter will die when the hail comes down upon them. [20]Those of Pharaoh's servants who feared the word of the LORD hurried their servants and their livestock off to shelter. [21]But those who did not pay attention to the word of the LORD left their servants and their livestock in the fields.

[22]The LORD then said to Moses: Stretch out your hand toward the sky, that hail may fall upon the entire land of Egypt, on human being and beast alike and all the vegetation of the fields in the land of Egypt. [23]So Moses stretched out his staff toward the sky, and the LORD sent forth peals of thunder and hail. Lightning flashed toward the earth, and the LORD rained down hail upon the land of Egypt. [24]There was hail and lightning flashing here and there through the hail, and the hail was so fierce that nothing like it had been seen in Egypt since it became a nation. [25]Throughout the land of Egypt the hail struck down everything in the fields, human being and beast alike; it struck down all the vegetation of the fields and splintered every tree in the fields. [26]Only in the land of Goshen, where the Israelites were, was there no hail.

[27]Then Pharaoh sent for Moses and Aaron and said to them, "I have sinned this time! The LORD is the just one, and I and my people are the ones at fault. [28]Pray to the LORD! Enough of the thunder and hail! I will let you go; you need stay no longer." [29]Moses replied to him, "As soon as I leave the city I will extend my hands to the LORD; the thunder will cease, and there will be no more hail so that you may know that the earth belongs to the LORD. [30]But as for you and your servants, I know that you do not yet fear the LORD God."

[31]Now the flax and the barley were ruined, because the barley was in ear and the flax in bud. [32]But the wheat and the spelt were not ruined, for they grow later.

[33]When Moses had left Pharaoh and gone out of the city, he extended his

hands to the LORD. The thunder and the hail ceased, and the rain no longer poured down upon the earth. [34]But Pharaoh, seeing that the rain and the hail and the thunder had ceased, sinned again and became obstinate, both he and his servants. [35]In the hardness of his heart, Pharaoh would not let the Israelites go, just as the LORD had said through Moses.

Eighth Plague: the Locusts. 10:1 Then the LORD said to Moses: Go to Pharaoh, for I have made him and his servants obstinate in order that I may perform these signs of mine among them [2]and that you may recount to your son and grandson how I made a fool of the Egyptians and what signs I did among them, so that you may know that I am the LORD.

[3]So Moses and Aaron went to Pharaoh and told him, "Thus says the LORD, the God of the Hebrews: How long will you refuse to submit to me? Let my people go to serve me. [4]For if you refuse to let my people go, tomorrow I will bring locusts into your territory. [5]They will cover the surface of the earth, so that the earth itself will not be visible. They will eat up the remnant you saved undamaged from the hail, as well as all the trees that are growing in your fields. [6]They will fill your houses and the houses of your servants and of all the Egyptians—something your parents and your grandparents have not seen from the day they appeared on this soil until today." With that he turned and left Pharaoh.

[7]But Pharaoh's servants said to him, "How long will he be a snare for us? Let the people go to serve the LORD, their God. Do you not yet realize that Egypt is being destroyed?" [8]So Moses and Aaron were brought back to Pharaoh, who said to them, "Go, serve the LORD, your God. But who exactly will go?" [9]Moses answered, "With our young and old we must go; with our sons and daughters, with our flocks and herds we must go. It is a pilgrimage feast of

the LORD for us." [10]"The LORD help you," Pharaoh replied, "if I let your little ones go with you! Clearly, you have some evil in mind. [11]By no means! Just you men go and serve the LORD. After all, that is what you have been asking for." With that they were driven from Pharaoh's presence.

[12]The LORD then said to Moses: Stretch out your hand over the land of Egypt for the locusts, that they may come upon it and eat up all the land's vegetation, whatever the hail has left. [13]So Moses stretched out his staff over the land of Egypt, and the LORD drove an east wind over the land all that day and all night. When it was morning, the east wind brought the locusts. [14]The locusts came up over the whole land of Egypt and settled down over all its territory. Never before had there been such a fierce swarm of locusts, nor will there ever be again. [15]They covered the surface of the whole land, so that it became black. They ate up all the vegetation in the land and all the fruit of the trees the hail had spared. Nothing green was left on any tree or plant in the fields throughout the land of Egypt.

[16]Pharaoh hurriedly summoned Moses and Aaron and said, "I have sinned against the LORD, your God, and against you. [17]But now, do forgive me my sin only this once, and pray to the LORD, your God, only to take this death from me." [18]When Moses left Pharaoh, he prayed to the LORD, [19]and the LORD caused the wind to shift to a very strong west wind, which took up the locusts and hurled them into the Red Sea. Not a single locust remained within the whole territory of Egypt. [20]Yet the LORD hardened Pharaoh's heart, and he would not let the Israelites go.

Ninth Plague: the Darkness. [21]Then the LORD said to Moses: Stretch out your hand toward the sky, that over the land of Egypt there may be such darkness that one can feel it. [22]So Moses stretched out his hand toward the sky, and there was dense darkness throughout the land of Egypt for three days. ²³People could not see one another, nor could they get up from where they were, for three days. But all the Israelites had light where they lived.

²⁴Pharaoh then summoned Moses and Aaron and said, "Go, serve the LORD. Only your flocks and herds will be detained. Even your little ones may go with you." ²⁵But Moses replied, "You also must give us sacrifices and burnt offerings to make to the LORD, our God. ²⁶Our livestock also must go with us. Not an animal must be left behind, for some of them we will select for service to the LORD, our God; but we will not know with which ones we are to serve the LORD until we arrive there." ²⁷But the LORD hardened Pharaoh's heart, and he was unwilling to let them go. ²⁸Pharaoh said to Moses, "Leave me, and see to it that you do not see my face again! For the day you do see my face you will die!" ²⁹Moses replied, "You are right! I will never see your face again."

☐ MARK 9:30-50

The Second Prediction of the Passion. 9:30 They left from there and began a journey through Galilee, but he did not wish anyone to know about it. ³¹He was teaching his disciples and telling them, "The Son of Man is to be handed over to men and they will kill him, and three days after his death he will rise." ³²But they did not understand the saying, and they were afraid to question him.

The Greatest in the Kingdom. ³³They came to Capernaum and, once inside the house, he began to ask them, "What were you arguing about on the way?" ³⁴But they remained silent. They had been discussing among themselves on the way who was the greatest. ³⁵Then he sat down, called the Twelve, and said to them, "If anyone wishes to be first, he shall be the last of all and the servant of all." ³⁶Taking a child he placed it in their midst, and putting his arms around it he said to them, ³⁷"Whoever receives one child such as this in my name, receives me; and whoever receives me, receives not me but the One who sent me."

Another Exorcist. ³⁸John said to him, "Teacher, we saw someone driving out demons in your name, and we tried to prevent him because he does not follow us." ³⁹Jesus replied, "Do not prevent him. There is no one who performs a mighty deed in my name who can at the same time speak ill of me. ⁴⁰For whoever is not against us is for us. ⁴¹Anyone who gives you a cup of water to drink because you belong to Christ, amen, I say to you, will surely not lose his reward.

Temptations to Sin. ⁴²"Whoever causes one of these little ones who believe [in me] to sin, it would be better for him if a great millstone were put around his neck and he were thrown into the sea. ⁴³If your hand causes you to sin, cut it off. It is better for you to enter into life maimed than with two hands to go into Gehenna, into the unquenchable fire. ⁴⁴ ⁴⁵And if your foot causes you to sin, cut it off. It is better for you to enter into life crippled than with two feet to be thrown into Gehenna. ⁴⁷And if your eye causes you to sin, pluck it out. Better for you to enter into the kingdom of God with one eye than with two eyes to be thrown into Gehenna, ⁴⁸where 'their worm does not die, and the fire is not quenched.'

The Simile of Salt. ⁴⁹"Everyone will be salted with fire. ⁵⁰Salt is good, but if salt becomes insipid, with what will you restore its flavor? Keep salt in yourselves and you will have peace with one another."

January 25

The Conversion of St. Paul

Heaven is filled with converted sinners of all kinds, and there is room for more.

— St. Joseph Cafasso

☐ EXODUS 11-12

Tenth Plague: the Death of the Firstborn. 11:1 Then the LORD spoke to Moses: One more plague I will bring upon Pharaoh and upon Egypt. After that he will let you depart. In fact, when he finally lets you go, he will drive you away. ²Instruct the people that every man is to ask his neighbor, and every woman her neighbor, for silver and gold articles and for clothing. ³The LORD indeed made the Egyptians well-disposed toward the people; Moses himself was very highly regarded by Pharaoh's servants and the people in the land of Egypt.

⁴Moses then said, "Thus says the LORD: About midnight I will go forth through Egypt. ⁵Every firstborn in the land of Egypt will die, from the firstborn of Pharaoh who sits on his throne to the firstborn of the slave-girl who is at the handmill, as well as all the firstborn of the animals. ⁶Then there will be loud wailing throughout the land of Egypt, such as has never been, nor will ever be again. ⁷But among all the Israelites, among human beings and animals alike, not even a dog will growl, so that you may know that the LORD distinguishes between Egypt and Israel. ⁸All these servants of yours will then come down to me and bow down before me, saying: Leave, you and all your followers! Then I will depart." With that he left Pharaoh's presence in hot anger.

⁹The LORD said to Moses: Pharaoh will not listen to you so that my wonders may be multiplied in the land of Egypt. ¹⁰Thus, although Moses and Aaron performed all these wonders in Pharaoh's presence, the LORD hardened Pharaoh's heart, and he would not let the Israelites go from his land.

The Passover Ritual Prescribed. 12:1 The LORD said to Moses and Aaron in the land of Egypt: ²This month will stand at the head of your calendar; you will reckon it the first month of the year. ³Tell the whole community of Israel: On the tenth of this month every family must procure for itself a lamb, one apiece for each household. ⁴If a household is too small for a lamb, it along with its nearest neighbor will procure one, and apportion the lamb's cost in proportion to the number of persons, according to what each household consumes. ⁵Your lamb must be a year-old male and without blemish. You may take it from either the sheep or the goats. ⁶You will keep it until the fourteenth day of this month, and then, with the whole community of Israel assembled, it will be slaughtered during the evening twilight. ⁷They will take some of its blood and apply it to the two doorposts and the lintel of the houses in which they eat it. ⁸They will consume its meat that same night, eating it roasted with unleavened bread and bitter herbs. ⁹Do not eat any of it raw or even boiled in water, but roasted, with its head and shanks and inner organs. ¹⁰You must not keep any of it beyond the morning; whatever is left over in the morning must be burned up.

¹¹This is how you are to eat it: with your loins girt, sandals on your feet and your staff in hand, you will eat it in a hurry. It is the LORD's Passover. ¹²For on this same night I will go through Egypt, striking down every firstborn in the land, human being and beast alike, and executing judgment on all the gods of Egypt—I, the

LORD! [13]But for you the blood will mark the houses where you are. Seeing the blood, I will pass over you; thereby, when I strike the land of Egypt, no destructive blow will come upon you.

[14]This day will be a day of remembrance for you, which your future generations will celebrate with pilgrimage to the LORD; you will celebrate it as a statute forever. [15]For seven days you must eat unleavened bread. From the very first day you will have your houses clear of all leaven. For whoever eats leavened bread from the first day to the seventh will be cut off from Israel. [16]On the first day you will hold a sacred assembly, and likewise on the seventh. On these days no sort of work shall be done, except to prepare the food that everyone needs. [17]Keep, then, the custom of the unleavened bread, since it was on this very day that I brought your armies out of the land of Egypt. You must observe this day throughout your generations as a statute forever. [18]From the evening of the fourteenth day of the first month until the evening of the twenty-first day of this month you will eat unleavened bread. [19]For seven days no leaven may be found in your houses; for anyone, a resident alien or a native, who eats leavened food will be cut off from the community of Israel. [20]You shall eat nothing leavened; wherever you dwell you may eat only unleavened bread.

Promulgation of the Passover. [21]Moses summoned all the elders of Israel and said to them, "Go and procure lambs for your families, and slaughter the Passover victims. [22]Then take a bunch of hyssop, and dipping it in the blood that is in the basin, apply some of this blood to the lintel and the two doorposts. And none of you shall go outdoors until morning. [23]For when the LORD goes by to strike down the Egyptians, seeing the blood on the lintel and the two doorposts, the LORD will pass over that door and not let the destroyer come into your houses to strike you down.

[24]"You will keep this practice forever as a statute for yourselves and your descendants. [25]Thus, when you have entered the land which the LORD will give you as he promised, you must observe this rite. [26]When your children ask you, 'What does this rite of yours mean?' [27]you will reply, 'It is the Passover sacrifice for the LORD, who passed over the houses of the Israelites in Egypt; when he struck down the Egyptians, he delivered our houses.'"

Then the people knelt and bowed down, [28]and the Israelites went and did exactly as the LORD had commanded Moses and Aaron.

Death of the Firstborn. [29]And so at midnight the LORD struck down every firstborn in the land of Egypt, from the firstborn of Pharaoh sitting on his throne to the firstborn of the prisoner in the dungeon, as well as all the firstborn of the animals. [30]Pharaoh arose in the night, he and all his servants and all the Egyptians; and there was loud wailing throughout Egypt, for there was not a house without its dead.

Permission to Depart. [31]During the night Pharaoh summoned Moses and Aaron and said, "Leave my people at once, you and the Israelites! Go and serve the LORD as you said. [32]Take your flocks, too, and your herds, as you said, and go; and bless me, too!"

[33]The Egyptians, in a hurry to send them away from the land, urged the people on, for they said, "All of us will die!" [34]The people, therefore, took their dough before it was leavened, in their kneading bowls wrapped in their cloaks on their shoulders. [35]And the Israelites did as Moses had commanded: they asked the Egyptians for articles of silver and gold and for clothing. [36]Indeed the LORD had made the Egyptians so well-disposed toward the people that they let them have whatever they asked for. And so they despoiled the Egyptians.

Departure from Egypt. [37]The Israelites set out from Rameses for Succoth, about six hundred thousand men on foot, not counting the children. [38]A crowd of mixed ancestry also went up with them, with livestock in great abundance, both flocks and herds. [39]The dough they had brought out of Egypt they baked into unleavened loaves. It was not leavened, because they had been driven out of Egypt and could not wait. They did not even prepare food for the journey.

[40]The time the Israelites had stayed in Egypt was four hundred and thirty years. [41]At the end of four hundred and thirty years, on this very date, all the armies of the LORD left the land of Egypt. [42]This was a night of vigil for the LORD, when he brought them out of the land of Egypt; so on this night all Israelites must keep a vigil for the LORD throughout their generations.

Law of the Passover. [43]The LORD said to Moses and Aaron: This is the Passover statute. No foreigner may eat of it. [44]However, every slave bought for money you will circumcise; then he may eat of it. [45]But no tenant or hired worker may eat of it. [46]It must be eaten in one house; you may not take any of its meat outside the house. You shall not break any of its bones. [47]The whole community of Israel must celebrate this feast. [48]If any alien residing among you would celebrate the Passover for the LORD, all his males must be circumcised, and then he may join in its celebration just like the natives. But no one who is uncircumcised may eat of it. [49]There will be one law for the native and for the alien residing among you.

[50]All the Israelites did exactly as the LORD had commanded Moses and Aaron. [51]On that same day the LORD brought the Israelites out of the land of Egypt company by company.

☐ MARK 10:1-16

Marriage and Divorce. 10:1 He set out from there and went into the district of Judea [and] across the Jordan. Again crowds gathered around him and, as was his custom, he again taught them. [2]The Pharisees approached and asked, "Is it lawful for a husband to divorce his wife?" They were testing him. [3]He said to them in reply, "What did Moses command you?" [4]They replied, "Moses permitted him to write a bill of divorce and dismiss her." [5]But Jesus told them, "Because of the hardness of your hearts he wrote you this commandment. [6]But from the beginning of creation, 'God made them male and female. [7]For this reason a man shall leave his father and mother [and be joined to his wife], [8]and the two shall become one flesh.' So they are no longer two but one flesh. [9]Therefore what God has joined together, no human being must separate." [10]In the house the disciples again questioned him about this. [11]He said to them, "Whoever divorces his wife and marries another commits adultery against her; [12]and if she divorces her husband and marries another, she commits adultery."

Blessing of the Children. [13]And people were bringing children to him that he might touch them, but the disciples rebuked them. [14]When Jesus saw this he became indignant and said to them, "Let the children come to me; do not prevent them, for the kingdom of God belongs to such as these. [15]Amen, I say to you, whoever does not accept the kingdom of God like a child will not enter it." [16]Then he embraced them and blessed them, placing his hands on them.

January 26

Sts. Timothy and Titus

It is not a sin to have riches, but to fix our hearts upon them.
— St. John Baptist de la Salle

☐ EXODUS 13-14

Consecration of Firstborn. 13:1 The LORD spoke to Moses and said: [2]Consecrate to me every firstborn; whatever opens the womb among the Israelites, whether of human being or beast, belongs to me.

[3]Moses said to the people, "Remember this day on which you came out of Egypt, out of a house of slavery. For it was with a strong hand that the LORD brought you out from there. Nothing made with leaven may be eaten. [4]This day on which you are going out is in the month of Abib. [5]Therefore, when the LORD, your God, has brought you into the land of the Canaanites, the Hittites, the Amorites, the Perrizites, the Girgashites, the Hivites, and the Jebusites, which he swore to your ancestors to give you, a land flowing with milk and honey, you will perform the following service in this month. [6]For seven days you will eat unleavened bread, and the seventh day will also be a festival to the LORD. [7]Unleavened bread may be eaten during the seven days, but nothing leavened and no leaven may be found in your possession in all your territory. [8]And on that day you will explain to your son, 'This is because of what the LORD did for me when I came out of Egypt.' [9]It will be like a sign on your hand and a reminder on your forehead, so that the teaching of the LORD will be on your lips: with a strong hand the LORD brought you out of Egypt. [10]You will keep this statute at its appointed time from year to year.

[11]"When the LORD, your God, has brought you into the land of the Canaanites, just as he swore to you and your ancestors, and gives it to you, [12]you will dedicate to the LORD every newborn that opens the womb; and every firstborn male of your animals will belong to the LORD. [13]Every firstborn of a donkey you will ransom with a sheep. If you do not ransom it, you will break its neck. Every human firstborn of your sons you must ransom. [14]And when your son asks you later on, 'What does this mean?' you will tell him, 'With a strong hand the LORD brought us out of Egypt, out of a house of slavery. [15]When Pharaoh stubbornly refused to let us go, the LORD killed every firstborn in the land of Egypt, the firstborn of human being and beast alike. That is why I sacrifice to the LORD every male that opens the womb, and why I ransom every firstborn of my sons.' [16]It will be like a sign on your hand and a band on your forehead that with a strong hand the LORD brought us out of Egypt."

Toward the Red Sea. [17]Now, when Pharaoh let the people go, God did not lead them by way of the Philistines' land, though this was the nearest; for God said: If the people see that they have to fight, they might change their minds and return to Egypt. [18]Instead, God rerouted them toward the Red Sea by way of the wilderness road, and the Israelites went up out of the land of Egypt arrayed for battle. [19]Moses also took Joseph's bones with him, for Joseph had made the Israelites take a solemn oath, saying, "God will surely take care of you, and you must bring my bones up with you from here."

[20]Setting out from Succoth, they camped at Etham near the edge of the wilderness.

[21]The LORD preceded them, in the daytime by means of a column of cloud to

show them the way, and at night by means of a column of fire to give them light. Thus they could travel both day and night. [22]Neither the column of cloud by day nor the column of fire by night ever left its place in front of the people.

14:1 Then the LORD spoke to Moses: [2]Speak to the Israelites: Let them turn about and camp before Pi-hahiroth, between Migdol and the sea. Camp in front of Baal-zephon, just opposite, by the sea. [3]Pharaoh will then say, "The Israelites are wandering about aimlessly in the land. The wilderness has closed in on them." [4]I will so harden Pharaoh's heart that he will pursue them. Thus I will receive glory through Pharaoh and all his army, and the Egyptians will know that I am the LORD.

This the Israelites did. [5]When it was reported to the king of Egypt that the people had fled, Pharaoh and his servants had a change of heart about the people. "What in the world have we done!" they said. "We have released Israel from our service!" [6]So Pharaoh harnessed his chariots and took his army with him. [7]He took six hundred select chariots and all the chariots of Egypt, with officers on all of them. [8]The LORD hardened the heart of Pharaoh, king of Egypt, so that he pursued the Israelites while they were going out in triumph. [9]The Egyptians pursued them—all Pharaoh's horses, his chariots, his horsemen, and his army—and caught up with them as they lay encamped by the sea, at Pi-hahiroth, in front of Baal-zephon.

Crossing the Red Sea. [10]Now Pharaoh was near when the Israelites looked up and saw that the Egyptians had set out after them. Greatly frightened, the Israelites cried out to the LORD. [11]To Moses they said, "Were there no burial places in Egypt that you brought us to die in the wilderness? What have you done to us, bringing us out of Egypt? [12]Did we not tell you this in Egypt, when we said, 'Leave us alone that we may serve the Egyptians'? Far better for us to serve the Egyptians than to die in the wilderness." [13]But Moses answered the people, "Do not fear! Stand your ground and see the victory the LORD will win for you today. For these Egyptians whom you see today you will never see again. [14]The LORD will fight for you; you have only to keep still."

[15]Then the LORD said to Moses: Why are you crying out to me? Tell the Israelites to set out. [16]And you, lift up your staff and stretch out your hand over the sea, and split it in two, that the Israelites may pass through the sea on dry land. [17]But I will harden the hearts of the Egyptians so that they will go in after them, and I will receive glory through Pharaoh and all his army, his chariots and his horsemen. [18]The Egyptians will know that I am the LORD, when I receive glory through Pharaoh, his chariots, and his horsemen.

[19]The angel of God, who had been leading Israel's army, now moved and went around behind them. And the column of cloud, moving from in front of them, took up its place behind them, [20]so that it came between the Egyptian army and that of Israel. And when it became dark, the cloud illumined the night; and so the rival camps did not come any closer together all night long. [21]Then Moses stretched out his hand over the sea; and the LORD drove back the sea with a strong east wind all night long and turned the sea into dry ground. The waters were split, [22]so that the Israelites entered into the midst of the sea on dry land, with the water as a wall to their right and to their left.

Rout of the Egyptians. [23]The Egyptians followed in pursuit after them—all Pharaoh's horses and chariots and horsemen—into the midst of the sea. [24]But during the watch just before dawn, the LORD looked down from a column of fiery cloud upon the Egyptian army and threw it into a panic; [25]and he so clogged their chariot wheels that they could drive only with difficulty. With that the Egyptians said, "Let us flee from Israel, because the LORD is fighting for them against Egypt."

²⁶Then the LORD spoke to Moses: Stretch out your hand over the sea, that the water may flow back upon the Egyptians, upon their chariots and their horsemen. ²⁷So Moses stretched out his hand over the sea, and at daybreak the sea returned to its normal flow. The Egyptians were fleeing head on toward it when the LORD cast the Egyptians into the midst of the sea. ²⁸As the water flowed back, it covered the chariots and the horsemen. Of all Pharaoh's army which had followed the Israelites into the sea, not even one escaped. ²⁹But the Israelites had walked on dry land through the midst of the sea, with the water as a wall to their right and to their left. ³⁰Thus the LORD saved Israel on that day from the power of Egypt. When Israel saw the Egyptians lying dead on the seashore ³¹and saw the great power that the LORD had shown against Egypt, the people feared the LORD. They believed in the LORD and in Moses his servant.

☐ MARK 10:17-34

The Rich Man. 10:17 As he was setting out on a journey, a man ran up, knelt down before him, and asked him, "Good teacher, what must I do to inherit eternal life?" ¹⁸Jesus answered him, "Why do you call me good? No one is good but God alone. ¹⁹You know the commandments: 'You shall not kill; you shall not commit adultery; you shall not steal; you shall not bear false witness; you shall not defraud; honor your father and your mother.'" ²⁰He replied and said to him, "Teacher, all of these I have observed from my youth." ²¹Jesus, looking at him, loved him and said to him, "You are lacking in one thing. Go, sell what you have, and give to [the] poor and you will have treasure in heaven; then come, follow me." ²²At that statement his face fell, and he went away sad, for he had many possessions.

²³Jesus looked around and said to his disciples, "How hard it is for those who have wealth to enter the kingdom of God!" ²⁴The disciples were amazed at his words. So Jesus again said to them in reply, "Children, how hard it is to enter the kingdom of God! ²⁵It is easier for a camel to pass through [the] eye of [a] needle than for one who is rich to enter the kingdom of God." ²⁶They were exceedingly astonished and said among themselves, "Then who can be saved?" ²⁷Jesus looked at them and said, "For human beings it is impossible, but not for God. All things are possible for God." ²⁸Peter began to say to him, "We have given up everything and followed you." ²⁹Jesus said, "Amen, I say to you, there is no one who has given up house or brothers or sisters or mother or father or children or lands for my sake and for the sake of the gospel ³⁰who will not receive a hundred times more now in this present age: houses and brothers and sisters and mothers and children and lands, with persecutions, and eternal life in the age to come. ³¹But many that are first will be last, and [the] last will be first."

The Third Prediction of the Passion. ³²They were on the way, going up to Jerusalem, and Jesus went ahead of them. They were amazed, and those who followed were afraid. Taking the Twelve aside again, he began to tell them what was going to happen to him. ³³"Behold, we are going up to Jerusalem, and the Son of Man will be handed over to the chief priests and the scribes, and they will condemn him to death and hand him over to the Gentiles ³⁴who will mock him, spit upon him, scourge him, and put him to death, but after three days he will rise."

January 27

St. Angela Merici

Disorder in society is the result of disorder in the family.
— St. Angela Merici

☐ **EXODUS 15-16**

15:1 Then Moses and the Israelites sang this song to the LORD:

I will sing to the LORD, for he is
gloriously triumphant;
horse and chariot he has cast into
the sea.
²My strength and my refuge is the LORD,
and he has become my savior.
This is my God, I praise him;
the God of my father, I extol him.
³The LORD is a warrior,
LORD is his name!
⁴Pharaoh's chariots and army he hurled
into the sea;
the elite of his officers were drowned
in the Red Sea.
⁵The flood waters covered them,
they sank into the depths like a stone.
⁶Your right hand, O LORD, magnificent
in power,
your right hand, O LORD, shattered
the enemy.
⁷In your great majesty you overthrew
your adversaries;
you loosed your wrath to consume
them like stubble.
⁸At the blast of your nostrils the waters
piled up,
the flowing waters stood like a
mound,
the flood waters foamed in the
midst of the sea.
⁹The enemy boasted, "I will pursue and
overtake them;
I will divide the spoils and have my
fill of them;
I will draw my sword; my hand will
despoil them!"

¹⁰When you blew with your breath, the
sea covered them;
like lead they sank in the mighty
waters.
¹¹Who is like you among the gods,
O LORD?
Who is like you, magnificent among
the holy ones?
Awe-inspiring in deeds of renown,
worker of wonders,
¹²when you stretched out your right
hand, the earth swallowed
them!
¹³In your love you led the people you
redeemed;
in your strength you guided them to
your holy dwelling.
¹⁴The peoples heard and quaked;
anguish gripped the dwellers in
Philistia.
¹⁵Then were the chieftains of Edom
dismayed,
the nobles of Moab seized by
trembling;
All the inhabitants of Canaan melted
away;
¹⁶terror and dread fell upon them.
By the might of your arm they became
silent like stone,
while your people, LORD, passed
over,
while the people whom you created
passed over.
¹⁷You brought them in, you planted
them
on the mountain that is your
own—
The place you made the base of your
throne, LORD,

the sanctuary, LORD, your hands established.
[18]May the LORD reign forever and ever!

[19]When Pharaoh's horses and chariots and horsemen entered the sea, the LORD made the waters of the sea flow back upon them, though the Israelites walked on dry land through the midst of the sea. [20]Then the prophet Miriam, Aaron's sister, took a tambourine in her hand, while all the women went out after her with tambourines, dancing; [21]and she responded to them:

Sing to the LORD, for he is gloriously triumphant;
horse and chariot he has cast into the sea.

At Marah and Elim. [22]Then Moses led Israel forward from the Red Sea, and they marched out to the wilderness of Shur. After traveling for three days through the wilderness without finding water, [23]they arrived at Marah, where they could not drink its water, because it was too bitter. Hence this place was called Marah. [24]As the people grumbled against Moses, saying, "What are we to drink?" [25]he cried out to the LORD, who pointed out to him a piece of wood. When he threw it into the water, the water became fresh.

It was here that God, in making statutes and ordinances for them, put them to the test. [26]He said: If you listen closely to the voice of the LORD, your God, and do what is right in his eyes: if you heed his commandments and keep all his statutes, I will not afflict you with any of the diseases with which I afflicted the Egyptians; for I, the LORD, am your healer.

[27]Then they came to Elim, where there were twelve springs of water and seventy palm trees, and they camped there near the water.

The Wilderness of Sin. 16:1 Having set out from Elim, the whole Israelite community came into the wilderness of Sin, which is between Elim and Sinai, on the fifteenth day of the second month after their departure from the land of Egypt. [2]Here in the wilderness the whole Israelite community grumbled against Moses and Aaron. [3]The Israelites said to them, "If only we had died at the LORD's hand in the land of Egypt, as we sat by our kettles of meat and ate our fill of bread! But you have led us into this wilderness to make this whole assembly die of famine!"

The Quail and the Manna. [4]Then the LORD said to Moses: I am going to rain down bread from heaven for you. Each day the people are to go out and gather their daily portion; thus will I test them, to see whether they follow my instructions or not. [5]On the sixth day, however, when they prepare what they bring in, let it be twice as much as they gather on the other days. [6]So Moses and Aaron told all the Israelites, "At evening you will know that it was the LORD who brought you out of the land of Egypt; [7]and in the morning you will see the glory of the LORD, when he hears your grumbling against him. But who are we that you should grumble against us?" [8]And Moses said, "When the LORD gives you meat to eat in the evening and in the morning your fill of bread, and hears the grumbling you utter against him, who then are we? Your grumbling is not against us, but against the LORD."

[9]Then Moses said to Aaron, "Tell the whole Israelite community: Approach the LORD, for he has heard your grumbling." [10]But while Aaron was speaking to the whole Israelite community, they turned in the direction of the wilderness, and there the glory of the LORD appeared in the cloud! [11]The LORD said to Moses: [12]I have heard the grumbling of the Israelites. Tell them: In the evening twilight you will eat meat, and in the morning you will have your fill of bread, and then you will know that I, the LORD, am your God.

¹³In the evening, quail came up and covered the camp. In the morning there was a layer of dew all about the camp, ¹⁴and when the layer of dew evaporated, fine flakes were on the surface of the wilderness, fine flakes like hoarfrost on the ground. ¹⁵On seeing it, the Israelites asked one another, "What is this?" for they did not know what it was. But Moses told them, "It is the bread which the LORD has given you to eat.

Regulations Regarding the Manna. ¹⁶"Now, this is what the LORD has commanded. Gather as much of it as each needs to eat, an omer for each person for as many of you as there are, each of you providing for those in your own tent." ¹⁷The Israelites did so. Some gathered a large and some a small amount. ¹⁸But when they measured it out by the omer, the one who had gathered a large amount did not have too much, and the one who had gathered a small amount did not have too little. They gathered as much as each needed to eat. ¹⁹Moses said to them, "Let no one leave any of it over until morning." ²⁰But they did not listen to Moses, and some kept a part of it over until morning, and it became wormy and stank. Therefore Moses was angry with them.

²¹Morning after morning they gathered it, as much as each needed to eat; but when the sun grew hot, it melted away. ²²On the sixth day they gathered twice as much food, two omers for each person. When all the leaders of the community came and reported this to Moses, ²³he told them, "That is what the LORD has prescribed. Tomorrow is a day of rest, a holy sabbath of the LORD. Whatever you want to bake, bake; whatever you want to boil, boil; but whatever is left put away and keep until the morning." ²⁴When they put it away until the morning, as Moses commanded, it did not stink nor were there worms in it. ²⁵Moses then said, "Eat it today, for today is the sabbath of the LORD. Today you will not find any in the field. ²⁶Six days you will gather it, but on the seventh day, the sabbath, it will not be there." ²⁷Still, on the seventh day some of the people went out to gather it, but they did not find any. ²⁸Then the LORD said to Moses: How long will you refuse to keep my commandments and my instructions? ²⁹Take note! The LORD has given you the sabbath. That is why on the sixth day he gives you food for two days. Each of you stay where you are and let no one go out on the seventh day. ³⁰After that the people rested on the seventh day.

³¹The house of Israel named this food manna. It was like coriander seed, white, and it tasted like wafers made with honey.

³²Moses said, "This is what the LORD has commanded. Keep a full omer of it for your future generations, so that they may see the food I gave you to eat in the wilderness when I brought you out of the land of Egypt." ³³Moses then told Aaron, "Take a jar and put a full omer of manna in it. Then place it before the LORD to keep it for your future generations." ³⁴As the LORD had commanded Moses, Aaron placed it in front of the covenant to keep it.

³⁵The Israelites ate the manna for forty years, until they came to settled land; they ate the manna until they came to the borders of Canaan. ³⁶(An omer is one tenth of an ephah.)

☐ MARK 10:35-52

Ambition of James and John. 10:35 Then James and John, the sons of Zebedee, came to him and said to him, "Teacher, we want you to do for us whatever we ask of you." ³⁶He replied, "What do you wish [me] to do for you?" ³⁷They answered him, "Grant that in your glory we may sit one at your right and the other at your left." ³⁸Jesus said to them, "You do not know what you are asking. Can you drink the cup that I drink or be baptized with the baptism with which I am baptized?" ³⁹They said to him, "We can." Jesus said to them, "The cup that I drink, you will drink, and with the baptism with which I am baptized, you will be baptized; ⁴⁰but to sit at my right or at my left is not mine to give but is for those for whom it has been prepared." ⁴¹When the ten heard this, they became indignant at James and John. ⁴²Jesus summoned them and said to them, "You know that those who are recognized as rulers over the Gentiles lord it over them, and their great ones make their authority over them felt. ⁴³But it shall not be so among you. Rather, whoever wishes to be great among you will be your servant; ⁴⁴whoever wishes to be first among you will be the slave of all. ⁴⁵For the Son of Man did not come to be served but to serve and to give his life as a ransom for many."

The Blind Bartimaeus. ⁴⁶They came to Jericho. And as he was leaving Jericho with his disciples and a sizable crowd, Bartimaeus, a blind man, the son of Timaeus, sat by the roadside begging. ⁴⁷On hearing that it was Jesus of Nazareth, he began to cry out and say, "Jesus, son of David, have pity on me." ⁴⁸And many rebuked him, telling him to be silent. But he kept calling out all the more, "Son of David, have pity on me." ⁴⁹Jesus stopped and said, "Call him." So they called the blind man, saying to him, "Take courage; get up, he is calling you." ⁵⁰He threw aside his cloak, sprang up, and came to Jesus. ⁵¹Jesus said to him in reply, "What do you want me to do for you?" The blind man replied to him, "Master, I want to see." ⁵²Jesus told him, "Go your way; your faith has saved you." Immediately he received his sight and followed him on the way.

January 28

St. Thomas Aquinas

It is one of the glories of the Scripture that it can embrace many meanings in a single passage.

— St. Thomas Aquinas

☐ EXODUS 17-18

Water from the Rock. 17:1 From the wilderness of Sin the whole Israelite community journeyed by stages, as the LORD directed, and encamped at Rephidim.

But there was no water for the people to drink, ²and so they quarreled with Moses and said, "Give us water to drink." Moses replied to them, "Why do you quarrel with me? Why do you put the LORD to a test?" ³Here, then, in their thirst for water, the people grumbled against Moses, saying, "Why then did you bring us up out of Egypt? To have us die of thirst with our children and our livestock?" ⁴So Moses cried out to the LORD, "What shall I do with this people? A little more and they will stone me!" ⁵The LORD answered Moses: Go on ahead of the people, and take along with you some of the elders of Israel, holding in your hand, as you go, the staff with which you struck the Nile. ⁶I will be standing there in front of you on the rock in Horeb. Strike the rock, and the water will flow from it for the people to drink.

Moses did this, in the sight of the elders of Israel. [7]The place was named Massah and Meribah, because the Israelites quarreled there and tested the LORD, saying, "Is the LORD in our midst or not?"

Battle with Amalek. [8]Then Amalek came and waged war against Israel in Rephidim. [9]So Moses said to Joshua, "Choose some men for us, and tomorrow go out and engage Amalek in battle. I will be standing on top of the hill with the staff of God in my hand." [10]Joshua did as Moses told him: he engaged Amalek in battle while Moses, Aaron, and Hur climbed to the top of the hill. [11]As long as Moses kept his hands raised up, Israel had the better of the fight, but when he let his hands rest, Amalek had the better of the fight. [12]Moses' hands, however, grew tired; so they took a rock and put it under him and he sat on it. Meanwhile Aaron and Hur supported his hands, one on one side and one on the other, so that his hands remained steady until sunset. [13]And Joshua defeated Amalek and his people with the sword.

[14]Then the LORD said to Moses: Write this down in a book as something to be remembered, and recite it to Joshua: I will completely blot out the memory of Amalek from under the heavens. [15]Moses built an altar there, which he named Yahweh-nissi; [16]for he said, "Take up the banner of the LORD! The LORD has a war against Amalek through the ages."

Meeting with Jethro. 18:1 Now Moses' father-in-law Jethro, the priest of Midian, heard of all that God had done for Moses and for his people Israel: how the LORD had brought Israel out of Egypt. [2]So his father-in-law Jethro took along Zipporah, Moses' wife—now this was after Moses had sent her back— [3]and her two sons. One of these was named Gershom; for he said, "I am a resident alien in a foreign land." [4]The other was named Eliezer; for he said, "The God of my father is my help; he has res-

cued me from Pharaoh's sword." [5]Together with Moses' wife and sons, then, his father-in-law Jethro came to him in the wilderness where he was encamped at the mountain of God, [6]and he sent word to Moses, "I, your father-in-law Jethro, am coming to you, along with your wife and her two sons."

[7]Moses went out to meet his father-in-law, bowed down, and then kissed him. Having greeted each other, they went into the tent. [8]Moses then told his father-in-law of all that the LORD had done to Pharaoh and the Egyptians for the sake of Israel, and of all the hardships that had beset them on their journey, and how the LORD had rescued them. [9]Jethro rejoiced over all the goodness that the LORD had shown Israel in rescuing them from the power of the Egyptians. [10]"Blessed be the LORD," he said, "who has rescued you from the power of the Egyptians and of Pharaoh. [11]Now I know that the LORD is greater than all the gods; for he rescued the people from the power of the Egyptians when they treated them arrogantly." [12]Then Jethro, the father-in-law of Moses, brought a burnt offering and sacrifices for God, and Aaron came with all the elders of Israel to share with Moses' father-in-law in the meal before God.

Appointment of Minor Judges. [13]The next day Moses sat in judgment for the people, while they stood around him from morning until evening. [14]When Moses' father-in-law saw all that he was doing for the people, he asked, "What is this business that you are conducting for the people? Why do you sit alone while all the people have to stand about you from morning till evening?" [15]Moses answered his father-in-law, "The people come to me to consult God. [16]Whenever they have a disagreement, they come to me to have me settle the matter between them and make known to them God's statutes and instructions."

[17]"What you are doing is not wise," Moses' father-in-law replied. [18]"You will surely wear yourself out, both you and these

people with you. The task is too heavy for you; you cannot do it alone. [19]Now, listen to me, and I will give you some advice, and may God be with you. Act as the people's representative before God, and bring their disputes to God. [20]Enlighten them in regard to the statutes and instructions, showing them how they are to conduct themselves and what they are to do. [21]But you should also look among all the people for able and God-fearing men, trustworthy men who hate dishonest gain, and set them over the people as commanders of thousands, of hundreds, of fifties, and of tens. [22]Let these render decisions for the people in all routine cases. Every important case they should refer to you, but every lesser case they can settle themselves. Lighten your burden by letting them bear it with you! [23]If you do this, and God so commands you, you will be able to stand the strain, and all these people, too, will go home content."

[24]Moses listened to his father-in-law and did all that he had said. [25]He picked out able men from all Israel and put them in charge of the people as commanders of thousands, of hundreds, of fifties, and of tens. [26]They rendered decisions for the people in all routine cases. The more difficult cases they referred to Moses, but all the lesser cases they settled themselves. [27]Then Moses said farewell to his father-in-law, who went off to his own country.

□ MARK 11:1-14

The Entry into Jerusalem. 11:1 When they drew near to Jerusalem, to Bethphage and Bethany at the Mount of Olives, he sent two of his disciples [2]and said to them, "Go into the village opposite you, and immediately on entering it, you will find a colt tethered on which no one has ever sat. Untie it and bring it here. [3]If anyone should say to you, 'Why are you doing this?' reply, 'The Master has need of it and will send it back here at once.'" [4]So they went off and found a colt tethered at a gate outside on the street, and they untied it. [5]Some of the bystanders said to them, "What are you doing, untying the colt?" [6]They answered them just as Jesus had told them to, and they permitted them to do it. [7]So they brought the colt to Jesus and put their cloaks over it. And he sat on it. [8]Many people spread their cloaks on the road, and others spread leafy branches that they had cut from the fields. [9]Those preceding him as well as those following kept crying out:

"Hosanna!
Blessed is he who comes in the
name of the Lord!
[10]Blessed is the kingdom of our
father David that is to come!
Hosanna in the highest!"

[11]He entered Jerusalem and went into the temple area. He looked around at everything and, since it was already late, went out to Bethany with the Twelve.

Jesus Curses a Fig Tree. [12]The next day as they were leaving Bethany he was hungry. [13]Seeing from a distance a fig tree in leaf, he went over to see if he could find anything on it. When he reached it he found nothing but leaves; it was not the time for figs. [14]And he said to it in reply, "May no one ever eat of your fruit again!" And his disciples heard it.

January 29

Faith furnishes prayer with wings, without which it cannot soar to heaven.

— St. John Climacus

☐ EXODUS 19-20

Arrival at Sinai. 19:1 In the third month after the Israelites' departure from the land of Egypt, on the first day, they came to the wilderness of Sinai. [2]After they made the journey from Rephidim and entered the wilderness of Sinai, they then pitched camp in the wilderness.

While Israel was encamped there in front of the mountain, [3]Moses went up to the mountain of God. Then the LORD called to him from the mountain, saying: This is what you will say to the house of Jacob; tell the Israelites: [4]You have seen how I treated the Egyptians and how I bore you up on eagles' wings and brought you to myself. [5]Now, if you obey me completely and keep my covenant, you will be my treasured possession among all peoples, though all the earth is mine. [6]You will be to me a kingdom of priests, a holy nation. That is what you must tell the Israelites. [7]So Moses went and summoned the elders of the people. When he set before them all that the LORD had ordered him to tell them, [8]all the people answered together, "Everything the LORD has said, we will do." Then Moses brought back to the LORD the response of the people.

[9]The LORD said to Moses: I am coming to you now in a dense cloud, so that when the people hear me speaking with you, they will also remain faithful to you.

When Moses, then, had reported the response of the people to the LORD, [10]the LORD said to Moses: Go to the people and have them sanctify themselves today and tomorrow. Have them wash their garments [11]and be ready for the third day; for on the third day the LORD will come down on Mount Sinai in the sight of all the people. [12]Set limits for the people all around, saying: Take care not to go up the mountain, or even to touch its edge. All who touch the mountain must be put to death. [13]No hand shall touch them, but they must be stoned to death or killed with arrows. Whether human being or beast, they must not be allowed to live. Only when the ram's horn sounds may they go up on the mountain. [14]Then Moses came down from the mountain to the people and had them sanctify themselves, and they washed their garments. [15]He said to the people, "Be ready for the third day. Do not approach a woman."

The Great Theophany. [16]On the morning of the third day there were peals of thunder and lightning, and a heavy cloud over the mountain, and a very loud blast of the shofar, so that all the people in the camp trembled. [17]But Moses led the people out of the camp to meet God, and they stationed themselves at the foot of the mountain. [18]Now Mount Sinai was completely enveloped in smoke, because the LORD had come down upon it in fire. The smoke rose from it as though from a kiln, and the whole mountain trembled violently. [19]The blast of the shofar grew louder and louder, while Moses was speaking and God was answering him with thunder.

[20]When the LORD came down upon Mount Sinai, to the top of the mountain, the LORD summoned Moses to the top of the mountain, and Moses went up. [21]Then the LORD told Moses: Go down and warn the people not to break through to the LORD in order to see him; otherwise many of them will be struck down. [22]For their

part, the priests, who approach the LORD must sanctify themselves; else the LORD will break out in anger against them. ²³But Moses said to the LORD, "The people cannot go up to Mount Sinai, for you yourself warned us, saying: Set limits around the mountain to make it sacred." ²⁴So the LORD said to him: Go down and come up along with Aaron. But do not let the priests and the people break through to come up to the LORD; else he will break out against them." ²⁵So Moses went down to the people and spoke to them.

The Ten Commandments. 20:1 Then God spoke all these words:

²I am the LORD your God, who brought you out of the land of Egypt, out of the house of slavery. ³You shall not have other gods beside me. ⁴You shall not make for yourself an idol or a likeness of anything in the heavens above or on the earth below or in the waters beneath the earth; ⁵you shall not bow down before them or serve them. For I, the LORD, your God, am a jealous God, inflicting punishment for their ancestors' wickedness on the children of those who hate me, down to the third and fourth generation; ⁶but showing love down to the thousandth generation of those who love me and keep my commandments.

⁷You shall not invoke the name of the LORD, your God, in vain. For the LORD will not leave unpunished anyone who invokes his name in vain.

⁸Remember the sabbath day—keep it holy. ⁹Six days you may labor and do all your work, ¹⁰but the seventh day is a sabbath of the LORD your God. You shall not do any work, either you, your son or your daughter, your male or female slave, your work animal, or the resident alien within your gates. ¹¹For in six days the LORD made the heavens and the earth, the sea and all that is in them; but on the seventh day he rested. That is why the LORD has blessed the sabbath day and made it holy.

¹²Honor your father and your mother, that you may have a long life in the land the LORD your God is giving you.

¹³You shall not kill.

¹⁴You shall not commit adultery.

¹⁵You shall not steal.

¹⁶You shall not bear false witness against your neighbor.

¹⁷You shall not covet your neighbor's house. You shall not covet your neighbor's wife, his male or female slave, his ox or donkey, or anything that belongs to your neighbor.

Moses Accepted as Mediator. ¹⁸Now as all the people witnessed the thunder and lightning, the blast of the shofar and the mountain smoking, they became afraid and trembled. So they took up a position farther away ¹⁹and said to Moses, "You speak to us, and we will listen; but do not let God speak to us, or we shall die." ²⁰Moses answered the people, "Do not be afraid, for God has come only to test you and put the fear of him upon you so you do not sin." ²¹So the people remained at a distance, while Moses approached the dark cloud where God was.

The Covenant Code. ²²The LORD said to Moses: This is what you will say to the Israelites: You have seen for yourselves that I have spoken to you from heaven. ²³You shall not make alongside of me gods of silver, nor shall you make for yourselves gods of gold. ²⁴An altar of earth make for me, and sacrifice upon it your burnt offerings and communion sacrifices, your sheep and your oxen. In every place where I cause my name to be invoked I will come to you and bless you. ²⁵But if you make an altar of stone for me, do not build it of cut stone, for by putting a chisel to it you profane it. ²⁶You shall not ascend to my altar by steps, lest your nakedness be exposed.

☐ MARK 11:15-33

Cleansing of the Temple. 11:15 They came to Jerusalem, and on entering the temple area he began to drive out those selling and buying there. He overturned the tables of the money changers and the seats of those who were selling doves. [16]He did not permit anyone to carry anything through the temple area. [17]Then he taught them saying, "Is it not written:

'My house shall be called a house of prayer for all peoples'?
But you have made it a den of thieves."

[18]The chief priests and the scribes came to hear of it and were seeking a way to put him to death, yet they feared him because the whole crowd was astonished at his teaching. [19]When evening came, they went out of the city.

The Withered Fig Tree. [20]Early in the morning, as they were walking along, they saw the fig tree withered to its roots. [21]Peter remembered and said to him, "Rabbi, look! The fig tree that you cursed has withered." [22]Jesus said to them in reply, "Have faith in God. [23]Amen, I say to you, whoever says to this mountain, 'Be lifted up and thrown into the sea,' and does not doubt in his heart but believes that what he says will happen, it shall be done for him. [24]Therefore I tell you, all that you ask for in prayer, believe that you will receive it and it shall be yours. [25]When you stand to pray, forgive anyone against whom you have a grievance, so that your heavenly Father may in turn forgive you your transgressions." [26]

The Authority of Jesus Questioned. [27]They returned once more to Jerusalem. As he was walking in the temple area, the chief priests, the scribes, and the elders approached him [28]and said to him, "By what authority are you doing these things? Or who gave you this authority to do them?" [29]Jesus said to them, "I shall ask you one question. Answer me, and I will tell you by what authority I do these things. [30]Was John's baptism of heavenly or of human origin? Answer me." [31]They discussed this among themselves and said, "If we say, 'Of heavenly origin,' he will say, '[Then] why did you not believe him?' [32]But shall we say, 'Of human origin'?"—they feared the crowd, for they all thought John really was a prophet. [33]So they said to Jesus in reply, "We do not know." Then Jesus said to them, "Neither shall I tell you by what authority I do these things."

January 30

Yoke yourself under the law of God, so that you may be in truth a free man.

— St. Ephraem the Syrian

☐ EXODUS 21-22

Laws Regarding Slaves. 21:1 These are the ordinances you shall lay before them. [2]When you purchase a Hebrew slave, he is to serve you for six years, but in the seventh year he shall leave as a free person without any payment. [3]If he comes into service alone, he shall leave alone; if he comes with a wife, his wife shall leave with him. [4]But if his master gives him a wife and she bears him sons or daughters, the woman and her children belong to her master and the man shall leave alone. [5]If, however, the slave declares, 'I love my master and my wife and children; I will not leave as a free person,' [6]his master shall bring him to God and there, at the door or doorpost, he shall pierce his ear with an awl, thus keeping him as his slave forever.

[7]When a man sells his daughter as a slave, she shall not go free as male slaves do. [8]But if she displeases her master, who had designated her for himself, he shall let her be redeemed. He has no right to sell her to a foreign people, since he has broken faith with her. [9]If he designates her for his son, he shall treat her according to the ordinance for daughters. [10]If he takes another wife, he shall not withhold her food, her clothing, or her conjugal rights. [11]If he does not do these three things for her, she may leave without cost, without any payment.

Personal Injury. [12]Whoever strikes someone a mortal blow must be put to death. [13]However, regarding the one who did not hunt another down, but God caused death to happen by his hand, I will set apart for you a place to which that one may flee. [14]But when someone kills a neighbor after maliciously scheming to do so, you must take him even from my altar and put him to death. [15]Whoever strikes father or mother shall be put to death.

[16]A kidnaper, whether he sells the person or the person is found in his possession, shall be put to death.

[17]Whoever curses father or mother shall be put to death.

[18]When men quarrel and one strikes the other with a stone or with his fist, not mortally, but enough to put him in bed, [19]the one who struck the blow shall be acquitted, provided the other can get up and walk around with the help of his staff. Still, he must compensate him for his recovery time and make provision for his complete healing. [20]When someone strikes his male or female slave with a rod so that the slave dies under his hand, the act shall certainly be avenged. [21]If, however, the slave survives for a day or two, he is not to be punished, since the slave is his own property.

[22]When men have a fight and hurt a pregnant woman, so that she suffers a miscarriage, but no further injury, the guilty one shall be fined as much as the woman's husband demands of him, and he shall pay in the presence of the judges. [23]But if injury ensues, you shall give life for life, [24]eye for eye, tooth for tooth, hand for hand, foot for foot, [25]burn for burn, wound for wound, stripe for stripe.

[26]When someone strikes his male or female slave in the eye and destroys the use of the eye, he shall let the slave go free in compensation for the eye. [27]If he knocks out a tooth of his male or female slave, he shall let the slave go free in compensation for the tooth.

[28]When an ox gores a man or a woman to death, the ox must be stoned; its meat may not be eaten. The owner of the ox, however, shall be free of blame. [29]But if an ox was previously in the habit of goring people and its owner, though warned, would not watch it; should it then kill a man or a woman, not only must the ox be stoned, but its owner also must be put to death. [30]If, however, a fine is imposed on him, he must pay in ransom for his life whatever amount is imposed on him. [31]This ordinance applies if it is a boy or a girl that the ox gores. [32]But if it is a male or a female slave that it gores, he must pay the owner of the slave thirty shekels of silver, and the ox must be stoned.

Property Damage. [33]When someone uncovers or digs a cistern and does not cover it over again, should an ox or a donkey fall into it, [34]the owner of the cistern must make good by restoring the value of the animal to its owner, but the dead animal he may keep.

[35]When one man's ox hurts another's ox and it dies, they shall sell the live ox and di-

vide this money as well as the dead animal equally between them. [36]But if it was known that the ox was previously in the habit of goring and its owner would not watch it, he must make full restitution, an ox for an ox; but the dead animal he may keep.

[37]When someone steals an ox or a sheep and slaughters or sells it, he shall restore five oxen for the one ox, and four sheep for the one sheep.

22:1 [If a thief is caught in the act of housebreaking and beaten to death, there is no bloodguilt involved. [2]But if after sunrise he is thus beaten, there is bloodguilt.] He must make full restitution. If he has nothing, he shall be sold to pay for his theft. [3]If what he stole is found alive in his possession, be it an ox, a donkey or a sheep, he shall make twofold restitution.

[4]When someone causes a field or a vineyard to be grazed over, by sending his cattle to graze in another's field, he must make restitution with the best produce of his own field or vineyard. [5]If a fire breaks out, catches on to thorn bushes, and consumes shocked grain, standing grain, or the field itself, the one who started the fire must make full restitution.

Trusts and Loans. [6]When someone gives money or articles to another for safekeeping and they are stolen from the latter's house, the thief, if caught, must make twofold restitution. [7]If the thief is not caught, the owner of the house shall be brought to God, to swear that he himself did not lay hands on his neighbor's property. [8]In every case of dishonest appropriation, whether it be about an ox, or a donkey, or a sheep, or a garment, or anything else that has disappeared, where another claims that the thing is his, the claim of both parties shall be brought before God; the one whom God convicts must make twofold restitution to the other.

[9]When someone gives an ass, or an ox, or a sheep, or any other animal to another for safekeeping, if it dies, or is maimed or snatched away, without anyone witnessing the fact, [10]there shall be an oath before the LORD between the two of them that the guardian did not lay hands on his neighbor's property; the owner must accept the oath, and no restitution is to be made. [11]But if the guardian has actually stolen from it, then he must make restitution to the owner. [12]If it has been killed by a wild beast, let him bring it as evidence; he need not make restitution for the mangled animal.

[13]When someone borrows an animal from a neighbor, if it is maimed or dies while the owner is not present, that one must make restitution. [14]But if the owner is present, that one need not make restitution. If it was hired, this was covered by the price of its hire.

Social Laws. [15]When a man seduces a virgin who is not betrothed, and lies with her, he shall make her his wife by paying the bride price. [16]If her father refuses to give her to him, he must still pay him the bride price for virgins.

[17]You shall not let a woman who practices sorcery live.

[18]Anyone who lies with an animal shall be put to death.

[19]Whoever sacrifices to any god, except to the LORD alone, shall be put under the ban.

[20]You shall not oppress or afflict a resident alien, for you were once aliens residing in the land of Egypt. [21]You shall not wrong any widow or orphan. [22]If ever you wrong them and they cry out to me, I will surely listen to their cry. [23]My wrath will flare up, and I will kill you with the sword; then your own wives will be widows, and your children orphans.

[24]If you lend money to my people, the poor among you, you must not be like a money lender; you must not demand interest from them. [25]If you take your neighbor's cloak as a pledge, you shall return it to him before sunset; [26]for this is his only covering;

it is the cloak for his body. What will he sleep in? If he cries out to me, I will listen; for I am compassionate.

[27]You shall not despise God, nor curse a leader of your people.

[28]You shall not delay the offering of your harvest and your press. You shall give me the firstborn of your sons. [29]You must do

☐ MARK 12:1-17

Parable of the Tenants. 12:1 He began to speak to them in parables. "A man planted a vineyard, put a hedge around it, dug a wine press, and built a tower. Then he leased it to tenant farmers and left on a journey. [2]At the proper time he sent a servant to the tenants to obtain from them some of the produce of the vineyard. [3]But they seized him, beat him, and sent him away empty-handed. [4]Again he sent them another servant. And that one they beat over the head and treated shamefully. [5]He sent yet another whom they killed. So, too, many others; some they beat, others they killed. [6]He had one other to send, a beloved son. He sent him to them last of all, thinking, 'They will respect my son.' [7]But those tenants said to one another, 'This is the heir. Come, let us kill him, and the inheritance will be ours.' [8]So they seized him and killed him, and threw him out of the vineyard. [9]What [then] will the owner of the vineyard do? He will come, put the tenants to death, and give the vineyard to others. [10]Have you not read this scripture passage:

'The stone that the builders rejected

the same with your oxen and your sheep; for seven days the firstling may stay with its mother, but on the eighth day you must give it to me.

[30]You shall be a people sacred to me. Flesh torn to pieces in the field you shall not eat; you must throw it to the dogs.

has become the cornerstone;
[11]by the Lord has this been done,
    and it is wonderful in our eyes'?"

[12]They were seeking to arrest him, but they feared the crowd, for they realized that he had addressed the parable to them. So they left him and went away.

Paying Taxes to the Emperor. [13]They sent some Pharisees and Herodians to him to ensnare him in his speech. [14]They came and said to him, "Teacher, we know that you are a truthful man and that you are not concerned with anyone's opinion. You do not regard a person's status but teach the way of God in accordance with the truth. Is it lawful to pay the census tax to Caesar or not? Should we pay or should we not pay?" [15]Knowing their hypocrisy he said to them, "Why are you testing me? Bring me a denarius to look at." [16]They brought one to him and he said to them, "Whose image and inscription is this?" They replied to him, "Caesar's." [17]So Jesus said to them, "Repay to Caesar what belongs to Caesar and to God what belongs to God." They were utterly amazed at him.

January 31

St. John Bosco

Never read books you aren't sure about morally, even supposing that these bad books are very well written from a literary point of view. Let me ask you this: Would you drink something you knew was poisoned just because it was offered to you in a golden cup?

— St. John Bosco

☐ EXODUS 23-24

23:1 You shall not repeat a false report. Do not join your hand with the wicked to be a witness supporting violence. ²You shall not follow the crowd in doing wrong. When testifying in a lawsuit, you shall not follow the crowd in perverting justice. ³You shall not favor the poor in a lawsuit.

⁴When you come upon your enemy's ox or donkey going astray, you must see to it that it is returned. ⁵When you notice the donkey of one who hates you lying down under its burden, you should not desert him; you must help him with it.

⁶You shall not pervert justice for the needy among you in a lawsuit. ⁷You shall keep away from anything dishonest. The innocent and the just you shall not put to death, for I will not acquit the guilty. ⁸Never take a bribe, for a bribe blinds the clear-sighted and distorts the words of the just. ⁹You shall not oppress a resident alien; you well know how it feels to be an alien, since you were once aliens yourselves in the land of Egypt.

Religious Laws. ¹⁰For six years you may sow your land and gather in its produce. ¹¹But the seventh year you shall let the land lie untilled and fallow, that the poor of your people may eat of it and their leftovers the wild animals may eat. So also shall you do in regard to your vineyard and your olive grove.

¹²For six days you may do your work, but on the seventh day you must rest, that your ox and your donkey may have rest, and that the son of your maidservant and the resident alien may be refreshed. ¹³Give heed to all that I have told you.

You shall not mention the name of any other god; it shall not be heard from your lips.

¹⁴Three times a year you shall celebrate a pilgrim feast to me. ¹⁵You shall keep the feast of Unleavened Bread. As I have commanded you, you must eat unleavened bread for seven days at the appointed time in the month of Abib, for it was then that you came out of Egypt. No one shall appear before me empty-handed. ¹⁶You shall also keep the feast of the grain harvest with the first fruits of the crop that you sow in the field; and finally, the feast of Ingathering at the end of the year, when you collect your produce from the fields. ¹⁷Three times a year shall all your men appear before the Lord God.

¹⁸You shall not offer the blood of my sacrifice with anything leavened; nor shall the fat of my feast be kept overnight till the next day. ¹⁹The choicest first fruits of your soil you shall bring to the house of the Lord, your God.

You shall not boil a young goat in its mother's milk.

Reward of Fidelity. ²⁰See, I am sending an angel before you, to guard you on the way and bring you to the place I have prepared. ²¹Be attentive to him and obey him. Do not rebel against him, for he will not forgive your sin. My authority is within him. ²²If you obey him and carry out all I tell you, I will be an enemy to your enemies and a foe to your foes.

[23]My angel will go before you and bring you to the Amorites, Hittites, Perizzites, Canaanites, Hivites and Jebusites; and I will wipe them out. [24]Therefore, you shall not bow down to their gods and serve them, nor shall you act as they do; rather, you must demolish them and smash their sacred stones. [25]You shall serve the Lord, your God; then he will bless your food and drink, and I will remove sickness from your midst; [26]no woman in your land will be barren or miscarry; and I will give you a full span of life.

[27]I will have the terror of me precede you, so that I will throw into panic every nation you reach. I will make all your enemies turn from you in flight, [28]and ahead of you I will send hornets to drive the Hivites, Canaanites and Hittites out of your way. [29]But I will not drive them all out before you in one year, lest the land become desolate and the wild animals multiply against you. [30]Little by little I will drive them out before you, until you have grown numerous enough to take possession of the land. [31]I will set your boundaries from the Red Sea to the sea of the Philistines, and from the wilderness to the Euphrates; all who dwell in this land I will hand over to you and you shall drive them out before you. [32]You shall not make a covenant with them or their gods. [33]They must not live in your land. For if you serve their gods, this will become a snare to you.

Ratification of the Covenant. 24:1 Moses himself was told: Come up to the Lord, you and Aaron, with Nadab, Abihu, and seventy of the elders of Israel. You shall bow down at a distance. [2]Moses alone is to come close to the Lord; the others shall not come close, and the people shall not come up with them.

[3]When Moses came to the people and related all the words and ordinances of the Lord, they all answered with one voice, "We will do everything that the Lord has told us." [4]Moses then wrote down all the words of the Lord and, rising early in the morning, he built at the foot of the mountain an altar and twelve sacred stones for the twelve tribes of Israel. [5]Then, having sent young men of the Israelites to offer burnt offerings and sacrifice young bulls as communion offerings to the Lord, [6]Moses took half of the blood and put it in large bowls; the other half he splashed on the altar. [7]Taking the book of the covenant, he read it aloud to the people, who answered, "All that the Lord has said, we will hear and do." [8]Then he took the blood and splashed it on the people, saying, "This is the blood of the covenant which the Lord has made with you according to all these words."

[9]Moses then went up with Aaron, Nadab, Abihu, and seventy elders of Israel, [10]and they beheld the God of Israel. Under his feet there appeared to be sapphire tilework, as clear as the sky itself. [11]Yet he did not lay a hand on these chosen Israelites. They saw God, and they ate and drank.

Moses on the Mountain. [12]The Lord said to Moses: Come up to me on the mountain and, while you are there, I will give you the stone tablets on which I have written the commandments intended for their instruction. [13]So Moses set out with Joshua, his assistant, and went up to the mountain of God. [14]He told the elders, "Wait here for us until we return to you. Aaron and Hur are with you. Anyone with a complaint should approach them." [15]Moses went up the mountain. Then the cloud covered the mountain. [16]The glory of the Lord settled upon Mount Sinai. The cloud covered it for six days, and on the seventh day he called to Moses from the midst of the cloud. [17]To the Israelites the glory of the Lord was seen as a consuming fire on the top of the mountain. [18]But Moses entered into the midst of the cloud and went up on the mountain. He was on the mountain for forty days and forty nights.

☐ MARK 12:18-34

The Question about the Resurrection. 12:18 Some Sadducees, who say there is no resurrection, came to him and put this question to him, [19]saying, "Teacher, Moses wrote for us, 'If someone's brother dies, leaving a wife but no child, his brother must take the wife and raise up descendants for his brother.' [20]Now there were seven brothers. The first married a woman and died, leaving no descendants. [21]So the second married her and died, leaving no descendants, and the third likewise. [22]And the seven left no descendants. Last of all the woman also died. [23]At the resurrection [when they arise] whose wife will she be? For all seven had been married to her." [24]Jesus said to them, "Are you not misled because you do not know the scriptures or the power of God? [25]When they rise from the dead, they neither marry nor are given in marriage, but they are like the angels in heaven. [26]As for the dead being raised, have you not read in the Book of Moses, in the passage about the bush, how God told him, 'I am the God of Abraham, [the] God of Isaac, and [the] God of Jacob'? [27]He is not God of the dead but of the living. You are greatly misled."

The Greatest Commandment. [28]One of the scribes, when he came forward and heard them disputing and saw how well he had answered them, asked him, "Which is the first of all the commandments?" [29]Jesus replied, "The first is this: 'Hear, O Israel! The Lord our God is Lord alone! [30]You shall love the Lord your God with all your heart, with all your soul, with all your mind, and with all your strength.' [31]The second is this: 'You shall love your neighbor as yourself.' There is no other commandment greater than these." [32]The scribe said to him, "Well said, teacher. You are right in saying, 'He is One and there is no other than he.' [33]And 'to love him with all your heart, with all your understanding, with all your strength, and to love your neighbor as yourself' is worth more than all burnt offerings and sacrifices." [34]And when Jesus saw that [he] answered with understanding, he said to him, "You are not far from the kingdom of God." And no one dared to ask him any more questions.

February 1

I would like a great lake of ale for the King of kings, and I would like for heaven's family to be drinking it through all eternity.

— ST. BRIGID

☐ EXODUS 25-26

Collection of Materials. 25:1 The LORD spoke to Moses: [2]Speak to the Israelites: Let them receive contributions for me. From each you shall receive the contribution that their hearts prompt them to give me. [3]These are the contributions you shall accept from them: gold, silver, and bronze; [4]violet, purple, and scarlet yarn; fine linen and goat hair; [5]rams' skins dyed red, and tahash skins; acacia wood; [6]oil for the light; spices for the anointing oil and for the fragrant incense; [7]onyx stones and other gems for mounting on the ephod and the breastpiece. [8]They are to make a sanctuary for me, that I may dwell in their midst. [9]According to all that I show you regarding the pattern of the tabernacle and the pattern of its furnishings, so you are to make it.

Plan of the Ark. [10]You shall make an ark of acacia wood, two and a half cubits long, one and a half cubits wide, and one and a half cubits high. [11]Plate it inside and outside with pure gold, and put a molding of gold around the top of it. [12]Cast four gold rings and put them on the four supports of the ark, two rings on one side and two on the opposite side. [13]Then make poles of acacia wood and plate them with gold. [14]These poles you are to put through the rings on the sides of the ark, for carrying it; [15]they must remain in the rings of the ark and never be withdrawn. [16]In the ark you are to put the covenant which I will give you.

[17]You shall then make a cover of pure gold, two and a half cubits long, and one and a half cubits wide. [18]Make two cherubim of beaten gold for the two ends of the cover; [19]make one cherub at one end, and the other at the other end, of one piece with the cover, at each end. [20]The cherubim shall have their wings spread out above, sheltering the cover with them; they shall face each other, with their faces looking toward the cover. [21]This cover you shall then place on top of the ark. In the ark itself you are to put the covenant which I will give you. [22]There I will meet you and there, from above the cover, between the two cherubim on the ark of the covenant, I will tell you all that I command you regarding the Israelites.

The Table. [23]You shall also make a table of acacia wood, two cubits long, a cubit wide, and a cubit and a half high. [24]Plate it with pure gold and make a molding of gold around it. [25]Make a frame for it, a handbreadth high, and make a molding of gold around the frame. [26]You shall also make four rings of gold for it and fasten them at the four corners, one at each leg. [27]The rings shall be alongside the frame as holders for the poles to carry the table. [28]These poles for carrying the table you shall make of acacia wood and plate with gold. [29]You shall make its plates and cups, as well as its pitchers and bowls for pouring libations; make them of pure gold. [30]On the table you shall always keep showbread set before me.

The Menorah. [31]You shall make a menorah of pure beaten gold—its shaft and branches—with its cups and knobs and petals springing directly from it. [32]Six branches are to extend from its sides, three branches on one side, and three on the other. [33]On one branch there are to be three cups, shaped like almond blossoms, each with its knob and petals; on the opposite branch there are to be three cups, shaped like almond blossoms, each with its knob and petals; and so for the six branches that extend from the menorah. [34]On the menorah there are to be four cups, shaped like almond blossoms, with their knobs and petals. [35]The six branches that go out from the menorah are to have a knob under each pair. [36]Their knobs and branches shall so spring from it that the whole will form a single piece of pure beaten gold. [37]You shall then make seven lamps for it and so set up the lamps that they give their light on the space in front of the menorah. [38]These, as well as the trimming shears and trays, must be of pure gold. [39]Use a talent of pure gold for the menorah and all these utensils. [40]See that you make them according to the pattern shown you on the mountain.

The Tent Cloth. 26:1 The tabernacle itself you shall make out of ten sheets woven of fine linen twined and of violet, purple, and scarlet yarn, with cherubim embroidered on them. [2]The length of each shall be twenty-eight cubits, and the width four cubits; all the sheets shall be of the same size. [3]Five of the sheets are to be joined one to another; and the same for the other five. [4]Make loops of violet yarn along the edge of the end sheet in one set, and the same along the edge of the end sheet in the other set. [5]Make fifty loops along the edge of the end sheet in the first set, and fifty loops along the edge of the corresponding sheet in the second set, and so placed that the loops are directly opposite each other. [6]Then make fifty clasps of gold and join the two sets of sheets, so that the tabernacle forms one whole.

[7]Also make sheets woven of goat hair for a tent over the tabernacle. Make eleven such sheets; [8]the length of each shall be thirty cubits, and the width four cubits: all eleven sheets shall be of the same size.

[9]Join five of the sheets into one set, and the other six sheets into another set. Use the sixth sheet double at the front of the tent. [10]Make fifty loops along the edge of the end sheet in one set, and fifty loops along the edge of the end sheet in the second set. [11]Also make fifty bronze clasps and put them into the loops, to join the tent into one whole. [12]There will be an extra half sheet of tent covering, which shall be allowed to hang down over the rear of the tabernacle. [13]Likewise, the sheets of the tent will have an extra cubit's length to be left hanging down on either side of the tabernacle to cover it. [14]Over the tent itself make a covering of rams' skins dyed red, and above that, a covering of tahash skins.

The Framework. [15]You shall make frames for the tabernacle, acacia-wood uprights. [16]The length of each frame is to be ten cubits, and its width one and a half cubits. [17]Each frame shall have two arms joined one to another; so you are to make all the frames of the tabernacle. [18]Make the frames of the tabernacle as follows: twenty frames on the south side, [19]with forty silver pedestals under the twenty frames, two pedestals under each frame for its two arms; [20]twenty frames on the other side of the tabernacle, the north side, [21]with their forty silver pedestals, two pedestals under each frame. [22]At the rear of the tabernacle, to the west, six frames, [23]and two frames for the corners of the tabernacle, at its rear. [24]These two shall be double at the bottom, and likewise double at the top, to the first ring. That is how both corner frames are to be made. [25]Thus, there shall be eight frames, with their sixteen silver pedestals, two pedestals under each frame. [26]Also make bars of acacia wood: five for the frames on one side of the tabernacle, [27]five for those on the other side, and five for those at the rear, to the west. [28]The center bar, at the middle of the frames, shall reach across from end to end. [29]Plate the frames with gold, and make gold rings on them as holders for the bars, which are also to be plated with gold. [30]You shall set up the tabernacle according to its plan, which you were shown on the mountain.

The Veils. [31]You shall make a veil woven of violet, purple, and scarlet yarn, and of fine linen twined, with cherubim embroidered on it. [32]It is to be hung on four gold-plated columns of acacia wood, which shall have gold hooks and shall rest on four silver pedestals. [33]Hang the veil from clasps. The ark of the covenant you shall bring inside, behind this veil which divides the holy place from the holy of holies. [34]Set the cover on the ark of the covenant in the holy of holies.

[35]Outside the veil you shall place the table and the menorah, the latter on the south side of the tabernacle, opposite the table, which is to be put on the north side. [36]For the entrance of the tent make a variegated curtain of violet, purple, and scarlet yarn and of fine linen twined. [37]Make five columns of acacia wood for this curtain; plate them with gold, with their hooks of gold; and cast five bronze pedestals for them.

☐ MARK 12:35-44

The Question about David's Son. 12:35 As Jesus was teaching in the temple area he said, "How do the scribes claim that the Messiah is the son of David? [36]David himself, inspired by the holy Spirit, said:

'The Lord said to my lord,
  "Sit at my right hand
    until I place your enemies under
      your feet."'

[37]David himself calls him 'lord'; so how is he his son?" [The] great crowd heard this with delight.

Denunciation of the Scribes. [38]In the course of his teaching he said, "Beware of the scribes, who like to go around in long robes and accept greetings in the marketplaces, [39]seats of honor in synagogues, and places of honor at banquets. [40]They devour the houses of widows and, as a pretext, recite lengthy prayers. They will receive a very severe condemnation."

The Poor Widow's Contribution. [41]He sat down opposite the treasury and observed how the crowd put money into the treasury. Many rich people put in large sums. [42]A poor widow also came and put in two small coins worth a few cents. [43]Calling his disciples to himself, he said to them, "Amen, I say to you, this poor widow put in more than all the other contributors to the treasury. [44]For they have all contributed from their surplus wealth, but she, from her poverty, has contributed all she had, her whole livelihood."

February 2

The Presentation of the Lord

In Christ, the greatness of God was not cast away, but the smallness of human nature was taken on.

— St. Thomas Aquinas

☐ EXODUS 27-28

The Altar for Burnt Offerings. 27:1 You shall make an altar of acacia wood, on a square, five cubits long and five cubits wide; it shall be three cubits high. ²At the four corners make horns that are of one piece with the altar. You shall then plate it with bronze. ³Make pots for removing the ashes, as well as shovels, basins, forks, and fire pans; all these utensils you shall make of bronze. ⁴Make for it a grating, a bronze network; make four bronze rings for it, one at each of its four corners. ⁵Put it down around the altar, on the ground. This network is to be half as high as the altar. ⁶You shall also make poles of acacia wood for the altar, and plate them with bronze. ⁷These poles are to be put through the rings, so that they are on either side of the altar when it is carried. ⁸Make the altar itself in the form of a hollow box. Just as it was shown you on the mountain, so it is to be made.

Court of the Tabernacle. ⁹You shall also make a court for the tabernacle. On the south side the court shall have hangings, of fine linen twined, a hundred cubits long, ¹⁰with twenty columns and twenty pedestals of bronze; the hooks and bands on the columns shall be of silver. ¹¹On the north side there shall be similar hangings, a hundred cubits long, with twenty columns and twenty pedestals of bronze; the hooks and bands on the columns shall be of silver. ¹²On the west side, across the width of the court, there shall be hangings, fifty cubits long, with ten columns and ten pedestals. ¹³The width of the court on the east side shall be fifty cubits. ¹⁴On one side there shall be hangings to the extent of fifteen cubits, with three columns and three pedestals; ¹⁵on the other side there shall be hangings to the extent of fifteen cubits, with three columns and three pedestals.

¹⁶At the gate of the court there shall be a variegated curtain, twenty cubits long, woven of violet, purple, and scarlet yarn and of fine linen twined. It shall have four columns and four pedestals.

¹⁷All the columns around the court shall have bands and hooks of silver, and pedestals of bronze. ¹⁸The court is to be one hundred cubits long, fifty cubits wide, and five cubits high. Fine linen twined must be used, and the pedestals must be of bronze. ¹⁹All the fittings of the tabernacle, whatever be their use, as well as all its tent pegs and all the tent pegs of the court, must be of bronze.

Oil for the Lamps. ²⁰You shall command the Israelites to bring you clear oil of crushed olives, to be used for the light, so that you may keep lamps burning always. ²¹From evening to morning Aaron and his sons shall maintain them before the Lord in the tent of meeting, outside the veil which hangs in front of the covenant. This shall be a perpetual statute for the Israelites throughout their generations.

The Priestly Vestments. 28:1 Have your brother Aaron, and with him his sons, brought to you, from among the Israelites, that they may be my priests: Nadab and Abihu, Eleazar and Ithamar, Aaron's sons. ²For the glorious adornment of your brother Aaron you shall have sacred vestments made. [3]Therefore, tell the various artisans whom I have endowed with skill to make vestments for Aaron to consecrate him as my priest. [4]These are the vestments they shall make: a breastpiece, an ephod, a robe, a brocade tunic, a turban, and a sash. In making these sacred vestments which your brother Aaron and his sons are to wear in serving as my priests, [5]they shall use gold, violet, purple, and scarlet yarn and fine linen.

The Ephod and Breastpiece. [6]The ephod they shall make of gold thread and of violet, purple, and scarlet yarn, embroidered on cloth of fine linen twined. [7]It shall have a pair of shoulder straps joined to its two upper ends. [8]The embroidered belt of the ephod shall extend out from it and, like it, be made of gold thread, of violet, purple, and scarlet yarn, and of fine linen twined.

[9]Get two onyx stones and engrave on them the names of the sons of Israel: [10]six of their names on one stone, and the names of the remaining six on the other stone, in the order of their birth. [11]As a gem-cutter engraves a seal, so shall you have the two stones engraved with the names of the sons of Israel and then mounted in gold filigree work. [12]Set these two stones on the shoulder straps of the ephod as memorial stones of the sons of Israel. Thus Aaron shall bear their names on his shoulders as a reminder before the LORD. [13]Make filigree rosettes of gold, [14]as well as two chains of pure gold, twisted like cords, and fasten the cordlike chains to the filigree rosettes.

[15]The breastpiece of decision you shall also have made, embroidered like the ephod with gold thread and violet, purple, and scarlet yarn on cloth of fine linen twined. [16]It is to be square when folded double, a span high and a span wide. [17]On it you shall mount four rows of precious stones: in the first row, a carnelian, a topaz, and an emerald; [18]in the second row, a garnet, a sapphire, and a beryl; [19]in the third row, a jacinth, an agate, and an am-

ethyst; [20]in the fourth row, a chrysolite, an onyx, and a jasper. These stones are to be mounted in gold filigree work, [21]twelve of them to match the names of the sons of Israel, each stone engraved like a seal with the name of one of the twelve tribes.

[22]When the chains of pure gold, twisted like cords, have been made for the breastpiece, [23]you shall then make two rings of gold for it and fasten them to the two upper ends of the breastpiece. [24]The gold cords are then to be fastened to the two rings at the upper ends of the breastpiece, [25]the other two ends of the cords being fastened in front to the two filigree rosettes which are attached to the shoulder straps of the ephod. [26]Make two other rings of gold and put them on the two lower ends of the breastpiece, on its edge that faces the ephod. [27]Then make two more rings of gold and fasten them to the bottom of the shoulder straps next to where they join the ephod in front, just above its embroidered belt. [28]Violet ribbons shall bind the rings of the breastpiece to the rings of the ephod, so that the breastpiece will stay right above the embroidered belt of the ephod and not swing loose from it.

[29]Whenever Aaron enters the sanctuary, he will thus bear the names of the sons of Israel on the breastpiece of decision over his heart as a constant reminder before the LORD. [30]In this breastpiece of decision you shall put the Urim and Thummim, that they may be over Aaron's heart whenever he enters the presence of the LORD. Thus he shall always bear the decisions for the Israelites over his heart in the presence of the LORD.

Other Vestments. [31]The robe of the ephod you shall make entirely of violet material. [32]It shall have an opening for the head in the center, and around this opening there shall be a selvage, woven as at the opening of a shirt, to keep it from being torn. [33]At the hem at the bottom you shall make pomegranates, woven of violet, purple, and scarlet yarn and fine linen twined, with gold bells between them; ³⁴a gold bell, a pomegranate, a gold bell, a pomegranate, all around the hem of the robe. ³⁵Aaron shall wear it when ministering, that its sound may be heard as he enters and leaves the LORD's presence in the sanctuary; else he will die.

³⁶You shall also make a plate of pure gold and engrave on it, as on a seal engraving, "Sacred to the LORD." ³⁷This plate is to be tied over the turban with a violet ribbon in such a way that it rests on the front of the turban, ³⁸over Aaron's forehead. Since Aaron bears whatever guilt the Israelites may incur in consecrating any of their sacred gifts, this plate must always be over his forehead, so that they may find favor with the LORD.

³⁹The tunic of fine linen shall be brocaded. The turban shall be made of fine linen. The sash shall be of variegated work. ⁴⁰Likewise, for the glorious adornment of Aaron's sons you shall have tunics and sashes and skullcaps made, for glorious splendor. ⁴¹With these you shall clothe your brother Aaron and his sons. Anoint and install them, consecrating them as my priests. ⁴²You must also make linen pants for them, to cover their naked flesh from their loins to their thighs. ⁴³Aaron and his sons shall wear them whenever they go into the tent of meeting or approach the altar to minister in the sanctuary, lest they incur guilt and die. This shall be a perpetual ordinance for him and for his descendants.

☐ MARK 13

The Destruction of the Temple Foretold. 13:1 As he was making his way out of the temple area one of his disciples said to him, "Look, teacher, what stones and what buildings!" ²Jesus said to him, "Do you see these great buildings? There will not be one stone left upon another that will not be thrown down."

The Signs of the End. ³As he was sitting on the Mount of Olives opposite the temple area, Peter, James, John, and Andrew asked him privately, ⁴"Tell us, when will this happen, and what sign will there be when all these things are about to come to an end?" ⁵Jesus began to say to them, "See that no one deceives you. ⁶Many will come in my name saying, 'I am he,' and they will deceive many. ⁷When you hear of wars and reports of wars do not be alarmed; such things must happen, but it will not yet be the end. ⁸Nation will rise against nation and kingdom against kingdom. There will be earthquakes from place to place and there will be famines. These are the beginnings of the labor pains.

The Coming Persecution. ⁹"Watch out for yourselves. They will hand you over to the courts. You will be beaten in synagogues. You will be arraigned before governors and kings because of me, as a witness before them. ¹⁰But the gospel must first be preached to all nations. ¹¹When they lead you away and hand you over, do not worry beforehand about what you are to say. But say whatever will be given to you at that hour. For it will not be you who are speaking but the holy Spirit. ¹²Brother will hand over brother to death, and the father his child; children will rise up against parents and have them put to death. ¹³You will be hated by all because of my name. But the one who perseveres to the end will be saved.

The Great Tribulation. ¹⁴"When you see the desolating abomination standing where he should not (let the reader understand), then those in Judea must flee to the mountains, ¹⁵[and] a person on a housetop must not go down or enter to get anything out of his house, ¹⁶and a person in a field must not return to get his cloak. ¹⁷Woe to pregnant women and nursing mothers in those days. [18]Pray that this does not happen in winter. [19]For those times will have tribulation such as has not been since the beginning of God's creation until now, nor ever will be. [20]If the Lord had not shortened those days, no one would be saved; but for the sake of the elect whom he chose, he did shorten the days. [21]If anyone says to you then, 'Look, here is the Messiah! Look, there he is!' do not believe it. [22]False messiahs and false prophets will arise and will perform signs and wonders in order to mislead, if that were possible, the elect. [23]Be watchful! I have told it all to you beforehand.

The Coming of the Son of Man. [24]"But in those days after that tribulation

the sun will be darkened,
      and the moon will not give its light,
[25]and the stars will be falling from the
      sky,
      and the powers in the heavens will
      be shaken.

[26]And then they will see 'the Son of Man coming in the clouds' with great power and glory, [27]and then he will send out the angels and gather [his] elect from the four winds, from the end of the earth to the end of the sky.

The Lesson of the Fig Tree. [28]"Learn a lesson from the fig tree. When its branch becomes tender and sprouts leaves, you know that summer is near. [29]In the same way, when you see these things happening, know that he is near, at the gates. [30]Amen, I say to you, this generation will not pass away until all these things have taken place. [31]Heaven and earth will pass away, but my words will not pass away.

Need for Watchfulness. [32]"But of that day or hour, no one knows, neither the angels in heaven, nor the Son, but only the Father. [33]Be watchful! Be alert! You do not know when the time will come. [34]It is like a man traveling abroad. He leaves home and places his servants in charge, each with his work, and orders the gatekeeper to be on the watch. [35]Watch, therefore; you do not know when the lord of the house is coming, whether in the evening, or at midnight, or at cockcrow, or in the morning. [36]May he not come suddenly and find you sleeping. [37]What I say to you, I say to all: 'Watch!'"

February 3

St. Aelred; St. Ansgar; St. Blase

One who speaks the Word of God to others should not aim at showing off his own knowledge, but rather at discerning how he can build up his hearers.

— St. Aelred

☐ EXODUS 29-30

Consecration of the Priests. 29:1 This is the rite you shall perform in consecrating them as my priests. Procure a young bull and two unblemished rams. [2]With bran flour make unleavened cakes mixed with oil, and unleavened wafers spread with oil, [3]and put them in a basket. Take the basket of them along with the bull and the two rams. [4]Aaron and his sons you shall also bring to the entrance of the tent of meeting, and there wash them with water. [5]Take the vestments and clothe Aaron with the tunic, the robe of the ephod, the ephod itself, and the breastpiece, fastening the embroidered belt of the ephod around him. [6]Put the turban on his head, the sacred diadem on the turban. [7]Then take the anointing oil and pour it on his head, and anoint him. [8]Bring forward his sons also and clothe them with the tunics, [9]gird them with the sashes, and tie the skullcaps on them. Thus shall the priesthood be theirs by a perpetual statute, and thus shall you install Aaron and his sons.

Installation Sacrifices. [10]Now bring forward the bull in front of the tent of meeting. There Aaron and his sons shall lay their hands on its head. [11]Then slaughter the bull before the LORD, at the entrance of the tent of meeting. [12]Take some of its blood and with your finger put it on the horns of the altar. All the rest of the blood you shall pour out at the base of the altar. [13]All the fat that covers its inner organs, as well as the lobe of its liver and its two kidneys, together with the fat that is on them, you shall take and burn on the altar. [14]But the meat and hide and dung of the bull you must burn up outside the camp, since this is a purification offering.

[15]Then take one of the rams, and after Aaron and his sons have laid their hands on its head, [16]slaughter it. The blood you shall take and splash on all the sides of the altar. [17]Cut the ram into pieces; you shall wash its inner organs and shanks and put them with the pieces and with the head. [18]Then you shall burn the entire ram on the altar, since it is a burnt offering, a sweet-smelling oblation to the LORD.

[19]After this take the other ram, and when Aaron and his sons have laid their hands on its head, [20]slaughter it. Some of its blood you shall take and put on the tip of Aaron's right ear and on the tips of his sons' right ears and on the thumbs of their right hands and the great toes of their right feet. Splash the rest of the blood on all the sides of the altar. [21]Then take some of the blood that is on the altar, together with some of the anointing oil, and sprinkle this on Aaron and his vestments, as well as on his sons and their vestments, that he and his sons and their vestments may be sacred.

[22]Now, from this ram you shall take its fat: its fatty tail, the fat that covers its inner organs, the lobe of its liver, its two kidneys with the fat that is on them, and its right thigh, since this is the ram for installation; [23]then, out of the basket of unleavened food that you have set before the LORD, you shall take one of the loaves of bread, one of the cakes made with oil, and one of the wafers. [24]All these things you shall put into the hands of Aaron and his sons, so that they may raise them as an elevated offering before the LORD. [25]After you receive them back from their hands, you shall burn them on top of the burnt offering on the altar as a sweet-smelling oblation to the LORD. [26]Finally, take the brisket of Aaron's installation ram and raise it as an elevated offering before the LORD; this is to be your own portion.

[27]Thus shall you set aside the brisket of whatever elevated offering is raised, as well as the thigh of whatever contribution is raised up, whether this be the installation ram or anything else belonging to Aaron or to his sons. [28]Such things are due to Aaron and his sons from the Israelites by a perpetual statute as a contribution. From their communion offerings, too, the Israelites shall make a contribution, their contribution to the LORD.

[29]The sacred vestments of Aaron shall be passed down to his sons after him, that in them they may be anointed and installed. [30]The son who succeeds him as priest and who is to enter the tent of meeting to minister in the sanctuary shall be clothed with them for seven days.

[31]You shall take the installation ram and boil its meat in a holy place. [32]At the entrance of the tent of meeting Aaron and his sons shall eat the meat of the ram and the

bread that is in the basket. [33]They themselves are to eat of these things by which atonement was made at their installation and consecration; but no unauthorized person may eat of them, since they are sacred. [34]If some of the meat of the installation sacrifice or some of the bread remains over on the next day, this remnant you must burn up; it is not to be eaten, since it is sacred.

[35]Carry out all these commands in regard to Aaron and his sons just as I have given them to you. Seven days you shall spend installing them, [36]sacrificing a bull each day as a purification offering, to make atonement. Thus you shall purify the altar by purging it, and you shall anoint it in order to consecrate it. [37]Seven days you shall spend in purging the altar and in consecrating it. Then the altar will be most sacred, and whatever touches it will become sacred.

[38]Now, this is what you shall regularly offer on the altar: two yearling lambs as the sacrifice established for each day; [39]one lamb in the morning and the other lamb at the evening twilight. [40]With the first lamb there shall be a tenth of an ephah of bran flour mixed with a fourth of a hin of oil of crushed olives and, as its libation, a fourth of a hin of wine. [41]The other lamb you shall offer at the evening twilight, with the same grain offering and libation as in the morning. You shall offer this as a sweet-smelling oblation to the LORD. [42]Throughout your generations this regular burnt offering shall be made before the LORD at the entrance of the tent of meeting, where I will meet you and speak to you.

[43]There, at the altar, I will meet the Israelites; hence, it will be made sacred by my glory. [44]Thus I will consecrate the tent of meeting and the altar, just as I also consecrate Aaron and his sons to be my priests. [45]I will dwell in the midst of the Israelites and will be their God. [46]They shall know that I, the LORD, am their God who brought them out of the land of Egypt, so that I, the LORD, their God, might dwell among them.

Altar of Incense. 30:1 For burning incense you shall make an altar of acacia wood, [2]with a square surface, a cubit long, a cubit wide, and two cubits high, with horns that are of one piece with it. [3]Its grate on top, its walls on all four sides, and its horns you shall plate with pure gold. Put a gold molding around it. [4]Underneath the molding you shall put gold rings, two on one side and two on the opposite side, as holders for the poles used in carrying it. [5]Make the poles, too, of acacia wood and plate them with gold. [6]This altar you are to place in front of the veil that hangs before the ark of the covenant where I will meet you.

[7]On it Aaron shall burn fragrant incense. Morning after morning, when he prepares the lamps, [8]and again in the evening twilight, when he lights the lamps, he shall burn incense. Throughout your generations this shall be the regular incense offering before the LORD. [9]On this altar you shall not offer up any profane incense, or any burnt offering or grain offering; nor shall you pour out a libation upon it. [10]Once a year Aaron shall purge its horns. Throughout your generations he is to purge it once a year with the blood of the atoning purification offering. This altar is most sacred to the LORD.

Census Tax. [11]The LORD also told Moses: [12]When you take a census of the Israelites who are to be enrolled, each one, as he is enrolled, shall give the LORD a ransom for his life, so that no plague may come upon them for being enrolled. [13]This is what everyone who is enrolled must pay: a half-shekel, according to the standard of the sanctuary shekel—twenty gerahs to the shekel—a half-shekel contribution to the LORD. [14]Everyone who is enrolled, of twenty years or more, must give the contribution to the LORD. [15]The rich need not give more, nor shall the poor give less, than a half-shekel in this contribution to the LORD to pay the ransom for their lives. [16]When you receive this ransom money from the Israelites, you shall donate it to the service of the tent of meeting, that there it may be a reminder of the Israelites before the LORD of the ransom paid for their lives.

The Basin. [17]The LORD told Moses: [18]For ablutions you shall make a bronze basin with a bronze stand. Place it between the tent of meeting and the altar, and put water in it. [19]Aaron and his sons shall use it in washing their hands and feet. [20]When they are about to enter the tent of meeting, they must wash with water, lest they die. Likewise when they approach the altar to minister, to offer an oblation to the LORD, [21]they must wash their hands and feet, lest they die. This shall be a perpetual statute for him and his descendants throughout their generations.

The Anointing Oil. [22]The LORD told Moses: [23]Take the finest spices: five hundred shekels of free-flowing myrrh; half that amount, that is, two hundred and fifty shekels, of fragrant cinnamon; two hundred and fifty shekels of fragrant cane; [24]five hundred shekels of cassia—all according to the standard of the sanctuary shekel; together with a hin of olive oil; [25]and blend them into sacred anointing oil, perfumed ointment expertly prepared. With this sacred anointing oil [26]you shall

anoint the tent of meeting and the ark of the covenant, [27]the table and all its utensils, the menorah and its utensils, the altar of incense [28]and the altar for burnt offerings with all its utensils, and the basin with its stand. [29]When you have consecrated them, they shall be most sacred; whatever touches them shall be sacred. [30]Aaron and his sons you shall also anoint and consecrate as my priests. [31]Tell the Israelites: As sacred anointing oil this shall belong to me throughout your generations. [32]It may not be used in any ordinary anointing of the body, nor may you make any other oil of a like mixture. It is sacred, and shall be treated as sacred by you. [33]Whoever prepares a perfume like this, or whoever puts any of this on an unauthorized person, shall be cut off from his people.

The Incense. [34]The LORD told Moses: Take these aromatic substances: storax and onycha and galbanum, these and pure frankincense in equal parts; [35]and blend them into incense. This fragrant powder, expertly prepared, is to be salted and so kept pure and sacred. [36]Grind some of it into fine dust and put this before the covenant in the tent of meeting where I will meet you. This incense shall be treated as most sacred by you. [37]You may not make incense of a like mixture for yourselves; you must treat it as sacred to the LORD. [38]Whoever makes an incense like this for his own enjoyment of its fragrance, shall be cut off from his people.

☐ MARK 14:1-16

The Conspiracy against Jesus. 14:1 The Passover and the Feast of Unleavened Bread were to take place in two days' time. So the chief priests and the scribes were seeking a way to arrest him by treachery and put him to death. [2]They said, "Not during the festival, for fear that there may be a riot among the people."

The Anointing at Bethany. [3]When he was in Bethany reclining at table in the house of Simon the leper, a woman came with an alabaster jar of perfumed oil, costly genuine spikenard. She broke the alabaster jar and poured it on his head. [4]There were some who were indignant. "Why has there been this waste of perfumed oil? [5]It could have been sold for more than three hundred days' wages and the money given to the poor." They were infuriated with her. [6]Jesus said, "Let her alone. Why do you make trouble for her? She has done a good thing for me. [7]The poor you will always have with you, and whenever you wish you can do good to them, but you will not always have me. [8]She has done what she could. She has anticipated anointing my body for burial. [9]Amen, I say to you, wherever the gospel is proclaimed to the whole world, what she has done will be told in memory of her."

The Betrayal by Judas. [10]Then Judas Iscariot, one of the Twelve, went off to the chief priests to hand him over to them. [11]When they heard him they were pleased and promised to pay him money. Then he looked for an opportunity to hand him over.

Preparations for the Passover. [12]On the first day of the Feast of Unleavened Bread, when they sacrificed the Passover lamb, his disciples said to him, "Where do you want us to go and prepare for you to eat the Passover?" [13]He sent two of his disciples and said to them, "Go into the city and a man will meet you, carrying a jar of water. Follow him. [14]Wherever he enters, say to the master of the house, 'The Teacher says, "Where is my guest room where I may eat the Passover with my disciples?"' [15]Then he will show you a large upper room furnished and ready. Make the preparations for us there." [16]The disciples then went off, entered the city, and found it just as he had told them; and they prepared the Passover.

February 4

St. Joseph of Leonissa

Every Christian must be a living book in which others can read the teaching of the Gospel.

— St. Joseph of Leonissa

☐ **EXODUS 31-32**

Choice of Artisans. 31:1 The LORD said to Moses: [2]See, I have singled out Bezalel, son of Uri, son of Hur, of the tribe of Judah, [3]and I have filled him with a divine spirit of skill and understanding and knowledge in every craft: [4]in the production of embroidery, in making things of gold, silver, or bronze, [5]in cutting and mounting precious stones, in carving wood, and in every other craft. [6]As his assistant I myself have appointed Oholiab, son of Ahisamach, of the tribe of Dan. I have also endowed all the experts with the necessary skill to make all the things I have commanded you: [7]the tent of meeting, the ark of the covenant with its cover, all the furnishings of the tent, [8]the table with its utensils, the pure gold menorah with all its utensils, the altar of incense, [9]the altar for burnt offerings with all its utensils, the basin with its stand, [10]the service cloths, the sacred vestments for Aaron the priest, the vestments for his sons in their ministry, [11]the anointing oil, and the fragrant incense for the sanctuary. According to all I have commanded you, so shall they do.

Sabbath Laws. [12]The LORD said to Moses: [13]You must also tell the Israelites: Keep my sabbaths, for that is to be the sign between you and me throughout the generations, to show that it is I, the LORD, who make you holy. [14]Therefore, you must keep the sabbath for it is holiness for you. Whoever desecrates it shall be put to death. If anyone does work on that day, that person must be cut off from the people. [15]Six days there are for doing work, but the seventh day is the sabbath of complete rest, holy to the LORD. Anyone who does work on the sabbath day shall be put to death. [16]So shall the Israelites observe the sabbath, keeping it throughout their generations as an everlasting covenant. [17]Between me and the Israelites it is to be an everlasting sign; for in six days the LORD made the heavens and the earth, but on the seventh day he rested at his ease.

[18]When the LORD had finished speaking to Moses on Mount Sinai, he gave him the two tablets of the covenant, the stone tablets inscribed by God's own finger.

The Golden Calf. 32:1 When the people saw that Moses was delayed in coming down from the mountain, they gathered around Aaron and said to him, "Come, make us a god who will go before us; as for that man Moses who brought us out of the land of Egypt, we do not know what has happened to him." [2]Aaron replied, "Take off the golden earrings that your wives, your sons, and your daughters are wearing, and bring them to me." [3]So all the people took off their earrings and brought them to Aaron. [4]He received their offering, and fashioning it with a tool, made a molten calf. Then they cried out, "These are your gods, Israel, who brought you up from the land of Egypt." [5]On seeing this, Aaron built an altar in front of the calf and proclaimed, "Tomorrow is a feast of the LORD." [6]Early the next day the people sacrificed burnt offerings and brought communion sacrifices. Then they sat down to eat and drink, and rose up to revel.

[7]Then the LORD said to Moses: Go down at once because your people, whom you brought out of the land of Egypt, have acted corruptly. [8]They have quickly turned aside from the way I commanded them, making for themselves a molten calf and bowing down to it, sacrificing to it and crying out, "These are your gods, Israel, who brought you up from the land of Egypt!" [9]I have seen this people, how stiff-necked they are, continued the LORD to Moses. [10]Let me alone, then, that my anger may burn against them to consume them. Then I will make of you a great nation.

[11]But Moses implored the LORD, his God, saying, "Why, O LORD, should your anger burn against your people, whom you brought out of the land of Egypt with great power and with a strong hand? [12]Why should the Egyptians say, 'With evil intent he brought them out, that he might kill them in the mountains and wipe them off the face of the earth'? Turn from your burning wrath; change your mind about punishing your people. [13]Remember your servants Abraham, Isaac, and Israel, and how you swore to them by your own self, saying, 'I will make your descendants as numerous as the stars in the sky; and all this land that I promised, I will give your descendants as their perpetual heritage.'" [14]So the LORD changed his mind about the punishment he had threatened to inflict on his people.

[15]Moses then turned and came down the mountain with the two tablets of the covenant in his hands, tablets that were written on both sides, front and back. [16]The tablets were made by God; the writing was the writing of God, engraved on the tablets. [17]Now, when Joshua heard the noise of the people shouting, he said to Moses, "That sounds like a battle in the camp." [18]But Moses answered,

"It is not the noise of victory,
   it is not the noise of defeat;
   the sound I hear is singing."

[19]As he drew near the camp, he saw the calf and the dancing. Then Moses' anger burned, and he threw the tablets down and broke them on the base of the mountain.

20Taking the calf they had made, he burned it in the fire and then ground it down to powder, which he scattered on the water and made the Israelites drink.

21Moses asked Aaron, "What did this people do to you that you should lead them into a grave sin?" 22Aaron replied, "Do not let my lord be angry. You know how the people are prone to evil. 23They said to me, 'Make us a god to go before us; as for this man Moses who brought us out of the land of Egypt, we do not know what has happened to him.' 24So I told them, 'Whoever is wearing gold, take it off.' They gave it to me, and I threw it into the fire, and this calf came out."

25Moses saw that the people were running wild because Aaron had lost control—to the secret delight of their foes. 26Moses stood at the gate of the camp and shouted, "Whoever is for the LORD, come to me!" All the Levites then rallied to him, 27and he told them, "Thus says the LORD, the God of Israel: Each of you put your sword on your hip! Go back and forth through the camp, from gate to gate, and kill your brothers, your friends, your neighbors!" 28The Levites did as Moses had commanded, and that day about three thousand of the people fell. 29Then Moses said, "Today you are installed as priests for the LORD, for you went against your own sons and brothers, to bring a blessing upon yourselves this day."

The Atonement. 30On the next day Moses said to the people, "You have committed a grave sin. Now I will go up to the LORD; perhaps I may be able to make atonement for your sin." 31So Moses returned to the LORD and said, "Ah, this people has committed a grave sin in making a god of gold for themselves! 32Now if you would only forgive their sin! But if you will not, then blot me out of the book that you have written." 33The LORD answered Moses: Only the one who has sinned against me will I blot out of my book. 34Now, go and lead the people where I have told you. See, my angel will go before you. When it is time for me to punish, I will punish them for their sin.

35Thus the LORD struck the people for making the calf, the one that Aaron made.

☐ MARK 14:17-42

The Betrayer. 14:17 When it was evening, he came with the Twelve. 18And as they reclined at table and were eating, Jesus said, "Amen, I say to you, one of you will betray me, one who is eating with me." 19They began to be distressed and to say to him, one by one, "Surely it is not I?" 20He said to them, "One of the Twelve, the one who dips with me into the dish. 21For the Son of Man indeed goes, as it is written of him, but woe to that man by whom the Son of Man is betrayed. It would be better for that man if he had never been born."

The Lord's Supper. 22While they were eating, he took bread, said the blessing, broke it, and gave it to them, and said, "Take it; this is my body." 23Then he took a cup, gave thanks, and gave it to them, and they all drank from it. 24He said to them, "This is my blood of the covenant, which will be shed for many. 25Amen, I say to you, I shall not drink again the fruit of the vine until the day when I drink it new in the kingdom of God." 26Then, after singing a hymn, they went out to the Mount of Olives.

Peter's Denial Foretold. 27Then Jesus said to them, "All of you will have your faith shaken, for it is written:

'I will strike the shepherd,
    and the sheep will be dispersed.'

28But after I have been raised up, I shall go before you to Galilee." 29Peter said to him,

"Even though all should have their faith shaken, mine will not be." [30]Then Jesus said to him, "Amen, I say to you, this very night before the cock crows twice you will deny me three times." [31]But he vehemently replied, "Even though I should have to die with you, I will not deny you." And they all spoke similarly.

The Agony in the Garden. [32]Then they came to a place named Gethsemane, and he said to his disciples, "Sit here while I pray." [33]He took with him Peter, James, and John, and began to be troubled and distressed. [34]Then he said to them, "My soul is sorrowful even to death. Remain here and keep watch." [35]He advanced a little and fell to the ground and prayed that if it were possible the hour might pass by him; [36]he

said, "Abba, Father, all things are possible to you. Take this cup away from me, but not what I will but what you will." [37]When he returned he found them asleep. He said to Peter, "Simon, are you asleep? Could you not keep watch for one hour? [38]Watch and pray that you may not undergo the test. The spirit is willing but the flesh is weak." [39]Withdrawing again, he prayed, saying the same thing. [40]Then he returned once more and found them asleep, for they could not keep their eyes open and did not know what to answer him. [41]He returned a third time and said to them, "Are you still sleeping and taking your rest? It is enough. The hour has come. Behold, the Son of Man is to be handed over to sinners. [42]Get up, let us go. See, my betrayer is at hand."

February 5

St. Agatha

Jesus Christ, Lord of all things! You see my heart; You know my desires. Possess all that I am — You alone. I am Your sheep; make me worthy to overcome the devil.

— St. Agatha

☐ EXODUS 33-34

33:1 The LORD spoke to Moses: Go! You and the people whom you have brought up from the land of Egypt are to go up from here to the land about which I swore to Abraham, Isaac, and Jacob: I will give it to your descendants. [2]Driving out the Canaanites, Amorites, Hittites, Perizzites, Hivites and Jebusites, I will send an angel before you [3]to a land flowing with milk and honey. But I myself will not go up in your company, because you are a stiff-necked people; otherwise I might consume you on the way. [4]When the people heard this painful news, they mourned, and no one wore any ornaments.

[5]The LORD spoke to Moses: Speak to the Israelites: You are a stiff-necked people. Were I to go up in your company even for a moment, I would destroy you. Now off with your ornaments! Let me think what to do with you. [6]So, from Mount Horeb onward, the Israelites stripped off their ornaments.

Moses' Intimacy with God. [7]Moses used to pitch a tent outside the camp at some distance. It was called the tent of meeting. Anyone who wished to consult the LORD would go to the tent of meeting outside the camp. [8]Whenever Moses went out to the tent, the people would all rise and stand at the entrance of their own tents, watching Moses until he entered the tent. ⁹As Moses entered the tent, the column of cloud would come down and stand at its entrance while the LORD spoke with Moses. ¹⁰On seeing the column of cloud stand at the entrance of the tent, all the people would rise and bow down at the entrance of their own tents. ¹¹The LORD used to speak to Moses face to face, as a person speaks to a friend. Moses would then return to the camp, but his young assistant, Joshua, son of Nun, never left the tent. ¹²Moses said to the LORD, "See, you are telling me: Lead this people. But you have not let me know whom you will send with me. Yet you have said: You are my intimate friend; You have found favor with me. ¹³Now, if I have found favor with you, please let me know your ways so that, in knowing you, I may continue to find favor with you. See, this nation is indeed your own people. ¹⁴The LORD answered: I myself will go along, to give you rest. ¹⁵Moses replied, "If you are not going yourself, do not make us go up from here. ¹⁶For how can it be known that I and your people have found favor with you, except by your going with us? Then we, your people and I, will be singled out from every other people on the surface of the earth." ¹⁷The LORD said to Moses: This request, too, which you have made, I will carry out, because you have found favor with me and you are my intimate friend.

¹⁸Then Moses said, "Please let me see your glory!" ¹⁹The LORD answered: I will make all my goodness pass before you, and I will proclaim my name, "LORD," before you; I who show favor to whom I will, I who grant mercy to whom I will. ²⁰But you cannot see my face, for no one can see me and live. ²¹Here, continued the LORD, is a place near me where you shall station yourself on the rock. ²²When my glory passes I will set you in the cleft of the rock and will cover you with my hand until I have passed by. ²³Then I will remove my hand, so that you may see my back; but my face may not be seen.

Renewal of the Tablets. 34:1 The LORD said to Moses: "Cut two stone tablets like the former, that I may write on them the words which were on the former tablets that you broke. ²Get ready for tomorrow morning, when you are to go up Mount Sinai and there present yourself to me on the top of the mountain. ³No one shall come up with you, and let no one even be seen on any part of the mountain; even the sheep and the cattle are not to graze in front of this mountain." ⁴Moses then cut two stone tablets like the former, and early the next morning he went up Mount Sinai as the LORD had commanded him, taking in his hand the two stone tablets.

⁵The LORD came down in a cloud and stood with him there and proclaimed the name, "LORD." ⁶So the LORD passed before him and proclaimed: The LORD, the LORD, a God gracious and merciful, slow to anger and abounding in love and fidelity, ⁷continuing his love for a thousand generations, and forgiving wickedness, rebellion, and sin; yet not declaring the guilty guiltless, but bringing punishment for their parents' wickedness on children and children's children to the third and fourth generation! ⁸Moses at once knelt and bowed down to the ground. ⁹Then he said, "If I find favor with you, Lord, please, Lord, come along in our company. This is indeed a stiff-necked people; yet pardon our wickedness and sins, and claim us as your own."

Religious Laws. ¹⁰The LORD said: Here is the covenant I will make. Before all your people I will perform marvels never before done in any nation anywhere on earth, so that all the people among whom you live may see the work of the LORD. Awe-inspiring are the deeds I will perform with you! ¹¹As for you, observe what I am commanding you today.

See, I am about to drive out before you the Amorites, Canaanites, Hittites, Perizzites, Hivites and Jebusites. [12]Take care not to make a covenant with the inhabitants of the land that you are to enter; lest they become a snare among you. [13]Tear down their altars; smash their sacred stones, and cut down their asherahs. [14]You shall not bow down to any other god, for the LORD— "Jealous" his name—is a jealous God. [15]Do not make a covenant with the inhabitants of the land; else, when they prostitute themselves with their gods and sacrifice to them, one of them may invite you and you may partake of the sacrifice. [16]And when you take their daughters as wives for your sons, and their daughters prostitute themselves with their gods, they will make your sons do the same.

[17]You shall not make for yourselves molten gods.

[18]You shall keep the festival of Unleavened Bread. For seven days at the appointed time in the month of Abib you are to eat unleavened bread, as I commanded you; for in the month of Abib you came out of Egypt.

[19]To me belongs every male that opens the womb among all your livestock, whether in the herd or in the flock. [20]The firstling of a donkey you shall redeem with a lamb; if you do not redeem it, you must break its neck. The firstborn among your sons you shall redeem.

No one shall appear before me empty-handed.

[21]Six days you may labor, but on the seventh day you shall rest; even during the seasons of plowing and harvesting you must rest.

[22]You shall keep the feast of Weeks with the first fruits of the wheat harvest, likewise, the feast of the Ingathering at the close of the year. [23]Three times a year all your men shall appear before the Lord, the LORD God of Israel. [24]Since I will drive out the nations before you and enlarge your territory, no one will covet your land when you go up three times a year to appear before the LORD, your God.

[25]You shall not offer me the blood of sacrifice with anything leavened, nor shall the sacrifice of the Passover feast be kept overnight for the next day.

[26]The choicest first fruits of your soil you shall bring to the house of the LORD, your God.

You shall not boil a young goat in its mother's milk.

Radiance of Moses' Face. [27]Then the LORD said to Moses: Write down these words, for in accordance with these words I have made a covenant with you and with Israel. [28]So Moses was there with the LORD for forty days and forty nights, without eating any food or drinking any water, and he wrote on the tablets the words of the covenant, the ten words.

[29]As Moses came down from Mount Sinai with the two tablets of the covenant in his hands, he did not know that the skin of his face had become radiant while he spoke with the LORD. [30]When Aaron, then, and the other Israelites saw Moses and noticed how radiant the skin of his face had become, they were afraid to come near him. [31]Only after Moses called to them did Aaron and all the leaders of the community come back to him. Moses then spoke to them. [32]Later, all the Israelites came up to him, and he enjoined on them all that the LORD had told him on Mount Sinai. [33]When Moses finished speaking with them, he put a veil over his face. [34]Whenever Moses entered the presence of LORD to speak with him, he removed the veil until he came out again. On coming out, he would tell the Israelites all that he had been commanded. [35]Then the Israelites would see that the skin of Moses' face was radiant; so he would again put the veil over his face until he went in to speak with the LORD.

☐ MARK 14:43-72

The Betrayal and Arrest of Jesus. 14:43
Then, while he was still speaking, Judas, one of the Twelve, arrived, accompanied by a crowd with swords and clubs who had come from the chief priests, the scribes, and the elders. [44]His betrayer had arranged a signal with them, saying, "The man I shall kiss is the one; arrest him and lead him away securely." [45]He came and immediately went over to him and said, "Rabbi." And he kissed him. [46]At this they laid hands on him and arrested him. [47]One of the bystanders drew his sword, struck the high priest's servant, and cut off his ear. [48]Jesus said to them in reply, "Have you come out as against a robber, with swords and clubs, to seize me? [49]Day after day I was with you teaching in the temple area, yet you did not arrest me; but that the scriptures may be fulfilled." [50]And they all left him and fled. [51]Now a young man followed him wearing nothing but a linen cloth about his body. They seized him, [52]but he left the cloth behind and ran off naked.

Jesus before the Sanhedrin. [53]They led Jesus away to the high priest, and all the chief priests and the elders and the scribes came together. [54]Peter followed him at a distance into the high priest's courtyard and was seated with the guards, warming himself at the fire. [55]The chief priests and the entire Sanhedrin kept trying to obtain testimony against Jesus in order to put him to death, but they found none. [56]Many gave false witness against him, but their testimony did not agree. [57]Some took the stand and testified falsely against him, alleging, [58]"We heard him say, 'I will destroy this temple made with hands and within three days I will build another not made with hands.'" [59]Even so their testimony did not agree. [60]The high priest rose before the assembly and questioned Jesus, saying, "Have you no answer? What are these men testifying against you?" [61]But he was silent and answered nothing. Again the high priest asked him and said to him, "Are you the Messiah, the son of the Blessed One?" [62]Then Jesus answered, "I am; and

'you will see the Son of Man
   seated at the right hand of the
      Power
and coming with the clouds of
   heaven.'"

[63]At that the high priest tore his garments and said, "What further need have we of witnesses? [64]You have heard the blasphemy. What do you think?" They all condemned him as deserving to die. [65]Some began to spit on him. They blindfolded him and struck him and said to him, "Prophesy!" And the guards greeted him with blows.

Peter's Denial of Jesus. [66]While Peter was below in the courtyard, one of the high priest's maids came along. [67]Seeing Peter warming himself, she looked intently at him and said, "You too were with the Nazarene, Jesus." [68]But he denied it saying, "I neither know nor understand what you are talking about." So he went out into the outer court. [Then the cock crowed.] [69]The maid saw him and began again to say to the bystanders, "This man is one of them." [70]Once again he denied it. A little later the bystanders said to Peter once more, "Surely you are one of them; for you too are a Galilean." [71]He began to curse and to swear, "I do not know this man about whom you are talking." [72]And immediately a cock crowed a second time. Then Peter remembered the word that Jesus had said to him, "Before the cock crows twice you will deny me three times." He broke down and wept.

February 6

St. Paul Miki and Companions

After Christ's example, I forgive my persecutors. I do not hate them. I ask God to have pity on all, and I hope my blood will fall on my fellow men as a fruitful rain.

— St. Paul Miki

☐ EXODUS 35-36

Sabbath Regulations. 35:1 Moses assembled the whole Israelite community and said to them, "These are the words the LORD has commanded to be observed. [2]On six days work may be done, but the seventh day shall be holy to you as the sabbath of complete rest to the LORD. Anyone who does work on that day shall be put to death. [3]You shall not even light a fire in any of your dwellings on the sabbath day."

Collection of Materials. [4]Moses said to the whole Israelite community, "This is what the LORD has commanded: [5]Receive from among you contributions for the LORD. Everyone, as his heart prompts him, shall bring, as a contribution to the LORD, gold, silver, and bronze; [6]violet, purple, and scarlet yarn; fine linen and goat hair; [7]rams' skins dyed red, and tahash skins; acacia wood; [8]oil for the light; spices for the anointing oil and for the fragrant incense; [9]onyx stones and other gems for mounting on the ephod and on the breastpiece.

Call for Artisans. [10]"Let every artisan among you come and make all that the LORD has commanded: [11]the tabernacle, with its tent, its covering, its clasps, its frames, its bars, its columns, and its pedestals; [12]the ark, with its poles, the cover, and the curtain veil; [13]the table, with its poles and all its utensils, and the showbread; [14]the menorah, with its utensils, the lamps, and the oil for the light; [15]the altar of incense, with its poles; the anointing oil, and the fragrant incense; the entrance curtain for the entrance of the tabernacle; [16]the altar for burnt offerings, with its bronze grating, its poles, and all its utensils; the basin, with its stand; [17]the hangings of the court, with their columns and pedestals; the curtain for the gate of the court; [18]the tent pegs for the tabernacle and for the court, with their ropes; [19]the service cloths for use in the sanctuary; the sacred vestments for Aaron, the priest, and the vestments for his sons in their ministry."

The Contribution. [20]When the whole Israelite community left Moses' presence, [21]all, as their hearts moved them and their spirit prompted, brought a contribution to the LORD for the work of the tent of meeting, for all its services, and for the sacred vestments. [22]Both the men and the women, all as their heart prompted them, brought brooches, earrings, rings, necklaces, and various other gold articles. Everyone who could presented an offering of gold to the LORD. [23]Everyone who happened to have violet, purple, or scarlet yarn, fine linen or goat hair, rams' skins dyed red or tahash skins, brought them. [24]Whoever could make a contribution of silver or bronze offered it to the LORD; and everyone who happened to have acacia wood for any part of the work, brought it. [25]All the women who were expert spinners brought handspun violet, purple, and scarlet yarn and fine linen thread. [26]All the women, as their hearts and skills moved them, spun goat hair. [27]The tribal leaders brought onyx stones and other gems for mounting on the ephod and on the breastpiece; [28]as well as spices, and oil for the light, anointing oil, and fragrant incense. [29]Every Israelite man and woman brought to the LORD such voluntary offerings as they thought best, for the various kinds of work which the LORD, through Moses, had commanded to be done.

The Artisans. [30]Moses said to the Israelites: "See, the LORD has singled out Bezalel, son of Uri, son of Hur, of the tribe of Judah, [31]and has filled him with a divine spirit of skill and understanding and knowledge in every craft: [32]in the production of embroidery, in making things of gold, silver, or bronze, [33]in cutting and mounting precious stones, in carving wood, and in every other craft. [34]He has also given both him and Oholiab, son of Ahisamach, of the tribe of Dan, the ability to teach others. [35]He has endowed them with skill to execute all types of work: engraving, embroidering, the making of variegated cloth of violet, purple, and scarlet yarn and fine linen thread, weaving, and all other arts and crafts.

36:1 "Bezalel, therefore, will set to work with Oholiab and with all the artisans whom the LORD has endowed with skill and understanding in knowing how to do all the work for the service of the sanctuary, just as the LORD has commanded."

[2]Moses then called Bezalel and Oholiab and all the other artisans whom the LORD had endowed with skill, men whose hearts moved them to come and do the work. [3]They received from Moses all the contributions which the Israelites had brought for the work to be done for the sanctuary service. Still, morning after morning the people continued to bring their voluntary offerings to Moses. [4]Thereupon all the artisans who were doing the work for the sanctuary came from the work each was doing, [5]and told Moses, "The people are bringing much more than is needed to carry out the work which the LORD has commanded us to do." [6]Moses, therefore, ordered a proclamation to be made throughout the camp: "Let neither man nor woman make any more contributions for the sanctuary." So the people stopped bringing their offerings; [7]there was already enough at hand, and more than enough, to complete the work to be done.

The Tent Cloth and Coverings. [8]The various artisans who were doing the work made the tabernacle with its ten sheets woven of fine linen twined, having cherubim embroidered on them with violet, purple, and scarlet yarn. [9]The length of each sheet was twenty-eight cubits, and the width four cubits; all the sheets were the same size. [10]Five of the sheets were joined together, edge to edge; and the other five sheets likewise, edge to edge. [11]Loops of violet yarn were made along the edge of the end sheet in the first set, and the same along the edge of the end sheet in the second set. [12]Fifty loops were thus put on one inner sheet, and fifty loops on the inner sheet in the other set, with the loops directly opposite each other. [13]Then fifty clasps of gold were made, with which the sheets were joined so that the tabernacle formed one whole.

[14]Sheets of goat hair were also woven as a tent over the tabernacle. Eleven such sheets were made. [15]The length of each sheet was thirty cubits and the width four cubits; all eleven sheets were the same size. [16]Five of these sheets were joined into one set, and the other six sheets into another set. [17]Fifty loops were made along the edge of the end sheet in one set, and fifty loops along the edge of the corresponding sheet in the other set. [18]Fifty bronze clasps were made with which the tent was joined so that it formed one whole. [19]A covering for the tent was made of rams' skins dyed red and, above that, a covering of tahash skins.

The Framework. [20]Frames were made for the tabernacle, acacia-wood uprights. [21]The length of each frame was ten cubits, and the width one and a half cubits. [22]Each frame had two arms, fastening them one to another. In this way all the frames of the tabernacle were made. [23]The frames for the tabernacle were made as follows: twenty frames on the south side, [24]with forty silver pedestals under the twenty frames, two pedestals under each frame for its two arms; [25]twenty frames on the other side of the tabernacle, the north side, [26]with their forty silver pedestals, two pedestals under each frame. [27]At the rear of the tabernacle, to the west, six frames were made, [28]and two frames were made for the corners of the tabernacle, at its rear. [29]These were double at the bottom, and likewise double at the top, to the first ring. That is how both corner frames were made. [30]Thus, there were eight frames, with their sixteen silver pedestals, two pedestals under each frame. [31]Bars of acacia wood were also made, five for the frames on one side of the tabernacle, [32]five for those on the other side, and five for those at the rear, to the west. [33]The center bar, at the middle of the frames, was made to reach across from end to end. [34]The frames were plated with gold, and gold rings were made on them as holders for the bars, which were also plated with gold.

The Veil. [35]The veil was made of violet, purple, and scarlet yarn, and of fine linen twined, with cherubim embroidered on it. [36]Four gold-plated columns of acacia wood, with gold hooks, were made for it, and four silver pedestals were cast for them.

[37]The curtain for the entrance of the tent was made of violet, purple, and scarlet yarn, and of fine linen twined, woven in a variegated manner. [38]Its five columns, with their hooks as well as their capitals and bands, were plated with gold; their five pedestals were of bronze.

☐ MARK 15:1-20

Jesus before Pilate. 15:1 As soon as morning came, the chief priests with the elders and the scribes, that is, the whole Sanhedrin, held a council. They bound Jesus, led him away, and handed him over to Pilate. [2]Pilate questioned him, "Are you the king of the Jews?" He said to him in reply, "You say so." [3]The chief priests accused him of many things. [4]Again Pilate questioned him, "Have you no answer? See how many things they accuse you of." [5]Jesus gave him no further answer, so that Pilate was amazed.

The Sentence of Death. [6]Now on the occasion of the feast he used to release to them one prisoner whom they requested. [7]A man called Barabbas was then in prison along with the rebels who had committed murder in a rebellion. [8]The crowd came forward and began to ask him to do for them as he was accustomed. [9]Pilate answered, "Do you want me to release to you the king of the Jews?" [10]For he knew that it was out of envy that the chief priests had handed him over. [11]But the chief priests stirred up the crowd to have him release Barabbas for them instead. [12]Pilate again said to them in reply, "Then what [do you want] me to do with [the man you call] the king of the Jews?" [13]They shouted again, "Crucify him." [14]Pilate said to them, "Why? What evil has he done?" They only shouted the louder, "Crucify him." [15]So Pilate, wishing to satisfy the crowd, released Barabbas to them and, after he had Jesus scourged, handed him over to be crucified.

Mockery by the Soldiers. [16]The soldiers led him away inside the palace, that is, the praetorium, and assembled the whole cohort. [17]They clothed him in purple and, weaving a crown of thorns, placed it on him. [18]They began to salute him with, "Hail, King of the Jews!" [19]and kept striking his head with a reed and spitting upon him. They knelt before him in homage. [20]And when they had mocked him, they stripped him of the purple cloak, dressed him in his own clothes, and led him out to crucify him.

February 7

St. Moses the Black

It is good not to hide your thoughts, but to talk them over with older believers who are discreet, devout, and more experienced.

— ST. MOSES THE BLACK

☐ EXODUS 37-38

The Ark. 37:1 Bezalel made the ark of acacia wood, two and a half cubits long, one and a half cubits wide, and one and a half cubits high. ²The inside and outside were plated with gold, and a molding of gold was put around it. ³Four gold rings were cast for its four supports, two rings on one side and two on the opposite side. ⁴Poles of acacia wood were made and plated with gold; ⁵these poles were put through the rings on the sides of the ark, for carrying it.

⁶The cover was made of pure gold, two and a half cubits long and one and a half cubits wide. ⁷Two cherubim of beaten gold were made for the two ends of the cover; ⁸one cherub was at one end, the other at the other end, made of one piece with the cover, at each end. ⁹The cherubim had their wings spread out above, sheltering the cover. They faced each other, with their faces looking toward the cover.

The Table. ¹⁰The table was made of acacia wood, two cubits long, a cubit wide, and a cubit and a half high. ¹¹It was plated with pure gold, and a molding of gold was put around it. ¹²A frame a handbreadth high was also put around it, with a molding of gold around the frame. ¹³Four rings of gold were cast for it and fastened at the four corners, one at each leg. ¹⁴The rings were alongside the frame as holders for the poles to carry the table. ¹⁵These poles for carrying the table were made of acacia wood and plated with gold. ¹⁶The vessels that were set on the table, its plates and cups, as well as its pitchers and bowls for pouring libations, were made of pure gold.

The Menorah. ¹⁷The menorah was made of pure beaten gold—its shaft and branches—with its cups and knobs and petals springing directly from it. ¹⁸Six branches extended from its sides, three branches on one side and three on the other. ¹⁹On one branch there were three cups, shaped like almond blossoms, each with its knob and petals; on the opposite branch there were three cups, shaped like almond blossoms, each with its knob and petals; and so for the six branches that extended from the menorah. ²⁰On the menorah there were four cups, shaped like almond blossoms, with their knobs and petals. ²¹The six branches that went out from the menorah had a knob under each pair. ²²The knobs and branches so sprang from it that the whole formed but a single piece of pure beaten gold. ²³Its seven lamps, as well as its trimming shears and trays, were made of pure gold. ²⁴A talent of pure gold was used for the menorah and its various utensils.

The Altar of Incense. ²⁵The altar of incense was made of acacia wood, on a square, a cubit long, a cubit wide, and two cubits high, having horns that sprang directly from it. ²⁶Its grate on top, its walls on all four sides, and its horns were plated with pure gold; and a gold molding was put around it. ²⁷Underneath the molding gold rings were placed, two on one side and two on the opposite side, as holders for the poles used in carrying it. ²⁸The poles, too, were made of acacia wood and plated with gold.

[29]The sacred anointing oil and the fragrant incense were prepared in their pure form by a perfumer.

The Altar for Burnt Offerings. 38:1 The altar for burnt offerings was made of acacia wood, on a square, five cubits long and five cubits wide; its height was three cubits. [2]At the four corners horns were made that sprang directly from the altar. It was then plated with bronze. [3]All the utensils of the altar, the pots, shovels, basins, forks and fire pans, were likewise made of bronze. [4]A grating, a bronze network, was made for the altar and placed around it, on the ground, half as high as the altar itself. [5]Four rings were cast for the four corners of the bronze grating, as holders for the poles, [6]which were made of acacia wood and plated with bronze. [7]The poles were put through the rings on the sides of the altar for carrying it. The altar was made in the form of a hollow box.

[8]The bronze basin, with its bronze stand, was made from the mirrors of the women who served at the entrance of the tent of meeting.

The Court of the Tabernacle. [9]The court was made as follows. On the south side the hangings of the court were of fine linen twined, a hundred cubits long, [10]with twenty columns and twenty pedestals of bronze, the hooks and bands of the columns being of silver. [11]On the north side there were similar hangings, a hundred cubits long, with twenty columns and twenty pedestals of bronze; the hooks and bands of the columns were of silver. [12]On the west side there were hangings, fifty cubits long, with ten columns and ten pedestals; the hooks and bands of the columns were of silver. [13]On the east side the court was fifty cubits. [14]On one side there were hangings to the extent of fifteen cubits, with three columns and three pedestals; [15]on the other side, beyond the gate of the court, there were likewise hangings to the extent of fifteen cubits, with three columns and three pedestals. [16]The hangings on all sides of the court were woven of fine linen twined. [17]The pedestals of the columns were of bronze, while the hooks and bands of the columns were of silver; the capitals were silver-plated, and all the columns of the court were banded with silver.

[18]At the gate of the court there was a variegated curtain, woven of violet, purple, and scarlet yarn and of fine linen twined, twenty cubits long and five cubits wide, in keeping with the hangings of the court. [19]There were four columns and four pedestals of bronze for it, while their hooks were of silver, and their capitals and their bands silver-plated. [20]All the tent pegs for the tabernacle and for the court around it were of bronze.

Amount of Metal Used. [21]The following is an account of the various amounts used on the tabernacle, the tabernacle of the covenant, drawn up at the command of Moses by the Levites under the direction of Ithamar, son of Aaron the priest. [22]However, it was Bezalel, son of Uri, son of Hur, of the tribe of Judah, who made all that the LORD commanded Moses, [23]and he was assisted by Oholiab, son of Ahisamach, of the tribe of Dan, who was an engraver, an embroiderer, and a weaver of variegated cloth of violet, purple, and scarlet yarn and of fine linen.

[24]All the gold used in the entire construction of the sanctuary, having previously been given as an offering, amounted to twenty-nine talents and seven hundred and thirty shekels, according to the standard of the sanctuary shekel. [25]The silver of those of the community who were enrolled was one hundred talents and one thousand seven hundred and seventy-five shekels, according to the standard of the sanctuary shekel; [26]one bekah apiece, that is, a half-shekel, according to the standard of the sanctuary shekel, was received from everyone who was enrolled, of twenty years or

more, namely, six hundred and three thousand five hundred and fifty men. [27]One hundred talents of silver were used for casting the pedestals of the sanctuary and the pedestals of the veil, one talent for each pedestal, or one hundred talents for the one hundred pedestals. [28]The remaining one thousand seven hundred and seventy-five shekels were used for making the hooks on the columns, for plating the capitals, and for banding them with silver. [29]The bronze, given as an offering, amounted to seventy talents and two thousand four hundred shekels. [30]With this were made the pedestals at the entrance of the tent of meeting, the bronze altar with its bronze gratings, and all the utensils of the altar, [31]the pedestals around the court, the pedestals at the gate of the court, and all the tent pegs for the tabernacle and for the court around it.

☐ MARK 15:21-47

The Way of the Cross. 15:21 They pressed into service a passer-by, Simon, a Cyrenian, who was coming in from the country, the father of Alexander and Rufus, to carry his cross.

The Crucifixion. [22]They brought him to the place of Golgotha (which is translated Place of the Skull). [23]They gave him wine drugged with myrrh, but he did not take it. [24]Then they crucified him and divided his garments by casting lots for them to see what each should take. [25]It was nine o'clock in the morning when they crucified him. [26]The inscription of the charge against him read, "The King of the Jews." [27]With him they crucified two revolutionaries, one on his right and one on his left. [28] [29]Those passing by reviled him, shaking their heads and saying, "Aha! You who would destroy the temple and rebuild it in three days, [30]save yourself by coming down from the cross." [31]Likewise the chief priests, with the scribes, mocked him among themselves and said, "He saved others; he cannot save himself. [32]Let the Messiah, the King of Israel, come down now from the cross that we may see and believe." Those who were crucified with him also kept abusing him.

The Death of Jesus. [33]At noon darkness came over the whole land until three in the afternoon. [34]And at three o'clock Jesus cried out in a loud voice, "*Eloi, Eloi, lema sabachthani?*" which is translated, "My God, my God, why have you forsaken me?" [35]Some of the bystanders who heard it said, "Look, he is calling Elijah." [36]One of them ran, soaked a sponge with wine, put it on a reed, and gave it to him to drink, saying, "Wait, let us see if Elijah comes to take him down." [37]Jesus gave a loud cry and breathed his last. [38]The veil of the sanctuary was torn in two from top to bottom. [39]When the centurion who stood facing him saw how he breathed his last he said, "Truly this man was the Son of God!" [40]There were also women looking on from a distance. Among them were Mary Magdalene, Mary the mother of the younger James and of Joses, and Salome. [41]These women had followed him when he was in Galilee and ministered to him. There were also many other women who had come up with him to Jerusalem.

The Burial of Jesus. [42]When it was already evening, since it was the day of preparation, the day before the sabbath, [43]Joseph of Arimathea, a distinguished member of the council, who was himself awaiting the kingdom of God, came and courageously went to Pilate and asked for the body of Jesus. [44]Pilate was amazed that he was already dead. He summoned the centurion and asked him if Jesus had already died. [45]And when he learned of it from the centurion, he gave the body to Joseph. [46]Having bought a linen cloth, he took him down, wrapped him in the linen cloth and laid him in a tomb that had been hewn out of the rock. Then he rolled a stone against the entrance to the tomb. [47]Mary Magdalene and Mary the mother of Joses watched where he was laid.

February 8

St. Jerome Emiliani

God wishes to test you like gold in the furnace. The dross is consumed by the fire, but the pure gold remains, and its value increases.

— St. Jerome Emiliani

☐ **EXODUS 39-40**

The Priestly Vestments. 39:1 With violet, purple, and scarlet yarn were woven the service cloths for use in the sanctuary, as well as the sacred vestments for Aaron, as the LORD had commanded Moses.

[2]The ephod was woven of gold thread and of violet, purple, and scarlet yarn and of fine linen twined. [3]Gold was first hammered into gold leaf and then cut up into threads, which were woven with the violet, purple, and scarlet yarn into an embroidered pattern on the fine linen. [4]Shoulder straps were made for it and joined to its two upper ends. [5]The embroidered belt on the ephod extended out from it, and like it, was made of gold thread, of violet, purple, and scarlet yarn, and of fine linen twined, as the LORD had commanded Moses. [6]The onyx stones were prepared and mounted in gold filigree work; they were engraved like seal engravings with the names of the sons of Israel. [7]These stones were set on the shoulder straps of the ephod as memorial stones of the sons of Israel, just as the LORD had commanded Moses.

[8]The breastpiece was embroidered like the ephod, with gold thread and violet, purple, and scarlet yarn on cloth of fine linen twined. [9]It was square and folded double, a span high and a span wide in its folded form. [10]Four rows of precious stones were mounted on it: in the first row a carnelian, a topaz, and an emerald; [11]in the second row, a garnet, a sapphire, and a beryl; [12]in the third row a jacinth, an agate, and an amethyst; [13]in the fourth row a chrysolite, an onyx, and a jasper. They were mounted in gold filigree work. [14]These stones were twelve, to match the names of the sons of Israel, and each stone was engraved like a seal with the name of one of the twelve tribes.

[15]Chains of pure gold, twisted like cords, were made for the breastpiece, [16]together with two gold filigree rosettes and two gold rings. The two rings were fastened to the two upper ends of the breastpiece. [17]The two gold chains were then fastened to the two rings at the ends of the breastpiece. [18]The other two ends of the two chains were fastened in front to the two filigree rosettes, which were attached to the shoulder straps of the ephod. [19]Two other gold rings were made and put on the two lower ends of the breastpiece, on the edge facing the ephod. [20]Two more gold rings were made and fastened to the bottom of the two shoulder straps next to where they joined the ephod in front, just above its embroidered belt. [21]Violet ribbons bound the rings of the

breastpiece to the rings of the ephod, so that the breastpiece stayed right above the embroidered belt of the ephod and did not swing loose from it. All this was just as the LORD had commanded Moses.

Other Vestments. ²²The robe of the ephod was woven entirely of violet yarn, ²³with an opening in its center like the opening of a shirt, with selvage around the opening to keep it from being torn. ²⁴At the hem of the robe pomegranates were made of violet, purple, and scarlet yarn and of fine linen twined; ²⁵bells of pure gold were also made and put between the pomegranates all around the hem of the robe: ²⁶a bell, a pomegranate, a bell, a pomegranate, all around the hem of the robe which was to be worn in performing the ministry—all this, just as the LORD had commanded Moses.

²⁷For Aaron and his sons there were also woven tunics of fine linen; ²⁸the turban of fine linen; the ornate skullcaps of fine linen; linen pants of fine linen twined; ²⁹and sashes of variegated work made of fine linen twined and of violet, purple, and scarlet yarn, as the LORD had commanded Moses. ³⁰The plate of the sacred diadem was made of pure gold and inscribed, as on a seal engraving: "Sacred to the LORD." ³¹It was tied over the turban with a violet ribbon, as the LORD had commanded Moses.

Presentation of the Work to Moses. ³²Thus the entire work of the tabernacle of the tent of meeting was completed. The Israelites did the work just as the LORD had commanded Moses; so it was done. ³³They then brought to Moses the tabernacle, the tent with all its furnishings, the clasps, the frames, the bars, the columns, the pedestals, ³⁴the covering of rams' skins dyed red, the covering of tahash skins, the curtain veil; ³⁵the ark of the covenant with its poles, the cover, ³⁶the table with all its utensils and the showbread, ³⁷the pure gold menorah with its lamps set up on it and with all its utensils, the oil for the light, ³⁸the golden altar, the anointing oil, the fragrant incense; the curtain for the entrance of the tent, ³⁹the altar of bronze with its bronze grating, its poles and all its utensils, the basin with its stand, ⁴⁰the hangings of the court with their columns and pedestals, the curtain for the gate of the court with its ropes and tent pegs, all the equipment for the service of the tabernacle of the tent of meeting; ⁴¹the service cloths for use in the sanctuary, the sacred vestments for Aaron the priest, and the vestments to be worn by his sons in their ministry. ⁴²Just as the LORD had commanded Moses, so the Israelites had carried out all the work. ⁴³So when Moses saw that all the work was done just as the LORD had commanded, he blessed them.

Setting up the Tabernacle. 40:1 Then the LORD said to Moses: ²On the first day of the first month you shall set up the tabernacle of the tent of meeting. ³Put the ark of the covenant in it, and screen off the ark with the veil. ⁴Bring in the table and set it. Then bring in the menorah and set up the lamps on it. ⁵Put the golden altar of incense in front of the ark of the covenant, and hang the curtain at the entrance of the tabernacle. ⁶Put the altar for burnt offerings in front of the entrance of the tabernacle of the tent of meeting. ⁷Place the basin between the tent of meeting and the altar, and put water in it. ⁸Set up the court round about, and put the curtain at the gate of the court.

⁹Take the anointing oil and anoint the tabernacle and everything in it, consecrating it and all its furnishings, so that it will be sacred. ¹⁰Anoint the altar for burnt offerings and all its utensils, consecrating it, so that it will be most sacred. ¹¹Likewise, anoint the basin with its stand, and thus consecrate it.

¹²Then bring Aaron and his sons to the entrance of the tent of meeting, and there wash them with water. ¹³Clothe Aaron with

the sacred vestments and anoint him, thus consecrating him as my priest. [14]Bring forward his sons also, and clothe them with the tunics. [15]As you have anointed their father, anoint them also as my priests. Thus, by being anointed, shall they receive a perpetual priesthood throughout all future generations.

[16]Moses did just as the LORD had commanded him. [17]On the first day of the first month of the second year the tabernacle was set up. [18]It was Moses who set up the tabernacle. He placed its pedestals, set up its frames, put in its bars, and set up its columns. [19]He spread the tent over the tabernacle and put the covering on top of the tent, as the LORD had commanded him. [20]He took the covenant and put it in the ark; he placed poles alongside the ark and set the cover upon it. [21]He brought the ark into the tabernacle and hung the curtain veil, thus screening off the ark of the covenant, as the LORD had commanded him. [22]He put the table in the tent of meeting, on the north side of the tabernacle, outside the veil, [23]and arranged the bread on it before the LORD, as the LORD had commanded him. [24]He placed the menorah in the tent of meeting, opposite the table, on the south side of the tabernacle, [25]and he set up the lamps before the LORD, as the LORD had commanded him. [26]He placed the golden altar in the tent of meeting, in front of the veil, [27]and on it he burned fragrant incense, as the LORD had commanded him. [28]He hung the curtain at the entrance of the tabernacle. [29]He put the altar for burnt offerings in front of the entrance of the tabernacle of the tent of meeting, and sacrificed burnt offerings and grain offerings on it, as the LORD had commanded him. [30]He placed the basin between the tent of meeting and the altar, and put water in it for washing. [31]Moses and Aaron and his sons used to wash their hands and feet there, [32]for they washed themselves whenever they went into the tent of meeting or approached the altar, as the LORD had commanded Moses. [33]Finally, he set up the court around the tabernacle and the altar and hung the curtain at the gate of the court.

Thus Moses finished all the work.

God's Presence in the Tabernacle. [34]Then the cloud covered the tent of meeting, and the glory of the LORD filled the tabernacle. [35]Moses could not enter the tent of meeting, because the cloud settled down upon it and the glory of the LORD filled the tabernacle. [36]Whenever the cloud rose from the tabernacle, the Israelites would set out on their journey. [37]But if the cloud did not lift, they would not go forward; only when it lifted did they go forward. [38]The cloud of the LORD was over the tabernacle by day, and fire in the cloud at night, in the sight of the whole house of Israel in all the stages of their journey.

☐ MARK 16

The Resurrection of Jesus. 16:1 When the sabbath was over, Mary Magdalene, Mary, the mother of James, and Salome bought spices so that they might go and anoint him. [2]Very early when the sun had risen, on the first day of the week, they came to the tomb. [3]They were saying to one another, "Who will roll back the stone for us from the entrance to the tomb?" [4]When they looked up, they saw that the stone had been rolled back; it was very large. [5]On entering the tomb they saw a young man sitting on the right side, clothed in a white robe, and they were utterly amazed. [6]He said to them, "Do not be amazed! You seek Jesus of Nazareth, the crucified. He has been raised; he is not here. Behold the place where they laid him. [7]But go and tell his disciples and Peter, 'He is going before you to Galilee; there you will see him, as he told you.'" [8]Then they went out and fled from the tomb, seized with trembling and bewilderment. They said nothing to anyone, for they were afraid.

The Appearance to Mary Magdalene. [[9]When he had risen, early on the first day of the week, he appeared first to Mary Magdalene, out of whom he had driven seven demons. [10]She went and told his companions who were mourning and weeping. [11]When they heard that he was alive and had been seen by her, they did not believe.

The Appearance to Two Disciples. [12]After this he appeared in another form to two of them walking along on their way to the country. [13]They returned and told the others; but they did not believe them either.

The Commissioning of the Eleven. [14][But] later, as the eleven were at table, he appeared to them and rebuked them for their unbelief and hardness of heart because they had not believed those who saw him

after he had been raised. [15]He said to them, "Go into the whole world and proclaim the gospel to every creature. [16]Whoever believes and is baptized will be saved; whoever does not believe will be condemned. [17]These signs will accompany those who believe: in my name they will drive out demons, they will speak new languages. [18]They will pick up serpents [with their hands], and if they drink any deadly thing, it will not harm them. They will lay hands on the sick, and they will recover."

The Ascension of Jesus. [19]So then the Lord Jesus, after he spoke to them, was taken up into heaven and took his seat at the right hand of God. [20]But they went forth and preached everywhere, while the Lord worked with them and confirmed the word through accompanying signs.]

[And they reported all the instructions briefly to Peter's companions. Afterwards Jesus himself, through them, sent forth from east to west the sacred and imperishable proclamation of eternal salvation. Amen.]

February 9

St. Miguel Febres Cordero

The heart is rich when it is content, and it is always content when its desires are fixed on God.

— St. Miguel Febres Cordero

☐ LEVITICUS 1-3

Burnt Offerings. 1:1 The LORD called Moses, and spoke to him from the tent of meeting: [2]Speak to the Israelites and tell them: When any one of you brings an offering of livestock to the LORD, you shall bring your offering from the herd or from the flock.

[3]If a person's offering is a burnt offering from the herd, the offering must be a male without blemish. The individual shall bring it to the entrance of the tent of meeting to

find favor with the LORD, [4]and shall lay a hand on the head of the burnt offering, so that it may be acceptable to make atonement for the one who offers it. [5]The bull shall then be slaughtered before the LORD, and Aaron's sons, the priests, shall offer its blood by splashing it on all the sides of the altar which is at the entrance of the tent of meeting. [6]Then the burnt offering shall be flayed and cut into pieces. [7]After Aaron's sons, the priests, have put burning embers on the altar and laid wood on them, [8]they shall lay the pieces of meat, together with the head and the suet, on top of the wood and the embers on the altar; [9]but the inner organs and the shanks shall be washed with water. The priest shall then burn all of it on the altar as a burnt offering, a sweet-smelling oblation to the LORD.

[10]If a person's burnt offering is from the flock, that is, a sheep or a goat, the offering must be a male without blemish. [11]It shall be slaughtered on the north side of the altar before the LORD, and Aaron's sons, the priests, shall splash its blood on all the sides of the altar. [12]When it has been cut into pieces, the priest shall lay these, together with the head and suet, on top of the wood and the embers on the altar; [13]but the inner organs and the shanks shall be washed with water. The priest shall then offer all of it, burning it on the altar. It is a burnt offering, a sweet-smelling oblation to the LORD.

[14]If a person offers a bird as a burnt offering to the LORD, the offering brought must be a turtledove or a pigeon. [15]Having brought it to the altar, the priest shall wring its head off and burn it on the altar. The blood shall be drained out against the side of the altar. [16]He shall remove its crissum by means of its feathers and throw it on the ash heap at the east side of the altar. [17]Then, having torn the bird open by its wings without separating the halves, the priest shall burn it on the altar, on the wood and the embers. It is a burnt offering, a sweet-smelling oblation to the LORD.

Grain Offerings. 2:1 When anyone brings a grain offering to the LORD, the offering must consist of bran flour. The offerer shall pour oil on it and put frankincense over it, [2]and bring it to Aaron's sons, the priests. A priest shall take a handful of the bran flour and oil, together with all the frankincense, and shall burn it on the altar as a token of the offering, a sweet-smelling oblation to the LORD. [3]The rest of the grain offering belongs to Aaron and his sons, a most holy portion from the oblations to the LORD.

[4]When you offer a grain offering baked in an oven, it must be in the form of unleavened cakes made of bran flour mixed with oil, or of unleavened wafers spread with oil. [5]If your offering is a grain offering that is fried on a griddle, it must be of bran flour mixed with oil and unleavened. [6]Break it into pieces, and pour oil over it. It is a grain offering. [7]If your offering is a grain offering that is prepared in a pan, it must be made of bran flour, fried in oil. [8]A grain offering that is made in any of these ways you shall bring to the LORD. It shall be presented to the priest, who shall take it to the altar. [9]The priest shall then remove from the grain offering a token and burn it on the altar as a sweet-smelling oblation to the LORD. [10]The rest of the grain offering belongs to Aaron and his sons, a most holy portion from the oblations to the LORD.

[11]Every grain offering that you present to the LORD shall be unleavened, for you shall not burn any leaven or honey as an oblation to the LORD. [12]Such you may present to the LORD in the offering of the first produce that is processed, but they are not to be placed on the altar for a pleasing odor. [13]You shall season all your grain offerings with salt. Do not let the salt of the covenant with your God be lacking from your grain offering. On every offering you shall offer salt.

[14]If you offer a grain offering of first ripe fruits to the LORD, you shall offer it in the form of fresh early grain, roasted by fire and crushed as a grain offering of your first ripe fruits. [15]You shall put oil on it and set frankincense on it. It is a grain offering. [16]The priest shall then burn some of the groats and oil, together with all the frankincense, as a token of the offering, an oblation to the LORD.

Communion Sacrifices. 3:1 If a person's offering is a communion sacrifice, if it is brought from the herd, be it a male or a female animal, it must be presented without blemish before the LORD. ²The one offering it shall lay a hand on the head of the offering. It shall then be slaughtered at the entrance of the tent of meeting. Aaron's sons, the priests, shall splash its blood on all the sides of the altar. ³From the communion sacrifice the individual shall offer as an oblation to the LORD the fat that covers the inner organs, and all the fat that adheres to them, ⁴as well as the two kidneys, with the fat on them near the loins, and the lobe of the liver, which is removed with the kidneys. ⁵Aaron's sons shall burn this on the altar with the burnt offering that is on the wood and the embers, as a sweet-smelling oblation to the LORD.

⁶If the communion sacrifice one offers to the LORD is from the flock, be it a male or a female animal, it must be presented without blemish. ⁷If one presents a lamb as an offering, that person shall bring it before the LORD, ⁸and after laying a hand on the head of the offering, it shall then be slaughtered before the tent of meeting. Aaron's sons shall splash its blood on all the sides of the altar. ⁹From the communion sacrifice the individual shall present as an oblation to the LORD its fat: the whole fatty tail, which is removed close to the spine, the fat that covers the inner organs, and all the fat that adheres to them, ¹⁰as well as the two kidneys, with the fat on them near the loins, and the lobe of the liver, which is removed with the kidneys. ¹¹The priest shall burn this on the altar as food, an oblation to the LORD.

¹²If a person's offering is a goat, the individual shall bring it before the LORD, ¹³and after laying a hand on its head, it shall then be slaughtered before the tent of meeting. Aaron's sons shall splash its blood on all the sides of the altar. ¹⁴From this the one sacrificing shall present an offering as an oblation to the LORD: the fat that covers the inner organs, and all the fat that adheres to them, ¹⁵as well as the two kidneys, with the fat on them near the loins, and the lobe of the liver, which is removed with the kidneys. ¹⁶The priest shall burn these on the altar as food, a sweet-smelling oblation.

All the fat belongs to the LORD. ¹⁷This shall be a perpetual ordinance for your descendants wherever they may dwell. You shall not eat any fat or any blood.

ROMANS 1:1-17

Greeting. 1:1 Paul, a slave of Christ Jesus, called to be an apostle and set apart for the gospel of God, ²which he promised previously through his prophets in the holy scriptures, ³the gospel about his Son, descended from David according to the flesh, ⁴but established as Son of God in power according to the spirit of holiness through resurrection from the dead, Jesus Christ our Lord. ⁵Through him we have received the grace of apostleship, to bring about the obedience of faith, for the sake of his name, among all the Gentiles, ⁶among whom are you also, who are called to belong to Jesus Christ; ⁷to all the beloved of God in Rome, called to be holy. Grace to you and peace from God our Father and the Lord Jesus Christ.

Thanksgiving. ⁸First, I give thanks to my God through Jesus Christ for all of you, because your faith is heralded throughout the world. ⁹God is my witness, whom I serve with my spirit in proclaiming the gospel of his Son, that I remember you constantly, ¹⁰always asking in my prayers that somehow by God's will I may at last find my way clear to come to you. ¹¹For I long to see you, that I may share with you some spiritual gift so that you may be strengthened, ¹²that is, that you and I may be mutually encouraged by one another's faith, yours and mine. [13]I do not want you to be unaware, brothers, that I often planned to come to you, though I was prevented until now, that I might harvest some fruit among you, too, as among the rest of the Gentiles. [14]To Greeks and non-Greeks alike, to the wise and the ignorant, I am under obligation; [15]that is why I am eager to preach the gospel also to you in Rome.

God's Power for Salvation. [16]For I am not ashamed of the gospel. It is the power of God for the salvation of everyone who believes: for Jew first, and then Greek. [17]For in it is revealed the righteousness of God from faith to faith; as it is written, "The one who is righteous by faith will live."

February 10

St. Scholastica

When we will have come to Judgment Day, we will then recognize the justice of all God's decisions.

— St. Augustine of Hippo

☐ LEVITICUS 4-6

Purification Offerings. 4:1 The Lord said to Moses: [2]Tell the Israelites: When a person inadvertently does wrong by violating any one of the Lord's prohibitions—

For the Anointed Priest. [3]If it is the anointed priest who thus does wrong and thereby makes the people guilty, he shall offer to the Lord an unblemished bull of the herd as a purification offering for the wrong he committed. [4]Bringing the bull to the entrance of the tent of meeting, before the Lord, he shall lay his hand on its head and slaughter it before the Lord. [5]The anointed priest shall then take some of the bull's blood and bring it into the tent of meeting, [6]where, dipping his finger in the blood, he shall sprinkle some of it seven times before the Lord, toward the veil of the sanctuary. [7]The priest shall also put some of the blood on the horns of the altar of fragrant incense which stands before Lord in the tent of meeting. The rest of the bull's blood he shall pour out at the base of the altar for burnt offerings which is at the entrance of the tent of meeting. [8]He shall remove all the fat of the bull of the purification offering: the fat that covers the inner organs, and all the fat that adheres to them, [9]as well as the two kidneys, with the fat on them near the loins, and the lobe of the liver, which is removed with the kidneys, [10]just as the fat pieces are removed from the ox of the communion sacrifice. The priest shall burn these on the altar for burnt offerings. [11]But the hide of the bull and its meat, with its head, shanks, inner organs and dung, [12]that is, the whole bull, shall be brought outside the camp to a clean place where the ashes are deposited and there be burned in a wood fire. At the place of the ash heap, there it must be burned.

For the Community. [13]If the whole community of Israel errs inadvertently and without even being aware of it violates any of the Lord's prohibitions, and thus are guilty, [14]when the wrong that was committed becomes known, the community shall offer a bull of the herd as a purification offering. They shall bring it before the tent of meeting. [15]The elders of the community shall lay their hands on the bull's head before the Lord. When the bull has been slaughtered before the Lord, [16]the anointed priest shall bring some of its blood into the tent of meeting, [17]and dipping his finger in the blood, he shall sprinkle it seven times before the Lord, toward the veil. [18]He shall also put some of the blood on the horns of the altar which is before the Lord in the tent of meeting. The rest of the blood he shall pour out at the base of the altar for burnt offerings which is at the entrance of the tent of meeting. [19]He shall remove all of its fat and burn it on the altar, [20]doing with this bull just as he did with the other bull of the purification offering; he will do the same thing. Thus the priest shall make atonement on their behalf, that they may be forgiven. [21]This bull shall also be brought outside the camp and burned, just as the first bull. It is a purification offering for the assembly.

For the Tribal Leader. [22]Should a tribal leader do wrong inadvertently by violating any one of the prohibitions of the Lord his God, and thus be guilty, [23]when he learns of the wrong he committed, he shall bring as his offering an unblemished male goat. [24]He shall lay his hand on its head and it shall be slaughtered in the place where the burnt offering is slaughtered, before the Lord. It is a purification offering. [25]The priest shall then take some of the blood of the purification offering on his finger and put it on the horns of the altar for burnt offerings. The rest of the blood he shall pour out at the base of the altar. [26]All of its fat he shall burn on the altar like the fat of the communion sacrifice. Thus the priest shall make atonement on the tribal leader's behalf for his wrong, that he may be forgiven.

For the General Populace. [27]If anyone of the general populace does wrong inadvertently by violating one of the Lord's prohibitions, and thus is guilty, [28]upon learning of the wrong committed, that person shall bring an unblemished she-goat as the offering for the wrong committed. [29]The wrongdoer shall lay a hand on the head of the purification offering, and the purification offering shall be slaughtered at the place of the burnt offerings. [30]The priest shall then take some of its blood on his finger and put it on the horns of the altar for burnt offerings. The rest of the blood he shall pour out at the base of the altar. [31]He shall remove all the fat, just as the fat is removed from the communion sacrifice. The priest shall burn it on the altar for a sweet odor to the Lord. Thus the priest shall make atonement, so that the individual may be forgiven.

[32]If, however, a person brings a lamb as a purification offering, that person shall bring an unblemished female, and [33]lay a hand on its head. It shall be slaughtered as a purification offering in the place where the burnt offering is slaughtered. [34]The priest shall then take some of the blood of the purification offering on his finger and put it on the horns of the altar for burnt offerings. The rest of the blood he shall pour out at the base of the altar. [35]He shall remove all its fat just as the fat is removed from the lamb of the communion sacrifice. The priest shall burn these on the altar with the other oblations for the Lord. Thus the priest shall make atonement on the person's behalf for the wrong committed, that the individual may be forgiven.

Special Cases for Purification Offerings. 5:1 If a person, either having seen or come to know something, does wrong by refusing as a witness under oath to give information, that individual shall bear the penalty; [2]or if someone, without being aware of it, touches any unclean thing, such as the carcass of an unclean wild animal, or an unclean domestic animal, or an unclean swarming creature, and thus is unclean and guilty; [3]or if someone, without being aware of it, touches some human uncleanness, whatever kind of uncleanness this may be, and then subsequently becomes aware of guilt; [4]or if someone, without being aware of it, rashly utters an oath with bad or good intent, whatever kind of oath this may be, and then subsequently becomes aware of guilt in regard to any of these matters— [5]when someone is guilty in regard to any of these matters, that person shall confess the wrong committed, [6]and make reparation to the LORD for the wrong committed: a female animal from the flock, a ewe lamb or a she-goat, as a purification offering. Thus the priest shall make atonement on the individual's behalf for the wrong.

[7]If, however, the person cannot afford an animal of the flock, that person shall bring to the LORD as reparation for the wrong committed two turtledoves or two pigeons, one for a purification offering and the other for a burnt offering. [8]The guilty party shall bring them to the priest, who shall offer the one for the purification offering first. Wringing its head at the neck, yet without breaking it off, [9]he shall sprinkle some of the blood of the purification offering against the side of the altar. The rest of the blood shall be drained out against the base of the altar. It is a purification offering. [10]The other bird he shall offer as a burnt offering according to procedure. Thus the priest shall make atonement on the person's behalf for the wrong committed, so that the individual may be forgiven.

[11]If the person is unable to afford even two turtledoves or two pigeons, that person shall bring as an offering for the wrong committed one tenth of an ephah of bran flour for a purification offering. The guilty party shall not put oil or place frankincense on it, because it is a purification offering. [12]The individual shall bring it to the priest, who shall take a handful as a token of the offering and burn it on the altar with the other oblations for the LORD. It is a purification offering. [13]Thus the priest shall make atonement on the person's behalf for the wrong committed in any of the above cases, so that the individual may be forgiven. The

rest of the offering, like the grain offering, shall belong to the priest.

Reparation Offerings. [14]The LORD said to Moses: [15]When a person commits sacrilege by inadvertently misusing any of the LORD's sacred objects, the wrongdoer shall bring to the LORD as reparation an unblemished ram from the flock, at the established value in silver shekels according to the sanctuary shekel, as a reparation offering. [16]The wrongdoer shall also restore what has been misused of the sacred objects, adding a fifth of its value, and give this to the priest. Thus the priest shall make atonement for the person with the ram of the reparation offering, so that the individual may be forgiven.

[17]If someone does wrong and violates one of the LORD's prohibitions without realizing it, that person is guilty and shall bear the penalty. [18]The individual shall bring to the priest an unblemished ram of the flock, at the established value, for a reparation offering. The priest shall then make atonement on the offerer's behalf for the error inadvertently and unknowingly committed so that the individual may be forgiven. [19]It is a reparation offering. The individual must make reparation to the LORD.

[20]The LORD said to Moses: [21]When someone does wrong and commits sacrilege against the LORD by deceiving a neighbor about a deposit or a pledge or a stolen article, or by otherwise retaining a neighbor's goods unjustly; [22]or if, having found a lost article, the person lies about it, swearing falsely about any of the things that a person may do wrong— [23]when someone has thus done wrong and is guilty, that person shall restore the thing that was stolen, the item unjustly retained, the item left as deposit, or the lost article that was found [24]or whatever else the individual swore falsely about. That person shall make full restitution of the thing itself, and add one fifth of its value to it, giving it to its owner at the time of reparation. [25]Then that person

shall bring to the priest as reparation to the LORD an unblemished ram of the flock, at the established value, as a reparation offering. [26]The priest shall make atonement on the person's behalf before the LORD, so that the individual may be forgiven for whatever was done to incur guilt.

The Daily Burnt Offering. 6:1 The LORD said to Moses: [2]Give Aaron and his sons the following command: This is the ritual for the burnt offering—the burnt offering that is to remain on the hearth of the altar all night until the next morning, while the fire is kept burning on the altar. [3]The priest, clothed in his linen robe and wearing linen pants underneath, shall take away the ashes to which the fire has reduced the burnt offering on the altar, and lay them at the side of the altar. [4]Then, having taken off these garments and put on other garments, he shall carry the ashes to a clean place outside the camp. [5]The fire on the altar is to be kept burning; it must not go out. Every morning the priest shall put firewood on it. On this he shall lay out the burnt offering and burn the fat of the communion offering. [6]The fire is to be kept burning continuously on the altar; it must not go out.

The Grain Offering. [7]This is the ritual of the grain offering. Aaron's sons shall offer it before the LORD, in front of the altar. [8]A priest shall then take from the grain offering a handful of bran flour and oil, together with all the frankincense that is on it, and this he shall burn on the altar as a token of the offering, a sweet aroma to the LORD. [9]The rest of it Aaron and his sons may eat; but it must be eaten unleavened in a sacred place: in the court of the tent of meeting they shall eat it. [10]It shall not be baked with leaven. I have given it to them as their portion from the oblations for the LORD; it is most holy, like the purification offering and the reparation offering. [11]Every male of Aaron's descendants may eat of it perpetually throughout your generations as their rightful due from the oblations for the LORD. Whatever touches the oblations becomes holy.

High Priest's Daily Grain Offering. [12]The LORD said to Moses: [13]This is the offering that Aaron and his sons shall present to the LORD on the day he is anointed: one tenth of an ephah of bran flour for the regular grain offering, half of it in the morning and half of it in the evening. [14]You shall bring it well kneaded and fried in oil on a griddle. Having broken the offering into pieces, you shall present it as a sweet aroma to the LORD. [15]The anointed priest descended from Aaron who succeeds him shall do likewise. This is the LORD's due forever. The offering shall be wholly burned. [16]Every grain offering of a priest shall be a whole offering; it may not be eaten.

Purification Offerings. [17]The LORD said to Moses: [18]Tell Aaron and his sons: This is the ritual for the purification offering. At the place where the burnt offering is slaughtered, there also, before the LORD, shall the purification offering be slaughtered. It is most holy. [19]The priest who offers the purification offering shall eat of it; it shall be eaten in a sacred place, in the court of the tent of meeting. [20]Whatever touches its flesh becomes holy. If any of its blood spatters on a garment, the stained part must be washed in a sacred place. [21]A clay vessel in which it has been boiled shall be broken; if it is boiled in a copper vessel, this shall be scoured afterward and rinsed with water. [22]Every male of the priestly line may eat it. It is most holy. [23]But no purification offering of which some blood has been brought into the tent of meeting to make atonement in the sanctuary shall be eaten; it must be burned with fire.

☐ ROMANS 1:18-32

Punishment of Idolaters. 1:18 The wrath of God is indeed being revealed from heaven against every impiety and wickedness of those who suppress the truth by their wickedness. [19]For what can be known about God is evident to them, because God made it evident to them. [20]Ever since the creation of the world, his invisible attributes of eternal power and divinity have been able to be understood and perceived in what he has made. As a result, they have no excuse; [21]for although they knew God they did not accord him glory as God or give him thanks. Instead, they became vain in their reasoning, and their senseless minds were darkened. [22]While claiming to be wise, they became fools [23]and exchanged the glory of the immortal God for the likeness of an image of mortal man or of birds or of four-legged animals or of snakes.

[24]Therefore, God handed them over to impurity through the lusts of their hearts for the mutual degradation of their bodies. [25]They exchanged the truth of God for a lie and revered and worshiped the creature rather than the creator, who is blessed forever. Amen. [26]Therefore, God handed them over to degrading passions. Their females exchanged natural relations for unnatural, [27]and the males likewise gave up natural relations with females and burned with lust for one another. Males did shameful things with males and thus received in their own persons the due penalty for their perversity. [28]And since they did not see fit to acknowledge God, God handed them over to their undiscerning mind to do what is improper. [29]They are filled with every form of wickedness, evil, greed, and malice; full of envy, murder, rivalry, treachery, and spite. They are gossips [30]and scandalmongers and they hate God. They are insolent, haughty, boastful, ingenious in their wickedness, and rebellious toward their parents. [31]They are senseless, faithless, heartless, ruthless. [32]Although they know the just decree of God that all who practice such things deserve death, they not only do them but give approval to those who practice them.

February 11

Our Lady of Lourdes

In dangers, in doubts, in difficulties, think of Mary, call upon Mary. Don't let her name depart from your lips; never allow it to leave your heart. And that you may more surely obtain the assistance of her prayer, don't neglect to walk in her footsteps.

— St. Bernard of Clairvaux

☐ LEVITICUS 7-9

Reparation Offerings. 7:1 This is the ritual for the reparation offering. It is most holy. [2]At the place where the burnt offering is slaughtered, the reparation offering shall also be slaughtered. Its blood shall be splashed on all the sides of the altar. [3]All of its fat shall be offered: the fatty tail, the fat that covers the inner organs, and all the fat that adheres to them, [4]as well as the two kidneys with the fat on them near the loins, and the lobe of the liver, which is removed with the kidneys. [5]The priest shall burn these on the altar as an oblation to the LORD. It is a reparation offering. [6]Every male of the priestly line may eat of it; but it must be eaten in a sacred place. It is most holy.

[7]Because the purification offering and the reparation offering are alike, both have the same ritual. The reparation offering belongs to the priest who makes atonement with it. [8]As for the priest who offers someone's burnt offering, to him belongs the hide of the burnt offering that is offered. [9]Also, every grain offering that is baked in an oven or made in a pan or on a griddle shall belong to the priest who offers it, [10]whereas all grain offerings that are mixed with oil or are dry shall belong to all of Aaron's sons without distinction.

Communion Sacrifices. [11]This is the ritual for the communion sacrifice that is offered to the LORD. [12]If someone offers it for thanksgiving, that person shall offer it with unleavened cakes mixed with oil, unleavened wafers spread with oil, and cakes made of bran flour mixed with oil and well kneaded. [13]One shall present this offering together with loaves of leavened bread along with the thanksgiving communion sacrifice. [14]From this the individual shall offer one bread of each type of offering as a contribution to the LORD; this shall belong to the priest who splashes the blood of the communion offering.

[15]The meat of the thanksgiving communion sacrifice shall be eaten on the day it is offered; none of it may be kept till the next morning. [16]However, if the sacrifice offered is a votive or a voluntary offering, it shall be eaten on the day the sacrifice is offered, and on the next day what is left over may be eaten. [17]But what is left over of the meat of the sacrifice on the third day must be burned in the fire. [18]If indeed any of the flesh of the communion sacrifice is eaten on the third day, it shall not be accepted; it will not be reckoned to the credit of the one offering it. Rather it becomes a desecrated meat. Anyone who eats of it shall bear the penalty.

[19]Should the meat touch anything unclean, it may not be eaten, but shall be burned in the fire. As for other meat, all who are clean may eat of it. [20]If, however, someone in a state of uncleanness eats the meat of a communion sacrifice belonging to the LORD, that person shall be cut off from the people. [21]Likewise, if someone touches anything unclean, whether it be human uncleanness or an unclean animal or an unclean loathsome creature, and then eats the meat of the communion sacrifice belonging to the LORD, that person, too, shall be cut off from the people.

Prohibition Against Blood and Fat. [22]The LORD said to Moses: [23]Tell the Israelites: You shall not eat the fat of any ox or sheep or goat. [24]Although the fat of an animal that has died a natural death or has been killed by wild beasts may be put to any other use, you may not eat it. [25]If anyone eats the fat of an animal from which an oblation is made to the LORD, that person shall be cut off from the people. [26]Wherever you dwell, you shall not eat any blood, whether of bird or of animal. [27]Every person who eats any blood shall be cut off from the people.

Portions from the Communion Sacrifice for Priests. [28]The LORD said to Moses: [29]Tell the Israelites: The person who offers a communion sacrifice to the LORD shall be the one to bring from it the offering to the LORD. [30]The offerer's own hands shall carry the oblations for the LORD: the person shall bring the fat together with the brisket, which is to be raised as an elevated offering before the LORD. [31]The priest shall burn the fat on the altar, but the brisket belongs to Aaron and his sons. [32]Moreover, from your communion sacrifices you shall give to the priest the right leg as a contribution. [33]The one among Aaron's sons who offers the blood and the fat of the communion offering shall have the right leg as his portion, ³⁴for from the communion sacrifices of the Israelites I have taken the brisket that is elevated and the leg that is a contribution, and I have given them to Aaron, the priest, and to his sons as their due from the Israelites forever.

³⁵This is the priestly share from the oblations for the LORD, allotted to Aaron and his sons on the day they were brought forth to be the priests of the LORD, ³⁶which the LORD ordered to be given them from the Israelites on the day they were anointed, as their due throughout their generations forever.

Summary. ³⁷This is the ritual for the burnt offering, the grain offering, the purification offering, the reparation offering, the ordination offering, and the communion sacrifice, ³⁸which the LORD enjoined on Moses at Mount Sinai at the time when he commanded the Israelites in the wilderness of Sinai to bring their offerings to the LORD.

Ordination of Aaron and His Sons. 8:1 The LORD said to Moses: ²Take Aaron along with his sons, the vestments, the anointing oil, the bull for a purification offering, the two rams, and the basket of unleavened bread, ³then assemble the whole community at the entrance of the tent of meeting. ⁴Moses did as the LORD had commanded. When the community had assembled at the entrance of the tent of meeting, ⁵Moses told them: "This is what the LORD has ordered to be done." ⁶Bringing forward Aaron and his sons, Moses first washed them with water. ⁷Then he put the tunic on Aaron, girded him with the sash, clothed him with the robe, placed the ephod on him, and girded him with the ephod's embroidered belt, fastening the ephod on him with it. ⁸He then set the breastpiece on him, putting the Urim and Thummim in it. ⁹He put the turban on his head, attaching the gold medallion, the sacred headband, on the front of the turban, as the LORD had commanded Moses to do.

¹⁰Taking the anointing oil, Moses anointed and consecrated the tabernacle and all that was in it. ¹¹Then he sprinkled some of the oil seven times on the altar, and anointed the altar, with all its utensils, and the laver, with its base, to consecrate them. ¹²He also poured some of the anointing oil on Aaron's head and anointed him, to consecrate him. ¹³Moses likewise brought forward Aaron's sons, clothed them with tunics, girded them with sashes, and put skullcaps on them, as the LORD had commanded him to do.

Ordination Sacrifices. ¹⁴He brought forward the bull for a purification offering, and Aaron and his sons laid their hands on its head. ¹⁵When it was slaughtered, Moses took the blood and with his finger he put it on the horns around the altar, thus purifying the altar. He poured out the rest of the blood at the base of the altar. Thus he consecrated it so that atonement could be made on it. ¹⁶Taking all the fat that was over the inner organs, as well as the lobe of the liver and the two kidneys with their fat, Moses burned them on the altar. ¹⁷The bull, however, with its hide and flesh and dung he burned in the fire outside the camp, as the LORD had commanded Moses to do.

¹⁸He next brought forward the ram of the burnt offering, and Aaron and his sons laid their hands on its head. ¹⁹When it was slaughtered, Moses splashed the blood on all sides of the altar. ²⁰After the ram was cut up into pieces, Moses burned the head, the cut-up pieces and the suet. ²¹After the inner organs and the shanks were washed with water, Moses burned these remaining parts of the ram on the altar. It was a burnt offering for a sweet aroma, an oblation to the LORD, as the LORD had commanded Moses.

²²Then he brought forward the second ram, the ordination ram, and Aaron

and his sons laid their hands on its head. [23]When it was slaughtered, Moses took some of its blood and put it on the lobe of Aaron's right ear, on the thumb of his right hand, and on the big toe of his right foot. [24]Moses had the sons of Aaron also come forward, and he put some of the blood on the lobes of their right ears, on the thumbs of their right hands, and on the big toes of their right feet. The rest of the blood he splashed on all the sides of the altar. [25]He then took the fat: the fatty tail and all the fat over the inner organs, the lobe of the liver and the two kidneys with their fat, and likewise the right thigh; [26]from the basket of unleavened bread that was set before the Lord he took one unleavened cake, one loaf of bread made with oil, and one wafer; these he placed on top of the portions of fat and the right thigh. [27]He then put all these things upon the palms of Aaron and his sons, whom he had raise them as an elevated offering before the Lord. [28]When Moses had removed them from their palms, he burned them on the altar with the burnt offering. They were an ordination offering for a sweet aroma, an oblation to the Lord. [29]He then took the brisket and raised it as an elevated offering before the Lord; this was Moses' own portion of the ordination ram, as the Lord had commanded Moses. [30]Taking some of the anointing oil and some of the blood that was on the altar, Moses sprinkled it upon Aaron and his vestments, as well as his sons and their vestments, thus consecrating both Aaron and his vestments and his sons and their vestments.

[31]Moses said to Aaron and his sons, "Boil the meat at the entrance of the tent of meeting, and there eat it with the bread that is in the basket of the ordination offering, in keeping with the command I have received: 'Aaron and his sons shall eat of it.' [32]What is left over of the meat and the bread you shall burn in the fire. [33]Moreover, you are not to depart from the entrance of the tent of meeting for seven days, until the days of your ordination are completed; for your ordination is to last for seven days. [34]What has been done today the Lord has commanded be done, to make atonement for you. [35]You must remain at the entrance of the tent of meeting day and night for seven days, carrying out the prescriptions of the Lord, so that you do not die, for this is the command I have received." [36]So Aaron and his sons did all that the Lord had commanded through Moses.

Octave of the Ordination. 9:1 On the eighth day Moses summoned Aaron and his sons, together with the elders of Israel, [2]and said to Aaron, "Take a calf of the herd for a purification offering and a ram for a burnt offering, both without blemish, and offer them before the Lord. [3]Tell the Israelites, too: Take a he-goat for a purification offering, a calf and a lamb, both unblemished yearlings, for a burnt offering, [4]and an ox and a ram for a communion sacrifice, to sacrifice before the Lord, along with a grain offering mixed with oil; for today the Lord will appear to you." [5]So they brought what Moses had ordered before the tent of meeting. When the whole community had come forward and stood before the Lord, [6]Moses said, "This is what the Lord orders you to do, that the glory of the Lord may appear to you. [7]Approach the altar," Moses then told Aaron, "and make your purification offering and your burnt offering in atonement for yourself and for your household; then make the offering of the people in atonement for them, as the Lord has commanded."

[8]Approaching the altar, Aaron first slaughtered the calf of the purification offering that was his own offering. [9]When his sons presented the blood to him, he dipped his finger in the blood and put it on the horns of the altar. The rest of the blood he poured out at the base of the altar. [10]He then burned on the altar the fat, the kidneys and

the lobe of the liver from the purification offering, as the LORD had commanded Moses; [11]but the flesh and the hide he burned in the fire outside the camp. [12]Then Aaron slaughtered the burnt offering. When his sons brought him the blood, he splashed it on all sides of the altar. [13]They then brought him the pieces and the head of the burnt offering, and he burned them on the altar. [14]Having washed the inner organs and the shanks, he burned these also with the burnt offering on the altar.

[15]Then he had the people's offering brought. Taking the goat that was for the people's purification offering, he slaughtered it and offered it as a purification offering as before. [16]Then he brought forward the burnt offering and offered it according to procedure. [17]He then presented the grain offering; taking a handful of it, he burned it on the altar, in addition to the morning burnt offering. [18]Finally he slaughtered the ox and the ram, the communion sacrifice of the people. When his sons brought him the blood, Aaron splashed it on all sides of the altar. [19]The portions of fat from the ox and from the ram, the fatty tail, the covering fat, the kidneys, and the lobe of the liver [20]they placed on top of the briskets. Aaron burned the fat pieces on the altar, [21]but the briskets and the right thigh he raised as an elevated offering before the LORD, as the LORD had commanded Moses.

Revelation of the Lord's Glory. [22]Aaron then raised his hands over the people and blessed them. When he came down from offering the purification offering, the burnt offering, and the communion offering, [23]Moses and Aaron went into the tent of meeting. On coming out they blessed the people. Then the glory of the LORD appeared to all the people. [24]Fire came forth from the LORD's presence and consumed the burnt offering and the fat on the altar. Seeing this, all the people shouted with joy and fell prostrate.

☐ ROMANS 2:1-16

God's Just Judgment. 2:1 Therefore, you are without excuse, every one of you who passes judgment. For by the standard by which you judge another you condemn yourself, since you, the judge, do the very same things. [2]We know that the judgment of God on those who do such things is true. [3]Do you suppose, then, you who judge those who engage in such things and yet do them yourself, that you will escape the judgment of God? [4]Or do you hold his priceless kindness, forbearance, and patience in low esteem, unaware that the kindness of God would lead you to repentance? [5]By your stubbornness and impenitent heart, you are storing up wrath for yourself for the day of wrath and revelation of the just judgment of God, [6]who will repay everyone according to his works: [7]eternal life to those who seek glory, honor, and immortality through perseverance in good works, [8]but wrath and fury to those who selfishly disobey the truth and obey wickedness. [9]Yes, affliction and distress will come upon every human being who does evil, Jew first and then Greek. [10]But there will be glory, honor, and peace for everyone who does good, Jew first and then Greek. [11]There is no partiality with God.

Judgment by the Interior Law. [12]All who sin outside the law will also perish without reference to it, and all who sin under the law will be judged in accordance with it. [13]For it is not those who hear the law who are just in the sight of God; rather, those who observe the law will be justified. [14]For when the Gentiles who do not have the law by nature observe the prescriptions of the law, they are a law for themselves even though they do not have the law. [15]They show that the demands of the law are written in their hearts, while their conscience also bears witness and their conflicting thoughts accuse or even defend them [16]on the day when, according to my gospel, God will judge people's hidden works through Christ Jesus.

February 12

Those who imagine they can attain to holiness by any wisdom or strength of their own will find themselves after many labors, and struggles, and weary efforts, only the farther from possessing it, and this in proportion to their certainty that they of themselves have gained it.

— ST. JOHN OF ÁVILA

☐ LEVITICUS 10–12

Nadab and Abihu. 10:1 Aaron's sons Nadab and Abihu took their censers and, putting incense on the fire they had set in them, they offered before the LORD unauthorized fire, such as he had not commanded. [2]Fire therefore came forth from the LORD's presence and consumed them, so that they died in the LORD's presence. [3]Moses then said to Aaron, "This is as the LORD said:

Through those near to me I will be
    sanctified;
    in the sight of all the people I will
        obtain glory."

But Aaron said nothing. [4]Then Moses summoned Mishael and Elzaphan, the sons of Aaron's uncle Uzziel, with the order, "Come, carry your kinsmen from before the sanctuary to a place outside the camp." [5]So they drew near and carried them by means of their tunics outside the camp, as Moses had commanded.

Conduct of the Priests. [6]Moses said to Aaron and his sons Eleazar and Ithamar, "Do not dishevel your hair or tear your garments, lest you die and bring God's wrath also on the whole community. While your kindred, the rest of the house of Israel, may mourn for those whom the LORD's fire has burned up, [7]you shall not go beyond the entrance of the tent of meeting, else you shall die; for the anointing oil of the LORD is upon you." So they did as Moses told them.

[8]The LORD said to Aaron: [9]When you are to go to the tent of meeting, you and your sons are forbidden, by a perpetual statute throughout your generations, to drink any wine or strong drink, lest you die. [10]You must be able to distinguish between what is sacred and what is profane, and between what is clean and what is unclean; [11]and you must be able to teach the Israelites all the statutes that the LORD has given them through Moses.

The Eating of the Priestly Portions. [12]Moses said to Aaron and his surviving sons, Eleazar and Ithamar, "Take the grain offering left over from the oblations to the LORD, and eat it beside the altar in the form of unleavened cakes, since it is most holy. [13]You must eat it in a sacred place because it is your and your sons' due from the oblations to the LORD; such is the command I have received. [14]The brisket of the elevated offering and the leg of the contribution, however, you and your sons and daughters may eat, in a clean place; for these have been assigned to you and your children as your due from the communion sacrifices of the Israelites. [15]The leg of the contribution and the brisket of the elevated offering shall be brought in with the oblations of fat to be raised as an elevated offering before the LORD. They shall belong to you and your children as your due forever, as the LORD has commanded."

[16]Moses inquired closely about the goat of the purification offering and discovered that it had all been burned. So he was angry with the surviving sons of Aaron, Eleazar and Ithamar, and said, [17]"Why did you not eat the purification offering in the sacred place, since it is most holy? It has been given to you that you might remove the guilt of the community and make atonement for them before the LORD. [18]Since its blood was not brought inside the sanctuary, you should certainly have eaten the offering in the sanctuary, as I was commanded." [19]Aaron answered Moses, "Even though they presented their purification offering and burnt offering before the LORD today, still this misfortune has befallen me. Had I then eaten of the purification offering today, would it have been pleasing to the LORD?" [20]On hearing this, Moses was satisfied.

Clean and Unclean Meats. 11:1 The LORD said to Moses and Aaron: [2]Speak to the Israelites and tell them: Of all land animals these are the ones you may eat: [3]Any animal that has hoofs you may eat, provided it is cloven-footed and chews the cud. [4]But you shall not eat any of the following from among those that only chew the cud or only have hoofs: the camel, which indeed chews the cud, but does not have hoofs and is therefore unclean for you; [5]the rock hyrax, which indeed chews the cud, but does not have hoofs and is therefore unclean for you; [6]the hare, which indeed chews the cud, but does not have hoofs and is therefore unclean for you; [7]and the pig, which does indeed have hoofs and is cloven-footed, but does not chew the cud and is therefore unclean for you. [8]You shall not eat their meat, and you shall not touch their carcasses; they are unclean for you.

[9]Of the various creatures that live in the water, you may eat the following: whatever in the seas or in river waters that has both fins and scales you may eat. [10]But of the creatures that swarm in the water or of animals that otherwise live in the water, whether in the sea or in the rivers, all those that lack either fins or scales are loathsome for you, [11]and shall always be loathsome to you. Their meat you shall not eat, and their carcasses you shall loathe. [12]Every water creature that lacks fins or scales is loathsome for you.

[13]Of the birds, these you shall loathe; they shall not be eaten, they are loathsome: the griffon vulture, the bearded vulture, the black vulture, [14]the kite, the various species of falcons, [15]the various species of crows, [16]the eagle owl, the kestrel, the long-eared owl, the various species of hawks, [17]the little owl, the cormorant, the screech owl, [18]the barn owl, the horned owl, the osprey, [19]the stork, the various species of herons, the hoopoe, and the bat.

[20]The various winged insects that walk on all fours are loathsome for you. [21]But of the various winged insects that walk on all fours you may eat those that have legs jointed above their feet for leaping on the ground; [22]hence of these you may eat the following: the various kinds of locusts, the various kinds of bald locusts, the various kinds of crickets, and the various kinds of grasshoppers. [23]All other winged insects that have four legs are loathsome for you.

[24]You become unclean by the following—anyone who touches their carcasses shall be unclean until evening, [25]and anyone who carries any part of their carcasses shall wash his garments and be unclean

until evening— [26]by all hoofed animals that are not cloven-footed or do not chew the cud; they are unclean for you; anyone who touches them becomes unclean. [27]Also by the various quadrupeds that walk on paws; they are unclean for you; anyone who touches their carcasses shall be unclean until evening, [28]and anyone who carries their carcasses shall wash his garments and be unclean until evening. They are unclean for you.

[29]Of the creatures that swarm on the ground, the following are unclean for you: the rat, the mouse, the various kinds of lizards, [30]the gecko, the spotted lizard, the agama, the skink, and the chameleon. [31]Among the various swarming creatures, these are unclean for you. Everyone who touches them when they are dead shall be unclean until evening. [32]Everything on which one of them falls when dead becomes unclean, including any article of wood, cloth, leather or goat hair—any article of which use can be made. It must be immersed in water and remain unclean until evening, when it again becomes clean. [33]Should any of these creatures fall into a clay vessel, everything in it becomes unclean, and the vessel itself you must break. [34]Any food that can be eaten which makes contact with water, and any liquid that may be drunk, in any such vessel become unclean. [35]Any object on which any part of their carcasses falls becomes unclean; if it is an oven or stove, this must be broken to pieces; they are unclean and shall always be unclean to you. [36]However, a spring or a cistern for collecting water remains clean; but whoever touches such an animal's carcass becomes unclean. [37]If any part of their carcasses falls on any sort of grain that is to be sown, it remains clean; [38]but if the grain has become moistened, it becomes unclean to you when any part of their carcasses falls on it.

[39]When one of the animals that you could otherwise eat dies of itself, anyone who touches its carcass shall be unclean until evening; [40]and anyone who eats any part of its carcass shall wash his garments and be unclean until evening; so also, anyone who carries its carcass shall wash his garments and be unclean until evening.

[41]All the creatures that swarm on the ground are loathsome and shall not be eaten. [42]Whether it crawls on its belly, goes on all fours, or has many legs—any creature that swarms on the earth—you shall not eat them; they are loathsome. [43]Do not make yourselves loathsome by any swarming creature nor defile yourselves with them and so become unclean by them. [44]For I, the LORD, am your God. You shall make and keep yourselves holy, because I am holy. You shall not make yourselves unclean, then, by any swarming creature that crawls on the ground. [45]Since I, the LORD, am the one who brought you up from the land of Egypt that I might be your God, you shall be holy, because I am holy.

[46]This is the instruction for land animals, birds, and all the creatures that move about in the water, as well as any animal that swarms on the ground, [47]that you may distinguish between the clean and the unclean, and between creatures that may be eaten and those that may not be eaten.

Uncleanness of Childbirth. 12:1 The LORD said to Moses: [2]Tell the Israelites: When a woman has a child, giving birth to a boy, she shall be unclean for seven days, with the same uncleanness as during her menstrual period. [3]On the eighth day, the flesh of the boy's foreskin shall be circumcised, [4]and then she shall spend thirty-three days more in a state of blood purity; she shall not touch anything sacred nor enter the sanctuary till the days of her purification are fulfilled. [5]If she gives birth to a girl, for fourteen days she shall be as unclean as during her menstrual period, after which she shall spend sixty-six days in a state of blood purity.

[6]When the days of her purification for a son or for a daughter are fulfilled, she shall bring to the priest at the entrance of the tent of meeting a yearling lamb for a burnt offering and a pigeon or a turtledove for a purification offering. [7]The priest shall offer them before the LORD to make atonement for her, and thus she will be clean again af-ter her flow of blood. Such is the ritual for the woman who gives birth to a child, male or female. [8]If, however, she cannot afford a lamb, she may take two turtledoves or two pigeons, the one for a burnt offering and the other for a purification offering. The priest shall make atonement for her, and thus she will again be clean.

☐ ROMANS 2:17-3:20

Judgment by the Mosaic Law. 2:17 Now if you call yourself a Jew and rely on the law and boast of God [18]and know his will and are able to discern what is important since you are instructed from the law, [19]and if you are confident that you are a guide for the blind and a light for those in darkness, [20]that you are a trainer of the foolish and teacher of the simple, because in the law you have the formulation of knowledge and truth— [21]then you who teach another, are you failing to teach yourself? You who preach against stealing, do you steal? [22]You who forbid adultery, do you commit adultery? You who detest idols, do you rob temples? [23]You who boast of the law, do you dishonor God by breaking the law? [24]For, as it is written, "Because of you the name of God is reviled among the Gentiles."

[25]Circumcision, to be sure, has value if you observe the law; but if you break the law, your circumcision has become uncircumcision. [26]Again, if an uncircumcised man keeps the precepts of the law, will he not be considered circumcised? [27]Indeed, those who are physically uncircumcised but carry out the law will pass judgment on you, with your written law and circumcision, who break the law. [28]One is not a Jew outwardly. True circumcision is not outward, in the flesh. [29]Rather, one is a Jew inwardly, and circumcision is of the heart, in the spirit, not the letter; his praise is not from human beings but from God.

Answers to Objections. 3:1 What advantage is there then in being a Jew? Or what is the value of circumcision? [2]Much, in every respect. [For] in the first place, they were entrusted with the utterances of God. [3]What if some were unfaithful? Will their infidelity nullify the fidelity of God? [4]Of course not! God must be true, though every human being is a liar, as it is written:

"That you may be justified in your words,
and conquer when you are judged."

[5]But if our wickedness provides proof of God's righteousness, what can we say? Is God unjust, humanly speaking, to inflict his wrath? [6]Of course not! For how else is God to judge the world? [7]But if God's truth redounds to his glory through my falsehood, why am I still being condemned as a sinner? [8]And why not say—as we are accused and as some claim we say—that we should do evil that good may come of it? Their penalty is what they deserve.

Universal Bondage to Sin. [9]Well, then, are we better off? Not entirely, for we have already brought the charge against Jews and Greeks alike that they are all under the domination of sin, [10]as it is written:

"There is no one just, not one,
[11]there is no one who understands,
there is no one who seeks God.
[12]All have gone astray; all alike are worthless;

there is not one who does good,
[there is not] even one.
[13]Their throats are open graves;
they deceive with their tongues;
the venom of asps is on their lips;
[14]their mouths are full of bitter
cursing.
[15]Their feet are quick to shed blood;
[16]ruin and misery are in their
ways,

[17]and the way of peace they know not.
[18]There is no fear of God before
their eyes."

[19]Now we know that what the law says is addressed to those under the law, so that every mouth may be silenced and the whole world stand accountable to God, [20]since no human being will be justified in his sight by observing the law; for through the law comes consciousness of sin.

February 13

Blessed Jordan of Saxony

The law that is perfect because it takes away all imperfections is charity. You find it written with a strange beauty when you gaze at Jesus your Savior stretched out like a sheet of parchment on the cross, inscribed with wounds, illustrated in His own loving blood. Where else is there a comparable book of love from which to read?

— BLESSED JORDAN OF SAXONY

☐ LEVITICUS 13-14

Scaly Infection. 13:1 The LORD said to Moses and Aaron: [2]When someone has on the skin a mark, lesion, or blotch which appears to develop into a scaly infection, the person shall be brought to Aaron, the priest, or to one of the priests among his sons. [3]If the priest, upon examination of the skin's infection, finds that the hair on the infection has turned white and the infection itself appears to be deeper than the skin, it is indeed a scaly infection; the priest, on seeing this, shall declare the person unclean. [4]If, however, the blotch on the skin is white, but does not seem to be deeper than the skin, nor has the hair turned white, the priest shall quarantine the afflicted person for seven days. [5]Should the priest, upon examination on the seventh day, find that the infection has remained unchanged in color and has not spread on the skin, the priest shall quarantine the person for another seven days. [6]Should the priest, upon examination again on the seventh day, find that the infection is now faded and has not spread on the skin, the priest shall declare the person clean; it was merely a scab. The person shall wash his garments and so become clean. [7]But if, after the person was examined by the priest and declared clean, the scab spreads at all on the skin, the person shall once more be examined by the priest. [8]Should the priest, upon examination, find that the scab has indeed spread on the skin, he shall declare the person unclean; it is a scaly infection.

[9]When someone is afflicted with a scaly infection, that person shall be brought to the priest. [10]Should the priest, upon exami-

nation, find that there is a white mark on the skin which has turned the hair white and that there is raw flesh in it, [11]it is a chronic scaly infection on the skin. The priest shall declare the person unclean without quarantine, since the individual is certainly unclean. [12]If the scaly infection breaks out on the skin and, as far as the priest can see, covers all the skin of the afflicted person from head to foot, [13]should the priest then, upon examination, find that the scaly infection does cover the whole body, he shall declare the afflicted person clean; since the person has turned completely white; that individual is clean. [14]But as soon as raw flesh appears, the individual is unclean; [15]on observing the raw flesh, the priest shall declare the person unclean, because raw flesh is unclean; it is a scaly infection. [16]If, however, the raw flesh again turns white, the person shall return to the priest; [17]should the latter, upon examination, find that the infection has indeed turned white, he shall declare the afflicted person clean; the individual is clean.

[18]If a boil appeared on a person's skin which later healed, [19]should now in the place of the boil a white mark or a reddish white blotch develop, the person shall be examined by the priest. [20]If the latter, upon examination, finds that it is deeper than the skin and that the hair has turned white, he shall declare the person unclean; it is a scaly infection that has broken out in the boil. [21]But if the priest, upon examination, finds that there is no white hair in it and that it is not deeper than the skin and is faded, the priest shall quarantine the person for seven days. [22]If it has then spread on the skin, the priest shall declare the person unclean; it is an infection. [23]But if the blotch remains the same without spreading, it is merely the scar of the boil; the priest shall therefore declare the person clean.

[24]If there was a burn on a person's skin, and the burned area now becomes a reddish white or a white blotch, [25]when the priest, upon examination, finds that the hair has turned white in the blotch and this seems to be deeper than the skin, it is a scaly infection that has broken out in the burn; the priest shall therefore declare the person unclean; it is a scaly infection. [26]But if the priest, upon examination, finds that there is no white hair in the blotch and that this is not deeper than the skin and is faded, the priest shall quarantine the person for seven days. [27]Should the priest, upon examination on the seventh day, find that it has spread at all on the skin, he shall declare the person unclean; it is a scaly infection. [28]But if the blotch remains the same without spreading on the skin and is faded, it is merely the spot of the burn; the priest shall therefore declare the person clean, since it is only the scar of the burn.

[29]When a man or a woman has an infection on the head or in the beard, [30]should the priest, upon examination, find that the infection appears to be deeper than the skin and that there is fine yellow hair in it, the priest shall declare the person unclean; it is a scall. It is a scaly infection of the head or beard. [31]But if the priest, upon examining the scall infection, finds that it does not appear to be deeper than the skin, though the hair in it may not be black, the priest shall quarantine the scall-stricken person for seven days. [32]Should the priest, upon examining the infection on the seventh day find that the scall has not spread and has no yellow hair in it and does not seem to be deeper than the skin, [33]the person shall shave, but not the scall spot. Then the priest shall quarantine the scall-diseased person for another seven days. [34]If the priest, upon examining the scall on the seventh day, finds that it has not spread on the skin and that it does not appear to be deeper than the skin, he shall declare the person clean; the latter shall wash his garments, and will thus be clean. [35]But if the scall spreads at all on the skin after the person has been declared clean— [36]should the priest, upon examination, find

that the scall has indeed spread on the skin, he need not look for yellow hair; the individual is unclean. [37]If, however, the scall has remained unchanged in color and black hair has grown in it, the disease has been healed; the person is clean, and the priest shall declare the individual clean.

[38]When the skin of a man or a woman is spotted with several white blotches, [39]if the priest, upon examination, finds that the blotches on the skin are pale white, it is only tetter that has broken out on the skin, and the person therefore is clean.

[40]When a man loses the hair of his head, he is simply bald on the crown and not unclean. [41]So too, if he loses the hair on the front of his head, he is simply bald on the forehead and not unclean. [42]But when there is a reddish white infection on his bald crown or bald forehead, it is a scaly infection that is breaking out there. [43]If the priest, upon examination, finds that the infection spot on the bald area on the crown or forehead has the same reddish white appearance as that of a scaly infection of the skin, [44]the man has a scaly infection and is unclean. The priest shall declare him unclean; his infection is on his head.

[45]The garments of one afflicted with a scaly infection shall be rent and the hair disheveled, and the mustache covered. The individual shall cry out, "Unclean, unclean!" [46]As long as the infection is present, the person shall be unclean. Being unclean, that individual shall dwell apart, taking up residence outside the camp.

Fungal Infection of Fabrics and Leather. [47]When a fungal infection is on a garment of wool or of linen, [48]or on the warp and woof of linen or wool, or on a hide or anything made of leather, [49]if the infection on the garment or hide, or on the warp or woof, or on any leather article is greenish or reddish, the thing is indeed a fungal infection and must be examined by the priest. [50]Having examined the infection, the priest shall quarantine the infected article for seven days. [51]If the priest, upon inspecting the infection on the seventh day, finds that it has spread on the garment, or on the warp or woof, or on the leather, whatever be its use, the infection is a harmful fungus; the article is unclean. [52]He shall therefore burn up the garment, or the warp or woof, be it of wool or linen, or any leather article which is infected; since it is a harmful fungus, it must be destroyed by fire. [53]But if the priest, upon examination, finds that it has not spread on the garment, or on the warp or woof, or on the leather article, [54]he shall give orders to have the infected article washed and then quarantined for another seven days. [55]If the priest, upon examination after the infection was washed, finds that it has not changed its color, even though it may not have spread, the article is unclean. You shall burn it with fire. It is a fray, be it on its inner or outer side. [56]But if the priest, upon examination, finds that the infection has faded after the washing, he shall cut it out of the garment, or the leather, or the warp or woof. [57]If, however, the infection again appears on the garment, or on the warp or woof, or on the leather article, it is still virulent and you shall burn the thing infected with fire. [58]But if, after the washing, the infection has disappeared from the garment, or the warp or woof, or the leather article, the thing shall be washed a second time, and thus it will be clean. [59]This is the instruction for a fungal infection on a garment of wool or linen, or on a warp or woof, or on any leather article, to determine whether it is clean or unclean.

Purification After Scaly Infection. 14:1 The LORD said to Moses: [2]This is the ritual for someone that had a scaly infection at the time of that person's purification. The individual shall be brought to the priest, [3]who is to go outside the camp. If the priest, upon inspection, finds that the scaly infection has healed in the afflicted person, [4]he shall order that two live, clean birds, as well as some cedar wood, scarlet yarn, and hyssop be obtained for the one who is to be purified. [5]The priest shall then order that one of the birds be slaughtered over an earthen vessel with fresh water in it. [6]Taking the living bird with the cedar wood, the scarlet yarn and the hyssop, the priest shall dip them, including the live bird, in the blood of the bird that was slaughtered over the fresh water, [7]and then sprinkle seven times on the person to be purified from the scaly infection. When he has thus purified that person, he shall let the living bird fly away over the countryside. [8]The person being purified shall then wash his garments, shave off all hair, and bathe in water, and so become clean. After this the person may come inside the camp, but shall still remain outside his or her tent for seven days. [9]On the seventh day this individual shall again shave off all hair, of the head, beard, and eyebrows—all hair must be shaved—and also wash his garments and bathe the body in water, and so become clean.

[10]On the eighth day the individual shall take two unblemished male lambs, one unblemished yearling ewe lamb, three tenths of an ephah of bran flour mixed with oil for a grain offering, and one log of oil. [11]The priest who performs the purification ceremony shall place the person who is being purified, as well as all these offerings, before the LORD at the entrance of the tent of meeting. [12]Taking one of the male lambs, the priest shall present it as a reparation offering, along with the log of oil, raising them as an elevated offering before the LORD. [13]This lamb shall be slaughtered in the sacred place where the purification offering and the burnt offering are slaughtered, because the reparation offering is like the purification offering; it belongs to the priest and is most holy. [14]Then the priest shall take some of the blood of the reparation offering and put it on the lobe of the right ear, the thumb of the right hand, and the big toe of the right foot of the person

being purified. [15]The priest shall also take the log of oil and pour some of it into the palm of his own left hand; [16]then, dipping his right finger in the oil on his left palm, he shall sprinkle some of it with his finger seven times before the LORD. [17]Of the oil left in his hand the priest shall put some on the lobe of the right ear, the thumb of the right hand, and the big toe of the right foot of the person being purified, over the blood of the reparation offering. [18]The rest of the oil in his hand the priest shall put on the head of the one being purified. Thus shall the priest make atonement for the individual before the LORD. [19]The priest shall next offer the purification offering, thus making atonement on behalf of the one being purified from the uncleanness. After this the burnt offering shall be slaughtered. [20]The priest shall offer the burnt offering and the grain offering on the altar before the LORD. Thus shall the priest make atonement for the person, and the individual will become clean.

Poor Person's Sacrifices. [21]If a person is poor and cannot afford so much, that person shall take one male lamb for a reparation offering, to be used as an elevated offering in atonement, one tenth of an ephah of bran flour mixed with oil for a grain offering, a log of oil, [22]and two turtledoves or pigeons, which the individual can more easily afford, the one as a purification offering and the other as a burnt offering. [23]On the eighth day of purification the person shall bring them to the priest, at the entrance of the tent of meeting before the LORD. [24]Taking the lamb of the reparation offering, along with the log of oil, the priest shall raise them as an elevated offering before the LORD. [25]When the lamb of the reparation offering has been slaughtered, the priest shall take some of its blood, and put it on the lobe of the right ear, on the thumb of the right hand, and on the big toe of the right foot of the person being purified. [26]The priest shall then pour some of the oil into the palm of his own left hand [27]and with his right finger sprinkle some of the oil in his left palm seven times before the LORD. [28]Some of the oil in his hand the priest shall also put on the lobe of the right ear, the thumb of the right hand, and the big toe of the right foot of the person being purified, where he had sprinkled the blood of the reparation offering. [29]The rest of the oil in his hand the priest shall put on the head of the one being purified. Thus shall he make atonement for the individual before the LORD. [30]Then, of the turtledoves or pigeons, such as the person can afford, [31]the priest shall offer one as a purification offering and the other as a burnt offering, along with the grain offering. Thus shall the priest make atonement before the LORD for the person who is being purified. [32]This is the ritual for one afflicted with a scaly infection who has insufficient means for purification.

Fungal Infection of Houses. [33]The LORD said to Moses and Aaron: [34]When you come into the land of Canaan, which I am giving you to possess, if I put a fungal infection in any house of the land you occupy, [35]the owner of the house shall come and report to the priest, "Something like an infection has appeared in my house." [36]The priest shall then order the house to be cleared out before he goes in to examine the infection, lest everything in the house become unclean. Only after this is he to go in to examine the house. [37]If the priest, upon inspection, finds that the infection on the walls of the house consists of greenish or reddish spots which seem to go deeper than the surface of the wall, [38]he shall go out of the house to the doorway and quarantine the house for seven days. [39]On the seventh day the priest shall return. If, upon inspection, he finds that the infection has spread on the walls, [40]he shall order the infected stones to be pulled out and cast in an unclean place outside the city. [41]The whole inside of the house shall then

be scraped, and the mortar that has been scraped off shall be dumped in an unclean place outside the city. [42]Then other stones shall be brought and put in the place of the old stones, and new mortar obtained and plastered on the house. [43]If the infection breaks out once more in the house after the stones have been pulled out and the house has been scraped and replastered, [44]the priest shall come; and if, upon inspection, he finds that the infection has spread in the house, it is a corrosive fungus in the house, and it is unclean. [45]It shall be pulled down, and all its stones, beams and mortar shall be hauled away to an unclean place outside the city. [46]Whoever enters a house while it is quarantined shall be unclean until evening. [47]Whoever sleeps or eats in such a house shall also wash his garments.

[48]If the priest finds, when he comes to the house, that the infection has in fact not spread in the house after the plastering, he shall declare the house clean, since the infection has been healed. [49]To purify the house, he shall take two birds, as well as cedar wood, scarlet yarn, and hyssop. [50]One of the birds he shall slaughter over an earthen vessel with fresh water in it. [51]Then, taking the cedar wood, the hyssop and the scarlet yarn, together with the living bird, he shall dip them all in the blood of the slaughtered bird and the fresh water, and sprinkle the house seven times. [52]Thus he shall purify the house with the bird's blood and the fresh water, along with the living bird, the cedar wood, the hyssop, and the scarlet yarn. [53]He shall then let the living bird fly away over the countryside outside the city. Thus he shall make atonement for the house, and it will be clean.

[54]This is the ritual for every kind of human scaly infection and scall, [55]and for fungus diseases in garments and houses— [56]for marks, lesions and blotches— [57]to give direction when there is a state of uncleanness and when a state of cleanness. This is the ritual for scaly infection.

☐ ROMANS 3:21-4:25

Justification apart from the Law. 3:21 But now the righteousness of God has been manifested apart from the law, though testified to by the law and the prophets, [22]the righteousness of God through faith in Jesus Christ for all who believe. For there is no distinction; [23]all have sinned and are deprived of the glory of God. [24]They are justified freely by his grace through the redemption in Christ Jesus, [25]whom God set forth as an expiation, through faith, by his blood, to prove his righteousness because of the forgiveness of sins previously committed, [26]through the forbearance of God—to prove his righteousness in the present time, that he might be righteous and justify the one who has faith in Jesus.

[27]What occasion is there then for boasting? It is ruled out. On what principle, that of works? No, rather on the principle of faith. [28]For we consider that a person is justified by faith apart from works of the law. [29]Does God belong to Jews alone? Does he not belong to Gentiles, too? Yes, also to Gentiles, [30]for God is one and will justify the circumcised on the basis of faith and the uncircumcised through faith. [31]Are we then annulling the law by this faith? Of course not! On the contrary, we are supporting the law.

Abraham Justified by Faith. 4:1 What then can we say that Abraham found, our ancestor according to the flesh? [2]Indeed, if Abraham was justified on the basis of his works, he has reason to boast; but this was not so in the sight of God. [3]For what does the scripture say? "Abraham believed God, and it was credited to him as righteousness." [4]A worker's wage is credited not as a gift, but as something due. [5]But when one does not work, yet believes in the one who justifies the ungodly, his faith is credited as righteousness. [6]So also David declares the blessedness of the person to whom God credits righteousness apart from works:

[7]"Blessed are they whose iniquities are
forgiven
and whose sins are covered.
[8]Blessed is the man whose sin the Lord
does not record."

[9]Does this blessedness apply only to the circumcised, or to the uncircumcised as well? Now we assert that "faith was credited to Abraham as righteousness." [10]Under what circumstances was it credited? Was he circumcised or not? He was not circumcised, but uncircumcised. [11]And he received the sign of circumcision as a seal on the righteousness received through faith while he was uncircumcised. Thus he was to be the father of all the uncircumcised who believe, so that to them [also] righteousness might be credited, [12]as well as the father of the circumcised who not only are circumcised, but also follow the path of faith that our father Abraham walked while still uncircumcised.

Inheritance through Faith. [13]It was not through the law that the promise was made to Abraham and his descendants that he would inherit the world, but through the righteousness that comes from faith. [14]For if those who adhere to the law are the heirs, faith is null and the promise is void. [15]For the law produces wrath; but where there is no law, neither is there violation. [16]For this reason, it depends on faith, so that it may be a gift, and the promise may be guaranteed to all his descendants, not to those who only adhere to the law but to those who follow the faith of Abraham, who is the father of all of us, [17]as it is written, "I have made you father of many nations." He is our father in the sight of God, in whom he believed, who gives life to the dead and calls into being what does not exist. [18]He believed, hoping against hope, that he would become "the father of many nations," according to what was said, "Thus shall your descendants be."

[19]He did not weaken in faith when he considered his own body as [already] dead (for he was almost a hundred years old) and the dead womb of Sarah. [20]He did not doubt God's promise in unbelief; rather, he was empowered by faith and gave glory to God [21]and was fully convinced that what he had promised he was also able to do. [22]That is why "it was credited to him as righteousness." [23]But it was not for him alone that it was written that "it was credited to him"; [24]it was also for us, to whom it will be credited, who believe in the one who raised Jesus our Lord from the dead, [25]who was handed over for our transgressions and was raised for our justification.

February 14

Sts. Cyril and Methodius

O Lord, my God, build up Your Church and gather all into unity. Make Your people known for the unity and profession of their faith.

— St. Cyril

☐ LEVITICUS 15-16

Sexual Uncleanness. 15:1 The LORD said to Moses and Aaron: [2]Speak to the Israelites and tell them: When any man has a genital discharge, he is thereby unclean. [3]Such is his uncleanness from this discharge, whether his body drains freely with the discharge or is blocked up from the discharge. His uncleanness is on him all the days that his body discharges or is blocked up from his discharge; this is his uncleanness. [4]Any bed on which the man with the discharge lies is unclean, and any article on which he sits is unclean. [5]Anyone who touches his bed shall wash his garments, bathe in water, and be unclean until evening. [6]Whoever sits on an article on which the man with the discharge was sitting shall wash his garments, bathe in water, and be unclean until evening. [7]Whoever touches the body of the man with the discharge shall wash his garments, bathe in water, and be unclean until evening. [8]If the man with the discharge spits on a clean person, the latter shall wash his garments, bathe in water, and be unclean until evening. [9]Any saddle on which the man with the discharge rides is unclean. [10]Whoever touches anything that was under him shall be unclean until evening; whoever carries any such thing shall wash his garments, bathe in water, and be unclean until evening. [11]Anyone whom the man with the discharge touches with his unrinsed hands shall wash his garments, bathe in water, and be unclean until evening. [12]Earthenware touched by the man with the discharge shall be broken; and every wooden article shall be rinsed with water.

[13]When a man with a discharge becomes clean of his discharge, he shall count seven days for his purification. Then he shall wash his garments and bathe his body in fresh water, and so he will be clean. [14]On the eighth day he shall take two turtledoves or two pigeons, and going before the LORD, to the entrance of the tent of meeting, he shall give them to the priest, [15]who shall offer them up, the one as a purification offering and the other as a burnt offering. Thus shall the priest make atonement before the LORD for the man because of his discharge.

¹⁶When a man has an emission of semen, he shall bathe his whole body in water and be unclean until evening. ¹⁷Any piece of cloth or leather with semen on it shall be washed with water and be unclean until evening.

¹⁸If a man has sexual relations with a woman, they shall both bathe in water and be unclean until evening.

¹⁹When a woman has a flow of blood from her body, she shall be in a state of menstrual uncleanness for seven days. Anyone who touches her shall be unclean until evening. ²⁰Anything on which she lies or sits during her menstrual period shall be unclean. ²¹Anyone who touches her bed shall wash his garments, bathe in water, and be unclean until evening. ²²Whoever touches any article on which she was sitting shall wash his garments, bathe in water, and be unclean until evening. ²³Whether an object is on the bed or on something she sat upon, when the person touches it, that person shall be unclean until evening. ²⁴If a man lies with her, he contracts her menstrual uncleanness and shall be unclean for seven days; every bed on which he then lies also becomes unclean.

²⁵When a woman has a flow of blood for several days outside her menstrual period, or when her flow continues beyond the ordinary period, as long as she suffers this unclean flow she shall be unclean, just as during her menstrual period. ²⁶Any bed on which she lies during such a flow becomes unclean, as it would during her menstrual period, and any article on which she sits becomes unclean just as during her menstrual period. ²⁷Anyone who touches them becomes unclean; that person shall wash his garments, bathe in water, and be unclean until evening.

²⁸When she becomes clean from her flow, she shall count seven days; after this she becomes clean. ²⁹On the eighth day she shall take two turtledoves or two pigeons and bring them to the priest at the entrance of the tent of meeting. ³⁰The priest shall offer one of them as a purification offering and the other as a burnt offering. Thus shall the priest make atonement before the Lord for her because of her unclean flow.

³¹You shall warn the Israelites of their uncleanness, lest they die through their uncleanness by defiling my tabernacle, which is in their midst.

³²This is the ritual for the man with a discharge, or who has an emission of semen, and thereby becomes unclean; ³³as well as for the woman who has her menstrual period; or one who has a discharge, male or female; and also for the man who lies with an unclean woman.

The Day of Atonement. 16:1 After the death of Aaron's two sons, who died when they encroached on the Lord's presence, the Lord spoke to Moses ²and said to him: Tell your brother Aaron that he is not to come whenever he pleases into the inner sanctuary, inside the veil, in front of the cover on the ark, lest he die, for I reveal myself in a cloud above the ark's cover. ³Only in this way may Aaron enter the inner sanctuary. He shall bring a bull of the herd for a purification offering and a ram for a burnt offering. ⁴He shall wear the sacred linen tunic, with the linen pants underneath, gird himself with the linen sash and put on the linen turban. But since these vestments are sacred, he shall not put them on until he has first bathed his body in water. ⁵From the Israelite community he shall receive two male goats for a purification offering and one ram for a burnt offering.

⁶Aaron shall offer the bull, his purification offering, to make atonement for himself and for his household. ⁷Taking the two male goats and setting them before the Lord at the entrance of the tent of meeting, ⁸he shall cast lots to determine which one is for the Lord and which for Azazel. ⁹The goat that is determined by lot for the Lord, Aaron shall present and offer up as

a purification offering. [10]But the goat determined by lot for Azazel he shall place before the LORD alive, so that with it he may make atonement by sending it off to Azazel in the desert.

[11]Thus shall Aaron offer his bull for the purification offering, to make atonement for himself and for his family. When he has slaughtered it, [12]he shall take a censer full of glowing embers from the altar before the LORD, as well as a double handful of finely ground fragrant incense, and bringing them inside the veil, [13]there before the LORD he shall put incense on the fire, so that a cloud of incense may shield the cover that is over the covenant, else he will die. [14]Taking some of the bull's blood, he shall sprinkle it with his finger on the front of the ark's cover and likewise sprinkle some of the blood with his finger seven times in front of the cover.

[15]Then he shall slaughter the goat of the people's purification offering, and bringing its blood inside the veil, he shall do with it as he did with the bull's blood, sprinkling it on the ark's cover and in front of it. [16]Thus he shall purge the inner sanctuary of all the Israelites' impurities and trespasses, including all their sins. He shall do the same for the tent of meeting, which is set up among them in the midst of their uncleanness. [17]No one else may be in the tent of meeting from the time he enters the inner sanctuary to make atonement until he departs. When he has made atonement for himself and his household, as well as for the whole Israelite assembly, [18]he shall come out to the altar before the LORD and purge it also. Taking some of the bull's and the goat's blood, he shall put it on the horns around the altar, [19]and with his finger sprinkle some of the blood on it seven times. Thus he shall purify it and sanctify it from the impurities of the Israelites.

The Scapegoat. [20]When he has finished purging the inner sanctuary, the tent of meeting and the altar, Aaron shall bring forward the live goat. [21]Laying both hands on its head, he shall confess over it all the iniquities of the Israelites and their trespasses, including all their sins, and so put them on the goat's head. He shall then have it led into the wilderness by an attendant. [22]The goat will carry off all their iniquities to an isolated region.

When the goat is dispatched into the wilderness, [23]Aaron shall go into the tent of meeting, strip off the linen vestments he had put on when he entered the inner sanctuary, and leave them in the tent of meeting. [24]After bathing his body with water in a sacred place, he shall put on his regular vestments, and then come out and offer his own and the people's burnt offering, in atonement for himself and for the people, [25]and also burn the fat of the purification offering on the altar.

[26]The man who led away the goat for Azazel shall wash his garments and bathe his body in water; only then may he enter the camp. [27]The bull and the goat of the purification offering whose blood was brought to make atonement in the inner sanctuary, shall be taken outside the camp, where their hides and flesh and dung shall be burned in the fire. [28]The one who burns them shall wash his garments and bathe his body in water; only then may he enter the camp.

The Fast. [29]This shall be an everlasting statute for you: on the tenth day of the seventh month every one of you, whether a native or a resident alien, shall humble yourselves and shall do no work. [30]For on this day atonement is made for you to make you clean; of all your sins you will be cleansed before the LORD. [31]It shall be a sabbath of complete rest for you, on which you must humble yourselves—an everlasting statute.

[32]This atonement is to be made by the priest who has been anointed and ordained to the priesthood in succession to his father. He shall wear the linen garments, the sacred vestments, [33]and purge the most

sacred part of the sanctuary, as well as the tent of meeting, and the altar. He shall also make atonement for the priests and all the people of the assembly. [34]This, then, shall be an everlasting statute for you: once a year atonement shall be made on behalf of the Israelites for all their sins. And Moses did as the LORD had commanded him.

☐ ROMANS 5

Faith, Hope, and Love. 5:1 Therefore, since we have been justified by faith, we have peace with God through our Lord Jesus Christ, [2]through whom we have gained access [by faith] to this grace in which we stand, and we boast in hope of the glory of God. [3]Not only that, but we even boast of our afflictions, knowing that affliction produces endurance, [4]and endurance, proven character, and proven character, hope, [5]and hope does not disappoint, because the love of God has been poured out into our hearts through the holy Spirit that has been given to us. [6]For Christ, while we were still helpless, yet died at the appointed time for the ungodly. [7]Indeed, only with difficulty does one die for a just person, though perhaps for a good person one might even find courage to die. [8]But God proves his love for us in that while we were still sinners Christ died for us. [9]How much more then, since we are now justified by his blood, will we be saved through him from the wrath. [10]Indeed, if, while we were enemies, we were reconciled to God through the death of his Son, how much more, once reconciled, will we be saved by his life. [11]Not only that, but we also boast of God through our Lord Jesus Christ, through whom we have now received reconciliation.

Humanity's Sin through Adam. [12]Therefore, just as through one person sin entered the world, and through sin, death, and thus death came to all, inasmuch as all sinned— [13]for up to the time of the law, sin was in the world, though sin is not accounted when there is no law. [14]But death reigned from Adam to Moses, even over those who did not sin after the pattern of the trespass of Adam, who is the type of the one who was to come.

Grace and Life through Christ. [15]But the gift is not like the transgression. For if by that one person's transgression the many died, how much more did the grace of God and the gracious gift of the one person Jesus Christ overflow for the many. [16]And the gift is not like the result of the one person's sinning. For after one sin there was the judgment that brought condemnation; but the gift, after many transgressions, brought acquittal. [17]For if, by the transgression of one person, death came to reign through that one, how much more will those who receive the abundance of grace and of the gift of justification come to reign in life through the one person Jesus Christ. [18]In conclusion, just as through one transgression condemnation came upon all, so through one righteous act acquittal and life came to all. [19]For just as through the disobedience of one person the many were made sinners, so through the obedience of one the many will be made righteous. [20]The law entered in so that transgression might increase but, where sin increased, grace overflowed all the more, [21]so that, as sin reigned in death, grace also might reign through justification for eternal life through Jesus Christ our Lord.

February 15

St. Claude de la Colombière

I vow never to do anything nor to leave anything undone because of what people think. It will establish in me a great interior peace.

— St. Claude de la Colombière

☐ LEVITICUS 17-18

Sacredness of Blood. 17:1 The LORD said to Moses: [2]Speak to Aaron and his sons, as well as to all the Israelites, and tell them: This is what the LORD has commanded: [3]Any Israelite who slaughters an ox or a sheep or a goat, whether in the camp or outside of it, [4]without first bringing it to the entrance of the tent of meeting to present it as an offering to the LORD in front of the LORD's tabernacle, shall be judged guilty of bloodshed —that individual has shed blood, and shall be cut off from the people. [5]This is so that such sacrifices as they used to offer in the open field the Israelites shall henceforth bring to the LORD at the entrance of the tent of meeting, to the priest, and sacrifice them there as communion sacrifices to the LORD. [6]The priest will splash the blood on the altar of the LORD at the entrance of the tent of meeting and burn the fat for an odor pleasing to the LORD. [7]No longer shall they offer their sacrifices to the demons with whom they prostituted themselves. This shall be an everlasting statute for them and their descendants.

[8]Tell them, therefore: Anyone, whether of the house of Israel or of the aliens residing among them, who offers a burnt offering or sacrifice [9]without bringing it to the entrance of the tent of meeting to offer it to the LORD, shall be cut off from the people. [10]As for anyone, whether of the house of Israel or of the aliens residing among them, who consumes any blood, I will set myself against that individual and will cut that person off from among the people, [11]since the life of the flesh is in the blood, and I have given it to you to make atonement on the altar for yourselves, because it is the blood as life that makes atonement. [12]That is why I have told the Israelites: No one among you, not even a resident alien, may consume blood.

[13]Anyone hunting, whether of the Israelites or of the aliens residing among them, who catches an animal or a bird that may be eaten, shall pour out its blood and cover it with earth, [14]since the life of all flesh is its blood. I have told the Israelites: You shall not consume the blood of any flesh. Since the life of all flesh is its blood, anyone who consumes it shall be cut off.

[15]Everyone, whether a native or an alien, who eats of an animal that died of itself or was killed by a wild beast, shall wash his garments, bathe in water, and be unclean until evening, and then become clean. [16]If one does not wash his garments and bathe, that person shall bear the penalty.

Laws Concerning Sexual Behavior. 18:1 The LORD said to Moses: [2]Speak to the Israelites and tell them: I, the LORD, am your God. [3]You shall not do as they do in the land of Egypt, where you once lived, nor shall you do as they do in the land of Canaan, where I am bringing you; do not conform to their customs. [4]My decrees you shall carry out, and my statutes you shall take care to follow. I, the LORD, am your God. [5]Keep, then, my statutes and decrees, for the person who carries them out will find life through them. I am the LORD.

[6]None of you shall approach a close relative to have sexual intercourse. I am the LORD. [7]You shall not disgrace your father by having intercourse with your mother. She is your own mother; you shall not have intercourse with her. [8]You shall not have intercourse with your father's wife, for that would be a disgrace to your father. [9]You shall not have intercourse with your sister, your father's daughter or your mother's daughter, whether she was born in your own household or born elsewhere. [10]You shall not have intercourse with your son's daughter or with your daughter's daughter, for that would be a disgrace to you. [11]You shall not have intercourse with the daughter whom your father's wife bore to him in his household, since she, too, is your sister. [12]You shall not have intercourse with your father's sister, since she is your father's relative. [13]You shall not have intercourse with your mother's sister, since she is your mother's relative. [14]You shall not disgrace your father's brother by having sexual relations with his wife, since she, too, is your aunt. [15]You shall not have intercourse with your daughter-in-law; she is your son's wife; you shall not have intercourse with her. [16]You shall not have intercourse with your brother's wife; that would be a disgrace to your brother. [17]You shall not have intercourse with a woman and also with her daughter, nor shall you marry and have intercourse with her son's daughter or her daughter's daughter; they are related to her. This would be shameful. [18]While your wife is still living you shall not marry her sister as her rival and have intercourse with her.

[19]You shall not approach a woman to have intercourse with her while she is in her menstrual uncleanness. [20]You shall not have sexual relations with your neighbor's wife, defiling yourself with her. [21]You shall not offer any of your offspring for immolation to Molech, thus profaning the name of your God. I am the LORD. [22]You shall not lie with a male as with a woman; such a thing is an abomination. [23]You shall not have sexual relations with an animal, defiling yourself with it; nor shall a woman set herself in front of an animal to mate with it; that is perverse.

[24]Do not defile yourselves by any of these things, because by them the nations whom I am driving out of your way have defiled themselves. [25]And so the land has become defiled, and I have punished it for its wickedness, and the land has vomited out its inhabitants. [26]You, however, must keep my statutes and decrees, avoiding all these abominations, both the natives and the aliens resident among you— [27]because the previous inhabitants did all these abominations and the land became defiled; [28]otherwise the land will vomit you out also for having defiled it, just as it vomited out the nations before you. [29]For whoever does any of these abominations shall be cut off from the people. [30]Heed my charge, then, not to observe the abominable customs that have been observed before your time, and thus become impure by them. I, the LORD, am your God.

☐ ROMANS 6

Freedom from Sin; Life in God. 6:1 What then shall we say? Shall we persist in sin that grace may abound? Of course not! [2]How can we who died to sin yet live in it? [3]Or are you unaware that we who were baptized into Christ Jesus were baptized into his death? [4]We were indeed buried with him through baptism into death, so that, just as Christ was raised from the dead by the glory of the Father, we too might live in newness of life.

[5]For if we have grown into union with him through a death like his, we shall also be united with him in the resurrection.

[6]We know that our old self was crucified with him, so that our sinful body might be done away with, that we might no longer be in slavery to sin. [7]For a dead person has been absolved from sin. [8]If, then, we have died with Christ, we believe that we shall also live with him. [9]We know that Christ, raised from the dead, dies no more; death no longer has power over him. [10]As to his death, he died to sin once and for all; as to his life, he lives for God. [11]Consequently, you too must think of yourselves as [being] dead to sin and living for God in Christ Jesus.

[12]Therefore, sin must not reign over your mortal bodies so that you obey their desires. [13]And do not present the parts of your bodies to sin as weapons for wickedness, but present yourselves to God as raised from the dead to life and the parts of your bodies to God as weapons for righteousness. [14]For sin is not to have any power over you, since you are not under the law but under grace.

[15]What then? Shall we sin because we are not under the law but under grace? Of course not! [16]Do you not know that if you present yourselves to someone as obedient slaves, you are slaves of the one you obey, either of sin, which leads to death, or of obedience, which leads to righteousness? [17]But thanks be to God that, although you were once slaves of sin, you have become obedient from the heart to the pattern of teaching to which you were entrusted. [18]Freed from sin, you have become slaves of righteousness. [19]I am speaking in human terms because of the weakness of your nature. For just as you presented the parts of your bodies as slaves to impurity and to lawlessness for lawlessness, so now present them as slaves to righteousness for sanctification. [20]For when you were slaves of sin, you were free from righteousness. [21]But what profit did you get then from the things of which you are now ashamed? For the end of those things is death. [22]But now that you have been freed from sin and have become slaves of God, the benefit that you have leads to sanctification, and its end is eternal life. [23]For the wages of sin is death, but the gift of God is eternal life in Christ Jesus our Lord.

February 16

No matter what efforts I make, I cannot die to myself without His grace. I am like a frog that, no matter how high it leaps, always finishes up back in the mud. O Lord, draw me after You; for unless You do, I cannot move even one step away from myself.

— BLESSED DOMINIC BARBERI

☐ LEVITICUS 19-20

Various Rules of Conduct. 19:1 The LORD said to Moses: [2]Speak to the whole Israelite community and tell them: Be holy, for I, the LORD your God, am holy. [3]Each of you revere your mother and father, and keep my sabbaths. I, the LORD, am your God.

[4]Do not turn aside to idols, nor make molten gods for yourselves. I, the LORD, am your God.

[5]When you sacrifice your communion sacrifice to the LORD, you shall sacrifice it so that it is acceptable on your behalf. [6]It

must be eaten on the day of your sacrifice or on the following day. Whatever is left over until the third day shall be burned in fire. [7]If any of it is eaten on the third day, it will be a desecrated offering and not be accepted; [8]whoever eats of it then shall bear the penalty for having profaned what is sacred to the LORD. Such a one shall be cut off from the people.

[9]When you reap the harvest of your land, you shall not be so thorough that you reap the field to its very edge, nor shall you gather the gleanings of your harvest. [10]Likewise, you shall not pick your vineyard bare, nor gather up the grapes that have fallen. These things you shall leave for the poor and the alien. I, the LORD, am your God.

[11]You shall not steal. You shall not deceive or speak falsely to one another. [12]You shall not swear falsely by my name, thus profaning the name of your God. I am the LORD.

[13]You shall not exploit your neighbor. You shall not commit robbery. You shall not withhold overnight the wages of your laborer. [14]You shall not insult the deaf, or put a stumbling block in front of the blind, but you shall fear your God. I am the LORD.

[15]You shall not act dishonestly in rendering judgment. Show neither partiality to the weak nor deference to the mighty, but judge your neighbor justly. [16]You shall not go about spreading slander among your people; nor shall you stand by idly when your neighbor's life is at stake. I am the LORD.

[17]You shall not hate any of your kindred in your heart. Reprove your neighbor openly so that you do not incur sin because of that person. [18]Take no revenge and cherish no grudge against your own people. You shall love your neighbor as yourself. I am the LORD.

[19]Keep my statutes: do not breed any of your domestic animals with others of a different species; do not sow a field of yours with two different kinds of seed; and do not put on a garment woven with two different kinds of thread.

[20]If a man has sexual relations with a female slave who has been acquired by another man but has not yet been redeemed or given her freedom, an investigation shall be made. They shall not be put to death, because she has not been freed. [21]The man shall bring to the entrance of the tent of meeting as his reparation to the LORD a ram as a reparation offering. [22]With the ram of the reparation offering the priest shall make atonement before the LORD for the wrong the man has committed, so that he will be forgiven for the wrong he has committed.

[23]When you come into the land and plant any fruit tree there, first look upon its fruit as if it were uncircumcised. For three years, it shall be uncircumcised for you; it may not be eaten. [24]In the fourth year, however, all of its fruit shall be dedicated to the LORD in joyous celebration. [25]Not until the fifth year may you eat its fruit, to increase the yield for you. I, the LORD, am your God.

[26]Do not eat anything with the blood still in it. Do not recite charms or practice soothsaying. [27]Do not clip your hair at the temples, nor spoil the edges of your beard. [28]Do not lacerate your bodies for the dead, and do not tattoo yourselves. I am the LORD.

[29]You shall not degrade your daughter by making a prostitute of her; otherwise the land will prostitute itself and become full of lewdness. [30]Keep my sabbaths, and reverence my sanctuary. I am the LORD.

[31]Do not turn to ghosts or consult spirits, by which you will be defiled. I, the LORD, am your God.

[32]Stand up in the presence of the aged, show respect for the old, and fear your God. I am the LORD.

[33]When an alien resides with you in your land, do not mistreat such a one. [34]You shall

treat the alien who resides with you no differently than the natives born among you; you shall love the alien as yourself; for you too were once aliens in the land of Egypt. I, the LORD, am your God.

³⁵Do not act dishonestly in using measures of length or weight or capacity. ³⁶You shall have a true scale and true weights, an honest ephah and an honest hin. I, the LORD, am your God, who brought you out of the land of Egypt. ³⁷Be careful, then, to observe all my statutes and decrees. I am the LORD.

Penalties for Various Sins. 20:1 The LORD said to Moses: ²Tell the Israelites: Anyone, whether an Israelite or an alien residing in Israel, who gives offspring to Molech shall be put to death. The people of the land shall stone that person. ³I myself will turn against and cut off that individual from among the people; for in the giving of offspring to Molech, my sanctuary was defiled and my holy name was profaned. ⁴If the people of the land condone the giving of offspring to Molech, by failing to put the wrongdoer to death, ⁵I myself will turn against that individual and his or her family, and I will cut off from their people both the wrongdoer and all who follow this person by prostituting themselves with Molech.

⁶Should anyone turn to ghosts and spirits and prostitute oneself with them, I will turn against that person and cut such a one off from among the people. ⁷Sanctify yourselves, then, and be holy; for I, the LORD, your God, am holy. ⁸Be careful, therefore, to observe my statutes. I, the LORD, make you holy.

⁹Anyone who curses father or mother shall be put to death; and having cursed father or mother, such a one will bear the bloodguilt. ¹⁰If a man commits adultery with his neighbor's wife, both the adulterer and the adulteress shall be put to death. ¹¹If a man disgraces his father by lying with his father's wife, the two of them shall be put to death; their bloodguilt is upon them. ¹²If a man lies with his daughter-in-law, both of them shall be put to death; they have done what is perverse; their bloodguilt is upon them. ¹³If a man lies with a male as with a woman, they have committed an abomination; the two of them shall be put to death; their bloodguilt is upon them. ¹⁴If a man marries a woman and her mother also, that is shameful conduct; the man and the two women as well shall be burned to death, so that shamefulness may not be found among you. ¹⁵If a man has sexual relations with an animal, the man shall be put to death, and you shall kill the animal. ¹⁶If a woman goes up to any animal to mate with it, you shall kill the woman and the animal; they shall both be put to death; their bloodguilt is upon them. ¹⁷If a man marries his sister, his father's daughter or his mother's daughter, and they have intercourse with each other, that is disgraceful; they shall be publicly cut off from the people; the man shall bear the penalty of having had intercourse with his own sister. ¹⁸If a man lies with a woman during her menstrual period and has intercourse with her, he has laid bare the source of her flow and she has uncovered it. The two of them shall be cut off from the people. ¹⁹You shall not have intercourse with your mother's sister or your father's sister, because that dishonors one's own flesh; they shall bear their penalty. ²⁰If a man lies with his uncle's wife, he disgraces his uncle; they shall bear the penalty; they shall die childless. ²¹If a man takes his brother's wife, it is severe defilement and he has disgraced his brother; they shall be childless.

²²Be careful to observe all my statutes and all my decrees; otherwise the land where I am bringing you to dwell will vomit you out. ²³Do not conform, therefore, to the customs of the nations whom I am driving out of your way, because all these things that they have done have filled me with disgust for them. ²⁴But to you I

have said: You shall take possession of their land. I am giving it to you to possess, a land flowing with milk and honey. I, the LORD, am your God, who have set you apart from other peoples. [25]You, too, must set apart, then, the clean animals from the unclean, and the clean birds from the unclean, so that you do not make yourselves detestable through any beast or bird or any creature which creeps on the ground that I have set apart for you as unclean. [26]To me, therefore, you shall be holy; for I, the LORD, am holy, and I have set you apart from other peoples to be my own.

[27]A man or a woman who acts as a medium or clairvoyant shall be put to death. They shall be stoned to death; their bloodguilt is upon them.

☐ ROMANS 7

Freedom from the Law. 7:1 Are you unaware, brothers (for I am speaking to people who know the law), that the law has jurisdiction over one as long as one lives? [2]Thus a married woman is bound by law to her living husband; but if her husband dies, she is released from the law in respect to her husband. [3]Consequently, while her husband is alive she will be called an adulteress if she consorts with another man. But if her husband dies she is free from that law, and she is not an adulteress if she consorts with another man.

[4]In the same way, my brothers, you also were put to death to the law through the body of Christ, so that you might belong to another, to the one who was raised from the dead in order that we might bear fruit for God. [5]For when we were in the flesh, our sinful passions, awakened by the law, worked in our members to bear fruit for death. [6]But now we are released from the law, dead to what held us captive, so that we may serve in the newness of the spirit and not under the obsolete letter.

Acquaintance with Sin through the Law. [7]What then can we say? That the law is sin? Of course not! Yet I did not know sin except through the law, and I did not know what it is to covet except that the law said, "You shall not covet." [8]But sin, finding an opportunity in the commandment, produced in me every kind of covetousness. Apart from the law sin is dead. [9]I once lived outside the law, but when the commandment came, sin became alive; [10]then I died, and the commandment that was for life turned out to be death for me. [11]For sin, seizing an opportunity in the commandment, deceived me and through it put me to death. [12]So then the law is holy, and the commandment is holy and righteous and good.

Sin and Death. [13]Did the good, then, become death for me? Of course not! Sin, in order that it might be shown to be sin, worked death in me through the good, so that sin might become sinful beyond measure through the commandment. [14]We know that the law is spiritual; but I am carnal, sold into slavery to sin. [15]What I do, I do not understand. For I do not do what I want, but I do what I hate. [16]Now if I do what I do not want, I concur that the law is good. [17]So now it is no longer I who do it, but sin that dwells in me. [18]For I know that good does not dwell in me, that is, in my flesh. The willing is ready at hand, but doing the good is not. [19]For I do not do the good I want, but I do the evil I do not want. [20]Now if [I] do what I do not want, it is no longer I who do it, but sin that dwells in me. [21]So, then, I discover the principle that when I want to do right, evil is at hand. [22]For I take delight in the law of God, in my inner self, [23]but I see in my members another principle at war with the law of my mind, taking me captive to the law of sin that dwells in my members. [24]Miserable one that I am! Who will deliver me from this mortal body? [25]Thanks be to God through Jesus Christ our Lord. Therefore, I myself, with my mind, serve the law of God but, with my flesh, the law of sin.

February 17

Seven Founders of the Order of Servites
(Servants of Mary)

To serve Mary and to be her courtier is the greatest honor one can possibly possess, for to serve the Queen of heaven is already to reign there, and to live under her commands is more than to govern.

— St. John of Damascus

☐ LEVITICUS 21–22

Sanctity of the Priesthood. 21:1 The LORD said to Moses: Speak to the priests, Aaron's sons, and tell them: None of you shall make himself unclean for any dead person among his kindred, [2]except for his nearest relatives, his mother or father, his son or daughter, his brother [3]or his unmarried sister, who is of his own family while she remains single; for these he may make himself unclean. [4]But as a husband among his kindred he shall not make himself unclean and thus profane himself.

[5]The priests shall not make bald the crown of their head, nor shave the edges of their beard, nor lacerate their body. [6]They shall be holy to their God, and shall not profane their God's name, since they offer the oblations of the LORD, the food of their God; so they must be holy.

[7]A priest shall not marry a woman debased by prostitution, nor a woman who has been divorced by her husband; for the priest is holy to his God. [8]Honor him as holy for he offers the food of your God; he shall be holy to you, because I, the LORD, am holy who make you holy.

[9]If a priest's daughter debases herself by prostitution, she thereby debases her father; she shall be burned with fire.

[10]The most exalted of the priests, upon whose head the anointing oil has been poured and who has been ordained to wear the special vestments, shall not dishevel his hair or rend his garments, [11]nor shall he go near any dead person. Not even for his father or mother may he thus become unclean; [12]nor shall he leave the sanctuary and profane the sanctuary of his God, for the consecration of the anointing oil of his God is upon him. I am the LORD.

[13]He shall marry only a woman who is a virgin. [14]He shall not marry a widow or a woman who has been divorced or one who has been debased by prostitution, but only a virgin, taken from his kindred, he shall marry, [15]so that he not profane his offspring among his kindred. I, the LORD, make him holy.

Priestly Blemishes. [16]The LORD said to Moses: [17]Say to Aaron: None of your descendants, throughout their generations, who has any blemish shall come forward to offer the food of his God. [18]Anyone who has any of the following blemishes may not come forward: he who is blind, or lame, or who has a split lip, or a limb too long, [19]or a broken leg or arm, [20]or who is a hunchback or dwarf or has a growth in the eye, or who is afflicted with sores, scabs, or crushed testicles. [21]No descendant of Aaron the priest who has any such blemish may draw near to offer the oblations of the Lord; on account of his blemish he may not draw near to offer the food of his God. [22]He may, however, eat the food of his God: of the most sacred as well as sacred offerings. [23]Only, he may not enter through the veil nor draw near to the altar on account of his blemish; he shall not profane my sacred precincts, for it is I, the Lord, who make them holy. [24]Moses, therefore, told this to Aaron and his sons and to all the Israelites.

Priestly Purity. 22:1 The Lord said to Moses: [2]Tell Aaron and his sons to treat with respect the sacred offerings which the Israelites consecrate to me; otherwise they will profane my holy name. I am the Lord. [3]Tell them: If any one of you, or of your descendants in any future generation, dares, while he is in a state of uncleanness, to draw near the sacred offerings which the Israelites consecrate to the Lord, such a one shall be cut off from my presence. I am the Lord. [4]No descendant of Aaron who is stricken with a scaly infection, or who suffers from a genital discharge, may eat of the sacred offerings, until he again becomes clean. Moreover, if anyone touches a person who has become unclean by contact with a corpse, or if anyone has had an emission of semen, [5]or if anyone touches any swarming creature whose uncleanness is contagious or any person whose uncleanness, of whatever kind it may be, is contagious—[6]the one who touches such as these shall be unclean until evening and may not eat of the sacred portions until he has first bathed his body in water. [7]Then, when the sun sets, he shall be clean. Only then may he eat of the sacred offerings, for they are his food. [8]He shall not make himself unclean by eating of any animal that has died of itself or has been killed by wild beasts. I am the Lord.

[9]They shall keep my charge so that they will not bear the punishment in this matter and die for their profanation. I am the Lord who makes them holy. [10]Neither an unauthorized person nor a priest's tenant or laborer may eat of any sacred offering. [11]But a slave whom a priest acquires by purchase or who is born in his house may eat of his food. [12]A priest's daughter who is married to an unauthorized person may not eat of the sacred contributions. [13]But if a priest's daughter is widowed or divorced and, having no children, returns to her father's house, she may then eat of her father's food as in her youth. No unauthorized person, however, may eat of it. [14]If such a one eats of a sacred offering through inadvertence, that person shall make restitution to the priest for the sacred offering, with an increment of one fifth of the amount. [15]The priests shall not allow the sacred offerings which the Israelites contribute to the Lord to be profaned [16]nor make them incur a penalty when they eat their sacred offerings. For I, the Lord, make them holy.

Unacceptable Victims. [17]The Lord said to Moses: [18]Speak to Aaron and his sons and to all the Israelites, and tell them: When anyone of the house of Israel, or any alien residing in Israel, who presents an offering, brings a burnt offering as a votive offering or as a voluntary offering to the Lord, [19]if it is to be acceptable for you, it must be an unblemished male of the herd, of the sheep or of the goats. [20]You shall not offer one that has any blemish, for such a one would not be acceptable on your behalf. [21]When anyone presents a communion sacrifice to the Lord from the herd or the flock in fulfillment of a vow, or as a voluntary offering, if it is to find acceptance, it must be unblemished; it shall not have any blemish. [22]One that is blind or lame or maimed, or one that has running lesions or sores or scabs, you shall not offer to the Lord; do not put such an animal on the altar as an oblation to the LORD. ²³An ox or a sheep that has a leg that is too long or is stunted you may indeed present as a voluntary offering, but it will not be acceptable as a votive offering. ²⁴One that has its testicles bruised or crushed or torn out or cut off you shall not offer to the LORD. You shall neither do this in your own land ²⁵nor receive from a foreigner any such animals to offer up as the food of your God; since they are deformed or blemished, they will not be acceptable on your behalf.

²⁶The LORD said to Moses: ²⁷When an ox or a lamb or a goat is born, it shall remain with its mother for seven days; only from the eighth day onward will it be acceptable, to be offered as an oblation to the LORD. ²⁸You shall not slaughter an ox or a sheep on one and the same day with its young. ²⁹Whenever you offer a thanksgiving sacrifice to the LORD, so offer it that it may be acceptable on your behalf; ³⁰it must be eaten on the same day; none of it shall be left over until morning. I am the LORD.

³¹Be careful to observe my commandments. I am the LORD. ³²Do not profane my holy name, that in the midst of the Israelites I may be hallowed. I, the LORD, make you holy, ³³who led you out of the land of Egypt to be your God. I am the LORD.

☐ ROMANS 8:1-27

The Flesh and the Spirit. 8:1 Hence, now there is no condemnation for those who are in Christ Jesus. ²For the law of the spirit of life in Christ Jesus has freed you from the law of sin and death. ³For what the law, weakened by the flesh, was powerless to do, this God has done: by sending his own Son in the likeness of sinful flesh and for the sake of sin, he condemned sin in the flesh, ⁴so that the righteous decree of the law might be fulfilled in us, who live not according to the flesh but according to the spirit. ⁵For those who live according to the flesh are concerned with the things of the flesh, but those who live according to the spirit with the things of the spirit. ⁶The concern of the flesh is death, but the concern of the spirit is life and peace. ⁷For the concern of the flesh is hostility toward God; it does not submit to the law of God, nor can it; ⁸and those who are in the flesh cannot please God. ⁹But you are not in the flesh; on the contrary, you are in the spirit, if only the Spirit of God dwells in you. Whoever does not have the Spirit of Christ does not belong to him. ¹⁰But if Christ is in you, although the body is dead because of sin, the spirit is alive because of righteousness. ¹¹If the Spirit of the one who raised Jesus from the dead dwells in you, the one who raised Christ from the dead will give life to your mortal bodies also, through his Spirit that dwells in you. ¹²Consequently, brothers, we are not debtors to the flesh, to live according to the flesh. ¹³For if you live according to the flesh, you will die, but if by the spirit you put to death the deeds of the body, you will live.

Children of God through Adoption. ¹⁴For those who are led by the Spirit of God are children of God. ¹⁵For you did not receive a spirit of slavery to fall back into fear, but you received a spirit of adoption, through which we cry, "Abba, Father!" ¹⁶The Spirit itself bears witness with our spirit that we are children of God, ¹⁷and if children, then heirs, heirs of God and joint heirs with Christ, if only we suffer with him so that we may also be glorified with him.

Destiny of Glory. ¹⁸I consider that the sufferings of this present time are as nothing compared with the glory to be revealed for us. ¹⁹For creation awaits with eager expectation the revelation of the children of God; ²⁰for creation was made subject to futility, not of its own accord but because of the one who subjected it, in hope [21]that creation itself would be set free from slavery to corruption and share in the glorious freedom of the children of God. [22]We know that all creation is groaning in labor pains even until now; [23]and not only that, but we ourselves, who have the firstfruits of the Spirit, we also groan within ourselves as we wait for adoption, the redemption of our bodies. [24]For in hope we were saved. Now hope that sees for itself is not hope.

For who hopes for what one sees? [25]But if we hope for what we do not see, we wait with endurance.

[26]In the same way, the Spirit too comes to the aid of our weakness; for we do not know how to pray as we ought, but the Spirit itself intercedes with inexpressible groanings. [27]And the one who searches hearts knows what is the intention of the Spirit, because it intercedes for the holy ones according to God's will.

February 18

Eternal Beauty! You act as if You could not live without Your creation, even though You are Life itself, and everything has its life from You and nothing can live without You. Why then are you so mad? Because You have fallen madly in love with what You have made!

— ST. CATHERINE OF SIENA

☐ LEVITICUS 23-24

Holy Days. 23:1 The LORD said to Moses: [2]Speak to the Israelites and tell them: The following are the festivals of the LORD, which you shall declare holy days. These are my festivals:

[3]For six days work may be done; but the seventh day is a sabbath of complete rest, a declared holy day; you shall do no work. It is the LORD's sabbath wherever you dwell.

Passover. [4]These are the festivals of the LORD, holy days which you shall declare at their proper time. [5]The Passover of the LORD falls on the fourteenth day of the first month, at the evening twilight. [6]The fifteenth day of this month is the LORD's feast of Unleavened Bread. For seven days you shall eat unleavened bread. [7]On the first of these days you will have a declared holy day; you shall do no heavy work. [8]On each of the seven days you shall offer an oblation to the LORD. Then on the seventh day you will have a declared holy day; you shall do no heavy work.

[9]The LORD said to Moses: [10]Speak to the Israelites and tell them: When you come into the land which I am giving you, and reap its harvest, you shall bring the first sheaf of your harvest to the priest, [11]who shall elevate the sheaf before the LORD that it may be acceptable on your behalf. On the day after the sabbath the priest shall do this. [12]On this day, when your sheaf is elevated, you shall offer to the LORD for a burnt offering an unblemished yearling lamb. [13]Its grain offering shall be two tenths of an ephah of bran flour mixed with oil, as a sweet-smelling oblation to the LORD; and its libation shall be a fourth of a hin of wine. [14]You shall not eat any bread or roasted grain or fresh kernels until this day,

when you bring the offering for your God. This shall be a perpetual statute throughout your generations wherever you dwell.

Pentecost. [15]Beginning with the day after the sabbath, the day on which you bring the sheaf for elevation, you shall count seven full weeks; [16]you shall count to the day after the seventh week, fifty days. Then you shall present a new grain offering to the LORD. [17]For the elevated offering of your first-ripened fruits to the LORD, you shall bring with you from wherever you live two loaves of bread made of two tenths of an ephah of bran flour and baked with leaven. [18]Besides the bread, you shall offer to the LORD a burnt offering of seven unblemished yearling lambs, one bull of the herd, and two rams, along with their grain offering and libations, as a sweet-smelling oblation to the LORD. [19]One male goat shall be sacrificed as a purification offering, and two yearling lambs as a communion sacrifice. [20]The priest shall elevate them— that is, the two lambs—with the bread of the first-ripened fruits as an elevated offering before the LORD; these shall be sacred to the LORD and belong to the priest. [21]On this same day you shall make a proclamation: there shall be a declared holy day for you; no heavy work may be done. This shall be a perpetual statute through all your generations wherever you dwell.

[22]When you reap the harvest of your land, you shall not be so thorough that you reap the field to its very edge, nor shall you gather the gleanings of your harvest. These things you shall leave for the poor and the alien. I, the LORD, am your God.

New Year's Day. [23]The LORD said to Moses: [24]Tell the Israelites: On the first day of the seventh month you will have a sabbath rest, with trumpet blasts as a reminder, a declared holy day; [25]you shall do no heavy work, and you shall offer an oblation to the LORD.

The Day of Atonement. [26]The LORD said to Moses: [27]Now the tenth day of this seventh month is the Day of Atonement. You will have a declared holy day. You shall humble yourselves and offer an oblation to the LORD. [28]On this day you shall not do any work, because it is the Day of Atonement, when atonement is made for you before the LORD, your God. [29]Those who do not humble themselves on this day shall be cut off from the people. [30]If anyone does any work on this day, I will remove that person from the midst of the people. [31]You shall do no work; this is a perpetual statute throughout your generations wherever you dwell; [32]it is a sabbath of complete rest for you. You shall humble yourselves. Beginning on the evening of the ninth of the month, you shall keep your sabbath from evening to evening.

The Feast of Booths. [33]The LORD said to Moses: [34]Tell the Israelites: The fifteenth day of this seventh month is the LORD's feast of Booths, which shall continue for seven days. [35]On the first day, a declared holy day, you shall do no heavy work. [36]For seven days you shall offer an oblation to the LORD, and on the eighth day you will have a declared holy day. You shall offer an oblation to the LORD. It is the festival closing. You shall do no heavy work.

[37]These, therefore, are the festivals of the LORD which you shall declare holy days, in order to offer as an oblation to the LORD burnt offerings and grain offerings, sacrifices and libations, as prescribed for each day, [38]in addition to the LORD's sabbaths, your donations, your various votive offerings, and the voluntary offerings that you present to the LORD.

[39]On the fifteenth day, then, of the seventh month, when you have gathered in the produce of the land, you shall celebrate the feast of the LORD for a whole week. The first and the eighth day shall be days of rest. [40]On the first day you shall gather fruit of majestic trees, branches of palms, and boughs of leafy trees and valley willows. Then for a week you shall make

merry before the LORD, your God. ⁴¹You shall keep this feast of the LORD for one whole week in the year. By perpetual statute throughout your generations in the seventh month of the year, you shall keep it. ⁴²You shall dwell in booths for seven days; every native-born Israelite shall dwell in booths, ⁴³that your descendants may realize that, when I led the Israelites out of the land of Egypt, I made them dwell in booths. I, the LORD, am your God.

⁴⁴Thus did Moses announce to the Israelites the festivals of the LORD.

The Sanctuary Light. 24:1 The LORD said to Moses: ²Order the Israelites to bring you clear oil of crushed olives for the light, so that you may keep the lamp burning regularly. ³In the tent of meeting, outside the veil that hangs in front of the covenant, Aaron shall set up the lamp to burn before the LORD regularly, from evening till morning, by a perpetual statute throughout your generations. ⁴He shall set up the lamps on the pure gold menorah to burn regularly before the LORD.

The Showbread. ⁵You shall take bran flour and bake it into twelve cakes, using two tenths of an ephah of flour for each cake. ⁶These you shall place in two piles, six in each pile, on the pure gold table before the LORD. ⁷With each pile put some pure frankincense, which shall serve as an oblation to the LORD, a token of the bread offering. ⁸Regularly on each sabbath day the bread shall be set out before the LORD on behalf of the Israelites by an everlasting covenant. ⁹It shall belong to Aaron and his sons, who must eat it in a sacred place, since it is most sacred, his as a perpetual due from the oblations to the LORD.

Punishment of Blasphemy. ¹⁰A man born of an Israelite mother and an Egyptian father went out among the Israelites, and in the camp a fight broke out between the son of the Israelite woman and an Israelite man. ¹¹The son of the Israelite woman uttered the LORD's name in a curse and blasphemed. So he was brought to Moses—now his mother's name was Shelomith, daughter of Dibri, of the tribe of Dan— ¹²and he was kept in custody till a decision from the LORD should settle the case for them. ¹³The LORD then said to Moses: ¹⁴Take the blasphemer outside the camp, and when all who heard him have laid their hands on his head, let the whole community stone him. ¹⁵Tell the Israelites: Anyone who blasphemes God shall bear the penalty; ¹⁶whoever utters the name of the LORD in a curse shall be put to death. The whole community shall stone that person; alien and native-born alike must be put to death for uttering the LORD's name in a curse.

¹⁷Whoever takes the life of any human being shall be put to death; ¹⁸whoever takes the life of an animal shall make restitution of another animal, life for a life. ¹⁹Anyone who inflicts a permanent injury on his or her neighbor shall receive the same in return: ²⁰fracture for fracture, eye for eye, tooth for tooth. The same injury that one gives another shall be inflicted in return. ²¹Whoever takes the life of an animal shall make restitution, but whoever takes a human life shall be put to death. ²²You shall have but one rule, for alien and native-born alike. I, the LORD, am your God.

²³When Moses told this to the Israelites, they took the blasphemer outside the camp and stoned him; they did just as the LORD commanded Moses.

☐ ROMANS 8:28-39

God's Indomitable Love in Christ. 8:28 We know that all things work for good for those who love God, who are called according to his purpose. [29]For those he foreknew he also predestined to be conformed to the image of his Son, so that he might be the firstborn among many brothers. [30]And those he predestined he also called; and those he called he also justified; and those he justified he also glorified.

[31]What then shall we say to this? If God is for us, who can be against us? [32]He who did not spare his own Son but handed him over for us all, how will he not also give us everything else along with him? [33]Who will bring a charge against God's chosen ones? It is God who acquits us. [34]Who will condemn? It is Christ [Jesus] who died, rather, was raised, who also is at the right hand of God, who indeed intercedes for us. [35]What will separate us from the love of Christ? Will anguish, or distress, or persecution, or famine, or nakedness, or peril, or the sword? [36]As it is written:

> "For your sake we are being slain all
>   the day;
> we are looked upon as sheep to be
>   slaughtered."

[37]No, in all these things we conquer overwhelmingly through him who loved us. [38]For I am convinced that neither death, nor life, nor angels, nor principalities, nor present things, nor future things, nor powers, [39]nor height, nor depth, nor any other creature will be able to separate us from the love of God in Christ Jesus our Lord.

February 19

The Creator has used the very will of the creature that was working in opposition to His will as an instrument for carrying out His will. The Supreme Good has thus turned to good account even what is evil. In a way unspeakably strange and wonderful, even what is done in opposition to God's will does not defeat His will.

— St. Augustine of Hippo

☐ LEVITICUS 25-26

The Sabbatical Year. 25:1 The LORD said to Moses on Mount Sinai: [2]Speak to the Israelites and tell them: When you enter the land that I am giving you, let the land, too, keep a sabbath for the LORD. [3]For six years you may sow your field, and for six years prune your vineyard, gathering in their produce. [4]But during the seventh year the land shall have a sabbath of complete rest, a sabbath for the LORD, when you may neither sow your field nor prune your vineyard. [5]The aftergrowth of your harvest you shall not reap, nor shall you pick the grapes of your untrimmed vines. It shall be a year of rest for the land. [6]While the land has its sabbath, all its produce will be food to eat for you yourself and for your male and female slave, for your laborer and the tenant who live with you, [7]and likewise for your livestock and for the wild animals on your land.

The Jubilee Year. [8]You shall count seven weeks of years—seven times seven years—such that the seven weeks of years amount to forty-nine years. [9]Then, on the tenth day of the seventh month let the ram's horn resound; on this, the Day of Atonement, the ram's horn blast shall resound throughout your land. [10]You shall treat this fiftieth year as sacred. You shall proclaim liberty in the land for all its inhabitants. It shall be a jubilee for you, when each of you shall return to your own property, each of you to your own family. [11]This fiftieth year is your year of jubilee; you shall not sow, nor shall you reap the aftergrowth or pick the untrimmed vines, [12]since this is the jubilee. It shall be sacred for you. You may only eat what the field yields of itself.

[13]In this year of jubilee, then, each of you shall return to your own property. [14]Therefore, when you sell any land to your neighbor or buy any from your neighbor, do not deal unfairly with one another. [15]On the basis of the number of years since the last jubilee you shall purchase the land from your neighbor; and so also, on the basis of the number of years of harvest, that person shall sell it to you. [16]When the years are many, the price shall be so much the more; when the years are few, the price shall be so much the less. For it is really the number of harvests that the person sells you. [17]Do not deal unfairly with one another, then; but stand in fear of your God. I, the LORD, am your God.

[18]Observe my statutes and be careful to keep my ordinances, so that you will dwell securely in the land. [19]The land will yield its fruit and you will eat your fill, and live there securely. [20]And if you say, "What shall we eat in the seventh year, if we do not sow or reap our crop?" [21]I will command such a blessing for you in the sixth year that there will be crop enough for three years, [22]and when you sow in the eighth year, you will still be eating from the old crop; even into the ninth year, until the crop comes in, you will still be eating from the old crop.

Redemption of Property. [23]The land shall not be sold irrevocably; for the land is mine, and you are but resident aliens and under my authority. [24]Therefore, in every part of the country that you occupy, you must permit the land to be redeemed. [25]When one of your kindred is reduced to poverty and has to sell some property, that person's closest relative, who has the duty to redeem it, shall come and redeem what the relative has sold. [26]If, however, the person has no relative to redeem it, but later on acquires sufficient means to redeem it, [27]the person shall calculate the years since the sale, return the balance to the one to whom it was sold, and thus regain the property. [28]But if the person does not acquire sufficient means to buy back the land, what was sold shall remain in the possession of the purchaser until the year of the jubilee, when it must be released and returned to the original owner.

[29]When someone sells a dwelling in a walled town, it can be redeemed up to a full year after its sale—the redemption period is one year. [30]But if such a house in a walled town has not been redeemed at the end of a full year, it shall belong irrevocably to the purchaser throughout the generations; it shall not be released in the jubilee. [31]However, houses in villages that are not encircled by walls shall be reckoned as part of the surrounding farm land; they may be redeemed, and in the jubilee they must be released.

[32]In levitical cities the Levites shall always have the right to redeem the houses in the cities that are in their possession. [33]As for levitical property that goes unredeemed—houses sold in cities of their possession shall be released in the jubilee; for the houses in levitical cities are their possession in the midst of the Israelites. [34]Moreover, the pasture land belonging to their

cities shall not be sold at all; it must always remain their possession.

[35]When one of your kindred is reduced to poverty and becomes indebted to you, you shall support that person like a resident alien; let your kindred live with you. [36]Do not exact interest in advance or accrued interest, but out of fear of God let your kindred live with you. [37]Do not give your money at interest or your food at a profit. [38]I, the LORD, am your God, who brought you out of the land of Egypt to give you the land of Canaan and to be your God.

[39]When your kindred with you, having been so reduced to poverty, sell themselves to you, do not make them work as slaves. [40]Rather, let them be like laborers or like your tenants, working with you until the jubilee year, [41]when, together with any children, they shall be released from your service and return to their family and to their ancestral property. [42]Since they are my servants, whom I brought out of the land of Egypt, they shall not sell themselves as slaves are sold. [43]Do not lord it over them harshly, but stand in fear of your God.

[44]The male and female slaves that you possess—these you shall acquire from the nations round about you. [45]You may also acquire them from among the resident aliens who reside with you, and from their families who are with you, those whom they bore in your land. These you may possess, [46]and bequeath to your children as their hereditary possession forever. You may treat them as slaves. But none of you shall lord it harshly over any of your fellow Israelites.

[47]When your kindred, having been so reduced to poverty, sell themselves to a resident alien who has become wealthy or to descendants of a resident alien's family, [48]even after having sold themselves, they still may be redeemed by one of their kindred, [49]by an uncle or cousin, or by some other relative from their family; or, having acquired the means, they may pay the redemption price themselves. [50]With the purchaser they shall compute the years from the sale to the jubilee, distributing the sale price over these years as though they had been hired as laborers. [51]The more years there are, the more of the sale price they shall pay back as the redemption price; [52]the fewer years there are before the jubilee year, the more they have as credit; in proportion to the years of service they shall pay the redemption price. [53]The tenant alien shall treat those who sold themselves as laborers hired on an annual basis, and the alien shall not lord it over them harshly before your very eyes. [54]And if they are not redeemed by these means, they shall nevertheless be released, together with any children, in the jubilee year. [55]For the Israelites belong to me as servants; they are my servants, whom I brought out of the land of Egypt, I, the LORD, your God.

The Reward of Obedience. 26:1 Do not make idols for yourselves. You shall not erect a carved image or a sacred stone for yourselves, nor shall you set up a carved stone for worship in your land; for I, the LORD, am your God. [2]Keep my sabbaths, and reverence my sanctuary. I am the LORD.

[3]If you live in accordance with my statutes and are careful to observe my commandments, [4]I will give you your rains in due season, so that the land will yield its crops, and the trees their fruit; [5]your threshing will last till vintage time, and your vintage till the time for sowing, and you will eat your fill of food, and live securely in your land. [6]I will establish peace in the land, and you will lie down to rest with no one to cause you anxiety. I will rid the country of ravenous beasts, and no sword shall sweep across your land. [7]You will rout your enemies, and they shall fall before your sword. [8]Five of you will put a hundred of your foes to flight, and a hundred of you will put to flight ten thousand,

till your enemies fall before your sword. ⁹I will look with favor upon you, and make you fruitful and numerous, as I carry out my covenant with you. ¹⁰You shall eat the oldest stored harvest, and have to discard it to make room for the new. ¹¹I will set my tabernacle in your midst, and will not loathe you. ¹²Ever present in your midst, I will be your God, and you will be my people; ¹³I, the Lord, am your God, who brought you out of the land of Egypt to be their slaves no more, breaking the bars of your yoke and making you walk erect.

The Punishment of Disobedience. ¹⁴But if you do not heed me and do not keep all these commandments, ¹⁵if you reject my statutes and loathe my decrees, refusing to obey all my commandments and breaking my covenant, ¹⁶then I, in turn, will do this to you: I will bring terror upon you—with consumption and fever to dim the eyes and sap the life. You will sow your seed in vain, for your enemies will consume the crop. ¹⁷I will turn against you, and you will be beaten down before your enemies and your foes will lord it over you. You will flee though no one pursues you.

¹⁸If even after this you do not obey me, I will increase the chastisement for your sins sevenfold, ¹⁹to break your proud strength. I will make the sky above you as hard as iron, and your soil as hard as bronze, ²⁰so that your strength will be spent in vain; your land will bear no crops, and its trees no fruit.

²¹If then you continue hostile, unwilling to obey me, I will multiply my blows sevenfold, as your sins deserve. ²²I will unleash wild beasts against you, to rob you of your children and wipe out your livestock, till your population dwindles away and your roads become deserted.

²³If, with all this, you still do not accept my discipline and continue hostile to me, ²⁴I, too, will continue to be hostile to you and I, for my part, will smite you for your sins sevenfold. ²⁵I will bring against you the sword, the avenger of my covenant. Though you then huddle together in your cities, I will send pestilence among you, till you are delivered to the enemy. ²⁶When I break your staff of bread, ten women will need but one oven for baking your bread, and they shall dole it out to you by weight; and though you eat, you shall not be satisfied.

²⁷If, despite all this, you disobey and continue hostile to me, ²⁸I will continue in my hostile rage toward you, and I myself will discipline you for your sins sevenfold, ²⁹till you begin to eat the flesh of your own sons and daughters. ³⁰I will demolish your high places, overthrow your incense stands, and cast your corpses upon the corpses of your idols. In my loathing of you, ³¹I will lay waste your cities and desolate your sanctuaries, refusing your sweet-smelling offerings. ³²So devastated will I leave the land that your enemies who come to live there will stand aghast at the sight of it. ³³And you I will scatter among the nations at the point of my drawn sword, leaving your countryside desolate and your cities deserted. ³⁴Then shall the land, during the time it lies waste, make up its lost sabbaths, while you are in the land of your enemies; then shall the land have rest and make up for its sabbaths ³⁵during all the time that it lies desolate, enjoying the rest that you would not let it have on your sabbaths when you lived there.

³⁶Those of you who survive in the lands of their enemies, I will make so faint-hearted that the sound of a driven leaf will pursue them, and they shall run as if from the sword, and fall though no one pursues them; ³⁷stumbling over one another as if to escape a sword, while no one is after them—so helpless will you be to take a stand against your foes! ³⁸You shall perish among the nations, swallowed up in your enemies' country. ³⁹Those of you who survive will waste away in the lands of their enemies, for their own and their ancestors' guilt.

⁴⁰They will confess their iniquity and the iniquity of their ancestors in their treachery against me and in their continued hostility toward me, ⁴¹so that I, too, had to be hostile to them and bring them into their enemies' land. Then, when their uncircumcised hearts are humbled and they make amends for their iniquity, ⁴²I will remember my covenant with Jacob, and also my covenant with Isaac; and also my covenant with Abraham I will remember. The land, too, I will remember. ⁴³The land will be forsaken by them, that in its desolation without them, it may make up its sabbaths, and that they, too, may make good the debt of their guilt for having spurned my decrees and loathed my statutes. ⁴⁴Yet even so, even while they are in their enemies' land, I will not reject or loathe them to the point of wiping them out, thus making void my covenant with them; for I, the LORD, am their God. ⁴⁵I will remember for them the covenant I made with their forebears, whom I brought out of the land of Egypt before the eyes of the nations, that I might be their God. I am the LORD.

⁴⁶These are the statutes, decrees and laws which the LORD established between himself and the Israelites through Moses on Mount Sinai.

☐ ROMANS 9

Paul's Love for Israel. 9:1 I speak the truth in Christ, I do not lie; my conscience joins with the holy Spirit in bearing me witness ²that I have great sorrow and constant anguish in my heart. ³For I could wish that I myself were accursed and separated from Christ for the sake of my brothers, my kin according to the flesh. ⁴They are Israelites; theirs the adoption, the glory, the covenants, the giving of the law, the worship, and the promises; ⁵theirs the patriarchs, and from them, according to the flesh, is the Messiah. God who is over all be blessed forever. Amen.

God's Free Choice. ⁶But it is not that the word of God has failed. For not all who are of Israel are Israel, ⁷nor are they all children of Abraham because they are his descendants; but "It is through Isaac that descendants shall bear your name." ⁸This means that it is not the children of the flesh who are the children of God, but the children of the promise are counted as descendants. ⁹For this is the wording of the promise, "About this time I shall return and Sarah will have a son." ¹⁰And not only that, but also when Rebecca had conceived children by one husband, our father Isaac—¹¹before they had yet been born or had done anything, good or bad, in order that God's elective plan might continue, ¹²not by works but by his call—she was told, "The older shall serve the younger." ¹³As it is written:

"I loved Jacob
but hated Esau."

¹⁴What then are we to say? Is there injustice on the part of God? Of course not! ¹⁵For he says to Moses:

"I will show mercy to whom I will,
I will take pity on whom I will."

¹⁶So it depends not upon a person's will or exertion, but upon God, who shows mercy. ¹⁷For the scripture says to Pharaoh, "This is why I have raised you up, to show my power through you that my name may be proclaimed throughout the earth." ¹⁸Consequently, he has mercy upon whom he wills, and he hardens whom he wills.

¹⁹You will say to me then, "Why [then] does he still find fault? For who can oppose his will?" ²⁰But who indeed are you, a human being, to talk back to God? Will what is made say to its maker, "Why have you

created me so?" ²¹Or does not the potter have a right over the clay, to make out of the same lump one vessel for a noble purpose and another for an ignoble one? ²²What if God, wishing to show his wrath and make known his power, has endured with much patience the vessels of wrath made for destruction? ²³This was to make known the riches of his glory to the vessels of mercy, which he has prepared previously for glory, ²⁴namely, us whom he has called, not only from the Jews but also from the Gentiles.

Witness of the Prophets. ²⁵As indeed he says in Hosea:

"Those who were not my people I will
    call 'my people,'
    and her who was not beloved I will
    call 'beloved.'
²⁶And in the very place where it was
    said to them, 'You are not my
    people,'
    there they shall be called children of
    the living God."

²⁷And Isaiah cries out concerning Israel, "Though the number of the Israelites were like the sand of the sea, only a remnant will be saved; ²⁸for decisively and quickly will the Lord execute sentence upon the earth." ²⁹And as Isaiah predicted:

"Unless the Lord of hosts had left us
    descendants,
    we would have become like Sodom
    and have been made like
    Gomorrah."

Righteousness Based on Faith. ³⁰What then shall we say? That Gentiles, who did not pursue righteousness, have achieved it, that is, righteousness that comes from faith; ³¹but that Israel, who pursued the law of righteousness, did not attain to that law? ³²Why not? Because they did it not by faith, but as if it could be done by works. They stumbled over the stone that causes stumbling, ³³as it is written:

"Behold, I am laying a stone in Zion
    that will make people stumble
    and a rock that will make them fall,
    and whoever believes in him shall not
    be put to shame."

February 20

Be sure that you first preach by the way you live. If you do not, people will notice that you say one thing, but live otherwise, and your words will bring only cynical laughter and a derisive shake of the head.

— St. Charles Borromeo

☐ LEVITICUS 27

Votive Offerings and Dedications. 27:1 The Lord said to Moses: ²Speak to the Israelites and tell them: When anyone makes a vow to the Lord with respect to the value of a human being, ³the value for males between the ages of twenty and sixty shall be fifty silver shekels, by the sanctuary shekel; ⁴and for a female, the value shall be thirty shekels. ⁵For persons between the ages of five and twenty, the value for a male shall be twenty shekels, and for a female, ten shekels. ⁶For persons between the ages of one month and five years, the value for a male shall be five silver shekels, and for a female, three shekels. [7]For persons of sixty or more, for a male the value shall be fifteen shekels, and ten shekels for a female. [8]However, if the one who made the vow is too poor to meet the sum, the person must be set before the priest, who shall determine a value; the priest will do this in keeping with the means of the one who made the vow.

[9]If the offering vowed to the LORD is an animal that may be sacrificed, every such animal given to the LORD becomes sacred. [10]The offerer shall not substitute or exchange another for it, either a worse or a better one. If the offerer exchanges one animal in place of another, both the original and its substitute shall become sacred. [11]If any unclean animal which is unfit for sacrifice to the LORD is vowed, it must be set before the priest, [12]who shall determine its value in keeping with its good or bad qualities, and the value set by the priest shall stand. [13]If the offerer wishes to redeem the animal, the person shall pay one fifth more than this valuation.

[14]When someone dedicates a house as sacred to the LORD, the priest shall determine its value in keeping with its good or bad qualities, and the value set by the priest shall stand. [15]A person dedicating a house who then wishes to redeem it shall pay one fifth more than the price thus established, and then it will again belong to that individual.

[16]If someone dedicates to the LORD a portion of hereditary land, its valuation shall be made according to the amount of seed required to sow it, the acreage sown with a homer of barley seed being valued at fifty silver shekels. [17]If the dedication of a field is made at the beginning of a jubilee period, the full valuation shall hold; [18]but if it is some time after this, the priest shall estimate its money value according to the number of years left until the next jubilee year, with a corresponding reduction on the valuation. [19]A person dedicating a field who then wishes to redeem it shall pay one fifth more than the price thus established, and so reclaim it. [20]If, instead of redeeming such a field, one sells it to another, it may no longer be redeemed; [21]but at the jubilee it shall be released as sacred to the LORD; like a field that is put under the ban, it shall become priestly property.

[22]If someone dedicates to the LORD a field that was purchased and was not part of hereditary property, [23]the priest shall compute its value in proportion to the number of years until the next jubilee, and on the same day the person shall pay the price thus established, a sacred donation to the LORD; [24]at the jubilee the field shall revert to the hereditary owner of this land from whom it had been purchased.

[25]Every valuation shall be made according to the standard of the sanctuary shekel. There are twenty gerahs to the shekel.

Irredeemable Offerings. [26]Note that a firstborn animal, which as such already belongs to the LORD, may not be dedicated. Whether an ox or a sheep, it is the LORD's. [27]But if it is an unclean animal, it may be redeemed by paying one fifth more than its value. If it is not redeemed, it shall be sold at its value.

[28]Note, also, that any possession which someone puts under the ban for the LORD, whether it is a human being, an animal, or a hereditary field, shall be neither sold nor redeemed; everything that is put under the ban becomes most holy to the LORD. [29]All human beings that are put under the ban cannot be redeemed; they must be put to death.

[30]All tithes of the land, whether in grain from the fields or in fruit from the trees, belong to the LORD; they are sacred to the LORD. [31]If someone wishes to redeem any of the tithes, the person shall pay one fifth more than their value. [32]The tithes of the herd and the flock, every tenth animal that passes under the herdsman's rod, shall be sacred to the LORD. [33]It shall not matter whether good ones or bad ones are thus chosen, and no exchange may be made.

If any exchange is made, both the original animal and its substitute become sacred and cannot be redeemed.

☐ ROMANS 10-11

10:1 Brothers, my heart's desire and prayer to God on their behalf is for salvation. [2]I testify with regard to them that they have zeal for God, but it is not discerning. [3]For, in their unawareness of the righteousness that comes from God and their attempt to establish their own [righteousness], they did not submit to the righteousness of God. [4]For Christ is the end of the law for the justification of everyone who has faith.

[5]Moses writes about the righteousness that comes from [the] law, "The one who does these things will live by them." [6]But the righteousness that comes from faith says, "Do not say in your heart, 'Who will go up into heaven?' (that is, to bring Christ down) [7]or 'Who will go down into the abyss?' (that is, to bring Christ up from the dead)." [8]But what does it say?

"The word is near you,
in your mouth and in your heart"

(that is, the word of faith that we preach), [9]for, if you confess with your mouth that Jesus is Lord and believe in your heart that God raised him from the dead, you will be saved. [10]For one believes with the heart and so is justified, and one confesses with the mouth and so is saved. [11]For the scripture says, "No one who believes in him will be put to shame." [12]For there is no distinction between Jew and Greek; the same Lord is Lord of all, enriching all who call upon him. [13]For "everyone who calls on the name of the Lord will be saved."

[14]But how can they call on him in whom they have not believed? And how can they believe in him of whom they have not heard? And how can they hear without someone to preach? [15]And how can people preach unless they are sent? As it is written, "How beautiful are the feet of those who bring [the] good news!" [16]But not everyone has heeded the good news; for Isaiah says, "Lord, who has believed what was heard from us?" [17]Thus faith comes from what is heard, and what is heard comes through the word of Christ. [18]But I ask, did they not hear? Certainly they did; for

"Their voice has gone forth to all the
    earth,
and their words to the ends of the
    world."

[19]But I ask, did not Israel understand? First Moses says:

"I will make you jealous of those who
    are not a nation;
with a senseless nation I will make
    you angry."

[20]Then Isaiah speaks boldly and says:

"I was found [by] those who were not
    seeking me;
I revealed myself to those who were
    not asking for me."

[21]But regarding Israel he says, "All day long I stretched out my hands to a disobedient and contentious people."

The Remnant of Israel. 11:1 I ask, then, has God rejected his people? Of course not! For I too am an Israelite, a descendant of Abraham, of the tribe of Benjamin. [2]God has not rejected his people whom he foreknew. Do you not know what the scripture says about Elijah, how he pleads with God against Israel? [3]"Lord, they have killed your prophets, they have torn down your altars,

[34]These are the commandments which the LORD gave Moses on Mount Sinai for the Israelites.

and I alone am left, and they are seeking my life." [4]But what is God's response to him? "I have left for myself seven thousand men who have not knelt to Baal." [5]So also at the present time there is a remnant, chosen by grace. [6]But if by grace, it is no longer because of works; otherwise grace would no longer be grace. [7]What then? What Israel was seeking it did not attain, but the elect attained it; the rest were hardened, [8]as it is written:

"God gave them a spirit of deep sleep,
　　eyes that should not see
　　and ears that should not hear,
down to this very day."

[9]And David says:

"Let their table become a snare and a
　　trap,
　　a stumbling block and a retribution
　　　for them;
[10]let their eyes grow dim so that they
　　may not see,
　　and keep their backs bent forever."

The Gentiles' Salvation. [11]Hence I ask, did they stumble so as to fall? Of course not! But through their transgression salvation has come to the Gentiles, so as to make them jealous. [12]Now if their transgression is enrichment for the world, and if their diminished number is enrichment for the Gentiles, how much more their full number.

[13]Now I am speaking to you Gentiles. Inasmuch then as I am the apostle to the Gentiles, I glory in my ministry [14]in order to make my race jealous and thus save some of them. [15]For if their rejection is the reconciliation of the world, what will their acceptance be but life from the dead? [16]If the firstfruits are holy, so is the whole batch of dough; and if the root is holy, so are the branches.

[17]But if some of the branches were broken off, and you, a wild olive shoot, were grafted in their place and have come to share in the rich root of the olive tree, [18]do not boast against the branches. If you do boast, consider that you do not support the root; the root supports you. [19]Indeed you will say, "Branches were broken off so that I might be grafted in." [20]That is so. They were broken off because of unbelief, but you are there because of faith. So do not become haughty, but stand in awe. [21]For if God did not spare the natural branches, [perhaps] he will not spare you either. [22]See, then, the kindness and severity of God: severity toward those who fell, but God's kindness to you, provided you remain in his kindness; otherwise you too will be cut off. [23]And they also, if they do not remain in unbelief, will be grafted in, for God is able to graft them in again. [24]For if you were cut from what is by nature a wild olive tree, and grafted, contrary to nature, into a cultivated one, how much more will they who belong to it by nature be grafted back into their own olive tree.

God's Irrevocable Call. [25]I do not want you to be unaware of this mystery, brothers, so that you will not become wise [in] your own estimation: a hardening has come upon Israel in part, until the full number of the Gentiles comes in, [26]and thus all Israel will be saved, as it is written:

"The deliverer will come out of Zion,
　　he will turn away godlessness from
　　　Jacob;
[27]and this is my covenant with them
　　when I take away their sins."

[28]In respect to the gospel, they are enemies on your account; but in respect to election, they are beloved because of the patriarchs. [29]For the gifts and the call of God are irrevocable.

Triumph of God's Mercy. [30]Just as you once disobeyed God but have now received mercy because of their disobedience, [31]so they have now disobeyed in order that, by virtue of the mercy shown to you, they too may [now] receive mercy. [32]For God delivered all to disobedience, that he might have mercy upon all.

[33]Oh, the depth of the riches and wisdom and knowledge of God! How inscrutable are his judgments and how unsearchable his ways!

[34]"For who has known the mind of the Lord

or who has been his counselor?"
[35]"Or who has given him anything that he may be repaid?"

[36]For from him and through him and for him are all things. To him be glory forever. Amen.

February 21

St. Peter Damian

Receive the Body and Blood of Christ very frequently. The sight of a Christian's lips red with the Blood of Christ terrifies the enemy. He immediately recognizes the sign of his own ruin. He cannot stand the instrument of divine victory by which he was taken captive and cast down.

— St. Peter Damian

☐ NUMBERS 1-3

The Census. 1:1 In the second year after the Israelites' departure from the land of Egypt, on the first day of the second month, the Lord said to Moses at the tent of meeting in the wilderness of Sinai: [2]Take a census of the whole community of the Israelites, by clans and ancestral houses, registering by name each male individually. [3]You and Aaron shall enroll in companies all the men in Israel of twenty years or more who are fit for military service.

Moses' Assistants. [4]With you there shall be a man from each tribe, each the head of his ancestral house. [5]These are the names of those who are to assist you:

from Reuben: Elizur, son of Shedeur;
[6]from Simeon: Shelumiel, son of Zurishaddai;
[7]from Judah: Nahshon, son of Amminadab;
[8]from Issachar: Nethanel, son of Zuar;
[9]from Zebulun: Eliab, son of Helon;
[10]for the descendants of Joseph: from Ephraim: Elishama, son of Ammihud;

and from Manasseh: Gamaliel, son of Pedahzur;
[11]from Benjamin: Abidan, son of Gideoni;
[12]from Dan: Ahiezer, son of Ammishaddai;
[13]from Asher: Pagiel, son of Ochran;
[14]from Gad: Eliasaph, son of Reuel;
[15]from Naphtali: Ahira, son of Enan.

[16]These were the elect of the community, leaders of their ancestral tribes, heads of the clans of Israel. [17]So Moses and Aaron took these men who had been designated by name, [18]and assembled the whole community on the first day of the second month. Every man of twenty years or more then registered individually his name and lineage according to clan and ancestral house, [19]as the Lord had commanded Moses. So he enrolled them in the wilderness of Sinai.

Count of the Twelve Tribes. [20]Of the descendants of Reuben, the firstborn of Israel, registered individually by name and lineage according to their clans and ancestral houses, every male of twenty years or more, everyone fit for military service: [21]those enrolled from the tribe of Reuben were forty-six thousand five hundred.

[22]Of the descendants of Simeon, registered individually by name and lineage according to their clans and ancestral houses, every male of twenty years or more, everyone fit for military service: [23]those enrolled from the tribe of Simeon were fifty-nine thousand three hundred.

[24]Of the descendants of Gad, registered by name and lineage according to their clans and ancestral houses, every male of twenty years or more, everyone fit for military service: [25]those enrolled from the tribe of Gad were forty-five thousand six hundred and fifty.

[26]Of the descendants of Judah, registered by name and lineage according to their clans and ancestral houses, every male of twenty years or more, everyone fit for military service: [27]those enrolled from the tribe of Judah were seventy-four thousand six hundred.

[28]Of the descendants of Issachar, registered by name and lineage according to their clans and ancestral houses, every male of twenty years or more, everyone fit for military service: [29]those enrolled from the tribe of Issachar were fifty-four thousand four hundred.

[30]Of the descendants of Zebulun, registered by name and lineage according to their clans and ancestral houses, every male of twenty years or more, everyone fit for military service: [31]those enrolled from the tribe of Zebulun were fifty-seven thousand four hundred.

[32]Of the descendants of Joseph:

Of the descendants of Ephraim, registered by name and lineage according to their clans and ancestral houses, every male of twenty years or more, everyone fit for military service: [33]those enrolled from the tribe of Ephraim were forty thousand five hundred.

[34]Of the descendants of Manasseh, registered by name and lineage according to their clans and ancestral houses, every male of twenty years or more, everyone fit for military service: [35]those enrolled from the tribe of Manasseh were thirty-two thousand two hundred.

[36]Of the descendants of Benjamin, registered by name and lineage according to their clans and ancestral houses, every male of twenty years or more, everyone fit for military service: [37]those enrolled from the tribe of Benjamin were thirty-five thousand four hundred.

[38]Of the descendants of Dan, registered by name and lineage according to their clans and ancestral houses, every male of twenty years or more, everyone fit for military service: [39]those enrolled from the tribe of Dan were sixty-two thousand seven hundred.

[40]Of the descendants of Asher, registered by name and lineage according to their clans and ancestral houses, every male of twenty years or more, everyone fit for military service: [41]those enrolled from the tribe of Asher were forty-one thousand five hundred.

[42]Of the descendants of Naphtali, registered by name and lineage according to their clans and ancestral houses, every male of twenty years or more, everyone fit for military service: [43]those enrolled from the tribe of Naphtali were fifty-three thousand four hundred.

[44]It was these who were enrolled, each according to his ancestral house, by Moses and Aaron and the twelve leaders of Israel. [45]The total enrollment of the Israelites of twenty years or more, according to their ancestral houses, everyone fit for military service in Israel— [46]the total enrollment was six hundred and three thousand, five hundred and fifty.

Levites Omitted in the Census. [47]Now the Levites were not enrolled by their ancestral tribe with the others. [48]For the LORD had told Moses, [49]The tribe of Levi alone you shall not enroll nor include in the census along with the other Israelites. [50]You are to give the Levites charge of the tabernacle of the covenant with all its equipment and all that belongs to it. It is they who shall carry the tabernacle with all its equipment and who shall be its ministers; and they shall camp all around the tabernacle. ⁵¹When the tabernacle is to move on, the Levites shall take it down; when the tabernacle is to be pitched, it is the Levites who shall set it up. Any unauthorized person who comes near it shall be put to death. ⁵²The other Israelites shall camp according to their companies, each in their own divisional camps, ⁵³but the Levites shall camp around the tabernacle of the covenant to ensure that God's wrath will not fall upon the Israelite community. The Levites shall keep guard over the tabernacle of the covenant. ⁵⁴The Israelites complied; they did just as the LORD had commanded Moses.

Arrangement of the Tribes. 2:1 The LORD said to Moses and Aaron: ²The Israelites shall camp, each in their own divisions, under the ensigns of their ancestral houses. They shall camp at some distance all around the tent of meeting.

³Encamped on the east side, toward the sunrise, shall be the divisional camp of Judah, arranged in companies. The leader of the Judahites is Nahshon, son of Amminadab, ⁴and the enrollment of his company is seventy-four thousand six hundred. ⁵Encamped beside it is the tribe of Issachar. The leader of the Issacharites is Nethanel, son of Zuar, ⁶and the enrollment of his company is fifty-four thousand four hundred. ⁷Also the tribe of Zebulun. The leader of the Zebulunites is Eliab, son of Helon, ⁸and the enrollment of his company is fifty-seven thousand four hundred. ⁹The total enrollment of the camp of Judah by companies is one hundred and eighty-six thousand four hundred. They shall be first on the march.

¹⁰The divisional camp of Reuben shall be on the south side, by companies. The leader of the Reubenites is Elizur, son of Shedeur, ¹¹and the enrollment of his company is forty-six thousand five hundred. ¹²Encamped beside it is the tribe of Simeon. The leader of the Simeonites is Shelumiel, son of Zurishaddai, ¹³and the enrollment of his company is fifty-nine thousand three hundred. ¹⁴Next is the tribe of Gad. The leader of the Gadites is Eliasaph, son of Reuel, ¹⁵and the enrollment of his company is forty-five thousand six hundred and fifty. ¹⁶The total enrollment of the camp of Reuben by companies is one hundred and fifty-one thousand four hundred and fifty. They shall be second on the march.

¹⁷Then the tent of meeting and the camp of the Levites shall set out in the midst of the divisions. As they camp, so also they will march, each in place, by their divisions.

¹⁸The divisional camp of Ephraim shall be on the west side, by companies. The leader of the Ephraimites is Elishama, son of Ammihud, ¹⁹and the enrollment of his company is forty thousand five hundred. ²⁰Beside it shall be the tribe of Manasseh. The leader of the Manassites is Gamaliel, son of Pedahzur, ²¹and the enrollment of his company is thirty-two thousand two hundred. ²²Also the tribe of Benjamin. The leader of the Benjaminites is Abidan, son of Gideoni, ²³and the enrollment of his company is thirty-five thousand four hundred. ²⁴The total enrollment of the camp of Ephraim by companies is one hundred and eight thousand one hundred. They shall be third on the march.

²⁵The divisional camp of Dan shall be on the north side, by companies. The leader of the Danites is Ahiezer, son of Ammishaddai, ²⁶and the enrollment of his company is sixty-two thousand seven hundred. ²⁷Encamped beside it shall be the tribe of Asher. The leader of the Asherites is Pagiel, son of Ochran, ²⁸and the enrollment of his company is forty-one thousand five hundred. ²⁹Also the tribe of Naphtali. The leader of the Naphtalites is Ahira, son of Enan, ³⁰and the enrollment of his company is fifty-three thousand four hundred.

[31]The total enrollment of the camp of Dan is one hundred and fifty-seven thousand six hundred. They shall be the last on the march, by divisions.

[32]These are the enrollments of the Israelites according to their ancestral houses. The total enrollment of the camps by companies is six hundred and three thousand five hundred and fifty. [33]The Levites, however, were not enrolled with the other Israelites, just as the LORD had commanded Moses. [34]The Israelites did just as the LORD had commanded Moses; both in camp and on the march they were in their own divisions, everyone by clan and according to ancestral house.

The Sons of Aaron. 3:1 These are the offspring of Aaron and Moses at the time the LORD spoke to Moses on Mount Sinai. [2]These are the names of Aaron's sons: Nadab, the firstborn, Abihu, Eleazar, and Ithamar. [3]These are the names of Aaron's sons, the anointed priests whom he ordained to serve as priests. [4]But Nadab and Abihu died in the presence of the LORD when they offered unauthorized fire before the LORD in the wilderness of Sinai; and they left no sons. So only Eleazar and Ithamar served as priests during the lifetime of their father Aaron.

Levites in Place of the Firstborn. [5]Now the LORD said to Moses: [6]Summon the tribe of Levi and station them before Aaron the priest to serve him. [7]They shall discharge his obligations and those of the whole community before the tent of meeting by maintaining the tabernacle. [8]They shall have responsibility for all the furnishings of the tent of meeting and discharge the obligations of the Israelites by maintaining the tabernacle. [9]You shall assign the Levites to Aaron and his sons; they have been assigned unconditionally to him from among the Israelites. [10]But you will appoint only Aaron and his descendants to exercise the priesthood. Any unauthorized person who comes near shall be put to death.

[11]The LORD said to Moses: [12]I hereby take the Levites from the Israelites in place of every firstborn that opens the womb among the Israelites. The Levites, therefore, are mine, [13]because every firstborn is mine. When I struck down all the firstborn in the land of Egypt, I consecrated to me every firstborn in Israel, human being and beast alike. They belong to me; I am the LORD.

Census of the Levites. [14]The LORD said to Moses in the wilderness of Sinai: [15]Enroll the Levites by their ancestral houses and clans, enrolling every male of a month or more. [16]Moses, therefore, enrolled them at the direction of the LORD, just as the LORD had charged.

[17]These were the sons of Levi by name: Gershon, Kohath and Merari. [18]These were the names of the sons of Gershon, by their clans: Libni and Shimei. [19]The sons of Kohath, by their clans, were Amram, Izhar, Hebron and Uzziel. [20]The sons of Merari, by their clans, were Mahli and Mushi. These were the clans of the Levites by their ancestral houses.

Duties of the Levitical Clans. [21]To Gershon belonged the clan of the Libnites and the clan of the Shimeites; these were the clans of the Gershonites. [22]Their enrollment, registering every male of a month or more, was seven thousand five hundred. [23]The clans of the Gershonites camped behind the tabernacle, to the west. [24]The leader of the ancestral house of the Gershonites was Eliasaph, son of Lael. [25]At the tent of meeting their responsibility was the tabernacle: the tent and its covering, the curtain at the entrance of the tent of meeting, [26]the hangings of the court, the curtain at the entrance of the court enclosing both the tabernacle and the altar, and the ropes—whatever pertained to their maintenance.

[27]To Kohath belonged the clans of the Amramites, the Izharites, the Hebronites,

and the Uzzielites; these were the clans of the Kohathites. ²⁸Their enrollment, registering every male of a month or more, was eight thousand three hundred. They were the ones who performed the duties of the sanctuary. ²⁹The clans of the Kohathites camped on the south side of the tabernacle. ³⁰And the leader of their ancestral house of the clan of the Kohathites was Elizaphan, son of Uzziel. ³¹Their responsibility was the ark, the table, the menorah, the altars, the utensils of the sanctuary with which the priests minister, the veil, and everything pertaining to their maintenance. ³²The chief of the leaders of the Levites, however, was Eleazar, son of Aaron the priest; he was in charge of those who performed the duties of the sanctuary.

³³To Merari belonged the clans of the Mahlites and the Mushites; these were the clans of Merari. ³⁴Their enrollment, registering every male of a month or more, was six thousand two hundred. ³⁵The leader of the ancestral house of the clans of Merari was Zuriel, son of Abihail. They camped at the north side of the tabernacle. ³⁶The Merarites were assigned responsibility for the boards of the tabernacle, its bars, columns, pedestals, and all its fittings—and everything pertaining to their maintenance, ³⁷as well as the columns of the surrounding court with their pedestals, pegs and ropes.

³⁸East of the tabernacle, that is, in front of the tent of meeting, toward the sunrise, were camped Moses and Aaron and the latter's sons, performing the duties of the sanctuary incumbent upon the Israelites. Any unauthorized person who came near was to be put to death.

³⁹The total enrollment of the Levites whom Moses and Aaron enrolled at the direction of the LORD, by clans, every male a month old or more, was twenty-two thousand.

Census and Ransom of Firstborn. ⁴⁰The LORD then said to Moses: Enroll every firstborn male of the Israelites a month old or more, and count the number of their names. ⁴¹Then take the Levites for me—I am the LORD—in place of all the firstborn of the Israelites, as well as the Levites' cattle, in place of all the firstborn among the cattle of the Israelites. ⁴²So Moses enrolled all the firstborn of the Israelites, as the LORD had commanded him. ⁴³All the firstborn males, registered by name, of a month or more, numbered twenty-two thousand two hundred and seventy-three.

⁴⁴The LORD said to Moses: ⁴⁵Take the Levites in place of all the firstborn of the Israelites, and the Levites' cattle in place of their cattle, that the Levites may belong to me. I am the LORD. ⁴⁶As a redemption-price for the two hundred and seventy-three firstborn of the Israelites over and above the number of the Levites, ⁴⁷you shall take five shekels for each individual, according to the sanctuary shekel, twenty gerahs to the shekel. ⁴⁸Give this money to Aaron and his sons as a redemption-price for the extra number. ⁴⁹So Moses took the redemption money for those over and above the ones redeemed by the Levites. ⁵⁰From the firstborn of the Israelites he took the money, one thousand three hundred and sixty-five shekels according to the sanctuary shekel. ⁵¹He then gave this redemption money to Aaron and his sons, at the direction of the LORD, just as the LORD had commanded Moses.

☐ ROMANS 12

Sacrifice of Body and Mind. 12:1 I urge you therefore, brothers, by the mercies of God, to offer your bodies as a living sacrifice, holy and pleasing to God, your spiritual worship. [2]Do not conform yourselves to this age but be transformed by the renewal of your mind, that you may discern what is the will of God, what is good and pleasing and perfect.

Many Parts in One Body. [3]For by the grace given to me I tell everyone among you not to think of himself more highly than one ought to think, but to think soberly, each according to the measure of faith that God has apportioned. [4]For as in one body we have many parts, and all the parts do not have the same function, [5]so we, though many, are one body in Christ and individually parts of one another. [6]Since we have gifts that differ according to the grace given to us, let us exercise them: if prophecy, in proportion to the faith; [7]if ministry, in ministering; if one is a teacher, in teaching; [8]if one exhorts, in exhortation; if one contributes, in generosity; if one is over others, with diligence; if one does acts of mercy, with cheerfulness.

Mutual Love. [9]Let love be sincere; hate what is evil, hold on to what is good; [10]love one another with mutual affection; anticipate one another in showing honor. [11]Do not grow slack in zeal, be fervent in spirit, serve the Lord. [12]Rejoice in hope, endure in affliction, persevere in prayer. [13]Contribute to the needs of the holy ones, exercise hospitality. [14]Bless those who persecute [you], bless and do not curse them. [15]Rejoice with those who rejoice, weep with those who weep. [16]Have the same regard for one another; do not be haughty but associate with the lowly; do not be wise in your own estimation. [17]Do not repay anyone evil for evil; be concerned for what is noble in the sight of all. [18]If possible, on your part, live at peace with all. [19]Beloved, do not look for revenge but leave room for the wrath; for it is written, "Vengeance is mine, I will repay, says the Lord." [20]Rather, "if your enemy is hungry, feed him; if he is thirsty, give him something to drink; for by so doing you will heap burning coals upon his head." [21]Do not be conquered by evil but conquer evil with good.

February 22

The Chair of St. Peter the Apostle

Peter: the leader of the choir, the mouth of all the apostles, the head of that company, the ruler of the whole world, the foundation of the Church, the ardent lover of Christ.
— St. John Chrysostom

☐ NUMBERS 4-5

Duties Further Defined. 4:1 The LORD said to Moses and Aaron: [2]Take a census among the Levites of the Kohathites, by clans and ancestral houses, [3]all between thirty and fifty years of age, who will join the personnel for doing tasks in the tent of meeting.

[4]This is the task of the Kohathites in the tent of meeting: the most sacred objects.

[5]In breaking camp, Aaron and his sons shall go in and take down the screening curtain and cover the ark of the covenant with it. [6]Over these they shall put a cover of yellow-orange skin, and on top of this spread an all-violet cloth and put the poles in place. [7]On the table of the Presence they shall spread a violet cloth and put on it the plates and cups, as well as the bowls and pitchers for libations; the established bread offering shall remain on the table. [8]Over these they shall spread a scarlet cloth and cover it with a covering of yellow-orange skin, and put the poles in place. [9]They shall use a violet cloth to cover the menorah of the light with its lamps, tongs, and trays, as well as the various containers of oil from which it is supplied. [10]The menorah with all its utensils they shall then put in a covering of yellow-orange skin, and place on a litter. [11]Over the golden altar they shall spread a violet cloth, and cover this also with a covering of yellow-orange skin, and put the poles in place. [12]Taking the utensils of the sanctuary service, they shall put them all in violet cloth and cover them with a covering of yellow-orange skin. They shall then place them on a litter. [13]After cleansing the altar of its ashes, they shall spread a purple cloth over it. [14]On this they shall put all the utensils with which it is served: the fire pans, forks, shovels, basins, and all the utensils of the altar. They shall then spread a covering of yellow-orange skin over this, and put the poles in place.

[15]Only after Aaron and his sons have finished covering the sacred objects and all their utensils on breaking camp, can the Kohathites enter to carry them. But they shall not touch the sacred objects; if they do they will die. These, then, are the objects in the tent of meeting that the Kohathites shall carry.

[16]Eleazar, son of Aaron the priest, shall be in charge of the oil for the light, the fragrant incense, the established grain offering, and the anointing oil. He shall be in charge of the whole tabernacle with all the sacred objects and utensils that are in it.

[17]The LORD said to Moses and Aaron: [18]Do not let the group of Kohathite clans perish from among the Levites. [19]That they may live and not die when they approach the most sacred objects, this is what you shall do for them: Aaron and his sons shall go in and assign to each of them his task and what he must carry; [20]but the Kohathites shall not go in to look upon the sacred objects even for an instant, or they will die.

[21]The LORD said to Moses: [22]Take a census of the Gershonites also, by ancestral houses and clans, [23]enrolling all between thirty and fifty years of age who will join the personnel to do the work in the tent of meeting. [24]This is the task of the clans of the Gershonites, what they must do and what they must carry: [25]they shall carry the curtains of the tabernacle, the tent of meeting with its covering and the outer wrapping of yellow-orange skin, the curtain at the entrance of the tent of meeting, [26]the hangings of the court, the curtain at the entrance to the gate of the court that encloses both the tabernacle and the altar, together with their ropes and all other objects necessary for their use. Whatever is to be done to maintain these things, they shall do. [27]The service of the Gershonites shall be entirely under the direction of Aaron and his sons, with regard to what they must carry and what they must do; you shall list for them by name what they are to carry. [28]This, then, is the task of the clans of the Gershonites in the tent of meeting; and they shall be under the supervision of Ithamar, son of Aaron the priest.

[29]The Merarites, too, you shall enroll by clans and ancestral houses, [30]enrolling all between thirty and fifty years of age who will join the personnel to maintain the tent of meeting. [31]This is what they shall be responsible for carrying, with respect to all their service in the tent of meeting: the

boards of the tabernacle with its bars, columns and pedestals, [32]and the columns of the surrounding court with their pedestals, pegs and ropes, including all their accessories and everything for their maintenance. You shall list by name the objects they shall be responsible for carrying. [33]This, then, is the task of the clans of the Merarites with respect to all their service in the tent of meeting under the supervision of Ithamar, son of Aaron the priest.

Number of Adult Levites. [34]So Moses and Aaron and the leaders of the community enrolled the Kohathites, by clans and ancestral houses, [35]all between thirty and fifty years of age who will join the personnel to work in the tent of meeting; [36]their enrollment by clans was two thousand seven hundred and fifty. [37]Such was the enrollment of the clans of the Kohathites, everyone who was to serve in the tent of meeting, whom Moses enrolled, together with Aaron, as the LORD directed through Moses.

[38]As for the enrollment of the Gershonites, by clans and ancestral houses, [39]all between thirty and fifty years of age who will join the personnel to work in the tent of meeting— [40]their enrollment by clans and ancestral houses was two thousand six hundred and thirty. [41]Such was the enrollment of the clans of the Gershonites, everyone who was to serve in the tent of meeting, whom Moses enrolled, together with Aaron, as the LORD directed.

[42]As for the enrollment of the clans of the Merarites, by clans and ancestral houses, [43]all from thirty up to fifty years of age who will join the personnel to work in the tent of meeting— [44]their enrollment by clans was three thousand two hundred. [45]Such was the enrollment of the clans of the Merarites, whom Moses enrolled, together with Aaron, as the LORD directed through Moses.

[46]As for the total enrollment of the Levites, which Moses and Aaron and the Israelite leaders had made, by clans and ancestral houses, [47]all between thirty and fifty years of age who were to undertake tasks of service or transport for the tent of meeting— [48]their total enrollment was eight thousand five hundred and eighty. [49]As the LORD directed through Moses, they gave each of them their assignments for service and for transport; just as the LORD had commanded Moses.

The Unclean Expelled. 5:1 The LORD said to Moses: [2]Order the Israelites to expel from camp everyone with a scaly infection, and everyone suffering from a discharge, and everyone who has become unclean by contact with a corpse. [3]Male and female alike, you shall expel them. You shall expel them from the camp so that they do not defile their camp, where I dwell in their midst. [4]This the Israelites did, expelling them from the camp; just as the LORD had commanded Moses, so the Israelites did.

Unjust Possession. [5]The LORD said to Moses: [6]Tell the Israelites: If a man or a woman commits any offense against another person, thus breaking faith with the LORD, and thereby becomes guilty, [7]that person shall confess the wrong that has been done, make restitution in full, and in addition give one fifth of its value to the one that has been wronged. [8]However, if there is no next of kin, one to whom restitution can be made, the restitution shall be made to the LORD and shall fall to the priest; this is apart from the ram of atonement with which the priest makes atonement for the guilty individual. [9]Likewise, every contribution among the sacred offerings that the Israelites present to the priest will belong to him. [10]Each shall possess his own sacred offerings; what is given to a priest shall be his.

Ordeal for Suspected Adultery. [11]The LORD said to Moses: [12]Speak to the Israelites and tell them: If a man's wife goes astray and becomes unfaithful to him [13]by virtue of a man having intercourse with her in secret from her husband and she is able to conceal the fact that she has defiled herself for lack of a witness who might have caught her in the act; [14]or if a man is overcome by a feeling of jealousy that makes him suspect his wife, and she has defiled herself; or if a man is overcome by a feeling of jealousy that makes him suspect his wife and she has not defiled herself— [15]then the man shall bring his wife to the priest as well as an offering on her behalf, a tenth of an ephah of barley meal. However, he shall not pour oil on it nor put frankincense over it, since it is a grain offering of jealousy, a grain offering of remembrance which recalls wrongdoing.

[16]The priest shall first have the woman come forward and stand before the LORD. [17]In an earthen vessel he shall take holy water, as well as some dust from the floor of the tabernacle and put it in the water. [18]Making the woman stand before the LORD, the priest shall uncover her head and place in her hands the grain offering of remembrance, that is, the grain offering of jealousy, while he himself shall hold the water of bitterness that brings a curse. [19]Then the priest shall adjure the woman, saying to her, "If no other man has had intercourse with you, and you have not gone astray by defiling yourself while under the authority of your husband, be immune to this water of bitterness that brings a curse. [20]But if you have gone astray while under the authority of your husband, and if you have defiled yourself and a man other than your husband has had intercourse with you"— [21]so shall the priest adjure the woman with this imprecation—"may the LORD make

you a curse and malediction among your people by causing your uterus to fall and your belly to swell! [22]May this water, then, that brings a curse, enter your bowels to make your belly swell and your uterus fall!" And the woman shall say, "Amen, amen!" [23]The priest shall put these curses in writing and shall then wash them off into the water of bitterness, [24]and he will have the woman drink the water of bitterness that brings a curse, so that the water that brings a curse may enter into her to her bitter hurt. [25]But first the priest shall take the grain offering of jealousy from the woman's hand, and having elevated the grain offering before the LORD, shall bring it to the altar, [26]where he shall take a handful of the grain offering as a token offering and burn it on the altar. Only then shall he have the woman drink the water. [27]Once he has had her drink the water, if she has defiled herself and been unfaithful to her husband, the water that brings a curse will enter into her to her bitter hurt, and her belly will swell and her uterus will fall, so that she will become a curse among her people. [28]If, however, the woman has not defiled herself, but is still pure, she will be immune and will still be fertile.

[29]This, then, is the ritual for jealousy when a woman goes astray while under the authority of her husband and defiles herself, [30]or when such a feeling of jealousy comes over a man that he becomes suspicious of his wife; he shall have her stand before the LORD, and the priest shall perform this entire ritual for her. [31]The man shall be free from punishment, but the woman shall bear her punishment.

☐ ROMANS 13

Obedience in Authority. 13:1 Let every person be subordinate to the higher authorities, for there is no authority except from God, and those that exist have been established by God. [2]Therefore, whoever resists authority opposes what God has appointed, and those who oppose it will bring judgment upon themselves. [3]For rulers are not a cause of fear to good conduct, but to evil. Do you wish to have no fear of authority? Then do what is good and you will receive approval from it, [4]for it is a servant of God for your good. But if you do evil, be afraid, for it does not bear the sword without purpose; it is the servant of God to inflict wrath on the evildoer. [5]Therefore, it is necessary to be subject not only because of the wrath but also because of conscience. [6]This is why you also pay taxes, for the authorities are ministers of God, devoting themselves to this very thing. [7]Pay to all their dues, taxes to whom taxes are due, toll to whom toll is due, respect to whom respect is due, honor to whom honor is due.

Love Fulfills the Law. [8]Owe nothing to anyone, except to love one another; for the one who loves another has fulfilled the law. [9]The commandments, "You shall not commit adultery; you shall not kill; you shall not steal; you shall not covet," and whatever other commandment there may be, are summed up in this saying, [namely] "You shall love your neighbor as yourself." [10]Love does no evil to the neighbor; hence, love is the fulfillment of the law.

Awareness of the End of Time. [11]And do this because you know the time; it is the hour now for you to awake from sleep. For our salvation is nearer now than when we first believed; [12]the night is advanced, the day is at hand. Let us then throw off the works of darkness [and] put on the armor of light; [13]let us conduct ourselves properly as in the day, not in orgies and drunkenness, not in promiscuity and licentiousness, not in rivalry and jealousy. [14]But put on the Lord Jesus Christ, and make no provision for the desires of the flesh.

February 23

St. Polycarp

Those who hypocritically call themselves Christians fool only empty-headed people.

— St. Polycarp

☐ **NUMBERS 6–7**

Laws Concerning Nazirites. 6:1 The Lord said to Moses: [2]Speak to the Israelites and tell them: When men or women solemnly take the nazirite vow to dedicate themselves to the Lord, [3]they shall abstain from wine and strong drink; they may neither drink wine vinegar, other vinegar, or any kind of grape juice, nor eat either fresh or dried grapes. [4]As long as they are nazirites they shall not eat anything of the produce of the grapevine; not even the seeds or the skins. [5]While they are under the nazirite vow, no razor shall touch their hair. Until the period of their dedication to the Lord is over, they shall be holy, letting the hair of their heads grow freely. [6]As long as they are dedicated to the Lord, they shall not come near a dead person. [7]Not even for their father or mother, sister or brother, should they defile themselves, when these die, since their heads bear their dedication to God. [8]As long as they are nazirites they are holy to the Lord.

[9]If someone dies very suddenly in their presence, defiling their dedicated heads, they shall shave their heads on the day of their purification, that is, on the seventh day. [10]On the eighth day they shall bring

two turtledoves or two pigeons to the priest at the entrance of the tent of meeting. [11]The priest shall offer up the one as a purification offering and the other as a burnt offering, thus making atonement for them for the sin they committed with respect to the corpse. On the same day they shall reconsecrate their heads [12]and rededicate themselves to the LORD for the period of their dedication, bringing a yearling lamb as a reparation offering. The previous period is not valid, because they defiled their dedicated heads.

[13]This is the ritual for the nazirites: When the period of their dedication is complete they shall go to the entrance of the tent of meeting, [14]bringing their offerings to the LORD, one unblemished yearling lamb for a burnt offering, one unblemished yearling ewe lamb for a purification offering, one unblemished ram as a communion offering, [15]and a basket of unleavened cakes of bran flour mixed with oil and of unleavened wafers spread with oil, along with their grain offerings and libations. [16]The priest shall present them before the LORD, and shall offer up the purification offering and the burnt offering for them. [17]He shall then offer up the ram as a communion sacrifice to the LORD, along with the basket of unleavened cakes, and the priest will offer the grain offering and libation. [18]Then at the entrance of the tent of meeting the nazirite shall shave his or her dedicated head, take the hair of the dedicated head, and put it in the fire under the communion sacrifice. [19]After the nazirite has shaved off the dedicated hair, the priest shall take a boiled shoulder of the ram, as well as one unleavened cake from the basket and one unleavened wafer, and shall put them in the hands of the nazirite. [20]The priest shall then elevate them as an elevated offering before the LORD. They are an offering belonging to the priest, along with the brisket of the elevated offering and the leg of the contribution. Only after this may the nazirite drink wine.

[21]This, then, is the law for the nazirites, that is, what they vow as their offering to the LORD in accord with their dedication, apart from anything else which their means may allow. In keeping with the vow they take so shall they do, according to the law of their dedication.

The Priestly Blessing. [22]The LORD said to Moses: [23]Speak to Aaron and his sons and tell them: This is how you shall bless the Israelites. Say to them:

[24]The LORD bless you and keep you!
[25]The LORD let his face shine upon you,
     and be gracious to you!
[26]The LORD look upon you kindly and
     give you peace!

[27]So shall they invoke my name upon the Israelites, and I will bless them.

Offerings of the Tribal Leaders. 7:1 Now, when Moses had completed the erection of the tabernacle, he anointed and consecrated it with all its equipment, as well as the altar with all its equipment. After he anointed and consecrated them, [2]an offering was made by the tribal leaders of Israel, who were heads of ancestral houses, the same leaders of the tribes who supervised those enrolled. [3]The offering they brought before the LORD consisted of six wagons for baggage and twelve oxen, that is, a wagon for every two tribal leaders, and an ox for each. These they presented before the tabernacle.

[4]The LORD then said to Moses: [5]Accept their offering, that these things may be put to use to maintain the tent of meeting. Assign them to the Levites, to each according to his duties. [6]So Moses accepted the wagons and oxen, and assigned them to the Levites. [7]He gave two wagons and four oxen to the Gershonites according to their duties, [8]and four wagons and eight oxen to the Merarites according to their duties, under the supervision of Ithamar, son of Aaron the priest. [9]He gave none to the

Kohathites, because they were responsible for maintenance of the sacred objects that had to be carried on their shoulders.

[10]For the dedication of the altar also, the tribal leaders brought offerings when it was anointed; the leaders presented their offering before the altar. [11]But the LORD said to Moses: Let one leader each day present his offering for the dedication of the altar.

[12]The one who presented his offering on the first day was Nahshon, son of Amminadab, of the tribe of Judah. [13]His offering consisted of one silver plate weighing a hundred and thirty shekels and one silver basin weighing seventy shekels according to the sanctuary shekel, both filled with bran flour mixed with oil for a grain offering; [14]one gold cup of ten shekels' weight filled with incense; [15]one bull from the herd, one ram, and one yearling lamb for a burnt offering; [16]one goat for a purification offering; [17]and two bulls, five rams, five he-goats, and five yearling lambs for a communion sacrifice. This was the offering of Nahshon, son of Amminadab.

[18]On the second day Nethanel, son of Zuar, tribal leader of Issachar, made his offering. [19]He presented as his offering one silver plate weighing a hundred and thirty shekels and one silver basin weighing seventy shekels according to the sanctuary shekel, both filled with bran flour mixed with oil for a grain offering; [20]one gold cup of ten shekels' weight filled with incense; [21]one bull from the herd, one ram, and one yearling lamb for a burnt offering; [22]one goat for a purification offering; [23]and two bulls, five rams, five he-goats, and five yearling lambs for a communion sacrifice. This was the offering of Nethanel, son of Zuar.

[24]On the third day it was the turn of the tribal leader of the Zebulunites, Eliab, son of Helon. [25]His offering consisted of one silver plate weighing a hundred and thirty shekels and one silver basin weighing seventy shekels according to the sanctuary shekel, both filled with bran flour mixed with oil for a grain offering; [26]one gold cup of ten shekels' weight filled with incense; [27]one bull from the herd, one ram, and one yearling lamb for a burnt offering; [28]one goat for a purification offering; [29]and two bulls, five rams, five he-goats, and five yearling lambs for a communion sacrifice. This was the offering of Eliab, son of Helon.

[30]On the fourth day it was the turn of the tribal leader of the Reubenites, Elizur, son of Shedeur. [31]His offering consisted of one silver plate weighing a hundred and thirty shekels and one silver basin weighing seventy shekels according to the sanctuary shekel, both filled with bran flour mixed with oil for a grain offering; [32]one gold cup of ten shekels' weight filled with incense; [33]one bull from the herd, one ram, and one yearling lamb for a burnt offering; [34]one goat for a purification offering; [35]and two bulls, five rams, five he-goats, and five yearling lambs for a communion sacrifice. This was the offering of Elizur, son of Shedeur.

[36]On the fifth day it was the turn of the tribal leader of the Simeonites, Shelumiel, son of Zurishaddai. [37]His offering consisted of one silver plate weighing a hundred and thirty shekels and one silver basin weighing seventy shekels according to the sanctuary shekel, both filled with bran flour mixed with oil for a grain offering; [38]one gold cup of ten shekels' weight filled with incense; [39]one bull from the herd, one ram, and one yearling lamb for a burnt offering; [40]one goat for a purification offering; [41]and two bulls, five rams, five he-goats, and five yearling lambs for a communion sacrifice. This was the offering of Shelumiel, son of Zurishaddai.

[42]On the sixth day it was the turn of the tribal leader of the Gadites, Eliasaph, son of Reuel. [43]His offering consisted of one silver plate weighing a hundred and thirty shekels and one silver basin weighing seventy shekels according to the sanctuary shekel, both filled with bran flour mixed with oil for a grain offering; [44]one gold cup

of ten shekels' weight filled with incense; [45]one bull from the herd, one ram, and one yearling lamb for a burnt offering; [46]one goat for a purification offering; [47]and two bulls, five rams, five he-goats, and five yearling lambs for a communion sacrifice. This was the offering of Eliasaph, son of Reuel.

[48]On the seventh day it was the turn of the tribal leader of the Ephraimites, Elishama, son of Ammihud. [49]His offering consisted of one silver plate weighing a hundred and thirty shekels and one silver basin weighing seventy shekels according to the sanctuary shekel, both filled with bran flour mixed with oil for a grain offering; [50]one gold cup of ten shekels' weight filled with incense; [51]one bull from the herd, one ram, and one yearling lamb for a burnt offering; [52]one goat for a purification offering; [53]and two bulls, five rams, five he-goats, and five yearling lambs for a communion sacrifice. This was the offering of Elishama, son of Ammihud.

[54]On the eighth day it was the turn of the tribal leader of the Manassites, Gamaliel, son of Pedahzur. [55]His offering consisted of one silver plate weighing a hundred and thirty shekels and one silver basin weighing seventy shekels according to the sanctuary shekel, both filled with bran flour mixed with oil for a grain offering; [56]one gold cup of ten shekels' weight filled with incense; [57]one bull from the herd, one ram, and one yearling lamb for a burnt offering; [58]one goat for a purification offering; [59]and two bulls, five rams, five he-goats, and five yearling lambs for a communion sacrifice. This was the offering of Gamaliel, son of Pedahzur.

[60]On the ninth day it was the turn of the tribal leader of the Benjaminites, Abidan, son of Gideoni. [61]His offering consisted of one silver plate weighing a hundred and thirty shekels and one silver basin weighing seventy shekels according to the sanctuary shekel, both filled with bran flour mixed with oil for a grain offering; [62]one gold cup

of ten shekels' weight filled with incense; [63]one bull from the herd, one ram, and one yearling lamb for a burnt offering; [64]one goat for a purification offering; [65]and two bulls, five rams, five he-goats, and five yearling lambs for a communion sacrifice. This was the offering of Abidan, son of Gideoni.

[66]On the tenth day it was the turn of the tribal leader of the Danites, Ahiezer, son of Ammishaddai. [67]His offering consisted of one silver plate weighing a hundred and thirty shekels and one silver basin weighing seventy shekels according to the sanctuary shekel, both filled with bran flour mixed with oil for a grain offering; [68]one gold cup of ten shekels' weight filled with incense; [69]one bull from the herd, one ram, and one yearling lamb for a burnt offering; [70]one goat for a purification offering; [71]and two bulls, five rams, five he-goats, and five yearling lambs for a communion sacrifice. This was the offering of Ahiezer, son of Ammishaddai.

[72]On the eleventh day it was the turn of the tribal leader of the Asherites, Pagiel, son of Ochran. [73]His offering consisted of one silver plate weighing one hundred and thirty shekels and one silver basin weighing seventy shekels according to the sanctuary shekel, both filled with bran flour mixed with oil for a grain offering; [74]one gold cup of ten shekels' weight filled with incense; [75]one bull from the herd, one ram, and one yearling lamb for a burnt offering; [76]one goat for a purification offering; [77]and two bulls, five rams, five he-goats, and five yearling lambs for a communion sacrifice. This was the offering of Pagiel, son of Ochran.

[78]On the twelfth day it was the turn of the tribal leader of the Naphtalites, Ahira, son of Enan. [79]His offering consisted of one silver plate weighing a hundred and thirty shekels and one silver basin weighing seventy shekels according to the sanctuary shekel, both filled with bran flour mixed with oil for a grain offering; [80]one gold cup of ten shekels' weight filled with

incense; [81]one bull from the herd, one ram, and one yearling lamb for a burnt offering; [82]one goat for a purification offering; [83]and two bulls, five rams, five he-goats, and five yearling lambs for a communion sacrifice. This was the offering of Ahira, son of Enan.

[84]These were the offerings for the dedication of the altar, given by the tribal leaders of Israel on the occasion of its anointing: twelve silver plates, twelve silver basins, and twelve gold cups. [85]Each silver plate weighed a hundred and thirty shekels, and each silver basin seventy, so that all the silver of these vessels amounted to two thousand four hundred shekels, according to the sanctuary shekel. [86]The twelve gold cups that were filled with incense weighed ten shekels apiece, according to the sanctuary shekel, so that all the gold of the cups amounted to one hundred and twenty shekels. [87]The animals for the burnt offerings were, in all, twelve bulls, twelve rams, and twelve yearling lambs, with their grain offerings; those for the purification offerings were twelve goats. [88]The animals for the communion sacrifices were, in all, twenty-four bulls, sixty rams, sixty he-goats, and sixty yearling lambs. These, then, were the offerings for the dedication of the altar after it was anointed.

The Voice. [89]When Moses entered the tent of meeting to speak with God, he heard the voice addressing him from above the cover on the ark of the covenant, from between the two cherubim; and so it spoke to him.

□ ROMANS 14

To Live and Die for Christ. 14:1 Welcome anyone who is weak in faith, but not for disputes over opinions. [2]One person believes that one may eat anything, while the weak person eats only vegetables. [3]The one who eats must not despise the one who abstains, and the one who abstains must not pass judgment on the one who eats; for God has welcomed him. [4]Who are you to pass judgment on someone else's servant? Before his own master he stands or falls. And he will be upheld, for the Lord is able to make him stand. [5][For] one person considers one day more important than another, while another person considers all days alike. Let everyone be fully persuaded in his own mind. [6]Whoever observes the day, observes it for the Lord. Also whoever eats, eats for the Lord, since he gives thanks to God; while whoever abstains, abstains for the Lord and gives thanks to God. [7]None of us lives for oneself, and no one dies for oneself. [8]For if we live, we live for the Lord, and if we die, we die for the Lord; so then, whether we live or die, we are the Lord's. [9]For this is why Christ died and came to life, that he might be Lord of both the dead and the living. [10]Why then do you judge your brother? Or you, why do you look down on your brother? For we shall all stand before the judgment seat of God; [11]for it is written:

"As I live, says the Lord, every knee
    shall bend before me,
    and every tongue shall give praise to
        God."

[12]So [then] each of us shall give an account of himself [to God].

Consideration for the Weak Conscience. [13]Then let us no longer judge one another, but rather resolve never to put a stumbling block or hindrance in the way of a brother. [14]I know and am convinced in the Lord Jesus that nothing is unclean in itself; still, it is unclean for someone who thinks it unclean. [15]If your brother is being hurt by what you eat, your conduct is no longer in accord with love. Do not because of your food destroy him for whom Christ died. [16]So do not let your good be reviled. [17]For the kingdom of God is not a matter of food and drink, but of righteousness, peace, and joy in the holy Spirit; [18]whoever serves Christ in this way is pleasing to God and approved by others. [19]Let us then pursue what leads to peace and to building up one another. [20]For the sake of food, do not destroy the work of God. Everything is indeed clean, but it is wrong for anyone to become a stumbling block by eating; [21]it is good not to eat meat or drink wine or do anything that causes your brother to stumble. [22]Keep the faith [that] you have to yourself in the presence of God; blessed is the one who does not condemn himself for what he approves. [23]But whoever has doubts is condemned if he eats, because this is not from faith; for whatever is not from faith is sin.

February 24

Whoever subjects himself to his neighbor in love can never be humiliated.

— St. Basil the Great

☐ NUMBERS 8-10

The Menorah. 8:1 The Lord said to Moses: [2]Speak to Aaron and say: "When you set up the menorah-lamps, have the seven lamps throw their light in front of the menorah." [3]Aaron did so, setting up the menorah-lamps to face the area in front of the menorah, just as the Lord had commanded Moses. [4]This is the construction of the menorah: hammered gold, from its base to its bowls it was hammered; according to the pattern which the Lord had shown Moses, so he made the menorah.

Purification of the Levites. [5]The Lord said to Moses: [6]Take the Levites from among the Israelites and cleanse them. [7]This is what you shall do to them to cleanse them. Sprinkle them with the water of purification, have them shave their whole bodies and wash their garments, and so cleanse themselves. [8]Then they shall take a bull from the herd, along with its grain offering of bran flour mixed with oil; and you shall take another bull from the herd for a purification offering. [9]Bringing the Levites before the tent of meeting, you shall assemble also the whole community of the Israelites. [10]When you have brought the Levites before the Lord, the Israelites shall lay their hands upon them. [11]Aaron shall then present the Levites before the Lord as an elevated offering from the Israelites, that they may perform the service of the Lord. [12]The Levites in turn shall lay their hands on the heads of the bulls, offering one as a purification offering and the other as a burnt offering to the Lord, to make atonement for the Levites. [13]Then you shall have the Levites stand before Aaron and his sons, and you shall present them as an elevated offering to the Lord; [14]thus you shall separate the Levites from the rest of the Israelites, and the Levites shall belong to me.

[15]Only then shall the Levites enter upon their service in the tent of meeting, when you have cleansed them and presented them as an elevated offering. [16]For they, among the Israelites, are totally dedicated to me; I have taken them for myself in place of everyone that opens the womb, the

firstborn of all the Israelites. ¹⁷Indeed, all the firstborn among the Israelites, human being and beast alike, belong to me; I consecrated them to myself on the day I killed all the firstborn in the land of Egypt. ¹⁸But I have taken the Levites in place of all the firstborn Israelites; ¹⁹and from among the Israelites I have given to Aaron and his sons these Levites, who are to be dedicated, to perform the service of the Israelites in the tent of meeting and to make atonement for them, so that no plague may strike among the Israelites should they come too near the sanctuary.

²⁰This, then, is what Moses and Aaron and the whole community of the Israelites did with respect to the Levites; the Israelites did exactly as the LORD had commanded Moses concerning them. ²¹When the Levites had purified themselves and washed their garments, Aaron presented them as an elevated offering before the LORD, and made atonement for them to cleanse them. ²²Only then did they enter upon their service in the tent of meeting under the supervision of Aaron and his sons. Exactly as the LORD had commanded Moses concerning the Levites, so it was done with regard to them.

Age Limits for Levitical Service. ²³The LORD said to Moses: ²⁴This is the rule for the Levites. Everyone twenty-five years old or more shall join the personnel in the service of the tent of meeting. ²⁵But everyone fifty on up shall retire from the work force and serve no more. ²⁶They shall assist their fellow Levites in the tent of meeting in performing their duties, but they shall not do the work. This, then, is how you are to regulate the duties of the Levites.

Second Passover. 9:1 The LORD said to Moses in the wilderness of Sinai, in the first month of the second year following their departure from the land of Egypt: ²Tell the Israelites to celebrate the Passover at the prescribed time. ³In the evening twilight of the fourteenth day of this month you shall celebrate it at its prescribed time, in accord with all its statutes and regulations. ⁴So Moses told the Israelites to celebrate the Passover, ⁵and they did celebrate the Passover on the fourteenth day of the first month during the evening twilight in the wilderness of Sinai. Just as the LORD had commanded Moses, so the Israelites did.

⁶There were some, however, who were unclean because of a human corpse and so could not celebrate the Passover that day. These men came up to Moses and Aaron that same day ⁷and they said to them, "Although we are unclean because of a human corpse, why should we be deprived of presenting the LORD's offering at its prescribed time along with other Israelites?" ⁸Moses answered them, "Wait so that I can learn what the LORD will command in your regard."

⁹The LORD then said to Moses: ¹⁰Speak to the Israelites: "If any one of you or of your descendants is unclean because of a human corpse, or is absent on a journey, you may still celebrate the LORD's Passover. ¹¹But you shall celebrate it in the second month, on the fourteenth day of that month during the evening twilight, eating it with unleavened bread and bitter herbs, ¹²and not leaving any of it over till morning, nor breaking any of its bones, but observing all the statutes of the Passover. ¹³However, anyone who is clean and not away on a journey, who yet fails to celebrate the Passover, shall be cut off from the people, for not presenting the LORD's offering at the prescribed time. That person shall bear the consequences of this sin.

¹⁴"If an alien who lives among you would celebrate the LORD's Passover, it shall be celebrated according to the statutes and regulations for the Passover. You shall have the same law for the resident alien as for the native of the land."

The Fiery Cloud. ¹⁵On the day when the tabernacle was erected, the cloud covered the tabernacle, the tent of the covenant; but from evening until morning it took on the appearance of fire over the tabernacle. [16]It was always so: during the day the cloud covered the tabernacle and at night had the appearance of fire. [17]Whenever the cloud rose from the tent, the Israelites would break camp; wherever the cloud settled, the Israelites would pitch camp. [18]At the direction of the LORD the Israelites broke camp, and at the LORD's direction they pitched camp. As long as the cloud stayed over the tabernacle, they remained in camp.

[19]Even when the cloud lingered many days over the tabernacle, the Israelites kept the charge of the LORD and would not move on. [20]Yet if it happened the cloud was over the tabernacle only for a few days, at the direction of the LORD they stayed in camp; and at the LORD's direction they broke camp. [21]If it happened the cloud remained there only from evening until morning, when the cloud rose in the morning, they would break camp. Whether the cloud lifted during the day or the night they would then break camp. [22]Whether the cloud lingered over the tabernacle for two days or for a month or longer, the Israelites remained in camp and did not break camp; but when it lifted, they broke camp. [23]At the direction of the LORD they pitched camp, and at the LORD's direction they broke camp; they kept the charge of the LORD, as the LORD directed them through Moses.

The Silver Trumpets. 10:1 The LORD said to Moses: [2]Make two trumpets of silver, making them of hammered silver, for you to use in summoning the community and in breaking camp. [3]When both are blown, the whole community shall gather round you at the entrance of the tent of meeting; [4]but when one of them is blown, only the tribal leaders, the heads of the clans of Israel, shall gather round you. [5]When you sound the signal, those encamped on the east side shall break camp; [6]when you sound a second signal, those encamped on the south side shall break camp; when you sound a third signal, those encamped on the west side shall break camp; when you sound a fourth signal, those encamped on the north side shall break camp. Thus shall the signal be sounded for them to break camp. [7]But in calling forth an assembly you are to blow a blast, without sounding the signal.

[8]The sons of Aaron, the priests, shall blow the trumpets; this is prescribed forever for you and your descendants. [9]When in your own land you go to war against an enemy that is attacking you, you shall sound the alarm on the trumpets, and you shall be remembered before the LORD, your God, and be saved from your foes. [10]And when you rejoice on your festivals, and your new-moon feasts, you shall blow the trumpets over your burnt offerings and your communion sacrifices, so that this serves as a reminder of you before your God. I, the LORD, am your God.

Departure from Sinai. [11]In the second year, on the twentieth day of the second month, the cloud rose from the tabernacle of the covenant, [12]and the Israelites moved on from the wilderness of Sinai by stages, until the cloud came to rest in the wilderness of Paran.

[13]The first time that they broke camp at the direction of the LORD through Moses, [14]the divisional camp of the Judahites, arranged in companies, was the first to set out. Over its whole company was Nahshon, son of Amminadab, [15]with Nethanel, son of Zuar, over the company of the tribe of Issacharites, [16]and Eliab, son of Helon, over the company of the tribe of Zebulunites. [17]Then, after the tabernacle was dismantled, the Gershonites and Merarites who carried the tabernacle set out. [18]The divisional camp of the Reubenites, arranged in companies, was the next to set out. Over its whole company was Elizur, son of Shedeur,

¹⁹with Shelumiel, son of Zurishaddai, over the company of the tribe of Simeonites, ²⁰and Eliasaph, son of Reuel, over the company of the tribe of Gadites. ²¹The Kohathites, who carried the sacred objects, then set out. Before their arrival the tabernacle would be erected. ²²The divisional camp of the Ephraimites set out next, arranged in companies. Over its whole company was Elishama, son of Ammihud, ²³with Gamaliel, son of Pedahzur, over the company of the tribe of Manassites, ²⁴and Abidan, son of Gideoni, over the company of the tribe of Benjaminites. ²⁵Finally, as rear guard for all the camps, the divisional camp of the Danites set out, arranged in companies. Over its whole company was Ahiezer, son of Ammishaddai, ²⁶with Pagiel, son of Ochran, over the company of the tribe of Asherites, ²⁷and Ahira, son of Enan, over the company of the tribe of Naphtalites. ²⁸This was the order of march for the Israelites, company by company, when they set out.

Hobab as Guide. ²⁹Moses said to Hobab, son of Reuel the Midianite, Moses' father-in-law, "We are setting out for the place concerning which the LORD has said,

'I will give it to you.' Come with us, and we will be generous toward you, for the LORD has promised prosperity to Israel." ³⁰But he answered, "No, I will not come. I am going instead to the land of my birth." ³¹Moses said, "Please, do not leave us; you know where we can camp in the wilderness, and you can serve as our guide. ³²If you come with us, we will share with you the prosperity the LORD will bestow on us."

Into the Wilderness. ³³From the mountain of the LORD they made a journey of three days, and the ark of the covenant of the LORD went before them for the three-day journey to seek out a resting place for them. ³⁴And the cloud of the LORD was over them by day when they set out from camp. ³⁵Whenever the ark set out, Moses would say,

"Arise, O LORD, may your enemies be
    scattered,
    and may those who hate you flee
        before you."

³⁶And when it came to rest, he would say,

"Bring back, O LORD, the myriads of
    Israel's troops!"

□ ROMANS 15

Patience and Self-Denial. 15:1 We who are strong ought to put up with the failings of the weak and not to please ourselves; ²let each of us please our neighbor for the good, for building up. ³For Christ did not please himself; but, as it is written, "The insults of those who insult you fall upon me." ⁴For whatever was written previously was written for our instruction, that by endurance and by the encouragement of the scriptures we might have hope. ⁵May the God of endurance and encouragement grant you to think in harmony with one another, in keeping with Christ Jesus, ⁶that with one accord you may with one voice glorify the God and Father of our Lord Jesus Christ.

God's Fidelity and Mercy. ⁷Welcome one another, then, as Christ welcomed you, for the glory of God. ⁸For I say that Christ became a minister of the circumcised to show God's truthfulness, to confirm the promises to the patriarchs, ⁹but so that the Gentiles might glorify God for his mercy. As it is written:

"Therefore, I will praise you among the
    Gentiles
    and sing praises to your name."

¹⁰And again it says:

"Rejoice, O Gentiles, with his people."

[11]And again:

"Praise the Lord, all you Gentiles,
and let all the peoples praise him."

[12]And again Isaiah says:

"The root of Jesse shall come,
raised up to rule the Gentiles;
in him shall the Gentiles hope."

[13]May the God of hope fill you with all joy and peace in believing, so that you may abound in hope by the power of the holy Spirit.

Apostle to the Gentiles. [14]I myself am convinced about you, my brothers, that you yourselves are full of goodness, filled with all knowledge, and able to admonish one another. [15]But I have written to you rather boldly in some respects to remind you, because of the grace given me by God [16]to be a minister of Christ Jesus to the Gentiles in performing the priestly service of the gospel of God, so that the offering up of the Gentiles may be acceptable, sanctified by the holy Spirit. [17]In Christ Jesus, then, I have reason to boast in what pertains to God. [18]For I will not dare to speak of anything except what Christ has accomplished through me to lead the Gentiles to obedience by word and deed, [19]by the power of signs and wonders, by the power of the Spirit [of God], so that from Jerusalem all the way around to Illyricum I have finished preaching the gospel of Christ. [20]Thus I aspire to proclaim the gospel not where Christ has already been named, so that I do not build on another's foundation, [21]but as it is written:

"Those who have never been told of
him shall see,
and those who have never heard of
him shall understand."

Paul's Plans; Need for Prayers. [22]That is why I have so often been prevented from coming to you. [23]But now, since I no longer have any opportunity in these regions and since I have desired to come to you for many years, [24]I hope to see you in passing as I go to Spain and to be sent on my way there by you, after I have enjoyed being with you for a time. [25]Now, however, I am going to Jerusalem to minister to the holy ones. [26]For Macedonia and Achaia have decided to make some contribution for the poor among the holy ones in Jerusalem; [27]they decided to do it, and in fact they are indebted to them, for if the Gentiles have come to share in their spiritual blessings, they ought also to serve them in material blessings. [28]So when I have completed this and safely handed over this contribution to them, I shall set out by way of you to Spain; [29]and I know that in coming to you I shall come in the fullness of Christ's blessing.

[30]I urge you, [brothers,] by our Lord Jesus Christ and by the love of the Spirit, to join me in the struggle by your prayers to God on my behalf, [31]that I may be delivered from the disobedient in Judea, and that my ministry for Jerusalem may be acceptable to the holy ones, [32]so that I may come to you with joy by the will of God and be refreshed together with you. [33]The God of peace be with all of you. Amen.

February 25

Heresies have often arisen and still arise because of this: Perverted minds have no peace, and faithless dissidents will not maintain unity. But the Lord endures and allows these things, while we still have the opportunity to choose freely, so that as the discernment of truth is testing our hearts and minds, the sound faith of those who are approved may shine clearly.

— St. Cyprian of Carthage

☐ NUMBERS 11-14

Discontent of the People. 11:1 Now the people complained bitterly in the hearing of the LORD; and when he heard it his wrath flared up, so that the LORD's fire burned among them and consumed the outskirts of the camp. ²But when the people cried out to Moses, he prayed to the LORD and the fire died out. ³Hence that place was called Taberah, because there the fire of the LORD burned among them.

⁴The riffraff among them were so greedy for meat that even the Israelites lamented again, "If only we had meat for food! ⁵We remember the fish we used to eat without cost in Egypt, and the cucumbers, the melons, the leeks, the onions, and the garlic. ⁶But now we are famished; we have nothing to look forward to but this manna."

⁷Manna was like coriander seed and had the appearance of bdellium. ⁸When they had gone about and gathered it up, the people would grind it between millstones or pound it in a mortar, then cook it in a pot and make it into loaves, with a rich creamy taste. ⁹At night, when the dew fell upon the camp, the manna also fell.

¹⁰When Moses heard the people, family after family, crying at the entrance of their tents, so that the LORD became very angry, he was grieved. ¹¹"Why do you treat your servant so badly?" Moses asked the LORD. "Why are you so displeased with me that you burden me with all this people? ¹²Was it I who conceived all this people? or was it I who gave them birth, that you tell me to carry them at my breast, like a nurse carrying an infant, to the land you have promised under oath to their fathers? ¹³Where can I get meat to give to all this people? For they are crying to me, 'Give us meat for our food.' ¹⁴I cannot carry all this people by myself, for they are too heavy for me. ¹⁵If this is the way you will deal with me, then please do me the favor of killing me at once, so that I need no longer face my distress."

The Seventy Elders. ¹⁶Then the LORD said to Moses: Assemble for me seventy of the elders of Israel, whom you know to be elders and authorities among the people, and bring them to the tent of meeting. When they are in place beside you, ¹⁷I will come down and speak with you there. I will also take some of the spirit that is on you and will confer it on them, that they may share the burden of the people with you. You will then not have to bear it by yourself.

¹⁸To the people, however, you shall say: "Sanctify yourselves for tomorrow, when you shall have meat to eat. For in the hearing of the LORD you have cried, 'If only we had meat for food! Oh, how well off we were in Egypt!' Therefore the LORD will give you meat to eat, ¹⁹and you will eat it, not for one day, or two days, or five, or ten, or twenty days, ²⁰but for a whole month— until it comes out of your very nostrils and becomes loathsome to you. For you have rejected the LORD who is in your midst,

and in his presence you have cried, 'Why did we ever leave Egypt?'"

²¹But Moses said, "The people around me include six hundred thousand soldiers; yet you say, 'I will give them meat to eat for a whole month.' ²²Can enough sheep and cattle be slaughtered for them? If all the fish of the sea were caught for them, would they have enough?" ²³The LORD answered Moses: Is this beyond the LORD's reach? You shall see now whether or not what I have said to you takes place.

The Spirit on the Elders. ²⁴So Moses went out and told the people what the LORD had said. Gathering seventy elders of the people, he had them stand around the tent. ²⁵The LORD then came down in the cloud and spoke to him. Taking some of the spirit that was on Moses, he bestowed it on the seventy elders; and as the spirit came to rest on them, they prophesied but did not continue.

²⁶Now two men, one named Eldad and the other Medad, had remained in the camp, yet the spirit came to rest on them also. They too had been on the list, but had not gone out to the tent; and so they prophesied in the camp. ²⁷So, when a young man ran and reported to Moses, "Eldad and Medad are prophesying in the camp," ²⁸Joshua, son of Nun, who from his youth had been Moses' aide, said, "My lord, Moses, stop them." ²⁹But Moses answered him, "Are you jealous for my sake? If only all the people of the LORD were prophets! If only the LORD would bestow his spirit on them!" ³⁰Then Moses retired to the camp, along with the elders of Israel.

The Quail. ³¹There arose a wind from the LORD that drove in quail from the sea and left them all around the camp site, to a distance of a day's journey and at a depth of two cubits upon the ground. ³²So all that day, all night, and all the next day the people set about to gather in the quail. Even the one who got the least gathered ten homers of them. Then they spread them out all around the camp. ³³But while the meat was still between their teeth, before it could be chewed, the LORD's wrath flared up against the people, and the LORD struck them with a very great plague. ³⁴So that place was named Kibroth-hattaavah, because it was there that the greedy people were buried.

³⁵From Kibroth-hattaavah the people set out for Hazeroth, where they stayed.

Jealousy of Aaron and Miriam. 12:1 Miriam and Aaron spoke against Moses on the pretext of the Cushite woman he had married; for he had in fact married a Cushite woman. ²They complained, "Is it through Moses alone that the LORD has spoken? Has he not spoken through us also?" And the LORD heard this. ³Now the man Moses was very humble, more than anyone else on earth. ⁴So at once the LORD said to Moses and Aaron and Miriam: Come out, you three, to the tent of meeting. And the three of them went. ⁵Then the LORD came down in a column of cloud, and standing at the entrance of the tent, called, "Aaron and Miriam." When both came forward, ⁶the LORD said: Now listen to my words:

If there are prophets among you,
in visions I reveal myself to them,
in dreams I speak to them;
⁷Not so with my servant Moses!
Throughout my house he is worthy of
trust:
⁸face to face I speak to him,
plainly and not in riddles.
The likeness of the LORD he beholds.

Why, then, do you not fear to speak against my servant Moses? ⁹And so the LORD's wrath flared against them, and he departed.

Miriam's Punishment. ¹⁰Now the cloud withdrew from the tent, and there was Miriam, stricken with a scaly infection, white as snow! When Aaron turned toward Miriam and saw her stricken with snow-white scales,

[11]he said to Moses, "Ah, my lord! Please do not charge us with the sin that we have foolishly committed! [12]Do not let her be like the stillborn baby that comes forth from its mother's womb with its flesh half consumed." [13]Then Moses cried to the LORD, "Please, not this! Please, heal her!" [14]But the LORD answered Moses: Suppose her father had spit in her face, would she not bear her shame for seven days? Let her be confined outside the camp for seven days; afterwards she may be brought back. [15]So Miriam was confined outside the camp for seven days, and the people did not start out again until she was brought back.

[16]After that the people set out from Hazeroth and encamped in the wilderness of Paran.

The Twelve Scouts. 13:1 The LORD said to Moses: [2]Send men to reconnoiter the land of Canaan, which I am giving the Israelites. You shall send one man from each ancestral tribe, every one a leader among them. [3]So Moses sent them from the wilderness of Paran, at the direction of the LORD. All of them were leaders among the Israelites. [4]These were their names:

from the tribe of Reuben, Shammua, son of Zaccur;

[5]from the tribe of Simeon, Shaphat, son of Hori;

[6]from the tribe of Judah, Caleb, son of Jephunneh;

[7]from the tribe of Issachar, Igal;

[8]for the Josephites, from the tribe of Ephraim, Hoshea, son of Nun;

[9]from the tribe of Benjamin, Palti, son of Raphu;

[10]from the tribe of Zebulun, Gaddiel, son of Sodi;

[11]for the Josephites, from the tribe of Manasseh, Gaddi, son of Susi;

[12]from the tribe of Dan, Ammiel, son of Gemalli;

[13]from the tribe of Asher, Sethur, son of Michael;

[14]from the tribe of Naphtali, Nahbi, son of Vophsi;

[15]from the tribe of Gad, Geuel, son of Machi.

[16]These are the names of the men whom Moses sent to reconnoiter the land. But Hoshea, son of Nun, Moses called Joshua.

[17]In sending them to reconnoiter the land of Canaan, Moses said to them, "Go up there in the Negeb, up into the highlands, [18]and see what kind of land it is and whether the people living there are strong or weak, few or many. [19]Is the country in which they live good or bad? Are the towns in which they dwell open or fortified? [20]Is the soil fertile or barren, wooded or clear? And do your best to get some of the fruit of the land." It was then the season for early grapes.

[21]So they went up and reconnoitered the land from the wilderness of Zin as far as where Rehob adjoins Lebo-hamath. [22]Going up by way of the Negeb, they reached Hebron, where Ahiman, Sheshai and Talmai, descendants of the Anakim, were. (Now Hebron had been built seven years before Zoan in Egypt.) [23]They also reached the Wadi Eshcol, where they cut down a branch with a single cluster of grapes on it, which two of them carried on a pole, as well as some pomegranates and figs. [24]It was because of the cluster the Israelites cut there that they called the place Wadi Eshcol.

Their Report. [25]They returned from reconnoitering the land forty days later. [26]Proceeding directly to Moses and Aaron and the whole community of the Israelites in the wilderness of Paran at Kadesh, they made a report to them and to the whole community, showing them the fruit of the land. [27]They told Moses: "We came to the land to which you sent us. It does indeed flow with milk and honey, and here is its fruit. [28]However, the people who are living in the land are powerful, and the towns are fortified and very large. Besides, we saw descendants of the Anakim there. [29]Amalekites live in the region of the Negeb; Hittites, Jebusites and Amorites dwell in the highlands, and Canaanites along the sea and the banks of the Jordan."

³⁰Caleb, however, quieted the people before Moses and said, "We ought to go up and seize the land, for we can certainly prevail over it." ³¹But the men who had gone up with him said, "We cannot attack these people; they are too strong for us." ³²They spread discouraging reports among the Israelites about the land they had reconnoitered, saying, "The land that we went through and reconnoitered is a land that consumes its inhabitants. And all the people we saw there are huge. ³³There we saw the Nephilim (the Anakim are from the Nephilim); in our own eyes we seemed like mere grasshoppers, and so we must have seemed to them."

Threats of Revolt. 14:1 At this, the whole community broke out with loud cries, and the people wept into the night. ²All the Israelites grumbled against Moses and Aaron, the whole community saying to them, "If only we had died in the land of Egypt," or "If only we would die here in the wilderness! ³Why is the Lord bringing us into this land only to have us fall by the sword? Our wives and little ones will be taken as spoil. Would it not be better for us to return to Egypt?" ⁴So they said to one another, "Let us appoint a leader and go back to Egypt."

⁵But Moses and Aaron fell prostrate before the whole assembled community of the Israelites; ⁶while Joshua, son of Nun, and Caleb, son of Jephunneh, who had been among those that reconnoitered the land, tore their garments ⁷and said to the whole community of the Israelites, "The land which we went through and reconnoitered is an exceedingly good land. ⁸If the Lord is pleased with us, he will bring us in to this land and give it to us, a land which flows with milk and honey. ⁹Only do not rebel against the Lord! You need not be afraid of the people of the land, for they are but food for us! Their protection has left them, but the Lord is with us. Do not fear them."

The Lord's Sentence. ¹⁰The whole community threatened to stone them. But the glory of the Lord appeared at the tent of meeting to all the Israelites. ¹¹And the Lord said to Moses: How long will this people spurn me? How long will they not trust me, despite all the signs I have performed among them? ¹²I will strike them with pestilence and disown them. Then I will make of you a nation greater and mightier than they.

¹³But Moses said to the Lord: "The Egyptians will hear of this, for by your power you brought out this people from among them. ¹⁴They will tell the inhabitants of this land, who have heard that you, Lord, are in the midst of this people; you, Lord, who directly revealed yourself! Your cloud stands over them, and you go before them by day in a column of cloud and by night in a column of fire. ¹⁵If now you slay this people all at once, the nations who have heard such reports of you will say, ¹⁶'The Lord was not able to bring this people into the land he swore to give them; that is why he slaughtered them in the wilderness.' ¹⁷Now then, may my Lord's forbearance be great, even as you have said, ¹⁸'The Lord is slow to anger and abounding in kindness, forgiving iniquity and rebellion; yet certainly not declaring the guilty guiltless, but punishing children to the third and fourth generation for their parents' iniquity.' ¹⁹Pardon, then, the iniquity of this people in keeping with your great kindness, even as you have forgiven them from Egypt until now."

²⁰The Lord answered: I pardon them as you have asked. ²¹Yet, by my life and the Lord's glory that fills the whole earth, ²²of all the people who have seen my glory and the signs I did in Egypt and in the wilderness, and who nevertheless have put me to the test ten times already and have not

obeyed me, ²³not one shall see the land which I promised on oath to their ancestors. None of those who have spurned me shall see it. ²⁴But as for my servant Caleb, because he has a different spirit and follows me unreservedly, I will bring him into the land which he entered, and his descendants shall possess it. ²⁵But now, since the Amalekites and Canaanites are living in the valleys, turn away tomorrow and set out into the wilderness by way of the Red Sea road.

²⁶The LORD also said to Moses and Aaron: ²⁷How long will this wicked community grumble against me? I have heard the grumblings of the Israelites against me. ²⁸Tell them: "By my life"—oracle of the LORD—"I will do to you just what I have heard you say. ²⁹Here in the wilderness your dead bodies shall fall. Of all your men of twenty years or more, enrolled in your registration, who grumbled against me, ³⁰not one of you shall enter the land where I solemnly swore to settle you, except Caleb, son of Jephunneh, and Joshua, son of Nun. ³¹Your little ones, however, who you said would be taken as spoil, I will bring in, and they shall know the land you rejected. ³²But as for you, your bodies shall fall here in the wilderness, ³³while your children will wander for forty years, suffering for your infidelity, till the last of you lies dead in the wilderness. ³⁴Corresponding to the number of days you spent reconnoitering the land—forty days—you shall bear your punishment one year for each day: forty years. Thus you will realize what it means to oppose me. ³⁵I, the LORD, have spoken; and I will surely do this to this entire wicked community that conspired against me: here in the wilderness they shall come to their end and there they will die."

³⁶And the men whom Moses had sent to reconnoiter the land and who on returning had set the whole community grumbling against him by spreading discouraging reports about the land— ³⁷these men who had spread discouraging reports about the land were struck down by the LORD and died. ³⁸Only Joshua, son of Nun, and Caleb, son of Jephunneh, survived of all the men who had gone to reconnoiter the land.

Unsuccessful Invasion. ³⁹When Moses repeated these words to all the Israelites, the people mourned greatly. ⁴⁰Early the next morning they started up high into the hill country, saying, "Here we are, ready to go up to the place that the LORD spoke of: for we did wrong." ⁴¹But Moses said, "Why are you now transgressing the LORD's order? This cannot succeed. ⁴²Do not go up, because the LORD is not in your midst; do not allow yourself to be struck down by your enemies. ⁴³For there the Amalekites and Canaanites will face you, and you will fall by the sword. You have turned back from following the LORD; therefore the LORD will not be with you."

⁴⁴Yet they dared to go up high into the hill country, even though neither the ark of the covenant of the LORD nor Moses left the camp. ⁴⁵And the Amalekites and Canaanites who dwelt in that hill country came down and defeated them, beating them back as far as Hormah.

☐ ROMANS 16

Phoebe Commended. 16:1 I commend to you Phoebe our sister, who is [also] a minister of the church at Cenchreae, ²that you may receive her in the Lord in a manner worthy of the holy ones, and help her in whatever she may need from you, for she has been a benefactor to many and to me as well.

Paul's Greetings. ³Greet Prisca and Aquila, my co-workers in Christ Jesus, ⁴who risked their necks for my life, to whom not only I am grateful but also all the churches of the Gentiles; [5]greet also the church at their house. Greet my beloved Epaenetus, who was the firstfruits in Asia for Christ. [6]Greet Mary, who has worked hard for you. [7]Greet Andronicus and Junia, my relatives and my fellow prisoners; they are prominent among the apostles and they were in Christ before me. [8]Greet Ampliatus, my beloved in the Lord. [9]Greet Urbanus, our co-worker in Christ, and my beloved Stachys. [10]Greet Apelles, who is approved in Christ. Greet those who belong to the family of Aristobulus. [11]Greet my relative Herodion. Greet those in the Lord who belong to the family of Narcissus. [12]Greet those workers in the Lord, Tryphaena and Tryphosa. Greet the beloved Persis, who has worked hard in the Lord. [13]Greet Rufus, chosen in the Lord, and his mother and mine. [14]Greet Asyncritus, Phlegon, Hermes, Patrobas, Hermas, and the brothers who are with them. [15]Greet Philologus, Julia, Nereus and his sister, and Olympas, and all the holy ones who are with them. [16]Greet one another with a holy kiss. All the churches of Christ greet you.

Against Factions. [17]I urge you, brothers, to watch out for those who create dissensions and obstacles, in opposition to the teaching that you learned; avoid them. [18]For such people do not serve our Lord Christ but their own appetites, and by fair and flattering speech they deceive the hearts of the innocent. [19]For while your obedience is known to all, so that I rejoice over you, I want you to be wise as to what is good, and simple as to what is evil; [20]then the God of peace will quickly crush Satan under your feet. The grace of our Lord Jesus be with you.

Greetings from Corinth. [21]Timothy, my co-worker, greets you; so do Lucius and Jason and Sosipater, my relatives. [22]I, Tertius, the writer of this letter, greet you in the Lord. [23]Gaius, who is host to me and to the whole church, greets you. Erastus, the city treasurer, and our brother Quartus greet you. [24]

Doxology. [25][Now to him who can strengthen you, according to my gospel and the proclamation of Jesus Christ, according to the revelation of the mystery kept secret for long ages [26]but now manifested through the prophetic writings and, according to the command of the eternal God, made known to all nations to bring about the obedience of faith, [27]to the only wise God, through Jesus Christ be glory forever and ever. Amen.]

February 26

Those who share in Christ's blood have taken their stand with angels, and archangels, and the powers from on high, clad in the royal uniform of Christ with spiritual weapons in their hands. Yet greater still than that: They are wearing the King himself!
— St. John Chrysostom

☐ NUMBERS 15-18

Secondary Offerings. 15:1 The LORD spoke to Moses: [2]Speak to the Israelites and say to them: When you enter the land that I am giving you for your settlements, [3]if you make to the LORD an oblation from the herd or from the flock—either a burnt offering or a sacrifice, to fulfill a vow, or as a voluntary offering, or for one of your festivals—to produce a pleasing aroma for the LORD, [4]the one presenting the offering shall also present to the LORD a grain offering, a tenth of a measure of bran flour mixed with a fourth of a hin of oil, [5]as well as wine for a libation, a fourth of a hin. You will do this with the burnt offering or the sacrifice, for each lamb. [6]Alternatively for a ram you shall make a grain offering of two tenths of a measure of bran flour mixed with a third of a hin of oil, [7]and for a libation, a third of a hin of wine, thereby presenting a pleasing aroma to the LORD. [8]If you make an offering from the herd—either a burnt offering, or a sacrifice, to fulfill a vow, or as a communion offering to the LORD, [9]with it a grain offering of three tenths of a measure of bran flour mixed with half a hin of oil will be presented; [10]and you will present for a libation, half a hin of wine—a sweet-smelling oblation to the LORD. [11]The same is to be done for each ox, ram, lamb or goat. [12]Whatever the number you offer, do the same for each of them.

[13]All the native-born shall make these offerings in this way, whenever they present a sweet-smelling oblation to the LORD. [14]Likewise, in any future generation, any alien residing with you or anyone else in your midst, who presents an oblation of pleasing aroma to the LORD, must do as you do. [15]There is but one statute for you and for the resident alien, a perpetual statute throughout your generations. You and the resident alien will be alike before the LORD; [16]you and the alien residing with you will have the same rule and the same application of it.

[17]The LORD spoke to Moses: [18]Speak to the Israelites and say to them: When you enter the land into which I am bringing you [19]and eat of the bread of the land, you shall offer the LORD a contribution. [20]A round loaf from your first batch of dough you shall offer as a contribution. Just like a contribution from the threshing floor you shall offer it. [21]Throughout your generations you shall give a contribution to the LORD from your first batch of dough.

Purification Offerings. [22]If through inadvertence you fail to do any of these commandments which the LORD has given to Moses— [23]anything the LORD commanded you through Moses from the time the LORD first gave the command down through your generations— [24]if it was done inadvertently without the community's knowledge, the whole community shall sacrifice one bull from the herd as a burnt offering of pleasing aroma to the LORD, along with its prescribed grain offering and libation, as well as one he-goat as a purification offering. [25]Then the priest shall make atonement for the whole Israelite community; and they will be forgiven, since it was inadvertence, and for their inadvertence they have brought their offering: an oblation to the LORD as well as their purification offering before the LORD. [26]Not only the whole Israelite community but also the aliens residing among you shall be forgiven, since the inadvertent fault affects all the people.

[27]If it is an individual who sins inadvertently, this person shall bring a yearling she-goat as a purification offering. [28]And the priest shall make atonement before the LORD for the one who erred, since the sin was inadvertent, making atonement for the person to secure forgiveness. [29]You shall have but one rule for the person who sins inadvertently, whether a native-born Israelite or an alien residing among you.

[30]But anyone who acts defiantly, whether a native or an alien, reviles the LORD, and shall be cut off from among the people. [31]For having despised the word of the LORD and broken his commandment, he must be cut off entirely and bear the punishment.

The Sabbath-breaker. [32]While the Israelites were in the wilderness, a man was discovered gathering wood on the sabbath day. [33]Those who caught him at it brought him to Moses and Aaron and the whole community. [34]But they put him in custody, for there was no clear decision as to what should be done with him. [35]Then the LORD said to Moses: This man shall be put to death; let the whole community stone him outside the camp. [36]So the whole community led him outside the camp and stoned him to death, as the LORD had commanded Moses.

Tassels on the Cloak. [37]The LORD said to Moses: [38]Speak to the Israelites and tell them that throughout their generations they are to make tassels for the corners of their garments, fastening a violet cord to each corner. [39]When you use these tassels, the sight of the cord will remind you of all the commandments of the LORD and you will do them, without prostituting yourself going after the desires of your hearts and your eyes. [40]Thus you will remember to do all my commandments and you will be holy to your God. [41]I, the LORD, am your God who brought you out of the land of Egypt to be your God: I, the LORD your God.

Rebellion of Korah. 16:1 Korah, son of Izhar, son of Kohath, son of Levi, and the Reubenites Dathan and Abiram, sons of Eliab, and On, son of Peleth, son of Reuben took [2]two hundred and fifty Israelites who were leaders in the community, members of the council and men of note, and confronted Moses. [3]Holding an assembly against Moses and Aaron, they said, "You go too far! The whole community, all of them, are holy; the LORD is in their midst. Why then should you set yourselves over the LORD's assembly?"

[4]When Moses heard this, he fell prostrate. [5]Then he said to Korah and to all his faction, "May the LORD make known tomorrow morning who belongs to him and who is the holy one and whom he will have draw near to him! The one whom he chooses, he will have draw near to him. [6]Do this: take your censers, Korah and all his faction, [7]and put fire in them and place incense in them before the LORD tomorrow. He whom the LORD then chooses is the holy one. You Levites go too far!"

[8]Moses also said to Korah, "Hear, now, you Levites! [9]Are you not satisfied that the God of Israel has singled you out from the community of Israel, to have you draw near him to maintain the LORD's tabernacle, and to attend upon the community and to serve them? [10]He has allowed you and your Levite kinsmen with you to approach him, and yet you seek the priesthood too. [11]It is therefore against the LORD that you and all your faction are conspiring. As for Aaron, what has he done that you should grumble against him?"

Rebellion of Dathan and Abiram. [12]Moses summoned Dathan and Abiram, sons of Eliab, but they answered, "We will not go. [13]Are you not satisfied that you have brought us here from a land flowing with milk and honey to have us perish in the wilderness, that now you must also lord it over us? [14]Far from bringing us to a land flowing with milk and honey, or giving us fields and vineyards for our inheritance, will you gouge out our eyes? No, we will not go."

[15]Then Moses became very angry and said to the LORD, "Pay no attention to their offering. I have never taken a single donkey from them, nor have I wronged any one of them."

Korah. [16]Moses said to Korah, "You and all your faction shall appear before the LORD tomorrow—you and they and Aaron too. [17]Then each of you take his own censer, put incense in it, and present it before the LORD, two hundred and fifty censers; and you and Aaron, each with his own censer, do the same." [18]So each of them took their censers, and laying incense on the fire they had put in them, they took their stand by the entrance of the tent of meeting along with Moses and Aaron. [19]Then, when Korah had assembled all the community against them at the entrance of the tent of meeting, the glory of the LORD appeared to the entire community, ²⁰and the LORD said to Moses and Aaron: ²¹Stand apart from this community, that I may consume them at once. ²²But they fell prostrate and exclaimed, "O God, God of the spirits of all living creatures, if one man sins will you be angry with the whole community?" ²³The LORD answered Moses: ²⁴Speak to the community and tell them: Withdraw from the area around the tent of Korah, Dathan and Abiram.

Punishment of Dathan and Abiram.
²⁵Moses, followed by the elders of Israel, arose and went to Dathan and Abiram. ²⁶Then he spoke to the community, "Move away from the tents of these wicked men and do not touch anything that is theirs: otherwise you too will be swept away because of all their sins." ²⁷So they withdrew from the area around the tents of Korah, Dathan and Abiram. When Dathan and Abiram had come out and were standing at the entrance of their tents with their wives, their children, and their little ones, ²⁸Moses said, "This is how you shall know that the LORD sent me to do all I have done, and that it was not of my own devising: ²⁹if these die an ordinary death, merely suffering the fate common to all humanity, the LORD has not sent me. ³⁰But if the LORD makes a chasm, and the ground opens its mouth and swallows them with all belonging to them, and they go down alive to Sheol, then you will know that these men have spurned the LORD." ³¹No sooner had he finished saying all this than the ground beneath them split open, ³²and the earth opened its mouth and swallowed them and their families and all of Korah's people with all their possessions. ³³They went down alive to Sheol with all belonging to them; the earth closed over them, and they disappeared from the assembly. ³⁴But all the Israelites near them fled at their shrieks, saying, "The earth might swallow us too!"

Punishment of Korah. ³⁵And fire from the LORD came forth which consumed the two hundred and fifty men who were offering the incense.

17:1 The LORD said to Moses: ²Tell Eleazar, son of Aaron the priest, to remove the censers from the embers; and scatter the fire some distance away, for they have become holy— ³the censers of those who sinned at the cost of their lives. Have them hammered into plates to cover the altar, because in being presented before the LORD they have become holy. In this way they shall serve as a sign to the Israelites. ⁴So taking the bronze censers which had been presented by those who were burned, Eleazar the priest had them hammered into a covering for the altar, ⁵just as the LORD had directed him through Moses. This was to be a reminder to the Israelites that no unauthorized person, no one who was not a descendant of Aaron, should draw near to offer incense before the LORD, lest he meet the fate of Korah and his faction.

⁶The next day the whole Israelite community grumbled against Moses and Aaron, saying, "You have killed the people of the LORD." ⁷But while the community was assembling against them, Moses and Aaron turned toward the tent of meeting, and the cloud now covered it and the glory of the LORD appeared. ⁸Then Moses and Aaron came to the front of the tent of meeting, ⁹and the LORD said to Moses: ¹⁰Remove yourselves from this community, that I may consume them at once. But they fell prostrate.

¹¹Then Moses said to Aaron, "Take your censer, put fire from the altar in it, lay incense on it, and bring it quickly to the community to make atonement for them; for wrath has come forth from the LORD and the plague has begun." ¹²Aaron took his censer just as Moses directed and ran in among the assembly, where the plague had already begun among the people. Then he offered the incense and made atonement

for the people, [13]while standing there between the living and the dead. And so the scourge was checked. [14]There were fourteen thousand seven hundred dead from the scourge, in addition to those who died because of Korah. [15]When the scourge had been checked, Aaron returned to Moses at the entrance of the tent of meeting.

Aaron's Staff. [16]The LORD now said to Moses: [17]Speak to the Israelites and get from them a staff for each ancestral house, twelve staffs in all, from all the leaders of their ancestral houses. Write each man's name on his staff; [18]and write Aaron's name on Levi's staff. For each head of an ancestral house shall have a staff. [19]Then deposit them in the tent of meeting, in front of the covenant, where I meet you. [20]The staff of the man whom I choose shall sprout. Thus I will rid myself of the Israelites' grumbling against you.

[21]So Moses spoke to the Israelites, and all their leaders gave him staffs, twelve in all, one from each leader of their ancestral houses; and Aaron's staff was among them. [22]Then Moses deposited the staffs before the LORD in the tent of the covenant. [23]The next day, when Moses entered the tent of the covenant, Aaron's staff, representing the house of Levi, had sprouted. It had put forth sprouts, produced blossoms, and borne ripe almonds! [24]So Moses brought out all the staffs from the LORD's presence to all the Israelites, and each one identified his own staff and took it. [25]Then the LORD said to Moses: Put back Aaron's staff in front of the covenant, for safe keeping as a sign to the rebellious, so that their grumbling against me may cease and they might not die. [26]Moses did this. Just as the LORD had commanded him, so he did.

Charge of the Sacred Things. [27]Then the Israelites exclaimed to Moses, "We will perish; we are lost, we are all lost! [28]Anyone who approaches the tabernacle of the LORD will die! Will there be no end to our perishing?"

18:1 The LORD said to Aaron: You and your sons as well as your ancestral house with you shall be responsible for any sin with respect to the sanctuary; but only you and your sons with you shall be responsible for any sin with respect to your priesthood. [2]You shall also present with you your kinsmen of the tribe of Levi, your ancestral tribe, that they may be joined to you and assist you, while you and your sons with you are in front of the tent of the covenant. [3]They shall discharge your obligations and those with respect to the whole tent; however, they shall not come near the utensils of the sanctuary or the altar, or else both they and you will die. [4]They will be joined to you to perform the duties associated with the tent of meeting, all the labor pertaining to the tent. But no unauthorized person shall come near you. [5]You shall perform the duties of the sanctuary and of the altar, that wrath may not fall again upon the Israelites.

[6]I hereby take your kinsmen, the Levites, from among the Israelites; they are a gift to you, dedicated to the LORD for the labor they perform for the tent of meeting. [7]But you and your sons with you must take care to exercise your priesthood in whatever concerns the altar and the area within the veil. I give you your priesthood as a gift. Any unauthorized person who comes near shall be put to death.

The Priests' Share of the Sacrifices. [8]The LORD said to Aaron: I hereby give to you charge of the contributions made to me, including the various holy offerings of the Israelites; I assign them to you and to your sons as a perquisite, a perpetual due. [9]This is what you shall have from the oblations that are most holy: every offering of theirs—namely, all their grain offerings, purification offerings, and reparation offerings which they must return to me—shall be most holy for you and for your sons. [10]You shall eat them in a most holy place; every male may partake of them. As holy, they belong to you.

[11]This also you shall have: the contributions that are their gifts, including the elevated offering of the Israelites; I assign them to you and to your sons and daughters with you as a perpetual due. All in your household who are clean may eat them. [12]I also assign to you all the best of the new oil and of the new wine and grain that they give to the LORD as their first produce that has been processed. [13]The first-ripened fruits of whatever is in their land, which they bring to the LORD, shall be yours; all of your household who are clean may eat them. [14]Whatever is under the ban in Israel shall be yours. [15]Every living thing that opens the womb, human being and beast alike, such as are to be offered to the LORD, shall be yours; but you must redeem the firstborn of human beings, as well as redeem the firstborn of unclean animals. [16]For the redemption price of a son, when he is a month old, you shall pay the equivalent of five silver shekels according to the sanctuary shekel, that is, twenty gerahs. [17]But the firstborn of cattle, or the firstborn of sheep or the firstborn of goats you shall not redeem; they are holy. Their blood you must splash on the altar and their fat you must burn as an oblation of pleasing aroma to the LORD. [18]Their meat, however, shall be yours, just as the brisket of the elevated offering and the right thigh belong to you. [19]As a perpetual due I assign to you and to your sons and daughters with you all the contributions of holy things which the Israelites set aside for the LORD; this is a covenant of salt to last forever before the LORD, for you and for your descendants with you. [20]Then the LORD said to Aaron: You shall not have any heritage in their land nor hold any portion among them; I will be your portion and your heritage among the Israelites.

Tithes Due the Levites. [21]To the Levites, however, I hereby assign all tithes in Israel as their heritage in recompense for the labor they perform, the labor pertaining to the tent of meeting. [22]The Israelites may no longer approach the tent of meeting, thereby incurring the penalty of death. [23]Only the Levites are to perform the labor pertaining to the tent of meeting, and they shall incur the penalty for the Israelites' sin; this is a permanent statute for all your generations. But they shall not have any heritage among the Israelites, [24]for I have assigned to the Levites as their heritage the tithes which the Israelites put aside as a contribution to the LORD. That is why I have said, they will not have any heritage among the Israelites.

Tithes Paid by the Levites. [25]The LORD said to Moses: [26]Speak to the Levites and say to them: When you take from the Israelites the tithes I have assigned you from them as your heritage, you are to make a contribution from them to the LORD, a tithe of the tithe; [27]and your contribution will be credited to you as if it were grain from the threshing floor or new wine from the vat. [28]Thus you too shall make a contribution to the LORD from all the tithes you take from the Israelites, handing over to Aaron the priest the contribution to the LORD. [29]From all the gifts to you, you shall make every contribution due to the LORD—from their best parts, that is the part to be consecrated from them.

[30]Say to them also: Once you have made your contribution from the best part, the rest of the tithe will be credited to the Levites as if it were produce of the threshing floor or the produce of the vat. [31]You and your households may eat it anywhere, since it is your recompense in exchange for labor in the tent of meeting. [32]You will incur no punishment when you contribute the best part of it. But do not profane the holy offerings of the Israelites or else you shall die.

☐ HEBREWS 1-2

1:1 In times past, God spoke in partial and various ways to our ancestors through the prophets; [2]in these last days, he spoke to us through a son, whom he made heir of all things and through whom he created the universe,

[3]who is the refulgence of his glory,
the very imprint of his being,
and who sustains all things by his
mighty word.
When he had accomplished
purification from sins,
he took his seat at the right hand of the
Majesty on high,
[4]as far superior to the angels
as the name he has inherited is more
excellent than theirs.

Messianic Enthronement. [5]For to which of the angels did God ever say:

"You are my son; this day I have
begotten you"?

Or again:

"I will be a father to him, and he shall
be a son to me"?

[6]And again, when he leads the first-born into the world, he says:

"Let all the angels of God worship him."

[7]Of the angels he says:

"He makes his angels winds
and his ministers a fiery flame";

[8]but of the Son:

"Your throne, O God, stands forever
and ever;
and a righteous scepter is the scepter
of your kingdom.
[9]You loved justice and hated wickedness;
therefore God, your God, anointed
you

with the oil of gladness above your
companions";

[10]and:

"At the beginning, O Lord, you
established the earth,
and the heavens are the works of
your hands.
[11]They will perish, but you remain;
and they will all grow old like a
garment.
[12]You will roll them up like a cloak,
and like a garment they will be
changed.
But you are the same, and your years
will have no end."

[13]But to which of the angels has he ever said:

"Sit at my right hand
until I make your enemies your
footstool"?

[14]Are they not all ministering spirits sent to serve, for the sake of those who are to inherit salvation?

Exhortation to Faithfulness. 2:1 Therefore, we must attend all the more to what we have heard, so that we may not be carried away. [2]For if the word announced through angels proved firm, and every transgression and disobedience received its just recompense, [3]how shall we escape if we ignore so great a salvation? Announced originally through the Lord, it was confirmed for us by those who had heard. [4]God added his testimony by signs, wonders, various acts of power, and distribution of the gifts of the holy Spirit according to his will.

Exaltation through Abasement. [5]For it was not to angels that he subjected the world to come, of which we are speaking. [6]Instead, someone has testified somewhere:

"What is man that you are mindful of
him,
  or the son of man that you care for
him?
[7]You made him for a little while lower
than the angels;
  you crowned him with glory and
honor,
[8]subjecting all things under his feet."

In "subjecting" all things [to him], he left
nothing not "subject to him." Yet at present
we do not see "all things subject to him,"
[9]but we do see Jesus "crowned with glory
and honor" because he suffered death, he
who "for a little while" was made "lower
than the angels," that by the grace of God
he might taste death for everyone.

[10]For it was fitting that he, for whom and
through whom all things exist, in bringing
many children to glory, should make the
leader to their salvation perfect through
suffering. [11]He who consecrates and those
who are being consecrated all have one
origin. Therefore, he is not ashamed to call
them "brothers," [12]saying:

"I will proclaim your name to my
brothers,
  in the midst of the assembly I will
praise you";

[13]and again:

"I will put my trust in him";

and again:

"Behold, I and the children God has
given me."

[14]Now since the children share in blood
and flesh, he likewise shared in them, that
through death he might destroy the one
who has the power of death, that is, the
devil, [15]and free those who through fear of
death had been subject to slavery all their
life. [16]Surely he did not help angels but
rather the descendants of Abraham; [17]there-
fore, he had to become like his brothers in
every way, that he might be a merciful and
faithful high priest before God to expiate
the sins of the people. [18]Because he himself
was tested through what he suffered, he is
able to help those who are being tested.

February 27

St. Gabriel Possenti

*I will attempt day by day to break my will into little pieces.
I want to do God's holy will, not my own!*

— St. Gabriel Possenti

☐ NUMBERS 19-21

Ashes of the Red Heifer. 19:1 The LORD
spoke to Moses and Aaron: [2]This is the
statute for the ritual which the LORD has
commanded. Tell the Israelites to procure
for you a red heifer without defect and free
from every blemish and on which no yoke
has ever been laid. [3]You will give it to Eleazar the priest, and it will be led outside
the camp and slaughtered in his presence.

[4]Eleazar the priest will take some of its
blood on his finger and sprinkle it seven
times toward the front of the tent of meeting. [5]Then the heifer will be burned in his
sight; it will be burned with its hide and
flesh, its blood and dung; [6]and the priest
will take cedar wood, hyssop and scarlet
yarn and throw them into the fire in which
the heifer is being burned. [7]The priest shall

then wash his garments and bathe his body in water, afterward he may enter the camp. The priest remains unclean until the evening. [8]Likewise, the one who burned the heifer shall wash his garments in water, bathe his body in water, and be unclean until evening. [9]Then somebody who is clean shall gather up the ashes of the heifer and deposit them in a clean place outside the camp. There they are to be kept to prepare purification water for the Israelite community. This is a purification offering. [10]The one who has gathered up the ashes of the heifer shall also wash his garments and be unclean until evening. This is a permanent statute, both for the Israelites and for the alien residing among them.

Use of the Ashes. [11]Those who touch the corpse of any human being will be unclean for seven days; [12]they shall purify themselves with the water on the third and on the seventh day, and then be clean. But if they fail to purify themselves on the third and on the seventh day, they will not become clean. [13]Those who touch the corpse of a human being who dies and who fail to purify themselves defile the tabernacle of the LORD and these persons shall be cut off from Israel. Since the purification water has not been splashed over them, they remain unclean: their uncleanness is still on them.

[14]This is the ritual: When someone dies in a tent, everyone who enters the tent, as well as everyone already in it, will be unclean for seven days; [15]and every open vessel with its lid unfastened will be unclean. [16]Moreover, everyone who in the open country touches a person who has been slain by the sword or who has died naturally, or who touches a human bone or a grave, will be unclean for seven days. [17]For anyone who is thus unclean, ashes shall be taken from the burnt purification offering, and spring water will be poured on them from a vessel. [18]Then someone who is clean will take hyssop, dip it in this water, and sprinkle it on the tent and on all the vessels and persons that were in it, or on the one who touched the bone, the slain person or the other corpse, or the grave. [19]The clean will sprinkle the unclean on the third and on the seventh day, and thus purify them on the seventh day. Then they will wash their garments and bathe in water, and in the evening be clean. [20]Those who become unclean and fail to purify themselves—those people will be cut off from the assembly, because they defile the sanctuary of the LORD. The purification water has not been splashed over them; they remain unclean. [21]This will be a permanent statute for you.

Those who sprinkle the purification water will wash their garments, and those who come in contact with the purification water will be unclean until evening. [22]Moreover, anything that the unclean person touches becomes unclean itself, and the one who touches such a person becomes unclean until evening.

Death of Miriam. 20:1 The Israelites, the whole community, arrived in the wilderness of Zin in the first month, and the people stayed at Kadesh. It was here that Miriam died, and here that she was buried.

Need for Water at Kadesh. [2]Since the community had no water, they held an assembly against Moses and Aaron. [3]The people quarreled with Moses, exclaiming, "Would that we had perished when our kindred perished before the LORD! [4]Why have you brought the LORD's assembly into this wilderness for us and our livestock to die here? [5]Why have you brought us up out of Egypt, only to bring us to this wretched place? It is not a place for grain nor figs nor vines nor pomegranates! And there is no water to drink!" [6]But Moses and Aaron went away from the assembly to the entrance of the tent of meeting, where they fell prostrate.

Sin of Moses and Aaron. Then the glory of the LORD appeared to them, [7]and the LORD said to Moses: [8]Take the staff and assemble the community, you and Aaron your brother, and in their presence command the rock to yield its waters. Thereby you will bring forth water from the rock for them, and supply the community and their livestock with water. [9]So Moses took the staff from its place before the LORD, as he was ordered. [10]Then Moses and Aaron gathered the assembly in front of the rock, where he said to them, "Just listen, you rebels! Are we to produce water for you out of this rock?" [11]Then, raising his hand, Moses struck the rock twice with his staff, and water came out in abundance, and the community and their livestock drank. [12]But the LORD said to Moses and Aaron: Because you did not have confidence in me, to acknowledge my holiness before the Israelites, therefore you shall not lead this assembly into the land I have given them.

[13]These are the waters of Meribah, where the Israelites quarreled with the LORD, and through which he displayed his holiness.

Edom's Refusal. [14]From Kadesh Moses sent messengers to the king of Edom: "Thus says your brother Israel: You know of all the hardships that have befallen us, [15]how our ancestors went down to Egypt, and we stayed in Egypt a long time, and the Egyptians treated us and our ancestors harshly. [16]When we cried to the LORD, he heard our cry and sent an angel who led us out of Egypt. Now here we are at Kadesh, a town at the edge of your territory. [17]Please let us pass through your land. We will not cross any fields or vineyards, nor drink any well water, but we will go straight along the King's Highway without turning to the right or to the left, until we have passed through your territory."

[18]But Edom answered him, "You shall not pass through here; if you do, I will advance against you with the sword." [19]The Israelites said to him, "We will go up along the highway. If we or our livestock drink any of your water, we will pay for it. It is noth-ing—just let us pass through on foot." [20]But Edom replied, "You shall not pass through," and advanced against them with a large and heavily armed force. [21]Therefore, since Edom refused to let Israel pass through their territory, Israel turned away from them.

Death of Aaron. [22]Setting out from Kadesh, the Israelites, the whole community, came to Mount Hor. [23]There at Mount Hor, on the border of the land of Edom, the LORD said to Moses and Aaron: [24]Let Aaron be gathered to his people, for he shall not enter the land I have given to the Israelites, because you both rebelled against my directions at the waters of Meribah. [25]Take Aaron and Eleazar his son and bring them up on Mount Hor. [26]Then strip Aaron of his garments and put them on Eleazar, his son; but there Aaron shall be gathered up in death.

[27]Moses did as the LORD commanded. When they had climbed Mount Hor in view of the whole community, [28]Moses stripped Aaron of his garments and put them on Eleazar his son. Then Aaron died there on top of the mountain. When Moses and Eleazar came down from the mountain, [29]all the community understood that Aaron had breathed his last; and for thirty days the whole house of Israel mourned Aaron.

Victory over Arad. 21:1 When the Canaanite, the king of Arad, who ruled over the Negeb, heard that the Israelites were coming along the way of Atharim, he engaged Israel in battle and took some of them captive. [2]Israel then made this vow to the LORD: "If you deliver this people into my hand, I will put their cities under the ban." [3]The LORD paid attention to Israel and delivered up the Canaanites, and they put them and their cities under the ban. Hence that place was named Hormah.

The Bronze Serpent. [4]From Mount Hor they set out by way of the Red Sea, to bypass the land of Edom, but the people's patience was worn out by the journey; [5]so the people complained against God and Moses, "Why have you brought us up from Egypt to die in the wilderness, where there is no food or water? We are disgusted with this wretched food!"

[6]So the LORD sent among the people seraph serpents, which bit the people so that many of the Israelites died. [7]Then the people came to Moses and said, "We have sinned in complaining against the LORD and you. Pray to the LORD to take the serpents from us." So Moses prayed for the people, [8]and the LORD said to Moses: Make a seraph and mount it on a pole, and everyone who has been bitten will look at it and recover. [9]Accordingly Moses made a bronze serpent and mounted it on a pole, and whenever the serpent bit someone, the person looked at the bronze serpent and recovered.

Journey Around Moab. [10]The Israelites moved on and encamped in Oboth. [11]Then they moved on from Oboth and encamped in Iye-abarim in the wilderness facing Moab on the east. [12]Moving on from there, they encamped in the Wadi Zered. [13]Moving on from there, they encamped on the other side of the Arnon, in the wilderness that extends from the territory of the Amorites; for the Arnon forms Moab's boundary, between Moab and the Amorites. [14]Hence it is said in the "Book of the Wars of the LORD":

> "Waheb in Suphah and the wadies,
> [15]Arnon and the wadi gorges
> That reach back toward the site of Ar
> and lean against the border of
> Moab."

[16]From there they went to Beer, which is the well of which the LORD said to Moses, Gather the people together so that I may give them water. [17]Then Israel sang this song:

> Spring up, O well!—so sing to it—
> [18]The well that the princes sank,
> that the nobles of the people dug,
> With their scepters and their
> staffs—
> from the wilderness, a gift.

[19]From Beer to Nahaliel, from Nahaliel to Bamoth, [20]from Bamoth to the valley in the country of Moab at the headland of Pisgah that overlooks Jeshimon.

Victory over Sihon. [21]Now Israel sent messengers to Sihon, king of the Amorites, with the message, [22]"Let us pass through your land. We will not turn aside into any field or vineyard, nor will we drink any well water, but we will go straight along the King's Highway until we have passed through your territory." [23]Sihon, however, would not permit Israel to pass through his territory, but mustered all his forces and advanced against Israel into the wilderness. When he reached Jahaz, he engaged Israel in battle. [24]But Israel put him to the sword, and took possession of his land from the Arnon to the Jabbok and as far as Jazer of the Ammonites, for Jazer is the boundary of the Ammonites. [25]Israel seized all the towns here, and Israel settled in all the towns of the Amorites, in Heshbon and all its dependencies. [26]For Heshbon was the city of Sihon, king of the Amorites, who had fought against the former king of Moab and had taken all his land from him as far as the Arnon. [27]That is why the poets say:

> "Come to Heshbon, let it be rebuilt,
> let Sihon's city be firmly
> constructed.
> [28]For fire went forth from Heshbon
> and a blaze from the city of
> Sihon;
> It consumed Ar of Moab
> and swallowed up the high places
> of the Arnon.
> [29]Woe to you, Moab!
> You are no more, people of
> Chemosh!
> He let his sons become fugitives
> and his daughters be taken captive
> by the Amorite king Sihon.

³⁰From Heshbon to Dibon their
dominion is no more;
Ar is laid waste; fires blaze as far as
Medeba."

³¹So Israel settled in the land of the Amorites. ³²Moses sent spies to Jazer; and the Israelites captured it with its dependencies and dispossessed the Amorites who were there.

Victory over Og. ³³Then they turned and went up along the road to Bashan. But Og, king of Bashan, advanced against them with all his forces to give battle at Edrei. ³⁴The LORD, however, said to Moses: Do not fear him; for into your hand I deliver him with all his forces and his land. You will do to him as you did to Sihon, king of the Amorites, who reigned in Heshbon. ³⁵So they struck him down with his sons and all his forces, until not a survivor was left to him, and they took possession of his land.

☐ HEBREWS 3

Jesus, Superior to Moses. 3:1 Therefore, holy "brothers," sharing in a heavenly calling, reflect on Jesus, the apostle and high priest of our confession, ²who was faithful to the one who appointed him, just as Moses was "faithful in [all] his house." ³But he is worthy of more "glory" than Moses, as the founder of a house has more "honor" than the house itself. ⁴Every house is founded by someone, but the founder of all is God. ⁵Moses was "faithful in all his house" as a "servant" to testify to what would be spoken, ⁶but Christ was faithful as a son placed over his house. We are his house, if [only] we hold fast to our confidence and pride in our hope.

Israel's Infidelity a Warning. ⁷Therefore, as the holy Spirit says:

"Oh, that today you would hear his
voice,
⁸'Harden not your hearts as at the
rebellion
in the day of testing in the desert,
⁹where your ancestors tested and
tried me
and saw my works ¹⁰for forty years.
Because of this I was provoked with
that generation
and I said, "They have always been
of erring heart,
and they do not know my ways."
¹¹As I swore in my wrath,
"They shall not enter into my rest."

¹²Take care, brothers, that none of you may have an evil and unfaithful heart, so as to forsake the living God. ¹³Encourage yourselves daily while it is still "today," so that none of you may grow hardened by the deceit of sin. ¹⁴We have become partners of Christ if only we hold the beginning of the reality firm until the end, ¹⁵for it is said:

"Oh, that today you would hear his
voice:
'Harden not your hearts as at the
rebellion.'"

¹⁶Who were those who rebelled when they heard? Was it not all those who came out of Egypt under Moses? ¹⁷With whom was he "provoked for forty years"? Was it not those who had sinned, whose corpses fell in the desert? ¹⁸And to whom did he "swear that they should not enter into his rest," if not to those who were disobedient? ¹⁹And we see that they could not enter for lack of faith.

February 28

Withdraw often into the depths of your being, and there with living faith rest on the breast of God, like a child, in the sacred silence of faith and holy love.

— ST. PAUL OF THE CROSS

☐ NUMBERS 22-24

22:1 Then the Israelites moved on and encamped in the plains of Moab on the other side of the Jordan opposite Jericho.

Balaam Summoned. ²Now Balak, son of Zippor, saw all that Israel did to the Amorites, ³and Moab feared the Israelites greatly because they were numerous. Moab was in dread of the Israelites. ⁴So Moab said to the elders of Midian, "Now this horde will devour everything around us as an ox devours the grass of the field." At that time Balak, son of Zippor, was king of Moab; ⁵and he sent messengers to Balaam, son of Beor, at Pethor on the river, in the land of the Ammonites, to summon him with these words, "A people has come out of Egypt! They have covered up the earth and are settling down opposite me! ⁶Now come, curse this people for me, since they are stronger than I am. Perhaps I may be able to defeat them and drive them out of the land. For I know that whoever you bless is blessed and whoever you curse is cursed." ⁷So the elders of Moab and the elders of Midian, themselves experts in divination, left and went to Balaam, to whom they gave Balak's message. ⁸He said to them, "Stay here overnight, and I will give you whatever answer the LORD gives me." So the princes of Moab lodged with Balaam.

⁹Then God came to Balaam and said: Who are these men with you? ¹⁰Balaam answered God, "Balak, son of Zippor, king of Moab, sent me the message: ¹¹'This people that has come out of Egypt has covered up the earth. Now come, lay a curse on them for me; perhaps I may be able to fight them and drive them out.'" ¹²But God said to Balaam: Do not go with them and do not curse this people, for they are blessed. ¹³The next morning Balaam arose and told the princes of Balak, "Go back to your own country, for the LORD has refused to let me go with you." ¹⁴So the princes of Moab went back to Balak with the report, "Balaam refused to come with us."

Second Appeal to Balaam. ¹⁵Balak yet again sent princes, who were more numerous and more distinguished than the others. ¹⁶On coming to Balaam they told him, "Thus says Balak, son of Zippor: Please do not refuse to come to me. ¹⁷I will reward you very handsomely and will do anything you ask of me. Come, lay a curse on this people for me." ¹⁸But Balaam replied to Balak's servants, "Even if Balak gave me his house full of silver and gold, I could not do anything, small or great, contrary to the command of the LORD, my God. ¹⁹But, you too stay here overnight, so that I may learn what else the LORD may say to me." ²⁰That night God came to Balaam and said to him: If these men have come to summon you, go back with them; yet only on the condition that you do exactly as I tell you. ²¹So the next morning when Balaam arose, he saddled his donkey, and went off with the princes of Moab.

The Talking Donkey. ²²But now God's anger flared up at him for going, and the angel of the LORD took up a position on the road as his adversary. As Balaam was riding along on his donkey, accompanied by two of his servants, ²³the donkey saw the angel of the LORD standing in the road with sword drawn. The donkey turned off the road and went into the field, and Balaam beat the donkey to bring her back on the road. [24]Then the angel of the LORD stood in a narrow lane between vineyards with a stone wall on each side. [25]When the donkey saw the angel of the LORD there, she pressed against the wall; and since she squeezed Balaam's leg against the wall, he beat her again. [26]Then the angel of the LORD again went ahead, and stood next in a passage so narrow that there was no room to move either to the right or to the left. [27]When the donkey saw the angel of the LORD there, she lay down under Balaam. Balaam's anger flared up and he beat the donkey with his stick.

[28]Then the LORD opened the mouth of the donkey, and she asked Balaam, "What have I done to you that you beat me these three times?" [29]"You have acted so willfully against me," said Balaam to the donkey, "that if I only had a sword at hand, I would kill you here and now." [30]But the donkey said to Balaam, "Am I not your donkey, on which you have always ridden until now? Have I been in the habit of treating you this way before?" "No," he replied.

[31]Then the LORD opened Balaam's eyes, so that he saw the angel of the LORD standing on the road with sword drawn; and he knelt and bowed down to the ground. [32]But the angel of the LORD said to him: "Why have you beaten your donkey these three times? I have come as an adversary because this rash journey of yours is against my will. [33]When the donkey saw me, she turned away from me these three times. If she had not turned away from me, you are the one I would have killed, though I would have spared her." [34]Then Balaam said to the angel of the LORD, "I have sinned. Yet I did not know that you took up a position to oppose my journey. Since it has displeased you, I will go back home." [35]But the angel of the LORD said to Balaam: "Go with the men; but you may say only what I tell you." So Balaam went on with the princes of Balak.

[36]When Balak heard that Balaam was coming, he went out to meet him at Ar-Moab on the border formed by the Arnon, at its most distant point. [37]And Balak said to Balaam, "Did I not send an urgent summons to you? Why did you not come to me? Did you think I could not reward you?" [38]Balaam answered Balak, "Well, I have come to you after all. But what power have I to say anything? I can speak only what God puts in my mouth." [39]Then Balaam went with Balak, and they came to Kiriath-huzoth. [40]Here Balak sacrificed oxen and sheep, and sent portions to Balaam and to the princes who were with him.

The First Oracle. [41]The next morning Balak took Balaam up on Bamoth-baal, and from there he could see some of the people.

23:1 Then Balaam said to Balak, "Build me seven altars here, and here prepare seven bulls and seven rams for me." [2]So Balak did as Balaam had ordered, and Balak and Balaam offered a bull and a ram on each altar. [3]Balaam said to Balak, "Stand here by your burnt offering while I go over there. Perhaps the LORD will meet me, and then I will tell you whatever he lets me see." And so he went out on the barren height. [4]Then God met Balaam, and Balak said to him: "I have erected the seven altars, and have offered a bull and a ram on each altar." [5]The LORD put an utterance in Balaam's mouth, and said: Go back to Balak, and speak accordingly. [6]So he went back to Balak, who was still standing by his burnt offering together with all the princes of Moab. [7]Then Balaam recited his poem:

> From Aram Balak has led me here,
>> Moab's king, from the mountains of Qedem:
> "Come, curse for me Jacob,
>> come, denounce Israel."
> [8]How can I lay a curse on the one
>> whom God has not cursed?

How denounce the one whom the
    LORD has not denounced?
[9]For from the top of the crags I see him,
    from the heights I behold him.
Here is a people that lives apart
    and does not reckon itself among
        the nations.
[10]Who has ever counted the dust of
    Jacob,
    who numbered Israel's dust-cloud?
May I die the death of the just,
    may my end be like theirs!

[11]"What have you done to me?" cried Balak to Balaam. "It was to lay a curse on my foes that I brought you here; but instead, you have blessed them!" [12]Balaam replied, "Is it not what the LORD puts in my mouth that I take care to repeat?"

The Second Oracle. [13]Then Balak said to him, "Please come with me to another place from which you can see them; but you will see only some, not all of them, and from there lay a curse on them for me." [14]So he brought him to a lookout post on the top of Pisgah, where he built seven altars and offered a bull and a ram on each of them. [15]Balaam then said to Balak, "Stand here by your burnt offering, while I seek a meeting over there." [16]Then the LORD met Balaam, and, having put an utterance in his mouth, said to him: Return to Balak, and speak accordingly. [17]So he went to Balak, who was still standing by his burnt offering together with the princes of Moab. When Balak asked him, "What did the LORD say?" [18]Balaam recited his poem:

Rise, Balak, and listen;
    give ear to my testimony, son of
        Zippor!
[19]God is not a human being who
    speaks falsely,
    nor a mortal, who feels regret.
Is God one to speak and not act,
    to decree and not bring it to pass?
[20]I was summoned to bless;
    I will bless; I cannot revoke it!

[21]Misfortune I do not see in Jacob,
    nor do I see misery in Israel.
The LORD, their God, is with them;
    among them is the war-cry of their
        King.
[22]They have the like of a wild ox's horns:
    God who brought them out of
        Egypt.
[23]No, there is no augury against Jacob,
    nor divination against Israel.
Now it is said of Jacob,
    of Israel, "Look what God has
        done!"
[24]Here is a people that rises up like a
    lioness,
    and gets up like a lion;
It does not rest till it has devoured its
    prey
    and has drunk the blood of the
        slain.

[25]"Neither lay a curse on them nor bless them," said Balak to Balaam. [26]But Balaam answered Balak, "Did I not tell you, 'Everything the LORD tells me I must do'?"

The Third Oracle. [27]Then Balak said to Balaam, "Come, let me bring you to another place; perhaps God will approve of your laying a curse on them for me from there." [28]So he took Balaam to the top of Peor, that overlooks Jeshimon. [29]Balaam then said to Balak, "Build me seven altars here; and here prepare for me seven bulls and seven rams." [30]And Balak did as Balaam had ordered, offering a bull and a ram on each altar.

24:1 Balaam, however, perceiving that the LORD was pleased to bless Israel, did not go aside as before to seek omens, but turned his gaze toward the wilderness. [2]When Balaam looked up and saw Israel encamped, tribe by tribe, the spirit of God came upon him, [3]and he recited his poem:

The oracle of Balaam, son of Beor,
    the oracle of the man whose eye is
        true,

⁴The oracle of one who hears what
   God says,
   and knows what the Most High
      knows,
Of one who sees what the Almighty
      sees,
   in rapture and with eyes unveiled:
⁵How pleasant are your tents, Jacob;
   your encampments, Israel!
⁶Like palm trees spread out,
   like gardens beside a river,
Like aloes the LORD planted,
   like cedars beside water;
⁷Water will drip from their buckets,
   their seed will have plentiful water;
Their king will rise higher than Agag
   and their dominion will be exalted.
⁸They have the like of a wild ox's horns:
   God who brought them out of
      Egypt.
They will devour hostile nations,
   break their bones, and crush their
      loins.
⁹Crouching, they lie like a lion,
   or like a lioness; who will arouse
      them?
Blessed are those who bless you,
   and cursed are those who curse you!

¹⁰In a blaze of anger at Balaam, Balak clapped his hands and said to him, "It was to lay a curse on my foes that I summoned you here; yet three times now you have actually blessed them! ¹¹Now flee to your home. I promised to reward you richly, but the LORD has withheld the reward from you!" ¹²Balaam replied to Balak, "Did I not even tell the messengers whom you sent to me, ¹³'Even if Balak gave me his house full of silver and gold, I could not of my own accord do anything, good or evil, contrary to the command of the LORD'? Whatever the LORD says I must say.

The Fourth Oracle. ¹⁴"But now that I am about to go to my own people, let me warn you what this people will do to your people in the days to come." ¹⁵Then he recited his poem:

The oracle of Balaam, son of Beor,
   the oracle of the man whose eye is
      true,
¹⁶The oracle of one who hears what
   God says,
   and knows what the Most High
      knows,
Of one who sees what the Almighty
      sees,
   in rapture and with eyes unveiled.
¹⁷I see him, though not now;
   I observe him, though not near:
A star shall advance from Jacob,
   and a scepter shall rise from Israel,
That will crush the brows of Moab,
   and the skull of all the Sethites,
¹⁸Edom will be dispossessed,
   and no survivor is left in Seir.
Israel will act boldly,
   ¹⁹and Jacob will rule his foes.

²⁰Upon seeing Amalek, Balaam recited his poem:

First of the nations is Amalek,
   but their end is to perish forever.

²¹Upon seeing the Kenites, he recited his poem:

Though your dwelling is safe,
   and your nest is set on a cliff;
²²Yet Kain will be destroyed
   when Asshur takes you captive.

²³Upon seeing [the Ishmaelites?] he recited his poem:

Alas, who shall survive of Ishmael,
   ²⁴to deliver them from the hands of
      the Kittim?
When they have conquered Asshur and
      conquered Eber,
They too shall perish forever.

²⁵Then Balaam set out on his journey home; and Balak also went his way.

☐ HEBREWS 4:1-13

The Sabbath Rest. 4:1 Therefore, let us be on our guard while the promise of entering into his rest remains, that none of you seem to have failed. [2]For in fact we have received the good news just as they did. But the word that they heard did not profit them, for they were not united in faith with those who listened. [3]For we who believed enter into [that] rest, just as he has said:

"As I swore in my wrath,
　'They shall not enter into my rest,'"

and yet his works were accomplished at the foundation of the world. [4]For he has spoken somewhere about the seventh day in this manner, "And God rested on the seventh day from all his works"; [5]and again, in the previously mentioned place, "They shall not enter into my rest." [6]Therefore, since it remains that some will enter into it, and those who formerly received the good news did not enter because of disobedience, [7]he once more set a day, "today," when long afterwards he spoke through David, as already quoted:

"Oh, that today you would hear his
　　voice:
'Harden not your hearts.'"

[8]Now if Joshua had given them rest, he would not have spoken afterwards of another day. [9]Therefore, a sabbath rest still remains for the people of God. [10]And whoever enters into God's rest, rests from his own works as God did from his. [11]Therefore, let us strive to enter into that rest, so that no one may fall after the same example of disobedience.

[12]Indeed, the word of God is living and effective, sharper than any two-edged sword, penetrating even between soul and spirit, joints and marrow, and able to discern reflections and thoughts of the heart. [13]No creature is concealed from him, but everything is naked and exposed to the eyes of him to whom we must render an account.

Our sins are nothing but a grain of sand alongside the great mountain of the mercy of God.

— St. John Vianney

☐ NUMBERS 25-28

Worship of Baal of Peor. 25:1 While Israel was living at Shittim, the people profaned themselves by prostituting themselves with the Moabite women. [2]These then invited the people to the sacrifices of their god, and the people ate of the sacrifices and bowed down to their god. [3]Israel thereby attached itself to the Baal of Peor, and the LORD's anger flared up against Israel. [4]The LORD said to Moses: Gather all the leaders of the people, and publicly execute them before the LORD, that the blazing wrath of the LORD may turn away from Israel. [5]So Moses told the Israelite judges, "Each of you kill those of his men who have attached themselves to the Baal of Peor."

Zeal of Phinehas. [6]At this a certain Israelite came and brought in a Midianite woman to his kindred in the view of Moses and of the whole Israelite community, while they were weeping at the entrance of the tent of meeting. [7]When Phinehas, son of Eleazar, son of Aaron the priest, saw this, he rose up from the assembly, and taking a spear in his hand, [8]followed the Israelite into the tent where he pierced the two of them, the Israelite and the woman. Thus the plague upon the Israelites was checked; [9]but the dead from the plague were twenty-four thousand.

[10]Then the LORD said to Moses: [11]Phinehas, son of Eleazar, son of Aaron the priest, has turned my anger from the Israelites by his being as jealous among them as I am; that is why I did not put an end to the Israelites in my jealousy. [12]Announce, therefore, that I hereby give him my covenant of peace, [13]which shall be for him and for his descendants after him the covenant of an everlasting priesthood, because he was jealous on behalf of his God and thus made expiation for the Israelites.

[14]The name of the slain Israelite, the one slain with the Midianite woman, was Zimri, son of Salu, prince of a Simeonite ancestral house. [15]The name of the slain Midianite woman was Cozbi, daughter of Zur, who was head of a clan, an ancestral house, in Midian.

Vengeance on the Midianites. [16]The LORD then said to Moses: [17]Treat the Midianites as enemies and strike them, [18]for they have been your enemies by the deceitful dealings they had with you regarding Peor and their kinswoman Cozbi, the daughter of a Midianite prince, who was slain at the time of the plague because of Peor.

The Second Census. [19]After the plague **26:1** the LORD said to Moses and Eleazar, son of Aaron the priest: [2]Take a census, by ancestral houses, throughout the community of the Israelites of all those of twenty years or more who are eligible for military service in Israel. [3]So on the plains of Moab along the Jordan at Jericho, Moses and Eleazar the priest enrolled them, [4]those of twenty years or more, as the LORD had commanded Moses.

The Israelites who came out of the land of Egypt were as follows:

[5]Reuben, the firstborn of Israel. The descendants of Reuben by their clans were: through Hanoch, the clan of the Hanochites; through Pallu, the clan of the Palluites; [6]through Hezron, the clan of the Hezronites; through Carmi, the clan of the Carmites. [7]These were the clans of the Reu-

benites, and those enrolled numbered forty-three thousand seven hundred and thirty.

[8]From Pallu descended Eliab. [9]The sons of Eliab were Nemuel, Dathan, and Abiram—the same Dathan and Abiram, ones designated by the community, who contended with Moses and Aaron as part of Korah's faction when they contended with the LORD. [10]The earth opened its mouth and swallowed them, along with Korah, as a warning. The faction was destroyed when the fire consumed two hundred and fifty men. [11]The descendants of Korah, however, did not die out.

[12]The descendants of Simeon by clans were: through Nemuel, the clan of the Nemuelites; through Jamin, the clan of the Jaminites; through Jachin, the clan of the Jachinites; [13]through Zerah, the clan of the Zerahites; through Shaul, the clan of the Shaulites. [14]These were the clans of the Simeonites, twenty-two thousand two hundred.

[15]The descendants of Gad by clans were: through Zephon, the clan of the Zephonites; through Haggi, the clan of the Haggites; through Shuni, the clan of the Shunites; [16]through Ozni, the clan of the Oznites; through Eri, the clan of the Erites; [17]through Arod, the clan of the Arodites; through Areli, the clan of the Arelites. [18]These were the clans of the descendants of Gad, of whom there were enrolled forty thousand five hundred.

[19]The sons of Judah were Er and Onan. Er and Onan died in the land of Canaan. [20]The descendants of Judah by their clans were: through Shelah, the clan of the Shelahites; through Perez, the clan of the Perezites; through Zerah, the clan of the Zerahites. [21]The descendants of Perez were: through Hezron, the clan of the Hezronites; through Hamul, the clan of the Hamulites. [22]These were the clans of Judah, of whom there were enrolled seventy-six thousand five hundred.

[23]The descendants of Issachar by their clans were: through Tola, the clan of the Tolaites; through Puvah, the clan of the Puvahites; [24]through Jashub, the clan of the Jashubites; through Shimron, the clan of the Shimronites. [25]These were the clans of Issachar, of whom there were enrolled sixty-four thousand three hundred.

[26]The descendants of Zebulun by their clans were: through Sered, the clan of the Seredites; through Elon, the clan of the Elonites; through Jahleel, the clan of the Jahleelites. [27]These were the clans of the Zebulunites, of whom there were enrolled sixty thousand five hundred.

[28]The sons of Joseph were Manasseh and Ephraim. [29]The descendants of Manasseh by clans were: through Machir, the clan of the Machirites. Now Machir begot Gilead: through Gilead, the clan of the Gileadites. [30]The descendants of Gilead were: through Iezer, the clan of the Iezrites; through Helek, the clan of the Helekites; [31]through Asriel, the clan of the Asrielites; through Shechem, the clan of the Shechemites; [32]through Shemida, the clan of the Shemidaites; through Hepher, the clan of the Hepherites. [33]As for Zelophehad, son of Hepher—he had no sons, but only daughters. The names of the daughters of Zelophehad were Mahlah, Noah, Hoglah, Milcah and Tirzah. [34]These were the clans of Manasseh, and those enrolled numbered fifty-two thousand seven hundred.

[35]These were the descendants of Ephraim by their clans: through Shuthelah, the clan of the Shuthelahites; through Becher, the clan of the Becherites; through Tahan, the clan of the Tahanites. [36]These were the descendants of Shuthelah: through Eran, the clan of the Eranites. [37]These were the clans of the Ephraimites, of whom there were enrolled thirty-two thousand five hundred. These were the descendants of Joseph by their clans.

[38]The descendants of Benjamin by their clans: through Bela, the clan of the Belaites; through Ashbel, the clan of the Ashbelites; through Ahiram, the clan of the

Ahiramites; [39]through Shupham, the clan of the Shuphamites; through Hupham, the clan of the Huphamites. [40]The sons of Bela were Ard and Naaman: through Ard, the clan of the Ardites; through Naaman, the clan of the Naamites. [41]These were the descendants of Benjamin by their clans, of whom there were enrolled forty-five thousand six hundred.

[42]These were the descendants of Dan by their clans: through Shuham the clan of the Shuhamites. These were the clans of Dan, [43]of whom there were enrolled sixty-four thousand four hundred.

[44]The descendants of Asher by their clans were: through Imnah, the clan of the Imnites; through Ishvi, the clan of the Ishvites; through Beriah, the clan of the Beriites; [45]through Heber, the clan of the Heberites; through Malchiel, the clan of the Malchielites. [46]The name of Asher's daughter was Serah. [47]These were the clans of the descendants of Asher, of whom there were enrolled fifty-three thousand four hundred.

[48]The descendants of Naphtali by their clans were: through Jahzeel, the clan of the Jahzeelites; through Guni, the clan of the Gunites; [49]through Jezer, the clan of the Jezerites; through Shillem, the clan of the Shillemites. [50]These were the clans of Naphtali, of whom there were enrolled forty-five thousand four hundred.

[51]These were the Israelites who were enrolled: six hundred and one thousand seven hundred and thirty.

Allotment of the Land. [52]The Lord said to Moses: [53]Among these the land shall be divided as their heritage in keeping with the number of people named. [54]To a large tribe you shall assign a large heritage, to a small tribe a small heritage, each receiving its heritage in proportion to the number enrolled in it. [55]But the land shall be divided by lot, all inheriting according to the lists of their ancestral tribes. [56]As the lot falls the heritage of each tribe, large or small, will be assigned.

Census of the Levites. [57]These were the Levites enrolled by clans: through Gershon, the clan of the Gershonites; through Kohath, the clan of the Kohathites; through Merari, the clan of the Merarites. [58]These were clans of Levi: the clan of the Libnites, the clan of the Hebronites, the clan of the Mahlites, the clan of the Mushites, the clan of the Korahites.

Now Kohath begot Amram, [59]whose wife was named Jochebed. She was the daughter of Levi, born to Levi in Egypt. To Amram she bore Aaron and Moses and Miriam their sister. [60]To Aaron were born Nadab and Abihu, Eleazar and Ithamar. [61]But Nadab and Abihu died when they offered unauthorized fire before the Lord. [62]The Levites enrolled were twenty-three thousand, every male one month or more of age. They were not enrolled with the other Israelites, however, for no heritage was given them among the Israelites.

[63]These, then, were those enrolled by Moses and Eleazar the priest, when they enrolled the Israelites on the plains of Moab along the Jordan at Jericho. [64]Among them there was not one of those who had been enrolled by Moses and Aaron the priest, when they enrolled the Israelites in the wilderness of Sinai. [65]For the Lord had told them that they would surely die in the wilderness, and not one of them was left except Caleb, son of Jephunneh, and Joshua, son of Nun.

Zelophehad's Daughters. 27:1 The daughters of Zelophehad, son of Hepher, son of Gilead, son of Machir, son of Manasseh, came forward. (Zelophehad belonged to the clans of Manasseh, son of Joseph.) The names of his daughters were Mahlah, Noah, Hoglah, Milcah and Tirzah. [2]Standing before Moses, Eleazar the priest, the princes, and the whole community at the entrance of the tent of meeting, they said: [3]"Our father died in the wilderness. Although he did not join the faction of those who conspired against the Lord,

Korah's faction, he died for his own sin without leaving any sons. [4]But why should our father's name be cut off from his clan merely because he had no son? Give us land among our father's kindred."

Laws Concerning Heiresses. [5]So Moses laid their case before the Lord, [6]and the Lord said to him: [7]The plea of Zelophehad's daughters is just; you shall give them hereditary land among their father's kindred and transfer their father's heritage to them. [8]Tell the Israelites: If a man dies without leaving a son, you shall transfer his heritage to his daughter; [9]if he has no daughter, you shall give his heritage to his brothers; [10]if he has no brothers, you shall give his heritage to his father's brothers; [11]if his father had no brothers, you shall give his heritage to his nearest relative in his clan, who shall then take possession of it. This will be the statutory procedure for the Israelites, as the Lord commanded Moses.

Joshua to Succeed Moses. [12]The Lord said to Moses: Go up into this mountain of the Abarim range and view the land that I have given to the Israelites. [13]When you have viewed it, you will be gathered to your people, as was Aaron your brother. [14]For in the rebellion of the community in the wilderness of Zin you both rebelled against my order to acknowledge my holiness before them by means of the water. (These were the waters of Meribah of Kadesh in the wilderness of Zin.)

[15]Then Moses said to the Lord, [16]"May the Lord, the God of the spirits of all humanity, set over the community someone [17]who will be their leader in battle and who will lead them out and bring them in, that the Lord's community may not be like sheep without a shepherd." [18]And the Lord replied to Moses: Take Joshua, son of Nun, a man of spirit, and lay your hand upon him. [19]Have him stand before Eleazar the priest and the whole community, and commission him in their sight. [20]Invest him with some of your own power, that the whole Israelite community may obey him. [21]He shall present himself to Eleazar the priest, who will seek for him the decision of the Urim in the Lord's presence; and as it directs, Joshua, all the Israelites with him, and the whole community will go out for battle; and as it directs, they will come in.

[22]Moses did as the Lord had commanded him. Taking Joshua and having him stand before Eleazar the priest and the whole community, [23]he laid his hands on him and commissioned him, as the Lord had directed through Moses.

General Sacrifices. 28:1 The Lord said to Moses: [2]Give the Israelites this commandment: At their prescribed times, you will be careful to present to me the food offerings that are due me, oblations of pleasing aroma to me.

Each Morning and Evening. [3]You will tell them therefore: This is the oblation which you will offer to the Lord: two unblemished yearling lambs each day as the regular burnt offering, [4]offering one lamb in the morning and the other during the evening twilight, [5]each with a grain offering of one tenth of an ephah of bran flour mixed with a fourth of a hin of oil of crushed olives. [6]This is the regular burnt offering that was made at Mount Sinai for a pleasing aroma, an oblation to the Lord. [7]And as the libation for the first lamb, you will make a libation to the Lord in the sanctuary of a fourth of a hin of strong drink. [8]The other lamb you will offer during the evening twilight, making the same grain offering and the same libation as in the morning, as an oblation of pleasing aroma to the Lord.

On the Sabbath. [9]On the sabbath day: two unblemished yearling lambs, with a grain offering of two tenths of an ephah of bran flour mixed with oil, and its libation. [10]This is the sabbath burnt offering each sabbath, in addition to the regular burnt offering and its libation.

At the New Moon Feast. [11]On your new moons you will offer as a burnt offering to the LORD two bulls of the herd, one ram, and seven unblemished yearling lambs, [12]with three tenths of an ephah of bran flour mixed with oil as the grain offering for each bull, two tenths of an ephah of bran flour mixed with oil as the grain offering for the ram, [13]and one tenth of an ephah of bran flour mixed with oil as the grain offering for each lamb, a burnt offering with a pleasing aroma, an oblation to the LORD. [14]Their libations will consist of a half a hin of wine for each bull, a third of a hin for the ram, and a fourth of a hin for each lamb. This is the burnt offering for the new moon, for every new moon through the months of the year. [15]Moreover, there will be one goat for a purification offering to the LORD; it will be offered in addition to the regular burnt offering and its libation.

At the Passover. [16]The fourteenth day of the first month is the Passover of the LORD, [17]and the fifteenth day of this month is the pilgrimage feast. For seven days unleavened bread is to be eaten. [18]On the first day you will declare a holy day, and you shall do no heavy work. [19]You will offer an oblation, a burnt offering to the LORD: two bulls of the herd, one ram, and seven yearling lambs that you are sure are unblemished. [20]Their grain offerings will be of bran flour mixed with oil; you will offer three tenths of an ephah for each bull and two tenths for the ram. [21]You will offer one tenth for each of the seven lambs; [22]and one goat as a purification offering to make atonement for yourselves. [23]These offerings you will make in addition to the morning burnt offering which is part of the regular burnt offering. [24]You will make exactly the same offerings each day for seven days as food offerings, oblations of pleasing aroma to the LORD; they will be offered in addition to the regular burnt offering with its libation. [25]On the seventh day you will declare a holy day: you shall do no heavy work.

At Pentecost. [26]On the day of first fruits, on your feast of Weeks, when you present to the LORD an offering of new grain, you will declare a holy day: you shall do no heavy work. [27]You will offer burnt offering for a pleasing aroma to the LORD: two bulls of the herd, one ram, and seven yearling lambs that you are sure are unblemished. [28]Their grain offerings will be of bran flour mixed with oil: three tenths of an ephah for each bull, two tenths for the ram, [29]and one tenth for each of the seven lambs. [30]One goat will be for a purification offering to make atonement for yourselves. [31]You will make these offerings, together with their libations, in addition to the regular burnt offering with its grain offering.

□ **HEBREWS 4:14-5:10**

Jesus, Compassionate High Priest. 4:14 Therefore, since we have a great high priest who has passed through the heavens, Jesus, the Son of God, let us hold fast to our confession. [15]For we do not have a high priest who is unable to sympathize with our weaknesses, but one who has similarly been tested in every way, yet without sin. [16]So let us confidently approach the throne of grace to receive mercy and to find grace for timely help.

5:1 Every high priest is taken from among men and made their representative before God, to offer gifts and sacrifices for sins. [2]He is able to deal patiently with the ignorant and erring, for he himself is beset by weakness [3]and so, for this reason, must make sin offerings for himself as well as for the people. [4]No one takes this honor upon himself but only when called by God, just as Aaron was. [5]In the same way, it was not Christ who glorified himself in becoming high priest, but rather the one who said to him:

"You are my son;
this day I have begotten you";

[6]just as he says in another place:

"You are a priest forever
according to the order of
Melchizedek."

[7]In the days when he was in the flesh, he offered prayers and supplications with loud cries and tears to the one who was able to save him from death, and he was heard because of his reverence. [8]Son though he was, he learned obedience from what he suffered; [9]and when he was made perfect, he became the source of eternal salvation for all who obey him, [10]declared by God high priest according to the order of Melchizedek.

March 2

Blessed Henry Suso

Worldly people often purchase hell at a very dear price by sacrificing themselves to please the world.

— BLESSED HENRY SUSO

☐ NUMBERS 29–32

On New Year's Day. 29:1 In the seventh month on the first day you will declare a holy day, and do no heavy work; it shall be a day on which you sound the trumpet. [2]You will offer a burnt offering for a pleasing aroma to the LORD: one bull of the herd, one ram, and seven unblemished yearling lambs. [3]Their grain offerings will be of bran flour mixed with oil: three tenths of an ephah for the bull, two tenths for the ram, [4]and one tenth for each of the seven lambs. [5]One goat will be a purification offering to make atonement for yourselves. [6]These are in addition to the burnt offering for the new moon with its grain offering, and in addition to the regular burnt offering with its grain offering, together with the libations prescribed for them, for a pleasing aroma, an oblation to the LORD.

On the Day of Atonement. [7]On the tenth day of this seventh month you will declare a holy day, humble yourselves, and do no sort of work. [8]You will offer a burnt offering to the LORD, a pleasing aroma: one

bull of the herd, one ram, and seven yearling lambs that you are sure are unblemished. [9]Their grain offerings of bran flour mixed with oil: three tenths of an ephah for the bull, two tenths for the one ram, [10]and one tenth for each of the seven lambs. [11]One goat will be a purification offering. These are in addition to the purification offering for purging, the regular burnt offering with its grain offering, and their libations.

On the Feast of Booths. [12]On the fifteenth day of the seventh month you will declare a holy day: you shall do no heavy work. For the following seven days you will celebrate a pilgrimage feast to the LORD. [13]You will offer a burnt offering, an oblation of pleasing aroma to the LORD: thirteen bulls of the herd, two rams, and fourteen yearling lambs that are unblemished. [14]Their grain offerings will be of bran flour mixed with oil: three tenths of an ephah for each of the thirteen bulls, two tenths for each of the two rams, [15]and one tenth for each of the fourteen lambs. ¹⁶One goat will be a purification offering. These are in addition to the regular burnt offering with its grain offering and libation.

¹⁷On the second day: twelve bulls of the herd, two rams, and fourteen unblemished yearling lambs, ¹⁸with the grain offerings and libations for the bulls, rams and lambs in their prescribed number, ¹⁹as well as one goat as a purification offering, besides the regular burnt offering with its grain offering and libation.

²⁰On the third day: eleven bulls, two rams, and fourteen unblemished yearling lambs, ²¹with the grain offerings and libations for the bulls, rams and lambs in their prescribed number, ²²as well as one goat for a purification offering, besides the regular burnt offering with its grain offering and libation.

²³On the fourth day: ten bulls, two rams, and fourteen unblemished yearling lambs, ²⁴the grain offerings and libations for the bulls, rams and lambs in their prescribed number, ²⁵as well as one goat as a purification offering, besides the regular burnt offering, its grain offering and libation.

²⁶On the fifth day: nine bulls, two rams, and fourteen unblemished yearling lambs, ²⁷with the grain offerings and libations for the bulls, rams and lambs in their prescribed number, ²⁸as well as one goat as a purification offering, besides the regular burnt offering with its grain offering and libation.

²⁹On the sixth day: eight bulls, two rams, and fourteen unblemished yearling lambs, ³⁰with the grain offerings and libations for the bulls, rams and lambs in their prescribed number, ³¹as well as one goat as a purification offering, besides the regular burnt offering, its grain offering and libation.

³²On the seventh day: seven bulls, two rams, and fourteen unblemished yearling lambs, ³³with the grain offerings and libations for the bulls, rams and lambs in their prescribed number, ³⁴as well as one goat as a purification offering, besides the regu-lar burnt offering, its grain offering and libation.

³⁵On the eighth day you will hold a public assembly: you shall do no heavy work. ³⁶You will offer a burnt offering, an oblation of pleasing aroma to the LORD: one bull, one ram, and seven unblemished yearling lambs, ³⁷with the grain offerings and libations for the bulls, rams and lambs in their prescribed number, ³⁸as well as one goat as a purification offering, besides the regular burnt offering with its grain offering and libation.

³⁹These are the offerings you will make to the LORD on your festivals, besides your votive or voluntary offerings of burnt offerings, grain offerings, libations, and communion offerings.

30:1 So Moses instructed the Israelites exactly as the LORD had commanded him.

Validity and Annulment of Vows. ²Moses said to the heads of the Israelite tribes, "This is what the LORD has commanded: ³When a man makes a vow to the LORD or binds himself under oath to a pledge, he shall not violate his word, but must fulfill exactly the promise he has uttered.

⁴"When a woman makes a vow to the LORD, or binds herself to a pledge, while still in her father's house in her youth, ⁵and her father learns of her vow or the pledge to which she bound herself and says nothing to her about it, then any vow or any pledge to which she bound herself remains valid. ⁶But if on the day he learns of it her father opposes her, then any vow or any pledge to which she bound herself becomes invalid; and the LORD will release her from it, since her father opposed her.

⁷"If she marries while under a vow or under a rash pledge to which she bound herself, ⁸and her husband learns of it, yet says nothing to her on the day he learns it, then the vows or the pledges to which she bound herself remain valid. ⁹But if on the day her husband learns of it he opposes her,

he thereby annuls the vow she had made or the rash pledge to which she had bound herself, and the LORD will release her from it. [10](The vow of a widow or of a divorced woman, however, any pledge to which such a woman binds herself, is valid.)

[11]"If it is in her husband's house that she makes a vow or binds herself under oath to a pledge, [12]and her husband learns of it yet says nothing to her to oppose her, then all her vows remain valid or any pledge to which she has bound herself. [13]But if on the day he learns of them her husband annuls them, then whatever she has expressly promised in her vows or in her pledge becomes invalid; since her husband has annulled them, the LORD will release her from them.

[14]"Any vow or any pledge that she makes under oath to humble herself, her husband may either confirm or annul. [15]But if her husband, day after day, says nothing at all to her, he thereby confirms all her vows or all the pledges incumbent upon her; he has confirmed them, because on the day he learned of them he said nothing to her. [16]If, however, he annuls them some time after he first learned of them, he will be responsible for her guilt."

[17]These are the statutes which the LORD commanded Moses concerning a husband and his wife, as well as a father and his daughter while she is still in her youth in her father's house.

Campaign Against the Midianites. 31:1 The LORD said to Moses: [2]Avenge the Israelites on the Midianites, and then you will be gathered to your people. [3]So Moses told the people, "Arm some men among you for the campaign, to attack Midian and to execute the LORD's vengeance on Midian. [4]From each of the tribes of Israel you will send a thousand men to the campaign." [5]From the contingents of Israel, therefore, a thousand men of each tribe were levied, so that there were twelve thousand men armed for war.

[6]Moses sent them out on the campaign, a thousand from each tribe, with Phinehas, son of Eleazar, the priest for the campaign, who had with him the sacred vessels and the trumpets for sounding the alarm. [7]They waged war against the Midianites, as the LORD had commanded Moses, and killed every male. [8]Besides those slain in battle, they killed the kings of Midian: Evi, Rekem, Zur, Hur and Reba, the five kings of Midian; and they also killed Balaam, son of Beor, with the sword. [9]But the Israelites took captive the women of the Midianites with their children, and all their herds and flocks and wealth as loot, [10]while they set on fire all the towns where they had settled and all their encampments. [11]Then they took all the plunder, with the people and animals they had captured, and brought the captives, together with the spoils and plunder, [12]to Moses and Eleazar the priest and to the Israelite community at their camp on the plains of Moab by the Jordan opposite Jericho.

Treatment of the Captives. [13]When Moses and Eleazar the priest, with all the leaders of the community, went outside the camp to meet them, [14]Moses became angry with the officers of the army, the commanders of thousands and the commanders of hundreds, who were returning from the military campaign. [15]"So you have spared all the women!" he exclaimed. [16]"These are the very ones who on Balaam's advice were behind the Israelites' unfaithfulness to the LORD in the affair at Peor, so that plague struck the LORD's community. [17]Now kill, therefore, every male among the children and kill every woman who has had sexual relations with a man. [18]But you may spare for yourselves all the girls who have not had sexual relations.

Purification After Combat. [19]"Moreover, remain outside the camp for seven days; every one of you who has killed anyone or touched someone killed will purify yourselves on the third and on the seventh day—both you and your captives. [20]You will also purify every garment, every article of leather, everything made of goats' hair, and every article of wood."

[21]Eleazar the priest told the soldiers who had taken part in the battle: "This is the prescribed ritual which the LORD has commanded Moses: [22]gold, silver, bronze, iron, tin and lead— [23]whatever can stand fire—you shall put into the fire, that it may become clean; however, it must also be purified with water of purification. But whatever cannot stand fire you must put into the water. [24]On the seventh day you will wash your garments, and then you will again be clean. After that you may enter the camp."

Division of the Spoils. [25]The LORD said to Moses: [26]With the help of Eleazar the priest and of the heads of the ancestral houses of the community, inventory all the spoils captured, human being and beast alike; [27]then divide the spoils between the warriors who went on the campaign and the whole community. [28]You will levy a tax for the LORD on the soldiers who went on the campaign: one out of every five hundred persons, oxen, donkeys, and sheep. [29]From their half you will take it and give it to Eleazar the priest as a contribution to the LORD. [30]From the Israelites' half you will take one captive from every fifty human beings, oxen, donkeys, and sheep—all the animals—and give them to the Levites, who perform the duties of the LORD's tabernacle. [31]So Moses and Eleazar the priest did this, as the LORD had commanded Moses.

Amount of the Plunder. [32]This plunder, what was left of the loot which the troops had taken, amounted to six hundred and seventy-five thousand sheep, [33]seventy-two thousand oxen, [34]sixty-one thousand donkeys, [35]and thirty-two thousand women who had not had sexual relations.

[36]The half-share that fell to those who had gone out on the campaign was in number: three hundred and thirty-seven thousand five hundred sheep, [37]of which six hundred and seventy-five fell as tax to the LORD; [38]thirty-six thousand oxen, of which seventy-two fell as tax to the LORD; [39]thirty thousand five hundred donkeys, of which sixty-one fell as tax to the LORD; [40]and sixteen thousand persons, of whom thirty-two persons fell as tax to the LORD. [41]Moses gave the taxes contributed to the LORD to Eleazar the priest, exactly as the LORD had commanded Moses.

[42]As for the Israelites' half, which Moses had taken from the men who had fought— [43]the community's half was three hundred and thirty-seven thousand five hundred sheep, [44]thirty-six thousand oxen, [45]thirty thousand five hundred donkeys, [46]and sixteen thousand persons. [47]From the Israelites' half, Moses took one captive from every fifty, from human being and beast alike, and gave them to the Levites, who performed the duties of the LORD's tabernacle, exactly as the LORD had commanded Moses.

Gifts of the Officers. [48]Then those who were officers over the contingents of the army, commanders of thousands and commanders of hundreds, came up to Moses [49]and said to him, "Your servants have counted the soldiers under our command, and not one of us is missing. [50]So, we have brought as an offering to the LORD articles of gold that each of us has picked up— anklets, bracelets, rings, earrings, or pendants—to make atonement for ourselves before the LORD." [51]Moses and Eleazar the priest accepted the gold from them, all fashioned pieces. [52]The gold that was given as a contribution to the LORD—from the commanders of thousands and the commanders of hundreds—amounted in all to sixteen thousand seven hundred and fifty shekels. [53]What the common soldiers had looted each one kept for himself. [54]So Moses and Eleazar the priest accepted the gold from the commanders of thousands and of hundreds, and put it in the tent of meeting as a reminder on behalf of the Israelites before the LORD.

Request of Gad and Reuben. 32:1 Now the Reubenites and Gadites had a very large number of livestock. Noticing that the land of Jazer and of Gilead was a place suited to livestock, [2]the Gadites and Reubenites came to Moses and Eleazar the priest and to the leaders of the community and said, [3]"The region of Ataroth, Dibon, Jazer, Nimrah, Heshbon, Elealeh, Sebam, Nebo and Baal-meon— [4]the land which the LORD has laid low before the community of Israel, is a land for livestock, and your servants have livestock." [5]They continued, "If we find favor with you, let this land be given to your servants as their possession. Do not make us cross the Jordan."

Moses' Rebuke. [6]But Moses answered the Gadites and Reubenites: "Are your kindred, then, to go to war, while you remain here? [7]Why do you wish to discourage the Israelites from crossing to the land the LORD has given them? [8]That is just what your ancestors did when I sent them from Kadesh-barnea to reconnoiter the land. [9]They went up to the Wadi Eshcol and reconnoitered the land, then so discouraged the Israelites that they would not enter the land the LORD had given them. [10]At that time the anger of the LORD flared up, and he swore: [11]None of the men twenty years old or more who have come up from Egypt will see the land I promised under oath to Abraham and Isaac and Jacob, because they have not followed me unreservedly— [12]except the Kenizzite Caleb, son of Jephunneh, the Kenizzite, and Joshua, son of Nun, since they have followed the LORD unreservedly. [13]So the anger of the LORD flared up against the Israelites and he made them wander in the wilderness forty years, until the whole generation that had done evil in the sight of the LORD had disappeared. [14]And now here you are, offspring of sinful stock, rising up in your ancestors' place to add still more to the LORD's blazing anger against the Israelites. [15]If you turn away from following him, he will again abandon them in the wilderness, and you will bring about the ruin of this entire people."

Counter Proposal. [16]But they approached him and said: "We will only build sheepfolds here for our flocks and towns for our families; [17]but we ourselves will march as troops in the vanguard before the Israelites, until we have led them to their destination. Meanwhile our families will remain in the fortified towns because of the land's inhabitants. [18]We will not return to our homes until all the Israelites have taken possession of their heritage. [19]But we will not claim any heritage with them across the Jordan and beyond, because we have received a heritage for ourselves on the eastern side of the Jordan."

Agreement Reached. [20]Moses said to them in reply: "If you do this—if you march as troops before the LORD into battle [21]and cross the Jordan in full force before the LORD until he has driven his enemies out of his way [22]and the land is subdued before the LORD, then you may return here, free from every obligation to the LORD and to Israel, and this land will be your possession before the LORD. [23]But if you do not do this, you will have sinned against the LORD, and you can be sure that the consequences of your sin will overtake you. [24]Build the towns, then, for your families, and the folds for your flocks, but fulfill what you have promised."

[25]The Gadites and Reubenites answered Moses, "Your servants will do as my lord commands. [26]While our wives and children, our livestock and other animals remain there in the towns of Gilead, [27]all your servants will go across as armed troops before the LORD to battle, just as my lord says."

[28]So Moses gave this command in their regard to Eleazar the priest, to Joshua, son

of Nun, and to the heads of the ancestral houses of the Israelite tribes: [29]He said to them, "If all the Gadites and Reubenites cross the Jordan with you in full force before the LORD into battle, the land will be subdued before you, and you will give them Gilead as a possession. [30]But if they will not go across in force with you before the LORD, you will bring their wives and children and livestock across before you into Canaan, and they will possess a holding among you in the land of Canaan."

[31]To this the Gadites and Reubenites replied, "We will do what the LORD has ordered your servants. [32]We ourselves will go across in force before the LORD into the land of Canaan, but we will retain our hereditary property on this side of the Jordan." [33]So Moses gave them—the Gadites and Reubenites, as well as half the tribe of Manasseh, son of Joseph—the kingdom of Sihon, king of the Amorites, and the kingdom of Og, king of Bashan, the land with its towns, and the districts of the surrounding towns.

[34]The Gadites rebuilt the cities of Dibon, Ataroth, Aroer, [35]Atroth-shophan, Jazer, Jogbehah, [36]Beth-nimrah and Beth-haran—fortified cities—and sheepfolds. [37]The Reubenites rebuilt Heshbon, Elealeh, Kiriathaim, [38]Nebo, Baal-meon (names to be changed!), and Sibmah. These towns, which they rebuilt, they called by their old names.

Other Conquests. [39]The descendants of Machir, son of Manasseh, went to Gilead and captured it, dispossessing the Amorites who were there. [40](Moses gave Gilead to Machir, son of Manasseh, and he settled there.) [41]Jair, a descendant of Manasseh, went and captured their tent villages, and called them Havvoth-jair. [42]Nobah went and captured Kenath with its dependencies and called it Nobah after his own name.

☐ HEBREWS 5:11–6:20

Exhortation to Spiritual Renewal. 5:11 About this we have much to say, and it is difficult to explain, for you have become sluggish in hearing. [12]Although you should be teachers by this time, you need to have someone teach you again the basic elements of the utterances of God. You need milk, [and] not solid food. [13]Everyone who lives on milk lacks experience of the word of righteousness, for he is a child. [14]But solid food is for the mature, for those whose faculties are trained by practice to discern good and evil.

6:1 Therefore, let us leave behind the basic teaching about Christ and advance to maturity, without laying the foundation all over again: repentance from dead works and faith in God, [2]instruction about baptisms and laying on of hands, resurrection of the dead and eternal judgment. [3]And we shall do this, if only God permits. [4]For it is impossible in the case of those who have once been enlightened and tasted the heavenly gift and shared in the holy Spirit [5]and tasted the good word of God and the powers of the age to come, [6]and then have fallen away, to bring them to repentance again, since they are recrucifying the Son of God for themselves and holding him up to contempt. [7]Ground that has absorbed the rain falling upon it repeatedly and brings forth crops useful to those for whom it is cultivated receives a blessing from God. [8]But if it produces thorns and thistles, it is rejected; it will soon be cursed and finally burned.

[9]But we are sure in your regard, beloved, of better things related to salvation, even though we speak in this way. [10]For God is not unjust so as to overlook your work and the love you have demonstrated for his

name by having served and continuing to serve the holy ones. [11]We earnestly desire each of you to demonstrate the same eagerness for the fulfillment of hope until the end, [12]so that you may not become sluggish, but imitators of those who, through faith and patience, are inheriting the promises.

God's Promise Immutable. [13]When God made the promise to Abraham, since he had no one greater by whom to swear, "he swore by himself," [14]and said, "I will indeed bless you and multiply" you. [15]And so, after patient waiting, he obtained the promise. [16]Human beings swear by someone greater than themselves; for them an oath serves as a guarantee and puts an end to all argument. [17]So when God wanted to give the heirs of his promise an even clearer demonstration of the immutability of his purpose, he intervened with an oath, [18]so that by two immutable things, in which it was impossible for God to lie, we who have taken refuge might be strongly encouraged to hold fast to the hope that lies before us. [19]This we have as an anchor of the soul, sure and firm, which reaches into the interior behind the veil, [20]where Jesus has entered on our behalf as forerunner, becoming high priest forever according to the order of Melchizedek.

March 3

St. Katharine Drexel

Teach children with joy. They will be attracted by joy to the Source of all joy, the heart of Jesus.

— St. Katharine Drexel

☐ NUMBERS 33-36

Stages of the Journey. 33:1 The following are the stages by which the Israelites went out by companies from the land of Egypt under the guidance of Moses and Aaron. [2]Moses recorded the starting points of the various stages at the direction of the Lord. These are the stages according to their starting points: [3]They set out from Rameses in the first month, on the fifteenth day of the first month. On the day after the Passover the Israelites went forth in triumph, in view of all Egypt, [4]while the Egyptians buried those whom the Lord had struck down, every firstborn; on their gods, too, the Lord executed judgments.

From Egypt to Sinai. [5]Setting out from Rameses, the Israelites camped at Succoth. [6]Setting out from Succoth, they camped at Etham near the edge of the wilderness. [7]Setting out from Etham, they turned back to Pi-hahiroth, which is opposite Baal-zephon, and they camped opposite Migdol. [8]Setting out from Pi-hahiroth, they crossed over through the sea into the wilderness, and after they traveled a three days' journey in the wilderness of Etham, they camped at Marah. [9]Setting out from Marah, they came to Elim; at Elim there were twelve springs of water and seventy palm trees, and they camped there. [10]Setting out from Elim, they camped beside the Red Sea. [11]Setting out from the Red Sea, they camped in the wilderness of Sin. [12]Setting out from the wilderness of Sin, they camped at Dophkah. [13]Setting out from Dophkah, they camped at Alush. [14]Setting out from Alush, they camped at Rephidim, where there was no water for the people to drink. [15]Setting out from Rephidim, they camped in the wilderness of Sinai.

From Sinai to Kadesh. [16]Setting out from the wilderness of Sinai, they camped at Kibroth-hattaavah. [17]Setting out from Kibroth-hattaavah, they camped at Hazeroth. [18]Setting out from Hazeroth, they camped at Rithmah. [19]Setting out from Rithmah, they camped at Rimmon-perez. [20]Setting out from Rimmon-perez, they camped at Libnah. [21]Setting out from Libnah, they camped at Rissah. [22]Setting out from Rissah, they camped at Kehelathah. [23]Setting out from Kehelathah, they camped at Mount Shepher. [24]Setting out from Mount Shepher, they camped at Haradah. [25]Setting out from Haradah, they camped at Makheloth. [26]Setting out from Makheloth, they camped at Tahath. [27]Setting out from Tahath, they camped at Terah. [28]Setting out from Terah, they camped at Mithkah. [29]Setting out from Mithkah, they camped at Hashmonah. [30]Setting out from Hashmonah, they camped at Moseroth. [31]Setting out from Moseroth, they camped at Bene-jaakan. [32]Setting out from Bene-jaakan, they camped at Mount Gidgad. [33]Setting out from Mount Gidgad, they camped at Jotbathah. [34]Setting out from Jotbathah, they camped at Abronah. [35]Setting out from Abronah, they camped at Ezion-geber. [36]Setting out from Ezion-geber, they camped in the wilderness of Zin, that is, Kadesh.

From Kadesh to the Plains of Moab. [37]Setting out from Kadesh, they camped at Mount Hor on the border of the land of Edom.

[38]Aaron the priest ascended Mount Hor at the Lord's direction, and there he died in the fortieth year after the departure of the Israelites from the land of Egypt, on the first day of the fifth month. [39]Aaron was a hundred and twenty-three years old when he died on Mount Hor.

[40]When the Canaanite, the king of Arad, who ruled over the Negeb in the land of Canaan, heard that the Israelites were coming....

[41]Setting out from Mount Hor, they camped at Zalmonah. [42]Setting out from Zalmonah, they camped at Punon. [43]Setting out from Punon, they camped at Oboth. [44]Setting out from Oboth, they camped at Iye-abarim on the border of Moab. [45]Setting out from Iye-abarim, they camped at Dibon-gad. [46]Setting out from Dibon-gad, they camped at Almon-diblathaim. [47]Setting out from Almon-diblathaim, they camped in the Abarim range opposite Nebo. [48]Setting out from the Abarim range, they camped on the plains of Moab by the Jordan opposite Jericho. [49]They camped by the Jordan on the plains of Moab extended from Beth-jeshimoth to Abel-shittim.

Conquest and Division of Canaan. [50]The Lord spoke to Moses on the plains of Moab by the Jordan opposite Jericho: [51]Speak to the Israelites and say to them: When you go across the Jordan into the land of Canaan, [52]dispossess all the inhabitants of the land before you; destroy all their stone figures, destroy all their molten images, and demolish all their high places. [53]You will take possession of the land and settle in it, for I have given you the land to possess. [54]You will apportion the land among yourselves by lot, clan by clan, assigning a large heritage to a large clan and a small heritage to a small clan. Wherever anyone's lot falls, there will his possession be; you will apportion these shares within your ancestral tribe.

[55]But if you do not dispossess the inhabitants of the land before you, those whom you allow to remain will become barbs in your eyes and thorns in your sides, and they will harass you in the land where you live, [56]and I will treat you as I had intended to treat them.

The Boundaries. 34:1 The Lord spoke to Moses: [2]Give the Israelites this order:

When you enter the land of Canaan, this is the territory that shall fall to you as your heritage—the land of Canaan with its boundaries:

³Your southern boundary will be at the wilderness of Zin along the border of Edom; on the east your southern boundary will begin at the end of the Salt Sea. ⁴Then your boundary will turn south of the Akrabbim Pass and cross Zin. Terminating south of Kadesh-barnea, it extends to Hazar-addar and crosses to Azmon. ⁵Then the boundary will turn from Azmon to the Wadi of Egypt and terminate at the Sea.

⁶For your western boundary you will have the Great Sea with its coast; this will be your western boundary.

⁷This will be your boundary on the north: from the Great Sea you will draw a line to Mount Hor, ⁸and draw it from Mount Hor to Lebo-hamath, with the boundary terminating at Zedad. ⁹Then the boundary extends to Ziphron and terminates at Hazar-enan. This will be your northern boundary.

¹⁰For your eastern boundary you will draw a line from Hazar-enan to Shepham. ¹¹From Shepham the boundary will go down to Riblah, east of Ain, and descending further, the boundary will strike the ridge on the east side of the Sea of Chinnereth; ¹²then the boundary will descend along the Jordan and terminate with the Salt Sea.

This will be your land, with the boundaries that surround it.

¹³Moses also gave this order to the Israelites: "This is the land, to be apportioned among you by lot, which the LORD has commanded to be given to the nine and a half tribes. ¹⁴For the tribe of the Reubenites according to their ancestral houses, and the tribe of the Gadites according to their ancestral houses, as well as half of the tribe of Manasseh, have already received their heritage; ¹⁵these two and a half tribes have received their heritage across the Jordan opposite Jericho, in the east, toward the sunrise."

Supervisors of the Allotment. ¹⁶The LORD spoke to Moses: ¹⁷These are the names of the men who shall apportion the land among you: Eleazar the priest, and Joshua, son of Nun; ¹⁸and you will designate one leader from each of the tribes to apportion the land. ¹⁹These are the names of the men:

from the tribe of Judah: Caleb, son of Jephunneh,
²⁰from the tribe of the Simeonites: Samuel, son of Ammihud;
²¹from the tribe of Benjamin: Elidad, son of Chislon;
²²from the tribe of the Danites: a leader, Bukki, son of Jogli;
²³for the descendants of Joseph: from the tribe of the Manassites: a leader, Hanniel, son of Ephod; and
²⁴from the tribe of the Ephraimites: a leader, Kemuel, son of Shiphtan;
²⁵from the tribe of the Zebulunites: a leader, Elizaphan, son of Parnach;
²⁶from the tribe of the Issacharites: a leader, Paltiel, son of Azzan;
²⁷from the tribe of the Asherites: a leader, Ahihud, son of Shelomi;
²⁸from the tribe of the Naphtalites: a leader, Pedahel, son of Ammihud.

²⁹These are the ones whom the LORD commanded to apportion to the Israelites their heritage in the land of Canaan.

Cities for the Levites. 35:1 The LORD spoke to Moses on the plains of Moab by the Jordan opposite Jericho: ²Command the Israelites out of the heritage they possess to give the Levites cities to dwell in; you will also give the Levites the pasture lands around the cities. ³The cities will be for them to dwell in, and the pasture lands will be for their cattle, their flocks, and all their other animals. ⁴The pasture lands of the cities to be assigned the Levites shall extend a thousand cubits out from the city walls in every direction. ⁵You will measure out two thousand cubits outside the city along the east side, two thousand cubits along the south side, two thousand cubits along the west side, and two thousand cubits along the north side, with the city lying in the center. These will be the pasture lands of their cities.

⁶Now these are the cities you will give to the Levites: the six cities of asylum which you must establish for the homicide to run to, and in addition forty-two other cities— ⁷a total of forty-eight cities with their pasture lands which you will assign to the Levites. ⁸In assigning the cities from what the Israelites possess, take more from a larger group and fewer from a smaller one, so that each will cede cities to the Levites in proportion to the heritage which it receives.

Cities of Asylum. ⁹The LORD spoke to Moses: ¹⁰Speak to the Israelites and say to them: When you go across the Jordan into the land of Canaan, ¹¹select for yourselves cities to serve as cities of asylum, where a homicide who has killed someone inadvertently may flee. ¹²These cities will serve you as places of asylum from the avenger of blood, so that a homicide will not be put to death until tried before the community. ¹³As for the cities you assign, you will have six cities of asylum: ¹⁴you will designate three cities beyond the Jordan, and you will designate three cities in the land of Canaan. These will be cities of asylum. ¹⁵These six cities will serve as places of asylum for the Israelites, and for the resident or transient aliens among them, so that anyone who has killed a person inadvertently may flee there.

Murder and Manslaughter. ¹⁶If someone strikes another with an iron instrument and causes death, that person is a murderer, and the murderer must be put to death. ¹⁷If someone strikes another with a death-dealing stone in the hand and death results, that person is a murderer, and the murderer

must be put to death. ¹⁸Or if someone strikes another with a death-dealing club in the hand and death results, that person is a murderer, and the murderer must be put to death. ¹⁹The avenger of blood is the one who will kill the murderer, putting the individual to death on sight.

²⁰If someone pushes another out of hatred, or throws something from an ambush, and death results, ²¹or strikes another with the hand out of enmity and death results, the assailant must be put to death as a murderer. The avenger of blood will kill the murderer on sight.

²²However, if someone pushes another without malice aforethought, or without lying in ambush throws some object at another, ²³or without seeing drops upon another some death-dealing stone and death results, although there was neither enmity nor malice— ²⁴then the community will judge between the assailant and the avenger of blood in accordance with these norms. ²⁵The community will deliver the homicide from the avenger of blood and the community will return the homicide to the city of asylum where the latter had fled; and the individual will stay there until the death of the high priest who has been anointed with sacred oil. ²⁶If the homicide leaves at all the bounds of the city of asylum to which flight had been made, ²⁷and is found by the avenger of blood beyond the bounds of the city of asylum, and the avenger of blood kills the homicide, the avenger incurs no bloodguilt; ²⁸for the homicide was required to stay in the city of asylum until the death of the high priest. Only after the death of the high priest may the homicide return to the land of the homicide's possession.

²⁹This is the statute for you throughout all your generations, wherever you live, for rendering judgment.

Judgment. ³⁰Whenever someone kills another, the evidence of witnesses is required to kill the murderer. A single witness does not suffice for putting a person to death.

No Indemnity. [31]You will not accept compensation in place of the life of a murderer who deserves to die, but that person must be put to death. [32]Nor will you accept compensation to allow one who has fled to a city of asylum to return to live in the land before the death of the high priest. [33]You will not pollute the land where you live. For bloodshed pollutes the land, and the land can have no expiation for the blood shed on it except through the blood of the one who shed it. [34]Do not defile the land in which you live and in the midst of which I dwell; for I the LORD dwell in the midst of the Israelites.

Inheritance of Daughters. 36:1 The heads of the ancestral houses in a clan of the descendants of Gilead, son of Machir, son of Manasseh—one of the Josephite clans—came up and spoke before Moses and Eleazar the priest and before the leaders who were the heads of the ancestral houses of the Israelites. [2]They said: "The LORD commanded my lord to apportion the land by lot for a heritage among the Israelites; and my lord was commanded by the LORD to give the heritage of Zelophehad our kinsman to his daughters. [3]But if they marry into one of the other Israelite tribes, their heritage will be withdrawn from our ancestral heritage and will be added to that of the tribe into which they marry; thus the heritage that fell to us by lot will be diminished. [4]When the Israelites celebrate the jubilee year, the heritage of these women will be added to that of the tribe into which they marry and their heritage will be withdrawn from that of our ancestral tribe."

[5]So Moses commanded the Israelites at the direction of the LORD: "The tribe of the Josephites are right in what they say. [6]This is what the LORD commands with regard to the daughters of Zelophehad: They may marry anyone they please, provided they marry into a clan of their ancestral tribe, [7]so that no heritage of the Israelites will pass from one tribe to another, but all the Israelites will retain their own ancestral heritage. [8]Every daughter who inherits property in any of the Israelite tribes will marry someone belonging to a clan of her own ancestral tribe, in order that all the Israelites may remain in possession of their own ancestral heritage. [9]Thus, no heritage will pass from one tribe to another, but all the Israelite tribes will retain their own ancestral heritage."

[10]The daughters of Zelophehad did exactly as the LORD commanded Moses. [11]Mahlah, Tirzah, Hoglah, Milcah and Noah, Zelophehad's daughters, married sons of their uncles on their father's side. [12]They married within the clans of the descendants of Manasseh, son of Joseph; hence their heritage remained in the tribe of their father's clan.

Conclusion. [13]These are the commandments and decisions which the LORD commanded the Israelites through Moses, on the plains of Moab beside the Jordan opposite Jericho.

☐ HEBREWS 7

Melchizedek, a Type of Christ. 7:1 This "Melchizedek, king of Salem and priest of God Most High," "met Abraham as he returned from his defeat of the kings" and "blessed him." [2]And Abraham apportioned to him "a tenth of everything." His name first means righteous king, and he was also "king of Salem," that is, king of peace. [3]Without father, mother, or ancestry, without beginning of days or end of life, thus made to resemble the Son of God, he remains a priest forever.

[4]See how great he is to whom the patriarch "Abraham [indeed] gave a tenth"

of his spoils. [5]The descendants of Levi who receive the office of priesthood have a commandment according to the law to exact tithes from the people, that is, from their brothers, although they also have come from the loins of Abraham. [6]But he who was not of their ancestry received tithes from Abraham and blessed him who had received the promises. [7]Unquestionably, a lesser person is blessed by a greater. [8]In the one case, mortal men receive tithes; in the other, a man of whom it is testified that he lives on. [9]One might even say that Levi himself, who receives tithes, was tithed through Abraham, [10]for he was still in his father's loins when Melchizedek met him.

[11]If, then, perfection came through the levitical priesthood, on the basis of which the people received the law, what need would there still have been for another priest to arise according to the order of Melchizedek, and not reckoned according to the order of Aaron? [12]When there is a change of priesthood, there is necessarily a change of law as well. [13]Now he of whom these things are said belonged to a different tribe, of which no member ever officiated at the altar. [14]It is clear that our Lord arose from Judah, and in regard to that tribe Moses said nothing about priests. [15]It is even more obvious if another priest is raised up after the likeness of Melchizedek, [16]who has become so, not by a law expressed in a commandment concerning physical descent but by the power of a life that cannot be destroyed. [17]For it is testified:

> "You are a priest forever
>   according to the order of
>   Melchizedek."

[18]On the one hand, a former commandment is annulled because of its weakness and uselessness, [19]for the law brought nothing to perfection; on the other hand, a better hope is introduced, through which we draw near to God. [20]And to the degree that this happened not without the taking of an oath—for others became priests without an oath, [21]but he with an oath, through the one who said to him:

> "The Lord has sworn, and he will not
>   repent:
>   'You are a priest forever'"—

[22]to that same degree has Jesus [also] become the guarantee of an [even] better covenant. [23]Those priests were many because they were prevented by death from remaining in office, [24]but he, because he remains forever, has a priesthood that does not pass away. [25]Therefore, he is always able to save those who approach God through him, since he lives forever to make intercession for them.

[26]It was fitting that we should have such a high priest: holy, innocent, undefiled, separated from sinners, higher than the heavens. [27]He has no need, as did the high priests, to offer sacrifice day after day, first for his own sins and then for those of the people; he did that once for all when he offered himself. [28]For the law appoints men subject to weakness to be high priests, but the word of the oath, which was taken after the law, appoints a son, who has been made perfect forever.

March 4

Teaching unsupported by grace may enter our ears, but it never reaches the heart. When God's grace does touch our innermost minds to bring understanding, then His Word, which is received by the ear, can sink deep into the heart.

— ST. ISIDORE OF SEVILLE

☐ DEUTERONOMY 1-3

Introduction. 1:1 These are the words that Moses spoke to all Israel beyond the Jordan in the wilderness, in the Arabah, opposite Suph, between Paran and Tophel, Laban, Hazeroth, and Dizahab. [2]It is a journey of eleven days from Horeb to Kadesh-barnea by way of the highlands of Seir.

[3]In the fortieth year, on the first day of the eleventh month, Moses spoke to the Israelites according to all that the LORD had commanded him to speak to them, [4]after he had defeated Sihon, king of the Amorites, who reigned in Heshbon, and Og, king of Bashan, who reigned in Ashtaroth and in Edrei. [5]Beyond the Jordan, in the land of Moab, Moses undertook to explain this law:

Departure from Horeb. [6]The LORD, our God, said to us at Horeb: You have stayed long enough at this mountain. [7]Leave here and go to the hill country of the Amorites and to all the surrounding regions, the Arabah, the mountains, the Shephelah, the Negeb and the seacoast—the land of the Canaanites and the Lebanon as far as the Great River, the Euphrates. [8]See, I have given that land over to you. Go now and possess the land that the LORD swore to your ancestors, Abraham, Isaac, and Jacob, to give to them and to their descendants after them.

Appointment of Elders. [9]At that time I said to you, "I am unable to carry you by myself. [10]The LORD, your God, has made you numerous, and now you are as numerous as the stars of the heavens. [11]May the LORD, the God of your ancestors, increase you a thousand times over, and bless you as he promised! [12]But how can I, by myself, bear the weight, the contentiousness of you? [13]Provide wise, discerning, and reputable persons for each of your tribes, that I may appoint them as your leaders." [14]You answered me, "What you have proposed is good." [15]So I took the leaders of your tribes, wise and reputable, and set them as leaders over you, commanders over thousands, over hundreds, over fifties and over tens, and other tribal officers. [16]I charged your judges at that time, "Listen to complaints among your relatives, and administer true justice to both parties even if one of them is a resident alien. [17]In rendering judgment, do not consider who a person is; give ear to the lowly and to the great alike, fearing no one, for the judgment is God's. Any case that is too difficult for you bring to me and I will hear it." [18]Thus I charged you, at that time, with all the things you were to do.

The Twelve Scouts. [19]Then we set out from Horeb and journeyed through that whole vast and fearful wilderness that you have seen, in the direction of the hill country of the Amorites, as the LORD, our God, had commanded; and we came to Kadesh-barnea. [20]I said to you, "You have come to the hill country of the Amorites, which the LORD, our God, is giving us. [21]See, the LORD, your God, has given this land over to you. Go up and take possession of it, as the LORD, the God of your ancestors, has promised you. Do not fear or be dismayed." ²²Then all of you approached me and said, "Let us send men ahead to spy out the land for us and report to us on the road we should follow and the cities we will come upon." ²³Agreeing with the proposal, I took twelve men from your number, one from each tribe. ²⁴They set out into the hill country as far as the Wadi Eshcol, and explored it. ²⁵Then, taking along some of the fruit of the land, they brought it down to us and reported, "The land the LORD, our God, is giving us is good."

Threats of Revolt. ²⁶But you refused to go up; you defied the command of the LORD, your God. ²⁷You set to murmuring in your tents, "Out of hatred for us the LORD has brought us out of the land of Egypt, to deliver us into the power of the Amorites and destroy us. ²⁸What shall we meet with up there? Our men have made our hearts melt by saying, 'The people are bigger and taller than we, and their cities are large and fortified to the sky; besides, we saw the Anakim there.'"

²⁹But I said to you, "Have no dread or fear of them. ³⁰The LORD, your God, who goes before you, is the one who will fight for you, just as he acted with you before your very eyes in Egypt, ³¹as well as in the wilderness, where you saw how the LORD, your God, carried you, as one carries his own child, all along your journey until you arrived at this place." ³²Despite this, you would not trust the LORD, your God, ³³who journeys before you to find you a place to camp—by night in the fire, and by day in the cloud, to show you the way to go. ³⁴When the LORD heard your words, he was angry, and took an oath: ³⁵Not a single one of this evil generation shall look upon the good land I swore to give to your ancestors, ³⁶except Caleb, son of Jephunneh. He shall see it, for to him and to his descendants I will give the land he trod upon, because he has fully followed the LORD.

³⁷The LORD was angered against me also on your account, and said, You shall not enter there either, ³⁸but Joshua, son of Nun, your attendant, shall enter. Encourage him, for he is the one who is to give Israel its possession. ³⁹Your little ones, who you said would become plunder, and your children, who as yet do not know good from evil— they shall enter there; to them I will give it, and they shall take possession of it. ⁴⁰But as for yourselves: turn back and proceed into the wilderness on the Red Sea road.

Unsuccessful Invasion. ⁴¹In reply you said to me, "We have sinned against the LORD. We will go up ourselves and fight, just as the LORD, our God, commanded us." And each of you girded on his weapons, making light of going up into the hill country. ⁴²But the LORD said to me, Warn them: Do not go up and fight—for I will not be in your midst—lest you be beaten down before your enemies. ⁴³I gave you this warning but you would not listen. You defied the LORD's command and arrogantly went off into the hill country. ⁴⁴Then the Amorites living in that hill country came out against you and put you to flight the way bees do, cutting you down in Seir as far as Hormah. ⁴⁵On your return you wept before the LORD, but the LORD did not listen to your voice or give ear to you. ⁴⁶That is why you had to stay as long as you did at Kadesh.

Northward Along Edom. 2:1 Then we turned and proceeded into the wilderness on the Red Sea road, as the LORD had told me, and circled around the highlands of Seir for a long time. ²Finally the LORD said to me, ³You have wandered round these highlands long enough; turn and go north. ⁴Command the people: You are now about to pass through the territory of your relatives, the descendants of Esau, who live in Seir. Though they are afraid of you, be very careful ⁵not to come in conflict with them, for I will not give you so much as a foot of their land, since I have already given Esau possession of the highlands of Seir. [6]You shall purchase from them with money the food you eat; even the water you drink you shall buy from them with money. [7]Surely, the LORD, your God, has blessed you in all your undertakings; he has been concerned about your journey through this vast wilderness. It is now forty years that the LORD, your God, has been with you, and you have lacked nothing. [8]So we passed by our relatives, the descendants of Esau who live in Seir, leaving behind us the Arabah route, Elath, and Ezion-geber.

Along Moab. Then we turned and passed on toward the wilderness of Moab. [9]And the LORD said to me, Do not show hostility to the Moabites or engage them in battle, for I will not give you possession of any of their land, since I have given Ar to the descendants of Lot as their possession. [10](Formerly the Emim lived there, a people great and numerous and as tall as the Anakim; [11]like the Anakim they are considered Rephaim, though the Moabites call them Emim. [12]In Seir, however, the former inhabitants were the Horites; the descendants of Esau dispossessed them, clearing them out of the way and dwelling in their place, just as Israel has done in the land of its possession which the LORD gave it.) [13]Now get ready to cross the Wadi Zered.

So we crossed the Wadi Zered. [14]Now thirty-eight years had elapsed between our departure from Kadesh-barnea and the crossing of the Wadi Zered; in the meantime the whole generation of soldiers had perished from the camp, as the LORD had sworn they should. [15]Indeed the LORD's own hand was against them, to rout them from the camp completely.

Along Ammon. [16]When at length death had put an end to all the soldiers among the people, [17]the LORD said to me, [18]You are now about to leave Ar and the territory of Moab behind. [19]As you come opposite the Ammonites, do not show hostility or come in conflict with them, for I will not give you possession of any land of the Ammonites, since I have given it to the descendants of Lot as their possession. [20](This also is considered a country of the Rephaim; formerly the Rephaim dwelt there. The Ammonites call them Zamzummim, [21]a people great and numerous and as tall as the Anakim. But these, too, the LORD cleared out of the way for the Ammonites, so that they dispossessed them and dwelt in their place. [22]He did the same for the descendants of Esau, who live in Seir, by clearing the Horites out of their way, so that they dispossessed them and dwelt in their place down to the present. [23]As for the Avvim, who once lived in villages in the vicinity of Gaza, the Caphtorim, migrating from Caphtor, cleared them away and dwelt in their place.)

Defeat of Sihon. [24]Advance now across the Wadi Arnon. I now deliver into your power Sihon, the Amorite king of Heshbon, and his land. Begin to take possession; engage him in battle. [25]This day I will begin to put a fear and dread of you into the peoples everywhere under heaven, so that at the mention of your name they will quake and tremble before you.

[26]So I sent messengers from the wilderness of Kedemoth to Sihon, king of Heshbon, with this offer of peace: [27]"Let me pass through your country. I will travel only on the road. I will not turn aside either to the right or to the left. [28]The food I eat you will sell me for money, and the water I drink, you will give me for money. Only let me march through, [29]as the descendants of Esau who dwell in Seir and the Moabites who dwell in Ar have done, until I cross the Jordan into the land the LORD, our God, is about to give us." [30]But Sihon, king of Heshbon, refused to let us pass through his land, because the LORD, your God, made him stubborn in mind and obstinate in heart that he might deliver him into your power, as indeed he has now done.

³¹Then the LORD said to me, Now that I have already begun to give over to you Sihon and his land, begin to take possession. ³²So Sihon and all his people advanced against us to join battle at Jahaz; ³³but since the LORD, our God, had given him over to us, we defeated him and his sons and all his people. ³⁴At that time we captured all his cities and put every city under the ban, men, women and children; we left no survivor. ³⁵Our only plunder was the livestock and the spoils of the captured cities. ³⁶From Aroer on the edge of the Wadi Arnon and from the town in the wadi itself, as far as Gilead, no city was too well fortified for us. All of them the LORD, our God, gave over to us. ³⁷However, just as the LORD, our God, commanded us, you did not encroach upon any of the Ammonite land, neither the region bordering on the Wadi Jabbok, nor the cities of the highlands.

Defeat of Og. 3:1 Then we turned and proceeded up the road to Bashan. But Og, king of Bashan, came out against us with all his people to give battle at Edrei. ²The LORD said to me, Do not be afraid of him, for I have delivered him into your power with all his people and his land. Do to him as you did to Sihon, king of the Amorites, who reigned in Heshbon. ³And thus the LORD, our God, delivered into our power also Og, king of Bashan, with all his people. We defeated him so completely that we left him no survivor. ⁴At that time we captured all his cities; there was no town we did not take: sixty cities in all, the whole region of Argob, the kingdom of Og in Bashan— ⁵all these cities were fortified with high walls and gates and bars—besides a great number of unwalled towns. ⁶As we had done to Sihon, king of Heshbon, so also here we put all the towns under the ban, men, women and children; ⁷but all the livestock and the spoils of each city we took as plunder for ourselves.

⁸And so at that time we took from the two kings of the Amorites beyond the Jordan the territory from the Wadi Arnon to Mount Hermon ⁹(the Sidonians call Hermon Sirion and the Amorites call it Senir), ¹⁰all the towns of the plateau, all of Gilead, and all of Bashan as far as Salecah and Edrei, towns of the kingdom of Og in Bashan. ¹¹(Og, king of Bashan, was the last remaining survivor of the Rephaim. He had a bed of iron, nine regular cubits long and four wide, which is still preserved in Rabbah of the Ammonites.)

Allotment of the Conquered Lands. ¹²As for the land we took possession of at that time, I gave Reuben and Gad the territory from Aroer, on the edge of the Wadi Arnon, halfway up into the highlands of Gilead, with its cities. ¹³The rest of Gilead and all of Bashan, the kingdom of Og, I gave to the half-tribe of Manasseh. (The whole Argob region, all that part of Bashan, was once called a land of the Rephaim. ¹⁴Jair, a Manassite, took all the region of Argob as far as the border of the Geshurites and Maacathites, and named them—Bashan, that is—after himself, Havvoth-jair, the name it bears today.) ¹⁵To Machir I gave Gilead, ¹⁶and to Reuben and Gad the territory from Gilead to the Wadi Arnon—the middle of the wadi being its boundary—and to the Wadi Jabbok, which is the border of the Ammonites, ¹⁷as well as the Arabah with the Jordan and its banks from Chinnereth to the Salt Sea of the Arabah, under the slopes of Pisgah on the east.

¹⁸At that time I charged you: The LORD, your God, has given you this land as your possession. But all your troops equipped for battle must cross over in the vanguard of your fellow Israelites. ¹⁹But your wives and children, as well as your livestock, of which I know you have a large number, shall remain behind in the towns I have given you, ²⁰until the LORD has settled your relatives as well, and they too possess the land which the LORD, your God, will give them on the other side of the Jordan. Then you may all return to the possessions I have given you.

²¹And I charged Joshua as well, "Your own eyes have seen all that the LORD, your God, has done to both these kings; so, too, will the LORD do to all the kingdoms into which you will cross over. ²²Do not fear them, for it is the LORD, your God, who will fight for you."

Moses Excluded from the Promised Land. ²³It was then that I entreated the LORD, ²⁴"Lord GOD, you have begun to show to your servant your greatness and your mighty hand. What god in heaven or on earth can perform deeds and powerful acts like yours? ²⁵Ah, let me cross over and see the good land beyond the Jordan, that

fine hill country, and the Lebanon!" ²⁶But the LORD was angry with me on your account and would not hear me. The LORD said to me, Enough! Speak to me no more of this. ²⁷Go up to the top of Pisgah and look out to the west, and to the north, and to the south, and to the east. Look well, for you shall not cross this Jordan. ²⁸Commission Joshua, and encourage and strengthen him, for it is he who will cross at the head of this people and he who will give them possession of the land you are to see.

²⁹So we remained in the valley opposite Beth-peor.

☐ HEBREWS 8:1-9:10

Heavenly Priesthood of Jesus. 8:1 The main point of what has been said is this: we have such a high priest, who has taken his seat at the right hand of the throne of the Majesty in heaven, ²a minister of the sanctuary and of the true tabernacle that the Lord, not man, set up. ³Now every high priest is appointed to offer gifts and sacrifices; thus the necessity for this one also to have something to offer. ⁴If then he were on earth, he would not be a priest, since there are those who offer gifts according to the law. ⁵They worship in a copy and shadow of the heavenly sanctuary, as Moses was warned when he was about to erect the tabernacle. For he says, "See that you make everything according to the pattern shown you on the mountain." ⁶Now he has obtained so much more excellent a ministry as he is mediator of a better covenant, enacted on better promises.

Old and New Covenants. ⁷For if that first covenant had been faultless, no place would have been sought for a second one. ⁸But he finds fault with them and says:

"Behold, the days are coming, says the Lord,

when I will conclude a new
  covenant with the house of
  Israel and the house of
  Judah.
⁹It will not be like the covenant I
  made with their fathers
the day I took them by the hand
  to lead them forth from the
  land of Egypt;
for they did not stand by my covenant
  and I ignored them, says the Lord.
¹⁰But this is the covenant I will
  establish with the house of
  Israel
after those days, says the Lord:
I will put my laws in their minds
  and I will write them upon their
  hearts.
I will be their God,
  and they shall be my people.
¹¹And they shall not teach, each one
  his fellow citizen
  and kinsman, saying, 'Know the
  Lord,'
for all shall know me,
  from least to greatest.
¹²For I will forgive their evildoing
  and remember their sins no more."

[13]When he speaks of a "new" covenant, he declares the first one obsolete. And what has become obsolete and has grown old is close to disappearing.

The Worship of the First Covenant. 9:1 Now [even] the first covenant had regulations for worship and an earthly sanctuary. [2]For a tabernacle was constructed, the outer one, in which were the lampstand, the table, and the bread of offering; this is called the Holy Place. [3]Behind the second veil was the tabernacle called the Holy of Holies, [4]in which were the gold altar of incense and the ark of the covenant entirely covered with gold. In it were the gold jar containing the manna, the staff of Aaron that had sprouted, and the tablets of the covenant. [5]Above it were the cherubim of glory overshadowing the place of expiation. Now is not the time to speak of these in detail.

[6]With these arrangements for worship, the priests, in performing their service, go into the outer tabernacle repeatedly, [7]but the high priest alone goes into the inner one once a year, not without blood that he offers for himself and for the sins of the people. [8]In this way the holy Spirit shows that the way into the sanctuary had not yet been revealed while the outer tabernacle still had its place. [9]This is a symbol of the present time, in which gifts and sacrifices are offered that cannot perfect the worshiper in conscience [10]but only in matters of food and drink and various ritual washings: regulations concerning the flesh, imposed until the time of the new order.

March 5

St. Mark the Ascetic

If we want to do something but cannot, then before God, who knows our hearts, it is the same as if we have done it. This is true whether the intended action is good or bad.

— St. Mark the Ascetic

☐ DEUTERONOMY 4-5

Advantages of Fidelity. 4:1 Now therefore, Israel, hear the statutes and ordinances I am teaching you to observe, that you may live, and may enter in and take possession of the land which the LORD, the God of your ancestors, is giving you. [2]In your observance of the commandments of the LORD, your God, which I am commanding you, you shall not add to what I command you nor subtract from it. [3]You have seen with your own eyes what the LORD did at Baal-peor: the LORD, your God, destroyed from your midst everyone who followed the Baal of Peor; [4]but you, who held fast to the LORD, your God, are all alive today. [5]See, I am teaching you the statutes and ordinances as the LORD, my God, has commanded me, that you may observe them in the land you are entering to possess. [6]Observe them carefully, for this is your wisdom and discernment in the sight of the peoples, who will hear of all these statutes and say, "This great nation is truly a wise and discerning people." [7]For what great nation is there that has gods so close to it as the LORD, our God, is to us whenever we call upon him? [8]Or what great nation has statutes and ordinances that are as just as this whole law which I am setting before you today? **Revelation at Horeb.** [9]However, be on your guard and be very careful not to forget the things your own eyes have seen, nor let them slip from your heart as long as you live, but make them known to your children and to your children's children, [10]that day you stood before the LORD, your God, at Horeb, when the LORD said to me: Assemble the people for me, that I may let them hear my words, that they may learn to fear me as long as they live in the land and may so teach their children. [11]You came near and stood at the foot of the mountain, while the mountain blazed to the heart of the heavens with fire and was enveloped in a dense black cloud. [12]Then the LORD spoke to you from the midst of the fire. You heard the sound of the words, but saw no form; there was only a voice. [13]He proclaimed to you his covenant, which he commanded you to keep: the ten words, which he wrote on two stone tablets. [14]At that time the LORD charged me to teach you the statutes and ordinances for you to observe in the land you are about to cross into and possess.

Danger of Idolatry. [15]Because you saw no form at all on the day the LORD spoke to you at Horeb from the midst of the fire, be strictly on your guard [16]not to act corruptly by fashioning an idol for yourselves to represent any figure, whether it be the form of a man or of a woman, [17]the form of any animal on the earth, the form of any bird that flies in the sky, [18]the form of anything that crawls on the ground, or the form of any fish in the waters under the earth. [19]And when you look up to the heavens and behold the sun or the moon or the stars, the whole heavenly host, do not be led astray into bowing down to them and serving them. These the LORD, your God, has apportioned to all the other nations under the heavens; [20]but you the LORD has taken and led out of that iron foundry, Egypt, that you might be his people, his heritage, as you are today. [21]But the LORD was angry with me on your account and swore that I should not cross the Jordan nor enter the good land which the LORD, your God, is giving you as a heritage. [22]I myself shall die in this country; I shall not cross the Jordan; but you are going to cross over and take possession of that good land. [23]Be careful, therefore, lest you forget the covenant which the LORD, your God, has made with you, and fashion for yourselves against his command an idol in any form whatsoever. [24]For the LORD, your God, is a consuming fire, a jealous God.

God's Fidelity and Love. [25]When you have children and children's children, and have grown old in the land, should you then act corruptly by fashioning an idol in the form of anything, and by this evil done in his sight provoke the LORD, your God, [26]I call heaven and earth this day to witness against you, that you shall all quickly perish from the land which you are crossing the Jordan to possess. You shall not live in it for any length of time but shall be utterly wiped out. [27]The LORD will scatter you among the peoples, and there shall remain but a handful of you among the nations to which the LORD will drive you. [28]There you shall serve gods that are works of human hands, of wood and stone, gods which can neither see nor hear, neither eat nor smell. [29]Yet when you seek the LORD, your God, from there, you shall indeed find him if you search after him with all your heart and soul. [30]In your distress, when all these things shall have come upon you, you shall finally return to the LORD, your God, and listen to his voice. [31]Since the LORD, your God, is a merciful God, he will not abandon or destroy you, nor forget the covenant with your ancestors that he swore to them.

[32]Ask now of the days of old, before your time, ever since God created humankind upon the earth; ask from one end of the sky to the other: Did anything so great

ever happen before? Was it ever heard of? ³³Did a people ever hear the voice of God speaking from the midst of fire, as you did, and live? ³⁴Or did any god venture to go and take a nation for himself from the midst of another nation, by testings, by signs and wonders, by war, with strong hand and outstretched arm, and by great terrors, all of which the LORD, your God, did for you in Egypt before your very eyes? ³⁵All this you were allowed to see that you might know that the LORD is God; there is no other. ³⁶Out of the heavens he let you hear his voice to discipline you; on earth he let you see his great fire, and you heard him speaking out of the fire. ³⁷For love of your ancestors he chose their descendants after them and by his presence and great power led you out of Egypt, ³⁸dispossessing before you nations greater and mightier than you, so as to bring you in and to give their land to you as a heritage, as it is today. ³⁹This is why you must now acknowledge, and fix in your heart, that the LORD is God in the heavens above and on earth below, and that there is no other. ⁴⁰And you must keep his statutes and commandments which I command you today, that you and your children after you may prosper, and that you may have long life on the land which the LORD, your God, is giving you forever.

Cities of Refuge. ⁴¹Then Moses set apart three cities in the region east of the Jordan, ⁴²to which a homicide might flee who killed a neighbor unintentionally, where there had been no hatred previously, so that the killer might flee to one of these cities and live: ⁴³Bezer in the wilderness, in the region of the plateau, for the Reubenites; Ramoth in Gilead for the Gadites; and Golan in Bashan for the Manassites.

Introduction. ⁴⁴This is the law which Moses set before the Israelites. ⁴⁵These are the decrees, and the statutes and ordinances which Moses proclaimed to the Israelites after they came out of Egypt, ⁴⁶beyond the Jordan in the valley opposite Beth-peor, in the land of Sihon, king of the Amorites, who reigned in Heshbon, whom Moses and the Israelites defeated after they came out of Egypt. ⁴⁷They took possession of his land and the land of Og, king of Bashan, as well—the land of these two kings of the Amorites in the region beyond the Jordan to the east: ⁴⁸from Aroer on the edge of the Wadi Arnon to Mount Sion (that is, Hermon) ⁴⁹and all the Arabah beyond the Jordan to the east, as far as the Arabah Sea under the slopes of Pisgah.

The Covenant at Horeb. 5:1 Moses summoned all Israel and said to them, Hear, O Israel, the statutes and ordinances which I proclaim in your hearing this day, that you may learn them and take care to observe them. ²The LORD, our God, made a covenant with us at Horeb; ³not with our ancestors did the LORD make this covenant, but with us, all of us who are alive here this day. ⁴Face to face, the LORD spoke with you on the mountain from the midst of the fire, ⁵while I was standing between the LORD and you at that time, to announce to you these words of the LORD, since you were afraid of the fire and would not go up the mountain:

The Decalogue. ⁶I am the LORD your God, who brought you out of the land of Egypt, out of the house of slavery. ⁷You shall not have other gods beside me. ⁸You shall not make for yourself an idol or a likeness of anything in the heavens above or on the earth below or in the waters beneath the earth; ⁹you shall not bow down before them or serve them. For I, the LORD, your God, am a jealous God, bringing punishment for their parents' wickedness on the children of those who hate me, down to the third and fourth generation, ¹⁰but showing love down to the thousandth generation of those who love me and keep my commandments.

¹¹You shall not invoke the name of the LORD, your God, in vain. For the LORD

will not leave unpunished anyone who invokes his name in vain.

¹²Observe the sabbath day—keep it holy, as the LORD, your God, commanded you. ¹³Six days you may labor and do all your work, ¹⁴but the seventh day is a sabbath of the LORD your God. You shall not do any work, either you, your son or your daughter, your male or female slave, your ox or donkey or any work animal, or the resident alien within your gates, so that your male and female slave may rest as you do. ¹⁵Remember that you too were once slaves in the land of Egypt, and the LORD, your God, brought you out from there with a strong hand and outstretched arm. That is why the LORD, your God, has commanded you to observe the sabbath day.

¹⁶Honor your father and your mother, as the LORD, your God, has commanded you, that you may have a long life and that you may prosper in the land the LORD your God is giving you.

¹⁷You shall not kill.

¹⁸You shall not commit adultery.

¹⁹You shall not steal.

²⁰You shall not bear dishonest witness against your neighbor.

²¹You shall not covet your neighbor's wife.

You shall not desire your neighbor's house or field, his male or female slave, his ox or donkey, or anything that belongs to your neighbor.

Moses as Mediator. ²²These words the LORD spoke with a loud voice to your entire assembly on the mountain from the midst of the fire and the dense black cloud, and added no more. He inscribed them on two stone tablets and gave them to me. ²³But when you heard the voice from the midst of the darkness, while the mountain was ablaze with fire, you came near to me, all your tribal heads and elders, ²⁴and said, "The LORD, our God, has indeed let us see his glory and his greatness, and we have heard his voice from the midst of the fire. Today we have found out that God may speak to a mortal and that person may still live. ²⁵Now, why should we die? For this great fire will consume us. If we hear the voice of the LORD, our God, any more, we shall die. ²⁶For what mortal has heard the voice of the living God speaking from the midst of fire, as we have, and lived? ²⁷You go closer and listen to all that the LORD, our God, will say, and then tell us what the LORD, our God, tells you; we will listen and obey."

²⁸The LORD heard your words as you were speaking to me and said to me, I have heard the words these people have spoken to you, which are all well said. ²⁹Would that they might always be of such a mind, to fear me and to keep all my commandments! Then they and their descendants would prosper forever. ³⁰Go, tell them: Return to your tents. ³¹Then you stand here near me and I will give you all the commandments, the statutes and the ordinances; you must teach them, that they may observe them in the land I am giving them to possess.

³²Be careful, therefore, to do as the LORD, your God, has commanded you, not turning aside to the right or to the left, ³³but following exactly the way that the LORD, your God, commanded you that you may live and prosper, and may have long life in the land which you are to possess.

☐ HEBREWS 9:11–10:18

Sacrifice of Jesus. 9:11 But when Christ came as high priest of the good things that have come to be, passing through the greater and more perfect tabernacle not made by hands, that is, not belonging to this creation, ¹²he entered once for all into the sanctuary, not with the blood of goats and calves but with his own blood, thus obtaining eternal redemption. [13]For if the blood of goats and bulls and the sprinkling of a heifer's ashes can sanctify those who are defiled so that their flesh is cleansed, [14]how much more will the blood of Christ, who through the eternal spirit offered himself unblemished to God, cleanse our consciences from dead works to worship the living God.

[15]For this reason he is mediator of a new covenant: since a death has taken place for deliverance from transgressions under the first covenant, those who are called may receive the promised eternal inheritance. [16]Now where there is a will, the death of the testator must be established. [17]For a will takes effect only at death; it has no force while the testator is alive. [18]Thus not even the first covenant was inaugurated without blood. [19]When every commandment had been proclaimed by Moses to all the people according to the law, he took the blood of calves [and goats], together with water and crimson wool and hyssop, and sprinkled both the book itself and all the people, [20]saying, "This is 'the blood of the covenant which God has enjoined upon you.'" [21]In the same way, he sprinkled also the tabernacle and all the vessels of worship with blood. [22]According to the law almost everything is purified by blood, and without the shedding of blood there is no forgiveness.

[23]Therefore, it was necessary for the copies of the heavenly things to be purified by these rites, but the heavenly things themselves by better sacrifices than these. [24]For Christ did not enter into a sanctuary made by hands, a copy of the true one, but heaven itself, that he might now appear before God on our behalf. [25]Not that he might offer himself repeatedly, as the high priest enters each year into the sanctuary with blood that is not his own; [26]if that were so, he would have had to suffer repeatedly from the foundation of the world. But now once for all he has appeared at the end of the ages to take away sin by his sacrifice. [27]Just as it is appointed that human beings die once, and after this the judgment, [28]so also Christ, offered once to take away the sins of many, will appear a second time, not to take away sin but to bring salvation to those who eagerly await him.

One Sacrifice instead of Many. 10:1 Since the law has only a shadow of the good things to come, and not the very image of them, it can never make perfect those who come to worship by the same sacrifices that they offer continually each year. [2]Otherwise, would not the sacrifices have ceased to be offered, since the worshipers, once cleansed, would no longer have had any consciousness of sins? [3]But in those sacrifices there is only a yearly remembrance of sins, [4]for it is impossible that the blood of bulls and goats take away sins. [5]For this reason, when he came into the world, he said:

"Sacrifice and offering you did not
 desire,
  but a body you prepared for me;
[6]holocausts and sin offerings you took
  no delight in.
[7]Then I said, 'As is written of me in
  the scroll,
Behold, I come to do your will,
  O God.'"

[8]First he says, "Sacrifices and offerings, holocausts and sin offerings, you neither desired nor delighted in." These are offered according to the law. [9]Then he says, "Behold, I come to do your will." He takes away the first to establish the second. [10]By this "will," we have been consecrated through the offering of the body of Jesus Christ once for all.

[11]Every priest stands daily at his ministry, offering frequently those same sacrifices that can never take away sins. [12]But this one offered one sacrifice for sins, and took his seat forever at the right hand of God; [13]now he waits until his enemies are

made his footstool. [14]For by one offering he has made perfect forever those who are being consecrated. [15]The holy Spirit also testifies to us, for after saying:

[16]"This is the covenant I will establish
    with them after those days, says
    the Lord:
'I will put my laws in their hearts,

and I will write them upon their
    minds,'"

[17]he also says:

"Their sins and their evildoing
    I will remember no more."

[18]Where there is forgiveness of these, there is no longer offering for sin.

March 6

St. Colette

We must faithfully keep what we have promised. If through human weakness we fail, we must always without delay arise again by means of holy penance, and give our attention to leading a good life and to dying a holy death.

— ST. COLETTE

☐ DEUTERONOMY 6-8

6:1 This then is the commandment, the statutes and the ordinances, which the LORD, your God, has commanded that you be taught to observe in the land you are about to cross into to possess, [2]so that you, that is, you, your child, and your grandchild, may fear the LORD, your God, by keeping, as long as you live, all his statutes and commandments which I enjoin on you, and thus have long life. [3]Hear then, Israel, and be careful to observe them, that it may go well with you and that you may increase greatly; for the LORD, the God of your ancestors, promised you a land flowing with milk and honey.

The Great Commandment. [4]Hear, O Israel! The LORD is our God, the LORD alone! [5]Therefore, you shall love the LORD, your God, with your whole heart, and with your whole being, and with your whole strength. [6]Take to heart these words which I command you today. [7]Keep repeating them to your children. Recite them when you are at home and when you are away, when you lie down and when you get up. [8]Bind them on your arm as a sign and let them be as a pendant on your forehead. [9]Write them on the doorposts of your houses and on your gates.

Fidelity in Prosperity. [10]When the LORD, your God, brings you into the land which he swore to your ancestors, to Abraham, Isaac, and Jacob, that he would give you, a land with fine, large cities that you did not build, [11]with houses full of goods of all sorts that you did not garner, with cisterns that you did not dig, with vineyards and olive groves that you did not plant; and when, therefore, you eat and are satisfied, [12]be careful not to forget the LORD, who brought you out of the land of Egypt, that house of slavery. [13]The LORD, your God, shall you fear; him shall you serve, and by his name shall you swear. [14]You shall not go after other gods, any of the gods of the surrounding peoples— [15]for the LORD, your

God who is in your midst, is a passionate God—lest the anger of the LORD, your God, flare up against you and he destroy you from upon the land.

[16]You shall not put the LORD, your God, to the test, as you did at Massah. [17]But keep the commandments of the LORD, your God, and the decrees and the statutes he has commanded you. [18]Do what is right and good in the sight of the LORD, that it may go well with you, and you may enter in and possess the good land which the LORD promised on oath to your ancestors, [19]driving all your enemies out of your way, as the LORD has promised.

Instruction to Children. [20]Later on, when your son asks you, "What do these decrees and statutes and ordinances mean?" which the LORD, our God, has enjoined on you, [21]you shall say to your son, "We were once slaves of Pharaoh in Egypt, but the LORD brought us out of Egypt with a strong hand [22]and wrought before our eyes signs and wonders, great and dire, against Egypt and against Pharaoh and his whole house. [23]He brought us from there to bring us in and give us the land he had promised on oath to our ancestors. [24]The LORD commanded us to observe all these statutes in fear of the LORD, our God, that we may always have as good a life as we have today. [25]This is our justice before the LORD, our God: to observe carefully this whole commandment he has enjoined on us."

Destruction of the Nations in the Land. 7:1 When the LORD, your God, brings you into the land which you are about to enter to possess, and removes many nations before you—the Hittites, Girgashites, Amorites, Canaanites, Perizzites, Hivites, and Jebusites, seven nations more numerous and powerful than you— [2]and when the LORD, your God, gives them over to you and you defeat them, you shall put them under the ban. Make no covenant with them and do not be gracious to them.

[3]You shall not intermarry with them, neither giving your daughters to their sons nor taking their daughters for your sons. [4]For they would turn your sons from following me to serving other gods, and then the anger of the LORD would flare up against you and he would quickly destroy you.

[5]But this is how you must deal with them: Tear down their altars, smash their sacred pillars, chop down their asherahs, and destroy their idols by fire. [6]For you are a people holy to the LORD, your God; the LORD, your God, has chosen you from all the peoples on the face of the earth to be a people specially his own. [7]It was not because you are more numerous than all the peoples that the LORD set his heart on you and chose you; for you are really the smallest of all peoples. [8]It was because the LORD loved you and because of his fidelity to the oath he had sworn to your ancestors, that the LORD brought you out with a strong hand and redeemed you from the house of slavery, from the hand of Pharaoh, king of Egypt. [9]Know, then, that the LORD, your God, is God: the faithful God who keeps covenant mercy to the thousandth generation toward those who love him and keep his commandments, [10]but who repays with destruction those who hate him; he does not delay with those who hate him, but makes them pay for it. [11]Therefore carefully observe the commandment, the statutes and the ordinances which I command you today.

Blessings of Obedience. [12]As your reward for heeding these ordinances and keeping them carefully, the LORD, your God, will keep with you the covenant mercy he promised on oath to your ancestors. [13]He will love and bless and multiply you; he will bless the fruit of your womb and the produce of your soil, your grain and wine and oil, the young of your herds and the offspring of your flocks, in the land which he swore to your ancestors he would give you. [14]You will be blessed above all peoples; no man or woman among you shall be childless nor shall your livestock be barren. ¹⁵The LORD will remove all sickness from you; he will not afflict you with any of the malignant diseases that you know from Egypt, but will leave them with all those who hate you.

¹⁶You shall consume all the peoples which the LORD, your God, is giving over to you. You are not to look on them with pity, nor serve their gods, for that would be a snare to you. ¹⁷If you say to yourselves, "These nations are more numerous than we. How can we dispossess them?" ¹⁸do not be afraid of them. Rather, remember clearly what the LORD, your God, did to Pharaoh and to all Egypt: ¹⁹the great testings which your own eyes have seen, the signs and wonders, the strong hand and outstretched arm with which the LORD, your God, brought you out. The same also will he do to all the peoples of whom you are now afraid. ²⁰Moreover, the LORD, your God, will send hornets among them, until those who are left and those who are hiding from you are destroyed. ²¹Therefore, do not be terrified by them, for the LORD, your God, who is in your midst, is a great and awesome God. ²²He will remove these nations before you little by little. You cannot finish with them quickly, lest the wild beasts become too numerous for you. ²³The LORD, your God, will give them over to you and throw them into utter panic until they are destroyed. ²⁴He will deliver their kings into your power, that you may make their names perish from under the heavens. No one will be able to stand up against you, till you have destroyed them. ²⁵The images of their gods you shall destroy by fire. Do not covet the silver or gold on them, nor take it for yourselves, lest you be ensnared by it; for it is an abomination to the LORD, your God. ²⁶You shall not bring any abominable thing into your house, so as to be, like it, under the ban; loathe and abhor it utterly for it is under the ban.

God's Care. 8:1 Be careful to observe this whole commandment that I enjoin on you today, that you may live and increase, and may enter in and possess the land which the LORD promised on oath to your ancestors. ²Remember how for these forty years the LORD, your God, has directed all your journeying in the wilderness, so as to test you by affliction, to know what was in your heart: to keep his commandments, or not. ³He therefore let you be afflicted with hunger, and then fed you with manna, a food unknown to you and your ancestors, so you might know that it is not by bread alone that people live, but by all that comes forth from the mouth of the LORD. ⁴The clothing did not fall from you in tatters, nor did your feet swell these forty years. ⁵So you must know in your heart that, even as a man disciplines his son, so the LORD, your God, disciplines you. ⁶Therefore, keep the commandments of the LORD, your God, by walking in his ways and fearing him.

Cautions About Prosperity. ⁷For the LORD, your God, is bringing you into a good country, a land with streams of water, with springs and fountains welling up in the hills and valleys, ⁸a land of wheat and barley, of vines and fig trees and pomegranates, of olive trees and of honey, ⁹a land where you will always have bread and where you will lack nothing, a land whose stones contain iron and in whose hills you can mine copper. ¹⁰But when you have eaten and are satisfied, you must bless the LORD, your God, for the good land he has given you. ¹¹Be careful not to forget the LORD, your God, by failing to keep his commandments and ordinances and statutes which I enjoin on you today: ¹²lest, when you have eaten and are satisfied, and have built fine houses and lived in them, ¹³and your herds and flocks have increased, your silver and gold has increased, and all your property has increased, ¹⁴you then become haughty of heart and forget the LORD, your God, who brought you out of the land of Egypt, that house of slavery; ¹⁵he guided you through the vast and terrible wilderness with its saraph serpents and scorpions, its parched and waterless ground; he brought forth water for you from the flinty rock [16]and fed you in the wilderness with manna, a food unknown to your ancestors, that he might afflict you and test you, but also make you prosperous in the end. [17]Otherwise, you might say in your heart, "It is my own power and the strength of my own hand that has got me this wealth." [18]Remember then the Lord, your God, for he is the one who gives you the power to get wealth, by fulfilling, as he has now done, the covenant he swore to your ancestors. [19]But if you do forget the Lord, your God, and go after other gods, serving and bowing down to them, I bear witness to you this day that you will perish utterly. [20]Like the nations which the Lord destroys before you, so shall you too perish for not listening to the voice of the Lord, your God.

☐ HEBREWS 10:19-39

Recalling the Past. 10:19 Therefore, brothers, since through the blood of Jesus we have confidence of entrance into the sanctuary [20]by the new and living way he opened for us through the veil, that is, his flesh, [21]and since we have "a great priest over the house of God," [22]let us approach with a sincere heart and in absolute trust, with our hearts sprinkled clean from an evil conscience and our bodies washed in pure water. [23]Let us hold unwaveringly to our confession that gives us hope, for he who made the promise is trustworthy. [24]We must consider how to rouse one another to love and good works. [25]We should not stay away from our assembly, as is the custom of some, but encourage one another, and this all the more as you see the day drawing near.

[26]If we sin deliberately after receiving knowledge of the truth, there no longer remains sacrifice for sins [27]but a fearful prospect of judgment and a flaming fire that is going to consume the adversaries. [28]Anyone who rejects the law of Moses is put to death without pity on the testimony of two or three witnesses. [29]Do you not think that a much worse punishment is due the one who has contempt for the Son of God, considers unclean the covenant-blood by which he was consecrated, and insults the spirit of grace? [30]We know the one who said:

"Vengeance is mine; I will repay,"

and again:

"The Lord will judge his people."

[31]It is a fearful thing to fall into the hands of the living God.

[32]Remember the days past when, after you had been enlightened, you endured a great contest of suffering. [33]At times you were publicly exposed to abuse and affliction; at other times you associated yourselves with those so treated. [34]You even joined in the sufferings of those in prison and joyfully accepted the confiscation of your property, knowing that you had a better and lasting possession. [35]Therefore, do not throw away your confidence; it will have great recompense. [36]You need endurance to do the will of God and receive what he has promised.

[37]"For, after just a brief moment,
    he who is to come shall come;
    he shall not delay.
[38]But my just one shall live by faith,
    and if he draws back I take no
        pleasure in him."

[39]We are not among those who draw back and perish, but among those who have faith and will possess life.

March 7

Sts. Perpetua and Felicity

Stand fast in the faith, and love one another, and don't let our suffering cause you to stumble.

— ST. PERPETUA (AT HER MARTYRDOM)

☐ DEUTERONOMY 9-11

Unmerited Success. 9:1 Hear, O Israel! You are now about to cross the Jordan to enter in and dispossess nations greater and stronger than yourselves, having large cities fortified to the heavens, ²the Anakim, a people great and tall. You yourselves know of them and have heard it said of them, "Who can stand up against the Anakim?" ³Know, then, today that it is the LORD, your God, who will cross over before you as a consuming fire; he it is who will destroy them and subdue them before you, so that you can dispossess and remove them quickly, as the LORD promised you. ⁴After the LORD, your God, has driven them out of your way, do not say in your heart, "It is because of my justice the LORD has brought me in to possess this land, and because of the wickedness of these nations the LORD is dispossessing them before me." ⁵No, it is not because of your justice or the integrity of your heart that you are going in to take possession of their land; but it is because of their wickedness that the LORD, your God, is dispossessing these nations before you and in order to fulfill the promise he made on oath to your ancestors, Abraham, Isaac, and Jacob. ⁶Know this, therefore: it is not because of your justice that the LORD, your God, is giving you this good land to possess, for you are a stiff-necked people.

The Golden Calf. ⁷Remember and do not forget how you angered the LORD, your God, in the wilderness. From the day you left the land of Egypt until you came to this place, you have been rebellious toward the LORD. ⁸At Horeb you so provoked the LORD that he was angry enough to destroy you, ⁹when I had gone up the mountain to receive the stone tablets of the covenant which the LORD made with you. Meanwhile I stayed on the mountain forty days and forty nights; I ate no food and drank no water. ¹⁰The LORD gave me the two stone tablets inscribed, by God's own finger, with a copy of all the words that the LORD spoke to you on the mountain from the midst of the fire on the day of the assembly. ¹¹Then, at the end of the forty days and forty nights, when the LORD had given me the two stone tablets, the tablets of the covenant, ¹²the LORD said to me, Go down from here now, quickly, for your people whom you have brought out of Egypt are acting corruptly; they have already turned aside from the way I commanded them and have made for themselves a molten idol. ¹³I have seen now how stiff-necked this people is, the LORD said to me. ¹⁴Let me be, that I may destroy them and blot out their name from under the heavens. I will then make of you a nation mightier and greater than they.

¹⁵When I had come down again from the blazing, fiery mountain, with the two tablets of the covenant in both my hands, ¹⁶I saw how you had sinned against the LORD, your God, by making for yourselves a molten calf. You had already turned aside from the way which the LORD had commanded you. ¹⁷I took hold of the two tablets and with both hands cast them from me and broke them before your eyes. ¹⁸Then, as before, I lay prostrate before the LORD for forty days and forty nights; I ate no food, I drank no water, because of all the sin you

had committed in the sight of the LORD, doing wrong and provoking him. [19]For I dreaded the fierce anger of the LORD against you: his wrath would destroy you. Yet once again the LORD listened to me. [20]With Aaron, too, the LORD was deeply angry, and would have destroyed him; but I prayed for Aaron also at that time. [21]Then, taking the calf, the sinful object you had made, I burnt it and ground it down to powder as fine as dust, which I threw into the wadi that went down the mountainside.

[22]At Taberah, at Massah, and at Kibroth-hattaavah likewise, you enraged the LORD. [23]And when the LORD sent you up from Kadesh-barnea saying, Go up and take possession of the land I have given you, you rebelled against this command of the LORD, your God, and would not believe him or listen to his voice. [24]You have been rebels against the LORD from the day I first knew you.

[25]Those forty days, then, and forty nights, I lay prostrate before the LORD, because he had threatened to destroy you. [26]And I prayed to the Lord and said: O Lord GOD, do not destroy your people, the heritage you redeemed in your greatness and have brought out of Egypt with your strong hand. [27]Remember your servants, Abraham, Isaac, and Jacob. Do not look upon the stubbornness of this people nor upon their wickedness and sin, [28]lest the land from which you have brought us say, "The LORD was not able to bring them into the land he promised them, and out of hatred for them, he brought them out to let them die in the wilderness." [29]They are your people and your heritage, whom you have brought out by your great power and with your outstretched arm.

10:1 At that time the LORD said to me, Cut two stone tablets like the first ones and come up the mountain to me. Also make an ark out of wood. [2]I will write upon the tablets the words that were on the tablets that you broke, and you shall place them in the ark. [3]So I made an ark of acacia wood, and cut two stone tablets like the first ones, and went up the mountain with the two tablets in my hand. [4]The LORD then wrote on the tablets, as he had written before, the ten words that the LORD had spoken to you on the mountain from the midst of the fire on the day of the assembly; and the LORD gave them to me. [5]Then I turned and came down from the mountain, and placed the tablets in the ark I had made. There they have remained, as the LORD commanded me.

[6]The Israelites set out from Beeroth Bene-jaakan for Moserah; Aaron died there and was buried. His son Eleazar succeeded him as priest. [7]From there they set out for Gudgodah, and from Gudgodah for Jotbathah, a region where there is water in the wadies. [8]At that time the LORD set apart the tribe of Levi to carry the ark of the covenant of the LORD, to stand before the LORD to minister to him, and to bless in his name, as they have done to this day. [9]For this reason, Levi has no hereditary portion with his relatives; the LORD himself is his portion, as the LORD, your God, promised him.

[10]Meanwhile I stayed on the mountain as I did before, forty days and forty nights, and once again the LORD listened to me. The LORD was unwilling to destroy you. [11]The LORD said to me, Go now and set out at the head of the people, that they may enter in and possess the land that I swore to their ancestors I would give them.

The Lord's Majesty and Compassion. [12]Now, therefore, Israel, what does the LORD, your God, ask of you but to fear the LORD, your God, to follow in all his ways, to love and serve the LORD, your God, with your whole heart and with your whole being, [13]to keep the commandments and statutes of the LORD that I am commanding you today for your own well-being? [14]Look, the heavens, even the highest heavens, belong to the LORD, your God, as well as the earth and everything on it. [15]Yet only on your ancestors did the LORD set his heart to love them. He chose you, their descendants, from all the peoples, as it is today. [16]Circumcise therefore the foreskins of your hearts, and be stiff-necked no longer. [17]For the LORD, your God, is the God of gods, the Lord of lords, the great God, mighty and awesome, who has no favorites, accepts no bribes, [18]who executes justice for the orphan and the widow, and loves the resident alien, giving them food and clothing. [19]So you too should love the resident alien, for that is what you were in the land of Egypt. [20]The LORD, your God, shall you fear, and him shall you serve; to him hold fast and by his name shall you swear. [21]He is your praise; he is your God, who has done for you those great and awesome things that your own eyes have seen. [22]Seventy strong your ancestors went down to Egypt, and now the LORD, your God, has made you as numerous as the stars of heaven.

Recalling the Wonders of the Lord. 11:1 Love the LORD, your God, therefore, and keep his charge, statutes, ordinances, and commandments always. [2]Recall today that it was not your children, who have neither known nor seen the discipline of the LORD, your God—his greatness, his strong hand and outstretched arm; [3]the signs and deeds he wrought in the midst of Egypt, on Pharaoh, king of Egypt, and on all his land; [4]what he did to the Egyptian army and to their horses and chariots, engulfing them in the waters of the Red Sea as they pursued you, so that the LORD destroyed them even to this day; [5]what he did for you in the wilderness until you came to this place; [6]and what he did to the Reubenites Dathan and Abiram, sons of Eliab, when the earth opened its mouth and swallowed them up out of the midst of Israel, with their families and tents and every living thing that belonged to them— [7]but it was you who saw with your own eyes all these great deeds that the LORD has done.

The Gift of Rain. [8]So keep all the commandments I give you today, that you may be strong enough to enter in and take possession of the land that you are crossing over to possess, [9]and that you may have long life on the land which the LORD swore to your ancestors he would give to them and their descendants, a land flowing with milk and honey. [10]The land you are to enter and possess is not like the land of Egypt from which you have come, where you would sow your seed and then water it by hand, as in a vegetable garden. [11]No, the land into which you are crossing to take possession is a land of mountains and valleys that drinks in rain from the heavens, [12]a land which the LORD, your God, looks after; the eyes of the LORD, your God, are upon it continually through the year, from beginning to end.

[13]If, then, you truly listen to my commandments which I give you today, loving and serving the LORD, your God, with your whole heart and your whole being, [14]I will give the seasonal rain to your land, the early rain and the late rain, that you may have your grain, wine and oil to gather in; [15]and I will bring forth grass in your fields for your animals. Thus you may eat and be satisfied. [16]But be careful lest your heart be so lured away that you serve other gods and bow down to them. [17]For then the anger of the LORD will flare up against you and he will close up the heavens, so that no rain will fall, and the soil will not yield its crops, and you will soon perish from the good land the LORD is giving you.

Need for Fidelity. [18]Therefore, take these words of mine into your heart and soul. Bind them on your arm as a sign, and let them be as a pendant on your forehead. [19]Teach them to your children, speaking of them when you are at home and when you are away, when you lie down and when you get up, [20]and write them on the doorposts of your houses and on your gates, [21]so that, as long as the heavens are above the earth, you and your children may live on in the land which the LORD swore to your ancestors he would give them.

²²For if you are careful to observe this entire commandment I am giving you, loving the LORD, your God, following his ways exactly, and holding fast to him, ²³the LORD will dispossess all these nations before you, and you will dispossess nations greater and mightier than yourselves. ²⁴Every place where you set foot shall be yours: from the wilderness and the Lebanon, from the Euphrates River to the Western Sea, shall be your territory. ²⁵None shall stand up against you; the LORD, your God, will spread the fear and dread of you through any land where you set foot, as he promised you.

Blessing and Curse. ²⁶See, I set before you this day a blessing and a curse: ²⁷a blessing for obeying the commandments of the LORD, your God, which I give you today; ²⁸a curse if you do not obey the commandments of the LORD, your God, but turn aside from the way I command you today, to go after other gods, whom you do not know. ²⁹When the LORD, your God, brings you into the land which you are to enter and possess, then on Mount Gerizim you shall pronounce the blessing, on Mount Ebal, the curse. ³⁰(These are beyond the Jordan, on the other side of the western road in the land of the Canaanites who live in the Arabah, opposite Gilgal beside the oak of Moreh.) ³¹Now you are about to cross the Jordan to enter and possess the land which the LORD, your God, is giving you. When, therefore, you take possession of it and settle there, ³²be careful to observe all the statutes and ordinances that I set before you today.

☐ HEBREWS 11

Faith of the Ancients. 11:1 Faith is the realization of what is hoped for and evidence of things not seen. ²Because of it the ancients were well attested. ³By faith we understand that the universe was ordered by the word of God, so that what is visible came into being through the invisible. ⁴By faith Abel offered to God a sacrifice greater than Cain's. Through this he was attested to be righteous, God bearing witness to his gifts, and through this, though dead, he still speaks. ⁵By faith Enoch was taken up so that he should not see death, and "he was found no more because God had taken him." Before he was taken up, he was attested to have pleased God. ⁶But without faith it is impossible to please him, for anyone who approaches God must believe that he exists and that he rewards those who seek him. ⁷By faith Noah, warned about what was not yet seen, with reverence built an ark for the salvation of his household. Through this he condemned the world and inherited the righteousness that comes through faith.

⁸By faith Abraham obeyed when he was called to go out to a place that he was to receive as an inheritance; he went out, not knowing where he was to go. ⁹By faith he sojourned in the promised land as in a foreign country, dwelling in tents with Isaac and Jacob, heirs of the same promise; ¹⁰for he was looking forward to the city with foundations, whose architect and maker is God. ¹¹By faith he received power to generate, even though he was past the normal age—and Sarah herself was sterile—for he thought that the one who had made the promise was trustworthy. ¹²So it was that there came forth from one man, himself as good as dead, descendants as numerous as the stars in the sky and as countless as the sands on the seashore.

¹³All these died in faith. They did not receive what had been promised but saw it and greeted it from afar and acknowledged

themselves to be strangers and aliens on earth, [14]for those who speak thus show that they are seeking a homeland. [15]If they had been thinking of the land from which they had come, they would have had opportunity to return. [16]But now they desire a better homeland, a heavenly one. Therefore, God is not ashamed to be called their God, for he has prepared a city for them.

[17]By faith Abraham, when put to the test, offered up Isaac, and he who had received the promises was ready to offer his only son, [18]of whom it was said, "Through Isaac descendants shall bear your name." [19]He reasoned that God was able to raise even from the dead, and he received Isaac back as a symbol. [20]By faith regarding things still to come Isaac blessed Jacob and Esau. [21]By faith Jacob, when dying, blessed each of the sons of Joseph and "bowed in worship, leaning on the top of his staff." [22]By faith Joseph, near the end of his life, spoke of the Exodus of the Israelites and gave instructions about his bones.

[23]By faith Moses was hidden by his parents for three months after his birth, because they saw that he was a beautiful child, and they were not afraid of the king's edict. [24]By faith Moses, when he had grown up, refused to be known as the son of Pharaoh's daughter; [25]he chose to be ill-treated along with the people of God rather than enjoy the fleeting pleasure of sin. [26]He considered the reproach of the Anointed greater wealth than the treasures of Egypt, for he was looking to the recompense. [27]By faith he left Egypt, not fearing the king's fury, for he persevered as if seeing the one who is invisible. [28]By faith he kept the Passover and sprinkled the blood, that the Destroyer of the firstborn might not touch them. [29]By faith they crossed the Red Sea as if it were dry land, but when the Egyptians attempted it they were drowned. [30]By faith the walls of Jericho fell after being encircled for seven days. [31]By faith Rahab the harlot did not perish with the disobedient, for she had received the spies in peace.

[32]What more shall I say? I have not time to tell of Gideon, Barak, Samson, Jephthah, of David and Samuel and the prophets, [33]who by faith conquered kingdoms, did what was righteous, obtained the promises; they closed the mouths of lions, [34]put out raging fires, escaped the devouring sword; out of weakness they were made powerful, became strong in battle, and turned back foreign invaders. [35]Women received back their dead through resurrection. Some were tortured and would not accept deliverance, in order to obtain a better resurrection. [36]Others endured mockery, scourging, even chains and imprisonment. [37]They were stoned, sawed in two, put to death at sword's point; they went about in skins of sheep or goats, needy, afflicted, tormented. [38]The world was not worthy of them. They wandered about in deserts and on mountains, in caves and in crevices in the earth.

[39]Yet all these, though approved because of their faith, did not receive what had been promised. [40]God had foreseen something better for us, so that without us they should not be made perfect.

March 8

Whether you like it or not, you will always grow apart from other human beings. But Christ is faithful and will always be with you.

— St. John of God

☐ DEUTERONOMY 12–14

One Center of Worship. 12:1 These are the statutes and ordinances which you must be careful to observe in the land which the LORD, the God of your ancestors, has given you to possess, throughout the time you live on its soil. ²Destroy entirely all the places where the nations you are to dispossess serve their gods, on the high mountains, on the hills, and under every green tree. ³Tear down their altars, smash their sacred pillars, burn up their asherahs, and chop down the idols of their gods, that you may destroy the very name of them from that place.

⁴That is not how you are to act toward the LORD, your God. ⁵Instead, you shall seek out the place which the LORD, your God, chooses out of all your tribes and designates as his dwelling to put his name there. There you shall go, ⁶bringing your burnt offerings and sacrifices, your tithes and personal contributions, your votive and voluntary offerings, and the firstlings of your herds and flocks. ⁷There, too, in the presence of the LORD, your God, you and your families shall eat and rejoice in all your undertakings, in which the LORD, your God, has blessed you.

⁸You shall not do as we are doing here today, everyone doing what is right in their own sight, ⁹since you have not yet reached your resting place, the heritage which the LORD, your God, is giving you. ¹⁰But after you have crossed the Jordan and dwell in the land which the LORD, your God, is giving you as a heritage, when he has given you rest from all your enemies round about

and you live there in security, ¹¹then to the place which the LORD, your God, chooses as the dwelling place for his name you shall bring all that I command you: your burnt offerings and sacrifices, your tithes and personal contributions, and every special offering you have vowed to the LORD. ¹²You shall rejoice in the presence of the LORD, your God, with your sons and daughters, your male and female slaves, as well as with the Levite within your gates, who has no hereditary portion with you.

¹³Be careful not to sacrifice your burnt offerings in any place you like, ¹⁴but offer them in the place which the LORD chooses in one of your tribal territories; there you shall do what I command you.

Profane and Sacred Slaughter. ¹⁵However, in any of your communities you may slaughter and eat meat freely, according to the blessing that the LORD, your God, has given you; the unclean as well as the clean may eat it, as they do the gazelle or the deer. ¹⁶Only, you shall not eat of the blood, but must pour it out on the ground like water. ¹⁷Moreover, you may not, in your own communities, partake of your tithe of grain or wine or oil, of the firstborn of your herd or flock, of any offering you have vowed, of your voluntary offerings, or of your personal contributions. ¹⁸These you must eat in the presence of the LORD, your God, in the place that the LORD, your God, chooses, along with your son and daughter, your male and female slave, and the Levite within your gates; and there, in the presence of the LORD, you shall rejoice in all your undertakings. [19]Be careful, also, that you do not neglect the Levite as long as you live in your land.

[20]After the LORD, your God, has enlarged your territory, as he promised you, and you think, "I will eat meat," as it is your desire to eat meat, you may eat it freely; [21]and if the place where the LORD, your God, chooses to put his name is too far, you may slaughter in the manner I have commanded you any of your herd or flock that the LORD has given you, and eat it freely in your own community. [22]You may eat it as you would the gazelle or the deer: the unclean and the clean eating it together. [23]But make sure that you do not eat of the blood; for blood is life; you shall not eat that life with the flesh. [24]Do not eat of the blood, therefore, but pour it out on the ground like water. [25]Do not eat of it, that you and your children after you may prosper for doing what is right in the sight of the LORD. [26]However, any sacred gifts or votive offerings that you may have, you shall bring with you to the place which the LORD chooses, [27]and there you must sacrifice your burnt offerings, both the flesh and the blood, on the altar of the LORD, your God; of your other sacrifices the blood indeed must be poured out against the altar of the LORD, your God, but their flesh you may eat.

[28]Be careful to heed all these words I command you today, that you and your descendants after you may forever prosper for doing what is good and right in the sight of the LORD, your God.

Warning Against Abominable Practices.
[29]When the LORD, your God, cuts down from before you the nations you are going in to dispossess, and you have dispossessed them and are settled in their land, [30]be careful that you not be trapped into following them after they have been destroyed before you. Do not inquire regarding their gods, "How did these nations serve their gods, so I might do the same." [31]You shall not worship the LORD, your God, that way, because they offered to their gods every abomination that the LORD detests, even burning their sons and daughters to their gods.

Penalties for Enticing to Idolatry. 13:1 Every word that I command you, you shall be careful to observe, neither adding to it nor subtracting from it.

[2]If there arises in your midst a prophet or a dreamer who promises you a sign or wonder, [3]saying, "Let us go after other gods," whom you have not known, "and let us serve them," and the sign or wonder foretold to you comes to pass, [4]do not listen to the words of that prophet or that dreamer; for the LORD, your God, is testing you to know whether you really love the LORD, your God, with all your heart and soul. [5]The LORD, your God, shall you follow, and him shall you fear; his commandments shall you observe, and to his voice shall you listen; him you shall serve, and to him you shall hold fast. [6]But that prophet or that dreamer shall be put to death, because, in order to lead you astray from the way which the LORD, your God, has commanded you to take, the prophet or dreamer has spoken apostasy against the LORD, your God, who brought you out of the land of Egypt and redeemed you from the house of slavery. Thus shall you purge the evil from your midst.

[7]If your brother, your father's child or your mother's child, your son or daughter, your beloved spouse, or your intimate friend entices you secretly, saying, "Come, let us serve other gods," whom you and your ancestors have not known, [8]any of the gods of the surrounding peoples, near to you or far away, from one end of the earth to the other: [9]do not yield or listen to any such person; show no pity or compassion and do not shield such a one, [10]but kill that person. Your hand shall be the first raised to put such a one to death; the hand of all the people shall follow. [11]You shall stone that person to death, for seeking to lead

you astray from the Lord, your God, who brought you out of the land of Egypt, out of the house of slavery. [12]And all Israel shall hear of it and fear, and never again do such evil as this in your midst.

[13]If you hear it said concerning one of the cities which the Lord, your God, gives you to dwell in, [14]that certain scoundrels have sprung up in your midst and have led astray the inhabitants of their city, saying, "Come, let us serve other gods," whom you have not known, [15]you must inquire carefully into the matter and investigate it thoroughly. If you find that it is true and an established fact that this abomination has been committed in your midst, [16]you shall put the inhabitants of that city to the sword, placing the city and all that is in it, even its livestock, under the ban. [17]Having heaped up all its spoils in the middle of its square, you shall burn the city with all its spoils as a whole burnt offering to the Lord, your God. Let it be a heap of ruins forever, never to be rebuilt. [18]You shall not hold on to anything that is under the ban; then the Lord will turn from his burning anger and show you mercy, and in showing you mercy multiply you as he swore to your ancestors, [19]because you have listened to the voice of the Lord, your God, keeping all his commandments, which I give you today, doing what is right in the sight of the Lord, your God.

Improper Mourning Rites. 14:1 You are children of the Lord, your God. You shall not gash yourselves nor shave the hair above your foreheads for the dead. [2]For you are a people holy to the Lord, your God; the Lord, your God, has chosen you from all the peoples on the face of the earth to be a people specially his own.

Clean and Unclean Animals. [3]You shall not eat any abominable thing. [4]These are the animals you may eat: the ox, the sheep, the goat, [5]the deer, the gazelle, the roebuck, the wild goat, the ibex, the ante-lope, and the mountain sheep. [6]Any among the animals that has divided hooves, with the foot cloven in two, and that chews the cud you may eat. [7]But you shall not eat any of the following that chew the cud or have cloven hooves: the camel, the hare, and the rock badger, which indeed chew the cud, but do not have divided hooves; they are unclean for you. [8]And the pig, which indeed has divided hooves, with cloven foot, but does not chew the cud, is unclean for you. Their flesh you shall not eat, and their dead bodies you shall not touch.

[9]These you may eat, of all that live in the water: whatever has both fins and scales you may eat, [10]but all those that lack either fins or scales you shall not eat; they are unclean for you.

[11]You may eat all clean birds. [12]But you shall not eat any of the following: the griffon vulture, the bearded vulture, the black vulture, [13]the various kites and falcons, [14]all kinds of crows, [15]the eagle owl, the kestrel, the long-eared owl, all species of hawks, [16]the little owl, the screech owl, the barn owl, [17]the horned owl, the osprey, the cormorant, [18]the stork, any kind of heron, the hoopoe, and the bat. [19]All winged insects are also unclean for you and shall not be eaten. [20]Any clean winged creatures you may eat.

[21]You shall not eat the carcass of any animal that has died of itself; but you may give it to a resident alien within your gates to eat, or you may sell it to a foreigner. For you are a people holy to the Lord, your God.

You shall not boil a young goat in its mother's milk.

Tithes. [22]Each year you shall tithe all the produce of your seed that grows in the field; [23]then in the place which the Lord, your God, chooses as the dwelling place of his name you shall eat in his presence the tithe of your grain, wine and oil, as well as the firstlings of your herd and flock, that you may learn always to fear the Lord, your God. [24]But if, when the Lord, your God, blesses you, the journey is too much for you and you are not able to bring your tithe, because the place which the LORD, your God, chooses to put his name is too far for you, ²⁵you may exchange the tithe for money, and with the money securely in hand, go to the place which the LORD, your God, chooses. ²⁶You may then exchange the money for whatever you desire, oxen or sheep, wine or beer, or anything else you want, and there in the presence of the LORD, your God, you shall consume it and rejoice, you and your household together.

☐ HEBREWS 12

God our Father. 12:1 Therefore, since we are surrounded by so great a cloud of witnesses, let us rid ourselves of every burden and sin that clings to us and persevere in running the race that lies before us ²while keeping our eyes fixed on Jesus, the leader and perfecter of faith. For the sake of the joy that lay before him he endured the cross, despising its shame, and has taken his seat at the right of the throne of God. ³Consider how he endured such opposition from sinners, in order that you may not grow weary and lose heart. ⁴In your struggle against sin you have not yet resisted to the point of shedding blood. ⁵You have also forgotten the exhortation addressed to you as sons:

"My son, do not disdain the discipline
    of the Lord
  or lose heart when reproved by him;
⁶for whom the Lord loves, he
    disciplines;
  he scourges every son he
    acknowledges."

⁷Endure your trials as "discipline"; God treats you as sons. For what "son" is there whom his father does not discipline? ⁸If you are without discipline, in which all have shared, you are not sons but bastards. ⁹Besides this, we have had our earthly fathers to discipline us, and we respected

²⁷But do not neglect the Levite within your gates, for he has no hereditary portion with you.

²⁸At the end of every third year you shall bring out all the tithes of your produce for that year and deposit them within your own communities, ²⁹that the Levite who has no hereditary portion with you, and also the resident alien, the orphan and the widow within your gates, may come and eat and be satisfied; so that the LORD, your God, may bless you in all that you undertake.

them. Should we not [then] submit all the more to the Father of spirits and live? ¹⁰They disciplined us for a short time as seemed right to them, but he does so for our benefit, in order that we may share his holiness. ¹¹At the time, all discipline seems a cause not for joy but for pain, yet later it brings the peaceful fruit of righteousness to those who are trained by it.

¹²So strengthen your drooping hands and your weak knees. ¹³Make straight paths for your feet, that what is lame may not be dislocated but healed.

Penalties of Disobedience. ¹⁴Strive for peace with everyone, and for that holiness without which no one will see the Lord. ¹⁵See to it that no one be deprived of the grace of God, that no bitter root spring up and cause trouble, through which many may become defiled, ¹⁶that no one be an immoral or profane person like Esau, who sold his birthright for a single meal. ¹⁷For you know that later, when he wanted to inherit his father's blessing, he was rejected because he found no opportunity to change his mind, even though he sought the blessing with tears.

¹⁸You have not approached that which could be touched and a blazing fire and gloomy darkness and storm ¹⁹and a trumpet blast and a voice speaking words such

that those who heard begged that no message be further addressed to them, [20]for they could not bear to hear the command: "If even an animal touches the mountain, it shall be stoned." [21]Indeed, so fearful was the spectacle that Moses said, "I am terrified and trembling." [22]No, you have approached Mount Zion and the city of the living God, the heavenly Jerusalem, and countless angels in festal gathering, [23]and the assembly of the firstborn enrolled in heaven, and God the judge of all, and the spirits of the just made perfect, [24]and Jesus, the mediator of a new covenant, and the sprinkled blood that speaks more eloquently than that of Abel.

[25]See that you do not reject the one who speaks. For if they did not escape when they refused the one who warned them on earth, how much more in our case if we turn away from the one who warns from heaven. [26]His voice shook the earth at that time, but now he has promised, "I will once more shake not only earth but heaven." [27]That phrase, "once more," points to [the] removal of shaken, created things, so that what is unshaken may remain. [28]Therefore, we who are receiving the unshakable kingdom should have gratitude, with which we should offer worship pleasing to God in reverence and awe. [29]For our God is a consuming fire.

March 9

St. Frances of Rome; St. Gregory of Nyssa

Truly barren is a secular education. It is always in labor, but never gives birth.

— St. Gregory of Nyssa

☐ DEUTERONOMY 15–18

Debts and the Poor. 15:1 At the end of every seven-year period you shall have a remission of debts, [2]and this is the manner of the remission. Creditors shall remit all claims on loans made to a neighbor, not pressing the neighbor, one who is kin, because the LORD's remission has been proclaimed. [3]You may press a foreigner, but you shall remit the claim on what your kin owes to you. [4]However, since the LORD, your God, will bless you abundantly in the land the LORD, your God, will give you to possess as a heritage, there shall be no one of you in need [5]if you but listen to the voice of the LORD, your God, and carefully observe this entire commandment which I enjoin on you today. [6]Since the LORD, your God, will bless you as he promised,

you will lend to many nations, and borrow from none; you will rule over many nations, and none will rule over you.

[7]If one of your kindred is in need in any community in the land which the LORD, your God, is giving you, you shall not harden your heart nor close your hand against your kin who is in need. [8]Instead, you shall freely open your hand and generously lend what suffices to meet that need. [9]Be careful not to entertain the mean thought, "The seventh year, the year of remission, is near," so that you would begrudge your kin who is in need and give nothing, and your kin would cry to the LORD against you and you would be held guilty. [10]When you give, give generously and not with a stingy heart; for that, the

LORD, your God, will bless you in all your works and undertakings. [11]The land will never lack for needy persons; that is why I command you: "Open your hand freely to your poor and to your needy kin in your land."

Hebrew Slaves. [12]If your kin, a Hebrew man or woman, sells himself or herself to you, he or she is to serve you for six years, but in the seventh year you shall release him or her as a free person. [13]When you release a male from your service, as a free person, you shall not send him away empty-handed, [14]but shall weigh him down with gifts from your flock and threshing floor and wine press; as the LORD, your God, has blessed you, so you shall give to him. [15]For remember that you too were slaves in the land of Egypt, and the LORD, your God, redeemed you. That is why I am giving you this command today. [16]But if he says to you, "I do not wish to leave you," because he loves you and your household, since he is well off with you, [17]you shall take an awl and put it through his ear into the door, and he shall be your slave forever. Your female slave, also, you shall treat in the same way. [18]Do not be reluctant when you let them go free, since the service they have given you for six years was worth twice a hired laborer's salary; and the LORD, your God, will bless you in everything you do.

Firstlings. [19]You shall consecrate to the LORD, your God, every male firstling born in your herd and in your flock. You shall not work the firstlings of your cattle, nor shear the firstlings of your flock. [20]In the presence of the LORD, your God, you shall eat them year after year, you and your household, in the place that the LORD will choose. [21]But if a firstling has any defect, lameness or blindness, any such serious defect, you shall not sacrifice it to the LORD, your God, [22]but in your own communities you may eat it, the unclean and the clean eating it together, as you would a gazelle or a deer. [23]Only, you must not eat of its blood; you shall pour it out on the ground like water.

Feast of the Passover. 16:1 Observe the month of Abib by keeping the Passover of the LORD, your God, since it was in the month of Abib that the LORD, your God, brought you out of Egypt by night. [2]You shall offer the Passover sacrifice from your flock and your herd to the LORD, your God, in the place the LORD will choose as the dwelling place of his name. [3]You shall not eat leavened bread with it. For seven days you shall eat with it only unleavened bread, the bread of affliction, so that you may remember as long as you live the day you left the land of Egypt; for in hurried flight you left the land of Egypt. [4]No leaven is to be found with you in all your territory for seven days, and none of the meat which you sacrificed on the evening of the first day shall be kept overnight for the next day.

[5]You may not sacrifice the Passover in any of the communities which the LORD, your God, gives you; [6]only at the place which the LORD, your God, will choose as the dwelling place of his name, and in the evening at sunset, at the very time when you left Egypt, shall you sacrifice the Passover. [7]You shall cook and eat it at the place the LORD, your God, will choose; then in the morning you may return to your tents. [8]For six days you shall eat unleavened bread, and on the seventh day there shall be a solemn assembly for the LORD, your God; on that day you shall do no work.

Feast of Weeks. [9]You shall count off seven weeks; begin to count the seven weeks from the day when the sickle is first put to the standing grain. [10]You shall then keep the feast of Weeks for the LORD, your God, and the measure of your own voluntary offering which you will give shall be in proportion to the blessing the LORD, your God, has given you. [11]You shall rejoice in the presence of the LORD, your God, together with your son and daughter, your male and female slave, and the Levite within your gates, as well as the resident alien, the orphan, and the widow among you, in the place which the LORD, your God, will choose as the dwelling place of his name. [12]Remember that you too were slaves in Egypt, so carry out these statutes carefully.

Feast of Booths. [13]You shall celebrate the feast of Booths for seven days, when you have gathered in the produce from your threshing floor and wine press. [14]You shall rejoice at your feast, together with your son and daughter, your male and female slave, and also the Levite, the resident alien, the orphan and the widow within your gates. [15]For seven days you shall celebrate this feast for the LORD, your God, in the place which the LORD will choose; since the LORD, your God, has blessed you in all your crops and in all your undertakings, you will be full of joy.

[16]Three times a year, then, all your males shall appear before the LORD, your God, in the place which he will choose: at the feast of Unleavened Bread, at the feast of Weeks, and at the feast of Booths. They shall not appear before the LORD empty-handed, [17]but each with his own gift, in proportion to the blessing which the LORD, your God, has given to you.

Justice. [18]In all the communities which the LORD, your God, is giving you, you shall appoint judges and officials throughout your tribes to administer true justice for the people. [19]You must not distort justice: you shall not show partiality; you shall not take a bribe, for a bribe blinds the eyes even of the wise and twists the words even of the just. [20]Justice, justice alone shall you pursue, so that you may live and possess the land the LORD, your God, is giving you.

Illicit Worship. [21]You shall not plant an asherah of any kind of wood next to the altar of the LORD, your God, which you will build; [22]nor shall you erect a sacred pillar, such as the LORD, your God, hates.

17:1 You shall not sacrifice to the LORD, your God, an ox or a sheep with any serious defect; that would be an abomination to the LORD, your God.

[2]If there is found in your midst, in any one of the communities which the LORD, your God, gives you, a man or a woman who does evil in the sight of the LORD, your God, and transgresses his covenant, [3]by going to serve other gods, by bowing down to them, to the sun or the moon or any of the host of heaven, contrary to my command; [4]and if you are told or hear of it, you must investigate it thoroughly. If the truth of the matter is established that this abomination has been committed in Israel, [5]you shall bring the man or the woman who has done this evil deed out to your gates and stone the man or the woman to death. [6]Only on the testimony of two or three witnesses shall a person be put to death; no one shall be put to death on the testimony of only one witness. [7]The hands of the witnesses shall be the first raised to put the person to death, and afterward the hands of all the people. Thus shall you purge the evil from your midst.

Judges. [8]If there is a case for judgment which proves too baffling for you to decide, in a matter of bloodshed or of law or of injury, matters of dispute within your gates, you shall then go up to the place which the LORD, your God, will choose, [9]to the levitical priests or to the judge who is in office at that time. They shall investigate the case and then announce to you the decision. [10]You shall act according to the decision they announce to you in the place which the LORD will choose, carefully observing everything as they instruct you. [11]You shall carry out the instruction they give you and the judgment they pronounce, without turning aside either to the right or left from the decision they announce to you. [12]Anyone who acts presumptuously and does not obey the priest who officiates there in the ministry of the LORD, your God, or the judge, shall die. Thus shall you purge the evil from Israel. [13]And all the people, on hearing of it, shall fear, and will never again act presumptuously.

The King. [14]When you have come into the land which the LORD, your God, is giving you, and have taken possession of it and settled in it, should you then decide, "I will set a king over me, like all the surrounding nations," [15]you may indeed set over you a king whom the LORD, your God, will choose. Someone from among your own kindred you may set over you as king; you may not set over you a foreigner, who is no kin of yours. [16]But he shall not have a great number of horses; nor shall he make his people go back again to Egypt to acquire many horses, for the LORD said to you, Do not go back that way again. [17]Neither shall he have a great number of wives, lest his heart turn away, nor shall he accumulate a vast amount of silver and gold. [18]When he is sitting upon his royal throne, he shall write a copy of this law upon a scroll from the one that is in the custody of the levitical priests. [19]It shall remain with him and he shall read it as long as he lives, so that he may learn to fear the LORD, his God, and to observe carefully all the words of this law and these statutes, [20]so that he does not exalt himself over his kindred or turn aside from this commandment to the right or to the left, and so that he and his descendants may reign long in Israel.

Priests. 18:1 The levitical priests, the whole tribe of Levi, shall have no hereditary portion with Israel; they shall eat the fire offerings of the LORD and the portions due to him. [2]They shall have no heritage among their kindred; the LORD himself is their heritage, as he has told them. [3]This shall be the due of the priests from the people: those who are offering a sacrifice, whether an ox or a sheep, shall give the priest the shoulder, the jowls and the stomach. [4]The first fruits of your grain, your wine, and your oil, as well as the first shearing of your flock, you shall also give him. [5]For the LORD, your God, has chosen him out of all your tribes to be in attendance to minister in the name of the LORD, him and his descendants for all time.

[6]When a Levite goes from one of your communities anywhere in Israel in which he has been residing, to visit, as his heart may desire, the place which the LORD will choose, [7]and ministers there in the name of the LORD, his God, like all his fellow Levites who stand before the LORD there, [8]he shall receive the same portions to eat, along with his stipends and patrimony.

Prophets. [9]When you come into the land which the LORD, your God, is giving you, you shall not learn to imitate the abominations of the nations there. [10]Let there not be found among you anyone who causes their son or daughter to pass through the fire, or practices divination, or is a soothsayer, augur, or sorcerer, [11]or who casts spells, consults ghosts and spirits, or seeks oracles from the dead. [12]Anyone who does such things is an abomination to the LORD, and because of such abominations the LORD, your God, is dispossessing them before you. [13]You must be altogether sincere with the LORD, your God. [14]Although these nations whom you are about to dispossess listen to their soothsayers and diviners, the LORD, your God, will not permit you to do so.

[15]A prophet like me will the LORD, your God, raise up for you from among your own kindred; that is the one to whom you shall listen. [16]This is exactly what you requested of the LORD, your God, at Horeb on the day of the assembly, when you said, "Let me not again hear the voice of the LORD, my God, nor see this great fire any more, or I will die." [17]And the LORD said to me, What they have said is good. [18]I will raise up for them a prophet like you from among their kindred, and will put my words into the mouth of the prophet; the prophet shall tell them all that I command.

¹⁹Anyone who will not listen to my words which the prophet speaks in my name, I myself will hold accountable for it. ²⁰But if a prophet presumes to speak a word in my name that I have not commanded, or speaks in the name of other gods, that prophet shall die.

☐ HEBREWS 13

13:1 Let mutual love continue. ²Do not neglect hospitality, for through it some have unknowingly entertained angels. ³Be mindful of prisoners as if sharing their imprisonment, and of the ill-treated as of yourselves, for you also are in the body. ⁴Let marriage be honored among all and the marriage bed be kept undefiled, for God will judge the immoral and adulterers. ⁵Let your life be free from love of money but be content with what you have, for he has said, "I will never forsake you or abandon you." ⁶Thus we may say with confidence:

"The Lord is my helper,
[and] I will not be afraid.
What can anyone do to me?"

⁷Remember your leaders who spoke the word of God to you. Consider the outcome of their way of life and imitate their faith. ⁸Jesus Christ is the same yesterday, today, and forever.

⁹Do not be carried away by all kinds of strange teaching. It is good to have our hearts strengthened by grace and not by foods, which do not benefit those who live by them. ¹⁰We have an altar from which those who serve the tabernacle have no right to eat. ¹¹The bodies of the animals whose blood the high priest brings into the sanctuary as a sin offering are burned outside the camp. ¹²Therefore, Jesus also suffered outside the gate, to consecrate the people by his own blood. ¹³Let us then go to him outside the camp, bearing the reproach that he bore. ¹⁴For here we have no lasting city, but we seek the one that is to come. ¹⁵Through him [then] let us continually offer God a sacrifice of praise, that is, the fruit of lips that confess his name. ¹⁶Do not neglect to do good and to share what you have; God is pleased by sacrifices of that kind.

¹⁷Obey your leaders and defer to them, for they keep watch over you and will have to give an account, that they may fulfill their task with joy and not with sorrow, for that would be of no advantage to you.

¹⁸Pray for us, for we are confident that we have a clear conscience, wishing to act rightly in every respect. ¹⁹I especially ask for your prayers that I may be restored to you very soon.

²⁰May the God of peace, who brought up from the dead the great shepherd of the sheep by the blood of the eternal covenant, Jesus our Lord, ²¹furnish you with all that is good, that you may do his will. May he carry out in you what is pleasing to him through Jesus Christ, to whom be glory forever [and ever]. Amen.

²²Brothers, I ask you to bear with this message of encouragement, for I have written to you rather briefly. ²³I must let you know that our brother Timothy has been set free. If he comes soon, I shall see you together with him. ²⁴Greetings to all your leaders and to all the holy ones. Those from Italy send you greetings. ²⁵Grace be with all of you.

March 10

God measures out affliction according to our need.
— St. John Chrysostom

☐ DEUTERONOMY 19-23

Cities of Refuge. 19:1 When the LORD, your God, cuts down the nations whose land the LORD, your God, is giving you, and you have dispossessed them and settled in their cities and houses, [2]you shall set apart three cities in the land the LORD, your God, is giving you to possess. [3]You shall measure the distances and divide into three regions the land of which the LORD, your God, is giving you possession, so that every homicide will be able to find a refuge.

[4]This is the case of a homicide who may take refuge there and live: when someone strikes down a neighbor unintentionally and not out of previous hatred. [5]For example, if someone goes with a neighbor to a forest to cut wood, wielding an ax to cut down a tree, and its head flies off the handle and hits the neighbor a mortal blow, such a person may take refuge in one of these cities and live. [6]Should the distance be too great, the avenger of blood might in hot anger pursue, overtake, and strike the killer dead, even though that one does not deserve the death penalty since there had been no previous hatred; [7]for this reason I command you: Set apart three cities.

[8]But if the LORD, your God, enlarges your territory, as he swore to your ancestors, and gives you all the land he promised your ancestors he would give, [9]because you carefully observe this whole commandment which I give you today, loving the LORD, your God, and ever walking in his ways, then add three more cities to these three. [10]Thus, in the land which the LORD, your God, is giving you as a heritage, innocent blood will not be shed and you will not become guilty of bloodshed.

[11]However, if someone, hating a neighbor, lies in wait, attacks, and strikes the neighbor dead, and then flees to one of these cities, [12]the elders of the killer's own city shall send and have the killer taken from there, to be handed over to the avenger of blood and slain. [13]Do not show pity, but purge from Israel the innocent blood, so that it may go well with you.

Removal of Landmarks. [14]You shall not move your neighbor's boundary markers erected by your forebears in the heritage that will be allotted to you in the land the LORD, your God, is giving you to possess.

False Witnesses. [15]One witness alone shall not stand against someone in regard to any crime or any offense that may have been committed; a charge shall stand only on the testimony of two or three witnesses.

[16]If a hostile witness rises against someone to accuse that person of wrongdoing, [17]the two parties in the dispute shall appear in the presence of the LORD, in the presence of the priests and judges in office at that time, [18]and the judges must investigate it thoroughly. If the witness is a false witness and has falsely accused the other, [19]you shall do to the false witness just as that false witness planned to do to the other. Thus shall you purge the evil from your midst. [20]The rest shall hear and be afraid, and never again do such an evil thing as this in your midst. [21]Do not show pity. Life for life, eye for eye, tooth for tooth, hand for hand, and foot for foot!

Courage in War. 20:1 When you go out to war against your enemies and you see horses and chariots and an army greater than your own, you shall not be afraid of them, for the

LORD, your God, who brought you up from the land of Egypt, will be with you.

[2]When you are drawing near to battle, the priest shall come forward and speak to the army, [3]and say to them, "Hear, O Israel! Today you are drawing near for battle against your enemies. Do not be weakhearted or afraid, alarmed or frightened by them. [4]For it is the LORD, your God, who goes with you to fight for you against your enemies and give you victory."

[5]Then the officials shall speak to the army: "Is there anyone who has built a new house and not yet dedicated it? Let him return home, lest he die in battle and another dedicate it. [6]Is there anyone who has planted a vineyard and not yet plucked its fruit? Let him return home, lest he die in battle and another pluck its fruit. [7]Is there anyone who has betrothed a woman and not yet married her? Let him return home, lest he die in battle and another marry her." [8]The officials shall continue to speak to the army: "Is there anyone who is afraid and weakhearted? Let him return home, or else he might make the hearts of his fellows melt as his does."

[9]When the officials have finished speaking to the army, military commanders shall be appointed over them.

Cities of the Enemy. [10]When you draw near a city to attack it, offer it terms of peace. [11]If it agrees to your terms of peace and lets you in, all the people to be found in it shall serve you in forced labor. [12]But if it refuses to make peace with you and instead joins battle with you, lay siege to it, [13]and when the LORD, your God, delivers it into your power, put every male in it to the sword; [14]but the women and children and livestock and anything else in the city— all its spoil—you may take as plunder for yourselves, and you may enjoy this spoil of your enemies, which the LORD, your God, has given you.

[15]That is how you shall deal with any city at a considerable distance from you, which does not belong to these nations here. [16]But in the cities of these peoples that the LORD, your God, is giving you as a heritage, you shall not leave a single soul alive. [17]You must put them all under the ban—the Hittites, Amorites, Canaanites, Perizzites, Hivites, and Jebusites—just as the LORD, your God, has commanded you, [18]so that they do not teach you to do all the abominations that they do for their gods, and you thus sin against the LORD, your God.

Trees of a Besieged City. [19]When you are at war with a city and have to lay siege to it for a long time before you capture it, you shall not destroy its trees by putting an ax to them. You may eat of them, but you must not cut them down. Are the trees of the field human beings, that they should be included in your siege? [20]However, those trees which you know are not fruit trees you may destroy. You may cut them down to build siegeworks against the city that is waging war with you, until it falls.

Absolution of Untraced Murder. 21:1 If the corpse of someone who has been slain is found lying in the open, in the land the LORD, your God, is giving you to possess, and it is not known who killed the person, [2]your elders and judges shall go out and measure the distances to the cities that are in the neighborhood of the corpse. [3]When it is established which city is nearest the corpse, the elders of that city shall take a heifer that has never been put to work or worn a yoke; [4]the elders of that city shall bring the heifer down to a wadi with an everflowing stream at a place that has not been plowed or sown, and shall break the heifer's neck there in the wadi. [5]The priests, the descendants of Levi, shall come forward, for the LORD, your God, has chosen them to minister to him and to bless in the name of the LORD, and every case of dispute or assault shall be for them to decide. [6]Then all the elders of that city nearest the corpse shall wash their hands over the heifer whose neck was broken in the wadi, [7]and shall declare, "Our hands did not shed this blood, and our eyes did not see the deed. [8]Absolve, O LORD, your people Israel, whom you have redeemed, and do not let the guilt of shedding innocent blood remain in the midst of your people Israel." Thus they shall be absolved from the guilt of bloodshed, [9]and you shall purge the innocent blood from your midst, and do what is right in the eyes of the LORD.

Marriage with a Female Captive. [10]When you go out to war against your enemies and the LORD, your God, delivers them into your power, so that you take captives, [11]if you see a beautiful woman among the captives and become so enamored of her that you wish to have her as a wife, [12]and so you take her home to your house, she must shave her head, cut her nails, [13]lay aside her captive's garb, and stay in your house, mourning her father and mother for a full month. After that, you may come to her, and you shall be her husband and she shall be your wife. [14]If later on you lose your liking for her, you shall give her her freedom, if she wishes it; you must not sell her for money. Do not enslave her, since you have violated her.

Rights of the Firstborn. [15]If a man has two wives, one loved and the other unloved, and if both the loved and the unloved bear him sons, but the firstborn is the son of the unloved wife: [16]when he comes to bequeath his property to his sons he may not consider as his firstborn the son of the wife he loves, in preference to the son of the wife he does not love, the firstborn. [17]On the contrary, he shall recognize as his firstborn the son of the unloved wife, giving him a double share of whatever he happens to own, since he is the first fruits of his manhood, and to him belong the rights of the firstborn.

The Stubborn and Rebellious Son. [18]If someone has a stubborn and rebellious son who will not listen to his father or mother, and will not listen to them even though they discipline him, [19]his father and mother shall take hold of him and bring him out to the elders at the gate of his home city, [20]where they shall say to the elders of the city, "This son of ours is a stubborn and rebellious fellow who will not listen to us; he is a glutton and a drunkard." [21]Then all his fellow citizens shall stone him to death. Thus shall you purge the evil from your midst, and all Israel will hear and be afraid.

Corpse of a Criminal. [22]If a man guilty of a capital offense is put to death and you hang him on a tree, [23]his corpse shall not remain on the tree overnight. You must bury it the same day; anyone who is hanged is a curse of God. You shall not defile the land which the LORD, your God, is giving you as a heritage.

Concern for the Neighbor. 22:1 You shall not see your neighbor's ox or sheep going astray and ignore it; you must bring it back. [2]If this neighbor does not live near you, or you do not know who the owner may be, take it to your own house and keep it with you until your neighbor claims it; then return it. [3]You shall do the same with a donkey; you shall do the same with a garment; and you shall do the same with anything else which your neighbor loses and you happen to find. You may not ignore them.

[4]You shall not see your neighbor's donkey or ox fallen on the road and ignore it; you must help in lifting it up.

Various Precepts. [5]A woman shall not wear a man's garment, nor shall a man put on a woman's clothing; for anyone who does such things is an abomination to the LORD, your God.

[6]If, while walking along, you come across a bird's nest with young birds or eggs in it, in any tree or on the ground, and the mother bird is sitting on them, you shall not take away the mother bird along with

her brood. [7]You must let the mother go, taking only her brood, in order that you shall prosper and have a long life.

[8]When you build a new house, put a parapet around the roof, so that you do not bring bloodguilt upon your house if someone falls off.

[9]You shall not sow your vineyard with two different kinds of seed, or else its produce shall become forfeit, both the crop you have sown and the yield of the vineyard. [10]You shall not plow with an ox and a donkey harnessed together. [11]You shall not wear cloth made from wool and linen woven together.

[12]You shall put tassels on the four corners of the cloak that you wrap around yourself.

Marriage Legislation. [13]If a man, after marrying a woman and having relations with her, comes to dislike her, [14]and accuses her of misconduct and slanders her by saying, "I married this woman, but when I approached her I did not find evidence of her virginity," [15]the father and mother of the young woman shall take the evidence of her virginity and bring it to the elders at the city gate. [16]There the father of the young woman shall say to the elders, "I gave my daughter to this man in marriage, but he has come to dislike her, [17]and now accuses her of misconduct, saying: 'I did not find evidence of your daughter's virginity.' But here is the evidence of my daughter's virginity!" And they shall spread out the cloth before the elders of the city. [18]Then these city elders shall take the man and discipline him, [19]and fine him one hundred silver shekels, which they shall give to the young woman's father, because the man slandered a virgin in Israel. She shall remain his wife, and he may not divorce her as long as he lives. [20]But if this charge is true, and evidence of the young woman's virginity is not found, [21]they shall bring the young woman to the entrance of her father's house and there the men of her town shall stone her to death, because she committed a shameful crime in Israel by prostituting herself in her father's house. Thus shall you purge the evil from your midst.

[22]If a man is discovered lying with a woman who is married to another, they both shall die, the man who was lying with the woman as well as the woman. Thus shall you purge the evil from Israel.

[23]If there is a young woman, a virgin who is betrothed, and a man comes upon her in the city and lies with her, [24]you shall bring them both out to the gate of the city and there stone them to death: the young woman because she did not cry out though she was in the city, and the man because he violated his neighbor's wife. Thus shall you purge the evil from your midst. [25]But if it is in the open fields that a man comes upon the betrothed young woman, seizes her and lies with her, only the man who lay with her shall die. [26]You shall do nothing to the young woman, since the young woman is not guilty of a capital offense. As when a man rises up against his neighbor and murders him, so in this case: [27]it was in the open fields that he came upon her, and though the betrothed young woman may have cried out, there was no one to save her.

[28]If a man comes upon a young woman, a virgin who is not betrothed, seizes her and lies with her, and they are discovered, [29]the man who lay with her shall give the young woman's father fifty silver shekels and she will be his wife, because he has violated her. He may not divorce her as long as he lives.

23:1 A man shall not marry his father's wife, nor shall he dishonor his father's bed.

Membership in the Assembly. [2]No one whose testicles have been crushed or whose penis has been cut off may come into the assembly of the LORD. [3]No one born of an illicit union may come into the assembly of the LORD, nor any descendant of such even to the tenth generation may come into the assembly of the LORD. [4]No Ammonite or

Moabite may ever come into the assembly of the LORD, nor may any of their descendants even to the tenth generation come into the assembly of the LORD, ⁵because they would not come to meet you with food and water on your journey after you left Egypt, and because they hired Balaam, son of Beor, from Pethor in Aram Naharaim, to curse you. ⁶The LORD, your God, would not listen to Balaam but turned his curse into a blessing for you, because the LORD, your God, loves you. ⁷Never seek their welfare or prosperity as long as you live. ⁸Do not abhor the Edomite: he is your brother. Do not abhor the Egyptian: you were a resident alien in his country. ⁹Children born to them may come into the assembly of the LORD in the third generation.

Cleanliness in Camp. ¹⁰When in camp during an expedition against your enemies, you shall keep yourselves from anything bad. ¹¹If one of you becomes unclean because of a nocturnal emission, he shall go outside the camp; he shall not come back into the camp. ¹²Toward evening, he shall bathe in water; then, when the sun has set, he may come back into the camp. ¹³Outside the camp you shall have a place set aside where you shall go. ¹⁴You shall keep a trowel in your equipment and, when you go outside to relieve yourself, you shall dig a hole with it and then cover up your excrement. ¹⁵Since the LORD, your God, journeys along in the midst of your camp to deliver you and to give your enemies over to you, your camp must be holy, so that he does not see anything indecent in your midst and turn away from you.

☐ 1 PETER 1:1-12

Greeting. 1:1 Peter, an apostle of Jesus Christ, to the chosen sojourners of the dispersion in Pontus, Galatia, Cappadocia, Asia, and Bithynia, ²in the foreknowledge of God the Father, through sanctification

Various Precepts. ¹⁶You shall not hand over to their master any slaves who have taken refuge with you from their master. ¹⁷Let them live among you in any place they choose, in any one of your communities that seems good to them. Do not oppress them.

¹⁸There shall be no temple prostitute among the Israelite women, nor a temple prostitute among the Israelite men. ¹⁹You shall not offer a prostitute's fee or a dog's pay as any kind of votive offering in the house of the LORD, your God; both these things are an abomination to the LORD, your God.

²⁰You shall not demand interest from your kindred on a loan of money or of food or of anything else which is loaned. ²¹From a foreigner you may demand interest, but you may not demand interest from your kindred, so that the LORD, your God, may bless you in all your undertakings on the land you are to enter and possess.

²²When you make a vow to the LORD, your God, you shall not delay in fulfilling it; for the LORD, your God, will surely require it of you and you will be held guilty. ²³Should you refrain from making a vow, you will not be held guilty. ²⁴But whatever your tongue utters you must be careful to do, just as you freely vowed to the LORD, your God, with your own mouth.

²⁵When you go through your neighbor's vineyard, you may eat as many grapes as you wish, until you are satisfied, but do not put them in your basket. ²⁶When you go through your neighbor's grainfield, you may pluck some of the ears with your hand, but do not put a sickle to your neighbor's grain.

by the Spirit, for obedience and sprinkling with the blood of Jesus Christ: may grace and peace be yours in abundance.

Blessing. ³Blessed be the God and Father of our Lord Jesus Christ, who in his great mercy gave us a new birth to a living hope through the resurrection of Jesus Christ from the dead, [4]to an inheritance that is imperishable, undefiled, and unfading, kept in heaven for you [5]who by the power of God are safeguarded through faith, to a salvation that is ready to be revealed in the final time. [6]In this you rejoice, although now for a little while you may have to suffer through various trials, [7]so that the genuineness of your faith, more precious than gold that is perishable even though tested by fire, may prove to be for praise, glory, and honor at the revelation of Jesus Christ. [8]Although you have not seen him you love him; even though you do not see him now yet believe in him, you rejoice with an indescribable and glorious joy, [9]as you attain the goal of [your] faith, the salvation of your souls.

[10]Concerning this salvation, prophets who prophesied about the grace that was to be yours searched and investigated it, [11]investigating the time and circumstances that the Spirit of Christ within them indicated when it testified in advance to the sufferings destined for Christ and the glories to follow them. [12]It was revealed to them that they were serving not themselves but you with regard to the things that have now been announced to you by those who preached the good news to you [through] the holy Spirit sent from heaven, things into which angels longed to look.

March 11

He who aspires to the grace of God must be pure, with a heart as innocent as a child's. Purity of heart is to God like a perfume, sweet and agreeable.

— St. Nicholas of Flüe

☐ DEUTERONOMY 24-25

Marriage Legislation. 24:1 When a man, after marrying a woman, is later displeased with her because he finds in her something indecent, and he writes out a bill of divorce and hands it to her, thus dismissing her from his house, [2]if on leaving his house she goes and becomes the wife of another man, [3]and the second husband, too, comes to dislike her and he writes out a bill of divorce and hands it to her, thus dismissing her from his house, or if this second man who has married her dies, [4]then her former husband, who dismissed her, may not again take her as his wife after she has become defiled. That would be an abomination before the Lord, and you shall not bring such guilt upon the land the Lord, your God, is giving you as a heritage.

[5]When a man is newly wed, he shall not go out on a military expedition, nor shall any duty be imposed on him. He shall be exempt for one year for the sake of his family, to bring joy to the wife he has married.

Pledges and Kidnappings. [6]No one shall take a hand mill or even its upper stone as a pledge for debt, for that would be taking as a pledge the debtor's life.

[7]If anyone is caught kidnapping a fellow Israelite, enslaving or selling the victim, that kidnapper shall be put to death. Thus shall you purge the evil from your midst.

Skin Diseases. [8]In an attack of scaly infection you shall be careful to observe exactly and to carry out all the instructions the levitical priests give you, as I have commanded them: observe them carefully. ⁹Remember what the LORD, your God, did to Miriam on the journey after you left Egypt.

Loans and Wages. ¹⁰When you make a loan of any kind to your neighbor, you shall not enter the neighbor's house to receive the pledge, ¹¹but shall wait outside until the person to whom you are making the loan brings the pledge outside to you. ¹²If the person is poor, you shall not sleep in the pledged garment, ¹³but shall definitely return it at sunset, so that your neighbor may sleep in the garment and bless you. That will be your justice before the LORD, your God.

¹⁴You shall not exploit a poor and needy hired servant, whether one of your own kindred or one of the resident aliens who live in your land, within your gates. ¹⁵On each day you shall pay the servant's wages before the sun goes down, since the servant is poor and is counting on them. Otherwise the servant will cry to the LORD against you, and you will be held guilty.

Individual Responsibility. ¹⁶Parents shall not be put to death for their children, nor shall children be put to death for their parents; only for one's own crime shall a person be put to death.

Rights of the Unprotected. ¹⁷You shall not deprive the resident alien or the orphan of justice, nor take the clothing of a widow as pledge. ¹⁸For, remember, you were slaves in Egypt, and the LORD, your God, redeemed you from there; that is why I command you to do this.

¹⁹When you reap the harvest in your field and overlook a sheaf in the field, you shall not go back to get it; let it be for the resident alien, the orphan, and the widow, so that the LORD, your God, may bless you in all your undertakings. ²⁰When you knock down the fruit of your olive trees, you shall not go over the branches a second time; let what remains be for the resident alien, the orphan, and the widow. ²¹When you pick your grapes, you shall not go over the vineyard a second time; let what remains be for the resident alien, the orphan, and the widow. ²²For remember that you were slaves in the land of Egypt; that is why I command you to do this.

Limits on Punishments. 25:1 When there is a dispute and the parties draw near for judgment, and a decision is given, declaring one party in the right and the other in the wrong, ²if the one in the wrong deserves whipping, the judge shall have him lie down and in the presence of the judge receive the number of lashes the crime warrants. ³Forty lashes may be given, but no more; or else, if more lashes are added to these many blows, your brother will be degraded in your sight.

Treatment of Oxen. ⁴You shall not muzzle an ox when it treads out grain.

Levirate Marriage. ⁵When brothers live together and one of them dies without a son, the widow of the deceased shall not marry anyone outside the family; but her husband's brother shall come to her, marrying her and performing the duty of a brother-in-law. ⁶The firstborn son she bears shall continue the name of the deceased brother, that his name may not be blotted out from Israel. ⁷But if a man does not want to marry his brother's wife, she shall go up to the elders at the gate and say, "My brother-in-law refuses to perpetuate his brother's name in Israel and does not intend to perform his duty toward me." ⁸Thereupon the elders of his city shall summon him and speak to him. If he persists in saying, "I do not want to marry her," ⁹his sister-in-law, in the presence of the elders, shall go up to him and strip his sandal from his foot and spit in his face, declaring, "This is how one should be treated who will not build up his brother's family!" ¹⁰And his name shall be called in Israel, "the house of the man stripped of his sandal."

Various Precepts. [11]When two men are fighting and the wife of one intervenes to save her husband from the blows of his opponent, if she stretches out her hand and seizes the latter by his genitals, [12]you shall chop off her hand; show no pity.

[13]You shall not keep two differing weights in your bag, one heavy and the other light; [14]nor shall you keep two different ephahs in your house, one large and the other small. [15]But use a full and just weight, a full and just ephah, so that you may have a long life on the land the LORD, your God, is giving you. [16]For everyone who does these things, everyone who does what is dishonest, is an abomination to the LORD, your God.

[17]Bear in mind what Amalek did to you on the journey after you left Egypt, [18]how he surprised you along the way, weak and weary as you were, and struck down at the rear all those who lagged behind; he did not fear God. [19]Therefore, when the LORD, your God, gives you rest from all your enemies round about in the land which the LORD, your God, is giving you to possess as a heritage, you shall blot out the memory of Amalek from under the heavens. Do not forget!

☐ 1 PETER 1:13-25

Obedience. 1:13 Therefore, gird up the loins of your mind, live soberly, and set your hopes completely on the grace to be brought to you at the revelation of Jesus Christ. [14]Like obedient children, do not act in compliance with the desires of your former ignorance [15]but, as he who called you is holy, be holy yourselves in every aspect of your conduct, [16]for it is written, "Be holy because I [am] holy."

Reverence. [17]Now if you invoke as Father him who judges impartially according to each one's works, conduct yourselves with reverence during the time of your sojourning, [18]realizing that you were ransomed from your futile conduct, handed on by your ancestors, not with perishable things like silver or gold [19]but with the precious blood of Christ as of a spotless unblemished lamb. [20]He was known before the foundation of the world but revealed in the final time for you, [21]who through him believe in God who raised him from the dead and gave him glory, so that your faith and hope are in God.

Mutual Love. [22]Since you have purified yourselves by obedience to the truth for sincere mutual love, love one another intensely from a [pure] heart. [23]You have been born anew, not from perishable but from imperishable seed, through the living and abiding word of God, [24]for:

"All flesh is like grass,
and all its glory like the flower of
the field;
the grass withers,
and the flower wilts;
[25]but the word of the Lord remains
forever."

This is the word that has been proclaimed to you.

March 12

St. Maximilian

My army is the army of God, and I cannot fight for this world.
— ST. MAXIMILIAN

☐ DEUTERONOMY 26-29

Thanksgiving for the Harvest. 26:1 When you have come into the land which the LORD, your God, is giving you as a heritage, and have taken possession and settled in it, ²you shall take some first fruits of the various products of the soil which you harvest from the land the LORD, your God, is giving you; put them in a basket and go to the place which the LORD, your God, will choose as the dwelling place for his name. ³There you shall go to the priest in office at that time and say to him, "Today I acknowledge to the LORD, my God, that I have indeed come into the land which the LORD swore to our ancestors to give us." ⁴The priest shall then take the basket from your hands and set it in front of the altar of the LORD, your God. ⁵Then you shall declare in the presence of the LORD, your God, "My father was a refugee Aramean who went down to Egypt with a small household and lived there as a resident alien. But there he became a nation great, strong and numerous. ⁶When the Egyptians maltreated and oppressed us, imposing harsh servitude upon us, ⁷we cried to the LORD, the God of our ancestors, and the LORD heard our cry and saw our affliction, our toil and our oppression. ⁸Then the LORD brought us out of Egypt with a strong hand and outstretched arm, with terrifying power, with signs and wonders, ⁹and brought us to this place, and gave us this land, a land flowing with milk and honey. ¹⁰Now, therefore, I have brought the first fruits of the products of the soil which you, LORD, have given me." You shall set them before the LORD, your God, and you shall bow down before the LORD, your God. ¹¹Then you and your household, together with the Levite and the resident aliens who live among you, shall celebrate with all these good things which the LORD, your God, has given you.

Declaration Concerning Tithes. ¹²When you have finished setting aside all the tithes of your produce in the third year, the year of the tithes, and have given them to the Levite, the resident alien, the orphan and the widow, that they may eat and be satisfied in your own communities, ¹³you shall declare before the LORD, your God, "I have purged my house of the sacred portion and I have given it to the Levite, the resident alien, the orphan and the widow, just as you have commanded me. I have not transgressed any of your commandments, nor forgotten any. ¹⁴I have not eaten any of the tithe while in mourning; I have not brought any of it while unclean; I have not offered any of it to the dead. I have thus obeyed the voice of the LORD, my God, and done just as you have commanded me. ¹⁵Look down, then, from heaven, your holy abode, and bless your people Israel and the fields you have given us, as you promised on oath to our ancestors, a land flowing with milk and honey."

The Covenant. ¹⁶This day the LORD, your God, is commanding you to observe these statutes and ordinances. Be careful, then, to observe them with your whole heart and with your whole being. ¹⁷Today you have accepted the LORD's agreement: he will be your God, and you will walk in his ways, observe his statutes, commandments, and ordinances, and obey his voice. ¹⁸And today the LORD has accepted your agreement: you will be a people specially his own, as he promised you, you will keep all his commandments, [19]and he will set you high in praise and renown and glory above all nations he has made, and you will be a people holy to the LORD, your God, as he promised.

The Altar on Mount Ebal. 27:1 Then Moses, with the elders of Israel, commanded the people, saying: Keep this whole commandment which I give you today. [2]On the day you cross the Jordan into the land which the LORD, your God, is giving you, set up some large stones and coat them with plaster. [3]Write on them, at the time you cross, all the words of this law, so that you may enter the land which the LORD, your God, is giving you, a land flowing with milk and honey, just as the LORD, the God of your ancestors, promised you. [4]When you cross the Jordan, on Mount Ebal you shall set up these stones concerning which I command you today, and coat them with plaster, [5]and you shall build there an altar to the LORD, your God, an altar made of stones that no iron tool has touched. [6]You shall build this altar of the LORD, your God, with unhewn stones, and shall offer on it burnt offerings to the LORD, your God. [7]You shall also offer communion sacrifices and eat them there, rejoicing in the presence of the LORD, your God. [8]On the stones you shall inscribe all the words of this law very clearly.

[9]Moses, with the levitical priests, then said to all Israel: Be silent, Israel, and listen! This day you have become the people of the LORD, your God. [10]You shall obey the voice of the LORD, your God, and keep his commandments and statutes which I am giving you today.

Preparation for Blessings and Curses. [11]That same day Moses commanded the people, saying: [12]When you cross the Jordan, these shall stand on Mount Gerizim to bless the people: Simeon, Levi, Judah, Issachar, Joseph and Benjamin. [13]And these shall stand on Mount Ebal for the curse: Reuben, Gad, Asher, Zebulun, Dan and Naphtali.

The Twelve Curses. [14]The Levites shall proclaim in a loud voice to all the Israelites: [15]"Cursed be anyone who makes a carved or molten idol, an abomination to the LORD, the work of a craftsman's hands, and sets it up in secret!" And all the people shall answer, "Amen!"

[16]"Cursed be anyone who dishonors father or mother!" And all the people shall answer, "Amen!"

[17]"Cursed be anyone who moves a neighbor's boundary markers!" And all the people shall answer, "Amen!"

[18]"Cursed be anyone who misleads the blind on their way!" And all the people shall answer, "Amen!"

[19]"Cursed be anyone who deprives the resident alien, the orphan or the widow of justice!" And all the people shall answer, "Amen!"

[20]"Cursed be anyone who has relations with his father's wife, for he dishonors his father's bed!" And all the people shall answer, "Amen!"

[21]"Cursed be anyone who has relations with any animal!" And all the people shall answer, "Amen!"

[22]"Cursed be anyone who has relations with his sister, whether his father's daughter or his mother's daughter!" And all the people shall answer, "Amen!"

[23]"Cursed be anyone who has relations with his mother-in-law!" And all the people shall answer, "Amen!"

[24]"Cursed be anyone who strikes down a neighbor in secret!" And all the people shall answer, "Amen!"

[25]"Cursed be anyone who accepts payment to kill an innocent person!" And all the people shall answer, "Amen!"

[26]"Cursed be anyone whose actions do not uphold the words of this law!" And all the people shall answer, "Amen!"

Blessings for Obedience. 28:1 Now, if you diligently obey the voice of the Lord, your God, carefully observing all his commandments which I give you today, the Lord, your God, will set you high above all the nations of the earth. ²All these blessings will come upon you and overwhelm you when you obey the voice of the Lord, your God:

³May you be blessed in the city,
and blessed in the country!
⁴Blessed be the fruit of your womb,
the produce of your soil and the
offspring of your livestock,
the issue of your herds and the
young of your flocks!
⁵Blessed be your grain basket and your
kneading bowl!
⁶May you be blessed in your coming in,
and blessed in your going out!

Victory and Prosperity. ⁷The Lord will beat down before you the enemies that rise up against you; they will come out against you from one direction, and flee before you in seven. ⁸The Lord will affirm the blessing upon you, on your barns and on all your undertakings; he will bless you in the land that the Lord, your God, is giving you. ⁹The Lord will establish you as a holy people, as he swore to you, if you keep the commandments of the Lord, your God, and walk in his ways. ¹⁰All the peoples of the earth will see that the name of the Lord is proclaimed over you, and they will be afraid of you. ¹¹The Lord will generously increase the fruit of your womb, the offspring of your livestock, and the produce of your soil, upon the land which the Lord swore to your ancestors he would give you. ¹²The Lord will open up for you his rich storehouse, the heavens, to give your land rain in due season and to bless all the works of your hands. You will lend to many nations but borrow from none. ¹³The Lord will make you the head not the tail, the top not the bottom, if you obey the commandments of the Lord, your God, which I am giving you today, observing them carefully, ¹⁴not turning aside, either to the right or to the left, from any of the words which I am giving you today, following other gods and serving them.

Curses for Disobedience. ¹⁵But if you do not obey the voice of the Lord, your God, carefully observing all his commandments and statutes which I give you today, all these curses shall come upon you and overwhelm you:

¹⁶May you be cursed in the city, and cursed in the country! ¹⁷Cursed be your grain basket and your kneading bowl! ¹⁸Cursed be the fruit of your womb, the produce of your soil and the offspring of your livestock, the issue of your herds and the young of your flocks! ¹⁹May you be cursed in your coming in, and cursed in your going out!

Sickness and Defeat. ²⁰The Lord will send on you a curse, panic, and frustration in everything you set your hand to, until you are speedily destroyed and perish for the evil you have done in forsaking me. ²¹The Lord will make disease cling to you until he has made an end of you from the land you are entering to possess. ²²The Lord will strike you with consumption, fever, and inflammation, with fiery heat and drought, with blight and mildew, that will pursue you until you perish. ²³The heavens over your heads will be like bronze and the earth under your feet like iron. ²⁴For rain the Lord will give your land powdery dust, which will come down upon you from the heavens until you are destroyed. ²⁵The Lord will let you be beaten down before your enemies; though you advance against them from one direction, you will flee before them in seven, so that you will become an object of horror to all the kingdoms of the earth. ²⁶Your corpses will become food for all the birds of the air and for the beasts of the field, with no one to frighten them off. ²⁷The Lord will strike you with Egyptian boils and with tumors, skin diseases and the itch, from none of which you can be cured. [28]And the LORD will strike you with madness, blindness and panic, [29]so that even at midday you will grope in the dark as though blind, unable to find your way.

Despoilment. You will be oppressed and robbed continually, with no one to come to your aid. [30]Though you betroth a wife, another will have her. Though you build a house, you will not live in it. Though you plant a vineyard, you will not pluck its fruits. [31]Your ox will be slaughtered before your eyes, but you will not eat its flesh. Your donkey will be stolen in your presence, but you will never get it back. Your flocks will be given to your enemies, with no one to come to your aid. [32]Your sons and daughters will be given to another people while you strain your eyes looking for them every day, having no power to do anything. [33]A people you do not know will consume the fruit of your soil and of all your labor, and you will be thoroughly oppressed and continually crushed, [34]until you are driven mad by what your eyes must look upon. [35]The LORD will strike you with malignant boils of which you cannot be cured, on your knees and legs, and from the soles of your feet to the crown of your head.

Exile. [36]The LORD will bring you, and your king whom you have set over you, to a nation which you and your ancestors have not known, and there you will serve other gods, of wood and stone, [37]and you will be a horror, a byword, a taunt among all the peoples to which the LORD will drive you.

Fruitless Labors. [38]Though you take out seed to your field, you will harvest but little, for the locusts will devour it. [39]Though you plant and cultivate vineyards, you will not drink or store up the wine, for the worms will eat them. [40]Though you have olive trees throughout your country, you will have no oil for ointment, for your olives will drop off. [41]Though you beget sons and daughters, they will not remain with you, for they will go into captivity. [42]Buzzing insects will take possession of all your trees

and the crops of your soil. [43]The resident aliens among you will rise above you higher and higher, while you sink lower and lower. [44]They will lend to you, not you to them. They will become the head, you the tail.

[45]All these curses will come upon you, pursuing you and overwhelming you, until you are destroyed, because you would not obey the voice of the LORD, your God, by keeping his commandments and statutes which he gave you. [46]They will be a sign and a wonder for you and your descendants for all time. [47]Since you would not serve the LORD, your God, with heartfelt joy for abundance of every kind, [48]in hunger and thirst, in nakedness and utter want, you will serve the enemies whom the LORD will send against you. He will put an iron yoke on your neck, until he destroys you.

Invasion and Siege. [49]The LORD will raise up against you a nation from afar, from the end of the earth, that swoops down like an eagle, a nation whose language you do not understand, [50]a nation of fierce appearance, that shows neither respect for the aged nor mercy for the young. [51]They will consume the offspring of your livestock and the produce of your soil, until you are destroyed; they will leave you no grain or wine or oil, no issue of herd, no young of flock, until they have brought about your ruin. [52]They will besiege you in each of your communities, until the great, fortified walls, in which you trust, come tumbling down all over your land. They will besiege you in every community throughout the land which the LORD, your God, has given you, [53]and because of the siege and the distress to which your enemy subjects you, you will eat the fruit of your womb, the flesh of your own sons and daughters whom the LORD, your God, has given you. [54]The most refined and fastidious man among you will begrudge his brother and his beloved wife and his surviving children, [55]any share in the flesh of his children that he himself is using for food because nothing else is left him—

such the siege and distress to which your enemy will subject you in all your communities. [56]The most fastidious woman among you, who would not venture to set the sole of her foot on the ground, so refined and fastidious is she, will begrudge her beloved husband and her son and daughter [57]the afterbirth that issues from her womb and the infants she brings forth because she secretly eats them for want of anything else—such the siege and distress to which your enemy will subject you in your communities.

Plagues. [58]If you are not careful to observe all the words of this law which is written in this book, and to fear this glorious and awesome name, the LORD, your God, [59]the LORD will bring upon you and your descendants wondrous calamities, severe and constant calamities, and malignant and constant sicknesses. [60]He will bring back upon you all the diseases of Egypt which you dread, and they will cling to you. [61]Even any sickness or calamity not written in this book of the law, that too the LORD will bring upon you until you are destroyed. [62]You who were numerous as the stars of the heavens will be left few in number, because you would not obey the voice of the LORD, your God.

Exile. [63]Just as the LORD once took delight in making you prosper and grow, so will the LORD now take delight in ruining and destroying you, and you will be plucked out of the land you are now entering to possess. [64]The LORD will scatter you among all the peoples from one end of the earth to the other, and there you will serve other gods, of wood and stone, which you and your ancestors have not known. [65]Among these nations you will find no rest, not even a resting place for the sole of your foot, for there the LORD will give you an anguished heart and wearied eyes and a trembling spirit. [66]Your life will hang in suspense and you will stand in dread both day and night, never sure of your life. [67]In the morning you will say, "Would that it were evening!" and in the evening you will say, "Would that it were morning!" because of the dread that your heart must feel and the sight that your eyes must see. [68]The LORD will send you back in ships to Egypt, by a route which I told you that you would never see again; and there you will offer yourselves for sale to your enemies as male and female slaves, but there will be no buyer.

[69]These are the words of the covenant which the LORD commanded Moses to make with the Israelites in the land of Moab, in addition to the covenant he made with them at Horeb.

Past Favors Recalled. 29:1 Moses summoned all Israel and said to them, You have seen with your own eyes all that the LORD did in the land of Egypt to Pharaoh and all his servants and to all his land, [2]the great testings your own eyes have seen, and those great signs and wonders. [3]But the LORD has not given you a heart to understand, or eyes to see, or ears to hear until this day. [4]I led you for forty years in the wilderness. Your clothes did not fall from you in tatters nor your sandals from your feet; [5]it was not bread that you ate, nor wine or beer that you drank—so that you might know that I, the LORD, am your God. [6]When you came to this place, Sihon, king of Heshbon, and Og, king of Bashan, came out to engage us in battle, but we defeated them [7]and took their land, and gave it as a heritage to the Reubenites, Gadites, and the half-tribe of Manasseh. [8]Observe carefully the words of this covenant, therefore, in order that you may succeed in whatever you do.

All Israel Bound by Covenant. [9]You are standing today, all of you, in the presence of the LORD, your God—your tribal heads, elders, and officials, all of the men of Israel, [10]your children, your wives, and the resident alien who lives in your camp, from those who cut wood to those who draw water for you— [11]to enter into the covenant of the LORD, your God, which the LORD, your God, is making with you today, with its curse, [12]so that he may establish you today as his people and he may be your God, as he promised you and as he swore to your ancestors, to Abraham, Isaac and Jacob. [13]But it is not with you alone that I am making this covenant, with its curse, [14]but with those who are standing here with us today in the presence of the LORD, our God, and with those who are not here with us today.

Warning Against Idolatry. [15]You know that we lived in the land of Egypt and that we passed through the nations, that you too passed through [16]and saw the loathsome things and idols of wood and stone, of gold and silver, that they possess. [17]There may be among you a man or woman, or a clan or tribe, whose heart is now turning away from the LORD, our God, to go and serve the gods of these nations; there may be among you a root bearing poison and wormwood; [18]if any such persons, after hearing the words of this curse, should congratulate themselves, saying in their hearts, "I am safe, even though I walk in stubbornness of heart," thereby sweeping away moist and dry alike, [19]the LORD will never consent to pardon them. Instead, the LORD's burning wrath will flare up against them; every curse written in this book will pounce on them, and the LORD will blot out their names from under the heavens.

[20]The LORD will single them out from all the tribes of Israel for doom, in keeping with all the curses of the covenant written in this book of the law.

Punishment for Idolatry. [21]Future generations, your descendants who will rise up after you, as well as the foreigners who will come here from distant lands, when they see the calamities of this land and the ills the LORD has inflicted upon it—[22]all its soil burned out by sulphur and salt, unsown and unfruitful, without a blade of grass, like the catastrophe of Sodom and Gomorrah, Admah and Zeboiim, which the LORD overthrew in his furious wrath— [23]they and all the nations will ask, "Why has the LORD dealt thus with this land? Why this great outburst of wrath?" [24]And they will say, "Because they abandoned the covenant of the LORD, the God of their ancestors, which he had made with them when he brought them out of the land of Egypt, [25]and they went and served other gods and bowed down to them, gods whom they did not know and whom he had not apportioned to them. [26]So the anger of the LORD flared up against this land and brought on it every curse written in this book. [27]The LORD uprooted them from their soil in anger, fury, and great wrath, and cast them out into another land, as they are today." [28]The hidden things belong to the LORD our God, but the revealed things are for us and for our children forever, to observe all the words of this law.

☐ 1 PETER 2:1-12

God's House and People. 2:1 Rid yourselves of all malice and all deceit, insincerity, envy, and all slander; [2]like newborn infants, long for pure spiritual milk so that through it you may grow into salvation, [3]for you have tasted that the Lord is good. [4]Come to him, a living stone, rejected by human beings but chosen and precious in the sight of God, [5]and, like living stones, let yourselves be built into a spiritual house to be a holy priesthood to offer spiritual sacrifices acceptable to God through Jesus Christ. [6]For it says in scripture:

"Behold, I am laying a stone in Zion,
    a cornerstone, chosen and precious,
and whoever believes in it shall not be
    put to shame."

[7]Therefore, its value is for you who have faith, but for those without faith:

"The stone which the builders rejected
    has become the cornerstone,"

[8]and

"A stone that will make people
        stumble,
    and a rock that will make them fall."

They stumble by disobeying the word, as is their destiny.

[9]But you are "a chosen race, a royal priesthood, a holy nation, a people of his own, so that you may announce the praises" of him who called you out of darkness into his wonderful light.

[10]Once you were "no people"
    but now you are God's people;
you "had not received mercy"
    but now you have received mercy.

Christian Examples. [11]Beloved, I urge you as aliens and sojourners to keep away from worldly desires that wage war against the soul. [12]Maintain good conduct among the Gentiles, so that if they speak of you as evildoers, they may observe your good works and glorify God on the day of visitation.

March 13

One must not think that a person who is suffering is not praying. He is offering up his sufferings to God, and many a time he is praying much more truly than one who goes away by himself and meditates his head off and, if he has squeezed out a few tears, thinks that is prayer.

— St. Teresa of Ávila

☐ DEUTERONOMY 30–32

Compassion for the Repentant. 30:1 When all these things, the blessing and the curse which I have set before you, come upon you, and you take them to heart in any of the nations where the Lord, your God, has dispersed you, [2]and return to the Lord, your God, obeying his voice, according to all that I am commanding you today, you and your children, with your whole heart and your whole being, [3]the Lord, your God, will restore your fortunes and will have compassion on you; he will again gather you from all the peoples where the Lord, your God, has scattered you. [4]Though you may have been dispersed to the farthest corner of the heavens, even from there will the Lord, your God, gather you; even from there will he bring you back. [5]The Lord, your God, will then bring you into the land your ancestors once possessed, that you may possess it; and he will make you more prosperous and numerous than your ancestors. [6]The Lord, your God, will circumcise your hearts and the hearts of your descendants, so that you will love the Lord, your God, with your whole heart and your whole being, in order that you may live. [7]The Lord, your God, will put all those curses on your enemies and the foes who pursued you. [8]You, however, shall again obey the voice of the Lord and observe all his commandments which I am giving you today. [9]Then the Lord, your God, will generously increase your undertakings, the fruit of your womb, the offspring of your livestock, and the produce of your soil; for the LORD, your God, will again take delight in your prosperity, just as he took delight in your ancestors', [10]because you will obey the voice of the LORD, your God, keeping the commandments and statutes that are written in this book of the law, when you return to the LORD, your God, with your whole heart and your whole being.

[11]For this command which I am giving you today is not too wondrous or remote for you. [12]It is not in the heavens, that you should say, "Who will go up to the heavens to get it for us and tell us of it, that we may do it?" [13]Nor is it across the sea, that you should say, "Who will cross the sea to get it for us and tell us of it, that we may do it?" [14]No, it is something very near to you, in your mouth and in your heart, to do it.

The Choice Before Israel. [15]See, I have today set before you life and good, death and evil. [16]If you obey the commandments of the LORD, your God, which I am giving you today, loving the LORD, your God, and walking in his ways, and keeping his commandments, statutes and ordinances, you will live and grow numerous, and the LORD, your God, will bless you in the land you are entering to possess. [17]If, however, your heart turns away and you do not obey, but are led astray and bow down to other gods and serve them, [18]I tell you today that you will certainly perish; you will not have a long life on the land which you are crossing the Jordan to enter and possess. [19]I call heaven and earth today to witness against you: I have set before you life and death, the blessing and the curse. Choose life, then, that you and your descendants may live, [20]by loving the LORD, your God, obeying his voice, and holding fast to him. For that will mean life for you, a long life for you to live on the land which the LORD swore to your ancestors, to Abraham, Isaac, and Jacob, to give to them.

The Lord's Leadership. 31:1 When Moses had finished speaking these words to all Israel, [2]he said to them, I am now one hundred and twenty years old and am no longer able to go out and come in; besides, the LORD has said to me, Do not cross this Jordan. [3]It is the LORD, your God, who will cross before you; he will destroy these nations before you, that you may dispossess them. (It is Joshua who will cross before you, as the LORD promised.) [4]The LORD will deal with them just as he dealt with Sihon and Og, the kings of the Amorites, and with their country, when he destroyed them. [5]When, therefore, the LORD delivers them up to you, you shall deal with them according to the whole commandment which I have given you. [6]Be strong and steadfast; have no fear or dread of them, for it is the LORD, your God, who marches with you; he will never fail you or forsake you.

Call of Joshua. [7]Then Moses summoned Joshua and in the presence of all Israel said to him, "Be strong and steadfast, for you shall bring this people into the land which the LORD swore to their ancestors he would give them; it is you who will give them possession of it. [8]It is the LORD who goes before you; he will be with you and will never fail you or forsake you. So do not fear or be dismayed."

The Reading of the Law. [9]When Moses had written down this law, he gave it to the levitical priests who carry the ark of the covenant of the LORD, and to all the elders of Israel. [10]Moses commanded them, saying, On the feast of Booths, at the prescribed time in the year for remission which comes at the end of every seven-year period, [11]when all Israel goes to appear before the LORD, your God, in the place which he will choose, you shall read this law aloud in the presence of all Israel. [12]Assemble the people—men, women and children, as well as the resident aliens who live in your communities—that they may hear and so learn to fear the LORD, your

God, and to observe carefully all the words of this law. ¹³Their children also, who do not know it yet, shall hear and learn to fear the LORD, your God, as long as you live on the land which you are about to cross the Jordan to possess.

Commission to Joshua. ¹⁴The LORD said to Moses, The time is now approaching for you to die. Summon Joshua, and present yourselves at the tent of meeting that I may commission him. So Moses and Joshua went and presented themselves at the tent of meeting. ¹⁵And the LORD appeared at the tent in a column of cloud; the column of cloud stood at the entrance of the tent.

A Command to Moses. ¹⁶The LORD said to Moses, Soon you will be at rest with your ancestors, and then this people will prostitute themselves by following the foreign gods among whom they will live in the land they are about to enter. They will forsake me and break the covenant which I have made with them. ¹⁷At that time my anger will flare up against them; I will forsake them and hide my face from them; they will become a prey to be devoured, and much evil and distress will befall them. At that time they will indeed say, "Is it not because our God is not in our midst that these evils have befallen us?" ¹⁸Yet I will surely hide my face at that time because of all the evil they have done in turning to other gods. ¹⁹Now, write out this song for yourselves. Teach it to the Israelites and have them recite it, so that this song may be a witness for me against the Israelites. ²⁰For when I have brought them into the land flowing with milk and honey which I promised on oath to their ancestors, and they have eaten and are satisfied and have grown fat, if they turn to other gods and serve them, despising me and breaking my covenant, ²¹then, when great evil and distress befall them, this song will speak to them as a witness, for it will not be forgotten if their descendants recite it. For I know what they are inclined to do even at the present time, before I have brought them into the land which I promised on oath. ²²So Moses wrote this song that same day, and he taught it to the Israelites.

Commission of Joshua. ²³Then he commissioned Joshua, son of Nun, and said to him, Be strong and steadfast, for it is you who will bring the Israelites into the land which I promised them on oath. I myself will be with you.

The Law Placed in the Ark. ²⁴When Moses had finished writing out on a scroll the words of this law in their entirety, ²⁵Moses gave the Levites who carry the ark of the covenant of the LORD this order: ²⁶Take this book of the law and put it beside the ark of the covenant of the LORD, your God, that there it may be a witness against you. ²⁷For I already know how rebellious and stiff-necked you will be. Why, even now, while I am alive among you, you have been rebels against the LORD! How much more, then, after I am dead! ²⁸Assemble all your tribal elders and your officials before me, that I may speak these words for them to hear and so may call heaven and earth to witness against them. ²⁹For I know that after my death you are sure to act corruptly and to turn aside from the way along which I commanded you, so that evil will befall you in time to come because you have done what is evil in the LORD's sight, and provoked him by your deeds.

The Song of Moses. ³⁰Then Moses recited the words of this song in their entirety, for the whole assembly of Israel to hear:

32:1 Give ear, O heavens, and let me speak;
　　let the earth hear the words of my
　　　　mouth!
²May my teaching soak in like the rain,
　　and my utterance drench like the dew,
Like a downpour upon the grass,
　　like a shower upon the crops.
³For I will proclaim the name of the
　　LORD,
　　praise the greatness of our God!

⁴The Rock—how faultless are his deeds,
  how right all his ways!
A faithful God, without deceit,
  just and upright is he!

⁵Yet his degenerate children have
    treated him basely,
  a twisted and crooked generation!
⁶Is this how you repay the LORD,
  so foolish and unwise a people?
Is he not your father who begot you,
  the one who made and established
    you?

⁷Remember the days of old,
  consider the years of generations
    past.
Ask your father, he will inform you,
  your elders, they will tell you:
⁸When the Most High allotted each
    nation its heritage,
  when he separated out human
    beings,
He set up the boundaries of the
    peoples
  after the number of the divine
    beings;
⁹But the LORD's portion was his
    people;
  his allotted share was Jacob.

¹⁰He found them in a wilderness,
  a wasteland of howling desert.
He shielded them, cared for them,
  guarded them as the apple of
    his eye.
¹¹As an eagle incites its nestlings,
  hovering over its young,
So he spread his wings, took them,
  bore them upon his pinions.
¹²The LORD alone guided them,
  no foreign god was with them.

¹³He had them mount the summits of
    the land,
  fed them the produce of its fields;
He suckled them with honey from the
    crags
  and olive oil from the flinty rock;

¹⁴Butter from cows and milk from
    sheep,
  with the best of lambs;
Bashan bulls and goats,
  with the cream of finest wheat;
  and the foaming blood of grapes
    you drank.

¹⁵So Jacob ate and was satisfied,
  Jeshurun grew fat and kicked;
  you became fat and gross and
    gorged.
They forsook the God who made them
  and scorned the Rock of their
    salvation.
¹⁶With strange gods they incited him,
  with abominations provoked him
    to anger.
¹⁷They sacrificed to demons, to
    "no-gods,"
  to gods they had never known,
Newcomers from afar,
  before whom your ancestors had
    never trembled.
¹⁸You were unmindful of the Rock that
    begot you,
  you forgot the God who gave you
    birth.

¹⁹The LORD saw and was filled with
    loathing,
  provoked by his sons and
    daughters.
²⁰He said, I will hide my face from
    them,
  and see what becomes of them.
For they are a fickle generation,
  children with no loyalty in them!
²¹Since they have incited me with a
    "no-god,"
  and provoked me with their empty
    idols,
I will incite them with a "no-people";
  with a foolish nation I will provoke
    them.
²²For by my wrath a fire is kindled
  that has raged to the depths of
    Sheol,

It has consumed the earth with its
  yield,
    and set on fire the foundations of
      the mountains.
²³I will heap evils upon them
  and exhaust all my arrows against
    them:
²⁴Emaciating hunger and consuming
  fever
    and bitter pestilence,
And the teeth of wild beasts I will send
  among them,
    with the venom of reptiles gliding in
      the dust.
²⁵Out in the street the sword shall
  bereave,
    and at home the terror
For the young man and the young
  woman alike,
    the nursing babe as well as the gray
      beard.
²⁶I said: I will make an end of them
  and blot out their name from
    human memory,
²⁷Had I not feared the provocation by
  the enemy,
    that their foes might misunderstand,
And say, "Our own hand won the
  victory;
    the LORD had nothing to do with
      any of it."
²⁸For they are a nation devoid of reason,
  having no understanding.
²⁹If they had insight they would realize
  this,
    they would understand their end:
³⁰"How could one rout a thousand,
  or two put ten thousand to flight,
Unless it was because their Rock sold
  them,
    the LORD delivered them up?"

³¹Indeed, their "rock" is not like our
  Rock;
    our enemies are fools.
³²For their vine is from the vine of Sodom,
  from the vineyards of Gomorrah.

Their grapes are grapes of poison,
  and their clusters are bitter.
³³Their wine is the venom of serpents,
  the cruel poison of vipers.
³⁴Is not this stored up with me,
  sealed up in my storehouses?
³⁵Vengeance is mine and recompense,
  for the time they lose their footing;
Because the day of their disaster is at
  hand
    and their doom is rushing upon
      them!

³⁶Surely, the LORD will do justice for
  his people;
    on his servants he will have pity.
When he sees their strength is gone,
  and neither bond nor free is left,
³⁷He will say, Where are their gods,
  the rock in whom they took refuge,
³⁸Who ate the fat of their sacrifices
  and drank the wine of their
    libations?
Let them rise up now and help you!
  Let them be your protection!
³⁹See now that I, I alone, am he,
  and there is no god besides me.
It is I who bring both death and life,
  I who inflict wounds and heal them,
    and from my hand no one can
      deliver.
⁴⁰For I raise my hand to the heavens
  and will say: As surely as I live
    forever,
⁴¹When I sharpen my flashing sword,
  and my hand lays hold of judgment,
With vengeance I will repay my foes
  and requite those who hate me.
⁴²I will make my arrows drunk with
  blood,
    and my sword shall devour flesh—
With the blood of the slain and the
  captured,
    from the long-haired heads of the
      enemy.

⁴³Exult with him, you heavens,
  bow to him, all you divine beings!

For he will avenge the blood of his
    servants,
  take vengeance on his foes;
He will requite those who hate him,
    and purge his people's land.

[44]So Moses, together with Hoshea, son of Nun, went and spoke all the words of this song in the hearing of the people.

Final Appeal. [45]When Moses had finished speaking all these words to all Israel, [46]he said to them, Take to heart all the words that I am giving in witness against you today, words you should command your children, that they may observe carefully every word of this law. [47]For this is no trivial matter for you, but rather your very life; by this word you will enjoy a long life on the land you are crossing the Jordan to possess.

Moses Looks upon Canaan. [48]On that very day the LORD said to Moses, [49]Ascend this mountain of the Abarim, Mount Nebo in the land of Moab facing Jericho, and view the land of Canaan, which I am giving to the Israelites as a possession. [50]Then you shall die on the mountain you are about to ascend, and shall be gathered to your people, just as your brother Aaron died on Mount Hor and there was gathered to his people, [51]because both of you broke faith with me among the Israelites at the waters of Meribath-kadesh in the wilderness of Zin: you did not manifest my holiness among the Israelites. [52]You may indeed see the land from a distance, but you shall not enter that land which I am giving to the Israelites.

☐ 1 PETER 2:13-25

Christian Citizens. 2:13 Be subject to every human institution for the Lord's sake, whether it be to the king as supreme [14]or to governors as sent by him for the punishment of evildoers and the approval of those who do good. [15]For it is the will of God that by doing good you may silence the ignorance of foolish people. [16]Be free, yet without using freedom as a pretext for evil, but as slaves of God. [17]Give honor to all, love the community, fear God, honor the king.

Christian Slaves. [18]Slaves, be subject to your masters with all reverence, not only to those who are good and equitable but also to those who are perverse. [19]For whenever anyone bears the pain of unjust suffering because of consciousness of God, that is a grace. [20]But what credit is there if you are patient when beaten for doing wrong? But if you are patient when you suffer for doing what is good, this is a grace before God. [21]For to this you have been called, because Christ also suffered for you, leaving you an example that you should follow in his footsteps.

[22]"He committed no sin,
    and no deceit was found in his
        mouth."

[23]When he was insulted, he returned no insult; when he suffered, he did not threaten; instead, he handed himself over to the one who judges justly. [24]He himself bore our sins in his body upon the cross, so that, free from sin, we might live for righteousness. By his wounds you have been healed. [25]For you had gone astray like sheep, but you have now returned to the shepherd and guardian of your souls.

March 14

Why, you words, did I ever let you go out? I have often been sorry that I spoke, but never that I kept quiet.

— ST. ARSENIUS

☐ DEUTERONOMY 33–34

Blessing upon the Tribes. 33:1 This is the blessing with which Moses, the man of God, blessed the Israelites before he died.
²He said:

The LORD came from Sinai
    and dawned on his people from
        Seir;
    he shone forth from Mount Paran.
With him were myriads of holy ones;
    at his right hand advanced the gods.
³Indeed, lover of the peoples,
    all the holy ones are at your side;
They follow at your heels,
    carry out your decisions.
⁴Moses charged us with the law,
    as a possession for the assembly of
        Jacob.
⁵A king arose in Jeshurun
    when the chiefs of the people
        assembled,
    and the tribes of Israel united.

⁶May Reuben live and not die out,
    but let his numbers be few.

⁷Of Judah he said this:

Hear, LORD, the voice of Judah,
    and bring him to his people.
His own hands defend his cause;
    be a help against his foes.

⁸Of Levi he said:

Give to Levi your Thummim,
    your Urim to your faithful one;
Him you tested at Massah,
    contended against him at the waters
        of Meribah.
⁹He said of his father and mother,
    "I have no regard for them";

His brothers he would not acknowledge,
    and his own children he did not
        recognize.
For they kept your words,
    and your covenant they upheld.
¹⁰They teach your ordinances to Jacob,
    your law to Israel.
They bring incense to your nostrils,
    and burnt offerings to your altar.
¹¹Bless, LORD, his strength,
    be pleased with the work of his hands.
Crush the loins of his adversaries
    and of his foes, that they may not
        rise.

¹²Of Benjamin he said:

The beloved of the LORD,
    he abides in safety beside him;
He shelters him all day long;
    the beloved abides at his breast.

¹³Of Joseph he said:

Blessed by the LORD is his land
    with the best of heaven above
    and of the abyss crouching beneath;
¹⁴With the best of the produce of the
        sun,
    and the choicest yield of the months;
¹⁵With the finest gifts of the ancient
        mountains
    and the best from the everlasting
        hills;
¹⁶With the best of the earth and its
        fullness,
    and the favor of the one who dwells
        on Sinai.
Let these come upon the head of Joseph
    and upon the brow of the prince
        among his brothers.

¹⁷His firstborn bull, majesty is his!
    His horns are the horns of a wild ox;
With them he gores the peoples,
    attacks the ends of the earth.
These are the myriads of Ephraim,
    and these the thousands of Manasseh.

¹⁸Of Zebulun he said:

Rejoice, Zebulun, in your expeditions,
    exult, Issachar, in your tents!
¹⁹They invite peoples to the mountain
    where they offer right sacrifices,
Because they suck up the abundance of
        the seas
    and the hidden treasures of the sand.

²⁰Of Gad he said:

Blessed be the one who has made Gad
        so vast!
    He lies there like a lion;
    he tears the arm, the head as well.
²¹He saw that the best should be his,
    for there the commander's portion
        was assigned;
    he came at the head of the people.
He carried out the justice of the LORD
    and his ordinances for Israel.

²²Of Dan he said:

Dan is a lion's cub,
    that springs away from a viper!

²³Of Naphtali he said:

Naphtali, abounding with favor,
    filled with the blessing of the LORD,
    take possession of the west and
        south.

²⁴Of Asher he said:

Most blessed of sons be Asher!
    May he be the favorite among his
        brothers,
    and may he dip his foot in oil!
²⁵May the bolts of your gates be iron
        and bronze;
    may your strength endure through
        all your days!

²⁶There is none like the God of
        Jeshurun,
    who rides the heavens in his power,
    who rides the clouds in his majesty;
²⁷The God of old is a refuge;
    a support are the arms of the
        Everlasting.
He drove the enemy out of your way
    and he said, "Destroy!"
²⁸Israel abides securely,
    Jacob dwells apart,
In a land of grain and wine,
    where the heavens drip with dew.
²⁹Happy are you, Israel! Who is like you,
    a people delivered by the LORD,
Your help and shield,
    and the sword of your glory.
Your enemies cringe before you;
    you stride upon their backs.

34:1 Then Moses went up from the plains of Moab to Mount Nebo, the peak of Pisgah which faces Jericho, and the LORD showed him all the land—Gilead, and as far as Dan, ²all Naphtali, the land of Ephraim and Manasseh, all the land of Judah as far as the Western Sea, ³the Negeb, the plain (the valley of Jericho, the City of Palms), and as far as Zoar. ⁴The LORD then said to him, This is the land about which I promised on oath to Abraham, Isaac, and Jacob, "I will give it to your descendants." I have let you see it with your own eyes, but you shall not cross over. ⁵So there, in the land of Moab, Moses, the servant of the LORD, died as the LORD had said; ⁶and he was buried in a valley in the land of Moab, opposite Beth-peor; to this day no one knows the place of his burial. ⁷Moses was one hundred and twenty years old when he died, yet his eyes were undimmed and his vigor unabated. ⁸The Israelites wept for Moses in the plains of Moab for thirty days, till they had completed the period of grief and mourning for Moses.

⁹Now Joshua, son of Nun, was filled with the spirit of wisdom, since Moses had

laid his hands upon him; and so the Israelites gave him their obedience, just as the LORD had commanded Moses.

[10]Since then no prophet has arisen in Israel like Moses, whom the LORD knew face to face, [11]in all the signs and wonders the LORD sent him to perform in the land of Egypt against Pharaoh and all his servants and against all his land, [12]and all the great might and the awesome power that Moses displayed in the sight of all Israel.

☐ 1 PETER 3:1-12

Christian Spouses. 3:1 Likewise, you wives should be subordinate to your husbands so that, even if some disobey the word, they may be won over without a word by their wives' conduct [2]when they observe your reverent and chaste behavior. [3]Your adornment should not be an external one: braiding the hair, wearing gold jewelry, or dressing in fine clothes, [4]but rather the hidden character of the heart, expressed in the imperishable beauty of a gentle and calm disposition, which is precious in the sight of God. [5]For this is also how the holy women who hoped in God once used to adorn themselves and were subordinate to their husbands; [6]thus Sarah obeyed Abraham, calling him "lord." You are her children when you do what is good and fear no intimidation.

[7]Likewise, you husbands should live with your wives in understanding, showing honor to the weaker female sex, since we are joint heirs of the gift of life, so that your prayers may not be hindered.

Christian Conduct. [8]Finally, all of you, be of one mind, sympathetic, loving toward one another, compassionate, humble. [9]Do not return evil for evil, or insult for insult; but, on the contrary, a blessing, because to this you were called, that you might inherit a blessing. [10]For:

> "Whoever would love life
>   and see good days
> must keep the tongue from evil
>   and the lips from speaking deceit,
> [11]must turn from evil and do good,
>   seek peace and follow after it.
> [12]For the eyes of the Lord are on the
>   righteous
>   and his ears turned to their prayer,
> but the face of the Lord is against
>   evildoers."

March 15

St. Louise de Marillac

Be diligent in serving the poor. Love the poor; honor them, my children, as you would honor Christ himself.

— ST. LOUISE DE MARILLAC

☐ JOSHUA 1-4

Divine Promise of Assistance. 1:1 After Moses, the servant of the LORD, had died, the LORD said to Moses' aide Joshua, son of Nun: [2]Moses my servant is dead. So now, you and the whole people with you, prepare to cross the Jordan to the land that I will give the Israelites. [3]Every place where you set foot I have given you, as I promised Moses.

[4]All the land of the Hittites, from the wilderness and the Lebanon east to the great river Euphrates and west to the Great Sea, will be your territory. [5]No one can withstand you as long as you live. As I was with Moses, I will be with you: I will not leave you nor forsake you. [6]Be strong and steadfast, so that you may give this people possession of the land I swore to their ancestors that I would give them. [7]Only be strong and steadfast, being careful to observe the entire law which Moses my servant enjoined on you. Do not swerve from it either to the right or to the left, that you may succeed wherever you go. [8]Do not let this book of the law depart from your lips. Recite it by day and by night, that you may carefully observe all that is written in it; then you will attain your goal; then you will succeed. [9]I command you: be strong and steadfast! Do not fear nor be dismayed, for the LORD, your God, is with you wherever you go.

[10]So Joshua commanded the officers of the people: [11]"Go through the camp and command the people, 'Prepare your provisions, for three days from now you shall cross the Jordan here, to march in and possess the land the LORD, your God, is giving as your possession.'"

The Transjordan Tribes. [12]Joshua addressed the Reubenites, the Gadites, and the half-tribe of Manasseh: [13]"Remember what Moses, the servant of the LORD, commanded you when he said, 'The LORD, your God, is about to give you rest; he will give you this land.' [14]Your wives, your children, and your livestock may remain in the land Moses gave you here beyond the Jordan. But all the warriors among you must cross over armed, ahead of your kindred, and you must help them [15]until the LORD has settled your kindred, and they like you possess the land the LORD, your God, is giving them. Afterward you may return and possess your own land, which Moses, the servant of the LORD, has given you east of the Jordan." [16]They answered Joshua, "We will do all you have commanded us, and we will go wherever you send us. [17]As completely as we obeyed Moses, we will obey you. Only, may the LORD, your God, be with you as God was with Moses. [18]Anyone who rebels against your orders and does not obey all your commands shall be put to death. Only be strong and steadfast."

Spies Saved by Rahab. 2:1 Then Joshua, son of Nun, secretly sent out two spies from Shittim, saying, "Go, reconnoiter the land and Jericho." When the two reached Jericho, they went into the house of a prostitute named Rahab, where they lodged. [2]But a report was brought to the king of Jericho: "Some men came here last night, Israelites, to spy out the land." [3]So the king of Jericho sent Rahab the order, "Bring out the men who have come to you and entered your house, for they have come to spy out the entire land." [4]The woman had taken the two men and hidden them, so she said, "True, the men you speak of came to me, but I did not know where they came from. [5]At dark, when it was time to close the gate, they left, and I do not know where they went. You will have to pursue them quickly to overtake them." [6]Now, she had led them to the roof, and hidden them among her stalks of flax spread out there. [7]But the pursuers set out along the way to the fords of the Jordan. As soon as they had left to pursue them, the gate was shut.

[8]Before the spies lay down, Rahab went up to them on the roof [9]and said: "I know that the LORD has given you the land, that a dread of you has come upon us, and that all the inhabitants of the land tremble with fear because of you. [10]For we have heard how the LORD dried up the waters of the Red Sea before you when you came out of Egypt, and what you did to Sihon and Og, the two kings of the Amorites beyond the Jordan, whom you destroyed under the ban. [11]We heard, and our hearts melted within us; everyone is utterly dispirited be-

cause of you, since the LORD, your God, is God in heaven above and on earth below. [12]Now then, swear to me by the LORD that, since I am showing kindness to you, you in turn will show kindness to my family. Give me a reliable sign [13]that you will allow my father and mother, brothers and sisters, and my whole family to live, and that you will deliver us from death." [14]"We pledge our lives for yours," they answered her. "If you do not betray our mission, we will be faithful in showing kindness to you when the LORD gives us the land."

[15]Then she let them down through the window with a rope; for she lived in a house built into the city wall. [16]"Go up into the hill country," she said, "that your pursuers may not come upon you. Hide there for three days, until they return; then you may go on your way." [17]They answered her, "We are free of this oath that you made us take, unless, [18]when we come into the land, you tie this scarlet cord in the window through which you are letting us down. Gather your father and mother, your brothers, and all your family into your house. [19]Should any of them pass outside the doors of your house, their blood will be on their own heads, and we will be guiltless. But if anyone in your house is harmed, their blood will be on our heads. [20]If, however, you betray our mission, we will be free of the oath you have made us take." [21]"Let it be as you say," she replied, and sent them away. When they were gone, she tied the scarlet cord in the window.

[22]They went up into the hill country, where they stayed three days until their pursuers, who had sought them all along the road without finding them, returned. [23]Then the two came back down from the hills, crossed the Jordan to Joshua, son of Nun, and told him all that had happened to them. [24]They assured Joshua, "The LORD has given all this land into our power; indeed, all the inhabitants of the land tremble with fear because of us."

Preparations for Crossing the Jordan. 3:1 Early the next morning, Joshua and all the Israelites moved from Shittim and came to the Jordan, where they stayed before crossing over. [2]Three days later the officers went through the camp [3]and issued these commands to the people: "When you see the ark of the covenant of the LORD, your God, which the levitical priests will carry, you must break camp and follow it, [4]that you may know the way to take, for you have not gone over this road before. But let there be a space of two thousand cubits between you and the ark: do not come nearer to it." [5]Joshua also said to the people, "Sanctify yourselves, for tomorrow the LORD will perform wonders among you." [6]And he told the priests, "Take up the ark of the covenant and cross ahead of the people"; so they took up the ark of the covenant and went before the people.

[7]Then the LORD said to Joshua: Today I will begin to exalt you in the sight of all Israel, that they may know that, as I was with Moses, so I will be with you. [8]Now command the priests carrying the ark of the covenant, "When you come to the edge of the waters of the Jordan, there take your stand."

[9]So Joshua said to the Israelites, "Come here and listen to the words of the LORD, your God." [10]He continued: "By this you will know that there is a living God in your midst: he will certainly dispossess before you the Canaanites, Hittites, Hivites, Perizzites, Girgashites, Amorites, and Jebusites. [11]The ark of the covenant of the Lord of the whole earth will cross the Jordan before you. [12]Now choose twelve men, one from each of the tribes of Israel. [13]When the soles of the feet of the priests carrying the ark of the LORD, the Lord of the whole earth, touch the waters of the Jordan, it will cease to flow; the water flowing down from upstream will halt in a single heap."

The Crossing Begun. [14]The people set out from their tents to cross the Jordan, with the priests carrying the ark of the covenant ahead of them. [15]When those bearing the ark came to the Jordan and the feet of the priests bearing the ark were immersed in the waters of the Jordan—which overflows all its banks during the entire season of the harvest— [16]the waters flowing from upstream halted, standing up in a single heap for a very great distance indeed, from Adam, a city in the direction of Zarethan; those flowing downstream toward the Salt Sea of the Arabah disappeared entirely. Thus the people crossed over opposite Jericho. [17]The priests carrying the ark of the covenant of the LORD stood on dry ground in the Jordan riverbed while all Israel crossed on dry ground, until the whole nation had completed the crossing of the Jordan.

Memorial Stones. 4:1 After the entire nation had completed the crossing of the Jordan, [2]the LORD said to Joshua: Choose twelve men from the people, one from each tribe, [3]and command them, "Take up twelve stones from this spot in the Jordan riverbed where the priests have been standing. Carry them over with you, and place them where you are to stay tonight."

[4]Summoning the twelve men he had selected from among the Israelites, one from each tribe, [5]Joshua said to them: "Go to the Jordan riverbed in front of the ark of the LORD, your God; lift to your shoulders one stone apiece, so that they will equal in number the tribes of the Israelites. [6]In the future, these are to be a sign among you. When your children ask you, 'What do these stones mean to you?' [7]you shall answer them, 'The waters of the Jordan ceased to flow before the ark of the covenant of the LORD when it crossed the Jordan.' Thus these stones are to serve as a perpetual memorial to the Israelites." [8]The twelve Israelites did as Joshua had commanded: they took up twelve stones from the Jordan riverbed as the LORD had said to Joshua, one

for each of the tribes of the Israelites. They carried them along to the camp site, and there they placed them. [9]Joshua set up the twelve stones that had been in the Jordan riverbed on the spot where the priests stood who were carrying the ark of the covenant. They are there to this day.

[10]The priests carrying the ark stood in the Jordan riverbed until everything had been done that the LORD had commanded Joshua to tell the people, just as Moses had commanded Joshua. The people crossed over quickly, [11]and when all the people had completed the crossing, the ark of the LORD also crossed; and the priests were now in front of them. [12]The Reubenites, Gadites, and half-tribe of Manasseh, armed, marched in the vanguard of the Israelites, as Moses had ordered. [13]About forty thousand troops, equipped for battle, crossed over before the LORD to the plains of Jericho for war.

[14]That day the LORD exalted Joshua in the sight of all Israel, and so during his whole life they feared him as they had feared Moses.

[15]Then the LORD said to Joshua: [16]Command the priests carrying the ark of the covenant to come up from the Jordan. [17]Joshua commanded the priests, "Come up from the Jordan," [18]and when the priests carrying the ark of the covenant of the LORD had come up from the Jordan riverbed, as the soles of their feet regained the dry ground, the waters of the Jordan resumed their course and as before overflowed all its banks.

[19]The people came up from the Jordan on the tenth day of the first month, and camped in Gilgal on the eastern limits of Jericho. [20]At Gilgal Joshua set up the twelve stones that had been taken from the Jordan, [21]saying to the Israelites, "In the future, when your children ask their parents, 'What do these stones mean?' [22]you shall inform them, 'Israel crossed the Jordan here on dry ground.' [23]For the LORD, your

God, dried up the waters of the Jordan in front of you until you crossed over, just as the LORD, your God, had done at the Red Sea, drying it up in front of us until we crossed over, ²⁴in order that all the peoples of the earth may know that the hand of the LORD is mighty, and that you may fear the LORD, your God, forever."

☐ 1 PETER 3:13-22

Christian Suffering. 3:13 Now who is going to harm you if you are enthusiastic for what is good? ¹⁴But even if you should suffer because of righteousness, blessed are you. Do not be afraid or terrified with fear of them, ¹⁵but sanctify Christ as Lord in your hearts. Always be ready to give an explanation to anyone who asks you for a reason for your hope, ¹⁶but do it with gentleness and reverence, keeping your conscience clear, so that, when you are maligned, those who defame your good conduct in Christ may themselves be put to shame. ¹⁷For it is better to suffer for doing good, if that be the will of God, than for doing evil.

¹⁸For Christ also suffered for sins once, the righteous for the sake of the unrighteous, that he might lead you to God. Put to death in the flesh, he was brought to life in the spirit. ¹⁹In it he also went to preach to the spirits in prison, ²⁰who had once been disobedient while God patiently waited in the days of Noah during the building of the ark, in which a few persons, eight in all, were saved through water. ²¹This prefigured baptism, which saves you now. It is not a removal of dirt from the body but an appeal to God for a clear conscience, through the resurrection of Jesus Christ, ²²who has gone into heaven and is at the right hand of God, with angels, authorities, and powers subject to him.

March 16

How long will the sun and moon, the stars, continue to give forth light? Who can tell? In God's own time — then shall come the Son of Man in great power and majesty to render to each according to his works.

— ST. KATHARINE DREXEL

☐ JOSHUA 5-9

Rites at Gilgal. 5:1 When all the kings of the Amorites to the west of the Jordan and all the kings of the Canaanites by the sea heard that the LORD had dried up the waters of the Jordan before the Israelites until they crossed over, their hearts melted and they were utterly dispirited because of the Israelites.

²On this occasion the LORD said to Joshua: Make flint knives and circumcise Israel for the second time. ³So Joshua made flint knives and circumcised the Israelites at Gibeath-haaraloth. ⁴This was the reason for the circumcision: Of all the people who had come out of Egypt, every male of military age had died in the wilderness during the journey after they came out of Egypt. ⁵Though all the men who came out were circumcised, none of those born in the wilder-

ness during the journey after the departure from Egypt were circumcised. [6]Now the Israelites wandered forty years in the wilderness, until all the warriors among the people that came forth from Egypt died off because they had not listened to the voice of the LORD. For the LORD swore that he would not let them see the land he had sworn to their ancestors to give us, a land flowing with milk and honey. [7]It was the children God raised up in their stead whom Joshua circumcised, for these were yet with foreskins, not having been circumcised on the journey. [8]When the circumcision of the entire nation was complete, they remained in camp where they were, until they recovered. [9]Then the LORD said to Joshua: Today I have removed the reproach of Egypt from you. Therefore the place is called Gilgal to the present day.

[10]While the Israelites were encamped at Gilgal on the plains of Jericho, they celebrated the Passover on the evening of the fourteenth day of the month. [11]On the day after the Passover they ate of the produce of the land in the form of unleavened cakes and parched grain. On that same day [12]after they ate of the produce of the land, the manna ceased. No longer was there manna for the Israelites, who that year ate of the yield of the land of Canaan.

Siege at Jericho. [13]While Joshua was near Jericho, he raised his eyes and saw one who stood facing him, drawn sword in hand. Joshua went up to him and asked, "Are you one of us or one of our enemies?" [14]He replied, "Neither. I am the commander of the army of the LORD: now I have come." Then Joshua fell down to the ground in worship, and said to him, "What has my lord to say to his servant?" [15]The commander of the army of the LORD replied to Joshua, "Remove your sandals from your feet, for the place on which you are standing is holy." And Joshua did so.

6:1 Now Jericho was in a state of siege because of the presence of the Israelites. No one left or entered. [2]And to Joshua the LORD said: I have delivered Jericho, its king, and its warriors into your power. [3]Have all the soldiers circle the city, marching once around it. Do this for six days, [4]with seven priests carrying ram's horns ahead of the ark. On the seventh day march around the city seven times, and have the priests blow the horns. [5]When they give a long blast on the ram's horns and you hear the sound of the horn, all the people shall shout aloud. The wall of the city will collapse, and the people shall attack straight ahead.

[6]Summoning the priests, Joshua, son of Nun, said to them, "Take up the ark of the covenant with seven of the priests carrying ram's horns in front of the ark of the LORD." [7]And he ordered the people, "Proceed and surround the city, with the picked troops marching ahead of the ark of the LORD." [8]When Joshua spoke to the people, the seven priests who carried the ram's horns before the LORD marched and blew their horns, and the ark of the covenant of the LORD followed them. [9]In front of the priests with the horns marched the picked troops; the rear guard followed the ark, and the blowing of horns was kept up continually as they marched. [10]But Joshua had commanded the people, "Do not shout or make any noise or outcry until I tell you, 'Shout!' Then you must shout." [11]So he had the ark of the LORD circle the city, going once around it, after which they returned to camp for the night.

[12]Early the next morning, Joshua had the priests take up the ark of the LORD. [13]The seven priests bearing the ram's horns marched in front of the ark of the LORD, blowing their horns. Ahead of these marched the picked troops, while the rear guard followed the ark of the LORD, and the blowing of horns was kept up continually. [14]On this second day they again marched around the city once before returning to camp; and for six days in all they did the same.

¹⁵On the seventh day, beginning at daybreak, they marched around the city seven times in the same manner; on that day only did they march around the city seven times. ¹⁶The seventh time around, the priests blew the horns and Joshua said to the people, "Now shout, for the LORD has given you the city. ¹⁷The city and everything in it is under the ban. Only Rahab the prostitute and all who are in the house with her are to live, because she hid the messengers we sent. ¹⁸But be careful not to covet or take anything that is under the ban; otherwise you will bring upon the camp of Israel this ban and the misery of it. ¹⁹All silver and gold, and the articles of bronze or iron, are holy to the LORD. They shall be put in the treasury of the LORD."

The Fall of Jericho. ²⁰As the horns blew, the people began to shout. When they heard the sound of the horn, they raised a tremendous shout. The wall collapsed, and the people attacked the city straight ahead and took it. ²¹They observed the ban by putting to the sword all living creatures in the city: men and women, young and old, as well as oxen, sheep and donkeys.

²²To the two men who had spied out the land, Joshua said, "Go into the prostitute's house and bring out the woman with all her family, as you swore to her you would do." ²³The spies entered and brought out Rahab, with her father, mother, brothers, and all her family; her entire family they led forth and placed outside the camp of Israel. ²⁴The city itself they burned with all that was in it; but the silver, gold, and articles of bronze and iron they placed in the treasury of the house of the LORD. ²⁵Because Rahab the prostitute had hidden the messengers whom Joshua had sent to reconnoiter Jericho, Joshua let her live, along with her father's house and all her family, who dwell in the midst of Israel to this day.

²⁶On that occasion Joshua imposed the oath: Cursed before the LORD be the man who attempts to rebuild this city, Jericho.

At the cost of his firstborn will he lay its foundation, and at the cost of his youngest son will he set up its gates.

²⁷Thus the LORD was with Joshua so that his fame spread throughout the land.

Defeat at Ai. 7:1 But the Israelites acted treacherously with regard to the ban; Achan, son of Carmi, son of Zabdi, son of Zerah of the tribe of Judah, took goods that were under the ban, and the anger of the LORD flared up against the Israelites.

²Joshua next sent men from Jericho to Ai, which is near Beth-aven and east of Bethel, with the order, "Go up and reconnoiter the land." When they had explored Ai, ³they returned to Joshua and advised, "Do not send all the people up; if only about two or three thousand go up, they can attack and overcome Ai. You need not tire all the people: the enemy there are few." ⁴About three thousand of the people made the attack, but they fled before the army at Ai, ⁵who killed some thirty-six of them. They pursued them from the city gate to the Shebarim, and defeated them on the descent, so that the confidence of the people melted away like water.

⁶Joshua, together with the elders of Israel, tore their garments and fell face down before the ark of the LORD until evening; and they threw dust on their heads. ⁷"Alas, Lord GOD," Joshua prayed, "why did you ever allow this people to cross over the Jordan, delivering us into the power of the Amorites, that they might destroy us? Would that we had been content to dwell on the other side of the Jordan. ⁸Please, Lord, what can I say, now that Israel has turned its back to its enemies? ⁹When the Canaanites and the other inhabitants of the land hear of it, they will close in around us and efface our name from the earth. What will you do for your great name?"

¹⁰The LORD replied to Joshua: Stand up. Why are you lying there? ¹¹Israel has sinned: they have transgressed the covenant which I enjoined on them. They have taken

goods subject to the ban. They have stolen and lied, placing the goods in their baggage. [12]If the Israelites cannot stand up to their enemies, but must turn their back to them, it is because they are under the ban. I will not continue to be with you unless you remove that which is banned from among you. [13]Get up, sanctify the people. Tell them, "Sanctify yourselves before tomorrow, for thus says the LORD, the God of Israel: That which is banned is in your midst, Israel. You cannot stand up to your enemies until you remove it from among you. [14]In the morning you must come forward by tribes. The tribe which the LORD designates shall come forward by clans; the clan which the LORD designates shall come forward by families; the family which the LORD designates shall come forward one by one. [15]Whoever is designated as having incurred the ban shall be destroyed by fire, with all that is his, because he has transgressed the covenant of the LORD and has committed a shameful crime in Israel."

Achan's Guilt and Punishment. [16]Early the next morning Joshua had Israel come forward by tribes, and the tribe of Judah was designated. [17]Then he had the clans of Judah come forward, and the clan of Zerah was designated. He had the clan of Zerah come forward by families, and Zabdi was designated. [18]Finally he had that family come forward one by one, and Achan, son of Carmi, son of Zabdi, son of Zerah of the tribe of Judah, was designated. [19]Joshua said to Achan, "My son, give glory to the LORD, the God of Israel, and praise him by telling me what you have done; do not hide it from me." [20]Achan answered Joshua, "I have indeed sinned against the LORD, the God of Israel. This is what I have done: [21]Among the spoils, I saw a beautiful Babylonian mantle, two hundred shekels of silver, and a bar of gold fifty shekels in weight; I coveted them and I took them. They are now hidden in the ground inside my tent, with the silver underneath." [22]Joshua sent messengers and

they ran to the tent and there they were, hidden in the tent, with the silver underneath. [23]They took them from the tent, brought them to Joshua and all the Israelites, and spread them out before the LORD.

[24]Then Joshua and all Israel took Achan, son of Zerah, with the silver, the mantle, and the bar of gold, and with his sons and daughters, his ox, his donkey and his sheep, his tent, and all his possessions, and led them off to the Valley of Achor. [25]Joshua said, "What misery have you caused us? May the LORD bring misery upon you today!" And all Israel stoned him to death. They burnt them with fire and they stoned them. [26]Over Achan they piled a great heap of stones, which remains to the present day. Then the LORD turned from his anger. That is why the place is called the Valley of Achor to this day.

Capture of Ai. 8:1 The LORD then said to Joshua: Do not be afraid or dismayed. Take all the army with you and prepare to attack Ai. I have delivered the king of Ai into your power, with his people, city, and land. [2]Do to Ai and its king what you did to Jericho and its king—except that you may take its spoil and livestock as plunder. Set an ambush behind the city. [3]So Joshua and all the soldiers prepared to attack Ai. Picking out thirty thousand warriors, Joshua sent them off by night [4]with these orders: "See that you ambush the city from the rear. Do not be very far from the city. All of you must be ready. [5]The rest of the people and I will come up to the city, and when they make a sortie against us as they did the last time, we will flee from them. [6]They will keep coming out after us until we have drawn them away from the city, for they will think, 'They are fleeing from us as they did the last time.' When we flee, [7]then you rise from ambush and take possession of the city, which the LORD, your God, will deliver into your power. [8]When you have taken the city, set it on fire in obedience to the LORD's command. These are my orders to you." [9]Then Joshua sent them away. They went to the place of ambush, taking up their position to the west of Ai, toward Bethel. Joshua, however, spent that night with the army.

[10]Early the next morning Joshua mustered the army and went up to Ai at its head, with the elders of Israel. [11]When all the troops he led were drawn up in position before the city, they pitched camp north of Ai, on the other side of the ravine. [12]He took about five thousand warriors and set them in ambush between Bethel and Ai, west of the city. [13]Thus the people took up their stations, with the main body north of the city and the ambush west of it, and Joshua waited overnight in the valley. [14]The king of Ai saw this, and he and all his army came out very early in the morning to engage Israel in battle at the place in front of the Arabah, not knowing that there was an ambush behind the city. [15]Joshua and the main body of the Israelites fled toward the wilderness, pretending defeat, [16]until the last of the soldiers in the city had been called out to pursue them. Since they were drawn away from the city, with everyone pursuing Joshua, [17]not a soldier remained in Ai or Bethel. They abandoned the city, leaving it open, as they pursued Israel.

[18]Then the LORD directed Joshua: Stretch out the javelin in your hand toward Ai, for I will deliver it into your power. Joshua stretched out the javelin in his hand toward the city, [19]and as soon as he did so, the men in ambush rose from their post, rushed in, captured the city, and immediately set it on fire. [20]By the time the army of Ai looked back, the smoke from the city was going up to the heavens. Escape in any direction was impossible, because the Israelites retreating toward the wilderness now turned on their pursuers; [21]for when Joshua and the main body of Israelites saw that the city had been taken by ambush and was going up in smoke, they struck back at the forces of Ai. [22]Since those in the city came out to intercept them, Ai's army was hemmed in by Israelites on both sides, who cut them down without any fugitives or survivors [23]except the king, whom they took alive and brought to Joshua.

[24]When Israel finished killing all the inhabitants of Ai in the open, who had pursued them into the wilderness, and all of them to the last man fell by the sword, then all Israel returned and put to the sword those inside the city. [25]There fell that day a total of twelve thousand men and women, the entire population of Ai. [26]Joshua kept the javelin in his hand stretched out until he had carried out the ban on all the inhabitants of Ai. [27]However, the Israelites took for themselves as plunder the livestock and the spoil of that city, according to the command of the LORD issued to Joshua. [28]Then Joshua destroyed Ai by fire, reducing it to an everlasting mound of ruins, as it remains today. [29]He had the king of Ai hanged on a tree until evening; then at sunset Joshua ordered the body removed from the tree and cast at the entrance of the city gate, where a great heap of stones was piled up over it, which remains to the present day.

Altar on Mount Ebal. [30]Later, on Mount Ebal, Joshua built to the LORD, the God of Israel, an altar [31]of unhewn stones on which no iron tool had been used, just as Moses, the servant of the LORD, had commanded the Israelites, as recorded in the book of the law. On this altar they sacrificed burnt offerings to the LORD and made communion sacrifices. [32]There, in the presence of the Israelites, Joshua inscribed upon the stones a copy of the law written by Moses. [33]And all Israel, resident alien and native alike, with their elders, officers and judges, stood on either side of the ark facing the levitical priests who were carrying the ark of the covenant of the LORD. Half of them were facing Mount Gerizim and half Mount Ebal, just as Moses, the servant of the LORD, had first commanded for the blessing of the people of Israel.

[34]Then were read aloud all the words of the law, the blessings and the curses, exactly as written in the book of the law. [35]Every single word that Moses had commanded, Joshua read aloud to the entire assembly, including the women and children, and the resident aliens among them.

Confederacy Against Israel. 9:1 When the news reached all the kings west of the Jordan, in the mountain regions and in the Shephelah, and all along the coast of the Great Sea as far as the Lebanon: Hittites, Amorites, Canaanites, Perizzites, Hivites, and Jebusites, [2]they gathered together to launch a common attack against Joshua and Israel.

The Gibeonite Deception. [3]On hearing what Joshua had done to Jericho and Ai, the inhabitants of Gibeon [4]formed their own scheme. They chose provisions for a journey, making use of old sacks for their donkeys, and old wineskins, torn and mended. [5]They wore old, patched sandals and shabby garments; and all the bread they took was dry and crumbly. [6]Thus they journeyed to Joshua in the camp at Gilgal, where they said to him and to the Israelites, "We have come from a far-off land; now, make a covenant with us." [7]But the Israelites replied to the Hivites, "You may be living in land that is ours. How, then, can we make a covenant with you?" [8]But they answered Joshua, "We are your servants." Then Joshua asked them, "Who are you? Where do you come from?" [9]They answered him, "Your servants have come from a far-off land, because of the fame of the LORD, your God. For we have heard reports of all that he did in Egypt [10]and all that he did to the two kings of the Amorites beyond the Jordan, Sihon, king of Heshbon, and Og, king of Bashan, who lived in Ashtaroth. [11]So our elders and all the inhabitants of our land said to us, 'Take along provisions for the journey and go to meet them. Say to them: "We are your servants; now make a covenant with us."' [12]This bread of ours was still warm when we brought it from home as provisions the day we left to come to you, but now it is dry and crumbly. [13]Here are our wineskins, which were new when we filled them, but now they are torn. Look at our garments and sandals; they are worn out from the very long journey." [14]Then the Israelite leaders partook of their provisions, without inquiring of the LORD. [15]So Joshua made peace with them and made a covenant to let them live, which the leaders of the community sealed with an oath.

Gibeonites Made Vassals. [16]Three days after the covenant was made, the Israelites heard that these people were from nearby, and would be living in Israel. [17]The third day on the road, the Israelites came to their cities of Gibeon, Chephirah, Beeroth, and Kiriath-jearim, [18]but did not attack them, because the leaders of the community had sworn to them by the LORD, the God of Israel. When the entire community grumbled against the leaders, [19]these all remonstrated with the community, "We have sworn to them by the LORD, the God of Israel, and so we cannot harm them. [20]Let us therefore let them live, and so deal with them that no wrath fall upon us because of the oath we have sworn to them." [21]Thus the leaders said to them, "Let them live, and become hewers of wood and drawers of water for the entire community." So the community did as the leaders advised them.

[22]Joshua summoned the Gibeonites and said to them, "Why did you deceive us and say, 'We live far off from you'?—You live among us! [23]Now are you accursed: every one of you shall always be a slave, hewers of wood and drawers of water, for the house of my God." [24]They answered Joshua, "Your servants were fully informed of how the LORD, your God, commanded Moses his servant that you be given the entire land and that all its inhabitants be destroyed before you. Since, therefore, at

your advance, we were in great fear for our lives, we acted as we did. [25]And now that we are in your power, do with us what is good and right in your eyes." [26]Joshua did what he had decided: while he saved them from being killed by the Israelites, [27]on that day he made them, as they still are, hewers of wood and drawers of water for the community and for the altar of the LORD, in the place the LORD would choose.

☐ 1 PETER 4:1-11

Christian Restraint. 4:1 Therefore, since Christ suffered in the flesh, arm yourselves also with the same attitude (for whoever suffers in the flesh has broken with sin), [2]so as not to spend what remains of one's life in the flesh on human desires, but on the will of God. [3]For the time that has passed is sufficient for doing what the Gentiles like to do: living in debauchery, evil desires, drunkenness, orgies, carousing, and wanton idolatry. [4]They are surprised that you do not plunge into the same swamp of profligacy, and they vilify you; [5]but they will give an account to him who stands ready to judge the living and the dead. [6]For this is why the gospel was preached even to the dead that, though condemned in the flesh in human estimation, they might live in the spirit in the estimation of God.

Christian Charity. [7]The end of all things is at hand. Therefore, be serious and sober for prayers. [8]Above all, let your love for one another be intense, because love covers a multitude of sins. [9]Be hospitable to one another without complaining. [10]As each one has received a gift, use it to serve one another as good stewards of God's varied grace. [11]Whoever preaches, let it be with the words of God; whoever serves, let it be with the strength that God supplies, so that in all things God may be glorified through Jesus Christ, to whom belong glory and dominion forever and ever. Amen.

March 17

St. Patrick of Ireland

Christ with me, Christ before me, Christ behind me, Christ within me, Christ below me, Christ above me, Christ at my right, Christ at my left, Christ in lying down, Christ in sitting, Christ in rising up, Christ in the heart of every man who thinks of me, Christ in the mouth of every man who speaks to me, Christ in every eye that sees me, Christ in every ear that hears me.

— ST. PATRICK OF IRELAND

☐ JOSHUA 10-14

The Siege of Gibeon. 10:1 Now when Adonizedek, king of Jerusalem, heard that Joshua had captured Ai and put it under the ban, and had done to that city and its king as he had done to Jericho and its king, and that the inhabitants of Gibeon had made their peace with Israel, remaining among them, [2]there was great fear abroad, because

Gibeon was a great city, like one of the royal cities, greater even than Ai, and all its men were warriors. ³So Adonizedek, king of Jerusalem, sent to Hoham, king of Hebron, Piram, king of Jarmuth, Japhia, king of Lachish, and Debir, king of Eglon, with this message: ⁴"Come and help me attack Gibeon, for it has made peace with Joshua and the Israelites." ⁵The five Amorite kings, of Jerusalem, Hebron, Jarmuth, Lachish, and Eglon, gathered with all their forces, and marched against Gibeon to make war on it. ⁶Thereupon, the Gibeonites sent an appeal to Joshua in his camp at Gilgal: "Do not abandon your servants. Come up here quickly and save us. Help us, because all the Amorite kings of the mountain country have joined together against us."

Joshua's Victory. ⁷So Joshua marched up from Gilgal with all his army and all his warriors. ⁸The LORD said to Joshua: Do not fear them, for I have delivered them into your power. Not one of them will be able to withstand you. ⁹After an all-night march from Gilgal, Joshua made a surprise attack upon them, ¹⁰and the LORD threw them into disorder before Israel. The Israelites inflicted a great slaughter on them at Gibeon and pursued them down the Beth-horon slope, attacking them as far as Azekah and Makkedah.

¹¹While they fled before Israel along the descent of Beth-horon, the LORD hurled great stones from the heavens above them all the way to Azekah, killing many. More died from these hailstones than the Israelites killed with the sword. ¹²It was then, when the LORD delivered up the Amorites to the Israelites, that Joshua prayed to the LORD, and said in the presence of Israel:

Sun, stand still at Gibeon,
    Moon, in the valley of Aijalon!
¹³The sun stood still,
    the moon stayed,
        while the nation took vengeance
            on its foes.

This is recorded in the Book of Jashar. The sun halted halfway across the heavens; not for an entire day did it press on. ¹⁴Never before or since was there a day like this, when the LORD obeyed the voice of a man; for the LORD fought for Israel. ¹⁵Then Joshua and all Israel returned to the camp at Gilgal.

Execution of Amorite Kings. ¹⁶The five kings who had fled hid in the cave at Makkedah. ¹⁷When Joshua was told, "The five kings have been found, hiding in the cave at Makkedah," ¹⁸he said, "Roll large stones to the mouth of the cave and post guards over it. ¹⁹But do not remain there yourselves. Pursue your enemies, and harry them in the rear. Do not allow them to reach their cities, for the LORD, your God, has delivered them into your power."

²⁰Once Joshua and the Israelites had finally inflicted the last blows in this very great slaughter, and the survivors had escaped from them into the fortified cities, ²¹all the army returned to Joshua and the camp at Makkedah in victory; no one uttered a sound against the Israelites. ²²Then Joshua said, "Open the mouth of the cave and bring me those five kings from the cave." ²³They did so; they brought out to him from the cave the five kings, of Jerusalem, Hebron, Jarmuth, Lachish, and Eglon. ²⁴When they brought the five kings out to Joshua, he summoned all the army of Israel and said to the commanders of the soldiers who had marched with him, "Come forward and put your feet on the necks of these kings." They came forward and put their feet upon their necks. ²⁵Then Joshua said to them, "Do not be afraid or dismayed, be firm and steadfast. This is what the LORD will do to all the enemies against whom you fight." ²⁶Thereupon Joshua struck and killed the kings, and hanged them on five trees, where they remained hanging until evening. ²⁷At sunset Joshua commanded that they be taken down from the trees and be thrown into

the cave where they had hidden; over the mouth of the cave large stones were placed, which remain until this very day.

Conquest of Southern Canaan. 28Makkedah, too, Joshua captured and put to the sword at that time. He put the city, its king, and every person in it under the ban, leaving no survivors. Thus he did to the king of Makkedah what he had done to the king of Jericho. 29Joshua then passed on with all Israel from Makkedah to Libnah, and attacked it, 30and the LORD delivered it, with its king, into the power of Israel. He put it to the sword with every person there, leaving no survivors. Thus he did to its king what he had done to the king of Jericho. 31Joshua next passed on with all Israel from Libnah to Lachish, where they set up a camp during the attack. 32The LORD delivered Lachish into the power of Israel, so that on the second day Joshua captured it and put it to the sword with every person in it, just as he had done to Libnah. 33At that time Horam, king of Gezer, came up to help Lachish, but Joshua defeated him and his people, leaving him no survivors. 34From Lachish, Joshua passed on with all Israel to Eglon; encamping near it, they attacked it 35and captured it the same day, putting it to the sword. On that day he put under the ban every person in it, just as he had done at Lachish. 36From Eglon, Joshua went up with all Israel to Hebron, which they attacked 37and captured. They put it to the sword with its king, all its cities, and every person there, leaving no survivors, just as Joshua had done to Eglon. He put it under the ban and every person in it. 38Then Joshua and all Israel turned back to Debir and attacked it, 39capturing it with its king and all its cities. They put them to the sword and put under the ban every person in it, leaving no survivors. Thus he did to Debir and its king what he had done to Hebron, as well as to Libnah and its king. 40Joshua conquered the entire land; the mountain regions, the Negeb, the Shephelah, and the mountain slopes, with all their kings. He left no survivors, but put under the ban every living being, just as the LORD, the God of Israel, had commanded. 41Joshua conquered them from Kadesh-barnea to Gaza, and all the land of Goshen to Gibeon. 42All these kings and their lands Joshua captured all at once, for the LORD, the God of Israel, fought for Israel. 43Thereupon Joshua with all Israel returned to the camp at Gilgal.

Northern Confederacy. 11:1 When Jabin, king of Hazor, learned of this, he sent a message to Jobab, king of Madon, to the king of Shimron, to the king of Achshaph, 2and to the northern kings in the mountain regions and in the Arabah near Chinneroth, in the Shephelah, and in Naphath-dor to the west. 3These were Canaanites to the east and west, Amorites, Hittites, Perizzites, and Jebusites in the mountain regions, and Hivites at the foot of Hermon in the land of Mizpah. 4They came out with all their troops, an army numerous as the sands on the seashore, and with a multitude of horses and chariots. 5All these kings made a pact and together they marched to the waters of Merom, where they encamped to fight against Israel.

6The LORD said to Joshua, "Do not fear them, for by this time tomorrow I will present them slain to Israel. You must hamstring their horses and burn their chariots." 7Joshua with his whole army came upon them suddenly at the waters of Merom and fell upon them. 8The LORD delivered them into the power of the Israelites, who defeated them and pursued them to Greater Sidon, to Misrephoth-maim, and eastward to the valley of Mizpeh. They struck them all down, leaving no survivors. 9Joshua did to them as the LORD had commanded: he hamstrung their horses and burned their chariots.

Conquest of Northern Canaan. 10At that time Joshua, turning back, captured

Hazor and struck down its king with the sword; for Hazor formerly was the chief of all those kingdoms. [11]He also struck down with the sword every person there, carrying out the ban, till none was left alive. Hazor itself he burned. [12]All the cities of those kings, and the kings themselves, Joshua captured and put to the sword, carrying out the ban on them, as Moses, the servant of the LORD, had commanded. [13]However, Israel did not destroy by fire any of the cities built on their mounds, except Hazor, which Joshua burned. [14]All the spoil and livestock of these cities the Israelites took as plunder; but the people they put to the sword, until they had destroyed the last of them, leaving none alive. [15]As the LORD had commanded his servant Moses, so Moses commanded Joshua, and Joshua acted accordingly. He left nothing undone that the LORD had commanded Moses should be done.

Survey of the Conquest. [16]So Joshua took all this land: the mountain regions, the entire Negeb, all the land of Goshen, the Shephelah, the Arabah, as well as the mountain regions and Shephelah of Israel, [17]from Mount Halak that rises toward Seir as far as Baal-gad in the Lebanon valley at the foot of Mount Hermon. All their kings he captured and put to death. [18]Joshua waged war against all these kings for a long time. [19]With the exception of the Hivites who lived in Gibeon, no city made peace with the Israelites; all were taken in battle. [20]For it was the LORD's doing to make their hearts obstinate to meet Israel in battle, that they might be put under the ban without mercy, and be destroyed as the LORD had commanded Moses.

[21]At that time Joshua penetrated the mountain regions and exterminated the Anakim in Hebron, Debir, Anab, the entire mountain region of Judah, and the entire mountain region of Israel. Joshua put them and their cities under the ban, [22]so that no Anakim were left in the land of the Israel-

ites. However, some survived in Gaza, in Gath, and in Ashdod. [23]Thus Joshua took the whole land, just as the LORD had said to Moses. Joshua gave it to Israel as their heritage, apportioning it among the tribes. And the land had rest from war.

Lists of Conquered Kings. 12:1 These are the kings of the land whom the Israelites conquered and whose lands they occupied, east of the Jordan, from the River Arnon to Mount Hermon, including all the eastern section of the Arabah: [2]First, Sihon, king of the Amorites, who lived in Heshbon. His domain extended from Aroer, which is on the bank of the Wadi Arnon, to include the wadi itself, and the land northward through half of Gilead to the Wadi Jabbok at the border with the Ammonites, [3]as well as the Arabah from the eastern side of the Sea of Chinnereth, as far south as the eastern side of the Salt Sea of the Arabah in the direction of Beth-jeshimoth, southward under the slopes of Pisgah. [4]Secondly, the border of Og, king of Bashan, a survivor of the Rephaim, who lived at Ashtaroth and Edrei. [5]He ruled over Mount Hermon, Salecah, and all Bashan as far as the boundary of the Geshurites and Maacathites, and over half of Gilead as far as the territory of Sihon, king of Heshbon. [6]It was Moses, the servant of the LORD, and the Israelites who conquered them; Moses, the servant of the LORD, gave possession of their land to the Reubenites, the Gadites, and the half-tribe of Manasseh.

[7]This is a list of the kings of the land whom Joshua and the Israelites conquered west of the Jordan, from Baal-gad in the Lebanon valley to Mount Halak which rises toward Seir; Joshua apportioned their land and gave possession of it to the tribes of Israel; [8]it included the mountain regions and Shephelah, the Arabah, the slopes, the wilderness, and the Negeb, belonging to the Hittites, Amorites, Canaanites, Perizzites, Hivites, and Jebusites: [9]The king of

Jericho, one; the king of Ai, which is near Bethel, one; [10]the king of Jerusalem, one; the king of Hebron, one; [11]the king of Jarmuth, one; the king of Lachish, one; [12]the king of Eglon, one; the king of Gezer, one; [13]the king of Debir, one; the king of Geder, one; [14]the king of Hormah, one; the king of Arad, one; [15]the king of Libnah, one; the king of Adullam, one; [16]the king of Makkedah, one; the king of Bethel, one; [17]the king of Tappuah, one; the king of Hepher, one; [18]the king of Aphek, one; the king of Lasharon, one; [19]the king of Madon, one; the king of Hazor, one; [20]the king of Shimron, one; the king of Achshaph, one; [21]the king of Taanach, one; the king of Megiddo, one; [22]the king of Kedesh, one; the king of Jokneam, at Carmel, one; [23]the king of Dor, in Naphath-dor, one; the king of Goyim at Gilgal, one; [24]and the king of Tirzah, one—thirty-one kings in all.

Division of Land Commanded. 13:1 When Joshua was old and advanced in years, the LORD said to him: Though now you are old and advanced in years, a very large part of the land still remains to be possessed. [2]This is the remaining land: all Geshur and all the districts of the Philistines [3](from the stream adjoining Egypt to the boundary of Ekron in the north is reckoned Canaanite territory, though held by the five lords of the Philistines in Gaza, Ashdod, Ashkelon, Gath, and Ekron); [4]also where the Avvim are in the south; all the land of the Canaanites from Mearah of the Sidonians to Aphek, and the boundaries of the Amorites; [5]and the Gebalite territory; and all the Lebanon on the east, from Baal-gad at the foot of Mount Hermon to Lebo-hamath. [6]All the inhabitants of the mountain regions between Lebanon and Misrephoth-maim, all Sidonians, I will drive out before the Israelites; at least include these areas in the division of the Israelite heritage, just as I have commanded you. [7]Now, therefore, apportion among the nine tribes and the half-tribe of Manasseh the land which is to be their heritage.

The Eastern Tribes. [8]Now the other half of the tribe of Manasseh, as well as the Reubenites and Gadites, had taken as their heritage what Moses, the servant of the LORD, had given them east of the Jordan: [9]from Aroer on the bank of the Wadi Arnon and the city in the wadi itself, through the tableland of Medeba and Dibon, [10]with the rest of the cities of Sihon, king of the Amorites, who reigned in Heshbon, to the boundary of the Ammonites; [11]also Gilead and the territory of the Geshurites and Maacathites, all Mount Hermon, and all Bashan as far as Salecah, [12]the entire kingdom in Bashan of Og, who was king at Ashtaroth and Edrei (he was a holdover from the remnant of the Rephaim). These Moses defeated and dispossessed. [13]But the Israelites did not dispossess the Geshurites and Maacathites, so that Geshur and Maacath dwell in the midst of Israel to this day. [14]However, Moses assigned no heritage to the tribe of Levi; the LORD, the God of Israel, is their heritage, as the LORD had promised them.

Reuben. [15]This is what Moses gave to the tribe of the Reubenites by their clans: [16]Their territory reached from Aroer, on the bank of the Wadi Arnon, and the city in the wadi itself, through the tableland about Medeba, [17]to include Heshbon and all its towns on the tableland, Dibon, Bamoth-baal, Beth-baal-meon, [18]Jahaz, Kedemoth, Mephaath, [19]Kiriathaim, Sibmah, Zereth-shahar on the knoll within the valley, [20]Beth-peor, the slopes of Pisgah, Beth-jeshimoth, [21]and the other cities of the tableland and of the whole kingdom of Sihon. This Amorite king, who reigned in Heshbon, Moses had defeated, with the princes of Midian, vassals of Sihon who were settled in the land: Evi, Rekem, Zur, Hur, and Reba; [22]Balaam, son of Beor, the diviner, the Israelites killed with the sword, together with those they struck down. [23]The boundary of the Reubenites was the Jordan. These cities and their villages were the heritage of the Reubenites by their clans.

Gad. [24]This is what Moses gave to the tribe of the Gadites by their clans: [25]Their territory included Jazer, all the cities of Gilead, and half the land of the Ammonites as far as Aroer, toward Rabbah [26](that is, from Heshbon to Ramath-mizpeh and Betonim, and from Mahanaim to the boundary of Lo-debar); [27]and in the Jordan valley: Beth-haram, Beth-nimrah, Succoth, Zaphon, the other part of the kingdom of Sihon, king of Heshbon, with the bank of the Jordan to the southeastern tip of the Sea of Chinnereth. [28]These cities and their villages were the heritage of the clans of the Gadites.

Manasseh. [29]This is what Moses gave to the half-tribe of Manasseh; the half-tribe of the Manassites, by their clans, had [30]territory including Mahanaim, all of Bashan, the entire kingdom of Og, king of Bashan, and all the villages of Jair, which are sixty cities in Bashan. [31]Half of Gilead, with Ashtaroth and Edrei, royal cities of Og in Bashan, fell to the descendants of Machir, son of Manasseh, to half the Machirites, by their clans.

[32]These are the heritages which Moses gave when he was in the plains of Moab, beyond the Jordan east of Jericho. [33]But Moses gave no heritage to the tribe of Levi: the LORD, the God of Israel, is their heritage, as he had promised them.

The Western Tribes. 14:1 These are the portions which the Israelites received as heritage in the land of Canaan. Eleazar the priest, Joshua, son of Nun, and the heads of families in the tribes of the Israelites determined [2]their heritage by lot, as the LORD had commanded through Moses concerning the remaining nine and a half tribes. [3]To two and a half tribes Moses had already given a heritage beyond the Jordan; to the Levites he had given no heritage among them: [4]the descendants of Joseph formed two tribes, Manasseh and Ephraim. But the Levites were given no share of the land except cities to live in, with their pasture lands for the herds and flocks.

[5]As the LORD had commanded Moses, so the Israelites did: they apportioned the land.

Caleb's Portion. [6]When the Judahites approached Joshua in Gilgal, the Kenizzite Caleb, son of Jephunneh, said to him: "You know the word the LORD spoke to Moses, the man of God, concerning you and concerning me in Kadesh-barnea. [7]I was forty years old when Moses, the servant of the LORD, sent me from Kadesh-barnea to reconnoiter the land; and I brought back to him a frank report. [8]My fellow scouts who went up with me made the people's confidence melt away, but I was completely loyal to the LORD, my God. [9]On that occasion Moses swore this oath, 'The land where you have set foot shall become your heritage and that of your descendants forever, because you have been completely loyal to the LORD, my God.' [10]Now, as he promised, the LORD has preserved me these forty-five years since the LORD spoke thus to Moses while Israel journeyed in the wilderness; and now I am eighty-five years old, [11]but I am still as strong today as I was the day Moses sent me forth, with no less vigor whether it be for war or for any other tasks. [12]Now give me this mountain region which the LORD promised me that day, as you yourself heard. True, the Anakim are there, with large fortified cities, but if the LORD is with me I shall be able to dispossess them, as the LORD promised." [13]Joshua blessed Caleb, son of Jephunneh, and gave him Hebron as his heritage. [14]Therefore Hebron remains the heritage of the Kenizzite Caleb, son of Jephunneh, to the present day, because he was completely loyal to the LORD, the God of Israel. [15]Hebron was formerly called Kiriath-arba, for Arba, the greatest among the Anakim. And the land had rest from war.

☐ 1 PETER 4:12-19

Trial of Persecution. 4:12 Beloved, do not be surprised that a trial by fire is occurring among you, as if something strange were happening to you. [13]But rejoice to the extent that you share in the sufferings of Christ, so that when his glory is revealed you may also rejoice exultantly. [14]If you are insulted for the name of Christ, blessed are you, for the Spirit of glory and of God rests upon you. [15]But let no one among you be made to suffer as a murderer, a thief, an evildoer, or as an intriguer. [16]But whoever is made to suffer as a Christian should not be ashamed but glorify God because of the name. [17]For it is time for the judgment to begin with the household of God; if it begins with us, how will it end for those who fail to obey the gospel of God?

[18]"And if the righteous one is barely saved,
where will the godless and the sinner appear?"

[19]As a result, those who suffer in accord with God's will hand their souls over to a faithful creator as they do good.

March 18

St. Cyril of Jerusalem

The purpose of clothing is to keep warm in winter and to cover your nakedness, not to serve your vanity.

— St. Cyril of Jerusalem

☐ JOSHUA 15-19

Boundaries of Judah. 15:1 The lot for the tribe of Judah by their clans fell toward the boundary of Edom, the wilderness of Zin in the Negeb, in the extreme south. [2]Their southern boundary ran from the end of the Salt Sea, from the tongue of land that faces the Negeb, [3]and went southward below the pass of Akrabbim, across through Zin, up to a point south of Kadesh-barnea, across to Hezron, and up to Addar; from there, looping around Karka, [4]it crossed to Azmon and then joined the Wadi of Egypt before coming out at the sea. (This is your southern boundary.) [5]The eastern boundary was the Salt Sea as far as the mouth of the Jordan.

The northern boundary climbed northward from the tongue of the sea, toward the mouth of the Jordan, [6]up to Beth-hoglah, and ran north of Beth-arabah, up to Eben-Bohan-ben-Reuben. [7]Thence the boundary climbed to Debir, north of the Valley of Achor, in the direction of the Gilgal that faces the pass of Adummim, on the south side of the wadi; from there it crossed to the waters of En-shemesh and emerged at En-rogel. [8]Climbing again to the Valley of Ben-hinnom on the southern flank of the Jebusites (that is, Jerusalem), the boundary rose to the top of the mountain at the northern end of the Valley of Rephaim, which bounds the Valley of Hinnom on the west. [9]From the top of the mountain it ran to the fountain of waters of Nephtoah, extended to the cities of Mount Ephron, and continued to Baalah, or Kiriath-jearim. [10]From Baalah the boundary curved westward to Mount Seir and passed north of the ridge of Mount Jearim (that is, Chesalon); it descended to Beth-shemesh, and ran across to Timnah. [11]It then extended along the northern flank of Ekron, continued through Shikkeron, and across to Mount Baalah, from there to include Jabneel, before it came out at the sea. [12]The western boundary was the Great Sea and its coast. This was the complete boundary of the Judahites by their clans.

Conquest by Caleb. [13]As the LORD had commanded, Joshua gave Caleb, son of Jephunneh, a portion among the Judahites, namely, Kiriath-arba (Arba was the father of Anak), that is, Hebron. [14]And Caleb dispossessed from there the three Anakim, the descendants of Anak: Sheshai, Ahiman, and Talmai. [15]From there he marched up against the inhabitants of Debir, which was formerly called Kiriath-sepher. [16]Caleb said, "To the man who attacks Kiriath-sepher and captures it, I will give my daughter Achsah in marriage." [17]Othniel captured it, the son of Caleb's brother Kenaz; so Caleb gave him his daughter Achsah in marriage. [18]When she came to him, she induced him to ask her father for some land. Then, as she alighted from the donkey, Caleb asked her, "What do you want?" [19]She answered, "Give me a present! Since you have assigned to me land in the Negeb, give me also pools of water." So he gave her the upper and the lower pools.

Cities of Judah. [20]This is the heritage of the tribe of Judahites by their clans: [21]The cities of the tribe of the Judahites in the extreme southern district toward Edom were: Kabzeel, Eder, Jagur, [22]Kinah, Dimonah, Adadah, [23]Kedesh, Hazor, and Ithnan; [24]Ziph, Telem, Bealoth, [25]Hazor-hadattah, and Kerioth-hezron (that is, Hazor); [26]Amam, Shema, Moladah, [27]Hazar-gaddah, Heshmon, Beth-pelet, [28]Hazar-shual, Beer-sheba, and Biziothiah; [29]Baalah, Iim, Ezem, [30]Eltolad, Chesil, Hormah, [31]Ziklag, Madmannah, Sansannah, [32]Lebaoth, Shilhim, and Ain and Rimmon; a total of twenty-nine cities with their villages.

[33]In the Shephelah: Eshtaol, Zorah, Ashnah, [34]Zanoah, Engannim, Tappuah, Enam, [35]Jarmuth, Adullam, Socoh, Azekah, [36]Shaaraim, Adithaim, Gederah, and Gederothaim; fourteen cities and their villages. [37]Zenan, Hadashah, Migdal-gad, [38]Dilean, Mizpeh, Joktheel, [39]Lachish, Bozkath, Eglon, [40]Cabbon, Lahmas, Chitlish, [41]Gederoth, Beth-dagon, Naamah, and Makkedah; sixteen cities and their villages. [42]Libnah, Ether, Ashan, [43]Iphtah, Ashnah, Nezib, [44]Keilah, Achzib, and Mareshah; nine cities and their villages. [45]Ekron and its towns and villages; [46]from Ekron to the sea, all the towns that lie alongside Ashdod, and their villages; [47]Ashdod and its towns and villages; Gaza and its towns and villages, as far as the Wadi of Egypt and the coast of the Great Sea.

[48]In the mountain regions: Shamir, Jattir, Socoh, [49]Dannah, Kiriath-sannah (that is, Debir), [50]Anab, Eshtemoh, Anim, [51]Goshen, Holon, and Giloh; eleven cities and their villages. [52]Arab, Dumah, Eshan, [53]Janim, Beth-tappuah, Aphekah, [54]Humtah, Kiriath-arba (that is, Hebron), and Zior; nine cities and their villages. [55]Maon, Carmel, Ziph, Juttah, [56]Jezreel, Jokdeam, Zanoah, [57]Kain, Gibeah, and Timnah; ten cities and their villages. [58]Halhul, Beth-zur, Gedor, [59]Maarath, Beth-anoth, and Eltekon; six cities and their villages. Tekoa, Ephrathah (that is, Bethlehem), Peor, Etam, Kulom, Tatam, Zores, Karim, Gallim, Bether, and Manoko; eleven cities and their villages. [60]Kiriath-baal (that is, Kiriath-jearim) and Rabbah; two cities and their villages.

[61]In the wilderness: Beth-arabah, Middin, Secacah, [62]Nibshan, Ir-hamelah, and En-gedi; six cities and their villages. [63]But the Jebusites who lived in Jerusalem the Judahites could not dispossess; so the Jebusites dwell in Jerusalem beside the Judahites to the present day.

The Joseph Tribes. 16:1 The lot that fell to the Josephites extended from the Jordan at Jericho to the waters of Jericho east of the wilderness; then the boundary went up from Jericho to the heights at Bethel. ²Leaving Bethel for Luz, it crossed the ridge to the border of the Archites at Ataroth, ³and descended westward to the border of the Japhletites, to that of the Lower Beth-horon, and to Gezer, and from there to the sea.

Ephraim. ⁴Within the heritage of Manasseh and Ephraim, sons of Joseph, ⁵the dividing line for the heritage of the Ephraimites by their clans ran from east of Ataroth-addar to Upper Beth-horon ⁶and thence to the sea. From Michmethath on the north, their boundary curved eastward around Taanath-shiloh, and continued east of it to Janoah; ⁷from there it descended to Ataroth and Naarah, and reaching Jericho, it ended at the Jordan. ⁸From Tappuah the boundary ran westward to the Wadi Kanah and ended at the sea. This was the heritage of the Ephraimites by their clans, ⁹including the villages that belonged to each city set aside for the Ephraimites within the heritage of the Manassites. ¹⁰But they did not dispossess the Canaanites living in Gezer; they live within Ephraim to the present day, though they have been put to forced labor.

Manasseh. 17:1 Now as for the lot that fell to the tribe of Manasseh as the firstborn of Joseph: since Manasseh's eldest son, Machir, the father of Gilead, was a warrior, who had already obtained Gilead and Bashan, ²the allotment was now made to the rest of the Manassites by their clans: the descendants of Abiezer, Helek, Asriel, Shechem, Hepher, and Shemida; these are the other male children of Manasseh, son of Joseph, by their clans.

³Furthermore, Zelophehad, son of Hepher, son of Gilead, son of Machir, son of Manasseh, had no sons, but only daughters, whose names were Mahlah, Noah, Hoglah, Milcah, and Tirzah. ⁴These presented themselves to Eleazar the priest, to Joshua, son of Nun, and to the leaders, saying, "The LORD commanded Moses to give us a heritage among our relatives." So in accordance with the command of the LORD a heritage was given them among their father's relatives. ⁵Thus ten shares fell to Manasseh apart from the land of Gilead and Bashan beyond the Jordan, ⁶since these female descendants of Manasseh received each a portion among his sons. The land of Gilead fell to the rest of the Manassites. ⁷Manasseh bordered on Asher. From Michmethath, near Shechem, another boundary ran southward to include the inhabitants of En-Tappuah, ⁸because the district of Tappuah belonged to Manasseh, although Tappuah itself was an Ephraimite city on the border of Manasseh. ⁹This same boundary continued down to the Wadi Kanah. The cities that belonged to Ephraim from among the cities in Manasseh were those to the south of that wadi; thus the territory of Manasseh ran north of the wadi and ended at the sea. ¹⁰The land on the south belonged to Ephraim and that on the north to Manasseh; with the sea as their common boundary, they reached Asher on the north and Issachar on the east.

¹¹Moreover, in Issachar and in Asher Manasseh was awarded Beth-shean and its towns, Ibleam and its towns, the inhabitants of Dor and its towns, the inhabitants of Endor and its towns, the inhabitants of Taanach and its towns, the inhabitants of Megiddo and its towns (the third is Naphath-dor). ¹²Since the Manassites were not able to dispossess these cities, the Canaanites continued to inhabit this region. ¹³When the Israelites grew stronger they put the Canaanites to forced labor, but they did not dispossess them.

Protest of Joseph Tribes. ¹⁴The descendants of Joseph said to Joshua, "Why have you given us only one lot and one share as our heritage? Our people are too many, because of the extent to which the LORD has blessed us." ¹⁵Joshua answered them, "If you are too many, go up to the forest and clear out a place for yourselves there in the land of the Perizzites and Rephaim, since the mountain regions of Ephraim are so narrow." ¹⁶For the Josephites said, "Our mountain regions are not enough for us; on the other hand, the Canaanites living in the valley region all have iron chariots, in particular those in Beth-shean and its towns, and those in the valley of Jezreel." ¹⁷Joshua therefore said to Ephraim and Manasseh, the house of Joseph, "You are a numerous people and very strong. You shall not have merely one share, ¹⁸for the mountain region which is now forest shall be yours when you clear it. Its adjacent land shall also be yours if, despite their strength and iron chariots, you dispossess the Canaanites."

18:1 The whole community of the Israelites assembled at Shiloh, where they set up the tent of meeting; and the land was subdued before them.

The Seven Remaining Portions. ²There remained seven tribes among the Israelites that had not yet received their heritage. ³Joshua therefore said to the Israelites, "How much longer will you put off taking steps to possess the land which the LORD, the God of your ancestors, has given you? ⁴Choose three representatives from each of your tribes; I will send them to go throughout the land and describe it for purposes of acquiring their heritage. When they return to me ⁵you shall divide it into seven parts. Judah is to retain its territory in the south, and the house of Joseph its territory in the north. ⁶You shall bring to me here the description of the land in seven sections. I will then cast lots for you here before the LORD, our God. ⁷For the Levites have no share among you, because the priesthood of the LORD is their heritage; while Gad, Reuben, and the half-tribe of Manasseh have already received the heritage east of the Jordan which Moses, the servant of the LORD, gave them."

⁸When those who were to describe the land were ready for their journey, Joshua commanded them, "Go throughout the land and describe it; return to me and I will cast lots for you here before the LORD in Shiloh." ⁹So they went through the land, described its cities in writing in seven sections, and returned to Joshua in the camp at Shiloh. ¹⁰Joshua then cast lots for them before the LORD in Shiloh, and divided up the land for the Israelites into their separate shares.

Benjamin. ¹¹One lot fell to the tribe of Benjaminites by their clans. The territory allotted them lay between the descendants of Judah and those of Joseph. ¹²Their northern boundary began at the Jordan and went over the northern flank of Jericho, up westward into the mountains, until it reached the wilderness of Beth-aven. ¹³From there it crossed over to the southern flank of Luz (that is, Bethel). Then it ran down to Ataroth-addar, on the mountaintop south of Lower Beth-horon. ¹⁴For the western border, the boundary line swung south from the mountaintop opposite Beth-horon until it reached Kiriath-baal (that is, Kiriath-jearim; this city belonged to the Judahites). This was the western boundary. ¹⁵The southern boundary began at the limits of Kiriath-jearim and projected to the spring at Nephtoah. ¹⁶It went down to the edge of the mountain on the north of the Valley of Rephaim, where it faces the Valley of Ben-hinnom; and continuing down the Valley of Hinnom along the southern flank of the Jebusites, reached En-rogel. ¹⁷Inclining to the north, it extended to En-shemesh, and thence to Geliloth, opposite the pass of Adummim. Then it dropped to Eben-Bohan-ben-Reuben, ¹⁸across the northern flank of the Arabah overlook, down into the Arabah. ¹⁹From there the boundary continued across the northern flank of Beth-hoglah and extended northward to the tongue of the Salt Sea, toward the southern end of the Jordan. This was the southern boundary. [20]The Jordan bounded it on the east. This was how the heritage of the Benjaminites by their clans was bounded on all sides.

[21]Now the cities belonging to the tribe of the Benjaminites by their clans were: Jericho, Beth-hoglah, Emek-keziz, [22]Beth-arabah, Zemaraim, Bethel, [23]Avvim, Parah, Ophra, [24]Chephar-ammoni, Ophni, and Geba; twelve cities and their villages. [25]Also Gibeon, Ramah, Beeroth, [26]Mizpeh, Chephirah, Mozah, [27]Rekem, Irpeel, Taralah, [28]Zela, Haeleph, the Jebusite city (that is, Jerusalem), Gibeah, and Kiriath; fourteen cities and their villages. This was the heritage of the clans of Benjaminites.

Simeon. **19:1** The second lot fell to Simeon. The heritage of the tribe of Simeonites by their clans lay within that of the Judahites. [2]For their heritage they received Beer-sheba, Shema, Moladah, [3]Hazar-shual, Balah, Ezem, [4]Eltolad, Bethul, Hormah, [5]Ziklag, Bethmar-caboth, Hazar-susah, [6]Beth-lebaoth, and Sharuhen; thirteen cities and their villages. [7]Also Ain, Rimmon, Ether, and Ashan; four cities and their villages, [8]besides all the villages around these cities as far as Baalath-beer (that is, Ramoth-negeb). This was the heritage of the tribe of the Simeonites by their clans. [9]This heritage of the Simeonites was within the confines of the Judahites; for since the portion of the latter was too large for them, the Simeonites obtained their heritage within it.

Zebulun. [10]The third lot fell to the Zebulunites by their clans. The boundary of their heritage was at Sarid. [11]Their boundary went up west and through Mareal, reaching Dabbesheth and the wadi that is near Jokneam. [12]From Sarid eastward it ran to the district of Chisloth-tabor, on to Daberath, and up to Japhia. [13]From there it continued eastward to Gath-hepher and to Eth-kazin, extended to Rimmon, and turned to Neah. [14]Skirting north of Han-

nathon, the boundary ended at the valley of Iphtahel. [15]Thus, with Kattath, Nahalal, Shimron, Idalah, and Bethlehem, there were twelve cities and their villages. [16]This was the heritage of the Zebulunites by their clans, these cities and their villages.

Issachar. [17]The fourth lot fell to Issachar. The territory of the Issacharites by their clans [18]included Jezreel, Chesulloth, Shunem, [19]Hapharaim, Shion, Anaharath, [20]Rabbith, Kishion, Ebez, [21]Remeth, En-gannim, En-haddah, and Beth-pazzez. [22]The boundary reached Tabor, Shahazumah, and Beth-shemesh, ending at the Jordan: sixteen cities and their villages. [23]This was the heritage of the Issacharites by their clans, these cities and their villages.

Asher. [24]The fifth lot fell to the Asherites by their clans. [25]Their territory included Helkath, Hali, Beten, Achshaph, [26]Allammelech, Amad, and Mishal, and reached Carmel on the west, and Shihor-libnath. [27]In the other direction, it ran eastward of Beth-dagon, reached Zebulun and the valley of Iphtahel; then north of Beth-emek and Neiel, it extended northward to Cabul, [28]Ebron, Rehob, Hammon, and Kanah, near Greater Sidon. [29]Then the boundary turned back to Ramah and to the fortress city of Tyre; thence it cut back to Hosah and ended at the sea. Thus, with Mahalab, Achzib, [30]Ummah, Acco, Aphek, and Rehob, there were twenty-two cities and their villages. [31]This was the heritage of the tribe of the Asherites by their clans, these cities and their villages.

Naphtali. [32]The sixth lot fell to the Naphtalites. [33]Their boundary extended from Heleph, from the oak at Zaanannim, including Adami-nekeb and Jabneel, to Lakkum, and ended at the Jordan. [34]In the opposite direction, westerly, it ran through Aznoth-tabor and from there extended to Hukkok; it reached Zebulun on the south, Asher on the west, and the Jordan on the east. [35]The fortified cities were Ziddim, Zer, Hammath, Rakkath, Chinnereth,

³⁶Adamah, Ramah, Hazor, ³⁷Kedesh, Edrei, En-hazor, ³⁸Yiron, Migdal-el, Horem, Beth-anath, and Beth-shemesh; nineteen cities and their villages. ³⁹This was the heritage of the tribe of the Naphtalites by their clans, these cities and their villages.

Dan. ⁴⁰The seventh lot fell to the tribe of Danites by their clans. ⁴¹Their heritage was the territory of Zorah, Eshtaol, Ir-shemesh, ⁴²Shaalabbin, Aijalon, Ithlah, ⁴³Elon, Timnah, Ekron, ⁴⁴Eltekoh, Gibbethon, Baalath, ⁴⁵Jehud, Bene-berak, Gath-rimmon, ⁴⁶Me-jarkon, and Rakkon, with the coast at Joppa. ⁴⁷But the territory of the Danites was too small for them; so the Danites marched up and attacked Leshem, which they captured and put to the sword. Once they had taken possession of Leshem, they dwelt there and named it after their ancestor Dan. ⁴⁸This was the heritage of the tribe of the Danites by their clans, these cities and their villages.

Joshua's City. ⁴⁹When the last of them had received the portions of the land they were to inherit, the Israelites assigned a heritage in their midst to Joshua, son of Nun. ⁵⁰According to the command of the LORD, they gave him the city he requested, Timnah-serah in the mountain region of Ephraim. He rebuilt the city and made it his home.

⁵¹These are the heritages which Eleazar the priest, Joshua, son of Nun, and the heads of families in the tribes of the Israelites apportioned by lot in the presence of the LORD, at the door of the tent of meeting in Shiloh. Thus they finished dividing the land.

☐ **1 PETER 5**

Advice to Presbyters. 5:1 So I exhort the presbyters among you, as a fellow presbyter and witness to the sufferings of Christ and one who has a share in the glory to be revealed. ²Tend the flock of God in your midst, [overseeing] not by constraint but willingly, as God would have it, not for shameful profit but eagerly. ³Do not lord it over those assigned to you, but be examples to the flock. ⁴And when the chief Shepherd is revealed, you will receive the unfading crown of glory.

Advice to the Community. ⁵Likewise, you younger members, be subject to the presbyters. And all of you, clothe yourselves with humility in your dealings with one another, for:

"God opposes the proud
but bestows favor on the humble."

⁶So humble yourselves under the mighty hand of God, that he may exalt you in due time. ⁷Cast all your worries upon him because he cares for you.

⁸Be sober and vigilant. Your opponent the devil is prowling around like a roaring lion looking for [someone] to devour. ⁹Resist him, steadfast in faith, knowing that your fellow believers throughout the world undergo the same sufferings. ¹⁰The God of all grace who called you to his eternal glory through Christ [Jesus] will himself restore, confirm, strengthen, and establish you after you have suffered a little. ¹¹To him be dominion forever. Amen.

¹²I write you this briefly through Silvanus, whom I consider a faithful brother, exhorting you and testifying that this is the true grace of God. Remain firm in it. ¹³The chosen one at Babylon sends you greeting, as does Mark, my son. ¹⁴Greet one another with a loving kiss. Peace to all of you who are in Christ.

March 19

St. Joseph

To other saints, it seems, the Lord has given the grace to help and support in a special need. But this glorious saint — I know from personal experience — helps in all need and distress, because our Lord Jesus wants to give us a signal that, just as He was subject to St. Joseph in His earthly life, so He wants to grant him all his requests in heaven.

— ST. TERESA OF ÁVILA

☐ JOSHUA 20-24

Cities of Refuge. 20:1 The LORD said to Joshua: ²Tell the Israelites: Designate for yourselves the cities of refuge of which I spoke to you through Moses, ³to which anyone guilty of inadvertent and unintentional homicide may flee for asylum from the avenger of blood. ⁴To one of these cities the killer shall flee, and standing at the entrance of the city gate, shall plead his case in the hearing of the elders of the city, who must receive him and assign him a place in which to live among them. ⁵Though the avenger of blood pursues him, they shall not deliver up to him the one who killed a neighbor unintentionally, when there had been no hatred previously. ⁶Once he has stood judgment before the community, he shall live on in that city until the death of the high priest who is in office at the time. Then the killer may return home to the city from where he originally fled.

List of Cities. ⁷So they set apart Kedesh in Galilee in the mountain region of Naphtali, Shechem in the mountain region of Ephraim, and Kiriath-arba (that is, Hebron) in the mountain region of Judah. ⁸And beyond the Jordan east of Jericho they designated Bezer in the wilderness on the tableland in the tribe of Reuben, Ramoth in Gilead in the tribe of Gad, and Golan in Bashan in the tribe of Manasseh. ⁹These are the designated cities to which any Israelite or alien residing among them

who had killed a person unintentionally might flee to escape death at the hand of the avenger of blood, until the killer could appear before the community.

Levitical Cities. 21:1 The heads of the Levite families approached Eleazar the priest, Joshua, son of Nun, and the heads of families of the other tribes of the Israelites ²at Shiloh in the land of Canaan, and said to them, "The LORD commanded, through Moses, that cities be given us to dwell in, with pasture lands for our livestock." ³Out of their own heritage, according to the command of the LORD, the Israelites gave the Levites the following cities with their pasture lands.

⁴When the first lot among the Levites fell to the clans of the Kohathites, the descendants of Aaron the priest obtained by lot from the tribes of Judah, Simeon, and Benjamin, thirteen cities. ⁵From the clans of the tribe of Ephraim, from the tribe of Dan, and from the half-tribe of Manasseh, the rest of the Kohathites obtained by lot ten cities. ⁶From the clans of the tribe of Issachar, from the tribe of Asher, from the tribe of Naphtali, and from the half-tribe of Manasseh, the Gershonites obtained by lot thirteen cities. ⁷From the tribes of Reuben, Gad, and Zebulun, the clans of the Merarites obtained twelve cities. ⁸These cities with their pasture lands the Israelites

gave by lot to the Levites, as the LORD had commanded through Moses.

Cities of the Priests. [9]From the tribes of the Judahites and Simeonites they gave the following cities [10]and assigned them to the descendants of Aaron in the Kohathite clan of the Levites, since the first lot fell to them: [11]first, Kiriath-arba (Arba was the father of Anak), that is, Hebron, in the mountain region of Judah, with the adjacent pasture lands, [12]although the open country and villages belonging to the city had been given to Caleb, son of Jephunneh, as his holding. [13]Thus to the descendants of Aaron the priest were given the city of refuge for homicides at Hebron, with its pasture lands; also, Libnah with its pasture lands, [14]Jattir with its pasture lands, Eshtemoa with its pasture lands, [15]Holon with its pasture lands, Debir with its pasture lands, [16]Ain with its pasture lands, Juttah with its pasture lands, and Beth-shemesh with its pasture lands: nine cities from these two tribes. [17]From the tribe of Benjamin they obtained Gibeon with its pasture lands, Geba with its pasture lands, [18]Anathoth with its pasture lands, and Almon with its pasture lands: four cities. [19]These cities which with their pasture lands belonged to the priestly descendants of Aaron, were thirteen in all.

Cities of the Other Kohathites. [20]The rest of the Kohathite clans among the Levites obtained by lot, from the tribe of Ephraim, four cities. [21]They were assigned, with its pasture lands, the city of refuge for homicides at Shechem in the mountain region of Ephraim; also Gezer with its pasture lands, [22]Kibzaim with its pasture lands, and Beth-horon with its pasture lands. [23]From the tribe of Dan they obtained Elteke with its pasture lands, Gibbethon with its pasture lands, [24]Aijalon with its pasture lands, and Gath-rimmon with its pasture lands: four cities. [25]From the half-tribe of Manasseh, Taanach with its pasture lands, and Gath-rimmon with its pasture lands: two cities. [26]These cities which with their pasture lands belonged to the rest of the Kohathite clans were ten in all.

Cities of the Gershonites. [27]The Gershonite clan of the Levites received from the half-tribe of Manasseh the city of refuge for homicides at Golan in Bashan, with its pasture lands; and also Beth-Astharoth with its pasture lands: two cities. [28]From the tribe of Issachar they obtained Kishion with its pasture lands, Daberath with its pasture lands, [29]Jarmuth with its pasture lands, and En-gannim with its pasture lands: four cities. [30]From the tribe of Asher, Mishal with its pasture lands, Abdon with its pasture lands, [31]Helkath with its pasture lands, and Rehob with its pasture lands: four cities. [32]From the tribe of Naphtali, the city of refuge for homicides at Kedesh in Galilee, with its pasture lands; also Hammath with its pasture lands, and Kartan with its pasture lands: three cities. [33]The cities which belonged to the Gershonite clans, with their pasture lands, were thirteen in all.

Cities of the Merarites. [34]The Merarite clans, the last of the Levites, received, from the tribe of Zebulun, Jokneam with its pasture lands, Kartah with its pasture lands, [35]Dimnah with its pasture lands, and Nahalal with its pasture lands: four cities. [36]Also, across the Jordan, from the tribe of Reuben, the city of refuge for homicides at Bezer with its pasture lands, Jahaz with its pasture lands, [37]Kedemoth with its pasture lands, and Mephaath with its pasture lands: four cities. [38]From the tribe of Gad, the city of refuge for homicides at Ramoth in Gilead with its pasture lands, Mahanaim with its pasture lands, [39]Heshbon with its pasture lands, and Jazer with its pasture lands: four cities in all. [40]The cities allotted to the Merarite clans, the last of the Levites, were therefore twelve in all.

[41]Thus the total number of cities within the territory of the Israelites which, with their pasture lands, belonged to the Levites, was forty-eight. [42]With each and every one

of these cities went the pasture lands round about it. ⁴³And so the LORD gave Israel the entire land he had sworn to their ancestors he would give them. Once they had taken possession of it, and dwelt in it, ⁴⁴the LORD gave them peace on every side, just as he had promised their ancestors. Not one of their enemies could withstand them; the LORD gave all their enemies into their power. ⁴⁵Not a single word of the blessing that the LORD had promised to the house of Israel failed; it all came true.

The Eastern Tribes Dismissed. 22:1 At that time Joshua summoned the Reubenites, the Gadites, and the half-tribe of Manasseh ²and said to them: "You have observed all that Moses, the servant of the LORD, commanded you, and have listened to my voice in everything I commanded you. ³For many years now, even until today, you have not abandoned your allies, but have taken care to observe the commands of the LORD, your God. ⁴Now that the LORD, your God, has settled your allies as he promised them, you may return to your tents, to your own land, which Moses, the servant of the LORD, gave you, across the Jordan. ⁵But be very careful to observe the commandment and the law which Moses, the servant of the LORD, commanded you: love the LORD, your God, follow him in all his ways, keep his commandments, hold fast to him, and serve him with your whole heart and your whole self." ⁶Joshua then blessed them and sent them away, and they went to their tents.

⁷(For, to half of the tribe of Manasseh Moses had assigned land in Bashan; and to the other half Joshua had given a portion along with their allies west of the Jordan.) When Joshua sent them away to their tents and blessed them, ⁸he said, "Now that you are returning to your own tents with great wealth, with abundant livestock, with silver, gold, bronze and iron, and with a very large supply of clothing, divide these spoils of your enemies with your allies there." ⁹So the Reubenites, the Gadites, and the half-tribe of Manasseh left the other Israelites at Shiloh in the land of Canaan and returned to the land of Gilead, their own land, which they had received according to the LORD's command through Moses.

The Altar Beside the Jordan. ¹⁰When the Reubenites, the Gadites, and the half-tribe of Manasseh came to the region of the Jordan in the land of Canaan, they built an altar there at the Jordan, an impressively large altar. ¹¹The other Israelites heard the report: "The Reubenites, the Gadites, and the half-tribe of Manasseh have built an altar" in the region of the Jordan facing the land of Canaan, across from the Israelites. ¹²When the Israelites heard this, they assembled at Shiloh, as the entire Israelite community to take military action against them.

Accusation of the Western Tribes. ¹³The Israelites sent Phinehas, son of Eleazar the priest, to the Reubenites, the Gadites, and the half-tribe of Manasseh in the land of Gilead, ¹⁴and with him ten leaders, one from each tribe of Israel, each one the head of an ancestral house among the clans of Israel. ¹⁵When these came to the Reubenites, the Gadites, and the half-tribe of Manasseh in the land of Gilead, they said to them: ¹⁶"Thus says the whole community of the LORD: What act of treachery is this you have committed against the God of Israel? This day you have turned from following the LORD; by building an altar of your own you have rebelled against the LORD this day. ¹⁷Is the iniquity of Peor not enough, by which we made ourselves impure, even to this day, and a plague came upon the community of the LORD? ¹⁸If today you turn away from following the LORD, and rebel against the LORD, tomorrow he will be angry with the whole community of Israel! ¹⁹If you consider the land you now possess unclean, cross over to the land the LORD possesses, where the tabernacle of the LORD stands, and share that with us. But do not rebel against the LORD, nor involve us in rebellion, by building an altar of your own in addition to the altar of the LORD, our God. ²⁰When Achan, son of Zerah, acted treacherously by violating the ban, was it not upon the entire community of Israel that wrath fell? Though he was but a single man, he did not perish alone for his guilt!"

Reply of the Eastern Tribes. ²¹The Reubenites, the Gadites, and the half-tribe of Manasseh replied to the heads of the Israelite clans: ²²"The LORD is the God of gods. The LORD, the God of gods, knows and Israel shall know. If now we have acted out of rebellion or treachery against the LORD, our God, do not try to save us this day, ²³and if we have built an altar of our own to turn from following the LORD, or to sacrifice burnt offerings, grain offerings, or communion sacrifices upon it, the LORD himself will exact the penalty. ²⁴We did it rather out of our anxious concern lest in the future your children should say to our children: 'What have you to do with the LORD, the God of Israel? ²⁵For the LORD has placed the Jordan as a boundary between you and us, you Reubenites and Gadites. You have no share in the LORD.' Thus your children would prevent ours from revering the LORD. ²⁶So we thought, 'Let us act for ourselves by building this altar of our own'—not for burnt offerings or sacrifice, ²⁷but as witness between us and you and our descendants, that we have the right to provide for the service of the LORD in his presence with our burnt offerings, sacrifices, and communion sacrifices. Now in the future your children cannot say to our children, 'You have no share in the LORD.' ²⁸Our thought was that, if in the future they should speak thus to us or to our descendants, we could answer: 'Look at the copy of the altar of the LORD which our ancestors made, not for burnt offerings or for sacrifices, but to witness between you and us.' ²⁹Far be it from us to rebel against the

LORD or to turn now from following the LORD by building an altar for burnt offering, grain offering, or sacrifice in addition to the altar of the LORD, our God, which stands before his tabernacle."

³⁰When Phinehas the priest and the leaders of the community, the heads of the Israelite clans, heard what the Reubenites, the Gadites, and the Manassites had to say, they were satisfied. ³¹Phinehas, son of Eleazar the priest, said to the Reubenites, the Gadites, and the Manassites, "Today we know that the LORD is in our midst. Since you have not rebelled against the LORD by this act of treachery, you have delivered the Israelites from the hand of the LORD."

³²Phinehas, son of Eleazar the priest, and the leaders returned from the Reubenites and the Gadites in the land of Gilead to the Israelites in the land of Canaan, and reported the matter to them. ³³The report satisfied the Israelites, who blessed God and decided not to take military action against the Reubenites and Gadites nor to ravage the land where they lived.

³⁴The Reubenites and the Gadites gave the altar its name as a witness among them that the LORD is God.

Joshua's Final Plea. 23:1 Many years later, after the LORD had given the Israelites rest from all their enemies round about them, and when Joshua was old and advanced in years, ²he summoned all Israel, including their elders, leaders, judges and officers, and said to them: "I am old and advanced in years. ³You have seen all that the LORD, your God, has done for you against all these nations; for it has been the LORD, your God, who fought for you. ⁴See, I have apportioned among your tribes as their heritage the nations that survive, as well as those I destroyed, between the Jordan and the Great Sea in the west. ⁵The LORD, your God, will drive them out and dispossess them at your approach, so that you will take possession of their land as the LORD, your

God, promised you. ⁶Therefore be strong and be careful to observe all that is written in the book of the law of Moses, never turning from it right or left, ⁷or mingling with these nations that survive among you. You must not invoke their gods by name, or swear by them, or serve them, or bow down to them, ⁸but you must hold fast to the LORD, your God, as you have done up to this day. ⁹At your approach the LORD has dispossessed great and strong nations; not one has withstood you up to this day. ¹⁰One of you puts to flight a thousand, because it is the LORD, your God, himself who fights for you, as he promised you. ¹¹As for you, take great care to love the LORD, your God. ¹²For if you ever turn away from him and join with the remnant of these nations that survive among you, by intermarrying and intermingling with them, ¹³know for certain that the LORD, your God, will no longer dispossess these nations at your approach. Instead they will be a snare and a trap for you, a scourge for your sides and thorns for your eyes, until you perish from this good land which the LORD, your God, has given you.

¹⁴"Today, as you see, I am going the way of all the earth. So now acknowledge with your whole heart and soul that not one of all the promises the LORD, your God, made concerning you has failed. Every one has come true for you; not one has failed. ¹⁵But just as every promise the LORD, your God, made to you has come true for you, so will he bring upon you every threat, even so far as to exterminate you from this good land which the LORD, your God, has given you. ¹⁶If you transgress the covenant of the LORD, your God, which he enjoined on you, to go and serve other gods and bow down to them, the anger of the LORD will flare up against you and you will quickly perish from the good land he has given you."

Covenant Ceremony. 24:1 Joshua gathered together all the tribes of Israel at Shechem, summoning the elders, leaders, judges, and officers of Israel. When they stood in ranks before God, ²Joshua addressed all the people: "Thus says the LORD, the God of Israel: In times past your ancestors, down to Terah, father of Abraham and Nahor, lived beyond the River and served other gods. ³But I brought your father Abraham from the region beyond the River and led him through the entire land of Canaan. I made his descendants numerous, and gave him Isaac. ⁴To Isaac I gave Jacob and Esau. To Esau I assigned the mountain region of Seir to possess, while Jacob and his children went down to Egypt.

⁵"Then I sent Moses and Aaron, and struck Egypt with the plagues and wonders that I wrought in her midst. Afterward I led you out. ⁶And when I led your ancestors out of Egypt, you came to the sea, and the Egyptians pursued your ancestors to the Red Sea with chariots and charioteers. ⁷When they cried out to the LORD, he put darkness between you and the Egyptians, upon whom he brought the sea so that it covered them. Your eyes saw what I did to Egypt. After you dwelt a long time in the wilderness, ⁸I brought you into the land of the Amorites who lived east of the Jordan. They fought against you, but I delivered them into your power. You took possession of their land, and I destroyed them at your approach. ⁹Then Balak, son of Zippor, king of Moab, prepared to war against Israel. He summoned Balaam, son of Beor, to curse you, ¹⁰but I would not listen to Balaam. Instead, he had to bless you, and I delivered you from his power. ¹¹Once you crossed the Jordan and came to Jericho, the citizens of Jericho fought against you, but I delivered them also into your power. ¹²And I sent the hornets ahead of you which drove them—the Amorites, Perizzites, Canaanites, Hittites, Girgashites, Hivites, and Jebusites—out of your way; it was not your sword or your bow. ¹³I gave you a land you did not till and cities you did not build,

to dwell in; you ate of vineyards and olive groves you did not plant.

[14]"Now, therefore, fear the LORD and serve him completely and sincerely. Cast out the gods your ancestors served beyond the River and in Egypt, and serve the LORD. [15]If it is displeasing to you to serve the LORD, choose today whom you will serve, the gods your ancestors served beyond the River or the gods of the Amorites in whose country you are dwelling. As for me and my household, we will serve the LORD."

[16]But the people answered, "Far be it from us to forsake the LORD to serve other gods. [17]For it was the LORD, our God, who brought us and our ancestors up out of the land of Egypt, out of the house of slavery. He performed those great signs before our very eyes and protected us along our entire journey and among all the peoples through whom we passed. [18]At our approach the LORD drove out all the peoples, including the Amorites who dwelt in the land. Therefore we also will serve the LORD, for he is our God."

[19]Joshua in turn said to the people, "You may not be able to serve the LORD, for he is a holy God; he is a passionate God who will not forgive your transgressions or your sins. [20]If you forsake the LORD and serve strange gods, he will then do evil to you and destroy you, after having done you good."

[21]But the people answered Joshua, "No! We will serve the LORD." [22]Joshua therefore said to the people, "You are witnesses against yourselves that you have chosen to serve the LORD." They replied, "We are witnesses!" [23]"Now, therefore, put away the foreign gods that are among you and turn your hearts to the LORD, the God of Israel." [24]Then the people promised Joshua, "We will serve the LORD, our God, and will listen to his voice."

[25]So Joshua made a covenant with the people that day and made statutes and ordinances for them at Shechem. [26]Joshua wrote these words in the book of the law of God. Then he took a large stone and set it up there under the terebinth that was in the sanctuary of the LORD. [27]And Joshua said to all the people, "This stone shall be our witness, for it has heard all the words which the LORD spoke to us. It shall be a witness against you, should you wish to deny your God." [28]Then Joshua dismissed the people, each to their own heritage.

Death of Joshua. [29]After these events, Joshua, son of Nun, servant of the LORD, died at the age of a hundred and ten, [30]and they buried him within the borders of his heritage at Timnath-serah in the mountain region of Ephraim north of Mount Gaash. [31]Israel served the LORD during the entire lifetime of Joshua, and of those elders who outlived Joshua and who knew all the work the LORD had done for Israel. [32]The bones of Joseph, which the Israelites had brought up from Egypt, were buried in Shechem in the plot of ground Jacob had bought from the sons of Hamor, father of Shechem, for a hundred pieces of money. This was a heritage of the descendants of Joseph. [33]When Eleazar, son of Aaron, also died, he was buried on the hill which had been given to his son Phinehas in the mountain region of Ephraim.

☐ 1 CORINTHIANS 1:1-25

Greeting. 1:1 Paul, called to be an apostle of Christ Jesus by the will of God, and Sosthenes our brother, [2]to the church of God that is in Corinth, to you who have been sanctified in Christ Jesus, called to be holy, with all those everywhere who call upon the name of our Lord Jesus Christ, their Lord and ours. [3]Grace to you and peace from God our Father and the Lord Jesus Christ.

Thanksgiving. ⁴I give thanks to my God always on your account for the grace of God bestowed on you in Christ Jesus, ⁵that in him you were enriched in every way, with all discourse and all knowledge, ⁶as the testimony to Christ was confirmed among you, ⁷so that you are not lacking in any spiritual gift as you wait for the revelation of our Lord Jesus Christ. ⁸He will keep you firm to the end, irreproachable on the day of our Lord Jesus [Christ]. ⁹God is faithful, and by him you were called to fellowship with his Son, Jesus Christ our Lord.

Groups and Slogans. ¹⁰I urge you, brothers, in the name of our Lord Jesus Christ, that all of you agree in what you say, and that there be no divisions among you, but that you be united in the same mind and in the same purpose. ¹¹For it has been reported to me about you, my brothers, by Chloe's people, that there are rivalries among you. ¹²I mean that each of you is saying, "I belong to Paul," or "I belong to Apollos," or "I belong to Cephas," or "I belong to Christ." ¹³Is Christ divided? Was Paul crucified for you? Or were you baptized in the name of Paul? ¹⁴I give thanks [to God] that I baptized none of you except Crispus and Gaius, ¹⁵so that no one can say you were baptized in my name. ¹⁶(I baptized the household of Stephanas also; beyond that I do not know whether I baptized anyone else.) ¹⁷For Christ did not send me to baptize but to preach the gospel, and not with the wisdom of human eloquence, so that the cross of Christ might not be emptied of its meaning.

Paradox of the Cross. ¹⁸The message of the cross is foolishness to those who are perishing, but to us who are being saved it is the power of God. ¹⁹For it is written:

> "I will destroy the wisdom of the wise,
>   and the learning of the learned I will
>   set aside."

²⁰Where is the wise one? Where is the scribe? Where is the debater of this age? Has not God made the wisdom of the world foolish? ²¹For since in the wisdom of God the world did not come to know God through wisdom, it was the will of God through the foolishness of the proclamation to save those who have faith. ²²For Jews demand signs and Greeks look for wisdom, ²³but we proclaim Christ crucified, a stumbling block to Jews and foolishness to Gentiles, ²⁴but to those who are called, Jews and Greeks alike, Christ the power of God and the wisdom of God. ²⁵For the foolishness of God is wiser than human wisdom, and the weakness of God is stronger than human strength.

March 20

As a ship cannot be built without nails, so a person cannot be saved without humility.

— St. Syncletica

☐ JUDGES 1-2

Canaanites in Palestine. 1:1 After the death of Joshua the Israelites consulted the LORD, asking, "Who shall be first among us to attack the Canaanites and to do battle with them?" ²The LORD answered: Judah shall attack: I have delivered the land into his power. ³Judah then said to his brother Simeon, "Come up with me into the territory allotted to me, and let us do battle with the Canaanites. I will likewise go with you into the territory allotted to you." So Simeon went with him.

⁴When Judah attacked, the Lord delivered the Canaanites and Perizzites into their power, and they struck down ten thousand of them in Bezek. ⁵They came upon Adonibezek in Bezek and fought against him. When they struck down the Canaanites and Perizzites, ⁶Adonibezek fled. They pursued him, and when they caught him, they cut off his thumbs and big toes. ⁷"Seventy kings," said Adonibezek, "used to pick up scraps under my table with their thumbs and big toes cut off. As I have done, so has God repaid me." He was brought to Jerusalem, and he died there. ⁸The Judahites fought against Jerusalem, captured it, and put it to the sword, setting the city itself on fire.

⁹Afterward the Judahites went down to fight against the Canaanites who lived in the mountain region, in the Negeb, and in the foothills. ¹⁰Judah also marched against the Canaanites who lived in Hebron, which was formerly called Kiriath-arba, and defeated Sheshai, Ahiman, and Talmai. ¹¹They marched from there against the inhabitants of Debir, which was formerly called Kiriath-sepher. ¹²Caleb said, "To the man who attacks Kiriath-sepher and captures it, I will give my daughter Achsah in marriage." ¹³Othniel captured it, the son of Caleb's younger brother Kenaz; so Caleb gave him his daughter Achsah in marriage. ¹⁴When she came to him, she induced him to ask her father for some land. Then, as she alighted from the donkey, Caleb asked her, "What do you want?" ¹⁵She answered, "Give me a present. Since you have put me in the land of the Negeb, give me pools of water." So Caleb gave her what she wanted, both the upper and the lower pool.

¹⁶The descendants of Hobab the Kenite, Moses' father-in-law, came up with the Judahites from the City of Palms to the wilderness of Arad, which is in the Negeb, and they settled among the Amalekites. ¹⁷Then Judah went with his brother Simeon, and they defeated the Canaanites who lived in Zephath. They put the city under the ban and renamed it Hormah. ¹⁸Judah captured Gaza with its territory, Ashkelon with its territory, Ekron with its territory, and Ashdod with its territory. ¹⁹The Lord was with Judah, so they gained possession of the mountain region. But they could not dispossess those who lived on the plain, because they had iron chariots. ²⁰As Moses had commanded, they gave Hebron to Caleb, who then drove the three sons of Anak away from there.

²¹As for the Jebusites dwelling in Jerusalem, the Benjaminites did not dispossess them, so that the Jebusites live with the Benjaminites in Jerusalem to the present day.

²²The house of Joseph, too, went up against Bethel, and the Lord was with them. ²³The house of Joseph reconnoitered Bethel, which formerly was called Luz. ²⁴The scouts saw a man coming out of the city and said to him, "Tell us the way into the city, and we will show you mercy." ²⁵He showed them the way into the city, and they put the city to the sword; but they let the man and his whole clan go free. ²⁶The man then went to the land of the Hittites, where he built a city and called it Luz, which is its name to this day.

²⁷Manasseh did not take possession of Beth-shean with its towns or of Taanach with its towns. Nor did they dispossess the inhabitants of Dor and its towns, those of Ibleam and its towns, or those of Megiddo and its towns. The Canaanites continued to live in this district. ²⁸When Israel grew stronger, they conscripted the Canaanites as laborers, but did not actually drive them out. ²⁹Ephraim did not drive out the Canaanites living in Gezer, and so the Canaanites lived among them in Gezer.

³⁰Nor did Zebulun dispossess the inhabitants of Kitron or those of Nahalol; the Canaanites lived among them and became forced laborers.

31Nor did Asher dispossess the inhabitants of Acco or those of Sidon, or take possession of Mahaleb, Achzib, Helbah, Aphik, or Rehob. 32So the Asherites settled among the Canaanite inhabitants of the land, for they had not dispossessed them.

33Nor did Naphtali drive out the inhabitants of Beth-shemesh or those of Beth-anath. They settled among the Canaanite inhabitants of the land and the inhabitants of Beth-shemesh and Beth-anath became forced laborers for them.

34The Amorites hemmed in the Danites in the mountain region, not permitting them to come down onto the plain. 35So the Amorites continued to live in Harheres, Aijalon, and Shaalbim, but as the power of the house of Joseph grew, they were conscripted as laborers.

36The territory of the Amorites extended from the Akrabbim pass, from Sela and upward.

Infidelities of the Israelites. 2:1 A messenger of the LORD went up from Gilgal to Bochim and said, I brought you up from Egypt and led you into the land which I promised on oath to your ancestors. I said, I will never break my covenant with you, 2but you must not make a covenant with the inhabitants of this land; you must pull down their altars. But you did not listen to me. Look what you have done! 3For I also said, I will not clear them out of your way; they will become traps for you, and their gods a snare for you.

4When the messenger of the LORD had spoken these things to all the Israelites, the people wept aloud. 5They named that place Bochim, and they offered sacrifice there to the LORD.

6Then Joshua dismissed the people, and the Israelites went, each to their own heritage, to take possession of the land. 7The people served the LORD during the entire lifetime of Joshua, and of those elders who outlived Joshua and who had seen all the great work the LORD had done for Israel. 8Joshua, son of Nun, the servant of the LORD, died at the age of a hundred and ten, 9and they buried him within the borders of his heritage at Timnath-heres in the mountain region of Ephraim north of Mount Gaash.

10When the rest of that generation were also gathered to their ancestors, and a later generation arose that did not know the LORD or the work he had done for Israel, 11the Israelites did what was evil in the sight of the LORD. They served the Baals, 12and abandoned the LORD, the God of their ancestors, the one who had brought them out of the land of Egypt. They followed other gods, the gods of the peoples around them, and bowed down to them, and provoked the LORD.

13Because they had abandoned the LORD and served Baal and the Astartes, 14the anger of the LORD flared up against Israel, and he delivered them into the power of plunderers who despoiled them. He sold them into the power of the enemies around them, and they were no longer able to withstand their enemies. 15Whenever they marched out, the hand of the LORD turned against them, as the LORD had said, and as the LORD had sworn to them; and they were in great distress. 16But the LORD raised up judges to save them from the power of their plunderers; 17but they did not listen to their judges either, for they prostituted themselves by following other gods, bowing down to them. They were quick to stray from the way their ancestors had taken, who obeyed the commandments of the LORD; but these did not. 18When the LORD raised up judges for them, he would be with the judge and save them from the power of their enemies as long as the judge lived. The LORD would change his mind when they groaned in their affliction under their oppressors. 19But when the judge died, they would again do worse than their ancestors, following other gods, serving and bowing down to them, relinquishing none of their evil practices or stubborn ways.

[20]The anger of the LORD flared up against Israel, and he said: Because this nation has transgressed my covenant, which I enjoined on their ancestors, and has not listened to me, [21]I for my part will not clear away for them any more of the nations Joshua left when he died. [22]They will be made to test Israel, to see whether or not they will keep to the way of the LORD and continue in it as their ancestors did. [23]Therefore the LORD allowed these nations to remain instead of expelling them immediately. He had not delivered them into the power of Joshua.

☐ 1 CORINTHIANS 1:26–2:16

The Corinthians and Paul. 1:26 Consider your own calling, brothers. Not many of you were wise by human standards, not many were powerful, not many were of noble birth. [27]Rather, God chose the foolish of the world to shame the wise, and God chose the weak of the world to shame the strong, [28]and God chose the lowly and despised of the world, those who count for nothing, to reduce to nothing those who are something, [29]so that no human being might boast before God. [30]It is due to him that you are in Christ Jesus, who became for us wisdom from God, as well as righteousness, sanctification, and redemption, [31]so that, as it is written, "Whoever boasts, should boast in the Lord."

2:1 When I came to you, brothers, proclaiming the mystery of God, I did not come with sublimity of words or of wisdom. [2]For I resolved to know nothing while I was with you except Jesus Christ, and him crucified. [3]I came to you in weakness and fear and much trembling, [4]and my message and my proclamation were not with persuasive (words of) wisdom, but with a demonstration of spirit and power, [5]so that your faith might rest not on human wisdom but on the power of God.

The True Wisdom. [6]Yet we do speak a wisdom to those who are mature, but not a wisdom of this age, nor of the rulers of this age who are passing away. [7]Rather, we speak God's wisdom, mysterious, hidden, which God predetermined before the ages for our glory, [8]and which none of the rulers of this age knew; for if they had known it, they would not have crucified the Lord of glory. [9]But as it is written:

"What eye has not seen, and ear has
    not heard,
and what has not entered the
        human heart,
what God has prepared for those
    who love him,"

[10]this God has revealed to us through the Spirit.

For the Spirit scrutinizes everything, even the depths of God. [11]Among human beings, who knows what pertains to a person except the spirit of the person that is within? Similarly, no one knows what pertains to God except the Spirit of God. [12]We have not received the spirit of the world but the Spirit that is from God, so that we may understand the things freely given us by God. [13]And we speak about them not with words taught by human wisdom, but with words taught by the Spirit, describing spiritual realities in spiritual terms.

[14]Now the natural person does not accept what pertains to the Spirit of God, for to him it is foolishness, and he cannot understand it, because it is judged spiritually. [15]The spiritual person, however, can judge everything but is not subject to judgment by anyone.

[16]For "who has known the mind of the Lord, so as to counsel him?" But we have the mind of Christ.

March 21

St. Nicholas of Flüe

Each state of life has its special duties; by accomplishing them, one may find happiness.

— St. Nicholas of Flüe

☐ JUDGES 3-5

3:1 These are the nations the Lord allowed to remain, so that through them he might test Israel, all those who had not experienced any of the Canaanite wars— ²to teach warfare to those generations of Israelites who had never experienced it: ³the five lords of the Philistines, and all the Canaanites, the Sidonians, and the Hivites who lived in the mountain region of the Lebanon between Baal-hermon and Lebo-hamath. ⁴These served as a test for Israel, to know whether they would obey the commandments the Lord had enjoined on their ancestors through Moses. ⁵So the Israelites settled among the Canaanites, Hittites, Amorites, Perizzites, Hivites, and Jebusites. ⁶They took their daughters in marriage, and gave their own daughters to their sons in marriage, and served their gods.

Othniel. ⁷Then the Israelites did what was evil in the sight of the Lord; they forgot the Lord, their God, and served the Baals and the Asherahs, ⁸and the anger of the Lord flared up against them. He sold them into the power of Cushan-rishathaim, king of Aram Naharaim; and the Israelites served Cushan-rishathaim for eight years. ⁹But when the Israelites cried out to the Lord, he raised up a savior for them, to save them. It was Othniel, son of Caleb's younger brother Kenaz. ¹⁰The spirit of the Lord came upon him, and he judged Israel. When he marched out to war, the Lord delivered Cushan-rishathaim, king of Aram, into his power, and his hold on Cushan-rishathaim was firm. ¹¹So the land was at rest for forty years, until Othniel, son of Kenaz, died.

Ehud. ¹²Again the Israelites did what was evil in the sight of the Lord, so he strengthened Eglon, king of Moab, against Israel because they did what was evil in the sight of the Lord. ¹³Taking the Ammonites and Amalek as allies, he went and defeated Israel, taking possession of the City of Palms. ¹⁴So the Israelites served Eglon, king of Moab, for eighteen years.

¹⁵But when the Israelites cried out to the Lord, he raised up for them a savior, Ehud, son of Gera, a Benjaminite who was left-handed. The Israelites would send their tribute to Eglon, king of Moab, by him. ¹⁶Ehud made himself a two-edged dagger a foot long, and strapped it under his clothes on his right thigh. ¹⁷He presented the tribute to Eglon, king of Moab; now Eglon was a very fat man. ¹⁸When he had finished presenting the tribute, he dismissed the troops who had carried the tribute. ¹⁹But he himself turned back at the sculptured stones near Gilgal, and said, "I have a secret message for you, O king." And the king said, "Silence!" Then when all his attendants had left his presence, ²⁰Ehud went in to him where he sat alone in his cool upper room. Ehud said, "I have a word from God for you." So the king rose from his throne. ²¹Then Ehud with his left hand drew the dagger from his right thigh, and thrust it into Eglon's belly. ²²The hilt also went in after the blade, and the fat closed over the blade because he did not withdraw the dagger from the body.

²³Then Ehud went out onto the porch, shutting the doors of the upper room on Eglon and locking them. ²⁴When Ehud

had left and the servants had come, they saw that the doors of the upper room were locked, and thought, "He must be easing himself in the cool chamber." ²⁵They waited until they were at a loss when he did not open the doors of the upper room. So they took the key and opened them, and there was their lord lying on the floor, dead.

²⁶During their delay Ehud escaped and, passing the sculptured stones, took refuge in Seirah. ²⁷On his arrival he sounded the horn in the mountain region of Ephraim, and the Israelites went down from the mountains with him as their leader. ²⁸"Follow me," he said to them, "for the Lord has delivered your enemies the Moabites into your power." So they followed him down and seized the fords of the Jordan against the Moabites, permitting no one to cross. ²⁹On that occasion they slew about ten thousand Moabites, all of them strong warriors. Not one escaped. ³⁰So Moab was brought under the power of Israel at that time; and the land had rest for eighty years.

Shamgar. ³¹After him there was Shamgar, son of Anath, who slew six hundred Philistines with an oxgoad. He, too, was a savior for Israel.

Deborah and Barak. 4:1 The Israelites again did what was evil in the sight of the Lord; Ehud was dead. ²So the Lord sold them into the power of the Canaanite king, Jabin, who reigned in Hazor. The general of his army was Sisera, who lived in Harosheth-ha-goiim. ³But the Israelites cried out to the Lord; for with his nine hundred iron chariots Jabin harshly oppressed the Israelites for twenty years.

⁴At that time the prophet Deborah, wife of Lappidoth, was judging Israel. ⁵She used to sit under Deborah's palm tree, between Ramah and Bethel in the mountain region of Ephraim, where the Israelites came up to her for judgment. ⁶She had Barak, son of Abinoam, summoned from Kedesh of Naphtali. She said to him, "This is what the Lord, the God of Israel, commands: Go, march against Mount Tabor, and take with you ten thousand men from Naphtali and Zebulun. ⁷I will draw Sisera, the general of Jabin's army, out to you at the Wadi Kishon, together with his chariots and troops, and I will deliver them into your power." ⁸But Barak answered her, "If you come with me, I will go; if you do not come with me, I will not go." ⁹"I will certainly go with you," she replied, "but you will not gain glory for the expedition on which you are setting out, for it is into a woman's power that the Lord is going to sell Sisera." So Deborah arose and went with Barak and journeyed with him to Kedesh.

¹⁰Barak summoned Zebulun and Naphtali to Kedesh, and ten thousand men followed him. Deborah also went up with him. ¹¹Now Heber the Kenite had detached himself from Cain, the descendants of Hobab, Moses' father-in-law, and had pitched his tent by the terebinth of Zaanannim, which was near Kedesh.

¹²It was reported to Sisera that Barak, son of Abinoam, had gone up to Mount Tabor. ¹³So Sisera called out all nine hundred of his iron chariots and all his forces from Harosheth-ha-goiim to the Wadi Kishon. ¹⁴Deborah then said to Barak, "Up! This is the day on which the Lord has delivered Sisera into your power. The Lord marches before you." So Barak went down Mount Tabor, followed by his ten thousand men. ¹⁵And the Lord threw Sisera and all his chariots and forces into a panic before Barak. Sisera himself dismounted from his chariot and fled on foot, ¹⁶but Barak pursued the chariots and the army as far as Harosheth-ha-goiim. The entire army of Sisera fell beneath the sword, not even one man surviving.

¹⁷Sisera fled on foot to the tent of Jael, wife of Heber the Kenite, for there was peace between Jabin, king of Hazor, and the family of Heber the Kenite. ¹⁸Jael went out to meet Sisera and said to him, "Turn

aside, my lord, turn aside with me; do not be afraid." So he went into her tent, and she covered him with a rug. ¹⁹He said to her, "Please give me a little water to drink. I am thirsty." So she opened a skin of milk, gave him a drink, and then covered him. ²⁰"Stand at the entrance of the tent," he said to her. "If anyone comes and asks, 'Is there someone here?' say, 'No!'" ²¹Jael, wife of Heber, got a tent peg and took a mallet in her hand. When Sisera was in a deep sleep from exhaustion, she approached him stealthily and drove the peg through his temple and down into the ground, and he died. ²²Then when Barak came in pursuit of Sisera, Jael went out to meet him and said to him, "Come, I will show you the man you are looking for." So he went in with her, and there lay Sisera dead, with the tent peg through his temple.

²³Thus on that day God humbled the Canaanite king, Jabin, before the Israelites; ²⁴their power weighed ever more heavily on him, until at length they finished off the Canaanite king, Jabin.

Song of Deborah. 5:1 On that day Deborah sang this song—and Barak, son of Abinoam:

²When uprising broke out in Israel,
    when the people rallied for duty—
        bless the LORD!
³Hear, O kings! Give ear, O princes!
    I will sing, I will sing to the LORD,
    I will make music to the LORD, the
        God of Israel.
⁴LORD, when you went out from Seir,
    when you marched from the plains
        of Edom,
The earth shook, the heavens poured,
    the clouds poured rain,
⁵The mountains streamed,
    before the LORD, the One of Sinai,
    before the LORD, the God of Israel.
⁶In the days of Shamgar, son of Anath,
    in the days of Jael, caravans ceased:

Those who traveled the roads
    now traveled by roundabout paths.
⁷Gone was freedom beyond the walls,
    gone indeed from Israel.
When I, Deborah, arose,
    when I arose, a mother in Israel.
⁸New gods were their choice;
    then war was at the gates.
No shield was to be found, no spear,
    among forty thousand in Israel!
⁹My heart is with the leaders of Israel,
    with the dedicated ones of the
        people—bless the LORD;
¹⁰Those who ride on white donkeys,
    seated on saddle rugs,
    and those who travel the road,
Sing of them
    ¹¹to the sounds of musicians at the
        wells.
There they recount the just deeds of
    the LORD,
    his just deeds bringing freedom to
        Israel.
¹²Awake, awake, Deborah!
    Awake, awake, strike up a song!
Arise, Barak!
    Take captive your captors, son of
        Abinoam!
¹³Then down went Israel against the
    mighty,
    the army of the LORD went down
        for him against the warriors.
¹⁴From Ephraim, their base in the
    valley;
    behind you, Benjamin, among your
        troops.
From Machir came down
    commanders,
    from Zebulun wielders of the
        marshal's staff.
¹⁵The princes of Issachar were with
    Deborah,
Issachar, faithful to Barak;
    in the valley they followed at his
        heels.
Among the clans of Reuben
    great were the searchings of heart!

16Why did you stay beside your hearths
   listening to the lowing of the herds?
Among the clans of Reuben
   great were the searchings of heart!
17Gilead stayed beyond the Jordan;
   Why did Dan spend his time in ships?
Asher remained along the shore,
   he stayed in his havens.
18Zebulun was a people who defied
   death,
   Naphtali, too, on the open heights!
19The kings came and fought;
   then they fought, those kings of
     Canaan,
At Taanach by the waters of Megiddo;
   no spoil of silver did they take.
20From the heavens the stars fought;
   from their courses they fought
     against Sisera.
21The Wadi Kishon swept them away;
   the wadi overwhelmed them, the
     Wadi Kishon.
   Trample down the strong!
22Then the hoofs of the horses
    hammered,
   the galloping, galloping of steeds.
23"Curse Meroz," says the messenger of
   the LORD,
   "curse, curse its inhabitants!
For they did not come when the LORD
   helped,
   the help of the LORD against the
     warriors."
24Most blessed of women is Jael,
   the wife of Heber the Kenite,
   blessed among tent-dwelling women!

25He asked for water, she gave him milk,
   in a princely bowl she brought him
     curds.
26With her hand she reached for the
    peg,
   with her right hand, the workman's
     hammer.
She hammered Sisera, crushed his
    head;
   she smashed, pierced his temple.
27At her feet he sank down, fell, lay still;
   down at her feet he sank and fell;
   where he sank down, there he fell,
    slain.

28From the window she looked down,
   the mother of Sisera peered through
     the lattice:
"Why is his chariot so long in coming?
   why are the hoofbeats of his chariots
    delayed?"
29The wisest of her princesses answers
   her;
   she even replies to herself,
30"They must be dividing the spoil they
    took:
   a slave woman or two for each man,
Spoil of dyed cloth for Sisera,
   spoil of ornate dyed cloth,
   a pair of ornate dyed cloths for my
     neck in the spoil."

31So perish all your enemies, O LORD!
   But may those who love you be like
    the sun rising in its might!

And the land was at rest for forty years.

☐ 1 CORINTHIANS 3

3:1 Brothers, I could not talk to you as spiritual people, but as fleshly people, as infants in Christ. 2I fed you milk, not solid food, because you were unable to take it. Indeed, you are still not able, even now, 3for you are still of the flesh. While there is jealousy and rivalry among you, are you not of the flesh, and behaving in an ordinary human way? 4Whenever someone says, "I belong to Paul," and another, "I belong to Apollos," are you not merely human?

The Role of God's Ministers. 5What is Apollos, after all, and what is Paul? Ministers through whom you became believers, just as the Lord assigned each one. ⁶I planted, Apollos watered, but God caused the growth. ⁷Therefore, neither the one who plants nor the one who waters is anything, but only God, who causes the growth. ⁸The one who plants and the one who waters are equal, and each will receive wages in proportion to his labor. ⁹For we are God's co-workers; you are God's field, God's building.

¹⁰According to the grace of God given to me, like a wise master builder I laid a foundation, and another is building upon it. But each one must be careful how he builds upon it, ¹¹for no one can lay a foundation other than the one that is there, namely, Jesus Christ. ¹²If anyone builds on this foundation with gold, silver, precious stones, wood, hay, or straw, ¹³the work of each will come to light, for the Day will disclose it. It will be revealed with fire, and the fire [itself] will test the quality of each one's work. ¹⁴If the work stands that someone built upon the foundation, that person will receive a wage. ¹⁵But if someone's work is burned up, that one will suffer loss; the person will be saved, but only as through fire. ¹⁶Do you not know that you are the temple of God, and that the Spirit of God dwells in you? ¹⁷If anyone destroys God's temple, God will destroy that person; for the temple of God, which you are, is holy.

¹⁸Let no one deceive himself. If any one among you considers himself wise in this age, let him become a fool so as to become wise. ¹⁹For the wisdom of this world is foolishness in the eyes of God, for it is written:

> "He catches the wise in their own ruses,"

²⁰and again:

> "The Lord knows the thoughts of the wise, that they are vain."

²¹So let no one boast about human beings, for everything belongs to you, ²²Paul or Apollos or Cephas, or the world or life or death, or the present or the future: all belong to you, ²³and you to Christ, and Christ to God.

March 22

Divine Scripture is the feast of wisdom, and the individual books are the various dishes.

— St. Ambrose of Milan

☐ JUDGES 6-8

The Call of Gideon. 6:1 The Israelites did what was evil in the sight of the Lord, who therefore delivered them into the power of Midian for seven years, ²so that Midian held Israel subject. From fear of Midian the Israelites made dens in the mountains, the caves, and the strongholds. ³For it used to be that whenever the Israelites had completed sowing their crops, Midian, Amalek, and the Kedemites would come up, ⁴encamp against them, and lay waste the produce of the land as far as the outskirts of Gaza, leaving no sustenance in Israel, and no sheep, ox, or donkey. ⁵For they would come up with their livestock, and their tents would appear as thick as locusts. They would be too many to count when they came into the land to lay it waste. ⁶Israel was reduced to utter poverty by Midian, and so the Israelites cried out to the Lord.

[7]When Israel cried out to the LORD because of Midian, [8]the LORD sent a prophet to the Israelites who said to them: Thus says the LORD, the God of Israel: I am the one who brought you up from Egypt; I brought you out of the house of slavery. [9]I rescued you from the power of Egypt and all your oppressors. I drove them out before you and gave you their land. [10]And I said to you: I, the LORD, am your God; you shall not fear the gods of the Amorites in whose land you are dwelling. But you did not listen to me.

[11]Then the messenger of the LORD came and sat under the terebinth in Ophrah that belonged to Joash the Abiezrite. Joash's son Gideon was beating out wheat in the wine press to save it from the Midianites, [12]and the messenger of the LORD appeared to him and said: The LORD is with you, you mighty warrior! [13]"My lord," Gideon said to him, "if the LORD is with us, why has all this happened to us? Where are his wondrous deeds about which our ancestors told us when they said, 'Did not the LORD bring us up from Egypt?' For now the LORD has abandoned us and has delivered us into the power of Midian." [14]The LORD turned to him and said: Go with the strength you have, and save Israel from the power of Midian. Is it not I who send you? [15]But he answered him, "Please, my Lord, how can I save Israel? My family is the poorest in Manasseh, and I am the most insignificant in my father's house." [16]The LORD said to him: I will be with you, and you will cut down Midian to the last man. [17]He answered him, "If you look on me with favor, give me a sign that you are the one speaking with me. [18]Please do not depart from here until I come to you and bring out my offering and set it before you." He answered: I will await your return.

[19]So Gideon went off and prepared a young goat and an ephah of flour in the form of unleavened cakes. Putting the meat in a basket and the broth in a pot, he brought them out to him under the terebinth and presented them. [20]The messenger of God said to him: Take the meat and unleavened cakes and lay them on this rock; then pour out the broth. When he had done so, [21]the messenger of the LORD stretched out the tip of the staff he held. When he touched the meat and unleavened cakes, a fire came up from the rock and consumed the meat and unleavened cakes. Then the messenger of the LORD disappeared from sight. [22]Gideon, now aware that it had been the messenger of the LORD, said, "Alas, Lord GOD, that I have seen the messenger of the LORD face to face!" [23]The LORD answered him: You are safe. Do not fear. You shall not die. [24]So Gideon built there an altar to the LORD and called it Yahweh-shalom. To this day it is still in Ophrah of the Abiezrites.

[25]That same night the LORD said to him: Take your father's bull, the bull fattened for seven years, and pull down your father's altar to Baal. As for the asherah beside it, cut it down [26]and build an altar to the LORD, your God, on top of this stronghold with the pile of wood. Then take the fattened bull and offer it as a whole-burnt sacrifice on the wood from the asherah you have cut down. [27]So Gideon took ten of his servants and did as the LORD had commanded him. But he was too afraid of his family and of the townspeople to do it by day; he did it at night. [28]Early the next morning the townspeople found that the altar of Baal had been dismantled, the asherah beside it cut down, and the fattened bull offered on the altar that was built. [29]They asked one another, "Who did this?" They inquired and searched until they were told, "Gideon, son of Joash, did it." [30]So the townspeople said to Joash, "Bring out your son that he may die, for he has dismantled the altar of Baal and cut down the asherah that was beside it." [31]But Joash replied to all who were standing around him, "Is it for you to take action for Baal, or be his savior?

Anyone who takes action for him shall be put to death by morning. If he is a god, let him act for himself, since his altar has been dismantled!" ³²So on that day Gideon was called Jerubbaal, because of the words, "Let Baal take action against him, since he dismantled his altar."

³³Then all Midian and Amalek and the Kedemites mustered and crossed over into the valley of Jezreel, where they encamped. ³⁴And Gideon was clothed with the spirit of the LORD, and he blew the horn summoning Abiezer to follow him. ³⁵He sent messengers throughout Manasseh, and they, too, were summoned to follow him; he also sent messengers throughout Asher, Zebulun, and Naphtali, and they advanced to meet the others. ³⁶Gideon said to God, "If indeed you are going to save Israel through me, as you have said, ³⁷I am putting this woolen fleece on the threshing floor, and if dew is on the fleece alone, while all the ground is dry, I shall know that you will save Israel through me, as you have said." ³⁸That is what happened. Early the next morning when he wrung out the fleece, he squeezed enough dew from it to fill a bowl. ³⁹Gideon then said to God, "Do not be angry with me if I speak once more. Let me make just one more test with the fleece. Let the fleece alone be dry, but let there be dew on all the ground." ⁴⁰That is what God did that night: the fleece alone was dry, but there was dew on all the ground.

Defeat of Midian. 7:1 Early the next morning Jerubbaal (that is, Gideon) encamped by the spring of Harod with all his soldiers. The camp of Midian was north of him, beside the hill of Moreh in the valley. ²The LORD said to Gideon: You have too many soldiers with you for me to deliver Midian into their power, lest Israel vaunt itself against me and say, "My own power saved me." ³So announce in the hearing of the soldiers, "If anyone is afraid or fearful, let him leave! Let him depart from Mount Gilead!" Twenty-two thousand of the soldiers left, but ten thousand remained. ⁴The LORD said to Gideon: There are still too many soldiers. Lead them down to the water and I will test them for you there. If I tell you that a certain man is to go with you, he must go with you. But no one is to go if I tell you he must not. ⁵When Gideon led the soldiers down to the water, the LORD said to him: Everyone who laps up the water as a dog does with its tongue you shall set aside by himself; and everyone who kneels down to drink raising his hand to his mouth you shall set aside by himself. ⁶Those who lapped up the water with their tongues numbered three hundred, but all the rest of the soldiers knelt down to drink the water. ⁷The LORD said to Gideon: By means of the three hundred who lapped up the water I will save you and deliver Midian into your power. So let all the other soldiers go home. ⁸They took up such supplies as the soldiers had with them, as well as their horns, and Gideon sent the rest of the Israelites to their tents, but kept the three hundred men. Now the camp of Midian was below him in the valley.

⁹That night the LORD said to Gideon: Go, descend on the camp, for I have delivered it into your power. ¹⁰If you are afraid to attack, go down to the camp with your aide Purah ¹¹and listen to what they are saying. After that you will have the courage to descend on the camp. So he went down with his aide Purah to the outposts of the armed men in the camp. ¹²The Midianites, Amalekites, and all the Kedemites were lying in the valley, thick as locusts. Their camels could not be counted, for they were as many as the sands on the seashore. ¹³When Gideon arrived, one man was telling another about a dream. "I had a dream," he said, "that a round loaf of barley bread was rolling into the camp of Midian. It came to a certain tent and struck it and turned it upside down, and the tent collapsed." ¹⁴"This can only be the sword

of the Israelite Gideon, son of Joash," the other replied. "God has delivered Midian and all the camp into his power." ¹⁵When Gideon heard the account of the dream and its explanation, he bowed down. Then returning to the camp of Israel, he said, "Arise, for the LORD has delivered the camp of Midian into your power."

¹⁶He divided the three hundred men into three companies, and provided them all with horns and with empty jars and torches inside the jars. ¹⁷"Watch me and follow my lead," he told them. "I shall go to the edge of the camp, and as I do, you must do also. ¹⁸When I and those with me blow horns, you too must blow horns all around the camp and cry out, 'For the LORD and for Gideon!'" ¹⁹So Gideon and the hundred men who were with him came to the edge of the camp at the beginning of the middle watch, just after the posting of the guards. They blew the horns and broke the jars they were holding. ²⁰When the three companies had blown their horns and broken their jars, they took the torches in their left hands, and in their right the horns they had been blowing, and cried out, "A sword for the LORD and for Gideon!" ²¹They all remained standing in place around the camp, while the whole camp began to run and shout and flee. ²²When they blew the three hundred horns, the LORD set the sword of one against another throughout the camp, and they fled as far as Beth-shittah in the direction of Zeredah, near the border of Abel-meholah at Tabbath.

²³The Israelites were called to arms from Naphtali, from Asher, and from all Manasseh, and they pursued Midian. ²⁴Gideon also sent messengers throughout the mountain region of Ephraim to say, "Go down to intercept Midian, and seize the water courses against them as far as Beth-barah, as well as the Jordan." So all the Ephraimites were called to arms, and they seized the water courses as far as Beth-barah, and the Jordan as well. ²⁵They captured the two princes of Midian, Oreb and Zeeb, killing Oreb at the rock of Oreb and Zeeb at the wine press of Zeeb. Then they pursued Midian, but they had the heads of Oreb and Zeeb brought to Gideon beyond the Jordan.

8:1 But the Ephraimites said to him, "What have you done to us, not summoning us when you went to fight against Midian?" And they quarreled bitterly with him. ²But he answered them, "What have I done in comparison with you? Is not the gleaning of Ephraim better than the vintage of Abiezer? ³It was into your power God delivered the princes of Midian, Oreb and Zeeb. What have I been able to do in comparison with you?" When he said this, their anger against him subsided.

⁴When Gideon reached the Jordan and crossed it, he and his three hundred men were exhausted and famished. ⁵So he said to the people of Succoth, "Will you give my followers some loaves of bread? They are exhausted, and I am pursuing Zebah and Zalmunna, kings of Midian." ⁶But the princes of Succoth replied, "Are the hands of Zebah and Zalmunna already in your possession, that we should give food to your army?" ⁷Gideon said, "Very well; when the LORD has delivered Zebah and Zalmunna into my power, I will thrash your bodies with desert thorns and briers." ⁸He went up from there to Penuel and made the same request of them, but the people of Penuel answered him as had the people of Succoth. ⁹So to the people of Penuel, too, he said, "When I return in peace, I will demolish this tower."

¹⁰Now Zebah and Zalmunna were in Karkor with their force of about fifteen thousand men; these were all who were left of the whole Kedemite army, a hundred and twenty thousand swordsmen having fallen. ¹¹Gideon went up by the route of the tent-dwellers east of Nobah and Jogbehah, and attacked the force when it felt secure. ¹²Zebah and Zalmunna fled and Gideon

pursued them. He captured the two kings of Midian, Zebah and Zalmunna, terrifying the entire force.

¹³Then Gideon, son of Joash, returned from battle by the pass of Heres. ¹⁴He captured a young man of Succoth and questioned him, and he wrote down for him the seventy-seven princes and elders of Succoth. ¹⁵So he went to the princes of Succoth and said, "Here are Zebah and Zalmunna, with whom you taunted me, 'Are the hands of Zebah and Zalmunna already in your possession, that we should give food to your weary men?'" ¹⁶He seized the elders of the city, and with desert thorns and briers he thrashed the people of Succoth. ¹⁷He also demolished the tower of Penuel and killed the people of the city.

¹⁸Then he said to Zebah and Zalmunna, "What about the men you killed at Tabor?" "They were all like you," they replied. "They appeared to be princes." ¹⁹"They were my brothers, my mother's sons," he said. "As the Lord lives, if you had spared their lives, I would not kill you." ²⁰Then he said to his firstborn, Jether, "Go, kill them." But the boy did not draw his sword, for he was afraid, for he was still a boy. ²¹Zebah and Zalmunna said, "Come, kill us yourself, for as a man is, so is his strength." So Gideon stepped forward and killed Zebah and Zalmunna. He also took the crescents that were on the necks of their camels.

²²The Israelites then said to Gideon, "Rule over us—you, your son, and your son's son—for you saved us from the power of Midian." ²³But Gideon answered them, "I will not rule over you, nor shall my son rule over you. The Lord must rule over you."

²⁴Gideon went on to say, "Let me make a request of you. Give me, each of you, a ring from his spoils." (Since they were Ishmaelites, the enemy had gold rings.) ²⁵"We will certainly give them," they replied, and they spread out a cloak into which everyone threw a ring from his spoils. ²⁶The gold rings he had requested weighed seventeen hundred gold shekels, apart from the crescents and pendants, the purple garments worn by the kings of Midian, and apart from the trappings that were on the necks of their camels. ²⁷Gideon made an ephod out of the gold and placed it in his city, Ophrah. All Israel prostituted themselves there, and it became a snare to Gideon and his household.

²⁸Midian was brought into subjection by the Israelites; they no longer held their heads high, and the land had rest for forty years, during the lifetime of Gideon.

Gideon's Son Abimelech. ²⁹Then Jerubbaal, son of Joash, went to live in his house. ³⁰Now Gideon had seventy sons, his own offspring, for he had many wives. ³¹His concubine who lived in Shechem also bore him a son, whom he named Abimelech. ³²At a good old age Gideon, son of Joash, died and was buried in the tomb of Joash his father in Ophrah of the Abiezrites. ³³But after Gideon was dead, the Israelites again prostituted themselves by following the Baals, making Baal-berith their god. ³⁴The Israelites did not remember the Lord, their God, who had delivered them from the power of their enemies all around them. ³⁵Nor were they loyal to the house of Jerubbaal (Gideon) for all the good he had done for Israel.

☐ 1 CORINTHIANS 4

4:1 Thus should one regard us: as servants of Christ and stewards of the mysteries of God. ²Now it is of course required of stewards that they be found trustworthy. ³It does not concern me in the least that I be judged by you or any human tribunal; I do not even pass judgment on myself; ⁴I am not conscious of anything against me, but I do not thereby stand acquitted; the one who judges me is the Lord. ⁵Therefore, do not make any judgment before the appointed time, until the Lord comes, for he will bring to light what is hidden in darkness and will manifest the motives of our hearts, and then everyone will receive praise from God.

Paul's Life as Pattern. ⁶I have applied these things to myself and Apollos for your benefit, brothers, so that you may learn from us not to go beyond what is written, so that none of you will be inflated with pride in favor of one person over against another. ⁷Who confers distinction upon you? What do you possess that you have not received? But if you have received it, why are you boasting as if you did not receive it? ⁸You are already satisfied; you have already grown rich; you have become kings without us! Indeed, I wish that you had become kings, so that we also might become kings with you.

⁹For as I see it, God has exhibited us apostles as the last of all, like people sentenced to death, since we have become a spectacle to the world, to angels and human beings alike. ¹⁰We are fools on Christ's account, but you are wise in Christ; we are weak, but you are strong; you are held in honor, but we in disrepute. ¹¹To this very hour we go hungry and thirsty, we are poorly clad and roughly treated, we wander about homeless ¹²and we toil, working with our own hands. When ridiculed, we bless; when persecuted, we endure; ¹³when slandered, we respond gently. We have become like the world's rubbish, the scum of all, to this very moment.

¹⁴I am writing you this not to shame you, but to admonish you as my beloved children. ¹⁵Even if you should have countless guides to Christ, yet you do not have many fathers, for I became your father in Christ Jesus through the gospel. ¹⁶Therefore, I urge you, be imitators of me. ¹⁷For this reason I am sending you Timothy, who is my beloved and faithful son in the Lord; he will remind you of my ways in Christ [Jesus], just as I teach them everywhere in every church.

¹⁸Some have become inflated with pride, as if I were not coming to you. ¹⁹But I will come to you soon, if the Lord is willing, and I shall ascertain not the talk of these inflated people but their power. ²⁰For the kingdom of God is not a matter of talk but of power. ²¹Which do you prefer? Shall I come to you with a rod, or with love and a gentle spirit?

March 23

St. Turibius de Mongrovejo

If a man preaches but does not practice what he preaches, he is like a well of water where everyone can quench his thirst and wash off his dirt, but which cannot clean away the filth and dung that is around it.

— St. Poemen

☐ JUDGES 9–12

9:1 Abimelech, son of Jerubbaal, went to his mother's kin in Shechem, and said to them and to the whole clan to which his mother's family belonged, ²"Put this question to all the lords of Shechem: 'Which is better for you: that seventy men, all Jerubbaal's sons, rule over you, or that one man rule over you?' You must remember that I am your own flesh and bone." ³When his mother's kin repeated these words on his behalf to all the lords of Shechem, they set their hearts on Abimelech, thinking, "He is our kin." ⁴They also gave him seventy pieces of silver from the temple of Baal-berith, with which Abimelech hired worthless men and outlaws as his followers. ⁵He then went to his father's house in Ophrah, and killed his brothers, the seventy sons of Jerubbaal, on one stone. Only the youngest son of Jerubbaal, Jotham, escaped, for he was hidden. ⁶Then all the lords of Shechem and all Beth-millo came together and made Abimelech king by the terebinth at the memorial pillar in Shechem.

⁷When this was reported to Jotham, he went and stood at the top of Mount Gerizim and cried out in a loud voice:

"Hear me, lords of Shechem,
  and may God hear you!
⁸One day the trees went out
  to anoint a king over themselves.
So they said to the olive tree,
  'Reign over us.'
⁹But the olive tree answered them,
  'Must I give up my rich oil,
  whereby gods and human beings
    are honored,
  and go off to hold sway over the
    trees?'
¹⁰Then the trees said to the fig tree,
  'Come; you reign over us!'
¹¹But the fig tree answered them,
  'Must I give up my sweetness
  and my sweet fruit,
  and go off to hold sway over the
    trees?'
¹²Then the trees said to the vine,
  'Come you, reign over us.'
¹³But the vine answered them,
  'Must I give up my wine
  that cheers gods and human beings,
  and go off to hold sway over the
    trees?'
¹⁴Then all the trees said to the buckthorn,
  'Come; you reign over us!'
¹⁵The buckthorn answered the trees,
  'If you are anointing me in good
    faith,
  to make me king over you,
  come, and take refuge in my shadow.
  But if not, let fire come from the
    buckthorn
  and devour the cedars of Lebanon.'

¹⁶"Now then, if you have acted in good faith and integrity in appointing Abimelech your king, if you have acted with good will toward Jerubbaal and his house, and if you have treated him as he deserved— ¹⁷for my father fought for you at the risk of his life when he delivered you from the power of Midian, ¹⁸but you have risen against my father's house today and killed his seventy sons upon one stone and made Abimelech, the son of his maidservant, king over the lords of Shechem, because he is your kin— ¹⁹if, then, you have acted in good faith and integrity toward Jerubbaal and his house today, then rejoice in Abimelech and may he in turn rejoice in you! ²⁰But if not, let fire come forth from Abimelech and devour the lords of Shechem and Beth-millo, and let fire come forth from the lords of Shechem and Beth-millo and devour Abimelech." ²¹Then Jotham fled and escaped to Beer, where he remained for fear of his brother Abimelech.

²²When Abimelech had ruled Israel for three years, ²³God put an evil spirit between Abimelech and the lords of Shechem, and the lords of Shechem broke faith with the house of Abimelech. ²⁴This was to repay the violence done to the seventy sons of Jerubbaal and to avenge their blood upon their brother Abimelech, who killed them, and upon the lords of Shechem, who encouraged him to kill his brothers. ²⁵The lords of Shechem then set men in ambush for him on the mountaintops, and they robbed all who passed them on the road. It was reported to Abimelech.

[26]Now Gaal, son of Ebed, and his kin came, and when they passed through Shechem, the lords of Shechem put their trust in him. [27]They went out into the fields, harvested the grapes from their vineyards, trod them out, and held a festival. Then they went to the temple of their god, where they ate and drank and cursed Abimelech. [28]Gaal, son of Ebed, said, "Who is Abimelech? And who is Shechem that we should serve him? Did not the son of Jerubbaal and his lieutenant Zebul serve the men of Hamor, father of Shechem? So why should we serve him? [29]Would that these troops were entrusted to my command! I would depose Abimelech. I would say to Abimelech, 'Get a larger army and come out!'"

[30]When Zebul, the ruler of the city, heard what Gaal, son of Ebed, had said, he was angry [31]and sent messengers to Abimelech in Arumah to say, "Gaal, son of Ebed, and his kin have come to Shechem and are stirring up the city against you. [32]So take action tonight, you and the troops who are with you, and set an ambush in the fields. [33]Promptly at sunrise tomorrow morning, make a raid on the city. When he and the troops who are with him come out against you, deal with him as best you can."

[34]During the night Abimelech went into action with all his soldiers and set up an ambush outside of Shechem in four companies. [35]Gaal, son of Ebed, went out and stood at the entrance of the city gate. When Abimelech and his soldiers rose from their place of ambush, [36]Gaal saw the soldiers and said to Zebul, "There are soldiers coming down from the mountaintops!" But Zebul answered him, "It is the shadow of the hills that you see as men." [37]But Gaal went on to say, "Soldiers are coming down from the region of Tabbur-haarez, and one company is coming by way of Elon-meonenim." [38]Zebul said to him, "Where now is your boast, when you said, 'Who is Abimelech that we should serve him?' Are these not the troops for whom you expressed contempt? Go out now and fight with them." [39]So Gaal went out at the head of the lords of Shechem to fight against Abimelech; [40]but when Abimelech went after him, he fled from him. Many fell slain right up to the entrance of the gate. [41]Abimelech returned to Arumah, and Zebul drove Gaal and his kin away so that they could no longer remain at Shechem.

[42]The next day, the army marched out into the field, and it was reported to Abimelech. [43]He divided the troops he had into three companies, and set up an ambush in the fields. He watched until he saw the army leave the city and then went on the attack against them. [44]Abimelech and the company with him rushed in and stood by the entrance of the city gate, while the other two companies rushed upon all who were in the field and attacked them. [45]That entire day Abimelech fought against the city. He captured it, killed the people who were in it, and demolished the city itself, sowing it with salt.

[46]When they heard of this, all the lords of the Migdal-shechem went into the crypt of the temple of El-berith. [47]It was reported to Abimelech that all the lords of the Migdal-shechem were gathered together. [48]So he went up Mount Zalmon with all his soldiers, took his ax in his hand, and cut down some brushwood. This he lifted to his shoulder, then said to the troops with him, "Hurry! Do just as you have seen me do." [49]So all the soldiers likewise cut down brushwood and, following Abimelech, placed it against the crypt. Then they set the crypt on fire over them, so that every one of the people of the Migdal-shechem, about a thousand men and women, perished.

[50]Abimelech proceeded to Thebez, encamped, and captured it. [51]Now there was a strong tower in the middle of the city, and all the men and women and all the lords of the city fled there, shutting themselves in and going up to the roof of the tower.

⁵²Abimelech came up to the tower and fought against it. When he came close to the entrance of the tower to set it on fire, ⁵³a certain woman cast the upper part of a millstone down on Abimelech's head, and it fractured his skull. ⁵⁴He immediately called his armor-bearer and said to him, "Draw your sword and put me to death so they will not say about me, 'A woman killed him.'" So his attendant ran him through and he died. ⁵⁵When the Israelites saw that Abimelech was dead, they all left for their homes.

⁵⁶Thus did God repay the evil that Abimelech had done to his father in killing his seventy brothers. ⁵⁷God also brought all the wickedness of the people of Shechem back on their heads, for the curse of Jotham, son of Jerubbaal, overtook them.

Tola. 10:1 After Abimelech, Tola, son of Puah, son of Dodo, a man of Issachar, rose up to save Israel; he lived in Shamir in the mountain region of Ephraim. ²When he had judged Israel twenty-three years, he died and was buried in Shamir.

Jair. ³Jair the Gileadite came after him and judged Israel twenty-two years. ⁴He had thirty sons who rode on thirty donkeys and possessed thirty cities in the land of Gilead (these are called Havvoth-jair to the present day). ⁵Jair died and was buried in Kamon.

Oppression by the Ammonites. ⁶The Israelites again did what was evil in the sight of the LORD, serving the Baals and Ashtarts, the gods of Aram, the gods of Sidon, the gods of Moab, the gods of the Ammonites, and the gods of the Philistines. Since they had abandoned the LORD and would not serve him, ⁷the LORD became angry with Israel and he sold them into the power of the Philistines and the Ammonites. ⁸For eighteen years they afflicted and oppressed the Israelites in Bashan, and all the Israelites in the Amorite land beyond the Jordan in Gilead. ⁹The Ammonites also

crossed the Jordan to fight against Judah, Benjamin and the house of Ephraim, so that Israel was in great distress.

¹⁰Then the Israelites cried out to the LORD, "We have sinned against you, for we have abandoned our God and served the Baals." ¹¹The LORD answered the Israelites: Did not the Egyptians, the Amorites, the Ammonites, the Philistines, ¹²the Sidonians, the Amalekites, and the Midianites oppress you? Yet when you cried out to me, and I saved you from their power, ¹³you still abandoned me and served other gods. Therefore I will save you no more. ¹⁴Go and cry out to the gods you have chosen; let them save you in your time of distress. ¹⁵But the Israelites said to the LORD, "We have sinned. Do to us whatever is good in your sight. Only deliver us this day!" ¹⁶And they cast out the foreign gods from their midst and served the LORD, so that he grieved over the misery of Israel.

¹⁷The Ammonites were called out for war and encamped in Gilead, while the Israelites assembled and encamped at Mizpah. ¹⁸The captains of the army of Gilead said to one another, "The one who begins the war against the Ammonites shall be leader of all the inhabitants of Gilead."

Jephthah. 11:1 Jephthah the Gileadite was a warrior. He was the son of a prostitute, fathered by Gilead. ²Gilead's wife had also borne him sons. When they grew up the sons of the wife had driven Jephthah away, saying to him, "You shall inherit nothing in our father's house, for you are the son of another woman." ³So Jephthah had fled from his brothers and taken up residence in the land of Tob. Worthless men had joined company with him, and went out with him on raids.

⁴Some time later, the Ammonites went to war with Israel. ⁵As soon as the Ammonites were at war with Israel, the elders of Gilead went to bring Jephthah from the land of Tob. ⁶"Come," they said to Jephthah, "be

our commander so that we can fight the Ammonites." ⁷"Are you not the ones who hated me and drove me from my father's house?" Jephthah replied to the elders of Gilead, "Why do you come to me now, when you are in distress?" ⁸The elders of Gilead said to Jephthah, "This is the reason we have come back to you now: if you go with us to fight against the Ammonites, you shall be the leader of all of the inhabitants of Gilead." ⁹Jephthah answered the elders of Gilead, "If you bring me back to fight against the Ammonites and the LORD delivers them up to me, I will be your leader." ¹⁰The elders of Gilead said to Jephthah, "The LORD is witness between us that we will do as you say." ¹¹So Jephthah went with the elders of Gilead, and the army made him their leader and commander. Jephthah gave all his orders in the presence of the LORD in Mizpah.

¹²Then he sent messengers to the king of the Ammonites to say, "What do you have against me that you come to fight with me in my land?" ¹³The king of the Ammonites answered the messengers of Jephthah, "Israel took away my land from the Arnon to the Jabbok and the Jordan when they came up from Egypt. Now restore it peaceably."

¹⁴Again Jephthah sent messengers to the king of the Ammonites, ¹⁵saying to him, "This is what Jephthah says: 'Israel did not take the land of Moab or the land of the Ammonites. ¹⁶For when they came up from Egypt, Israel went through the wilderness to the Red Sea and came to Kadesh. ¹⁷Israel then sent messengers to the king of Edom saying, "Let me pass through your land." But the king of Edom did not give consent. They also sent to the king of Moab, but he too was unwilling. So Israel remained in Kadesh. ¹⁸Then they went through the wilderness, and bypassing the land of Edom and the land of Moab, they arrived east of the land of Moab and encamped across the Arnon. Thus they did not enter the territory of Moab, for the Arnon is the boundary of Moab. ¹⁹Then Israel sent messengers to the Amorite king Sihon, who was king of Heshbon. Israel said to him, "Let me pass through your land to my own place." ²⁰But Sihon refused to let Israel pass through his territory. He gathered all his soldiers, and they encamped at Jahaz and fought Israel. ²¹But the LORD, the God of Israel, delivered Sihon and his entire army into the power of Israel, who defeated them and occupied all the land of the Amorites who lived in that region. ²²They occupied all of the Amorite territory from the Arnon to the Jabbok and the wilderness to the Jordan. ²³Now, then, it was the LORD, the God of Israel, who dispossessed the Amorites for his people, Israel. And you are going to dispossess them? ²⁴Should you not take possession of that which your god Chemosh gave you to possess, and should we not take possession of all that the LORD, our God, has dispossessed for us? ²⁵Now, then, are you any better than Balak, son of Zippor, king of Moab? Did he ever quarrel with Israel or make war against them? ²⁶Israel has dwelt in Heshbon and its villages, Aroer and its villages, and all the cities on the banks of the Arnon for three hundred years. Why did you not recover them during that time? ²⁷As for me, I have not sinned against you, but you wrong me by making war against me. Let the LORD, who is judge, decide this day between the Israelites and the Ammonites!'" ²⁸But the king of the Ammonites paid no heed to the message Jephthah sent him.

Jephthah's Vow. ²⁹The spirit of the LORD came upon Jephthah. He passed through Gilead and Manasseh, and through Mizpah of Gilead as well, and from Mizpah of Gilead he crossed over against the Ammonites. ³⁰Jephthah made a vow to the LORD. "If you deliver the Ammonites into my power," he said, ³¹"whoever comes out of the doors of my house to meet me when I return from the Ammonites in peace shall belong to the LORD. I shall offer him up as a burnt offering."

³²Jephthah then crossed over against the Ammonites to fight against them, and the Lord delivered them into his power. ³³He inflicted a very severe defeat on them from Aroer to the approach of Minnith—twenty cities in all—and as far as Abel-keramin. So the Ammonites were brought into subjection by the Israelites. ³⁴When Jephthah returned to his house in Mizpah, it was his daughter who came out to meet him, with tambourine-playing and dancing. She was his only child: he had neither son nor daughter besides her. ³⁵When he saw her, he tore his garments and said, "Ah, my daughter! You have struck me down and brought calamity upon me. For I have made a vow to the Lord and I cannot take it back." ³⁶"Father," she replied, "you have made a vow to the Lord. Do with me as you have vowed, because the Lord has taken vengeance for you against your enemies the Ammonites." ³⁷Then she said to her father, "Let me have this favor. Do nothing for two months, that I and my companions may go wander in the mountains to weep for my virginity." ³⁸"Go," he replied, and sent her away for two months. So she departed with her companions and wept for her virginity in the mountains. ³⁹At the end of the two months she returned to her father, and he did to her as he had vowed. She had not had relations with any man.

It became a custom in Israel ⁴⁰for Israelite women to go yearly to mourn the daughter of Jephthah the Gileadite for four days of the year.

The Shibboleth Incident. 12:1 The men of Ephraim were called out, and they crossed over to Zaphon. They said to Jephthah, "Why did you go to fight with the Ammonites without calling us to go with you? We will burn your house on top of you." ²Jephthah answered them, "My soldiers and I were engaged in a contest with the Ammonites. They were pressing us hard, and I cried out to you, but you did not come to save me from their power. ³When I saw that you were not coming to save me, I took my life in my own hand and crossed over against the Ammonites, and the Lord delivered them into my power. Why, then, should you come up against me this day to fight with me?"

⁴Then Jephthah gathered together all the men of Gilead and fought against Ephraim. The men of Gilead defeated Ephraim, ⁵and Gilead seized the fords of the Jordan against Ephraim. When any of the fleeing Ephraimites said, "Let me pass," the men of Gilead would say to him, "Are you an Ephraimite?" If he answered, "No!" ⁶they would ask him to say "Shibboleth." If he said "Sibboleth," not pronouncing it exactly right, they would seize him and kill him at the fords of the Jordan. Forty-two thousand Ephraimites fell at that time.

⁷Jephthah judged Israel for six years, and Jephthah the Gileadite died and was buried in his city in Gilead.

Ibzan. ⁸After him Ibzan of Bethlehem judged Israel. ⁹He had thirty sons and thirty daughters whom he gave in marriage outside the family, while bringing in thirty wives for his sons from outside the family. He judged Israel for seven years. ¹⁰Ibzan died and was buried in Bethlehem.

Elon. ¹¹After him Elon the Zebulunite judged Israel; he judged Israel for ten years. ¹²Elon the Zebulunite died and was buried at Aijalon in the land of Zebulun.

Abdon. ¹³After him Abdon, son of Hillel, the Pirathonite, judged Israel. ¹⁴He had forty sons and thirty grandsons, who rode on seventy donkeys. He judged Israel for eight years. ¹⁵Abdon, son of Hillel, the Pirathonite, died and was buried in Pirathon in the land of Ephraim in the mountain region of the Amalekites.

☐ 1 CORINTHIANS 5

A Case of Incest. 5:1 It is widely reported that there is immorality among you, and immorality of a kind not found even among pagans—a man living with his father's wife. ²And you are inflated with pride. Should you not rather have been sorrowful? The one who did this deed should be expelled from your midst. ³I, for my part, although absent in body but present in spirit, have already, as if present, pronounced judgment on the one who has committed this deed, ⁴in the name of [our] Lord Jesus: when you have gathered together and I am with you in spirit with the power of the Lord Jesus, ⁵you are to deliver this man to Satan for the destruction of his flesh, so that his spirit may be saved on the day of the Lord.

⁶Your boasting is not appropriate. Do you not know that a little yeast leavens all the dough? ⁷Clear out the old yeast, so that you may become a fresh batch of dough, inasmuch as you are unleavened. For our paschal lamb, Christ, has been sacrificed. ⁸Therefore let us celebrate the feast, not with the old yeast, the yeast of malice and wickedness, but with the unleavened bread of sincerity and truth.

⁹I wrote you in my letter not to associate with immoral people, ¹⁰not at all referring to the immoral of this world or the greedy and robbers or idolaters; for you would then have to leave the world. ¹¹But I now write to you not to associate with anyone named a brother, if he is immoral, greedy, an idolater, a slanderer, a drunkard, or a robber, not even to eat with such a person. ¹²For why should I be judging outsiders? Is it not your business to judge those within? ¹³God will judge those outside. "Purge the evil person from your midst."

March 24

Don't tell me that the body is the cause of sin: After all, if the body is the cause of sin, how is it that a corpse doesn't sin? The body of itself doesn't sin — rather, the soul sins through the body. The body is the soul's instrument, its cloak and garment.

— St. Cyril of Jerusalem

☐ JUDGES 13-16

The Birth of Samson. 13:1 The Israelites again did what was evil in the sight of the LORD, who therefore delivered them into the power of the Philistines for forty years.

²There was a certain man from Zorah, of the clan of the Danites, whose name was Manoah. His wife was barren and had borne no children. ³An angel of the LORD appeared to the woman and said to her: Though you are barren and have had no children, you will conceive and bear a son.

⁴Now, then, be careful to drink no wine or beer and to eat nothing unclean, ⁵for you will conceive and bear a son. No razor shall touch his head, for the boy is to be a nazirite for God from the womb. It is he who will begin to save Israel from the power of the Philistines.

⁶The woman went and told her husband, "A man of God came to me; he had the appearance of an angel of God, fearsome indeed. I did not ask him where he

came from, nor did he tell me his name. [7]But he said to me, 'You will conceive and bear a son. So drink no wine or beer, and eat nothing unclean. For the boy shall be a nazirite for God from the womb, until the day of his death.'" [8]Manoah then prayed to the Lord. "Please, my Lord," he said, "may the man of God whom you sent return to us to teach us what to do for the boy who is to be born."

[9]God heard the prayer of Manoah, and the angel of God came again to the woman as she was sitting in the field; but her husband Manoah was not with her. [10]The woman ran quickly and told her husband. "The man who came to me the other day has appeared to me," she said to him; [11]so Manoah got up and followed his wife. When he reached the man, he said to him, "Are you the one who spoke to my wife?" I am, he answered. [12]Then Manoah asked, "Now, when what you say comes true, what rules must the boy follow? What must he do?" [13]The angel of the Lord answered Manoah: Your wife must be careful about all the things of which I spoke to her. [14]She must not eat anything that comes from the vine, she must not drink wine or beer, and she must not eat anything unclean. Let her observe all that I have commanded her. [15]Then Manoah said to the angel of the Lord, "Permit us to detain you, so that we may prepare a young goat for you." [16]But the angel of the Lord answered Manoah: Though you detained me, I would not eat your food. But if you want to prepare a burnt offering, then offer it up to the Lord. For Manoah did not know that he was the angel of the Lord. [17]Then Manoah said to the angel of the Lord, "What is your name, that we may honor you when your words come true?" [18]The angel of the Lord answered him: Why do you ask my name? It is wondrous. [19]Then Manoah took a young goat with a grain offering and offered it on the rock to the Lord, who works wonders. While Manoah and his wife were looking on, [20]as the flame rose to the heavens from the altar, the angel of the Lord ascended in the flame of the altar. When Manoah and his wife saw this, they fell on their faces to the ground; [21]but the angel of the Lord was seen no more by Manoah and his wife. Then Manoah, realizing that it was the angel of the Lord, [22]said to his wife, "We will certainly die, for we have seen God." [23]But his wife said to him, "If the Lord had meant to kill us, he would not have accepted a burnt offering and grain offering from our hands! Nor would he have let us see all this, or hear what we have heard."

[24]The woman bore a son and named him Samson, and when the boy grew up the Lord blessed him. [25]The spirit of the Lord came upon him for the first time in Mahaneh-dan, between Zorah and Eshtaol.

Marriage of Samson. 14:1 Samson went down to Timnah where he saw one of the Philistine women. [2]On his return he told his father and mother, "I saw in Timnah a woman, a Philistine. Get her for me as a wife." [3]His father and mother said to him, "Is there no woman among your kinsfolk or among all your people, that you must go and take a woman from the uncircumcised Philistines?" But Samson answered his father, "Get her for me, for she is the one I want." [4]Now his father and mother did not know that this had been brought about by the Lord, who was seeking an opportunity against the Philistines; for at that time they ruled over Israel.

[5]So Samson went down to Timnah with his father and mother. When he turned aside to the vineyards of Timnah, a young lion came roaring out toward him. [6]But the spirit of the Lord rushed upon Samson, and he tore the lion apart barehanded, as one tears a young goat. Without telling his father or mother what he had done, [7]he went down and spoke to the woman. He

liked her. ⁸Later, when he came back to marry her, he turned aside to look at the remains of the lion, and there was a swarm of bees in the lion's carcass, and honey. ⁹So he scooped the honey out into his hands and ate it as he went along. When he came to his father and mother, he gave them some to eat, but he did not tell them that he had scooped the honey from the lion's carcass.

¹⁰His father also went down to the woman, and Samson gave a feast there, since it was customary for the young men to do this. ¹¹Out of their fear of him, they brought thirty men to be his companions. ¹²Samson said to them, "Let me propose a riddle to you. If within the seven days of the feast you solve it for me, I will give you thirty linen tunics and thirty sets of garments. ¹³But if you cannot answer it for me, you must give me thirty tunics and thirty sets of garments." "Propose your riddle," they responded, "and we will listen to it." ¹⁴So he said to them,

"Out of the eater came food,
    out of the strong came sweetness."

For three days they were unable to answer the riddle, ¹⁵and on the fourth day they said to Samson's wife, "Trick your husband into solving the riddle for us, or we will burn you and your family. Did you invite us here to reduce us to poverty?" ¹⁶So Samson's wife wept at his side and said, "You just hate me! You do not love me! You proposed a riddle to my people, but did not tell me the answer." He said to her, "If I did not tell even my father or my mother, must I tell you?" ¹⁷But she wept beside him during the seven days the feast lasted, and on the seventh day, he told her the answer, because she pressed him, and she explained the riddle to her people.

¹⁸On the seventh day, before the sun set, the men of the city said to him,

"What is sweeter than honey,
    what is stronger than a lion?"

He replied to them,

"If you had not plowed with my heifer,
    you would not have solved my
        riddle."

¹⁹The spirit of the LORD rushed upon him, and he went down to Ashkelon, where he killed thirty of their men and stripped them; he gave their garments to those who had answered the riddle. Then he went off to his own family in anger, ²⁰and Samson's wife was married to the companion who had been his best man.

Samson Defeats the Philistines. 15:1 After some time, in the season of the wheat harvest, Samson visited his wife, bringing a young goat. But when he said, "Let me go into my wife's room," her father would not let him go in. ²He said, "I thought you hated her, so I gave her to your best man. Her younger sister is better; you may have her instead." ³Samson said to him, "This time I am guiltless if I harm the Philistines." ⁴So Samson went and caught three hundred jackals, and turning them tail to tail, he took some torches and tied one between each pair of tails. ⁵He then kindled the torches and set the jackals loose in the standing grain of the Philistines, thus burning both the shocks and standing grain, the vineyards and olive groves.

⁶When the Philistines asked, "Who has done this?" they were told, "Samson, the son-in-law of the Timnite, because his wife was taken and given to his best man." So the Philistines went up and destroyed her and her family by fire. ⁷Samson said to them, "If this is how you act, I will not stop until I have taken revenge on you." ⁸And he struck them hip and thigh—a great slaughter. Then he went down and stayed in a cleft of the crag of Etam.

⁹The Philistines went up and encamped in Judah, deploying themselves against Lehi. ¹⁰When the men of Judah asked, "Why have you come up against us?" they

answered, "To take Samson prisoner; to do to him as he has done to us." [11]Three thousand men of Judah went down to the cleft of the crag of Etam and said to Samson, "Do you not know that the Philistines are our rulers? Why, then, have you done this to us?" He answered them, "As they have done to me, so have I done to them." [12]They said to him, "We have come down to bind you and deliver you to the Philistines." Samson said to them, "Swear to me that you will not attack me yourselves." [13]"No," they replied, "we will only bind you and hand you over to them. We will certainly not kill you." So they bound him with two new ropes and brought him up from the crag. [14]When he reached Lehi, and the Philistines came shouting to meet him, the spirit of the LORD rushed upon him: the ropes around his arms became like flax that is consumed by fire, and his bonds melted away from his hands. [15]Coming upon the fresh jawbone of an ass, he reached out, grasped it, and with it killed a thousand men. [16]Then Samson said,

"With the jawbone of an ass
    I have piled them in a heap;
With the jawbone of an ass
    I have slain a thousand men."

[17]As he finished speaking he threw the jawbone from him; and so that place was named Ramath-lehi. [18]Being very thirsty, he cried to the LORD and said, "You have put this great victory into the hand of your servant. Must I now die of thirst and fall into the hands of the uncircumcised?" [19]Then God split the cavity in Lehi, and water issued from it, and Samson drank till his spirit returned and he revived. Hence it is called En-hakkore in Lehi to this day.

[20]Samson judged Israel for twenty years in the days of the Philistines.

16:1 Once Samson went to Gaza, where he saw a prostitute and visited her. [2]The people of Gaza were told, "Samson has come here," and they surrounded him with an ambush at the city gate all night long. And all the night they waited, saying, "At morning light we will kill him." [3]Samson lay there until midnight. Then he rose at midnight, seized the doors of the city gate and the two gateposts, and tore them loose, bar and all. He hoisted them on his shoulders and carried them to the top of the ridge opposite Hebron.

Samson and Delilah. [4]After that he fell in love with a woman in the Wadi Sorek whose name was Delilah. [5]The lords of the Philistines came up to her and said, "Trick him and find out where he gets his great strength, and how we may overcome and bind him so as to make him helpless. Then for our part, we will each give you eleven hundred pieces of silver."

[6]So Delilah said to Samson, "Tell me where you get your great strength and how you may be bound so as to be made helpless." [7]"If they bind me with seven fresh bowstrings that have not dried," Samson answered her, "I shall grow weaker and be like anyone else." [8]So the lords of the Philistines brought her seven fresh bowstrings that had not dried, and she bound him with them. [9]She had men lying in wait in the room, and she said to him, "The Philistines are upon you, Samson!" But he snapped the bowstrings as a thread of tow is snapped by a whiff of flame; and his strength remained unexplained.

[10]Delilah said to Samson, "You have mocked me and told me lies. Now tell me how you may be bound." [11]"If they bind me tight with new ropes, with which no work has been done," he answered her, "I shall grow weaker and be like anyone else." [12]So Delilah took new ropes and bound him with them. Then she said to him, "The Philistines are upon you, Samson!" For there were men lying in wait in the room. But he snapped the ropes off his arms like thread.

[13]Delilah said to Samson again, "Up to now you have mocked me and told me lies.

Tell me how you may be bound." He said to her, "If you weave the seven locks of my hair into the web and fasten them with the pin, I shall grow weaker and be like anyone else." [14]So when he went to bed, Delilah took the seven locks of his hair and wove them into the web, and fastened them with the pin. Then she said, "The Philistines are upon you, Samson!" Awakening from his sleep, he pulled out both the loom and the web.

[15]Then she said to him, "How can you say 'I love you' when your heart is not mine? Three times already you have mocked me, and not told me where you get your great strength!" [16]She pressed him continually and pestered him till he was deathly weary of it. [17]So he told her all that was in his heart and said, "No razor has touched my head, for I have been a nazirite for God from my mother's womb. If I am shaved, my strength will leave me, and I shall grow weaker and be like anyone else." [18]When Delilah realized that he had told her all that was in his heart, she summoned the lords of the Philistines, saying, "Come up this time, for he has told me all that is in his heart." So the lords of the Philistines came to her and brought the money with them. [19]She put him to sleep on her lap, and called for a man who shaved off the seven locks of his hair. He immediately became helpless, for his strength had left him. [20]When she said "The Philistines are upon you, Samson!" he woke from his sleep and thought, "I will go out as I have done time and again and shake myself free." He did not realize that the Lord had left him. [21]But the Philistines seized him and gouged out his eyes. Then they brought him down to Gaza and bound him with bronze fetters, and he was put to grinding grain in the prison. [22]But the hair of his head began to grow as soon as it was shaved.

The Death of Samson. [23]The lords of the Philistines assembled to offer a great sacrifice to their god Dagon and to celebrate. They said, "Our god has delivered Samson our enemy into our power." [24]When the people saw him, they praised their god. For they said,

> "Our god has delivered into our power
> our enemy, the ravager of our land,
> the one who has multiplied our
> slain."

[25]When their spirits were high, they said, "Call Samson that he may amuse us." So they called Samson from the prison, and he provided amusement for them. They made him stand between the columns, [26]and Samson said to the attendant who was holding his hand, "Put me where I may touch the columns that support the temple, so that I may lean against them." [27]The temple was full of men and women: all the lords of the Philistines were there, and from the roof about three thousand men and women looked on as Samson provided amusement. [28]Samson cried out to the Lord and said, "Lord God, remember me! Strengthen me only this once that I may avenge myself on the Philistines at one blow for my two eyes." [29]Samson grasped the two middle columns on which the temple rested and braced himself against them, one at his right, the other at his left. [30]Then saying, "Let me die with the Philistines!" Samson pushed hard, and the temple fell upon the lords and all the people who were in it. Those he killed by his dying were more than those he had killed during his lifetime.

[31]His kinsmen and all his father's house went down and bore him up for burial in the grave of Manoah his father between Zorah and Eshtaol. He had judged Israel for twenty years.

☐ 1 CORINTHIANS 6

Lawsuits before Unbelievers. 6:1 How can any one of you with a case against another dare to bring it to the unjust for judgment instead of to the holy ones? [2]Do you not know that the holy ones will judge the world? If the world is to be judged by you, are you unqualified for the lowest law courts? [3]Do you not know that we will judge angels? Then why not everyday matters? [4]If, therefore, you have courts for everyday matters, do you seat as judges people of no standing in the church? [5]I say this to shame you. Can it be that there is not one among you wise enough to be able to settle a case between brothers? [6]But rather brother goes to court against brother, and that before unbelievers?

[7]Now indeed [then] it is, in any case, a failure on your part that you have lawsuits against one another. Why not rather put up with injustice? Why not rather let yourselves be cheated? [8]Instead, you inflict injustice and cheat, and this to brothers. [9]Do you not know that the unjust will not inherit the kingdom of God? Do not be deceived; neither fornicators nor idolaters nor adulterers nor boy prostitutes nor sodomites [10]nor thieves nor the greedy nor drunkards nor slanderers nor robbers will inherit the kingdom of God. [11]That is what some of you used to be; but now you have had yourselves washed, you were sanctified, you were justified in the name of the Lord Jesus Christ and in the Spirit of our God.

Sexual Immorality. [12]"Everything is lawful for me," but not everything is beneficial. "Everything is lawful for me," but I will not let myself be dominated by anything. [13]"Food for the stomach and the stomach for food," but God will do away with both the one and the other. The body, however, is not for immorality, but for the Lord, and the Lord is for the body; [14]God raised the Lord and will also raise us by his power.

[15]Do you not know that your bodies are members of Christ? Shall I then take Christ's members and make them the members of a prostitute? Of course not! [16][Or] do you not know that anyone who joins himself to a prostitute becomes one body with her? For "the two," it says, "will become one flesh." [17]But whoever is joined to the Lord becomes one spirit with him. [18]Avoid immorality. Every other sin a person commits is outside the body, but the immoral person sins against his own body. [19]Do you not know that your body is a temple of the holy Spirit within you, whom you have from God, and that you are not your own? [20]For you have been purchased at a price. Therefore, glorify God in your body.

March 25

The Annunciation of the Lord

May He make us children of God, He who for our sakes wished to become a Child of man.

— St. Augustine of Hippo

☐ JUDGES 17-19

Micah and the Levite. 17:1 There was a man from the mountain region of Ephraim whose name was Micah. ²He said to his mother, "The eleven hundred pieces of silver that were taken from you, about which you pronounced a curse and even said it in my hearing—I have that silver. I took it. So now I will restore it to you." Then his mother said, "May my son be blessed by the LORD!" ³When he restored the eleven hundred pieces of silver to his mother, she said, "I consecrate the silver to the LORD from my own hand on behalf of my son to make an idol overlaid with silver." ⁴So when he restored the silver to his mother, she took two hundred pieces and gave them to the silversmith, who made of them an idol overlaid with silver. So it remained in the house of Micah. ⁵The man Micah had a shrine, and he made an ephod and teraphim, and installed one of his sons, who became his priest. ⁶In those days there was no king in Israel; everyone did what was right in their own eyes.

⁷There was a young man from Bethlehem of Judah, from the clan of Judah; he was a Levite residing there. ⁸The man set out from the city, Bethlehem of Judah, to take up residence wherever he could find a place. On his journey he came into the mountain region of Ephraim as far as the house of Micah. ⁹"Where do you come from?" Micah asked him. He answered him, "I am a Levite, from Bethlehem in Judah, and I am on my way to take up residence wherever I can find a place." ¹⁰"Stay with me," Micah said to him. "Be father and priest to me, and I will give you

ten silver pieces a year, a set of garments, and your living." He pressed the Levite, ¹¹and he agreed to stay with the man. The young man became like one of his own sons. ¹²Micah installed the Levite, and the young man became his priest, remaining in the house of Micah. ¹³Then Micah said, "Now I know that the LORD will prosper me, since I have the Levite as my priest."

Migration of the Danites. 18:1 In those days there was no king in Israel. In those days the tribe of the Danites were in search of a heritage to dwell in, for up to that time no heritage had been allotted to them among the tribes of Israel.

²So the Danites sent from their clans five powerful men of Zorah and Eshtaol, to reconnoiter the land and scout it. "Go, scout the land," they were told. They went into the mountain region of Ephraim, and they spent the night there. ³While they were near the house of Micah, they recognized the voice of the young Levite, so they turned aside. They asked him, "Who brought you here? What are you doing here? What is your interest here?" ⁴"This is what Micah has done for me," he replied to them. "He has hired me and I have become his priest." ⁵They said to him, "Consult God, that we may know whether the journey we are making will lead to success." ⁶The priest said to them, "Go in peace! The journey you are making is under the eye of the LORD."

⁷So the five men went on and came to Laish. They saw the people there living securely after the manner of the Sidonians,

quiet and trusting, with no lack of any natural resource. They were distant from the Sidonians and had no dealings with the Arameans. ⁸When the five returned to their kin in Zorah and Eshtaol, they were asked, "What do you have to report?" ⁹They replied, "Come, let us attack them, for we have seen the land and it is very good. Are you going to hesitate? Do not be slow to go in and take possession of the land! ¹⁰When you go you will come to a trusting people. The land stretches out in both directions, and God has indeed given it into your power—a place where no natural resource is lacking."

¹¹So six hundred of the clan of the Danites, men armed with weapons of war, set out from Zorah and Eshtaol. ¹²They marched up into Judah and encamped near Kiriath-jearim; for this reason the place is called Mahaneh-dan to this day (it lies west of Kiriath-jearim).

¹³From there they passed on into the mountain region of Ephraim and came to the house of Micah. ¹⁴Then the five men who had gone to reconnoiter the land spoke up and said to their kindred, "Do you know that in these houses there are an ephod, teraphim, and an idol overlaid with silver? Now decide what you must do!" ¹⁵So turning in that direction, they went to the house of the young Levite at the home of Micah and greeted him. ¹⁶The six hundred Danites stationed themselves at the entrance of the gate armed with weapons of war. ¹⁷The five men who had gone to reconnoiter the land went up ¹⁸and entered the house of Micah with the priest standing there. They took the idol, the ephod, the teraphim and the metal image. When the priest said to them, "What are you doing?" ¹⁹they said to him, "Be still! Put your hand over your mouth! Come with us and be our father and priest. Is it better for you to be priest for the family of one man or to be priest for a tribe and a clan in Israel?" ²⁰The priest, agreeing, took the ephod, the teraphim, and the idol, and went along with the troops. ²¹As they turned to depart, they placed their little ones, their livestock, and their goods at the head of the column.

²²When the Danites had gone some distance from the house of Micah, Micah and the men in the houses nearby mustered and overtook them. ²³They called to the Danites, who turned and said to Micah, "What do you want that you have called this muster?" ²⁴"You have taken my god, which I made for myself, and you have gone off with my priest as well," he answered. "What is left for me? How, then, can you ask me, 'What do you want?'" ²⁵The Danites said to him, "Do not let your voice be heard near us, or aggravated men will attack you, and you will have forfeited your life and the lives of your family!" ²⁶Then the Danites went on their way, and Micah, seeing that they were too strong for him, turned back and went home.

²⁷Having taken what Micah had made and his priest, they marched against Laish, a quiet and trusting people; they put them to the sword and destroyed the city by fire. ²⁸No one came to their aid, since the city was far from Sidon and they had no dealings with the Arameans; the city was in the valley that belongs to Beth-rehob. The Danites then rebuilt the city and occupied it. ²⁹They named it Dan after their ancestor Dan, who was born to Israel. But Laish was the name of the city formerly. ³⁰The Danites set up the idol for themselves, and Jonathan, son of Gershom, son of Moses, and his descendants were priests for the tribe of the Danites until the time the land went into captivity. ³¹They maintained the idol Micah had made as long as the house of God was in Shiloh.

The Levite from Ephraim. 19:1 In those days, when there was no king in Israel, there was a Levite residing in remote parts of the mountain region of Ephraim who had taken for himself a concubine from

Bethlehem of Judah. ²But his concubine spurned him and left him for her father's house in Bethlehem of Judah, where she stayed for some four months. ³Her husband then set out with his servant and a pair of donkeys, and went after her to soothe her and bring her back. He arrived at her father's house, and when the young woman's father saw him, he came out joyfully to meet him. ⁴His father-in-law, the young woman's father, urged him to stay, and so he spent three days eating and drinking and passing the night there. ⁵On the fourth day they rose early in the morning and he prepared to go. But the young woman's father said to his son-in-law, "Fortify yourself with a little food; you can go later on." ⁶So they stayed and the two men ate and drank together. Then the young woman's father said to the husband, "Why not decide to spend the night here and enjoy yourself?" ⁷The man made a move to go, but when his father-in-law pressed him he went back and spent the night there.

⁸On the fifth morning he rose early to depart, but the young woman's father said, "Fortify yourself!" He coaxed him, and he tarried until the afternoon, and the two of them ate. ⁹Then when the husband was ready to go with his concubine and servant, the young woman's father said to him, "See, the day is wearing on toward evening. Stay for the night. See, the day is coming to an end. Spend the night here and enjoy yourself. Early tomorrow you can start your journey home." ¹⁰The man, however, refused to stay another night; he and his concubine set out with a pair of saddled donkeys, and traveled until they came opposite Jebus, which is Jerusalem. ¹¹Since they were near Jebus with the day far gone, the servant said to his master, "Come, let us turn off to this city of the Jebusites and spend the night in it." ¹²But his master said to him, "We will not turn off to a foreigner's city, where there are no Israelites. We will go on to Gibeah. ¹³Come," he said to his servant, "let us make for some other place and spend the night in either Gibeah or Ramah." ¹⁴So they continued on their way until the sun set on them when they were opposite Gibeah of Benjamin.

¹⁵There they turned off to enter Gibeah for the night. The man went in and sat down in the town square, but no one took them inside to spend the night. ¹⁶In the evening, however, an old man came from his work in the field; he was from the mountain region of Ephraim, though he was living in Gibeah where the local people were Benjaminites. ¹⁷When he noticed the traveler in the town square, the old man asked, "Where are you going, and where have you come from?" ¹⁸He said to him, "We are traveling from Bethlehem of Judah far up into the mountain region of Ephraim, where I am from. I have been to Bethlehem of Judah, and now I am going home; but no one has taken me into his house. ¹⁹We have straw and fodder for our donkeys, and bread and wine for myself and for your maidservant and the young man who is with your servant; there is nothing else we need." ²⁰"Rest assured," the old man said to him, "I will provide for all your needs, but do not spend the night in the public square." ²¹So he led them to his house and mixed fodder for the donkeys. Then they washed their feet, and ate and drank.

The Outrage at Gibeah. ²²While they were enjoying themselves, the men of the city, a bunch of scoundrels, surrounded the house and beat on the door. They said to the old man who was the owner of the house, "Bring out the man who has come into your house, so that we may get intimate with him." ²³The man who was the owner of the house went out to them and said, "No, my brothers; do not be so wicked. This man has come into my house; do not commit this terrible crime. ²⁴Instead, let me bring out my virgin daughter and this man's concubine. Humiliate them, or do whatever you want; but against him do not commit such a terrible crime." [25]But the men would not listen to him. So the man seized his concubine and thrust her outside to them. They raped her and abused her all night until morning, and let her go as the sun was coming up. [26]At the approach of morning the woman came and collapsed at the entrance of the house in which her husband was, and lay there until morning. [27]When her husband rose in the morning and opened the door of the house to start out again on his journey, there was the woman, his concubine, collapsed at the entrance of the house with her hands on the threshold. [28]"Come, let us go," he said to her, but there was no answer. So the man placed her on a donkey and started out again for home.

[29]On reaching home, he got a knife and took hold of the body of his concubine. He cut her up limb by limb into twelve pieces and sent them throughout the territory of Israel. [30]He instructed the men whom he sent, "Thus you shall say to all the men of Israel: 'Has such a thing ever happened from the day the Israelites came up from the land of Egypt to this day? Take note of it; form a plan and give orders.'"

☐ 1 CORINTHIANS 7:1-24

Advice to the Married. 7:1 Now in regard to the matters about which you wrote: "It is a good thing for a man not to touch a woman," [2]but because of cases of immorality every man should have his own wife, and every woman her own husband. [3]The husband should fulfill his duty toward his wife, and likewise the wife toward her husband. [4]A wife does not have authority over her own body, but rather her husband, and similarly a husband does not have authority over his own body, but rather his wife. [5]Do not deprive each other, except perhaps by mutual consent for a time, to be free for prayer, but then return to one another, so that Satan may not tempt you through your lack of self-control. [6]This I say by way of concession, however, not as a command. [7]Indeed, I wish everyone to be as I am, but each has a particular gift from God, one of one kind and one of another.

[8]Now to the unmarried and to widows, I say: it is a good thing for them to remain as they are, as I do, [9]but if they cannot exercise self-control they should marry, for it is better to marry than to be on fire. [10]To the married, however, I give this instruction (not I, but the Lord): A wife should not separate from her husband [11]—and if she does separate she must either remain single or become reconciled to her husband— and a husband should not divorce his wife.

[12]To the rest I say (not the Lord): if any brother has a wife who is an unbeliever, and she is willing to go on living with him, he should not divorce her; [13]and if any woman has a husband who is an unbeliever, and he is willing to go on living with her, she should not divorce her husband. [14]For the unbelieving husband is made holy through his wife, and the unbelieving wife is made holy through the brother. Otherwise your children would be unclean, whereas in fact they are holy.

[15]If the unbeliever separates, however, let him separate. The brother or sister is not bound in such cases; God has called you to peace. [16]For how do you know, wife, whether you will save your husband; or how do you know, husband, whether you will save your wife?

The Life That the Lord Has Assigned. [17]Only, everyone should live as the Lord has assigned, just as God called each one. I give this order in all the churches. [18]Was someone called after he had been circumcised? He should not try to undo his circumcision. Was an uncircumcised person called?

He should not be circumcised. [19]Circumcision means nothing, and uncircumcision means nothing; what matters is keeping God's commandments. [20]Everyone should remain in the state in which he was called.

[21]Were you a slave when you were called? Do not be concerned but, even if you can gain your freedom, make the most of it.

[22]For the slave called in the Lord is a freed person in the Lord, just as the free person who has been called is a slave of Christ. [23]You have been purchased at a price. Do not become slaves to human beings. [24]Brothers, everyone should continue before God in the state in which he was called.

March 26

The state of marriage is one that requires more virtue and constancy than any other. It is a perpetual exercise in mortification.

— St. Francis de Sales

☐ JUDGES 20-21

Assembly of Israelites. 20:1 So all the Israelites came out as one, from Dan to Beer-sheba including the land of Gilead, and the assembly gathered to the LORD at Mizpah. [2]The leaders of all the people, all the staff-bearers of Israel, presented themselves in the assembly of the people of God—four hundred thousand foot soldiers who carried swords. [3]Meanwhile, the Benjaminites heard that the Israelites had gone up to Mizpah. The Israelites asked, "How did this evil thing happen?" [4]and the Levite, the husband of the murdered woman, testified: "It was at Gibeah of Benjamin, which my concubine and I had entered for the night. [5]The lords of Gibeah rose up against me and surrounded me in the house at night. I was the one they intended to kill, but they abused my concubine and she died. [6]So I took my concubine and cut her up and sent her through every part of the territory of Israel, because of the terrible thing they had done in Israel. [7]So now, all you Israelites, give your judgment and counsel in this matter." [8]All the people rose as one to say, "None of us will leave for our tents or return to our homes. [9]Now as for

Gibeah, this is what we will do: We will go up against it by lot, [10]taking from all the tribes of Israel ten men for every hundred, a hundred for every thousand, a thousand for every ten thousand, and procuring supplies for the soldiers who will go to exact from Gibeah of Benjamin the full measure of the terrible thing it committed in Israel."

[11]So all the men of Israel gathered against the city, united as one. [12]The tribes of Israel sent men throughout the tribe of Benjamin to say, "What is this evil that has occurred among you? [13]Now give up the men, the scoundrels who are in Gibeah, that we may put them to death and thus purge the evil from Israel." But the Benjaminites refused to listen to their kindred, the Israelites. [14]Instead, the Benjaminites assembled from their cities at Gibeah, to march out to battle with the Israelites. [15]On that day the Benjaminites mustered from their cities twenty-six thousand swordsmen, in addition to the inhabitants of Gibeah, who mustered seven hundred picked men [16]who were left-handed, every one of them able to sling a stone at a hair without missing. [17]The men of Israel, without Benjamin,

mustered four hundred thousand swordsmen, all of them warriors. [18]They went up to Bethel and consulted God. When the Israelites asked, "Who shall go up first for us to do battle with the Benjaminites?" the LORD said: Judah first. [19]The Israelites rose in the morning and encamped against Gibeah.

War with Benjamin. [20]The men of Israel marched out to do battle with Benjamin and drew up in battle array against them at Gibeah. [21]The Benjaminites marched out of Gibeah that day and felled twenty-two thousand men of Israel. [22]But the army of the men of Israel took courage and again drew up for battle in the place where they had drawn up on the previous day. [23]Then the Israelites went up and wept before the LORD until evening. "Shall I again engage my brother Benjamin in battle?" they asked the LORD; and the LORD answered: Attack! [24]When the Israelites drew near to the Benjaminites on the second day, [25]Benjamin marched out of Gibeah against them again and felled eighteen thousand Israelites, all of them swordsmen. [26]So the entire Israelite army went up and entered Bethel, where they sat weeping before the LORD. They fasted that day until evening and presented burnt offerings and communion offerings before the LORD. [27]The Israelites consulted the LORD (for the ark of the covenant of the LORD was there in those days, [28]and Phinehas, son of Eleazar, son of Aaron, was standing in his presence in those days), and asked, "Shall I again go out to battle with my brother Benjamin, or shall I stop?" The LORD said: Attack! For tomorrow I will deliver him into your power. [29]So Israel set men in ambush around Gibeah.

[30]When the Israelites went up against the Benjaminites on the third day, they drew up against Gibeah as on other occasions. [31]When the Benjaminites marched out to meet the army, they began, as on other occasions, to strike down some of the troops along the highways, one of which goes up to Bethel and one to Gibeah in the open country; about thirty Israelites were slain. [32]The Benjaminites thought, "They are routed before us as previously." The Israelites, however, were thinking, "We will flee and draw them out from the city onto the highways." [33]And then all the men of Israel rose from their places, forming up at Baal-tamar, and the Israelites in ambush rushed from their place west of Gibeah [34]and advanced against Gibeah with ten thousand picked men from all Israel. The fighting was severe, but no one knew that a disaster was closing in. [35]The LORD defeated Benjamin before Israel; and on that day the Israelites killed twenty-five thousand one hundred men of Benjamin, all of them swordsmen.

[36]Then the Benjaminites saw that they were defeated. The men of Israel gave ground to Benjamin, trusting in the ambush they had set at Gibeah. [37]Then the men in ambush, having made a sudden dash against Gibeah, marched in and put the whole city to the sword. [38]The arrangement the men of Israel had with the men in ambush was that they would send up a smoke signal from the city, [39]and the men of Israel would then wheel about in the battle. Benjamin, having begun by killing off some thirty of the men of Israel, thought, "Surely they are completely routed before us, as in the earlier fighting." [40]But when the signal, the column of smoke, began to rise up from the city, Benjamin looked back and there was the whole city going up in smoke toward heaven. [41]Then when the men of Israel wheeled about, the men of Benjamin were thrown into confusion, for they realized that disaster was closing in on them. [42]They retreated before the men of Israel in the direction of the wilderness, but the fighting kept pace with them, and those who had been in the city were spreading destruction in between. [43]They surrounded the men of Benjamin, pursued them from Nohah and drove them along to a point

east of Gibeah. ⁴⁴Eighteen thousand from Benjamin fell, all of them warriors. ⁴⁵They turned and fled into the wilderness to the crag of Rimmon. The Israelites picked off five thousand men on the highways and kept pace with them as far as Gidom, where they struck down another two thousand of them. ⁴⁶The total of those from Benjamin who fell that day was twenty-five thousand swordsmen, all of them warriors. ⁴⁷Six hundred men turned and fled into the wilderness to the crag of Rimmon, where they remained for four months.

⁴⁸Then the men of Israel turned back against the Benjaminites, putting them to the sword—the inhabitants of the cities, the livestock, and all they came upon. Moreover they destroyed by fire all the cities they came upon.

Ensuring a Future for Benjamin. 21:1
The men of Israel took an oath at Mizpah: "None of us will give his daughter in marriage to anyone from Benjamin." ²So the people went to Bethel and remained there before God until evening, raising their voices in bitter weeping. ³They said, "Lord, God of Israel, why has this happened in Israel that today one tribe of Israel should be lacking?" ⁴Early the next day the people built an altar there and offered burnt offerings and communion offerings. ⁵Then the Israelites asked, "Are there any among all the tribes of Israel who did not come up to the Lord for the assembly?" For there was a solemn oath that anyone who did not go up to the Lord at Mizpah should be put to death.

⁶The Israelites were disconsolate over their brother Benjamin and said, "Today one tribe has been cut off from Israel. ⁷What can we do about wives for the survivors, since we have sworn by the Lord not to give them any of our daughters in marriage?" ⁸And when they asked, "Is there one among the tribes of Israel who did not come up to the Lord in Mizpah?" they found

that none of the men of Jabesh-gilead had come to the encampment for the assembly. ⁹A roll call of the people was taken, and none of the inhabitants of Jabesh-gilead was present. ¹⁰So the assembly sent twelve thousand warriors there with orders, "Go put the inhabitants of Jabesh-gilead to the sword. ¹¹This is what you are to do: Every male and every woman who has had relations with a male you shall put under the ban." ¹²Finding among the inhabitants of Jabesh-gilead four hundred young virgin women, who had not had relations with a man, they brought them to the camp at Shiloh, in the land of Canaan. ¹³Then the whole assembly sent word to the Benjaminites at the crag of Rimmon, offering them peace. ¹⁴So Benjamin returned at that time, and they were given as wives the women of Jabesh-gilead who had been spared; but these proved to be not enough for them.

¹⁵The people had regrets about Benjamin because the Lord had made a breach among the tribes of Israel. ¹⁶The elders of the assembly said, "What shall we do for wives for the survivors? For the women of Benjamin have been annihilated." ¹⁷They said, "There must be heirs for the survivors of Benjamin, so that a tribe will not be wiped out from Israel. ¹⁸Yet we cannot give them any of our daughters in marriage." For the Israelites had taken an oath, "Cursed be he who gives a wife to Benjamin!" ¹⁹Then they thought of the yearly feast of the Lord at Shiloh, north of Bethel, east of the highway that goes up from Bethel to Shechem, and south of Lebonah. ²⁰And they instructed the Benjaminites, "Go and set an ambush in the vineyards. ²¹When you see the women of Shiloh come out to join in the dances, come out of the vineyards and catch a wife for each of you from the women of Shiloh; then go on to the land of Benjamin. ²²When their fathers or their brothers come to complain to us, we shall say to them, 'Release them to us as a kindness, since

we did not take a woman for every man in battle. Nor did you yourselves give your daughters to them, thus incurring guilt.'"

²³The Benjaminites did this; they carried off wives for each of them from the dancers they had seized, and they went back each to his own heritage, where they rebuilt the cities and settled them. ²⁴At that time the Israelites dispersed from there for their own tribes and clans; they set out from there each to his own heritage.

²⁵In those days there was no king in Israel; everyone did what was right in their own sight.

☐ 1 CORINTHIANS 7:25-40

Advice to Virgins and Widows. 7:25 Now in regard to virgins, I have no commandment from the Lord, but I give my opinion as one who by the Lord's mercy is trustworthy. ²⁶So this is what I think best because of the present distress: that it is a good thing for a person to remain as he is. ²⁷Are you bound to a wife? Do not seek a separation. Are you free of a wife? Then do not look for a wife. ²⁸If you marry, however, you do not sin, nor does an unmarried woman sin if she marries; but such people will experience affliction in their earthly life, and I would like to spare you that.

²⁹I tell you, brothers, the time is running out. From now on, let those having wives act as not having them, ³⁰those weeping as not weeping, those rejoicing as not rejoicing, those buying as not owning, ³¹those using the world as not using it fully. For the world in its present form is passing away.

³²I should like you to be free of anxieties. An unmarried man is anxious about the things of the Lord, how he may please the Lord. ³³But a married man is anxious about the things of the world, how he may please his wife, ³⁴and he is divided. An unmarried woman or a virgin is anxious about the things of the Lord, so that she may be holy in both body and spirit. A married woman, on the other hand, is anxious about the things of the world, how she may please her husband. ³⁵I am telling you this for your own benefit, not to impose a restraint upon you, but for the sake of propriety and adherence to the Lord without distraction.

³⁶If anyone thinks he is behaving improperly toward his virgin, and if a critical moment has come and so it has to be, let him do as he wishes. He is committing no sin; let them get married. ³⁷The one who stands firm in his resolve, however, who is not under compulsion but has power over his own will, and has made up his mind to keep his virgin, will be doing well. ³⁸So then, the one who marries his virgin does well; the one who does not marry her will do better.

³⁹A wife is bound to her husband as long as he lives. But if her husband dies, she is free to be married to whomever she wishes, provided that it be in the Lord. ⁴⁰She is more blessed, though, in my opinion, if she remains as she is, and I think that I too have the Spirit of God.

March 27

A small thing is not small when it leads to something great; and it is no small matter to forsake the ancient tradition of the Church that was upheld by all those who were called before us, whose conduct we should observe, and whose faith we should imitate.

— St. John of Damascus

☐ RUTH

Naomi in Moab. 1:1 Once back in the time of the judges there was a famine in the land; so a man from Bethlehem of Judah left home with his wife and two sons to reside on the plateau of Moab. ²The man was named Elimelech, his wife Naomi, and his sons Mahlon and Chilion; they were Ephrathites from Bethlehem of Judah. Some time after their arrival on the plateau of Moab, ³Elimelech, the husband of Naomi, died, and she was left with her two sons. ⁴They married Moabite women, one named Orpah, the other Ruth. When they had lived there about ten years, ⁵both Mahlon and Chilion died also, and the woman was left with neither her two boys nor her husband.

⁶She and her daughters-in-law then prepared to go back from the plateau of Moab because word had reached her there that the Lord had seen to his people's needs and given them food. ⁷She and her two daughters-in-law left the place where they had been living. On the road back to the land of Judah, ⁸Naomi said to her daughters-in-law, "Go back, each of you to your mother's house. May the Lord show you the same kindness as you have shown to the deceased and to me. ⁹May the Lord guide each of you to find a husband and a home in which you will be at rest." She kissed them good-bye, but they wept aloud, ¹⁰crying, "No! We will go back with you, to your people." ¹¹Naomi replied, "Go back, my daughters. Why come with me? Have I other sons in my womb who could become your husbands? ¹²Go, my daugh-

ters, for I am too old to marry again. Even if I had any such hope, or if tonight I had a husband and were to bear sons, ¹³would you wait for them and deprive yourselves of husbands until those sons grew up? No, my daughters, my lot is too bitter for you, because the Lord has extended his hand against me." ¹⁴Again they wept aloud; then Orpah kissed her mother-in-law good-bye, but Ruth clung to her.

¹⁵"See now," she said, "your sister-in-law has gone back to her people and her god. Go back after your sister-in-law!" ¹⁶But Ruth said, "Do not press me to go back and abandon you!

Wherever you go I will go,
    wherever you lodge I will lodge.
Your people shall be my people
    and your God, my God.
¹⁷Where you die I will die,
    and there be buried.

May the Lord do thus to me, and more, if even death separates me from you!" ¹⁸Naomi then ceased to urge her, for she saw she was determined to go with her.

The Return to Bethlehem. ¹⁹So they went on together until they reached Bethlehem. On their arrival there, the whole town was excited about them, and the women asked: "Can this be Naomi?" ²⁰But she said to them, "Do not call me Naomi ['Sweet']. Call me Mara ['Bitter'], for the Almighty has made my life very bitter. ²¹I went away full, but the Lord has brought me back empty. Why should you call me 'Sweet,' since the Lord has brought me to trial, and the Almighty has pronounced evil sentence on me." [22]Thus it was that Naomi came back with her Moabite daughter-in-law Ruth, who accompanied her back from the plateau of Moab. They arrived in Bethlehem at the beginning of the barley harvest.

The Meeting. 2:1 Naomi had a powerful relative named Boaz, through the clan of her husband Elimelech. [2]Ruth the Moabite said to Naomi, "I would like to go and glean grain in the field of anyone who will allow me." Naomi said to her, "Go ahead, my daughter." [3]So she went. The field she entered to glean after the harvesters happened to be the section belonging to Boaz, of the clan of Elimelech. [4]Soon, along came Boaz from Bethlehem and said to the harvesters, "The LORD be with you," and they replied, "The LORD bless you." [5]Boaz asked the young man overseeing his harvesters, "Whose young woman is this?" [6]The young man overseeing the harvesters answered, "She is the young Moabite who came back with Naomi from the plateau of Moab. [7]She said, 'I would like to gather the gleanings into sheaves after the harvesters.' Ever since she came this morning she has remained here until now, with scarcely a moment's rest."

[8]Boaz then spoke to Ruth, "Listen, my daughter. Do not go to glean in anyone else's field; you are not to leave here. Stay here with my young women. [9]Watch to see which field is to be harvested, and follow them. Have I not commanded the young men to do you no harm? When you are thirsty, go and drink from the vessels the young people have filled." [10]Casting herself prostrate upon the ground, she said to him, "Why should I, a foreigner, be favored with your attention?" [11]Boaz answered her: "I have had a complete account of what you have done for your mother-in-law after your husband's death; you have left your father and your mother and the land of your birth, and have come to a people whom previously you did not know. [12]May

the LORD reward what you have done! May you receive a full reward from the LORD, the God of Israel, under whose wings you have come for refuge." [13]She said, "May I prove worthy of your favor, my lord. You have comforted me. You have spoken to the heart of your servant—and I am not even one of your servants!" [14]At mealtime Boaz said to her, "Come here and have something to eat; dip your bread in the sauce." Then as she sat near the harvesters, he handed her some roasted grain and she ate her fill and had some left over. [15]As she rose to glean, Boaz instructed his young people: "Let her glean among the sheaves themselves without scolding her, [16]and even drop some handfuls and leave them for her to glean; do not rebuke her."

[17]She gleaned in the field until evening, and when she beat out what she had gleaned it came to about an ephah of barley, [18]which she took into the town and showed to her mother-in-law. Next she brought out what she had left over from the meal and gave it to her. [19]So her mother-in-law said to her, "Where did you glean today? Where did you go to work? May the one who took notice of you be blessed!" Then she told her mother-in-law with whom she had worked. "The man at whose place I worked today is named Boaz," she said. [20]"May he be blessed by the LORD, who never fails to show kindness to the living and to the dead," Naomi exclaimed to her daughter-in-law. She continued, "This man is a near relative of ours, one of our redeemers." [21]"He even told me," added Ruth the Moabite, "Stay with my young people until they complete my entire harvest." [22]"You would do well, my daughter," Naomi rejoined, "to work with his young women; in someone else's field you might be insulted." [23]So she stayed gleaning with Boaz's young women until the end of the barley and wheat harvests.

Ruth Again Presents Herself. When Ruth was back with her mother-in-law, **3:1**

Naomi said to her, "My daughter, should I not be seeking a pleasing home for you? [2]Now! Is not Boaz, whose young women you were working with, a relative of ours? This very night he will be winnowing barley at the threshing floor. [3]Now, go bathe and anoint yourself; then put on your best attire and go down to the threshing floor. Do not make yourself known to the man before he has finished eating and drinking. [4]But when he lies down, take note of the place where he lies; then go uncover a place at his feet and you lie down. He will then tell you what to do." [5]"I will do whatever you say," Ruth replied. [6]She went down to the threshing floor and did just as her mother-in-law had instructed her.

[7]Boaz ate and drank to his heart's content, and went to lie down at the edge of the pile of grain. She crept up, uncovered a place at his feet, and lay down. [8]Midway through the night, the man gave a start and groped about, only to find a woman lying at his feet. [9]"Who are you?" he asked. She replied, "I am your servant Ruth. Spread the wing of your cloak over your servant, for you are a redeemer." [10]He said, "May the LORD bless you, my daughter! You have been even more loyal now than before in not going after the young men, whether poor or rich. [11]Now rest assured, my daughter, I will do for you whatever you say; all my townspeople know you to be a worthy woman. [12]Now, I am in fact a redeemer, but there is another redeemer closer than I. [13]Stay where you are for tonight, and tomorrow, if he will act as redeemer for you, good. But if he will not, as the LORD lives, I will do it myself. Lie there until morning." [14]So she lay at his feet until morning, but rose before anyone could recognize another, for Boaz had said, "Let it not be known that this woman came to the threshing floor." [15]Then he said to her, "Take off the shawl you are wearing; hold it firmly." When she did so, he poured out six measures of barley and helped her lift the bundle; then he himself left for the town.

[16]She, meanwhile, went home to her mother-in-law, who asked, "How did things go, my daughter?" So she told her all the man had done for her, [17]and concluded, "He gave me these six measures of barley and said, 'Do not go back to your mother-in-law empty.'" [18]Naomi then said, "Wait here, my daughter, until you learn what happens, for the man will not rest, but will settle the matter today."

Boaz Marries Ruth. 4:1 Boaz went to the gate and took a seat there. Along came the other redeemer of whom he had spoken. Boaz called to him by name, "Come, sit here." And he did so. [2]Then Boaz picked out ten of the elders of the town and asked them to sit nearby. When they had done this, [3]he said to the other redeemer: "Naomi, who has come back from the plateau of Moab, is putting up for sale the piece of land that belonged to our kinsman Elimelech. [4]So I thought I would inform you. Before those here present, including the elders of my people, purchase the field; act as redeemer. But if you do not want to do it, tell me so, that I may know, for no one has a right of redemption prior to yours, and mine is next." He answered, "I will act as redeemer."

[5]Boaz continued, "When you acquire the field from Naomi, you also acquire responsibility for Ruth the Moabite, the widow of the late heir, to raise up a family for the deceased on his estate." [6]The redeemer replied, "I cannot exercise my right of redemption for that would endanger my own estate. You do it in my place, for I cannot." [7]Now it used to be the custom in Israel that, to make binding a contract of redemption or exchange, one party would take off a sandal and give it to the other. This was the form of attestation in Israel. [8]So the other redeemer, in saying to Boaz, "Acquire it for yourself," drew off his sandal. [9]Boaz then said to the elders and to all the people, "You are witnesses today that I

have acquired from Naomi all the holdings of Elimelech, Chilion and Mahlon. [10]I also acquire Ruth the Moabite, the widow of Mahlon, as my wife, in order to raise up a family for her late husband on his estate, so that the name of the deceased may not perish from his people and his place. Do you witness this today?" [11]All those at the gate, including the elders, said, "We do. May the LORD make this woman come into your house like Rachel and Leah, who between them built up the house of Israel. Prosper in Ephrathah! Bestow a name in Bethlehem! [12]With the offspring the LORD will give you from this young woman, may your house become like the house of Perez, whom Tamar bore to Judah."

[13]Boaz took Ruth. When they came together as husband and wife, the LORD enabled her to conceive and she bore a son. [14]Then the women said to Naomi, "Blessed is the LORD who has not failed to provide you today with a redeemer. May he become famous in Israel! [15]He will restore your life and be the support of your old age, for his mother is the daughter-in-law who loves you. She is worth more to you than seven sons!" [16]Naomi took the boy, cradled him against her breast, and cared for him. [17]The neighbor women joined the celebration: "A son has been born to Naomi!" They named him Obed. He was the father of Jesse, the father of David.

[18]These are the descendants of Perez: Perez was the father of Hezron, [19]Hezron was the father of Ram, Ram was the father of Amminadab, [20]Amminadab was the father of Nahshon, Nahshon was the father of Salma, [21]Salma was the father of Boaz, Boaz was the father of Obed, [22]Obed was the father of Jesse, and Jesse became the father of David.

☐ 1 CORINTHIANS 8

Knowledge Insufficient. 8:1 Now in regard to meat sacrificed to idols: we realize that "all of us have knowledge"; knowledge inflates with pride, but love builds up. [2]If anyone supposes he knows something, he does not yet know as he ought to know. [3]But if one loves God, one is known by him.

[4]So about the eating of meat sacrificed to idols: we know that "there is no idol in the world," and that "there is no God but one." [5]Indeed, even though there are so-called gods in heaven and on earth (there are, to be sure, many "gods" and many "lords"), [6]yet for us there is

one God, the Father,
from whom all things are and for
whom we exist,
and one Lord, Jesus Christ,
through whom all things are and
through whom we exist.

Practical Rules. [7]But not all have this knowledge. There are some who have been so used to idolatry up until now that, when they eat meat sacrificed to idols, their conscience, which is weak, is defiled.

[8]Now food will not bring us closer to God. We are no worse off if we do not eat, nor are we better off if we do. [9]But make sure that this liberty of yours in no way becomes a stumbling block to the weak. [10]If someone sees you, with your knowledge, reclining at table in the temple of an idol, may not his conscience too, weak as it is, be "built up" to eat the meat sacrificed to idols? [11]Thus through your knowledge, the weak person is brought to destruction, the brother for whom Christ died. [12]When you sin in this way against your brothers and wound their consciences, weak as they are, you are sinning against Christ. [13]Therefore, if food causes my brother to sin, I will never eat meat again, so that I may not cause my brother to sin.

March 28

When I see the need for divine teaching and how hungry people are to hear it, I tremble to be off and running throughout the world, preaching the Word of God. I have no rest, my soul finds no other relief, than to rush about and preach.

— St. Anthony Mary Claret

☐ 1 SAMUEL 1-2

Elkanah and His Family at Shiloh. 1:1 There was a certain man from Ramathaim, a Zuphite from the hill country of Ephraim. His name was Elkanah, the son of Jeroham, son of Elihu, son of Tohu, son of Zuph, an Ephraimite. [2]He had two wives, one named Hannah, the other Peninnah; Peninnah had children, but Hannah had no children. [3]Each year this man went up from his city to worship and offer sacrifice to the Lord of hosts at Shiloh, where the two sons of Eli, Hophni and Phinehas, were ministering as priests of the Lord. [4]When the day came for Elkanah to offer sacrifice, he used to give portions to his wife Peninnah and to all her sons and daughters, [5]but he would give a double portion to Hannah because he loved her, though the Lord had closed her womb. [6]Her rival, to upset her, would torment her constantly, since the Lord had closed her womb. [7]Year after year, when she went up to the house of the Lord, Peninnah would provoke her, and Hannah would weep and refuse to eat. [8]Elkanah, her husband, would say to her: "Hannah, why are you weeping? Why are you not eating? Why are you so miserable? Am I not better for you than ten sons?"

Hannah's Prayer. [9]Hannah rose after one such meal at Shiloh, and presented herself before the Lord; at the time Eli the priest was sitting on a chair near the doorpost of the Lord's temple. [10]In her bitterness she prayed to the Lord, weeping freely, [11]and made this vow: "O Lord of hosts, if you look with pity on the hardship of your servant, if you remember me and do not forget me, if you give your handmaid a male child, I will give him to the Lord all the days of his life. No razor shall ever touch his head." [12]As she continued praying before the Lord, Eli watched her mouth, [13]for Hannah was praying silently; though her lips were moving, her voice could not be heard. Eli, thinking she was drunk, [14]said to her, "How long will you make a drunken spectacle of yourself? Sober up from your wine!" [15]"No, my lord!" Hannah answered. "I am an unhappy woman. I have had neither wine nor liquor; I was only pouring out my heart to the Lord. [16]Do not think your servant a worthless woman; my prayer has been prompted by my deep sorrow and misery." [17]Eli said, "Go in peace, and may the God of Israel grant you what you have requested." [18]She replied, "Let your servant find favor in your eyes," and left. She went to her quarters, ate and drank with her husband, and no longer appeared downhearted. [19]Early the next morning they worshiped before the Lord, and then returned to their home in Ramah. When they returned Elkanah had intercourse with his wife Hannah, and the Lord remembered her.

Hannah Bears a Son. [20]She conceived and, at the end of her pregnancy, bore a son whom she named Samuel. "Because I asked the Lord for him. [21]The next time her husband Elkanah was going up with the rest of his household to offer the customary sacrifice to the Lord and to fulfill his vows, [22]Hannah did not go, explaining to her husband, "Once the child is weaned,

I will take him to appear before the Lord and leave him there forever." [23]Her husband Elkanah answered her: "Do what you think best; wait until you have weaned him. Only may the Lord fulfill his word!" And so she remained at home and nursed her son until she had weaned him.

Hannah Presents Samuel to the Lord. [24]Once he was weaned, she brought him up with her, along with a three-year-old bull, an ephah of flour, and a skin of wine, and presented him at the house of the Lord in Shiloh. [25]After they had slaughtered the bull, they brought the child to Eli. [26]Then Hannah spoke up: "Excuse me, my lord! As you live, my lord, I am the woman who stood here near you, praying to the Lord. [27]I prayed for this child, and the Lord granted my request. [28]Now I, in turn, give him to the Lord; as long as he lives, he shall be dedicated to the Lord." Then they worshiped there before the Lord.

2:1 And Hannah prayed:

"My heart exults in the Lord,
my horn is exalted by my God.
I have swallowed up my enemies;
I rejoice in your victory.
[2]There is no Holy One like the Lord;
there is no Rock like our God.
[3]Speak boastfully no longer,
Do not let arrogance issue from
your mouths.
For an all-knowing God is the Lord,
a God who weighs actions.
[4]"The bows of the mighty are broken,
while the tottering gird on strength.
[5]The well-fed hire themselves out for
bread,
while the hungry no longer have to
toil.
The barren wife bears seven sons,
while the mother of many
languishes.
[6]"The Lord puts to death and gives
life,

casts down to Sheol and brings up
again.
[7]The Lord makes poor and makes rich,
humbles, and also exalts.
[8]He raises the needy from the dust;
from the ash heap lifts up the poor,
To seat them with nobles
and make a glorious throne their
heritage.

"For the pillars of the earth are the
Lord's,
and he has set the world upon
them.
[9]He guards the footsteps of his faithful
ones,
but the wicked shall perish in the
darkness;
for not by strength does one prevail.
[10]The Lord's foes shall be shattered;
the Most High in heaven thunders;
the Lord judges the ends of the
earth.
May he give strength to his king,
and exalt the horn of his anointed!"

[11]When Elkanah returned home to Ramah, the child remained in the service of the Lord under the priest Eli.

Wickedness of Eli's Sons. [12]Now the sons of Eli were wicked; they had respect neither for the Lord [13]nor for the priests' duties toward the people. When someone offered a sacrifice, the priest's servant would come with a three-pronged fork, while the meat was still boiling, [14]and would thrust it into the basin, kettle, caldron, or pot. Whatever the fork brought up, the priest would take for himself. They treated all the Israelites who came to the sanctuary at Shiloh in this way. [15]In fact, even before the fat was burned, the priest's servant would come and say to the one offering the sacrifice, "Give me some meat to roast for the priest. He will not accept boiled meat from you, only raw meat." [16]And if this one protested, "Let the fat be burned first, then take whatever you wish," he would reply, "No, give it to me now, or else I will take it by force." ¹⁷Thus the young men sinned grievously in the presence of the LORD, treating the offerings to the LORD with disdain.

The Lord Rewards Hannah. ¹⁸Meanwhile the boy Samuel, wearing a linen ephod, was serving in the presence of the LORD. ¹⁹His mother used to make a little garment for him, which she would bring him each time she went up with her husband to offer the customary sacrifice. ²⁰And Eli would bless Elkanah and his wife, as they were leaving for home. He would say, "May the LORD repay you with children from this woman for the gift she has made to the LORD!" ²¹The LORD favored Hannah so that she conceived and gave birth to three more sons and two daughters, while young Samuel grew up in the service of the LORD.

Eli's Futile Rebuke. ²²When Eli was very old, he kept hearing how his sons were treating all Israel, and that they were behaving promiscuously with the women serving at the entry of the meeting tent. ²³So he said to them: "Why are you doing such things? I hear from everyone that your behavior is depraved. ²⁴Stop this, my sons! The report that I hear the LORD's people spreading is not good. ²⁵If someone sins against another, anyone can intercede for the sinner with the LORD; but if anyone sins against the LORD, who can intercede for the sinner?" But they disregarded their father's warning, since the LORD wanted them dead. ²⁶Meanwhile, young Samuel was growing in stature and in worth in the estimation of the LORD and the people.

The Fate of Eli's House. ²⁷A man of God came to Eli and said to him: "Thus says the LORD: I went so far as to reveal myself to your father's house when they were in Egypt as slaves to the house of Pharaoh. ²⁸I chose them out of all the tribes of Israel to be my priests, to go up to my altar, to burn incense, and to wear the ephod in my presence; and I assigned all the fire offerings of the Israelites to your father's house. ²⁹Why do you stare greedily at my sacrifices and at the offerings that I have prescribed? Why do you honor your sons more than you honor me, fattening yourselves with the choicest part of every offering of my people Israel? ³⁰This, therefore, is the oracle of the LORD, the God of Israel: I said in the past that your family and your father's house should minister in my presence forever. But now—oracle of the LORD: Far be it from me! I will honor those who honor me, but those who despise me shall be cursed. ³¹Yes, the days are coming when I will break your strength and the strength of your father's house, so that no one in your family lives to old age. ³²You shall witness, like a disappointed rival, all the benefits enjoyed by Israel, but no member of your household shall ever grow old. ³³I will leave you one man at my altar to wear out his eyes and waste his strength, but the rest of your family shall die by the sword. ³⁴This is a sign for you—what happens to your two sons, Hophni and Phinehas. Both of them will die on the same day. ³⁵I will choose a faithful priest who shall do what I have in heart and mind. I will establish a lasting house for him and he shall serve in the presence of my anointed forever. ³⁶Then whoever is left of your family will grovel before him for a piece of silver or a loaf of bread, saying: Please assign me a priestly function, that I may have a crust of bread to eat."

☐ 1 CORINTHIANS 9:1-18

Paul's Rights as an Apostle. 9:1 Am I not free? Am I not an apostle? Have I not seen Jesus our Lord? Are you not my work in the Lord? [2]Although I may not be an apostle for others, certainly I am for you, for you are the seal of my apostleship in the Lord.

[3]My defense against those who would pass judgment on me is this. [4]Do we not have the right to eat and drink? [5]Do we not have the right to take along a Christian wife, as do the rest of the apostles, and the brothers of the Lord, and Cephas? [6]Or is it only myself and Barnabas who do not have the right not to work? [7]Who ever serves as a soldier at his own expense? Who plants a vineyard without eating its produce? Or who shepherds a flock without using some of the milk from the flock? [8]Am I saying this on human authority, or does not the law also speak of these things? [9]It is written in the law of Moses, "You shall not muzzle an ox while it is treading out the grain." Is God concerned about oxen, [10]or is he not really speaking for our sake? It was written for our sake, because the plowman should plow in hope, and the thresher in hope of receiving a share. [11]If we have sown spiri-tual seed for you, is it a great thing that we reap a material harvest from you? [12]If others share this rightful claim on you, do not we still more?

Reason for Not Using His Rights. Yet we have not used this right. On the contrary, we endure everything so as not to place an obstacle to the gospel of Christ. [13]Do you not know that those who perform the temple services eat [what] belongs to the temple, and those who minister at the altar share in the sacrificial offerings? [14]In the same way, the Lord ordered that those who preach the gospel should live by the gospel.

[15]I have not used any of these rights, however, nor do I write this that it be done so in my case. I would rather die. Certainly no one is going to nullify my boast. [16]If I preach the gospel, this is no reason for me to boast, for an obligation has been imposed on me, and woe to me if I do not preach it! [17]If I do so willingly, I have a recompense, but if unwillingly, then I have been entrusted with a stewardship. [18]What then is my recompense? That, when I preach, I offer the gospel free of charge so as not to make full use of my right in the gospel.

March 29

The Lord gives a man grace of speech in proportion to the sincerity with which his audience wishes to hear him.

— St. Moses the Black

☐ 1 SAMUEL 3-4

Revelation to Samuel. 3:1 During the time young Samuel was minister to the LORD under Eli, the word of the LORD was scarce and vision infrequent. [2]One day Eli was asleep in his usual place. His eyes had lately grown so weak that he could not see. [3]The lamp of God was not yet extinguished, and Samuel was sleeping in the temple of the LORD where the ark of God was. [4]The LORD called to Samuel, who answered, "Here I am." [5]He ran to Eli and said, "Here I am. You called me." "I did not call you," Eli answered. "Go back to sleep." So he went back to sleep. [6]Again the LORD called Samuel, who rose and went to Eli. "Here I am," he said. "You called me." But he answered, "I did not call you, my son. Go back to sleep."

[7]Samuel did not yet recognize the LORD, since the word of the LORD had not yet been revealed to him. [8]The LORD called Samuel again, for the third time. Getting up and going to Eli, he said, "Here I am. You called me." Then Eli understood that the LORD was calling the youth. [9]So he said to Samuel, "Go to sleep, and if you are called, reply, 'Speak, LORD, for your servant is listening.'" When Samuel went to sleep in his place, [10]the LORD came and stood there, calling out as before: Samuel, Samuel! Samuel answered, "Speak, for your servant is listening." [11]The LORD said to Samuel: I am about to do something in Israel that will make the ears of everyone who hears it ring. [12]On that day I will carry out against Eli everything I have said about his house, beginning to end. [13]I announce to him that I am condemning his house once and for all, because of this crime: though he knew his sons were blaspheming God, he did not reprove them. [14]Therefore, I swear to Eli's house: No sacrifice or offering will ever expiate its crime. [15]Samuel then slept until morning, when he got up early and opened the doors of the temple of the LORD. He was afraid to tell Eli the vision, [16]but Eli called to him, "Samuel, my son!" He replied, "Here I am." [17]Then Eli asked, "What did he say to you? Hide nothing from me! May God do thus to you, and more, if you hide from me a single thing he told you." [18]So Samuel told him everything, and held nothing back. Eli answered, "It is the LORD. What is pleasing in the LORD's sight, the LORD will do."

Samuel Acknowledged as Prophet. [19]Samuel grew up, and the LORD was with him, not permitting any word of his to go unfulfilled. [20]Thus all Israel from Dan to Beer-sheba came to know that Samuel was a trustworthy prophet of the LORD. [21]The LORD continued to appear at Shiloh, manifesting himself to Samuel at Shiloh through his word. Samuel's word spread throughout Israel.

Defeat of the Israelites. 4:1 At that time, the Philistines gathered for an attack on Israel. Israel went out to engage them in battle and camped at Ebenezer, while the Philistines camped at Aphek. [2]The Philistines then drew up in battle formation against Israel. After a fierce struggle Israel was defeated by the Philistines, who killed about four thousand men on the battlefield. [3]When the troops retired to the camp, the elders of Israel said, "Why has the LORD permitted us to be defeated today by the Philistines? Let us fetch the ark of the LORD from Shiloh that it may go into battle among us and save us from the grasp of our enemies."

Loss of the Ark. [4]So the people sent to Shiloh and brought from there the ark of the LORD of hosts, who is enthroned upon the cherubim. The two sons of Eli, Hophni and Phinehas, accompanied the ark of God. [5]When the ark of the LORD arrived in the camp, all Israel shouted so loudly that the earth shook. [6]The Philistines, hearing the uproar, asked, "What does this loud shouting in the camp of the Hebrews mean?" On learning that the ark of the LORD had come into the camp, [7]the Philistines were frightened, crying out, "Gods have come to their camp. Woe to us! This has never happened before. [8]Woe to us! Who can deliver us from the power of these mighty gods? These are the gods who struck the Egyptians with various plagues in the desert. [9]Take courage and act like soldiers, Philistines; otherwise you will become slaves to the Hebrews, as they were your slaves. Fight like soldiers!" [10]The

Philistines fought and Israel was defeated; everyone fled to their own tents. It was a disastrous defeat; Israel lost thirty thousand foot soldiers. [11]The ark of God was captured, and Eli's two sons, Hophni and Phinehas, were dead.

Death of Eli. [12]A Benjaminite fled from the battlefield and reached Shiloh that same day, with his clothes torn and his head covered with dirt. [13]When he arrived, Eli was sitting in his chair beside the gate, watching the road, for he was troubled at heart about the ark of God. The man, however, went into the city to announce his news; then the whole city cried out. [14]When Eli heard the uproar, he wondered why there was such commotion. Just then the man rushed up to inform him. [15]Eli was ninety-eight years old, and his eyes would not focus. So he could not see. [16]The man said to Eli: "I have come from the battlefield; today I fled from there." He asked, "What happened, my son?" [17]And the messenger answered: "Israel fled from the Philistines; in fact, the troops suffered heavy losses. Your two sons, Hophni and Phinehas, are dead, and the ark of God has been captured." [18]At this mention of the ark of God, Eli fell backward from his chair into the gateway; he died of a broken neck since he was an old man and heavy. He had judged Israel for forty years.

[19]His daughter-in-law, the wife of Phinehas, was pregnant and about to give birth. When she heard the news about the capture of the ark of God and the deaths of her father-in-law and her husband, she crouched down in labor, and gave birth. [20]She was about to die when the women standing around her said to her, "Do not be afraid, you have given birth to a son." Yet she neither answered nor paid any attention. [21]She named the child Ichabod, saying, "Gone is the glory from Israel," referring to the capture of the ark of God and to her father-in-law and her husband. [22]She said, "Gone is the glory from Israel," because the ark of God had been captured.

☐ 1 CORINTHIANS 9:19-27

All Things to All. 9:19 Although I am free in regard to all, I have made myself a slave to all so as to win over as many as possible. [20]To the Jews I became like a Jew to win over Jews; to those under the law I became like one under the law—though I myself am not under the law—to win over those under the law. [21]To those outside the law I became like one outside the law—though I am not outside God's law but within the law of Christ—to win over those outside the law. [22]To the weak I became weak, to win over the weak. I have become all things to all, to save at least some. [23]All this I do for the sake of the gospel, so that I too may have a share in it.

[24]Do you not know that the runners in the stadium all run in the race, but only one wins the prize? Run so as to win. [25]Every athlete exercises discipline in every way. They do it to win a perishable crown, but we an imperishable one. [26]Thus I do not run aimlessly; I do not fight as if I were shadowboxing. [27]No, I drive my body and train it, for fear that, after having preached to others, I myself should be disqualified.

March 30

St. John Climacus

A tool that is in good condition may sharpen one that is not in good condition, and a fervent brother may save the person who is only lukewarm about his faith.

— St. John Climacus

☐ 1 SAMUEL 5-7

The Ark in the Temple of Dagon. 5:1 The Philistines, having captured the ark of God, transferred it from Ebenezer to Ashdod. ²They then took the ark of God and brought it into the temple of Dagon, placing it beside Dagon. ³When the people of Ashdod rose early the next morning, Dagon was lying face down on the ground before the ark of the Lord. So they picked Dagon up and put him back in his place. ⁴But early the next morning, when they arose, Dagon lay face down on the ground before the ark of the Lord, his head and hands broken off and lying on the threshold, his trunk alone intact. ⁵For this reason, neither the priests of Dagon nor any others who enter the temple of Dagon tread on the threshold of Dagon in Ashdod to this very day.

The Ark Is Carried About. ⁶Now the hand of the Lord weighed heavily on the people of Ashdod, ravaging them and afflicting the city and its vicinity with tumors. ⁷On seeing how matters stood, the people of Ashdod decided, "The ark of the God of Israel must not remain with us, for his hand weighs heavily on us and Dagon our god." ⁸So they summoned all the Philistine leaders and inquired of them, "What shall we do with the ark of the God of Israel?" The people of Gath replied, "Let them move the ark of the God of Israel to us." So they moved the ark of the God of Israel to Gath. ⁹But after it had been brought there, the hand of the Lord was against the city, resulting in utter turmoil: the Lord afflicted its inhabitants, young and old, and tumors broke out on them. ¹⁰The ark of God was next sent to Ekron; but as it entered that city, the people there cried out, "Why have they brought the ark of the God of Israel here to kill us and our kindred?" ¹¹Then they, too, sent a summons to all the Philistine leaders and pleaded: "Send away the ark of the God of Israel. Send it back to its place so it does not kill us and our kindred." A deadly panic had seized the whole city, since the hand of God lay heavy upon it. ¹²Those who escaped death were afflicted with tumors. Thus the outcry from the city went up to the heavens.

The Ark Is Returned. 6:1 The ark of the Lord had been in the land of the Philistines seven months ²when they summoned priests and diviners to ask, "What shall we do with the ark of the Lord? Tell us what we should send back with it." ³They replied: "If you intend to send back the ark of the God of Israel, you must not send it alone, but must, by all means, make amends to God through a reparation offering. Then you will be healed, and will learn why God continues to afflict you." ⁴When asked further, "What reparation offering should be our amends to God?" they replied: "Five golden tumors and five golden mice to correspond to the number of Philistine leaders, since the same plague has struck all of you and your leaders. ⁵Therefore, make images of the tumors and of the mice that are devastating your land and so give glory to the God of Israel. Perhaps then God will lift his hand from you, your gods, and your land. ⁶Why should you become stubborn, the way the Egyptians and Pharaoh were stubborn? Was it not after he had dealt ruthlessly with them that the Israelites were released and departed? ⁷So now set to work and make a new cart. Then take two milk cows that have not borne the yoke; hitch them to the cart, but drive their calves indoors away from them. ⁸You shall next take the ark of the LORD and place it on the cart, putting the golden articles that you are offering as reparation for your guilt in a box beside it. Start it on its way, and let it go. ⁹Then watch! If it goes up to Beth-shemesh along the route to the LORD's territory, then it was the LORD who brought this great calamity upon us; if not, we will know that it was not the LORD's hand, but a bad turn, that struck us."

The Ark in Beth-shemesh. ¹⁰They acted upon this advice. Taking two milk cows, they hitched them to the cart but shut up their calves indoors. ¹¹Then they placed the ark of the LORD on the cart, along with the box containing the golden mice and the images of the tumors. ¹²The cows went straight for the route to Beth-shemesh and continued along this road, mooing as they went, turning neither right nor left. The Philistine leaders followed them as far as the border of Beth-shemesh. ¹³The people of Beth-shemesh were harvesting the wheat in the valley. They looked up and rejoiced when they saw the ark. ¹⁴The cart came to the field of Joshua the Beth-shemite and stopped there. At a large stone in the field, the wood of the cart was split up and the cows were offered as a burnt offering to the LORD. ¹⁵The Levites, meanwhile, had taken down the ark of God and the box beside it, with the golden articles, and had placed them on the great stone. The people of Beth-shemesh also offered other burnt offerings and sacrifices to the LORD that day. ¹⁶After witnessing this, the five Philistine leaders returned to Ekron the same day.

¹⁷The golden tumors the Philistines sent back as a reparation offering to the LORD were as follows: one for Ashdod, one for Gaza, one for Ashkelon, one for Gath, and one for Ekron. ¹⁸The golden mice, however, corresponded to the number of all the cities of the Philistines belonging to the five leaders, including fortified cities and open villages. The large stone on which the ark of the LORD was placed is still in the field of Joshua the Beth-shemite at the present time.

Penalty for Irreverence. ¹⁹The descendants of Jeconiah did not join in the celebration with the inhabitants of Beth-shemesh when they saw the ark of the LORD, and seventy of them were struck down. The people mourned over this great calamity which the LORD had inflicted upon them. ²⁰The men of Beth-shemesh asked, "Who can stand in the presence of the LORD, this Holy God? To whom can the ark go so that we are rid of it?" ²¹They then sent messengers to the inhabitants of Kiriath-jearim, saying, "The Philistines have returned the ark of the LORD; come down and get it."

7:1 So the inhabitants of Kiriath-jearim came for the ark of the LORD and brought it into the house of Abinadab on the hill, appointing his son Eleazar as guardian of the ark of the LORD.

Samuel the Judge. ²From the day the ark came to rest in Kiriath-jearim, a long time, twenty years, elapsed, and the whole house of Israel turned to the LORD. ³Then Samuel addressed the whole house of Israel: "If you would return to the LORD with your whole heart, remove your foreign gods and your Astartes, fix your hearts on the LORD, and serve him alone, then the LORD will deliver you from the hand of the Philistines." ⁴So the Israelites removed their Baals and Astartes, and served the LORD alone. ⁵Samuel then gave orders, "Gather all Israel to Mizpah, that I may pray to the

LORD for you." [6]When they had gathered at Mizpah, they drew water and poured it out on the ground before the LORD, and they fasted that day, saying, "We have sinned against the LORD." It was at Mizpah that Samuel began to judge the Israelites.

Rout of the Philistines. [7]When the Philistines heard that the Israelites had gathered at Mizpah, their leaders went up against Israel. Hearing this, the Israelites became afraid of the Philistines [8]and appealed to Samuel, "Do not stop crying out to the LORD our God for us, to save us from the hand of the Philistines." [9]Samuel therefore took an unweaned lamb and offered it whole as a burnt offering to the LORD. He cried out to the LORD for Israel, and the LORD answered him. [10]While Samuel was sacrificing the burnt offering, the Philistines drew near for battle with Israel. That day, however, the LORD thundered loudly against the Philistines, and threw them into such confusion that they were defeated by Israel. [11]Thereupon the Israelites rushed out from Mizpah and pursued the Philistines, striking them down even beyond Beth-car. [12]Samuel then took a stone and placed it between Mizpah and Jeshanah; he named it Ebenezer, explaining, "As far as this place the LORD has been our help." [13]Thus were the Philistines subdued, never again to enter the territory of Israel, for the hand of the LORD was against them as long as Samuel lived. [14]The cities from Ekron to Gath which the Philistines had taken from Israel were restored to them. Israel also freed the territory of these cities from Philistine domination. There was also peace between Israel and the Amorites.

[15]Samuel judged Israel as long as he lived. [16]He made a yearly circuit, passing through Bethel, Gilgal and Mizpah and judging Israel at each of these places. [17]Then he used to return to Ramah, for that was his home. There, too, he judged Israel and built an altar to the LORD.

☐ 1 CORINTHIANS 10

Warning against Overconfidence. 10:1 I do not want you to be unaware, brothers, that our ancestors were all under the cloud and all passed through the sea, [2]and all of them were baptized into Moses in the cloud and in the sea. [3]All ate the same spiritual food, [4]and all drank the same spiritual drink, for they drank from a spiritual rock that followed them, and the rock was the Christ. [5]Yet God was not pleased with most of them, for they were struck down in the desert.

[6]These things happened as examples for us, so that we might not desire evil things, as they did. [7]And do not become idolaters, as some of them did, as it is written, "The people sat down to eat and drink, and rose up to revel." [8]Let us not indulge in immorality as some of them did, and twenty-three thousand fell within a single day. [9]Let us not test Christ as some of them did, and suffered death by serpents. [10]Do not grumble as some of them did, and suffered death by the destroyer. [11]These things happened to them as an example, and they have been written down as a warning to us, upon whom the end of the ages has come. [12]Therefore, whoever thinks he is standing secure should take care not to fall. [13]No trial has come to you but what is human. God is faithful and will not let you be tried beyond your strength; but with the trial he will also provide a way out, so that you may be able to bear it.

Warning against Idolatry. [14]Therefore, my beloved, avoid idolatry. [15]I am speaking as to sensible people; judge for yourselves what I am saying. [16]The cup of blessing that we bless, is it not a participation in the blood of Christ? The bread that we break, is it not a participation in the body of Christ? [17]Because the loaf of bread is one, we, though many, are one body, for we all partake of the one loaf.

[18]Look at Israel according to the flesh; are not those who eat the sacrifices participants in the altar? [19]So what am I saying? That meat sacrificed to idols is anything? Or that an idol is anything? [20]No, I mean that what they sacrifice, [they sacrifice] to demons, not to God, and I do not want you to become participants with demons. [21]You cannot drink the cup of the Lord and also the cup of demons. You cannot partake of the table of the Lord and of the table of demons. [22]Or are we provoking the Lord to jealous anger? Are we stronger than he?

Seek the Good of Others. [23]"Everything is lawful," but not everything is beneficial. "Everything is lawful," but not everything builds up. [24]No one should seek his own advantage, but that of his neighbor. [25]Eat anything sold in the market, without raising questions on grounds of conscience, [26]for "the earth and its fullness are the Lord's." [27]If an unbeliever invites you and you want to go, eat whatever is placed before you, without raising questions on grounds of conscience. [28]But if someone says to you, "This was offered in sacrifice," do not eat it on account of the one who called attention to it and on account of conscience; [29]I mean not your own conscience, but the other's. For why should my freedom be determined by someone else's conscience? [30]If I partake thankfully, why am I reviled for that over which I give thanks?

[31]So whether you eat or drink, or whatever you do, do everything for the glory of God. [32]Avoid giving offense, whether to Jews or Greeks or the church of God, [33]just as I try to please everyone in every way, not seeking my own benefit but that of the many, that they may be saved.

March 31

Since Christ himself, then, has declared and said of the Bread, "This is My Body," who will dare any longer to doubt? And when He himself has affirmed and said, "This is My Blood," who can ever hesitate and say it is not His Blood?

— St. Cyril of Jerusalem

☐ 1 SAMUEL 8–10

Request for a King. 8:1 In his old age Samuel appointed his sons judges over Israel. [2]His firstborn was named Joel, his second son, Abijah; they judged at Beersheba. [3]His sons did not follow his example, but looked to their own gain, accepting bribes and perverting justice. [4]Therefore all the elders of Israel assembled and went to Samuel at Ramah [5]and said to him, "Now that you are old, and your sons do not follow your example, appoint a king over us, like all the nations, to rule us."

[6]Samuel was displeased when they said, "Give us a king to rule us." But he prayed to the Lord. [7]The Lord said: Listen to whatever the people say. You are not the one they are rejecting. They are rejecting me as their king. [8]They are acting toward you just as they have acted from the day I brought them up from Egypt to this very day, deserting me

to serve other gods. ⁹Now listen to them; but at the same time, give them a solemn warning and inform them of the rights of the king who will rule them.

The Governance of the King. ¹⁰Samuel delivered the message of the LORD in full to those who were asking him for a king. ¹¹He told them: "The governance of the king who will rule you will be as follows: He will take your sons and assign them to his chariots and horses, and they will run before his chariot. ¹²He will appoint from among them his commanders of thousands and of hundreds. He will make them do his plowing and harvesting and produce his weapons of war and chariotry. ¹³He will use your daughters as perfumers, cooks, and bakers. ¹⁴He will take your best fields, vineyards, and olive groves, and give them to his servants. ¹⁵He will tithe your crops and grape harvests to give to his officials and his servants. ¹⁶He will take your male and female slaves, as well as your best oxen and donkeys, and use them to do his work. ¹⁷He will also tithe your flocks. As for you, you will become his slaves. ¹⁸On that day you will cry out because of the king whom you have chosen, but the LORD will not answer you on that day."

Persistent Demand. ¹⁹The people, however, refused to listen to Samuel's warning and said, "No! There must be a king over us. ²⁰We too must be like all the nations, with a king to rule us, lead us in warfare, and fight our battles." ²¹Samuel listened to all the concerns of the people and then repeated them to the LORD. ²²The LORD said: Listen to them! Appoint a king to rule over them. Then Samuel said to the people of Israel, "Return, each one of you, to your own city."

Saul. 9:1 There was a powerful man from Benjamin named Kish, who was the son of Abiel, son of Zeror, son of Becorath, son of Aphiah, a Benjaminite. ²He had a son named Saul, who was a handsome young man. There was no other Israelite more handsome than Saul; he stood head and shoulders above the people.

The Lost Donkeys. ³Now the donkeys of Saul's father, Kish, had wandered off. Kish said to his son Saul, "Take one of the servants with you and go out and hunt for the donkeys." ⁴So they went through the hill country of Ephraim, and through the land of Shalishah. Not finding them there, they continued through the land of Shaalim without success. They also went through the land of Benjamin, but they failed to find the animals. ⁵When they came to the land of Zuph, Saul said to the servant who was with him, "Come, let us turn back, lest my father forget about the donkeys and become anxious about us." ⁶The servant replied, "Listen! There is a man of God in this city, a man held in high esteem; everything he says comes true. Let us go there now! Perhaps he can advise us about the journey we have undertaken." ⁷But Saul said to his servant, "If we go, what can we offer the man? The food in our bags has run out; we have no present to give the man of God. What else do we have?" ⁸Again the servant answered Saul, "I have a quarter shekel of silver. If I give that to the man of God, he will advise us about the journey." ⁹(In former times in Israel, anyone who went to consult God used to say, "Come, let us go to the seer." For the one who is now called prophet was formerly called seer.) ¹⁰Saul then said to his servant, "You are right! Come on, let us go!" So they headed toward the city where the man of God lived.

Meeting the Young Women. ¹¹As they were going up the path to the city, they met some young women coming out to draw water and they asked them, "Is the seer in town?" ¹²The young women answered, "Yes, there—straight ahead. Hurry now; just today he came to the city, because the people have a sacrifice today on the high place. ¹³When you enter the city, you may reach him before he goes up to the high place to eat. The people will not eat until he arrives; only after he blesses the sacrifice will the invited guests eat. Go up immediately, for you should find him right now."

Saul Meets Samuel. [14]So they went up to the city. As they entered it—there was Samuel coming toward them on his way to the high place. [15]The day before Saul's arrival, the LORD had revealed to Samuel: [16]At this time tomorrow I will send you a man from the land of Benjamin whom you are to anoint as ruler of my people Israel. He shall save my people from the hand of the Philistines. I have looked upon my people; their cry has come to me. [17]When Samuel caught sight of Saul, the LORD assured him: This is the man I told you about; he shall govern my people. [18]Saul met Samuel in the gateway and said, "Please tell me where the seer lives." [19]Samuel answered Saul: "I am the seer. Go up ahead of me to the high place and eat with me today. In the morning, before letting you go, I will tell you everything on your mind. [20]As for your donkeys that were lost three days ago, do not worry about them, for they have been found. Whom should Israel want if not you and your father's family?" [21]Saul replied: "Am I not a Benjaminite, from the smallest of the tribes of Israel, and is not my clan the least among the clans of the tribe of Benjamin? Why say such things to me?"

The Meal. [22]Samuel then took Saul and his servant and brought them into the room. He seated them at the head of the guests, of whom there were about thirty. [23]He said to the cook, "Bring the portion I gave you and told you to put aside." [24]So the cook took up the leg and what went with it, and placed it before Saul. Samuel said: "This is a reserved portion that is set before you. Eat, for it was kept for you until this time; I explained that I was inviting some guests." Thus Saul dined with Samuel that day. [25]When they came down from the high place into the city, a mattress was spread for Saul on the roof, [26]and he slept there.

Saul's Anointing. At daybreak Samuel called to Saul on the roof, "Get up, and I will send you on your way." Saul got up, and he and Samuel went outside the city together. [27]As they were approaching the edge of the town, Samuel said to Saul, "Tell the servant to go on ahead of us, but you stay here for a moment, that I may give you a word from God."

10:1 Then, from a flask he had with him, Samuel poured oil on Saul's head and kissed him, saying: "The LORD anoints you ruler over his people Israel. You are the one who will govern the LORD's people and save them from the power of their enemies all around them.

The Signs Foretold. "This will be the sign for you that the LORD has anointed you ruler over his heritage: [2]When you leave me today, you will meet two men near Rachel's tomb at Zelzah in the territory of Benjamin. They will say to you, 'The donkeys you went to look for have been found. Now your father is no longer worried about the donkeys, but is anxious about you and says: What shall I do about my son?' [3]Farther on, when you arrive at the oak of Tabor, three men will meet you as they go up to God at Bethel; one will be bringing three young goats, another three loaves of bread, and the third a skin of wine. [4]They will greet you and offer you two elevated offerings of bread, which you should accept from them. [5]After that you will come to Gibeath-elohim, where the Philistine garrison is located. As you enter that city, you will meet a band of prophets coming down from the high place. They will be preceded by lyres, tambourines, flutes, and harps, and will be in prophetic ecstasy. [6]The spirit of the LORD will rush upon you, and you will join them in their prophetic ecstasy and will become a changed man. [7]When these signs have come to pass, do whatever lies to hand, because God is with you. [8]Now go down ahead of me to Gilgal, for I shall come down to you, to offer burnt offerings and to sacrifice communion offerings. Wait seven days until I come to you; I shall then tell you what you must do."

The Signs Come to Pass. ⁹As Saul turned to leave Samuel, God changed his heart. That very day all these signs came to pass.... ¹⁰From there they arrived at Gibeah, where a band of prophets met Saul, and the spirit of God rushed upon him, so that he joined them in their prophetic ecstasy. ¹¹When all who had known him previously saw him in a prophetic state among the prophets, they said to one another, "What has happened to the son of Kish? Is Saul also among the prophets?" ¹²And someone from that district responded, "And who is their father?" Thus the saying arose, "Is Saul also among the prophets?" ¹³When he came out of the prophetic ecstasy, he went home.

Silence About the Kingship. ¹⁴Saul's uncle asked him and his servant, "Where have you been?" Saul replied, "Looking for the donkeys. When we could not find them, we went to Samuel." ¹⁵Saul's uncle said, "Tell me, then, what Samuel said to you." ¹⁶Saul said to his uncle, "He assured us that the donkeys had been found." But Saul told him nothing about what Samuel had said about the kingship.

Saul Chosen King. ¹⁷Samuel called the people together to the LORD at Mizpah ¹⁸and addressed the Israelites: "Thus says the LORD, the God of Israel: It was I who brought Israel up from Egypt and delivered you from the power of the Egyptians and from the power of all the kingdoms that oppressed you. ¹⁹But today you have rejected your God, who saves you from all your evils and calamities, by saying, 'No! You must appoint a king over us.' Now, therefore, take your stand before the LORD according to your tribes and families." ²⁰So Samuel had all the tribes of Israel come forward, and the tribe of Benjamin was chosen. ²¹Next he had the tribe of Benjamin come forward by clans, and the clan of Matri was chosen, and finally Saul, son of Kish, was chosen. But when they went to look for him, he was nowhere to be found. ²²Again they consulted the LORD, "Is there still someone else to come forward?" The LORD answered: He is hiding among the baggage. ²³They ran to bring him from there; when he took his place among the people, he stood head and shoulders above all the people. ²⁴Then Samuel addressed all the people, "Do you see the man whom the LORD has chosen? There is no one like him among all the people!" Then all the people shouted out, "Long live the king!"

²⁵Samuel next explained to the people the rules of the monarchy, wrote them in a book, and placed them before the presence of the LORD. Samuel then sent the people back to their own homes. ²⁶Saul also went home to Gibeah, accompanied by warriors whose hearts the LORD had touched. ²⁷But some worthless people said, "How can this fellow save us?" They despised him and brought him no tribute.

☐ 1 CORINTHIANS 11

11:1 Be imitators of me, as I am of Christ.

²I praise you because you remember me in everything and hold fast to the traditions, just as I handed them on to you.

Man and Woman. ³But I want you to know that Christ is the head of every man, and a husband the head of his wife, and God the head of Christ. ⁴Any man who prays or prophesies with his head covered brings shame upon his head. ⁵But any woman who prays or prophesies with her head unveiled brings shame upon her head, for it is one and the same thing as if she had had her head shaved. ⁶For if a woman does not have her head veiled, she may as well have her hair cut off. But if it is shameful for a woman to have her hair cut off or her head shaved, then she should wear a veil.

[7]A man, on the other hand, should not cover his head, because he is the image and glory of God, but woman is the glory of man. [8]For man did not come from woman, but woman from man; [9]nor was man created for woman, but woman for man; [10]for this reason a woman should have a sign of authority on her head, because of the angels. [11]Woman is not independent of man or man of woman in the Lord. [12]For just as woman came from man, so man is born of woman; but all things are from God.

[13]Judge for yourselves: is it proper for a woman to pray to God with her head unveiled? [14]Does not nature itself teach you that if a man wears his hair long it is a disgrace to him, [15]whereas if a woman has long hair it is her glory, because long hair has been given [her] for a covering? [16]But if anyone is inclined to be argumentative, we do not have such a custom, nor do the churches of God.

An Abuse at Corinth. [17]In giving this instruction, I do not praise the fact that your meetings are doing more harm than good. [18]First of all, I hear that when you meet as a church there are divisions among you, and to a degree I believe it; [19]there have to be factions among you in order that [also] those who are approved among you may become known. [20]When you meet in one place, then, it is not to eat the Lord's supper, [21]for in eating, each one goes ahead with his own supper, and one goes hungry while another gets drunk. [22]Do you not have houses in which you can eat and drink? Or do you show contempt for the church of God and make those who have nothing feel ashamed? What can I say to you? Shall I praise you? In this matter I do not praise you.

Tradition of the Institution. [23]For I received from the Lord what I also handed on to you, that the Lord Jesus, on the night he was handed over, took bread, [24]and, after he had given thanks, broke it and said, "This is my body that is for you. Do this in remembrance of me." [25]In the same way also the cup, after supper, saying, "This cup is the new covenant in my blood. Do this, as often as you drink it, in remembrance of me." [26]For as often as you eat this bread and drink the cup, you proclaim the death of the Lord until he comes.

[27]Therefore whoever eats the bread or drinks the cup of the Lord unworthily will have to answer for the body and blood of the Lord. [28]A person should examine himself, and so eat the bread and drink the cup. [29]For anyone who eats and drinks without discerning the body, eats and drinks judgment on himself. [30]That is why many among you are ill and infirm, and a considerable number are dying. [31]If we discerned ourselves, we would not be under judgment; [32]but since we are judged by [the] Lord, we are being disciplined so that we may not be condemned along with the world.

[33]Therefore, my brothers, when you come together to eat, wait for one another. [34]If anyone is hungry, he should eat at home, so that your meetings may not result in judgment. The other matters I shall set in order when I come.

St. Melito of Sardis

Christ rose from the dead, and cried aloud: "Who will contend with Me? Let him confront Me. I have freed the condemned, brought the dead back to life, raised men from their graves. Who has anything to say against Me? I am the Christ. I have destroyed death, triumphed over the enemy, trampled hell underfoot, bound the strong one, and taken men up to the heights of heaven."

— ST. MELITO OF SARDIS

☐ 1 SAMUEL 11–14

Defeat of the Ammonites. 11:1 About a month later, Nahash the Ammonite went up and besieged Jabesh-gilead. All the people of Jabesh begged Nahash, "Make a treaty with us, and we will serve you." ²But Nahash the Ammonite replied, "This is my condition for making a treaty with you: I will gouge out the right eye of every man, and thus bring shame on all Israel." ³The elders of Jabesh said to him: "Give us seven days to send messengers throughout the territory of Israel. If there is no one to save us, we will surrender to you." ⁴When the messengers arrived at Gibeah of Saul and reported the news in the people's hearing, they all wept aloud. ⁵Just then Saul came in from the field, behind his oxen. "Why are the people weeping?" he asked. They repeated the message of the inhabitants of Jabesh for him. ⁶As he listened to this report, the spirit of God rushed upon him and he became very angry. ⁷Taking a yoke of oxen, he cut them into pieces and sent them throughout the territory of Israel by messengers saying, "If anyone does not come out to follow Saul and Samuel, the same thing will be done to his oxen!" The dread of the LORD came upon the people and they went forth as one. ⁸When Saul reviewed them in Bezek, there were three hundred thousand Israelites and seventy thousand Judahites.

⁹To the messengers who had come he said, "Tell the inhabitants of Jabesh-gilead that tomorrow, when the sun grows hot, they will be saved." The messengers went and reported this to the inhabitants of Jabesh, and they rejoiced. ¹⁰The men of Jabesh said to Nahash, "Tomorrow we will surrender to you, and you may do with us whatever you want." ¹¹The next day, Saul arranged his troops in three companies and invaded the camp during the dawn watch. They slaughtered Ammonites until the day had gotten hot; by then the survivors were so scattered that no two of them were left together.

Saul Accepted as King. ¹²The people then said to Samuel: "Who questioned whether Saul should rule over us? Hand them over and we will put them to death." ¹³But Saul objected, "No one will be put to death this day, for today the LORD has rescued Israel." ¹⁴Samuel said to the people, "Come, let us go to Gilgal to renew the kingship there." ¹⁵So all the people went to Gilgal, and there they made Saul king in the LORD's presence. They also sacrificed communion offerings there before the LORD, and Saul and all the Israelites rejoiced greatly.

Samuel's Integrity. 12:1 Samuel addressed all Israel: "I have granted your request in every respect," he said. "I have set a king over you ²and now the king will lead you. As for me, I am old and gray, and my sons are among you. I was your leader from my youth to the present day. ³Here I stand! Answer me in the presence of the LORD and the LORD's anointed. Whose ox have I taken? Whose donkey have I taken? Whom have I cheated? Whom have I wronged? From whom have I accepted a bribe and shut my eyes because of it? I will make restitution to you." ⁴They replied, "You have neither cheated us, nor oppressed us, nor accepted anything from anyone." ⁵So he said to them, "The LORD is witness against you this day, and the LORD's anointed is witness, that you have found nothing in my possession." "The LORD is witness," they said.

Samuel Admonishes the People. ⁶Samuel continued: "The LORD is witness, who appointed Moses and Aaron and brought your ancestors up from the land of Egypt. ⁷Now take your stand, that I may judge you in the presence of the LORD according to all the gracious acts that the LORD has done for you and your ancestors. ⁸When Jacob and his sons went to Egypt and the Egyptians oppressed them, your ancestors cried out to the LORD. The LORD then sent Moses and Aaron to bring them out of Egypt and settled them in this place. ⁹But they forgot the LORD their God; and so the LORD sold them into the power of Sisera, the captain of the army of Hazor, the power of the Philistines, and the power of the king of Moab, who made war against them. ¹⁰They cried out to the LORD and said, 'We have sinned because we abandoned the LORD and served the Baals and Astartes. Now deliver us from the power of our enemies, and we will serve you.' ¹¹The LORD sent Jerubbaal, Barak, Jephthah, and Samuel; he delivered you from the power of your enemies on every side, so that you could live in security. ¹²Yet, when you saw Nahash, king of the Ammonites, advancing against you, you said to me, 'No! A king must rule us,' even though the LORD your God is your king.

Warnings for People and King. ¹³"Now here is the king you chose. See! The LORD has given you a king. ¹⁴If you fear and serve the LORD, if you listen to the voice of the LORD and do not rebel against the LORD's command, if both you and the king, who rules over you, follow the LORD your God—well and good. ¹⁵But if you do not listen to the voice of the LORD and if you rebel against the LORD's command, the hand of the LORD will be against you and your king. ¹⁶Now then, stand ready to witness the great marvel the LORD is about to accomplish before your eyes. ¹⁷Are we not in the harvest time for wheat? Yet I will call upon the LORD, and he will send thunder and rain. Thus you will see and understand how great an evil it is in the eyes of the LORD that you have asked for a king." ¹⁸Samuel called upon the LORD, and the LORD sent thunder and rain that day.

Assistance Promised. Then all the people feared the LORD and Samuel. ¹⁹They said to Samuel, "Pray to the LORD your God for us, your servants, that we may not die for having added to all our other sins the evil of asking for a king." ²⁰"Do not fear," Samuel answered them. "You have indeed committed all this evil! Yet do not turn from the LORD, but serve him with your whole heart. ²¹Do not turn aside to gods who are nothing, who cannot act and deliver. They are nothing. ²²For the sake of his own great name the LORD will not abandon his people, since the LORD has decided to make you his people. ²³As for me, far be it from me to sin against the LORD by ceasing to pray for you and to teach you the good and right way. ²⁴But you must fear the LORD and serve him faithfully with all your heart, for you have seen the great things the LORD has done among you. ²⁵If instead you continue to do evil, both you and your king shall be swept away."

13:1 [Saul was… years old when he became king and he reigned… -two years over Israel.]

Saul Offers Sacrifice. ²Saul chose three thousand of Israel, of whom two thousand remained with him in Michmash and in the hill country of Bethel, and one thousand were with Jonathan in Gibeah of Benjamin. He sent the rest of the army back to their tents. [3]Now Jonathan struck the Philistine garrison in Gibeah, and the Philistines got word of it. Then Saul sounded the horn throughout the land, saying, "Let the Hebrews hear!" [4]Then all Israel heard the report, "Saul has struck the garrison of the Philistines! Israel has become odious to the Philistines!" Then the army was called up to Saul in Gilgal. [5]The Philistines also assembled for battle against Israel, with thirty thousand chariots, six thousand horsemen, and foot soldiers as numerous as the sand on the seashore. They came up and encamped in Michmash, east of Beth-aven. [6]When the soldiers saw they were in danger because the army was hardpressed, they hid themselves in caves, thickets, rocks, caverns, and cisterns. [7]Other Hebrews crossed the Jordan into the land of Gad and Gilead. Saul, however, held out in Gilgal, all his army trembling in fear behind him. [8]He waited seven days, until the appointed time Samuel had set, but Samuel did not come, and the army deserted Saul. [9]He then said, "Bring me the burnt offering and communion offerings!" Then he sacrificed the burnt offering.

King Saul Reproved. [10]As he finished sacrificing the burnt offering, there came Samuel! So Saul went out toward him in order to greet him. [11]Samuel asked him, "What have you done?" Saul explained: "When I saw that the army was deserting me and you did not come on the appointed day, and that the Philistines were assembling at Michmash, [12]I said to myself, 'Now the Philistines will come down against me at Gilgal, and I have not yet sought the LORD's blessing.' So I thought I should sacrifice the burnt offering." [13]Samuel replied to Saul: "You have acted foolishly! Had you kept the command the LORD your God gave you, the LORD would now establish your kingship in Israel forever; [14]but now

your kingship shall not endure. The LORD has sought out a man after his own heart to appoint as ruler over his people because you did not observe what the LORD commanded you."

Philistine Invasion. [15]Then Samuel set out from Gilgal and went his own way; but what was left of the army went up after Saul to meet the soldiers, going from Gilgal to Gibeah of Benjamin. Saul then counted the soldiers he had with him, about six hundred. [16]Saul, his son Jonathan, and the soldiers they had with them were now occupying Geba of Benjamin, and the Philistines were encamped at Michmash. [17]Meanwhile, raiders left the camp of the Philistines in three bands. One band took the Ophrah road toward the district of Shual; [18]another turned in the direction of Beth-horon; and the third took the road for Geba that overlooks the Valley of the Hyenas toward the desert.

Disarmament of Israel. [19]Not a single smith was to be found anywhere in Israel, for the Philistines had said, "Otherwise the Hebrews will make swords or spears." [20]All Israel, therefore, had to go down to the Philistines to sharpen their plowshares, mattocks, axes, and sickles. [21]The price for the plowshares and mattocks was two thirds of a shekel, and a third of a shekel for sharpening the axes and for setting the ox-goads. [22]And so on the day of battle neither sword nor spear could be found in the hand of any of the soldiers with Saul or Jonathan. Only Saul and his son Jonathan had them.

Jonathan's Exploit. [23]An outpost of the Philistines had pushed forward to the pass of Michmash.

14:1 One day Jonathan, son of Saul, said to his armor-bearer, "Come, let us go over to the Philistine outpost on the other side." But he did not inform his father— [2]Saul was sitting under the pomegranate tree in Migron on the outskirts of Gibeah; with him were about six hundred men. [3]Ahijah, son of Ahitub, brother of Ichabod, the son of Phinehas, son of Eli, the priest of the LORD at Shiloh, was wearing the ephod—nor did the soldiers know that Jonathan had gone. ⁴Flanking the ravine through which Jonathan intended to cross to the Philistine outpost were rocky crags on each side, one named Bozez and the other Seneh. ⁵One crag was to the north, toward Michmash; the other to the south, toward Geba. ⁶Jonathan said to his armor-bearer: "Come, let us go over to that outpost of the uncircumcised. Perhaps the LORD will help us, because it is no more difficult for the LORD to grant victory by means of a few than it is by means of many." ⁷His armor-bearer replied, "Do whatever you think best; I am with you in whatever you decide." ⁸Jonathan continued: "When we cross over to those men, we will be visible to them. ⁹If they say to us, 'Stay there until we can come to you,' we will stop where we are; we will not go up to them. ¹⁰But if they say, 'Come up to us,' we will go up, because the LORD has delivered them into our hand. That will be our sign." ¹¹When the two of them came into the view of the Philistine outpost, the Philistines remarked, "Look, some Hebrews are coming out of the holes where they have been hiding." ¹²The men of the outpost called to Jonathan and his armor-bearer. "Come up here," they said, "and we will teach you a lesson." So Jonathan said to his armor-bearer, "Climb up after me, for the LORD has delivered them into the hand of Israel." ¹³Jonathan clambered up with his armor-bearer behind him. As the Philistines fell before Jonathan, his armor-bearer, who followed him, would finish them off. ¹⁴In this first attack Jonathan and his armor-bearer killed about twenty men within half a furlong. ¹⁵Then terror spread through the camp and the countryside; all the soldiers in the outpost and in the raiding parties shuddered in terror. The earth shook with an awesome shuddering.

Rout of the Philistines. ¹⁶Saul's sentinels in Gibeah of Benjamin saw that the enemy camp had scattered and were running in all directions. ¹⁷Saul said to those around him, "Count the troops and find out if any of us are missing." When they had taken the count, they found Jonathan and his armor-bearer missing. ¹⁸Saul then said to Ahijah, "Bring the ephod here." (Ahijah was wearing the ephod before the Israelites at that time.) ¹⁹While Saul was speaking to the priest, the uproar in the Philistine camp kept increasing. So he said to the priest, "Withdraw your hand." ²⁰And Saul and all his men rallied and rushed into the fight, where the Philistines, wholly confused, were thrusting swords at one another. ²¹The Hebrews who had previously sided with the Philistines and had gone up with them to their camp turned to join the Israelites under Saul and Jonathan. ²²Likewise, all the Israelites who were hiding in the hill country of Ephraim, hearing that the Philistines were fleeing, kept after them in the battle. ²³ Thus the LORD saved Israel that day.

Saul's Oath. The battle continued past Beth-aven. ²⁴Even though the Israelites were exhausted that day, Saul laid an oath on them, saying, "Cursed be the one who takes food before evening, before I am able to avenge myself on my enemies." So none of the people tasted food. ²⁵Now there was a honeycomb lying on the ground, ²⁶and when the soldiers came to the comb the honey was flowing; yet no one raised a hand from it to his mouth, because the people feared the oath.

Violation of the Oath. ²⁷Jonathan, who had not heard that his father had put the people under oath, thrust out the end of the staff he was holding and dipped it into the honeycomb. Then he raised it to his mouth and his eyes brightened. ²⁸At this, one of the soldiers spoke up: "Your father put the people under a strict oath, saying, 'Cursed be the one who takes food today!'

As a result the people are weakened." ²⁹Jonathan replied: "My father brings trouble to the land. Look how bright my eyes are because I had this little taste of honey. ³⁰What is more, if the army had eaten freely of the enemy's plunder when they came across it today, surely the slaughter of the Philistines would have been the greater by now!"

Consuming the Blood. ³¹After the Philistines were routed that day from Michmash to Aijalon, the people were completely exhausted. ³²So the army pounced upon the plunder and took sheep, oxen, and calves, slaughtering them on the ground and eating the meat with the blood in it. ³³Informed that the army was sinning against the LORD by eating the meat with blood in it, Saul said: "You have broken faith. Roll a large stone here for me." ³⁴He continued: "Mingle with the people and tell each of them, 'Bring an ox or sheep to me. Slaughter them here and then eat. But you must not sin against the LORD by eating meat with blood in it.'" So that night they all brought whatever oxen they had seized, and they slaughtered them there; ³⁵and Saul built an altar to the LORD—this was the first time he built an altar to the LORD.

Jonathan in Danger of Death. ³⁶Then Saul said, "Let us go down in pursuit of the Philistines by night, to plunder them until daybreak and leave no one alive." They replied, "Do what you think best." But the priest said, "Let us consult God." ³⁷So Saul inquired of God: "Shall I go down in pursuit of the Philistines? Will you deliver them into the hand of Israel?" But he received no answer on this occasion. ³⁸"All officers of the army," Saul announced, "come forward. Find out how this sin was committed today. ³⁹As the LORD lives who has given victory to Israel, even if my son Jonathan has committed it, he shall surely die!" But none of the people answered him. ⁴⁰So he said to all Israel, "Stand on one side, and my son Jonathan and I will stand on the other." The people responded, "Do what you think best." ⁴¹And Saul said to the LORD, the God of Israel: "Why did you not answer your servant this time? If the blame for this resides in me or my son Jonathan, LORD, God of Israel, respond with Urim; but if this guilt is in your people Israel, respond with Thummim." Jonathan and Saul were designated, and the people went free. ⁴²Saul then said, "Cast lots between me and my son Jonathan." And Jonathan was designated. ⁴³Saul said to Jonathan, "Tell me what you have done." Jonathan replied, "I only tasted a little honey from the end of the staff I was holding. Am I to die for this?" ⁴⁴Saul declared, "May God do thus to me, and more, if you do not indeed die, Jonathan!"

Rescue of Jonathan. ⁴⁵But the soldiers protested to Saul: "Is Jonathan to die, the man who won this great victory for Israel? This must not be! As the LORD lives, not a single hair of his head shall fall to the ground, for God was with him in what he did today!" Thus the soldiers rescued Jonathan and he did not die. ⁴⁶After that Saul gave up the pursuit of the Philistines, who returned to their own territory.

Saul's Victories. ⁴⁷After taking possession of the kingship over Israel, Saul waged war on its enemies all around—Moab, the Ammonites, Edom, the kings of Zobah, and the Philistines. Wherever he turned, he was successful ⁴⁸and fought bravely. He defeated Amalek and delivered Israel from the hand of those who were plundering them.

Saul's Family. ⁴⁹The sons of Saul were Jonathan, Ishvi, and Malchishua; the name of his firstborn daughter was Merob; the name of the younger was Michal. ⁵⁰The name of Saul's wife was Ahinoam, daughter of Ahimaaz. The name of his general was Abner, son of Ner, Saul's uncle; ⁵¹Kish, Saul's father, and Ner, Abner's father, were sons of Abiel.

⁵²There was heavy fighting with the Philistines during Saul's lifetime. Whenever Saul saw any strong or brave man, he took him into his service.

☐ 1 CORINTHIANS 12:1-11

Unity and Variety. 12:1 Now in regard to spiritual gifts, brothers, I do not want you to be unaware. [2]You know how, when you were pagans, you were constantly attracted and led away to mute idols. [3]Therefore, I tell you that nobody speaking by the spirit of God says, "Jesus be accursed." And no one can say, "Jesus is Lord," except by the holy Spirit.

[4]There are different kinds of spiritual gifts but the same Spirit; [5]there are different forms of service but the same Lord; [6]there are different workings but the same God who produces all of them in every-one. [7]To each individual the manifestation of the Spirit is given for some benefit. [8]To one is given through the Spirit the expression of wisdom; to another the expression of knowledge according to the same Spirit; [9]to another faith by the same Spirit; to another gifts of healing by the one Spirit; [10]to another mighty deeds; to another prophecy; to another discernment of spirits; to another varieties of tongues; to another interpretation of tongues. [11]But one and the same Spirit produces all of these, distributing them individually to each person as he wishes.

April 2

St. Francis of Paola

Take pains to refrain from sharp words. Pardon one another so that later on you will not remember the injury. The recollection of an injury is itself wrong. It adds to our anger, nurtures our sins, and hates what is good. It is a rusty arrow and poison for the soul. It puts all virtue to flight.

— ST. FRANCIS OF PAOLA

☐ 1 SAMUEL 15-17

Disobedience of Saul. 15:1 Samuel said to Saul: "It was I the LORD sent to anoint you king over his people Israel. Now, therefore, listen to the message of the LORD. [2]Thus says the LORD of hosts: I will punish what Amalek did to the Israelites when he barred their way as they came up from Egypt. [3]Go, now, attack Amalek, and put under the ban everything he has. Do not spare him; kill men and women, children and infants, oxen and sheep, camels and donkeys."

[4]Saul alerted the army, and at Telaim reviewed two hundred thousand foot soldiers and ten thousand men of Judah. [5]Saul went to the city of Amalek and set up an ambush in the wadi. [6]He warned the Kenites: "Leave Amalek, turn aside and come down so I will not have to destroy you with them, for you were loyal to the Israelites when they came up from Egypt." After the Kenites left, [7]Saul routed Amalek from Havilah to the approaches of Shur, on the frontier of Egypt. [8]He took Agag, king of Amalek, alive, but the rest of the people he destroyed by the sword, putting them under the ban. [9]He and his troops spared Agag and the best of the fat sheep and oxen, and the lambs. They refused to put

under the ban anything that was worthwhile, destroying only what was worthless and of no account.

Samuel Rebukes Saul. [10]Then the word of the Lord came to Samuel: [11]I regret having made Saul king, for he has turned from me and has not kept my command. At this Samuel grew angry and cried out to the Lord all night. [12]Early in the morning he went to meet Saul, but was informed that Saul had gone to Carmel, where he set up a monument in his own honor, and that on his return he had gone down to Gilgal. [13]When Samuel came to him, Saul greeted him: "The Lord bless you! I have kept the command of the Lord." [14]But Samuel asked, "What, then, is this bleating of sheep that comes to my ears, the lowing of oxen that I hear?" [15]Saul replied: "They were brought from Amalek. The people spared the best sheep and oxen to sacrifice to the Lord, your God; but the rest we destroyed, putting them under the ban." [16]Samuel said to Saul: "Stop! Let me tell you what the Lord said to me last night." "Speak!" he replied. [17]Samuel then said: "Though little in your own eyes, are you not chief of the tribes of Israel? The Lord anointed you king of Israel [18]and sent you on a mission, saying: Go and put the sinful Amalekites under a ban of destruction. Fight against them until you have exterminated them. [19]Why then have you disobeyed the Lord? You have pounced on the spoil, thus doing what was evil in the Lord's sight." [20]Saul explained to Samuel: "I did indeed obey the Lord and fulfill the mission on which the Lord sent me. I have brought back Agag, the king of Amalek, and, carrying out the ban, I have destroyed the Amalekites. [21]But from the spoil the army took sheep and oxen, the best of what had been banned, to sacrifice to the Lord your God in Gilgal." [22]But Samuel said:

"Does the Lord delight in burnt
offerings and sacrifices
as much as in obedience to the
Lord's command?
Obedience is better than sacrifice,
to listen, better than the fat of rams.
[23]For a sin of divination is rebellion,
and arrogance, the crime of idolatry.
Because you have rejected the word of
the Lord,
the Lord in turn has rejected you
as king."

Rejection of Saul. [24]Saul admitted to Samuel: "I have sinned, for I have transgressed the command of the Lord and your instructions. I feared the people and obeyed them. [25]Now forgive my sin, and return with me, that I may worship the Lord." [26]But Samuel said to Saul, "I will not return with you, because you rejected the word of the Lord and the Lord has rejected you as king of Israel." [27]As Samuel turned to go, Saul seized a loose end of his garment, and it tore off. [28]So Samuel said to him: "The Lord has torn the kingdom of Israel from you this day, and has given it to a neighbor of yours, who is better than you. [29]The Glory of Israel neither deceives nor repents, for he is not a mortal who repents." [30]But Saul answered: "I have sinned, yet honor me now before the elders of my people and before Israel. Return with me that I may worship the Lord your God." [31]And so Samuel returned with him, and Saul worshiped the Lord.

Samuel Executes Agag. [32]Afterward Samuel commanded, "Bring Agag, king of Amalek, to me." Agag came to him struggling and saying, "So it is bitter death!" [33]And Samuel said,

"As your sword has made women
childless,
so shall your mother be childless
among women."

Then he cut Agag to pieces before the Lord in Gilgal. [34]Samuel departed for Ramah, while Saul went up to his home in Gibeah of Saul. [35]Never again, as long as he lived, did Samuel see Saul. Yet he grieved over Saul, because the LORD repented that he had made him king of Israel.

Samuel Is Sent to Bethlehem. 16:1 The LORD said to Samuel: How long will you grieve for Saul, whom I have rejected as king of Israel? Fill your horn with oil, and be on your way. I am sending you to Jesse of Bethlehem, for from among his sons I have decided on a king. [2]But Samuel replied: "How can I go? Saul will hear of it and kill me." To this the LORD answered: Take a heifer along and say, "I have come to sacrifice to the LORD." [3]Invite Jesse to the sacrifice, and I myself will tell you what to do; you are to anoint for me the one I point out to you.

Samuel Anoints David. [4]Samuel did as the LORD had commanded him. When he entered Bethlehem, the elders of the city came trembling to meet him and asked, "Is your visit peaceful, O seer?" [5]He replied: "Yes! I have come to sacrifice to the LORD. So purify yourselves and celebrate with me today." He also had Jesse and his sons purify themselves and invited them to the sacrifice. [6]As they came, he looked at Eliab and thought, "Surely the anointed is here before the LORD." [7]But the LORD said to Samuel: Do not judge from his appearance or from his lofty stature, because I have rejected him. God does not see as a mortal, who sees the appearance. The LORD looks into the heart. [8]Then Jesse called Abinadab and presented him before Samuel, who said, "The LORD has not chosen him." [9]Next Jesse presented Shammah, but Samuel said, "The LORD has not chosen this one either." [10]In the same way Jesse presented seven sons before Samuel, but Samuel said to Jesse, "The LORD has not chosen any one of these." [11]Then Samuel asked Jesse, "Are these all the sons you have?" Jesse replied, "There is still the youngest, but he is tending the sheep." Samuel said to Jesse, "Send

for him; we will not sit down to eat until he arrives here." [12]Jesse had the young man brought to them. He was ruddy, a youth with beautiful eyes, and good looking. The LORD said: There—anoint him, for this is the one! [13]Then Samuel, with the horn of oil in hand, anointed him in the midst of his brothers, and from that day on, the spirit of the LORD rushed upon David. Then Samuel set out for Ramah.

David Wins Saul's Approval. [14]The spirit of the LORD had departed from Saul, and he was tormented by an evil spirit from the LORD. [15]So the servants of Saul said to him: "Look! An evil spirit from God is tormenting you. [16]If your lordship will order it, we, your servants here attending to you, will look for a man skilled in playing the harp. When the evil spirit from God comes upon you, he will play and you will feel better." [17]Saul then told his servants, "Find me a good harpist and bring him to me." [18]One of the servants spoke up: "I have observed that a son of Jesse of Bethlehem is a skillful harpist. He is also a brave warrior, an able speaker, and a handsome young man. The LORD is certainly with him."

David Made Armor-Bearer. [19]Accordingly, Saul dispatched messengers to ask Jesse to send him his son David, who was with the flock. [20]Then Jesse took five loaves of bread, a skin of wine, and a young goat, and sent them to Saul with his son David. [21]Thus David came to Saul and entered his service. Saul became very fond of him and made him his armor-bearer. [22]Saul sent Jesse the message, "Let David stay in my service, for he meets with my approval." [23]Whenever the spirit from God came upon Saul, David would take the harp and play, and Saul would be relieved and feel better, for the evil spirit would leave him.

The Challenge of Goliath. 17:1 The Philistines rallied their forces for battle at Socoh in Judah and camped between Socoh and Azekah at Ephes-dammim. [2]Saul and the

Israelites rallied and camped in the valley of the Elah, drawing up their battle line to meet the Philistines. [3]The Philistines were stationed on one hill and the Israelites on an opposite hill, with a valley between them.

[4]A champion named Goliath of Gath came out from the Philistine camp; he was six cubits and a span tall. [5]He had a bronze helmet on his head and wore a bronze breastplate of scale armor weighing five thousand shekels, [6]bronze greaves, and had a bronze scimitar slung from his shoulders. [7]The shaft of his javelin was like a weaver's beam, and its iron head weighed six hundred shekels. His shield-bearer went ahead of him. [8]He stood and shouted to the ranks of Israel: "Why come out in battle formation? I am a Philistine, and you are Saul's servants. Choose one of your men, and have him come down to me. [9]If he beats me in combat and kills me, we will be your vassals; but if I beat him and kill him, you shall be our vassals and serve us." [10]The Philistine continued: "I defy the ranks of Israel today. Give me a man and let us fight together." [11]When Saul and all Israel heard this challenge of the Philistine, they were stunned and terrified.

David Comes to the Camp. [12]David was the son of an Ephrathite named Jesse from Bethlehem in Judah who had eight sons. In the days of Saul Jesse was old and well on in years. [13]The three oldest sons of Jesse had followed Saul to war; the names of these three sons who had gone off to war were Eliab the firstborn; Abinadab the second; and Shammah the third. [14]David was the youngest. While the three oldest had joined Saul, [15]David would come and go from Saul's presence to tend his father's sheep at Bethlehem.

[16]Meanwhile the Philistine came forward and took his stand morning and evening for forty days.

[17]Now Jesse said to his son David: "Take this ephah of roasted grain and these ten loaves for your brothers, and bring them quickly to your brothers in the camp. [18]Also take these ten cheeses for the field officer. Greet your brothers and bring home some token from them. [19]Saul and your brothers, together with all Israel, are at war with the Philistines in the valley of the Elah." [20]Early the next morning, having left the flock with a shepherd, David packed up and set out, as Jesse had commanded him. He reached the barricade of the camp just as the army, on their way to the battleground, were shouting their battle cry. [21]The Israelites and the Philistines drew up opposite each other in battle array. [22]David entrusted what he had brought to the keeper of the baggage and hastened to the battle line, where he greeted his brothers. [23]While he was talking with them, the Philistine champion, by name Goliath of Gath, came up from the ranks of the Philistines and spoke as before, and David listened. [24]When the Israelites saw the man, they all retreated before him, terrified. [25]The Israelites had been saying: "Do you see this man coming up? He comes up to insult Israel. The king will make whoever kills him a very wealthy man. He will give his daughter to him and declare his father's family exempt from taxes in Israel." [26]David now said to the men standing near him: "How will the man who kills this Philistine and frees Israel from disgrace be rewarded? Who is this uncircumcised Philistine that he should insult the armies of the living God?" [27]They repeated the same words to him and said, "That is how the man who kills him will be rewarded." [28]When Eliab, his oldest brother, heard him speaking with the men, he grew angry with David and said: "Why did you come down? With whom have you left those sheep in the wilderness? I know your arrogance and dishonest heart. You came down to enjoy the battle!" [29]David protested, "What have I done now? I was only talking." [30]He turned from him to another and asked the same question; and everyone gave him the same

answer as before. [31]The words that David had spoken were overheard and reported to Saul, who sent for him.

David Challenges Goliath. [32]Then David spoke to Saul: "My lord should not lose heart. Let your servant go and fight this Philistine." [33]But Saul answered David, "You cannot go up against this Philistine and fight with him, for you are only a youth, while he has been a warrior from his youth." [34]Then David told Saul: "Your servant used to tend his father's sheep, and whenever a lion or bear came to carry off a sheep from the flock, [35]I would chase after it, attack it, and snatch the prey from its mouth. If it attacked me, I would seize it by the throat, strike it, and kill it. [36]Your servant has killed both a lion and a bear. This uncircumcised Philistine will be as one of them, because he has insulted the armies of the living God."

[37]David continued: "The same LORD who delivered me from the claws of the lion and the bear will deliver me from the hand of this Philistine." Saul answered David, "Go! the LORD will be with you."

Preparation for the Encounter. [38]Then Saul dressed David in his own tunic, putting a bronze helmet on his head and arming him with a coat of mail. [39]David also fastened Saul's sword over the tunic. He walked with difficulty, however, since he had never worn armor before. He said to Saul, "I cannot go in these, because I am not used to them." So he took them off. [40]Then, staff in hand, David selected five smooth stones from the wadi and put them in the pocket of his shepherd's bag. With his sling in hand, he approached the Philistine.

David's Victory. [41]With his shield-bearer marching before him, the Philistine advanced closer and closer to David. [42]When he sized David up and saw that he was youthful, ruddy, and handsome in appearance, he began to deride him. [43]He said to David, "Am I a dog that you come against me with a staff?" Then the Philistine cursed David by his gods [44]and said to him, "Come here to me, and I will feed your flesh to the birds of the air and the beasts of the field." [45]David answered him: "You come against me with sword and spear and scimitar, but I come against you in the name of the LORD of hosts, the God of the armies of Israel whom you have insulted. [46]Today the LORD shall deliver you into my hand; I will strike you down and cut off your head. This very day I will feed your dead body and the dead bodies of the Philistine army to the birds of the air and the beasts of the field; thus the whole land shall learn that Israel has a God. [47]All this multitude, too, shall learn that it is not by sword or spear that the LORD saves. For the battle belongs to the LORD, who shall deliver you into our hands."

[48]The Philistine then moved to meet David at close quarters, while David ran quickly toward the battle line to meet the Philistine. [49]David put his hand into the bag and took out a stone, hurled it with the sling, and struck the Philistine on the forehead. The stone embedded itself in his brow, and he fell on his face to the ground. [50]Thus David triumphed over the Philistine with sling and stone; he struck the Philistine dead, and did it without a sword in his hand. [51]Then David ran and stood over him; with the Philistine's own sword which he drew from its sheath he killed him, and cut off his head.

Flight of the Philistines. When the Philistines saw that their hero was dead, they fled. [52]Then the men of Israel and Judah sprang up with a battle cry and pursued them to the approaches of Gath and to the gates of Ekron, and Philistines fell wounded along the road from Shaaraim as far as Gath and Ekron. [53]When they returned from their pursuit of the Philistines, the Israelites looted their camp. [54]David took the head of the Philistine and brought it to Jerusalem; but he kept Goliath's armor in his own tent.

David Presented to Saul. [55]As Saul watched David go out to meet the Philistine, he asked his general Abner, "Abner, whose son is that young man?" Abner replied, "On your life, O king, I have no idea." [56]And the king said, "Find out whose son the lad is." [57]So when David returned from slaying the Philistine, Abner escorted him into Saul's presence. David was still holding the Philistine's head. [58]Saul then asked him, "Whose son are you, young man?" David replied, "I am the son of your servant Jesse of Bethlehem."

☐ 1 CORINTHIANS 12:12-31

One Body, Many Parts. 12:12 As a body is one though it has many parts, and all the parts of the body, though many, are one body, so also Christ. [13]For in one Spirit we were all baptized into one body, whether Jews or Greeks, slaves or free persons, and we were all given to drink of one Spirit.

[14]Now the body is not a single part, but many. [15]If a foot should say, "Because I am not a hand I do not belong to the body," it does not for this reason belong any less to the body. [16]Or if an ear should say, "Because I am not an eye I do not belong to the body," it does not for this reason belong any less to the body. [17]If the whole body were an eye, where would the hearing be? If the whole body were hearing, where would the sense of smell be? [18]But as it is, God placed the parts, each one of them, in the body as he intended. [19]If they were all one part, where would the body be? [20]But as it is, there are many parts, yet one body. [21]The eye cannot say to the hand, "I do not need you," nor again the head to the feet, "I do not need you." [22]Indeed, the parts of the body that seem to be weaker are all the more necessary, [23]and those parts of the body that we consider less honorable we surround with greater honor, and our less presentable parts are treated with greater propriety, [24]whereas our more presentable parts do not need this. But God has so constructed the body as to give greater honor to a part that is without it, [25]so that there may be no division in the body, but that the parts may have the same concern for one another. [26]If [one] part suffers, all the parts suffer with it; if one part is honored, all the parts share its joy.

Application to Christ. [27]Now you are Christ's body, and individually parts of it. [28]Some people God has designated in the church to be, first, apostles; second, prophets; third, teachers; then, mighty deeds; then, gifts of healing, assistance, administration, and varieties of tongues. [29]Are all apostles? Are all prophets? Are all teachers? Do all work mighty deeds? [30]Do all have gifts of healing? Do all speak in tongues? Do all interpret? [31]Strive eagerly for the greatest spiritual gifts.

The Way of Love. But I shall show you a still more excellent way.

April 3

St. Richard of Chichester

O most merciful Redeemer,
Friend, and Brother,
May I know Thee more clearly,
Love Thee more dearly,
Follow Thee more nearly,
Day by day.

— St. Richard of Chichester

☐ 1 SAMUEL 18-20

David and Jonathan. 18:1 By the time David finished speaking with Saul, Jonathan's life became bound up with David's life; he loved him as his very self. ²Saul retained David on that day and did not allow him to return to his father's house. ³Jonathan and David made a covenant, because Jonathan loved him as his very self. ⁴Jonathan took off the cloak he was wearing and handed it over to David, along with his military dress, even his sword, bow, and belt. ⁵David then carried out successfully every mission on which Saul sent him. So Saul put him in charge of his soldiers; this met with the approval of the whole army, even Saul's officers.

Saul's Jealousy. ⁶At the approach of Saul and David, on David's return after striking down the Philistine, women came out from all the cities of Israel to meet Saul the king, singing and dancing, with tambourines, joyful songs, and stringed instruments. ⁷The women played and sang:

"Saul has slain his thousands,
    David his tens of thousands."

⁸Saul was very angry and resentful of the song, for he thought: "They give David tens of thousands, but only thousands to me. All that remains for him is the kingship." ⁹From that day on, Saul kept a jealous eye on David.

¹⁰The next day an evil spirit from God rushed upon Saul, and he raged in his house. David was in attendance, playing the harp as at other times, while Saul was holding his spear. ¹¹Saul poised the spear, thinking, "I will nail David to the wall!" But twice David escaped him. ¹²Saul then began to fear David because the Lord was with him but had turned away from Saul. ¹³Saul sent him out of his presence and appointed him a field officer. So David led the people on their military expeditions ¹⁴and prospered in all his ways, for the Lord was with him. ¹⁵Seeing how he prospered, Saul feared David. ¹⁶But all Israel and Judah loved David, since he led them on their expeditions.

Saul Plots Against David. ¹⁷Saul said to David, "Look, I will give you my older daughter, Merob, in marriage if you become my warrior and fight the battles of the Lord." Saul thought, "I will not lay a hand on him. Let the hand of the Philistines strike him." ¹⁸But David answered Saul: "Who am I? And who are my kindred or my father's clan in Israel that I should become the king's son-in-law?" ¹⁹But when the time came for Saul's daughter Merob to be given to David, she was given as wife to Adriel the Meholathite instead.

²⁰Now Saul's daughter Michal loved David. When this was reported to Saul,

he was pleased. ²¹He thought, "I will offer her to him as a trap, so that the hand of the Philistines may strike him." So for the second time Saul said to David, "You shall become my son-in-law today." ²²Saul then ordered his servants, "Speak to David privately and say: The king favors you, and all his officers love you. You should become son-in-law to the king." ²³But when Saul's servants mentioned this to David, he said: "Is becoming the king's son-in-law a trivial matter in your eyes? I am poor and insignificant." ²⁴When his servants reported David's answer to him, ²⁵Saul commanded them, "Say this to David: The king desires no other price for the bride than the foreskins of one hundred Philistines, that he may thus take vengeance on his enemies." Saul intended to have David fall into the hands of the Philistines. ²⁶When the servants reported this offer to David, he was pleased with the prospect of becoming the king's son-in-law. Before the year was up, ²⁷David arose and went with his men and slew two hundred Philistines. He brought back their foreskins and counted them out before the king that he might become the king's son-in-law. So Saul gave him his daughter Michal as wife. ²⁸Then Saul realized that the LORD was with David and that his own daughter Michal loved David. ²⁹So Saul feared David all the more and was his enemy ever after.

³⁰The Philistine chiefs continued to make forays, but each time they took the field, David was more successful against them than any of Saul's other officers, and his name was held in great esteem.

Persecution of David. 19:1 Saul discussed his intention to kill David with his son Jonathan and with all his servants. But Saul's son Jonathan, who was very fond of David, ²told him: "My father Saul is trying to kill you. Therefore, please be on your guard tomorrow morning; stay out of sight and remain in hiding. ³I, however, will go out and stand beside my father in the countryside where you are, and will speak to him about you. If I learn anything, I will let you know."

⁴Jonathan then spoke well of David to his father Saul, telling him: "The king should not harm his servant David. He has not harmed you, but has helped you very much by his deeds. ⁵When he took his life in his hands and killed the Philistine, and the LORD won a great victory for all Israel, you were glad to see it. Why, then, should you become guilty of shedding innocent blood by killing David without cause?" ⁶Saul heeded Jonathan's plea and swore, "As the LORD lives, he shall not be killed." ⁷So Jonathan summoned David and repeated the whole conversation to him. He then brought David to Saul, and David served him as before.

David Escapes from Saul. ⁸When war broke out again, David went out to fight against the Philistines and inflicted such a great defeat upon them that they fled from him. ⁹Then an evil spirit from the LORD came upon Saul as he was sitting in his house with spear in hand while David was playing the harp nearby. ¹⁰Saul tried to pin David to the wall with the spear, but David eluded Saul, and the spear struck only the wall, while David got away safely.

¹¹The same night, Saul sent messengers to David's house to guard it, planning to kill him in the morning. David's wife Michal informed him, "Unless you run for your life tonight, tomorrow you will be killed." ¹²Then Michal let David down through a window, and he made his escape in safety. ¹³Michal took the teraphim and laid it in the bed, putting a tangle of goat's hair at its head and covering it with a blanket. ¹⁴When Saul sent officers to arrest David, she said, "He is sick." ¹⁵Saul, however, sent the officers back to see David and commanded them, "Bring him up to me in his bed, that I may kill him." ¹⁶But when the messengers entered, they found

the teraphim in the bed, with the tangle of goat's hair at its head. [17]Saul asked Michal: "Why did you lie to me like this? You have helped my enemy to get away!" Michal explained to Saul: "He threatened me, saying 'Let me go or I will kill you.'"

David and Saul in Ramah. [18]When David got safely away, he went to Samuel in Ramah, informing him of all that Saul had done to him. Then he and Samuel went to stay in Naioth. [19]When Saul was told that David was at Naioth in Ramah, [20]he sent officers to arrest David. But when they saw the band of prophets presided over by Samuel in a prophetic state, the spirit of God came upon them and they too fell into the prophetic ecstasy. [21]Informed of this, Saul sent other messengers, who also fell into the prophetic ecstasy. For the third time Saul sent messengers, but they too fell into a prophetic ecstasy.

Saul Among the Prophets. [22]Finally Saul went to Ramah himself. Arriving at the large cistern in Secu, he asked, "Where are Samuel and David?" Someone answered, "At Naioth in Ramah." [23]As he walked from there to Naioth in Ramah, the spirit of God came upon him also, and he continued on, acting like a prophet until he reached Naioth in Ramah. [24]Then he, too, stripped himself of his garments and remained in a prophetic state in the presence of Samuel; all that day and night he lay naked. That is why they say, "Is Saul also among the prophets?"

David Consults with Jonathan. 20:1 David fled from Naioth in Ramah, and went to Jonathan. "What have I done?" he asked him. "What crime or what offense does your father hold against me that he seeks my life?" [2]Jonathan answered him: "Heaven forbid that you should die! My father does nothing, great or small, without telling me. Why, then, should my father conceal this from me? It cannot be true!" [3]But David replied: "Your father is well aware that I am favored with your friendship, so he has decided, 'Jonathan must not know about this or he will be grieved.' Nevertheless, as the LORD lives and as you live, there is only a step between me and death." [4]Jonathan then said to David, "I will do whatever you say." [5]David answered: "Tomorrow is the new moon, when I should in fact dine with the king. Let me go and hide in the open country until evening. [6]If it turns out that your father misses me, say, 'David urged me to let him go on short notice to his city Bethlehem, because his whole clan is holding its seasonal sacrifice there.' [7]If he says, 'Very well,' your servant is safe. But if he becomes quite angry, you can be sure he has planned some harm. [8]Do this kindness for your servant because of the LORD's covenant into which you brought us: if I am guilty, kill me yourself! Why should you give me up to your father?" [9]But Jonathan answered: "Not I! If ever I find out that my father is determined to harm you, I will certainly let you know." [10]David then asked Jonathan, "Who will tell me if your father gives you a harsh answer?"

Mutual Agreement. [11]Jonathan replied to David, "Come, let us go out into the field." When they were out in the open country together, [12]Jonathan said to David: "As the LORD, the God of Israel, lives, I will sound out my father about this time tomorrow. Whether he is well disposed toward David or not, I will inform you. [13]Should it please my father to bring any harm upon you, may the LORD do thus to Jonathan and more, if I do not inform you of it and send you on your way in peace. May the LORD be with you even as he was with my father. [14]Only this: if I am still alive, may you show me the kindness of the LORD. But if I die, [15]never cut off your kindness from my house. And when the LORD cuts off all the enemies of David from the face of the land, [16]the name of Jonathan must never be cut off from the family of David, or the LORD will make you answer for it."

¹⁷And in his love for David, Jonathan renewed his oath to him, because he loved him as he loved himself.

¹⁸Jonathan then said to him: "Tomorrow is the new moon; you will be missed, since your place will be vacant. ¹⁹On the third day you will be missed all the more. Go to the spot where you hid on the other occasion and wait near the mound there. ²⁰On the third day of the month I will shoot arrows to the side of it, as though aiming at a target. ²¹I will then send my attendant to recover the arrows. If in fact I say to him, 'Look, the arrow is this side of you; pick it up,' come, for you are safe. As the LORD lives, there will be nothing to fear. ²²But if I say to the boy, 'Look, the arrow is beyond you,' go, for the LORD sends you away. ²³However, in the matter which you and I have discussed, the LORD shall be between you and me forever." ²⁴So David hid in the open country.

David's Absence. On the day of the new moon, when the king sat down at the feast to dine, ²⁵he took his usual place against the wall. Jonathan sat facing him, while Abner sat at the king's side. David's place was vacant. ²⁶Saul, however, said nothing that day, for he thought, "He must have become unclean by accident." ²⁷On the next day, the second day of the month, David's place was still vacant. So Saul asked his son Jonathan, "Why has the son of Jesse not come to table yesterday or today?" ²⁸Jonathan explained to Saul: "David pleaded with me to let him go to Bethlehem. ²⁹'Please let me go,' he begged, 'for we are having a clan sacrifice in our city, and my brothers insist on my presence. Now then, if you think well of me, give me leave to visit my brothers.' That is why he has not come to the king's table." ³⁰But Saul grew angry with Jonathan and said to him: "Son of a rebellious woman, do I not know that, to your own disgrace and to the disgrace of your mother's nakedness, you are the companion of Jesse's son? ³¹For as long as the son of Jesse lives upon the earth, you cannot make good your claim to the kingship! Now send for him, and bring him to me, for he must die." ³²But Jonathan argued with his father Saul: "Why should he die? What has he done?" ³³At this Saul brandished his spear to strike him, and thus Jonathan learned that his father was determined to kill David. ³⁴Jonathan sprang up from the table in a rage and ate nothing that second day of the month, because he was grieved on David's account, and because his father had humiliated him.

Jonathan's Farewell. ³⁵The next morning Jonathan, accompanied by a young boy, went out into the field for his appointment with David. ³⁶There he said to the boy, "Run and find the arrows." And as the boy ran, he shot an arrow past him. ³⁷When the boy made for the spot where Jonathan had shot the arrow, Jonathan called after him, "The arrow is farther on!" ³⁸Again he called to the boy, "Hurry, be quick, don't delay!" Jonathan's boy picked up the arrow and brought it to his master. ³⁹The boy suspected nothing; only Jonathan and David knew what was meant. ⁴⁰Then Jonathan gave his weapons to his boy and said to him, "Go, take them to the city." ⁴¹When the boy had gone, David rose from beside the mound and fell on his face to the ground three times in homage. They kissed each other and wept aloud together. ⁴²At length Jonathan said to David, "Go in peace, in keeping with what the two of us have sworn by the name of the LORD: 'The LORD shall be between you and me, and between your offspring and mine forever.'"

☐ 1 CORINTHIANS 13

13:1 If I speak in human and angelic tongues but do not have love, I am a resounding gong or a clashing cymbal. ²And if I have the gift of prophecy and comprehend all mysteries and all knowledge; if I have all faith so as to move mountains but do not have love, I am nothing. ³If I give away everything I own, and if I hand my body over so that I may boast but do not have love, I gain nothing.

⁴Love is patient, love is kind. It is not jealous, [love] is not pompous, it is not inflated, ⁵it is not rude, it does not seek its own interests, it is not quick-tempered, it does not brood over injury, ⁶it does not rejoice over wrongdoing but rejoices with the truth. ⁷It bears all things, believes all things, hopes all things, endures all things.

⁸Love never fails. If there are prophecies, they will be brought to nothing; if tongues, they will cease; if knowledge, it will be brought to nothing. ⁹For we know partially and we prophesy partially, ¹⁰but when the perfect comes, the partial will pass away. ¹¹When I was a child, I used to talk as a child, think as a child, reason as a child; when I became a man, I put aside childish things. ¹²At present we see indistinctly, as in a mirror, but then face to face. At present I know partially; then I shall know fully, as I am fully known. ¹³So faith, hope, love remain, these three; but the greatest of these is love.

April 4

St. Isidore of Seville

If a man wants to be always in God's company, he must pray regularly and read spiritual books regularly. When we pray, we talk to God; when we read, God talks to us.

— ST. ISIDORE OF SEVILLE

☐ 1 SAMUEL 21-25

21:1 Then David departed on his way, while Jonathan went back into the city.

The Holy Bread. ²David went to Ahimelech, the priest of Nob, who came trembling to meet him. He asked, "Why are you alone? Is there no one with you?" ³David answered the priest: "The king gave me a commission and told me, 'Do not let anyone know anything about the business on which I have sent you or the commission I have given you.' For that reason I have arranged a particular meeting place with my men. ⁴Now what do you have on hand? Give me five loaves, or whatever you can find." ⁵But the priest replied to David, "I have no ordinary bread on hand, only holy bread; if the men have abstained from women, you may eat some of that." ⁶David answered the priest: "We have indeed stayed away from women. In the past whenever I went out on a campaign, all the young men were consecrated—even for an ordinary campaign. All the more so are they consecrated with their weapons today!" ⁷So the priest gave him holy bread, for no other bread was on hand except the showbread which had been removed from before the LORD and replaced by fresh bread when it was taken away. ⁸One of Saul's servants was there that day, detained before the LORD;

his name was Doeg the Edomite, the chief of Saul's shepherds.

The Sword of Goliath. ⁹David then asked Ahimelech: "Do you have a spear or a sword on hand? I brought along neither my sword nor my weapons, because the king's business was urgent." ¹⁰The priest replied: "The sword of Goliath the Philistine, whom you killed in the Valley of Elah, is here wrapped in a garment behind an ephod. If you wish to take it, do so; there is no sword here except that one." "There is none like it," David cried, "give it to me!"

David a Fugitive. ¹¹That same day David fled from Saul, going to Achish, king of Gath. ¹²But the servants of Achish said to him, "Is this not David, the king of the land? Is it not for him that during their dances they sing out,

'Saul has slain his thousands,
David his tens of thousands'?"

¹³David took note of these remarks and became very much afraid of Achish, king of Gath. ¹⁴So, he feigned insanity in front of them and acted like a madman in their custody, drumming on the doors of the gate and drooling onto his beard. ¹⁵Finally Achish said to his servants: "You see the man is mad. Why did you bring him to me? ¹⁶Do I not have enough madmen, that you bring this one to rant in my presence? Should this fellow come into my house?"

22:1 David left Gath and escaped to the cave of Adullam. When his brothers and the rest of his family heard about it, they came down to him there. ²He was joined by all those in difficulties or in debt, or embittered, and became their leader. About four hundred men were with him.

³From there David went to Mizpeh of Moab and said to the king of Moab, "Let my father and mother stay with you, until I learn what God will do for me." ⁴He left them with the king of Moab; they stayed with him as long as David remained in the stronghold.

⁵But Gad the prophet said to David: "Do not remain in the stronghold! Leave! Go to the land of Judah." And so David left and went to the forest of Hereth.

Doeg Betrays Ahimelech. ⁶Now Saul heard that David and his men had been located. At the time he was sitting in Gibeah under a tamarisk tree on the high place, holding his spear, while all his servants stood by him. ⁷So he said to them: "Listen, men of Benjamin! Will the son of Jesse give all of you fields and vineyards? Will he appoint any of you an officer over a thousand or a hundred men? ⁸Is that why you have all conspired against me? Why no one told me that my son had made a pact with the son of Jesse? None of you has shown compassion for me by revealing to me that my son has incited my servant to ambush me, as is the case today." ⁹Then Doeg the Edomite, who was standing with Saul's officers, spoke up: "I saw the son of Jesse come to Ahimelech, son of Ahitub, in Nob. ¹⁰He consulted the LORD for him, furnished him with provisions, and gave him the sword of Goliath the Philistine."

Slaughter of the Priests. ¹¹So the king summoned Ahimelech the priest, son of Ahitub, and all his family, the priests in Nob. They all came to the king. ¹²"Listen, son of Ahitub!" Saul declared. "Yes, my lord," he replied. ¹³Saul questioned him, "Why have you conspired against me with the son of Jesse by giving him food and a sword and by consulting God for him, that he might rise up against me in ambush, as is the case today?" ¹⁴Ahimelech answered the king: "Who among all your servants is as loyal as David, the king's son-in-law, captain of your bodyguard, and honored in your own house? ¹⁵Is this the first time I have consulted God for him? No indeed! Let not the king accuse his servant or anyone in my family of such a thing. Your servant knows nothing at all, great or small, about the whole matter." ¹⁶But the king said, "You shall certainly die, Ahimelech, with all your family." [17]The king then commanded his guards standing by him: "Turn and kill the priests of the LORD, for they gave David a hand. They knew he was a fugitive and yet failed to inform me." But the king's servants refused to raise a hand to strike the priests of the LORD.

[18]The king therefore commanded Doeg, "You, turn and kill the priests!" So Doeg the Edomite himself turned and killed the priests that day—eighty-five who wore the linen ephod. [19]Saul also put the priestly city of Nob to the sword, including men and women, children and infants, and oxen, donkeys and sheep.

Abiathar Escapes. [20]One son of Ahimelech, son of Ahitub, named Abiathar, escaped and fled to David. [21]When Abiathar told David that Saul had slain the priests of the LORD, [22]David said to him: "I knew that day, when Doeg the Edomite was there, that he would certainly tell Saul. I am responsible for the slaughter of all your family. [23]Stay with me. Do not be afraid; whoever seeks your life must seek my life also. You are under my protection."

Keilah Liberated. 23:1 David was informed that the Philistines were attacking Keilah and plundering the threshing floors. [2]So he consulted the LORD, asking, "Shall I go and attack these Philistines?" The LORD answered, Go, attack them, and free Keilah. [3]But David's men said to him: "Even in Judah we have reason to fear. How much more so if we go to Keilah against the forces of the Philistines!" [4]Again David consulted the LORD, who answered: Go down to Keilah, for I will deliver the Philistines into your power. [5]So David went with his men to Keilah and fought against the Philistines. He drove off their cattle and inflicted a severe defeat on them, and freed the inhabitants of Keilah.

[6]Abiathar, son of Ahimelech, who had fled to David, went down with David to Keilah, taking the ephod with him.

Flight from Keilah. [7]When Saul was told that David had entered Keilah, he thought: "God has put him in my hand, for he has boxed himself in by entering a city with gates and bars." [8]Saul then called all the army to war, in order to go down to Keilah and besiege David and his men. [9]When David found out that Saul was planning to harm him, he said to the priest Abiathar, "Bring the ephod here." [10]"LORD God of Israel," David prayed, "your servant has heard that Saul plans to come to Keilah, to destroy the city on my account. [11]Will they hand me over? Will Saul come down as your servant has heard? LORD God of Israel, tell your servant." The LORD answered: He will come down. [12]David then asked, "Will the citizens of Keilah deliver me and my men into the hand of Saul?" The LORD answered: They will deliver you. [13]So David and his men, about six hundred in number, left Keilah and wandered from place to place. When Saul was informed that David had fled from Keilah, he did not go forth.

David and Jonathan in Horesh. [14]David now lived in the strongholds in the wilderness, or in the barren hill country near Ziph. Though Saul sought him continually, the LORD did not deliver David into his hand. [15]While David was in the wilderness of Ziph at Horesh he was afraid that Saul had come out to seek his life. [16]Then Saul's son, Jonathan, came down to David at Horesh and encouraged him in the LORD. [17]He said to him: "Have no fear, my father Saul shall not lay a hand to you. You shall be king of Israel and I shall be second to you. Even my father Saul knows this." [18]The two of them made a covenant before the LORD in Horesh, where David remained, while Jonathan returned to his home.

Treachery of the Ziphites. [19]Some of the Ziphites went up to Saul in Gibeah and said, "David is hiding among us in the strongholds at Horesh on the hill of

Hachilah, south of Jeshimon. ²⁰Therefore, whenever the king wishes to come down, let him do so. It will be our task to deliver him into the king's hand." ²¹Saul replied: "The LORD bless you for your compassion toward me. ²²Go now and make sure once more! Take note of the place where he sets foot for I am told that he is very cunning. ²³Look around and learn in which of all the various hiding places he is holding out. Then come back to me with reliable information, and I will go with you. If he is in the region, I will track him down out of all the families of Judah." ²⁴So they went off to Ziph ahead of Saul. At this time David and his men were in the wilderness below Maon, in the Arabah south of the wasteland.

Escape from Saul. ²⁵When Saul and his men came looking for him, David got word of it and went down to the gorge in the wilderness below Maon. Saul heard of this and pursued David into the wilderness below Maon. ²⁶As Saul moved along one side of the gorge, David and his men took to the other. David was anxious to escape Saul, while Saul and his men were trying to outflank David and his men in order to capture them. ²⁷Then a messenger came to Saul, saying, "Come quickly, because the Philistines have invaded the land." ²⁸Saul interrupted his pursuit of David and went to meet the Philistines. This is how that place came to be called the Rock of Divisions.

David Spares Saul. 24:1 David then went up from there and stayed in the strongholds of Engedi. ²When Saul returned from the pursuit of the Philistines, he was told that David was in the desert near Engedi. ³So Saul took three thousand of the best men from all Israel and went in search of David and his men in the direction of the wild goat crags. ⁴When he came to the sheepfolds along the way, he found a cave, which he entered to relieve himself. David and his men were occupying the inmost recesses of the cave.

⁵David's servants said to him, "This is the day about which the LORD said to you: I will deliver your enemy into your hand; do with him as you see fit." So David moved up and stealthily cut off an end of Saul's robe. ⁶Afterward, however, David regretted that he had cut off an end of Saul's robe. ⁷He said to his men, "The LORD forbid that I should do such a thing to my master, the LORD's anointed, to lay a hand on him, for he is the LORD's anointed." ⁸With these words David restrained his men and would not permit them to attack Saul. Saul then left the cave and went on his way. ⁹David also stepped out of the cave, calling to Saul, "My lord the king!" When Saul looked back, David bowed, his face to the ground in homage, ¹⁰and asked Saul: "Why do you listen to those who say, 'David is trying to harm you'? ¹¹You see for yourself today that the LORD just now delivered you into my hand in the cave. I was told to kill you, but I took pity on you instead. I decided, 'I will not raise a hand against my master, for he is the LORD's anointed.' ¹²Look here, my father. See the end of your robe which I hold. I cut off an end of your robe and did not kill you. Now see and be convinced that I plan no harm and no rebellion. I have done you no wrong, though you are hunting me down to take my life. ¹³May the LORD judge between me and you. May the LORD exact justice from you in my case. I shall not lay a hand on you. ¹⁴As the old proverb says, 'From the wicked comes wickedness.' Thus I will not lay a hand on you. ¹⁵What is the king of Israel attacking? What are you pursuing? A dead dog! A single flea! ¹⁶The LORD will be the judge to decide between us. May the LORD see this, defend my cause, and give me justice against you!"

Saul's Remorse. ¹⁷When David finished saying these things to Saul, Saul answered, "Is that your voice, my son David?" And he wept freely. ¹⁸Saul then admitted to

David: "You are more in the right than I am. You have treated me graciously, while I have treated you badly. [19]You have declared this day how you treated me graciously: the LORD delivered me into your hand and you did not kill me. [20]For if someone comes upon an enemy, do they send them graciously on their way? So may the LORD reward you graciously for what you have done this day. [21]And now, since I know that you will certainly become king and that the kingship over Israel shall come into your possession, [22]swear to me by the LORD that you will not cut off my descendants and that you will not blot out my name from my father's house." [23]David gave Saul his oath and Saul returned home, while David and his men went up to the stronghold.

Death of Samuel. 25:1 Samuel died, and all Israel gathered to mourn him; they buried him at his home in Ramah. Then David went down to the wilderness of Paran.

  Nabal and Abigail. [2]There was a man of Maon who had property in Carmel; he was very wealthy, owning three thousand sheep and a thousand goats. At the time, he was present for the shearing of his flock in Carmel. [3]The man's name was Nabal and his wife was Abigail. The woman was intelligent and attractive, but Nabal, a Calebite, was harsh and bad-mannered. [4]While in the wilderness, David heard that Nabal was shearing his flock, [5]so he sent ten young men, instructing them: "Go up to Carmel. Pay Nabal a visit and greet him in my name. [6]Say to him, 'Peace be with you, my brother, and with your family, and with all who belong to you. [7]I have just heard that shearers are with you. Now, when your shepherds were with us, we did them no injury, neither did they miss anything while they were in Carmel. [8]Ask your servants and they will tell you. Look kindly on these young men, since we come at a festival time. Please give your servants and your son David whatever you can.'"

[9]When David's young men arrived, they delivered the entire message to Nabal in David's name, and then waited. [10]But Nabal answered the servants of David: "Who is David? Who is the son of Jesse? Nowadays there are many servants who run away from their masters. [11]Must I take my bread, my wine, my meat that I have slaughtered for my own shearers, and give them to men who come from who knows where?" [12]So David's young men retraced their steps and on their return reported to him all that had been said. [13]Thereupon David said to his men, "Let everyone strap on his sword." And everyone did so, and David put on his own sword. About four hundred men went up after David, while two hundred remained with the baggage.

[14]Abigail, Nabal's wife, was informed of this by one of the servants, who said: "From the wilderness David sent messengers to greet our master, but he screamed at them. [15]Yet these men were very good to us. We were not harmed, neither did we miss anything all the while we were living among them during our stay in the open country. [16]Day and night they were a wall of protection for us, the whole time we were pasturing the sheep near them. [17]Now, see what you can do, for you must realize that otherwise disaster is in store for our master and for his whole house. He is such a scoundrel that no one can talk to him." [18]Abigail quickly got together two hundred loaves, two skins of wine, five dressed sheep, five seahs of roasted grain, a hundred cakes of pressed raisins, and two hundred cakes of pressed figs, and loaded them on donkeys. [19]She then said to her servants, "Go on ahead; I will follow you." But to her husband Nabal she said nothing.

[20]Hidden by the mountain, she came down riding on a donkey, as David and his men were coming down from the opposite direction. When she met them, [21]David had just been saying: "Indeed, it was in vain that I guarded all this man's

possessions in the wilderness, so that nothing of his was missing. He has repaid good with evil. ²²May God do thus to David, and more, if by morning I leave a single male alive among all those who belong to him." ²³As soon as Abigail saw David, she dismounted quickly from the donkey and, falling down, bowed low to the ground before David in homage.

²⁴As she fell at his feet she said: "My lord, let the blame be mine. Please let your maidservant speak to you; listen to the words of your maidservant. ²⁵My lord, do not pay any attention to that scoundrel Nabal, for he is just like his name. His name means fool, and he acts the fool. I, your maidservant, did not see the young men whom my lord sent. ²⁶Now, therefore, my lord, as the LORD lives, and as you live, the LORD has kept you from shedding blood and from avenging yourself by your own hand. May your enemies and those who seek to harm my lord become as Nabal! ²⁷Accept this gift, then, which your maidservant has brought for my lord, and let it be given to the young men who follow my lord. ²⁸Please forgive the offense of your maidservant, for the LORD shall certainly establish a lasting house for my lord, because my lord fights the battles of the LORD. Let no evil be found in you your whole life long. ²⁹If any adversary pursues you to seek your life, may the life of my lord be bound in the bundle of the living in the care of the LORD your God; may God hurl out the lives of your enemies as from the hollow of a sling. ³⁰And when the LORD fulfills for my lord the promise of success he has made concerning you, and appoints you as ruler over Israel, ³¹you shall not have any regrets or burdens on your conscience, my lord, for having shed innocent blood or for having rescued yourself. When the LORD bestows good on my lord, remember your maidservant." ³²David said to Abigail: "Blessed is the LORD, the God of Israel, who sent you to meet me today. ³³Blessed is your good judgment and blessed are you yourself. Today you have prevented me from shedding blood and rescuing myself with my own hand. ³⁴Otherwise, as the LORD, the God of Israel, lives, who has kept me from harming you, if you had not come so promptly to meet me, by dawn Nabal would not have had so much as one male left alive." ³⁵David then took from her what she had brought him and said to her: "Go to your home in peace! See, I have listened to your appeal and have granted your request."

Nabal's Death. ³⁶When Abigail came to Nabal, he was hosting a banquet in his house like that of a king, and Nabal was in a festive mood and very drunk. So she said not a word to him until daybreak the next morning. ³⁷But then, when Nabal was sober, his wife told him what had happened. At this his heart died within him, and he became like a stone. ³⁸About ten days later the LORD struck Nabal and he died. ³⁹Hearing that Nabal was dead, David said: "Blessed be the LORD, who has defended my cause against the insult from Nabal, and who restrained his servant from doing evil, but has repaid Nabal for his evil deeds."

David Marries Abigail and Ahinoam. David then sent a proposal of marriage to Abigail. ⁴⁰When David's servants came to Abigail in Carmel, they said to her, "David has sent us to make his proposal of marriage to you." ⁴¹Rising and bowing to the ground, she answered, "Let your maidservant be the slave who washes the feet of my lord's servants." ⁴²She got up immediately, mounted a donkey, and followed David's messengers, with her five maids attending her. She became his wife. ⁴³David also married Ahinoam of Jezreel. Thus both of them were his wives. ⁴⁴But Saul gave David's wife Michal, Saul's own daughter, to Palti, son of Laish, who was from Gallim.

☐ 1 CORINTHIANS 14

Prophecy Greater than Tongues. 14:1 Pursue love, but strive eagerly for the spiritual gifts, above all that you may prophesy. [2]For one who speaks in a tongue does not speak to human beings but to God, for no one listens; he utters mysteries in spirit. [3]On the other hand, one who prophesies does speak to human beings, for their building up, encouragement, and solace. [4]Whoever speaks in a tongue builds himself up, but whoever prophesies builds up the church. [5]Now I should like all of you to speak in tongues, but even more to prophesy. One who prophesies is greater than one who speaks in tongues, unless he interprets, so that the church may be built up.

[6]Now, brothers, if I should come to you speaking in tongues, what good will I do you if I do not speak to you by way of revelation, or knowledge, or prophecy, or instruction? [7]Likewise, if inanimate things that produce sound, such as flute or harp, do not give out the tones distinctly, how will what is being played on flute or harp be recognized? [8]And if the bugle gives an indistinct sound, who will get ready for battle? [9]Similarly, if you, because of speaking in tongues, do not utter intelligible speech, how will anyone know what is being said? For you will be talking to the air. [10]It happens that there are many different languages in the world, and none is meaningless; [11]but if I do not know the meaning of a language, I shall be a foreigner to one who speaks it, and one who speaks it a foreigner to me. [12]So with yourselves: since you strive eagerly for spirits, seek to have an abundance of them for building up the church.

Need for Interpretation. [13]Therefore, one who speaks in a tongue should pray to be able to interpret. [14][For] if I pray in a tongue, my spirit is at prayer but my mind is unproductive. [15]So what is to be done? I will pray with the spirit, but I will also pray with the mind. I will sing praise with the spirit, but I will also sing praise with the mind. [16]Otherwise, if you pronounce a blessing [with] the spirit, how shall one who holds the place of the uninstructed say the "Amen" to your thanksgiving, since he does not know what you are saying? [17]For you may be giving thanks very well, but the other is not built up. [18]I give thanks to God that I speak in tongues more than any of you, [19]but in the church I would rather speak five words with my mind, so as to instruct others also, than ten thousand words in a tongue.

Functions of These Gifts. [20]Brothers, stop being childish in your thinking. In respect to evil be like infants, but in your thinking be mature. [21]It is written in the law:

"By people speaking strange tongues
    and by the lips of foreigners
I will speak to this people,
    and even so they will not listen
        to me,

says the Lord." [22]Thus, tongues are a sign not for those who believe but for unbelievers, whereas prophecy is not for unbelievers but for those who believe.

[23]So if the whole church meets in one place and everyone speaks in tongues, and then uninstructed people or unbelievers should come in, will they not say that you are out of your minds? [24]But if everyone is prophesying, and an unbeliever or uninstructed person should come in, he will be convinced by everyone and judged by everyone, [25]and the secrets of his heart will be disclosed, and so he will fall down and worship God, declaring, "God is really in your midst."

Rules of Order. [26]So what is to be done, brothers? When you assemble, one has a psalm, another an instruction, a revelation, a tongue, or an interpretation. Everything should be done for building up. [27]If anyone speaks in a tongue, let it be two or at most three, and each in turn, and one should interpret. ²⁸But if there is no interpreter, the person should keep silent in the church and speak to himself and to God.

²⁹Two or three prophets should speak, and the others discern. ³⁰But if a revelation is given to another person sitting there, the first one should be silent. ³¹For you can all prophesy one by one, so that all may learn and all be encouraged. ³²Indeed, the spirits of prophets are under the prophets' control, ³³since he is not the God of disorder but of peace.

As in all the churches of the holy ones, ³⁴women should keep silent in the churches, for they are not allowed to speak, but should be subordinate, as even the law says. ³⁵But if they want to learn anything, they should ask their husbands at home. For it is improper for a woman to speak in the church. ³⁶Did the word of God go forth from you? Or has it come to you alone?

³⁷If anyone thinks that he is a prophet or a spiritual person, he should recognize that what I am writing to you is a commandment of the Lord. ³⁸If anyone does not acknowledge this, he is not acknowledged. ³⁹So, (my) brothers, strive eagerly to prophesy, and do not forbid speaking in tongues, ⁴⁰but everything must be done properly and in order.

April 5

St. Vincent Ferrer

If you truly want to help the soul of your neighbor, you should approach God first with all your heart. Ask Him simply to fill you with charity, the greatest of all virtues; with it, you can accomplish what you desire.

— ST. VINCENT FERRER

☐ 1 SAMUEL 26-31

David Spares Saul Again. 26:1 Men from Ziph came to Saul in Gibeah, reporting that David was hiding on the hill of Hachilah at the edge of Jeshimon. ²So Saul went down to the wilderness of Ziph with three thousand of the best warriors of Israel, to search for David in the wilderness of Ziph. ³Saul camped beside the road on the hill of Hachilah, at the edge of Jeshimon. David, who was living in the wilderness, saw that Saul had come into the wilderness after him ⁴and sent out scouts, who confirmed Saul's arrival. ⁵David then went to the place where Saul was encamped and saw the spot where Saul and his general, Abner, son of Ner, had their sleeping quarters. Saul was lying within the camp, and all his soldiers were bivouacked around him. ⁶David asked Ahimelech the Hittite, and Abishai, son of Zeruiah and brother of Joab, "Who will go down into the camp with me to Saul?" Abishai replied, "I will." ⁷So David and Abishai reached Saul's soldiers by night, and there was Saul lying asleep within the camp, his spear thrust into the ground at his head and Abner and his troops sleeping around him.

⁸Abishai whispered to David: "God has delivered your enemy into your hand today. Let me nail him to the ground with one thrust of the spear; I will not need to strike him twice!" ⁹But David said to Abishai, "Do not harm him, for who can

lay a hand on the LORD's anointed and remain innocent? [10]As the LORD lives," David declared, "only the LORD can strike him: either when the time comes for him to die, or when he goes out and perishes in battle. [11]But the LORD forbid that I lay a hand on the LORD's anointed! Now take the spear at his head and the water jug, and let us be on our way." [12]So David took the spear and the water jug from their place at Saul's head, and they withdrew without anyone seeing or knowing or awakening. All remained asleep, because a deep slumber from the LORD had fallen upon them.

David Taunts Abner. [13]Crossing over to an opposite slope, David stood on a distant hilltop. With a great distance between them [14]David called to the army and to Abner, son of Ner, "Will you not answer, Abner?" Then Abner shouted back, "Who is it that calls me?" [15]David said to Abner: "Are you not a man? Who in Israel is your equal? Why were you not guarding your lord the king when one of his subjects came to assassinate the king, your lord? [16]What you have done is not right. As the LORD lives, you people deserve death because you have not guarded your lord, the anointed of the LORD. Go, look: where are the king's spear and the water jug that was at his head?"

Saul Admits His Guilt. [17]Saul recognized David's voice and asked, "Is that your voice, David my son?" David answered, "Yes, my lord the king." [18]He continued: "Why does my lord pursue his servant? What have I done? What evil am I planning? [19]Please, now, let my lord the king listen to the words of his servant. If the LORD has incited you against me, may an offering please the LORD. But if it is the people who have done so, may they be cursed before the LORD. They have driven me away so that today I have no share in the LORD's heritage, but am told: 'Go serve other gods!' [20]Do not let my blood spill on the ground far from the presence of the LORD. For the king of Israel has come out to seek a single flea as if he were hunting partridge in the mountains." [21]Then Saul said: "I have done wrong. Come back, David, my son! I will not harm you again, because you considered my life precious today even though I have been a fool and have made a serious mistake." [22]But David answered: "Here is the king's spear. Let an attendant come over to get it. [23]The LORD repays everyone's righteousness and faithfulness. Although the LORD delivered you into my hands today, I could not lay a hand on the LORD's anointed. [24]Just as I regarded your life as precious today, so may the LORD regard my life as precious and deliver me from all dangers." [25]Then Saul said to David: "Blessed are you, my son David! You shall certainly succeed in whatever you undertake." David went his way, and Saul returned to his place.

David Flees to the Philistines. 27:1 David said to himself: "I shall perish some day at the hand of Saul. I have no choice but to escape to the land of the Philistines; then Saul will give up his continual search for me throughout the land of Israel, and I will be out of his reach." [2]Accordingly, David departed with his six hundred soldiers and went over to Achish, son of Maoch, king of Gath. [3]David and his men lived in Gath with Achish; each one had his family, and David had his two wives, Ahinoam from Jezreel and Abigail, the widow of Nabal from Carmel. [4]When Saul learned that David had fled to Gath, he no longer searched for him.

[5]David said to Achish: "If I meet with your approval, let me have a place to live in one of the country towns. Why should your servant live with you in the royal city?" [6]That same day Achish gave him Ziklag, which has, therefore, belonged to the kings of Judah up to the present time. [7]In all, David lived a year and four months in Philistine territory.

David Raids Israel's Foes. [8]David and his men went out on raids against the Geshurites, Girzites, and Amalekites—

peoples living in the land between Telam, on the approach to Shur, and the land of Egypt. [9]In attacking the land David would not leave a man or woman alive, but would carry off sheep, oxen, donkeys, camels, and clothes. Then he would return to Achish, [10]who would ask, "Against whom did you raid this time?" David would reply, "Against the Negeb of Judah," or "Against the Negeb of Jerahmeel," or "Against the Negeb of the Kenites." [11]David never left a man or woman alive to be brought to Gath. He thought, "They will betray us and say, 'This is what David did.'" This was his custom as long as he lived in Philistine territory. [12]Achish trusted David, thinking, "His people Israel must certainly detest him. I shall have him as my vassal forever."

28:1 In those days the Philistines mustered their military forces to fight against Israel. So Achish said to David, "You realize, of course, that you and your warriors must march out for battle with me." [2]David answered Achish, "Good! Now you shall learn what your servant can do." Then Achish said to David, "I shall appoint you as my permanent bodyguard."

[3]Now, Samuel was dead. All Israel had mourned him and buried him in his city, Ramah. Meanwhile Saul had driven mediums and diviners out of the land.

Saul in Despair. [4]The Philistines rallied and, coming to Shunem, they encamped. Saul, too, mustered all Israel; they camped on Gilboa. [5]When Saul saw the Philistine camp, he grew afraid and lost heart completely. [6]He consulted the LORD; but the LORD gave no answer, neither in dreams nor by Urim nor through prophets. [7]Then Saul said to his servants, "Find me a medium through whom I can seek counsel." His servants answered him, "There is a woman in Endor who is a medium."

The Medium at Endor. [8]So he disguised himself, putting on other clothes, and set out with two companions. They came to the woman at night, and Saul said to her, "Divine for me; conjure up the spirit I tell you." [9]But the woman answered him, "You know what Saul has done, how he expelled the mediums and diviners from the land. Then why are you trying to entrap me and get me killed?" [10]But Saul swore to her by the LORD, "As the LORD lives, you shall incur no blame for this." [11]"Whom do you want me to conjure up?" the woman asked him. "Conjure up Samuel for me," he replied.

Samuel Appears. [12]When the woman saw Samuel, she shrieked at the top of her voice and said to Saul, "Why have you deceived me? You are Saul!" [13]But the king said to her, "Do not be afraid. What do you see?" "I see a god rising from the earth," she replied. [14]"What does he look like?" asked Saul. "An old man is coming up wrapped in a robe," she replied. Saul knew that it was Samuel, and so he bowed his face to the ground in homage.

Saul's Doom. [15]Samuel then said to Saul, "Why do you disturb me by conjuring me up?" Saul replied: "I am in great distress, for the Philistines are waging war against me and God has turned away from me. Since God no longer answers me through prophets or in dreams, I have called upon you to tell me what I should do." [16]To this Samuel said: "But why do you ask me, if the LORD has abandoned you for your neighbor? [17]The LORD has done to you what he declared through me: he has torn the kingdom from your hand and has given it to your neighbor David.

[18]"Because you disobeyed the LORD's directive and would not carry out his fierce anger against Amalek, the LORD has done this to you today. [19]Moreover, the LORD will deliver Israel, and you as well, into the hands of the Philistines. By tomorrow you and your sons will be with me, and the LORD will have delivered the army of Israel into the hands of the Philistines."

[20]Immediately Saul fell full length on the ground, in great fear because of Samuel's

message. He had no strength left, since he had eaten nothing all that day and night. ²¹Then the woman came to Saul and, seeing that he was quite terror-stricken, said to him: "Remember, your maidservant obeyed you: I took my life in my hands and carried out the request you made of me. ²²Now you, in turn, please listen to your maidservant. Let me set out a bit of food for you to eat, so that you are strong enough to go on your way." ²³But he refused, saying, "I will not eat." However, when his servants joined the woman in urging him, he listened to their entreaties, got up from the ground, and sat on a couch. ²⁴The woman had a stall-fed calf in the house, which she now quickly slaughtered. Then taking flour, she kneaded it and baked unleavened bread. ²⁵She set the meal before Saul and his servants, and they ate. Then they got up and left the same night.

David's Aid Rejected. 29:1 Now the Philistines had mustered all their forces in Aphek, and the Israelites were encamped at the spring in Jezreel. ²As the Philistine lords were marching their units of a hundred and a thousand, David and his warriors were marching in the rear guard with Achish. ³The Philistine commanders asked, "What are those Hebrews doing here?" Achish answered them: "Why, that is David, the officer of Saul, king of Israel. He has been with me for a year or two, and from the day he came over to me until now I have never found fault in him." ⁴But the Philistine commanders were angered at this and said to him: "Send that man back! Let him return to the place you picked out for him. He must not go down into battle with us; during the battle he might become our enemy. For how else can he win back his master's favor, if not at the expense of our soldiers? ⁵Is this not the David for whom they sing during their dances,

'Saul has slain his thousands,
David his tens of thousands'?"

⁶So Achish summoned David and said to him: "As the LORD lives, you are honest, and I would want you with me in all my battles. To this day I have found nothing wrong with you since you came to me. But in the view of the chiefs you are not welcome. ⁷Leave peacefully, now, and do nothing that might displease the Philistine chiefs." ⁸But David said to Achish: "What have I done? What fault have you found in your servant from the day I entered your service until today, that I cannot go to fight against the enemies of my lord the king?" ⁹"I recognize," Achish answered David, "that you are trustworthy, like an angel of God. But the Philistine commanders are saying, 'He must not go with us into battle.' ¹⁰So the first thing tomorrow, you and your lord's servants who came with you, go to the place I picked out for you. Do not take to heart their worthless remarks; for you have been valuable in my service. But make an early morning start, as soon as it grows light, and be on your way." ¹¹So David and his warriors left early in the morning to return to the land of the Philistines, and the Philistines went on up to Jezreel.

Ziklag in Ruins. 30:1 Before David and his men reached Ziklag on the third day, the Amalekites had raided the Negeb and Ziklag. They stormed Ziklag, and set it on fire. ²They took captive the women and all who were in the city, young and old, killing no one, and they herded them off when they left. ³David and his men arrived at the city to find it burned to the ground and their wives, sons, and daughters taken captive. ⁴Then David and those who were with him wept aloud until they could weep no more. ⁵David's two wives, Ahinoam of Jezreel and Abigail, the widow of Nabal from Carmel, had also been carried off. ⁶Now David found himself in great danger, for the soldiers spoke of stoning him, so bitter were they over the fate of their sons and daughters. David took courage in the LORD his God [7]and said to Abiathar, the priest, son of Ahimelech, "Bring me the ephod!" When Abiathar brought him the ephod, [8]David inquired of the LORD, "Shall I pursue these raiders? Can I overtake them?" The LORD answered him: Go in pursuit, for you will certainly overtake them and bring about a rescue.

Raid on the Amalekites. [9]So David went off with his six hundred as far as the Wadi Besor, where those who were to remain behind halted. [10]David continued the pursuit with four hundred, but two hundred were too exhausted to cross the Wadi Besor and remained behind. [11]An Egyptian was found in the open country and brought to David. They gave him food to eat and water to drink; [12]they also offered a cake of pressed figs and two cakes of pressed raisins. When he had eaten, he revived, for he had not taken food nor drunk water for three days and three nights. [13]Then David asked him, "To whom do you belong? Where did you come from?" "I am an Egyptian, the slave of an Amalekite," he replied. "My master abandoned me three days ago because I fell sick. [14]We raided the Negeb of the Cherethites, the territory of Judah, and the Negeb of Caleb; and we set Ziklag on fire." [15]David then asked him, "Will you lead me down to these raiders?" He answered, "Swear to me by God that you will not kill me or hand me over to my master, and I will lead you down to the raiders." [16]So he led them down, and there were the Amalekites lounging all over the ground, eating, drinking, and celebrating because of all the rich plunder they had taken from the land of the Philistines and from the land of Judah.

The Plunder Recovered. [17]From dawn to sundown the next day David attacked them, allowing no one to escape except four hundred young men, who mounted their camels and fled. [18]David recovered everything the Amalekites had taken, and he rescued his two wives. [19]Nothing was missing, small or great, plunder or sons or daughters, of all that the Amalekites had taken. David brought back everything. [20]Moreover, David took all the sheep and oxen, and as they drove these before him, they shouted, "This is David's plunder!"

Division of the Plunder. [21]When David came to the two hundred men who had been too exhausted to follow him, whom he had left behind at the Wadi Besor, they came out to meet David and the men with him. As David approached, he greeted them. [22]But all the greedy and worthless among those who had accompanied David said, "Since they did not accompany us, we will not give them anything from the plunder, except for each man's wife and children." [23]But David said: "You must not do this, my brothers, after what the LORD has given us. The LORD has protected us and delivered into our hands the raiders that came against us. [24]Who could agree with this proposal of yours? Rather, the share of the one who goes down to battle shall be the same as that of the one who remains with the baggage—they share alike." [25]And from that day forward he made this a law and a custom in Israel, as it still is today.

David's Gifts to Judah. [26]When David came to Ziklag, he sent part of the plunder to his friends, the elders of Judah, saying, "This is a gift to you from the plunder of the enemies of the LORD," namely, [27]to those in Bethel, Ramoth-negeb, Jattir, [28]Aroer, Siphmoth, Eshtemoa, [29]Racal, Jerahmeelite cities and Kenite cities, [30]Hormah, Borashan, Athach, [31]Hebron, and to all the places that David and his men had frequented.

Death of Saul and His Sons. 31:1 Now the Philistines went to war against Israel, and the Israelites fled before them, and fell, slain on Mount Gilboa. [2]The Philistines pressed hard after Saul and his sons. When the Philistines had struck down Jonathan, Abinadab, and Malchishua, sons of Saul, [3]the fury of the battle converged on Saul. Then the archers hit him, and he was severely wounded. ⁴Saul said to his armor-bearer, "Draw your sword and run me through; otherwise these uncircumcised will come and abuse me." But the armor-bearer, badly frightened, refused, so Saul took his own sword and fell upon it. ⁵When the armor-bearer saw that Saul was dead, he too fell upon his sword and died with him. ⁶Thus Saul, his three sons, and his armor-bearer died together on that same day. ⁷When the Israelites on the slope of the valley and those along the Jordan saw that the men of Israel had fled and that Saul and his sons were dead, they abandoned their cities and fled. Then the Philistines came and lived in those cities.

⁸On the following day, when the Philistines came to strip the slain, they found Saul and his three sons fallen on Mount Gilboa. ⁹They cut off Saul's head and stripped him of his armor; these they sent throughout the land of the Philistines to bring the good news to the temple of their idols and to the people. ¹⁰They put his armor in the temple of Astarte but impaled his body on the wall of Beth-shan.

Burial of Saul. ¹¹When the inhabitants of Jabesh-gilead heard what the Philistines had done to Saul, ¹²all their warriors set out and traveled through the night; they removed the bodies of Saul and his sons from the wall of Beth-shan, and, returning to Jabesh, burned them. ¹³Then they took their bones and buried them under the tamarisk tree in Jabesh, and fasted for seven days.

☐ 1 CORINTHIANS 15

The Gospel Teaching. 15:1 Now I am reminding you, brothers, of the gospel I preached to you, which you indeed received and in which you also stand. ²Through it you are also being saved, if you hold fast to the word I preached to you, unless you believed in vain. ³For I handed on to you as of first importance what I also received: that Christ died for our sins in accordance with the scriptures; ⁴that he was buried; that he was raised on the third day in accordance with the scriptures; ⁵that he appeared to Cephas, then to the Twelve. ⁶After that, he appeared to more than five hundred brothers at once, most of whom are still living, though some have fallen asleep. ⁷After that he appeared to James, then to all the apostles. ⁸Last of all, as to one born abnormally, he appeared to me. ⁹For I am the least of the apostles, not fit to be called an apostle, because I persecuted the church of God. ¹⁰But by the grace of God I am what I am, and his grace to me has not been ineffective. Indeed, I have toiled harder than all of them; not I, however, but the grace of God [that is] with me. ¹¹Therefore, whether it be I or they, so we preach and so you believed.

Results of Denial. ¹²But if Christ is preached as raised from the dead, how can some among you say there is no resurrection of the dead? ¹³If there is no resurrection of the dead, then neither has Christ been raised. ¹⁴And if Christ has not been raised, then empty [too] is our preaching; empty, too, your faith. ¹⁵Then we are also false witnesses to God, because we testified against God that he raised Christ, whom he did not raise if in fact the dead are not raised. ¹⁶For if the dead are not raised, neither has Christ been raised, ¹⁷and if Christ has not been raised, your faith is vain; you are still in your sins. ¹⁸Then those who have fallen asleep in Christ have perished. ¹⁹If for this life only we have hoped in Christ, we are the most pitiable people of all.

Christ the Firstfruits. ²⁰But now Christ has been raised from the dead, the firstfruits of those who have fallen asleep. ²¹For since death came through a human being, the resurrection of the dead came also through a human being. [22]For just as in Adam all die, so too in Christ shall all be brought to life, [23]but each one in proper order: Christ the firstfruits; then, at his coming, those who belong to Christ; [24]then comes the end, when he hands over the kingdom to his God and Father, when he has destroyed every sovereignty and every authority and power. [25]For he must reign until he has put all his enemies under his feet. [26]The last enemy to be destroyed is death, [27]for "he subjected everything under his feet." But when it says that everything has been subjected, it is clear that it excludes the one who subjected everything to him. [28]When everything is subjected to him, then the Son himself will [also] be subjected to the one who subjected everything to him, so that God may be all in all.

Practical Arguments. [29]Otherwise, what will people accomplish by having themselves baptized for the dead? If the dead are not raised at all, then why are they having themselves baptized for them?

[30]Moreover, why are we endangering ourselves all the time? [31]Every day I face death; I swear it by the pride in you [brothers] that I have in Christ Jesus our Lord. [32]If at Ephesus I fought with beasts, so to speak, what benefit was it to me? If the dead are not raised:

"Let us eat and drink,
    for tomorrow we die."

[33]Do not be led astray:

"Bad company corrupts good morals."

[34]Become sober as you ought and stop sinning. For some have no knowledge of God; I say this to your shame.

[35]But someone may say, "How are the dead raised? With what kind of body will they come back?"

The Resurrection Body. [36]You fool! What you sow is not brought to life unless it dies. [37]And what you sow is not the body that is to be but a bare kernel of wheat, perhaps, or of some other kind; [38]but God gives it a body as he chooses, and to each of the seeds its own body. [39]Not all flesh is the same, but there is one kind for human beings, another kind of flesh for animals, another kind of flesh for birds, and another for fish. [40]There are both heavenly bodies and earthly bodies, but the brightness of the heavenly is one kind and that of the earthly another. [41]The brightness of the sun is one kind, the brightness of the moon another, and the brightness of the stars another. For star differs from star in brightness.

[42]So also is the resurrection of the dead. It is sown corruptible; it is raised incorruptible. [43]It is sown dishonorable; it is raised glorious. It is sown weak; it is raised powerful. [44]It is sown a natural body; it is raised a spiritual body. If there is a natural body, there is also a spiritual one.

[45]So, too, it is written, "The first man, Adam, became a living being," the last Adam a life-giving spirit. [46]But the spiritual was not first; rather the natural and then the spiritual. [47]The first man was from the earth, earthly; the second man, from heaven. [48]As was the earthly one, so also are the earthly, and as is the heavenly one, so also are the heavenly. [49]Just as we have borne the image of the earthly one, we shall also bear the image of the heavenly one.

The Resurrection Event. [50]This I declare, brothers: flesh and blood cannot inherit the kingdom of God, nor does corruption inherit incorruption. [51]Behold, I tell you a mystery. We shall not all fall asleep, but we will all be changed, [52]in an instant, in the blink of an eye, at the last trumpet. For the trumpet will sound, the dead will be raised incorruptible, and we shall be changed. [53]For that which is corruptible must clothe itself with incorruptibility, and that which is mortal must clothe itself with immortality. [54]And when this which is corruptible clothes itself with incorruptibility and this which is mortal clothes itself with immortality, then the word that is written shall come about:

"Death is swallowed up in victory.
[55]Where, O death, is your victory?
Where, O death, is your sting?"

[56]The sting of death is sin, and the power of sin is the law. [57]But thanks be to God who gives us the victory through our Lord Jesus Christ.

[58]Therefore, my beloved brothers, be firm, steadfast, always fully devoted to the work of the Lord, knowing that in the Lord your labor is not in vain.

April 6

Blessed Zefirino Agostini

Do not be dismayed by toil or suffering, nor by the meager fruit of your labors. Remember that God rewards not according to results, but effort.

— BLESSED ZEFIRINO AGOSTINI

☐ 2 SAMUEL 1-3

Report of Saul's Death. 1:1 After the death of Saul, David returned from his victory over the Amalekites and stayed in Ziklag two days. [2]On the third day a man came from the field of battle, one of Saul's people, with his garments torn and his head covered with dirt. Going to David, he fell to the ground in homage. [3]David asked him, "Where have you come from?" He replied, "From the Israelite camp: I have escaped." [4]"What happened?" David said. "Tell me." He answered that the soldiers had fled the battle and many of them had fallen and were dead; and that Saul and his son Jonathan were dead. [5]Then David said to the youth who was reporting to him, "How do you know that Saul and his son Jonathan are dead?" [6] The youth reporting to him replied: "I happened to find myself on Mount Gilboa and saw Saul leaning on his spear, with chariots and horsemen closing in on him. [7]He turned around and saw me, and called me to him. When I said, 'Here I am,' [8]he asked me, 'Who are you?'

and I replied, 'An Amalekite.' [9]Then he said to me, 'Stand over me, please, and put me to death, for I am in great suffering, but still alive.' [10]So I stood over him and put him to death, for I knew that he could not survive his wound. I removed the crown from his head and the armlet from his arm and brought them here to my lord."

[11]David seized his garments and tore them, and so did all the men who were with him. [12]They mourned and wept and fasted until evening for Saul and his son Jonathan, and for the people of the LORD and the house of Israel, because they had fallen by the sword. [13]David said to the youth who had reported to him, "Where are you from?" He replied, "I am the son of a resident alien, an Amalekite." [14]David said to him, "How is it that you were not afraid to put forth your hand to desecrate the LORD's anointed?" [15]David then called one of the attendants and said to him, "Come, strike him down"; so he struck him and he died. [16]David said to him,

"Your blood is on your head, for you testified against yourself when you said, 'I put the LORD's anointed to death.'"

Lament for Saul and Jonathan. ¹⁷Then David chanted this lament for Saul and his son Jonathan ¹⁸(he commanded that it be taught to the Judahites; it is recorded in the Book of Jashar):

¹⁹Alas! the glory of Israel,
　　slain upon your heights!
How can the warriors have fallen!
²⁰Do not report it in Gath,
　　as good news in Ashkelon's streets,
Lest Philistine women rejoice,
　　lest the women of the
　　　　uncircumcised exult!
²¹O mountains of Gilboa,
　　upon you be neither dew nor rain,
　　nor surging from the deeps!
Defiled there the warriors' shields,
　　the shield of Saul—no longer
　　　　anointed with oil!
²²From the blood of the slain,
　　from the bodies of the warriors,
The bow of Jonathan did not turn
　　back,
　　nor the sword of Saul return
　　　　unstained.
²³Saul and Jonathan, beloved and dear,
　　separated neither in life nor death,
　　swifter than eagles, stronger than
　　　　lions!
²⁴Women of Israel, weep over Saul,
　　who clothed you in scarlet and in
　　　　finery,
　　covered your clothing with
　　　　ornaments of gold.
²⁵How can the warriors have fallen
　　in the thick of battle!
Jonathan—slain upon your heights!
²⁶I grieve for you, Jonathan my brother!
　　Most dear have you been to me;
More wondrous your love to me
　　than the love of women.
²⁷How can the warriors have fallen,
　　the weapons of war have perished!

David Is Anointed King. 2:1 After this, David inquired of the LORD, "Shall I go up into one of the cities of Judah?" The LORD replied to him: Go up. Then David asked, "Where shall I go?" He replied: To Hebron. ²So David went up there, with his two wives, Ahinoam of Jezreel and Abigail, the wife of Nabal of Carmel. ³David also brought up his men with their families, and they dwelt in the towns of Hebron. ⁴Then the men of Judah came there and anointed David king over the house of Judah.

A report reached David that the people of Jabesh-gilead had buried Saul. ⁵So David sent messengers to the people of Jabesh-gilead and said to them: "May you be blessed by the LORD for having done this kindness to your lord Saul in burying him. ⁶And now may the LORD show you kindness and fidelity. For my part, I will show generosity to you for having done this. ⁷So take courage and prove yourselves valiant, for though your lord Saul is dead, the house of Judah has anointed me king over them."

Ishbaal King of Israel. ⁸Abner, son of Ner, captain of Saul's army, took Ishbaal, son of Saul, and brought him over to Mahanaim, ⁹where he made him king over Gilead, the Asherites, Jezreel, Ephraim, Benjamin, and the rest of Israel. ¹⁰Ishbaal, son of Saul, was forty years old when he became king over Israel, and he reigned two years; but the house of Judah followed David. ¹¹In all, David was king in Hebron over the house of Judah seven years and six months.

Combat near Gibeon. ¹²Now Abner, son of Ner, and the servants of Ishbaal, Saul's son, set out from Mahanaim for Gibeon. ¹³Joab, son of Zeruiah, and the servants of David also set out and encountered them at the pool of Gibeon. And they sat down, one group on one side of the pool and the other on the opposite side. ¹⁴Then Abner said to Joab, "Let the young men rise and perform for us." Joab replied, "All right." ¹⁵So they rose and were counted off: twelve of the Benjaminites of Ishbaal, son of Saul, and twelve of David's servants. [16]Then each one grasped his opponent's head and thrust his sword into his opponent's side, and they all fell down together. And so that place was named the Field of the Sides; it is in Gibeon.

Death of Asahel. [17]The battle that day was very fierce, and Abner and the men of Israel were defeated by David's servants. [18]The three sons of Zeruiah were there— Joab, Abishai, and Asahel. Asahel, who was as fleet of foot as a gazelle in the open field, [19]set out after Abner, turning neither right nor left in his pursuit. [20]Abner turned around and said, "Is that you, Asahel?" He replied, "Yes." [21]Abner said to him, "Turn right or left; seize one of the young men and take what you can strip from him." But Asahel would not stop pursuing him. [22]Once more Abner said to Asahel: "Stop pursuing me! Why must I strike you to the ground? How could I show my face to your brother Joab?" [23]Still he refused to stop. So Abner struck him in the abdomen with the heel of his spear, and the weapon protruded from his back. He fell there and died on the spot. All who came to the place where Asahel had fallen and died, halted. [24]But Joab and Abishai continued the pursuit of Abner. The sun had gone down when they came to the hill of Ammah which lies east of the valley toward the wilderness near Geba.

Truce Between Joab and Abner. [25]Here the Benjaminites rallied around Abner, forming a single group, and made a stand on a hilltop. [26]Then Abner called to Joab and said: "Must the sword devour forever? Do you not know that afterward there will be bitterness? How long before you tell the people to stop pursuing their brothers?" [27]Joab replied, "As God lives, if you had not spoken, it would be morning before the people would be stopped from pursuing their brothers." [28]Joab then sounded the horn, and all the people came to a halt,

pursuing Israel no farther and fighting no more. [29]Abner and his men marched all night long through the Arabah, crossed the Jordan, marched all through the morning, and came to Mahanaim. [30]Joab, coming from the pursuit of Abner, assembled all the men. Nineteen other servants of David were missing, besides Asahel. [31]But David's servants had struck down and killed three hundred and sixty men of Benjamin, followers of Abner. [32]They took up Asahel and buried him in his father's tomb in Bethlehem. Joab and his men made an all-night march, and dawn found them in Hebron.

3:1 There followed a long war between the house of Saul and the house of David, in which David grew ever stronger, but the house of Saul ever weaker.

Sons Born in Hebron. [2] Sons were born to David in Hebron: his firstborn, Amnon, of Ahinoam from Jezreel; [3]the second, Chileab, of Abigail the wife of Nabal of Carmel; the third, Absalom, son of Maacah, who was the daughter of Talmai, king of Geshur; [4]the fourth, Adonijah, son of Haggith; the fifth, Shephatiah, son of Abital; [5]and the sixth, Ithream, by David's wife Eglah. These were born to David in Hebron.

Ishbaal and Abner Quarrel. [6]During the war between the house of Saul and the house of David, Abner was gaining power in the house of Saul. [7]Now Saul had had a concubine, Rizpah, the daughter of Aiah. And Ishbaal, son of Saul, said to Abner, "Why have you slept with my father's concubine?" [8]Enraged at the words of Ishbaal, Abner said, "Am I a dog's head from Judah? As of today, I have been loyal to the house of Saul your father, to his brothers and his friends, and I have kept you out of David's clutches; and today you charge me with a crime involving a woman! [9]May God do thus to Abner, and more, if I do not carry out for David what the LORD swore to him— [10]that is, take away the kingdom from the house of Saul and establish the throne of David over Israel as well as Judah, from Dan to Beer-sheba." [11]Ishbaal was no longer able to say a word to Abner, he feared him so.

Abner and David Reconciled. [12]Then Abner sent messengers to David in Telam, where he was at the moment, to say, "Make a covenant with me, and you have me on your side, to bring all Israel over to you." [13]He replied, "Good, I will make a covenant with you. But one thing I require of you. You must not appear before me unless you bring back Michal, Saul's daughter, when you come to present yourself to me." [14]At the same time David sent messengers to Ishbaal, son of Saul, to say, "Give me my wife Michal, whom I betrothed by paying a hundred Philistine foreskins." [15]Ishbaal sent for her and took her away from her husband Paltiel, son of Laish, [16]who followed her weeping as far as Bahurim. But Abner said to him, "Go back!" So he turned back.

[17]Abner then had a word with the elders of Israel: "For some time you have been wanting David as your king. [18]Now take action, for the LORD has said of David: By David my servant I will save my people Israel from the power of the Philistines and from the power of all their enemies." [19]Abner also spoke with Benjamin, and then went to speak with David in Hebron concerning all that would be agreeable to Israel and to the whole house of Benjamin. [20]When Abner, accompanied by twenty men, came to David in Hebron, David prepared a feast for Abner and for the men who were with him. [21]Then Abner said to David, "I will now go to assemble all Israel for my lord the king, that they may make a covenant with you; you will then be king over all whom you wish to rule." So David let Abner go on his way in peace.

Death of Abner. [22]Just then David's servants and Joab were coming in from an expedition, bringing much plunder with them. Abner, having been dismissed by David, was no longer with him in Hebron but had gone on his way in peace. [23]When Joab and the whole force he had with him arrived, he was informed, "Abner, son of Ner, came to David, and he let him go on his way in peace." [24]So Joab went to the king and said: "What have you done? Abner came to you! Why did you let him get away? [25]Don't you know Abner? He came to trick you, to learn your comings and goings, to learn everything you do." [26]Joab then left David and sent messengers after Abner to bring him back from the cistern of Sirah; but David did not know. [27]When Abner returned to Hebron, Joab took him aside within the city gate to speak with him privately. There he stabbed him in the abdomen, and he died for the blood of Asahel, Joab's brother. [28]Later David heard of it and said: "Before the LORD, I and my kingdom are forever innocent. [29]May the blood of Abner, son of Ner, be on the head of Joab and all his family. May Joab's family never be without one suffering from a discharge, or one with a skin disease, or a man who holds the distaff, or one falling by the sword, or one in need of food!" [30]Joab and Abishai his brother had been lying in wait for Abner because he killed Asahel their brother in battle at Gibeon.

David Mourns Abner. [31]Then David said to Joab and to all the people who were with him, "Tear your garments, put on sackcloth, and mourn over Abner." King David himself followed the bier. [32]When they had buried Abner in Hebron, the king wept aloud at the grave of Abner, and all the people wept. [33]And the king sang this lament over Abner:

> Should Abner have died like a fool?
> [34]Your hands were not bound with
>   chains,
>   nor your feet placed in fetters;
> As one falls before the wicked, you fell.

And all the people continued to weep for him. [35]Then they went to console David with food while it was still day. But David swore, "May God do thus to me, and more, if before the sun goes down I eat bread or anything else." ³⁶All the people noted this with approval, just as everything the king did met with their approval. ³⁷So on that day all the people and all Israel came to know that it was not the king's doing that Abner, son of Ner, was put to death. ³⁸The king then said to his servants: "Do you not know that a prince, a great man, has fallen today in Israel. ³⁹Although I am the anointed king, I am weak this day, and these men, the sons of Zeruiah, are too ruthless for me. May the LORD repay the evildoer in accordance with his evil deed."

☐ 1 CORINTHIANS 16

The Collection. 16:1 Now in regard to the collection for the holy ones, you also should do as I ordered the churches of Galatia. ²On the first day of the week each of you should set aside and save whatever one can afford, so that collections will not be going on when I come. ³And when I arrive, I shall send those whom you have approved with letters of recommendation to take your gracious gift to Jerusalem. ⁴If it seems fitting that I should go also, they will go with me.

Paul's Travel Plans. ⁵I shall come to you after I pass through Macedonia (for I am going to pass through Macedonia), ⁶and perhaps I shall stay or even spend the winter with you, so that you may send me on my way wherever I may go. ⁷For I do not wish to see you now just in passing, but I hope to spend some time with you, if the Lord permits. ⁸I shall stay in Ephesus until Pentecost, ⁹because a door has opened for me wide and productive for work, but there are many opponents.

¹⁰If Timothy comes, see that he is without fear in your company, for he is doing the work of the Lord just as I am. ¹¹Therefore no one should disdain him. Rather, send him on his way in peace that he may come to me, for I am expecting him with the brothers. ¹²Now in regard to our brother Apollos, I urged him strongly to go to you with the brothers, but it was not at all his will that he go now. He will go when he has an opportunity.

Exhortation and Greetings. ¹³Be on your guard, stand firm in the faith, be courageous, be strong. ¹⁴Your every act should be done with love.

¹⁵I urge you, brothers—you know that the household of Stephanas is the firstfruits of Achaia and that they have devoted themselves to the service of the holy ones— ¹⁶be subordinate to such people and to everyone who works and toils with them. ¹⁷I rejoice in the arrival of Stephanas, Fortunatus, and Achaicus, because they made up for your absence, ¹⁸for they refreshed my spirit as well as yours. So give recognition to such people.

¹⁹The churches of Asia send you greetings. Aquila and Prisca together with the church at their house send you many greetings in the Lord. ²⁰All the brothers greet you. Greet one another with a holy kiss.

²¹I, Paul, write you this greeting in my own hand. ²²If anyone does not love the Lord, let him be accursed. *Marana tha.* ²³The grace of the Lord Jesus be with you. ²⁴My love to all of you in Christ Jesus.

April 7

*Children should never be taken to church in dress that would
not be thought good enough for appearing before company.*
— ST. JOHN BAPTIST DE LA SALLE

☐ 2 SAMUEL 4-7

Death of Ishbaal. 4:1 When Ishbaal, son of Saul, heard that Abner was dead in Hebron, he lost his resolve and all Israel was alarmed. ²Ishbaal, son of Saul, had two company leaders named Baanah and Rechab, sons of Rimmon the Beerothite, of the tribe of Benjamin—Beeroth, too, was ascribed to Benjamin: ³the Beerothites fled to Gittaim, where they have been resident aliens to this day. ⁴(Jonathan, son of Saul, had a son with crippled feet. He was five years old when the news about Saul and Jonathan came from Jezreel; his nurse took him and fled, but in their hasty flight, he fell and became lame. His name was Meribbaal.) ⁵The sons of Rimmon the Beerothite, Rechab and Baanah, came into the house of Ishbaal during the heat of the day, while he was lying on his bed in the afternoon. ⁶The gatekeeper of the house had dozed off while sifting wheat, and was asleep. So Rechab and his brother Baanah slipped past her ⁷and entered the house while Ishbaal was lying asleep in his bedroom. They struck and killed him, and cut off his head. Then, taking the head, they traveled on the Arabah road all night long.

The Murder Avenged. ⁸They brought the head of Ishbaal to David in Hebron and said to the king: "This is the head of Ishbaal, son of your enemy Saul, who sought your life. Thus has the LORD this day avenged my lord the king on Saul and his posterity." ⁹But David replied to Rechab and his brother Baanah, sons of Rimmon the Beerothite: "As the LORD lives, who rescued me from every distress: ¹⁰the man who reported to me, 'Saul is dead,' and

thought he was bringing good news, that man I seized and killed in Ziglag: that was the reward I gave him. ¹¹How much more now, when wicked men have slain an innocent man in bed at home, must I require his blood from you and purge you from the land!" ¹²So at David's command, the young men killed them and cut off their hands and feet, hanging them up near the pool in Hebron. But he took the head of Ishbaal and buried it in Abner's grave in Hebron.

David King of Israel. 5:1 All the tribes of Israel came to David in Hebron, and they said: "Look! We are your bone and your flesh. ²In days past, when Saul was still our king, you were the one who led Israel out in all its battles and brought it back. And the LORD said to you: You shall shepherd my people Israel; you shall be ruler over Israel." ³Then all the elders of Israel came to the king in Hebron, and at Hebron King David made a covenant with them in the presence of the LORD; and they anointed David king over Israel. ⁴David was thirty years old when he became king, and he reigned forty years: ⁵in Hebron he was king over Judah seven years and six months, and in Jerusalem he was king thirty-three years over all Israel and Judah.

Capture of Zion. ⁶ Then the king and his men went to Jerusalem against the Jebusites who inhabited the land. They told David, "You shall not enter here: the blind and the lame will drive you away!" which was their way of saying, "David shall not enter here." ⁷David nevertheless captured the fortress of Zion, which is the City of

David. [8]On that day David said: "All who wish to strike at the Jebusites must attack through the water shaft. The lame and the blind shall be the personal enemies of David." That is why it is said, "The blind and the lame shall not enter the palace." [9]David took up residence in the fortress which he called the City of David. David built up the city on all sides, from the Millo toward the center. [10]David became ever more powerful, for the LORD of hosts was with him. [11]Hiram, king of Tyre, sent envoys to David along with cedar wood, and carpenters and masons, who built a house for David. [12]David now knew that the LORD had truly established him as king over Israel and had exalted his kingdom for the sake of his people Israel.

David's Family in Jerusalem. [13]David took more concubines and wives in Jerusalem after he had come from Hebron, and more sons and daughters were born to him. [14]These are the names of those who were born to him in Jerusalem: Shammua, Shobab, Nathan, Solomon, [15]Ibhar, Elishua, Nepheg, Japhia, [16]Elishama, Beeliada, and Eliphelet.

Rout of the Philistines. [17]When the Philistines had heard that David was anointed king over Israel, they marched out in force to come after him. When David heard this, he went down to the refuge. [18]Meanwhile the Philistines had come and deployed themselves in the valley of Rephaim. [19]David inquired of the LORD, "Shall I attack the Philistines, and will you deliver them into my power?" The LORD answered David: Attack, for I will surely deliver the Philistines into your power. [20]So David went to Baal-perazim, and he defeated them there. He said, "The LORD has broken through my enemies before me just as water breaks through a dam." Therefore that place was called Baal-perazim. [21]The Philistines abandoned their gods there, and David and his men carried them away. [22]Once again the Philistines came up and deployed themselves in the valley of Rephaim, [23]and again David inquired of the LORD, who replied: Do not attack the front—circle behind them and come against them near the balsam trees. [24]When you hear the sound of marching in the tops of the balsam trees, act decisively, for then the LORD has already gone before you to strike the army of the Philistines. [25]David did as the LORD commanded him, and routed the Philistines from Gibeon as far as Gezer.

The Ark Brought to Jerusalem. 6:1 David again assembled all the picked men of Israel, thirty thousand in number. [2]Then David and all the people who were with him set out for Baala of Judah to bring up from there the ark of God, which bears the name "the LORD of hosts enthroned above the cherubim." [3]They transported the ark of God on a new cart and took it away from the house of Abinadab on the hill. Uzzah and Ahio, sons of Abinadab, were guiding the cart, [4]with Ahio walking before it, [5]while David and all the house of Israel danced before the LORD with all their might, with singing, and with lyres, harps, tambourines, sistrums, and cymbals. [6]As they reached the threshing floor of Nodan, Uzzah stretched out his hand to the ark of God and steadied it, for the oxen were tipping it. [7]Then the LORD became angry with Uzzah; God struck him on that spot, and he died there in God's presence. [8]David was angry because the LORD's wrath had broken out against Uzzah. Therefore that place has been called Perez-uzzah even to this day. [9]David became frightened of the LORD that day, and he said, "How can the ark of the LORD come to me?" [10]So David was unwilling to take the ark of the LORD with him into the City of David. David deposited it instead at the house of Obed-edom the Gittite. [11]The ark of the LORD remained in the house of Obed-edom the Gittite for three months, and the LORD blessed Obed-edom and all his household. ¹² When it was reported to King David that the LORD had blessed the household of Obed-edom and all that he possessed because of the ark of God, David went to bring up the ark of God from the house of Obed-edom into the City of David with joy. ¹³As soon as the bearers of the ark of the LORD had advanced six steps, he sacrificed an ox and a fatling. ¹⁴Then David came dancing before the LORD with abandon, girt with a linen ephod. ¹⁵David and all the house of Israel were bringing up the ark of the LORD with shouts of joy and sound of horn. ¹⁶As the ark of the LORD was entering the City of David, Michal, daughter of Saul, looked down from her window, and when she saw King David jumping and dancing before the LORD, she despised him in her heart. ¹⁷ They brought in the ark of the LORD and set it in its place within the tent which David had pitched for it. Then David sacrificed burnt offerings and communion offerings before the LORD. ¹⁸When David had finished sacrificing burnt offerings and communion offerings, he blessed the people in the name of the LORD of hosts, ¹⁹and distributed among all the people, the entire multitude of Israel, to every man and every woman, one loaf of bread, one piece of meat, and one raisin cake. Then all the people returned to their homes.

²⁰When David went home to bless his own house, Michal, the daughter of Saul, came out to meet him and said, "How well the king of Israel has honored himself today, exposing himself to the view of the slave girls of his followers, as a commoner might expose himself!" ²¹But David replied to Michal: "I was dancing before the LORD. As the LORD lives, who chose me over your father and all his house when he appointed me ruler over the LORD's people, Israel, not only will I make merry before the LORD, ²²but I will demean myself even more. I will be lowly in your eyes, but in the eyes of the slave girls you spoke of I will be somebody." ²³Saul's daughter Michal was childless to the day she died.

The Oracle of Nathan. 7:1 After the king had taken up residence in his house, and the LORD had given him rest from his enemies on every side, ²the king said to Nathan the prophet, "Here I am living in a house of cedar, but the ark of God dwells in a tent!" ³Nathan answered the king, "Whatever is in your heart, go and do, for the LORD is with you." ⁴But that same night the word of the LORD came to Nathan: ⁵Go and tell David my servant, Thus says the LORD: Is it you who would build me a house to dwell in? ⁶I have never dwelt in a house from the day I brought Israel up from Egypt to this day, but I have been going about in a tent or a tabernacle. ⁷As long as I have wandered about among the Israelites, did I ever say a word to any of the judges whom I commanded to shepherd my people Israel: Why have you not built me a house of cedar?

⁸Now then, speak thus to my servant David, Thus says the LORD of hosts: I took you from the pasture, from following the flock, to become ruler over my people Israel. ⁹I was with you wherever you went, and I cut down all your enemies before you. And I will make your name like that of the greatest on earth. ¹⁰I will assign a place for my people Israel and I will plant them in it to dwell there; they will never again be disturbed, nor shall the wicked ever again oppress them, as they did at the beginning, ¹¹and from the day when I appointed judges over my people Israel. I will give you rest from all your enemies. Moreover, the LORD also declares to you that the LORD will make a house for you: ¹² when your days have been completed and you rest with your ancestors, I will raise up your offspring after you, sprung from your loins, and I will establish his kingdom. ¹³He it is who shall build a house for my

name, and I will establish his royal throne forever. ¹⁴I will be a father to him, and he shall be a son to me. If he does wrong, I will reprove him with a human rod and with human punishments; ¹⁵but I will not withdraw my favor from him as I withdrew it from Saul who was before you. ¹⁶Your house and your kingdom are firm forever before me; your throne shall be firmly established forever. ¹⁷In accordance with all these words and this whole vision Nathan spoke to David.

David's Thanksgiving. ¹⁸Then King David went in and sat in the LORD's presence and said, "Who am I, Lord GOD, and what is my house, that you should have brought me so far? ¹⁹And yet even this is too little in your sight, Lord GOD! For you have made a promise regarding your servant's house reaching into the future, and giving guidance to the people, Lord GOD! ²⁰What more can David say to you? You know your servant, Lord GOD! ²¹For your servant's sake and as you have had at heart, you have brought about this whole magnificent disclosure to your servant. ²²Therefore, great are you, Lord GOD! There is no one like you, no God but you, as we have always heard. ²³What other nation on earth is there like your people Israel? What god has ever led a nation, redeeming it as his people and making a name by great and awesome deeds, as you drove out the nations and their gods before your people, whom you redeemed for yourself from Egypt? ²⁴You have established for yourself your people Israel as your people forever, and you, LORD, have become their God. ²⁵Now, LORD God, confirm the promise that you have spoken concerning your servant and his house forever. Bring about what you have promised ²⁶so that your name may be forever great. People will say: 'The LORD of hosts is God over Israel,' when the house of your servant David is established in your presence. ²⁷Because you, LORD of hosts, God of Israel, have revealed to your servant, 'I will build you a house,' your servant now finds the courage to make this prayer before you. ²⁸Since you, Lord GOD, are truly God and your words are truth and you have made this generous promise to your servant, ²⁹do, then, bless the house of your servant, that it may be in your presence forever—since you, Lord GOD, have promised, and by your blessing the house of your servant shall be blessed forever."

☐ MATTHEW 1:1-17

The Genealogy of Jesus. 1:1 The book of the genealogy of Jesus Christ, the son of David, the son of Abraham.

²Abraham became the father of Isaac, Isaac the father of Jacob, Jacob the father of Judah and his brothers. ³Judah became the father of Perez and Zerah, whose mother was Tamar. Perez became the father of Hezron, Hezron the father of Ram, ⁴Ram the father of Amminadab. Amminadab became the father of Nahshon, Nahshon the father of Salmon, ⁵Salmon the father of Boaz, whose mother was Rahab. Boaz became the father of Obed, whose mother was Ruth. Obed became the father of Jesse, ⁶Jesse the father of David the king.

David became the father of Solomon, whose mother had been the wife of Uriah. ⁷Solomon became the father of Rehoboam, Rehoboam the father of Abijah, Abijah the father of Asaph. ⁸Asaph became the father of Jehoshaphat, Jehoshaphat the father of Joram, Joram the father of Uzziah. ⁹Uzziah became the father of Jotham, Jotham the father of Ahaz, Ahaz the father of Hezekiah. ¹⁰Hezekiah became the father of Manasseh, Manasseh the father of Amos, Amos the father of Josiah. ¹¹Josiah became the father of Jechoniah and his brothers at the time of the Babylonian exile.

[12]After the Babylonian exile, Jechoniah became the father of Shealtiel, Shealtiel the father of Zerubbabel, [13]Zerubbabel the father of Abiud. Abiud became the father of Eliakim, Eliakim the father of Azor, [14]Azor the father of Zadok. Zadok became the father of Achim, Achim the father of Eliud, [15]Eliud the father of Eleazar. Eleazar be-

came the father of Matthan, Matthan the father of Jacob, [16]Jacob the father of Joseph, the husband of Mary. Of her was born Jesus who is called the Messiah.

[17]Thus the total number of generations from Abraham to David is fourteen generations; from David to the Babylonian exile, fourteen generations; from the Babylonian exile to the Messiah, fourteen generations.

April 8

St. Julie Billiart

I ought to die of shame to think I have not already died of gratitude to my good God.

— St. Julie Billiart

☐ 2 SAMUEL 8-10

Summary of David's Wars. 8:1 After this, David defeated the Philistines and subdued them; and David took… from the Philistines. [2]He also defeated Moab and measured them with a line. Making them lie down on the ground, he measured two lengths of line for death, and a full length for life. Thus the Moabites became subject to David, paying tribute. [3] David then defeated Hadadezer, son of Rehob, king of Zobah, when he went to re-establish his dominion at the River. [4]David captured from him one thousand seven hundred horsemen and twenty thousand foot soldiers. David hamstrung all the chariot horses, but left one hundred for his chariots. [5]The Arameans of Damascus came to help Hadadezer, king of Zobah, but David also defeated twenty-two thousand of them in Aram. [6]David then placed garrisons in the Damascus region of Aram, and the Arameans became David's subjects, paying tribute. The LORD brought David victory in all his undertakings. [7]David took the golden shields that were carried by Hadadezer's at-

tendants and brought them to Jerusalem. (These Shishak, king of Egypt, took away when he came to Jerusalem in the days of Rehoboam, son of Solomon.) [8]From Tebah and Berothai, cities of Hadadezer, King David removed a very large quantity of bronze. [9]When Toi, king of Hamath, heard that David had defeated the entire army of Hadadezer, [10]Toi sent his son Hadoram to wish King David well and to congratulate him on having waged a victorious war against Hadadezer; for Hadadezer had been at war with Toi. Hadoram also brought with him articles of silver, gold, and bronze. [11]These also King David consecrated to the LORD along with the silver and gold that he had taken for this purpose from all the nations he had subdued: [12]from Edom, Moab, the Ammonites, the Philistines, and Amalek, and from the spoils of Hadadezer, son of Rehob, king of Zobah.

[13]On his return, David made a name for himself by defeating eighteen thousand Edomites in the Valley of Salt. [14]He set up

garrisons in Edom, and all the Edomites became David's subjects. Thus the LORD brought David victory in all his undertakings.

David's Officials. [15]David was king over all Israel; he dispensed justice and right to all his people. [16]Joab, son of Zeruiah, was in command of the army. Jehoshaphat, son of Ahilud, was chancellor. [17]Zadok, son of Ahitub, and Ahimelech, son of Abiathar, were priests. Shavsha was scribe. [18]Benaiah, son of Jehoiada, was in command of the Cherethites and the Pelethites; and David's sons were priests.

David and Meribbaal. 9:1 David asked, "Is there any survivor of Saul's house to whom I may show kindness for the sake of Jonathan?" [2]Now there was an official of the house of Saul named Ziba. He was summoned to David, and the king asked him, "Are you Ziba?" He replied, "Your servant." [3]Then the king asked, "Is there any survivor of Saul's house to whom I may show God's kindness?" Ziba answered the king, "There is still Jonathan's son, the one whose feet are crippled." [4]The king asked him, "Where is he?" and Ziba answered the king, "He is in the house of Machir, son of Ammiel, in Lodebar." [5]So King David sent for him and had him brought from the house of Machir, son of Ammiel, from Lodebar. [6]When Meribbaal, son of Jonathan, son of Saul, came to David, he fell face down in homage. David said, "Meribbaal," and he answered, "Your servant." [7]"Do not be afraid," David said to him, "I will surely be kind to you for the sake of Jonathan your father. I will restore to you all the lands of Saul your grandfather, and you shall eat at my table always." [8]Bowing low, he answered, "What am I, your servant, that you should pay attention to a dead dog like me?" [9]The king then called Ziba, Saul's attendant, and said to him: "All that belonged to Saul and to his entire house, I am giving to your lord's son. [10]You and your

sons and servants must till the land for him. You shall bring in the produce, which shall be food for your lord's household to eat. But Meribbaal, your lord's son, shall always eat at my table." Now Ziba had fifteen sons and twenty servants. [11]Ziba answered the king, "Whatever my lord the king commands his servant, so shall your servant do." And so Meribbaal ate at David's table like one of the king's sons. [12]Meribbaal had a young son whose name was Mica; and all the tenants of Ziba's household worked for Meribbaal. [13]But Meribbaal lived in Jerusalem, because he always ate at the king's table. He was lame in both feet.

Campaigns Against Ammon. 10:1 After this, the king of the Ammonites died, and Hanun his son succeeded him as king. [2]David said, "I will show kindness to Hanun, the son of Nahash, as his father showed kindness to me." Therefore David sent his servants to Hanun to console him concerning his father. But when David's servants had entered the land of the Ammonites, [3]the Ammonite princes said to their lord Hanun, "Do you think David is doing this—sending you these consolers—to honor your father? Is it not rather to explore the city, to spy on it, and to overthrow it, that David has sent his servants to you?" [4]So Hanun seized David's servants, shaved off half their beards, cut away the lower halves of their garments at the buttocks, and sent them away. [5]David was told of it and he sent word for them to be intercepted, for the men had been greatly disgraced. "Remain at Jericho," the king told them, "until your beards have grown again; then come back here."

[6]When the Ammonites realized that they were in bad odor with David, they sent for and hired twenty thousand Aramean foot soldiers from Beth-rehob and Zobah, as well as the king of Maacah with one thousand men, and twelve thousand men from Tob.

⁷When David heard of this, he sent Joab and his whole army of warriors against them. ⁸The Ammonites marched out and lined up for battle at the entrance of their city gate, while the Arameans of Zobah and Rehob and the men of Tob and Maacah remained apart in the open field. ⁹When Joab saw that there was a battle line both in front of and behind him, he chose some of the best fighters of Israel and lined them up against the Arameans; ¹⁰the rest of the army he placed under the command of his brother Abishai and lined up to oppose the Ammonites. ¹¹And he said, "If the Arameans prove too strong for me, you must come and save me; and if the Ammonites prove too strong for you, I will come to save you. ¹²Hold firm and let us show ourselves courageous for the sake of our people and the cities of our God; and may the LORD do what is good in his sight." ¹³Joab therefore advanced with his men for battle with the Arameans, but they fled before him. ¹⁴And when the Ammonites saw that the Arameans had fled, they too fled before Abishai, and reentered their city. Joab then ceased his attack on the Ammonites and came to Jerusalem. ¹⁵ Seeing themselves vanquished by Israel, the Arameans held a full muster of troops. ¹⁶Hadadezer sent for and brought Arameans from beyond the River. They came to Helam, with Shobach, the captain of Hadadezer's army, at their head. ¹⁷When this was reported to David, he gathered all Israel together, crossed the Jordan, and went to Helam. The Arameans drew up in formation against David and gave battle. ¹⁸But the Arameans fled before Israel, and David killed seven hundred of their chariot fighters and forty thousand of their foot soldiers. He struck down Shobach, commander of the army, and he died on the field. ¹⁹When Hadadezer's vassal kings saw themselves vanquished by Israel, they made peace with the Israelites and became their subjects. After this, the Arameans were afraid to give further aid to the Ammonites.

☐ MATTHEW 1:18-25

The Birth of Jesus. 1:18 Now this is how the birth of Jesus Christ came about. When his mother Mary was betrothed to Joseph, but before they lived together, she was found with child through the holy Spirit. ¹⁹Joseph her husband, since he was a righteous man, yet unwilling to expose her to shame, decided to divorce her quietly. ²⁰Such was his intention when, behold, the angel of the Lord appeared to him in a dream and said, "Joseph, son of David, do not be afraid to take Mary your wife into your home. For it is through the holy Spirit that this child has been conceived in her. ²¹She will bear a son and you are to name him Jesus, because he will save his people from their sins." ²²All this took place to fulfill what the Lord had said through the prophet:

²³"Behold, the virgin shall be with
child and bear a son,
and they shall name him
Emmanuel,"

which means "God is with us." ²⁴When Joseph awoke, he did as the angel of the Lord had commanded him and took his wife into his home. ²⁵He had no relations with her until she bore a son, and he named him Jesus.

April 9

The One who is our very Life descended into our world, and bore our death, and slew it with the abundance of His own life. Thundering, He called out to us to return to Him in heaven.

— St. Augustine of Hippo

☐ **2 SAMUEL 11-13**

David's Sin. 11:1 At the turn of the year, the time when kings go to war, David sent out Joab along with his officers and all Israel, and they laid waste the Ammonites and besieged Rabbah. David himself remained in Jerusalem. [2] One evening David rose from his bed and strolled about on the roof of the king's house. From the roof he saw a woman bathing; she was very beautiful. [3] David sent people to inquire about the woman and was told, "She is Bathsheba, daughter of Eliam, and wife of Uriah the Hittite, Joab's armor-bearer." [4] Then David sent messengers and took her. When she came to him, he took her to bed, at a time when she was just purified after her period; and she returned to her house. [5] But the woman had become pregnant; she sent a message to inform David, "I am pregnant."

[6] So David sent a message to Joab, "Send me Uriah the Hittite." Joab sent Uriah to David. [7] And when he came, David asked him how Joab was, how the army was, and how the war was going, and Uriah answered that all was well. [8] David then said to Uriah, "Go down to your house and bathe your feet." Uriah left the king's house, and a portion from the king's table was sent after him. [9] But Uriah slept at the entrance of the king's house with the other officers of his lord, and did not go down to his own house. [10] David was told, "Uriah has not gone down to his house." So he said to Uriah, "Have you not come from a journey? Why, then, did you not go down to your house?" [11] Uriah answered David, "The ark and Israel and Judah are staying in tents, and my lord Joab and my lord's servants are encamped in the open field. Can I go home to eat and to drink and to sleep with my wife? As the LORD lives and as you live, I will do no such thing." [12] Then David said to Uriah, "Stay here today also, and tomorrow I will send you back." So Uriah stayed in Jerusalem that day. On the following day, [13] David summoned him, and he ate and drank with David, who got him drunk. But in the evening he went out to sleep on his bed among his lord's servants, and did not go down to his house. [14] The next morning David wrote a letter to Joab which he sent by Uriah. [15] This is what he wrote in the letter: "Place Uriah up front, where the fighting is fierce. Then pull back and leave him to be struck down dead." [16] So while Joab was besieging the city, he assigned Uriah to a place where he knew the defenders were strong. [17] When the men of the city made a sortie against Joab, some officers of David's army fell, and Uriah the Hittite also died.

[18] Then Joab sent David a report of all the details of the battle, [19] instructing the messenger, "When you have finished giving the king all the details of the battle, [20] the king may become angry and say to you: 'Why did you go near the city to fight? Did you not know that they would shoot from the wall above? [21] Who killed Abimelech, son of Jerubbaal? Was it not a woman who threw a millstone down on him from the wall above, so that he died in Thebez? Why did you go near the wall?' Then you in turn are to say, 'Your servant Uriah the Hittite is also dead.'" [22] The messenger set out, and on his arrival he

reported to David everything Joab had sent him to tell. ²³He told David: "The men had the advantage over us and came out into the open against us, but we pushed them back to the entrance of the city gate. ²⁴Then the archers shot at your servants from the wall above, and some of the king's servants died; and your servant Uriah the Hittite is also dead." ²⁵David said to the messenger: "This is what you shall say to Joab: 'Do not let this be a great evil in your sight, for the sword devours now here and now there. Strengthen your attack on the city and destroy it.' Encourage him."

²⁶When the wife of Uriah heard that her husband had died, she mourned her lord. ²⁷But once the mourning was over, David sent for her and brought her into his house. She became his wife and bore him a son. But in the sight of the LORD what David had done was evil.

Nathan's Parable. **12:1** The LORD sent Nathan to David, and when he came to him, he said: "Tell me how you judge this case: In a certain town there were two men, one rich, the other poor. ²The rich man had flocks and herds in great numbers. ³But the poor man had nothing at all except one little ewe lamb that he had bought. He nourished her, and she grew up with him and his children. Of what little he had she ate; from his own cup she drank; in his bosom she slept; she was like a daughter to him. ⁴Now, a visitor came to the rich man, but he spared his own flocks and herds to prepare a meal for the traveler who had come to him: he took the poor man's ewe lamb and prepared it for the one who had come to him." ⁵David grew very angry with that man and said to Nathan: "As the LORD lives, the man who has done this deserves death! ⁶He shall make fourfold restitution for the lamb because he has done this and was unsparing." ⁷Then Nathan said to David: "You are the man!

Nathan's Indictment. "Thus says the LORD God of Israel: I anointed you king over Israel. I delivered you from the hand of Saul. ⁸I gave you your lord's house and your lord's wives for your own. I gave you the house of Israel and of Judah. And if this were not enough, I could count up for you still more. ⁹Why have you despised the LORD and done what is evil in his sight? You have cut down Uriah the Hittite with the sword; his wife you took as your own, and him you killed with the sword of the Ammonites. ¹⁰Now, therefore, the sword shall never depart from your house, because you have despised me and have taken the wife of Uriah the Hittite to be your wife. ¹¹Thus says the LORD: I will bring evil upon you out of your own house. I will take your wives before your very eyes, and will give them to your neighbor: he shall lie with your wives in broad daylight. ¹²You have acted in secret, but I will do this in the presence of all Israel, in the presence of the sun itself."

David's Repentance. ¹³Then David said to Nathan, "I have sinned against the LORD." Nathan answered David: "For his part, the LORD has removed your sin. You shall not die, ¹⁴but since you have utterly spurned the LORD by this deed, the child born to you will surely die." ¹⁵Then Nathan returned to his house.

The LORD struck the child that the wife of Uriah had borne to David, and it became desperately ill. ¹⁶David pleaded with God on behalf of the child. He kept a total fast, and spent the night lying on the ground clothed in sackcloth. ¹⁷The elders of his house stood beside him to get him to rise from the ground; but he would not, nor would he take food with them. ¹⁸On the seventh day, the child died. David's servants were afraid to tell him that the child was dead, for they said: "When the child was alive, we spoke to him, but he would not listen to what we said. How can we tell him the child is dead? He may do some harm!" ¹⁹But David noticed his servants whispering among themselves and realized that the child was dead. He asked his servants, "Is the child dead?" They said, "Yes." [20]Rising from the ground, David washed and anointed himself, and changed his clothes. Then he went to the house of the LORD and worshiped. He returned to his own house and asked for food; they set it before him, and he ate. [21]His servants said to him: "What is this you are doing? While the child was living, you fasted and wept and kept vigil; now that the child is dead, you rise and take food." [22]He replied: "While the child was living, I fasted and wept, thinking, 'Who knows? The LORD may grant me the child's life.' [23]But now he is dead. Why should I fast? Can I bring him back again? I shall go to him, but he will not return to me." [24]Then David consoled Bathsheba his wife. He went and slept with her; and she conceived and bore him a son, who was named Solomon. The LORD loved him [25]and sent the prophet Nathan to name him Jedidiah, on behalf of the LORD.

End of the Ammonite War. [26]Joab fought against Rabbah of the Ammonites and captured that royal city. [27]He sent messengers to David to say: "I have fought against Rabbah and have taken the water-city. [28]Therefore, assemble the rest of the soldiers, join the siege against the city, and capture it, lest I be the one to capture the city and mine be the name people mention, not yours." [29]So David assembled the rest of the soldiers, went to Rabbah, fought against it, and captured it. [30]He took the crown of Milcom from the idol's head, a talent of gold in weight, with precious stones; this crown David wore on his own head. He also brought out a great amount of spoil from the city. [31]He deported the people of the city and set them to work with saws, iron picks, and iron axes, or put them to work at the brickmold. He dealt thus with all the cities of the Ammonites. Then David and his whole army returned to Jerusalem.

Amnon's Rape of Tamar. 13:1 After this, the following occurred. David's son Absa-lom had a beautiful sister named Tamar, and David's son Amnon loved her. [2]He was in such anguish over his sister Tamar that he became sick; she was a virgin, and Amnon thought it impossible to do anything to her. [3]Now Amnon had a friend named Jonadab, son of David's brother Shimeah, who was very clever. [4]He asked him, "Prince, why are you so dejected morning after morning? Why not tell me?" So Amnon said to him, "I am in love with Tamar, my brother Absalom's sister." [5]Then Jonadab replied, "Lie down on your bed and pretend to be sick. When your father comes to visit you, say to him, 'Please let my sister Tamar come and encourage me to take food. If she prepares something in my presence, for me to see, I will eat it from her hand.'" [6]So Amnon lay down and pretended to be sick. When the king came to visit him, Amnon said to the king, "Please let my sister Tamar come and prepare some fried cakes before my eyes, that I may take food from her hand."

[7]David then sent home a message to Tamar, "Please go to the house of your brother Amnon and prepare some food for him." [8]Tamar went to the house of her brother Amnon, who was in bed. Taking dough and kneading it, she twisted it into cakes before his eyes and fried the cakes. [9]Then she took the pan and set out the cakes before him. But Amnon would not eat; he said, "Have everyone leave me." When they had all left him, [10]Amnon said to Tamar, "Bring the food into the bedroom, that I may have it from your hand." So Tamar picked up the cakes she had prepared and brought them to her brother Amnon in the bedroom. [11]But when she brought them close to him so he could eat, he seized her and said to her, "Come! Lie with me, my sister!" [12]But she answered him, "No, my brother! Do not force me! This is not done in Israel. Do not commit this terrible crime. [13]Where would I take my shame? And you would be labeled a fool in Israel.

So please, speak to the king; he will not keep me from you." ¹⁴But he would not listen to her; he was too strong for her: he forced her down and raped her. ¹⁵Then Amnon felt intense hatred for her; the hatred he felt for her far surpassed the love he had had for her. Amnon said to her, "Get up, leave." ¹⁶She replied, "No, brother, because sending me away would be far worse than this evil thing you have done to me." He would not listen to her, ¹⁷but called the youth who was his attendant and said, "Send this girl outside, away from me, and bar the door after her." ¹⁸Now she had on a long tunic, for that is how virgin princesses dressed in olden days. When his attendant put her out and barred the door after her, ¹⁹Tamar put ashes on her head and tore the long tunic in which she was clothed. Then, putting her hands to her head, she went away crying loudly. ²⁰Her brother Absalom said to her: "Has your brother Amnon been with you? Keep still now, my sister; he is your brother. Do not take this so to heart." So Tamar remained, devastated, in the house of her brother Absalom. ²¹King David, when he heard of the whole affair, became very angry. He would not, however, antagonize Amnon, his high-spirited son; he loved him, because he was his firstborn. ²²And Absalom said nothing, good or bad, to Amnon; but Absalom hated Amnon for having humiliated his sister Tamar.

Absalom's Plot. ²³Two years went by. It was sheep-shearing time for Absalom in Baal-hazor near Ephraim, and Absalom invited all the king's sons. ²⁴Absalom went to the king and said: "Your servant has hired the shearers. Please, may the king come with all his servants to your servant." ²⁵But the king said to Absalom, "No, my son, all of us should not go lest we be a burden to you." And though Absalom urged him, he would not go but began to bid him goodbye. ²⁶Absalom then said, "If not you, then please let my brother Amnon come with us." The king asked him, "Why should he

go with you?" ²⁷But at Absalom's urging, the king sent Amnon and with him all his other sons. Absalom prepared a banquet fit for a king. ²⁸ But Absalom had instructed his attendants: "Now watch! When Amnon is merry with wine and I say to you, 'Kill Amnon,' put him to death. Do not be afraid, for it is I who order you to do it. Be strong and act like warriors."

Death of Amnon. ²⁹When the attendants did to Amnon as Absalom had commanded, all the king's other sons rose up, mounted their mules, and fled. ³⁰While they were still on the road, a report reached David: "Absalom has killed all the king's sons and not one of them is left." ³¹The king stood up, tore his garments, and lay on the ground. All his servants standing by him also tore their garments. ³²But Jonadab, son of David's brother Shimeah, spoke up: "Let not my lord think that all the young men, the king's sons, have been killed! Amnon alone is dead, for Absalom was set on this ever since Amnon humiliated his sister Tamar. ³³Now let my lord the king not take so to heart that report, 'All the king's sons are dead.' Amnon alone is dead." ³⁴Meanwhile, Absalom had taken flight. Then the servant on watch looked out and saw a large group coming down the slope from the direction of Bahurim. He came in and reported this to the king: "I saw some men coming down the mountainside from the direction of Bahurim." ³⁵So Jonadab said to the king: "There! The king's sons have come. It is as your servant said." ³⁶No sooner had he finished speaking than the king's sons came in, weeping aloud. The king, too, and all his servants wept very bitterly. ³⁷But Absalom, who had taken flight, went to Talmai, son of Ammihud, king of Geshur, ³⁸and stayed in Geshur for three years. ³⁹All that time the king continued to mourn his son; but his intention of going out against Absalom abated as he was consoled over the death of Amnon.

☐ MATTHEW 2:1-12

The Visit of the Magi. 2:1 When Jesus was born in Bethlehem of Judea, in the days of King Herod, behold, magi from the east arrived in Jerusalem, [2]saying, "Where is the newborn king of the Jews? We saw his star at its rising and have come to do him homage." [3]When King Herod heard this, he was greatly troubled, and all Jerusalem with him. [4]Assembling all the chief priests and the scribes of the people, he inquired of them where the Messiah was to be born. [5]They said to him, "In Bethlehem of Judea, for thus it has been written through the prophet:

> [6]'And you, Bethlehem, land of Judah,
>   are by no means least among the
>   rulers of Judah;
> since from you shall come a ruler,
>   who is to shepherd my people
>   Israel.'"

[7]Then Herod called the magi secretly and ascertained from them the time of the star's appearance. [8]He sent them to Bethlehem and said, "Go and search diligently for the child. When you have found him, bring me word, that I too may go and do him homage." [9]After their audience with the king they set out. And behold, the star that they had seen at its rising preceded them, until it came and stopped over the place where the child was. [10]They were overjoyed at seeing the star, [11]and on entering the house they saw the child with Mary his mother. They prostrated themselves and did him homage. Then they opened their treasures and offered him gifts of gold, frankincense, and myrrh. [12]And having been warned in a dream not to return to Herod, they departed for their country by another way.

April 10

Blessed be the Babe who made human nature young again!
— St. Ephraem

☐ 2 SAMUEL 14-16

The Wise Woman of Tekoa. 14:1 Now Joab, son of Zeruiah, knew how the king felt toward Absalom. [2]Joab sent to Tekoa and brought from there a wise woman, to whom he said: "Pretend to be in mourning. Put on mourning apparel and do not anoint yourself with oil, that you may appear to be a woman who has long been mourning someone dead. [3]Then go to the king and speak to him in this manner." And Joab told her what to say.

[4]So the woman of Tekoa went to the king and fell to the ground in homage, say-ing, "Help, O king!" [5]The king said to her, "What do you want?" She replied: "Alas, I am a widow; my husband is dead. [6]Your servant had two sons, who quarreled in the field, with no one to part them, and one of them struck his brother and killed him. [7]Then the whole clan confronted your servant and demanded: 'Give up the one who struck down his brother. We must put him to death for the life of his brother whom he has killed; we must do away with the heir also.' Thus they will quench my remaining hope and leave my husband neither name

nor posterity upon the earth." [8]The king then said to the woman: "Go home. I will issue a command on your behalf." [9]The woman of Tekoa answered him, "Upon me and my family be the blame, my lord king; the king and his throne are innocent." [10]Then the king said, "If anyone says a word to you, have him brought to me, and he shall not touch you again." [11]But she said, "Please, let the king remember the LORD your God, that the avenger of blood may not go too far in destruction and that my son may not be done away with." He replied, "As the LORD lives, not a hair of your son shall fall to the ground."

[12]But the woman continued, "Please let your servant say still another word to my lord the king." He replied, "Speak." [13]So the woman said: "Why, then, do you think the way you do against the people of God? In pronouncing as he has, the king shows himself guilty, in not bringing back his own banished son. [14]We must indeed die; we are then like water that is poured out on the ground and cannot be gathered up. Yet, though God does not bring back to life, he does devise means so as not to banish anyone from him. [15]And now, if I have presumed to speak to the king of this matter, it is because the people have given me cause to fear. And so your servant thought: 'Let me speak to the king. Perhaps he will grant the petition of his servant. [16]For the king must surely listen and rescue his servant from the grasp of one who would destroy both me and my son from the heritage of God.' [17]And your servant says, 'Let the word of my lord the king lead to rest; indeed, my lord the king is like an angel of God, discerning good and evil. The LORD your God be with you.'"

[18]The king answered the woman, "Now do not conceal from me anything I may ask you!" The woman said, "Let my lord the king speak." [19]So the king asked, "Is the hand of Joab with you in all this?" And the woman answered: "As you live, my lord the king, it is just as my lord has said, and not otherwise. It was your servant Joab who instructed me and told your servant all these things she was to say. [20]Your servant Joab did this in order to approach the matter in a roundabout way. But my lord is wise with the wisdom of an angel of God, knowing all things on earth."

Absalom's Return. [21]Then the king said to Joab: "I am granting this request. Go and bring back young Absalom." [22]Falling to the ground in homage and blessing the king, Joab said, "This day your servant knows that I am in good favor with you, my lord king, since the king has granted the request of your servant." [23]Joab then went off to Geshur and brought Absalom to Jerusalem. [24]But the king said, "Let him go off to his own house; he shall not appear before me." So Absalom went off to his house and did not appear before the king.

[25]In all Israel there was no man more praised for his beauty than Absalom, flawless from the sole of his foot to the crown of his head. [26]When he shaved his head—as he used to do at the end of every year, because his hair became too heavy for him—the hair weighed two hundred shekels according to the royal standard. [27]Absalom had three sons born to him, besides a daughter named Tamar, who was a beautiful woman.

Absalom Is Pardoned. [28]Absalom lived in Jerusalem for two years without appearing before the king. [29]Then he sent a message asking Joab to send him to the king, but Joab would not come to him. Although he asked him a second time, Joab would not come. [30]He therefore instructed his servants: "You see Joab's field that borders mine, where he has barley. Go, set it on fire." And so Absalom's servants set the field on fire. Joab's farmhands came to him with torn garments and told him, "Absalom's servants set your field on fire." [31]Joab went to Absalom in his house and asked him, "Why have your servants set my field on fire?" [32]Absalom answered Joab: "I sent you a message: Come here, that I may send you to the king to say: 'Why did I come back from Geshur? I would be better off if I were still there!' Now, let me appear before the king. If I am guilty, let him put me to death." [33]Joab went to the king and reported this. The king then called Absalom; he came to him and in homage fell on his face to the ground before the king. Then the king kissed Absalom.

Absalom's Ambition. 15:1 After this, Absalom provided himself with chariots, horses, and a retinue of fifty. [2]Moreover, Absalom used to rise early and stand alongside the road leading to the gate. If someone had a lawsuit to be decided by the king, Absalom would call to him and say, "From what city are you?" And when he replied, "Your servant is of such and such a tribe of Israel," [3]Absalom would say to him, "Your case is good and just, but there is no one to hear you in the king's name." [4]And he would continue: "If only I could be appointed judge in the land! Then everyone who has a lawsuit to be decided might come to me and I would render him justice." [5]Whenever a man approached him to show homage, he would extend his hand, hold him, and kiss him. [6]By behaving in this way toward all the Israelites who came to the king for judgment, Absalom was stealing the heart of Israel.

Conspiracy in Hebron. [7]After a period of four years, Absalom said to the king: "Please let me go to Hebron and fulfill a vow I made to the LORD. [8]For while living in Geshur in Aram, your servant made this vow: 'If the LORD ever brings me back to Jerusalem, I will worship him in Hebron.'" [9]The king said to him, "Go in peace," and he went off to Hebron. [10]Then Absalom sent agents throughout the tribes of Israel to say, "When you hear the sound of the horn, say, 'Absalom is king in Hebron!'" [11]Two hundred men had accompanied Absalom from Jerusalem. They had been invited and went in all innocence, knowing nothing. [12]Absalom also sent to Ahithophel the Gilonite, David's counselor, an invitation to come from his town, Giloh, for the sacrifices he was about to offer. So the conspiracy gained strength, and the people with Absalom increased in numbers.

David Flees Jerusalem. [13]An informant came to David with the report, "The Israelites have given their hearts to Absalom, and they are following him." [14]At this, David said to all his servants who were with him in Jerusalem: "Get up, let us flee, or none of us will escape from Absalom. Leave at once, or he will quickly overtake us, and then bring disaster upon us, and put the city to the sword." [15]The king's servants answered him, "Whatever our lord the king chooses to do, we are your servants." [16]Then the king set out, accompanied by his entire household, except for ten concubines whom he left behind to care for the palace. [17]As the king left the city, with all his officers accompanying him, they halted opposite the ascent of the Mount of Olives, at a distance, [18]while the whole army marched past him.

David and Ittai. As all the Cherethites and Pelethites, and the six hundred Gittites who had entered his service from that city, were passing in review before the king, [19]the king said to Ittai the Gittite: "Why should you also go with us? Go back and stay with the king, for you are a foreigner and you, too, are an exile from your own country. [20]You came only yesterday, and today shall I have you wander off with us wherever I have to go? Return and take your brothers with you, and may the LORD show you kindness and fidelity." [21]But Ittai answered the king, "As the LORD lives, and as my lord the king lives, your servant shall be wherever my lord the king is, whether for death or for life." [22]So the king said to Ittai, "Go, then, march on." And Ittai the Gittite, with all his men and all the dependents that were with him, marched on. [23]The whole land wept aloud as the last of the soldiers went by, and the king crossed the Wadi Kidron with all the soldiers moving on ahead of him by way of the ascent of the Mount of Olives, toward the wilderness.

David and the Priests. 24Zadok, too, and all the Levites bearing the ark of the covenant of God set down the ark of God until the whole army had finished marching out of the city; and Abiathar came up. 25Then the king said to Zadok: "Take the ark of God back to the city. If I find favor with the LORD, he will bring me back and permit me to see it and its lodging place. 26But if he should say, 'I am not pleased with you,' I am ready; let him do to me as he sees fit." 27The king also said to Zadok the priest: "Look, you and Abiathar return to the city in peace, and both your sons with you, your own son Ahimaaz, and Abiathar's son Jonathan. 28Remember, I shall be waiting at the fords near the wilderness until a report from you comes to me." 29So Zadok and Abiathar took the ark of God back to Jerusalem and remained there.

30As David went up the ascent of the Mount of Olives, he wept without ceasing. His head was covered, and he was walking barefoot. All those who were with him also had their heads covered and were weeping as they went. 31When David was told, "Ahithophel is among the conspirators with Absalom," he said, "O LORD, turn the counsel of Ahithophel to folly!"

David and Hushai. 32When David reached the top, where God was worshiped, Hushai the Archite was there to meet him, with garments torn and dirt upon his head. 33David said to him: "If you come with me, you will be a burden to me; 34but if you return to the city and say to Absalom, 'Let me be your servant, O king; I was formerly your father's servant, but now I will be yours,' you will thwart for me the counsel of Ahithophel. 35You will have the priests Zadok and Abiathar there with you. If you hear anything from the king's house, you shall report it to the priests Zadok and Abiathar, 36who have there with them their two sons, Zadok's son Ahimaaz and Abiathar's son Jonathan. Through them you shall send on to me whatever you hear." 37So David's friend Hushai went into the city, Jerusalem, as Absalom was about to enter it.

David and Ziba. 16:1 David went a little beyond the top and Ziba, the servant of Meribbaal, was there to meet him with saddled donkeys laden with two hundred loaves of bread, an ephah of cakes of pressed raisins, an ephah of summer fruits, and a skin of wine. 2The king said to Ziba, "What are you doing with all this?" Ziba replied: "The donkeys are for the king's household to ride on. The bread and summer fruits are for your servants to eat, and the wine to drink when they grow weary in the wilderness." 3Then the king said, "And where is your lord's son?" Ziba answered the king, "He is staying in Jerusalem, for he said, 'Today the house of Israel will restore to me my father's kingdom.'" 4The king therefore said to Ziba, "So! Everything Meribbaal had is yours." Then Ziba said: "I pay you homage, my lord the king. May I find favor with you!"

David and Shimei. 5As King David was approaching Bahurim, there was a man coming out; he was of the same clan as the house of Saul, and his name was Shimei, son of Gera. He kept cursing as he came out, 6and throwing stones at David and at all King David's officers, even though all the soldiers, including the royal guard, were on David's right and on his left. 7Shimei was saying as he cursed: "Get out! Get out! You man of blood, you scoundrel! 8The LORD has paid you back for all the blood shed from the family of Saul, whom you replaced as king, and the LORD has handed over the kingdom to your son Absalom. And now look at you: you suffer ruin because you are a man of blood." 9Abishai, son of Zeruiah, said to the king: "Why should this dead dog curse my lord the king? Let me go over and take off his head." [10]But the king replied: "What business is it of mine or of yours, sons of Zeruiah, that he curses? Suppose the LORD has told him to curse David; who then will dare to say, 'Why are you doing this?'" [11]Then David said to Abishai and to all his servants: "If my own son, who came forth from my loins, is seeking my life, how much more might this Benjaminite do so! Let him alone and let him curse, for the LORD has told him to. [12]Perhaps the LORD will look upon my affliction and repay me with good for the curses he is uttering this day." [13]David and his men continued on the road, while Shimei kept up with them on the hillside, all the while cursing and throwing stones and dirt as he went. [14]The king and all the soldiers with him arrived at the Jordan tired out, and stopped there to rest.

Absalom's Counselors. [15]In the meantime Absalom, with all the Israelites, entered Jerusalem, and Ahithophel was with him. [16]When David's friend Hushai the Archite came to Absalom, he said to him: "Long live the king! Long live the king!" [17]But Absalom asked Hushai: "Is this your devotion to your friend? Why did you not go with your friend?" [18]Hushai replied to Absalom: "On the contrary, I am his whom the LORD and all this people and all Israel have chosen, and with him I will stay. [19]Furthermore, as I was in attendance upon your father, so will I be before you. Whom should I serve, if not his son?"

[20]Then Absalom said to Ahithophel, "Offer your counsel on what we should do." [21]Ahithophel replied to Absalom: "Go to your father's concubines, whom he left behind to take care of the palace. When all Israel hears how odious you have made yourself to your father, all those on your side will take courage." [22]So a tent was pitched on the roof for Absalom, and Absalom went to his father's concubines in view of all Israel.

Counsel of Ahithophel. [23]Now the counsel given by Ahithophel at that time was as though one sought the word of God. Such was all the counsel of Ahithophel both to David and to Absalom.

☐ MATTHEW 2:13-23

The Flight to Egypt. 2:13 When they had departed, behold, the angel of the Lord appeared to Joseph in a dream and said, "Rise, take the child and his mother, flee to Egypt, and stay there until I tell you. Herod is going to search for the child to destroy him." [14]Joseph rose and took the child and his mother by night and departed for Egypt. [15]He stayed there until the death of Herod, that what the Lord had said through the prophet might be fulfilled, "Out of Egypt I called my son."

The Massacre of the Infants. [16]When Herod realized that he had been deceived by the magi, he became furious. He ordered the massacre of all the boys in Bethlehem and its vicinity two years old and under, in accordance with the time he had ascertained from the magi. [17]Then was fulfilled what had been said through Jeremiah the prophet:

[18]"A voice was heard in Ramah,
    sobbing and loud lamentation;
Rachel weeping for her children,
    and she would not be consoled,
    since they were no more."

The Return from Egypt. [19]When Herod had died, behold, the angel of the Lord appeared in a dream to Joseph in Egypt [20]and said, "Rise, take the child and his mother and go to the land of Israel, for those who sought the child's life are dead." [21]He rose, took the child and his mother, and went to the land of Israel. [22]But when he heard that Archelaus was ruling over Judea in place of his father Herod, he was afraid to go back there. And because he had been warned in a dream, he departed for the region of Galilee. [23]He went and dwelt in a town called Nazareth, so that what had been spoken through the prophets might be fulfilled, "He shall be called a Nazorean."

April 11

St. Stanislaus; St. Gemma Galgani

Even if I were to see the gates of hell open and to stand on the brink of the abyss, I should not despair, I should not lose hope of mercy, because I should trust in You, my God.

— St. Gemma Galgani

☐ 2 SAMUEL 17-19

17:1 Ahithophel went on to say to Absalom: "Let me choose twelve thousand men and be off in pursuit of David tonight. [2]If I come upon him when he is weary and discouraged, I shall cause him panic, and all the people with him will flee, and I shall strike down the king alone. [3]Then I can bring back the rest of the people to you, as a bride returns to her husband. It is the death of only one man you are seeking; then all the people will be at peace." [4]This plan sounded good to Absalom and to all the elders of Israel.

Counsel of Hushai. [5]Then Absalom said, "Now call Hushai the Archite also; let us hear what he too has to say." [6]When Hushai came to Absalom, Absalom said to him: "This is Ahithophel's plan. Shall we follow his plan? If not, give your own." [7]Hushai replied to Absalom, "This time Ahithophel has not given good counsel." [8]And he went on to say: "You know that your father and his men are warriors, and that they are as fierce as a bear in the wild robbed of her cubs. Moreover, since your father is a skilled fighter, he will not spend the night with the army. [9]Even now he lies hidden in one of the caves or in one of his

other places. And if some of our soldiers should fall at the first attack, whoever hears of it will say, 'Absalom's followers have been slaughtered.' [10]Then even the brave man with the heart of a lion—his heart will melt. For all Israel knows that your father is a fighter and those who are with him are brave. [11]This is what I counsel: Let all Israel be assembled, from Dan to Beer-sheba, as numerous as the sands by the sea, and you yourself go with them. [12]We can then attack him wherever we find him, settling down upon him as dew alights on the ground. None shall survive—neither he nor any of his followers. [13]And if he retires into a city, all Israel shall bring ropes to that city and we can drag it into the gorge, so that not even a pebble of it can be found." [14]Then Absalom and all the Israelites said, "The counsel of Hushai the Archite is better than the counsel of Ahithophel." For the Lord had commanded that Ahithophel's good counsel should be thwarted, so that he might bring Absalom to ruin.

David Told of the Plan. [15]Then Hushai said to the priests Zadok and Abiathar: "This is the counsel Ahithophel gave Absalom and the elders of Israel, and this is what

I counseled. ¹⁶So send a warning to David immediately: 'Do not spend the night at the fords near the wilderness, but cross over without fail. Otherwise the king and all the people with him will be destroyed.'" ¹⁷Now Jonathan and Ahimaaz were staying at En-rogel. A maidservant was to come with information for them, and they in turn were to go and report to King David. They could not risk being seen entering the city, ¹⁸but an attendant did see them and informed Absalom. They hurried on their way and reached the house of a man in Bahurim who had a cistern in his courtyard. They let themselves down into it, ¹⁹and the woman took the cover and spread it over the mouth of the cistern, strewing crushed grain on the cover so that nothing could be noticed. ²⁰When Absalom's servants came to the woman at the house, they asked, "Where are Ahimaaz and Jonathan?" The woman replied, "They went by a short while ago toward the water." They searched, but found no one, and so returned to Jerusalem. ²¹As soon as they left, Ahimaaz and Jonathan came up out of the cistern and went on to report to King David. They said to him: "Leave! Cross the water at once, for Ahithophel has given such and such counsel in regard to you." ²²So David and all his people moved on and crossed the Jordan. By daybreak, there was no one left who had not crossed.

²³When Ahithophel saw that his counsel was not acted upon, he saddled his donkey and departed, going to his home in his own city. Then, having left orders concerning his household, he hanged himself. And so he died and was buried in his father's tomb.

²⁴Now David had arrived at Mahanaim while Absalom crossed the Jordan accompanied by all the Israelites. ²⁵Absalom had put Amasa in command of the army in Joab's place. Amasa was the son of an Ishmaelite named Ithra, who had married Abigail, daughter of Jesse and sister of Joab's mother Zeruiah. ²⁶Israel and Absalom encamped in the land of Gilead.

²⁷When David came to Mahanaim, Shobi, son of Nahash from Rabbah of the Ammonites, Machir, son of Ammiel from Lodebar, and Barzillai, the Gileadite from Rogelim, ²⁸brought beds and covers, basins and pottery, as well as wheat, barley, flour, roasted grain, beans, lentils, ²⁹honey, and butter and cheese from the flocks and herds, for David and those who were with him to eat; for they said, "The people will be hungry and tired and thirsty in the wilderness."

Preparation for Battle. 18:1 After mustering the troops he had with him, David placed officers in command of units of a thousand and units of a hundred. ²David then divided the troops three ways, a third under Joab, a third under Abishai, son of Zeruiah and brother of Joab, and a third under Ittai the Gittite. The king said to the troops, "I intend to go out with you myself." ³But they replied: "You must not come out with us. For if we flee, no one will care; even if half of us die, no one will care. But you are worth ten thousand of us. Therefore it is better that we have you to help us from the city." ⁴The king said to them, "I will do what you think best." So the king stood by the gate as all the soldiers marched out in units of a hundred and a thousand. ⁵But the king gave this command to Joab, Abishai, and Ittai: "Be gentle with young Absalom for my sake." All the soldiers heard as the king gave commands to the various leaders with regard to Absalom.

Defeat of Absalom's Forces. ⁶David's army then took the field against Israel, and a battle was fought in the forest near Mahanaim. ⁷The forces of Israel were defeated by David's servants, and the casualties there that day were heavy—twenty thousand men. ⁸The battle spread out over that entire region, and the forest consumed more combatants that day than did the sword.

Death of Absalom. ⁹Absalom unexpectedly came up against David's servants.

He was mounted on a mule, and, as the mule passed under the branches of a large oak tree, his hair caught fast in the tree. He hung between heaven and earth while the mule under him kept going. ¹⁰Someone saw this and reported to Joab, "I saw Absalom hanging from an oak tree." ¹¹Joab said to the man who told him this: "If you saw him, why did you not strike him to the ground on the spot? Then it would have been my duty to give you fifty pieces of silver and a belt." ¹²But the man replied to Joab: "Even if I already held a thousand pieces of silver in my two hands, I would not lay a hand on the king's son, for in our hearing the king gave you and Abishai and Ittai a command: 'Protect the youth Absalom for my sake.' ¹³Had I been disloyal and killed him, it would all have come out before the king, and you would stand aloof." ¹⁴Joab replied, "I will not waste time with you in this way." And taking three pikes in hand, he thrust for the heart of Absalom. He was still alive in the tree. ¹⁵When ten of Joab's young armor-bearers closed in on Absalom, and killed him with further blows, ¹⁶Joab then sounded the horn, and the soldiers turned back from the pursuit of the Israelites, because Joab called them to halt. ¹⁷They took Absalom and cast him into a deep pit in the forest, and built up a very large mound of stones over him. And all the Israelites fled to their own tents.

¹⁸During his lifetime Absalom had taken a pillar and set it up for himself in the King's Valley, for he said, "I have no son to perpetuate my name." The pillar which he named for himself is called Absalom's Monument to the present day.

David Told of Absalom's Death. ¹⁹Then Ahimaaz, son of Zadok, said, "Let me run to take the good news to the king that the LORD has set him free from the power of his enemies." ²⁰But Joab said to him: "You are not the man to bring the news today. On some other day you may take the good news, but today you would not be bringing good news, for in fact the king's son is dead." ²¹Then Joab said to a Cushite, "Go, tell the king what you have seen." The Cushite bowed to Joab and ran off. ²²But Ahimaaz, son of Zadok, said to Joab again, "Come what may, permit me also to run after the Cushite." Joab replied: "Why do you want to run, my son? You will receive no reward." ²³But he insisted, "Come what may, I want to run." Joab said to him, "Run." Ahimaaz took the way of the Jordan plain and outran the Cushite.

²⁴Now David was sitting between the two gates, and a lookout mounted to the roof of the gate above the city wall, where he looked out and saw a man running all alone. ²⁵The lookout shouted to inform the king, who said, "If he is alone, he has good news to report." As he kept coming nearer, ²⁶the lookout spied another runner. From his place atop the gate he cried out, "There is another man running by himself." And the king responded, "He, too, is bringing good news." ²⁷Then the lookout said, "I notice that the first one runs like Ahimaaz, son of Zadok." The king replied, "He is a good man; he comes with good news." ²⁸Then Ahimaaz called out and greeted the king. With face to the ground he paid homage to the king and said, "Blessed be the LORD your God, who has delivered up the men who rebelled against my lord the king." ²⁹But the king asked, "Is young Absalom safe?" And Ahimaaz replied, "I saw a great disturbance when the king's servant Joab sent your servant on, but I do not know what it was." ³⁰The king said, "Step aside and remain in attendance here." So he stepped aside and remained there. ³¹When the Cushite came in, he said, "Let my lord the king receive the good news that this day the LORD has freed you from the power of all who rose up against you." ³²But the king asked the Cushite, "Is young Absalom all right?" The Cushite replied, "May the enemies of my lord the king and all who rebel against you with evil intent be as that young man!"

19:1 The king was shaken, and went up to the room over the city gate and wept. He said as he wept, "My son Absalom! My son, my son Absalom! If only I had died instead of you, Absalom, my son, my son!"

Joab Reproves David. ²Joab was told, "The king is weeping and mourning for Absalom," ³and that day's victory was turned into mourning for the whole army when they heard, "The king is grieving for his son." ⁴The soldiers stole into the city that day like men shamed by flight in battle. ⁵Meanwhile the king covered his face and cried out in a loud voice, "My son Absalom! Absalom! My son, my son!" ⁶So Joab went to the king's residence and said: "Though they saved your life and your sons' and daughters' lives, and the lives of your wives and your concubines, you have put all your servants to shame today ⁷by loving those who hate you and hating those who love you. For you have announced today that officers and servants are nothing to you. Indeed I am now certain that if Absalom were alive today and all of us dead, that would be fine with you. ⁸Now then, get up! Go out and speak kindly to your servants. I swear by the LORD that if you do not go out, not a single man will remain with you overnight, and this will be a far greater disaster for you than any that has come upon you from your youth until now." ⁹So the king got up and sat at the gate. When all the people were told, "The king is sitting at the gate," they came into his presence.

The Reconciliation. Now the Israelites had fled to their separate tents, ¹⁰but throughout the tribes of Israel all the people were arguing among themselves, saying to one another: "The king delivered us from the grasp of our enemies, and it was he who rescued us from the grasp of the Philistines. Now, he has fled the country before Absalom, ¹¹but Absalom, whom we anointed over us, has died in battle. Why, then, should you remain silent about restoring the king to his palace?" When the talk of all Israel reached the king, ¹²David sent word to the priests Zadok and Abiathar: "Say to the elders of Judah: 'Why should you be last to restore the king to his palace? ¹³You are my brothers, you are my bone and flesh. Why should you be last to restore the king?' ¹⁴Also say to Amasa: 'Are you not my bone and flesh? May God do thus to me, and more, if you do not become commander of my army permanently in place of Joab.'" ¹⁵He won the hearts of the Judahites all together, and so they sent a message to the king: "Return, with all your servants."

David and Shimei. ¹⁶So the king returned, and when he reached the Jordan, Judah had come to Gilgal to meet him and to bring him across the Jordan. ¹⁷Shimei, son of Gera, the Benjaminite from Bahurim, hurried down with the Judahites to meet King David, ¹⁸accompanied by a thousand men from Benjamin. Ziba, too, the servant of the house of Saul, accompanied by his fifteen sons and twenty servants, hastened to the Jordan before the king. ¹⁹They crossed over the ford to bring the king's household over and to do whatever he wished. When Shimei, son of Gera, crossed the Jordan, he fell down before the king ²⁰and said to him: "May my lord not hold me guilty; do not remember or take to heart the wrong that your servant did the day my lord the king left Jerusalem. ²¹For your servant knows that I have done wrong. But I now am the first of the whole house of Joseph to come down today to meet my lord the king." ²²But Abishai, son of Zeruiah, countered: "Shimei must be put to death for this. He cursed the anointed of the LORD." ²³David replied: "What has come between you and me, sons of Zeruiah, that you would become my adversaries this day? Should anyone die today in Israel? Am I not aware that today I am king over Israel?" ²⁴Then the king said to Shimei, "You shall not die." And the king gave him his oath.

David and Meribbaal. [25]Meribbaal, son of Saul, also went down to meet the king. He had not cared for his feet nor trimmed his mustache nor washed his clothes from the day the king left until he returned safely. [26]When he came from Jerusalem to meet the king, the king asked him, "Why did you not go with me, Meribbaal?" [27]He replied: "My lord king, my servant deceived me. For your servant said to him, 'Saddle the donkey for me, that I may ride on it and go with the king'; your servant is lame. [28]But he slandered your servant before my lord the king. But my lord the king is like an angel of God. Do whatever seems good to you. [29]For though my father's entire house deserved only death from my lord the king, yet you placed your servant among those who eat at your table. What right do I still have to make further appeal to the king?" [30]But the king said to him: "Why do you go on talking? I say, 'You and Ziba shall divide the property.'" [31]Meribbaal answered the king, "Indeed let him take it all, now that my lord the king has returned safely to his house."

David and Barzillai. [32]Barzillai the Gileadite also came down from Rogelim and escorted the king to the Jordan for his crossing, taking leave of him at the Jordan. [33]It was Barzillai, a very old man of eighty, who had provided for the king during his stay in Mahanaim; he was a very great man. [34]The king said to Barzillai, "Cross over with me, and I will provide for your old age as my guest in Jerusalem." [35]But Barzillai answered the king: "How much longer have I to live, that I should go up to Jerusalem with the king? [36]I am now eighty years old. Can I distinguish between good and evil? Can your servant taste what he eats and drinks, or still hear the voices of men and women singers? Why should your servant be any further burden to my lord the king? [37]In escorting the king across the Jordan, your servant is doing little enough! Why should the king give me this reward? [38]Please let your servant go back to die in my own city by the tomb of my father and mother. Here is your servant Chimham. Let him cross over with my lord the king. Do for him whatever seems good to you." [39]Then the king said to him, "Chimham shall cross over with me, and for him I will do whatever seems good to you. And anything else you would like me to do for you, I will do." [40]Then all the people crossed over the Jordan but the king remained; he kissed Barzillai and bade him farewell as he returned to his own place. [41]Finally the king crossed over to Gilgal, accompanied by Chimham.

Israel and Judah Quarrel. All of the people of Judah and half of the people of Israel had escorted the king across. [42]But then all these Israelites began coming to the king and saying, "Why did our brothers the Judahites steal you away and bring the king and his household across the Jordan, along with all David's men?" [43]All the Judahites replied to the men of Israel: "Because the king is our relative. Why are you angry over this? Have we had anything to eat at the king's expense? Or have portions from his table been given to us?" [44]The Israelites answered the Judahites: "We have ten shares in the king. Also, we are the firstborn rather than you. Why do you slight us? Were we not first to speak of restoring our king?" Then the Judahites in turn spoke even more fiercely than the Israelites.

☐ MATTHEW 3:1-12

The Preaching of John the Baptist. 3:1
In those days John the Baptist appeared, preaching in the desert of Judea [2][and] saying, "Repent, for the kingdom of heaven is at hand!" [3]It was of him that the prophet Isaiah had spoken when he said:

"A voice of one crying out in the desert,
'Prepare the way of the Lord,
make straight his paths.'"

[4]John wore clothing made of camel's hair and had a leather belt around his waist. His food was locusts and wild honey. [5]At that time Jerusalem, all Judea, and the whole region around the Jordan were going out to him [6]and were being baptized by him in the Jordan River as they acknowledged their sins.

[7]When he saw many of the Pharisees and Sadducees coming to his baptism, he said to them, "You brood of vipers! Who warned you to flee from the coming wrath? [8]Produce good fruit as evidence of your repentance. [9]And do not presume to say to yourselves, 'We have Abraham as our father.' For I tell you, God can raise up children to Abraham from these stones. [10]Even now the ax lies at the root of the trees. Therefore every tree that does not bear good fruit will be cut down and thrown into the fire. [11]I am baptizing you with water, for repentance, but the one who is coming after me is mightier than I.

I am not worthy to carry his sandals. He will baptize you with the holy Spirit and fire. [12]His winnowing fan is in his hand. He will clear his threshing floor and gather his wheat into his barn, but the chaff he will burn with unquenchable fire."

April 12

The Lord was baptized, not to be cleansed himself, but to cleanse the waters, so that those waters, cleansed by the flesh of Christ that knew no sin, might have the power of baptism.

— St. Ambrose of Milan

☐ 2 SAMUEL 20-22

Sheba's Rebellion. 20:1 Now a scoundrel named Sheba, the son of Bichri, a Benjaminite, happened to be there. He sounded the horn and cried out,

"We have no share in David,
nor any heritage in the son of Jesse.
Everyone to your tents, O Israel!"

[2]So all the Israelites left David to follow Sheba, son of Bichri. But the Judahites, from the Jordan to Jerusalem, remained loyal to their king. [3]David came to his house in Jerusalem, and the king took the ten concubines whom he had left behind to care for the palace and placed them under guard. He provided for them, but never again saw them. And so they remained shut away to the day of their death, lifelong widows.

Amasa's Death. [4]Then the king said to Amasa: "Summon the Judahites for me within three days. Then present yourself here." [5]Accordingly Amasa set out to summon Judah, but delayed beyond the time set for him. [6]Then David said to Abishai: "Sheba, son of Bichri, may now do us more harm than Absalom did. Take your lord's servants and pursue him, lest he find fortified cities and take shelter while we look on." [7]So Joab and the Cherethites and Pelethites and all the warriors marched out behind Abishai from Jerusalem to campaign in pursuit of Sheba, son of Bichri. [8]They were at the great stone in Gibeon when Amasa met them. Now Joab had a belt over his tunic, from which was slung a sword in its sheath at his thigh; the sword would slide out downwards. [9]Joab asked Amasa, "Is everything all right, my brother?" and with his right hand held Amasa's beard as if to kiss him. [10]And since Amasa was not on his guard against the sword in Joab's other hand, Joab stabbed him in the abdomen with it, so that his entrails burst forth to the ground, and he died; there was no second thrust. Then Joab and Abishai his brother pursued Sheba, son of Bichri. [11]One of Joab's attendants stood by Amasa and said, "Let him who favors Joab and is for David follow Joab." [12]Amasa lay covered with blood in the middle of the highroad, and the man noticed that all the soldiers were stopping. So he rolled Amasa away from the road to the field and spread a garment over him, because he saw how all who came upon him were stopping. [13]When he had been removed from the road, everyone went on after Joab in pursuit of Sheba, son of Bichri.

Joab Pursues Sheba. [14]Sheba had passed through all the tribes of Israel to Abel Beth-maacah. Then all the Bichrites assembled and they too entered the city after him. [15]So all Joab's troops came and besieged him in Abel Beth-maacah. They built up a mound against the city, so that it stood against the rampart, and were battering the wall to knock it down. [16]Then a wise woman from the city called out, "Listen, listen! Tell Joab, 'Come here, so I can speak with you.'" [17]When Joab had come near her, the woman said, "Are you Joab?"

And he replied, "Yes." She said to him, "Listen to what your servant has to say." He replied, "I am listening." [18]Then she went on to say: "There is a saying from long ago, 'Let them ask if they will in Abel or in Dan whether loyalty is finished [19]or ended in Israel.' You are seeking to batter down a city that is a mother in Israel. Why do you wish to swallow up the heritage of the LORD?" [20]Joab answered, "Not at all, not at all! I do not wish to swallow or batter anything. [21]That is not the case at all. A man from the hill country of Ephraim, whose name is Sheba, son of Bichri, has rebelled against King David. Give him up, just him, and I will withdraw from the city." Then the woman said to Joab, "His head shall be thrown to you across the wall." [22]In her wisdom, the woman went to all the people, and they cut off the head of Sheba, son of Bichri, and threw it out to Joab. He then sounded the horn, and they scattered from the city to their own tents, while Joab returned to Jerusalem to the king.

David's Officials. [23]Joab was in command of the whole army of Israel. Benaiah, son of Jehoiada, was in command of the Cherethites and Pelethites. [24]Adoram was in charge of the forced labor. Jehoshaphat, son of Ahilud, was the chancellor. [25]Shawsha was the scribe. Zadok and Abiathar were priests. [26]Ira the Jairite was also David's priest.

Gibeonite Vengeance. 21:1 In David's time there was a famine for three years, year after year. David sought the presence of the LORD, who said: There is bloodguilt on Saul and his family because he put the Gibeonites to death. [2]So the king called the Gibeonites and spoke to them. (Now the Gibeonites were not Israelites, but survivors of the Amorites; and although the Israelites had given them their oath, Saul had sought to kill them off in his zeal for the Israelites and for Judah.) [3]David said to the Gibeonites, "What must I do for you and how must

I make atonement, that you may bless the heritage of the LORD?" ⁴The Gibeonites answered him, "We have no claim against Saul and his house for silver or gold, nor is it our place to put anyone to death in Israel." Then he said, "I will do for you whatever you propose." ⁵They said to the king, "As for the man who was exterminating us and who intended to destroy us that we might have no place in all the territory of Israel, ⁶let seven men from among his descendants be given to us, that we may execute them before the LORD in Gibeon, on the LORD's mountain." The king replied, "I will give them up." ⁷The king, however, spared Meribbaal, son of Jonathan, son of Saul, because of the LORD's oath that formed a bond between David and Saul's son Jonathan. ⁸But the king took Armoni and Meribbaal, the two sons that Aiah's daughter Rizpah had borne to Saul, and the five sons of Saul's daughter Merob that she had borne to Adriel, son of Barzillai the Meholathite, ⁹and delivered them into the power of the Gibeonites, who then executed them on the mountain before the LORD. The seven fell at the one time; they were put to death during the first days of the harvest—that is, at the beginning of the barley harvest.

¹⁰Then Rizpah, Aiah's daughter, took sackcloth and spread it out for herself on the rock from the beginning of the harvest until rain came down on them from the heavens, fending off the birds of the heavens from settling on them by day, and the wild animals by night. ¹¹When David was informed of what Rizpah, Aiah's daughter, the concubine of Saul, had done, ¹²he went and obtained the bones of Saul and of his son Jonathan from the citizens of Jabesh-gilead, who had stolen them away secretly from the public square of Beth-shan, where the Philistines had hanged them at the time they defeated Saul on Gilboa. ¹³When he had brought up from there the bones of Saul and of his son Jonathan, the bones of those who had been executed were also gathered up. ¹⁴Then the bones of Saul and of his son Jonathan were buried in the land of Benjamin, at Zela, in the tomb of his father Kish. After all that the king commanded had been carried out, God granted relief to the land.

Exploits in Philistine Wars. ¹⁵There was another battle between the Philistines and Israel. David went down with his servants and fought the Philistines, but David grew tired. ¹⁶Dadu, a descendant of the Rephaim, whose bronze spear weighed three hundred shekels, was about to take him captive. Dadu was girt with a new sword and thought he would kill David, ¹⁷but Abishai, son of Zeruiah, came to help him, and struck and killed the Philistine. Then David's men swore to him, "You must not go out to battle with us again, lest you quench the lamp of Israel."

¹⁸After this, there was another battle with the Philistines, in Gob. On that occasion Sibbecai the Hushathite struck down Saph, a descendant of the Rephaim. ¹⁹There was another battle with the Philistines, in Gob, and Elhanan, son of Jair from Bethlehem, killed Goliath of Gath, whose spear shaft was like a weaver's beam. ²⁰There was another battle, at Gath, and there was a giant, who had six fingers on each hand and six toes on each foot—twenty-four in all. He too was descended from the Rephaim. ²¹And when he insulted Israel, Jonathan, son of David's brother Shimei, struck him down. ²²These four were descended from the Rephaim in Gath, and they fell at the hands of David and his servants.

Song of Thanksgiving. 22:1 David proclaimed the words of this song to the LORD when the LORD had rescued him from the grasp of all his enemies and from the grasp of Saul. ²He said:

O LORD, my rock, my fortress, my
    deliverer,
³my God, my rock of refuge!

My shield, my saving horn,
  my stronghold, my refuge,
  my savior, from violence you keep
    me safe.
⁴Praised be the LORD, I exclaim!
  I have been delivered from my
    enemies.

⁵The breakers of death surged round
    about me,
  the menacing floods terrified me;
⁶The cords of Sheol tightened;
  the snares of death lay in wait
    for me.
⁷In my distress I called out: LORD!
  I cried out to my God;
From his temple he heard my voice,
  my cry reached his ears.

⁸The earth rocked and shook;
  the foundations of the heavens
    trembled;
  they shook as his wrath flared up.
⁹Smoke rose in his nostrils,
  a devouring fire from his mouth;
  it kindled coals into flame.
¹⁰He parted the heavens and came
    down,
  a dark cloud under his feet.
¹¹Mounted on a cherub he flew,
  borne along on the wings of the
    wind.
¹²He made darkness the cover about
    him,
  a mass of water, heavy
    thunderheads.
¹³From the brightness of his presence
  coals were kindled to flame.
¹⁴The LORD thundered from heaven;
  the Most High made his voice
    resound.
¹⁵He let fly arrows and scattered them;
  lightning, and dispersed them.
¹⁶Then the bed of the sea appeared;
  the world's foundations lay bare,
At the roar of the LORD,
  at the storming breath of his
    nostrils.

¹⁷He reached down from on high and
    seized me,
  drew me out of the deep waters.
¹⁸He rescued me from my mighty
    enemy,
  from foes too powerful for me.
¹⁹They attacked me on a day of distress,
  but the LORD came to my support.
²⁰He set me free in the open;
  he rescued me because he loves me.

²¹The LORD acknowledged my
    righteousness;
  rewarded my clean hands.
²²For I kept the ways of the LORD;
  I was not disloyal to my God.
²³His laws were all before me,
  his decrees I did not cast aside.
²⁴I was honest toward him;
  I was on guard against sin.
²⁵So the LORD rewarded my
    righteousness,
  the cleanness of my hands in his
    sight.
²⁶Toward the faithful you are faithful;
  to the honest you are honest;
²⁷Toward the sincere you are sincere;
  but to the perverse you are devious.
²⁸Humble people you save,
  though on the haughty your eyes
    look down.
²⁹You are my lamp, O LORD!
  My God brightens the darkness
    about me.
³⁰With you I can rush an armed band,
  with my God to help I can leap a
    wall.
³¹God's way is unerring;
  the LORD's promise is tried and true;
  he is a shield for all who trust in
    him.

³²Truly, who is God except the LORD?
  Who but our God is the rock?
³³This God who girded me with might,
  kept my way unerring,
³⁴Who made my feet swift as a deer's,
  set me safe on the heights,

35Who trained my hands for war,
my arms to bend even a bow of
bronze.

36You have given me your protecting
shield,
and your help has made me great.
37You gave me room to stride;
my feet never stumbled.
38I pursued my enemies and overtook
them;
I did not turn back till I destroyed
them.
39I struck them down, and they did not
rise;
they fell dead at my feet.
40You girded me with strength for war;
subdued adversaries at my feet.
41My foes you put to flight before me;
those who hated me I destroyed.
42They cried for help, but no one saved
them,
cried to the LORD but got no
answer.
43I ground them fine as the dust of the
earth;
like mud in the streets I trod them
down.

44You rescued me from the strife of my
people;
you made me head over nations.
A people I had not known became my
slaves;
45Foreigners cringed before me;
as soon as they heard of me they
obeyed.
46Their courage failed;
they came trembling from their
fortresses.
47The LORD lives! Blessed be my rock!
Exalted be God, the rock of my
salvation.
48O God who granted me vindication,
subdued peoples under me,
49and helped me escape from my
enemies,
Truly you have exalted me above my
adversaries,
from the violent you have rescued me.
50Thus I will proclaim you, LORD,
among the nations;
I will sing the praises of your name.
51You have given great victories to your
king,
and shown kindness to your anointed,
to David and his posterity forever.

☐ MATTHEW 3:13-17

The Baptism of Jesus. 3:13 Then Jesus came from Galilee to John at the Jordan to be baptized by him. 14John tried to prevent him, saying, "I need to be baptized by you, and yet you are coming to me?" 15Jesus said to him in reply, "Allow it now, for thus it is fitting for us to fulfill all righteousness." Then he allowed him. 16After Jesus was baptized, he came up from the water and behold, the heavens were opened [for him], and he saw the Spirit of God descending like a dove [and] coming upon him. 17And a voice came from the heavens, saying, "This is my beloved Son, with whom I am well pleased."

April 13

Pope St. Martin I

As the pilot of a vessel is tested in the storm, the wrestler is tested in the ring, the soldier in the battle, and the hero in adversity: so is the Christian tested in temptation.

— St. Basil the Great

☐ **2 SAMUEL 23-24**

The Last Words of David. 23:1 These are the last words of David:

> The oracle of David, son of Jesse;
>> the oracle of the man God raised up,
> Anointed of the God of Jacob,
>> favorite of the Mighty One of Israel.
> [2]The spirit of the LORD spoke through me;
>> his word was on my tongue.
> [3]The God of Israel spoke;
>> of me the Rock of Israel said,
> "One who rules over humankind with justice,
>> who rules in the fear of God,
> [4]Is like the light at sunrise
>> on a cloudless morning,
>> making the land's vegetation glisten after rain."
> [5]Is not my house firm before God?
>> He has made an eternal covenant with me,
>> set forth in detail and secured.
> Will he not bring to fruition
>> all my salvation and my every desire?
> [6]But the wicked are all like thorns to be cast away;
>> they cannot be taken up by hand.
> [7]One wishing to touch them
>> must be armed with iron or the shaft of a spear.
> They must be utterly consumed by fire.

David's Warriors. [8]These are the names of David's warriors. Ishbaal, the son of Hachamoni, chief of the Three. He bran-dished his spear over eight hundred whom he had slain in a single encounter. [9]Next to him was Eleazar, the son of Dodo the Ahohite, one of the Three warriors with David at Ephes-dammim, when they insulted the Philistines who had massed there for battle. The Israelites had retreated, [10]but he stood there and struck down the Philistines until his hand grew tired from clutching the sword. The LORD brought about a great victory on that day; the army turned back to rejoin Eleazar, but only to strip the slain. [11]Next to him was Shammah, son of Agee the Hararite. The Philistines had assembled at Lehi, where there was a plot of land full of lentils. The people were fleeing before the Philistines, [12]but he took his stand in the middle of the plot, kept it safe, and cut down the Philistines. Thus the LORD brought about a great victory. Such deeds as these the Three warriors performed.

[13]Three of the Thirty chiefs went down to David in the cave of Adullam during the harvest, while a Philistine clan was encamped in the Valley of Rephaim. [14]David was then in the stronghold, and there was a garrison of Philistines in Bethlehem. [15]Now David had a craving and said, "If only someone would give me a drink of water from the cistern by the gate of Bethlehem!" [16]Thereupon the three warriors broke through the encampment of the Philistines, drew water from the cistern by the gate of Bethlehem, and carried it back to David. But he refused to drink it, and instead poured it out to the LORD, [17]saying: "The LORD forbid that I do such a thing!

Could I drink the blood of these men who went at the risk of their lives?" So he refused to drink it.

¹⁸Abishai, the brother of Joab, son of Zeruiah, was the chief of the Thirty; he brandished his spear over three hundred whom he had slain. He made a name among the Thirty, ¹⁹but was more famous than any of the Thirty, becoming their leader. However, he did not attain to the Three.

²⁰Benaiah, son of Jehoiada, a valiant man of mighty deeds, from Kabzeel, killed the two sons of Ariel of Moab. Also, he went down and killed the lion in the cistern on a snowy day. ²¹He likewise slew an Egyptian, a huge man. The Egyptian carried a spear, but Benaiah came against him with a staff; he wrested the spear from the Egyptian's hand, and killed him with that spear. ²²Such deeds as these Benaiah, the son of Jehoiada, performed; and he made a name among the Thirty warriors ²³but was more famous than any of the Thirty. However, he did not attain to the Three. David put him in charge of his bodyguard. ²⁴Asahel, brother of Joab, was among the Thirty; Elhanan, son of Dodo, from Bethlehem; ²⁵Shammah, from En-harod; Elika, from En-harod; ²⁶Helez, from Beth-pelet; Ira, son of Ikkesh, from Tekoa; ²⁷Abiezer, from Anathoth; Sibbecai, from Husha; ²⁸Zalmon, from Ahoh; Maharai, from Netophah; ²⁹Heled, son of Baanah, from Netophah; Ittai, son of Ribai, from Gibeah of Benjamin; ³⁰Benaiah, from Pirathon; Hiddai, from the valley of Gaash; ³¹Abibaal, from Beth-arabah; Azmaveth, from Bahurim; ³²Eliahba, from Shaalbon; Jashen the Gunite; Jonathan, ³³son of Shammah the Hararite; Ahiam, son of Sharar the Hararite; ³⁴Eliphelet, son of Ahasbai, from Beth-maacah; Eliam, son of Ahithophel, from Gilo; ³⁵Hezrai, from Carmel; Paarai the Arbite; ³⁶Igal, son of Nathan, from Zobah; Bani the Gadite; ³⁷Zelek the Ammonite; Naharai, from Beeroth, the armor-bearer of Joab, son of Zeruiah; ³⁸Ira, from Jattir; Gareb, from Jattir; ³⁹Uriah the Hittite—thirty-seven in all.

David's Census; the Plague. 24:1 The Lord's anger against Israel flared again, and he incited David against them: "Go, take a census of Israel and Judah." ²The king therefore said to Joab and the leaders of the army who were with him, "Tour all the tribes of Israel from Dan to Beer-sheba and register the people, that I may know their number." ³But Joab replied to the king: "May the Lord your God increase the number of people a hundred-fold for my lord the king to see it with his own eyes. But why does it please my lord to do a thing of this kind?" ⁴However, the king's command prevailed over Joab and the leaders of the army, so they left the king's presence in order to register the people of Israel. ⁵Crossing the Jordan, they began near Aroer, south of the city in the wadi, and turned in the direction of Gad toward Jazer. ⁶They continued on to Gilead and to the district below Mount Hermon. Then they proceeded to Dan; from there they turned toward Sidon, ⁷going to the fortress of Tyre and to all the cities of the Hivites and Canaanites, and ending up in the Negeb of Judah, at Beer-sheba. ⁸Thus they toured the whole land, reaching Jerusalem again after nine months and twenty days. ⁹Joab then reported the census figures to the king: of men capable of wielding a sword, there were in Israel eight hundred thousand, and in Judah five hundred thousand.

¹⁰Afterward, however, David regretted having numbered the people. David said to the Lord: "I have sinned grievously in what I have done. Take away, Lord, your servant's guilt, for I have acted very foolishly." ¹¹When David rose in the morning, the word of the Lord came to the prophet Gad, David's seer, saying: ¹²Go, tell David: Thus says the Lord: I am offering you three options; choose one of them, and I will

give you that. [13]Gad then went to David to inform him. He asked: "Should three years of famine come upon your land; or three months of fleeing from your enemy while he pursues you; or is it to be three days of plague in your land? Now consider well: what answer am I to give to him who sent me?" [14]David answered Gad: "I am greatly distressed. But let us fall into the hand of God, whose mercy is great, rather than into human hands." [15]Thus David chose the plague. At the time of the wheat harvest it broke out among the people. The LORD sent plague over Israel from morning until the time appointed, and from Dan to Beer-sheba seventy thousand of the people died. [16]But when the angel stretched forth his hand toward Jerusalem to destroy it, the LORD changed his mind about the calamity, and said to the angel causing the destruction among the people: Enough now! Stay your hand. The angel of the LORD was then standing at the threshing floor of Araunah the Jebusite. [17]When David saw the angel who was striking the people, he said to the LORD: "It is I who have sinned; it is I, the shepherd, who have done wrong. But these sheep, what have they done? Strike me and my father's family!"

David Offers Sacrifices. [18]On the same day Gad went to David and said to him, "Go and set up an altar to the LORD on the threshing floor of Araunah the Jebusite." [19]According to Gad's word, David went up as the LORD had commanded. [20]Now Araunah looked down and saw the king and his servants coming toward him while he was threshing wheat. So he went out and bowed down before the king, his face to the ground. [21]Then Araunah asked, "Why does my lord the king come to his servant?" David replied, "To buy the threshing floor from you, to build an altar to the LORD, that the plague may be withdrawn from the people." [22]But Araunah said to David: "Let my lord the king take it and offer up what is good in his sight. See, here are the oxen for burnt offerings, and the threshing sledges and the yokes of oxen for wood. [23]All this does Araunah give to the king." Araunah then said to the king, "May the LORD your God accept your offering." [24]The king, however, replied to Araunah, "No, I will buy it from you at the proper price, for I cannot sacrifice to the LORD my God burnt offerings that cost me nothing." So David bought the threshing floor and the oxen for fifty silver shekels. [25]Then David built an altar to the LORD there, and sacrificed burnt offerings and communion offerings. The LORD granted relief to the land, and the plague was withdrawn from Israel.

☐ MATTHEW 4:1-11

The Temptation of Jesus. 4:1 Then Jesus was led by the Spirit into the desert to be tempted by the devil. [2]He fasted for forty days and forty nights, and afterwards he was hungry. [3]The tempter approached and said to him, "If you are the Son of God, command that these stones become loaves of bread." [4]He said in reply, "It is written:

'One does not live by bread alone,
    but by every word that comes forth
        from the mouth of God.'"

[5]Then the devil took him to the holy city, and made him stand on the parapet of the temple, [6]and said to him, "If you are the Son of God, throw yourself down. For it is written:

'He will command his angels
        concerning you'
    and 'with their hands they will
        support you,
    lest you dash your foot against a
        stone.'"

[7]Jesus answered him, "Again it is written, 'You shall not put the Lord, your God, to the test.'" [8]Then the devil took him up to a very high mountain, and showed him all the kingdoms of the world in their magnificence, [9]and he said to him, "All these I shall give to you, if you will prostrate yourself and worship me." [10]At this, Jesus said to him, "Get away, Satan! It is written:

'The Lord, your God, shall you worship and him alone shall you serve.'"

[11]Then the devil left him and, behold, angels came and ministered to him.

April 14

Good virtuous folks feel more pleasure in the sorrow over their sins and the affliction of their penance than wretches feel in the fulfilling of their foul pleasure.

— St. Thomas More

☐ 1 KINGS 1-3

David's Old Age. 1:1 When King David was old and advanced in years, though they covered him with blankets he could not get warm. [2]His servants therefore said to him, "Let a young virgin be sought to attend my lord the king, and to nurse him. If she sleeps with you, my lord the king will be warm." [3]So they sought for a beautiful girl throughout the territory of Israel, and found Abishag the Shunamite. So they brought her to the king. [4]The girl was very beautiful indeed, and she nursed the king and took care of him. But the king did not have relations with her.

Adonijah's Ambition. [5]Adonijah, son of Haggith, boasted, "I shall be king!" and he provided himself with chariots, horses, and a retinue of fifty to go before him. [6]Yet his father would never antagonize him by asking, "Why are you doing this?" Adonijah was also very handsome, and next in age to Absalom by the same mother. [7]He consulted with Joab, son of Zeruiah, and with Abiathar the priest, and they became Adonijah's supporters. [8]However, Zadok the priest, Benaiah, son of Jehoiada, Nathan the prophet, Shimei and Rei, and David's warriors did not support Adonijah.

[9]Adonijah slaughtered sheep, oxen, and fatlings at the stone Zoheleth near En-rogel and invited all his brothers, the king's sons, and all the royal officials of Judah; [10]but he did not invite Nathan the prophet, or Benaiah, or the warriors, or Solomon his brother.

Solomon Proclaimed King. [11]Then Nathan said to Bathsheba, Solomon's mother: "Have you not heard that Adonijah, son of Haggith, has become king, and our lord David does not know? [12]Come now, let me advise you so that you may save your life and the life of your son Solomon. [13]Go, visit King David, and say to him, 'Did you not, my lord king, swear to your handmaid: Your son Solomon shall be king after me; it is he who shall sit upon my throne? Why, then, has Adonijah become king?' [14]And while you are still there speaking to the king, I will come in after you and confirm your words."

[15]So Bathsheba visited the king in his room. The king was very old, and Abishag the Shunamite was caring for the king. [16]Bathsheba bowed in homage to the king. The king said to her, "What do you wish?" [17]She answered him: "My lord, you swore

to your servant by the LORD, your God, 'Solomon your son will be king after me; it is he who shall sit upon my throne.' ¹⁸But now Adonijah has become king, and you, my lord king, do not know it. ¹⁹He has sacrificed bulls, fatlings, and sheep in great numbers; he has invited all the king's sons, Abiathar the priest, and Joab, the commander of the army, but not your servant Solomon. ²⁰Now, my lord king, all Israel is looking to you to declare to them who is to sit upon the throne of my lord the king after him. ²¹If this is not done, when my lord the king rests with his ancestors, I and my son Solomon will be considered criminals."

²²While she was still speaking to the king, Nathan the prophet came in. ²³They told the king, "Nathan the prophet is here." He entered the king's presence and did him homage, bowing to the floor. ²⁴Then Nathan said: "My lord king, did you say, 'Adonijah shall be king after me and shall sit upon my throne'? ²⁵For today he went down and sacrificed bulls, fatlings, and sheep in great numbers; he invited all the king's sons, the commanders of the army, and Abiathar the priest, and even now they are eating and drinking in his company and saying, 'Long live King Adonijah!' ²⁶But me, your servant, he did not invite; nor Zadok the priest, nor Benaiah, son of Jehoiada, nor your servant Solomon. ²⁷If this was done by order of my lord the king, you did not tell me, your servant, who is to sit upon the throne of my lord the king after him."

²⁸King David answered, "Call Bathsheba here." When she entered the king's presence and stood before him, ²⁹the king swore, "As the LORD lives, who has redeemed my life from all distress, ³⁰this very day I will fulfill the oath I swore to you by the LORD, the God of Israel, 'Your son Solomon shall be king after me and shall sit upon my throne in my place.'" ³¹Bowing to the floor in homage to the king, Bathsheba said, "May my lord, King David, live forever!"

³²Then King David said, "Call Zadok the priest, Nathan the prophet, and Benaiah, son of Jehoiada." When they had entered the king's presence, ³³he said to them: "Take with you the royal officials. Mount my son Solomon upon my own mule and escort him down to Gihon. ³⁴There Zadok the priest and Nathan the prophet shall anoint him king over Israel, and you shall blow the ram's horn and cry, 'Long live King Solomon!' ³⁵When you come back up with him, he is to go in and sit upon my throne. It is he that shall be king in my place: him I designate ruler of Israel and of Judah." ³⁶Benaiah, son of Jehoiada, answered the king: "So be it! May the LORD, the God of my lord the king, so decree! ³⁷As the LORD has been with my lord the king, so may he be with Solomon, and make his throne even greater than that of my lord, King David!"

³⁸So Zadok the priest, Nathan the prophet, Benaiah, son of Jehoiada, and the Cherethites and Pelethites went down, and mounting Solomon on King David's mule, escorted him to Gihon. ³⁹Then Zadok the priest took the horn of oil from the tent and anointed Solomon. They blew the ram's horn and all the people shouted, "Long live King Solomon!" ⁴⁰Then all the people went up after him, playing flutes and rejoicing so much the earth split with their shouting.

Adonijah Submits to Solomon. ⁴¹Adonijah and all the guests who were with him heard it, just as they ended their banquet. When Joab heard the sound of the ram's horn, he asked, "Why this uproar in the city?" ⁴²As he was speaking, Jonathan, son of Abiathar the priest, arrived. Adonijah said, "Come, you are a man of worth and must bring good news." ⁴³Jonathan answered Adonijah, "Hardly! Our lord, King David, has made Solomon king. ⁴⁴The king sent with him Zadok the priest, Nathan the prophet, Benaiah, son of Jehoiada, and the Cherethites and Pelethites, and they mounted him upon the king's own mule. ⁴⁵Zadok the priest and Nathan the prophet anointed him king at Gihon, and they went up from there rejoicing, so that the city is in an uproar. That is the noise you hear. ⁴⁶Moreover, Solomon has taken his seat on the royal throne, ⁴⁷and moreover the king's servants have come to pay their respects to our lord, King David, saying, 'May your God make Solomon's name more famous than your name, his throne greater than your throne!' And the king in his bed did homage. ⁴⁸This is what the king said: 'Blessed be the LORD, the God of Israel, who has this day provided one to sit upon my throne, so that I see it with my own eyes.'" ⁴⁹All the guests of Adonijah got up trembling, and went each their way, ⁵⁰but Adonijah, in fear of Solomon, got up and went to grasp the horns of the altar.

⁵¹It was reported to Solomon: "Adonijah, in fear of King Solomon, is clinging to the horns of the altar and saying, 'Let King Solomon first swear that he will not kill me, his servant, with the sword.'" ⁵²Solomon answered, "If he proves worthy, not a hair of his shall fall to the ground. But if evil is found in him, he shall die." ⁵³King Solomon sent to have him brought down from the altar, and he came and paid homage to King Solomon. Solomon then said to him, "Go to your house."

David's Last Instructions and Death. 2:1 When the time of David's death drew near, he gave these instructions to Solomon his son: ²"I am going the way of all the earth. Be strong and be a man! ³Keep the mandate of the LORD, your God, walking in his ways and keeping his statutes, commands, ordinances, and decrees as they are written in the law of Moses, that you may succeed in whatever you do, and wherever you turn, ⁴and that the LORD may fulfill the word he spoke concerning me: If your sons so conduct themselves that they walk before me in faithfulness with their whole heart and soul, there shall never be wanting someone of your line on the throne of Israel.

⁵"You yourself know what Joab, son of Zeruiah, did to me—what he did to the two commanders of Israel's armies, Abner, son of Ner, and Amasa, son of Jether: he killed them and brought the blood of war into a time of peace, and put the blood of war on the belt about his waist and the sandal on his foot. ⁶Act with all the wisdom you possess; do not let his gray head go down to Sheol in peace. ⁷But be true to the sons of Barzillai the Gileadite, and have them among those who eat at your table. For they were loyal to me when I was fleeing from your brother Absalom. ⁸You also have with you Shimei, son of Gera, the Benjaminite of Bahurim, who cursed me bitterly the day I was going to Mahanaim. When he came down to meet me at the Jordan, I swore to him by the LORD: 'I will not kill you by the sword.' ⁹But you must not let him go unpunished. You are wise; you will know what to do to send his gray head down to Sheol in blood."

¹⁰David rested with his ancestors and was buried in the City of David. ¹¹David was king over Israel for forty years: he was king seven years in Hebron and thirty-three years in Jerusalem.

The Kingdom Made Secure. ¹²Then Solomon sat on the throne of David his father, and his kingship was established.

¹³Adonijah, son of Haggith, came to Bathsheba, the mother of Solomon. "Do you come in peace?" she asked. "In peace," he answered, ¹⁴and he added, "I have something to say to you." She replied, "Speak." ¹⁵So he said: "You know that the kingship was mine, and all Israel expected me to be king. But the kingship passed me by and went to my brother; by the LORD's will it went to him. ¹⁶But now there is one favor I would ask of you. Do not refuse me." And she said, "Speak on." ¹⁷He said, "Please ask King Solomon, who will not refuse you,

to give me Abishag the Shunamite to be my wife." ¹⁸Bathsheba replied, "Very well, I will speak to the king for you."

¹⁹Then Bathsheba went to King Solomon to speak to him for Adonijah, and the king stood up to meet her and paid her homage. Then he sat down upon his throne, and a throne was provided for the king's mother, who sat at his right. ²⁰She said, "There is one small favor I would ask of you. Do not refuse me." The king said to her, "Ask it, my mother, for I will not refuse you." ²¹So she said, "Let Abishag the Shunamite be given to your brother Adonijah to be his wife." ²²King Solomon answered his mother, "And why do you ask that Abishag the Shunamite be given to Adonijah? Ask the kingship for him as well, for he is my older brother! Ask for him, for Abiathar the priest, for Joab, son of Zeruiah!" ²³And King Solomon swore by the Lord: "May God do thus to me and more, if Adonijah has not spoken this word at the cost of his life. ²⁴And now, as the Lord lives, who has established me and set me on the throne of David my father and made for me a house as he promised, this day shall Adonijah be put to death." ²⁵Then King Solomon sent Benaiah, son of Jehoiada, who struck him dead.

²⁶The king said to Abiathar the priest: "Go to your estate in Anathoth. Though you deserve to die, I will not put you to death at this time, because you carried the ark of the Lord God before David my father and shared in all the hardships my father endured." ²⁷So Solomon dismissed Abiathar from the office of priest of the Lord, thus fulfilling the word the Lord had spoken in Shiloh against the house of Eli.

²⁸When the news came to Joab, since he had sided with Adonijah, though not with Absalom, he fled to the tent of the Lord and clung to the horns of the altar. ²⁹King Solomon was told, "Joab has fled to the tent of the Lord and is by the altar." He sent Benaiah, son of Jehoiada, with the order, "Go, strike him down." ³⁰Benaiah went to the tent of the Lord and said to him, "The king says, 'Come out.'" But he answered, "No! I will die here." Benaiah reported to the king, "This is what Joab said to me in reply." ³¹The king answered him: "Do as he has said. Strike him down and bury him, and remove from me and from my father's house the blood which Joab shed without provocation. ³²The Lord will bring blood upon his own head, because he struck down two men better and more just than himself, and slew them with the sword without my father David's knowledge: Abner, son of Ner, commander of Israel's army, and Amasa, son of Jether, commander of Judah's army. ³³Their blood will be upon the head of Joab and his descendants. But upon David and his descendants, upon his house and his throne, there shall be peace forever from the Lord." ³⁴Benaiah, son of Jehoiada, went back, struck him down and killed him; he was buried in his house in the wilderness. ³⁵The king appointed Benaiah, son of Jehoiada, over the army in his place; Zadok the priest the king put in place of Abiathar.

³⁶Then the king summoned Shimei and said to him: "Build yourself a house in Jerusalem and stay there. Do not go anywhere else. ³⁷For the day you leave, and cross the Wadi Kidron, be certain you shall surely die. Your blood shall be upon your own head." ³⁸Shimei answered the king: "I accept. Your servant will do just as my lord the king has said." So Shimei stayed in Jerusalem for a long time. ³⁹But three years later, two of Shimei's servants ran away to Achish, son of Maacah, king of Gath, and Shimei was told, "Your servants are in Gath." ⁴⁰So Shimei rose, saddled his donkey, and went to Achish in Gath in search of his servants; and Shimei returned from Gath with his servants. ⁴¹When Solomon was told that Shimei had gone from Jerusalem to Gath, and had returned, ⁴²the king summoned Shimei and said to him: "Did I

not have you swear by the LORD and warn you clearly, 'The day you leave and go anywhere else, be certain you shall surely die'? And you answered, 'I accept and obey.' ⁴³Why, then, have you not kept the oath of the LORD and the command that I gave you?" ⁴⁴And the king said to Shimei: "In your heart you know very well the evil that you did to David my father. Now the LORD is bringing your own evil upon your head. ⁴⁵But King Solomon shall be blessed, and David's throne shall be established before the LORD forever." ⁴⁶The king then gave the order to Benaiah, son of Jehoiada, who went out and struck him dead.

And the royal power was established in Solomon's hand.

Early Promise of Solomon's Reign. 3:1 Solomon allied himself by marriage with Pharaoh, king of Egypt. He married the daughter of Pharaoh and brought her to the City of David, until he should finish building his own house, and the house of the LORD, and the wall around Jerusalem. ²The people were sacrificing on the high places, however, for up to that time no house had been built for the name of the LORD. ³Although Solomon loved the LORD, walking in the statutes of David his father, he offered sacrifice and burned incense on the high places.

⁴The king went to Gibeon to sacrifice there, because that was the great high place. Upon its altar Solomon sacrificed a thousand burnt offerings. ⁵In Gibeon the LORD appeared to Solomon in a dream at night. God said: Whatever you ask I shall give you. ⁶Solomon answered: "You have shown great kindness to your servant, David my father, because he walked before you with fidelity, justice, and an upright heart; and you have continued this great kindness toward him today, giving him a son to sit upon his throne. ⁷Now, LORD, my God, you have made me, your servant, king to succeed David my father; but I am a mere youth, not knowing at all how to act— ⁸I, your servant, among the people you have chosen, a people so vast that it cannot be numbered or counted. ⁹Give your servant, therefore, a listening heart to judge your people and to distinguish between good and evil. For who is able to give judgment for this vast people of yours?"

¹⁰The Lord was pleased by Solomon's request. ¹¹So God said to him: Because you asked for this—you did not ask for a long life for yourself, nor for riches, nor for the life of your enemies—but you asked for discernment to know what is right— ¹²I now do as you request. I give you a heart so wise and discerning that there has never been anyone like you until now, nor after you will there be anyone to equal you. ¹³In addition, I give you what you have not asked for: I give you such riches and glory that among kings there will be no one like you all your days. ¹⁴And if you walk in my ways, keeping my statutes and commandments, as David your father did, I will give you a long life. ¹⁵Solomon awoke; it was a dream! He went to Jerusalem, stood before the ark of the covenant of the Lord, sacrificed burnt offerings and communion offerings, and gave a feast for all his servants.

Solomon's Listening Heart. ¹⁶Later, two prostitutes came to the king and stood before him. ¹⁷One woman said: "By your leave, my lord, this woman and I live in the same house, and I gave birth in the house while she was present. ¹⁸On the third day after I gave birth, this woman also gave birth. We were alone; no one else was in the house with us; only the two of us were in the house. ¹⁹This woman's son died during the night when she lay on top of him. ²⁰So in the middle of the night she got up and took my son from my side, as your servant was sleeping. Then she laid him in her bosom and laid her dead son in my bosom. ²¹I rose in the morning to nurse my son, and he was dead! But when I examined him in the morning light, I saw it was not the son I had borne." [22]The other woman answered, "No! The living one is my son, the dead one is yours." But the first kept saying, "No! the dead one is your son, the living one is mine!" Thus they argued before the king. [23]Then the king said: "One woman claims, 'This, the living one, is my son, the dead one is yours.' The other answers, 'No! The dead one is your son, the living one is mine.'" [24]The king continued, "Get me a sword." When they brought the sword before the king, [25]he said, "Cut the living child in two, and give half to one woman and half to the other." [26]The woman whose son was alive, because she was stirred with compassion for her son, said to the king, "Please, my lord, give her the living baby—do not kill it!" But the other said, "It shall be neither mine nor yours. Cut it in two!" [27]The king then answered, "Give her the living baby! Do not kill it! She is the mother." [28]When all Israel heard the judgment the king had given, they were in awe of him, because they saw that the king had in him the wisdom of God for giving right judgment.

☐ MATTHEW 4:12-17

The Beginning of the Galilean Ministry.
4:12 When he heard that John had been arrested, he withdrew to Galilee. [13]He left Nazareth and went to live in Capernaum by the sea, in the region of Zebulun and Naphtali, [14]that what had been said through Isaiah the prophet might be fulfilled:

[15]"Land of Zebulun and land of
  Naphtali,
the way to the sea, beyond the Jordan,
  Galilee of the Gentiles,
[16]the people who sit in darkness
  have seen a great light,
on those dwelling in a land
  overshadowed by death
  light has arisen."

[17]From that time on, Jesus began to preach and say, "Repent, for the kingdom of heaven is at hand."

April 15

A good vocation is simply a firm and constant will in which the person who is called must serve God in the way and in the places to which almighty God has called him.

— St. Francis de Sales

☐ 1 KINGS 4-6

Solomon's Riches: Domestic Affairs. 4:1
Solomon was king over all Israel, [2]and these were the officials he had in his service:

Azariah, son of Zadok, the priest;
[3]Elihoreph and Ahijah, sons of Shisha, scribes;
Jehoshaphat, son of Ahilud, the chancellor;
[4]Benaiah, son of Jehoiada, in charge of the army;
Zadok and Abiathar, priests;
[5]Azariah, son of Nathan, in charge of the governors;

Zabud, son of Nathan, priest and companion to the king;
⁶Ahishar, master of the palace; and Adoniram, son of Abda, in charge of the forced labor.

⁷Solomon had twelve governors over all Israel who supplied food for the king and his household, each having to provide for one month in the year. ⁸Their names were:

the son of Hur in the hill country of Ephraim;
⁹the son of Deker in Makaz, Shaalbim, Beth-shemesh, and Elon Beth-hanan;
¹⁰the son of Hesed in Arubboth, as well as in Socoh and the whole region of Hepher;
¹¹the son of Abinadab, in all Naphath-dor; he was married to Taphath, Solomon's daughter;
¹²Baana, son of Ahilud, in Taanach and Megiddo and all Beth-shean near Zarethan below Jezreel, from Beth-shean to Abel-meholah to beyond Jokmeam;
¹³the son of Geber in Ramoth-gilead, having charge of the villages of Jair, son of Manasseh, in Gilead; and of the district of Argob in Bashan— sixty large walled cities with gates barred with bronze;
¹⁴Ahinadab, son of Iddo, in Ma-hanaim;
¹⁵Ahimaaz, in Naphtali; he was married to Basemath, another daughter of Solomon;
¹⁶Baana, son of Hushai, in Asher and Aloth;
¹⁷Jehoshaphat, son of Paruah, in Issachar;
¹⁸Shimei, son of Ela, in Benjamin;
¹⁹Geber, son of Uri, in the land of Gilead, the land of Sihon, king of the Amorites, and of Og, king of Bashan.

There was one governor besides, in the land of Judah. ²⁰Judah and Israel were as numerous as the sands by the sea; they ate and drank and rejoiced.

Solomon's Riches: International Affairs. 5:1 Solomon ruled over all the kingdoms from the River to the land of the Philistines, down to the border of Egypt; they paid Solomon tribute and served him as long as he lived. ²Solomon's provisions for each day were thirty kors of fine flour, sixty kors of meal, ³ten fatted oxen, twenty pasture-fed oxen, and a hundred sheep, not counting harts, gazelles, roebucks, and fatted fowl. ⁴He had dominion over all the land west of the River, from Tiphsah to Gaza, and all its kings, and he had peace on all his borders round about. ⁵Thus Judah and Israel lived in security, everyone under their own vine and fig tree from Dan to Beer-sheba, as long as Solomon lived.

Solomon's Riches: Chariots and Horses. ⁶Solomon had forty thousand stalls for horses for chariots and twelve thousand horsemen. ⁷The governors, one for each month, provided food for King Solomon and for all the guests at King Solomon's table. They left nothing unprovided. ⁸For the chariot horses and draft animals also, each brought his quota of barley and straw to the required place.

Solomon's Renown. ⁹Moreover, God gave Solomon wisdom, exceptional understanding, and knowledge, as vast as the sand on the seashore. ¹⁰Solomon's wisdom surpassed that of all the peoples of the East and all the wisdom of Egypt. ¹¹He was wiser than anyone else—wiser than Ethan the Ezrahite, or Heman, Chalcol, and Darda, the musicians—and his fame spread throughout the neighboring peoples. ¹²Solomon also uttered three thousand proverbs, and his songs numbered a thousand and five. ¹³He spoke of plants, from the cedar on Lebanon to the hyssop growing out of the wall, and he spoke about beasts, birds, reptiles, and fishes. ¹⁴People from all nations came to hear Solomon's wisdom, sent by all the kings of the earth who had heard of his wisdom.

Preparations for the Temple. [15]When Hiram, king of Tyre, heard that Solomon had been anointed king in place of his father, he sent an embassy to him; for Hiram had always been David's friend. [16]Solomon sent back this message to Hiram: [17]"You know that David my father, because of the wars that beset him, could not build a house for the name of the LORD his God until such time as the LORD should put his enemies under the soles of his feet. [18]But now the LORD, my God, has given me rest on all sides, without adversary or misfortune. [19]So I intend to build a house for the name of the LORD, my God, as the LORD said to David my father: Your son whom I will put upon your throne in your place shall build the house for my name. [20]Give orders, then, to have cedars from the Lebanon cut down for me. My servants shall accompany yours, and I will pay you whatever you say for your servants' wages. For you know that there is no one among us who is skilled in cutting timber like the Sidonians." [21]When Hiram had heard the words of Solomon, he was overjoyed, and said, "Blessed be the LORD this day, who has given David a wise son over this numerous people." [22]Hiram then sent word to Solomon, "I have heard the proposal you sent me, and I will provide all the cedars and fir trees you desire. [23]My servants shall bring them down from the Lebanon to the sea, and I will arrange them into rafts in the sea and bring them wherever you say. There I will break up the rafts, and you shall take the lumber. You, for your part, shall furnish the provisions I desire for my household." [24]So Hiram continued to provide Solomon with all the cedars and fir trees he desired, [25]while Solomon gave Hiram twenty thousand kors of wheat to provide for his household, and twenty kors of hand-pressed oil. Solomon gave Hiram all

this every year. [26]The LORD gave Solomon wisdom as he promised him. So there was peace between Hiram and Solomon, and the two of them made a covenant.

[27]King Solomon raised thirty thousand forced laborers from all Israel. [28]He sent them to the Lebanon for a month in relays of ten thousand, so that they spent one month in the Lebanon and two months at home. Adoniram was in charge of the forced labor. [29]Solomon had seventy thousand carriers and eighty thousand stonecutters in the mountain, [30]in addition to three thousand three hundred overseers answerable to Solomon, who were in charge of the work and directed the people engaged in the work. [31]By order of the king, fine, large blocks of stone were quarried to give the house a foundation of hewn stone. [32]Solomon's and Hiram's builders, along with others from Gebal, shaped them, and prepared the wood and stones for building the house.

Building of the Temple. 6:1 In the four hundred and eightieth year after the Israelites went forth from the land of Egypt, in the fourth year of Solomon's reign over Israel, in the month of Ziv (the second month), he began to build the house of the LORD.

[2]The house which King Solomon built for the LORD was sixty cubits long, twenty wide, and thirty high. [3]The porch in front of the nave of the house was twenty cubits from side to side along the width of the house, and ten cubits deep in front of the house. [4]Windows with closed lattices were made for the house, [5]and adjoining the wall of the house he built a substructure around its walls that enclosed the nave and the inner sanctuary, and he made side chambers all around. [6]The lowest story was five cubits wide, the middle one six cubits wide, the third seven cubits wide, because he put recesses along the outside of the house to avoid fastening anything

into the walls of the house. [7]The house was built of stone dressed at the quarry, so that no hammer or ax, no iron tool, was to be heard in the house during its construction. [8]The entrance to the middle story was on the south side of the house; stairs led up to the middle story and from the middle story to the third. [9]When he had finished building the house, it was roofed in with rafters and boards of cedar. [10]He built the substructure five cubits high all along the outside of the house, to which it was joined by cedar beams.

[11]The word of the LORD came to Solomon: [12]As to this house you are building— if you walk in my statutes, carry out my ordinances, and observe all my commands, walking in them, I will fulfill toward you my word which I spoke to David your father. [13]I will dwell in the midst of the Israelites and will not forsake my people Israel.

[14]When Solomon finished building the house, [15]its inside walls were lined with cedar paneling: he covered the interior with wood from floor to ceiling, and he covered its floor with fir planking. [16]At the rear of the house a space of twenty cubits was set off by cedar panels from the floor to the ceiling, enclosing the inner sanctuary, the holy of holies. [17]The house was forty cubits long, that is, the nave, the part in front. [18]The cedar in the interior of the house was carved in the form of gourds and open flowers; all was of cedar, and no stone was to be seen.

[19]In the innermost part of the house he set up the inner sanctuary to house the ark of the LORD's covenant. [20]In front of the inner sanctuary (it was twenty cubits long, twenty wide, and twenty high, and he covered it with pure gold), he made an altar of cedar. [21]Solomon covered the interior of the house with pure gold, and he drew golden chains across in front of the inner sanctuary, and covered it with gold. [22]He covered the whole house with gold, until the whole house was done, and the whole altar that belonged to the inner sanctuary he covered with gold. [23]In the inner sanctuary he made two cherubim, each ten cubits high, made of pine. [24]Each wing of a cherub was five cubits so that the span from wing tip to wing tip was ten cubits. [25]The second cherub was also ten cubits: the two cherubim were identical in size and shape; [26]the first cherub was ten cubits high, and so was the second. [27]He placed the cherubim in the inmost part of the house; the wings of the cherubim were spread wide, so that one wing of the first touched the side wall and the wing of the second touched the other wall; the wings pointing to the middle of the room touched each other. [28]He overlaid the cherubim with gold.

[29]The walls of the house on all sides of both the inner and the outer rooms had carved figures of cherubim, palm trees, and open flowers. [30]The floor of the house of both the inner and the outer rooms was overlaid with gold. [31]At the entrance of the inner sanctuary, doors of pine were made; the doorframes had five-sided posts. [32]The two doors were of pine, with carved figures of cherubim, palm trees, and open flowers. The doors were overlaid with gold, and the cherubim and the palm trees were also covered with beaten gold. [33]He did the same at the entrance to the nave, where the doorposts were of pine and were four-sided. [34]The two doors were of fir wood, each door consisting of two panels hinged together; [35]and he carved cherubim, palm trees, and open flowers, and plated them with gold. [36]He walled off the inner court with three courses of hewn stones and one course of cedar beams.

[37]The foundations of the LORD's house were laid in the month of Ziv in the fourth year, [38]and it was finished, in all particulars, exactly according to plan, in the month of Bul, the eighth month, in the eleventh year. Thus Solomon built it in seven years.

☐ MATTHEW 4:18-25

The Call of the First Disciples. 4:18 As he was walking by the Sea of Galilee, he saw two brothers, Simon who is called Peter, and his brother Andrew, casting a net into the sea; they were fishermen. ¹⁹He said to them, "Come after me, and I will make you fishers of men." ²⁰At once they left their nets and followed him. ²¹He walked along from there and saw two other brothers, James, the son of Zebedee, and his brother John. They were in a boat, with their father Zebedee, mending their nets. He called them, ²²and immediately they left their boat and their father and followed him.

Ministering to a Great Multitude. ²³He went around all of Galilee, teaching in their synagogues, proclaiming the gospel of the kingdom, and curing every disease and illness among the people. ²⁴His fame spread to all of Syria, and they brought to him all who were sick with various diseases and racked with pain, those who were possessed, lunatics, and paralytics, and he cured them. ²⁵And great crowds from Galilee, the Decapolis, Jerusalem, and Judea, and from beyond the Jordan followed him.

April 16

St. Bernadette Soubirous

Let the crucifix be not only in my eyes and on my breast, but in my heart.

— St. Bernadette Soubirous

☐ 1 KINGS 7-9

7:1 To finish the building of his own house Solomon took thirteen years. ²He built the House of the Forest of Lebanon one hundred cubits long, fifty wide, and thirty high; it was supported by four rows of cedar columns, with cedar beams upon the columns. ³Moreover, it had a ceiling of cedar above the rafters resting on the columns; these rafters numbered forty-five, fifteen to a row. ⁴There were lattices in three rows, each row facing the next, ⁵and all the openings and doorposts were squared with lintels, each facing across from the next. ⁶He also made the Porch of Columns, fifty cubits long and thirty wide. The porch extended across the front, and there were columns with a canopy in front of them. ⁷He also made the Porch of the Throne where he gave judgment—

that is, the Porch of Judgment; it was paneled with cedar from floor to ceiling beams. ⁸The house in which he lived was in another court, set in deeper than the Porch and of the same construction. (Solomon made a house like this Porch for Pharaoh's daughter, whom he had married.) ⁹All these buildings were of fine stones, hewn to size and trimmed front and back with a saw, from the foundation to the bonding course and outside as far as the great court. ¹⁰The foundation was made of fine, large blocks, some ten cubits and some eight cubits. ¹¹Above were fine stones hewn to size, and cedar wood. ¹²The great court had three courses of hewn stones all around and a course of cedar beams. So also were the inner court of the house of the LORD and its porch.

[13]King Solomon brought Hiram from Tyre. [14]He was a bronze worker, the son of a widow from the tribe of Naphtali; his father had been from Tyre. He was endowed with wisdom, understanding, and knowledge for doing any work in bronze. He came to King Solomon and did all his metal work.

[15]He fashioned two bronze columns, each eighteen cubits high and twelve cubits in circumference. [16]He also made two capitals cast in bronze, to be placed on top of the columns, each of them five cubits high. [17]There were meshes made like netting and braid made like chains for the capitals on top of the columns, seven for each capital. [18]He also cast pomegranates, two rows around each netting to cover the capital on top of the columns. [19]The capitals on top of the columns (in the porch) were made like lilies, four cubits high. [20]And the capitals on the two columns, both above and adjoining the bulge where it crossed out of the netting, had two hundred pomegranates in rows around each capital. [21]He set up the columns at the temple porch; one he set up to the south, and called it Jachin, and the other to the north, and called it Boaz. [22]The top of the columns was made like a lily. Thus the work on the columns was completed.

[23]Then he made the molten sea; it was made with a circular rim, and measured ten cubits across, five in height, and thirty in circumference. [24]Under the brim, gourds encircled it for ten cubits around the compass of the sea; the gourds were in two rows and were cast in one mold with the sea. [25]This rested on twelve oxen, three facing north, three facing west, three facing south, and three facing east, with their haunches all toward the center; upon them was set the sea. [26]It was a handbreadth thick, and its brim resembled that of a cup, being lily-shaped. Its capacity was two thousand baths.

[27]He also made ten stands of bronze, each four cubits long, four wide, and three high. [28]When these stands were constructed, panels were set within the framework. [29]On the panels within the frames there were lions, oxen, and cherubim; and on the frames likewise, above and below the lions and oxen, there were wreaths in hammered relief. [30]Each stand had four bronze wheels and bronze axles. The four legs of each stand had cast braces, which were under the basin; they had wreaths on each side. [31]The mouth of the basin was inside, and a cubit above, the crown, whose opening was round, made like a receptacle, a cubit and a half in depth. There was carved work at the opening, on panels that were square, not circular. [32]The four wheels were below the paneling, and the axletrees of the wheels and the stand were of one piece. Each wheel was a cubit and a half high. [33]The wheels were constructed like chariot wheels; their axletrees, rims, spokes, and hubs were all cast. [34]The four braces reached the four corners of each stand, and formed part of the stand. [35]At the top of the stand there was a raised collar half a cubit high, and the handles and panels on top of the stand formed part of it. [36]On the flat ends of the handles and on the panels, wherever there was a bare space, cherubim, lions, and palm trees were carved, as well as wreaths all around. [37]This was how he made the ten stands, all of the same casting, the same size, the same shape. [38]He made ten bronze basins, each four cubits in diameter with a capacity of forty baths, one basin atop each of the ten stands.

[39]He placed the stands, five on the south side of the house and five on the north. The sea he placed off to the southeast from the south side of the house.

[40]When Hiram had made the pots, shovels, and bowls, he finished all his work for King Solomon in the house of the LORD: [41]two columns; two nodes for the capitals on top of the columns; two pieces of netting covering the two nodes for the capitals on top of the columns;

⁴²four hundred pomegranates in double rows on both pieces of netting that covered the two nodes of the capitals on top of the columns; ⁴³ten stands; ten basins on the stands; ⁴⁴one sea; twelve oxen supporting the sea; ⁴⁵pots, shovels, and bowls. All these articles which Hiram made for King Solomon in the house of the LORD were of burnished bronze. ⁴⁶The king had them cast in the neighborhood of the Jordan, between Succoth and Zarethan, in thick clay molds. ⁴⁷Solomon did not weigh all the articles because they were so numerous; the weight of the bronze, therefore, was not determined.

⁴⁸Solomon made all the articles that were for the house of the LORD: the golden altar; the table on which the showbread lay; ⁴⁹the lampstands of pure gold, five to the right and five to the left before the inner sanctuary; their flowers, lamps, and tongs of gold; ⁵⁰basins, snuffers, bowls, cups, and firepans of pure gold; hinges of gold for the doors of the innermost part of the house, or holy of holies, and for the doors of the outer room, the nave. ⁵¹When all the work undertaken by King Solomon in the house of the LORD was completed, he brought in the votive offerings of his father David, and put the silver, gold, and other articles in the treasuries of the house of the LORD.

Dedication of the Temple. 8:1 Then Solomon assembled the elders of Israel and all the heads of the tribes, the princes in the ancestral houses of the Israelites. They came to King Solomon in Jerusalem, to bring up the ark of the LORD's covenant from the city of David (which is Zion). ²All the people of Israel assembled before King Solomon during the festival in the month of Ethanim (the seventh month). ³When all the elders of Israel had arrived, the priests took up the ark; ⁴and they brought up the ark of the LORD and the tent of meeting with all the sacred vessels that were in the tent. The priests and Levites brought them up. ⁵King Solomon and the entire community of Israel, gathered for the occasion before the ark, sacrificed sheep and oxen too many to number or count. ⁶The priests brought the ark of the covenant of the LORD to its place, the inner sanctuary of the house, the holy of holies, beneath the wings of the cherubim. ⁷The cherubim had their wings spread out over the place of the ark, sheltering the ark and its poles from above. ⁸The poles were so long that their ends could be seen from the holy place in front of the inner sanctuary. They cannot be seen from outside, but they remain there to this day. ⁹There was nothing in the ark but the two stone tablets which Moses had put there at Horeb, when the LORD made a covenant with the Israelites after they went forth from the land of Egypt. ¹⁰When the priests left the holy place, the cloud filled the house of the LORD ¹¹so that the priests could no longer minister because of the cloud, since the glory of the LORD had filled the house of the LORD. ¹²Then Solomon said,

> "The LORD intends to dwell in the dark cloud;
> ¹³I have indeed built you a princely house,
> the base for your enthronement forever."

¹⁴The king turned and blessed the whole assembly of Israel, while the whole assembly of Israel stood. ¹⁵He said: "Blessed be the LORD, the God of Israel, who with his own mouth spoke a promise to David my father and by his hand fulfilled it, saying: ¹⁶Since the day I brought my people Israel out of Egypt, I have not chosen a city out of any tribe of Israel for the building of a house, that my name might be there; but I have chosen David to rule my people Israel. ¹⁷When David my father wished to build a house for the name of the LORD, the God of Israel, ¹⁸the LORD said to him: In wishing to build a house for my name, you did well. ¹⁹But it is not you who will

build the house, but your son, who comes from your loins; he shall build the house for my name. ²⁰Now the LORD has fulfilled the word he spoke: I have succeeded David my father, and I sit on the throne of Israel, as the LORD has spoken, and I have built this house for the name of the LORD, the God of Israel. ²¹I have provided there a place for the ark in which is the covenant of the LORD that he made with our ancestors when he brought them out of the land of Egypt."

Solomon's Prayer. ²²Solomon stood before the altar of the LORD in the presence of the whole assembly of Israel, and stretching forth his hands toward heaven, ²³he said, "LORD, God of Israel, there is no God like you in heaven above or on earth below; you keep covenant and love toward your servants who walk before you with their whole heart, ²⁴the covenant that you kept toward your servant, David my father, what you promised him; your mouth has spoken and your hand has fulfilled this very day. ²⁵And now, LORD, God of Israel, keep toward your servant, David my father, what you promised: There shall never be wanting someone from your line to sit before me on the throne of Israel, provided that your descendants keep to their way, walking before me as you have. ²⁶Now, God of Israel, may the words you spoke to your servant, David my father, be confirmed.

²⁷"Is God indeed to dwell on earth? If the heavens and the highest heavens cannot contain you, how much less this house which I have built! ²⁸Regard kindly the prayer and petition of your servant, LORD, my God, and listen to the cry of supplication which I, your servant, utter before you this day. ²⁹May your eyes be open night and day toward this house, the place of which you said, My name shall be there; listen to the prayer your servant makes toward this place. ³⁰Listen to the petition of your servant and of your people Israel which they offer toward this place. Listen, from the place of your enthronement, heaven, listen and forgive.

³¹"If someone sins in some way against a neighbor and is required to take an oath sanctioned by a curse, and comes and takes the oath before your altar in this house, ³²listen in heaven; act and judge your servants. Condemn the wicked, requiting their ways; acquit the just, rewarding their justice.

³³"When your people Israel are defeated by an enemy because they sinned against you, and then they return to you, praise your name, pray to you, and entreat you in this house, ³⁴listen in heaven and forgive the sin of your people Israel, and bring them back to the land you gave their ancestors.

³⁵"When the heavens are closed, so that there is no rain, because they have sinned against you, but they pray toward this place and praise your name, and turn from their sin because you have afflicted them, ³⁶listen in heaven and forgive the sin of your servants, your people Israel (for you teach them the good way in which they should walk). Give rain to this land of yours which you have given to your people as their heritage.

³⁷"If there is famine in the land or pestilence; or if blight comes, or mildew, or locusts, or caterpillars; if an enemy of your people presses upon them in the land and at their gates; whatever plague or sickness there may be; ³⁸whatever prayer or petition any may make, any of your people Israel, who know heartfelt remorse and stretch out their hands toward this house, ³⁹listen in heaven, the place of your enthronement; forgive and take action. Render to each and all according to their ways, you who know every heart; for it is you alone who know the heart of every human being. ⁴⁰So may they revere you as long as they live on the land you gave our ancestors.

⁴¹"To the foreigners, likewise, who are not of your people Israel, but who come from a distant land for the sake of your name ⁴²(since people will hear of your great

name and your mighty hand and your outstretched arm), when they come and pray toward this house, ⁴³listen in heaven, the place of your enthronement. Do all that the foreigner asks of you, that all the peoples of the earth may know your name, may revere you as do your people Israel, and may know that your name has been invoked upon this house that I have built.

⁴⁴"When your people go out to war against their enemies, by whatever way you send them, and they pray to the LORD toward the city you have chosen and the house I have built for your name, ⁴⁵listen in heaven to their prayer and petition, and uphold their cause.

⁴⁶"When they sin against you (for there is no one who does not sin), and in your anger against them you deliver them to an enemy, so that their captors carry them off to the land of the enemy, far or near, ⁴⁷and they have a change of heart in the land of their captivity and they turn and entreat you in the land of their captors and say, 'We have sinned and done wrong; we have been wicked'; ⁴⁸if with their whole heart and soul they turn back to you in the land of their enemies who took them captive, and pray to you toward the land you gave their ancestors, the city you have chosen, and the house I have built for your name, ⁴⁹listen in heaven, your dwelling place, to their prayer and petition, and uphold their cause. ⁵⁰Forgive your people who have sinned against you and all the offenses they have committed against you, and grant them mercy in the sight of their captors, so that these will be merciful to them. ⁵¹For they are your people and your heritage, whom you brought out of Egypt, from the midst of the iron furnace.

⁵²"Thus may your eyes be open to the petition of your servant and to the petition of your people Israel; thus may you listen to them whenever they call upon you. ⁵³For you have set them apart from all the peoples of the earth to be your heritage, as you declared through Moses your servant when you brought our ancestors out of Egypt, Lord my GOD."

⁵⁴After Solomon finished offering this entire prayer and petition to the LORD, he rose from before the altar of the LORD, where he had been kneeling, hands outstretched toward heaven. ⁵⁵He stood and blessed the whole assembly of Israel, saying in a loud voice: ⁵⁶"Blessed be the LORD who has given rest to his people Israel, just as he promised. Not a single word has gone unfulfilled of the entire gracious promise he made through Moses his servant. ⁵⁷May the LORD, our God, be with us as he was with our ancestors and may he not forsake us nor cast us off. ⁵⁸May he draw our hearts to himself, that we may walk in his ways and keep the commands, statutes, and ordinances that he enjoined on our ancestors. ⁵⁹May these words of mine, the petition I have offered before the LORD, our God, be present to the LORD our God day and night, that he may uphold the cause of his servant and the cause of his people Israel as each day requires, ⁶⁰so that all the peoples of the earth may know that the LORD is God and there is no other. ⁶¹Your heart must be wholly devoted to the LORD, our God, observing his statutes and keeping his commandments, as on this day."

⁶²The king and all Israel with him offered sacrifices before the LORD. ⁶³Solomon offered as communion offerings to the LORD twenty-two thousand oxen and one hundred twenty thousand sheep. Thus the king and all the Israelites dedicated the house of the LORD. ⁶⁴On that day the king consecrated the middle of the court facing the house of the LORD; he offered there the burnt offerings, the grain offerings, and the fat of the communion offerings, because the bronze altar before the LORD was too small to hold the burnt offering, the grain offering, and the fat of the communion offering. ⁶⁵On this occasion Solomon and all Israel with him, a great assembly from Lebo-hamath to the Wadi of Egypt,

celebrated the festival before the LORD, our God, for seven days. ⁶⁶On the eighth day he dismissed the people, who blessed the king and went to their tents, rejoicing and glad of heart because of all the blessings the LORD had given to David his servant and to his people Israel.

Promise and Warning to Solomon. 9:1 After Solomon finished building the house of the LORD, the house of the king, and everything else that he wanted to do, ²the LORD appeared to Solomon a second time, as he had appeared to him in Gibeon. ³The LORD said to him: I have heard the prayer of petition which you offered in my presence. I have consecrated this house which you have built and I set my name there forever; my eyes and my heart shall be there always. ⁴As for you, if you walk before me as David your father did, wholeheartedly and uprightly, doing all that I have commanded you, keeping my statutes and ordinances, ⁵I will establish your royal throne over Israel forever, as I promised David your father: There shall never be wanting someone from your line on the throne of Israel. ⁶But if ever you and your descendants turn from following me, fail to keep my commandments and statutes which I set before you, and proceed to serve other gods and bow down to them, ⁷I will cut off Israel from the land I gave them and repudiate the house I have consecrated for my name. Israel shall become a proverb and a byword among all nations, ⁸and this house shall become a heap of ruins. Every passerby shall gasp in horror and ask, "Why has the LORD done such things to this land and to this house?" ⁹And the answer will come: "Because they abandoned the LORD, their God, who brought their ancestors out of the land of Egypt, and they embraced other gods, bowing down to them and serving them. That is why the LORD has brought upon them all this evil."

After Building the Temple. ¹⁰After the twenty years during which Solomon built the two houses, the house of the LORD and the house of the king—¹¹Hiram, king of Tyre, supplying Solomon with all the cedar wood, fir wood, and gold he wished, and King Solomon giving Hiram in return twenty cities in the land of Galilee— ¹²Hiram left Tyre to see the cities Solomon had given him, but he was not satisfied with them. ¹³So he said, "What are these cities you have given me, my brother?" And he called them the land of Cabul, as they are called to this day. ¹⁴Hiram, however, had sent King Solomon one hundred and twenty talents of gold.

¹⁵This is an account of the conscript labor force King Solomon raised in order to build the house of the LORD, his own house, Millo, the wall of Jerusalem, Hazor, Megiddo, Gezer ¹⁶(Pharaoh, king of Egypt, had come up and taken Gezer and, after destroying it by fire and slaying all the Canaanites living in the city, had given it as a farewell gift to his daughter, Solomon's wife; ¹⁷Solomon then rebuilt Gezer), Lower Beth-horon, ¹⁸Baalath, Tamar in the desert of Judah, ¹⁹all his cities for supplies, cities for chariots and cities for cavalry, and whatever Solomon desired to build in Jerusalem, in Lebanon, and in the entire land under his dominion. ²⁰All the people who were left of the Amorites, Hittites, Perizzites, Hivites, and Jebusites, who were not Israelites— ²¹those of their descendants who were left in the land and whom the Israelites had not been able to destroy under the ban—these Solomon conscripted as forced laborers, as they are to this day. ²²But Solomon made none of the Israelites forced laborers, for they were his fighting force, his ministers, commanders, adjutants, chariot officers, and cavalry. ²³There were five hundred fifty overseers answerable to Solomon's governors for the work, directing the people engaged in the work.

²⁴As soon as Pharaoh's daughter went up from the City of David to her house, which he had built for her, Solomon built Millo. ²⁵Three times a year Solomon used to offer

burnt offerings and communion offerings on the altar which he had built to the LORD, and to burn incense before the LORD.

Thus he completed the temple.

Solomon's Gifts. ²⁶King Solomon also built a fleet at Ezion-geber, which is near Elath on the shore of the Red Sea in the land of Edom. ²⁷To this fleet Hiram sent his own servants, expert sailors, with the servants of Solomon. ²⁸They went to Ophir, and obtained four hundred and twenty talents of gold and brought it to King Solomon.

☐ MATTHEW 5:1-16

The Sermon on the Mount. 5:1 When he saw the crowds, he went up the mountain, and after he had sat down, his disciples came to him. ²He began to teach them, saying:

The Beatitudes. ³"Blessed are the poor
  in spirit,
    for theirs is the kingdom of heaven.
⁴Blessed are they who mourn,
    for they will be comforted.
⁵Blessed are the meek,
    for they will inherit the land.
⁶Blessed are they who hunger and thirst
    for righteousness,
    for they will be satisfied.
⁷Blessed are the merciful,
    for they will be shown mercy.
⁸Blessed are the clean of heart,
    for they will see God.
⁹Blessed are the peacemakers,
    for they will be called children of
      God.

¹⁰Blessed are they who are persecuted
    for the sake of righteousness,
    for theirs is the kingdom of heaven.

¹¹Blessed are you when they insult you and persecute you and utter every kind of evil against you [falsely] because of me. ¹²Rejoice and be glad, for your reward will be great in heaven. Thus they persecuted the prophets who were before you.

The Similes of Salt and Light. ¹³"You are the salt of the earth. But if salt loses its taste, with what can it be seasoned? It is no longer good for anything but to be thrown out and trampled underfoot. ¹⁴You are the light of the world. A city set on a mountain cannot be hidden. ¹⁵Nor do they light a lamp and then put it under a bushel basket; it is set on a lampstand, where it gives light to all in the house. ¹⁶Just so, your light must shine before others, that they may see your good deeds and glorify your heavenly Father."

April 17

Imagine your anger to be a kind of wild beast, because it too has ferocious teeth and claws, and if you don't tame it, it will devastate all things. It not only hurts the body; it even corrupts the health of the soul, devouring, rending, tearing to pieces all its strength, and making it useless for everything.

— St. John Chrysostom

☐ **1 KINGS 10-12**

Solomon's Listening Heart: the Queen of Sheba. 10:1 The queen of Sheba, having heard a report of Solomon's fame, came to test him with subtle questions. ²She arrived in Jerusalem with a very numerous retinue, and with camels bearing spices, a large amount of gold, and precious stones. She came to Solomon and spoke to him about everything that she had on her mind. ³King Solomon explained everything she asked about, and there was nothing so obscure that the king could not explain it to her. ⁴When the queen of Sheba witnessed Solomon's great wisdom, the house he had built, ⁵the food at his table, the seating of his ministers, the attendance and dress of his waiters, his servers, and the burnt offerings he offered in the house of the LORD, it took her breath away. ⁶"The report I heard in my country about your deeds and your wisdom is true," she told the king. ⁷"I did not believe the report until I came and saw with my own eyes that not even the half had been told me. Your wisdom and prosperity surpass the report I heard. ⁸Happy are your servants, happy these ministers of yours, who stand before you always and listen to your wisdom. ⁹Blessed be the LORD, your God, who has been pleased to place you on the throne of Israel. In his enduring love for Israel, the LORD has made you king to carry out judgment and justice." ¹⁰Then she gave the king one hundred and twenty gold talents, a very large quantity of spices, and precious stones. Never again did any-

one bring such an abundance of spices as the queen of Sheba gave to King Solomon. ¹¹Hiram's fleet, which used to bring gold from Ophir, also brought from there a very large quantity of almug wood and precious stones. ¹²With this wood the king made supports for the house of the LORD and for the house of the king, and harps and lyres for the singers. Never again was any such almug wood brought or seen to the present day.

¹³King Solomon gave the queen of Sheba everything she desired and asked for, besides what King Solomon gave her from Solomon's royal bounty. Then she returned with her servants to her own country.

Solomon's Riches: Domestic Affairs. ¹⁴The gold that came to Solomon in one year weighed six hundred and sixty-six gold talents, ¹⁵in addition to what came from the tolls on travelers, from the traffic of merchants, and from all the kings of Arabia and the governors of the country. ¹⁶King Solomon made two hundred shields of beaten gold (six hundred shekels of gold went into each shield) ¹⁷and three hundred bucklers of beaten gold (three minas of gold went into each buckler); and the king put them in the house of the Forest of Lebanon. ¹⁸The king made a large ivory throne, and overlaid it with refined gold. ¹⁹The throne had six steps, a back with a round top, and an arm on each side of the seat, with two lions standing next to the arms, ²⁰and twelve other lions standing there on the steps, two to a step, one on either side of each step. Nothing like this was made in any other kingdom. ²¹All King Solomon's drinking vessels were gold, and all the utensils in the house of the Forest of Lebanon were pure gold. There was no silver, for in Solomon's time silver was reckoned as nothing. ²²For the king had a fleet of Tarshish ships at sea with Hiram's fleet. Once every three years the fleet of Tarshish ships would come with a cargo of gold, silver, ivory, apes, and peacocks.

Solomon's Renown. ²³Thus King Solomon surpassed all the kings of the earth in riches and wisdom. ²⁴And the whole world sought audience with Solomon, to hear the wisdom God had put into his heart. ²⁵They all brought their yearly tribute: vessels of silver and gold, garments, weapons, spices, horses and mules—what was due each year.

Solomon's Riches: Chariots and Horses. ²⁶Solomon amassed chariots and horses; he had one thousand four hundred chariots and twelve thousand horses; these he allocated among the chariot cities and to the king's service in Jerusalem. ²⁷The king made silver as common in Jerusalem as stones, and cedars as numerous as the sycamores of the Shephelah. ²⁸Solomon's horses were imported from Egypt and from Cilicia, where the king's merchants purchased them. ²⁹A chariot imported from Egypt cost six hundred shekels of silver, a horse one hundred and fifty shekels; they were exported at these rates to all the Hittite and Aramean kings.

The End of Solomon's Reign. 11:1 King Solomon loved many foreign women besides the daughter of Pharaoh—Moabites, Ammonites, Edomites, Sidonians, Hittites— ²from nations of which the LORD had said to the Israelites: You shall not join with them and they shall not join with you, lest they turn your hearts to their gods. But Solomon held them close in love. ³He had as wives seven hundred princesses and three hundred concubines, and they turned his heart.

⁴When Solomon was old his wives had turned his heart to follow other gods, and his heart was not entirely with the LORD, his God, as the heart of David his father had been. ⁵Solomon followed Astarte, the goddess of the Sidonians, and Milcom, the abomination of the Ammonites. ⁶Solomon did what was evil in the sight of the LORD, and he did not follow the LORD unreservedly as David his father had done. ⁷Solomon then built a high place to Chemosh, the abomination of Moab, and to Molech, the abomination of the Ammonites, on the mountain opposite Jerusalem. ⁸He did the same for all his foreign wives who burned incense and sacrificed to their gods.

⁹The LORD became angry with Solomon, because his heart turned away from the LORD, the God of Israel, who had appeared to him twice ¹⁰and commanded him not to do this very thing, not to follow other gods. But he did not observe what the LORD commanded. ¹¹So the LORD said to Solomon: Since this is what you want, and you have not kept my covenant and the statutes which I enjoined on you, I will surely tear the kingdom away from you and give it to your servant. ¹²But I will not do this during your lifetime, for the sake of David your father; I will tear it away from your son's hand. ¹³Nor will I tear away the whole kingdom. I will give your son one tribe for the sake of David my servant and for the sake of Jerusalem, which I have chosen.

Threats to Solomon's Kingdom. ¹⁴The LORD then raised up an adversary against Solomon: Hadad the Edomite, who was of the royal line in Edom. ¹⁵Earlier, when David had conquered Edom, Joab, the commander of the army, while going to bury the slain, killed every male in Edom. ¹⁶Joab and all Israel remained there six months until they had killed off every male in Edom. ¹⁷But Hadad, with some Edomite servants of his father, fled toward Egypt. Hadad was then a young boy. [18]They left Midian and came to Paran; they gathered men from Paran and came to Egypt, to Pharaoh, king of Egypt; he gave Hadad a house, appointed him rations, and assigned him land. [19]Hadad won great favor with Pharaoh, so that he gave him in marriage his sister-in-law, the sister of Queen Tahpenes, his own wife. [20]Tahpenes' sister bore Hadad a son, Genubath. Tahpenes weaned him in Pharaoh's palace. And Genubath lived in Pharaoh's house, with Pharaoh's own sons. [21]When Hadad in Egypt heard that David rested with his ancestors and that Joab, the commander of the army, was dead, he said to Pharaoh, "Give me leave to return to my own land." [22]Pharaoh said to him, "What do you lack with me, that you are seeking to return to your own land?" He answered, "Nothing, but please let me go!"

[23]God raised up against Solomon another adversary, Rezon, the son of Eliada, who had fled from his lord, Hadadezer, king of Zobah, [24]when David was slaughtering them. Rezon gathered men about him and became leader of a marauding band. They went to Damascus, settled there, and made him king in Damascus. [25]Rezon was an adversary of Israel as long as Solomon lived, in addition to the harm done by Hadad, and he felt contempt for Israel. He became king over Aram.

Ahijah Announces Jeroboam's Kingship. [26]Solomon had a servant, Jeroboam, son of Nebat, an Ephraimite from Zeredah with a widowed mother named Zeruah. He rebelled against the king. [27]This is how he came to rebel. King Solomon was building Millo, closing up the breach of the City of David, his father. [28]Jeroboam was a very able man, and when Solomon saw that the young man was also a good worker, he put him in charge of all the carriers conscripted from the house of Joseph.

[29]At that time Jeroboam left Jerusalem, and the prophet Ahijah the Shilonite met him on the road. The prophet was wearing a new cloak, and when the two were alone in the open country, [30]Ahijah took off his new cloak, tore it into twelve pieces, [31]and said to Jeroboam: "Take ten pieces for yourself. Thus says the LORD, the God of Israel: I am about to tear the kingdom out of Solomon's hand and will give you ten of the tribes. [32]He shall have one tribe for the sake of my servant David, and for the sake of Jerusalem, the city I have chosen out of all the tribes of Israel. [33]For they have forsaken me and have bowed down to Astarte, goddess of the Sidonians, Chemosh, god of Moab, and Milcom, god of the Ammonites. They have not walked in my ways or done what is right in my eyes, according to my statutes and my ordinances, as David his father did. [34]Yet I will not take any of the kingdom from Solomon himself, but will keep him a prince as long as he lives, for the sake of David my servant, whom I have chosen, who kept my commandments and statutes.

[35]But I will take the kingdom from his son's hand and give it to you—that is, the ten tribes. [36]I will give his son one tribe, that David my servant may always have a holding before me in Jerusalem, the city I have chosen, to set my name there. [37]You I will take and you shall reign over all that you desire and shall become king of Israel. [38]If, then, you heed all that I command you, walking in my ways, and do what is right in my eyes by keeping my statutes and my commandments like David my servant, I will be with you. I will build a lasting house for you, just as I did for David; I will give Israel to you. [39]I will humble David's line for this, but not forever."

[40]When Solomon tried to have Jeroboam killed, Jeroboam fled to Shishak, king of Egypt. He remained in Egypt until Solomon's death.

[41]The rest of the acts of Solomon, with all that he did and his wisdom, are recorded in the book of the acts of Solomon.

454 • April 17

⁴²Solomon was king in Jerusalem over all Israel for forty years. ⁴³Solomon rested with his ancestors and was buried in the City of David, his father, and Rehoboam his son succeeded him as king.

Political Disunity. 12:1 Rehoboam went to Shechem, where all Israel had come to make him king. ²When Jeroboam, son of Nebat, heard about it, he was still in Egypt. He had fled from King Solomon and remained in Egypt, ³and they sent for him.

Then Jeroboam and the whole assembly of Israel came and they said to Rehoboam, ⁴"Your father put a heavy yoke on us. If you now lighten the harsh servitude and the heavy yoke your father imposed on us, we will be your servants." ⁵He answered them, "Come back to me in three days," and the people went away.

⁶King Rehoboam asked advice of the elders who had been in his father Solomon's service while he was alive, and asked, "How do you advise me to answer this people?" ⁷They replied, "If today you become the servant of this people and serve them, and give them a favorable answer, they will be your servants forever." ⁸But he ignored the advice the elders had given him, and asked advice of the young men who had grown up with him and were in his service. ⁹He said to them, "What answer do you advise that we should give this people, who have told me, 'Lighten the yoke your father imposed on us'?" ¹⁰The young men who had grown up with him replied, "This is what you must say to this people who have told you, 'Your father made our yoke heavy; you lighten it for us.' You must say, 'My little finger is thicker than my father's loins. ¹¹My father put a heavy yoke on you, but I will make it heavier. My father beat you with whips, but I will beat you with scorpions.'" ¹²Jeroboam and the whole people came back to King Rehoboam on the third day, as the king had instructed them: "Come back to me in three days."

¹³Ignoring the advice the elders had given him, the king gave the people a harsh answer. ¹⁴He spoke to them as the young men had advised: "My father made your yoke heavy, but I will make it heavier. My father beat you with whips, but I will beat you with scorpions." ¹⁵The king did not listen to the people, for this turn of events was from the LORD: he fulfilled the word the LORD had spoken through Ahijah the Shilonite to Jeroboam, son of Nebat. ¹⁶When all Israel saw that the king did not listen to them, the people answered the king:

"What share have we in David?
   We have no heritage in the son of
      Jesse.
To your tents, Israel!
   Now look to your own house,
      David."

So Israel went off to their tents. ¹⁷But Rehoboam continued to reign over the Israelites who lived in the cities of Judah.

¹⁸King Rehoboam then sent out Adoram, who was in charge of the forced labor, but all Israel stoned him to death. King Rehoboam then managed to mount his chariot and flee to Jerusalem. ¹⁹And so Israel has been in rebellion against the house of David to this day. ²⁰When all Israel heard that Jeroboam had returned, they summoned him to an assembly and made him king over all Israel. None remained loyal to the house of David except the tribe of Judah alone.

Divine Approval. ²¹On his arrival in Jerusalem, Rehoboam assembled all the house of Judah and the tribe of Benjamin—one hundred and eighty thousand elite warriors—to wage war against the house of Israel, to restore the kingdom to Rehoboam, son of Solomon. ²²However, the word of God came to Shemaiah, a man of God: ²³Say to Rehoboam, son of Solomon, king of Judah, and to all the house of Judah and to Benjamin, and to the rest of the people: ²⁴Thus says the LORD: You must not go out to war against your fellow Israelites. Return home, each of you, for it is I who have brought this about. They obeyed the word of the LORD and turned back, according to the word of the LORD.

²⁵Jeroboam built up Shechem in the hill country of Ephraim and lived there. Then he left it and built up Penuel.

Jeroboam's Cultic Innovations. ²⁶Jeroboam thought to himself: "Now the kingdom will return to the house of David. ²⁷If this people go up to offer sacrifices in the house of the LORD in Jerusalem, the hearts of this people will return to their master, Rehoboam, king of Judah, and they will kill me and return to Rehoboam, king of Judah." ²⁸The king took counsel, made two calves of gold, and said to the people: "You have been going up to Jerusalem long enough. Here are your gods, O Israel, who

brought you up from the land of Egypt." ²⁹And he put one in Bethel, the other in Dan. ³⁰This led to sin, because the people frequented these calves in Bethel and in Dan. ³¹He also built temples on the high places and made priests from among the common people who were not Levites.

Divine Disapproval. ³²Jeroboam established a feast in the eighth month on the fifteenth day of the month like the pilgrimage feast in Judah, and he went up to the altar. He did this in Bethel, sacrificing to the calves he had made. He stationed in Bethel the priests of the high places he had built. ³³Jeroboam went up to the altar he built in Bethel on the fifteenth day of the eighth month, the month he arbitrarily chose. He established a feast for the Israelites, and he went up to the altar to burn incense.

☐ MATTHEW 5:17-30

Teaching about the Law. 5:17 "Do not think that I have come to abolish the law or the prophets. I have come not to abolish but to fulfill. ¹⁸Amen, I say to you, until heaven and earth pass away, not the smallest letter or the smallest part of a letter will pass from the law, until all things have taken place. ¹⁹Therefore, whoever breaks one of the least of these commandments and teaches others to do so will be called least in the kingdom of heaven. But whoever obeys and teaches these commandments will be called greatest in the kingdom of heaven. ²⁰I tell you, unless your righteousness surpasses that of the scribes and Pharisees, you will not enter into the kingdom of heaven.

Teaching about Anger. ²¹"You have heard that it was said to your ancestors, 'You shall not kill; and whoever kills will be liable to judgment.' ²²But I say to you, whoever is angry with his brother will be liable to judgment, and whoever says to his

brother, 'Raqa,' will be answerable to the Sanhedrin, and whoever says, 'You fool,' will be liable to fiery Gehenna. ²³Therefore, if you bring your gift to the altar, and there recall that your brother has anything against you, ²⁴leave your gift there at the altar, go first and be reconciled with your brother, and then come and offer your gift. ²⁵Settle with your opponent quickly while on the way to court with him. Otherwise your opponent will hand you over to the judge, and the judge will hand you over to the guard, and you will be thrown into prison. ²⁶Amen, I say to you, you will not be released until you have paid the last penny.

Teaching about Adultery. ²⁷"You have heard that it was said, 'You shall not commit adultery.' ²⁸But I say to you, everyone who looks at a woman with lust has already committed adultery with her in his heart. ²⁹If your right eye causes you to sin, tear it out and throw it away. It is better for you to lose one of your members than to have your whole body thrown into Gehenna. [30]And if your right hand causes you to sin, cut it off and throw it away. It is better for you to lose one of your members than to have your whole body go into Gehenna."

April 18

You don't love in your enemies what they are, but what you would have them to become.

— St. Augustine of Hippo

☐ 1 KINGS 13–15

13:1 A man of God came from Judah to Bethel by the word of the LORD, while Jeroboam was standing at the altar to burn incense. [2]He cried out against the altar by the word of the LORD: "Altar, altar, thus says the LORD: A child shall be born to the house of David, Josiah by name, who shall slaughter upon you the priests of the high places who burn incense upon you, and they shall burn human bones upon you." [3]He also gave a sign that same day and said: "This is the sign that the LORD has spoken: The altar shall be torn apart and the ashes on it shall be scattered." [4]When the king heard the word of the man of God which he was crying out against the altar in Bethel, Jeroboam stretched forth his hand from the altar and said, "Seize him!" But the hand he stretched forth against him withered, so that he could not draw it back. [5](The altar was torn apart and the ashes from the altar were scattered, in accordance with the sign the man of God gave by the word of the LORD.)

[6]Then the king said to the man of God, "Entreat the LORD, your God, and intercede for me that my hand may be restored." So the man of God entreated the LORD, and the king's hand was restored as it was before. [7]The king told the man of God, "Come with me to the house for some refreshment so that I may give you a pres-

ent." [8]The man of God said to the king, "If you gave me half your palace, I would not go with you, nor eat bread or drink water in this place. [9]For I was instructed by the word of the LORD: Do not eat bread or drink water, and do not return by the way you came." [10]So he departed by another road and did not go back the way he had come to Bethel.

Prophetic Disunity. [11]There was an old prophet living in Bethel, whose son came and told him all that the man of God had done that day in Bethel. When his sons repeated to their father the words the man of God had spoken to the king, [12]the father asked them, "Which way did he go?" So his sons pointed out to him the road taken by the man of God who had come from Judah. [13]Then he said to his sons, "Saddle the donkey for me." When they had saddled it, he mounted [14]and followed the man of God, whom he found seated under a terebinth. When he asked him, "Are you the man of God who came from Judah?" he answered, "Yes." [15]Then he said, "Come home with me and have some bread." [16]"I cannot return with you or go with you, and I cannot eat bread or drink water with you in this place," he answered, [17]"for I was told by the word of the LORD: You shall not eat bread or drink water there, and do not go back the way you came." [18]But he said to him, "I, too, am a prophet like you, and an angel told me by the word of the LORD: Bring him back with you to your house to eat bread and drink water." But he was lying to him. [19]So he went back with him, and ate bread and drank water in his house. [20]But while they were sitting at table, the word of the LORD came to the prophet who had brought him back, [21]and he cried out to the man of God who had come from Judah: "Thus says the LORD: Because you rebelled against the charge of the LORD and did not keep the command which the LORD, your God, gave you, [22]but returned and ate bread and drank water in the place where he told you, Do not eat bread or drink water, your corpse shall not be brought to the grave of your ancestors." [23]After he had eaten bread and drunk, they saddled for him the donkey that belonged to the prophet who had brought him back, [24]and he set out. But a lion met him on the road, and killed him. His body lay sprawled on the road, and the donkey remained standing by it, and so did the lion. [25]Some passersby saw the body lying in the road, with the lion standing beside it, and carried the news to the city where the old prophet lived. [26]On hearing it, the prophet who had brought him back from his journey said: "It is the man of God who rebelled against the charge of the LORD. The LORD has delivered him to a lion, which mangled and killed him, according to the word which the LORD had spoken to him." [27]Then he said to his sons, "Saddle the donkey for me," and they saddled it. [28]He went off and found the body sprawled on the road with the donkey and the lion standing beside it. The lion had not eaten the body nor had it harmed the donkey. [29]The prophet lifted up the body of the man of God and put it on the donkey, and brought him back to the city to mourn and to bury him. [30]He laid the man's body in his own grave, and they mourned over it: "Alas, my brother!" [31]After he had buried him, he said to his sons, "When I die, bury me in the grave where the man of God is buried. Lay my bones beside his. [32]For the word which he proclaimed by the word of the LORD against the altar in Bethel and against all the temples on the high places in the cities of Samaria shall certainly come to pass."

[33]Even after this, Jeroboam did not turn from his evil way, but again made priests for the high places from among the common people. Whoever desired it was installed as a priest of the high places. [34]This is the account of the sin of the house of Jeroboam for which it was to be cut off and destroyed from the face of the earth.

Ahijah Announces Jeroboam's Downfall. **14:1** At that time Abijah, son of Jeroboam, took sick. [2]So Jeroboam said to his wife, "Go and disguise yourself so that no one will recognize you as Jeroboam's wife. Then go to Shiloh, where you will find Ahijah the prophet. It was he who spoke the word that made me king over this people. [3]Take along ten loaves, some cakes, and a jar of honey, and go to him. He will tell you what will happen to the child." [4]The wife of Jeroboam did so. She left and went to Shiloh and came to the house of Ahijah.

Now Ahijah could not see because age had dimmed his sight. [5]But the LORD said to Ahijah: Jeroboam's wife is coming to consult you about her son, for he is sick. Thus and so you must tell her. When she comes, she will be in disguise. [6]So Ahijah, hearing the sound of her footsteps as she entered the door, said, "Come in, wife of Jeroboam. Why are you in disguise? For my part, I have been commissioned to give you bitter news. [7]Go, tell Jeroboam, 'Thus says the LORD, the God of Israel: I exalted you from among the people and made you ruler of my people Israel. [8]I tore the kingdom away from the house of David and gave it to you. Yet you have not been like my servant David, who kept my commandments and followed me with his whole heart, doing only what is right in my sight. [9]You have done more evil than all who were before you: you have gone and made for yourself other gods and molten images to provoke me; but me you have cast behind your back. [10]Therefore, I am bringing evil upon the house of Jeroboam:

I will cut off from Jeroboam's line every male
    —bond or free—in Israel;
I will burn up what is left of the house of Jeroboam
    as dung is burned, completely.
[11]Anyone of Jeroboam's line who dies in the city,
    dogs will devour;
anyone who dies in the field,
    the birds of the sky will devour.

For the LORD has spoken!' [12]As for you, leave, and go home! As you step inside the city, the child will die, [13]and all Israel will mourn him and bury him, for he alone of Jeroboam's line will be laid in the grave, since in him alone of Jeroboam's house has something pleasing to the LORD, the God of Israel, been found. [14]The LORD will raise up for himself a king over Israel who will cut off the house of Jeroboam—today, at this very moment! [15]The LORD will strike Israel like a reed tossed about in the water and will pluck out Israel from this good land which he gave their ancestors, and will scatter them beyond the River, because they made asherahs for themselves, provoking the LORD. [16]He will give up Israel because of the sins Jeroboam has committed and caused Israel to commit." [17]So Jeroboam's wife left and went back; when she came to Tirzah and crossed the threshold of her house, the child died. [18]He was buried and all Israel mourned him, according to the word of the LORD spoken through his servant Ahijah the prophet.

[19]The rest of the acts of Jeroboam, how he fought and how he reigned, these are recorded in the book of the chronicles of the kings of Israel. [20]The length of Jeroboam's reign was twenty-two years. He rested with his ancestors, and Nadab his son succeeded him as king.

Reign of Rehoboam. [21]Rehoboam, son of Solomon, became king in Judah. Rehoboam was forty-one years old when he became king, and he reigned seventeen years in Jerusalem, the city in which, out of all the tribes of Israel, the LORD chose to set his name. His mother's name was Naamah the Ammonite.

[22]Judah did evil in the LORD's sight and they angered him even more than their ancestors had done. [23]They, too, built for themselves high places, sacred pillars, and asherahs, upon every high hill and under every green tree. [24]There were also pagan priests in the land. Judah imitated all the abominable practices of the nations whom the LORD had driven out of the Israelites' way. [25]In the fifth year of King Rehoboam, Shishak, king of Egypt, attacked Jerusalem. [26]He took everything, including the treasures of the house of the LORD and the treasures of the house of the king, even the gold shields Solomon had made. [27]To replace them, King Rehoboam made bronze shields, which he entrusted to the officers of the guard on duty at the entrance of the royal house. [28]Whenever the king visited the house of the LORD, those on duty would carry the shields, and then return them to the guardroom.

[29]The rest of the acts of Rehoboam, with all that he did, are recorded in the book of the chronicles of the kings of Judah. [30]There was war between Rehoboam and Jeroboam all their days. [31]Rehoboam rested with his ancestors; he was buried with his ancestors in the City of David. His mother's name was Naamah the Ammonite. His son Abijam succeeded him as king.

Reign of Abijam. 15:1 In the eighteenth year of King Jeroboam, son of Nebat, Abijam became king of Judah; ²he reigned three years in Jerusalem. His mother's name was Maacah, daughter of Abishalom.

³He followed all the sins his father had committed before him, and his heart was not entirely with the LORD, his God, as was the heart of David his father. ⁴Yet for David's sake the LORD, his God, gave him a holding in Jerusalem, raising up his son after him and permitting Jerusalem to endure, ⁵because David had done what was right in the sight of the LORD and did not disobey any of his commands as long as he lived, except in the case of Uriah the Hittite.

⁶There was war between Rehoboam and Jeroboam all their days. ⁷The rest of the acts of Abijam, with all that he did, are recorded in the book of the chronicles of the kings of Judah. There was war between Abijam and Jeroboam. ⁸Abijam rested with his ancestors; they buried him in the City of David, and his son Asa succeeded him as king.

Reign of Asa. ⁹In the twentieth year of Jeroboam, king of Israel, Asa, king of Judah, became king; ¹⁰he reigned forty-one years in Jerusalem. His mother's name was Maacah, daughter of Abishalom. ¹¹Asa did what was right in the sight of the LORD like David his father, ¹²banishing the pagan priests from the land and removing all the idols his ancestors had made. ¹³He also deposed his grandmother Maacah from her position as queen mother, because she had made an outrageous object for Asherah. Asa cut down this object and burned it in the Wadi Kidron. ¹⁴The high places did not disappear; yet Asa's heart was entirely with the LORD as long as he lived. ¹⁵He brought into the house of the LORD his father's and his own votive offerings of silver and gold and various vessels. ¹⁶There was war between Asa and Baasha, king of Israel, all their days. ¹⁷Baasha, king of Israel, attacked Judah and fortified Ramah to blockade Asa, king of Judah. ¹⁸Asa then took all the silver and gold remaining in the treasuries of the house of the LORD and the house of the king. Entrusting them to his ministers, King Asa sent them to Ben-hadad, son of Tabrimmon, son of Hezion, king of Aram, who ruled in Damascus. He said: ¹⁹"There is a treaty between you and me, as there was between your father and my father. I am sending you a present of silver and gold. Go, break your treaty with Baasha, king of Israel, that he may withdraw from me." ²⁰Ben-hadad agreed with King Asa and sent the leaders of his troops against the cities of Israel. They attacked Ijon, Dan, Abel-beth-maacah, and all Chinnereth, besides all the land of Naphtali. ²¹When Baasha heard of it, he left off fortifying Ramah, and stayed in Tirzah. ²²Then King Asa summoned all Judah without exception, and they carried away the stones and beams with which Baasha was fortifying Ramah. With them King Asa built Geba of Benjamin and Mizpah. ²³All the rest of the acts of Asa, with all his valor and all that he did, and the cities he built, are recorded in the book of the chronicles of the kings of Judah. But in his old age, Asa had an infirmity in his feet. ²⁴Asa rested with his ancestors; he was buried with his ancestors in the City of David his father, and his son Jehoshaphat succeeded him as king.

Reign of Nadab. ²⁵Nadab, son of Jeroboam, became king of Israel in the second year of Asa, king of Judah. For two years he reigned over Israel.

²⁶He did what was evil in the LORD's sight, walking in the way of his father and the sin he had caused Israel to commit. ²⁷Baasha, son of Ahijah, of the house of Issachar, plotted against him and struck him down at Gibbethon of the Philistines, which Nadab and all Israel were besieging. ²⁸Baasha killed him in the third year of Asa, king of Judah, and succeeded him as king. ²⁹Once he was king, he killed the entire house of Jeroboam, not leaving a single soul but destroying Jeroboam utterly, ac-

cording to the word of the LORD spoken through his servant, Ahijah the Shilonite, ³⁰because of the sins Jeroboam committed and caused Israel to commit, by which he provoked the LORD, the God of Israel, to anger.

³¹The rest of the acts of Nadab, with all that he did, are recorded in the book of the chronicles of the kings of Israel. ³²There was war between Asa and Baasha, king of Israel, all their days.

Reign of Baasha. ³³In the third year of Asa, king of Judah, Baasha, son of Ahijah, became king of all Israel in Tirzah for twenty-four years.

³⁴He did what was evil in the LORD's sight, walking in the way of Jeroboam and the sin he had caused Israel to commit.

☐ MATTHEW 5:31-48

Teaching about Divorce. 5:31 "It was also said, 'Whoever divorces his wife must give her a bill of divorce.' ³²But I say to you, whoever divorces his wife (unless the marriage is unlawful) causes her to commit adultery, and whoever marries a divorced woman commits adultery.

Teaching about Oaths. ³³"Again you have heard that it was said to your ancestors, 'Do not take a false oath, but make good to the Lord all that you vow.' ³⁴But I say to you, do not swear at all; not by heaven, for it is God's throne; ³⁵nor by the earth, for it is his footstool; nor by Jerusalem, for it is the city of the great King. ³⁶Do not swear by your head, for you cannot make a single hair white or black. ³⁷Let your 'Yes' mean 'Yes,' and your 'No' mean 'No.' Anything more is from the evil one.

Teaching about Retaliation. ³⁸"You have heard that it was said, 'An eye for an eye and a tooth for a tooth.' ³⁹But I say to you, offer no resistance to one who is evil. When someone strikes you on (your) right cheek, turn the other one to him as well. ⁴⁰If anyone wants to go to law with you over your tunic, hand him your cloak as well. ⁴¹Should anyone press you into service for one mile, go with him for two miles. ⁴²Give to the one who asks of you, and do not turn your back on one who wants to borrow.

Love of Enemies. ⁴³"You have heard that it was said, 'You shall love your neighbor and hate your enemy.' ⁴⁴But I say to you, love your enemies, and pray for those who persecute you, ⁴⁵that you may be children of your heavenly Father, for he makes his sun rise on the bad and the good, and causes rain to fall on the just and the unjust. ⁴⁶For if you love those who love you, what recompense will you have? Do not the tax collectors do the same? ⁴⁷And if you greet your brothers only, what is unusual about that? Do not the pagans do the same? ⁴⁸So be perfect, just as your heavenly Father is perfect."

April 19

We don't say "My Father, who art in heaven," nor "Give me this day my daily bread"; nor does each one ask that only his own debt should be forgiven him; nor does he request for himself alone that he may not be led into temptation and may be delivered from evil. Our prayer is public and common; and when we pray, we pray not for one, but for the whole people, because we the whole people are one.

— St. Cyprian of Carthage

☐ 1 KINGS 16-18

16:1 The word of the Lord came to Jehu, son of Hanani, against Baasha: ²Inasmuch as I exalted you from the dust and made you ruler of my people Israel, but you have walked in the way of Jeroboam and have caused my people Israel to sin, provoking me to anger by their sins, ³I will burn up what is left of Baasha and his house; I will make your house like that of Jeroboam, son of Nebat:

⁴One of Baasha's line who dies in the city,
    dogs will devour;
One who dies in the field,
    the birds of the sky will devour.

⁵The rest of the acts of Baasha, what he did and his valor, are recorded in the book of the chronicles of the kings of Israel. ⁶Baasha rested with his ancestors; he was buried in Tirzah, and his son Elah succeeded him as king. ⁷(Through the prophet Jehu, son of Hanani, the word of the Lord came against Baasha and his house, because of all the evil Baasha did in the sight of the Lord, provoking him to anger by his deeds so that he became like the house of Jeroboam, and because of what he destroyed.)

Reign of Elah. ⁸In the twenty-sixth year of Asa, king of Judah, Elah, son of Baasha, became king of Israel in Tirzah for two years.

⁹His servant Zimri, commander of half his chariots, plotted against him. As he was in Tirzah, drinking to excess in the house of Arza, master of his palace in Tirzah, ¹⁰Zimri entered; he struck and killed him in the twenty-seventh year of Asa, king of Judah, and succeeded him as king. ¹¹Once he was king, seated on the throne, he killed the whole house of Baasha, not sparing a single male relative or friend of his. ¹²Zimri destroyed the entire house of Baasha, according to the word the Lord spoke against Baasha through Jehu the prophet, ¹³because of all the sins which Baasha and his son Elah committed and caused Israel to commit, provoking the Lord, the God of Israel, to anger by their idols.

¹⁴The rest of the acts of Elah, with all that he did, are recorded in the book of the chronicles of the kings of Israel.

Reign of Zimri. ¹⁵In the twenty-seventh year of Asa, king of Judah, Zimri became king for seven days in Tirzah.

The army was encamped at Gibbethon of the Philistines ¹⁶when they heard, "Zimri has formed a conspiracy and has killed the king." So that day in the camp all Israel made Omri, commander of the army, king of Israel. ¹⁷Omri and all Israel with him marched up from Gibbethon and besieged Tirzah. ¹⁸When Zimri saw that the city was captured, he entered the citadel of the king's house and burned it down over him.

He died [19]because of the sins he had committed, doing what was evil in the LORD's sight by walking in the way of Jeroboam and the sin he had caused Israel to commit.

[20]The rest of the acts of Zimri, with the conspiracy he carried out, are recorded in the book of the chronicles of the kings of Israel.

Civil War. [21]At that time the people of Israel were divided in two, half following Tibni, son of Ginath, to make him king, and half for Omri. [22]The partisans of Omri prevailed over those of Tibni, son of Ginath, Tibni died and Omri became king.

Reign of Omri. [23]In the thirty-first year of Asa, king of Judah, Omri became king of Israel for twelve years; the first six of them he reigned in Tirzah.

[24]He then bought the mountain of Samaria from Shemer for two silver talents and built upon the mountain the city he named Samaria, after Shemer, the former owner. [25]But Omri did what was evil in the LORD's sight, more than any of his predecessors. [26]In every way he imitated the sinful conduct of Jeroboam, son of Nebat, and the sin he had caused Israel to commit, thus provoking the LORD, the God of Israel, to anger by their idols.

[27]The rest of the acts of Omri, what he did and his valor, are recorded in the book of the chronicles of the kings of Israel. [28]Omri rested with his ancestors; he was buried in Samaria, and Ahab his son succeeded him as king.

Reign of Ahab. [29]Ahab, son of Omri, became king of Israel in the thirty-eighth year of Asa, king of Judah. Ahab, son of Omri, reigned over Israel in Samaria for twenty-two years.

[30]Ahab, son of Omri, did what was evil in the LORD's sight more than any of his predecessors. [31]It was not enough for him to follow the sins of Jeroboam, son of Nebat. He even married Jezebel, daughter of Ethbaal, king of the Sidonians, and began to serve Baal, and worship him. [32]Ahab set up an altar to Baal in the house of Baal which he built in Samaria, [33]and also made an asherah. Ahab did more to provoke the LORD, the God of Israel, to anger than any of the kings of Israel before him. [34]During his reign, Hiel from Bethel rebuilt Jericho. At the cost of Abiram, his firstborn son, he laid the foundation, and at the cost of Segub, his youngest son, he set up the gates, according to the word of the LORD spoken through Joshua, son of Nun.

Elijah Proclaims a Drought. 17:1 Elijah the Tishbite, from Tishbe in Gilead, said to Ahab: "As the LORD, the God of Israel, lives, whom I serve, during these years there shall be no dew or rain except at my word." [2]The word of the LORD came to Elijah: [3]Leave here, go east and hide in the Wadi Cherith, east of the Jordan. [4]You shall drink of the wadi, and I have commanded ravens to feed you there. [5]So he left and did as the LORD had commanded. He left and remained by the Wadi Cherith, east of the Jordan. [6]Ravens brought him bread and meat in the morning, and bread and meat in the evening, and he drank from the wadi.

[7]After some time, however, the wadi ran dry, because no rain had fallen in the land. [8]So the word of the LORD came to him: [9]Arise, go to Zarephath of Sidon and stay there. I have commanded a widow there to feed you. [10]He arose and went to Zarephath. When he arrived at the entrance of the city, a widow was there gathering sticks; he called out to her, "Please bring me a small cupful of water to drink." [11]She left to get it, and he called out after her, "Please bring along a crust of bread." [12]She said, "As the LORD, your God, lives, I have nothing baked; there is only a handful of flour in my jar and a little oil in my jug. Just now I was collecting a few sticks, to go in and prepare something for myself and my son; when we have eaten it, we shall die." [13]Elijah said to her, "Do not be afraid. Go and do as you have said. But first make

me a little cake and bring it to me. Afterwards you can prepare something for yourself and your son. ¹⁴For the LORD, the God of Israel, says: The jar of flour shall not go empty, nor the jug of oil run dry, until the day when the LORD sends rain upon the earth." ¹⁵She left and did as Elijah had said. She had enough to eat for a long time—he and she and her household. ¹⁶The jar of flour did not go empty, nor the jug of oil run dry, according to the word of the LORD spoken through Elijah.

¹⁷Some time later the son of the woman, the owner of the house, fell sick, and his sickness grew more severe until he stopped breathing. ¹⁸So she said to Elijah, "Why have you done this to me, man of God? Have you come to me to call attention to my guilt and to kill my son?" ¹⁹Elijah said to her, "Give me your son." Taking him from her lap, he carried him to the upper room where he was staying, and laid him on his own bed. ²⁰He called out to the LORD: "LORD, my God, will you afflict even the widow with whom I am staying by killing her son?" ²¹Then he stretched himself out upon the child three times and he called out to the LORD: "LORD, my God, let the life breath return to the body of this child." ²²The LORD heard the prayer of Elijah; the life breath returned to the child's body and he lived. ²³Taking the child, Elijah carried him down into the house from the upper room and gave him to his mother. Elijah said, "See! Your son is alive." ²⁴The woman said to Elijah, "Now indeed I know that you are a man of God, and it is truly the word of the LORD that you speak."

Elijah Ends the Drought. 18:1 Long afterward, in the third year, the word of the LORD came to Elijah: Go, present yourself to Ahab, that I may send rain upon the earth. ²So Elijah went to present himself to Ahab.

Now the famine in Samaria was severe, ³and Ahab had summoned Obadiah, master of his palace, who greatly revered the LORD. ⁴When Jezebel was slaughtering the prophets of the LORD, Obadiah took a hundred prophets, hid them away by fifties in caves, and supplied them with food and water. ⁵Ahab said to Obadiah, "Go through the land to all sources of water and to all the wadis. We may find grass and keep the horses and mules alive, so that we shall not have to slaughter any of the beasts." ⁶Dividing the land to explore between them, Ahab went one way by himself, Obadiah another way by himself. ⁷As Obadiah was on his way, Elijah met him. Recognizing him, Obadiah fell prostrate and asked, "Is it you, my lord Elijah?" ⁸He said to him, "Yes. Go tell your lord, 'Elijah is here!'" ⁹But Obadiah said, "What sin has your servant committed, that you are handing me over to Ahab to be killed? ¹⁰As the LORD, your God, lives, there is no nation or kingdom where my lord has not sent in search of you. When they replied, 'He is not here,' he made each kingdom and nation swear they could not find you. ¹¹And now you say, 'Go tell your lord: Elijah is here!' ¹²After I leave you, the spirit of the LORD will carry you to some place I do not know, and when I go to inform Ahab and he does not find you, he will kill me—though your servant has revered the LORD from his youth! ¹³Have you not been told, my lord, what I did when Jezebel was murdering the prophets of the LORD—that I hid a hundred of the prophets of the LORD, fifty each in caves, and supplied them with food and water? ¹⁴And now you say, 'Go tell your lord: Elijah is here!' He will kill me!" ¹⁵Elijah answered, "As the LORD of hosts lives, whom I serve, I will present myself to him today."

¹⁶So Obadiah went to meet Ahab and informed him, and Ahab came to meet Elijah. ¹⁷When Ahab saw Elijah, he said to him, "Is it you, you disturber of Israel?" ¹⁸He answered, "It is not I who disturb Israel, but you and your father's house, by

forsaking the commands of the LORD and you by following the Baals. ¹⁹Now summon all Israel to me on Mount Carmel, as well as the four hundred and fifty prophets of Baal and the four hundred prophets of Asherah who eat at Jezebel's table." ²⁰So Ahab summoned all the Israelites and had the prophets gather on Mount Carmel.

²¹Elijah approached all the people and said, "How long will you straddle the issue? If the LORD is God, follow him; if Baal, follow him." But the people did not answer him. ²²So Elijah said to the people, "I am the only remaining prophet of the LORD, and there are four hundred and fifty prophets of Baal. ²³Give us two young bulls. Let them choose one, cut it into pieces, and place it on the wood, but start no fire. I shall prepare the other and place it on the wood, but shall start no fire. ²⁴You shall call upon the name of your gods, and I will call upon the name of the LORD. The God who answers with fire is God." All the people answered, "We agree!"

²⁵Elijah then said to the prophets of Baal, "Choose one young bull and prepare it first, for there are more of you. Call upon your gods, but do not start the fire." ²⁶Taking the young bull that was turned over to them, they prepared it and called upon Baal from morning to noon, saying, "Baal, answer us!" But there was no sound, and no one answering. And they hopped around the altar they had prepared. ²⁷When it was noon, Elijah taunted them: "Call louder, for he is a god; he may be busy doing his business, or may be on a journey. Perhaps he is asleep and must be awakened." ²⁸They called out louder and slashed themselves with swords and spears according to their ritual until blood gushed over them. ²⁹Noon passed and they remained in a prophetic state until the time for offering sacrifice. But there was no sound, no one answering, no one listening.

³⁰Then Elijah said to all the people, "Come here to me." When they drew near to him, he repaired the altar of the LORD which had been destroyed. ³¹He took twelve stones, for the number of tribes of the sons of Jacob, to whom the LORD had said: Israel shall be your name. ³²He built the stones into an altar to the name of the LORD, and made a trench around the altar large enough for two measures of grain. ³³When he had arranged the wood, he cut up the young bull and laid it on the wood. ³⁴He said, "Fill four jars with water and pour it over the burnt offering and over the wood." "Do it again," he said, and they did it again. "Do it a third time," he said, and they did it a third time. ³⁵The water flowed around the altar; even the trench was filled with the water. ³⁶At the time for offering sacrifice, Elijah the prophet came forward and said, "LORD, God of Abraham, Isaac, and Israel, let it be known this day that you are God in Israel and that I am your servant and have done all these things at your command. ³⁷Answer me, LORD! Answer me, that this people may know that you, LORD, are God and that you have turned their hearts back to you." ³⁸The LORD's fire came down and devoured the burnt offering, wood, stones, and dust, and lapped up the water in the trench. ³⁹Seeing this, all the people fell prostrate and said, "The LORD is God! The LORD is God!" ⁴⁰Then Elijah said to them, "Seize the prophets of Baal. Let none of them escape!" They seized them, and Elijah brought them down to the Wadi Kishon and there he slaughtered them. ⁴¹Elijah then said to Ahab, "Go up, eat and drink, for there is the sound of a heavy rain." ⁴²So Ahab went up to eat and drink, while Elijah went up to the top of Carmel, crouched down to the earth, and put his head between his knees. ⁴³He said to his servant, "Go up and look out to sea." He went up and looked, but reported, "There is nothing." Seven times he said, "Go look again!" ⁴⁴And the seventh time the youth reported, "There is a cloud as small as a

man's hand rising from the sea." Elijah said, "Go and say to Ahab, 'Harness up and go down the mountain before the rain stops you.'" [45]All at once the sky grew dark with clouds and wind, and a heavy rain fell. Ahab mounted his chariot and headed for Jezreel. [46]But the hand of the LORD was on Elijah. He girded up his clothing and ran before Ahab as far as the approaches to Jezreel.

☐ MATTHEW 6:1-18

Teaching about Almsgiving. 6:1 "[But] take care not to perform righteous deeds in order that people may see them; otherwise, you will have no recompense from your heavenly Father. [2]When you give alms, do not blow a trumpet before you, as the hypocrites do in the synagogues and in the streets to win the praise of others. Amen, I say to you, they have received their reward. [3]But when you give alms, do not let your left hand know what your right is doing, [4]so that your almsgiving may be secret. And your Father who sees in secret will repay you.

Teaching about Prayer. [5]"When you pray, do not be like the hypocrites, who love to stand and pray in the synagogues and on street corners so that others may see them. Amen, I say to you, they have received their reward. [6]But when you pray, go to your inner room, close the door, and pray to your Father in secret. And your Father who sees in secret will repay you. [7]In praying, do not babble like the pagans, who think that they will be heard because of their many words. [8]Do not be like them. Your Father knows what you need before you ask him.

The Lord's Prayer. [9]"This is how you are to pray:

Our Father in heaven,
   hallowed be your name,
  [10]your kingdom come,
your will be done,
   on earth as in heaven.
[11]Give us today our daily bread;
[12]and forgive us our debts,
   as we forgive our debtors;
[13]and do not subject us to the final test,
   but deliver us from the evil one.

[14]If you forgive others their transgressions, your heavenly Father will forgive you. [15]But if you do not forgive others, neither will your Father forgive your transgressions.

Teaching about Fasting. [16]"When you fast, do not look gloomy like the hypocrites. They neglect their appearance, so that they may appear to others to be fasting. Amen, I say to you, they have received their reward. [17]But when you fast, anoint your head and wash your face, [18]so that you may not appear to others to be fasting, except to your Father who is hidden. And your Father who sees what is hidden will repay you."

April 20

When we throw earth upon the fire burning in a stove, we extinguish it. In the same way, worldly cares, and every kind of attachment to something — however small and insignificant — destroy the warmth of the heart that was there at the beginning.
— St. Simeon the New Theologian

☐ 1 KINGS 19-22

Flight to Horeb. 19:1 Ahab told Jezebel all that Elijah had done—that he had murdered all the prophets by the sword. ²Jezebel then sent a messenger to Elijah and said, "May the gods do thus to me and more, if by this time tomorrow I have not done with your life what was done to each of them." ³Elijah was afraid and fled for his life, going to Beer-sheba of Judah. He left his servant there ⁴and went a day's journey into the wilderness, until he came to a solitary broom tree and sat beneath it. He prayed for death: "Enough, Lord! Take my life, for I am no better than my ancestors." ⁵He lay down and fell asleep under the solitary broom tree, but suddenly a messenger touched him and said, "Get up and eat!" ⁶He looked and there at his head was a hearth cake and a jug of water. After he ate and drank, he lay down again, ⁷but the angel of the Lord came back a second time, touched him, and said, "Get up and eat or the journey will be too much for you!" ⁸He got up, ate, and drank; then strengthened by that food, he walked forty days and forty nights to the mountain of God, Horeb.

⁹There he came to a cave, where he took shelter. But the word of the Lord came to him: Why are you here, Elijah? ¹⁰He answered: "I have been most zealous for the Lord, the God of hosts, but the Israelites have forsaken your covenant. They have destroyed your altars and murdered your prophets by the sword. I alone remain, and they seek to take my life." ¹¹Then the Lord said: Go out and stand on the mountain before the Lord; the Lord will pass by. There was a strong and violent wind rending the mountains and crushing rocks before the Lord—but the Lord was not in the wind; after the wind, an earthquake— but the Lord was not in the earthquake; ¹²after the earthquake, fire—but the Lord was not in the fire; after the fire, a light silent sound.

¹³When he heard this, Elijah hid his face in his cloak and went out and stood at the entrance of the cave. A voice said to him, Why are you here, Elijah? ¹⁴He replied, "I have been most zealous for the Lord, the God of hosts, but the Israelites have forsaken your covenant. They have destroyed your altars and murdered your prophets by the sword. I alone remain, and they seek to take my life." ¹⁵The Lord said to him: Go back! Take the desert road to Damascus. When you arrive, you shall anoint Hazael as king of Aram. ¹⁶You shall also anoint Jehu, son of Nimshi, as king of Israel, and Elisha, son of Shaphat of Abel-meholah, as prophet to succeed you. ¹⁷Anyone who escapes the sword of Hazael, Jehu will kill. Anyone who escapes the sword of Jehu, Elisha will kill. ¹⁸But I will spare seven thousand in Israel—every knee that has not bent to Baal, every mouth that has not kissed him.

¹⁹Elijah set out, and came upon Elisha, son of Shaphat, as he was plowing with twelve yoke of oxen; he was following the twelfth. Elijah went over to him and threw his cloak on him. ²⁰Elisha left the oxen, ran after Elijah, and said, "Please, let me kiss

my father and mother good-bye, and I will follow you." Elijah answered, "Go back! What have I done to you?" [21]Elisha left him and, taking the yoke of oxen, slaughtered them; he used the plowing equipment for fuel to boil their flesh, and gave it to the people to eat. Then he left and followed Elijah to serve him.

Ahab's Victories over Aram. 20:1 Ben-hadad, king of Aram, gathered all his forces and, accompanied by thirty-two kings with horses and chariotry, set out to besiege and attack Samaria. [2]He sent messengers to Ahab, king of Israel, within the city, [3]and said to him, "This is Ben-hadad's message: 'Your silver and gold are mine, and your wives and your fine children are mine.'" [4]The king of Israel answered, "Just as you say, my lord king, I and all I have are yours." [5]But the messengers came again and said, "This is Ben-hadad's message: 'I sent you word: Give me your silver and gold, your wives and your children. [6]But now I say: At this time tomorrow I will send my servants to you, and they shall ransack your house and the houses of your servants. They shall seize and take away whatever you consider valuable.'" [7]The king of Israel then summoned all the elders of the land and said: "Understand clearly that this man is intent on evil. When he sent to me for my wives and children, my silver and my gold, I did not refuse him." [8]All the elders and all the people said to him, "Do not listen. Do not give in." [9]Accordingly he directed the messengers of Ben-hadad, "Say this: 'To my lord the king: I will do all that you demanded of your servant the first time. But this I cannot do.'" The messengers left and reported this. [10]Ben-hadad then responded, "May the gods do thus to me and more, if there will remain enough dust in Samaria to make handfuls for all my followers." [11]The king of Israel replied, "Tell him, 'Let not one who puts on armor boast like one who takes it off.'" [12]Ben-hadad was drinking in the pavilions with the kings when he heard this reply. He commanded his servants, "Get ready!"; and they got ready to storm the city.

[13]Then a prophet came up to Ahab, king of Israel, and said: "The LORD says, Do you see all this vast army? Today I am giving it into your power, that you may know that I am the LORD." [14]But Ahab asked, "Through whom will it be given over?" He answered, "The LORD says, Through the aides of the provincial governors." Then Ahab asked, "Who is to attack?" He replied, "You are." [15]So Ahab mustered the aides of the provincial governors, two hundred thirty-two of them. Behind them he mustered all the Israelite soldiery, who numbered seven thousand in all. [16]They marched out at noon, while Ben-hadad was drinking heavily in the pavilions with the thirty-two kings who were his allies. [17]When the aides of the provincial governors marched out first, Ben-hadad received word, "Some men have marched out of Samaria." [18]He answered, "Whether they have come out for peace or for war, take them alive." [19]But when these had come out of the city—the aides of the provincial governors with the army following them— [20]each of them struck down his man. The Arameans fled with Israel pursuing them, while Ben-hadad, king of Aram, escaped on a chariot horse. [21]Then the king of Israel went out and destroyed the horses and chariots. Thus he inflicted a severe defeat on Aram.

[22]Then the prophet approached the king of Israel and said to him: "Go, regroup your forces. Understand clearly what you must do, for at the turning of the year the king of Aram will attack you." [23]Meanwhile the servants of the king of Aram said to him: "Their gods are mountain gods. That is why they defeated us. But if we fight them on level ground, we shall be sure to defeat them. [24]This is what you must do: Take the kings from their posts and put prefects in their places. [25]Raise an army as large as the army

you have lost, horse for horse, chariot for chariot. Let us fight them on level ground, and we shall surely defeat them." He took their advice and did this. ²⁶At the turning of the year, Ben-hadad mustered Aram and went up to Aphek to fight against Israel. ²⁷The Israelites, too, were mustered and supplied with provisions; then they went out to meet the enemy. The Israelites, encamped opposite, looked like little flocks of goats, while Aram covered the land. ²⁸A man of God approached and said to the king of Israel: "The LORD says, Because Aram has said the LORD is a god of mountains, not a god of plains, I will give all this vast army into your power that you may know I am the LORD." ²⁹They were encamped opposite each other for seven days. On the seventh day battle was joined, and the Israelites struck down one hundred thousand foot soldiers of Aram in one day. ³⁰The survivors fled into the city of Aphek, where the wall collapsed on twenty-seven thousand of them. Ben-hadad, too, fled, and took refuge within the city, in an inner room.

³¹His servants said to him: "We have heard that the kings of the house of Israel are merciful kings. Allow us, therefore, to garb ourselves in sackcloth, with cords around our heads, and go out to the king of Israel. Perhaps he will spare your life." ³²Dressed in sackcloth girded at the waist and wearing cords around their heads, they went to the king of Israel and said, "Your servant Ben-hadad says, 'Spare my life!'" He asked, "Is he still alive? He is my brother." ³³Hearing this as a good omen, the men quickly took him at his word and said, "Ben-hadad is your brother." He answered, "Go and get him." When Ben-hadad came out to him, the king had him mount his chariot. ³⁴Ben-hadad said to him, "The cities my father took from your father I will restore, and you may set up bazaars for yourself in Damascus, as my father did in Samaria." Ahab replied, "For my part, I will set you free on those terms."

So he made a covenant with him and then set him free.

Prophetic Condemnation. ³⁵Acting on the word of the LORD, one of the guild prophets said to his companion, "Strike me." But he refused to strike him. ³⁶Then he said to him, "Since you did not obey the voice of the LORD, a lion will attack you when you leave me." When he left him, a lion came upon him and attacked him. ³⁷Then the prophet met another man and said, "Strike me." The man struck him a blow and wounded him. ³⁸The prophet went on and waited for the king on the road, disguising himself with a bandage over his eyes. ³⁹As the king was passing, he called out to the king and said: "Your servant went into the thick of the battle, and suddenly someone turned and brought me a man and said, 'Guard this man. If he is missing, you shall have to pay for his life with your life or pay out a talent of silver.' ⁴⁰But while your servant was occupied here and there, the man disappeared." The king of Israel said to him, "That is your sentence. You have decided it yourself." ⁴¹He quickly removed the bandage from his eyes, and the king of Israel recognized him as one of the prophets. ⁴²He said to him: "The LORD says, Because you have set free the man I put under the ban, your life shall pay for his life, your people for his people." ⁴³Disturbed and angry, the king of Israel set off for home and entered Samaria.

Seizure of Naboth's Vineyard. 21:1 Naboth the Jezreelite had a vineyard in Jezreel next to the palace of Ahab, king of Samaria. Some time later, ²Ahab said to Naboth, "Give me your vineyard to be my vegetable garden, since it is close by, next to my house. I will give you a better vineyard in exchange, or, if you prefer, I will give you its value in money." ³Naboth said to Ahab, "The LORD forbid that I should give you my ancestral heritage." ⁴Ahab went home disturbed and angry at the answer

Naboth the Jezreelite had given him: "I will not give you my ancestral heritage." Lying down on his bed, he turned away and would not eat. ⁵His wife Jezebel came to him and said to him, "Why are you so sullen that you will not eat?" ⁶He answered her, "Because I spoke to Naboth the Jezreelite and said to him, 'Sell me your vineyard, or, if you prefer, I will give you a vineyard in exchange.' But he said, 'I will not give you my vineyard.'" ⁷Jezebel his wife said to him, "What a king of Israel you are! Get up! Eat and be cheerful. I will give you the vineyard of Naboth the Jezreelite."

⁸So she wrote letters in Ahab's name and, having sealed them with his seal, sent them to the elders and to the nobles who lived in the same city with Naboth. ⁹This is what she wrote in the letters: "Proclaim a fast and set Naboth at the head of the people. ¹⁰Next, set two scoundrels opposite him to accuse him: 'You have cursed God and king.' Then take him out and stone him to death."

¹¹His fellow citizens—the elders and the nobles who dwelt in his city—did as Jezebel had ordered in the letters she sent them. ¹²They proclaimed a fast and set Naboth at the head of the people. ¹³Two scoundrels came in and sat opposite Naboth, and the scoundrels accused him in the presence of the people, "Naboth has cursed God and king." And they led him out of the city and stoned him to death. ¹⁴Then they sent word to Jezebel: "Naboth has been stoned to death."

¹⁵When Jezebel learned that Naboth had been stoned to death, she said to Ahab, "Go, take possession of the vineyard of Naboth the Jezreelite which he refused to sell you, because Naboth is not alive, but dead." ¹⁶When Ahab heard that Naboth was dead, he started on his way down to the vineyard of Naboth the Jezreelite, to take possession of it.

Prophetic Condemnation. ¹⁷Then the word of the LORD came to Elijah the Tishbite: ¹⁸Go down to meet Ahab, king of Israel, who is in Samaria. He will be in the vineyard of Naboth, where he has gone to take possession. ¹⁹Tell him: "Thus says the LORD: After murdering, do you also take possession?" And tell him, "Thus says the LORD: In the place where the dogs licked up the blood of Naboth, the dogs shall lick up your blood, too."

²⁰Ahab said to Elijah, "Have you found me out, my enemy?" He said, "I have found you. Because you have given yourself up to doing evil in the LORD's sight, ²¹I am bringing evil upon you: I will consume you and will cut off every male belonging to Ahab, whether bond or free, in Israel. ²²I will make your house like that of Jeroboam, son of Nebat, and like the house of Baasha, son of Ahijah, because you have provoked me by leading Israel into sin."

²³Against Jezebel, too, the LORD declared: The dogs shall devour Jezebel in the confines of Jezreel.

²⁴Anyone of Ahab's line who dies in the city,
    dogs will devour;
Anyone who dies in the field,
    the birds of the sky will devour.

²⁵Indeed, no one gave himself up to the doing of evil in the sight of the LORD as did Ahab, urged on by his wife Jezebel. ²⁶He became completely abominable by going after idols, just as the Amorites had done, whom the LORD drove out of the Israelites' way.

²⁷When Ahab heard these words, he tore his garments and put on sackcloth over his bare flesh. He fasted, slept in the sackcloth, and went about subdued. ²⁸Then the word of the LORD came to Elijah the Tishbite, ²⁹Have you seen how Ahab has humbled himself before me? Since he has humbled himself before me, I will not bring the evil in his time. I will bring the evil upon his house in his son's time.

Ahab's Defeat by Aram. 22:1 Three years passed without war between Aram and

Israel. ²In the third year, however, King Jehoshaphat of Judah came down to the king of Israel. ³The king of Israel said to his servants, "Do you not know that Ramoth-gilead is ours and we are doing nothing to take it from the king of Aram?" ⁴He asked Jehoshaphat, "Will you come with me to fight against Ramoth-gilead?" Jehoshaphat answered the king of Israel, "You and I are as one, and your people and my people, your horses and my horses as well."

Prophetic Condemnation. ⁵Jehoshaphat also said to the king of Israel, "Seek the word of the LORD at once." ⁶The king of Israel assembled the prophets, about four hundred of them, and asked, "Shall I go to fight against Ramoth-gilead or shall I refrain?" They said, "Attack. The Lord will give it into the power of the king." ⁷But Jehoshaphat said, "Is there no other prophet of the LORD here we might consult?" ⁸The king of Israel answered, "There is one other man through whom we might consult the LORD; but I hate him because he prophesies not good but evil about me. He is Micaiah, son of Imlah." Jehoshaphat said, "Let not the king say that." ⁹So the king of Israel called an official and said to him, "Get Micaiah, son of Imlah, at once."

¹⁰The king of Israel and Jehoshaphat, king of Judah, were seated, each on his throne, clothed in their robes of state in the square at the entrance of the gate of Samaria, and all the prophets were prophesying before them. ¹¹Zedekiah, son of Chenaanah, made himself two horns of iron and said, "The LORD says, With these you shall gore Aram until you have destroyed them." ¹²The other prophets prophesied in a similar vein, saying: "Attack Ramoth-gilead and conquer! The LORD will give it into the power of the king."

¹³Meanwhile, the messenger who had gone to call Micaiah said to him, "Look now, the prophets are unanimously predicting good for the king. Let your word be the same as any of theirs; speak a good word." ¹⁴Micaiah said, "As the LORD lives, I shall speak whatever the LORD tells me."

¹⁵When he came to the king, the king said to him, "Micaiah, shall we go to fight at Ramoth-gilead, or shall we refrain?" He said, "Attack and conquer! The LORD will give it into the power of the king." ¹⁶But the king answered him, "How many times must I adjure you to tell me nothing but the truth in the name of the LORD?" ¹⁷So Micaiah said:

"I see all Israel
    scattered on the mountains,
    like sheep without a shepherd,
And the LORD saying,
    These have no master!
    Let each of them go back home in
        peace."

¹⁸The king of Israel said to Jehoshaphat, "Did I not tell you, he does not prophesy good about me, but only evil?" ¹⁹Micaiah continued: "Therefore hear the word of the LORD: I saw the LORD seated on his throne, with the whole host of heaven standing to his right and to his left. ²⁰The LORD asked: Who will deceive Ahab, so that he will go up and fall on Ramoth-gilead? And one said this, another that, ²¹until this spirit came forth and stood before the LORD, saying, 'I will deceive him.' The LORD asked: How? ²²He answered, 'I will go forth and become a lying spirit in the mouths of all his prophets.' The LORD replied: You shall succeed in deceiving him. Go forth and do this. ²³So now, the LORD has put a lying spirit in the mouths of all these prophets of yours; the LORD himself has decreed evil against you."

²⁴Thereupon Zedekiah, son of Chenaanah, came up and struck Micaiah on the cheek, saying, "Has the spirit of the LORD, then, left me to speak with you?" ²⁵Micaiah said, "You shall find out on the day you go into an inner room to hide." ²⁶The king of Israel then said, "Seize Micaiah and take him back to Amon, prefect of the city, and

to Joash, the king's son, ²⁷and say, 'This is the king's order: Put this man in prison and feed him scanty rations of bread and water until I come back in safety.'" ²⁸But Micaiah said, "If you return in safety, the LORD has not spoken through me." (He also said, "Hear, O peoples, all of you.")

Ahab at Ramoth-gilead. ²⁹The king of Israel and Jehoshaphat, king of Judah, went up to Ramoth-gilead, ³⁰and the king of Israel said to Jehoshaphat, "I will disguise myself and go into battle, but you put on your own robes." So the king of Israel disguised himself and entered the battle. ³¹In the meantime the king of Aram had given his thirty-two chariot commanders the order, "Do not fight with anyone, great or small, except the king of Israel alone."

³²When the chariot commanders saw Jehoshaphat, they cried out, "There is the king of Israel!" and wheeled to fight him. But Jehoshaphat cried out, ³³and the chariot commanders, seeing that he was not the king of Israel, turned away from him. ³⁴But someone drew his bow at random, and hit the king of Israel between the joints of his breastplate. He ordered his charioteer, "Rein about and take me out of the ranks, for I am wounded."

³⁵The battle grew fierce during the day, and the king, who was propped up in his chariot facing the Arameans, died in the evening. The blood from his wound flowed to the bottom of the chariot. ³⁶At sunset a cry went through the army, "Every man to his city, every man to his land!"

³⁷And so the king died, and came back to Samaria, and they buried him there. ³⁸When they washed out the chariot at the pool of Samaria, the dogs licked up his blood and prostitutes bathed there, as the LORD had prophesied.

³⁹The rest of the acts of Ahab, with all that he did, including the ivory house he built and all the cities he built, are recorded in the book of the chronicles of the kings of Israel. ⁴⁰Ahab rested with his ancestors, and his son Ahaziah succeeded him as king.

Reign of Jehoshaphat. ⁴¹Jehoshaphat, son of Asa, became king of Judah in the fourth year of Ahab, king of Israel. ⁴²Jehoshaphat was thirty-five years old when he became king, and he reigned twenty-five years in Jerusalem. His mother's name was Azubah, daughter of Shilhi.

⁴³He walked in the way of Asa his father unceasingly, doing what was right in the LORD's sight. ⁴⁴Nevertheless, the high places did not disappear, and the people still sacrificed on the high places and burned incense there. ⁴⁵Jehoshaphat also made peace with the king of Israel.

⁴⁶The rest of the acts of Jehoshaphat, with his valor, what he did and how he fought, are recorded in the book of the chronicles of the kings of Judah. ⁴⁷He removed from the land the rest of the pagan priests who had remained in the reign of Asa his father. ⁴⁸There was no king in Edom, but an appointed regent. ⁴⁹Jehoshaphat made Tarshish ships to go to Ophir for gold; but in fact the ships did not go, because they were wrecked at Ezion-geber. ⁵⁰That was the time when Ahaziah, son of Ahab, had said to Jehoshaphat, "Let my servants accompany your servants in the ships." But Jehoshaphat would not agree. ⁵¹Jehoshaphat rested with his ancestors; he was buried with his ancestors in the City of David his father, and his son Jehoram succeeded him as king.

Reign of Ahaziah. ⁵²Ahaziah, son of Ahab, became king over Israel in Samaria in the seventeenth year of Jehoshaphat, king of Judah; he reigned two years over Israel.

⁵³He did what was evil in the sight of the LORD, walking in the way of his father, his mother, and Jeroboam, son of Nebat, who caused Israel to sin. ⁵⁴He served Baal and worshiped him, thus provoking the LORD, the God of Israel, just as his father had done.

☐ MATTHEW 6:19-34

Treasure in Heaven. 6:19 "Do not store up for yourselves treasures on earth, where moth and decay destroy, and thieves break in and steal. ²⁰But store up treasures in heaven, where neither moth nor decay destroys, nor thieves break in and steal. ²¹For where your treasure is, there also will your heart be.

The Light of the Body. ²²"The lamp of the body is the eye. If your eye is sound, your whole body will be filled with light; ²³but if your eye is bad, your whole body will be in darkness. And if the light in you is darkness, how great will the darkness be.

God and Money. ²⁴"No one can serve two masters. He will either hate one and love the other, or be devoted to one and despise the other. You cannot serve God and mammon.

Dependence on God. ²⁵"Therefore I tell you, do not worry about your life, what you will eat [or drink], or about your body, what you will wear. Is not life more than food and the body more than clothing? ²⁶Look

at the birds in the sky; they do not sow or reap, they gather nothing into barns, yet your heavenly Father feeds them. Are not you more important than they? ²⁷Can any of you by worrying add a single moment to your life-span? ²⁸Why are you anxious about clothes? Learn from the way the wild flowers grow. They do not work or spin. ²⁹But I tell you that not even Solomon in all his splendor was clothed like one of them. ³⁰If God so clothes the grass of the field, which grows today and is thrown into the oven tomorrow, will he not much more provide for you, O you of little faith? ³¹So do not worry and say, 'What are we to eat?' or 'What are we to drink?' or 'What are we to wear?' ³²All these things the pagans seek. Your heavenly Father knows that you need them all. ³³But seek first the kingdom (of God) and his righteousness, and all these things will be given you besides. ³⁴Do not worry about tomorrow; tomorrow will take care of itself. Sufficient for a day is its own evil."

April 21

St. Anselm

God has promised pardon to the one who repents, but He has not promised repentance to the one who sins.

— ST. ANSELM

☐ 2 KINGS 1-3

Reign of Ahaziah, Continued. 1:1 After Ahab's death, Moab rebelled against Israel.

²Ahaziah fell through the lattice of his roof terrace at Samaria and was injured. So he sent out messengers with the instructions: "Go and inquire of Baalzebub, the god of Ekron, whether I shall recover from this injury."

³Meanwhile, the messenger of the LORD said to Elijah the Tishbite: Go and meet the messengers of Samaria's king, and tell them: "Is it because there is no God in Israel that you are going to inquire of Baalzebub, the god of Ekron?" ⁴For this, the LORD says: You shall not leave the bed upon which you lie; instead, you shall die. And Elijah departed.

[5]The messengers then returned to Ahaziah, who asked them, "Why have you returned?" [6]They answered, "A man met us and said to us, 'Go back to the king who sent you and tell him: The LORD says: Is it because there is no God in Israel that you are sending to inquire of Baalzebub, the god of Ekron? For this you shall not leave the bed upon which you lie; instead, you shall die.'" [7]The king asked them, "What was the man like who met you and said these things to you?" [8]They replied, "He wore a hairy garment with a leather belt around his waist." "It is Elijah the Tishbite!" he exclaimed.

[9]Then the king sent a captain with his company of fifty men after Elijah. The prophet was seated on a hilltop when he found him. He said, "Man of God, the king commands you, 'Come down.'" [10]Elijah answered the captain, "Well, if I am a man of God, may fire come down from heaven and consume you and your fifty men." And fire came down from heaven and consumed him and his fifty men. [11]The king sent another captain with his company of fifty men after Elijah. He shouted up and said, "Man of God, the king says, 'Come down immediately!'" [12]Elijah answered them, "If I am a man of God, may fire come down from heaven and consume you and your fifty men." And divine fire came down from heaven and consumed him and his fifty men. [13]The king sent a third captain with his company of fifty men. When the third captain had climbed the hill, he fell to his knees before Elijah, pleading with him. He said, "Man of God, let my life and the lives of these fifty men, your servants, count for something in your sight! [14]Already fire has come down from heaven, consuming the first two captains with their companies of fifty men. But now, let my life count for something in your sight!" [15]Then the messenger of the LORD said to Elijah: Go down with him; you need not be afraid of him. So Elijah left and went down with him to the king.

[16]He declared to the king: "Thus says the LORD: Because you sent messengers to inquire of Baalzebub, the god of Ekron—do you think there is no God in Israel to inquire of?—you shall not leave the bed upon which you lie; instead you shall die."

[17]Ahaziah died according to the word of the LORD spoken by Elijah. Since he had no son, Joram succeeded him as king, in the second year of Joram, son of Jehoshaphat, king of Judah.

[18]The rest of the acts of Ahaziah, which he did, are recorded in the book of chronicles of the kings of Israel.

Elijah's Journey. 2:1 When the LORD was about to take Elijah up to heaven in a whirlwind, he and Elisha were on their way from Gilgal.

[2]Elijah said to Elisha, "Stay here, please. The LORD has sent me on to Bethel." Elisha replied, "As the LORD lives, and as you yourself live, I will not leave you." So they went down to Bethel. [3]The guild prophets who were in Bethel went out to Elisha and asked him, "Do you know that today the LORD will take your master from you?" He replied, "Yes, I know that. Be still."

[4]Elijah said to him, "Elisha, stay here, please. The LORD has sent me on to Jericho." Elisha replied, "As the LORD lives, and as you yourself live, I will not leave you." So they came to Jericho. [5]The guild prophets who were in Jericho approached Elisha and asked him, "Do you know that today the LORD will take your master from you?" He replied, "Yes, I know that. Be still."

[6]Elijah said to him, "Stay here, please. The LORD has sent me on to the Jordan." Elisha replied, "As the LORD lives, and as you yourself live, I will not leave you." So the two went on together. [7]Fifty of the guild prophets followed and stood facing them at a distance, while the two of them stood next to the Jordan.

Elisha Succeeds Elijah. [8]Elijah took his mantle, rolled it up and struck the water: it divided, and the two of them crossed over on dry ground.

⁹When they had crossed over, Elijah said to Elisha, "Request whatever I might do for you, before I am taken from you." Elisha answered, "May I receive a double portion of your spirit." ¹⁰He replied, "You have asked something that is not easy. Still, if you see me taken up from you, your wish will be granted; otherwise not." ¹¹As they walked on still conversing, a fiery chariot and fiery horses came between the two of them, and Elijah went up to heaven in a whirlwind, ¹²and Elisha saw it happen. He cried out, "My father! my father! Israel's chariot and steeds!" Then he saw him no longer.

He gripped his own garment, tore it into two pieces, ¹³and picked up the mantle which had fallen from Elijah. Then he went back and stood at the bank of the Jordan. ¹⁴Wielding the mantle which had fallen from Elijah, he struck the water and said, "The LORD, the God of Elijah—where is he now?" He struck the water: it divided, and he crossed over.

Elisha's Journey. ¹⁵The guild prophets in Jericho, who were on the other side, saw him and said, "The spirit of Elijah rests on Elisha." They went to meet him, bowing to the ground before him. ¹⁶They said, "Among your servants are fifty brave men. Let them go in search of your master. Perhaps the spirit of the LORD has lifted him up and left him on some mountain or in some valley." He answered, "Do not send them." ¹⁷But they kept urging him, until he was embarrassed and said, "Send them." So they sent the fifty men, who searched for three days without finding him. ¹⁸When they returned to Elisha in Jericho, where he was staying, he said to them, "Did I not tell you not to go?"

¹⁹The inhabitants of the city complained to Elisha, "The site of the city is fine indeed, as my lord can see, but the water is bad and the land sterile." ²⁰Elisha said,

"Bring me a new bowl and put salt into it." When they had brought it to him, ²¹he went out to the spring and threw salt into it, saying, "Thus says the LORD: I have purified this water. Never again shall death or sterility come from it." ²²And the water has stayed pure even to this day, according to the word Elisha had spoken.

²³From there Elisha went up to Bethel. While he was on the way, some little boys came out of the city and jeered at him: "Go away, baldy; go away, baldy!" ²⁴The prophet turned and saw them, and he cursed them in the name of the LORD. Then two she-bears came out of the woods and tore forty-two of the children to pieces.

²⁵From there he went to Mount Carmel, and returned to Samaria from there.

Reign of Joram of Israel. 3:1 Joram, son of Ahab, became king over Israel in Samaria in the eighteenth year of Jehoshaphat, king of Judah, and he reigned twelve years.

²He did what was evil in the LORD's sight, though not like his father and mother. He did away with the pillar of Baal that his father had made, ³but he still held fast unceasingly to the sins which Jeroboam, son of Nebat, caused Israel to commit.

War Against Moab: Drought. ⁴Now Mesha, king of Moab, who raised sheep, used to pay the king of Israel as tribute a hundred thousand lambs and the wool of a hundred thousand rams. ⁵But when Ahab died, the king of Moab rebelled against the king of Israel. ⁶King Joram set out from Samaria and mustered all Israel. ⁷Then he sent Jehoshaphat, the king of Judah, the message: "The king of Moab has rebelled against me. Will you come with me to Moab to fight?" He replied, "I will. You and I are as one, your people and my people, and your horses and my horses as well." ⁸He said, "By what route shall we attack?" and the other said, "By way of the wilderness of Edom."

⁹So the king of Israel set out, accompanied by the king of Judah and the king of Edom. After a roundabout journey of seven days the water gave out for the army and for the animals with them. ¹⁰The king of Israel exclaimed, "Alas! The LORD has called three kings together only to deliver us into the power of Moab." ¹¹But Jehoshaphat asked, "Is there no prophet of the LORD here through whom we may inquire of the LORD?" One of the servants of the king of Israel replied, "Elisha, son of Shaphat, who poured water on the hands of Elijah, is here." ¹²Jehoshaphat agreed, "He has the word of the LORD." So the king of Israel, along with Jehoshaphat and the king of Edom, went down to Elisha. ¹³Elisha asked the king of Israel, "What do you want with me? Go to the prophets of your father and to the prophets of your mother." The king of Israel replied, "No, the LORD has called these three kings together only to deliver us into the power of Moab." ¹⁴Then Elisha said, "As the LORD of hosts lives, whom I serve, were it not that I respect Jehoshaphat, the king of Judah, I should neither look at you nor notice you at all. ¹⁵Now get me a minstrel." When the minstrel played, the hand of the LORD came upon Elisha, ¹⁶and he announced: "Thus says the LORD: Provide many catch basins in this wadi. ¹⁷For the LORD says: Though you will see neither wind nor rain, yet this wadi will be filled with water for you to drink, and for your livestock and pack animals. ¹⁸And since the LORD does not consider this enough, he will also deliver Moab into your power. ¹⁹You shall destroy every fortified city and every choice city, fell every fruit tree, stop up all the springs, and ruin every fertile field with stones."

²⁰In the morning, at the time of the sacrifice, water came from the direction of Edom and filled the land.

²¹Meanwhile, all Moab had heard that the kings had come to war against them; troops from the youngest on up were mobilized and stationed at the border. ²²When they rose early that morning, the sun was shining across the water. The Moabites saw the water as red as blood, ²³and said, "This is blood! The kings have fought among themselves and killed one another. Quick! To the spoils, Moab!" ²⁴But when they reached the camp of Israel, the Israelites rose up and attacked the Moabites, who fled from them. They ranged through the countryside destroying Moab— ²⁵leveling the cities, each one casting the stones onto every fertile field and filling it, stopping up every spring, felling every fruit tree, until only the stones of Kir-hareseth remained. Then the slingers surrounded and attacked it. ²⁶When he saw that the battle was going against him, the king of Moab took seven hundred swordsmen to break through to the king of Edom, but he failed. ²⁷So he took his firstborn, who was to succeed him as king, and offered him as a burnt offering upon the wall. The wrath against Israel was so great that they gave up the siege and returned to their own land.

☐ MATTHEW 7:1-23

Judging Others. 7:1 "Stop judging, that you may not be judged. ²For as you judge, so will you be judged, and the measure with which you measure will be measured out to you. ³Why do you notice the splinter in your brother's eye, but do not perceive the wooden beam in your own eye? ⁴How can you say to your brother, 'Let me remove that splinter from your eye,' while the wooden beam is in your eye? ⁵You hypocrite, remove the wooden beam from your eye first; then you will see clearly to remove the splinter from your brother's eye.

Pearls before Swine. [6]"Do not give what is holy to dogs, or throw your pearls before swine, lest they trample them underfoot, and turn and tear you to pieces.

The Answer to Prayers. [7]"Ask and it will be given to you; seek and you will find; knock and the door will be opened to you. [8]For everyone who asks, receives; and the one who seeks, finds; and to the one who knocks, the door will be opened. [9]Which one of you would hand his son a stone when he asks for a loaf of bread, [10]or a snake when he asks for a fish? [11]If you then, who are wicked, know how to give good gifts to your children, how much more will your heavenly Father give good things to those who ask him.

The Golden Rule. [12]"Do to others whatever you would have them do to you. This is the law and the prophets.

The Narrow Gate. [13]"Enter through the narrow gate; for the gate is wide and the road broad that leads to destruction, and those who enter through it are many. [14]How narrow the gate and constricted the road that leads to life. And those who find it are few.

False Prophets. [15]"Beware of false prophets, who come to you in sheep's clothing, but underneath are ravenous wolves. [16]By their fruits you will know them. Do people pick grapes from thornbushes, or figs from thistles? [17]Just so, every good tree bears good fruit, and a rotten tree bears bad fruit. [18]A good tree cannot bear bad fruit, nor can a rotten tree bear good fruit. [19]Every tree that does not bear good fruit will be cut down and thrown into the fire. [20]So by their fruits you will know them.

The True Disciple. [21]"Not everyone who says to me, 'Lord, Lord,' will enter the kingdom of heaven, but only the one who does the will of my Father in heaven. [22]Many will say to me on that day, 'Lord, Lord, did we not prophesy in your name? Did we not drive out demons in your name? Did we not do mighty deeds in your name?' [23]Then I will declare to them solemnly, 'I never knew you. Depart from me, you evildoers.'"

April 22

Blessed Maria Gabriella

I saw in front of me a big cross. I thought that my sacrifice was nothing in comparison to His.

— BLESSED MARIA GABRIELLA

☐ 2 KINGS 4-6:23

The Widow's Oil. 4:1 A certain woman, the widow of one of the guild prophets, cried out to Elisha: "My husband, your servant, is dead. You know that he revered the LORD, yet now his creditor has come to take my two children into servitude." [2]Elisha answered her, "What am I to do for you? Tell me what you have in the house." She replied, "This servant of yours has nothing in the house but a jug of oil." [3]He said, "Go out, borrow vessels from all your neighbors—as many empty vessels as you can. [4]Then come back and close the door on yourself and your children; pour the oil into all the vessels, and as each is filled, set it aside." [5]So she went out. She closed the door on herself and her children and, as they handed her the vessels, she would pour in oil. [6]When all the vessels were filled, she said to her son, "Bring me another vessel." He answered, "There is none left." And then the oil stopped. [7]She went and told the man of God, who said, "Go sell the oil to pay off your creditor; with what remains, you and your children can live."

Elisha Raises the Shunammite's Son.
[8]One day Elisha came to Shunem, where there was a woman of influence, who pressed him to dine with her. Afterward, whenever he passed by, he would stop there to dine. [9]So she said to her husband, "I know that he is a holy man of God. Since he visits us often, [10]let us arrange a little room on the roof and furnish it for him with a bed, table, chair, and lamp, so that when he comes to us he can stay there."

[11]One day Elisha arrived and stayed in the room overnight. [12]Then he said to his servant Gehazi, "Call this Shunammite woman." He did so, and when she stood before Elisha, [13]he told Gehazi, "Say to her, 'You have troubled yourself greatly for us; what can we do for you? Can we say a good word for you to the king or to the commander of the army?'" She replied, "I am living among my own people." [14]Later Elisha asked, "What can we do for her?" Gehazi answered, "She has no son, and her husband is old." [15]Elisha said, "Call her." He did so, and when she stood at the door, [16]Elisha promised, "This time next year you will be cradling a baby son." She said, "My lord, you are a man of God; do not deceive your servant." [17]Yet the woman conceived, and by the same time the following year she had given birth to a son, as Elisha had promised; [18]and the child grew up healthy.

One day the boy went out to his father among the reapers. [19]He said to his father, "My head! My head!" And his father said to the servant, "Carry him to his mother." [20]The servant picked him up and carried him to his mother; he sat in her lap until noon, and then died. [21]She went upstairs and laid him on the bed of the man of God. Closing the door on him, she went out [22]and called to her husband, "Let me have one of the servants and a donkey. I must go quickly to the man of God, and I will be back." [23]He asked, "Why are you going to him today? It is neither the new moon nor the sabbath." But she said, "It is all right." [24]When the donkey was saddled, she said to her servant, "Lead on! Do not stop my donkey unless I tell you." [25]She kept going till she reached the man of God on Mount Carmel. When he saw her at a distance, the man of God said to his servant Gehazi: "There is the Shunammite! [26]Hurry to meet her, and ask if everything is all right with her, with her husband, and with the boy." "Everything is all right," she replied. [27]But when she reached the man of God on the mountain, she clasped his feet. Gehazi came near to push her away, but the man of God said: "Let her alone, she is in bitter anguish; the LORD hid it from me and did not let me know." [28]She said, "Did I ask my lord for a son? Did I not say, 'Do not mislead me'?" [29]He said to Gehazi, "Get ready for a journey. Take my staff with you and be off; if you meet anyone, give no greeting, and if anyone greets you, do not answer. Lay my staff upon the boy." [30]But the boy's mother cried out: "As the LORD lives and as you yourself live, I will not release you." So he started back with her.

[31]Meanwhile, Gehazi had gone on ahead and had laid the staff upon the boy, but there was no sound, no response. He returned to meet Elisha and told him, "The boy has not awakened." [32]When Elisha reached the house, he found the boy dead, lying on the bed. [33]He went in, closed the door on them both, and prayed to the LORD. [34]Then he lay upon the child on the bed, placing his mouth upon the child's mouth, his eyes upon the eyes, and his hands upon the hands. As Elisha stretched himself over the child, the boy's flesh became warm. [35]He arose, paced up

and down the room, and then once more stretched himself over him, and the boy sneezed seven times and opened his eyes. ³⁶Elisha summoned Gehazi and said, "Call the Shunammite." He called her, and she came to him, and Elisha said to her, "Take your son." ³⁷She came in and fell at his feet in homage; then she took her son and left.

The Poisoned Stew. ³⁸When Elisha returned to Gilgal, there was a famine in the land. Once, when the guild prophets were seated before him, he said to his servant, "Put the large pot on, and make some vegetable stew for the guild prophets." ³⁹Someone went out into the field to gather herbs and found a wild vine, from which he picked a sackful of poisonous wild gourds. On his return he cut them up into the pot of vegetable stew without anybody's knowing it. ⁴⁰The stew was served, but when they began to eat it, they cried, "Man of God, there is death in the pot!" And they could not eat it. ⁴¹He said, "Bring some meal." He threw it into the pot and said, "Serve it to the people to eat." And there was no longer anything harmful in the pot.

The Barley Loaves. ⁴²A man came from Baal-shalishah bringing the man of God twenty barley loaves made from the first fruits, and fresh grain in the ear. Elisha said, "Give it to the people to eat." ⁴³But his servant objected, "How can I set this before a hundred?" Elisha again said, "Give it to the people to eat, for thus says the LORD: You will eat and have some left over." ⁴⁴He set it before them, and when they had eaten, they had some left over, according to the word of the LORD.

Elisha Cures Naaman's Leprosy. 5:1 Naaman, the army commander of the king of Aram, was highly esteemed and respected by his master, for through him the LORD had brought victory to Aram. But valiant as he was, the man was a leper. ²Now the Arameans had captured from the land of Israel in a raid a little girl, who became the servant of Naaman's wife. ³She said to her mistress, "If only my master would present himself to the prophet in Samaria! He would cure him of his leprosy."

⁴Naaman went and told his master, "This is what the girl from the land of Israel said." ⁵The king of Aram said, "Go. I will send along a letter to the king of Israel." So Naaman set out, taking along ten silver talents, six thousand gold pieces, and ten festal garments.

⁶He brought the king of Israel the letter, which read: "With this letter I am sending my servant Naaman to you, that you may cure him of his leprosy." ⁷When he read the letter, the king of Israel tore his garments and exclaimed: "Am I a god with power over life and death, that this man should send someone for me to cure him of leprosy? Take note! You can see he is only looking for a quarrel with me!" ⁸When Elisha, the man of God, heard that the king of Israel had torn his garments, he sent word to the king: "Why have you torn your garments? Let him come to me and find out that there is a prophet in Israel."

⁹Naaman came with his horses and chariot and stopped at the door of Elisha's house. ¹⁰Elisha sent him the message: "Go and wash seven times in the Jordan, and your flesh will heal, and you will be clean." ¹¹But Naaman went away angry, saying, "I thought that he would surely come out to me and stand there to call on the name of the LORD his God, and would move his hand over the place, and thus cure the leprous spot. ¹²Are not the rivers of Damascus, the Abana and the Pharpar, better than all the waters of Israel? Could I not wash in them and be cleansed?" With this, he turned about in anger and left.

¹³But his servants came up and reasoned with him: "My father, if the prophet told you to do something extraordinary, would you not do it? All the more since he told you, 'Wash, and be clean'?" ¹⁴So Naaman went down and plunged into the Jordan

seven times, according to the word of the man of God. His flesh became again like the flesh of a little child, and he was clean.

[15]He returned with his whole retinue to the man of God. On his arrival he stood before him and said, "Now I know that there is no God in all the earth, except in Israel. Please accept a gift from your servant." [16]Elisha replied, "As the LORD lives whom I serve, I will not take it." And despite Naaman's urging, he still refused. [17]Naaman said: "If you will not accept, please let me, your servant, have two mule-loads of earth, for your servant will no longer make burnt offerings or sacrifices to any other god except the LORD. [18]But may the LORD forgive your servant this: when my master enters the temple of Rimmon to bow down there, as he leans upon my arm, I too must bow down in the temple of Rimmon. When I bow down in the temple of Rimmon, may the LORD please forgive your servant this." [19]Elisha said to him, "Go in peace."

Naaman had gone some distance [20]when Gehazi, the servant of Elisha, the man of God, thought to himself: "My master was too easy on this Aramean Naaman, not accepting what he brought. As the LORD lives, I will run after him and get something out of him." [21]So Gehazi hurried after Naaman. Seeing that someone was running after him, Naaman alighted from his chariot to wait for him. He asked, "Is everything all right?" [22]Gehazi replied, "Yes, but my master sent me to say, 'Two young men have just come to me, guild prophets from the hill country of Ephraim. Please give them a talent of silver and two festal garments.'" [23]Naaman said, "I insist! Take two talents," and he pressed him. He tied up two silver talents in bags and gave them, with two festal garments, to two of his servants, who carried them before Gehazi. [24]When he reached the hill, Gehazi received these things, appropriated them for his house, and sent the men on their way.

[25]He went in and stood by Elisha his master, who asked him, "Where have you been, Gehazi?" He answered, "Your servant has not gone anywhere." [26]But Elisha said to him: "Was I not present in spirit when someone got down from his chariot to wait for you? Is this a time to take money or to take garments, olive orchards or vineyards, sheep or cattle, male or female servants? [27]The leprosy of Naaman shall cling to you and your descendants forever." And Gehazi went out, a leper with skin like snow.

The Lost Ax. 6:1 The guild prophets once said to Elisha: "This place where we live with you is too cramped for us. [2]Let us go to the Jordan, where by getting one beam apiece we can build ourselves a place to live." Elisha said, "Go." [3]One of them requested, "Please agree to accompany your servants." He replied, "Yes, I will come."

[4]So he went with them, and when they arrived at the Jordan they began to cut down trees. [5]While one of them was felling a tree trunk, the iron ax blade slipped into the water. He cried out, "Oh, no, master! It was borrowed!" [6]"Where did it fall?" asked the man of God. When he pointed out the spot, Elisha cut off a stick, threw it into the water, and brought the iron to the surface. [7]He said, "Pick it up." And the man stretched out his hand and grasped it.

The Aramean Ambush. [8]When the king of Aram was waging war on Israel, he would make plans with his servants: "I will bivouac at such and such a place." [9]But the man of God would send word to the king of Israel, "Be careful! Do not pass by this place, for Aram will attack there." [10]So the king of Israel would send word to the place which the man of God had indicated, and alert it; then they would be on guard. This happened several times.

[11]Greatly disturbed over this, the king of Aram called together his officers and asked them, "Will you not tell me who among us is for the king of Israel?" [12]"No one, my lord

king," answered one of the officers. "The Israelite prophet Elisha can tell the king of Israel the very words you speak in your bedroom." [13]He said, "Go, find out where he is, so that I may take him captive."

Informed that Elisha was in Dothan, [14]he sent there a strong force with horses and chariots. They arrived by night and encircled the city. [15]Early the next morning, when the servant of the man of God arose and went out, he saw the force with its horses and chariots surrounding the city. "Alas!" he said to Elisha. "What shall we do, my lord?" [16]Elisha answered, "Do not be afraid. Our side outnumbers theirs." [17]Then he prayed, "O LORD, open his eyes, that he may see." And the LORD opened the eyes of the servant, and he saw that the mountainside was filled with fiery chariots and horses around Elisha.

[18]When the Arameans came down to get him, Elisha prayed to the LORD, "Strike this people blind, I pray you." And the LORD struck them blind, according to Elisha's word. [19]Then Elisha said to them: "This is the wrong road, and this is the wrong city. Follow me! I will take you to the man you want." And he led them to Samaria. [20]When they entered Samaria, Elisha prayed, "O LORD, open their eyes that they may see." The LORD opened their eyes, and they saw that they were inside Samaria. [21]When the king of Israel saw them, he asked, "Shall I kill them, my father? Shall I kill them?" [22]Elisha replied, "You must not kill them. Do you slay those whom you have taken captive with your sword or bow? Serve them a meal. Let them eat and drink, and then go back to their master." [23]The king spread a great feast for them. When they had eaten and drunk he sent them away, and they went back to their master. No more Aramean raiders came into the land of Israel.

☐ MATTHEW 7:24-29

The Two Foundations. 7:24 "Everyone who listens to these words of mine and acts on them will be like a wise man who built his house on rock. [25]The rain fell, the floods came, and the winds blew and buffeted the house. But it did not collapse; it had been set solidly on rock. [26]And everyone who listens to these words of mine but does not act on them will be like a fool who built his house on sand. [27]The rain fell, the floods came, and the winds blew and buffeted the house. And it collapsed and was completely ruined."

[28]When Jesus finished these words, the crowds were astonished at his teaching, [29]for he taught them as one having authority, and not as their scribes.

April 23

St. George

St. George was a man who abandoned one army for another: He gave up the rank of a Roman tribune to enlist as a soldier for Christ. Eager to encounter the enemy, he first stripped away his worldly wealth by giving all he had to the poor. Then, free and unencumbered, bearing the shield of faith, he plunged into the thick of the battle, an ardent soldier for Christ.

— ST. PETER DAMIEN

☐ 2 KINGS 6:24-7:20

War Against Aram: Famine. 6:24 After this, Ben-hadad, king of Aram, mustered his whole army and laid siege to Samaria. ²⁵Because of the siege the famine in Samaria was so severe that a donkey's head sold for eighty pieces of silver, and a fourth of a kab of "dove droppings" for five pieces of silver.

²⁶One day, as the king of Israel was walking on the city wall, a woman cried out to him, "Save us, my lord king!" ²⁷He replied, "If the LORD does not save you, where could I find means to save you? On the threshing floor? In the wine press?" ²⁸Then the king asked her, "What is your trouble?" She replied: "This woman said to me, 'Give up your son that we may eat him today; then tomorrow we will eat my son.' ²⁹So we boiled my son and ate him. The next day I said to her, 'Now give up your son that we may eat him.' But she hid her son." ³⁰When the king heard the woman's words, he tore his garments. And as he was walking on the wall, the people saw that he was wearing sackcloth underneath, next to his skin.

³¹The king exclaimed, "May God do thus to me, and more, if the head of Elisha, son of Shaphat, stays on him today!"

³²Meanwhile, Elisha was sitting in his house in conference with the elders. The king had sent one of his courtiers; but before the messenger reached him, Elisha said to the elders: "Do you know that this murderer is sending someone to cut off my head? When the messenger comes, see that you close the door and hold it fast against him. His master's footsteps are echoing behind him." ³³While Elisha was still speaking, the messenger came down to him and said, "This evil is from the LORD. Why should I trust in the LORD any longer?"

7:1 Elisha replied: "Hear the word of the LORD! Thus says the LORD: At this time tomorrow a seah of fine flour will sell for a shekel, and two seahs of barley for a shekel, in the market of Samaria." ²But the adjutant, upon whose arm the king leaned, answered the man of God, "Even if the LORD were to make windows in heaven, how could this happen?" Elisha said, "You shall see it with your own eyes, but you shall not eat of it."

³At the city gate four lepers were asking one another, "Why should we sit here until we die? ⁴If we decide to go into the city, we shall die there, for there is famine in the city. If we remain here, we shall die too. So come, let us desert to the camp of the Arameans. If they let us live, we live; if they kill us, we die." ⁵At twilight they left for the Arameans; but when they reached the edge of the camp, no one was there. ⁶The Lord had caused the army of the Arameans to hear the sound of chariots and horses, the sound of a large army, and they had reasoned among

themselves, "The king of Israel has hired the kings of the Hittites and the kings of Egypt to fight us." [7]Then in the twilight they had fled, abandoning their tents, their horses, and their donkeys, the whole camp just as it was, and fleeing for their lives.

[8]After the lepers reached the edge of the camp, they went first into one tent, ate and drank, and took silver, gold, and clothing from it, and went out and hid them. Back they came into another tent, took things from it, and again went out and hid them. [9]Then they said to one another: "We are not doing right. This is a day of good news, and we are keeping silent. If we wait until morning breaks, we will be blamed. So come, let us go and inform the palace." [10]They came and summoned the city gatekeepers. They said, "We went to the camp of the Arameans, but no one was there—not a human voice, only the horses and donkeys tethered, and the tents just as they were left." [11]The gatekeepers announced this and it was reported within the palace.

[12]Though it was night, the king got up; he said to his servants, "Let me tell you what the Arameans have done to us. Knowing that we are starving, they have left their camp to hide in the field. They are thinking, 'The Israelites will leave the city and we will take them alive and enter it.'" [13]One of his servants, however, suggested: "Let some of us take five of the horses remaining in the city—they are just like the whole throng of Israel that has reached its limit—and let us send scouts to investigate." [14]They took two chariots, and horses, and the king sent them to reconnoiter the Aramean army with the order, "Go and find out." [15]They followed the Arameans as far as the Jordan, and the whole route was strewn with garments and other objects that the Arameans had thrown away in their haste. The messengers returned and told the king. [16]The people went out and plundered the camp of the Arameans.

Then a seah of fine flour sold for a shekel and two seahs of barley for a shekel, according to the word of the LORD. [17]The king had put in charge of the gate the officer upon whose arm he leaned; but the people trampled him to death at the gate, just as the man of God had predicted when the messenger came down to him. [18]This was in accordance with the word the man of God spoke to the king: "Two seahs of barley will sell for a shekel, and a seah of fine flour for a shekel at this time tomorrow in the market of Samaria." [19]The adjutant had answered the man of God, "Even if the LORD were to make windows in heaven, how could this happen?" And Elisha had replied, "You shall see it with your own eyes, but you shall not eat of it." [20]And that is what happened to him, for the people trampled him to death at the gate.

☐ MATTHEW 8:1-22

The Cleansing of a Leper. 8:1 When Jesus came down from the mountain, great crowds followed him. [2]And then a leper approached, did him homage, and said, "Lord, if you wish, you can make me clean." [3]He stretched out his hand, touched him, and said, "I will do it. Be made clean." His leprosy was cleansed immediately. [4]Then Jesus said to him, "See that you tell no one, but go show yourself to the priest, and offer the gift that Moses prescribed; that will be proof for them."

The Healing of a Centurion's Servant. [5]When he entered Capernaum, a centurion approached him and appealed to him, [6]saying, "Lord, my servant is lying at home paralyzed, suffering dreadfully." [7]He said to him, "I will come and cure him." [8]The centurion said in reply, "Lord, I am not worthy to have you enter under my roof;

only say the word and my servant will be healed. [9]For I too am a person subject to authority, with soldiers subject to me. And I say to one, 'Go,' and he goes; and to another, 'Come here,' and he comes; and to my slave, 'Do this,' and he does it." [10]When Jesus heard this, he was amazed and said to those following him, "Amen, I say to you, in no one in Israel have I found such faith. [11]I say to you, many will come from the east and the west, and will recline with Abraham, Isaac, and Jacob at the banquet in the kingdom of heaven, [12]but the children of the kingdom will be driven out into the outer darkness, where there will be wailing and grinding of teeth." [13]And Jesus said to the centurion, "You may go; as you have believed, let it be done for you." And at that very hour [his] servant was healed.

The Cure of Peter's Mother-in-Law.
[14]Jesus entered the house of Peter, and saw his mother-in-law lying in bed with a fever.

[15]He touched her hand, the fever left her, and she rose and waited on him.

Other Healings. [16]When it was evening, they brought him many who were possessed by demons, and he drove out the spirits by a word and cured all the sick, [17]to fulfill what had been said by Isaiah the prophet:

"He took away our infirmities
and bore our diseases."

The Would-be Followers of Jesus.
[18]When Jesus saw a crowd around him, he gave orders to cross to the other side. [19]A scribe approached and said to him, "Teacher, I will follow you wherever you go." [20]Jesus answered him, "Foxes have dens and birds of the sky have nests, but the Son of Man has nowhere to rest his head." [21]Another of [his] disciples said to him, "Lord, let me go first and bury my father." [22]But Jesus answered him, "Follow me, and let the dead bury their dead."

April 24

St. Fidelis of Sigmaringen

It is because of faith that we exchange the present for the future.

— St. Fidelis of Sigmaringen

☐ **2 KINGS 8-10**

The Shunammite's Return. 8:1 Elisha once said to the woman whose son he had restored to life: "Get ready! Leave with your household and live wherever you can, because the LORD has decreed a seven-year famine which is coming upon the land." [2]The woman got ready and did as the man of God said, setting out with her household, and living in the land of the Philistines for seven years.

[3]At the end of the seven years, the woman returned from the land of the Philistines and went out to the king to appeal for her house and her field. [4]The king was talking with Gehazi, the servant of the man of God: "Tell me all the great things that Elisha has done." [5]Just as he was telling the king how his master had restored a dead person to life, the very woman whose son Elisha had restored to life came to the king appealing for her house and field. Gehazi said, "My lord king, this is the woman, and this is that son of hers whom Elisha restored to life." [6]The king questioned the woman, and she told him her story. With that the king placed an official at her

disposal, saying, "Restore all her property to her, with all that the field produced from the day she left the land until now."

Elisha and Hazael of Aram. ⁷Elisha came to Damascus at a time when Ben-hadad, king of Aram, lay sick. When he was told, "The man of God has come here," ⁸the king said to Hazael, "Take a gift with you and go call on the man of God. Consult the LORD through him, 'Will I recover from this sickness?'" ⁹Hazael went to visit him, carrying a present, and with forty camel loads of the best goods of Damascus. On his arrival, he stood before Elisha and said, "Your son Ben-hadad, king of Aram, has sent me to you to ask, 'Will I recover from my sickness?'" ¹⁰Elisha answered, "Go and tell him, 'You will surely recover.' But the LORD has showed me that he will surely die." ¹¹Then he stared him down until he became ill at ease. The man of God wept, ¹²and Hazael asked, "Why are you weeping, my lord?" Elisha replied, "Because I know the evil that you will inflict upon the Israelites. You will burn their fortresses, you will slay their youth with the sword, you will dash their little children to pieces, you will rip open their pregnant women." ¹³Hazael exclaimed, "How can your servant, a dog like me, do anything so important?" Elisha replied, "The LORD has showed you to me as king over Aram."

¹⁴Hazael left Elisha and returned to his master, who asked, "What did Elisha tell you?" Hazael replied, "He said, 'You will surely recover.'" ¹⁵The next day, however, Hazael took a cloth, dipped it in water, and spread it over the king's face, so that he died. And Hazael succeeded him as king.

Reign of Joram of Judah. ¹⁶In the fifth year of Joram, son of Ahab, king of Israel, Joram, son of Jehoshaphat, king of Judah, became king. ¹⁷He was thirty-two years old when he became king, and he reigned eight years in Jerusalem.

¹⁸He walked in the way of the kings of Israel as the house of Ahab had done, since the daughter of Ahab was his wife; and he did what was evil in the LORD's sight. ¹⁹Even so, the LORD was unwilling to destroy Judah, for the sake of his servant David. For he had promised David that he would leave him a holding in the LORD's presence for all time. ²⁰During Joram's reign, Edom revolted against the rule of Judah and installed a king of its own. ²¹Thereupon Joram with all his chariots crossed over to Zair. He arose by night and broke through the Edomites when they had surrounded him and the commanders of his chariots. Then his army fled homeward. ²²To this day Edom has been in revolt against the rule of Judah. Libnah also revolted at that time.

²³The rest of the acts of Joram, with all that he did, are recorded in the book of the chronicles of the kings of Judah. ²⁴Joram rested with his ancestors; he was buried with his ancestors in the City of David, and his son Ahaziah succeeded him as king.

Reign of Ahaziah of Judah. ²⁵In the twelfth year of Joram, son of Ahab, king of Israel, Ahaziah, son of Joram, king of Judah, became king. ²⁶Ahaziah was twenty-two years old when he became king, and he reigned one year in Jerusalem. His mother's name was Athaliah, daughter of Omri, king of Israel.

²⁷He walked in the way of the house of Ahab and did what was evil in the LORD's sight like the house of Ahab, since he was related to them by marriage. ²⁸He joined Joram, son of Ahab, in battle against Hazael, king of Aram, at Ramoth-gilead, where the Arameans wounded Joram. ²⁹King Joram returned to Jezreel to be healed of the wounds which the Arameans had inflicted on him at Ramah in his battle against Hazael, king of Aram. Then Ahaziah, son of Joram, king of Judah, went down to Jezreel to visit Joram, son of Ahab, for he was sick.

Elisha and Jehu of Israel. 9:1 Elisha the prophet called one of the guild prophets and said to him: "Get ready for a journey. Take this flask of oil with you, and go to Ramoth-gilead. ²When you get there, look for Jehu, son of Jehoshaphat, son of Nimshi. Enter and take him away from his companions and bring him into an inner chamber. ³From the flask you have, pour oil on his head, and say, 'Thus says the LORD: I anoint you king over Israel.' Then open the door and flee without delay."

⁴The aide (the prophet's aide) went to Ramoth-gilead. ⁵When he arrived, the commanders of the army were in session. He said, "I have a message for you, commander." Jehu asked, "For which one of us?" "For you, commander," he answered. ⁶Jehu got up and went into the house. Then the prophet's aide poured the oil on his head and said, "Thus says the LORD, the God of Israel: I anoint you king over the people of the LORD, over Israel. ⁷You shall destroy the house of Ahab your master; thus will I avenge the blood of my servants the prophets, and the blood of all the other servants of the LORD shed by Jezebel. ⁸The whole house of Ahab shall perish:

I will cut off from Ahab's line every male,
whether bond or free in Israel.

⁹I will make the house of Ahab like that of Jeroboam, son of Nebat, and like that of Baasha, son of Ahijah. ¹⁰In the confines of Jezreel, the dogs shall devour Jezebel so that no one can bury her." Then he opened the door and fled.

¹¹When Jehu rejoined his master's servants, they asked him, "Is all well? Why did that madman come to you?" He replied, "You know that kind of man and his talk." ¹²But they said, "Tell us another lie!" So he told them, "This is what the prophet's aide said to me, 'Thus says the LORD: I anoint you king over Israel.'" ¹³At once each took his garment, spread it under Jehu on the bare steps, blew the horn, and cried out, "Jehu is king!"

Death of Joram of Israel. ¹⁴Jehu, son of Jehoshaphat, son of Nimshi, formed a conspiracy against Joram. (Joram, with all Israel, had been besieging Ramoth-gilead against Hazael, king of Aram, ¹⁵but had returned to Jezreel to be healed of the wounds the Arameans had inflicted on him in the battle against Hazael, king of Aram.) Jehu said to them, "If this is what you really want, see that no one escapes from the city to report in Jezreel."

¹⁶Then Jehu mounted his chariot and drove to Jezreel, where Joram lay ill and Ahaziah, king of Judah, had come to visit him. ¹⁷The watchman standing on the tower in Jezreel saw the troop of Jehu coming and reported, "I see chariots." Joram said, "Get a driver and send him to meet them and to ask whether all is well." ¹⁸So a horseman went out to meet him and said, "The king asks, 'Is everything all right?'" Jehu said, "What does it matter to you how things are? Get behind me." The watchman reported to the king, "The messenger has reached them, but is not returning." ¹⁹Joram sent a second horseman, who went to them and said, "The king asks, 'Is everything all right?'" "What does it matter to you how things are?" Jehu replied. "Get behind me." ²⁰The watchman reported, "He has reached them, but is not returning. The driving is like that of Jehu, son of Nimshi; he drives like a madman." ²¹"Hitch up my chariot," said Joram, and they hitched up his chariot. Then Joram, king of Israel, and Ahaziah, king of Judah, set out, each in his own chariot, to meet Jehu. They reached him near the plot of ground of Naboth the Jezreelite.

²²When Joram recognized Jehu, he asked, "Is everything all right, Jehu?" Jehu replied, "How could everything be all right as long as all the harlotry and sorcery of your mother Jezebel continues?" ²³Joram reined about and fled, crying to Ahaziah, "Treason, Ahaziah!" ²⁴But Jehu had drawn his bow and he shot Joram between the

shoulders, so that the arrow went through his heart and he collapsed in his chariot. [25]Then Jehu said to his adjutant Bidkar, "Take him and throw him into the plot of ground in the field of Naboth the Jezreelite. For remember when you and I were driving teams behind Ahab his father, the LORD delivered this oracle against him: [26]As surely as I saw yesterday the blood of Naboth and the blood of his sons—oracle of the LORD—I will repay you for it in that very plot of ground—oracle of the LORD. So now take him and throw him into this plot of ground, in keeping with the word of the LORD."

Death of Ahaziah of Judah. [27]Seeing what was happening, Ahaziah, king of Judah, fled toward Beth-haggan. Jehu pursued him, shouting, "Him too!" They struck him as he rode through the pass of Gur near Ibleam, but he continued his flight as far as Megiddo and died there. [28]His servants brought him in a chariot to Jerusalem and they buried him in his grave with his ancestors in the City of David. [29]In the eleventh year of Joram, son of Ahab, Ahaziah became king over Judah.

Death of Jezebel. [30]Jehu came to Jezreel, and when Jezebel heard of it, she shadowed her eyes, adorned her hair, and looked down from her window. [31]As Jehu came through the gate, she cried out, "Is all well, you Zimri, murderer of your master?" [32]Jehu looked up to the window and shouted, "Who is on my side? Who?" At this, two or three eunuchs looked down toward him. [33]"Throw her down," he ordered. They threw her down, and some of her blood spurted against the wall and against the horses. Jehu trod over her body [34]and, after eating and drinking, he said: "Attend to that accursed woman and bury her; for she was the daughter of a king." [35]But when they went to bury her, they found nothing of her but the skull, the feet, and the hands. [36]They returned to Jehu, and when they told him, he said, "This is the word of the LORD spoke through his servant Elijah the Tishbite: In the confines of Jezreel the dogs shall devour the flesh of Jezebel. [37]The corpse of Jezebel shall be like dung in the field in the confines of Jezreel, so that no one can say: This was Jezebel."

Death of the Sons of Ahab of Israel. 10:1 Ahab had seventy sons in Samaria. Jehu wrote letters and sent them to Samaria, to the elders who were rulers of Jezreel and to Ahab's guardians. Jehu wrote: [2]"Since your master's sons are with you, as well as his chariots, horses, fortified city, and weaponry, when this letter reaches you [3]decide which is the best and the fittest of your master's sons, place him on his father's throne, and fight for your master's house." [4]They were overcome with fright and said, "If the two kings could not withstand him, how can we?" [5]So the master of the palace and the chief of the city, along with the elders and the guardians, sent this message to Jehu: "We are your servants, and we will do everything you tell us. We will proclaim no one king; do whatever you think best." [6]So Jehu wrote them a second letter: "If you are on my side and will obey me, bring along the heads of your master's sons and come to me in Jezreel at this time tomorrow." (The seventy princes were in the care of prominent men of the city, who were rearing them.)

[7]When the letter arrived, they took the princes and slew all seventy of them, put their heads in baskets, and sent them to Jehu in Jezreel. [8]A messenger came in and told him, "They have brought the heads of the princes." He said, "Pile them in two heaps at the gate of the city until morning."

[9]In the morning he came outside, stood there, and said to all the people: "You are guiltless, for it was I who conspired against my lord and slew him. But who killed all these? [10]Know that not a single word which the LORD has spoken against the house of Ahab shall fail. The LORD has accomplished

what he decreed through his servant Elijah." [11](And so Jehu slew all who were left of the house of Ahab in Jezreel, as well as all his powerful supporters, intimates, and priests, leaving him no survivor.) [12]Then he went back inside.

Death of the Relatives of Ahaziah of Judah. He set out for Samaria and, at Beth-eked-haroim on the way, [13]Jehu came across relatives of Ahaziah, king of Judah. "Who are you?" he asked, and they said, "We are relatives of Ahaziah. We are going down to visit the princes and the family of the queen mother." [14]"Take them alive," Jehu ordered. They were taken alive, forty-two in number, then slain at the pit of Beth-eked. Not one of them survived.

[15]When he set out from there, Jehu met Jehonadab, son of Rechab, on the road. He greeted him and asked, "Are you with me wholeheartedly, as I am with you?" "Yes," he replied. "If you are, give me your hand." He gave him his hand, and he had him mount his chariot, [16]and said, "Come with me and see my zeal for the LORD." And they took him along in his chariot.

Slaughter of the Worshipers of Baal. [17]When he arrived in Samaria, Jehu slew all who were left of Ahab's line in Samaria, doing away with them completely, according to the word the LORD spoke to Elijah. [18]Jehu gathered all the people together and said to them: "Ahab served Baal to some extent, but Jehu will serve him yet more. [19]Now summon for me all Baal's prophets, all his servants, and all his priests. See that no one is absent, for I have a great sacrifice for Baal. Whoever is absent shall not live." This Jehu did as a ruse, so that he might destroy the servants of Baal.

[20]Jehu said further, "Proclaim a solemn assembly in honor of Baal." They did so, [21]and Jehu sent word of it throughout all Israel. All the servants of Baal came; there was no one who did not come; they came to the temple of Baal, and it was filled from wall to wall. [22]Then Jehu said to the custodian of the wardrobe, "Bring out garments for all the servants of Baal." When he had brought out the garments for them, [23]Jehu, with Jehonadab, son of Rechab, entered the temple of Baal and said to the servants of Baal, "Search and be sure that there is no one who serves the LORD here with you, but only servants of Baal." [24]Then they proceeded to offer sacrifices and burnt offerings. Now Jehu had stationed eighty troops outside with this warning, "Any of you who lets someone escape of those whom I shall deliver into your hands shall pay life for life."

[25]As soon as he finished offering the burnt offering, Jehu said to the guards and aides, "Go in and slay them. Let no one escape." So the guards and aides put them to the sword and cast them out. Afterward they went into the inner shrine of the temple of Baal, [26]and took out the pillars of the temple of Baal. They burned the shrine, [27]tore down the pillar of Baal, tore down the temple of Baal, and turned it into a latrine, as it remains today.

[28]Thus Jehu destroyed Baal in Israel.

Death of Jehu of Israel. [29]However, Jehu did not desist from the sins which Jeroboam, son of Nebat, had caused Israel to commit, the golden calves at Bethel and at Dan.

[30]The LORD said to Jehu: Because you have done well what is right in my eyes, and have done to the house of Ahab all that was in my heart, your sons to the fourth generation shall sit upon the throne of Israel. [31]But Jehu was not careful to walk in the law of the LORD, the God of Israel, with all his heart, since he did not desist from the sins which Jeroboam had caused Israel to commit. [32]At that time the LORD began to dismember Israel. Hazael defeated the Israelites throughout their territory [33]east of the Jordan (all the land of Gilead, of the Gadites, Reubenites, and Manassites), from Aroer on the wadi Arnon up through Gilead and Bashan.

[34]The rest of the acts of Jehu, with all that he did and all his valor, are recorded in the book of the chronicles of the kings of Israel. [35]Jehu rested with his ancestors and was buried in Samaria, and his son Jehoahaz succeeded him as king. [36]The length of Jehu's reign over Israel was twenty-eight years in Samaria.

☐ MATTHEW 8:23-9:8

The Calming of the Storm at Sea. 8:23 He got into a boat and his disciples followed him. [24]Suddenly a violent storm came up on the sea, so that the boat was being swamped by waves; but he was asleep. [25]They came and woke him, saying, "Lord, save us! We are perishing!" [26]He said to them, "Why are you terrified, O you of little faith?" Then he got up, rebuked the winds and the sea, and there was great calm. [27]The men were amazed and said, "What sort of man is this, whom even the winds and the sea obey?"

The Healing of the Gadarene Demoniacs. [28]When he came to the other side, to the territory of the Gadarenes, two demoniacs who were coming from the tombs met him. They were so savage that no one could travel by that road. [29]They cried out, "What have you to do with us, Son of God? Have you come here to torment us before the appointed time?" [30]Some distance away a herd of many swine was feeding. [31]The demons pleaded with him, "If you drive us out, send us into the herd of swine." [32]And he said to them, "Go then!" They came out and entered the swine, and the whole herd rushed down the steep bank into the sea where they drowned. [33]The swineherds ran away, and when they came to the town they reported everything, including what had happened to the demoniacs. [34]Thereupon the whole town came out to meet Jesus, and when they saw him they begged him to leave their district.

The Healing of a Paralytic. 9:1 He entered a boat, made the crossing, and came into his own town. [2]And there people brought to him a paralytic lying on a stretcher. When Jesus saw their faith, he said to the paralytic, "Courage, child, your sins are forgiven." [3]At that, some of the scribes said to themselves, "This man is blaspheming." [4]Jesus knew what they were thinking, and said, "Why do you harbor evil thoughts? [5]Which is easier, to say, 'Your sins are forgiven,' or to say, 'Rise and walk'? [6]But that you may know that the Son of Man has authority on earth to forgive sins"—he then said to the paralytic, "Rise, pick up your stretcher, and go home." [7]He rose and went home. [8]When the crowds saw this they were struck with awe and glorified God who had given such authority to human beings.

April 25

St. Mark; Our Lady of Good Counsel

As sailors are guided by a star to the port, so Christians are guided to heaven by Mary.

— St. Thomas Aquinas

☐ 2 KINGS 11-12

Death of the Heirs of Ahaziah of Judah.
11:1 When Athaliah, the mother of Ahaziah, saw that her son was dead, she began to kill off the whole royal family. ²But Jehosheba, daughter of King Joram and sister of Ahaziah, took Joash, Ahaziah's son, and spirited him away, along with his nurse, from the bedroom where the princes were about to be slain. He was concealed from Athaliah, and so he did not die. ³For six years he remained hidden with her in the house of the LORD, while Athaliah ruled as queen over the land.

Death of Athaliah. ⁴But in the seventh year, Jehoiada summoned the captains of the Carians and of the guards. He had them come to him in the house of the LORD, made a covenant with them, exacted an oath from them in the house of the LORD, and then showed them the king's son. ⁵He gave them these orders: "This is what you must do: one third of you who come on duty on the sabbath shall guard the king's house; ⁶another third shall be at the gate Sur; and the last third shall be at the gate behind the guards. You shall guard the palace on all sides, ⁷while the two of your divisions who are going off duty that week shall keep guard over the house of the LORD for the king. ⁸You shall surround the king, each with drawn weapons, and anyone who tries to approach the guard detail is to be killed; stay with the king, wherever he goes."

⁹The captains did just as Jehoiada the priest commanded. Each took his troops, both those going on duty for the week and those going off duty that week, and came to Jehoiada the priest. ¹⁰He gave the captains King David's spear and quivers, which were in the house of the LORD. ¹¹And the guards, with drawn weapons, lined up from the southern to the northern limit of the enclosure, surrounding the altar and the temple on the king's behalf. ¹²Then Jehoiada brought out the king's son and put the crown and the testimony upon him. They proclaimed him king and anointed him, clapping their hands and shouting, "Long live the king!"

¹³When Athaliah heard the noise made by the people, she came before them in the house of the LORD. ¹⁴When she saw the king standing by the column, as was the custom, and the captains and trumpeters near the king, and all the people of the land rejoicing and blowing trumpets, Athaliah tore her garments and cried out, "Treason, treason!" ¹⁵Then Jehoiada the priest instructed the captains in command of the force: "Escort her with a guard detail. If anyone follows her, let him die by the sword." For the priest had said, "She must not die in the house of the LORD." ¹⁶So they seized her, and when she reached the Horse Gate of the king's house, she was put to death.

¹⁷Then Jehoiada made a covenant between the LORD and the king and the people, by which they would be the LORD's people; and another between the king and the people. ¹⁸Thereupon all the people of the land went to the temple of Baal and demolished it. They shattered its altars and images completely, and slew Mattan, the priest of Baal, before the altars. Jehoiada the priest appointed a detachment for the house of the LORD, ¹⁹and took the captains,

the Carians, the guards, and all the people of the land, and they led the king down from the house of the LORD; they came through the guards' gate to the king's house, and Joash took his seat on the royal throne. [20]All the people of the land rejoiced and the city was quiet, now that Athaliah had been slain with the sword at the king's house.

Reign of Joash of Judah. 12:1 Joash was seven years old when he became king. [2]In the seventh year of Jehu, Joash became king, and he reigned forty years in Jerusalem. His mother's name was Zibiah, from Beer-sheba.

[3]Joash did what was right in the LORD's sight as long as he lived, because Jehoiada the priest guided him, [4]though the high places did not disappear; the people continued to sacrifice and to burn incense on the high places.

[5]Joash said to the priests: "All the funds for sacred purposes that are brought to the house of the LORD—the census tax, personal redemption money—and all funds that are freely brought to the house of the LORD, [6]the priests may take for themselves, each from his own vendor. However, they must make whatever repairs on the temple may prove necessary." [7]Nevertheless, as late as the twenty-third year of the reign of King Joash, the priests had not made needed repairs on the temple. [8]Accordingly, King Joash summoned the priest Jehoiada and the other priests. He asked, "Why do you not repair the temple? You must no longer take funds from your vendors, but you shall turn them over for the repairs." [9]So the priests agreed that they would neither take funds from the people nor make the repairs on the temple.

[10]Jehoiada the priest then took a chest, bored a hole in its lid, and set it beside the altar, on the right as one entered the house of the LORD. The priests who kept the doors would put into it all the silver that was brought to the house of the LORD. [11]When they noticed that there was a large amount of silver in the chest, the royal scribe would come up with the high priest, and they would gather up and weigh all the silver that was in the house of the LORD. [12]The amount thus realized they turned over to the workers assigned to the house of the LORD. They in turn would pay it to the carpenters and builders working in the house of the LORD, [13]and to the masons and stone cutters, and for the purchase of the wood and hewn stone used in repairing the breaches, and for any other expenses that were necessary to repair the house of the LORD. [14]None of the valuables brought to the house of the LORD were used there to make silver basins, snuffers, bowls, trumpets, or any gold or silver article. [15]Instead, they were given to the workers, and with them they repaired the house of the LORD. [16]Moreover, no reckoning was asked of those who were provided with the funds to give to the workers, because they held positions of trust. [17]The funds from reparation offerings and from purification offerings, however, were not brought to the house of the LORD; they belonged to the priests.

[18]Then Hazael, king of Aram, came up and attacked Gath. When he had taken it, Hazael resolved to go on to attack Jerusalem. [19]Joash, king of Judah, took all the sacred offerings presented by his forebears, Jehoshaphat, Jehoram, and Ahaziah, kings of Judah, as well as his own, and all the gold there was in the treasuries of the house of the LORD and the king's house, and sent them to King Hazael of Aram, who then turned away from Jerusalem.

[20]The rest of the acts of Joash, with all that he did, are recorded in the book of the chronicles of the kings of Judah. [21]Certain of his officials entered into a conspiracy and struck Joash down at Beth-millo. [22]Jozacar, son of Shimeath, and Jehozabad, son of Shomer, were the officials who struck and killed him. He was buried with his ancestors in the City of David, and his son Amaziah succeeded him as king.

☐ MATTHEW 9:9-13

The Call of Matthew. 9:9 As Jesus passed on from there, he saw a man named Matthew sitting at the customs post. He said to him, "Follow me." And he got up and followed him. [10]While he was at table in his house, many tax collectors and sinners came and sat with Jesus and his disciples. [11]The Pharisees saw this and said to his disciples, "Why does your teacher eat with tax collectors and sinners?" [12]He heard this and said, "Those who are well do not need a physician, but the sick do. [13]Go and learn the meaning of the words, 'I desire mercy, not sacrifice.' I did not come to call the righteous but sinners."

April 26

They alone can truly feast who have first fasted.
— BLESSED JOHN HENRY NEWMAN

☐ 2 KINGS 13-15

Reign of Jehoahaz of Israel. 13:1 In the twenty-third year of Joash, son of Ahaziah, king of Judah, Jehoahaz, son of Jehu, became king over Israel in Samaria for seventeen years.

[2]He did what was evil in the LORD's sight: he did not depart from following the sins that Jeroboam, son of Nebat, had caused Israel to commit. [3]The LORD was angry with Israel and for a long time gave them into the power of Hazael, king of Aram, and of Ben-hadad, son of Hazael. [4]Then Jehoahaz entreated the LORD, who heard him, since he saw the oppression to which the king of Aram had subjected Israel. [5]So the LORD gave Israel a savior, and the Israelites, freed from the power of Aram, dwelt in their own tents as formerly. [6]Nevertheless, they did not desist from the sins the house of Jeroboam had caused Israel to commit, but persisted in them. The Asherah remained even in Samaria. [7]No army was left to Jehoahaz, except fifty horses with ten chariots and ten thousand foot soldiers, since the king of Aram had destroyed them and trampled them like dust.

[8]The rest of the acts of Jehoahaz, with all that he did and his valor, are recorded in the book of the chronicles of the kings of Israel. [9]Jehoahaz rested with his ancestors; he was buried in Samaria and his son Joash succeeded him as king.

Reign of Joash of Israel. [10]In the thirty-seventh year of Joash, king of Judah, Joash, son of Jehoahaz, became king over Israel in Samaria sixteen years.

[11]He did what was evil in the LORD's sight; he did not desist from any of the sins Jeroboam, son of Nebat, had caused Israel to commit, but persisted in them.

[12]The rest of the acts of Joash, with all that he did and his valor, and how he fought with Amaziah, king of Judah, are recorded in the book of the chronicles of the kings of Israel. [13]Joash rested with his ancestors. Then Jeroboam sat on his throne. Joash was buried in Samaria with the kings of Israel.

Elisha's Deathbed Prophecy. [14]When Elisha was suffering from the sickness of which he was to die, Joash, king of Israel, went down to weep over him. "My father, my father!" he exclaimed, "Israel's chariot and steeds!" [15]Elisha said to him, "Take bow and arrows," and he took bow and arrows. [16]Elisha said to the king of Israel, "Rest your hand on the bow," and he rested his hand on it. Elisha placed his hands over the king's hands [17]and said, "Open the window toward the east." He opened it. Elisha said, "Shoot," and he shot. He said,

"An arrow of victory for the LORD!
  An arrow of victory over Aram!
You will beat Aram at Aphek and finish him!"

[18]Then he said to the king of Israel, "Take the arrows," which he did. Elisha said to the king of Israel, "Beat the ground!" He beat the ground three times and stopped. [19]The man of God became angry with him and said, "You should have beat five or six times. You would have beaten Aram and finished him. Now you will beat Aram only three times."

[20]And so Elisha died and was buried.

At that time of year, bands of Moabites used to raid the land. [21]Once some people were burying a man, when suddenly they saw such a raiding band. So they cast the man into the grave of Elisha, and everyone went off. But when the man came in contact with the bones of Elisha, he came back to life and got to his feet.

[22]King Hazael of Aram oppressed Israel all the days of Jehoahaz. [23]But the LORD was gracious with Israel and looked on them with compassion because of his covenant with Abraham, Isaac, and Jacob. He was unwilling to destroy them or to cast them out from his presence even up to now. [24]So when King Hazael of Aram died and his son Ben-hadad succeeded him as king, [25]Joash, son of Jehoahaz, took back from Ben-hadad, son of Hazael, the cities Hazael had taken in battle from Jehoahaz, his father. Three times Joash beat him, and thus recovered the cities of Israel.

Reign of Amaziah of Judah. 14:1 In the second year of Joash, son of Jehoahaz, king of Israel, Amaziah, son of Joash, king of Judah, became king. [2]He was twenty-five years old when he became king, and he reigned twenty-nine years in Jerusalem. His mother's name was Jehoaddin, from Jerusalem.

[3]He did what was right in the LORD's eyes, though not like David his father. He did just as his father Joash had done, [4]though the high places did not disappear, and the people continued to sacrifice and to burn incense on the high places.

[5]When Amaziah had the kingdom firmly in hand, he struck down the officials who had struck down the king, his father. [6]But their children he did not put to death, according to what is written in the book of the law of Moses, which the LORD commanded: "Parents shall not be put to death for their children, nor shall children be put to death for their parents; only for one's own crimes shall a person be put to death."

[7]Amaziah struck down ten thousand Edomites in the Salt Valley. He took Sela in battle and renamed it Joktheel, the name it has to this day.

[8]Then Amaziah sent messengers to Joash, son of Jehoahaz, son of Jehu, king of Israel, with this message: "Come, let us meet face to face." [9]Joash, king of Israel, sent this reply to Amaziah, king of Judah: "A thistle of Lebanon sent word to a cedar of Lebanon, 'Give your daughter to my son in marriage,' but an animal of Lebanon passed by and trampled the thistle underfoot. [10]You have indeed struck down Edom, and your heart is lifted up; enjoy your glory, but stay home! Why bring misfortune and failure on yourself and on Judah with you?" [11]But Amaziah did not listen. So Joash, king of Israel, advanced, and he and Amaziah, king of Judah, met face to face at Beth-shemesh of Judah, [12]and Judah was defeated by Israel, and all fled to their tents. [13]But Amaziah, king of Judah, son of Joash, son of Ahaziah, was captured by Joash, king of Israel, at Beth-

shemesh. When they came to Jerusalem Joash tore down the wall of Jerusalem, from the Gate of Ephraim to the Corner Gate, four hundred cubits. [14]He took all the gold and silver and all the vessels found in the house of the LORD and in the treasuries of the king's house, and hostages as well. Then he returned to Samaria.

[15]The rest of the acts of Joash, what he did and his valor, and how he made war against Amaziah, king of Judah, are recorded in the book of the chronicles of the kings of Israel. [16]Joash rested with his ancestors; he was buried in Samaria with the kings of Israel, and his son Jeroboam succeeded him as king.

[17]Amaziah, son of Joash, king of Judah, survived Joash, son of Jehoahaz, king of Israel, by fifteen years. [18]The rest of the acts of Amaziah are recorded in the book of the chronicles of the kings of Judah. [19]When a conspiracy was formed against him in Jerusalem, he fled to Lachish. But he was pursued to Lachish and killed there. [20]He was brought back on horses and was buried in Jerusalem with his ancestors in the City of David. [21]Thereupon all the people of Judah took Azariah, who was only sixteen years old, and made him king to succeed Amaziah, his father. [22]It was he who rebuilt Elath and restored it to Judah, after the king rested with his ancestors.

Reign of Jeroboam II of Israel. [23]In the fifteenth year of Amaziah, son of Joash, king of Judah, Jeroboam, son of Joash, king of Israel, became king in Samaria for forty-one years.

[24]He did evil in the LORD's sight; he did not desist from any of the sins that Jeroboam, son of Nebat, had caused Israel to commit. [25]He restored the boundaries of Israel from Lebo-hamath to the sea of the Arabah, as the LORD, the God of Israel, had foretold through his servant, the prophet Jonah, son of Amittai, from Gath-hepher. [26]For the LORD saw the very bitter affliction of Israel, where there was neither bond nor free, no one at all to help Israel. [27]Since the LORD had not resolved to wipe out the name of Israel from under the heavens, he saved them through Jeroboam, son of Joash.

[28]The rest of the acts of Jeroboam, with all that he did and his valor, how he fought, and how he regained Damascus and Hamath for Israel, are recorded in the book of the chronicles of the kings of Israel. [29]Jeroboam rested with his ancestors, the kings of Israel, and his son Zechariah succeeded him as king.

Reign of Azariah of Judah. 15:1 In the twenty-seventh year of Jeroboam, king of Israel, Azariah, son of Amaziah, king of Judah, became king. [2]He was sixteen years old when he became king, and he reigned fifty-two years in Jerusalem. His mother's name was Jecholiah, from Jerusalem.

[3]He did what was right in the LORD's sight, just as his father Amaziah had done, [4]though the high places did not disappear, and the people continued to sacrifice and to burn incense on the high places. [5]The LORD afflicted the king, and he was a leper until the day he died. He lived in a house apart, while Jotham, the king's son, was master of the palace and ruled the people of the land.

[6]The rest of the acts of Azariah, and all that he did, are recorded in the book of the chronicles of the kings of Judah. [7]Azariah rested with his ancestors, and was buried with them in the City of David, and his son Jotham succeeded him as king.

Reign of Zechariah of Israel. [8]In the thirty-eighth year of Azariah, king of Judah, Zechariah, son of Jeroboam, became king over Israel in Samaria for six months.

[9]He did what was evil in the LORD's sight, as his ancestors had done, and did not desist from the sins that Jeroboam, son of Nebat, had caused Israel to commit. [10]Shallum, son of Jabesh, plotted against him and struck him down at Ibleam. He killed him and reigned in his place.

¹¹As for the rest of the acts of Zechariah, these are recorded in the book of the chronicles of the kings of Israel. ¹²This was the word the LORD had spoken to Jehu: Sons of your line to the fourth generation shall sit upon the throne of Israel; and so it was.

Reign of Shallum of Israel. ¹³Shallum, son of Jabesh, became king in the thirty-ninth year of Uzziah, king of Judah; he reigned one month in Samaria.

¹⁴Menahem, son of Gadi, came up from Tirzah to Samaria, and struck down Shallum, son of Jabesh, in Samaria. He killed him and reigned in his place.

¹⁵As for the rest of the acts of Shallum, with the conspiracy he carried out, these are recorded in the book of the chronicles of the kings of Israel. ¹⁶At that time, Menahem attacked Tappuah, all its inhabitants, and its whole district as far as Tirzah, because they did not let him in. He attacked them; he even ripped open all their pregnant women.

Reign of Menahem of Israel. ¹⁷In the thirty-ninth year of Azariah, king of Judah, Menahem, son of Gadi, became king over Israel for ten years in Samaria. ¹⁸He did what was evil in the LORD's sight as long as he lived, not desisting from the sins that Jeroboam, son of Nebat, had caused Israel to commit. ¹⁹Pul, king of Assyria, came against the land. But Menahem gave Pul a thousand talents of silver to have his help in holding onto his kingdom. ²⁰Menahem paid out silver on behalf of Israel, that is, for all the people of substance, by giving the king of Assyria fifty shekels of silver for each one. So the king of Assyria went home and did not stay in the land.

²¹The rest of the acts of Menahem, with all that he did, are recorded in the book of the chronicles of the kings of Israel. ²²Menahem rested with his ancestors, and his son Pekahiah succeeded him as king.

Reign of Pekahiah of Israel. ²³In the fiftieth year of Azariah, king of Judah, Pekahiah, son of Menahem, became king over Israel in Samaria for two years.

²⁴He did what was evil in the LORD's sight, not desisting from the sins that Jeroboam, son of Nebat, had caused Israel to commit. ²⁵His adjutant Pekah, son of Remaliah, conspired against him, and struck him down at Samaria within the palace stronghold; he had with him fifty men from Gilead. He killed him and reigned in his place. ²⁶As for the rest of the acts of Pekahiah, with all that he did, these are recorded in the book of the chronicles of the kings of Israel.

Reign of Pekah of Israel. ²⁷In the fifty-second year of Azariah, king of Judah, Pekah, son of Remaliah, became king over Israel in Samaria for twenty years.

²⁸He did what was evil in the LORD's sight, not desisting from the sins that Jeroboam, son of Nebat, had caused Israel to commit. ²⁹In the days of Pekah, king of Israel, Tiglath-pileser, king of Assyria, came and took Ijon, Abel-beth-maacah, Janoah, Kedesh, Hazor, Gilead, and Galilee—all the land of Naphtali—deporting the inhabitants to Assyria. ³⁰Hoshea, son of Elah, carried out a conspiracy against Pekah, son of Remaliah; he struck and killed him, and succeeded him as king in the twentieth year of Jotham, son of Uzziah.

³¹As for the rest of the acts of Pekah, with all that he did, these are recorded in the book of the chronicles of the kings of Israel.

Reign of Jotham of Judah. ³²In the second year of Pekah, son of Remaliah, king of Israel, Jotham, son of Uzziah, king of Judah, became king. ³³He was twenty-five years old when he became king, and he reigned sixteen years in Jerusalem. His mother's name was Jerusha, daughter of Zadok.

³⁴He did what was right in the LORD's sight, just as his father Uzziah had done, ³⁵though the high places did not disappear, and the people continued to sacrifice and

to burn incense on the high places. It was he who built the Upper Gate of the LORD's house. ³⁶The rest of the acts of Jotham, with what he did, are recorded in the book of the chronicles of the kings of Judah. ³⁷It was at that time that the LORD began to unleash Rezin, king of Aram, and Pekah, son of Remaliah, against Judah. ³⁸Jotham rested with his ancestors; he was buried with his ancestors in the City of David his father, and his son Ahaz succeeded him as king.

☐ MATTHEW 9:14-17

The Question about Fasting. 9:14 Then the disciples of John approached him and said, "Why do we and the Pharisees fast [much], but your disciples do not fast?" ¹⁵Jesus answered them, "Can the wedding guests mourn as long as the bridegroom is with them? The days will come when the bridegroom is taken away from them, and then they will fast. ¹⁶No one patches an old cloak with a piece of unshrunken cloth, for its fullness pulls away from the cloak and the tear gets worse. ¹⁷People do not put new wine into old wineskins. Otherwise the skins burst, the wine spills out, and the skins are ruined. Rather, they pour new wine into fresh wineskins, and both are preserved."

April 27

St. Zita

All devotion that leads to sloth is false. We must love work.
— St. Zita

☐ 2 KINGS 16-18

Reign of Ahaz of Judah. 16:1 In the seventeenth year of Pekah, son of Remaliah, Ahaz, son of Jotham, king of Judah, became king. ²Ahaz was twenty years old when he became king, and he reigned sixteen years in Jerusalem.

He did not do what was right in the sight of the LORD his God, as David his father had done. ³He walked in the way of the kings of Israel; he even immolated his child by fire, in accordance with the abominable practices of the nations whom the LORD had dispossessed before the Israelites. ⁴Further, he sacrificed and burned incense on the high places, on hills, and under every green tree.

⁵Then Rezin, king of Aram, and Pekah, son of Remaliah, king of Israel, came up to Jerusalem to attack it. Although they besieged Ahaz, they were unable to do battle. ⁶(In those days Rezin, king of Aram, recovered Elath for Aram, and drove the Judahites out of it. The Edomites then entered Elath, which they have occupied until the present.) ⁷Meanwhile, Ahaz sent messengers to Tiglath-pileser, king of Assyria, with the plea: "I am your servant and your son. Come up and rescue me from the power of the king of Aram and the king of Israel, who are attacking me." ⁸Ahaz took the silver and gold that were in the house

of the LORD and in the treasuries of the king's house and sent them as a present to the king of Assyria. ⁹The king of Assyria listened to him and moved against Damascus, captured it, deported its inhabitants to Kir, and put Rezin to death.

¹⁰King Ahaz went to Damascus to meet Tiglath-pileser, king of Assyria. When he saw the altar in Damascus, King Ahaz sent to Uriah the priest a model of the altar and a detailed design of its construction. ¹¹Uriah the priest built an altar according to the plans which King Ahaz sent him from Damascus, and had it completed by the time King Ahaz returned from Damascus. ¹²On his arrival from Damascus, the king inspected the altar; the king approached the altar, went up ¹³and sacrificed his burnt offering and grain offering, pouring out his libation, and sprinkling the blood of his communion offerings on the altar. ¹⁴The bronze altar that stood before the LORD he brought from the front of the temple—that is, from the space between the new altar and the house of the LORD—and set it on the north side of his altar. ¹⁵King Ahaz commanded Uriah the priest, "Upon the large altar sacrifice the morning burnt offering and the evening grain offering, the king's burnt offering and grain offering, and the burnt offering and grain offering of the people of the land. Their libations you must sprinkle on it along with all the blood of burnt offerings and sacrifices. But the old bronze altar shall be mine for consultation." ¹⁶Uriah the priest did just as King Ahaz had commanded. ¹⁷King Ahaz detached the panels from the stands and removed the basins from them; he also took down the bronze sea from the bronze oxen that supported it, and set it on a stone pavement. ¹⁸In deference to the king of Assyria he removed the sabbath canopy that had been set up in the house of the LORD and the king's outside entrance to the temple.

¹⁹The rest of the acts of Ahaz, with what he did, are recorded in the book of the chronicles of the kings of Judah. ²⁰Ahaz rested with his ancestors; he was buried with his ancestors in the City of David, and his son Hezekiah succeeded him as king.

Reign of Hoshea of Israel. 17:1 In the twelfth year of Ahaz, king of Judah, Hoshea, son of Elah, became king in Samaria over Israel for nine years.

²He did what was evil in the LORD's sight, yet not to the extent of the kings of Israel before him. ³Shalmaneser, king of Assyria, advanced against him, and Hoshea became his vassal and paid him tribute. ⁴But the king of Assyria found Hoshea guilty of conspiracy for sending messengers to the king of Egypt at Sais, and for failure to pay the annual tribute to the king of Assyria. So the king of Assyria arrested and imprisoned him. ⁵Then the king of Assyria occupied the whole land and attacked Samaria, which he besieged for three years.

Israelites Deported. ⁶In Hoshea's ninth year, the king of Assyria took Samaria, deported the Israelites to Assyria, and settled them in Halah, and at the Habor, a river of Gozan, and in the cities of the Medes. ⁷This came about because the Israelites sinned against the LORD, their God, who had brought them up from the land of Egypt, from under the hand of Pharaoh, king of Egypt. They venerated other gods, ⁸they followed the rites of the nations whom the LORD had dispossessed before the Israelites and those that the kings of Israel had practiced. ⁹They adopted unlawful practices toward the LORD, their God. They built high places in all their cities, from guard post to garrisoned town. ¹⁰They set up pillars and asherahs for themselves on every high hill and under every green tree. ¹¹They burned incense there, on all the high places, like the nations whom the LORD had sent into exile at their coming. They did evil things that provoked the LORD, ¹²and served idols, although the LORD had told them: You must not do this.

[13]The LORD warned Israel and Judah by every prophet and seer: Give up your evil ways and keep my commandments and statutes, in accordance with the entire law which I enjoined on your ancestors and which I sent you by my servants the prophets. [14]But they did not listen. They grew as stiff-necked as their ancestors, who had not believed in the LORD, their God. [15]They rejected his statutes, the covenant he had made with their ancestors, and the warnings he had given them. They followed emptiness and became empty; they followed the surrounding nations whom the LORD had commanded them not to imitate. [16]They abandoned all the commandments of the LORD, their God: they made for themselves two molten calves; they made an asherah; they bowed down to all the host of heaven; they served Baal. [17]They immolated their sons and daughters by fire. They practiced augury and divination. They surrendered themselves to doing what was evil in the LORD's sight, and provoked him.

[18]The LORD became enraged, and removed them from his presence. Only the tribe of Judah was left. [19]Even the people of Judah did not keep the commandments of the LORD, their God, but followed the rites practiced by Israel. [20]So the LORD rejected the entire people of Israel: he afflicted them and delivered them over to plunderers, finally casting them from his presence. [21]When he tore Israel away from the house of David, they made Jeroboam, son of Nebat, king; but Jeroboam lured the Israelites away from the LORD, causing them to commit a great sin. [22]The Israelites imitated Jeroboam in all the sins he committed; they would not depart from them. [23]Finally, the LORD removed Israel from his presence, just as he had declared through all his servants, the prophets. Thus Israel went into exile from their native soil to Assyria until this very day.

Foreigners Deported to Israel. [24]The king of Assyria brought people from Babylon, Cuthah, Avva, Hamath, and Sepharvaim, and settled them in the cities of Samaria in place of the Israelites. They took possession of Samaria and dwelt in its cities. [25]When they first settled there, they did not venerate the LORD, so he sent lions among them that killed some of them. [26]A report reached the king of Assyria: "The nations you deported and settled in the cities of Samaria do not know the proper worship of the god of the land, so he has sent lions among them that are killing them, since they do not know the law of the god of the land." [27]The king of Assyria gave the order, "Send back some of the priests you deported, to go there and settle, to teach them the proper worship of the god of the land." [28]So one of the priests who had been deported from Samaria returned and settled in Bethel, and began to teach them how to venerate the LORD.

[29]Thus each of these nations continued to make its own gods, setting them up in the shrines of the high places the Samarians had made: each nation in the cities in which they dwelt. [30]The Babylonians made Sukkot-Benot; the people of Cuth made Nergal; those from Hamath made Ashima; [31]those from Avva made Nibhaz and Tartak; and those from Sepharvaim immolated their children by fire to their city gods, King Hadad and King Anu. [32]At the same time, they were venerating the LORD, appointing from their own number priests for the high places to officiate for them in the shrines on the high places. [33]They were both venerating the LORD and serving their own gods. They followed the custom of the nations from among whom they had been deported.

[34]To this very day they continue to act according to their former customs, not venerating the LORD nor observing the statutes and regulations, the law and commandment, that the LORD enjoined on the descendants of Jacob, whom he had named Israel. [35]When the LORD made a covenant

with them, he commanded them: You must not venerate other gods, nor bow down to them, nor serve them, nor offer sacrifice to them, ³⁶but only to the LORD, who brought you up from the land of Egypt with great power and outstretched arm. Him shall you venerate, to him shall you bow down, and to him shall you offer sacrifice. ³⁷You must be careful always to observe the statutes and ordinances, the law and commandment, which he wrote for you; you must not venerate other gods. ³⁸The covenant I made with you, you must not forget; you must not venerate other gods. ³⁹You must venerate only the LORD, your God; it is he who will deliver you from the power of all your enemies. ⁴⁰But they did not listen; they continued to act according to their former customs.

⁴¹But these nations were both venerating the LORD and serving their own idols. Their children and children's children are still acting like their ancestors, to this very day.

Reign of Hezekiah. 18:1 In the third year of Hoshea, son of Elah, king of Israel, Hezekiah, son of Ahaz, king of Judah, became king. ²He was twenty-five years old when he became king, and he reigned twenty-nine years in Jerusalem. His mother's name was Abi, daughter of Zechariah.

³He did what was right in the LORD's sight, just as David his father had done. ⁴It was he who removed the high places, shattered the pillars, cut down the asherah, and smashed the bronze serpent Moses had made, because up to that time the Israelites were burning incense to it. (It was called Nehushtan.) ⁵He put his trust in the LORD, the God of Israel; and neither before nor after him was there anyone like him among all the kings of Judah. ⁶Hezekiah held fast to the LORD and never turned away from following him, but observed the commandments the LORD had given Moses. ⁷The LORD was with him, and he succeeded in all he set out to do. He rebelled against the king of Assyria and did not serve him. ⁸It was he who struck the Philistines as far as Gaza, and all its territory from guard post to garrisoned town.

⁹In the fourth year of King Hezekiah, which was the seventh year of Hoshea, son of Elah, king of Israel, Shalmaneser, king of Assyria, attacked Samaria and laid siege to it, ¹⁰and after three years they captured it. In the sixth year of Hezekiah, the ninth year of Hoshea, king of Israel, Samaria was taken. ¹¹The king of Assyria then deported the Israelites to Assyria and led them off to Halah, and the Habor, a river of Gozan, and the cities of the Medes. ¹²This happened because they did not obey the LORD, their God, but violated his covenant; they did not obey nor do all that Moses, the servant of the LORD, commanded.

Sennacherib and Hezekiah. ¹³In the fourteenth year of King Hezekiah, Sennacherib, king of Assyria, attacked all the fortified cities of Judah and captured them. ¹⁴Hezekiah, king of Judah, sent this message to the king of Assyria at Lachish: "I have done wrong. Leave me, and whatever you impose on me I will bear." The king of Assyria exacted three hundred talents of silver and thirty talents of gold from Hezekiah, king of Judah. ¹⁵Hezekiah gave him all the funds there were in the house of the LORD and in the treasuries of the king's house. ¹⁶At the same time, Hezekiah removed the nave doors and the uprights of the house of the LORD, which the king of Judah had ordered to be overlaid with gold, and gave them to the king of Assyria. ¹⁷The king of Assyria sent the general, the lord chamberlain, and the commander from Lachish with a great army to King Hezekiah at Jerusalem. They went up and came to Jerusalem, to the conduit of the upper pool on the highway of the fuller's field, where they took their stand. ¹⁸They called for the king, but Eliakim, son of Hilkiah, the master of the palace, came out, along with Shebnah the scribe and the chancellor Joah, son of Asaph.

[19]The commander said to them, "Tell Hezekiah, 'Thus says the great king, the king of Assyria: On what do you base this trust of yours? [20]Do you think mere words substitute for strategy and might in war? In whom, then, do you place your trust, that you rebel against me? [21]Do you trust in Egypt, that broken reed of a staff, which pierces the hand of anyone who leans on it? That is what Pharaoh, king of Egypt, is to all who trust in him. [22]Or do you people say to me, "It is in the LORD our God we trust!"? Is it not he whose high places and altars Hezekiah has removed, commanding Judah and Jerusalem, "Worship before this altar in Jerusalem"?'

[23]"Now, make a wager with my lord, the king of Assyria: I will give you two thousand horses if you are able to put riders on them. [24]How then can you turn back even a captain, one of the least servants of my lord, trusting, as you do, in Egypt for chariots and horses? [25]Did I come up to destroy this place without the LORD? The LORD himself said to me: Go up and destroy that land!'"

[26]Then Eliakim, son of Hilkiah, and Shebnah and Joah said to the commander: "Please speak to your servants in Aramaic; we understand it. Do not speak to us in the language of Judah within earshot of the people who are on the wall." [27]But the commander replied: "Was it to your lord and to you that my lord sent me to speak these words? Was it not rather to those sitting on the wall, who, with you, will have to eat their own excrement and drink their urine?"

[28]Then the commander stepped forward and cried out in a loud voice in the language of Judah, "Listen to the words of the great king, the king of Assyria. [29]Thus says the king: Do not let Hezekiah deceive you, for he cannot rescue you from my hand. [30]And do not let Hezekiah induce you to trust in the LORD, saying, 'The LORD will surely rescue us, and this city will not be handed over to the king of Assyria.' [31]Do not listen to Hezekiah, for thus says the king of Assyria: Make peace with me, and surrender to me! Eat, each of you, from your vine, each from your own fig tree. Drink water, each from your own well, [32]until I arrive and take you to a land like your own, a land of grain and wine, a land of bread and vineyards, a land of rich olives and honey. Live, and do not die! And do not listen to Hezekiah when he would incite you by saying, 'The LORD will rescue us.' [33]Has any of the gods of the nations ever rescued his land from the power of the king of Assyria? [34]Where are the gods of Hamath and Arpad? Where are the gods of Sepharvaim, Hena, and Ivvah? Did they indeed rescue Samaria from my power? [35]Which of the gods for all these lands ever rescued his land from my power? Will the LORD then rescue Jerusalem from my power?" [36]But the people remained silent and did not answer at all, for the king's command was, "Do not answer him."

[37]Then the master of the palace, Eliakim, son of Hilkiah, Shebnah the scribe, and the chancellor Joah, son of Asaph, came to Hezekiah with their garments torn, and reported to him the words of the commander.

☐ MATTHEW 9:18-26

The Official's Daughter and the Woman with a Hemorrhage. 9:18 While he was saying these things to them, an official came forward, knelt down before him, and said, "My daughter has just died. But come, lay your hand on her, and she will live." [19]Jesus rose and followed him, and so did his disciples. [20]A woman suffering hemorrhages for twelve years came up behind him and touched the tassel on his cloak.

²¹She said to herself, "If only I can touch his cloak, I shall be cured." ²²Jesus turned around and saw her, and said, "Courage, daughter! Your faith has saved you." And from that hour the woman was cured.

²³When Jesus arrived at the official's house and saw the flute players and the crowd who were making a commotion, ²⁴he said, "Go away! The girl is not dead but sleeping." And they ridiculed him. ²⁵When the crowd was put out, he came and took her by the hand, and the little girl arose. ²⁶And news of this spread throughout all that land.

April 28

St. Peter Chanel; St. Louis de Montfort

Do with your adversities as the merchant does with his merchandise: Make a profit on every item. Don't allow the loss of the tiniest fragment of the true cross. It may be only the sting of a horsefly or the prick of a pin that annoys you; it may be a neighbor's little eccentricities, some unintended slight, the insignificant loss of a penny, some small restlessness of soul, a light pain in your limbs. Make a profit on every item as the grocer does, and you'll soon be wealthy in God.

— ST. LOUIS DE MONTFORT

☐ 2 KINGS 19-20

Hezekiah and Isaiah. 19:1 When King Hezekiah heard this, he tore his garments, covered himself with sackcloth, and went into the house of the LORD. ²He sent Eliakim, the master of the palace, Shebnah the scribe, and the elders of the priests, covered with sackcloth, to tell the prophet Isaiah, son of Amoz, ³"Thus says Hezekiah:

A day of distress and rebuke,
  a day of disgrace is this day!
Children are due to come forth,
  but the strength to give birth is
    lacking.

⁴Perhaps the LORD, your God, will hear all the words of the commander, whom his lord, the king of Assyria, sent to taunt the living God, and will rebuke him for the words which the LORD, your God, has heard. So lift up a prayer for the remnant that is here." ⁵When the servants of King Hezekiah had come to Isaiah, ⁶he said to them, "Tell this to your lord: Thus says the LORD: Do not be frightened by the words you have heard, by which the deputies of the king of Assyria have blasphemed me. ⁷I am putting in him such a spirit that when he hears a report he will return to his land. I will make him fall by the sword in his land."

⁸When the commander, on his return, heard that the king of Assyria had withdrawn from Lachish, he found him besieging Libnah.

Sennacherib, Hezekiah, and Isaiah. ⁹The king of Assyria heard a report: "Tirhakah, king of Ethiopia, has come out to fight against you." Again he sent messengers to Hezekiah to say: ¹⁰"Thus shall you say to Hezekiah, king of Judah: Do not let your God in whom you trust deceive you by saying, 'Jerusalem will not be handed over to the king of Assyria.' ¹¹You, certainly, have heard what the kings of Assyria have done to all the lands: they put them under the ban! And are you to be rescued? ¹²Did the gods of the nations whom my fathers destroyed deliver them—Gozan, Haran, Rezeph, or the Edenites in Telassar? ¹³Where are the king of Hamath, the king of Arpad, or the kings of the cities Sepharvaim, Hena and Ivvah?"

¹⁴Hezekiah took the letter from the hand of the messengers and read it; then he went up to the house of the LORD, and spreading it out before the LORD, ¹⁵Hezekiah prayed in the LORD's presence: "LORD, God of Israel, enthroned on the cherubim! You alone are God over all the kingdoms of the earth. It is you who made the heavens and the earth. ¹⁶Incline your ear, LORD, and listen! Open your eyes, LORD, and see! Hear the words Sennacherib has sent to taunt the living God. ¹⁷Truly, O LORD, the kings of Assyria have laid waste the nations and their lands. ¹⁸They gave their gods to the fire—they were not gods at all, but the work of human hands—wood and stone, they destroyed them. ¹⁹Therefore, LORD, our God, save us from this man's power, that all the kingdoms of the earth may know that you alone, LORD, are God."

²⁰Then Isaiah, son of Amoz, sent this message to Hezekiah: "Thus says the LORD, the God of Israel, to whom you have prayed concerning Sennacherib, king of Assyria: I have listened! ²¹This is the word the LORD has spoken concerning him:

She despises you, laughs you to scorn,
    the virgin daughter Zion!
Behind you she wags her head,
    daughter Jerusalem.
²²Whom have you insulted and
        blasphemed,
    at whom have you raised your voice
And lifted up your eyes on high?
    At the Holy One of Israel!
²³Through the mouths of your
        messengers

you insulted the Lord when you
        said,
'With my many chariots I went up
    to the tops of the peaks,
    to the recesses of Lebanon,
To cut down its lofty cedars,
    its choice cypresses;
I reached to the farthest shelter,
    the forest ranges.
²⁴I myself dug wells
    and drank foreign waters,
Drying up all the rivers of Egypt
    beneath the soles of my feet.'

²⁵"Have you not heard?
    A long time ago I prepared it,
    from days of old I planned it.
Now I have brought it about:
You are here to reduce
    fortified cities to heaps of ruins,
²⁶Their people powerless,
    dismayed and distraught.
They are plants of the field,
    green growth,
    thatch on the rooftops,
Grain scorched by the east wind.
²⁷I know when you stand or sit,
    when you come or go
    and how you rage against me.
²⁸Because you rage against me,
    and your smugness has reached
        my ears,
I will put my hook in your nose
    and my bit in your mouth,
And make you leave by the way you
        came.

²⁹"This shall be a sign for you:
This year you shall eat the
        aftergrowth,
    next year, what grows of itself;
But in the third year, sow and reap,
    plant vineyards and eat their
        fruit!
³⁰The remaining survivors of the house
        of Judah
    shall again strike root below
    and bear fruit above.

³¹For out of Jerusalem shall come a
remnant,
and from Mount Zion, survivors.
The zeal of the LORD of hosts shall do
this.

³²"Therefore, thus says the LORD about
the king:

He shall not come as far as this city,
nor shoot there an arrow,
nor confront it with a shield,
Nor cast up a siege-work against it.
³³By the way he came he shall leave,
never coming as far as this city,
oracle of the LORD.
³⁴I will shield and save this city
for my own sake and the sake of
David my servant."

³⁵That night the angel of the LORD went
forth and struck down one hundred and
eighty-five thousand men in the Assyrian
camp. Early the next morning, there they
were, dead, all those corpses! ³⁶So Sennacherib, the king of Assyria, broke camp,
departed, returned home, and stayed in
Nineveh.

³⁷When he was worshiping in the tem-
ple of his god Nisroch, his sons Adram-
melech and Sharezer struck him down with
the sword and fled into the land of Ararat.
His son Esarhaddon reigned in his place.

End of Hezekiah's Reign. 20:1 In those
days, when Hezekiah was mortally ill, the
prophet Isaiah, son of Amoz, came and
said to him: "Thus says the LORD: Put
your house in order, for you are about to
die; you shall not recover." ²He turned his
face to the wall and prayed to the LORD:
³"Ah, LORD, remember how faithfully and
wholeheartedly I conducted myself in your
presence, doing what was good in your
sight!" And Hezekiah wept bitterly. ⁴Be-
fore Isaiah had left the central courtyard,
the word of the LORD came to him: ⁵Go
back and tell Hezekiah, the leader of my

people: "Thus says the LORD, the God of
David your father:

I have heard your prayer;
I have seen your tears.
Now I am healing you.
On the third day you shall go up
to the house of the LORD.
⁶I will add to your life fifteen years.
I will rescue you and this city
from the hand of the king of Assyria;
I will be a shield to this city
for my own sake and the sake of
David my servant."

⁷Then Isaiah said, "Bring a poultice of figs
and apply it to the boil for his recovery."
⁸Hezekiah asked Isaiah, "What is the sign
that the LORD will heal me and that I shall
go up to the house of the LORD on the
third day?" ⁹Isaiah replied, "This will be
the sign for you from the LORD that he will
carry out the word he has spoken: Shall
the shadow go forward or back ten steps?"
¹⁰"It is easy for the shadow to advance ten
steps," Hezekiah answered. "Rather, let it
go back ten steps." ¹¹So Isaiah the prophet
invoked the LORD. He made the shadow
go back the ten steps it had descended on
the staircase to the terrace of Ahaz.

¹²At that time, Berodach-baladan, son
of Baladan, king of Babylon, sent letters
and gifts to Hezekiah when he heard that
he had been ill. ¹³Hezekiah listened to the
envoys and then showed off his whole treasury: his silver, gold, spices and perfumed
oil, his armory, and everything in his storerooms; there was nothing in his house or
in all his realm that Hezekiah did not show
them. ¹⁴Then Isaiah the prophet came to
King Hezekiah and asked him: "What did
these men say to you? Where did they come
from?" Hezekiah replied, "They came from
a distant land, from Babylon." ¹⁵He asked,
"What did they see in your house?" Hezekiah answered, "They saw everything in my
house. There is nothing in my storerooms
that I did not show them." ¹⁶Then Isaiah

said to Hezekiah: "Hear the word of the LORD: [17]The time is coming when all that is in your house, everything that your ancestors have stored up until this day, shall be carried off to Babylon; nothing shall be left, says the LORD. [18]Some of your own descendants, your offspring, your progeny, shall be taken and made attendants in the palace of the king of Babylon." [19]Hezekiah replied to Isaiah, "The word of the LORD which you have spoken is good." For he thought, "There will be peace and stability in my lifetime."

[20]The rest of the acts of Hezekiah, with all his valor, and how he constructed the pool and conduit and brought water into the city, are recorded in the book of the chronicles of the kings of Judah. [21]Hezekiah rested with his ancestors, and his son Manasseh succeeded him as king.

☐ MATTHEW 9:27-34

The Healing of Two Blind Men. 9:27 And as Jesus passed on from there, two blind men followed [him], crying out, "Son of David, have pity on us!" [28]When he entered the house, the blind men approached him and Jesus said to them, "Do you believe that I can do this?" "Yes, Lord," they said to him. [29]Then he touched their eyes and said, "Let it be done for you according to your faith." [30]And their eyes were opened. Jesus warned them sternly, "See that no one knows about this." [31]But they went out and spread word of him through all that land.

The Healing of a Mute Person. [32]As they were going out, a demoniac who could not speak was brought to him, [33]and when the demon was driven out the mute person spoke. The crowds were amazed and said, "Nothing like this has ever been seen in Israel." [34]But the Pharisees said, "He drives out demons by the prince of demons."

April 29

St. Catherine of Siena

Since the Church began aiming more at worldly things than at spiritual, things have gone from bad to worse.

— ST. CATHERINE OF SIENA

☐ 2 KINGS 21-23

Reign of Manasseh. 21:1 Manasseh was twelve years old when he became king, and he reigned fifty-five years in Jerusalem. His mother's name was Hephzibah.

[2]He did what was evil in the LORD's sight, following the abominable practices of the nations whom the LORD had dispossessed before the Israelites. [3]He rebuilt the high places which Hezekiah his father had destroyed. He set up altars to Baal and also made an asherah, as Ahab, king of Israel, had done. He bowed down to the whole host of heaven and served them. [4]He built altars in the house of the LORD, of which the LORD had said: In Jerusalem I will set my name. [5]And he built altars for the whole host of heaven in the two courts of the house of the LORD. [6]He immolated his

child by fire. He practiced soothsaying and divination, and reintroduced the consulting of ghosts and spirits.

He did much evil in the LORD's sight and provoked him to anger. ⁷The Asherah idol he had made, he placed in the LORD's house, of which the LORD had said to David and to his son Solomon: In this house and in Jerusalem, which I have chosen out of all the tribes of Israel, I shall set my name forever. ⁸I will no longer make Israel step out of the land I gave their ancestors, provided that they are careful to observe all I have commanded them and the entire law which Moses my servant enjoined upon them. ⁹But they did not listen.

Manasseh misled them into doing even greater evil than the nations the LORD had destroyed at the coming of the Israelites. ¹⁰Then the LORD spoke through his servants the prophets: ¹¹"Because Manasseh, king of Judah, has practiced these abominations, and has done greater evil than all that was done by the Amorites before him, and has led Judah into sin by his idols, ¹²therefore, thus says the LORD, the God of Israel: I am about to bring such evil on Jerusalem and Judah that, when any hear of it, their ears shall ring: ¹³I will measure Jerusalem with the same cord as I did Samaria, and with the plummet I used for the house of Ahab. I will wipe Jerusalem clean as one wipes a dish, wiping it inside and out. ¹⁴I will cast off the survivors of my inheritance. I will deliver them into enemy hands, to become prey and booty for all their enemies, ¹⁵because they have done what is evil in my sight and provoked me from the day their ancestors came forth from Egypt until this very day." ¹⁶Manasseh shed so much innocent blood that it filled the length and breadth of Jerusalem, in addition to the sin he caused Judah to commit by doing what was evil in the LORD's sight.

¹⁷The rest of the acts of Manasseh, with all that he did and the sin he committed, are recorded in the book of the chronicles of the kings of Judah. ¹⁸Manasseh rested with his ancestors; he was buried in his palace garden, the garden of Uzza, and his son Amon succeeded him as king.

Reign of Amon. ¹⁹Amon was twenty-two years old when he became king, and he reigned two years in Jerusalem. His mother's name was Meshullemeth, daughter of Haruz, from Jotbah.

²⁰He did what was evil in the LORD's sight, as his father Manasseh had done. ²¹He walked in all the ways of his father; he served the idols his father had served, and bowed down to them. ²²He abandoned the LORD, the God of his ancestors, and did not walk in the way of the LORD.

²³Officials of Amon plotted against him and killed the king in his palace, ²⁴but the people of the land then slew all who had plotted against King Amon, and the people of the land made his son Josiah king in his stead. ²⁵The rest of the acts of Amon, which he did, are recorded in the book of the chronicles of the kings of Judah. ²⁶He was buried in his own grave in the garden of Uzza, and his son Josiah succeeded him as king.

Reign of Josiah. 22:1 Josiah was eight years old when he became king, and he reigned thirty-one years in Jerusalem. His mother's name was Jedidah, daughter of Adaiah, from Bozkath.

²He did what was right in the LORD's sight, walking in the way of David his father, not turning right or left.

The Book of the Law. ³In his eighteenth year, King Josiah sent the scribe Shaphan, son of Azaliah, son of Meshullam, to the house of the LORD with these orders: ⁴"Go to the high priest Hilkiah and have him calculate the valuables that have been brought to the house of the LORD, which the doorkeepers have collected from the people. ⁵Then have him turn them over to the master workers in the house of the

LORD, and have them give them to the ordinary workers who are in the house of the LORD to repair its breaches: [6]to the carpenters, the builders, and the masons, and to purchase wood and hewn stone. [7]No reckoning shall be asked of them regarding the funds provided to them, because they hold positions of trust."

[8]The high priest Hilkiah informed the scribe Shaphan, "I have found the book of the law in the temple of the LORD." Hilkiah gave the book to Shaphan, who read it. [9]Then the scribe Shaphan went to the king and reported, "Your servants have smelted down the silver deposited in the temple and have turned it over to the master workers in the house of the LORD." [10]The scribe Shaphan also informed the king, "Hilkiah the priest has given me a book," and then Shaphan read it in the presence of the king. [11]When the king heard the words of the book of the law, he tore his garments.

[12]The king then issued this command to Hilkiah the priest, Ahikam, son of Shaphan, Achbor, son of Micaiah, Shaphan the scribe, and Asaiah the king's servant: [13]"Go, consult the LORD for me, for the people, and for all Judah, about the words of this book that has been found, for the rage of the LORD has been set furiously ablaze against us, because our ancestors did not obey the words of this book, nor do what is written for us." [14]So Hilkiah the priest, Ahikam, Achbor, Shaphan, and Asaiah went to Huldah the prophet, wife of Shallum, son of Tikvah, son of Harhas, keeper of the wardrobe; she lived in Jerusalem, in the Second Quarter. When they had spoken to her, [15]she said to them, "Thus says the LORD, the God of Israel: Say to the man who sent you to me, [16]Thus says the LORD: I am about to bring evil upon this place and upon its inhabitants—all the words of the book which the king of Judah has read. [17]Because they have abandoned me and have burned incense to other gods, provoking me by all the works of their hands, my rage is ablaze against this place and it cannot be extinguished.

[18]"But to the king of Judah who sent you to consult the LORD, give this response: Thus says the LORD, the God of Israel: As for the words you have heard, [19]because you were heartsick and have humbled yourself before the LORD when you heard what I have spoken concerning this place and its inhabitants, that they would become a desolation and a curse; and because you tore your garments and wept before me, I in turn have heard, oracle of the LORD. [20]I will therefore gather you to your ancestors; you shall go to your grave in peace, and your eyes shall not see all the evil I am about to bring upon this place." This they reported to the king.

23:1 The king then had all the elders of Judah and of Jerusalem summoned before him. [2]The king went up to the house of the LORD with all the people of Judah and all the inhabitants of Jerusalem: priests, prophets, and all the people, great and small. He read aloud to them all the words of the book of the covenant that had been found in the house of the LORD. [3]The king stood by the column and made a covenant in the presence of the LORD to follow the LORD and to observe his commandments, statutes, and decrees with his whole heart and soul, and to re-establish the words of the covenant written in this book. And all the people stood by the covenant.

Josiah's Religious Reform. [4]Then the king commanded the high priest Hilkiah, his assistant priests, and the doorkeepers to remove from the temple of the LORD all the objects that had been made for Baal, Asherah, and the whole host of heaven. These he burned outside Jerusalem on the slopes of the Kidron; their ashes were carried to Bethel. [5]He also put an end to the idolatrous priests whom the kings of Judah had appointed to burn incense on the high places in the cities of Judah and in the vicinity of Jerusalem, as well as those who burned incense to Baal, to the sun, moon, and signs of the zodiac, and to the whole host of heaven. [6]From the house of the LORD he also removed the Asherah to the Wadi Kidron, outside Jerusalem; he burned it and beat it to dust, in the Wadi Kidron, and scattered its dust over the graveyard of the people of the land. [7]He tore down the apartments of the cult prostitutes in the house of the LORD, where the women wove garments for the Asherah. [8]He brought in all the priests from the cities of Judah, and then defiled, from Geba to Beer-sheba, the high places where they had offered incense. He also tore down the high places of the gates, which were at the entrance of the Gate of Joshua, governor of the city, north of the city gate. [9](The priests of the high places could not function at the altar of the LORD in Jerusalem; but they, along with their relatives, ate the unleavened bread.)

[10]The king also defiled Topheth in the Valley of Ben-hinnom, so that there would no longer be any immolation of sons or daughters by fire in honor of Molech. [11]He did away with the horses which the kings of Judah had dedicated to the sun; these were at the entrance of the house of the LORD, near the chamber of Nathan-melech the official, which was in the large building. The chariots of the sun he destroyed by fire. [12]He also demolished the altars made by the kings of Judah on the roof (the roof terrace of Ahaz), and the altars made by Manasseh in the two courts of the LORD's house. He pulverized them and threw the dust into the Wadi Kidron. [13]The king defiled the high places east of Jerusalem, south of the Mount of the Destroyer, which Solomon, king of Israel, had built in honor of Astarte, the Sidonian horror, of Chemosh, the Moabite horror, and of Milcom, the Ammonites' abomination. [14]He broke to pieces the pillars, cut down the asherahs, and filled the places where they had been with human bones.

[15]Likewise the altar which was at Bethel, the high place built by Jeroboam, son of Nebat, who caused Israel to sin—this same altar and high place he tore down and burned, grinding the high place to powder and burning the asherah. [16]When Josiah turned and saw the graves there on the mountainside, he ordered the bones taken from the graves and burned on the altar, and thus defiled it, according to the LORD's word proclaimed by the man of God as Jeroboam stood by the altar on the feast day. When the king looked up and saw the grave of the man of God who had proclaimed these words, [17]he asked, "What is that marker I see?" The people of the city replied, "The grave of the man of God who came from Judah and proclaimed the very things you have done to the altar in Bethel." [18]"Let him be," he said, "let no one move his bones." So they left his bones undisturbed together with the bones of the prophet who had come from Samaria. [19]Josiah also removed all the temples on the high places in the cities of Samaria which the kings of Israel had built, provoking the LORD; he did the very same to them as he had done in Bethel. [20]He slaughtered upon the altars all the priests of the high places that were there, and burned human bones upon them. Then he returned to Jerusalem.

[21]The king issued a command to all the people: "Observe the Passover of the LORD, your God, as it is written in this book of the covenant." [22]No Passover such as this had been observed during the period when the judges ruled Israel, or during the entire period of the kings of Israel and the kings of Judah, [23]until the eighteenth year of King Josiah, when this Passover of the LORD was kept in Jerusalem.

[24]Further, Josiah purged the consultation of ghosts and spirits, with the household gods, idols, and all the other horrors to be seen in the land of Judah and in Jerusalem, so that he might carry out the words of the law that were written in the book

that Hilkiah the priest had found in the house of the LORD.

²⁵Before him there had been no king who turned to the LORD as he did, with his whole heart, his whole being, and his whole strength, in accord with the entire law of Moses; nor did any king like him arise after him. ²⁶Yet the LORD did not turn from his fiercely burning anger against Judah, because of all the provocations that Manasseh had given. ²⁷The LORD said: Even Judah will I put out of my sight as I did Israel. I will reject this city, Jerusalem, which I chose, and the house of which I said: There shall my name be.

²⁸The rest of the acts of Josiah, with all that he did, are recorded in the book of the chronicles of the kings of Judah. ²⁹In his time Pharaoh Neco, king of Egypt, went up toward the Euphrates River against the king of Assyria. King Josiah set out to meet him, but was slain at Megiddo at the first encounter. ³⁰His servants brought his body on a chariot from Megiddo to Jerusalem, where they buried him in his own grave. Then the people of the land took Jehoahaz, son of Josiah, anointed him, and proclaimed him king to succeed his father.

Reign of Jehoahaz. ³¹Jehoahaz was twenty-three years old when he became king, and he reigned three months in Jerusalem. His mother's name was Hamutal, daughter of Jeremiah, from Libnah. ³²He did what was evil in the LORD's sight, just as his ancestors had done. ³³Pharaoh Neco took him prisoner at Riblah in the land of Hamath, thus ending his reign in Jerusalem. He imposed a fine upon the land of a hundred talents of silver and a talent of gold. ³⁴Pharaoh Neco then made Eliakim, son of Josiah, king in place of Josiah his father; he changed his name to Jehoiakim. Jehoahaz he took away with him to Egypt, where he died. ³⁵Jehoiakim gave the silver and gold to Pharaoh, but taxed the land to raise the amount Pharaoh demanded. He exacted the silver and gold from the people of the land, from each proportionately, to pay Pharaoh Neco.

Reign of Jehoiakim. ³⁶Jehoiakim was twenty-five years old when he became king, and he reigned eleven years in Jerusalem. His mother's name was Zebidah, daughter of Pedaiah, from Rumah. ³⁷He did what was evil in the LORD's sight, just as his ancestors had done.

☐ MATTHEW 9:35–11:1

The Compassion of Jesus. 9:35 Jesus went around to all the towns and villages, teaching in their synagogues, proclaiming the gospel of the kingdom, and curing every disease and illness. ³⁶At the sight of the crowds, his heart was moved with pity for them because they were troubled and abandoned, like sheep without a shepherd. ³⁷Then he said to his disciples, "The harvest is abundant but the laborers are few; ³⁸so ask the master of the harvest to send out laborers for his harvest."

The Mission of the Twelve. 10:1 Then he summoned his twelve disciples and gave them authority over unclean spirits to drive them out and to cure every disease and every illness. ²The names of the twelve apostles are these: first, Simon called Peter, and his brother Andrew; James, the son of Zebedee, and his brother John; ³Philip and Bartholomew, Thomas and Matthew the tax collector; James, the son of Alphaeus, and Thaddeus; ⁴Simon the Cananean, and Judas Iscariot who betrayed him.

The Commissioning of the Twelve. ⁵Jesus sent out these twelve after instructing them thus, "Do not go into pagan territory or enter a Samaritan town. ⁶Go rather to the lost sheep of the house of Israel.

[7]As you go, make this proclamation: 'The kingdom of heaven is at hand.' [8]Cure the sick, raise the dead, cleanse lepers, drive out demons. Without cost you have received; without cost you are to give. [9]Do not take gold or silver or copper for your belts; [10]no sack for the journey, or a second tunic, or sandals, or walking stick. The laborer deserves his keep. [11]Whatever town or village you enter, look for a worthy person in it, and stay there until you leave. [12]As you enter a house, wish it peace. [13]If the house is worthy, let your peace come upon it; if not, let your peace return to you. [14]Whoever will not receive you or listen to your words—go outside that house or town and shake the dust from your feet. [15]Amen, I say to you, it will be more tolerable for the land of Sodom and Gomorrah on the day of judgment than for that town.

Coming Persecutions. [16]"Behold, I am sending you like sheep in the midst of wolves; so be shrewd as serpents and simple as doves. [17]But beware of people, for they will hand you over to courts and scourge you in their synagogues, [18]and you will be led before governors and kings for my sake as a witness before them and the pagans. [19]When they hand you over, do not worry about how you are to speak or what you are to say. You will be given at that moment what you are to say. [20]For it will not be you who speak but the Spirit of your Father speaking through you. [21]Brother will hand over brother to death, and the father his child; children will rise up against parents and have them put to death. [22]You will be hated by all because of my name, but whoever endures to the end will be saved. [23]When they persecute you in one town, flee to another. Amen, I say to you, you will not finish the towns of Israel before the Son of Man comes. [24]No disciple is above his teacher, no slave above his master. [25]It is enough for the disciple that he become like his teacher, for the slave that he become like his master. If they have called the master of the house Beelzebul, how much more those of his household!

Courage under Persecution. [26]"Therefore do not be afraid of them. Nothing is concealed that will not be revealed, nor secret that will not be known. [27]What I say to you in the darkness, speak in the light; what you hear whispered, proclaim on the housetops. [28]And do not be afraid of those who kill the body but cannot kill the soul; rather, be afraid of the one who can destroy both soul and body in Gehenna. [29]Are not two sparrows sold for a small coin? Yet not one of them falls to the ground without your Father's knowledge. [30]Even all the hairs of your head are counted. [31]So do not be afraid; you are worth more than many sparrows. [32]Everyone who acknowledges me before others I will acknowledge before my heavenly Father. [33]But whoever denies me before others, I will deny before my heavenly Father.

Jesus; A Cause of Division. [34]"Do not think that I have come to bring peace upon the earth. I have come to bring not peace but the sword. [35]For I have come to set

a man against his father,
  a daughter against her mother,
and a daughter-in-law against her
    mother-in-law;
  [36]and one's enemies will be those of
    his household.'

The Conditions of Discipleship. [37]"Whoever loves father or mother more than me is not worthy of me, and whoever loves son or daughter more than me is not worthy of me; [38]and whoever does not take up his cross and follow after me is not worthy of me. [39]Whoever finds his life will lose it, and whoever loses his life for my sake will find it.

Rewards. [40]"Whoever receives you receives me, and whoever receives me receives the one who sent me. [41]Whoever receives a prophet because he is a prophet will receive a prophet's reward, and whoever receives a righteous man because he is righteous will receive a righteous man's reward. [42]And whoever gives only a cup of cold water to one of these little ones to drink because he is a disciple—amen, I say to you, he will surely not lose his reward."

11:1 When Jesus finished giving these commands to his twelve disciples, he went away from that place to teach and to preach in their towns.

April 30

Blessed Marie of the Incarnation

We crush the head of the serpent when we scorn and trample underfoot the glory of the world, the praises, the vanities, and all the other pomps of pride.

— BLESSED MARIE OF THE INCARNATION

☐ 2 KINGS 24-25

24:1 During Jehoiakim's reign Nebuchadnezzar, king of Babylon, attacked, and Jehoiakim became his vassal for three years. Then Jehoiakim turned and rebelled against him. ²The LORD loosed against him bands of Chaldeans, Arameans, Moabites, and Ammonites; he unleashed them against Judah to destroy him, according to the LORD's word spoken through his servants the prophets. ³This befell Judah because the LORD had stated that he would put them out of his sight for the sins Manasseh had committed in all that he did, ⁴and especially because of the innocent blood he shed; he filled Jerusalem with innocent blood, and the LORD would not forgive.

⁵The rest of the acts of Jehoiakim, with all that he did, are recorded in the book of the chronicles of the kings of Judah. ⁶Jehoiakim rested with his ancestors, and his son Jehoiachin succeeded him as king. ⁷The king of Egypt did not again leave his own land, for the king of Babylon had taken all that belonged to the king of Egypt from the wadi of Egypt to the Euphrates River.

Reign of Jehoiachin. ⁸Jehoiachin was eighteen years old when he became king, and he reigned three months in Jerusalem.

His mother's name was Nehushta, daughter of Elnathan, from Jerusalem.

⁹He did what was evil in the LORD's sight, just as his father had done.

¹⁰At that time officers of Nebuchadnezzar, king of Babylon, attacked Jerusalem, and the city came under siege. ¹¹Nebuchadnezzar, king of Babylon, himself arrived at the city while his officers were besieging it. ¹²Then Jehoiachin, king of Judah, together with his mother, his ministers, officers, and functionaries, surrendered to the king of Babylon, who, in the eighth year of his reign, took him captive. ¹³He carried off all the treasures of the house of the LORD and the treasures of the king's house, and broke up all the gold utensils that Solomon, king of Israel, had provided in the house of the LORD, as the LORD had decreed. ¹⁴He deported all Jerusalem: all the officers and warriors of the army, ten thousand in number, and all the artisans and smiths. Only the lowliest of the people of the land were left. ¹⁵He deported Jehoiachin to Babylon, and the king's mother, his wives, his functionaries, and the chiefs of the land he led captive from Jerusalem to Babylon. ¹⁶All seven thousand soldiers of the army, and a thousand artisans and smiths, all of

them trained warriors, these too the king of Babylon brought captive to Babylon. [17]In place of Jehoiachin the king of Babylon made Mattaniah, Jehoiachin's uncle, king; he changed his name to Zedekiah.

Reign of Zedekiah. [18]Zedekiah was twenty-one years old when he became king, and he reigned eleven years in Jerusalem. His mother's name was Hamutal, daughter of Jeremiah, from Libnah.

[19]He did what was evil in the sight of the LORD, just as Jehoiakim had done. [20]This befell Jerusalem and Judah because the LORD was so angry that he cast them out of his sight.

Zedekiah rebelled against the king of Babylon.

25:1 In the tenth month of the ninth year of Zedekiah's reign, on the tenth day of the month, Nebuchadnezzar, king of Babylon, and his whole army advanced against Jerusalem, encamped around it, and built siege walls on every side. [2]The siege of the city continued until the eleventh year of Zedekiah. [3]On the ninth day of the month, when famine had gripped the city, and the people of the land had no more food, [4]the city walls were breached. That night, all the soldiers came to the gate between the two walls near the king's garden (the Chaldeans had the city surrounded), while the king went toward the Arabah. [5]But the Chaldean army pursued the king and overtook him in the desert near Jericho, abandoned by his whole army. [6]The king was therefore arrested and brought to Riblah to the king of Babylon, who pronounced sentence on him. [7]They slew Zedekiah's sons before his eyes; then they put out his eyes, bound him with fetters, and brought him to Babylon.

[8]On the seventh day of the fifth month (this was in the nineteenth year of Nebuchadnezzar, king of Babylon), Nebuzaradan, captain of the bodyguard, came to Jerusalem as the agent of the king of Babylon. [9]He burned the house of the LORD, the house of the king, and all the houses of Jerusalem (every noble house); he destroyed them by fire. [10]The Chaldean troops who were with the captain of the guard tore down the walls that surrounded Jerusalem, [11]and Nebuzaradan, captain of the guard, led into exile the last of the army remaining in the city, and those who had deserted to the king of Babylon, and the last of the commoners. [12]But some of the country's poor the captain of the guard left behind as vinedressers and farmers.

[13]The bronze columns that belonged to the house of the LORD, and the stands and the bronze sea in the house of the LORD, the Chaldeans broke into pieces; they carried away the bronze to Babylon. [14]They took also the pots, the shovels, the snuffers, the cups and all the bronze articles used for service. [15]The fire pans and the bowls that were of solid gold or silver the captain of the guard also carried off. [16]The two columns, the one bronze sea, and the stands, which Solomon had made for the house of the LORD—the weight in bronze of all these articles was never calculated. [17]Each of the columns was eighteen cubits high; a bronze capital three cubits high surmounted each column, and a netting with pomegranates encircled the capital, all of bronze; and they were duplicated on the other column, on the netting.

[18]The captain of the guard also took Seraiah, the chief priest, Zephaniah, an assistant priest, and the three doorkeepers. [19]And from the city he took one officer who was a commander of soldiers, five courtiers in the personal service of the king who were still in the city, the scribe in charge of the army who mustered the people of the land, and sixty of the people of the land still remaining in the city. [20]The captain of the guard, Nebuzaradan, arrested these and brought them to the king of Babylon at Riblah, and [21]the king of Babylon struck them down and put them to death in Riblah, in the land of Hamath.

And thus Judah went into exile from their native soil.

Governorship of Gedaliah. ²²As for the people whom he had allowed to remain in the land of Judah, Nebuchadnezzar, king of Babylon, appointed Gedaliah, son of Ahikam, son of Shaphan, over them. ²³Hearing that the king of Babylon had appointed Gedaliah over them, all the army commanders and the troops came to him at Mizpah: Ishmael, son of Nethaniah, Johanan, son of Kareah, Seraiah, son of Tanhumeth the Netophathite, and Jaazaniah, son of the Maakite, each with his troops. ²⁴Gedaliah gave the commanders and their troops his oath. He said to them, "Do not be afraid of the Chaldean officials. Remain in the country and serve the king of Babylon, so that all will be well with you."

²⁵But in the seventh month Ishmael, son of Nethaniah, son of Elishama, of royal descent, came with ten others, attacked Gedaliah and killed him, along with the Judahites and Chaldeans who were in Mizpah with him. ²⁶Then all the people, great and small, left with the army commanders and went to Egypt for fear of the Chaldeans.

Release of Jehoiachin. ²⁷In the thirty-seventh year of the exile of Jehoiachin, king of Judah, on the twenty-seventh day of the twelfth month, Evil-merodach, king of Babylon, in the inaugural year of his own reign, raised up Jehoiachin, king of Judah, from prison. ²⁸He spoke kindly to him and gave him a throne higher than that of the other kings who were with him in Babylon. ²⁹Jehoiachin took off his prison garb; he ate regularly in the king's presence as long as he lived; ³⁰and for his allowance the king granted him a regular allowance, in fixed daily amounts, for as long as he lived.

☐ MATTHEW 11:2-24

The Messengers from John the Baptist. **11:2** When John heard in prison of the works of the Messiah, he sent his disciples to him ³with this question, "Are you the one who is to come, or should we look for another?" ⁴Jesus said to them in reply, "Go and tell John what you hear and see: ⁵the blind regain their sight, the lame walk, lepers are cleansed, the deaf hear, the dead are raised, and the poor have the good news proclaimed to them. ⁶And blessed is the one who takes no offense at me."

Jesus' Testimony to John. ⁷As they were going off, Jesus began to speak to the crowds about John, "What did you go out to the desert to see? A reed swayed by the wind? ⁸Then what did you go out to see? Someone dressed in fine clothing? Those who wear fine clothing are in royal palaces. ⁹Then why did you go out? To see a prophet? Yes, I tell you, and more than a prophet. ¹⁰This is the one about whom it is written:

'Behold, I am sending my messenger
  ahead of you;
he will prepare your way before
  you.'

¹¹Amen, I say to you, among those born of women there has been none greater than John the Baptist; yet the least in the kingdom of heaven is greater than he. ¹²From the days of John the Baptist until now, the kingdom of heaven suffers violence, and the violent are taking it by force. ¹³All the prophets and the law prophesied up to the time of John. ¹⁴And if you are willing to accept it, he is Elijah, the one who is to come. ¹⁵Whoever has ears ought to hear.

¹⁶"To what shall I compare this generation? It is like children who sit in marketplaces and call to one another, ¹⁷'We played

the flute for you, but you did not dance, we sang a dirge but you did not mourn.' [18]For John came neither eating nor drinking, and they said, 'He is possessed by a demon.' [19]The Son of Man came eating and drinking and they said, 'Look, he is a glutton and a drunkard, a friend of tax collectors and sinners.' But wisdom is vindicated by her works."

Reproaches to Unrepentant Towns. [20]Then he began to reproach the towns where most of his mighty deeds had been done, since they had not repented. [21]"Woe to you, Chorazin! Woe to you, Bethsaida! For if the mighty deeds done in your midst had been done in Tyre and Sidon, they would long ago have repented in sackcloth and ashes. [22]But I tell you, it will be more tolerable for Tyre and Sidon on the day of judgment than for you. [23]And as for you, Capernaum:

'Will you be exalted to heaven?
You will go down to the
netherworld.'

For if the mighty deeds done in your midst had been done in Sodom, it would have remained until this day. [24]But I tell you, it will be more tolerable for the land of Sodom on the day of judgment than for you."

St. Joseph the Worker

Without work, it's impossible to have fun.
— St. Thomas Aquinas

☐ 1 CHRONICLES 1-3

From Adam to Abraham. 1:1 Adam, Seth, Enosh, ²Kenan, Mahalalel, Jared, ³Enoch, Methuselah, Lamech, ⁴Noah, Shem, Ham, and Japheth. ⁵The sons of Japheth were Gomer, Magog, Madai, Javan, Tubal, Meshech, and Tiras. ⁶The sons of Gomer were Ashkenaz, Riphath, and Togarmah. ⁷The sons of Javan were Elishah, Tarshish, the Kittim, and the Rodanim.

⁸The sons of Ham were Cush, Mizraim, Put, and Canaan. ⁹The sons of Cush were Seba, Havilah, Sabta, Raama, and Sabteca. The sons of Raama were Sheba and Dedan. ¹⁰Cush became the father of Nimrod, who was the first to be a warrior on the earth. ¹¹Mizraim became the father of the Ludim, Anamim, Lehabim, Naphtuhim, ¹²Pathrusim, Casluhim, and Caphtorim, from whom the Philistines sprang. ¹³Canaan became the father of Sidon, his firstborn, and Heth, ¹⁴and the Jebusites, the Amorites, the Girgashites, ¹⁵the Hivites, the Arkites, the Sinites, ¹⁶the Arvadites, the Zemarites, and the Hamathites.

¹⁷The sons of Shem were Elam, Asshur, Arpachshad, Lud, and Aram. The sons of Aram were Uz, Hul, Gether, and Mash. ¹⁸Arpachshad became the father of Shelah, and Shelah became the father of Eber. ¹⁹Two sons were born to Eber; the first was named Peleg (for in his time the world was divided), and his brother was named Joktan. ²⁰Joktan became the father of Almodad, Sheleph, Hazarmaveth, Jerah, ²¹Hadoram, Uzal, Diklah, ²²Ebal, Abimael, Sheba, ²³Ophir, Havilah, and Jobab; all these were the sons of Joktan.

²⁴Shem, Arpachshad, Shelah, ²⁵Eber, Peleg, Reu, ²⁶Serug, Nahor, Terah, ²⁷Abram, that is, Abraham.

From Abraham to Jacob. ²⁸The sons of Abraham were Isaac and Ishmael. ²⁹These were their generations:

Nebaioth, the firstborn of Ishmael, then Kedar, Adbeel, Mibsam, ³⁰Mishma, Dumah, Massa, Hadad, Tema, ³¹Jetur, Naphish, and Kedemah. These were the sons of Ishmael.

³²The sons of Keturah, Abraham's concubine: she bore Zimran, Jokshan, Medan, Midian, Ishbak, and Shuah. The sons of Jokshan were Sheba and Dedan. ³³The sons of Midian were Ephah, Epher, Hanoch, Abida, and Eldaah. All these were the sons of Keturah.

³⁴Abraham begot Isaac. The sons of Isaac were Esau and Israel.

³⁵The descendants of Esau were Eliphaz, Reuel, Jeush, Jalam, and Korah. ³⁶The descendants of Eliphaz were Teman, Omar, Zephi, Gatam, Kenaz, Timna, and Amalek. ³⁷The descendants of Reuel were Nahath, Zerah, Shammah, and Mizzah.

³⁸The sons of Seir were Lotan, Shobal, Zibeon, Anah, Dishon, Ezer, and Dishan. ³⁹The sons of Lotan were Hori and Homam; Timna was the sister of Lotan. ⁴⁰The sons of Shobal were Alian, Manahath, Ebal, Shephi, and Onam. The sons of Zibeon were Aiah and Anah. ⁴¹The sons of Anah: Dishon. The sons of Dishon were Hemdan, Eshban, Ithran, and Cheran. ⁴²The sons of Ezer were Bilhan, Zaavan, and Jaakan. The sons of Dishan were Uz and Aran.

⁴³The kings who reigned in the land of Edom before the Israelites had kings were the following: Bela, son of Beor, the name of whose city was Dinhabah. ⁴⁴When Bela

died, Jobab, son of Zerah, from Bozrah, succeeded him as king. ⁴⁵When Jobab died, Husham, from the land of the Temanites, succeeded him as king. ⁴⁶Husham died and Hadad, son of Bedad, succeeded him as king. He overthrew the Midianites on the Moabite plateau, and the name of his city was Avith. ⁴⁷Hadad died and Samlah of Masrekah succeeded him as king. ⁴⁸Samlah died and Shaul from Rehoboth on the Euphrates succeeded him as king. ⁴⁹When Shaul died, Baalhanan, son of Achbor, succeeded him as king. ⁵⁰Baalhanan died and Hadad succeeded him as king. The name of his city was Pai, and his wife's name was Mehetabel. She was the daughter of Matred, who was the daughter of Mezahab. ⁵¹After Hadad died, there were chiefs in Edom: the chiefs of Timna, Aliah, Jetheth, ⁵²Oholibamah, Elah, Pinon, ⁵³Kenaz, Teman, Mibzar, ⁵⁴Magdiel, and Iram were the chiefs of Edom.

2:1 These were the sons of Israel: Reuben, Simeon, Levi, Judah, Issachar, Zebulun, ²Dan, Joseph, Benjamin, Naphtali, Gad, and Asher.

Judah. ³The sons of Judah were: Er, Onan, and Shelah; these three Bathshua, a Canaanite woman, bore to him. But Judah's firstborn, Er, was wicked in the sight of the LORD, so he took his life. ⁴Judah's daughter-in-law Tamar bore him Perez and Zerah, so that he had five sons in all.

⁵The sons of Perez were Hezron and Hamul. ⁶The sons of Zerah were Zimri, Ethan, Heman, Calcol, and Darda—five in all. ⁷The sons of Zimri: Carmi. The sons of Carmi: Achar, who brought trouble upon Israel by violating the ban. ⁸The sons of Ethan: Azariah. ⁹The sons born to Hezron were Jerahmeel, Ram, and Chelubai.

¹⁰Ram became the father of Amminadab, and Amminadab became the father of Nahshon, a prince of the Judahites. ¹¹Nahshon became the father of Salmah. Salmah became the father of Boaz. ¹²Boaz became the father of Obed. Obed became the father of Jesse. ¹³Jesse became the father of Eliab, his firstborn, of Abinadab, the second son, Shimea, the third, ¹⁴Nethanel, the fourth, Raddai, the fifth, ¹⁵Ozem, the sixth, and David, the seventh. ¹⁶Their sisters were Zeruiah and Abigail. Zeruiah had three sons: Abishai, Joab, and Asahel. ¹⁷Abigail bore Amasa, whose father was Jether the Ishmaelite.

¹⁸By his wife Azubah, Caleb, son of Hezron, became the father of a daughter, Jerioth. Her sons were Jesher, Shobab, and Ardon. ¹⁹When Azubah died, Caleb married Ephrath, who bore him Hur. ²⁰Hur became the father of Uri, and Uri became the father of Bezalel. ²¹Then Hezron had relations with the daughter of Machir, the father of Gilead, whom he married when he was sixty years old. She bore him Segub. ²²Segub became the father of Jair, who possessed twenty-three cities in the land of Gilead. ²³Geshur and Aram took from them the villages of Jair, that is, Kenath and its towns, sixty cities in all, which had belonged to the sons of Machir, the father of Gilead. ²⁴After the death of Hezron, Caleb had relations with Ephrathah, the widow of his father Hezron, and she bore him Ashhur, the father of Tekoa.

²⁵The sons of Jerahmeel, the firstborn of Hezron, were Ram, the firstborn, then Bunah, Oren, and Ozem, his brothers. ²⁶Jerahmeel also had another wife, named Atarah, who was the mother of Onam. ²⁷The sons of Ram, the firstborn of Jerahmeel, were Maaz, Jamin, and Eker. ²⁸The sons of Onam were Shammai and Jada. The sons of Shammai were Nadab and Abishur. ²⁹Abishur's wife, who was named Abihail, bore him Ahban and Molid. ³⁰The sons of Nadab were Seled and Appaim. Seled died childless. ³¹The sons of Appaim: Ishi. The sons of Ishi: Sheshan. The sons of Sheshan: Ahlai. ³²The sons of Jada, the brother of Shammai, were Jether and Jonathan. Jether died childless. ³³The sons

of Jonathan were Peleth and Zaza. These were the sons of Jerahmeel. ³⁴Sheshan had no sons, only daughters; he had an Egyptian slave named Jarha. ³⁵Sheshan gave his daughter in marriage to his slave Jarha, and she bore him Attai. ³⁶Attai became the father of Nathan. Nathan became the father of Zabad. ³⁷Zabad became the father of Ephlal. Ephlal became the father of Obed. ³⁸Obed became the father of Jehu. Jehu became the father of Azariah. ³⁹Azariah became the father of Helez. Helez became the father of Eleasah. ⁴⁰Eleasah became the father of Sismai. Sismai became the father of Shallum. ⁴¹Shallum became the father of Jekamiah. Jekamiah became the father of Elishama.

⁴²The sons of Caleb, the brother of Jerahmeel: Mesha his firstborn, who was the father of Ziph. Then the sons of Mareshah, who was the father of Hebron. ⁴³The sons of Hebron were Korah, Tappuah, Rekem, and Shema. ⁴⁴Shema became the father of Raham, who was the father of Jorkeam. Rekem became the father of Shammai. ⁴⁵The son of Shammai: Maon, who was the father of Beth-zur. ⁴⁶Ephah, Caleb's concubine, bore Haran, Moza, and Gazez. Haran became the father of Gazez. ⁴⁷The sons of Jahdai were Regem, Jotham, Geshan, Pelet, Ephah, and Shaaph. ⁴⁸Maacah, Caleb's concubine, bore Sheber and Tirhanah. ⁴⁹She also bore Shaaph, the father of Madmannah, Sheva, the father of Machbenah, and the father of Gibea. Achsah was Caleb's daughter.

⁵⁰These were sons of Caleb, sons of Hur, the firstborn of Ephrathah: Shobal, the father of Kiriath-jearim, ⁵¹Salma, the father of Bethlehem, and Hareph, the father of Bethgader. ⁵²The sons of Shobal, the father of Kiriath-jearim, were Reaiah, half of the Manahathites, ⁵³and the clans of Kiriath-jearim: the Ithrites, the Puthites, the Shumathites, and the Mishraites. From these the Zorahites and the Eshtaolites derived. ⁵⁴The sons of Salma were Bethlehem, the Netophathites, Atroth-beth-Joab, half of the Manahathites, and the Zorites. ⁵⁵The clans of the Sopherim dwelling in Jabez were the Tirathites, the Shimeathites, and the Sucathites. They were the Kenites, who descended from Hammath, the ancestor of the Rechabites.

3:1 These were the sons of David born to him in Hebron: the firstborn, Amnon, by Ahinoam of Jezreel; the second, Daniel, by Abigail of Carmel; ²the third, Absalom, son of Maacah, who was the daughter of Talmai, king of Geshur; the fourth, Adonijah, son of Haggith; ³the fifth, Shephatiah, by Abital; the sixth, Ithream, by his wife Eglah. ⁴Six in all were born to him in Hebron, where he reigned seven years and six months. Then he reigned thirty-three years in Jerusalem. ⁵In Jerusalem the following were born to him: Shimea, Shobab, Nathan, Solomon—four by Bathsheba, the daughter of Ammiel; ⁶Ibhar, Elishua, Eliphelet, ⁷Nogah, Nepheg, Japhia, ⁸Elishama, Eliada, and Eliphelet—nine. ⁹All these were sons of David, in addition to other sons by concubines; and Tamar was their sister.

¹⁰The son of Solomon was Rehoboam, whose son was Abijah, whose son was Asa, whose son was Jehoshaphat, ¹¹whose son was Joram, whose son was Ahaziah, whose son was Joash, ¹²whose son was Amaziah, whose son was Azariah, whose son was Jotham, ¹³whose son was Ahaz, whose son was Hezekiah, whose son was Manasseh, ¹⁴whose son was Amon, whose son was Josiah. ¹⁵The sons of Josiah were: the firstborn Johanan; the second, Jehoiakim; the third, Zedekiah; the fourth, Shallum. ¹⁶The sons of Jehoiakim were: Jeconiah, his son; Zedekiah, his son.

¹⁷The sons of Jeconiah the captive were: Shealtiel, ¹⁸Malchiram, Pedaiah, Shenazzar, Jekamiah, Hoshama, and Nedabiah. ¹⁹The sons of Pedaiah were Zerubbabel and Shimei. The sons of Zerubbabel were

Meshullam and Hananiah; Shelomith was their sister. [20]The sons of Meshullam were Hashubah, Ohel, Berechiah, Hasadiah, Jushabhesed—five. [21]The sons of Hananiah were Pelatiah, Jeshaiah, Rephaiah, Arnan, Obadiah, and Shecaniah. [22]The sons of Shecaniah were Shemaiah, Hattush, Igal, Bariah, Neariah, Shaphat—six. [23]The sons of Neariah were Elioenai, Hizkiah, and Azrikam—three. [24]The sons of Elioenai were Hodaviah, Eliashib, Pelaiah, Akkub, Johanan, Delaiah, and Anani—seven.

☐ MATTHEW 11:25-30

The Praise of the Father. 11:25 At that time Jesus said in reply, "I give praise to you, Father, Lord of heaven and earth, for although you have hidden these things from the wise and the learned you have revealed them to the childlike. [26]Yes, Father, such has been your gracious will. [27]All things have been handed over to me by my Father. No one knows the Son except the Father, and no one knows the Father except the Son and anyone to whom the Son wishes to reveal him.

The Gentle Mastery of Christ. [28]"Come to me, all you who labor and are burdened, and I will give you rest. [29]Take my yoke upon you and learn from me, for I am meek and humble of heart; and you will find rest for your selves. [30]For my yoke is easy, and my burden light."

May 2

St. Athanasius

If we were to think each day that we had to die that day, we would never sin at all. If in the morning we imagined that we would never last till evening, and if at evening we thought that we would never see morning, we would never sin.

— St. Athanasius

☐ 1 CHRONICLES 4-6

4:1 The sons of Judah were: Perez, Hezron, Carmi, Hur, and Shobal. [2]Reaiah, the son of Shobal, became the father of Jahath, and Jahath became the father of Ahumai and Lahad. These were the clans of the Zorathites.

[3]These were the sons of Hareph, the father of Etam: Jezreel, Ishma, and Idbash; their sister was named Hazzelelponi. [4]Penuel was the father of Gedor, and Ezer the father of Hushah. These were the sons of Hur, the firstborn of Ephrathah, the father of Bethlehem.

[5]Ashhur, the father of Tekoa, had two wives, Helah and Naarah. [6]Naarah bore him Ahuzzam, Hepher, the Temenites, and the Ahashtarites. These were the sons of Naarah. [7]The sons of Helah were Zereth, Izhar, Ethnan, and Koz. [8]Koz became the father of Anub and Zobebah, as well as of the clans of Aharhel, son of Harum. [9]Jabez was the most distinguished of his brothers. His mother had named him Jabez, saying, "I bore him with pain." [10]Jabez prayed to the God of Israel: "Oh, that you may truly

bless me and extend my boundaries! May your hand be with me and make me free of misfortune, without pain!" And God granted his prayer.

[11]Chelub, the brother of Shuhah, became the father of Mehir, who was the father of Eshton. [12]Eshton became the father of Bethrapha, Paseah, and Tehinnah, the father of the city of Nahash. These were the men of Recah.

[13]The sons of Kenaz were Othniel and Seraiah. The sons of Othniel were Hathath and Meonothai; [14]Meonothai became the father of Ophrah. Seraiah became the father of Joab, the father of Geharashim, so called because they were artisans. [15]The sons of Caleb, son of Jephunneh, were Ir, Elah, and Naam. The sons of Elah: Kenaz. [16]The sons of Jehallelel were Ziph, Ziphah, Tiria, and Asarel. [17]The sons of Ezrah were Jether, Mered, Epher, and Jalon. Jether became the father of Miriam, Shammai, and Ishbah, the father of Eshtemoa. [18]Mered's Egyptian wife bore Jered, the father of Gedor, Heber, the father of Soco, and Jekuthiel, the father of Zanoah. These were the sons of Bithiah, the daughter of Pharaoh, whom Mered married. [19]The sons of his Jewish wife, the sister of Naham, the father of Keilah, were Shimon the Garmite and Ishi the Maacathite. [20]The sons of Shimon were Amnon, Rinnah, Benhanan, and Tilon. The son of Ishi was Zoheth and the son of Zoheth....

[21]The sons of Shelah, son of Judah, were: Er, the father of Lecah; Laadah, the father of Mareshah; the clans of the linen weavers' guild in Bethashbea; [22]Jokim; the people of Cozeba; and Joash and Saraph, who held property in Moab, but returned to Bethlehem. (These are events of old.) [23]They were potters and inhabitants of Netaim and Gederah, where they lived in the king's service.

Simeon. [24]The sons of Simeon were Nemuel, Jamin, Jachin, Zerah, and Shaul, [25]whose son was Shallum, whose son was Mibsam, whose son was Mishma. [26]The sons of Mishma were his son Hammuel, whose son was Zaccur, whose son was Shimei. [27]Shimei had sixteen sons and six daughters. His brothers, however, did not have many sons, and as a result all their clans did not equal the number of the Judahites.

[28]They dwelt in Beer-sheba, Moladah, Hazar-shual, [29]Bilhah, Ezem, Tolad, [30]Bethuel, Hormah, Ziklag, [31]Beth-marcaboth, Hazar-susim, Bethbiri, and Shaaraim. Until the reign of David, these were their cities [32]and their villages. Etam, also, and Ain, Rimmon, Tochen, and Ashan—five cities, [33]together with all their outlying villages as far as Baal. Here is where they dwelt, and so it was inscribed of them in their family records.

[34]Meshobab, Jamlech, Joshah, son of Amaziah, [35]Joel, Jehu, son of Joshibiah, son of Seraiah, son of Asiel, [36]Elioenai, Jaakobah, Jeshohaiah, Asaiah, Adiel, Jesimiel, Benaiah, [37]Ziza, son of Shiphi, son of Allon, son of Jedaiah, son of Shimri, son of Shemaiah— [38]these just named were princes in their clans, and their ancestral houses spread out to such an extent [39]that they went to the approaches of Gedor, east of the valley, seeking pasture for their flocks. [40]They found abundant and good pastures, and the land was spacious, quiet, and peaceful—for the Hamites dwelt there formerly. [41]They who have just been listed by name set out during the reign of Hezekiah, king of Judah, and attacked their tents and also the Meunites who were there. They put them under the ban that is still in force to this day and dwelt in their place because they found pasture there for their flocks.

[42]Five hundred of them (the Simeonites) went to Mount Seir, with Pelatiah, Neariah, Rephaiah, and Uzziel, sons of Ishi, at their head. [43]They attacked the surviving Amalekites who had escaped, and have lived there to the present day.

Reuben. 5:1 The sons of Reuben, the first-born of Israel. (He was indeed the first-born, but because he defiled the couch of his father his birthright was given to the sons of Joseph, son of Israel, so that he is not listed in the family records according to his birthright. [2]Judah, in fact, became powerful among his brothers, so that the ruler came from him, though the birthright had been Joseph's.) [3]The sons of Reuben, the firstborn of Israel, were Hanoch, Pallu, Hezron, and Carmi. [4]His son was Joel, whose son was Shemaiah, whose son was Gog, whose son was Shimei, [5]whose son was Micah, whose son was Reaiah, whose son was Baal, [6]whose son was Beerah, whom Tilgath-pileser, the king of Assyria, took into exile; he was a prince of the Reubenites. [7]His brothers who belonged to his clans, when they were listed in the family records according to their descendants, were: Jeiel, the chief, and Zechariah, [8]and Bela, son of Azaz, son of Shema, son of Joel. The Reubenites lived in Aroer and as far as Nebo and Baal-meon; [9]toward the east they dwelt as far as the wilderness which extends from the Euphrates River, for they had much livestock in the land of Gilead. [10]In Saul's time they waged war with the Hagrites, and when they had defeated them they dwelt in their tents throughout the region east of Gilead.

Gad. [11]The Gadites lived alongside them in the land of Bashan as far as Salecah. [12]Joel was chief, Shapham was second in command, and Janai was judge in Bashan. [13]Their brothers, according to their ancestral houses, were: Michael, Meshullam, Sheba, Jorai, Jacan, Zia, and Eber—seven. [14]These were the sons of Abihail, son of Huri, son of Jaroah, son of Gilead, son of Michael, son of Jeshishai, son of Jahdo, son of Buz. [15]Ahi, son of Abdiel, son of Guni, was the head of their ancestral houses. [16]They dwelt in Gilead, in Bashan and its towns, and in all the pasture lands of Sirion to the borders. [17]All were listed in the family records in the time of Jotham, king of Judah, and of Jeroboam, king of Israel.

[18]The Reubenites, Gadites, and the half-tribe of Manasseh were warriors, men who bore shield and sword and who drew the bow, trained in warfare—forty-four thousand seven hundred and sixty men fit for military service. [19]When they waged war against the Hagrites and against Jetur, Naphish, and Nodab, [20]they received help so that the Hagrites and all who were with them were delivered into their power. For during the battle they cried out to God, and he heard them because they had put their trust in him. [21]Along with one hundred thousand persons they also captured their livestock: fifty thousand camels, two hundred fifty thousand sheep, and two thousand donkeys. [22]Many were slain and fell; for "From God the victory." They dwelt in their place until the time of the exile.

The Half-tribe of Manasseh. [23]The half-tribe of Manasseh lived in the land of Bashan as far as Baal-hermon, Senir, and Mount Hermon; they were numerous. [24]The following were the heads of their ancestral houses: Epher, Ishi, Eliel, Azriel, Jeremiah, Hodaviah, and Jahdiel—men who were warriors, famous men, and heads over their ancestral houses.

[25]However, they acted treacherously toward the God of their ancestors by prostituting themselves to follow the gods of the peoples of the land, whom God had destroyed before them. [26]Therefore the God of Israel stirred up against them the anger of Pul, king of Assyria, and the anger of Tilgath-pilneser [sic], king of Assyria, who deported the Reubenites, the Gadites, and the half-tribe of Manasseh and brought them to Halah, Habor, and Hara, and to the river Gozan, where they have remained to this day.

Levi. [27]The sons of Levi were Gershon, Kohath, and Merari. [28]The sons of Kohath were Amram, Izhar, Hebron, and Uzziel.

²⁹The children of Amram were Aaron, Moses, and Miriam. The sons of Aaron were Nadab, Abihu, Eleazar, and Ithamar. ³⁰Eleazar became the father of Phinehas. Phinehas became the father of Abishua. ³¹Abishua became the father of Bukki. Bukki became the father of Uzzi. ³²Uzzi became the father of Zerahiah. Zerahiah became the father of Meraioth. ³³Meraioth became the father of Amariah. Amariah became the father of Ahitub. ³⁴Ahitub became the father of Zadok. Zadok became the father of Ahimaaz. ³⁵Ahimaaz became the father of Azariah. Azariah became the father of Johanan. ³⁶Johanan became the father of Azariah, who served as priest in the temple Solomon built in Jerusalem. ³⁷Azariah became the father of Amariah. Amariah became the father of Ahitub. ³⁸Ahitub became the father of Zadok. Zadok became the father of Shallum. ³⁹Shallum became the father of Hilkiah. Hilkiah became the father of Azariah. ⁴⁰Azariah became the father of Seraiah. Seraiah became the father of Jehozadak. ⁴¹Jehozadak was one of those who went into the exile which the LORD inflicted on Judah and Jerusalem through Nebuchadnezzar.

6:1 The sons of Levi were Gershon, Kohath, and Merari. ²The sons of Gershon were named Libni and Shimei. ³The sons of Kohath were Amram, Izhar, Hebron, and Uzziel. ⁴The sons of Merari were Mahli and Mushi.

These were the clans of Levi, according to their ancestors. ⁵Of Gershon: his son Libni, whose son was Jahath, whose son was Zimmah, ⁶whose son was Joah, whose son was Iddo, whose son was Zerah, whose son was Jetherai.

⁷The sons of Kohath: his son Amminadab, whose son was Korah, whose son was Assir, ⁸whose son was Elkanah, whose son was Ebiasaph, whose son was Assir, ⁹whose son was Tahath, whose son was Uriel, whose son was Uzziah, whose son was Shaul. ¹⁰The sons of Elkanah were Amasai and Ahimoth, ¹¹whose son was Elkanah, whose son was Zophai, whose son was Nahath, ¹²whose son was Eliab, whose son was Jeroham, whose son was Elkanah, whose son was Samuel. ¹³The sons of Samuel were Joel, the firstborn, and Abijah, the second.

¹⁴The sons of Merari: Mahli, whose son was Libni, whose son was Shimei, whose son was Uzzah, ¹⁵whose son was Shimea, whose son was Haggiah, whose son was Asaiah.

¹⁶The following were established by David for the service of song in the LORD's house at the time when the ark had a resting place. ¹⁷They served as singers before the tabernacle of the tent of meeting until Solomon built the house of the LORD in Jerusalem, and they performed their services according to the order prescribed for them. ¹⁸Those who so performed are the following, together with their sons.

Among the Kohathites: Heman, the chanter, son of Joel, son of Samuel, ¹⁹son of Elkanah, son of Jeroham, son of Eliel, son of Toah, ²⁰son of Zuph, son of Elkanah, son of Mahath, son of Amasi, ²¹son of Elkanah, son of Joel, son of Azariah, son of Zephaniah, ²²son of Tahath, son of Assir, son of Ebiasaph, son of Korah, ²³son of Izhar, son of Kohath, son of Levi, son of Israel.

²⁴His brother Asaph stood at his right hand. Asaph was the son of Berechiah, son of Shimea, ²⁵son of Michael, son of Baaseiah, son of Malchijah, ²⁶son of Ethni, son of Zerah, son of Adaiah, ²⁷son of Ethan, son of Zimmah, son of Shimei, ²⁸son of Jahath, son of Gershon, son of Levi.

²⁹Their brothers, the Merarites, stood at the left: Ethan, son of Kishi, son of Abdi, son of Malluch, ³⁰son of Hashabiah, son of Amaziah, son of Hilkiah, ³¹son of Amzi, son of Bani, son of Shemer, ³²son of Mahli, son of Mushi, son of Merari, son of Levi.

³³Their brother Levites were appointed to all the other services of the tabernacle of the house of God. ³⁴However, it was Aaron

and his sons who made the sacrifice on the altar for burnt offerings and on the altar of incense; they alone had charge of the holy of holies and of making atonement for Israel, as Moses, the servant of God, had commanded.

[35]These were the sons of Aaron: his son Eleazar, whose son was Phinehas, whose son was Abishua, [36]whose son was Bukki, whose son was Uzzi, whose son was Zerahiah, [37]whose son was Meraioth, whose son was Amariah, whose son was Ahitub, [38]whose son was Zadok, whose son was Ahimaaz.

[39]The following were their dwelling places, by encampments in their territories. To the sons of Aaron who belonged to the clan of the Kohathites, since the lot fell to them, [40]was assigned Hebron in the land of Judah, with its adjacent pasture lands. [41]However, the open country and the villages belonging to the city had been given to Caleb, the son of Jephunneh. [42]There were assigned to the sons of Aaron: Hebron a city of refuge, Libnah with its pasture lands, Jattir with its pasture lands, Eshtemoa with its pasture lands, [43]Holon with its pasture lands, Debir with its pasture lands, [44]Ashan with its pasture lands, Jetta with its pasture lands, and Beth-shemesh with its pasture lands. [45]Also from the tribe of Benjamin: Gibeon with its pasture lands, Geba with its pasture lands, Almon with its pasture lands, Anathoth with its pasture lands. In all, they had thirteen cities with their pasture lands. [49]The Israelites assigned these cities with their pasture lands to the Levites, [50]designating them by name and assigning them by lot from the tribes of the Judahites, Simeonites, and Benjaminites.

[46]The other Kohathites obtained ten cities by lot for their clans from the tribe of Ephraim, from the tribe of Dan, and from the half-tribe of Manasseh. [47]The clans of the Gershonites obtained thirteen cities from the tribes of Issachar, Asher, and Naphtali, and from the half-tribe of Manasseh in Bashan. [48]The clans of the Merarites obtained twelve cities by lot from the tribes of Reuben, Gad, and Zebulun.

[51]The clans of the Kohathites obtained cities by lot from the tribe of Ephraim. [52]They were assigned cities of refuge: Shechem in the mountain region of Ephraim, with its pasture lands, Gezer with its pasture lands, [53]Kibzaim with its pasture lands, and Beth-horon with its pasture lands. [54]From the tribe of Dan: Elteke with its pasture lands, Gibbethon with its pasture lands, Aijalon with its pasture lands, and Gath-rimmon with its pasture lands. [55]From the half-tribe of Manasseh: Taanach with its pasture lands and Ibleam with its pasture lands. These belonged to the rest of the Kohathite clan.

[56]The clans of the Gershonites received from the half-tribe of Manasseh: Golan in Bashan with its pasture lands and Ashtaroth with its pasture lands. [57]From the tribe of Issachar: Kedesh with its pasture lands, Daberath with its pasture lands, [58]Ramoth with its pasture lands, and Engannim with its pasture lands. [59]From the tribe of Asher: Mashal with its pasture lands, Abdon with its pasture lands, [60]Hilkath with its pasture lands, and Rehob with its pasture lands. [61]From the tribe of Naphtali: Kedesh in Galilee with its pasture lands, Hammon with its pasture lands, and Kiriathaim with its pasture lands.

[62]The rest of the Merarites received from the tribe of Zebulun: Jokneam with its pasture lands, Kartah with its pasture lands, Rimmon with its pasture lands, and Tabor with its pasture lands. [63]Across the Jordan at Jericho (that is, east of the Jordan) they received from the tribe of Reuben: Bezer in the desert with its pasture lands, Jahzah with its pasture lands, [64]Kedemoth with its pasture lands, and Mephaath with its pasture lands. [65]From the tribe of Gad: Ramoth in Gilead with its pasture lands, Mahanaim with its pasture lands, [66]Heshbon with its pasture lands, and Jazer with its pasture lands.

☐ MATTHEW 12:1-21

Picking Grain on the Sabbath. 12:1 At that time Jesus was going through a field of grain on the sabbath. His disciples were hungry and began to pick the heads of grain and eat them. ²When the Pharisees saw this, they said to him, "See, your disciples are doing what is unlawful to do on the sabbath." ³He said to them, "Have you not read what David did when he and his companions were hungry, ⁴how he went into the house of God and ate the bread of offering, which neither he nor his companions but only the priests could lawfully eat? ⁵Or have you not read in the law that on the sabbath the priests serving in the temple violate the sabbath and are innocent? ⁶I say to you, something greater than the temple is here. ⁷If you knew what this meant, 'I desire mercy, not sacrifice,' you would not have condemned these innocent men. ⁸For the Son of Man is Lord of the sabbath."

The Man with a Withered Hand. ⁹Moving on from there, he went into their synagogue. ¹⁰And behold, there was a man there who had a withered hand. They questioned him, "Is it lawful to cure on the sabbath?" so that they might accuse him. ¹¹He said to them, "Which one of you who has a sheep that falls into a pit on the sabbath will not take hold of it and lift it out? ¹²How much more valuable a person is than a sheep. So it is lawful to do good on the sabbath." ¹³Then he said to the man, "Stretch out your hand." He stretched it out, and it was restored as sound as the other. ¹⁴But the Pharisees went out and took counsel against him to put him to death.

The Chosen Servant. ¹⁵When Jesus realized this, he withdrew from that place. Many [people] followed him, and he cured them all, ¹⁶but he warned them not to make him known. ¹⁷This was to fulfill what had been spoken through Isaiah the prophet:

> ¹⁸"Behold, my servant whom I have
> chosen,
> my beloved in whom I delight;
> I shall place my spirit upon him,
> and he will proclaim justice to the
> Gentiles.
> ¹⁹He will not contend or cry out,
> nor will anyone hear his voice in
> the streets.
> ²⁰A bruised reed he will not break,
> a smoldering wick he will not quench,
> until he brings justice to victory.
> ²¹And in his name the Gentiles will
> hope."

May 3

Sts. Philip and James

Whoever has been called to the preaching of the Gospel should obey instantly and without delay.

— St. Basil the Great

☐ 1 CHRONICLES 7-9:34

Issachar. 7:1 The sons of Issachar were Tola, Puah, Jashub, and Shimron: four. ²The sons of Tola were Uzzi, Rephaiah, Jeriel, Jahmai, Ibsam, and Shemuel, heads of the ancestral houses of Tola, mighty warriors in their generations. In the time of David they numbered twenty-two thousand six hundred. ³The sons of Uzzi: Izarahiah.

The sons of Izarahiah were Michael, Obadiah, Joel, and Isshiah. All five of these were chiefs. ⁴Along with them, in their generations, according to ancestral houses, were thirty-six thousand men in organized military troops, since they had more wives and children ⁵than their fellow tribesmen. In all the clans of Issachar there was a total of eighty-seven thousand warriors listed in their family records.

Benjamin. ⁶The sons of Benjamin were Bela, Becher, and Jediael—three. ⁷The sons of Bela were Ezbon, Uzzi, Uzziel, Jerimoth, and Iri—five. They were heads of their ancestral houses and warriors. Their family records listed twenty-two thousand and thirty-four. ⁸The sons of Becher were Zemirah, Joash, Eliezer, Elioenai, Omri, Jeremoth, Abijah, Anathoth, and Alemeth—all these were sons of Becher. ⁹Their family records listed twenty thousand two hundred of their kindred who were heads of their ancestral houses and warriors. ¹⁰The sons of Jediael: Bilhan. The sons of Bilhan were Jeush, Benjamin, Ehud, Chenaanah, Zethan, Tarshish, and Ahishahar. ¹¹All these were sons of Jediael, heads of ancestral houses and warriors. They numbered seventeen thousand two hundred men fit for military service... ¹²Shupham and Hupham.

Dan, Naphtali and Manasseh. The sons of Dan: Hushim. ¹³The sons of Naphtali were Jahziel, Guni, Jezer, and Shallum. These were sons of Bilhah. ¹⁴The sons of Manasseh, whom his Aramean concubine bore: she bore Machir, the father of Gilead. ¹⁵Machir took a wife whose name was Maacah; his sister's name was Molecheth. Manasseh's second son was named Zelophehad, who had only daughters. ¹⁶Maacah, Machir's wife, bore a son whom she named Peresh. He had a brother named Sheresh, whose sons were Ulam and Rakem. ¹⁷The sons of Ulam: Bedan. These were the sons of Gilead, the son of Machir, the son of Manasseh. ¹⁸His sister Molecheth bore Ishhod, Abiezer, and Mahlah. ¹⁹The sons of Shemida were Ahian, Shechem, Likhi, and Aniam.

Ephraim. ²⁰The sons of Ephraim: Shuthelah, whose son was Bered, whose son was Tahath, whose son was Eleadah, whose son was Tahath, ²¹whose son was Zabad. Ephraim's son Shuthelah, and Ezer and Elead, who were born in the land, were killed by the inhabitants of Gath because they had gone down to take away their livestock. ²²Their father Ephraim mourned a long time, but after his relatives had come and comforted him, ²³he had relations with his wife, who conceived and bore a son whom he named Beriah, since evil had befallen his house. ²⁴He had a daughter, Sheerah, who built Lower and Upper Beth-horon and Uzzen-sheerah. ²⁵Zabad's son was Rephah, whose son was Resheph, whose son was Telah, whose son was Tahan, ²⁶whose son was Ladan, whose son was Ammihud, whose son was Elishama, ²⁷whose son was Nun, whose son was Joshua.

²⁸Their property and their dwellings were in Bethel and its towns, Naaran to the east, Gezer and its towns to the west, and also Shechem and its towns as far as Ayyah and its towns. ²⁹Manasseh, however, had possession of Beth-shean and its towns, Taanach and its towns, Megiddo and its towns, and Dor and its towns. In these dwelt the sons of Joseph, the son of Israel.

Asher. ³⁰The sons of Asher were Imnah, Ishvah, Ishvi, and Beriah; their sister was Serah. ³¹Beriah's sons were Heber and Malchiel, who was the father of Birzaith. ³²Heber became the father of Japhlet, Shomer, Hotham, and their sister Shua. ³³The sons of Japhlet were Pasach, Bimhal, and Ashvath; these were the sons of Japhlet. ³⁴The sons of Shomer were Ahi, Rohgah, Jehubbah, and Aram. ³⁵The sons of his brother Hotham were Zophah, Imna, Shelesh, and Amal. ³⁶The sons of Zophah were Suah, Harnepher, Shual, Beri, Imrah, ³⁷Bezer, Hod, Shamma, Shilshah, Ithran, and Beera. [38]The sons of Jether were Jephunneh, Pispa, and Ara. [39]The sons of Ulla were Arah, Hanniel, and Rizia. [40]All these were sons of Asher, heads of ancestral houses, distinguished men, warriors, and chiefs among the princes. Their family records numbered twenty-six thousand men fit for military service.

Benjamin. 8:1 Benjamin became the father of Bela, his firstborn, Ashbel, the second son, Aharah, the third, [2]Nohah, the fourth, and Rapha, the fifth. [3]The sons of Bela were Addar and Gera, the father of Ehud. [4]The sons of Ehud were Abishua, Naaman, Ahoah, [5]Gera, Shephuphan, and Huram. [6]These were the sons of Ehud, family heads over those who dwelt in Geba and were deported to Manahath. [7]Also Naaman, Ahijah, and Gera. The last, who led them into exile, became the father of Uzza and Ahihud. [8]Shaharaim became a father on the Moabite plateau after he had put away his wives Hushim and Baara. [9]By his wife Hodesh he begot Jobab, Zibia, Mesha, Malcam, [10]Jeuz, Sachia, and Mirmah. These were his sons, family heads. [11]By Hushim he begot Abitub and Elpaal. [12]The sons of Elpaal were Eber, Misham, Shemed (who built Ono and Lod with its nearby towns), [13]and Beriah, and Shema. They were family heads of those who dwelt in Aijalon, and they put the inhabitants of Gath to flight. [14]Their relatives were Elpaal, Shashak, and Jeremoth. [15]Zebadiah, Arad, Eder, [16]Michael, Ishpah, and Joha were the sons of Beriah. [17]Zebadiah, Meshullam, Hizki, Heber, [18]Ishmerai, Izliah, and Jobab were the sons of Elpaal. [19]Jakim, Zichri, Zabdi, [20]Elienai, Zillethai, Eliel, [21]Adaiah, Beraiah, and Shimrath were the sons of Shimei. [22]Ishpan, Eber, Eliel, [23]Abdon, Zichri, Hanan, [24]Hananiah, Elam, Anthothijah, [25]Iphdeiah, and Penuel were the sons of Shashak. [26]Shamsherai, Shehariah, Athaliah, [27]Jaareshiah, Elijah, and Zichri were the sons of Jeroham. [28]These were family heads in their generations, chiefs who dwelt in Jerusalem.

[29]In Gibeon dwelt Jeiel, the founder of Gibeon, whose wife's name was Maacah; [30]also his firstborn son, Abdon, and Zur, Kish, Baal, Ner, Nadab, [31]Gedor, Ahio, Zecher, and Mikloth. [32]Mikloth became the father of Shimeah. These, too, dwelt with their relatives in Jerusalem, opposite their fellow tribesmen. [33]Ner became the father of Kish, and Kish became the father of Saul. Saul became the father of Jonathan, Malchishua, Abinadab, and Eshbaal. [34]The son of Jonathan was Meribbaal, and Meribbaal became the father of Micah. [35]The sons of Micah were Pithon, Melech, Tarea, and Ahaz. [36]Ahaz became the father of Jehoaddah, and Jehoaddah became the father of Alemeth, Azmaveth, and Zimri. Zimri became the father of Moza. [37]Moza became the father of Binea, whose son was Raphah, whose son was Eleasah, whose son was Azel. [38]Azel had six sons, whose names were Azrikam, his firstborn, Ishmael, Sheariah, Azariah, Obadiah, and Hanan; all these were the sons of Azel. [39]The sons of Eshek, his brother, were Ulam, his firstborn, Jeush, the second son, and Eliphelet, the third. [40]The sons of Ulam were warriors, skilled with the bow, and they had many sons and grandsons: one hundred and fifty. All these were the sons of Benjamin.

9:1 Thus all Israel was listed in family lists, and these are recorded in the book of the kings of Israel.

Now Judah had been exiled to Babylon because of its treachery. [2]The first to settle again in their cities and dwell there were certain Israelites, the priests, the Levites, and the temple servants.

Jerusalemites. [3]In Jerusalem lived Judahites and Benjaminites; also Ephraimites and Manassites. [4]Among the Judahites was Uthai, son of Ammihud, son of Omri, son of Imri, son of Bani, one of the sons of Perez, son of Judah. [5]Among the Shelanites were Asaiah, the firstborn, and his sons. [6]Among the Zerahites were Jeuel and six hundred and ninety of their relatives. [7]Among the Benjaminites were Sallu, son of Meshullam, son of Hodaviah, son of Hassenuah, [8]as well as Ibneiah, son of Jeroham; Elah, son of Uzzi, son of Michri; Meshullam, son of Shephatiah, son of Reuel, son of Ibnijah. [9]Their kindred of various families were nine hundred and fifty-six. All those named were heads of their ancestral houses.

[10]Among the priests were Jedaiah; Jehoiarib; Jachin; [11]Azariah, son of Hilkiah, son of Meshullam, son of Zadok, son of Meraioth, son of Ahitub, the ruler of the house of God; [12]Adaiah, son of Jeroham, son of Pashhur, son of Malchijah; Maasai, son of Adiel, son of Jahzerah, son of Meshullam, son of Meshillemith, son of Immer. [13]Their brothers, heads of their ancestral houses, were one thousand seven hundred and sixty, valiant in the work of the service of the house of God.

[14]Among the Levites were Shemaiah, son of Hasshub, son of Azrikam, son of Hashabiah, one of the sons of Merari; [15]Bakbakkar; Heresh; Galal; Mattaniah, son of Mica, son of Zichri, a descendant of Asaph; [16]Obadiah, son of Shemaiah, son of Galal, a descendant of Jeduthun; and Berechiah, son of Asa, son of Elkanah, whose family lived in the villages of the Netophathites.

[17]The gatekeepers were Shallum, Akkub, Talmon, Ahiman, and their brothers; Shallum was the chief. [18]Previously they had stood guard at the king's gate on the east side; now they became gatekeepers for the encampments of the Levites. [19]Shallum, son of Kore, son of Ebiasaph, a descendant of Korah, and his brothers of the same ancestral house of the Korahites had as their assigned task the guarding of the threshold of the tent, just as their fathers had guarded the entrance to the encampment of the LORD. [20]Phinehas, son of Eleazar, had been their chief in times past; the LORD was with him. [21]Zechariah, son of Meshelemiah, guarded the gate of the tent of meeting. [22]In all, those who were chosen for gatekeepers at the threshold were two hundred and twelve. They were inscribed in the family records of their villages. David and Samuel the seer had established them in their position of trust. [23]Thus they and their sons kept guard over the gates of the house of the LORD, the house which was then a tent. [24]The gatekeepers were stationed at the four sides, to the east, the west, the north, and the south. [25]Their brothers who lived in their own villages took turns in assisting them for seven-day periods, [26]while the four chief gatekeepers were on permanent duty. These were the Levites who also had charge of the chambers and treasures of the house of God. [27]They would spend the night near the house of God, for it was in their charge and they had the duty of opening it each morning.

[28]Some of them had charge of the vessels used there, tallying them as they were brought in and taken out. [29]Others were appointed to take care of the utensils and all the sacred vessels, as well as the fine flour, the wine, the oil, the frankincense, and the spices. [30]It was the sons of priests, however, who mixed the spiced ointments. [31]Mattithiah, one of the Levites, the firstborn of Shallum the Korahite, was entrusted with preparing the cakes. [32]Benaiah the Kohathite, one of their brothers, was in charge of setting out the showbread each sabbath.

[33]These were the singers and the gatekeepers, family heads over the Levites. They stayed in the chambers when free of duty, for day and night they had to be ready for service. [34]These were the levitical family heads by their generations, chiefs who dwelt in Jerusalem.

☐ MATTHEW 12:22-37

Jesus and Beelzebul. 12:22 Then they brought to him a demoniac who was blind and mute. He cured the mute person so that he could speak and see. [23]All the crowd was astounded, and said, "Could this perhaps be the Son of David?" [24]But when the Pharisees heard this, they said, "This man drives out demons only by the power of Beelzebul, the prince of demons." [25]But he knew what they were thinking and said to them, "Every kingdom divided against itself will be laid waste, and no town or house divided against itself will stand. [26]And if Satan drives out Satan, he is divided against himself; how, then, will his kingdom stand? [27]And if I drive out demons by Beelzebul, by whom do your own people drive them out? Therefore they will be your judges. [28]But if it is by the Spirit of God that I drive out demons, then the kingdom of God has come upon you. [29]How can anyone enter a strong man's house and steal his property, unless he first ties up the strong man? Then he can plunder his house. [30]Whoever is not with me is against me, and whoever does not gather with me scatters. [31]Therefore, I say to you, every sin and blasphemy will be forgiven people, but blasphemy against the Spirit will not be forgiven. [32]And whoever speaks a word against the Son of Man will be forgiven; but whoever speaks against the holy Spirit will not be forgiven, either in this age or in the age to come.

A Tree and Its Fruits. [33]"Either declare the tree good and its fruit is good, or declare the tree rotten and its fruit is rotten, for a tree is known by its fruit. [34]You brood of vipers, how can you say good things when you are evil? For from the fullness of the heart the mouth speaks. [35]A good person brings forth good out of a store of goodness, but an evil person brings forth evil out of a store of evil. [36]I tell you, on the day of judgment people will render an account for every careless word they speak. [37]By your words you will be acquitted, and by your words you will be condemned."

May 4

If God has given you the power, go ahead and work a miracle; that's why He gave you the power. But don't think that those who have never worked a miracle aren't part of the kingdom of God.

— St. Augustine of Hippo

☐ 1 CHRONICLES 9:35-12:41

Genealogy of Saul. 9:35 Jeiel, the founder of Gibeon, dwelt in Gibeon; his wife's name was Maacah. [36]His firstborn son was Abdon; then came Zur, Kish, Baal, Ner, Nadab, [37]Gedor, Ahio, Zechariah, and Mikloth. [38]Mikloth became the father of Shimeam. These, too, with their relatives, dwelt opposite their relatives in Jerusalem. [39]Ner became the father of Kish, and Kish became the father of Saul. Saul became the father of Jonathan, Malchishua, Abinadab, and Eshbaal. [40]The son of Jonathan was Meribbaal, and Meribbaal became the father of Micah. [41]The sons of Micah were Pithon,

Melech, Tahrea, and Ahaz. [42]Ahaz became the father of Jehoaddah, and Jehoaddah became the father of Alemeth, Azmaveth, and Zimri. Zimri became the father of Moza. [43]Moza became the father of Binea, whose son was Rephaiah, whose son was Eleasah, whose son was Azel. [44]Azel had six sons, whose names were Azrikam, his firstborn, Ishmael, Sheariah, Azariah, Obadiah, and Hanan; these were the sons of Azel.

Death of Saul and His Sons. 10:1 Now the Philistines went to war against Israel, and Israel fled before them, and they fell, slain on Mount Gilboa. [2]The Philistines pressed hard after Saul and his sons. When the Philistines had struck down Jonathan, Abinadab, and Malchishua, sons of Saul, [3]the fury of the battle converged on Saul. Then the archers hit him, and he was severely wounded.

[4]Saul said to his armor-bearer, "Draw your sword and run me through; otherwise these uncircumcised will come and abuse me." But the armor-bearer, badly frightened, refused, so Saul took his own sword and fell upon it. [5]When the armor-bearer saw that Saul was dead, he too fell upon his sword and died. [6]Thus Saul, and his three sons, his whole house, died together. [7]When all the Israelites in the valley saw that Saul and his sons had fled and that they had died, they abandoned their cities and fled. Then the Philistines came and lived in those cities.

[8]On the following day, when the Philistines came to strip the slain, they found Saul and his sons fallen on Mount Gilboa. [9]They stripped him, and took his head and his armor; these they sent throughout the land of the Philistines to bring the good news to their idols and to the people. [10]They put his armor in the temple of their gods, but his skull they impaled at the temple of Dagon.

Burial of Saul. [11]When all the inhabitants of Jabesh-gilead heard all that the Philistines had done to Saul, [12]all their warriors set out, recovered the corpses of Saul and his sons, and brought them to Jabesh. They buried their bones under the oak of Jabesh, and fasted for seven days.

[13]Thus Saul died because of his treason against the LORD in disobeying his word, and also because he had sought counsel from a ghost, [14]rather than from the LORD. Therefore the LORD took his life, and turned his kingdom over to David, the son of Jesse.

David Is Made King. 11:1 Then all Israel gathered around David in Hebron, and they said: "Look! We are your bone and your flesh. [2]In days past, when Saul was still the king, it was you who led Israel in all its battles. And now the LORD, your God, has said to you: You shall shepherd my people Israel; you shall be ruler over my people Israel." [3]Then all the elders of Israel came to the king at Hebron, and at Hebron David made a covenant with them in the presence of the LORD; and they anointed David king over Israel, in accordance with the word of the LORD given through Samuel.

Jerusalem Captured. [4]Then David and all Israel went to Jerusalem, that is, Jebus, where the inhabitants of the land were called Jebusites. [5]The inhabitants of Jebus said to David, "You shall not enter here." David nevertheless captured the fortress of Zion, which is the City of David. [6]David said, "Whoever strikes the Jebusites first shall be made chief and captain." Joab, the son of Zeruiah, was the first to attack; and so he became chief. [7]David took up residence in the fortress, which therefore was called the City of David. [8]He built up the city on all sides, from the Millo all the way around, while Joab restored the rest of the city. [9]David became ever more powerful, for the LORD of hosts was with him.

David's Warriors. [10]These were David's chief warriors who, together with all Israel, supported him in his reign in order to make him king, according to the LORD's word concerning Israel.

[11]Here is the list of David's warriors:

Ishbaal, the son of Hachamoni, chief of the Three. He brandished his spear over three hundred, whom he had slain in a single encounter.

¹²Next to him was Eleazar, the son of Dodo the Ahohite, one of the Three warriors. ¹³He was with David at Pas-dammim, where the Philistines had massed for battle. There was a plot of land full of barley. The people were fleeing before the Philistines, ¹⁴but he took his stand in the middle of the plot, kept it safe, and cut down the Philistines. Thus the LORD brought about a great victory.

¹⁵Three of the Thirty chiefs went down to the rock, to David, who was in the cave of Adullam while the Philistines were encamped in the valley of Rephaim. ¹⁶David was then in the stronghold, and a Philistine garrison was at Bethlehem. ¹⁷David had a strong craving, and said, "If only someone would give me a drink of water from the cistern by the gate of Bethlehem!" ¹⁸Thereupon the Three broke through the encampment of the Philistines, drew water from the cistern by the gate of Bethlehem, and carried it back to David. But David refused to drink it. Instead, he poured it out to the LORD, ¹⁹saying, "God forbid that I should do such a thing! Could I drink the blood of these men who risked their lives? For at the risk of their lives they brought it." So he refused to drink it. Such deeds as these the Three warriors performed.

²⁰Abishai, the brother of Joab, was the chief of the Thirty; he brandished his spear over three hundred, whom he had slain. He made a name beside the Three, ²¹but was twice as famous as any of the Thirty, becoming their leader. However, he did not attain to the Three.

²²Benaiah, son of Jehoiada, a valiant man of mighty deeds, from Kabzeel, killed the two sons of Ariel of Moab. Also, he went down and killed the lion in the cistern on a snowy day. ²³He likewise slew the Egyptian, a huge man five cubits tall. The Egyptian carried a spear that was like a weaver's beam, but Benaiah came against him with a staff; he wrested the spear from the Egyptian's hand, and killed him with that spear. ²⁴Such deeds as these Benaiah, the son of Jehoiada, performed, and he made a name beside the Three warriors, ²⁵but was more famous than any of the Thirty. However, he did not attain to the Three. David put him in charge of his bodyguard.

²⁶Also these warriors: Asahel, the brother of Joab; Elhanan, son of Dodo, from Bethlehem; ²⁷Shammoth, from En-harod; Helez, from Beth-pelet; ²⁸Ira, son of Ikkesh, from Tekoa; Abiezer, from Anathoth; ²⁹Sibbecai, from Husha; Ilai, from Ahoh; ³⁰Maharai, from Netophah; Heled, son of Baanah, from Netophah; ³¹Ithai, son of Ribai, from Gibeah of Benjamin; Benaiah, from Pirathon; ³²Hurai, from Nahale-gaash; Abiel, from Beth-arabah; ³³Azmaveth, from Bahurim; Eliahba, from Shaalbon; ³⁴Jashen the Gunite; Jonathan, son of Shagee the Hararite; ³⁵Ahiam, son of Sachar the Hararite; Elipheleth, son of ³⁶Ahasbai, from Beth-maacah; Ahijah, from Gilo; ³⁷Hezro, from Carmel; Naarai, the son of Ezbai; ³⁸Joel, brother of Nathan, from Rehob, the Gadite; ³⁹Zelek the Ammonite; Naharai, from Beeroth, the armor-bearer of Joab, son of Zeruiah; ⁴⁰Ira, from Jattir; Gareb, from Jattir; ⁴¹Uriah the Hittite; Zabad, son of Ahlai, ⁴²and, in addition to the Thirty, Adina, son of Shiza, the Reubenite, chief of the tribe of Reuben; ⁴³Hanan, son of Maacah; Joshaphat the Mithnite; ⁴⁴Uzzia, the Ashterathite; Shama and Jeiel, sons of Hotham, from Aroer; ⁴⁵Jediael, son of Shimri, and Joha, his brother, the Tizite; ⁴⁶Eliel the Mahavite; Jeribai and Joshaviah, sons of Elnaam; Ithmah, from Moab; ⁴⁷Eliel, Obed, and Jaasiel the Mezobian.

David's Early Followers. 12:1 The following men came to David in Ziklag while he was still under banishment from Saul, son of Kish; they, too, were among the warriors who helped him in his battles. ²They were archers who could use either the right or the left hand, both in slinging stones and in shooting arrows with the bow. They were some of Saul's kinsmen, from Benjamin. ³Ahiezer was their chief, along with Joash, both sons of Shemaah of Gibeah; also Jeziel and Pelet, sons of Azmaveth; Beracah; Jehu, from Anathoth; ⁴Ishmaiah the Gibeonite, a warrior among the Thirty, and over the Thirty; ⁵Jeremiah; Jahaziel; Johanan; Jozabad from Gederah; ⁶Eluzai; Jerimoth; Bealiah; Shemariah; Shephatiah the Haruphite; ⁷Elkanah, Isshiah, Azarel, Joezer, and Jashobeam, who were Korahites; ⁸Joelah and Zebadiah, sons of Jeroham, from Gedor.

⁹Some of the Gadites also went over to David when he was at the stronghold in the wilderness. They were valiant warriors, experienced soldiers equipped with shield and spear, fearsome as lions, swift as gazelles on the mountains. ¹⁰Ezer was their chief, Obadiah was second, Eliab third, ¹¹Mishmannah fourth, Jeremiah fifth, ¹²Attai sixth, Eliel seventh, ¹³Johanan eighth, Elzabad ninth, ¹⁴Jeremiah tenth, and Machbannai eleventh. ¹⁵These Gadites were army commanders, the lesser over hundreds and the greater over thousands. ¹⁶It was they who crossed over the Jordan in the first month, when it was overflowing both its banks, and chased away all who were in the valleys to the east and to the west.

¹⁷Some Benjaminites and Judahites also came to David at the stronghold. ¹⁸David went out to meet them and addressed them in these words: "If you come peacefully, to help me, I am of a mind to have you join me. But if you have come to betray me to my enemies though my hands have done no wrong, may the God of our ancestors see and punish you." ¹⁹Then a spirit clothed Amasai, the chief of the Thirty, and he answered David:

"We are yours, O David,
    we are with you, son of Jesse.
Peace, peace to you,
    and peace to him who helps you;
    may your God be your helper!"

So David received them and placed them among the leaders of his troops.

²⁰Men from Manasseh also deserted to David when he came with the Philistines to battle against Saul. However, he did not help the Philistines, for their lords took counsel and sent him home, saying, "At the cost of our heads he will desert to his master Saul." ²¹As he was returning to Ziklag, therefore, these deserted to him from Manasseh: Adnah, Jozabad, Jediael, Michael, Jozabad, Elihu, and Zillethai, chiefs of thousands of Manasseh. ²²They helped David by taking charge of his troops, for they were all warriors and became commanders of his army. ²³And from day to day men kept coming to David's help until there was a vast encampment, like God's own encampment.

The Assembly at Hebron. ²⁴This is the muster of the detachments of armed troops that came to David at Hebron to bring Saul's kingdom over to him, as the Lord had ordained. ²⁵Judahites bearing shields and spears: six thousand eight hundred armed troops. ²⁶Of the Simeonites, warriors fit for battle: seven thousand one hundred. ²⁷Of the Levites: four thousand six hundred, ²⁸along with Jehoiada, leader of the line of Aaron, with another three thousand seven hundred, ²⁹and Zadok, a young warrior, with twenty-two princes of his father's house. ³⁰Of the Benjaminites, the kinsmen of Saul: three thousand—until this time, most of them had kept their allegiance to the house of Saul. ³¹Of the Ephraimites: twenty thousand eight hundred warriors, men renowned in their ancestral houses. ³²Of the half-tribe of Manasseh: eighteen thousand, designated by name to come and make David king. ³³Of the Issacharites, their chiefs who were endowed with an understanding of the times and who knew what Israel had to do: two hundred chiefs, together with all their kinsmen under their command. [34]From Zebulun, men fit for military service, set in battle array with every kind of weapon for war: fifty thousand men rallying with a single purpose. [35]From Naphtali: one thousand captains, and with them, armed with shield and lance, thirty-seven thousand men. [36]Of the Danites, set in battle array: twenty-eight thousand six hundred. [37]From Asher, fit for military service and set in battle array: forty thousand. [38]From the other side of the Jordan, of the Reubenites, Gadites, and the half-tribe of Manasseh, men equipped with every kind of weapon of war: one hundred and twenty thousand.

[39]All these soldiers, drawn up in battle order, came to Hebron with the resolute intention of making David king over all Israel. The rest of Israel was likewise of one mind to make David king. [40]They remained with David for three days, eating and drinking, for their relatives had prepared for them. [41]Moreover, their neighbors from as far as Issachar, Zebulun, and Naphtali came bringing food on donkeys, camels, mules, and oxen—provisions in great quantity of meal, pressed figs, raisins, wine, oil, oxen, and sheep. For there was rejoicing in Israel.

☐ MATTHEW 12:38-45

The Demand for a Sign. 12:38 Then some of the scribes and Pharisees said to him, "Teacher, we wish to see a sign from you." [39]He said to them in reply, "An evil and unfaithful generation seeks a sign, but no sign will be given it except the sign of Jonah the prophet. [40]Just as Jonah was in the belly of the whale three days and three nights, so will the Son of Man be in the heart of the earth three days and three nights. [41]At the judgment, the men of Nineveh will arise with this generation and condemn it, because they repented at the preaching of Jonah; and there is something greater than Jonah here. [42]At the judgment the queen of the south will arise with this generation and condemn it, because she came from the ends of the earth to hear the wisdom of Solomon; and there is something greater than Solomon here.

The Return of the Unclean Spirit. [43]"When an unclean spirit goes out of a person it roams through arid regions searching for rest but finds none. [44]Then it says, 'I will return to my home from which I came.' But upon returning, it finds it empty, swept clean, and put in order. [45]Then it goes and brings back with itself seven other spirits more evil than itself, and they move in and dwell there; and the last condition of that person is worse than the first. Thus it will be with this evil generation."

May 5

Take the holy, gentle will of God as your spouse, wedded each moment by the ring of faith in which are set all the jewels of hope and love.

— St. Paul of the Cross

☐ 1 CHRONICLES 13-16

Transfer of the Ark. 13:1 After David had taken counsel with his commanders of thousands and of hundreds, that is, with every leader, [2]he said to the whole assembly of Israel: "If it seems good to you, and is so decreed by the LORD our God, let us send to the rest of our kindred from all the districts of Israel, and also the priests and the Levites from their cities with pasture lands, that they may join us; [3]and let us bring the ark of our God here among us, for in the days of Saul we did not consult it." [4]And the whole assembly agreed to do it, for it seemed right in the eyes of all the people.

[5]Then David assembled all Israel, from Shihor of Egypt to Lebo-hamath, to bring the ark of God from Kiriath-jearim. [6]David and all Israel went up to Baalah, that is, to Kiriath-jearim, of Judah, to bring up from there the ark of God, which was known by the name "LORD enthroned upon the cherubim." [7]They transported the ark of God on a new cart from the house of Abinadab; Uzzah and Ahio were guiding the cart, [8]while David and all Israel danced before God with all their might, with singing, and with lyres, harps, tambourines, cymbals, and trumpets.

[9]As they reached the threshing floor of Chidon, Uzzah stretched out his hand to steady the ark, for the oxen were tipping it. [10]Then the LORD became angry with Uzzah and struck him, because he had laid his hand on the ark; he died there in God's presence. [11]David was angry because the LORD's anger had broken out against Uzzah. Therefore that place has been called Perez-uzzah even to this day.

[12]David was afraid of God that day, and he said, "How can I bring in the ark of God to me?" [13]Therefore he did not take the ark with him into the City of David, but deposited it instead at the house of Obed-edom the Gittite. [14]The ark of God remained in the house of Obed-edom with his family for three months, and the LORD blessed Obed-edom's household and all that he possessed.

David in Jerusalem. 14:1 Hiram, king of Tyre, sent envoys to David along with cedar wood, and masons and carpenters to build him a house. [2]David now knew that the LORD had truly established him as king over Israel, for his kingdom was greatly exalted for the sake of his people Israel. [3]David took other wives in Jerusalem and became the father of more sons and daughters. [4]These are the names of those who were born to him in Jerusalem: Shammua, Shobab, Nathan, Solomon, [5]Ibhar, Elishua, Elpelet, [6]Nogah, Nepheg, Japhia, [7]Elishama, Beeliada, and Eliphelet.

The Philistine Wars. [8]When the Philistines had heard that David was anointed king over all Israel, they marched out in force looking for him. But when David heard of this, he went out against them. [9]Meanwhile the Philistines had come and raided the valley of Rephaim. [10]David inquired of God, "Shall I attack the Philistines, and will you deliver them into my power?" The LORD answered him, "Attack, for I have delivered them into your power." [11]So they attacked, at Baal-perazim, and David defeated them there. Then David said, "By my hand God has broken through my enemies just as water breaks through a dam." Therefore that place was called Baal-perazim. [12]The Philistines abandoned their gods there, and David ordered them to be burnt.

[13]Once again the Philistines raided the valley, [14]and again David inquired of God. But God answered him: Do not try to pursue them, but go around them and come against them near the balsam trees. [15]When you hear the sound of marching in the tops of the balsam trees, then go forth to battle, for God has already gone before you to strike the army of the Philistines. [16]David did as God commanded him, and they routed the Philistine army from Gibeon to Gezer.

[17]Thus David's fame was spread abroad through every land, and the LORD put the fear of him on all the nations.

Preparations for Moving the Ark. 15:1 David built houses for himself in the City of David and prepared a place for the ark of God, pitching a tent for it there. [2]At that time he said, "No one may carry the ark of God except the Levites, for the LORD chose them to carry the ark of the LORD and to minister to him forever." [3]Then David assembled all Israel to Jerusalem to bring up the ark of the LORD to its place, which he had prepared for it. [4]David also convened the sons of Aaron and the Levites: [5]of the sons of Kohath, Uriel, their chief, and one hundred and twenty of his brothers; [6]of the sons of Merari, Asaiah, their chief, and two hundred and twenty of his brothers; [7]of the sons of Gershon, Joel, their chief, and one hundred and thirty of his brothers; [8]of the sons of Elizaphan, Shemaiah, their chief, and two hundred of his brothers; [9]of the sons of Hebron, Eliel, their chief, and eighty of his brothers; [10]of the sons of Uzziel, Amminadab, their chief, and one hundred and twelve of his brothers.

[11]David summoned the priests Zadok and Abiathar, and the Levites Uriel, Asaiah, Joel, Shemaiah, Eliel, and Amminadab, [12]and said to them: "You heads of the levitical houses, sanctify yourselves along with your brothers to bring up the ark of the LORD, the God of Israel, to the place which I have prepared for it. [13]Because you were not with us the first time, the LORD our God broke out against us, for we did not seek him aright." [14]Accordingly, the priests and the Levites sanctified themselves to bring up the ark of the LORD, the God of Israel. [15]The Levites carried the ark of God on their shoulders with poles, as Moses had commanded according to the word of the LORD.

[16]David commanded the commanders of the Levites to appoint their brothers as singers and to play on musical instruments, harps, lyres, and cymbals, to make a loud sound of rejoicing. [17]Therefore the Levites appointed Heman, son of Joel, and, among his brothers, Asaph, son of Berechiah; and among the sons of Merari, their brothers, Ethan, son of Kushaiah; [18]and, together with these, their brothers of the second rank: the gatekeepers Zechariah, Uzziel, Shemiramoth, Jehiel, Unni, Eliab, Benaiah, Maaseiah, Mattithiah, Eliphelehu, Mikneiah, Obed-edom, and Jeiel. [19]The singers, Heman, Asaph, and Ethan, sounded brass cymbals. [20]Zechariah, Uzziel, Shemiramoth, Jehiel, Unni, Eliab, Maaseiah, and Benaiah played on harps set to "Alamoth." [21]But Mattithiah, Eliphelehu, Mikneiah, Obed-edom, and Jeiel led the song on lyres set to "sheminith." [22]Chenaniah was the chief of the Levites in the singing; he directed the singing, for he was skillful. [23]Berechiah and Elkanah were gatekeepers before the ark. [24]The priests, Shebaniah, Joshaphat, Nethanel, Amasai, Zechariah, Benaiah, and Eliezer, sounded the trumpets before the ark of God. Obed-edom and Jeiel were also gatekeepers before the ark.

The Ark Comes to Jerusalem. [25]Thus David, the elders of Israel, and the commanders of thousands went to bring up the ark of the covenant of the LORD with joy from the house of Obed-edom. ²⁶While God helped the Levites to carry the ark of the covenant of the LORD, they sacrificed seven bulls and seven rams. ²⁷David was vested in a robe of fine linen, as were all the Levites who carried the ark, the singers, and Chenaniah, the leader of song; David was also wearing a linen ephod. ²⁸Thus all Israel brought up the ark of the covenant of the LORD with joyful shouting, to the sound of horns, trumpets, and cymbals, and the music of harps and lyres. ²⁹But as the ark of the covenant of the LORD was entering the City of David, Michal, daughter of Saul, looked down from her window, and when she saw King David leaping and dancing, she despised him in her heart.

16:1 They brought in the ark of God and set it within the tent which David had pitched for it. Then they sacrificed burnt offerings and communion offerings to God. ²When David had finished sacrificing the burnt offerings and communion offerings, he blessed the people in the name of the LORD, ³and distributed to every Israelite, to every man and every woman, a loaf of bread, a piece of meat, and a raisin cake.

David's Directives for the Levites. ⁴He then appointed certain Levites to minister before the ark of the LORD, to celebrate, thank, and praise the LORD, the God of Israel. ⁵Asaph was their chief, and second to him were Zechariah, Uzziel, Shemiramoth, Jehiel, Mattithiah, Eliab, Benaiah, Obed-edom, and Jeiel. These were to play on harps and lyres, while Asaph was to sound the cymbals, ⁶and the priests Benaiah and Jahaziel were to be the regular trumpeters before the ark of the covenant of God.

⁷On that same day, David appointed Asaph and his brothers to sing for the first time these praises of the LORD:

⁸Give thanks to the LORD, invoke his name;

make known among the peoples his deeds.
⁹Sing praise, play music;
   proclaim all his wondrous deeds.
¹⁰Glory in his holy name;
   rejoice, O hearts that seek the LORD!
¹¹Rely on the mighty LORD;
   constantly seek his face.
¹²Recall the wondrous deeds he has done,
   his signs, and his words of judgment,
¹³You sons of Israel, his servants,
   offspring of Jacob, the chosen ones!
¹⁴The LORD is our God;
   who rules the whole earth.
¹⁵He remembers forever his covenant
   the pact imposed for a thousand generations—
¹⁶Which was made with Abraham,
   confirmed by oath to Isaac,
¹⁷And ratified as binding for Jacob,
   an everlasting covenant for Israel:
¹⁸"To you will I give the land of Canaan,
   your own allotted heritage."
¹⁹When they were few in number,
   a handful, and strangers there,
²⁰Wandering from nation to nation,
   from one kingdom to another,
²¹He let no one oppress them;
   for their sake he rebuked kings:
²²"Do not touch my anointed,
   to my prophets do no harm."
²³Sing to the LORD, all the earth,
   announce his salvation, day after day.
²⁴Tell his glory among the nations;
   among all peoples, his wondrous deeds.
²⁵For great is the LORD and highly to be praised;
   to be feared above all gods.
²⁶For the gods of the nations all do nothing,
   but the LORD made the heavens.

27Splendor and majesty go before him;
  power and rejoicing are in his holy
    place.
28Give to the LORD, you families of
    nations,
  give to the LORD glory and might;
29Give to the LORD the glory due his
    name!
Bring gifts, and come before him;
  bow down to the LORD, splendid
    in holiness.
30Tremble before him, all the earth;
  the world will surely stand fast,
    never to be moved.
31Let the heavens be glad and the earth
    rejoice;
  let them say among the nations:
    The LORD is king.
32Let the sea and what fills it resound;
  let the plains be joyful and all that
    is in them!
33Then let all the trees of the forest
    exult
  before the LORD, who comes,
  who comes to rule the earth.
34Give thanks to the LORD, who is
    good,
  whose love endures forever;
35And say, "Save us, O God, our
    savior,
  gather us and deliver us from
    among the nations,

That we may give thanks to your holy
    name
  and glory in praising you."
36Blessed be the LORD, the God of
    Israel,
  from everlasting to everlasting!
Let all the people say, Amen!
  Hallelujah.

37Then David left Asaph and his brothers there before the ark of the covenant of the LORD to minister before the ark regularly according to the daily ritual; 38he also left there Obed-edom and sixty-eight of his brothers, including Obed-edom, son of Jeduthun, and Hosah, to be gatekeepers.

39But the priest Zadok and his priestly brothers he left before the tabernacle of the LORD on the high place at Gibeon, 40to make burnt offerings to the LORD on the altar for burnt offerings regularly, morning and evening, and to do all that is written in the law of the LORD which he commanded Israel. 41With them were Heman and Jeduthun and the others who were chosen and designated by name to give thanks to the LORD, "whose love endures forever," 42with trumpets and cymbals for accompaniment, and instruments for sacred song. The sons of Jeduthun kept the gate.

43Then all the people departed, each to their own homes, and David returned to bless his household.

☐ MATTHEW 12:46–50

The True Family of Jesus. 12:46 While he was still speaking to the crowds, his mother and his brothers appeared outside, wishing to speak with him. 47[Someone told him, "Your mother and your brothers are standing outside, asking to speak with you."] 48But he said in reply to the one who told him, "Who is my mother? Who are my brothers?" 49And stretching out his hand toward his disciples, he said, "Here are my mother and my brothers. 50For whoever does the will of my heavenly Father is my brother, and sister, and mother."

May 6

Do you know that often a root has split a rock when allowed to remain in it? Give no place to the seed of evil, seeing that it will break up your faith.

— St. Cyril of Jerusalem

☐ 1 CHRONICLES 17-20

The Oracle of Nathan. 17:1 After David had taken up residence in his house, he said to Nathan the prophet, "See, I am living in a house of cedar, but the ark of the covenant of the Lord is under tentcloth." ²Nathan replied to David, "Whatever is in your heart, go and do, for God is with you."

³But that same night the word of God came to Nathan: ⁴Go and tell David my servant, Thus says the Lord: It is not you who are to build the house for me to dwell in. ⁵For I have never dwelt in a house, from the day I brought Israel up, even to this day, but I have been lodging in tent or tabernacle. ⁶As long as I have wandered about with all Israel, did I ever say a word to any of the judges of Israel whom I commanded to shepherd my people, Why have you not built me a house of cedar? ⁷Now then, speak thus to my servant David, Thus says the Lord of hosts: I took you from the pasture, from following the flock, to become ruler over my people Israel. ⁸I was with you wherever you went, and I cut down all your enemies before you. I will make your name like that of the greatest on the earth. ⁹I will assign a place for my people Israel and I will plant them in it to dwell there; they will never again be disturbed, nor shall the wicked ever again oppress them, as they did at the beginning, ¹⁰and during all the time when I appointed judges over my people Israel. And I will subdue all your enemies. Moreover, I declare to you that the Lord will build you a house: ¹¹when your days have been completed and you must join your ancestors, I will raise up your offspring after you who will be one of your own sons, and I will establish his kingdom. ¹²He it is who shall build me a house, and I will establish his throne forever. ¹³I will be a father to him, and he shall be a son to me, and I will not withdraw my favor from him as I withdrew it from the one who was before you; ¹⁴but I will maintain him in my house and in my kingdom forever, and his throne shall be firmly established forever.

¹⁵In accordance with all these words and this whole vision Nathan spoke to David.

David's Thanksgiving. ¹⁶Then King David came in and sat in the Lord's presence, and said: "Who am I, Lord God, and what is my house, that you should have brought me so far? ¹⁷And yet, even this is too little in your sight, O God! For you have made a promise regarding your servant's house reaching into the future, and you have looked on me as henceforth the most notable of men, Lord God. ¹⁸What more can David say to you? You have known your servant. ¹⁹Lord, for your servant's sake and in keeping with your purpose, you have done this great thing. ²⁰Lord, there is no one like you, no God but you, just as we have always heard.

²¹"Is there, like your people Israel, whom you redeemed from Egypt, another nation on earth whom a god went to redeem as his people? You won for yourself a name for great and awesome deeds by driving out the nations before your people. ²²You made your people Israel your own forever, and you, Lord, became their God. ²³Now, Lord, may the promise that you have spoken concerning your servant and his house remain firm forever. Bring about

what you have promised, [24]that your name, LORD of hosts, God of Israel, may be great and abide forever, while the house of your servant is established in your presence. [25]"Because you, my God, have revealed to your servant that you will build him a house, your servant dares to pray before you. [26]Since you, LORD, are truly God and have made this generous promise to your servant, [27]do, then, bless the house of your servant, that it may be in your presence forever—since it is you, LORD, who blessed it, it is blessed forever."

David's Victories. 18:1 After this, David defeated the Philistines and subdued them; and he took Gath and its towns away from the Philistines. [2]He also defeated Moab, and the Moabites became David's subjects, paying tribute.

[3]David then defeated Hadadezer, king of Zobah, toward Hamath, who was on his way to set up his victory stele at the river Euphrates. [4]David captured from him one thousand chariots, seven thousand horsemen, and twenty thousand foot soldiers. David hamstrung all the chariot horses, but left one hundred for his chariots. [5]The Arameans of Damascus came to help Hadadezer, king of Zobah, but David also defeated twenty-two thousand of their men in Aram. [6]Then David set up garrisons in the Damascus region of Aram, and the Arameans became David's subjects, paying tribute. Thus the LORD made David victorious in all his campaigns.

[7]David took the golden shields that were carried by Hadadezer's attendants and brought them to Jerusalem. [8]David likewise took away from Tibhath and Cun, cities of Hadadezer, large quantities of bronze; Solomon later used it to make the bronze sea and the pillars and the vessels of bronze.

[9]When Tou, king of Hamath, heard that David had defeated the entire army of Hadadezer, king of Zobah, [10]he sent his son Hadoram to wish King David well and to congratulate him on having waged a victorious war against Hadadezer; for Hadadezer had been at war with Tou. He also brought gold, silver and bronze articles of every sort. [11]These also King David consecrated to the LORD along with all the silver and gold that he had taken from the nations: from Edom, Moab, the Ammonites, the Philistines, and Amalek.

[12]Abishai, the son of Zeruiah, also defeated eighteen thousand Edomites in the Valley of Salt. [13]He set up garrisons in Edom, and all the Edomites became David's subjects. Thus the LORD brought David victory in all his undertakings.

David's Officials. [14]David was king over all Israel; he dispensed justice and right to all his people. [15]Joab, son of Zeruiah, was in command of the army; Jehoshaphat, son of Ahilud, was chancellor; [16]Zadok, son of Ahitub, and Ahimelech, son of Abiathar, were priests; Shavsha was scribe; [17]Benaiah, son of Jehoiada, was in command of the Cherethites and the Pelethites; and David's sons were the chief assistants to the king.

Campaigns Against Ammon. 19:1 Afterward Nahash, king of the Ammonites, died and his son succeeded him as king. [2]David said, "I will show kindness to Hanun, the son of Nahash, for his father showed kindness to me." Therefore he sent envoys to console him over his father. But when David's servants had entered the land of the Ammonites to console Hanun, [3]the Ammonite princes said to Hanun, "Do you think David is doing this—sending you these consolers—to honor your father? Have not his servants rather come to you to explore the land, spying it out for its overthrow?" [4]So Hanun seized David's servants and had them shaved and their garments cut off halfway at the hips. Then he sent them away. [5]David was told about the men, and he sent word for them to be intercepted, for the men had been greatly disgraced. "Remain at Jericho," the king told them, "until your beards have grown again; then come back here."

⁶When the Ammonites realized that they had put themselves in bad odor with David, Hanun and the Ammonites sent a thousand talents of silver to hire chariots and horsemen from Aram Naharaim, from Aram-maacah, and from Zobah. ⁷They hired thirty-two thousand chariots along with the king of Maacah and his army, who came and encamped before Medeba. The Ammonites also assembled from their cities and came out for war.

⁸When David heard of this, he sent Joab and his whole army of warriors against them. ⁹The Ammonites marched out and lined up for battle at the entrance of the city, while the kings who had come to their help remained apart in the open field. ¹⁰When Joab saw that there was a battle line both in front of and behind him, he chose some of the best fighters among the Israelites and lined them up against the Arameans; ¹¹the rest of the army, which he placed under the command of his brother Abishai, then lined up to oppose the Ammonites. ¹²And he said: "If the Arameans prove too strong for me, you must come and save me; and if the Ammonites prove too strong for you, I will save you. ¹³Hold firm and let us show ourselves courageous for the sake of our people and the cities of our God; and may the LORD do what is good in his sight." ¹⁴Joab therefore advanced with his men to engage the Arameans in battle; but they fled before him. ¹⁵And when the Ammonites saw that the Arameans had fled, they too fled before his brother Abishai, and entered their city. Joab then came to Jerusalem.

¹⁶Seeing themselves vanquished by Israel, the Arameans sent messengers to bring out the Arameans from beyond the Euphrates, with Shophach, the commander of Hadadezer's army, at their head. ¹⁷When this was reported to David, he gathered all Israel together, crossed the Jordan, and met them. With the army of David drawn up to fight the Arameans, they gave battle. ¹⁸But the Arameans fled before Israel, and David killed seven thousand of their chariot fighters and forty thousand of their foot soldiers; he also put to death Shophach, the commander of the army. ¹⁹When the vassals of Hadadezer saw themselves vanquished by Israel, they made peace with David and became his subjects. After this, the Arameans refused to come to the aid of the Ammonites.

20:1 At the turn of the year, the time when kings go to war, Joab led the army out in force, laid waste the land of the Ammonites, and went on to besiege Rabbah; David himself remained in Jerusalem. When Joab had attacked Rabbah and destroyed it, ²David took the crown of Milcom from the idol's head. It was found to weigh a talent of gold, with precious stones on it; this crown David wore on his own head. He also brought out a great amount of spoil from the city. ³He deported the people of the city and set them to work with saws, iron picks, and axes. David dealt thus with all the cities of the Ammonites. Then David and his whole army returned to Jerusalem.

Victories over the Philistines. ⁴Afterward there was another battle with the Philistines, at Gezer. At that time, Sibbecai the Hushathite struck down Sippai, one of the descendants of the Rephaim, and the Philistines were subdued.

⁵There was another battle with the Philistines, and Elhanan, the son of Jair, slew Lahmi, the brother of Goliath of Gath, whose spear shaft was like a weaver's beam.

⁶There was another battle, at Gath, and there was a giant, who had six fingers to each hand and six toes to each foot; twenty-four in all. He too was descended from the Rephaim. ⁷He defied Israel, and Jonathan, the son of Shimea, David's brother, slew him. ⁸These were the descendants of the Rephaim of Gath who died at the hands of David and his servants.

☐ MATTHEW 13:1-23

The Parable of the Sower. 13:1 On that day, Jesus went out of the house and sat down by the sea. ²Such large crowds gathered around him that he got into a boat and sat down, and the whole crowd stood along the shore. ³And he spoke to them at length in parables, saying: "A sower went out to sow. ⁴And as he sowed, some seed fell on the path, and birds came and ate it up. ⁵Some fell on rocky ground, where it had little soil. It sprang up at once because the soil was not deep, ⁶and when the sun rose it was scorched, and it withered for lack of roots. ⁷Some seed fell among thorns, and the thorns grew up and choked it. ⁸But some seed fell on rich soil, and produced fruit, a hundred or sixty or thirtyfold. ⁹Whoever has ears ought to hear."

The Purpose of Parables. ¹⁰The disciples approached him and said, "Why do you speak to them in parables?" ¹¹He said to them in reply, "Because knowledge of the mysteries of the kingdom of heaven has been granted to you, but to them it has not been granted. ¹²To anyone who has, more will be given and he will grow rich; from anyone who has not, even what he has will be taken away. ¹³This is why I speak to them in parables, because 'they look but do not see and hear but do not listen or understand.' ¹⁴Isaiah's prophecy is fulfilled in them, which says:

'You shall indeed hear but not
    understand
    you shall indeed look but never see.

¹⁵Gross is the heart of this people,
    they will hardly hear with their
        ears, they have closed their
        eyes, lest they see with their
        eyes
    and hear with their ears
    and understand with their heart and
        be converted,
    and I heal them.'

The Privilege of Discipleship. ¹⁶"But blessed are your eyes, because they see, and your ears, because they hear. ¹⁷Amen, I say to you, many prophets and righteous people longed to see what you see but did not see it, and to hear what you hear but did not hear it.

The Explanation of the Parable of the Sower. ¹⁸"Hear then the parable of the sower. ¹⁹The seed sown on the path is the one who hears the word of the kingdom without understanding it, and the evil one comes and steals away what was sown in his heart. ²⁰The seed sown on rocky ground is the one who hears the word and receives it at once with joy. ²¹But he has no root and lasts only for a time. When some tribulation or persecution comes because of the word, he immediately falls away. ²²The seed sown among thorns is the one who hears the word, but then worldly anxiety and the lure of riches choke the word and it bears no fruit. ²³But the seed sown on rich soil is the one who hears the word and understands it, who indeed bears fruit and yields a hundred or sixty or thirtyfold."

May 7

> *If you would heed the Word of life, cut yourself off from evil things. The hearing of the Word profits nothing to the one who is busy with sins.*
>
> — St. Ephraem

☐ 1 CHRONICLES 21-24

David's Census; the Plague. 21:1 A satan rose up against Israel, and he incited David to take a census of Israel. ²David therefore said to Joab and to the other generals of the army, "Go, number the Israelites from Beer-sheba to Dan, and report back to me that I may know their number." ³But Joab replied: "May the Lord increase his people a hundredfold! My lord king, are not all of them my lord's subjects? Why does my lord seek to do this thing? Why should he bring guilt upon Israel?" ⁴However, the king's command prevailed over Joab, who departed and traversed all of Israel, and then returned to Jerusalem. ⁵Joab reported the census figures to David: of men capable of wielding a sword, there were in all Israel one million one hundred thousand, and in Judah four hundred and seventy thousand. ⁶Levi and Benjamin, however, he did not include in the census, for the king's command was repugnant to Joab. ⁷This command was evil in the sight of God, and he struck Israel. ⁸Then David said to God, "I have sinned greatly in doing this thing. Take away your servant's guilt, for I have acted very foolishly."

⁹Then the Lord spoke to Gad, David's seer, in these words: ¹⁰Go, tell David: Thus says the Lord: I am laying out three options; choose one of them, and I will inflict it on you. ¹¹Accordingly, Gad went to David and said to him: "Thus says the Lord: Decide now— ¹²will it be three years of famine; or three months of fleeing your enemies, with the sword of your foes ever at your back; or three days of the Lord's own sword, a plague in the land, with the Lord's destroying angel in every part of Israel? Now consider: What answer am I to give him who sent me?" ¹³Then David said to Gad: "I am in serious trouble. But let me fall into the hand of the Lord, whose mercy is very great, rather than into hands of men."

¹⁴Therefore the Lord sent a plague upon Israel, and seventy thousand Israelites died. ¹⁵God also sent an angel to Jerusalem to destroy it; but as the angel was on the point of destroying it, the Lord saw and changed his mind about the calamity, and said to the destroying angel, "Enough now! Stay your hand!"

Ornan's Threshing Floor. The angel of the Lord was then standing by the threshing floor of Ornan the Jebusite. ¹⁶When David raised his eyes, he saw the angel of the Lord standing between earth and heaven, drawn sword in hand stretched out against Jerusalem. David and the elders, clothed in sackcloth, fell face down, ¹⁷and David prayed to God: "Was it not I who ordered the census of the people? I am the one who sinned, I did this wicked thing. But these sheep, what have they done? O Lord, my God, strike me and my father's family, but do not afflict your people with this plague!"

¹⁸Then the angel of the Lord commanded Gad to tell David to go up and set up an altar to the Lord on the threshing floor of Ornan the Jebusite. ¹⁹David went up at the word of Gad, which he spoke in the name of the Lord. ²⁰Ornan turned around and saw the king; his four sons who were with him hid themselves, but Ornan

kept on threshing wheat. ²¹But as David came toward Ornan, he looked up and saw that it was David, and left the threshing floor and bowed down before David, his face to the ground. ²²David said to Ornan: "Sell me the site of this threshing floor, that I may build on it an altar to the LORD. Sell it to me at its full price, that the plague may be withdrawn from the people." ²³But Ornan said to David: "Take it as your own, and let my lord the king do what is good in his sight. See, I also give you the oxen for the burnt offerings, the threshing sledges for the wood, and the wheat for the grain offering. I give it all to you." ²⁴But King David replied to Ornan: "No! I will buy it from you properly, at its full price. I will not take what is yours for the LORD, nor bring burnt offerings that cost me nothing." ²⁵So David paid Ornan six hundred shekels of gold for the place.

Altar for Burnt Offerings. ²⁶David then built an altar there to the LORD, and sacrificed burnt offerings and communion offerings. He called upon the LORD, who answered him by sending down fire from heaven upon the altar for burnt offerings. ²⁷Then the LORD gave orders to the angel to return his sword to its sheath.

²⁸Once David saw that the LORD had answered him at the threshing floor of Ornan the Jebusite, he continued to offer sacrifices there. ²⁹The tabernacle of the LORD, which Moses had made in the wilderness, and the altar for burnt offerings were at that time on the high place at Gibeon. ³⁰But David could not go into his presence to inquire of God, for he was fearful of the sword of the angel of the LORD.

22:1 Thus David said, "This is the house of the LORD God, and this is the altar for burnt offerings for Israel." ²David then ordered that the resident aliens in the land of Israel should be brought together, and he appointed them stonecutters to hew out stone blocks for building the house of God.

³David also laid up large stores of iron to make nails for the doors of the gates, and clamps, together with so much bronze that it could not be weighed, ⁴and cedar trees without number. The Sidonians and Tyrians brought great stores of cedar logs to David. ⁵David said: "My son Solomon is young and inexperienced; but the house that is to be built for the LORD must be made so magnificent that it will be renowned and glorious in all lands. Therefore I will make preparations for it." Thus before his death David laid up materials in abundance.

Charge to Solomon. ⁶Then he summoned his son Solomon and commanded him to build a house for the LORD, the God of Israel. ⁷David said to Solomon: "My son, it was my purpose to build a house myself for the name of the LORD, my God. ⁸But this word of the LORD came to me: You have shed much blood, and you have waged great wars. You may not build a house for my name, because you have shed too much blood upon the earth in my sight. ⁹However, a son will be born to you. He will be a peaceful man, and I will give him rest from all his enemies on every side. For Solomon shall be his name, and in his time I will bestow peace and tranquility on Israel. ¹⁰It is he who shall build a house for my name; he shall be a son to me, and I will be a father to him, and I will establish the throne of his kingship over Israel forever.

¹¹"Now, my son, the LORD be with you, and may you succeed in building the house of the LORD your God, as he has said you shall. ¹²But may the LORD give you prudence and discernment when he gives you command over Israel, so that you keep the law of the LORD, your God. ¹³Only then shall you succeed, if you are careful to observe the statutes and ordinances which the LORD commanded Moses for Israel. Be strong and steadfast; do not fear or be dismayed. ¹⁴See, with great effort I have laid up for the house of the LORD a hundred

thousand talents of gold, a million talents of silver, and bronze and iron in such great quantities that they cannot be weighed. I have also laid up wood and stones, to which you must add. [15]Moreover, you have available workers, stonecutters, masons, carpenters, and experts in every craft, [16]without number, skilled with gold, silver, bronze, and iron. Set to work, therefore, and the LORD be with you!"

Charge to the Officials. [17]David also commanded all of the officials of Israel to help his son Solomon: [18]"Is not the LORD your God with you? Has he not given you rest on every side? Indeed, he has delivered the inhabitants of the land into my power, and the land is subdued before the LORD and his people. [19]Therefore, devote your hearts and souls to seeking the LORD your God. Proceed to build the sanctuary of the LORD God, that the ark of the covenant of the LORD and God's sacred vessels may be brought into the house built for the name of the LORD."

The Levitical Divisions. 23:1 When David had grown old and was near the end of his days, he made his son Solomon king over Israel. [2]He then gathered together all the officials of Israel, along with the priests and the Levites.

[3]The Levites thirty years old and above were counted, and their total number was found to be thirty-eight thousand. [4]Of these, twenty-four thousand were to direct the service of the house of the LORD, six thousand were to be officials and judges, [5]four thousand were to be gatekeepers, and four thousand were to praise the LORD with the instruments which [David] had devised for praise. [6]David apportioned them into divisions according to the sons of Levi: Gershon, Kohath, and Merari.

[7]To the Gershonites belonged Ladan and Shimei. [8]The sons of Ladan: Jehiel the chief, then Zetham and Joel; three in all. [9]The sons of Shimei were Shelomoth, Haziel, and Haran; three. These were the heads of the families of Ladan. [10]The sons of Shimei were Jahath, Zizah, Jeush, and Beriah; these were the sons of Shimei, four in all. [11]Jahath was the chief and Zizah was second to him; but Jeush and Beriah had few sons, and therefore they were classed as a single family, exercising a single office.

[12]The sons of Kohath: Amram, Izhar, Hebron, and Uzziel; four in all. [13]The sons of Amram were Aaron and Moses. Aaron was set apart to be consecrated as most holy, he and his sons forever, to offer sacrifice before the LORD, to minister to him, and to bless in his name forever. [14]As for Moses, however, the man of God, his sons were counted as part of the tribe of Levi. [15]The sons of Moses were Gershom and Eliezer. [16]The sons of Gershom: Shubael the chief. [17]The sons of Eliezer were Rehabiah the chief—Eliezer had no other sons, but the sons of Rehabiah were very numerous. [18]The sons of Izhar: Shelomith the chief. [19]The sons of Hebron: Jeriah, the chief, Amariah, the second, Jahaziel, the third, and Jekameam, the fourth. [20]The sons of Uzziel: Micah, the chief, and Isshiah, the second.

[21]The sons of Merari: Mahli and Mushi. The sons of Mahli: Eleazar and Kish. [22]Eleazar died leaving no sons, only daughters; the sons of Kish, their kinsmen, married them. [23]The sons of Mushi: Mahli, Eder, and Jeremoth; three in all.

[24]These were the sons of Levi according to their ancestral houses, the family heads as they were enrolled one by one according to their names. They performed the work of the service of the house of the LORD beginning at twenty years of age.

[25]David said: "The LORD, the God of Israel, has given rest to his people, and has taken up his dwelling in Jerusalem forever. [26]Henceforth the Levites need not carry the tabernacle or any of the equipment for its service." [27]For by David's last words the Levites were enlisted from the time they were twenty years old. [28]Their duty is to

assist the sons of Aaron in the service of the house of the LORD, having charge of the courts, the chambers, and the preservation of everything holy: they take part in the service of the house of God. ²⁹They also have charge of the showbread, of the fine flour for the grain offering, of the wafers of unleavened bread, and of the baking and mixing, and of all measures of quantity and size. ³⁰They are to be present every morning to offer thanks and to praise the LORD, and likewise in the evening; ³¹and at every sacrifice of burnt offerings to the LORD on sabbaths, new moons, and feast days, in such numbers as are prescribed, they must always be present before the LORD ³²and observe what is prescribed for them concerning the tent of meeting, the sanctuary, and the sons of Aaron, their kinsmen, in the service of the house of the LORD.

The Priestly Divisions. 24:1 There were also divisions for the sons of Aaron. The sons of Aaron were Nadab, Abihu, Eleazar, and Ithamar. ²Nadab and Abihu died before their father, leaving no sons; therefore only Eleazar and Ithamar served as priests. ³David, with Zadok, a descendant of Eleazar, and Ahimelech, a descendant of Ithamar, apportioned them their offices in the priestly service. ⁴But since the sons of Eleazar were found to be more numerous by male heads than those of Ithamar, the former were divided into sixteen groups, and the latter into eight groups, each under its family heads. ⁵Their functions were assigned impartially by lot, for there were officers of the holy place, and officers of God, descended both from Eleazar and from Ithamar. ⁶The scribe Shemaiah, son of Nethanel, a Levite, recorded them in the presence of the king, and of the officials, of Zadok the priest, and of Ahimelech, son of Abiathar, and of the heads of the ancestral houses of the priests and of the Levites, listing two successive family groups from Eleazar before each one from Ithamar.

⁷The first lot fell to Jehoiarib, the second to Jedaiah, ⁸the third to Harim, the fourth to Seorim, ⁹the fifth to Malchijah, the sixth to Mijamin, ¹⁰the seventh to Hakkoz, the eighth to Abijah, ¹¹the ninth to Jeshua, the tenth to Shecaniah, ¹²the eleventh to Eliashib, the twelfth to Jakim, ¹³the thirteenth to Huppah, the fourteenth to Ishbaal, ¹⁴the fifteenth to Bilgah, the sixteenth to Immer, ¹⁵the seventeenth to Hezir, the eighteenth to Happizzez, ¹⁶the nineteenth to Pethahiah, the twentieth to Jehezkel, ¹⁷the twenty-first to Jachin, the twenty-second to Gamul, ¹⁸the twenty-third to Delaiah, the twenty-fourth to Maaziah. ¹⁹This was the appointed order of their service when they functioned in the house of the LORD according to the precepts given them by Aaron, their father, as the LORD, the God of Israel, had commanded him.

Other Levites. ²⁰Of the remaining Levites, there were Shubael, of the sons of Amram, and Jehdeiah, of the sons of Shubael; ²¹Isshiah, the chief, of the sons of Rehabiah; ²²Shelomith of the Izharites, and Jahath of the sons of Shelomith. ²³The sons of Hebron were Jeriah, the chief, Amariah, the second, Jahaziel, the third, Jekameam, the fourth. ²⁴The sons of Uzziel were Micah; Shamir, of the sons of Micah; ²⁵Isshiah, the brother of Micah; and Zechariah, a descendant of Isshiah. ²⁶The sons of Merari were Mahli, Mushi, and the sons of his son Uzziah. ²⁷The sons of Merari through his son Uzziah: Shoham, Zaccur, and Ibri. ²⁸The sons of Mahli were Eleazar, who had no sons, ²⁹and Jerahmeel, of the sons of Kish. ³⁰The sons of Mushi were Mahli, Eder, and Jerimoth.

These were the sons of the Levites according to their ancestral houses. ³¹They too, in the same manner as their kinsmen, the sons of Aaron, cast lots in the presence of King David, Zadok, Ahimelech, and the heads of the priestly and levitical families; the more important family did so in the same way as the less important one.

☐ MATTHEW 13:24-43

The Parable of the Weeds among the Wheat. 13:24 He proposed another parable to them. "The kingdom of heaven may be likened to a man who sowed good seed in his field. 25While everyone was asleep his enemy came and sowed weeds all through the wheat, and then went off. 26When the crop grew and bore fruit, the weeds appeared as well. 27The slaves of the householder came to him and said, 'Master, did you not sow good seed in your field? Where have the weeds come from?' 28He answered, 'An enemy has done this.' His slaves said to him, 'Do you want us to go and pull them up?' 29He replied, 'No, if you pull up the weeds you might uproot the wheat along with them. 30Let them grow together until harvest; then at harvest time I will say to the harvesters, "First collect the weeds and tie them in bundles for burning; but gather the wheat into my barn."'

The Parable of the Mustard Seed. 31He proposed another parable to them. "The kingdom of heaven is like a mustard seed that a person took and sowed in a field. 32It is the smallest of all the seeds, yet when full-grown it is the largest of plants. It becomes a large bush, and the 'birds of the sky come and dwell in its branches.'"

The Parable of the Yeast. 33He spoke to them another parable. "The kingdom of heaven is like yeast that a woman took and mixed with three measures of wheat flour until the whole batch was leavened."

The Use of Parables. 34All these things Jesus spoke to the crowds in parables. He spoke to them only in parables, 35to fulfill what had been said through the prophet:

"I will open my mouth in parables,
  I will announce what has lain
        hidden from the foundation
        [of the world]."

The Explanation of the Parable of the Weeds. 36Then, dismissing the crowds, he went into the house. His disciples approached him and said, "Explain to us the parable of the weeds in the field." 37He said in reply, "He who sows good seed is the Son of Man, 38the field is the world, the good seed the children of the kingdom. The weeds are the children of the evil one, 39and the enemy who sows them is the devil. The harvest is the end of the age, and the harvesters are angels. 40Just as weeds are collected and burned [up] with fire, so will it be at the end of the age. 41The Son of Man will send his angels, and they will collect out of his kingdom all who cause others to sin and all evildoers. 42They will throw them into the fiery furnace, where there will be wailing and grinding of teeth. 43Then the righteous will shine like the sun in the kingdom of their Father. Whoever has ears ought to hear."

May 8

Just as the Gospel extends itself like mustard seed, and prevails like leaven, so it is precious like a pearl, and affords full abundance like a treasure. The Lord's parables teach us, then, not only that we are to strip ourselves of everything else, and cling to the Gospel, but also that we are to do so with joy.

— St. John Chrysostom

☐ 1 CHRONICLES 25-29

The Singers. 25:1 David and the leaders of the liturgy set apart for the service the sons of Asaph, Heman, and Jeduthun, who prophesied to the accompaniment of lyres and harps and cymbals.

This is the list of those who performed this service: [2]Of the sons of Asaph: Zaccur, Joseph, Nethaniah, and Asharelah, sons of Asaph, under the direction of Asaph, who prophesied under the guidance of the king. [3]Of Jeduthun, these sons of Jeduthun: Gedaliah, Zeri, Jeshaiah, Shimei, Hashabiah, and Mattithiah; six, under the direction of their father Jeduthun, who prophesied to the accompaniment of a lyre, to give thanks and praise to the Lord. [4]Of Heman, these sons of Heman: Bukkiah, Mattaniah, Uzziel, Shubael, and Jerimoth; Hananiah, Hanani, Eliathah, Giddalti, Romamti-ezer, Joshbekashah, Mallothi, Hothir, and Mahazioth. [5]All these were the sons of Heman, the king's seer for divine matters; to exalt him God gave Heman fourteen sons and three daughters. [6]All these, whether of Asaph, Jeduthun, or Heman, were under their fathers' direction in the singing in the house of the Lord to the accompaniment of cymbals, harps and lyres, serving in the house of God, under the guidance of the king. [7]Their number, together with that of their kinsmen who were trained in singing to the Lord, all of them skilled men, was two hundred and eighty-eight. [8]They cast lots for their functions equally, young and old, master and pupil alike.

[9]The first lot fell to Asaph, to the family of Joseph; he and his sons and his kinsmen were twelve. Gedaliah was the second; he and his kinsmen and his sons were twelve. [10]The third was Zaccur, his sons, and his kinsmen: twelve. [11]The fourth fell to Izri, his sons, and his kinsmen: twelve. [12]The fifth was Nethaniah, his sons, and his kinsmen: twelve. [13]The sixth was Bukkiah, his sons, and his kinsmen: twelve. [14]The seventh was Jesarelah, his sons, and his kinsmen: twelve. [15]The eighth was Jeshaiah, his sons, and his kinsmen: twelve. [16]The ninth was Mattaniah, his sons, and his kinsmen: twelve. [17]The tenth was Shimei, his sons, and his kinsmen: twelve. [18]The eleventh was Uzziel, his sons, and his kinsmen: twelve. [19]The twelfth fell to Hashabiah, his sons, and his kinsmen: twelve. [20]The thirteenth was Shubael, his sons, and his kinsmen: twelve. [21]The fourteenth was Mattithiah, his sons, and his kinsmen: twelve. [22]The fifteenth fell to Jeremoth, his sons, and his kinsmen: twelve. [23]The sixteenth fell to Hananiah, his sons, and his kinsmen: twelve. [24]The seventeenth fell to Joshbekashah, his sons, and his kinsmen: twelve. [25]The eighteenth fell to Hanani, his sons, and his kinsmen: twelve. [26]The nineteenth fell to Mallothi, his sons, and his kinsmen: twelve. [27]The twentieth fell to Eliathah, his sons, and his kinsmen: twelve. [28]The twenty-first fell to Hothir, his sons, and his kinsmen: twelve. [29]The twenty-second fell to Giddalti, his sons,

and his kinsmen: twelve. ³⁰The twenty-third fell to Mahazioth, his sons, and his kinsmen: twelve. ³¹The twenty-fourth fell to Romamti-ezer, his sons, and his kinsmen: twelve.

Divisions of Gatekeepers. 26:1 As for the divisions of gatekeepers: Of the Korahites was Meshelemiah, the son of Kore, one of the sons of Abiasaph. ²Meshelemiah's sons: Zechariah, the firstborn, Jediael, the second son, Zebadiah, the third, Jathniel, the fourth, ³Elam, the fifth, Jehohanan, the sixth, Eliehoenai, the seventh. ⁴Obed-edom's sons: Shemaiah, the firstborn, Jehozabad, a second son, Joah, the third, Sachar, the fourth, Nethanel, the fifth, ⁵Ammiel, the sixth, Issachar, the seventh, Peullethai, the eighth, for God blessed him. ⁶To his son Shemaiah were born sons who ruled over their family, for they were warriors. ⁷The sons of Shemaiah were Othni, Rephael, Obed, and Elzabad; also his kinsmen who were men of substance, Elihu and Semachiah. ⁸All these were the sons of Obed-edom, who, together with their sons and their kinsmen, were men of substance, fit for the service. Of Obed-edom, sixty-two. ⁹Of Meshelemiah, eighteen sons and kinsmen, men of substance.

¹⁰Hosah, a descendant of Merari, had these sons: Shimri, the chief (for though he was not the firstborn, his father made him chief), ¹¹Hilkiah, the second son, Tebaliah, the third, Zechariah, the fourth. All the sons and kinsmen of Hosah were thirteen.

¹²To these divisions of the gatekeepers, by their chief men, were assigned watches for them to minister in the house of the LORD, for each group in the same way. ¹³They cast lots for each gate, small and large families alike. ¹⁴When the lot was cast for the east side, it fell to Meshelemiah. Then they cast lots for his son Zechariah, a prudent counselor, and the north side fell to his lot. ¹⁵To Obed-edom fell the south side, and to his sons the storehouse. ¹⁶To Hosah fell the west side with the Shallecheth gate at the ascending highway. For each family, watches were established. ¹⁷On the east, six watched each day, on the north, four each day, on the south, four each day, and at the storehouse they were two and two; ¹⁸as for the large building on the west, there were four at the highway and two at the large building. ¹⁹These were the classes of the gatekeepers, sons of Korah and Merari.

Treasurers. ²⁰Their brother Levites had oversight of the treasuries of the house of God and the treasuries of votive offerings. ²¹Among the sons of Ladan the Gershonite, the family heads were sons of Jehiel: ²²the sons of Jehiel, Zetham and his brother Joel, who oversaw the treasures of the house of the LORD. ²³Of the Amramites, Izharites, Hebronites, and Uzzielites, ²⁴Shubael, son of Gershom, son of Moses, was principal overseer of the treasures. ²⁵His associate was of the line of Eliezer, whose son was Rehabiah, whose son was Jeshaiah, whose son was Joram, whose son was Zichri, whose son was Shelomith. ²⁶This Shelomith and his kinsmen oversaw all the treasures of the votive offerings dedicated by King David, the heads of the families, the commanders of thousands and of hundreds, and the commanders of the army; ²⁷what came from wars and from spoils, they dedicated for the support of the house of the LORD. ²⁸Also, whatever Samuel the seer, Saul, son of Kish, Abner, son of Ner, Joab, son of Zeruiah, and all others had consecrated, was under the charge of Shelomith and his kinsmen.

Magistrates. ²⁹Among the Izharites, Chenaniah and his sons were in charge of Israel's civil affairs as officials and judges. ³⁰Among the Hebronites, Hashabiah and his kinsmen, one thousand seven hundred men of substance, had the administration of Israel on the western side of the Jordan for all the work of the LORD and the service of the king. ³¹Among the Hebronites,

Jerijah was their chief according to their family records. In the fortieth year of David's reign search was made, and there were found among them warriors at Jazer of Gilead. [32]His kinsmen were also men of substance, two thousand seven hundred heads of families. King David appointed them to the administration of the Reubenites, the Gadites, and the half-tribe of Manasseh for everything pertaining to God and to the king.

Army Commanders. 27:1 This is the list of the Israelite family heads, commanders of thousands and of hundreds, and other officers who served the king in all that pertained to the divisions, of twenty-four thousand men each, that came and went month by month throughout the year. [2]Over the first division for the first month was Ishbaal, son of Zabdiel, and in his division were twenty-four thousand men; [3]a descendant of Perez, he was chief over all the commanders of the army for the first month. [4]Over the division of the second month was Eleazar, son of Dodo, from Ahoh, and in his division were twenty-four thousand men. [5]The third army commander, for the third month, was Benaiah, son of Jehoiada the chief priest, and in his division were twenty-four thousand men. [6]This Benaiah was a warrior among the Thirty and over the Thirty. His son Ammizabad was over his division. [7]Fourth, for the fourth month, was Asahel, brother of Joab, and after him his son Zebadiah, and in his division were twenty-four thousand men. [8]Fifth, for the fifth month, was the commander Shamhuth, a descendant of Zerah, and in his division were twenty-four thousand men. [9]Sixth, for the sixth month, was Ira, son of Ikkesh, from Tekoa, and in his division were twenty-four thousand men. [10]Seventh, for the seventh month, was Hellez, from Beth-pelet, of the Ephraimites, and in his division were twenty-four thousand men. [11]Eighth, for the eighth month, was Sibbecai the Hushathite, a descendant of Zerah, and in his division were twenty-four thousand men. [12]Ninth, for the ninth month, was Abiezer from Anathoth, of Benjamin, and in his division were twenty-four thousand men. [13]Tenth, for the tenth month, was Maharai from Netophah, a descendant of Zerah, and in his division were twenty-four thousand men. [14]Eleventh, for the eleventh month, was Benaiah the Pirathonite, of the Ephraimites, and in his division were twenty-four thousand men. [15]Twelfth, for the twelfth month, was Heldai the Netophathite, of the family of Othniel, and in his division were twenty-four thousand men.

Tribal Leaders. [16]Over the tribes of Israel, for the Reubenites the leader was Eliezer, son of Zichri; for the Simeonites, Shephatiah, son of Maacah; [17]for Levi, Hashabiah, son of Kemuel; for Aaron, Zadok; [18]for Judah, Eliab, one of David's brothers; for Issachar, Omri, son of Michael; [19]for Zebulun, Ishmaiah, son of Obadiah; for Naphtali, Jeremoth, son of Azriel; [20]for the Ephraimites, Hoshea, son of Azaziah; for the half-tribe of Manasseh, Joel, son of Pedaiah; [21]for the half-tribe of Manasseh in Gilead, Iddo, son of Zechariah; for Benjamin, Jaasiel, son of Abner; [22]for Dan, Azarel, son of Jeroham. These were the commanders of the tribes of Israel.

[23]David did not count those who were twenty years of age or younger, for the LORD had promised to multiply Israel like the stars of the heavens. [24]Joab, son of Zeruiah, began to take the census, but he did not complete it, for because of it wrath fell upon Israel. Therefore the number was not recorded in the book of chronicles of King David.

Overseers. [25]Over the treasuries of the king was Azmaveth, the son of Adiel. Over the treasuries in the country, the cities, the villages, and the towers was Jonathan, son of Uzziah. [26]Over the farm workers who tilled the soil was Ezri, son of Chelub. ²⁷Over the vineyards was Shimei from Ramah, and over their produce for the wine cellars was Zabdi the Shiphmite. ²⁸Over the olive trees and sycamores of the Shephelah was Baalhanan the Gederite, and over the stores of oil was Joash. ²⁹Over the cattle that grazed in Sharon was Shitrai the Sharonite, and over the cattle in the valleys was Shaphat, the son of Adlai; ³⁰over the camels was Obil the Ishmaelite; over the donkeys was Jehdeiah the Meronothite; ³¹and over the flocks was Jaziz the Hagrite. All these were the overseers of King David's possessions.

David's Court. ³²Jonathan, David's uncle and a man of intelligence, was counselor and scribe; he and Jehiel, the son of Hachmoni, attended the king's sons. ³³Ahithophel was also the king's counselor, and Hushai the Archite was the king's friend. ³⁴After Ahithophel came Jehoiada, the son of Benaiah, and Abiathar. The commander of the king's army was Joab.

The Assembly at Jerusalem. 28:1 David assembled at Jerusalem all the commanders of Israel, the tribal commanders, the commanders of the divisions who were in the service of the king, the commanders of thousands and of hundreds, those in command of all the king's estates and possessions, and his sons, together with the courtiers, the warriors, and every person of substance. ²King David rose to his feet and said: "Hear me, my kinsmen and my people. It was my purpose to build a house of repose myself for the ark of the covenant of the LORD, the footstool for the feet of our God; and I was preparing to build it. ³But God said to me, You may not build a house for my name, for you are a man who waged wars and shed blood. ⁴However, the LORD, the God of Israel, chose me from all my father's family to be king over Israel forever. For he chose Judah as leader, then one family of Judah, that of my father; and finally, among all the sons of my father, it pleased him to make me king over all Israel. ⁵And of all my sons—for the LORD has given me many sons—he has chosen my son Solomon to sit on the throne of the LORD's kingship over Israel. ⁶For he said to me: It is your son Solomon who shall build my house and my courts, for I have chosen him for my son, and I will be a father to him. ⁷I will establish his kingdom forever, if he perseveres in carrying out my commandments and ordinances as he does now. ⁸Therefore, in the sight of all Israel, the assembly of the LORD, and in the hearing of our God: keep and carry out all the commandments of the LORD, your God, that you may continue to possess this good land and afterward leave it as an inheritance to your children forever.

⁹"As for you, Solomon, my son, know the God of your father and serve him with a whole heart and a willing soul, for the LORD searches all hearts and understands all the mind's thoughts. If you search for him, he will be found; but if you abandon him, he will cast you off forever. ¹⁰See, then! The LORD has chosen you to build a house as his sanctuary. Be strong and set to work."

Temple Plans Given to Solomon. ¹¹Then David gave to his son Solomon the design of the portico and of the house itself, with its storerooms, its upper rooms and inner chambers, and the shrine containing the cover of the ark. ¹²He provided also the design for all else that he had in mind by way of courts for the house of the LORD, with the surrounding compartments for the treasuries of the house of God and the treasuries for the votive offerings, ¹³as well as for the divisions of the priests and Levites, for all the work of the service of the house of the LORD, and for all the liturgical vessels of the house of the LORD. ¹⁴He specified the weight of gold to be used in the golden vessels for the various services and the weight of silver to be used in the silver vessels for the various services; ¹⁵likewise for the golden menorahs and their lamps he specified the weight of gold for each menorah and its lamps, and for the silver menorahs he specified the weight of silver for each menorah and its lamps, depending on the use to which each menorah was to be put. ¹⁶He specified the weight of gold for each table that was to hold the showbread, and the silver for the silver tables; ¹⁷the pure gold for the forks, basins, and pitchers; the weight of gold for each golden bowl and the weight of silver for each silver bowl; ¹⁸the refined gold, and its weight, to be used for the altar of incense; and, finally, gold to fashion the chariot: the cherubim spreading their wings and covering the ark of the covenant of the LORD. ¹⁹All this he wrote down, by the hand of the LORD, to make him understand it— the working out of the whole design.

²⁰Then David said to his son Solomon: "Be strong and steadfast, and go to work; do not fear or be dismayed, for the LORD God, my God, is with you. He will not fail you or abandon you before you have completed all the work for the service of the house of the LORD. ²¹The divisions of the priests and Levites are ready for all the service of the house of God; they will be with you in all the work with all those who are eager to show their skill in every kind of craftsmanship. Also the commanders and all the people will do everything that you command."

Offerings for the Temple. 29:1 King David then said to the whole assembly: "My son Solomon, whom alone God has chosen, is still young and inexperienced; the work, however, is great, for this palace is not meant for human beings, but for the LORD God. ²For this reason I have stored up for the house of my God, as far as I was able, gold for what will be made of gold, silver for what will be made of silver, bronze for what will be made of bronze, iron for what will be made of iron, wood for what will be made of wood, onyx stones and settings for them, carnelian and mosaic stones, every other kind of precious stone, and great quantities of marble. ³But now, because of the delight I take in the house of my God, in addition to all that I stored up for the holy house, I give to the house of my God my personal fortune in gold and silver: ⁴three thousand talents of Ophir gold, and seven thousand talents of refined silver, for overlaying the walls of the rooms, ⁵for the various utensils to be made of gold and silver, and for every work that is to be done by artisans. Now, who else will contribute generously and consecrate themselves this day to the LORD?"

⁶Then the heads of the families, the tribal commanders of Israel, the commanders of thousands and of hundreds, and those who had command of the king's affairs came forward willingly ⁷and contributed for the service of the house of God five thousand talents and ten thousand darics of gold, ten thousand talents of silver, eighteen thousand talents of bronze, and one hundred thousand talents of iron. ⁸Those who had precious stones gave them into the keeping of Jehiel the Gershonite for the treasury of the house of the LORD. ⁹The people rejoiced over these free-will offerings, for they had been contributed to the LORD wholeheartedly. King David also rejoiced greatly.

David's Prayer. ¹⁰Then David blessed the LORD in the sight of the whole assembly. David said:

"Blessed are you, LORD,
    God of Israel our father,
    from eternity to eternity.
¹¹Yours, LORD, are greatness and might,
    majesty, victory, and splendor.
For all in heaven and on earth is yours;
    yours, LORD, is kingship;
    you are exalted as head over all.
¹²Riches and glory are from you,
    and you have dominion over all.
In your hand are power and might;
    it is yours to give greatness and
      strength to all.

[13]Therefore, our God, we give you thanks and we praise the majesty of your name.

[14]"But who am I, and who are my people, that we should have the means to contribute so freely? For everything is from you, and what we give is what we have from you. [15]For before you we are strangers and travelers, like all our ancestors. Our days on earth are like a shadow, without a future. [16]Lord our God, all this wealth that we have brought together to build you a house for your holy name comes from you and is entirely yours. [17]I know, my God, that you put hearts to the test and that you take pleasure in integrity. With a whole heart I have willingly given all these things, and now with joy I have seen your people here present also giving to you generously. [18]Lord, God of our ancestors Abraham, Isaac, and Israel, keep such thoughts in the hearts and minds of your people forever, and direct their hearts toward you. [19]Give to my son Solomon a wholehearted desire to keep your commandments, precepts, and statutes, that he may carry out all these plans and build the palace for which I have made preparation."

[20]Then David told the whole assembly, "Now bless the Lord your God!" And the whole assembly blessed the Lord, the God of their ancestors, bowing down in homage before the Lord and before the king. [21]On the following day they brought sacrifices and burnt offerings to the Lord, a thousand bulls, a thousand rams, and a thousand lambs, together with their libations and many other sacrifices for all Israel; [22]and on that day they ate and drank in the Lord's presence with great rejoicing.

Solomon Anointed. Then for a second time they proclaimed David's son Solomon king, and they anointed him for the Lord as ruler, and Zadok as priest. [23]Thereafter Solomon sat on the throne of the Lord as king succeeding his father David; he prospered, and all Israel obeyed him. [24]All the commanders and warriors, and also all the other sons of King David, swore allegiance to King Solomon. [25]And the Lord exalted Solomon greatly in the eyes of all Israel, giving him a glorious reign such as had not been enjoyed by any king over Israel before him.

David's Death. [26]Thus David, the son of Jesse, had reigned over all Israel. [27]He was king over Israel for forty years: he was king seven years in Hebron and thirty-three years in Jerusalem. [28]He died at a ripe old age, rich in years and wealth and glory, and his son Solomon succeeded him as king.

[29]Now the deeds of King David, first and last, are recorded in the history of Samuel the seer, the history of Nathan the prophet, and the history of Gad the seer, [30]together with the particulars of his reign and valor, and of the events that affected him and all Israel and all the kingdoms of the earth.

☐ MATTHEW 13:44-53

More Parables. 13:44 "The kingdom of heaven is like a treasure buried in a field, which a person finds and hides again, and out of joy goes and sells all that he has and buys that field. [45]Again, the kingdom of heaven is like a merchant searching for fine pearls. [46]When he finds a pearl of great price, he goes and sells all that he has and buys it. [47]Again, the kingdom of heaven is like a net thrown into the sea, which collects fish of every kind. [48]When it is full they haul it ashore and sit down to put what is good into buckets. What is bad they throw away. [49]Thus it will be at the end of the age. The angels will go out and separate the wicked from the righteous [50]and throw them into the fiery furnace, where there will be wailing and grinding of teeth.

Treasures New and Old. ⁵¹"Do you understand all these things?" They answered, "Yes." ⁵²And he replied, "Then every scribe who has been instructed in the kingdom of heaven is like the head of a household who brings from his storeroom both the new and the old." ⁵³When Jesus finished these parables, he went away from there.

May 9

St. Pachomius

Say to your hands: "O hands, the time will come when you will be unable to move, and when you will never be clasped in each other again. Why then, before that time comes, don't you stretch yourselves out to the Lord in prayer?"

— ST. PACHOMIUS

☐ 2 CHRONICLES 1-4

Solomon at Gibeon. 1:1 Solomon, son of David, strengthened his hold on the kingdom, for the LORD, his God, was with him, making him ever greater. ²Solomon summoned all Israel, the commanders of thousands and of hundreds, the judges, the princes of all Israel, and the family heads; ³and, accompanied by the whole assembly, Solomon went to the high place at Gibeon, because the tent of meeting of God, made in the wilderness by Moses, the LORD's servant, was there. ⁴David had, however, brought up the ark of God from Kiriath-jearim to Jerusalem, where he had provided a place and pitched a tent for it; ⁵the bronze altar made by Bezalel, son of Uri, son of Hur, he put in front of the tabernacle of the LORD. There Solomon and the assembly sought out the LORD, ⁶and Solomon offered sacrifice in the LORD's presence on the bronze altar at the tent of meeting; he sacrificed a thousand burnt offerings upon it.

⁷That night God appeared to Solomon and said to him: Whatever you ask, I will give you. ⁸Solomon answered God: "You have shown great favor to David my father, and you have made me king to succeed him. ⁹Now, LORD God, may your word to David my father be confirmed, for you have made me king over a people as numerous as the dust of the earth. ¹⁰Give me, therefore, wisdom and knowledge to govern this people, for otherwise who could rule this vast people of yours?" ¹¹God then replied to Solomon: Because this has been your wish—you did not ask for riches, treasures, and glory, or the life of those who hate you, or even for a long life for yourself, but you have asked for wisdom and knowledge in order to rule my people over whom I have made you king— ¹²wisdom and knowledge are given you. I will also give you riches, treasures, and glory, such as kings before you never had, nor will those who come after you.

Solomon's Wealth. ¹³Solomon returned to Jerusalem from the high place at Gibeon, from before the tent of meeting, and became king over Israel. ¹⁴Solomon amassed chariots and horses: he had one thousand four hundred chariots and twelve thousand horses; these he allocated among the chariot cities and to the king's service in Jerusalem. ¹⁵The king made silver and gold as common in Jerusalem as stones, and cedars as numerous as the sycamores of the Shephelah. ¹⁶Solomon's horses were imported from Egypt and Cilicia, where the king's agents purchased them at the prevailing price. ¹⁷A chariot imported from Egypt cost six hundred shekels of silver, a horse one hundred and fifty shekels; so they were exported to all the Hittite and Aramean kings.

Preparations for the Temple. ¹⁸Solomon gave orders for the building of a house for the name of the LORD and also a king's house for himself.

2:1 Solomon conscripted seventy thousand men to carry stones and eighty thousand to cut the stones in the mountains, and over these he placed three thousand six hundred overseers. ²Moreover, Solomon sent this message to Huram, king of Tyre: "As you dealt with David my father, and sent him cedars to build a house for his dwelling— ³now I am going to build a house for the name of the LORD, my God, and to consecrate it to him, for the burning of fragrant incense in his presence, for the perpetual display of the showbread, for burnt offerings morning and evening, and for the sabbaths, new moons, and festivals of the LORD, our God: such is Israel's perpetual obligation. ⁴And the house I am going to build must be great, for our God is greater than all other gods. ⁵Yet who is really able to build him a house, since the heavens and even the highest heavens cannot contain him? And who am I that I should build him a house, unless it be to offer incense in his presence? ⁶Now, send me men skilled at work in gold, silver, bronze, and iron, in purple, crimson, and violet fabrics, and who know how to do engraved work, to join the skilled craftsmen who are with me in Judah and Jerusalem, whom David my father appointed. ⁷Also send me boards of cedar, cypress and cabinet wood from Lebanon, for I realize that your servants know how to cut the wood of Lebanon.

My servants will work with yours ⁸in order to prepare for me a great quantity of wood, since the house I intend to build must be great and wonderful. ⁹I will furnish as food for your servants, the woodcutters, twenty thousand kors of wheat, twenty thousand kors of barley, twenty thousand baths of wine, and twenty thousand baths of oil."

¹⁰Huram, king of Tyre, wrote an answer which he sent to Solomon: "Because the LORD loves his people, he has placed you over them as king." ¹¹He added: "Blessed be the LORD, the God of Israel, who made heaven and earth, for having given King David a wise son of intelligence and understanding, who will build a house for the LORD and also his own royal house. ¹²I am now sending you a craftsman of great skill, Huram-abi, ¹³son of a Danite woman and of a father from Tyre; he knows how to work with gold, silver, bronze, and iron, with stone and wood, with purple, violet, fine linen, and crimson, and also how to do all kinds of engraved work and to devise every type of design that may be given him and your craftsmen and the craftsmen of my lord David your father. ¹⁴And now, let my lord send to his servants the wheat, barley, oil, and wine which he has promised. ¹⁵For our part, we will cut trees on Lebanon, as many as you need, and send them down to you in rafts to the port of Joppa, whence you may take them up to Jerusalem."

¹⁶Thereupon Solomon took a census of all the alien men resident in the land of Israel (following the census David his father had taken of them); they were found to number one hundred fifty-three thousand six hundred. ¹⁷Of these he made seventy thousand carriers and eighty thousand cutters in the mountains, and three thousand six hundred overseers to keep the people working.

Building of the Temple. 3:1 Then Solomon began to build the house of the LORD in Jerusalem on Mount Moriah, which had been shown to David his father, in the place David had prepared, the threshing floor of Ornan the Jebusite. ²He began to build in the second month of the fourth year of his reign. ³These were the specifications laid down by Solomon for building the house of God: the length was sixty cubits according to the old measure, and the width was twenty cubits; ⁴the front porch along the width of the house was also twenty cubits, and it was twenty cubits high. He covered its interior with pure gold. ⁵The nave he overlaid with cypress wood and overlaid that with fine gold, embossing on it palms and chains. ⁶He also covered the house with precious stones for splendor; the gold was from Parvaim. ⁷The house, its beams and thresholds, as well as its walls and its doors, he overlaid with gold, and he engraved cherubim upon the walls. ⁸He also made the room of the holy of holies. Its length corresponded to the width of the house, twenty cubits, and its width was also twenty cubits. He overlaid it with fine gold to the amount of six hundred talents. ⁹The weight of the nails was fifty gold shekels. The upper chambers he likewise overlaid with gold.

¹⁰For the room of the holy of holies he made two cherubim of carved workmanship, which were then covered with gold. ¹¹The wings of the cherubim spanned twenty cubits: one wing of each cherub, five cubits in length, extended to a wall of the house, while the other wing, also five cubits in length, touched the corresponding wing of the other cherub. ¹²The wing of the cherub, five cubits, touched the wall of the house, and the other wing, five cubits, was joined to the wing of the other cherub. ¹³The combined wingspread of the two cherubim was thus twenty cubits. They stood upon their own feet, facing toward the nave. ¹⁴He made the veil of violet, purple, crimson, and fine linen, and had cherubim embroidered upon it.

¹⁵In front of the house he set two columns thirty-five cubits high; the capital of each was five cubits. ¹⁶He devised chains in the form of a collar with which he encircled the capitals of the columns, and he made a hundred pomegranates which he set on the chains. ¹⁷He set up the columns to correspond with the nave, one for the right side and the other for the left, and he called the one to the right Jachin and the one to the left Boaz.

4:1 Then he made a bronze altar twenty cubits long, twenty cubits wide and ten cubits high. ²He also made the molten sea. It was made with a circular rim, and measured ten cubits across, five in height, and thirty in circumference. ³Under the brim a ring of figures of oxen encircled it for ten cubits, all the way around the compass of the sea; there were two rows of oxen cast in one mold with the sea. ⁴This rested on twelve oxen, three facing north, three facing west, three facing south, and three facing east, with their haunches all toward the center; upon them was set the sea. ⁵It was a handbreadth thick, and its brim resembled that of a cup, being lily-shaped. It had a capacity of three thousand baths.

⁶Then he made ten basins for washing, placing five of them to the right and five to the left. In these the victims for the burnt offerings were washed; but the sea was for the priests to wash in.

⁷He made the menorahs of gold, ten of them as was prescribed, and placed them in the nave, five to the right and five to the left. ⁸He made ten tables and had them set in the nave, five to the right and five to the left; and he made a hundred golden bowls. ⁹He made the court of the priests and the great courtyard and the gates of the courtyard; the gates he covered with bronze. ¹⁰The sea he placed off to the southeast from the south side of the house.

¹¹When Huram had made the pots, shovels, and bowls, he finished all his work for King Solomon in the house of God: ¹²two columns; two nodes for the

capitals on top of the columns; and two pieces of netting covering the two nodes for the capitals on top of the columns; [13]four hundred pomegranates in double rows on both pieces of netting that covered the two nodes of the capitals on top of the columns. [14]He made the stands, and the basins on the stands; [15]one sea, and the twelve oxen under it; [16]pots, shovels, forks, and all the articles Huram-abi made for King Solomon for the house of the LORD; they were of burnished bronze. [17]The king had them cast in the neighborhood of the Jordan, between Succoth and Zeredah, in thick clay molds. [18]Solomon made all these vessels, so many in number that the weight of the bronze could not be determined.

[19]Solomon made all the articles that were for the house of God: the golden altar, the tables on which the showbread lay, [20]the menorahs and their lamps of pure gold which were to burn as prescribed before the inner sanctuary, [21]flowers, lamps, and gold tongs (this was of purest gold), [22]snuffers, bowls, cups, and firepans of pure gold. As for the entrance to the house, its inner doors to the holy of holies, as well as the doors to the nave of the temple, were of gold.

☐ MATTHEW 13:54-58

The Rejection at Nazareth. 13:54 He came to his native place and taught the people in their synagogue. They were astonished and said, "Where did this man get such wisdom and mighty deeds? [55]Is he not the carpenter's son? Is not his mother named Mary and his brothers James, Joseph, Simon, and Judas? [56]Are not his sisters all with us? Where did this man get all this?" [57]And they took offense at him. But Jesus said to them, "A prophet is not without honor except in his native place and in his own house." [58]And he did not work many mighty deeds there because of their lack of faith.

May 10

St. John of Ávila; St. Damien Joseph de Veuster

One act of thanksgiving to God when things are going wrong is worth a thousand thanks when things are going the way we want them to go.

— ST. JOHN OF ÁVILA

☐ 2 CHRONICLES 5-7

Dedication of the Temple. 5:1 When all the work undertaken by Solomon for the house of the LORD was completed, he brought in the votive offerings of David his father, putting the silver, the gold, and other articles in the treasuries of the house of God. [2]Then Solomon assembled the elders of Israel and all the heads of the tribes, the princes in the ancestral houses of the Israelites, to Jerusalem to bring up the ark of the LORD's covenant from the City of David, which is Zion. [3]All the people of Israel assembled before the king during the festival of the seventh month. [4]When all the elders of Israel had arrived, the Levites took up the ark; [5]and they brought up the ark and the tent of meeting with all the sacred vessels that were in the tent. The levitical priests brought them up.

⁶King Solomon and the entire community of Israel, gathered for the occasion before the ark, sacrificed sheep and oxen too many to number or count. ⁷The priests brought the ark of the covenant of the LORD to its place: the inner sanctuary of the house, the holy of holies, beneath the wings of the cherubim. ⁸The cherubim had their wings spread out over the place of the ark, covering the ark and its poles from above. ⁹The poles were so long that their ends could be seen from the holy place in front of the inner sanctuary. (They cannot be seen from outside, but they remain there to this day.) ¹⁰There was nothing in the ark but the two tablets which Moses had put there at Horeb when the LORD made a covenant with the Israelites after they went forth from Egypt.

¹¹When the priests left the holy place (all the priests who were present had purified themselves regardless of the rotation of their various divisions), ¹²the Levites who were singers, all who belonged to Asaph, Heman, Jeduthun, and their sons and brothers, clothed in fine linen, with cymbals, harps, and lyres, stood east of the altar, and with them a hundred and twenty priests blowing trumpets.

¹³When the trumpeters and singers were heard as a single voice praising and giving thanks to the LORD, and when they raised the sound of the trumpets, cymbals, and other musical instruments to "Praise the LORD, who is so good, whose love endures forever," the cloud filled the house of the LORD. ¹⁴The priests could no longer minister because of the cloud, since the glory of the LORD had filled the house of God.

6:1 Then Solomon said:

"The LORD intends to dwell in the dark cloud;
²I have built you a princely house,
the base for your enthronement forever."

³The king turned and blessed the whole assembly of Israel, while the whole assembly of Israel stood. ⁴He said: "Blessed be the LORD, the God of Israel, who with his own mouth spoke a promise to David my father and by his hand fulfilled it, saying: ⁵Since the day I brought my people out of the land of Egypt, I have not chosen a city out of any tribe of Israel for the building of a house, that my name might be there; nor have I chosen any man to be ruler of my people Israel; ⁶but now I have chosen Jerusalem, that my name may be there, and I have chosen David to rule my people Israel. ⁷When David my father wished to build a house for the name of the LORD, the God of Israel, ⁸the LORD said to him: In wishing to build a house for my name, you did well. ⁹But it is not you who will build the house, but your son, who comes from your loins: he shall build the house for my name.

¹⁰"Now the LORD has fulfilled the word he spoke. I have succeeded David my father, and I sit on the throne of Israel, as the LORD has said, and I have built this house for the name of the LORD, the God of Israel. ¹¹I have placed there the ark, in which is the covenant of the LORD that he made with the Israelites."

Solomon's Prayer. ¹²Then he stood before the altar of the LORD in the presence of the whole assembly of Israel and stretched forth his hands. ¹³Solomon had made a bronze platform five cubits long, five cubits wide, and three cubits high, which he had placed in the middle of the courtyard. Having ascended it, Solomon knelt in the presence of the whole assembly of Israel and stretched forth his hands toward heaven. ¹⁴He said: "LORD, God of Israel, there is no God like you in heaven or on earth; you keep the covenant and love toward your servants who walk before you with their whole heart, ¹⁵the covenant that you kept toward your servant, David my father. That which you promised him, your mouth has spoken and your hand has fulfilled this very day. [16]And now, LORD, God of Israel, keep toward your servant, David my father, what you promised: There shall never be wanting someone from your line to sit before me on the throne of Israel, provided that your descendants keep to their way, walking by my law, as you have. [17]Now, LORD, God of Israel, may the words which you spoke to David your servant be confirmed.

[18]"Is God indeed to dwell with human beings on earth? If the heavens and the highest heavens cannot contain you, how much less this house which I have built! [19]Regard kindly the prayer and petition of your servant, LORD, my God, and listen to the cry of supplication which I, your servant, utter before you. [20]May your eyes be open day and night toward this house, the place where you have decreed your name shall be; listen to the prayer your servant makes toward this place. [21]Listen to the petition of your servant and of your people Israel which they offer toward this place. Listen, from the place of your enthronement, heaven, and listen and forgive.

[22]"If someone sins against a neighbor and is required to take an oath sanctioned by a curse, and comes and takes the oath before your altar in this house, [23]listen in heaven: act and judge your servants. Condemn the wicked, requiting their ways; acquit the just, rewarding their justice. [24]When your people Israel are defeated by an enemy because they have sinned against you, and then they turn, praise your name, pray to you, and entreat you in this house, [25]listen from heaven and forgive the sin of your people Israel, and bring them back to the land you gave them and their ancestors. [26]When the heavens are closed so that there is no rain, because they have sinned against you, but they pray toward this place and praise your name, and turn from their sin because you have afflicted them, [27]listen in heaven and forgive the sin of your servants, your people Israel. (For you teach them the good way in which they should walk.) Give rain upon this land of yours which you have given to your people as their heritage.

[28]"If there is famine in the land or pestilence; or if blight comes, or mildew, or locusts swarm, or caterpillars; when their enemies besiege them at any of their gates; whatever plague or sickness there may be; [29]whatever prayer of petition any may make, any of your people Israel, who know affliction and pain and stretch out their hands toward this house, [30]listen from heaven, the place of your enthronement, and forgive. Render to each and all according to their ways, you who know every heart; for it is you alone who know the heart of every human being. [31]So may they revere you and walk in your ways as long as they live on the land you gave our ancestors.

[32]"To the foreigners, likewise, who are not of your people Israel, but who come from a distant land for the sake of your great name, your mighty hand and outstretched arm, and come in prayer to this house, [33]listen from heaven, the place of your enthronement. Do all that the foreigner asks of you, that all the peoples of the earth may know your name, may revere you as do your people Israel, and may know that your name has been invoked upon this house that I have built.

[34]"When your people go out to war against their enemies, by whatever way you send them, and they pray to you toward the city you have chosen and the house I have built for your name, [35]listen from heaven to their prayer and petition, and uphold their cause. [36]When they sin against you (for there is no one who does not sin), and in your anger against them you deliver them to an enemy, so that their captors carry them off to another land, far or near, [37]and they have a change of heart in the land of their captivity and they turn

and entreat you in the land of their captors and say, 'We have sinned and done wrong; we have been wicked,' [38]if with all their heart and soul they turn back to you in the land of those who took them captive, and pray toward their land which you gave their ancestors, the city you have chosen, and the house which I have built for your name, [39]listen from heaven, the place of your enthronement, to their prayer and petitions, and uphold their cause. Forgive your people who have sinned against you. [40]Now, my God, may your eyes be open and your ears be attentive to the prayer of this place. [41]And now:

> "Arise, Lord God, come to your
> resting place,
> you and your majestic ark.
> Your priests, Lord God, will be
> clothed with salvation,
> your faithful ones rejoice in good
> things.
> [42]Lord God, do not reject the plea of
> your anointed,
> remember the devotion of David,
> your servant."

7:1 When Solomon had ended his prayer, fire came down from heaven and consumed the burnt offerings and the sacrifices, and the glory of the Lord filled the house. [2]But the priests could not enter the house of the Lord, for the glory of the Lord filled the house of the Lord. [3]All the Israelites looked on while the fire came down and the glory of the Lord was upon the house, and they fell down upon the pavement with their faces to the earth and worshiped, praising the Lord, "who is so good, whose love endures forever." [4]The king and all the people offered sacrifices before the Lord. [5]King Solomon offered as sacrifice twenty-two thousand oxen, and one hundred twenty thousand sheep.

End of the Dedication. Thus the king and all the people dedicated the house of God. [6]The priests were standing at their stations, as were the Levites, with the musical instruments of the Lord which King David had made to give thanks to the Lord, "whose love endures forever," when David offered praise through them. The priests opposite them blew the trumpets and all Israel stood.

[7]Then Solomon consecrated the middle of the court facing the house of the Lord; he offered there the burnt offerings and the fat of the communion offerings, since the bronze altar which Solomon had made could not hold the burnt offering, the grain offering, and the fat.

[8]On this occasion Solomon and with him all Israel, a great assembly from Lebo-hamath to the Wadi of Egypt, celebrated the festival for seven days. [9]On the eighth day they held a solemn assembly, for they had celebrated the dedication of the altar for seven days and the feast for seven days. [10]On the twenty-third day of the seventh month he dismissed the people to their tents, rejoicing and glad of heart because of all the blessings the Lord had given to David, to Solomon, and to his people Israel. [11]Solomon finished building the house of the Lord, the house of the king, and everything else he wanted to do in regard to the house of the Lord and his own house.

God's Promise to Solomon. [12]The Lord appeared to Solomon during the night and said to him: I have heard your prayer, and I have chosen this place for my house of sacrifice. [13]If I close heaven so that there is no rain, if I command the locust to devour the land, if I send pestilence among my people, [14]if then my people, upon whom my name has been pronounced, humble themselves and pray, and seek my face and turn from their evil ways, I will hear them from heaven and pardon their sins and heal their land. [15]Now, therefore, my eyes shall be open and my ears attentive to the prayer of this place; [16]now I have chosen and consecrated this house that my name may be there forever; my eyes and my heart shall be there always.

[17]As for you, if you walk before me as David your father did, doing all that I have commanded you and keeping my statutes and ordinances, [18]I will establish the throne of your kingship as I covenanted with David your father when I said, There shall never be wanting someone from your line as ruler in Israel. [19]But if ever you turn away and forsake my commandments and statutes which I set before you, and proceed to serve other gods, and bow down to them, [20]I will uproot the people from the land I gave and repudiate the house I have consecrated for my name. I will make it a proverb and a byword among all nations. [21]And this house which is so exalted—every passerby shall be horrified and ask: "Why has the LORD done such things to this land and to this house?" [22]And the answer will come: "Because they abandoned the LORD, the God of their ancestors, who brought them out of the land of Egypt, and they embraced other gods, bowing down to them and serving them. That is why he has brought upon them all this evil."

☐ MATTHEW 14:1-12

Herod's Opinion of Jesus. 14:1 At that time Herod the tetrarch heard of the reputation of Jesus [2]and said to his servants, "This man is John the Baptist. He has been raised from the dead; that is why mighty powers are at work in him."

The Death of John the Baptist. [3]Now Herod had arrested John, bound [him], and put him in prison on account of Herodias, the wife of his brother Philip, [4]for John had said to him, "It is not lawful for you to have her." [5]Although he wanted to kill him, he feared the people, for they regarded him as a prophet. [6]But at a birthday celebration for Herod, the daughter of Herodias performed a dance before the guests and delighted Herod [7]so much that he swore to give her whatever she might ask for. [8]Prompted by her mother, she said, "Give me here on a platter the head of John the Baptist." [9]The king was distressed, but because of his oaths and the guests who were present, he ordered that it be given, [10]and he had John beheaded in the prison. [11]His head was brought in on a platter and given to the girl, who took it to her mother. [12]His disciples came and took away the corpse and buried him; and they went and told Jesus.

May 11

St. Francis di Girolamo

Procure for yourself a good ship of war, well furnished with guns, in order to make war upon sin, and strike terror into the powers of hell.

— ST. FRANCIS DI GIROLAMO

☐ 2 CHRONICLES 8-10

Public Works. 8:1 After the twenty years during which Solomon built the house of the LORD and his own house, [2]he built up the cities which Huram had given him, and settled Israelites there. [3]Then Solomon went to Hamath of Zoba and conquered it. [4]He built Tadmor in the wilderness and all the supply cities, which he built in Hamath. [5]He built Upper Beth-horon and Lower Beth-horon, fortified cities with walls, gates, and bars; [6]also Baalath, all the supply cities belonging to Solomon, and all the cities for the chariots, the cities for horses, and whatever else Solomon desired to build in Jerusalem, in Lebanon, and in the entire land under his dominion. [7]All the people who were left of the Hittites, Amorites, Perizzites, Hivites, and Jebusites who were not Israelites— [8]those of their descendants who were left in the land and whom the Israelites had not destroyed—Solomon conscripted as forced laborers, as they are to this day. [9]But Solomon made none of the Israelites forced laborers for his works, for they were his fighting force, commanders, adjutants, chariot officers, and cavalry. [10]They were also King Solomon's two hundred and fifty overseers who directed the people.

Solomon's Piety. [11]Solomon brought the daughter of Pharaoh up from the City of David to the house which he had built for her, for he said, "No wife of mine shall dwell in the house of David, king of Israel, for the places where the ark of the LORD has come are holy."

[12]In those times Solomon sacrificed burnt offerings to the LORD upon the altar of the LORD which he had built in front of the porch, [13]as was required to be done day by day according to the command of Moses, especially on the sabbaths, at the new moons, and on the fixed festivals three times a year: on the feast of the Unleavened Bread, the feast of Weeks, and the feast of Booths.

[14]And according to the ordinance of David his father he appointed the various divisions of the priests for their service, and the Levites according to their functions of praise and attendance upon the priests, as the daily duty required. The gatekeepers by their divisions stood guard at each gate, since such was the command of David, the man of God. [15]There was no deviation from the king's command in whatever related to the priests and Levites or the treasuries. [16]All of Solomon's work was carried out successfully from the day the foundation of the house of the LORD was laid until its completion. The house of the LORD was finished.

Glories of the Court. [17]In those times Solomon went to Ezion-geber and to Elath on the seashore of the land of Edom. [18]Huram had his servants send him ships and his own servants, expert seamen; they went with Solomon's servants to Ophir, and obtained there four hundred and fifty talents of gold and brought it to King Solomon.

The Queen of Sheba. 9:1 The queen of Sheba, having heard a report of Solomon's fame, came to Jerusalem to test him with subtle questions, accompanied by a very numerous retinue and by camels bearing spices, a large amount of gold, and precious stones. She came to Solomon and spoke to him about everything that she had on her mind. [2]Solomon explained to her everything she asked about, and there was nothing so obscure that Solomon could not explain it to her.

[3]When the queen of Sheba witnessed Solomon's great wisdom, the house he had built, [4]the food at his table, the seating of his ministers, the attendance and dress of his waiters, his cupbearers and their dress, and the burnt offerings he sacrificed in the house of the LORD, it took her breath away. [5]"The report I heard in my country about your deeds and your wisdom is true," she told the king. [6]"I did not believe the report until I came and saw with my own eyes that not even the half of your great wisdom had been told me. You have surpassed the report I heard. [7]Happy your servants, happy these ministers of yours, who stand before you always and listen to your wisdom. [8]Blessed be the LORD, your God, who was pleased to set you on his throne as king for the LORD, your God. In the love your God has for Israel, to establish them

forever, he has made you king over them to carry out judgment and justice." [9]Then she gave the king one hundred and twenty gold talents, a very large quantity of spices, and precious stones. Never again did anyone bring such an abundance of spices as the queen of Sheba gave to King Solomon. [10]The servants of Huram and of Solomon who brought gold from Ophir also brought cabinet wood and precious stones. [11]With the cabinet wood the king made stairs for the house of the LORD and the house of the king, and harps and lyres for the chanters. The like of these had not been seen before in the land of Judah.

[12]King Solomon gave the queen of Sheba everything she desired and asked for, more than she had brought to the king. Then she returned with her servants to her own country.

[13]The gold that came to Solomon in one year weighed six hundred and sixty-six gold talents, [14]in addition to what came from the tolls on travelers and what the merchants brought. All the kings of Arabia also, and the governors of the country, brought gold and silver to Solomon.

[15]King Solomon made two hundred large shields of beaten gold (six hundred shekels of gold went into each shield) [16]and three hundred bucklers of beaten gold (three hundred shekels of gold went into each buckler); and the king put them in the house of the Forest of Lebanon.

[17]The king made a large ivory throne, and overlaid it with fine gold. [18]The throne had six steps; a footstool of gold was fastened to the throne, and there was an arm on each side of the seat, with two lions standing next to the arms, [19]and twelve other lions standing there on the steps, two to a step. Nothing like this was made in any other kingdom. [20]All King Solomon's drinking vessels were gold, and all the utensils in the house of the Forest of Lebanon were pure gold. There was no silver, for in Solomon's time silver was reckoned as nothing. [21]For the king had ships that went to Tarshish with the servants of Huram. Once every three years the fleet of Tarshish ships would come with a cargo of gold, silver, ivory, apes, and monkeys.

Solomon's Renown. [22]Thus King Solomon surpassed all the kings of the earth in riches and wisdom.

[23]All the kings of the earth sought audience with Solomon, to hear the wisdom God had put into his heart. [24]They all brought their tribute: vessels of silver and gold, garments, weapons, spices, horses, and mules—what was due each year. [25]Solomon had four thousand stalls for horses, chariots, and twelve thousand horses; these he allocated among the chariot cities and to the king's service in Jerusalem. [26]He was ruler over all the kings from the River to the land of the Philistines and down to the border of Egypt. [27]The king made silver as common in Jerusalem as stones, and cedars as numerous as the sycamores of the Shephelah. [28]Solomon's horses were imported from Egypt and from all the lands.

The Death of Solomon. [29]The remainder of the acts of Solomon, first and last, are recorded in the acts of Nathan the prophet, in the prophecy of Ahijah the Shilonite, and in the visions of Iddo the seer concerning Jeroboam, son of Nebat. [30]Solomon was king in Jerusalem over all Israel for forty years. [31]Solomon rested with his ancestors and was buried in the City of David, his father, and Rehoboam his son succeeded him as king.

Division of the Kingdom. 10:1 Rehoboam went to Shechem, where all Israel had come to make him king. [2]When Jeroboam, son of Nebat, heard about it, he was in Egypt where he had fled from King Solomon; and he returned from Egypt. [3]They sent for him; Jeroboam and all Israel came and said to Rehoboam: [4]"Your father put on us a heavy yoke. If you now lighten the harsh servitude and the heavy yoke your father imposed on us, we will be your servants." [5]He answered them, "Come back to me in three days," and the people went away.

[6]King Rehoboam asked advice of the elders who had been in his father Solomon's service while he was still alive, and asked, "How do you advise me to answer this people?" [7]They replied, "If you will deal kindly with this people and please them, giving them a favorable reply, they will be your servants forever." [8]But he ignored the advice the elders had given him and asked advice of the young men who had grown up with him and were in his service. [9]He said to them, "What answer do you advise us to give this people, who have told me, 'Lighten the yoke your father imposed on us'?" [10]The young men who had grown up with him replied: "This is what you must say to this people who have told you, 'Your father laid a heavy yoke on us; lighten it for us.' You must say, 'My little finger is thicker than my father's loins. [11]My father put a heavy yoke on you; I will make it heavier. My father beat you with whips; I will use scorpions!'"

[12]On the third day, Jeroboam and the whole people came back to King Rehoboam as the king had instructed them: "Come back to me in three days." [13]Ignoring the advice

the elders had given him, King Rehoboam gave the people a harsh answer. [14]He spoke to them as the young men had advised: "My father laid a heavy yoke on you; I will make it heavier. My father beat you with whips; I will use scorpions." [15]The king did not listen to the people, for this turn of events was from God: the LORD fulfilled the word he had spoken through Ahijah the Shilonite to Jeroboam, the son of Nebat.

[16]When all Israel saw that the king did not listen to them, the people answered the king:

"What share have we in David?
    We have no heritage in the son of
        Jesse.
Everyone to your tents, Israel!
    Now look to your own house,
        David!"

So all Israel went off to their tents, [17]but the Israelites who lived in the cities of Judah had Rehoboam as their king. [18]King Rehoboam then sent out Hadoram, who was in charge of the forced labor, but the Israelites stoned him to death. King Rehoboam, however, managed to mount his chariot and flee to Jerusalem. [19]And so Israel has been in rebellion against the house of David to this day.

☐ MATTHEW 14:13-21

The Return of the Twelve and the Feeding of the Five Thousand. 14:13 When Jesus heard of it, he withdrew in a boat to a deserted place by himself. The crowds heard of this and followed him on foot from their towns. [14]When he disembarked and saw the vast crowd, his heart was moved with pity for them, and he cured their sick. [15]When it was evening, the disciples approached him and said, "This is a deserted place and it is already late; dismiss the crowds so that they can go to the villages and buy food for themselves." [16][Jesus] said to them, "There is no need

for them to go away; give them some food yourselves." [17]But they said to him, "Five loaves and two fish are all we have here." [18]Then he said, "Bring them here to me," [19]and he ordered the crowds to sit down on the grass. Taking the five loaves and the two fish, and looking up to heaven, he said the blessing, broke the loaves, and gave them to the disciples, who in turn gave them to the crowds. [20]They all ate and were satisfied, and they picked up the fragments left over—twelve wicker baskets full. [21]Those who ate were about five thousand men, not counting women and children.

May 12

Where there is no room for the poor, neither is there room for me.

— St. Candida Maria de Jesus

☐ 2 CHRONICLES 11-14

11:1 On his arrival in Jerusalem, Rehoboam assembled the house of Judah and Benjamin—one hundred and eighty thousand elite warriors—to wage war against Israel and restore the kingdom to Rehoboam. ²However, the word of the LORD came to Shemaiah, a man of God: ³Say to Rehoboam, son of Solomon, king of Judah, and to all the Israelites in Judah and Benjamin: ⁴"Thus says the LORD: You must not go out to war against your kinsmen. Return home, each of you, for it is I who have brought this about." They obeyed the word of the LORD and turned back from going against Jeroboam.

Rehoboam's Works. ⁵Rehoboam took up residence in Jerusalem and built fortified cities in Judah. ⁶He built up Bethlehem, Etam, Tekoa, ⁷Beth-zur, Soco, Adullam, ⁸Gath, Mareshah, Ziph, ⁹Adoraim, Lachish, Azekah, ¹⁰Zorah, Aijalon, and Hebron; these were fortified cities in Judah and Benjamin. ¹¹Then he strengthened the fortifications and put commanders in them, along with supplies of food, oil, and wine. ¹²In every city were shields and spears, and he made them very strong. Thus Judah and Benjamin remained his.

Refugees from the North. ¹³Now the priests and Levites throughout Israel presented themselves to him from all parts of their land, ¹⁴for the Levites left their assigned pasture lands and their holdings and came to Judah and Jerusalem, because Jeroboam and his sons rejected them as priests of the LORD. ¹⁵In their place, he himself appointed priests for the high places as well as for the satyrs and calves he had made. ¹⁶After them, all those, of every tribe of Israel, who set their hearts to seek the LORD, the God of Israel, came to Jerusalem to sacrifice to the LORD, the God of their ancestors. ¹⁷Thus they strengthened the kingdom of Judah and made Rehoboam, son of Solomon, prevail for three years; for they walked in the way of David and Solomon three years.

Rehoboam's Family. ¹⁸Rehoboam married Mahalath, daughter of Jerimoth, son of David and of Abihail, daughter of Eliab, son of Jesse. ¹⁹She bore him sons: Jehush, Shemariah, and Zaham. ²⁰After her, he married Maacah, daughter of Absalom, who bore him Abijah, Attai, Ziza, and Shelomith. ²¹Rehoboam loved Maacah, daughter of Absalom, more than all his other wives and concubines; he had taken eighteen wives and sixty concubines, and he fathered twenty-eight sons and sixty daughters. ²²Rehoboam put Abijah, son of Maacah, first among his brothers, as leader, for he intended to make him king. ²³He acted prudently, distributing his various sons throughout all the districts of Judah and Benjamin, in all the fortified cities; and he gave them generous provisions and sought an abundance of wives for them.

Rehoboam's Apostasy. 12:1 Once Rehoboam had established himself as king and was firmly in charge, he abandoned the law of the LORD, and so did all Israel with him. ²So in the fifth year of King Rehoboam, Shishak, king of Egypt, attacked Jerusalem, for they had acted treacherously toward the LORD. ³He had twelve hundred chariots and sixty thousand horsemen, and there was no counting the army that came with him from Egypt—Libyans, Sukkites, and Ethiopians. ⁴They captured the fortified cities of Judah and came as far as Jerusalem. ⁵Then Shemaiah the prophet came to Rehoboam and the commanders of Judah who had gathered at Jerusalem because of Shishak, and said to them: "Thus says the LORD: You have abandoned me, and so I have abandoned you to the power of Shishak."

⁶Then the commanders of Israel and the king humbled themselves saying, "The LORD is in the right." ⁷When the LORD saw that they had humbled themselves, the word of the LORD came to Shemaiah: Because they have humbled themselves, I will not destroy them; I will give them some deliverance, and my wrath shall not be poured out upon Jerusalem through Shishak. ⁸But they shall be his servants. Then they will know what it is to serve me and what it is to serve the kingdoms of the earth. ⁹Thereupon Shishak, king of Egypt, attacked Jerusalem and took away the treasures of the house of the LORD and the treasures of the house of the king. He took everything, including the gold shields that Solomon had made. ¹⁰To replace them, King Rehoboam made bronze shields, which he entrusted to the officers of the attendants on duty at the entrance of the king's house. ¹¹Whenever the king visited the house of the LORD, the attendants would carry them, and then return them to the guardroom. ¹²Because he had humbled himself, the anger of the LORD turned from him so as not to destroy him completely; in Judah, moreover, there was some good.

¹³King Rehoboam was firmly in power in Jerusalem and continued to rule. Rehoboam was forty-one years old when he became king, and he reigned seventeen years in Jerusalem, the city in which, out of all the tribes of Israel, the LORD chose to set his name. His mother's name was Naamah, the Ammonite. ¹⁴He did evil, for he had not set his heart to seek the LORD. ¹⁵The acts of Rehoboam, first and last, are recorded in the history of Shemaiah the prophet and of Iddo the seer (his family record). There were wars between Rehoboam and Jeroboam all their days. ¹⁶Rehoboam rested with his ancestors; he was buried in the City of David. His son Abijah succeeded him as king.

War Between Abijah and Jeroboam. 13:1 In the eighteenth year of King Jeroboam, Abijah became king of Judah; ²he reigned three years in Jerusalem. His mother was named Micaiah, daughter of Uriel of Gibeah. There was war between Abijah and Jeroboam.

³Abijah joined battle with a force of four hundred thousand picked warriors, while Jeroboam lined up against him in battle with eight hundred thousand picked and valiant warriors. ⁴Abijah stood on Mount Zemaraim, which is in the highlands of Ephraim, and said: "Listen to me, Jeroboam and all Israel! ⁵Do you not know that the LORD, the God of Israel, has given David kingship over Israel forever, to him and to his sons, by a covenant of salt? ⁶Yet Jeroboam, son of Nebat, the servant of Solomon, son of David, arose and rebelled against his lord! ⁷Worthless men, scoundrels, joined him and overcame Rehoboam, son of Solomon, when Rehoboam was young and inexperienced, and no match for them. ⁸But now, do you think you are a match for the kingdom of the LORD led by the descendants of David, simply because you are a huge multitude and have with you the golden calves which Jeroboam made you for gods? ⁹Have you not expelled the priests of the LORD, the sons of Aaron, and the Levites, and made for yourselves priests like the peoples of other lands? Everyone who comes to consecrate himself with a young bull and seven rams becomes a priest of no-gods. ¹⁰But as

for us, the LORD is our God, and we have not abandoned him. The priests ministering to the LORD are sons of Aaron, and the Levites also have their offices. [11]They sacrifice burnt offerings to the LORD and fragrant incense morning after morning and evening after evening; they set out the showbread on the pure table, and the lamps of the golden menorah burn evening after evening; for we observe our duties to the LORD, our God, but you have abandoned him. [12]See, God is with us, at our head, and his priests are here with trumpets to sound the attack against you. Israelites, do not fight against the LORD, the God of your ancestors, for you will not succeed!"

[13]But Jeroboam had an ambush go around them to come at them from the rear; so that while his army faced Judah, his ambush lay behind them. [14]When Judah turned and saw that they had to battle on both fronts, they cried out to the LORD and the priests sounded the trumpets. [15]Then the Judahites shouted; and when they shouted, God struck down Jeroboam and all Israel before Abijah and Judah. [16]The Israelites fled before Judah, and God delivered them into their power. [17]Abijah and his people inflicted a severe defeat upon them; five hundred thousand picked men of Israel fell slain. [18]The Israelites were humbled on that occasion, while the Judahites were victorious because they relied on the LORD, the God of their ancestors. [19]Abijah pursued Jeroboam and seized cities from him: Bethel and its dependencies, Jeshanah and its dependencies, and Ephron and its dependencies. [20]Jeroboam did not regain power during Abijah's time; the LORD struck him down and he died, [21]while Abijah continued to grow stronger. He married fourteen wives and fathered twenty-two sons and sixteen daughters.

Death of Abijah. [22]The rest of the acts of Abijah, his deeds and his words, are recorded in the midrash of the prophet Iddo. [23]Abijah rested with his ancestors; they buried him in the City of David and his son Asa succeeded him as king. During his time, the land had ten years of peace.

Asa's Initial Reforms. 14:1 Asa did what was good and right in the sight of the LORD, his God. [2]He removed the illicit altars and the high places, smashed the sacred pillars, and cut down the asherahs. [3]He told Judah to seek the LORD, the God of their ancestors, and to observe the law and the commandment. [4]He removed the high places and incense stands from all the cities of Judah, and under him the kingdom had peace. [5]He built fortified cities in Judah, for the land had peace and no war was waged against him during these years, because the LORD had given him rest. [6]He said to Judah: "Let us build these cities and surround them with walls, towers, gates and bars. The land is still ours, for we have sought the LORD, our God; we sought him, and he has given us rest on every side." So they built and prospered.

The Ethiopian Invasion. [7]Asa had an army of three hundred thousand shield- and lance-bearers from Judah, and from Benjamin two hundred and eighty thousand who carried bucklers and were archers, all of them valiant warriors. [8]Zerah the Ethiopian advanced against them with a force of one million men and three hundred chariots, and he came as far as Mareshah. [9]Asa went out to meet him and they drew up for battle in the valley of Zephathah, near Mareshah. [10]Asa called upon the LORD, his God: "LORD, there is none like you to help the powerless against the strong. Help us, LORD, our God, for we rely on you, and in your name we have come against this multitude. You are the LORD, our God; do not let men prevail against you." [11]And so the LORD defeated the Ethiopians before Asa and Judah, and the Ethiopians fled. [12]Asa and those with him pursued them as far as Gerar, and the Ethiopians fell until there were no survivors, for they were crushed before the LORD and his army, which carried away enormous spoils. [13]Then the Judahites conquered all the cities around Gerar, for the fear of the LORD was upon them; they plundered all the cities, for there was much plunder in them. [14]They also attacked the tents of the cattle-herders and carried off a great number of sheep and camels. Then they returned to Jerusalem.

☐ MATTHEW 14:22-36

The Walking on the Water. 14:22 Then he made the disciples get into the boat and precede him to the other side, while he dismissed the crowds. [23]After doing so, he went up on the mountain by himself to pray. When it was evening he was there alone. [24]Meanwhile the boat, already a few miles offshore, was being tossed about by the waves, for the wind was against it. [25]During the fourth watch of the night, he came toward them, walking on the sea. [26]When the disciples saw him walking on the sea they were terrified. "It is a ghost," they said, and they cried out in fear. [27]At once [Jesus] spoke to them, "Take courage, it is I; do not be afraid." [28]Peter said to him in reply, "Lord, if it is you, command me to come to you on the water." [29]He said, "Come." Peter got out of the boat and began to walk on the water toward Jesus. [30]But when he saw how [strong] the wind was he became frightened; and, beginning to sink, he cried out, "Lord, save me!" [31]Immediately Jesus stretched out his hand and caught him, and said to him, "O you of little faith, why did you doubt?" [32]After they got into the boat, the wind died down. [33]Those who were in the boat did him homage, saying, "Truly, you are the Son of God."

The Healings at Gennesaret. [34]After making the crossing, they came to land at Gennesaret. [35]When the men of that place recognized him, they sent word to all the surrounding country. People brought to him all those who were sick [36]and begged him that they might touch only the tassel on his cloak, and as many as touched it were healed.

May 13

Our Lady of Fátima

If the hurricanes of temptation rise against you, or you are running upon the rocks of trouble, look to the star — call on Mary!
— ST. BERNARD OF CLAIRVAUX

☐ 2 CHRONICLES 15-19

Further Reforms. 15:1 The spirit of God came upon Azariah, son of Oded. [2]He went forth to meet Asa and said to him: "Hear me, Asa and all Judah and Benjamin! The LORD is with you when you are with him, and if you seek him he will be found; but if you abandon him, he will abandon you. [3]For a long time Israel was without a true God, without a priest-teacher, without instruction, [4]but when in their distress they turned to the LORD, the God of Israel, and sought him, he was found by them. [5]At that time there was no peace for anyone to go or come; rather, there were many terrors upon the inhabitants of the lands. [6]Nation crushed nation and city crushed city, for God overwhelmed them with every kind of distress. [7]But as for you, be strong and do not slack off, for there shall be a reward for what you do."

[8]When Asa heard these words and the prophecy (Oded the prophet), he was encouraged to remove the detestable idols from the whole land of Judah and Benjamin and from the cities he had taken in the highlands of Ephraim, and to restore the altar of the LORD which was before the vestibule of the LORD. [9]Then he gathered all Judah and Benjamin, together with those of Ephraim, Manasseh, and Simeon who were resident with them; for many had defected to him from Israel when they saw that the LORD, his God, was with him. [10]They gathered at Jerusalem in the third month of the fifteenth year of Asa's reign, [11]and sacrificed to the LORD on that day seven hundred oxen and seven thousand sheep from the spoils they had brought. [12]They entered into a covenant to seek the LORD, the God of their ancestors, with all their heart and soul; [13]and everyone who would not seek the LORD, the God of Israel, was to be put to death, from least to greatest, man or woman. [14]They swore an oath to the LORD with a loud voice, with shouting and with trumpets and horns. [15]All Judah rejoiced over the oath, for they had sworn it with their whole heart and sought him with complete desire. The LORD was found by them, and gave them rest on every side.

[16]He also deposed Maacah, the mother of King Asa, from her position as queen mother because she had made an obscene object for Asherah; Asa cut down this object, smashed it, and burnt it in the Wadi Kidron. [17]The high places did not disappear from Israel, yet Asa's heart was undivided as long as he lived. [18]He brought into the house of God his father's and his own votive offerings: silver, gold, and vessels.

[19]There was no war until the thirty-fifth year of Asa's reign.

Asa's Infidelity. 16:1 In the thirty-sixth year of Asa's reign, Baasha, king of Israel, attacked Judah and fortified Ramah to block all movement for Asa, king of Judah. [2]Asa then brought out silver and gold from the treasuries of the house of the LORD and the house of the king and sent them to Ben-hadad, king of Aram, who ruled in Damascus. He said: [3]"There is a treaty between you and me, as there was between your father and my father. I am sending you silver and gold. Go, break your treaty with Baasha, king of Israel, that he may withdraw from me." [4]Ben-hadad agreed with King Asa and sent the leaders of his troops against the cities of Israel. They attacked Ijon, Dan, Abel-maim, besides all the store cities of Naphtali. [5]When Baasha heard of it, he left off fortifying Ramah, putting an end to his work. [6]Then King Asa commandeered all Judah and they carried away the stones and beams with which Baasha was fortifying Ramah. With them he fortified Geba and Mizpah.

[7]At that time Hanani the seer came to Asa, king of Judah, and said to him: "Because you relied on the king of Aram and did not rely on the LORD, your God, the army of the king of Aram has escaped your power. [8]Were not the Ethiopians and Libyans a vast army, with great numbers of chariots and horses? And yet, because you relied on the LORD, he delivered them into your power. [9]The eyes of the LORD roam over the whole earth, to encourage those who are devoted to him wholeheartedly. You have acted foolishly in this matter, for from now on you will have wars." [10]But Asa became angry with the seer and imprisoned him in the stocks, so greatly was he enraged at him over this. Asa also oppressed some of his people at this time.

[11]Now the acts of Asa, first and last, are recorded in the book of the kings of Judah

and Israel. [12]In the thirty-ninth year of his reign, Asa contracted disease in his feet; it became worse, but even with this disease he did not seek the LORD, only physicians. [13]Asa rested with his ancestors; he died in the forty-first year of his reign. [14]They buried him in the tomb he had hewn for himself in the City of David, after laying him on a couch that was filled with spices and various kinds of aromatics compounded into an ointment; and they kindled a huge fire for him.

Jehoshaphat's Zeal for the Law. 17:1 His son Jehoshaphat succeeded him as king and strengthened his position against Israel. [2]He placed armed forces in all the fortified cities of Judah, and set garrisons in the land of Judah and in the cities of Ephraim which Asa his father had taken. [3]The LORD was with Jehoshaphat, for he walked in the earlier ways of David his father, and did not seek the Baals. [4]Rather, he sought the God of his father and walked in his commands, and not the practices of Israel. [5]Through him, the LORD made the kingdom secure, and all Judah gave Jehoshaphat gifts, so that great wealth and glory was his. [6]Thus he was encouraged to follow the LORD's ways, and once again he removed the high places and the asherahs from Judah.

[7]In the third year of his reign he sent his officials, Ben-hail, Obadiah, Zechariah, Nethanel, and Micaiah, to teach in the cities of Judah. [8]With them he sent the Levites Shemaiah, Nethaniah, Zebadiah, Asahel, Shemiramoth, Jehonathan, Adonijah, and Tobijah, together with Elishama and Jehoram the priests. [9]They taught in Judah, having with them the book of the law of the LORD; they traveled through all the cities of Judah and taught among the people.

His Power. [10]Now the fear of the LORD was upon all the kingdoms of the countries surrounding Judah, so that they did not war against Jehoshaphat. [11]Some of the Philistines brought Jehoshaphat gifts and a tribute of silver; the Arabians also brought him a flock of seven thousand seven hundred rams and seven thousand seven hundred he-goats.

[12]Jehoshaphat grew ever greater. He built strongholds and store cities in Judah. [13]He carried out many works in the cities of Judah, and he had soldiers, valiant warriors, in Jerusalem. [14]This was their mustering according to their ancestral houses. From Judah, the commanders of thousands: Adnah the commander, and with him three hundred thousand valiant warriors. [15]Next to him, Jehohanan the commander, and with him two hundred eighty thousand. [16]Next to him, Amasiah, son of Zichri, who offered himself to the LORD, and with him two hundred thousand valiant warriors. [17]From Benjamin: Eliada, a valiant warrior, and with him two hundred thousand armed with bow and buckler. [18]Next to him, Jehozabad, and with him one hundred and eighty thousand equipped for war. [19]These attended the king; in addition to those whom the king had stationed in the fortified cities throughout all Judah.

Alliance with Israel. 18:1 Jehoshaphat therefore had wealth and glory in abundance; but he became related to Ahab by marriage. [2]After some years he went down to Ahab at Samaria; Ahab slaughtered numerous sheep and oxen for him and for the people with him, and incited him to go up against Ramoth-gilead. [3]Ahab, king of Israel, asked Jehoshaphat, king of Judah, "Will you come with me to Ramoth-gilead?" He answered, "You and I are as one, and your people and my people as well. We will be with you in the battle." [4]Jehoshaphat also said to the king of Israel, "Seek the word of the LORD at once."

Prophets in Conflict. [5]The king of Israel assembled the prophets, four hundred of them, and asked, "Shall we go to fight against Ramoth-gilead, or shall I refrain?" They said, "Attack. God will give it into the power of the king." [6]But Jehoshaphat said, "Is there no other prophet of the LORD here we might consult?" [7]The king of Israel answered, "There is one other man through whom we may consult the LORD; but I hate him, because he prophesies not good but always evil about me. He is Micaiah, son of Imlah." Jeshoshaphat said, "Let not the king say that." [8]So the king of Israel called an official, and said to him, "Get Micaiah, son of Imlah, at once." [9]The king of Israel and Jehoshaphat, king of Judah, were seated, each on his throne, clothed in their robes of state in the square at the entrance of the gate of Samaria, and all the prophets were prophesying before them.

[10]Zedekiah, son of Chenaanah, made himself two horns of iron and said: "The LORD says: With these you shall gore Aram until you have destroyed them." [11]The other prophets prophesied in the same vein, saying: "Attack Ramoth-gilead, and conquer! The LORD will give it into the power of the king." [12]Meanwhile the messenger who had gone to call Micaiah said to him: "Look now, the words of the prophets are as one in speaking good for the king. Let your word be at one with theirs; speak a good word." [13]Micaiah said, "As the LORD lives, I shall speak whatever my God says."

[14]When he came to the king, the king said to him, "Micah, shall we go to fight at Ramoth-gilead, or shall I refrain?" He said, "Attack and conquer! They will be delivered into your power." [15]But the king answered him, "How many times must I adjure you to tell me nothing but the truth in the name of the LORD?" [16]So Micaiah said:

"I see all Israel
    scattered on the mountains,
    like sheep without a shepherd,
And the LORD saying,
    These have no masters!

Let each of them go back home in
    peace."

[17]The king of Israel said to Jehoshaphat, "Did I not tell you, he does not prophesy good about me, but only evil?" [18]Micaiah continued: "Therefore hear the word of the LORD. I saw the LORD seated on his throne, with the whole host of heaven standing to his right and to his left. [19]The LORD asked: Who will deceive Ahab, king of Israel, so that he will go up and fall on Ramoth-gilead? And one said this, another that, [20]until this spirit came forth and stood before the LORD, saying, 'I will deceive him.' The LORD asked: How? [21]He answered, 'I will go forth and become a lying spirit in the mouths of all his prophets.' The LORD replied: You shall succeed in deceiving him. Go forth and do this. [22]So now the LORD has put a lying spirit in the mouths of these prophets of yours; but the LORD himself has decreed evil against you."

[23]Thereupon Zedekiah, son of Chenaanah, came up and struck Micaiah on the cheek, saying, "Has the spirit of the LORD, then, passed from me to speak with you?" [24]Micaiah said, "You shall find out on the day you go into an innermost room to hide." [25]The king of Israel then said: "Seize Micaiah and take him back to Amon, prefect of the city, and to Joash the king's son, [26]and say, 'This is the king's order: Put this man in prison and feed him scanty rations of bread and water until I come back in safety!'" [27]But Micaiah said, "If ever you return in safety, the LORD has not spoken through me." (He also said, "Hear, O peoples, all of you!")

Ahab's Death. [28]The king of Israel and Jehoshaphat, king of Judah, went up to Ramoth-gilead, [29]and the king of Israel said to Jehoshaphat, "I will disguise myself and go into battle. But you, put on your own robes." So the king of Israel disguised himself and they entered the battle. [30]In the meantime, the king of Aram had given his chariot commanders the order, "Fight with no one, great or small, except the king of Israel alone." [31]When the chariot commanders saw Jehoshaphat, they thought, "There is the king of Israel!" and wheeled to fight him. But Jehoshaphat cried out and the LORD helped him; God induced them to leave him alone. [32]The chariot commanders, seeing that he was not the king of Israel, turned away from him. [33]But someone drew his bow at random and hit the king of Israel between the joints of his breastplate. He ordered his charioteer, "Rein about and take me out of the ranks, for I am wounded." [34]The battle grew fierce during the day, and the king of Israel braced himself up in his chariot facing the Arameans until evening. He died as the sun was setting.

Jehoshaphat Rebuked. 19:1 Jehoshaphat king of Judah returned in safety to his house in Jerusalem. [2]Jehu the seer, son of Hanani, went out to meet King Jehoshaphat and said to him: "Should you help the wicked and love those who hate the LORD? For this reason, wrath is upon you from the LORD. [3]Yet some good has been found in you, since you have removed the asherahs from the land and have set your heart to seek God."

Judges Appointed. [4]Jehoshaphat dwelt in Jerusalem; but he went out again among the people from Beer-sheba to the highlands of Ephraim and brought them back to the LORD, the God of their ancestors. [5]He appointed judges in the land, in all the fortified cities of Judah, city by city, [6]and he said to them: "Take care what you do, for the judgment you give is not human but divine; for when it comes to judgment God will be with you. [7]And now, let the fear of the LORD be upon you. Act carefully, for with the LORD, our God, there is no injustice, no partiality, no bribe-taking." [8]In Jerusalem also, Jehoshaphat appointed some Levites and priests and some of the family heads of Israel for the LORD's judgment and the disputes of those who dwell in Jerusalem. [9]He gave them this command: "Thus you shall act: in the fear of the LORD, with fidelity and with an undivided heart. [10]And in every dispute that comes to you from your kin living in their cities, whether it concerns bloodguilt or questions of law, command, statutes, or ordinances, warn them lest they incur guilt before the LORD and his wrath come upon you and your kin. Do that and you shall not incur guilt. [11]See now, Amariah is chief priest over you for everything that pertains to the LORD, and Zebadiah, son of Ishmael, is leader of the house of Judah in all that pertains to the king; and the Levites will be your officials. Take firm action, and the LORD will be with the good."

☐ MATTHEW 15:1-20

The Tradition of the Elders. 15:1 Then Pharisees and scribes came to Jesus from Jerusalem and said, [2]"Why do your disciples break the tradition of the elders? They do not wash [their] hands when they eat a meal." [3]He said to them in reply, "And why do you break the commandment of God for the sake of your tradition? [4]For God said, 'Honor your father and your mother,' and 'Whoever curses father or mother shall die.' [5]But you say, 'Whoever says to father or mother, "Any support you might have had from me is dedicated to God," [6]need not honor his father.' You have nullified the word of God for the sake of your tradition. [7]Hypocrites, well did Isaiah prophesy about you when he said:

[8]"This people honors me with their lips,
  but their hearts are far from me;

⁹in vain do they worship me,
    teaching as doctrines human
      precepts.'"

¹⁰He summoned the crowd and said to them, "Hear and understand. ¹¹It is not what enters one's mouth that defiles that person; but what comes out of the mouth is what defiles one." ¹²Then his disciples approached and said to him, "Do you know that the Pharisees took offense when they heard what you said?" ¹³He said in reply, "Every plant that my heavenly Father has not planted will be uprooted. ¹⁴Let them alone; they are blind guides (of the blind).

If a blind person leads a blind person, both will fall into a pit." ¹⁵Then Peter said to him in reply, "Explain [this] parable to us." ¹⁶He said to them, "Are even you still without understanding? ¹⁷Do you not realize that everything that enters the mouth passes into the stomach and is expelled into the latrine? ¹⁸But the things that come out of the mouth come from the heart, and they defile. ¹⁹For from the heart come evil thoughts, murder, adultery, unchastity, theft, false witness, blasphemy. ²⁰These are what defile a person, but to eat with unwashed hands does not defile."

May 14

St. Matthias; St. Mary Mazzarello

Sometimes by making too much of the little things we miss the big things.

— St. Mary Mazzarello

☐ 2 CHRONICLES 20–24

Invasion from Edom. 20:1 After this the Moabites, the Ammonites, and with them some Meunites came to fight against Jehoshaphat. ²Jehoshaphat was told: "A great multitude is coming against you from across the sea, from Edom; they are already in Hazazon-tamar" (which is En-gedi). ³Frightened, Jehoshaphat resolved to consult the Lord. He proclaimed a fast throughout all Judah. ⁴Then Judah gathered to seek the Lord's help; from every one of the cities of Judah they came to seek the Lord.

Jehoshaphat's Prayer. ⁵Jehoshaphat stood up in the assembly of Judah and Jerusalem in the house of the Lord before the new court, ⁶and he said: "Lord, God of our ancestors, are you not God in heaven, and do you not rule over all the kingdoms of the nations? In your hand is power and might, and no one can withstand you. ⁷Was

it not you, our God, who dispossessed the inhabitants of this land before your people Israel and gave it forever to the descendants of Abraham, your friend? ⁸They have dwelt in it and they built in it a sanctuary for your name. They have said: ⁹'If evil comes upon us, the sword of judgment, or pestilence, or famine, we will stand before this house and before you, for your name is in this house, and we will cry out to you in our affliction, and you will hear and save!' ¹⁰And now, see the Ammonites, Moabites, and those of Mount Seir whom you did not allow Israel to invade when they came from the land of Egypt, but instead they passed them by and did not destroy them: ¹¹See how they are now repaying us by coming to drive us out of the possession you have given us. ¹²O our God, will you not bring judgment on them? We are powerless before this vast multitude that is coming against us. We ourselves do not know what to do, so our eyes are turned toward you."

Victory Prophesied. [13]All Judah was standing before the LORD, with their little ones, their wives, and their children. [14]And the spirit of the LORD came upon Jahaziel, son of Zechariah, son of Benaiah, son of Jeiel, son of Mattaniah, a Levite of the clan of Asaph, in the midst of the assembly, [15]and he said: "Pay attention, all of Judah, inhabitants of Jerusalem, and King Jehoshaphat! The LORD says to you: Do not fear or be dismayed at the sight of this vast multitude, for the battle is not yours but God's. [16]Go down against them tomorrow. You will see them coming up by the ascent of Ziz, and you will come upon them at the end of the wadi which opens on the wilderness of Jeruel. [17]You will not have to fight in this encounter. Take your places, stand firm, and see the salvation of the LORD; he will be with you, Judah and Jerusalem. Do not fear or be dismayed. Tomorrow go out to meet them, and the LORD will be with you." [18]Then Jehoshaphat knelt down with his face to the ground, and all Judah and the inhabitants of Jerusalem fell down before the LORD in worship. [19]Levites from among the Kohathites and Korahites stood up to sing the praises of the LORD, the God of Israel, their voices ever louder.

The Invaders Destroyed. [20]Early in the morning they went out to the wilderness of Tekoa. As they were going out, Jehoshaphat halted and said: "Listen to me, Judah and inhabitants of Jerusalem! Let your faith in the LORD, your God, be firm, and you will be firm. Have faith in his prophets and you will succeed." [21]After taking counsel with the people, he appointed some to sing to the LORD and some to praise the holy Splendor as it went forth at the head of the army. They sang: "Give thanks to the LORD, whose love endures forever." [22]At the moment they began their jubilant praise, the LORD laid an ambush against the Ammonites, Moabites, and those of Mount Seir who were coming against Judah, so that they were defeated. [23]For the Ammonites and Moabites set upon the inhabitants of Mount Seir and exterminated them according to the ban. And when they had finished with the inhabitants of Seir, each helped to destroy the other.

[24]When Judah came to the watchtower of the wilderness and looked toward the throng, there were only corpses fallen on the ground, with no survivors. [25]Jehoshaphat and his people came to gather the spoils, and they found an abundance of cattle and personal property, garments and precious vessels. They took so much that they were unable to carry it all; it took them three days to gather the spoils, there was so much of it. [26]On the fourth day they held an assembly in the Valley of Berakah—for there they blessed the LORD; that is why the place is called the Valley of Berakah to this day. [27]Then all the men of Judah and Jerusalem, with Jehoshaphat at their head, returned to Jerusalem with joy; for the LORD had given them joy over their enemies. [28]They came to Jerusalem, with harps, lyres, and trumpets, to the house of the LORD. [29]And the fear of God came upon all the kingdoms of the surrounding lands when they heard how the LORD had fought against the enemies of Israel. [30]Thereafter Jehoshaphat's kingdom had peace, for his God gave him rest on every side.

Jehoshaphat's Other Deeds. [31]Thus Jehoshaphat reigned over Judah. He was thirty-five years old when he became king, and he reigned twenty-five years in Jerusalem. His mother's name was Azubah, daughter of Shilhi. [32]He walked in the way of Asa his father unceasingly, doing what was right in the LORD's sight. [33]Nevertheless, the high places did not disappear and the people had not yet set their hearts on the God of their ancestors.

[34]The rest of the acts of Jehoshaphat, first and last, are recorded in the chronicle

of Jehu, son of Hanani, which was incorporated into the book of the kings of Israel. ³⁵After this, Jehoshaphat king of Judah joined with Ahaziah king of Israel—he acted wickedly. ³⁶He joined with him in building ships to go to Tarshish; the fleet was built at Ezion-geber. ³⁷But Eliezer, son of Dodavahu from Mareshah, prophesied against Jehoshaphat. He said: "Because you have joined with Ahaziah, the LORD will shatter your work." And the ships were wrecked and were unable to sail to Tarshish.

21:1 Jehoshaphat rested with his ancestors; he was buried with them in the City of David. Jehoram, his son, succeeded him as king. ²He had brothers, Jehoshaphat's sons: Azariah, Jehiel, Zechariah, Azariah, Michael, and Shephatiah; all these were sons of King Jehoshaphat of Judah. ³Their father gave them many gifts of silver, gold, and precious objects, together with fortified cities in Judah, but the kingship he gave to Jehoram because he was the firstborn.

Jehoram's Evil Deeds. ⁴When Jehoram had acceded to his father's kingdom and was firmly in power, he killed all his brothers with the sword, and also some of the princes of Israel. ⁵Jehoram was thirty-two years old when he became king, and he reigned eight years in Jerusalem. ⁶He walked in the way of the kings of Israel as the house of Ahab had done, since the daughter of Ahab was his wife; and he did what was evil in the LORD's sight. ⁷Even so, the LORD was unwilling to destroy the house of David because of the covenant he had made with David and because of his promise to leave him and his sons a holding for all time.

⁸During his time Edom revolted against the rule of Judah and installed its own king. ⁹Thereupon Jehoram with his officers and all his chariots crossed over. He arose by night and broke through the Edomites when they had surrounded him and the commanders of his chariots. ¹⁰To this day

Edom has been in revolt against the rule of Judah. Libnah also revolted at that time against his rule because he had abandoned the LORD, the God of his ancestors. ¹¹He also set up high places in the mountains of Judah, prostituting the inhabitants of Jerusalem, leading Judah astray.

Jehoram Punished. ¹²A letter came to him from Elijah the prophet with this message: "Thus says the LORD, the God of David your father: Because you have not walked in the way of your father Jehoshaphat, nor of Asa, king of Judah, ¹³but instead have walked in the way of the kings of Israel, leading Judah and the inhabitants of Jerusalem into prostitution, like the harlotries of the house of Ahab, and because you have killed your brothers of your father's house, who were better than you, ¹⁴the LORD will strike your people, your children, your wives, and all that is yours with a great plague. ¹⁵You shall have severe pains from a disease in your bowels, which will fall out because of the disease, day after day."

¹⁶Then the LORD stirred up against Jehoram the animosity of the Philistines and of the Arabians who were neighbors of the Ethiopians. ¹⁷They came up against Judah, breached it, and carried away all the wealth found in the king's house, along with his sons and his wives. He was left with only one son, Jehoahaz, his youngest. ¹⁸After these events, the LORD afflicted him with a disease of the bowels for which there was no cure. ¹⁹Some time later, after a period of two years had elapsed, his bowels fell out because of the disease and he died in great pain. His people did not make a fire for him as they had for his ancestors. ²⁰He was thirty-two years old when he became king, and he reigned eight years in Jerusalem. He departed unloved; and they buried him in the City of David, though not in the tombs of the kings.

Ahaziah. 22:1 Then the inhabitants of Jerusalem made Ahaziah, his youngest son, king to succeed him, since all the older sons had been killed by the band that had come into the camp with the Arabians. Thus Ahaziah, son of Jehoram, reigned as the king of Judah. ²Ahaziah was twenty-two years old when he became king, and he reigned one year in Jerusalem. His mother's name was Athaliah, daughter of Omri. ³He, too, walked in the ways of the house of Ahab, because his mother was his counselor in doing evil. ⁴To his own destruction, he did what was evil in the sight of the LORD, like the house of Ahab, since they were his counselors after the death of his father.

⁵He was also following their counsel when he joined Jehoram, son of Ahab, king of Israel, in battle against Hazael, king of Aram, at Ramoth-gilead, where the Arameans wounded Jehoram. ⁶He returned to Jezreel to be healed of the wounds that had been inflicted on him at Ramah in his battle against Hazael, king of Aram. Then Ahaziah, son of Jehoram, king of Judah, went down to Jezreel to visit Jehoram, son of Ahab, for he was sick. ⁷Now from God came Ahaziah's downfall, that he should join Jehoram; for after his arrival he rode out with Jehoram to Jehu, son of Nimshi, whom the LORD had anointed to cut down the house of Ahab. ⁸While Jehu was executing judgment on the house of Ahab, he also came upon the princes of Judah and the nephews of Ahaziah who were his attendants, and he killed them. ⁹Then he looked for Ahaziah himself. They caught him hiding in Samaria and brought him to Jehu, who put him to death. They buried him, for they said, "He was the grandson of Jehoshaphat, who sought the LORD with his whole heart." Now the house of Ahaziah did not retain the power of kingship.

Usurpation of Athaliah. ¹⁰When Athaliah, the mother of Ahaziah, saw that her son was dead, she began to kill off the whole royal family of the house of Judah. ¹¹But Jehosheba, a daughter of the king, took Joash, Ahaziah's son, and spirited him away from among the king's sons who were about to be slain, and put him and his nurse in a bedroom. In this way Jehosheba, the daughter of King Jehoram, a sister of Ahaziah and wife of Jehoiada the priest, concealed the child from Athaliah, so that she did not put him to death. ¹²For six years he remained hidden with them in the house of God, while Athaliah ruled as queen over the land.

Athaliah Overthrown. 23:1 In the seventh year, Jehoiada took courage and brought into covenant with himself the captains: Azariah, son of Jehoram; Ishmael, son of Jehohanan; Azariah, son of Obed; Maaseiah, son of Adaiah; and Elishaphat, son of Zichri. ²They journeyed about Judah, gathering the Levites from all the cities of Judah and also the heads of the Israelite families, and they came to Jerusalem. ³The whole assembly made a covenant with the king in the house of God. Jehoiada said to them: "Here is the king's son who must reign, as the LORD promised concerning the sons of David. ⁴This is what you must do: a third of your number, both priests and Levites, who come on duty on the sabbath must guard the thresholds, ⁵another third must be at the king's house, and the final third at the Foundation Gate, when all the people will be in the courts of the LORD's house. ⁶Let no one enter the LORD's house except the priests and those Levites who are ministering. They may enter because they are holy; but all the other people must observe the prescriptions of the LORD. ⁷The Levites shall surround the king on all sides, each with drawn weapon. Whoever tries to enter the house is to be killed. Stay with the king wherever he goes."

⁸The Levites and all Judah did just as Jehoiada the priest commanded. Each took his troops, both those going on duty for the week and those going off duty that week, since Jehoiada the priest had not dismissed

any of the divisions. ⁹Jehoiada the priest gave to the captains the spears, shields, and bucklers of King David which were in the house of God. ¹⁰He stationed all the people, each with spear in hand, from the southern to the northern limit of the enclosure, surrounding the altar and the temple on the king's behalf. ¹¹Then they brought out the king's son and put the crown and the testimony upon him, and proclaimed him king. Jehoiada and his sons anointed him, and they cried, "Long live the king!"

¹²When Athaliah heard the noise of the people running and acclaiming the king, she came before them in the house of the LORD. ¹³When she saw the king standing by his column at the entrance, the captains and the trumpeters near the king, and all the people of the land rejoicing and blowing trumpets, while the singers with their musical instruments were leading the acclaim, Athaliah tore her garments, saying, "Treason! treason!" ¹⁴Then Jehoiada the priest brought out the captains in command of the force: "Escort her with a guard detail. If anyone follows her, let him die by the sword." For the priest had said, "You must not put her to death in the house of the LORD." ¹⁵So they seized her, and when she reached the Horse Gate of the royal palace, they put her to death.

¹⁶Then Jehoiada made a covenant between himself and all the people and the king, that they should be the LORD's people. ¹⁷Thereupon all the people went to the temple of Baal and demolished it. They shattered its altars and images completely, and killed Mattan, the priest of Baal, before the altars. ¹⁸Then Jehoiada gave the charge of the LORD's house into the hands of the levitical priests, to whom David had assigned turns in the LORD's house for sacrificing the burnt offerings of the LORD, as is written in the law of Moses, with rejoicing and song, as David had provided. ¹⁹Moreover, he stationed guards at the gates of the LORD's house so that no one unclean in any respect might enter. ²⁰Then he took the captains, the nobles, the rulers among the people, and all the people of the land, and led the king out of the LORD's house; they came within the upper gate of the king's house, and seated the king upon the royal throne. ²¹All the people of the land rejoiced and the city was quiet, now that Athaliah had been slain with the sword.

The Temple Restored. 24:1 Joash was seven years old when he became king, and he reigned forty years in Jerusalem. His mother's name was Zibiah, from Beersheba. ²Joash did what was right in the LORD's sight as long as Jehoiada the priest lived. ³Jehoiada provided him with two wives, and he became the father of sons and daughters.

⁴After some time, Joash decided to restore the house of the LORD. ⁵He gathered together the priests and Levites and said to them: "Go out to all the cities of Judah and gather money from all Israel that you may repair the house of your God over the years. You must hurry this project." But the Levites did not. ⁶Then the king summoned Jehoiada, who was in charge, and said to him: "Why have you not required the Levites to bring in from Judah and Jerusalem the tax levied by Moses, the servant of the LORD, and by the assembly of Israel, for the tent of the testimony?" ⁷For the wicked Athaliah and her sons had damaged the house of God and had even turned over to the Baals the holy things of the LORD's house.

⁸At the king's command, therefore, they made a chest, which they put outside the gate of the LORD's house. ⁹They had it proclaimed throughout Judah and Jerusalem that the tax which Moses, the servant of God, had imposed on Israel in the wilderness should be brought to the LORD. ¹⁰All the princes and the people rejoiced; they brought what was asked and cast it into the chest until it was filled. ¹¹Whenever the chest was brought to the royal officials by

the Levites and they noticed that there was a large amount of money, the royal scribe and an overseer for the chief priest would come up, empty the chest, and then take it back and return it to its place. This they did day after day until they had collected a large sum of money. [12]Then the king and Jehoiada gave it to the workers in charge of the labor on the LORD's house, who hired masons and carpenters to restore the LORD's house, and also iron- and bronze-smiths to repair it. [13]The workers labored, and the task of restoration progressed under their hands. They restored the house of God according to its original form, and reinforced it. [14]After they had finished, they brought the rest of the money to the king and to Jehoiada, who had it made into utensils for the house of the LORD, utensils for the service and the burnt offerings, and basins and other gold and silver utensils. They sacrificed burnt offerings in the LORD's house continually all the days of Jehoiada. [15]Jehoiada grew old, full of years, and died; he was a hundred and thirty years old. [16]They buried him in the City of David with the kings, because of the good he had done in Israel, especially for God and his house.

Joash's Apostasy. [17]After the death of Jehoiada, the princes of Judah came and paid homage to the king; then the king listened to them. [18]They abandoned the house of the LORD, the God of their ancestors, and began to serve the asherahs and the idols; and because of this crime of theirs, wrath came upon Judah and Jerusalem. [19]Although prophets were sent to them to turn them back to the LORD and to warn them, the people would not listen.

[20]Then the spirit of God clothed Zechariah, son of Jehoiada the priest. He took his stand above the people and said to them: "Thus says God, Why are you transgressing the LORD's commands, so that you cannot prosper? Because you have abandoned the LORD, he has abandoned you." [21]But they conspired against him, and at the king's command they stoned him in the court of the house of the LORD. [22]Thus King Joash was unmindful of the devotion shown him by Jehoiada, Zechariah's father, and killed the son. As he was dying, he said, "May the LORD see and avenge."

Joash Punished. [23]At the turn of the year a force of Arameans came up against Joash. They invaded Judah and Jerusalem, killed all the princes of the people, and sent all their spoil to the king of Damascus. [24]Though the Aramean force was small, the LORD handed over a very large force into their power, because Judah had abandoned the LORD, the God of their ancestors. So judgment was meted out to Joash. [25]After the Arameans had departed from him, abandoning him to his many injuries, his servants conspired against him because of the murder of the son of Jehoiada the priest. They killed him on his sickbed. He was buried in the City of David, but not in the tombs of the kings.

[26]Those who conspired against him were Zabad, son of Shimeath from Ammon, and Jehozabad, son of Shimrith from Moab. [27]An account of his sons, the great tribute imposed on him, and his rebuilding of the house of God is written in the midrash of the book of the kings. His son Amaziah succeeded him as king.

☐ MATTHEW 15:21-31

The Canaanite Woman's Faith. 15:21 Then Jesus went from that place and withdrew to the region of Tyre and Sidon. [22]And behold, a Canaanite woman of that district came and called out, "Have pity on me, Lord, Son of David! My daughter is tormented by a demon." [23]But he did not say a word in answer to her. His disciples came and asked him, "Send her away, for she keeps calling out after us." ²⁴He said in reply, "I was sent only to the lost sheep of the house of Israel." ²⁵But the woman came and did him homage, saying, "Lord, help me." ²⁶He said in reply, "It is not right to take the food of the children and throw it to the dogs." ²⁷She said, "Please, Lord, for even the dogs eat the scraps that fall from the table of their masters." ²⁸Then Jesus said to her in reply, "O woman, great is your faith! Let it be done for you as you wish." And her daughter was healed from that hour.

The Healing of Many People. ²⁹Moving on from there Jesus walked by the Sea of Galilee, went up on the mountain, and sat down there. ³⁰Great crowds came to him, having with them the lame, the blind, the deformed, the mute, and many others. They placed them at his feet, and he cured them. ³¹The crowds were amazed when they saw the mute speaking, the deformed made whole, the lame walking, and the blind able to see, and they glorified the God of Israel.

May 15

St. Isidore the Farmer

The farmer rejoices when the heavy rain of a thunderstorm comes. He's not worrying about the present, but awaiting the future. He pays no attention to the thunder, but instead thinks of the harvest to come. In the same way should we focus, not on our present tribulation, but on the benefit that may arise from it — the fruit that it will bring forth.

— St. John Chrysostom

☐ 2 CHRONICLES 25-28

Amaziah's Good Start. 25:1 Amaziah was twenty-five years old when he became king, and he reigned twenty-nine years in Jerusalem. His mother's name was Jehoaddan, from Jerusalem. ²He did what was right in the LORD's sight, though not wholeheartedly. ³When he had the kingdom firmly in hand, he struck down the officials who had struck down the king, his father. ⁴But their children he did not put to death, for he acted according to what is written in the law, in the Book of Moses, which the LORD commanded: "Parents shall not be put to death for their children, nor shall children be put to death for their parents; they shall each die for their own sin."

⁵Amaziah gathered Judah and placed them, out of all Judah and Benjamin according to their ancestral houses, under leaders of thousands and of hundreds. When he made a count of those twenty years old and over, he found that there were three hundred thousand picked men fit for war, capable of handling lance and shield. ⁶He also hired a hundred thousand valiant warriors from Israel for a hundred talents of silver. ⁷But a man of God came to him and said: "O king, let not the army of Israel go with you, for the LORD is not with Israel—with any Ephraimite. ⁸Instead, go on your own, strongly prepared for the battle; why should the LORD hinder you in the face of

the enemy: for with God is power to help or to hinder." [9]Amaziah answered the man of God, "But what is to be done about the hundred talents that I paid for the troops of Israel?" The man of God replied, "The LORD can give you much more than that." [10]Amaziah then disbanded the troops that had come to him from Ephraim, and sent them home. But they became furiously angry with Judah, and returned home blazing with anger.

[11]Amaziah now assumed command of his army. They proceeded to the Valley of Salt, where they killed ten thousand men of Seir. [12]The Judahites also brought back another ten thousand alive, led them to the summit of Sela, and then threw them down from that rock so that their bodies split open. [13]Meanwhile, the troops Amaziah had dismissed from going into battle with him raided the cities of Judah from Samaria to Beth-horon. They struck down three thousand of the inhabitants and carried off much plunder.

Amaziah's Apostasy. [14]When Amaziah returned from his conquest of the Edomites he brought back with him the gods of the people of Seir. He set these up as his own gods; he bowed down before them and offered sacrifice to them. [15]Then the anger of the LORD blazed out against Amaziah, and he sent a prophet to him who said: "Why have you sought this people's gods that could not deliver their own people from your power?" [16]While he was still speaking, however, the king said to him: "Have you been appointed the king's counselor? Stop! Why should you have to be killed?" Therefore the prophet stopped. But he said, "I know that God's counsel is your destruction, for by doing this you have refused to listen to my counsel."

Amaziah Punished. [17]Having taken counsel, Amaziah, king of Judah, sent word to Joash, son of Jehoahaz, son of Jehu, the king of Israel, saying, "Come, let us meet face to face." [18]Joash, king of Israel, sent

this reply to Amaziah, king of Judah: "A thistle of Lebanon sent word to a cedar of Lebanon, 'Give your daughter to my son in marriage,' but an animal of Lebanon passed by and trampled the thistle underfoot. [19]You are thinking,

'See, I have struck down Edom!'
Your heart is lifted up,
And glories in it. Stay home!
Why bring misfortune and failure
on yourself and on Judah with
you?"

[20]But Amaziah did not listen; for it was God's doing that they be handed over because they sought the gods of Edom.

[21]So Joash, king of Israel, advanced, and he and Amaziah, king of Judah, met face to face at Beth-shemesh of Judah, [22]and Judah was defeated by Israel, and all fled to their tents. [23]But Amaziah, king of Judah, son of Joash, son of Jehoahaz, was captured by Joash, king of Israel, at Beth-shemesh. Joash brought him to Jerusalem and tore down the wall of Jerusalem from the Gate of Ephraim to the Corner Gate, four hundred cubits. [24]He took all the gold and silver and all the vessels found in the house of God with Obed-edom, and in the treasuries of the king's house, and hostages as well. Then he returned to Samaria.

[25]Amaziah, son of Joash, king of Judah, survived Joash, son of Jehoahaz, king of Israel, by fifteen years. [26]The rest of the acts of Amaziah, first and last, are recorded in the book of the kings of Judah and Israel. [27]Now from the time that Amaziah turned away from the LORD, a conspiracy was formed against him in Jerusalem, and he fled to Lachish. But he was pursued to Lachish and killed there. [28]He was brought back on horses and was buried with his ancestors in the City of Judah.

Uzziah's Projects. 26:1 All the people of Judah took Uzziah, who was only sixteen years old, and made him king to succeed

Amaziah his father. [2]It was he who rebuilt Elath and restored it to Judah, after the king rested with his ancestors. [3]Uzziah was sixteen years old when he became king, and he reigned fifty-two years in Jerusalem. His mother's name was Jecoliah, from Jerusalem. [4]He did what was right in the LORD's sight, just as his father Amaziah had done.

[5]He was prepared to seek God as long as Zechariah lived, who taught him to fear God; and as long as he sought the LORD, God made him prosper. [6]He went out and fought the Philistines and razed the walls of Gath, Jabneh, and Ashdod, and built cities in the district of Ashdod and in Philistia. [7]God helped him against the Philistines, against the Arabians who dwelt in Gurbaal, and against the Meunites. [8]The Ammonites paid tribute to Uzziah and his fame spread as far as Egypt, for he grew stronger and stronger. [9]Moreover, Uzziah built towers in Jerusalem at the Corner Gate, at the Valley Gate, and at the Angle, and he fortified them. [10]He built towers in the wilderness and dug numerous cisterns, for he had many cattle. He had plowmen in the Shephelah and the plains, farmers and vinedressers in the highlands and the garden land. He was a lover of the soil.

[11]Uzziah also had a standing army of fit soldiers divided into bands according to the number in which they were mustered by Jeiel the scribe and Maaseiah the recorder, under the command of Hananiah, one of the king's officials. [12]The entire number of family heads over these valiant warriors was two thousand six hundred, [13]and at their disposal was a mighty army of three hundred seven thousand five hundred fighting men of great valor to help the king against his enemies. [14]Uzziah provided for them— for the entire army—bucklers, lances, helmets, breastplates, bows, and slingstones. [15]He also built machines in Jerusalem, devices designed to stand on the towers and at the angles of the walls to shoot arrows and cast large stones. His name spread far and wide; the help he received was wondrous, so strong did he become.

Pride and Fall. [16]But after he had become strong, he became arrogant to his own destruction and acted treacherously with the LORD, his God. He entered the temple of the LORD to make an offering on the altar of incense. [17]But Azariah the priest, and with him eighty other priests of the LORD, courageous men, followed him. [18]They stood up to King Uzziah, saying to him: "It is not for you, Uzziah, to burn incense to the LORD, but for the priests, the sons of Aaron, who have been consecrated for this purpose. Leave the sanctuary, for you have acted treacherously and no longer have a part in the glory that comes from the LORD God." [19]Uzziah, who was holding a censer for burning the incense, became angry. But at the very moment he showed his anger to the priests, while they were looking at him in the house of the LORD beside the altar of incense, leprosy broke out on his forehead. [20]Azariah the chief priest and all the other priests examined him, and when they saw that his forehead was leprous, they rushed him out. He let himself be expelled, for the LORD had afflicted him. [21]King Uzziah remained a leper till the day he died. As a leper he lived in a house apart, for he was excluded from the house of the LORD. Therefore his son Jotham was master of the palace and ruled the people of the land.

[22]The rest of the acts of Uzziah, first and last, were written by Isaiah the prophet, son of Amoz. [23]Uzziah rested with his ancestors and was buried with them in the field adjoining the royal cemetery, for they said, "He was a leper." His son Jotham succeeded him as king.

Jotham. 27:1 Jotham was twenty-five years old when he became king, and he reigned sixteen years in Jerusalem. His mother's name was Jerusha, daughter of Zadok. [2]He did what was right in the LORD's sight, just as his father Uzziah had done, though he did not enter the temple of the LORD. The people, however, continued to act corruptly.

³It was he who built the Upper Gate of the LORD's house and did much construction on the wall of Ophel. ⁴Moreover, he built cities in the hill country of Judah, and in the wooded areas he set up fortresses and towers. ⁵He fought with the king of the Ammonites and conquered them. That year the Ammonites paid him one hundred talents of silver, together with ten thousand kors of wheat and ten thousand of barley. They brought the same to him also in the second and in the third year. ⁶Thus Jotham continued to grow strong because he made sure to walk before the LORD, his God. ⁷The rest of the acts of Jotham, his wars and his activities, are recorded in the book of the kings of Israel and Judah. ⁸He was twenty-five years old when he became king, and he reigned sixteen years in Jerusalem. ⁹Jotham rested with his ancestors and was buried in the City of David, and his son Ahaz succeeded him as king.

Ahaz's Misdeeds. 28:1 Ahaz was twenty years old when he became king, and he reigned sixteen years in Jerusalem. He did not do what was right in the sight of the LORD as David his father had done. ²He walked in the ways of the kings of Israel and even made molten idols for the Baals. ³Moreover, he offered sacrifice in the Valley of Ben-hinnom, and immolated his children by fire in accordance with the abominable practices of the nations whom the LORD had dispossessed before the Israelites. ⁴He sacrificed and burned incense on the high places, on hills, and under every green tree.

Ahaz Punished. ⁵Therefore the LORD, his God, delivered him into the power of the king of Aram. The Arameans defeated him and carried away captive a large number of his people, whom they brought to Damascus. He was also delivered into the power of the king of Israel, who defeated him with great slaughter. ⁶For Pekah, son of Remaliah, killed one hundred and twenty thousand of Judah in a single day, all of them valiant men, because they had abandoned the LORD, the God of their ancestors. ⁷Zichri, an Ephraimite warrior, killed Maaseiah, the king's son, and Azrikam, the master of the palace, and also Elkanah, who was second to the king. ⁸The Israelites took away as captives two hundred thousand of their kinfolk's wives, sons, and daughters; they also took from them much plunder, which they brought to Samaria.

Oded's Prophecy. ⁹In Samaria there was a prophet of the LORD by the name of Oded. He went out to meet the army returning to Samaria and said to them: "It was because the LORD, the God of your ancestors, was angry with Judah that he delivered them into your power. You, however, have killed them with a fury that has reached up to heaven. ¹⁰And now you are planning to subjugate the people of Judah and Jerusalem as your slaves and bondwomen. Are not you yourselves, therefore, guilty of a crime against the LORD, your God? ¹¹Now listen to me: send back the captives you have carried off from among your kin, for the burning anger of the LORD is upon you."

¹²At this, some of the Ephraimite leaders, Azariah, son of Johanan, Berechiah, son of Meshillemoth, Jehizkiah, son of Shallum, and Amasa, son of Hadlai, themselves stood up in opposition to those who had returned from the war. ¹³They said to them: "Do not bring the captives here, for what you are planning will make us guilty before the LORD and increase our sins and our guilt. Great is our guilt, and there is burning anger upon Israel." ¹⁴Therefore the soldiers left their captives and the plunder before the princes and the whole assembly. ¹⁵Then the men just named proceeded to help the captives. All of them who were

naked they clothed from the spoils; they clothed them, put sandals on their feet, gave them food and drink, anointed them, and all who were weak they set on donkeys. They brought them to Jericho, the City of Palms, to their kinfolk. Then they returned to Samaria.

Further Sins of Ahaz. ¹⁶At that time King Ahaz sent an appeal for help to the kings of Assyria. ¹⁷The Edomites had returned, attacked Judah, and carried off captives. ¹⁸The Philistines too had raided the cities of the Shephelah and the Negeb of Judah; they captured Beth-shemesh, Aijalon, Gederoth, Soco and its dependencies, Timnah and its dependencies, and Gimzo and its dependencies, and settled there. ¹⁹For the LORD had brought Judah low because of Ahaz, king of Israel, who let Judah go its own way and committed treachery against the LORD. ²⁰Tiglath-pileser, king of Assyria, did indeed come to him, but to oppress him rather than to lend strength. ²¹Though Ahaz plundered the LORD's house and the houses of the king and the princes to pay off the king of Assyria, it was no help to him.

²²While he was already in distress, the same King Ahaz increased his treachery to the LORD. ²³He sacrificed to the gods of Damascus who had defeated him, saying, "Since it was the gods of the kings of Aram who helped them, I will sacrifice to them that they may help me also." However, they only furthered his downfall and that of all Israel. ²⁴Ahaz gathered up the utensils of God's house and broke them in pieces. He closed the doors of the LORD's house and made altars for himself in every corner of Jerusalem. ²⁵In every city throughout Judah he set up high places to offer sacrifice to other gods. Thus he provoked the LORD, the God of his ancestors, to anger.

²⁶The rest of his words and his deeds, first and last, are recorded in the book of the kings of Judah and Israel. ²⁷Ahaz rested with his ancestors and was buried in Jerusalem—in the city, for they did not bring him to the tombs of the kings of Israel. His son Hezekiah succeeded him as king.

☐ MATTHEW 15:32-39

The Feeding of the Four Thousand. 15:32 Jesus summoned his disciples and said, "My heart is moved with pity for the crowd, for they have been with me now for three days and have nothing to eat. I do not want to send them away hungry, for fear they may collapse on the way." ³³The disciples said to him, "Where could we ever get enough bread in this deserted place to satisfy such a crowd?" ³⁴Jesus said to them, "How many loaves do you have?" "Seven," they replied, "and a few fish." ³⁵He ordered the crowd to sit down on the ground. ³⁶Then he took the seven loaves and the fish, gave thanks, broke the loaves, and gave them to the disciples, who in turn gave them to the crowds. ³⁷They all ate and were satisfied. They picked up the fragments left over—seven baskets full. ³⁸Those who ate were four thousand men, not counting women and children. ³⁹And when he had dismissed the crowds, he got into the boat and came to the district of Magadan.

May 16

Only he who rules well is worthy of the name of king.
— St. John Nepomucene

☐ 2 CHRONICLES 29-32

Hezekiah's Reforms. 29:1 Hezekiah was twenty-five years old when he became king, and he reigned twenty-nine years in Jerusalem. His mother's name was Abijah, daughter of Zechariah. [2]He did what was right in the Lord's sight, just as David his father had done. [3]In the first month of the first year of his reign, he opened the doors of the Lord's house and repaired them. [4]He summoned the priests and Levites, gathering them in the open space to the east, [5]and said to them: "Listen to me, you Levites! Sanctify yourselves now and sanctify the house of the Lord, the God of your ancestors, and clean out the filth from the sanctuary. [6]Our ancestors acted treacherously and did what was evil in the eyes of the Lord, our God. They abandoned him, turned away their faces from the Lord's dwelling, and turned their backs on him. [7]They also closed the doors of the vestibule, extinguished the lamps, and failed to burn incense and sacrifice burnt offerings in the sanctuary to the God of Israel. [8]Therefore the anger of the Lord has come upon Judah and Jerusalem; he has made them an object of terror, horror, and hissing, as you see with your own eyes. [9]For our ancestors fell by the sword, and our sons, our daughters, and our wives have been taken captive because of this. [10]Now, I intend to make a covenant with the Lord, the God of Israel, that his burning anger may turn away from us. [11]My sons, do not be negligent any longer, for it is you whom the Lord has chosen to stand before him, to minister to him, to be his ministers and to offer incense."

[12]Then the Levites arose: Mahath, son of Amasai, and Joel, son of Azariah, of the Kohathites; of the descendants of Merari: Kish, son of Abdi, and Azariah, son of Jehallel; of the Gershonites: Joah, son of Zimmah, and Eden, son of Joah; [13]of the sons of Elizaphan: Shimri and Jeuel; of the sons of Asaph: Zechariah and Mattaniah; [14]of the sons of Heman: Jehuel and Shimei; of the sons of Jeduthun: Shemiah and Uzziel. [15]They gathered their kinfolk together and sanctified themselves; then they came as the king had ordered, in keeping with the words of the Lord, to cleanse the Lord's house.

[16]The priests entered the interior of the Lord's house to cleanse it. Whatever they found in the Lord's temple that was unclean they brought out to the court of the Lord's house, where the Levites took it from them and carried it out to the Wadi Kidron. [17]They began the work of consecration on the first day of the first month, and on the eighth day of the month they reached the vestibule of the Lord; they consecrated the Lord's house over an eight-day period, and on the sixteenth day of the first month, they had finished.

[18]Then they went inside to King Hezekiah and said: "We have cleansed the entire house of the Lord, the altar for burnt offerings with all its utensils, and the table for the showbread with all its utensils. [19]We have restored and consecrated all the articles which King Ahaz had thrown away during his reign because of his treachery; they are now before the Lord's altar."

The Rite of Expiation. [20]Then King Hezekiah hastened to convoke the princes of the city and went up to the Lord's house. [21]Seven bulls, seven rams, seven lambs, and seven he-goats were presented as a purification offering for the kingdom, for the sanctuary, and for Judah. Hezekiah ordered the sons of Aaron, the priests, to offer them on the altar of the LORD. ²²They slaughtered the bulls, and the priests collected the blood and splashed it on the altar. Then they slaughtered the rams and splashed the blood on the altar; then they slaughtered the lambs and splashed the blood on the altar. ²³Then the he-goats for the purification offering were led before the king and the assembly, who laid their hands upon them. ²⁴The priests then slaughtered them and offered their blood on the altar to atone for the sin of all Israel. For the king had said, "The burnt offering and the purification offering are for all Israel."

²⁵He stationed the Levites in the LORD's house with cymbals, harps, and lyres, according to the command of David, of Gad the king's seer, and of Nathan the prophet; for this command was from the LORD through his prophets. ²⁶The Levites were stationed with the instruments of David, and the priests with the trumpets. ²⁷Then Hezekiah ordered the burnt offering to be sacrificed on the altar. At the very moment the burnt offering began, they also began the song of the LORD, to the accompaniment of the trumpets and the instruments of David, king of Israel. ²⁸The entire assembly bowed down, and the song was sung and the trumpets sounded until the burnt offering had been completed. ²⁹Once the burnt offering was completed, the king and all who were with him knelt and worshiped. ³⁰King Hezekiah and the princes then told the Levites to sing the praises of the LORD in the words of David and of Asaph the seer. They sang praises till their joy was full, then fell down and worshiped. ³¹Hezekiah then said: "You have dedicated yourselves to the LORD. Approach, and bring forward the sacrifices and thank offerings for the house of the LORD." Then the assembly brought forward the sacrifices

and thank offerings and all their voluntary burnt offerings. ³²The number of burnt offerings that the assembly brought forward was seventy oxen, one hundred rams, and two hundred lambs: all of these as a burnt offering to the LORD. ³³As consecrated gifts there were six hundred oxen and three thousand sheep. ³⁴Since there were too few priests to skin all the victims for the burnt offerings, their fellow Levites assisted them until the task was completed and the priests had sanctified themselves. The Levites, in fact, were more careful than the priests to sanctify themselves. ³⁵The burnt offerings were indeed many, along with the fat of the communion offerings and the libations for the burnt offerings. Thus the service of the house of the LORD was reestablished. ³⁶Hezekiah and all the people rejoiced over what God had re-established for the people, and at how suddenly this had been done.

Invitation to Passover. 30:1 Hezekiah sent word to all Israel and Judah, and even wrote letters to Ephraim and Manasseh, saying that they should come to the house of the LORD in Jerusalem to celebrate the Passover to the LORD, the God of Israel. ²The king, his princes, and the entire assembly in Jerusalem had agreed to celebrate the Passover during the second month. ³They could not celebrate it at the regular time because the priests had not sanctified themselves in sufficient numbers, and the people were not gathered at Jerusalem. ⁴This seemed right to the king and the entire assembly, ⁵and they issued a decree to be proclaimed throughout all Israel from Beer-sheba to Dan, that everyone should come to celebrate the Passover to the LORD, the God of Israel, in Jerusalem; for not many had kept it in the prescribed manner. ⁶By the king's command, the couriers, with the letters written by the king and his princes, went through all Israel and Judah. They said: "Israelites, return to the LORD, the God of Abraham,

Isaac, and Israel, that he may return to you, the remnant left from the hands of the Assyrian kings. [7]Do not be like your ancestors and your kin who acted treacherously toward the LORD, the God of their ancestors, so that he handed them over to desolation, as you yourselves now see. [8]Do not be stiff-necked, as your ancestors were; stretch out your hands to the LORD and come to his sanctuary that he has consecrated forever, and serve the LORD, your God, that he may turn his burning anger from you. [9]If you return to the LORD, your kinfolk and your children will find mercy with their captors and return to this land. The LORD, your God, is gracious and merciful and he will not turn away his face from you if you return to him."

[10]So the couriers passed from city to city in the land of Ephraim and Manasseh and as far as Zebulun, but they were derided and scoffed at. [11]Nevertheless, some from Asher, Manasseh, and Zebulun humbled themselves and came to Jerusalem. [12]In Judah, however, the hand of God brought it about that the people were of one heart to carry out the command of the king and the princes by the word of the LORD. [13]Thus many people gathered in Jerusalem to celebrate the feast of Unleavened Bread in the second month; it was a very great assembly.

Passover Celebrated. [14]They proceeded to remove the altars that were in Jerusalem as well as all the altars of incense, and cast them into the Wadi Kidron. [15]They slaughtered the Passover on the fourteenth day of the second month. The priests and Levites were shamed into sanctifying themselves and brought burnt offerings into the house of the LORD. [16]They stood in the places prescribed for them according to the law of Moses, the man of God. The priests splashed the blood given them by the Levites; [17]for many in the assembly had not sanctified themselves, and the Levites were in charge of slaughtering the Passover victims for all who were unclean so as to consecrate them to the LORD. [18]The greater part of the people, in fact, chiefly from Ephraim, Manasseh, Issachar, and Zebulun, had not cleansed themselves. Nevertheless they ate the Passover, contrary to the prescription; because Hezekiah prayed for them, saying, "May the good LORD grant pardon to [19]all who have set their heart to seek God, the LORD, the God of their ancestors, even though they are not clean as holiness requires." [20]The LORD heard Hezekiah and healed the people.

[21]Thus the Israelites who were in Jerusalem celebrated the feast of Unleavened Bread with great rejoicing for seven days, and the Levites and the priests sang the praises of the LORD day after day with all their strength. [22]Hezekiah spoke encouragingly to all the Levites who had shown themselves well skilled in the service of the LORD. And when they had completed the seven days of festival, sacrificing communion offerings and singing praises to the LORD, the God of their ancestors, [23]the whole assembly agreed to celebrate another seven days. So with joy they celebrated seven days more. [24]King Hezekiah of Judah had contributed a thousand bulls and seven thousand sheep to the assembly, and the princes a thousand bulls and ten thousand sheep. The priests sanctified themselves in great numbers, [25]and the whole assembly of Judah rejoiced, together with the priests and Levites and the rest of the assembly that had come from Israel, as well as the resident aliens from the land of Israel and those that lived in Judah. [26]There was great rejoicing in Jerusalem, for since the days of Solomon, son of David, king of Israel, there had been nothing like it in the city. [27]Then the levitical priests rose and blessed the people; their voice was heard and their prayer reached heaven, God's holy dwelling.

Liturgical Reforms. 31:1 After all this was over, those Israelites who had been present went forth to the cities of Judah and smashed the sacred pillars, cut down the asherahs, and tore down the high places and altars throughout Judah, Benjamin, Ephraim, and Manasseh, until they were all destroyed. Then the Israelites returned to their cities, each to his own possession.

²Hezekiah re-established the divisions of the priests and the Levites according to their former divisions, assigning to each priest and Levite his proper service, whether in regard to burnt offerings or communion offerings, thanksgiving or praise, or ministering in the gates of the encampment of the LORD. ³From his own wealth the king allotted a portion for burnt offerings, those of morning and evening and those on sabbaths, new moons, and festivals, as is written in the law of the LORD. ⁴He also commanded the people living in Jerusalem to provide for the support of the priests and Levites, that they might firmly adhere to the law of the LORD.

⁵As soon as the order was promulgated, the Israelites brought, in great quantities, the best of their grain, wine, oil, and honey, and all the produce of the fields; they gave a generous tithe of everything. ⁶Israelites and Judahites living in other cities of Judah also brought in tithes of oxen, sheep, and votive offerings consecrated to the LORD, their God; these they brought in and heaped up in piles. ⁷It was in the third month that they began to establish these heaps, and they completed them in the seventh month. ⁸When Hezekiah and the princes had come and seen the piles, they blessed the LORD and his people Israel. ⁹Then Hezekiah questioned the priests and the Levites concerning the piles, ¹⁰and the priest Azariah, head of the house of Zadok, answered him, "Since they began to bring the offerings to the house of the LORD, we have eaten, been satisfied, and had much left over, for the LORD has blessed his people. This great supply is what was left over."

¹¹Hezekiah then gave orders that chambers be constructed in the house of the LORD. When this had been done, ¹²they deposited the offerings, tithes, and votive offerings there for safekeeping. The overseer of these things was Conaniah the Levite, and his brother Shimei was second in command. ¹³Jehiel, Azaziah, Nahath, Asahel, Jerimoth, Jozabad, Eliel, Ismachiah, Mahath, and Benaiah were supervisors subject to Conaniah the Levite and his brother Shimei by appointment of King Hezekiah and of Azariah, the prefect of the house of God. ¹⁴Kore, the son of Imnah, a Levite and the keeper of the eastern gate, was in charge of the voluntary offerings made to God; he distributed the offerings made to the LORD and the most holy of the votive offerings. ¹⁵Under him in the priestly cities were Eden, Miniamin, Jeshua, Shemaiah, Amariah, and Shecaniah, who faithfully made the distribution to their brothers, great and small alike, according to their divisions.

¹⁶There was also a register by ancestral houses of males three years of age and over, for all priests who were eligible to enter the house of the LORD according to the daily schedule to fulfill their service in the order of their divisions. ¹⁷The priests were inscribed in their family records according to their ancestral houses, as were the Levites twenty years of age and over according to their various offices and divisions. ¹⁸A distribution was also made to all who were inscribed in the family records, for their little ones, wives, sons and daughters—thus for the entire assembly, since they were to sanctify themselves by sharing faithfully in the votive offerings. ¹⁹The sons of Aaron, the priests who lived on the lands attached to their cities, had in every city men designated by name to distribute portions to every male of the priests and to every Levite listed in the family records.

²⁰Hezekiah did this in all Judah. He did what was good, upright, and faithful before the LORD, his God. ²¹Everything that he undertook, for the service of the house of

God or for the law and the commandment, was to seek his God. He did this with all his heart, and he prospered.

Sennacherib's Invasion. 32:1 But after all this and all Hezekiah's fidelity, there came Sennacherib, king of Assyria. He invaded Judah and besieged the fortified cities, intending to breach and take them. [2]When Hezekiah saw that Sennacherib was coming with the intention of attacking Jerusalem, [3]he took the advice of his princes and warriors to stop the waters of the springs outside the city; they promised their help. [4]A large force was gathered and stopped all the springs and also the stream running nearby. For they said, "Why should the kings of Assyria come and find an abundance of water?" [5]He then looked to his defenses: he rebuilt the wall where it was broken down, raised towers upon it, and built another wall outside. He strengthened the Millo of the City of David and made a great number of spears and shields. [6]Then he appointed army commanders over the people. He gathered them together in his presence in the open space at the gate of the city and encouraged them with these words: [7]"Be strong and steadfast; do not be afraid or dismayed because of the king of Assyria and all the horde coming with him, for there is more with us than with him. [8]He has only an arm of flesh, but we have the LORD, our God, to help us and to fight our battles." And the people took confidence from the words of Hezekiah, king of Judah.

Threat of Sennacherib. [9]After this, while Sennacherib, king of Assyria, himself remained at Lachish with all his forces, he sent his officials to Jerusalem with this message for Hezekiah, king of Judah, and all the Judahites who were in Jerusalem: [10]"Thus says Sennacherib, king of Assyria: In what are you trusting, now that you are under siege in Jerusalem? [11]Is not Hezekiah deceiving you, delivering you

over to a death of famine and thirst, by his claim that 'the LORD, our God, will rescue us from the grasp of the king of Assyria'? [12]Has not this same Hezekiah removed the Lord's own high places and altars and commanded Judah and Jerusalem, 'You shall bow down before one altar only, and on it alone you shall offer incense'? [13]Do you not know what my fathers and I have done to all the peoples of other lands? Were the gods of the nations in those lands able to rescue their lands from my hand? [14]Who among all the gods of those nations which my fathers put under the ban was able to rescue their people from my hand? Will your god, then, be able to rescue you from my hand? [15]Let not Hezekiah mislead you further and deceive you in any such way. Do not believe him! Since no other god of any other nation or kingdom has been able to rescue his people from my hand or the hands of my fathers, how much the less shall your god rescue you from my hand!"

[16]His officials said still more against the LORD God and against his servant Hezekiah, [17]for he had written letters to deride the LORD, the God of Israel, speaking of him in these terms: "As the gods of the nations in other lands have not rescued their people from my hand, neither shall Hezekiah's god rescue his people from my hand." [18]In a loud voice they shouted in the language of Judah to the people of Jerusalem who were on the wall, to frighten and terrify them so that they might capture their city. [19]They spoke of the God of Israel as though he were one of the gods of the other peoples of the earth, a work of human hands. [20]But because of this, King Hezekiah and Isaiah the prophet, son of Amoz, prayed and cried out to heaven.

Sennacherib's Defeat. [21]Then the LORD sent an angel, who destroyed every warrior, leader, and commander in the camp of the Assyrian king, so that he had to return shamefaced to his own country. And when he entered the temple of his god, some of his own offspring struck him down there with the sword. [22]Thus the LORD saved Hezekiah and the inhabitants of Jerusalem from the hand of Sennacherib, king of Assyria, as from every other power; he gave them rest on every side. [23]Many brought gifts for the LORD to Jerusalem and costly objects for Hezekiah, king of Judah, who thereafter was exalted in the eyes of all the nations.

Hezekiah's Later Reign. [24]In those days Hezekiah became mortally ill. He prayed to the LORD, who answered him by giving him a sign. [25]Hezekiah, however, did not respond with like generosity, for he had become arrogant. Therefore wrath descended upon him and upon Judah and Jerusalem. [26]But then Hezekiah humbled himself for his pride—both he and the inhabitants of Jerusalem; and therefore the wrath of the LORD did not come upon them during the time of Hezekiah.

[27]Hezekiah possessed very great wealth and glory. He made treasuries for his silver, gold, precious stones, spices, jewels, and other precious things of all kinds; [28]also storehouses for the harvest of grain, for wine and oil, and barns for the various kinds of cattle and flocks. [29]He built cities for himself, and he acquired sheep and oxen in great numbers, for God gave him very great riches. [30]This same Hezekiah stopped the upper outlet for water from Gihon and redirected it underground westward to the City of David. Hezekiah prospered in all his works. [31]Nevertheless, in respect to the ambassadors of the Babylonian officials who were sent to him to investigate the sign that had occurred in the land, God abandoned him as a test, to know all that was in his heart.

[32]The rest of Hezekiah's acts, including his good deeds, are recorded in the vision of Isaiah the prophet, son of Amoz, and in the book of the kings of Judah and Israel. [33]Hezekiah rested with his ancestors; he was buried at the approach to the tombs of the descendants of David. All Judah and the inhabitants of Jerusalem paid him honor at his death. His son Manasseh succeeded him as king.

☐ MATTHEW 16:1-12

The Demand for a Sign. 16:1 The Pharisees and Sadducees came and, to test him, asked him to show them a sign from heaven. [2]He said to them in reply, "[In the evening you say, 'Tomorrow will be fair, for the sky is red'; [3]and, in the morning, 'Today will be stormy, for the sky is red and threatening.' You know how to judge the appearance of the sky, but you cannot judge the signs of the times.] [4]An evil and unfaithful generation seeks a sign, but no sign will be given it except the sign of Jonah." Then he left them and went away.

The Leaven of the Pharisees and Sadducees. [5]In coming to the other side of the sea, the disciples had forgotten to bring bread. [6]Jesus said to them, "Look out, and beware of the leaven of the Pharisees and Sadducees." [7]They concluded among themselves, saying, "It is because we have brought no bread." [8]When Jesus became aware of this he said, "You of little faith, why do you conclude among yourselves that it is because you have no bread? [9]Do you not yet understand, and do you not remember the five loaves for the five thousand, and how many wicker baskets you took up? [10]Or the seven loaves for the four thousand, and how many baskets you took up? [11]How do you not comprehend that I was not speaking to you about bread? Beware of the leaven of the Pharisees and Sadducees." [12]Then they understood that he was not telling them to beware of the leaven of bread, but of the teaching of the Pharisees and Sadducees.

May 17

Reckon up the priests from the days that Peter sat, and in their ancestral ranks note who succeeded whom; for that is the Rock over which the gates of hell shall never prevail.

— St. Augustine of Hippo

☐ 2 CHRONICLES 33–36

Manasseh's Impiety. 33:1 Manasseh was twelve years old when he became king, and he reigned fifty-five years in Jerusalem. ²He did what was evil in the Lord's sight, following the abominable practices of the nations whom the Lord dispossessed before the Israelites. ³He rebuilt the high places which Hezekiah his father had torn down. He set up altars to the Baals, and also made asherahs. He bowed down to the whole host of heaven and served them. ⁴He built altars in the house of the Lord, of which the Lord had said: In Jerusalem shall my name be forever; ⁵and he built altars to the whole host of heaven in the two courts of the house of the Lord. ⁶It was he, too, who immolated his children by fire in the Valley of Ben-hinnom. He practiced soothsaying and divination, and reintroduced the consulting of ghosts and spirits.

He did much evil in the Lord's sight and provoked him to anger. ⁷An idol he had made he placed in the house of God, of which God had said to David and to his son Solomon: In this house and in Jerusalem, which I have chosen out of all the tribes of Israel, I shall set my name forever. ⁸I will no longer make Israel step out of the land I assigned to your ancestors, provided that they are careful to observe all I commanded them, the entire law, the statutes, and the ordinances given by Moses. ⁹Manasseh misled Judah and the inhabitants of Jerusalem into doing even greater evil than the nations the Lord had destroyed at the coming of the Israelites. ¹⁰The Lord spoke to Manasseh and his people, but they paid no attention.

Manasseh's Conversion. ¹¹Therefore the Lord brought against them the army commanders of the Assyrian king; they captured Manasseh with hooks, shackled him with chains, and transported him to Babylon. ¹²In his distress, he began to appease the Lord, his God. He humbled himself abjectly before the God of his ancestors, ¹³and prayed to him. The Lord let himself be won over: he heard his prayer and restored him to his kingdom in Jerusalem. Then Manasseh knew that the Lord is indeed God.

¹⁴Afterward he built an outer wall for the City of David to the west of Gihon in the valley, extending to the Fish Gate and encircling Ophel; he built it very high. He stationed army officers in all the fortified cities of Judah. ¹⁵He removed the foreign gods and the idol from the Lord's house and all the altars he had built on the mount of the Lord's house and in Jerusalem, and cast them outside the city. ¹⁶He restored the altar of the Lord, and sacrificed on it communion offerings and thank offerings, and commanded Judah to serve the Lord, the God of Israel. ¹⁷Though the people continued to sacrifice on the high places, they now did so to the Lord, their God.

¹⁸The rest of the acts of Manasseh, his prayer to his God, and the words of the seers who spoke to him in the name of the Lord, the God of Israel, are written in the chronicles of the kings of Israel. ¹⁹His prayer and how his supplication was heard, all his sins and his treachery, the sites where he built high places and set up asherahs and carved images before he humbled himself,

all this is recorded in the chronicles of his seers. [20]Manasseh rested with his ancestors and was buried in his own palace. His son Amon succeeded him as king.

Reign of Amon. [21]Amon was twenty-two years old when he became king, and he reigned two years in Jerusalem. [22]He did what was evil in the LORD's sight, as his father Manasseh had done. Amon offered sacrifice to all the idols his father Manasseh had made, and served them. [23]Moreover, he did not humble himself before the LORD as his father Manasseh had humbled himself; on the contrary, Amon only increased his guilt. [24]His officials plotted against him and put him to death in his palace, [25]but the people of the land then slew all who had plotted against King Amon, and the people of the land made his son Josiah king in his stead.

Josiah's Reforms. 34:1 Josiah was eight years old when he became king, and he reigned thirty-one years in Jerusalem. [2]He did what was right in the LORD's sight, walking in the way of David his father, not turning right or left. [3]In the eighth year of his reign, while he was still a youth, he began to seek after the God of David his father. Then in his twelfth year he began to purify Judah and Jerusalem of the high places, the asherahs, and the carved and molten images. [4]In his presence, the altars of the Baals were torn down; the incense stands erected above them he broke down; the asherahs and the carved and molten images he smashed and beat into dust, which he scattered over the tombs of those who had sacrificed to them; [5]and the bones of the priests he burned upon their altars. Thus he purified Judah and Jerusalem. [6]He did likewise in the cities of Manasseh, Ephraim, Simeon, and in the ruined villages of the surrounding country as far as Naphtali; [7]he tore down the altars and asherahs, and the carved images he beat into dust, and broke down the incense stands

throughout the land of Israel. Then he returned to Jerusalem.

The Temple Restored. [8]In the eighteenth year of his reign, in order to purify the land and the temple, he sent Shaphan, son of Azaliah, Maaseiah, the ruler of the city, and Joah, son of Joahaz, the chancellor, to restore the house of the LORD, his God. [9]They came to Hilkiah the high priest and turned over the money brought to the house of God which the Levites, the guardians of the threshold, had collected from Manasseh, Ephraim, and all the remnant of Israel, as well as from all of Judah, Benjamin, and the inhabitants of Jerusalem. [10]They turned it over to the master workers in the house of the LORD, and these in turn used it to pay the workers in the LORD's house who were restoring and repairing it. [11]They also gave it to the carpenters and the masons to buy hewn stone and timber for the tie beams and rafters of the buildings which the kings of Judah had allowed to fall into ruin. [12]The men worked faithfully at their task; their overseers were Jahath and Obadiah, Levites of the line of Merari, and Zechariah and Meshullam, of the Kohathites, who directed them. All those Levites who were skillful with musical instruments [13]were in charge of the men who carried the burdens, and they directed all the workers in every kind of labor. Some of the other Levites were scribes, officials, and gatekeepers.

The Finding of the Law. [14]When they brought out the money that had been deposited in the house of the LORD, Hilkiah the priest found the book of the law of the LORD given through Moses. [15]He reported this to Shaphan the scribe, saying, "I have found the book of the law in the house of the LORD." Hilkiah gave the book to Shaphan, [16]who brought it to the king at the same time that he made his report to him. He said, "Your servants are doing everything that has been entrusted to them; [17]they have smelted down the silver deposited in the LORD's house and have turned it over to the overseers and the workers." [18]Then Shaphan the scribe also informed the king, "Hilkiah the priest has given me a book," and then Shaphan read it in the presence of the king.

[19]When the king heard the words of the law, he tore his garments. [20]The king then issued this command to Hilkiah, to Ahikam, son of Shaphan, to Abdon, son of Michah, to Shaphan the scribe, and to Asaiah, the king's servant: [21]"Go, consult the LORD for me and for those who are left in Israel and Judah, about the words of the book that has been found, for the anger of the LORD burns furiously against us, because our ancestors did not keep the word of the LORD and have not done all that is written in this book." [22]Then Hilkiah and others from the king went to Huldah the prophet, wife of Shallum, son of Tokhath, son of Hasrah, keeper of the wardrobe; she lived in Jerusalem, in the Second Quarter. They spoke to her as they had been instructed, [23]and she said to them: "Thus says the LORD, the God of Israel: Say to the man who sent you to me, [24]Thus says the LORD: I am about to bring evil upon this place and upon its inhabitants, all the curses written in the book that was read before the king of Judah. [25]Because they have abandoned me and have burned incense to other gods, provoking me by all the works of their hands, my anger burns against this place and it cannot be extinguished.

[26]"But to the king of Judah who sent you to consult the LORD, give this response: Thus says the LORD, the God of Israel: As for the words you have heard, [27]because you were heartsick and have humbled yourself before God when you heard his words concerning this place and its inhabitants; because you humbled yourself before me, tore your garments, and wept before me, I in turn have heard—oracle of the LORD. [28]I will gather you to your ancestors and you shall go to your grave in peace, and your eyes shall not see all the evil I am about to bring upon this place and upon its inhabitants."

This they reported to the king.

Covenant Renewal. [29]The king then had all the elders of Judah and of Jerusalem summoned before him. [30]The king went up to the house of the LORD with all the people of Judah and the inhabitants of Jerusalem: priests, Levites, and all the people, great and small. He read aloud to them all the words of the book of the covenant that had been found in the house of the LORD. [31]The king stood by the column and made a covenant in the presence of the LORD to follow the LORD and to observe his commandments, statutes, and decrees with his whole heart and soul, carrying out the words of the covenant written in this book. [32]He thereby committed all who were in Jerusalem and Benjamin, and the inhabitants of Jerusalem acted according to the covenant of God, the God of their ancestors. [33]Josiah removed every abomination from all the territories belonging to the Israelites, and he obliged all who were in Israel to serve the LORD, their God. During his lifetime they did not turn away from following the LORD, the God of their ancestors.

The Passover. 35:1 Josiah celebrated in Jerusalem a Passover to honor the LORD; the Passover sacrifice was slaughtered on the fourteenth day of the first month. [2]He reappointed the priests to their duties and confirmed them in the service of the LORD's house. [3]He said to the Levites who were to instruct all Israel, and who were consecrated to the LORD: "Put the holy ark in the house built by Solomon, son of David, king of Israel. It shall no longer be a burden on your shoulders. Serve now the LORD, your God, and his people Israel. [4]Prepare yourselves by your ancestral houses and your divisions according to the prescriptions of David, king of Israel, and the prescriptions of his son Solomon. [5]Stand in the sanctuary according to the branches of the ancestral houses of your kin, the common people, so that the distribution of the Levites and the families may be the same. [6]Slaughter the Passover sacrifice, sanctify yourselves, and be at the disposition of your kin, that all may be done according to the word of the LORD given through Moses."

[7]Josiah contributed to the common people a flock of lambs and young goats, thirty thousand in number, each to serve as a Passover victim for all who were present, and also three thousand oxen; these were from the king's property. [8]His princes also gave a voluntary offering to the people, the priests, and the Levites. Hilkiah, Zechariah, and Jehiel, prefects of the house of God, gave to the priests two thousand six hundred Passover victims along with three hundred oxen. [9]Conaniah and his brothers Shemaiah, Nethanel, Hashabiah, Jehiel, and Jozabad, the rulers of the Levites, contributed to the Levites five thousand Passover victims, together with five hundred oxen.

[10]When the service had been arranged, the priests took their places, as did the Levites in their divisions according to the king's command. [11]The Passover sacrifice was slaughtered, whereupon the priests splashed some of the blood and the Levites proceeded with the skinning. [12]They separated out what was destined for the burnt offering and gave it to various groups of the ancestral houses of the common people to offer to the LORD, as is written in the book of Moses. They did the same with the oxen. [13]They cooked the Passover on the fire as prescribed, and also cooked the sacred portions in pots, caldrons, and pans, then brought them quickly to all the common people. [14]Afterward they prepared the Passover for themselves and for the priests. Indeed the priests, the sons of Aaron, were busy sacrificing burnt offerings and the fatty portions until night; therefore the Levites prepared for themselves and for the priests, the sons of Aaron. [15]The singers, the sons of Asaph, were at their posts as commanded by David and by Asaph, Heman, and Jeduthun, the king's seer. The gatekeepers were at every gate; there was no need for them to leave their stations, for their fellow Levites prepared for them. [16]Thus the entire service of the LORD was arranged that day so that the Passover could be celebrated and the burnt offerings sacrificed on the altar of the LORD, as King Josiah had commanded. [17]The Israelites who were present on that occasion kept the Passover and the feast of the Unleavened Bread for seven days. [18]No such Passover had been observed in Israel since the time of Samuel the prophet; no king of Israel had observed a Passover like that celebrated by Josiah, the priests, and Levites, all of Judah and Israel that were present, and the inhabitants of Jerusalem. [19]It was in the eighteenth year of Josiah's reign that this Passover was observed.

Josiah's End. [20]After Josiah had done all this to restore the temple, Neco, king of Egypt, came up to fight at Carchemish on the Euphrates, and Josiah went out to meet him. [21]Neco sent messengers to him, saying: "What quarrel is between us, king of Judah? I have not come against you this day, for my war is with another kingdom, and God has told me to hasten. Do not interfere with God who is with me; let him not destroy you." [22]But Josiah would not withdraw from him, for he was seeking a pretext to fight with him. Therefore he would not listen to the words of Neco that came from the mouth of God, but went out to fight in the plain of Megiddo. [23]Then the archers shot King Josiah, who said to his servants, "Take me away, I am seriously wounded." [24]His servants took him from his own chariot, placed him in the one he had in reserve, and brought him to Jerusalem, where he died. He was buried in the tombs of his ancestors, and all Judah and Jerusalem mourned him. [25]Jeremiah also composed a lamentation for Josiah, which is recited to this day by all the male and female singers in their lamentations for Josiah. These have been made an ordinance for Israel, and can be found written in the Lamentations.

[26]The rest of the acts of Josiah, his good deeds in accord with what is written in the law of the LORD, [27]and his words, first and last, are recorded in the book of the kings of Israel and Judah.

Jehoahaz. 36:1 The people of the land took Jehoahaz, son of Josiah, and made him king in Jerusalem to succeed his father. [2]Jehoahaz was twenty-three years old when he became king, and he reigned three months in Jerusalem. [3]The king of Egypt deposed him in Jerusalem and fined the land one hundred talents of silver and a talent of gold. [4]Then the king of Egypt made Eliakim, the brother of Jehoahaz, king over Judah and Jerusalem, changing his name to Jehoiakim. Neco took Jehoahaz his brother away and brought him to Egypt.

Jehoiakim. [5]Jehoiakim was twenty-five years old when he became king, and he reigned eleven years in Jerusalem. He did what was evil in the sight of the LORD, his God. [6]Nebuchadnezzar, king of Babylon, attacked and bound him in chains to take him to Babylon. [7]Nebuchadnezzar also carried away to Babylon some of the vessels of the house of the LORD and put them in his palace in Babylon. [8]The rest of the acts of Jehoiakim, the abominable things that he did, and what therefore happened to him, are recorded in the book of the kings of Israel and Judah. His son Jehoiachin succeeded him as king.

Jehoiachin. [9]Jehoiachin was eighteen years old when he became king, and he reigned three months and ten days in Jerusalem. He did what was evil in the LORD's sight. [10]At the turn of the year, King Ne-buchadnezzar sent for him and had him brought to Babylon, along with precious vessels from the house of the LORD. He made his brother Zedekiah king over Judah and Jerusalem.

Zedekiah. [11]Zedekiah was twenty-one years old when he became king, and he reigned eleven years in Jerusalem. [12]He did what was evil in the sight of the LORD, his God, and he did not humble himself before Jeremiah the prophet, who spoke for the LORD. [13]He also rebelled against King Nebuchadnezzar, who had made him swear by God. He became stiff-necked and hardened his heart rather than return to the LORD, the God of Israel. [14]Likewise all the princes of Judah, the priests, and the people added treachery to treachery, practicing all the abominations of the nations and defiling the LORD's house which he had consecrated in Jerusalem.

The Fall of Judah. [15]Early and often the LORD, the God of their ancestors, sent his messengers to them, for he had compassion on his people and his dwelling place. [16]But they mocked God's messengers, despised his words, and scoffed at his prophets, until the LORD's anger against his people blazed up beyond remedy. [17]Then he brought up against them the king of the Chaldeans, who killed their young men with the sword in their own sanctuary, with compassion for neither young men nor young women, neither the old nor the infirm; all of them he delivered into his power. [18]All the utensils of the house of God, large and small, the treasures of the LORD's house, and the treasures of the king and his princes, all these he brought to Babylon. [19]They burnt the house of God, tore down the walls of Jerusalem, burnt down all its palaces, and destroyed all its precious objects. [20]Those who escaped the sword he carried captive to Babylon, where they became servants to him and his sons until the Persian kingdom came to power. [21]All this was to fulfill the word of the LORD spoken by Jeremiah: Until the land has retrieved its lost sabbaths, during all the time it lies waste it shall have rest while seventy years are fulfilled.

Decree of Cyrus. ²²In the first year of Cyrus, king of Persia, in order to realize the word of the LORD spoken by Jeremiah, the LORD roused the spirit of Cyrus, King of Persia, to spread this proclamation throughout his kingdom, both by word of mouth and in writing: ²³"Thus says Cyrus, king of Persia: The LORD, the God of heaven, has given to me all the kingdoms of the earth. He has also charged me to build him a house in Jerusalem, which is in Judah. All among you, therefore, who belong to his people, may their God be with them; let them go up."

☐ MATTHEW 16:13-20

Peter's Confession about Jesus. 16:13 When Jesus went into the region of Caesarea Philippi he asked his disciples, "Who do people say that the Son of Man is?" ¹⁴They replied, "Some say John the Baptist, others Elijah, still others Jeremiah or one of the prophets." ¹⁵He said to them, "But who do you say that I am?" ¹⁶Simon Peter said in reply, "You are the Messiah, the Son of the living God." ¹⁷Jesus said to him in reply, "Blessed are you, Simon son of Jonah. For flesh and blood has not revealed this to you, but my heavenly Father. ¹⁸And so I say to you, you are Peter, and upon this rock I will build my church, and the gates of the netherworld shall not prevail against it. ¹⁹I will give you the keys to the kingdom of heaven. Whatever you bind on earth shall be bound in heaven; and whatever you loose on earth shall be loosed in heaven." ²⁰Then he strictly ordered his disciples to tell no one that he was the Messiah.

May 18

Pope St. John I

Be proud that you are helping God to bear the cross, and don't grasp at comforts. It is only mercenaries who expect to be paid by the day. Serve Him without pay.

— ST. TERESA OF ÁVILA

☐ EZRA 1-3

The Decree of Cyrus. 1:1 In the first year of Cyrus, king of Persia, in order to fulfill the word of the LORD spoken by Jeremiah, the LORD stirred up the spirit of Cyrus king of Persia to issue a proclamation throughout his entire kingdom, both by word of mouth and in writing: ²"Thus says Cyrus, king of Persia: 'All the kingdoms of the earth the LORD, the God of heaven, has given to me, and he has charged me to build him a house in Jerusalem, which is in Judah. ³Those among you who belong to any part of his people, may their God be with them! Let them go up to Jerusalem in Judah to build the house of the LORD the God of Israel, that is, the God who is in Jerusalem. ⁴Let all those who have survived, in whatever place they may have lived, be assisted by the people of that place with silver, gold, goods, and livestock, together with voluntary offerings for the house of God in Jerusalem.'"

[5]Then the heads of ancestral houses of Judah and Benjamin and the priests and Levites—everyone, that is, whose spirit had been stirred up by God—prepared to go up to build the house of the LORD in Jerusalem. [6]All their neighbors gave them help in every way, with silver, gold, goods, livestock, and many precious gifts, besides all their voluntary offerings. [7]King Cyrus, too, had the vessels of the house of the LORD brought forth that Nebuchadnezzar had taken from Jerusalem and placed in the house of his god. [8]Cyrus, king of Persia, had them brought forth by the treasurer Mithredath, who counted them out to Sheshbazzar, prince of Judah. [9]This was the inventory: baskets of goldware, thirty; baskets of silverware, one thousand and twenty-nine; [10]golden bowls, thirty; silver bowls, four hundred and ten; other vessels, one thousand. [11]Total of the gold and silver vessels: five thousand four hundred. All these Sheshbazzar took with him when the exiles were brought up from Babylon to Jerusalem.

A Census of the Returned Exiles. 2:1 These are the inhabitants of the province who returned from the captivity of the exiles, whom Nebuchadnezzar, king of Babylon, had carried away to Babylon, and who came back to Jerusalem and Judah, to their various cities [2](those who returned with Zerubbabel, Jeshua, Nehemiah, Seraiah, Reelaiah, Mordecai, Bilshan, Mispar, Bigvai, Rehum, and Baanah):

The census of the people of Israel: [3]descendants of Parosh, two thousand one hundred and seventy-two; [4]descendants of Shephatiah, three hundred and seventy-two; [5]descendants of Arah, seven hundred and seventy-five; [6]descendants of Pahathmoab, who were descendants of Jeshua and Joab, two thousand eight hundred and twelve; [7]descendants of Elam, one thousand two hundred and fifty-four; [8]descendants of Zattu, nine hundred and forty-five; [9]descendants of Zaccai, seven hundred and sixty; [10]descendants of Bani, six hundred and forty-two; [11]descendants of Bebai, six hundred and twenty-three; [12]descendants of Azgad, one thousand two hundred and twenty-two; [13]descendants of Adonikam, six hundred and sixty-six; [14]descendants of Bigvai, two thousand and fifty-six; [15]descendants of Adin, four hundred and fifty-four; [16]descendants of Ater, who were descendants of Hezekiah, ninety-eight; [17]descendants of Bezai, three hundred and twenty-three; [18]descendants of Jorah, one hundred and twelve; [19]descendants of Hashum, two hundred and twenty-three; [20]descendants of Gibeon, ninety-five; [21]descendants of Bethlehem, one hundred and twenty-three; [22]people of Netophah, fifty-six; [23]people of Anathoth, one hundred and twenty-eight; [24]people of Beth-azmaveth, forty-two; [25]people of Kiriath-jearim, Chephirah, and Beeroth, seven hundred and forty-three; [26]people of Ramah and Geba, six hundred and twenty-one; [27]people of Michmas, one hundred and twenty-two; [28]people of Bethel and Ai, two hundred and twenty-three; [29]descendants of Nebo, fifty-two; [30]descendants of Magbish, one hundred and fifty-six; [31]descendants of the other Elam, one thousand two hundred and fifty-four; [32]descendants of Harim, three hundred and twenty; [33]descendants of Lod, Hadid, and Ono, seven hundred and twenty-five; [34]descendants of Jericho, three hundred and forty-five; [35]descendants of Senaah, three thousand six hundred and thirty.

[36]The priests: descendants of Jedaiah, of the house of Jeshua, nine hundred and seventy-three; [37]descendants of Immer, one thousand and fifty-two; [38]descendants of Pashhur, one thousand two hundred and forty-seven; [39]descendants of Harim, one thousand and seventeen.

[40]The Levites: descendants of Jeshua and Kadmiel, of the descendants of Hodaviah, seventy-four.

[41]The singers: descendants of Asaph, one hundred and twenty-eight.

[42]The gatekeepers: descendants of Shallum, descendants of Ater, descendants of Talmon, descendants of Akkub, descendants of Hatita, descendants of Shobai, one hundred and thirty-nine in all.

[43]The temple servants: descendants of Ziha, descendants of Hasupha, descendants of Tabbaoth, [44]descendants of Keros, descendants of Siaha, descendants of Padon, [45]descendants of Lebanah, descendants of Hagabah, descendants of Akkub, [46]descendants of Hagab, descendants of Shamlai, descendants of Hanan, [47]descendants of Giddel, descendants of Gahar, descendants of Reaiah, [48]descendants of Rezin, descendants of Nekoda, descendants of Gazzam, [49]descendants of Uzza, descendants of Paseah, descendants of Besai, [50]descendants of Asnah, descendants of the Meunites, descendants of the Nephusites, [51]descendants of Bakbuk, descendants of Hakupha, descendants of Harhur, [52]descendants of Bazluth, descendants of Mehida, descendants of Harsha, [53]descendants of Barkos, descendants of Sisera, descendants of Temah, [54]descendants of Neziah, descendants of Hatipha.

[55]Descendants of Solomon's servants: descendants of Sotai, descendants of Hassophereth, descendants of Peruda, [56]descendants of Jaalah, descendants of Darkon, descendants of Giddel, [57]descendants of Shephatiah, descendants of Hattil, descendants of Pochereth-hazzebaim, descendants of Ami. [58]The total of the temple servants together with the descendants of Solomon's servants was three hundred and ninety-two.

[59]The following who returned from Telmelah, Tel-harsha, Cherub, Addan, and Immer were unable to prove that their ancestral houses and their descent were Israelite: [60]descendants of Delaiah, descendants of Tobiah, descendants of Nekoda, six hundred and fifty-two. [61]Also, of the priests: descendants of Habaiah, descendants of Hakkoz, descendants of Barzillai (he had married one of the daughters of Barzillai the Gileadite and was named after him). [62]These searched their family records, but their names could not be found there, and they were excluded from the priesthood. [63]The governor ordered them not to partake of the most holy foods until there should be a priest to consult the Urim and Thummim.

[64]The entire assembly taken together came to forty-two thousand three hundred and sixty, [65]not counting their male and female servants, who numbered seven thousand three hundred and thirty-seven. They also had two hundred male and female singers. [66]Their horses numbered seven hundred and thirty-six, their mules two hundred and forty-five, [67]their camels four hundred and thirty-five, their donkeys six thousand seven hundred and twenty.

[68]When they arrived at the house of the LORD in Jerusalem, some of the heads of ancestral houses made voluntary offerings for the house of God, to rebuild it in its place. [69]According to their means they contributed to the treasury for the temple service: sixty-one thousand drachmas of gold, five thousand minas of silver, and one hundred priestly robes. [70]The priests, the Levites, and some of the people took up residence in Jerusalem; the singers, the gatekeepers, and the temple servants settled in their cities. Thus all the Israelites settled in their cities.

Restoration of Worship. 3:1 Now when the seventh month came, after the Israelites had settled in their cities, the people gathered as one in Jerusalem. [2]Then Jeshua, son of Jozadak, together with his kinsmen the priests, and Zerubbabel, son of Shealtiel, together with his kinsmen, began building the altar of the God of Israel in order to offer on it the burnt offerings prescribed in the law of Moses, the man of God. [3]They set the altar on its foundations, for they lived in fear of the peoples of the lands, and offered burnt offerings to the LORD on it, both morning and evening. ⁴They also kept the feast of Booths in the manner prescribed, and they offered the daily burnt offerings in the proper number required for each day. ⁵Thereafter they offered regular burnt offerings, the sacrifices prescribed for the new moons and all the festivals sacred to the LORD, and those which anyone might bring as a voluntary offering to the LORD.

Laying the Foundations of the Temple. ⁶From the first day of the seventh month they reinstituted the burnt offering to the LORD, though the foundation of the LORD's temple had not yet been laid. ⁷Then they hired stonecutters and carpenters, and sent food and drink and oil to the Sidonians and Tyrians that they might ship cedar trees from the Lebanon to the port of Joppa, as Cyrus, king of Persia, had authorized. ⁸In the year after their coming to the house of God in Jerusalem, in the second month, Zerubbabel, son of Shealtiel, and Jeshua, son of Jozadak, together with the rest of their kinsmen, the priests and Levites and all who had come from the captivity to Jerusalem, began by appointing the Levites twenty years of age and over

to supervise the work on the house of the LORD. ⁹Jeshua and his sons and kinsmen, with Kadmiel and Binnui, son of Hodaviah, and their sons and their kindred, the Levites, together undertook to supervise those who were engaged in the work on the house of God. ¹⁰While the builders were laying the foundation of the LORD's temple, the priests in their vestments were stationed with trumpets and the Levites, sons of Asaph, with cymbals to praise the LORD in the manner laid down by David, king of Israel. ¹¹They alternated in songs of praise and thanksgiving to the LORD, "for he is good, for his love for Israel endures forever"; and all the people raised a great shout of joy, praising the LORD because the foundation of the LORD's house had been laid. ¹²Many of the priests, Levites, and heads of ancestral houses, who were old enough to have seen the former house, cried out in sorrow as they watched the foundation of the present house being laid. Many others, however, lifted up their voices in shouts of joy. ¹³No one could distinguish the sound of the joyful shouting from the sound of those who were weeping; for the people raised a mighty clamor which was heard far away.

☐ MATTHEW 16:21-28

The First Prediction of the Passion. **16:21** From that time on, Jesus began to show his disciples that he must go to Jerusalem and suffer greatly from the elders, the chief priests, and the scribes, and be killed and on the third day be raised. ²²Then Peter took him aside and began to rebuke him, "God forbid, Lord! No such thing shall ever happen to you." ²³He turned and said to Peter, "Get behind me, Satan! You are an obstacle to me. You are thinking not as God does, but as human beings do."

The Conditions of Discipleship. ²⁴Then Jesus said to his disciples, "Whoever

wishes to come after me must deny himself, take up his cross, and follow me. ²⁵For whoever wishes to save his life will lose it, but whoever loses his life for my sake will find it. ²⁶What profit would there be for one to gain the whole world and forfeit his life? Or what can one give in exchange for his life? ²⁷For the Son of Man will come with his angels in his Father's glory, and then he will repay everyone according to his conduct. ²⁸Amen, I say to you, there are some standing here who will not taste death until they see the Son of Man coming in his kingdom."

May 19

Whoever doesn't seek the cross of Christ doesn't seek the glory of Christ.

— St. John of the Cross

☐ EZRA 4-6

Outside Interference. 4:1 When the enemies of Judah and Benjamin heard that the exiles were building a temple for the LORD, the God of Israel, [2]they approached Zerubbabel and the heads of ancestral houses and said to them, "Let us build with you, for we seek your God just as you do, and we have sacrificed to him since the days of Esarhaddon, king of Assyria, who brought us here." [3]But Zerubbabel, Jeshua, and the rest of the heads of ancestral houses of Israel answered them, "It is not your responsibility to build with us a house for our God, but we alone must build it for the LORD, the God of Israel, as Cyrus king of Persia has commanded us." [4]Thereupon the local inhabitants discouraged the people of Judah and frightened them off from building. [5]They also bribed counselors to work against them and to frustrate their plans during all the years of Cyrus, king of Persia, and even into the reign of Darius, king of Persia.

Later Hostility. [6]In the reign of Ahasuerus, at the beginning of his reign, they prepared a written accusation against the inhabitants of Judah and Jerusalem.

[7]Again, in the time of Artaxerxes, Tabeel and the rest of his fellow officials, in concert with Mithredath, wrote to Artaxerxes, king of Persia. The document was written in Aramaic and was accompanied by a translation.

[8]Then Rehum, the governor, and Shimshai, the scribe, wrote the following letter against Jerusalem to King Artaxerxes: [9]"Rehum, the governor, Shimshai, the scribe, and their fellow officials, judges, legates, and agents from among the Persians, Urukians, Babylonians, Susians (that is, Elamites), [10]and the other peoples whom the great and illustrious Osnappar transported and settled in the city of Samaria and elsewhere in the province West-of-Euphrates, as follows...." [11]This is a copy of the letter that they sent to him:

"To King Artaxerxes, your servants, the men of West-of-Euphrates, as follows: [12]Let it be known to the king that the Jews who came up from you to us have arrived at Jerusalem and are now rebuilding this rebellious and evil city. They are completing its walls, and the foundations have already been laid. [13]Now let it be known to the king that if this city is rebuilt and its walls completed, they will no longer pay taxes, tributes, or tolls; eventually the throne will be harmed. [14]Now, since we eat the salt of the palace and it is not fitting for us to look on while the king is being dishonored, we have sent this message to inform the king, [15]so that inquiry may be made in the historical records of your fathers. In the historical records you will discover and verify that this is a rebellious city, harmful to kings and provinces; its people have been acting seditiously there since ancient times. That is why this city was destroyed. [16]We therefore inform the king, that if this city is rebuilt and its walls completed again, you will thereupon not have a portion in the province West-of-Euphrates."

[17]The king sent this answer: "To Rehum, the governor, Shimshai, the scribe, and their fellow officials living in Samaria and elsewhere in the province West-of-Euphrates, greetings: [18]The communication which you sent us has been read in translation in

my presence. [19]When at my command inquiry was made, it was verified that from ancient times this city has risen up against kings and that rebellion and sedition have been fostered there. [20]Powerful kings once ruled in Jerusalem who controlled all West-of-Euphrates, and taxes, tributes, and tolls were paid to them. [21]Give orders, therefore, to stop these men. This city may not be rebuilt until a further decree has been issued by me. [22]Take care that you do not neglect this matter. Why should evil increase to harm the throne?"

[23]As soon as a copy of King Artaxerxes' letter had been read before Rehum, the governor, Shimshai, the scribe, and their fellow officials, they immediately went to the Jews in Jerusalem and stopped their work by force of arms. [24]As a result, work on the house of God in Jerusalem ceased. This interruption lasted until the second year of the reign of Darius, king of Persia.

The Work Resumed Under Darius; Further Problems. 5:1 Then the prophets Haggai and Zechariah, son of Iddo, began to prophesy to the Jews in Judah and Jerusalem in the name of the God of Israel. [2]Thereupon Zerubbabel, son of Shealtiel, and Jeshua, son of Jozadak, began again to build the house of God in Jerusalem, with the prophets of God giving them support. [3]At that time Tattenai, governor of West-of-Euphrates, came to them, along with Shethar-bozenai, and their fellow officials, and asked of them: "Who issued the decree for you to build this house and complete this edifice? [4]What are the names of the men who are building this structure?" [5]But the eye of their God was upon the elders of the Jews, and they were not delayed during the time a report went to Darius and a written order came back concerning this matter.

[6]A copy of the letter which Tattenai, governor of West-of-Euphrates, along with Shethar-bozenai and their fellow officials from West-of-Euphrates, sent to King Darius; [7]they sent him a report in which was written the following:

"To King Darius, all good wishes! [8]Let it be known to the king that we have visited the province of Judah and the house of the great God: it is being rebuilt of cut stone and the walls are being reinforced with timber; the work is being carried out diligently, prospering under their hands. [9]We then questioned the elders, addressing to them the following words: 'Who issued the decree for you to build this house and complete this edifice?' [10]We also asked them their names, in order to give you a list of the men who are their leaders. [11]This was their answer to us: 'We are the servants of the God of heaven and earth, and we are rebuilding the house built here many years ago, which a great king of Israel built and completed. [12]But because our ancestors provoked the wrath of the God of heaven, he delivered them into the power of the Chaldean, Nebuchadnezzar, king of Babylon, who destroyed this house and exiled the people to Babylon. [13]However, in the first year of Cyrus, king of Babylon, King Cyrus issued a decree for the rebuilding of this house of God. [14]Moreover, the gold and silver vessels of the house of God, which Nebuchadnezzar had taken from the temple in Jerusalem and carried off to the temple in Babylon, King Cyrus ordered to be removed from the temple in Babylon, and they were given to a certain Sheshbazzar, whom he named governor. [15]He commanded him: Take these vessels and deposit them in the temple of Jerusalem, and let the house of God be rebuilt on its former site. [16]Then this same Sheshbazzar came and laid the foundations of the house of God in Jerusalem. Since that time to the present the building has been going on, and is not yet completed.' [17]Now, if it please the king, let a search be made in the royal archives of Babylon to discover whether a decree really was issued by King Cyrus for the rebuilding of this house of God in Jerusalem. And may the king's decision in this matter be communicated to us."

The Decree of Darius. 6:1 Thereupon King Darius issued an order to search the archives in which the treasures were stored in Babylon. [2]However, a scroll was found in Ecbatana, the stronghold in the province of Media, containing the following text: "Memorandum. [3]In the first year of his reign, King Cyrus issued a decree: With regard to the house of God in Jerusalem: the house is to be rebuilt as a place for offering sacrifices and bringing burnt offerings. Its height is to be sixty cubits and its width sixty cubits. [4]It shall have three courses of cut stone for each one of timber. The costs are to be borne by the royal house. [5]Also, let the gold and silver vessels of the house of God which Nebuchadnezzar took from the temple of Jerusalem and brought to Babylon be sent back; let them be returned to their place in the temple of Jerusalem and deposited in the house of God."

[6]"Now, therefore, Tattenai, governor of West-of-Euphrates, and Shethar-bozenai, and you, their fellow officials in West-of-Euphrates, stay away from there. [7]Let the governor and the elders of the Jews continue the work on that house of God; they are to rebuild it on its former site. [8]I also issue this decree concerning your dealing with these elders of the Jews in the rebuilding of that house of God: Let these men be repaid for their expenses, in full and without delay from the royal revenue, deriving from the taxes of West-of-Euphrates, so that the work not be interrupted. [9]Whatever else is required—young bulls, rams, and lambs for burnt offerings to the God of heaven, wheat, salt, wine, and oil, according to the requirements of the priests who are in Jerusalem—let that be delivered to them day by day without fail, [10]that they may continue to offer sacrifices of pleasing odor to the God of heaven and pray for the life of the king and his sons. [11]I also issue this decree: if any man alters this edict, a beam is to be taken from his house, and he is to be lifted up and impaled on it; and his house is to be reduced to rubble for this offense. [12]And may the God who causes his name to dwell there overthrow every king or people who may undertake to alter this decree or to destroy this house of God in Jerusalem. I, Darius, have issued this decree; let it be diligently executed."

The Task Finally Completed. [13]Then Tattenai, the governor of West-of-Euphrates, and Shethar-bozenai, and their fellow officials carried out with all diligence the instructions King Darius had sent them. [14]The elders of the Jews continued to make progress in the building, supported by the message of the prophets, Haggai and Zechariah, son of Iddo. They finished the building according to the command of the God of Israel and the decrees of Cyrus and Darius, and of Artaxerxes, king of Persia. [15]They completed this house on the third day of the month Adar, in the sixth year of the reign of King Darius. [16]The Israelites—priests, Levites, and the other returned exiles—celebrated the dedication of this house of God with joy. [17]For the dedication of this house of God, they offered one hundred bulls, two hundred rams, and four hundred lambs, together with twelve he-goats as a sin offering for all Israel, in keeping with the number of the tribes of Israel. [18]Finally, they set up the priests in their classes and the Levites in their divisions for the service of God in Jerusalem, as is prescribed in the book of Moses.

The Passover. [19]The returned exiles kept the Passover on the fourteenth day of the first month. [20]The Levites, every one of whom had purified himself for the occasion, sacrificed the Passover for all the exiles, for their colleagues the priests, and for themselves. [21]The Israelites who had returned from the exile and all those who had separated themselves from the uncleanness of the Gentiles in the land shared in it, seeking the LORD, the God of Israel. ²²They joyfully kept the feast of Unleavened Bread for seven days, for the LORD had filled them with joy by making the king of Assyria favorable to them, so that he gave them help in their work on the house of God, the God of Israel.

☐ MATTHEW 17:1-13

The Transfiguration of Jesus. 17:1 After six days Jesus took Peter, James, and John his brother, and led them up a high mountain by themselves. ²And he was transfigured before them; his face shone like the sun and his clothes became white as light. ³And behold, Moses and Elijah appeared to them, conversing with him. ⁴Then Peter said to Jesus in reply, "Lord, it is good that we are here. If you wish, I will make three tents here, one for you, one for Moses, and one for Elijah." ⁵While he was still speaking, behold, a bright cloud cast a shadow over them, then from the cloud came a voice that said, "This is my beloved Son, with whom I am well pleased; listen to him." ⁶When the disciples heard this, they fell prostrate and were very much afraid.

⁷But Jesus came and touched them, saying, "Rise, and do not be afraid." ⁸And when the disciples raised their eyes, they saw no one else but Jesus alone.

The Coming of Elijah. ⁹As they were coming down from the mountain, Jesus charged them, "Do not tell the vision to anyone until the Son of Man has been raised from the dead." ¹⁰Then the disciples asked him, "Why do the scribes say that Elijah must come first?" ¹¹He said in reply, "Elijah will indeed come and restore all things; ¹²but I tell you that Elijah has already come, and they did not recognize him but did to him whatever they pleased. So also will the Son of Man suffer at their hands." ¹³Then the disciples understood that he was speaking to them of John the Baptist.

May 20

St. Bernardine of Siena

Faith means battles. If there are no contests, it is because there are none who desire to contend.

— ST. AMBROSE OF MILAN

☐ EZRA 7-10

Ezra, Priest and Scribe. 7:1 After these events, during the reign of Artaxerxes, king of Persia, Ezra, son of Seraiah, son of Azariah, son of Hilkiah, ²son of Shallum, son of Zadok, son of Ahitub, ³son of Amariah, son of Azariah, son of Meraioth, ⁴son of Zerahiah, son of Uzzi, son of Bukki, ⁵son of Abishua, son of Phinehas, son of Eleazar, son of Aaron, the high priest— ⁶this Ezra came up from Babylon. He was a scribe, well-versed in the law of Moses given by the LORD, the God of Israel. The king granted him all that he requested, because the hand of the LORD, his God, was over him.

⁷Some of the Israelites and some priests, Levites, singers, gatekeepers, and temple servants also came up to Jerusalem in the

seventh year of King Artaxerxes. [8]Ezra came to Jerusalem in the fifth month of that seventh year of the king. [9]On the first day of the first month he began the journey up from Babylon, and on the first day of the fifth month he arrived at Jerusalem, for the favoring hand of his God was over him. [10]Ezra had set his heart on the study and practice of the law of the LORD and on teaching statutes and ordinances in Israel.

The Decree of Artaxerxes. [11]This is a copy of the rescript which King Artaxerxes gave to Ezra the priest-scribe, the scribe versed in matters concerning the LORD's commandments and statutes for Israel:

[12]"Artaxerxes, king of kings, to Ezra the priest, scribe of the law of the God of heaven, greetings! And now, [13]I have issued this decree, that anyone in my kingdom belonging to the people of Israel, its priests or Levites, who is willing to go up to Jerusalem with you, may go, [14]for you are the one sent by the king and his seven counselors to supervise Judah and Jerusalem with regard to the law of your God which is in your possession, [15]and to bring the silver and gold which the king and his counselors have freely contributed to the God of Israel, whose dwelling is in Jerusalem, [16]as well as all the silver and gold which you may receive throughout the province of Babylon, together with the voluntary offerings the people and priests freely contribute for the house of their God in Jerusalem. [17]Therefore, you must use this money with all diligence to buy bulls, rams, lambs, and the grain offerings and libations proper to these, and offer them on the altar of the house of your God in Jerusalem. [18]You and your kinsmen may do whatever seems best to you with the remainder of the silver and gold, as your God wills. [19]The vessels given to you for the service of the house of your God you are to deposit before the God of Jerusalem. [20]Whatever else you may be required to supply for the needs of the house of your God, you may draw from the royal treasury. [21]I, Artaxerxes the king, issue this decree to all the treasurers of West-of-Euphrates: Whatever Ezra the priest, scribe of the law of the God of heaven, requests of you, let it be done with all diligence, [22]within these limits: silver, one hundred talents; wheat, one hundred kors; wine, one hundred baths; oil, one hundred baths; salt, without limit. [23]Let everything that is decreed by the God of heaven be carried out exactly for the house of the God of heaven, that wrath may not come upon the realm of the king and his sons. [24]We also inform you that it is not permitted to impose taxes, tributes, or tolls on any priest, Levite, singer, gatekeeper, temple servant, or any other servant of that house of God.

[25]"As for you, Ezra, in accordance with the wisdom of your God which is in your possession, appoint magistrates and judges to administer justice to all the people in West-of-Euphrates, to all, that is, who know the laws of your God. Instruct those who do not know these laws. [26]All who will not obey the law of your God and the law of the king, let judgment be executed upon them with all diligence, whether death, or corporal punishment, or confiscation of goods, or imprisonment."

Ezra Prepares for the Journey. [27]Blessed be the LORD, the God of our ancestors, who put it into the heart of the king thus to glorify the house of the LORD in Jerusalem, [28]and who let me find favor with the king, with his counselors, and with all the most influential royal officials. I therefore took courage and, with the hand of the LORD, my God, over me, I gathered together Israelite leaders to make the return journey with me.

Ezra's Caravan. 8:1 These are the heads of the ancestral houses and the genealogies of those who returned with me from Babylon during the reign of King Artaxerxes:

[2]Of the descendants of Phinehas, Gershon; of the descendants of Ithamar, Dan-

iel; of the descendants of David, Hattush, [3]son of Shecaniah; of the descendants of Parosh, Zechariah, and with him one hundred and fifty males were enrolled; [4]of the descendants of Pahath-moab, Eliehoenai, son of Zerahiah, and with him two hundred males; [5]of the descendants of Zattu, Shecaniah, son of Jahaziel, and with him three hundred males; [6]of the descendants of Adin, Ebed, son of Jonathan, and with him fifty males; [7]of the descendants of Elam, Jeshaiah, son of Athaliah, and with him seventy males; [8]of the descendants of Shephatiah, Zebadiah, son of Michael, and with him eighty males; [9]of the descendants of Joab, Obadiah, son of Jehiel, and with him two hundred and eighteen males; [10]of the descendants of Bani, Shelomoth, son of Josiphiah, and with him one hundred and sixty males; [11]of the descendants of Bebai, Zechariah, son of Bebai, and with him twenty-eight males; [12]of the descendants of Azgad, Johanan, son of Hakkatan, and with him one hundred and ten males; [13]of the descendants of Adonikam, younger sons, whose names were Eliphelet, Jeiel, and Shemaiah, and with them sixty males; [14]of the descendants of Bigvai, Uthai, son of Zakkur, and with him seventy males.

Final Preparations for the Journey. [15]I assembled them by the river that flows toward Ahava, where we camped for three days. There I perceived that both laymen and priests were present, but I could not discover a single Levite. [16]So I sent for discerning leaders, Eliezer, Ariel, Shemaiah, Jarib, Elnathan, Nathan, Zechariah, and Meshullam, [17]with a command for Iddo, the leader in the place Casiphia, instructing them what to say to Iddo and his kinsmen, and to the temple servants in Casiphia, in order to procure for us ministers for the house of our God. [18]Since the favoring hand of our God was over us, they sent to us a well-instructed man, one of the descendants of Mahli, son of Levi, son of Israel, namely Sherebiah, with his sons

and kinsmen, eighteen men. [19]They also sent us Hashabiah, and with him Jeshaiah, descendants of Merari, and their kinsmen and their sons, twenty men. [20]Of the temple servants, those whom David and the princes appointed to serve the Levites, there were two hundred and twenty. All these were enrolled by name.

[21]Then I proclaimed a fast, there by the river of Ahava, that we might humble ourselves before our God to seek from him a safe journey for ourselves, our children, and all our possessions. [22]For I was ashamed to ask the king for troops and horsemen to protect us against enemies along the way, since we had said to the king, "The favoring hand of our God is over all who seek him, but his fierce anger is against all who forsake him." [23]So we fasted, seeking this from our God, and it was granted. [24]Next I selected twelve of the priestly leaders along with Sherebiah, Hashabiah, and ten of their kinsmen, [25]and I weighed out before them the silver and the gold and the vessels offered for the house of our God by the king, his counselors, his officials, and all the Israelites of that region. [26]I weighed out into their hands these amounts: silver, six hundred and fifty talents; silver vessels, one hundred; gold, one hundred talents; [27]twenty golden bowls valued at a thousand darics; two vases of excellent polished bronze, as precious as gold. [28]I addressed them in these words: "You are consecrated to the LORD, and the vessels are also consecrated; the silver and the gold are a voluntary offering to the LORD, the God of your ancestors. [29]Watch over them carefully until you weigh them out in Jerusalem in the presence of the chief priests and Levites and the leaders of ancestral houses of Israel, in the chambers of the house of the LORD." [30]The priests and the Levites then took over the silver, the gold, and the vessels that had been weighed out, to bring them to Jerusalem, to the house of our God.

Arrival in Jerusalem. [31]We set out from the river of Ahava on the twelfth day of the first month to go to Jerusalem. The hand of our God remained over us, and he protected us from enemies and robbers along the way. ³²We arrived in Jerusalem, where we rested for three days. ³³On the fourth day, the silver, the gold, and the vessels were weighed out in the house of our God and given to the priest Meremoth, son of Uriah, with whom was Eleazar, son of Phinehas; they were assisted by the Levites Jozabad, son of Jeshua, and Noadiah, son of Binnui. ³⁴Everything was in order as to number and weight, and the total weight was registered. At that same time, ³⁵those who had returned from the captivity, the exiles, offered as burnt offerings to the God of Israel twelve bulls for all Israel, ninety-six rams, seventy-seven lambs, and twelve goats as sin offerings: all these as a burnt offering to the LORD. ³⁶Finally, the orders of the king were presented to the king's satraps and to the governors in West-of-Euphrates, who gave their support to the people and to the house of God.

The Crisis of Mixed Marriages. 9:1 When these matters had been concluded, the leaders approached me with this report: "Neither the Israelite laymen nor the priests nor the Levites have kept themselves separate from the peoples of the lands and their abominations—Canaanites, Hittites, Perizzites, Jebusites, Ammonites, Moabites, Egyptians, and Amorites— ²for they have taken some of their daughters as wives for themselves and their sons, thus intermingling the holy seed with the peoples of the lands. Furthermore, the leaders and rulers have taken a prominent part in this apostasy!"

Ezra's Reaction. ³When I had heard this, I tore my cloak and my mantle, plucked hair from my head and beard, and sat there devastated. ⁴Around me gathered all who were in dread of the sentence of the God of Israel on the apostasy of the exiles, while I remained devastated until the evening sacrifice. ⁵Then, at the time of the evening sacrifice, I rose in my wretchedness, and with cloak and mantle torn I fell on my knees, stretching out my hands to the LORD, my God.

A Penitential Prayer. ⁶I said: "My God, I am too ashamed and humiliated to raise my face to you, my God, for our wicked deeds are heaped up above our heads and our guilt reaches up to heaven. ⁷From the time of our ancestors even to this day our guilt has been great, and for our wicked deeds we have been delivered, we and our kings and our priests, into the hands of the kings of foreign lands, to the sword, to captivity, to pillage, and to disgrace, as is the case today.

⁸"And now, only a short time ago, mercy came to us from the LORD, our God, who left us a remnant and gave us a stake in his holy place; thus our God has brightened our eyes and given us relief in our slavery. ⁹For slaves we are, but in our slavery our God has not abandoned us; rather, he has turned the good will of the kings of Persia toward us. Thus he has given us new life to raise again the house of our God and restore its ruins, and has granted us a protective wall in Judah and Jerusalem. ¹⁰But now, our God, what can we say after all this? For we have abandoned your commandments, ¹¹which you gave through your servants the prophets: The land which you are entering to take as your possession is a land unclean with the filth of the peoples of the lands, with the abominations with which they have filled it from one end to the other by their uncleanness. ¹²Do not, then, give your daughters to their sons in marriage, and do not take their daughters for your sons. Never promote their welfare and prosperity; thus you will grow strong, enjoy the produce of the land, and leave it as an inheritance to your children forever.

¹³"After all that has come upon us for our evil deeds and our great guilt—though you, our God, have made less of our sinful-

ness than it deserved and have allowed us to survive as we do— [14]shall we again violate your commandments by intermarrying with these abominable peoples? Would you not become so angered with us as to destroy us without remnant or survivor? [15]Lord, God of Israel, you are just; yet we have been spared, the remnant we are today. Here we are before you in our sins. Because of all this, we can no longer stand in your presence."

Response to the Crisis. 10:1 While Ezra prayed and acknowledged their guilt, weeping and prostrate before the house of God, a very large assembly of Israelites gathered about him, men, women, and children; and the people wept profusely. [2]Then Shecaniah, the son of Jehiel, one of the descendants of Elam, made this appeal to Ezra: "We have indeed betrayed our God by taking as wives foreign women of the peoples of the land. Yet in spite of this there still remains a hope for Israel. [3]Let us therefore enter into a covenant before our God to dismiss all our foreign wives and the children born of them, in keeping with what you, my lord, advise, and those who are in dread of the commandments of our God. Let it be done according to the law! [4]Rise, then, for this is your duty! We are with you, so have courage and act!"

[5]Ezra stood and demanded an oath from the leaders of the priests, from the Levites and from all Israel that they would do as had been proposed; and they swore it. [6]Then Ezra left his place before the house of God and entered the chamber of Johanan, son of Eliashib, where he spent the night neither eating food nor drinking water, for he was in mourning over the apostasy of the exiles. [7]A proclamation was made throughout Judah and Jerusalem that all the exiles should gather together in Jerusalem, [8]and that whoever failed to appear within three days would, according to the judgment of the leaders and elders, suffer the confiscation of all his possessions, and would be excluded from the assembly of the exiles.

[9]All the men of Judah and Benjamin gathered together in Jerusalem within the three-day period: it was in the ninth month, on the twentieth day of the month. All the people, sitting in the open place before the house of God, were trembling both over the matter at hand and because it was raining. [10]Then Ezra, the priest, stood up and said to them: "Your apostasy in taking foreign women as wives has added to Israel's guilt. [11]But now, give praise to the Lord, the God of your ancestors, and do his will: separate yourselves from the peoples of the land and from the foreign women." [12]In answer, the whole assembly cried out with a loud voice: "Yes, it is our duty to do as you say! [13]But the people are numerous and it is the rainy season, so that we cannot remain outside; besides, this is not a task that can be performed in a single day or even two, for those of us who have sinned in this regard are many. [14]Let our leaders represent the whole assembly; then let all those in our cities who have taken foreign women for wives appear at appointed times, accompanied by the elders and magistrates of each city in question, till we have turned away from us our God's burning anger over this affair." [15]Only Jonathan, son of Asahel, and Jahzeiah, son of Tikvah, were against this proposal, with Meshullam and Shabbethai the Levite supporting them.

[16]The exiles did as agreed. Ezra the priest appointed as his assistants men who were heads of ancestral houses, one for each ancestral house, all of them designated by name. They held sessions to examine the matter, beginning with the first day of the tenth month. [17]By the first day of the first month they had finished dealing with all the men who had taken foreign women for wives.

The List of Transgressors. [18]Among the priests, the following were found to have taken foreign women for wives: Of the descendants of Jeshua, son of Jozadak, and his kinsmen: Maaseiah, Eliezer, Jarib, and Gedaliah. ¹⁹They pledged themselves to dismiss their wives, and as a guilt offering for their guilt they gave a ram from the flock. ²⁰Of the descendants of Immer: Hanani and Zebadiah; ²¹of the descendants of Harim: Maaseiah, Elijah, Shemaiah, Jehiel, and Uzziah; ²²of the descendants of Pashhur: Elioenai, Maaseiah, Ishmael, Nethanel, Jozabad, and Elasah.

²³Of the Levites: Jozabad, Shimei, Kelaiah (also called Kelita), Pethahiah, Judah, and Eliezer.

²⁴Of the singers: Eliashib; of the gatekeepers: Shallum, Telem, and Uri.

²⁵Of the people of Israel: Of the descendants of Parosh: Ramiah, Izziah, Malchijah, Mijamin, Eleazar, Malchijah, and Benaiah; ²⁶of the descendants of Elam: Mattaniah, Zechariah, Jehiel, Abdi, Jeremoth, and Elijah; ²⁷of the descendants of Zattu: Elioenai, Eliashib, Mattaniah, Jeremoth, Zabad, and Aziza; ²⁸of the descendants of Bebai: Jehohanan, Hananiah, Zabbai, and Athlai; ²⁹of the descendants of Bani: Meshullam, Malluch, Adaiah, Jashub, Sheal, and Jeremoth; ³⁰of the descendants of Pahath-moab: Adna, Chelal, Benaiah, Maaseiah, Mattaniah, Bezalel, Binnui, and Manasseh; ³¹of the descendants of Harim: Eliezer, Isshijah, Malchijah, Shemaiah, Shimeon, ³²Benjamin, Malluch, Shemariah; ³³of the descendants of Hashum: Mattenai, Mattattah, Zabad, Eliphelet, Jeremai, Manasseh, Shimei; ³⁴of the descendants of Begui: Maadai, Amram, Uel, ³⁵Benaiah, Bedeiah, Cheluhi, ³⁶Vaniah, Meremoth, Eliashib, ³⁷Mattaniah, Mattenai, and Jaasu; ³⁸of the descendants of Binnui: Shimei, ³⁹Shelemiah, Nathan, and Adaiah; ⁴⁰of the descendants of Zachai: Shashai, Sharai, ⁴¹Azarel, Shelemiah, Shemariah, ⁴²Shallum, Amariah, Joseph; ⁴³of the descendants of Nebo: Jeiel, Mattithiah, Zabad, Zebina, Jaddai, Joel, Benaiah.

⁴⁴All these had taken foreign wives; but they sent them away, both the women and their children.

☐ MATTHEW 17:14-21

The Healing of a Boy with a Demon. 17:14 When they came to the crowd a man approached, knelt down before him, ¹⁵and said, "Lord, have pity on my son, for he is a lunatic and suffers severely; often he falls into fire, and often into water. ¹⁶I brought him to your disciples, but they could not cure him." ¹⁷Jesus said in reply, "O faithless and perverse generation, how long will I be with you? How long will I endure you? Bring him here to me." ¹⁸Jesus rebuked him and the demon came out of him, and from that hour the boy was cured. ¹⁹Then the disciples approached Jesus in private and said, "Why could we not drive it out?" ²⁰He said to them, "Because of your little faith. Amen, I say to you, if you have faith the size of a mustard seed, you will say to this mountain, 'Move from here to there,' and it will move. Nothing will be impossible for you." ²¹

May 21

St. Christopher Magallanes and Companions;
St. Eugene de Mazenod

I am a priest, a priest of Jesus Christ. That says it all.
— St. Eugene de Mazenod

☐ NEHEMIAH 1-3

Nehemiah Hears Bad News. 1:1 The words of Nehemiah, son of Hacaliah.

In the month Kislev of the twentieth year, I was in the citadel of Susa ²when Hanani, one of my brothers, came with other men from Judah. I asked them about the Jews, the remnant preserved after the captivity, and about Jerusalem. ³They answered me: "The survivors of the captivity there in the province are in great distress and under reproach. The wall of Jerusalem has been breached, its gates gutted by fire." ⁴When I heard this report, I began to weep and continued mourning for several days, fasting and praying before the God of heaven.

⁵I prayed: "LORD, God of heaven, great and awesome God, you preserve your covenant of mercy with those who love you and keep your commandments. ⁶May your ears be attentive, and your eyes open, to hear the prayer that I, your servant, now offer in your presence day and night for your servants the Israelites, confessing the sins we have committed against you, I and my ancestral house included. ⁷We have greatly offended you, not keeping the commandments, the statutes, and the ordinances you entrusted to your servant Moses. ⁸But remember the admonition which you addressed to Moses, your servant, when you said: If you prove faithless, I will scatter you among the peoples; ⁹but if you return to me and carefully keep my commandments, even though your outcasts have been driven to the farthest corner of the world, I will gather them from there, and bring them back to the place I have chosen as the dwelling place for my name. ¹⁰They are your servants, your people, whom you freed by your great might and strong hand. ¹¹LORD, may your ears be attentive to the prayer of your servant and that of all your servants who willingly revere your name. Grant success to your servant this day, and let him find favor with this man"—for I was cupbearer to the king.

Appointment by the King. 2:1 In the month Nisan of the twentieth year of King Artaxerxes, when the wine was in my charge, I took some and offered it to the king. Because I had never before been sad in his presence, ²the king asked me, "Why do you look sad? If you are not sick, you must be sad at heart." Though I was seized with great fear, ³I answered the king: "May the king live forever! How could I not look sad when the city where my ancestors are buried lies in ruins, and its gates consumed by fire?" ⁴The king asked me, "What is it, then, that you wish?" I prayed to the God of heaven ⁵and then answered the king: "If it please the king, and if your servant is deserving of your favor, send me to Judah, to the city where my ancestors are buried, that I may rebuild it." ⁶Then the king, with the queen seated beside him, asked me, "How long will your journey take and when will you return?" My answer was acceptable to the king and he agreed to let me go; I set a date for my return.

⁷I asked the king further: "If it please the king, let letters be given to me for the governors of West-of-Euphrates, that they may give me safe-conduct till I arrive in Judah; ⁸also a letter for Asaph, the keeper of the royal woods, that he may give me timber

to make beams for the gates of the temple citadel, for the city wall and the house that I will occupy." Since I enjoyed the good favor of my God, the king granted my requests. [9]Thus I proceeded to the governors of West-of-Euphrates and presented the king's letters to them. The king also sent with me army officers and cavalry.

[10]When Sanballat the Horonite and Tobiah the Ammonite official had heard of this, they were very much displeased that someone had come to improve the lot of the Israelites.

Circuit of the City. [11]When I arrived in Jerusalem, and had been there three days, [12]I set out by night with only a few other men and with no other animals but my own mount (for I had not told anyone what my God had inspired me to do for Jerusalem). [13]I rode out at night by the Valley Gate, passed by the Dragon Spring, and came to the Dung Gate, observing how the walls of Jerusalem were breached and its gates consumed by fire. [14]Then I passed over to the Fountain Gate and to the King's Pool. Since there was no room here for my mount to pass with me astride, [15]I continued on foot up the wadi by night, inspecting the wall all the while, until I once more reached the Valley Gate, by which I went back in. [16]The magistrates knew nothing of where I had gone or what I was doing, for as yet I had disclosed nothing to the Jews, neither to the priests, nor to the nobles, nor to the magistrates, nor to the others who were to do the work.

Decision to Rebuild the City Wall. [17]Afterward I said to them: "You see the trouble we are in: how Jerusalem lies in ruins and its gates have been gutted by fire. Come, let us rebuild the wall of Jerusalem, so that we may no longer be a reproach!" [18]Then I explained to them how God had shown his gracious favor to me, and what the king had said to me. They replied, "Let us begin building!" And they undertook the work with vigor.

[19]When they heard about this, Sanballat the Horonite, Tobiah the Ammonite official, and Geshem the Arab mocked and ridiculed us. "What are you doing?" they asked. "Are you rebelling against the king?" [20]My answer to them was this: "It is the God of heaven who will grant us success. We, his servants, shall set about the rebuilding; but you have neither share nor claim nor memorial in Jerusalem."

List of Workers. 3:1 Eliashib the high priest and his priestly kinsmen took up the task of rebuilding the Sheep Gate. They consecrated it and set up its doors, its bolts, and its bars, then continued the rebuilding to the Tower of the Hundred, the Tower of Hananel. [2]At their side the men of Jericho were rebuilding, and next to them was Zaccur, son of Imri. [3]The Fish Gate was rebuilt by the people of Hassenaah; they timbered it and set up its doors, its bolts, and its bars. [4]At their side Meremoth, son of Uriah, son of Hakkoz, carried out the work of repair; next to him was Meshullam, son of Berechiah, son of Meshezabel; and next to him was Zadok, son of Baana. [5]Next to him the Tekoites carried out the work of repair; however, some of their most powerful men would not submit to the labor asked by their masters. [6]The Mishneh Gate was repaired by Joiada, son of Paseah; and Meshullam, son of Besodeiah; they timbered it and set up its doors, its bolts, and its bars. [7]At their side Melatiah the Gibeonite did the repairing, together with Jadon the Meronothite, and the men of Gibeon and of Mizpah, who were under the jurisdiction of the governor of West-of-Euphrates. [8]Next to them the work of repair was carried out by Uzziel, son of Harhaiah, a member of the goldsmiths' guild, and at his side was Hananiah, one of the perfumers' guild. They restored Jerusalem as far as the Broad Wall. [9]Next to them the work of repair carried out by Rephaiah, son of Hur, administrator of half the district of Jerusalem, [10]and at his side was Jedaiah, son of Harumaph, who repaired opposite his own house. Next to him Hattush, son of Hashabneiah, carried out the work of repair. [11]The adjoining sector, as far as the Oven Tower, was repaired by Malchijah, son of Harim, and Hasshub, son of Pahath-moab. [12]At their side the work of repair was carried out by Shallum, son of Hallohesh, administrator of half the district of Jerusalem, together with his daughters. [13]The Valley Gate was repaired by Hanun and the inhabitants of Zanoah; they rebuilt it and set up its doors, its bolts, and its bars. They also repaired a thousand cubits of the wall up to the Dung Gate. [14]The Dung Gate was repaired by Malchijah, son of Rechab, administrator of the district of Beth-haccherem; he rebuilt it and set up its doors, its bolts, and its bars. [15]The Fountain Gate was repaired by Shallum, son of Colhozeh, administrator of the district of Mizpah; he rebuilt it, roofed it, and set up its doors, its bolts, and its bars. He also repaired the wall of the Aqueduct Pool near the King's Garden as far as the steps that lead down from the City of David. [16]After him, the work of repair was carried out by Nehemiah, son of Azbuk, administrator of half the district of Beth-zur, to a place opposite the tombs of David, as far as the Artificial Pool and the barracks.

[17]After him, these Levites carried out the work of repair: Rehum, son of Bani, and next to him, for his own district, was Hashabiah, administrator of half the district of Keilah. [18]After him, their kinsmen carried out the work of repair: Binnui, son of Henadad, administrator of half the district of Keilah; [19]next to him Ezer, son of Jeshua, administrator of Mizpah, who repaired the adjoining sector, the Corner, opposite the ascent to the arsenal. [20]After him, Baruch, son of Zabbai, repaired the adjoining sector from the Corner to the entrance of the house of Eliashib, the high priest. [21]After him, Meremoth, son of Uriah, son of Hakkoz, repaired the adjoining sector from the entrance of Eliashib's house to its end.

[22]After him, the work of repair was carried out by the priests, men of the surrounding country. [23]After them, Benjamin and Hasshub carried out the repair in front of their houses; after them, Azariah, son of Maaseiah, son of Ananiah, made the repairs alongside his house. [24]After him, Binnui, son of Henadad, repaired the adjoining sector from the house of Azariah to the Corner (that is, to the Angle). [25]After him, Palal, son of Uzai, carried out the work of repair opposite the Corner and the tower projecting from the Upper Palace at the quarters of the guard. After him, Pedaiah, son of Parosh, carried out the work of repair [26]to a point opposite the Water Gate on the east, and the projecting tower. [27]After him, the Tekoites repaired the adjoining sector opposite the great projecting tower, to the wall of Ophel.

[28]Above the Horse Gate the priests carried out the work of repair, each opposite his own house. [29]After them Zadok, son of Immer, carried out the repair opposite his house, and after him the repair was carried out by Shemaiah, son of Shecaniah, keeper of the East Gate. [30]After him, Hananiah, son of Shelemiah, and Hanun, the sixth son of Zalaph, repaired the adjoining sector; after them, Meshullam, son of Berechiah, repaired the place opposite his own lodging. [31]After him, Malchijah, a member of the goldsmiths' guild, carried out the work of repair as far as the quarters of the temple servants and the merchants, in front of the Gate of Inspection and as far as the upper chamber of the Angle. [32]Between the upper chamber of the Angle and the Sheep Gate, the goldsmiths and the merchants carried out the work of repair.

Opposition from Judah's Enemies. [33]When Sanballat heard that we were rebuilding the wall, he became angry and very much incensed. He ridiculed the Jews, [34]saying in the presence of his associates and the troops of Samaria: "What are these miserable Jews trying to do? Will they complete their restoration in a single day? Will they recover these stones, burnt as they are, from the heaps of dust?" [35]Tobiah the Ammonite was beside him, and he said: "Whatever they are building—if a fox attacks it, it will breach their wall of stones!" [36]Hear, our God, how we were mocked! Turn back their reproach upon their own heads and deliver them up as plunder in a land of captivity! [37]Do not hide their crime and do not let their sin be blotted out in your sight, for they insulted the builders to their faces! [38]We, however, continued to build the wall, and soon it was completed up to half its height. The people worked enthusiastically.

☐ MATTHEW 17:22-27

The Second Prediction of the Passion. **17:22** As they were gathering in Galilee, Jesus said to them, "The Son of Man is to be handed over to men, [23]and they will kill him, and he will be raised on the third day." And they were overwhelmed with grief.

Payment of the Temple Tax. [24]When they came to Capernaum, the collectors of the temple tax approached Peter and said, "Doesn't your teacher pay the temple tax?" [25]"Yes," he said. When he came into the house, before he had time to speak, Jesus asked him, "What is your opinion, Simon? From whom do the kings of the earth take tolls or census tax? From their subjects or from foreigners?" [26]When he said, "From foreigners," Jesus said to him, "Then the subjects are exempt. [27]But that we may not offend them, go to the sea, drop in a hook, and take the first fish that comes up. Open its mouth and you will find a coin worth twice the temple tax. Give that to them for me and for you."

May 22

St. Rita of Cascia

What is impossible to God? Not what is difficult to His power, but whatever is contrary to His nature.

— St. Ambrose of Milan

☐ NEHEMIAH 4-6

4:1 When Sanballat, Tobiah, the Arabs, the Ammonites, and the Ashdodites heard that the restoration of the walls of Jerusalem was progressing—for the gaps were beginning to be closed up—they became extremely angry. [2]They all plotted together to come and fight against Jerusalem and to throw us into confusion. [3]We prayed to our God and posted a watch against them day and night for fear of what they might do. [4]Meanwhile the Judahites were saying:

> "Slackened is the bearers' strength,
> there is no end to the rubbish;
> Never will we be able
> to rebuild the wall."

[5]Our enemies thought, "Before they are aware of it or see us, we will come into

their midst, kill them, and put an end to the work."

⁶When the Jews who lived near them had come to us from one place after another, and had told us ten times over that they were about to attack us, ⁷I stationed guards down below, behind the wall, near the exposed points, assigning them by family groups with their swords, spears, and bows. ⁸I made an inspection, then addressed these words to the nobles, the magistrates, and the rest of the people: "Do not fear them! Keep in mind the LORD, who is great and to be feared, and fight for your kindred, your sons and daughters, your wives and your homes." ⁹When our enemies realized that we had been warned and that God had upset their plan, we all went back, each to our own task at the wall.

¹⁰From that time on, however, only half my work force took a hand in the work, while the other half, armed with spears, bucklers, bows, and breastplates, stood guard behind the whole house of Judah ¹¹as they rebuilt the wall. The load carriers, too, were armed; each worked with one hand and held a weapon with the other. ¹²Every builder, while working, had a sword tied at his side. A trumpeter stood beside me, ¹³for I had said to the nobles, the magistrates, and the rest of the people: "Our work is scattered and extensive, and we are widely separated from one another along the wall; ¹⁴wherever you hear the trumpet sound, join us there; our God will fight with us." ¹⁵Thus we went on with the work, half with spears in hand, from daybreak till the stars came out.

¹⁶At the same time I told the people to spend the nights inside Jerusalem, each with an attendant, so that they might serve as a guard by night and a working force by day. ¹⁷Neither I, nor my kindred, nor any of my attendants, nor any of the bodyguard that accompanied me took off our clothes; everyone kept a weapon at hand.

Social and Economic Problems. 5:1 Then there rose a great outcry of the people and their wives against certain of their Jewish kindred. ²Some said: "We are forced to pawn our sons and daughters in order to get grain to eat that we may live." ³Others said: "We are forced to pawn our fields, our vineyards, and our houses, that we may have grain during the famine." ⁴Still others said: "To pay the king's tax we have borrowed money on our fields and vineyards. ⁵And though these are our own kindred, and our children are as good as theirs, we have had to reduce our sons and daughters to slavery, and violence has been done to some of our daughters! Yet we can do nothing about it, for our fields and vineyards belong to others."

⁶I was extremely angry when I heard the reasons for their complaint. ⁷After some deliberation, I called the nobles and magistrates to account, saying to them, "You are exacting interest from your own kindred!" I then rebuked them severely, ⁸saying to them: "As far as we were able, we bought back our Jewish kindred who had been sold to Gentiles; you, however, are selling your own kindred, to have them bought back by us." They remained silent, for they could find no answer. ⁹I continued: "What you are doing is not good. Should you not conduct yourselves out of fear of our God rather than fear of the reproach of our Gentile enemies? ¹⁰I myself, my kindred, and my attendants have lent the people money and grain without charge. Let us put an end to this usury! ¹¹Return to them this very day their fields, vineyards, olive groves, and houses, together with the interest on the money, the grain, the wine, and the oil that you have lent them." ¹²They answered: "We will return everything and exact nothing further from them. We will do just what you ask." Then I called for the priests to administer an oath to them that they would do as they had promised. ¹³I shook out the folds of my garment, saying, "Thus may God shake from home and fortune every man who fails to keep this

promise, and may he thus be shaken out and emptied!" And the whole assembly answered, "Amen," and praised the LORD. Then the people did as they had promised.

Nehemiah's Record. [14]Moreover, from the time that King Artaxerxes appointed me governor in the land of Judah, from his twentieth to his thirty-second year—during these twelve years neither I nor my kindred lived off the governor's food allowance. [15]The earlier governors, my predecessors, had laid a heavy burden on the people, taking from them each day forty silver shekels for their food; then, too, their attendants oppressed the people. But I, because I feared God, did not do this. [16]In addition, though I had acquired no land of my own, I did my part in this work on the wall, and all my attendants were gathered there for the work. [17]Though I set my table for a hundred and fifty persons, Jews and magistrates, as well as the neighboring Gentiles who came to us, [18]and though the daily preparations were made at my expense—one ox, six choice sheep, poultry—besides all kinds of wine in abundance every ten days, despite this I did not claim the governor's allowance, for the labor lay heavy upon this people. [19]Keep in mind, my God, to my credit all that I did for this people.

Plots Against Nehemiah. 6:1 When it had been reported to Sanballat, Tobiah, Geshem the Arab, and our other enemies that I had rebuilt the wall and that there was no breach left in it (though up to that time I had not yet set up the doors in the gates), [2]Sanballat and Geshem sent me this message: "Come, let us hold council together at Chephirim in the plain of Ono." They were planning to do me harm. [3]I sent messengers to them with this reply: "I am engaged in a great enterprise and am unable to come down. Why should the work stop, while I leave it to come down to you?" [4]Four times they sent me

this same proposal, and each time I gave the same reply. [5]Then, the fifth time, Sanballat sent me the same message by one of his servants, who bore an unsealed letter [6]containing this text: "Among the nations it has been reported—Gashmu is witness to this—that you and the Jews are planning a rebellion; that for this reason you are rebuilding the wall; and that you are to be their king. [7]Also, that you have set up prophets in Jerusalem to proclaim you king of Judah. Now, since matters like these will reach the ear of the king, come, let us hold council together." [8]I sent him this answer: "Nothing of what you report is happening; rather, it is the invention of your own mind." [9]They were all trying to intimidate us, thinking, "They will be discouraged from continuing with the work, and it will never be completed." But instead, I then redoubled my efforts.

[10]I went to the house of Shemaiah, son of Delaiah, son of Mehetabel, who was confined to his house, and he said: "Let us meet in the house of God, inside the temple building; let us lock the doors of the temple. For they are coming to kill you—by night they are coming to kill you." [11]My answer was: "A man like me take flight? Should a man like me enter the temple to save his life? I will not go!" [12]For on consideration, it was plain to me that God had not sent him; rather, because Tobiah and Sanballat had bribed him, he voiced this prophecy concerning me, [13]that I might act on it out of fear and commit this sin. Then they would have had a shameful story with which to discredit me. [14]Keep in mind Tobiah and Sanballat, my God, because of these things they did; keep in mind as well Noadiah the woman prophet and the other prophets who were trying to intimidate me.

Completion of the Work. [15]The wall was finished on the twenty-fifth day of Elul; the work had taken fifty-two days. [16]When all our enemies had heard of this, and all the neighboring Gentiles round about had taken note of it, they were very discouraged, for they knew that it was with our God's help that this work had been completed. ¹⁷At that same time, however, many letters were going to Tobiah from the nobles of Judah, and Tobiah's letters were reaching them, ¹⁸for many in Judah were in league with him, since he was the son-in-law of Shecaniah, son of Arah, and his son Jehohanan had married the daughter of Meshullam, son of Berechiah. ¹⁹They would praise his good deeds in my presence and relate to him whatever I said; and Tobiah sent letters trying to intimidate me.

☐ MATTHEW 18:1-9

The Greatest in the Kingdom. 18:1 At that time the disciples approached Jesus and said, "Who is the greatest in the kingdom of heaven?" ²He called a child over, placed it in their midst, ³and said, "Amen, I say to you, unless you turn and become like children, you will not enter the kingdom of heaven. ⁴Whoever humbles himself like this child is the greatest in the kingdom of heaven. ⁵And whoever receives one child such as this in my name receives me.

Temptations to Sin. ⁶"Whoever causes one of these little ones who believe in me to sin, it would be better for him to have a great millstone hung around his neck and to be drowned in the depths of the sea. ⁷Woe to the world because of things that cause sin! Such things must come, but woe to the one through whom they come! ⁸If your hand or foot causes you to sin, cut it off and throw it away. It is better for you to enter into life maimed or crippled than with two hands or two feet to be thrown into eternal fire. ⁹And if your eye causes you to sin, tear it out and throw it away. It is better for you to enter into life with one eye than with two eyes to be thrown into fiery Gehenna."

May 23

My Lord, if it is necessary to give the children a whipping or two to convert them, please do it, as long as their souls are saved in the end.

— St. Pio of Pietrelcina

☐ NEHEMIAH 7-9

7:1 Now that the wall had been rebuilt, I had the doors set up, and the gatekeepers, the singers, and the Levites were put in charge of them. ²Over Jerusalem I placed Hanani, my brother, and Hananiah, the commander of the citadel, who was more trustworthy and God-fearing than most. ³I said to them: "The gates of Jerusalem are not to be opened until the sun is hot, and while the sun is still shining they shall shut and bar the doors. Appoint as sentinels the inhabitants of Jerusalem, some at their watch posts, and others in front of their own houses."

Census of the Province. ⁴Now, the city was quite wide and spacious, but its population was small, and none of the houses had been rebuilt. ⁵When my God had inspired me to gather together the nobles, the magistrates, and the people, and to examine their family records, I came upon the family list of those who had returned in the earliest period. There I found the following written:

⁶These are the inhabitants of the province who returned from the captivity of the exiles whom Nebuchadnezzar, king of Babylon, had carried away, and who came back to Jerusalem and Judah, to their own cities: ⁷They returned with Zerubbabel, Jeshua, Nehemiah, Azariah, Raamiah, Nahamani, Mordecai, Bilshan, Mispereth, Bigvai, Nehum, and Baanah.

The census of the people of Israel: ⁸descendants of Parosh, two thousand one hundred and seventy-two; ⁹descendants of Shephatiah, three hundred and seventy-two; ¹⁰descendants of Arah, six hundred and fifty-two; ¹¹descendants of Pahath-moab who were descendants of Jeshua and Joab, two thousand eight hundred and eighteen; ¹²descendants of Elam, one thousand two hundred and fifty-four; ¹³descendants of Zattu, eight hundred and forty-five; ¹⁴descendants of Zaccai, seven hundred and sixty; ¹⁵descendants of Binnui, six hundred and forty-eight; ¹⁶descendants of Bebai, six hundred and twenty-eight; ¹⁷descendants of Azgad, two thousand three hundred and twenty-two; ¹⁸descendants of Adonikam, six hundred and sixty-seven; ¹⁹descendants of Bigvai, two thousand and sixty-seven; ²⁰descendants of Adin, six hundred and fifty-five; ²¹descendants of Ater who were descendants of Hezekiah, ninety-eight; ²²descendants of Hashum, three hundred and twenty-eight; ²³descendants of Bezai, three hundred and twenty-four; ²⁴descendants of Hariph, one hundred and twelve; ²⁵descendants of Gibeon, ninety-five; ²⁶people of Bethlehem and Netophah, one hundred and eighty-eight; ²⁷people of Anathoth, one hundred and twenty-eight; ²⁸people of Beth-azmaveth, forty-two; ²⁹people of Kiriath-jearim, Chephirah, and Beeroth,

seven hundred and forty-three; ³⁰people of Ramah and Geba, six hundred and twenty-one; ³¹people of Michmas, one hundred and twenty-two; ³²people of Bethel and Ai, one hundred and twenty-three; ³³people of Nebo, fifty-two; ³⁴descendants of the other Elam, one thousand two hundred and fifty-four; ³⁵descendants of Harim, three hundred and twenty; ³⁶descendants of Jericho, three hundred and forty-five; ³⁷descendants of Lod, Hadid, and Ono, seven hundred and twenty-one; ³⁸descendants of Senaah, three thousand nine hundred and thirty.

³⁹The priests: descendants of Jedaiah of the house of Jeshua, nine hundred and seventy-three; ⁴⁰descendants of Immer, one thousand and fifty-two; ⁴¹descendants of Pashhur, one thousand two hundred and forty-seven; ⁴²descendants of Harim, one thousand and seventeen.

⁴³The Levites: descendants of Jeshua, Kadmiel of the descendants of Hodeviah, seventy-four.

⁴⁴The singers: descendants of Asaph, one hundred and forty-eight.

⁴⁵The gatekeepers: descendants of Shallum, descendants of Ater, descendants of Talmon, descendants of Akkub, descendants of Hatita, descendants of Shobai, one hundred and thirty-eight.

⁴⁶The temple servants: descendants of Ziha, descendants of Hasupha, descendants of Tabbaoth, ⁴⁷descendants of Keros, descendants of Sia, descendants of Padon, ⁴⁸descendants of Lebana, descendants of Hagaba, descendants of Shalmai, ⁴⁹descendants of Hanan, descendants of Giddel, descendants of Gahar, ⁵⁰descendants of Reaiah, descendants of Rezin, descendants of Nekoda, ⁵¹descendants of Gazzam, descendants of Uzza, descendants of Paseah, ⁵²descendants of Besai, descendants of the Meunites, descendants of the Nephusites, ⁵³descendants of Bakbuk, descendants of Hakupha, descendants of Harhur, ⁵⁴descendants of Bazlith, descendants of Mehida, descendants of Harsha, ⁵⁵descendants

of Barkos, descendants of Sisera, descendants of Temah, ⁵⁶descendants of Neziah, descendants of Hatipha.

⁵⁷Descendants of Solomon's servants: descendants of Sotai, descendants of Sophereth, descendants of Perida, ⁵⁸descendants of Jaala, descendants of Darkon, descendants of Giddel, ⁵⁹descendants of Shephatiah, descendants of Hattil, descendants of Pochereth-hazzebaim, descendants of Amon. ⁶⁰The total of the temple servants and the descendants of Solomon's servants was three hundred and ninety-two.

⁶¹The following who returned from Tel-melah, Tel-harsha, Cherub, Addon, and Immer were unable to prove that their ancestral houses and their descent were Israelite: ⁶²descendants of Delaiah, descendants of Tobiah, descendants of Nekoda, six hundred and forty-two. ⁶³Also, of the priests: descendants of Hobaiah, descendants of Hakkoz, descendants of Barzillai (he had married one of the daughters of Barzillai the Gileadite and was named after him). ⁶⁴These men searched their family records, but their names could not be found written there; hence they were disqualified from the priesthood, ⁶⁵and the governor ordered them not to partake of the most holy foods until there should be a priest to consult the Urim and Thummim.

⁶⁶The entire assembly taken together came to forty-two thousand three hundred and sixty, ⁶⁷not counting their male and female servants, who were seven thousand three hundred and thirty-seven. They also had two hundred male and female singers. Their horses were seven hundred and thirty-six, their mules two hundred and forty-five, ⁶⁸their camels four hundred and thirty-five, their donkeys six thousand seven hundred and twenty.

⁶⁹Certain of the heads of ancestral houses contributed to the temple service. The governor put into the treasury one thousand drachmas of gold, fifty basins, thirty vestments for priests, and five hundred minas of silver. ⁷⁰Some of the heads of ancestral houses contributed to the treasury for the temple service: twenty thousand drachmas of gold and two thousand two hundred minas of silver. ⁷¹The contributions of the rest of the people amounted to twenty thousand drachmas of gold, two thousand minas of silver, and sixty-seven vestments for priests.

⁷²The priests, the Levites, the gatekeepers, the singers, the temple servants, and all Israel took up residence in their cities.

Ezra Reads the Law. 8:1 Now when the seventh month came, the whole people gathered as one in the square in front of the Water Gate, and they called upon Ezra the scribe to bring forth the book of the law of Moses which the LORD had commanded for Israel. ²On the first day of the seventh month, therefore, Ezra the priest brought the law before the assembly, which consisted of men, women, and those children old enough to understand. ³In the square in front of the Water Gate, Ezra read out of the book from daybreak till midday, in the presence of the men, the women, and those children old enough to understand; and all the people listened attentively to the book of the law. ⁴Ezra the scribe stood on a wooden platform that had been made for the occasion; at his right side stood Mattithiah, Shema, Anaiah, Uriah, Hilkiah, and Maaseiah, and on his left Pedaiah, Mishael, Malchijah, Hashum, Hashbaddanah, Zechariah, Meshullam. ⁵Ezra opened the scroll so that all the people might see it, for he was standing higher than any of the people. When he opened it, all the people stood. ⁶Ezra blessed the LORD, the great God, and all the people, their hands raised high, answered, "Amen, amen!" Then they knelt down and bowed before the LORD, their faces to the ground. ⁷The Levites Jeshua, Bani, Sherebiah, Jamin, Akkub, Shabbethai, Hodiah, Maaseiah, Kelita, Azariah, Jozabad, Hanan, and

Pelaiah explained the law to the people, who remained in their places. ⁸Ezra read clearly from the book of the law of God, interpreting it so that all could understand what was read. ⁹Then Nehemiah, that is, the governor, and Ezra the priest-scribe, and the Levites who were instructing the people said to all the people: "Today is holy to the Lᴏʀᴅ your God. Do not lament, do not weep!"—for all the people were weeping as they heard the words of the law. ¹⁰He continued: "Go, eat rich foods and drink sweet drinks, and allot portions to those who had nothing prepared; for today is holy to our Lᴏʀᴅ. Do not be saddened this day, for rejoicing in the Lᴏʀᴅ is your strength!" ¹¹And the Levites quieted all the people, saying, "Silence! Today is holy, do not be saddened." ¹²Then all the people began to eat and drink, to distribute portions, and to celebrate with great joy, for they understood the words that had been explained to them.

The Feast of Booths. ¹³On the second day, the heads of ancestral houses of the whole people, and also the priests and the Levites, gathered around Ezra the scribe to study the words of the law. ¹⁴They found it written in the law commanded by the Lᴏʀᴅ through Moses that the Israelites should dwell in booths during the feast of the seventh month; ¹⁵and that they should have this proclamation made throughout their cities and in Jerusalem: "Go out into the hill country and bring in branches of olive, oleaster, myrtle, palm, and other trees in leaf, to make booths, as it is written." ¹⁶The people went out and brought in branches with which they made booths for themselves, on the roof of their houses, in their courtyards, in the courts of the house of God, and in the squares of the Water Gate and the Gate of Ephraim. ¹⁷So the entire assembly of the returned exiles made booths and dwelt in them. Now the Israelites had done nothing of this sort from the days of Jeshua, son of Nun, until this

occasion; therefore there was very great joy. ¹⁸Ezra read from the book of the law of God day after day, from the first day to the last. They kept the feast for seven days, and the solemn assembly on the eighth day, as was required.

Public Confession of Sin. 9:1 On the twenty-fourth day of this month, the Israelites gathered together while fasting and wearing sackcloth, their heads covered with dust. ²Those of Israelite descent separated themselves from all who were of foreign extraction, then stood forward and confessed their sins and the guilty deeds of their ancestors. ³When they had taken their places, they read from the book of the law of the Lᴏʀᴅ their God, for a fourth of the day, and during another fourth they made their confession and bowed down before the Lᴏʀᴅ their God. ⁴Standing on the platform of the Levites were Jeshua, Binnui, Kadmiel, Shebaniah, Bunni, Sherebiah, Bani, and Chenani, who cried out to the Lᴏʀᴅ their God, with a loud voice. ⁵The Levites Jeshua, Kadmiel, Bani, Hashabneiah, Sherebiah, Hodiah, Shebaniah, and Pethahiah said,

"Arise, bless the Lᴏʀᴅ, your God,
    from eternity to eternity!"
"And may they bless your glorious
    name,
      which is exalted above all blessing
        and praise."
⁶"You are the Lᴏʀᴅ, you alone;
You made the heavens,
    the highest heavens and all their host,
The earth and all that is upon it,
    the seas and all that is in them.
To all of them you give life,
    the heavenly hosts bow down before
      you.
⁷You are the Lᴏʀᴅ God
    who chose Abram,
Who brought him from Ur of the
    Chaldees,

who named him Abraham.
⁸You found his heart faithful in your
    sight,
    you made the covenant with him
To give the land of the Canaanites,
    Hittites, Amorites,
Perizzites, Jebusites, and Girgashites
    to him and his descendants.
You fulfilled your promises,
    for you are just.
⁹You saw the affliction of our ancestors
    in Egypt,
    you heard their cry by the Red Sea;
¹⁰You worked signs and wonders
    against Pharaoh,
    against all his servants and the
      people of his land,
Because you knew of their insolence
    toward them;
    thus you made for yourself a name
      even to this day.
¹¹The sea you divided before them,
    on dry ground they passed through
      the midst of the sea;
Their pursuers you hurled into the
    depths,
    like a stone into the mighty waters.
¹²With a column of cloud you led them
    by day,
    and by night with a column of fire,
To light the way of their journey,
    the way in which they must travel.
¹³On Mount Sinai you came down,
    you spoke with them from heaven;
You gave them just ordinances, true
    laws,
    good statutes and commandments;
¹⁴Your holy sabbath you made known
    to them,
    commandments, statutes, and law
      you prescribed for them,
    by the hand of Moses your servant.
¹⁵Food from heaven you gave them in
    their hunger,
    water from a rock you sent them in
      their thirst.

You told them to enter and occupy the
    land
    which you had sworn to give them.
¹⁶But they, our ancestors, proved to be
    insolent;
    they were obdurate and did not
      obey your commandments.
¹⁷They refused to obey and no longer
    remembered
    the wonders you had worked for
      them.
They were obdurate and appointed a
    leader
    in order to return to their slavery in
      Egypt.
But you are a forgiving God, gracious
    and merciful,
    slow to anger and rich in mercy;
    you did not forsake them.
¹⁸Though they made for themselves a
    molten calf,
    and proclaimed, 'Here is your God
      who brought you up from
      Egypt,'
    and were guilty of great insults,
¹⁹Yet in your great mercy
    you did not forsake them in the
      desert.
By day the column of cloud did not
    cease to lead them on their
      journey,
    by night the column of fire did not
      cease to light the way they
      were to travel.
²⁰Your good spirit you bestowed on
    them,
    to give them understanding;
Your manna you did not withhold
    from their mouths,
    and you gave them water in their
      thirst.
²¹Forty years in the desert you
    sustained them:
    they did not want;
Their garments did not become worn,
    and their feet did not swell.

²²You gave them kingdoms and
    peoples,
  which you divided among them as
    border lands.
They possessed the land of Sihon, king
    of Heshbon,
  and the land of Og, king of Bashan.
²³You made their children as numerous
    as the stars of the heavens,
  and you brought them into the land
  which you had commanded their
    ancestors to enter and possess.
²⁴The children went in to possess the
    land;
  you humbled before them the
    Canaanite inhabitants
  and gave them into their power,
Their kings and the peoples of the
    land,
  to do with them as they wished.
²⁵They captured fortified cities and
    fertile land;
  they took possession of houses filled
    with all good things,
Cisterns already dug, vineyards, olive
    groves,
  and fruit trees in abundance.
They ate and had their fill,
  fattened and feasted on your great
    goodness.
²⁶But they were contemptuous and
    rebelled against you:
  they cast your law behind their
    backs.
They murdered your prophets
  who bore witness against them to
    bring them back to you:
  they were guilty of great insults.
²⁷Therefore you gave them into the
    power of their enemies,
  who oppressed them.
But in the time of their oppression
    they would cry out to you,
  and you would hear them from
    heaven,
And according to your great mercy give
    them saviors

to deliver them from the power of
    their enemies.
²⁸As soon as they had relief,
  they would go back to doing evil in
    your sight.
Again you abandoned them to the
    power of their enemies,
  who crushed them.
Once again they cried out to you, and
    you heard them from heaven
  and delivered them according to
    your mercy, many times over.
²⁹You bore witness against them,
  to bring them back to your law.
But they were insolent
  and would not obey your
    commandments;
They sinned against your ordinances,
  which give life to those who keep
    them.
They turned stubborn backs, stiffened
    their necks,
  and would not obey.
³⁰You were patient with them for many
    years,
  bearing witness against them
    through your spirit, by means
    of your prophets;
Still they would not listen.
  Therefore you delivered them into
    the power of the peoples of
    the lands.
³¹Yet in your great mercy you did not
    completely destroy them
  and did not forsake them, for you
    are a gracious and merciful
    God.
³²Now, our God, great, mighty, and
    awesome God,
  who preserves the covenant of mercy,
  do not discount all the hardship
    that has befallen us,
Our kings, our princes, our priests,
  our prophets, our ancestors, and
    your entire people,
  from the time of the kings of Assyria
    until this day!

³³In all that has come upon us you have
　　been just,
　　for you kept faith while we have
　　　done evil.
³⁴Yes, our kings, our princes, our
　　priests, and our ancestors
　　have not kept your law;
They paid no attention to your
　　commandments
　　and the warnings which you gave
　　　them.
³⁵While they were still in their
　　kingdom,
　　in the midst of the many good
　　　things that you had given
　　　them

And in the wide, fertile land
　　that you had spread out before
　　　them,
They did not serve you
　　nor turn away from their evil deeds.
³⁶Today we are slaves!
　　As for the land which you gave our
　　　ancestors
That they might eat its fruits and good
　　things—
　　see, we have become slaves upon it!
³⁷Its rich produce goes to the kings
　　you set over us because of our sins,
Who rule over our bodies and our
　　cattle as they please.
　　We are in great distress!"

☐ MATTHEW 18:10-20

The Parable of the Lost Sheep. 18:10 "See that you do not despise one of these little ones, for I say to you that their angels in heaven always look upon the face of my heavenly Father. ^{11, 12}What is your opinion? If a man has a hundred sheep and one of them goes astray, will he not leave the ninety-nine in the hills and go in search of the stray? ¹³And if he finds it, amen, I say to you, he rejoices more over it than over the ninety-nine that did not stray. ¹⁴In just the same way, it is not the will of your heavenly Father that one of these little ones be lost.

A Brother Who Sins. ¹⁵"If your brother sins [against you], go and tell him his fault between you and him alone. If he listens to you, you have won over your brother. ¹⁶If he does not listen, take one or two others along with you, so that 'every fact may be established on the testimony of two or three witnesses.' ¹⁷If he refuses to listen to them, tell the church. If he refuses to listen even to the church, then treat him as you would a Gentile or a tax collector. ¹⁸Amen, I say to you, whatever you bind on earth shall be bound in heaven, and whatever you loose on earth shall be loosed in heaven. ¹⁹Again, [amen,] I say to you, if two of you agree on earth about anything for which they are to pray, it shall be granted to them by my heavenly Father. ²⁰ For where two or three are gathered together in my name, there am I in the midst of them."

May 24

St. Vincent of Lerins

Keep the talent of the Catholic faith pure and unalloyed. What has been faithfully entrusted, keep in your possession and hand it on faithfully. You've received gold, so give gold. Don't substitute one thing for another; don't impudently put lead in place of gold, or try to deceive with brass. I don't want the appearance of gold, but the real thing.

— St. Vincent of Lerins

☐ NEHEMIAH 10-13

Signatories to the Pact. 10:1 In view of all this, we are entering into a firm pact, which we are putting into writing. On the sealed document appear the names of our princes, our Levites, and our priests.

²On the sealed document: the governor Nehemiah, son of Hacaliah, and Zedekiah. ³Seraiah, Azariah, Jeremiah, ⁴Pashhur, Amariah, Malchijah, ⁵Hattush, Shebaniah, Malluch, ⁶Harim, Meremoth, Obadiah, ⁷Daniel, Ginnethon, Baruch, ⁸Meshullam, Abijah, Mijamin, ⁹Maaziah, Bilgai, Shemaiah: these are the priests.

¹⁰The Levites: Jeshua, son of Azaniah; Binnui, of the descendants of Henadad; Kadmiel; ¹¹and their kinsmen Shebaniah, Hodiah, Kelita, Pelaiah, Hanan, ¹²Mica, Rehob, Hashabiah, ¹³Zaccur, Sherebiah, Shebaniah, ¹⁴Hodiah, Bani, Beninu.

¹⁵The leaders of the people: Parosh, Pahath-moab, Elam, Zattu, Bani, ¹⁶Bunni, Azgad, Bebai, ¹⁷Adonijah, Bigvai, Adin, ¹⁸Ater, Hezekiah, Azzur, ¹⁹Hodiah, Hashum, Bezai, ²⁰Hariph, Anathoth, Nebai, ²¹Magpiash, Meshullam, Hezir, ²²Meshezabel, Zadok, Jaddua, ²³Pelatiah, Hanan, Anaiah, ²⁴Hoshea, Hananiah, Hasshub, ²⁵Hallhohesh, Pilha, Shobek, ²⁶Rehum, Hashabnah, Maaseiah, ²⁷Ahiah, Hanan, Anan, ²⁸Malluch, Harim, Baanah.

Provisions of the Pact. ²⁹The rest of the people, priests, Levites, gatekeepers, singers, temple servants, and all others who have separated themselves from the local inhabitants in favor of the law of God, with their wives, their sons, their daughters, all who are of the age of discretion, ³⁰join their influential kindred, and with the sanction of a curse take this oath to follow the law of God given through Moses, the servant of God, and to observe carefully all the commandments of the LORD, our Lord, his ordinances and his statutes.

³¹We will not marry our daughters to the local inhabitants, and we will not accept their daughters for our sons.

³²When the local inhabitants bring in merchandise or any kind of grain for sale on the sabbath day, we will not buy from them on the sabbath or on any other holy day. In the seventh year we will forgo the produce, and forgive every kind of debt.

³³We impose these commandments on ourselves: to give a third of a shekel each year for the service of the house of our God, ³⁴for the showbread, the daily grain offering, the daily burnt offering, for the sabbaths, new moons, and festivals, for the holy offerings and sin offerings to make atonement for Israel, for every service of the house of our God. ³⁵We, priests, Levites, and people, have determined by lot concerning the procurement of wood: it is to be brought to the house of our God by each of our ancestral houses at stated times each year, to be burnt on the altar of the LORD, our God, as the law prescribes. ³⁶We have agreed to bring each year to the

house of the LORD the first fruits of our fields and of our fruit trees, of every kind; [37]also, as is prescribed in the law, to bring to the house of our God, to the priests who serve in the house of our God, the firstborn of our children and our animals, including the firstborn of our flocks and herds. [38]The first batch of our dough, and our offerings of the fruit of every tree, of wine and oil, we will bring to the priests, to the chambers of the house of our God. The tithe of our fields we will bring to the Levites; they, the Levites, shall take the tithe in all the cities of our service. [39]An Aaronite priest shall be with the Levites when they take the tithe, and the Levites shall bring the tithe of the tithes to the house of our God, to the chambers of the treasury. [40]For to these chambers the Israelites and Levites bring the offerings of grain, wine, and oil; there also are housed the vessels of the sanctuary, and the ministering priests, the gatekeepers, and the singers. We will not neglect the house of our God.

Resettlement of Jerusalem. 11:1 The administrators took up residence in Jerusalem, and the rest of the people cast lots to bring one man in ten to reside in Jerusalem, the holy city, while the other nine would remain in the other cities. [2]The people blessed all those who willingly agreed to take up residence in Jerusalem.

[3]These are the heads of the province who took up residence in Jerusalem. In the cities of Judah dwelt Israelites, priests, Levites, temple servants, and the descendants of Solomon's servants, each on the property they owned in their own cities.

[4]In Jerusalem dwelt both Judahites and Benjaminites. Of the Judahites: Athaiah, son of Uzziah, son of Zechariah, son of Amariah, son of Shephatiah, son of Mehallalel, of the sons of Perez; [5]Maaseiah, son of Baruch, son of Colhozeh, son of Hazaiah, son of Adaiah, son of Joiarib, son of Zechariah, a son of the Shelanites. [6]The total of the descendants of Perez who dwelt in Jerusalem was four hundred and sixty-eight people of substance.

[7]These were the Benjaminites: Sallu, son of Meshullam, son of Joed, son of Pedaiah, son of Kolaiah, son of Maaseiah, son of Ithiel, son of Jeshaiah, [8]and his kinsmen, warriors, nine hundred and twenty-eight in number. [9]Joel, son of Zichri, was their commander, and Judah, son of Hassenuah, was second in command of the city.

[10]Among the priests were: Jedaiah; Joiarib; Jachin; [11]Seraiah, son of Hilkiah, son of Meshullam, son of Zadok, son of Meraioth, son of Ahitub, the ruler of the house of God, [12]and their kinsmen who carried out the temple service, eight hundred and twenty-two; Adaiah, son of Jeroham, son of Pelaliah, son of Amzi, son of Zechariah, son of Pashhur, son of Malchijah, [13]and his kinsmen, heads of ancestral houses, two hundred and forty-two; and Amasai, son of Azarel, son of Ahzai, son of Meshillemoth, son of Immer, [14]and his kinsmen, warriors, one hundred and twenty-eight. Their commander was Zabdiel, son of Haggadol.

[15]Among the Levites were Shemaiah, son of Hasshub, son of Azrikam, son of Hashabiah, son of Bunni; [16]Shabbethai and Jozabad, levitical chiefs who were placed over the external affairs of the house of God; [17]Mattaniah, son of Micah, son of Zabdi, son of Asaph, director of the psalms, who led the thanksgiving at prayer; Bakbukiah, second in rank among his kinsmen; and Abda, son of Shammua, son of Galal, son of Jeduthun. [18]The total of the Levites in the holy city was two hundred and eighty-four.

[19]The gatekeepers were Akkub, Talmon, and their kinsmen, who kept watch over the gates; one hundred and seventy-two in number.

[20]The rest of Israel, including priests and Levites, were in all the other cities of Judah in their own inheritances.

²¹The temple servants lived on Ophel. Ziha and Gishpa were in charge of the temple servants.

²²The prefect of the Levites in Jerusalem was Uzzi, son of Bani, son of Hashabiah, son of Mattaniah, son of Micah; he was one of the descendants of Asaph, the singers appointed to the service of the house of God— ²³for they had been appointed by royal decree, and there was a fixed schedule for the singers assigning them their daily duties.

²⁴Pethahiah, son of Meshezabel, a descendant of Zerah, son of Judah, was royal deputy in all affairs that concerned the people.

Other Settlements. ²⁵As concerns their villages with their fields: Judahites lived in Kiriath-arba and its dependencies, in Dibon and its dependencies, in Jekabzeel and its villages, ²⁶in Jeshua, Moladah, Beth-pelet, ²⁷in Hazarshual, in Beer-sheba and its dependencies, ²⁸in Ziklag, in Meconah and its dependencies, ²⁹in En-rimmon, Zorah, Jarmuth, ³⁰Zanoah, Adullam, and their villages, Lachish and its fields, Azekah and its dependencies. They were settled from Beer-sheba to Ge-hinnom.

³¹Benjaminites were in Geba, Michmash, Aija, Bethel and its dependencies, ³²Anathoth, Nob, Ananiah, ³³Hazor, Ramah, Gittaim, ³⁴Hadid, Zeboim, Neballat, ³⁵Lod, Ono, and the Valley of the Artisans. ³⁶Some divisions of the Levites from Judah were attached to Benjamin.

Priests and Levites at the Time of Zerubbabel. 12:1 The following are the priests and Levites who returned with Zerubbabel, son of Shealtiel, and Jeshua: Seraiah, Jeremiah, Ezra, ²Amariah, Malluch, Hattush, ³Shecaniah, Rehum, Meremoth, ⁴Iddo, Ginnethon, Abijah, ⁵Mijamin, Maadiah, Bilgah, ⁶Shemaiah, and Joiarib, Jedaiah, ⁷Sallu, Amok, Hilkiah, Jedaiah. These were the priestly heads and their kinsmen in the days of Jeshua.

⁸The Levites were Jeshua, Binnui, Kadmiel, Sherebiah, Judah, Mattaniah, who, together with his kinsmen, was in charge of the thanksgiving hymns, ⁹while Bakbukiah and Unno and their kinsmen ministered opposite them by turns.

High Priests. ¹⁰Jeshua became the father of Joiakim, Joiakim the father of Eliashib, and Eliashib the father of Joiada; ¹¹Joiada the father of Johanan, and Johanan the father of Jaddua.

Priests and Levites Under Joiakim. ¹²In the days of Joiakim these were the priestly family heads: for Seraiah, Meraiah; for Jeremiah, Hananiah; ¹³for Ezra, Meshullam; for Amariah, Jehohanan; ¹⁴for Malluchi, Jonathan; for Shebaniah, Joseph; ¹⁵for Harim, Adna; for Meremoth, Helkai; ¹⁶for Iddo, Zechariah; for Ginnethon, Meshullam; ¹⁷for Abijah, Zichri; for Miamin, … ; for Moadiah, Piltai; ¹⁸for Bilgah, Shammua; for Shemaiah, Jehonathan; ¹⁹and for Joiarib, Mattenai; for Jedaiah, Uzzi; ²⁰for Sallu, Kallai; for Amok, Eber; ²¹for Hilkiah, Hashabiah; for Jedaiah, Nethanel.

²²In the time of Eliashib, Joiada, Johanan, and Jaddua, the heads of ancestral houses of the priests were written down in the Book of Chronicles, up until the reign of Darius the Persian. ²³The sons of Levi: the family heads were written down in the Book of Chronicles, up until the time of Johanan, the son of Eliashib.

²⁴The heads of the Levites were Hashabiah, Sherebiah, Jeshua, Binnui, Kadmiel. Their kinsmen who stood opposite them to sing praises and thanksgiving in fulfillment of the command of David, the man of God, one section opposite the other, ²⁵were Mattaniah, Bakbukiah, Obadiah.

Meshullam, Talmon, and Akkub were gatekeepers. They guarded the storerooms at the gates.

²⁶All these lived in the time of Joiakim, son of Jeshua, son of Jozadak (and in the time of Nehemiah the governor and of Ezra the priest-scribe).

Dedication of the Wall. [27]At the dedication of the wall of Jerusalem, the Levites were sought out wherever they lived and were brought to Jerusalem to celebrate a joyful dedication with thanksgiving hymns and the music of cymbals, harps, and lyres. [28]The levitical singers gathered together from the region about Jerusalem, from the villages of the Netophathites, [29]from Bethgilgal, and from the plains of Geba and Azmaveth (for the singers had built themselves settlements about Jerusalem). [30]The priests and Levites first purified themselves, then they purified the people, the gates, and the wall.

[31]I had the administrators of Judah go up on the wall, and I arranged two great choirs. The first of these proceeded to the right, along the top of the wall, in the direction of the Dung Gate, [32]followed by Hoshaiah and half the administrators of Judah, [33]along with Azariah, Ezra, Meshullam, [34]Judah, Benjamin, Shemaiah, and Jeremiah, [35]priests with the trumpets, and also Zechariah, son of Jonathan, son of Shemaiah, son of Mattaniah, son of Micaiah, son of Zaccur, son of Asaph, [36]and his kinsmen Shemaiah, Azarel, Milalai, Gilalai, Maai, Nethanel, Judah, and Hanani, with the musical instruments of David, the man of God. Ezra the scribe was at their head. [37]At the Fountain Gate they went straight up by the steps of the City of David and continued along the top of the wall above the house of David until they came to the Water Gate on the east.

[38]The second choir proceeded to the left, followed by myself and the other half of the administrators, along the top of the wall past the Oven Tower as far as the Broad Wall, [39]then past the Ephraim Gate to the Mishneh Gate, the Fish Gate, the Tower of Hananel, and the Hundred Tower, as far as the Sheep Gate. They came to a halt at the Prison Gate.

[40]Both choirs took up a position in the house of God; I, too, and half the magistrates with me, [41]together with the priests Eliakim, Maaseiah, Minjamin, Micaiah, Elioenai, Zechariah, Hananiah, with the trumpets, [42]and Maaseiah, Shemaiah, Eleazar, Uzzi, Jehohanan, Malchijah, Elam, and Ezer. The singers were heard under the leadership of Jezrahiah. [43]Great sacrifices were offered on that day, and they rejoiced, for God had given them cause for great rejoicing. The women and the children joined in, and the rejoicing at Jerusalem could be heard from far off.

[44]At that time men were appointed over the chambers set aside for stores, offerings, first fruits, and tithes; in them they were to collect from the fields of the various cities the portions legally assigned to the priests and Levites. For Judah rejoiced in its appointed priests and Levites [45]who carried out the ministry of their God and the ministry of purification (as did the singers and the gatekeepers) in accordance with the prescriptions of David and Solomon, his son. [46]For in the days of David and Asaph, long ago, there were leaders of singers for songs of praise and thanksgiving to God. [47]All Israel, in the days of Zerubbabel and in the days of Nehemiah, gave the singers and the gatekeepers their portions, according to their daily needs. They made their consecrated offering to the Levites, and the Levites made theirs to the descendants of Aaron.

13:1 At that time, when the book of Moses was being read in the hearing of the people, it was found written there: "No Ammonite or Moabite may ever be admitted into the assembly of God; [2]for they did not meet the Israelites with food and water, but they hired Balaam to curse them, though our God turned the curse into a blessing." [3]When they had heard the law, they separated all those of mixed descent from Israel.

Reform in the Temple. [4]Before this, the priest Eliashib, who had been placed in charge of the chambers of the house of our God and who was an associate of Tobiah, [5]had set aside for the latter's use a large chamber in which had previously been stored the grain offerings, incense and vessels, the tithes in grain, wine, and oil allotted to the Levites, singers, and gatekeepers, and the offerings due the priests. [6]During all this time I had not been in Jerusalem, for in the thirty-second year of Artaxerxes, king of Babylon, I had gone back to the king. After a suitable period of time, however, I asked leave of the king [7]and returned to Jerusalem, where I discovered the evil thing that Eliashib had done for Tobiah, in setting aside for him a chamber in the courts of the house of God. [8]This displeased me very much, so I had all of Tobiah's household goods thrown outside the chamber. [9]Then I gave orders to purify the chambers, and I brought back the vessels of the house of God, the grain offerings, and the incense.

[10]I learned, too, that the portions due the Levites were no longer being given, so that the Levites and the singers who should have been carrying out the services had deserted to their own fields. [11]I reprimanded the magistrates, demanding, "Why is the house of God neglected?" Then I brought the Levites together and had them resume their stations. [12]All Judah once more brought in the tithes of grain, wine, and oil to the storerooms. [13]In charge of the storerooms I appointed Shelemiah the priest, Zadok the scribe, and Pedaiah, one of the Levites, together with Hanan, son of Zaccur, son of Mattaniah, as their assistant; for they were considered trustworthy. It was their duty to make the distribution to their kinsmen. [14]Remember this to my credit, my God! Do not forget the good deeds I have done for the house of my God and its services!

Sabbath Observance. [15]In those days I perceived that people in Judah were treading the wine presses on the sabbath; that they were bringing in sheaves of grain, loading them on their donkeys, together with wine, grapes, figs, and every other kind of load, and bringing them to Jerusalem on the sabbath day. I warned them to sell none of these provisions. [16]In Jerusalem itself the Tyrians residing there were importing fish and every other kind of merchandise and selling it to the Judahites on the sabbath. [17]I reprimanded the nobles of Judah, demanding: "What is this evil thing you are doing, profaning the sabbath day? [18]Did not your ancestors act in this same way, with the result that our God has brought all this evil upon us and upon this city? Would you add to the wrath against Israel by once more profaning the sabbath?"

[19]When the shadows were falling on the gates of Jerusalem before the sabbath, I ordered the doors to be closed and prohibited their reopening until after the sabbath. I posted some of my own people at the gates so that no load might enter on the sabbath day. [20]The merchants and sellers of various kinds of merchandise spent the night once or twice outside Jerusalem, [21]but then I warned them: "Why do you spend the night alongside the wall? If you keep this up, I will beat you!" From that time on, they did not return on the sabbath. [22]Then I ordered the Levites to purify themselves and to watch the gates, so that the sabbath day might be kept holy. This, too, remember in my favor, my God, and have mercy on me in accordance with your great mercy!

Mixed Marriages. [23]Also in those days I saw Jews who had married women of Ashdod, Ammon, or Moab. [24]Of their children, half spoke the language of Ashdod, or of one of the other peoples, and none of them knew how to speak the language of Judah. [25]So I reprimanded and cursed them; I beat some of their men and pulled out their hair; and I adjured them by God: "You shall not marry your daughters to their sons nor accept any of their daughters for your sons or for yourselves! [26]Did not Solomon, the king of Israel, sin because of them? Though among the many nations there was no king like him, and though he was beloved of his God and God had made him king over all Israel, yet even he was led into sin by foreign women. ²⁷Must it also be heard of you that you have done this same terrible evil, betraying our God by marrying foreign women?"

²⁸One of the sons of Joiada, son of Eliashib the high priest, was the son-in-law of Sanballat the Horonite! I drove him from my presence. ²⁹Remember against them, my God, how they defiled the priesthood and the covenant of the priesthood and the Levites!

³⁰So I cleansed them of all foreign contamination. I established the various functions for the priests and Levites, so that each had an appointed task. ³¹I also provided for the procurement of wood at stated times and for the first fruits. Remember this in my favor, my God!

☐ MATTHEW 18:21-35

The Parable of the Unforgiving Servant. 18:21 Then Peter approaching asked him, "Lord, if my brother sins against me, how often must I forgive him? As many as seven times?" ²²Jesus answered, "I say to you, not seven times but seventy-seven times. ²³That is why the kingdom of heaven may be likened to a king who decided to settle accounts with his servants. ²⁴When he began the accounting, a debtor was brought before him who owed him a huge amount. ²⁵Since he had no way of paying it back, his master ordered him to be sold, along with his wife, his children, and all his property, in payment of the debt. ²⁶At that, the servant fell down, did him homage, and said, 'Be patient with me, and I will pay you back in full.' ²⁷Moved with compassion the master of that servant let him go and forgave him the loan. ²⁸When that servant had left, he found one of his fellow servants who owed him a much smaller amount. He seized him and started to choke him, demanding, 'Pay back what you owe.' ²⁹Falling to his knees, his fellow servant begged him, 'Be patient with me, and I will pay you back.' ³⁰But he refused. Instead, he had him put in prison until he paid back the debt. ³¹Now when his fellow servants saw what had happened, they were deeply disturbed, and went to their master and reported the whole affair. ³²His master summoned him and said to him, 'You wicked servant! I forgave you your entire debt because you begged me to. ³³Should you not have had pity on your fellow servant, as I had pity on you?' ³⁴Then in anger his master handed him over to the torturers until he should pay back the whole debt. ³⁵So will my heavenly Father do to you, unless each of you forgives his brother from his heart."

May 25

St. Mary Magdalene de Pazzi; St. Bede the Venerable; Pope St. Gregory VII

Never utter in your neighbor's absence what you wouldn't say in his presence.

— St. Mary Magdalene de Pazzi

☐ TOBIT 1–3

Tobit. 1:1 This book tells the story of Tobit, son of Tobiel, son of Hananiel, son of Aduel, son of Gabael, son of Raphael, son of Raguel, of the family of Asiel and the tribe of Naphtali. ²During the days of Shalmaneser, king of the Assyrians, he was taken captive from Thisbe, which is south of Kedesh Naphtali in upper Galilee, above and to the west of Asher, north of Phogor.

His Virtue. ³I, Tobit, have walked all the days of my life on paths of fidelity and righteousness. I performed many charitable deeds for my kindred and my people who had been taken captive with me to Nineveh, in the land of the Assyrians. ⁴When I lived as a young man in my own country, in the land of Israel, the entire tribe of my ancestor Naphtali broke away from the house of David, my ancestor, and from Jerusalem, the city that had been singled out of all Israel's tribes that all Israel might offer sacrifice there. It was the place where the temple, God's dwelling, had been built and consecrated for all generations to come. ⁵All my kindred, as well as the house of Naphtali, my ancestor, used to offer sacrifice on every hilltop in Galilee to the calf that Jeroboam, king of Israel, had made in Dan.

⁶But I alone used to go often to Jerusalem for the festivals, as was prescribed for all Israel by longstanding decree. Bringing with me the first fruits of crops, the firstlings of the flock, the tithes of livestock, and the first shearings of sheep, I used to hasten to Jerusalem ⁷and present them to the priests, Aaron's sons, at the altar. To the Levites ministering in Jerusalem I used to give the tithe of grain, wine, olive oil, pomegranates, figs, and other fruits. Six years in a row, I used to give a second tithe in money, which each year I would go to pay in Jerusalem. ⁸The third-year tithe I gave to orphans, widows, and converts who had joined the Israelites. Every third year I would bring them this offering, and we ate it in keeping with the decree laid down in the Mosaic law concerning it, and according to the commands of Deborah, the mother of my father Tobiel; for my father had died and left me an orphan.

⁹When I reached manhood, I married Anna, a woman of our ancestral family. By her I had a son whom I named Tobiah. ¹⁰Now, after I had been deported to the Assyrians and came as a captive to Nineveh, all my kindred and my people used to eat the food of the Gentiles, ¹¹but I refrained from eating that Gentile food. ¹²Because I was mindful of God with all my heart, ¹³the Most High granted me favor and status with Shalmaneser, so that I became purchasing agent for all his needs. ¹⁴Until he died, I would go to Media to buy goods for him there. I also deposited pouches of silver worth ten talents in trust with my kinsman Gabael, son of Gabri, who lived at Rages, in the land of Media. ¹⁵When Shalmaneser died and his son Sennacherib came to rule in his stead, the roads to Media became unsafe, so I could no longer go to Media.

Courage in Burying the Dead. ¹⁶In the days of Shalmaneser I had performed many charitable deeds for my kindred, members of my people. [17]I would give my bread to the hungry and clothing to the naked. If I saw one of my people who had died and been thrown behind the wall of Nineveh, I used to bury him. [18]Sennacherib returned from Judea, having fled during the days of the judgment enacted against him by the King of Heaven because of the blasphemies he had uttered; whomever he killed I buried. For in his rage he killed many Israelites, but I used to take their bodies away by stealth and bury them. So when Sennacherib looked for them, he could not find them. [19]But a certain Ninevite went and informed the king about me, that I was burying them, and I went into hiding. When I realized that the king knew about me and that I was being hunted to be put to death, I became afraid and took flight. [20]All my property was confiscated; I was left with nothing. All that I had was taken to the king's palace, except for my wife Anna and my son Tobiah.

[21]But forty days did not pass before two of the king's sons assassinated him and fled to the mountains of Ararat. A son of his, Esarhaddon, succeeded him as king. He put Ahiqar, my kinsman Anael's son, in charge of all the credit accounts of his kingdom, and he took control over the entire administration. [22]Then Ahiqar interceded on my behalf, and I returned to Nineveh. Ahiqar had been chief cupbearer, keeper of the signet ring, treasury accountant, and credit accountant under Sennacherib, king of the Assyrians; and Esarhaddon appointed him as Second to himself. He was, in fact, my nephew, of my father's house, and of my own family.

2:1 Thus under King Esarhaddon I returned to my home, and my wife Anna and my son Tobiah were restored to me. Then on our festival of Pentecost, the holy feast of Weeks, a fine dinner was prepared for me, and I reclined to eat. [2]The table was set for me, and the dishes placed before me were many. So I said to my son Tobiah: "Son, go out and bring in whatever poor person you find among our kindred exiled here in Nineveh who may be a sincere worshiper of God to share this meal with me. Indeed, son, I shall wait for you to come back."

[3]Tobiah went out to look for some poor person among our kindred, but he came back and cried, "Father!" I said to him, "Here I am, son." He answered, "Father, one of our people has been murdered! He has been thrown out into the market place, and there he lies strangled." [4]I sprang to my feet, leaving the dinner untouched, carried the dead man from the square, and put him in one of the rooms until sundown, so that I might bury him. [5]I returned and washed and in sorrow ate my food. [6]I remembered the oracle pronounced by the prophet Amos against Bethel:

"I will turn your feasts into mourning,
    and all your songs into dirges."

[7]Then I wept. At sunset I went out, dug a grave, and buried him.

[8]My neighbors mocked me, saying: "Does he have no fear? Once before he was hunted, to be executed for this sort of deed, and he ran away; yet here he is again burying the dead!"

Tobit's Blindness. [9]That same night I washed and went into my courtyard, where I lay down to sleep beside the wall. Because of the heat I left my face uncovered. [10]I did not know that sparrows were perched on the wall above me; their warm droppings settled in my eyes, causing white scales on them. I went to doctors for a cure, but the more they applied ointments, the more my vision was obscured by the white scales, until I was totally blind. For four years I was unable to see, and all my kindred were distressed at my condition. Ahiqar, however, took care of me for two years, until he left for Elam.

[11]At that time my wife Anna worked for hire at weaving cloth, doing the kind

of work women do. [12]When she delivered the material to her employers, they would pay her a wage. On the seventh day of the month of Dystrus, she finished the woven cloth and delivered it to her employers. They paid her the full salary and also gave her a young goat for a meal. [13]On entering my house, the goat began to bleat. So I called to my wife and said: "Where did this goat come from? It was not stolen, was it? Give it back to its owners; we have no right to eat anything stolen!" [14]But she said to me, "It was given to me as a bonus over and above my wages." Yet I would not believe her and told her to give it back to its owners. I flushed with anger at her over this. So she retorted: "Where are your charitable deeds now? Where are your righteous acts? Look! All that has happened to you is well known!"

3:1 Then sad at heart, I groaned and wept aloud. With sobs I began to pray:

Tobit's Prayer for Death. [2]"You are righteous, Lord,
and all your deeds are just;
All your ways are mercy and fidelity;
you are judge of the world.
[3]And now, Lord, be mindful of me
and look with favor upon me.
Do not punish me for my sins,
or for my inadvertent offenses,
or for those of my ancestors.

"They sinned against you,
[4]and disobeyed your
commandments.
So you handed us over to plunder,
captivity, and death,
to become an object lesson, a
byword, and a reproach
in all the nations among whom you
scattered us.

[5]"Yes, your many judgments are right
in dealing with me as my sins,
and those of my ancestors, deserve.

For we have neither kept your
commandments,
nor walked in fidelity before you.

[6]"So now, deal with me as you please;
command my life breath to be taken
from me,
that I may depart from the face of
the earth and become dust.
It is better for me to die than to live,
because I have listened to
undeserved reproaches,
and great is the grief within me.

"Lord, command that I be released
from such anguish;
let me go to my everlasting abode;
Do not turn your face away from
me, Lord.
For it is better for me to die
than to endure so much misery in
life,
and to listen to such reproaches!"

Sarah Falsely Accused. [7]On that very day, at Ecbatana in Media, it so happened that Raguel's daughter Sarah also had to listen to reproaches from one of her father's maids. [8]For she had been given in marriage to seven husbands, but the wicked demon Asmodeus kept killing them off before they could have intercourse with her, as is prescribed for wives. The maid said to her: "You are the one who kills your husbands! Look! You have already been given in marriage to seven husbands, but you do not bear the name of a single one of them. [9]Why do you beat us? Because your husbands are dead? Go, join them! May we never see son or daughter of yours!"

[10]That day Sarah was sad at heart. She went in tears to an upstairs room in her father's house and wanted to hang herself. But she reconsidered, saying to herself: "No! May people never reproach my father and say to him, 'You had only one beloved daughter, but she hanged herself because of her misfortune.' And thus would I bring

my father laden with sorrow in his old age to Hades. It is far better for me not to hang myself, but to beg the Lord that I might die, and no longer have to listen to such reproaches in my lifetime."

[11]At that same time, with hands outstretched toward the window, she implored favor:

Sarah's Prayer for Death. "Blessed are you, merciful God!
Blessed be your holy and honorable name forever!
May all your works forever bless you.
[12]Now to you, Lord, I have turned my face
and have lifted up my eyes.
[13]Bid me to depart from the earth,
never again to listen to such reproaches.

[14]"You know, Master, that I am clean of any defilement with a man.
[15]I have never sullied my own name
or my father's name in the land of my captivity.

"I am my father's only daughter,
and he has no other child to be his heir,

Nor does he have a kinsman or close relative
whose wife I should wait to become.
Seven husbands of mine have already died.
Why then should I live any longer?
But if it does not please you, Lord, to take my life,
look favorably upon me and have pity on me,
that I may never again listen to such reproaches!"

An Answer to Prayer. [16]At that very time, the prayer of both of them was heard in the glorious presence of God. [17]So Raphael was sent to heal them both: to remove the white scales from Tobit's eyes, so that he might again see with his own eyes God's light; and to give Sarah, the daughter of Raguel, as a wife to Tobiah, the son of Tobit, and to rid her of the wicked demon Asmodeus. For it fell to Tobiah's lot to claim her before any others who might wish to marry her.

At that very moment Tobit turned from the courtyard to his house, and Raguel's daughter Sarah came down from the upstairs room.

☐ MATTHEW 19:1-12

Marriage and Divorce. 19:1 When Jesus finished these words, he left Galilee and went to the district of Judea across the Jordan. [2]Great crowds followed him, and he cured them there. [3]Some Pharisees approached him, and tested him, saying, "Is it lawful for a man to divorce his wife for any cause whatever?" [4]He said in reply, "Have you not read that from the beginning the Creator 'made them male and female' [5]and said, 'For this reason a man shall leave his father and mother and be joined to his wife, and the two shall become one flesh'? [6]So they are no longer two, but one flesh. Therefore, what God has joined together, no human being must separate." [7]They said to him, "Then why did Moses command that the man give the woman a bill of divorce and dismiss [her]?" [8]He said to them, "Because of the hardness of your hearts Moses allowed you to divorce your wives, but from the beginning it was not so. [9]I say to you, whoever divorces his wife (unless the marriage is unlawful) and marries another commits adultery." [10][His] disciples said to him, "If that is the case of a man with his wife, it is better not to marry." ¹¹He answered, "Not all can accept [this] word, but only those to whom that is granted. ¹²Some are incapable of marriage because they were born so; some, because they were made so by others; some, because they have renounced marriage for the sake of the kingdom of heaven. Whoever can accept this ought to accept it."

May 26

St. Philip Neri

It is an old custom of the saints of God to have some little prayers ready and to be frequently darting them up to heaven during the day, lifting their minds to God out of the mire of this world. He who adopts this plan will obtain great fruits with little pains.

— St. Philip Neri

☐ TOBIT 4-6

A Father's Instruction. 4:1 That same day Tobit remembered the money he had deposited in trust with Gabael at Rages in Media. ²He thought to himself, "Now that I have asked for death, why should I not call my son Tobiah and let him know about this money before I die?" ³So he called his son Tobiah; and when he came, he said to him: "Son, when I die, give me a decent burial. Honor your mother, and do not abandon her as long as she lives. Do whatever pleases her, and do not grieve her spirit in any way. ⁴Remember, son, how she went through many dangers for you while you were in her womb. When she dies, bury her in the same grave with me.

⁵"Through all your days, son, keep the Lord in mind, and do not seek to sin or to transgress the commandments. Perform righteous deeds all the days of your life, and do not tread the paths of wickedness. ⁶For those who act with fidelity, all who practice righteousness, will prosper in their affairs.

⁷"Give alms from your possessions. Do not turn your face away from any of the poor, so that God's face will not be turned away from you. ⁸Give in proportion to what you own. If you have great wealth, give alms out of your abundance; if you have but little, do not be afraid to give alms even of that little. ⁹You will be storing up a goodly treasure for yourself against the day of adversity. ¹⁰For almsgiving delivers from death and keeps one from entering into Darkness. ¹¹Almsgiving is a worthy offering in the sight of the Most High for all who practice it.

¹²"Be on your guard, son, against every kind of fornication, and above all, marry a woman of your own ancestral family. Do not marry a foreign woman, one who is not of your father's tribe, because we are descendants of the prophets, who were the first to speak the truth. Noah prophesied first, then Abraham, Isaac, and Jacob, our ancestors from the beginning of time. Son, remember that all of them took wives from among their own kindred and were blessed in their children, and that their posterity would inherit the land. ¹³Therefore, son, love your kindred. Do not act arrogantly toward any of them, the sons and daughters of your people, by refusing to take a wife for yourself from among them. For in

arrogance there is ruin and great instability. In idleness there is loss and dire poverty, for idleness is the mother of famine.

[14]"Do not keep with you overnight the wages of those who have worked for you, but pay them at once. If you serve God thus, you will receive your reward. Be on your guard, son, in everything you do; be wise in all that you say and discipline yourself in all your conduct. [15]Do to no one what you yourself hate. Do not drink wine till you become drunk or let drunkenness accompany you on your way.

[16]"Give to the hungry some of your food, and to the naked some of your clothing. Whatever you have left over, give away as alms; and do not let your eye begrudge the alms that you give. [17]Pour out your wine and your bread on the grave of the righteous, but do not share them with sinners.

[18]"Seek counsel from every wise person, and do not think lightly of any useful advice. [19]At all times bless the Lord, your God, and ask him that all your paths may be straight and all your endeavors and plans may prosper. For no other nation possesses good counsel, but it is the Lord who gives all good things. Whomever the Lord chooses to raise is raised; and whomever the Lord chooses to cast down is cast down to the recesses of Hades. So now, son, keep in mind these my commandments, and never let them be erased from your heart.

[20]"Now, I must tell you, son, that I have deposited in trust ten talents of silver with Gabael, the son of Gabri, at Rages in Media. [21]Do not fear, son, that we have lived in poverty. You will have great wealth, if you fear God, avoid all sin, and do what is good before the Lord your God."

The Angel Raphael. 5:1 Then Tobiah replied to his father Tobit: "Everything that you have commanded me, father, I shall do. [2]But how will I be able to get that money from him, since he does not know

me, and I do not know him? What sign can I give him so that he will recognize and trust me, and give me the money? I do not even know the roads to Media, in order to go there." [3]Tobit answered his son Tobiah: "He gave me his bond, and I gave him mine; I divided his into two parts, and each of us took one part; I put one part with the money. It is twenty years since I deposited that money! So, son, find yourself a trustworthy person who will make the journey with you, and we will give him wages when you return; but bring back that money from Gabael while I am still alive."

[4]Tobiah went out to look for someone who would travel with him to Media, someone who knew the way. He went out and found the angel Raphael standing before him (though he did not know that this was an angel of God). [5]Tobiah said to him, "Where do you come from, young man?" He replied, "I am an Israelite, one of your kindred. I have come here to work." Tobiah said to him, "Do you know the way to Media?" [6]"Yes," he replied, "I have been there many times. I know the place well and am acquainted with all the routes. I have often traveled to Media; I used to stay with our kinsman Gabael, who lives at Rages in Media. It is a good two days' journey from Ecbatana to Rages, for Rages is situated in the mountains, but Ecbatana is in the middle of the plain." [7]Tobiah said to him, "Wait for me, young man, till I go in and tell my father; for I need you to make the journey with me. I will pay you your wages." [8]He replied, "Very well, I will wait; but do not be long."

[9]Tobiah went in and informed his father Tobit: "I have found someone of our own Israelite kindred who will go with me!" Tobit said, "Call the man in, so that I may find out from what family and tribe he comes, and whether he is trustworthy enough to travel with you, son."

[10]Tobiah went out to summon him, saying, "Young man, my father is calling for you." When Raphael entered the house,

Tobit greeted him first. He replied, "Joyful greetings to you!" Tobit answered, "What joy is left for me? Here I am, a blind man who cannot see the light of heaven, but must remain in darkness, like the dead who no longer see the light! Though alive, I am among the dead. I can hear people's voices, but I do not see them." The young man said, "Take courage! God's healing is near; so take courage!" Tobit then said: "My son Tobiah wants to go to Media. Can you go with him to show him the way? I will pay you your wages, brother." He answered: "Yes, I will go with him, and I know all the routes. I have often traveled to Media and crossed all its plains so I know well the mountains and all its roads." [11]Tobit asked him, "Brother, tell me, please, from what family and tribe are you?" [12]He replied, "Why? What need do you have for a tribe? Aren't you looking for a hired man?" Tobit replied, "I only want to know, brother, whose son you truly are and what your name is."

[13]He answered, "I am Azariah, son of the great Hananiah, one of your own kindred." [14]Tobit exclaimed: "Welcome! God save you, brother! Do not be provoked with me, brother, for wanting to learn the truth about your family. It turns out that you are a kinsman, from a noble and good line! I knew Hananiah and Nathan, the two sons of the great Shemeliah. They used to go to Jerusalem with me, where we would worship together. They were not led astray; your kindred are good people. You are certainly of good lineage. So welcome!"

[15]Then he added: "For each day I will give you a drachma as wages, as well as expenses for you and for my son. So go with my son, and [16]I will even add a bonus to your wages!" The young man replied: "I will go with him. Do not fear. In good health we will leave you, and in good health we will return to you, for the way is safe." [17]Tobit said, "Blessing be upon you, brother." Then he called his son and said to him: "Son, prepare whatever you need for the journey, and set out with your kinsman. May God in heaven protect you on the way and bring you back to me safe and sound; may his angel accompany you for your safety, son."

Tobiah left to set out on his journey, and he kissed his father and mother. Tobit said to him, "Have a safe journey." [18]But his mother began to weep and she said to Tobit: "Why have you sent my child away? Is he not the staff of our hands, as he goes in and out before us? [19]Do not heap money upon money! Rather relinquish it in exchange for our child! [20]What the Lord has given us to live on is certainly enough for us." [21]Tobit reassured her: "Do not worry! Our son will leave in good health and come back to us in good health. Your own eyes will see the day when he returns to you safe and sound. So, do not worry; do not fear for them, my sister. [22]For a good angel will go with him, his journey will be successful, and he will return in good health." **6:1** Then she stopped weeping.

On the Way to Rages. 6:2 When the young man left home, accompanied by the angel, the dog followed Tobiah out and went along with them. Both journeyed along, and when the first night came, they camped beside the Tigris River. [3]When the young man went down to wash his feet in the Tigris River, a large fish leaped out of the water and tried to swallow his foot. He shouted in alarm. [4]But the angel said to the young man, "Grab the fish and hold on to it!" He seized the fish and hauled it up on dry land. [5]The angel then told him: "Slit the fish open and take out its gall, heart, and liver, and keep them with you; but throw away the other entrails. Its gall, heart, and liver are useful for medicine." [6]After Tobiah had slit the fish open, he put aside the gall, heart, and liver. Then he roasted and ate part of the fish; the rest he salted and kept for the journey.

Raphael's Instructions. Afterward the two of them traveled on together till they drew near to Media. [7]Then the young man asked the angel this question: "Brother Azariah, what medicine is in the fish's heart, liver, and gall?" [8]He answered: "As for the fish's heart and liver, if you burn them to make smoke in the presence of a man or a woman who is afflicted by a demon or evil spirit, any affliction will flee and never return. [9]As for the gall, if you apply it to the eyes of one who has white scales, blowing right into them, sight will be restored."

[10]When they had entered Media and were getting close to Ecbatana, [11]Raphael said to the young man, "Brother Tobiah!" He answered, "Here I am!" Raphael continued, "Tonight we must stay in the house of Raguel, who is a relative of yours. He has a beautiful daughter named Sarah, [12]but no other son or daughter apart from Sarah. Since you are Sarah's closest relative, you more than any other have the right to marry her. Moreover, her father's estate is rightfully yours to inherit. The girl is wise, courageous, and very beautiful; and her father is a good man who loves her dearly." [13]He continued: "You have the right to marry her. So listen to me, brother. Tonight I will speak to her father about the girl so that we may take her as your bride. When we return from Rages, we will have the wedding feast for her. I know that Raguel cannot keep her from you or promise her to another man; he would incur the death penalty as decreed in the Book of Moses. For he knows that you, more than anyone else, have the right to marry his daughter. Now listen to me, brother; we will speak about this girl tonight, so that we may arrange her engagement to you. Then when we return from Rages, we will take her and bring her back with us to your house."

[14]But Tobiah said to Raphael in reply, "Brother Azariah, I have heard that she has already been given in marriage to seven husbands, and that they have died in the bridal chamber. On the very night they approached her, they would die. I have also heard it said that it was a demon that killed them. [15]So now I too am afraid of this demon, because it is in love with her and does not harm her; but it kills any man who wishes to come close to her. I am my father's only child. If I should die, I would bring the life of my father and mother down to their grave in sorrow over me; they have no other son to bury them!"

[16]Raphael said to him: "Do you not remember your father's commands? He ordered you to marry a woman from your own ancestral family. Now listen to me, brother; do not worry about that demon. Take Sarah. I know that tonight she will be given to you as your wife! [17]When you go into the bridal chamber, take some of the fish's liver and the heart, and place them on the embers intended for incense, and an odor will be given off. [18]As soon as the demon smells the odor, it will flee and never again show itself near her. Then when you are about to have intercourse with her, both of you must first get up to pray. Beg the Lord of heaven that mercy and protection be granted you. Do not be afraid, for she was set apart for you before the world existed. You will save her, and she will go with you. And I assume that you will have children by her, and they will be like brothers for you. So do not worry."

When Tobiah heard Raphael's words that she was his kinswoman, and of the lineage of his ancestral house, he loved her deeply, and his heart was truly set on her.

☐ MATTHEW 19:13-30

Blessing of the Children. 19:13 Then children were brought to him that he might lay his hands on them and pray. The disciples rebuked them, [14]but Jesus said, "Let the children come to me, and do not prevent them; for the kingdom of heaven belongs to such as these." [15]After he placed his hands on them, he went away.

The Rich Young Man. [16]Now someone approached him and said, "Teacher, what good must I do to gain eternal life?" [17]He answered him, "Why do you ask me about the good? There is only One who is good. If you wish to enter into life, keep the commandments." [18]He asked him, "Which ones?" And Jesus replied, " 'You shall not kill; you shall not commit adultery; you shall not steal; you shall not bear false witness; [19]honor your father and your mother'; and 'you shall love your neighbor as yourself.' " [20]The young man said to him, "All of these I have observed. What do I still lack?" [21]Jesus said to him, "If you wish to be perfect, go, sell what you have and give to [the] poor, and you will have treasure in heaven. Then come, follow me." [22]When the young man heard this statement, he went away sad, for he had many possessions. [23]Then Jesus said to his disciples, "Amen, I say to you, it will be hard for one who is rich to enter the kingdom of heaven. [24]Again I say to you, it is easier for a camel to pass through the eye of a needle than for one who is rich to enter the kingdom of God." [25]When the disciples heard this, they were greatly astonished and said, "Who then can be saved?" [26]Jesus looked at them and said, "For human beings this is impossible, but for God all things are possible." [27]Then Peter said to him in reply, "We have given up everything and followed you. What will there be for us?" [28]Jesus said to them, "Amen, I say to you that you who have followed me, in the new age, when the Son of Man is seated on his throne of glory, will yourselves sit on twelve thrones, judging the twelve tribes of Israel. [29]And everyone who has given up houses or brothers or sisters or father or mother or children or lands for the sake of my name will receive a hundred times more, and will inherit eternal life. [30]But many who are first will be last, and the last will be first."

May 27

St. Augustine of Canterbury

Nothing seems tiresome or painful when you are working for a Master who pays well, who rewards even a cup of cold water given for love of Him.

— St. Dominic Savio

☐ TOBIT 7-9

At the House of Raguel. 7:1 When they entered Ecbatana, Tobiah said, "Brother Azariah, bring me straight to the house of our kinsman Raguel." So he did, and they came to the house of Raguel, whom they found seated by his courtyard gate. They greeted him first, and he answered, "Many greetings to you, brothers! Welcome! You have come in peace! Now enter in peace!" And he brought them into his house. [2]He said to his wife Edna, "How this young man resembles Tobit, the son of my uncle!" [3]So Edna asked them, saying, "Where are you from, brothers?" They answered, "We are descendants of Naphtali, now captives in Nineveh." [4]She said to them, "Do you know our kinsman Tobit?" They answered her, "Indeed, we do know him!" She asked, "Is he well?" [5]They answered, "Yes, he is alive and well." Then Tobiah said, "He is my father!" [6]Raguel jumped up, kissed him, and broke into tears. [7]Then, finding words, he said, "A blessing upon you, son! You are the son of a good and noble father. What a terrible misfortune that a man so righteous and charitable has been afflicted with blindness!" He embraced his kinsman Tobiah and continued to weep. [8]His wife Edna also wept for Tobit; and their daughter Sarah also began to weep.

Marriage of Tobiah and Sarah. [9]Afterward, Raguel slaughtered a ram from the flock and gave them a warm reception. When they had washed, bathed, and reclined to eat and drink, Tobiah said to Raphael, "Brother Azariah, ask Raguel to give me my kinswoman Sarah." [10]Raguel overheard the words; so he said to the young man: "Eat and drink and be merry tonight, for no man has a greater right to marry my daughter Sarah than you, brother. Besides, not even I have the right to give her to anyone but you, because you are my closest relative. However, son, I must frankly tell you the truth. [11]I have given her in marriage to seven husbands who were kinsmen of ours, and all died on the very night they approached her. But now, son, eat and drink. The Lord will look after you both." Tobiah answered, "I will neither eat nor drink anything here until you settle what concerns me."

Raguel said to him: "I will do it. She is yours as decreed by the Book of Moses. It has been decided in heaven that she be given to you! Take your kinswoman; from now on you are her brother, and she is your sister. She is given to you today and here ever after. May the Lord of heaven prosper you both tonight, son, and grant you mercy and peace." [12]Then Raguel called his daughter Sarah, and she came to him. He took her by the hand and gave her to Tobiah with these words: "Take her according to the law. According to the decree written in the Book of Moses I give her to be your wife. Take her and bring her safely to your father. And may the God of heaven grant both of you a safe journey in peace!" [13]He then called her mother and told her to bring writing materials. He wrote out a copy of a marriage contract stating that he gave Sarah to Tobiah as his wife as decreed by the law of Moses. Her mother brought the material, and he drew up the contract, to which he affixed his seal.

[14]Afterward they began to eat and drink. [15]Later Raguel called his wife Edna and said, "My sister, prepare the other bedroom and bring Sarah there." [16]She went, made the bed in the room, as he had told her, and brought Sarah there. After she had cried over her, she wiped away her tears and said, [17]"Take courage, my daughter! May the Lord of heaven grant you joy in place of your grief! Courage, my daughter!" Then she left.

Expulsion of the Demon. 8:1 When they had finished eating and drinking, they wanted to retire. So they brought the young man out and led him to the bedroom. [2]Tobiah, mindful of Raphael's instructions, took the fish's liver and heart from the bag where he had them, and put them on the embers intended for incense. [3]The odor of the fish repulsed the demon, and it fled to the upper regions of Egypt; Raphael went in pursuit of it and there bound it hand and foot. Then Raphael returned immediately.

[4]When Sarah's parents left the bedroom and closed the door behind them, Tobiah

rose from bed and said to his wife, "My sister, come, let us pray and beg our Lord to grant us mercy and protection." ⁵She got up, and they started to pray and beg that they might be protected. He began with these words:

"Blessed are you, O God of our
        ancestors;
    blessed be your name forever and
        ever!
Let the heavens and all your creation
    bless you forever.
⁶You made Adam, and you made his
    wife Eve
    to be his helper and support;
    and from these two the human race
        has come.
You said, 'It is not good for the man to
    be alone;
    let us make him a helper like
        himself.'
⁷Now, not with lust,
    but with fidelity I take this
        kinswoman as my wife.
Send down your mercy on me and on
    her,
    and grant that we may grow old
        together.
    Bless us with children."

⁸They said together, "Amen, amen!" ⁹Then they went to bed for the night.

But Raguel got up and summoned his servants. They went out with him and dug a grave, ¹⁰for he said, "Perhaps Tobiah will die; then we would be a laughingstock and an object of mockery." ¹¹When they had finished digging the grave, Raguel went back into the house and called his wife, ¹²saying, "Send one of the maids in to see whether he is alive. If he has died, let us bury him without anyone knowing about it." ¹³They sent the maid, lit a lamp, and opened the bedroom door; she went in and found them sleeping together. ¹⁴The maid came out and told them that Tobiah was alive, and that nothing was wrong. ¹⁵Then they praised the God of heaven in these words:

"Blessed are you, God, with every pure
    blessing!
    Let all your chosen ones bless you
        forever!
¹⁶Blessed are you, for you have made
    me happy;
    what I feared did not happen.
Rather you have dealt with us
    according to your abundant mercy.
¹⁷Blessed are you, for you have shown
    mercy
    toward two only children.
Grant them, Master, mercy and
    protection,
    and bring their lives to fulfillment
    with happiness and mercy."

¹⁸Then Raguel told his servants to fill in the grave before dawn.

Wedding Feast. ¹⁹He asked his wife to bake many loaves of bread; he himself went out to the herd and brought two steers and four rams, which he ordered to be slaughtered. So they began to prepare the feast. ²⁰He summoned Tobiah and said to him, "For fourteen days you shall not stir from here, but shall remain here eating and drinking with me; you shall bring joy to my daughter's afflicted spirit. ²¹Now take half of what I own here; go back in good health to your father. The other half will be yours when I and my wife die. Take courage, son! I am your father, and Edna is your mother; we belong to you and to your sister both now and forever. So take courage, son!"

The Money Recovered. 9:1 Then Tobiah called Raphael and said to him: ²"Brother Azariah, take along with you from here four servants and two camels and travel to Rages. Go to Gabael's house and give him this bond. Get the money and then bring him along with you to the wedding celebration. ³For you know that my father will be counting the days. If I should delay even by a single day, I would cause him intense grief. [4]You have witnessed the oath that Raguel has sworn; I cannot violate his oath." [5]So Raphael, together with the four servants and two camels, traveled to Rages in Media, where they stayed at Gabael's house. Raphael gave Gabael his bond and told him about Tobit's son Tobiah, that he had married and was inviting him to the wedding celebration. Gabael got up and counted out for him the moneybags with their seals, and they packed them on the camels.

[6]The following morning they both got an early start and traveled to the wedding celebration. When they entered Raguel's house, they found Tobiah reclining at table. He jumped up and greeted Gabael, who wept and blessed him, exclaiming: "Good and noble child, son of a good and noble, righteous and charitable man, may the Lord bestow a heavenly blessing on you and on your wife, and on your wife's father and mother. Blessed be God, because I have seen the very image of my cousin Tobit!"

☐ MATTHEW 20:1-16

The Workers in the Vineyard. 20:1 "The kingdom of heaven is like a landowner who went out at dawn to hire laborers for his vineyard. [2]After agreeing with them for the usual daily wage, he sent them into his vineyard. [3]Going out about nine o'clock, he saw others standing idle in the marketplace, [4]and he said to them, 'You too go into my vineyard, and I will give you what is just.' [5]So they went off. [And] he went out again around noon, and around three o'clock, and did likewise. [6]Going out about five o'clock, he found others standing around, and said to them, 'Why do you stand here idle all day?' [7]They answered, 'Because no one has hired us.' He said to them, 'You too go into my vineyard.' [8]When it was evening the owner of the vineyard said to his foreman, 'Summon the laborers and give them their pay, beginning with the last and ending with the first.' [9]When those who had started about five o'clock came, each received the usual daily wage. [10]So when the first came, they thought that they would receive more, but each of them also got the usual wage. [11]And on receiving it they grumbled against the landowner, [12]saying, 'These last ones worked only one hour, and you have made them equal to us, who bore the day's burden and the heat.' [13]He said to one of them in reply, 'My friend, I am not cheating you. Did you not agree with me for the usual daily wage? [14]Take what is yours and go. What if I wish to give this last one the same as you? [15][Or] am I not free to do as I wish with my own money? Are you envious because I am generous?' [16]Thus, the last will be first, and the first will be last."

May 28

To argue over who is more noble is nothing more than to dispute whether dirt is better for making bricks or for making mortar. O my God! What an insignificant matter!

— St. Teresa of Ávila

☐ TOBIT 10-14

Anxiety of the Parents. 10:1 Meanwhile, day by day, Tobit was keeping track of the time Tobiah would need to go and to return. When the number of days was reached and his son did not appear, [2]he said, "Could it be that he has been detained there? Or perhaps Gabael has died, and there is no one to give him the money?" [3]And he began to grieve. [4]His wife Anna said, "My son has perished and is no longer among the living!" And she began to weep aloud and to wail over her son: [5]"Alas, child, light of my eyes, that I have let you make this journey!" [6]But Tobit kept telling her: "Be still, do not worry, my sister; he is safe! Probably they have to take care of some unexpected business there. The man who is traveling with him is trustworthy and one of our kindred. So do not grieve over him, my sister. He will be here soon." [7]But she retorted, "You be still, and do not try to deceive me! My son has perished!" She would rush out and keep watch every day at the road her son had taken. She ate nothing. After the sun had set, she would go back home to wail and cry the whole night through, getting no sleep at all.

Departure from Ecbatana. Now when the fourteen days of the wedding celebration, which Raguel had sworn to hold for his daughter, had come to an end, Tobiah went to him and said: "Send me off, now, since I know that my father and mother do not believe they will ever see me again. So I beg you, father, let me depart and go back to my own father. I have already told you how I left him." [8]Raguel said to Tobiah: "Stay, son, stay with me. I am sending messengers to your father Tobit, and they will give him news of you." [9]But Tobiah insisted, "No, I beg you to send me back to my father."

[10]Raguel then promptly handed over to Tobiah his wife Sarah, together with half of all his property: male and female slaves, oxen and sheep, donkeys and camels, clothing, money, and household goods. [11]He saw them safely off. Embracing Tobiah, he said to him: "Farewell, son. Have a safe journey. May the Lord of heaven grant prosperity to you and to your wife Sarah. And may I see children of yours before I die!" [12]Then he said to his daughter Sarah, "My daughter, honor your father-in-law and your mother-in-law, because from now on they are as much your parents as the ones who brought you into the world. Go in peace, daughter; let me hear a good report about you as long as I live." Finally he said good-bye to them and let them go.

Edna also said to Tobiah: "My child and beloved kinsman, may the Lord bring you back safely, and may I live long enough to see children of you and of my daughter Sarah before I die. Before the Lord, I entrust my daughter to your care. Never cause her grief all the days of your life. Go in peace, son. From now on I am your mother, and Sarah is your sister. Together may we all prosper throughout the days of our lives." She kissed them both and saw them safely off.

[13]Tobiah left Raguel, full of happiness and joy, and he blessed the Lord of heaven and earth, the King of all, for making his journey so successful. Finally he blessed

Raguel and his wife Edna, and added, "I have been commanded by the Lord to honor you all the days of your life!"

Homeward Journey. 11:1 As they drew near to Kaserin, which is opposite Nineveh, [2]Raphael said: "You know how we left your father. [3]Let us hurry on ahead of your wife to prepare the house while they are still on the way." [4]So both went on ahead together, and Raphael said to him, "Take the gall in your hand!" And the dog ran along behind them.

[5]Meanwhile, Anna sat watching the road by which her son was to come. [6]When she saw him coming, she called to his father, "Look, your son is coming, and the man who traveled with him!"

[7]Raphael said to Tobiah before he came near to his father: "I know that his eyes will be opened. [8]Apply the fish gall to his eyes, and the medicine will make the white scales shrink and peel off from his eyes; then your father will have sight again and will see the light of day."

Sight Restored. [9]Then Anna ran up to her son, embraced him, and said to him, "Now that I have seen you again, son, I am ready to die!" And she sobbed aloud. [10]Tobit got up and stumbled out through the courtyard gate to meet his son. Tobiah went up to him [11]with the fish gall in his hand and blew into his eyes. Holding him firmly, he said, "Courage, father." Then he applied the medicine to his eyes, and it made them sting. [12, 13]Tobiah used both hands to peel the white scales from the corners of his eyes. Tobit saw his son and threw his arms around him. [14]Weeping, he exclaimed, "I can see you, son, the light of my eyes!" Then he prayed,

"Blessed be God,
blessed be his great name,
and blessed be all his holy angels.
May his great name be with us,
and blessed be all the angels
throughout all the ages.

[15]God it was who afflicted me,
and God who has had mercy on me.
Now I see my son Tobiah!"

Then Tobit went back in, rejoicing and praising God with full voice. Tobiah related to his father how his journey had been a success; that he had brought back the money; and that he had married Raguel's daughter Sarah, who was about to arrive, for she was near the gate of Nineveh.

[16]Rejoicing and blessing God, Tobit went out to the gate of Nineveh to meet his daughter-in-law. When the people of Nineveh saw him coming, walking along briskly, with no one leading him by the hand, they were amazed. [17]Before them all Tobit proclaimed how God had shown mercy to him and opened his eyes. When Tobit came up to Sarah, the wife of his son Tobiah, he blessed her and said: "Welcome, my daughter! Blessed be your God for bringing you to us, daughter! Blessed are your father and your mother. Blessed be my son Tobiah, and blessed be you, daughter! Welcome to your home with blessing and joy. Come in, daughter!" That day there was joy for all the Jews who lived in Nineveh. [18]Ahiqar and his nephew Nadin were also on hand to rejoice with Tobit. Tobiah's wedding feast was celebrated with joy for seven days, and many gifts were given to him.

Raphael's Wages. 12:1 When the wedding celebration came to an end, Tobit called his son Tobiah and said to him, "Son, see to it that you pay his wages to the man who made the journey with you and give him a bonus too." [2]Tobiah said: "Father, how much shall I pay him? It would not hurt to give him half the wealth he brought back with me. [3]He led me back safe and sound, healed my wife, brought the money back with me, and healed you. How much should I pay him?" [4]Tobit answered, "It is only fair, son, that he should receive half of all that he brought back." ⁵So Tobiah called Raphael and said, "Take as your wages half of all that you have brought back, and farewell!"

Exhortation. ⁶Raphael called the two of them aside privately and said to them: "Bless God and give him thanks before all the living for the good things he has done for you, by blessing and extolling his name in song. Proclaim before all with due honor the deeds of God, and do not be slack in thanking him. ⁷A king's secret should be kept secret, but one must declare the works of God and give thanks with due honor. Do good, and evil will not overtake you. ⁸Prayer with fasting is good. Almsgiving with righteousness is better than wealth with wickedness. It is better to give alms than to store up gold, ⁹for almsgiving saves from death, and purges all sin. Those who give alms will enjoy a full life, ¹⁰but those who commit sin and do evil are their own worst enemies.

Raphael's Identity. ¹¹"I shall now tell you the whole truth and conceal nothing at all from you. I have already said to you, 'A king's secret should be kept secret, but one must declare the works of God with due honor.' ¹²Now when you, Tobit, and Sarah prayed, it was I who presented the record of your prayer before the Glory of the Lord; and likewise whenever you used to bury the dead. ¹³When you did not hesitate to get up and leave your dinner in order to go and bury that dead man, ¹⁴I was sent to put you to the test. At the same time, however, God sent me to heal you and your daughter-in-law Sarah. ¹⁵I am Raphael, one of the seven angels who stand and serve before the Glory of the Lord."

¹⁶Greatly shaken, the two of them fell prostrate in fear. ¹⁷But Raphael said to them: "Do not fear; peace be with you! Bless God now and forever. ¹⁸As for me, when I was with you, I was not acting out of any favor on my part, but by God's will. So bless God every day; give praise with song. ¹⁹Even though you saw me eat and drink, I did not eat or drink anything; what you were seeing was a vision. ²⁰So now bless the Lord on earth and give thanks to God. Look, I am ascending to the one who sent me. Write down all that has happened to you." And he ascended. ²¹They stood up but were no longer able to see him. ²²They kept blessing God and singing his praises, and they continued to give thanks for these marvelous works that God had done, because an angel of God appeared to them.

13:1 Then Tobit spoke and composed a song of joyful praise; he said:

Blessed be God who lives forever,
    because his kingship lasts for all ages.
²For he afflicts and shows mercy,
    casts down to the depths of Hades,
    brings up from the great abyss.
What is there that can snatch from his hand?

³Give thanks to him, you Israelites, in the presence of the nations,
    for though he has scattered you among them,
⁴even there recount his greatness.
Exalt him before every living being,
    because he is your Lord, and he is your God,
    our Father and God forever and ever!
⁵He will afflict you for your iniquities,
    but will have mercy on all of you.
He will gather you from all the nations among whom you have been scattered.

⁶When you turn back to him with all your heart,
    and with all your soul do what is right before him,
Then he will turn to you,
    and will hide his face from you no longer.

Now consider what he has done for
   you,
   and give thanks with full voice.
Bless the Lord of righteousness,
   and exalt the King of the ages.

In the land of my captivity I give thanks,
   and declare his power and majesty
      to a sinful nation.
According to your heart do what is
   right before him:
   perhaps there will be pardon for you.

⁷As for me, I exalt my God,
   my soul exalts the King of
      heaven,
   and rejoices all the days of my life.
Let all sing praise to his greatness,
   ⁸let all speak and give thanks in
      Jerusalem.

⁹Jerusalem, holy city,
   he will afflict you for the works of
      your hands,
   but will again pity the children of
      the righteous.
¹⁰Give thanks to the Lord with
   righteousness,
   and bless the King of the ages,
   so that your tabernacle may be
      rebuilt in you with joy.
May he gladden within you all who
   are captives;
   may he cherish within you all who
      are distressed
   for all generations to come.

¹¹A bright light will shine to the limits
   of the earth.
   Many nations will come to you
      from afar,
And inhabitants of all the ends of the
   earth
   to your holy name,
Bearing in their hands gifts for the
   King of heaven.
Generation after generation will offer
   joyful worship in you;

your name will be great forever
   and ever.
¹²Cursed be all who despise you and
   revile you;
   cursed be all who hate you and
      speak a harsh word against
      you;
   cursed be all who destroy you
   and pull down your walls,
And all who overthrow your towers
   and set fire to your homes.
But blessed forever be all those who
   respect you.

¹³Go, then, rejoice and exult over the
   children of the righteous,
   for they will all be gathered
      together
   and will bless the Lord of the ages.
¹⁴Happy are those who love you,
   and happy are those who rejoice
      in your peace.
Happy too are all who grieve
   over all your afflictions,
For they will rejoice over you
   and behold all your joy forever.

¹⁵My soul, bless the Lord, the great
   King;
   ¹⁶for Jerusalem will be rebuilt as his
      house forever.
Happy too will I be if a remnant of my
   offspring survives
   to see your glory and to give thanks
      to the King of heaven!

The gates of Jerusalem will be built
   with sapphire and emerald,
   and all your walls with precious
      stones.
The towers of Jerusalem will be built
   with gold,
   and their battlements with purest
      gold.
¹⁷The streets of Jerusalem will be
   paved
   with rubies and stones of Ophir;

[18]The gates of Jerusalem will sing
   hymns of gladness,
and all its houses will cry out,
   Hallelujah!
Blessed be the God of Israel for all ages!
For in you the blessed will bless the
   holy name forever and ever.

Parting Advice. 14:1 So the words of Tobit's hymn of praise came to an end. Tobit died in peace at the age of a hundred and twelve and was buried with honor in Nineveh. [2]He was fifty-eight years old when he lost his eyesight, and after he recovered it he lived in prosperity, giving alms; he continued to fear God and give thanks to the divine Majesty.

[3]As he was dying, he summoned his son Tobiah and Tobiah's seven sons, and commanded him, "Son, take your children [4]and flee into Media, for I believe God's word that Nahum spoke against Nineveh. It will all happen and will overtake Assyria and Nineveh; indeed all that was said by Israel's prophets whom God sent will come to pass. Not one of all their words will remain unfulfilled, but everything will take place in the time appointed for it. So it will be safer in Media than in Assyria or Babylon. For I know and believe that whatever God has said will be accomplished. It will happen, and not a single word of the prophecies will fail.

As for our kindred who dwell in the land of Israel, they will all be scattered and taken into captivity from the good land. All the land of Israel will become a wilderness; even Samaria and Jerusalem will be a wilderness! For a time, the house of God will be desolate and will be burned. [5]But God will again have mercy on them and bring them back to the land of Israel. They will build the house again, but it will not be like the first until the era when the appointed times will be completed. Afterward all of them will return from their captivity, and they will rebuild Jerusalem with due honor. In it the house of God will also be rebuilt, just as the prophets of Israel said of it. [6]All the nations of the world will turn and reverence God in truth; all will cast away their idols, which have deceitfully led them into error. [7]They will bless the God of the ages in righteousness. All the Israelites truly mindful of God, who are to be saved in those days, will be gathered together and will come to Jerusalem; in security will they dwell forever in the land of Abraham, which will be given to them. Those who love God sincerely will rejoice, but those who commit sin and wickedness will disappear completely from the land.

[8, 9]"Now, my children, I give you this command: serve God sincerely and do what is pleasing in his sight; you must instruct your children to do what is right and to give alms, to be mindful of God and at all times to bless his name sincerely and with all their strength. Now, as for you, son, leave Nineveh; do not stay here. [10]The day you bury your mother next to me, do not even stay overnight within the confines of the city. For I see that there is much wickedness in it, and much treachery is practiced in it, and people are not ashamed. See, my son, all that Nadin did to Ahiqar, the very one who reared him. Was not Ahiqar brought down alive into the earth? Yet God made Nadin's disgraceful crime rebound against him. Ahiqar came out again into the light, but Nadin went into the everlasting darkness, for he had tried to kill Ahiqar. Because Ahiqar had given alms he escaped from the deadly trap Nadin had set for him. But Nadin fell into the deadly trap himself, and it destroyed him. [11]So, my children, see what almsgiving does, and also what wickedness does—it kills! But now my spirit is about to leave me."

Death of Tobit and Tobiah. They laid him on his bed, and he died; and he was buried with honor. [12]When Tobiah's mother died, he buried her next to his father. He then departed with his wife and children for Media, where he settled in Ecbatana with his father-in-law Raguel. [13]He took respectful care of his aging father-in-law and mother-in-law; and he buried them at Ecbatana in Media. Then he inherited Raguel's estate as well as that of his father Tobit. [14]He died highly respected at the age of one hundred seventeen. [15]But before he died, he saw and heard of the destruction of Nineveh. He saw the inhabitants of the city being led captive into Media by Cyaxares, the king of Media. Tobiah blessed God for all that he had done against the Ninevites and Assyrians. Before dying he rejoiced over Nineveh, and he blessed the Lord God forever and ever.

☐ MATTHEW 20:17-28

The Third Prediction of the Passion. 20:17 As Jesus was going up to Jerusalem, he took the twelve [disciples] aside by themselves, and said to them on the way, [18]"Behold, we are going up to Jerusalem, and the Son of Man will be handed over to the chief priests and the scribes, and they will condemn him to death, [19]and hand him over to the Gentiles to be mocked and scourged and crucified, and he will be raised on the third day."

The Request of James and John. [20]Then the mother of the sons of Zebedee approached him with her sons and did him homage, wishing to ask him for something. [21]He said to her, "What do you wish?" She answered him, "Command that these two sons of mine sit, one at your right and the other at your left, in your kingdom." [22]Jesus said in reply, "You do not know what you are asking. Can you drink the cup that I am going to drink?" They said to him, "We can." [23]He replied, "My cup you will indeed drink, but to sit at my right and at my left [, this] is not mine to give but is for those for whom it has been prepared by my Father." [24]When the ten heard this, they became indignant at the two brothers. [25]But Jesus summoned them and said, "You know that the rulers of the Gentiles lord it over them, and the great ones make their authority over them felt. [26]But it shall not be so among you. Rather, whoever wishes to be great among you shall be your servant; [27]whoever wishes to be first among you shall be your slave. [28]Just so, the Son of Man did not come to be served but to serve and to give his life as a ransom for many."

May 29

Man, blinded and bowed, sits in darkness and cannot see the light of heaven unless grace with righteousness comes to his aid.
— St. Bonaventure

☐ JUDITH 1-3

Nebuchadnezzar Against Arphaxad. 1:1 It was the twelfth year of the reign of Nebuchadnezzar, who ruled over the Assyrians in the great city of Nineveh. At that time Arphaxad was ruling over the Medes in Ecbatana. [2]Around Ecbatana he built a wall of hewn stones, three cubits thick and six cubits long. He made the walls seventy cubits high and fifty cubits wide. [3]At its gates he raised towers one hundred cubits high with foundations sixty cubits wide. [4]He made its gates seventy cubits high and forty cubits wide to allow passage of his mighty forces, with his infantry in formation. [5]At that time King Nebuchadnezzar waged war against King Arphaxad in the vast plain that borders Ragau. [6]Rallying to him were all who lived in the hill country, all who lived along the Euphrates, the Tigris, and the Hydaspes, as well as Arioch, king of the Elamites, in the plains. Thus many nations joined the ranks of the Chelodites.

[7]Then Nebuchadnezzar, king of the Assyrians, contacted all the inhabitants of Persia and all who lived in the west, the inhabitants of Cilicia and Damascus, Lebanon and Antilebanon, and all who lived along the seacoast, [8]the peoples of Carmel, Gilead, Upper Galilee, and the vast plain of Esdraelon, [9]and all in Samaria and its cities, and west of the Jordan as far as Jerusalem, Bethany, Chelous, Kadesh, and the river of Egypt; Tahpanhes, Raamses, all the land of Goshen, [10]Tanis, Memphis and beyond, and all the inhabitants of Egypt as far as the borders of Ethiopia.

[11]But all the inhabitants of the whole land made light of the summons of Nebuchadnezzar, king of the Assyrians, and would not join him in the war. They were not afraid of him, since he was only a single opponent. So they sent back his envoys empty-handed and disgraced. [12]Then Nebuchadnezzar fell into a violent rage against all the land, and swore by his throne and his kingdom that he would take revenge on all the territories of Cilicia, Damascus, and Syria, and would destroy with his sword all the inhabitants of Moab, Ammon, the whole of Judea, and all those living in Egypt as far as the coasts of the two seas.

Defeat of Arphaxad. [13]In the seventeenth year he mustered his forces against King Arphaxad and was victorious in his campaign. He routed the whole force of Arphaxad, his entire cavalry, and all his chariots, [14]and took possession of his cities. He pressed on to Ecbatana, took its towers, sacked its marketplaces, and turned its glory into shame. [15]He captured Arphaxad in the mountains of Ragau, ran him through with spears, and utterly destroyed him once and for all. [16]Then he returned to Nineveh with all his consolidated forces, a very great multitude of warriors; and there he and his forces relaxed and feasted for one hundred and twenty days.

Revenge Planned Against the Western Nations. 2:1 In the eighteenth year, on the twenty-second day of the first month, there was a discussion in the palace of Nebuchadnezzar, king of the Assyrians, about taking revenge on all the land, as he had threatened. [2]He summoned all his attendants and officers, laid before them his secret plan, and with his own lips recounted in full detail the wickedness of all the land. [3]They decided to destroy all who had refused to obey the order he had issued.

[4]When he had fully recounted his plan, Nebuchadnezzar, king of the Assyrians, summoned Holofernes, the ranking general of his forces, second only to himself in command, and said to him: [5]"Thus says the great king, the lord of all the earth: Go forth from my presence, take with you men of proven valor, one hundred and twenty thousand infantry and twelve thousand cavalry, [6]and proceed against all the land of the west, because they disobeyed the order I issued. [7]Tell them to have earth and water ready, for I will come against them in my wrath; I will cover all the land with the feet of my soldiers, to whom I will deliver them as spoils. [8]Their wounded will fill their ravines and wadies, the swelling river will be choked with their dead; [9]and I will deport them as exiles to the very ends of the earth.

[10]"Go before me and take possession of all their territories for me. If they surrender to you, guard them for me until the day of their sentencing. [11]As for those who

disobey, show them no mercy, but deliver them up to slaughter and plunder in all the land you occupy. [12]For as I live, and by the strength of my kingdom, what I have spoken I will accomplish by my own hand. [13]Do not disobey a single one of the orders of your lord; fulfill them exactly as I have commanded you, and do it without delay."

Campaigns of Holofernes. [14]So Holofernes left the presence of his lord, and summoned all the commanders, generals, and officers of the Assyrian forces. [15]He mustered one hundred and twenty thousand picked troops, as his lord had commanded, and twelve thousand mounted archers, [16]and drew them up as a vast force organized for battle. [17]He took along a very large number of camels, donkeys, and mules for carrying their supplies; innumerable sheep, cattle, and goats for their food; [18]abundant provisions for each man, and much gold and silver from the royal palace.

[19]Then he and all his forces set out on their expedition in advance of King Nebuchadnezzar, to overrun all the lands of the western region with their chariots, cavalry, and picked infantry. [20]A huge, irregular force, too many to count, like locusts, like the dust of the earth, went along with them.

[21]After a three-day march from Nineveh, they reached the plain of Bectileth, and camped opposite Bectileth near the mountains to the north of Upper Cilicia. [22]From there Holofernes took all his forces, the infantry, cavalry, and chariots, and marched into the hill country. [23]He devastated Put and Lud, and plundered all the Rassisites and the Ishmaelites on the border of the wilderness toward the south of the Chelleans. [24]Then, following the Euphrates, he went through Mesopotamia, and battered down every fortified city along the Wadi Abron, until he reached the sea. [25]He seized the territory of Cilicia, and cut down everyone who resisted him. Then he proceeded to the southern borders of Japheth, toward Arabia. [26]He surrounded all the Midianites, burned their tents, and sacked their encampments. [27]Descending to the plain of Damascus at the time of the wheat harvest, he set fire to all their fields, destroyed their flocks and herds, looted their cities, devastated their plains, and put all their young men to the sword.

[28]Fear and dread of him fell upon all the inhabitants of the coastland, upon those in Sidon and Tyre, and those who dwelt in Sur and Ocina, and the inhabitants of Jamnia. Those in Azotus and Ascalon also feared him greatly.

Submission of the Vassal Nations. 3:1 So they sent messengers to him to sue for peace in these words: [2]"We, the servants of Nebuchadnezzar the great king, lie prostrate before you; do with us as you will. [3]See, our dwellings and all our land and every wheat field, our flocks and herds, and all our encampments are at your disposal; make use of them as you please. [4]Our cities and their inhabitants are also at your service; come and deal with them as you see fit."

[5]After the spokesmen had reached Holofernes and given him this message, [6]he went down with his forces to the seacoast, stationed garrisons in the fortified cities, and took selected men from them as auxiliaries. [7]The people of these cities and all the inhabitants of the countryside received him with garlands and dancing to the sound of timbrels. [8]But he devastated their whole territory and cut down their sacred groves, for he was allowed to destroy all the gods of the land, so that every nation might worship only Nebuchadnezzar, and all their tongues and tribes should invoke him as a god. [9]At length Holofernes reached Esdraelon in the neighborhood of Dothan, the approach to the main ridge of the Judean mountains; [10]he set up his camp between Geba and Scythopolis, and stayed there a whole month to replenish all the supplies of his forces.

☐ MATTHEW 20:29-34

The Healing of Two Blind Men. 20:29 As they left Jericho, a great crowd followed him. [30]Two blind men were sitting by the roadside, and when they heard that Jesus was passing by, they cried out, "[Lord,] Son of David, have pity on us!" [31]The crowd warned them to be silent, but they called out all the more, "Lord, Son of David, have pity on us!" [32]Jesus stopped and called them and said, "What do you want me to do for you?" [33]They answered him, "Lord, let our eyes be opened." [34]Moved with pity, Jesus touched their eyes. Immediately they received their sight, and followed him.

May 30

St. Joan of Arc

About Jesus Christ and the Church, I simply know that they are just one thing, and we shouldn't complicate the matter.

— ST. JOAN OF ARC

☐ JUDITH 4-6

Israel Prepares for War. 4:1 When the Israelites who lived in Judea heard of all that Holofernes, the ranking general of Nebuchadnezzar king of the Assyrians, had done to the nations, and how he had looted all their shrines and utterly destroyed them, [2]they were in very great fear of him, and greatly alarmed for Jerusalem and the temple of the Lord, their God. [3]Now, they had only recently returned from exile, and all the people of Judea were just now reunited, and the vessels, the altar, and the temple had been purified from profanation. [4]So they sent word to the whole region of Samaria, to Kona, Beth-horon, Belmain, and Jericho, to Choba and Aesora, and to the valley of Salem. [5]The people there secured all the high hilltops, fortified the villages on them, and since their fields had recently been harvested, stored up provisions in preparation for war.

[6]Joakim, who was high priest in Jerusalem in those days, wrote to the inhabitants of Bethulia and Betomesthaim, which is opposite Esdraelon, facing the plain near Dothan, [7]and instructed them to keep firm hold of the mountain passes, since these offered access to Judea. It would be easy to stop those advancing, as the approach was only wide enough for two at a time. [8]The Israelites carried out the orders given them by Joakim, the high priest, and the senate of the whole people of Israel, in session in Jerusalem.

Israel at Prayer. [9]All the men of Israel cried to God with great fervor and humbled themselves. [10]They, along with their wives, and children, and domestic animals, every resident alien, hired worker, and purchased slave, girded themselves with sackcloth. [11]And all the Israelite men, women, and children who lived in Jerusalem fell prostrate in front of the temple and sprinkled ashes on their heads, spreading out their sackcloth before the Lord. [12]The altar, too, they draped in sackcloth; and with one accord they cried out fervently to the God of Israel not to allow their children to be seized, their wives to be taken captive, the cities of their inheritance to be ruined, or the sanctuary to be profaned and mocked for the nations to gloat over.

¹³The Lord heard their cry and saw their distress. The people continued fasting for many days throughout Judea and before the sanctuary of the Lord Almighty in Jerusalem. ¹⁴Also girded with sackcloth, Joakim, the high priest, and all the priests in attendance before the Lord, and those who ministered to the Lord offered the daily burnt offering, the votive offerings, and the voluntary offerings of the people. ¹⁵With ashes upon their turbans, they cried to the Lord with all their strength to look with favor on the whole house of Israel.

Achior in the Assyrian War Council. 5:1

It was reported to Holofernes, the ranking general of the Assyrian forces, that the Israelites were ready for battle, had blocked the mountain passes, fortified the high hilltops, and placed roadblocks in the plains. ²In great anger he summoned all the rulers of Moab, the governors of Ammon, and all the satraps of the coastland ³and said to them: "Now tell me, you Canaanites, what sort of people is this that lives in the hill country? Which cities do they inhabit? How large is their force? In what does their power and strength consist? Who has set himself up as their king and the leader of their army? ⁴Why have they alone of all the inhabitants of the west refused to come out to meet me?"

⁵Then Achior, the leader of all the Ammonites, said to him: "My lord, please listen to a report from your servant. I will tell you the truth about this people that lives in the hill country near here. No lie shall escape your servant's lips.

⁶"These people are descendants of the Chaldeans. ⁷They formerly lived in Mesopotamia, for they did not wish to follow the gods of their ancestors who were in the land of the Chaldeans. ⁸Since they abandoned the way of their ancestors, and worshiped the God of heaven, the God whom they had come to know, their ancestors expelled them from the presence of their gods. So they fled to Mesopotamia and lived there a long time. ⁹Their God told them to leave the place where they were living and go to the land of Canaan. Here they settled, and grew very rich in gold, silver, and a great abundance of livestock. ¹⁰Later, when famine had gripped the land of Canaan, they went down into Egypt. They stayed there as long as they found sustenance and there they grew into such a great multitude that the number of their people could not be counted. ¹¹The king of Egypt, however, rose up against them, and shrewdly forced them to labor at brickmaking; they were oppressed and made into slaves. ¹²But they cried to their God, and he struck the whole land of Egypt with plagues for which there was no remedy. So the Egyptians drove them out. ¹³Then God dried up the Red Sea before them ¹⁴and led them along the route to Sinai and Kadesh-barnea. They drove out all the inhabitants of the wilderness ¹⁵and settled in the land of the Amorites. By their strength they destroyed all the Heshbonites, crossed the Jordan, and took possession of all the hill country. ¹⁶They drove out before them the Canaanites, the Perizzites, the Jebusites, the Shechemites, and all the Gergesites, and they lived there a long time.

¹⁷"As long as the Israelites did not sin in the sight of their God, they prospered, for their God, who hates wickedness, was with them. ¹⁸But when they abandoned the way he had prescribed for them, they were utterly destroyed by frequent wars, and finally taken as captives into foreign lands. The temple of their God was razed to the ground, and their cities were occupied by their enemies. ¹⁹But now they have returned to their God, and they have come back from the Diaspora where they were scattered. They have reclaimed Jerusalem, where their sanctuary is, and have settled again in the hill country, because it was unoccupied.

[20]"So now, my master and lord, if these people are inadvertently at fault, or if they are sinning against their God, and if we verify this offense of theirs, then we will be able to go up and conquer them. [21]But if they are not a guilty nation, then let my lord keep his distance; otherwise their Lord and God will shield them, and we will be mocked in the eyes of all the earth."

[22]Now when Achior had finished saying these things, all the people standing round about the tent murmured; and the officers of Holofernes and all the inhabitants of the seacoast and of Moab alike said he should be cut to pieces. [23]"We are not afraid of the Israelites," they said, "for they are a powerless people, incapable of a strong defense. [24]Therefore let us attack, master Holofernes. They will become fodder for your great army."

6:1 When the noise of the crowd surrounding the council had subsided, Holofernes, the ranking general of the Assyrian forces, said to Achior, in the presence of the whole throng of foreigners, of the Moabites, and of the Ammonite mercenaries: [2]"Who are you, Achior and the mercenaries of Ephraim, to prophesy among us as you have done today, and to tell us not to fight against the people of Israel because their God shields them? Who is God beside Nebuchadnezzar? He will send his force and destroy them from the face of the earth. Their God will not save them; [3]but we, the servants of Nebuchadnezzar, will strike them down with one blow, for they will be unable to withstand the force of our cavalry. [4]We will overwhelm them with it, and their mountains shall be drunk with their blood, and their plains filled with their corpses. Not a trace of them shall survive our attack; they will utterly perish. So says King Nebuchadnezzar, lord of all the earth. For he has spoken, and his words will not be in vain. [5]As for you, Achior, you Ammonite mercenary, for saying these things

in a moment of perversity, you will not see my face after today, until I have taken revenge on this people that came out of Egypt. [6]Then at my return, the sword of my army or the spear of my attendants will pierce your sides, and you will fall among their wounded. [7]My servants will now conduct you to the hill country, and leave you at one of the cities beside the passes. [8]You will not die until you are destroyed together with them. [9]If you still harbor the hope that they will not be taken, then there is no need for you to be downcast. I have spoken, and not one of my words will fail to be fulfilled."

[10]Then Holofernes ordered the servants who were standing by in his tent to seize Achior, conduct him to Bethulia, and hand him over to the Israelites. [11]So the servants seized him and took him out of the camp into the plain. From the plain they led him up into the hill country until they reached the springs below Bethulia.

[12]When the men of the city saw them, they seized their weapons and ran out of the city to the top of the hill, and all the slingers kept them from coming up by hurling stones at them. [13]So, taking cover below the hill, they bound Achior and left him lying at the foot of the hill; then they returned to their lord.

Achior in Bethulia. [14]The Israelites came down from their city and found him, untied him, and brought him into Bethulia. They placed him before the rulers of the city, [15]who in those days were Uzziah, son of Micah of the tribe of Simeon, and Chabris, son of Gothoniel, and Charmis, son of Melchiel. [16]They then convened all the elders of the city, and all their young men, as well as the women, gathered in haste at the place of assembly. They placed Achior in the center of the people, and Uzziah questioned him about what had happened. [17]He replied by giving them an account of what was said in the council of Holofernes, and of all his own words among the Assyrian rulers, and of all the boasting threats of Holofernes against the house of Israel. [18]At this the people fell prostrate and worshiped God, and they cried out: [19]"Lord, God of heaven, look at their arrogance! Have mercy on our people in their abject state, and look with favor this day on the faces of those who are consecrated to you." [20]Then they reassured Achior and praised him highly. [21]Uzziah brought him from the place of assembly to his home, where he gave a banquet for the elders. That whole night they called upon the God of Israel for help.

☐ MATTHEW 21:1-11

The Entry into Jerusalem. 21:1 When they drew near Jerusalem and came to Bethphage on the Mount of Olives, Jesus sent two disciples, [2]saying to them, "Go into the village opposite you, and immediately you will find an ass tethered, and a colt with her. Untie them and bring them here to me. [3]And if anyone should say anything to you, reply, 'The master has need of them.' Then he will send them at once." [4]This happened so that what had been spoken through the prophet might be fulfilled:

[5]"Say to daughter Zion,
  'Behold, your king comes to you,
  meek and riding on an ass,
  and on a colt, the foal of a beast of
    burden.'"

[6]The disciples went and did as Jesus had ordered them. [7]They brought the ass and the colt and laid their cloaks over them, and he sat upon them. [8]The very large crowd spread their cloaks on the road, while others cut branches from the trees and strewed them on the road. [9]The crowds preceding him and those following kept crying out and saying:

"Hosanna to the Son of David;
  blessed is he who comes in the name
    of the Lord;
  hosanna in the highest."

[10]And when he entered Jerusalem the whole city was shaken and asked, "Who is this?" [11]And the crowds replied, "This is Jesus the prophet, from Nazareth in Galilee."

May 31

The Visitation of the Blessed Virgin Mary to Elizabeth

The One whom the heavens cannot contain, the womb of one woman bore. She ruled our Ruler; she carried the One in whom we are; she gave milk to our Bread.

— St. Augustine of Hippo

☐ JUDITH 7-9

The Campaign Against Israel. 7:1 The following day Holofernes ordered his whole army, and all the troops who had come to join him, to break camp and move against Bethulia, seize the passes into the hills, and make war on the Israelites. [2]That same day all their fighting men went into action. Their forces numbered a hundred and seventy thousand infantry and twelve thousand cavalry, not counting the baggage train or the men who accompanied it on foot, a very great army. [3]They encamped at the spring in the valley near Bethulia, and spread crosswise toward Dothan as far as Balbaim, and lengthwise from Bethulia to Cyamon, which faces Esdraelon.

[4]When the Israelites saw how many there were, they were greatly distressed and said to one another, "Soon they will strip the whole land bare. Neither the high mountains nor the valleys nor the hills will bear their weight." [5]Yet they all seized their weapons, lighted fires on their towers, and kept watch throughout the night.

The Siege of Bethulia. [6]On the second day Holofernes led out all his cavalry in the sight of the Israelites who were in Bethulia. [7]He reconnoitered the ascents to their city and located their springs of water; these he seized, stationing armed detachments around them, while he himself returned to his troops.

[8]All the rulers of the Edomites, all the leaders of the Moabites, together with the generals of the coastal region, came to Holofernes and said: [9]"Master, please listen to what we have to say, that there may be no losses among your forces. [10]These Israelite troops do not rely on their spears, but on the height of the mountains where they dwell, for it is not easy to reach the summit of their mountains. [11]Therefore, master, do not attack them in regular formation, and not a single one of your troops will fall. [12]Stay in your camp, and spare every man of your force. Have some of your servants keep control of the spring of water that flows out at the base of the mountain, [13]for that is where the inhabitants of Bethulia get their water. Then thirst will destroy them, and they will surrender their city. Meanwhile, we and our troops will go up to the nearby hilltops and encamp there to guard against anyone's leaving the city. [14]They and their wives and children will languish with hunger, and even before the sword strikes them they will be laid low in the streets where they live. [15]Thus you will render them dire punishment for their rebellion and their refusal to meet you peacefully."

[16]Their words pleased Holofernes and all his attendants, and he ordered their proposal to be carried out. [17]So the Ammonites moved camp, together with five thousand Assyrians. They encamped in the valley and held the water supply and the springs of the Israelites. [18]The Edomites and the Ammonites went up and encamped in the hill country opposite Dothan; and they sent some of their men to the southeast opposite Egrebel, near Chusi, which is on Wadi Mochmur. The rest of the Assyrian army was encamped in the plain, covering all the land. Their tents and equipment were spread out in profusion everywhere, and they formed a vast multitude.

The Distress of the Israelites. [19]The Israelites cried to the Lord, their God, for they were disheartened, since all their enemies had them surrounded, and there was no way of escaping from them. [20]The whole Assyrian army, infantry, chariots, and cavalry, kept them thus surrounded for thirty-four days. All the reservoirs of water failed the inhabitants of Bethulia, [21]and the cisterns ran dry, so that on no day did they have enough water to drink, for their drinking water was rationed. [22]Their children were listless, and the women and youths were fainting from thirst and were collapsing in the streets and gateways of the city, with no strength left in them.

[23]So all the people, including youths, women, and children, went in a crowd to Uzziah and the rulers of the city. They cried out loudly and said before all the elders: [24]"May God judge between you and us! You have done us grave injustice in not making peace with the Assyrians. [25]There is no one to help us now! God has sold us into their hands by laying us prostrate before them

in thirst and utter exhaustion. ²⁶So now, summon them and deliver the whole city as plunder to the troops of Holofernes and to all his forces; ²⁷we would be better off to become their prey. Although we would be made slaves, at least we would live, and not have to see our little ones dying before our eyes, and our wives and children breathing their last. ²⁸We adjure you by heaven and earth and by our God, the Lord of our ancestors, who is punishing us for our sins and the sins of our ancestors, that this very day you do as we have proposed."

²⁹All in the assembly with one accord broke into shrill wailing and cried loudly to the Lord their God. ³⁰But Uzziah said to them, "Courage, my brothers and sisters! Let us endure patiently five days more for the Lord our God to show mercy toward us; for God will not utterly forsake us. ³¹But if these days pass and help does not come to us, I will do as you say." ³²Then he dismissed the people. The men returned to their posts on the walls and towers of the city, the women and children went back to their homes. Throughout the city they were in great misery.

Description of Judith. 8:1 Now in those days Judith, daughter of Merari, son of Ox, son of Joseph, son of Oziel, son of Elkiah, son of Ananias, son of Gideon, son of Raphain, son of Ahitub, son of Elijah, son of Hilkiah, son of Eliab, son of Nathanael, son of Salamiel, son of Sarasadai, son of Simeon, son of Israel, heard of this. ²Her husband, Manasseh, of her own tribe and clan, had died at the time of the barley harvest. ³While he was supervising those who bound the sheaves in the field, he was overcome by the heat; and he collapsed on his bed and died in Bethulia, his native city. He was buried with his ancestors in the field between Dothan and Balamon. ⁴Judith was living as a widow in her home for three years and four months. ⁵She set up a tent for herself on the roof of her house, put sackcloth about her waist, and wore widow's clothing. ⁶She fasted all the days of her widowhood, except sabbath eves and sabbaths, new moon eves and new moons, feastdays and holidays of the house of Israel. ⁷She was beautiful in appearance and very lovely to behold. Her husband, Manasseh, had left her gold and silver, male and female servants, livestock and fields, which she was maintaining. ⁸No one had a bad word to say about her, for she feared God greatly.

Judith and the Elders. ⁹So when Judith heard of the harsh words that the people, discouraged by their lack of water, had spoken against their ruler, and of all that Uzziah had said to them in reply, swearing that he would hand over the city to the Assyrians at the end of five days, ¹⁰she sent her maid who was in charge of all her things to summon Uzziah, Chabris, and Charmis, the elders of her city. ¹¹When they came, she said to them: "Listen to me, you rulers of the people of Bethulia. What you said to the people today is not right. You pronounced this oath, made between God and yourselves, and promised to hand over the city to our enemies unless within a certain time the Lord comes to our aid. ¹²Who are you to put God to the test today, setting yourselves in the place of God in human affairs? ¹³And now it is the Lord Almighty you are putting to the test, but you will never understand anything! ¹⁴You cannot plumb the depths of the human heart or grasp the workings of the human mind; how then can you fathom God, who has made all these things, or discern his mind, or understand his plan?

"No, my brothers, do not anger the Lord our God. ¹⁵For if he does not plan to come to our aid within the five days, he has it equally within his power to protect us at such time as he pleases, or to destroy us in the sight of our enemies. ¹⁶Do not impose conditions on the plans of the Lord our God. God is not like a human being to be moved by threats, nor like a mortal to be cajoled.

¹⁷"So while we wait for the salvation that comes from him, let us call upon him to help us, and he will hear our cry if it pleases him. ¹⁸For there has not risen among us in recent generations, nor does there exist today, any tribe, or clan, or district, or city of ours that worships gods made by hands, as happened in former days. ¹⁹It was for such conduct that our ancestors were handed over to the sword and to pillage, and fell with great destruction before our enemies. ²⁰But since we acknowledge no other god but the Lord, we hope that he will not disdain us or any of our people. ²¹If we are taken, then all Judea will fall, our sanctuary will be plundered, and God will demand an account from us for their profanation. ²²For the slaughter of our kindred, for the taking of exiles from the land, and for the devastation of our inheritance, he will hold us responsible among the nations. Wherever we are enslaved, we will be a scandal and a reproach in the eyes of our masters. ²³Our servitude will not work to our advantage, but the Lord our God will turn it to disgrace.

²⁴"Therefore, my brothers, let us set an example for our kindred. Their lives depend on us, and the defense of the sanctuary, the temple, and the altar rests with us. ²⁵Besides all this, let us give thanks to the Lord our God for putting us to the test as he did our ancestors. ²⁶Recall how he dealt with Abraham, and how he tested Isaac, and all that happened to Jacob in Syrian Mesopotamia while he was tending the flocks of Laban, his mother's brother. ²⁷He has not tested us with fire, as he did them, to try their hearts, nor is he taking vengeance on us. But the Lord chastises those who are close to him in order to admonish them."

²⁸Then Uzziah said to her: "All that you have said you have spoken truthfully, and no one can deny your words. ²⁹For today is not the first time your wisdom has been evident, but from your earliest days all the people have recognized your understanding, for your heart's disposition is right. ³⁰The people, however, were so thirsty that they forced us to do for them as we have promised, and to bind ourselves by an oath that we cannot break. ³¹But now, since you are a devout woman, pray for us that the Lord may send rain to fill up our cisterns. Then we will no longer be fainting from thirst."

³²Then Judith said to them: "Listen to me! I will perform a deed that will go down from generation to generation among our descendants. ³³Stand at the city gate tonight to let me pass through with my maid; and within the days you have specified before you will surrender the city to our enemies, the Lord will deliver Israel by my hand. ³⁴You must not inquire into the affair, for I will not tell you what I am doing until it has been accomplished." ³⁵Uzziah and the rulers said to her, "Go in peace, and may the Lord God go before you to take vengeance upon our enemies!" ³⁶Then they withdrew from the tent and returned to their posts.

The Prayer of Judith. 9:1 Judith fell prostrate, put ashes upon her head, and uncovered the sackcloth she was wearing. Just as the evening incense was being offered in the temple of God in Jerusalem, Judith cried loudly to the Lord: ²"Lord, God of my father Simeon, into whose hand you put a sword to take revenge upon the foreigners who had defiled a virgin by violating her, shaming her by uncovering her thighs, and dishonoring her by polluting her womb. You said, 'This shall not be done!' Yet they did it. ³Therefore you handed over their rulers to slaughter; and you handed over to bloodshed the bed in which they lay deceived, the same bed that had felt the shame of their own deceiving. You struck down the slaves together with their masters, and the masters upon their thrones. [4]Their wives you handed over to plunder, and their daughters to captivity, and all the spoils you divided among your favored children, who burned with zeal for you and in their abhorrence of the defilement of their blood called on you for help. O God, my God, hear me also, a widow.

[5]"It is you who were the author of those events and of what preceded and followed them. The present and the future you have also planned. Whatever you devise comes into being. [6]The things you decide come forward and say, 'Here we are!' All your ways are in readiness, and your judgment is made with foreknowledge.

[7]"Here are the Assyrians, a vast force, priding themselves on horse and chariot, boasting of the power of their infantry, trusting in shield and spear, bow and sling. They do not know that you are the Lord who crushes wars; [8]Lord is your name. Shatter their strength in your might, and crush their force in your wrath. For they have resolved to profane your sanctuary, to defile the tent where your glorious name resides, and to break off the horns of your altar with the sword. [9]See their pride, and send forth your fury upon their heads. Give me, a widow, a strong hand to execute my plan. [10]By the deceit of my lips, strike down slave together with ruler, and ruler together with attendant. Crush their arrogance by the hand of a female.

[11]"Your strength is not in numbers, nor does your might depend upon the powerful. You are God of the lowly, helper of those of little account, supporter of the weak, protector of those in despair, savior of those without hope.

[12]"Please, please, God of my father, God of the heritage of Israel, Master of heaven and earth, Creator of the waters, King of all you have created, hear my prayer! [13]Let my deceitful words wound and bruise those who have planned dire things against your covenant, your holy temple, Mount Zion, and the house your children possess. [14]Make every nation and every tribe know clearly that you are God, the God of all power and might, and that there is no other who shields the people of Israel but you alone."

☐ MATTHEW 21:12-17

The Cleansing of the Temple. 21:12 Jesus entered the temple area and drove out all those engaged in selling and buying there. He overturned the tables of the money changers and the seats of those who were selling doves. [13]And he said to them, "It is written:

'My house shall be a house of prayer,'
but you are making it a den of
thieves."

[14]The blind and the lame approached him in the temple area, and he cured them.

[15]When the chief priests and the scribes saw the wondrous things he was doing, and the children crying out in the temple area, "Hosanna to the Son of David," they were indignant [16]and said to him, "Do you hear what they are saying?" Jesus said to them, "Yes; and have you never read the text, 'Out of the mouths of infants and nurslings you have brought forth praise'?" [17]And leaving them, he went out of the city to Bethany, and there he spent the night.

June 1

All truth, wherever it is found, belongs to us as Christians.
— St. Justin Martyr

☐ JUDITH 10-13

Judith Prepares to Depart. 10:1 As soon as Judith had ceased her prayer to the God of Israel and finished all these words, [2]she rose from the ground. She called her maid and they went down into the house, which she used only on sabbaths and feast days. [3]She took off the sackcloth she had on, laid aside the garments of her widowhood, washed her body with water, and anointed herself with rich ointment. She arranged her hair, put on a diadem, and dressed in the festive attire she had worn while her husband, Manasseh, was living. [4]She chose sandals for her feet, and put on her anklets, bracelets, rings, earrings, and all her other jewelry. Thus she made herself very beautiful, to entice the eyes of all the men who should see her.

[5]She gave her maid a skin of wine and a jug of oil. She filled a bag with roasted grain, dried fig cakes, and pure bread. She wrapped all her dishes and gave them to the maid to carry.

[6]Then they went out to the gate of the city of Bethulia and found Uzziah and the elders of the city, Chabris and Charmis, standing there. [7]When they saw Judith transformed in looks and differently dressed, they were very much astounded at her beauty and said to her, [8]"May the God of our ancestors grant you favor and make your design successful, for the glory of the Israelites and the exaltation of Jerusalem." [9]Judith bowed down to God.

Judith and Her Maid Leave Bethulia. Then she said to them, "Order the gate of the city opened for me, that I may go to accomplish the matters we discussed." So they ordered the young men to open the gate for her, as she had requested, [10]and they did so. Then Judith and her maidservant went out. The men of the city kept her in view as she went down the mountain and crossed the valley; then they lost sight of her.

[11]As Judith and her maid walked directly across the valley, they encountered the Assyrian patrol. [12]The men took her in custody and asked her, "To what people do you belong? Where do you come from, and where are you going?" She replied: "I am a daughter of the Hebrews, and I am fleeing from them, because they are about to be delivered up to you as prey. [13]I have come to see Holofernes, the ranking general of your forces, to give him a trustworthy report; in his presence I will show him the way by which he can ascend and take possession of the whole hill country without a single one of his men suffering injury or loss of life."

[14]When the men heard her words and gazed upon her face, which appeared marvelously beautiful to them, they said to her, [15]"By hastening down to see our master, you have saved your life. Now go to his tent; some of us will accompany you to hand you over to him. [16]When you stand before him, have no fear in your heart; give him the report you have given us, and he will treat you well." [17]So they selected a hundred of their men as an escort for her and her maid, and these conducted them to the tent of Holofernes.

[18]As the news of her arrival spread among the tents, a crowd gathered in the camp. They came and stood around her as she waited outside the tent of Holofernes,

while he was being informed about her. [19]They marveled at her beauty, regarding the Israelites with wonder because of her, and they said to one another, "Who can despise this people who have such women among them? It is not good to leave one of their men alive, for if any were to be spared they could beguile the whole earth."

Judith Meets Holofernes. [20]Then the guards of Holofernes and all his attendants came out and ushered her into the tent. [21]Holofernes was reclining on his bed under a canopy woven of purple, gold, emeralds, and other precious stones. [22]When they announced her to him, he came out to the front part of the tent, preceded by silver lamps. [23]When Judith came before Holofernes and his attendants, they all marveled at the beauty of her face. She fell prostrate and paid homage to him, but his servants raised her up.

11:1 Then Holofernes said to her: "Take courage, woman! Have no fear in your heart! I have never harmed anyone who chose to serve Nebuchadnezzar, king of all the earth. [2]As for your people who live in the hill country, I would never have raised my spear against them, had they not insulted me. They have brought this upon themselves. [3]But now tell me why you have fled from them and come to us? In any case, you have come to safety. Take courage! Your life is spared tonight and for the future. [4]No one at all will harm you. Rather, you will be well treated, as are the servants of my lord, King Nebuchadnezzar."

[5]Judith answered him: "Listen to the words of your servant, and let your maidservant speak in your presence! I will say nothing false to my lord this night. [6]If you follow the words of your maidservant, God will successfully perform a deed through you, and my lord will not fail to achieve his designs. [7]I swear by the life of Nebuchadnezzar, king of all the earth, and by the power of him who has sent you to guide all living things, that not only do human beings serve him through you; but even the wild animals, and the cattle, and the birds of the air, because of your strength, will live for Nebuchadnezzar and his whole house. [8]Indeed, we have heard of your wisdom and cleverness. The whole earth is aware that you above all others in the kingdom are able, rich in experience, and distinguished in military strategy.

[9]"As for Achior's speech in your council, we have heard it. When the men of Bethulia rescued him, he told them all he had said to you. [10]So then, my lord and master, do not disregard his word, but bear it in mind, for it is true. Indeed our people are not punished, nor does the sword prevail against them, except when they sin against their God. [11]But now their sin has caught up with them, by which they will bring the wrath of their God upon them when they do wrong; so that my lord will not be repulsed and fail, but death will overtake them. [12]Because their food has given out and all their water is running low, they have decided to kill their animals, and are determined to consume all the things which God in his laws has forbidden them to eat. [13]They have decided that they would use the first fruits of grain and the tithes of wine and oil, which they had consecrated and reserved for the priests who minister in the presence of our God in Jerusalem—things which the people should not so much as touch with their hands. [14]They have sent messengers to Jerusalem to bring back permission from the senate, for even there people have done these things. [15]On the very day when the response reaches them and they act upon it, they will be handed over to you for destruction.

[16]"As soon as I, your servant, learned all this, I fled from them. God has sent me to perform with you such deeds as will astonish people throughout the whole earth who hear of them. [17]Your servant is, indeed, a God-fearing woman, serving the God of

heaven night and day. Now I will remain with you, my lord; but each night your servant will go out into the valley and pray to God. He will tell me when they have committed their offenses. [18]Then I will come and let you know, so that you may march out with all your forces, and not one of them will be able to withstand you. [19]I will lead you through the heart of Judea until you come to Jerusalem, and there in its center I will set up your throne. You will drive them like sheep that have no shepherd, and not even a dog will growl at you. This was told to me in advance and announced to me, and I have been sent to tell you."

[20]Her words pleased Holofernes and all his attendants. They marveled at her wisdom and exclaimed, [21]"No other woman from one end of the earth to the other looks so beautiful and speaks so wisely!" [22]Then Holofernes said to her: "God has done well in sending you ahead of your people, to bring victory to our hands, and destruction to those who have despised my lord. [23]You are not only beautiful in appearance, but you are also eloquent. If you do as you have said, your God will be my God; you will live in the palace of King Nebuchadnezzar and be renowned throughout the whole earth."

12:1 Then he ordered them to lead her into the room where his silver dinnerware was kept, and ordered them to set a table for her with his own delicacies to eat and his own wine to drink. [2]But Judith said, "I cannot eat any of them, because it would be a scandal. Besides, I will have enough with the things I brought with me." [3]Holofernes asked her, "But if your provisions give out, where can we get more of the same to provide for you? None of your people are with us." [4]Judith answered him, "As surely as you live, my lord, your servant will not use up her supplies before the Lord accomplishes by my hand what he has determined."

[5]Then the attendants of Holofernes led her to her tent, where she slept until the middle of the night. Toward the early morning watch, she rose [6]and sent this message to Holofernes, "Give orders, my lord, to let your servant go out for prayer." [7]So Holofernes ordered his guards not to hinder her. Thus she stayed in the camp three days. Each night she went out to the valley of Bethulia, where she bathed herself at the spring of the camp. [8]After bathing, she prayed to the Lord, the God of Israel, to direct her way for the triumph of her people. [9]Then she returned purified to the tent and remained there until her food was brought to her toward evening.

Judith at the Banquet of Holofernes. [10]On the fourth day Holofernes gave a banquet for his servants alone, to which he did not invite any of the officers. [11]And he said to Bagoas, the eunuch in charge of his personal affairs, "Go and persuade the Hebrew woman in your care to come and to eat and drink with us. [12]It would bring shame on us to be with such a woman without enjoying her. If we do not seduce her, she will laugh at us."

[13]So Bagoas left the presence of Holofernes, and came to Judith and said, "So lovely a maidservant should not be reluctant to come to my lord to be honored by him, to enjoy drinking wine with us, and to act today like one of the Assyrian women who serve in the palace of Nebuchadnezzar." [14]Judith replied, "Who am I to refuse my lord? Whatever is pleasing to him I will promptly do. This will be a joy for me until the day of my death."

[15]So she proceeded to put on her festive garments and all her finery. Meanwhile her servant went ahead and spread out on the ground opposite Holofernes the fleece Bagoas had furnished for her daily use in reclining while eating. [16]Then Judith came in and reclined. The heart of Holofernes was in rapture over her and his passion was aroused. He was burning with the desire

to possess her, for he had been biding his time to seduce her from the day he saw her. ¹⁷Holofernes said to her, "Drink and be happy with us!" ¹⁸Judith replied, "I will gladly drink, my lord, for today is the greatest day of my whole life." ¹⁹She then took the things her servant had prepared and ate and drank in his presence. ²⁰Holofernes, charmed by her, drank a great quantity of wine, more than he had ever drunk on any day since he was born.

Judith Beheads Holofernes. 13:1 When it grew late, his servants quickly withdrew. Bagoas closed the tent from the outside and dismissed the attendants from their master's presence. They went off to their beds, for they were all tired because the banquet had lasted so long. ²Judith was left alone in the tent with Holofernes, who lay sprawled on his bed, for he was drunk with wine. ³Judith had ordered her maidservant to stand outside the bedchamber and to wait, as on the other days, for her to come out; she had said she would be going out for her prayer. She had also said this same thing to Bagoas.

⁴When all had departed, and no one, small or great, was left in the bedchamber, Judith stood by Holofernes' bed and prayed silently, "O Lord, God of all might, in this hour look graciously on the work of my hands for the exaltation of Jerusalem. ⁵Now is the time for aiding your heritage and for carrying out my design to shatter the enemies who have risen against us." ⁶She went to the bedpost near the head of Holofernes, and taking his sword from it, ⁷she drew close to the bed, grasped the hair of his head, and said, "Strengthen me this day, Lord, God of Israel!" ⁸Then with all her might she struck his neck twice and cut off his head. ⁹She rolled his body off the bed and took the canopy from its posts. Soon afterward, she came out and handed over the head of Holofernes to her maid, ¹⁰who put it into her food bag. Then the two went out together for prayer as they were accustomed to do.

Judith and Her Maid Return to Bethulia. They passed through the camp, and skirting that valley, went up the mountain to Bethulia, and approached its gates. ¹¹From a distance, Judith shouted to the guards at the gates: "Open! Open the gate! God, our God, is with us. Once more he has shown his strength in Israel and his power against the enemy, as he has today!"

Judith Displays the Head of Holofernes. ¹²When the citizens heard her voice, they hurried down to their city gate and summoned the elders of the city. ¹³All the people, from the least to the greatest, hurriedly assembled, for her return seemed unbelievable. They opened the gate and welcomed the two women. They made a fire for light and gathered around the two. ¹⁴Judith urged them with a loud voice: "Praise God, give praise! Praise God, who has not withdrawn his mercy from the house of Israel, but has shattered our enemies by my hand this very night!" ¹⁵Then she took the head out of the bag, showed it to them, and said: "Here is the head of Holofernes, the ranking general of the Assyrian forces, and here is the canopy under which he lay in his drunkenness. The Lord struck him down by the hand of a female! ¹⁶Yet I swear by the Lord, who has protected me in the way I have walked, that it was my face that seduced Holofernes to his ruin, and that he did not defile me with sin or shame."

¹⁷All the people were greatly astonished. They bowed down and worshiped God, saying with one accord, "Blessed are you, our God, who today have humiliated the enemies of your people." ¹⁸Then Uzziah said to her, "Blessed are you, daughter, by the Most High God, above all the women on earth; and blessed be the Lord God, the creator of heaven and earth, who guided your blow at the head of the leader of our enemies. ¹⁹Your deed of hope will never be

forgotten by those who recall the might of God. [20]May God make this redound to your everlasting honor, rewarding you with blessings, because you risked your life when our people were being oppressed, and you averted our disaster, walking in the straight path before our God." And all the people answered, "Amen! Amen!"

☐ MATTHEW 21:18-27

The Cursing of the Fig Tree. 21:18 When he was going back to the city in the morning, he was hungry. [19]Seeing a fig tree by the road, he went over to it, but found nothing on it except leaves. And he said to it, "May no fruit ever come from you again." And immediately the fig tree withered. [20]When the disciples saw this, they were amazed and said, "How was it that the fig tree withered immediately?" [21]Jesus said to them in reply, "Amen, I say to you, if you have faith and do not waver, not only will you do what has been done to the fig tree, but even if you say to this mountain, 'Be lifted up and thrown into the sea,' it will be done. [22]Whatever you ask for in prayer with faith, you will receive."

The Authority of Jesus Questioned. [23]When he had come into the temple area, the chief priests and the elders of the people approached him as he was teaching and said, "By what authority are you doing these things? And who gave you this authority?" [24]Jesus said to them in reply, "I shall ask you one question, and if you answer it for me, then I shall tell you by what authority I do these things. [25]Where was John's baptism from? Was it of heavenly or of human origin?" They discussed this among themselves and said, "If we say 'Of heavenly origin,' he will say to us, 'Then why did you not believe him?' [26]But if we say, 'Of human origin,' we fear the crowd, for they all regard John as a prophet." [27]So they said to Jesus in reply, "We do not know." He himself said to them, "Neither shall I tell you by what authority I do these things."

June 2

Sts. Marcellinus and Peter

You must refuse nothing you recognize to be God's will.

— St. Jane Frances de Chantal

☐ JUDITH 14-16

Judith's Plan of Attack. 14:1 Then Judith said to them: "Listen to me, my brothers and sisters. Take this head and hang it on the parapet of your wall. [2]At daybreak, when the sun rises on the earth, each of you seize your weapons, and let all the able-bodied men rush out of the city under command of a captain, as if about to go down into the valley against the Assyrian patrol, but without going down. [3]The Assyrians will seize their weapons and hurry to their camp to awaken the generals of the army. When they run to the tent of Holofernes and do not find him, panic will seize them, and they will flee before you. [4]Then you and all the other inhabitants of the whole territory of Israel will pursue them and strike them down in their tracks. [5]But before doing this, summon for me Achior the Ammonite, that he may see and recognize the one who despised the house of Israel and sent him here to meet his death."

Achior's Conversion. [6]So they called Achior from the house of Uzziah. When he came and saw the head of Holofernes in the hand of one of the men in the assembly of the people, he collapsed in a faint. [7]Then, after they lifted him up, he threw himself at the feet of Judith in homage, saying: "Blessed are you in every tent of Judah! In every nation, all who hear your name will be struck with terror. [8]But now, tell me all that you did during these days." So Judith told him, in the midst of the people, all that she had done, from the day she left until the time she began speaking to them. [9]When she had finished her account, the people cheered loudly, so that the city resounded with shouts of joy. [10]Now Achior, seeing all that the God of Israel had done, believed firmly in God. He circumcised the flesh of his foreskin and he has been united with the house of Israel to the present day.

Panic in the Assyrian Camp. [11]At daybreak they hung the head of Holofernes on the wall. Then all the Israelite men took up their weapons and went out by groups to the mountain passes. [12]When the Assyrians saw them, they notified their commanders, who, in turn, went to their generals, their division leaders, and all their other leaders. [13]They came to the tent of Holofernes and said to the one in charge of all his things, "Awaken our lord, for the slaves have dared come down against us in battle, to their utter destruction." [14]So Bagoas went in and knocked at the entry of the tent, presuming that Holofernes was sleeping with Judith. [15]When no one answered, he parted the curtains, entered the bedchamber, and found him thrown on the floor dead, with his head gone! [16]He cried out loudly, weeping, groaning, and howling, and tore his garments. [17]Then he entered the tent where Judith had her quarters; and, not finding her, he rushed out to the troops and cried: [18]"The slaves have duped us! One Hebrew woman has brought shame on the house of King Nebuchadnezzar. Look! Holofernes on the ground—without a head!"

[19]When the leaders of the Assyrian forces heard these words, they tore their tunics and were overcome with great distress. Their loud cries and shouts were heard throughout the camp.

15:1 On hearing what had happened, those still in their tents were horrified. [2]Overcome with fear and dread, no one kept ranks any longer. They scattered in all directions, and fled along every path, both through the valley and in the hill country. [3]Those who were stationed in the hill country around Bethulia also took to flight. Then the Israelites, every warrior among them, came charging down upon them.

[4]Uzziah sent messengers to Betomasthaim, to Choba and Kona, and to the whole territory of Israel to report what had happened and to urge them all to attack the enemy and destroy them. [5]On hearing this, all the Israelites, with one accord, attacked them and cut them down as far as Choba. Even those from Jerusalem and the rest of the hill country took part in this, for they too had been notified of the happenings in the camp of their enemy. The Gileadites and the Galileans struck the enemy's flanks with great slaughter, even beyond Damascus and its borders. [6]The remaining people of Bethulia swept down on the camp of the Assyrians, plundered it, and acquired great riches. [7]The Israelites, when they returned from the slaughter, took possession of what was left. Even the towns and villages in the hill country and on the plain got an enormous quantity of spoils, for there was a tremendous amount of it.

Israel Celebrates Judith's Victory. [8]Then the high priest Joakim and the senate of the Israelites who lived in Jerusalem came to see for themselves the good things that the Lord had done for Israel, and to meet and congratulate Judith. ⁹When they came to her, all with one accord blessed her, saying:

"You are the glory of Jerusalem!
    You are the great pride of Israel!
    You are the great boast of our nation!
¹⁰By your own hand you have done all
        this.
    You have done good things for Israel,
    and God is pleased with them.
May the Almighty Lord bless you
        forever!"

And all the people said, "Amen!"

¹¹For thirty days all the people plundered the camp, giving Judith the tent of Holofernes, with all his silver, his beds, his dishes, and all his furniture. She took them and loaded her mule, hitched her carts, and loaded these things on them.

¹²All the women of Israel gathered to see her, and they blessed her and performed a dance in her honor. She took branches in her hands and distributed them to the women around her, ¹³and she and the other women crowned themselves with olive leaves. Then, at the head of all the people, she led the women in the dance, while the men of Israel followed, bearing their weapons, wearing garlands and singing songs of praise. ¹⁴Judith led all Israel in this song of thanksgiving, and the people loudly sang this hymn of praise:

16:1 And Judith sang:

"Strike up a song to my God with
        tambourines,
    sing to the Lord with cymbals;
Improvise for him a new song,
    exalt and acclaim his name.
²For the Lord is a God who crushes
        wars;
    he sets his encampment among his
        people;
    he delivered me from the hands of
        my pursuers.

³"The Assyrian came from the
        mountains of the north,
    with myriads of his forces he came;
Their numbers blocked the wadis,
    their cavalry covered the hills.
⁴He threatened to burn my territory,
    put my youths to the sword,
Dash my infants to the ground,
    seize my children as plunder.
    And carry off my virgins as spoil.

⁵"But the Lord Almighty thwarted
        them,
    by the hand of a female!
⁶Not by youths was their champion
        struck down,
    nor did Titans bring him low,
    nor did tall giants attack him;
But Judith, the daughter of Merari,
    by the beauty of her face brought
        him down.
⁷She took off her widow's garb
    to raise up the afflicted in Israel.
She anointed her face with fragrant oil;
    ⁸fixed her hair with a diadem,
    and put on a linen robe to beguile
        him.
⁹Her sandals ravished his eyes,
    her beauty captivated his mind,
    the sword cut through his neck!

¹⁰"The Persians trembled at her
        boldness,
    the Medes were daunted at her
        daring.
¹¹When my lowly ones shouted,
    and my weak ones cried out,
The enemy was terrified,
    screamed and took to flight.
¹²Sons of maidservants pierced them
        through;
    wounded them like deserters'
        children.
    They perished before the ranks of
        my Lord.

¹³"I will sing a new song to my God.
    O Lord, great are you and glorious,

marvelous in power and
unsurpassable.
[14]Let your every creature serve you;
for you spoke, and they were made.
You sent forth your spirit, and it
created them;
no one can resist your voice.
[15]For the mountains to their bases
are tossed with the waters;
the rocks, like wax, melt before your
glance.

"But to those who fear you,
you will show mercy.
[16]Though the sweet fragrance of every
sacrifice is a trifle,
and the fat of all burnt offerings but
little in your sight,
one who fears the Lord is forever
great.

[17]"Woe to the nations that rise against
my people!
the Lord Almighty will requite
them;
in the day of judgment he will
punish them:
He will send fire and worms into their
flesh,
and they will weep and suffer
forever."

[18]When they arrived at Jerusalem, they
worshiped God. As soon as the people
were purified, they offered their burnt offerings, voluntary offerings, and donations. [19]Judith dedicated to God all the things of Holofernes that the people had given her, putting under the ban the canopy that she herself had taken from his bedchamber. [20]For three months the people continued their celebration in Jerusalem before the sanctuary, and Judith remained with them.

The Renown and Death of Judith. [21]When those days were over, all of them returned to their inheritance. Judith went back to Bethulia and remained on her estate. For the rest of her life she was renowned throughout the land. [22]Many wished to marry her, but she gave herself to no man all the days of her life from the time her husband, Manasseh, died and was gathered to his people. [23]Her fame continued to increase, and she lived in the house of her husband, reaching the advanced age of one hundred and five. She set her maid free. And when she died in Bethulia, they buried her in the cave of her husband, Manasseh; [24]and the house of Israel mourned her for seven days. Before she died, she distributed her property to the relatives of her husband, Manasseh, and to her own relatives.

[25]During the lifetime of Judith and for a long time after her death, no one ever again spread terror among the Israelites.

☐ MATTHEW 21:28–46

The Parable of the Two Sons. 21:28 "What is your opinion? A man had two sons. He came to the first and said, 'Son, go out and work in the vineyard today.' [29]He said in reply, 'I will not,' but afterwards he changed his mind and went. [30]The man came to the other son and gave the same order. He said in reply, 'Yes, sir,' but did not go. [31]Which of the two did his father's will?" They answered, "The first." Jesus said to them, "Amen, I say to you, tax collectors and prostitutes are entering the kingdom of God before you. [32]When John came to you in the way of righteousness, you did not believe him; but tax collectors and prostitutes did. Yet even when you saw that, you did not later change your minds and believe him.

The Parable of the Tenants. [33]"Hear another parable. There was a landowner who planted a vineyard, put a hedge around it, dug a wine press in it, and built a tower.

Then he leased it to tenants and went on a journey. ³⁴When vintage time drew near, he sent his servants to the tenants to obtain his produce. ³⁵But the tenants seized the servants and one they beat, another they killed, and a third they stoned. ³⁶Again he sent other servants, more numerous than the first ones, but they treated them in the same way. ³⁷Finally, he sent his son to them, thinking, 'They will respect my son.' ³⁸But when the tenants saw the son, they said to one another, 'This is the heir. Come, let us kill him and acquire his inheritance.' ³⁹They seized him, threw him out of the vineyard, and killed him. ⁴⁰What will the owner of the vineyard do to those tenants when he comes?" ⁴¹They answered him, "He will put those wretched men to a wretched death and lease his vineyard to other ten-ants who will give him the produce at the proper times." ⁴²Jesus said to them, "Did you never read in the scriptures:

'The stone that the builders rejected
    has become the cornerstone;
by the Lord has this been done,
    and it is wonderful in our eyes'?

⁴³Therefore, I say to you, the kingdom of God will be taken away from you and given to a people that will produce its fruit. ⁴⁴[The one who falls on this stone will be dashed to pieces; and it will crush anyone on whom it falls.]" ⁴⁵When the chief priests and the Pharisees heard his parables, they knew that he was speaking about them. ⁴⁶And although they were attempting to arrest him, they feared the crowds, for they regarded him as a prophet.

June 3

St. Charles Lwanga and Companions

Bless the martyrs heartily, that you may be a martyr by inten-tion. Thus, even though you depart this life without persecutor, fire, or lash, you will still be found worthy of the same reward.

— St. Basil the Great

☐ ESTHER A, 1-3, B

Dream of Mordecai. A:1 In the second year of the reign of Ahasuerus the great, on the first day of Nisan, Mordecai, son of Jair, son of Shimei, son of Kish, of the tribe of Benjamin, had a dream. ²He was a Jew re-siding in the city of Susa, a prominent man who served at the king's court, ³and one of the captives whom Nebuchadnezzar, king of Babylon, had taken from Jerusalem with Jeconiah, king of Judah.

⁴This was his dream. There was noise and tumult, thunder and earthquake—confu-sion upon the earth. ⁵Two great dragons advanced, both poised for combat. They uttered a mighty cry, ⁶and at their cry ev-ery nation prepared for war, to fight against the nation of the just. ⁷It was a dark and gloomy day. Tribulation and distress, evil and great confusion, lay upon the earth. ⁸The whole nation of the just was shaken with fear at the evils to come upon them, and they expected to perish. ⁹Then they cried out to God, and from their crying there arose, as though from a tiny spring, a

mighty river, a flood of water. [10]The light of the sun broke forth; the lowly were exalted and they devoured the boastful.

[11]Having seen this dream and what God intended to do, Mordecai awoke. He kept it in mind, and tried in every way, until night, to understand its meaning.

Mordecai Thwarts an Assassination. [12]Mordecai lodged in the courtyard with Bigthan and Teresh, two eunuchs of the king who guarded the courtyard. [13]He overheard them plotting, investigated their plans, and discovered that they were preparing to assassinate King Ahasuerus. So he informed the king about them. [14]The king had the two eunuchs questioned and, upon their confession, put to death. [15]Then the king had these things recorded; Mordecai, too, put them into writing. [16]The king also appointed Mordecai to serve at the court, and rewarded him for his actions.

[17]Haman, however, son of Hammedatha, a Bougean, who was held in high honor by the king, sought to harm Mordecai and his people because of the two eunuchs of the king.

The Banquet of Ahasuerus. 1:1 During the reign of Ahasuerus—the same Ahasuerus who ruled over a hundred and twenty-seven provinces from India to Ethiopia— [2]while he was occupying the royal throne in the royal precinct of Susa, [3]in the third year of his reign, he gave a feast for all his officials and ministers: the Persian and Median army officers, the nobles, and the governors of the provinces. [4]For as many as a hundred and eighty days, he displayed the glorious riches of his kingdom and the resplendent wealth of his royal estate.

[5]At the end of this time the king gave a feast of seven days in the garden court of the royal palace for all the people, great and small, who were in the royal precinct of Susa. [6]There were white cotton draperies and violet hangings, held by cords of fine crimson linen from silver rings on marble pillars. Gold and silver couches were on a mosaic pavement, which was of porphyry, marble, mother-of-pearl, and colored stones. [7]Drinks were served in a variety of golden cups, and the royal wine flowed freely, as befitted the king's liberality. [8]By ordinance of the king the drinking was unstinted, for he had instructed all the stewards of his household to comply with the good pleasure of everyone. [9]Queen Vashti also gave a feast for the women in the royal palace of King Ahasuerus.

Refusal of Vashti. [10]On the seventh day, when the king was merry with wine, he instructed Mehuman, Biztha, Harbona, Bigtha, Abagtha, Zethar, and Carkas, the seven eunuchs who attended King Ahasuerus, [11]to bring Queen Vashti into his presence wearing the royal crown, that he might display her beauty to the populace and the officials, for she was lovely to behold. [12]But Queen Vashti refused to come at the royal order issued through the eunuchs. At this the king's wrath flared up, and he burned with fury. [13]He conferred with the sages who understood the times, because the king's business was conducted in general consultation with lawyers and jurists. [14]He summoned Carshena, Shethar, Admatha, Tarshish, Meres, Marsena, and Memucan, the seven Persian and Median officials who were in the king's personal service and held first rank in the realm, [15]and asked them, "What is to be done by law with Queen Vashti for disobeying the order of King Ahasuerus issued through the eunuchs?"

[16]In the presence of the king and of the officials, Memucan answered: "Queen Vashti has not wronged the king alone, but all the officials and the populace throughout the provinces of King Ahasuerus. [17]For the queen's conduct will become known to all the women, and they will look with disdain upon their husbands when it is reported, 'King Ahasuerus commanded that Queen Vashti be ushered into his presence, but she would not come.' [18]This very day

the Persian and Median noblewomen who hear of the queen's conduct will recount it to all the royal officials, and disdain and rancor will abound. [19]If it please the king, let an irrevocable royal decree be issued by him and inscribed among the laws of the Persians and Medes, forbidding Vashti to come into the presence of King Ahasuerus and authorizing the king to give her royal dignity to one more worthy than she. [20]Thus, when the decree that the king will issue is published throughout his realm, vast as it is, all wives will honor their husbands, from the greatest to the least."

[21]This proposal pleased the king and the officials, and the king acted on the advice of Memucan. [22]He sent letters to all the royal provinces, to each province in its own script and to each people in its own language, to the effect that every man should be lord in his own home.

The Search for a New Queen. 2:1 After this, when King Ahasuerus' wrath had cooled, he thought over what Vashti had done and what had been decreed against her. [2]Then the king's personal attendants suggested: "Let beautiful young virgins be sought for the king. [3]Let the king appoint emissaries in all the provinces of his realm to gather all beautiful young virgins into the harem in the royal precinct of Susa. Under the care of the royal eunuch Hegai, guardian of the women, let cosmetics be given them. [4]Then the young woman who pleases the king shall reign in place of Vashti." This suggestion pleased the king, and he acted accordingly.

[5]There was in the royal precinct of Susa a certain Jew named Mordecai, son of Jair, son of Shimei, son of Kish, a Benjaminite, [6]who had been exiled from Jerusalem with the captives taken with Jeconiah, king of Judah, whom Nebuchadnezzar, king of Babylon, had deported. [7]He became foster father to his cousin Hadassah, that is, Esther, when she lost both father and mother.

The young woman was beautifully formed and lovely to behold. On the death of her father and mother, Mordecai adopted her as his own daughter.

[8]When the king's order and decree had been proclaimed and many young women brought together to the royal precinct of Susa under the care of Hegai, Esther also was brought in to the royal palace under the care of Hegai, guardian of the women. [9]The young woman pleased him and won his favor. So he promptly furnished her with cosmetics and provisions. Then choosing seven maids for her from the royal palace, he transferred both her and her maids to the best place in the harem. [10]Esther did not reveal her nationality or family, for Mordecai had commanded her not to do so.

[11]Day by day Mordecai would walk about in front of the court of the harem to learn how Esther was faring and what was to become of her.

[12]After the twelve months' preparation decreed for the women, each one went in turn to visit King Ahasuerus. During this period of beautifying treatment, six months were spent with oil of myrrh, and the other six months with perfumes and cosmetics. [13]Then, when each one was to visit the king, she was allowed to take with her from the harem to the royal palace whatever she chose. [14]She would go in the evening and return in the morning to a second harem under the care of the royal eunuch Shaashgaz, guardian of the concubines. She could not return to the king unless he was pleased with her and had her summoned by name. [15]As for Esther, daughter of Abihail and adopted daughter of his nephew Mordecai, when her turn came to visit the king, she did not ask for anything but what the royal eunuch Hegai, guardian of the women, suggested. And she won the admiration of all who saw her.

Ahasuerus Chooses Esther. [16]Esther was led to King Ahasuerus in his palace in the tenth month, Tebeth, in the seventh year of his reign. ¹⁷The king loved Esther more than all other women, and of all the virgins she won his favor and good will. So he placed the royal crown on her head and made her queen in place of Vashti. ¹⁸Then the king gave a great feast in honor of Esther to all his officials and servants, granting a holiday to the provinces and bestowing gifts with royal generosity.

Mordecai Thwarts an Assassination. ¹⁹As was said, from the time the virgins had been brought together, and while Mordecai was passing his time at the king's gate, ²⁰Esther had not revealed her family or nationality, because Mordecai had told her not to; and Esther continued to follow Mordecai's instructions, just as she had when she was being brought up by him. ²¹During the time that Mordecai spent at the king's gate, Bigthan and Teresh, two of the royal eunuchs who guarded the entrance, became angry and plotted to assassinate King Ahasuerus. ²²When the plot became known to Mordecai, he told Queen Esther, who in turn informed the king in Mordecai's name. ²³The matter was investigated and verified, and both of them were impaled on stakes. This was written in the annals in the king's presence.

Mordecai Refuses to Honor Haman. 3:1 After these events King Ahasuerus promoted Haman, son of Hammedatha the Agagite, to high rank, seating him above all his fellow officials. ²All the king's servants who were at the royal gate would kneel and bow down to Haman, for that is what the king had ordered in his regard. Mordecai, however, would not kneel and bow down. ³The king's servants who were at the royal gate said to Mordecai, "Why do you disobey the king's order?" ⁴When they had reminded him day after day and he would not listen to them, they informed Haman, to see whether Mordecai's explanation would prevail, since he had told them that he was a Jew.

Haman's Reprisal. ⁵When Haman observed that Mordecai would not kneel and bow down to him, he was filled with anger. ⁶But he thought it was beneath him to attack only Mordecai. Since they had told Haman of Mordecai's nationality, he sought to destroy all the Jews, Mordecai's people, throughout the realm of King Ahasuerus. ⁷In the first month, Nisan, in the twelfth year of King Ahasuerus, the *pur*, or lot, was cast in Haman's presence to determine the day and the month for the destruction of Mordecai's people on a single day, and the lot fell on the thirteenth day of the twelfth month, Adar.

Decree Against the Jews. ⁸Then Haman said to King Ahasuerus: "Dispersed among the nations throughout the provinces of your kingdom, there is a certain people living apart. Their laws differ from those of every other people and they do not obey the laws of the king; so it is not proper for the king to tolerate them. ⁹If it please the king, let a decree be issued to destroy them; and I will deliver to the procurators ten thousand silver talents for deposit in the royal treasury." ¹⁰The king took the signet ring from his hand and gave it to Haman, son of Hammedatha the Agagite, the enemy of the Jews. ¹¹The king said to Haman, "The silver is yours, as well as the people, to do with as you please."

¹²So the royal scribes were summoned on the thirteenth day of the first month, and they wrote, at the dictation of Haman, an order to the royal satraps, the governors of every province, and the officials of every people, to each province in its own script and to each people in its own language. It was written in the name of King Ahasuerus and sealed with the royal signet ring. ¹³Letters were sent by couriers to all the royal provinces, to destroy, kill and annihilate all the Jews, young and old, including women and children in one day, the thirteenth day of the twelfth month, Adar, and to seize their goods as spoil.

B:1 This is a copy of the letter:

"The great King Ahasuerus writes to the satraps of the hundred and twenty-seven provinces from India to Ethiopia, and the governors subordinate to them, as follows: [2]When I came to rule many peoples and to hold sway over the whole world, not being carried away by a sense of my own authority but always acting fairly and with mildness, I determined to provide for my subjects a life of lasting tranquility; and, by making my kingdom civilized and safe for travel to its farthest borders, to restore the peace desired by all people. [3]When I consulted my counselors as to how this might be accomplished, Haman, who excels among us in discretion, who is outstanding for constant good will and steadfast loyalty, and who has gained a place in the kingdom second only to me, [4]brought it to our attention that, mixed among all the nations throughout the world, there is one people of ill will, which by its laws is opposed to every other people and continually disregards the decrees of kings, so that the unity of empire blamelessly designed by us cannot be established. [5]"Having noted, therefore, that this nation, and it alone, is continually at variance with all people, lives by divergent and alien laws, is inimical to our government, and does all the harm it can to undermine the stability of the kingdom, [6]we hereby decree that all those who are indicated to you in the letters of Haman, who is in charge of the administration and is a second father to us, shall, together with their wives and children, be utterly destroyed by the swords of their enemies, without any pity or mercy, on the fourteenth day of the twelfth month, Adar, of the current year; [7]so that when these people, whose present ill will is of long standing, have gone down into Hades by a violent death on a single day, they may leave our government completely stable and undisturbed for the future."

3:14 A copy of the decree to be promulgated as law in every province was published to all the peoples, that they might be prepared for that day. [15]The couriers set out in haste at the king's command; meanwhile, the decree was promulgated in the royal precinct of Susa. The king and Haman then sat down to drink, but the city of Susa was thrown into confusion.

☐ MATTHEW 22:1-14

The Parable of the Wedding Feast. 22:1 Jesus again in reply spoke to them in parables, saying, [2]"The kingdom of heaven may be likened to a king who gave a wedding feast for his son. [3]He dispatched his servants to summon the invited guests to the feast, but they refused to come. [4]A second time he sent other servants, saying, 'Tell those invited: "Behold, I have prepared my banquet, my calves and fattened cattle are killed, and everything is ready; come to the feast."' [5]Some ignored the invitation and went away, one to his farm, another to his business. [6]The rest laid hold of his servants, mistreated them, and killed them. [7]The king was enraged and sent his troops, destroyed those murderers, and burned their city. [8]Then he said to his servants, 'The feast is ready, but those who were invited were not worthy to come. [9]Go out, therefore, into the main roads and invite to the feast whomever you find.' [10]The servants went out into the streets and gathered all they found, bad and good alike, and the hall was filled with guests. [11]But when the king came in to meet the guests he saw a man there not dressed in a wedding garment. [12]He said to him, 'My friend, how is it that you came in here without a wedding garment?' But he was reduced to silence. [13]Then the king said to his attendants, 'Bind his hands and feet, and cast him into the darkness outside, where there will be wailing and grinding of teeth.' [14]Many are invited, but few are chosen."

June 4

Blessed Mary Elizabeth Hesselblad

Dear Lord, I do not ask to see the path. In darkness, in anguish and in fear, I will hang on tightly to Your hand, and I will close my eyes, so that You know how much trust I place in You, Spouse of my soul.

— BLESSED MARY ELIZABETH HESSELBLAD

☐ ESTHER 4, C, D, 5

Mordecai Exhorts Esther. 4:1 When Mordecai learned all that was happening, he tore his garments, put on sackcloth and ashes, and went through the city crying out loudly and bitterly, [2]till he came before the royal gate, which no one clothed in sackcloth might enter. [3]Likewise in each of the provinces, wherever the king's decree and law reached, the Jews went into deep mourning, with fasting, weeping, and lament; most of them lay on sackcloth and ashes.

[4]Esther's maids and eunuchs came and told her. Overwhelmed with anguish, the queen sent garments for Mordecai to put on, so that he might take off his sackcloth; but he refused. [5]Esther then summoned Hathach, one of the king's eunuchs whom he had placed at her service, and commanded him to find out what this action of Mordecai meant and the reason for it. [6]So Hathach went out to Mordecai in the public square in front of the royal gate, [7]and Mordecai recounted all that had happened to him, as well as the exact amount of silver Haman had promised to pay to the royal treasury for the slaughter of the Jews. [8]He also gave him a copy of the written decree for their destruction that had been promulgated in Susa, to show and explain to Esther. Hathach was to instruct her to go to the king and to plead and intercede with him on behalf of her people.

[9]Hathach returned to Esther and told her what Mordecai had said. [10]Then Esther replied to Hathach and gave him this message for Mordecai: [11]"All the servants of the king and the people of his provinces know that any man or woman who goes to the king in the inner court without being summoned is subject to the same law—death. Only if the king extends the golden scepter will such a person live. Now as for me, I have not been summoned to the king for thirty days."

[12]When Esther's words were reported to Mordecai, [13]he had this reply brought to her: "Do not imagine that you are safe in the king's palace, you alone of all the Jews. [14]Even if you now remain silent, relief and deliverance will come to the Jews from another source; but you and your father's house will perish. Who knows—perhaps it was for a time like this that you became queen?"

[15]Esther sent back to Mordecai the response: [16]"Go and assemble all the Jews

who are in Susa; fast on my behalf, all of you, not eating or drinking night or day for three days. I and my maids will also fast in the same way. Thus prepared, I will go to the king, contrary to the law. If I perish, I perish!" [17]Mordecai went away and did exactly as Esther had commanded.

Prayer of Mordecai. C:1 Recalling all that the Lord had done, Mordecai prayed to the Lord [2]and said: "Lord, Lord, King and Ruler of all, everything is in your power, and there is no one to oppose you when it is your will to save Israel. [3]You made heaven and earth and every wonderful thing under heaven. [4]You are Lord of all, and there is no one who can resist you, the Lord. [5]You know all things. You know, Lord, that it was not out of insolence or arrogance or desire for glory that I acted thus in not bowing down to the arrogant Haman. [6]I would have gladly kissed the soles of his feet for the salvation of Israel. [7]But I acted as I did so as not to place the honor of a mortal above that of God. I will not bow down to anyone but you, my Lord. It is not out of arrogance that I am acting thus. [8]And now, Lord God, King, God of Abraham, spare your people, for our enemies regard us with deadly envy and are bent upon destroying the inheritance that was yours from the beginning. [9]Do not spurn your portion, which you redeemed for yourself out of the land of Egypt. [10]Hear my prayer; have pity on your inheritance and turn our mourning into feasting, that we may live to sing praise to your name, Lord. Do not silence the mouths of those who praise you."

[11]All Israel, too, cried out with all their strength, for death was staring them in the face.

Prayer of Esther. [12]Queen Esther, seized with mortal anguish, fled to the Lord for refuge. [13]Taking off her splendid garments, she put on garments of distress and mourning. In place of her precious ointments she covered her head with dung and ashes. She afflicted her body severely and in place of her festive adornments, her tangled hair covered her.

[14]Then she prayed to the Lord, the God of Israel, saying: "My Lord, you alone are our King. Help me, who am alone and have no help but you, [15]for I am taking my life in my hand. [16]From birth, I have heard among my people that you, Lord, chose Israel from among all nations, and our ancestors from among all their forebears, as a lasting inheritance, and that you fulfilled all your promises to them. [17]But now we have sinned in your sight, and you have delivered us into the hands of our enemies, [18]because we worshiped their gods. You are just, O Lord. [19]But now they are not satisfied with our bitter servitude, but have sworn an oath to their idols [20]to do away with the decree you have pronounced, to destroy your inheritance, to close the mouths of those who praise you, to extinguish the glory of your house and your altar, [21]to open the mouths of the nations to acclaim their worthless gods, and to extol a mortal king forever.

[22]"Lord, do not relinquish your scepter to those who are nothing. Do not let our foes gloat over our ruin, but turn their own counsel against them and make an example of the one who began this against us. [23]Be mindful of us, Lord. Make yourself known in the time of our distress and give me courage, King of gods and Ruler of every power. [24]Put in my mouth persuasive words in the presence of the lion, and turn his heart to hatred for our enemy, so that he and his co-conspirators may perish. [25]Save us by your power, and help me, who am alone and have no one but you, Lord.

[26]"You know all things. You know that I hate the pomp of the lawless, and abhor the bed of the uncircumcised or of any foreigner. [27]You know that I am under constraint, that I abhor the sign of grandeur that rests on my head when I appear in

public. I abhor it like a polluted rag, and do not wear it in private. [28]I, your servant, have never eaten at the table of Haman, nor have I graced the banquet of the king or drunk the wine of libations. [29]From the day I was brought here till now, your servant has had no joy except in you, Lord, God of Abraham. [30]O God, whose power is over all, hear the voice of those in despair. Save us from the power of the wicked, and deliver me from my fear."

Esther Goes to Ahasuerus. D:1 On the third day, ending her prayers, she took off her prayer garments and arrayed herself in her splendid attire. [2]In making her appearance, after invoking the all-seeing God and savior, she took with her two maids; [3]on the one she leaned gently for support, [4]while the other followed her, bearing her train. [5]She glowed with perfect beauty and her face was as joyous as it was lovely, though her heart was pounding with fear. [6]She passed through all the portals till she stood before the king, who was seated on his royal throne, clothed in full robes of state, and covered with gold and precious stones, so that he inspired great awe. [7]As he looked up in extreme anger, his features fiery and majestic, the queen staggered, turned pale and fainted, collapsing against the maid in front of her. [8]But God changed the king's anger to gentleness. In great anxiety he sprang from his throne, held her in his arms until she recovered, and comforted her with reassuring words. [9]"What is it, Esther?" he said to her. "I am your brother. Take courage! [10]You shall not die; this order of ours applies only to our subjects. [11]Come near!" [12]Raising the golden scepter, he touched her neck with it, embraced her, and said, "Speak to me." [13]She replied: "I saw you, my lord, as an angel of God, and my heart was shaken by fear of your majesty. [14]For you are awesome, my lord, though your countenance is full of mercy." [15]As she said this, she

fainted. [16]The king was shaken and all his attendants tried to revive her.

5:1 [Now on the third day, Esther put on her royal garments and stood in the inner courtyard, looking toward the royal palace, while the king was seated on his royal throne in the audience chamber, facing the palace doorway. [2]When he saw Queen Esther standing in the courtyard, she won his favor and he extended toward her the golden scepter he held. She came up to him, and touched the top of the scepter.]

[3]Then the king said to her, "What is it, Queen Esther? What is your request? Even if it is half of my kingdom, it shall be granted you." [4]Esther replied, "If it please your majesty, come today with Haman to a banquet I have prepared." [5]The king ordered, "Have Haman make haste to fulfill the wish of Esther."

First Banquet of Esther. So the king went with Haman to the banquet Esther had prepared. [6]During the drinking of the wine, the king said to Esther, "Whatever you ask for shall be granted, and whatever request you make shall be honored, even if it is for half my kingdom." [7]Esther replied: "This is my petition and request: [8]if I have found favor with the king and if it pleases your majesty to grant my petition and honor my request, let the king come with Haman tomorrow to a banquet I will prepare; and tomorrow I will do as the king asks."

Haman's Plot Against Mordecai. [9]That day Haman left happy and in good spirits. But when he saw that Mordecai at the royal gate did not rise, and showed no fear of him, he was filled with anger toward him. [10]Haman restrained himself, however, and went home, where he summoned his friends and his wife Zeresh. [11]He recounted the greatness of his riches, the large number of his sons, and how the king had promoted him and placed him above the officials and royal servants. [12]"Moreover," Haman added, "Queen Esther invited no one but me to come with the king to the banquet she prepared; again tomorrow I am to be her guest with the king. [13]Yet none of this satisfies me as long as I continue to see the Jew Mordecai sitting at the royal gate." [14]His wife Zeresh and all his

☐ MATTHEW 22:15-22

Paying Taxes to the Emperor. 22:15 Then the Pharisees went off and plotted how they might entrap him in speech. [16]They sent their disciples to him, with the Herodians, saying, "Teacher, we know that you are a truthful man and that you teach the way of God in accordance with the truth. And you are not concerned with anyone's opinion, for you do not regard a person's status. [17]Tell us, then, what is your opinion: Is it lawful to pay the census tax to Caesar

friends said to him, "Have a stake set up, fifty cubits in height, and in the morning ask the king to have Mordecai impaled on it. Then go to the banquet with the king in good spirits." This suggestion pleased Haman, and he had the stake erected.

or not?" [18]Knowing their malice, Jesus said, "Why are you testing me, you hypocrites? [19]Show me the coin that pays the census tax." Then they handed him the Roman coin. [20]He said to them, "Whose image is this and whose inscription?" [21]They replied, "Caesar's." At that he said to them, "Then repay to Caesar what belongs to Caesar and to God what belongs to God." [22]When they heard this they were amazed, and leaving him they went away.

June 5

St. Boniface

The Church is like a great ship being pounded by the waves of life's different stresses. Our duty is not to abandon ship, but to keep her on her course.

— ST. BONIFACE

☐ ESTHER 6, 7, 8, E

Mordecai's Reward from the King. 6:1 That night the king, unable to sleep, asked that the chronicle of notable events be brought in. While this was being read to him, [2]the passage occurred in which Mordecai reported Bigthan and Teresh, two of the royal eunuchs who guarded the entrance, for seeking to assassinate King Ahasuerus. [3]The king asked, "What was done to honor and exalt Mordecai for this?" The king's attendants replied, "Nothing was done for him."

[4]"Who is in the court?" the king asked. Now Haman had entered the outer court of the king's palace to suggest to the king that Mordecai should be impaled on the stake he had raised for him. [5]The king's attendants answered him, "Haman is waiting in the court." The king said, "Let him come in." [6]When Haman entered, the king said to him, "What should be done for the man whom the king wishes to reward?" Now Haman thought to himself, "Whom would the king wish to honor more than

me?" [7]So he replied to the king: "For the man whom the king wishes to honor [8]there should be brought the royal robe the king wore and the horse the king rode with the royal crest placed on its head. [9]The robe and the horse should be given to one of the noblest of the king's officials, who must clothe the man the king wishes to reward, have him ride on the horse in the public square of the city, and cry out before him, 'This is what is done for the man whom the king wishes to honor!'" [10]Then the king said to Haman: "Hurry! Take the robe and horse as you have proposed, and do this for the Jew Mordecai, who is sitting at the royal gate. Do not omit anything you proposed." [11]So Haman took the robe and horse, clothed Mordecai, had him ride in the public square of the city, and cried out before him, "This is what is done for the man whom the king wishes to honor!"

[12]Mordecai then returned to the royal gate, while Haman hurried home grieving, with his head covered. [13]When he told his wife Zeresh and all his friends everything that had happened to him, his advisers and his wife Zeresh said to him, "If Mordecai, before whom you are beginning to fall, is of Jewish ancestry, you will not prevail against him, but will surely be defeated by him."

Esther's Second Banquet. [14]While they were speaking with him, the king's eunuchs arrived and hurried Haman off to the banquet Esther had prepared.

7:1 So the king and Haman went to the banquet with Queen Esther. [2]Again, on this second day, as they were drinking wine, the king said to Esther, "Whatever you ask, Queen Esther, shall be granted you. Whatever request you make, even for half the kingdom, shall be honored." [3]Queen Esther replied: "If I have found favor with you, O king, and if it pleases your majesty, I ask that my life be spared, and I beg that you spare the lives of my people. [4]For we have been sold, I and my people,

to be destroyed, killed, and annihilated. If we were only to be sold into slavery I would remain silent, for then our distress would not have been worth troubling the king." [5]King Ahasuerus said to Queen Esther, "Who and where is the man who has dared to do this?" [6]Esther replied, "The enemy oppressing us is this wicked Haman." At this, Haman was seized with dread of the king and queen.

[7]The king left the banquet in anger and went into the garden of the palace, but Haman stayed to beg Queen Esther for his life, since he saw that the king had decided on his doom. [8]When the king returned from the palace garden to the banquet hall, Haman had thrown himself on the couch on which Esther was reclining; and the king exclaimed, "Will he also violate the queen while she is with me in my own house!" Scarcely had the king spoken when the face of Haman was covered over.

Punishment of Haman. [9]Harbona, one of the eunuchs who attended the king, said, "At the house of Haman stands a stake fifty cubits high. Haman made it for Mordecai, who gave the report that benefited the king." The king answered, "Impale him on it." [10]So they impaled Haman on the stake he had set up for Mordecai, and the anger of the king abated.

8:1 That day King Ahasuerus gave the house of Haman, enemy of the Jews, to Queen Esther; and Mordecai was admitted to the king's presence, for Esther had revealed his relationship to her. [2]The king removed his signet ring that he had taken away from Haman, and gave it to Mordecai; and Esther put Mordecai in charge of the house of Haman.

The Second Royal Decree. [3]Esther again spoke to the king. She fell at his feet and tearfully implored him to revoke the harm done by Haman the Agagite and the plan he had devised against the Jews. [4]The king stretched forth the golden scepter to

Esther. So she rose and, standing before him, [5]said: "If it seems good to the king and if I have found favor with him, if the thing seems right to the king and I am pleasing in his eyes, let a document be issued to revoke the letters that the schemer Haman, son of Hammedatha the Agagite, wrote for the destruction of the Jews in all the royal provinces. [6]For how can I witness the evil that is to befall my people, and how can I behold the destruction of my kindred?"

[7]King Ahasuerus then said to Queen Esther and to the Jew Mordecai: "Now that I have given Esther the house of Haman, and they have impaled him on the stake because he was going to attack the Jews, [8]you in turn may write in the king's name what you see fit concerning the Jews and seal the letter with the royal signet ring." For a decree written in the name of the king and sealed with the royal signet ring cannot be revoked.

[9]At that time, on the twenty-third day of the third month, Sivan, the royal scribes were summoned. Exactly as Mordecai dictated, they wrote to the Jews and to the satraps, governors, and officials of the hundred and twenty-seven provinces from India to Ethiopia: to each province in its own script and to each people in its own language, and to the Jews in their own script and language. [10]These letters, which he wrote in the name of King Ahasuerus and sealed with the royal signet ring, he sent by mounted couriers riding thoroughbred royal steeds. [11]In these letters the king authorized the Jews in each and every city to gather and defend their lives, to destroy, kill, and annihilate every armed group of any nation or province that might attack them, along with their wives and children, and to seize their goods as spoil [12]on a single day throughout the provinces of King Ahasuerus, the thirteenth day of the twelfth month, Adar.

E:1 The following is a copy of the letter:

"The great King Ahasuerus to the governors of the provinces in the hundred and twenty-seven satrapies from India to Ethiopia, and to those who are loyal to our government: Greetings!

[2]"Many have become more ambitious the more they were showered with honors through the bountiful generosity of their patrons. [3]Not only do they seek to do harm to our subjects but, incapable of dealing with such greatness, they even begin plotting against their own benefactors. [4]Not only do they drive out gratitude from among humankind but, with the arrogant boastfulness of those to whom goodness has no meaning, they suppose they will escape the stern judgment of the all-seeing God.

[5]"Often, too, the fair speech of friends entrusted with the administration of affairs has induced many placed in authority to become accomplices in the shedding of innocent blood, and has involved them in irreparable calamities [6]by deceiving with malicious slander the sincere good will of rulers. [7]This can be verified in the ancient stories that have been handed down to us, but more fully when you consider the wicked deeds perpetrated in your midst by the pestilential influence of those undeserving of authority. [8]We must provide for the future, so as to render the kingdom undisturbed and peaceful for all people, [9]taking advantage of changing conditions and always deciding matters coming to our attention with equitable treatment.

[10]"For instance, Haman, son of Hammedatha, a Macedonian, certainly not of Persian blood, and very different from us in generosity, was hospitably received by us. [11]He benefited so much from the good will we have toward all peoples that he was proclaimed 'our father,' before whom everyone was to bow down; and he attained a position second only to the royal throne. [12]But, unable to control his arrogance, he strove to deprive us of kingdom

and of life, [13]and by weaving intricate webs of deceit he demanded the destruction of Mordecai, our savior and constant benefactor, and of Esther, our blameless royal consort, together with their whole nation. [14]For by such measures he hoped to catch us defenseless and to transfer the rule of the Persians to the Macedonians. [15]But we find that the Jews, who were doomed to extinction by this archcriminal, are not evildoers, but rather are governed by very just laws [16]and are the children of the Most High, the living God of majesty, who has maintained the kingdom in a flourishing condition for us and for our forebears.

[17]"You will do well, then, to ignore the letter sent by Haman, son of Hammedatha, [18]for he who composed it has been impaled, together with his entire household, before the gates of Susa. Thus swiftly has God, who governs all, brought just punishment upon him.

[19]"You shall exhibit a copy of this letter publicly in every place to certify that the Jews may follow their own laws [20]and that you may help them on the day set for their ruin, the thirteenth day of the twelfth month, Adar, to defend themselves against those who attack them. [21]For God, the ruler of all, has turned that day from one of destruction of the chosen people into one of joy for them. [22]Therefore, you too must celebrate this memorable day among your designated feasts with all rejoicing, [23]so that both now and in the future it may be a celebration of deliverance for us and for Persians of good will, but for those who plot against us a reminder of destruction.

[24]"Every city and province without exception that does not observe this decree shall be ruthlessly destroyed with fire and sword, so that it will be left not merely untrodden by people, but even shunned by wild beasts and birds forever."

8:13 A copy of the letter to be promulgated as law in each and every province was published among all the peoples, so that the Jews might be prepared on that day to avenge themselves on their enemies. [14]Couriers mounted on royal steeds sped forth in haste at the king's order, and the decree was promulgated in the royal precinct of Susa.

[15]Mordecai left the king's presence clothed in a royal robe of violet and of white cotton, with a large crown of gold and a mantle of fine crimson linen. The city of Susa shouted with joy, [16]and for the Jews there was splendor and gladness, joy and triumph. [17]In each and every province and in each and every city, wherever the king's order arrived, there was merriment and joy, banqueting and feasting for the Jews. And many of the peoples of the land identified themselves as Jews, for fear of the Jews fell upon them.

☐ MATTHEW 22:23-33

The Question about the Resurrection.
22:23 On that day Sadducees approached him, saying that there is no resurrection. They put this question to him, [24]saying, "Teacher, Moses said, 'If a man dies without children, his brother shall marry his wife and raise up descendants for his brother.' [25]Now there were seven brothers among us. The first married and died and, having no descendants, left his wife to his brother. [26]The same happened with the second and the third, through all seven. [27]Finally the woman died. [28]Now at the resurrection, of the seven, whose wife will she be? For they all had been married to her." [29]Jesus said to them in reply, "You are misled because you do not know the scriptures or the power of God. [30]At the resurrection

they neither marry nor are given in marriage but are like the angels in heaven. [31]And concerning the resurrection of the dead, have you not read what was said to you by God, [32]'I am the God of Abraham, the God of Isaac, and the God of Jacob'? He is not the God of the dead but of the living." [33]When the crowds heard this, they were astonished at his teaching.

June 6

Blessed Maria Karlowska

We must make Christ more visible to others than we are ourselves.

— BLESSED MARIA KARLOWSKA

☐ ESTHER 9, 10, F

The Massacre Reversed. 9:1 When the day arrived on which the order decreed by the king was to be carried out, the thirteenth day of the twelfth month, Adar, on which the enemies of the Jews had expected to overpower them, the situation was reversed: the Jews overpowered those who hated them. [2]The Jews mustered in their cities throughout the provinces of King Ahasuerus to attack those who sought to do them harm, and no one could withstand them, for fear of them fell upon all the peoples. [3]Moreover, all the officials of the provinces, the satraps, governors, and royal procurators supported the Jews out of fear of Mordecai; [4]for Mordecai was powerful in the royal palace, and the report was spreading through all the provinces that he was continually growing in power.

[5]The Jews struck down all their enemies with the sword, killing and destroying them; they did to those who hated them as they pleased. [6]In the royal precinct of Susa, the Jews killed and destroyed five hundred people. [7]They also killed Parshandatha, Dalphon, Aspatha, [8]Poratha, Adalia, Aridatha, [9]Parmashta, Arisai, Aridai, and Vaizatha, [10]the ten sons of Haman, son of Hammedatha, the foe of the Jews. However, they did not engage in plundering.

[11]On the same day, when the number of those killed in the royal precinct of Susa was reported to the king, [12]he said to Queen Esther: "In the royal precinct of Susa the Jews have killed and destroyed five hundred people, as well as the ten sons of Haman. What must they have done in the other royal provinces! You shall again be granted whatever you ask, and whatever you request shall be honored." [13]So Esther said, "If it pleases your majesty, let the Jews in Susa be permitted again tomorrow to act according to today's decree, and let the ten sons of Haman be impaled on stakes." [14]The king then gave an order that this be done, and the decree was published in Susa. So the ten sons of Haman were impaled, [15]and the Jews in Susa mustered again on the fourteenth of the month of Adar and killed three hundred people in Susa. However, they did not engage in plundering.

[16]The other Jews, who dwelt in the royal provinces, also mustered and defended themselves, and obtained rest from their enemies. They killed seventy-five thousand

of those who hated them, but they did not engage in plunder. [17]This happened on the thirteenth day of the month of Adar.

The Feast of Purim. On the fourteenth of the month they rested, and made it a day of feasting and rejoicing.

[18]The Jews in Susa, however, mustered on the thirteenth and fourteenth of the month. But on the fifteenth they rested, and made it a day of joyful banqueting. [19]That is why the rural Jews, who dwell in villages, celebrate the fourteenth of the month of Adar as a day of joyful banqueting, a holiday on which they send food to one another.

[20]Mordecai recorded these events and sent letters to all the Jews, both near and far, in all the provinces of King Ahasuerus. [21]He ordered them to celebrate every year both the fourteenth and the fifteenth of the month of Adar [22]as the days on which the Jews obtained rest from their enemies and as the month which was turned for them from sorrow into joy, from mourning into celebration. They were to observe these days with joyful banqueting, sending food to one another and gifts to the poor. [23]The Jews adopted as a custom what they had begun doing and what Mordecai had written to them.

Summary of the Story. [24]Haman, son of Hammedatha the Agagite, the foe of all the Jews, had planned to destroy them and had cast the *pur*, or lot, for the time of their defeat and destruction. [25]Yet, when the plot became known to the king, the king ordered in writing that the wicked plan Haman had devised against the Jews should instead be turned against Haman and that he and his sons should be impaled on stakes. [26]And so these days have been named Purim after the word *pur*.

Thus, because of all that was contained in this letter, and because of what they had witnessed and experienced in this event, [27]the Jews established and adopted as a custom for themselves, their descendants, and all who should join them, the perpetual obligation of celebrating these two days every year in the manner prescribed by this letter, and at the time appointed. [28]These days were to be commemorated and kept in every generation, by every clan, in every province, and in every city. These days of Purim were never to be neglected among the Jews, nor forgotten by their descendants.

Esther and Mordecai Act in Concert. [29]Queen Esther, daughter of Abihail, and Mordecai the Jew, wrote to confirm with full authority this second letter about Purim, [30]and Mordecai sent documents concerning peace and security to all the Jews in the hundred and twenty-seven provinces of Ahasuerus' kingdom. [31]Thus were established, for their appointed time, these days of Purim which Mordecai the Jew and Queen Esther had designated for the Jews, just as they had previously enjoined upon themselves and upon their descendants the duty of fasting and supplication. [32]The command of Esther confirmed these prescriptions for Purim and was recorded in the book.

The Rise of Mordecai Completed. 10:1 King Ahasuerus levied a tax on the land and on the islands of the sea. [2]All the acts of his power and valor, as well as a detailed account of the greatness of Mordecai, whom the king promoted, are recorded in the chronicles of the kings of Media and Persia. [3]The Jew Mordecai was next in rank to King Ahasuerus, in high standing among the Jews, popular with many of his kindred, seeking the good of his people and speaking out on behalf of the welfare of all its descendants.

Mordecai's Dream Fulfilled. F:1 Then Mordecai said: "This is the work of God. [2]I recall the dream I had about these very things, and not a single detail has been left unfulfilled— [3]the tiny spring that grew into a river, and there was light, and sun, and many waters. The river is Esther, whom the king married and made queen. [4]The two dragons are myself and Haman. [5]The nations are those who assembled to destroy the name of the Jews, [6]but my people is Israel, who cried to God and was saved.

"The Lord saved his people and delivered us from all these evils. God worked signs and great wonders, such as have not occurred among the nations. [7]For this purpose he arranged two lots: one for the people of God, the second for all the other nations. [8]These two lots were fulfilled in the hour, the time, and the day of judgment before God and among all the nations. [9]God remembered his people and rendered justice to his inheritance.

[10]"Gathering together with joy and happiness before God, they shall celebrate these days on the fourteenth and fifteenth of the month Adar throughout all future generations of his people Israel."

Colophon. [11]In the fourth year of the reign of Ptolemy and Cleopatra, Dositheus, who said he was a priest and Levite, and his son Ptolemy brought the present letter of Purim, saying that it was genuine and that Lysimachus, son of Ptolemy, of the community of Jerusalem, had translated it.

☐ MATTHEW 22:34-46

The Greatest Commandment. 22:34 When the Pharisees heard that he had silenced the Sadducees, they gathered together, [35]and one of them [a scholar of the law] tested him by asking, [36]"Teacher, which commandment in the law is the greatest?" [37]He said to him, "You shall love the Lord, your God, with all your heart, with all your soul, and with all your mind. [38]This is the greatest and the first commandment. [39]The second is like it: You shall love your neighbor as yourself. [40]The whole law and the prophets depend on these two commandments."

The Question about David's Son. [41]While the Pharisees were gathered together, Jesus questioned them, [42]saying, "What is your opinion about the Messiah? Whose son is he?" They replied, "David's." [43]He said to them, "How, then, does David, inspired by the Spirit, call him 'lord,' saying:

[44]"The Lord said to my lord,
  "Sit at my right hand
  until I place your enemies under
      your feet'"?

[45]If David calls him 'lord,' how can he be his son?" [46]No one was able to answer him a word, nor from that day on did anyone dare to ask him any more questions.

June 7

Humility is to the various virtues what the chain is in a rosary. Take away the chain, and the beads are scattered; remove humility, and all virtues vanish.

— St. John Vianney

☐ 1 MACCABEES 1-2

From Alexander to Antiochus. 1:1 After Alexander the Macedonian, Philip's son, who came from the land of Kittim, had defeated Darius, king of the Persians and Medes, he became king in his place, having first ruled in Greece. ²He fought many battles, captured fortresses, and put the kings of the earth to death. ³He advanced to the ends of the earth, gathering plunder from many nations; the earth fell silent before him, and his heart became proud and arrogant. ⁴He collected a very strong army and won dominion over provinces, nations, and rulers, and they paid him tribute.

⁵But after all this he took to his bed, realizing that he was going to die. ⁶So he summoned his noblest officers, who had been brought up with him from his youth, and divided his kingdom among them while he was still alive. ⁷Alexander had reigned twelve years when he died.

⁸So his officers took over his kingdom, each in his own territory, ⁹and after his death they all put on diadems, and so did their sons after them for many years, multiplying evils on the earth.

¹⁰There sprang from these a sinful offshoot, Antiochus Epiphanes, son of King Antiochus, once a hostage at Rome. He became king in the one hundred and thirty-seventh year of the kingdom of the Greeks.

Lawless Jews. ¹¹In those days there appeared in Israel transgressors of the law who seduced many, saying: "Let us go and make a covenant with the Gentiles all around us; since we separated from them, many evils have come upon us." ¹²The proposal was agreeable; ¹³some from among the people promptly went to the king, and he authorized them to introduce the ordinances of the Gentiles. ¹⁴Thereupon they built a gymnasium in Jerusalem according to the Gentile custom. ¹⁵They disguised their circumcision and abandoned the holy covenant; they allied themselves with the Gentiles and sold themselves to wrongdoing.

Antiochus in Egypt. ¹⁶When his kingdom seemed secure, Antiochus undertook to become king of the land of Egypt and to rule over both kingdoms. ¹⁷He invaded Egypt with a strong force, with chariots, elephants and cavalry, and with a large fleet, ¹⁸to make war on Ptolemy, king of Egypt. Ptolemy was frightened at his presence and fled, and many were wounded and fell dead. ¹⁹The fortified cities in the land of Egypt were captured, and Antiochus plundered the land of Egypt.

Robbery of the Temple. ²⁰After Antiochus had defeated Egypt in the one hundred and forty-third year, he returned and went up against Israel and against Jerusalem with a strong force. ²¹He insolently entered the sanctuary and took away the golden altar, the lampstand for the light with all its utensils, ²²the offering table, the cups and bowls, the golden censers, and the curtain. The cornices and the golden ornament on the facade of the temple—he stripped it all off. ²³And he took away the silver and gold and the precious vessels; he also took all the hidden treasures he could find. ²⁴Taking all this, he went back to his own country. He shed much blood and spoke with great arrogance.

²⁵And there was great mourning
    throughout all Israel,
    ²⁶and the rulers and the elders
        groaned.
Young women and men languished,
    and the beauty of the women faded.
²⁷Every bridegroom took up
    lamentation,
    while the bride sitting in her
        chamber mourned,
²⁸And the land quaked on account of
    its inhabitants,
    and all the house of Jacob was
        clothed with shame.

Attack and Occupation. ²⁹Two years later, the king sent the Mysian commander to the cities of Judah, and he came to Jerusalem with a strong force. ³⁰He spoke to them deceitfully in peaceful terms, and they believed him. Then he attacked the city suddenly, in a great onslaught, and destroyed many of the people in Israel. ³¹He plundered the city and set fire to it, demolished its houses and its surrounding walls. ³²And they took captive the women and children, and seized the animals. ³³Then they built up the City of David with a high, strong wall and strong towers, and it became their citadel. ³⁴There they installed a sinful race, transgressors of the law, who fortified themselves inside it. ³⁵They stored up weapons and provisions, depositing there the plunder they had collected from Jerusalem, and they became a great snare.

³⁶The citadel became an ambush
    against the sanctuary,
    and a wicked adversary to Israel at
        all times.
³⁷They shed innocent blood around the
    sanctuary;
    they defiled the sanctuary.
³⁸Because of them the inhabitants of
    Jerusalem fled away,
    she became the abode of strangers.
She became a stranger to her own
    offspring,
    and her children forsook her.
³⁹Her sanctuary became desolate as a
    wilderness;
    her feasts were turned into mourning,
Her sabbaths to shame,
    her honor to contempt.
⁴⁰As her glory had been, so great was
    her dishonor:
    her exaltation was turned into
        mourning.

Religious Persecution. ⁴¹Then the king wrote to his whole kingdom that all should be one people, ⁴²and abandon their particular customs. All the Gentiles conformed to the command of the king, ⁴³and many Israelites delighted in his religion; they sacrificed to idols and profaned the sabbath.

⁴⁴The king sent letters by messenger to Jerusalem and to the cities of Judah, ordering them to follow customs foreign to their land; ⁴⁵to prohibit burnt offerings, sacrifices, and libations in the sanctuary, to profane the sabbaths and feast days, ⁴⁶to desecrate the sanctuary and the sacred ministers, ⁴⁷to build pagan altars and temples and shrines, to sacrifice swine and unclean animals, ⁴⁸to leave their sons uncircumcised, and to defile themselves with every kind of impurity and abomination; ⁴⁹so that they might forget the law and change all its ordinances. ⁵⁰Whoever refused to act according to the command of the king was to be put to death.

⁵¹In words such as these he wrote to his whole kingdom. He appointed inspectors over all the people, and he ordered the cities of Judah to offer sacrifices, each city in turn. ⁵²Many of the people, those who abandoned the law, joined them and committed evil in the land. ⁵³They drove Israel into hiding, wherever places of refuge could be found.

⁵⁴On the fifteenth day of the month Kislev, in the year one hundred and forty-five, the king erected the desolating abomination upon the altar of burnt offerings,

and in the surrounding cities of Judah they built pagan altars. [55]They also burned incense at the doors of houses and in the streets. [56]Any scrolls of the law that they found they tore up and burned. [57]Whoever was found with a scroll of the covenant, and whoever observed the law, was condemned to death by royal decree. [58]So they used their power against Israel, against those who were caught, each month, in the cities. [59]On the twenty-fifth day of each month they sacrificed on the pagan altar that was over the altar of burnt offerings. [60]In keeping with the decree, they put to death women who had their children circumcised, [61]and they hung their babies from their necks; their families also and those who had circumcised them were killed.

[62]But many in Israel were determined and resolved in their hearts not to eat anything unclean; [63]they preferred to die rather than to be defiled with food or to profane the holy covenant; and they did die. [64]And very great wrath came upon Israel.

Mattathias and His Sons. 2:1 In those days Mattathias, son of John, son of Simeon, a priest of the family of Joarib, left Jerusalem and settled in Modein. [2]He had five sons: John, who was called Gaddi; [3]Simon, who was called Thassi; [4]Judas, who was called Maccabeus; [5]Eleazar, who was called Avaran; and Jonathan, who was called Apphus. [6]When he saw the sacrileges that were being committed in Judah and in Jerusalem, [7]he said:

"Woe is me! Why was I born
    to see the ruin of my people,
    the ruin of the holy city—
To dwell there
    as it was given into the hands of
        enemies,
    the sanctuary into the hands of
        strangers?
[8]Her temple has become like a man
    disgraced,

[9]her glorious vessels carried off as
    spoils,
Her infants murdered in her streets,
    her youths by the sword of the
        enemy.
[10]What nation has not taken its share
    of her realm,
    and laid its hand on her spoils?
[11]All her adornment has been taken
    away.
    Once free, she has become a slave.
[12]We see our sanctuary laid waste,
    our beauty, our glory.
    The Gentiles have defiled them!
[13]Why are we still alive?"

[14]Then Mattathias and his sons tore their garments, put on sackcloth, and mourned bitterly.

Pagan Worship Refused and Resisted. [15]The officers of the king in charge of enforcing the apostasy came to the city of Modein to make them sacrifice. [16]Many of Israel joined them, but Mattathias and his sons drew together. [17]Then the officers of the king addressed Mattathias: "You are a leader, an honorable and great man in this city, supported by sons and kindred. [18]Come now, be the first to obey the king's command, as all the Gentiles and Judeans and those who are left in Jerusalem have done. Then you and your sons shall be numbered among the King's Friends, and you and your sons shall be honored with silver and gold and many gifts."

[19]But Mattathias answered in a loud voice: "Although all the Gentiles in the king's realm obey him, so that they forsake the religion of their ancestors and consent to the king's orders, [20]yet I and my sons and my kindred will keep to the covenant of our ancestors. [21]Heaven forbid that we should forsake the law and the commandments. [22]We will not obey the words of the king by departing from our religion in the slightest degree."

[23]As he finished saying these words, a certain Jew came forward in the sight of

all to offer sacrifice on the altar in Modein according to the king's order. [24]When Mattathias saw him, he was filled with zeal; his heart was moved and his just fury was aroused; he sprang forward and killed him upon the altar. [25]At the same time, he also killed the messenger of the king who was forcing them to sacrifice, and he tore down the altar. [26]Thus he showed his zeal for the law, just as Phinehas did with Zimri, son of Salu.

[27]Then Mattathias cried out in the city, "Let everyone who is zealous for the law and who stands by the covenant follow me!" [28]Then he and his sons fled to the mountains, leaving behind in the city all their possessions.

[29]At that time many who sought righteousness and justice went out into the wilderness to settle there, [30]they and their children, their wives and their animals, because misfortunes pressed so hard on them. [31]It was reported to the officers and soldiers of the king who were in the City of David, in Jerusalem, that those who had flouted the king's order had gone out to secret refuges in the wilderness. [32]Many hurried out after them, and having caught up with them, camped opposite and prepared to attack them on the sabbath. [33]The pursuers said to them, "Enough of this! Come out and obey the king's command, and you will live." [34]But they replied, "We will not come out, nor will we obey the king's command to profane the sabbath." [35]Then the enemy attacked them at once. [36]But they did not retaliate; they neither threw stones, nor blocked up their secret refuges. [37]They said, "Let us all die in innocence; heaven and earth are our witnesses that you destroy us unjustly." [38]So the officers and soldiers attacked them on the sabbath, and they died with their wives, their children and their animals, to the number of a thousand persons.

[39]When Mattathias and his friends heard of it, they mourned deeply for them.

[40]They said to one another, "If we all do as our kindred have done, and do not fight against the Gentiles for our lives and our laws, they will soon destroy us from the earth." [41]So on that day they came to this decision: "Let us fight against anyone who attacks us on the sabbath, so that we may not all die as our kindred died in their secret refuges."

[42]Then they were joined by a group of Hasideans, mighty warriors of Israel, all of them devoted to the law. [43]And all those who were fleeing from the persecutions joined them and supported them. [44]They gathered an army and struck down sinners in their wrath and the lawless in their anger, and the survivors fled to the Gentiles for safety. [45]Mattathias and his friends went about and tore down the pagan altars; [46]they also forcibly circumcised any uncircumcised boys whom they found in the territory of Israel. [47]They put to flight the arrogant, and the work prospered in their hands. [48]They saved the law from the hands of the Gentiles and of the kings and did not let the sinner triumph.

Farewell of Mattathias. [49]When the time came for Mattathias to die, he said to his sons: "Arrogance and scorn have now grown strong; it is a time of disaster and violent wrath. [50]Therefore, my children, be zealous for the law and give your lives for the covenant of our ancestors.

[51]"Remember the deeds that our
　　ancestors did in their times,
　and you shall win great honor and
　　　an everlasting name.
[52]Was not Abraham found faithful in
　　trial,
　and it was credited to him as
　　　righteousness?
[53]Joseph, when in distress, kept the
　　commandment,
　and he became master of Egypt.
[54]Phinehas our ancestor, for his
　　burning zeal,

received the covenant of an
everlasting priesthood.
⁵⁵Joshua, for executing his commission,
became a judge in Israel.
⁵⁶Caleb, for bearing witness before the
assembly,
received an inheritance in the land.
⁵⁷David, for his loyalty,
received as a heritage a throne of
eternal kingship.
⁵⁸Elijah, for his burning zeal for the
law,
was taken up to heaven.
⁵⁹Hananiah, Azariah and Mishael, for
their faith,
were saved from the fire.
⁶⁰Daniel, for his innocence,
was delivered from the mouths of
lions.
⁶¹And so, consider this from generation
to generation,
that none who hope in Heaven shall
fail in strength.
⁶²Do not fear the words of sinners,

for their glory ends in corruption
and worms.
⁶³Today exalted, tomorrow not to be
found,
they have returned to dust,
their schemes have perished.
⁶⁴Children! be courageous and strong
in keeping the law,
for by it you shall be honored.

⁶⁵"Here is your brother Simeon who I know is a wise counselor; listen to him always, and he will be a father to you. ⁶⁶And Judas Maccabeus, a mighty warrior from his youth, shall be the leader of your army and wage the war against the nations. ⁶⁷Gather about you all who observe the law, and avenge your people. ⁶⁸Pay back the Gentiles what they deserve, and observe the precepts of the law."

⁶⁹Then he blessed them, and he was gathered to his ancestors. ⁷⁰He died in the year one hundred and forty-six, and was buried in the tombs of his ancestors in Modein, and all Israel mourned him greatly.

☐ MATTHEW 23:1-12

Denunciation of the Scribes and Pharisees. 23:1 Then Jesus spoke to the crowds and to his disciples, ²saying, "The scribes and the Pharisees have taken their seat on the chair of Moses. ³Therefore, do and observe all things whatsoever they tell you, but do not follow their example. For they preach but they do not practice. ⁴They tie up heavy burdens [hard to carry] and lay them on people's shoulders, but they will not lift a finger to move them. ⁵All their works are performed to be seen. They widen their phylacteries and lengthen their tassels. ⁶They love places of honor at banquets, seats of honor in synagogues, ⁷greetings in marketplaces, and the salutation 'Rabbi.' ⁸As for you, do not be called 'Rabbi.' You have but one teacher, and you are all brothers. ⁹Call no one on earth your father; you have but one Father in heaven. ¹⁰Do not be called 'Master'; you have but one master, the Messiah. ¹¹The greatest among you must be your servant. ¹²Whoever exalts himself will be humbled; but whoever humbles himself will be exalted."

June 8

Whoever bids other folks to do right, but gives an evil example by acting the opposite way, is like a foolish weaver who weaves quickly with one hand and unravels the cloth just as quickly with the other.

— St. Thomas More

☐ 1 MACCABEES 3-5

Judas and His Early Victories. 3:1 Then his son Judas, who was called Maccabeus, took his place. ²All his brothers and all who had joined his father supported him, and they gladly carried on Israel's war.

³He spread abroad the glory of his
people,
and put on his breastplate like a
giant.
He armed himself with weapons of
war;
he fought battles and protected the
camp with his sword.
⁴In his deeds he was like a lion,
like a young lion roaring for prey.
⁵He pursued the lawless, hunting them
out,
and those who troubled his people
he destroyed by fire.
⁶The lawless were cowed by fear of him,
and all evildoers were dismayed.
By his hand deliverance was happily
achieved,
⁷and he afflicted many kings.
He gave joy to Jacob by his deeds,
and his memory is blessed forever.
⁸He went about the cities of Judah
destroying the renegades there.
He turned away wrath from Israel,
⁹was renowned to the ends of the
earth;
and gathered together those who
were perishing.

¹⁰Then Apollonius gathered together the Gentiles, along with a large army from Samaria, to fight against Israel. ¹¹When Judas learned of it, he went out to meet him and struck and killed him. Many fell wounded, and the rest fled. ¹²They took their spoils, and Judas took the sword of Apollonius and fought with it the rest of his life.

¹³But Seron, commander of the Syrian army, heard that Judas had mustered an assembly of faithful men ready for war. ¹⁴So he said, "I will make a name for myself and win honor in the kingdom. I will wage war against Judas and his followers, who have despised the king's command." ¹⁵And again a large company of renegades advanced with him to help him take revenge on the Israelites.

¹⁶When he reached the ascent of Beth horon, Judas went out to meet him with a few men. ¹⁷But when they saw the army coming against them, they said to Judas: "How can we, few as we are, fight such a strong host as this? Besides, we are weak since we have not eaten today." ¹⁸But Judas said: "Many are easily hemmed in by a few; in the sight of Heaven there is no difference between deliverance by many or by few; ¹⁹for victory in war does not depend upon the size of the army, but on strength that comes from Heaven. ²⁰With great presumption and lawlessness they come against us to destroy us and our wives and children and to despoil us; ²¹but we are fighting for our lives and our laws. ²²He will crush them before us; so do not fear them." ²³When he finished speaking, he rushed suddenly upon Seron and his army, who were crushed before him. ²⁴He pursued Seron down the descent of Beth-horon into

the plain. About eight hundred of their men fell, and the rest fled to the land of the Philistines. ²⁵Then Judas and his brothers began to be feared, and dread fell upon the Gentiles about them. ²⁶His fame reached the king, and the Gentiles talked about the battles of Judas.

The King's Strategy. ²⁷When King Antiochus heard these reports, he was filled with rage; so he ordered that all the forces of his kingdom be gathered, a very strong army. ²⁸He opened his treasury, gave his soldiers a year's pay, and commanded them to be prepared for anything. ²⁹But then he saw that this exhausted the money in his treasury; moreover the tribute from the province was small because of the dissension and distress he had brought upon the land by abolishing the laws which had been in effect from of old. ³⁰He feared that, as had happened once or twice, he would not have enough for his expenses and for the gifts that he was accustomed to give with a lavish hand—more so than all previous kings. ³¹Greatly perplexed, he decided to go to Persia and levy tribute on those provinces, and so raise a large sum of money.

³²He left Lysias, a noble of royal descent, in charge of the king's affairs from the Euphrates River to the frontier of Egypt, ³³and commissioned him to take care of his son Antiochus until his return. ³⁴He entrusted to him half of his forces, and the elephants, and gave him instructions concerning everything he wanted done. As for the inhabitants of Judea and Jerusalem, ³⁵Lysias was to send an army against them to crush and destroy the power of Israel and the remnant of Jerusalem and efface their memory from the place. ³⁶He was to settle foreigners in all their territory and distribute their land by lot. ³⁷The king took the remaining half of the army and set out from Antioch, his capital, in the year one hundred and forty-seven; he crossed the Euphrates River and went through the provinces beyond.

Preparations for Battle. ³⁸Lysias chose Ptolemy, son of Dorymenes, and Nicanor and Gorgias, powerful men among the King's Friends, ³⁹and with them he sent forty thousand foot soldiers and seven thousand cavalry to invade and ravage the land of Judah according to the king's orders. ⁴⁰Setting out with their whole force, they came and pitched their camp near Emmaus in the plain. ⁴¹When the merchants of the region heard of their prowess, they came to the camp, bringing a huge sum of silver and gold, along with fetters, to buy the Israelites as slaves. A force from Edom and from Philistia joined with them.

⁴²Judas and his brothers saw that evils had multiplied and that armies were encamped within their territory. They learned of the orders which the king had given to destroy and utterly wipe out the people. ⁴³So they said to one another, "Let us raise our people from their ruin and fight for them and for our sanctuary!"

⁴⁴The assembly gathered together to prepare for battle and to pray and ask for mercy and compassion.

⁴⁵Jerusalem was uninhabited, like a
wilderness;
    not one of her children came in or
        went out.
The sanctuary was trampled on,
    and foreigners were in the citadel;
    it was a habitation for Gentiles.
Joy had disappeared from Jacob,
    and the flute and the harp were
        silent.

⁴⁶Thus they assembled and went to Mizpah near Jerusalem, because formerly at Mizpah there was a place of prayer for Israel. ⁴⁷That day they fasted and wore sackcloth; they sprinkled ashes on their heads and tore their garments. ⁴⁸They unrolled the scroll of the law, to learn about the things for which the Gentiles consulted the images of their idols. ⁴⁹They brought with them the priestly garments, the first fruits, and the tithes;

and they brought forward the nazirites who had completed the time of their vows. ⁵⁰And they cried aloud to Heaven: "What shall we do with these, and where shall we take them? ⁵¹For your sanctuary has been trampled on and profaned, and your priests are in mourning and humbled. ⁵²Now the Gentiles are gathered together against us to destroy us. You know what they plot against us. ⁵³How shall we be able to resist them unless you help us?" ⁵⁴Then they blew the trumpets and cried out loudly.

⁵⁵After this Judas appointed officers for the people, over thousands, over hundreds, over fifties, and over tens. ⁵⁶He proclaimed that those who were building houses, or were just married, or were planting vineyards, and those who were afraid, could each return home, according to the law. ⁵⁷Then the army moved off, and they camped to the south of Emmaus. ⁵⁸Judas said: "Arm yourselves and be brave; in the morning be ready to fight these Gentiles who have assembled against us to destroy us and our sanctuary. ⁵⁹It is better for us to die in battle than to witness the evils befalling our nation and our sanctuary. ⁶⁰Whatever is willed in heaven will be done."

Victory over Gorgias. 4:1 Now Gorgias took five thousand infantry and a thousand picked cavalry, and this detachment set out at night ²in order to fall upon the camp of the Jews in a surprise attack. Some from the citadel were his guides. ³Judas heard of it and himself set out with his soldiers to attack the king's army at Emmaus ⁴while these forces were still scattered away from the camp. ⁵During the night Gorgias came into the camp of Judas, and found no one there; so he sought them in the mountains, saying, "They are fleeing from us."

⁶But at daybreak Judas appeared in the plain with three thousand men; furthermore they lacked the helmets and swords they wanted. ⁷They saw the army of the Gentiles, strong, breastplated, and flanked with cavalry, and made up of experienced soldiers. ⁸Judas said to the men with him: "Do not fear their numbers or dread their attack. ⁹Remember how our ancestors were saved in the Red Sea, when Pharaoh pursued them with an army. ¹⁰So now let us cry to Heaven in the hope that he will favor us, remember the covenant with our ancestors, and destroy this army before us today. ¹¹All the Gentiles shall know that there is One who redeems and delivers Israel."

¹²When the foreigners looked up and saw them marching toward them, ¹³they came out of their camp for battle. The men with Judas blew the trumpet, and ¹⁴joined the battle. They crushed the Gentiles, who fled toward the plain. ¹⁵Their whole rear guard fell by the sword, and they were pursued as far as Gazara and the plains of Idumaea, to Azotus and Jamnia. About three thousand of their men fell.

¹⁶When Judas and the army returned from the pursuit, ¹⁷he said to the people: "Do not be greedy for plunder; for there is a fight ahead of us, ¹⁸and Gorgias and his army are near us on the mountain. But now stand firm against our enemies and fight them. Afterward you can freely take the plunder."

¹⁹As Judas was finishing this speech, a detachment appeared, looking down from the mountain. ²⁰They saw that their army had been put to flight and their camp was burning. The smoke they saw revealed what had happened. ²¹When they realized this, they completely lost heart; and when they also saw the army of Judas in the plain ready to attack, ²²they all fled to the land of the foreigners.

²³Then Judas went back to plunder the camp, and they took much gold and silver, cloth dyed blue and marine purple, and great treasure. ²⁴As they returned, they were singing hymns and glorifying Heaven, "who is good, whose mercy endures forever." ²⁵Thus Israel experienced a great deliverance that day.

Victory over Lysias. [26]But those of the foreigners who had escaped went and told Lysias all that had occurred. [27]When he heard it he was disturbed and discouraged, because things had not turned out in Israel as he intended and as the king had ordered.

[28]So the following year he gathered together sixty thousand picked men and five thousand cavalry, to fight them. [29]They came into Idumea and camped at Bethzur, and Judas met them with ten thousand men. [30]Seeing that the army was strong, he prayed thus:

"Blessed are you, Savior of Israel, who crushed the attack of the mighty one by the hand of your servant David and delivered the foreign camp into the hand of Jonathan, the son of Saul, and his armorbearer. [31]Give this army into the hands of your people Israel; make them ashamed of their troops and their cavalry. [32]Strike them with cowardice, weaken the boldness of their strength, and let them tremble at their own destruction. [33]Strike them down by the sword of those who love you, that all who know your name may sing your praise."

[34]Then they engaged in battle, and about five thousand of Lysias' army fell in hand-to-hand fighting. [35]When Lysias saw the tide of the battle turning, and the increased boldness of Judas, whose men were ready either to live or to die nobly, he withdrew to Antioch and began to recruit mercenaries so as to return to Judea with greater numbers.

Purification and Rededication of the Temple. [36]Then Judas and his brothers said, "Now that our enemies have been crushed, let us go up to purify the sanctuary and rededicate it." [37]So the whole army assembled, and went up to Mount Zion. [38]They found the sanctuary desolate, the altar desecrated, the gates burnt, weeds growing in the courts as in a thicket or on some mountain, and the priests' chambers demolished. [39]Then they tore their garments and made great lamentation; they sprinkled their heads with ashes [40]and prostrated themselves. And when the signal was given with trumpets, they cried out to Heaven.

[41]Judas appointed men to attack those in the citadel, while he purified the sanctuary. [42]He chose blameless priests, devoted to the law; [43]these purified the sanctuary and carried away the stones of the defilement to an unclean place. [44]They deliberated what ought to be done with the altar for burnt offerings that had been desecrated. [45]They decided it best to tear it down, lest it be a lasting shame to them that the Gentiles had defiled it; so they tore down the altar. [46]They stored the stones in a suitable place on the temple mount, until the coming of a prophet who could determine what to do with them. [47]Then they took uncut stones, according to the law, and built a new altar like the former one. [48]They also repaired the sanctuary and the interior of the temple and consecrated the courts. [49]They made new sacred vessels and brought the lampstand, the altar of incense, and the table into the temple. [50]Then they burned incense on the altar and lighted the lamps on the lampstand, and these illuminated the temple. [51]They also put loaves on the table and hung up the curtains. Thus they finished all the work they had undertaken.

[52]They rose early on the morning of the twenty-fifth day of the ninth month, that is, the month of Kislev, in the year one hundred and forty-eight, [53]and offered sacrifice according to the law on the new altar for burnt offerings that they had made. [54]On the anniversary of the day on which the Gentiles had desecrated it, on that very day it was rededicated with songs, harps, lyres, and cymbals. [55]All the people prostrated themselves and adored and praised Heaven, who had given them success.

[56]For eight days they celebrated the dedication of the altar and joyfully offered burnt offerings and sacrifices of deliverance and praise. [57]They ornamented the facade of the temple with gold crowns and shields;

they repaired the gates and the priests' chambers and furnished them with doors. [58]There was great joy among the people now that the disgrace brought by the Gentiles was removed. [59]Then Judas and his brothers and the entire assembly of Israel decreed that every year for eight days, from the twenty-fifth day of the month Kislev, the days of the dedication of the altar should be observed with joy and gladness on the anniversary.

[60]At that time they built high walls and strong towers around Mount Zion, to prevent the Gentiles from coming and trampling it as they had done before. [61]Judas also placed a garrison there to protect it, and likewise fortified Beth-zur, that the people might have a stronghold facing Idumea.

Victories over Hostile Neighbors. 5:1 When the nations round about heard that the altar had been rebuilt and the sanctuary restored as before, they were enraged. [2]So they decided to destroy the descendants of Jacob who were among them, and they began to kill and eradicate the people. [3]Then Judas attacked the Edomites at Akrabattene in Idumea, because they were blockading Israel; he dealt them a heavy blow, humbled and despoiled them. [4]He also remembered the malice of the Baeanites, who had become a snare and a stumbling block to the people by ambushing them along the roads. [5]He forced them to take refuge in towers, which he besieged; he put them under the ban and burned down their towers along with all who were in them. [6]Then he crossed over to the Ammonites, where he found a strong army and a large body of people with Timothy as their leader. [7]He fought many battles with them, routed them, and struck them down. [8]After seizing Jazer and its villages, he returned to Judea.

Liberation of Jews in Galilee and Gilead. [9]The Gentiles in Gilead assembled to destroy the Israelites who were in their territory; these then fled to the stronghold of Dathema. [10]They sent a letter to Judas and his brothers saying: "The Gentiles around us have assembled against us to destroy us, [11]and they are preparing to come and seize this stronghold to which we have fled. Timothy is the leader of their army. [12]Come at once to rescue us from them, for many of us have fallen. [13]All our kindred who were in the territory of the Tobiads have been killed; the Gentiles have captured their wives, their children and their goods, and they have slain there about a thousand men."

[14]While they were reading this letter, suddenly other messengers, with garments torn, arrived from Galilee to deliver a similar message: [15]that "the inhabitants of Ptolemais, Tyre, and Sidon, and the whole of Gentile Galilee have joined forces to destroy us." [16]When Judas and the people heard this, a great assembly convened to consider what they should do for their kindred who were in distress and being attacked by enemies.

[17]Judas said to his brother Simon: "Choose men for yourself, and go, rescue your kindred in Galilee; my brother Jonathan and I will go to Gilead."

[18]He left Joseph, son of Zechariah, and Azariah, leader of the people, with the rest of the army in Judea to guard it. [19]He commanded them, "Take charge of these people, but do not join battle against the Gentiles until we return." [20]Three thousand men were allotted to Simon to go into Galilee, and eight thousand men to Judas, for Gilead.

[21]Simon went into Galilee and fought many battles with the Gentiles. They were crushed before him, [22]and he pursued them to the very gate of Ptolemais. About three thousand of the Gentiles fell, and he gathered their spoils. [23]He took with him the Jews who were in Galilee and in Arbatta, with their wives and children and all that they had, and brought them to Judea with great rejoicing.

²⁴Judas Maccabeus and his brother Jonathan crossed the Jordan and marched for three days through the wilderness. ²⁵There they met some Nabateans, who received them peaceably and told them all that had happened to their kindred in Gilead: ²⁶"Many of them are shut up in Bozrah, in Bosor near Alema, in Chaspho, Maked, and Carnaim"—all of these are large, fortified cities— ²⁷"and some are shut up in other cities of Gilead. Tomorrow their enemies plan to attack the strongholds and to seize and destroy all these people in one day."

²⁸Thereupon Judas suddenly changed direction with his army, marched across the wilderness to Bozrah, and captured the city. He put every male to the sword, took all their spoils, and set fire to the city. ²⁹He led his army from that place by night, and they marched toward the stronghold. ³⁰When morning came, they looked ahead and saw a countless multitude, with ladders and machines for capturing the stronghold, beginning to attack. ³¹When Judas perceived that the struggle had begun and that the noise of the battle was resounding to heaven with trumpet blasts and loud shouting, ³²he said to the men of his army, "Fight for our kindred today." ³³He came up behind them with three columns blowing their trumpets and crying out in prayer. ³⁴When the army of Timothy realized that it was Maccabeus, they fled before him, and he inflicted on them a great defeat. About eight thousand of their men fell that day.

³⁵Then he turned toward Alema and attacked and captured it; he killed every male, took spoils, and burned it down. ³⁶From there he moved on and took Chaspho, Maked, Bosor, and the other cities of Gilead.

³⁷After these events Timothy assembled another army and camped opposite Raphon, on the other side of the wadi. ³⁸Judas sent men to spy on the camp, and they reported to him: "All the Gentiles around us have rallied to him, making a very large force; ³⁹they have also hired Arabians to help them, and have camped beyond the wadi, ready to attack you." So Judas went forward to meet them.

⁴⁰As Judas and his army were approaching the flowing wadi, Timothy said to the officers of his army: "If he crosses over to us first, we shall not be able to resist him; he will certainly defeat us. ⁴¹But if he is hesitant and camps on the other side of the river, we will cross over to him and defeat him." ⁴²But when Judas reached the flowing wadi, he stationed the officers of the people beside it and gave them this order: "Do not allow anyone to encamp; all must go into battle." ⁴³He was the first to cross to the attack, with all the people behind him, and all the Gentiles were crushed before them. They threw away their arms and fled to the temple enclosure at Carnaim. ⁴⁴But Judas' troops captured the city and burnt the temple enclosure with all who were in it. So Carnaim was subdued, and Judas met with no more resistance.

Return to Jerusalem. ⁴⁵Then Judas assembled all the Israelites, great and small, who were in Gilead, with their wives and children and their goods, a very large company, to go into the land of Judah. ⁴⁶When they reached Ephron, a large and strongly fortified city along the way, they found it impossible to go around it on either the right or the left; they would have to march right through it. ⁴⁷But the people in the city shut them out and blocked up the gates with stones. ⁴⁸Then Judas sent them this peaceful message: "Let us cross your territory in order to reach our own; no one will harm you; we will only march through." But they would not open to him. ⁴⁹So Judas ordered a proclamation to be made in the camp that everyone should take up positions where they were. ⁵⁰When the men of the army took up their positions, he assaulted the city all that day and night, and it was delivered into his hand. ⁵¹He put every male to the sword, leveled the city, took spoils and passed through it over the slain.

⁵²Then they crossed the Jordan to the great plain in front of Beth-shan; ⁵³and Judas kept gathering the stragglers and encouraging the people the whole way, until he reached the land of Judah. ⁵⁴They ascended Mount Zion in joy and gladness and sacrificed burnt offerings, because not one of them had fallen; they had returned in safety.

Joseph and Azariah Defeated. ⁵⁵In those days when Judas and Jonathan were in the land of Gilead, and Simon his brother was in Galilee opposite Ptolemais, ⁵⁶Joseph, son of Zechariah, and Azariah, the leaders of the army, heard about the brave deeds and the fighting that they were doing. ⁵⁷They said, "Let us also make a name for ourselves by going out and fighting against the Gentiles around us." ⁵⁸They gave orders to those of their army who were with them, and marched against Jamnia. ⁵⁹But Gorgias and his men came out of the city to meet them in battle. ⁶⁰Joseph and Azariah were routed and were pursued to the frontiers of Judea, and about two thousand Israelites fell that day. ⁶¹It was a great setback for the people, because they had not obeyed Judas and his brothers, thinking that they would do brave deeds. ⁶²But they were not of the family through whom Israel's deliverance was given.

Victories at Hebron and Azotus. ⁶³The valiant Judas and his brothers were greatly honored in all Israel and among all the Gentiles, wherever their name was heard; ⁶⁴and people gathered about them and praised them.

⁶⁵Then Judas and his brothers went out and attacked the Edomites in the land toward the south; he took Hebron and its villages, and he destroyed its strongholds and burned the towers around it. ⁶⁶He then set out for the land of the foreigners and passed through Marisa. ⁶⁷On that day some priests fell in battle who had gone out rashly to fight in their desire to do brave deeds. ⁶⁸Judas then turned toward Azotus in the land of the foreigners. He destroyed their altars and burned the carved images of their gods; and after plundering their cities he returned to the land of Judah.

☐ MATTHEW 23:13-24

23:13 "Woe to you, scribes and Pharisees, you hypocrites. You lock the kingdom of heaven before human beings. You do not enter yourselves, nor do you allow entrance to those trying to enter. ¹⁴

¹⁵"Woe to you, scribes and Pharisees, you hypocrites. You traverse sea and land to make one convert, and when that happens you make him a child of Gehenna twice as much as yourselves.

¹⁶"Woe to you, blind guides, who say, 'If one swears by the temple, it means nothing, but if one swears by the gold of the temple, one is obligated.' ¹⁷Blind fools, which is greater, the gold, or the temple that made the gold sacred? ¹⁸And you say, 'If one swears by the altar, it means nothing, but if one swears by the gift on the altar, one is obligated.' ¹⁹You blind ones, which is greater, the gift, or the altar that makes the gift sacred? ²⁰One who swears by the altar swears by it and all that is upon it; ²¹one who swears by the temple swears by it and by him who dwells in it; ²²one who swears by heaven swears by the throne of God and by him who is seated on it.

²³"Woe to you, scribes and Pharisees, you hypocrites. You pay tithes of mint and dill and cummin, and have neglected the weightier things of the law: judgment and mercy and fidelity. [But] these you should have done, without neglecting the others. ²⁴Blind guides, who strain out the gnat and swallow the camel!"

June 9

St. Ephraem

The seaman stores up drinking water in his vessel; in the midst of the salty sea he lays up and keeps it, the sweet in the midst of the bitter. In the same way, amidst the floods of sin, keep the water of baptism.

— ST. EPHRAEM

☐ 1 MACCABEES 6-9

6:1 As King Antiochus passed through the eastern provinces, he heard that in Persia there was a city, Elam, famous for its wealth in silver and gold, ²and that its temple was very rich, containing gold helmets, breastplates, and weapons left there by the first king of the Greeks, Alexander, son of Philip, king of Macedon. ³He went therefore and tried to capture and loot the city. But he could not do so, because his plan became known to the people of the city ⁴who rose up in battle against him. So he fled and in great dismay withdrew from there to return to Babylon.

⁵While he was in Persia, a messenger brought him news that the armies that had gone into the land of Judah had been routed; ⁶that Lysias had gone at first with a strong army and been driven back; that the people of Judah had grown strong by reason of the arms, wealth, and abundant spoils taken from the armies they had cut down; ⁷that they had pulled down the abomination which he had built upon the altar in Jerusalem; and that they had surrounded with high walls both the sanctuary, as it had been before, and his city of Beth-zur.

⁸When the king heard this news, he was astonished and very much shaken. Sick with grief because his designs had failed, he took to his bed. ⁹There he remained many days, assailed by waves of grief, for he thought he was going to die. ¹⁰So he called in all his Friends and said to them: "Sleep has departed from my eyes, and my heart sinks from anxiety. ¹¹I said to myself: 'Into what tribulation have I come, and in what floods of sorrow am I now! Yet I was kindly and beloved in my rule.' ¹²But I now recall the evils I did in Jerusalem, when I carried away all the vessels of silver and gold that were in it, and for no cause gave orders that the inhabitants of Judah be destroyed. ¹³I know that this is why these evils have overtaken me; and now I am dying, in bitter grief, in a foreign land."

¹⁴Then he summoned Philip, one of his Friends, and put him in charge of his whole kingdom. ¹⁵He gave him his diadem, his robe, and his signet ring, so that he might guide the king's son Antiochus and bring him up to be king. ¹⁶So King Antiochus died there in the one hundred and forty-ninth year. ¹⁷When Lysias learned that the king was dead, he set up the king's son Antiochus, whom he had reared as a child, to be king in his place; and he gave him the title Eupator.

Siege of the Citadel. ¹⁸Those in the citadel were hemming Israel in around the sanctuary, continually trying to harm them and to strengthen the Gentiles. ¹⁹And so Judas planned to destroy them, and assembled the people to besiege them. ²⁰So in the one hundred and fiftieth year they assembled and besieged the citadel, for which purpose he constructed platforms and siege engines. ²¹But some of the besieged escaped, and some renegade Israelites joined them. ²²They went to the king and said: "How long will you fail to do justice and to avenge our kindred? [23]We agreed to serve your father and to follow his orders and obey his edicts. [24]And for this our own people have become our enemies; they have put to death as many of us as they could find and have seized our inheritances. [25]They have acted aggressively not only against us, but throughout their whole territory. [26]Look! Today they have besieged the citadel in Jerusalem in order to capture it, and they have fortified the sanctuary and Beth-zur. [27]Unless you act quickly to prevent them, they will do even worse things than these, and you will not be able to stop them."

[28]When the king heard this he was enraged, and he called together all his Friends, the officers of his army, and the commanders of the cavalry. [29]Mercenary forces also came to him from other kingdoms and from the islands of the seas. [30]His army numbered a hundred thousand footsoldiers, twenty thousand cavalry, and thirty-two elephants trained for war. [31]They passed through Idumea and camped before Beth-zur. For many days they attacked it; they constructed siege engines, but the besieged made a sortie and burned these, and they fought bravely.

Battle of Beth-zechariah. [32]Then Judas marched away from the citadel and moved his camp to Beth-zechariah, opposite the king's camp. [33]The king, rising before dawn, moved his force hastily along the road to Beth-zechariah; and the troops prepared for battle and sounded the trumpet. [34]They made the elephants drunk on the juice of grapes and mulberries to get them ready to fight. [35]The beasts were distributed along the phalanxes, each elephant having assigned to it a thousand men in coats of mail, with bronze helmets on their heads, and five hundred picked cavalry. [36]These accompanied the beast wherever it was; wherever it moved, they moved too and never left it. [37]Each elephant was outfitted with a strong wooden tower, fastened to it by a harness; each tower held three soldiers who fought from it, besides the Indian driver. [38]The remaining cavalry were stationed on one or the other of the two flanks of the army, to harass the enemy and to be protected by the phalanxes. [39]When the sun shone on the gold and bronze shields, the mountains gleamed with their brightness and blazed like flaming torches. [40]Part of the king's army spread out along the heights, while some were on low ground, and they marched forward steadily in good order. [41]All who heard the noise of their numbers, the tramp of their marching, and the clanging of the arms, trembled; for the army was very great and strong.

[42]Judas with his army advanced to fight, and six hundred men of the king's army fell. [43]Eleazar, called Avaran, saw one of the beasts covered with royal armor and bigger than any of the others, and so he thought the king was on it. [44]He gave up his life to save his people and win an everlasting name for himself. [45]He dashed courageously up to it in the middle of the phalanx, killing men right and left, so that they parted before him. [46]He ran under the elephant, stabbed it and killed it. The beast fell to the ground on top of him, and he died there. [47]But when Judas' troops saw the strength of the royal army and the ardor of its forces, they retreated from them.

The Siege of Jerusalem. [48]Some of the king's army went up to Jerusalem to attack them, and the king established camps in Judea and at Mount Zion. [49]He made peace with the people of Beth-zur, and they evacuated the city, because they had no food there to enable them to withstand a siege, for that was a sabbath year in the land. [50]The king took Beth-zur and stationed a garrison there to hold it. [51]For many days he besieged the sanctuary, setting up platforms and siege engines, firethrowers, catapults and mechanical bows for shooting arrows and projectiles. [52]The defenders countered by setting up siege engines of their own, and kept up the fight a long time. ⁵³But there were no provisions in the storerooms, because it was the seventh year, and the reserves had been eaten up by those who had been rescued from the Gentiles and brought to Judea. ⁵⁴Few men remained in the sanctuary because the famine was too much for them; the rest scattered, each to his own home.

Peace Treaty. ⁵⁵Lysias heard that Philip, whom King Antiochus, before his death, had appointed to train his son Antiochus to be king, ⁵⁶had returned from Persia and Media with the army that accompanied the king, and that he was seeking to take over the government. ⁵⁷So he hastily decided to withdraw. He said to the king, the leaders of the army, and the soldiers: "We are growing weaker every day, our provisions are scanty, the place we are besieging is strong, and it is our duty to take care of the affairs of the kingdom. ⁵⁸Therefore let us now come to terms with these people and make peace with them and all their nation. ⁵⁹Let us grant them freedom to live according to their own laws as formerly; it was on account of their laws, which we abolished, that they became enraged and did all these things."

⁶⁰The proposal pleased the king and the leaders; he sent peace terms to the Jews, and they accepted. ⁶¹So the king and the leaders swore an oath to them, and on these terms the Jews evacuated the fortification. ⁶²But when the king entered Mount Zion and saw how the place was fortified, he broke the oath he had sworn and gave orders to tear down the encircling wall. ⁶³Then he departed in haste and returned to Antioch, where he found Philip in control of the city. He fought against him and took the city by force.

Expedition of Bacchides and Alcimus. 7:1 In the one hundred and fifty-first year, Demetrius, son of Seleucus, set out from Rome, arrived with a few men at a coastal city, and began to rule there. ²As he was entering the royal palace of his ancestors, the soldiers seized Antiochus and Lysias to bring them to him. ³When he was informed of this, he said, "Do not show me their faces." ⁴So the soldiers killed them, and Demetrius assumed the royal throne.

⁵Then all the lawless men and renegades of Israel came to him. They were led by Alcimus, who desired to be high priest. ⁶They made this accusation to the king against the people: "Judas and his brothers have destroyed all your friends and have driven us out of our land. ⁷So now, send a man whom you trust to go and see all the destruction Judas has wrought on us and on the king's territory, and let him punish them and all their supporters."

⁸So the king chose Bacchides, one of the King's Friends, who ruled the province of West-of-Euphrates, a great man in the kingdom, and faithful to the king. ⁹He sent him and the renegade Alcimus, to whom he granted the high priesthood, with orders to take revenge on the Israelites. ¹⁰They set out and, on arriving in the land of Judah with a great army, sent messengers who spoke deceitfully to Judas and his brothers in peaceful terms. ¹¹But these paid no attention to their words, seeing that they had come with a great army.

¹²A group of scribes, however, gathered about Alcimus and Bacchides to ask for a just agreement. ¹³The Hasideans were the first among the Israelites to seek peace with them, ¹⁴for they said, "A priest of the line of Aaron has come with the army, and he will not do us any wrong." ¹⁵He spoke with them peacefully and swore to them, "We will not seek to injure you or your friends." ¹⁶So they trusted him. But he arrested sixty of them and killed them in one day, according to the words that he wrote:

¹⁷"The flesh of your faithful,
and their blood they have spilled all
around about Jerusalem,
and no one was left to bury them."

[18]Then fear and dread of them came upon all the people, who said: "There is no truth or justice among them; they violated the agreement and the oath that they swore."

[19]Bacchides withdrew from Jerusalem and camped in Beth-zaith. He had many of the men who deserted to him arrested and some of the people. He killed them and threw them into a great cistern. [20]He handed the province over to Alcimus, leaving troops to help him, while he himself returned to the king.

[21]Alcimus struggled to maintain his high priesthood, [22]and all those who were troubling the people gathered about him. They took possession of the land of Judah and caused great distress in Israel. [23]When Judas saw all the evils that Alcimus and those with him were bringing upon the Israelites, even more than the Gentiles had, [24]he went about all the borders of Judea and took revenge on the men who had deserted, preventing them from going out into the country. [25]But when Alcimus saw that Judas and his followers were gaining strength and realized that he could not resist them, he returned to the king and accused them of grave crimes.

Defeat of Nicanor. [26]Then the king sent Nicanor, one of his honored officers, who was a bitter enemy of Israel, with orders to destroy the people. [27]Nicanor came to Jerusalem with a large force and deceitfully sent to Judas and his brothers this peaceable message: [28]"Let there be no fight between me and you. I will come with a few men to meet you face to face in peace."

[29]So he came to Judas, and they greeted one another peaceably. But Judas' enemies were prepared to seize him. [30]When he became aware that Nicanor had come to him with deceit in mind, Judas was afraid of him and would not meet him again. [31]When Nicanor saw that his plan had been discovered, he went out to fight Judas near Capharsalama. [32]About five hundred men of Nicanor's army fell; the rest fled to the City of David.

[33]After this, Nicanor went up to Mount Zion. Some of the priests from the sanctuary and some of the elders of the people came out to greet him peaceably and to show him the burnt offering that was being sacrificed for the king. [34]But he mocked and ridiculed them, defiled them, and spoke arrogantly. [35]In a rage he swore: "If Judas and his army are not delivered to me at once, when I return victorious I will burn this temple down." He went away in great anger. [36]The priests, however, went in and stood before the altar and the sanctuary. They wept and said: [37]"You have chosen this house to bear your name, to be a house of prayer and supplication for your people. [38]Take revenge on this man and his army, and let them fall by the sword. Remember their blasphemies, and do not let them continue."

[39]Nicanor left Jerusalem and camped at Beth-horon, where the Syrian army joined him. [40]But Judas camped in Adasa with three thousand men. Here Judas uttered this prayer: [41]"When they who were sent by the king blasphemed, your angel went out and killed a hundred and eighty-five thousand of them. [42]In the same way, crush this army before us today, and let the rest know that Nicanor spoke wickedly against your sanctuary; judge him according to his wickedness."

[43]The armies met in battle on the thirteenth day of the month Adar. Nicanor's army was crushed, and he himself was the first to fall in the battle. [44]When his army saw that Nicanor had fallen, they threw down their weapons and fled. [45]The Jews pursued them a day's journey from Adasa to near Gazara, blowing the trumpets behind them as signals. [46]From all the surrounding villages of Judea people came out and outflanked them. They turned them back, and all the enemies fell by the sword; not a single one escaped.

[47]Then the Jews collected the spoils and the plunder; they cut off Nicanor's head

and his right arm, which he had lifted up so arrogantly. These they brought and displayed in the sight of Jerusalem. [48]The people rejoiced greatly, and observed that day as a day of much joy. [49]They decreed that it should be observed every year on the thirteenth of Adar. [50]And so for a few days the land of Judah was at rest.

Eulogy of the Romans. 8:1 Judas had heard of the reputation of the Romans. They were valiant fighters and acted amiably to all who took their side. They established a friendly alliance with all who applied to them. [2]He was also told of their battles and the brave deeds that they performed against the Gauls, conquering them and forcing them to pay tribute; [3]and what they did in Spain to get possession of the silver and gold mines there. [4]By planning and persistence they subjugated the whole region, although it was very remote from their own. They also subjugated the kings who had come against them from the far corners of the earth until they crushed them and inflicted on them severe defeat. The rest paid tribute to them every year. [5]Philip and Perseus, king of the Macedonians, and the others who opposed them in battle they overwhelmed and subjugated. [6]Antiochus the Great, king of Asia, who fought against them with a hundred and twenty elephants and with cavalry and chariots and a very great army, was defeated by them. [7]They took him alive and obliged him and the kings who succeeded him to pay a heavy tribute, to give hostages and to cede [8]Lycia, Mysia, and Lydia from among their best provinces. The Romans took these from him and gave them to King Eumenes. [9]When the Greeks planned to come and destroy them, [10]the Romans discovered it, and sent against the Greeks a single general who made war on them. Many were wounded and fell, and the Romans took their wives and children captive. They plundered them, took possession of their land, tore down their strongholds and reduced them to slavery even to this day. [11]All the other kingdoms and islands that had ever opposed them they destroyed and enslaved; with their friends, however, and those who relied on them, they maintained friendship. [12]They subjugated kings both near and far, and all who heard of their fame were afraid of them. [13]Those whom they wish to help and to make kings, they make kings; and those whom they wish, they depose; and they were greatly exalted. [14]Yet with all this, none of them put on a diadem or wore purple as a display of grandeur. [15]But they made for themselves a senate chamber, and every day three hundred and twenty men took counsel, deliberating on all that concerned the people and their well-being. [16]They entrust their government to one man every year, to rule over their entire land, and they all obey that one, and there is no envy or jealousy among them.

Treaty with the Romans. [17]So Judas chose Eupolemus, son of John, son of Accos, and Jason, son of Eleazar, and sent them to Rome to establish friendship and alliance with them. [18]He did this to lift the yoke from Israel, for it was obvious that the kingdom of the Greeks was subjecting them to slavery. [19]After making a very long journey to Rome, the envoys entered the senate chamber and spoke as follows: [20]"Judas, called Maccabeus, and his brothers, with the Jewish people, have sent us to you to establish alliance and peace with you, and to be enrolled among your allies and friends." [21]The proposal pleased the Romans, [22]and this is a copy of the reply they inscribed on bronze tablets and sent to Jerusalem, to remain there with the Jews as a record of peace and alliance:

[23]"May it be well with the Romans and the Jewish nation at sea and on land forever; may sword and enemy be far from them. [24]But if war is first made on Rome, or any of its allies in any of their dominions,

²⁵the Jewish nation will fight along with them wholeheartedly, as the occasion shall demand; ²⁶and to those who wage war they shall not give or provide grain, weapons, money, or ships, as seems best to Rome. They shall fulfill their obligations without receiving any recompense. ²⁷In the same way, if war is made first on the Jewish nation, the Romans will fight along with them willingly, as the occasion shall demand, ²⁸and to those who attack them there shall not be given grain, weapons, money, or ships, as seems best to Rome. They shall fulfill their obligations without deception. ²⁹On these terms the Romans have made an agreement with the Jewish people. ³⁰But if both parties hereafter agree to add or take away anything, they shall do as they choose, and whatever they shall add or take away shall be valid.

³¹"Moreover, concerning the wrongs that King Demetrius is doing to them, we have written to him thus: 'Why have you made your yoke heavy upon our friends and allies the Jews? ³²If they petition against you again, we will enforce justice and make war on you by sea and land.'"

Death of Judas. 9:1 When Demetrius heard that Nicanor and his army had fallen in battle, he again sent Bacchides and Alcimus into the land of Judah, along with the right wing of his army. ²They took the road to Galilee, and camping opposite the ascent at Arbela, they captured it and killed many people. ³In the first month of the one hundred and fifty-second year, they encamped against Jerusalem. ⁴Then they set out for Berea with twenty thousand men and two thousand cavalry. ⁵Judas, with three thousand picked men, had camped at Elasa. ⁶When they saw the great number of the troops, they were very much afraid, and many slipped away from the camp, until only eight hundred of them remained.

⁷When Judas saw that his army was melting away just as the battle was imminent, he was brokenhearted, because he had no time to gather them together. ⁸In spite of his discouragement he said to those who remained: "Let us go forward to meet our enemies; perhaps we can put up a good fight against them." ⁹They tried to dissuade him, saying: "We certainly cannot. Let us save our own lives now, and come back with our kindred, and then fight against them. Now we are too few." ¹⁰But Judas said: "Far be it from me to do such a thing as to flee from them! If our time has come, let us die bravely for our kindred and not leave a stain upon our honor!"

¹¹Then the army of Bacchides moved out of camp and took its position for combat. The cavalry were divided into two squadrons, and the slingers and the archers came on ahead of the army, and in the front line were all the best warriors. Bacchides was on the right wing. ¹²Flanked by the two squadrons, the phalanx attacked as they blew their trumpets. Those who were on Judas' side also blew their trumpets. ¹³The earth shook with the noise of the armies, and the battle raged from morning until evening.

¹⁴When Judas saw that Bacchides was on the right, with the main force of his army, all the most stouthearted rallied to him, ¹⁵and the right wing was crushed; Judas pursued them as far as the mountain slopes. ¹⁶But when those on the left wing saw that the right wing was crushed, they closed in behind Judas and those with him. ¹⁷The battle became intense, and many on both sides fell wounded. ¹⁸Then Judas fell, and the rest fled.

¹⁹Jonathan and Simon took their brother Judas and buried him in the tomb of their ancestors at Modein. ²⁰All Israel wept for him with great lamentation. They mourned for him many days, and they said, ²¹"How the mighty one has fallen, the savior of Israel!" ²²The other acts of Judas, his battles, the brave deeds he performed, and his greatness have not been recorded; but they were very many.

Jonathan Succeeds Judas. [23]After the death of Judas, the lawless raised their heads in every part of Israel, and all kinds of evildoers appeared. [24]In those days there was a very great famine, and the country deserted to them. [25]Bacchides chose renegades and made them masters of the country. [26]These sought out and hunted down the friends of Judas and brought them to Bacchides, who punished and derided them. [27]There was great tribulation in Israel, the like of which had not been since the time prophets ceased to appear among them.

[28]Then all the friends of Judas came together and said to Jonathan: [29]"Ever since your brother Judas died, there has been no one like him to lead us against our enemies, both Bacchides and those of our nation who are hostile to us. [30]Now therefore we have chosen you today to be our ruler and leader in his place, to fight our battle." [31]From that moment Jonathan accepted the leadership, and took the place of Judas his brother.

Bacchides Pursues Jonathan. [32]When Bacchides learned of it, he sought to kill him. [33]But Jonathan and his brother Simon and all who were with him discovered this, and they fled to the wilderness of Tekoa and camped by the waters of the pool of Asphar. [34]

[35]Jonathan sent his brother as leader of the convoy to implore his friends, the Nabateans, to let them deposit with them their great quantity of baggage. [36]But the tribe of Jambri from Medaba made a raid and seized and carried off John and everything he had.

[37]After this, word was brought to Jonathan and his brother Simon: "The tribe of Jambri are celebrating a great wedding, and with a large escort they are bringing the bride, the daughter of one of the great princes of Canaan, from Nadabath." [38]Remembering the blood of John their brother, they went up and hid themselves under cover of the mountain. [39]As they watched there appeared a noisy throng with much baggage; then the bridegroom and his friends and kinsmen had come out to meet them with tambourines and musicians with their instruments. [40]Jonathan and his party rose up against them from their ambush and killed them. Many fell wounded; the rest fled toward the mountain; all their spoils were taken. [41]Thus the wedding was turned into mourning, and the sound of their music into lamentation. [42]Having taken their revenge for the blood of their brother, they returned to the marshes of the Jordan.

[43]When Bacchides heard of it, he came on the sabbath to the banks of the Jordan with a large force. [44]Then Jonathan said to his companions, "Let us rise up now and fight for our lives, for today is not like yesterday and the day before. [45]The battle is before us, behind us are the waters of the Jordan, on either side of us, marsh and thickets; there is no way of escape. [46]Cry out now to Heaven so that you may be delivered from the hand of our enemies." [47]When they joined battle, Jonathan raised his hand to strike Bacchides, but Bacchides backed away from him. [48]Jonathan and those with him jumped into the Jordan and swam across to the other side, but the enemy did not pursue them across the Jordan. [49]About a thousand men on Bacchides' side fell that day.

[50]On returning to Jerusalem, Bacchides built strongholds in Judea: the Jericho fortress, as well as Emmaus, Beth-horon, Bethel, Timnath, Pharathon, and Tephon, with high walls and gates and bars. [51]In each he put a garrison to harass Israel. [52]He fortified the city of Beth-zur, Gazara and the citadel, and put troops in them and stores of provisions. [53]He took as hostages the sons of the leading people of the country and put them in custody in the citadel at Jerusalem.

[54]In the one hundred and fifty-third year, in the second month, Alcimus ordered

the wall of the inner court of the sanctuary to be torn down, thus destroying the work of the prophets. But he only began to tear it down. ⁵⁵Just at that time Alcimus was stricken, and his work was interrupted; his mouth was closed and he was paralyzed, so that he could no longer utter a word or give orders concerning his household. ⁵⁶Alcimus died in great agony at that time. ⁵⁷Seeing that Alcimus was dead, Bacchides returned to the king, and the land of Judah was at rest for two years.

⁵⁸Then all the lawless took counsel and said: "Jonathan and those with him are living in peace and security. Now then, let us have Bacchides return, and he will capture all of them in a single night." ⁵⁹So they went and took counsel with him. ⁶⁰When Bacchides was setting out with a large force, he sent letters secretly to all his allies in Judea, telling them to seize Jonathan and his companions. They were not able to do this, however, because their plan became known. ⁶¹In fact, Jonathan's men seized about fifty of the men of the country who were leaders in the conspiracy and put them to death.

⁶²Then Jonathan and those with him, along with Simon, withdrew to Bethbasi in the wilderness; he rebuilt its ruins and fortified it. ⁶³When Bacchides learned of this, he gathered together his whole force and sent word to those who were in Judea.

⁶⁴He came and camped before Bethbasi, and constructing siege engines, he fought against it for many days.

⁶⁵Leaving his brother Simon in the city, Jonathan, accompanied by a small group of men, went out into the countryside. ⁶⁶He struck down Odomera and his kindred and the tribe of Phasiron in their encampment; these men had begun to attack and they were going up with their forces. ⁶⁷Simon and those with him then sallied forth from the city and set fire to the siege engines. ⁶⁸They fought against Bacchides, and he was crushed. They caused him great distress, because the enterprise he had planned was in vain. ⁶⁹He was enraged with the lawless men who had advised him to invade the province. He killed many of them and resolved to return to his own country.

⁷⁰Jonathan learned of this and sent ambassadors to agree on peace with him and to obtain the release of the prisoners. ⁷¹He agreed to do as Jonathan asked. He swore an oath to him that he would never try to do him any harm for the rest of his life; ⁷²and he released to him the prisoners he had previously taken from the land of Judah. Thereupon he returned to his own land and never came into their territory again. ⁷³Then the sword ceased from Israel. Jonathan settled in Michmash; he began to judge the people and he eliminated the renegades from Israel.

☐ MATTHEW 23:25-39

23:25 "Woe to you, scribes and Pharisees, you hypocrites. You cleanse the outside of cup and dish, but inside they are full of plunder and self-indulgence. ²⁶Blind Pharisee, cleanse first the inside of the cup, so that the outside also may be clean.

²⁷"Woe to you, scribes and Pharisees, you hypocrites. You are like whitewashed tombs, which appear beautiful on the outside, but inside are full of dead men's bones and every kind of filth. ²⁸Even so, on the outside you appear righteous, but inside you are filled with hypocrisy and evildoing.

²⁹"Woe to you, scribes and Pharisees, you hypocrites. You build the tombs of the prophets and adorn the memorials of the righteous, ³⁰and you say, 'If we had lived in the days of our ancestors, we would not have joined them in shedding the prophets' blood.' ³¹Thus you bear witness against

yourselves that you are the children of those who murdered the prophets; ³²now fill up what your ancestors measured out! ³³You serpents, you brood of vipers, how can you flee from the judgment of Gehenna? ³⁴Therefore, behold, I send to you prophets and wise men and scribes; some of them you will kill and crucify, some of them you will scourge in your synagogues and pursue from town to town, ³⁵so that there may come upon you all the righteous blood shed upon earth, from the righteous blood of Abel to the blood of Zechariah, the son of Barachiah, whom you mur-

dered between the sanctuary and the altar. ³⁶Amen, I say to you, all these things will come upon this generation.

The Lament over Jerusalem. ³⁷"Jerusalem, Jerusalem, you who kill the prophets and stone those sent to you, how many times I yearned to gather your children together, as a hen gathers her young under her wings, but you were unwilling! ³⁸Behold, your house will be abandoned, desolate. ³⁹I tell you, you will not see me again until you say, 'Blessed is he who comes in the name of the Lord.'"

June 10

Blessed Edward Poppe

According to the divine plan, action must be fed with prayer. The interior life is the wellspring of the apostolate.

— BLESSED EDWARD POPPE

☐ **1 MACCABEES 10–13**

Jonathan Becomes High Priest. 10:1 In the one hundred and sixtieth year, Alexander Epiphanes, son of Antiochus, came up and took Ptolemais. They accepted him as king and he began to reign there. ²When King Demetrius heard of it, he mustered a very large army and marched out to engage him in battle. ³Demetrius sent a letter to Jonathan written in peaceful terms, to exalt him; ⁴for he said: "Let us be the first to make peace with him, before he makes peace with Alexander against us, ⁵since he will remember all the wrongs we have done to him, his brothers, and his nation."

⁶So Demetrius authorized him to gather an army and procure arms as his ally; and he ordered that the hostages in the citadel be released to him. ⁷Accordingly Jonathan went to Jerusalem and read the letter to all the people and to those who were in the

citadel. ⁸They were struck with fear when they heard that the king had given him authority to gather an army. ⁹Those in the citadel released the hostages to Jonathan, and he gave them back to their parents. ¹⁰Thereafter Jonathan dwelt in Jerusalem, and began to build and restore the city. ¹¹He ordered those doing the work to build the walls and to encircle Mount Zion with square stones for its fortification, and they did so. ¹²The foreigners in the strongholds that Bacchides had built took flight; ¹³all of them left their places and returned to their own lands. ¹⁴Only in Beth-zur did some remain of those who had abandoned the law and the commandments, for it was a place of refuge.

¹⁵King Alexander heard of the promises that Demetrius had made to Jonathan; he was also told of the battles and brave deeds

of Jonathan and his brothers and of the troubles that they had endured. [16]He said, "Shall we ever find another man like him? Let us now make him our friend and ally." [17]So he sent Jonathan a letter written in these terms: [18]"King Alexander sends greetings to his brother Jonathan. [19]We have heard of you, that you are a mighty warrior and worthy to be our friend. [20]We have therefore appointed you today to be high priest of your nation; you are to be called the King's Friend, and you are to look after our interests and preserve friendship with us." He also sent him a purple robe and a crown of gold. [21]Jonathan put on the sacred vestments in the seventh month of the one hundred and sixtieth year at the feast of Booths, and he gathered an army and procured many weapons.

A Letter from Demetrius to Jonathan. [22]When Demetrius heard of these things, he was distressed and said: [23]"Why have we allowed Alexander to get ahead of us by gaining the friendship of the Jews and thus strengthening himself? [24]I too will write them encouraging words and offer honors and gifts, so that they may support me." [25]So he sent them this message: "King Demetrius sends greetings to the Jewish nation. [26]We have heard how you have kept the treaty with us and continued in our friendship and not gone over to our enemies, and we are glad. [27]Continue, therefore, to keep faith with us, and we will reward you with favors in return for what you do in our behalf. [28]We will grant you many exemptions and will bestow gifts on you.

[29]"I now free you and exempt all the Jews from the tribute, the salt tax, and the crown levies. [30]Instead of collecting the third of the grain and the half of the fruit of the trees that should be my share, I renounce the right from this day forward. Neither now nor in the future will I collect them from the land of Judah or from the three districts annexed from Samaria. [31]Let Jerusalem and her territory, her tithes and her tolls, be sacred and free from tax. [32]I also yield my authority over the citadel in Jerusalem, and I transfer it to the high priest, that he may put in it such men as he shall choose to guard it. [33]Every Jew who has been carried into captivity from the land of Judah into any part of my kingdom I set at liberty without ransom; and let all their taxes, even those on their cattle, be canceled.

[34]Let all feast days, sabbaths, new moon festivals, appointed days, and the three days that precede each feast day, and the three days that follow, be days of immunity and exemption for all Jews in my kingdom. [35]No one will have authority to exact payment from them or to harass any of them in any matter.

[36]"Let thirty thousand Jews be enrolled in the king's army and allowances be given them, as is due to all the king's soldiers. [37]Let some of them be stationed in the king's principal strongholds, and of these let some be given positions of trust in the affairs of the kingdom. Let their superiors and their rulers be chosen from among them, and let them follow their own laws, as the king has commanded in the land of Judah.

[38]"Let the three districts that have been added to Judea from the province of Samaria be annexed to Judea so that they may be under one rule and obey no other authority than the high priest. [39]Ptolemais and its confines I give as a present to the sanctuary in Jerusalem for the necessary expenses of the sanctuary. [40]I make a yearly personal grant of fifteen thousand silver shekels out of the royal revenues, taken from appropriate places. [41]All the additional funds that the officials did not hand over as they had done in the first years shall henceforth be handed over for the services of the temple. [42]Moreover, the dues of five thousand silver shekels that used to be taken from the revenue of the sanctuary every year shall be canceled, since these funds belong to the priests who perform the ser-

vices. [43]All who take refuge in the temple of Jerusalem or in any of its precincts, because of money they owe the king, or because of any other debt, shall be released, together with all the goods they possess in my kingdom. [44]The cost of rebuilding and restoring the structures of the sanctuary shall be covered out of the royal revenue. [45]Likewise the cost of building the walls of Jerusalem and fortifying it all around, and of building walls in Judea, shall be donated from the royal revenue."

[46]When Jonathan and the people heard these words, they neither believed nor accepted them, for they remembered the great evil that Demetrius had done in Israel, and the great tribulation he had brought upon them. [47]They therefore decided in favor of Alexander, for he had been the first to address them peaceably, and they remained his allies for the rest of his life.

[48]Then King Alexander gathered together a large army and encamped opposite Demetrius. [49]The two kings joined battle, and when the army of Demetrius fled, Alexander pursued him, and overpowered his soldiers. [50]He pressed the battle hard until sunset, and Demetrius fell that day.

Treaty of Ptolemy and Alexander. [51]Alexander sent ambassadors to Ptolemy, king of Egypt, with this message: [52]"Now that I have returned to my realm, taken my seat on the throne of my ancestors, and established my rule by crushing Demetrius and gaining control of my country— [53]for I engaged him in battle, he and his army were crushed by us, and we assumed his royal throne— [54]let us now establish friendship with each other. Give me now your daughter for my wife; and as your son-in-law, I will give to you and to her gifts worthy of you."

[55]King Ptolemy answered in these words: "Happy the day on which you returned to the land of your ancestors and took your seat on their royal throne! [56]I will do for you what you have written; but meet me in Ptolemais, so that we may see each other, and I will become your father-in-law as you have proposed."

[57]So Ptolemy with his daughter Cleopatra set out from Egypt and came to Ptolemais in the one hundred and sixty-second year. [58]There King Alexander met him, and Ptolemy gave him his daughter Cleopatra in marriage. Their wedding was celebrated at Ptolemais with great splendor according to the custom of kings.

[59]King Alexander also wrote to Jonathan to come and meet him. [60]So he went with pomp to Ptolemais, where he met the two kings and gave them and their friends silver and gold and many gifts and thus won their favor. [61]Some villainous men of Israel, transgressors of the law, united against him to accuse him, but the king paid no heed to them. [62]The king ordered Jonathan to be divested of his garments and to be clothed in royal purple; and so it was done. [63]The king also had him seated at his side. He said to his magistrates: "Go with him to the center of the city and make a proclamation that no one is to bring charges against him on any grounds or be troublesome to him for any reason." [64]When his accusers saw the honor paid to him according to the king's proclamation, and him clothed in purple, they all fled. [65]And so the king honored him, enrolling him among his Chief Friends, and he made him governor and chief of the province. [66]So Jonathan returned in peace and happiness to Jerusalem.

Jonathan Defeats Apollonius. [67]In the one hundred and sixty-fifth year, Demetrius, son of Demetrius, came from Crete to the land of his ancestors. [68]When King Alexander heard of it he was greatly troubled, and returned to Antioch. [69]Demetrius set Apollonius over Coelesyria. Having gathered a large army, Apollonius encamped at Jamnia. From there he sent this message to Jonathan the high priest:

[70]"You are the only one who resists us. I am laughed at and put to shame on your account. Why are you exercising author-

ity against us in the mountains? [71]If you have confidence in your forces, come down now to us in the plain, and let us test each other's strength there; for the forces of the cities are on my side. [72]Inquire and find out who I am and who the others are who are helping me. People are saying that you cannot make a stand against us because your ancestors were twice put to flight in their own land. [73]Now you too will be unable to withstand our cavalry and such a force as this in the plain, where there is not a stone or a pebble or a place to flee."

[74]When Jonathan heard the message of Apollonius, he was provoked. Choosing ten thousand men, he set out from Jerusalem, and Simon his brother joined him to help him. [75]He encamped near Joppa, but the people of the city shut him out because Apollonius had a garrison in Joppa. When they attacked it, [76]the people of the city became afraid and opened the gates, and so Jonathan took possession of Joppa.

[77]When Apollonius heard of it, he drew up three thousand cavalry and a large force of infantry. He marched toward Azotus as though he were going on through, but at the same time he was advancing into the plain, because he had such a large number of cavalry to rely on. [78]Jonathan pursued him toward Azotus, and the armies engaged in battle. [79]Apollonius, however, had left a thousand cavalry in hiding behind them. [80]Jonathan discovered that there was an ambush behind him; his army was surrounded. From morning until evening they showered his troops with arrows. [81]But his troops held their ground, as Jonathan had commanded, while the enemy's horses became tired out.

[82]Then Simon brought forward his force, and engaged the phalanx in battle. Since the cavalry were exhausted, the phalanx was crushed by him and fled, [83]while the cavalry too were scattered over the plain. They fled to Azotus and entered Beth-dagon, the temple of their idol, to save themselves. [84]But Jonathan burned and plundered Azotus with its neighboring towns, and destroyed by fire both the temple of Dagon and those who had taken refuge in it. [85]Those who fell by the sword, together with those who were burned alive, came to about eight thousand.

[86]Then Jonathan left there and encamped at Askalon, and the people of that city came out to meet him with great pomp. [87]Jonathan and those with him then returned to Jerusalem, with much spoil. [88]When King Alexander heard of these events, he accorded new honors to Jonathan. [89]He sent him a gold buckle, such as is usually given to King's Kinsmen; he also gave him Ekron and all its territory as a possession.

Alliance of Ptolemy and Demetrius II. 11:1 Then the king of Egypt gathered forces as numerous as the sands of the seashore, and many ships; and he sought by deceit to take Alexander's kingdom and add it to his own. [2]He set out for Syria with peaceful words, and the people in the cities opened their gates to welcome him, as King Alexander had ordered them to do, since Ptolemy was his father-in-law. [3]But when Ptolemy entered the cities, he stationed a garrison of troops in each one.

[4]As they neared Azotus, they showed him the temple of Dagon destroyed by fire, Azotus and its suburbs demolished, corpses lying about, and the charred bodies of those burned in the war, for they had heaped them up along his route. [5]They told the king what Jonathan had done in order to denigrate him; but the king said nothing. [6]Jonathan met the king with pomp at Joppa, and they greeted each other and spent the night there. [7]Jonathan accompanied the king as far as the river called Eleutherus and then returned to Jerusalem.

[8]And so King Ptolemy took possession of the cities along the seacoast as far as Seleucia by the sea, plotting evil schemes

against Alexander all the while. [9]He sent ambassadors to King Demetrius, saying: "Come, let us make a covenant with each other; I will give you my daughter whom Alexander has married, and you shall reign over your father's kingdom. [10]I regret that I gave him my daughter, for he has sought to kill me." [11]He was criticizing Alexander, however, because he coveted his kingdom. [12]After taking his daughter away, Ptolemy gave her to Demetrius and broke with Alexander; the enmity between them was now evident. [13]Then Ptolemy entered Antioch and assumed the crown of Asia; thus he set upon his head two crowns, that of Egypt and that of Asia.

[14]Now King Alexander was in Cilicia at that time, because the people of that region had revolted. [15]When Alexander heard the news, he came against Ptolemy in battle. Ptolemy marched out and met him with a strong force and routed him. [16]When Alexander fled to Arabia to seek protection, King Ptolemy was triumphant. [17]Zabdiel the Arabian cut off Alexander's head and sent it to Ptolemy. [18]But three days later King Ptolemy himself died, and his troops in the strongholds were killed by the inhabitants of the strongholds. [19]Thus Demetrius became king in the one hundred and sixty-seventh year.

Alliance of Jonathan and Demetrius II. [20]In those days Jonathan gathered together the people of Judea to attack the citadel in Jerusalem, and they set up many siege engines against it. [21]But some transgressors of the law, enemies of their own nation, went to the king and informed him that Jonathan was besieging the citadel. [22]When Demetrius heard this, he was enraged; and as soon as he heard it, he set out and came to Ptolemais. He wrote to Jonathan to discontinue the siege and to meet him for a conference at Ptolemais as soon as possible.

[23]On hearing this, Jonathan ordered the siege to continue. He selected some elders and priests of Israel and put himself at risk. [24]Taking with him silver, gold and apparel, and many other presents, he went to the king at Ptolemais, and found favor with him. [25]Although certain renegades of his own nation kept on bringing charges against him, [26]the king treated him just as his predecessors had done and exalted him in the presence of all his Friends. [27]He confirmed him in the high priesthood and in the other honors he had previously held, and had him enrolled among his Chief Friends.

[28]Jonathan asked the king to exempt Judea and the three districts of Samaria from tribute, promising him in return three hundred talents. [29]The king agreed and wrote a letter to Jonathan about all these matters as follows:

[30]"King Demetrius sends greetings to his brother Jonathan and to the Jewish nation. [31]We are sending you, for your information, a copy of the letter that we wrote to Lasthenes our Kinsman concerning you. [32]'King Demetrius sends greetings to his father Lasthenes. [33]Upon the Jewish nation, who are our friends and observe their obligations to us, we have decided to bestow benefits because of the good will they show us. [34]Therefore we confirm their possession, not only of the territory of Judea, but also of the three districts of Aphairema, Lydda, and Ramathaim. These districts, together with all their dependencies, are hereby transferred from Samaria to Judea for those who offer sacrifices in Jerusalem in lieu of the royal taxes the king used to receive yearly from the produce of earth and trees. [35]From payment of the other things that would henceforth be due to us, namely, the tithes and taxes, as well as the salt tax, and the crown tax—from all these we grant them release. [36]Henceforth and forever not one of these provisions shall ever be revoked. [37]See to it, therefore, that a copy of these instructions be made and given to Jonathan. Let it be displayed on the holy mountain in a conspicuous place.'"

The Intrigue of Trypho. [38]When King Demetrius saw that the land was peaceful under his rule and that he had no opposition, he dismissed his entire army, each to his own home, except the foreign troops which he had hired from the islands of the nations. So all the soldiers who had served under his predecessors became hostile to him. [39]When a certain Trypho, who had previously supported Alexander, saw that all the troops were grumbling against Demetrius, he went to Imalkue the Arabian, who was raising Alexander's young son Antiochus. [40]Trypho kept urging Imalkue to hand over the boy to him, so that he might succeed his father as king. He told him of all that Demetrius had done and of the hostility his soldiers had for him; and he remained there for many days.

Jonathan Aids Demetrius II. [41]Meanwhile Jonathan sent the request to King Demetrius to withdraw the troops in the citadel from Jerusalem and from the other strongholds, for they were constantly waging war on Israel. [42]Demetrius, in turn, sent this word to Jonathan: "I will do not only this for you and your nation, but I will greatly honor you and your nation when I find the opportunity. [43]Now, therefore, you will do well to send men to fight for me, because all my troops have revolted."

[44]So Jonathan sent three thousand good fighting men to him at Antioch. When they came to the king, he was delighted over their arrival. [45]The populace, one hundred and twenty thousand strong, massed in the center of the city in an attempt to kill the king. [46]So the king took refuge in the palace, while the populace gained control of the main streets of the city and prepared for battle. [47]Then the king called the Jewish force to his aid. They all rallied around him and spread out through the city. On that day they killed about a hundred thousand in the city. [48]At the same time, they set the city on fire and took much spoil. Thus they saved the king. [49]When the populace saw that the Jewish force controlled the city, they lost courage and cried out to the king in supplication, [50]"Extend the hand of friendship to us, and make the Jews stop attacking us and the city." [51]So they threw down their weapons and made peace. The Jews thus gained honor in the eyes of the king and all his subjects, and they became renowned throughout his kingdom. Finally they returned to Jerusalem with much plunder.

[52]But when King Demetrius was sure of his royal throne, and the land was peaceful under his rule, [53]he broke all his promises and became estranged from Jonathan. Instead of repaying Jonathan for all the favors he had received from him, he caused him much distress.

Alliance of Jonathan and Antiochus VI. [54]After this, Trypho returned and brought with him the young boy Antiochus, who became king and put on the diadem. [55]All the soldiers whom Demetrius had discharged rallied around Antiochus and fought against Demetrius, who was routed and fled. [56]Trypho captured the elephants and occupied Antioch. [57]Then young Antiochus wrote to Jonathan: "I confirm you in the high priesthood and appoint you ruler over the four districts, and to be one of the King's Friends." [58]He also sent him gold dishes and a table service, gave him the right to drink from gold cups, to dress in royal purple, and to wear a gold buckle. [59]Likewise, he made Jonathan's brother Simon governor of the region from the Ladder of Tyre to the borders of Egypt.

Campaigns of Jonathan and Simon. [60]Jonathan set out and traveled through the province of West-of-Euphrates and its cities, and all the forces of Syria espoused his cause as allies. When he arrived at Askalon, the citizens welcomed him with pomp. [61]But when he set out for Gaza, the people of Gaza shut him out. So he besieged it, and burned and plundered its suburbs. [62]Then the people of Gaza appealed to

Jonathan, and he granted them terms of peace. He took the sons of their leaders as hostages and sent them to Jerusalem. He then traveled on through the province as far as Damascus.

⁶³Jonathan heard that the generals of Demetrius had come with a strong force to Kadesh in Galilee, intending to remove him from office. ⁶⁴So he went to meet them, leaving his brother Simon in the province. ⁶⁵Simon encamped against Bethzur, attacked it for many days, and shut in the inhabitants. ⁶⁶They appealed to him, and he granted them terms of peace. He expelled them from the city, took possession of it, and put a garrison there.

⁶⁷Meanwhile, Jonathan and his army pitched their camp near the waters of Gennesaret, and at daybreak they went to the plain of Hazor. ⁶⁸There the army of the foreigners met him on the plain. Having first detached an ambush in the mountains, this army mounted a frontal attack. ⁶⁹Then those in ambush rose out of their places and joined in the battle. ⁷⁰All of Jonathan's men fled; no one stayed except the army commanders Mattathias, son of Absalom, and Judas, son of Chalphi. ⁷¹Jonathan tore his clothes, threw dust on his head, and prayed. ⁷²Then he went back to the battle and routed them, and they fled. ⁷³Those of his men who were running away saw it and returned to him; and with him they pursued the enemy as far as their camp in Kadesh, and there they encamped. ⁷⁴About three thousand of the foreign troops fell on that day. Then Jonathan returned to Jerusalem.

Alliances with Rome and Sparta. 12:1 When Jonathan saw that the time was right, he chose men and sent them to Rome to confirm and renew the friendship with the Romans. ²He also sent letters to the Spartans and other places to the same effect.

³After reaching Rome, the men entered the senate chamber and said, "The high priest Jonathan and the Jewish people have sent us to renew the friendship and alliance of earlier times with them." ⁴The Romans gave them letters addressed to authorities in various places, with the request to provide them with safe conduct to the land of Judah.

⁵This is a copy of the letter that Jonathan wrote to the Spartans: ⁶"Jonathan the high priest, the senate of the nation, the priests, and the rest of the Jewish people send greetings to their brothers the Spartans. ⁷Long ago a letter was sent to the high priest Onias from Arius, who then reigned over you, stating that you are our brothers, as the attached copy shows. ⁸Onias welcomed the envoy with honor and received the letter, which spoke clearly of alliance and friendship. ⁹Though we have no need of these things, since we have for our encouragement the holy books that are in our possession, ¹⁰we have ventured to send word to you for the renewal of brotherhood and friendship, lest we become strangers to you; a long time has passed since you sent your message to us. ¹¹We, on our part, have unceasingly remembered you in the sacrifices and prayers that we offer on our feasts and other appropriate days, as it is right and proper to remember brothers. ¹²We likewise rejoice in your renown. ¹³But many tribulations and many wars have beset us, and the kings around us have attacked us. ¹⁴We did not wish to be troublesome to you and to the rest of our allies and friends in these wars. ¹⁵For we have the help of Heaven for our support, and we have been saved from our enemies, and our enemies have been humbled. ¹⁶So we have chosen Numenius, son of Antiochus, and Antipater, son of Jason, and we have sent them to the Romans to renew with them the friendship and alliance of earlier times. ¹⁷We have also ordered them to come to you and greet you, and to deliver to you our letter concerning the renewal of our brotherhood. ¹⁸Therefore kindly send us an answer on this matter."

[19]This is a copy of the letter that they sent to Onias: [20]"Arius, king of the Spartans, sends greetings to Onias the high priest. [21]A document has been found stating that the Spartans and the Jews are brothers and that they are of the family of Abraham. [22]Now that we have learned this, kindly write to us about your welfare. [23]We, for our part, declare to you that your animals and your possessions are ours, and ours are yours. We have, therefore, given orders that you should be told of this."

More Campaigns of Jonathan and Simon. [24]Then Jonathan heard that the officers of Demetrius had returned to attack him with a stronger army than before. [25]So he set out from Jerusalem and met them in the territory of Hamath, giving them no opportunity to enter his province. [26]The spies he had sent into their camp came back and reported to him that the enemy were preparing to attack them that night. [27]Therefore, when the sun set, Jonathan ordered his men to keep watch, with their weapons at the ready for battle, throughout the night; and he set outposts around the camp. [28]When the enemy heard that Jonathan and his men were ready for battle, their hearts sank with fear and dread. They lighted fires in their camp and then withdrew. [29]But because Jonathan and his men were watching the campfires burning, they did not know until the morning what had happened. [30]Then Jonathan pursued them, but he could not overtake them, for they had crossed the river Eleutherus. [31]So Jonathan turned aside against the Arabians who are called Zabadeans, and he struck them down and plundered them. [32]Then he broke camp, marched on toward Damascus and traveled through the whole region.

[33]Simon also set out and traveled as far as Askalon and its neighboring strongholds. He then turned to Joppa and took it by surprise, [34]for he heard that its people intended to hand over the stronghold to the supporters of Demetrius. He left a garrison there to guard it.

[35]When Jonathan returned, he assembled the elders of the people, and with them he made plans for building strongholds in Judea, [36]for making the walls of Jerusalem still higher, and for erecting a high barrier between the citadel and the city, to separate it from the city and isolate it, so that its garrison could neither buy nor sell. [37]The people therefore gathered together to build up the city, for part of the wall of the eastern valley had collapsed. And Jonathan repaired the quarter called Chaphenatha. [38]Simon likewise built up Adida in the Shephelah, and fortified it by installing gates and bars.

Capture of Jonathan. [39]Then Trypho sought to become king of Asia, assume the diadem, and do violence to King Antiochus. [40]But he was afraid that Jonathan would not permit him, but would fight against him. Looking for a way to seize and kill him, he set out and came to Beth-shan. [41]Jonathan marched out to meet him with forty thousand picked fighting men and came to Beth-shan. [42]But when Trypho saw that Jonathan had arrived with a large army he was afraid to do him violence. [43]Instead, he received him with honor, introduced him to all his friends, and gave him presents. He also ordered his friends and soldiers to obey him as they would himself. [44]Then he said to Jonathan: "Why have you put all these people to so much trouble when we are not at war? [45]Now pick out a few men to stay with you, send the rest to their homes, and then come with me to Ptolemais. I will hand it over to you together with other strongholds and the remaining troops, as well as all the officials; then I will turn back and go home. That is why I came here."

[46]Jonathan trusted him and did as he said. He dismissed his troops, and they returned to the land of Judah. [47]But he kept with him three thousand men, of whom he left two thousand in Galilee while one

thousand accompanied him. ⁴⁸Then as soon as Jonathan entered Ptolemais, the people of Ptolemais closed the gates and seized him; all who had entered with him, they killed with the sword.

⁴⁹Then Trypho sent soldiers and cavalry to Galilee and the Great Plain to destroy all Jonathan's men. ⁵⁰These, upon learning that Jonathan had been captured and killed along with his companions, encouraged one another and went out in close formation, ready to fight. ⁵¹As their pursuers saw that they were ready to fight for their lives, they turned back. ⁵²Thus all Jonathan's men came safely into the land of Judah. They mourned Jonathan and those who were with him. They were in great fear, and all Israel fell into deep mourning. ⁵³All the nations round about sought to crush them. They said, "Now that they have no leader or helper, let us make war on them and wipe out their memory from the earth."

Simon as Leader. 13:1 When Simon heard that Trypho was gathering a large army to invade and ravage the land of Judah, ²and saw that the people were trembling with terror, he went up to Jerusalem. There he assembled the people ³and exhorted them in these words: "You know what I, my brothers, and my father's house have done for the laws and the sanctuary; what battles and hardships we have seen. ⁴For the sake of this, for the sake of Israel, all my brothers have perished, and I alone am left. ⁵Far be it from me, then, to save my own life in any time of distress, for I am not better than my brothers. ⁶But I will avenge my nation and the sanctuary, as well as your wives and children, for out of hatred all the Gentiles have united to crush us."

⁷As the people heard these words, their spirit was rekindled. ⁸They shouted in reply: "You are our leader in place of your brothers Judas and Jonathan. ⁹Fight our battles, and we will do everything that you tell us." ¹⁰So Simon mustered all the men able to fight, and hastening to complete the walls of Jerusalem, fortified it on every side. ¹¹He sent Jonathan, son of Absalom, to Joppa with a strong force; Jonathan drove out the occupants and remained there.

Trypho's Deceit. ¹²Then Trypho moved from Ptolemais with a large army to invade the land of Judah, bringing Jonathan with him as a prisoner. ¹³Simon encamped at Adida, facing the plain. ¹⁴When Trypho learned that Simon had succeeded his brother Jonathan, and that he intended to fight him, he sent ambassadors to him with this message: ¹⁵"It was on account of the money your brother Jonathan owed the royal treasury in connection with the offices that he held, that we have detained him. ¹⁶Now send a hundred talents of silver, and two of his sons as hostages to guarantee that when he is set free he will not revolt against us, and we will release him."

¹⁷Simon knew that they were speaking deceitfully to him. Nevertheless, for fear of provoking much hostility among the people, he sent for the money and the boys, ¹⁸lest the people say "Jonathan perished because I would not send Trypho the money and the boys." ¹⁹So he sent the boys and the hundred talents; but Trypho broke his promise and would not release Jonathan.

²⁰Next Trypho moved to invade and ravage the country. His troops went around by the road that leads to Adora, but Simon and his army moved along opposite him everywhere he went. ²¹The people in the citadel kept sending emissaries to Trypho, pressing him to come to them by way of the wilderness, and to send them provisions. ²²Although Trypho got all his cavalry ready to go, there was a very heavy snowfall that night, and he could not go on account of the snow. So he left for Gilead. ²³When he was approaching Baskama, he had Jonathan killed and buried him there. ²⁴Then Trypho returned to his own land.

Jonathan's Tomb. ²⁵Simon sent for the remains of his brother Jonathan, and buried him in Modein, the city of his ancestors. [26]All Israel bewailed him with solemn lamentation, mourning over him for many days. [27]Then Simon erected over the tomb of his father and his brothers a monument of stones, polished front and back, and raised high enough to be seen at a distance. [28]He set up seven pyramids facing one another for his father and his mother and his four brothers. [29]For the pyramids he devised a setting of massive columns, which he adorned with suits of armor as a perpetual memorial, and next to the armor carved ships, which could be seen by all who sailed the sea. [30]This tomb which he built at Modein is there to the present day.

Alliance of Simon and Demetrius II. [31]Trypho dealt treacherously with the young King Antiochus. He killed him [32]and became king in his place, putting on the crown of Asia. Thus he brought much evil on the land. [33]Simon, for his part, built up the strongholds of Judea, fortifying them all around with high towers, thick walls, and gates with bars, and he stored up provisions in the strongholds. [34]Simon also chose men and sent them to King Demetrius to obtain for the land an exemption from taxation, since Trypho did nothing but plunder. [35]King Demetrius replied favorably and sent him the following letter:

[36]"King Demetrius sends greetings to Simon, high priest and friend of kings, and to the elders and the Jewish people. [37]We have received the gold crown and the palm branch that you sent. We are ready to make a lasting peace with you and to write to our officials to grant you exemption. [38]Whatever decrees we have made in your regard remain in force, and the strongholds that you have built you may keep. [39]We pardon any oversights and offenses committed up to now, as well as the crown tax that you owe. Any other tax that used to be collected in Jerusalem shall no longer be collected there. [40]Any of you qualified for enrollment in our service may be enrolled. Let there be peace between us."

[41]Thus in the one hundred and seventieth year, the yoke of the Gentiles was removed from Israel, [42]and the people began to write in their records and contracts, "In the first year of Simon, great high priest, governor, and leader of the Jews."

Simon Captures Gazara. [43]In those days Simon besieged Gazara and surrounded it with troops. He made a siege machine, brought it up against the city, and attacked and captured one of the towers. [44]Those in the siege machine leaped down into the city and a great tumult arose there. [45]Those in the city, together with their wives and children, went up on the wall, with their garments rent, and cried out in loud voices, begging Simon to grant them terms of peace. [46]They said, "Treat us not according to our evil deeds but according to your mercy." [47]So Simon came to terms with them and did not attack them. He expelled them from the city, however, and he purified the houses in which there were idols. Then he entered the city with hymns and songs of praise. [48]After removing from it everything that was impure, he settled there people who observed the law. He improved its fortifications and built himself a residence.

Simon Captures the Citadel. [49]The people in the citadel in Jerusalem were prevented from going out into the country and back to buy or sell; they suffered greatly from hunger, and many of them died of starvation. [50]They finally cried out to Simon, and he gave them terms of peace. He expelled them from the citadel and cleansed it of impurities. [51]On the twenty-third day of the second month, in the one hundred and seventy-first year, the Jews entered the citadel with shouts of praise, the waving of palm branches, the playing of harps and cymbals and lyres, and the singing of hymns and canticles, because a great enemy of Israel had been crushed. [52]Simon decreed that this day should be celebrated every year with rejoicing. He also strengthened the fortifications of the temple mount alongside the citadel, and he and his people dwelt there. [53]Seeing that his son John was now a grown man, Simon made him commander of all his soldiers, and he dwelt in Gazara.

☐ MATTHEW 24:1-14

The Destruction of the Temple Foretold. **24:1** Jesus left the temple area and was going away, when his disciples approached him to point out the temple buildings. [2]He said to them in reply, "You see all these things, do you not? Amen, I say to you, there will not be left here a stone upon another stone that will not be thrown down."

The Beginning of Calamities. [3]As he was sitting on the Mount of Olives, the disciples approached him privately and said, "Tell us, when will this happen, and what sign will there be of your coming, and of the end of the age?" [4]Jesus said to them in reply, "See that no one deceives you. [5]For many will come in my name, saying, 'I am the Messiah,' and they will deceive many. [6]You will hear of wars and reports of wars; see that you are not alarmed, for these things must happen, but it will not yet be the end. [7]Nation will rise against nation, and kingdom against kingdom; there will be famines and earthquakes from place to place. [8]All these are the beginning of the labor pains. [9]Then they will hand you over to persecution, and they will kill you. You will be hated by all nations because of my name. [10]And then many will be led into sin; they will betray and hate one another. [11]Many false prophets will arise and deceive many; [12]and because of the increase of evildoing, the love of many will grow cold. [13]But the one who perseveres to the end will be saved. [14]And this gospel of the kingdom will be preached throughout the world as a witness to all nations, and then the end will come."

June 11

St. Barnabas; St. Paula Frassinetti

Don't permit your miseries or defects to depress you. Rather, let them be steps by which you descend into the deep mine where we find the precious gem of holy humility.

— St. Paula Frassinetti

☐ 1 MACCABEES 14-16

Capture of Demetrius II. 14:1 In the one hundred and seventy-second year, King Demetrius assembled his army and marched into Media to obtain help so that he could fight Trypho. [2]When Arsaces, king of Persia and Media, heard that Demetrius had entered his territory, he sent one of his generals to take him alive. [3]The general went forth and attacked the army of Demetrius; he captured him and brought him to Arsaces, who put him under guard.

Praise of Simon. [4]The land was at rest
all the days of Simon,
who sought the good of his nation.
His rule delighted his people
and his glory all his days.
[5]As his crowning glory he took Joppa
for a port
and made it a gateway to the isles of
the sea.
[6]He enlarged the borders of his nation
and gained control of the country.
[7]He took many prisoners of war
and made himself master of Gazara,
Beth-zur, and the citadel.
He cleansed the citadel of its
impurities;
there was no one to withstand him.
[8]The people cultivated their land in
peace;
the land yielded its produce,
the trees of the field their fruit.
[9]Old men sat in the squares,
all talking about the good times,
while the young men put on the
glorious raiment of war.
[10]He supplied the cities with food
and equipped them with means of
defense,
till his glorious name reached the
ends of the earth.
[11]He brought peace to the land,
and Israel was filled with great joy.
[12]Every one sat under his vine and fig
tree,
with no one to disturb them.
[13]No attacker was left in the land;
the kings in those days were
crushed.
[14]He strengthened all the lowly among
his people
and was zealous for the law;
he destroyed the lawless and the
wicked.
[15]The sanctuary he made splendid
and multiplied its furnishings.

Alliance with Rome and Sparta. [16]When
people in Rome and even in Sparta heard
that Jonathan had died, they were deeply
grieved. [17]But when they heard that his
brother Simon had become high priest in
his place and was master of the territory
and its cities, [18]they sent him inscribed
tablets of bronze to renew with him the
friendship and alliance that they had established with his brothers Judas and Jonathan. [19]These were read before the assembly
in Jerusalem.

[20]This is a copy of the letter that the
Spartans sent: "The rulers and the city of
the Spartans send greetings to Simon the
high priest, the elders, the priests, and the
rest of the Jewish people, our brothers.
[21]The ambassadors sent to our people have
informed us of your glory and renown, and
we rejoiced at their coming. [22]In accordance
with what they said we have recorded the
following in the public decrees: Numenius,
son of Antiochus, and Antipater, son of Jason, ambassadors of the Jews, have come
to us to renew their friendship with us.
[23]The people have resolved to receive these
men with honor, and to deposit a copy of
their words in the public archives, so that
the people of Sparta may have a record of
them. A copy of this decree has been made
for Simon the high priest."

[24]After this, Simon sent Numenius to
Rome with a large gold shield weighing a
thousand minas, to confirm the alliance
with the Romans.

Official Honors for Simon. [25]When the
people heard of these things, they said, "How
shall we thank Simon and his sons? [26]He and
his brothers and his father's house have stood
firm and repulsed Israel's enemies, and so
have established its freedom." So they made
an inscription on bronze tablets, which they
affixed to pillars on Mount Zion.

[27]The following is a copy of the inscription: "On the eighteenth day of Elul, in

the one hundred and seventy-second year, that is, the third year under Simon the great high priest in Asaramel, [28]in a great assembly of priests, people, rulers of the nation, and elders of the region, the following proclamation was made to us:

[29]"Since there have often been wars in our country, Simon, son of the priest Mattathias, descendant of Joarib, and his brothers have put themselves in danger and resisted the enemies of their nation, so that their sanctuary and law might be maintained, and they have thus brought great glory to their nation. [30]Jonathan rallied the nation, became their high priest, and was gathered to his people. [31]When their enemies sought to invade and ravage their country and to violate their sanctuary, [32]Simon rose up and fought for his nation, spending large sums of his own money to equip his nation's forces and give them their pay. [33]He fortified the cities of Judea, especially the border city of Beth-zur, formerly the site of the enemy's weaponry, and he stationed there a garrison of Jewish soldiers. [34]He also fortified Joppa by the sea and Gazara on the border of Azotus, a place previously occupied by the enemy; these cities he settled with Jews and furnished them with all that was necessary for their restoration. [35]When the people saw Simon's fidelity and the glory he planned to bring to his nation, they made him their leader and high priest because of all he had accomplished and the justice and fidelity he had shown his nation. In every way he sought to exalt his people.

[36]"In his time and under his guidance they succeeded in driving the Gentiles out of their country and those in the City of David in Jerusalem, who had built for themselves a citadel from which they used to sally forth to defile the environs of the sanctuary and inflict grave injury on its purity. [37]In this citadel he stationed Jewish soldiers, and he strengthened its fortifications for the security of the land and the city, while he also built up the wall of Jerusalem to a greater height.

[38]Consequently, King Demetrius confirmed him in the high priesthood, [39]made him one of his Friends, and conferred great honor on him. [40]This was because he had heard that the Romans had addressed the Jews as friends, allies, and brothers, that they had received Simon's envoys with honor, [41]and that the Jewish people and their priests had decided the following: Simon shall be their leader and high priest forever until a trustworthy prophet arises. [42]He shall act as governor over them, and shall have charge of the sanctuary, to make regulations concerning its functions and concerning the country, its weapons and strongholds. [43]He shall be obeyed by all. All contracts in the country shall be written in his name, and he shall be clothed in purple and gold. [44]It shall not be lawful for any of the people or priests to nullify any of these decisions, or to contradict the orders given by him, or to convene an assembly in the country without his consent, to be clothed in purple or wear a gold buckle. [45]Whoever acts otherwise or violates any of these prescriptions shall be liable to punishment.

[46]"Thus all the people approved of granting Simon the right to act in accord with these decisions, [47]and Simon accepted and agreed to be high priest, governor, and ethnarch of the Jewish people and priests, and to have authority over all.'"

[48]It was decreed that this inscription should be engraved on bronze tablets, to be set up in a conspicuous place in the precincts of the sanctuary, [49]and that copies of it should be deposited in the treasury, where they would be available to Simon and his sons.

Letter of Antiochus VII. 15:1 Antiochus, son of King Demetrius, sent a letter from the islands of the sea to Simon, the priest and ethnarch of the Jews, and to all the nation, [2]which read as follows:

"King Antiochus sends greetings to Simon, the high priest and ethnarch, and to the Jewish nation. ³Whereas certain villains have gained control of the kingdom of our ancestors, I intend to reclaim it, that I may restore it to its former state. I have recruited a large number of mercenary troops and equipped warships. ⁴I intend to make a landing in the country so that I may take revenge on those who have ruined our country and laid waste many cities in my kingdom.

⁵"Now, therefore, I confirm to you all the tax exemptions that the kings before me granted you and whatever other privileges they conceded to you. ⁶I authorize you to coin your own money, as legal tender in your country. ⁷Jerusalem and its sanctuary shall be free. All the weapons you have prepared and all the strongholds you have built and now occupy shall remain in your possession. ⁸All debts, present or future, due to the royal treasury shall be canceled for you, now and for all time. ⁹When we establish our kingdom, we will greatly honor you and your nation and the temple, so that your glory will be manifest in all the earth."

¹⁰In the one hundred and seventy-fourth year Antiochus invaded the land of his ancestors, and all the troops rallied to him, so that few were left with Trypho. ¹¹Pursued by Antiochus, Trypho fled to Dor, by the sea, ¹²realizing what troubles had come upon him now that his soldiers had deserted him. ¹³Antiochus encamped before Dor with a hundred and twenty thousand infantry and eight thousand cavalry. ¹⁴While he surrounded the city, his ships closed from the sea, so that he pressed it hard by land and sea and let no one go in or out.

Roman Alliance Renewed. ¹⁵Meanwhile, Numenius and his companions came from Rome with letters containing this message to various kings and countries: ¹⁶"Lucius, Consul of the Romans, sends greetings to King Ptolemy. ¹⁷Ambassadors of the Jews, our friends and allies, have come to us to renew their earlier friendship and alliance. They had been sent by Simon the high priest and the Jewish people, ¹⁸and they brought with them a gold shield of a thousand minas. ¹⁹Therefore we have decided to write to various kings and countries, that they are not to venture to harm them, or wage war against them or their cities or their country, and are not to assist those who fight against them. ²⁰We have also decided to accept the shield from them. ²¹If, then, any troublemakers from their country take refuge with you, hand them over to Simon the high priest, so that he may punish them according to their law."

²²The consul sent identical letters to Kings Demetrius, Attalus, Ariarthes and Arsaces; ²³to all the countries— Sampsames, the Spartans, Delos, Myndos, Sicyon, Caria, Samos, Pamphylia, Lycia, Halicarnassus, Rhodes, Phaselis, Cos, Side, Aradus, Gortyna, Cnidus, Cyprus, and Cyrene. ²⁴A copy of the letter was also sent to Simon the high priest.

Hostility from Antiochus VII. ²⁵When King Antiochus encamped before Dor, he assaulted it continuously both with troops and with the siege engines he had made. He blockaded Trypho by preventing anyone from going in or out. ²⁶Simon sent to Antiochus' support two thousand elite troops, together with silver and gold and much equipment. ²⁷But he refused to accept the aid; in fact, he broke all the agreements he had previously made with Simon and became hostile toward him.

²⁸He sent Athenobius, one of his Friends, to confer with Simon and say: "You are occupying Joppa and Gazara and the citadel of Jerusalem; these are cities of my kingdom. ²⁹You have laid waste their territories, done great harm to the land, and taken possession of many districts in my kingdom. ³⁰Now, therefore, give up the cities you have seized and the tribute money of the districts you control outside the territory of Judea; ³¹or instead, pay me five hundred talents of silver for the devas-

tation you have caused and five hundred talents more for the tribute money of the cities. If you do not do this, we will come and make war on you."

³²So Athenobius, the king's Friend, came to Jerusalem and on seeing the splendor of Simon's court, the gold and silver plate on the sideboard, and his rich display, he was amazed. When he gave him the king's message, ³³Simon said to him in reply: "It is not foreign land we have taken nor have we seized the property of others, but only our ancestral heritage which for a time had been unjustly held by our enemies. ³⁴Now that we have the opportunity, we are holding on to the heritage of our ancestors. ³⁵As for Joppa and Gazara, which you demand, those cities were doing great harm to our people and our country. For these we will give you a hundred talents." Athenobius made no reply, ³⁶but returned to the king in anger. When he told him of Simon's words, of his splendor, and of all he had seen, the king fell into a violent rage.

Victory over Cendebeus. ³⁷Trypho had boarded a ship and escaped to Orthosia. ³⁸Then the king appointed Cendebeus commander-in-chief of the seacoast, and gave him infantry and cavalry forces. ³⁹He ordered him to encamp against Judea and to fortify Kedron and strengthen its gates, so that he could wage war on the people. Meanwhile the king went in pursuit of Trypho. ⁴⁰When Cendebeus came to Jamnia, he began to harass the people and to make incursions into Judea, where he took people captive and massacred them. ⁴¹As the king ordered, he fortified Kedron and stationed cavalry and infantry there, so that they could go out and patrol the roads of Judea.

16:1 John then went up from Gazara and told his father Simon what Cendebeus was doing. ²Simon called his two oldest sons, Judas and John, and said to them: "I and my brothers and my father's house have fought the wars of Israel from our youth until today, and many times we succeeded in saving Israel. ³I have now grown old, but you, by the mercy of Heaven, have come to maturity. Take my place and my brother's, and go out and fight for our nation; and may the help of Heaven be with you!"

⁴John then mustered in the land twenty thousand warriors and cavalry. Setting out against Cendebeus, they spent the night at Modein, ⁵rose early, and marched into the plain. There, facing them, was an immense army of foot soldiers and cavalry, and between the two armies was a wadi. ⁶John and his people took their position against the enemy. Seeing that his people were afraid to cross the wadi, John crossed first. When his men saw this, they crossed over after him. ⁷Then he divided his infantry and put his cavalry in the center, for the enemy's cavalry were very numerous. ⁸They blew the trumpets, and Cendebeus and his army were routed; many of them fell wounded, and the rest fled toward the stronghold. ⁹It was then that John's brother Judas fell wounded; but John pursued them until Cendebeus reached Kedron, which he had fortified. ¹⁰Some took refuge in the towers on the plain of Azotus, but John set fire to these, and about two thousand of the enemy perished. He then returned to Judea in peace.

Murder of Simon and His Sons. ¹¹Ptolemy, son of Abubus, had been appointed governor of the plain of Jericho, and he had much silver and gold, ¹²being the son-in-law of the high priest. ¹³But his heart became proud and he was determined to get control of the country. So he made treacherous plans to do away with Simon and his sons. ¹⁴As Simon was inspecting the cities of the country and providing for their needs, he and his sons Mattathias and Judas went down to Jericho in the one hundred and seventy-seventh year, in the eleventh month (that is, the month Shebat). ¹⁵The son of Abubus gave them a deceitful welcome in the little stronghold called Dok which he had built. He served them a sumptuous banquet, but he had his men hidden there. [16]Then, when Simon and his sons were drunk, Ptolemy and his men sprang up, weapons in hand, rushed upon Simon in the banquet hall, and killed him, his two sons, and some of his servants. [17]By this vicious act of treachery he repaid good with evil.

[18]Then Ptolemy wrote a report and sent it to the king, asking him to send troops to help him and to turn over to him their country and its cities. [19]He sent other men to Gazara to do away with John. To the army officers he sent letters inviting them to come to him so that he might present them with silver, gold, and gifts. [20]He also sent others to seize Jerusalem and the temple mount. [21]But someone ran ahead and brought word to John at Gazara that his father and his brothers had perished, and "Ptolemy has sent men to kill you also." [22]On hearing this, John was utterly astounded. When the men came to kill him, he seized them and put them to death, for he knew that they sought to kill him.

[23]Now the rest of the acts of John, his wars and the brave deeds he performed, his rebuilding of the walls, and all his achievements— [24]these are recorded in the chronicle of his high priesthood, from the time that he succeeded his father as high priest.

☐ MATTHEW 24:15-28

The Great Tribulation. 24:15 "When you see the desolating abomination spoken of through Daniel the prophet standing in the holy place (let the reader understand), [16]then those in Judea must flee to the mountains, [17]a person on the housetop must not go down to get things out of his house, [18]a person in the field must not return to get his cloak. [19]Woe to pregnant women and nursing mothers in those days. [20]Pray that your flight not be in winter or on the sabbath, [21]for at that time there will be great tribulation, such as has not been since the beginning of the world until now, nor ever will be. [22]And if those days had not been shortened, no one would be saved; but for the sake of the elect they will be shortened. [23]If anyone says to you then, 'Look, here is the Messiah!' or, 'There he is!' do not believe it. [24]False messiahs and false prophets will arise, and they will perform signs and wonders so great as to deceive, if that were possible, even the elect. [25]Behold, I have told it to you beforehand. [26]So if they say to you, 'He is in the desert,' do not go out there; if they say, 'He is in the inner rooms,' do not believe it. [27]For just as lightning comes from the east and is seen as far as the west, so will the coming of the Son of Man be. [28]Wherever the corpse is, there the vultures will gather."

June 12

Whatever has been prophesied in Scripture is coming to pass, and as the end of the world approaches, it tests both men and the times.

— St. Cyprian of Carthage

☐ 2 MACCABEES 1-2

Letter 1: 124 B.C. 1:1 The Jews in Jerusalem and in the land of Judea send greetings to their kindred, the Jews in Egypt, and wish them true peace! ²May God do good to you and remember his covenant with his faithful servants, Abraham, Isaac and Jacob, ³give to all of you a heart to worship him and to do his will wholeheartedly and with a willing spirit, ⁴open your heart to his law and commandments and grant you peace, ⁵hear your prayers, and be reconciled to you, and never forsake you in time of adversity. ⁶Even now we are praying for you here.

⁷In the reign of Demetrius, the one hundred and sixty-ninth year, we Jews wrote to you during the height of the distress that overtook us in those years after Jason and his followers revolted against the holy land and the kingdom, ⁸set fire to the gatehouse and shed innocent blood. But we prayed to the Lord, and our prayer was heard; we offered sacrifices and fine flour; we lighted the lamps and set out the loaves of bread. ⁹We are now reminding you to celebrate the feast of Booths in the month of Kislev. ¹⁰Dated in the one hundred and eighty-eighth year.

Letter 2: 164 B.C. The people of Jerusalem and Judea, the senate, and Judas send greetings and good wishes to Aristobulus, teacher of King Ptolemy and member of the family of the anointed priests, and to the Jews in Egypt. ¹¹Since we have been saved by God from grave dangers, we give him great thanks as befits those who fought against the king; ¹²for it was God who drove out those who fought against the holy city. ¹³When their leader arrived in Persia with his seemingly irresistible army, they were cut to pieces in the temple of the goddess Nanea through a deceitful stratagem employed by Nanea's priests. ¹⁴On the pretext of marrying the goddess, Antiochus with his Friends had come to the place to get its great treasures as a dowry. ¹⁵When the priests of Nanea's temple had displayed the treasures and Antiochus with a few attendants had come inside the wall of the temple precincts, the priests locked the temple as soon as he entered. ¹⁶Then they opened a hidden trapdoor in the ceiling, and hurling stones at the leader and his companions, struck them down. They dismembered the bodies, cut off their heads and tossed them to the people outside. ¹⁷Forever blessed be our God, who has thus punished the impious!

¹⁸Since we shall be celebrating the purification of the temple on the twenty-fifth day of the month Kislev, we thought it right to inform you, that you too may celebrate the feast of Booths and of the fire that appeared when Nehemiah, the rebuilder of the temple and the altar, offered sacrifices. ¹⁹For when our ancestors were being led into captivity in Persia, devout priests at the time took some of the fire from the altar and hid it secretly in the hollow of a dry cistern, making sure that the place would be unknown to anyone. ²⁰Many years later, when it so pleased God, Nehemiah, commissioned by the king of Persia, sent the descendants of the priests who had hidden the fire to look for it. ²¹When they informed us that they could not find any fire, but only a thick liquid, he ordered them to scoop some out and bring it. After the material for the sacrifices had been prepared, Nehemiah ordered the

priests to sprinkle the wood and what lay on it with the liquid. ²²This was done, and when at length the sun, which had been clouded over, began to shine, a great fire blazed up, so that everyone marveled. ²³While the sacrifice was being burned, the priests recited a prayer, and all present joined in with them. Jonathan led and the rest responded with Nehemiah.

²⁴The prayer was as follows: "Lord, Lord God, creator of all things, awesome and strong, just and merciful, the only king and benefactor, ²⁵who alone are gracious, just, almighty, and eternal, Israel's savior from all evil, who chose our ancestors and sanctified them: ²⁶accept this sacrifice on behalf of all your people Israel and guard and sanctify your portion. ²⁷Gather together our scattered people, free those who are slaves among the Gentiles, look kindly on those who are despised and detested, and let the Gentiles know that you are our God. ²⁸Punish those who lord it over us and in their arrogance oppress us. ²⁹Plant your people in your holy place, as Moses said."

³⁰Then the priests sang hymns. ³¹After the sacrifice was consumed, Nehemiah ordered the rest of the liquid to be poured upon large stones. ³²As soon as this was done, a flame blazed up, but its light was lost in the brilliance coming from the altar. ³³When the event became known and the king of the Persians was told that, in the very place where the exiled priests had hidden the fire, a liquid was found with which Nehemiah and his people had burned the sacrifices, ³⁴the king, after verifying the fact, fenced the place off and declared it sacred. ³⁵To those whom the king favored, he distributed many benefits he received. ³⁶Nehemiah and his companions called the liquid nephthar, meaning purification, but most people named it naphtha.

2:1 In the records it will be found that Jeremiah the prophet ordered the deportees to take some of the fire with them as in-

dicated, ²and that the prophet, in giving them the law, directed the deportees not to forget the commandments of the Lord or be led astray in their thoughts, when seeing the gold and silver idols and their adornments. ³With other similar words he exhorted them that the law should not depart from their hearts.

⁴The same document also tells how the prophet, in virtue of an oracle, ordered that the tent and the ark should accompany him, and how he went to the very mountain that Moses climbed to behold God's inheritance. ⁵When Jeremiah arrived there, he found a chamber in a cave in which he put the tent, the ark, and the altar of incense; then he sealed the entrance. ⁶Some of those who followed him came up intending to mark the path, but they could not find it. ⁷When Jeremiah heard of this, he reproved them: "The place is to remain unknown until God gathers his people together again and shows them mercy. ⁸Then the Lord will disclose these things, and the glory of the Lord and the cloud will be seen, just as they appeared in the time of Moses and of Solomon when he prayed that the place might be greatly sanctified."

⁹It is also related how Solomon in his wisdom offered a sacrifice for the dedication and the completion of the temple. ¹⁰Just as Moses prayed to the Lord and fire descended from the sky and consumed the sacrifices, so also Solomon prayed and fire came down and consumed the burnt offerings. ¹¹Moses had said, "Because it had not been eaten, the purification offering was consumed." ¹²Solomon also celebrated the feast in the same way for eight days.

¹³These same things are also told in the records and in Nehemiah's memoirs, as well as how he founded a library and collected the books about the kings and the prophets, the books of David, and the royal letters about votive offerings. ¹⁴In like manner Judas also collected for us all the books that had been scattered because of the war,

and we now have them in our possession. [15]If you need them, send messengers to get them for you.

[16]As we are about to celebrate the purification, we are writing: you should celebrate the feast days. [17]It is God who has saved all his people and has restored to all of them their inheritance, the kingdom, the priesthood, and the sacred rites, [18]as he promised through the law. For we hope in God, that he will soon have mercy on us and gather us together from everywhere under the heavens to his holy place, for he has rescued us from great perils and has purified the place.

[19]This is the story of Judas Maccabeus and his brothers, of the purification of the great temple, the dedication of the altar, [20]the campaigns against Antiochus Epiphanes and his son Eupator, [21]and of the heavenly manifestations accorded to the heroes who fought bravely for the Jewish people. Few as they were, they plundered the whole land, put to flight the barbarian hordes, [22]regained possession of the temple renowned throughout the world, and liberated the city. They re-established the laws that were in danger of being abolished, while the Lord favored them with every kindness. [23]All this, detailed by Jason of Cyrene in five volumes, we will try to condense into a single book.

[24]For in view of the flood of data, and the difficulties encountered, given such abundant material, by those who wish to plunge into accounts of the history, [25]we have aimed to please those who prefer simply to read, to make it easy for the studious who wish to commit things to memory, and to be helpful to all. [26]For us who have undertaken the labor of making this digest, the task, far from being easy, is one of sweat and of sleepless nights. [27]Just so, the preparation of a festive banquet is no light matter for one who seeks to give enjoyment to others. Similarly, to win the gratitude of many we will gladly endure this labor, [28]leaving the responsibility for exact details to the historian, and confining our efforts to presenting only a summary outline. [29]As the architect of a new house must pay attention to the whole structure, while the one who undertakes the decoration and the frescoes has to be concerned only with what is needed for ornamentation, so I think it is with us. [30]To enter into questions and examine them from all sides and to be busy about details is the task of the historian; [31]but one who is making an adaptation should be allowed to aim at brevity of expression and to forgo complete treatment of the matter. [32]Here, then, let us begin our account without adding to what has already been said; it would be silly to lengthen the preface to the history and then cut short the history itself.

☐ MATTHEW 24:29-51

The Coming of the Son of Man. 24:29 "Immediately after the tribulation of those days,

> the sun will be darkened,
> and the moon will not give its light,
> and the stars will fall from the sky,
> and the powers of the heavens will
> be shaken.

[30]And then the sign of the Son of Man will appear in heaven, and all the tribes of the earth will mourn, and they will see the Son of Man coming upon the clouds of heaven with power and great glory. [31]And he will send out his angels with a trumpet blast, and they will gather his elect from the four winds, from one end of the heavens to the other.

The Lesson of the Fig Tree. [32]"Learn a lesson from the fig tree. When its branch becomes tender and sprouts leaves, you know that summer is near. [33]In the same way, when you see all these things, know that he is near, at the gates. [34]Amen, I say to you, this generation will not pass away until all these things have taken place. [35]Heaven and earth will pass away, but my words will not pass away.

The Unknown Day and Hour. [36]"But of that day and hour no one knows, neither the angels of heaven, nor the Son, but the Father alone. [37]For as it was in the days of Noah, so it will be at the coming of the Son of Man. [38]In [those] days before the flood, they were eating and drinking, marrying and giving in marriage, up to the day that Noah entered the ark. [39]They did not know until the flood came and carried them all away. So will it be [also] at the coming of the Son of Man. [40]Two men will be out in the field; one will be taken, and one will be left. [41]Two women will be grinding at the mill; one will be taken, and one will be left. [42]Therefore, stay awake! For you do not know on which day your Lord will come. [43]Be sure of this: if the master of the house had known the hour of night when the thief was coming, he would have stayed awake and not let his house be broken into. [44]So too, you also must be prepared, for at an hour you do not expect, the Son of Man will come.

The Faithful or the Unfaithful Servant. [45]"Who, then, is the faithful and prudent servant, whom the master has put in charge of his household to distribute to them their food at the proper time? [46]Blessed is that servant whom his master on his arrival finds doing so. [47]Amen, I say to you, he will put him in charge of all his property. [48]But if that wicked servant says to himself, 'My master is long delayed,' [49]and begins to beat his fellow servants, and eat and drink with drunkards, [50]the servant's master will come on an unexpected day and at an unknown hour [51]and will punish him severely and assign him a place with the hypocrites, where there will be wailing and grinding of teeth."

June 13

St. Anthony of Padua

If things created are so full of loveliness, how resplendent with beauty must be the One who made them! The wisdom of the Worker is apparent in His handiwork.

— St. Anthony of Padua

☐ 2 MACCABEES 3–4

Heliodorus' Arrival in Jerusalem. 3:1 While the holy city lived in perfect peace and the laws were strictly observed because of the piety of the high priest Onias and his hatred of evil, [2]the kings themselves honored the place and glorified the temple with the most magnificent gifts. [3]Thus Seleucus, king of Asia, defrayed from his own revenues all the expenses necessary for the liturgy of sacrifice.

[4]But a certain Simon, of the priestly clan of Bilgah, who had been appointed superintendent of the temple, had a quarrel with the high priest about the administration of the city market. [5]Since he could not prevail against Onias, he went to Apollonius of Tarsus, who at that time was governor of Coelesyria and Phoenicia, [6]and reported to him that the treasury in Jerusalem was full of such untold riches that the sum total of

the assets was past counting and that since they did not belong to the account of the sacrifices, it would be possible for them to fall under the authority of the king.

⁷When Apollonius had an audience with the king, he informed him about the riches that had been reported to him. The king chose his chief minister Heliodorus and sent him with instructions to seize those riches. ⁸So Heliodorus immediately set out on his journey, ostensibly to visit the cities of Coelesyria and Phoenicia, but in reality to carry out the king's purpose.

⁹When he arrived in Jerusalem and had been graciously received by the high priest of the city, he told him about the information that had been given, and explained the reason for his presence, and he inquired if these things were really true. ¹⁰The high priest explained that there were deposits for widows and orphans, ¹¹and some was the property of Hyrcanus, son of Tobias, a man who occupied a very high position. Contrary to the misrepresentations of the impious Simon, the total amounted only to four hundred talents of silver and two hundred of gold. ¹²It was utterly unthinkable to defraud those who had placed their trust in the sanctity of the place and in the sacred inviolability of a temple venerated all over the world.

Heliodorus' Plan To Rob the Temple. ¹³But Heliodorus, because of the orders he had from the king, said that in any case this money must be confiscated for the royal treasury. ¹⁴So on the day he had set he went in to take an inventory of the funds. There was no little anguish throughout the city. ¹⁵Priests prostrated themselves before the altar in their priestly robes, and called toward heaven for the one who had given the law about deposits to keep the deposits safe for those who had made them. ¹⁶Whoever saw the appearance of the high priest was pierced to the heart, for the changed complexion of his face revealed his mental anguish. ¹⁷The terror and bodily trembling that had come over the man clearly showed those who saw him the pain that lodged in his heart. ¹⁸People rushed out of their houses and crowded together making common supplication, because the place was in danger of being profaned. ¹⁹Women, girded with sackcloth below their breasts, filled the streets. Young women secluded indoors all ran, some to the gates, some to the walls, others peered through the windows— ²⁰all of them with hands raised toward heaven, making supplication. ²¹It was pitiful to see the populace prostrate everywhere and the high priest full of dread and anguish. ²²While they were imploring the almighty Lord to keep the deposits safe and secure for those who had placed them in trust, ²³Heliodorus went on with his plan.

God Protects the Temple. ²⁴But just as Heliodorus was arriving at the treasury with his bodyguards, the Lord of spirits and all authority produced an apparition so great that those who had been bold enough to accompany Heliodorus were panic-stricken at God's power and fainted away in terror. ²⁵There appeared to them a richly caparisoned horse, mounted by a fearsome rider. Charging furiously, the horse attacked Heliodorus with its front hooves. The rider was seen wearing golden armor. ²⁶Then two other young men, remarkably strong, strikingly handsome, and splendidly attired, appeared before him. Standing on each side of him, they flogged him unceasingly, inflicting innumerable blows. ²⁷Suddenly he fell to the ground, enveloped in great darkness. His men picked him up and laid him on a stretcher. ²⁸They carried away helpless the man who a moment before had entered that treasury under arms with a great retinue and his whole bodyguard. They clearly recognized the sovereign power of God.

The Restoration and Testimony of Heliodorus. ²⁹As Heliodorus lay speechless because of God's action and deprived of any hope of recovery, ³⁰the people praised the Lord who had marvelously glorified his own place; and the temple, charged so shortly before with fear and commotion, was filled with joy and gladness, now that the almighty Lord had appeared. [31]Quickly some of the companions of Heliodorus begged Onias to call upon the Most High to spare the life of one who was about to breathe his last. [32]The high priest, suspecting that the king might think that Heliodorus had suffered some foul play at the hands of the Jews, offered a sacrifice for the man's recovery. [33]While the high priest was offering the sacrifice of atonement, the same young men dressed in the same clothing again appeared and stood before Heliodorus. "Be very grateful to the high priest Onias," they told him. "It is for his sake that the Lord has spared your life. [34]Since you have been scourged by Heaven, proclaim to all God's great power." When they had said this, they disappeared.

[35]After Heliodorus had offered a sacrifice to the Lord and made most solemn vows to the one who had spared his life, he bade Onias farewell, and returned with his soldiers to the king. [36]Before all he gave witness to the deeds of the most high God that he had seen with his own eyes. [37]When the king asked Heliodorus what sort of person would be suitable to be sent to Jerusalem next, he answered: [38]"If you have an enemy or one who is plotting against the government, send him there, and you will get him back with a flogging, if indeed he survives at all; for there is certainly some divine power about the place. [39]The one whose dwelling is in heaven watches over that place and protects it, and strikes down and destroys those who come to harm it." [40]This was how the matter concerning Heliodorus and the preservation of the treasury turned out.

Simon Accuses Onias. 4:1 The Simon mentioned above as the informer about the funds against his own country slandered Onias as the one who incited Heliodorus and instigated the whole miserable affair. [2]He dared to brand as a schemer against the government the man who was the benefactor of the city, the protector of his compatriots, and a zealous defender of the laws. [3]When Simon's hostility reached such a pitch that murders were being committed by one of his henchmen, [4]Onias saw that the opposition was serious and that Apollonius, son of Menestheus, the governor of Coelesyria and Phoenicia, was abetting Simon's wickedness. [5]So he had recourse to the king, not as an accuser of his compatriots, but as one looking to the general and particular good of all the people. [6]He saw that without royal attention it would be impossible to have a peaceful government, and that Simon would not desist from his folly.

Jason as High Priest. [7]But Seleucus died, and when Antiochus surnamed Epiphanes succeeded him on the throne, Onias' brother Jason obtained the high priesthood by corrupt means: [8]in an interview, he promised the king three hundred and sixty talents of silver, as well as eighty talents from another source of income. [9]Besides this he would undertake to pay a hundred and fifty more, if he was given authority to establish a gymnasium and a youth center for it and to enroll Jerusalemites as citizens of Antioch.

[10]When Jason received the king's approval and came into office, he immediately initiated his compatriots into the Greek way of life. [11]He set aside the royal concessions granted to the Jews through the mediation of John, father of Eupolemus (that Eupolemus who would later go on an embassy to the Romans to establish friendship and alliance with them); he set aside the lawful practices and introduced customs contrary to the law. [12]With perverse delight he established a gymnasium at the very foot of the citadel, where he induced the noblest young men to wear the Greek hat. [13]The craze for Hellenism and the adoption of foreign customs reached such

a pitch, through the outrageous wickedness of Jason, the renegade and would-be high priest, ¹⁴that the priests no longer cared about the service of the altar. Disdaining the temple and neglecting the sacrifices, they hastened, at the signal for the games, to take part in the unlawful exercises at the arena. ¹⁵What their ancestors had regarded as honors they despised; what the Greeks esteemed as glory they prized highly. ¹⁶For this reason they found themselves in serious trouble: the very people whose manner of life they emulated, and whom they desired to imitate in everything, became their enemies and oppressors. ¹⁷It is no light matter to flout the laws of God, as subsequent events will show.

¹⁸When the quinquennial games were held at Tyre in the presence of the king, ¹⁹the vile Jason sent representatives of the Antiochians of Jerusalem, to bring three hundred silver drachmas for the sacrifice to Hercules. But the bearers themselves decided that the money should not be spent on a sacrifice, as that was not right, but should be used for some other purpose. ²⁰So the contribution meant for the sacrifice to Hercules by the sender, was in fact applied to the construction of triremes by those who brought it.

²¹When Apollonius, son of Menestheus, was sent to Egypt for the coronation of King Philometor, Antiochus learned from him that the king was opposed to his policies. He took measures for his own security; so after going to Joppa, he proceeded to Jerusalem. ²²There he was received with great pomp by Jason and the people of the city, who escorted him with torchlights and acclamations; following this, he led his army into Phoenicia.

Menelaus as High Priest. ²³Three years later Jason sent Menelaus, brother of the aforementioned Simon, to deliver the money to the king, and to complete negotiations on urgent matters. ²⁴But after his introduction to the king, he flattered him with such an air of authority that he secured the high priesthood for himself, outbidding Jason by three hundred talents of silver. ²⁵He returned with the royal commission, but with nothing that made him worthy of the high priesthood; he had the temper of a cruel tyrant and the rage of a wild beast. ²⁶So Jason, who had cheated his own brother and now saw himself cheated by another man, was driven out as a fugitive to the country of the Ammonites. ²⁷But Menelaus, who obtained the office, paid nothing of the money he had promised to the king, ²⁸in spite of the demand of Sostratus, the commandant of the citadel, whose duty it was to collect the taxes. For this reason, both were summoned before the king. ²⁹Menelaus left his brother Lysimachus as his deputy in the high priesthood, while Sostratus left Crates, commander of the Cypriots.

Murder of Onias. ³⁰While these things were taking place, the people of Tarsus and Mallus rose in revolt, because their cities had been given as a gift to Antiochis, the king's concubine. ³¹So the king hastened off to settle the affair, leaving Andronicus, one of his nobles, as his deputy. ³²Menelaus, for his part, thinking this a good opportunity, stole some gold vessels from the temple and presented them to Andronicus; he had already sold other vessels in Tyre and in the neighboring cities. ³³When Onias had clear evidence, he accused Menelaus publicly, after withdrawing to the inviolable sanctuary at Daphne, near Antioch. ³⁴Thereupon Menelaus approached Andronicus privately and urged him to seize Onias. So Andronicus went to Onias, treacherously reassuring him by offering his right hand in oath, and persuaded him, in spite of his suspicions, to leave the sanctuary. Then, with no regard for justice, he immediately put him to death.

³⁵As a result, not only the Jews, but many people of other nations as well, were indignant and angry over the unjust murder of the man. ³⁶When the king returned

from the region of Cilicia, the Jews of the city, together with the Greeks who detested the crime, went to see him about the murder of Onias. [37]Antiochus was deeply grieved and full of pity; he wept as he recalled the prudence and noble conduct of the deceased. [38]Inflamed with anger, he immediately stripped Andronicus of his purple robe, tore off his garments, and had him led through the whole city to the very place where he had committed the outrage against Onias; and there he put the murderer to death. Thus the Lord rendered him the punishment he deserved.

More Outrages. [39]Many acts of sacrilege had been committed by Lysimachus in the city with the connivance of Menelaus. When word spread, the people assembled in protest against Lysimachus, because a large number of gold vessels had been stolen. [40]As the crowds, now thoroughly enraged, began to riot, Lysimachus launched an unjustified attack against them with about three thousand armed men under the leadership of a certain Auranus, a man as advanced in folly as he was in years. [41]Seeing Lysimachus' attack, people picked up stones, pieces of wood or handfuls of the ashes lying there and threw them in wild confusion at Lysimachus and his men. [42]As a result, they wounded many of them and even killed a few, while they put all to flight. The temple robber himself they killed near the treasury.

[43]Charges about this affair were brought against Menelaus. [44]When the king came to Tyre, three men sent by the senate pleaded the case before him. [45]But Menelaus, seeing himself on the losing side, promised Ptolemy, son of Dorymenes, a substantial sum of money if he would win the king over. [46]So Ptolemy took the king aside into a colonnade, as if to get some fresh air, and persuaded him to change his mind. [47]Menelaus, who was the cause of all the trouble, the king acquitted of the charges, while he condemned to death those poor men who would have been declared innocent even if they had pleaded their case before Scythians. [48]Thus, those who had prosecuted the case on behalf of the city, the people, and the sacred vessels, quickly suffered unjust punishment. [49]For this reason, even Tyrians, detesting the crime, provided sumptuously for their burial. [50]But Menelaus, thanks to the greed of those in power, remained in office, where he grew in wickedness, scheming greatly against his fellow citizens.

☐ **MATTHEW 25:1-13**

The Parable of the Ten Virgins. 25:1 "Then the kingdom of heaven will be like ten virgins who took their lamps and went out to meet the bridegroom. [2]Five of them were foolish and five were wise. [3]The foolish ones, when taking their lamps, brought no oil with them, [4]but the wise brought flasks of oil with their lamps. [5]Since the bridegroom was long delayed, they all became drowsy and fell asleep. [6]At midnight, there was a cry, 'Behold, the bridegroom! Come out to meet him!' [7]Then all those virgins got up and trimmed their lamps. [8]The foolish ones said to the wise, 'Give us some of your oil, for our lamps are going out.' [9]But the wise ones replied, 'No, for there may not be enough for us and you. Go instead to the merchants and buy some for yourselves.' [10]While they went off to buy it, the bridegroom came and those who were ready went into the wedding feast with him. Then the door was locked. [11]Afterwards the other virgins came and said, 'Lord, Lord, open the door for us!' [12]But he said in reply, 'Amen, I say to you, I do not know you.' [13]Therefore, stay awake, for you know neither the day nor the hour."

June 14

The fullness of life that God rightly expects from His children means that they have to have a careful concern for the quality of their everyday work, because it is this work, even in its most minor aspects, which they must sanctify.

— St. Josemaría Escrivá

☐ 2 MACCABEES 5-6

Jason's Revolt. 5:1 About this time Antiochus sent his second expedition into Egypt. ²It then happened that all over the city, for nearly forty days, there appeared horsemen, clothed in garments of a golden weave, charging in midair—companies fully armed with lances and drawn swords; ³squadrons of cavalry in battle array, charges and countercharges on this side and that, with brandished shields and bristling spears, flights of arrows and flashes of gold ornaments, together with armor of every sort. ⁴Therefore all prayed that this vision might be a good omen.

⁵But when a false rumor circulated that Antiochus was dead, Jason gathered at least a thousand men and suddenly attacked the city. As the defenders on the walls were forced back and the city was finally being taken, Menelaus took refuge in the citadel. ⁶For his part, Jason continued the merciless slaughter of his fellow citizens, not realizing that triumph over one's own kindred is the greatest calamity; he thought he was winning a victory over his enemies, not over his own people. ⁷Even so, he did not gain control of the government, but in the end received only disgrace for his treachery, and once again took refuge in the country of the Ammonites. ⁸At length he met a miserable end. Called to account before Aretas, ruler of the Arabians, he fled from city to city, hunted by all, hated as an apostate from the laws, abhorred as the executioner of his country and his compatriots. Driven into Egypt, ⁹he set out by sea for the Lacedaemonians, among whom he hoped to find protection because of his relations with them. He who had exiled so many from their country perished in exile; ¹⁰and he who had cast out so many to lie unburied went unmourned and without a funeral of any kind, nor any place in the tomb of his ancestors.

Revenge by Antiochus. ¹¹When these happenings were reported to the king, he thought that Judea was in revolt. Raging like a wild animal, he set out from Egypt and took Jerusalem by storm. ¹²He ordered his soldiers to cut down without mercy those whom they met and to slay those who took refuge in their houses. ¹³There was a massacre of young and old, a killing of women and children, a slaughter of young women and infants. ¹⁴In the space of three days, eighty thousand were lost, forty thousand meeting a violent death, and the same number being sold into slavery.

¹⁵Not satisfied with this, the king dared to enter the holiest temple in the world; Menelaus, that traitor both to the laws and to his country, served as guide. ¹⁶He laid his impure hands on the sacred vessels and swept up with profane hands the votive offerings made by other kings for the advancement, the glory, and the honor of the place. ¹⁷Antiochus became puffed up in spirit, not realizing that it was because of the sins of the city's inhabitants that the Sovereign Lord was angry for a little while: hence the disregard of the place. ¹⁸If they had not become entangled in so many sins, this man, like that Heliodorus sent by King Seleucus to inspect the treasury,

would have been flogged and turned back from his presumptuous act as soon as he approached. ¹⁹The Lord, however, had not chosen the nation for the sake of the place, but the place for the sake of the nation. ²⁰Therefore, the place itself, having shared in the nation's misfortunes, afterward participated in their good fortune; and what the Almighty had forsaken in wrath was restored in all its glory, once the great Sovereign Lord became reconciled.

²¹Antiochus carried off eighteen hundred talents from the temple and hurried back to Antioch, thinking in his arrogance that he could make the land navigable and the sea passable on foot, so carried away was he with pride. ²²He left governors to harass the nation: at Jerusalem, Philip, a Phrygian by birth, and in character more barbarous than the man who appointed him; ²³at Mount Gerizim, Andronicus; and besides these, Menelaus, who lorded it over his fellow citizens more than the others. Out of hatred for the Jewish citizens, ²⁴the king sent Apollonius, commander of the Mysians, at the head of an army of twenty-two thousand, with orders to kill all the grown men and sell the women and children into slavery. ²⁵When this man arrived in Jerusalem, he pretended to be peacefully disposed and waited until the holy day of the sabbath; then, finding the Jews refraining from work, he ordered his men to parade fully armed. ²⁶All those who came out to watch, he massacred, and running through the city with armed men, he cut down a large number of people.

²⁷But Judas Maccabeus and about nine others withdrew to the wilderness to avoid sharing in defilement; there he and his companions lived like the animals in the hills, eating what grew wild.

Abolition of Judaism. 6:1 Not long after this the king sent an Athenian senator to force the Jews to abandon the laws of their ancestors and live no longer by the laws of God, ²also to profane the temple in Jerusalem and dedicate it to Olympian Zeus, and the one on Mount Gerizim to Zeus the Host to Strangers, as the local inhabitants were wont to be. ³This was a harsh and utterly intolerable evil. ⁴The Gentiles filled the temple with debauchery and revelry; they amused themselves with prostitutes and had intercourse with women even in the sacred courts. They also brought forbidden things into the temple, ⁵so that the altar was covered with abominable offerings prohibited by the laws.

⁶No one could keep the sabbath or celebrate the traditional feasts, nor even admit to being a Jew. ⁷Moreover, at the monthly celebration of the king's birthday the Jews, from bitter necessity, had to partake of the sacrifices, and when the festival of Dionysus was celebrated, they were compelled to march in his procession, wearing wreaths of ivy.

⁸Following upon a vote of the citizens of Ptolemais, a decree was issued ordering the neighboring Greek cities to adopt the same measures, obliging the Jews to partake of the sacrifices ⁹and putting to death those who would not consent to adopt the customs of the Greeks. It was obvious, therefore, that disaster had come upon them. ¹⁰Thus, two women who were arrested for having circumcised their children were publicly paraded about the city with their babies hanging at their breasts and then thrown down from the top of the city wall. ¹¹Others, who had assembled in nearby caves to observe the seventh day in secret, were betrayed to Philip and all burned to death. In their respect for the holiness of that day, they refrained from defending themselves.

God's Purpose. ¹²Now I urge those who read this book not to be disheartened by these misfortunes, but to consider that these punishments were meant not for the ruin but for the correction of our nation. ¹³It is, in fact, a sign of great kindness to punish the impious promptly instead of letting them go for long. [14]Thus, in dealing with other nations, the Sovereign Lord patiently waits until they reach the full measure of their sins before punishing them; but with us he has decided to deal differently, [15]in order that he may not have to punish us later, when our sins have reached their fullness. [16]Therefore he never withdraws his mercy from us. Although he disciplines us with misfortunes, he does not abandon his own people. [17]Let these words suffice for recalling this truth. Without further ado we must go on with our story.

Martyrdom of Eleazar. [18]Eleazar, one of the foremost scribes, a man advanced in age and of noble appearance, was being forced to open his mouth to eat pork. [19]But preferring a glorious death to a life of defilement, he went forward of his own accord to the instrument of torture, [20]spitting out the meat as they should do who have the courage to reject food unlawful to taste even for love of life.

[21]Those in charge of that unlawful sacrifice took the man aside, because of their long acquaintance with him, and privately urged him to bring his own provisions that he could legitimately eat, and only to pretend to eat the sacrificial meat prescribed by the king. [22]Thus he would escape death, and be treated kindly because of his old friendship with them. [23]But he made up his mind in a noble manner, worthy of his years, the dignity of his advanced age, the merited distinction of his gray hair, and of the admirable life he had lived from childhood. Above all loyal to the holy laws given by God, he swiftly declared, "Send me to Hades!"

[24]"At our age it would be unbecoming to make such a pretense; many of the young would think the ninety-year-old Eleazar had gone over to an alien religion. [25]If I dissemble to gain a brief moment of life, they would be led astray by me, while I would bring defilement and dishonor on my old age. [26]Even if, for the time being, I avoid human punishment, I shall never, whether alive or dead, escape the hand of the Almighty. [27]Therefore, by bravely giving up life now, I will prove myself worthy of my old age, [28]and I will leave to the young a noble example of how to die willingly and nobly for the revered and holy laws."

He spoke thus, and went immediately to the instrument of torture. [29]Those who shortly before had been kindly disposed, now became hostile toward him because what he had said seemed to them utter madness. [30]When he was about to die under the blows, he groaned, saying: "The Lord in his holy knowledge knows full well that, although I could have escaped death, I am not only enduring terrible pain in my body from this scourging, but also suffering it with joy in my soul because of my devotion to him." [31]This is how he died, leaving in his death a model of nobility and an unforgettable example of virtue not only for the young but for the whole nation.

☐ MATTHEW 25:14-30

The Parable of the Talents. 25:14 "It will be as when a man who was going on a journey called in his servants and entrusted his possessions to them. [15]To one he gave five talents; to another, two; to a third, one—to each according to his ability. Then he went away. Immediately [16]the one who received five talents went and traded with them, and made another five. [17]Likewise, the one who received two made another two. [18]But the man who received one went off and dug a hole in the ground and buried his master's money. [19]After a long time the master of those servants came back and settled accounts with them. [20]The one who had received five talents came forward bringing the additional five. He said, 'Master, you gave me five talents. See, I have made five more.' ²¹His master said to him, 'Well done, my good and faithful servant. Since you were faithful in small matters, I will give you great responsibilities. Come, share your master's joy.' ²²[Then] the one who had received two talents also came forward and said, 'Master, you gave me two talents. See, I have made two more.' ²³His master said to him, 'Well done, my good and faithful servant. Since you were faithful in small matters, I will give you great responsibilities. Come, share your master's joy.' ²⁴Then the one who had received the one talent came forward and said, 'Master, I knew you were a demanding person, harvesting where you did not plant and gathering where you did not scatter; ²⁵so out of fear I went off and buried your talent in the ground. Here it is back.' ²⁶His master said to him in reply, 'You wicked, lazy servant! So you knew that I harvest where I did not plant and gather where I did not scatter? ²⁷Should you not then have put my money in the bank so that I could have got it back with interest on my return? ²⁸Now then! Take the talent from him and give it to the one with ten. ²⁹For to everyone who has, more will be given and he will grow rich; but from the one who has not, even what he has will be taken away. ³⁰And throw this useless servant into the darkness outside, where there will be wailing and grinding of teeth.'"

June 15

St. Germaine Cousin

Dear God, please don't let me be too hungry or too thirsty. Help me to please my mother. And help me to please You.

— St. Germaine Cousin

☐ 2 MACCABEES 7–8

Martyrdom of a Mother and Her Seven Sons. 7:1 It also happened that seven brothers with their mother were arrested and tortured with whips and scourges by the king to force them to eat pork in violation of God's law. ²One of the brothers, speaking for the others, said: "What do you expect to learn by questioning us? We are ready to die rather than transgress the laws of our ancestors."

³At that the king, in a fury, gave orders to have pans and caldrons heated. ⁴These were quickly heated, and he gave the order to cut out the tongue of the one who had spoken for the others, to scalp him and cut off his hands and feet, while the rest of his brothers and his mother looked on. ⁵When he was completely maimed but still breathing, the king ordered them to carry him to the fire and fry him. As a cloud of smoke spread from the pan, the brothers and their mother encouraged one another to die nobly, with these words: ⁶"'The Lord God is looking on and truly has compassion on us, as Moses declared in his song, when he openly bore witness, saying, 'And God will have compassion on his servants.'"

⁷After the first brother had died in this manner, they brought the second to be made sport of. After tearing off the skin and hair of his head, they asked him, "Will you eat the pork rather than have your body tortured limb by limb?" ⁸Answering in the language of his ancestors, he said,

"Never!" So he in turn suffered the same tortures as the first. [9]With his last breath he said: "You accursed fiend, you are depriving us of this present life, but the King of the universe will raise us up to live again forever, because we are dying for his laws."

[10]After him the third suffered their cruel sport. He put forth his tongue at once when told to do so, and bravely stretched out his hands, [11]as he spoke these noble words: "It was from Heaven that I received these; for the sake of his laws I disregard them; from him I hope to receive them again." [12]Even the king and his attendants marveled at the young man's spirit, because he regarded his sufferings as nothing.

[13]After he had died, they tortured and maltreated the fourth brother in the same way. [14]When he was near death, he said, "It is my choice to die at the hands of mortals with the hope that God will restore me to life; but for you, there will be no resurrection to life."

[15]They next brought forward the fifth brother and maltreated him. [16]Looking at the king, he said: "Mortal though you are, you have power over human beings, so you do what you please. But do not think that our nation is forsaken by God. [17]Only wait, and you will see how his great power will torment you and your descendants."

[18]After him they brought the sixth brother. When he was about to die, he said: "Have no vain illusions. We suffer these things on our own account, because we have sinned against our God; that is why such shocking things have happened. [19]Do not think, then, that you will go unpunished for having dared to fight against God."

[20]Most admirable and worthy of everlasting remembrance was the mother who, seeing her seven sons perish in a single day, bore it courageously because of her hope in the Lord. [21]Filled with a noble spirit that stirred her womanly reason with manly emotion, she exhorted each of them in the language of their ancestors with these words: [22]"I do not know how you came to be in my womb; it was not I who gave you breath and life, nor was it I who arranged the elements you are made of. [23]Therefore, since it is the Creator of the universe who shaped the beginning of humankind and brought about the origin of everything, he, in his mercy, will give you back both breath and life, because you now disregard yourselves for the sake of his law."

[24]Antiochus, suspecting insult in her words, thought he was being ridiculed. As the youngest brother was still alive, the king appealed to him, not with mere words, but with promises on oath, to make him rich and happy if he would abandon his ancestral customs: he would make him his Friend and entrust him with high office. [25]When the youth paid no attention to him at all, the king appealed to the mother, urging her to advise her boy to save his life. [26]After he had urged her for a long time, she agreed to persuade her son. [27]She leaned over close to him and, in derision of the cruel tyrant, said in their native language: "Son, have pity on me, who carried you in my womb for nine months, nursed you for three years, brought you up, educated and supported you to your present age. [28]I beg you, child, to look at the heavens and the earth and see all that is in them; then you will know that God did not make them out of existing things. In the same way humankind came into existence. [29]Do not be afraid of this executioner, but be worthy of your brothers and accept death, so that in the time of mercy I may receive you again with your brothers."

[30]She had scarcely finished speaking when the youth said: "What is the delay? I will not obey the king's command. I obey the command of the law given to our ancestors through Moses. [31]But you, who have contrived every kind of evil for the Hebrews, will not escape the hands of God. [32]We, indeed, are suffering because

of our sins. ³³Though for a little while our living Lord has been angry, correcting and chastising us, he will again be reconciled with his servants. ³⁴But you, wretch, most vile of mortals, do not, in your insolence, buoy yourself up with unfounded hopes, as you raise your hand against the children of heaven. ³⁵You have not yet escaped the judgment of the almighty and all-seeing God. ³⁶Our brothers, after enduring brief pain, have drunk of never-failing life, under God's covenant. But you, by the judgment of God, shall receive just punishments for your arrogance. ³⁷Like my brothers, I offer up my body and my life for our ancestral laws, imploring God to show mercy soon to our nation, and by afflictions and blows to make you confess that he alone is God. ³⁸Through me and my brothers, may there be an end to the wrath of the Almighty that has justly fallen on our whole nation."

³⁹At that, the king became enraged and treated him even worse than the others, since he bitterly resented the boy's contempt. ⁴⁰Thus he too died undefiled, putting all his trust in the Lord. ⁴¹Last of all, after her sons, the mother was put to death. ⁴²Enough has been said about the sacrificial meals and the excessive cruelties.

Resistance from Judas Maccabeus. 8:1 Judas Maccabeus and his companions entered the villages secretly, summoned their kindred, and enlisted others who had remained faithful to Judaism. Thus they assembled about six thousand men. ²They implored the Lord to look kindly upon this people, who were being oppressed by all; to have pity on the sanctuary, which was profaned by renegades; ³to have mercy on the city, which was being destroyed and was about to be leveled to the ground; to listen to the blood that cried out to him; ⁴to remember the criminal slaughter of innocent children and the blasphemies uttered against his name; and to manifest his hatred of evil.

⁵Once Maccabeus got his men organized, the Gentiles could not withstand him, for the Lord's wrath had now changed to mercy. ⁶Coming by surprise upon towns and villages, he set them on fire. He captured strategic positions, and put to flight not a few of the enemy. ⁷He preferred the nights as being especially favorable for such attacks. Soon talk of his valor spread everywhere.

First Victory over Nicanor. ⁸When Philip saw that Judas was gaining ground little by little and that his successful advances were becoming more frequent, he wrote to Ptolemy, governor of Coelesyria and Phoenicia, to come to the aid of the king's interests. ⁹Ptolemy promptly selected Nicanor, son of Patroclus, one of the Chief Friends, and sent him at the head of at least twenty thousand armed men of various nations to wipe out the entire Jewish nation. With him he associated Gorgias, a general, experienced in the art of war. ¹⁰Nicanor planned to raise the two thousand talents of tribute owed by the king to the Romans by selling captured Jews into slavery. ¹¹So he immediately sent word to the coastal cities, inviting them to buy Jewish slaves and promising to deliver ninety slaves for a talent—little anticipating the punishment that was to fall upon him from the Almighty.

¹²When Judas learned of Nicanor's advance and informed his companions about the approach of the army, ¹³those who were fearful and those who lacked faith in God's justice deserted and got away. ¹⁴But the others sold everything they had left, and at the same time entreated the Lord to deliver those whom the ungodly Nicanor had sold before even capturing them. ¹⁵They entreated the Lord to do this, if not for their sake, at least for the sake of the covenants made with their ancestors, and because they themselves invoked his holy and glorious name. ¹⁶Maccabeus assembled his forces, six thousand strong, and exhorted them not to be panic-stricken before the

enemy, nor to fear the very large number of Gentiles unjustly attacking them, but to fight nobly. [17]They were to keep before their eyes the lawless outrage perpetrated by the Gentiles against the holy place and the affliction of the humiliated city, as well as the subversion of their ancestral way of life. [18]He said, "They trust in weapons and acts of daring, but we trust in almighty God, who can by a mere nod destroy not only those who attack us but even the whole world." [19]He went on to tell them of the times when help had been given their ancestors: both the time of Sennacherib, when a hundred and eighty-five thousand of his men perished, [20]and the time of the battle in Babylonia against the Galatians, when only eight thousand Jews fought along with four thousand Macedonians; yet when the Macedonians were hard pressed, the eight thousand, by the help they received from Heaven, destroyed one hundred and twenty thousand and took a great quantity of spoils. [21]With these words he encouraged them and made them ready to die for their laws and their country.

Then Judas divided his army into four, [22]placing his brothers, Simon, Joseph, and Jonathan, each over a division, assigning them fifteen hundred men apiece. [23]There was also Eleazar. After reading to them from the holy book and giving them the watchword, "The help of God," Judas himself took charge of the first division and joined in battle with Nicanor. [24]With the Almighty as their ally, they killed more than nine thousand of the enemy, wounded and disabled the greater part of Nicanor's army, and put all of them to flight. [25]They also seized the money of those who had come to buy them as slaves. When they had pursued the enemy for some time, they were obliged to return by reason of the late hour. [26]It was the day before the sabbath, and for that reason they could not continue the pursuit. [27]They collected the enemy's weapons and stripped them of their spoils, and then observed the sabbath with fervent praise and thanks to the Lord who kept them safe for that day on which he allotted them the beginning of his mercy. [28]After the sabbath, they gave a share of the spoils to those who were tortured and to widows and orphans; the rest they divided among themselves and their children. [29]When this was done, they made supplication in common, imploring the merciful Lord to be completely reconciled with his servants.

Other Victories. [30]They also challenged the forces of Timothy and Bacchides, killed more than twenty thousand of them, and captured some very high fortresses. They divided the considerable plunder, allotting half to themselves and the rest to victims of torture, orphans, widows, and the aged. [31]They collected the enemies' weapons and carefully stored them in strategic places; the rest of the spoils they carried to Jerusalem. [32]They also killed the commander of Timothy's forces, a most wicked man, who had done great harm to the Jews. [33]While celebrating the victory in their ancestral city, they burned both those who had set fire to the sacred gates and Callisthenes, who had taken refuge in a little house; so he received the reward his wicked deeds deserved.

[34]The thrice-accursed Nicanor, who had brought the thousand slave dealers to buy the Jews, [35]after being humbled through the Lord's help by those whom he had thought of no account, laid aside his fine clothes and fled alone across country like a runaway slave, until he reached Antioch. He was eminently successful in destroying his own army. [36]So he who had promised to provide tribute for the Romans by the capture of the people of Jerusalem proclaimed that the Jews had a champion, and that because they followed the laws laid down by him, they were unharmed.

☐ MATTHEW 25:31-46

The Judgment of the Nations. 25:31 "When the Son of Man comes in his glory, and all the angels with him, he will sit upon his glorious throne, ³²and all the nations will be assembled before him. And he will separate them one from another, as a shepherd separates the sheep from the goats. ³³He will place the sheep on his right and the goats on his left. ³⁴Then the king will say to those on his right, 'Come, you who are blessed by my Father. Inherit the kingdom prepared for you from the foundation of the world. ³⁵For I was hungry and you gave me food, I was thirsty and you gave me drink, a stranger and you welcomed me, ³⁶naked and you clothed me, ill and you cared for me, in prison and you visited me.' ³⁷Then the righteous will answer him and say, 'Lord, when did we see you hungry and feed you, or thirsty and give you drink? ³⁸When did we see you a stranger and welcome you, or naked and clothe you? ³⁹When did we see you ill or in prison, and visit you?' ⁴⁰And the king will say to them in reply, 'Amen, I say to you, whatever you did for one of these least brothers of mine, you did for me.' ⁴¹Then he will say to those on his left, 'Depart from me, you accursed, into the eternal fire prepared for the devil and his angels. ⁴²For I was hungry and you gave me no food, I was thirsty and you gave me no drink, ⁴³a stranger and you gave me no welcome, naked and you gave me no clothing, ill and in prison, and you did not care for me.' ⁴⁴Then they will answer and say, 'Lord, when did we see you hungry or thirsty or a stranger or naked or ill or in prison, and not minister to your needs?' ⁴⁵He will answer them, 'Amen, I say to you, what you did not do for one of these least ones, you did not do for me.' ⁴⁶And these will go off to eternal punishment, but the righteous to eternal life."

June 16

If God allows some people to pile up riches instead of making themselves poor as Jesus did, it is so they may use what He has entrusted to them as loyal servants, in accordance with the Master's will, to do spiritual and temporal good to others.

— BLESSED CHARLES DE FOUCAULD

☐ 2 MACCABEES 9-11

Punishment and Death of Antiochus IV. 9:1 About that time Antiochus retreated in disgrace from the region of Persia. ²He had entered the city called Persepolis and attempted to rob the temples and gain control of the city. Thereupon the people had swift recourse to arms, and Antiochus' forces were routed, so that in the end Antiochus was put to flight by the people of that region and forced to beat a shameful retreat. ³On his arrival in Ecbatana, he learned what had happened to Nicanor and to Timothy's forces. ⁴Overcome with anger, he planned to make the Jews suffer for the injury done by those who had put him to flight. Therefore he ordered his charioteer to drive without stopping until he finished the journey. Yet the condemnation of Heaven rode with him, because he said in his arrogance, "I will make Jerusalem the common graveyard of Jews as soon as I arrive there."

⁵So the all-seeing Lord, the God of Israel, struck him down with an incurable and invisible blow; for scarcely had he uttered those words when he was seized with excruciating pains in his bowels and sharp internal torment, ⁶a fit punishment for him who had tortured the bowels of others with many barbarous torments. ⁷Far from giving up his insolence, he was all the more filled with arrogance. Breathing fire in his rage against the Jews, he gave orders to drive even faster. As a result he hurtled from the speeding chariot, and every part of his body was racked by the violent fall. ⁸Thus he who previously, in his superhuman presumption, thought he could command the waves of the sea, and imagined he could weigh the mountaintops in his scales, was now thrown to the ground and had to be carried on a litter, clearly manifesting to all the power of God. ⁹The body of this impious man swarmed with worms, and while he was still alive in hideous torments, his flesh rotted off, so that the entire army was sickened by the stench of his corruption. ¹⁰Shortly before, he had thought that he could reach the stars of heaven, and now, no one could endure to transport the man because of this intolerable stench.

¹¹At last, broken in spirit, he began to give up his excessive arrogance, and to gain some understanding, under the scourge of God, for he was racked with pain unceasingly. ¹²When he could no longer bear his own stench, he said, "It is right to be subject to God, and not to think one's mortal self equal to God." ¹³Then this vile man vowed to him who would never again show him mercy, the Sovereign Lord, ¹⁴that the holy city, toward which he had been hurrying with the intention of leveling it to the ground and making it a common graveyard, he would now set free; ¹⁵that the Jews, whom he had judged not even worthy of burial, but fit only to be thrown out with their children to be eaten by vultures and wild animals—all of them he would make equal to the Athenians; ¹⁶that he would adorn with the finest offerings the holy temple which he had previously despoiled, restore all the sacred vessels many times over, and provide from his own revenues the expenses required for the sacrifices. ¹⁷Besides all this, he would become a Jew himself and visit every inhabited place to proclaim there the power of God. ¹⁸But since his sufferings were not lessened, for God's just judgment had come upon him, he lost hope for himself and wrote the following letter to the Jews in the form of a supplication. It read thus:

¹⁹"To the worthy Jewish citizens, Antiochus, king and general, sends hearty greetings and best wishes for their health and prosperity. ²⁰If you and your children are well and your affairs are going as you wish, I thank God very much, for my hopes are in heaven. ²¹Now that I am ill, I recall with affection your esteem and goodwill. On returning from the regions of Persia, I fell victim to a troublesome illness; so I thought it necessary to form plans for the general security of all. ²²I do not despair about my health, since I have much hope of recovering from my illness. ²³Nevertheless, I know that my father, whenever he went on campaigns in the hinterland, would name his successor, ²⁴so that, if anything unexpected happened or any unwelcome news came, the people throughout the realm would know to whom the government had been entrusted, and so not be disturbed. ²⁵I am also bearing in mind that the neighboring rulers, especially those on the borders of our kingdom, are on the watch for opportunities and waiting to see what will happen. I have therefore appointed as king my son Antiochus, whom I have often before entrusted and commended to most of you, when I made hurried visits to the outlying provinces. I have written to him what is

written here. [26]Therefore I beg and entreat each of you to remember the general and individual benefits you have received, and to continue to show goodwill toward me and my son. [27]I am confident that, following my policy, he will treat you with equity and kindness in his relations with you."

[28]So this murderer and blasphemer, after extreme sufferings, such as he had inflicted on others, died a miserable death in the mountains of a foreign land. [29]His foster brother Philip brought the body home; but fearing Antiochus' son, he later withdrew into Egypt, to Ptolemy Philometor.

Purification of the Temple. 10:1 When Maccabeus and his companions, under the Lord's leadership, had recovered the temple and the city, [2]they destroyed the altars erected by the foreigners in the marketplace and the sacred shrines. [3]After purifying the temple, they made another altar. Then, with fire struck from flint, they offered sacrifice for the first time in two years, burned incense, and lighted lamps. They also set out the showbread. [4]When they had done this, they prostrated themselves and begged the Lord that they might never again fall into such misfortunes, and that if they should sin at any time, he might chastise them with moderation and not hand them over to blasphemous and barbarous Gentiles. [5]On the anniversary of the day on which the temple had been profaned by the foreigners, that is, the twenty-fifth of the same month Kislev, the purification of the temple took place. [6]The Jews celebrated joyfully for eight days as on the feast of Booths, remembering how, a little while before, they had spent the feast of Booths living like wild animals in the mountains and in caves. [7]Carrying rods entwined with leaves, beautiful branches and palms, they sang hymns of grateful praise to him who had successfully brought about the purification of his own place. [8]By public decree and vote they prescribed that the whole Jewish nation should celebrate these days every year. [9]Such was the end of Antiochus surnamed Epiphanes.

Accession of Antiochus V. [10]Now we shall relate what happened under Antiochus Eupator, the son of that godless man, and shall give a summary of the chief evils caused by the wars. [11]When Eupator succeeded to the kingdom, he put a certain Lysias in charge of the government as commander-in-chief of Coelesyria and Phoenicia. [12]Ptolemy, called Macron, had taken the lead in treating the Jews fairly because of the previous injustice that had been done them, and he endeavored to have peaceful relations with them. [13]As a result, he was accused before Eupator by the King's Friends. In fact, on all sides he heard himself called a traitor for having abandoned Cyprus, which Philometor had entrusted to him, and for having gone over to Antiochus Epiphanes. Since he could not command the respect due to his high office, he ended his life by taking poison.

Victory over the Idumeans. [14]When Gorgias became governor of the region, he employed foreign troops and used every opportunity to attack the Jews. [15]At the same time the Idumeans, who held some strategic strongholds, were harassing the Jews; they welcomed fugitives from Jerusalem and endeavored to continue the war. [16]Maccabeus and his companions, after public prayers asking God to be their ally, moved quickly against the strongholds of the Idumeans. [17]Attacking vigorously, they gained control of the places, drove back all who were fighting on the walls, and cut down those who opposed them, killing no fewer than twenty thousand. [18]When at least nine thousand took refuge in two very strong towers, well equipped to sustain a siege, [19]Maccabeus left Simon and Joseph, along with Zacchaeus and his forces, in sufficient numbers to besiege them, while he himself went off to places where he was more urgently needed. [20]But some of those in Simon's force who were lovers of money let themselves be bribed by some of those in the towers; on receiving seventy thousand drachmas, they allowed a number of them to escape. [21]When Maccabeus was told what had happened, he assembled the rulers of the people and accused those men of having sold their kindred for money by setting their enemies free to fight against them. [22]So he put them to death as traitors, and without delay captured the two towers. [23]As he was successful at arms in all his undertakings, he destroyed more than twenty thousand in the two strongholds.

Victory over Timothy. [24]Timothy, who had previously been defeated by the Jews, gathered a tremendous force of foreign troops and collected a large number of cavalry from Asia; then he appeared in Judea, ready to conquer it by force. [25]At his approach, Maccabeus and his companions made supplication to God, sprinkling earth upon their heads and girding their loins in sackcloth. [26]Lying prostrate at the foot of the altar, they begged him to be gracious to them, and to be an enemy to their enemies, and a foe to their foes, as the law declares. [27]After the prayer, they took up their weapons and advanced a considerable distance from the city, halting when they were close to the enemy. [28]As soon as dawn broke, the armies joined battle, the one having as pledge of success and victory not only their valor but also their reliance on the Lord, and the other taking fury as their leader in the fight.

[29]In the midst of the fierce battle, there appeared to the enemy five majestic men from the heavens riding on golden-bridled horses, leading the Jews. [30]They surrounded Maccabeus, and shielding him with their own armor, kept him from being wounded. They shot arrows and hurled thunderbolts at the enemy, who were bewildered and blinded, routed in utter confusion. [31]Twenty thousand five hundred of their foot soldiers and six hundred cavalry were slain.

[32]Timothy, however, fled to a well-fortified stronghold called Gazara, where Chaereas was in command. [33]For four days Maccabeus and his forces eagerly besieged the fortress. [34]Those inside, relying on the strength of the place, kept repeating outrageous blasphemies and uttering abominable words. [35]When the fifth day dawned, twenty young men in the army of Maccabeus, angered over such blasphemies, bravely stormed the wall and with savage fury cut down everyone they encountered. [36]Similarly, others climbed up and swung around on the defenders; they put the towers to the torch, spread the fire and burned the blasphemers alive. Still others broke down the gates and let in the rest of the troops, who took possession of the city. [37]Timothy had hidden in a cistern, but they killed him, along with his brother Chaereas, and Apollophanes. [38]On completing these exploits, they blessed, with hymns of grateful praise, the Lord who shows great kindness to Israel and grants them victory.

Defeat of Lysias. 11:1 Very soon afterward, Lysias, guardian and kinsman of the king and head of the government, being greatly displeased at what had happened, [2]mustered about eighty thousand infantry and all his cavalry and marched against the Jews. His plan was to make their city a Greek settlement; [3]to levy tribute on the temple, as he did on the shrines of the other nations; and to put the high priesthood up for sale every year. [4]He did not take God's power into account at all, but felt exultant confidence in his myriads of foot soldiers, his thousands of cavalry, and his eighty elephants. [5]So he invaded Judea, and when he reached Beth-zur, a fortified place about five stadia from Jerusalem, launched a strong attack against it.

[6]When Maccabeus and his companions learned that Lysias was besieging the strongholds, they and all the people begged the Lord with lamentations and tears to send a

good angel to save Israel. [7]Maccabeus himself was the first to take up arms, and he exhorted the others to join him in risking their lives to help their kindred. Then they resolutely set out together. [8]Suddenly, while they were still near Jerusalem, a horseman appeared at their head, clothed in white garments and brandishing gold weapons. [9]Then all of them together thanked the merciful God, and their hearts were filled with such courage that they were ready to assault not only human beings but even the most savage beasts, or even walls of iron. [10]Now that the Lord had shown mercy toward them, they advanced in battle order with the aid of their heavenly ally. [11]Hurling themselves upon the enemy like lions, they laid low eleven thousand foot soldiers and sixteen hundred cavalry, and put all the rest to flight. [12]Most of those who survived were wounded and disarmed, while Lysias himself escaped only by shameful flight.

Peace Negotiations. [13]But Lysias was not a stupid man. He reflected on the defeat he had suffered, and came to realize that the Hebrews were invincible because the mighty God was their ally. He therefore sent a message [14]persuading them to settle everything on just terms, and promising to persuade the king also, and to induce him to become their friend. [15]Maccabeus, solicitous for the common good, agreed to all that Lysias proposed; and the king granted on behalf of the Jews all the written requests of Maccabeus to Lysias.

[16]These are the terms of the letter which Lysias wrote to the Jews: "Lysias sends greetings to the Jewish people. [17]John and Absalom, your envoys, have presented your signed communication and asked about the matters contained in it. [18]Whatever had to be referred to the king I called to his attention, and the things that were acceptable he has granted. [19]If you maintain your loyalty to the government, I will endeavor to further your interests in the future. [20]On the details of these matters I have authorized my representatives, as well as your envoys, to confer with you. [21]Farewell." The one hundred and forty-eighth year, the twenty-fourth of Dioscorinthius.

[22]The king's letter read thus: "King Antiochus sends greetings to his brother Lysias. [23]Now that our father has taken his place among the gods, we wish the subjects of our kingdom to be undisturbed in conducting their own affairs. [24]We have heard that the Jews do not agree with our father's change to Greek customs but prefer their own way of life. They are petitioning us to let them retain their own customs. [25]Since we desire that this people too should be undisturbed, our decision is that their temple be restored to them and that they live in keeping with the customs of their ancestors. [26]Accordingly, please send them messengers to give them our assurances of friendship, so that, when they learn of our decision, they may have nothing to worry about but may contentedly go about their own business."

[27]The king's letter to the people was as follows: "King Antiochus sends greetings to the Jewish senate and to the rest of the Jews. [28]If you are well, it is what we desire. We too are in good health. [29]Menelaus has told us of your wish to return home and attend to your own affairs. [30]Therefore, those who return by the thirtieth of Xanthicus will have our assurance of full permission [31]to observe their dietary and other laws, just as before, and none of the Jews shall be molested in any way for faults committed through ignorance. [32]I have also sent Menelaus to reassure you. [33]Farewell." In the one hundred and forty-eighth year, the fifteenth of Xanthicus.

[34]The Romans also sent them a letter as follows: "Quintus Memmius and Titus Manius, legates of the Romans, send greetings to the Jewish people. [35]What Lysias, kinsman of the king, has granted you, we also approve. [36]But for the matters that he decided should be submitted to the king,

send someone to us immediately with your decisions so that we may present them to your advantage, for we are on our way to Antioch. ³⁷Make haste, then, to send us those who can inform us of your preference. ³⁸Farewell." In the one hundred and forty-eighth year, the fifteenth of Xanthicus.

☐ MATTHEW 26:1-19

The Conspiracy against Jesus. 26:1 When Jesus finished all these words, he said to his disciples, ²"You know that in two days' time it will be Passover, and the Son of Man will be handed over to be crucified." ³Then the chief priests and the elders of the people assembled in the palace of the high priest, who was called Caiaphas, ⁴and they consulted together to arrest Jesus by treachery and put him to death. ⁵But they said, "Not during the festival, that there may not be a riot among the people."

The Anointing at Bethany. ⁶Now when Jesus was in Bethany in the house of Simon the leper, ⁷a woman came up to him with an alabaster jar of costly perfumed oil, and poured it on his head while he was reclining at table. ⁸When the disciples saw this, they were indignant and said, "Why this waste? ⁹It could have been sold for much, and the money given to the poor." ¹⁰Since Jesus knew this, he said to them, "Why do you make trouble for the woman? She has done a good thing for me. ¹¹The poor you will always have with you; but you will not always have me. ¹²In pouring this perfumed oil upon my body, she did it to prepare me for burial. ¹³Amen, I say to you, wherever this gospel is proclaimed in the whole world, what she has done will be spoken of, in memory of her."

The Betrayal by Judas. ¹⁴Then one of the Twelve, who was called Judas Iscariot, went to the chief priests ¹⁵and said, "What are you willing to give me if I hand him over to you?" They paid him thirty pieces of silver, ¹⁶and from that time on he looked for an opportunity to hand him over.

Preparations for the Passover. ¹⁷On the first day of the Feast of Unleavened Bread, the disciples approached Jesus and said, "Where do you want us to prepare for you to eat the Passover?" ¹⁸He said, "Go into the city to a certain man and tell him, 'The teacher says, "My appointed time draws near; in your house I shall celebrate the Passover with my disciples."'" ¹⁹The disciples then did as Jesus had ordered, and prepared the Passover.

June 17

Do not, therefore, regard the Bread and Wine as simply that, for they are, according to the Master's declaration, the Body and Blood of Christ. Even though the senses suggest to you the other, let faith make you firm. Do not judge in this matter by taste, but be fully assured by faith, not doubting that you have been deemed worthy of the Body and Blood of Christ.

— St. Cyril of Jerusalem

☐ 2 MACCABEES 12-13

Incidents at Joppa and Jamnia. 12:1 After these agreements were made, Lysias returned to the king, and the Jews went about their farming. ²But some of the local governors, Timothy and Apollonius, son of Gennaeus, as also Hieronymus and Demophon, to say nothing of Nicanor, the commander of the Cyprians, would not allow them to live in peace and quiet.

³Some people of Joppa also committed this outrage: they invited the Jews who lived among them, together with their wives and children, to embark on boats which they had provided. There was no hint of enmity toward them. ⁴This was done by public vote of the city. When the Jews, wishing to live on friendly terms and not suspecting anything, accepted the invitation, the people of Joppa took them out to sea and drowned at least two hundred of them.

⁵As soon as Judas heard of the barbarous deed perpetrated against his compatriots, he summoned his men; ⁶and after calling upon God, the just judge, he marched against the murderers of his kindred. In a night attack he set the harbor on fire, burned the boats, and put to the sword those who had taken refuge there. ⁷Because the gates of the town were shut, he withdrew, intending to come back later and wipe out the entire population of Joppa.

⁸On hearing that the people of Jamnia planned in the same way to wipe out the Jews who lived among them, ⁹he attacked the Jamnians by night, setting fire to the harbor and the fleet, so that the glow of the flames was visible as far as Jerusalem, thirty miles away.

More Victories by Judas. ¹⁰When the Jews had gone about a mile from there in the march against Timothy, they were attacked by Arabians numbering at least five thousand foot soldiers and five hundred cavalry. ¹¹After a hard fight, Judas and his companions, with God's help, were victorious. The defeated nomads begged Judas to give pledges of friendship, and they promised to supply the Jews with livestock and to be of service to them in any other way. ¹²Realizing that they could indeed be useful in many respects, Judas agreed to make peace with them. After the pledges of friendship had been exchanged, the Arabians withdrew to their tents.

¹³He also attacked a certain city called Caspin, fortified with earthworks and walls and inhabited by a mixed population of Gentiles. ¹⁴Relying on the strength of their walls and their supply of provisions, the besieged treated Judas and his men with contempt, insulting them and even uttering blasphemies and profanity. ¹⁵But Judas and his men invoked the aid of the great Sovereign of the world, who, in the days of Joshua, overthrew Jericho without battering rams or siege engines; then they furiously stormed the walls. ¹⁶Capturing the city by the will of God, they inflicted

such indescribable slaughter on it that the adjacent pool, which was about a quarter of a mile wide, seemed to be filled with the blood that flowed into it.

[17]When they had gone on some ninety miles, they reached Charax, where there were certain Jews known as Toubians. [18]But they did not find Timothy in that region, for he had already departed from there without having done anything except to leave behind in one place a very strong garrison. [19]But Dositheus and Sosipater, two of Maccabeus' captains, marched out and destroyed the force of more than ten thousand men that Timothy had left in the stronghold. [20]Meanwhile, Maccabeus divided his army into cohorts, with a commander over each cohort, and went in pursuit of Timothy, who had a force of a hundred and twenty thousand foot soldiers and twenty-five hundred cavalry. [21]When Timothy learned of the approach of Judas, he sent on ahead of him the women and children, as well as the baggage, to a place called Karnion, which was hard to besiege and even hard to reach because of the difficult terrain of that region. [22]But when Judas' first cohort appeared, the enemy was overwhelmed with fear and terror at the manifestation of the all-seeing One. Scattering in every direction, they rushed away in such headlong flight that in many cases they wounded one another, pierced by the points of their own swords. [23]Judas pressed the pursuit vigorously, putting the sinners to the sword and destroying as many as thirty thousand men.

[24]Timothy himself fell into the hands of those under Dositheus and Sosipater; but with great cunning, he begged them to spare his life and let him go, because he had in his power the parents and relatives of many of them, and would show them no consideration. [25]When he had fully confirmed his solemn pledge to restore them unharmed, they let him go for the sake of saving their relatives.

[26]Judas then marched to Karnion and the shrine of Atargatis, where he killed twenty-five thousand people. [27]After the defeat and destruction of these, he moved his army to Ephron, a fortified city inhabited by Lysias and people of many nationalities. Robust young men took up their posts in defense of the walls, from which they fought valiantly; inside were large supplies of war machines and missiles. [28]But the Jews, invoking the Sovereign who powerfully shatters the might of enemies, got possession of the city and slaughtered twenty-five thousand of the people in it.

[29]Then they set out from there and hastened on to Scythopolis, seventy-five miles from Jerusalem. [30]But when the Jews who lived there testified to the goodwill shown by the Scythopolitans and to their kind treatment even in times of adversity, [31]Judas and his men thanked them and exhorted them to be well disposed to their nation in the future also. Finally they arrived in Jerusalem, shortly before the feast of Weeks.

[32]After this feast, also called Pentecost, they lost no time in marching against Gorgias, governor of Idumea, [33]who opposed them with three thousand foot soldiers and four hundred cavalry. [34]In the ensuing battle, a few of the Jews were slain. [35]A man called Dositheus, a powerful horseman and one of Bacenor's men, caught hold of Gorgias, grasped his military cloak and dragged him along by brute strength, intending to capture the vile wretch alive, when a Thracian horseman attacked Dositheus and cut off his arm at the shoulder. Then Gorgias fled to Marisa.

[36]After Esdris and his men had been fighting for a long time and were weary, Judas called upon the Lord to show himself their ally and leader in the battle. [37]Then, raising a battle cry in his ancestral language, and with hymns, he charged Gorgias' men when they were not expecting it and put them to flight.

Expiation for the Dead. [38]Judas rallied his army and went to the city of Adullam. As the seventh day was approaching, they purified themselves according to custom and kept the sabbath there. [39]On the following day, since the task had now become urgent, Judas and his companions went to gather up the bodies of the fallen and bury them with their kindred in their ancestral tombs. [40]But under the tunic of each of the dead they found amulets sacred to the idols of Jamnia, which the law forbids the Jews to wear. So it was clear to all that this was why these men had fallen. [41]They all therefore praised the ways of the Lord, the just judge who brings to light the things that are hidden. [42]Turning to supplication, they prayed that the sinful deed might be fully blotted out. The noble Judas exhorted the people to keep themselves free from sin, for they had seen with their own eyes what had happened because of the sin of those who had fallen. [43]He then took up a collection among all his soldiers, amounting to two thousand silver drachmas, which he sent to Jerusalem to provide for an expiatory sacrifice. In doing this he acted in a very excellent and noble way, inasmuch as he had the resurrection in mind; [44]for if he were not expecting the fallen to rise again, it would have been superfluous and foolish to pray for the dead. [45]But if he did this with a view to the splendid reward that awaits those who had gone to rest in godliness, it was a holy and pious thought. [46]Thus he made atonement for the dead that they might be absolved from their sin.

Death of Menelaus. 13:1 In the one hundred and forty-ninth year, Judas and his men learned that Antiochus Eupator was invading Judea with a large force, [2]and that with him was Lysias, his guardian, who was in charge of the government. They led a Greek army of one hundred and ten thousand foot soldiers, fifty-three hundred cavalry, twenty-two elephants, and three hundred chariots armed with scythes.

[3]Menelaus also joined them, and with great duplicity kept urging Antiochus on, not for the welfare of his country, but in the hope of being established in office. [4]But the King of kings aroused the anger of Antiochus against the scoundrel. When the king was shown by Lysias that Menelaus was to blame for all the trouble, he ordered him to be taken to Beroea and executed there in the customary local method. [5]There is at that place a tower seventy-five feet high, full of ashes, with a circular rim sloping down steeply on all sides toward the ashes. [6]Anyone guilty of sacrilege or notorious for certain other crimes is brought up there and then hurled down to destruction. [7]In such a manner was Menelaus, that transgressor of the law, fated to die, deprived even of burial. [8]It was altogether just that he who had committed so many sins against the altar with its pure fire and ashes, in ashes should meet his death.

Battle near Modein. [9]The king was advancing, his mind full of savage plans for inflicting on the Jews things worse than those they suffered in his father's time. [10]When Judas learned of this, he urged the people to call upon the Lord day and night, now more than ever, to help them when they were about to be deprived of their law, their country, and their holy temple; [11]and not to allow this people, which had just begun to revive, to be subjected again to blasphemous Gentiles. [12]When they had all joined in doing this, and had implored the merciful Lord continuously with weeping and fasting and prostrations for three days, Judas encouraged them and told them to stand ready.

[13]After a private meeting with the elders, he decided that, before the king's army could invade Judea and take possession of the city, the Jews should march out and settle the matter with God's help. [14]Leaving the outcome to the Creator of the world, and exhorting his followers to fight nobly to death for the laws, the temple, the city,

the country, and the government, he encamped near Modein. [15]Giving his troops the battle cry "God's Victory," he made a night attack on the king's pavilion with a picked force of the bravest young men and killed about two thousand in the camp. He also stabbed the lead elephant and its rider. [16]Finally they withdrew in triumph, having filled the camp with terror and confusion. [17]Day was just breaking when this was accomplished with the help and protection of the Lord.

Treaty with Antiochus V. [18]The king, having had a taste of the Jews' boldness, tried to take their positions by a stratagem. [19]So he marched against Beth-zur, a strong fortress of the Jews; but he was driven back, checked, and defeated. [20]Judas sent supplies to the men inside, [21]but Rhodocus, of the Jewish army, betrayed military secrets to the enemy. He was found out, arrested, and imprisoned. [22]The king made a second attempt by negotiating with the people of Beth-zur. After giving them his pledge and receiving theirs, he withdrew [23]and attacked Judas' men. But he was defeated. Next he heard that Philip, who was left in charge of the government in Antioch, had rebelled. Dismayed, he negotiated with the Jews, submitted to their terms, and swore to observe all their rights. Having come to this agreement, he offered a sacrifice, and honored the sanctuary and the place with a generous donation. [24]He received Maccabeus, and left Hegemonides as governor of the territory from Ptolemais to the region of the Gerrhenes. [25]When he came to Ptolemais, the people of Ptolemais were angered by the peace treaty; in fact they were so indignant that they wanted to annul its provisions. [26]But Lysias took the platform, defended the treaty as well as he could and won them over by persuasion. After calming them and gaining their goodwill, he returned to Antioch. That is the story of the king's attack and withdrawal.

☐ MATTHEW 26:20-46

The Betrayer. 26:20 When it was evening, he reclined at table with the Twelve. [21]And while they were eating, he said, "Amen, I say to you, one of you will betray me." [22]Deeply distressed at this, they began to say to him one after another, "Surely it is not I, Lord?" [23]He said in reply, "He who has dipped his hand into the dish with me is the one who will betray me. [24]The Son of Man indeed goes, as it is written of him, but woe to that man by whom the Son of Man is betrayed. It would be better for that man if he had never been born." [25]Then Judas, his betrayer, said in reply, "Surely it is not I, Rabbi?" He answered, "You have said so."

The Lord's Supper. [26]While they were eating, Jesus took bread, said the blessing, broke it, and giving it to his disciples said, "Take and eat; this is my body." [27]Then he took a cup, gave thanks, and gave it to them, saying, "Drink from it, all of you, [28]for this is my blood of the covenant, which will be shed on behalf of many for the forgiveness of sins. [29]I tell you, from now on I shall not drink this fruit of the vine until the day when I drink it with you new in the kingdom of my Father." [30]Then, after singing a hymn, they went out to the Mount of Olives.

Peter's Denial Foretold. [31]Then Jesus said to them, "This night all of you will have your faith in me shaken, for it is written:

'I will strike the shepherd,
and the sheep of the flock will be
dispersed';

[32]but after I have been raised up, I shall go before you to Galilee." [33]Peter said to him in reply, "Though all may have their faith in you shaken, mine will never be." [34]Jesus

said to him, "Amen, I say to you, this very night before the cock crows, you will deny me three times." [35]Peter said to him, "Even though I should have to die with you, I will not deny you." And all the disciples spoke likewise.

The Agony in the Garden. [36]Then Jesus came with them to a place called Gethsemane, and he said to his disciples, "Sit here while I go over there and pray." [37]He took along Peter and the two sons of Zebedee, and began to feel sorrow and distress. [38]Then he said to them, "My soul is sorrowful even to death. Remain here and keep watch with me." [39]He advanced a little and fell prostrate in prayer, saying, "My Father, if it is possible, let this cup pass from me; yet, not as I will, but as you will." [40]When he returned to his disciples he found them asleep. He said to Peter, "So you could not keep watch with me for one hour? [41]Watch and pray that you may not undergo the test. The spirit is willing, but the flesh is weak." [42]Withdrawing a second time, he prayed again, "My Father, if it is not possible that this cup pass without my drinking it, your will be done!" [43]Then he returned once more and found them asleep, for they could not keep their eyes open. [44]He left them and withdrew again and prayed a third time, saying the same thing again. [45]Then he returned to his disciples and said to them, "Are you still sleeping and taking your rest? Behold, the hour is at hand when the Son of Man is to be handed over to sinners. [46]Get up, let us go. Look, my betrayer is at hand."

June 18

The Church has always taught that all our penance without Christ's passion is not worth a pea.

— St. Thomas More

☐ 2 MACCABEES 14–15

14:1 Three years later, Judas and his companions learned that Demetrius, son of Seleucus, had sailed into the port of Tripolis with a powerful army and a fleet, [2]and that he had occupied the country, after doing away with Antiochus and his guardian Lysias.

[3]A certain Alcimus, a former high priest, who had willfully incurred defilement before the time of the revolt, realized that there was no way for him to be safe and regain access to the holy altar. [4]So he went to King Demetrius around the one hundred and fifty-first year and presented him with a gold crown and a palm branch, as well as some of the customary olive branches from the temple. On that day he kept quiet. [5]But he found an opportunity to further his mad scheme when he was invited to the council by Demetrius and questioned about the dispositions and intentions of the Jews. He replied: [6]"Those Jews called Hasideans, led by Judas Maccabeus, are warmongers, who stir up sedition and keep the kingdom from enjoying peace. [7]For this reason, now that I am deprived of my ancestral dignity, that is to say, the high priesthood, I have come here, [8]first, out of my genuine concern for the king's interests, and second, out of consideration for my own compatriots, since our entire nation is suffering no little affliction from the rash conduct of the people just mentioned. [9]When you

have informed yourself in detail on these matters, O king, provide for our country and its hard-pressed people with the same gracious consideration that you show toward all. [10]As long as Judas is around, it is impossible for the government to enjoy peace." [11]When he had said this, the other Friends who were hostile to Judas quickly added fuel to Demetrius' indignation.

Dealings with Nicanor. [12]The king immediately chose Nicanor, who had been in command of the elephants, and appointed him governor of Judea. He sent him off [13]with orders to put Judas to death, to disperse his followers, and to set up Alcimus as high priest of the great temple. [14]The Gentiles from Judea, who had fled before Judas, flocked to Nicanor, thinking that the misfortunes and calamities of the Jews would mean prosperity for themselves.

[15]When the Jews heard of Nicanor's coming, and that the Gentiles were rallying to him, they sprinkled themselves with earth and prayed to him who established his people forever, and who always comes to the aid of his heritage by manifesting himself. [16]At their leader's command, they set out at once from there and came upon the enemy at the village of Adasa. [17]Judas' brother Simon had engaged Nicanor, but he suffered a slight setback because of the sudden appearance of the enemy.

[18]However, when Nicanor heard of the valor of Judas and his companions, and the great courage with which they fought for their country, he shrank from deciding the issue by bloodshed. [19]So he sent Posidonius, Theodotus and Mattathias to exchange pledges of friendship. [20]After a long discussion of the terms, each leader communicated them to his troops; and when general agreement was expressed, they assented to the treaty. [21]A day was set on which the leaders would meet by themselves. From each side a chariot came forward, and thrones were set in place. [22]Judas had posted armed men in readiness at strategic points for fear that the enemy might suddenly commit some treachery. But the conference was held in the proper way.

[23]Nicanor stayed on in Jerusalem, where he did nothing out of place. He disbanded the throngs of people who gathered around him; [24]and he always kept Judas in his company, for he felt affection for the man. [25]He urged him to marry and have children; so Judas married and settled into an ordinary life.

Nicanor's Threat Against Judas. [26]When Alcimus saw their mutual goodwill, he took the treaty that had been made, went to Demetrius, and said that Nicanor was plotting against the government, for he had appointed Judas, that conspirator against the kingdom, as his successor. [27]Stirred up by the villain's slander, the king became enraged. He wrote to Nicanor, stating that he was displeased with the treaty, and ordering him to send Maccabeus at once as a prisoner to Antioch. [28]When this message reached Nicanor he was dismayed and troubled at the thought of annulling his agreement with a man who had done no wrong. [29]However, there was no way of opposing the king, so he watched for an opportunity to carry out this order by a stratagem. [30]But Maccabeus, noticing that Nicanor was more harsh in his dealings with him, and acting with unaccustomed rudeness when they met, concluded that this harshness was not a good sign. So he gathered together not a few of his men, and went into hiding from Nicanor.

[31]When Nicanor realized that he had been cleverly outwitted by the man, he went to the great and holy temple, at a time when the priests were offering the customary sacrifices, and ordered them to surrender Judas. [32]As they declared under oath that they did not know where the man they sought was, [33]he stretched out his right arm toward the temple and swore this oath: "If you do not hand Judas over to me as prisoner, I will level this shrine of God to the

ground; I will tear down the altar, and erect here a splendid temple to Dionysus."

[34]With these words he went away. The priests stretched out their hands toward heaven, calling upon the unfailing defender of our nation in these words: [35]"Lord of all, though you are in need of nothing, you were pleased to have a temple for your dwelling place among us. [36]Therefore, Holy One, Lord of all holiness, preserve forever undefiled this house, which has been so recently purified."

Martyrdom of Razis. [37]A certain Razis, one of the elders of Jerusalem, was denounced to Nicanor as a patriot. A man highly regarded, he was called a father of the Jews because of his goodwill toward them. [38]In the days before the revolt, he had been convicted of being a Jew, and had risked body and soul in his ardent zeal for Judaism. [39]Nicanor, to show his disdain for the Jews, sent more than five hundred soldiers to arrest him. [40]He thought that by arresting that man he would deal the Jews a hard blow.

[41]But when the troops, on the point of capturing the tower, were forcing the outer gate and calling for fire to set the door ablaze, Razis, now caught on all sides, turned his sword against himself, [42]preferring to die nobly rather than fall into the hands of vile men and suffer outrages unworthy of his noble birth. [43]In the excitement of the struggle he failed to strike exactly. So while the troops rushed in through the doors, he gallantly ran up to the top of the wall and courageously threw himself down into the crowd. [44]But as they quickly drew back and left an opening, he fell into the middle of the empty space. [45]Still breathing, and inflamed with anger, he got up and ran through the crowd, with blood gushing from his frightful wounds. Then, standing on a steep rock, [46]as he lost the last of his blood, he tore out his entrails and flung them with both hands into the crowd, calling upon the Lord of life and of

spirit to give these back to him again. Such was the manner of his death.

Nicanor's Arrogance. 15:1 When Nicanor learned that Judas and his companions were in the territory of Samaria, he decided he could attack them in complete safety on the day of rest. [2]The Jews who were forced to accompany him pleaded, "Do not massacre them so savagely and barbarously, but show respect for the day which the All-seeing has exalted with holiness above all other days." [3]At this the thrice-accursed wretch asked if there was a ruler in heaven who prescribed the keeping of the sabbath day. [4]They replied, "It is the living Lord, the ruler in heaven, who commands the observance of the sabbath day." [5]Then he said, "I, the ruler on earth, command you to take up arms and carry out the king's business." Nevertheless he did not succeed in carrying out his cruel plan.

[6]In his utter boastfulness and arrogance Nicanor had determined to erect a public victory monument over Judas and his companions. [7]But Maccabeus remained confident, fully convinced that he would receive help from the Lord. [8]He urged his men not to fear the attack of the Gentiles, but mindful of the help they had received in the past from Heaven, to expect now the victory that would be given them by the Almighty. [9]By encouraging them with words from the law and the prophets, and by reminding them of the battles they had already won, he filled them with fresh enthusiasm. [10]Having stirred up their courage, he gave his orders and pointed out at the same time the perfidy of the Gentiles and their violation of oaths. [11]When he had armed each of them, not so much with the security of shield and spear as with the encouragement of noble words, he cheered them all by relating a dream, a kind of waking vision, worthy of belief.

[12]What he saw was this: Onias, the former high priest, a noble and good man,

modest in bearing, gentle in manner, distinguished in speech, and trained from childhood in all that belongs to excellence, was praying with outstretched arms for the whole Jewish community. [13]Then in the same way another man appeared, distinguished by his white hair and dignity, and with an air of wondrous and majestic authority. [14]Onias then said of him, "This is a man who loves his fellow Jews and fervently prays for the people and the holy city—the prophet of God, Jeremiah." [15]Stretching out his right hand, Jeremiah presented a gold sword to Judas. As he gave it to him he said, [16]"Accept this holy sword as a gift from God; with it you shall shatter your adversaries."

[17]Encouraged by Judas' words, so noble and capable of instilling valor and stirring young hearts to courage, they determined not merely to march, but to charge gallantly and decide the issue by hand-to-hand combat with the utmost courage, since city, sanctuary and temple were in danger. [18]They were not so much concerned about wives and children, or family and relations; their first and foremost fear was for the consecrated sanctuary. [19]Those who were left in the city suffered no less an agony, anxious as they were about the battle in the open country. [20]Everyone now awaited the decisive moment. The enemy were already drawing near with their troops drawn up in battle line, their beasts placed in strategic positions, and their cavalry stationed on the flanks.

Defeat of Nicanor. [21]Maccabeus, surveying the hosts before him, the variety of weaponry, and the fierceness of their beasts, stretched out his hands toward heaven and called upon the Lord who works wonders; for he knew that it is not weapons but the Lord's decision that brings victory to those who deserve it. [22]Calling upon God, he spoke in this manner: "You, master, sent your angel in the days of King Hezekiah of Judea, and he slew a hundred and eighty-five thousand men of Sennacherib's camp. [23]And now, Sovereign of the heavens, send a good angel to spread fear and trembling ahead of us. [24]By the might of your arm may those be struck down who have blasphemously come against your holy people!" With these words he ended his prayer.

[25]Nicanor and his troops advanced to the sound of trumpets and battle songs. [26]But Judas and his troops met the enemy with supplication and prayers. [27]Fighting with their hands and praying to God with their hearts, they laid low at least thirty-five thousand, and rejoiced greatly over this manifestation of God's power. [28]When the battle was over and they were joyfully departing, they discovered Nicanor fallen there in all his armor; [29]so they raised tumultuous shouts in their ancestral language in praise of the divine Sovereign.

[30]Then Judas, that man who was ever in body and soul the chief defender of his fellow citizens, and had maintained from youth his affection for his compatriots, ordered Nicanor's head and right arm up to the shoulder to be cut off and taken to Jerusalem. [31]When he arrived there, he assembled his compatriots, stationed the priests before the altar, and sent for those in the citadel. [32]He showed them the vile Nicanor's head and the wretched blasphemer's arm that had been boastfully stretched out against the holy dwelling of the Almighty. [33]He cut out the tongue of the godless Nicanor, saying he would feed it piecemeal to the birds and would hang up the other wages of his folly opposite the temple. [34]At this, everyone looked toward heaven and praised the Lord who manifests himself: "Blessed be the one who has preserved undefiled his own place!" [35]Judas hung Nicanor's head and arm on the wall of the citadel, a clear and evident sign to all of the Lord's help. [36]By public vote it was unanimously decreed never to let this day pass unobserved, but to celebrate the thirteenth day of the twelfth month, called

Adar in Aramaic, the eve of Mordecai's Day.

Compiler's Apology. [37]Since Nicanor's doings ended in this way, with the city remaining in the possession of the Hebrews from that time on, I will bring my story to an end here too. [38]If it is well written and to the point, that is what I wanted; if it is poorly done and mediocre, that is the best I could do. [39]Just as it is unpleasant to drink wine by itself or just water, whereas wine mixed with water makes a delightful and pleasing drink, so a skillfully composed story delights the ears of those who read the work. Let this, then, be the end.

☐ MATTHEW 26:47-75

The Betrayal and Arrest of Jesus. 26:47 While he was still speaking, Judas, one of the Twelve, arrived, accompanied by a large crowd, with swords and clubs, who had come from the chief priests and the elders of the people. [48]His betrayer had arranged a sign with them, saying, "The man I shall kiss is the one; arrest him." [49]Immediately he went over to Jesus and said, "Hail, Rabbi!" and he kissed him. [50]Jesus answered him, "Friend, do what you have come for." Then stepping forward they laid hands on Jesus and arrested him. [51]And behold, one of those who accompanied Jesus put his hand to his sword, drew it, and struck the high priest's servant, cutting off his ear. [52]Then Jesus said to him, "Put your sword back into its sheath, for all who take the sword will perish by the sword. [53]Do you think that I cannot call upon my Father and he will not provide me at this moment with more than twelve legions of angels? [54]But then how would the scriptures be fulfilled which say that it must come to pass in this way?" [55]At that hour Jesus said to the crowds, "Have you come out as against a robber, with swords and clubs to seize me? Day after day I sat teaching in the temple area, yet you did not arrest me. [56]But all this has come to pass that the writings of the prophets may be fulfilled." Then all the disciples left him and fled.

Jesus before the Sanhedrin. [57]Those who had arrested Jesus led him away to Caiaphas the high priest, where the scribes and the elders were assembled. [58]Peter was following him at a distance as far as the high priest's courtyard, and going inside he sat down with the servants to see the outcome. [59]The chief priests and the entire Sanhedrin kept trying to obtain false testimony against Jesus in order to put him to death, [60]but they found none, though many false witnesses came forward. Finally two came forward [61]who stated, "This man said, 'I can destroy the temple of God and within three days rebuild it.'" [62]The high priest rose and addressed him, "Have you no answer? What are these men testifying against you?" [63]But Jesus was silent. Then the high priest said to him, "I order you to tell us under oath before the living God whether you are the Messiah, the Son of God." [64]Jesus said to him in reply, "You have said so. But I tell you:

> From now on you will see 'the Son of Man
> seated at the right hand of the Power'
> and 'coming on the clouds of heaven.'"

[65]Then the high priest tore his robes and said, "He has blasphemed! What further need have we of witnesses? You have now heard the blasphemy; [66]what is your opinion?" They said in reply, "He deserves to die!" [67]Then they spat in his face and struck him, while some slapped him, [68]saying,

"Prophesy for us, Messiah: who is it that struck you?"

Peter's Denial of Jesus. [69]Now Peter was sitting outside in the courtyard. One of the maids came over to him and said, "You too were with Jesus the Galilean." [70]But he denied it in front of everyone, saying, "I do not know what you are talking about!" [71]As he went out to the gate, another girl saw him and said to those who were there, "This man was with Jesus the Nazorean."

[72]Again he denied it with an oath, "I do not know the man!" [73]A little later the bystanders came over and said to Peter, "Surely you too are one of them; even your speech gives you away." [74]At that he began to curse and to swear, "I do not know the man." And immediately a cock crowed. [75]Then Peter remembered the word that Jesus had spoken: "Before the cock crows you will deny me three times." He went out and began to weep bitterly.

June 19

St. Romuald

Realize above all that you are in God's presence. Empty yourself completely and sit waiting, content with the grace of God, like a chick that tastes nothing and eats nothing except what its mother gives it.

— St. Romuald

☐ JOB 1–3

Job's Piety. 1:1 In the land of Uz there was a blameless and upright man named Job, who feared God and avoided evil. [2]Seven sons and three daughters were born to him; [3]and he had seven thousand sheep, three thousand camels, five hundred yoke of oxen, five hundred she-donkeys, and a very large household, so that he was greater than anyone in the East. [4]His sons used to take turns giving feasts, sending invitations to their three sisters to eat and drink with them. [5]And when each feast had run its course, Job would send for them and sanctify them, rising early and offering sacrifices for every one of them. For Job said, "It may be that my children have sinned and cursed God in their hearts." Job did this habitually.

The Interview Between the Lord and the Satan. [6]One day, when the sons of God came to present themselves before the

LORD, the satan also came among them. [7]The LORD said to the satan, "Where have you been?" Then the satan answered the LORD and said, "Roaming the earth and patrolling it." [8]The LORD said to the satan, "Have you noticed my servant Job? There is no one on earth like him, blameless and upright, fearing God and avoiding evil." [9]The satan answered the LORD and said, "Is it for nothing that Job is God-fearing? [10]Have you not surrounded him and his family and all that he has with your protection? You have blessed the work of his hands, and his livestock are spread over the land. [11]But now put forth your hand and touch all that he has, and surely he will curse you to your face." [12]The LORD said to the satan, "Very well, all that he has is in your power; only do not lay a hand on him." So the satan went forth from the presence of the LORD.

The First Trial. ¹³One day, while his sons and daughters were eating and drinking wine in the house of their eldest brother, ¹⁴a messenger came to Job and said, "The oxen were plowing and the donkeys grazing beside them, ¹⁵and the Sabeans carried them off in a raid. They put the servants to the sword, and I alone have escaped to tell you." ¹⁶He was still speaking when another came and said, "God's fire has fallen from heaven and struck the sheep and the servants and consumed them; I alone have escaped to tell you." ¹⁷He was still speaking when another came and said, "The Chaldeans formed three columns, seized the camels, carried them off, and put the servants to the sword; I alone have escaped to tell you." ¹⁸He was still speaking when another came and said, "Your sons and daughters were eating and drinking wine in the house of their eldest brother, ¹⁹and suddenly a great wind came from across the desert and smashed the four corners of the house. It fell upon the young people and they are dead; I alone have escaped to tell you."

Job's Reaction. ²⁰Then Job arose and tore his cloak and cut off his hair. He fell to the ground and worshiped. ²¹He said,

> "Naked I came forth from my mother's
> > womb,
> > and naked shall I go back there.
> The LORD gave and the LORD has taken
> > away;
> > blessed be the name of the LORD!"

²²In all this Job did not sin, nor did he charge God with wrong.

The Second Interview. 2:1 One day, when the sons of God came to present themselves before the LORD, the satan also came with them. ²The LORD said to the satan, "Where have you been?" Then the satan answered the LORD and said, "Roaming the earth and patrolling it." ³The LORD said to the satan, "Have you noticed my servant Job? There is no one on earth like him, blameless and upright, fearing God and avoiding evil. He still holds fast to his innocence although you incited me against him to ruin him for nothing." ⁴The satan answered the LORD and said, "Skin for skin! All that a man has he will give for his life. ⁵But put forth your hand and touch his bone and his flesh. Then surely he will curse you to your face." ⁶And the LORD said to the satan, "He is in your power; only spare his life."

The Second Trial. ⁷So the satan went forth from the presence of the LORD and struck Job with severe boils from the soles of his feet to the crown of his head.

Job's Reaction. ⁸He took a potsherd to scrape himself, as he sat among the ashes. ⁹Then his wife said to him, "Are you still holding to your innocence? Curse God and die!" ¹⁰But he said to her, "You speak as foolish women do. We accept good things from God; should we not accept evil?" Through all this, Job did not sin in what he said.

Job's Three Friends. ¹¹Now when three of Job's friends heard of all the misfortune that had come upon him, they set out each one from his own place: Eliphaz from Teman, Bildad from Shuh, and Zophar from Naamath. They met and journeyed together to give him sympathy and comfort. ¹²But when, at a distance, they lifted up their eyes and did not recognize him, they began to weep aloud; they tore their cloaks and threw dust into the air over their heads. ¹³Then they sat down upon the ground with him seven days and seven nights, but none of them spoke a word to him; for they saw how great was his suffering.

Job's Complaint. 3:1 After this, Job opened his mouth and cursed his day. ²Job spoke out and said:

> ³Perish the day on which I was born,
> > the night when they said, "The child
> > is a boy!"
> ⁴May that day be darkness:

may God above not care for it,
may light not shine upon it!
⁵May darkness and gloom claim it,
clouds settle upon it,
blackness of day affright it!
⁶May obscurity seize that night;
may it not be counted among the
days of the year,
nor enter into the number of the
months!
⁷May that night be barren;
let no joyful outcry greet it!
⁸Let them curse it who curse the Sea,
those skilled at disturbing
Leviathan!
⁹May the stars of its twilight be darkened;
may it look for daylight, but have
none,
nor gaze on the eyes of the dawn,
¹⁰Because it did not keep shut the
doors of the womb
to shield my eyes from trouble!
¹¹Why did I not die at birth,
come forth from the womb and
expire?
¹²Why did knees receive me,
or breasts nurse me?
¹³For then I should have lain down and
been tranquil;
had I slept, I should then have been
at rest
¹⁴With kings and counselors of the
earth

who rebuilt what were ruins
¹⁵Or with princes who had gold
and filled their houses with silver.
¹⁶Or why was I not buried away like a
stillborn child,
like babies that have never seen the
light?
¹⁷There the wicked cease from
troubling,
there the weary are at rest.
¹⁸The captives are at ease together,
and hear no overseer's voice.
¹⁹Small and great are there;
the servant is free from the master.
²⁰Why is light given to the toilers,
life to the bitter in spirit?
²¹They wait for death and it does not
come;
they search for it more than for
hidden treasures.
²²They rejoice in it exultingly,
and are glad when they find the
grave:
²³A man whose path is hidden from
him,
one whom God has hemmed in!
²⁴For to me sighing comes more readily
than food;
my groans well forth like water.
²⁵For what I feared overtakes me;
what I dreaded comes upon me.
²⁶I have no peace nor ease;
I have no rest, for trouble has come!

☐ MATTHEW 27:1-31

Jesus before Pilate. 27:1 When it was morning, all the chief priests and the elders of the people took counsel against Jesus to put him to death. ²They bound him, led him away, and handed him over to Pilate, the governor.

The Death of Judas. ³Then Judas, his betrayer, seeing that Jesus had been condemned, deeply regretted what he had done. He returned the thirty pieces of silver to the chief priests and elders, ⁴saying, "I have sinned in betraying innocent blood." They said, "What is that to us? Look to it yourself." ⁵Flinging the money into the temple, he departed and went off and hanged himself. ⁶The chief priests gathered up the money, but said, "It is not lawful to deposit this in the temple treasury, for it is the price of blood." ⁷After consultation, they used it to buy the potter's field as a burial place for foreigners. [8]That is why that field even today is called the Field of Blood. [9]Then was fulfilled what had been said through Jeremiah the prophet, "And they took the thirty pieces of silver, the value of a man with a price on his head, a price set by some of the Israelites, [10]and they paid it out for the potter's field just as the Lord had commanded me."

Jesus Questioned by Pilate. [11]Now Jesus stood before the governor, and he questioned him, "Are you the king of the Jews?" Jesus said, "You say so." [12]And when he was accused by the chief priests and elders, he made no answer. [13]Then Pilate said to him, "Do you not hear how many things they are testifying against you?" [14]But he did not answer him one word, so that the governor was greatly amazed.

The Sentence of Death. [15]Now on the occasion of the feast the governor was accustomed to release to the crowd one prisoner whom they wished. [16]And at that time they had a notorious prisoner called [Jesus] Barabbas. [17]So when they had assembled, Pilate said to them, "Which one do you want me to release to you, [Jesus] Barabbas, or Jesus called Messiah?" [18]For he knew that it was out of envy that they had handed him over. [19]While he was still seated on the bench, his wife sent him a message, "Have nothing to do with that righteous man. I suffered much in a dream today because of him." [20]The chief priests and the elders persuaded the crowds to ask for Barabbas but to destroy Jesus. [21]The governor said to them in reply, "Which of the two do you want me to release to you?" They answered, "Barabbas!" [22]Pilate said to them, "Then what shall I do with Jesus called Messiah?" They all said, "Let him be crucified!" [23]But he said, "Why? What evil has he done?" They only shouted the louder, "Let him be crucified!" [24]When Pilate saw that he was not succeeding at all, but that a riot was breaking out instead, he took water and washed his hands in the sight of the crowd, saying, "I am innocent of this man's blood. Look to it yourselves." [25]And the whole people said in reply, "His blood be upon us and upon our children." [26]Then he released Barabbas to them, but after he had Jesus scourged, he handed him over to be crucified.

Mockery by the Soldiers. [27]Then the soldiers of the governor took Jesus inside the praetorium and gathered the whole cohort around him. [28]They stripped off his clothes and threw a scarlet military cloak about him. [29]Weaving a crown out of thorns, they placed it on his head, and a reed in his right hand. And kneeling before him, they mocked him, saying, "Hail, King of the Jews!" [30]They spat upon him and took the reed and kept striking him on the head. [31]And when they had mocked him, they stripped him of the cloak, dressed him in his own clothes, and led him off to crucify him.

June 20

Make a little bouquet of the sufferings of Jesus and carry them in the bosom of the soul.

— ST. PAUL OF THE CROSS

☐ JOB 4-7

Eliphaz's First Speech. 4:1 Then Eliphaz the Temanite answered and said:

²If someone attempts a word with you,
would you mind?
How can anyone refrain from
speaking?
³Look, you have instructed many,
and made firm their feeble hands.
⁴Your words have upheld the stumbler;
you have strengthened faltering
knees.
⁵But now that it comes to you, you are
impatient;
when it touches you, you are
dismayed.
⁶Is not your piety a source of
confidence,
and your integrity of life your hope?
⁷Reflect now, what innocent person
perishes?
Where are the upright destroyed?
⁸As I see it, those who plow mischief
and sow trouble will reap them.
⁹By the breath of God they perish,
and by the blast of his wrath they
are consumed.
¹⁰Though the lion roars, though the
king of beasts cries out,
yet the teeth of the young lions are
broken;
¹¹The old lion perishes for lack of prey,
and the cubs of the lioness are
scattered.
¹²A word was stealthily brought to me,
my ear caught a whisper of it.
¹³In my thoughts during visions of the
night,
when deep sleep falls on mortals,

¹⁴Fear came upon me, and shuddering,
that terrified me to the bone.
¹⁵Then a spirit passed before me,
and the hair of my body stood on
end.
¹⁶It paused, but its likeness I could not
recognize;
a figure was before my eyes,
in silence I heard a voice:
¹⁷"Can anyone be more in the right
than God?
Can mortals be more blameless than
their Maker?
¹⁸Look, he puts no trust in his servants,
and even with his messengers he
finds fault.
¹⁹How much more with those who
dwell in houses of clay,
whose foundation is in the dust,
who are crushed more easily than a
moth!
²⁰Morning or evening they may be
shattered;
unnoticed, they perish forever.
²¹The pegs of their tent are plucked up;
they die without knowing wisdom."

5:1 Call now! Will anyone respond to
you?
To which of the holy ones will you
turn?
²Surely impatience kills the fool
and indignation slays the simpleton.
³I have seen a fool spreading his roots,
but I cursed his household
suddenly:
⁴May his children be far from safety;
may they be crushed at the gate
without a rescuer.

⁵What they have reaped may the
    hungry eat up,
  or God take away by blight,
  or the thirsty swallow their
    substance.
⁶For not from dust does mischief come,
  nor from the soil does trouble sprout.
⁷Human beings beget mischief
  as sparks fly upward.
⁸In your place, I would appeal to God,
  and to God I would state my plea.
⁹He does things great and
    unsearchable,
  things marvelous and innumerable.
¹⁰He gives rain upon the earth
  and sends water upon the fields;
¹¹He sets up the lowly on high,
  and those who mourn are raised to
    safety.
¹²He frustrates the plans of the cunning,
  so that their hands achieve no
    success;
¹³He catches the wise in their own ruses,
  and the designs of the crafty are
    routed.
¹⁴They meet with darkness in the
    daytime,
  at noonday they grope as though it
    were night.
¹⁵But he saves the poor from the sword
    of their mouth,
  from the hand of the mighty.
¹⁶Thus the needy have hope,
  and iniquity closes its mouth.
¹⁷Happy the one whom God reproves!
  The Almighty's discipline do not
    reject.
¹⁸For he wounds, but he binds up;
  he strikes, but his hands give
    healing.
¹⁹Out of six troubles he will deliver you,
  and at the seventh no evil shall
    touch you.
²⁰In famine he will deliver you from
    death,
  and in war from the power of the
    sword;

²¹From the scourge of the tongue you
    shall be hidden,
  and you shall not fear approaching
    ruin.
²²At ruin and want you shall laugh;
  the beasts of the earth, do not fear.
²³With the stones of the field shall your
    covenant be,
  and the wild beasts shall be at peace
    with you.
²⁴And you shall know that your tent is
    secure;
  taking stock of your household, you
    shall miss nothing.
²⁵You shall know that your descendants
    are many,
  and your offspring like the grass of
    the earth.
²⁶You shall approach the grave in full
    vigor,
  as a shock of grain comes in at its
    season.
²⁷See, this we have searched out; so it is!
  This we have heard, and you should
    know.

Job's First Reply. 6:1 Then Job answered
and said:

²Ah, could my anguish but be
    measured
  and my calamity laid with it in the
    scales,
³They would now outweigh the sands
    of the sea!
  Because of this I speak without
    restraint.
⁴For the arrows of the Almighty are
    in me,
  and my spirit drinks in their poison;
  the terrors of God are arrayed
    against me.
⁵Does the wild donkey bray when it
    has grass?
  Does the ox low over its fodder?
⁶Can anything insipid be eaten without
    salt?

Is there flavor in the white of an
  egg?
⁷I refuse to touch them;
  they are like loathsome food to me.
⁸Oh, that I might have my request,
  and that God would grant what I
    long for:
⁹Even that God would decide to crush
    me,
    that he would put forth his hand
      and cut me off!
¹⁰Then I should still have consolation
  and could exult through
    unremitting pain,
  because I have not transgressed the
    commands of the Holy One.
¹¹What strength have I that I should
    endure,
  and what is my limit that I should
    be patient?
¹²Have I the strength of stones,
  or is my flesh of bronze?
¹³Have I no helper,
  and has my good sense deserted me?
¹⁴A friend owes kindness to one in
    despair,
  though he has forsaken the fear of
    the Almighty.
¹⁵My companions are undependable as
    a wadi,
  as watercourses that run dry in the
    wadies;
¹⁶Though they may be black with ice,
  and with snow heaped upon them,
¹⁷Yet once they flow, they cease to be;
  in the heat, they disappear from
    their place.
¹⁸Caravans wander from their routes;
  they go into the wasteland and
    perish.
¹⁹The caravans of Tema search,
  the companies of Sheba have hopes;
²⁰They are disappointed, though they
    were confident;
  they come there and are frustrated.
²¹It is thus that you have now become
    for me;

you see a terrifying thing and are
    afraid.
²²Have I said, "Give me something,
  make a bribe on my behalf from
    your possessions"?
²³Or "Deliver me from the hand of the
    enemy,
  redeem me from oppressors"?
²⁴Teach me, and I will be silent;
  make me understand how I have
    erred.
²⁵How painful honest words can be;
  yet how unconvincing is your
    argument!
²⁶Do you consider your words as proof,
  but the sayings of a desperate man
    as wind?
²⁷You would even cast lots for the
    orphan,
  and would barter over your friend!
²⁸Come, now, give me your attention;
  surely I will not lie to your face.
²⁹Think it over; let there be no
    injustice.
  Think it over; I still am right.
³⁰Is there insincerity on my tongue,
  or cannot my taste discern falsehood?

7:1 Is not life on earth a drudgery,
  its days like those of a hireling?
²Like a slave who longs for the shade,
  a hireling who waits for wages,
³So I have been assigned months of
    futility,
  and troubled nights have been
    counted off for me.
⁴When I lie down I say, "When shall I
    arise?"
  then the night drags on;
  I am filled with restlessness until the
    dawn.
⁵My flesh is clothed with worms and
    scabs;
  my skin cracks and festers;
⁶My days are swifter than a weaver's
    shuttle;
  they come to an end without hope.

⁷Remember that my life is like the
wind;
my eye will not see happiness again.
⁸The eye that now sees me shall no
more behold me;
when your eye is on me, I shall be
gone.
⁹As a cloud dissolves and vanishes,
so whoever goes down to Sheol shall
not come up.
¹⁰They shall not return home again;
their place shall know them no more.
¹¹My own utterance I will not restrain;
I will speak in the anguish of my
spirit;
I will complain in the bitterness of
my soul.
¹²Am I the Sea, or the dragon,
that you place a watch over me?
¹³When I say, "My bed shall comfort me,
my couch shall ease my complaint,"
¹⁴Then you frighten me with dreams
and terrify me with visions,

¹⁵So that I should prefer strangulation
and death rather than my existence.
¹⁶I waste away: I will not live forever;
let me alone, for my days are but a
breath.
¹⁷What are human beings, that you
make much of them,
or pay them any heed?
¹⁸You observe them every morning
and try them at every moment!
¹⁹How long before you look away
from me,
and let me alone till I swallow my
spit?
²⁰If I sin, what do I do to you,
O watcher of mortals?
Why have you made me your target?
Why should I be a burden for you?
²¹Why do you not pardon my offense,
or take away my guilt?
For soon I shall lie down in the dust;
and should you seek me I shall be
gone.

☐ MATTHEW 27:32–66

The Way of the Cross. 27:32 As they were going out, they met a Cyrenian named Simon; this man they pressed into service to carry his cross.

The Crucifixion. ³³And when they came to a place called Golgotha (which means Place of the Skull), ³⁴they gave Jesus wine to drink mixed with gall. But when he had tasted it, he refused to drink. ³⁵After they had crucified him, they divided his garments by casting lots; ³⁶then they sat down and kept watch over him there. ³⁷And they placed over his head the written charge against him: This is Jesus, the King of the Jews. ³⁸Two revolutionaries were crucified with him, one on his right and the other on his left. ³⁹Those passing by reviled him, shaking their heads ⁴⁰and saying, "You who would destroy the temple and rebuild it in three days, save yourself, if you are the Son of God, [and] come down from the cross!" ⁴¹Likewise the chief priests with the scribes and elders mocked him and said, ⁴²"He saved others; he cannot save himself. So he is the king of Israel! Let him come down from the cross now, and we will believe in him. ⁴³He trusted in God; let him deliver him now if he wants him. For he said, 'I am the Son of God.'" ⁴⁴The revolutionaries who were crucified with him also kept abusing him in the same way.

The Death of Jesus. ⁴⁵From noon onward, darkness came over the whole land until three in the afternoon. ⁴⁶And about three o'clock Jesus cried out in a loud voice, *Eli, Eli, lema sabachthani?* which means, "My God, my God, why have you forsaken me?" ⁴⁷Some of the bystanders who heard it said, "This one is calling for Elijah." ⁴⁸Immediately one of them ran to get a sponge; he soaked it in wine, and putting it on a reed, gave it to him to drink. [49]But the rest said, "Wait, let us see if Elijah comes to save him." [50]But Jesus cried out again in a loud voice, and gave up his spirit. [51]And behold, the veil of the sanctuary was torn in two from top to bottom. The earth quaked, rocks were split, [52]tombs were opened, and the bodies of many saints who had fallen asleep were raised. [53]And coming forth from their tombs after his resurrection, they entered the holy city and appeared to many. [54]The centurion and the men with him who were keeping watch over Jesus feared greatly when they saw the earthquake and all that was happening, and they said, "Truly, this was the Son of God!" [55]There were many women there, looking on from a distance, who had followed Jesus from Galilee, ministering to him. [56]Among them were Mary Magdalene and Mary the mother of James and Joseph, and the mother of the sons of Zebedee.

The Burial of Jesus. [57]When it was evening, there came a rich man from Arimathea named Joseph, who was himself a disciple of Jesus. [58]He went to Pilate and asked for the body of Jesus; then Pilate ordered it to be handed over. [59]Taking the body, Joseph wrapped it [in] clean linen [60]and laid it in his new tomb that he had hewn in the rock. Then he rolled a huge stone across the entrance to the tomb and departed. [61]But Mary Magdalene and the other Mary remained sitting there, facing the tomb.

The Guard at the Tomb. [62]The next day, the one following the day of preparation, the chief priests and the Pharisees gathered before Pilate [63]and said, "Sir, we remember that this impostor while still alive said, 'After three days I will be raised up.' [64]Give orders, then, that the grave be secured until the third day, lest his disciples come and steal him and say to the people, 'He has been raised from the dead.' This last imposture would be worse than the first." [65]Pilate said to them, "The guard is yours; go secure it as best you can." [66]So they went and secured the tomb by fixing a seal to the stone and setting the guard.

June 21

St. Aloysius Gonzaga

Of what use are riches in eternity?
— St. Aloysius Gonzaga

☐ JOB 8–10

Bildad's First Speech. 8:1 Bildad the Shuhite answered and said:

[2]How long will you utter such things?
The words from your mouth are a
mighty wind!
[3]Does God pervert judgment,
does the Almighty pervert justice?
[4]If your children have sinned against him
and he has left them in the grip of
their guilt,

[5]Still, if you yourself have recourse to
God
and make supplication to the
Almighty,
[6]Should you be blameless and upright,
surely now he will rouse himself for
you
and restore your rightful home.
[7]Though your beginning was small,
your future will flourish indeed.

⁸Inquire of the former generations,
pay attention to the experience of
their ancestors—
⁹As we are but of yesterday and have no
knowledge,
because our days on earth are but a
shadow—
¹⁰Will they not teach you and tell you
and utter their words of
understanding?
¹¹Can the papyrus grow up without
mire?
Can the reed grass flourish without
water?
¹²While it is yet green and uncut,
it withers quicker than any grass.
¹³So is the end of everyone who forgets
God,
and so shall the hope of the godless
perish.
¹⁴His confidence is but a gossamer
thread,
his trust is a spider's house.
¹⁵He shall lean upon his house, but it
shall not stand;
he shall cling to it, but it shall not
endure.
¹⁶He thrives in full sun,
and over his garden his shoots go
forth;
¹⁷About a heap of stones his roots are
entwined;
among the rocks he takes hold.
¹⁸Yet if one tears him from his place,
it will disown him: "I have never
seen you!"
¹⁹There he lies rotting beside the road,
and out of the soil another sprouts.
²⁰Behold, God will not cast away the
upright;
neither will he take the hand of the
wicked.
²¹Once more will he fill your mouth
with laughter
and your lips with rejoicing.
²²Those who hate you shall be clothed
with shame,

and the tent of the wicked shall be
no more.

Job's Second Reply. 9:1 Then Job answered and said:

²I know well that it is so;
but how can anyone be in the right
before God?
³Should one wish to contend with him,
he could not answer him once in a
thousand times.
⁴God is wise in heart and mighty in
strength;
who has withstood him and
remained whole?
⁵He removes the mountains before
they know it;
he overturns them in his anger.
⁶He shakes the earth out of its place,
and the pillars beneath it tremble.
⁷He commands the sun, and it does
not rise;
he seals up the stars.
⁸He alone stretches out the heavens
and treads upon the back of the sea.
⁹He made the Bear and Orion,
the Pleiades and the constellations
of the south;
¹⁰He does things great and
unsearchable,
things marvelous and innumerable.
¹¹Should he come near me, I do not see
him;
should he pass by, I am not aware
of him;
¹²Should he seize me forcibly, who can
resist?
Who can say to him, "What are you
doing?"
¹³He is God and he does not relent;
the helpers of Rahab bow beneath
him.
¹⁴How then could I give him any
answer,
or choose out arguments against
him!

¹⁵Even though I were right, I could not answer,
  but should rather beg for what was due me.
¹⁶If I appealed to him and he answered me,
  I could not believe that he would listen to me;
¹⁷With a storm he might overwhelm me,
  and multiply my wounds for nothing;
¹⁸He would not allow me to draw breath,
  but might fill me with bitter griefs.
¹⁹If it be a question of strength, he is mighty;
  or of judgment, who will call him to account?
²⁰Though I were right, my own mouth might condemn me;
  were I innocent, it might put me in the wrong.
²¹I am innocent, but I cannot know it;
  I despise my life.
²²It is all one! therefore I say:
  Both the innocent and the wicked he destroys.
²³When the scourge slays suddenly,
  he scoffs at the despair of the innocent.
²⁴The earth is given into the hands of the wicked;
  he covers the faces of its judges.
  If it is not he, who then is it?
²⁵My days are swifter than a runner,
  they flee away; they see no happiness;
²⁶They shoot by like skiffs of reed,
  like an eagle swooping upon its prey.
²⁷If I say: I will forget my complaining,
  I will lay aside my sadness and be of good cheer,
²⁸Then I am in dread of all my pains;
  I know that you will not hold me innocent.

²⁹It is I who will be accounted guilty;
  why then should I strive in vain?
³⁰If I should wash myself with soap
  and cleanse my hands with lye,
³¹Yet you would plunge me in the ditch,
  so that my garments would abhor me.
³²For he is not a man like myself, that I should answer him,
  that we should come together in judgment.
³³Would that there were an arbiter between us,
  who could lay his hand upon us both
³⁴and withdraw his rod from me,
So that his terrors did not frighten me;
  ³⁵that I might speak without being afraid of him.
Since this is not the case with me,
  10:1 I loathe my life.

I will give myself up to complaint;
  I will speak from the bitterness of my soul.
²I will say to God: Do not put me in the wrong!
  Let me know why you oppose me.
³Is it a pleasure for you to oppress,
  to spurn the work of your hands,
  and shine on the plan of the wicked?
⁴Have you eyes of flesh?
  Do you see as mortals see?
⁵Are your days like the days of a mortal,
  and are your years like a human lifetime,
⁶That you seek for guilt in me
  and search after my sins,
⁷Even though you know that I am not wicked,
  and that none can deliver me out of your hand?
⁸Your hands have formed me and fashioned me;

will you then turn and destroy me?
⁹Oh, remember that you fashioned me
    from clay!
  Will you then bring me down to
    dust again?
¹⁰Did you not pour me out like milk,
  and thicken me like cheese?
¹¹With skin and flesh you clothed me,
  with bones and sinews knit me
    together.
¹²Life and love you granted me,
  and your providence has preserved
    my spirit.
¹³Yet these things you have hidden in
  your heart;
  I know they are your purpose:
¹⁴If I should sin, you would keep a
  watch on me,
  and from my guilt you would not
    absolve me.
¹⁵If I should be wicked, alas for me!
  even if righteous, I dare not hold up
    my head,
  sated with shame, drenched in
    affliction!

¹⁶Should it lift up, you hunt me like a
  lion:
  repeatedly you show your wondrous
    power against me,
¹⁷You renew your attack upon me
  and multiply your harassment of
    me;
  in waves your troops come against
    me.
¹⁸Why then did you bring me forth
  from the womb?
  I should have died and no eye have
    seen me.
¹⁹I should be as though I had never
  lived;
  I should have been taken from the
    womb to the grave.
²⁰Are not my days few? Stop!
  Let me alone, that I may recover a
    little
²¹Before I go whence I shall not return,
  to the land of darkness and of
    gloom,
²²The dark, disordered land
  where darkness is the only light.

☐ MATTHEW 28

The Resurrection of Jesus. 28:1 After the sabbath, as the first day of the week was dawning, Mary Magdalene and the other Mary came to see the tomb. ²And behold, there was a great earthquake; for an angel of the Lord descended from heaven, approached, rolled back the stone, and sat upon it. ³His appearance was like lightning and his clothing was white as snow. ⁴The guards were shaken with fear of him and became like dead men. ⁵Then the angel said to the women in reply, "Do not be afraid! I know that you are seeking Jesus the crucified. ⁶He is not here, for he has been raised just as he said. Come and see the place where he lay. ⁷Then go quickly and tell his disciples, 'He has been raised from the dead, and he is going before you to Gali-lee; there you will see him.' Behold, I have told you." ⁸Then they went away quickly from the tomb, fearful yet overjoyed, and ran to announce this to his disciples. ⁹And behold, Jesus met them on their way and greeted them. They approached, embraced his feet, and did him homage. ¹⁰Then Jesus said to them, "Do not be afraid. Go tell my brothers to go to Galilee, and there they will see me."

The Report of the Guard. ¹¹While they were going, some of the guard went into the city and told the chief priests all that had happened. ¹²They assembled with the elders and took counsel; then they gave a large sum of money to the soldiers, ¹³telling them, "You are to say, 'His disciples came by night and stole him while we were asleep.' ¹⁴And if this gets to the ears of the governor, we will satisfy [him] and keep you out of trouble." ¹⁵The soldiers took the money and did as they were instructed. And this story has circulated among the Jews to the present [day].

The Commissioning of the Disciples. ¹⁶The eleven disciples went to Galilee, to the mountain to which Jesus had ordered them. ¹⁷When they saw him, they worshiped, but they doubted. ¹⁸Then Jesus approached and said to them, "All power in heaven and on earth has been given to me. ¹⁹Go, therefore, and make disciples of all nations, baptizing them in the name of the Father, and of the Son, and of the holy Spirit, ²⁰teaching them to observe all that I have commanded you. And behold, I am with you always, until the end of the age."

June 22

St. Paulinus of Nola; St. John Fisher and St. Thomas More

We must have such great love for the truth that our words will take on the character of oaths.

— ST. PAULINUS OF NOLA

☐ JOB 11–14

Zophar's First Speech. 11:1 And Zophar the Naamathite answered and said:

²Should not many words be answered,
  or must the garrulous man
    necessarily be right?
³Shall your babblings keep others
    silent,
  and shall you deride and no one
    give rebuke?
⁴Shall you say: "My teaching is pure,
  and I am clean in your sight"?
⁵But oh, that God would speak,
  and open his lips against you,
⁶And tell you the secrets of wisdom,
  for good sense has two sides;
So you might learn that God
  overlooks some of your sinfulness.
⁷Can you find out the depths of God?
  or find out the perfection of the
    Almighty?
⁸It is higher than the heavens; what can
    you do?
  It is deeper than Sheol; what can
    you know?

⁹It is longer than the earth in measure,
  and broader than the sea.
¹⁰If he should seize and imprison
  or call to judgment, who then could
    turn him back?
¹¹For he knows the worthless
  and sees iniquity; will he then
    ignore it?
¹²An empty head will gain
    understanding,
  when a colt of a wild jackass is born
    human.
¹³If you set your heart aright
  and stretch out your hands toward
    him,
¹⁴If iniquity is in your hand, remove it,
  and do not let injustice dwell in
    your tent,
¹⁵Surely then you may lift up your face
    in innocence;
  you may stand firm and unafraid.
¹⁶For then you shall forget your misery,
  like water that has ebbed away you
    shall regard it.

¹⁷Then your life shall be brighter than
the noonday;
its gloom shall become like the
morning,
¹⁸And you shall be secure, because
there is hope;
you shall look round you and lie
down in safety;
¹⁹you shall lie down and no one will
disturb you.
Many shall entreat your favor,
²⁰but the wicked, looking on, shall
be consumed with envy.
Escape shall be cut off from them,
their only hope their last breath.

Job's Third Reply. 12:1 Then Job answered
and said:

²No doubt you are the people
with whom wisdom shall die!
³But I have intelligence as well as you;
I do not fall short of you;
for who does not know such things
as these?
⁴I have become the sport of my
neighbors:
"The one whom God answers when
he calls upon him,
The just, the perfect man," is a
laughingstock;
⁵The undisturbed esteem my downfall
a disgrace
such as awaits unsteady feet;
⁶Yet the tents of robbers are prosperous,
and those who provoke God are
secure,
whom God has in his power.
⁷But now ask the beasts to teach you,
the birds of the air to tell you;
⁸Or speak to the earth to instruct you,
and the fish of the sea to inform
you.
⁹Which of all these does not know
that the hand of God has done this?
¹⁰In his hand is the soul of every living
thing,

and the life breath of all mortal flesh.
¹¹Does not the ear judge words
as the mouth tastes food?
¹²So with old age is wisdom,
and with length of days
understanding.
¹³With him are wisdom and might;
his are counsel and understanding.
¹⁴If he knocks a thing down, there is no
rebuilding;
if he imprisons, there is no release.
¹⁵He holds back the waters and there is
drought;
he sends them forth and they
overwhelm the land.
¹⁶With him are strength and prudence;
the misled and the misleaders are
his.
¹⁷He sends counselors away barefoot,
makes fools of judges.
¹⁸He loosens the belt of kings,
ties a waistcloth on their loins.
¹⁹He sends priests away barefoot,
leads the powerful astray.
²⁰He silences the trusted adviser,
takes discretion from the elders.
²¹He pours shame on nobles,
the waistband of the strong he
loosens.
²²He uncovers deep things from the
darkness,
brings the gloom into the light.
²³He makes nations great and destroys
them,
spreads peoples abroad and
abandons them.
²⁴He takes understanding from the
leaders of the land,
makes them wander in a pathless
desert.
²⁵They grope in the darkness without
light;
he makes them wander like
drunkards.

13:1 All this my eye has seen;
my ear has heard and perceived it.

²What you know, I also know;
 I do not fall short of you.
³But I would speak with the Almighty;
 I want to argue with God.
⁴But you gloss over falsehoods,
 you are worthless physicians, every
  one of you!
⁵Oh, that you would be altogether
  silent;
 that for you would be wisdom!
⁶Hear now my argument
 and listen to the accusations from
  my lips.
⁷Is it for God that you speak falsehood?
 Is it for him that you utter deceit?
⁸Is it for him that you show partiality?
 Do you make accusations on behalf
  of God?
⁹Will it be well when he shall search
  you out?
 Can you deceive him as you do a
  mere human being?
¹⁰He will openly rebuke you
 if in secret you show partiality.
¹¹Surely his majesty will frighten you
 and dread of him fall upon you.
¹²Your reminders are ashy maxims,
 your fabrications mounds of clay.
¹³Be silent! Let me alone that I may
  speak,
 no matter what happens to me.
¹⁴I will carry my flesh between my
  teeth,
 and take my life in my hand.
¹⁵Slay me though he might, I will wait
  for him;
 I will defend my conduct before
  him.
¹⁶This shall be my salvation:
 no impious man can come into his
  presence.
¹⁷Pay close attention to my speech,
 give my statement a hearing.
¹⁸Behold, I have prepared my case,
 I know that I am in the right.
¹⁹If anyone can make a case against me,
 then I shall be silent and expire.

²⁰Two things only do not use against
  me,
 then from your presence I need not
  hide:
²¹Withdraw your hand far from me,
 do not let the terror of you frighten
  me.
²²Then call me, and I will respond;
 or let me speak first, and answer me.
²³What are my faults and my sins?
 My misdeed, my sin make known
  to me!
²⁴Why do you hide your face
 and consider me your enemy?
²⁵Will you harass a wind-driven leaf
 or pursue a withered straw?
²⁶For you draw up bitter indictments
  against me,
 and punish in me the faults of my
  youth.
²⁷You put my feet in the stocks;
 you watch all my paths
 and trace out all my footsteps,
²⁸Though I wear out like a leather
  bottle,
 like a garment the moth has
  consumed.

14:1 Man born of woman
 is short-lived and full of trouble,
²Like a flower that springs up and fades,
 swift as a shadow that does not
  abide.
³Upon such a one will you set your
  eyes,
 bringing me into judgment before
  you?
⁴Can anyone make the unclean clean?
 No one can.
⁵Since his days are determined—
 you know the number of his
  months;
 you have fixed the limit which he
  cannot pass—
⁶Look away from him and let him be,
 while, like a hireling, he completes
  his day.

7For a tree there is hope;
    if it is cut down, it will sprout again,
    its tender shoots will not cease.
8Even though its root grow old in the
    earth
    and its stump die in the dust,
9Yet at the first whiff of water it sprouts
    and puts forth branches like a
      young plant.
10But when a man dies, all vigor leaves
    him;
    when a mortal expires, where then
      is he?
11As when the waters of a lake fail,
    or a stream shrivels and dries up,
12So mortals lie down, never to rise.
    Until the heavens are no more, they
      shall not awake,
    nor be roused out of their sleep.
13Oh, that you would hide me in
    Sheol,
    shelter me till your wrath is past,
    fix a time to remember me!
14If a man were to die, and live again,
    all the days of my drudgery I would
      wait
    for my relief to come.

15You would call, and I would answer
    you;
    you would long for the work of
      your hands.
16Surely then you would count my
    steps,
    and not keep watch for sin in me.
17My misdeeds would be sealed up in a
    pouch,
    and you would cover over my guilt.
18Mountains fall and crumble,
    rocks move from their place,
19And water wears away stone,
    and floods wash away the soil of the
      land—
    so you destroy the hope of mortals!
20You prevail once for all against them
    and they pass on;
    you dismiss them with changed
      appearance.
21If their children are honored, they are
    not aware of it;
    or if disgraced, they do not know
      about them.
22Only for themselves, their pain;
    only for themselves, their
      mourning.

☐ 1 TIMOTHY 1

Greeting. 1:1 Paul, an apostle of Christ Jesus by command of God our savior and of Christ Jesus our hope, 2to Timothy, my true child in faith: grace, mercy, and peace from God the Father and Christ Jesus our Lord.

Warning against False Doctrine. 3I repeat the request I made of you when I was on my way to Macedonia, that you stay in Ephesus to instruct certain people not to teach false doctrines 4or to concern themselves with myths and endless genealogies, which promote speculations rather than the plan of God that is to be received by faith. 5The aim of this instruction is love from a pure heart, a good conscience, and a sin-cere faith. 6Some people have deviated from these and turned to meaningless talk, 7wanting to be teachers of the law, but without understanding either what they are saying or what they assert with such assurance.

8We know that the law is good, provided that one uses it as law, 9with the understanding that law is meant not for a righteous person but for the lawless and unruly, the godless and sinful, the unholy and profane, those who kill their fathers or mothers, murderers, 10the unchaste, sodomites, kidnapers, liars, perjurers, and whatever else is opposed to sound teaching, 11according to the glorious gospel of the blessed God, with which I have been entrusted.

Gratitude for God's Mercy. ¹²I am grateful to him who has strengthened me, Christ Jesus our Lord, because he considered me trustworthy in appointing me to the ministry. ¹³I was once a blasphemer and a persecutor and an arrogant man, but I have been mercifully treated because I acted out of ignorance in my unbelief. ¹⁴Indeed, the grace of our Lord has been abundant, along with the faith and love that are in Christ Jesus. ¹⁵This saying is trustworthy and deserves full acceptance: Christ Jesus came into the world to save sinners. Of these I am the foremost. ¹⁶But for that reason I was mercifully treated, so that in me, as the foremost, Christ Jesus might display all his patience as an example for those who would come to believe in him for everlasting life. ¹⁷To the king of ages, incorruptible, invisible, the only God, honor and glory forever and ever. Amen.

Responsibility of Timothy. ¹⁸I entrust this charge to you, Timothy, my child, in accordance with the prophetic words once spoken about you. Through them may you fight a good fight ¹⁹by having faith and a good conscience. Some, by rejecting conscience, have made a shipwreck of their faith, ²⁰among them Hymenaeus and Alexander, whom I have handed over to Satan to be taught not to blaspheme.

June 23

St. Joseph Cafasso

We are born to love, we live to love, and we will die to love still more.

— St. Joseph Cafasso

☐ JOB 15–17

Second Speech of Eliphaz. 15:1 Then Eliphaz the Temanite answered and said:

²Does a wise man answer with windy opinions,
  or puff himself up with the east wind?
³Does he argue in speech that does not avail,
  and in words that are to no profit?
⁴You in fact do away with piety,
  you lessen devotion toward God,
⁵Because your wickedness instructs your mouth,
  and you choose to speak like the crafty.
⁶Your own mouth condemns you, not I;
  your own lips refute you.

⁷Were you the first to be born?
  Were you brought forth before the hills?
⁸Do you listen in on God's council
  and restrict wisdom to yourself?
⁹What do you know that we do not know,
  or understand that we do not?
¹⁰There are gray-haired old men among us,
  more advanced in years than your father.
¹¹Are the consolations of God not enough for you,
  and speech that deals gently with you?
¹²Why does your heart carry you away,
  and why do your eyes flash,

¹³So that you turn your anger against
    God
    and let such words escape your
        mouth!
¹⁴How can any mortal be blameless,
    anyone born of woman be
        righteous?
¹⁵If in his holy ones God places no
        confidence,
    and if the heavens are not without
        blame in his sight,
¹⁶How much less so is the abominable
        and corrupt:
    people who drink in iniquity like
        water!
¹⁷I will show you, if you listen to me;
    what I have seen I will tell—
¹⁸What the wise relate
    and have not contradicted since the
        days of their ancestors,
¹⁹To whom alone the land was given,
    when no foreigner moved among
        them:
²⁰The wicked is in torment all his days,
    and limited years are in store for the
        ruthless;
²¹The sound of terrors is in his ears;
    when all is prosperous, a spoiler
        comes upon him.
²²He despairs of escaping the darkness,
    and looks ever for the sword;
²³A wanderer, food for vultures,
    he knows destruction is imminent.
²⁴A day of darkness fills him with
        dread;
    distress and anguish overpower him,
    like a king expecting an attack.
²⁵Because he has stretched out his hand
        against God
    and arrogantly challenged the
        Almighty,
²⁶Rushing defiantly against him,
    with the stout bosses of his shields.
²⁷Although he has covered his face with
        his crassness,
    padded his loins with blubber,
²⁸He shall dwell in ruined cities,

in houses that are deserted,
    crumbling into rubble.
²⁹He shall not be rich, his possessions
        shall not endure;
    his property shall not spread over
        the land.
³⁰A flame shall sear his early growth,
    and with the wind his blossoms
        shall disappear.
³¹Let him not trust in his height, misled,
    even though his height be like the
        palm tree.
³²He shall wither before his time,
    his branches no longer green.
³³He shall be like a vine that sheds its
        grapes unripened,
    like an olive tree casting off its
        blossom.
³⁴For the breed of the impious shall be
        sterile,
    and fire shall consume the tents of
        extortioners.
³⁵They conceive malice, bring forth
        deceit,
    give birth to fraud.

Job's Fourth Reply. 16:1 Then Job answered and said:

²I have heard this sort of thing many
        times.
    Troublesome comforters, all of you!
³Is there no end to windy words?
    What sickness makes you rattle on?
⁴I also could talk as you do,
    were you in my place.
I could declaim over you,
    or wag my head at you;
⁵I could strengthen you with talk,
    with mere chatter give relief.
⁶If I speak, my pain is not relieved;
    if I stop speaking, nothing changes.
⁷But now he has exhausted me;
    you have stunned all my
        companions.
⁸You have shriveled me up; it is a
        witness,

my gauntness rises up to testify
    against me;
⁹His wrath tears and assails me,
    he gnashes his teeth against me;
My enemy looks daggers at me.
    ¹⁰They gape at me with their mouths;
They strike me on the cheek with
    insults;
    they are all enlisted against me.
¹¹God has given me over to the
    impious;
    into the hands of the wicked he has
    cast me.
¹²I was in peace, but he dislodged me,
    seized me by the neck, dashed me to
    pieces.
He has set me up for a target;
    ¹³his arrows strike me from all
    directions.
He pierces my sides without mercy,
    pours out my gall upon the ground.
¹⁴He pierces me, thrust upon thrust,
    rushes at me like a warrior.
¹⁵I have sewn sackcloth on my skin,
    laid my horn low in the dust.
¹⁶My face is inflamed with weeping,
    darkness covers my eyes,
¹⁷Although my hands are free from
    violence,
    and my prayer sincere.
¹⁸O earth, do not cover my blood,
    nor let my outcry come to rest!
¹⁹Even now my witness is in heaven,
    my advocate is on high.
²⁰My friends it is who wrong me;
    before God my eyes shed tears,
²¹That justice may be done for a mortal
    with God:
    as for a man with his neighbor.
²²For my years are numbered,
    and I go the road of no return.

17:1 My spirit is broken, my days finished,
    my burial at hand.

²Surely mockers surround me,
    at their provocation, my eyes grow
    dim.
³Put up a pledge for me with you:
    who is there to give surety for me?
⁴You darken their minds to knowledge;
    therefore you will not exalt them.
⁵For a share of property he informs on
    friends,
    while the eyes of his children grow
    dim.
⁶I am made a byword of the people;
    I am one at whom people spit.
⁷My eyes are blind with anguish,
    and my whole frame is like a
    shadow.
⁸The upright are astonished at this,
    the innocent aroused against the
    wicked.
⁹The righteous holds to his way,
    the one with clean hands increases
    in strength.
¹⁰But turn now, and come on again;
    I do not find a wise man among
    you!
¹¹My days pass by, my plans are at an
    end,
    the yearning of my heart.
¹²They would change the night into day;
    where there is darkness they talk of
    approaching light.
¹³If my only hope is dwelling in Sheol,
    and spreading my couch in
    darkness,
¹⁴If I am to say to the pit, "You are my
    father,"
    and to the worm "my mother," "my
    sister,"
¹⁵Where then is my hope,
    my happiness, who can see it?
¹⁶Will they descend with me into
    Sheol?
    Shall we go down together into the
    dust?

☐ 1 TIMOTHY 2

Prayer and Conduct. 2:1 First of all, then, I ask that supplications, prayers, petitions, and thanksgivings be offered for everyone, [2]for kings and for all in authority, that we may lead a quiet and tranquil life in all devotion and dignity. [3]This is good and pleasing to God our savior, [4]who wills everyone to be saved and to come to knowledge of the truth.

[5]For there is one God.
There is also one mediator between
    God and the human race,
Christ Jesus, himself human,
[6]who gave himself as ransom for all.

This was the testimony at the proper time. [7]For this I was appointed preacher and apostle (I am speaking the truth, I am not lying), teacher of the Gentiles in faith and truth.

[8]It is my wish, then, that in every place the men should pray, lifting up holy hands, without anger or argument. [9]Similarly, [too,] women should adorn themselves with proper conduct, with modesty and self-control, not with braided hairstyles and gold ornaments, or pearls, or expensive clothes, [10]but rather, as befits women who profess reverence for God, with good deeds. [11]A woman must receive instruction silently and under complete control. [12]I do not permit a woman to teach or to have authority over a man. She must be quiet. [13]For Adam was formed first, then Eve. [14]Further, Adam was not deceived, but the woman was deceived and transgressed. [15]But she will be saved through motherhood, provided women persevere in faith and love and holiness, with self-control.

June 24

The Birth of St. John the Baptist

Those who, to please their listeners, avoid giving a forthright declaration of the will of God become the slaves of those they would please, and abandon the service of God.
— ST. BASIL THE GREAT

☐ JOB 18-21

Bildad's Second Speech. 18:1 Then Bildad the Shuhite answered and said:

[2]When will you put an end to words?
    Reflect, and then we can have
        discussion.
[3]Why are we accounted like beasts,
    equal to them in your sight?
[4]You who tear yourself in your anger—
    shall the earth be neglected on your
        account
    or the rock be moved out of its place?

[5]Truly, the light of the wicked is
        extinguished;
    the flame of his fire casts no light.
[6]In his tent light is darkness;
    the lamp above him goes out.
[7]His vigorous steps are hemmed in,
    his own counsel casts him down.
[8]A net catches him by the feet,
    he wanders into a pitfall.
[9]A trap seizes him by the heel,
    a snare lays hold of him.

¹⁰A noose is hidden for him on the
    ground,
    a netting for him on the path.
¹¹On every side terrors frighten him;
    they harry him at each step.
¹²His strength is famished,
    disaster is ready at his side,
¹³His skin is eaten to the limbs,
    the firstborn of Death eats his
      limbs.
¹⁴He is plucked from the security of his
    tent;
    and marched off to the king of
      terrors.
¹⁵Fire lodges in his tent,
    over his abode brimstone is scattered.
¹⁶Below, his roots dry up,
    and above, his branches wither.
¹⁷His memory perishes from the earth,
    and he has no name in the
      countryside.
¹⁸He is driven from light into darkness,
    and banished from the world.
¹⁹He has neither offshoot nor offspring
    among his people,
    no survivor where once he dwelt.
²⁰Those who come after shall be
    appalled at his fate;
    those who went before are seized
      with horror.
²¹So is it then with the dwelling of the
    impious;
    such is the place of the one who
      does not know God!

Job's Fifth Reply. 19:1 Then Job answered
and said:

²How long will you afflict my spirit,
    grind me down with words?
³These ten times you have humiliated
    me,
    have assailed me without shame!
⁴Even if it were true that I am at fault,
    my fault would remain with me;
⁵If truly you exalt yourselves at my
    expense,

    and use my shame as an argument
      against me,
⁶Know then that it is God who has
    dealt unfairly with me,
    and compassed me round with his
      net.
⁷If I cry out "Violence!" I am not
    answered.
    I shout for help, but there is no
      justice.
⁸He has barred my way and I cannot
    pass;
    veiled my path in darkness;
⁹He has stripped me of my glory,
    taken the diadem from my brow.
¹⁰He breaks me down on every side,
    and I am gone;
    he has uprooted my hope like a tree.
¹¹He has kindled his wrath against me;
    he counts me one of his enemies.
¹²His troops advance as one;
    they build up their road to attack
      me,
    encamp around my tent.
¹³My family has withdrawn from me,
    my friends are wholly estranged.
¹⁴My relatives and companions neglect
    me,
    my guests have forgotten me.
¹⁵Even my maidservants consider me a
    stranger;
    I am a foreigner in their sight.
¹⁶I call my servant, but he gives no
    answer,
    though I plead aloud with him.
¹⁷My breath is abhorrent to my wife;
    I am loathsome to my very children.
¹⁸Even young children despise me;
    when I appear, they speak against
      me.
¹⁹All my intimate friends hold me in
    horror;
    those whom I loved have turned
      against me!
²⁰My bones cling to my skin,
    and I have escaped by the skin of
      my teeth.

²¹Pity me, pity me, you my friends,
> for the hand of God has struck me!
²²Why do you pursue me like God,
> and prey insatiably upon me?
²³Oh, would that my words were
> written down!
> Would that they were inscribed in a
> record:
²⁴That with an iron chisel and with lead
> they were cut in the rock forever!
²⁵As for me, I know that my vindicator
> lives,
> and that he will at last stand forth
> upon the dust.
²⁶This will happen when my skin has
> been stripped off,
> and from my flesh I will see God:
²⁷I will see for myself,
> my own eyes, not another's, will
> behold him:
> my inmost being is consumed with
> longing.
²⁸But you who say, "How shall we
> persecute him,
> seeing that the root of the matter is
> found in him?"
²⁹Be afraid of the sword for yourselves,
> for your anger is a crime deserving
> the sword;
> that you may know that there is a
> judgment.

Zophar's Second Speech. 20:1 Then Zophar the Naamathite answered and said:

²So now my thoughts provide an
> answer for me,
> because of the feelings within me.
³A rebuke that puts me to shame I hear,
> and from my understanding a spirit
> gives me a reply.
⁴Do you not know this: from of old,
> since human beings were placed
> upon the earth,
⁵The triumph of the wicked is short
> and the joy of the impious but for a
> moment?

⁶Though his pride mount up to the
> heavens
> and his head reach to the clouds,
⁷Yet he perishes forever like the dung
> he uses for fuel,
> and onlookers say, "Where is he?"
⁸Like a dream he takes flight and
> cannot be found;
> he fades away like a vision of the
> night.
⁹The eye which saw him does so no
> more;
> nor shall his dwelling again behold
> him.
¹⁰His sons will restore to the poor,
> and his hands will yield up his riches.
¹¹Though his bones are full of youthful
> vigor,
> it shall lie with him in the dust.
¹²Though wickedness is sweet in his
> mouth,
> and he hides it under his tongue,
¹³Though he retains it and will not let
> it go
> but keeps it still within his mouth,
¹⁴Yet in his stomach the food shall
> turn;
> it shall be venom of asps inside him.
¹⁵The riches he swallowed he shall
> vomit up;
> God shall make his belly disgorge
> them.
¹⁶The poison of asps he shall drink in;
> the viper's fangs shall slay him.
¹⁷He shall see no streams of oil,
> no torrents of honey or milk.
¹⁸He shall give back his gains, never
> used;
> like his profit from trade, never
> enjoyed.
¹⁹Because he has oppressed and
> neglected the poor,
> and stolen a house he did not build;
²⁰For he has known no quiet in his
> greed,
> in his treasure he cannot save
> himself.

²¹None of his survivors will consume it,
  therefore his prosperity shall not
  endure.
²²When he has more than enough,
  distress shall be his,
  every sort of trouble shall come
  upon him.
²³When he has filled his belly,
  God shall send against him the fury
  of his wrath
  and rain down his missiles upon
  him.
²⁴Should he escape an iron weapon,
  a bronze bow shall pierce him
  through;
²⁵The dart shall come out of his back,
  a shining point out of his gall-
  bladder:
  terrors fall upon him.
²⁶Complete darkness is in store for his
  treasured ones;
  a fire unfanned shall consume him;
  any survivor in his tent shall be
  destroyed.
²⁷The heavens shall reveal his guilt,
  and the earth rise up against him.
²⁸The flood shall sweep away his house,
  torrents in the day of God's anger.
²⁹This is the portion of the wicked,
  the heritage appointed him by God.

Job's Sixth Reply. 21:1 Then Job answered
and said:

²At least listen to my words,
  and let that be the consolation you
  offer.
³Bear with me while I speak;
  and after I have spoken, you can
  mock!
⁴Is my complaint toward any human
  being?
  Why should I not be impatient?
⁵Look at me and be appalled,
  put your hands over your mouths.
⁶When I think of it, I am dismayed,
  and shuddering seizes my flesh.

⁷Why do the wicked keep on living,
  grow old, become mighty in power?
⁸Their progeny is secure in their sight;
  their offspring are before their eyes.
⁹Their homes are safe, without fear,
  and the rod of God is not upon
  them.
¹⁰Their bulls breed without fail;
  their cows calve and do not miscarry.
¹¹They let their young run free like
  sheep,
  their children skip about.
¹²They sing along with drum and lyre,
  and make merry to the sound of the
  pipe.
¹³They live out their days in prosperity,
  and tranquilly go down to Sheol.
¹⁴Yet they say to God, "Depart from us,
  for we have no desire to know your
  ways!
¹⁵What is the Almighty that we should
  serve him?
  And what do we gain by praying to
  him?"
¹⁶Their happiness is not in their own
  hands.
  The designs of the wicked are far
  from me!
¹⁷How often is the lamp of the wicked
  put out?
  How often does destruction come
  upon them,
  the portion God allots in his anger?
¹⁸Let them be like straw before the
  wind,
  like chaff the storm carries away!
¹⁹"God is storing up the man's misery
  for his children"?—
  let him requite the man himself so
  that he knows it!
²⁰Let his own eyes behold his calamity,
  and the wrath of the Almighty let
  him drink!
²¹For what interest has he in his family
  after him,
  when the number of his months is
  finished?

²²Can anyone teach God knowledge,
    seeing that he judges those on high?
²³One dies in his full vigor,
    wholly at ease and content;
²⁴His figure is full and nourished,
    his bones are moist with marrow.
²⁵Another dies with a bitter spirit,
    never having tasted happiness.
²⁶Alike they lie down in the dust,
    and worms cover them both.
²⁷See, I know your thoughts,
    and the arguments you plot
        against me.
²⁸For you say, "Where is the house of
        the great,
    and where the dwelling place of the
        wicked?"
²⁹Have you not asked the wayfarers

and do you not acknowledge the
    witness they give?
³⁰On the day of calamity the evil man
        is spared,
    on the day that wrath is released.
³¹Who will charge him to his face
        about his conduct,
    and for what he has done who will
        repay him?
³²He is carried to the grave
    and at his tomb they keep watch.
³³Sweet to him are the clods of the
        valley.
    All humankind will follow after him,
    and countless others before him.
³⁴How empty the consolation you offer
        me!
    Your arguments remain a fraud.

☐ 1 TIMOTHY 3

Qualifications of Various Ministers. 3:1
This saying is trustworthy: whoever aspires
to the office of bishop desires a noble task.
²Therefore, a bishop must be irreproachable, married only once, temperate, self-
controlled, decent, hospitable, able to
teach, ³not a drunkard, not aggressive,
but gentle, not contentious, not a lover of
money. ⁴He must manage his own household well, keeping his children under control with perfect dignity; ⁵for if a man does
not know how to manage his own household, how can he take care of the church
of God? ⁶He should not be a recent convert, so that he may not become conceited
and thus incur the devil's punishment. ⁷He
must also have a good reputation among
outsiders, so that he may not fall into disgrace, the devil's trap.

⁸Similarly, deacons must be dignified,
not deceitful, not addicted to drink, not
greedy for sordid gain, ⁹holding fast to the
mystery of the faith with a clear conscience.
¹⁰Moreover, they should be tested first;

then, if there is nothing against them, let
them serve as deacons. ¹¹Women, similarly,
should be dignified, not slanderers, but temperate and faithful in everything. ¹²Deacons
may be married only once and must manage their children and their households well.
¹³Thus those who serve well as deacons gain
good standing and much confidence in their
faith in Christ Jesus.

The Mystery of Our Religion. ¹⁴I am
writing you about these matters, although
I hope to visit you soon. ¹⁵But if I should
be delayed, you should know how to behave in the household of God, which is the
church of the living God, the pillar and
foundation of truth. ¹⁶Undeniably great is
the mystery of devotion,

Who was manifested in the flesh,
vindicated in the spirit,
seen by angels,
proclaimed to the Gentiles,
believed in throughout the world,
taken up in glory.

June 25

Let us live soberly. For through our bodily senses, whether we wish it or not, robbers come in. The inside of the house is sure to be blackened when the smoke that is climbing up the outer walls finds the windows open.

— St. Syncletica

☐ JOB 22-24

Eliphaz's Third Speech. 22:1 Then Eliphaz the Temanite answered and said:

²Can a man be profitable to God?
  Can a wise man be profitable to him?
³Does it please the Almighty that you
      are just?
  Does he gain if your ways are perfect?
⁴Is it because of your piety that he
      reproves you—
  that he enters into judgment with
      you?
⁵Is not your wickedness great,
  your iniquity endless?
⁶You keep your relatives' goods in
      pledge unjustly,
  leave them stripped naked of their
      clothing.
⁷To the thirsty you give no water to
      drink,
  and from the hungry you withhold
      bread;
⁸As if the land belonged to the
      powerful,
  and only the privileged could dwell
      in it!
⁹You sent widows away empty-handed,
  and the resources of orphans are
      destroyed.
¹⁰Therefore snares are round about you,
  sudden terror makes you panic,
¹¹Or darkness—you cannot see!
  A deluge of waters covers you.
¹²Does not God, in the heights of the
      heavens,
  behold the top of the stars, high
      though they are?

¹³Yet you say, "What does God know?
  Can he judge through the thick
      darkness?
¹⁴Clouds hide him so that he cannot
      see
  as he walks around the circuit of the
      heavens!"
¹⁵Do you indeed keep to the ancient
      way
  trodden by the worthless?
¹⁶They were snatched before their time;
  their foundations a river swept away.
¹⁷They said to God, "Let us alone!"
  and, "What can the Almighty do
      to us?"
¹⁸Yet he had filled their houses with
      good things.
  The designs of the wicked are far
      from me!
¹⁹The just look on and are glad,
  and the innocent deride them:
²⁰"Truly our enemies are destroyed,
  and what was left to them, fire has
      consumed!"
²¹Settle with him and have peace.
  That way good shall come to you:
²²Receive instruction from his mouth,
  and place his words in your heart.
²³If you return to the Almighty, you
      will be restored;
  if you put iniquity far from your
      tent,
²⁴And treat raw gold as dust,
  the fine gold of Ophir as pebbles in
      the wadi,
²⁵Then the Almighty himself shall be
      your gold

and your sparkling silver.
²⁶For then you shall delight in the
Almighty,
you shall lift up your face toward
God.
²⁷Entreat him and he will hear you,
and your vows you shall fulfill.
²⁸What you decide shall succeed for you,
and upon your ways light shall
shine.
²⁹For when they are brought low, you
will say, "It is pride!"
But downcast eyes he saves.
³⁰He will deliver whoever is innocent;
you shall be delivered if your hands
are clean.

Job's Seventh Reply. 23:1 Then Job answered and said:

²Today especially my complaint is
bitter,
his hand is heavy upon me in my
groanings.
³Would that I knew how to find him,
that I might come to his dwelling!
⁴I would set out my case before him,
fill my mouth with arguments;
⁵I would learn the words he would
answer me,
understand what he would say to me.
⁶Would he contend against me with his
great power?
No, he himself would heed me!
⁷There an upright man might argue
with him,
and I would once and for all be
delivered from my judge.
⁸But if I go east, he is not there;
or west, I cannot perceive him;
⁹The north enfolds him, and I cannot
catch sight of him;
The south hides him, and I cannot
see him.
¹⁰Yet he knows my way;
if he tested me, I should come forth
like gold.

¹¹My foot has always walked in his
steps;
I have kept his way and not turned
aside.
¹²From the commands of his lips I have
not departed;
the words of his mouth I have
treasured in my heart.
¹³But once he decides, who can
contradict him?
What he desires, that he does.
¹⁴For he will carry out what is
appointed for me,
and many such things he has in
store.
¹⁵Therefore I am terrified before him;
when I take thought, I dread him.
¹⁶For it is God who has made my heart
faint,
the Almighty who has terrified me.
¹⁷Yes, would that I had vanished in
darkness,
hidden by the thick gloom before me.

24:1 Why are times not set by the
Almighty,
and why do his friends not see his
days?
²People remove landmarks;
they steal herds and pasture them.
³The donkeys of orphans they drive
away;
they take the widow's ox for a
pledge.
⁴They force the needy off the road;
all the poor of the land are driven
into hiding.
⁵Like wild donkeys in the wilderness,
they go forth to their task of seeking
prey;
the steppe provides food for their
young;
⁶They harvest fodder in the field,
and glean in the vineyard of the
wicked.
⁷They pass the night naked, without
clothing;

they have no covering against the
cold;
[8]They are drenched with rain from the
mountains,
and for want of shelter they cling to
the rock.
[9]Orphans are snatched from the breast,
infants of the needy are taken in
pledge.
[10]They go about naked, without
clothing,
and famished, they carry the
sheaves.
[11]Between the rows they press out the
oil;
they tread the wine presses, yet are
thirsty.
[12]In the city the dying groan,
and the souls of the wounded cry
out.
Yet God does not treat it as a
disgrace!
[13]They are rebels against the light:
they do not recognize its ways;
they do not stay in its paths.
[14]When there is no light the murderer
rises,
to kill the poor and needy;
in the night he acts like a thief.
[15]The eye of the adulterer watches for
the twilight;
he says, "No eye will see me."
He puts a mask over his face;
[16]in the dark he breaks into houses;
By day they shut themselves in;

they do not know the light.
[17]Indeed, for all of them morning is
deep darkness;
then they recognize the terrors of
deep darkness.
[18]He is swift on the surface of the
water:
their portion in the land is accursed,
they do not turn aside by way of the
vineyards.
[19]Drought and heat snatch away the
snow waters,
Sheol, those who have sinned.
[20]May the womb forget him,
may the worm find him sweet,
may he no longer be remembered;
And may wickedness be broken like a
tree.
[21]May his companion be barren,
unable to give birth,
may his widow not prosper!
[22]He sustains the mighty by his
strength,
to him who rises without assurance
of his life
[23]he gives safety and support,
and his eyes are on their ways.
[24]They are exalted for a while, and then
are no more;
laid low, like everyone else they are
gathered up;
like ears of grain they shrivel.
[25]If this be not so, who can make me
a liar,
and reduce my words to nothing?

☐ 1 TIMOTHY 4

False Asceticism. 4:1 Now the Spirit ex-
plicitly says that in the last times some will
turn away from the faith by paying attention
to deceitful spirits and demonic instructions [2]through the hypocrisy of liars with
branded consciences. [3]They forbid marriage
and require abstinence from foods that God
created to be received with thanksgiving

by those who believe and know the truth.
[4]For everything created by God is good, and
nothing is to be rejected when received with
thanksgiving, [5]for it is made holy by the in-
vocation of God in prayer.

Counsel to Timothy. [6]If you will give
these instructions to the brothers, you
will be a good minister of Christ Jesus,

nourished on the words of the faith and of the sound teaching you have followed. [7]Avoid profane and silly myths. Train yourself for devotion, [8]for, while physical training is of limited value, devotion is valuable in every respect, since it holds a promise of life both for the present and for the future. [9]This saying is trustworthy and deserves full acceptance. [10]For this we toil and struggle, because we have set our hope on the living God, who is the savior of all, especially of those who believe.

[11]Command and teach these things. [12]Let no one have contempt for your youth, but set an example for those who believe, in speech, conduct, love, faith, and purity. [13]Until I arrive, attend to the reading, exhortation, and teaching. [14]Do not neglect the gift you have, which was conferred on you through the prophetic word with the imposition of hands of the presbyterate. [15]Be diligent in these matters, be absorbed in them, so that your progress may be evident to everyone. [16]Attend to yourself and to your teaching; persevere in both tasks, for by doing so you will save both yourself and those who listen to you.

June 26

St. Josemaría Escrivá

Why lose your temper if by doing so you offend God, annoy other people, give yourself a bad time . . . and in the end have to find it again?

— St. Josemaría Escrivá

☐ JOB 25–28

Bildad's Third Speech. 25:1 Then Bildad the Shuhite answered and said:

[2]Dominion and dread are his
  who brings about harmony in his
    heavens.
[3]Is there any numbering of his troops?
  Yet on which of them does his light
    not rise?
[4]How can anyone be in the right
    against God,
  or how can any born of woman be
    innocent?
[5]Even the moon is not bright
  and the stars are not clean in his
    eyes,
[6]How much less a human being, who is
    but a worm,
  a mortal, who is only a maggot?

Job's Reply. 26:1 Then Job answered and said:

[2]What help you give to the powerless,
  what strength to the feeble arm!
[3]How you give counsel to one without
    wisdom;
  how profuse is the advice you offer!
[4]With whose help have you uttered
    those words,
  whose breath comes forth from you?
[5]The shades beneath writhe in terror,
  the waters, and their inhabitants.
[6]Naked before him is Sheol,
  and Abaddon has no covering.
[7]He stretches out Zaphon over the
    void,
  and suspends the earth over nothing
    at all;

[8]He binds up the waters in his clouds,
  yet the cloud is not split by their
    weight;
[9]He holds back the appearance of the
    full moon
  by spreading his clouds before it.
[10]He has marked out a circle on the
    surface of the deep
  as the boundary of light and
    darkness.
[11]The pillars of the heavens tremble
  and are stunned at his thunderous
    rebuke;
[12]By his power he stilled Sea,
  by his skill he crushed Rahab;
[13]By his wind the heavens were made
    clear,
  his hand pierced the fleeing serpent.
[14]Lo, these are but the outlines of his
    ways,
  and what a whisper of a word we
    hear of him:
  Who can comprehend the thunder
    of his power?

Job's Reply. 27:1 Job took up his theme
again and said:

  [2]As God lives, who takes away my
    right,
    the Almighty, who has made my life
      bitter,
  [3]So long as I still have life breath in me,
    the breath of God in my nostrils,
  [4]My lips shall not speak falsehood,
    nor my tongue utter deceit!
  [5]Far be it from me to account you right;
    till I die I will not renounce my
      innocence.
  [6]My justice I maintain and I will not
    relinquish it;
    my heart does not reproach me for
      any of my days.
  [7]Let my enemy be as the wicked
    and my adversary as the unjust!
  [8]For what hope has the impious when
    he is cut off,

when God requires his life?
  [9]Will God then listen to his cry
    when distress comes upon him,
  [10]If he delights in the Almighty
    and calls upon God constantly?
  [11]I will teach you what is in God's hand,
    and the way of the Almighty I will
      not conceal.
  [12]Look, you yourselves have all seen it;
    why do you spend yourselves in
      empty words!
  [13]This is the portion of the wicked with
      God,
    the heritage oppressors receive from
      the Almighty:
  [14]Though his children be many, the
      sword awaits them.
    His descendants shall want for
      bread.
  [15]His survivors shall be buried in death;
    their widows shall not weep.
  [16]Though he heap up silver like dust
    and store away mounds of clothing,
  [17]What he has stored the righteous
      shall wear,
    and the innocent shall divide the
      silver.
  [18]He builds his house as of cobwebs,
    or like a booth put up by a
      watchman.
  [19]He lies down a rich man, one last
      time;
    he opens his eyes—nothing is there.
  [20]Terrors flood over him like water,
    at night the tempest carries him off.
  [21]The east wind seizes him and he is
      gone;
    it sweeps him from his place;
  [22]It hurls itself at him without pity,
    as he tries to flee from its power.
  [23]It claps its hands at him,
    and whistles at him from its place.

Where Is Wisdom to be Found? 28:1
There is indeed a mine for silver,
  and a place for refining gold.
[2]Iron is taken from the earth,

and copper smelted out of stone.
³He sets a boundary for the darkness;
  the farthest confines he explores.
⁴He breaks open a shaft far from
    habitation,
  unknown to human feet;
  suspended, far from people, they
    sway.
⁵The earth, though out of it comes
    forth bread,
  is in fiery upheaval underneath.
⁶Its stones are the source of lapis lazuli,
  and there is gold in its dust.
⁷The path no bird of prey knows,
  nor has the hawk's eye seen it.
⁸The proud beasts have not trodden it,
  nor has the lion gone that way.
⁹He sets his hand to the flinty rock,
  and overturns the mountains at
    their root.
¹⁰He splits channels in the rocks;
  his eyes behold all that is precious.
¹¹He dams up the sources of the
    streams,
  and brings hidden things to light.
¹²As for wisdom—where can she be
    found?
  Where is the place of understanding?
¹³Mortals do not know her path,
  nor is she to be found in the land of
    the living.
¹⁴The Deep says, "She is not in me";
  and the Sea says, "She is not with
    me."
¹⁵Solid gold cannot purchase her,
  nor can her price be paid with silver.
¹⁶She cannot be bought with gold of
    Ophir,

with precious onyx or lapis lazuli,
¹⁷Gold or crystal cannot equal her,
  nor can golden vessels be exchanged
    for her.
¹⁸Neither coral nor crystal should be
    thought of;
  the value of wisdom surpasses
    pearls.
¹⁹Ethiopian topaz does not equal her,
  nor can she be weighed out for pure
    gold.
²⁰As for wisdom, where does she come
    from?
  Where is the place of
    understanding?
²¹She is hidden from the eyes of every
    living thing;
  even from the birds of the air she is
    concealed.
²²Abaddon and Death say,
  "Only by rumor have we heard of
    her."
²³But God understands the way to her;
  it is he who knows her place.
²⁴For he beholds the ends of the earth
  and sees all that is under the
    heavens.
²⁵When he weighed out the wind,
  and measured out the waters;
²⁶When he made a rule for the rain
  and a path for the thunderbolts,
²⁷Then he saw wisdom and appraised
    her,
  established her, and searched her
    out.
²⁸And to mortals he said:
  See: the fear of the Lord is wisdom;
  and avoiding evil is understanding.

☐ 1 TIMOTHY 5

5:1 Do not rebuke an older man, but appeal to him as a father. Treat younger men as brothers, ²older women as mothers, and younger women as sisters with complete purity.

Rules for Widows. ³Honor widows who are truly widows. ⁴But if a widow has children or grandchildren, let these first learn to perform their religious duty to their own family and to make recompense to their parents, for this is pleasing to God. [5]The real widow, who is all alone, has set her hope on God and continues in supplications and prayers night and day. [6]But the one who is self-indulgent is dead while she lives. [7]Command this, so that they may be irreproachable. [8]And whoever does not provide for relatives and especially family members has denied the faith and is worse than an unbeliever.

[9]Let a widow be enrolled if she is not less than sixty years old, married only once, [10]with a reputation for good works, namely, that she has raised children, practiced hospitality, washed the feet of the holy ones, helped those in distress, involved herself in every good work. [11]But exclude younger widows, for when their sensuality estranges them from Christ, they want to marry [12]and will incur condemnation for breaking their first pledge. [13]And furthermore, they learn to be idlers, going about from house to house, and not only idlers but gossips and busybodies as well, talking about things that ought not to be mentioned. [14]So I would like younger widows to marry, have children, and manage a home, so as to give the adversary no pretext for maligning us. [15]For some have already turned away to follow Satan. [16]If any woman believer has widowed relatives, she must assist them; the church is not to be burdened, so that it will be able to help those who are truly widows.

Rules for Presbyters. [17]Presbyters who preside well deserve double honor, especially those who toil in preaching and teaching. [18]For the scripture says, "You shall not muzzle an ox when it is threshing," and, "A worker deserves his pay." [19]Do not accept an accusation against a presbyter unless it is supported by two or three witnesses. [20]Reprimand publicly those who do sin, so that the rest also will be afraid. [21]I charge you before God and Christ Jesus and the elect angels to keep these rules without prejudice, doing nothing out of favoritism. [22]Do not lay hands too readily on anyone, and do not share in another's sins. Keep yourself pure. [23]Stop drinking only water, but have a little wine for the sake of your stomach and your frequent illnesses. [24]Some people's sins are public, preceding them to judgment; but other people are followed by their sins. [25]Similarly, good works are also public; and even those that are not cannot remain hidden.

June 27

St. Cyril of Alexandria

Even if we make images of pious men, it is not so that we might adore them as gods, but that when we see them, we might be prompted to imitate them. And if we make images of Christ, it is so that our minds might soar aloft in yearning for Him.

— St. Cyril of Alexandria

☐ JOB 29-31

29:1 Job took up his theme again and said:

[2]Oh, that I were as in the months past,
  as in the days when God watched
    over me:

[3]While he kept his lamp shining above
    my head,
  and by his light I walked through
    darkness;

⁴As I was in my flourishing days,
   when God sheltered my tent;
⁵When the Almighty was still with me,
   and my children were round about
      me;
⁶When my footsteps were bathed in
      cream,
   and the rock flowed with streams
      of oil.
⁷Whenever I went out to the gate of
      the city
   and took my seat in the square,
⁸The young men saw me and withdrew,
   and the elders rose up and stood;
⁹Officials refrained from speaking
   and covered their mouths with their
      hands;
¹⁰The voice of the princes was silenced,
   and their tongues stuck to the roofs
      of their mouths.
¹¹The ear that heard blessed me;
   the eye that saw acclaimed me.
¹²For I rescued the poor who cried out
      for help,
   the orphans, and the unassisted;
¹³The blessing of those in extremity
      came upon me,
   and the heart of the widow I made
      joyful.
¹⁴I wore my righteousness like a
      garment;
   justice was my robe and my turban.
¹⁵I was eyes to the blind,
   and feet to the lame was I.
¹⁶I was a father to the poor;
   the complaint of the stranger I
      pursued,
¹⁷And I broke the jaws of the wicked
      man;
   from his teeth I forced the prey.
¹⁸I said: "In my own nest I shall grow
      old;
   I shall multiply years like the
      phoenix.
¹⁹My root is spread out to the waters;
   the dew rests by night on my
      branches.

²⁰My glory is fresh within me,
   and my bow is renewed in my
      hand!"
²¹For me they listened and waited;
   they were silent for my counsel.
²²Once I spoke, they said no more,
   but received my pronouncement
      drop by drop.
²³They waited for me as for the rain;
   they drank in my words like the
      spring rains.
²⁴When I smiled on them they could
      not believe it;
   they would not let the light of my
      face be dimmed.
²⁵I decided their course and sat at their
      head,
   I lived like a king among the troops,
      like one who comforts mourners.

30:1 But now they hold me in derision
   who are younger than I,
Whose fathers I should have disdained
   to rank with the dogs of my flock.
²Such strength as they had meant
      nothing to me;
   their vigor had perished.
³In want and emaciating hunger
      they fled to the parched lands:
   to the desolate wasteland by night.
⁴They plucked saltwort and shrubs;
   the roots of the broom plant were
      their food.
⁵They were banished from the
      community,
   with an outcry like that against a
      thief—
⁶To dwell on the slopes of the wadies,
   in caves of sand and stone;
⁷Among the bushes they brayed;
   under the nettles they huddled
      together.
⁸Irresponsible, of no account,
   they were driven out of the land.
⁹Yet now they sing of me in mockery;
   I have become a byword among
      them.

¹⁰They abhor me, they stand aloof,
  they do not hesitate to spit in my
    face!
¹¹Because he has loosened my
  bowstring and afflicted me,
  they have thrown off restraint in my
    presence.
¹²On my right the young rabble rise up;
  they trip my feet,
  they build their approaches for my
    ruin.
¹³They tear up my path,
  they promote my ruin,
  no helper is there against them.
¹⁴As through a wide breach they
    advance;
  amid the uproar they come on in
    waves;
¹⁵terrors roll over me.
My dignity is driven off like the wind,
  and my well-being vanishes like a
    cloud.
¹⁶And now my life ebbs away from me,
  days of affliction have taken hold
    of me.
¹⁷At night he pierces my bones,
  my sinews have no rest.
¹⁸With great difficulty I change my
    clothes,
  the collar of my tunic fits around
    my waist.
¹⁹He has cast me into the mire;
  I have become like dust and ashes.
²⁰I cry to you, but you do not answer
    me;
  I stand, but you take no notice.
²¹You have turned into my tormentor,
  and with your strong hand you
    attack me.
²²You raise me up and drive me before
    the wind;
  I am tossed about by the tempest.
²³Indeed I know that you will return
    me to death
  to the house destined for everyone
    alive.
²⁴Yet should not a hand be held out

to help a wretched person in
    distress?
²⁵Did I not weep for the hardships of
    others;
  was not my soul grieved for the
    poor?
²⁶Yet when I looked for good, evil
    came;
  when I expected light, darkness
    came.
²⁷My inward parts seethe and will not
    be stilled;
  days of affliction have overtaken me.
²⁸I go about in gloom, without the sun;
  I rise in the assembly and cry for
    help.
²⁹I have become a brother to jackals,
  a companion to ostriches.
³⁰My blackened skin falls away from me;
  my very frame is scorched by the
    heat.
³¹My lyre is tuned to mourning,
  and my reed pipe to sounds of
    weeping.

31:1 I made a covenant with my eyes
  not to gaze upon a virgin.
²What portion comes from God above,
  what heritage from the Almighty on
    high?
³Is it not calamity for the unrighteous,
  and woe for evildoers?
⁴Does he not see my ways,
  and number all my steps?
⁵If I have walked in falsehood
  and my foot has hastened to deceit,
⁶Let God weigh me in the scales of
    justice;
  thus will he know my innocence!
⁷If my steps have turned out of the
    way,
  and my heart has followed my eyes,
  or any stain clings to my hands,
⁸Then may I sow, but another eat,
  and may my produce be rooted up!
⁹If my heart has been enticed toward a
    woman,

and I have lain in wait at my
neighbor's door;

[10]Then may my wife grind for another,
and may others kneel over her!

[11]For that would be heinous,
a crime to be condemned,

[12]A fire that would consume down to
Abaddon
till it uprooted all my crops.

[13]Had I refused justice to my
manservant
or to my maidservant, when they
had a complaint against me,

[14]What then should I do when God
rises up?
What could I answer when he
demands an account?

[15]Did not he who made me in the belly
make him?
Did not the same One fashion us in
the womb?

[16]If I have denied anything that the
poor desired,
or allowed the eyes of the widow to
languish

[17]While I ate my portion alone,
with no share in it for the
fatherless,

[18]Though like a father he has reared me
from my youth,
guiding me even from my mother's
womb—

[19]If I have seen a wanderer without
clothing,
or a poor man without covering,

[20]Whose limbs have not blessed me
when warmed with the fleece of my
sheep;

[21]If I have raised my hand against the
innocent
because I saw that I had supporters
at the gate—

[22]Then may my arm fall from the
shoulder,
my forearm be broken at the elbow!

[23]For I dread calamity from God,
and his majesty will overpower me.

[24]Had I put my trust in gold
or called fine gold my security;

[25]Or had I rejoiced that my wealth
was great,
or that my hand had acquired
abundance—

[26]Had I looked upon the light as it
shone,
or the moon in the splendor of its
progress,

[27]And had my heart been secretly
enticed
to blow them a kiss with my hand,

[28]This too would be a crime for
condemnation,
for I should have denied God
above.

[29]Had I rejoiced at the destruction of
my enemy
or exulted when evil came upon
him,

[30]Even though I had not allowed my
mouth to sin
by invoking a curse against his
life—

[31]Had not the men of my tent
exclaimed,
"Who has not been filled with his
meat!"

[32]No stranger lodged in the street,
for I opened my door to
wayfarers—

[33]Had I, all too human, hidden my
sins
and buried my guilt in my bosom

[34]Because I feared the great multitude
and the scorn of the clans terrified
me—
then I should have remained silent,
and not come out of doors!

[35]Oh, that I had one to hear my case:
here is my signature: let the
Almighty answer me!
Let my accuser write out his
indictment!

[36]Surely, I should wear it on my
shoulder

or put it on me like a diadem;
[37]Of all my steps I should give him an
   account;
   like a prince I should present myself
   before him.
[38]If my land has cried out against me
   till its furrows wept together;

[39]If I have eaten its strength without
   payment
   and grieved the hearts of its tenants;
[40]Then let the thorns grow instead of
   wheat
   and stinkweed instead of barley!

The words of Job are ended.

□ 1 TIMOTHY 6

Rules for Slaves. 6:1 Those who are under the yoke of slavery must regard their masters as worthy of full respect, so that the name of God and our teaching may not suffer abuse. [2]Those whose masters are believers must not take advantage of them because they are brothers but must give better service because those who will profit from their work are believers and are beloved.

Teach and urge these things. [3]Whoever teaches something different and does not agree with the sound words of our Lord Jesus Christ and the religious teaching [4]is conceited, understanding nothing, and has a morbid disposition for arguments and verbal disputes. From these come envy, rivalry, insults, evil suspicions, [5]and mutual friction among people with corrupted minds, who are deprived of the truth, supposing religion to be a means of gain. [6]Indeed, religion with contentment is a great gain. [7]For we brought nothing into the world, just as we shall not be able to take anything out of it. [8]If we have food and clothing, we shall be content with that. [9]Those who want to be rich are falling into temptation and into a trap and into many foolish and harmful desires, which plunge them into ruin and destruction. [10]For the love of money is the root of all evils, and some people in their desire for it have strayed from the faith and have pierced themselves with many pains.

Exhortations to Timothy. [11]But you, man of God, avoid all this. Instead, pursue righteousness, devotion, faith, love, patience, and gentleness. [12]Compete well for the faith. Lay hold of eternal life, to which you were called when you made the noble confession in the presence of many witnesses. [13]I charge [you] before God, who gives life to all things, and before Christ Jesus, who gave testimony under Pontius Pilate for the noble confession, [14]to keep the commandment without stain or reproach until the appearance of our Lord Jesus Christ [15]that the blessed and only ruler will make manifest at the proper time, the King of kings and Lord of lords, [16]who alone has immortality, who dwells in unapproachable light, and whom no human being has seen or can see. To him be honor and eternal power. Amen.

Right Use of Wealth. [17]Tell the rich in the present age not to be proud and not to rely on so uncertain a thing as wealth but rather on God, who richly provides us with all things for our enjoyment. [18]Tell them to do good, to be rich in good works, to be generous, ready to share, [19]thus accumulating as treasure a good foundation for the future, so as to win the life that is true life.

[20]O Timothy, guard what has been entrusted to you. Avoid profane babbling and the absurdities of so-called knowledge. [21]By professing it, some people have deviated from the faith.

Grace be with all of you.

June 28

St. Irenaeus

The Church is the entrance to life; all the others are thieves and robbers.

— St. Irenaeus

☐ JOB 32-34

32:1 Then the three men ceased to answer Job, because in his own eyes he was in the right. ²But the anger of Elihu, son of Barachel the Buzite, of the clan of Ram, was kindled. He was angry with Job for considering himself rather than God to be in the right. ³He was angry also with the three friends because they had not found a good answer and had not condemned Job. ⁴But since these men were older than he, Elihu bided his time before addressing Job. ⁵When, however, Elihu saw that there was no reply in the mouths of the three men, his wrath was inflamed. ⁶So Elihu, son of Barachel the Buzite, answered and said:

I am young and you are very old;
   therefore I held back and was afraid
   to declare to you my knowledge.
⁷I thought, days should speak,
   and many years teach wisdom!
⁸But there is a spirit in human beings,
   the breath of the Almighty, that
      gives them understanding.
⁹It is not those of many days who are
      wise,
   nor the aged who understand the
      right.
¹⁰Therefore I say, listen to me;
   I also will declare my knowledge!
¹¹Behold, I have waited for your words,
   have given ear to your arguments,
   as you searched out what to say.
¹²Yes, I followed you attentively:
   And look, none of you has
      convicted Job,
   not one could refute his statements.
¹³So do not say, "We have met wisdom;

God can vanquish him but no
      mortal!"
¹⁴For had he addressed his words
      to me,
   I would not then have answered
      him with your words.
¹⁵They are dismayed, they make no
      more reply;
   words fail them.
¹⁶Must I wait? Now that they speak no
      more,
   and have ceased to make reply,
¹⁷I too will speak my part;
   I also will declare my knowledge!
¹⁸For I am full of words;
   the spirit within me compels me.
¹⁹My belly is like unopened wine,
   like wineskins ready to burst.
²⁰Let me speak and obtain relief;
   let me open my lips, and reply.
²¹I would not be partial to anyone,
   nor give flattering titles to any.
²²For I know nothing of flattery;
   if I did, my Maker would soon take
      me away.

33:1 Therefore, O Job, hear my
      discourse;
   listen to all my words.
²Behold, now I open my mouth;
   my tongue and voice form words.
³I will state directly what is in my
      mind,
   my lips shall speak knowledge
      clearly;
⁴For the spirit of God made me,
   the breath of the Almighty keeps me
      alive.

⁵If you are able, refute me;
  draw up your arguments and take
    your stand.
⁶Look, I am like you before God,
  I too was pinched from clay.
⁷Therefore fear of me should not
    dismay you,
  nor should I weigh heavily upon
    you.
⁸But you have said in my hearing,
  as I listened to the sound of your
    words:
⁹"I am clean, without transgression;
  I am innocent, there is no guilt
    in me.
¹⁰Yet he invents pretexts against me
  and counts me as an enemy.
¹¹He puts my feet in the stocks,
  watches all my paths!"
¹²In this you are not just, let me tell
    you;
  for God is greater than mortals.
¹³Why, then, do you make complaint
    against him
  that he gives no reply to their
    words?
¹⁴For God does speak, once,
  even twice, though you do not
    see it:
¹⁵In a dream, in a vision of the night,
  when deep sleep falls upon mortals
  as they slumber in their beds.
¹⁶It is then he opens their ears
  and with a warning, terrifies them,
¹⁷By turning mortals from acting
  and keeping pride away from a
    man,
¹⁸He holds his soul from the pit,
  his life from passing to the grave.
¹⁹Or he is chastened on a bed of pain,
  suffering continually in his bones,
²⁰So that to his appetite food is
    repulsive,
  his throat rejects the choicest
    nourishment.
²¹His flesh is wasted, it cannot be seen;
  bones, once invisible, appear;

²²His soul draws near to the pit,
  his life to the place of the dead.
²³If then there be a divine messenger,
  a mediator, one out of a thousand,
  to show him what is right,
²⁴He will take pity on him and say,
  "Deliver him from going down to
    the pit;
  I have found him a ransom."
²⁵Then his flesh shall become soft as a
    boy's;
  he shall be again as in the days of his
    youth.
²⁶He shall pray and God will favor
    him;
  he shall see God's face with
    rejoicing;
  for he restores a person's
    righteousness.
²⁷He shall sing before all and say,
  "I sinned and did wrong,
  yet I was not punished accordingly.
²⁸He delivered me from passing to the
    pit,
  and my life sees light."
²⁹See, all these things God does,
  two, even three times, for a man,
³⁰Bringing back his soul from the pit
  to the light, in the light of the
    living.
³¹Be attentive, Job, listen to me!
  Be silent and I will speak.
³²If you have anything to say, then
    answer me.
  Speak out! I should like to see you
    justified.
³³If not, then you listen to me;
  be silent, and I will teach you
    wisdom.

34:1 Then Elihu answered and said:

²Hear my discourse, you that are wise;
  you that have knowledge, listen
    to me!
³For the ear tests words,
  as the palate tastes food.

⁴Let us choose what is right;
let us determine among ourselves
what is good.
⁵For Job has said, "I am innocent,
but God has taken away what is my
right.
⁶I declare the judgment on me to be a
lie;
my arrow-wound is incurable,
sinless though I am."
⁷What man is like Job?
He drinks in blasphemies like water,
⁸Keeps company with evildoers
and goes along with the wicked,
⁹When he says, "There is no profit
in pleasing God."
¹⁰Therefore, you that have
understanding, hear me:
far be it from God to do
wickedness;
far from the Almighty to do wrong!
¹¹Rather, he requites mortals for their
conduct,
and brings home to them their way
of life.
¹²Surely, God cannot act wickedly,
the Almighty cannot pervert justice.
¹³Who gave him charge over the earth,
or who set all the world in its place?
¹⁴If he were to set his mind to it,
gather to himself his spirit and
breath,
¹⁵All flesh would perish together,
and mortals return to dust.
¹⁶Now you—understand, hear this!
Listen to the words I speak!
¹⁷Can an enemy of justice be in
control,
will you condemn the supreme Just
One,
¹⁸Who says to a king, "You are
worthless!"
and to nobles, "You are wicked!"
¹⁹Who neither favors the person of
princes,
nor respects the rich more than the
poor?

For they are all the work of his hands;
²⁰in a moment they die, even at
midnight.
People are shaken, and pass away,
the powerful are removed without
lifting a hand;
²¹For his eyes are upon our ways,
and all our steps he sees.
²²There is no darkness so dense
that evildoers can hide in it.
²³For no one has God set a time
to come before him in judgment.
²⁴Without inquiry he shatters the
mighty,
and appoints others in their place,
²⁵Thus he discerns their works;
overnight they are crushed.
²⁶Where the wicked are, he strikes them,
in a place where all can see,
²⁷Because they turned away from him
and did not understand his ways
at all:
²⁸And made the cry of the poor reach
him,
so that he heard the cry of the
afflicted.
²⁹If he is silent, who then can
condemn?
If he hides his face, who then can
behold him,
whether nation or individual?
³⁰Let an impious man not rule,
nor those who ensnare their people.
³¹Should anyone say to God,
"I accept my punishment; I will
offend no more;
³²What I cannot see, teach me:
if I have done wrong, I will do so no
more,"
³³Would you then say that God must
punish,
when you are disdainful?
It is you who must choose, not I;
speak, therefore, what you know.
³⁴Those who understand will say to me,
all the wise who hear my views:
³⁵"Job speaks without knowledge,

his words make no sense.

³⁶Let Job be tested to the limit,
since his answers are those of the
impious;

³⁷For he is adding rebellion to his sin
by brushing off our arguments
and addressing many words to
God."

☐ TITUS 1

Greeting. 1:1 Paul, a slave of God and apostle of Jesus Christ for the sake of the faith of God's chosen ones and the recognition of religious truth, ²in the hope of eternal life that God, who does not lie, promised before time began, ³who indeed at the proper time revealed his word in the proclamation with which I was entrusted by the command of God our savior, ⁴to Titus, my true child in our common faith: grace and peace from God the Father and Christ Jesus our savior.

Titus in Crete. ⁵For this reason I left you in Crete so that you might set right what remains to be done and appoint presbyters in every town, as I directed you, ⁶on condition that a man be blameless, married only once, with believing children who are not accused of licentiousness or rebellious. ⁷For a bishop as God's steward must be blameless, not arrogant, not irritable, not a drunkard, not aggressive, not greedy for sordid gain, ⁸but hospitable, a lover of goodness, temperate, just, holy, and self-controlled, ⁹holding fast to the true mes-

sage as taught so that he will be able both to exhort with sound doctrine and to refute opponents. ¹⁰For there are also many rebels, idle talkers and deceivers, especially the Jewish Christians. ¹¹It is imperative to silence them, as they are upsetting whole families by teaching for sordid gain what they should not. ¹²One of them, a prophet of their own, once said,

"Cretans have always been liars, vicious
beasts, and lazy gluttons."

¹³That testimony is true. Therefore, admonish them sharply, so that they may be sound in the faith, ¹⁴instead of paying attention to Jewish myths and regulations of people who have repudiated the truth. ¹⁵To the clean all things are clean, but to those who are defiled and unbelieving nothing is clean; in fact, both their minds and their consciences are tainted. ¹⁶They claim to know God, but by their deeds they deny him. They are vile and disobedient and unqualified for any good deed.

June 29

Sts. Peter and Paul

When a fire is lit to clear a field, it burns off all the dry and useless weeds and thorns. When the sun rises and darkness is dispelled, robbers, night prowlers, and burglars hide away. In the same way, when the apostle Paul's voice was raised to preach the Gospel to the nations, like a great clap of thunder in the sky, his preaching was a blazing fire carrying all before it. It was the sun rising in full glory.

— St. Bernardine of Siena

☐ JOB 35–37

35:1 Then Elihu answered and said:

²Do you think it right to say,
   "I am in the right, not God"?
³When you ask what it profits you,
   "What advantage do I have from
      not sinning?"
⁴I have words for a reply to you
   and your friends as well.
⁵Look up to the skies and see;
   behold the heavens high above
      you.
⁶If you sin, what do you do to God?
   Even if your offenses are many, how
      do you affect him?
⁷If you are righteous, what do you give
      him,
   or what does he receive from your
      hand?
⁸Your wickedness affects only someone
      like yourself,
   and your justice, only a fellow
      human being.
⁹In great oppression people cry out;
   they call for help because of the
      power of the great,
¹⁰No one says, "Where is God, my
      Maker,
   who gives songs in the night,
¹¹Teaches us more than the beasts of
      the earth,
   and makes us wiser than the birds of
      the heavens?"

¹²Though thus they cry out, he does
      not answer
   because of the pride of the wicked.
¹³But it is idle to say God does not
      hear
   or that the Almighty does not take
      notice.
¹⁴Even though you say, "You take no
      notice of it,"
   the case is before him; with
      trembling wait upon him.
¹⁵But now that you have done
      otherwise, God's anger punishes,
   nor does he show much concern
      over a life.
¹⁶Yet Job to no purpose opens his
      mouth,
   multiplying words without
      knowledge.

36:1 Elihu continued and said:

²Wait a little and I will instruct you,
   for there are still words to be said
      for God.
³I will assemble arguments from afar,
   and for my maker I will establish
      what is right.
⁴For indeed, my words are not a lie;
   one perfect in knowledge is before
      you.
⁵Look, God is great, not disdainful;
   his strength of purpose is great.

He does not preserve the life of the
    wicked.
⁶He establishes the right of the poor;
    he does not divert his eyes from the
        just
⁷But he seats them upon thrones
    with kings, exalted forever.
⁸If they are bound with fetters,
    held fast by bonds of affliction,
⁹He lets them know what they have
        done,
    and how arrogant are their sins.
¹⁰He opens their ears to correction
    and tells them to turn back from
        evil.
¹¹If they listen and serve him,
    they spend their days in prosperity,
    their years in happiness.
¹²But if they do not listen, they pass to
        the grave,
    they perish for lack of knowledge.
¹³The impious in heart lay up anger;
    they do not cry for help when he
        binds them;
¹⁴They will die young—
    their life among the reprobate.
¹⁵But he saves the afflicted through
        their affliction,
    and opens their ears through
        oppression.
¹⁶He entices you from distress,
    to a broad place without constraint;
    what rests on your table is rich food.
¹⁷Though you are full of the judgment
        of the wicked,
    judgment and justice will be
        maintained.
¹⁸Let not anger at abundance entice you,
    nor great bribery lead you astray.
¹⁹Will your wealth equip you against
        distress,
    or all your exertions of strength?
²⁰Do not long for the night,
    when peoples vanish in their place.
²¹Be careful; do not turn to evil;
    for this you have preferred to
        affliction.

²²Look, God is exalted in his power.
    What teacher is there like him?
²³Who prescribes for him his way?
    Who says, "You have done wrong"?
²⁴Remember, you should extol his work,
    which people have praised in song.
²⁵All humankind beholds it;
    everyone views it from afar.
²⁶See, God is great beyond our
        knowledge,
    the number of his years past
        searching out.
²⁷He holds in check the waterdrops
    that filter in rain from his flood,
²⁸Till the clouds flow with them
    and they rain down on all
        humankind.
²⁹Can anyone understand the spreading
        clouds,
    the thunderings from his tent?
³⁰Look, he spreads his light over it,
    it covers the roots of the sea.
³¹For by these he judges the nations,
    and gives food in abundance.
³²In his hands he holds the lightning,
    and he commands it to strike the
        mark.
³³His thunder announces him
    and incites the fury of the storm.

37:1 At this my heart trembles
    and leaps out of its place.
²Listen to his angry voice
    and the rumble that comes forth
        from his mouth!
³Everywhere under the heavens he
        sends it,
    with his light, to the ends of the
        earth.
⁴Again his voice roars,
    his majestic voice thunders;
    he does not restrain them when his
        voice is heard.
⁵God thunders forth marvels with his
        voice;
    he does great things beyond our
        knowing.

⁶He says to the snow, "Fall to the
earth";
likewise to his heavy, drenching
rain.
⁷He shuts up all humankind indoors,
so that all people may know his
work.
⁸The wild beasts take to cover
and remain quiet in their dens.
⁹Out of its chamber the tempest comes
forth;
from the north winds, the cold.
¹⁰With his breath God brings the frost,
and the broad waters congeal.
¹¹The clouds too are laden with
moisture,
the storm-cloud scatters its light.
¹²He it is who changes their rounds,
according to his plans,
to do all that he commands them
across the inhabited world.
¹³Whether for punishment or mercy,
he makes it happen.
¹⁴Listen to this, Job!
Stand and consider the marvels of
God!
¹⁵Do you know how God lays his
command upon them,
and makes the light shine forth
from his clouds?
¹⁶Do you know how the clouds are
banked,
the marvels of him who is perfect in
knowledge?
¹⁷You, who swelter in your clothes
when calm lies over the land from
the south,
¹⁸Can you with him spread out the
firmament of the skies,
hard as a molten mirror?
¹⁹Teach us then what we shall say to
him;
we cannot, for the darkness, make
our plea.
²⁰Will he be told about it when I
speak?
Can anyone talk when he is being
destroyed?
²¹Rather, it is as the light that cannot
be seen
while it is obscured by the clouds,
till the wind comes by and sweeps
them away.
²²From Zaphon the golden splendor
comes,
surrounding God's awesome
majesty!
²³The Almighty! We cannot find him,
preeminent in power and judgment,
abundant in justice, who never
oppresses.
²⁴Therefore people fear him;
none can see him, however wise
their hearts.

☐ TITUS 2

Christian Behavior. 2:1 As for yourself,
you must say what is consistent with sound
doctrine, namely, ²that older men should
be temperate, dignified, self-controlled,
sound in faith, love, and endurance. ³Similarly, older women should be reverent in
their behavior, not slanderers, not addicted
to drink, teaching what is good, ⁴so that
they may train younger women to love
their husbands and children, ⁵to be self-controlled, chaste, good homemakers, under the control of their husbands, so that
the word of God may not be discredited.

⁶Urge the younger men, similarly, to
control themselves, ⁷showing yourself as a
model of good deeds in every respect, with
integrity in your teaching, dignity, ⁸and
sound speech that cannot be criticized, so
that the opponent will be put to shame
without anything bad to say about us.

⁹Slaves are to be under the control of
their masters in all respects, giving them

satisfaction, not talking back to them [10]or stealing from them, but exhibiting complete good faith, so as to adorn the doctrine of God our savior in every way.

Transformation of Life. [11]For the grace of God has appeared, saving all [12]and training us to reject godless ways and worldly desires and to live temperately, justly, and devoutly in this age, [13]as we await the blessed hope, the appearance of the glory of the great God and of our savior Jesus Christ, [14]who gave himself for us to deliver us from all lawlessness and to cleanse for himself a people as his own, eager to do what is good.

[15]Say these things. Exhort and correct with all authority. Let no one look down on you.

June 30

The First Martyrs of the Church of Rome

The martyrs were bound, imprisoned, scourged, racked, burned, torn apart, butchered — and they multiplied.

— St. Augustine of Hippo

☐ JOB 38-42

38:1 Then the Lord answered Job out of the storm and said:

[2]Who is this who darkens counsel
    with words of ignorance?
[3]Gird up your loins now, like a man;
    I will question you, and you tell me
        the answers!
[4]Where were you when I founded the
        earth?
    Tell me, if you have understanding.
[5]Who determined its size? Surely you
        know?
    Who stretched out the measuring
        line for it?
[6]Into what were its pedestals sunk,
    and who laid its cornerstone,
[7]While the morning stars sang together
    and all the sons of God shouted for
        joy?
[8]Who shut within doors the sea,
    when it burst forth from the womb,
[9]When I made the clouds its garment
    and thick darkness its swaddling
        bands?

[10]When I set limits for it
    and fastened the bar of its door,
[11]And said: Thus far shall you come but
        no farther,
    and here shall your proud waves
        stop?
[12]Have you ever in your lifetime
        commanded the morning
    and shown the dawn its place
[13]For taking hold of the ends of the
        earth,
    till the wicked are shaken from it?
[14]The earth is changed as clay by the
        seal,
    and dyed like a garment;
[15]But from the wicked their light is
        withheld,
    and the arm of pride is shattered.
[16]Have you entered into the sources of
        the sea,
    or walked about on the bottom of
        the deep?
[17]Have the gates of death been shown
        to you,

or have you seen the gates of
darkness?
[18]Have you comprehended the breadth
of the earth?
Tell me, if you know it all.
[19]What is the way to the dwelling of
light,
and darkness—where is its place?
[20]That you may take it to its territory
and know the paths to its home?
[21]You know, because you were born
then,
and the number of your days is
great!
[22]Have you entered the storehouses of
the snow,
and seen the storehouses of the hail
[23]Which I have reserved for times of
distress,
for a day of war and battle?
[24]What is the way to the parting of the
winds,
where the east wind spreads over the
earth?
[25]Who has laid out a channel for the
downpour
and a path for the thunderstorm
[26]To bring rain to uninhabited land,
the unpeopled wilderness;
[27]To drench the desolate wasteland
till the desert blooms with verdure?
[28]Has the rain a father?
Who has begotten the drops of dew?
[29]Out of whose womb comes the ice,
and who gives the hoarfrost its birth
in the skies,
[30]When the waters lie covered as
though with stone
that holds captive the surface of the
deep?
[31]Have you tied cords to the Pleiades,
or loosened the bonds of Orion?
[32]Can you bring forth the Mazzaroth
in their season,
or guide the Bear with her children?
[33]Do you know the ordinances of the
heavens;

can you put into effect their plan on
the earth?
[34]Can you raise your voice to the
clouds,
for them to cover you with a deluge
of waters?
[35]Can you send forth the lightnings on
their way,
so that they say to you, "Here we
are"?
[36]Who gives wisdom to the ibis,
and gives the rooster understanding?
[37]Who counts the clouds with wisdom?
Who tilts the water jars of heaven
[38]So that the dust of earth is fused into
a mass
and its clods stick together?
[39]Do you hunt the prey for the lion
or appease the hunger of young
lions,
[40]While they crouch in their dens,
or lie in ambush in the thicket?
[41]Who provides nourishment for the
raven
when its young cry out to God,
wandering about without food?

39:1 Do you know when mountain
goats are born,
or watch for the birth pangs of deer,
[2]Number the months that they must
fulfill,
or know when they give birth,
[3]When they crouch down and drop
their young,
when they deliver their progeny?
[4]Their offspring thrive and grow in the
open,
they leave and do not return.
[5]Who has given the wild donkey his
freedom,
and who has loosed the wild ass
from bonds?
[6]I have made the wilderness his home
and the salt flats his dwelling.
[7]He scoffs at the uproar of the city,
hears no shouts of a driver.

⁸He ranges the mountains for pasture,
and seeks out every patch of green.
⁹Will the wild ox consent to serve you,
or pass the nights at your manger?
¹⁰Will you bind the wild ox with a rope
in the furrow,
and will he plow the valleys after
you?
¹¹Will you depend on him for his great
strength
and leave to him the fruits of your
toil?
¹²Can you rely on him to bring in your
grain
and gather in the yield of your
threshing floor?
¹³The wings of the ostrich flap away;
her plumage is lacking in feathers.
¹⁴When she abandons her eggs on the
ground
and lets them warm in the sand,
¹⁵She forgets that a foot may crush
them,
that the wild beasts may trample
them;
¹⁶She cruelly disowns her young
and her labor is useless; she has no
fear.
¹⁷For God has withheld wisdom from
her
and given her no share in
understanding.
¹⁸Yet when she spreads her wings high,
she laughs at a horse and rider.
¹⁹Do you give the horse his strength,
and clothe his neck with a mane?
²⁰Do you make him quiver like a
locust,
while his thunderous snorting
spreads terror?
²¹He paws the valley, he rejoices in his
strength,
and charges into battle.
²²He laughs at fear and cannot be
terrified;
he does not retreat from the sword.
²³Around him rattles the quiver,
flashes the spear and the javelin.
²⁴Frenzied and trembling he devours
the ground;
he does not hold back at the sound
of the trumpet;
²⁵at the trumpet's call he cries, "Aha!"
Even from afar he scents the battle,
the roar of the officers and the
shouting.
²⁶Is it by your understanding that the
hawk soars,
that he spreads his wings toward the
south?
²⁷Does the eagle fly up at your
command
to build his nest up high?
²⁸On a cliff he dwells and spends the
night,
on the spur of cliff or fortress.
²⁹From there he watches for his food;
his eyes behold it afar off.
³⁰His young ones greedily drink blood;
where the slain are, there is he.

40:1 The Lord then answered Job and said:

²Will one who argues with the
Almighty be corrected?
Let him who would instruct God
give answer!

³Then Job answered the Lord and said:

⁴Look, I am of little account; what can
I answer you?
I put my hand over my mouth.
⁵I have spoken once, I will not reply;
twice, but I will do so no more.

⁶Then the Lord answered Job out of the
storm and said:

⁷Gird up your loins now, like a man.
I will question you, and you tell me
the answers!
⁸Would you refuse to acknowledge my
right?
Would you condemn me that you
may be justified?

⁹Have you an arm like that of God,
  or can you thunder with a voice like
      his?
¹⁰Adorn yourself with grandeur and
      majesty,
  and clothe yourself with glory and
      splendor.
¹¹Let loose the fury of your wrath;
  look at everyone who is proud and
      bring them down.
¹²Look at everyone who is proud, and
      humble them.
  Tear down the wicked in their place,
    ¹³bury them in the dust together;
  in the hidden world imprison them.
¹⁴Then will I too praise you,
  for your own right hand can save
      you.
¹⁵Look at Behemoth, whom I made
      along with you,
  who feeds on grass like an ox.
¹⁶See the strength in his loins,
  the power in the sinews of his belly.
¹⁷He carries his tail like a cedar;
  the sinews of his thighs are like
      cables.
¹⁸His bones are like tubes of bronze;
  his limbs are like iron rods.
¹⁹He is the first of God's ways,
  only his maker can approach him
      with a sword.
²⁰For the mountains bring him
      produce,
  and all wild animals make sport
      there.
²¹Under lotus trees he lies,
  in coverts of the reedy swamp.
²²The lotus trees cover him with their
      shade;
  all about him are the poplars in the
      wadi.
²³If the river grows violent, he is not
      disturbed;
  he is tranquil though the Jordan
      surges about his mouth.
²⁴Who can capture him by his eyes,
  or pierce his nose with a trap?

²⁵Can you lead Leviathan about with
      a hook,
  or tie down his tongue with a rope?
²⁶Can you put a ring into his nose,
  or pierce through his cheek with a
      gaff?
²⁷Will he then plead with you, time
      after time,
  or address you with tender words?
²⁸Will he make a covenant with you
  that you may have him as a slave
      forever?
²⁹Can you play with him, as with a
      bird?
  Can you tie him up for your little
      girls?
³⁰Will the traders bargain for him?
  Will the merchants divide him up?
³¹Can you fill his hide with barbs,
  or his head with fish spears?
³²Once you but lay a hand upon him,
  no need to recall any other conflict!

41:1 Whoever might vainly hope to
      do so
  need only see him to be overthrown.
²No one is fierce enough to arouse him;
  who then dares stand before me?
³Whoever has assailed me, I will pay
      back—
  Everything under the heavens is
      mine.
⁴I need hardly mention his limbs,
  his strength, and the fitness of his
      equipment.
⁵Who can strip off his outer garment,
  or penetrate his double armor?
⁶Who can force open the doors of his
      face,
  close to his terrible teeth?
⁷Rows of scales are on his back,
  tightly sealed together;
⁸They are fitted so close to each other
  that no air can come between them;
⁹So joined to one another
  that they hold fast and cannot be
      parted.

¹⁰When he sneezes, light flashes forth;
 his eyes are like the eyelids of the
 dawn.
¹¹Out of his mouth go forth torches;
 sparks of fire leap forth.
¹²From his nostrils comes smoke
 as from a seething pot or bowl.
¹³His breath sets coals afire;
 a flame comes from his mouth.
¹⁴Strength abides in his neck,
 and power leaps before him.
¹⁵The folds of his flesh stick together,
 it is cast over him and immovable.
¹⁶His heart is cast as hard as stone;
 cast as the lower millstone.
¹⁷When he rises up, the gods are afraid;
 when he crashes down, they fall back.
¹⁸Should a sword reach him, it will not
 avail;
 nor will spear, dart, or javelin.
¹⁹He regards iron as chaff,
 and bronze as rotten wood.
²⁰No arrow will put him to flight;
 slingstones used against him are but
 straw.
²¹Clubs he regards as straw;
 he laughs at the crash of the spear.
²²Under him are sharp pottery
 fragments,
 spreading a threshing sledge upon
 the mire.
²³He makes the depths boil like a pot;
 he makes the sea like a perfume
 bottle.
²⁴Behind him he leaves a shining path;
 you would think the deep had white
 hair.
²⁵Upon the earth there is none like him,
 he was made fearless.
²⁶He looks over all who are haughty,
 he is king over all proud beasts.

42:1 Then Job answered the LORD and said:

²I know that you can do all things,
 and that no purpose of yours can be
 hindered.

³"Who is this who obscures counsel
 with ignorance?"
I have spoken but did not understand;
 things too marvelous for me, which
 I did not know.
⁴"Listen, and I will speak;
 I will question you, and you tell me the
 answers."
⁵By hearsay I had heard of you,
 but now my eye has seen you.
⁶Therefore I disown what I have said,
 and repent in dust and ashes.

Job's Restoration. ⁷And after the LORD had spoken these words to Job, the LORD said to Eliphaz the Temanite, "My anger blazes against you and your two friends! You have not spoken rightly concerning me, as has my servant Job. ⁸So now take seven bulls and seven rams, and go to my servant Job, and sacrifice a burnt offering for yourselves, and let my servant Job pray for you. To him I will show favor, and not punish your folly, for you have not spoken rightly concerning me, as has my servant Job." ⁹Then Eliphaz the Temanite, and Bildad the Shuhite, and Zophar the Naamathite, went and did as the LORD had commanded them. The LORD showed favor to Job.

¹⁰The LORD also restored the prosperity of Job, after he had prayed for his friends; the LORD even gave to Job twice as much as he had before. ¹¹Then all his brothers and sisters came to him, and all his former acquaintances, and they dined with him in his house. They consoled and comforted him for all the evil the LORD had brought upon him, and each one gave him a piece of money and a gold ring.

¹²Thus the LORD blessed the later days of Job more than his earlier ones. Now he had fourteen thousand sheep, six thousand camels, a thousand yoke of oxen, and a thousand she-donkeys. ¹³He also had seven sons and three daughters: ¹⁴the first daughter he called Jemimah, the second Keziah,

and the third Keren-happuch. [15]In all the land no other women were as beautiful as the daughters of Job; and their father gave them an inheritance among their brothers.

[16]After this, Job lived a hundred and forty years; and he saw his children, his grandchildren, and even his great-grandchildren. [17]Then Job died, old and full of years.

☐ TITUS 3

3:1 Remind them to be under the control of magistrates and authorities, to be obedient, to be open to every good enterprise. [2]They are to slander no one, to be peaceable, considerate, exercising all graciousness toward everyone. [3]For we ourselves were once foolish, disobedient, deluded, slaves to various desires and pleasures, living in malice and envy, hateful ourselves and hating one another.

[4]But when the kindness and generous
    love
of God our savior appeared,
[5]not because of any righteous deeds we
    had done
but because of his mercy,
he saved us through the bath of rebirth
    and renewal by the holy Spirit,
[6]whom he richly poured out on us
    through Jesus Christ our savior,
[7]so that we might be justified by his
    grace
    and become heirs in hope of eternal
    life.

[8]This saying is trustworthy.

Advice to Titus. I want you to insist on these points, that those who have believed in God be careful to devote themselves to good works; these are excellent and beneficial to others. [9]Avoid foolish arguments, genealogies, rivalries, and quarrels about the law, for they are useless and futile. [10]After a first and second warning, break off contact with a heretic, [11]realizing that such a person is perverted and sinful and stands self-condemned.

Directives, Greetings, and Blessing. [12]When I send Artemas to you, or Tychicus, try to join me at Nicopolis, where I have decided to spend the winter. [13]Send Zenas the lawyer and Apollos on their journey soon, and see to it that they have everything they need. [14]But let our people, too, learn to devote themselves to good works to supply urgent needs, so that they may not be unproductive.

[15]All who are with me send you greetings. Greet those who love us in the faith.

Grace be with all of you.

July 1

As iron is fashioned by the fire and on an anvil, so in the fire of suffering and under the weight of trials, our souls receive the form that Our Lord desires for them to have.

— St. Madeleine Sophie Barat

☐ PSALMS 1-5

True Happiness in God's Law. 1:1

Blessed is the man who does not walk
  in the counsel of the wicked,
Nor stand in the way of sinners,
  nor sit in company with scoffers.
²Rather, the law of the LORD is his joy;
  and on his law he meditates day and
    night.
³He is like a tree
  planted near streams of water,
  that yields its fruit in season;
Its leaves never wither;
  whatever he does prospers.

⁴But not so are the wicked, not so!
  They are like chaff driven by the
    wind.
⁵Therefore the wicked will not arise at
    the judgment,
  nor will sinners in the assembly of
    the just.
⁶Because the LORD knows the way of
    the just,
  but the way of the wicked leads to
    ruin.

A Psalm for a Royal Coronation. 2:1

Why do the nations protest
  and the peoples conspire in vain?
²Kings on earth rise up
  and princes plot together
  against the LORD and against his
    anointed one:
³"Let us break their shackles
  and cast off their chains from us!"
⁴The one enthroned in heaven laughs;
  the Lord derides them,

⁵Then he speaks to them in his anger,
  in his wrath he terrifies them:
⁶"I myself have installed my king
  on Zion, my holy mountain."
⁷I will proclaim the decree of the
    LORD,
  he said to me, "You are my son;
  today I have begotten you.
⁸Ask it of me,
  and I will give you the nations as
    your inheritance,
  and, as your possession, the ends of
    the earth.
⁹With an iron rod you will shepherd
    them,
  like a potter's vessel you will shatter
    them."
¹⁰And now, kings, give heed;
  take warning, judges on earth.
¹¹Serve the LORD with fear;
  exult with trembling,
Accept correction
  lest he become angry and you perish
    along the way
  when his anger suddenly blazes up.
Blessed are all who take refuge in him!

Threatened but Trusting. 3:1 A psalm of
David, when he fled from his son Absalom.

²How many are my foes, LORD!
  How many rise against me!
³How many say of me,
  "There is no salvation for him in God."
    Selah
⁴But you, LORD, are a shield around me;
  my glory, you keep my head high.

⁵With my own voice I will call out to
the LORD,
and he will answer me from his holy
mountain.
Selah

⁶I lie down and I fall asleep,
[and] I will wake up, for the LORD
sustains me.
⁷I do not fear, then, thousands of
people
arrayed against me on every side.

⁸Arise, LORD! Save me, my God!
For you strike the cheekbone of all
my foes;
you break the teeth of the wicked.
⁹Salvation is from the LORD!
May your blessing be upon your
people!
Selah

Trust in God. 4:1 For the leader; with
stringed instruments. A psalm of David.

²Answer me when I call, my saving
God.
When troubles hem me in, set me
free;
take pity on me, hear my prayer.

³How long, O people, will you be hard
of heart?
Why do you love what is worthless,
chase after lies?
Selah

⁴Know that the LORD works wonders
for his faithful one;
The LORD hears when I call out to
him.
⁵Tremble and sin no more;
weep bitterly within your hearts,
wail upon your beds,
⁶Offer fitting sacrifices
and trust in the LORD.

⁷Many say, "May we see better times!
LORD, show us the light of your
face!"
Selah

⁸But you have given my heart more joy
than they have when grain and wine
abound.
⁹In peace I will lie down and fall asleep,
for you alone, LORD, make me
secure.

Prayer for Divine Help. 5:1 For the leader;
with wind instruments. A psalm of David.

²Give ear to my words, O LORD;
understand my sighing.
³Attend to the sound of my cry,
my king and my God!
For to you I will pray, LORD;
⁴in the morning you will hear my
voice;
in the morning I will plead before
you and wait.

⁵You are not a god who delights in evil;
no wicked person finds refuge with
you;
⁶the arrogant cannot stand before
your eyes.
You hate all who do evil;
⁷you destroy those who speak falsely.
A bloody and fraudulent man
the LORD abhors.

⁸But I, through the abundance of your
mercy,
will enter into your house.
I will bow down toward your holy
sanctuary
out of fear of you.
⁹LORD, guide me in your justice
because of my foes;
make straight your way before me.

¹⁰For there is no sincerity in their mouth;
their heart is corrupt.
Their throat is an open grave;
on their tongue are subtle lies.
¹¹Declare them guilty, God;
make them fall by their own
devices.
Drive them out for their many sins;
for they have rebelled against you.

¹²Then all who trust in you will be glad
and forever shout for joy.
You will protect them and those will
rejoice in you

who love your name.
¹³For you, LORD, bless the just one;
you surround him with favor like a
shield.

☐ 2 CORINTHIANS 1:1-2:4

Greeting. 1:1 Paul, an apostle of Christ Jesus by the will of God, and Timothy our brother, to the church of God that is in Corinth, with all the holy ones throughout Achaia: ²grace to you and peace from God our Father and the Lord Jesus Christ.

Thanksgiving. ³Blessed be the God and Father of our Lord Jesus Christ, the Father of compassion and God of all encouragement, ⁴who encourages us in our every affliction, so that we may be able to encourage those who are in any affliction with the encouragement with which we ourselves are encouraged by God. ⁵For as Christ's sufferings overflow to us, so through Christ does our encouragement also overflow. ⁶If we are afflicted, it is for your encouragement and salvation; if we are encouraged, it is for your encouragement, which enables you to endure the same sufferings that we suffer. ⁷Our hope for you is firm, for we know that as you share in the sufferings, you also share in the encouragement.

⁸We do not want you to be unaware, brothers, of the affliction that came to us in the province of Asia; we were utterly weighed down beyond our strength, so that we despaired even of life. ⁹Indeed, we had accepted within ourselves the sentence of death, that we might trust not in ourselves but in God who raises the dead. ¹⁰He rescued us from such great danger of death, and he will continue to rescue us; in him we have put our hope [that] he will also rescue us again, ¹¹as you help us with prayer, so that thanks may be given by many on our behalf for the gift granted us through the prayers of many.

Paul's Sincerity and Constancy. ¹²For our boast is this, the testimony of our conscience that we have conducted ourselves in the world, and especially toward you, with the simplicity and sincerity of God, [and] not by human wisdom but by the grace of God. ¹³For we write you nothing but what you can read and understand, and I hope that you will understand completely, ¹⁴as you have come to understand us partially, that we are your boast as you also are ours, on the day of [our] Lord Jesus.

¹⁵With this confidence I formerly intended to come to you so that you might receive a double favor, ¹⁶namely, to go by way of you to Macedonia, and then to come to you again on my return from Macedonia, and have you send me on my way to Judea. ¹⁷So when I intended this, did I act lightly? Or do I make my plans according to human considerations, so that with me it is "yes, yes" and "no, no"? ¹⁸As God is faithful, our word to you is not "yes" and "no." ¹⁹For the Son of God, Jesus Christ, who was proclaimed to you by us, Silvanus and Timothy and me, was not "yes" and "no," but "yes" has been in him. ²⁰For however many are the promises of God, their Yes is in him; therefore, the Amen from us also goes through him to God for glory. ²¹But the one who gives us security with you in Christ and who anointed us is God; ²²he has also put his seal upon us and given the Spirit in our hearts as a first installment.

Paul's Change of Plan. ²³But I call upon God as witness, on my life, that it is to spare you that I have not yet gone to Corinth. ²⁴Not that we lord it over your faith; rather, we work together for your joy, for you stand firm in the faith.

2:1 For I decided not to come to you again in painful circumstances. ²For if I inflict pain upon you, then who is there to cheer me except the one pained by me? ³And I wrote as I did so that when I came I might not be pained by those in whom I should have rejoiced, confident about all of you that my joy is that of all of you. ⁴For out of much affliction and anguish of heart I wrote to you with many tears, not that you might be pained but that you might know the abundant love I have for you.

July 2

One must deal with some sinners as with snails: Put them first in cool water until they come out, and then cook them little by little before they realize what's happening to them.

— St. Anthony Mary Claret

☐ PSALMS 6–10

Prayer in Distress. 6:1 For the leader; with stringed instruments, "upon the eighth."
   A psalm of David.

²Do not reprove me in your anger,
   Lord,
      nor punish me in your wrath.
³Have pity on me, Lord, for I am weak;
      heal me, Lord, for my bones are
         shuddering.
⁴My soul too is shuddering greatly—
      and you, Lord, how long…?
⁵Turn back, Lord, rescue my soul;
      save me because of your mercy.
⁶For in death there is no remembrance
      of you.
   Who praises you in Sheol?

⁷I am wearied with sighing;
      all night long I drench my bed with
         tears;
   I soak my couch with weeping.
⁸My eyes are dimmed with sorrow,
      worn out because of all my foes.

⁹Away from me, all who do evil!
   The Lord has heard the sound of
      my weeping.
¹⁰The Lord has heard my plea;

   The Lord will receive my prayer.
¹¹My foes will all be disgraced and will
      shudder greatly;
      they will turn back in sudden
         disgrace.

God the Vindicator. 7:1 A plaintive song of David, which he sang to the Lord concerning Cush, the Benjaminite.

²Lord my God, in you I trusted;
      save me; rescue me from all who
         pursue me,
³Lest someone maul me like a lion,
      tear my soul apart with no one to
         deliver.

⁴Lord my God, if I have done this,
      if there is guilt on my hands,
⁵If I have maltreated someone treating
      me equitably—
   or even despoiled my oppressor
         without cause—
⁶Then let my enemy pursue and
         overtake my soul,
      trample my life to the ground,
      and lay my honor in the dust.
                                    Selah

7Rise up, LORD, in your anger;
    be aroused against the outrages of
      my oppressors.
    Stir up the justice, my God, you
      have commanded.
8Have the assembly of the peoples
      gather about you;
    and return on high above them,
    9the LORD will pass judgment on
      the peoples.
Judge me, LORD, according to my
      righteousness,
    and my integrity.
10Let the malice of the wicked end.
    Uphold the just one,
    O just God,
    who tries hearts and minds.

11God is a shield above me
    saving the upright of heart.
12God is a just judge, powerful and
      patient,
    not exercising anger every day.
13If one does not repent,
    God sharpens his sword,
    strings and readies the bow,
14Prepares his deadly shafts,
    makes arrows blazing thunderbolts.
15Consider how one conceives
      iniquity;
    is pregnant with mischief,
    and gives birth to deception.
16He digs a hole and bores it deep,
    but he falls into the pit he has made.
17His malice turns back upon his head;
    his violence falls on his own skull.
18I will thank the LORD in accordance
    with his justice;
    I will sing the name of the LORD
      Most High.

Divine Majesty and Human Dignity. 8:1
For the leader; "upon the *gittith*." A psalm
of David.

2O LORD, our Lord,
    how awesome is your name through
      all the earth!

I will sing of your majesty above the
      heavens
3with the mouths of babes and
      infants.
You have established a bulwark against
      your foes,
    to silence enemy and avenger.

4When I see your heavens, the work of
      your fingers,
    the moon and stars that you set in
      place—
5What is man that you are mindful of
      him,
    and a son of man that you care for him?
6Yet you have made him little less than
      a god,
    crowned him with glory and honor.
7You have given him rule over the
      works of your hands,
    put all things at his feet:
8All sheep and oxen,
    even the beasts of the field,
9The birds of the air, the fish of the sea,
    and whatever swims the paths of the
      seas.

10O LORD, our Lord,
    how awesome is your name through
      all the earth!

Thanksgiving for Victory and Prayer for Justice. 9:1 For the leader; according to *Muth Labben*. A psalm of David.

2I will praise you, LORD, with all my
      heart;
    I will declare all your wondrous
      deeds.
3I will delight and rejoice in you;
    I will sing hymns to your name,
      Most High.
4When my enemies turn back,
    they stumble and perish before you.

5For you upheld my right and my
      cause,
    seated on your throne, judging
      justly.

⁶You rebuked the nations, you
  destroyed the wicked;
  their name you blotted out for all
  time.
⁷The enemies have been ruined forever;
  you destroyed their cities;
  their memory has perished.

⁸The LORD rules forever,
  has set up his throne for judgment.
⁹It is he who judges the world with
  justice,
  who judges the peoples with fairness.
¹⁰The LORD is a stronghold for the
  oppressed,
  a stronghold in times of trouble.
¹¹Those who know your name trust in
  you;
  you never forsake those who seek
  you, LORD.

¹²Sing hymns to the LORD enthroned
  on Zion;
  proclaim his deeds among the
  nations!
¹³For the avenger of bloodshed
  remembers,
  does not forget the cry of the
  afflicted.

¹⁴Be gracious to me, LORD;
  see how my foes afflict me!
  You alone can raise me from the
  gates of death.
¹⁵Then I will declare all your praises,
  sing joyously of your salvation
  in the gates of daughter Zion.

¹⁶The nations fall into the pit they dig;
  in the snare they hide, their own
  foot is caught.
¹⁷The LORD is revealed in making
  judgments:
  by the deeds they do the wicked are
  trapped.
              Higgaion. Selah

¹⁸To Sheol the wicked will depart,
  all the nations that forget God.

¹⁹For the needy will never be forgotten,
  nor will the hope of the afflicted
  ever fade.
²⁰Arise, LORD, let no mortal prevail;
  let the nations be judged in your
  presence.
²¹Strike them with terror, LORD;
  show the nations they are only
  human.
              Selah

10:1 Why, LORD, do you stand afar
  and pay no heed in times of
  trouble?
²Arrogant scoundrels pursue the poor;
  they trap them by their cunning
  schemes.

³The wicked even boast of their greed;
  these robbers curse and scorn the
  LORD.
⁴In their insolence the wicked boast:
  "God does not care; there is no God."
⁵Yet their affairs always succeed;
  they ignore your judgment on high;
  they sneer at all who oppose them.
⁶They say in their hearts, "We will
  never fall;
  never will we see misfortune."
⁷Their mouths are full of oaths,
  violence, and lies;
  discord and evil are under their
  tongues.
⁸They wait in ambush near towns;
  their eyes watch for the helpless
  to murder the innocent in secret.
⁹They lurk in ambush like lions in a
  thicket,
  hide there to trap the poor,
  snare them and close the net.
¹⁰The helpless are crushed, laid low;
  they fall into the power of the
  wicked,
¹¹Who say in their hearts, "God has
  forgotten,
  shows no concern, never bothers to
  look."

¹²Rise up, LORD! God, lift up your
  hand!
  Do not forget the poor!
¹³Why should the wicked scorn God,
  say in their hearts, "God does not
    care"?
¹⁴But you do see;
  you take note of misery and sorrow;
  you take the matter in hand.
To you the helpless can entrust their
    cause;
  you are the defender of orphans.
¹⁵Break the arm of the wicked and
    depraved;

make them account for their crimes;
  let none of them survive.
¹⁶The LORD is king forever;
  the nations have vanished from his
    land.
¹⁷You listen, LORD, to the needs of the
    poor;
  you strengthen their heart and
    incline your ear.
¹⁸You win justice for the orphaned and
    oppressed;
  no one on earth will cause terror
    again.

☐ 2 CORINTHIANS 2:5-17

The Offender. 2:5 If anyone has caused pain, he has caused it not to me, but in some measure (not to exaggerate) to all of you. ⁶This punishment by the majority is enough for such a person, ⁷so that on the contrary you should forgive and encourage him instead, or else the person may be overwhelmed by excessive pain. ⁸Therefore, I urge you to reaffirm your love for him. ⁹For this is why I wrote, to know your proven character, whether you were obedient in everything. ¹⁰Whomever you forgive anything, so do I. For indeed what I have forgiven, if I have forgiven anything, has been for you in the presence of Christ, ¹¹so that we might not be taken advantage of by Satan, for we are not unaware of his purposes.

Paul's Anxiety. ¹²When I went to Troas for the gospel of Christ, although a door was opened for me in the Lord, ¹³I had no relief in my spirit because I did not find my brother Titus. So I took leave of them and went on to Macedonia.

Ministers of a New Covenant. ¹⁴But thanks be to God, who always leads us in triumph in Christ and manifests through us the odor of the knowledge of him in every place. ¹⁵For we are the aroma of Christ for God among those who are being saved and among those who are perishing, ¹⁶to the latter an odor of death that leads to death, to the former an odor of life that leads to life. Who is qualified for this? ¹⁷For we are not like the many who trade on the word of God; but as out of sincerity, indeed as from God and in the presence of God, we speak in Christ.

July 3

St. Thomas

The disbelief of Thomas has done more for our faith than the faith of the other disciples. As he touches Christ and is won over to belief, every doubt is cast aside and our faith is strengthened.

— POPE ST. GREGORY THE GREAT

☐ PSALMS 11–15

Confidence in the Presence of God. 11:1
For the leader. Of David.

In the LORD I take refuge;
how can you say to me,
"Flee like a bird to the mountains!
²See how the wicked string their bows,
fit their arrows to the string
to shoot from the shadows at the
upright of heart.
³If foundations are destroyed,
what can the just one do?"

⁴The LORD is in his holy temple;
The LORD's throne is in heaven.
God's eyes keep careful watch;
they test the children of Adam.
⁵The LORD tests the righteous and the
wicked,
hates those who love violence,
⁶And rains upon the wicked
fiery coals and brimstone,
a scorching wind their allotted cup.
⁷The LORD is just and loves just deeds;
the upright will see his face.

Prayer Against Evil Tongues. 12:1 For the
leader; "upon the eighth." A psalm of David.

²Help, LORD, for no one loyal remains;
the faithful have vanished from the
children of men.
³They tell lies to one another,
speak with deceiving lips and a
double heart.

⁴May the LORD cut off all deceiving lips,
and every boastful tongue,

⁵Those who say, "By our tongues we
prevail;
when our lips speak, who can lord it
over us?"

⁶"Because they rob the weak, and the
needy groan,
I will now arise," says the LORD;
"I will grant safety to whoever longs
for it."

⁷The promises of the LORD are sure,
silver refined in a crucible,
silver purified seven times.
⁸You, O LORD, protect us always;
preserve us from this generation.
⁹On every side the wicked roam;
the shameless are extolled by the
children of men.

Prayer for Help. 13:1 For the leader. A
psalm of David.

²How long, LORD? Will you utterly
forget me?
How long will you hide your face
from me?
³How long must I carry sorrow in my
soul,
grief in my heart day after day?
How long will my enemy triumph
over me?

⁴Look upon me, answer me, LORD,
my God!
Give light to my eyes lest I sleep in
death,
⁵Lest my enemy say, "I have prevailed,"

lest my foes rejoice at my downfall.

⁶But I trust in your mercy.
Grant my heart joy in your salvation,
I will sing to the LORD,
for he has dealt bountifully with me!

A Lament over Widespread Corruption.
14:1 For the leader. Of David.

The fool says in his heart,
"There is no God."
Their deeds are loathsome and corrupt;
not one does what is good.
²The LORD looks down from heaven
upon the children of men,
To see if even one is wise,
if even one seeks God.
³All have gone astray;
all alike are perverse.
Not one does what is good,
not even one.

⁴Will these evildoers never learn?
They devour my people as they
devour bread;
they do not call upon the LORD.
⁵They have good reason, then, to fear;
God is with the company of the just.
⁶They would crush the hopes of the poor,

but the poor have the LORD as their
refuge.

⁷Oh, that from Zion might come
the salvation of Israel!
Jacob would rejoice, and Israel be glad
when the LORD restores his people!

The Righteous Israelite. **15:1** A psalm of David.

LORD, who may abide in your tent?
Who may dwell on your holy
mountain?

²Whoever walks without blame,
doing what is right,
speaking truth from the heart;
³Who does not slander with his
tongue,
does no harm to a friend,
never defames a neighbor;
⁴Who disdains the wicked,
but honors those who fear the LORD;
Who keeps an oath despite the cost,
⁵lends no money at interest,
accepts no bribe against the
innocent.
Whoever acts like this
shall never be shaken.

☐ 2 CORINTHIANS 3

3:1 Are we beginning to commend our-selves again? Or do we need, as some do, letters of recommendation to you or from you? ²You are our letter, written on our hearts, known and read by all, ³shown to be a letter of Christ administered by us, written not in ink but by the Spirit of the living God, not on tablets of stone but on tablets that are hearts of flesh.

⁴Such confidence we have through Christ toward God. ⁵Not that of ourselves we are qualified to take credit for anything as coming from us; rather, our qualification comes from God, ⁶who has indeed quali-fied us as ministers of a new covenant, not of letter but of spirit; for the letter brings death, but the Spirit gives life.

Contrast with the Old Covenant. ⁷Now if the ministry of death, carved in letters on stone, was so glorious that the Israelites could not look intently at the face of Moses because of its glory that was go-ing to fade, ⁸how much more will the min-istry of the Spirit be glorious? ⁹For if the ministry of condemnation was glorious, the ministry of righteousness will abound much more in glory. ¹⁰Indeed, what was endowed with glory has come to have no glory in this respect because of the glory that surpasses it. [11]For if what was going to fade was glorious, how much more will what endures be glorious.

[12]Therefore, since we have such hope, we act very boldly [13]and not like Moses, who put a veil over his face so that the Israelites could not look intently at the cessation of what was fading. [14]Rather, their thoughts were rendered dull, for to this present day the same veil remains unlifted when they read the old covenant, because through Christ it is taken away. [15]To this day, in fact, whenever Moses is read, a veil lies over their hearts, [16]but whenever a person turns to the Lord the veil is removed. [17]Now the Lord is the Spirit, and where the Spirit of the Lord is, there is freedom. [18]All of us, gazing with unveiled face on the glory of the Lord, are being transformed into the same image from glory to glory, as from the Lord who is the Spirit.

July 4

St. Elizabeth of Portugal

The world would have peace if only the men of politics would follow the Gospels.

— St. Bridget of Sweden

☐ PSALMS 16-20

God the Supreme Good. 16:1 A *miktam* of David.

Keep me safe, O God;
   in you I take refuge.
[2]I say to the Lord,
   you are my Lord,
   you are my only good.
[3]As for the holy ones who are in the land,
   they are noble,
   in whom is all my delight.
[4]They multiply their sorrows
   who court other gods.
Blood libations to them I will not pour out,
   nor will I take their names upon my lips.
[5]Lord, my allotted portion and my cup,
   you have made my destiny secure.
[6]Pleasant places were measured out for me;
   fair to me indeed is my inheritance.

[7]I bless the Lord who counsels me;
   even at night my heart exhorts me.
[8]I keep the Lord always before me;
   with him at my right hand, I shall never be shaken.
[9]Therefore my heart is glad, my soul rejoices;
   my body also dwells secure,
[10]For you will not abandon my soul to Sheol,
   nor let your devout one see the pit.
[11]You will show me the path to life,
   abounding joy in your presence,
   the delights at your right hand forever.

Prayer for Rescue from Persecutors. 17:1 A prayer of David.

Hear, Lord, my plea for justice;
   pay heed to my cry;
Listen to my prayer
   from lips without guile.
[2]From you let my vindication come;
   your eyes see what is right.
[3]You have tested my heart,

searched it in the night.
You have tried me by fire,
　but find no malice in me.
My mouth has not transgressed
　⁴as others often do.
As your lips have instructed me,
　I have kept from the way of the
　　lawless.
⁵My steps have kept to your paths;
　my feet have not faltered.

⁶I call upon you; answer me, O God.
　Turn your ear to me; hear my speech.
⁷Show your wonderful mercy,
　you who deliver with your right arm
　those who seek refuge from their foes.
⁸Keep me as the apple of your eye;
　hide me in the shadow of your wings
　⁹from the wicked who despoil me.

My ravenous enemies press upon me;
　¹⁰they close their hearts,
　they fill their mouths with proud
　　roaring.
¹¹Their steps even now encircle me;
　they watch closely, keeping low to
　　the ground,
¹²Like lions eager for prey,
　like a young lion lurking in ambush.
¹³Rise, O Lord, confront and cast
　　them down;
　rescue my soul from the wicked.
¹⁴Slay them with your sword;
　with your hand, Lord, slay them;
　snatch them from the world in their
　　prime.
Their bellies are being filled with your
　　friends;
　their children are satisfied too,
　for they share what is left with their
　　young.
¹⁵I am just—let me see your face;
　when I awake, let me be filled with
　　your presence.

A King's Thanksgiving for Victory. **18:1**
For the leader. Of David, the servant of the
Lord, who sang to the Lord the words of

this song after the Lord had rescued him
from the clutches of all his enemies and
from the hand of Saul. ²He said:

I love you, Lord, my strength,
　³Lord, my rock, my fortress, my
　　deliverer,
My God, my rock of refuge,
　my shield, my saving horn, my
　　stronghold!
⁴Praised be the Lord, I exclaim!
　I have been delivered from my
　　enemies.

⁵The cords of death encompassed me;
　the torrents of destruction terrified
　　me.
⁶The cords of Sheol encircled me;
　the snares of death lay in wait
　　for me.
⁷In my distress I called out: Lord!
　I cried out to my God.
From his temple he heard my voice;
　my cry to him reached his ears.
⁸The earth rocked and shook;
　the foundations of the mountains
　　trembled;
　they shook as his wrath flared up.
⁹Smoke rose from his nostrils,
　a devouring fire from his mouth;
　it kindled coals into flame.
¹⁰He parted the heavens and came
　　down,
　a dark cloud under his feet.
¹¹Mounted on a cherub he flew,
　borne along on the wings of the
　　wind.
¹²He made darkness his cloak around
　　him;
　his canopy, water-darkened
　　stormclouds.
¹³From the gleam before him, his
　　clouds passed,
　hail and coals of fire.
¹⁴The Lord thundered from heaven;
　the Most High made his voice
　　resound.

¹⁵He let fly his arrows and scattered
  them;
    shot his lightning bolts and
      dispersed them.
¹⁶Then the bed of the sea appeared;
    the world's foundations lay bare,
At your rebuke, O Lord,
    at the storming breath of your
      nostrils.
¹⁷He reached down from on high and
  seized me;
    drew me out of the deep waters.
¹⁸He rescued me from my mighty
  enemy,
    from foes too powerful for me.
¹⁹They attacked me on my day of
  distress,
    but the Lord was my support.
²⁰He set me free in the open;
    he rescued me because he loves me.
²¹The Lord acknowledged my
  righteousness,
    rewarded my clean hands.
²²For I kept the ways of the Lord;
    I was not disloyal to my God.
²³For his laws were all before me,
    his decrees I did not cast aside.
²⁴I was honest toward him;
    I was on guard against sin.
²⁵So the Lord rewarded my
  righteousness,
    the cleanness of my hands in his sight.
²⁶Toward the faithful you are faithful;
    to the honest man you are honest;
²⁷Toward the pure, you are pure;
    but to the perverse you are devious.
²⁸For humble people you save;
    haughty eyes you bring low.
²⁹For you, Lord, give light to my lamp;
    my God brightens my darkness.
³⁰With you I can rush an armed band,
    with my God to help I can leap a wall.
³¹God's way is unerring;
    The Lord's promise is refined;
      he is a shield for all who take refuge
        in him.

³²Truly, who is God except the Lord?
    Who but our God is the rock?
³³This God who girded me with might,
    kept my way unerring,
³⁴Who made my feet like a deer's,
    and set me on the heights,
³⁵Who trained my hands for war,
    my arms to string a bow of bronze.
³⁶You have given me your saving shield;
    your right hand has upheld me;
      your favor made me great.
³⁷You made room for my steps beneath
  me;
    my ankles never twisted.
³⁸I pursued my enemies and overtook
  them;
    I did not turn back till I destroyed
      them.
³⁹I decimated them; they could not rise;
    they fell at my feet.
⁴⁰You girded me with valor for war,
    subjugated my opponents beneath
      me.
⁴¹You made my foes expose their necks
  to me;
    those who hated me I silenced.
⁴²They cried for help, but no one saved
  them;
    cried to the Lord but received no
      answer.
⁴³I ground them to dust before the
  wind;
    I left them like mud in the streets.
⁴⁴You rescued me from the strife of
  peoples;
    you made me head over nations.
A people I had not known served me;
    ⁴⁵as soon as they heard of me they
      obeyed.
Foreigners submitted before me;
    ⁴⁶foreigners cringed;
      they came cowering from their
        dungeons.

⁴⁷The Lord lives! Blessed be my rock!
    Exalted be God, my savior!
⁴⁸O God who granted me vengeance,

made peoples subject to me,
⁴⁹and saved me from my enemies,
Truly you have elevated me above my
    opponents,
    from a man of lawlessness you have
      rescued me.
⁵⁰Thus I will praise you, LORD, among
    the nations;
    I will sing praises to your name.
⁵¹You have given great victories to your
    king,
    and shown mercy to his anointed,
    to David and his posterity forever.

God's Glory in the Heavens and in the Law. 19:1 For the leader. A psalm of David.

²The heavens declare the glory of God;
    the firmament proclaims the works
      of his hands.
³Day unto day pours forth speech;
    night unto night whispers
      knowledge.
⁴There is no speech, no words;
    their voice is not heard;
⁵A report goes forth through all the
    earth,
    their messages, to the ends of the
      world.
He has pitched in them a tent for the
    sun;
⁶it comes forth like a bridegroom
    from his canopy,
    and like a hero joyfully runs its
      course.
⁷From one end of the heavens it comes
    forth;
    its course runs through to the other;
    nothing escapes its heat.

⁸The law of the LORD is perfect,
    refreshing the soul.
The decree of the LORD is trustworthy,
    giving wisdom to the simple.
⁹The precepts of the LORD are right,
    rejoicing the heart.
The command of the LORD is clear,
    enlightening the eye.

¹⁰The fear of the LORD is pure,
    enduring forever.
The statutes of the LORD are true,
    all of them just;
¹¹More desirable than gold,
    than a hoard of purest gold,
Sweeter also than honey
    or drippings from the comb.
¹²By them your servant is warned;
    obeying them brings much reward.
¹³Who can detect trespasses?
    Cleanse me from my inadvertent
      sins.
¹⁴Also from arrogant ones restrain your
    servant;
    let them never control me.
Then shall I be blameless,
    innocent of grave sin.
¹⁵Let the words of my mouth be
    acceptable,
    the thoughts of my heart before you,
    LORD, my rock and my redeemer.

Prayer for the King in Time of War. 20:1 For the leader. A psalm of David.

²The LORD answer you in time of
    distress;
    the name of the God of Jacob
      defend you!
³May he send you help from the
    sanctuary,
    from Zion be your support.
⁴May he remember your every offering,
    graciously accept your burnt offering,
              Selah
⁵Grant what is in your heart,
    fulfill your every plan.
⁶May we shout for joy at your victory,
    raise the banners in the name of our
      God.
    The LORD grant your every petition!

⁷Now I know the LORD gives victory
    to his anointed.
He will answer him from the holy
    heavens

with a strong arm that brings
victory.
⁸Some rely on chariots, others on horses,
but we on the name of the LORD
our God.

⁹They collapse and fall,
but we stand strong and firm.
¹⁰LORD, grant victory to the king;
answer when we call upon you.

☐ 2 CORINTHIANS 4:1-15

Integrity in the Ministry. 4:1 Therefore, since we have this ministry through the mercy shown us, we are not discouraged. ²Rather, we have renounced shameful, hidden things; not acting deceitfully or falsifying the word of God, but by the open declaration of the truth we commend ourselves to everyone's conscience in the sight of God. ³And even though our gospel is veiled, it is veiled for those who are perishing, ⁴in whose case the god of this age has blinded the minds of the unbelievers, so that they may not see the light of the gospel of the glory of Christ, who is the image of God. ⁵For we do not preach ourselves but Jesus Christ as Lord, and ourselves as your slaves for the sake of Jesus. ⁶For God who said, "Let light shine out of darkness," has shone in our hearts to bring to light the knowledge of the glory of God on the face of [Jesus] Christ.

The Paradox of the Ministry. ⁷But we hold this treasure in earthen vessels, that the surpassing power may be of God and not from us. ⁸We are afflicted in every way, but not constrained; perplexed, but not driven to despair; ⁹persecuted, but not abandoned; struck down, but not destroyed; ¹⁰always carrying about in the body the dying of Jesus, so that the life of Jesus may also be manifested in our body. ¹¹For we who live are constantly being given up to death for the sake of Jesus, so that the life of Jesus may be manifested in our mortal flesh.

¹²So death is at work in us, but life in you. ¹³Since, then, we have the same spirit of faith, according to what is written, "I believed, therefore I spoke," we too believe and therefore speak, ¹⁴knowing that the one who raised the Lord Jesus will raise us also with Jesus and place us with you in his presence. ¹⁵Everything indeed is for you, so that the grace bestowed in abundance on more and more people may cause the thanksgiving to overflow for the glory of God.

July 5

St. Anthony Mary Zaccaria

We should love and feel compassion for those who oppose us, since they harm themselves and do us good, and adorn us with crowns of everlasting glory.

— St. Anthony Mary Zaccaria

☐ PSALMS 21–25

Thanksgiving and Assurances for the King. **21:1** For the leader. A psalm of David.

²Lord, the king finds joy in your power;
in your victory how greatly he rejoices!
³You have granted him his heart's desire;
you did not refuse the request of his lips.

Selah

⁴For you welcomed him with goodly blessings;
you placed on his head a crown of pure gold.
⁵He asked life of you;
you gave it to him,
length of days forever.
⁶Great is his glory in your victory;
majesty and splendor you confer upon him.
⁷You make him the pattern of blessings forever,
you gladden him with the joy of your face.
⁸For the king trusts in the Lord,
stands firm through the mercy of the Most High.

⁹Your hand will find all your enemies;
your right hand will find your foes!
¹⁰At the time of your coming
you will make them a fiery furnace.
Then the Lord in his anger will consume them,
devour them with fire.
¹¹Even their descendants you will wipe out from the earth,
their offspring from the human race.

¹²Though they intend evil against you,
devising plots, they will not succeed,
¹³For you will put them to flight;
you will aim at their faces with your bow.

¹⁴Arise, Lord, in your power!
We will sing and chant the praise of your might.

The Prayer of an Innocent Person. **22:1** For the leader; according to "The deer of the dawn." A psalm of David.

²My God, my God, why have you abandoned me?
Why so far from my call for help,
from my cries of anguish?
³My God, I call by day, but you do not answer;
by night, but I have no relief.
⁴Yet you are enthroned as the Holy One;
you are the glory of Israel.
⁵In you our fathers trusted;
they trusted and you rescued them.
⁶To you they cried out and they escaped;
in you they trusted and were not disappointed.
⁷But I am a worm, not a man,
scorned by men, despised by the people.
⁸All who see me mock me;
they curl their lips and jeer;
they shake their heads at me:
⁹"He relied on the Lord—let him deliver him;
if he loves him, let him rescue him."

¹⁰For you drew me forth from the womb,
made me safe at my mother's breasts.
¹¹Upon you I was thrust from the
womb;
since my mother bore me you are
my God.
¹²Do not stay far from me,
for trouble is near,
and there is no one to help.

¹³Many bulls surround me;
fierce bulls of Bashan encircle me.
¹⁴They open their mouths against me,
lions that rend and roar.
¹⁵Like water my life drains away;
all my bones are disjointed.
My heart has become like wax,
it melts away within me.
¹⁶As dry as a potsherd is my throat;
my tongue cleaves to my palate;
you lay me in the dust of death.
¹⁷Dogs surround me;
a pack of evildoers closes in on me.
They have pierced my hands and my
feet
¹⁸I can count all my bones.
They stare at me and gloat;
¹⁹they divide my garments among
them;
for my clothing they cast lots.
²⁰But you, LORD, do not stay far off;
my strength, come quickly to
help me.
²¹Deliver my soul from the sword,
my life from the grip of the dog.
²²Save me from the lion's mouth,
my poor life from the horns of wild
bulls.
²³Then I will proclaim your name to
my brethren;
in the assembly I will praise you:
²⁴"You who fear the LORD, give praise!
All descendants of Jacob, give
honor;
show reverence, all descendants of
Israel!
²⁵For he has not spurned or disdained
the misery of this poor wretch,
Did not turn away from me,
but heard me when I cried out.
²⁶I will offer praise in the great
assembly;
my vows I will fulfill before those
who fear him.
²⁷The poor will eat their fill;
those who seek the LORD will offer
praise.
May your hearts enjoy life forever!"

²⁸All the ends of the earth
will remember and turn to the LORD;
All the families of nations
will bow low before him.
²⁹For kingship belongs to the LORD,
the ruler over the nations.
³⁰All who sleep in the earth
will bow low before God;
All who have gone down into the dust
will kneel in homage.
³¹And I will live for the LORD;
my descendants will serve you.
³²The generation to come will be told
of the Lord,
that they may proclaim to a people
yet unborn
the deliverance you have brought.

The Lord, Shepherd and Host. 23:1 A
psalm of David.

The LORD is my shepherd;
there is nothing I lack.
²In green pastures he makes me lie down;
to still waters he leads me;
³he restores my soul.
He guides me along right paths
for the sake of his name.
⁴Even though I walk through the valley
of the shadow of death,
I will fear no evil, for you are with me;
your rod and your staff comfort me.

⁵You set a table before me
in front of my enemies;
You anoint my head with oil;

my cup overflows.
[6]Indeed, goodness and mercy will
pursue me
all the days of my life;
I will dwell in the house of the Lord
for endless days.

The Glory of God in Procession to Zion.
24:1 A psalm of David.

The earth is the Lord's and all it holds,
the world and those who dwell in it.
[2]For he founded it on the seas,
established it over the rivers.

[3]Who may go up the mountain of the
Lord?
Who can stand in his holy place?
[4]"The clean of hand and pure of heart,
who has not given his soul to useless
things,
what is vain.
[5]He will receive blessings from the Lord,
and justice from his saving God.
[6]Such is the generation that seeks him,
that seeks the face of the God of
Jacob."

Selah

[7]Lift up your heads, O gates;
be lifted, you ancient portals,
that the king of glory may enter.
[8]Who is this king of glory?
The Lord, strong and mighty,
The Lord, mighty in war.
[9]Lift up your heads, O gates;
rise up, you ancient portals,
that the king of glory may enter.
[10]Who is this king of glory?
The Lord of hosts, he is the king of
glory.

Selah

Confident Prayer for Forgiveness and Guidance.
25:1 Of David.

To you, O Lord, I lift up my soul,
[2]my God, in you I trust;
do not let me be disgraced;

do not let my enemies gloat over me.
[3]No one is disgraced who waits for you,
but only those who are treacherous
without cause.
[4]Make known to me your ways, Lord;
teach me your paths.
[5]Guide me by your fidelity and teach me,
for you are God my savior,
for you I wait all the day long.
[6]Remember your compassion and your
mercy, O Lord,
for they are ages old.
[7]Remember no more the sins of my
youth;
remember me according to your
mercy,
because of your goodness, Lord.

[8]Good and upright is the Lord,
therefore he shows sinners the way,
[9] He guides the humble in
righteousness,
and teaches the humble his way.
[10]All the paths of the Lord are mercy
and truth
toward those who honor his
covenant and decrees.
[11]For the sake of your name, Lord,
pardon my guilt, though it is great.
[12]Who is the one who fears the Lord?
God shows him the way he should
choose.
[13] He will abide in prosperity,
and his descendants will inherit the
land.
[14]The counsel of the Lord belongs to
those who fear him;
and his covenant instructs them.
[15]My eyes are ever upon the Lord,
who frees my feet from the snare.
[16]Look upon me, have pity on me,
for I am alone and afflicted.
[17]Relieve the troubles of my heart;
bring me out of my distress.
[18] Look upon my affliction and
suffering;
take away all my sins.

[19]See how many are my enemies,
  see how fiercely they hate me.
[20]Preserve my soul and rescue me;
  do not let me be disgraced, for in
    you I seek refuge.

[21]Let integrity and uprightness preserve
    me;
  I wait for you, O LORD.
[22]Redeem Israel, O God,
  from all its distress!

☐ 2 CORINTHIANS 4:16–5:10

4:16 Therefore, we are not discouraged; rather, although our outer self is wasting away, our inner self is being renewed day by day. [17]For this momentary light affliction is producing for us an eternal weight of glory beyond all comparison, [18]as we look not to what is seen but to what is unseen; for what is seen is transitory, but what is unseen is eternal.

Our Future Destiny. 5:1 For we know that if our earthly dwelling, a tent, should be destroyed, we have a building from God, a dwelling not made with hands, eternal in heaven. [2]For in this tent we groan, longing to be further clothed with our heavenly habitation [3]if indeed, when we have taken it off, we shall not be found naked. [4]For while we are in this tent we groan and are weighed down, because we do not wish to be unclothed but to be further clothed, so that what is mortal may be swallowed up by life. [5]Now the one who has prepared us for this very thing is God, who has given us the Spirit as a first installment.

[6]So we are always courageous, although we know that while we are at home in the body we are away from the Lord, [7]for we walk by faith, not by sight. [8]Yet we are courageous, and we would rather leave the body and go home to the Lord. [9]Therefore, we aspire to please him, whether we are at home or away. [10]For we must all appear before the judgment seat of Christ, so that each one may receive recompense, according to what he did in the body, whether good or evil.

July 6

St. Maria Goretti

*He loves, He hopes, He waits. Our Lord prefers to wait himself
for the sinner for years rather than keep us waiting an instant.*
— ST. MARIA GORETTI

☐ PSALMS 26–30

Prayer of Innocence. 26:1 Of David.

Judge me, LORD!
  For I have walked in my integrity.
In the LORD I trust;
  I do not falter.
[2]Examine me, Lord, and test me;
  search my heart and mind.

[3]Your mercy is before my eyes;
  I walk guided by your faithfulness.

[4]I do not sit with worthless men,
  nor with hypocrites do I mingle.
[5]I hate an evil assembly;
  with the wicked I do not sit.
[6]I will wash my hands in innocence

so that I may process around your
    altar, Lord,
[7]To hear the sound of thanksgiving,
    and recount all your wondrous
      deeds.
[8]Lord, I love the refuge of your house,
    the site of the dwelling-place of your
      glory.

[9]Do not take me away with sinners,
    nor my life with the men of blood,
[10]In whose hands there is a plot,
    their right hands full of bribery.
[11]But I walk in my integrity;
    redeem me, be gracious to me!
[12]My foot stands on level ground;
    in assemblies I will bless the LORD.

Trust in God. 27:1 Of David.

The LORD is my light and my salvation;
    whom should I fear?
The LORD is my life's refuge;
    of whom should I be afraid?
[2]When evildoers come at me
    to devour my flesh,
These my enemies and foes
    themselves stumble and fall.
[3]Though an army encamp against me,
    my heart does not fear;
Though war be waged against me,
    even then do I trust.

[4]One thing I ask of the LORD;
    this I seek:
To dwell in the LORD's house
    all the days of my life,
To gaze on the LORD's beauty,
    to visit his temple.
[5]For God will hide me in his shelter
    in time of trouble,
He will conceal me in the cover of his
      tent;
    and set me high upon a rock.
[6]Even now my head is held high
    above my enemies on every side!
I will offer in his tent
    sacrifices with shouts of joy;

I will sing and chant praise to the
    LORD.

[7]Hear my voice, LORD, when I call;
    have mercy on me and answer me.
[8]"Come," says my heart, "seek his face";
    your face, LORD, do I seek!
[9]Do not hide your face from me;
    do not repel your servant in anger.
You are my salvation; do not cast me
      off;
    do not forsake me, God my savior!
[10]Even if my father and mother
      forsake me,
    The LORD will take me in.

[11]LORD, show me your way;
    lead me on a level path
    because of my enemies.
[12]Do not abandon me to the desire of
      my foes;
malicious and lying witnesses have
      risen against me.
[13]I believe I shall see the LORD's
      goodness
    in the land of the living.
[14]Wait for the LORD, take courage;
    be stouthearted, wait for the LORD!

Petition and Thanksgiving. 28:1 Of David.

To you, LORD, I call;
    my Rock, do not be deaf to me,
Do not be silent toward me,
    so that I join those who go down to
      the pit.
[2]Hear the sound of my pleading when
    I cry to you for help
    when I lift up my hands toward
      your holy place.
[3]Do not drag me off with the wicked,
    with those who do wrong,
Who speak peace to their neighbors
    though evil is in their hearts.
[4]Repay them for their deeds,
    for the evil that they do.
For the work of their hands repay them;
    give them what they deserve.

⁵Because they do not understand the
Lord's works,
the work of his hands,
He will tear them down,
never to rebuild them.

⁶Blessed be the Lord,
who has heard the sound of my
pleading.
⁷The Lord is my strength and my shield,
in whom my heart trusts.
I am helped, so my heart rejoices;
with my song I praise him.

⁸Lord, you are a strength for your
people,
the saving refuge of your anointed.
⁹Save your people, bless your
inheritance;
pasture and carry them forever!

The Lord of Majesty Acclaimed as King of the World. 29:1 A psalm of David.

Give to the Lord, you sons of God,
give to the Lord glory and might;
²Give to the Lord the glory due his
name.
Bow down before the Lord's holy
splendor!

³The voice of the Lord is over the
waters;
the God of glory thunders,
the Lord, over the mighty waters.
⁴The voice of the Lord is power;
the voice of the Lord is splendor.
⁵The voice of the Lord cracks the
cedars;
The Lord splinters the cedars of
Lebanon,
⁶Makes Lebanon leap like a calf,
and Sirion like a young bull.
⁷The voice of the Lord strikes with
fiery flame;
⁸the voice of the Lord shakes the
desert;
The Lord shakes the desert of
Kadesh.

⁹The voice of the Lord makes the deer
dance
and strips the forests bare.
All in his Temple say, "Glory!"

¹⁰The Lord sits enthroned above the
flood!
The Lord reigns as king forever!
¹¹May the Lord give might to his
people;
may the Lord bless his people with
peace!

Thanksgiving for Deliverance. 30:1 A psalm. A song for the dedication of the Temple. Of David.

²I praise you, Lord, for you raised me up
and did not let my enemies rejoice
over me.
³O Lord, my God,
I cried out to you for help and you
healed me.
⁴Lord, you brought my soul up from
Sheol;
you let me live, from going down to
the pit.

⁵Sing praise to the Lord, you faithful;
give thanks to his holy memory.
⁶For his anger lasts but a moment;
his favor a lifetime.
At dusk weeping comes for the night;
but at dawn there is rejoicing.

⁷Complacent, I once said,
"I shall never be shaken."
⁸Lord, you showed me favor,
established for me mountains of
virtue.
But when you hid your face
I was struck with terror.
⁹To you, Lord, I cried out;
with the Lord I pleaded for mercy:
¹⁰"What gain is there from my
lifeblood,
from my going down to the grave?
Does dust give you thanks
or declare your faithfulness?

[11]Hear, O LORD, have mercy on me;
LORD, be my helper."

[12]You changed my mourning into
dancing;
you took off my sackcloth

and clothed me with gladness.
[13]So that my glory may praise you
and not be silent.
O LORD, my God,
forever will I give you thanks.

☐ 2 CORINTHIANS 5:11-21

The Ministry of Reconciliation. 5:11 Therefore, since we know the fear of the Lord, we try to persuade others; but we are clearly apparent to God, and I hope we are also apparent to your consciousness. [12]We are not commending ourselves to you again but giving you an opportunity to boast of us, so that you may have something to say to those who boast of external appearance rather than of the heart. [13]For if we are out of our minds, it is for God; if we are rational, it is for you. [14]For the love of Christ impels us, once we have come to the conviction that one died for all; therefore, all have died. [15]He indeed died for all, so that those who live might no longer live for themselves but for him who for their sake died and was raised.

[16]Consequently, from now on we regard no one according to the flesh; even if we

once knew Christ according to the flesh, yet now we know him so no longer. [17]So whoever is in Christ is a new creation: the old things have passed away; behold, new things have come. [18]And all this is from God, who has reconciled us to himself through Christ and given us the ministry of reconciliation, [19]namely, God was reconciling the world to himself in Christ, not counting their trespasses against them and entrusting to us the message of reconciliation. [20]So we are ambassadors for Christ, as if God were appealing through us. We implore you on behalf of Christ, be reconciled to God. [21]For our sake he made him to be sin who did not know sin, so that we might become the righteousness of God in him.

July 7

If I had to advise parents, I should tell them to take great care about the people with whom their children associate. Much harm may result from bad company, and we are inclined by nature to follow what is worse rather than what is better.

— ST. ELIZABETH ANN SETON

☐ PSALMS 31-35

Prayer in Distress and Thanksgiving for Escape. 31:1 For the leader. A psalm of David.

[2]In you, LORD, I take refuge;
let me never be put to shame.
In your righteousness deliver me;

[3]incline your ear to me;
make haste to rescue me!
Be my rock of refuge,
a stronghold to save me.
[4]For you are my rock and my fortress;

for your name's sake lead me and
    guide me.
⁵Free me from the net they have set
    for me,
for you are my refuge.
⁶Into your hands I commend my spirit;
    you will redeem me, LORD, God of
    truth.
⁷You hate those who serve worthless
    idols,
but I trust in the LORD.
⁸I will rejoice and be glad in your mercy,
    once you have seen my misery,
    [and] gotten to know the distress of
    my soul.
⁹You will not abandon me into enemy
    hands,
but will set my feet in a free and
    open space.

¹⁰Be gracious to me, LORD, for I am in
    distress;
affliction is wearing down my eyes,
    my throat and my insides.
¹¹My life is worn out by sorrow,
    and my years by sighing.
My strength fails in my affliction;
    my bones are wearing down.
¹²To all my foes I am a thing of scorn,
    and especially to my neighbors
    a horror to my friends.
When they see me in public,
    they quickly shy away.
¹³I am forgotten, out of mind like the
    dead;
I am like a worn-out tool.
¹⁴I hear the whispers of the crowd;
    terrors are all around me.
They conspire together against me;
    they plot to take my life.
¹⁵But I trust in you, LORD;
    I say, "You are my God."
¹⁶My destiny is in your hands;
    rescue me from my enemies,
    from the hands of my pursuers.
¹⁷Let your face shine on your servant;
    save me in your mercy.

¹⁸Do not let me be put to shame,
    for I have called to you, LORD.
Put the wicked to shame;
    reduce them to silence in Sheol.
¹⁹Strike dumb their lying lips,
    which speak arrogantly against the
    righteous
    in contempt and scorn.

²⁰How great is your goodness, Lord,
    stored up for those who fear you.
You display it for those who trust you,
    in the sight of the children of Adam.
²¹You hide them in the shelter of your
    presence,
safe from scheming enemies.
You conceal them in your tent,
    away from the strife of tongues.
²²Blessed be the LORD,
    marvelously he showed to me
    his mercy in a fortified city.
²³Though I had said in my alarm,
    "I am cut off from your eyes."
Yet you heard my voice, my cry for
    mercy,
    when I pleaded with you for help.
²⁴Love the LORD, all you who are
    faithful to him.
The LORD protects the loyal,
    but repays the arrogant in full.
²⁵Be strong and take heart,
    all who hope in the LORD.

***Remission of Sin.* 32:1** Of David. A *maskil.*

Blessed is the one whose fault is removed,
    whose sin is forgiven.
²Blessed is the man to whom the LORD
    imputes no guilt,
    in whose spirit is no deceit.

³Because I kept silent, my bones wasted
    away;
I groaned all day long.
⁴For day and night your hand was
    heavy upon me;
my strength withered as in dry
    summer heat.

Selah

⁵Then I declared my sin to you;
  my guilt I did not hide.
I said, "I confess my transgression to
    the LORD,"
  and you took away the guilt of my
    sin.

Selah

⁶Therefore every loyal person should
    pray to you
  in time of distress.
Though flood waters threaten,
  they will never reach him.
⁷You are my shelter; you guard me
    from distress;
  with joyful shouts of deliverance
    you surround me.

Selah

⁸I will instruct you and show you the
    way you should walk,
  give you counsel with my eye upon
    you.
⁹Do not be like a horse or mule,
    without understanding;
  with bit and bridle their temper is
    curbed,
  else they will not come to you.

¹⁰Many are the sorrows of the wicked one,
  but mercy surrounds the one who
    trusts in the LORD.
¹¹Be glad in the LORD and rejoice, you
    righteous;
  exult, all you upright of heart.

Praise of God's Power and Providence.

33:1 Rejoice, you righteous, in the LORD;
  praise from the upright is fitting.
²Give thanks to the LORD on the harp;
  on the ten-stringed lyre offer praise.
³Sing to him a new song;
  skillfully play with joyful chant.
⁴For the LORD's word is upright;
  all his works are trustworthy.
⁵He loves justice and right.
  The earth is full of the mercy of the
    LORD.

⁶By the LORD's word the heavens were
    made;
  by the breath of his mouth all their
    host.
⁷He gathered the waters of the sea as a
    mound;
  he sets the deep into storage vaults.

⁸Let all the earth fear the LORD;
  let all who dwell in the world show
    him reverence.
⁹For he spoke, and it came to be,
  commanded, and it stood in place.
¹⁰The LORD foils the plan of nations,
  frustrates the designs of peoples.
¹¹But the plan of the LORD stands forever,
  the designs of his heart through all
    generations.
¹²Blessed is the nation whose God is
    the LORD,
  the people chosen as his inheritance.

¹³From heaven the LORD looks down
  and observes the children of Adam,
¹⁴From his dwelling place he surveys
  all who dwell on earth.
¹⁵The One who fashioned together
    their hearts
  is the One who knows all their works.

¹⁶A king is not saved by a great army,
  nor a warrior delivered by great
    strength.
¹⁷Useless is the horse for safety;
  despite its great strength, it cannot
    be saved.
¹⁸Behold, the eye of the LORD is upon
    those who fear him,
  upon those who count on his mercy,
¹⁹To deliver their soul from death,
  and to keep them alive through
    famine.

²⁰Our soul waits for the LORD,
  he is our help and shield.
²¹For in him our hearts rejoice;
  in his holy name we trust.
²²May your mercy, LORD, be upon us;
  as we put our hope in you.

Thanksgiving to God Who Delivers the Just. 34:1 Of David, when he feigned madness before Abimelech, who drove him out and he went away.

²I will bless the LORD at all times;
  his praise shall be always in my
    mouth.
³My soul will glory in the LORD;
  let the poor hear and be glad.
⁴Magnify the LORD with me;
  and let us exalt his name together.

⁵I sought the LORD, and he answered me,
  delivered me from all my fears.
⁶Look to him and be radiant,
  and your faces may not blush for
    shame.
⁷This poor one cried out and the LORD
    heard,
  and from all his distress he saved him.
⁸The angel of the LORD encamps
  around those who fear him, and he
    saves them.
⁹Taste and see that the LORD is good;
  blessed is the stalwart one who takes
    refuge in him.
¹⁰Fear the LORD, you his holy ones;
  nothing is lacking to those who fear
    him.
¹¹The rich grow poor and go hungry,
  but those who seek the LORD lack
    no good thing.

¹²Come, children, listen to me;
  I will teach you fear of the LORD.
¹³Who is the man who delights in life,
  who loves to see the good days?
¹⁴Keep your tongue from evil,
  your lips from speaking lies.
¹⁵Turn from evil and do good;
  seek peace and pursue it.
¹⁶The eyes of the LORD are directed
    toward the righteous
  and his ears toward their cry.
¹⁷The LORD's face is against evildoers
  to wipe out their memory from the
    earth.

¹⁸The righteous cry out, the LORD hears
  and he rescues them from all their
    afflictions.
¹⁹The LORD is close to the
    brokenhearted,
  saves those whose spirit is crushed.
²⁰Many are the troubles of the
    righteous,
  but the LORD delivers him from
    them all.
²¹He watches over all his bones;
  not one of them shall be broken.
²²Evil will slay the wicked;
  those who hate the righteous are
    condemned.
²³The LORD is the redeemer of the souls
    of his servants;
  and none are condemned who take
    refuge in him.

Prayer for Help Against Unjust Enemies. 35:1 Of David.

Oppose, O LORD, those who oppose me;
  war upon those who make war
    upon me.
²Take up the shield and buckler;
  rise up in my defense.
³Brandish lance and battle-ax
  against my pursuers.
Say to my soul,
  "I am your salvation."
⁴Let those who seek my life
  be put to shame and disgrace.
Let those who plot evil against me
  be turned back and confounded.
⁵Make them like chaff before the wind,
  with the angel of the LORD driving
    them on.
⁶Make their way slippery and dark,
  with the angel of the LORD pursuing
    them.
⁷Without cause they set their snare
    for me;
  without cause they dug a pit for me.
⁸Let ruin overtake them unawares;
  let the snare they have set catch them;

let them fall into the pit they have
dug.
⁹Then I will rejoice in the LORD,
exult in God's salvation.
¹⁰My very bones shall say,
"O LORD, who is like you,
Who rescue the afflicted from the
powerful,
the afflicted and needy from the
despoiler?"

¹¹Malicious witnesses rise up,
accuse me of things I do not know.
¹²They repay me evil for good;
my soul is desolate.
¹³Yet I, when they were ill, put on
sackcloth,
afflicted myself with fasting,
sobbed my prayers upon my bosom.
¹⁴I went about in grief as for my brother,
bent in mourning as for my mother.
¹⁵Yet when I stumbled they gathered
with glee,
gathered against me and I did not
know it.
They slandered me without ceasing;
¹⁶without respect they mocked me,
gnashed their teeth against me.

¹⁷O Lord, how long will you look on?
Restore my soul from their
destruction,
my very life from lions!
¹⁸Then I will thank you in the great
assembly;
I will praise you before the mighty
throng.

¹⁹Do not let lying foes rejoice over me,
my undeserved enemies wink
knowingly.
²⁰They speak no words of peace,
but against the quiet in the land
they fashion deceitful speech.
²¹They open wide their mouths
against me.
They say, "Aha! Good!
Our eyes have seen it!"
²²You see this, LORD; do not be silent;
Lord, do not withdraw from me.
²³Awake, be vigilant in my defense,
in my cause, my God and my Lord.
²⁴Defend me because you are just, LORD;
my God, do not let them rejoice
over me.
²⁵Do not let them say in their hearts,
"Aha! Our soul!"
Do not let them say,
"We have devoured that one!"
²⁶Put to shame and confound
all who relish my misfortune.
Clothe with shame and disgrace
those who lord it over me.
²⁷But let those who favor my just cause
shout for joy and be glad.
May they ever say, "Exalted be the
LORD
who delights in the peace of his
loyal servant."
²⁸Then my tongue shall recount your
justice,
declare your praise, all the day long.

☐ 2 CORINTHIANS 6:1-7:1

The Experience of the Ministry. 6:1
Working together, then, we appeal to you
not to receive the grace of God in vain. ²For
he says:

"In an acceptable time I heard you,
and on the day of salvation I helped
you."

Behold, now is a very acceptable time;
behold, now is the day of salvation. ³We
cause no one to stumble in anything, in
order that no fault may be found with our
ministry; ⁴on the contrary, in everything
we commend ourselves as ministers of
God, through much endurance, in afflic-

812 • July 8

tions, hardships, constraints, [5]beatings, imprisonments, riots, labors, vigils, fasts; [6]by purity, knowledge, patience, kindness, in a holy spirit, in unfeigned love, [7]in truthful speech, in the power of God; with weapons of righteousness at the right and at the left; [8]through glory and dishonor, insult and praise. We are treated as deceivers and yet are truthful; [9]as unrecognized and yet acknowledged; as dying and behold we live; as chastised and yet not put to death; [10]as sorrowful yet always rejoicing; as poor yet enriching many; as having nothing and yet possessing all things.

[11]We have spoken frankly to you, Corinthians; our heart is open wide. [12]You are not constrained by us; you are constrained by your own affections. [13]As recompense in kind (I speak as to my children), be open yourselves.

Call to Holiness. [14]Do not be yoked with those who are different, with unbelievers. For what partnership do righteousness and lawlessness have? Or what fellowship does light have with darkness? [15]What accord has Christ with Beliar? Or what has a believer in common with an unbeliever? [16]What agreement has the temple of God with idols? For we are the temple of the living God; as God said:

"I will live with them and move among
        them,
    and I will be their God
    and they shall be my people.
[17]Therefore, come forth from them
    and be separate," says the Lord,
"and touch nothing unclean;
    then I will receive you
[18]and I will be a father to you,
    and you shall be sons and daughters
        to me,
says the Lord Almighty."

7:1 Since we have these promises, beloved, let us cleanse ourselves from every defilement of flesh and spirit, making holiness perfect in the fear of God.

July 8

St. Jeanne-Marie Kerguin and Companions
Do not be afraid of death. Death is only God passing by.
— St. Jeanne-Marie Kerguin

☐ PSALMS 36–39

***Human Wickedness and Divine Providence.* 36:1** For the leader. Of David, the servant of the LORD.

[2]Sin directs the heart of the wicked man;
    his eyes are closed to the fear of God.
[3]For he lives with the delusion:
    his guilt will not be known and hated.
[4]Empty and false are the words of his
        mouth;
    he has ceased to be wise and do
        good.

[5]On his bed he hatches plots;
    he sets out on a wicked way;
    he does not reject evil.
[6]LORD, your mercy reaches to heaven;
    your fidelity, to the clouds.
[7]Your justice is like the highest
        mountains;
    your judgments, like the mighty
        deep;
    human being and beast you sustain,
    LORD.

[8]How precious is your mercy, O God!
The children of Adam take refuge in
the shadow of your wings.
[9]They feast on the rich food of your
house;
from your delightful stream you
give them drink.
[10]For with you is the fountain of life,
and in your light we see light.
[11]Show mercy on those who know you,
your just defense to the upright of
heart.
[12]Do not let the foot of the proud
overtake me,
nor the hand of the wicked disturb
me.
[13]There make the evildoers fall;
thrust them down, unable to rise.

The Fate of Sinners and the Reward of the Just. 37:1 Of David.

Aleph. Do not be provoked by
evildoers;
do not envy those who do wrong.
[2]Like grass they wither quickly;
like green plants they wilt away.

Beth. [3]Trust in the LORD and do good
that you may dwell in the land and
live secure.
[4]Find your delight in the LORD
who will give you your heart's desire.

Gimel. [5]Commit your way to the LORD;
trust in him and he will act
[6]And make your righteousness shine
like the dawn,
your justice like noonday.

Daleth. [7]Be still before the LORD;
wait for him.
Do not be provoked by the prosperous,
nor by malicious schemers.

He. [8]Refrain from anger; abandon wrath;
do not be provoked; it brings only
harm.
[9]Those who do evil will be cut off,

but those who wait for the LORD
will inherit the earth.

Waw. [10]Wait a little, and the wicked
will be no more;
look for them and they will not be
there.
[11]But the poor will inherit the earth,
will delight in great prosperity.

Zayin. [12]The wicked plot against the
righteous
and gnash their teeth at them;
[13]But my Lord laughs at them,
because he sees that their day is
coming.

Heth. [14]The wicked unsheath their
swords;
they string their bows
To fell the poor and oppressed,
to slaughter those whose way is
upright.
[15]Their swords will pierce their own
hearts;
their bows will be broken.

Teth. [16]Better the meagerness of the
righteous one
than the plenty of the wicked.
[17]The arms of the wicked will be
broken,
while the LORD will sustain the
righteous.

Yodh. [18]The LORD knows the days of
the blameless;
their heritage lasts forever.
[19]They will not be ashamed when times
are bad;
in days of famine they will be satisfied.

Kaph. [20]The wicked perish,
enemies of the LORD;
They shall be consumed like fattened
lambs;
like smoke they disappear.

Lamedh. [21]The wicked one borrows
but does not repay;

the righteous one is generous and
    gives.
22For those blessed by the Lord will
    inherit the earth,
but those accursed will be cut off.

Mem. 23The valiant one whose steps
    are guided by the LORD,
who will delight in his way,
24May stumble, but he will never fall,
    for the LORD holds his hand.

Nun. 25Neither in my youth, nor now
    in old age
have I seen the righteous one
    abandoned
or his offspring begging for bread.
26 All day long he is gracious and lends,
    and his offspring become a blessing.

Samekh. 27Turn from evil and do good,
    that you may be settled forever.
28For the LORD loves justice
    and does not abandon the faithful.

Ayin. When the unjust are destroyed,
    and the offspring of the wicked
    cut off,
29The righteous will inherit the earth
    and dwell in it forever.

Pe. 30The mouth of the righteous utters
    wisdom;
his tongue speaks what is right.
31God's teaching is in his heart;
    his steps do not falter.

Sadhe. 32The wicked spies on the
    righteous
and seeks to kill him.
33But the LORD does not abandon him
    in his power,
nor let him be condemned when
    tried.

Qoph. 34Wait eagerly for the LORD,
    and keep his way;
He will raise you up to inherit the earth;
    you will see when the wicked are cut
    off.

Resh. 35I have seen a ruthless
    scoundrel,
spreading out like a green cedar.
36When I passed by again, he was gone;
    though I searched, he could not be
    found.

Shin. 37Observe the person of integrity
    and mark the upright;
Because there is a future for a man
    of peace.
38Sinners will be destroyed together;
    the future of the wicked will be
    cut off.

Taw. 39The salvation of the righteous is
    from the LORD,
their refuge in a time of distress.
40The LORD helps and rescues them,
    rescues and saves them from the
    wicked,
because they take refuge in him.

Prayer of an Afflicted Sinner. 38:1 A
psalm of David. For remembrance.

2LORD, do not punish me in your
    anger;
in your wrath do not chastise me!
3Your arrows have sunk deep in me;
    your hand has come down upon me.
4There is no wholesomeness in my flesh
    because of your anger;
there is no health in my bones
    because of my sin.
5My iniquities overwhelm me,
    a burden too heavy for me.

6Foul and festering are my sores
    because of my folly.
7I am stooped and deeply bowed;
    every day I go about mourning.
8My loins burn with fever;
    there is no wholesomeness in my
    flesh.
9I am numb and utterly crushed;
    I wail with anguish of heart.
10My Lord, my deepest yearning is
    before you;

my groaning is not hidden from you.
[11]My heart shudders, my strength
forsakes me;
the very light of my eyes has failed.
[12]Friends and companions shun my
disease;
my neighbors stand far off.
[13]Those who seek my life lay snares
for me;
they seek my misfortune, they speak
of ruin;
they plot treachery every day.

[14]But I am like the deaf, hearing nothing,
like the mute, I do not open my
mouth.
[15]I am even like someone who does not
hear,
who has no answer ready.
[16]LORD, it is for you that I wait;
O Lord, my God, you respond.
[17]For I have said that they would gloat
over me,
exult over me if I stumble.

[18]I am very near to falling;
my wounds are with me always.
[19]I acknowledge my guilt
and grieve over my sin.
[20]My enemies live and grow strong,
those who hate me grow numerous
fraudulently,
[21]Repaying me evil for good,
accusing me for pursuing good.
[22]Do not forsake me, O LORD;
my God, be not far from me!
[23]Come quickly to help me,
my Lord and my salvation!

The Vanity of Life. 39:1 For the leader, for
Jeduthun. A psalm of David.

[2]I said, "I will watch my ways,
lest I sin with my tongue;

I will keep a muzzle on my mouth."
[3]Mute and silent before the wicked,
I refrain from good things.
But my sorrow increases;
[4]my heart smolders within me.
In my sighing a fire blazes up,
and I break into speech:

[5]LORD, let me know my end, the
number of my days,
that I may learn how frail I am.
[6]To be sure, you establish the expanse
of my days;
indeed, my life is as nothing before
you.
Every man is but a breath.
Selah
[7]Man goes about as a mere phantom;
they hurry about, although in vain;
he heaps up stores without knowing
for whom.
[8]And now, LORD, for what do I wait?
You are my only hope.
[9]From all my sins deliver me;
let me not be the taunt of fools.

[10]I am silent and do not open my mouth
because you are the one who did this.
[11]Take your plague away from me;
I am ravaged by the touch of your
hand.
[12]You chastise man with rebukes for sin;
like a moth you consume his
treasures.
Every man is but a breath.
Selah
[13]Listen to my prayer, LORD, hear my
cry;
do not be deaf to my weeping!
For I am with you like a foreigner,
a refugee, like my ancestors.
[14]Turn your gaze from me, that I may
smile
before I depart to be no more.

☐ 2 CORINTHIANS 7:2-16

7:2 Make room for us; we have not wronged anyone, or ruined anyone, or taken advantage of anyone. ³I do not say this in condemnation, for I have already said that you are in our hearts, that we may die together and live together. ⁴I have great confidence in you, I have great pride in you; I am filled with encouragement, I am overflowing with joy all the more because of all our affliction.

Paul's Joy in Macedonia. ⁵For even when we came into Macedonia, our flesh had no rest, but we were afflicted in every way—external conflicts, internal fears. ⁶But God, who encourages the downcast, encouraged us by the arrival of Titus, ⁷and not only by his arrival but also by the encouragement with which he was encouraged in regard to you, as he told us of your yearning, your lament, your zeal for me, so that I rejoiced even more. ⁸For even if I saddened you by my letter, I do not regret it; and if I did regret it ([for] I see that that letter saddened you, if only for a while), ⁹I rejoice now, not because you were saddened, but because you were saddened into repentance; for you were saddened in a godly way, so that you did not suffer loss in anything because of us. ¹⁰For godly sorrow produces a salutary repentance without regret, but worldly sorrow produces death. ¹¹For behold what earnestness this godly sorrow has produced for you, as well as readiness for a defense, and indignation, and fear, and yearning, and zeal, and punishment. In every way you have shown yourselves to be innocent in the matter. ¹²So then even though I wrote to you, it was not on account of the one who did the wrong, or on account of the one who suffered the wrong, but in order that your concern for us might be made plain to you in the sight of God. ¹³For this reason we are encouraged.

And besides our encouragement, we rejoice even more because of the joy of Titus, since his spirit has been refreshed by all of you. ¹⁴For if I have boasted to him about you, I was not put to shame. No, just as everything we said to you was true, so our boasting before Titus proved to be the truth. ¹⁵And his heart goes out to you all the more, as he remembers the obedience of all of you, when you received him with fear and trembling. ¹⁶I rejoice, because I have confidence in you in every respect.

July 9

St. Augustine Zhao Rong and Companions;
St. Veronica Giuliani

Love makes the heart leap and dance. Love makes it exult and be festive. Love makes it sing and be silent as it pleases. Love grants it rest and enables it to act. Love possesses it and gives it everything. Love takes it over completely and dwells in it. And Holy Communion is a mansion of love.

— St. Veronica Giuliani

☐ PSALMS 40-44

Gratitude and Prayer for Help. **40:1** For the leader. A psalm of David.

²Surely, I wait for the LORD;
    who bends down to me and hears
        my cry,
³Draws me up from the pit of
        destruction,
    out of the muddy clay,
Sets my feet upon rock,
    steadies my steps,
⁴And puts a new song in my mouth,
    a hymn to our God.
Many shall look on in fear
    and they shall trust in the LORD.
⁵Blessed the man who sets
his security in the LORD,
who turns not to the arrogant
    or to those who stray after
        falsehood.
⁶You, yes you, O LORD, my God,
    have done many wondrous deeds!
And in your plans for us
    there is none to equal you.
Should I wish to declare or tell them,
    too many are they to recount.
⁷Sacrifice and offering you do not want;
    you opened my ears.
Holocaust and sin-offering you do not
        request;
    ⁸so I said, "See; I come
with an inscribed scroll written
        upon me.
⁹I delight to do your will, my God;

your law is in my inner being!"
¹⁰When I sing of your righteousness
    in a great assembly,
See, I do not restrain my lips;
    as you, LORD, know.
¹¹I do not conceal your righteousness
    within my heart;
I speak of your loyalty and your
        salvation.
    I do not hide your mercy or
            faithfulness from a great
            assembly.
¹²LORD, may you not withhold
your compassion from me;
May your mercy and your faithfulness
    continually protect me.

¹³But evils surround me
    until they cannot be counted.
My sins overtake me,
    so that I can no longer see.
They are more numerous than the hairs
        of my head;
    my courage fails me.
¹⁴LORD, graciously rescue me!
    Come quickly to help me, LORD!
¹⁵May those who seek to destroy my
        life
    be shamed and confounded.
Turn back in disgrace
    those who desire my ruin.
¹⁶Let those who say to me "Aha!"
    Be made desolate on account of
        their shame.

¹⁷While those who seek you
    rejoice and be glad in you.
May those who long for your salvation
    always say, "The LORD is great."
¹⁸Though I am afflicted and poor,
    my Lord keeps me in mind.
You are my help and deliverer;
    my God, do not delay!

Thanksgiving After Sickness. 41:1 For the leader. A psalm of David.

²Blessed the one concerned for the poor;
    on a day of misfortune, the LORD
        delivers him.
³The LORD keeps and preserves him,
    makes him blessed in the land,
    and does not betray him to his
        enemies.
⁴The LORD sustains him on his sickbed,
    you turn down his bedding
        whenever he is ill.

⁵Even I have said, "LORD, take note
    of me;
    heal me, although I have sinned
        against you.
⁶My enemies say bad things against me:
    'When will he die and his name be
        forgotten?'
⁷When someone comes to visit me, he
    speaks without sincerity.
    His heart stores up malice;
    when he leaves, he gossips.
⁸All those who hate me whisper
        together against me;
    they imagine the worst about me:
⁹ 'He has had ruin poured over him;
    that one lying down will never rise
        again.'
¹⁰Even my trusted friend,
    who ate my bread,
    has raised his heel against me.
¹¹"But you, LORD, take note of me to
    raise me up
    that I may repay them."

¹²By this I will know you are pleased
    with me,
    that my enemy no longer shouts in
        triumph over me.
¹³In my integrity may you support me
    and let me stand in your presence
        forever.
¹⁴Blessed be the LORD, the God of Israel,
    from all eternity and forever.
    Amen. Amen.

**Longing for God's Presence in the Temple.
42:1** For the leader. A *maskil* of the Korahites.

²As the deer longs for streams of water,
    so my soul longs for you, O God.
³My soul thirsts for God, the living God.
    When can I enter and see the face
        of God?
⁴My tears have been my bread day and
    night,
    as they ask me every day, "Where is
        your God?"
⁵Those times I recall
    as I pour out my soul,
When I would cross over to the shrine
    of the Mighty One,
    to the house of God,
Amid loud cries of thanksgiving,
    with the multitude keeping festival.
⁶Why are you downcast, my soul;
    why do you groan within me?
Wait for God, for I shall again praise
    him,
    my savior and my God.

⁷My soul is downcast within me;
    therefore I remember you
From the land of the Jordan and
        Hermon,
    from Mount Mizar,
⁸Deep calls to deep
    in the roar of your torrents,
    and all your waves and breakers
        sweep over me.
⁹ By day may the LORD send his mercy,

and by night may his righteousness
be with me!
I will pray to the God of my life,
¹⁰I will say to God, my rock:
"Why do you forget me?
Why must I go about mourning
with the enemy oppressing me?"
¹¹It shatters my bones, when my
adversaries reproach me,
when they say to me every day:
"Where is your God?"
¹²Why are you downcast, my soul,
why do you groan within me?
Wait for God, for I shall again praise him,
my savior and my God.

43:1 Grant me justice, O God;
defend me from a faithless people;
from the deceitful and unjust
rescue me.
²You, O God, are my strength.
Why then do you spurn me?
Why must I go about mourning,
with the enemy oppressing me?
³Send your light and your fidelity,
that they may be my guide;
Let them bring me to your holy
mountain,
to the place of your dwelling,
⁴That I may come to the altar of God,
to God, my joy, my delight.
Then I will praise you with the harp,
O God, my God.
⁵Why are you downcast, my soul?
Why do you groan within me?
Wait for God, for I shall again praise
him,
my savior and my God.

God's Past Favor and Israel's Present Need.
44:1 For the leader. A *maskil* of the Korahites.

²O God, we have heard with our own
ears;
our ancestors have told us
The deeds you did in their days,
with your own hand in days of old:

³You rooted out nations to plant them,
crushed peoples and expelled them.
⁴Not with their own swords did they
conquer the land,
nor did their own arms bring victory;
It was your right hand, your own arm,
the light of your face for you
favored them.
⁵You are my king and my God,
who bestows victories on Jacob.
⁶Through you we batter our foes;
through your name we trample our
adversaries.
⁷Not in my bow do I trust,
nor does my sword bring me victory.
⁸You have brought us victory over our
enemies,
shamed those who hate us.
⁹In God we have boasted all the day
long;
your name we will praise forever.
Selah

¹⁰But now you have rejected and
disgraced us;
you do not march out with our
armies.
¹¹You make us retreat before the foe;
those who hate us plunder us at will.
¹²You hand us over like sheep to be
slaughtered,
scatter us among the nations.
¹³You sell your people for nothing;
you make no profit from their sale.
¹⁴You make us the reproach of our
neighbors,
the mockery and scorn of those
around us.
¹⁵You make us a byword among the
nations;
the peoples shake their heads at us.
¹⁶All day long my disgrace is before me;
shame has covered my face
¹⁷At the sound of those who taunt and
revile,
at the sight of the enemy and
avenger.

¹⁸All this has come upon us,
  though we have not forgotten you,
  nor been disloyal to your covenant.
¹⁹Our hearts have not turned back,
  nor have our steps strayed from
      your path.
²⁰Yet you have left us crushed,
  desolate in a place of jackals;
  you have covered us with a shadow
      of death.
²¹If we had forgotten the name of our
      God,
  stretched out our hands to another
      god,
²²Would not God have discovered this,

God who knows the secrets of the
    heart?
²³For you we are slain all the day long,
  considered only as sheep to be
      slaughtered.

²⁴Awake! Why do you sleep, O Lord?
  Rise up! Do not reject us forever!
²⁵Why do you hide your face;
  why forget our pain and misery?
²⁶For our soul has been humiliated in
      the dust;
  our belly is pressed to the earth.
²⁷Rise up, help us!
  Redeem us in your mercy.

☐ 2 CORINTHIANS 8

Generosity in Giving. 8:1 We want you to know, brothers, of the grace of God that has been given to the churches of Macedonia, ²for in a severe test of affliction, the abundance of their joy and their profound poverty overflowed in a wealth of generosity on their part. ³For according to their means, I can testify, and beyond their means, spontaneously, ⁴they begged us insistently for the favor of taking part in the service to the holy ones, ⁵and this, not as we expected, but they gave themselves first to the Lord and to us through the will of God, ⁶so that we urged Titus that, as he had already begun, he should also complete for you this gracious act also. ⁷Now as you excel in every respect, in faith, discourse, knowledge, all earnestness, and in the love we have for you, may you excel in this gracious act also.

⁸I say this not by way of command, but to test the genuineness of your love by your concern for others. ⁹For you know the gracious act of our Lord Jesus Christ, that for your sake he became poor although he was rich, so that by his poverty you might become rich. ¹⁰And I am giving counsel in this matter, for it is appropriate for you who began not only to act but to act willingly last year: ¹¹complete it now, so that your eager willingness may be matched by your completion of it out of what you have. ¹²For if the eagerness is there, it is acceptable according to what one has, not according to what one does not have; ¹³not that others should have relief while you are burdened, but that as a matter of equality ¹⁴your surplus at the present time should supply their needs, so that their surplus may also supply your needs, that there may be equality. ¹⁵As it is written:

"Whoever had much did not have
    more,
  and whoever had little did not have
    less."

Titus and His Collaborators. ¹⁶But thanks be to God who put the same concern for you into the heart of Titus, ¹⁷for he not only welcomed our appeal but, since he is very concerned, he has gone to you of his own accord. ¹⁸With him we have sent the brother who is praised in all the churches for his preaching of the gospel. ¹⁹And not only that, but he has also been appointed our traveling companion by the churches in this gracious work administered by us for the glory of the Lord [himself] and for the expression of our eagerness. [20]This we desire to avoid, that anyone blame us about this lavish gift administered by us, [21]for we are concerned for what is honorable not only in the sight of the Lord but also in the sight of others. [22]And with them we have sent our brother whom we often tested in many ways and found earnest, but who is now much more earnest because of his great confidence in you. [23]As for Titus, he is my partner and co-worker for you; as for our brothers, they are apostles of the churches, the glory of Christ. [24]So give proof before the churches of your love and of our boasting about you to them.

July 10

If you are not yet capable of laying down your life for your brother, you are at least capable of sharing some of your goods with him. For if you cannot even give out of your abundance to someone in need, how could you possibly lay down your life for anyone?

— St. Augustine of Hippo

☐ PSALMS 45-49

Song for a Royal Wedding. 45:1 For the leader; according to "Lilies." A *maskil* of the Korahites. A love song.

[2]My heart is stirred by a noble theme,
as I sing my ode to the king.
My tongue is the pen of a nimble
scribe.

[3]You are the most handsome of men;
fair speech has graced your lips,
for God has blessed you forever.
[4]Gird your sword upon your hip,
mighty warrior!
In splendor and majesty ride on
triumphant!
[5]In the cause of truth, meekness, and
justice
may your right hand show your
wondrous deeds.
[6]Your arrows are sharp;
peoples will cower at your feet;
the king's enemies will lose heart.
[7]Your throne, O God, stands forever;
your royal scepter is a scepter for
justice.
[8]You love justice and hate wrongdoing;
therefore God, your God, has
anointed you
with the oil of gladness above your
fellow kings.
[9]With myrrh, aloes, and cassia
your robes are fragrant.
From ivory-paneled palaces
stringed instruments bring you joy.
[10]Daughters of kings are your lovely
wives;
a princess arrayed in Ophir's gold
comes to stand at your right hand.

[11]Listen, my daughter, and understand;
pay me careful heed.
Forget your people and your father's
house,
[12]that the king might desire your
beauty.
He is your lord;
[13]honor him, daughter of Tyre.

Then the richest of the people
will seek your favor with gifts.
¹⁴All glorious is the king's daughter as
she enters,
her raiment threaded with gold;
¹⁵In embroidered apparel she is led to
the king.
The maids of her train are presented
to the king.
¹⁶They are led in with glad and joyous
acclaim;
they enter the palace of the king.

---

¹⁷The throne of your fathers your sons
will have;
you shall make them princes
through all the land.
¹⁸I will make your name renowned
through all generations;
thus nations shall praise you forever.

God, the Protector of Zion. 46:1 For the
leader. A song of the Korahites. According
to *alamoth.*

²God is our refuge and our strength,
an ever-present help in distress.
³Thus we do not fear, though earth be
shaken
and mountains quake to the depths
of the sea,
⁴Though its waters rage and foam
and mountains totter at its surging.
Selah

⁵Streams of the river gladden the city
of God,
the holy dwelling of the Most High.
⁶God is in its midst; it shall not be
shaken;
God will help it at break of day.
⁷Though nations rage and kingdoms
totter,
he utters his voice and the earth melts.
⁸The LORD of hosts is with us;
our stronghold is the God of Jacob.
Selah

⁹Come and see the works of the LORD,

who has done fearsome deeds on
earth;
¹⁰Who stops wars to the ends of the
earth,
breaks the bow, splinters the spear,
and burns the shields with fire;
¹¹"Be still and know that I am God!
I am exalted among the nations,
exalted on the earth."
¹²The LORD of hosts is with us;
our stronghold is the God of Jacob.
Selah

The Ruler of All the Nations. 47:1 For the
leader. A psalm of the Korahites.

²All you peoples, clap your hands;
shout to God with joyful cries.
³For the LORD, the Most High, is to
be feared,
the great king over all the earth,
⁴Who made people subject to us,
nations under our feet,
⁵Who chose our heritage for us,
the glory of Jacob, whom he loves.
Selah

⁶God has gone up with a shout;
the LORD, amid trumpet blasts.
⁷Sing praise to God, sing praise;
sing praise to our king, sing praise.

⁸For God is king over all the earth;
sing hymns of praise.
⁹God rules over the nations;
God sits upon his holy throne.
¹⁰The princes of the peoples assemble
with the people of the God of
Abraham.
For the shields of the earth belong to
God,
highly exalted.

The Splendor of the Invincible City. 48:1
A psalm of the Korahites. A song.

²Great is the LORD and highly praised
in the city of our God:
His holy mountain,

³fairest of heights,
the joy of all the earth,
Mount Zion, the heights of Zaphon,
the city of the great king.

⁴God is in its citadel,
renowned as a stronghold.
⁵See! The kings assembled,
together they advanced.
⁶When they looked they were
astounded;
terrified, they were put to flight!
⁷Trembling seized them there,
anguish, like a woman's labor,
⁸As when the east wind wrecks
the ships of Tarshish!

⁹What we had heard we have now seen
in the city of the LORD of hosts,
In the city of our God,
which God establishes forever.

Selah

¹⁰We ponder, O God, your mercy
within your temple
¹¹Like your name, O God,
so is your praise to the ends of the
earth.
Your right hand is fully victorious.
¹²Mount Zion is glad!
The daughters of Judah rejoice
because of your judgments!

¹³Go about Zion, walk all around it,
note the number of its towers.
¹⁴Consider the ramparts, examine its
citadels,
that you may tell future generations:
¹⁵That this is God,
our God for ever and ever.
He will lead us until death.

Confidence in God Rather than in Riches.
49:1 For the leader. A psalm of the Korahites.
²Hear this, all you peoples!
Give ear, all who inhabit the world,
³You of lowly birth or high estate,
rich and poor together.

⁴My mouth shall speak words of
wisdom,
my heart shall offer insights.
⁵I will turn my ear to a riddle,
expound my question on a lyre.

⁶Why should I fear in evil days,
with the iniquity of my assailants
surrounding me,
⁷Of those who trust in their wealth
and boast of their abundant riches?
⁸No man can ransom even a brother,
or pay to God his own ransom.
⁹The redemption of his soul is costly;
and he will pass away forever.
¹⁰Will he live on forever, then,
and never see the Pit of Corruption?
¹¹Indeed, he will see that the wise die,
and the fool will perish together
with the senseless,
and they leave their wealth to others.
¹²Their tombs are their homes forever,
their dwellings through all
generations,
"They named countries after
themselves"
¹³—but man does not abide in
splendor.
He is like the beasts—they perish.

¹⁴This is the way of those who trust in
themselves,
and the end of those who take
pleasure in their own mouth.

Selah

¹⁵Like a herd of sheep they will be put
into Sheol,
and Death will shepherd them.
Straight to the grave they descend,
where their form will waste away,
Sheol will be their palace.
¹⁶But God will redeem my life,
will take me from the hand of
Sheol.

Selah

¹⁷Do not fear when a man becomes rich,
when the wealth of his house grows
great.

¹⁸At his death he will not take along
   anything,
   his glory will not go down after him.
¹⁹During his life his soul uttered
   blessings;
   "They will praise you, for you do
   well for yourself."

²⁰But he will join the company of his
   fathers,
   never again to see the light.
²¹In his prime, man does not
   understand.
   He is like the beasts—they perish.

☐ 2 CORINTHIANS 9

God's Indescribable Gift. 9:1 Now about the service to the holy ones, it is superfluous for me to write to you, ²for I know your eagerness, about which I boast of you to the Macedonians, that Achaia has been ready since last year; and your zeal has stirred up most of them. ³Nonetheless, I sent the brothers so that our boast about you might not prove empty in this case, so that you might be ready, as I said, ⁴for fear that if any Macedonians come with me and find you not ready we might be put to shame (to say nothing of you) in this conviction. ⁵So I thought it necessary to encourage the brothers to go on ahead to you and arrange in advance for your promised gift, so that in this way it might be ready as a bountiful gift and not as an exaction.

⁶Consider this: whoever sows sparingly will also reap sparingly, and whoever sows bountifully will also reap bountifully. ⁷Each must do as already determined, without sadness or compulsion, for God loves a cheerful giver. ⁸Moreover, God is able to make every grace abundant for you, so that in all things, always having all you need, you may have an abundance for every good work. ⁹As it is written:

"He scatters abroad, he gives to the
   poor;
   his righteousness endures forever."

¹⁰The one who supplies seed to the sower and bread for food will supply and multiply your seed and increase the harvest of your righteousness.

¹¹You are being enriched in every way for all generosity, which through us produces thanksgiving to God, ¹²for the administration of this public service is not only supplying the needs of the holy ones but is also overflowing in many acts of thanksgiving to God. ¹³Through the evidence of this service, you are glorifying God for your obedient confession of the gospel of Christ and the generosity of your contribution to them and to all others, ¹⁴while in prayer on your behalf they long for you, because of the surpassing grace of God upon you. ¹⁵Thanks be to God for his indescribable gift!

July 11

Receive counsel in everything you do, and you won't be sorry when you've done it.

— St. Benedict

☐ PSALMS 50-54

The Acceptable Sacrifice. 50:1 A psalm of Asaph.

The God of gods, the Lord,
  has spoken and summoned the earth
  from the rising of the sun to its setting.
²From Zion, the perfection of beauty,
God shines forth.
³Our God comes and will not be silent!
  Devouring fire precedes him,
  it rages strongly around him.
⁴He calls to the heavens above
  and to the earth to judge his people:
⁵"Gather my loyal ones to me,
  those who made a covenant with me
  by sacrifice."
⁶The heavens proclaim his
  righteousness,
  for God himself is the judge.

Selah

⁷"Listen, my people, I will speak;
  Israel, I will testify against you;
  God, your God, am I.
⁸Not for your sacrifices do I rebuke you,
  your burnt offerings are always
  before me.
⁹I will not take a bullock from your
  house,
  or he-goats from your folds.
¹⁰For every animal of the forest is mine,
  beasts by the thousands on my
  mountains.
¹¹I know every bird in the heights;
  whatever moves in the wild is mine.
¹²Were I hungry, I would not tell you,
  for mine is the world and all that
  fills it.
¹³Do I eat the flesh of bulls

or drink the blood of he-goats?
¹⁴Offer praise as your sacrifice to God;
  fulfill your vows to the Most High.
¹⁵Then call on me on the day of
  distress;
  I will rescue you, and you shall
  honor me."

¹⁶But to the wicked God says:
  "Why do you recite my
  commandments
  and profess my covenant with your
  mouth?
¹⁷You hate discipline;
  you cast my words behind you!
¹⁸If you see a thief, you run with him;
  with adulterers you throw in your
  lot.
¹⁹You give your mouth free rein for evil;
  you yoke your tongue to deceit.
²⁰You sit and speak against your brother,
  slandering your mother's son.
²¹When you do these things should I
  be silent?
  Do you think that I am like you?
  I accuse you, I lay out the matter
  before your eyes.

²²"Now understand this, you who
  forget God,
  lest I start ripping apart and there
  be no rescuer.
²³Those who offer praise as a sacrifice
  honor me;
  I will let him whose way is steadfast
  look upon the salvation of God."

The Miserere: Prayer of Repentance. 51:1
For the leader. A psalm of David, ²when

Nathan the prophet came to him after he had gone in to Bathsheba.

³Have mercy on me, God, in accord
    with your merciful love;
    in your abundant compassion blot
        out my transgressions.
⁴Thoroughly wash away my guilt;
    and from my sin cleanse me.
⁵For I know my transgressions;
    my sin is always before me.
⁶Against you, you alone have I sinned;
    I have done what is evil in your eyes
So that you are just in your word,
    and without reproach in your
        judgment.
⁷Behold, I was born in guilt,
    in sin my mother conceived me.
⁸Behold, you desire true sincerity;
    and secretly you teach me wisdom.
⁹Cleanse me with hyssop, that I may
        be pure;
    wash me, and I will be whiter than
        snow.
¹⁰You will let me hear gladness and joy;
    the bones you have crushed will
        rejoice.
¹¹Turn away your face from my sins;
    blot out all my iniquities.
¹²A clean heart create for me, God;
    renew within me a steadfast spirit.
¹³Do not drive me from before your face,
    nor take from me your holy spirit.
¹⁴Restore to me the gladness of your
        salvation;
    uphold me with a willing spirit.
¹⁵I will teach the wicked your ways,
    that sinners may return to you.
¹⁶Rescue me from violent bloodshed,
        God, my saving God,
    and my tongue will sing joyfully of
        your justice.
¹⁷Lord, you will open my lips;
    and my mouth will proclaim your
        praise.
¹⁸For you do not desire sacrifice or I
    would give it;

a burnt offering you would not accept.
¹⁹My sacrifice, O God, is a contrite spirit;
    a contrite, humbled heart, O God,
        you will not scorn.
²⁰Treat Zion kindly according to your
        good will;
    build up the walls of Jerusalem.
²¹Then you will desire the sacrifices of
        the just,
    burnt offering and whole offerings;
    then they will offer up young bulls
        on your altar.

The Deceitful Tongue. 52:1 For the leader. A *maskil* of David, ²when Doeg the Edomite entered and reported to Saul, saying to him: "David has entered the house of Ahimelech."

³Why do you glory in what is evil, you
    who are mighty by the mercy of
    God?
All day long
⁴you are thinking up intrigues;
    your tongue is like a sharpened razor,
    you worker of deceit.
⁵You love evil more than good,
    lying rather than saying what is right.
                                    Selah

⁶You love all the words that create
        confusion,
    you deceitful tongue.

⁷God too will strike you down forever,
    he will lay hold of you and pluck
        you from your tent,
    uproot you from the land of the
        living.
                                    Selah
⁸The righteous will see and they will fear;
    but they will laugh at him:
⁹"Behold the man! He did not take
        God as his refuge,
    but he trusted in the abundance of
        his wealth,
    and grew powerful through his
        wickedness."

¹⁰But I, like an olive tree flourishing in
the house of God,
I trust in God's mercy forever and
ever.
¹¹I will thank you forever
for what you have done.
I will put my hope in your name—for
it is good,
—in the presence of those devoted
to you.

A Lament over Widespread Corruption.
53:1 For the leader; according to *Mahalath*.
A *maskil* of David.

²The fool says in his heart,
"There is no God."
They act corruptly and practice injustice;
there is none that does good.
³God looks out from the heavens
upon the children of Adam,
To see if there is a discerning person
who is seeking God.
⁴All have gone astray;
each one is altogether perverse.
There is not one who does what is
good, not even one.

⁵Do they not know better, those who
do evil,
who feed upon my people as they
feed upon bread?
Have they not called upon God?
⁶They are going to fear his name with
great fear,
though they had not feared it before.

For God will scatter the bones
of those encamped against you.
They will surely be put to shame,
for God has rejected them.
⁷Who will bring forth from Zion
the salvation of Israel?
When God reverses the captivity of his
people
Jacob will rejoice and Israel will be
glad.

Confident Prayer in Great Peril. **54:1**
For the leader. On stringed instruments. A
maskil of David, ²when the Ziphites came
and said to Saul, "David is hiding among us."

³O God, by your name save me.
By your strength defend my cause.
⁴O God, hear my prayer.
Listen to the words of my mouth.
⁵Strangers have risen against me;
the ruthless seek my life;
they do not keep God before them.
Selah

⁶God is present as my helper;
the Lord sustains my life.
⁷Turn back the evil upon my foes;
in your faithfulness, destroy them.
⁸Then I will offer you generous
sacrifice
and give thanks to your name,
LORD, for it is good.
⁹Because it has rescued me from every
trouble,
and my eyes look down on my foes.

☐ 2 CORINTHIANS 10

Accusation of Weakness. **10:1** Now I my-
self, Paul, urge you through the gentleness
and clemency of Christ, I who am humble
when face to face with you, but brave toward you when absent, ²I beg you that,
when present, I may not have to be brave
with that confidence with which I intend
to act boldly against some who consider
us as acting according to the flesh. ³For,
although we are in the flesh, we do not
battle according to the flesh, ⁴for the weapons of our battle are not of flesh but are
enormously powerful, capable of destroying fortresses. We destroy arguments ⁵and
every pretension raising itself against the
knowledge of God, and take every thought

captive in obedience to Christ, ⁶and we are ready to punish every disobedience, once your obedience is complete.

⁷Look at what confronts you. Whoever is confident of belonging to Christ should consider that as he belongs to Christ, so do we. ⁸And even if I should boast a little too much of our authority, which the Lord gave for building you up and not for tearing you down, I shall not be put to shame. ⁹May I not seem as one frightening you through letters. ¹⁰For someone will say, "His letters are severe and forceful, but his bodily presence is weak, and his speech contemptible." ¹¹Such a person must understand that what we are in word through letters when absent, that we also are in action when present.

¹²Not that we dare to class or compare ourselves with some of those who recommend themselves. But when they measure themselves by one another and compare themselves with one another, they are without understanding. ¹³But we will not boast beyond measure but will keep to the limits God has apportioned us, namely, to reach even to you. ¹⁴For we are not overreaching ourselves, as though we did not reach you; we indeed first came to you with the gospel of Christ. ¹⁵We are not boasting beyond measure, in other people's labors; yet our hope is that, as your faith increases, our influence among you may be greatly enlarged, within our proper limits, ¹⁶so that we may preach the gospel even beyond you, not boasting of work already done in another's sphere. ¹⁷"Whoever boasts, should boast in the Lord." ¹⁸For it is not the one who recommends himself who is approved, but the one whom the Lord recommends.

July 12

I urge you, therefore — not I, but the love of Jesus Christ — eat only Christian food. Keep away from strange fare, by which I mean heresy. For heretics mix Jesus Christ with their teachings, speaking things unworthy of belief. It is as if they were giving a deadly poison mixed with sweetened wine, so that the unsuspecting victim readily accepts it and drinks his own death with fatal pleasure.

— St. Ignatius of Antioch

☐ PSALMS 55-60

A Lament over Betrayal. 55:1 For the leader. On stringed instruments. A *maskil* of David.

²Listen, God, to my prayer;
do not hide from my pleading;
³hear me and give answer.
I rock with grief; I groan
⁴at the uproar of the enemy,
the clamor of the wicked.

They heap trouble upon me,
savagely accuse me.
⁵My heart pounds within me;
death's terrors fall upon me.
⁶Fear and trembling overwhelm me;
shuddering sweeps over me.
⁷I say, "If only I had wings like a dove
that I might fly away and find rest.
⁸Far away I would flee;

I would stay in the desert.
⁹"I would soon find a shelter
  from the raging wind and storm."

¹⁰Lord, check and confuse their tongues.
  For I see violence and strife in the city
    ¹¹making rounds on its walls day
      and night.
Within are mischief and trouble;
  ¹²treachery is in its midst;
  oppression and fraud never leave its
    streets.
¹³For it is not an enemy that reviled me—
  that I could bear—
Not a foe who viewed me with
    contempt,
  from that I could hide.
¹⁴But it was you, my other self,
  my comrade and friend,
¹⁵You, whose company I enjoyed,
  at whose side I walked
  in the house of God.

¹⁶Let death take them;
  let them go down alive to Sheol,
  for evil is in their homes and bellies.
¹⁷But I will call upon God,
  and the Lord will save me.
¹⁸At dusk, dawn, and noon
  I will grieve and complain,
  and my prayer will be heard.
¹⁹He will redeem my soul in peace
  from those who war against me,
  though there are many who
    oppose me.
²⁰God, who sits enthroned forever,
  will hear me and afflict them.
                    Selah
For they will not mend their ways;
  they have no fear of God.
²¹He stretched out his hand at his friends
  and broke his covenant.
²²Softer than butter is his speech,
  but war is in his heart.
Smoother than oil are his words,
  but they are unsheathed swords.
²³Cast your care upon the Lord,
  who will give you support.

He will never allow
  the righteous to stumble.
²⁴But you, God, will bring them down
  to the pit of destruction.
These bloodthirsty liars
  will not live half their days,
  but I put my trust in you.

Trust in God. 56:1 For the director. According to *Yonath elem rehoqim*. A *miktam* of David, when the Philistines seized him at Gath.

²Have mercy on me, God,
  for I am treated harshly;
  attackers press me all the day.
³My foes treat me harshly all the day;
  yes, many are my attackers.
O Most High,⁴when I am afraid,
  in you I place my trust.
⁵I praise the word of God;
  I trust in God, I do not fear.
  What can mere flesh do to me?

⁶All the day they foil my plans;
  their every thought is of evil
    against me.
⁷They hide together in ambush;
  they watch my every step;
  they lie in wait for my life.
⁸They are evil; watch them, God!
  Cast the nations down in your anger!
⁹My wanderings you have noted;
  are my tears not stored in your flask,
  recorded in your book?
¹⁰My foes turn back when I call on you.
  This I know: God is on my side.
¹¹I praise the word of God,
  I praise the word of the Lord.
¹²In God I trust, I do not fear.
  What can man do to me?

¹³I have made vows to you, God;
  with offerings I will fulfill them,
¹⁴For you have snatched me from death,
  kept my feet from stumbling,
That I may walk before God
  in the light of the living.

Confident Prayer for Deliverance. **57:1**
For the director. Do not destroy. A *miktam*
of David, when he fled from Saul into a cave.

²Have mercy on me, God,
    have mercy on me.
In you I seek refuge.
In the shadow of your wings I seek refuge
    till harm pass by.
³I call to God Most High,
    to God who provides for me.
⁴May God send help from heaven to
    save me,
    shame those who trample upon me.
    May God send fidelity and mercy.
                                    Selah
⁵I must lie down in the midst of lions
    hungry for human prey.
Their teeth are spears and arrows;
    their tongue, a sharpened sword.
⁶Be exalted over the heavens, God;
    may your glory appear above all the
        earth.

⁷They have set a trap for my feet;
    my soul is bowed down;
They have dug a pit before me.
    May they fall into it themselves!
                                    Selah
⁸My heart is steadfast, God,
    my heart is steadfast.
I will sing and chant praise.
⁹Awake, my soul;
    awake, lyre and harp!
I will wake the dawn.
¹⁰I will praise you among the peoples,
    Lord;
I will chant your praise among the
    nations.
¹¹For your mercy towers to the heavens;
    your faithfulness reaches to the skies.
¹²Exalt yourself over the heavens, God;
    may your glory appear above all the
        earth.

The Dethroning of Unjust Rulers. **58:1**
For the leader. Do not destroy. A *miktam*
of David.

²Do you indeed pronounce justice,
    O gods;
    do you judge fairly you children of
        Adam?
³No, you freely engage in crime;
    your hands dispense violence to the
        earth.
⁴The wicked have been corrupt since
    birth;
    liars from the womb, they have gone
        astray.
⁵Their venom is like the venom of a
    snake,
    like that of a serpent stopping its ears,
⁶So as not to hear the voice of the
    charmer
    or the enchanter with cunning spells.

⁷O God, smash the teeth in their mouths;
    break the fangs of these lions, LORD!
⁸Make them vanish like water flowing
    away;
    trodden down, let them wither like
        grass.
⁹Let them dissolve like a snail that
    oozes away,
    like an untimely birth that never
        sees the sun.
¹⁰Suddenly, like brambles or thistles,
    have the whirlwind snatch them away.
¹¹Then the just shall rejoice to see the
    vengeance
    and bathe their feet in the blood of
        the wicked.
¹²Then people will say:
    "Truly there is a reward for the just;
    there is a God who is judge on earth!"

Complaint Against Bloodthirsty Enemies.
59:1 For the director. Do not destroy. A
miktam of David, when Saul sent people
to watch his house and kill him.

²Rescue me from my enemies, my God;
    lift me out of reach of my foes.
³Deliver me from evildoers;
    from the bloodthirsty save me.

⁴They have set an ambush for my life;
    the powerful conspire against me.
For no offense or misdeed of mine, Lord,
    ⁵for no fault they hurry to take up
        arms.
Come near and see my plight!
    ⁶You, Lord God of hosts, are the
        God of Israel!
Awake! Punish all the nations.
    Have no mercy on these worthless
        traitors.
                                        Selah

⁷Each evening they return,
    growling like dogs, prowling the city.
⁸Their mouths pour out insult;
    sharp words are on their lips.
    They say: "Who is there to hear?"
⁹But you, Lord, laugh at them;
    you deride all the nations.
¹⁰My strength, for you I watch;
    you, God, are my fortress,
    ¹¹my loving God.

May God go before me,
    and show me my fallen foes.
¹²Slay them, God,
    lest they deceive my people.
Shake them by your power;
    Lord, our shield, bring them down.
¹³For the sinful words of their mouths
        and lips
    let them be caught in their pride.
For the lies they have told under oath
    ¹⁴destroy them in anger,
    destroy till they are no more.
Then people will know God rules over
        Jacob,
    yes, even to the ends of the earth.
                                        Selah

¹⁵Each evening they return,
    growling like dogs, prowling the city.
¹⁶They roam about as scavengers;
    if they are not filled, they howl.

¹⁷But I shall sing of your strength,
    extol your mercy at dawn,
For you are my fortress,
    my refuge in time of trouble.

¹⁸My strength, your praise I will sing;
    you, God, are my fortress, my
        loving God.

Lament After Defeat in Battle. **60:1** For
the leader; according to "The Lily of...." A
miktam of David (for teaching), ²when he
fought against Aram-Naharaim and Aram-
Zobah; and Joab, coming back, killed twelve
thousand Edomites in the Valley of Salt.

³O God, you rejected us, broke our
        defenses;
    you were angry but now revive us.
⁴You rocked the earth, split it open;
    repair the cracks for it totters.
⁵You made your people go through
        hardship,
    made us stagger from the wine you
        gave us.
⁶Raise up a banner for those who
        revere you,
    a refuge for them out of bow shot.
                                        Selah

⁷Help with your right hand and
        answer us
    that your loved ones may escape.

⁸In the sanctuary God promised:
    "I will exult, will apportion Shechem;
    the valley of Succoth I will measure
        out.
⁹Gilead is mine, mine is Manasseh;
    Ephraim is the helmet for my head,
    Judah, my own scepter.
¹⁰Moab is my washbowl;
    upon Edom I cast my sandal.
I will triumph over Philistia."

¹¹Who will bring me to the fortified city?
    Who will lead me into Edom?
¹²Was it not you who rejected us, God?
    Do you no longer march with our
        armies?
¹³Give us aid against the foe;
    worthless is human help.
¹⁴We will triumph with the help of God,
    who will trample down our foes.

☐ 2 CORINTHIANS 11:1-15

Preaching without Charge. 11:1 If only you would put up with a little foolishness from me! Please put up with me. ²For I am jealous of you with the jealousy of God, since I betrothed you to one husband to present you as a chaste virgin to Christ. ³But I am afraid that, as the serpent deceived Eve by his cunning, your thoughts may be corrupted from a sincere [and pure] commitment to Christ. ⁴For if someone comes and preaches another Jesus than the one we preached, or if you receive a different spirit from the one you received or a different gospel from the one you accepted, you put up with it well enough. ⁵For I think that I am not in any way inferior to these "superapostles." ⁶Even if I am untrained in speaking, I am not so in knowledge; in every way we have made this plain to you in all things.

⁷Did I make a mistake when I humbled myself so that you might be exalted, because I preached the gospel of God to you without charge? ⁸I plundered other churches by accepting from them in order to minister to you. ⁹And when I was with you and in need, I did not burden anyone, for the brothers who came from Macedonia supplied my needs. So I refrained and will refrain from burdening you in any way. ¹⁰By the truth of Christ in me, this boast of mine shall not be silenced in the regions of Achaia. ¹¹And why? Because I do not love you? God knows I do!

¹²And what I do I will continue to do, in order to end this pretext of those who seek a pretext for being regarded as we are in the mission of which they boast. ¹³For such people are false apostles, deceitful workers, who masquerade as apostles of Christ. ¹⁴And no wonder, for even Satan masquerades as an angel of light. ¹⁵So it is not strange that his ministers also masquerade as ministers of righteousness. Their end will correspond to their deeds.

July 13

St. Henry; St. Teresa of the Andes

There will never be any separation between our souls. I will live in Him. Search for Jesus, and in Him you'll find me. There, the three of us will continue our intimate conversations, the ones we'll be carrying on there forever in eternity.

— St. Teresa of the Andes (to a friend)

☐ PSALMS 61-66

Prayer of the King in Time of Danger.
61:1 For the leader; with stringed instruments. Of David.

²Hear my cry, O God,
  listen to my prayer!
³From the ends of the earth I call;
  my heart grows faint.

Raise me up, set me on a rock,
  ⁴for you are my refuge,
  a tower of strength against the foe.
⁵Let me dwell in your tent forever,
  take refuge in the shelter of your
    wings.
Selah

⁶For you, O God, have heard my
    vows,
  you have granted me the heritage of
    those who revere your name.
⁷Add days to the life of the king;
  may his years be as from generation
    to generation;
⁸May he reign before God forever;
  send your love and fidelity to
    preserve him—
⁹I will duly sing to your name forever,
  fulfill my vows day after day.

Trust in God Alone. 62:1 For the leader;
'al Jeduthun. A psalm of David.

²My soul rests in God alone,
  from whom comes my salvation.
³God alone is my rock and salvation,
  my fortress; I shall never fall.
⁴How long will you set yourself against
    a man?
  You shall all be destroyed,
Like a sagging wall
  or a tumbled down fence!
⁵Even highly placed people
  plot to overthrow him.
They delight in lies;
  they bless with their mouths,
  but inwardly they curse.

                              Selah

⁶My soul, be at rest in God alone,
  from whom comes my hope.
⁷God alone is my rock and my salvation,
  my fortress; I shall not fall.
⁸My deliverance and honor are with God,
  my strong rock;
  my refuge is with God.
⁹Trust God at all times, my people!
  Pour out your hearts to God our
    refuge!

                              Selah

¹⁰Mortals are a mere breath,
  the sons of man but an illusion;
On a balance they rise;
  together they weigh nothing.

¹¹Do not trust in extortion;
  in plunder put no empty hope.
On wealth that increases,
  do not set your heart.
¹²One thing God has said;
  two things I have heard:
Strength belongs to God;
  ¹³so too, my Lord, does mercy,
For you repay each man
  according to his deeds.

Ardent Longing for God. 63:1 A psalm of
David, when he was in the wilderness of
Judah.

²O God, you are my God—
  it is you I seek!
For you my body yearns;
  for you my soul thirsts,
In a land parched, lifeless,
  and without water.
³I look to you in the sanctuary
  to see your power and glory.
⁴For your love is better than life;
  my lips shall ever praise you!

⁵I will bless you as long as I live;
  I will lift up my hands, calling on
    your name.
⁶My soul shall be sated as with choice
    food,
  with joyous lips my mouth shall
    praise you!
⁷I think of you upon my bed,
  I remember you through the
    watches of the night
⁸You indeed are my savior,
  and in the shadow of your wings I
    shout for joy.
⁹My soul clings fast to you;
  your right hand upholds me.

¹⁰But those who seek my life will come
    to ruin;
  they shall go down to the depths of
    the netherworld!
¹¹Those who would hand over my
  life to the sword shall

become the prey of jackals!
12 But the king shall rejoice in God;
all who swear by the Lord shall exult,
but the mouths of liars will be shut!

Treacherous Conspirators Punished by God. 64:1 For the leader. A psalm of David.

2O God, hear my anguished voice;
from a dreadful foe protect my life.
3Hide me from the malicious crowd,
the mob of evildoers.
4They sharpen their tongues like swords,
bend their bows of poison words.
5They shoot at the innocent from
ambush,
they shoot him in a moment and do
not fear.
6They resolve on their wicked plan;
they conspire to set snares;
they say: "Who will see us?"
7They devise wicked schemes,
conceal the schemes they devise;
the designs of their hearts are hidden.

8God shoots an arrow at them;
in a moment they are struck down.
9They are brought down by their own
tongues;
all who see them flee.
10Every person fears and proclaims
God's actions,
they ponder his deeds.
11The righteous rejoices and takes
refuge in the LORD;
all the upright give praise.

Thanksgiving for God's Blessings. 65:1 For the leader. A psalm of David. A song.

2To you we owe our hymn of praise,
O God on Zion;
To you our vows must be fulfilled,
3you who hear our prayers.
To you all flesh must come
4with its burden of wicked deeds.
We are overcome by our sins;
only you can pardon them.

5Blessed the one whom you will choose
and bring
to dwell in your courts.
May we be filled with the good things
of your house,
your holy temple!

6You answer us with awesome deeds of
justice,
O God our savior,
The hope of all the ends of the earth
and of those far off across the sea.
7You are robed in power,
you set up the mountains by your
might.
8You still the roaring of the seas,
the roaring of their waves,
the tumult of the peoples.
9Distant peoples stand in awe of your
marvels;
the places of morning and evening
you make resound with joy.
10You visit the earth and water it,
make it abundantly fertile.
God's stream is filled with water;
you supply their grain.
Thus do you prepare it:
11you drench its plowed furrows,
and level its ridges.
With showers you keep it soft,
blessing its young sprouts.
12You adorn the year with your bounty;
your paths drip with fruitful rain.
13The meadows of the wilderness also
drip;
the hills are robed with joy.
14The pastures are clothed with flocks,
the valleys blanketed with grain;
they cheer and sing for joy.

Praise of God, Israel's Deliverer. 66:1 For the leader. A song; a psalm.

2Shout joyfully to God, all the earth;
sing of his glorious name;
give him glorious praise.
3Say to God: "How awesome your deeds!

Before your great strength your
enemies cringe.
[4]All the earth falls in worship before you;
they sing of you, sing of your name!"
Selah

[5]Come and see the works of God,
awesome in deeds before the
children of Adam.
[6]He changed the sea to dry land;
through the river they passed on foot.
There we rejoiced in him,
[7]who rules by his might forever,
His eyes are fixed upon the nations.
Let no rebel rise to challenge!
Selah

[8]Bless our God, you peoples;
loudly sound his praise,
[9]Who has kept us alive
and not allowed our feet to slip.
[10]You tested us, O God,
tried us as silver tried by fire.
[11]You led us into a snare;
you bound us at the waist as captives.
[12]You let captors set foot on our neck;

we went through fire and water;
then you led us out to freedom.

[13]I will bring burnt offerings to your
house;
to you I will fulfill my vows,
[14]Which my lips pronounced
and my mouth spoke in my distress.
[15]Burnt offerings of fatlings I will offer
you
and sacrificial smoke of rams;
I will sacrifice oxen and goats.
Selah

[16]Come and hear, all you who fear God,
while I recount what has been done
for me.
[17]I called to him with my mouth;
praise was upon my tongue.
[18]Had I cherished evil in my heart,
the Lord would not have heard.
[19]But God did hear
and listened to my voice in prayer.
[20]Blessed be God, who did not reject
my prayer
and refuse his mercy.

☐ 2 CORINTHIANS 11:16-33

Paul's Boast: His Labors. 11:16 I repeat, no one should consider me foolish; but if you do, accept me as a fool, so that I too may boast a little. [17]What I am saying I am not saying according to the Lord but as in foolishness, in this boastful state. [18]Since many boast according to the flesh, I too will boast. [19]For you gladly put up with fools, since you are wise yourselves. [20]For you put up with it if someone enslaves you, or devours you, or gets the better of you, or puts on airs, or slaps you in the face. [21]To my shame I say that we were too weak!

But what anyone dares to boast of (I am speaking in foolishness) I also dare. [22]Are they Hebrews? So am I. Are they Israelites? So am I. Are they descendants of Abraham? So am I. [23]Are they ministers of Christ? (I am talking like an insane person.) I am still more, with far greater labors, far more imprisonments, far worse beatings, and numerous brushes with death. [24]Five times at the hands of the Jews I received forty lashes minus one. [25]Three times I was beaten with rods, once I was stoned, three times I was shipwrecked, I passed a night and a day on the deep; [26]on frequent journeys, in dangers from rivers, dangers from robbers, dangers from my own race, dangers from Gentiles, dangers in the city, dangers in the wilderness, dangers at sea, dangers among false brothers; [27]in toil and hardship, through many sleepless nights, through hunger and thirst, through frequent fastings, through cold and exposure. [28]And apart from these things, there is the daily pressure upon me of my anxiety for all the churches. [29]Who is weak, and I am not weak? Who is led to sin, and I am not indignant?

Paul's Boast: His Weakness. [30]If I must boast, I will boast of the things that show my weakness. [31]The God and Father of the Lord Jesus knows, he who is blessed forever, that I do not lie. [32]At Damascus, the governor under King Aretas guarded the city of Damascus, in order to seize me, [33]but I was lowered in a basket through a window in the wall and escaped his hands.

July 14

Blessed Kateri Tekakwitha; St. Camillus de Lellis

I don't put a penny's value on this life if only Our Lord will give me a tiny corner in Paradise.

— St. Camillus de Lellis

☐ PSALMS 67–70

***Harvest Thanks and Petition.* 67:1** For the leader; with stringed instruments. A psalm; a song.

[2]May God be gracious to us and bless us;
may his face shine upon us.
Selah
[3]So shall your way be known upon the earth,
your victory among all the nations.
[4]May the peoples praise you, God;
may all the peoples praise you!

[5]May the nations be glad and rejoice;
for you judge the peoples with fairness,
you guide the nations upon the earth.
Selah
[6]May the peoples praise you, God;
may all the peoples praise you!

[7]The earth has yielded its harvest;
God, our God, blesses us.
[8]May God bless us still;
that the ends of the earth may revere him.

***The Exodus and Conquest, Pledge of Future Help.* 68:1** For the leader. A psalm of David; a song.

[2]May God arise;
may his enemies be scattered;
may those who hate him flee before him.
[3]As the smoke is dispersed, disperse them;
as wax is melted by fire,
so may the wicked perish before God.
[4]Then the just will be glad;
they will rejoice before God;
they will celebrate with great joy.

[5]Sing to God, praise his name;
exalt the rider of the clouds.
Rejoice before him
whose name is the Lord.
[6]Father of the fatherless, defender of widows—
God in his holy abode,
[7]God gives a home to the forsaken,
who leads prisoners out to prosperity,
while rebels live in the desert.

[8]God, when you went forth before your people,
when you marched through the desert,
Selah
[9]The earth quaked, the heavens poured, before God, the One of Sinai,

before God, the God of Israel.
¹⁰You poured abundant rains, God,
  your inheritance was weak and you
    repaired it.
¹¹Your creatures dwelt in it;
  you will establish it in your goodness
    for the poor, O God.

¹²The Lord announced:
  "Those bringing news are a great
    Army.
¹³The kings of the armies are in
    desperate flight.
Every household will share the spoil,
  ¹⁴though you lie down among the
    sheepfolds,
  you shall be covered with silver as
    the wings of a dove,
  her feathers bright as fine gold."
¹⁵When the Almighty routs the kings
    there,
  it will be as when snow fell on
    Zalmon.

¹⁶You mountain of God, mountain of
    Bashan,
  you rugged mountain, mountain of
    Bashan,
¹⁷You rugged mountains, why look
    with envy
  at the mountain where God has
    chosen to dwell,
  where the LORD resides forever?
¹⁸God's chariots were myriad,
    thousands upon thousands;
  from Sinai the Lord entered the
    holy place.
¹⁹You went up to its lofty height;
  you took captives, received slaves as
    tribute,
  even rebels, for the LORD God to
    dwell.

²⁰Blessed be the Lord day by day,
  God, our salvation, who carries us.
                                    Selah
²¹Our God is a God who saves;
  escape from death is the LORD God's.

²²God will crush the heads of his
    enemies,
  the hairy scalp of the one who walks
    in sin.
²³The Lord has said:
  "Even from Bashan I will fetch them,
  fetch them even from the depths of
    the sea.
²⁴You will wash your feet in your
    enemy's blood;
  the tongues of your dogs will lap
    it up."

²⁵Your procession comes into view,
    O God,
  your procession into the holy place,
    my God and king.
²⁶The singers go first, the harpists
    follow;
  in their midst girls sound the
    timbrels.
²⁷In your choirs, bless God;
  LORD, Israel's fountain.
²⁸In the lead is Benjamin, few in number;
  there the princes of Judah, a large
    throng,
  the princes of Zebulun, the princes
    of Naphtali, too.

²⁹Summon again, O God, your power,
  the divine power you once showed
    for us,
³⁰From your temple on behalf of
    Jerusalem,
  that kings may bring you tribute.
³¹Roar at the wild beast of the reeds,
  the herd of mighty bulls, the calves
    of the peoples;
  trampling those who lust after silver
  scatter the peoples that delight in war.
³²Let bronze be brought from Egypt,
  Ethiopia hurry its hands to God.

³³You kingdoms of the earth, sing to
    God;
  chant the praises of the Lord,
                                    Selah

³⁴Who rides the heights of the ancient
    heavens,
  Who sends forth his voice as a
    mighty voice?
³⁵Confess the power of God,
  whose majesty protects Israel,
  whose power is in the sky.
³⁶Awesome is God in his holy place,
  the God of Israel,
  who gives power and strength to his
    people.
Blessed be God!

A Cry of Anguish in Great Distress. 69:1

For the leader; according to "Lilies." Of
David.

²Save me, God,
  for the waters have reached my neck.
³I have sunk into the mire of the deep,
  where there is no foothold.
I have gone down to the watery depths;
  the flood overwhelms me.
⁴I am weary with crying out;
  my throat is parched.
My eyes fail,
  from looking for my God.
⁵More numerous than the hairs of my
    head
  are those who hate me without
    cause.
Those who would destroy me are mighty,
  my enemies without reason.
Must I now restore
  what I did not steal?

⁶God, you know my folly;
  my faults are not hidden from you.
⁷Let those who wait in hope for you,
  Lord of hosts,
  not be shamed because of me.
Let those who seek you, God of Israel,
  not be disgraced because of me.
⁸For it is on your account I bear insult,
  that disgrace covers my face.
⁹I have become an outcast to my
    kindred,
  a stranger to my mother's children.

¹⁰Because zeal for your house has
    consumed me,
  I am scorned by those who scorn you.
¹¹When I humbled my spirit with
    fasting,
  this led only to scorn.
¹²When I clothed myself in sackcloth;
  I became a byword for them.
¹³Those who sit in the gate gossip
    about me;
  drunkards make me the butt of
    songs.

¹⁴But I will pray to you, Lord,
  at a favorable time.
God, in your abundant kindness,
    answer me
  with your sure deliverance.
¹⁵Rescue me from the mire,
  and do not let me sink.
Rescue me from those who hate me
  and from the watery depths.
¹⁶Do not let the flood waters
    overwhelm me,
  nor the deep swallow me,
  nor the pit close its mouth over me.
¹⁷Answer me, Lord, in your generous
    love;
  in your great mercy turn to me.
¹⁸Do not hide your face from your
    servant;
  hasten to answer me, for I am in
    distress.
¹⁹Come and redeem my life;
  because of my enemies ransom me.
²⁰You know my reproach, my shame,
    my disgrace;
  before you stand all my foes.
²¹Insult has broken my heart, and I
    despair;
  I looked for compassion, but there
    was none,
  for comforters, but found none.
²²Instead they gave me poison for my
    food;
  and for my thirst they gave me
    vinegar.

²³May their own table be a snare for
them,
and their communion offerings a
trap.
²⁴Make their eyes so dim they cannot
see;
keep their backs ever feeble.
²⁵Pour out your wrath upon them;
let the fury of your anger overtake
them.
²⁶Make their camp desolate,
with none to dwell in their tents.
²⁷For they pursued the one you struck,
added to the pain of the one you
wounded.
²⁸Heap punishment upon their
punishment;
let them gain from you no
vindication.
²⁹May they be blotted from the book
of life;
not registered among the just!

³⁰But here I am miserable and in pain;
let your saving help protect me,
God,
³¹That I may praise God's name in song
and glorify it with thanksgiving.
³²That will please the LORD more than
oxen,
more than bulls with horns and
hooves:
³³"See, you lowly ones, and be glad;
you who seek God, take heart!

³⁴For the LORD hears the poor,
and does not spurn those in
bondage.
³⁵Let the heaven and the earth praise
him,
the seas and whatever moves in
them!"

³⁶For God will rescue Zion,
and rebuild the cities of Judah.
They will dwell there and possess it;
³⁷the descendants of God's servants will
inherit it;
those who love God's name will
dwell in it.

Prayer for Divine Help. 70:1 For the
leader; of David. For remembrance.
²Graciously rescue me, God!
Come quickly to help me, LORD!
³Let those who seek my life
be confused and put to shame.
Let those who desire my ruin
turn back in disgrace.
⁴Let those who say "Aha!"
turn back in their shame.
⁵But may all who seek you
rejoice and be glad in you,
Those who long for your help
always say, "God be glorified!"
⁶I am miserable and poor.
God, come to me quickly!
You are my help and deliverer.
LORD, do not delay!

☐ 2 CORINTHIANS 12:1-10

12:1 I must boast; not that it is profitable,
but I will go on to visions and revelations of
the Lord. ²I know someone in Christ who,
fourteen years ago (whether in the body
or out of the body I do not know, God
knows), was caught up to the third heaven.
³And I know that this person (whether
in the body or out of the body I do not
know, God knows) ⁴was caught up into
Paradise and heard ineffable things, which

no one may utter. ⁵About this person I will
boast, but about myself I will not boast,
except about my weaknesses. ⁶Although if
I should wish to boast, I would not be foolish, for I would be telling the truth. But I
refrain, so that no one may think more of
me than what he sees in me or hears from
me ⁷because of the abundance of the revelations. Therefore, that I might not become
too elated, a thorn in the flesh was given to

me, an angel of Satan, to beat me, to keep me from being too elated. [8]Three times I begged the Lord about this, that it might leave me, [9]but he said to me, "My grace is sufficient for you, for power is made perfect in weakness." I will rather boast most gladly of my weaknesses, in order that the power of Christ may dwell with me. [10]Therefore, I am content with weaknesses, insults, hardships, persecutions, and constraints, for the sake of Christ; for when I am weak, then I am strong.

July 15

St. Bonaventure

In God alone is there ultimate and true delight, and in all our delights it is this delight that we are seeking.

— ST. BONAVENTURE

☐ PSALMS 71–75

Prayer in Time of Old Age. 71:1 In
you, LORD, I take refuge;
let me never be put to shame.
[2]In your justice rescue and deliver me;
listen to me and save me!
[3]Be my rock of refuge,
my stronghold to give me safety;
for you are my rock and fortress.
[4]My God, rescue me from the hand of
the wicked,
from the clutches of the evil and
violent.
[5]You are my hope, Lord;
my trust, GOD, from my youth.
[6]On you I have depended since birth;
from my mother's womb you are
my strength;
my hope in you never wavers.
[7]I have become a portent to many,
but you are my strong refuge!
[8]My mouth shall be filled with your
praise,
shall sing your glory every day.

[9]Do not cast me aside in my old age;
as my strength fails, do not forsake
me.
[10]For my enemies speak against me;

they watch and plot against me.
[11]They say, "God has abandoned him.
Pursue, and seize him!
No one will come to the rescue!"
[12]God, be not far from me;
my God, hasten to help me.
[13]Bring to a shameful end
those who attack me;
Cover with contempt and scorn
those who seek my ruin.
[14]I will always hope in you
and add to all your praise.
[15]My mouth shall proclaim your just
deeds,
day after day your acts of deliverance,
though I cannot number them all.
[16]I will speak of the mighty works of
the Lord;
O GOD, I will tell of your singular
justice.
[17]God, you have taught me from my
youth;
to this day I proclaim your
wondrous deeds.
[18]Now that I am old and gray,
do not forsake me, God,
That I may proclaim your might

to all generations yet to come,
Your power ¹⁹and justice, God,
 to the highest heaven.
You have done great things;
 O God, who is your equal?
²⁰Whatever bitter afflictions you sent me,
 you would turn and revive me.
From the watery depths of the earth
 once more raise me up.
²¹Restore my honor;
 turn and comfort me,
²²That I may praise you with the lyre
 for your faithfulness, my God,
And sing to you with the harp,
 O Holy One of Israel!
²³My lips will shout for joy as I sing
 your praise;
 my soul, too, which you have
 redeemed.
²⁴Yes, my tongue shall recount
 your justice day by day.
For those who sought my ruin
 have been shamed and disgraced.

A Prayer for the King. 72:1 Of Solomon.

²O God, give your judgment to the king;
 your justice to the king's son;
That he may govern your people with
 justice,
 your oppressed with right judgment,
³That the mountains may yield their
 bounty for the people,
 and the hills great abundance,
⁴That he may defend the oppressed
 among the people,
 save the children of the poor and
 crush the oppressor.

⁵May they fear you with the sun,
 and before the moon, through all
 generations.
⁶May he be like rain coming down
 upon the fields,
 like showers watering the earth,
⁷That abundance may flourish in his
 days,

great bounty, till the moon be no
 more.
⁸May he rule from sea to sea,
 from the river to the ends of the
 earth.
⁹May his foes kneel before him,
 his enemies lick the dust.
¹⁰May the kings of Tarshish and the
 islands bring tribute,
 the kings of Sheba and Seba offer
 gifts.
¹¹May all kings bow before him,
 all nations serve him.
¹²For he rescues the poor when they
 cry out,
 the oppressed who have no one to
 help.
¹³He shows pity to the needy and the
 poor
 and saves the lives of the poor.
¹⁴From extortion and violence he
 redeems them,
 for precious is their blood in his
 sight.

¹⁵Long may he live, receiving gold from
 Sheba,
 prayed for without cease, blessed
 day by day.
¹⁶May wheat abound in the land,
 flourish even on the mountain
 heights.
May his fruit be like that of Lebanon,
 and flourish in the city like the
 grasses of the land.
¹⁷May his name be forever;
 as long as the sun, may his name
 endure.
May the tribes of the earth give
 blessings with his name;
 may all the nations regard him as
 favored.
¹⁸Blessed be the LORD God, the God
 of Israel,
 who alone does wonderful deeds.
¹⁹Blessed be his glorious name forever;
 may he fill all the earth with his glory.

Amen and amen.

20The end of the psalms of David, son of Jesse.

The Trial of the Just. 73:1 A psalm of Asaph.

How good God is to the upright,
  to those who are pure of heart!
2But, as for me, my feet had almost stumbled;
  my steps had nearly slipped,
3Because I was envious of the arrogant
  when I saw the prosperity of the wicked.
4For they suffer no pain;
  their bodies are healthy and sleek.
5They are free of the burdens of life;
  they are not afflicted like others.
6Thus pride adorns them as a necklace;
  violence clothes them as a robe.
7Out of such blindness comes sin;
  evil thoughts flood their hearts.
8They scoff and spout their malice;
  from on high they utter threats.
9They set their mouths against the heavens,
  their tongues roam the earth.
10So my people turn to them
  and drink deeply of their words.
11They say, "Does God really know?"
  "Does the Most High have any knowledge?"
12Such, then, are the wicked,
  always carefree, increasing their wealth.

13Is it in vain that I have kept my heart pure,
  washed my hands in innocence?
14For I am afflicted day after day,
  chastised every morning.
15Had I thought, "I will speak as they do,"
  I would have betrayed this
    generation of your children.
16Though I tried to understand all this,
  it was too difficult for me,
17Till I entered the sanctuary of God
and came to understand their end.

18You set them, indeed, on a slippery road;
  you hurl them down to ruin.
19How suddenly they are devastated;
  utterly undone by disaster!
20They are like a dream after waking, Lord,
  dismissed like shadows when you arise.

21Since my heart was embittered
  and my soul deeply wounded,
22I was stupid and could not understand;
  I was like a brute beast in your presence.
23Yet I am always with you;
  you take hold of my right hand.
24With your counsel you guide me,
  and at the end receive me with honor.
25Whom else have I in the heavens?
  None beside you delights me on earth.
26Though my flesh and my heart fail,
  God is the rock of my heart, my portion forever.
27But those who are far from you perish;
  you destroy those unfaithful to you.
28As for me, to be near God is my good,
  to make the Lord GOD my refuge.
I shall declare all your works
  in the gates of daughter Zion.

Prayer at the Destruction of the Temple. 74:1 A maskil of Asaph.

Why, God, have you cast us off forever?
  Why does your anger burn against
    the sheep of your pasture?
2Remember your people, whom you acquired of old,
  the tribe you redeemed as your own heritage,
  Mount Zion where you dwell.
3Direct your steps toward the utter destruction,

everything the enemy laid waste in
the sanctuary.

⁴Your foes roared triumphantly in the
place of your assembly;
they set up their own tokens of
victory.

⁵They hacked away like a forester
gathering boughs,
swinging his ax in a thicket of trees.

⁶They smashed all its engraved work,
struck it with ax and pick.

⁷They set your sanctuary on fire,
profaned your name's abode by
razing it to the ground.

⁸They said in their hearts, "We will
destroy them all!
Burn all the assembly-places of God
in the land!"

⁹Even so we have seen no signs for us,
there is no prophet any more,
no one among us who knows for
how long.

¹⁰How long, O God, will the enemy
jeer?
Will the enemy revile your name
forever?

¹¹Why draw back your hand,
why hold back your right hand
within your bosom?

¹²Yet you, God, are my king from of
old,
winning victories throughout the
earth.

¹³You stirred up the sea by your might;
you smashed the heads of the
dragons on the waters.

¹⁴You crushed the heads of Leviathan,
gave him as food to the sharks.

¹⁵You opened up springs and torrents,
brought dry land out of the
primeval waters.

¹⁶Yours the day and yours the night
too;
you set the moon and sun in place.

¹⁷You fixed all the limits of the earth;
summer and winter you made.

¹⁸Remember how the enemy has
jeered, LORD,
how a foolish people has reviled
your name.

¹⁹Do not surrender to wild animals
those who praise you;
do not forget forever the life of your
afflicted.

²⁰Look to your covenant,
for the recesses of the land
are full of the haunts of violence.

²¹Let not the oppressed turn back in
shame;
may the poor and needy praise your
name.

²²Arise, God, defend your cause;
remember the constant jeering of
the fools.

²³Do not forget the clamor of your foes,
the unceasing uproar of your
enemies.

God the Judge of the World. 75:1 For the
leader. Do not destroy! A psalm of Asaph;
a song.

²We thank you, God, we give thanks;
we call upon your name,
we declare your wonderful deeds.
[You said:]

³"I will choose the time;
I will judge fairly.

⁴Though the earth and all its
inhabitants quake,
I make steady its pillars."

Selah

⁵So I say to the boastful: "Do not
boast!"
to the wicked: "Do not raise your
horns!

⁶Do not raise your horns against
heaven!
Do not speak with a stiff neck!"

⁷For judgment comes not from east or
from west,
not from the wilderness or the
mountains,

⁸But from God who decides,
    who brings some low and raises
      others high.
⁹Yes, a cup is in the Lord's hand,
    foaming wine, fully spiced.
When God pours it out,
    they will drain it even to the dregs;
    all the wicked of the earth will drink.

¹⁰But I will rejoice forever;
    I will sing praise to the God of
      Jacob,
¹¹[Who has said:]
"I will cut off all the horns of the
    wicked,
    but the horns of the righteous will
      be exalted."

☐ 2 CORINTHIANS 12:11–13:13

Selfless Concern for the Church. 12:11 I have been foolish. You compelled me, for I ought to have been commended by you. For I am in no way inferior to these "superapostles," even though I am nothing. ¹²The signs of an apostle were performed among you with all endurance, signs and wonders, and mighty deeds. ¹³In what way were you less privileged than the rest of the churches, except that on my part I did not burden you? Forgive me this wrong!

¹⁴Now I am ready to come to you this third time. And I will not be a burden, for I want not what is yours, but you. Children ought not to save for their parents, but parents for their children. ¹⁵I will most gladly spend and be utterly spent for your sakes. If I love you more, am I to be loved less? ¹⁶But granted that I myself did not burden you, yet I was crafty and got the better of you by deceit. ¹⁷Did I take advantage of you through any of those I sent to you? ¹⁸I urged Titus to go and sent the brother with him. Did Titus take advantage of you? Did we not walk in the same spirit? And in the same steps?

Final Warnings and Appeals. ¹⁹Have you been thinking all along that we are defending ourselves before you? In the sight of God we are speaking in Christ, and all for building you up, beloved. ²⁰For I fear that when I come I may find you not such as I wish, and that you may find me not as you wish; that there may be rivalry, jealousy, fury, selfishness, slander, gossip, conceit, and disorder. ²¹I fear that when I come again my God may humiliate me before you, and I may have to mourn over many of those who sinned earlier and have not repented of the impurity, immorality, and licentiousness they practiced.

13:1 This third time I am coming to you. "On the testimony of two or three witnesses a fact shall be established." ²I warned those who sinned earlier and all the others, and I warn them now while absent, as I did when present on my second visit, that if I come again I will not be lenient, ³since you are looking for proof of Christ speaking in me. He is not weak toward you but powerful in you. ⁴For indeed he was crucified out of weakness, but he lives by the power of God. So also we are weak in him, but toward you we shall live with him by the power of God.

⁵Examine yourselves to see whether you are living in faith. Test yourselves. Do you not realize that Jesus Christ is in you?—unless, of course, you fail the test. ⁶I hope you will discover that we have not failed. ⁷But we pray to God that you may not do evil, not that we may appear to have passed the test but that you may do what is right, even though we may seem to have failed. ⁸For we cannot do anything against the truth, but only for the truth. ⁹For we rejoice when we are weak but you are strong. What we pray for is your improvement.

¹⁰I am writing this while I am away, so that when I come I may not have to be se-

vere in virtue of the authority that the Lord has given me to build up and not to tear down.

[11]Finally, brothers, rejoice. Mend your ways, encourage one another, agree with one another, live in peace, and the God of love and peace will be with you. [12]Greet one another with a holy kiss. All the holy ones greet you.

[13]The grace of the Lord Jesus Christ and the love of God and the fellowship of the holy Spirit be with all of you.

July 16

Our Lady of Mount Carmel

Invisible in His own nature, He became visible in ours. Beyond our grasp, He chose to come within our grasp. Existing before time began, He began to exist at a moment in time. Incapable of suffering as God, He did not refuse to be a man, capable of suffering. Immortal, He chose to be subject to the laws of death.

— POPE ST. LEO THE GREAT

☐ PSALMS 76-79

God Defends Zion. 76:1 For the leader; a psalm with stringed instruments. A song of Asaph.

[2]Renowned in Judah is God,
   whose name is great in Israel.
[3]On Salem is God's tent, his shelter on
      Zion.
   [4]There the flashing arrows were
         shattered,
      shield, sword, and weapons of war.
                                  Selah

[5]Terrible and awesome are you,
   stronger than the ancient mountains.
[6]Despoiled are the stouthearted;
   they sank into sleep;
   the hands of all the men of valor
         have failed.
[7]At your roar, O God of Jacob,
   chariot and steed lay still.
[8]You, terrible are you;
   who can stand before you and your
         great anger?

[9]From the heavens you pronounced
         sentence;
   the earth was terrified and reduced
         to silence,
[10]When you arose, O God, for
         judgment
   to save the afflicted of the land.
                                  Selah
[11]Surely the wrath of man will give you
         thanks;
   the remnant of your furor will keep
         your feast.
[12]Make and keep vows to the LORD
         your God.
   May all around him bring gifts to
         the one to be feared,
[13]Who checks the spirit of princes,
   who is fearful to the kings of earth.

Confidence in God During National Distress. 77:1 For the leader; According to *Jeduthun*. A psalm of Asaph.

[2]I cry aloud to God,

I cry to God to hear me.
³On the day of my distress I seek the
Lord;
by night my hands are stretched out
unceasingly;
I refuse to be consoled.
⁴When I think of God, I groan;
as I meditate, my spirit grows faint.
Selah

⁵You have kept me from closing my
eyes in sleep;
I am troubled and cannot speak.
⁶I consider the days of old;
the years long past ⁷I remember.
At night I ponder in my heart;
and as I meditate, my spirit probes:
⁸"Will the Lord reject us forever,
never again show favor?
⁹Has God's mercy ceased forever?
The promise to go unfulfilled for
future ages?
¹⁰Has God forgotten how to show mercy,
in anger withheld his compassion?"
Selah

¹¹ I conclude: "My sorrow is this,
the right hand of the Most High has
abandoned us."

¹²I will recall the deeds of the LORD;
yes, recall your wonders of old.
¹³I will ponder all your works;
on your exploits I will meditate.
¹⁴Your way, God, is holy;
what god is as great as our God?
¹⁵You are the God who does wonders;
among the peoples you have
revealed your might.
¹⁶With your mighty arm you redeemed
your people,
the children of Jacob and Joseph.
Selah

¹⁷The waters saw you, God;
the waters saw you and lashed about,
even the deeps of the sea trembled.
¹⁸The clouds poured down their rains;
the thunderheads rumbled;
your arrows flashed back and forth.

¹⁹The thunder of your chariot wheels
resounded;
your lightning lit up the world;
the earth trembled and quaked.
²⁰Through the sea was your way;
your path, through the mighty
waters,
though your footsteps were unseen.
²¹You led your people like a flock
by the hand of Moses and Aaron.

A New Beginning in Zion and David.
78:1 A *maskil* of Asaph.

Attend, my people, to my teaching;
listen to the words of my mouth.
²I will open my mouth in a parable,
unfold the puzzling events of the past.
³What we have heard and know;
things our ancestors have recounted
to us.
⁴We do not keep them from our
children;
we recount them to the next
generation,
The praiseworthy deeds of the LORD
and his strength,
the wonders that he performed.
⁵God made a decree in Jacob,
established a law in Israel:
Which he commanded our ancestors,
they were to teach their children;
⁶That the next generation might come
to know,
children yet to be born.
In turn they were to recount them to
their children,
⁷that they too might put their
confidence in God,
And not forget God's deeds,
but keep his commandments.
⁸They were not to be like their ancestors,
a rebellious and defiant generation,
A generation whose heart was not
constant,
and whose spirit was not faithful to
God.

⁹The ranks of Ephraimite archers,
  retreated on the day of battle.
¹⁰They did not keep God's covenant;
  they refused to walk according to
    his law.
¹¹They forgot his deeds,
  the wonders that he had shown them.

¹²In the sight of their ancestors God
    did wonders,
  in the land of Egypt, the plain of
    Zoan.
¹³He split the sea and led them across,
  making the waters stand like walls.
¹⁴He led them with a cloud by day,
  all night with the light of fire.
¹⁵He split rocks in the desert,
  gave water to drink, abundant as the
    deeps of the sea.
¹⁶He made streams flow from crags,
  caused rivers of water to flow down.
¹⁷But they went on sinning against him,
  rebelling against the Most High in
    the desert.
¹⁸They tested God in their hearts,
  demanding the food they craved.
¹⁹They spoke against God, and said,
  "Can God spread a table in the
    wilderness?
²⁰True, when he struck the rock,
  water gushed forth,
  the wadies flooded.
But can he also give bread,
  or provide meat to his people?"
²¹The LORD heard and grew angry;
  fire blazed up against Jacob;
  anger flared up against Israel.
²²For they did not believe in God,
  did not trust in his saving power.
²³So he commanded the clouds above;
  and opened the doors of heaven.
²⁴God rained manna upon them for
    food;
  grain from heaven he gave them.
²⁵Man ate the bread of the angels;
  food he sent in abundance.
²⁶He stirred up the east wind in the skies;

by his might God brought on the
    south wind.
²⁷He rained meat upon them like dust,
  winged fowl like the sands of the sea,
²⁸They fell down in the midst of their
    camp,
  all round their dwellings.
²⁹They ate and were well filled;
  he gave them what they had craved.
³⁰But while they still wanted more,
  and the food was still in their mouths,
³¹God's anger flared up against them,
  and he made a slaughter of their
    strongest,
  laying low the youth of Israel.
³²In spite of all this they went on sinning,
  they did not believe in his wonders.
³³God ended their days abruptly,
  their years in sudden death.
³⁴When he slew them, they began to
    seek him;
  they again looked for God.
³⁵They remembered that God was their
    rock,
  God Most High, their redeemer.
³⁶But they deceived him with their
    mouths,
  lied to him with their tongues.
³⁷Their hearts were not constant toward
    him;
  they were not faithful to his
    covenant.
³⁸But God being compassionate
    forgave their sin;
  he did not utterly destroy them.
Time and again he turned back his anger,
  unwilling to unleash all his rage.
³⁹He remembered that they were flesh,
  a breath that passes on and does not
    return.

⁴⁰How often they rebelled against God
    in the wilderness,
  grieved him in the wasteland.
⁴¹Again and again they tested God,
  provoked the Holy One of Israel.
⁴²They did not remember his power,

the day he redeemed them from the
foe,
43When he performed his signs in
Egypt,
his wonders in the plain of Zoan.
44God turned their rivers to blood;
their streams they could not drink.
45He sent swarms of insects that
devoured them,
frogs that destroyed them.
46He gave their harvest to the
caterpillar,
the fruits of their labor to the locust.
47He killed their vines with hail,
their sycamores with frost.
48He exposed their cattle to plague,
their flocks to pestilence.
49He let loose against them the heat of
his anger,
wrath, fury, and distress,
a band of deadly messengers.
50He cleared a path for his anger;
he did not spare them from death,
but delivered their animals to the
plague.
51He struck all the firstborn of Egypt,
the first fruits of their vigor in the
tents of Ham.
52Then God led forth his people like
sheep,
guided them like a flock through
the wilderness.
53He led them on secure and unafraid,
while the sea enveloped their
enemies.
54And he brought them to his holy
mountain,
the hill his right hand had won.
55He drove out the nations before
them,
allotted them as their inherited
portion,
and settled in their tents the tribes
of Israel.
56But they tested and rebelled against
God Most High,
his decrees they did not observe.

57They turned disloyal, faithless like
their ancestors;
they proved false like a slack bow.
58They enraged him with their high
places,
and with their idols provoked him
to jealous anger.
59God heard and grew angry;
he rejected Israel completely.
60He forsook the shrine at Shiloh,
the tent he set up among human
beings.
61He gave up his might into captivity,
his glorious ark into the hands of
the foe.
62God delivered his people to the
sword;
he was enraged against his heritage.
63Fire consumed their young men;
their young women heard no
wedding songs.
64Their priests fell by the sword;
their widows made no lamentation.
65Then the Lord awoke as from sleep,
like a warrior shouting from the
effects of wine.
66He put his foes to flight;
everlasting shame he dealt them.
67He rejected the tent of Joseph,
chose not the tribe of Ephraim.
68God chose the tribe of Judah,
Mount Zion which he loved.
69He built his shrine like the heavens,
like the earth which he founded
forever.
70He chose David his servant,
took him from the sheepfolds.
71From tending ewes God brought
him,
to shepherd Jacob, his people,
Israel, his heritage.
72He shepherded them with a pure
heart;
with skilled hands he guided them.

A Prayer for Jerusalem. 79:1 A psalm of
Asaph.

O God, the nations have invaded your
      inheritance;
   they have defiled your holy temple;
   they have laid Jerusalem in ruins.
²They have left the corpses of your
      servants
      as food for the birds of the sky,
   the flesh of those devoted to you for
      the beasts of the earth.
³They have poured out their blood like
      water
      all around Jerusalem,
   and no one is left to do the burying.
⁴We have become the reproach of our
      neighbors,
   the scorn and derision of those
      around us.

⁵How long, LORD? Will you be angry
      forever?
   Will your jealous anger keep
      burning like fire?
⁶Pour out your wrath on nations that
      do not recognize you,
   on kingdoms that do not call on
      your name,
⁷For they have devoured Jacob,
   laid waste his dwelling place.
⁸Do not remember against us the
      iniquities of our forefathers;

let your compassion move quickly
      ahead of us,
   for we have been brought very low.

⁹Help us, God our savior,
   on account of the glory of your
      name.
Deliver us, pardon our sins
   for your name's sake.
¹⁰Why should the nations say,
   "Where is their God?"
Before our eyes make known to the
      nations
   that you avenge the blood of your
      servants which has been
      poured out.

¹¹Let the groaning of the imprisoned
      come in before you;
   in accord with the greatness of your
      arm
   preserve those doomed to die.
¹²Turn back sevenfold into the bosom
      of our neighbors
   the insult with which they insulted
      you, Lord.
¹³Then we, your people, the sheep of
      your pasture,
   will give thanks to you forever;
   from generation to generation
   we will recount your praise.

☐ JOHN 1:1-18

1:1 In the beginning was the Word,
   and the Word was with God,
   and the Word was God.
²He was in the beginning with God.
³All things came to be through him,
   and without him nothing came to be.
What came to be ⁴through him was
      life,
   and this life was the light of the
      human race;
⁵the light shines in the darkness,
   and the darkness has not overcome it.

⁶A man named John was sent from God.
⁷He came for testimony, to testify to the
light, so that all might believe through
him. ⁸He was not the light, but came to
testify to the light. ⁹The true light, which
enlightens everyone, was coming into the
world.

   ¹⁰He was in the world,
   and the world came to be through
      him,
   but the world did not know him.

[11]He came to what was his own,
  but his own people did not accept
    him.

[12]But to those who did accept him he gave power to become children of God, to those who believe in his name, [13]who were born not by natural generation nor by human choice nor by a man's decision but of God.

[14]And the Word became flesh
  and made his dwelling among us,
  and we saw his glory,

the glory as of the Father's only Son,
  full of grace and truth.

[15]John testified to him and cried out, saying, "This was he of whom I said, 'The one who is coming after me ranks ahead of me because he existed before me.'" [16]From his fullness we have all received, grace in place of grace, [17]because while the law was given through Moses, grace and truth came through Jesus Christ. [18]No one has ever seen God. The only Son, God, who is at the Father's side, has revealed him.

July 17

Baptism is ransom, forgiveness of debts, death of sin, regeneration of the soul, a resplendent garment, an unbreakable seal, a chariot to heaven, a royal protector, a gift of adoption.
— St. Basil the Great

☐ PSALMS 80-84

Prayer to Restore God's Vineyard. 80:1
For the leader; according to "Lilies." *Eduth.*
A psalm of Asaph.

[2]O Shepherd of Israel, lend an ear,
  you who guide Joseph like a flock!
Seated upon the cherubim, shine forth
  [3]upon Ephraim, Benjamin, and
    Manasseh.
Stir up your power, and come to save us.
  [4]O God, restore us;
  light up your face and we shall be
    saved.

[5]Lord of hosts,
  how long will you smolder in anger
  while your people pray?
[6]You have fed them the bread of tears,
  made them drink tears in great
    measure.
[7]You have left us to be fought over by
  our neighbors;

our enemies deride us.
[8]O God of hosts, restore us;
  light up your face and we shall be
    saved.

[9]You brought a vine out of Egypt;
  you drove out nations and planted it.
[10]You cleared out what was before it;
  it took deep root and filled the land.
[11]The mountains were covered by its
    shadow,
  the cedars of God by its branches.
[12] It sent out its boughs as far as the sea,
  its shoots as far as the river.
[13]Why have you broken down its walls,
  so that all who pass along the way
    pluck its fruit?
[14]The boar from the forest strips the vine;
  the beast of the field feeds upon it.
[15]Turn back again, God of hosts;
  look down from heaven and see;

Visit this vine,
  16the stock your right hand has
      planted,
  and the son whom you made strong
      for yourself.
17Those who would burn or cut it
      down—
  may they perish at your rebuke.
18May your hand be with the man on
      your right,
  with the son of man whom you
      made strong for yourself.
19Then we will not withdraw from you;
  revive us, and we will call on your
      name.
20LORD God of hosts, restore us;
  light up your face and we shall be
      saved.

An Admonition to Fidelity. **81:1** For the
leader; "upon the *gittith*." Of Asaph.

2Sing joyfully to God our strength;
  raise loud shouts to the God of Jacob!
3Take up a melody, sound the timbrel,
  the pleasant lyre with a harp.
4Blow the shofar at the new moon,
  at the full moon, on our solemn feast.
5For this is a law for Israel,
  an edict of the God of Jacob,
6He made it a decree for Joseph
  when he came out of the land of
      Egypt.

7I heard a tongue I did not know:
  "I removed his shoulder from the
      burden;
  his hands moved away from the
      basket.
8In distress you called and I rescued you;
  I answered you in secret with
      thunder;
At the waters of Meribah I tested you:
9"Listen, my people, I will testify
  against you
  If only you will listen to me, Israel!

10There shall be no foreign god among
      you;
  you shall not bow down to an alien
      god.
11I am the LORD your God,
  who brought you up from the land
      of Egypt.
  Open wide your mouth that I may
      fill it.'
12But my people did not listen to my
      words;
  Israel would not submit to me.
13So I thrust them away to the hardness
      of their heart;
  'Let them walk in their own
      machinations.'
14O that my people would listen to me,
  that Israel would walk in my ways,
15In a moment I would humble their
      foes,
  and turn back my hand against their
      oppressors.
16Those who hate the LORD will try
      flattering him,
  but their fate is fixed forever.
17But Israel I will feed with the finest
      wheat,
  I will satisfy them with honey from
      the rock."

The Downfall of Unjust Gods. **82:1** A
psalm of Asaph.

God takes a stand in the divine
      council,
  gives judgment in the midst of the
      gods.
2"How long will you judge unjustly
  and favor the cause of the wicked?
                                      Selah
3"Defend the lowly and fatherless;
  render justice to the afflicted and
      needy.
4Rescue the lowly and poor;
  deliver them from the hand of the
      wicked."

⁵The gods neither know nor understand,
  wandering about in darkness,
  and all the world's foundations shake.
⁶I declare: "Gods though you be,
  offspring of the Most High all of you,
⁷Yet like any mortal you shall die;
  like any prince you shall fall."
⁸Arise, O God, judge the earth,
  for yours are all the nations.

Prayer Against a Hostile Alliance. 83:1 A song; a psalm of Asaph.

²God, do not be silent;
  God, do not be deaf or remain
    unmoved!
³See how your enemies rage;
  your foes proudly raise their heads.
⁴They conspire against your people,
  plot against those you protect.
⁵They say, "Come, let us wipe them out
    as a nation;
  let Israel's name be remembered no
    more!"
⁶They scheme with one mind,
  they have entered into a covenant
    against you:
⁷The tents of Edom and the
    Ishmaelites,
  of Moab and the Hagrites,
⁸Gebal, Ammon, and Amalek,
  Philistia and the inhabitants of Tyre.
⁹Assyria, too, in league with them,
  backs the descendants of Lot.
                            Selah

¹⁰Deal with them as with Midian;
  as with Sisera and Jabin at the wadi
    Kishon,
¹¹Those destroyed at Endor,
  who became dung for the ground.
¹²Make their nobles like Oreb and Zeeb,
  all their princes like Zebah and
    Zalmunna,
¹³Who made a plan together,
  "Let us take for ourselves the
    pastures of God."
¹⁴My God, make them like tumbleweed,

into chaff flying before the wind.
¹⁵As a fire raging through a forest,
  a flame setting mountains ablaze,
¹⁶Pursue them with your tempest;
  terrify them with your storm-wind.
¹⁷Cover their faces with shame,
  till they seek your name, LORD.
¹⁸Let them be ashamed and terrified
    forever;
  let them perish in disgrace.
¹⁹Let them know that your name is
    LORD,
  you alone are the Most High over
    all the earth.

Prayer of a Pilgrim to Jerusalem. 84:1 For the leader; "upon the *gittith*." A psalm of the Korahites.

²How lovely your dwelling,
  O LORD of hosts!
³My soul yearns and pines
  for the courts of the LORD.
My heart and flesh cry out
  for the living God.
⁴As the sparrow finds a home
  and the swallow a nest to settle her
    young,
My home is by your altars,
  LORD of hosts, my king and my God!
⁵Blessed are those who dwell in your
    house!
  They never cease to praise you.
                            Selah

⁶Blessed the man who finds refuge in
    you,
  in their hearts are pilgrim roads.
⁷As they pass through the Baca valley,
  they find spring water to drink.
  The early rain covers it with blessings.

⁸They will go from strength to strength
  and see the God of gods on Zion.

⁹LORD God of hosts, hear my prayer;
  listen, God of Jacob.
                            Selah

[10]O God, watch over our shield;
 look upon the face of your anointed.

[11]Better one day in your courts
 than a thousand elsewhere.
Better the threshold of the house of my
 God
 than a home in the tents of the
 wicked.

[12]For a sun and shield is the LORD
 God,
 bestowing all grace and glory.
The LORD withholds no good thing
 from those who walk without
 reproach.
[13]O LORD of hosts,
 blessed the man who trusts in you!

☐ JOHN 1:19-51

John the Baptist's Testimony to Himself.
1:19 And this is the testimony of John.
When the Jews from Jerusalem sent priests
and Levites [to him] to ask him, "Who are
you?" [20]he admitted and did not deny it,
but admitted, "I am not the Messiah." [21]So
they asked him, "What are you then? Are
you Elijah?" And he said, "I am not." "Are
you the Prophet?" He answered, "No." [22]So
they said to him, "Who are you, so we can
give an answer to those who sent us? What
do you have to say for yourself?" [23]He said:

"I am 'the voice of one crying out in
 the desert,
"Make straight the way of the Lord,'"

as Isaiah the prophet said." [24]Some Pharisees were also sent. [25]They asked him, "Why
then do you baptize if you are not the Messiah or Elijah or the Prophet?" [26]John answered them, "I baptize with water; but
there is one among you whom you do not
recognize, [27]the one who is coming after
me, whose sandal strap I am not worthy to
untie." [28]This happened in Bethany across
the Jordan, where John was baptizing.

John the Baptist's Testimony to Jesus.
[29]The next day he saw Jesus coming toward
him and said, "Behold, the Lamb of God,
who takes away the sin of the world. [30]He
is the one of whom I said, 'A man is coming
after me who ranks ahead of me because he
existed before me.' [31]I did not know him,
but the reason why I came baptizing with
water was that he might be made known

to Israel." [32]John testified further, saying,
"I saw the Spirit come down like a dove
from the sky and remain upon him. [33]I did
not know him, but the one who sent me to
baptize with water told me, 'On whomever
you see the Spirit come down and remain,
he is the one who will baptize with the holy
Spirit.' [34]Now I have seen and testified that
he is the Son of God."

The First Disciples. [35]The next day
John was there again with two of his disciples, [36]and as he watched Jesus walk by,
he said, "Behold, the Lamb of God." [37]The
two disciples heard what he said and followed Jesus. [38]Jesus turned and saw them
following him and said to them, "What
are you looking for?" They said to him,
"Rabbi" (which translated means Teacher),
"where are you staying?" [39]He said to them,
"Come, and you will see." So they went
and saw where he was staying, and they
stayed with him that day. It was about four
in the afternoon. [40]Andrew, the brother of
Simon Peter, was one of the two who heard
John and followed Jesus. [41]He first found
his own brother Simon and told him, "We
have found the Messiah" (which is translated Anointed). [42]Then he brought him to
Jesus. Jesus looked at him and said, "You
are Simon the son of John; you will be
called Cephas" (which is translated Peter).

[43]The next day he decided to go to Galilee, and he found Philip. And Jesus said to
him, "Follow me." [44]Now Philip was from
Bethsaida, the town of Andrew and Peter.

⁴⁵Philip found Nathanael and told him, "We have found the one about whom Moses wrote in the law, and also the prophets, Jesus, son of Joseph, from Nazareth." ⁴⁶But Nathanael said to him, "Can anything good come from Nazareth?" Philip said to him, "Come and see." ⁴⁷Jesus saw Nathanael coming toward him and said of him, "Here is a true Israelite. There is no duplicity in him." ⁴⁸Nathanael said to him, "How do you know me?" Jesus answered and said to him, "Before Philip called you, I saw you under the fig tree." ⁴⁹Nathanael answered him, "Rabbi, you are the Son of God; you are the King of Israel." ⁵⁰Jesus answered and said to him, "Do you believe because I told you that I saw you under the fig tree? You will see greater things than this." ⁵¹And he said to him, "Amen, amen, I say to you, you will see the sky opened and the angels of God ascending and descending on the Son of Man."

July 18

St. Pambo

Marriage has three blessings. The first is children, to be received and raised for God's service. The second is the loyal faithfulness by which each serves the other. The third is the Sacrament of Matrimony, which signifies the inseparable union of Christ with His Church.

— ST. THOMAS AQUINAS

☐ PSALMS 85–89

Prayer for Divine Favor. 85:1 For the leader. A psalm of the Korahites.

²You once favored, LORD, your land,
    restored the captives of Jacob.
³You forgave the guilt of your people,
    pardoned all their sins.   *Selah*

⁴You withdrew all your wrath,
    turned back from your burning anger.

⁵Restore us, God of our salvation;
    let go of your displeasure with us.
⁶Will you be angry with us forever,
    prolong your anger for all generations?
⁷Certainly you will again restore our life,
    that your people may rejoice in you.
⁸Show us, LORD, your mercy;
    grant us your salvation.

⁹I will listen for what God, the LORD,
    has to say;

surely he will speak of peace
To his people and to his faithful.
    May they not turn to foolishness!
¹⁰Near indeed is his salvation for those
        who fear him;
    glory will dwell in our land.
¹¹Love and truth will meet;
    justice and peace will kiss.
¹²Truth will spring from the earth;
    justice will look down from heaven.
¹³Yes, the LORD will grant his bounty;
    our land will yield its produce.
¹⁴Justice will march before him,
    and make a way for his footsteps.

Prayer in Time of Distress. 86:1 A prayer of David.

Incline your ear, LORD, and answer me,
    for I am poor and oppressed.
²Preserve my life, for I am devoted;

save your servant who trusts in you.
You are my God; ³be gracious to me,
    Lord;
    to you I call all the day.
⁴Gladden the soul of your servant;
    to you, Lord, I lift up my soul.
⁵Lord, you are good and forgiving,
    most merciful to all who call on you.
⁶Lord, hear my prayer;
    listen to my cry for help.
⁷On the day of my distress I call to you,
    for you will answer me.

⁸None among the gods can equal you,
    O Lord;
    nor can their deeds compare to yours.
⁹All the nations you have made shall
    come
    to bow before you, Lord,
    and give honor to your name.
¹⁰For you are great and do wondrous
    deeds;
    and you alone are God.

¹¹Teach me, Lord, your way
    that I may walk in your truth,
    single-hearted and revering your
    name.
¹²I will praise you with all my heart,
    glorify your name forever, Lord my
    God.
¹³Your mercy to me is great;
    you have rescued me from the
    depths of Sheol.
¹⁴O God, the arrogant have risen
    against me;
    a ruthless band has sought my life;
    to you they pay no heed.
¹⁵But you, Lord, are a compassionate
    and gracious God,
    slow to anger, abounding in mercy
    and truth.
¹⁶Turn to me, be gracious to me;
    give your strength to your servant;
    save the son of your handmaid.
¹⁷Give me a sign of your favor:
    make my enemies see, to their
    confusion,
    that you, Lord, help and comfort me.

Zion the True Birthplace. **87:1** A psalm of
the Korahites. A song.
    His foundation is on holy mountains,
    ²The Lord loves the gates of Zion
    more than any dwelling in Jacob.
³Glorious things are said of you,
    O city of God!

                            Selah

⁴Rahab and Babylon I count
    among those who know me.
See, Philistia and Tyre, with Ethiopia,
    "This one was born there."
⁵And of Zion it will be said:
    "Each one was born in it."
The Most High will establish it;
    ⁶the Lord notes in the register of
        the peoples:
    "This one was born there."

                            Selah

⁷So singers and dancers:
    "All my springs are in you."

A Despairing Lament. **88:1** A song; a
psalm of the Korahites. For the leader; according to *Mahalath*. For singing; a *maskil*
of Heman the Ezrahite.
    ²Lord, the God of my salvation, I call
        out by day;
    at night I cry aloud in your presence.
³Let my prayer come before you;
    incline your ear to my cry.
⁴For my soul is filled with troubles;
    my life draws near to Sheol.
⁵I am reckoned with those who go
        down to the pit;
    I am like a warrior without strength.
⁶My couch is among the dead,
    like the slain who lie in the grave.
You remember them no more;
    they are cut off from your influence.
⁷You plunge me into the bottom of the
        pit,
    into the darkness of the abyss.
⁸Your wrath lies heavy upon me;

all your waves crash over me.

Selah

⁹Because of you my acquaintances
shun me;
you make me loathsome to them;
Caged in, I cannot escape;
¹⁰my eyes grow dim from trouble.

All day I call on you, LORD;
I stretch out my hands to you.
¹¹Do you work wonders for the dead?
Do the shades arise and praise you?

Selah

¹²Is your mercy proclaimed in the
grave,
your faithfulness among those who
have perished?
¹³Are your marvels declared in the
darkness,
your righteous deeds in the land of
oblivion?

¹⁴But I cry out to you, LORD;
in the morning my prayer comes
before you.
¹⁵Why do you reject my soul, LORD,
and hide your face from me?
¹⁶I have been mortally afflicted since
youth;
I have borne your terrors and I am
made numb.
¹⁷Your wrath has swept over me;
your terrors have destroyed me.
¹⁸All day they surge round like a
flood;
from every side they encircle me.
¹⁹Because of you friend and neighbor
shun me;
my only friend is darkness.

A Lament over God's Promise to David.
89:1 A *maskil* of Ethan the Ezrahite.

²I will sing of your mercy forever, LORD
proclaim your faithfulness through
all ages.
³For I said, "My mercy is established
forever;

my faithfulness will stand as long as
the heavens.
⁴I have made a covenant with my
chosen one;
I have sworn to David my servant:
⁵I will make your dynasty stand forever
and establish your throne through
all ages."

Selah

⁶The heavens praise your marvels,
LORD,
your loyalty in the assembly of the
holy ones.
⁷Who in the skies ranks with the
LORD?
Who is like the LORD among the
sons of the gods?
⁸A God dreaded in the council of the
holy ones,
greater and more awesome than all
those around him!
⁹LORD, God of hosts, who is like you?
Mighty LORD, your faithfulness
surrounds you.
¹⁰You rule the raging sea;
you still its swelling waves.
¹¹You crush Rahab with a mortal
blow;
with your strong arm you scatter
your foes.
¹²Yours are the heavens, yours the
earth;
you founded the world and
everything in it.
¹³Zaphon and Amanus you created;
Tabor and Hermon rejoice in your
name.
¹⁴You have a mighty arm.
Your hand is strong; your right hand
is ever exalted.
¹⁵Justice and judgment are the
foundation of your throne;
mercy and faithfulness march before
you.
¹⁶Blessed the people who know the war
cry,

who walk in the radiance of your
    face, LORD.
¹⁷In your name they sing joyfully all
    the day;
    they rejoice in your righteousness.
¹⁸You are their majestic strength;
    by your favor our horn is exalted.
¹⁹Truly the LORD is our shield,
    the Holy One of Israel, our king!

²⁰Then you spoke in vision;
    to your faithful ones you said:
"I have set a leader over the warriors;
    I have raised up a chosen one from
    the people.
²¹I have chosen David, my servant;
    with my holy oil I have anointed
    him.
²²My hand will be with him;
    my arm will make him strong.
²³No enemy shall outwit him,
    nor shall the wicked defeat him.
²⁴I will crush his foes before him,
    strike down those who hate him.
²⁵My faithfulness and mercy will be
    with him;
    through my name his horn will be
    exalted.
²⁶I will set his hand upon the sea,
    his right hand upon the rivers.
²⁷He shall cry to me, 'You are my
    father,
    my God, the Rock of my
    salvation!'
²⁸I myself make him the firstborn,
    Most High over the kings of the
    earth.
²⁹Forever I will maintain my mercy
    for him;
    my covenant with him stands firm.
³⁰I will establish his dynasty forever,
    his throne as the days of the
    heavens.
³¹If his descendants forsake my
    teaching,
    do not follow my decrees,
³²If they fail to observe my statutes,

    do not keep my commandments,
³³I will punish their crime with a rod
    and their guilt with blows.
³⁴But I will not take my mercy from
    him,
    nor will I betray my bond of
    faithfulness.
³⁵I will not violate my covenant;
    the promise of my lips I will not
    alter.
³⁶By my holiness I swore once for all:
    I will never be false to David.
³⁷His dynasty will continue forever,
    his throne, like the sun before me.
³⁸Like the moon it will stand eternal,
    forever firm like the sky!"
                    Selah

³⁹But now you have rejected and
    spurned,
    been enraged at your anointed.
⁴⁰You renounced the covenant with
    your servant,
    defiled his crown in the dust.
⁴¹You broke down all city walls,
    left his strongholds in ruins.
⁴²All who pass through seize
    plunder;
    his neighbors deride him.
⁴³You have exalted the right hand of
    his foes,
    have gladdened all his enemies.
⁴⁴You turned back his sharp sword,
    did not support him in battle.
⁴⁵You brought to an end his
    splendor,
    hurled his throne to the ground.
⁴⁶You cut short the days of his youth,
    covered him with shame.
                    Selah
⁴⁷How long, LORD? Will you hide
    forever?
    Must your wrath smolder like fire?
⁴⁸Remember how brief life is,
    how frail the sons of man you have
    created!

⁴⁹What is man, that he should live and
not see death?
Who can deliver his soul from the
power of Sheol?
Selah
⁵⁰Where are your former mercies, Lord,
that you swore to David in your
faithfulness?

⁵¹Remember, Lord, the insults to your
servants,
how I have borne in my bosom the
slander of the nations.
⁵²Your enemies, LORD, insult;
they insult each step of your
anointed.
⁵³Blessed be the LORD forever! Amen
and amen!

☐ JOHN 2

The Wedding at Cana. 2:1 On the third day there was a wedding in Cana in Galilee, and the mother of Jesus was there. ²Jesus and his disciples were also invited to the wedding. ³When the wine ran short, the mother of Jesus said to him, "They have no wine." ⁴[And] Jesus said to her, "Woman, how does your concern affect me? My hour has not yet come." ⁵His mother said to the servers, "Do whatever he tells you." ⁶Now there were six stone water jars there for Jewish ceremonial washings, each holding twenty to thirty gallons. ⁷Jesus told them, "Fill the jars with water." So they filled them to the brim. ⁸Then he told them, "Draw some out now and take it to the headwaiter." So they took it. ⁹And when the headwaiter tasted the water that had become wine, without knowing where it came from (although the servers who had drawn the water knew), the headwaiter called the bridegroom ¹⁰and said to him, "Everyone serves good wine first, and then when people have drunk freely, an inferior one; but you have kept the good wine until now." ¹¹Jesus did this as the beginning of his signs in Cana in Galilee and so revealed his glory, and his disciples began to believe in him.

¹²After this, he and his mother, [his] brothers, and his disciples went down to Capernaum and stayed there only a few days.

Cleansing of the Temple. ¹³Since the Passover of the Jews was near, Jesus went up to Jerusalem. ¹⁴He found in the temple area those who sold oxen, sheep, and doves, as well as the money-changers seated there. ¹⁵He made a whip out of cords and drove them all out of the temple area, with the sheep and oxen, and spilled the coins of the money-changers and overturned their tables, ¹⁶and to those who sold doves he said, "Take these out of here, and stop making my Father's house a marketplace." ¹⁷His disciples recalled the words of scripture, "Zeal for your house will consume me." ¹⁸At this the Jews answered and said to him, "What sign can you show us for doing this?" ¹⁹Jesus answered and said to them, "Destroy this temple and in three days I will raise it up." ²⁰The Jews said, "This temple has been under construction for forty-six years, and you will raise it up in three days?" ²¹But he was speaking about the temple of his body. ²²Therefore, when he was raised from the dead, his disciples remembered that he had said this, and they came to believe the scripture and the word Jesus had spoken.

²³While he was in Jerusalem for the feast of Passover, many began to believe in his name when they saw the signs he was doing. ²⁴But Jesus would not trust himself to them because he knew them all, ²⁵and did not need anyone to testify about human nature. He himself understood it well.

July 19

O Lord, You have freed us from the fear of death. You have made the end of life here the beginning of a true life for us. For a time, You give rest to our bodies in sleep, and you awaken us again with the trumpet. The dust from which You fashioned us with Your hands You give back to the earth for safekeeping. And You will call it back, transforming our mortal and graceless remains with immortality and grace.

— St. Macrina

☐ PSALMS 90-96

***God's Eternity and Human Frailty.* 90:1**
A prayer of Moses, the man of God.

Lord, you have been our refuge
through all generations.
²Before the mountains were born,
the earth and the world brought
forth,
from eternity to eternity you are God.
³You turn humanity back into dust,
saying, "Return, you children of
Adam!"
⁴A thousand years in your eyes
are merely a day gone by,
Before a watch passes in the night,
⁵you wash them away;
They sleep,
and in the morning they sprout
again like an herb.
⁶In the morning it blooms only to pass
away;
in the evening it is wilted and
withered.

⁷Truly we are consumed by your anger,
filled with terror by your wrath.
⁸You have kept our faults before you,
our hidden sins in the light of your
face.
⁹Our life ebbs away under your wrath;
our years end like a sigh.
¹⁰Seventy is the sum of our years,
or eighty, if we are strong;

Most of them are toil and sorrow;
they pass quickly, and we are gone.
¹¹Who comprehends the strength of
your anger?
Your wrath matches the fear it inspires.
¹²Teach us to count our days aright,
that we may gain wisdom of heart.
¹³Relent, O Lord! How long?
Have pity on your servants!
¹⁴Fill us at daybreak with your mercy,
that all our days we may sing for joy.
¹⁵Make us glad as many days as you
humbled us,
for as many years as we have seen
trouble.
¹⁶Show your deeds to your servants,
your glory to their children.
¹⁷May the favor of the Lord our God
be ours.
Prosper the work of our hands!
Prosper the work of our hands!

***Security Under God's Protection.* 91:1**
You who dwell in the shelter of
the Most High,
who abide in the shade of the
Almighty,
²Say to the Lord, "My refuge and
fortress,
my God in whom I trust."
³He will rescue you from the fowler's
snare,

from the destroying plague,
⁴He will shelter you with his pinions,
    and under his wings you may take
      refuge;
    his faithfulness is a protecting shield.
⁵You shall not fear the terror of the
    night
    nor the arrow that flies by day,
⁶Nor the pestilence that roams in
    darkness,
    nor the plague that ravages at noon.
⁷Though a thousand fall at your side,
    ten thousand at your right hand,
    near you it shall not come.
⁸You need simply watch;
the punishment of the wicked you
    will see.

⁹Because you have the LORD for your
    refuge
    and have made the Most High your
      stronghold,
¹⁰No evil shall befall you,
    no affliction come near your tent.
¹¹For he commands his angels with
    regard to you,
    to guard you wherever you go.
¹²With their hands they shall support
    you,
    lest you strike your foot against a
      stone.
¹³You can tread upon the asp and the
    viper,
    trample the lion and the dragon.

¹⁴Because he clings to me I will deliver
    him;
    because he knows my name I will
      set him on high.
¹⁵He will call upon me and I will answer;
    I will be with him in distress;
    I will deliver him and give him honor.
¹⁶With length of days I will satisfy
    him,
    and fill him with my saving power.

A Hymn of Thanksgiving for God's Fidelity. **92:1** A psalm. A sabbath song.

²It is good to give thanks to the LORD,
    to sing praise to your name, Most
      High,
³To proclaim your love at daybreak,
    your faithfulness in the night,
⁴With the ten-stringed harp,
    with melody upon the lyre.
⁵For you make me jubilant, LORD, by
    your deeds;
    at the works of your hands I shout
      for joy.

⁶How great are your works, LORD!
    How profound your designs!
⁷A senseless person cannot know this;
    a fool cannot comprehend.
⁸Though the wicked flourish like grass
    and all sinners thrive,
They are destined for eternal destruction;
    ⁹but you, LORD, are forever on high.
¹⁰Indeed your enemies, LORD,
    indeed your enemies shall perish;
    all sinners shall be scattered.

¹¹You have given me the strength of a
    wild ox;
    you have poured rich oil upon me.
¹²My eyes look with glee on my wicked
    enemies;
    my ears shall hear what happens to
      my wicked foes.
¹³The just shall flourish like the palm tree,
    shall grow like a cedar of Lebanon.
¹⁴Planted in the house of the LORD,
    they shall flourish in the courts of
      our God.
¹⁵They shall bear fruit even in old age,
    they will stay fresh and green,
¹⁶To proclaim: "The LORD is just;
    my rock, in whom there is no wrong."

God Is a Mighty King. **93:1** The LORD
    is king, robed with majesty;
    the LORD is robed, girded with might.
The world will surely stand in place,

never to be moved.
²Your throne stands firm from of old;
    you are from everlasting.
³The flood has raised up, LORD;
    the flood has raised up its roar;
    the flood has raised its pounding
        waves.
⁴More powerful than the roar of many
        waters,
    more powerful than the breakers of
        the sea,
    powerful in the heavens is the LORD.
⁵Your decrees are firmly established;
    holiness befits your house, LORD,
    for all the length of days.

**A Prayer for Deliverance from the
Wicked.** 94:1 LORD, avenging God,
    avenging God, shine forth!
²Rise up, O judge of the earth;
    give the proud what they deserve!

³How long, LORD, shall the wicked,
    how long shall the wicked glory?
⁴How long will they mouth haughty
        speeches,
    go on boasting, all these evildoers?
⁵They crush your people, LORD,
    torment your very own.
⁶They kill the widow and alien;
    the orphan they murder.
⁷They say, "The LORD does not see;
    the God of Jacob takes no notice."

⁸Understand, you stupid people!
    You fools, when will you be wise?
⁹Does the one who shaped the ear not
        hear?
    The one who formed the eye not see?
¹⁰Does the one who guides nations not
        rebuke?
    The one who teaches man not have
        knowledge?
¹¹The LORD knows the plans of man;
    they are like a fleeting breath.

¹²Blessed the one whom you guide,
    LORD,

    whom you teach by your instruction,
¹³To give rest from evil days,
    while a pit is being dug for the wicked.
¹⁴For the LORD will not forsake his
        people,
    nor abandon his inheritance.
¹⁵Judgment shall again be just,
    and all the upright of heart will
        follow it.

¹⁶Who will rise up for me against the
        wicked?
    Who will stand up for me against
        evildoers?
¹⁷If the LORD were not my help,
    I would long have been silent in the
        grave.
¹⁸When I say, "My foot is slipping,"
    your mercy, LORD, holds me up.
¹⁹When cares increase within me,
    your comfort gives me joy.

²⁰Can unjust judges be your allies,
    those who create burdens by decree,
²¹Those who conspire against the just
    and condemn the innocent to death?
²²No, the LORD is my secure height,
    my God, my rock of refuge,
²³Who will turn back their evil upon
        them
    and destroy them for their wickedness.
    Surely the LORD our God will
        destroy them!

A Call to Praise and Obedience.
95:1 Come, let us sing joyfully to the
    LORD;
    cry out to the rock of our salvation.
²Let us come before him with a song of
        praise,
    joyfully sing out our psalms.
³For the LORD is the great God,
    the great king over all gods,
⁴Whose hand holds the depths of the
        earth;
    who owns the tops of the mountains.
⁵The sea and dry land belong to God,

who made them, formed them by hand.

[6]Enter, let us bow down in worship;
let us kneel before the LORD who made us.
[7]For he is our God,
we are the people he shepherds,
the sheep in his hands.

Oh, that today you would hear his voice:
[8]Do not harden your hearts as at Meribah,
as on the day of Massah in the desert.
[9]There your ancestors tested me;
they tried me though they had seen my works.
[10]Forty years I loathed that generation;
I said: "This people's heart goes astray;
they do not know my ways."
[11]Therefore I swore in my anger:
"They shall never enter my rest."

God of the Universe. **96:1** Sing to the LORD a new song;
sing to the LORD, all the earth.
[2]Sing to the LORD, bless his name;
proclaim his salvation day after day.
[3]Tell his glory among the nations;
among all peoples, his marvelous deeds.

[4]For great is the LORD and highly to be praised,
to be feared above all gods.
[5]For the gods of the nations are idols,
but the LORD made the heavens.
[6]Splendor and power go before him;
power and grandeur are in his holy place.

[7]Give to the LORD, you families of nations,
give to the LORD glory and might;
[8]give to the LORD the glory due his name!
Bring gifts and enter his courts;
[9]bow down to the LORD, splendid in holiness.
Tremble before him, all the earth;
[10]declare among the nations: The LORD is king.
The world will surely stand fast, never to be shaken.
He rules the peoples with fairness.

[11]Let the heavens be glad and the earth rejoice;
let the sea and what fills it resound;
[12]let the plains be joyful and all that is in them.
Then let all the trees of the forest rejoice
[13]before the LORD who comes,
who comes to govern the earth,
To govern the world with justice
and the peoples with faithfulness.

☐ JOHN 3:1-21

Nicodemus. 3:1 Now there was a Pharisee named Nicodemus, a ruler of the Jews. [2]He came to Jesus at night and said to him, "Rabbi, we know that you are a teacher who has come from God, for no one can do these signs that you are doing unless God is with him." [3]Jesus answered and said to him, "Amen, amen, I say to you, no one can see the kingdom of God without being born from above." [4]Nicodemus said to him, "How can a person once grown old be born again? Surely he cannot reenter his mother's womb and be born again, can he?" [5]Jesus answered, "Amen, amen, I say to you, no one can enter the kingdom of God without being born of water and Spirit. [6]What is born of flesh is flesh and what is born of spirit is spirit. [7]Do not be amazed that I told you, 'You must be born from above.' [8]The wind blows where it wills, and you can hear the sound it makes, but you do not know where it comes from or where it goes; so it is with everyone who is born of the Spirit." [9]Nicodemus answered and said to him, "How can this happen?" [10]Jesus answered and said to him, "You are the teacher of Israel and you do not understand this? [11]Amen, amen, I say to you, we speak of what we know and we testify to what we have seen, but you people do not accept our testimony. [12]If I tell you about earthly things and you do not believe, how will you believe if I tell you about heavenly things? [13]No one has gone up to heaven except the one who has come down from heaven, the Son of Man. [14]And just as Moses lifted up the serpent in the desert, so must the Son of Man be lifted up, [15]so that everyone who believes in him may have eternal life."

[16]For God so loved the world that he gave his only Son, so that everyone who believes in him might not perish but might have eternal life. [17]For God did not send his Son into the world to condemn the world, but that the world might be saved through him. [18]Whoever believes in him will not be condemned, but whoever does not believe has already been condemned, because he has not believed in the name of the only Son of God. [19]And this is the verdict, that the light came into the world, but people preferred darkness to light, because their works were evil. [20]For everyone who does wicked things hates the light and does not come toward the light, so that his works might not be exposed. [21]But whoever lives the truth comes to the light, so that his works may be clearly seen as done in God.

July 20

St. Apollinarius; Blessed Gregory Lopez

If I were to die in a few hours, I would do nothing more than I do now. For now I am actually giving to God all that I have. I cannot give more unless God in His mercy bestows it on me.

— BLESSED GREGORY LOPEZ

☐ PSALMS 97-102

The Divine Ruler of All. **97:1** The
> LORD is king; let the earth rejoice;
> let the many islands be glad.
[2]Cloud and darkness surround him;
> justice and right are the foundation
> of his throne.
[3]Fire goes before him,
> consuming his foes on every side.
[4]His lightening illumines the world;
> the earth sees and trembles.
[5]The mountains melt like wax before
> the LORD,
> before the Lord of all the earth.
[6]The heavens proclaim his justice;
> all peoples see his glory.

[7]All who serve idols are put to shame,
> who glory in worthless things;
> all gods bow down before him.
[8]Zion hears and is glad,
> and the daughters of Judah rejoice
> because of your judgments,
> O LORD.
[9]For you, LORD, are the Most High
> over all the earth,
> exalted far above all gods.
[10]You who love the LORD, hate evil,
> he protects the souls of the
> faithful,
> rescues them from the hand of the
> wicked.

¹¹Light dawns for the just,
   and gladness for the honest of heart.
¹²Rejoice in the LORD, you just,
   and give thanks at the remembrance
      of his holiness.

The Coming of God. 98:1 A psalm.

Sing a new song to the LORD,
   for he has done marvelous deeds.
His right hand and holy arm
   have won the victory.
²The LORD has made his victory known;
   has revealed his triumph in the sight
      of the nations,
³He has remembered his mercy and
      faithfulness
   toward the house of Israel.
All the ends of the earth have seen
   the victory of our God.

⁴Shout with joy to the LORD, all the
      earth;
   break into song; sing praise.
⁵Sing praise to the LORD with the lyre,
   with the lyre and melodious song.
⁶With trumpets and the sound of the
      horn
   shout with joy to the King, the LORD.

⁷Let the sea and what fills it resound,
   the world and those who dwell
      there.
⁸Let the rivers clap their hands,
   the mountains shout with them for
      joy,
⁹Before the LORD who comes,
   who comes to govern the earth,
To govern the world with justice
   and the peoples with fairness.

The Holy King. 99:1 The LORD is
      king, the peoples tremble;
   he is enthroned on the cherubim,
      the earth quakes.
²Great is the LORD in Zion,
   exalted above all the peoples.

³Let them praise your great and
      awesome name:
   Holy is he!

⁴O mighty king, lover of justice,
   you have established fairness;
   you have created just rule in Jacob.
⁵Exalt the LORD, our God;
   bow down before his footstool;
   holy is he!

⁶Moses and Aaron were among his
      priests,
   Samuel among those who called on
      his name;
   they called on the LORD, and he
      answered them.
⁷From the pillar of cloud he spoke to
      them;
   they kept his decrees, the law he had
      given them.
⁸O LORD, our God, you answered
      them;
   you were a forgiving God to them,
   though you punished their
      offenses.
⁹Exalt the LORD, our God;
   bow down before his holy
      mountain;
   holy is the LORD, our God.

Processional Hymn. 100:1 A psalm of
thanksgiving.

Shout joyfully to the LORD, all you lands;
   ²serve the LORD with gladness;
   come before him with joyful song.
³Know that the LORD is God,
   he made us, we belong to him,
   we are his people, the flock he
      shepherds.
⁴Enter his gates with thanksgiving,
   his courts with praise.
Give thanks to him, bless his name;
   ⁵good indeed is the LORD,
His mercy endures forever,
   his faithfulness lasts through every
      generation.

Norm of Life for Rulers. **101:1** A psalm of David.

I sing of mercy and justice;
   to you, Lord, I sing praise.
²I study the the way of integrity;
   when will you come to me?
I act with integrity of heart
   within my household.
³I do not allow into my presence
      anything base.
   I hate wrongdoing;
   I will have no part of it.
⁴May the devious heart keep far
      from me;
   the wicked I will not acknowledge.
⁵Whoever slanders a neighbor in secret
   I will reduce to silence.
Haughty eyes and arrogant hearts
   I cannot endure.

⁶I look to the faithful of the land
   to sit at my side.
Whoever follows the way of integrity
   is the one to enter my service.
⁷No one who practices deceit
   can remain within my house.
No one who speaks falsely
   can last in my presence.
⁸Morning after morning I clear all the
      wicked from the land,
   to rid the city of the Lord of all
      doers of evil.

Prayer in Time of Distress. **102:1** The prayer of one afflicted and wasting away whose anguish is poured out before the Lord.

²Lord, hear my prayer;
   let my cry come to you.
³Do not hide your face from me
   in the day of my distress.
Turn your ear to me;
   when I call, answer me quickly.
⁴For my days vanish like smoke;
   my bones burn away as in a furnace.
⁵My heart is withered, dried up like grass,
      too wasted to eat my food.
⁶From my loud groaning
   I become just skin and bones.
⁷I am like a desert owl,
   like an owl among the ruins.
⁸I lie awake and moan,
   like a lone sparrow on the roof.
⁹All day long my enemies taunt me;
   in their rage, they make my name a
      curse.
¹⁰I eat ashes like bread,
   mingle my drink with tears.
¹¹Because of your furious wrath,
   you lifted me up just to cast me
      down.
¹²My days are like a lengthening shadow;
   I wither like the grass.

¹³But you, Lord, are enthroned forever;
   your renown is for all generations.
¹⁴You will again show mercy to Zion;
   now is the time for pity;
   the appointed time has come.
¹⁵Its stones are dear to your servants;
   its dust moves them to pity.
¹⁶The nations shall fear your name,
      Lord,
   all the kings of the earth, your glory,
¹⁷Once the Lord has rebuilt Zion
   and appeared in glory,
¹⁸Heeding the plea of the lowly,
   not scorning their prayer.
¹⁹Let this be written for the next
      generation,
   for a people not yet born,
   that they may praise the Lord:
²⁰"The Lord looked down from the
      holy heights,
   viewed the earth from heaven,
²¹To attend to the groaning of the
      prisoners,
   to release those doomed to die."
²²Then the Lord's name will be
      declared on Zion,
   his praise in Jerusalem,
²³When peoples and kingdoms gather
   to serve the Lord.

²⁴He has shattered my strength in mid-
course,
has cut short my days.
²⁵I plead, O my God,
do not take me in the midst of
my days.
Your years last through all generations.
²⁶Of old you laid the earth's foundations;
the heavens are the work of your
hands.

²⁷They perish, but you remain;
they all wear out like a garment;
Like clothing you change them and
they are changed,
²⁸but you are the same, your years
have no end.
²⁹May the children of your servants
live on;
may their descendants live in your
presence.

☐ JOHN 3:22-36

Final Witness of the Baptist. 3:22 After
this, Jesus and his disciples went into the
region of Judea, where he spent some time
with them baptizing. ²³John was also baptizing in Aenon near Salim, because there
was an abundance of water there, and
people came to be baptized, ²⁴for John had
not yet been imprisoned. ²⁵Now a dispute
arose between the disciples of John and a
Jew about ceremonial washings. ²⁶So they
came to John and said to him, "Rabbi, the
one who was with you across the Jordan,
to whom you testified, here he is baptizing
and everyone is coming to him." ²⁷John answered and said, "No one can receive anything except what has been given him from
heaven. ²⁸You yourselves can testify that I
said [that] I am not the Messiah, but that I
was sent before him. ²⁹The one who has the
bride is the bridegroom; the best man, who
stands and listens to him, rejoices greatly
at the bridegroom's voice. So this joy of
mine has been made complete. ³⁰He must
increase; I must decrease."

The One from Heaven. ³¹The one who
comes from above is above all. The one
who is of the earth is earthly and speaks
of earthly things. But the one who comes
from heaven [is above all]. ³²He testifies to
what he has seen and heard, but no one
accepts his testimony. ³³Whoever does
accept his testimony certifies that God is
trustworthy. ³⁴For the one whom God sent
speaks the words of God. He does not ration his gift of the Spirit. ³⁵The Father loves
the Son and has given everything over to
him. ³⁶Whoever believes in the Son has
eternal life, but whoever disobeys the Son
will not see life, but the wrath of God remains upon him.

July 21

St. Lawrence of Brindisi

God's Word is light to the mind and fire to the will so that a person may know and love the Lord. To the inner man who lives by the Spirit, it is bread and water, but a bread sweeter than any honey from the comb, and water more delicious than milk or wine.

— ST. LAWRENCE OF BRINDISI

☐ PSALMS 103-106

Praise of Divine Goodness. 103:1
Of David.

Bless the LORD, my soul;
all my being, bless his holy name!
²Bless the LORD, my soul;
and do not forget all his gifts,
³Who pardons all your sins,
and heals all your ills,
⁴Who redeems your life from the pit,
and crowns you with mercy and
compassion,
⁵Who fills your days with good things,
so your youth is renewed like the
eagle's.

⁶The LORD does righteous deeds,
brings justice to all the oppressed.
⁷He made known his ways to Moses,
to the Israelites his deeds.
⁸Merciful and gracious is the LORD,
slow to anger, abounding in mercy.
⁹He will not always accuse,
and nurses no lasting anger;
¹⁰He has not dealt with us as our sins
merit,
nor requited us as our wrongs deserve.

¹¹For as the heavens tower over the earth,
so his mercy towers over those who
fear him.
¹²As far as the east is from the west,
so far has he removed our sins from
us.
¹³As a father has compassion on his
children,

so the LORD has compassion on
those who fear him.
¹⁴For he knows how we are formed,
remembers that we are dust.
¹⁵As for man, his days are like the grass;
he blossoms like a flower in the field.
¹⁶A wind sweeps over it and it is gone;
its place knows it no more.
¹⁷But the LORD's mercy is from age to
age,
toward those who fear him.
His salvation is for the children's
children
¹⁸of those who keep his covenant,
and remember to carry out his
precepts.

¹⁹The LORD has set his throne in heaven;
his dominion extends over all.
²⁰Bless the LORD, all you his angels,
mighty in strength, acting at his
behest,
obedient to his command.
²¹Bless the LORD, all you his hosts,
his ministers who carry out his will.
²²Bless the LORD, all his creatures,
everywhere in his domain.
Bless the LORD, my soul!

Praise of God the Creator. 104:1 Bless
the LORD, my soul!
LORD, my God, you are great indeed!
You are clothed with majesty and
splendor,
²robed in light as with a cloak.

You spread out the heavens like a tent;
    ³setting the beams of your chambers
        upon the waters.
You make the clouds your chariot;
    traveling on the wings of the wind.
⁴You make the winds your messengers;
    flaming fire, your ministers.

⁵You fixed the earth on its foundation,
    so it can never be shaken.
⁶The deeps covered it like a garment;
    above the mountains stood the waters.
⁷At your rebuke they took flight;
    at the sound of your thunder they
        fled.
⁸They rushed up the mountains, down
        the valleys
    to the place you had fixed for them.
⁹You set a limit they cannot pass;
    never again will they cover the earth.

¹⁰You made springs flow in wadies
    that wind among the mountains.
¹¹They give drink to every beast of the
        field;
    here wild asses quench their thirst.
¹²Beside them the birds of heaven nest;
    among the branches they sing.
¹³You water the mountains from your
        chambers;
    from the fruit of your labor the
        earth abounds.
¹⁴You make the grass grow for the cattle
    and plants for people's work
    to bring forth food from the earth,
¹⁵wine to gladden their hearts,
    oil to make their faces shine,
    and bread to sustain the human heart.
¹⁶The trees of the LORD drink their fill,
    the cedars of Lebanon, which you
        planted.
¹⁷There the birds build their nests;
    the stork in the junipers, its home.
¹⁸The high mountains are for wild goats;
    the rocky cliffs, a refuge for badgers.

¹⁹You made the moon to mark the
    seasons,

the sun that knows the hour of its
    setting.
²⁰You bring darkness and night falls,
    then all the animals of the forest
        wander about.
²¹Young lions roar for prey;
    they seek their food from God.
²²When the sun rises, they steal away
    and settle down in their dens.
²³People go out to their work,
    to their labor till evening falls.

²⁴How varied are your works, LORD!
    In wisdom you have made them all;
    the earth is full of your creatures.
²⁵There is the sea, great and wide!
    It teems with countless beings,
    living things both large and small.
²⁶There ships ply their course
    and Leviathan, whom you formed
        to play with.

²⁷All of these look to you
    to give them food in due time.
²⁸When you give it to them, they gather;
    when you open your hand, they are
        well filled.
²⁹When you hide your face, they panic.
    Take away their breath, they perish
    and return to the dust.
³⁰Send forth your spirit, they are created
    and you renew the face of the earth.

³¹May the glory of the LORD endure
        forever;
    may the LORD be glad in his works!
³²Who looks at the earth and it trembles,
    touches the mountains and they
        smoke!
³³I will sing to the LORD all my life;
    I will sing praise to my God while
        I live.
³⁴May my meditation be pleasing to him;
    I will rejoice in the LORD.
³⁵May sinners vanish from the earth,
    and the wicked be no more.
    Bless the LORD, my soul! Hallelujah!

God's Fidelity to the Promise. **105:1**

Give thanks to the LORD, invoke
his name;
    make known among the peoples his
        deeds!
[2]Sing praise to him, play music;
    proclaim all his wondrous deeds!
[3]Glory in his holy name;
    let hearts that seek the LORD rejoice!
[4]Seek out the LORD and his might;
    constantly seek his face.
[5]Recall the wondrous deeds he has
        done,
    his wonders and words of judgment,
[6]You descendants of Abraham his
        servant,
    offspring of Jacob the chosen one!

[7]He the LORD, is our God
    whose judgments reach through all
        the earth.
[8]He remembers forever his covenant,
    the word he commanded for a
        thousand generations,
[9]Which he made with Abraham,
    and swore to Isaac,
[10]And ratified in a statute for Jacob,
    an everlasting covenant for Israel:
[11]"To you I give the land of Canaan,
    your own allotted inheritance."

[12]When they were few in number,
    a handful, and strangers there,
[13]Wandering from nation to nation,
    from one kingdom to another people,
[14]He let no one oppress them;
    for their sake he rebuked kings:
[15]"Do not touch my anointed ones,
    to my prophets do no harm."

[16]Then he called down a famine on the
        land,
    destroyed the grain that sustained
        them.
[17]He had sent a man ahead of them,
    Joseph, sold as a slave.
[18]They shackled his feet with chains;
    collared his neck in iron,

[19]Till his prediction came to pass,
    and the word of the LORD proved
        him true.
[20]The king sent and released him;
    the ruler of peoples set him free.
[21]He made him lord over his
        household,
    ruler over all his possessions,
[22]To instruct his princes as he desired,
    to teach his elders wisdom.

[23]Then Israel entered Egypt;
    Jacob sojourned in the land of
        Ham.
[24]God greatly increased his people,
    made them more numerous than
        their foes.
[25]He turned their hearts to hate his
        people,
    to treat his servants deceitfully.
[26]He sent his servant Moses,
    and Aaron whom he had chosen.
[27]They worked his signs in Egypt
    and wonders in the land of Ham.
[28]He sent darkness and it grew dark,
    but they rebelled against his word.
[29]He turned their waters into blood
    and killed their fish.
[30]Their land swarmed with frogs,
    even the chambers of their kings.
[31]He spoke and there came swarms of
        flies,
    gnats through all their country.
[32]For rain he gave them hail,
    flashes of lightning throughout their
        land.
[33]He struck down their vines and fig
        trees,
    shattered the trees of their country.
[34]He spoke and the locusts came,
    grasshoppers without number.
[35]They devoured every plant in the
        land;
    they devoured the crops of their
        fields.
[36]He struck down every firstborn in the
        land,

the first fruits of all their vigor.
³⁷He brought his people out,
 laden with silver and gold;
 no one among the tribes stumbled.
³⁸Egypt rejoiced when they left,
 for fear had seized them.

³⁹He spread a cloud out as a cover,
 and made a fire to light up the
  night.
⁴⁰They asked and he brought them
  quail;
 with bread from heaven he filled
  them.
⁴¹He split the rock and water gushed
  forth;
 it flowed through the desert like a
  river.
⁴²For he remembered his sacred
  promise
 to Abraham his servant.
⁴³He brought his people out with joy,
 his chosen ones with shouts of
  triumph.
⁴⁴He gave them the lands of the
  nations,
 they took possession of the wealth
  of the peoples,
⁴⁵That they might keep his statutes
 and observe his teachings.
Hallelujah!

Israel's Confession of Sin. 106:1

Hallelujah!

Give thanks to the Lord, who is good,
 whose mercy endures forever.
²Who can recount the mighty deeds of
  the Lord,
 proclaim in full God's praise?
³Blessed those who do what is right,
 whose deeds are always just.
⁴Remember me, Lord, as you favor
  your people;
 come to me with your saving help,
⁵That I may see the prosperity of your
  chosen ones,
 rejoice in the joy of your people,

and glory with your heritage.
⁶We have sinned like our ancestors;
 we have done wrong and are guilty.

⁷Our ancestors in Egypt
 did not attend to your wonders.
They did not remember your manifold
  mercy;
 they defied the Most High at the
  Red Sea.
⁸Yet he saved them for his name's sake
 to make his power known.
⁹He roared at the Red Sea and it
  dried up.
He led them through the deep as
  through a desert.
¹⁰He rescued them from hostile hands,
 freed them from the power of the
  enemy.
¹¹The waters covered their oppressors;
 not one of them survived.
¹²Then they believed his words
 and sang his praise.

¹³But they soon forgot all he had done;
 they had no patience for his plan.
¹⁴In the desert they gave in to their
  cravings,
 tempted God in the wasteland.
¹⁵So he gave them what they asked
 and sent a wasting disease against
  them.

¹⁶In the camp they challenged Moses
 and Aaron, the holy one of the
  Lord.
¹⁷The earth opened and swallowed
  Dathan,
 it closed on the followers of Abiram.
¹⁸Against their company the fire
  blazed;
 flames consumed the wicked.

¹⁹At Horeb they fashioned a calf,
 worshiped a metal statue.
²⁰They exchanged their glory
 for the image of a grass-eating bull.
²¹They forgot the God who had saved
  them,

who had done great deeds in Egypt,
22Amazing deeds in the land of Ham,
fearsome deeds at the Red Sea.
23He would have decreed their
destruction,
had not Moses, his chosen one,
Withstood him in the breach
to turn back his destroying anger.

24Next they despised the beautiful
land;
they did not believe the promise.
25In their tents they complained;
they did not heed the voice of the
LORD.
26So with raised hand he swore
he would destroy them in the
desert,
27And scatter their descendants among
the nations,
disperse them in foreign lands.
28They joined in the rites of Baal of
Peor,
ate food sacrificed to the dead.
29They provoked him by their actions,
and a plague broke out among
them.
30Then Phinehas rose to intervene,
and the plague was brought to a
halt.
31This was counted for him as a
righteous deed
for all generations to come.
32At the waters of Meribah they
angered God,
and Moses suffered because of them.
33They so embittered his spirit
that rash words crossed his lips.
34They did not destroy the peoples
as the LORD had commanded them,
35But mingled with the nations
and imitated their ways.
36They served their idols

and were ensnared by them.
37They sacrificed to demons
their own sons and daughters,
38Shedding innocent blood,
the blood of their own sons and
daughters,
Whom they sacrificed to the idols of
Canaan,
desecrating the land with
bloodshed.
39They defiled themselves by their
actions,
became adulterers by their conduct.
40So the LORD grew angry with his
people,
abhorred his own heritage.
41He handed them over to the nations,
and their adversaries ruled over
them.
42Their enemies oppressed them,
kept them under subjection.
43Many times did he rescue them,
but they kept rebelling and
scheming
and were brought low by their own
guilt.
44Still God had regard for their
affliction
when he heard their wailing.
45For their sake he remembered his
covenant
and relented in his abundant mercy,
46Winning for them compassion
from all who held them captive.
47Save us, LORD, our God;
gather us from among the nations
That we may give thanks to your holy
name
and glory in praising you.
48Blessed be the LORD, the God of
Israel,
from everlasting to everlasting!
Let all the people say, Amen!
Hallelujah!

☐ JOHN 4:1-42

4:1 Now when Jesus learned that the Pharisees had heard that Jesus was making and baptizing more disciples than John [2](although Jesus himself was not baptizing, just his disciples), [3]he left Judea and returned to Galilee.

The Samaritan Woman. [4]He had to pass through Samaria. [5]So he came to a town of Samaria called Sychar, near the plot of land that Jacob had given to his son Joseph. [6]Jacob's well was there. Jesus, tired from his journey, sat down there at the well. It was about noon.

[7]A woman of Samaria came to draw water. Jesus said to her, "Give me a drink." [8]His disciples had gone into the town to buy food. [9]The Samaritan woman said to him, "How can you, a Jew, ask me, a Samaritan woman, for a drink?" (For Jews use nothing in common with Samaritans.) [10]Jesus answered and said to her, "If you knew the gift of God and who is saying to you, 'Give me a drink,' you would have asked him and he would have given you living water." [11][The woman] said to him, "Sir, you do not even have a bucket and the well is deep; where then can you get this living water? [12]Are you greater than our father Jacob, who gave us this well and drank from it himself with his children and his flocks?" [13]Jesus answered and said to her, "Everyone who drinks this water will be thirsty again; [14]but whoever drinks the water I shall give will never thirst; the water I shall give will become in him a spring of water welling up to eternal life." [15]The woman said to him, "Sir, give me this water, so that I may not be thirsty or have to keep coming here to draw water."

[16]Jesus said to her, "Go call your husband and come back." [17]The woman answered and said to him, "I do not have a husband." Jesus answered her, "You are right in saying, 'I do not have a husband.' [18]For you have had five husbands, and the one you have now is not your husband. What you have said is true." [19]The woman said to him, "Sir, I can see that you are a prophet. [20]Our ancestors worshiped on this mountain; but you people say that the place to worship is in Jerusalem." [21]Jesus said to her, "Believe me, woman, the hour is coming when you will worship the Father neither on this mountain nor in Jerusalem. [22]You people worship what you do not understand; we worship what we understand, because salvation is from the Jews. [23]But the hour is coming, and is now here, when true worshipers will worship the Father in Spirit and truth; and indeed the Father seeks such people to worship him. [24]God is Spirit, and those who worship him must worship in Spirit and truth." [25]The woman said to him, "I know that the Messiah is coming, the one called the Anointed; when he comes, he will tell us everything." [26]Jesus said to her, "I am he, the one who is speaking with you."

[27]At that moment his disciples returned, and were amazed that he was talking with a woman, but still no one said, "What are you looking for?" or "Why are you talking with her?" [28]The woman left her water jar and went into the town and said to the people, [29]"Come see a man who told me everything I have done. Could he possibly be the Messiah?" [30]They went out of the town and came to him. [31]Meanwhile, the disciples urged him, "Rabbi, eat." [32]But he said to them, "I have food to eat of which you do not know." [33]So the disciples said to one another, "Could someone have brought him something to eat?" [34]Jesus said to them, "My food is to do the will of the one who sent me and to finish his work. [35]Do you not say, 'In four months the harvest will be here'? I tell you, look up and see the fields ripe for the harvest. [36]The reaper is already receiving his payment and gathering crops for eternal life, so that the

sower and reaper can rejoice together. [37]For here the saying is verified that 'One sows and another reaps.' [38]I sent you to reap what you have not worked for; others have done the work, and you are sharing the fruits of their work."

[39]Many of the Samaritans of that town began to believe in him because of the word of the woman who testified, "He told me everything I have done." [40]When the Samaritans came to him, they invited him to stay with them; and he stayed there two days. [41]Many more began to believe in him because of his word, [42]and they said to the woman, "We no longer believe because of your word; for we have heard for ourselves, and we know that this is truly the savior of the world."

July 22

St. Mary Magdalene

The Magdalene, most of all, is the model I like to follow. That boldness of hers, which would be so amazing if it weren't the boldness of a lover, won the heart of Jesus, and how it fascinates mine!

— St. Thérèse of Lisieux

☐ PSALMS 107-111

God the Savior of Those in Distress.
107:1 "Give thanks to the LORD for he is good,
his mercy endures forever!"
[2]Let that be the prayer of the LORD's redeemed,
those redeemed from the hand of the foe,
[3]Those gathered from foreign lands,
from east and west, from north and south.

[4]Some had lost their way in a barren desert;
found no path toward a city to live in.
[5]They were hungry and thirsty;
their life was ebbing away.
[6]In their distress they cried to the LORD,
who rescued them in their peril,
[7]Guided them by a direct path
so they reached a city to live in.
[8]Let them thank the LORD for his mercy,

such wondrous deeds for the children of Adam.
[9]For he satisfied the thirsty,
filled the hungry with good things.

[10]Some lived in darkness and gloom,
imprisoned in misery and chains.
[11]Because they rebelled against God's word,
and scorned the counsel of the Most High,
[12]He humbled their hearts through hardship;
they stumbled with no one to help.
[13]In their distress they cried to the LORD,
who saved them in their peril;
[14]He brought them forth from darkness and the shadow of death
and broke their chains asunder.
[15]Let them thank the LORD for his mercy,
such wondrous deeds for the children of Adam.

¹⁶For he broke down the gates of bronze
    and snapped the bars of iron.

¹⁷Some fell sick from their wicked ways,
    afflicted because of their sins.
¹⁸They loathed all manner of food;
    they were at the gates of death.
¹⁹In their distress they cried to the LORD,
    who saved them in their peril,
²⁰Sent forth his word to heal them,
    and snatched them from the grave.
²¹Let them thank the LORD for his
      mercy,
    such wondrous deeds for the
      children of Adam.
²²Let them offer a sacrifice in thanks,
    recount his works with shouts of joy.

²³Some went off to sea in ships,
    plied their trade on the deep waters.
²⁴They saw the works of the LORD,
    the wonders of God in the deep.
²⁵He commanded and roused a storm
      wind;
    it tossed the waves on high.
²⁶They rose up to the heavens, sank to
      the depths;
    their hearts trembled at the danger.
²⁷They reeled, staggered like drunkards;
    their skill was of no avail.
²⁸In their distress they cried to the LORD,
    who brought them out of their
      peril;
²⁹He hushed the storm to silence,
    the waves of the sea were stilled.
³⁰They rejoiced that the sea grew calm,
    that God brought them to the
      harbor they longed for.
³¹Let them thank the LORD for his
      mercy,
    such wondrous deeds for the
      children of Adam.
³²Let them extol him in the assembly of
      the people,
    and praise him in the council of the
      elders.

³³God changed rivers into desert,

springs of water into thirsty ground,
³⁴Fruitful land into a salty waste,
    because of the wickedness of its
      people.
³⁵He changed the desert into pools of
      water,
    arid land into springs of water,
³⁶And settled the hungry there;
    they built a city to live in.
³⁷They sowed fields and planted
      vineyards,
    brought in an abundant harvest.
³⁸God blessed them, and they increased
      greatly,
    and their livestock did not decrease.
³⁹But he poured out contempt on
      princes,
    made them wander trackless wastes,
⁴⁰Where they were diminished and
      brought low
    through misery and cruel
      oppression.
⁴¹While he released the poor man from
      affliction,
    and increased their families like
      flocks.
⁴²The upright saw this and rejoiced;
    all wickedness shut its mouth.
⁴³Whoever is wise will take note of
      these things,
    and ponder the merciful deeds of
      the LORD.

Prayer for Victory. 108:1 A song; a psalm
of David.

²My heart is steadfast, God;
    my heart is steadfast.
    Let me sing and chant praise.
³Awake, lyre and harp!
    I will wake the dawn.
⁴I will praise you among the peoples,
    LORD;
    I will chant your praise among the
      nations.
⁵For your mercy is greater than the
      heavens;

your faithfulness, to the skies.
⁶Appear on high over the heavens, God;
  your glory above all the earth.
⁷Help with your right hand and
    answer us
  that your loved ones may escape.

⁸God speaks in his holiness:
  "I will exult, I will apportion
    Shechem;
  the valley of Succoth I will measure
    out.
⁹Gilead is mine, mine is Manasseh;
  Ephraim is the helmet for my head,
  Judah, my scepter.
¹⁰Moab is my washbowl;
  upon Edom I cast my sandal;
  I will shout in triumph over Philistia."

¹¹Who will bring me to the fortified
    city?
  Who will lead me into Edom?
¹²Was it not you who rejected us, God?
  Do you no longer march with our
    armies?
¹³Give us aid against the foe;
  worthless is human help.
¹⁴We will triumph with the help of God,
  who will trample down our foes.

Prayer of a Person Falsely Accused. 109:1
For the leader. A psalm of David.

²O God, whom I praise, do not be
    silent,
  for wicked and treacherous mouths
    attack me.
They speak against me with lying
    tongues;
  ³with hateful words they surround
    me,
  attacking me without cause.
⁴In return for my love they slander me,
  even though I prayed for them.
⁵They repay me evil for good,
  hatred for my love.
⁶Appoint an evil one over him,

an accuser to stand at his right
    hand,
⁷That he may be judged and found
    guilty,
  that his plea may be in vain.
⁸May his days be few;
  may another take his office.
⁹May his children be fatherless,
  his wife, a widow.
¹⁰May his children wander and beg,
  driven from their hovels.
¹¹May the usurer snare all he owns,
  strangers plunder all he earns.
¹²May no one treat him with mercy
  or pity his fatherless children.
¹³May his posterity be destroyed,
  their name rooted out in the next
    generation.
¹⁴May his fathers' guilt be mentioned
    to the LORD;
  his mother's sin not rooted out.
¹⁵May their guilt be always before the
    LORD,
  till their memory is banished from
    the earth,
¹⁶For he did not remember to show
    mercy,
  but hounded the wretched poor
  and brought death to the
    brokenhearted.
¹⁷He loved cursing; may it come upon
    him;
  he hated blessing; may none come
    to him.
¹⁸May cursing clothe him like a robe;
  may it enter his belly like water,
  his bones like oil.
¹⁹May it be near as the clothes he wears,
  as the belt always around him.
²⁰May this be the reward for my
    accusers from the LORD,
  for those speaking evil against me.
²¹But you, LORD, are my Lord,
  deal kindly with me for your name's
    sake;
  in your great mercy rescue me.

²²For I am poor and needy;
 my heart is pierced within me.
²³Like a lengthening shadow I am gone,
 I am shaken off like the locust.
²⁴My knees totter from fasting;
 my flesh has wasted away.
²⁵I have become a mockery to them;
 when they see me, they shake their
 heads.
²⁶Help me, Lord, my God;
 save me in your mercy.
²⁷Make them know this is your hand,
 that you, Lord, have done this.
²⁸Though they curse, may you bless;
 arise, shame them, that your servant
 may rejoice.
²⁹Clothe my accusers with disgrace;
 make them wear their shame like a
 mantle.
³⁰I will give fervent thanks to the Lord;
 before a crowd I will praise him.
³¹For he stands at the right hand of the
 poor
 to save him from those who pass
 judgment on him.

God Appoints the King both King and Priest. 110:1 A psalm of David.

The Lord says to my lord:
 "Sit at my right hand,
 while I make your enemies your
 footstool."
²The scepter of your might:
 the Lord extends your strong
 scepter from Zion.
 Have dominion over your enemies!
³Yours is princely power from the day
 of your birth.
 In holy splendor before the daystar,
 like dew I begot you.
⁴The Lord has sworn and will not waver:
 "You are a priest forever in the
 manner of Melchizedek."
⁵At your right hand is the Lord,
 who crushes kings on the day of his
 wrath,
⁶Who judges nations, heaps up corpses,
 crushes heads across the wide earth,
⁷Who drinks from the brook by the
 wayside
 and thus holds high his head.

Praise of God for Goodness to Israel. 111:1

Hallelujah!

I will praise the Lord with all my heart
 in the assembled congregation of
 the upright.
²Great are the works of the Lord,
 studied by all who delight in them.
³Majestic and glorious is his work,
 his righteousness endures forever.
⁴He won renown for his wondrous
 deeds;
 gracious and merciful is the Lord.
⁵He gives food to those who fear him,
 he remembers his covenant forever.
⁶He showed his powerful deeds to his
 people,
 giving them the inheritance of the
 nations.
⁷The works of his hands are true and
 just,
 reliable all his decrees,
⁸Established forever and ever,
 to be observed with truth and equity.
⁹He sent release to his people,
 decreed his covenant forever;
 holy and fearsome is his name.
¹⁰The fear of the Lord is the beginning
 of wisdom;
 prudent are all who practice it.
 His praise endures forever.

☐ JOHN 4:43–5:18

Return to Galilee. 4:43 After the two days, he left there for Galilee. ⁴⁴For Jesus himself testified that a prophet has no honor in his native place. ⁴⁵When he came into Galilee, the Galileans welcomed him, since they had seen all he had done in Jerusalem at the feast; for they themselves had gone to the feast.

Second Sign at Cana. ⁴⁶Then he returned to Cana in Galilee, where he had made the water wine. Now there was a royal official whose son was ill in Capernaum. ⁴⁷When he heard that Jesus had arrived in Galilee from Judea, he went to him and asked him to come down and heal his son, who was near death. ⁴⁸Jesus said to him, "Unless you people see signs and wonders, you will not believe." ⁴⁹The royal official said to him, "Sir, come down before my child dies." ⁵⁰Jesus said to him, "You may go; your son will live." The man believed what Jesus said to him and left. ⁵¹While he was on his way back, his slaves met him and told him that his boy would live. ⁵²He asked them when he began to recover. They told him, "The fever left him yesterday, about one in the afternoon." ⁵³The father realized that just at that time Jesus had said to him, "Your son will live," and he and his whole household came to believe. ⁵⁴[Now] this was the second sign Jesus did when he came to Galilee from Judea.

Cure on a Sabbath. 5:1 After this, there was a feast of the Jews, and Jesus went up to Jerusalem. ²Now there is in Jerusalem at the Sheep [Gate] a pool called in Hebrew Bethesda, with five porticoes. ³In these lay a large number of ill, blind, lame, and crippled. ⁴ ⁵One man was there who had been ill for thirty-eight years. ⁶When Jesus saw him lying there and knew that he had been ill for a long time, he said to him, "Do you want to be well?" ⁷The sick man answered him, "Sir, I have no one to put me into the pool when the water is stirred up; while I am on my way, someone else gets down there before me." ⁸Jesus said to him, "Rise, take up your mat, and walk." ⁹Immediately the man became well, took up his mat, and walked.

Now that day was a sabbath. ¹⁰So the Jews said to the man who was cured, "It is the sabbath, and it is not lawful for you to carry your mat." ¹¹He answered them, "The man who made me well told me, 'Take up your mat and walk.'" ¹²They asked him, "Who is the man who told you, 'Take it up and walk'?" ¹³The man who was healed did not know who it was, for Jesus had slipped away, since there was a crowd there. ¹⁴After this Jesus found him in the temple area and said to him, "Look, you are well; do not sin any more, so that nothing worse may happen to you." ¹⁵The man went and told the Jews that Jesus was the one who had made him well. ¹⁶Therefore, the Jews began to persecute Jesus because he did this on a sabbath. ¹⁷But Jesus answered them, "My Father is at work until now, so I am at work." ¹⁸For this reason the Jews tried all the more to kill him, because he not only broke the sabbath but he also called God his own father, making himself equal to God.

July 23

St. Bridget of Sweden

If we saw an angel clearly, we would die of pleasure.
— St. Bridget of Sweden

☐ **PSALMS 112-118**

The Blessings of the Just. **112:1** Hallelujah!

Blessed the man who fears the LORD,
  who greatly delights in his
    commands.
[2]His descendants shall be mighty in the
    land,
  a generation of the upright will be
    blessed.
[3]Wealth and riches shall be in his house;
  his righteousness shall endure
    forever.
[4]Light shines through the darkness for
    the upright;
  gracious, compassionate, and
    righteous.
[5]It is good for the man gracious in
    lending,
  who conducts his affairs with justice.
[6]For he shall never be shaken;
  the righteous shall be remembered
    forever.
[7]He shall not fear an ill report;
  his heart is steadfast, trusting the
    LORD.
[8]His heart is tranquil, without fear,
  till at last he looks down on his foes.
[9]Lavishly he gives to the poor;
  his righteousness shall endure
    forever;
  his horn shall be exalted in honor.
[10]The wicked sees and is angry;
  gnashes his teeth and wastes away;
  the desire of the wicked come to
    nothing.

Praise of God's Care for the Poor. **113:1**
Hallelujah!

Praise, you servants of the LORD,
  praise the name of the LORD.
[2]Blessed be the name of the LORD
  both now and forever.
[3]From the rising of the sun to its setting
  let the name of the LORD be praised.

[4]High above all nations is the LORD;
  above the heavens his glory.
[5]Who is like the LORD our God,
  enthroned on high,
[6]looking down on heaven and earth?
[7]He raises the needy from the dust,
  lifts the poor from the ash heap,
[8]Seats them with princes,
  the princes of the people,
[9]Gives the childless wife a home,
  the joyful mother of children.
  Hallelujah!

The Lord's Wonders at the Exodus.
114:1 When Israel came forth from
    Egypt,
  the house of Jacob from an alien
    people,
[2]Judah became God's sanctuary,
  Israel, God's domain.
[3]The sea saw and fled;
  the Jordan turned back.
[4]The mountains skipped like rams;
  the hills, like lambs.
[5]Why was it, sea, that you fled?
  Jordan, that you turned back?
[6]Mountains, that you skipped like rams?
  You hills, like lambs?
[7]Tremble, earth, before the Lord,
  before the God of Jacob,
[8]Who turned the rock into pools of
    water,
  flint into a flowing spring.

The Greatness of the True God. 115:1

Not to us, Lord, not to us
  but to your name give glory
  because of your mercy and
    faithfulness.
[2]Why should the nations say,
  "Where is their God?"
[3]Our God is in heaven
  and does whatever he wills.

[4]Their idols are silver and gold,
  the work of human hands.
[5]They have mouths but do not speak,
  eyes but do not see.
[6]They have ears but do not hear,
  noses but do not smell.
[7]They have hands but do not feel,
  feet but do not walk;
  they produce no sound from their
    throats.
[8]Their makers will be like them,
  and anyone who trusts in them.

[9]The house of Israel trusts in the Lord,
  who is their help and shield.
[10]The house of Aaron trusts in the Lord,
  who is their help and shield.
[11]Those who fear the Lord trust in the
    Lord,
  who is their help and shield.
[12]The Lord remembers us and will
    bless us,
  will bless the house of Israel,
  will bless the house of Aaron,
[13]Will bless those who fear the Lord,
  small and great alike.
[14]May the Lord increase your number,
  yours and your descendants.
[15]May you be blessed by the Lord,
  maker of heaven and earth.
[16]The heavens belong to the Lord,
  but he has given the earth to the
    children of Adam.
[17]The dead do not praise the Lord,
  not all those go down into silence.
[18]It is we who bless the Lord,
  both now and forever.
Hallelujah!

Thanksgiving to God Who Saves from Death. 116:1

I love the Lord, who
    listened
  to my voice in supplication,
[2]Who turned an ear to me
  on the day I called.
[3]I was caught by the cords of death;
  the snares of Sheol had seized me;
  I felt agony and dread.
[4]Then I called on the name of the Lord,
  "O Lord, save my life!"

[5]Gracious is the Lord and righteous;
  yes, our God is merciful.
[6]The Lord protects the simple;
  I was helpless, but he saved me.
[7]Return, my soul, to your rest;
  the Lord has been very good to you.
[8]For my soul has been freed from death,
  my eyes from tears, my feet from
    stumbling.
[9]I shall walk before the Lord
  in the land of the living.

[10]I kept faith, even when I said,
  "I am greatly afflicted!"
[11]I said in my alarm,
  "All men are liars!"
[12]How can I repay the Lord
  for all the great good done for me?
[13]I will raise the cup of salvation
  and call on the name of the Lord.
[14]I will pay my vows to the Lord
  in the presence of all his people.
[15]Dear in the eyes of the Lord
  is the death of his devoted.
[16]Lord, I am your servant,
  your servant, the child of your
    maidservant;
  you have loosed my bonds.
[17]I will offer a sacrifice of praise
  and call on the name of the Lord.
[18]I will pay my vows to the Lord
  in the presence of all his people,
[19]In the courts of the house of the
    Lord,
  in your midst, O Jerusalem.
Hallelujah!

The Nations Called To Praise. 117:1

Praise the Lord, all you nations!
Extol him, all you peoples!
²His mercy for us is strong;
the faithfulness of the Lord is
forever.
Hallelujah!

Hymn of Thanksgiving. 118:1

Give thanks to the Lord, for he is
good,
his mercy endures forever.
²Let Israel say:
his mercy endures forever.
³Let the house of Aaron say,
his mercy endures forever.
⁴Let those who fear the Lord say,
his mercy endures forever.

⁵In danger I called on the Lord;
the Lord answered me and set me
free.
⁶The Lord is with me; I am not afraid;
what can mortals do against me?
⁷The Lord is with me as my helper;
I shall look in triumph on my foes.
⁸Better to take refuge in the Lord
than to put one's trust in mortals.
⁹Better to take refuge in the Lord
than to put one's trust in princes.

¹⁰All the nations surrounded me;
in the Lord's name I cut them off.
¹¹They surrounded me on every side;
in the Lord's name I cut them off.
¹²They surrounded me like bees;
they burned up like fire among
thorns;
in the Lord's name I cut them off.
¹³I was hard pressed and falling,
but the Lord came to my help.
¹⁴The Lord, my strength and might,
has become my savior.

¹⁵The joyful shout of deliverance
is heard in the tents of the
righteous:
"The Lord's right hand works
valiantly;
¹⁶the Lord's right hand is raised;
the Lord's right hand works
valiantly."
¹⁷I shall not die but live
and declare the deeds of the Lord.
¹⁸The Lord chastised me harshly,
but did not hand me over to death.

¹⁹Open the gates of righteousness;
I will enter and thank the Lord.
²⁰This is the Lord's own gate,
through it the righteous enter.
²¹I thank you for you answered me;
you have been my savior.
²²The stone the builders rejected
has become the cornerstone.
²³By the Lord has this been done;
it is wonderful in our eyes.
²⁴This is the day the Lord has made;
let us rejoice in it and be glad.
²⁵Lord, grant salvation!
Lord, grant good fortune!

²⁶Blessed is he
who comes in the name of the
Lord.
We bless you from the house of the
Lord.
²⁷The Lord is God and has
enlightened us.
Join in procession with leafy branches
up to the horns of the altar.

²⁸You are my God, I give you thanks;
my God, I offer you praise.
²⁹Give thanks to the Lord, for he is
good,
his mercy endures forever.

☐ JOHN 5:19-30

The Work of the Son. 5:19 Jesus answered and said to them, "Amen, amen, I say to you, a son cannot do anything on his own, but only what he sees his father doing; for what he does, his son will do also. [20]For the Father loves his Son and shows him everything that he himself does, and he will show him greater works than these, so that you may be amazed. [21]For just as the Father raises the dead and gives life, so also does the Son give life to whomever he wishes. [22]Nor does the Father judge anyone, but he has given all judgment to his Son, [23]so that all may honor the Son just as they honor the Father. Whoever does not honor the Son does not honor the Father who sent him. [24]Amen, amen, I say to you, whoever hears my word and believes in the one who sent me has eternal life and will not come to condemnation, but has passed from death to life. [25]Amen, amen, I say to you, the hour is coming and is now here when the dead will hear the voice of the Son of God, and those who hear will live. [26]For just as the Father has life in himself, so also he gave to his Son the possession of life in himself. [27]And he gave him power to exercise judgment, because he is the Son of Man. [28]Do not be amazed at this, because the hour is coming in which all who are in the tombs will hear his voice [29]and will come out, those who have done good deeds to the resurrection of life, but those who have done wicked deeds to the resurrection of condemnation.

[30]"I cannot do anything on my own; I judge as I hear, and my judgment is just, because I do not seek my own will but the will of the one who sent me."

July 24

St. Sharbel Makhluf

Study your heart in the light of the Holy Scriptures, and you will know therein who you were, who you are, and who you ought to be.

— St. Fulgence of Ruspe

☐ PSALM 119

A Prayer to God, the Lawgiver. 119:1
Aleph. Blessed those whose way is blameless,
　who walk by the law of the Lord.
[2]Blessed those who keep his testimonies,
　who seek him with all their heart.
[3]They do no wrong;
　they walk in his ways.
[4]You have given them the command
　to observe your precepts with care.
[5]May my ways be firm
　in the observance of your statutes!
[6]Then I will not be ashamed
　to ponder all your commandments.
[7]I will praise you with sincere heart
　as I study your righteous judgments.
[8]I will observe your statutes;
　do not leave me all alone.

Beth. [9]How can the young keep his
　way without fault?
　Only by observing your words.

[10]With all my heart I seek you;
   do not let me stray from your
      commandments.
[11]In my heart I treasure your promise,
   that I may not sin against you.
[12]Blessed are you, O Lord;
   teach me your statutes.
[13]With my lips I recite
   all the judgments you have spoken.
[14]I find joy in the way of your
      testimonies
   more than in all riches.
[15]I will ponder your precepts
   and consider your paths.
[16]In your statutes I take delight;
   I will never forget your word.

Gimel. [17]Be kind to your servant that I
      may live,
   that I may keep your word.
[18]Open my eyes to see clearly
   the wonders of your law.
[19]I am a sojourner in the land;
   do not hide your commandments
      from me.
[20]At all times my soul is stirred
   with longing for your judgments.
[21]With a curse you rebuke the proud
   who stray from your commandments.
[22]Free me from disgrace and contempt,
   for I keep your testimonies.
[23]Though princes meet and talk
      against me,
   your servant meditates on your
      statutes.
[24]Your testimonies are my delight;
   they are my counselors.

Daleth. [25]My soul clings to the dust;
   give me life in accord with your word.
[26]I disclosed my ways and you
      answered me;
   teach me your statutes.
[27]Make me understand the way of your
      precepts;
   I will ponder your wondrous deeds.
[28]My soul is depressed;
   lift me up acccording to your word.

[29]Lead me from the way of deceit;
   favor me with your law.
[30]The way of loyalty I have chosen;
   I have kept your judgments.
[31]I cling to your testimonies, Lord;
   do not let me come to shame.
[32]I will run the way of your
      commandments,
   for you will broaden my heart.

He. [33]Lord, teach me the way of your
      statutes;
   I shall keep them with care.
[34]Give me understanding to keep your
      law,
   to observe it with all my heart.
[35]Lead me in the path of your
      commandments,
   for that is my delight.
[36]Direct my heart toward your
      testimonies
   and away from gain.
[37]Avert my eyes from what is
      worthless;
   by your way give me life.
[38]For your servant, fulfill your promise
   made to those who fear you.
[39]Turn away from me the taunts I
      dread,
   for your judgments are good.
[40]See how I long for your precepts;
   in your righteousness give me life.

Waw. [41]Let your mercy come to me,
      Lord,
   salvation in accord with your promise.
[42]Let me answer my taunters with a
      word,
   for I trust in your word.
[43]Do not take the word of truth from
      my mouth,
   for in your judgments is my hope.
[44]I will keep your law always,
   for all time and forever.
[45]I will walk freely in an open space
   because I cherish your precepts.
[46]I will speak openly of your
      testimonies

without fear even before kings.
⁴⁷I delight in your commandments,
which I dearly love.
⁴⁸I lift up my hands to your
commandments;
I study your statutes, which I love.

Zayin. ⁴⁹Remember your word to your
servant
by which you give me hope.
⁵⁰This is my comfort in affliction,
your promise that gives me life.
⁵¹Though the arrogant utterly scorn me,
I do not turn from your law.
⁵²When I recite your judgments of old
I am comforted, LORD.
⁵³Rage seizes me because of the wicked;
they forsake your law.
⁵⁴Your statutes become my songs
wherever I make my home.
⁵⁵Even at night I remember your name
in observance of your law, LORD.
⁵⁶This is my good fortune,
for I have kept your precepts.

Heth. ⁵⁷My portion is the LORD;
I promise to observe your words.
⁵⁸I entreat you with all my heart:
have mercy on me in accord with
your promise.
⁵⁹I have examined my ways
and turned my steps to your
testimonies.
⁶⁰I am prompt, I do not hesitate
in observing your commandments.
⁶¹Though the snares of the wicked
surround me,
your law I do not forget.
⁶²At midnight I rise to praise you
because of your righteous judgments.
⁶³I am the friend of all who fear you,
of all who observe your precepts.
⁶⁴The earth, LORD, is filled with your
mercy;
teach me your statutes.

Teth. ⁶⁵You have treated your servant
well,

according to your word, O LORD.
⁶⁶Teach me wisdom and knowledge,
for in your commandments I trust.
⁶⁷Before I was afflicted I went astray,
but now I hold to your promise.
⁶⁸You are good and do what is good;
teach me your statutes.
⁶⁹The arrogant smear me with lies,
but I keep your precepts with all my
heart.
⁷⁰Their hearts are gross and fat;
as for me, your law is my delight.
⁷¹It was good for me to be afflicted,
in order to learn your statutes.
⁷²The law of your mouth is more
precious to me
than heaps of silver and gold.

Yodh. ⁷³Your hands made me and
fashioned me;
give me understanding to learn your
commandments.
⁷⁴Those who fear you rejoice to see me,
because I hope in your word.
⁷⁵I know, LORD, that your judgments
are righteous;
though you afflict me, you are
faithful.
⁷⁶May your mercy comfort me
in accord with your promise to your
servant.
⁷⁷Show me compassion that I may live,
for your law is my delight.
⁷⁸Shame the proud for leading me
astray with falsehood,
that I may study your testimonies.
⁷⁹Let those who fear you turn to me,
those who acknowledge your
testimonies.
⁸⁰May I be wholehearted toward your
statutes,
that I may not be put to shame.

Kaph. ⁸¹My soul longs for your
salvation;
I put my hope in your word.
⁸²My eyes long to see your promise.
When will you comfort me?

83I am like a wineskin shriveled by
    smoke,
  but I have not forgotten your statutes.
84How long can your servant survive?
  When will your judgment doom my
    foes?
85The arrogant have dug pits for me;
  defying your law.
86All your commandments are
    steadfast.
  Help me! I am pursued without
    cause.
87They have almost put an end to me
    on earth,
  but I do not forsake your precepts.
88In your mercy give me life,
  to observe the testimonies of your
    mouth.

Lamedh. 89Your word, LORD, stands
    forever;
  it is firm as the heavens.
90Through all generations your truth
    endures;
  fixed to stand firm like the earth.
91By your judgments they stand firm to
    this day,
  for all things are your servants.
92Had your law not been my delight,
  I would have perished in my
    affliction.
93I will never forget your precepts;
  through them you give me life.
94I am yours; save me,
  for I cherish your precepts.
95The wicked hope to destroy me,
  but I seek to understand your
    testimonies.
96I have seen the limits of all perfection,
  but your commandment is without
    bounds.

Mem. 97How I love your law, Lord!
  I study it all day long.
98Your commandment makes me wiser
    than my foes,
  as it is forever with me.

99I have more insight than all my
    teachers,
  because I ponder your testimonies.
100I have more understanding than my
    elders,
  because I keep your precepts.
101I keep my steps from every evil path,
  that I may observe your word.
102From your judgments I do not turn,
  for you have instructed me.
103How sweet to my tongue is your
    promise,
  sweeter than honey to my mouth!
104Through your precepts I gain
    understanding;
  therefore I hate all false ways.

Nun. 105Your word is a lamp for my feet,
  a light for my path.
106I make a solemn vow
  to observe your righteous judgments.
107I am very much afflicted, LORD;
  give me life in accord with your word.
108Accept my freely offered praise;
  LORD, teach me your judgments.
109My life is always at risk,
  but I do not forget your law.
110The wicked have set snares for me,
  but from your precepts I do not
    stray.
111Your testimonies are my heritage
    forever;
  they are the joy of my heart.
112My heart is set on fulfilling your
    statutes;
  they are my reward forever.

Samekh. 113I hate every hypocrite;
  your law I love.
114You are my refuge and shield;
  in your word I hope.
115Depart from me, you wicked,
  that I may keep the commandments
    of my God.
116Sustain me by your promise that I
    may live;
  do not disappoint me in my hope.
117Strengthen me that I may be safe,

ever to contemplate your statutes.
¹¹⁸You reject all who stray from your
statutes,
for vain is their deceit.
¹¹⁹Like dross you regard all the wicked
on earth;
therefore I love your testimonies.
¹²⁰My flesh shudders with dread of you;
I fear your judgments.

Ayin. ¹²¹I have fulfilled your righteous
judgment;
do not abandon me to my
oppressors.
¹²²Guarantee your servant's welfare;
do not let the arrogant oppress me.
¹²³My eyes long to see your salvation
and the promise of your
righteousness.
¹²⁴Act with mercy toward your servant;
teach me your statutes.
¹²⁵I am your servant; give me
discernment
that I may know your testimonies.
¹²⁶It is time for the LORD to act;
they have disobeyed your law.
¹²⁷Truly I love your commandments
more than gold, more than the
finest gold.
¹²⁸Thus, I follow all your precepts;
every wrong way I hate.

Pe. ¹²⁹Wonderful are your testimonies;
therefore I keep them.
¹³⁰The revelation of your words sheds
light,
gives understanding to the simple.
¹³¹I sigh with open mouth,
yearning for your commandments.
¹³²Turn to me and be gracious,
according to your judgment for
those who love your name.
¹³³Steady my feet in accord with your
promise;
do not let iniquity lead me.
¹³⁴Free me from human oppression,
that I may observe your precepts.
¹³⁵Let your face shine upon your servant;

teach me your statutes.
¹³⁶My eyes shed streams of tears
because your law is not observed.

Sadhe. ¹³⁷You are righteous, LORD,
and just are your judgments.
¹³⁸You have given your testimonies in
righteousness
and in surpassing faithfulness.
¹³⁹I am consumed with rage,
because my foes forget your words.
¹⁴⁰Your servant loves your promise;
it has been proved by fire.
¹⁴¹Though belittled and despised,
I do not forget your precepts.
¹⁴²Your justice is forever right,
your law true.
¹⁴³Though distress and anguish come
upon me,
your commandments are my delight.
¹⁴⁴Your testimonies are forever
righteous;
give me understanding that I may
live.
¹⁴⁵I call with all my heart, O LORD;
answer me that I may keep your
statutes.
¹⁴⁶I call to you to save me
that I may observe your testimonies.
¹⁴⁷I rise before dawn and cry out;
I put my hope in your words.
¹⁴⁸My eyes greet the night watches
as I meditate on your promise.
¹⁴⁹Hear my voice in your mercy, O
LORD;
by your judgment give me life.
¹⁵⁰Malicious persecutors draw near me;
they are far from your law.
¹⁵¹You are near, O LORD;
reliable are all your commandments.
¹⁵²Long have I known from your
testimonies
that you have established them
forever.

Resh. ¹⁵³Look at my affliction and
rescue me,
for I have not forgotten your law.

¹⁵⁴Take up my cause and redeem me;
    for the sake of your promise give
        me life.
¹⁵⁵Salvation is far from sinners
    because they do not cherish your
        statutes.
¹⁵⁶Your compassion is great, O Lord;
    in accord with your judgments, give
        me life.
¹⁵⁷Though my persecutors and foes are
        many,
    I do not turn from your testimonies.
¹⁵⁸I view the faithless with loathing
    because they do not heed your
        promise.
¹⁵⁹See how I love your precepts, Lord;
    in your mercy give me life.
¹⁶⁰Your every word is enduring;
    all your righteous judgments are
        forever.

Shin. ¹⁶¹Princes persecute me without
        reason,
    but my heart reveres only your word.
¹⁶²I rejoice at your promise,
    as one who has found rich spoil.
¹⁶³Falsehood I hate and abhor;
    your law I love.
¹⁶⁴Seven times a day I praise you
    because your judgments are
        righteous.
¹⁶⁵Lovers of your law have much peace;

for them there is no stumbling
        block.
¹⁶⁶I look for your salvation, Lord,
    and I fulfill your commandments.
¹⁶⁷I observe your testimonies;
    I love them very much.
¹⁶⁸I observe your precepts and
        testimonies;
    all my ways are before you.

Taw. ¹⁶⁹Let my cry come before you,
    Lord;
    in keeping with your word, give me
        understanding.
¹⁷⁰Let my prayer come before you;
    rescue me according to your promise.
¹⁷¹May my lips pour forth your praise,
    because you teach me your statutes.
¹⁷²May my tongue sing of your
        promise,
    for all your commandments are
        righteous.
¹⁷³Keep your hand ready to help me,
    for I have chosen your precepts.
¹⁷⁴I long for your salvation, Lord;
    your law is my delight.
¹⁷⁵Let my soul live to praise you;
    may your judgments give me help.
¹⁷⁶I have wandered like a lost sheep;
    seek out your servant,
    for I do not forget your
        commandments.

☐ JOHN 5:31-47

Witnesses to Jesus. 5:31 "If I testify on my own behalf, my testimony cannot be verified. ³²But there is another who testifies on my behalf, and I know that the testimony he gives on my behalf is true. ³³You sent emissaries to John, and he testified to the truth. ³⁴I do not accept testimony from a human being, but I say this so that you may be saved. ³⁵He was a burning and shining lamp, and for a while you were content to rejoice in his light. ³⁶But I have testimony greater than John's. The works that the Father gave me to accomplish, these works that I perform testify on my behalf that the Father has sent me. ³⁷Moreover, the Father who sent me has testified on my behalf. But you have never heard his voice nor seen his form, ³⁸and you do not have his word remaining in you, because you do not believe in the one whom he has sent. ³⁹You search the scriptures, because you think you have eternal life through them; even they testify on my behalf. ⁴⁰But you do not want to come to me to have life.

Unbelief of Jesus' Hearers. [41]"I do not accept human praise; [42]moreover, I know that you do not have the love of God in you. [43]I came in the name of my Father, but you do not accept me; yet if another comes in his own name, you will accept him. [44]How can you believe, when you accept praise from one another and do not seek the praise that comes from the only God? [45]Do not think that I will accuse you before the Father: the one who will accuse you is Moses, in whom you have placed your hope. [46]For if you had believed Moses, you would have believed me, because he wrote about me. [47]But if you do not believe his writings, how will you believe my words?"

July 25

St. James

No one can be a Catholic without a simple faith that what the Church declares in God's name is God's Word, and therefore true. A man must simply believe that the Church is the oracle of God; he must be as certain of her mission as he is of the mission of the apostles.

—BLESSED JOHN HENRY NEWMAN

☐ PSALMS 120-127

Prayer of a Returned Exile. **120:1** A song of ascents.

The LORD answered me
  when I called in my distress:
[2]LORD, deliver my soul from lying lips,
  from a treacherous tongue.

[3]What will he inflict on you,
  O treacherous tongue,
  and what more besides?
[4]A warrior's arrows
  sharpened with coals of brush wood!

[5]Alas, I am a foreigner in Meshech,
  I live among the tents of Kedar!
[6]Too long do I live
  among those who hate peace.
[7]When I speak of peace,
  they are for war.

The Lord My Guardian. **121:1** A song of ascents.

I raise my eyes toward the mountains.

From whence shall come my help?
[2]My help comes from the LORD,
  the maker of heaven and earth.

[3]He will not allow your foot to slip;
  or your guardian to sleep.
[4]Behold, the guardian of Israel
  never slumbers nor sleeps.
[5]The LORD is your guardian;
  the LORD is your shade
  at your right hand.
[6]By day the sun will not strike you,
  nor the moon by night.
[7]The LORD will guard you from all evil;
  he will guard your soul.
[8]The LORD will guard your coming and
  going
  both now and forever.

A Pilgrim's Prayer for Jerusalem. **122:1** A song of ascents. Of David.

I rejoiced when they said to me,
  "Let us go to the house of the LORD."

²And now our feet are standing
　　within your gates, Jerusalem.
³Jerusalem, built as a city,
　　walled round about.
⁴There the tribes go up,
　　the tribes of the LORD,
As it was decreed for Israel,
　　to give thanks to the name of the LORD.
⁵There are the thrones of justice,
　　the thrones of the house of David.

⁶For the peace of Jerusalem pray:
　　"May those who love you prosper!
⁷May peace be within your ramparts,
　　prosperity within your towers."
⁸For the sake of my brothers and
　　friends I say,
　　"Peace be with you."
⁹For the sake of the house of the LORD,
　　our God,
　　I pray for your good.

Reliance on the Lord. **123:1** A song of ascents.

To you I raise my eyes,
　　to you enthroned in heaven.
²Yes, like the eyes of servants
　　on the hand of their masters,
Like the eyes of a maid
　　on the hand of her mistress,
So our eyes are on the LORD our God,
　　till we are shown favor.
³Show us favor, LORD, show us favor,
　　for we have our fill of contempt.
⁴Our souls are more than sated
　　with mockery from the insolent,
　　with contempt from the arrogant.

God, the Rescuer of the People. **124:1** A song of ascents. Of David.

Had not the LORD been with us,
　　let Israel say,
²Had not the LORD been with us,
　　when people rose against us,
³Then they would have swallowed us alive,
　　for their fury blazed against us.

⁴Then the waters would have engulfed us,
　　the torrent overwhelmed us;
⁵then seething water would have
　　drowned us.
⁶Blessed is the LORD, who did not
　　leave us
　　to be torn by their teeth.
⁷We escaped with our lives like a bird
　　from the fowler's snare;
　　the snare was broken,
　　and we escaped.
⁸Our help is in the name of the LORD,
　　the maker of heaven and earth.

Israel's Protector. **125:1** A song of ascents.

Those trusting in the LORD are like
　　Mount Zion,
　　unshakable, forever enduring.
²As mountains surround Jerusalem,
　　the LORD surrounds his people
　　both now and forever.

³The scepter of the wicked will not prevail
　　in the land allotted to the just,
Lest the just themselves
　　turn their hands to evil.

⁴Do good, LORD, to the good,
　　to those who are upright of heart.
⁵But those who turn aside to crooked
　　ways
　　may the LORD send down with the
　　evildoers.
　　Peace upon Israel!

The Reversal of Zion's Fortunes. **126:1** A song of ascents.

When the LORD restored the captives
　　of Zion,
　　we thought we were dreaming.
²Then our mouths were filled with
　　laughter;
　　our tongues sang for joy.
Then it was said among the nations,
　　"The LORD had done great things
　　for them."
³The LORD has done great things for us;

Oh, how happy we were!
⁴Restore our captives, LORD,
like the dry stream beds of the Negeb.

⁵Those who sow in tears
will reap with cries of joy.
⁶Those who go forth weeping,
carrying sacks of seed,
Will return with cries of joy,
carrying their bundled sheaves.

The Need of God's Blessing. 127:1 A song of ascents. Of Solomon.

Unless the LORD build the house,
they labor in vain who build.
Unless the LORD guard the city,

in vain does the guard keep watch.
²It is vain for you to rise early
and put off your rest at night,
To eat bread earned by hard toil—
all this God gives to his beloved in
sleep.

³Certainly sons are a gift from the LORD,
the fruit of the womb, a reward.
⁴Like arrows in the hand of a warrior
are the sons born in one's youth.
⁵Blessed is the man who has filled his
quiver with them.
He will never be shamed
for he will destroy his foes at the gate.

☐ JOHN 6:1-24

Multiplication of the Loaves. 6:1 After this, Jesus went across the Sea of Galilee [of Tiberias]. ²A large crowd followed him, because they saw the signs he was performing on the sick. ³Jesus went up on the mountain, and there he sat down with his disciples. ⁴The Jewish feast of Passover was near. ⁵When Jesus raised his eyes and saw that a large crowd was coming to him, he said to Philip, "Where can we buy enough food for them to eat?" ⁶He said this to test him, because he himself knew what he was going to do. ⁷Philip answered him, "Two hundred days' wages worth of food would not be enough for each of them to have a little [bit]." ⁸One of his disciples, Andrew, the brother of Simon Peter, said to him, ⁹"There is a boy here who has five barley loaves and two fish; but what good are these for so many?" ¹⁰Jesus said, "Have the people recline." Now there was a great deal of grass in that place. So the men reclined, about five thousand in number. ¹¹Then Jesus took the loaves, gave thanks, and distributed them to those who were reclining, and also as much of the fish as they wanted. ¹²When they had had their fill, he said to his

disciples, "Gather the fragments left over, so that nothing will be wasted." ¹³So they collected them, and filled twelve wicker baskets with fragments from the five barley loaves that had been more than they could eat. ¹⁴When the people saw the sign he had done, they said, "This is truly the Prophet, the one who is to come into the world." ¹⁵Since Jesus knew that they were going to come and carry him off to make him king, he withdrew again to the mountain alone.

Walking on the Water. ¹⁶When it was evening, his disciples went down to the sea, ¹⁷embarked in a boat, and went across the sea to Capernaum. It had already grown dark, and Jesus had not yet come to them. ¹⁸The sea was stirred up because a strong wind was blowing. ¹⁹When they had rowed about three or four miles, they saw Jesus walking on the sea and coming near the boat, and they began to be afraid. ²⁰But he said to them, "It is I. Do not be afraid." ²¹They wanted to take him into the boat, but the boat immediately arrived at the shore to which they were heading.

The Bread of Life Discourse. ²²The next day, the crowd that remained across the sea saw that there had been only one boat there, and that Jesus had not gone along with his disciples in the boat, but only his disciples had left. ²³Other boats came from Tiberias near the place where they had eaten the bread when the Lord gave thanks. ²⁴When the crowd saw that neither Jesus nor his disciples were there, they themselves got into boats and came to Capernaum looking for Jesus.

July 26

Sts. Joachim and Anne; Blessed Titus Brandsma

Just as many grains collected into one and ground and mingled together make one loaf, so in Christ, who is the heavenly Bread, we know there is one Body, in which our whole company is joined and united.

— ST. HILARY OF POITIERS

☐ PSALMS 128-136

The Blessed Home of the Just. **128:1** A song of ascents.

Blessed are all who fear the LORD,
and who walk in his ways.
²What your hands provide you will enjoy;
you will be blessed and prosper:
³Your wife will be like a fruitful vine within your home,
Your children like young olive plants around your table.
⁴Just so will the man be blessed who fears the LORD.

⁵May the LORD bless you from Zion;
may you see Jerusalem's prosperity all the days of your life,
⁶and live to see your children's children.
Peace upon Israel!

Against Israel's Enemies. **129:1** A song of ascents.

Viciously have they attacked me from my youth,
let Israel say now.

²Viciously have they attacked me from my youth,
yet they have not prevailed against me.
³Upon my back the plowers plowed,
as they traced their long furrows.
⁴But the just LORD cut me free from the ropes of the wicked.

⁵May they recoil in disgrace,
all who hate Zion.
⁶May they be like grass on the rooftops withered in early growth,
⁷Never to fill the reaper's hands,
nor the arms of the binders of sheaves,
⁸And with none passing by to call out:
"The blessing of the LORD be upon you!
We bless you in the name of the LORD!"

Prayer for Pardon and Mercy. **130:1** A song of ascents.

Out of the depths I call to you, LORD;
²Lord, hear my cry!
May your ears be attentive

to my cry for mercy.
³If you, LORD, keep account of sins,
  Lord, who can stand?
⁴But with you is forgiveness
  and so you are revered.
⁵I wait for the LORD,
  my soul waits
  and I hope for his word.
⁶My soul looks for the Lord
  more than sentinels for daybreak.
More than sentinels for daybreak,
  ⁷let Israel hope in the LORD,
For with the LORD is mercy,
  with him is plenteous redemption,
⁸And he will redeem Israel
  from all its sins.

Humble Trust in God. 131:1 A song of ascents. Of David.

LORD, my heart is not proud;
  nor are my eyes haughty.
I do not busy myself with great matters,
  with things too sublime for me.
²Rather, I have stilled my soul,
Like a weaned child to its mother,
  weaned is my soul.
³Israel, hope in the LORD,
  now and forever.

The Covenant Between David and God. 132:1 A song of ascents.

Remember, O LORD, for David
  all his hardships;
²How he swore an oath to the LORD,
  vowed to the Mighty One of Jacob:
³"I will not enter the house where I live,
  nor lie on the couch where I sleep;
⁴I will give my eyes no sleep,
  my eyelids no rest,
⁵Till I find a place for the LORD,
  a dwelling for the Mighty One of
    Jacob."
⁶"We have heard of it in Ephrathah;
  we have found it in the fields of Jaar.
⁷Let us enter his dwelling;

let us worship at his footstool."
⁸"Arise, LORD, come to your resting
    place,
  you and your mighty ark.
⁹Your priests will be clothed with justice;
  your devout will shout for joy."
¹⁰For the sake of David your servant,
  do not reject your anointed.

¹¹The LORD swore an oath to David in
    truth,
  he will never turn back from it:
"Your own offspring I will set upon
    your throne.
¹²If your sons observe my covenant,
  and my decrees I shall teach them,
Their sons, in turn,
  shall sit forever on your throne."
¹³Yes, the LORD has chosen Zion,
  desired it for a dwelling:
¹⁴"This is my resting place forever;
  here I will dwell, for I desire it.
¹⁵I will bless Zion with provisions;
  its poor I will fill with bread.
¹⁶I will clothe its priests with salvation;
  its devout shall shout for joy.
¹⁷There I will make a horn sprout for
    David;
  I will set a lamp for my anointed.
¹⁸His foes I will clothe with shame,
  but on him his crown shall shine."

A Vision of a Blessed Community. 133:1 A song of ascents. Of David.

How good and how pleasant it is,
  when brothers dwell together as one!
²Like fine oil on the head,
  running down upon the beard,
Upon the beard of Aaron,
  upon the collar of his robe.
³Like dew of Hermon coming down
  upon the mountains of Zion.
There the LORD has decreed a blessing,
  life for evermore!

Exhortation to the Night Watch to Bless God. 134:1 A song of ascents.

O come, bless the LORD,
    all you servants of the LORD
You who stand in the house of the LORD
    throughout the nights.
²Lift up your hands toward the
      sanctuary,
    and bless the LORD.
³May the LORD bless you from Zion,
    the Maker of heaven and earth.

Praise of God, the Ruler and Benefactor of Israel. 135:1 Hallelujah!

Praise the name of the LORD!
    Praise, you servants of the LORD,
²Who stand in the house of the LORD,
    in the courts of the house of our God!
³Praise the LORD, for the LORD is good!
    Sing to his name, for it brings joy!
⁴For the LORD has chosen Jacob for
      himself,
    Israel as his treasured possession.

⁵For I know that the LORD is great,
    that our Lord is greater than all gods.
⁶Whatever the LORD desires
    he does in heaven and on earth,
    in the seas and all the depths.
⁷It is he who raises storm clouds from
      the end of the earth,
    makes lightning for the rain,
    and brings forth wind from his
      storehouse.

⁸He struck down Egypt's firstborn,
    of human being and beast alike,
⁹And sent signs and wonders against
      you, Egypt,
    against Pharaoh and all his servants.
¹⁰It is he who struck down many
      nations,
    and slew mighty kings—
¹¹Sihon, king of the Amorites,
    and Og, king of Bashan,
    all the kings of Canaan—
¹²And made their land a heritage,
    a heritage for Israel his people.
¹³O LORD, your name is forever,

your renown, from generation to
    generation!
¹⁴For the LORD defends his people,
    shows mercy to his servants.

¹⁵The idols of the nations are silver and
    gold,
    the work of human hands.
¹⁶They have mouths but do not speak;
    they have eyes but do not see;
¹⁷They have ears but do not hear;
    nor is there breath in their mouths.
¹⁸Their makers will become like them,
    and anyone who trusts in them.

¹⁹House of Israel, bless the LORD!
    House of Aaron, bless the LORD!
²⁰House of Levi, bless the LORD!
    You who fear the LORD, bless the
    LORD!
²¹Blessed be the LORD from Zion,
    who dwells in Jerusalem!
    Hallelujah!

Hymn of Thanksgiving for God's Everlasting Mercy. 136:1

Praise the LORD, for he is good;
    for his mercy endures forever;
²Praise the God of gods;
    for his mercy endures forever;
³Praise the Lord of lords;
    for his mercy endures forever;

⁴Who alone has done great wonders,
    for his mercy endures forever;
⁵Who skillfully made the heavens,
    for his mercy endures forever;
⁶Who spread the earth upon the waters,
    for his mercy endures forever;
⁷Who made the great lights,
    for his mercy endures forever;
⁸The sun to rule the day,
    for his mercy endures forever;
⁹The moon and stars to rule the night,
    for his mercy endures forever;

¹⁰Who struck down the firstborn of
      Egypt,
    for his mercy endures forever;

[11] And led Israel from their midst,
  for his mercy endures forever;
[12] With mighty hand and outstretched arm,
  for his mercy endures forever;
[13] Who split in two the Red Sea,
  for his mercy endures forever;
[14] And led Israel through its midst,
  for his mercy endures forever;
[15] But swept Pharaoh and his army into the Red Sea,
  for his mercy endures forever;
[16] Who led the people through the desert,
  for his mercy endures forever;

[17] Who struck down great kings,
  for his mercy endures forever;
[18] Slew powerful kings,
  for his mercy endures forever;

[19] Sihon, king of the Amorites,
  for his mercy endures forever;
[20] Og, king of Bashan,
  for his mercy endures forever;
[21] And made their lands a heritage,
  for his mercy endures forever;
[22] A heritage for Israel, his servant,
  for his mercy endures forever.

[23] The Lord remembered us in our low estate,
  for his mercy endures forever;
[24] Freed us from our foes,
  for his mercy endures forever;
[25] And gives bread to all flesh,
  for his mercy endures forever.

[26] Praise the God of heaven,
  for his mercy endures forever.

☐ JOHN 6:25-59

6:25 And when they found him across the sea they said to him, "Rabbi, when did you get here?" [26] Jesus answered them and said, "Amen, amen, I say to you, you are looking for me not because you saw signs but because you ate the loaves and were filled. [27] Do not work for food that perishes but for the food that endures for eternal life, which the Son of Man will give you. For on him the Father, God, has set his seal." [28] So they said to him, "What can we do to accomplish the works of God?" [29] Jesus answered and said to them, "This is the work of God, that you believe in the one he sent." [30] So they said to him, "What sign can you do, that we may see and believe in you? What can you do? [31] Our ancestors ate manna in the desert, as it is written:

'He gave them bread from heaven
  to eat.'"

[32] So Jesus said to them, "Amen, amen, I say to you, it was not Moses who gave the bread from heaven; my Father gives you the true bread from heaven. [33] For the bread of God is that which comes down from heaven and gives life to the world."

[34] So they said to him, "Sir, give us this bread always." [35] Jesus said to them, "I am the bread of life; whoever comes to me will never hunger, and whoever believes in me will never thirst. [36] But I told you that although you have seen [me], you do not believe. [37] Everything that the Father gives me will come to me, and I will not reject anyone who comes to me, [38] because I came down from heaven not to do my own will but the will of the one who sent me. [39] And this is the will of the one who sent me, that I should not lose anything of what he gave me, but that I should raise it [on] the last day. [40] For this is the will of my Father, that everyone who sees the Son and believes in him may have eternal life, and I shall raise him [on] the last day."

[41] The Jews murmured about him because he said, "I am the bread that came down from heaven," [42] and they said, "Is

this not Jesus, the son of Joseph? Do we not know his father and mother? Then how can he say, 'I have come down from heaven'?" [43]Jesus answered and said to them, "Stop murmuring among yourselves. [44]No one can come to me unless the Father who sent me draw him, and I will raise him on the last day. [45]It is written in the prophets:

'They shall all be taught by God.'

Everyone who listens to my Father and learns from him comes to me. [46]Not that anyone has seen the Father except the one who is from God; he has seen the Father. [47]Amen, amen, I say to you, whoever believes has eternal life. [48]I am the bread of life. [49]Your ancestors ate the manna in the desert, but they died; [50]this is the bread that comes down from heaven so that one may eat it and not die. [51]I am the living bread that came down from heaven; whoever eats this bread will live forever; and the bread that I will give is my flesh for the life of the world."

[52]The Jews quarreled among themselves, saying, "How can this man give us [his] flesh to eat?" [53]Jesus said to them, "Amen, amen, I say to you, unless you eat the flesh of the Son of Man and drink his blood, you do not have life within you. [54]Whoever eats my flesh and drinks my blood has eternal life, and I will raise him on the last day. [55]For my flesh is true food, and my blood is true drink. [56]Whoever eats my flesh and drinks my blood remains in me and I in him. [57]Just as the living Father sent me and I have life because of the Father, so also the one who feeds on me will have life because of me. [58]This is the bread that came down from heaven. Unlike your ancestors who ate and still died, whoever eats this bread will live forever." [59]These things he said while teaching in the synagogue in Capernaum.

July 27

With regard to doing the will of the Lord, even if someone should be scandalized by what we do, we must not let that hamper our freedom of action.

— St. Basil the Great

☐ PSALMS 137–141

Sorrow and Hope in Exile. 137:1
By the rivers of Babylon
　there we sat weeping
　　when we remembered Zion.
[2]On the poplars in its midst
　we hung up our harps.
[3]For there our captors asked us
　for the words of a song;
Our tormentors, for joy:
　"Sing for us a song of Zion!"
[4]But how could we sing a song of the
　Lord

in a foreign land?
[5]If I forget you, Jerusalem,
　may my right hand forget.
[6]May my tongue stick to my palate
　if I do not remember you,
If I do not exalt Jerusalem
　beyond all my delights.

[7]Remember, Lord, against Edom
　that day at Jerusalem.
They said: "Level it, level it
　down to its foundations!"

[8]Desolate Daughter Babylon, you shall
be destroyed,
blessed the one who pays you back
what you have done us!
[9]Blessed the one who seizes your children
and smashes them against the rock.

Hymn of a Grateful Heart.

138:1 Of David.

I thank you, Lord, with all my heart;
in the presence of the angels to you
I sing.
[2]I bow low toward your holy temple;
I praise your name for your mercy
and faithfulness.
For you have exalted over all
your name and your promise.
[3]On the day I cried out, you answered;
you strengthened my spirit.

[4]All the kings of earth will praise you,
Lord,
when they hear the words of your
mouth.
[5]They will sing of the ways of the Lord:
"How great is the glory of the Lord!"
[6]The Lord is on high, but cares for the
lowly
and knows the proud from afar.
[7]Though I walk in the midst of dangers,
you guard my life when my enemies
rage.
You stretch out your hand;
your right hand saves me.
[8]The Lord is with me to the end.
Lord, your mercy endures forever.
Never forsake the work of your hands!

The All-knowing and Ever-present God.

139:1 For the leader. A psalm of David.

Lord, you have probed me, you know
me:
[2]you know when I sit and stand;
you understand my thoughts from
afar.
[3]You sift through my travels and my rest;
with all my ways you are familiar.
[4]Even before a word is on my tongue,
Lord, you know it all.
[5]Behind and before you encircle me
and rest your hand upon me.
[6]Such knowledge is too wonderful
for me,
far too lofty for me to reach.

[7]Where can I go from your spirit?
From your presence, where can I flee?
[8]If I ascend to the heavens, you are
there;
if I lie down in Sheol, there you are.
[9]If I take the wings of dawn
and dwell beyond the sea,
[10]Even there your hand guides me,
your right hand holds me fast.
[11]If I say, "Surely darkness shall hide me,
and night shall be my light"—
[12]Darkness is not dark for you,
and night shines as the day.
Darkness and light are but one.

[13]You formed my inmost being;
you knit me in my mother's womb.
[14]I praise you, because I am
wonderfully made;
wonderful are your works!
My very self you know.
[15]My bones are not hidden from you,
When I was being made in secret,
fashioned in the depths of the earth.
[16]Your eyes saw me unformed;
in your book all are written down;
my days were shaped, before one
came to be.

[17]How precious to me are your designs,
O God;
how vast the sum of them!
[18]Were I to count them, they would
outnumber the sands;
when I complete them, still you are
with me.
[19]When you would destroy the wicked,
O God,
the bloodthirsty depart from me!

²⁰Your foes who conspire a plot against
you
are exalted in vain.
²¹Do I not hate, LORD, those who hate
you?
Those who rise against you, do I not
loathe?
²²With fierce hatred I hate them,
enemies I count as my own.

²³Probe me, God, know my heart;
try me, know my thoughts.
²⁴See if there is a wicked path in me;
lead me along an ancient path.

Prayer for Deliverance from the Wicked.

140:1 For the leader. A psalm of David.

²Deliver me, LORD, from the wicked;
preserve me from the violent,
³From those who plan evil in their hearts,
who stir up conflicts every day,
⁴Who sharpen their tongue like a
serpent,
venom of asps upon their lips.
Selah

⁵Keep me, LORD, from the clutches of
the wicked;
preserve me from the violent,
who plot to trip me up.
⁶The arrogant have set a trap for me;
they have spread out ropes for a net,
laid snares for me by the wayside.
Selah

⁷I say to the LORD: You are my God;
listen, LORD, to the words of my pleas.
⁸LORD, my master, my strong deliverer,
you cover my head on the day of
armed conflict.
⁹LORD, do not grant the desires of the
wicked one;
do not let his plot succeed.
Selah

¹⁰Those who surround me raise their
heads;
may the mischief they threaten
overwhelm them.

¹¹Drop burning coals upon them;
cast them into the watery pit never
more to rise.
¹²Slanderers will not survive on earth;
evil will hunt down the man of
violence to overthrow him.
¹³For I know the LORD will take up the
cause of the needy,
justice for the poor.
¹⁴Then the righteous will give thanks to
your name;

Prayer for Deliverance from the Wicked.

141:1 A psalm of David.

LORD, I call to you; hasten to me;
listen to my plea when I call.
²Let my prayer be incense before you;
my uplifted hands an evening
offering.
³Set a guard, LORD, before my mouth,
keep watch over the door of my lips.
⁴Do not let my heart incline to evil,
to perform deeds in wickedness.
On the delicacies of evildoers
let me not feast.
⁵Let a righteous person strike me; it is
mercy if he reproves me.
Do not withhold oil from my head
while my prayer opposes their evil
deeds.
⁶May their leaders be cast over the cliff,
so that they hear that my speeches
are pleasing.
⁷Like the plowing and breaking up of
the earth,
our bones are strewn at the mouth
of Sheol.
⁸For my eyes are upon you, O LORD,
my Lord;
in you I take refuge; do not take
away my soul.
⁹Guard me from the trap they have set
for me,
from the snares of evildoers.
¹⁰Let the wicked fall into their own nets,
while only I pass over them safely.

☐ JOHN 6:60-71

The Words of Eternal Life. 6:60 Then many of his disciples who were listening said, "This saying is hard; who can accept it?" 61Since Jesus knew that his disciples were murmuring about this, he said to them, "Does this shock you? 62What if you were to see the Son of Man ascending to where he was before? 63It is the spirit that gives life, while the flesh is of no avail. The words I have spoken to you are spirit and life. 64But there are some of you who do not believe." Jesus knew from the beginning the ones who would not believe and the one who would betray him. 65And he said, "For this reason I have told you that no one can come to me unless it is granted him by my Father."

66As a result of this, many [of] his disciples returned to their former way of life and no longer accompanied him. 67Jesus then said to the Twelve, "Do you also want to leave?" 68Simon Peter answered him, "Master, to whom shall we go? You have the words of eternal life. 69We have come to believe and are convinced that you are the Holy One of God." 70Jesus answered them, "Did I not choose you twelve? Yet is not one of you a devil?" 71He was referring to Judas, son of Simon the Iscariot; it was he who would betray him, one of the Twelve.

July 28

If there is anyone who is not enlightened by the sublime magnificence of created things, he is blind. If there is anyone who, seeing all these works of God, does not praise Him, he is dumb. If there is anyone who, from so many signs, cannot perceive God, that man is foolish.

— St. Bonaventure

☐ PSALMS 142-145

A Prayer in Time of Trouble. **142:1** A *maskil* of David, when he was in the cave. A prayer.

2With my own voice I cry to the LORD;
    with my own voice I beseech the
      LORD.
3Before him I pour out my complaint,
    tell of my distress in front of him.
4When my spirit is faint within me,
    you know my path.
As I go along this path,
    they have hidden a trap for me.
5I look to my right hand to see
    that there is no one willing to
      acknowledge me.

My escape has perished;
    no one cares for me.
6I cry out to you, LORD,
    I say, You are my refuge,
    my portion in the land of the living.
7Listen to my cry for help,
    for I am brought very low.
Rescue me from my pursuers,
    for they are too strong for me.
8Lead my soul from prison,
    that I may give thanks to your name.
Then the righteous shall gather
      around me
    because you have been good to me.

A Prayer in Distress. **143:1** A psalm of David.

Lord, hear my prayer;
  in your faithfulness listen to my
    pleading;
  answer me in your righteousness.
²Do not enter into judgment with your
    servant;
  before you no one can be just.
³The enemy has pursued my soul;
  he has crushed my life to the ground.
He has made me dwell in darkness
  like those long dead.
⁴My spirit is faint within me;
  my heart despairs.
⁵I remember the days of old;
  I ponder all your deeds;
  the works of your hands I recall.
⁶I stretch out my hands toward you,
  my soul to you like a parched land.
                                        Selah
⁷Hasten to answer me, Lord;
  for my spirit fails me.
Do not hide your face from me,
  lest I become like those descending
    to the pit.
⁸In the morning let me hear of your
    mercy,
  for in you I trust.
Show me the path I should walk,
  for I entrust my life to you.
⁹Rescue me, Lord, from my foes,
  for I seek refuge in you.
¹⁰Teach me to do your will,
  for you are my God.
May your kind spirit guide me
  on ground that is level.
¹¹For your name's sake, Lord, give me
    life;
  in your righteousness lead my soul
    out of distress.
¹²In your mercy put an end to my foes;
  all those who are oppressing my soul,
  for I am your servant.

A Prayer for Victory and Prosperity.
144:1 Of David.

Blessed be the Lord, my rock,
  who trains my hands for battle,
  my fingers for war;
²My safeguard and my fortress,
  my stronghold, my deliverer,
My shield, in whom I take refuge,
  who subdues peoples under me.
³Lord, what is man that you take
    notice of him;
  the son of man, that you think of him?
⁴Man is but a breath,
  his days are like a passing shadow.
⁵Lord, incline your heavens and come
    down;
  touch the mountains and make
    them smoke.
⁶Flash forth lightning and scatter my
    foes;
  shoot your arrows and rout them.
⁷Reach out your hand from on high;
  deliver me from the many waters;
  rescue me from the hands of foreign
    foes.
⁸Their mouths speak untruth;
  their right hands are raised in lying
    oaths.
⁹O God, a new song I will sing to you;
  on a ten-stringed lyre I will play for
    you.
¹⁰You give victory to kings;
  you delivered David your servant.
From the menacing sword ¹¹deliver me;
  rescue me from the hands of foreign
    foes.
Their mouths speak untruth;
  their right hands are raised in lying
    oaths.
¹²May our sons be like plants
  well nurtured from their youth,
Our daughters, like carved columns,
  shapely as those of the temple.
¹³May our barns be full
  with every kind of store.

May our sheep increase by thousands,
by tens of thousands in our fields;
may our oxen be well fattened.
[14]May there be no breach in the walls,
no exile, no outcry in our streets.
[15]Blessed the people so fortunate;
blessed the people whose God is the
LORD.

The Greatness and Goodness of God.
145:1 Praise. Of David.

I will extol you, my God and king;
I will bless your name forever and
ever.
[2]Every day I will bless you;
I will praise your name forever and
ever.
[3]Great is the LORD and worthy of
much praise,
whose grandeur is beyond
understanding.
[4]One generation praises your deeds to
the next
and proclaims your mighty works.
[5]They speak of the splendor of your
majestic glory,
tell of your wonderful deeds.
[6]They speak of the power of your
awesome acts
and recount your great deeds.
[7]They celebrate your abounding
goodness
and joyfully sing of your justice.
[8]The LORD is gracious and merciful,
slow to anger and abounding in mercy.

[9]The LORD is good to all,
compassionate toward all your works.
[10]All your works give you thanks, LORD
and your faithful bless you.
[11]They speak of the glory of your reign
and tell of your mighty works,
[12]Making known to the sons of men
your mighty acts,
the majestic glory of your rule.
[13]Your reign is a reign for all ages,
your dominion for all generations.
The LORD is trustworthy in all his words,
and loving in all his works.
[14]The LORD supports all who are falling
and raises up all who are bowed down.
[15]The eyes of all look hopefully to you;
you give them their food in due
season.
[16]You open wide your hand
and satisfy the desire of every living
thing.
[17]The LORD is just in all his ways,
merciful in all his works.
[18]The LORD is near to all who call upon
him,
to all who call upon him in truth.
[19]He fulfills the desire of those who fear
him;
he hears their cry and saves them.
[20]The LORD watches over all who love
him,
but all the wicked he destroys.
[21]My mouth will speak the praises of
the LORD;
all flesh will bless his holy name
forever and ever.

☐ JOHN 7:1-13

The Feast of Tabernacles. 7:1 After this, Jesus moved about within Galilee; but he did not wish to travel in Judea, because the Jews were trying to kill him. [2]But the Jewish feast of Tabernacles was near. [3]So his brothers said to him, "Leave here and go to Judea, so that your disciples also may see the works you are doing. [4]No one works in secret if he wants to be known publicly. If you do these things, manifest yourself to the world." [5]For his brothers did not believe in him. [6]So Jesus said to them, "My time is not yet here, but the time is always right for you. [7]The world cannot hate you, but it hates me, because I testify to it that its works are evil. [8]You go up to the feast. I am not going up to this feast, because my time has not yet been fulfilled." [9]After he had said this, he stayed on in Galilee.

[10]But when his brothers had gone up to the feast, he himself also went up, not openly but [as it were] in secret. [11]The Jews were looking for him at the feast and saying, "Where is he?" [12]And there was considerable murmuring about him in the crowds. Some said, "He is a good man," [while] others said, "No; on the contrary, he misleads the crowd." [13]Still, no one spoke openly about him because they were afraid of the Jews.

July 29

St. Martha

You must lovingly leave some work to others and not seek to have all the crowns.

— St. Francis de Sales

☐ PSALMS 146-150

Trust in God the Creator and Redeemer.
146:1 Hallelujah!
[2]Praise the LORD, my soul;
  I will praise the LORD all my life,
  sing praise to my God while I live.
[3]Put no trust in princes,
  in children of Adam powerless to
    save.
[4]Who breathing his last, returns to
    the earth;
  that day all his planning comes to
    nothing.
[5]Blessed the one whose help is the God
    of Jacob,
  whose hope is in the LORD, his God,
[6]The maker of heaven and earth,
  the seas and all that is in them,
Who keeps faith forever,
  [7]secures justice for the oppressed,
  who gives bread to the hungry.
The LORD sets prisoners free;
  [8]the LORD gives sight to the blind.
The LORD raises up those who are
    bowed down;
  the LORD loves the righteous.
[9]The LORD protects the resident alien,

comes to the aid of the orphan and
    the widow,
  but thwarts the way of the wicked.
[10]The LORD shall reign forever,
  your God, Zion, through all
    generations!
Hallelujah!

God's Word Restores Jerusalem. **147:1**
Hallelujah!

How good to sing praise to our God;
  how pleasant to give fitting praise.
[2]The LORD rebuilds Jerusalem,
  and gathers the dispersed of Israel,
[3]Healing the brokenhearted,
  and binding up their wounds.
[4]He numbers the stars,
  and gives to all of them their names.
[5]Great is our Lord, vast in power,
  with wisdom beyond measure.
[6]The LORD gives aid to the poor,
  but casts the wicked to the ground.

[7]Sing to the LORD with thanksgiving;
  with the lyre make music to our God,
[8]Who covers the heavens with clouds,

provides rain for the earth,
  makes grass sprout on the
    mountains,
⁹Who gives animals their food
  and young ravens what they cry for.
¹⁰He takes no delight in the strength of
    horses,
  no pleasure in the runner's stride.
¹¹Rather the LORD takes pleasure in
    those who fear him,
  those who put their hope in his
    mercy.

¹²Glorify the LORD, Jerusalem;
  Zion, offer praise to your God,
¹³For he has strengthened the bars of
    your gates,
  blessed your children within you.
¹⁴He brings peace to your borders,
  and satisfies you with finest wheat.
¹⁵He sends his command to earth;
  his word runs swiftly!
¹⁶Thus he makes the snow like wool,
  and spreads the frost like ash;
¹⁷He disperses hail like crumbs.
  Who can withstand his cold?
¹⁸Yet when again he issues his
    command, it melts them;
  he raises his winds and the waters
    flow.
¹⁹He proclaims his word to Jacob,
  his statutes and laws to Israel.
²⁰He has not done this for any other
    nation;
  of such laws they know nothing.
Hallelujah!

All Creation Summoned to Praise. 148:1
Hallelujah!

Praise the LORD from the heavens;
  praise him in the heights.
²Praise him, all you his angels;
  give praise, all you his hosts.
³Praise him, sun and moon;
  praise him, all shining stars.
⁴Praise him, highest heavens,
  you waters above the heavens.

⁵Let them all praise the LORD's name;
  for he commanded and they were
    created,
⁶Assigned them their station forever,
  set an order that will never change.

⁷Praise the LORD from the earth,
  you sea monsters and all the deeps
    of the sea;
⁸Lightning and hail, snow and thick
    clouds,
  storm wind that fulfills his
    command;
⁹Mountains and all hills,
  fruit trees and all cedars;
¹⁰Animals wild and tame,
  creatures that crawl and birds that fly;
¹¹Kings of the earth and all peoples,
  princes and all who govern on earth;
¹²Young men and women too,
  old and young alike.
¹³Let them all praise the LORD's name,
  for his name alone is exalted,
  His majesty above earth and heaven.
¹⁴He has lifted high the horn of his
    people;
  to the praise of all his faithful,
  the Israelites, the people near to him.
Hallelujah!

Praise God with Song and Sword. 149:1
Hallelujah!

Sing to the LORD a new song,
  his praise in the assembly of the
    faithful.
²Let Israel be glad in its maker,
  the people of Zion rejoice in their
    king.
³Let them praise his name in dance,
  make music with tambourine and
    lyre.
⁴For the LORD takes delight in his people,
  honors the poor with victory.
⁵Let the faithful rejoice in their glory,
  cry out for joy on their couches,
⁶With the praise of God in their
    mouths,

and a two-edged sword in their
hands,
⁷To bring retribution on the nations,
punishment on the peoples,
⁸To bind their kings in shackles,
their nobles in chains of iron,
⁹To execute the judgments decreed for
them—
such is the glory of all God's faithful.
Hallelujah!

Final Doxology. **150:1** Hallelujah!

Praise God in his holy sanctuary;

give praise in the mighty dome of
heaven.
²Give praise for his mighty deeds,
praise him for his great majesty.
³Give praise with blasts upon the horn,
praise him with harp and lyre.
⁴Give praise with tambourines and
dance,
praise him with strings and pipes.
⁵Give praise with crashing cymbals,
praise him with sounding cymbals.
⁶Let everything that has breath
give praise to the LORD!
Hallelujah!

☐ JOHN 7:14-36

The First Dialogue. 7:14 When the feast was already half over, Jesus went up into the temple area and began to teach. ¹⁵The Jews were amazed and said, "How does he know scripture without having studied?" ¹⁶Jesus answered them and said, "My teaching is not my own but is from the one who sent me. ¹⁷Whoever chooses to do his will shall know whether my teaching is from God or whether I speak on my own. ¹⁸Whoever speaks on his own seeks his own glory, but whoever seeks the glory of the one who sent him is truthful, and there is no wrong in him. ¹⁹Did not Moses give you the law? Yet none of you keeps the law. Why are you trying to kill me?" ²⁰The crowd answered, "You are possessed! Who is trying to kill you?" ²¹Jesus answered and said to them, "I performed one work and all of you are amazed ²²because of it. Moses gave you circumcision—not that it came from Moses but rather from the patriarchs—and you circumcise a man on the sabbath. ²³If a man can receive circumcision on a sabbath so that the law of Moses may not be broken, are you angry with me because I made a whole person well on a sabbath? ²⁴Stop judging by appearances, but judge justly."

²⁵So some of the inhabitants of Jerusalem said, "Is he not the one they are trying to kill? ²⁶And look, he is speaking openly and they say nothing to him. Could the authorities have realized that he is the Messiah? ²⁷But we know where he is from. When the Messiah comes, no one will know where he is from." ²⁸So Jesus cried out in the temple area as he was teaching and said, "You know me and also know where I am from. Yet I did not come on my own, but the one who sent me, whom you do not know, is true. ²⁹I know him, because I am from him, and he sent me." ³⁰So they tried to arrest him, but no one laid a hand upon him, because his hour had not yet come. ³¹But many of the crowd began to believe in him, and said, "When the Messiah comes, will he perform more signs than this man has done?"

Officers Sent to Arrest Jesus. ³²The Pharisees heard the crowd murmuring about him to this effect, and the chief priests and the Pharisees sent guards to arrest him. ³³So Jesus said, "I will be with you only a little while longer, and then I will go to the one who sent me. ³⁴You will look for me but not find [me], and where I am you cannot come." ³⁵So the Jews said to one another, "Where is he going that we will not find him? Surely he is not going to the dispersion among the Greeks to teach the Greeks, is he? [36]What is the meaning of his saying, 'You will look for me and not find [me], and where I am you cannot come'?"

July 30

St. Peter Chrysologus

If you want to party with the devil, you can't celebrate with Christ.

— St. Peter Chrysologus

☐ PROVERBS 1-4

Purpose of the Proverbs of Solomon.
1:1 The proverbs of Solomon, the
son of David,
king of Israel:
[2]That people may know wisdom and
discipline,
may understand intelligent sayings;
[3]May receive instruction in wise conduct,
in what is right, just and fair;
[4]That resourcefulness may be imparted
to the naive,
knowledge and discretion to the
young.
[5]The wise by hearing them will advance
in learning,
the intelligent will gain sound
guidance,
[6]To comprehend proverb and byword,
the words of the wise and their
riddles.
[7]Fear of the Lord is the beginning of
knowledge;
fools despise wisdom and discipline.

**The Path of the Wicked: Greed and
Violence.** [8]Hear, my son, your
father's instruction,
and reject not your mother's teaching;
[9]A graceful diadem will they be for
your head;
a pendant for your neck.

[10]My son, should sinners entice you,
[11]do not go if they say, "Come along
with us!
Let us lie in wait for blood,
unprovoked, let us trap the innocent;
[12]Let us swallow them alive, like Sheol,
whole, like those who go down to
the pit!
[13]All kinds of precious wealth shall we
gain,
we shall fill our houses with booty;
[14]Cast in your lot with us,
we shall all have one purse!"
[15]My son, do not walk in the way with
them,
hold back your foot from their path!
[16][For their feet run to evil,
they hasten to shed blood.]
[17]In vain a net is spread
right under the eyes of any bird—
[18]They lie in wait for their own blood,
they set a trap for their own lives.
[19]This is the way of everyone greedy for
loot:
it takes away their lives.

Wisdom in Person Gives a Warning.
[20]Wisdom cries aloud in the
street,
in the open squares she raises her
voice;

²¹Down the crowded ways she calls out,
  at the city gates she utters her words:
²²"How long, you naive ones, will you
  love naivete,
  ²³How long will you turn away at
  my reproof?
[The arrogant delight in their arrogance,
  and fools hate knowledge.]
  Lo! I will pour out to you my spirit,
  I will acquaint you with my words:
²⁴'Because I called and you refused,
  extended my hand and no one took
  notice;
²⁵Because you disdained all my counsel,
  and my reproof you ignored—
²⁶I, in my turn, will laugh at your doom;
  will mock when terror overtakes you;
²⁷When terror comes upon you like a
  storm,
  and your doom approaches like a
  whirlwind;
  when distress and anguish befall you.'
²⁸Then they will call me, but I will not
  answer;
  they will seek me, but will not find
  me,
²⁹Because they hated knowledge,
  and the fear of the LORD they did
  not choose.
³⁰They ignored my counsel,
  they spurned all my reproof;
³¹Well, then, they shall eat the fruit of
  their own way,
  and with their own devices be glutted.
³²For the straying of the naive kills them,
  the smugness of fools destroys them.
³³But whoever obeys me dwells in
  security,
  in peace, without fear of harm."

The Blessings of Wisdom. 2:1 My
  son, if you receive my words
  and treasure my commands,
²Turning your ear to wisdom,
  inclining your heart to
  understanding;
³Yes, if you call for intelligence,
  and to understanding raise your
  voice;
⁴If you seek her like silver,
  and like hidden treasures search her
  out,
⁵Then will you understand the fear of
  the LORD;
  the knowledge of God you will find;
⁶For the LORD gives wisdom,
  from his mouth come knowledge
  and understanding;
⁷He has success in store for the upright,
  is the shield of those who walk
  honestly,
⁸Guarding the paths of justice,
  protecting the way of his faithful
  ones,
⁹Then you will understand what is
  right and just,
  what is fair, every good path;
¹⁰For wisdom will enter your heart,
  knowledge will be at home in your
  soul,
¹¹Discretion will watch over you,
  understanding will guard you;
¹²Saving you from the way of the
  wicked,
  from those whose speech is perverse.
¹³From those who have left the straight
  paths
  to walk in the ways of darkness,
¹⁴Who delight in doing evil
  and celebrate perversity;
¹⁵Whose ways are crooked,
  whose paths are devious;
¹⁶Saving you from a stranger,
  from a foreign woman with her
  smooth words,
¹⁷One who forsakes the companion of
  her youth
  and forgets the covenant of her God;
¹⁸For her path sinks down to death,
  and her footsteps lead to the shades.
¹⁹None who enter there come back,
  or gain the paths of life.
²⁰Thus you may walk in the way of the
  good,

and keep to the paths of the just.
²¹For the upright will dwell in the land,
　people of integrity will remain in it;
²²But the wicked will be cut off from
　the land,
　the faithless will be rooted out of it.

Confidence in God Leads to Prosperity.

3:1 My son, do not
　forget my teaching,
　take to heart my commands;
²For many days, and years of life,
　and peace, will they bring you.
³Do not let love and fidelity forsake you;
　bind them around your neck;
　write them on the tablet of your
　heart.
⁴Then will you win favor and esteem
　before God and human beings.
⁵Trust in the LORD with all your heart,
　on your own intelligence do not rely;
⁶In all your ways be mindful of him,
　and he will make straight your paths.
⁷Do not be wise in your own eyes,
　fear the LORD and turn away from
　evil;
⁸This will mean health for your flesh
　and vigor for your bones.
⁹Honor the LORD with your wealth,
　with first fruits of all your produce;
¹⁰Then will your barns be filled with
　plenty,
　with new wine your vats will overflow.
¹¹The discipline of the LORD, my son,
　do not spurn;
　do not disdain his reproof;
¹²For whom the LORD loves he reproves,
　as a father, the son he favors.

The Benefits of Finding Wisdom.

¹³Happy the one who finds
　wisdom,
　the one who gains understanding!
¹⁴Her profit is better than profit in
　silver,
　and better than gold is her revenue;
¹⁵She is more precious than corals,

　and no treasure of yours can
　compare with her.
¹⁶Long life is in her right hand,
　in her left are riches and honor;
¹⁷Her ways are pleasant ways,
　and all her paths are peace;
¹⁸She is a tree of life to those who grasp
　her,
　and those who hold her fast are
　happy.
¹⁹The LORD by wisdom founded the
　earth,
　established the heavens by
　understanding;
²⁰By his knowledge the depths are split,
　and the clouds drop down dew.

Justice Toward One's Neighbor Brings Blessing.

²¹My son, do
　not let these slip from your sight:
　hold to deliberation and planning;
²²So will they be life to your soul,
　and an adornment for your neck.
²³Then you may go your way securely;
　your foot will never stumble;
²⁴When you lie down, you will not be
　afraid,
　when you rest, your sleep will be
　sweet.
²⁵Do not be afraid of sudden terror,
　of the ruin of the wicked when it
　comes;
²⁶For the LORD will be your confidence,
　and will keep your foot from the
　snare.
²⁷Do not withhold any goods from the
　owner
　when it is in your power to act.
²⁸Say not to your neighbor, "Go, come
　back tomorrow,
　and I will give it to you," when all
　the while you have it.
²⁹Do not plot evil against your
　neighbors,
　when they live at peace with you.
³⁰Do not contend with someone
　without cause,

with one who has done you no harm.
³¹Do not envy the violent
and choose none of their ways:
³²To the Lord the devious are an
abomination,
but the upright are close to him.
³³The curse of the Lord is on the house
of the wicked,
but the dwelling of the just he
blesses;
³⁴Those who scoff, he scoffs at,
but the lowly he favors.
³⁵The wise will possess glory,
but fools will bear shame.

The Teacher as Model Disciple. 4:1
Hear, O children, a father's
instruction,
be attentive, that you may gain
understanding!
²Yes, excellent advice I give you;
my teaching do not forsake.
³When I was my father's child,
tender, the darling of my mother,
⁴He taught me and said to me:
"Let your heart hold fast my words:
keep my commands, and live!
⁵Get wisdom, get understanding!
Do not forget or turn aside from the
words of my mouth.
⁶Do not forsake her, and she will
preserve you;
love her, and she will safeguard you;
⁷The beginning of wisdom is: get
wisdom;
whatever else you get, get
understanding.
⁸Extol her, and she will exalt you;
she will bring you honors if you
embrace her;
⁹She will put on your head a graceful
diadem;
a glorious crown will she bestow on
you."

The Two Ways. ¹⁰Hear, my son, and
receive my words,

and the years of your life shall be
many.
¹¹On the way of wisdom I direct you,
I lead you on straight paths.
¹²When you walk, your step will not be
impeded,
and should you run, you will not
stumble.
¹³Hold fast to instruction, never let it go;
keep it, for it is your life.
¹⁴The path of the wicked do not enter,
nor walk in the way of the evil;
¹⁵Shun it, do not cross it,
turn aside from it, pass on.
¹⁶For they cannot rest unless they have
done evil;
if they do not trip anyone they lose
sleep.
¹⁷For they eat the bread of wickedness
and drink the wine of violence.
¹⁸But the path of the just is like shining
light,
that grows in brilliance till perfect day.
¹⁹The way of the wicked is like darkness;
they do not know on what they
stumble.

**With Your Whole Being Heed My
Words and Live.** ²⁰My son, to
my words be attentive,
to my sayings incline your ear;
²¹Let them not slip from your sight,
keep them within your heart;
²²For they are life to those who find
them,
bringing health to one's whole
being.
²³With all vigilance guard your heart,
for in it are the sources of life.
²⁴Dishonest mouth put away from you,
deceitful lips put far from you.
²⁵Let your eyes look straight ahead
and your gaze be focused forward.
²⁶Survey the path for your feet,
and all your ways will be sure.
²⁷Turn neither to right nor to left,
keep your foot far from evil.

☐ JOHN 7:37-52

Rivers of Living Water. 7:37 On the last and greatest day of the feast, Jesus stood up and exclaimed, "Let anyone who thirsts come to me and drink. [38]Whoever believes in me, as scripture says:

'Rivers of living water will flow from
within him.'"

[39]He said this in reference to the Spirit that those who came to believe in him were to receive. There was, of course, no Spirit yet, because Jesus had not yet been glorified.

Discussion about the Origins of the Messiah. [40]Some in the crowd who heard these words said, "This is truly the Prophet." [41]Others said, "This is the Messiah." But others said, "The Messiah will not come from Galilee, will he? [42]Does not scripture say that the Messiah will be of David's family and come from Bethlehem, the village where David lived?" [43]So a division occurred in the crowd because of him. [44]Some of them even wanted to arrest him, but no one laid hands on him.

[45]So the guards went to the chief priests and Pharisees, who asked them, "Why did you not bring him?" [46]The guards answered, "Never before has anyone spoken like this one."

[47]So the Pharisees answered them, "Have you also been deceived? [48]Have any of the authorities or the Pharisees believed in him? [49]But this crowd, which does not know the law, is accursed." [50]Nicodemus, one of their members who had come to him earlier, said to them, [51]"Does our law condemn a person before it first hears him and finds out what he is doing?" [52]They answered and said to him, "You are not from Galilee also, are you? Look and see that no prophet arises from Galilee."

July 31

St. Ignatius of Loyola

In times of deep discouragement you should never make a change, but stand firm in the resolutions and decisions that guided you the day before the discouragement.

— ST. IGNATIUS OF LOYOLA

☐ PROVERBS 5-8

Warning Against Adultery. 5:1 My
    son, to my wisdom be attentive,
    to understanding incline your ear,
[2]That you may act discreetly,
    and your lips guard what you know.
[3]Indeed, the lips of the stranger drip
    honey,
    and her mouth is smoother than oil;
[4]But in the end she is as bitter as
    wormwood,
    as sharp as a two-edged sword.

[5]Her feet go down to death,
    her steps reach Sheol;
[6]Her paths ramble, you know not where,
    lest you see before you the road to life.
[7]So now, children, listen to me,
    do not stray from the words of my
        mouth.
[8]Keep your way far from her,
    do not go near the door of her house,
[9]Lest you give your honor to others,
    and your years to a merciless one;

¹⁰Lest outsiders take their fill of your
wealth,
and your hard-won earnings go to
another's house;
¹¹And you groan in the end,
when your flesh and your body are
consumed;
¹²And you say, "Oh, why did I hate
instruction,
and my heart spurn reproof!
¹³Why did I not listen to the voice of
my teachers,
incline my ear to my instructors!
¹⁴I am all but ruined,
in the midst of the public assembly!"
¹⁵Drink water from your own cistern,
running water from your own well.
¹⁶Should your water sources be
dispersed abroad,
streams of water in the streets?
¹⁷Let them be yours alone,
not shared with outsiders;
¹⁸Let your fountain be blessed and have
joy of the wife of your youth,
¹⁹your lovely hind, your graceful doe.
Of whose love you will ever have your
fill,
and by her ardor always be
intoxicated.
²⁰Why then, my son, should you be
intoxicated with a stranger,
and embrace another woman?
²¹Indeed, the ways of each person are
plain to the LORD's sight;
all their paths he surveys;
²²By their own iniquities the wicked
will be caught,
in the meshes of their own sin they
will be held fast;
²³They will die from lack of discipline,
lost because of their great folly.

Miscellaneous Proverbs

Against Going Surety for One's Neighbor.
6:1 My son, if you
have become surety to your
neighbor,

given your hand in pledge to another,
²You have been snared by the utterance
of your lips,
caught by the words of your mouth;
³So do this, my son, to free yourself,
since you have fallen into your
neighbor's power:
Go, hurry, rouse your neighbor!
⁴Give no sleep to your eyes,
nor slumber to your eyelids;
⁵Free yourself like a gazelle from the
hunter,
or like a bird from the hand of the
fowler.

The Ant and the Sluggard at Harvest.
⁶Go to the ant, O sluggard,
study her ways and learn wisdom;
⁷For though she has no chief,
no commander or ruler,
⁸She procures her food in the summer,
stores up her provisions in the
harvest.
⁹How long, O sluggard, will you lie
there?
when will you rise from your sleep?
¹⁰A little sleep, a little slumber,
a little folding of the arms to rest—
¹¹Then poverty will come upon you
like a robber,
and want like a brigand.

The Scoundrel.
¹²Scoundrels, villains,
are they
who deal in crooked talk.
¹³Shifty of eye,
feet ever moving,
pointing with fingers,
¹⁴They have perversity in their hearts,
always plotting evil,
sowing discord.
¹⁵Therefore their doom comes suddenly;
in an instant they are crushed
beyond cure.

What the Lord Rejects.
¹⁶There are six
things the LORD hates,
yes, seven are an abomination to him;

[17]Haughty eyes, a lying tongue,
hands that shed innocent blood,
[18]A heart that plots wicked schemes,
feet that are quick to run to evil,
[19]The false witness who utters lies,
and the one who sows discord
among kindred.

Warning Against Adultery. [20]Observe,
my son, your father's command,
and do not reject your mother's
teaching;
[21]Keep them fastened over your heart
always,
tie them around your neck.
[22]When you lie down they will watch
over you,
when you wake, they will share your
concerns;
wherever you turn, they will guide
you.
[23]For the command is a lamp, and the
teaching a light,
and a way to life are the reproofs
that discipline,
[24]Keeping you from another's wife,
from the smooth tongue of the
foreign woman.
[25]Do not lust in your heart after her
beauty,
do not let her captivate you with her
glance!
[26]For the price of a harlot
may be scarcely a loaf of bread,
But a married woman
is a trap for your precious life.
[27]Can a man take embers into his bosom,
and his garments not be burned?
[28]Or can a man walk on live coals,
and his feet not be scorched?
[29]So with him who sleeps with
another's wife—
none who touches her shall go
unpunished.
[30]Thieves are not despised
if out of hunger they steal to satisfy
their appetite.

[31]Yet if caught they must pay back
sevenfold,
yield up all the wealth of their house.
[32]But those who commit adultery have
no sense;
those who do it destroy themselves.
[33]They will be beaten and disgraced,
and their shame will not be wiped
away;
[34]For passion enrages the husband,
he will have no pity on the day of
vengeance;
[35]He will not consider any restitution,
nor be satisfied by your many bribes.

The Seduction. 7:1 My son, keep my
words,
and treasure my commands.
[2]Keep my commands and live,
and my teaching as the apple of
your eye;
[3]Bind them on your fingers,
write them on the tablet of your
heart.
[4]Say to Wisdom, "You are my sister!"
Call Understanding, "Friend!"
[5]That they may keep you from a
stranger,
from the foreign woman with her
smooth words.
[6]For at the window of my house,
through my lattice I looked out
[7]And I saw among the naive,
I observed among the young men,
a youth with no sense,
[8]Crossing the street near the corner,
then walking toward her house,
[9]In the twilight, at dusk of day,
in the very dark of night.
[10]Then the woman comes to meet him,
dressed like a harlot, with secret
designs.
[11]She is raucous and unruly,
her feet cannot stay at home;
[12]Now she is in the streets, now in the
open squares,
lurking in ambush at every corner.

¹³Then she grabs him, kisses him,
and with an impudent look says to
him:
¹⁴"I owed peace offerings,
and today I have fulfilled my vows;
¹⁵So I came out to meet you,
to look for you, and I have found
you!
¹⁶With coverlets I have spread my couch,
with brocaded cloths of Egyptian
linen;
¹⁷I have sprinkled my bed with myrrh,
with aloes, and with cinnamon.
¹⁸Come, let us drink our fill of love,
until morning, let us feast on love!
¹⁹For my husband is not at home,
he has gone on a long journey;
²⁰A bag of money he took with him,
he will not return home till the full
moon."
²¹She wins him over by repeated urging,
with her smooth lips she leads him
astray.
²²He follows her impulsively,
like an ox that goes to slaughter;
Like a stag that bounds toward the net,
²³till an arrow pierces its liver;
Like a bird that rushes into a snare,
unaware that his life is at stake.
²⁴So now, children, listen to me,
be attentive to the words of my
mouth!
²⁵Do not let your heart turn to her ways,
do not go astray in her paths;
²⁶For many are those she has struck
down dead,
numerous, those she has slain.
²⁷Her house is a highway to Sheol,
leading down into the chambers of
death.

The Discourse of Wisdom. 8:1 Does
not Wisdom call,
and Understanding raise her voice?
²On the top of the heights along the
road,
at the crossroads she takes her stand;

³By the gates at the approaches of the
city,
in the entryways she cries aloud:
⁴"To you, O people, I call;
my appeal is to you mortals.
⁵You naive ones, gain prudence,
you fools, gain sense.
⁶Listen! for noble things I speak;
my lips proclaim honest words.
⁷Indeed, my mouth utters truth,
and my lips abhor wickedness.
⁸All the words of my mouth are
sincere,
none of them wily or crooked;
⁹All of them are straightforward to the
intelligent,
and right to those who attain
knowledge.
¹⁰Take my instruction instead of silver,
and knowledge rather than choice
gold.
¹¹[For Wisdom is better than corals,
and no treasures can compare with
her.]
¹²I, Wisdom, dwell with prudence,
and useful knowledge I have.
¹³[The fear of the Lord is hatred of
evil;]
Pride, arrogance, the evil way,
and the perverse mouth I hate.
¹⁴Mine are counsel and advice;
Mine is strength; I am
understanding.
¹⁵By me kings reign,
and rulers enact justice;
¹⁶By me princes govern,
and nobles, all the judges of the earth.
¹⁷Those who love me I also love,
and those who seek me find me.
¹⁸With me are riches and honor,
wealth that endures, and
righteousness.
¹⁹My fruit is better than gold, even
pure gold,
and my yield than choice silver.
²⁰On the way of righteousness I walk,
along the paths of justice,

²¹Granting wealth to those who love me,
and filling their treasuries.

²²"The LORD begot me, the beginning
of his works,
the forerunner of his deeds of long
ago;
²³From of old I was formed,
at the first, before the earth.
²⁴When there were no deeps I was
brought forth,
when there were no fountains or
springs of water;
²⁵Before the mountains were settled
into place,
before the hills, I was brought forth;
²⁶When the earth and the fields were
not yet made,
nor the first clods of the world.
²⁷When he established the heavens,
there was I,
when he marked out the vault over
the face of the deep;
²⁸When he made firm the skies above,
when he fixed fast the springs of the
deep;
²⁹When he set for the sea its limit,
so that the waters should not
transgress his command;
When he fixed the foundations of earth,
³⁰then was I beside him as artisan;
I was his delight day by day,
playing before him all the while,
³¹Playing over the whole of his earth,
having my delight with human
beings.
³²Now, children, listen to me;
happy are they who keep my ways.
³³Listen to instruction and grow wise,
do not reject it!
³⁴Happy the one who listens to me,
attending daily at my gates,
keeping watch at my doorposts;
³⁵For whoever finds me finds life,
and wins favor from the LORD;
³⁶But those who pass me by do violence
to themselves;
all who hate me love death."

□ JOHN 7:53–8:11

A Woman Caught in Adultery. 7:53 [Then each went to his own house, **8:1**while Jesus went to the Mount of Olives. ²But early in the morning he arrived again in the temple area, and all the people started coming to him, and he sat down and taught them. ³Then the scribes and the Pharisees brought a woman who had been caught in adultery and made her stand in the middle. ⁴They said to him, "Teacher, this woman was caught in the very act of committing adultery. ⁵Now in the law, Moses commanded us to stone such women. So what do you say?" ⁶They said this to test him, so that they could have some charge to bring against him. Jesus bent down and began to write on the ground with his finger. ⁷But when they continued asking him, he straightened up and said to them, "Let the one among you who is without sin be the first to throw a stone at her." ⁸Again he bent down and wrote on the ground. ⁹And in response, they went away one by one, beginning with the elders. So he was left alone with the woman before him. ¹⁰Then Jesus straightened up and said to her, "Woman, where are they? Has no one condemned you?" ¹¹She replied, "No one, sir." Then Jesus said, "Neither do I condemn you. Go, [and] from now on do not sin any more."]

August 1

St. Alphonsus Liguori

It is almost certain that excess in eating is the cause of almost all the diseases of the body, but its effects on the soul are even more disastrous.

— St. Alphonsus Liguori

☐ PROVERBS 9-12

The Two Women Invite Passersby to Their Banquets

Woman Wisdom Issues Her Invitation. 9:1 Wisdom has built her house,
she has set up her seven columns;
²She has prepared her meat, mixed her wine,
yes, she has spread her table.
³She has sent out her maidservants;
she calls
from the heights out over the city:
⁴"Let whoever is naive turn in here;
to any who lack sense I say,
⁵Come, eat of my food,
and drink of the wine I have mixed!
⁶Forsake foolishness that you may live;
advance in the way of understanding."

Miscellaneous Aphorisms. ⁷Whoever corrects the arrogant earns insults;
and whoever reproves the wicked incurs opprobrium.
⁸Do not reprove the arrogant, lest they hate you;
reprove the wise, and they will love you.
⁹Instruct the wise, and they become still wiser;
teach the just, and they advance in learning.
¹⁰The beginning of wisdom is fear of the Lord,
and knowledge of the Holy One is understanding.

¹¹For by me your days will be multiplied
and the years of your life increased.
¹²If you are wise, wisdom is to your advantage;
if you are arrogant, you alone shall bear it.

Woman Folly Issues Her Invitation.
¹³Woman Folly is raucous,
utterly foolish; she knows nothing.
¹⁴She sits at the door of her house
upon a seat on the city heights,
¹⁵Calling to passersby
as they go on their way straight ahead:
¹⁶"Let those who are naive turn in here,
to those who lack sense I say,
¹⁷Stolen water is sweet,
and bread taken secretly is pleasing!"
¹⁸Little do they know that the shades are there,
that her guests are in the depths of Sheol!

10:1 The Proverbs of Solomon:
A wise son gives his father joy,
but a foolish son is a grief to his mother.
²Ill-gotten treasures profit nothing,
but justice saves from death.
³The Lord does not let the just go hungry,
but the craving of the wicked he thwarts.
⁴The slack hand impoverishes,
but the busy hand brings riches.
⁵A son who gathers in summer is a credit;

a son who slumbers during harvest,
a disgrace.
⁶Blessings are for the head of the just;
but the mouth of the wicked
conceals violence.
⁷The memory of the just serves as
blessing,
but the name of the wicked will rot.
⁸A wise heart accepts commands,
but a babbling fool will be
overthrown.
⁹Whoever walks honestly walks
securely,
but one whose ways are crooked will
fare badly.
¹⁰One who winks at a fault causes
trouble,
but one who frankly reproves
promotes peace.
¹¹The mouth of the just is a fountain
of life,
but the mouth of the wicked
conceals violence.
¹²Hatred stirs up disputes,
but love covers all offenses.
¹³On the lips of the intelligent is found
wisdom,
but a rod for the back of one
without sense.
¹⁴The wise store up knowledge,
but the mouth of a fool is imminent
ruin.
¹⁵The wealth of the rich is their strong
city;
the ruin of the poor is their poverty.
¹⁶The labor of the just leads to life,
the gains of the wicked, to futility.
¹⁷Whoever follows instruction is in the
path to life,
but whoever disregards reproof goes
astray.
¹⁸Whoever conceals hatred has lying
lips,
and whoever spreads slander is a
fool.
¹⁹Where words are many, sin is not
wanting;

but those who restrain their lips do
well.
²⁰Choice silver is the tongue of the just;
the heart of the wicked is of little
worth.
²¹The lips of the just nourish many,
but fools die for want of sense.
²²It is the LORD's blessing that brings
wealth,
and no effort can substitute for it.
²³Crime is the entertainment of the
fool;
but wisdom is for the person of
understanding.
²⁴What the wicked fear will befall them,
but the desire of the just will be
granted.
²⁵When the tempest passes, the wicked
are no more;
but the just are established forever.
²⁶As vinegar to the teeth, and smoke to
the eyes,
are sluggards to those who send them.
²⁷Fear of the LORD prolongs life,
but the years of the wicked are cut
short.
²⁸The hope of the just brings joy,
but the expectation of the wicked
perishes.
²⁹The LORD is a stronghold to those
who walk honestly,
downfall for evildoers.
³⁰The just will never be disturbed,
but the wicked will not abide in the
land.
³¹The mouth of the just yields wisdom,
but the perverse tongue will be cut off.
³²The lips of the just know favor,
but the mouth of the wicked,
perversion.

11:1 False scales are an abomination to
the LORD,
but an honest weight, his delight.
²When pride comes, disgrace comes;
but with the humble is wisdom.
³The honesty of the upright guides them;

the faithless are ruined by their
duplicity.
⁴Wealth is useless on a day of wrath,
but justice saves from death.
⁵The justice of the honest makes their
way straight,
but by their wickedness the wicked
fall.
⁶The justice of the upright saves them,
but the faithless are caught in their
own intrigue.
⁷When a person dies, hope is
destroyed;
expectation pinned on wealth is
destroyed.
⁸The just are rescued from a tight spot,
but the wicked fall into it instead.
⁹By a word the impious ruin their
neighbors,
but through their knowledge the
just are rescued.
¹⁰When the just prosper, the city
rejoices;
when the wicked perish, there is
jubilation.
¹¹Through the blessing of the upright
the city is exalted,
but through the mouth of the
wicked it is overthrown.
¹²Whoever reviles a neighbor lacks
sense,
but the intelligent keep silent.
¹³One who slanders reveals secrets,
but a trustworthy person keeps a
confidence.
¹⁴For lack of guidance a people falls;
security lies in many counselors.
¹⁵Harm will come to anyone going
surety for another,
but whoever hates giving pledges is
secure.
¹⁶A gracious woman gains esteem,
and ruthless men gain wealth.
¹⁷Kindly people benefit themselves,
but the merciless harm themselves.
¹⁸The wicked make empty profits,

but those who sow justice have a
sure reward.
¹⁹Justice leads toward life,
but pursuit of evil, toward death.
²⁰The crooked in heart are an
abomination to the LORD,
but those who walk blamelessly are
his delight.
²¹Be assured, the wicked shall not go
unpunished,
but the offspring of the just shall
escape.
²²Like a golden ring in a swine's snout
is a beautiful woman without
judgment.
²³The desire of the just ends only in
good;
the expectation of the wicked is
wrath.
²⁴One person is lavish yet grows still
richer;
another is too sparing, yet is the
poorer.
²⁵Whoever confers benefits will be
amply enriched,
and whoever refreshes others will be
refreshed.
²⁶Whoever hoards grain, the people
curse,
but blessings are on the head of one
who distributes it!
²⁷Those who seek the good seek favor,
but those who pursue evil will have
evil come upon them.
²⁸Those who trust in their riches will
fall,
but like green leaves the just will
flourish.
²⁹Those who trouble their household
inherit the wind,
and fools become slaves to the wise
of heart.
³⁰The fruit of justice is a tree of life,
and one who takes lives is a sage.
³¹If the just are recompensed on the
earth,

how much more the wicked and the sinner!

12:1 Whoever loves discipline loves knowledge,
but whoever hates reproof is stupid.
[2]A good person wins favor from the Lord,
but the schemer he condemns.
[3]No one is made secure by wickedness,
but the root of the just will never be disturbed.
[4]A woman of worth is the crown of her husband,
but a disgraceful one is like rot in his bones.
[5]The plans of the just are right;
the designs of the wicked are deceit.
[6]The words of the wicked are a deadly ambush,
but the speech of the upright saves them.
[7]Overthrow the wicked and they are no more,
but the house of the just stands firm.
[8]For their good sense people are praised,
but the perverse of heart are despised.
[9]Better to be slighted and have a servant
than put on airs and lack bread.
[10]The just take care of their livestock,
but the compassion of the wicked is cruel.
[11]Those who till their own land have food in plenty,
but those who engage in idle pursuits lack sense.
[12]A wicked person desires the catch of evil people,
but the root of the righteous will bear fruit.
[13]By the sin of their lips the wicked are ensnared,
but the just escape from a tight spot.
[14]From the fruit of their mouths people have their fill of good,
and the works of their hands come back upon them.
[15]The way of fools is right in their own eyes,
but those who listen to advice are the wise.
[16]Fools immediately show their anger,
but the shrewd conceal contempt.
[17]Whoever speaks honestly testifies truly,
but the deceitful make lying witnesses.
[18]The babble of some people is like sword thrusts,
but the tongue of the wise is healing.
[19]Truthful lips endure forever,
the lying tongue, for only a moment.
[20]Deceit is in the heart of those who plot evil,
but those who counsel peace have joy.
[21]No harm befalls the just,
but the wicked are overwhelmed with misfortune.
[22]Lying lips are an abomination to the Lord,
but those who are truthful, his delight.
[23]The shrewd conceal knowledge,
but the hearts of fools proclaim folly.
[24]The diligent hand will govern,
but sloth makes for forced labor.
[25]Worry weighs down the heart,
but a kind word gives it joy.
[26]The just act as guides to their neighbors,
but the way of the wicked leads them astray.
[27]Sloth does not catch its prey,
but the wealth of the diligent is splendid.
[28]In the path of justice is life,
but the way of abomination leads to death.

☐ JOHN 8:12-30

The Light of the World. 8:12 Jesus spoke to them again, saying, "I am the light of the world. Whoever follows me will not walk in darkness, but will have the light of life." [13]So the Pharisees said to him, "You testify on your own behalf, so your testimony cannot be verified." [14]Jesus answered and said to them, "Even if I do testify on my own behalf, my testimony can be verified, because I know where I came from and where I am going. But you do not know where I come from or where I am going. [15]You judge by appearances, but I do not judge anyone. [16]And even if I should judge, my judgment is valid, because I am not alone, but it is I and the Father who sent me. [17]Even in your law it is written that the testimony of two men can be verified. [18]I testify on my behalf and so does the Father who sent me." [19]So they said to him, "Where is your father?" Jesus answered, "You know neither me nor my Father. If you knew me, you would know my Father also." [20]He spoke these words while teaching in the treasury in the temple area. But no one arrested him, because his hour had not yet come.

Jesus, the Father's Ambassador. [21]He said to them again, "I am going away and you will look for me, but you will die in your sin. Where I am going you cannot come." [22]So the Jews said, "He is not going to kill himself, is he, because he said, 'Where I am going you cannot come'?" [23]He said to them, "You belong to what is below, I belong to what is above. You belong to this world, but I do not belong to this world. [24]That is why I told you that you will die in your sins. For if you do not believe that I AM, you will die in your sins." [25]So they said to him, "Who are you?" Jesus said to them, "What I told you from the beginning. [26]I have much to say about you in condemnation. But the one who sent me is true, and what I heard from him I tell the world." [27]They did not realize that he was speaking to them of the Father. [28]So Jesus said (to them), "When you lift up the Son of Man, then you will realize that I AM, and that I do nothing on my own, but I say only what the Father taught me. [29]The one who sent me is with me. He has not left me alone, because I always do what is pleasing to him." [30]Because he spoke this way, many came to believe in him.

August 2

St. Peter Julian Eymard; St. Eusebius of Vercelli

Henceforth my motto shall be: Give me the Eucharist, or let me die!

— St. Peter Julian Eymard

☐ PROVERBS 13-15

13:1 A wise son loves correction,
 but the scoffer heeds no rebuke.
[2]From the fruit of the mouth one
 enjoys good things,
but from the throat of the
 treacherous comes violence.

[3]Those who guard their mouths
 preserve themselves;
those who open wide their lips
 bring ruin.
[4]The appetite of the sluggard craves but
 has nothing,

but the appetite of the diligent is
amply satisfied.
⁵The just hate deceitful words,
but the wicked are odious and
disgraceful.
⁶Justice guards one who walks honestly,
but sin leads the wicked astray.
⁷One acts rich but has nothing;
another acts poor but has great
wealth.
⁸People's riches serve as ransom for
their lives,
but the poor do not even hear a
threat.
⁹The light of the just gives joy,
but the lamp of the wicked goes
out.
¹⁰The stupid sow discord by their
insolence,
but wisdom is with those who take
counsel.
¹¹Wealth won quickly dwindles away,
but gathered little by little, it grows.
¹²Hope deferred makes the heart sick,
but a wish fulfilled is a tree of life.
¹³Whoever despises the word must pay
for it,
but whoever reveres the command
will be rewarded.
¹⁴The teaching of the wise is a fountain
of life,
turning one from the snares of
death.
¹⁵Good sense brings favor,
but the way of the faithless is their
ruin.
¹⁶The shrewd always act prudently
but the foolish parade folly.
¹⁷A wicked messenger brings on
disaster,
but a trustworthy envoy is a healing
remedy.
¹⁸Poverty and shame befall those who
let go of discipline,
but those who hold on to reproof
receive honor.
¹⁹Desire fulfilled delights the soul,

but turning from evil is an
abomination to fools.
²⁰Walk with the wise and you become
wise,
but the companion of fools fares
badly.
²¹Misfortune pursues sinners,
but the just shall be recompensed
with good.
²²The good leave an inheritance to their
children's children,
but the wealth of the sinner is stored
up for the just.
²³The tillage of the poor yields
abundant food,
but possessions are swept away for
lack of justice.
²⁴Whoever spares the rod hates the
child,
but whoever loves will apply
discipline.
²⁵When the just eat, their hunger is
appeased;
but the belly of the wicked suffers
want.

14:1 Wisdom builds her house,
but Folly tears hers down with her
own hands.
²Those who walk uprightly fear the
LORD,
but those who are devious in their
ways spurn him.
³In the mouth of the fool is a rod for
pride,
but the lips of the wise preserve
them.
⁴Where there are no oxen, the crib is
clean;
but abundant crops come through
the strength of the bull.
⁵A trustworthy witness does not lie,
but one who spouts lies makes a
lying witness.
⁶The scoffer seeks wisdom in vain,
but knowledge is easy for the
intelligent.

⁷Go from the face of the fool;
 you get no knowledge from such
  lips.
⁸The wisdom of the shrewd enlightens
  their way,
 but the folly of fools is deceit.
⁹The wicked scorn a guilt offering,
 but the upright find acceptance.
¹⁰The heart knows its own bitterness,
 and its joy no stranger shares.
¹¹The house of the wicked will be
  destroyed,
 but the tent of the upright will
  flourish.
¹²Sometimes a way seems right,
 but the end of it leads to death!
¹³Even in laughter the heart may be
  sad,
 and the end of joy may be sorrow.
¹⁴From their own ways turncoats are
  sated,
 from their own actions, the loyal.
¹⁵The naive believe everything,
 but the shrewd watch their steps.
¹⁶The wise person is cautious and turns
  from evil;
 the fool is reckless and gets
  embroiled.
¹⁷The quick-tempered make fools of
  themselves,
 and schemers are hated.
¹⁸The simple have folly as an
  adornment,
 but the shrewd wear knowledge as a
  crown.
¹⁹The malicious bow down before the
  good,
 and the wicked, at the gates of the
  just.
²⁰Even by their neighbors the poor are
  despised,
 but a rich person's friends are many.
²¹Whoever despises the hungry comes
  up short,
 but happy the one who is kind to
  the poor!
²²Do not those who plan evil go astray?

But those who plan good win
  steadfast loyalty.
²³In all labor there is profit,
 but mere talk tends only to loss.
²⁴The crown of the wise is wealth;
 the diadem of fools is folly.
²⁵The truthful witness saves lives,
 but whoever utters lies is a betrayer.
²⁶The fear of the LORD is a strong
  defense,
 a refuge even for one's children.
²⁷The fear of the LORD is a fountain of
  life,
 turning one from the snares of death.
²⁸A multitude of subjects is the glory of
  the king;
 but if his people are few, a prince is
  ruined.
²⁹Long-suffering results in great
  wisdom;
 a short temper raises folly high.
³⁰A tranquil mind gives life to the
  body,
 but jealousy rots the bones.
³¹Those who oppress the poor revile
  their Maker,
 but those who are kind to the needy
  honor him.
³²The wicked are overthrown by their
  wickedness,
 but the just find a refuge in their
  integrity.
³³Wisdom can remain silent in the
  discerning heart,
 but among fools she must make
  herself known.
³⁴Justice exalts a nation,
 but sin is a people's disgrace.
³⁵The king favors the skillful servant,
 but the shameless one incurs his
  wrath.

15:1 A mild answer turns back wrath,
 but a harsh word stirs up anger.
²The tongue of the wise pours out
  knowledge,
 but the mouth of fools spews folly.

³The eyes of the Lord are in every
place,
keeping watch on the evil and the
good.
⁴A soothing tongue is a tree of life,
but a perverse one breaks the spirit.
⁵The fool spurns a father's instruction,
but whoever heeds reproof is
prudent.
⁶In the house of the just there are
ample resources,
but the harvest of the wicked is in
peril.
⁷The lips of the wise spread knowledge,
but the heart of fools is not
steadfast.
⁸The sacrifice of the wicked is an
abomination to the Lord,
but the prayer of the upright is his
delight.
⁹The way of the wicked is an
abomination to the Lord,
but he loves one who pursues
justice.
¹⁰Discipline seems bad to those going
astray;
one who hates reproof will die.
¹¹Sheol and Abaddon lie open before
the Lord;
how much more the hearts of
mortals!
¹²Scoffers do not love reproof;
to the wise they will not go.
¹³A glad heart lights up the face,
but an anguished heart breaks the
spirit.
¹⁴The discerning heart seeks
knowledge,
but the mouth of fools feeds on
folly.
¹⁵All the days of the poor are evil,
but a good heart is a continual feast.
¹⁶Better a little with fear of the Lord
than a great fortune with anxiety.
¹⁷Better a dish of herbs where love is
than a fatted ox and hatred with it.
¹⁸The ill-tempered stir up strife,

but the patient settle disputes.
¹⁹The way of the sluggard is like a
thorn hedge,
but the path of the diligent is a
highway.
²⁰A wise son gives his father joy,
but a fool despises his mother.
²¹Folly is joy to the senseless,
but the person of understanding
goes the straight way.
²²Plans fail when there is no counsel,
but they succeed when advisers are
many.
²³One has joy from an apt response;
a word in season, how good it is!
²⁴The path of life leads upward for the
prudent,
turning them from Sheol below.
²⁵The Lord pulls down the house of
the proud,
but preserves intact the widow's
landmark.
²⁶The schemes of the wicked are an
abomination to the Lord,
but gracious words are pure.
²⁷The greedy tear down their own
house,
but those who hate bribes will live.
²⁸The heart of the just ponders a
response,
but the mouth of the wicked spews
evil.
²⁹The Lord is far from the wicked,
but hears the prayer of the just.
³⁰A cheerful glance brings joy to the
heart;
good news invigorates the bones.
³¹The ear that listens to salutary
reproof
is at home among the wise.
³²Those who disregard discipline hate
themselves,
but those who heed reproof acquire
understanding.
³³The fear of the Lord is training for
wisdom,
and humility goes before honors.

☐ JOHN 8:31-59

Jesus and Abraham. 8:31 Jesus then said to those Jews who believed in him, "If you remain in my word, you will truly be my disciples, ³²and you will know the truth, and the truth will set you free." ³³They answered him, "We are descendants of Abraham and have never been enslaved to anyone. How can you say, 'You will become free'?" ³⁴Jesus answered them, "Amen, amen, I say to you, everyone who commits sin is a slave of sin. ³⁵A slave does not remain in a household forever, but a son always remains. ³⁶So if a son frees you, then you will truly be free. ³⁷I know that you are descendants of Abraham. But you are trying to kill me, because my word has no room among you. ³⁸I tell you what I have seen in the Father's presence; then do what you have heard from the Father."

³⁹They answered and said to him, "Our father is Abraham." Jesus said to them, "If you were Abraham's children, you would be doing the works of Abraham. ⁴⁰But now you are trying to kill me, a man who has told you the truth that I heard from God; Abraham did not do this. ⁴¹You are doing the works of your father!" [So] they said to him, "We are not illegitimate. We have one Father, God." ⁴²Jesus said to them, "If God were your Father, you would love me, for I came from God and am here; I did not come on my own, but he sent me. ⁴³Why do you not understand what I am saying? Because you cannot bear to hear my word. ⁴⁴You belong to your father the devil and you willingly carry out your father's desires. He was a murderer from the beginning and does not stand in truth, because there is no truth in him. When he tells a lie, he speaks in character, because he is a liar and the father of lies. ⁴⁵But because I speak the truth, you do not believe me. ⁴⁶Can any of you charge me with sin? If I am telling the truth, why do you not believe me? ⁴⁷Whoever belongs to God hears the words of God; for this reason you do not listen, because you do not belong to God."

⁴⁸The Jews answered and said to him, "Are we not right in saying that you are a Samaritan and are possessed?" ⁴⁹Jesus answered, "I am not possessed; I honor my Father, but you dishonor me. ⁵⁰I do not seek my own glory; there is one who seeks it and he is the one who judges. ⁵¹Amen, amen, I say to you, whoever keeps my word will never see death." ⁵²(So) the Jews said to him, "Now we are sure that you are possessed. Abraham died, as did the prophets, yet you say, 'Whoever keeps my word will never taste death.' ⁵³Are you greater than our father Abraham, who died? Or the prophets, who died? Who do you make yourself out to be?" ⁵⁴Jesus answered, "If I glorify myself, my glory is worth nothing; but it is my Father who glorifies me, of whom you say, 'He is our God.' ⁵⁵You do not know him, but I know him. And if I should say that I do not know him, I would be like you a liar. But I do know him and I keep his word. ⁵⁶Abraham your father rejoiced to see my day; he saw it and was glad. ⁵⁷So the Jews said to him, "You are not yet fifty years old and you have seen Abraham?" ⁵⁸Jesus said to them, "Amen, amen, I say to you, before Abraham came to be, I AM." ⁵⁹So they picked up stones to throw at him; but Jesus hid and went out of the temple area.

August 3

So blind are we in this mortal life, and so unaware of what will happen — so uncertain even of how we will think tomorrow — that God could not take vengeance on a man more easily in this world than by granting his own foolish wishes.

— ST. THOMAS MORE

☐ PROVERBS 16-18

16:1 Plans are made in human hearts,
but from the LORD comes the
tongue's response.
²All one's ways are pure in one's own
eyes,
but the measurer of motives is the
LORD.
³Entrust your works to the LORD,
and your plans will succeed.
⁴The LORD has made everything for a
purpose,
even the wicked for the evil day.
⁵Every proud heart is an abomination
to the LORD;
be assured that none will go
unpunished.
⁶By steadfast loyalty guilt is expiated,
and by the fear of the LORD evil is
avoided.
⁷When the LORD is pleased with
someone's ways,
he makes even enemies be at peace
with them.
⁸Better a little with justice,
than a large income with injustice.
⁹The human heart plans the way,
but the LORD directs the steps.
¹⁰An oracle is upon the king's lips,
no judgment of his mouth is false.
¹¹Balance and scales belong to the
LORD;
every weight in the sack is his
concern.
¹²Wrongdoing is an abomination to
kings,
for by justice the throne endures.
¹³The king takes delight in honest lips,

and whoever speaks what is right he
loves.
¹⁴The king's wrath is a messenger of
death,
but a wise person can pacify it.
¹⁵A king's smile means life,
and his favor is like a rain cloud in
spring.
¹⁶How much better to get wisdom than
gold!
To get understanding is preferable
to silver.
¹⁷The path of the upright leads away
from misfortune;
those who attend to their way guard
their lives.
¹⁸Pride goes before disaster,
and a haughty spirit before a fall.
¹⁹It is better to be humble with the
poor
than to share plunder with the
proud.
²⁰Whoever ponders a matter will be
successful;
happy the one who trusts in the
LORD!
²¹The wise of heart is esteemed for
discernment,
and pleasing speech gains a
reputation for learning.
²²Good sense is a fountain of life to
those who have it,
but folly is the training of fools.
²³The heart of the wise makes for
eloquent speech,
and increases the learning on their
lips.

²⁴Pleasing words are a honeycomb,
  sweet to the taste and invigorating
    to the bones.
²⁵Sometimes a way seems right,
  but the end of it leads to death!
²⁶The appetite of workers works for
    them,
  for their mouths urge them on.
²⁷Scoundrels are a furnace of evil,
  and their lips are like a scorching
    fire.
²⁸Perverse speech sows discord,
  and talebearing separates bosom
    friends.
²⁹The violent deceive their neighbors,
  and lead them into a way that is not
    good.
³⁰Whoever winks an eye plans
    perversity;
  whoever purses the lips does evil.
³¹Gray hair is a crown of glory;
  it is gained by a life that is just.
³²The patient are better than warriors,
  and those who rule their temper,
    better than the conqueror of
    a city.
³³Into the bag the lot is cast,
  but from the LORD comes every
    decision.

17:1 Better a dry crust with quiet
  than a house full of feasting with
    strife.
²A wise servant will rule over an
    unworthy son,
  and will share the inheritance of the
    children.
³The crucible for silver, and the furnace
    for gold,
  but the tester of hearts is the LORD.
⁴The evildoer gives heed to wicked
    lips,
  the liar, to a mischievous tongue.
⁵Whoever mocks the poor reviles their
    Maker;
  whoever rejoices in their misfortune
    will not go unpunished.

⁶Children's children are the crown of
    the elderly,
  and the glory of children is their
    parentage.
⁷Fine words ill fit a fool;
  how much more lying lips, a noble!
⁸A bribe seems a charm to its user;
  at every turn it brings success.
⁹Whoever overlooks an offense fosters
    friendship,
  but whoever gossips about it
    separates friends.
¹⁰A single reprimand does more for a
    discerning person
  than a hundred lashes for a fool.
¹¹The wicked pursue only rebellion,
  and a merciless messenger is sent
    against them.
¹²Face a bear robbed of her cubs,
  but never fools in their folly!
¹³If you return evil for good,
  evil will not depart from your
    house.
¹⁴The start of strife is like the opening
    of a dam;
  check a quarrel before it bursts
    forth!
¹⁵Whoever acquits the wicked, whoever
    condemns the just—
  both are an abomination to the
    LORD.
¹⁶Of what use is money in the hands
    of fools
  when they have no heart to acquire
    wisdom?
¹⁷A friend is a friend at all times,
  and a brother is born for the time of
    adversity.
¹⁸Those without sense give their hands
    in pledge,
  becoming surety for their neighbors.
¹⁹Those who love an offense love a
    fight;
  those who build their gate high
    court disaster.
²⁰The perverse in heart come to no
    good,

and the double-tongued fall into
 trouble.
²¹Whoever conceives a fool has grief;
 the father of a numskull has no joy.
²²A joyful heart is the health of the
 body,
 but a depressed spirit dries up the
 bones.
²³A guilty person takes out a bribe from
 the pocket,
 thus perverting the course of justice.
²⁴On the countenance of a discerning
 person is wisdom,
 but the eyes of a fool are on the ends
 of the earth.
²⁵A foolish son is vexation to his father,
 and bitter sorrow to her who bore
 him.
²⁶It is wrong to fine an innocent
 person,
 but beyond reason to scourge
 nobles.
²⁷Those who spare their words are truly
 knowledgeable,
 and those who are discreet are
 intelligent.
²⁸Even fools, keeping silent, are
 considered wise;
 if they keep their lips closed,
 intelligent.

18:1 One who is alienated seeks a
 pretext,
 with all persistence picks a quarrel.
²Fools take no delight in
 understanding,
 but only in displaying what they
 think.
³With wickedness comes contempt,
 and with disgrace, scorn.
⁴The words of one's mouth are deep
 waters,
 the spring of wisdom, a running
 brook.
⁵It is not good to favor the guilty,
 nor to reject the claim of the just.
⁶The lips of fools walk into a fight,

and their mouths are asking for a
 beating.
⁷The mouths of fools are their ruin;
 their lips are a deadly snare.
⁸The words of a talebearer are like
 dainty morsels:
 they sink into one's inmost being.
⁹Those slack in their work
 are kin to the destroyer.
¹⁰The name of the Lᴏʀᴅ is a strong
 tower;
 the just run to it and are safe.
¹¹The wealth of the rich is their strong
 city;
 they fancy it a high wall.
¹²Before disaster the heart is haughty,
 but before honor is humility.
¹³Whoever answers before listening,
 theirs is folly and shame.
¹⁴One's spirit supports one when ill,
 but a broken spirit who can bear?
¹⁵The heart of the intelligent acquires
 knowledge,
 and the ear of the wise seeks
 knowledge.
¹⁶Gifts clear the way for people,
 winning access to the great.
¹⁷Those who plead the case first seem
 to be in the right;
 then the opponent comes and cross-
 examines them.
¹⁸The lot puts an end to disputes,
 and decides a controversy between
 the mighty.
¹⁹A brother offended is more
 unyielding than a stronghold;
 such strife is more daunting than
 castle gates.
²⁰With the fruit of one's mouth one's
 belly is filled,
 with the produce of one's lips one is
 sated.
²¹Death and life are in the power of the
 tongue;
 those who choose one shall eat its
 fruit.
²²To find a wife is to find happiness,

a favor granted by the LORD.
²³The poor implore,
    but the rich answer harshly.

²⁴There are friends who bring ruin,
    but there are true friends more loyal
        than a brother.

☐ JOHN 9

The Man Born Blind. 9:1 As he passed by he saw a man blind from birth. ²His disciples asked him, "Rabbi, who sinned, this man or his parents, that he was born blind?" ³Jesus answered, "Neither he nor his parents sinned; it is so that the works of God might be made visible through him. ⁴We have to do the works of the one who sent me while it is day. Night is coming when no one can work. ⁵While I am in the world, I am the light of the world." ⁶When he had said this, he spat on the ground and made clay with the saliva, and smeared the clay on his eyes, ⁷and said to him, "Go wash in the Pool of Siloam" (which means Sent). So he went and washed, and came back able to see.

⁸His neighbors and those who had seen him earlier as a beggar said, "Isn't this the one who used to sit and beg?" ⁹Some said, "It is," but others said, "No, he just looks like him." He said, "I am." ¹⁰So they said to him, "[So] how were your eyes opened?" ¹¹He replied, "The man called Jesus made clay and anointed my eyes and told me, 'Go to Siloam and wash.' So I went there and washed and was able to see." ¹²And they said to him, "Where is he?" He said, "I don't know."

¹³They brought the one who was once blind to the Pharisees. ¹⁴Now Jesus had made clay and opened his eyes on a sabbath. ¹⁵So then the Pharisees also asked him how he was able to see. He said to them, "He put clay on my eyes, and I washed, and now I can see." ¹⁶So some of the Pharisees said, "This man is not from God, because he does not keep the sabbath." [But] others said, "How can a sinful man do such signs?" And there was a division among them. ¹⁷So they said to the blind man again, "What do you have to say about him, since he opened your eyes?" He said, "He is a prophet."

¹⁸Now the Jews did not believe that he had been blind and gained his sight until they summoned the parents of the one who had gained his sight. ¹⁹They asked them, "Is this your son, who you say was born blind? How does he now see?" ²⁰His parents answered and said, "We know that this is our son and that he was born blind. ²¹We do not know how he sees now, nor do we know who opened his eyes. Ask him, he is of age; he can speak for himself." ²²His parents said this because they were afraid of the Jews, for the Jews had already agreed that if anyone acknowledged him as the Messiah, he would be expelled from the synagogue. ²³For this reason his parents said, "He is of age; question him."

²⁴So a second time they called the man who had been blind and said to him, "Give God the praise! We know that this man is a sinner." ²⁵He replied, "If he is a sinner, I do not know. One thing I do know is that I was blind and now I see." ²⁶So they said to him, "What did he do to you? How did he open your eyes?" ²⁷He answered them, "I told you already and you did not listen. Why do you want to hear it again? Do you want to become his disciples, too?" ²⁸They ridiculed him and said, "You are that man's disciple; we are disciples of Moses! ²⁹We know that God spoke to Moses, but we do not know where this one is from." ³⁰The man answered and said to them, "This is what is so amazing, that you do not know where he is from, yet he opened my eyes. ³¹We know that God does not listen to sinners, but if one is devout and does his will,

he listens to him. ³²It is unheard of that anyone ever opened the eyes of a person born blind. ³³If this man were not from God, he would not be able to do anything." ³⁴They answered and said to him, "You were born totally in sin, and are you trying to teach us?" Then they threw him out.

³⁵When Jesus heard that they had thrown him out, he found him and said, "Do you believe in the Son of Man?" ³⁶He answered and said, "Who is he, sir, that I may believe in him?" ³⁷Jesus said to him,

"You have seen him and the one speaking with you is he." ³⁸He said, "I do believe, Lord," and he worshiped him. ³⁹Then Jesus said, "I came into this world for judgment, so that those who do not see might see, and those who do see might become blind."

⁴⁰Some of the Pharisees who were with him heard this and said to him, "Surely we are not also blind, are we?" ⁴¹Jesus said to them, "If you were blind, you would have no sin; but now you are saying, 'We see,' so your sin remains."

August 4

St. John Vianney

The one who is suffering from a slight illness has no need to go and see a doctor; she can get well alone. But if it is a serious illness, if it is a dangerous wound, then the doctor must be called in, and after the doctor come the medicines. When we have fallen into some grave sin, we must go to the doctor, who is the priest, and take the medicine, which is confession.

— St. John Vianney

☐ PROVERBS 19-21

19:1 Better to be poor and walk in integrity
  than rich and crooked in one's ways.
²Desire without knowledge is not good;
  and whoever acts hastily, blunders.
³Their own folly leads people astray;
  in their hearts they rage against the
    Lord.
⁴Wealth adds many friends,
  but the poor are left friendless.
⁵The false witness will not go
    unpunished,
  and whoever utters lies will not
    escape.
⁶Many curry favor with a noble;
  everybody is a friend of a gift giver.
⁷All the kin of the poor despise them;

how much more do their friends
    shun them!
⁸Those who gain sense truly love
    themselves;
  those who preserve understanding
    will find success.
⁹The false witness will not go
    unpunished,
  and whoever utters lies will perish.
¹⁰Luxury is not befitting a fool;
  much less should a slave rule over
    princes.
¹¹It is good sense to be slow to anger,
  and an honor to overlook an
    offense.
¹²The king's wrath is like the roar of a
    lion,

but his favor, like dew on the grass."
¹³The foolish son is ruin to his father,
and a quarrelsome wife is water
constantly dripping.
¹⁴Home and possessions are an
inheritance from parents,
but a prudent wife is from the LORD.
¹⁵Laziness brings on deep sleep,
and the sluggard goes hungry.
¹⁶Those who keep commands keep
their lives,
but those who despise these ways
will die.
¹⁷Whoever cares for the poor lends to
the LORD,
who will pay back the sum in full.
¹⁸Discipline your son, for there is hope;
but do not be intent on his death.
¹⁹A wrathful person bears the penalty;
after one rescue, you will have it to
do again.
²⁰Listen to counsel and receive
instruction,
that you may eventually become
wise.
²¹Many are the plans of the human
heart,
but it is the decision of the LORD
that endures.
²²What is desired of a person is fidelity;
rather be poor than a liar.
²³The fear of the LORD leads to life;
one eats and sleeps free from any
harm.
²⁴The sluggard buries a hand in the
dish;
not even lifting it to the mouth.
²⁵Beat a scoffer and the naive learn a
lesson;
rebuke the intelligent and they gain
knowledge.
²⁶Whoever mistreats a father or drives
away a mother,
is a shameless and disgraceful child.
²⁷My son, stop attending to correction;
start straying from words of
knowledge.

²⁸An unprincipled witness scoffs at
justice,
and the mouth of the wicked pours
out iniquity.
²⁹Rods are prepared for scoffers,
and blows for the backs of fools.

20:1 Wine is arrogant, strong drink is
riotous;
none who are intoxicated by them
are wise.
²The terror of a king is like the roar of
a lion;
those who incur his anger forfeit
their lives.
³A person gains honor by avoiding
strife,
while every fool starts a quarrel.
⁴In seedtime sluggards do not plow;
when they look for the harvest, it is
not there.
⁵The intention of the human heart is
deep water,
but the intelligent draw it forth.
⁶Many say, "My loyal friend,"
but who can find someone worthy
of trust?
⁷The just walk in integrity;
happy are their children after them!
⁸A king seated on the throne of
judgment
dispels all evil with his glance.
⁹Who can say, "I have made my heart
clean,
I am cleansed of my sin"?
¹⁰Varying weights, varying measures,
are both an abomination to the LORD.
¹¹In their actions even children can
playact
though their deeds be blameless and
right.
¹²The ear that hears, the eye that sees—
the LORD has made them both.
¹³Do not love sleep lest you be reduced
to poverty;
keep your eyes open, have your fill
of food.

¹⁴"Bad, bad!" says the buyer,
then goes away only to boast.
¹⁵One can put on gold and abundant
jewels,
but wise lips are the most precious
ornament.
¹⁶Take the garment of the one who
became surety for a stranger;
if for foreigners, exact the pledge!
¹⁷Bread earned by deceit is sweet,
but afterward the mouth is filled
with gravel.
¹⁸Plans made with advice succeed;
with wise direction wage your war.
¹⁹A slanderer reveals secrets;
so have nothing to do with a
babbler!
²⁰Those who curse father or mother—
their lamp will go out in the dead
of night.
²¹Possessions greedily guarded at the
outset
will not be blessed in the end.
²²Do not say, "I will repay evil!"
Wait for the LORD, who will help
you.
²³Varying weights are an abomination
to the LORD,
and false scales are not good.
²⁴Our steps are from the LORD;
how, then, can mortals understand
their way?
²⁵It is a trap to pledge rashly a sacred
gift,
and after a vow, then to reflect.
²⁶A wise king winnows the wicked,
and threshes them under the
cartwheel.
²⁷A lamp from the LORD is human life-
breath;
it searches through the inmost being.
²⁸His steadfast loyalty safeguards the
king,
and he upholds his throne by
justice.
²⁹The glory of the young is their
strength,

and the dignity of the old is gray
hair.
³⁰Evil is cleansed away by bloody
lashes,
and a scourging to the inmost being.

21:1 A king's heart is channeled water
in the hand of the LORD;
God directs it where he pleases.
²All your ways may be straight in your
own eyes,
but it is the LORD who weighs
hearts.
³To do what is right and just
is more acceptable to the LORD than
sacrifice.
⁴Haughty eyes and a proud heart—
the lamp of the wicked will fail.
⁵The plans of the diligent end in profit,
but those of the hasty end in loss.
⁶Trying to get rich by lying
is chasing a bubble over deadly
snares.
⁷The violence of the wicked will sweep
them away,
because they refuse to do what is
right.
⁸One's path may be winding and
unfamiliar,
but one's conduct is blameless and
right.
⁹It is better to dwell in a corner of the
housetop
than in a mansion with a
quarrelsome woman.
¹⁰The soul of the wicked desires evil;
their neighbor finds no pity in their
eyes.
¹¹When scoffers are punished the naive
become wise;
when the wise succeed, they gain
knowledge.
¹²The Righteous One appraises the
house of the wicked,
bringing down the wicked to ruin.
¹³Those who shut their ears to the cry
of the poor

will themselves call out and not be
answered.
[14]A secret gift allays anger,
and a present concealed, violent
wrath.
[15]When justice is done it is a joy for the
just,
downfall for evildoers.
[16]Whoever strays from the way of good
sense
will abide in the assembly of the
shades.
[17]The lover of pleasure will suffer want;
the lover of wine and perfume will
never be rich.
[18]The wicked serve as ransom for the
just,
and the faithless for the upright.
[19]It is better to dwell in a wilderness
than with a quarrelsome wife and
trouble.
[20]Precious treasure and oil are in the
house of the wise,
but the fool consumes them.
[21]Whoever pursues justice and kindness
will find life and honor.
[22]The wise person storms the city of the
mighty,

and overthrows the stronghold in
which they trust.
[23]Those who guard mouth and tongue
guard themselves from trouble.
[24]Proud, boastful—scoffer is the name:
those who act with overbearing
pride.
[25]The desire of sluggards will slay them,
for their hands refuse to work.
[26]Some are consumed with avarice all
the day,
but the just give unsparingly.
[27]The sacrifice of the wicked is an
abomination,
the more so when they offer it with
bad intent.
[28]The false witness will perish,
but one who listens will give lasting
testimony.
[29]The face of the wicked hardens,
but the upright maintains a straight
course.
[30]No wisdom, no understanding,
no counsel prevail against the
Lord.
[31]The horse is equipped for the day of
battle,
but victory is the Lord's.

☐ JOHN 10:1-21

The Good Shepherd. 10:1 "Amen, amen,
I say to you, whoever does not enter a
sheepfold through the gate but climbs over
elsewhere is a thief and a robber. [2]But whoever enters through the gate is the shepherd
of the sheep. [3]The gatekeeper opens it for
him, and the sheep hear his voice, as he
calls his own sheep by name and leads them
out. [4]When he has driven out all his own,
he walks ahead of them, and the sheep follow him, because they recognize his voice.
[5]But they will not follow a stranger; they
will run away from him, because they do
not recognize the voice of strangers." [6]Al-
though Jesus used this figure of speech,

they did not realize what he was trying to
tell them.
[7]So Jesus said again, "Amen, amen, I
say to you, I am the gate for the sheep. [8]All
who came [before me] are thieves and robbers, but the sheep did not listen to them.
[9]I am the gate. Whoever enters through me
will be saved, and will come in and go out
and find pasture. [10]A thief comes only to
steal and slaughter and destroy; I came so
that they might have life and have it more
abundantly. [11]I am the good shepherd. A
good shepherd lays down his life for the
sheep. [12]A hired man, who is not a shepherd and whose sheep are not his own, sees

a wolf coming and leaves the sheep and runs away, and the wolf catches and scatters them. [13]This is because he works for pay and has no concern for the sheep. [14]I am the good shepherd, and I know mine and mine know me, [15]just as the Father knows me and I know the Father; and I will lay down my life for the sheep. [16]I have other sheep that do not belong to this fold. These also I must lead, and they will hear my voice, and there will be one flock, one shepherd. [17]This is why the Father loves me, because I lay down my life in order to take it up again. [18]No one takes it from me, but I lay it down on my own. I have power to lay it down, and power to take it up again. This command I have received from my Father."

[19]Again there was a division among the Jews because of these words. [20]Many of them said, "He is possessed and out of his mind; why listen to him?" [21]Others said, "These are not the words of one possessed; surely a demon cannot open the eyes of the blind, can he?"

August 5

Dedication of the Basilica of St. Mary Major

Far be it that anyone should try to defraud holy Mary of her privileges of divine grace and of her special glory. For by a certain singular favor of our Lord and God, and of her Son, she must be confessed to be the most true and most blessed Mother of God.

— St. Vincent of Lerins

☐ PROVERBS 22-24

22:1 A good name is more desirable
than great riches,
and high esteem, than gold and
silver.
[2]Rich and poor have a common bond:
the LORD is the maker of them all.
[3]The astute see an evil and hide,
while the naive continue on and pay
the penalty.
[4]The result of humility and fear of the
LORD
is riches, honor and life.
[5]Thorns and snares are on the path of
the crooked;
those who would safeguard their
lives will avoid them.
[6]Train the young in the way they
should go;

even when old, they will not swerve
from it.
[7]The rich rule over the poor,
and the borrower is the slave of the
lender.
[8]Those who sow iniquity reap calamity,
and the rod used in anger will fail.
[9]The generous will be blessed,
for they share their food with the
poor.
[10]Expel the arrogant and discord goes
too;
strife and insult cease.
[11]The LORD loves the pure of heart;
the person of winning speech has a
king for a friend.
[12]The eyes of the LORD watch over the
knowledgeable,

but he defeats the projects of the
faithless.

¹³The sluggard says, "A lion is outside;
I might be slain in the street."

¹⁴The mouth of the foreign woman is a
deep pit;
whoever incurs the LORD's anger
will fall into it.

¹⁵Folly is bound to the heart of a youth,
but the rod of discipline will drive
it out.

¹⁶Oppressing the poor for enrichment,
giving to the rich: both are sheer
loss.

¹⁷The Words of the Wise:
Incline your ear, and hear my words,
and let your mind attend to my
teaching;

¹⁸For it will be well if you hold them
within you,
if they all are ready on your lips.

¹⁹That your trust may be in the LORD,
I make them known to you today—
yes, to you.

²⁰Have I not written for you thirty
sayings,
containing counsels and knowledge,

²¹To teach you truly
how to give a dependable report to
one who sends you?

²²Do not rob the poor because they are
poor,
nor crush the needy at the gate;

²³For the LORD will defend their cause,
and will plunder those who plunder
them.

²⁴Do not be friendly with hotheads,
nor associate with the wrathful,

²⁵Lest you learn their ways,
and become ensnared.

²⁶Do not be one of those who give their
hand in pledge,
those who become surety for debts;

²⁷For if you are unable to pay,
your bed will be taken from under
you.

²⁸Do not remove the ancient landmark
that your ancestors set up.

²⁹Do you see those skilled at their
work?
They will stand in the presence of
kings,
but not in the presence of the
obscure.

23:1 When you sit down to dine with
a ruler,
mark well the one who is before
you;

²Stick the knife in your gullet
if you have a ravenous appetite.

³Do not desire his delicacies;
it is food that deceives.

⁴Do not wear yourself out to gain
wealth,
cease to be worried about it;

⁵When your glance flits to it, it is
gone!
For assuredly it grows wings,
like the eagle that flies toward
heaven.

⁶Do not take food with unwilling
hosts,
and do not desire their delicacies;

⁷For like something stuck in the throat
is that food.
"Eat and drink," they say to you,
but their hearts are not with you;

⁸The little you have eaten you will
vomit up,
and you will have wasted your
agreeable words.

⁹Do not speak in the hearing of fools;
they will despise the wisdom of your
words.

¹⁰Do not remove the ancient landmark,
nor invade the fields of the
fatherless;

¹¹For their redeemer is strong;
he will defend their cause against
you.

¹²Apply your heart to instruction,
and your ear to words of knowledge.

¹³Do not withhold discipline from
    youths;
  if you beat them with the rod, they
    will not die.
¹⁴Beat them with the rod,
  and you will save them from Sheol.
¹⁵My son, if your heart is wise,
  my heart also will rejoice;
¹⁶And my inmost being will exult,
  when your lips speak what is right.
¹⁷Do not let your heart envy sinners,
  but only those who always fear the
    LORD;
¹⁸For you will surely have a future,
  and your hope will not be cut off.
¹⁹Hear, my son, and be wise,
  and guide your heart in the right
    way.
²⁰Do not join with wine bibbers,
  nor with those who glut themselves
    on meat.
²¹For drunkards and gluttons come to
    poverty,
  and lazing about clothes one in rags.
²²Listen to your father who begot you,
  do not despise your mother when
    she is old.
²³Buy truth and do not sell:
  wisdom, instruction, understanding!
²⁴The father of a just person will exult
    greatly;
  whoever begets a wise son will
    rejoice in him.
²⁵Let your father and mother rejoice;
  let her who bore you exult.
²⁶My son, give me your heart,
  and let your eyes keep to my ways,
²⁷For the harlot is a deep pit,
  and the foreign woman a narrow
    well;
²⁸Yes, she lies in wait like a robber,
  and increases the number of the
    faithless.
²⁹Who scream? Who shout?
  Who have strife? Who have anxiety?
Who have wounds for nothing?
  Who have bleary eyes?

³⁰Whoever linger long over wine,
  whoever go around quaffing wine.
³¹Do not look on the wine when it is
    red,
  when it sparkles in the cup.
It goes down smoothly,
  ³²but in the end it bites like a
    serpent,
  and stings like an adder.
³³Your eyes behold strange sights,
  and your heart utters incoherent
    things;
³⁴You are like one sleeping on the high
    seas,
  sprawled at the top of the mast.
³⁵"They struck me, but it did not pain
    me;
  they beat me, but I did not feel it.
When can I get up,
  when can I go out and get more?"

24:1 Do not envy the wicked,
  nor desire to be with them;
²For their hearts plot violence,
  and their lips speak of foul play.
³By wisdom a house is built,
  by understanding it is established;
⁴And by knowledge its rooms are filled
  with every precious and pleasing
    possession.
⁵The wise are more powerful than the
    strong,
  and the learned, than the mighty,
⁶For by strategy war is waged,
  and victory depends on many
    counselors.
⁷Wise words are beyond fools' reach,
  in the assembly they do not open
    their mouth;
⁸As they calculate how to do evil,
  people brand them troublemakers.
⁹The scheme of a fool gains no
    acceptance,
  the scoffer is an abomination to the
    community.
¹⁰Did you fail in a day of adversity,
  did your strength fall short?

[11]Did you fail to rescue those who were
being dragged off to death,
those tottering, those near death,
[12]because you said, "We didn't know
about it"?
Surely, the Searcher of hearts knows
and will repay all according to their
deeds.
[13]If you eat honey, my son, because it
is good,
if pure honey is sweet to your taste,
[14]Such, you must know, is wisdom to
your soul.
If you find it, you will have a future,
and your hope will not be cut off.
[15]Do not lie in wait at the abode of the
just,
do not ravage their dwelling places;
[16]Though the just fall seven times, they
rise again,
but the wicked stumble from only
one mishap.
[17]Do not rejoice when your enemies fall,
and when they stumble, do not let
your heart exult,
[18]Lest the LORD see it, be displeased
with you,
and withdraw his wrath from your
enemies.
[19]Do not be provoked at evildoers,
do not envy the wicked;
[20]For the evil have no future,
the lamp of the wicked will be put
out.
[21]My son, fear the LORD and the king;
have nothing to do with those who
hate them;
[22]For disaster will issue suddenly,

and calamity from them both, who
knows when?
[23]These also are Words of the Wise:
To show partiality in judgment is not
good.
[24]Whoever says to the guilty party,
"You are innocent,"
will be cursed by nations, scorned
by peoples;
[25]But those who render just verdicts
will fare well,
and on them will come the blessing
of prosperity.
[26]An honest reply—
a kiss on the lips.
[27]Complete your outdoor tasks,
and arrange your work in the field;
afterward you can build your house.
[28]Do not testify falsely against your
neighbor
and so deceive with your lips.
[29]Do not say, "As they did to me, so
will I do to them;
I will repay them according to their
deeds."
[30]I passed by the field of a sluggard,
by the vineyard of one with no
sense;
[31]It was all overgrown with thistles;
its surface was covered with nettles,
and its stone wall broken down.
[32]As I gazed at it, I reflected;
I saw and learned a lesson:
[33]A little sleep, a little slumber,
a little folding of the arms to rest—
[34]Then poverty will come upon you
like a robber,
and want like a brigand.

☐ JOHN 10:22-42

Feast of the Dedication. 10:22 The feast of the Dedication was then taking place in Jerusalem. It was winter. [23]And Jesus walked about in the temple area on the Portico of Solomon. [24]So the Jews gathered around him and said to him, "How long are you going to keep us in suspense? If you are the Messiah, tell us plainly." [25]Jesus answered them, "I told you and you do not believe. The works I do in my Father's name testify to me. ²⁶But you do not believe, because you are not among my sheep. ²⁷My sheep hear my voice; I know them, and they follow me. ²⁸I give them eternal life, and they shall never perish. No one can take them out of my hand. ²⁹My Father, who has given them to me, is greater than all, and no one can take them out of the Father's hand. ³⁰The Father and I are one."

³¹The Jews again picked up rocks to stone him. ³²Jesus answered them, "I have shown you many good works from my Father. For which of these are you trying to stone me?" ³³The Jews answered him, "We are not stoning you for a good work but for blasphemy. You, a man, are making yourself God." ³⁴Jesus answered them, "Is it not written in your law, 'I said, "You are gods"'? ³⁵If it calls them gods to whom the word of God came, and scripture cannot be set aside, ³⁶can you say that the one whom the Father has consecrated and sent into the world blasphemes because I said, 'I am the Son of God'? ³⁷If I do not perform my Father's works, do not believe me; ³⁸but if I perform them, even if you do not believe me, believe the works, so that you may realize [and understand] that the Father is in me and I am in the Father." ³⁹[Then] they tried again to arrest him; but he escaped from their power.

⁴⁰He went back across the Jordan to the place where John first baptized, and there he remained. ⁴¹Many came to him and said, "John performed no sign, but everything John said about this man was true." ⁴²And many there began to believe in him.

August 6

The Transfiguration of the Lord

Grace is nothing else but a certain beginning of glory in us.
— St. Thomas Aquinas

☐ PROVERBS 25-27

25:1 These also are proverbs of Solomon. The servants of Hezekiah, king of Judah, transmitted them.

²It is the glory of God to conceal a
matter,
and the glory of kings to fathom a
matter.
³Like the heavens in height, and the
earth in depth,
the heart of kings is unfathomable.
⁴Remove the dross from silver,
and it comes forth perfectly
purified;
⁵Remove the wicked from the presence
of the king,
and his throne is made firm through
justice.

⁶Claim no honor in the king's presence,
nor occupy the place of superiors;
⁷For it is better to be told, "Come up
closer!"
than to be humbled before the prince.
⁸What your eyes have seen
do not bring forth too quickly
against an opponent;
For what will you do later on
when your neighbor puts you to
shame?
⁹Argue your own case with your
neighbor,
but the secrets of others do not
disclose;
¹⁰Lest, hearing it, they reproach you,
and your ill repute never ceases.

¹¹Golden apples in silver settings
are words spoken at the proper
time.
¹²A golden earring or a necklace of fine
gold—
one who gives wise reproof to a
listening ear.
¹³Like the coolness of snow in the heat
of the harvest
are faithful messengers for those
who send them,
lifting the spirits of their masters.
¹⁴Clouds and wind but no rain—
the one who boasts of a gift not
given.
¹⁵By patience is a ruler persuaded,
and a soft tongue can break a bone.
¹⁶If you find honey, eat only what you
need,
lest you have your fill and vomit it
up.
¹⁷Let your foot be seldom in your
neighbors' house,
lest they have their fill of you—and
hate you.
¹⁸A club, sword, or sharp arrow—
the one who bears false witness
against a neighbor.
¹⁹A bad tooth or an unsteady foot—
a trust betrayed in time of trouble.
²⁰Like the removal of clothes on a cold
day, or vinegar on soda,
is the one who sings to a troubled
heart.
²¹If your enemies are hungry, give them
food to eat,
if thirsty, give something to drink;
²²For live coals you will heap on their
heads,
and the LORD will vindicate you.
²³The north wind brings rain,
and a backbiting tongue, angry
looks.
²⁴It is better to dwell in a corner of the
housetop
than in a mansion with a
quarrelsome wife.

²⁵Cool water to one faint from thirst
is good news from a far country.
²⁶A trampled fountain or a polluted
spring—
a just person fallen before the wicked.
²⁷To eat too much honey is not good;
nor to seek honor after honor.
²⁸A city breached and left defenseless
are those who do not control their
temper.

26:1 Like snow in summer, like rain in
harvest,
honor for a fool is out of place.
²Like the sparrow in its flitting, like the
swallow in its flight,
a curse uncalled-for never lands.
³The whip for the horse, the bridle for
the ass,
and the rod for the back of fools.
⁴Do not answer fools according to their
folly,
lest you too become like them.
⁵Answer fools according to their folly,
lest they become wise in their own
eyes.
⁶Those who send messages by a fool
cut off their feet; they drink down
violence.
⁷A proverb in the mouth of a fool
hangs limp, like crippled legs.
⁸Giving honor to a fool
is like entangling a stone in the sling.
⁹A thorn stuck in the hand of a
drunkard
is a proverb in the mouth of fools.
¹⁰An archer wounding all who pass by
is anyone who hires a drunken fool.
¹¹As dogs return to their vomit,
so fools repeat their folly.
¹²You see those who are wise in their
own eyes?
There is more hope for fools than
for them.
¹³The sluggard says, "There is a lion in
the street,
a lion in the middle of the square!"

¹⁴The door turns on its hinges
and sluggards, on their beds.
¹⁵The sluggard buries a hand in the
dish,
too weary to lift it to the mouth.
¹⁶In their own eyes sluggards are wiser
than seven who answer with good
judgment.
¹⁷Whoever meddles in the quarrel of
another
is one who grabs a passing dog by
the ears.
¹⁸Like a crazed archer
scattering firebrands and deadly
arrows,
¹⁹Such are those who deceive their
neighbor,
and then say, "I was only joking."
²⁰Without wood the fire dies out;
without a talebearer strife subsides.
²¹Charcoal for coals, wood for fire—
such are the quarrelsome,
enkindling strife.
²²The words of a talebearer are like
dainty morsels:
they sink into one's inmost being.
²³Like a glazed finish on earthenware
are smooth lips and a wicked heart.
²⁴With their lips enemies pretend,
but inwardly they maintain deceit;
²⁵When they speak graciously, do not
trust them,
for seven abominations are in their
hearts.
²⁶Hatred can be concealed by pretense,
but malice will be revealed in the
assembly.
²⁷Whoever digs a pit falls into it;
and a stone comes back upon the
one who rolls it.
²⁸The lying tongue is its owner's enemy,
and the flattering mouth works
ruin.

27:1 Do not boast about tomorrow,
for you do not know what any day
may bring forth.

²Let another praise you, not your own
mouth;
a stranger, not your own lips.
³Stone is heavy, and sand a burden,
but a fool's provocation is heavier
than both.
⁴Anger is cruel, and wrath
overwhelming,
but before jealousy who can stand?
⁵Better is an open rebuke
than a love that remains hidden.
⁶Trustworthy are the blows of a friend,
dangerous, the kisses of an enemy.
⁷One who is full spurns honey;
but to the hungry, any bitter thing
is sweet.
⁸Like a bird far from the nest
so is anyone far from home.
⁹Perfume and incense bring joy to the
heart,
but by grief the soul is torn asunder.
¹⁰Do not give up your own friend and
your father's friend;
do not resort to the house of your
kindred when trouble strikes.
Better a neighbor near than kin far
away.
¹¹Be wise, my son, and bring joy to my
heart,
so that I can answer whoever taunts
me.
¹²The astute see an evil and hide;
the naive continue on and pay the
penalty.
¹³Take the garment of the one who
became surety for a stranger;
if for a foreign woman, exact the
pledge!
¹⁴Those who greet their neighbor
with a loud voice in the early
morning,
a curse can be laid to their charge.
¹⁵For a persistent leak on a rainy day
the match is a quarrelsome wife;
¹⁶Whoever would hide her hides a
stormwind
and cannot tell north from south.

¹⁷Iron is sharpened by iron;
    one person sharpens another.
¹⁸Those who tend a fig tree eat its fruit;
    so those attentive to their master
        will be honored.
¹⁹As face mirrors face in water,
    so the heart reflects the person.
²⁰Sheol and Abaddon can never be
    satisfied;
    so the eyes of mortals can never be
        satisfied.
²¹The crucible for silver, the furnace for
    gold,
    so you must assay the praise you
        receive.
²²Though you pound fools with a pestle,
    their folly never leaves them.
²³Take good care of your flocks,
    give careful attention to your herds;
²⁴For wealth does not last forever,
    nor even a crown from age to age.
²⁵When the grass comes up and the
    new growth appears,
    and the mountain greens are
        gathered in,
²⁶The lambs will provide you with
    clothing,
    and the goats, the price of a field,
²⁷And there will be ample goat's milk
    for your food,
    food for your house, sustenance for
        your maidens.

☐ JOHN 11:1-44

The Raising of Lazarus. 11:1 Now a man was ill, Lazarus from Bethany, the village of Mary and her sister Martha. ²Mary was the one who had anointed the Lord with perfumed oil and dried his feet with her hair; it was her brother Lazarus who was ill. ³So the sisters sent word to him, saying, "Master, the one you love is ill." ⁴When Jesus heard this he said, "This illness is not to end in death, but is for the glory of God, that the Son of God may be glorified through it." ⁵Now Jesus loved Martha and her sister and Lazarus. ⁶So when he heard that he was ill, he remained for two days in the place where he was. ⁷Then after this he said to his disciples, "Let us go back to Judea." ⁸The disciples said to him, "Rabbi, the Jews were just trying to stone you, and you want to go back there?" ⁹Jesus answered, "Are there not twelve hours in a day? If one walks during the day, he does not stumble, because he sees the light of this world. ¹⁰But if one walks at night, he stumbles, because the light is not in him." ¹¹He said this, and then told them, "Our friend Lazarus is asleep, but I am going to awaken him." ¹²So the disciples said to him, "Master, if he is asleep, he will be saved." ¹³But Jesus was talking about his death, while they thought that he meant ordinary sleep. ¹⁴So then Jesus said to them clearly, "Lazarus has died. ¹⁵And I am glad for you that I was not there, that you may believe. Let us go to him." ¹⁶So Thomas, called Didymus, said to his fellow disciples, "Let us also go to die with him."

¹⁷When Jesus arrived, he found that Lazarus had already been in the tomb for four days. ¹⁸Now Bethany was near Jerusalem, only about two miles away. ¹⁹And many of the Jews had come to Martha and Mary to comfort them about their brother. ²⁰When Martha heard that Jesus was coming, she went to meet him; but Mary sat at home. ²¹Martha said to Jesus, "Lord, if you had been here, my brother would not have died. ²²[But] even now I know that whatever you ask of God, God will give you." ²³Jesus said to her, "Your brother will rise." ²⁴Martha said to him, "I know he will rise, in the resurrection on the last day." ²⁵Jesus told her, "I am the resurrection and the life; whoever believes in me, even if he dies, will live, ²⁶and everyone who lives and believes

in me will never die. Do you believe this?" [27]She said to him, "Yes, Lord. I have come to believe that you are the Messiah, the Son of God, the one who is coming into the world."

[28]When she had said this, she went and called her sister Mary secretly, saying, "The teacher is here and is asking for you." [29]As soon as she heard this, she rose quickly and went to him. [30]For Jesus had not yet come into the village, but was still where Martha had met him. [31]So when the Jews who were with her in the house comforting her saw Mary get up quickly and go out, they followed her, presuming that she was going to the tomb to weep there. [32]When Mary came to where Jesus was and saw him, she fell at his feet and said to him, "Lord, if you had been here, my brother would not have died." [33]When Jesus saw her weeping and the Jews who had come with her weeping, he became perturbed and deeply troubled, [34]and said, "Where have you laid him?" They said to him, "Sir, come and see."

[35]And Jesus wept. [36]So the Jews said, "See how he loved him." [37]But some of them said, "Could not the one who opened the eyes of the blind man have done something so that this man would not have died?"

[38]So Jesus, perturbed again, came to the tomb. It was a cave, and a stone lay across it. [39]Jesus said, "Take away the stone." Martha, the dead man's sister, said to him, "Lord, by now there will be a stench; he has been dead for four days." [40]Jesus said to her, "Did I not tell you that if you believe you will see the glory of God?" [41]So they took away the stone. And Jesus raised his eyes and said, "Father, I thank you for hearing me. [42]I know that you always hear me; but because of the crowd here I have said this, that they may believe that you sent me." [43]And when he had said this, he cried out in a loud voice, "Lazarus, come out!" [44]The dead man came out, tied hand and foot with burial bands, and his face was wrapped in a cloth. So Jesus said to them, "Untie him and let him go."

August 7

Pope St. Sixtus II and Companions; St. Cajetan

Christ's Church is one, His see is one, founded by the voice of the Lord on Peter. No other altar can be set up, no other priesthood instituted apart from that one altar and that one priesthood. Whoever gathers elsewhere, scatters.

— St. Cyprian of Carthage

☐ PROVERBS 28–31

28:1 The wicked flee though none pursue;
   but the just, like a lion, are confident.
[2]If a land is rebellious, its princes will be many;
   but with an intelligent and wise ruler there is stability.

[3]One who is poor and extorts from the lowly
   is a devastating rain that leaves no food.
[4]Those who abandon instruction praise the wicked,
   but those who keep instruction oppose them.

⁵The evil understand nothing of justice,
  but those who seek the LORD
      understand everything.
⁶Better to be poor and walk in integrity
  than rich and crooked in one's ways.
⁷Whoever heeds instruction is a wise
      son,
  but whoever joins with wastrels
      disgraces his father.
⁸Whoever amasses wealth by interest
  and overcharge
  gathers it for the one who is kind to
      the poor.
⁹Those who turn their ears from
      hearing instruction,
  even their prayer is an abomination.
¹⁰Those who mislead the upright into
  an evil way
  will themselves fall into their own
      pit,
  but the blameless will attain
      prosperity.
¹¹The rich are wise in their own eyes,
  but the poor who are intelligent see
      through them.
¹²When the just triumph, there is great
      glory;
  but when the wicked prevail, people
      hide.
¹³Those who conceal their sins do not
      prosper,
  but those who confess and forsake
      them obtain mercy.
¹⁴Happy those who always fear;
  but those who harden their hearts
      fall into evil.
¹⁵A roaring lion or a ravenous bear
  is a wicked ruler over a poor people.
¹⁶The less prudent the rulers, the more
      oppressive their deeds.
  Those who hate ill-gotten gain
      prolong their days.
¹⁷Though a person burdened with
      blood guilt is in flight even to the
      grave,
  let no one offer support.
¹⁸Whoever walks blamelessly is safe,

but one whose ways are crooked
      falls into a pit.
¹⁹Those who cultivate their land will
      have plenty of food,
  but those who engage in idle
      pursuits will have plenty of
      want.
²⁰The trustworthy will be richly
      blessed;
  but whoever hastens to be rich will
      not go unpunished.
²¹To show partiality is never good:
  for even a morsel of bread one may
      do wrong.
²²Misers hurry toward wealth,
  not knowing that want is coming
      toward them.
²³Whoever rebukes another wins more
      favor
  than one who flatters with the
      tongue.
²⁴Whoever defrauds father or mother
  and says, "It is no sin,"
  is a partner to a brigand.
²⁵The greedy person stirs up strife,
  but the one who trusts in the LORD
      will prosper.
²⁶Those who trust in themselves are
      fools,
  but those who walk in wisdom are
      safe.
²⁷Those who give to the poor have no
      lack,
  but those who avert their eyes,
      many curses.
²⁸When the wicked prevail, people
      hide;
  but at their fall the just abound.

29:1 Those stiff-necked in the face of
      reproof
  in an instant will be shattered
      beyond cure.
²When the just flourish, the people
      rejoice;
  but when the wicked rule, the
      people groan.

³Whoever loves wisdom gives joy to his
  father,
  but whoever consorts with harlots
    squanders his wealth.
⁴By justice a king builds up the land;
  but one who raises taxes tears it
    down.
⁵Those who speak flattery to their
    neighbor
  cast a net at their feet.
⁶The sin of the wicked is a trap,
  but the just run along joyfully.
⁷The just care for the cause of the poor;
  the wicked do not understand such
    care.
⁸Scoffers enflame the city,
  but the wise calm the fury.
⁹If a wise person disputes with a fool,
  there is railing and ridicule but no
    resolution.
¹⁰The bloodthirsty hate the blameless,
  but the upright seek his life.
¹¹Fools give vent to all their anger;
  but the wise, biding their time,
    control it.
¹²If rulers listen to lying words,
  their servants all become wicked.
¹³The poor and the oppressor meet:
  the LORD gives light to the eyes of
    both.
¹⁴If a king is honestly for the rights of
    the poor,
  his throne stands firm forever.
¹⁵The rod of correction gives wisdom,
  but uncontrolled youths disgrace
    their mothers.
¹⁶When the wicked increase, crime
    increases;
  but the just will behold their
    downfall.
¹⁷Discipline your children, and they
    will bring you comfort,
  and give delight to your soul.
¹⁸Without a vision the people lose
    restraint;
  but happy is the one who follows
    instruction.

¹⁹Not by words alone can servants be
    trained;
  for they understand but do not
    respond.
²⁰Do you see someone hasty in
    speech?
  There is more hope for a fool!
²¹If servants are pampered from
    childhood
  they will turn out to be stubborn.
²²The ill-tempered stir up strife,
  and the hotheaded cause many sins.
²³Haughtiness brings humiliation,
  but the humble of spirit acquire
    honor.
²⁴Partners of a thief hate themselves;
  they hear the imprecation but do
    not testify.
²⁵Fear of others becomes a snare,
  but the one who trusts in the LORD
    is safe.
²⁶Many curry favor with a ruler,
  but it is from the LORD that one
    receives justice.
²⁷An abomination to the just, the
    evildoer;
  an abomination to the wicked, one
    whose way is straight.

30:1 The words of Agur, son of Jakeh the
Massaite:

  The pronouncement of mortal man: "I
    am weary, O God;
  I am weary, O God, and I am
    exhausted.
²I am more brute than human being,
  without even human intelligence;
³Neither have I learned wisdom,
  nor have I the knowledge of the
    Holy One.
⁴Who has gone up to heaven and come
    down again—
  who has cupped the wind in the
    hollow of the hand?
Who has bound up the waters in a
    cloak—

who has established all the ends of
the earth?
What is that person's name, or the
name of his son?"

⁵Every word of God is tested;
he is a shield to those who take
refuge in him.
⁶Add nothing to his words,
lest he reprimand you, and you be
proved a liar.

⁷Two things I ask of you,
do not deny them to me before I
die:
⁸Put falsehood and lying far from me,
give me neither poverty nor riches;
provide me only with the food I
need;
⁹Lest, being full, I deny you,
saying, "Who is the LORD?"
Or, being in want, I steal,
and profane the name of my God.

¹⁰Do not criticize servants to their
master,
lest they curse you, and you have to
pay the penalty.
¹¹There are some who curse their
fathers,
and do not bless their mothers.
¹²There are some pure in their own eyes,
yet not cleansed of their filth.
¹³There are some—how haughty their
eyes!
how overbearing their glance!
¹⁴There are some—their teeth are
swords,
their teeth are knives,
Devouring the needy from the earth,
and the poor from the human race.
¹⁵The leech has two daughters:
"Give," and "Give."
Three things never get their fill,
four never say, "Enough!"
¹⁶Sheol, a barren womb,
land that never gets its fill of water,
and fire, which never says,
"Enough!"

¹⁷The eye that mocks a father,
or scorns the homage due a mother,
Will be plucked out by brook ravens;
devoured by a brood of vultures.
¹⁸Three things are too wonderful for me,
yes, four I cannot understand:
¹⁹The way of an eagle in the sky,
the way of a serpent upon a rock,
The way of a ship on the high seas,
and the way of a man with a woman.
²⁰This is the way of an adulterous
woman:
she eats, wipes her mouth,
and says, "I have done no wrong."
²¹Under three things the earth trembles,
yes, under four it cannot bear up:
²²Under a slave who becomes king,
and a fool who is glutted with food;
²³Under an unloved woman who is wed,
and a maidservant who displaces her
mistress.
²⁴Four things are among the smallest
on the earth,
and yet are exceedingly wise:
²⁵Ants—a species not strong,
yet they store up their food in the
summer;
²⁶Badgers—a species not mighty,
yet they make their home in the crags;
²⁷Locusts—they have no king,
yet they march forth in formation;
²⁸Lizards—you can catch them with
your hands,
yet they find their way into kings'
palaces.
²⁹Three things are stately in their stride,
yes, four are stately in their carriage:
³⁰The lion, mightiest of beasts,
retreats before nothing;
³¹The strutting cock, and the he-goat,
and the king at the head of his
people.
³²If you have foolishly been proud
or presumptuous—put your hand
on your mouth;
³³For as the churning of milk produces
curds,

and the pressing of the nose
produces blood,
the churning of anger produces
strife.

31:1 The words of Lemuel, king of Massa,
the instruction his mother taught him:

²What are you doing, my son!
what are you doing, son of my
womb;
what are you doing, son of my vows!
³Do not give your vigor to women,
or your strength to those who ruin
kings.
⁴It is not for kings, Lemuel,
not for kings to drink wine;
strong drink is not for princes,
⁵Lest in drinking they forget what has
been decreed,
and violate the rights of any who are
in need.
⁶Give strong drink to anyone who is
perishing,
and wine to the embittered;
⁷When they drink, they will forget
their misery,
and think no more of their troubles.
⁸Open your mouth in behalf of the
mute,
and for the rights of the destitute;
⁹Open your mouth, judge justly,
defend the needy and the poor!

¹⁰Who can find a woman of worth?
Far beyond jewels is her value.
¹¹Her husband trusts her judgment;
he does not lack income.
¹²She brings him profit, not loss,
all the days of her life.
¹³She seeks out wool and flax
and weaves with skillful hands.
¹⁴Like a merchant fleet,
she secures her provisions from afar.
¹⁵She rises while it is still night,
and distributes food to her
household,
a portion to her maidservants.

¹⁶She picks out a field and acquires it;
from her earnings she plants a
vineyard.
¹⁷She girds herself with strength;
she exerts her arms with vigor.
¹⁸She enjoys the profit from her
dealings;
her lamp is never extinguished at
night.
¹⁹She puts her hands to the distaff,
and her fingers ply the spindle.
²⁰She reaches out her hands to the poor,
and extends her arms to the needy.
²¹She is not concerned for her
household when it snows—
all her charges are doubly clothed.
²²She makes her own coverlets;
fine linen and purple are her
clothing.
²³Her husband is prominent at the city
gates
as he sits with the elders of the land.
²⁴She makes garments and sells them,
and stocks the merchants with belts.
²⁵She is clothed with strength and
dignity,
and laughs at the days to come.
²⁶She opens her mouth in wisdom;
kindly instruction is on her tongue.
²⁷She watches over the affairs of her
household,
and does not eat the bread of
idleness.
²⁸Her children rise up and call her
blessed;
her husband, too, praises her:
²⁹"Many are the women of proven
worth,
but you have excelled them all."
³⁰Charm is deceptive and beauty
fleeting;
the woman who fears the LORD is to
be praised.
³¹Acclaim her for the work of her
hands,
and let her deeds praise her at the
city gates.

☐ JOHN 11:45-57

Session of the Sanhedrin. 11:45 Now many of the Jews who had come to Mary and seen what he had done began to believe in him. ⁴⁶But some of them went to the Pharisees and told them what Jesus had done. ⁴⁷So the chief priests and the Pharisees convened the Sanhedrin and said, "What are we going to do? This man is performing many signs. ⁴⁸If we leave him alone, all will believe in him, and the Romans will come and take away both our land and our nation." ⁴⁹But one of them, Caiaphas, who was high priest that year, said to them, "You know nothing, ⁵⁰nor do you consider that it is better for you that one man should die instead of the people, so that the whole nation may not perish." ⁵¹He did not say this on his own, but since he was high priest for that year, he prophesied that Jesus was going to die for the nation, ⁵²and not only for the nation, but also to gather into one the dispersed children of God. ⁵³So from that day on they planned to kill him.

⁵⁴So Jesus no longer walked about in public among the Jews, but he left for the region near the desert, to a town called Ephraim, and there he remained with his disciples.

The Last Passover. ⁵⁵Now the Passover of the Jews was near, and many went up from the country to Jerusalem before Passover to purify themselves. ⁵⁶They looked for Jesus and said to one another as they were in the temple area, "What do you think? That he will not come to the feast?" ⁵⁷For the chief priests and the Pharisees had given orders that if anyone knew where he was, he should inform them, so that they might arrest him.

August 8

St. Dominic

A man who governs his passions is master of the world. We must either command them, or be commanded by them. It is better to be a hammer than an anvil.

— St. Dominic

☐ ECCLESIASTES 1-3

1:1 The words of David's son, Qoheleth, king in Jerusalem:

²Vanity of vanities, says Qoheleth,
  vanity of vanities! All things are
    vanity!

Vanity of Human Toil. ³What profit
  have we from all the toil
  which we toil at under the sun?

⁴One generation departs and another
    generation comes,
  but the world forever stays.
⁵The sun rises and the sun sets;
  then it presses on to the place where
    it rises.
⁶Shifting south, then north,
  back and forth shifts the wind,
    constantly shifting its course.
⁷All rivers flow to the sea,

yet never does the sea become full.
To the place where they flow,
   the rivers continue to flow.
[8]All things are wearisome,
   too wearisome for words.
The eye is not satisfied by seeing
   nor has the ear enough of hearing.

[9]What has been, that will be; what has been done, that will be done. Nothing is new under the sun! [10]Even the thing of which we say, "See, this is new!" has already existed in the ages that preceded us. [11]There is no remembrance of past generations; nor will future generations be remembered by those who come after them.

Twofold Introduction. [12]I, Qoheleth, was king over Israel in Jerusalem, [13]and I applied my mind to search and investigate in wisdom all things that are done under the sun.

A bad business God has given
   to human beings to be busied with.

[14]I have seen all things that are done under the sun, and behold, all is vanity and a chase after wind.

[15]What is crooked cannot be made
   straight,
   and you cannot count what is not
      there.

[16]Though I said to myself, "See, I have greatly increased my wisdom beyond all who were before me in Jerusalem, and my mind has broad experience of wisdom and knowledge," [17]yet when I applied my mind to know wisdom and knowledge, madness and folly, I learned that this also is a chase after wind.

[18]For in much wisdom there is much
   sorrow;
   whoever increases knowledge
      increases grief.

Study of Pleasure-seeking. 2:1 I said in my heart, "Come, now, let me try you with pleasure and the enjoyment of good things." See, this too was vanity. [2]Of laughter I said: "Mad!" and of mirth: "What good does this do?" [3]Guided by wisdom, I probed with my mind how to beguile my senses with wine and take up folly, until I should understand what is good for human beings to do under the heavens during the limited days of their lives.

[4]I undertook great works; I built myself houses and planted vineyards; [5]I made gardens and parks, and in them set out fruit trees of all sorts. [6]And I constructed for myself reservoirs to water a flourishing woodland. [7]I acquired male and female slaves, and had slaves who were born in my house. I also owned vast herds of cattle and flocks of sheep, more than all who had been before me in Jerusalem. [8]I amassed for myself silver and gold, and the treasures of kings and provinces. I provided for myself male and female singers and delights of men, many women. [9]I accumulated much more than all others before me in Jerusalem; my wisdom, too, stayed with me. [10]Nothing that my eyes desired did I deny them, nor did I deprive myself of any joy; rather, my heart rejoiced in the fruit of all my toil. This was my share for all my toil. [11]But when I turned to all the works that my hands had wrought, and to the fruit of the toil for which I had toiled so much, see! all was vanity and a chase after wind. There is no profit under the sun. [12]What about one who succeeds a king? He can do only what has already been done.

Study of Wisdom and Folly. I went on to the consideration of wisdom, madness and folly. [13]And I saw that wisdom has as much profit over folly as light has over darkness.

[14]Wise people have eyes in their heads,
   but fools walk in darkness.

Yet I knew that the same lot befalls both. [15]So I said in my heart, if the fool's lot is to befall me also, why should I be wise? Where is the profit? And in my heart I decided that this too is vanity. [16]The wise person will have no more abiding remembrance than the fool; for in days to come both will have been forgotten. How is it that the wise person dies like the fool! [17]Therefore I detested life, since for me the work that is done under the sun is bad; for all is vanity and a chase after wind.

To Others the Profits. [18]And I detested all the fruits of my toil under the sun, because I must leave them to the one who is to come after me. [19]And who knows whether that one will be wise or a fool? Yet that one will take control of all the fruits of my toil and wisdom under the sun. This also is vanity. [20]So my heart turned to despair over all the fruits of my toil under the sun. [21]For here is one who has toiled with wisdom and knowledge and skill, and that one's legacy must be left to another who has not toiled for it. This also is vanity and a great evil. [22]For what profit comes to mortals from all the toil and anxiety of heart with which they toil under the sun? [23]Every day sorrow and grief are their occupation; even at night their hearts are not at rest. This also is vanity.

[24]There is nothing better for mortals than to eat and drink and provide themselves with good things from their toil. Even this, I saw, is from the hand of God. [25]For who can eat or drink apart from God? [26]For to the one who pleases God, he gives wisdom and knowledge and joy; but to the one who displeases, God gives the task of gathering possessions for the one who pleases God. This also is vanity and a chase after wind.

No One Can Determine the Right Time To Act. 3:1 There is an appointed time for everything, and a time for every affair under the heavens.
[2]A time to give birth, and a time to die;
a time to plant, and a time to uproot the plant.

[3]A time to kill, and a time to heal;
a time to tear down, and a time to build.
[4]A time to weep, and a time to laugh;
a time to mourn, and a time to dance.
[5]A time to scatter stones, and a time to gather them;
a time to embrace, and a time to be far from embraces.
[6]A time to seek, and a time to lose;
a time to keep, and a time to cast away.
[7]A time to rend, and a time to sew;
a time to be silent, and a time to speak.
[8]A time to love, and a time to hate;
a time of war, and a time of peace.

[9]What profit have workers from their toil? [10]I have seen the business that God has given to mortals to be busied about. [11]God has made everything appropriate to its time, but has put the timeless into their hearts so they cannot find out, from beginning to end, the work which God has done. [12]I recognized that there is nothing better than to rejoice and to do well during life. [13]Moreover, that all can eat and drink and enjoy the good of all their toil—this is a gift of God. [14]I recognized that whatever God does will endure forever; there is no adding to it, or taking from it. Thus has God done that he may be revered. [15]What now is has already been; what is to be, already is: God retrieves what has gone by.

The Problem of Retribution. [16]And still under the sun in the judgment place I saw wickedness, and wickedness also in the seat of justice. [17]I said in my heart, both the just and the wicked God will judge, since a time is set for every affair and for every work. [18]I said in my heart: As for human beings, it is God's way of testing them and of showing that they are in themselves like beasts. [19]For the lot of mortals and the lot of beasts is the same lot: The one dies as well as the other. Both have the same life breath. Human beings have no advantage over beasts, but all is vanity. [20]Both go to the same place; both were made from the dust, and to the dust they both return. [21]Who knows if the life breath of mortals goes upward and the life breath of beasts goes earthward? [22]And I saw that there is nothing better for mortals than to rejoice in their work; for this is their lot. Who will let them see what is to come after them?

☐ JOHN 12:1-19

The Anointing at Bethany. 12:1 Six days before Passover Jesus came to Bethany, where Lazarus was, whom Jesus had raised from the dead. [2]They gave a dinner for him there, and Martha served, while Lazarus was one of those reclining at table with him. [3]Mary took a liter of costly perfumed oil made from genuine aromatic nard and anointed the feet of Jesus and dried them with her hair; the house was filled with the fragrance of the oil. [4]Then Judas the Iscariot, one [of] his disciples, and the one who would betray him, said, [5]"Why was this oil not sold for three hundred days' wages and given to the poor?" [6]He said this not because he cared about the poor but because he was a thief and held the money bag and used to steal the contributions. [7]So Jesus said, "Leave her alone. Let her keep this for the day of my burial. [8]You always have the poor with you, but you do not always have me."

[9][The] large crowd of the Jews found out that he was there and came, not only because of Jesus, but also to see Lazarus, whom he had raised from the dead. [10]And the chief priests plotted to kill Lazarus too, [11]because many of the Jews were turning away and believing in Jesus because of him.

The Entry into Jerusalem. [12]On the next day, when the great crowd that had come to the feast heard that Jesus was coming to Jerusalem, [13]they took palm branches and went out to meet him, and cried out:

> "Hosanna!
> Blessed is he who comes in the name of the Lord,
> [even] the king of Israel."

[14]Jesus found an ass and sat upon it, as is written:

> [15]"Fear no more, O daughter Zion;
> see, your king comes, seated upon an ass's colt."

[16]His disciples did not understand this at first, but when Jesus had been glorified they remembered that these things were written about him and that they had done this for him. [17]So the crowd that was with him when he called Lazarus from the tomb and raised him from death continued to testify. [18]This was [also] why the crowd went to meet him, because they heard that he had done this sign. [19]So the Pharisees said to one another, "You see that you are gaining nothing. Look, the whole world has gone after him."

August 9

St. Teresa Benedicta of the Cross (Edith Stein)

Whenever you seek truth, you seek God, whether or not you know it.

— St. Teresa Benedicta of the Cross

☐ ECCLESIASTES 4-9

Vanity of Toil. 4:1 Again I saw all the oppressions that take place under the sun: the tears of the victims with none to comfort them! From the hand of their oppressors comes violence, and there is none to comfort them! ²And those now dead, I declared more fortunate in death than are the living to be still alive. ³And better off than both is the yet unborn, who has not seen the wicked work that is done under the sun. ⁴Then I saw that all toil and skillful work is the rivalry of one person with another. This also is vanity and a chase after wind.

⁵"Fools fold their arms
  and consume their own flesh"—
⁶Better is one handful with tranquility
  than two with toil and a chase after
    wind!

Companions and Successors. ⁷Again I saw this vanity under the sun: ⁸those all alone with no companion, with neither child nor sibling—with no end to all their toil, and no satisfaction from riches. For whom do I toil and deprive myself of good things? This also is vanity and a bad business. ⁹Two are better than one: They get a good wage for their toil. ¹⁰If the one falls, the other will help the fallen one. But woe to the solitary person! If that one should fall, there is no other to help. ¹¹So also, if two sleep together, they keep each other warm. How can one alone keep warm? ¹²Where one alone may be overcome, two together can resist. A three-ply cord is not easily broken.

¹³Better is a poor but wise youth than an old but foolish king who no longer knows caution; ¹⁴for from a prison house he came forth to reign; despite his kingship he was born poor. ¹⁵I saw all the living, those who move about under the sun, with the second youth who will succeed him. ¹⁶There is no end to all this people, to all who were before them; yet the later generations will not have joy in him. This also is vanity and a chase after wind.

Vanity of Many Words. ¹⁷Guard your step when you go to the house of God. Draw near for obedience, rather than for the fools' offering of sacrifice; for they know not how to keep from doing evil.

5:1 Be not hasty in your utterance and let not your heart be quick to utter a promise in God's presence. God is in heaven and you are on earth; therefore let your words be few.

²As dreams come along with many cares,
  so a fool's voice along with a
    multitude of words.

³When you make a vow to God, delay not its fulfillment. For God has no pleasure in fools; fulfill what you have vowed. ⁴It is better not to make a vow than make it and not fulfill it. ⁵Let not your utterances make you guilty, and say not before his representative, "It was a mistake." Why should God be angered by your words and destroy the works of your hands? ⁶Despite many dreams, futilities, and a multitude of words, fear God!

Gain and Loss of Goods. ⁷If you see oppression of the poor, and violation of rights and justice in the realm, do not be astonished by the fact, for the high official has another higher than he watching him and above these are others higher still—. [8]But profitable for a land in such circumstances is a king concerned about cultivation.

[9]The covetous are never satisfied with money, nor lovers of wealth with their gain; so this too is vanity. [10]Where there are great riches, there are also many to devour them. Of what use are they to the owner except as a feast for the eyes alone? [11]Sleep is sweet to the laborer, whether there is little or much to eat; but the abundance of the rich allows them no sleep.

[12]This is a grievous evil which I have seen under the sun: riches hoarded by their owners to their own hurt. [13]Should the riches be lost through some misfortune, they may have offspring when they have no means. [14]As they came forth from their mother's womb, so again shall they return, naked as they came, having nothing from their toil to bring with them. [15]This too is a grievous evil, that they go just as they came. What then does it profit them to toil for the wind? [16]All their days they eat in gloom with great vexation, sickness and resentment.

[17]Here is what I see as good: It is appropriate to eat and drink and prosper from all the toil one toils at under the sun during the limited days of life God gives us; for this is our lot. [18]Those to whom God gives riches and property, and grants power to partake of them, so that they receive their lot and find joy in the fruits of their toil: This is a gift from God. [19]For they will hardly dwell on the shortness of life, because God lets them busy themselves with the joy of their heart.

Limited Worth of Enjoyment. 6:1 There is another evil I have seen under the sun, and it weighs heavily upon humankind: [2]There is one to whom God gives riches and property and honor, and who lacks nothing the heart could desire; yet God does not grant the power to partake of them, but a stranger devours them. This is vanity and a dire plague. [3]Should one have a hundred children and live many years, no matter to what great age, still if one has not the full benefit of those goods, I proclaim that the child born dead, even if left unburied, is more fortunate. [4]Though it came in vain and goes into darkness and its name is enveloped in darkness, [5]though it has not seen the sun or known anything, yet the dead child has more peace. [6]Should such a one live twice a thousand years and not enjoy those goods, do not both go to the same place?

[7]All human toil is for the mouth, yet the appetite is never satisfied. [8]What profit have the wise compared to fools, or what profit have the lowly in knowing how to conduct themselves in life? [9]"What the eyes see is better than what the desires wander after." This also is vanity and a chase after wind.

[10]Whatever is, was long ago given its name, and human nature is known; mortals cannot contend in judgment with One who is stronger. [11]For the more words, the more vanity; what profit is there for anyone? [12]For who knows what is good for mortals in life, the limited days of their vain life, spent like a shadow? Because who can tell them what will come afterward under the sun?

Critique of Sages on the Day of Adversity. 7:1 A good name is
 better than good ointment,
and the day of death than the day
 of birth.
[2]It is better to go to the house of
 mourning
than to the house of feasting,
For that is the end of every mortal,
 and the living should take it to
 heart.
[3]Sorrow is better than laughter;
 when the face is sad, the heart grows
 wise.
[4]The heart of the wise is in the house of
 mourning,
 but the heart of fools is in the house
 of merriment.

⁵It is better to listen to the rebuke of
the wise
than to listen to the song of fools;
⁶For as the crackling of thorns under
a pot,
so is the fool's laughter.
This also is vanity.
⁷Extortion can make a fool out of the
wise,
and a bribe corrupts the heart.
⁸Better is the end of a thing than its
beginning;
better is a patient spirit than a lofty
one.
⁹Do not let anger upset your spirit,
for anger lodges in the bosom of a
fool.

¹⁰Do not say: How is it that former times were better than these? For it is not out of wisdom that you ask about this.

¹¹Wisdom is as good as an inheritance
and profitable to those who see the
sun.

¹²For the protection of wisdom is as the protection of money; and knowledge is profitable because wisdom gives life to those who possess it.

¹³Consider the work of God. Who can make straight what God has made crooked? ¹⁴On a good day enjoy good things, and on an evil day consider: Both the one and the other God has made, so that no one may find the least fault with him.

Critique of Sages on Justice and Wickedness. ¹⁵I have seen all manner of things in my vain days: the just perishing in their justice, and the wicked living long in their wickedness. ¹⁶"Be not just to excess, and be not overwise. Why work your own ruin? ¹⁷Be not wicked to excess, and be not foolish. Why should you die before your time?" ¹⁸It is good to hold to this rule, and not to let that one go; but the one who fears God will succeed with both.

¹⁹Wisdom is a better defense for the wise than ten princes in the city, ²⁰yet there is no one on earth so just as to do good and never sin. ²¹Do not give your heart to every word that is spoken; you may hear your servant cursing you, ²²for your heart knows that you have many times cursed others.

²³All these things I probed in wisdom. I said, "I will acquire wisdom"; but it was far beyond me. ²⁴What exists is far-reaching; it is deep, very deep: Who can find it out? ²⁵I turned my heart toward knowledge; I sought and pursued wisdom and its design, and I recognized that wickedness is foolishness and folly is madness.

Critique of Advice on Women. ²⁶More bitter than death I find the woman who is a hunter's trap, whose heart is a snare, whose hands are prison bonds. The one who pleases God will be delivered from her, but the one who displeases will be entrapped by her. ²⁷See, this have I found, says Qoheleth, adding one to one to find the sum. ²⁸What my soul still seeks and has yet to find is this: "One man out of a thousand have I found, but a woman among them all I have not found." ²⁹But this alone I have found: God made humankind honest, but they have pursued many designs.

Critique of Advice To Heed Authority. 8:1 Who is like the
wise person,
and who knows the explanation of
things?
Wisdom illumines the face
and transforms a grim countenance.

²Observe the command of the king, in view of your oath to God. ³Be not hasty to withdraw from the king; do not persist in an unpleasant situation, for he does whatever he pleases. ⁴His word is sovereign, and who can say to him, "What are you doing?"

⁵"Whoever observes a command knows no harm, and the wise heart knows times and judgments." ⁶Yes, there is a time and

a judgment for everything. But it is a great evil for mortals [7]that they are ignorant of what is to come; for who will make known to them how it will be? [8]No one is master of the breath of life so as to retain it, and none has mastery of the day of death. There is no exemption in wartime, nor does wickedness deliver those who practice it. [9]All these things I saw and I applied my heart to every work that is done under the sun, while one person tyrannizes over another for harm.

The Problem of Retribution. [10]Meanwhile I saw the wicked buried. They would come and go from the holy place. But those were forgotten in the city who had acted justly. This also is vanity. [11]Because the sentence against an evil deed is not promptly executed, the human heart is filled with the desire to commit evil— [12]because the sinner does evil a hundred times and survives. Though indeed I know that it shall be well with those who fear God, for their reverence toward him; [13]and that it shall not be well with the wicked, who shall not prolong their shadowy days, for their lack of reverence toward God.

[14]This is a vanity that occurs on earth: There are those who are just but are treated as though they had done evil, and those who are wicked but are treated as though they had done justly. This, too, I say is vanity. [15]Therefore I praised joy, because there is nothing better for mortals under the sun than to eat and to drink and to be joyful; this will accompany them in their toil through the limited days of life God gives them under the sun.

[16]I applied my heart to know wisdom and to see the business that is done on earth, though neither by day nor by night do one's eyes see sleep, [17]and I saw all the work of God: No mortal can find out the work that is done under the sun. However much mortals may toil in searching, no one finds it out; and even if the wise claim to know, they are unable to find it out.

9:1 All this I have kept in my heart and all this I examined: The just, the wise, and their deeds are in the hand of God. Love from hatred mortals cannot tell; both are before them. [2]Everything is the same for everybody: the same lot for the just and the wicked, for the good, for the clean and the unclean, for the one who offers sacrifice and the one who does not. As it is for the good, so it is for the sinner; as it is for the one who takes an oath, so it is for the one who fears an oath. [3]Among all the things that are done under the sun, this is the worst, that there is one lot for all. Hence the hearts of human beings are filled with evil, and madness is in their hearts during life; and afterward—to the dead!

[4]For whoever is chosen among all the living has hope: "A live dog is better off than a dead lion." [5]For the living know that they are to die, but the dead no longer know anything. There is no further recompense for them, because all memory of them is lost. [6]For them, love and hatred and rivalry have long since perished. Never again will they have part in anything that is done under the sun.

[7]Go, eat your bread with joy and drink your wine with a merry heart, because it is now that God favors your works. [8]At all times let your garments be white, and spare not the perfume for your head. [9]Enjoy life with the wife you love, all the days of the vain life granted you under the sun. This is your lot in life, for the toil of your labors under the sun. [10]Anything you can turn your hand to, do with what power you have; for there will be no work, no planning, no knowledge, no wisdom in Sheol where you are going.

The Time of Misfortune Is Not Known. [11]Again I saw under the sun that the race is not won by the swift, nor the battle by the valiant, nor a livelihood by the wise, nor riches by the shrewd, nor favor by the experts; for a time of misfortune comes to all alike. [12]Human beings no more know their own time than fish taken in the fatal net or birds trapped in the snare; like these, mortals are caught when an evil time suddenly falls upon them.

The Uncertain Future and the Sages. [13]On the other hand I saw this wise deed under the sun, which I thought magnificent. [14]Against a small city with few inhabitants advanced a mighty king, who surrounded it and threw up great siegeworks about it. [15]But in the city lived a man who, though poor, was wise, and he

☐ JOHN 12:20-50

The Coming of Jesus' Hour. 12:20 Now there were some Greeks among those who had come up to worship at the feast. [21]They came to Philip, who was from Bethsaida in Galilee, and asked him, "Sir, we would like to see Jesus." [22]Philip went and told Andrew; then Andrew and Philip went and told Jesus. [23]Jesus answered them, "The hour has come for the Son of Man to be glorified. [24]Amen, amen, I say to you, unless a grain of wheat falls to the ground and dies, it remains just a grain of wheat; but if it dies, it produces much fruit. [25]Whoever loves his life loses it, and whoever hates his life in this world will preserve it for eternal life. [26]Whoever serves me must follow me, and where I am, there also will my servant be. The Father will honor whoever serves me.

[27]"I am troubled now. Yet what should I say? 'Father, save me from this hour'? But it was for this purpose that I came to this hour. [28]Father, glorify your name." Then a voice came from heaven, "I have glorified it and will glorify it again." [29]The crowd there heard it and said it was thunder; but others said, "An angel has spoken to him." [30]Jesus answered and said, "This voice did not come for my sake but for yours. [31]Now is the time of judgment on this world; now the ruler of this world will be driven out.

delivered it through his wisdom. Yet no one remembered this poor man. [16]Though I had said, "Wisdom is better than force," yet the wisdom of the poor man is despised and his words go unheeded.

[17]The quiet words of the wise are better heeded
　　than the shout of a ruler of fools.
[18]Wisdom is better than weapons of war,
　　but one bungler destroys much good.

[32]And when I am lifted up from the earth, I will draw everyone to myself." [33]He said this indicating the kind of death he would die. [34]So the crowd answered him, "We have heard from the law that the Messiah remains forever. Then how can you say that the Son of Man must be lifted up? Who is this Son of Man?" [35]Jesus said to them, "The light will be among you only a little while. Walk while you have the light, so that darkness may not overcome you. Whoever walks in the dark does not know where he is going. [36]While you have the light, believe in the light, so that you may become children of the light."

Unbelief and Belief among the Jews. After he had said this, Jesus left and hid from them. [37]Although he had performed so many signs in their presence they did not believe in him, [38]in order that the word which Isaiah the prophet spoke might be fulfilled:

"Lord, who has believed our preaching,
　　to whom has the might of the Lord been revealed?"

[39]For this reason they could not believe, because again Isaiah said:

[40]"He blinded their eyes
　　and hardened their heart,

so that they might not see with their
eyes
and understand with their heart and
be converted,
and I would heal them."

[41]Isaiah said this because he saw his glory and spoke about him. [42]Nevertheless, many, even among the authorities, believed in him, but because of the Pharisees they did not acknowledge it openly in order not to be expelled from the synagogue. [43]For they preferred human praise to the glory of God.

Recapitulation. [44]Jesus cried out and said, "Whoever believes in me believes not only in me but also in the one who sent me, [45]and whoever sees me sees the one who sent me. [46]I came into the world as light, so that everyone who believes in me might not remain in darkness. [47]And if anyone hears my words and does not observe them, I do not condemn him, for I did not come to condemn the world but to save the world. [48]Whoever rejects me and does not accept my words has something to judge him: the word that I spoke, it will condemn him on the last day, [49]because I did not speak on my own, but the Father who sent me commanded me what to say and speak. [50]And I know that his commandment is eternal life. So what I say, I say as the Father told me."

August 10

St. Lawrence

If you should ask me what are the ways of God, I would tell you that the first is humility, the second is humility, and the third is still humility. Not that there are no other precepts to give, but if humility does not precede all that we do, our efforts are fruitless.

— ST. AUGUSTINE OF HIPPO

☐ ECCLESIASTES 10-12

10:1 Dead flies corrupt and spoil the
perfumer's oil;
more weighty than wisdom or
wealth is a little folly!
[2]The wise heart turns to the right;
the foolish heart to the left.

[3]Even when walking in the street the fool, lacking understanding, calls everyone a fool.

[4]Should the anger of a ruler burst upon you, do not yield your place; for calmness abates great offenses.

[5]I have seen under the sun another evil, like a mistake that proceeds from a tyrant: [6]a fool put in high position, while the great and the rich sit in lowly places. [7]I have seen slaves on horseback, while princes went on foot like slaves.

[8]Whoever digs a pit may fall into it,
and whoever breaks through a wall,
a snake may bite.
[9]Whoever quarries stones may be hurt
by them,
and whoever chops wood is in
danger from it.

[10]If the ax becomes dull, and the blade is not sharpened, then effort must be increased. But the advantage of wisdom is success.

[11]If the snake bites before it is charmed,
then there is no advantage in a
charmer.
[12]Words from the mouth of the wise
win favor,
but the lips of fools consume them.
[13]The beginning of their words is folly,
and the end of their talk is utter
madness;
[14]yet fools multiply words.
No one knows what is to come,
for who can tell anyone what will be?
[15]The toil of fools wearies them,
so they do not know even the way
to town.

No One Knows What Evil Will Come.
[16]Woe to you, O land,
whose king is a youth,
and whose princes feast in the
morning!
[17]Happy are you, O land, whose king is
of noble birth,
and whose princes dine at the right
time—
for vigor and not in drinking bouts.
[18]Because of laziness, the rafters sag;
when hands are slack, the house leaks.
[19]A feast is made for merriment
and wine gives joy to the living,
but money answers for everything.
[20]Even in your thoughts do not curse
the king,
nor in the privacy of your bedroom
curse the rich;
For the birds of the air may carry your
voice,
a winged creature may tell what you
say.

[11:1] Send forth your bread upon the
face of the waters;
after a long time you may find it
again.
[2]Make seven, or even eight portions;
you know not what misfortune may
come upon the earth.

No One Knows What Good Will Come.
[3]When the clouds are full,
they pour out rain upon the earth.
Whether a tree falls to the south or to
the north,
wherever it falls, there shall it lie.
[4]One who pays heed to the wind will
never sow,
and one who watches the clouds
will never reap.
[5]Just as you do not know how the life
breath
enters the human frame in the
mother's womb,
So you do not know the work of God,
who is working in everything.
[6]In the morning sow your seed,
and at evening do not let your hand
be idle:
For you do not know which of the two
will be successful,
or whether both alike will turn out
well.

Poem on Youth and Old Age.
[7]Light is sweet! and it is pleasant for the eyes to see the sun. [8]However many years mortals may live, let them, as they enjoy them all, remember that the days of darkness will be many. All that is to come is vanity.

[9]Rejoice, O youth, while you are young
and let your heart be glad in the
days of your youth.
Follow the ways of your heart,
the vision of your eyes;
Yet understand regarding all this
that God will bring you to
judgment.
[10]Banish misery from your heart
and remove pain from your body,
for youth and black hair are fleeting.

[12:1] Remember your Creator in the
days of your youth,
before the evil days come
And the years approach of which you
will say,

"I have no pleasure in them";
[2]Before the sun is darkened
and the light and the moon and the
stars
and the clouds return after the rain;
[3]When the guardians of the house
tremble,
and the strong men are bent;
When the women who grind are idle
because they are few,
and those who look through the
windows grow blind;
[4]When the doors to the street are shut,
and the sound of the mill is low;
When one rises at the call of a bird,
and all the daughters of song are
quiet;
[5]When one is afraid of heights,
and perils in the street;
When the almond tree blooms,
and the locust grows sluggish
and the caper berry is without
effect,
Because mortals go to their lasting
home,
and mourners go about the streets;
[6]Before the silver cord is snapped

and the golden bowl is broken,
And the pitcher is shattered at the spring,
and the pulley is broken at the well,
[7]And the dust returns to the earth as it
once was,
and the life breath returns to God
who gave it.
[8]Vanity of vanities, says Qoheleth,
all things are vanity!

Epilogue. [9]Besides being wise, Qoheleth taught the people knowledge, and weighed, scrutinized and arranged many proverbs. [10]Qoheleth sought to find appropriate sayings, and to write down true sayings with precision. [11]The sayings of the wise are like goads; like fixed spikes are the collected sayings given by one shepherd. [12]As to more than these, my son, beware. Of the making of many books there is no end, and in much study there is weariness for the flesh.

[13]The last word, when all is heard: Fear God and keep his commandments, for this concerns all humankind; [14]because God will bring to judgment every work, with all its hidden qualities, whether good or bad.

☐ JOHN 13:1-17

The Washing of the Disciples' Feet. 13:1 Before the feast of Passover, Jesus knew that his hour had come to pass from this world to the Father. He loved his own in the world and he loved them to the end. [2]The devil had already induced Judas, son of Simon the Iscariot, to hand him over. So, during supper, [3]fully aware that the Father had put everything into his power and that he had come from God and was returning to God, [4]he rose from supper and took off his outer garments. He took a towel and tied it around his waist. [5]Then he poured water into a basin and began to wash the disciples' feet and dry them with the towel around his waist. [6]He came

to Simon Peter, who said to him, "Master, are you going to wash my feet?" [7]Jesus answered and said to him, "What I am doing, you do not understand now, but you will understand later." [8]Peter said to him, "You will never wash my feet." Jesus answered him, "Unless I wash you, you will have no inheritance with me." [9]Simon Peter said to him, "Master, then not only my feet, but my hands and head as well." [10]Jesus said to him, "Whoever has bathed has no need except to have his feet washed, for he is clean all over; so you are clean, but not all." [11]For he knew who would betray him; for this reason, he said, "Not all of you are clean."

[12]So when he had washed their feet [and] put his garments back on and reclined at table again, he said to them, "Do you realize what I have done for you? [13]You call me 'teacher' and 'master,' and rightly so, for indeed I am. [14]If I, therefore, the master and teacher, have washed your feet, you ought to wash one another's feet. [15]I have given you a model to follow, so that as I have done for you, you should also do. [16]Amen, amen, I say to you, no slave is greater than his master nor any messenger greater than the one who sent him. [17]If you understand this, blessed are you if you do it."

August 11

St. Clare of Assisi

Our body is not made of iron. Our strength is not that of stone.
Live and hope in the Lord, and let your service be reasonable.

— St. Clare of Assisi

☐ SONG OF SONGS 1–4

1:1 The Song of Songs, which is Solomon's.

The Woman Speaks of Her Lover.
    [2]Let him kiss me with kisses of
      his mouth,
  for your love is better than wine,
    [3]better than the fragrance of your
      perfumes.
Your name is a flowing perfume—
therefore young women love you.
    [4]Draw me after you! Let us run!
  The king has brought me to his bed
    chambers.
Let us exult and rejoice in you;
    let us celebrate your love: it is
      beyond wine!
Rightly do they love you!

Love's Boast. [5]I am black and
  beautiful,
  Daughters of Jerusalem—
Like the tents of Qedar,
  like the curtains of Solomon.
  [6]Do not stare at me because I am so
    black,
  because the sun has burned me.
The sons of my mother were angry
  with me;
  they charged me with the care of the
    vineyards:

my own vineyard I did not take care
  of.

Love's Inquiry. [7]Tell me, you whom
  my soul loves,
  where you shepherd, where you give
    rest at midday.
Why should I be like one wandering
  after the flocks of your companions?
[8]If you do not know,
  most beautiful among women,
Follow the tracks of the flock
  and pasture your lambs
  near the shepherds' tents.

Love's Vision. [9]To a mare among
  Pharaoh's chariotry
I compare you, my friend:
[10]Your cheeks lovely in pendants,
  your neck in jewels.
[11]We will make pendants of gold for you,
  and ornaments of silver.

How Near Is Love! [12]While the king
  was upon his couch,
  my spikenard gave forth its fragrance.
[13]My lover is to me a sachet of myrrh;
  between my breasts he lies.
[14]My lover is to me a cluster of henna
  from the vineyards of En-gedi.

¹⁵How beautiful you are, my friend,
  how beautiful! your eyes are doves!
¹⁶How beautiful you are, my lover—
  handsome indeed!
Verdant indeed is our couch;
  ¹⁷the beams of our house are cedars,
  our rafters, cypresses.

2:1 I am a flower of Sharon,
  a lily of the valleys.
²Like a lily among thorns,
  so is my friend among women.
³Like an apple tree among the trees of
    the woods,
  so is my lover among men.
In his shadow I delight to sit,
  and his fruit is sweet to my taste.
⁴He brought me to the banquet hall
  and his glance at me signaled love.
⁵Strengthen me with raisin cakes,
  refresh me with apples,
  for I am sick with love.
⁶His left hand is under my head
  and his right arm embraces me.
⁷I adjure you, Daughters of Jerusalem,
  by the gazelles and the does of the
    field,
Do not awaken, or stir up love
  until it is ready.

Her Lover's Visit Remembered. ⁸The
    sound of my lover! here he comes
  springing across the mountains,
  leaping across the hills.
⁹My lover is like a gazelle
  or a young stag.
See! He is standing behind our wall,
  gazing through the windows,
  peering through the lattices.
¹⁰My lover speaks and says to me,
  "Arise, my friend, my beautiful one,
    and come!
¹¹For see, the winter is past,
  the rains are over and gone.
¹²The flowers appear on the earth,
  the time of pruning the vines has
    come,

and the song of the turtledove is
  heard in our land.
¹³The fig tree puts forth its figs,
  and the vines, in bloom, give forth
    fragrance.
Arise, my friend, my beautiful one,
  and come!
¹⁴My dove in the clefts of the rock,
  in the secret recesses of the cliff,
Let me see your face,
  let me hear your voice,
For your voice is sweet,
  and your face is lovely."
¹⁵Catch us the foxes, the little foxes
  that damage the vineyards; for our
    vineyards are in bloom!
¹⁶My lover belongs to me and I to him;
  he feeds among the lilies.
¹⁷Until the day grows cool and the
    shadows flee,
  roam, my lover,
Like a gazelle or a young stag
  upon the rugged mountains.

Loss and Discovery. 3:1 On my bed at
    night I sought him
  whom my soul loves—
I sought him but I did not find him.
²"Let me rise then and go about the city,
  through the streets and squares;
Let me seek him whom my soul loves."
  I sought him but I did not find him.
³The watchmen found me,
  as they made their rounds in the city:
  "Him whom my soul loves—have
    you seen him?"
⁴Hardly had I left them
  when I found him whom my soul
    loves.
I held him and would not let him go
  until I had brought him to my
    mother's house,
  to the chamber of her who
    conceived me.
⁵I adjure you, Daughters of Jerusalem,
  by the gazelles and the does of the
    field,

Do not awaken or stir up love
  until it is ready.

Solomon's Wedding Procession.
    [6]Who is this coming up from the
      desert,
  like columns of smoke
Perfumed with myrrh and frankincense,
  with all kinds of exotic powders?
[7]See! it is the litter of Solomon;
  sixty valiant men surround it,
  of the valiant men of Israel:
[8]All of them expert with the sword,
  skilled in battle,
Each with his sword at his side
  against the terrors of the night.
[9]King Solomon made himself an
    enclosed litter
  of wood from Lebanon.
[10]He made its columns of silver,
  its roof of gold,
Its seat of purple cloth,
  its interior lovingly fitted.
Daughters of Jerusalem, [11]go out
  and look upon King Solomon
In the crown with which his mother
    has crowned him
  on the day of his marriage,
  on the day of the joy of his heart.

The Beauty of the Woman. 4:1 How
    beautiful you are, my friend,
  how beautiful you are!
Your eyes are doves
  behind your veil.
Your hair is like a flock of goats
  streaming down Mount Gilead.
[2]Your teeth are like a flock of ewes to
    be shorn,
  that come up from the washing,
All of them big with twins,
  none of them barren.
[3]Like a scarlet strand, your lips,
  and your mouth—lovely!
Like pomegranate halves, your cheeks
  behind your veil.
[4]Like a tower of David, your neck,

built in courses,
A thousand shields hanging upon it,
  all the armor of warriors.
[5]Your breasts are like two fawns,
  twins of a gazelle
  feeding among the lilies.
[6]Until the day grows cool
  and the shadows flee,
  I shall go to the mountain of myrrh,
  to the hill of frankincense.
[7]You are beautiful in every way, my friend,
  there is no flaw in you!
[8]With me from Lebanon, my bride!
  With me from Lebanon, come!
Descend from the peak of Amana,
  from the peak of Senir and Hermon,
From the lairs of lions,
  from the leopards' heights.
[9]You have ravished my heart, my sister,
    my bride;
  you have ravished my heart with
      one glance of your eyes,
  with one bead of your necklace.
[10]How beautiful is your love,
  my sister, my bride,
How much better is your love than wine,
  and the fragrance of your perfumes
      than any spice!
[11]Your lips drip honey, my bride,
  honey and milk are under your tongue;
And the fragrance of your garments
  is like the fragrance of Lebanon.

The Lover's Garden. [12]A garden
    enclosed, my sister, my bride,
  a garden enclosed, a fountain sealed!
[13]Your branches are a grove of
    pomegranates,
  with fruits of choicest yield:
Henna with spikenard,
[14]spikenard and saffron,
Sweet cane and cinnamon,
  with all kinds of frankincense;
Myrrh and aloes,
  with all the finest spices;
[15]A garden fountain, a well of living
    water,

streams flowing from Lebanon.
¹⁶Awake, north wind!
Come, south wind!
Blow upon my garden

that its perfumes may spread abroad.
Let my lover come to his garden
and eat its fruits of choicest yield.

☐ JOHN 13:18-38

13:18 "I am not speaking of all of you. I know those whom I have chosen. But so that the scripture might be fulfilled, 'The one who ate my food has raised his heel against me.' ¹⁹From now on I am telling you before it happens, so that when it happens you may believe that I AM. ²⁰Amen, amen, I say to you, whoever receives the one I send receives me, and whoever receives me receives the one who sent me."

Announcement of Judas's Betrayal. ²¹When he had said this, Jesus was deeply troubled and testified, "Amen, amen, I say to you, one of you will betray me." ²²The disciples looked at one another, at a loss as to whom he meant. ²³One of his disciples, the one whom Jesus loved, was reclining at Jesus' side. ²⁴So Simon Peter nodded to him to find out whom he meant. ²⁵He leaned back against Jesus' chest and said to him, "Master, who is it?" ²⁶Jesus answered, "It is the one to whom I hand the morsel after I have dipped it." So he dipped the morsel and [took it and] handed it to Judas, son of Simon the Iscariot. ²⁷After he took the morsel, Satan entered him. So Jesus said to him, "What you are going to do, do quickly." ²⁸[Now] none of those reclining at table realized why he said this to him.

²⁹Some thought that since Judas kept the money bag, Jesus had told him, "Buy what we need for the feast," or to give something to the poor. ³⁰So he took the morsel and left at once. And it was night.

The New Commandment. ³¹When he had left, Jesus said, "Now is the Son of Man glorified, and God is glorified in him. ³²[If God is glorified in him,] God will also glorify him in himself, and he will glorify him at once. ³³My children, I will be with you only a little while longer. You will look for me, and as I told the Jews, 'Where I go you cannot come,' so now I say it to you. ³⁴I give you a new commandment: love one another. As I have loved you, so you also should love one another. ³⁵This is how all will know that you are my disciples, if you have love for one another."

Peter's Denial Predicted. ³⁶Simon Peter said to him, "Master, where are you going?" Jesus answered [him], "Where I am going, you cannot follow me now, though you will follow later." ³⁷Peter said to him, "Master, why can't I follow you now? I will lay down my life for you." ³⁸Jesus answered, "Will you lay down your life for me? Amen, amen, I say to you, the cock will not crow before you deny me three times."

August 12

Holy Spirit, Spirit of truth, You are the Reward of the saints, the Comforter of souls, Light in the darkness, Riches to the poor, Treasure to lovers, Food for the hungry, Comfort to those who are wandering. To sum up, You are the One in whom all treasures are contained.

— St. Mary Magdalene de' Pazzi

☐ SONG OF SONGS 5–8

5:1 I have come to my garden, my
    sister, my bride;
    I gather my myrrh with my spices,
I eat my honeycomb with my honey,
I drink my wine with my milk.
Eat, friends; drink!
    Drink deeply, lovers!

A Fruitless Search. ²I was sleeping, but
    my heart was awake.
The sound of my lover knocking!
"Open to me, my sister, my friend,
    my dove, my perfect one!
For my head is wet with dew,
    my hair, with the moisture of the
        night."
³I have taken off my robe,
    am I then to put it on?
I have bathed my feet,
    am I then to soil them?
⁴My lover put his hand in through the
    opening:
    my innermost being trembled
        because of him.
⁵I rose to open for my lover,
    my hands dripping myrrh:
My fingers, flowing myrrh
    upon the handles of the lock.
⁶I opened for my lover—
    but my lover had turned and gone!
At his leaving, my soul sank.
I sought him, but I did not find him;
    I called out after him, but he did
        not answer me.
⁷The watchmen found me,
    as they made their rounds in the city;

They beat me, they wounded me,
    they tore off my mantle,
    the watchmen of the walls.
⁸I adjure you, Daughters of Jerusalem,
    if you find my lover
What shall you tell him?
    that I am sick with love.

The Lost Lover Described. ⁹How does
    your lover differ from any other
        lover,
    most beautiful among women?
How does your lover differ from any
        other,
    that you adjure us so?
¹⁰My lover is radiant and ruddy;
    outstanding among thousands.
¹¹His head is gold, pure gold,
    his hair like palm fronds,
    as black as a raven.
¹²His eyes are like doves
    beside streams of water,
Bathing in milk,
    sitting by brimming pools.
¹³His cheeks are like beds of spices
    yielding aromatic scents;
his lips are lilies
    that drip flowing myrrh.
¹⁴His arms are rods of gold
    adorned with gems;
His loins, a work of ivory
    covered with sapphires.
¹⁵His legs, pillars of alabaster,
    resting on golden pedestals.
His appearance, like the Lebanon,
    imposing as the cedars.

[16]His mouth is sweetness itself;
  he is delightful in every way.
Such is my lover, and such my friend,
  Daughters of Jerusalem!

The Lost Lover Found. 6:1 Where has
    your lover gone,
  most beautiful among women?
Where has your lover withdrawn
  that we may seek him with you?
[2]My lover has come down to his garden,
  to the beds of spices,
To feed in the gardens
  and to gather lilies.
[3]I belong to my lover, and my lover
    belongs to me;
  he feeds among the lilies.

The Beauty of the Woman. [4]Beautiful
  as Tirzah are you, my friend;
  fair as Jerusalem,
  fearsome as celestial visions!
[5]Turn your eyes away from me,
  for they stir me up.
Your hair is like a flock of goats
  streaming down from Gilead.
[6]Your teeth are like a flock of ewes
  that come up from the washing,
All of them big with twins,
  none of them barren.
[7]Like pomegranate halves,
  your cheeks behind your veil.
[8]Sixty are the queens, eighty the
    concubines,
  and young women without number—
[9]One alone is my dove, my perfect one,
  her mother's special one,
  favorite of the one who bore her.
Daughters see her and call her happy,
  queens and concubines, and they
    praise her:
[10]"Who is this that comes forth like the
    dawn,
  beautiful as the white moon, pure as
    the blazing sun,
  fearsome as celestial visions?"

Love's Meeting. [11]To the walnut grove
    I went down,
  to see the young growth of the valley;
To see if the vines were in bloom,
  if the pomegranates had blossomed.
[12]Before I knew it, my desire had made
    me
  the blessed one of the prince's people.

The Beauty of the Beloved. 7:1 Turn,
    turn, O Shulammite!
  turn, turn that we may gaze upon you!
How can you gaze upon the Shulammite
  as at the dance of the two camps?
[2]How beautiful are your feet in sandals,
  O noble daughter!
Your curving thighs like jewels,
  the product of skilled hands.
[3]Your valley, a round bowl
  that should never lack mixed wine.
Your belly, a mound of wheat,
  encircled with lilies.
[4]Your breasts are like two fawns,
  twins of a gazelle.
[5]Your neck like a tower of ivory;
  your eyes, pools in Heshbon
  by the gate of Bath-rabbim.
Your nose like the tower of Lebanon
  that looks toward Damascus.
[6]Your head rises upon you like Carmel;
  your hair is like purple;
  a king is caught in its locks.

Love's Desires. [7]How beautiful you
    are, how fair,
  my love, daughter of delights!
[8]Your very form resembles a date-palm,
  and your breasts, clusters.
[9]I thought, "Let me climb the date-palm!
  Let me take hold of its branches!
Let your breasts be like clusters of the
    vine
  and the fragrance of your breath like
    apples,
[10]And your mouth like the best wine—
  that flows down smoothly for my
    lover,

gliding over my lips and teeth.
¹¹I belong to my lover,
and his yearning is for me.
¹²Come, my lover! Let us go out to the fields,
let us pass the night among the henna.
¹³Let us go early to the vineyards, and see if the vines are in bloom,
If the buds have opened,
if the pomegranates have blossomed;
There will I give you my love.
¹⁴The mandrakes give forth fragrance,
and over our doors are all choice fruits;
Fruits both fresh and dried, my lover,
have I kept in store for you.

8:1 Would that you were a brother to me,
nursed at my mother's breasts!
If I met you out of doors, I would kiss you
and none would despise me.
²I would lead you, bring you to my mother's house,
where you would teach me,
Where I would give you to drink
spiced wine, my pomegranate juice.
³His left hand is under my head,
and his right arm embraces me.
⁴I adjure you, Daughters of Jerusalem,
do not awaken or stir up love
until it is ready!

The Return from the Desert. ⁵Who is this coming up from the desert,
leaning upon her lover?
Beneath the apple tree I awakened you;
there your mother conceived you;
there she who bore you conceived.

True Love. ⁶Set me as a seal upon your heart,

as a seal upon your arm;
For Love is strong as Death,
longing is fierce as Sheol.
Its arrows are arrows of fire,
flames of the divine.
⁷Deep waters cannot quench love,
nor rivers sweep it away.
Were one to offer all the wealth of his house for love,
he would be utterly despised.

An Answer to the Brothers. ⁸"We have a little sister;
she has no breasts as yet.
What shall we do for our sister
on the day she is spoken for?
⁹If she is a wall,
we will build upon her a silver turret;
But if she is a door,
we will board her up with cedar planks."
¹⁰I am a wall,
and my breasts are like towers.
I became in his eyes
as one who brings peace.

A Boast. ¹¹Solomon had a vineyard at Baal-hamon;
he gave over the vineyard to caretakers.
For its fruit one would have to pay
a thousand silver pieces.
¹²My vineyard is at my own disposal;
the thousand pieces are for you, Solomon,
and two hundred for the caretakers of its fruit.

The Lovers' Yearnings. ¹³You who dwell in the gardens,
my companions are listening for your voice—
let me hear it!
¹⁴Swiftly, my lover,
be like a gazelle or a young stag
upon the mountains of spices.

☐ JOHN 14:1-21

Last Supper Discourses. 14:1 "Do not let your hearts be troubled. You have faith in God; have faith also in me. [2]In my Father's house there are many dwelling places. If there were not, would I have told you that I am going to prepare a place for you? [3]And if I go and prepare a place for you, I will come back again and take you to myself, so that where I am you also may be. [4]Where [I] am going you know the way." [5]Thomas said to him, "Master, we do not know where you are going; how can we know the way?" [6]Jesus said to him, "I am the way and the truth and the life. No one comes to the Father except through me. [7]If you know me, then you will also know my Father. From now on you do know him and have seen him." [8]Philip said to him, "Master, show us the Father, and that will be enough for us." [9]Jesus said to him, "Have I been with you for so long a time and you still do not know me, Philip? Whoever has seen me has seen the Father. How can you say, 'Show us the Father'? [10]Do you not believe that I am in the Father and the Father is in me? The words that I speak to you I do not speak on my own. The Father who dwells in me is doing his works. [11]Believe me that I am in the Father and the Father is in me, or else, believe because of the works themselves. [12]Amen, amen, I say to you, whoever believes in me will do the works that I do, and will do greater ones than these, because I am going to the Father. [13]And whatever you ask in my name, I will do, so that the Father may be glorified in the Son. [14]If you ask anything of me in my name, I will do it.

The Advocate. [15]"If you love me, you will keep my commandments. [16]And I will ask the Father, and he will give you another Advocate to be with you always, [17]the Spirit of truth, which the world cannot accept, because it neither sees nor knows it. But you know it, because it remains with you, and will be in you. [18]I will not leave you orphans; I will come to you. [19]In a little while the world will no longer see me, but you will see me, because I live and you will live. [20]On that day you will realize that I am in my Father and you are in me and I in you. [21]Whoever has my commandments and observes them is the one who loves me. And whoever loves me will be loved by my Father, and I will love him and reveal myself to him."

August 13

Pope St. Pontian and St. Hippolytus;
St. Maximus the Confessor

To harbor no envy, no anger, no resentment against an offender is still not to have charity for him. It is possible, without any charity, to avoid rendering evil for evil. But to render, spontaneously, good for evil — that is what belongs to a perfect spiritual love.

— St. Maximus the Confessor

☐ WISDOM 1–4:19

Exhortation to Righteousness, the Key to Life. 1:1 Love righteousness,
you who judge the earth;
think of the Lord in goodness,
and seek him in integrity of heart;
²Because he is found by those who do not test him,
and manifests himself to those who do not disbelieve him.
³For perverse counsels separate people from God,
and his power, put to the proof, rebukes the foolhardy;
⁴Because into a soul that plots evil wisdom does not enter,
nor does she dwell in a body under debt of sin.
⁵For the holy spirit of discipline flees deceit
and withdraws from senseless counsels
and is rebuked when unrighteousness occurs.

⁶For wisdom is a kindly spirit,
yet she does not acquit blasphemous lips;
Because God is the witness of the inmost self
and the sure observer of the heart
and the listener to the tongue.
⁷For the spirit of the Lord fills the world,
is all-embracing, and knows whatever is said.

⁸Therefore those who utter wicked things will not go unnoticed,
nor will chastising condemnation pass them by.
⁹For the devices of the wicked shall be scrutinized,
and the sound of their words shall reach the Lord,
for the chastisement of their transgressions;
¹⁰Because a jealous ear hearkens to everything,
and discordant grumblings are not secret.
¹¹Therefore guard against profitless grumbling,
and from calumny withhold your tongues;
For a stealthy utterance will not go unpunished,
and a lying mouth destroys the soul.

¹²Do not court death by your erring way of life,
nor draw to yourselves destruction by the works of your hands.
¹³Because God did not make death,
nor does he rejoice in the destruction of the living.
¹⁴For he fashioned all things that they might have being,
and the creatures of the world are wholesome;

There is not a destructive drug among
  them
  nor any domain of Hades on earth,
[15]For righteousness is undying.

**The Wicked Reject Immortality and
Righteousness Alike.** [16]It was
  the wicked who with hands and
  words invited death,
  considered it a friend, and pined for it,
  and made a covenant with it,
  Because they deserve to be allied
  with it.

2:1 For, not thinking rightly, they said
  among themselves:
"Brief and troubled is our lifetime;
  there is no remedy for our dying,
  nor is anyone known to have come
  back from Hades.
[2]For by mere chance were we born,
  and hereafter we shall be as though
  we had not been;
Because the breath in our nostrils is
  smoke,
  and reason a spark from the beating
  of our hearts,
[3]And when this is quenched, our body
  will be ashes
  and our spirit will be poured abroad
  like empty air.
[4]Even our name will be forgotten in time,
  and no one will recall our deeds.
So our life will pass away like the traces
  of a cloud,
  and will be dispersed like a mist
Pursued by the sun's rays
  and overpowered by its heat.
[5]For our lifetime is the passing of a
  shadow;
  and our dying cannot be deferred
  because it is fixed with a seal; and
  no one returns.
[6]Come, therefore, let us enjoy the good
  things that are here,
  and make use of creation with
  youthful zest.

[7]Let us have our fill of costly wine and
  perfumes,
  and let no springtime blossom pass
  us by;
[8]let us crown ourselves with
  rosebuds before they wither.
[9]Let no meadow be free from our
  wantonness;
  everywhere let us leave tokens of our
  merriment,
  for this is our portion, and this our
  lot.
[10]Let us oppress the righteous poor;
  let us neither spare the widow
  nor revere the aged for hair grown
  white with time.
[11]But let our strength be our norm of
  righteousness;
  for weakness proves itself useless.

[12]Let us lie in wait for the righteous one,
  because he is annoying to us;
  he opposes our actions,
Reproaches us for transgressions of the
  law
  and charges us with violations of
  our training.
[13]He professes to have knowledge of God
  and styles himself a child of the LORD.
[14]To us he is the censure of our thoughts;
  merely to see him is a hardship for us,
[15]Because his life is not like that of
  others,
  and different are his ways.
[16]He judges us debased;
  he holds aloof from our paths as
  from things impure.
He calls blest the destiny of the righteous
  and boasts that God is his Father.

[17]Let us see whether his words be true;
  let us find out what will happen to
  him in the end.
[18]For if the righteous one is the son of
  God, God will help him
  and deliver him from the hand of
  his foes.

19With violence and torture let us put
him to the test
that we may have proof of his
gentleness
and try his patience.
20Let us condemn him to a shameful
death;
for according to his own words,
God will take care of him."

21These were their thoughts, but they
erred;
for their wickedness blinded them,
22And they did not know the hidden
counsels of God;
neither did they count on a
recompense for holiness
nor discern the innocent souls' reward.
23For God formed us to be imperishable;
the image of his own nature he
made us.
24But by the envy of the devil, death
entered the world,
and they who are allied with him
experience it.

The Hidden Counsels of God
A. ON SUFFERING. 3:1 The souls of
the righteous are in the hand of
God,
and no torment shall touch them.
2They seemed, in the view of the
foolish, to be dead;
and their passing away was thought
an affliction
3and their going forth from us, utter
destruction.
But they are in peace.
4For if to others, indeed, they seem
punished,
yet is their hope full of immortality;
5Chastised a little, they shall be greatly
blessed,
because God tried them
and found them worthy of himself.
6As gold in the furnace, he proved them,

and as sacrificial offerings he took
them to himself.
7In the time of their judgment they
shall shine
and dart about as sparks through
stubble;
8They shall judge nations and rule over
peoples,
and the LORD shall be their King
forever.
9Those who trust in him shall
understand truth,
and the faithful shall abide with him
in love:
Because grace and mercy are with his
holy ones,
and his care is with the elect.
10But the wicked shall receive a
punishment to match their
thoughts,
since they neglected righteousness
and forsook the LORD.
11For those who despise wisdom and
instruction are doomed.
Vain is their hope, fruitless their labors,
and worthless their works.
12Their wives are foolish and their
children wicked,
accursed their brood.

B. ON CHILDLESSNESS. 13Yes,
blessed is she who, childless and
undefiled,
never knew transgression of the
marriage bed;
for she shall bear fruit at the
judgment of souls.
14So also the eunuch whose hand
wrought no misdeed,
who held no wicked thoughts
against the LORD—
For he shall be given fidelity's choice
reward
and a more gratifying heritage in the
LORD's temple.
15For the fruit of noble struggles is a
glorious one;

and unfailing is the root of
understanding.

¹⁶But the children of adulterers will
remain without issue,
and the progeny of an unlawful bed
will disappear.

¹⁷For should they attain long life, they
will be held in no esteem,
and dishonored will their old age be
in the end;

¹⁸Should they die abruptly, they will
have no hope
nor comfort in the day of scrutiny;

¹⁹for dire is the end of the wicked
generation.

4:1 Better is childlessness with virtue;
for immortal is the memory of virtue,
acknowledged both by God and
human beings.

²When it is present people imitate it,
and they long for it when it is gone;
Forever it marches crowned in
triumph,
victorious in unsullied deeds of valor.

³But the numerous progeny of the
wicked shall be of no avail;
their spurious offshoots shall not
strike deep root
nor take firm hold.

⁴For even though their branches
flourish for a time,
they are unsteady and shall be
rocked by the wind
and, by the violence of the winds,
uprooted;

⁵Their twigs shall be broken off untimely,
their fruit useless, unripe for eating,
fit for nothing.

⁶For children born of lawless unions
give evidence of the wickedness of
their parents, when they are
examined.

C. ON EARLY DEATH. ⁷But the
righteous one, though he die
early, shall be at rest.

⁸For the age that is honorable comes
not with the passing of time,
nor can it be measured in terms of
years.

⁹Rather, understanding passes for gray
hair,
and an unsullied life is the
attainment of old age.

¹⁰The one who pleased God was loved,
living among sinners, was
transported—

¹¹Snatched away, lest wickedness
pervert his mind
or deceit beguile his soul;

¹²For the witchery of paltry things
obscures what is right
and the whirl of desire transforms
the innocent mind.

¹³Having become perfect in a short
while,
he reached the fullness of a long
career;

¹⁴for his soul was pleasing to the
LORD,
therefore he sped him out of the
midst of wickedness.
But the people saw and did not
understand,
nor did they take that consideration
into account.

¹⁶Yes, the righteous one who has died
will condemn
the sinful who live;
And youth, swiftly completed, will
condemn
the many years of the unrighteous
who have grown old.

¹⁷For they will see the death of the wise
one
and will not understand what the
LORD intended,
or why he kept him safe.

¹⁸They will see, and hold him in
contempt;
but the LORD will laugh them to
scorn.

¹⁹And they shall afterward become
   dishonored corpses
  and an unceasing mockery among
   the dead.
For he shall strike them down
  speechless and prostrate

and rock them to their foundations;
They shall be utterly laid waste
  and shall be in grief
  and their memory shall perish.

☐ JOHN 14:22-31

14:22 Judas, not the Iscariot, said to him, "Master, [then] what happened that you will reveal yourself to us and not to the world?" ²³Jesus answered and said to him, "Whoever loves me will keep my word, and my Father will love him, and we will come to him and make our dwelling with him. ²⁴Whoever does not love me does not keep my words; yet the word you hear is not mine but that of the Father who sent me.

²⁵"I have told you this while I am with you. ²⁶The Advocate, the holy Spirit that the Father will send in my name—he will teach you everything and remind you of all that [I] told you. ²⁷Peace I leave with you; my peace I give to you. Not as the world gives do I give it to you. Do not let your hearts be troubled or afraid. ²⁸You heard me tell you, 'I am going away and I will come back to you.' If you loved me, you would rejoice that I am going to the Father; for the Father is greater than I. ²⁹And now I have told you this before it happens, so that when it happens you may believe. ³⁰I will no longer speak much with you, for the ruler of the world is coming. He has no power over me, ³¹but the world must know that I love the Father and that I do just as the Father has commanded me. Get up, let us go."

August 14

St. Maximilian Mary Kolbe

No one in the world can change Truth. What we can do and should do is to seek truth and to serve it when we have found it. The real conflict is the inner conflict. Beyond armies of occupation and extermination camps, there are two irreconcilable enemies in the depth of every soul: good and evil, sin and love. What use are the victories on the battlefield if we ourselves are defeated in our innermost personal selves?

— ST. MAXIMILIAN MARY KOLBE

☐ WISDOM 4:20-8:18

The Judgment of the Wicked. 4:20
  Fearful shall they come, at the
   counting up of their sins,
  and their lawless deeds shall convict
   them to their face.

5:1 Then shall the righteous one with
   great assurance confront
  his oppressors who set at nought his
   labors.
²Seeing this, the wicked shall be shaken
  with dreadful fear,

and be amazed at the unexpected
salvation.
³They shall say among themselves, rueful
and groaning through anguish of
spirit:

"This is the one whom once we held as
a laughingstock
and as a type for mockery,
⁴fools that we were!
His life we accounted madness,
and death dishonored.
⁵See how he is accounted among the
heavenly beings;
how his lot is with the holy ones!
⁶We, then, have strayed from the way
of truth,
and the light of righteousness did
not shine for us,
and the sun did not rise for us.
⁷We were entangled in the thorns of
mischief and of ruin;
we journeyed through trackless
deserts,
but the way of the LORD we never
knew.
⁸What did our pride avail us?
What have wealth and its
boastfulness afforded us?
⁹All of them passed like a shadow
and like a fleeting rumor;
¹⁰Like a ship traversing the heaving water:
when it has passed, no trace can be
found,
no path of its keel in the waves.
¹¹Or like a bird flying through the air;
no evidence of its course is to be
found—
But the fluid air, lashed by the beating
of pinions,
and cleft by the rushing force
Of speeding wings, is traversed;
and afterward no mark of passage
can be found in it.
¹²Or as, when an arrow has been shot
at a mark,

the parted air straightway flows
together again
so that none discerns the way it
went—
¹³Even so, once born, we abruptly came
to nought
and held no sign of virtue to display,
but were consumed in our
wickedness."

¹⁴Yes, the hope of the wicked is like
chaff borne by the wind,
and like fine, storm-driven snow;
Like smoke scattered by the wind,
and like the passing memory of the
nomad camping for a single day.
¹⁵But the righteous live forever,
and in the LORD is their recompense,
and the thought of them is with the
Most High.
¹⁶Therefore shall they receive the
splendid crown,
the beautiful diadem, from the hand
of the LORD,
For he will shelter them with his right
hand,
and protect them with his arm.
¹⁷He shall take his zeal for armor
and arm creation to requite the enemy,
¹⁸Shall put on righteousness for a
breastplate,
wear sure judgment for a helmet,
¹⁹Shall take invincible holiness for a
shield,
²⁰and sharpen his sudden anger for
a sword.
The universe will war with him against
the foolhardy;
²¹Well-aimed bolts of lightning will go
forth
and from the clouds will leap to the
mark as from a well-drawn bow;
²²and as from a sling, wrathful
hailstones shall be hurled.
The waters of the sea will be enraged
and flooding rivers will overwhelm
them;

[23]A mighty wind will confront them
and winnow them like a tempest;
Thus lawlessness will lay waste the
whole earth
and evildoing overturn the thrones
of the mighty.

Exhortation to Seek Wisdom. 6:1

Hear, therefore, kings, and
understand;
learn, you magistrates of the earth's
expanse!
[2]Give ear, you who have power over
multitudes
and lord it over throngs of peoples!
[3]Because authority was given you by
the Lord
and sovereignty by the Most High,
who shall probe your works and
scrutinize your counsels!
[4]Because, though you were ministers of
his kingdom, you did not judge
rightly,
and did not keep the law,
nor walk according to the will of God,
[5]Terribly and swiftly he shall come
against you,
because severe judgment awaits the
exalted—
[6]For the lowly may be pardoned out of
mercy
but the mighty shall be mightily put
to the test.
[7]For the Ruler of all shows no partiality,
nor does he fear greatness,
Because he himself made the great as
well as the small,
and provides for all alike;
[8]but for those in power a rigorous
scrutiny impends.

[9]To you, therefore, O princes, are my
words addressed
that you may learn wisdom and that
you may not fall away.
[10]For those who keep the holy precepts
hallowed will be found holy,

and those learned in them will have
ready a response.
[11]Desire therefore my words;
long for them and you will be
instructed.

[12]Resplendent and unfading is Wisdom,
and she is readily perceived by those
who love her,
and found by those who seek her.
[13]She hastens to make herself known to
those who desire her;
[14]one who watches for her at dawn
will not be disappointed,
for she will be found sitting at the
gate.
[15]For setting your heart on her is the
perfection of prudence,
and whoever keeps vigil for her is
quickly free from care;
[16]Because she makes her rounds,
seeking those worthy of her,
and graciously appears to them on
the way,
and goes to meet them with full
attention.

[17]For the first step toward Wisdom is
an earnest desire for discipline;
[18]then, care for discipline is love of her;
love means the keeping of her laws;
To observe her laws is the basis for
incorruptibility;
[19]and incorruptibility makes one
close to God;
[20]thus the desire for Wisdom leads
to a kingdom.
[21]If, then, you find pleasure in throne
and scepter, you princes of peoples,
honor Wisdom, that you may reign
as kings forever.

[22]Now what wisdom is, and how she
came to be I shall proclaim;
and I shall conceal no secrets from
you,
But from the very beginning I shall
search out

and bring to light knowledge of her;
I shall not diverge from the truth.
[23]Neither shall I admit consuming
jealousy to my company,
because that can have no fellowship
with Wisdom.
[24]A multitude of the wise is the safety
of the world,
and a prudent king, the stability of
the people;
[25]so take instruction from my
words, to your profit.

Solomon Is Like All Others. 7:1 I too
am a mortal, the same as all the rest,
and a descendant of the first one
formed of earth.
And in my mother's womb I was
molded into flesh
[2]in a ten-month period—body and
blood,
from the seed of a man, and the
pleasure that accompanies
marriage.
[3]And I too, when born, inhaled the
common air,
and fell upon the kindred earth;
wailing, I uttered that first sound
common to all.
[4]In swaddling clothes and with
constant care I was nurtured.
[5]For no king has any different origin or
birth;
[6]one is the entry into life for all,
and in one same way they leave it.

**Solomon Prayed and Wisdom and
Riches Came to Him.** [7]Therefore
I prayed, and prudence was given
me;
I pleaded and the spirit of Wisdom
came to me.
[8]I preferred her to scepter and throne,
And deemed riches nothing in
comparison with her,
[9]nor did I liken any priceless gem
to her;

Because all gold, in view of her, is a bit
of sand,
and before her, silver is to be
accounted mire.
[10]Beyond health and beauty I loved her,
And I chose to have her rather than the
light,
because her radiance never ceases.
[11]Yet all good things together came to
me with her,
and countless riches at her hands;
[12]I rejoiced in them all, because
Wisdom is their leader,
though I had not known that she is
their mother.

**Solomon Prays for Help to Speak
Worthily of Wisdom.** [13]Sincerely
I learned about her, and
ungrudgingly do I share—
her riches I do not hide away;
[14]For she is an unfailing treasure;
those who gain this treasure win the
friendship of God,
being commended by the gifts that
come from her discipline.
[15]Now God grant I speak suitably
and value these endowments at their
worth:
For he is the guide of Wisdom
and the director of the wise.
[16]For both we and our words are in his
hand,
as well as all prudence and
knowledge of crafts.
[17]For he gave me sound knowledge of
what exists,
that I might know the structure of
the universe and the force of
its elements,
[18]The beginning and the end and the
midpoint of times,
the changes in the sun's course and
the variations of the seasons,
[19]Cycles of years, positions of stars,
[20]natures of living things, tempers of
beasts,

Powers of the winds and thoughts of
  human beings,
  uses of plants and virtues of roots—
²¹Whatever is hidden or plain I learned,
  ²²for Wisdom, the artisan of all,
    taught me.

**Nature and Incomparable Dignity of
  Wisdom.** For in her is a spirit
  intelligent, holy, unique,
Manifold, subtle, agile,
  clear, unstained, certain,
Never harmful, loving the good, keen,
  ²³unhampered, beneficent, kindly,
Firm, secure, tranquil,
  all-powerful, all-seeing,
And pervading all spirits,
  though they be intelligent, pure and
    very subtle.

²⁴For Wisdom is mobile beyond all
  motion,
  and she penetrates and pervades all
    things by reason of her purity.
²⁵For she is a breath of the might of God
  and a pure emanation of the glory
    of the Almighty;
  therefore nothing defiled can enter
    into her.
²⁶For she is the reflection of eternal light,
  the spotless mirror of the power of
    God,
  the image of his goodness.
²⁷Although she is one, she can do all
    things,
  and she renews everything while
    herself perduring;
Passing into holy souls from age to age,
  she produces friends of God and
    prophets.
²⁸For God loves nothing so much as the
  one who dwells with Wisdom.
²⁹For she is fairer than the sun
  and surpasses every constellation of
    the stars.
Compared to light, she is found more
    radiant;
  ³⁰though night supplants light,

wickedness does not prevail over
  Wisdom.

8:1 Indeed, she spans the world from
  end to end mightily
  and governs all things well.

Wisdom, the Source of Blessings.
  ²Her I loved and sought after
    from my youth;
  I sought to take her for my bride
  and was enamored of her beauty.
³She adds to nobility the splendor of
    companionship with God;
  even the Ruler of all loved her.
⁴For she leads into the understanding
    of God,
  and chooses his works.
⁵If riches are desirable in life,
  what is richer than Wisdom, who
    produces all things?
⁶And if prudence is at work,
  who in the world is a better artisan
    than she?
⁷Or if one loves righteousness,
  whose works are virtues,
She teaches moderation and prudence,
  righteousness and fortitude,
  and nothing in life is more useful
    than these.
⁸Or again, if one yearns for wide
    experience,
  she knows the things of old, and
    infers the things to come.
She understands the turns of phrases
  and the solutions of riddles;
  signs and wonders she knows in
    advance
  and the outcome of times and ages.

**Wisdom as Solomon's Counselor and
  Comfort.** ⁹So I determined to
    take her to live with me,
  knowing that she would be my
    counselor while all was well,
  and my comfort in care and grief.

¹⁰Because of her I have glory among
    the multitudes,
    and esteem from the elders, though
        I am but a youth.
¹¹I shall become keen in judgment,
    and shall be a marvel before rulers.
¹²They will wait while I am silent and
        listen when I speak;
    and when I shall speak the more,
        they will put their hands upon their
        mouths.
¹³Because of her I shall have immortality
    and leave to those after me an
        everlasting memory.
¹⁴I shall govern peoples, and nations
        will be my subjects—
    ¹⁵tyrannical princes, hearing of me,
        will be afraid;
    in the assembly I shall appear noble,
        and in war courageous.

¹⁶Entering my house, I shall take my
    repose beside her;
For association with her involves no
    bitterness
    and living with her no grief,
    but rather joy and gladness.

Wisdom is a Gift of God. ¹⁷Reflecting
    on these things,
    and considering in my heart
That immortality lies in kinship with
    Wisdom,
    ¹⁸great delight in love of her,
    and unfailing riches in the works of
        her hands;
And that in associating with her there
    is prudence,
    and fair renown in sharing her
        discourses,
I went about seeking to take her for
    my own.

☐ JOHN 15:1-17

The Vine and the Branches. 15:1 "I am the true vine, and my Father is the vine grower. ²He takes away every branch in me that does not bear fruit, and every one that does he prunes so that it bears more fruit. ³You are already pruned because of the word that I spoke to you. ⁴Remain in me, as I remain in you. Just as a branch cannot bear fruit on its own unless it remains on the vine, so neither can you unless you remain in me. ⁵I am the vine, you are the branches. Whoever remains in me and I in him will bear much fruit, because without me you can do nothing. ⁶Anyone who does not remain in me will be thrown out like a branch and wither; people will gather them and throw them into a fire and they will be burned. ⁷If you remain in me and my words remain in you, ask for whatever you want and it will be done for you. ⁸By this is my Father glorified, that you bear much fruit and become my disciples. ⁹As the Father loves me, so I also love you. Remain in my love. ¹⁰If you keep my commandments, you will remain in my love, just as I have kept my Father's commandments and remain in his love.

¹¹"I have told you this so that my joy may be in you and your joy may be complete. ¹²This is my commandment: love one another as I love you. ¹³No one has greater love than this, to lay down one's life for one's friends. ¹⁴You are my friends if you do what I command you. ¹⁵I no longer call you slaves, because a slave does not know what his master is doing. I have called you friends, because I have told you everything I have heard from my Father. ¹⁶It was not you who chose me, but I who chose you and appointed you to go and bear fruit that will remain, so that whatever you ask the Father in my name he may give you. ¹⁷This I command you: love one another."

August 15

The Assumption of the Blessed Virgin Mary

And who, I ask, could believe that the ark of holiness, the dwelling place of the Word of God, the temple of the Holy Spirit, could be reduced to ruin? My soul is filled with horror at the thought that this virginal flesh that had begotten God, had brought Him into the world, had nourished and carried Him, could have been turned into ashes or given over to be the food of worms.

— St. Robert Bellarmine

☐ WISDOM 8:19–12:27

8:19 Now, I was a well-favored child,
   and I came by a noble nature;
   ²⁰or rather, being noble, I attained
      an unblemished body.
²¹And knowing that I could not
      otherwise possess her unless God
      gave it—
   and this, too, was prudence, to
      know whose gift she is—
I went to the Lord and besought him,
   and said with all my heart:

Solomon's Prayer. 9:1 God of my
      ancestors, Lord of mercy,
   you who have made all things by
      your word
²And in your wisdom have established
      humankind
   to rule the creatures produced by you,
³And to govern the world in holiness
      and righteousness,
   and to render judgment in integrity
      of heart:
⁴Give me Wisdom, the consort at your
      throne,
   and do not reject me from among
      your children;
⁵For I am your servant, the child of
      your maidservant,
   a man weak and short-lived
   and lacking in comprehension of
      judgment and of laws.

⁶Indeed, though one be perfect among
      mortals,
   if Wisdom, who comes from you,
      be lacking,
   that one will count for nothing.

⁷You have chosen me king over your
      people
   and magistrate over your sons and
      daughters.
⁸You have bid me build a temple on
      your holy mountain
   and an altar in the city that is your
      dwelling place,
   a copy of the holy tabernacle which
      you had established from of
      old.
⁹Now with you is Wisdom, who knows
      your works
   and was present when you made the
      world;
Who understands what is pleasing in
      your eyes
   and what is conformable with your
      commands.
¹⁰Send her forth from your holy heavens
   and from your glorious throne
      dispatch her
That she may be with me and work
      with me,
   that I may know what is pleasing to
      you.
¹¹For she knows and understands all
      things,

and will guide me prudently in my
    affairs
and safeguard me by her glory;
[12]Thus my deeds will be acceptable,
    and I will judge your people justly
    and be worthy of my father's throne.

[13]For who knows God's counsel,
    or who can conceive what the Lord
      intends?
[14]For the deliberations of mortals are
      timid,
    and uncertain our plans.
[15]For the corruptible body burdens the
      soul
    and the earthly tent weighs down the
      mind with its many concerns.
[16]Scarcely can we guess the things on
      earth,
    and only with difficulty grasp what
      is at hand;
    but things in heaven, who can
      search them out?
[17]Or who can know your counsel,
    unless you give Wisdom
    and send your holy spirit from on
      high?
[18]Thus were the paths of those on earth
      made straight,
    and people learned what pleases you,
    and were saved by Wisdom.

Wisdom Preserves Her Followers.
10:1 She preserved the first-
      formed father of the world
    when he alone had been created;
And she raised him up from his fall,
    [2]and gave him power to rule all
      things.
[3]But when an unrighteous man
      withdrew from her in his anger,
    he perished through his fratricidal
      wrath.
[4]When on his account the earth was
      flooded, Wisdom again saved it,
    piloting the righteous man on
      frailest wood.

[5]She, when the nations were sunk in
      universal wickedness,
    knew the righteous man, kept him
      blameless before God,
    and preserved him resolute against
      pity for his child.
[6]She rescued a righteous man from
      among the wicked who were
      being destroyed,
    when he fled as fire descended upon
      the Pentapolis—
[7]Where as a testimony to its wickedness,
    even yet there remain a smoking
      desert,
Plants bearing fruit that never ripens,
    and the tomb of a disbelieving soul,
      a standing pillar of salt.
[8]For those who forsook Wisdom
    not only were deprived of
      knowledge of the good,
But also left the world a memorial of
      their folly,
    so that they could not even be
      hidden in their fall.
[9]But Wisdom rescued from tribulations
    those who served her.

[10]She, when a righteous man fled from
      his brother's anger,
    guided him in right ways,
Showed him the kingdom of God
    and gave him knowledge of holy
      things;
She prospered him in his labors
    and made abundant the fruit of his
      works,
[11]Stood by him against the greed of his
      defrauders,
    and enriched him;
[12]She preserved him from foes,
    and secured him against ambush,
And she gave him the prize for his hard
      struggle
    that he might know that devotion
      to God is mightier than all
      else.

¹³She did not abandon a righteous man
    when he was sold,
  but rescued him from sin.
¹⁴She went down with him into the
    dungeon,
  and did not desert him in his bonds,
Until she brought him the scepter of
    royalty
  and authority over his oppressors,
Proved false those who had defamed him,
  and gave him eternal glory.

¹⁵The holy people and their blameless
    descendants—it was she
  who rescued them from the nation
    that oppressed them.
¹⁶She entered the soul of the Lord's
    servant,
  and withstood fearsome kings with
    signs and wonders;
  ¹⁷she gave the holy ones the reward
    of their labors,
Conducted them by a wondrous road,
  became a shelter for them by day
  a starry flame by night.
¹⁸She took them across the Red Sea
  and brought them through the deep
    waters.
¹⁹Their enemies she overwhelmed,
  and churned them up from the
    bottom of the depths.
²⁰Therefore the righteous despoiled the
    wicked;
  and they sang of your holy name,
    Lord,
  and praised in unison your
    conquering hand,
²¹Because Wisdom opened the mouths
    of the mute,
  and gave ready speech to infants.

11:1 She prospered their affairs
    through the holy prophet.

²They journeyed through the
    uninhabited desert,
  and in lonely places they pitched
    their tents;

³they withstood enemies and
    warded off their foes.
⁴When they thirsted, they called upon
    you,
  and water was given them from the
    sheer rock,
  a quenching of their thirst from the
    hard stone.
⁵For by the things through which their
    foes were punished
  they in their need were benefited.

**First Example: Water Punishes the
Egyptians and Benefits the
Israelites.** ⁶Instead of a river's
    perennial source,
  troubled with impure blood
⁷as a rebuke to the decree for the
    slaying of infants,
You gave them abundant water beyond
    their hope,
  ⁸after you had shown by the thirst
    they experienced
  how you punished their adversaries.
⁹For when they had been tried, though
    only mildly chastised,
  they recognized how the wicked,
    condemned in anger, were
    being tormented.
¹⁰You tested your own people,
    admonishing them as a father;
  but as a stern king you probed and
    condemned the wicked.
¹¹Those near and far were equally
    afflicted:
  ¹²for a twofold grief took hold of them
  and a groaning at the remembrance
    of the ones who had departed.
¹³For when they heard that the cause of
    their own torments
  was a benefit to these others, they
    recognized the Lord.
¹⁴For though they had mocked and
    rejected him who had been cast
    out and abandoned long ago,
  in the final outcome, they marveled
    at him,

since their thirst proved unlike that
of the righteous.

Second Example: Animals Punish the Egyptians and Benefit the Israelites. [15]In return for their
senseless, wicked thoughts,
which misled them into worshiping
dumb serpents and worthless
insects,
You sent upon them swarms of dumb
creatures for vengeance;
[16]that they might recognize that one
is punished by the very things
through which one sins.

Digression on God's Mercy. [17]For
not without means was your
almighty hand,
that had fashioned the universe
from formless matter,
to send upon them many bears or
fierce lions,
[18]Or newly created, wrathful, unknown
beasts
breathing forth fiery breath,
Or pouring out roaring smoke,
or flashing terrible sparks from their
eyes.
[19]Not only could these attack and
completely destroy them;
even their frightful appearance itself
could slay.
[20]Even without these, they could have
been killed at a single blast,
pursued by justice
and winnowed by your mighty
spirit.
But you have disposed all things by
measure and number and weight.
[21]For great strength is always present
with you;
who can resist the might of your arm?
[22]Indeed, before you the whole
universe is like a grain from a
balance,
or a drop of morning dew come
down upon the earth.

[23]But you have mercy on all, because
you can do all things;
and you overlook sins for the sake of
repentance.
[24]For you love all things that are
and loathe nothing that you have
made;
for you would not fashion what you
hate.
[25]How could a thing remain, unless
you willed it;
or be preserved, had it not been
called forth by you?
[26]But you spare all things, because they
are yours,
O Ruler and Lover of souls,

12:1 for your imperishable spirit is in
all things!
[2]Therefore you rebuke offenders little
by little,
warn them, and remind them of the
sins they are committing,
that they may abandon their
wickedness and believe in
you, Lord!

[3]For truly, the ancient inhabitants of
your holy land,
[4]whom you hated for deeds most
odious—
works of sorcery and impious
sacrifices;
[5]These merciless murderers of children,
devourers of human flesh,
and initiates engaged in a blood
ritual,
[6]and parents who took with their
own hands defenseless lives,
You willed to destroy by the hands of
our ancestors,
[7]that the land that is dearest of all
to you
might receive a worthy colony of
God's servants.
[8]But even these you spared, since they
were but mortals

and sent wasps as forerunners of
    your army
that they might exterminate them
    by degrees.

⁹Not that you were without power to
    have the wicked vanquished in
    battle by the righteous,
    or wiped out at once by terrible
        beasts or by one decisive word;
¹⁰But condemning them by degrees, you
    gave them space for repentance.
You were not unaware that their
    origins were wicked
    and their malice ingrained,
And that their dispositions would
    never change;
    ¹¹for they were a people accursed
        from the beginning.
Neither out of fear for anyone
    did you grant release from their sins.
¹²For who can say to you, "What have
    you done?"
    or who can oppose your decree?
Or when peoples perish, who can
    challenge you, their maker;
    or who can come into your presence
        to vindicate the unrighteous?
¹³For neither is there any god besides
    you who have the care of all,
    that you need show you have not
        unjustly condemned;
¹⁴Nor can any king or prince confront
    you on behalf of those you have
    punished.

¹⁵But as you are righteous, you govern
    all things righteously;
    you regard it as unworthy of your
        power
    to punish one who has incurred no
        blame.
¹⁶For your might is the source of
    righteousness;
    your mastery over all things makes
        you lenient to all.

¹⁷For you show your might when
    the perfection of your power is
    disbelieved;
    and in those who know you, you
        rebuke insolence.
¹⁸But though you are master of might,
    you judge with clemency,
    and with much lenience you
        govern us;
    for power, whenever you will,
        attends you.

¹⁹You taught your people, by these deeds,
    that those who are righteous must
    be kind;
And you gave your children reason to
    hope
    that you would allow them to
        repent for their sins.
²⁰For these were enemies of your
    servants, doomed to death;
    yet, while you punished them with
        such solicitude and indulgence,
    granting time and opportunity to
        abandon wickedness,
²¹With what exactitude you judged
    your children,
    to whose ancestors you gave the sworn
        covenants of goodly promises!
²²Therefore to give us a lesson you
    punish our enemies with
    measured deliberation
    so that we may think earnestly of
        your goodness when we
        judge,
    and, when being judged, we may
        look for mercy.

Second Example Resumed. ²³Hence
    those unrighteous who lived a
    life of folly,
    you tormented through their own
        abominations.
²⁴For they went far astray in the paths
    of error,
    taking for gods the worthless and
        disgusting among beasts,
    being deceived like senseless infants.

²⁵Therefore as though upon
  unreasoning children,
    you sent your judgment on them as
      a mockery;
²⁶But they who took no heed of a
    punishment which was but
      child's play
    were to experience a condemnation
      worthy of God.

²⁷For by the things through which they
    suffered distress,
      being tortured by the very things
        they deemed gods,
  They saw and recognized the true God
      whom formerly they had refused
        to know;
    with this, their final condemnation
      came upon them.

☐ JOHN 15:18-27

The World's Hatred. 15:18 "If the world hates you, realize that it hated me first. ¹⁹If you belonged to the world, the world would love its own; but because you do not belong to the world, and I have chosen you out of the world, the world hates you. ²⁰Remember the word I spoke to you, 'No slave is greater than his master.' If they persecuted me, they will also persecute you. If they kept my word, they will also keep yours. ²¹And they will do all these things to you on account of my name, because they do not know the one who sent me. ²²If I had not come and spoken to them, they would have no sin; but as it is they have no excuse for their sin. ²³Whoever hates me also hates my Father. ²⁴If I had not done works among them that no one else ever did, they would not have sin; but as it is, they have seen and hated both me and my Father. ²⁵But in order that the word written in their law might be fulfilled, 'They hated me without cause.'

²⁶"When the Advocate comes whom I will send you from the Father, the Spirit of truth that proceeds from the Father, he will testify to me. ²⁷And you also testify, because you have been with me from the beginning."

August 16

St. Stephen of Hungary

Be strong, lest prosperity lift you up too much or adversity cast you down. Be humble in this life, so that God may raise you up in the next.

— St. Stephen of Hungary

☐ WISDOM 13-16

Digression on False Worship
A. NATURE WORSHIP. 13:1 Foolish
    by nature were all who were in
      ignorance of God,
  and who from the good things seen
      did not succeed in knowing
        the one who is,

and from studying the works did
      not discern the artisan;
²Instead either fire, or wind, or the
      swift air,
    or the circuit of the stars, or the
      mighty water,

or the luminaries of heaven, the
governors of the world, they
considered gods.
³Now if out of joy in their beauty they
thought them gods,
let them know how far more
excellent is the Lord than these;
for the original source of beauty
fashioned them.
⁴Or if they were struck by their might
and energy,
let them realize from these things
how much more powerful is
the one who made them.
⁵For from the greatness and the beauty
of created things
their original author, by analogy, is
seen.
⁶But yet, for these the blame is less;
For they have gone astray perhaps,
though they seek God and wish to
find him.
⁷For they search busily among his works,
but are distracted by what they see,
because the things seen are fair.
⁸But again, not even these are pardonable.
⁹For if they so far succeeded in knowledge
that they could speculate about the
world,
how did they not more quickly find
its Lord?

B. IDOLATRY. ¹⁰But wretched are they,
and in dead things are their hopes,
who termed gods things made by
human hands:
Gold and silver, the product of art, and
images of beasts,
or useless stone, the work of an
ancient hand.

The Carpenter and Wooden Idols.
¹¹A carpenter may cut down a
suitable tree
and skillfully scrape off all its bark,
And deftly plying his art
produce something fit for daily use,

¹²And use the scraps from his
handiwork
in preparing his food, and have his fill;
¹³Then the good-for-nothing refuse
from these remnants,
crooked wood grown full of knots,
he takes and carves to occupy his
spare time.
This wood he models with mindless
skill,
and patterns it on the image of a
human being
¹⁴or makes it resemble some
worthless beast.
When he has daubed it with red and
crimsoned its surface with red
stain,
and daubed over every blemish in it,
¹⁵He makes a fitting shrine for it
and puts it on the wall, fastening it
with a nail.
¹⁶Thus he provides for it lest it fall down,
knowing that it cannot help itself;
for, truly, it is an image and needs
help.
¹⁷But when he prays about his goods or
marriage or children,
he is not ashamed to address the
thing without a soul.
For vigor he invokes the powerless;
¹⁸for life he entreats the dead;
For aid he beseeches the wholly
incompetent;
for travel, something that cannot
even walk;
¹⁹For profit in business and success
with his hands
he asks power of a thing with hands
utterly powerless.

14:1 Again, one preparing for a voyage
and about to traverse the wild
waves
cries out to wood more unsound
than the boat that bears him.
²For the urge for profits devised this
latter,

and Wisdom the artisan produced it.

³But your providence, O Father!
    guides it,
  for you have furnished even in the
      sea a road,
  and through the waves a steady path,
⁴Showing that you can save from any
    danger,
  so that even one without skill may
    embark.
⁵But you will that the products of your
    Wisdom be not idle;
  therefore people trust their lives
      even to most frail wood,
  and were safe crossing the waves on
      a raft.
⁶For of old, when the proud giants
      were being destroyed,
  the hope of the universe, who took
      refuge on a raft,
  left to the world a future for the
      human family, under the
      guidance of your hand.
⁷For blest is the wood through which
    righteousness comes about;
⁸but the handmade idol is accursed,
    and its maker as well:
  he for having produced it, and the
    corruptible thing, because it
    was termed a god.
⁹Equally odious to God are the evildoer
    and the evil deed;
¹⁰and the thing made will be
    punished with its maker.
¹¹Therefore upon even the idols of the
    nations shall a judgment come,
  since they became abominable
      among God's works,
  Snares for human souls
    and a trap for the feet of the senseless.

The Origin and Evils of Idolatry.
    ¹²For the source of wantonness is
      the devising of idols;
  and their invention, a corruption
      of life.

¹³For in the beginning they were not,
    nor can they ever continue;
¹⁴for from human emptiness they
      came into the world,
  and therefore a sudden end is
      devised for them.
¹⁵For a father, afflicted with untimely
    mourning,
  made an image of the child so
      quickly taken from him,
  And now honored as a god what once
      was dead
  and handed down to his household
      mysteries and sacrifices.
¹⁶Then, in the course of time, the
      impious practice gained strength
      and was observed as law,
  and graven things were worshiped
      by royal decrees.
¹⁷People who lived so far away that
      they could not honor him in his
      presence
  copied the appearance of the distant
      king
  And made a public image of him they
      wished to honor,
  out of zeal to flatter the absent one
      as though present.
¹⁸And to promote this observance among
    those to whom it was strange,
  the artisan's ambition provided a
      stimulus.
¹⁹For he, perhaps in his determination
      to please the ruler,
  labored over the likeness to the best
      of his skill;
²⁰And the masses, drawn by the charm
      of the workmanship,
  soon took as an object of worship
      the one who shortly before was
      honored as a human being.
²¹And this became a snare for the world,
    that people enslaved to either grief
      or tyranny
  conferred the incommunicable
      Name on stones and wood.

²²Then it was not enough for them to
err in their knowledge of God;
but even though they live in a great
war resulting from ignorance,
they call such evils peace.
²³For while they practice either child
sacrifices or occult mysteries,
or frenzied carousing in exotic rites,
²⁴They no longer respect either lives or
purity of marriage;
but they either waylay and kill each
other, or aggrieve each other
by adultery.
²⁵And all is confusion—blood and
murder, theft and guile,
corruption, faithlessness, turmoil,
perjury,
²⁶Disturbance of good people, neglect
of gratitude,
besmirching of souls, unnatural lust,
disorder in marriage, adultery and
shamelessness.
²⁷For the worship of infamous idols
is the reason and source and
extreme of all evil.
²⁸For they either go mad with
enjoyment, or prophesy lies,
or live lawlessly or lightly perjure
themselves.
²⁹For as their trust is in lifeless idols,
they expect no harm when they
have sworn falsely.
³⁰But on both counts justice shall
overtake them:
because they thought perversely of
God by devoting themselves
to idols,
and because they deliberately swore
false oaths, despising piety.
³¹For it is not the might of those by
whom they swear,
but the just retribution of sinners,
that ever follows upon the
transgression of the wicked.

15:1 But you, our God, are good and
true,
slow to anger, and governing all
with mercy.
²For even if we sin, we are yours, and
know your might;
but we will not sin, knowing that
we belong to you.
³For to know you well is complete
righteousness,
and to know your might is the root
of immortality.
⁴For the evil creation of human fancy
did not deceive us,
nor the fruitless labor of painters,
A form smeared with varied colors,
⁵the sight of which arouses yearning
in a fool,
till he longs for the inanimate form
of a dead image.
⁶Lovers of evil things, and worthy of
such hopes
are they who make them and long
for them and worship them.

The Potter's Clay Idols. ⁷For the
potter, laboriously working the
soft earth,
molds for our service each single
article:
He fashions out of the same clay
both the vessels that serve for clean
purposes
and their opposites, all alike;
As to what shall be the use of each
vessel of either class
the worker in clay is the judge.
⁸With misspent toil he molds a
meaningless god from the
selfsame clay,
though he himself shortly before
was made from the earth,
And is soon to go whence he was
taken,
when the life that was lent him is
demanded back.
⁹But his concern is not that he is to die

nor that his span of life is brief;
Rather, he vies with goldsmiths and
    silversmiths
    and emulates molders of bronze,
    and takes pride in fashioning
        counterfeits.
[10]Ashes his heart is! more worthless
    than earth is his hope,
    more ignoble than clay his life;
[11]Because he knew not the one who
    fashioned him,
    and breathed into him a quickening
        soul,
    and infused a vital spirit.
[12]Instead, he esteemed our life a mere
    game,
    and our span of life a holiday for gain;
"For one must," says he, "make a profit
    in every way, be it even from evil."
[13]For more than anyone else he knows
    that he is sinning,
    when out of earthen stuff he creates
        fragile vessels and idols alike.

[14]But most stupid of all and worse than
    senseless in mind,
    are the enemies of your people who
        enslaved them.
[15]For they esteemed all the idols of the
    nations as gods,
    which cannot use their eyes to see,
    nor nostrils to breathe the air,
Nor ears to hear,
    nor fingers on their hands for feeling;
    even their feet are useless to walk with.
[16]For it was a mere human being who
    made them;
    one living on borrowed breath who
        fashioned them.
For no one is able to fashion a god like
    himself;
[17]he is mortal, and what he makes
    with lawless hands is dead.
For he is better than the things he
    worships;
    he at least lives, but never his idols.

Second Example Resumed. [18]Besides,
    they worship the most loathsome
    beasts—
    as regards stupidity, these are worse
    than the rest,
[19]For beasts are neither good-looking
    nor desirable;
    they have escaped both the approval
    of God and his blessing.

16:1 Therefore they were fittingly
    punished by similar creatures,
    and were tormented by a swarm of
    insects.
[2]Instead of this punishment, you
    benefited your people
    with a novel dish, the delight they
    craved,
    by providing quail for their food,
[3]So that those others, when they
    desired food,
    should lose their appetite even for
    necessities,
    since the creatures sent to plague
    them were so loathsome,
While these, after a brief period of
    privation,
    partook of a novel dish.
[4]For inexorable want had to come
    upon those oppressors;
    but these needed only to be shown
    how their enemies were being
    tormented.

[5]For when the dire venom of beasts
    came upon them
    and they were dying from the bite
    of crooked serpents,
    your anger endured not to the end.
[6]But as a warning, for a short time they
    were terrorized,
    though they had a sign of salvation,
    to remind them of the precept
    of your law.
[7]For the one who turned toward it was
    saved,
    not by what was seen,
    but by you, the savior of all.

⁸By this also you convinced our foes
    that you are the one who delivers
        from all evil.
⁹For the bites of locusts and of flies
    slew them,
    and no remedy was found to save
        their lives
    because they deserved to be
        punished by such means;
¹⁰But not even the fangs of poisonous
    reptiles overcame your children,
    for your mercy came forth and
        healed them.
¹¹For as a reminder of your injunctions,
    they were stung,
    and swiftly they were saved,
Lest they should fall into deep
    forgetfulness
    and become unresponsive to your
        beneficence.
¹²For indeed, neither herb nor
    application cured them,
    but your all-healing word, O LORD!
¹³For you have dominion over life and
    death;
    you lead down to the gates of Hades
        and lead back.
¹⁴Human beings, however, may kill
    another with malice,
    but they cannot bring back the
        departed spirit,
    or release the soul that death has
        confined.
¹⁵Your hand no one can escape.

Third Example: A Rain of Manna for Israel Instead of the Plague of Storms. ¹⁶For the wicked who
    refused to know you
    were punished by the might of your
        arm,
Were pursued by unusual rains and
    hailstorms and unremitting
        downpours,
    and were consumed by fire.
¹⁷For against all expectation, in water
    which quenches everything,

the fire grew more active;
For the universe fights on behalf of the
    righteous.
¹⁸Then the flame was tempered
    so that the beasts that were sent
        upon the wicked might not be
        burnt up,
    but that these might see and know
        that they were struck by the
        judgment of God;
¹⁹And again, even in the water, fire
    blazed beyond its strength
    so as to consume the produce of the
        wicked land.
²⁰Instead of this, you nourished your
    people with food of angels
    and furnished them bread from
        heaven, ready to hand,
    untoiled-for,
    endowed with all delights and
        conforming to every taste.
²¹For this substance of yours revealed
    your sweetness toward your
        children,
    and serving the desire of the one
        who received it,
    was changed to whatever flavor each
        one wished.
²²Yet snow and ice withstood fire and
    were not melted,
    so that they might know that their
        enemies' fruits
Were consumed by a fire that blazed in
    the hail
    and flashed lightning in the rain.
²³But this fire, again, in order that the
    righteous might be nourished,
    forgot even its proper strength;
²⁴For your creation, serving you, its
    maker,
    grows tense for punishment against
        the wicked,
    but is relaxed in benefit for those
        who trust in you.
²⁵Therefore at that very time,
    transformed in all sorts of ways,

it was serving your all-nourishing
bounty
according to what they needed and
desired;
²⁶That your children whom you loved
might learn, O LORD,
that it is not the various kinds of
fruits that nourish,
but your word that preserves those
who believe you!

²⁷For what was not destroyed by fire,
melted when merely warmed by a
momentary sunbeam;
²⁸To make known that one must give
you thanks before sunrise,
and turn to you at daybreak.
²⁹For the hope of the ungrateful melts
like a wintry frost
and runs off like useless water.

☐ JOHN 16:1-15

16:1 "I have told you this so that you may not fall away. ²They will expel you from the synagogues; in fact, the hour is coming when everyone who kills you will think he is offering worship to God. ³They will do this because they have not known either the Father or me. ⁴I have told you this so that when their hour comes you may remember that I told you.

Jesus' Departure; Coming of the Advocate. "I did not tell you this from the beginning, because I was with you. ⁵But now I am going to the one who sent me, and not one of you asks me, 'Where are you going?' ⁶But because I told you this, grief has filled your hearts. ⁷But I tell you the truth, it is better for you that I go. For if I do not go, the Advocate will not come to you. But if I go, I will send him to you. ⁸And when he comes he will convict the world in regard to sin and righteousness and condemnation: ⁹sin, because they do not believe in me; ¹⁰righteousness, because I am going to the Father and you will no longer see me; ¹¹condemnation, because the ruler of this world has been condemned.

¹²"I have much more to tell you, but you cannot bear it now. ¹³But when he comes, the Spirit of truth, he will guide you to all truth. He will not speak on his own, but he will speak what he hears, and will declare to you the things that are coming. ¹⁴He will glorify me, because he will take from what is mine and declare it to you. ¹⁵Everything that the Father has is mine; for this reason I told you that he will take from what is mine and declare it to you."

August 17 ———————————————————————

We set forth our petitions before God, not in order to make known to Him our needs and desires, but rather so that we ourselves may realize that in these things it is necessary to turn to God for help.

— St. Thomas Aquinas

☐ WISDOM 17–19

Fourth Example: Darkness Afflicts the Egyptians, While the Israelites Have Light. 17:1 For great are your judgments, and hard to describe;
therefore the unruly souls went astray.
²For when the lawless thought to enslave the holy nation,
they themselves lay shackled with darkness, fettered by the long night,
confined beneath their own roofs as exiles from the eternal providence.
³For they, who supposed their secret sins were hid
under the dark veil of oblivion,
Were scattered in fearful trembling, terrified by apparitions.
⁴For not even their inner chambers kept them unafraid,
for crashing sounds on all sides terrified them,
and mute phantoms with somber looks appeared.
⁵No fire had force enough to give light, nor did the flaming brilliance of the stars
succeed in lighting up that gloomy night.
⁶But only intermittent, fearful fires flashed through upon them;
And in their terror they thought beholding these was worse
than the times when that sight was no longer to be seen.
⁷And mockeries of their magic art failed,
and there was a humiliating refutation of their vaunted shrewdness.
⁸For they who undertook to banish fears and terrors from the sick soul
themselves sickened with ridiculous fear.
⁹For even though no monstrous thing frightened them,
they shook at the passing of insects and the hissing of reptiles,
¹⁰And perished trembling,
reluctant to face even the air that they could nowhere escape.
¹¹For wickedness, of its nature cowardly, testifies in its own condemnation,
and because of a distressed conscience, always magnifies misfortunes.
¹²For fear is nought but the surrender of the helps that come from reason;
¹³and the more one's expectation is of itself uncertain,
the more one makes of not knowing the cause that brings on torment.
¹⁴So they, during that night, powerless though it was,
since it had come upon them from the recesses of a powerless Hades,
while all sleeping the same sleep,
¹⁵Were partly smitten by fearsome apparitions
and partly stricken by their souls' surrender;

for fear overwhelmed them, sudden
and unexpected.
[16]Thus, then, whoever was there fell
into that prison without bars and
was kept confined.
[17]For whether one was a farmer, or a
shepherd,
or a worker at tasks in the wasteland,
Taken unawares, each served out the
inescapable sentence;
[18]for all were bound by the one
bond of darkness.
And were it only the whistling wind,
or the melodious song of birds in
the spreading branches,
Or the steady sound of rushing water,
[19]or the rude crash of overthrown
rocks,
Or the unseen gallop of bounding
animals,
or the roaring cry of the fiercest
beasts,
Or an echo resounding from the
hollow of the hills—
these sounds, inspiring terror,
paralyzed them.
[20]For the whole world shone with
brilliant light
and continued its works without
interruption;
[21]But over them alone was spread
oppressive night,
an image of the darkness that was
about to come upon them.
Yet they were more a burden to
themselves than was the
darkness.

18:1 But your holy ones had very great
light;
And those others, who heard their
voices but did not see their forms,
counted them blest for not having
suffered;
[2]And because they who formerly had
been wronged did not harm
them, they thanked them,

and because of the difference
between them, pleaded with
them.
[3]Instead of this, you furnished the
flaming pillar,
a guide on the unknown way,
and the mild sun for an honorable
migration.
[4]For they deserved to be deprived
of light and imprisoned by
darkness,
they had kept your children confined,
through whom the imperishable
light of the law was to be
given to the world.

**Fifth Example: Death of the
Egyptian Firstborn; the
Israelites Are Spared.** [5]When
they determined to put to death
the infants of the holy ones,
and when a single boy had been cast
forth and then saved,
As a reproof you carried off a multitude
of their children
and made them perish all at once in
the mighty water.
[6]That night was known beforehand to
our ancestors,
so that, with sure knowledge of
the oaths in which they put
their faith, they might have
courage.
[7]The expectation of your people
was the salvation of the righteous and
the destruction of their foes.
[8]For by the same means with which
you punished our adversaries,
you glorified us whom you had
summoned.
[9]For in secret the holy children of the
good were offering sacrifice
and carried out with one mind the
divine institution,
So that your holy ones should share
alike the same blessings and
dangers,

once they had sung the ancestral
hymns of praise.
¹⁰But the discordant cry of their
enemies echoed back,
and the piteous wail of mourning for
children was borne to them.
¹¹And the slave was smitten with the
same retribution as the master;
even the commoner suffered the
same as the king.
¹²And all alike by one common form
of death
had countless dead;
For the living were not even sufficient
for the burial,
since at a single instant their most
valued offspring had been
destroyed.
¹³For though they disbelieved at every
turn on account of sorceries,
at the destruction of the firstborn
they acknowledged that this
people was God's son.
¹⁴For when peaceful stillness
encompassed everything
and the night in its swift course was
half spent,
¹⁵Your all-powerful word from heaven's
royal throne
leapt into the doomed land,
¹⁶a fierce warrior bearing the sharp
sword of your inexorable
decree,
And alighted, and filled every place
with death,
and touched heaven, while standing
upon the earth.
¹⁷Then, at once, visions in horrible
dreams perturbed them
and unexpected fears assailed them;
¹⁸And cast half-dead, one here, another
there,
they revealed why they were dying.
¹⁹For the dreams that disturbed them
had proclaimed this beforehand,
lest they perish unaware of why they
endured such evil.

²⁰The trial of death touched even the
righteous,
and in the desert a plague struck the
multitude;
Yet not for long did the anger last.
²¹For the blameless man hastened to be
their champion,
bearing the weapon of his special
office,
prayer and the propitiation of
incense;
He withstood the wrath and put a stop
to the calamity,
showing that he was your servant.
²²He overcame the bitterness
not by bodily strength, not by force
of arms;
But by word he overcame the smiter,
recalling the sworn covenants with
their ancestors.
²³For when corpses had already fallen
one on another in heaps,
he stood in the midst and checked
the anger,
and cut off its way to the living.
²⁴For on his full-length robe was the
whole world,
and ancestral glories were carved on
the four rows of stones,
and your grandeur was on the
crown upon his head.
²⁵To these the destroyer yielded, these
he feared;
for this sole trial of anger sufficed.

19:1 But merciless wrath assailed the
wicked until the end,
for God knew beforehand what they
were yet to do:
²That though they themselves had
agreed to the departure
and had anxiously sent them on
their way,
they would regret it and pursue
them.
³For while they were still engaged in
funeral rites

and mourning at the burials of the
dead,
They adopted another senseless plan:
those whom they had driven out
with entreaties
they now pursued as fugitives.
⁴For a compulsion appropriate to this
ending drew them on,
and made them forget what had
befallen them,
That they might complete the torments
of their punishment,
⁵and your people might experience a
glorious journey
while those others met an
extraordinary death.

⁶For all creation, in its several kinds,
was being made over anew,
serving your commands, that your
children might be preserved
unharmed.
⁷The cloud overshadowed their camp;
and out of what had been water, dry
land was seen emerging:
Out of the Red Sea an unimpeded
road,
and a grassy plain out of the mighty
flood.
⁸Over this crossed the whole nation
sheltered by your hand,
and they beheld stupendous wonders.
⁹For they ranged about like horses,
and leapt like lambs,
praising you, LORD, their deliverer.
¹⁰For they were still mindful of what
had happened in their sojourn:
how instead of the young of animals
the land brought forth gnats,
and instead of fishes the river
swarmed with countless frogs.
¹¹And later they saw also a new kind
of bird
when, prompted by desire, they
asked for pleasant foods;
¹²For to appease them quail came to
them from the sea.

¹³And the punishments came upon the
sinners
not without forewarnings from the
violence of the thunderbolts.

For they justly suffered for their own
misdeeds,
since they treated their guests with
the more grievous hatred.
¹⁴For those others did not receive
unfamiliar visitors,
but these were enslaving beneficent
guests.
¹⁵And not that only; but what
punishment was to be theirs
since they received strangers
unwillingly!
¹⁶Yet these, after welcoming them with
festivities,
oppressed with awful toils
those who had shared with them the
same rights.
¹⁷And they were struck with blindness,
as those others had been at the
doors of the righteous man—
When, surrounded by yawning
darkness,
each sought the entrance of his own
door.

¹⁸For the elements, in ever-changing
harmony,
like strings of the harp, produce
new melody,
while the flow of music steadily
persists.
And this can be perceived exactly from
a review of what took place.
¹⁹For land creatures were changed into
water creatures,
and those that swam went over on
land.
²⁰Fire in water maintained its own
strength,
and water forgot its quenching
nature;
²¹Flames, by contrast, neither
consumed the flesh

of the perishable animals that went
about in them,
nor melted the icelike, quick-melting
kind of ambrosial food.

☐ JOHN 16:16-33

16:16 "A little while and you will no longer see me, and again a little while later and you will see me." ¹⁷So some of his disciples said to one another, "What does this mean that he is saying to us, 'A little while and you will not see me, and again a little while and you will see me,' and 'Because I am going to the Father'?" ¹⁸So they said, "What is this 'little while' [of which he speaks]? We do not know what he means." ¹⁹Jesus knew that they wanted to ask him, so he said to them, "Are you discussing with one another what I said, 'A little while and you will not see me, and again a little while and you will see me'? ²⁰Amen, amen, I say to you, you will weep and mourn, while the world rejoices; you will grieve, but your grief will become joy. ²¹When a woman is in labor, she is in anguish because her hour has arrived; but when she has given birth to a child, she no longer remembers the pain because of her joy that a child has been born into the world. ²²So you also are now in anguish. But I will see you again, and your hearts will rejoice, and no one will take your joy away from you. ²³On that day you will not question me about anything. Amen, amen, I say to you, whatever you ask the Father in my name he will give you.

²⁴Until now you have not asked anything in my name; ask and you will receive, so that your joy may be complete.

²⁵"I have told you this in figures of speech. The hour is coming when I will no longer speak to you in figures but I will tell you clearly about the Father. ²⁶On that day you will ask in my name, and I do not tell you that I will ask the Father for you. ²⁷For the Father himself loves you, because you have loved me and have come to believe that I came from God. ²⁸I came from the Father and have come into the world. Now I am leaving the world and going back to the Father." ²⁹His disciples said, "Now you are talking plainly, and not in any figure of speech. ³⁰Now we realize that you know everything and that you do not need to have anyone question you. Because of this we believe that you came from God." ³¹Jesus answered them, "Do you believe now? ³²Behold, the hour is coming and has arrived when each of you will be scattered to his own home and you will leave me alone. But I am not alone, because the Father is with me. ³³I have told you this so that you might have peace in me. In the world you will have trouble, but take courage, I have conquered the world."

August 18

St. Jane Frances de Chantal

Hell is full of the talented, but heaven, of the energetic.
— St. Jane Frances de Chantal

☐ SIRACH: FOREWORD-3:29

Inasmuch as many and great truths have been given to us through the Law, the prophets, and the authors who followed them, for which the instruction and wisdom of Israel merit praise, it is the duty of those who read the scriptures not only to become knowledgeable themselves but also to use their love of learning in speech and in writing to help others less familiar. So my grandfather Jesus, who had long devoted himself to the study of the law, the prophets, and the rest of the books of our ancestors, and had acquired great familiarity with them, was moved to write something himself regarding instruction and wisdom. He did this so that those who love learning might, by accepting what he had written, make even greater progress in living according to the Law.

You are invited therefore to read it with good will and attention, with indulgence for any failure on our part, despite earnest efforts, in the interpretation of particular passages. For words spoken originally in Hebrew do not have the same effect when they are translated into another language. That is true not only of this book but of the Law itself, the prophecies, and the rest of the books, which differ no little when they are read in the original.

I arrived in Egypt in the thirty-eighth year of the reign of King Euergetes, and while there, I had access to no little learning. I therefore considered it my duty to devote some diligence and industry to the translation of this book. During this time I applied my skill for many sleepless hours to complete the book and publish it for those living abroad who wish to acquire learning and are disposed to live their lives according to the Law.

God's Gift of Wisdom. 1:1 All
wisdom is from the Lord
and remains with him forever.
²The sands of the sea, the drops of rain,
the days of eternity—who can
count them?
³Heaven's height, earth's extent,
the abyss and wisdom—who can
explore them?
⁴Before all other things wisdom was
created
and prudent understanding, from
eternity.
⁶The root of wisdom—to whom has it
been revealed?
Her subtleties—who knows them?
⁸There is but one, wise and truly
awesome,
seated upon his throne—the Lord.
⁹It is he who created her,
saw her and measured her,
Poured her forth upon all his works,
¹⁰upon every living thing according
to his bounty,
lavished her upon those who love
him.

Fear of the Lord Is Wisdom. ¹¹The fear
of the Lord is glory and exultation,
gladness and a festive crown.
¹²The fear of the Lord rejoices the heart,
giving gladness, joy, and long life.
¹³Those who fear the Lord will be
happy at the end,
even on the day of death they will
be blessed.

[14]The beginning of wisdom is to fear
the Lord;
she is created with the faithful in the
womb.
[15]With the godly she was created from
of old,
and with their descendants she will
keep faith.

[16]The fullness of wisdom is to fear the
Lord;
she inebriates them with her fruits.
[17]Their entire house she fills with
choice foods,
their granaries with her produce.

[18]The crown of wisdom is the fear of
the Lord,
flowering with peace and perfect
health.
[19]Knowledge and full understanding
she rains down;
she heightens the glory of those who
possess her.

[20]The root of wisdom is to fear the Lord;
her branches are long life.
[21]The fear of the Lord drives away sins;
where it abides it turns back all anger.
[22]Unjust anger can never be justified;
anger pulls a person to utter ruin.
[23]Until the right time, the patient
remain calm,
then cheerfulness comes back to
them.
[24]Until the right time they hold back
their words;
then the lips of many will tell of
their good sense.
[25]Among wisdom's treasures is the
model for knowledge;
but godliness is an abomination to
the sinner.
[26]If you desire wisdom, keep the
commandments,
and the Lord will bestow her upon
you;

[27]For the fear of the Lord is wisdom
and discipline;
faithfulness and humility are his
delight.
[28]Do not disobey the fear of the Lord,
do not approach it with duplicity of
heart.
[29]Do not be a hypocrite before others;
over your lips keep watch.
[30]Do not exalt yourself lest you fall
and bring dishonor upon yourself;

For then the Lord will reveal your secrets
and cast you down in the midst of
the assembly.
Because you did not approach the fear
of the Lord,
and your heart was full of deceit.

Trust in God. 2:1 My child, when you
come to serve the Lord,
prepare yourself for trials.
[2]Be sincere of heart and steadfast,
and do not be impetuous in time of
adversity.
[3]Cling to him, do not leave him,
that you may prosper in your last
days.
[4]Accept whatever happens to you;
in periods of humiliation be
patient.
[5]For in fire gold is tested,
and the chosen, in the crucible of
humiliation.
[6]Trust in God, and he will help you;
make your ways straight and hope
in him.
[7]You that fear the Lord, wait for his
mercy,
do not stray lest you fall.
[8]You that fear the Lord, trust in him,
and your reward will not be lost.
[9]You that fear the Lord, hope for good
things,
for lasting joy and mercy.

[10]Consider the generations long past
and see:
has anyone trusted in the Lord and
been disappointed?
Has anyone persevered in his fear and
been forsaken?
has anyone called upon him and
been ignored?
[11]For the Lord is compassionate and
merciful;
forgives sins and saves in time of
trouble.
[12]Woe to timid hearts and drooping
hands,
to the sinner who walks a double
path!
[13]Woe to the faint of heart! For they do
not trust,
and therefore have no shelter!
[14]Woe to you that have lost hope!
what will you do at the Lord's
visitation?

[15]Those who fear the Lord do not
disobey his words;
those who love him keep his ways.
[16]Those who fear the Lord seek to
please him;
those who love him are filled with
his law.
[17]Those who fear the Lord prepare their
hearts
and humble themselves before him.

[18]Let us fall into the hands of the Lord
and not into the hands of mortals,
For equal to his majesty is his mercy;
and equal to his name are his works.

Responsibilities to Parents. 3:1
Children, listen to me, your father;
act accordingly, that you may be safe.
[2]For the Lord sets a father in honor
over his children
and confirms a mother's authority
over her sons.

[3]Those who honor their father atone
for sins;
[4]they store up riches who respect
their mother.
[5]Those who honor their father will
have joy in their own children,
and when they pray they are heard.
[6]Those who respect their father will live
a long life;
those who obey the Lord honor
their mother.

[7]Those who fear the Lord honor their
father,
and serve their parents as masters.
[8]In word and deed honor your father,
that all blessings may come to you.
[9]A father's blessing gives a person firm
roots,
but a mother's curse uproots the
growing plant.
[10]Do not glory in your father's disgrace,
for that is no glory to you!
[11]A father's glory is glory also for oneself;
they multiply sin who demean their
mother.

[12]My son, be steadfast in honoring
your father;
do not grieve him as long as he lives.
[13]Even if his mind fails, be considerate
of him;
do not revile him because you are in
your prime.
[14]Kindness to a father will not be
forgotten;
it will serve as a sin offering—it will
take lasting root.
[15]In time of trouble it will be recalled
to your advantage,
like warmth upon frost it will melt
away your sins.
[16]Those who neglect their father are
like blasphemers;
those who provoke their mother are
accursed by their Creator.

Humility. ¹⁷My son, conduct your
affairs with humility,
and you will be loved more than a
giver of gifts.
¹⁸Humble yourself the more, the
greater you are,
and you will find mercy in the sight
of God.
²⁰For great is the power of the Lord;
by the humble he is glorified.
²¹What is too sublime for you, do not
seek;
do not reach into things that are
hidden from you.
²²What is committed to you, pay heed to;
what is hidden is not your concern.
²³In matters that are beyond you do
not meddle,
when you have been shown more
than you can understand.

²⁴Indeed, many are the conceits of
human beings;
evil imaginations lead them astray.

Docility. ²⁵Without the pupil of the
eye, light is missing;
without knowledge, wisdom is
missing.
²⁶A stubborn heart will fare badly in
the end;
those who love danger will perish
in it.
²⁷A stubborn heart will have many a
hurt;
adding sin to sin is madness.
²⁸When the proud are afflicted, there is
no cure;
for they are offshoots of an evil plant.
²⁹The mind of the wise appreciates
proverbs,
and the ear that listens to wisdom
rejoices.

☐ JOHN 17:1-19

The Prayer of Jesus. 17:1 When Jesus had said this, he raised his eyes to heaven and said, "Father, the hour has come. Give glory to your son, so that your son may glorify you, ²just as you gave him authority over all people, so that he may give eternal life to all you gave him. ³Now this is eternal life, that they should know you, the only true God, and the one whom you sent, Jesus Christ. ⁴I glorified you on earth by accomplishing the work that you gave me to do. ⁵Now glorify me, Father, with you, with the glory that I had with you before the world began.

⁶"I revealed your name to those whom you gave me out of the world. They belonged to you, and you gave them to me, and they have kept your word. ⁷Now they know that everything you gave me is from you, ⁸because the words you gave to me I have given to them, and they accepted them and truly understood that I came from you, and they have believed that you sent me. ⁹I pray for them. I do not pray for the world but for the ones you have given me, because they are yours, ¹⁰and everything of mine is yours and everything of yours is mine, and I have been glorified in them. ¹¹And now I will no longer be in the world, but they are in the world, while I am coming to you. Holy Father, keep them in your name that you have given me, so that they may be one just as we are. ¹²When I was with them I protected them in your name that you gave me, and I guarded them, and none of them was lost except the son of destruction, in order that the scripture might be fulfilled. ¹³But now I am coming to you. I speak this in the world so that they may share my joy completely. ¹⁴I gave them your word, and the world hated them, because they do not belong to the world any more than I belong to the world. ¹⁵I do not ask that you take them out of the

world but that you keep them from the evil one. [16]They do not belong to the world any more than I belong to the world. [17]Consecrate them in the truth. Your word is truth. [18]As you sent me into the world, so I sent them into the world. [19]And I consecrate myself for them, so that they also may be consecrated in truth."

August 19

St. John Eudes

Sin is a cruel murder, a frightful act of God-murder, a ghastly annihilation of all things. It is murder because it is the only cause of death, both of the body and of the soul of man. It is God-murder because sin and the sinner caused Christ to die on the cross, and the sinner continues this crucifixion of Jesus, day by day, within himself.

— St. John Eudes

☐ SIRACH 3:30–6:37

Alms for the Poor. 3:30 As water quenches a flaming fire,
so almsgiving atones for sins.
[31]The kindness people have done crosses their paths later on;
should they stumble, they will find support.

4:1 My child, do not mock the life of the poor;
do not keep needy eyes waiting.
[2]Do not grieve the hungry,
nor anger the needy.
[3]Do not aggravate a heart already angry,
nor delay giving to the needy.
[4]A beggar's request do not reject;
do not turn your face away from the poor.
[5]From the needy do not turn your eyes;
do not give them reason to curse you.
[6]If in their pain they cry out bitterly,
their Rock will hear the sound of their cry.

Social Conduct. [7]Endear yourself to the assembly;
before the city's ruler bow your head.
[8]Give a hearing to the poor,
and return their greeting with deference;
[9]Deliver the oppressed from their oppressors;
right judgment should not be repugnant to you.
[10]Be like a father to orphans,
and take the place of a husband to widows.
Then God will call you his child,
and he will be merciful to you and deliver you from the pit.

The Rewards of Wisdom. [11]Wisdom teaches her children
and admonishes all who can understand her.
[12]Those who love her love life;
those who seek her out win the Lord's favor.
[13]Those who hold her fast will attain glory,
and they shall abide in the blessing of the Lord.

¹⁴Those who serve her serve the Holy
One;
  those who love her the Lord loves.

¹⁵"Whoever obeys me will judge nations;
  whoever listens to me will dwell in
    my inmost chambers.
¹⁶If they remain faithful, they will
    possess me;
  their descendants too will inherit me.

¹⁷"I will walk with them in disguise,
  and at first I will test them with trials.
Fear and dread I will bring upon them
  and I will discipline them with my
    constraints.
When their hearts are fully with me,
  ¹⁸then I will set them again on the
    straight path
  and reveal my secrets to them.
¹⁹But if they turn away from me, I will
    abandon them
  and deliver them over to robbers."

Sincerity and Justice. ²⁰My son, watch
    for the right time; fear what is evil;
  do not bring shame upon yourself.
²¹There is a shame heavy with guilt,
  and a shame that brings glory and
    respect.
²²Show no favoritism to your own
    discredit;
  let no one intimidate you to your
    own downfall.
²³Do not refrain from speaking at the
    proper time,
  and do not hide your wisdom;
²⁴For wisdom becomes known through
    speech,
  and knowledge through the tongue's
    response.
²⁵Never speak against the truth,
  but of your own ignorance be
    ashamed.
²⁶Do not be ashamed to acknowledge
    your sins,
  and do not struggle against a
    rushing stream.

²⁷Do not abase yourself before a fool;
  do not refuse to do so before rulers.
²⁸Even to the death, fight for what is
    right,
  and the Lord will do battle for you.

²⁹Do not be haughty in your speech,
  or lazy and slack in your deeds.
³⁰Do not be like a lion at home,
  or sly and suspicious with your
    servants.
³¹Do not let your hand be open to
    receive,
  but clenched when it is time to give.

Against Presumption. 5:1 Do not rely
    on your wealth,
  or say, "I have the power."
²Do not rely on your strength
  in following the desires of your
    heart.
³Do not say, "Who can prevail against
    me?"
  for the Lord will exact punishment.
⁴Do not say, "I have sinned, yet what
    has happened to me?"
  for the Lord is slow to anger!
⁵Do not be so confident of forgiveness
  that you add sin upon sin.
⁶Do not say, "His mercy is great;
  my many sins he will forgive."
For mercy and anger alike are with him;
  his wrath comes to rest on the wicked.
⁷Do not delay turning back to the Lord,
  do not put it off day after day.
For suddenly his wrath will come
    forth;
  at the time of vengeance, you will
    perish.
⁸Do not rely on deceitful wealth,
  for it will be no help on the day of
    wrath.

Use and Abuse of the Tongue. ⁹Do
    not winnow in every wind,
  nor walk in every path.
¹⁰Be steadfast regarding your
    knowledge,

and let your speech be consistent.
¹¹Be swift to hear,
but slow to answer.
¹²If you can, answer your neighbor;
if not, place your hand over your
mouth!
¹³Honor and dishonor through
speaking!
The tongue can be your downfall.
¹⁴Do not be called double-tongued;
and with your tongue do not
slander a neighbor.
For shame has been created for the
thief,
and sore disgrace for the double-
tongued.
¹⁵In little or in much, do not act
corruptly;

6:1 Do not be a foe instead of a
friend.
A bad name, disgrace, and dishonor
you will inherit.
Thus the wicked, the double-
tongued!

Unruly Passions. ²Do not fall into the
grip of your passion,
lest like fire it consume your
strength.
³It will eat your leaves and destroy your
fruits,
and you will be left like a dry tree.
⁴For fierce passion destroys its owner
and makes him the sport of his
enemies.
True Friendship. ⁵Pleasant speech
multiplies friends,
and gracious lips, friendly greetings.
⁶Let those who are friendly to you be
many,
but one in a thousand your confidant.
⁷When you gain friends, gain them
through testing,
and do not be quick to trust them.
⁸For there are friends when it suits
them,

but they will not be around in time
of trouble.
⁹Another is a friend who turns into an
enemy,
and tells of the quarrel to your
disgrace.
¹⁰Others are friends, table companions,
but they cannot be found in time of
affliction.
¹¹When things go well, they are your
other self,
and lord it over your servants.
¹²If disaster comes upon you, they turn
against you
and hide themselves.
¹³Stay away from your enemies,
and be on guard with your friends.
¹⁴Faithful friends are a sturdy shelter;
whoever finds one finds a treasure.
¹⁵Faithful friends are beyond price,
no amount can balance their worth.
¹⁶Faithful friends are life-saving
medicine;
those who fear God will find them.
¹⁷Those who fear the Lord enjoy stable
friendship,
for as they are, so will their
neighbors be.

Blessings of Wisdom. ¹⁸My child,
from your youth choose
discipline;
and when you have gray hair you
will find wisdom.
¹⁹As though plowing and sowing, draw
close to her;
then wait for her bountiful crops.
For in cultivating her you will work
but little,
and soon you will eat her fruit.

²⁰She is rough ground to the fool!
The stupid cannot abide her.
²¹She will be like a burdensome stone
to them,
and they will not delay in casting
her aside.
²²For discipline is like her name,

she is not accessible to many.

²³Listen, my child, and take my advice;
do not refuse my counsel.
²⁴Put your feet into her fetters,
and your neck under her yoke.
²⁵Bend your shoulders and carry her
and do not be irked at her bonds.
²⁶With all your soul draw close to her;
and with all your strength keep her
ways.
²⁷Inquire and search, seek and find;
when you get hold of her, do not let
her go.
²⁸Thus at last you will find rest in her,
and she will become your joy.

²⁹Her fetters will be a place of strength;
her snare, a robe of spun gold.
³⁰Her yoke will be a gold ornament;
her bonds, a purple cord.
³¹You will wear her as a robe of glory,
and bear her as a splendid crown.

☐ JOHN 17:20-26

17:20 "I pray not only for them, but also for those who will believe in me through their word, ²¹so that they may all be one, as you, Father, are in me and I in you, that they also may be in us, that the world may believe that you sent me. ²²And I have given them the glory you gave me, so that they may be one, as we are one, ²³I in them and you in me, that they may be brought to perfection as one, that the world may know that you sent me, and that you loved them

³²If you wish, my son, you can be wise;
if you apply yourself, you can be
shrewd.
³³If you are willing to listen, you can
learn;
if you pay attention, you can be
instructed.

³⁴Stand in the company of the elders;
stay close to whoever is wise.
³⁵Be eager to hear every discourse;
let no insightful saying escape you.
³⁶If you see the intelligent, seek them
out;
let your feet wear away their
doorsteps!

³⁷Reflect on the law of the Most High,
and let his commandments be your
constant study.
Then he will enlighten your mind,
and make you wise as you desire.

even as you loved me. ²⁴Father, they are your gift to me. I wish that where I am they also may be with me, that they may see my glory that you gave me, because you loved me before the foundation of the world. ²⁵Righteous Father, the world also does not know you, but I know you, and they know that you sent me. ²⁶I made known to them your name and I will make it known, that the love with which you loved me may be in them and I in them."

August 20

The saints have no need of honor from us; neither does our devotion add the slightest thing to what is theirs. Clearly, if we venerate their memory, it serves us, not them. But I tell you, when I think of them, I feel myself inflamed by tremendous yearning.

— St. Bernard of Clairvaux

☐ SIRACH 7-10

Conduct Toward God and Neighbor.
7:1 Do no evil, and evil will not
overtake you;
²avoid wickedness, and it will turn
away from you.
³Do not sow in the furrows of injustice,
lest you harvest it sevenfold.
⁴Do not seek from God authority
or from the king a place of honor.
⁵Do not parade your righteousness
before the LORD,
and before the king do not flaunt
your wisdom.
⁶Do not seek to become a judge
if you do not have the strength to
root out crime,
Lest you show fear in the presence of
the prominent
and mar your integrity.
⁷Do not be guilty of any evil before the
city court
or disgrace yourself before the
assembly.
⁸Do not plot to repeat a sin;
even for one, you will not go
unpunished.
⁹Do not say, "He will appreciate my
many gifts;
the Most High God will accept my
offerings."
¹⁰Do not be impatient in prayer
or neglect almsgiving.
¹¹Do not ridicule the embittered;
Remember: there is One who exalts
and humbles.

¹²Do not plot mischief against your
relative
or against your friend and
companion.
¹³Refuse to tell lie after lie,
for it never results in good.
¹⁴Do not babble in the assembly of the
elders
or repeat the words of your prayer.
¹⁵Do not hate hard work;
work was assigned by God.
¹⁶Do not esteem yourself more than
your compatriots;
remember, his wrath will not delay.
¹⁷More and more, humble your pride;
what awaits mortals is worms.

**Duties of Family Life, Religion and
Charity.** ¹⁸Do not barter a friend
for money,
or a true brother for the gold of
Ophir.
¹⁹Do not reject a sensible wife;
a gracious wife is more precious
than pearls.
²⁰Do not mistreat a servant who works
faithfully,
or laborers who devote themselves
to their task.
²¹Love wise servants as yourself;
do not refuse them freedom.
²²Do you have livestock? Look after
them;
if they are dependable, keep them.
²³Do you have sons? Correct them

and cure their stubbornness in their
early youth.
²⁴Do you have daughters? Keep them
chaste,
and do not be indulgent to them.
²⁵Give your daughter in marriage, and
a worry comes to an end;
but give her to a sensible man.
²⁶Do you have a wife? Do not mistreat
her,
but do not trust the wife you hate.

²⁷With your whole heart honor your
father;
your mother's birth pangs do not
forget.
²⁸Remember, of these parents you were
born;
what can you give them for all they
gave you?

²⁹With all your soul fear God
and revere his priests.
³⁰With all your strength love your Maker
and do not neglect his ministers.
³¹Honor God and respect the priest;
give him his portion as you have
been commanded:
First fruits and contributions,
his portion of victims and holy
offerings.

³²To the poor also extend your hand,
that your blessing may be complete.
³³Give your gift to all the living,
and do not withhold your kindness
from the dead.
³⁴Do not avoid those who weep,
but mourn with those who mourn.
³⁵Do not hesitate to visit the sick,
because for such things you will be
loved.

³⁶In whatever you do, remember your
last days,
and you will never sin.

Prudence in Dealing with Others. 8:1
Do not contend with the mighty,
lest you fall into their power.
²Do not quarrel with the rich,
lest they pay out the price of your
downfall.
For gold has unsettled many,
and wealth perverts the character of
princes.

³Do not quarrel with loud-mouths,
or heap wood upon their fire.
⁴Do not associate with the senseless,
lest your ancestors be insulted.

⁵Do not reproach one who turns away
from sin;
remember, we all are guilty.
⁶Do not insult one who is old,
for some of us will also grow old.
⁷Do not rejoice when someone dies;
remember, we are all to be
gathered in.

⁸Do not neglect the discourse of the
wise,
but busy yourself with their proverbs;
For in this way you will acquire the
training
to stand in the presence of princes.
⁹Do not reject the tradition of the
elders
which they have heard from their
ancestors;
For from it you will learn
how to answer when the need arises.

¹⁰Do not kindle the coals of sinners,
lest you be burned in their flaming
fire.
¹¹Do not give ground before
scoundrels;
it will set them in ambush against
you.
¹²Do not lend to one more powerful
than yourself;
or if you lend, count it as lost.
¹³Do not give collateral beyond your
means;
consider any collateral a debt you
must pay.

¹⁴Do not go to court against a judge,
  for the case will be settled in his favor.
¹⁵Do not travel with the ruthless
  lest they weigh you down with
    calamity;
For they will only go their own way,
  and through their folly you will also
    perish.
¹⁶Do not defy the quick-tempered,
  or ride with them through the desert.
For bloodshed is nothing to them;
  when there is no one to help, they
    will destroy you.

¹⁷Do not take counsel with simpletons,
  for they cannot keep a confidence.
¹⁸Before a stranger do nothing that
    should be kept secret,
  for you do not know what it will
    produce later on.
¹⁹Open your heart to no one,
  do not banish your happiness.

Advice Concerning Women. 9:1 Do
    not be jealous of the wife of your
    bosom,
  lest you teach her to do evil against
    you.
²Do not give a woman power over you
  to trample on your dignity.
³Do not go near a strange woman,
  lest you fall into her snares.
⁴Do not dally with a singer,
  lest you be captivated by her charms.
⁵Do not entertain any thoughts about
    a virgin,
  lest you be enmeshed in damages
    for her.
⁶Do not give yourself to a prostitute
  lest you lose your inheritance.
⁷Do not look around the streets of the
    city
  or wander through its squares.
⁸Avert your eyes from a shapely woman;
  do not gaze upon beauty that is not
    yours;

Through woman's beauty many have
    been ruined,
  for love of it burns like fire.
⁹Never recline at table with a married
    woman,
  or drink intoxicants with her,
Lest your heart be drawn to her
  and you go down in blood to the
    grave.

Choice of Friends. ¹⁰Do not abandon
    old friends;
  new ones cannot equal them.
A new friend is like new wine—
  when it has aged, you drink it with
    pleasure.
¹¹Do not envy the wicked
  for you do not know when their day
    will come.
¹²Do not delight in the pleasures of the
    ungodly;
  remember, they will not die
    unpunished.

¹³Keep away from those who have
    power to kill,
  and you will not be filled with the
    dread of death.
But if you come near them, do not
    offend them,
  lest they take away your life.
Know that you are stepping among
    snares
  and walking over a net.
¹⁴As best you can, answer your neighbor,
  and associate with the wise.
¹⁵With the learned exchange ideas;
  and let all your conversation be about
    the law of the Most High.
¹⁶Take the righteous for your table
    companions;
  and let your glory be in the fear of
    God.

Concerning Rulers. ¹⁷Work by skilled
    hands will earn praise;
  but the people's leader is proved
    wise by his words.

¹⁸Loud mouths are feared in their city,
and whoever is reckless in speech is
hated.

10:1 A wise magistrate gives stability to
his people,
and government by the intelligent is
well ordered.
²As the people's judge, so the officials;
as the head of a city, so the
inhabitants.
³A reckless king destroys his people,
but a city grows through the
intelligence of its princes.
⁴Sovereignty over the earth is in the
hand of God,
who appoints the right person for
the right time.
⁵Sovereignty over everyone is in the
hand of God,
who imparts his majesty to the ruler.

The Sin of Pride. ⁶No matter what the
wrong, never harm your neighbor
or go the way of arrogance.
⁷Odious to the Lord and to mortals is
pride,
and for both oppression is a crime.
⁸Sovereignty is transferred from one
people to another
because of the lawlessness of the
proud.
⁹Why are dust and ashes proud?
Even during life the body decays.
¹⁰A slight illness—the doctor jests;
a king today—tomorrow he is dead.
¹¹When a people die,
they inherit corruption and worms,
gnats and maggots.

¹²The beginning of pride is stubbornness
in withdrawing the heart from one's
Maker.
¹³For sin is a reservoir of insolence,
a source which runs over with vice;
Because of it God sends unheard-of
afflictions
and strikes people with utter ruin.

¹⁴God overturns the thrones of the
proud
and enthrones the lowly in their place.
¹⁵God plucks up the roots of the proud,
and plants the lowly in their place.
¹⁶The Lord lays waste the lands of the
nations,
and destroys them to the very
foundations of the earth.
¹⁷He removes them from the earth,
destroying them,
erasing their memory from the world.
¹⁸Insolence does not befit mortals,
nor impudent anger those born of
women.

True Glory. ¹⁹Whose offspring can be
honorable? Human offspring.
Those who fear the LORD are
honorable offspring.
Whose offspring can be disgraceful?
Human offspring.
Those who transgress the
commandment are disgraceful
offspring.
²⁰Among relatives their leader is
honored;
but whoever fears God is honored
among God's people.
²²Resident alien, stranger, foreigner,
pauper—
their glory is the fear of the LORD.
²³It is not right to despise anyone wise
but poor,
nor proper to honor the lawless.

²⁴The prince, the ruler, the judge are in
honor;
but none is greater than the one
who fears God.
²⁵When the free serve a wise slave,
the wise will not complain.
²⁶Do not flaunt your wisdom in
managing your affairs,
or boast in your time of need.
²⁷Better the worker who has goods in
plenty
than the boaster who has no food.

²⁸My son, with humility have self-
esteem;
and give yourself the esteem you
deserve.
²⁹Who will acquit those who condemn
themselves?
Who will honor those who disgrace
themselves?

³⁰The poor are honored for their
wisdom;
the rich are honored for their
wealth.
³¹Honored in poverty, how much more
so in wealth!
Disgraced in wealth, in poverty how
much the more!

☐ JOHN 18:1-27

Jesus Arrested. 18:1 When he had said this, Jesus went out with his disciples across the Kidron valley to where there was a garden, into which he and his disciples entered. ²Judas his betrayer also knew the place, because Jesus had often met there with his disciples. ³So Judas got a band of soldiers and guards from the chief priests and the Pharisees and went there with lanterns, torches, and weapons. ⁴Jesus, knowing everything that was going to happen to him, went out and said to them, "Whom are you looking for?" ⁵They answered him, "Jesus the Nazorean." He said to them, "I AM." Judas his betrayer was also with them. ⁶When he said to them, "I AM," they turned away and fell to the ground. ⁷So he again asked them, "Whom are you looking for?" They said, "Jesus the Nazorean." ⁸Jesus answered, "I told you that I AM. So if you are looking for me, let these men go." ⁹This was to fulfill what he had said, "I have not lost any of those you gave me." ¹⁰Then Simon Peter, who had a sword, drew it, struck the high priest's slave, and cut off his right ear. The slave's name was Malchus. ¹¹Jesus said to Peter, "Put your sword into its scabbard. Shall I not drink the cup that the Father gave me?"

¹²So the band of soldiers, the tribune, and the Jewish guards seized Jesus, bound him, ¹³and brought him to Annas first. He was the father-in-law of Caiaphas, who was high priest that year. ¹⁴It was Caiaphas who had counseled the Jews that it was better that one man should die rather than the people.

Peter's First Denial. ¹⁵Simon Peter and another disciple followed Jesus. Now the other disciple was known to the high priest, and he entered the courtyard of the high priest with Jesus. ¹⁶But Peter stood at the gate outside. So the other disciple, the acquaintance of the high priest, went out and spoke to the gatekeeper and brought Peter in. ¹⁷Then the maid who was the gatekeeper said to Peter, "You are not one of this man's disciples, are you?" He said, "I am not." ¹⁸Now the slaves and the guards were standing around a charcoal fire that they had made, because it was cold, and were warming themselves. Peter was also standing there keeping warm.

The Inquiry before Annas. ¹⁹The high priest questioned Jesus about his disciples and about his doctrine. ²⁰Jesus answered him, "I have spoken publicly to the world. I have always taught in a synagogue or in the temple area where all the Jews gather, and in secret I have said nothing. ²¹Why ask me? Ask those who heard me what I said to them. They know what I said." ²²When he had said this, one of the temple guards standing there struck Jesus and said, "Is this the way you answer the high priest?" ²³Jesus answered him, "If I have spoken wrongly, testify to the wrong; but if I have spoken rightly, why do you strike me?" ²⁴Then Annas sent him bound to Caiaphas the high priest.

Peter Denies Jesus Again. ²⁵Now Simon Peter was standing there keeping warm. And they said to him, "You are not one of his disciples, are you?" He denied it and said, "I am not." ²⁶One of the slaves of the high priest, a relative of the one whose ear Peter had cut off, said, "Didn't I see you in the garden with him?" ²⁷Again Peter denied it. And immediately the cock crowed.

August 21

Pope St. Pius X

Holy Communion is the shortest and safest way to heaven. There are others: innocence, but that is for little children; penance, but we are afraid of it; generous endurance for the trials of life, but when they come we weep and ask to be spared. The surest, easiest, shortest way is the Eucharist.

— POPE ST. PIUS X

☐ SIRACH 11-14:2

11:1 The wisdom of the poor lifts their
    head high
    and sets them among princes.
²Do not praise anyone for good looks;
    or despise anyone because of
      appearance.
³The bee is least among winged
    creatures,
    but it reaps the choicest of harvests.
⁴Do not mock the one who wears only
    a loin-cloth,
    or scoff at a person's bitter day.
For strange are the deeds of the LORD,
    hidden from mortals his work.
⁵Many are the oppressed who rise to
    the throne;
    some that none would consider
      wear a crown.
⁶Many are the exalted who fall into
    utter disgrace,
    many the honored who are given
      into the power of the few.

Moderation and Patience. ⁷Before
    investigating, do not find fault;
    examine first, then criticize.

⁸Before listening, do not say a word,
    interrupt no one in the midst of
      speaking.
⁹Do not dispute about what is not your
    concern;
    in the quarrels of the arrogant do
      not take part.
¹⁰My son, why increase your anxiety,
    since whoever is greedy for wealth
      will not be blameless?
Even if you chase after it, you will
    never overtake it;
    and by fleeing you will not escape.
¹¹One may work and struggle and drive,
    and fall short all the same.
¹²Others go their way broken-down
    drifters,
    with little strength and great misery—
Yet the eye of the LORD looks favorably
    upon them,
    shaking them free of the stinking
      mire.
¹³He lifts up their heads and exalts them
    to the amazement of the many.

¹⁴Good and evil, life and death,

poverty and riches—all are from the LORD.

17The Lord's gift remains with the devout;
  his favor brings lasting success.
18Some become rich through a miser's life,
  and this is their allotted reward:
19When they say: "I have found rest,
  now I will feast on my goods,"
They do not know how long it will be
  till they die and leave them to others.

20My child, stand by your agreement
    and attend to it,
  grow old while doing your work.
21Do not marvel at the works of a sinner,
  but trust in the LORD and wait for his light;
For it is easy in the eyes of the LORD
  suddenly, in an instant, to make the poor rich.

22God's blessing is the lot of the righteous,
  and in due time their hope bears fruit.
23Do not say: "What do I need?
  What further benefits can be mine?"
24Do not say: "I am self-sufficient.
  What harm can come to me now?"
25The day of prosperity makes one forget adversity;
  the day of adversity makes one forget prosperity.
26For it is easy for the Lord on the day of death
  to repay mortals according to their conduct.
27A time of affliction brings forgetfulness of past delights;
  at the end of life one's deeds are revealed.
28Call none happy before death,
  for how they end, they are known.

Care in Choosing Friends. 29Not everyone should be brought into your house,
for many are the snares of the crafty.
30Like a decoy partridge in a cage, so is the heart of the proud,
  and like a spy they will pick out the weak spots.
31For they lie in wait to turn good into evil,
  and to praiseworthy deeds they attach blame.
32One spark kindles many coals;
  a sinner lies in wait for blood.
33Beware of scoundrels, for they breed only evil,
  and they may give you a lasting stain.
34Admit strangers into your home, and they will stir up trouble
  and make you a stranger to your own family.

12:1 If you do good, know for whom you are doing it,
  and your kindness will have its effect.
2Do good to the righteous and reward will be yours,
  if not from them, from the LORD.
3No good comes to those who give comfort to the wicked,
  nor is it an act of mercy that they do.
4Give to the good but refuse the sinner;
5refresh the downtrodden but give nothing to the proud.
No arms for combat should you give them,
  lest they use these against you;
Twofold evil you will obtain for every good deed you do for them.
6For God also hates sinners,
  and takes vengeance on evildoers.

8In prosperity we cannot know our friends;
  in adversity an enemy will not remain concealed.
9When one is successful even an enemy is friendly;
  but in adversity even a friend disappears.

¹⁰Never trust your enemies,
    for their wickedness is like corrosion
        in bronze.
¹¹Even though they act deferentially
    and peaceably toward you,
    take care to be on your guard
        against them.
Treat them as those who reveal secrets,
    and be certain that in the end there
        will still be envy.
¹²Do not let them stand near you,
    lest they push you aside and take
        your place.
Do not let them sit at your right hand,
    or they will demand your seat,
And in the end you will appreciate my
    advice,
    when you groan with regret, as I
        warned.

¹³Who pities a snake charmer when he
    is bitten,
    or anyone who goes near a wild beast?
¹⁴So it is with the companion of the
    proud,
    who is involved in their sins:
¹⁵While you stand firm, they make no
    move;
    but if you slip, they cannot hold back.
¹⁶With their lips enemies speak sweetly,
    but in their heart they scheme to
        plunge you into the abyss.
Though enemies have tears in their eyes,
    given the chance, they will never
        have enough of your blood.
¹⁷If evil comes upon you, you will find
    them at hand;
    pretending to help, they will trip
        you up,
¹⁸Then they will shake their heads and
    clap their hands
    and hiss repeatedly, and show their
        true faces.

Caution Regarding Associates. 13:1
    Touch pitch and you blacken
        your hand;

associate with scoundrels and you
    learn their ways.
²Do not lift a weight too heavy for you,
    or associate with anyone wealthier
        than you.
How can the clay pot go with the
    metal cauldron?
    When they knock together, the pot
        will be smashed:
³The rich do wrong and boast of it,
    while the poor are wronged and beg
        forgiveness.
⁴As long as the rich can use you they
    will enslave you,
    but when you are down and out
        they will abandon you.
⁵As long as you have anything they will
    live with you,
    but they will drain you dry without
        remorse.
⁶When they need you they will deceive
    you
    and smile at you and raise your
        hopes;
    they will speak kindly to you and
        say, "What do you need?"
⁷They will embarrass you at their
    dinner parties,
    and finally laugh at you.
Afterwards, when they see you, they
    will pass you by,
    and shake their heads at you.
⁸Be on guard: do not act too boldly;
    do not be like those who lack sense.
⁹When the influential draw near, keep
    your distance;
    then they will urge you all the more.
¹⁰Do not draw too close, lest you be
    rebuffed,
    but do not keep too far away lest
        you be regarded as an enemy.
¹¹Do not venture to be free with them,
    do not trust their many words;
For by prolonged talk they will test you,
    and though smiling they will probe
        you.

¹²Mercilessly they will make you a
    laughingstock,
  and will not refrain from injury or
    chains.
¹³Be on your guard and take care
  never to accompany lawless people.

¹⁵Every living thing loves its own kind,
  and we all love someone like
    ourselves.
¹⁶Every living being keeps close to its
    own kind;
  and people associate with their own
    kind.
¹⁷Is a wolf ever allied with a lamb?
  So the sinner with the righteous.
¹⁸Can there be peace between the
    hyena and the dog?
  Or peace between the rich and the
    poor?
¹⁹Wild donkeys of the desert are lion's
    prey;
  likewise the poor are feeding
    grounds for the rich.
²⁰Humility is an abomination to the
    proud;
  and the poor are an abomination to
    the rich.
²¹When the rich stumble they are
    supported by friends;
  when the poor trip they are pushed
    down by friends.
²²When the rich speak they have many
    supporters;

though what they say is repugnant,
  it wins approval.
When the poor speak people say,
  "Come, come, speak up!"
though they are talking sense, they
  get no hearing.
²³When the rich speak all are silent,
  their wisdom people extol to the
    clouds.
When the poor speak people say:
  "Who is that?"
If they stumble, people knock them
  down.
²⁴Wealth is good where there is no
    sin;
  but poverty is evil by the standards
    of the proud.
²⁵The heart changes one's face,
  either for good or for evil.
²⁶The sign of a good heart is a radiant
    face;
  withdrawn and perplexed is the
    toiling schemer.

14:1 Happy those whose mouth causes
    them no grief,
  those who are not stung by remorse
    for sin.
²Happy are those whose conscience
    does not reproach them,
  those who have not lost hope.

☐ JOHN 18:28–19:16

The Trial before Pilate. 18:28 Then they brought Jesus from Caiaphas to the praetorium. It was morning. And they themselves did not enter the praetorium, in order not to be defiled so that they could eat the Passover. ²⁹So Pilate came out to them and said, "What charge do you bring [against] this man?" ³⁰They answered and said to him, "If he were not a criminal, we would not have handed him over to you." ³¹At this, Pilate said to them, "Take him yourselves, and judge him according to your law." The Jews answered him, "We do not have the right to execute anyone," ³²in order that the word of Jesus might be fulfilled that he said indicating the kind of death he would die. ³³So Pilate went back into the praetorium and summoned Jesus and said to him, "Are you the King of the Jews?" ³⁴Jesus answered, "Do you say this on your own or have others told you about me?" ³⁵Pilate answered, "I am not a Jew, am I? Your own nation and the chief priests handed you over to me. What have you done?" ³⁶Jesus answered, "My kingdom does not belong to this world. If my kingdom did belong to this world, my attendants [would] be fighting to keep me from being handed over to the Jews. But as it is, my kingdom is not here." ³⁷So Pilate said to him, "Then you are a king?" Jesus answered, "You say I am a king. For this I was born and for this I came into the world, to testify to the truth. Everyone who belongs to the truth listens to my voice." ³⁸Pilate said to him, "What is truth?"

When he had said this, he again went out to the Jews and said to them, "I find no guilt in him. ³⁹But you have a custom that I release one prisoner to you at Passover. Do you want me to release to you the King of the Jews?" ⁴⁰They cried out again, "Not this one but Barabbas!" Now Barabbas was a revolutionary.

19:1 Then Pilate took Jesus and had him scourged. ²And the soldiers wove a crown out of thorns and placed it on his head, and clothed him in a purple cloak, ³and they came to him and said, "Hail, King of the Jews!" And they struck him repeatedly. ⁴Once more Pilate went out and said to them, "Look, I am bringing him out to you, so that you may know that I find no guilt in him." ⁵So Jesus came out, wearing the crown of thorns and the purple cloak. And he said to them, "Behold, the man!" ⁶When the chief priests and the guards saw him they cried out, "Crucify him, crucify him!" Pilate said to them, "Take him yourselves and crucify him. I find no guilt in him." ⁷The Jews answered, "We have a law, and according to that law he ought to die, because he made himself the Son of God." ⁸Now when Pilate heard this statement, he became even more afraid, ⁹and went back into the praetorium and said to Jesus, "Where are you from?" Jesus did not answer him. ¹⁰So Pilate said to him, "Do you not speak to me? Do you not know that I have power to release you and I have power to crucify you?" ¹¹Jesus answered [him], "You would have no power over me if it had not been given to you from above. For this reason the one who handed me over to you has the greater sin." ¹²Consequently, Pilate tried to release him; but the Jews cried out, "If you release him, you are not a Friend of Caesar. Everyone who makes himself a king opposes Caesar."

¹³When Pilate heard these words he brought Jesus out and seated him on the judge's bench in the place called Stone Pavement, in Hebrew, Gabbatha. ¹⁴It was preparation day for Passover, and it was about noon. And he said to the Jews, "Behold, your king!" ¹⁵They cried out, "Take him away, take him away! Crucify him!" Pilate said to them, "Shall I crucify your king?" The chief priests answered, "We have no king but Caesar." ¹⁶Then he handed him over to them to be crucified.

August 22

The Queenship of Mary

No one has access to the Almighty as His mother has; none has merit such as hers. Her Son will deny her nothing that she asks; and herein lies her power. While she defends the Church, neither height nor depth, neither men nor evil spirits, neither great monarchs, nor craft of man, nor popular violence, can avail to harm us; for human life is short, but Mary reigns above, a Queen forever.

— Blessed John Henry Newman

☐ SIRACH 14:3-18:33

The Use of Wealth. 14:3 Wealth is not
appropriate for the mean-spirited;
to misers, what use is gold?
⁴What they deny themselves they
collect for someone else,
and strangers will live sumptuously
on their possessions.
⁵To whom will they be generous that
are stingy with themselves
and do not enjoy what is their own?
⁶None are worse than those who are
stingy with themselves;
they punish their own avarice.
⁷If ever they do good, it is by mistake;
in the end they reveal their meanness.
⁸Misers are evil people,
they turn away and disregard others.
⁹The greedy see their share as not
enough;
greedy injustice dries up the soul.
¹⁰The eye of the miserly is rapacious for
food,
but there is none of it on their own
table.
¹¹My son, if you have the means, treat
yourself well,
and enjoy life as best you can.
¹²Remember that death does not
delay,
and you have not been told the
grave's appointed time.
¹³Before you die, be good to your friends;

give them a share in what you possess.
¹⁴Do not deprive yourself of good
things now
or let a choice portion escape you.
¹⁵Will you not leave your riches to
others,
and your earnings to be divided by
lot?
¹⁶Give and take, treat yourself well,
for in Sheol there are no joys to
seek.
¹⁷All flesh grows old like a garment;
the age-old law is: everyone must
die.
¹⁸As with the leaves growing on a
luxuriant tree—
one falls off and another sprouts—
So with the generations of flesh and
blood:
one dies and another flourishes.
¹⁹All human deeds surely perish;
the works they do follow after them.

**The Search for Wisdom and Her
Blessings.** ²⁰Happy those who
meditate on Wisdom,
and fix their gaze on knowledge;
²¹Who ponder her ways in their heart,
and understand her paths;
²²Who pursue her like a scout,
and watch at her entry way;
²³Who peep through her windows,
and listen at her doors;

²⁴Who encamp near her house
and fasten their tent pegs next to
her walls;
²⁵Who pitch their tent beside her,
and dwell in a good place;
²⁶Who build their nest in her leaves,
and lodge in her branches;
²⁷Who take refuge from the heat in her
shade
and dwell in her home.

15:1 Whoever fears the LORD will do
this;
whoever is practiced in the Law will
come to Wisdom.
²She will meet him like a mother;
like a young bride she will receive
him,
³She will feed him with the bread of
learning,
and give him the water of
understanding to drink.
⁴He will lean upon her and not fall;
he will trust in her and not be put
to shame.
⁵She will exalt him above his neighbors,
and in the assembly she will make
him eloquent.
⁶Joy and gladness he will find,
and an everlasting name he will
inherit.
⁷The worthless will not attain her,
and the haughty will not behold her.
⁸She is far from the impious;
liars never think of her.
⁹Praise is unseemly on the lips of sinners,
for it has not been allotted to them
by God.
¹⁰But praise is uttered by the mouth of
the wise,
and its rightful owner teaches it.

Free Will. ¹¹Do not say: "It was God's
doing that I fell away,"
for what he hates he does not do.
¹²Do not say: "He himself has led me
astray,"

for he has no need of the wicked.
¹³Abominable wickedness the LORD hates
and he does not let it happen to
those who fear him.

¹⁴God in the beginning created human
beings
and made them subject to their own
free choice.
¹⁵If you choose, you can keep the
commandments;
loyalty is doing the will of God.
¹⁶Set before you are fire and water;
to whatever you choose, stretch out
your hand.
¹⁷Before everyone are life and death,
whichever they choose will be given
them.

¹⁸Immense is the wisdom of the LORD;
mighty in power, he sees all things.
¹⁹The eyes of God behold his works,
and he understands every human
deed.
²⁰He never commands anyone to sin,
nor shows leniency toward deceivers.

God's Punishment of Sinners. 16:1
Do not yearn for worthless
children,
or rejoice in wicked offspring.
²Even if they be many, do not rejoice
in them
if they do not have fear of the LORD.
³Do not count on long life for them,
or have any hope for their future.
For one can be better than a thousand;
rather die childless than have
impious children!
⁴Through one wise person a city can be
peopled;
but through a clan of rebels it
becomes desolate.

⁵Many such things my eye has seen,
and even more than these my ear
has heard.
⁶Against a sinful band fire is kindled,

upon a godless people wrath blazes.
⁷He did not forgive the princes of old
who rebelled long ago in their might.
⁸He did not spare the neighbors of Lot,
abominable in their pride.
⁹He did not spare the doomed people,
dispossessed because of their sin;
¹⁰Nor the six hundred thousand foot
soldiers,
sent to their graves for the arrogance
of their hearts.
¹¹Had there been but one stiff-necked
person,
it would be a wonder had he gone
unpunished.
For mercy and anger alike are with him;
he remits and forgives, but also
pours out wrath.
¹²Great as his mercy is his punishment;
he judges people, each according to
their deeds.
¹³Criminals do not escape with their
plunder;
the hope of the righteous, God
never leaves unfulfilled.
¹⁴Whoever does good has a reward;
each receives according to their
deeds.

¹⁷Do not say: "I am hidden from God;
and on high who remembers me?
Among so many people I am
unknown;
what am I in the world of spirits?
¹⁸Look, the heavens and the highest
heavens,
the abyss and the earth tremble at
his visitation.
¹⁹The roots of the mountains and the
earth's foundations—
at his mere glance they quiver and
quake.
²⁰Of me, therefore, he will take no
notice;
with my ways who will be
concerned?
²¹If I sin, no eye will see me;

if all in secret I act deceitfully, who
is to know?
²²Who tells him about just deeds?
What can I expect for doing my
duty?"
²³Such the thoughts of the senseless;
only the foolish entertain them.

Divine Wisdom Seen in Creation.
²⁴Listen to me, my son, and take
my advice,
and apply your mind to my words,
²⁵While I pour out my spirit by
measure
and impart knowledge with care.
²⁶When at the first God created his
works
and, as he made them, assigned
their tasks,
²⁷He arranged for all time what they
were to do,
their domains from generation to
generation.
They were not to go hungry or grow
weary,
or ever cease from their tasks.
²⁸Never does a single one crowd its
neighbor,
or do any ever disobey his word.
²⁹Then the Lord looked upon the earth,
and filled it with his blessings.
³⁰Its surface he covered with every kind
of living creature
which must return into it again.

Creation of Human Beings. 17:1 The
Lord created human beings from
the earth,
and makes them return to earth
again.
²A limited number of days he gave
them,
but granted them authority over
everything on earth.
³He endowed them with strength like
his own,
and made them in his image.

⁴He put fear of them in all flesh,
  and gave them dominion over beasts
    and birds.
⁶Discernment, tongues, and eyes,
  ears, and a mind for thinking he
    gave them.
⁷With knowledge and understanding
  he filled them;
  good and evil he showed them.
⁸He put fear of him into their hearts
  to show them the grandeur of his
    works,
⁹That they might describe the wonders
  of his deeds
    ¹⁰and praise his holy name.
¹¹He set before them knowledge,
  and allotted to them the law of life.
¹²An everlasting covenant he made
  with them,
  and his commandments he revealed
    to them.
¹³His majestic glory their eyes beheld,
  his glorious voice their ears heard.
¹⁴He said to them, "Avoid all evil";
  to each of them he gave precepts
    about their neighbor.
¹⁵Their ways are ever known to him,
  they cannot be hidden from his eyes.
¹⁷Over every nation he appointed a
  ruler,
  but Israel is the Lord's own portion.
¹⁹All their works are clear as the sun to
  him,
  and his eyes are ever upon their ways.
²⁰Their iniquities cannot be hidden
  from him,
  all their sins are before the Lord.
²²Human goodness is like a signet ring
  with God,
  and virtue he keeps like the apple of
    his eye.
²³Later he will rise up and repay them,
  requiting each one as they deserve.

Appeal for a Return to God. ²⁴But to
  the penitent he provides a way
  back

and encourages those who are losing
  hope!
²⁵Turn back to the Lord and give up
  your sins,
  pray before him and make your
    offenses few.
²⁶Turn again to the Most High and
  away from iniquity,
  and hate intensely what he loathes.
²⁷Who in Sheol can glorify the Most
  High
  in place of the living who offer their
    praise?
²⁸The dead can no more give praise
  than those who have never lived;
  they who are alive and well glorify
    the Lord.
²⁹How great is the mercy of the Lord,
  and his forgiveness for those who
    return to him!
³⁰For not everything is within human
  reach,
  since human beings are not
    immortal.
³¹Is anything brighter than the sun? Yet
  it can be eclipsed.
  How worthless then the thoughts of
    flesh and blood!
³²God holds accountable the hosts of
  highest heaven,
  while all mortals are dust and ashes.

The Divine Power and Mercy. 18:1
  He who lives forever created the
    whole universe;
  ²the Lord alone is just.
⁴To whom has he given power to
  describe his works,
  and who can search out his mighty
    deeds?
⁵Who can measure his majestic power,
  or fully recount his mercies?
⁶No one can lessen, increase,
  or fathom the wonders of the Lord.
⁷When mortals finish, they are only
  beginning,

and when they stop they are still
bewildered.
[8]What are mortals? What are they
worth?
What is good in them, and what is
evil?
[9]The number of their days seems great
if it reaches a hundred years.
[10]Like a drop of water from the sea and
a grain of sand,
so are these few years among the
days of eternity.
[11]That is why the Lord is patient with
them
and pours out his mercy on them.
[12]He sees and understands that their
death is wretched,
and so he forgives them all the more.
[13]Their compassion is for their neighbor,
but the Lord's compassion reaches
all flesh,
Reproving, admonishing, teaching,
and turning them back, as a
shepherd his flock.
[14]He has compassion on those who
accept his discipline,
who are eager for his precepts.

The Need for Prudence. [15]My child,
add no reproach to your charity,
or spoil any gift by harsh words.
[16]Does not the dew give relief from the
scorching heat?
So a word can be better than a gift.
[17]Indeed does not a word count more
than a good gift?
But both are offered by a kind
person.
[18]The fool is ungracious and abusive,
and a grudging gift makes the eyes
smart.
[19]Before you speak, learn;
before you get sick, prepare the cure.
[20]Before you are judged, examine
yourself,
and at the time of scrutiny you will
have forgiveness.

[21]Before you fall ill, humble yourself;
and when you have sinned, show
repentance.
Do not delay forsaking your sins;
do not neglect to do so until you are
in distress.
[22]Let nothing prevent the prompt
payment of your vows;
do not wait until death to fulfill
them.
[23]Before making a vow prepare
yourself;
do not be like one who puts the
Lord to the test.
[24]Think of wrath on the day of death,
the time of vengeance when he will
hide his face.
[25]Think of the time of hunger in the
time of plenty,
poverty and need in the day of
wealth.
[26]Between morning and evening there
is a change of time;
before the Lord all things are fleeting.
[27]The wise are discreet in all things;
where sin is rife they keep
themselves from wrongdoing.
[28]Every wise person teaches wisdom,
and those who know her declare her
praise;
[29]Those skilled in words become wise
themselves,
and pour forth apt proverbs.

Self-Control. [30]Do not let your
passions be your guide,
but keep your desires in check.
[31]If you allow yourself to satisfy your
passions,
they will make you the laughingstock
of your enemies.
[32]Take no pleasure in too much luxury
which brings on poverty redoubled.
[33]Do not become a glutton and a
drunkard
with nothing in your purse.

☐ JOHN 19:17-42

The Crucifixion of Jesus. So they took Jesus, **19:17** and carrying the cross himself he went out to what is called the Place of the Skull, in Hebrew, Golgotha. [18]There they crucified him, and with him two others, one on either side, with Jesus in the middle. [19]Pilate also had an inscription written and put on the cross. It read, "Jesus the Nazorean, the King of the Jews." [20]Now many of the Jews read this inscription, because the place where Jesus was crucified was near the city; and it was written in Hebrew, Latin, and Greek. [21]So the chief priests of the Jews said to Pilate, "Do not write 'The King of the Jews,' but that he said, 'I am the King of the Jews.'" [22]Pilate answered, "What I have written, I have written."

[23]When the soldiers had crucified Jesus, they took his clothes and divided them into four shares, a share for each soldier. They also took his tunic, but the tunic was seamless, woven in one piece from the top down. [24]So they said to one another, "Let's not tear it, but cast lots for it to see whose it will be," in order that the passage of scripture might be fulfilled [that says]:

"They divided my garments among
    them,
and for my vesture they cast lots."

This is what the soldiers did. [25]Standing by the cross of Jesus were his mother and his mother's sister, Mary the wife of Clopas, and Mary of Magdala. [26]When Jesus saw his mother and the disciple there whom he loved, he said to his mother, "Woman, behold, your son." [27]Then he said to the disciple, "Behold, your mother." And from that hour the disciple took her into his home.

[28]After this, aware that everything was now finished, in order that the scripture might be fulfilled, Jesus said, "I thirst." [29]There was a vessel filled with common wine. So they put a sponge soaked in wine on a sprig of hyssop and put it up to his mouth. [30]When Jesus had taken the wine, he said, "It is finished." And bowing his head, he handed over the spirit.

The Blood and Water. [31]Now since it was preparation day, in order that the bodies might not remain on the cross on the sabbath, for the sabbath day of that week was a solemn one, the Jews asked Pilate that their legs be broken and they be taken down. [32]So the soldiers came and broke the legs of the first and then of the other one who was crucified with Jesus. [33]But when they came to Jesus and saw that he was already dead, they did not break his legs, [34]but one soldier thrust his lance into his side, and immediately blood and water flowed out. [35]An eyewitness has testified, and his testimony is true; he knows that he is speaking the truth, so that you also may [come to] believe. [36]For this happened so that the scripture passage might be fulfilled:

"Not a bone of it will be broken."

[37]And again another passage says:

"They will look upon him whom they
    have pierced."

The Burial of Jesus. [38]After this, Joseph of Arimathea, secretly a disciple of Jesus for fear of the Jews, asked Pilate if he could remove the body of Jesus. And Pilate permitted it. So he came and took his body. [39]Nicodemus, the one who had first come to him at night, also came bringing a mixture of myrrh and aloes weighing about one hundred pounds. [40]They took the body of Jesus and bound it with burial cloths along with the spices, according to the Jewish burial custom. [41]Now in the place where he had been crucified there was a garden, and in the garden a new tomb, in which no one had yet been buried. [42]So they laid Jesus there because of the Jewish preparation day; for the tomb was close by.

August 23

St. Rose of Lima

Apart from the cross there is no other ladder by which we may get to heaven.

— St. Rose of Lima

☐ SIRACH 19-22

19:1 Whoever does this grows no richer;
those who waste the little they have
will be stripped bare.
²Wine and women make the heart
lustful,
and the companion of prostitutes
becomes reckless.
³Rottenness and worms will possess him,
and the reckless will be snatched
away.
⁴Whoever trusts others too quickly has
a shallow mind,
and those who sin wrong themselves.

The Proper Use of Speech. ⁵Whoever
gloats over evil will be destroyed,
⁶and whoever repeats gossip has no
sense.
⁷Never repeat gossip,
and no one will reproach you.
⁸Tell nothing to friend or foe;
and unless it be a sin for you, do not
reveal a thing.
⁹For someone may have heard you and
watched you,
and in time come to hate you.
¹⁰Let anything you hear die with you;
never fear, it will not make you
burst!
¹¹Having heard something, the fool
goes into labor,
like a woman giving birth to a child.
¹²Like an arrow stuck in a fool's thigh,
so is gossip in the belly of a fool.
¹³Admonish your friend—he may not
have done it;
and if he did, that he may not do it
again.

¹⁴Admonish your neighbor—he may
not have said it;
and if he did, that he may not say it
again.
¹⁵Admonish your friend—often it may
be slander;
do not believe every story.
¹⁶Then, too, a person can slip and not
mean it;
who has not sinned with his tongue?
¹⁷Admonish your neighbor before you
break with him;
and give due place to the Law of the
Most High.

How to Recognize True Wisdom.
²⁰All wisdom is fear of the LORD;
and in all wisdom, the observance
of the Law.
²²The knowledge of wickedness is not
wisdom,
nor is there prudence in the counsel
of sinners.
²³There is a shrewdness that is detestable,
while the fool may be free from sin.
²⁴Better are the God-fearing who have
little understanding
than those of great intelligence who
violate the Law.

²⁵There is a shrewdness keen but
dishonest,
and there are those who are
duplicitous to win a judgment.
²⁶There is the villain bowed in grief,
but full of deceit within.
²⁷He hides his face and pretends not to
hear,

but when not observed, he will take
advantage of you:
²⁸Even if his lack of strength keeps him
from sinning,
when he finds the right time he will
do harm.
²⁹People are known by their appearance;
the sensible are recognized as such
when first met.
³⁰One's attire, hearty laughter, and gait
proclaim him for what he is.

Conduct of the Wise and the Foolish.
20:1 There is an admonition that
is untimely,
but the silent person is the wise one.
²It is much better to admonish than to
lose one's temper;
³one who admits a fault will be kept
from disgrace.
⁴Like a eunuch lusting to violate a
young woman
is the one who does right under
compulsion.
⁵One is silent and is thought wise;
another, for being talkative, is
disliked.
⁶One is silent, having nothing to say;
another is silent, biding his time.
⁷The wise remain silent till the right
time comes,
but a boasting fool misses the
proper time.
⁸Whoever talks too much is detested;
whoever pretends to authority is
hated.
⁹There is the misfortune that brings
success;
and there is the gain that turns into
loss.
¹⁰There is the gift that profits you
nothing,
and there is the gift that must be
paid back double.
¹¹There is the loss for the sake of glory,

and there is the one who rises above
humble circumstances.
¹²There is one who buys much for little,
but pays for it seven times over.
¹³The wise make themselves beloved by
a few words,
but the courtesies of fools are wasted.
¹⁴A gift from a fool will do you no good,
for in his eyes this one gift is equal
to many.
¹⁵He gives little, criticizes often,
and opens his mouth like a town
crier.
He lends today and asks for it tomorrow;
such a person is hateful.
¹⁶A fool says, "I have no friends
nor thanks for my generosity."
Those who eat his bread have a
mocking tongue.
¹⁷How many will ridicule him, and
how often!
¹⁸A slip on the floor is better than a slip
of the tongue;
in like manner the downfall of the
wicked comes quickly.
¹⁹A coarse person, an untimely story;
the ignorant are always ready to
offer it.
²⁰A proverb spoken by a fool is
unwelcome,
for he does not tell it at the proper
time.
²¹There is a person whose poverty
prevents him from sinning,
but when he takes his rest he has no
regrets.
²²There is a person who is destroyed
through shame,
and ruined by foolish posturing.
²³There is one who promises a friend
out of shame,
and so makes an enemy needlessly.
²⁴A lie is a foul blot in a person,
yet it is always on the lips of the
ignorant.

²⁵A thief is better than an inveterate
liar,
yet both will suffer ruin.
²⁶A liar's way leads to dishonor,
and his shame remains ever with him.
²⁷The wise gain promotion with few
words,
the prudent please the great.
²⁸Those who work the land have
abundant crops,
and those who please the great are
pardoned their faults.
²⁹Favors and gifts blind the eyes;
like a muzzle over the mouth they
silence reproofs.
³⁰Hidden wisdom and unseen treasure—
what value has either?
³¹Better are those who hide their folly
than those who hide their wisdom.

Dangers from Sin. 21:1 My child, if
you have sinned, do so no more,
and for your past sins pray to be
forgiven.
²Flee from sin as from a serpent
that will bite you if you go near it;
Its teeth, lion's teeth,
destroying human lives.
³All lawlessness is like a two-edged
sword;
when it cuts, there is no healing.
⁴Panic and pride wipe out wealth;
so too the house of the proud is
uprooted.
⁵Prayer from the lips of the poor is
heard at once,
and justice is quickly granted them.
⁶Whoever hates correction walks the
sinner's path,
but whoever fears the Lord repents
in his heart.
⁷Glib speakers are widely known,
but when they slip the sensible
perceive it.
⁸Those who build their houses with
someone else's money

are like those who collect stones for
their funeral mounds.
⁹A band of criminals is like a bundle
of tow;
they will end in a flaming fire.
¹⁰The path of sinners is smooth stones,
but its end is the pit of Sheol.

The Wise and Foolish: A Contrast.
¹¹Those who keep the Law
control their thoughts;
perfect fear of the Lord is wisdom.
¹²One who is not clever can never be
taught,
but there is a cleverness filled with
bitterness.
¹³The knowledge of the wise wells up
like a flood,
and their counsel like a living spring.
¹⁴A fool's mind is like a broken jar:
it cannot hold any knowledge at all.
¹⁵When the intelligent hear a wise
saying,
they praise it and add to it.
The wanton hear it with distaste
and cast it behind their back.
¹⁶A fool's chatter is like a load on a
journey,
but delight is to be found on the
lips of the intelligent.
¹⁷The views of the prudent are sought
in an assembly,
and their words are taken to heart.
¹⁸Like a house in ruins is wisdom to a
fool;
to the stupid, knowledge is
incomprehensible chatter.
¹⁹To the senseless, education is fetters
on the feet,
like manacles on the right hand.
²⁰Fools raise their voice in laughter,
but the prudent at most smile
quietly.
²¹Like a gold ornament is education to
the wise,

like a bracelet on the right arm.

²²A fool steps boldly into a house,
    while the well-bred are slow to make
        an entrance.
²³A boor peeps through the doorway of
    a house,
    but the educated stay outside.
²⁴It is rude for one to listen at a door;
    the discreet person would be
        overwhelmed by the disgrace.

²⁵The lips of the arrogant talk of what
    is not their concern,
    but the discreet carefully weigh their
        words.
²⁶The mind of fools is in their mouths,
    but the mouth of the wise is in their
        mind.
²⁷When the godless curse their adversary,
    they really curse themselves.
²⁸Slanderers sully themselves,
    and are hated by their neighbors.

On Laziness and Foolishness. 22:1

    The sluggard is like a filthy stone;
    everyone hisses at his disgrace.
²The sluggard is like a lump of dung;
    whoever touches it shakes it off the
        hands.

³An undisciplined child is a disgrace to
    its father;
    if it be a daughter, she brings him to
        poverty.
⁴A thoughtful daughter obtains a
    husband of her own;
    a shameless one is her father's grief.
⁵A hussy shames her father and her
    husband;
    she is despised by both.

⁶Like music at the time of mourning is
    ill-timed talk,
    but lashes and discipline are at all
        times wisdom.
⁹Teaching a fool is like gluing a broken
    pot,
    or rousing another from deep sleep.

¹⁰Whoever talks with a fool talks to
    someone asleep;
    when it is over, he says, "What was
        that?"

¹¹Weep over the dead, for their light
    has gone out;
    weep over the fool, for sense has left
        him.
Weep but less bitterly over the dead,
    for they are at rest;
    worse than death is the life of a fool.
¹²Mourning for the dead, seven days—
    but for the wicked fool, a whole
        lifetime.

¹³Do not talk much with the stupid,
    or visit the unintelligent.
Beware of them lest you have trouble
    and be spattered when they shake
        themselves off.
Avoid them and you will find rest
    and not be wearied by their lack of
        sense.
¹⁴What is heavier than lead?
    What is its name but "Fool"?
¹⁵Sand, salt, and an iron weight
    are easier to bear than the stupid
        person.

¹⁶A wooden beam firmly bonded into a
    building
    is not loosened by an earthquake;
So the mind firmly resolved after
    careful deliberation
    will not be afraid at any time.
¹⁷The mind solidly backed by
    intelligent thought
    is like a stucco decoration on a
        smooth wall.
¹⁸Small stones lying on an open height
    will not remain when the wind
        blows;
So a timid mind based on foolish plans
    cannot stand up to fear of any kind.

The Preservation of Friendship.

¹⁹Whoever jabs the eye brings
    tears;

whoever pierces the heart bares its
    feelings.
20Whoever throws a stone at birds
    drives them away;
    whoever insults a friend breaks up
        the friendship.
21Should you draw a sword against a
    friend,
    do not despair, for it can be undone.
22Should you open your mouth against
    a friend,
    do not worry, for you can be
        reconciled.
But a contemptuous insult, a
    confidence broken,
    or a treacherous attack will drive
        any friend away.

23Win your neighbor's trust while he is
    poor,
    so that you may rejoice with him in
        his prosperity.
In time of trouble remain true to him,
    so that you may share in his
        inheritance when it comes.
24The billowing smoke of a furnace
    precedes the fire,
    so insults precede bloodshed.
25I am not ashamed to shelter a friend,
    and I will not hide from him.
26But if harm should come to me
    because of him,
    all who hear of it will beware of
        him.

Prayer. 27Who will set a guard over my
    mouth,
    an effective seal on my lips,
That I may not fail through them,
    and my tongue may not destroy me?

☐ JOHN 20:1-18

The Empty Tomb. 20:1 On the first day of the week, Mary of Magdala came to the tomb early in the morning, while it was still dark, and saw the stone removed from the tomb. 2So she ran and went to Simon Peter and to the other disciple whom Jesus loved, and told them, "They have taken the Lord from the tomb, and we don't know where they put him." 3So Peter and the other disciple went out and came to the tomb. 4They both ran, but the other disciple ran faster than Peter and arrived at the tomb first; 5he bent down and saw the burial cloths there, but did not go in. 6When Simon Peter arrived after him, he went into the tomb and saw the burial cloths there, 7and the cloth that had covered his head, not with the burial cloths but rolled up in a separate place. 8Then the other disciple also went in, the one who had arrived at the tomb first, and he saw and believed. 9For they did not yet understand the scripture that he had to rise from the dead. 10Then the disciples returned home.

The Appearance to Mary of Magdala. 11But Mary stayed outside the tomb weeping. And as she wept, she bent over into the tomb 12and saw two angels in white sitting there, one at the head and one at the feet where the body of Jesus had been. 13And they said to her, "Woman, why are you weeping?" She said to them, "They have taken my Lord, and I don't know where they laid him." 14When she had said this, she turned around and saw Jesus there, but did not know it was Jesus. 15Jesus said to her, "Woman, why are you weeping? Whom are you looking for?" She thought it was the gardener and said to him, "Sir, if you carried him away, tell me where you laid him, and I will take him." 16Jesus said to her, "Mary!" She turned and said to him in Hebrew, "Rabbouni," which means Teacher. 17Jesus said to her, "Stop holding on to me, for I have not yet ascended to the Father. But go to my brothers and tell them, 'I am going to my Father and your Father, to my God and your God.'" [18]Mary of Magdala went and announced to the disciples, "I have seen the Lord," and what he told her.

August 24

St. Bartholomew

We should not seek from others for the truth that can easily be received from the Church. There the apostles, like a rich man making a deposit, fully bestowed upon her all that belongs to the truth, so that whoever wishes may receive from her the water of life.

— St. Irenaeus of Lyons

☐ SIRACH 23-25

23:1 Lord, Father and Master of my life,
  do not abandon me to their designs,
  do not let me fall because of them!

[2]Who will apply the lash to my thoughts,
  and to my mind the rod of discipline,
That my failings may not be spared
  or the sins of my heart overlooked?
[3]Otherwise my failings may increase,
  and my sins be multiplied;
And I fall before my adversaries,
  and my enemy rejoice over me?
[4]Lord, Father and God of my life,
  do not give me haughty eyes;
[5]remove evil desire from my heart.
[6]Let neither gluttony nor lust overcome me;
  do not give me up to shameless desires.

Proper Use of the Tongue. [7]Listen,
  my children, to instruction concerning the mouth,
  for whoever keeps it will not be ensnared.
[8]Through the lips the sinner is caught;

by them the reviler and the arrogant
  are tripped up.
[9]Do not accustom your mouth to oaths,
  or habitually utter the Holy Name.
[10]Just as a servant constantly under scrutiny
  will not be without bruises,
So one who swears continually by the Holy Name
  will never remain free from sin.
[11]Those who swear many oaths heap up offenses;
  and the scourge will never be far from their houses.
If they swear in error, guilt is incurred;
  if they neglect their obligation, the sin is doubly great.
If they swear without reason they cannot be declared innocent,
  for their households will be filled with calamities.

[12]There are words comparable to death;
  may they never be heard in the inheritance of Jacob.
To the devout all such words are foreign;
  they do not wallow in sin.

¹³Do not accustom your mouth to
coarse talk,
for it involves sinful speech.
¹⁴Keep your father and mother in mind
when you sit among the mighty,
Lest you forget yourself in their presence
and disgrace your upbringing.
Then you will wish you had never been
born
and will curse the day of your birth.
¹⁵Those accustomed to using abusive
language
will never acquire discipline as long
as they live.

Sins of the Flesh. ¹⁶Two types of
people multiply sins,
and a third draws down wrath:
Burning passion is like a blazing fire,
not to be quenched till it burns
itself out;
One unchaste with his kindred
never stops until fire breaks forth.
¹⁷To the unchaste all bread is sweet;
he is never through till he dies.

¹⁸The man who dishonors his marriage
bed
says to himself, "Who can see me?
Darkness surrounds me, walls hide me,
no one sees me. Who can stop me
from sinning?"
He is not mindful of the Most High,
¹⁹fearing only human eyes.
He does not realize that the eyes of the
Lord,
ten thousand times brighter than
the sun,
Observe every step taken
and peer into hidden corners.
²⁰The one who knows all things before
they exist
still knows them all after they are
made.
²¹Such a man will be denounced in the
streets of the city;
and where he least suspects it, he
will be apprehended.

²²So it is with the woman unfaithful to
her husband,
who offers him an heir by another
man.
²³First of all, she has disobeyed the law
of the Most High;
second, she has wronged her
husband;
Third, through her wanton adultery
she has brought forth children by
another man.
²⁴Such a woman will be dragged before
the assembly,
and her punishment will extend to
her children.
²⁵Her children will not take root;
her branches will not bring forth
fruit.
²⁶She will leave behind an accursed
memory;
her disgrace will never be blotted out.

²⁷Thus all who dwell on the earth shall
know,
all who remain in the world shall
understand,
That nothing is better than the fear of
the Lord,
nothing sweeter than obeying the
commandments of the Lord.

Praise of Wisdom. 24:1 Wisdom sings
her own praises,
among her own people she
proclaims her glory.
²In the assembly of the Most High she
opens her mouth,
in the presence of his host she tells
of her glory:
³"From the mouth of the Most High I
came forth,
and covered the earth like a mist.
⁴In the heights of heaven I dwelt,
and my throne was in a pillar of
cloud.
⁵The vault of heaven I compassed alone,
and walked through the deep abyss.

⁶Over waves of the sea, over all the land,
  over every people and nation I held
  sway.
⁷Among all these I sought a resting
  place.
  In whose inheritance should I abide?

⁸"Then the Creator of all gave me his
  command,
  and my Creator chose the spot for
  my tent.
He said, 'In Jacob make your dwelling,
  in Israel your inheritance.'
⁹Before all ages, from the beginning, he
  created me,
  and through all ages I shall not cease
  to be.
¹⁰In the holy tent I ministered before
  him,
  and so I was established in Zion.
¹¹In the city he loves as he loves me, he
  gave me rest;
  in Jerusalem, my domain.
¹²I struck root among the glorious
  people,
  in the portion of the Lord, his
  heritage.

¹³"Like a cedar in Lebanon I grew tall,
  like a cypress on Mount Hermon;
¹⁴I grew tall like a palm tree in Engedi,
  like rosebushes in Jericho;
Like a fair olive tree in the field,
  like a plane tree beside water I grew
  tall.
¹⁵Like cinnamon and fragrant cane,
  like precious myrrh I gave forth
  perfume;
Like galbanum and onycha and mastic,
  like the odor of incense in the holy
  tent.

¹⁶"I spread out my branches like a
  terebinth,
  my branches so glorious and so
  graceful.
¹⁷I bud forth delights like a vine;

my blossoms are glorious and rich
  fruit.
¹⁹Come to me, all who desire me,
  and be filled with my fruits.
²⁰You will remember me as sweeter
  than honey,
  better to have than the honeycomb.
²¹Those who eat of me will hunger still,
  those who drink of me will thirst for
  more.
²²Whoever obeys me will not be put to
  shame,
  and those who serve me will never
  go astray."

²³All this is the book of the covenant of
  the Most High God,
  the Law which Moses commanded us
  as a heritage for the community of
  Jacob.
²⁵It overflows, like the Pishon, with
  wisdom,
  and like the Tigris at the time of
  first fruits.
²⁶It runs over, like the Euphrates, with
  understanding,
  and like the Jordan at harvest time.
²⁷It floods like the Nile with
  instruction,
  like the Gihon at vintage time.
²⁸The first human being never finished
  comprehending wisdom,
  nor will the last succeed in
  fathoming her.
²⁹For deeper than the sea are her
  thoughts,
  and her counsels, than the great
  abyss.

³⁰Now I, like a stream from a river,
  and like water channeling into a
  garden—
³¹I said, "I will water my plants,
  I will drench my flower beds."
Then suddenly this stream of mine
  became a river,
  and this river of mine became a sea.

³²Again I will make my teachings shine
　　forth like the dawn;
　I will spread their brightness afar off.
³³Again I will pour out instruction like
　　prophecy
　　and bestow it on generations yet to
　　　come.

Those Who Are Worthy of Praise. 25:1
　　　With three things I am delighted,
　　for they are pleasing to the Lord and
　　　to human beings:
Harmony among relatives, friendship
　　among neighbors,
　　and a wife and a husband living
　　　happily together.
²Three kinds of people I hate,
　　and I loathe their manner of life:
A proud pauper, a rich liar,
　　and a lecherous old fool.

³In your youth you did not gather.
　　How will you find anything in your
　　　old age?
⁴How appropriate is sound judgment
　　in the gray-haired,
　　and good counsel in the elderly!
⁵How appropriate is wisdom in the aged,
　　understanding and counsel in the
　　　venerable!
⁶The crown of the elderly, wide
　　experience;
　　their glory, the fear of the Lord.

⁷There are nine who come to mind as
　　blessed,
　　a tenth whom my tongue proclaims:
The man who finds joy in his children,
　　and the one who lives to see the
　　　downfall of his enemies.
⁸Happy the man who lives with a
　　sensible woman,
　　and the one who does not plow with
　　　an ox and a donkey combined.
Happy the one who does not sin with
　　the tongue,
　　who does not serve an inferior.
⁹Happy the one who finds a friend,
　　who speaks to attentive ears.
¹⁰How great is the one who finds
　　wisdom,
　　but none is greater than the one
　　　who fears the Lord.
¹¹Fear of the Lord surpasses all else.
　　To whom can we compare the one
　　　who has it?

Wicked and Virtuous Women. ¹³Any
　　wound, but not a wound of the
　　heart!
　Any wickedness, but not the
　　wickedness of a woman!
¹⁴Any suffering, but not suffering from
　　one's foes!
　Any vengeance, but not the
　　vengeance of one's enemies!
¹⁵There is no poison worse than that of
　　a serpent,
　　no venom greater than that of a
　　woman.
¹⁶I would rather live with a dragon or
　　a lion
　　than live with a wicked woman.
¹⁷A woman's wicked disposition
　　changes her appearance,
　　and makes her face as dark as a bear.
¹⁸When her husband sits among his
　　neighbors,
　　a bitter sigh escapes him unawares.

¹⁹There is hardly an evil like that in a
　　woman;
　　may she fall to the lot of the sinner!
²⁰Like a sandy hill to aged feet
　　is a garrulous wife to a quiet husband.
²¹Do not be enticed by a woman's
　　beauty,
　　or be greedy for her wealth.
²²Harsh is the slavery and great the
　　shame
　　when a wife supports her husband.

²³Depressed mind, gloomy face,
　　and a wounded heart—a wicked
　　woman.
Drooping hands and quaking knees,

any wife who does not make her
husband happy.
²⁴With a woman sin had a beginning,
and because of her we all die.
²⁵Allow water no outlet,
and no boldness of speech to a
wicked woman.
²⁶If she does not go along as you direct,
cut her away from you.

☐ JOHN 20:19-31

Appearance to the Disciples. 20:19 On the evening of that first day of the week, when the doors were locked, where the disciples were, for fear of the Jews, Jesus came and stood in their midst and said to them, "Peace be with you." ²⁰When he had said this, he showed them his hands and his side. The disciples rejoiced when they saw the Lord. ²¹[Jesus] said to them again, "Peace be with you. As the Father has sent me, so I send you." ²²And when he had said this, he breathed on them and said to them, "Receive the holy Spirit. ²³Whose sins you forgive are forgiven them, and whose sins you retain are retained."

Thomas. ²⁴Thomas, called Didymus, one of the Twelve, was not with them when Jesus came. ²⁵So the other disciples said to him, "We have seen the Lord." But he said to them, "Unless I see the mark of the nails in his hands and put my finger into the nailmarks and put my hand into his side, I will not believe." ²⁶Now a week later his disciples were again inside and Thomas was with them. Jesus came, although the doors were locked, and stood in their midst and said, "Peace be with you." ²⁷Then he said to Thomas, "Put your finger here and see my hands, and bring your hand and put it into my side, and do not be unbelieving, but believe." ²⁸Thomas answered and said to him, "My Lord and my God!" ²⁹Jesus said to him, "Have you come to believe because you have seen me? Blessed are those who have not seen and have believed."

Conclusion. ³⁰Now Jesus did many other signs in the presence of [his] disciples that are not written in this book. ³¹But these are written that you may [come to] believe that Jesus is the Messiah, the Son of God, and that through this belief you may have life in his name.

August 25

St. Louis; St. Joseph Calasanz

You should permit yourself to be tormented by every kind of martyrdom before you would allow yourself to commit a mortal sin.

— St. Louis

☐ SIRACH 26-29

26:1 Happy the husband of a good wife;
the number of his days will be
doubled.
²A loyal wife brings joy to her husband,
and he will finish his years in peace.
³A good wife is a generous gift
bestowed upon him who fears the
Lord.

⁴Whether rich or poor, his heart is
content,
a smile ever on his face.

⁵There are three things I dread,
and a fourth which terrifies me:
Public slander, the gathering of a mob,
and false accusation—all harder to
bear than death.
⁶A wife jealous of another wife is
heartache and mourning;
everyone feels the lash of her tongue.

⁷A wicked wife is a chafing yoke;
taking hold of her is like grasping a
scorpion.
⁸A drunken wife arouses great anger,
for she does not hide her shame.
⁹By her haughty stare and her eyelids
an unchaste wife can be recognized.

¹⁰Keep a strict watch over an unruly
wife,
lest, finding an opportunity, she
use it;
¹¹Watch out for her impudent eye,
and do not be surprised if she
betrays you:
¹²As a thirsty traveler opens his mouth
and drinks from any water nearby,
So she sits down before every tent peg
and opens her quiver for every arrow.

¹³A gracious wife delights her husband;
her thoughtfulness puts flesh on his
bones.
¹⁴A silent wife is a gift from the Lord;
nothing is worth more than her self-
discipline.
¹⁵A modest wife is a supreme blessing;
no scales can weigh the worth of her
chastity.
¹⁶The sun rising in the Lord's heavens—
the beauty of a good wife in her
well-ordered home.
¹⁷The light which shines above the holy
lampstand—
a beautiful face on a stately figure.
¹⁸Golden columns on silver bases—

so her shapely legs and steady feet.

Dangers to Integrity and Friendship.
²⁸Two things bring grief to my
heart,
and a third arouses my anger:
The wealthy reduced to want,
the intelligent held in contempt,
And those who pass from righteousness
to sin—
the Lord prepares them for the sword.

²⁹A merchant can hardly keep from
wrongdoing,
nor can a shopkeeper stay free from
sin;

27:1 For the sake of profit many sin,
and the struggle for wealth blinds
the eyes.
²A stake will be driven between fitted
stones—
sin will be wedged in between
buying and selling.
³Unless one holds fast to the fear of the
Lord,
with sudden swiftness will one's
house be thrown down.

⁴When a sieve is shaken, the husks
appear;
so do people's faults when they speak.
⁵The furnace tests the potter's vessels;
the test of a person is in
conversation.
⁶The fruit of a tree shows the care it has
had;
so speech discloses the bent of a
person's heart.
⁷Praise no one before he speaks,
for it is then that people are tested.

⁸If you strive after justice, you will
attain it,
and wear it like a splendid robe.
⁹Birds nest with their own kind,
and honesty comes to those who
work at it.
¹⁰A lion lies in wait for prey,

so does sin for evildoers.

[11]The conversation of the godly is
always wisdom,
but the fool changes like the moon.
[12]Limit the time you spend among the
stupid,
but frequent the company of the
thoughtful.
[13]The conversation of fools is offensive,
and their laughter is wanton sin.
[14]Their oath-filled talk makes the hair
stand on end,
and their brawls make one stop the
ears.
[15]The wrangling of the proud ends in
bloodshed,
and their cursing is painful to hear.

[16]Whoever betrays a secret destroys
confidence,
and will never find a congenial
friend.
[17]Cherish your friend, keep faith with
him;
but if you betray his secrets, do not
go after him;
[18]For as one might kill another,
you have killed your neighbor's
friendship.
[19]Like a bird released from your hand,
you have let your friend go and
cannot recapture him.
[20]Do not go after him, for he is far away,
and has escaped like a gazelle from
a snare.
[21]For a wound can be bandaged, and
an insult forgiven,
but whoever betrays secrets does
hopeless damage.

Malice, Anger and Vengeance.
[22]Whoever has shifty eyes plots
mischief
and those who know him will keep
their distance;
[23]In your presence he uses honeyed talk,
and admires your words,

But later he changes his tone
and twists the words to your ruin.
[24]I have hated many things but not as
much as him,
and the Lord hates him as well.
[25]A stone falls back on the head of the
one who throws it high,
and a treacherous blow causes many
wounds.
[26]Whoever digs a pit falls into it,
and whoever lays a snare is caught
in it.
[27]The evil anyone does will recoil on him
without knowing how it came upon
him.

[28]Mockery and abuse will befall the
arrogant,
and vengeance lies in wait for them
like a lion.
[29]Those who rejoice in the downfall
of the godly will be caught in a
snare,
and pain will consume them before
they die.
[30]Wrath and anger, these also are
abominations,
yet a sinner holds on to them.

28:1 The vengeful will face the Lord's
vengeance;
indeed he remembers their sins in
detail.

[2]Forgive your neighbor the wrong done
to you;
then when you pray, your own sins
will be forgiven.
[3]Does anyone nourish anger against
another
and expect healing from the LORD?
[4]Can one refuse mercy to a sinner like
oneself,
yet seek pardon for one's own sins?
[5]If a mere mortal cherishes wrath,
who will forgive his sins?
[6]Remember your last days and set
enmity aside;

remember death and decay, and
cease from sin!
⁷Remember the commandments
and do not be angry with your
neighbor;
remember the covenant of the Most
High, and overlook faults.

⁸Avoid strife and your sins will be fewer,
for the hot-tempered kindle strife;
⁹The sinner disrupts friendships
and sows discord among those who
are at peace.
¹⁰The more the wood, the greater the
fire,
the more the cruelty, the fiercer the
strife;
The greater the strength, the sterner the
anger,
the greater the wealth, the greater
the wrath.
¹¹Pitch and resin make fire flare up,
and a hasty quarrel provokes
bloodshed.

The Evil Tongue. ¹²If you blow on a
spark, it turns into flame,
if you spit on it, it dies out;
yet both you do with your mouth!
¹³Cursed be gossips and the double-
tongued,
for they destroy the peace of many.
¹⁴A meddlesome tongue subverts many,
and makes them refugees among
peoples.
It destroys strong cities,
and overthrows the houses of the
great.
¹⁵A meddlesome tongue drives virtuous
women from their homes,
and robs them of the fruit of their
toil.
¹⁶Whoever heed it will find no rest,
nor will they dwell in peace.

¹⁷A blow from a whip raises a welt,
but a blow from the tongue will
break bones.

¹⁸Many have fallen by the edge of the
sword,
but not as many as by the tongue.
¹⁹Happy the one who is sheltered
from it,
and has not endured its wrath;
Who has not borne its yoke
nor been bound with its chains.
²⁰For its yoke is a yoke of iron,
and its chains are chains of bronze;
²¹The death it inflicts is an evil death,
even Sheol is preferable to it.
²²It will have no power over the godly,
nor will they be burned in its flame.
²³But those who forsake the Lord will
fall victim to it,
as it burns among them
unquenchably;
It will hurl itself against them like a
lion,
and like a leopard, it will tear them
to pieces.
²⁴As you fence in your property with
thorns,
so make a door and a bolt for your
mouth.
²⁵As you lock up your silver and gold,
so make balances and scales for your
words.
²⁶Take care not to slip by your tongue
and fall victim to one lying in
ambush.

Loans, Alms and Surety. 29:1 The
merciful lend to their neighbor,
by holding out a helping hand, they
keep the commandments.
²Lend to your neighbor in his time of
need,
and pay back your neighbor in time.
³Keep your promise and be honest with
him,
and at all times you will find what
you need.
⁴Many borrowers ask for a loan
and cause trouble for those who
help them.

⁵Till he gets a loan, he kisses the
  lender's hand
and speaks softly of his creditor's
  money,
But at time of payment, delays,
  makes excuses, and finds fault with
  the timing.
⁶If he can pay, the lender will recover
  barely half,
  and will consider that a windfall.
If he cannot pay, the lender is cheated
  of his money
  and acquires an enemy at no extra
  charge;
With curses and insults the borrower
  will repay,
  and instead of honor will repay with
  abuse.
⁷Many refuse to lend, not out of
  meanness,
  but from fear of being cheated
  needlessly.

⁸But with those in humble
  circumstances be patient;
  do not keep them waiting for your
  alms.
⁹Because of the commandment, help
  the poor,
  and in their need, do not send them
  away empty-handed.
¹⁰Lose your money for relative or
  friend;
  do not hide it under a stone to rot.
¹¹Dispose of your treasure according to
  the commandments of the Most
  High,
  and that will profit you more than
  the gold.
¹²Store up almsgiving in your treasury,
  and it will save you from every evil.
¹³Better than a mighty shield and a
  sturdy spear
  it will fight for you against the enemy.

¹⁴A good person will be surety for a
  neighbor,

but whoever has lost a sense of
  shame will fail him.
¹⁵Do not forget the kindness of your
  backer,
  for he has given his very life for you.
¹⁶A sinner will turn the favor of a
  pledge into misfortune,
¹⁷and the ungrateful will abandon
  his rescuer.
¹⁸Going surety has ruined many who
  were prosperous
  and tossed them about like waves
  of the sea;
It has exiled the prominent
  and sent them wandering through
  foreign lands.
¹⁹The sinner will come to grief through
  surety,
  and whoever undertakes too much
  will fall into lawsuits.
²⁰Help your neighbor according to
  your means,
  but take care lest you fall yourself.

Frugality and Its Rewards. ²¹Life's
  prime needs are water, bread, and
  clothing,
  and also a house for decent privacy.
²²Better is the life of the poor under the
  shadow of their own roof
  than sumptuous banquets among
  strangers.
²³Whether little or much, be content
  with what you have:
  then you will hear no reproach as a
  parasite.
²⁴It is a miserable life to go from house
  to house,
  for where you are a guest you dare
  not open your mouth.
²⁵You will entertain and provide drink
  without being thanked;
  besides, you will hear these bitter
  words:
²⁶"Come here, you parasite, set the
  table,
  let me eat the food you have there!

²⁷Go away, you parasite, for one more worthy;
for my relative's visit I need the room!"

²⁸Painful things to a sensitive person are rebuke as a parasite and insults from creditors.

☐ JOHN 21

The Appearance to the Seven Disciples. 21:1 After this, Jesus revealed himself again to his disciples at the Sea of Tiberias. He revealed himself in this way. ²Together were Simon Peter, Thomas called Didymus, Nathanael from Cana in Galilee, Zebedee's sons, and two others of his disciples. ³Simon Peter said to them, "I am going fishing." They said to him, "We also will come with you." So they went out and got into the boat, but that night they caught nothing. ⁴When it was already dawn, Jesus was standing on the shore; but the disciples did not realize that it was Jesus. ⁵Jesus said to them, "Children, have you caught anything to eat?" They answered him, "No." ⁶So he said to them, "Cast the net over the right side of the boat and you will find something." So they cast it, and were not able to pull it in because of the number of fish. ⁷So the disciple whom Jesus loved said to Peter, "It is the Lord." When Simon Peter heard that it was the Lord, he tucked in his garment, for he was lightly clad, and jumped into the sea. ⁸The other disciples came in the boat, for they were not far from shore, only about a hundred yards, dragging the net with the fish. ⁹When they climbed out on shore, they saw a charcoal fire with fish on it and bread. ¹⁰Jesus said to them, "Bring some of the fish you just caught." ¹¹So Simon Peter went over and dragged the net ashore full of one hundred fifty-three large fish. Even though there were so many, the net was not torn. ¹²Jesus said to them, "Come, have breakfast." And none of the disciples dared to ask him, "Who are you?" because they realized it was the Lord. ¹³Jesus came over and took the bread and gave it to them, and in like manner the fish. ¹⁴This was now the third time Jesus was revealed to his disciples after being raised from the dead.

Jesus and Peter. ¹⁵When they had finished breakfast, Jesus said to Simon Peter, "Simon, son of John, do you love me more than these?" He said to him, "Yes, Lord, you know that I love you." He said to him, "Feed my lambs." ¹⁶He then said to him a second time, "Simon, son of John, do you love me?" He said to him, "Yes, Lord, you know that I love you." He said to him, "Tend my sheep." ¹⁷He said to him the third time, "Simon, son of John, do you love me?" Peter was distressed that he had said to him a third time, "Do you love me?" and he said to him, "Lord, you know everything; you know that I love you." [Jesus] said to him, "Feed my sheep. ¹⁸Amen, amen, I say to you, when you were younger, you used to dress yourself and go where you wanted; but when you grow old, you will stretch out your hands, and someone else will dress you and lead you where you do not want to go." ¹⁹He said this signifying by what kind of death he would glorify God. And when he had said this, he said to him, "Follow me."

The Beloved Disciple. ²⁰Peter turned and saw the disciple following whom Jesus loved, the one who had also reclined upon his chest during the supper and had said, "Master, who is the one who will betray you?" ²¹When Peter saw him, he said to Jesus, "Lord, what about him?" ²²Jesus said to him, "What if I want him to remain until I come? What concern is it of yours? You follow me." ²³So the word spread among the brothers that that disciple would not die. But Jesus had not told him that he would not die, just "What if I want him to remain until I come? [What concern is it of yours?]"

Conclusion. ²⁴It is this disciple who testifies to these things and has written them, and we know that his testimony is true.

²⁵There are also many other things that Jesus did, but if these were to be described individually, I do not think the whole world would contain the books that would be written.

August 26

Just as those who are born in the body need to be fortified so that the body may become operative, even so those who are reborn in the spirit need to be fortified by the Holy Spirit. For this reason, so that they might become strong, the apostles received the Holy Spirit after Christ's ascension. This power is conferred in the Sacrament of Confirmation.

— St. Thomas Aquinas

☐ SIRACH 30-33

The Training of Children. 30:1
Whoever loves a son will chastise
　　him often,
that he may be his joy when he
　　grows up.
²Whoever disciplines a son will benefit
　　from him,
and boast of him among
　　acquaintances.
³Whoever educates a son will make his
　　enemy jealous,
and rejoice in him among his friends.
⁴At the father's death, he will seem not
　　dead,
for he leaves after him one like
　　himself,
⁵Whom he looked upon through life
　　with joy,
and in death, without regret.
⁶Against his enemies he has left an
　　avenger,
and one to repay his friends with
　　kindness.

⁷Whoever spoils a son will have
　　wounds to bandage,
and will suffer heartache at every
　　cry.
⁸An untamed horse turns out stubborn;
and a son left to himself grows up
　　unruly.
⁹Pamper a child and he will be a terror
　　for you,
indulge him, and he will bring you
　　grief.
¹⁰Do not laugh with him lest you share
　　sorrow with him,
and in the end you will gnash your
　　teeth.
¹¹Do not give him his own way in his
　　youth,
and do not ignore his follies.
¹²Bow down his head in his youth,
beat his sides while he is still young,
Lest he become stubborn and disobey
　　you,
and leave you disconsolate.
¹³Discipline your son and make heavy
　　his yoke,
lest you be offended by his
　　shamelessness.

Health and Cheerfulness. [14]Better the
poor in vigorous health
than the rich with bodily ills.
[15]I would rather have bodily health
than any gold,
and contentment of spirit than pearls.
[16]No riches are greater than a healthy
body;
and no happiness than a joyful heart.
[17]Better is death than a wretched life,
everlasting sleep than constant
illness.
[18]Good things set before one who
cannot eat
are like food offerings placed before
a tomb.
[19]What good is an offering to an idol
that can neither eat nor smell?
So it is with the one being punished by
the Lord,
[20]who groans at what his eyes behold.

[21]Do not give in to sadness,
or torment yourself deliberately.
[22]Gladness of heart is the very life of a
person,
and cheerfulness prolongs his days.
[23]Distract yourself and renew your
courage,
drive resentment far away from you;
For grief has killed many,
and nothing is to be gained from
resentment.
[24]Envy and anger shorten one's days,
and anxiety brings on premature
old age.
[25]Those who are cheerful and merry at
table
benefit from their food.

The Proper Attitude Toward Riches.
31:1 Wakefulness over wealth
wastes away the flesh,
and anxiety over it drives away
sleep.
[2]Wakeful anxiety banishes slumber;

more than a serious illness it
disturbs repose.
[3]The rich labor to pile up wealth,
and if they rest, it is to enjoy
pleasure;
[4]The poor labor for a meager living,
and if they ever rest, they become
needy.
[5]The lover of gold will not be free from
sin;
whoever pursues money will be led
astray by it.
[6]Many have come to ruin for the sake
of gold,
yet destruction lay before their very
eyes;
[7]It is a stumbling block for fools;
any simpleton will be ensnared by it.

[8]Happy the rich person found without
fault,
who does not turn aside after wealth.
[9]Who is he, that we may praise him?
For he has done wonders among his
people.
[10]Who has been tested by gold and
been found perfect?
Let it be for him his glory;
Who could have sinned but did not,
and could have done evil but did
not?
[11]So his good fortune is secure,
and the assembly will recount his
praises.

Table Etiquette. [12]Are you seated at
the table of the great?
Bring to it no greedy gullet,
Nor say, "How much food there is
here!"
[13]Remember that the greedy eye is
evil.
What has been created more greedy
than the eye?
Therefore, it weeps for any cause.
[15]Recognize that your neighbor feels as
you do,

and keep in mind everything you dislike.

¹⁴Toward what he looks at, do not put out a hand;
nor reach for the same dish when he does.

¹⁶Eat, like anyone else, what is set before you,
but do not eat greedily, lest you be despised.

¹⁷Be the first to stop, as befits good manners;
and do not gorge yourself, lest you give offense.

¹⁸If there are many with you at table,
do not be the first to stretch out your hand.

¹⁹Does not a little suffice for a well-bred person?
When he lies down, he does not wheeze.

²⁰Moderate eating ensures sound slumber
and a clear mind on rising the next day.
The distress of sleeplessness and of nausea and colic are with the glutton!

²¹Should you have eaten too much,
get up to vomit and you will have relief.

²²Listen to me, my child, and do not scorn me;
later you will find my advice good.
In whatever you do, be moderate,
and no sickness will befall you.

²³People bless one who is generous with food,
and this testimony to his goodness is lasting.

²⁴The city complains about one who is stingy with food,
and this testimony to his stinginess is lasting.

²⁵Let not wine be the proof of your strength,
for wine has been the ruin of many.

²⁶As the furnace tests the work of the smith,
so does wine the hearts of the insolent.

²⁷Wine is very life to anyone,
if taken in moderation.
Does anyone really live who lacks the wine
which from the beginning was created for joy?

²⁸Joy of heart, good cheer, and delight
is wine enough, drunk at the proper time.

²⁹Headache, bitterness, and disgrace
is wine drunk amid anger and strife.

³⁰Wine in excess is a snare for the fool;
it lessens strength and multiplies wounds.

³¹Do not wrangle with your neighbor when wine is served,
nor despise him while he is having a good time;
Say no harsh words to him
nor distress him by making demands.

32:1 If you are chosen to preside at a dinner, do not be puffed up,
but with the guests be as one of them;
Take care of them first and then sit down;
²see to their needs, and then take your place,
To share in their joy
and receive a wreath for a job well done.

³You who are older, it is your right to speak,
but temper your knowledge and do not interrupt the singing.

⁴Where there is entertainment, do not pour out discourse,
and do not display your wisdom at the wrong time.

⁵Like a seal of carnelian in a setting of gold:

a concert of music at a banquet of
  wine.
[6]A seal of emerald in a work of gold:
  the melody of music with delicious
  wine.
[7]Speak, young man, only when
  necessary,
  when they have asked you more
  than once.
[8]Be brief, say much in few words;
  be knowledgeable and yet quiet.
[9]When among elders do not be forward,
  and with officials do not be too
  insistent.
[10]The lightning that flashes before a
  hailstorm:
  the esteem that shines on modesty.
[11]Leave in good time and do not be the
  last;
  go home quickly without delay.
[12]There enjoy doing as you wish,
  but do not sin through words of
  pride.
[13]Above all, bless your Maker,
  who showers his favors upon you.

The Providence of God. [14]Whoever
  seeks God must accept discipline;
  and whoever resorts to him obtains
  an answer.
[15]Whoever seeks the law will master it,
  but the hypocrite will be ensnared
  by it.
[16]Whoever fears the LORD will
  understand what is right,
  and out of obscurity he will draw
  forth a course of action.
[17]The lawless turn aside warnings
  and distort the law to suit their
  purpose.
[18]The sensible will not neglect direction;
  the proud and insolent are deterred
  by no fear.
[19]Do nothing without deliberation;
  then once you have acted, have no
  regrets.
[20]Do not go on a way set with snares,
  and do not stumble on the same
  thing twice.
[21]Do not trust the road, because of
  bandits;
  [22]be careful on your paths.
[23]Whatever you do, be on your guard,
  for whoever does so keeps the
  commandments.
[24]Whoever keeps the law preserves
  himself;
  and whoever trusts in the LORD
  shall not be put to shame.

33:1 No evil can harm the one who
  fears the LORD;
  through trials, again and again he is
  rescued.
[2]Whoever hates the law is without
  wisdom,
  and is tossed about like a boat in a
  storm.
[3]The prudent trust in the word of the
  LORD,
  and the law is dependable for them
  as a divine oracle.
[4]Prepare your words and then you will
  be listened to;
  draw upon your training, and give
  your answer.
[5]Like the wheel of a cart is the mind of
  a fool,
  and his thoughts like a turning axle.
[6]A mocking friend is like a stallion
  that neighs, no matter who the rider
  may be.
[7]Why is one day more important than
  another,
  when the same sun lights up every
  day of the year?
[8]By the LORD's knowledge they are
  kept distinct;
  and he designates the seasons and
  feasts.
[9]Some he exalts and sanctifies,
  and others he lists as ordinary days.
[10]Likewise, all people are of clay,

and from earth humankind was
formed;
¹¹In the fullness of his knowledge the
Lord distinguished them,
and he designated their different
ways.
¹²Some he blessed and exalted,
and some he sanctified and drew to
himself.
Others he cursed and brought low,
and expelled them from their place.
¹³Like clay in the hands of a potter,
to be molded according to his
pleasure,
So are people in the hands of their
Maker,
to be dealt with as he decides.
¹⁴As evil contrasts with good, and
death with life,
so are sinners in contrast with the
godly.
¹⁵See now all the works of the Most
High:
they come in pairs, one the opposite
of the other.

¹⁶Now I am the last to keep vigil,
like a gleaner following the grape-
pickers;
¹⁷Since by the Lord's blessing I have
made progress
till like a grape-picker I have filled
my wine press,
¹⁸Consider that not for myself only
have I labored,
but for all who seek instruction.

Property and Servants. ¹⁹Listen to me,
leaders of the people;
rulers of the congregation, pay heed!
^{20a}Let neither son nor wife, neither
brother nor friend,
have power over you as long as you
live.
²¹While breath of life is still in you,

let no one take your place.
^{20b}Do not give your wealth to another,
lest you must plead for support
yourself.
²²Far better that your children plead
with you
than that you should look for a
handout from them.
²³Keep control over all your affairs;
bring no stain on your honor.
²⁴When your few days reach their limit,
at the time of death distribute your
inheritance.

²⁵Fodder and whip and loads for a
donkey;
food, correction and work for a
slave.
²⁶Make a slave work, and he will look
for rest;
let his hands be idle and he will seek
to be free.
²⁷The yoke and harness will bow the
neck;
and for a wicked slave, punishment
in the stocks.
²⁸Force him to work that he be not idle,
²⁹for idleness teaches much mischief.
³⁰Put him to work, as is fitting for him;
and if he does not obey, load him
with chains.
But never lord it over any human being,
and do nothing unjust.
³¹If you have but one slave, treat him
like yourself,
for you have acquired him with
your life's blood;
If you have but one slave, deal with
him as a brother,
for you need him as you need your
life.
³²If you mistreat him and he runs away,
³³in what direction will you look for
him?

☐ ACTS 1

The Promise of the Spirit. 1:1 In the first book, Theophilus, I dealt with all that Jesus did and taught [2]until the day he was taken up, after giving instructions through the holy Spirit to the apostles whom he had chosen. [3]He presented himself alive to them by many proofs after he had suffered, appearing to them during forty days and speaking about the kingdom of God. [4]While meeting with them, he enjoined them not to depart from Jerusalem, but to wait for "the promise of the Father about which you have heard me speak; [5]for John baptized with water, but in a few days you will be baptized with the holy Spirit."

The Ascension of Jesus. [6]When they had gathered together they asked him, "Lord, are you at this time going to restore the kingdom to Israel?" [7]He answered them, "It is not for you to know the times or seasons that the Father has established by his own authority. [8]But you will receive power when the holy Spirit comes upon you, and you will be my witnesses in Jerusalem, throughout Judea and Samaria, and to the ends of the earth." [9]When he had said this, as they were looking on, he was lifted up, and a cloud took him from their sight. [10]While they were looking intently at the sky as he was going, suddenly two men dressed in white garments stood beside them. [11]They said, "Men of Galilee, why are you standing there looking at the sky? This Jesus who has been taken up from you into heaven will return in the same way as you have seen him going into heaven." [12]Then they returned to Jerusalem from the mount called Olivet, which is near Jerusalem, a sabbath day's journey away.

The First Community in Jerusalem. [13]When they entered the city they went to the upper room where they were staying, Peter and John and James and Andrew, Philip and Thomas, Bartholomew and Matthew, James son of Alphaeus, Simon the Zealot, and Judas son of James. [14]All these devoted themselves with one accord to prayer, together with some women, and Mary the mother of Jesus, and his brothers.

The Choice of Judas's Successor. [15]During those days Peter stood up in the midst of the brothers (there was a group of about one hundred and twenty persons in the one place). He said, [16]"My brothers, the scripture had to be fulfilled which the holy Spirit spoke beforehand through the mouth of David, concerning Judas, who was the guide for those who arrested Jesus. [17]He was numbered among us and was allotted a share in this ministry. [18]He bought a parcel of land with the wages of his iniquity, and falling headlong, he burst open in the middle, and all his insides spilled out. [19]This became known to everyone who lived in Jerusalem, so that the parcel of land was called in their language 'Akeldama,' that is, Field of Blood. [20]For it is written in the Book of Psalms:

'Let his encampment become desolate,
    and may no one dwell in it.'

And:

'May another take his office.'

[21]Therefore, it is necessary that one of the men who accompanied us the whole time the Lord Jesus came and went among us, [22]beginning from the baptism of John until the day on which he was taken up from us, become with us a witness to his resurrection." [23]So they proposed two, Joseph called Barsabbas, who was also known as Justus, and Matthias. [24]Then they prayed, "You, Lord, who know the hearts of all, show which one of these two you have chosen [25]to take the place in this apostolic ministry from which Judas turned away to go to his own place." [26]Then they gave lots to them, and the lot fell upon Matthias, and he was counted with the eleven apostles.

August 27 ———————————————

When I die, put this body away anywhere. Don't let care about it disturb you. I ask only this of you, that you remember me at the altar of the Lord, wherever you may be. Nothing is far from God. I need not fear that He will not know where to raise me up at the end of the world.

— St. Monica

☐ **SIRACH 34-36**

Trust in the Lord and Not in Dreams. 34:1 Empty and false
    are the hopes of the senseless,
and dreams give wings to fools.
²Like one grasping at shadows or
    chasing the wind,
so anyone who believes in dreams.
³What is seen in dreams is a reflection,
    the likeness of a face looking at
    itself.
⁴How can the unclean produce what is
    clean?
    How can the false produce what is
    true?
⁵Divination, omens, and dreams are
    unreal;
    what you already expect, the mind
    fantasizes.
⁶Unless they are specially sent by the
    Most High,
do not fix your heart on them.
⁷For dreams have led many astray,
    and those who put their hope in
    them have perished.
⁸Without such deceptions the Law will
    be fulfilled,
and in the mouth of the faithful is
    complete wisdom.

⁹A much-traveled person knows many
    things;
    and one with much experience
    speaks sense.
¹⁰An inexperienced person knows little,

¹¹whereas with travel one adds to
    resourcefulness.
¹²I have seen much in my travels,
    and learned more than I could ever
    say.
¹³Often I was in danger of death,
    but by these experiences I was saved.
¹⁴Living is the spirit of those who fear
    the Lord,
¹⁵for their hope is in their savior.
¹⁶Whoever fear the Lord are afraid of
    nothing
    and are never discouraged, for he is
    their hope.
¹⁷Happy the soul that fears the Lord!
¹⁸In whom does he trust, and who is
    his support?
¹⁹The eyes of the Lord are upon those
    who love him;
    he is their mighty shield and strong
    support,
A shelter from the heat, a shade from
    the noonday sun,
    a guard against stumbling, a help
    against falling.
²⁰He lifts up spirits, brings a sparkle to
    the eyes,
gives health and life and blessing.

True Worship of God. ²¹Ill-gotten
    goods offered in sacrifice are
    tainted.
²²Presents from the lawless do not
    win God's favor.

²³The Most High is not pleased with
the gifts of the godless,
nor for their many sacrifices does he
forgive their sins.
²⁴One who slays a son in his father's
presence—
whoever offers sacrifice from the
holdings of the poor.
²⁵The bread of charity is life itself for
the needy;
whoever withholds it is a murderer.
²⁶To take away a neighbor's living is to
commit murder;
²⁷to deny a laborer wages is to shed
blood.

²⁸If one builds up and another tears
down,
what do they gain but trouble?
²⁹If one prays and another curses,
whose voice will God hear?
³⁰If one again touches a corpse after
bathing,
what does he gain by the
purification?
³¹So one who fasts for sins,
but goes and commits them again:
Who will hear his prayer,
what is gained by mortification?

35:1 To keep the law is to make many
offerings;
²whoever observes the
commandments sacrifices a
peace offering.
³By works of charity one offers fine flour,
⁴and one who gives alms presents a
sacrifice of praise.
⁵To refrain from evil pleases the Lord,
and to avoid injustice is atonement.

⁶Do not appear before the Lord empty-
handed,
⁷for all that you offer is in
fulfillment of the precepts.
⁸The offering of the just enriches the
altar:
a sweet odor before the Most High.

⁹The sacrifice of the just is accepted,
never to be forgotten.
¹⁰With a generous spirit pay homage to
the Lord,
and do not spare your freewill gifts.
¹¹With each contribution show a
cheerful countenance,
and pay your tithes in a spirit of joy.
¹²Give to the Most High as he has
given to you,
generously, according to your means.
¹³For he is a God who always repays
and will give back to you sevenfold.

¹⁴But offer no bribes; these he does not
accept!
¹⁵Do not trust in sacrifice of the
fruits of extortion,
For he is a God of justice,
who shows no partiality.
¹⁶He shows no partiality to the weak
but hears the grievance of the
oppressed.
¹⁷He does not forsake the cry of the
orphan,
nor the widow when she pours out
her complaint.
¹⁸Do not the tears that stream down
her cheek
¹⁹cry out against the one that causes
them to fall?
²⁰Those who serve God to please him
are accepted;
their petition reaches the clouds.
²¹The prayer of the lowly pierces the
clouds;
it does not rest till it reaches its goal;
Nor will it withdraw till the Most High
responds,
²²judges justly and affirms the right.

God indeed will not delay,
and like a warrior, will not be still
Till he breaks the backs of the merciless
²³and wreaks vengeance upon the
nations;
Till he destroys the scepter of the proud,
and cuts off the staff of the wicked;

²⁴Till he requites everyone according to
their deeds,
and repays them according to their
thoughts;
²⁵Till he defends the cause of his
people,
and makes them glad by his
salvation.
²⁶Welcome is his mercy in time of
distress
as rain clouds in time of drought.

A Prayer for God's People. 36:1 Come
to our aid, O God of the universe,
²and put all the nations in dread of
you!
³Raise your hand against the foreign
people,
that they may see your mighty deeds.
⁴As you have used us to show them
your holiness,
so now use them to show us your
glory.
⁵Thus they will know, as we know,
that there is no God but you.

⁶Give new signs and work new
wonders;
⁷show forth the splendor of your
right hand and arm.
⁸Rouse your anger, pour out wrath;
⁹humble the enemy, scatter the foe.
¹⁰Hasten the ending, appoint the time,
and let people proclaim your
mighty deeds.
¹¹Let raging fire consume the fugitive,
and your people's oppressors meet
destruction.
¹²Crush the heads of the hostile rulers
who say, "There is no one besides me."

¹³Gather all the tribes of Jacob,
¹⁶that they may inherit the land as
in days of old.
¹⁷Show mercy to the people called by
your name:
Israel, whom you named your
firstborn.

¹⁸Take pity on your holy city:
Jerusalem, your dwelling place.
¹⁹Fill Zion with your majesty,
your temple with your glory.

²⁰Give evidence of your deeds of old;
fulfill the prophecies spoken in your
name.
²¹Reward those who have hoped in you,
and let your prophets be proved
true.
²²Hear the prayer of your servants,
according to your good will toward
your people.
Thus all the ends of the earth will know
that you are the eternal God.

Choice of Associates. ²³The throat can
swallow any food,
yet some foods are more agreeable
than others.
²⁴The palate tests delicacies put forward
as gifts,
so does a keen mind test deceitful
tidbits.
²⁵One with a tortuous heart brings
about grief,
but an experienced person can turn
the tables on him.

²⁶A woman will accept any man as
husband,
but one woman will be preferable to
another.
²⁷A woman's beauty makes her
husband's face light up,
for it surpasses all else that delights
the eye.
²⁸And if, besides, her speech is
soothing,
her husband's lot is beyond that of
mortal men.
²⁹A wife is her husband's richest
treasure,
a help like himself and a staunch
support.
³⁰A vineyard with no hedge will be
overrun;

and a man with no wife becomes a
    homeless wanderer.
³¹Who will trust an armed band
    that shifts from city to city?

Or a man who has no nest,
    who lodges wherever night
        overtakes him?

☐ ACTS 2

The Coming of the Spirit. 2:1 When the
time for Pentecost was fulfilled, they were
all in one place together. ²And suddenly
there came from the sky a noise like a strong
driving wind, and it filled the entire house
in which they were. ³Then there appeared
to them tongues as of fire, which parted
and came to rest on each one of them. ⁴And
they were all filled with the holy Spirit and
began to speak in different tongues, as the
Spirit enabled them to proclaim.

⁵Now there were devout Jews from every
nation under heaven staying in Jerusalem.
⁶At this sound, they gathered in a large
crowd, but they were confused because
each one heard them speaking in his own
language. ⁷They were astounded, and in
amazement they asked, "Are not all these
people who are speaking Galileans? ⁸Then
how does each of us hear them in his own
native language? ⁹We are Parthians, Medes,
and Elamites, inhabitants of Mesopotamia,
Judea and Cappadocia, Pontus and Asia,
¹⁰Phrygia and Pamphylia, Egypt and the
districts of Libya near Cyrene, as well as
travelers from Rome, ¹¹both Jews and converts to Judaism, Cretans and Arabs, yet we
hear them speaking in our own tongues of
the mighty acts of God." ¹²They were all
astounded and bewildered, and said to one
another, "What does this mean?" ¹³But
others said, scoffing, "They have had too
much new wine."

Peter's Speech at Pentecost. ¹⁴Then
Peter stood up with the Eleven, raised his
voice, and proclaimed to them, "You who
are Jews, indeed all of you staying in Jerusalem. Let this be known to you, and listen
to my words. ¹⁵These people are not drunk,
as you suppose, for it is only nine o'clock in
the morning. ¹⁶No, this is what was spoken
through the prophet Joel:

¹⁷'It will come to pass in the last days,'
        God says,
    'that I will pour out a portion of my
        spirit upon all flesh.
Your sons and your daughters shall
        prophesy,
    your young men shall see visions,
    your old men shall dream dreams.
¹⁸Indeed, upon my servants and my
        handmaids
    I will pour out a portion of my
        spirit in those days,
    and they shall prophesy.
¹⁹And I will work wonders in the
        heavens above
    and signs on the earth below:
    blood, fire, and a cloud of smoke.
²⁰The sun shall be turned to darkness,
    and the moon to blood,
    before the coming of the great and
        splendid day of the Lord,
²¹and it shall be that everyone shall be
        saved who calls on
    the name of the Lord.'

²²You who are Israelites, hear these words.
Jesus the Nazorean was a man commended to you by God with mighty deeds,
wonders, and signs, which God worked
through him in your midst, as you yourselves know. ²³This man, delivered up by
the set plan and foreknowledge of God,
you killed, using lawless men to crucify
him. ²⁴But God raised him up, releasing

him from the throes of death, because it was impossible for him to be held by it. [25]For David says of him:

'I saw the Lord ever before me,
   with him at my right hand I shall
      not be disturbed.
[26]Therefore my heart has been glad and
   my tongue has exulted;
my flesh, too, will dwell in hope,
[27]because you will not abandon my
      soul to the netherworld,
   nor will you suffer your holy one to
      see corruption.
[28]You have made known to me the
   paths of life;
   you will fill me with joy in your
      presence.'

[29]My brothers, one can confidently say to you about the patriarch David that he died and was buried, and his tomb is in our midst to this day. [30]But since he was a prophet and knew that God had sworn an oath to him that he would set one of his descendants upon his throne, [31]he foresaw and spoke of the resurrection of the Messiah, that neither was he abandoned to the netherworld nor did his flesh see corruption. [32]God raised this Jesus; of this we are all witnesses. [33]Exalted at the right hand of God, he received the promise of the holy Spirit from the Father and poured it forth, as you (both) see and hear. [34]For David did not go up into heaven, but he himself said:

'The Lord said to my Lord, "Sit at my
   right hand
[35]until I make your enemies your
      footstool,"'

[36]Therefore let the whole house of Israel know for certain that God has made him both Lord and Messiah, this Jesus whom you crucified."

[37]Now when they heard this, they were cut to the heart, and they asked Peter and the other apostles, "What are we to do, my brothers?" [38]Peter [said] to them, "Repent and be baptized, every one of you, in the name of Jesus Christ for the forgiveness of your sins; and you will receive the gift of the holy Spirit. [39]For the promise is made to you and to your children and to all those far off, whomever the Lord our God will call." [40]He testified with many other arguments, and was exhorting them, "Save yourselves from this corrupt generation." [41]Those who accepted his message were baptized, and about three thousand persons were added that day.

Communal Life. [42]They devoted themselves to the teaching of the apostles and to the communal life, to the breaking of the bread and to the prayers. [43]Awe came upon everyone, and many wonders and signs were done through the apostles. [44]All who believed were together and had all things in common; [45]they would sell their property and possessions and divide them among all according to each one's need. [46]Every day they devoted themselves to meeting together in the temple area and to breaking bread in their homes. They ate their meals with exultation and sincerity of heart, [47]praising God and enjoying favor with all the people. And every day the Lord added to their number those who were being saved.

August 28

St. Augustine of Hippo

God has deemed it better to bring good out of evil than to permit evil at all.

— St. Augustine of Hippo

☐ SIRACH 37-39

37:1 Every friend declares friendship,
but there are friends who are friends
in name only.
[2] Is it not a sorrow unto death
when your other self becomes your
enemy?
[3] "Alas, my companion! Why were you
created
to fill the earth with deceit?"
[4] A harmful friend will look to your
table,
but in time of trouble he stands aloof.
[5] A good friend will fight with you
against the foe,
and against your enemies he will
hold up your shield.
[6] Do not forget your comrade during
the battle,
and do not neglect him when you
distribute your spoils.

[7] Every counselor points out a way,
but some counsel ways of their own.
[8] Watch out when one offers advice;
find out first of all what he wants.
For he also may be thinking of
himself—
Why should the opportunity fall to
him?
[9] He may tell you how good your way
will be,
and then stand by to see you
impoverished.
[10] Seek no advice from your father-in-law,
and from one who is envious of you,
keep your intentions hidden.
[11] Seek no advice from a woman about
her rival,

from a coward about war,
from a merchant about business,
from a buyer about value,
from a miser about generosity,
from a cruel person about well-
being,
from a worthless worker about his
work,
from a seasonal laborer about the
harvest,
from an idle slave about a great
task—
pay no attention to any advice they
give.

[12] Instead, associate with a religious
person,
who you know keeps the
commandments;
Who is like-minded with yourself
and will grieve for you if you fall.
[13] Then, too, heed your own heart's
counsel;
for there is nothing you can depend
on more.
[14] The heart can reveal your situation
better than seven sentinels on a
tower.
[15] Then with all this, pray to God
to make your steps firm in the true
path.

Wisdom and Temperance. [16] A word is
the source of every deed;
a thought, of every act.
[17] The root of all conduct is the heart;
[18] four branches it shoots forth:
Good and evil, death and life,

and their absolute mistress is the
tongue.
¹⁹One may be wise and benefit many,
yet appear foolish to himself.
²⁰One may be wise, but if his words are
rejected,
he will be deprived of all enjoyment.
²²When one is wise to his own
advantage,
the fruits of knowledge are seen in
his own person.
²³When one is wise to the advantage of
people,
the fruits of knowledge are lasting.
²⁴One wise for himself has full
enjoyment,
and all who see him praise him.
²⁵The days of one's life are numbered,
but the life of Israel, days without
number.
²⁶One wise among the people wins a
heritage of glory,
and his name lives on and on.

²⁷My son, while you are well, govern
your appetite,
and see that you do not allow it
what is bad for you.
²⁸For not everything is good for
everyone,
nor is everything suited to every taste.
²⁹Do not go to excess with any
enjoyment,
neither become a glutton for choice
foods;
³⁰For sickness comes with overeating,
and gluttony brings on nausea.
³¹Through lack of self-control many
have died,
but the abstemious one prolongs
life.

Sickness and Death. 38:1 Make
friends with the doctor, for he is
essential to you;
God has also established him in his
profession.

²From God the doctor has wisdom,
and from the king he receives
sustenance.
³Knowledge makes the doctor
distinguished,
and gives access to those in
authority.
⁴God makes the earth yield healing
herbs
which the prudent should not
neglect;
⁵Was not the water sweetened by a
twig,
so that all might learn his power?
⁶He endows people with knowledge,
to glory in his mighty works,
⁷Through which the doctor eases pain,
⁸and the druggist prepares his
medicines.
Thus God's work continues without
cease
in its efficacy on the surface of the
earth.

⁹My son, when you are ill, do not delay,
but pray to God, for it is he who
heals.
¹⁰Flee wickedness and purify your
hands;
cleanse your heart of every sin.
¹¹Offer your sweet-smelling oblation
and memorial,
a generous offering according to
your means.
¹²Then give the doctor his place
lest he leave; you need him too,
¹³For there are times when recovery is
in his hands.
¹⁴He too prays to God
That his diagnosis may be correct
and his treatment bring about a
cure.
¹⁵Whoever is a sinner before his Maker
will be defiant toward the doctor.

¹⁶My son, shed tears for one who is
dead
with wailing and bitter lament;

As is only proper, prepare the body,
 and do not absent yourself from the
  burial.
¹⁷Weeping bitterly, mourning fully,
 pay your tribute of sorrow, as
  deserved:
A day or two, to prevent gossip;
 then compose yourself after your
  grief.
¹⁸For grief can bring on death,
 and heartache can sap one's
  strength.
¹⁹When a person is carried away,
  sorrow is over;
 and the life of the poor one is
  grievous to the heart.
²⁰Do not turn your thoughts to him
  again;
 cease to recall him; think rather of
  the end.
²¹Do not recall him, for there is no
  hope of his return;
 you do him no good, and you harm
  yourself.
²²Remember that his fate will also be
  yours;
 for him it was yesterday, for you
  today.
²³With the dead at rest, let memory
  cease;
 be consoled, once the spirit has gone.

**Vocations of the Skilled Worker and
 the Scribe.** ²⁴The scribe's wisdom
  increases wisdom;
 whoever is free from toil can
  become wise.
²⁵How can one become learned who
  guides the plow,
 and thrills in wielding the goad like
  a lance,
Who guides the ox and urges on the
  bullock,
 and whose every concern is for cattle?
²⁶His concern is to plow furrows,
 and he is careful to fatten the
  livestock.

²⁷So with every engraver and designer
 who, laboring night and day,
Fashions carved seals,
 and whose concern is to vary the
  pattern.
His determination is to produce a
  lifelike impression,
 and he is careful to finish the work.
²⁸So too the smith sitting by the anvil,
 intent on the iron he forges.
The flame from the fire sears his flesh,
 yet he toils away in the furnace heat.
The clang of the hammer deafens his
  ears;
 his eyes are on the object he is
  shaping.
His determination is to finish the
  work,
 and he is careful to perfect it in
  detail.
²⁹So also the potter sitting at his labor,
 revolving the wheel with his feet.
He is always concerned for his
  products,
 and turns them out in quantity.
³⁰With his hands he molds the clay,
 and with his feet softens it.
His determination is to complete the
  glazing,
 and he is careful to fire the kiln.

³¹All these are skilled with their hands,
 each one an expert at his own work;
³²Without them no city could be
  lived in,
 and wherever they stay, they do not
  go hungry.
But they are not sought out for the
  council of the people,
 ³³nor are they prominent in the
  assembly.
They do not sit on the judge's bench,
 nor can they understand law and
  justice.
They cannot expound discipline or
 judgment,

nor are they found among the rulers.
[34]Yet they maintain the fabric of the
world,
and their concern is for exercise of
their skill.

How different the person who devotes
himself
to the study of the law of the Most
High!

39:1 He explores the wisdom of all the
ancients
and is occupied with the prophecies;
[2]He preserves the discourses of the
famous,
and goes to the heart of involved
sayings;
[3]He seeks out the hidden meaning of
proverbs,
and is busied with the enigmas
found in parables.
[4]He is in attendance on the great,
and appears before rulers.
He travels among the peoples of
foreign lands
to test what is good and evil among
people.
[5]His care is to rise early
to seek the Lord his Maker,
to petition the Most High,
To open his mouth in prayer,
to ask pardon for his sins.
[6]If it pleases the Lord Almighty,
he will be filled with the spirit of
understanding;
He will pour forth his words of wisdom
and in prayer give praise to the Lord.
[7]He will direct his knowledge and his
counsel,
as he meditates upon God's
mysteries.
[8]He will show the wisdom of what he
has learned
and glory in the Law of the Lord's
covenant.

[9]Many will praise his understanding;
his name can never be blotted out;
Unfading will be his memory,
through all generations his name
will live;
[10]Peoples will speak of his wisdom,
and the assembly will declare his
praise.
[11]While he lives he is one out of a
thousand,
and when he dies he leaves a good
name.

Praise of God the Creator. [12]Once
more I will set forth my theme
to shine like the moon in its
fullness!
[13]Listen to me, my faithful children:
open up your petals,
like roses planted near running
waters;
[14]Send up the sweet odor of incense,
break forth in blossoms like the lily.
Raise your voices in a chorus of praise;
bless the Lord for all his works!
[15]Proclaim the greatness of his name,
loudly sing his praises,
With music on the harp and all
stringed instruments;
sing out with joy as you proclaim:

[16]The works of God are all of them
good;
he supplies for every need in its own
time.
[17]At his word the waters become still as
in a flask;
he had but to speak and the
reservoirs were made.
[18]He has but to command and his will
is done;
nothing can limit his saving action.
[19]The works of all humankind are
present to him;
nothing is hidden from his eyes.
[20]His gaze spans all the ages:
is there any limit to his saving
action?

To him, nothing is small or
insignificant,
and nothing too wonderful or hard
for him.
²¹No cause then to say: "What is the
purpose of this?"
Everything is chosen to satisfy a need.

²²His blessing overflows like the Nile;
like the Euphrates it enriches the
surface of the earth.
²³Even so, his wrath dispossesses the
nations
and turns fertile land into a salt
marsh.
²⁴For the virtuous his paths are level,
to the haughty they are clogged
with stones.
²⁵Good things for the good he provided
from the beginning,
but for the wicked good things and
bad.
²⁶Chief of all needs for human life
are water and fire, iron and salt,
The heart of the wheat, milk and
honey,
the blood of the grape, and oil, and
clothing.
²⁷For the good all these are good,
but for the wicked they turn out
evil.

²⁸There are stormwinds created to
punish;

in their fury they can dislodge
mountains.
In a time of destruction they hurl their
force
and calm the anger of their Maker.
²⁹Fire and hail, famine and disease:
these too were created for
punishment.
³⁰Ravenous beasts, scorpions, vipers,
and the avenging sword to
exterminate the wicked:
All these were created to meet a need,
and are kept in his storehouse for
the proper time.
³¹When he commands them, they
rejoice,
in their assigned tasks they do not
disobey his command.

³²That is why from the first I took my
stand,
and wrote down as my theme:
³³The works of God are all of them
good;
he supplies for every need in its own
time.
³⁴There is no cause then to say: "This is
not as good as that";
for each shows its worth at the
proper time.
³⁵So now with full heart and voice
proclaim
and bless his name!

☐ ACTS 3

Cure of a Crippled Beggar. 3:1 Now Peter and John were going up to the temple area for the three o'clock hour of prayer. ²And a man crippled from birth was carried and placed at the gate of the temple called "the Beautiful Gate" every day to beg for alms from the people who entered the temple. ³When he saw Peter and John about to go into the temple, he asked for alms. ⁴But Peter looked intently at him, as did John, and said, "Look at us." ⁵He paid attention to them, expecting to receive something from them. ⁶Peter said, "I have neither silver nor gold, but what I do have I give you: in the name of Jesus Christ the Nazorean, [rise and] walk." ⁷Then Peter took him by the right hand and raised him up, and immediately his feet and ankles grew strong. ⁸He leaped up, stood, and walked around, and went into the temple with them, walking and jumping and praising God. ⁹When all the people saw him walking and praising God, ¹⁰they recognized him as the one who used to sit begging at the Beautiful Gate of the temple, and they were filled with amazement and astonishment at what had happened to him.

Peter's Speech. ¹¹As he clung to Peter and John, all the people hurried in amazement toward them in the portico called "Solomon's Portico." ¹²When Peter saw this, he addressed the people, "You Israelites, why are you amazed at this, and why do you look so intently at us as if we had made him walk by our own power or piety? ¹³The God of Abraham, [the God] of Isaac, and [the God] of Jacob, the God of our ancestors, has glorified his servant Jesus whom you handed over and denied in Pilate's presence, when he had decided to release him. ¹⁴You denied the Holy and Righteous One and asked that a murderer be released to you. ¹⁵The author of life you put to death, but God raised him from the dead; of this we are witnesses. ¹⁶And by faith in his name, this man, whom you see and know, his name has made strong, and the faith that comes through it has given him this perfect health, in the presence of all of you. ¹⁷Now I know, brothers, that you acted out of ignorance, just as your leaders did; ¹⁸but God has thus brought to fulfillment what he had announced beforehand through the mouth of all the prophets, that his Messiah would suffer. ¹⁹Repent, therefore, and be converted, that your sins may be wiped away, ²⁰and that the Lord may grant you times of refreshment and send you the Messiah already appointed for you, Jesus, ²¹whom heaven must receive until the times of universal restoration of which God spoke through the mouth of his holy prophets from of old. ²²For Moses said:

'A prophet like me will the Lord, your God, raise up for you
from among your own kinsmen;
to him you shall listen in all that he may say to you.
²³Everyone who does not listen to that prophet
will be cut off from the people.'

²⁴Moreover, all the prophets who spoke, from Samuel and those afterwards, also announced these days. ²⁵You are the children of the prophets and of the covenant that God made with your ancestors when he said to Abraham, 'In your offspring all the families of the earth shall be blessed.' ²⁶For you first, God raised up his servant and sent him to bless you by turning each of you from your evil ways."

August 29

The Martyrdom of St. John the Baptist

There is no doubt that blessed John suffered imprisonment and chains as a witness to our Redeemer, whose forerunner he was, and gave his life for Him. His persecutor had demanded not that he should deny Christ, but only that he should keep silent about the truth. Nevertheless, he died for Christ. Doesn't Christ say: "I am the truth"? Therefore, because John shed his blood for the truth, he surely died for Christ.

— ST. BEDE THE VENERABLE

☐ SIRACH 40–42

Joys and Miseries of Life. 40:1 A great anxiety has God allotted,
and a heavy yoke, to the children of Adam,
From the day they leave their mother's womb
until the day they return to the mother of all the living.
²Troubled thoughts and fear of heart are theirs
and anxious foreboding until death.
³Whether one sits on a lofty throne
or grovels in dust and ashes,
⁴Whether one wears a splendid crown
or is clothed in the coarsest of garments—
⁵There is wrath and envy, trouble and dread,
terror of death, fury and strife.
Even when one lies on his bed to rest,
his cares disturb his sleep at night.
⁶So short is his rest it seems like none,
till in his dreams he struggles as he did by day,
Troubled by the visions of his mind,
like a fugitive fleeing from the pursuer.
⁷As he reaches safety, he wakes up,
astonished that there was nothing to fear.
⁸To all flesh, human being and beast,
but for sinners seven times more,

⁹Come plague and bloodshed, fiery heat and drought,
plunder and ruin, famine and death.
¹⁰For the wicked evil was created,
and because of them destruction hastens.
¹¹All that is of earth returns to earth,
and what is from above returns above.
¹²All that comes from bribes or injustice will be wiped out,
but loyalty remains forever.
¹³Wealth from injustice is like a flooding wadi,
like a mighty stream with lightning and thunder,
¹⁴Which, in its rising, rolls along the stones,
but suddenly, once and for all, comes to an end.
¹⁵The offshoot of violence will not flourish,
for the root of the godless is on sheer rock.
¹⁶They are like reeds on riverbanks,
withered before all other plants;
¹⁷But goodness, like eternity, will never be cut off,
and righteousness endures forever.
¹⁸Wealth or wages can make life sweet,

but better than either, finding a
treasure.
[19]A child or a city will preserve one's
name,
but better than either, finding
wisdom.
Cattle and orchards make a person
flourish;
but better than either, a devoted
wife.
[20]Wine and strong drink delight the
soul,
but better than either, love of
friends.
[21]Flute and harp offer sweet melody,
but better than either, a pure
tongue.
[22]Grace and beauty delight the eye,
but better than either, the produce
of the field.
[23]A friend and a neighbor are timely
guides,
but better than either, a sensible
wife.
[24]Relatives and helpers for times of
stress;
but better than either, charity that
rescues.
[25]Gold and silver make one's way secure,
but better than either, sound
judgment.
[26]Wealth and vigor make the heart
exult,
but better than either, fear of God.
In the fear of the Lord there is no want;
whoever has it need seek no other
support.
[27]The fear of God is a paradise of
blessings;
its canopy is over all that is glorious.
[28]My son, do not live the life of a
beggar;
better to die than to beg.
[29]When one has to look to a stranger's
table,
life is not worth living.

The delicacies offered bring revulsion
of spirit,
and to the intelligent, inward
torture.
[30]In the mouth of the shameless
begging is sweet,
but within him it burns like fire.

41:1 O death! How bitter is the
thought of you
for the one at peace in his home,
For the one who is serene and always
successful,
who can still enjoy life's pleasures.
[2]O death! How welcome is your
sentence
to the weak, failing in strength,
Stumbling and tripping on everything,
with sight gone and hope lost.
[3]Do not fear death's decree for you;
remember, it embraces those before
you and those to come.
[4]This decree for all flesh is from God;
why then should you reject a law of
the Most High?
Whether one has lived a thousand
years, a hundred, or ten,
in Sheol there are no arguments
about life.

[5]The children of sinners are a reprobate
line,
and witless offspring are in the
homes of the wicked.
[6]The inheritance of children of sinners
will perish,
and on their offspring will be
perpetual disgrace.
[7]Children curse their wicked father,
for they suffer disgrace because of
him.
[8]Woe to you, O wicked people,
who forsake the Law of the Most
High.
[9]If you have children, calamity will be
theirs;

and if you beget them, it will be
only for groaning.
When you stumble, there is lasting joy;
and when you die, you become a
curse.
¹⁰All that is nought returns to nought,
so too the godless—from void to
void.

¹¹The human body is a fleeting thing,
but a virtuous name will never be
annihilated.
¹²Have respect for your name, for it
will stand by you
more than thousands of precious
treasures.
¹³The good things of life last a number
of days,
but a good name, for days without
number.

True and False Shame. ¹⁴ᵇHidden
wisdom and concealed treasure,
of what value is either?
¹⁵Better is the person who hides his
folly
than the one who hides his wisdom.
¹⁴ᵃMy children, listen to instruction
about shame;
¹⁶ᵃjudge of disgrace according to my
rules,
¹⁶ᵇNot every kind of shame is shameful,
nor is every kind of disgrace to be
recognized.
¹⁷Before father and mother be ashamed
of immorality,
before prince and ruler, of
falsehood;
¹⁸Before master and mistress, of deceit;
before the public assembly, of crime;
Before associate and friend, of
disloyalty,
¹⁹and in the place where you settle,
of theft.
Be ashamed of breaking an oath or a
covenant,
and of stretching your elbow at
dinner;

Of refusing to give when asked,
²¹of rebuffing your own relatives;
Of defrauding another of his appointed
share,
²⁰ᵃof failing to return a greeting;
²¹ᶜOf gazing at a man's wife,
²⁰ᵇof entertaining thoughts about
another woman;
²²Of trifling with a servant girl you have,
of violating her bed;
Of using harsh words with friends,
of following up your gifts with
insults;

42:1 Of repeating what you hear,
of betraying any secret.
Be ashamed of the right things,
and you will find favor in the sight
of all.

But of these things do not be ashamed,
lest you sin to save face:
²Of the Law of the Most High and his
precepts,
or of justice that acquits the
ungodly;
³Of sharing the expenses of a business
or a journey,
of dividing an inheritance or
property;
⁴Of accuracy of scales and balances,
of tested measures and weights;
Of acquiring much or little,
⁵of bargaining in dealing with a
merchant;
Of constant training of children,
of beating the sides of a wicked
servant;
⁶Of a seal to keep a foolish wife at
home,
of a key where there are many hands;
⁷Of numbering every deposit,
of recording all that is taken in and
given out;
⁸Of chastisement for the silly and the
foolish,
for the aged and infirm answering
for wanton conduct.

Thus you will be truly refined
and recognized by all as discreet.

A Father's Care for His Daughter. ⁹A
daughter is a treasure that keeps
her father wakeful,
and worry over her drives away
sleep:
Lest in her youth she remain
unmarried,
or when she is married, lest she be
childless;
¹⁰While unmarried, lest she be defiled,
or in her husband's house, lest she
prove unfaithful;
Lest she become pregnant in her
father's house,
or be sterile in that of her husband.
¹¹My son, keep a close watch on your
daughter,
lest she make you a laughingstock
for your enemies,
A byword in the city and the assembly
of the people,
an object of derision in public
gatherings.
See that there is no lattice in her room,
or spot that overlooks the
approaches to the house.
¹²Do not let her reveal her beauty to
any male,
or spend her time with married
women;
¹³For just as moths come from garments,
so a woman's wickedness comes
from a woman.
¹⁴Better a man's harshness than a
woman's indulgence,
a frightened daughter than any
disgrace.

The Works of God in Nature. ¹⁵Now
will I recall God's works;
what I have seen, I will describe.

By the LORD's word his works were
brought into being;
he accepts the one who does his will.
¹⁶As the shining sun is clear to all,
so the glory of the LORD fills all his
works;
¹⁷Yet even God's holy ones must fail
in recounting the wonders of the
LORD,
Though God has given his hosts the
strength
to stand firm before his glory.
¹⁸He searches out the abyss and
penetrates the heart;
their secrets he understands.
For the Most High possesses all
knowledge,
and sees from of old the things that
are to come.
¹⁹He makes known the past and the
future,
and reveals the deepest secrets.
²⁰He lacks no understanding;
no single thing escapes him.
²¹He regulates the mighty deeds of his
wisdom;
he is from all eternity one and the
same,
With nothing added, nothing taken
away;
no need of a counselor for him!
²²How beautiful are all his works,
delightful to gaze upon and a joy to
behold!
²³Everything lives and abides forever;
and to meet each need all things are
preserved.
²⁴All of them differ, one from another,
yet none of them has he made in
vain;
²⁵For each in turn, as it comes, is good;
can one ever see enough of their
splendor?

☐ ACTS 4

4:1 While they were still speaking to the people, the priests, the captain of the temple guard, and the Sadducees confronted them, [2]disturbed that they were teaching the people and proclaiming in Jesus the resurrection of the dead. [3]They laid hands on them and put them in custody until the next day, since it was already evening. [4]But many of those who heard the word came to believe and (the) number of men grew to [about] five thousand.

Before the Sanhedrin. [5]On the next day, their leaders, elders, and scribes were assembled in Jerusalem, [6]with Annas the high priest, Caiaphas, John, Alexander, and all who were of the high-priestly class. [7]They brought them into their presence and questioned them, "By what power or by what name have you done this?" [8]Then Peter, filled with the holy Spirit, answered them, "Leaders of the people and elders: [9]If we are being examined today about a good deed done to a cripple, namely, by what means he was saved, [10]then all of you and all the people of Israel should know that it was in the name of Jesus Christ the Nazorean whom you crucified, whom God raised from the dead; in his name this man stands before you healed. [11]He is 'the stone rejected by you, the builders, which has become the cornerstone.' [12]There is no salvation through anyone else, nor is there any other name under heaven given to the human race by which we are to be saved."

[13]Observing the boldness of Peter and John and perceiving them to be uneducated, ordinary men, they were amazed, and they recognized them as the companions of Jesus. [14]Then when they saw the man who had been cured standing there with them, they could say nothing in reply. [15]So they ordered them to leave the Sanhedrin, and conferred with one another, saying, [16]"What are we to do with these men? Everyone living in Jerusalem knows that a remarkable sign was done through them, and we cannot deny it. [17]But so that it may not be spread any further among the people, let us give them a stern warning never again to speak to anyone in this name."

[18]So they called them back and ordered them not to speak or teach at all in the name of Jesus. [19]Peter and John, however, said to them in reply, "Whether it is right in the sight of God for us to obey you rather than God, you be the judges. [20]It is impossible for us not to speak about what we have seen and heard." [21]After threatening them further, they released them, finding no way to punish them, on account of the people who were all praising God for what had happened. [22]For the man on whom this sign of healing had been done was over forty years old.

Prayer of the Community. [23]After their release they went back to their own people and reported what the chief priests and elders had told them. [24]And when they heard it, they raised their voices to God with one accord and said, "Sovereign Lord, maker of heaven and earth and the sea and all that is in them, [25]you said by the holy Spirit through the mouth of our father David, your servant:

'Why did the Gentiles rage
  and the peoples entertain folly?
[26]The kings of the earth took their
    stand
  and the princes gathered together
  against the Lord and against his
    anointed.'

[27]Indeed they gathered in this city against your holy servant Jesus whom you anointed, Herod and Pontius Pilate, together with the Gentiles and the peoples of Israel, [28]to do what your hand and [your] will had long ago planned to take place. [29]And now, Lord, take note of their threats, and enable your servants to speak your word with all

boldness, [30]as you stretch forth [your] hand to heal, and signs and wonders are done through the name of your holy servant Jesus." [31]As they prayed, the place where they were gathered shook, and they were all filled with the holy Spirit and continued to speak the word of God with boldness.

Life in the Christian Community. [32]The community of believers was of one heart and mind, and no one claimed that any of his possessions was his own, but they had everything in common. [33]With great power the apostles bore witness to the res-urrection of the Lord Jesus, and great favor was accorded them all. [34]There was no needy person among them, for those who owned property or houses would sell them, bring the proceeds of the sale, [35]and put them at the feet of the apostles, and they were distributed to each according to need.

[36]Thus Joseph, also named by the apostles Barnabas (which is translated "son of encouragement"), a Levite, a Cypriot by birth, [37]sold a piece of property that he owned, then brought the money and put it at the feet of the apostles.

August 30

The saints rejoiced at injuries and persecutions, because in for-giving them they had something to present to God when they prayed to Him.

— St. Teresa of Ávila

☐ SIRACH 43–44

43:1 The beauty of the celestial height
and the pure firmament,
heaven itself manifests its glory.
[2]The sun at its rising shines at its
fullest,
a wonderful instrument, the work
of the Most High!
[3]At noon it scorches the earth,
and who can bear its fiery heat?
[4]Like a blazing furnace of solid metal,
the sun's rays set the mountains
aflame;
Its fiery tongue consumes the world;
the eyes are burned by its fire.
[5]Great indeed is the LORD who made it,
at whose orders it urges on its
steeds.
[6]It is the moon that marks the
changing seasons,
governing the times, their lasting
sign.

[7]By it we know the sacred seasons and
pilgrimage feasts,
a light which wanes in its course:
[8]The new moon like its name renews
itself;
how wondrous it is when it changes:
A military signal for the waterskins on
high,
it paves the firmament with its
brilliance,
[9]The beauty of the heavens and the
glory of the stars,
a shining ornament in the heights
of God.
[10]By the LORD's command the moon
keeps its appointed place,
and does not fade as the stars keep
watch.
[11]Behold the rainbow! Then bless its
Maker,
for majestic indeed is its splendor;

¹²It spans the heavens with its glory,
  the hand of God has stretched it out
    in power.
¹³His rebuke marks out the path for
    the hail,
  and makes the flashes of his
    judgment shine forth.
¹⁴For his own purposes he opens the
    storehouse
  and makes the rain clouds fly like
    vultures.
¹⁵His might gives the clouds their
    strength,
  and breaks off the hailstones.
¹⁶The thunder of his voice makes the
    earth writhe;
  by his power he shakes the
    mountains.
¹⁷A word from him drives on the south
    wind,
  whirlwind, hurricane, and
    stormwind.
He makes the snow fly like birds;
  it settles down like swarms of locusts.
¹⁸Its shining whiteness blinds the eyes,
  the mind marvels at its steady fall.
¹⁹He scatters frost like salt;
  it shines like blossoms on the
    thornbush.
²⁰He sends cold northern blasts
  that harden the ponds like solid
    ground,
Spreads a crust over every body of
    water,
  and clothes each pool with a coat of
    armor.
²¹When mountain growth is scorched
    by heat,
  and flowering plains as by fire,
²²The dripping clouds restore them all,
  and the scattered dew enriches the
    parched land.
²³His is the plan that calms the deep,
  and plants the islands in the sea.
²⁴Those who go down to the sea
  recount its extent,
and when we hear them we are
    thunderstruck;
²⁵In it are his creatures, stupendous,
    amazing,
  all kinds of life, and the monsters of
    the deep.
²⁶For him each messenger succeeds,
  and at his bidding accomplishes his
    will.
²⁷More than this we need not add;
  let the last word be, he is the all!
²⁸Let us praise him the more, since we
    cannot fathom him,
  for greater is he than all his works;
²⁹Awesome indeed is the LORD,
  and wonderful his power.
³⁰Lift up your voices to glorify the
    LORD
  as much as you can, for there is still
    more.
Extol him with renewed strength,
  do not grow weary, for you cannot
    fathom him.
³¹For who has seen him and can
    describe him?
  Who can praise him as he is?
³²Beyond these, many things lie
    hidden;
  only a few of his works have I seen.
³³It is the LORD who has made all
    things;
  to those who fear him he gives
    wisdom.

Praise of Israel's Great Ancestors.
  44:1 I will now praise the godly,
  our ancestors, in their own time,
²The abounding glory of the Most
    High's portion,
  his own part, since the days of old.
³Subduers of the land in kingly fashion,
  renowned for their might,
Counselors in their prudence,
  seers of all things in prophecy,
⁴Resolute princes of the flock,
  lawgivers and their rules,

Sages skilled in composition,
    authors of sharp proverbs,
⁵Composers of melodious psalms,
    writers of lyric poems;
⁶Stalwart, solidly established,
    at peace in their own estates—
⁷All these were glorious in their time,
    illustrious in their day.
⁸Some of them left behind a name
    so that people recount their praises.
⁹Of others no memory remains,
    for when they perished, they perished,
As if they had never lived,
    they and their children after them.
¹⁰Yet these also were godly;
    their virtues have not been forgotten.
¹¹Their wealth remains in their families,
    their heritage with their
        descendants.
¹²Through God's covenant their family
        endures,
    and their offspring for their sake.
¹³And for all time their progeny will
        endure,
    their glory will never be blotted out;
¹⁴Their bodies are buried in peace,
    but their name lives on and on.
¹⁵At gatherings their wisdom is retold,
    and the assembly proclaims their
        praises.

The Early Ancestors. ¹⁶[ENOCH walked
    with the LORD and was taken,
    that succeeding generations might
        learn by his example.]
¹⁷NOAH, found just and perfect,
    renewed the race in the time of
        devastation.
Because of his worth there were
    survivors,

and with a sign to him the deluge
    ended.
¹⁸A lasting covenant was made with him,
    that never again would all flesh be
        destroyed.
¹⁹ABRAHAM, father of many peoples,
    kept his glory without stain:
²⁰He observed the Most High's
        command,
    and entered into a covenant with
        him;
In his own flesh he incised the
        ordinance,
    and when tested was found loyal.
²¹For this reason, God promised him
        with an oath
    to bless the nations through his
        descendants,
To make him numerous as grains of
        dust,
    and to exalt his posterity like the
        stars,
Giving them an inheritance from sea
        to sea,
    and from the River to the ends of
        the earth.
²²For ISAAC, too, he renewed the same
        promise
    because of Abraham, his father.
The covenant with all his forebears was
        confirmed,
²³and the blessing rested upon the
        head of ISRAEL.
God acknowledged him as the
        firstborn,
    and gave him his inheritance.
He fixed the boundaries for his tribes
    and their division into twelve.

☐ ACTS 5

Ananias and Sapphira. 5:1 A man named
Ananias, however, with his wife Sapphira,
sold a piece of property. ²He retained for
himself, with his wife's knowledge, some of
the purchase price, took the remainder, and
put it at the feet of the apostles. ³But Peter
said, "Ananias, why has Satan filled your
heart so that you lied to the holy Spirit

and retained part of the price of the land? [4]While it remained unsold, did it not remain yours? And when it was sold, was it not still under your control? Why did you contrive this deed? You have lied not to human beings, but to God." [5]When Ananias heard these words, he fell down and breathed his last, and great fear came upon all who heard of it. [6]The young men came and wrapped him up, then carried him out and buried him.

[7]After an interval of about three hours, his wife came in, unaware of what had happened. [8]Peter said to her, "Tell me, did you sell the land for this amount?" She answered, "Yes, for that amount." [9]Then Peter said to her, "Why did you agree to test the Spirit of the Lord? Listen, the footsteps of those who have buried your husband are at the door, and they will carry you out." [10]At once, she fell down at his feet and breathed her last. When the young men entered they found her dead, so they carried her out and buried her beside her husband. [11]And great fear came upon the whole church and upon all who heard of these things.

Signs and Wonders of the Apostles. [12]Many signs and wonders were done among the people at the hands of the apostles. They were all together in Solomon's portico. [13]None of the others dared to join them, but the people esteemed them. [14]Yet more than ever, believers in the Lord, great numbers of men and women, were added to them. [15]Thus they even carried the sick out into the streets and laid them on cots and mats so that when Peter came by, at least his shadow might fall on one or another of them. [16]A large number of people from the towns in the vicinity of Jerusalem also gathered, bringing the sick and those disturbed by unclean spirits, and they were all cured.

Trial before the Sanhedrin. [17]Then the high priest rose up and all his companions, that is, the party of the Sadducees, and, filled with jealousy, [18]laid hands upon the apostles and put them in the public jail. [19]But during the night, the angel of the Lord opened the doors of the prison, led them out, and said, [20]"Go and take your place in the temple area, and tell the people everything about this life." [21]When they heard this, they went to the temple early in the morning and taught. When the high priest and his companions arrived, they convened the Sanhedrin, the full senate of the Israelites, and sent to the jail to have them brought in. [22]But the court officers who went did not find them in the prison, so they came back and reported, [23]"We found the jail securely locked and the guards stationed outside the doors, but when we opened them, we found no one inside." [24]When they heard this report, the captain of the temple guard and the chief priests were at a loss about them, as to what this would come to. [25]Then someone came in and reported to them, "The men whom you put in prison are in the temple area and are teaching the people." [26]Then the captain and the court officers went and brought them in, but without force, because they were afraid of being stoned by the people.

[27]When they had brought them in and made them stand before the Sanhedrin, the high priest questioned them, [28]"We gave you strict orders [did we not?] to stop teaching in that name. Yet you have filled Jerusalem with your teaching and want to bring this man's blood upon us." [29]But Peter and the apostles said in reply, "We must obey God rather than men. [30]The God of our ancestors raised Jesus, though you had him killed by hanging him on a tree. [31]God exalted him at his right hand as leader and savior to grant Israel repentance and forgiveness of sins. [32]We are witnesses of these things, as is the holy Spirit that God has given to those who obey him."

[33]When they heard this, they became infuriated and wanted to put them to death. [34]But a Pharisee in the Sanhedrin named

Gamaliel, a teacher of the law, respected by all the people, stood up, ordered the men to be put outside for a short time, [35]and said to them, "Fellow Israelites, be careful what you are about to do to these men. [36]Some time ago, Theudas appeared, claiming to be someone important, and about four hundred men joined him, but he was killed, and all those who were loyal to him were disbanded and came to nothing. [37]After him came Judas the Galilean at the time of the census. He also drew people after him, but he too perished and all who were loyal to him were scattered. [38]So now I tell you, have nothing to do with these men, and let them go. For if this endeavor or this activity is of human origin, it will destroy itself. [39]But if it comes from God, you will not be able to destroy them; you may even find yourselves fighting against God." They were persuaded by him. [40]After recalling the apostles, they had them flogged, ordered them to stop speaking in the name of Jesus, and dismissed them. [41]So they left the presence of the Sanhedrin, rejoicing that they had been found worthy to suffer dishonor for the sake of the name. [42]And all day long, both at the temple and in their homes, they did not stop teaching and proclaiming the Messiah, Jesus.

August 31

Deacons must avoid all reproach as they would beware of fire.
— St. Ignatius of Antioch

☐ SIRACH 45–46

Praise of Moses, Aaron, and Phinehas.
45:1 From him came the man
who would win the favor of all the
living:
Dear to God and human beings,
Moses, whose memory is a blessing.
[2]God made him like the angels in
honor,
and strengthened him with fearful
powers.
[3]At his words God performed signs
and sustained him in the king's
presence.
He gave him the commandments for
his people,
and revealed to him his glory.
[4]Because of his trustworthiness and
meekness
God selected him from all flesh;
[5]He let him hear his voice,
and led him into the cloud,
Where he handed over the
commandments,
the law of life and understanding,
That he might teach his precepts to
Jacob,
his judgments and decrees to Israel.

[6]He also raised up, like Moses in
holiness,
his brother Aaron, of the tribe of
Levi.
[7]He made his office perpetual
and bestowed on him priesthood for
his people;
He established him in honor
and crowned him with lofty
majesty.
[8]He clothed him in splendid garments,
and adorned him with glorious
vestments:
Breeches, tunic, and robe
[9]with pomegranates at the hem

And a rustle of bells round about,
    whose pleasing sound at each step
Would make him heard within the
    sanctuary,
    a reminder for the people;
[10]The sacred vestments of gold, violet,
    and crimson, worked with
    embroidery;
The breastpiece for decision, the ephod
    and cincture
[11]with scarlet yarn, the work of the
    weaver;
Precious stones with seal engravings
    in golden settings, the work of the
    jeweler,
To commemorate in incised letters
    each of the tribes of Israel;
[12]On his turban a diadem of gold,
    its plate engraved with the sacred
    inscription—
Majestic, glorious, renowned for
    splendor,
    a delight to the eyes, supremely
    beautiful.
[13]Before him, no one had been adorned
    with these,
    nor may they ever be worn by any
    other
Except his sons and them alone,
    generation after generation, for all
    time.
[14]His grain offering is wholly burnt
    as an established offering twice each
    day;
[15]For Moses ordained him
    and anointed him with the holy oil,
In a lasting covenant with him and his
    family,
    as permanent as the heavens,
That he should serve God in the
    priesthood
    and bless the people in his name.
[16]He chose him from all the living
    to sacrifice burnt offerings and
    choice portions,
To burn incense, sweet odor as a
    memorial,

and to atone for the people of Israel.
[17]He gave to him the laws,
    and authority to prescribe and to
    judge:
To teach precepts to the people,
    and judgments to the Israelites.
[18]Strangers rose in anger against him,
    grew jealous of him in the desert—
The followers of Dathan and Abiram,
    and the band of Korah in their
    defiance.
[19]When the LORD saw this he became
    angry,
    and destroyed them in his burning
    wrath.
He brought against them a marvel,
    and consumed them in flaming fire.
[20]Then he increased the glory of Aaron
    and bestowed upon him his
    inheritance:
The sacred offerings he allotted to him,
    with the showbread as his portion;
[21]The oblations of the LORD are his
    food,
    a gift to him and his descendants.
[22]But he holds no land among the
    people
    nor shares with them their heritage;
For the LORD himself is his portion
    and inheritance
    among the Israelites.

[23]PHINEHAS too, the son of Eleazar,
    was the courageous third of his line
When, zealous for the God of all,
    he met the crisis of his people
And, at the prompting of his noble
    heart,
    atoned for the children of Israel.
[24]Therefore, on him also God conferred
    the right,
    in a covenant of friendship, to
    provide for the sanctuary,
So that he and his descendants
    should possess the high priesthood
    forever.
[25]For even his covenant with David,

the son of Jesse of the tribe of Judah,
Was an individual heritage through
    one son alone;
    but the heritage of Aaron is for all
      his descendants.

So now bless the LORD
    who has crowned you with glory!
²⁶May he grant you wisdom of heart
    to govern his people in justice,
Lest the benefits you confer should be
    forgotten,
    or your authority, throughout all
      time.

Joshua, Caleb, the Judges, and Samuel.

46:1 Valiant warrior was
    JOSHUA, son of Nun,
    aide to Moses in the prophetic
      office,
Formed to be, as his name implies,
    the great savior of God's chosen ones,
To punish the enemy
    and to give to Israel their heritage.
²What glory was his when he raised his
    hand,
    to brandish his sword against the
      city!
³Who could withstand him
    when he fought the battles of the
      LORD?
⁴Was it not by that same hand the sun
    stopped,
    so that one day became two?
⁵He called upon the Most High God
    when his enemies beset him on all
      sides,
And God Most High answered him
    with hailstones of tremendous
      power,
⁶That rained down upon the hostile
    army
    till on the slope he destroyed the foe;
That all the doomed nations might
    know
    the LORD was watching over his
      people's battles.

He was indeed a devoted follower of
    God
⁷and showed himself loyal in Moses'
    lifetime.
He and CALEB, son of Jephunneh,
    when they opposed the rebel
      assembly,
Averted God's anger from the people
    and suppressed the wicked
      complaint.
⁸Because of this, these two alone were
    spared
    from the six hundred thousand
      infantry,
To lead the people into their heritage,
    the land flowing with milk and
      honey.
⁹The strength God gave to Caleb
    remained with him even in old age
Till he won his way onto the summits
    of the land;
    his family too received a heritage,
¹⁰That all the offspring of Jacob might
    know
    how good it is to be a devoted
      follower of the LORD.

¹¹The JUDGES, each one of them,
    whose hearts were not deceived,
Who did not abandon God—
    may their memory be ever blessed!
¹²May their bones flourish with new
    life where they lie,
    and their names receive fresh luster
      in their children!
¹³Beloved of his people, dear to his
    Maker,
    pledged in a vow from his mother's
      womb,
As one consecrated to the LORD in the
    prophetic office,
    was SAMUEL, the judge who offered
      sacrifice.
At God's word he established the
    kingdom
    and anointed princes to rule the
      people.

¹⁴By the law of the LORD he judged the
congregation,
and visited the encampments of
Jacob.
¹⁵As a trustworthy prophet he was
sought out
and his words proved him to be a
true seer.
¹⁶He, too, called upon the mighty Lord
when his enemies pressed him on
every side,
and offered up a suckling lamb.
¹⁷Then the LORD thundered from
heaven,
and the tremendous roar of his
voice was heard.

¹⁸He brought low the rulers of the
enemy
and destroyed all the lords of the
Philistines.
¹⁹When Samuel neared the end of life,
he testified before the LORD and his
anointed prince,
"No bribe or secret gift have I taken
from anyone!"
and no one could accuse him.
²⁰Even after death his guidance was
sought;
he made known to the king his fate.
From the grave he spoke in prophecy
to put an end to wickedness.

☐ ACTS 6

The Need for Assistants. 6:1 At that time,
as the number of disciples continued to
grow, the Hellenists complained against
the Hebrews because their widows were
being neglected in the daily distribution.
²So the Twelve called together the community of the disciples and said, "It is not
right for us to neglect the word of God to
serve at table. ³Brothers, select from among
you seven reputable men, filled with the
Spirit and wisdom, whom we shall appoint
to this task, ⁴whereas we shall devote ourselves to prayer and to the ministry of the
word." ⁵The proposal was acceptable to the
whole community, so they chose Stephen,
a man filled with faith and the holy Spirit,
also Philip, Prochorus, Nicanor, Timon,
Parmenas, and Nicholas of Antioch, a convert to Judaism. ⁶They presented these men
to the apostles who prayed and laid hands
on them. ⁷The word of God continued to
spread, and the number of the disciples in
Jerusalem increased greatly; even a large
group of priests were becoming obedient
to the faith.

Accusation against Stephen. ⁸Now
Stephen, filled with grace and power, was
working great wonders and signs among
the people. ⁹Certain members of the so-
called Synagogue of Freedmen, Cyrenians,
and Alexandrians, and people from Cilicia
and Asia, came forward and debated with
Stephen, ¹⁰but they could not withstand
the wisdom and the spirit with which he
spoke. ¹¹Then they instigated some men
to say, "We have heard him speaking blasphemous words against Moses and God."
¹²They stirred up the people, the elders,
and the scribes, accosted him, seized him,
and brought him before the Sanhedrin.
¹³They presented false witnesses who testified, "This man never stops saying things
against [this] holy place and the law. ¹⁴For
we have heard him claim that this Jesus the
Nazorean will destroy this place and change
the customs that Moses handed down to
us." ¹⁵All those who sat in the Sanhedrin
looked intently at him and saw that his face
was like the face of an angel.

September 1

Wisdom is the foundation, and righteousness is the work without which a foundation cannot stand.

— St. Ambrose of Milan

☐ SIRACH 47–49

Nathan, David, and Solomon. 47:1
After him came Nathan
who served in David's presence.
²Like the choice fat of sacred offerings,
so was David in Israel.
³He played with lions as though they
were young goats,
and with bears, like lambs of the flock.
⁴As a youth he struck down the giant
and wiped out the people's disgrace;
His hand let fly the slingstone
that shattered the pride of Goliath.
⁵For he had called upon the Most High
God,
who gave strength to his right arm
To defeat the skilled warrior
and establish the might of his people.
⁶Therefore the women sang his praises
and honored him for "the tens of
thousands."
When he received the royal crown, he
battled
⁷and subdued the enemy on every
side.
He campaigned against the hostile
Philistines
and shattered their power till our
own day.
⁸With his every deed he offered thanks
to God Most High, in words of
praise.
With his whole heart he loved his Maker
⁹and daily had his praises sung;
¹⁰He added beauty to the feasts
and solemnized the seasons of each
year
⁹ᵇWith string music before the altar,
providing sweet melody for the
psalms

¹⁰ᵇSo that when the Holy Name was
praised,
before daybreak the sanctuary
would resound.
¹¹The Lord forgave him his sins
and exalted his strength forever;
He conferred on him the rights of
royalty
and established his throne in Israel.

¹²Because of his merits he had as
successor
a wise son, who lived in security:
¹³Solomon reigned during an era of
peace,
for God brought rest to all his
borders.
He built a house to the name of God,
and established a lasting sanctuary.
¹⁴How wise you were when you were
young,
overflowing with instruction, like
the Nile in flood!
¹⁵Your understanding covered the
whole earth,
and, like a sea, filled it with
knowledge.
¹⁶Your fame reached distant coasts,
and you were beloved for your
peaceful reign.
¹⁷With song and proverb and riddle,
and with your answers, you
astounded the nations.
¹⁸You were called by that glorious name
which was conferred upon Israel.
Gold you gathered like so much iron;
you heaped up silver as though it
were lead.
¹⁹But you abandoned yourself to women

and gave them dominion over your
  body.
²⁰You brought a stain upon your glory,
  shame upon your marriage bed,
Wrath upon your descendants,
  and groaning upon your deathbed.
²¹Thus two governments came into
  being,
    when in Ephraim kingship was
    usurped.
²²But God does not withdraw his mercy,
  nor permit even one of his promises
  to fail.
He does not uproot the posterity of the
  chosen,
    nor destroy the offspring of his friends.
So he gave to Jacob a remnant,
  to David a root from his own family.

Rehoboam and Jeroboam. ²³Solomon
  finally slept with his ancestors,
    and left behind him one of his sons,
Broad in folly, narrow in sense,
  whose policy made the people rebel.
Then arose the one who should not be
  remembered,
    the sinner who led Israel into sin,
Who brought ruin to Ephraim
  ²⁴and caused them to be exiled from
  their land.

Elijah and Elisha. ²⁵Their sinfulness
  grew more and more,
and they gave themselves to every evil

48:1 Until like fire a prophet appeared,
  his words a flaming furnace.
²The staff of life, their bread, he
  shattered,
    and in his zeal he made them few in
  number.
³By God's word he shut up the heavens
  and three times brought down fire.
⁴How awesome are you, ELIJAH!
  Whose glory is equal to yours?
⁵You brought a dead body back to life
  from Sheol, by the will of the LORD.
⁶You sent kings down to destruction,

and nobles, from their beds of
  sickness.
⁷You heard threats at Sinai,
  at Horeb avenging judgments.
⁸You anointed the agent of these
  punishments,
    the prophet to succeed in your place.
⁹You were taken aloft in a whirlwind,
  in a chariot with fiery horses.
¹⁰You are destined, it is written, in time
  to come
    to put an end to wrath before the
    day of the LORD,
To turn back the hearts of parents
  toward their children,
    and to re-establish the tribes of Israel.
¹¹Blessed is the one who shall have seen
  you before he dies!

¹²When Elijah was enveloped in the
  whirlwind,
ELISHA was filled with his spirit;
He worked twice as many marvels,
  and every utterance of his mouth
    was wonderful.
During his lifetime he feared no one,
  nor was anyone able to intimidate
  his will.
¹³Nothing was beyond his power;
  and from where he lay buried, his
    body prophesied.
¹⁴In life he performed wonders,
  and after death, marvelous deeds.
¹⁵Despite all this the people did not
  repent,
    nor did they give up their sins,
Until they were uprooted from their
  land
    and scattered all over the earth.

Judah. But Judah remained, a tiny
  people,
  with its ruler from the house of David.
¹⁶Some of them did what was right,
  but others were extremely sinful.

Hezekiah and Isaiah. ¹⁷HEZEKIAH
  fortified his city

and had water brought into it;
With bronze tools he cut through the
rocks
and dammed up a mountain site for
water.
¹⁸During his reign Sennacherib led an
invasion
and sent his adjutant;
He shook his fist at Zion
and blasphemed God in his pride.
¹⁹The people's hearts melted within them,
and they were in anguish like that of
childbirth.
²⁰But they called upon the Most High
God
and lifted up their hands to him;
He heard the prayer they uttered,
and saved them through Isaiah.
²¹God struck the camp of the Assyrians
and routed them with a plague.
²²For Hezekiah did what was right
and held fast to the paths of David,
As ordered by the illustrious prophet
Isaiah, who saw truth in visions.
²³In his lifetime he turned back the sun
and prolonged the life of the king.
²⁴By his powerful spirit he looked into
the future
and consoled the mourners of Zion;
²⁵He foretold what would happen till
the end of time,
hidden things yet to be fulfilled.

Josiah and the Prophets. 49:1 The name
Josiah is like blended incense,
made lasting by a skilled perfumer.
Precious is his memory, like honey to
the taste,
like music at a banquet.
²For he grieved over our betrayals,
and destroyed the abominable idols.
³He kept his heart fixed on God,
and in times of lawlessness practiced
virtue.
⁴Except for David, Hezekiah, and Josiah,
they all were wicked;

They abandoned the Law of the Most
High,
these kings of Judah, right to the
very end.
⁵So he gave over their power to others,
their glory to a foreign nation
⁶Who burned the holy city
and left its streets desolate,
⁷As foretold by Jeremiah. They
mistreated him
who even in the womb had been
made a prophet,
To root out, pull down, and destroy,
and then to build and to plant.
⁸Ezekiel beheld a vision
and described the different creatures
of the chariot;
⁹He also referred to Job,
who always persevered in the right
path.
¹⁰Then, too, the Twelve Prophets—
may their bones flourish with new
life where they lie!—
They gave new strength to Jacob
and saved him with steadfast hope.

The Heroes After the Exile. ¹¹How to
extol Zerubbabel?
He was like a signet ring on the
right hand,
¹²And Jeshua, Jozadak's son?
In their time they rebuilt the altar
And erected the holy temple,
destined for everlasting glory.
¹³Exalted be the memory of Nehemiah!
He rebuilt our ruined walls,
Restored our shattered defenses,
and set up gates and bars.

The Earliest Patriarchs. ¹⁴Few on earth
have been created like Enoch;
he also was taken up bodily.
¹⁵Was ever a man born like Joseph?
Even his dead body was provided for.
¹⁶Glorious, too, were Shem and Seth
and Enosh;
but beyond that of any living being
was the splendor of Adam.

☐ ACTS 7

Stephen's Discourses. 7:1 Then the high priest asked, "Is this so?" ²And he replied, "My brothers and fathers, listen. The God of glory appeared to our father Abraham while he was in Mesopotamia, before he had settled in Haran, ³and said to him, 'Go forth from your land and [from] your kinsfolk to the land that I will show you.' ⁴So he went forth from the land of the Chaldeans and settled in Haran. And from there, after his father died, he made him migrate to this land where you now dwell. ⁵Yet he gave him no inheritance in it, not even a foot's length, but he did promise to give it to him and his descendants as a possession, even though he was childless. ⁶And God spoke thus, 'His descendants shall be aliens in a land not their own, where they shall be enslaved and oppressed for four hundred years; ⁷but I will bring judgment on the nation they serve,' God said, 'and after that they will come out and worship me in this place.' ⁸Then he gave him the covenant of circumcision, and so he became the father of Isaac, and circumcised him on the eighth day, as Isaac did Jacob, and Jacob the twelve patriarchs.

⁹"And the patriarchs, jealous of Joseph, sold him into slavery in Egypt; but God was with him ¹⁰and rescued him from all his afflictions. He granted him favor and wisdom before Pharaoh, the king of Egypt, who put him in charge of Egypt and [of] his entire household. ¹¹Then a famine and great affliction struck all Egypt and Canaan, and our ancestors could find no food; ¹²but when Jacob heard that there was grain in Egypt, he sent our ancestors there a first time. ¹³The second time, Joseph made himself known to his brothers, and Joseph's family became known to Pharaoh. ¹⁴Then Joseph sent for his father Jacob, inviting him and his whole clan, seventy-five persons; ¹⁵and Jacob went down to Egypt. And he and our ancestors died ¹⁶and were brought back to Shechem and placed in the tomb that Abraham had purchased for a sum of money from the sons of Hamor at Shechem.

¹⁷"When the time drew near for the fulfillment of the promise that God pledged to Abraham, the people had increased and become very numerous in Egypt, ¹⁸until another king who knew nothing of Joseph came to power [in Egypt]. ¹⁹He dealt shrewdly with our people and oppressed [our] ancestors by forcing them to expose their infants, that they might not survive. ²⁰At this time Moses was born, and he was extremely beautiful. For three months he was nursed in his father's house; ²¹but when he was exposed, Pharaoh's daughter adopted him and brought him up as her own son. ²²Moses was educated [in] all the wisdom of the Egyptians and was powerful in his words and deeds.

²³"When he was forty years old, he decided to visit his kinsfolk, the Israelites. ²⁴When he saw one of them treated unjustly, he defended and avenged the oppressed man by striking down the Egyptian. ²⁵He assumed [his] kinsfolk would understand that God was offering them deliverance through him, but they did not understand. ²⁶The next day he appeared to them as they were fighting and tried to reconcile them peacefully, saying, 'Men, you are brothers. Why are you harming one another?' ²⁷Then the one who was harming his neighbor pushed him aside, saying, 'Who appointed you ruler and judge over us? ²⁸Are you thinking of killing me as you killed the Egyptian yesterday?' ²⁹Moses fled when he heard this and settled as an alien in the land of Midian, where he became the father of two sons.

³⁰"Forty years later, an angel appeared to him in the desert near Mount Sinai in the flame of a burning bush. ³¹When Moses saw it, he was amazed at the sight, and as

he drew near to look at it, the voice of the Lord came, [32]'I am the God of your fathers, the God of Abraham, of Isaac, and of Jacob.' Then Moses, trembling, did not dare to look at it. [33]But the Lord said to him, 'Remove the sandals from your feet, for the place where you stand is holy ground. [34]I have witnessed the affliction of my people in Egypt and have heard their groaning, and I have come down to rescue them. Come now, I will send you to Egypt.' [35]This Moses, whom they had rejected with the words, 'Who appointed you ruler and judge?' God sent as [both] ruler and deliverer, through the angel who appeared to him in the bush. [36]This man led them out, performing wonders and signs in the land of Egypt, at the Red Sea, and in the desert for forty years. [37]It was this Moses who said to the Israelites, 'God will raise up for you, from among your own kinsfolk, a prophet like me.' [38]It was he who, in the assembly in the desert, was with the angel who spoke to him on Mount Sinai and with our ancestors, and he received living utterances to hand on to us.

[39]"Our ancestors were unwilling to obey him; instead, they pushed him aside and in their hearts turned back to Egypt, [40]saying to Aaron, 'Make us gods who will be our leaders. As for that Moses who led us out of the land of Egypt, we do not know what has happened to him.' [41]So they made a calf in those days, offered sacrifice to the idol, and reveled in the works of their hands. [42]Then God turned and handed them over to worship the host of heaven, as it is written in the book of the prophets:

'Did you bring me sacrifices and offerings
    for forty years in the desert, O house of Israel?
[43]No, you took up the tent of Moloch
    and the star of (your) god Rephan,
    the images that you made to worship.

So I shall take you into exile beyond Babylon.'

[44]"Our ancestors had the tent of testimony in the desert just as the One who spoke to Moses directed him to make it according to the pattern he had seen. [45]Our ancestors who inherited it brought it with Joshua when they dispossessed the nations that God drove out from before our ancestors, up to the time of David, [46]who found favor in the sight of God and asked that he might find a dwelling place for the house of Jacob. [47]But Solomon built a house for him. [48]Yet the Most High does not dwell in houses made by human hands. As the prophet says:

[49]'The heavens are my throne,
    the earth is my footstool.
What kind of house can you build for me?
    says the Lord,
or what is to be my resting place?
[50]Did not my hand make all these things?'

Conclusion. [51]"You stiff-necked people, uncircumcised in heart and ears, you always oppose the holy Spirit; you are just like your ancestors. [52]Which of the prophets did your ancestors not persecute? They put to death those who foretold the coming of the righteous one, whose betrayers and murderers you have now become. [53]You received the law as transmitted by angels, but you did not observe it."

Stephen's Martyrdom. [54]When they heard this, they were infuriated, and they ground their teeth at him. [55]But he, filled with the holy Spirit, looked up intently to heaven and saw the glory of God and Jesus standing at the right hand of God, [56]and he said, "Behold, I see the heavens opened and the Son of Man standing at the right hand of God." [57]But they cried out in a loud voice, covered their ears, and rushed upon him together. [58]They threw him out of the city, and began to stone him. The witnesses laid down their cloaks at the feet of a young man named Saul. [59]As they were stoning Stephen, he called out, "Lord Jesus, receive my spirit." [60]Then he fell to his knees and cried out in a loud voice, "Lord, do not hold this sin against them"; and when he said this, he fell asleep.

September 2

Blessed Solomon Le Clerq

As for us, we hold to what we believed ten and twenty years ago; to what our forefathers believed one hundred years ago, and one thousand years ago, and to that which the whole Catholic world has always believed.

— BLESSED SOLOMON LE CLERQ

☐ SIRACH 50-51

Simeon, Son of Jochanan. 50:1
Greatest of his family, the glory
of his people,
was SIMEON the priest, son of
Jochanan,
In whose time the house of God was
renovated,
in whose days the temple was
reinforced.
[2]In his time also the retaining wall was
built
with powerful turrets for the temple
precincts.
[3]In his time the reservoir was dug,
a pool as vast as the sea.
[4]He protected the people against
brigands
and strengthened the city against
the enemy.
[5]How splendid he was as he looked out
from the tent,
as he came from behind the veil!
[6]Like a star shining among the clouds,
like the full moon at the festal
season;
[7]Like sun shining upon the temple of
the King,
like a rainbow appearing in the
cloudy sky;
[8]Like blossoms on the branches in
springtime,
like a lily by running waters;
Like a green shoot on Lebanon in
summer,
[9]like the fire of incense at sacrifice;
Like a vessel of hammered gold,
studded with all kinds of precious
stones;
[10]Like a luxuriant olive tree heavy with
fruit,
a plant with branches abounding
in oil;
[11]Wearing his glorious robes,
and vested in sublime magnificence,
As he ascended the glorious altar
and lent majesty to the court of the
sanctuary.
[12]When he received the portions from
the priests
while he stood before the sacrificial
wood,
His sons stood round him like a garland,
like young cedars on Lebanon;
And like poplars by the brook they
surrounded him,

¹³all the sons of Aaron in their glory,
With the offerings to the LORD in their
    hands,
    in the presence of the whole
        assembly of Israel.
¹⁴Once he had completed the service at
    the altar
    and arranged the sacrificial hearth
        for the Most High,
¹⁵And had stretched forth his hand for
    the cup,
    to offer blood of the grape,
And poured it out at the foot of the altar,
    a sweet-smelling odor to God the
        Most High,
¹⁶Then the sons of Aaron would sound
    a blast,
    the priests, on their trumpets of
        beaten metal;
A blast to resound mightily
    as a reminder before the Most High.
¹⁷All the people with one accord
    would fall with face to the ground
In adoration before the Most High,
    before the Holy One of Israel.

¹⁸Then hymns would re-echo,
    and over the throng sweet strains of
        praise resound.
¹⁹All the people of the land would
    shout for joy,
    praying to the Merciful One,
As the high priest completed the
    service at the altar
    by presenting to God the fitting
        sacrifice.
²⁰Then coming down he would raise
    his hands
    over all the congregation of Israel;
The blessing of the LORD would be
    upon his lips,
    the name of the LORD would be his
        glory.
²¹The people would again fall down
    to receive the blessing of the Most
        High.

²²And now, bless the God of all,

who has done wonders on earth;
Who fosters growth from the womb,
    fashioning it according to his will!
²³May he grant you a wise heart
    and abide with you in peace;
²⁴May his goodness toward Simeon last
    forever;
    may he fulfill for him the covenant
        with Phinehas
So that it may not be abrogated for him
    or his descendants while the heavens
        last.

Epilogue. ²⁵My whole being loathes
    two nations,
    the third is not even a people:
²⁶The inhabitants of Seir and Philistia,
    and the foolish people who dwell in
        Shechem.

²⁷Wise instruction, appropriate
    proverbs,
    I have written in this book—
I, Yeshua Ben Eleazar Ben Sira—
    as they poured forth from my heart's
        understanding.
²⁸Happy those who meditate upon
    these things;
    wise those who take them to heart!
²⁹If they put them into practice, they
    can cope with anything,
    for the fear of the LORD is their
        lamp.

A Prayer of Thanksgiving. 51:1 I give
    you thanks, LORD and King,
    I praise you, God my savior!
I declare your name, refuge of my life,
    ²because you have ransomed my life
        from death;
You held back my body from the pit,
    and delivered my foot from the
        power of Sheol.

You have preserved me from the
    scourge of the slanderous tongue,
    and from the lips of those who went
        over to falsehood.

You were with me against those who
 rise up against me;
 ³You have rescued me according to
  your abundant mercy
From the snare of those who look for
 my downfall,
  and from the power of those who
   seek my life.

From many dangers you have saved me,
 ⁴from flames that beset me on every
  side,
From the midst of fire till there was not
 a whiff of it,
 ⁵from the deep belly of Sheol,
From deceiving lips and painters of lies,
 ⁶from the arrows of a treacherous
  tongue.

I was at the point of death,
 my life was nearing the depths of
  Sheol;
⁷I turned every way, but there was no
 one to help;
 I looked for support but there was
  none.
⁸Then I remembered the mercies of the
 Lord,
 his acts of kindness through ages past;
For he saves those who take refuge in
 him,
 and rescues them from every evil.

⁹So I raised my voice from the grave;
 from the gates of Sheol I cried for
  help.
¹⁰I called out: Lord, you are my Father,
 my champion, my savior!
Do not abandon me in time of trouble,
 in the midst of storms and dangers.
¹¹I will always praise your name
 and remember you in prayer!

Then the Lord heard my voice,
 and listened to my appeal.
¹²He saved me from every evil
 and preserved me in time of trouble.
For this reason I thank and praise him;
 I bless the name of the Lord.

Ben Sira's Pursuit of Wisdom.
 ¹³When I was young and
  innocent,
 I sought wisdom.
¹⁴She came to me in her beauty,
 and until the end I will cultivate her.

¹⁵As the blossoms yielded to ripening
 grapes,
 the heart's joy,
My feet kept to the level path
 because from earliest youth I was
  familiar with her.

¹⁶In the short time I paid heed,
 I met with great instruction.
¹⁷Since in this way I have profited,
 I will give my Teacher grateful praise.

¹⁸I resolved to tread her paths;
 I have been jealous for the good and
  will not turn back.
¹⁹I burned with desire for her,
 never relenting.
I became preoccupied with her,
 never weary of extolling her.

I spread out my hands to the heavens
 and I came to know her secrets.
²⁰For her I purified my hands;
 in cleanness I attained to her.

At first acquaintance with her, I gained
 understanding
 such that I will never forsake her.
²¹My whole being was stirred to seek
 her;
 therefore I have made her my prize
  possession.
²²The Lord has rewarded me with lips,
 with a tongue for praising him.

²³Come aside to me, you untutored,
 and take up lodging in the house of
  instruction;
²⁴How long will you deprive yourself of
 wisdom's food,
 how long endure such bitter thirst?
²⁵I open my mouth and speak of her:
 gain wisdom for yourselves at no cost.

²⁶Take her yoke upon your neck;
  that your mind may receive her
    teaching.
For she is close to those who seek her,
  and the one who is in earnest finds
    her.

²⁷See for yourselves! I have labored only
    a little,
  but have found much.
²⁸Acquire but a little instruction,

and you will win silver and gold
    through her.

²⁹May your soul rejoice in God's mercy;
  do not be ashamed to give him
    praise.
³⁰Work at your tasks in due season,
  and in his own time God will give
    you your reward.

☐ ACTS 8

8:1 Now Saul was consenting to his execution.

Persecution of the Church. On that day, there broke out a severe persecution of the church in Jerusalem, and all were scattered throughout the countryside of Judea and Samaria, except the apostles. ²Devout men buried Stephen and made a loud lament over him. ³Saul, meanwhile, was trying to destroy the church; entering house after house and dragging out men and women, he handed them over for imprisonment.

Philip in Samaria. ⁴Now those who had been scattered went about preaching the word. ⁵Thus Philip went down to [the] city of Samaria and proclaimed the Messiah to them. ⁶With one accord, the crowds paid attention to what was said by Philip when they heard it and saw the signs he was doing. ⁷For unclean spirits, crying out in a loud voice, came out of many possessed people, and many paralyzed and crippled people were cured. ⁸There was great joy in that city.

Simon the Magician. ⁹A man named Simon used to practice magic in the city and astounded the people of Samaria, claiming to be someone great. ¹⁰All of them, from the least to the greatest, paid attention to him, saying, "This man is the 'Power of God' that is called 'Great.'" ¹¹They paid attention to him because he had astounded them by his magic for a long time, ¹²but once they began to believe Philip as he preached the good news about the kingdom of God and the name of Jesus Christ, men and women alike were baptized. ¹³Even Simon himself believed and, after being baptized, became devoted to Philip; and when he saw the signs and mighty deeds that were occurring, he was astounded.

¹⁴Now when the apostles in Jerusalem heard that Samaria had accepted the word of God, they sent them Peter and John, ¹⁵who went down and prayed for them, that they might receive the holy Spirit, ¹⁶for it had not yet fallen upon any of them; they had only been baptized in the name of the Lord Jesus. ¹⁷Then they laid hands on them and they received the holy Spirit.

¹⁸When Simon saw that the Spirit was conferred by the laying on of the apostles' hands, he offered them money ¹⁹and said, "Give me this power too, so that anyone upon whom I lay my hands may receive the holy Spirit." ²⁰But Peter said to him, "May your money perish with you, because you thought that you could buy the gift of God with money. ²¹You have no share or lot in this matter, for your heart is not upright before God. ²²Repent of this wickedness of yours and pray to the Lord that, if possible, your intention may be forgiven. ²³For I see that you are filled with bitter gall and are in the bonds of iniquity." ²⁴Simon

said in reply, "Pray for me to the Lord, that nothing of what you have said may come upon me." [25]So when they had testified and proclaimed the word of the Lord, they returned to Jerusalem and preached the good news to many Samaritan villages.

Philip and the Ethiopian. [26]Then the angel of the Lord spoke to Philip, "Get up and head south on the road that goes down from Jerusalem to Gaza, the desert route." [27]So he got up and set out. Now there was an Ethiopian eunuch, a court official of the Candace, that is, the queen of the Ethiopians, in charge of her entire treasury, who had come to Jerusalem to worship, [28]and was returning home. Seated in his chariot, he was reading the prophet Isaiah. [29]The Spirit said to Philip, "Go and join up with that chariot." [30]Philip ran up and heard him reading Isaiah the prophet and said, "Do you understand what you are reading?" [31]He replied, "How can I, unless someone instructs me?" So he invited Philip to get in and sit with him. [32]This was the scripture passage he was reading:

"Like a sheep he was led to the
slaughter,

and as a lamb before its shearer is
silent,
so he opened not his mouth.
[33]In (his) humiliation justice was
denied him.
Who will tell of his posterity?
For his life is taken from the earth."

[34]Then the eunuch said to Philip in reply, "I beg you, about whom is the prophet saying this? About himself, or about someone else?" [35]Then Philip opened his mouth and, beginning with this scripture passage, he proclaimed Jesus to him. [36]As they traveled along the road they came to some water, and the eunuch said, "Look, there is water. What is to prevent my being baptized?" [37] [38]Then he ordered the chariot to stop, and Philip and the eunuch both went down into the water, and he baptized him. [39]When they came out of the water, the Spirit of the Lord snatched Philip away, and the eunuch saw him no more, but continued on his way rejoicing. [40]Philip came to Azotus, and went about proclaiming the good news to all the towns until he reached Caesarea.

September 3

Pope St. Gregory the Great

The only true riches are those that make us rich in virtue. So if you want to be rich, beloved, love true riches. If you aspire to the heights of real honor, strive to reach the kingdom of heaven. If you value status and fame, hasten to be enrolled in the heavenly court of the angels.

— POPE ST. GREGORY THE GREAT

☐ ISAIAH 1-2

1:1 The vision which Isaiah, son of Amoz, saw concerning Judah and Jerusalem in the days of Uzziah, Jotham, Ahaz and Hezekiah, kings of Judah.

Accusation and Appeal. [2]Hear, O
heavens, and listen, O earth,
for the LORD speaks:
Sons have I raised and reared,

but they have rebelled against me!
³An ox knows its owner,
and an ass, its master's manger;
But Israel does not know,
my people has not understood.
⁴Ah! Sinful nation, people laden with
wickedness,
evil offspring, corrupt children!
They have forsaken the LORD,
spurned the Holy One of Israel,
apostatized,
⁵Why would you yet be struck,
that you continue to rebel?
The whole head is sick,
the whole heart faint.
⁶From the sole of the foot to the head
there is no sound spot in it;
Just bruise and welt and oozing wound,
not drained, or bandaged,
or eased with salve.
⁷Your country is waste,
your cities burnt with fire;
Your land—before your eyes
strangers devour it,
a waste, like the devastation of
Sodom.
⁸And daughter Zion is left
like a hut in a vineyard,
Like a shed in a melon patch,
like a city blockaded.
⁹If the LORD of hosts had not
left us a small remnant,
We would have become as Sodom,
would have resembled Gomorrah.

¹⁰Hear the word of the LORD,
princes of Sodom!
Listen to the instruction of our God,
people of Gomorrah!
¹¹What do I care for the multitude of
your sacrifices?
says the LORD.
I have had enough of whole-burnt rams
and fat of fatlings;
In the blood of calves, lambs, and goats
I find no pleasure.
¹²When you come to appear before me,

who asks these things of you?
¹³Trample my courts no more!
To bring offerings is useless;
incense is an abomination to me.
New moon and sabbath, calling
assemblies—
festive convocations with
wickedness—
these I cannot bear.
¹⁴Your new moons and festivals I detest;
they weigh me down, I tire of the
load.
¹⁵When you spread out your hands,
I will close my eyes to you;
Though you pray the more,
I will not listen.
Your hands are full of blood!
¹⁶Wash yourselves clean!
Put away your misdeeds from before
my eyes;
cease doing evil;
¹⁷learn to do good.
Make justice your aim: redress the
wronged,
hear the orphan's plea, defend the
widow.

¹⁸Come now, let us set things right,
says the LORD:
Though your sins be like scarlet,
they may become white as snow;
Though they be red like crimson,
they may become white as wool.
¹⁹If you are willing, and obey,
you shall eat the good things of the
land;
²⁰But if you refuse and resist,
you shall be eaten by the sword:
for the mouth of the LORD has
spoken!

The Purification of Jerusalem. ²¹How
she has become a prostitute,
the faithful city, so upright!
Justice used to lodge within her,
but now, murderers.
²²Your silver is turned to dross,
your wine is mixed with water.

²³Your princes are rebels
   and comrades of thieves;
Each one of them loves a bribe
   and looks for gifts.
The fatherless they do not defend,
   the widow's plea does not reach them.
²⁴Now, therefore, says the Lord,
   the LORD of hosts, the Mighty One
      of Israel:
Ah! I will take vengeance on my foes
   and fully repay my enemies!
²⁵I will turn my hand against you,
   and refine your dross in the furnace,
      removing all your alloy.
²⁶I will restore your judges as at first,
   and your counselors as in the
      beginning;
After that you shall be called
   city of justice, faithful city.
²⁷Zion shall be redeemed by justice,
   and her repentant ones by
      righteousness.
²⁸Rebels and sinners together shall be
      crushed,
   those who desert the LORD shall be
      consumed.

Judgment on the Sacred Groves.
   ²⁹You shall be ashamed of the
      terebinths which you desired,
   and blush on account of the gardens
      which you chose.
³⁰You shall become like a terebinth
      whose leaves wither,
   like a garden that has no water.
³¹The strong tree shall turn to tinder,
   and the one who tends it shall
      become a spark;
Both of them shall burn together,
   and there shall be none to quench
      them.

2:1 This is what Isaiah, son of Amoz, saw concerning Judah and Jerusalem.

Zion, the Royal City of God. ²In
      days to come,
The mountain of the LORD's house

shall be established as the highest
      mountain
   and raised above the hills.
All nations shall stream toward it.
   ³Many peoples shall come and say:
"Come, let us go up to the LORD's
      mountain,
   to the house of the God of Jacob,
That he may instruct us in his ways,
   and we may walk in his paths."
For from Zion shall go forth
      instruction,
   and the word of the LORD from
      Jerusalem.
⁴He shall judge between the nations,
   and set terms for many peoples.
They shall beat their swords into
      plowshares
   and their spears into pruning hooks;
One nation shall not raise the sword
      against another,
   nor shall they train for war again.
⁵House of Jacob, come,
   let us walk in the light of the LORD!

**The Lord's Day of Judgment on
Pride.** ⁶You have abandoned
      your people,
   the house of Jacob!
Because they are filled with diviners,
   and soothsayers, like the Philistines;
   with foreigners they clasp hands.
⁷Their land is full of silver and gold,
   there is no end to their treasures;
Their land is full of horses,
   there is no end to their chariots.
⁸Their land is full of idols;
   they bow down to the works of their
      hands,
   what their fingers have made.
⁹So all shall be abased,
   each one brought low.
   Do not pardon them!
¹⁰Get behind the rocks,
   hide in the dust,
From the terror of the LORD
   and the splendor of his majesty!

[11]The eyes of human pride shall be
lowered,
the arrogance of mortals shall be
abased,
and the LORD alone will be exalted,
on that day.
[12]For the LORD of hosts will have his day
against all that is proud and arrogant,
against all that is high, and it will be
brought low;
[13]Yes, against all the cedars of Lebanon
and against all the oaks of Bashan,
[14]Against all the lofty mountains
and all the high hills,
[15]Against every lofty tower
and every fortified wall,
[16]Against all the ships of Tarshish
and all stately vessels.
[17]Then human pride shall be abased,
the arrogance of mortals brought low,
And the LORD alone will be exalted on
that day.

[18]The idols will vanish completely.
[19]People will go into caves in the rocks
and into holes in the earth,
At the terror of the LORD
and the splendor of his majesty,
as he rises to overawe the earth.
[20]On that day people shall throw to
moles and bats
their idols of silver and their idols
of gold
which they made for themselves to
worship.
[21]And they shall go into caverns in the
rocks
and into crevices in the cliffs,
At the terror of the LORD
and the splendor of his majesty,
as he rises to overawe the earth.
[22]As for you, stop worrying about
mortals,
in whose nostrils is but a breath;
for of what worth are they?

☐ ACTS 9

Saul's Conversion. 9:1 Now Saul, still breathing murderous threats against the disciples of the Lord, went to the high priest [2]and asked him for letters to the synagogues in Damascus, that, if he should find any men or women who belonged to the Way, he might bring them back to Jerusalem in chains. [3]On his journey, as he was nearing Damascus, a light from the sky suddenly flashed around him. [4]He fell to the ground and heard a voice saying to him, "Saul, Saul, why are you persecuting me?" [5]He said, "Who are you, sir?" The reply came, "I am Jesus, whom you are persecuting. [6]Now get up and go into the city and you will be told what you must do." [7]The men who were traveling with him stood speechless, for they heard the voice but could see no one. [8]Saul got up from the ground, but when he opened his eyes he could see nothing; so they led him by the hand and brought him to Damascus. [9]For three days he was unable to see, and he neither ate nor drank.

Saul's Baptism. [10]There was a disciple in Damascus named Ananias, and the Lord said to him in a vision, "Ananias." He answered, "Here I am, Lord." [11]The Lord said to him, "Get up and go to the street called Straight and ask at the house of Judas for a man from Tarsus named Saul. He is there praying, [12]and [in a vision] he has seen a man named Ananias come in and lay [his] hands on him, that he may regain his sight." [13]But Ananias replied, "Lord, I have heard from many sources about this man, what evil things he has done to your holy ones in Jerusalem. [14]And here he has authority from the chief priests to imprison all who call upon your name." [15]But the Lord said to him, "Go, for this man is a chosen instrument of mine to carry my name before Gentiles, kings, and Israelites, [16]and I will show him what he will have to suffer for my name." [17]So Ananias went and entered the house; laying his hands on him, he said, "Saul, my brother, the Lord has sent me, Jesus who appeared to you on the way by which you came, that you may regain your sight and be filled with the holy Spirit." [18]Immediately things like scales fell from his eyes and he regained his sight. He got up and was baptized, [19]and when he had eaten, he recovered his strength.

Saul Preaches in Damascus. He stayed some days with the disciples in Damascus, [20]and he began at once to proclaim Jesus in the synagogues, that he is the Son of God. [21]All who heard him were astounded and said, "Is not this the man who in Jerusalem ravaged those who call upon this name, and came here expressly to take them back in chains to the chief priests?" [22]But Saul grew all the stronger and confounded [the] Jews who lived in Damascus, proving that this is the Messiah.

Saul Visits Jerusalem. [23]After a long time had passed, the Jews conspired to kill him, [24]but their plot became known to Saul. Now they were keeping watch on the gates day and night so as to kill him, [25]but his disciples took him one night and let him down through an opening in the wall, lowering him in a basket.

[26]When he arrived in Jerusalem he tried to join the disciples, but they were all afraid of him, not believing that he was a disciple. [27]Then Barnabas took charge of him and brought him to the apostles, and he reported to them how on the way he had seen the Lord and that he had spoken to him, and how in Damascus he had spoken out boldly in the name of Jesus. [28]He moved about freely with them in Jerusalem, and spoke out boldly in the name of the Lord. [29]He also spoke and debated with the Hellenists, but they tried to kill him.

[30]And when the brothers learned of this, they took him down to Caesarea and sent him on his way to Tarsus.

The Church at Peace. [31]The church throughout all Judea, Galilee, and Samaria was at peace. It was being built up and walked in the fear of the Lord, and with the consolation of the holy Spirit it grew in numbers.

Peter Heals Aeneas at Lydda. [32]As Peter was passing through every region, he went down to the holy ones living in Lydda. [33]There he found a man named Aeneas, who had been confined to bed for eight years, for he was paralyzed. [34]Peter said to him, "Aeneas, Jesus Christ heals you. Get up and make your bed." He got up at once. [35]And all the inhabitants of Lydda and Sharon saw him, and they turned to the Lord.

Peter Restores Tabitha to Life. [36]Now in Joppa there was a disciple named Tabitha (which translated means Dorcas). She was completely occupied with good deeds and almsgiving. [37]Now during those days she fell sick and died, so after washing her, they laid [her] out in a room upstairs. [38]Since Lydda was near Joppa, the disciples, hearing that Peter was there, sent two men to him with the request, "Please come to us without delay." [39]So Peter got up and went with them. When he arrived, they took him to the room upstairs where all the widows came to him weeping and showing him the tunics and cloaks that Dorcas had made while she was with them. [40]Peter sent them all out and knelt down and prayed. Then he turned to her body and said, "Tabitha, rise up." She opened her eyes, saw Peter, and sat up. [41]He gave her his hand and raised her up, and when he had called the holy ones and the widows, he presented her alive. [42]This became known all over Joppa, and many came to believe in the Lord. [43]And he stayed a long time in Joppa with Simon, a tanner.

September 4

God is One and Christ is One, and one is His Church, and the faith is one, and His people welded together by the glue of concord into a solid unity of body. Unity cannot be rent asunder; nor can the one body of the Church, through the division of its structure, be divided into separate pieces.

— St. Cyprian of Carthage

☐ ISAIAH 3-4

Judgment on Jerusalem and Judah.

3:1 The Lord, the LORD of hosts,
will take away from Jerusalem and
    from Judah
Support and staff—
    all support of bread,
    all support of water:
²Hero and warrior,
    judge and prophet, diviner and elder,
³The captain of fifty and the nobleman,
    counselor, skilled magician, and
        expert charmer.
⁴I will place boys as their princes;
    the fickle will govern them,
⁵And the people will oppress one another,
    yes, each one the neighbor.
The child will be insolent toward the
    elder,
    and the base toward the honorable.
⁶When anyone seizes a brother
    in their father's house, saying,
"You have clothes! Be our ruler,
    and take in hand this ruin!"—
⁷He will cry out in that day:
"I cannot be a healer,
    when there is neither bread nor
        clothing in my own house!
You will not make me a ruler of the
        people!"
⁸Jerusalem has stumbled, Judah has
        fallen;
    for their speech and deeds affront
        the LORD,
    a provocation in the sight of his
        majesty.

⁹Their very look bears witness against
        them;
    they boast of their sin like Sodom,
They do not hide it.
    Woe to them!
    They deal out evil to themselves.
¹⁰Happy the just, for it will go well with
        them,
    the fruit of their works they will eat.
¹¹Woe to the wicked! It will go ill with
        them,
    with the work of their hands they
        will be repaid.
¹²My people—infants oppress them,
    women rule over them!
My people, your leaders deceive you,
    they confuse the paths you should
        follow.
¹³The LORD rises to accuse,
    stands to try his people.
¹⁴The Lord enters into judgment
    with the people's elders and princes:
You, you who have devoured the
        vineyard;
    the loot wrested from the poor is in
        your houses.
¹⁵What do you mean by crushing my
        people,
    and grinding down the faces of the
        poor?
    says the Lord, the GOD of hosts.

The Haughty Women of Zion. ¹⁶The
LORD said:

Because the daughters of Zion are
    haughty,
  and walk with necks outstretched,
Ogling and mincing as they go,
  their anklets tinkling with every step,
¹⁷The Lord shall cover the scalps of
    Zion's daughters with scabs,
  and the LORD shall lay bare their
    heads.
¹⁸On that day the LORD will do away with
the finery of the anklets, sunbursts, and
crescents; ¹⁹the pendants, bracelets, and
veils; ²⁰the headdresses, bangles, cinctures,
perfume boxes, and amulets; ²¹the signet rings, and the nose rings; ²²the court
dresses, wraps, cloaks, and purses; ²³the lace
gowns, linen tunics, turbans, and shawls.

²⁴Instead of perfume there will be stench,
  instead of a girdle, a rope,
And instead of elaborate coiffure,
    baldness;
  instead of a rich gown, a sackcloth
    skirt.
Then, instead of beauty, shame.
²⁵Your men will fall by the sword,
  and your champions, in war;
²⁶Her gates will lament and mourn,
  as the city sits desolate on the
    ground.

4:1 Seven women will take hold of one
man

on that day, saying:
"We will eat our own food
  and wear our own clothing;
Only let your name be given us,
  put an end to our disgrace!"

Jerusalem Purified. ²On that day,
The branch of the LORD will be beauty
    and glory,
  and the fruit of the land will be
    honor and splendor
  for the survivors of Israel.
³Everyone who remains in Zion,
  everyone left in Jerusalem
Will be called holy:
  everyone inscribed for life in
    Jerusalem.
⁴When the Lord washes away
  the filth of the daughters of Zion,
And purges Jerusalem's blood from her
    midst
  with a blast of judgment, a searing
    blast,
⁵Then will the LORD create,
  over the whole site of Mount Zion
  and over her place of assembly,
A smoking cloud by day
  and a light of flaming fire by night.
⁶For over all, his glory will be shelter
    and protection:
  shade from the parching heat
    of day,
  refuge and cover from storm and rain.

☐ ACTS 10

The Vision of Cornelius. 10:1 Now in
Caesarea there was a man named Cornelius, a centurion of the Cohort called the
Italica, ²devout and God-fearing along
with his whole household, who used to
give alms generously to the Jewish people
and pray to God constantly. ³One afternoon about three o'clock, he saw plainly
in a vision an angel of God come in to him
and say to him, "Cornelius." ⁴He looked
intently at him and, seized with fear, said,

"What is it, sir?" He said to him, "Your
prayers and almsgiving have ascended as a
memorial offering before God. ⁵Now send
some men to Joppa and summon one Simon who is called Peter. ⁶He is staying
with another Simon, a tanner, who has a
house by the sea." ⁷When the angel who
spoke to him had left, he called two of
his servants and a devout soldier from his
staff, ⁸explained everything to them, and
sent them to Joppa.

The Vision of Peter. [9]The next day, while they were on their way and nearing the city, Peter went up to the roof terrace to pray at about noontime. [10]He was hungry and wished to eat, and while they were making preparations he fell into a trance. [11]He saw heaven opened and something resembling a large sheet coming down, lowered to the ground by its four corners. [12]In it were all the earth's four-legged animals and reptiles and the birds of the sky. [13]A voice said to him, "Get up, Peter. Slaughter and eat." [14]But Peter said, "Certainly not, sir. For never have I eaten anything profane and unclean." [15]The voice spoke to him again, a second time, "What God has made clean, you are not to call profane." [16]This happened three times, and then the object was taken up into the sky.

[17]While Peter was in doubt about the meaning of the vision he had seen, the men sent by Cornelius asked for Simon's house and arrived at the entrance. [18]They called out inquiring whether Simon, who is called Peter, was staying there. [19]As Peter was pondering the vision, the Spirit said [to him], "There are three men here looking for you. [20]So get up, go downstairs, and accompany them without hesitation, because I have sent them." [21]Then Peter went down to the men and said, "I am the one you are looking for. What is the reason for your being here?" [22]They answered, "Cornelius, a centurion, an upright and God-fearing man, respected by the whole Jewish nation, was directed by a holy angel to summon you to his house and to hear what you have to say." [23]So he invited them in and showed them hospitality.

The next day he got up and went with them, and some of the brothers from Joppa went with him. [24]On the following day he entered Caesarea. Cornelius was expecting them and had called together his relatives and close friends. [25]When Peter entered, Cornelius met him and, falling at his feet, paid him homage. [26]Peter, however, raised him up, saying, "Get up. I myself am also a human being." [27]While he conversed with him, he went in and found many people gathered together [28]and said to them, "You know that it is unlawful for a Jewish man to associate with, or visit, a Gentile, but God has shown me that I should not call any person profane or unclean. [29]And that is why I came without objection when sent for. May I ask, then, why you summoned me?"

[30]Cornelius replied, "Four days ago at this hour, three o'clock in the afternoon, I was at prayer in my house when suddenly a man in dazzling robes stood before me and said, [31]'Cornelius, your prayer has been heard and your almsgiving remembered before God. [32]Send therefore to Joppa and summon Simon, who is called Peter. He is a guest in the house of Simon, a tanner, by the sea.' [33]So I sent for you immediately, and you were kind enough to come. Now therefore we are all here in the presence of God to listen to all that you have been commanded by the Lord."

Peter's Speech. [34]Then Peter proceeded to speak and said, "In truth, I see that God shows no partiality. [35]Rather, in every nation whoever fears him and acts uprightly is acceptable to him. [36]You know the word [that] he sent to the Israelites as he proclaimed peace through Jesus Christ, who is Lord of all, [37]what has happened all over Judea, beginning in Galilee after the baptism that John preached, [38]how God anointed Jesus of Nazareth with the holy Spirit and power. He went about doing good and healing all those oppressed by the devil, for God was with him. [39]We are witnesses of all that he did both in the country of the Jews and [in] Jerusalem. They put him to death by hanging him on a tree. [40]This man God raised [on] the third day and granted that he be visible, [41]not to all the people, but to us, the witnesses chosen by God in advance, who ate and drank with him after he rose from the dead. [42]He commissioned us to preach to the people and testify that he is the one appointed by God as judge of the living and the dead. [43]To him all the prophets bear witness, that everyone who believes in him will receive forgiveness of sins through his name."

The Baptism of Cornelius. [44]While Peter was still speaking these things, the holy Spirit fell upon all who were listening to the word. [45]The circumcised believers who had accompanied Peter were astounded that the gift of the holy Spirit should have been poured out on the Gentiles also, [46]for they could hear them speaking in tongues and glorifying God. Then Peter responded, [47]"Can anyone withhold the water for baptizing these people, who have received the holy Spirit even as we have?" [48]He ordered them to be baptized in the name of Jesus Christ. [49]Then they invited him to stay for a few days.

September 5

Blessed Teresa of Calcutta

It is a great poverty to decide that a child must die so that you might live as you wish.

— BLESSED TERESA OF CALCUTTA

☐ ISAIAH 5-6

The Song of the Vineyard. 5:1 Now
    let me sing of my friend,
  my beloved's song about his vineyard.
My friend had a vineyard
    on a fertile hillside;
[2]He spaded it, cleared it of stones,
    and planted the choicest vines;
Within it he built a watchtower,
    and hewed out a wine press.
Then he waited for the crop of grapes,
    but it yielded rotten grapes.
[3]Now, inhabitants of Jerusalem, people
    of Judah,
    judge between me and my vineyard:
[4]What more could be done for my
    vineyard
    that I did not do?
Why, when I waited for the crop of
    grapes,
    did it yield rotten grapes?
[5]Now, I will let you know
    what I am going to do to my
      vineyard:

Take away its hedge, give it to grazing,
    break through its wall, let it be
      trampled!
[6]Yes, I will make it a ruin:
    it shall not be pruned or hoed,
    but will be overgrown with thorns
      and briers;
I will command the clouds
    not to rain upon it.
[7]The vineyard of the LORD of hosts is
    the house of Israel,
    the people of Judah, his cherished
      plant;
He waited for judgment, but see,
    bloodshed!
    for justice, but hark, the outcry!

Oracles of Reproach. [8]Ah! Those who
    join house to house,
    who connect field with field,
Until no space remains, and you alone
    dwell
    in the midst of the land!

⁹In my hearing the LORD of hosts has
  sworn:
  Many houses shall be in ruins,
  houses large and fine, with nobody
    living there.
¹⁰Ten acres of vineyard
  shall yield but one bath;
And a homer of seed
  shall yield but an ephah.
¹¹Ah! Those who rise early in the
    morning
  in pursuit of strong drink,
lingering late
  inflamed by wine,
¹²Banqueting on wine with harp and lyre,
  timbrel and flute,
But the deed of the LORD they do not
    regard,
  the work of his hands they do not see!
¹³Therefore my people go into exile
  for lack of understanding,
Its nobles starving,
  its masses parched with thirst.
¹⁴Therefore Sheol enlarges its throat
  and opens its mouth beyond
    measure;
Down into it go nobility and masses,
  tumult and revelry.
¹⁵All shall be abased, each one brought
    low,
  and the eyes of the haughty lowered,
¹⁶But the LORD of hosts shall be exalted
    by judgment,
  by justice the Holy God shown holy.
¹⁷Lambs shall graze as at pasture,
  young goats shall eat in the ruins of
    the rich.
¹⁸Ah! Those who tug at guilt with cords
    of perversity,
  and at sin as if with cart ropes!
¹⁹Who say, "Let him make haste,
  let him speed his work, that we may
    see it;
On with the plan of the Holy One of
    Israel!
  let it come to pass, that we may
    know it!"

²⁰Ah! Those who call evil good, and
    good evil,
  who change darkness to light, and
    light into darkness,
  who change bitter to sweet, and
    sweet into bitter!
²¹Ah! Those who are wise in their own
    eyes,
  prudent in their own view!
²²Ah! Those who are champions at
    drinking wine,
  masters at mixing drink!
²³Those who acquit the guilty for bribes,
  and deprive the innocent of justice!
²⁴Therefore, as the tongue of fire licks
    up stubble,
  as dry grass shrivels in the flame,
Their root shall rot
  and their blossom scatter like dust;
For they have rejected the instruction
    of the LORD of hosts,
  and scorned the word of the Holy
    One of Israel.

²⁵Therefore the wrath of the LORD
    blazes against his people,
  he stretches out his hand to strike
    them;
The mountains quake,
  their corpses shall be like refuse in
    the streets.
For all this, his wrath is not turned
    back,
  his hand is still outstretched.

Invasion. ²⁶He will raise a signal to a far-
    off nation,
  and whistle for it from the ends of
    the earth.
  Then speedily and promptly they
    will come.
²⁷None among them is weary, none
    stumbles,
  none will slumber, none will sleep.
None with waist belt loose,
  none with sandal thong broken.
²⁸Their arrows are sharp,
  and all their bows are bent,

The hooves of their horses like flint,
    and their chariot wheels like the
      whirlwind.
29They roar like the lion,
    like young lions, they roar;
They growl and seize the prey,
    they carry it off and none can
      rescue.
30They will growl over it, on that day,
    like the growling of the sea,
Look to the land—
    darkness closing in,
    the light dark with clouds!

The Sending of Isaiah. 6:1 In the year King Uzziah died, I saw the Lord seated on a high and lofty throne, with the train of his garment filling the temple. 2Seraphim were stationed above; each of them had six wings: with two they covered their faces, with two they covered their feet, and with two they hovered. 3One cried out to the other:

  "Holy, holy, holy is the LORD of hosts!
    All the earth is filled with his glory!"

4At the sound of that cry, the frame of the door shook and the house was filled with smoke. 5Then I said, "Woe is me, I am doomed! For I am a man of unclean lips, living among a people of unclean lips, and my eyes have seen the King, the LORD of hosts!" 6Then one of the seraphim flew to me, holding an ember which he had taken with tongs from the altar.

7He touched my mouth with it. "See," he said, "now that this has touched your lips, your wickedness is removed, your sin purged."
8Then I heard the voice of the Lord saying, "Whom shall I send? Who will go for us?" "Here I am," I said; "send me!" 9And he replied: Go and say to this people:

  Listen carefully, but do not understand!
  Look intently, but do not perceive!
10Make the heart of this people
    sluggish,
  dull their ears and close their eyes;
Lest they see with their eyes, and hear
    with their ears,
    and their heart understand,
    and they turn and be healed.

11"How long, O Lord?" I asked. And he replied:

  Until the cities are desolate,
    without inhabitants,
  Houses, without people,
    and the land is a desolate waste.
12Until the LORD sends the people far
    away,
  and great is the desolation in the
    midst of the land.
13If there remain a tenth part in it,
    then this in turn shall be laid waste;
As with a terebinth or an oak
    whose trunk remains when its leaves
      have fallen.
  Holy offspring is the trunk.

☐ ACTS 11

The Baptism of the Gentiles Explained. 11:1 Now the apostles and the brothers who were in Judea heard that the Gentiles too had accepted the word of God. 2So when Peter went up to Jerusalem the circumcised believers confronted him, 3saying, "You entered the house of uncircumcised people and ate with them." 4Peter began and explained it to them step by step, saying, 5"I was at prayer in the city of Joppa when in a trance I had a vision, something resembling a large sheet coming down, lowered from the sky by its four corners, and it came to me. 6Looking intently into it, I observed and saw the four-legged animals of the earth, the wild beasts, the reptiles, and the birds of the sky. [7]I also heard a voice say to me, 'Get up, Peter. Slaughter and eat.' [8]But I said, 'Certainly not, sir, because nothing profane or unclean has ever entered my mouth.' [9]But a second time a voice from heaven answered, 'What God has made clean, you are not to call profane.' [10]This happened three times, and then everything was drawn up again into the sky. [11]Just then three men appeared at the house where we were, who had been sent to me from Caesarea. [12]The Spirit told me to accompany them without discriminating. These six brothers also went with me, and we entered the man's house. [13]He related to us how he had seen (the) angel standing in his house, saying, 'Send someone to Joppa and summon Simon, who is called Peter, [14]who will speak words to you by which you and all your household will be saved.' [15]As I began to speak, the holy Spirit fell upon them as it had upon us at the beginning, [16]and I remembered the word of the Lord, how he had said, 'John baptized with water but you will be baptized with the holy Spirit.' [17]If then God gave them the same gift he gave to us when we came to believe in the Lord Jesus Christ, who was I to be able to hinder God?" [18]When they heard this, they stopped objecting and glorified God, saying, "God has then granted life-giving repentance to the Gentiles too."

The Church at Antioch. [19]Now those who had been scattered by the persecution that arose because of Stephen went as far as Phoenicia, Cyprus, and Antioch, preaching the word to no one but Jews. [20]There were some Cypriots and Cyrenians among them, however, who came to Antioch and began to speak to the Greeks as well, proclaiming the Lord Jesus. [21]The hand of the Lord was with them and a great number who believed turned to the Lord. [22]The news about them reached the ears of the church in Jerusalem, and they sent Barnabas [to go] to Antioch. [23]When he arrived and saw the grace of God, he rejoiced and encouraged them all to remain faithful to the Lord in firmness of heart, [24]for he was a good man, filled with the holy Spirit and faith. And a large number of people was added to the Lord. [25]Then he went to Tarsus to look for Saul, [26]and when he had found him he brought him to Antioch. For a whole year they met with the church and taught a large number of people, and it was in Antioch that the disciples were first called Christians.

The Prediction of Agabus. [27]At that time some prophets came down from Jerusalem to Antioch, [28]and one of them named Agabus stood up and predicted by the Spirit that there would be a severe famine all over the world, and it happened under Claudius. [29]So the disciples determined that, according to ability, each should send relief to the brothers who lived in Judea. [30]This they did, sending it to the presbyters in care of Barnabas and Saul.

September 6

So valuable to heaven is the dignity of the human soul that every member of the human race has a guardian angel from the moment the person begins to be.

— ST. JEROME

☐ ISAIAH 7–8

Crisis in Judah. 7:1 In the days of Ahaz, king of Judah, son of Jotham, son of Uzziah, Rezin, king of Aram, and Pekah, king of Israel, son of Remaliah, went up to attack Jerusalem, but they were not able to conquer it. ²When word came to the house of David that Aram had allied itself with Ephraim, the heart of the king and heart of the people trembled, as the trees of the forest tremble in the wind.

³Then the LORD said to Isaiah: Go out to meet Ahaz, you and your son Shear-jashub, at the end of the conduit of the upper pool, on the highway to the fuller's field, ⁴and say to him: Take care you remain calm and do not fear; do not let your courage fail before these two stumps of smoldering brands, the blazing anger of Rezin and the Arameans and of the son of Remaliah— ⁵because Aram, with Ephraim and the son of Remaliah, has planned evil against you. They say, ⁶"Let us go up against Judah, tear it apart, make it our own by force, and appoint the son of Tabeel king there."

⁷Thus says the Lord GOD:
It shall not stand, it shall not be!
⁸The head of Aram is Damascus,
   and the head of Damascus is
      Rezin;
⁹The head of Ephraim is Samaria,
   and the head of Samaria is the son
      of Remaliah.
Within sixty-five years,
   Ephraim shall be crushed, no longer
      a nation.
Unless your faith is firm,
   you shall not be firm!

Emmanuel. ¹⁰Again the LORD spoke to Ahaz: ¹¹Ask for a sign from the LORD, your God; let it be deep as Sheol, or high as the sky! ¹²But Ahaz answered, "I will not ask! I will not tempt the LORD!" ¹³Then he said: Listen, house of David! Is it not enough that you weary human beings? Must you also weary my God? ¹⁴Therefore the Lord himself will give you a sign; the young woman, pregnant and about to bear a son, shall name him Emmanuel. ¹⁵Curds and honey he will eat so that he may learn to reject evil and choose good; ¹⁶for before the child learns to reject evil and choose good, the land of those two kings whom you dread shall be deserted.

¹⁷The LORD shall bring upon you and your people and your father's house such days as have not come since Ephraim seceded from Judah (the king of Assyria). ¹⁸On that day

The LORD shall whistle
   for the fly in the farthest streams of
      Egypt,
   and for the bee in the land of
      Assyria.
¹⁹All of them shall come and settle
   in the steep ravines and in the rocky
      clefts,
   on all thornbushes and in all
      pastures.

²⁰On that day the Lord shall shave with the razor hired from across the River (the king of Assyria) the head, and the hair of the feet; it shall also shave off the beard. ²¹On that day a man shall keep alive a young cow or a couple of sheep, ²²and from

their abundant yield of milk he shall eat curds; curds and honey shall be the food of all who are left in the land. ²³On that day every place where there were a thousand vines worth a thousand pieces of silver shall become briers and thorns. ²⁴One shall have to go there with bow and arrows, for all the country shall be briers and thorns. ²⁵But as for all the hills which were hoed with a mattock, for fear of briers and thorns you will not go there; they shall become a place for cattle to roam and sheep to trample.

A Son of Isaiah. 8:1 The LORD said to me: Take a large tablet, and inscribe on it with an ordinary stylus, "belonging to Maher-shalal-hash-baz," ²and call reliable witnesses for me, Uriah the priest, and Zechariah, son of Jeberechiah.

³Then I went to the prophetess and she conceived and bore a son. The LORD said to me: Name him Maher-shalal-hash-baz, ⁴for before the child learns to say, "My father, my mother," the wealth of Damascus and the spoils of Samaria shall be carried off by the king of Assyria.

The Choice: The Lord or Assyria. ⁵Again the LORD spoke to me:

⁶Because this people has rejected
   the waters of Shiloah that flow gently,
And melts with fear at the display of
   Rezin and Remaliah's son,
⁷Therefore the Lord is bringing up
   against them
   the waters of the River, great and
   mighty,
   the king of Assyria and all his glory.
It shall rise above all its channels,
   and overflow all its banks.
⁸It shall roll on into Judah,
   it shall rage and pass on—
   up to the neck it shall reach.
But his outspread wings will fill
   the width of your land, Emmanuel!
⁹Band together, O peoples, but be
   shattered!

Give ear, all you distant lands!
Arm yourselves, but be shattered!
   Arm yourselves, but be
   shattered!
¹⁰Form a plan, it shall be thwarted;
   make a resolve, it shall not be
   carried out,
   for "With us is God!"

Disciples of Isaiah. ¹¹For thus said the LORD—his hand strong upon me—warning me not to walk in the way of this people:

¹²Do not call conspiracy what this
   people calls conspiracy,
   nor fear what they fear, nor feel dread.
¹³But conspire with the LORD of hosts;
   he shall be your fear, he shall be
   your dread.
¹⁴He shall be a snare,
   a stone for injury,
A rock for stumbling
   to both the houses of Israel,
A trap and a snare
   to those who dwell in Jerusalem;
¹⁵And many among them shall stumble;
   fallen and broken;
   snared and captured.

¹⁶Bind up my testimony, seal the instruction with my disciples. ¹⁷I will trust in the LORD, who is hiding his face from the house of Jacob; yes, I will wait for him. ¹⁸Here am I and the children whom the LORD has given me: we are signs and portents in Israel from the LORD of hosts, who dwells on Mount Zion.

¹⁹And when they say to you, "Inquire of ghosts and soothsayers who chirp and mutter; should not a people inquire of their gods, consulting the dead on behalf of the living, ²⁰for instruction and testimony?" Surely, those who speak like this are the ones for whom there is no dawn.

²¹He will pass through it hard-pressed
   and hungry,
   and when hungry, shall become
   enraged,

and curse king and gods.
He will look upward,
   [22]and will gaze at the earth,
But will see only distress and
      darkness,
   oppressive gloom,
   murky, without light.

The Promise of Salvation Under a New Davidic King. [23]There is no gloom where there had been distress. Where once he degraded the land of Zebulun and the land of Naphtali, now he has glorified the way of the Sea, the land across the Jordan, Galilee of the Nations.

☐ ACTS 12

Herod's Persecution of the Christians. **12:1** About that time King Herod laid hands upon some members of the church to harm them. [2]He had James, the brother of John, killed by the sword, [3]and when he saw that this was pleasing to the Jews he proceeded to arrest Peter also. (It was [the] feast of Unleavened Bread.) [4]He had him taken into custody and put in prison under the guard of four squads of four soldiers each. He intended to bring him before the people after Passover. [5]Peter thus was being kept in prison, but prayer by the church was fervently being made to God on his behalf.

[6]On the very night before Herod was to bring him to trial, Peter, secured by double chains, was sleeping between two soldiers, while outside the door guards kept watch on the prison. [7]Suddenly the angel of the Lord stood by him and a light shone in the cell. He tapped Peter on the side and awakened him, saying, "Get up quickly." The chains fell from his wrists. [8]The angel said to him, "Put on your belt and your sandals." He did so. Then he said to him, "Put on your cloak and follow me." [9]So he followed him out, not realizing that what was happening through the angel was real; he thought he was seeing a vision. [10]They passed the first guard, then the second, and came to the iron gate leading out to the city, which opened for them by itself. They emerged and made their way down an alley, and suddenly the angel left him. [11]Then Peter recovered his senses and said, "Now I know for certain that [the] Lord sent his angel and rescued me from the hand of Herod and from all that the Jewish people had been expecting." [12]When he realized this, he went to the house of Mary, the mother of John who is called Mark, where there were many people gathered in prayer. [13]When he knocked on the gateway door, a maid named Rhoda came to answer it. [14]She was so overjoyed when she recognized Peter's voice that, instead of opening the gate, she ran in and announced that Peter was standing at the gate. [15]They told her, "You are out of your mind," but she insisted that it was so. But they kept saying, "It is his angel." [16]But Peter continued to knock, and when they opened it, they saw him and were astounded. [17]He motioned to them with his hand to be quiet and explained [to them] how the Lord had led him out of the prison, and said, "Report this to James and the brothers." Then he left and went to another place. [18]At daybreak there was no small commotion among the soldiers over what had become of Peter. [19]Herod, after instituting a search but not finding him, ordered the guards tried and executed. Then he left Judea to spend some time in Caesarea.

Herod's Death. [20]He had long been very angry with the people of Tyre and Sidon, who now came to him in a body. After winning over Blastus, the king's chamberlain, they sued for peace because their country was supplied with food from the king's territory. [21]On an appointed day, Herod, attired in royal robes, [and] seated on the rostrum, addressed them publicly. ²²The assembled crowd cried out, "This is the voice of a god, not of a man." ²³At once the angel of the Lord struck him down because he did not ascribe the honor to God, and he was eaten by worms and breathed his last. ²⁴But the word of God continued to spread and grow.

Mission of Barnabas and Saul. ²⁵After Barnabas and Saul completed their relief mission, they returned to Jerusalem, taking with them John, who is called Mark.

September 7

The Holy Spirit longs to find the gates of our heart, so that He may enter in and dwell there, and sanctify it; and He goes round about to all the gates to see where He may enter.

— ST. EPHRAEM THE SYRIAN

☐ ISAIAH 9–10

9:1 The people who walked in darkness
　　have seen a great light;
Upon those who lived in a land of gloom
　　a light has shone.
²You have brought them abundant joy
　　and great rejoicing;
They rejoice before you as people
　　rejoice at harvest,
　　as they exult when dividing the spoils.
³For the yoke that burdened them,
　　the pole on their shoulder,
The rod of their taskmaster,
　　you have smashed, as on the day of
　　　　Midian.
⁴For every boot that tramped in battle,
　　every cloak rolled in blood,
　　will be burned as fuel for fire.
⁵For a child is born to us, a son is given
　　to us;
　　upon his shoulder dominion rests.
They name him Wonder-Counselor,
　　God-Hero,
　　Father-Forever, Prince of Peace.
⁶His dominion is vast
　　and forever peaceful,
Upon David's throne, and over his
　　kingdom,
　　which he confirms and sustains

By judgment and justice,
　　both now and forever.
The zeal of the LORD of hosts will do
　　this!

Judgment on the Northern Kingdom. ⁷The Lord has sent a word against Jacob,
　　and it falls upon Israel;
⁸And all the people know it—
　　Ephraim and those who dwell in
　　　　Samaria—
　　those who say in arrogance and
　　　　pride of heart,
⁹"Bricks have fallen,
　　but we will rebuild with cut stone;
Sycamores have been felled,
　　but we will replace them with cedars."
¹⁰So the LORD raises up their foes
　　against them
　　and stirs up their enemies to
　　　　action—
¹¹Aram from the east and the
　　　　Philistines from the west—
　　they devour Israel with open
　　　　mouth.
For all this, his wrath is not turned back,
　　and his hand is still outstretched!

¹²The people do not turn back to the
one who struck them,
nor do they seek the LORD of hosts.
¹³So the LORD cuts off from Israel head
and tail,
palm branch and reed in one day.
¹⁴(The elder and the noble are the head,
the prophet who teaches falsehood
is the tail.)
¹⁵Those who lead this people lead them
astray,
and those who are led are swallowed
up.
¹⁶That is why the Lord does not spare
their young men,
and their orphans and widows he
does not pity;
For they are totally impious and wicked,
and every mouth speaks folly.
For all this, his wrath is not turned
back,
his hand is still outstretched!
¹⁷For wickedness burns like fire,
devouring brier and thorn;
It kindles the forest thickets,
which go up in columns of smoke.
¹⁸At the wrath of the LORD of hosts the
land quakes,
and the people are like fuel for fire;
no one spares his brother.
¹⁹They hack on the right, but remain
hungry;
they devour on the left, but are not
filled.
Each devours the flesh of the
neighbor;
²⁰Manasseh devours Ephraim, and
Ephraim Manasseh,
together they turn on Judah.
For all this, his wrath is not turned
back,
his hand is still outstretched!

Perversion of Justice. 10:1 Ah! Those
who enact unjust statutes,
who write oppressive decrees,
²Depriving the needy of judgment,
robbing my people's poor of justice,
Making widows their plunder,
and orphans their prey!
³What will you do on the day of
punishment,
when the storm comes from afar?
To whom will you flee for help?
Where will you leave your wealth,
⁴Lest it sink beneath the captive
or fall beneath the slain?
For all this, his wrath is not turned back,
his hand is still outstretched!

Judgment on Assyria. ⁵Ah! Assyria,
the rod of my wrath,
the staff I wield in anger.
⁶Against an impious nation I send him,
and against a people under my
wrath I order him
To seize plunder, carry off loot,
and to trample them like the mud
of the street.
⁷But this is not what he intends,
nor does he have this in mind;
Rather, it is in his heart to destroy,
to make an end of not a few
nations.
⁸For he says, "Are not my commanders
all kings?"
⁹ "Is not Calno like Carchemish,
Or Hamath like Arpad,
or Samaria like Damascus?
¹⁰Just as my hand reached out to
idolatrous kingdoms
that had more images than
Jerusalem and Samaria—
¹¹Just as I treated Samaria and her idols,
shall I not do to Jerusalem and her
graven images?"

¹²But when the LORD has brought to an
end all his work on Mount Zion and in
Jerusalem,

I will punish the utterance
of the king of Assyria's proud heart,
and the boastfulness of his haughty
eyes.

¹³For he says:
"By my own power I have done it,
   and by my wisdom, for I am
      shrewd.
I have moved the boundaries of
      peoples,
   their treasures I have pillaged,
   and, like a mighty one, I have
      brought down the enthroned.
¹⁴My hand has seized, like a nest,
   the wealth of nations.
As one takes eggs left alone,
   so I took in all the earth;
No one fluttered a wing,
   or opened a mouth, or chirped!"
¹⁵Will the ax boast against the one who
      hews with it?
   Will the saw exalt itself above the
      one who wields it?
As if a rod could sway the one who
      lifts it,
   or a staff could lift the one who is
      not wood!
¹⁶Therefore the Lord, the LORD of
      hosts,
   will send lcanness among his fat
      ones,
And under his glory there will be a
      kindling
   like the kindling of fire.
¹⁷The Light of Israel will become a fire,
   the Holy One, a flame,
That burns and consumes its briers
   and its thorns in a single day.
¹⁸And the glory of its forests and
      orchards
   will be consumed, soul and body,
   and it will be like a sick man who
      wastes away.
¹⁹And the remnant of the trees in his
      forest
   will be so few,
   that any child can record them.
²⁰On that day
The remnant of Israel,
   the survivors of the house of Jacob,
will no more lean upon the one who
      struck them;
But they will lean upon the LORD,
   the Holy One of Israel, in truth.
²¹A remnant will return, the remnant
      of Jacob,
   to the mighty God.
²²Though your people, O Israel,
   were like the sand of the sea,
Only a remnant of them will return;
   their destruction is decreed,
   as overflowing justice demands.

²³For the Lord, the GOD of hosts, is about
to carry out the destruction decreed in the
midst of the whole land.

²⁴Therefore thus says the Lord, the GOD
of hosts: My people, who dwell in Zion,
do not fear the Assyrian, though he strikes
you with a rod, and raises his staff against
you as did the Egyptians. ²⁵For just a brief
moment more, and my wrath shall be over,
and my anger shall be set for their destruction. ²⁶Then the LORD of hosts will raise
against them a scourge such as struck Midian at the rock of Oreb; and he will raise his
staff over the sea as he did in Egypt. ²⁷On
that day,

His burden shall be taken from your
      shoulder,
   and his yoke shattered from your
      neck.

The March of an Enemy Army. He
      has come up from Rimmon,
²⁸he has reached Aiath, passed
      through Migron,
   at Michmash he has stored his
      supplies.
²⁹He has crossed the ravine,
   at Geba he has camped for the
      night.
Ramah trembles,
   Gibeah of Saul has fled.
³⁰Cry and shriek, Bath-Gallim!
   Hearken, Laishah! Answer her,
      Anathoth!

³¹Madmenah is in flight,
    the inhabitants of Gebim seek
      refuge.
³²Even today he will halt at Nob,
    he will shake his fist at the mount of
      daughter Zion,
    the hill of Jerusalem!
³³Now the Lord, the LORD of hosts,

    is about to lop off the boughs with
      terrible violence;
The tall of stature shall be felled,
    and the lofty ones shall be brought
      low;
³⁴He shall hack down the forest
    thickets with an ax,
    and Lebanon in its splendor shall fall.

☐ ACTS 13

13:1 Now there were in the church at Antioch prophets and teachers: Barnabas, Symeon who was called Niger, Lucius of Cyrene, Manaen who was a close friend of Herod the tetrarch, and Saul. ²While they were worshiping the Lord and fasting, the holy Spirit said, "Set apart for me Barnabas and Saul for the work to which I have called them." ³Then, completing their fasting and prayer, they laid hands on them and sent them off.

First Mission Begins in Cyprus. ⁴So they, sent forth by the holy Spirit, went down to Seleucia and from there sailed to Cyprus. ⁵When they arrived in Salamis, they proclaimed the word of God in the Jewish synagogues. They had John also as their assistant. ⁶When they had traveled through the whole island as far as Paphos, they met a magician named Bar-Jesus who was a Jewish false prophet. ⁷He was with the proconsul Sergius Paulus, a man of intelligence, who had summoned Barnabas and Saul and wanted to hear the word of God. ⁸But Elymas the magician (for that is what his name means) opposed them in an attempt to turn the proconsul away from the faith. ⁹But Saul, also known as Paul, filled with the holy Spirit, looked intently at him ¹⁰and said, "You son of the devil, you enemy of all that is right, full of every sort of deceit and fraud. Will you not stop twisting the straight paths of [the] Lord? ¹¹Even now the hand of the Lord is upon you. You will be blind, and unable to see the sun for a time." Immediately a dark mist fell upon him, and he went about seeking people to lead him by the hand. ¹²When the proconsul saw what had happened, he came to believe, for he was astonished by the teaching about the Lord.

Paul's Arrival at Antioch in Pisidia. ¹³From Paphos, Paul and his companions set sail and arrived at Perga in Pamphylia. But John left them and returned to Jerusalem. ¹⁴They continued on from Perga and reached Antioch in Pisidia. On the sabbath they entered (into) the synagogue and took their seats. ¹⁵After the reading of the law and the prophets, the synagogue officials sent word to them, "My brothers, if one of you has a word of exhortation for the people, please speak."

Paul's Address in the Synagogue. ¹⁶So Paul got up, motioned with his hand, and said, "Fellow Israelites and you others who are God-fearing, listen. ¹⁷The God of this people Israel chose our ancestors and exalted the people during their sojourn in the land of Egypt. With uplifted arm he led them out of it ¹⁸and for about forty years he put up with them in the desert. ¹⁹When he had destroyed seven nations in the land of Canaan, he gave them their land as an inheritance ²⁰at the end of about four hundred and fifty years. After these things he provided judges up to Samuel [the] prophet. ²¹Then they asked for a king. God gave them Saul, son of Kish, a man from the tribe of Benjamin, for forty years.

²²Then he removed him and raised up David as their king; of him he testified, 'I have found David, son of Jesse, a man after my own heart; he will carry out my every wish.' ²³From this man's descendants God, according to his promise, has brought to Israel a savior, Jesus. ²⁴John heralded his coming by proclaiming a baptism of repentance to all the people of Israel; ²⁵and as John was completing his course, he would say, 'What do you suppose that I am? I am not he. Behold, one is coming after me; I am not worthy to unfasten the sandals of his feet.'

²⁶"My brothers, children of the family of Abraham, and those others among you who are God-fearing, to us this word of salvation has been sent. ²⁷The inhabitants of Jerusalem and their leaders failed to recognize him, and by condemning him they fulfilled the oracles of the prophets that are read sabbath after sabbath. ²⁸For even though they found no grounds for a death sentence, they asked Pilate to have him put to death, ²⁹and when they had accomplished all that was written about him, they took him down from the tree and placed him in a tomb. ³⁰But God raised him from the dead, ³¹and for many days he appeared to those who had come up with him from Galilee to Jerusalem. These are [now] his witnesses before the people. ³²We ourselves are proclaiming this good news to you that what God promised our ancestors ³³he has brought to fulfillment for us, (their) children, by raising up Jesus, as it is written in the second psalm, 'You are my son; this day I have begotten you.' ³⁴And that he raised him from the dead never to return to corruption he declared in this way, 'I shall give you the benefits assured to David.' ³⁵That is why he also says in another psalm, 'You will not suffer your holy one to see corruption.' ³⁶Now David, after he had served the will of God in his lifetime, fell asleep, was gathered to his ancestors, and did see corruption. ³⁷But the one whom God raised up did not see corruption. ³⁸You must know, my brothers, that through him forgiveness of sins is being proclaimed to you, [and] in regard to everything from which you could not be justified under the law of Moses, ³⁹in him every believer is justified. ⁴⁰Be careful, then, that what was said in the prophets not come about:

⁴¹'Look on, you scoffers,
  be amazed and disappear.
For I am doing a work in your days,
  a work that you will never believe
  even if someone tells you.'"

⁴²As they were leaving, they invited them to speak on these subjects the following sabbath. ⁴³After the congregation had dispersed, many Jews and worshipers who were converts to Judaism followed Paul and Barnabas, who spoke to them and urged them to remain faithful to the grace of God.

Address to the Gentiles. ⁴⁴On the following sabbath almost the whole city gathered to hear the word of the Lord. ⁴⁵When the Jews saw the crowds, they were filled with jealousy and with violent abuse contradicted what Paul said. ⁴⁶Both Paul and Barnabas spoke out boldly and said, "It was necessary that the word of God be spoken to you first, but since you reject it and condemn yourselves as unworthy of eternal life, we now turn to the Gentiles. ⁴⁷For so the Lord has commanded us, 'I have made you a light to the Gentiles, that you may be an instrument of salvation to the ends of the earth.'"

⁴⁸The Gentiles were delighted when they heard this and glorified the word of the Lord. All who were destined for eternal life came to believe, ⁴⁹and the word of the Lord continued to spread through the whole region. ⁵⁰The Jews, however, incited the women of prominence who were worshipers and the leading men of the city, stirred up a persecution against Paul and Barnabas, and expelled them from their territory. ⁵¹So they shook the dust from their feet in protest against them and went to Iconium. ⁵²The disciples were filled with joy and the holy Spirit.

September 8

The Nativity of the Blessed Virgin Mary

Today, on the birthday of Mary, the reformation of our nature begins; the aging world is transformed anew to the divine likeness and receives the beginnings of a second formation by God.

— St. Andrew of Crete

☐ ISAIAH 11-12

The Ideal Davidic King. 11:1 But
a shoot shall sprout from the
stump of Jesse,
and from his roots a bud shall
blossom.
²The spirit of the Lord shall rest upon
him:
a spirit of wisdom and of
understanding,
A spirit of counsel and of strength,
a spirit of knowledge and of fear of
the Lord,
³and his delight shall be the fear of
the Lord.
Not by appearance shall he judge,
nor by hearsay shall he decide,
⁴But he shall judge the poor with
justice,
and decide fairly for the land's
afflicted.
He shall strike the ruthless with the rod
of his mouth,
and with the breath of his lips he
shall slay the wicked.
⁵Justice shall be the band around his
waist,
and faithfulness a belt upon his hips.
⁶Then the wolf shall be a guest of the
lamb,
and the leopard shall lie down with
the young goat;
The calf and the young lion shall
browse together,
with a little child to guide them.
⁷The cow and the bear shall graze,
together their young shall lie down;

the lion shall eat hay like the ox.
⁸The baby shall play by the viper's den,
and the child lay his hand on the
adder's lair.
⁹They shall not harm or destroy on all
my holy mountain;
for the earth shall be filled with
knowledge of the Lord,
as water covers the sea.

Restoration. ¹⁰On that day,
The root of Jesse,
set up as a signal for the peoples—
Him the nations will seek out;
his dwelling shall be glorious.
¹¹On that day,
The Lord shall again take it in hand
to reclaim the remnant of his people
that is left from Assyria and Egypt,
Pathros, Ethiopia, and Elam,
Shinar, Hamath, and the isles of the
sea.
¹²He shall raise a signal to the nations
and gather the outcasts of Israel;
The dispersed of Judah he shall
assemble
from the four corners of the earth.
¹³The envy of Ephraim shall pass away,
and those hostile to Judah shall be
cut off;
Ephraim shall not envy Judah,
and Judah shall not be hostile to
Ephraim;
¹⁴But they shall swoop down on the
foothills
of the Philistines to the west,

together they shall plunder the
 people of the east;
Edom and Moab shall be their
 possessions,
 and the Ammonites their subjects.
[15]The LORD shall dry up the tongue of
 the Sea of Egypt,
 and wave his hand over the
   Euphrates with his fierce wind,
And divide it into seven streamlets,
 so that it can be crossed in sandals.
[16]There shall be a highway for the
 remnant of his people
 that is left from Assyria,
As there was for Israel
 when it came up from the land of
   Egypt.

Song of Thanksgiving. 12:1 On
 that day, you will say:
I give you thanks, O LORD;
 though you have been angry with me,

your anger has abated, and you have
 consoled me.
[2]God indeed is my salvation;
 I am confident and unafraid.
For the LORD is my strength and my
 might,
 and he has been my salvation.
[3]With joy you will draw water
 from the fountains of salvation,
[4]And you will say on that day:
 give thanks to the LORD, acclaim his
  name;
Among the nations make known his
 deeds,
 proclaim how exalted is his name.
[5]Sing praise to the LORD for he has
 done glorious things;
 let this be known throughout all the
  earth.
[6]Shout with exultation, City of Zion,
 for great in your midst
 is the Holy One of Israel!

☐ ACTS 14

Paul and Barnabas at Iconium. 14:1 In Iconium they entered the Jewish synagogue together and spoke in such a way that a great number of both Jews and Greeks came to believe, [2]although the disbelieving Jews stirred up and poisoned the minds of the Gentiles against the brothers. [3]So they stayed for a considerable period, speaking out boldly for the Lord, who confirmed the word about his grace by granting signs and wonders to occur through their hands. [4]The people of the city were divided: some were with the Jews; others, with the apostles. [5]When there was an attempt by both the Gentiles and the Jews, together with their leaders, to attack and stone them, [6]they realized it and fled to the Lycaonian cities of Lystra and Derbe and to the surrounding countryside, [7]where they continued to proclaim the good news.

 Paul and Barnabas at Lystra. [8]At Lystra there was a crippled man, lame from birth, who had never walked. [9]He listened to Paul speaking, who looked intently at him, saw that he had the faith to be healed, [10]and called out in a loud voice, "Stand up straight on your feet." He jumped up and began to walk about. [11]When the crowds saw what Paul had done, they cried out in Lycaonian, "The gods have come down to us in human form." [12]They called Barnabas "Zeus" and Paul "Hermes," because he was the chief speaker. [13]And the priest of Zeus, whose temple was at the entrance to the city, brought oxen and garlands to the gates, for he together with the people intended to offer sacrifice.

 [14]The apostles Barnabas and Paul tore their garments when they heard this and rushed out into the crowd, shouting, [15] "Men, why are you doing this? We are of the same nature as you, human beings. We proclaim to you good news that you should turn from these idols to the living God,

'who made heaven and earth and sea and all that is in them.' ¹⁶In past generations he allowed all Gentiles to go their own ways; ¹⁷yet, in bestowing his goodness, he did not leave himself without witness, for he gave you rains from heaven and fruitful seasons, and filled you with nourishment and gladness for your hearts." ¹⁸Even with these words, they scarcely restrained the crowds from offering sacrifice to them.

¹⁹However, some Jews from Antioch and Iconium arrived and won over the crowds. They stoned Paul and dragged him out of the city, supposing that he was dead. ²⁰But when the disciples gathered around him, he got up and entered the city. On the following day he left with Barnabas for Derbe.

End of the First Mission. ²¹After they had proclaimed the good news to that city and made a considerable number of disciples, they returned to Lystra and to Iconium and to Antioch. ²²They strengthened the spirits of the disciples and exhorted them to persevere in the faith, saying, "It is necessary for us to undergo many hardships to enter the kingdom of God." ²³They appointed presbyters for them in each church and, with prayer and fasting, commended them to the Lord in whom they had put their faith. ²⁴Then they traveled through Pisidia and reached Pamphylia. ²⁵After proclaiming the word at Perga they went down to Attalia. ²⁶From there they sailed to Antioch, where they had been commended to the grace of God for the work they had now accomplished. ²⁷And when they arrived, they called the church together and reported what God had done with them and how he had opened the door of faith to the Gentiles. ²⁸Then they spent no little time with the disciples.

September 9

St. Peter Claver

Since gold and silver, which are only corruptible metals, are purified and tested by fire, it is but reasonable that our faith, which surpasses all the riches of the world, should be tried.

— St. Peter Claver

☐ ISAIAH 13-14

Babylon. 13:1 An oracle concerning Babylon; a vision of Isaiah, son of Amoz.

²Upon the bare mountains set up a
    signal;
    cry out to them,
Beckon for them to enter
    the gates of the nobles.
³I have commanded my consecrated
    ones,
I have summoned my warriors,
    eager and bold to carry out my
    anger.

⁴Listen! the rumble on the mountains:
    that of an immense throng!
Listen! the noise of kingdoms, nations
    assembled!
The Lord of hosts is mustering
    an army for battle.
⁵They come from a far-off country,
    and from the end of the heavens,
The Lord and the instruments of his
    wrath,
    to destroy all the land.
⁶Howl, for the day of the Lord is near;

as destruction from the Almighty it
 comes.
[7]Therefore all hands fall helpless,
 every human heart melts,
 [8]and they are terrified,
Pangs and sorrows take hold of them,
 like a woman in labor they writhe;
They look aghast at each other,
 their faces aflame.
[9]Indeed, the day of the Lord comes,
 cruel, with wrath and burning anger;
To lay waste the land
 and destroy the sinners within it!
[10]The stars of the heavens and their
 constellations
 will send forth no light;
The sun will be dark at its rising,
 and the moon will not give its light.
[11]Thus I will punish the world for its evil
 and the wicked for their guilt.
I will put an end to the pride of the
 arrogant,
 the insolence of tyrants I will
 humble.
[12]I will make mortals more rare than
 pure gold,
 human beings, than the gold of
 Ophir.
[13]For this I will make the heavens
 tremble
 and the earth shall be shaken from
 its place,
At the wrath of the Lord of hosts
 on the day of his burning anger.
[14]Like a hunted gazelle,
 or a flock that no one gathers,
They shall turn each to their own
 people
 and flee each to their own land.
[15]Everyone who is taken shall be run
 through;
 and everyone who is caught shall
 fall by the sword.
[16]Their infants shall be dashed to pieces
 in their sight;
 their houses shall be plundered
 and their wives ravished.

[17]I am stirring up against them the
 Medes,
 who think nothing of silver
 and take no delight in gold.
[18]With their bows they shall shatter the
 young men,
And the fruit of the womb they shall
 not spare,
 nor shall their eye take pity on
 children.
[19]And Babylon, the jewel of kingdoms,
 the glory and pride of the Chaldeans,
Shall become like Sodom and
 Gomorrah,
 overthrown by God.
[20]It shall never be inhabited,
 nor dwelt in, from age to age;
Arabians shall not pitch their tents
 there,
 nor shepherds rest their flocks there.
[21]But desert demons shall rest there
 and owls shall fill the houses;
There ostriches shall dwell,
 and satyrs shall dance.
[22]Wild dogs shall dwell in its castles,
 and jackals in its luxurious palaces.
Its time is near at hand
 and its days shall not be prolonged.

Restoration of Israel. 14:1 But the Lord
will take pity on Jacob and again choose
Israel, and will settle them on their own
land; foreigners will join them and attach
themselves to the house of Jacob. [2]The nations will take them and bring them to
their place, and the house of Israel will
possess them as male and female slaves on
the Lord's land; they will take captive their
captors and rule over their oppressors.

Downfall of the King of Babylon. [3]On
the day when the Lord gives you rest from
your sorrow and turmoil, from the hard
service with which you served, [4]you will
take up this taunt-song against the king of
Babylon:

How the oppressor has come to an end!

how the turmoil has ended!

⁵The LORD has broken the rod of the
wicked,
the staff of the tyrants

⁶That struck the peoples in wrath
with relentless blows;
That ruled the nations in anger,
with boundless persecution.

⁷The whole earth rests peacefully,
song breaks forth;

⁸The very cypresses rejoice over you,
the cedars of Lebanon:
"Now that you are laid to rest,
no one comes to cut us down."

⁹Below, Sheol is all astir
preparing for your coming;
Awakening the shades to greet you,
all the leaders of the earth;
Making all the kings of the nations
rise from their thrones.

¹⁰All of them speak out
and say to you,
"You too have become weak like us,
you are just like us!

¹¹Down to Sheol your pomp is
brought,
the sound of your harps.
Maggots are the couch beneath you,
worms your blanket."

¹²How you have fallen from the
heavens,
O Morning Star, son of the dawn!
How you have been cut down to the
earth,
you who conquered nations!

¹³In your heart you said:
"I will scale the heavens;
Above the stars of God
I will set up my throne;
I will take my seat on the Mount of
Assembly,
on the heights of Zaphon.

¹⁴I will ascend above the tops of the
clouds;
I will be like the Most High!"

¹⁵No! Down to Sheol you will be
brought

to the depths of the pit!

¹⁶When they see you they will stare,
pondering over you:
"Is this the man who made the earth
tremble,
who shook kingdoms?

¹⁷Who made the world a wilderness,
razed its cities,
and gave captives no release?"

¹⁸All the kings of the nations lie in
glory,
each in his own tomb;

¹⁹But you are cast forth without burial,
like loathsome carrion,
Covered with the slain, with those
struck by the sword,
a trampled corpse,
Going down to the very stones of the
pit.

²⁰You will never be together with
them in the grave,
For you have ruined your land,
you have slain your people!
Let him never be named,
that offshoot of evil!

²¹Make ready to slaughter his sons
for the guilt of their fathers;
Lest they rise and possess the earth,
and fill the breadth of the world
with cities.

²²I will rise up against them, says the
LORD of hosts, and cut off from Babylon
name and remnant, progeny and offspring,
says the LORD. ²³I will make it a haunt of
hoot owls and a marshland; I will sweep it
with the broom of destruction, oracle of
the LORD of hosts.

God's Plan for Assyria. ²⁴The LORD
of hosts has sworn:
As I have resolved,
so shall it be;
As I have planned,
so shall it stand:

²⁵To break the Assyrian in my land
and trample him on my
mountains;

Then his yoke shall be removed from
them,
and his burden from their shoulder.
²⁶This is the plan proposed for the
whole earth,
and this the hand outstretched over
all the nations.
²⁷The LORD of hosts has planned;
who can thwart him?
His hand is stretched out;
who can turn it back?

Philistia. ²⁸In the year that King Ahaz
died, there came this oracle:

²⁹Do not rejoice, Philistia, not one of
you,
that the rod which struck you is
broken;

For out of the serpent's root shall come
an adder,
its offspring shall be a flying saraph.
³⁰In my pastures the poor shall graze,
and the needy lie down in safety;
But I will kill your root with famine
that shall slay even your remnant.
³¹Howl, O gate; cry out, O city!
Philistia, all of you melts away!
For there comes a smoke from the
north,
without a straggler in its ranks.
³²What will one answer the messengers
of the nations?
"The LORD has established Zion,
and in her the afflicted of his people
find refuge."

☐ ACTS 15

Council of Jerusalem. 15:1 Some who
had come down from Judea were instructing the brothers, "Unless you are circumcised according to the Mosaic practice,
you cannot be saved." ²Because there arose
no little dissension and debate by Paul and
Barnabas with them, it was decided that
Paul, Barnabas, and some of the others
should go up to Jerusalem to the apostles
and presbyters about this question. ³They
were sent on their journey by the church,
and passed through Phoenicia and Samaria telling of the conversion of the
Gentiles, and brought great joy to all the
brothers. ⁴When they arrived in Jerusalem,
they were welcomed by the church, as well
as by the apostles and the presbyters, and
they reported what God had done with
them. ⁵But some from the party of the
Pharisees who had become believers stood
up and said, "It is necessary to circumcise
them and direct them to observe the Mosaic law."

⁶The apostles and the presbyters met
together to see about this matter. ⁷After

much debate had taken place, Peter got up
and said to them, "My brothers, you are
well aware that from early days God made
his choice among you that through my
mouth the Gentiles would hear the word
of the gospel and believe. ⁸And God, who
knows the heart, bore witness by granting
them the holy Spirit just as he did us. ⁹He
made no distinction between us and them,
for by faith he purified their hearts. ¹⁰Why,
then, are you now putting God to the test
by placing on the shoulders of the disciples
a yoke that neither our ancestors nor we
have been able to bear? ¹¹On the contrary,
we believe that we are saved through the
grace of the Lord Jesus, in the same way
as they." ¹²The whole assembly fell silent,
and they listened while Paul and Barnabas
described the signs and wonders God had
worked among the Gentiles through them.

James on Dietary Law. ¹³After they had
fallen silent, James responded, "My brothers, listen to me. ¹⁴Symeon has described
how God first concerned himself with acquiring from among the Gentiles a people

for his name. [15]The words of the prophets agree with this, as is written:

[16]'After this I shall return
and rebuild the fallen hut of David;
from its ruins I shall rebuild it
and raise it up again,
[17]so that the rest of humanity may seek out the Lord,
even all the Gentiles on whom my name is invoked.
Thus says the Lord who accomplishes these things,
[18]known from of old.'

[19]It is my judgment, therefore, that we ought to stop troubling the Gentiles who turn to God, [20]but tell them by letter to avoid pollution from idols, unlawful marriage, the meat of strangled animals, and blood. [21]For Moses, for generations now, has had those who proclaim him in every town, as he has been read in the synagogues every sabbath."

Letter of the Apostles. [22]Then the apostles and presbyters, in agreement with the whole church, decided to choose representatives and to send them to Antioch with Paul and Barnabas. The ones chosen were Judas, who was called Barsabbas, and Silas, leaders among the brothers. [23]This is the letter delivered by them: "The apostles and the presbyters, your brothers, to the brothers in Antioch, Syria, and Cilicia of Gentile origin: greetings. [24]Since we have heard that some of our number [who went out] without any mandate from us have upset you with their teachings and disturbed your peace of mind, [25]we have with one accord decided to choose representatives and to send them to you along with our beloved Barnabas and Paul, [26]who have dedicated their lives to the name of our Lord Jesus Christ. [27]So we are sending Judas and Silas who will also convey this same message by word of mouth: [28]'It is the decision of the holy Spirit and of us not to place on you any burden beyond these necessities, [29]namely, to abstain from meat sacrificed to idols, from blood, from meats of strangled animals, and from unlawful marriage. If you keep free of these, you will be doing what is right. Farewell.'"

Delegates at Antioch. [30]And so they were sent on their journey. Upon their arrival in Antioch they called the assembly together and delivered the letter. [31]When the people read it, they were delighted with the exhortation. [32]Judas and Silas, who were themselves prophets, exhorted and strengthened the brothers with many words. [33]After they had spent some time there, they were sent off with greetings of peace from the brothers to those who had commissioned them. [34] [35]But Paul and Barnabas remained in Antioch, teaching and proclaiming with many others the word of the Lord.

Paul and Barnabas Separate. [36]After some time, Paul said to Barnabas, "Come, let us make a return visit to see how the brothers are getting on in all the cities where we proclaimed the word of the Lord." [37]Barnabas wanted to take with them also John, who was called Mark, [38]but Paul insisted that they should not take with them someone who had deserted them at Pamphylia and who had not continued with them in their work. [39]So sharp was their disagreement that they separated. Barnabas took Mark and sailed to Cyprus. [40]But Paul chose Silas and departed after being commended by the brothers to the grace of the Lord. [41]He traveled through Syria and Cilicia bringing strength to the churches.

September 10

If you were the handsomest and the richest man in the world, and could work wonders and drive out devils, all that would be something extrinsic to you; it would not belong to you, and you could not boast of it. But there is one thing of which we can boast: We can boast of our humiliations and in taking up daily the holy cross of our Lord Jesus Christ.

— St. Francis of Assisi

☐ ISAIAH 15-16

Moab. 15:1 Oracle on Moab:
Laid waste in a night,
  Ar of Moab is destroyed;
Laid waste in a night,
  Kir of Moab is destroyed.
²Daughter Dibon has gone up
  to the high places to weep;
Over Nebo and over Medeba
  Moab is wailing.
Every head is shaved,
  every beard sheared off.
³In the streets they wear sackcloth,
  and on the rooftops;
In the squares
  everyone wails, streaming with tears.
⁴Heshbon and Elealeh cry out,
  they are heard as far as Jahaz.
At this the loins of Moab tremble,
  his soul quivers within him;
⁵My heart cries out for Moab,
  his fugitives reach Zoar,
  Eglath-shelishiyah:
The ascent of Luhith
  they ascend weeping;
On the way to Horonaim
  they utter rending cries;
⁶The waters of Nimrim
  have become a waste,
The grass is withered,
  new growth is gone,
  nothing is green.
⁷So now whatever they have acquired
  or stored away
they carry across the Wadi of the
  Poplars.

⁸The cry has gone round
  the territory of Moab;
As far as Eglaim his wailing,
  even at Beer-elim his wailing.
⁹The waters of Dimon are filled with
  blood,
  but I will bring still more upon
    Dimon:
Lions for those who are fleeing from
  Moab
  and for those who remain in the
    land!

16:1 Send them forth, hugging the earth
like reptiles,
  from Sela across the desert,
  to the mount of daughter Zion.
²Like flushed birds,
  like scattered nestlings,
Are the daughters of Moab
  at the fords of the Arnon.
³Offer counsel, take their part;
  at high noon make your shade like
    the night;
Hide the outcasts,
  do not betray the fugitives.
⁴Let the outcasts of Moab live with
  you,
  be their shelter from the destroyer.
When there is an end to the oppressor,
  when destruction has ceased,
  and the marauders have vanished
    from the land,
⁵A throne shall be set up in mercy,
  and on it shall sit in fidelity,

in David's tent,
A judge upholding right,
   prompt to do justice.
[6]We have heard of the pride of Moab,
   how very proud he is,
Of his haughtiness, pride, and
   arrogance
   that his empty words do not match.
[7]Therefore let Moab wail,
   let everyone wail for Moab;
For the raisin cakes of Kir-hareseth
   let them sigh, stricken with grief.
[8]The terraced slopes of Heshbon
   languish,
   the vines of Sibmah,
Whose clusters once overpowered
   the lords of nations,
Reaching as far as Jazer
   winding through the wilderness,
Whose branches spread forth,
   crossing over the sea.
[9]Therefore I weep with Jazer
   for the vines of Sibmah;
I drench you with my tears,

Heshbon and Elealeh;
For on your summer fruits and harvests
   the battle cry has fallen.
[10]From the orchards are taken away
   joy and gladness,
In the vineyards there is no singing,
   no shout of joy;
In the wine presses no one treads
   grapes,
   the vintage shout is stilled.
[11]Therefore for Moab
   my heart moans like a lyre,
   my inmost being for Kir-hareseth.
[12]When Moab wears himself out on the
   high places,
   and enters his sanctuary to pray,
   it shall avail him nothing.

[13]That is the word the LORD spoke against Moab in times past. [14]But now the LORD speaks: In three years, like the years of a hired laborer, the glory of Moab shall be empty despite all its great multitude; and the remnant shall be very small and weak.

☐ ACTS 16

Paul in Lycaonia: Timothy. 16:1 He reached (also) Derbe and Lystra where there was a disciple named Timothy, the son of a Jewish woman who was a believer, but his father was a Greek. [2]The brothers in Lystra and Iconium spoke highly of him, [3]and Paul wanted him to come along with him. On account of the Jews of that region, Paul had him circumcised, for they all knew that his father was a Greek. [4]As they traveled from city to city, they handed on to the people for observance the decisions reached by the apostles and presbyters in Jerusalem. [5]Day after day the churches grew stronger in faith and increased in number.

Through Asia Minor. [6]They traveled through the Phrygian and Galatian territory because they had been prevented by the holy Spirit from preaching the message in the province of Asia. [7]When they came to Mysia, they tried to go on into Bithynia, but the Spirit of Jesus did not allow them, [8]so they crossed through Mysia and came down to Troas. [9]During [the] night Paul had a vision. A Macedonian stood before him and implored him with these words, "Come over to Macedonia and help us." [10]When he had seen the vision, we sought passage to Macedonia at once, concluding that God had called us to proclaim the good news to them.

Into Europe. [11]We set sail from Troas, making a straight run for Samothrace, and on the next day to Neapolis, [12]and from there to Philippi, a leading city in that district of Macedonia and a Roman colony. We spent some time in that city. [13]On the sabbath we went outside the city gate along the river where we thought there would be a place of prayer. We sat and spoke with the women who had gathered there. [14]One of them, a woman named Lydia, a dealer in purple cloth, from the city of Thyatira, a worshiper of God, listened, and the Lord opened her heart to pay attention to what Paul was saying. [15]After she and her household had been baptized, she offered us an invitation, "If you consider me a believer in the Lord, come and stay at my home," and she prevailed on us.

Imprisonment at Philippi. [16]As we were going to the place of prayer, we met a slave girl with an oracular spirit, who used to bring a large profit to her owners through her fortune-telling. [17]She began to follow Paul and us, shouting, "These people are slaves of the Most High God, who proclaim to you a way of salvation." [18]She did this for many days. Paul became annoyed, turned, and said to the spirit, "I command you in the name of Jesus Christ to come out of her." Then it came out at that moment.

[19]When her owners saw that their hope of profit was gone, they seized Paul and Silas and dragged them to the public square before the local authorities. [20]They brought them before the magistrates and said, "These people are Jews and are disturbing our city [21]and are advocating customs that are not lawful for us Romans to adopt or practice." [22]The crowd joined in the attack on them, and the magistrates had them stripped and ordered them to be beaten with rods. [23]After inflicting many blows on them, they threw them into prison and instructed the jailer to guard them securely. [24]When he received these instructions, he put them in the innermost cell and secured their feet to a stake.

Deliverance from Prison. [25]About midnight, while Paul and Silas were praying and singing hymns to God as the prisoners listened, [26]there was suddenly such a severe earthquake that the foundations of the jail shook; all the doors flew open, and the chains of all were pulled loose. [27]When the jailer woke up and saw the prison doors wide open, he drew [his] sword and was about to kill himself, thinking that the prisoners had escaped. [28]But Paul shouted out in a loud voice, "Do no harm to yourself; we are all here." [29]He asked for a light and rushed in and, trembling with fear, he fell down before Paul and Silas. [30]Then he brought them out and said, "Sirs, what must I do to be saved?" [31]And they said, "Believe in the Lord Jesus and you and your household will be saved." [32]So they spoke the word of the Lord to him and to everyone in his house. [33]He took them in at that hour of the night and bathed their wounds; then he and all his family were baptized at once. [34]He brought them up into his house and provided a meal and with his household rejoiced at having come to faith in God.

[35]But when it was day, the magistrates sent the lictors with the order, "Release those men." [36]The jailer reported the[se] words to Paul, "The magistrates have sent orders that you be released. Now, then, come out and go in peace." [37]But Paul said to them, "They have beaten us publicly, even though we are Roman citizens and have not been tried, and have thrown us into prison. And now, are they going to release us secretly? By no means. Let them come themselves and lead us out." [38]The lictors reported these words to the magistrates, and they became alarmed when they heard that they were Roman citizens. [39]So they came and placated them, and led them out and asked that they leave the city. [40]When they had come out of the prison, they went to Lydia's house where they saw and encouraged the brothers, and then they left.

September 11

St. Jean Gabriel Perboyre

Many people have difficulty in finding a meditation book. But I have found nothing so good as my own heart and the heart of Jesus. Why is it that we so often change the subject of our meditation? Only one thing is necessary: Jesus Christ. Think unceasingly of Him.

— St. Jean Gabriel Perboyre

☐ ISAIAH 17–18

Damascus. 17:1 Oracle on Damascus:
See, Damascus shall cease to be a city
　and become a pile of ruins;
²Her cities shall be forever abandoned,
　for flocks to lie in undisturbed.
³The fortress shall vanish from Ephraim
　and dominion from Damascus;
The remnant of Aram shall become
　like the glory
of the Israelites—
　oracle of the LORD of hosts.
⁴On that day
The glory of Jacob shall fade,
　and his full body shall grow thin.
⁵Like the reaper's mere armful of stalks,
　when he gathers the standing grain;
Or as when one gleans the ears
　in the Valley of Rephaim.
⁶Only gleanings shall be left in it,
　as when an olive tree has been
　　beaten—
Two or three olives at the very top,
　four or five on its most fruitful
　　branches—
oracle of the LORD, the God of Israel.
⁷On that day people shall turn to their
　maker,
their eyes shall look to the Holy
　One of Israel.
⁸They shall not turn to the altars, the
　work of their hands,
nor shall they look to what their
　fingers have made:
the asherahs or the incense stands.

⁹On that day his strong cities shall be
　like those abandoned by the Hivites
　　and Amorites
When faced with the Israelites;
　and there shall be desolation.
¹⁰Truly, you have forgotten the God
　who saves you,
the Rock, your refuge, you have not
　remembered.
Therefore, though you plant plants for
　the Pleasant One,
　and set out cuttings for a foreign one,
¹¹Though you make them grow the day
　you plant them
and make them blossom the
　morning you set them out,
The harvest shall disappear on a day of
　sickness
and incurable pain.
¹²Ah! the roaring of many peoples—
　a roar like the roar of the seas!
The thundering of nations—
　thunder like the thundering of
　　mighty waters!
¹³But God shall rebuke them,
　and they shall flee far away,
Driven like chaff on the mountains
　before a wind,
　like tumbleweed before a storm.
¹⁴At evening, there is terror,
　but before morning, they are gone!
Such is the portion of those who
　despoil us,
the lot of those who plunder us.

Ethiopia. 18:1 Ah! Land of buzzing
insects,
beyond the rivers of Ethiopia,
²Sending ambassadors by sea,
in papyrus boats on the waters!
Go, swift messengers,
to a nation tall and bronzed,
To a people dreaded near and far,
a nation strong and conquering,
whose land is washed by rivers.
³All you who inhabit the world,
who dwell on earth,
When the signal is raised on the
mountain, look!
When the trumpet blows, listen!
⁴For thus says the LORD to me:
I will be quiet, looking on from
where I dwell,
Like the shimmering heat in
sunshine,
like a cloud of dew at harvest time.

⁵Before the vintage, when the flowering
has ended,
and the blooms are succeeded by
ripening grapes,
Then comes the cutting of branches
with pruning hooks,
and the discarding of the lopped-off
shoots.
⁶They shall all be left to the mountain
vultures
and to the beasts of the earth;
The vultures shall summer on them,
all the beasts of the earth shall
winter on them.

⁷Then will gifts be brought to the LORD of hosts—to the place of the name of the LORD of hosts, Mount Zion—from a people tall and bronzed, from a people dreaded near and far, a nation strong and conquering, whose land is washed by rivers.

☐ ACTS 17

Paul in Thessalonica. 17:1 When they took the road through Amphipolis and Apollonia, they reached Thessalonica, where there was a synagogue of the Jews. ²Following his usual custom, Paul joined them, and for three sabbaths he entered into discussions with them from the scriptures, ³expounding and demonstrating that the Messiah had to suffer and rise from the dead, and that "This is the Messiah, Jesus, whom I proclaim to you." ⁴Some of them were convinced and joined Paul and Silas; so, too, a great number of Greeks who were worshipers, and not a few of the prominent women. ⁵But the Jews became jealous and recruited some worthless men loitering in the public square, formed a mob, and set the city in turmoil. They marched on the house of Jason, intending to bring them before the people's assembly. ⁶When they could not find them, they dragged Jason and some of the brothers before the city

magistrates, shouting, "These people who have been creating a disturbance all over the world have now come here, ⁷and Jason has welcomed them. They all act in opposition to the decrees of Caesar and claim instead that there is another king, Jesus." ⁸They stirred up the crowd and the city magistrates who, upon hearing these charges, ⁹took a surety payment from Jason and the others before releasing them.

Paul in Beroea. ¹⁰The brothers immediately sent Paul and Silas to Beroea during the night. Upon arrival they went to the synagogue of the Jews. ¹¹These Jews were more fair-minded than those in Thessalonica, for they received the word with all willingness and examined the scriptures daily to determine whether these things were so. ¹²Many of them became believers, as did not a few of the influential Greek women and men. ¹³But when the Jews of Thessalonica learned that the word of

God had now been proclaimed by Paul in Beroea also, they came there too to cause a commotion and stir up the crowds. [14]So the brothers at once sent Paul on his way to the seacoast, while Silas and Timothy remained behind. [15]After Paul's escorts had taken him to Athens, they came away with instructions for Silas and Timothy to join him as soon as possible.

Paul in Athens. [16]While Paul was waiting for them in Athens, he grew exasperated at the sight of the city full of idols. [17]So he debated in the synagogue with the Jews and with the worshipers, and daily in the public square with whoever happened to be there. [18]Even some of the Epicurean and Stoic philosophers engaged him in discussion. Some asked, "What is this scavenger trying to say?" Others said, "He sounds like a promoter of foreign deities," because he was preaching about 'Jesus' and 'Resurrection.' [19]They took him and led him to the Areopagus and said, "May we learn what this new teaching is that you speak of? [20]For you bring some strange notions to our ears; we should like to know what these things mean." [21]Now all the Athenians as well as the foreigners residing there used their time for nothing else but telling or hearing something new.

Paul's Speech at the Areopagus. [22]Then Paul stood up at the Areopagus and said:

"You Athenians, I see that in every respect you are very religious. [23]For as I walked around looking carefully at your shrines, I even discovered an altar inscribed, 'To an Unknown God.' What therefore you unknowingly worship, I proclaim to you. [24]The God who made the world and all that is in it, the Lord of heaven and earth, does not dwell in sanctuaries made by human hands, [25]nor is he served by human hands because he needs anything. Rather it is he who gives to everyone life and breath and everything. [26]He made from one the whole human race to dwell on the entire surface of the earth, and he fixed the ordered seasons and the boundaries of their regions, [27]so that people might seek God, even perhaps grope for him and find him, though indeed he is not far from any one of us. [28]For 'In him we live and move and have our being,' as even some of your poets have said, 'For we too are his offspring.' [29]Since therefore we are the offspring of God, we ought not to think that the divinity is like an image fashioned from gold, silver, or stone by human art and imagination. [30]God has overlooked the times of ignorance, but now he demands that all people everywhere repent [31]because he has established a day on which he will 'judge the world with justice' through a man he has appointed, and he has provided confirmation for all by raising him from the dead."

[32]When they heard about resurrection of the dead, some began to scoff, but others said, "We should like to hear you on this some other time." [33]And so Paul left them. [34]But some did join him, and became believers. Among them were Dionysius, a member of the Court of the Areopagus, a woman named Damaris, and others with them.

September 12

If a man begins to continue in his sins, despair is born of the multitude of those sins, and obstinacy is begotten of despair. God does not compel anyone to be obstinate; obstinacy results rather from His indulgence and forgiveness. It was not divine power, but divine patience, that hardened Pharaoh.

— St. Caesarius of Arles

☐ ISAIAH 19-20

Egypt. 19:1 Oracle on Egypt:
See, the LORD is riding on a swift cloud
  on his way to Egypt;
The idols of Egypt tremble before him,
  the hearts of the Egyptians melt
    within them.
²I will stir up Egypt against Egypt:
  brother will war against brother,
Neighbor against neighbor,
  city against city, kingdom against
    kingdom.
³The courage of the Egyptians shall ebb
    away within them,
  and I will bring their counsel to
    nought;
They shall consult idols and charmers,
  ghosts and clairvoyants.
⁴I will deliver Egypt
  into the power of a cruel master,
A harsh king who shall rule over
    them—
  oracle of the Lord, the LORD of hosts.
⁵The waters shall be drained from the
    sea,
  the river shall parch and dry up;
⁶Its streams shall become foul,
  and the canals of Egypt shall
    dwindle and parch.
Reeds and rushes shall wither away,
  ⁷and bulrushes on the bank of the
    Nile;
All the sown land along the Nile
  shall dry up and blow away, and be
    no more.
⁸The fishermen shall mourn and lament,

all who cast hook in the Nile;
Those who spread their nets in the water
  shall pine away.
⁹The linen-workers shall be
    disappointed,
  the combers and weavers shall turn
    pale;
¹⁰The spinners shall be crushed,
  all the hired laborers shall be
    despondent.
¹¹Utter fools are the princes of Zoan!
  the wisest of Pharaoh's advisers give
    stupid counsel.
How can you say to Pharaoh,
  "I am a descendant of wise men, of
    ancient kings"?
¹²Where then are your wise men?
  Let them tell you and make known
What the LORD of hosts has planned
    against Egypt.
¹³The princes of Zoan have become
    fools,
  the princes of Memphis have been
    deceived.
The chiefs of its tribes
  have led Egypt astray.
¹⁴The LORD has prepared among them
  a spirit of dizziness,
And they have made Egypt stagger in
    whatever she does,
  as a drunkard staggers in his vomit.
¹⁵Egypt shall accomplish nothing—
  neither head nor tail, palm branch
    nor reed, shall accomplish
    anything.

[16]On that day the Egyptians shall be like women, trembling with fear, because of the LORD of hosts shaking his fist at them. [17]And the land of Judah shall be a terror to the Egyptians. Every time they think of Judah, they shall stand in dread because of the plan the LORD of hosts has in mind for them.

[18]On that day there shall be five cities in the land of Egypt that speak the language of Canaan and swear by the LORD of hosts; one shall be called "City of the Sun."

[19]On that day there shall be an altar to the LORD at the center of Egypt, and a sacred pillar to the LORD near its boundary. [20]This will be a sign and witness to the LORD of hosts in the land of Egypt, so that when they cry out to the LORD because of their oppressors, he will send them a savior to defend and deliver them. [21]The LORD shall make himself known to Egypt, and the Egyptians shall know the LORD in that day; they shall offer sacrifices and oblations, make vows to the LORD and fulfill them. [22]Although the LORD shall smite Egypt severely, he shall heal them; they shall turn to the LORD and he shall be moved by their entreaty and heal them.

[23]On that day there shall be a highway from Egypt to Assyria; the Assyrians shall enter Egypt, and the Egyptians enter Assyria, and the Egyptians shall worship with the Assyrians.

[24]On that day Israel shall be a third party with Egypt and Assyria, a blessing in the midst of the earth, [25]when the LORD of hosts gives this blessing: "Blessed be my people Egypt, and the work of my hands Assyria, and my heritage, Israel."

Isaiah's Warning Against Trust in Egypt and Ethiopia. 20:1 In the year the general sent by Sargon, king of Assyria, came to Ashdod, fought against it, and captured it— [2]at that time the LORD had spoken through Isaiah, the son of Amoz: Go and take off the sackcloth from your waist, and remove the sandals from your feet. This he did, walking naked and barefoot. [3]Then the LORD said: Just as my servant Isaiah has gone naked and barefoot for three years as a sign and portent against Egypt and Ethiopia, [4]so shall the king of Assyria lead away captives from Egypt, and exiles from Ethiopia, young and old, naked and barefoot, with buttocks uncovered, the shame of Egypt. [5]They shall be dismayed and ashamed because of Ethiopia, their hope, and because of Egypt, their boast. [6]The inhabitants of this coastland shall say on that day, "See what has happened to those we hoped in, to whom we fled for help and deliverance from the king of Assyria! What escape is there for us now?"

☐ ACTS 18

Paul in Corinth. 18:1 After this he left Athens and went to Corinth. [2]There he met a Jew named Aquila, a native of Pontus, who had recently come from Italy with his wife Priscilla because Claudius had ordered all the Jews to leave Rome. He went to visit them [3]and, because he practiced the same trade, stayed with them and worked, for they were tentmakers by trade. [4]Every sabbath, he entered into discussions in the synagogue, attempting to convince both Jews and Greeks.

[5]When Silas and Timothy came down from Macedonia, Paul began to occupy himself totally with preaching the word, testifying to the Jews that the Messiah was Jesus. [6]When they opposed him and reviled him, he shook out his garments and said to them, "Your blood be on your heads! I am clear of responsibility. From now on I will

go to the Gentiles." [7]So he left there and went to a house belonging to a man named Titus Justus, a worshiper of God; his house was next to a synagogue. [8]Crispus, the synagogue official, came to believe in the Lord along with his entire household, and many of the Corinthians who heard believed and were baptized. [9]One night in a vision the Lord said to Paul, "Do not be afraid. Go on speaking, and do not be silent, [10]for I am with you. No one will attack and harm you, for I have many people in this city." [11]He settled there for a year and a half and taught the word of God among them.

Accusations before Gallio. [12]But when Gallio was proconsul of Achaia, the Jews rose up together against Paul and brought him to the tribunal, [13]saying, "This man is inducing people to worship God contrary to the law." [14]When Paul was about to reply, Gallio spoke to the Jews, "If it were a matter of some crime or malicious fraud, I should with reason hear the complaint of you Jews; [15]but since it is a question of arguments over doctrine and titles and your own law, see to it yourselves. I do not wish to be a judge of such matters." [16]And he drove them away from the tribunal. [17]They all seized Sosthenes, the synagogue official, and beat him in full view of the tribunal. But none of this was of concern to Gallio.

Return to Syrian Antioch. [18]Paul remained for quite some time, and after saying farewell to the brothers he sailed for Syria, together with Priscilla and Aquila. At Cenchreae he had his hair cut because he had taken a vow. [19]When they reached Ephesus, he left them there, while he entered the synagogue and held discussions with the Jews. [20]Although they asked him to stay for a longer time, he did not consent, [21]but as he said farewell he promised, "I shall come back to you again, God willing." Then he set sail from Ephesus. [22]Upon landing at Caesarea, he went up and greeted the church and then went down to Antioch. [23]After staying there some time, he left and traveled in orderly sequence through the Galatian country and Phrygia, bringing strength to all the disciples.

Apollos. [24]A Jew named Apollos, a native of Alexandria, an eloquent speaker, arrived in Ephesus. He was an authority on the scriptures. [25]He had been instructed in the Way of the Lord and, with ardent spirit, spoke and taught accurately about Jesus, although he knew only the baptism of John. [26]He began to speak boldly in the synagogue; but when Priscilla and Aquila heard him, they took him aside and explained to him the Way (of God) more accurately. [27]And when he wanted to cross to Achaia, the brothers encouraged him and wrote to the disciples there to welcome him. After his arrival he gave great assistance to those who had come to believe through grace. [28]He vigorously refuted the Jews in public, establishing from the scriptures that the Messiah is Jesus.

September 13

Scatter what you have, then, so that you may not lose; give away, so that you may keep; lay out, so that you may save; spend, so that you may gain. If your treasures are to be hoarded, don't be the one who hoards them, for in doing so you will surely be throwing them away. Instead, entrust them to God, for no one can steal them from Him. Lend to Him who gives an interest greater than the principal.

— St. John Chrysostom

☐ ISAIAH 21-22

Fall of Babylon. 21:1 Oracle on the
wastelands by the sea:
Like whirlwinds sweeping through the
Negeb,
it comes from the desert,
from the fearful land.
²A harsh vision has been announced
to me:
"The traitor betrays,
the despoiler spoils.
Go up, O Elam; besiege, O Media;
put an end to all its groaning!"
³Therefore my loins are filled with
anguish,
pangs have seized me like those of a
woman in labor;
I am too bewildered to hear,
too dismayed to look.
⁴My mind reels,
shuddering assails me;
The twilight I yearned for
he has turned into dread.
⁵They set the table,
spread out the rugs;
they eat, they drink.
Rise up, O princes,
oil the shield!
⁶For thus my Lord said to me:
Go, station a watchman,
let him tell what he sees.
⁷If he sees a chariot,
a pair of horses,

Someone riding a donkey,
someone riding a camel,
Then let him pay heed,
very close heed.
⁸Then the watchman cried,
"On the watchtower, my Lord,
I stand constantly by day;
And I stay at my post
through all the watches of the night.
⁹Here he comes—
a single chariot,
a pair of horses—
He calls out and says,
'Fallen, fallen is Babylon!
All the images of her gods
are smashed to the ground!'"
¹⁰To you, who have been threshed,
beaten on my threshing floor,
What I have heard
from the LORD of hosts,
The God of Israel,
I have announced to you.

Dumah. ¹¹Oracle on Dumah:
They call to me from Seir,
"Watchman, how much longer the
night?
Watchman, how much longer the
night?"
¹²The watchman replies,
"Morning has come, and again night.
If you will ask, ask; come back
again."

In the Steppe. ¹³Oracle: in the steppe:
In the thicket in the steppe you will
  spend the night,
  caravans of Dedanites.
¹⁴Meet the thirsty, bring them water,
  inhabitants of the land of Tema,
  greet the fugitives with bread.
¹⁵For they have fled from the sword,
  from the drawn sword;
From the taut bow,
  from the thick of battle.

¹⁶For thus the Lord has said to me: In another year, like the years of a hired laborer, all the glory of Kedar shall come to an end. ¹⁷Few of Kedar's stalwart archers shall remain, for the LORD, the God of Israel, has spoken.

The Valley of Vision. 22:1 Oracle
  on the Valley of Vision:
What is the matter with you now, that
  you have gone up,
  all of you, to the housetops,
²You who were full of noise,
  tumultuous city,
  exultant town?
Your slain are not slain with the sword,
  nor killed in battle.
³All your leaders fled away together,
  they were captured without use of
    bow;
All who were found were captured
    together,
  though they had fled afar off.
⁴That is why I say: Turn away from me,
  let me weep bitterly;
Do not try to comfort me
  for the ruin of the daughter of my
    people.
⁵It is a day of panic, rout and confusion,
  from the Lord, the GOD of hosts, in
    the Valley of Vision
Walls crash;
  a cry for help to the mountains.
⁶Elam takes up the quiver,
  Aram mounts the horses
  and Kir uncovers the shields.

⁷Your choice valleys are filled with
  chariots,
  horses are posted at the gates—
⁸and shelter over Judah is removed.

On that day you looked to the weapons in the House of the Forest; ⁹you saw that the breaches in the City of David were many; you collected the water of the lower pool. ¹⁰You numbered the houses of Jerusalem, tearing some down to strengthen the wall; ¹¹you made a reservoir between the two walls for the water of the old pool. But you did not look to the city's Maker, nor consider the one who fashioned it long ago.

¹²On that day the Lord,
  the GOD of hosts, called
For weeping and mourning,
  for shaving the head and wearing
    sackcloth.
¹³But look! instead, there was
  celebration and joy,
  slaughtering cattle and butchering
    sheep,
Eating meat and drinking wine:
  "Eat and drink, for tomorrow we die!"

¹⁴This message was revealed in my hearing from the LORD of hosts:

  This iniquity will not be forgiven
    you until you die,
  says the Lord, the GOD of hosts.

Shebna and Eliakim. ¹⁵Thus says the
  Lord, the GOD of hosts:
Up, go to that official,
  Shebna, master of the palace,
¹⁶"What have you here? Whom have
    you here,
  that you have hewn for yourself a
    tomb here,
Hewing a tomb on high,
  carving a resting place in the rock?"
¹⁷The LORD shall hurl you down
  headlong, mortal man!
He shall grip you firmly,
¹⁸And roll you up and toss you like a ball

into a broad land.
There you will die, there with the
chariots you glory in,
you disgrace to your master's house!
¹⁹I will thrust you from your office
and pull you down from your station.
²⁰On that day I will summon my servant
Eliakim, son of Hilkiah;
²¹I will clothe him with your robe,
gird him with your sash,
confer on him your authority.
He shall be a father to the inhabitants
of Jerusalem,
and to the house of Judah.
²²I will place the key of the House of
David on his shoulder;

what he opens, no one will shut,
what he shuts, no one will open.
²³I will fix him as a peg in a firm place,
a seat of honor for his ancestral
house;
²⁴On him shall hang all the glory of his
ancestral house:
descendants and offspring,
all the little dishes, from bowls to
jugs.

²⁵On that day, says the LORD of hosts, the peg fixed in a firm place shall give way, break off and fall, and the weight that hung on it shall be done away with; for the LORD has spoken.

☐ ACTS 19

Paul in Ephesus. 19:1 While Apollos was in Corinth, Paul traveled through the interior of the country and came (down) to Ephesus where he found some disciples. ²He said to them, "Did you receive the holy Spirit when you became believers?" They answered him, "We have never even heard that there is a holy Spirit." ³He said, "How were you baptized?" They replied, "With the baptism of John." ⁴Paul then said, "John baptized with a baptism of repentance, telling the people to believe in the one who was to come after him, that is, in Jesus." ⁵When they heard this, they were baptized in the name of the Lord Jesus. ⁶And when Paul laid [his] hands on them, the holy Spirit came upon them, and they spoke in tongues and prophesied. ⁷Altogether there were about twelve men.

⁸He entered the synagogue, and for three months debated boldly with persuasive arguments about the kingdom of God. ⁹But when some in their obstinacy and disbelief disparaged the Way before the assembly, he withdrew and took his disciples with him and began to hold daily discussions in the lecture hall of Tyrannus.

¹⁰This continued for two years with the result that all the inhabitants of the province of Asia heard the word of the Lord, Jews and Greeks alike. ¹¹So extraordinary were the mighty deeds God accomplished at the hands of Paul ¹²that when face cloths or aprons that touched his skin were applied to the sick, their diseases left them and the evil spirits came out of them.

The Jewish Exorcists. ¹³Then some itinerant Jewish exorcists tried to invoke the name of the Lord Jesus over those with evil spirits, saying, "I adjure you by the Jesus whom Paul preaches." ¹⁴When the seven sons of Sceva, a Jewish high priest, tried to do this, ¹⁵the evil spirit said to them in reply, "Jesus I recognize, Paul I know, but who are you?" ¹⁶The person with the evil spirit then sprang at them and subdued them all. He so overpowered them that they fled naked and wounded from that house. ¹⁷When this became known to all the Jews and Greeks who lived in Ephesus, fear fell upon them all, and the name of the Lord Jesus was held in great esteem. ¹⁸Many of those who had become believers came forward and openly acknowledged their former practices. ¹⁹Moreover, a large number of those who had practiced magic collected their books and burned them in public. They calculated their value and found it to be fifty thousand silver pieces. ²⁰Thus did the word of the Lord continue to spread with influence and power.

Paul's Plans. ²¹When this was concluded, Paul made up his mind to travel through Macedonia and Achaia, and then to go on to Jerusalem, saying, "After I have been there, I must visit Rome also." ²²Then he sent to Macedonia two of his assistants, Timothy and Erastus, while he himself stayed for a while in the province of Asia.

The Riot of the Silversmiths. ²³About that time a serious disturbance broke out concerning the Way. ²⁴There was a silversmith named Demetrius who made miniature silver shrines of Artemis and provided no little work for the craftsmen. ²⁵He called a meeting of these and other workers in related crafts and said, "Men, you know well that our prosperity derives from this work. ²⁶As you can now see and hear, not only in Ephesus but throughout most of the province of Asia this Paul has persuaded and misled a great number of people by saying that gods made by hands are not gods at all. ²⁷The danger grows, not only that our business will be discredited, but also that the temple of the great goddess Artemis will be of no account, and that she whom the whole province of Asia and all the world worship will be stripped of her magnificence."

²⁸When they heard this, they were filled with fury and began to shout, "Great is Artemis of the Ephesians!" ²⁹The city was filled with confusion, and the people rushed with one accord into the theater, seizing Gaius and Aristarchus, the Macedonians, Paul's traveling companions. ³⁰Paul wanted to go before the crowd, but the disciples would not let him, ³¹and even some of the Asiarchs who were friends of his sent word to him advising him not to venture into the theater. ³²Meanwhile, some were shouting one thing, others something else; the assembly was in chaos, and most of the people had no idea why they had come together. ³³Some of the crowd prompted Alexander, as the Jews pushed him forward, and Alexander signaled with his hand that he wished to explain something to the gathering. ³⁴But when they recognized that he was a Jew, they all shouted in unison, for about two hours, "Great is Artemis of the Ephesians!" ³⁵Finally the town clerk restrained the crowd and said, "You Ephesians, what person is there who does not know that the city of the Ephesians is the guardian of the temple of the great Artemis and of her image that fell from the sky? ³⁶Since these things are undeniable, you must calm yourselves and not do anything rash. ³⁷The men you brought here are not temple robbers, nor have they insulted our goddess. ³⁸If Demetrius and his fellow craftsmen have a complaint against anyone, courts are in session, and there are proconsuls. Let them bring charges against one another. ³⁹If you have anything further to investigate, let the matter be settled in the lawful assembly, ⁴⁰for, as it is, we are in danger of being charged with rioting because of today's conduct. There is no cause for it. We shall [not] be able to give a reason for this demonstration." With these words he dismissed the assembly.

September 14

The Triumph of the Holy Cross

The Cross: once as the tree of torture known; now the bright gate to Jesus' throne.

— St. Peter Damian

☐ ISAIAH 23-24

Tyre and Sidon. 23:1 Oracle on Tyre:
Wail, ships of Tarshish,
  for your port is destroyed;
From the land of the Kittim
  the news reaches them.
²Silence! you who dwell on the coast,
  you merchants of Sidon,
Whose messengers crossed the sea
  ³over the deep waters,
Whose revenue was the grain of
    Shihor, the harvest of the Nile,
  you who were the merchant among
    the nations.
⁴Be ashamed, Sidon, fortress on the
    sea,
  for the sea has spoken,
"I have not been in labor, nor given
    birth,
  nor raised young men,
  nor reared young women."
⁵When the report reaches Egypt
  they shall be in anguish at the report
    about Tyre.
⁶Pass over to Tarshish,
  wail, you who dwell on the coast!
⁷Is this your exultant city,
  whose origin is from old,
Whose feet have taken her
  to dwell in distant lands?
⁸Who has planned such a thing
  against Tyre, the bestower of crowns,
Whose merchants are princes,
  whose traders are the earth's
    honored men?
⁹The LORD of hosts has planned it,
  to disgrace the height of all beauty,
  to degrade all the honored of the
    earth.

¹⁰Cross to your own land,
  ship of Tarshish;
  the harbor is no more.
¹¹His hand he stretches out over the
    sea,
  he shakes kingdoms;
The LORD commanded the destruction
  of Canaan's strongholds:
¹²Crushed, you shall exult no more,
  virgin daughter Sidon.
Arise, pass over to the Kittim,
  even there you shall find no rest.
¹³Look at the land of the Chaldeans,
  the people that has ceased to be.
Assyria founded it for ships,
  raised its towers,
Only to tear down its palaces,
  and turn it into a ruin.
¹⁴Lament, ships of Tarshish,
  for your stronghold is destroyed.

¹⁵On that day, Tyre shall be forgotten for seventy years, the lifetime of one king. At the end of seventy years, the song about the prostitute will be Tyre's song:

¹⁶Take a harp, go about the city,
  forgotten prostitute;
Pluck the strings skillfully, sing many
    songs,
  that you may be remembered.

¹⁷At the end of the seventy years the LORD shall visit Tyre. She shall return to her hire and serve as prostitute with all the world's kingdoms on the face of the earth. ¹⁸But her merchandise and her hire shall be sacred to the LORD. It shall not be stored up or laid away; instead, her merchandise

shall belong to those who dwell before the LORD, to eat their fill and clothe themselves in choice attire.

Judgment upon the World and the Lord's Enthronement on Mount Zion.

24:1 See! The LORD is about
to empty the earth and lay it waste;
he will twist its surface,
and scatter its inhabitants:
²People and priest shall fare alike:
servant and master,
Maid and mistress,
buyer and seller,
Lender and borrower,
creditor and debtor.
³The earth shall be utterly laid waste,
utterly stripped,
for the LORD has decreed this word.
⁴The earth mourns and fades,
the world languishes and fades;
both heaven and earth languish.
⁵The earth is polluted because of its
inhabitants,
for they have transgressed laws,
violated statutes,
broken the ancient covenant.
⁶Therefore a curse devours the earth,
and its inhabitants pay for their guilt;
Therefore they who dwell on earth
have dwindled,
and only a few are left.
⁷The new wine mourns, the vine
languishes,
all the merry-hearted groan.
⁸Stilled are the cheerful timbrels,
ended the shouts of the jubilant,
stilled the cheerful harp.
⁹They no longer drink wine and sing;
strong brew is bitter to those who
drink it.
¹⁰Broken down is the city of chaos,
every house is shut against entry.
¹¹In the streets they cry out for lack of
wine;
all joy has grown dim,
cheer is exiled from the land.
¹²In the city nothing remains but
desolation,
gates battered into ruins.
¹³For thus it shall be in the midst of the
earth,
among the peoples,
As when an olive tree has been beaten,
as with a gleaning when the vintage
is done.
¹⁴These shall lift up their voice,
they shall sing for joy in the majesty
of the LORD,
they shall shout from the western sea:
¹⁵"Therefore, in the east
give glory to the LORD!
In the coastlands of the sea,
to the name of the LORD, the God
of Israel!"
¹⁶From the end of the earth we hear
songs:
"Splendor to the Just One!"
But I said, "I am wasted, wasted away.
Woe is me! The traitors betray;
with treachery have the traitors
betrayed!
¹⁷Terror, pit, and trap
for you, inhabitant of the earth!
¹⁸One who flees at the sound of terror
will fall into the pit;
One who climbs out of the pit
will be caught in the trap.
For the windows on high are open
and the foundations of the earth
shake.
¹⁹The earth will burst asunder,
the earth will be shaken apart,
the earth will be convulsed.
²⁰The earth will reel like a drunkard,
sway like a hut;
Its rebellion will weigh it down;
it will fall, never to rise again."
²¹On that day the LORD will punish
the host of the heavens in the heavens,
and the kings of the earth on the
earth.
²²They will be gathered together
like prisoners into a pit;

They will be shut up in a dungeon,
    and after many days they will be
      punished.
²³Then the moon will blush

and the sun be ashamed,
For the Lord of hosts will reign
    on Mount Zion and in Jerusalem,
    glorious in the sight of the elders.

□ ACTS 20

Journey to Macedonia and Greece. 20:1 When the disturbance was over, Paul had the disciples summoned and, after encouraging them, he bade them farewell and set out on his journey to Macedonia. ²As he traveled throughout those regions, he provided many words of encouragement for them. Then he arrived in Greece, ³where he stayed for three months. But when a plot was made against him by the Jews as he was about to set sail for Syria, he decided to return by way of Macedonia.

Return to Troas. ⁴Sopater, the son of Pyrrhus, from Beroea, accompanied him, as did Aristarchus and Secundus from Thessalonica, Gaius from Derbe, Timothy, and Tychicus and Trophimus from Asia ⁵who went on ahead and waited for us at Troas. ⁶We sailed from Philippi after the feast of Unleavened Bread, and rejoined them five days later in Troas, where we spent a week.

Eutychus Restored to Life. ⁷On the first day of the week when we gathered to break bread, Paul spoke to them because he was going to leave on the next day, and he kept on speaking until midnight. ⁸There were many lamps in the upstairs room where we were gathered, ⁹and a young man named Eutychus who was sitting on the window sill was sinking into a deep sleep as Paul talked on and on. Once overcome by sleep, he fell down from the third story and when he was picked up, he was dead. ¹⁰Paul went down, threw himself upon him, and said as he embraced him, "Don't be alarmed; there is life in him." ¹¹Then he returned upstairs, broke the bread, and ate; after a long conversation that lasted until daybreak, he departed. ¹²And they took the boy away alive and were immeasurably comforted.

Journey to Miletus. ¹³We went ahead to the ship and set sail for Assos where we were to take Paul on board, as he had arranged, since he was going overland. ¹⁴When he met us in Assos, we took him aboard and went on to Mitylene. ¹⁵We sailed away from there on the next day and reached a point off Chios, and a day later we reached Samos, and on the following day we arrived at Miletus. ¹⁶Paul had decided to sail past Ephesus in order not to lose time in the province of Asia, for he was hurrying to be in Jerusalem, if at all possible, for the day of Pentecost.

Paul's Farewell Speech at Miletus. ¹⁷From Miletus he had the presbyters of the church at Ephesus summoned. ¹⁸When they came to him, he addressed them, "You know how I lived among you the whole time from the day I first came to the province of Asia. ¹⁹I served the Lord with all humility and with the tears and trials that came to me because of the plots of the Jews, ²⁰and I did not at all shrink from telling you what was for your benefit, or from teaching you in public or in your homes. ²¹I earnestly bore witness for both Jews and Greeks to repentance before God and to faith in our Lord Jesus. ²²But now, compelled by the Spirit, I am going to Jerusalem. What will happen to me there I do not know, ²³except that in one city after another the holy Spirit has been warning me that imprisonment and hardships await me. ²⁴Yet I consider life of no importance to me, if only I may finish my course and the ministry that I received from the Lord

Jesus, to bear witness to the gospel of God's grace.

[25]"But now I know that none of you to whom I preached the kingdom during my travels will ever see my face again. [26]And so I solemnly declare to you this day that I am not responsible for the blood of any of you, [27]for I did not shrink from proclaiming to you the entire plan of God. [28]Keep watch over yourselves and over the whole flock of which the holy Spirit has appointed you overseers, in which you tend the church of God that he acquired with his own blood. [29]I know that after my departure savage wolves will come among you, and they will not spare the flock. [30]And from your own group, men will come forward perverting the truth to draw the disciples away after them. [31]So be vigilant and remember that for three years, night and day, I unceasingly admonished each of you with tears. [32]And now I commend you to God and to that gracious word of his that can build you up and give you the inheritance among all who are consecrated. [33]I have never wanted anyone's silver or gold or clothing. [34]You know well that these very hands have served my needs and my companions. [35]In every way I have shown you that by hard work of that sort we must help the weak, and keep in mind the words of the Lord Jesus who himself said, 'It is more blessed to give than to receive.'"

[36]When he had finished speaking he knelt down and prayed with them all. [37]They were all weeping loudly as they threw their arms around Paul and kissed him, [38]for they were deeply distressed that he had said that they would never see his face again. Then they escorted him to the ship.

September 15

Our Lady of Sorrows; St. Catherine of Genoa

Blessed Mother dear, lend me your heart. I look for it each day to pour my troubles into.

— St. Gemma Galgani

☐ ISAIAH 25–26:19

Praise for God's Deliverance and the Celebration in Zion. 25:1

O Lord, you are my God,
    I extol you, I praise your name;
For you have carried out your
        wonderful plans of old,
    faithful and true.
[2]For you have made the city a heap,
    the fortified city a ruin,
The castle of the insolent, a city no more,
    not ever to be rebuilt.
[3]Therefore a strong people will honor
        you,
    ruthless nations will fear you.

[4]For you have been a refuge to the
        poor,
    a refuge to the needy in their
        distress;
Shelter from the rain,
    shade from the heat.
When the blast of the ruthless was like
        a winter rain,
    [5]the roar of strangers like heat in the
        desert,
You subdued the heat with the shade of
        a cloud,
    the rain of the tyrants was
        vanquished.

⁶On this mountain the LORD of hosts
will provide for all peoples
A feast of rich food and choice wines,
juicy, rich food and pure, choice
wines.
⁷On this mountain he will destroy
the veil that veils all peoples,
The web that is woven over all nations.
⁸He will destroy death forever.
The Lord GOD will wipe away
the tears from all faces;
The reproach of his people he will
remove
from the whole earth; for the LORD
has spoken.
⁹On that day it will be said:
"Indeed, this is our God; we looked to
him, and he saved us!
This is the LORD to whom we
looked;
let us rejoice and be glad that he has
saved us!"

Judgment on Moab. ¹⁰For the hand
of the LORD will rest on this
mountain,
but Moab will be trodden down
as straw is trodden down in the mire.
¹¹He will spread out his hands in its
midst,
as a swimmer spreads out his hands
to swim;
His pride will be brought low
despite his strokes.
¹²The high-walled fortress he will raze,
bringing it low, leveling it to the
ground, to the very dust.

Judah's Praise and Prayer for Deliverance.
26:1 On that day this song shall be sung in
the land of Judah:

"A strong city have we;
he sets up victory as our walls and
ramparts.
²Open up the gates
that a righteous nation may enter,
one that keeps faith.

³With firm purpose you maintain
peace;
in peace, because of our trust in you."
⁴Trust in the LORD forever!
For the LORD is an eternal Rock.
⁵He humbles those who dwell on high,
the lofty city he brings down,
Brings it down to the ground,
levels it to the dust.
⁶The feet of the needy trample on it—
the feet of the poor.
⁷The way of the just is smooth;
the path of the just you make level.
⁸The course of your judgments, LORD,
we await;
your name and your memory are
the desire of our souls.
⁹My soul yearns for you at night,
yes, my spirit within me seeks you
at dawn;
When your judgment comes upon the
earth,
the world's inhabitants learn justice.
¹⁰The wicked, when spared, do not
learn justice;
in an upright land they act
perversely,
and do not see the majesty of the
LORD.
¹¹LORD, your hand is raised high,
but they do not perceive it;
Let them be put to shame when they
see your zeal for your people:
let the fire prepared for your
enemies consume them.
¹²LORD, you will decree peace for us,
for you have accomplished all we
have done.
¹³LORD, our God, lords other than you
have ruled us;
only because of you can we call
upon your name.
¹⁴Dead they are, they cannot live,
shades that cannot rise;
Indeed, you have punished and
destroyed them,
and wiped out all memory of them.

¹⁵You have increased the nation, LORD,
you have increased the nation, have
added to your glory,
you have extended far all the
boundaries of the land.
¹⁶LORD, oppressed by your punishment,
we cried out in anguish under your
discipline.
¹⁷As a woman about to give birth
writhes and cries out in pain,
so were we before you, LORD.
¹⁸We conceived and writhed in pain,
giving birth only to wind;
Salvation we have not achieved for the
earth,
no inhabitants for the world were
born.
¹⁹But your dead shall live, their corpses
shall rise!
Awake and sing, you who lie in the
dust!
For your dew is a dew of light,
and you cause the land of shades to
give birth.

☐ ACTS 21:1-39

Arrival at Tyre. 21:1 When we had taken leave of them we set sail, made a straight run for Cos, and on the next day for Rhodes, and from there to Patara. ²Finding a ship crossing to Phoenicia, we went on board and put out to sea. ³We caught sight of Cyprus but passed by it on our left and sailed on toward Syria and put in at Tyre where the ship was to unload cargo. ⁴There we sought out the disciples and stayed for a week. They kept telling Paul through the Spirit not to embark for Jerusalem. ⁵At the end of our stay we left and resumed our journey. All of them, women and children included, escorted us out of the city, and after kneeling on the beach to pray, ⁶we bade farewell to one another. Then we boarded the ship, and they returned home.

Arrival at Ptolemais and Caesarea. ⁷We continued the voyage and came from Tyre to Ptolemais, where we greeted the brothers and stayed a day with them. ⁸On the next day we resumed the trip and came to Caesarea, where we went to the house of Philip the evangelist, who was one of the Seven, and stayed with him. ⁹He had four virgin daughters gifted with prophecy. ¹⁰We had been there several days when a prophet named Agabus came down from Judea. ¹¹He came up to us, took Paul's belt, bound his own feet and hands with it, and said, "Thus says the holy Spirit: This is the way the Jews will bind the owner of this belt in Jerusalem, and they will hand him over to the Gentiles." ¹²When we heard this, we and the local residents begged him not to go up to Jerusalem. ¹³Then Paul replied, "What are you doing, weeping and breaking my heart? I am prepared not only to be bound but even to die in Jerusalem for the name of the Lord Jesus." ¹⁴Since he would not be dissuaded we let the matter rest, saying, "The Lord's will be done."

Paul and James in Jerusalem. ¹⁵After these days we made preparations for our journey, then went up to Jerusalem. ¹⁶Some of the disciples from Caesarea came along to lead us to the house of Mnason, a Cypriot, a disciple of long standing, with whom we were to stay. ¹⁷When we reached Jerusalem the brothers welcomed us warmly. ¹⁸The next day, Paul accompanied us on a visit to James, and all the presbyters were present. ¹⁹He greeted them, then proceeded to tell them in detail what God had accomplished among the Gentiles through his ministry. ²⁰They praised God when they heard it but said to him, "Brother, you see how many thousands of believers there are from among the Jews, and they are all zealous observers of the law. ²¹They have been informed that you are teaching all the Jews who live among the Gentiles to abandon Moses and that you are telling them not to circumcise their children or to observe their customary practices. ²²What is to be done? They will surely hear that you have arrived. ²³So do what we tell you. We have four men who have taken a vow. ²⁴Take these men and purify yourself with them, and pay their expenses that they may have their heads shaved. In this way everyone will know that there is nothing to the reports they have been given about you but that you yourself live in observance of the law. ²⁵As for the Gentiles who have come to believe, we sent them our decision that they abstain from meat sacrificed to idols, from blood, from the meat of strangled animals, and from unlawful marriage." ²⁶So Paul took the men, and on the next day after purifying himself together with them entered the temple to give notice of the day when the purification would be completed and the offering made for each of them.

Paul's Arrest. ²⁷When the seven days were nearly completed, the Jews from the province of Asia noticed him in the temple, stirred up the whole crowd, and laid hands on him, ²⁸shouting, "Fellow Israelites, help us. This is the man who is teaching everyone everywhere against the people and the law and this place, and what is more, he has even brought Greeks into the temple and defiled this sacred place." ²⁹For they had previously seen Trophimus the Ephesian in the city with him and supposed that Paul had brought him into the temple. ³⁰The whole city was in turmoil with people rushing together. They seized Paul and dragged him out of the temple, and immediately the gates were closed. ³¹While they were trying to kill him, a report reached the cohort commander that all Jerusalem was rioting. ³²He immediately took soldiers and centurions and charged down on them. When they saw the commander and the soldiers they stopped beating Paul. ³³The cohort commander came forward, arrested him, and ordered him to be secured with two chains; he tried to find out who he might be and what he had done. ³⁴Some in the mob shouted one thing, others something else; so, since he was unable to ascertain the truth because of the uproar, he ordered Paul to be brought into the compound. ³⁵When he reached the steps, he was carried by the soldiers because of the violence of the mob, ³⁶for a crowd of people followed and shouted, "Away with him!"

³⁷Just as Paul was about to be taken into the compound, he said to the cohort commander, "May I say something to you?" He replied, "Do you speak Greek? ³⁸So then you are not the Egyptian who started a revolt some time ago and led the four thousand assassins into the desert?" ³⁹Paul answered, "I am a Jew, of Tarsus in Cilicia, a citizen of no mean city; I request you to permit me to speak to the people."

September 16

Sts. Cornelius and Cyprian of Carthage

Whatever a man prefers to God, he makes a god to himself.
— ST. CYPRIAN OF CARTHAGE

☐ ISAIAH 26:20-28:29

The Lord's Response. 26:20 Go, my
    people, enter your chambers,
    and close the doors behind you;
Hide yourselves for a brief moment,
    until the wrath is past.
[21]See, the LORD goes forth from his place,
    to punish the wickedness of the
        earth's inhabitants;
The earth will reveal the blood shed
    upon it,
    and no longer conceal the slain.

**The Judgment and Deliverance of
    Israel. 27:1** On that day,
The LORD will punish with his sword
    that is cruel, great, and strong,
Leviathan the fleeing serpent,
    Leviathan the coiled serpent;
    he will slay the dragon in the sea.

[2]On that day—
The pleasant vineyard, sing about it!
[3]I, the LORD, am its keeper,
    I water it every moment;
Lest anyone harm it,
    night and day I guard it.
[4]I am not angry.
    But if I were to find briers and thorns,
In battle I would march against it;
    I would burn it all.
[5]But if it holds fast to my refuge,
    it shall have peace with me;
    it shall have peace with me.

[6]In days to come Jacob shall take root,
    Israel shall sprout and blossom,
    covering all the world with fruit.
[7]Was he smitten as his smiter was
    smitten?
    Was he slain as his slayer was slain?

[8]Driving out and expelling, he
    struggled against it,
    carrying it off with his cruel wind
        on a day of storm.
[9]This, then, shall be the expiation of
    Jacob's guilt,
    this the result of removing his sin:
He shall pulverize all the stones of the
    altars
    like pieces of chalk;
    no asherahs or incense altars shall
        stand.
[10]For the fortified city shall be desolate,
    an abandoned pasture, a forsaken
        wilderness;
There calves shall graze, there they shall
    lie down,
    and consume its branches.
[11]When its boughs wither, they shall be
    broken off;
    and women shall come to kindle
        fires with them.
For this is not an understanding people;
    therefore their maker shall not spare
        them;
    their creator shall not be gracious to
        them.
[12]On that day,
The LORD shall beat out grain
    from the channel of the Euphrates
        to the Wadi of Egypt,
    and you shall be gleaned one by
        one, children of Israel.
[13]On that day,
A great trumpet shall blow,
    and the lost in the land of Assyria
    and the outcasts in the land of Egypt
Shall come and worship the LORD
    on the holy mountain, in Jerusalem.

The Fate of Samaria. 28:1 Ah! majestic
garland
of the drunkards of Ephraim,
Fading blooms of his glorious beauty,
at the head of the fertile valley,
upon those stupefied with wine.
[2]See, the LORD has a strong one, a
mighty one,
who, like an onslaught of hail, a
destructive storm,
Like a flood of water, great and
overflowing,
levels to the ground with violence;
[3]With feet that will trample
the majestic garland of the
drunkards of Ephraim.
[4]The fading blooms of his glorious
beauty
at the head of the fertile valley
Will be like an early fig before summer:
whoever sees it,
swallows it as soon as it is in hand.
[5]On that day the LORD of hosts
will be a glorious crown
And a brilliant diadem
for the remnant of his people,
[6]A spirit of judgment
for the one who sits in judgment,
And strength for those
who turn back the battle at the gate.

Against Judah. [7]But these also stagger
from wine
and stumble from strong drink:
Priest and prophet stagger from strong
drink,
overpowered by wine;
They are confused by strong drink,
they stagger in their visions,
they totter when giving judgment.
[8]Yes, all the tables
are covered with vomit,
with filth, and no place left clean.
[9]"To whom would he impart
knowledge?
To whom would he convey the message?
To those just weaned from milk,

those weaned from the breast?
[10]For he says,
'Command on command, command
on command,
rule on rule, rule on rule,
here a little, there a little!'"
[11]Yes, with stammering lips and in a
strange language
he will speak to this people,
[12]to whom he said:
"This is the resting place,
give rest to the weary;
And this is the place of repose"—
but they refused to hear.
[13]So for them the word of the LORD
shall be:
"Command on command,
command on command,
Rule on rule, rule on rule,
here a little, there a little!"
So that when they walk, they shall
stumble backward,
broken, ensnared, and captured.
[14]Therefore, hear the word of the
LORD, you scoffers,
who rule this people in Jerusalem:
[15]You have declared, "We have made a
covenant with death,
with Sheol we have made a pact;
When the raging flood passes through,
it will not reach us;
For we have made lies our refuge,
and in falsehood we have found a
hiding place,"—
[16]Therefore, thus says the Lord GOD:
See, I am laying a stone in Zion,
a stone that has been tested,
A precious cornerstone as a sure
foundation;
whoever puts faith in it will not waver.
[17]I will make judgment a measuring
line,
and justice a level.—
Hail shall sweep away the refuge of lies,
and waters shall flood the hiding
place.

¹⁸Your covenant with death shall be
canceled
and your pact with Sheol shall not
stand.
When the raging flood passes through,
you shall be beaten down by it.
¹⁹Whenever it passes, it shall seize you;
morning after morning it shall pass,
by day and by night.
Sheer terror
to impart the message!
²⁰For the bed shall be too short to
stretch out in,
and the cover too narrow to wrap in.
²¹For the LORD shall rise up as on
Mount Perazim,
bestir himself as in the Valley of
Gibeon,
To carry out his work—strange his work!
to perform his deed—alien his deed!
²²Now, cease scoffing,
lest your bonds be tightened,
For I have heard a decree of destruction
from the Lord, the GOD of hosts,
for the whole land.

The Parable of the Farmer. ²³Give ear
and hear my voice,

pay attention and hear my word:
²⁴Is the plowman forever plowing in
order to sow,
always loosening and harrowing the
field?
²⁵When he has leveled the surface,
does he not scatter caraway and sow
cumin,
Put in wheat and barley,
with spelt as its border?
²⁶His God has taught him this rule,
he has instructed him.
²⁷For caraway is not threshed with a
sledge,
nor does a cartwheel roll over
cumin.
But caraway is beaten out with a staff,
and cumin with a rod.
²⁸Grain is crushed for bread, but not
forever;
though he thresh it thoroughly,
and drive his cartwheel and horses
over it,
he does not pulverize it.
²⁹This too comes from the LORD of hosts;
wonderful is his counsel and great
his wisdom.

☐ ACTS 21:40-22:29

21:40 When he had given his permission,
Paul stood on the steps and motioned with
his hand to the people; and when all was
quiet he addressed them in Hebrew.

**Paul's Defense before the Jerusalem
Jews. 22:1** "My brothers and fathers, listen to what I am about to say to you in my
defense." ²When they heard him addressing them in Hebrew they became all the
more quiet. And he continued, ³"I am a
Jew, born in Tarsus in Cilicia, but brought
up in this city. At the feet of Gamaliel I
was educated strictly in our ancestral law
and was zealous for God, just as all of you
are today. ⁴I persecuted this Way to death,

binding both men and women and delivering them to prison. ⁵Even the high priest
and the whole council of elders can testify
on my behalf. For from them I even received letters to the brothers and set out
for Damascus to bring back to Jerusalem in
chains for punishment those there as well.
⁶"On that journey as I drew near to Damascus, about noon a great light from the
sky suddenly shone around me. ⁷I fell to
the ground and heard a voice saying to me,
'Saul, Saul, why are you persecuting me?' ⁸I
replied, 'Who are you, sir?' And he said to
me, 'I am Jesus the Nazorean whom you are
persecuting.' ⁹My companions saw the light
but did not hear the voice of the one who

spoke to me. [10]I asked, 'What shall I do, sir?' The Lord answered me, 'Get up and go into Damascus, and there you will be told about everything appointed for you to do.' [11]Since I could see nothing because of the brightness of that light, I was led by hand by my companions and entered Damascus.

[12]"A certain Ananias, a devout observer of the law, and highly spoken of by all the Jews who lived there, [13]came to me and stood there and said, 'Saul, my brother, regain your sight.' And at that very moment I regained my sight and saw him. [14]Then he said, 'The God of our ancestors designated you to know his will, to see the Righteous One, and to hear the sound of his voice; [15]for you will be his witness before all to what you have seen and heard. [16]Now, why delay? Get up and have yourself baptized and your sins washed away, calling upon his name.'

[17]"After I had returned to Jerusalem and while I was praying in the temple, I fell into a trance [18]and saw the Lord saying to me, 'Hurry, leave Jerusalem at once, because they will not accept your testimony about me.' [19]But I replied, 'Lord, they themselves know that from synagogue to synagogue I used to imprison and beat those who believed in you. [20]And when the blood of your witness Stephen was being shed, I myself stood by giving my approval and keeping guard over the cloaks of his murderers.' [21]Then he said to me, 'Go, I shall send you far away to the Gentiles.'"

Paul Imprisoned. [22]They listened to him until he said this, but then they raised their voices and shouted, "Take such a one as this away from the earth. It is not right that he should live." [23]And as they were yelling and throwing off their cloaks and flinging dust into the air, [24]the cohort commander ordered him to be brought into the compound and gave instruction that he be interrogated under the lash to determine the reason why they were making such an outcry against him. [25]But when they had stretched him out for the whips, Paul said to the centurion on duty, "Is it lawful for you to scourge a man who is a Roman citizen and has not been tried?" [26]When the centurion heard this, he went to the cohort commander and reported it, saying, "What are you going to do? This man is a Roman citizen." [27]Then the commander came and said to him, "Tell me, are you a Roman citizen?" "Yes," he answered. [28]The commander replied, "I acquired this citizenship for a large sum of money." Paul said, "But I was born one." [29]At once those who were going to interrogate him backed away from him, and the commander became alarmed when he realized that he was a Roman citizen and that he had had him bound.

September 17

St. Robert Bellarmine; St. Hildegard of Bingen

The school of Christ is the school of charity. On the last day, when the general examination takes place, there will be no question at all on the text of Aristotle, the aphorisms of Hippocrates, or the paragraphs of Justinian. Charity will be the whole syllabus.

— St. Robert Bellarmine

☐ ISAIAH 29–30

Judgment and Deliverance of Jerusalem. 29:1 Ah! Ariel, Ariel,
city where David encamped!
Let year follow year,
and feast follow feast,
²But I will bring distress upon Ariel,
and there will be mourning and
moaning.
You shall be to me like Ariel:
³I will encamp like David against
you;
I will circle you with outposts
and set up siege works against you.
⁴You shall speak from beneath the earth,
and from the dust below, your
words shall come.
Your voice shall be that of a ghost from
the earth,
and your words shall whisper from
the dust.
⁵The horde of your arrogant shall be
like fine dust,
a horde of tyrants like flying chaff.
Then suddenly, in an instant,
⁶you shall be visited by the Lord of
hosts,
With thunder, earthquake, and great
noise,
whirlwind, storm, and the flame of
consuming fire.
⁷Then like a dream,
a vision of the night,
Shall be the horde of all the nations
who make war against Ariel:
All the outposts, the siege works
against it,

all who distress it.
⁸As when a hungry man dreams he is
eating
and awakens with an empty stomach,
Or when a thirsty man dreams he is
drinking
and awakens faint, his throat
parched,
So shall the horde of all the nations be,
who make war against Mount Zion.

Blindness and Perversity. ⁹Stupefy
yourselves and stay stupid;
blind yourselves and stay blind!
You who are drunk, but not from wine,
who stagger, but not from strong
drink!
¹⁰For the Lord has poured out on you
a spirit of deep sleep.
He has shut your eyes (the prophets)
and covered your heads (the seers).

¹¹For you the vision of all this has become like the words of a sealed scroll. When it is handed to one who can read, with the request, "Read this," the reply is, "I cannot, because it is sealed." ¹²When the scroll is handed to one who cannot read, with the request, "Read this," the reply is, "I cannot read."

¹³The Lord said:
Since this people draws near with
words only
and honors me with their lips alone,
though their hearts are far from me,
And fear of me has become

mere precept of human teaching,
¹⁴Therefore I will again deal with this
people
in surprising and wondrous fashion:
The wisdom of the wise shall perish,
the prudence of the prudent shall
vanish.
¹⁵Ah! You who would hide a plan
too deep for the LORD!
Who work in the dark, saying,
"Who sees us, who knows us?"
¹⁶Your perversity is as though the potter
were taken to be the clay:
As though what is made should say of
its maker,
"He did not make me!"
Or the vessel should say of the potter,
"He does not understand."

Redemption. ¹⁷Surely, in a very little
while,
Lebanon shall be changed into an
orchard,
and the orchard be considered a
forest!
¹⁸On that day the deaf shall hear
the words of a scroll;
And out of gloom and darkness,
the eyes of the blind shall see.
¹⁹The lowly shall again find joy in the
LORD,
the poorest rejoice in the Holy One
of Israel.
²⁰For the tyrant shall be no more,
the scoffer shall cease to be;
All who are ready for evil shall be cut off,
²¹those who condemn with a mere
word,
Who ensnare the defender at the gate,
and leave the just with an empty
claim.
²²Therefore thus says the LORD,
the God of the house of Jacob,
who redeemed Abraham:
No longer shall Jacob be ashamed,
no longer shall his face grow pale.
²³For when his children see

the work of my hands in his midst,
They shall sanctify my name;
they shall sanctify the Holy One of
Jacob,
be in awe of the God of Israel.
²⁴Those who err in spirit shall acquire
understanding,
those who find fault shall receive
instruction.

**Oracle on the Futility of an Alliance
with Egypt. 30:1** Ah! Rebellious
children,
oracle of the LORD,
Who carry out a plan that is not mine,
who make an alliance I did not
inspire,
thus adding sin upon sin;
²They go down to Egypt,
without asking my counsel,
To seek strength in Pharaoh's protection
and take refuge in Egypt's shadow.
³Pharaoh's protection shall become
your shame,
refuge in Egypt's shadow your
disgrace.
⁴When his princes are at Zoan
and his messengers reach Hanes,
⁵All shall be ashamed
of a people that gain them nothing,
Neither help nor benefit,
but only shame and reproach.
⁶Oracle on the Beasts of the Negeb.
Through the distressed and troubled
land
of the lioness and roaring lion,
of the viper and flying saraph,
They carry their riches on the backs of
donkeys
and their treasures on the humps of
camels
To a people good for nothing,
⁷to Egypt whose help is futile and
vain.
Therefore I call her
"Rahab Sit-still."

8Now come, write it on a tablet they
can keep,
inscribe it on a scroll;
That in time to come it may be
an eternal witness.
9For this is a rebellious people,
deceitful children,
Children who refuse
to listen to the instruction of the
LORD;
10Who say to the seers, "Do not see";
to the prophets, "Do not prophesy
truth for us;
speak smooth things to us, see
visions that deceive!
11Turn aside from the way! Get out of
the path!
Let us hear no more
of the Holy One of Israel!"
12Therefore, thus says the Holy One of
Israel:
Because you reject this word,
And put your trust in oppression and
deceit,
and depend on them,
13This iniquity of yours shall be
like a descending rift
Bulging out in a high wall
whose crash comes suddenly, in an
instant,
14Crashing like a potter's jar
smashed beyond rescue,
And among its fragments cannot be
found
a sherd to scoop fire from the
hearth
or dip water from the cistern.
15For thus said the Lord GOD,
the Holy One of Israel:
By waiting and by calm you shall be
saved,
in quiet and in trust shall be your
strength.
But this you did not will.
16"No," you said,
"Upon horses we will flee."
Very well, you shall flee!

"Upon swift steeds we will ride."
Very well, swift shall be your pursuers!
17A thousand shall tremble at the threat
of one—
if five threaten, you shall flee.
You will then be left like a flagstaff on a
mountaintop,
like a flag on a hill.

Zion's Future Deliverance. 18Truly, the
LORD is waiting to be gracious
to you,
truly, he shall rise to show you mercy;
For the LORD is a God of justice:
happy are all who wait for him!
19Yes, people of Zion, dwelling in
Jerusalem,
you shall no longer weep;
He will be most gracious to you when
you cry out;
as soon as he hears he will answer
you.
20The Lord will give you bread in
adversity
and water in affliction.
No longer will your Teacher hide
himself,
but with your own eyes you shall see
your Teacher,
21And your ears shall hear a word
behind you:
"This is the way; walk in it,"
when you would turn to the right or
the left.
22You shall defile your silver-plated idols
and your gold-covered images;
You shall throw them away like filthy
rags,
you shall say, "Get out!"
23He will give rain for the seed
you sow in the ground,
And the bread that the soil produces
will be rich and abundant.
On that day your cattle will graze
in broad meadows;
24The oxen and the donkeys that till the
ground

will eat silage tossed to them
with shovel and pitchfork.
[25]Upon every high mountain and lofty
hill
there will be streams of running water.
On the day of the great slaughter,
when the towers fall,
[26]The light of the moon will be like the
light of the sun,
and the light of the sun will be
seven times greater,
like the light of seven days,
On the day the LORD binds up the
wounds of his people
and heals the bruises left by his blows.

Divine Judgment on Assyria. [27]See,
the name of the LORD is coming
from afar,
burning with anger, heavy with threat,
His lips filled with fury,
tongue like a consuming fire,
[28]Breath like an overflowing torrent
that reaches up to the neck!
He will winnow the nations with a
destructive winnowing
and bridle the jaws of the peoples to
send them astray.
[29]For you, there will be singing
as on a night when a feast is observed,

And joy of heart
as when one marches along with a
flute
Going to the mountain of the LORD,
to the Rock of Israel.
[30]The LORD will make his glorious
voice heard,
and reveal his arm coming down
In raging fury and flame of consuming
fire,
in tempest, and rainstorm, and hail.
[31]For at the voice of the LORD, Assyria
will be shattered,
as he strikes with the rod;
[32]And every sweep of the rod of his
punishment,
which the LORD will bring down on
him,
Will be accompanied by timbrels and
lyres,
while he wages war against him.
[33]For his tophet has long been ready,
truly it is prepared for the king;
His firepit made both deep and wide,
with fire and firewood in
abundance,
And the breath of the LORD, like a
stream of sulfur,
setting it afire.

☐ ACTS 22:30–23:35

Paul before the Sanhedrin. 22:30 The
next day, wishing to determine the truth
about why he was being accused by the
Jews, he freed him and ordered the chief
priests and the whole Sanhedrin to convene. Then he brought Paul down and
made him stand before them.

23:1 Paul looked intently at the Sanhedrin
and said, "My brothers, I have conducted
myself with a perfectly clear conscience
before God to this day." [2]The high priest
Ananias ordered his attendants to strike
his mouth. [3]Then Paul said to him, "God

will strike you, you whitewashed wall. Do
you indeed sit in judgment upon me according to the law and yet in violation of
the law order me to be struck?" [4]The attendants said, "Would you revile God's high
priest?" [5]Paul answered, "Brothers, I did
not realize he was the high priest. For it is
written, 'You shall not curse a ruler of your
people.'"
[6]Paul was aware that some were Sadducees and some Pharisees, so he called
out before the Sanhedrin, "My brothers, I
am a Pharisee, the son of Pharisees; [I] am
on trial for hope in the resurrection of the

dead." [7]When he said this, a dispute broke out between the Pharisees and Sadducees, and the group became divided. [8]For the Sadducees say that there is no resurrection or angels or spirits, while the Pharisees acknowledge all three. [9]A great uproar occurred, and some scribes belonging to the Pharisee party stood up and sharply argued, "We find nothing wrong with this man. Suppose a spirit or an angel has spoken to him?" [10]The dispute was so serious that the commander, afraid that Paul would be torn to pieces by them, ordered his troops to go down and rescue him from their midst and take him into the compound. [11]The following night the Lord stood by him and said, "Take courage. For just as you have borne witness to my cause in Jerusalem, so you must also bear witness in Rome."

Transfer to Caesarea. [12]When day came, the Jews made a plot and bound themselves by oath not to eat or drink until they had killed Paul. [13]There were more than forty who formed this conspiracy. [14]They went to the chief priests and elders and said, "We have bound ourselves by a solemn oath to taste nothing until we have killed Paul. [15]You, together with the Sanhedrin, must now make an official request to the commander to have him bring him down to you, as though you meant to investigate his case more thoroughly. We on our part are prepared to kill him before he arrives." [16]The son of Paul's sister, however, heard about the ambush; so he went and entered the compound and reported it to Paul. [17]Paul then called one of the centurions and requested, "Take this young man to the commander; he has something to report to him." [18]So he took him and brought him to the commander and explained, "The prisoner Paul called me and asked that I bring this young man to you; he has something to say to you." [19]The commander took him by the hand, drew him aside, and asked him privately, "What is it you have to report to me?" [20]He replied, "The Jews have conspired to ask you to bring Paul down to the Sanhedrin tomorrow, as though they meant to inquire about him more thoroughly, [21]but do not believe them. More than forty of them are lying in wait for him; they have bound themselves by oath not to eat or drink until they have killed him. They are now ready and only wait for your consent." [22]As the commander dismissed the young man he directed him, "Tell no one that you gave me this information."

[23]Then he summoned two of the centurions and said, "Get two hundred soldiers ready to go to Caesarea by nine o'clock tonight, along with seventy horsemen and two hundred auxiliaries. [24]Provide mounts for Paul to ride and give him safe conduct to Felix the governor." [25]Then he wrote a letter with this content: [26]"Claudius Lysias to his excellency the governor Felix, greetings. [27]This man, seized by the Jews and about to be murdered by them, I rescued after intervening with my troops when I learned that he was a Roman citizen. [28]I wanted to learn the reason for their accusations against him so I brought him down to their Sanhedrin. [29]I discovered that he was accused in matters of controversial questions of their law and not of any charge deserving death or imprisonment. [30]Since it was brought to my attention that there will be a plot against the man, I am sending him to you at once, and have also notified his accusers to state (their case) against him before you."

[31]So the soldiers, according to their orders, took Paul and escorted him by night to Antipatris. [32]The next day they returned to the compound, leaving the horsemen to complete the journey with him. [33]When they arrived in Caesarea they delivered the letter to the governor and presented Paul to him. [34]When he had read it and asked to what province he belonged, and learned that he was from Cilicia, [35]he said, "I shall hear your case when your accusers arrive." Then he ordered that he be held in custody in Herod's praetorium.

September 18

Obedience is a little dog that leads the blind.
— St. Joseph of Cupertino

☐ ISAIAH 31-32

Against the Egyptian Alliance. 31:1 Ah!
Those who go down to Egypt for help,
   who rely on horses;
   Who put their trust in chariots because
      of their number,
      and in horsemen because of their
      combined power,
   But look not to the Holy One of Israel
   nor seek the LORD!
²Yet he too is wise and will bring
      disaster;
   he will not turn from his threats.
He will rise up against the house of the
   wicked
   and against those who help evildoers.
³The Egyptians are human beings, not
   God,
   their horses flesh, not spirit;
When the LORD stretches forth his
      hand,
   the helper shall stumble, the one
      helped shall fall,
   and both of them shall perish
      together.
⁴For thus says the LORD to me:
As a lion or its young
   growling over the prey,
With a band of shepherds
   assembled against it,
Is neither dismayed by their shouts
   nor cowed by their noise,
So shall the LORD of hosts come down
   to wage war upon Mount Zion,
      upon its height.
⁵Like hovering birds, so the LORD of
   hosts
   shall shield Jerusalem,
To shield and deliver,
   to spare and rescue.

⁶Return, O Israelites, to him whom you
have utterly deserted. ⁷On that day each
one of you shall reject his idols of silver and
gold, which your hands have made.

⁸Assyria shall fall by a sword, not
   wielded by human being,
   no mortal sword shall devour him;
He shall flee before the sword,
   and his young men shall be
      impressed as laborers.
⁹He shall rush past his crag in panic,
   and his princes desert the standard
      in terror,
Says the LORD who has a fire in Zion
   and a furnace in Jerusalem.

The Kingdom of Justice. 32:1 See, a
   king will reign justly
   and princes will rule rightly.
²Each of them will be like a shelter
      from the wind,
   a refuge from the rain.
They will be like streams of water in a
   dry country,
   like the shade of a great rock in a
      parched land.
³The eyes of those who see will not be
   closed;
   the ears of those who hear will be
      attentive.
⁴The hasty of heart shall take thought
   to know,
   and tongues of stutterers shall speak
      readily and clearly.
⁵No more will the fool be called noble,
   nor the deceiver be considered
      honorable.
⁶For the fool speaks folly,

his heart plans evil:
Godless actions,
  perverse speech against the LORD,
Letting the hungry go empty
  and the thirsty without drink.
⁷The deceits of the deceiver are evil,
  he plans devious schemes:
To ruin the poor with lies,
  and the needy when they plead their
    case.
⁸But the noble plan noble deeds,
  and in noble deeds they persist.

The Women of Jerusalem. ⁹You
    women so complacent, rise up
    and hear my voice,
  daughters so confident, give heed to
    my words.
¹⁰In a little more than a year
  your confidence will be shaken;
For the vintage will fail,
  no fruit harvest will come in.
¹¹Tremble, you who are so complacent!
  Shudder, you who are so confident!
Strip yourselves bare,
  with only a loincloth for cover.
¹²Beat your breasts
  for the pleasant fields,
  for the fruitful vine;
¹³For the soil of my people,
  overgrown with thorns and briers;

For all the joyful houses,
  the exultant city.
¹⁴The castle will be forsaken,
  the noisy city deserted;
Citadel and tower will become
    wasteland forever,
  the joy of wild donkeys, the pasture
    of flocks;
¹⁵Until the spirit from on high
  is poured out on us.
And the wilderness becomes a garden
    land
  and the garden land seems as
    common as forest.
¹⁶Then judgment will dwell in the
    wilderness
  and justice abide in the garden land.
¹⁷The work of justice will be peace;
  the effect of justice, calm and
    security forever.
¹⁸My people will live in peaceful country,
  in secure dwellings and quiet resting
    places.
¹⁹And the forest will come down
    completely,
  the city will be utterly laid low.
²⁰Happy are you who sow beside every
    stream,
  and let the ox and the donkey go
    freely!

☐ ACTS 24

Trial before Felix. 24:1 Five days later the high priest Ananias came down with some elders and an advocate, a certain Tertullus, and they presented formal charges against Paul to the governor. ²When he was called, Tertullus began to accuse him, saying, "Since we have attained much peace through you, and reforms have been accomplished in this nation through your provident care, ³we acknowledge this in every way and everywhere, most excellent Felix, with all gratitude. ⁴But in order not to detain you further, I ask you to give us a brief hearing with your custom-ary graciousness. ⁵We found this man to be a pest; he creates dissension among Jews all over the world and is a ringleader of the sect of the Nazoreans. ⁶He even tried to desecrate our temple, but we arrested him. ⁷ ⁸If you examine him you will be able to learn from him for yourself about everything of which we are accusing him." ⁹The Jews also joined in the attack and asserted that these things were so.

¹⁰Then the governor motioned to him to speak and Paul replied, "I know that you have been a judge over this nation for many

years and so I am pleased to make my defense before you. [11]As you can verify, not more than twelve days have passed since I went up to Jerusalem to worship. [12]Neither in the temple, nor in the synagogues, nor anywhere in the city did they find me arguing with anyone or instigating a riot among the people. [13]Nor can they prove to you the accusations they are now making against me. [14]But this I do admit to you, that according to the Way, which they call a sect, I worship the God of our ancestors and I believe everything that is in accordance with the law and written in the prophets. [15]I have the same hope in God as they themselves have that there will be a resurrection of the righteous and the unrighteous. [16]Because of this, I always strive to keep my conscience clear before God and man. [17]After many years, I came to bring alms for my nation and offerings. [18]While I was so engaged, they found me, after my purification, in the temple without a crowd or disturbance. [19]But some Jews from the province of Asia, who should be here before you to make whatever accusation they might have against me— [20]or let these men themselves state what crime they discovered when I stood before the Sanhedrin, [21]unless it was my one outcry as I stood among them, that 'I am on trial before you today for the resurrection of the dead.'"

[22]Then Felix, who was accurately informed about the Way, postponed the trial, saying, "When Lysias the commander comes down, I shall decide your case." [23]He gave orders to the centurion that he should be kept in custody but have some liberty, and that he should not prevent any of his friends from caring for his needs.

Captivity in Caesarea. [24]Several days later Felix came with his wife Drusilla, who was Jewish. He had Paul summoned and listened to him speak about faith in Christ Jesus. [25]But as he spoke about righteousness and self-restraint and the coming judgment, Felix became frightened and said, "You may go for now; when I find an opportunity I shall summon you again." [26]At the same time he hoped that a bribe would be offered him by Paul, and so he sent for him very often and conversed with him.

[27]Two years passed and Felix was succeeded by Porcius Festus. Wishing to ingratiate himself with the Jews, Felix left Paul in prison.

September 19

St. Januarius; St. Alonso de Orozco

Do not go jumping about from one book of spiritual reading to another, nor begin by reading the end. We enjoy variety in what we read, but perseverance in reading is what brings us profit.
— St. Alonso de Orozco

☐ ISAIAH 33-34

Overthrow of Assyria. 33:1 Ah! You
  destroyer never destroyed,
  betrayer never betrayed!
When you have finished destroying,
  you will be destroyed;

when you have stopped betraying,
  you will be betrayed.
[2]Lord, be gracious to us; for you we wait.
  Be our strength every morning,
  our salvation in time of trouble!

³At the roaring sound, peoples flee;
  when you rise in your majesty,
    nations are scattered.
⁴Spoil is gathered up as caterpillars
    gather,
  an onrush like the rush of locusts.
⁵The LORD is exalted, enthroned on
    high;
  he fills Zion with right and justice.
⁶That which makes her seasons certain,
  her wealth, salvation, wisdom, and
    knowledge,
  is the fear of the LORD, her treasure.
⁷See, the men of Ariel cry out in the
    streets,
  the messengers of Shalem weep
    bitterly.
⁸The highways are desolate,
  travelers have quit the paths,
Covenants are broken, witnesses
    spurned;
  yet no one gives it a thought.
⁹The country languishes in mourning,
  Lebanon withers with shame;
Sharon is like the Arabah,
  Bashan and Carmel are stripped bare.
¹⁰Now I will rise up, says the LORD,
  now exalt myself,
  now lift myself up.
¹¹You conceive dry grass, bring forth
    stubble;
  my spirit shall consume you like
    fire.
¹²The peoples shall be burned to lime,
  thorns cut down to burn in fire.
¹³Hear, you who are far off, what I have
    done;
  you who are near, acknowledge my
    might.
¹⁴In Zion sinners are in dread,
  trembling grips the impious:
"Who of us can live with consuming
    fire?
  who of us can live with everlasting
    flames?"
¹⁵Whoever walks righteously and
    speaks honestly,

who spurns what is gained by
    oppression,
Who waves off contact with a bribe,
  who stops his ears so as not to hear
    of bloodshed,
  who closes his eyes so as not to look
    on evil—
¹⁶That one shall dwell on the heights,
  with fortresses of rock for
    stronghold,
  food and drink in steady supply.
¹⁷Your eyes will see a king in his
    splendor,
  they will look upon a vast land.
¹⁸Your mind will dwell on the terror:
  "Where is the one who counted,
    where the one who weighed?
  Where the one who counted the
    towers?"
¹⁹You shall no longer see a defiant
    people,
  a people of speech too obscure to
    comprehend,
  stammering in a tongue not
    understood.
²⁰Look to Zion, the city of our festivals;
  your eyes shall see Jerusalem
  as a quiet abode, a tent not to be
    struck,
Whose pegs will never be pulled up,
  nor any of its ropes severed.
²¹Indeed the LORD in majesty will be
    there for us
  a place of rivers and wide streams
  on which no galley may go,
  where no majestic ship may pass.
²²For the LORD is our judge,
  the LORD is our lawgiver,
  the LORD is our king;
  he it is who will save us.
²³The rigging hangs slack;
  it cannot hold the mast in place,
  nor keep the sail spread out.
Then the blind will divide great spoils
  and the lame will carry off the loot.
²⁴No one who dwells there will say, "I
    am sick";

the people who live there will be forgiven their guilt.

Judgment upon Edom. 34:1 Come near, nations, and listen;
be attentive, you peoples!
Let the earth and what fills it listen,
the world and all it produces.
²The LORD is angry with all the nations,
enraged against all their host;
He has placed them under the ban,
given them up to slaughter.
³Their slain shall be cast out,
their corpses shall send up a stench;
the mountains shall run with their blood,
⁴All the host of heaven shall rot;
the heavens shall be rolled up like a scroll.
All their host shall wither away,
as the leaf wilts on the vine,
or as the fig withers on the tree.
⁵When my sword has drunk its fill in the heavens,
it shall come down upon Edom for judgment,
upon a people under my ban.
⁶The LORD has a sword sated with blood,
greasy with fat,
With the blood of lambs and goats,
with the fat of rams' kidneys;
For the LORD has a sacrifice in Bozrah,
a great slaughter in the land of Edom.
⁷Wild oxen shall be struck down with fatlings,
and bullocks with bulls;
Their land shall be soaked with blood,
and their soil greasy with fat.
⁸For the LORD has a day of vengeance,
a year of requital for the cause of Zion.
⁹Edom's streams shall be changed into pitch,
its soil into sulfur,
and its land shall become burning pitch;
¹⁰Night and day it shall not be quenched,
its smoke shall rise forever.
From generation to generation it shall lie waste,
never again shall anyone pass through it.
¹¹But the desert owl and hoot owl shall possess it,
the screech owl and raven shall dwell in it.
The LORD will stretch over it the measuring line of chaos,
the plumb line of confusion.
¹²Its nobles shall be no more,
nor shall kings be proclaimed there;
all its princes are gone.
¹³Its castles shall be overgrown with thorns,
its fortresses with thistles and briers.
It shall become an abode for jackals,
a haunt for ostriches.
¹⁴Wildcats shall meet with desert beasts,
satyrs shall call to one another;
There shall the lilith repose,
and find for herself a place to rest.
¹⁵There the hoot owl shall nest and lay eggs,
hatch them out and gather them in her shadow;
There shall the kites assemble,
each with its mate.
¹⁶Search through the book of the LORD and read:
not one of these shall be lacking,
For the mouth of the LORD has ordered it,
and his spirit gathers them there.
¹⁷It is he who casts the lot for them;
his hand measures off their portions;
They shall possess it forever,
and dwell in it from generation to generation.

☐ ACTS 25

Appeal to Caesar. 25:1 Three days after his arrival in the province, Festus went up from Caesarea to Jerusalem [2]where the chief priests and Jewish leaders presented him their formal charges against Paul. They asked him [3]as a favor to have him sent to Jerusalem, for they were plotting to kill him along the way. [4]Festus replied that Paul was being held in custody in Caesarea and that he himself would be returning there shortly. [5]He said, "Let your authorities come down with me, and if this man has done something improper, let them accuse him."

[6]After spending no more than eight or ten days with them, he went down to Caesarea, and on the following day took his seat on the tribunal and ordered that Paul be brought in. [7]When he appeared, the Jews who had come down from Jerusalem surrounded him and brought many serious charges against him, which they were unable to prove. [8]In defending himself Paul said, "I have committed no crime either against the Jewish law or against the temple or against Caesar." [9]Then Festus, wishing to ingratiate himself with the Jews, said to Paul in reply, "Are you willing to go up to Jerusalem and there stand trial before me on these charges?" [10]Paul answered, "I am standing before the tribunal of Caesar; this is where I should be tried. I have committed no crime against the Jews, as you very well know. [11]If I have committed a crime or done anything deserving death, I do not seek to escape the death penalty; but if there is no substance to the charges they are bringing against me, then no one has the right to hand me over to them. I appeal to Caesar." [12]Then Festus, after conferring with his council, replied, "You have appealed to Caesar. To Caesar you will go."

Paul before King Agrippa. [13]When a few days had passed, King Agrippa and Bernice arrived in Caesarea on a visit to Festus. [14]Since they spent several days there, Festus referred Paul's case to the king, saying, "There is a man here left in custody by Felix. [15]When I was in Jerusalem the chief priests and the elders of the Jews brought charges against him and demanded his condemnation. [16]I answered them that it was not Roman practice to hand over an accused person before he has faced his accusers and had the opportunity to defend himself against their charge. [17]So when (they) came together here, I made no delay; the next day I took my seat on the tribunal and ordered the man to be brought in. [18]His accusers stood around him, but did not charge him with any of the crimes I suspected. [19]Instead they had some issues with him about their own religion and about a certain Jesus who had died but who Paul claimed was alive. [20]Since I was at a loss how to investigate this controversy, I asked if he were willing to go to Jerusalem and there stand trial on these charges. [21]And when Paul appealed that he be held in custody for the Emperor's decision, I ordered him held until I could send him to Caesar." [22]Agrippa said to Festus, "I too should like to hear this man." He replied, "Tomorrow you will hear him."

[23]The next day Agrippa and Bernice came with great ceremony and entered the audience hall in the company of cohort commanders and the prominent men of the city and, by command of Festus, Paul was brought in. [24]And Festus said, "King Agrippa and all you here present with us, look at this man about whom the whole Jewish populace petitioned me here and in Jerusalem, clamoring that he should live no longer. [25]I found, however, that he had done nothing deserving death, and so when he appealed to the Emperor, I decided to send him. [26]But I have nothing definite to write about him to our sovereign; therefore

I have brought him before all of you, and particularly before you, King Agrippa, so that I may have something to write as a result of this investigation. [27]For it seems senseless to me to send up a prisoner without indicating the charges against him."

September 20

Sts. Andrew Kim Taegon, Paul Chong Hasang, and Companions

Since the Lord of heaven is the Father of all mankind and the Lord of all creation, how can you ask me to betray Him? Even in this world anyone who betrays his own father or mother will not be forgiven. All the more may I never betray him who is the Father of us all!

— St. Teresa Kwon

☐ ISAIAH 35-36

Israel's Deliverance. 35:1 The wilderness
  and the parched land will exult;
  the Arabah will rejoice and bloom;
[2]Like the crocus it shall bloom
  abundantly,
  and rejoice with joyful song.
The glory of Lebanon will be given
  to it,
  the splendor of Carmel and Sharon;
They will see the glory of the Lord,
  the splendor of our God.
[3]Strengthen hands that are feeble,
  make firm knees that are weak,
[4]Say to the fearful of heart:
  Be strong, do not fear!
Here is your God,
  he comes with vindication;
With divine recompense
  he comes to save you.
[5]Then the eyes of the blind shall see,
  and the ears of the deaf be opened;
[6]Then the lame shall leap like a stag,
  and the mute tongue sing for joy.
For waters will burst forth in the
  wilderness,
  and streams in the Arabah.
[7]The burning sands will become pools,

  and the thirsty ground, springs of
  water;
The abode where jackals crouch
  will be a marsh for the reed and
  papyrus.
[8]A highway will be there,
  called the holy way;
No one unclean may pass over it,
  but it will be for his people;
  no traveler, not even fools, shall go
  astray on it.
[9]No lion shall be there,
  nor any beast of prey approach,
  nor be found.
But there the redeemed shall walk,
[10]And the ransomed of the Lord shall
  return,
  and enter Zion singing,
  crowned with everlasting joy;
They meet with joy and gladness,
  sorrow and mourning flee away.

Invasion of Sennacherib. 36:1 In the fourteenth year of King Hezekiah, Sennacherib, king of Assyria, went up against all the fortified cities of Judah and captured them. [2]From Lachish the king of Assyria sent his commander with a great army to King Hezekiah in Jerusalem. When he stopped at the conduit of the upper pool, on the highway of the fuller's field, ³there came out to him the master of the palace, Eliakim, son of Hilkiah, and Shebna the scribe, and the chancellor, Joah, son of Asaph. ⁴The commander said to them, "Tell Hezekiah: Thus says the great king, the king of Assyria: On what do you base this trust of yours? ⁵Do you think mere words substitute for strategy and might in war? In whom, then, do you place your trust, that you rebel against me? ⁶Do you trust in Egypt, that broken reed of a staff which pierces the hand of anyone who leans on it? That is what Pharaoh, king of Egypt, is to all who trust in him. ⁷Or do you say to me: It is in the LORD, our God, we trust? Is it not he whose high places and altars Hezekiah has removed, commanding Judah and Jerusalem, 'Worship before this altar'?

⁸"Now, make a wager with my lord, the king of Assyria: I will give you two thousand horses, if you are able to put riders on them. ⁹How then can you turn back even a captain, one of the least servants of my lord, trusting, as you do, in Egypt for chariots and horses? ¹⁰Did I come up to destroy this land without the LORD? The LORD himself said to me, Go up and destroy that land!"

¹¹Then Eliakim and Shebna and Joah said to the commander, "Please speak to your servants in Aramaic; we understand it. Do not speak to us in the language of Judah within earshot of the people who are on the wall."

¹²But the commander replied, "Was it to your lord and to you that my lord sent me to speak these words? Was it not rather to those sitting on the wall, who, with you, will have to eat their own excrement and drink their own urine?" ¹³Then the commander stepped forward and cried out in a loud voice in the language of Judah, "Listen to the words of the great king, the king of Assyria. ¹⁴Thus says the king: Do not let Hezekiah deceive you, for he cannot rescue you. ¹⁵And do not let Hezekiah induce you to trust in the LORD, saying, 'The LORD will surely rescue us, and this city will not be handed over to the king of Assyria.' ¹⁶Do not listen to Hezekiah, for thus says the king of Assyria:

Make peace with me
    and surrender to me!
Eat, each of you, from your vine,
    each from your own fig tree.
Drink water, each from your own well,
    ¹⁷until I arrive and take you
    to a land like your own,
A land of grain and wine,
    a land of bread and vineyards.

¹⁸Do not let Hezekiah seduce you by saying, 'The LORD will rescue us.' Has any of the gods of the nations rescued his land from the power of the king of Assyria? ¹⁹Where are the gods of Hamath and Arpad? Where are the gods of Sepharvaim? Where are the gods of Samaria? Have they saved Samaria from my power? ²⁰Who among all the gods of these lands ever rescued their land from my power, that the LORD should save Jerusalem from my power?" ²¹But they remained silent and did not answer at all, for the king's command was, "Do not answer him."

²²Then the master of the palace, Eliakim, son of Hilkiah, Shebna the scribe, and the chancellor Joah, son of Asaph, came to Hezekiah with their garments torn, and reported to him the words of the commander.

☐ ACTS 26

King Agrippa Hears Paul. 26:1 Then Agrippa said to Paul, "You may now speak on your own behalf." So Paul stretched out his hand and began his defense. [2]"I count myself fortunate, King Agrippa, that I am to defend myself before you today against all the charges made against me by the Jews, [3]especially since you are an expert in all the Jewish customs and controversies. And therefore I beg you to listen patiently. [4]My manner of living from my youth, a life spent from the beginning among my people and in Jerusalem, all [the] Jews know. [5]They have known about me from the start, if they are willing to testify, that I have lived my life as a Pharisee, the strictest party of our religion. [6]But now I am standing trial because of my hope in the promise made by God to our ancestors. [7]Our twelve tribes hope to attain to that promise as they fervently worship God day and night; and on account of this hope I am accused by Jews, O king. [8]Why is it thought unbelievable among you that God raises the dead? [9]I myself once thought that I had to do many things against the name of Jesus the Nazorean, [10]and I did so in Jerusalem. I imprisoned many of the holy ones with the authorization I received from the chief priests, and when they were to be put to death I cast my vote against them. [11]Many times, in synagogue after synagogue, I punished them in an attempt to force them to blaspheme; I was so enraged against them that I pursued them even to foreign cities.

[12]"On one such occasion I was traveling to Damascus with the authorization and commission of the chief priests. [13]At midday, along the way, O king, I saw a light from the sky, brighter than the sun, shining around me and my traveling companions. [14]We all fell to the ground and I heard a voice saying to me in Hebrew, 'Saul, Saul, why are you persecuting me? It is hard for you to kick against the goad.' [15]And I said, 'Who are you, sir?' And the Lord replied, 'I am Jesus whom you are persecuting. [16]Get up now, and stand on your feet. I have appeared to you for this purpose, to appoint you as a servant and witness of what you have seen [of me] and what you will be shown. [17]I shall deliver you from this people and from the Gentiles to whom I send you, [18]to open their eyes that they may turn from darkness to light and from the power of Satan to God, so that they may obtain forgiveness of sins and an inheritance among those who have been consecrated by faith in me.'

[19]"And so, King Agrippa, I was not disobedient to the heavenly vision. [20]On the contrary, first to those in Damascus and in Jerusalem and throughout the whole country of Judea, and then to the Gentiles, I preached the need to repent and turn to God, and to do works giving evidence of repentance. [21]That is why the Jews seized me [when I was] in the temple and tried to kill me. [22]But I have enjoyed God's help to this very day, and so I stand here testifying to small and great alike, saying nothing different from what the prophets and Moses foretold, [23]that the Messiah must suffer and that, as the first to rise from the dead, he would proclaim light both to our people and to the Gentiles."

Reactions to Paul's Speech. [24]While Paul was so speaking in his defense, Festus said in a loud voice, "You are mad, Paul; much learning is driving you mad." [25]But Paul replied, "I am not mad, most excellent Festus; I am speaking words of truth and reason. [26]The king knows about these matters and to him I speak boldly, for I cannot believe that [any] of this has escaped his notice; this was not done in a corner. [27]King Agrippa, do you believe the prophets? I know you believe." [28]Then Agrippa said to Paul, "You will soon persuade me to play the Christian." ²⁹Paul replied, "I would pray to God that sooner or later not only you but all who listen to me today might become as I am except for these chains."

³⁰Then the king rose, and with him the governor and Bernice and the others who sat with them. ³¹And after they had withdrawn they said to one another, "This man is doing nothing [at all] that deserves death or imprisonment." ³²And Agrippa said to Festus, "This man could have been set free if he had not appealed to Caesar."

September 21

St. Matthew

There is no reason for surprise that Matthew the tax collector abandoned earthly wealth as soon as the Lord commanded him. Nor should one be amazed that neglecting his wealth, he joined a band of men whose Leader had, on Matthew's assessment, no riches at all. For Matthew understood that Christ, who was summoning him away from earthly possessions, had the everlasting treasures of heaven to give.

— St. Bede the Venerable

☐ ISAIAH 37-39

37:1 When King Hezekiah heard this, he tore his garments, covered himself with sackcloth, and went into the house of the Lord. ²He sent Eliakim, the master of the palace, and Shebna the scribe, and the elders of the priests, covered with sackcloth, to tell the prophet Isaiah, son of Amoz,

³"Thus says Hezekiah:
A day of distress and rebuke,
   a day of disgrace is this day!
Children are due to come forth,
   but the strength to give birth is
      lacking.

⁴Perhaps the Lord, your God, will hear the words of the commander, whom his lord, the king of Assyria, sent to taunt the living God, and will rebuke him for the words which the Lord, your God, has heard. So lift up a prayer for the remnant that is here."

⁵When the servants of King Hezekiah had come to Isaiah, ⁶he said to them: "Tell this to your lord: Thus says the Lord: Do not be frightened by the words you have heard, by which the deputies of the king of Assyria have blasphemed me.

⁷I am putting in him such a spirit
   that when he hears a report
   he will return to his land.
I will make him fall by the sword in
   his land."

⁸When the commander, on his return, heard that the king of Assyria had withdrawn from Lachish, he found him besieging Libnah. ⁹The king of Assyria heard a report: "Tirhakah, king of Ethiopia, has come out to fight against you." Again he sent messengers to Hezekiah to say: ¹⁰"Thus shall you say to Hezekiah, king of Judah: Do not let your God in whom you trust deceive you by saying, 'Jerusalem will not be handed over to the king of Assyria.' ¹¹You, certainly, have heard what the kings of Assyria have done to all the lands: they

put them under the ban! And are you to be delivered? [12]Did the gods of the nations whom my fathers destroyed deliver them—Gozan, Haran, Rezeph, and the Edenites in Telassar? [13]Where are the king of Hamath, the king of Arpad, or a king of the cities Sepharvaim, Hena or Ivvah?"

[14]Hezekiah took the letter from the hand of the messengers and read it; then he went up to the house of the Lord, and spreading it out before the Lord, [15]Hezekiah prayed to the Lord:

[16]"Lord of hosts, God of Israel,
    enthroned on the cherubim!
You alone are God
    over all the kingdoms of the earth.
It is you who made
    the heavens and the earth.
[17]Incline your ear, Lord, and listen!
    open your eyes, Lord, and see!
Hear all the words Sennacherib has sent
    to taunt the living God.
[18]Truly, O Lord,
    the kings of Assyria have laid waste
    the nations and their lands.
[19]They gave their gods to the fire
    —they were not gods at all,
    but the work of human hands—
Wood and stone, they destroyed them.
[20]Therefore, Lord, our God,
    save us from this man's power,
That all the kingdoms of the earth may know
    that you alone, Lord, are God."

[21]Then Isaiah, son of Amoz, sent this message to Hezekiah: "Thus says the Lord, the God of Israel, to whom you have prayed concerning Sennacherib, king of Assyria: I have listened! [22]This is the word the Lord has spoken concerning him:

She despises you, laughs you to scorn,
    the virgin daughter Zion;
Behind you she wags her head,
    daughter Jerusalem.

[23]Whom have you insulted and blasphemed,
    at whom have you raised your voice
And lifted up your eyes on high?
    At the Holy One of Israel!
[24]Through the mouths of your messengers
    you have insulted the Lord when you said:
'With my many chariots I went up
    to the tops of the peaks,
    to the recesses of Lebanon,
To cut down its lofty cedars,
    its choice cypresses;
I reached the farthest shelter,
    the forest ranges.
[25]I myself dug wells
    and drank foreign water;
Drying up all the rivers of Egypt
    beneath the soles of my feet.'
[26]Have you not heard?
    A long time ago I prepared it,
    from days of old I planned it,
Now I have brought it about:
    You are here to reduce
    fortified cities to heaps of ruins,
[27]Their people powerless,
    dismayed and distraught,
They are plants of the field,
    green growth,
    thatch on the rooftops,
Grain scorched by the east wind.
[28]I know when you stand or sit,
    when you come or go,
    and how you rage against me.
[29]Because you rage against me
    and your smugness has reached my ears,
I will put my hook in your nose
    and my bit in your mouth,
And make you leave by the way you came.
[30]This shall be a sign for you:
This year you shall eat the aftergrowth,
    next year, what grows of itself;
But in the third year, sow and reap,
    plant vineyards and eat their fruit!

³¹The remaining survivors of the house
of Judah
 shall again strike root below
  and bear fruit above.
³²For out of Jerusalem shall come a
remnant,
 and from Mount Zion, survivors.
The zeal of the LORD of hosts shall do
 this.

³³Therefore, thus says the LORD about
the king of Assyria:

He shall not come as far as this city,
 nor shoot there an arrow,
 nor confront it with a shield,
Nor cast up a siege-work against it.
³⁴By the way he came he shall leave,
 never coming as far as this city,
 oracle of the LORD.
³⁵I will shield and save this city
 for my own sake and the sake of
  David my servant."

³⁶Then the angel of the LORD went forth
and struck down one hundred and eighty-
five thousand in the Assyrian camp. Early
the next morning, there they were, all those
corpses, dead! ³⁷So Sennacherib, the king
of Assyria, broke camp, departed, returned
home, and stayed in Nineveh.

³⁸When he was worshiping in the temple of his god Nisroch, his sons Adram-
melech and Sharezer struck him down with
the sword and fled into the land of Ararat.
His son Esarhaddon reigned in his place.

Sickness and Recovery of Hezekiah. 38:1
In those days, when Hezekiah was mortally
ill, the prophet Isaiah, son of Amoz, came
and said to him: "Thus says the LORD: Put
your house in order, for you are about to die;
you shall not recover." ²Hezekiah turned his
face to the wall and prayed to the LORD:

³"Ah, LORD, remember how faithfully
and wholeheartedly I conducted myself
in your presence, doing what was good in
your sight!" And Hezekiah wept bitterly.

⁴Then the word of the LORD came to Isaiah: ⁵Go, tell Hezekiah: Thus says the LORD,
the God of your father David: I have heard
your prayer; I have seen your tears. Now I
will add fifteen years to your life. ⁶I will rescue you and this city from the hand of the
king of Assyria; I will be a shield to this city.
⁷This will be the sign for you from the
LORD that the LORD will carry out the
word he has spoken: ⁸See, I will make the
shadow cast by the sun on the stairway to
the terrace of Ahaz go back the ten steps it
has advanced. So the sun came back the ten
steps it had advanced.

Hezekiah's Hymn of Thanksgiving.
⁹The song of Hezekiah, king of Judah, after
he had been sick and had recovered from
his illness:

¹⁰In the noontime of life I said,
 I must depart!
To the gates of Sheol I have been
 consigned
  for the rest of my years.
¹¹I said, I shall see the LORD no more
 in the land of the living.
Nor look on any mortals
 among those who dwell in the world.
¹²My dwelling, like a shepherd's tent,
 is struck down and borne away
  from me;
You have folded up my life, like a
 weaver
 who severs me from the last thread.
From morning to night you make an
 end of me;
¹³I cry out even until the dawn.
Like a lion he breaks all my bones;
 from morning to night you make an
  end of me.
¹⁴Like a swallow I chirp;
 I moan like a dove.
My eyes grow weary looking
 heavenward:
  Lord, I am overwhelmed; go
   security for me!
¹⁵What am I to say or tell him?

He is the one who has done it!
All my sleep has fled,
    because of the bitterness of my soul.
[16]Those live whom the LORD protects;
    yours is the life of my spirit.
You have given me health and restored
    my life!
[17]Peace in place of bitterness!
You have preserved my life
    from the pit of destruction;
Behind your back
    you cast all my sins.
[18]For it is not Sheol that gives you thanks,
    nor death that praises you;
Neither do those who go down into
    the pit
    await your kindness.
[19]The living, the living give you thanks,
    as I do today.
Parents declare to their children,
    O God, your faithfulness.
[20]The LORD is there to save us.
    We shall play our music
In the house of the LORD
    all the days of our life.

[21]Then Isaiah said, "Bring a poultice of figs and apply it to the boil for his recovery." [22]Hezekiah asked, "What is the sign that I shall go up to the house of the LORD?"

Embassy from Merodach-baladan. 39:1 At that time Merodach-baladan, son of Baladan, king of Babylon, sent letters and gifts to Hezekiah, when he heard that he had been sick and had recovered. [2]Hezekiah was pleased at their coming, and then showed the messengers his treasury, the silver and gold, the spices and perfumed oil, his whole armory, and everything in his storerooms; there was nothing in his house or in all his realm that Hezekiah did not show them.

[3]Then Isaiah the prophet came to King Hezekiah and asked him, "What did these men say to you? Where did they come from?" Hezekiah replied, "They came to me from a distant land, from Babylon." [4]He asked, "What did they see in your house?" Hezekiah answered, "They saw everything in my house. There is nothing in my storerooms that I did not show them." [5]Then Isaiah said to Hezekiah, "Hear the word of the LORD of hosts: [6]The time is coming when all that is in your house, everything that your ancestors have stored up until this day, shall be carried off to Babylon; nothing shall be left, says the LORD. [7]Some of your own descendants, your progeny, shall be taken and made attendants in the palace of the king of Babylon." [8]Hezekiah replied to Isaiah, "The word of the LORD which you have spoken is good." For he thought, "There will be peace and stability in my lifetime."

☐ ACTS 27

Departure for Rome. 27:1 When it was decided that we should sail to Italy, they handed Paul and some other prisoners over to a centurion named Julius of the Cohort Augusta. [2]We went on board a ship from Adramyttium bound for ports in the province of Asia and set sail. Aristarchus, a Macedonian from Thessalonica, was with us. [3]On the following day we put in at Sidon where Julius was kind enough to allow Paul to visit his friends who took care of him. [4]From there we put out to sea and sailed around the sheltered side of Cyprus because of the headwinds, [5]and crossing the open sea off the coast of Cilicia and Pamphylia we came to Myra in Lycia.

Storm and Shipwreck. [6]There the centurion found an Alexandrian ship that was sailing to Italy and put us on board. [7]For many days we made little headway, arriving at Cnidus only with difficulty, and because the wind would not permit us to continue our course we sailed for the sheltered side of Crete off Salmone. [8]We sailed past it with difficulty and reached a place called Fair Havens, near which was the city of Lasea.

[9]Much time had now passed and sailing had become hazardous because the time of the fast had already gone by, so Paul warned them, [10]"Men, I can see that this voyage will result in severe damage and heavy loss not only to the cargo and the ship, but also to our lives." [11]The centurion, however, paid more attention to the pilot and to the owner of the ship than to what Paul said. [12]Since the harbor was unfavorably situated for spending the winter, the majority planned to put out to sea from there in the hope of reaching Phoenix, a port in Crete facing west-northwest, there to spend the winter.

[13]A south wind blew gently, and thinking they had attained their objective, they weighed anchor and sailed along close to the coast of Crete. [14]Before long an offshore wind of hurricane force called a "Northeaster" struck. [15]Since the ship was caught up in it and could not head into the wind we gave way and let ourselves be driven. [16]We passed along the sheltered side of an island named Cauda and managed only with difficulty to get the dinghy under control. [17]They hoisted it aboard, then used cables to undergird the ship. Because of their fear that they would run aground on the shoal of Syrtis, they lowered the drift anchor and were carried along in this way. [18]We were being pounded by the storm so violently that the next day they jettisoned some cargo, [19]and on the third day with their own hands they threw even the ship's tackle overboard. [20]Neither the sun nor the stars were visible for many days, and no small storm raged. Finally, all hope of our surviving was taken away.

[21]When many would no longer eat, Paul stood among them and said, "Men, you should have taken my advice and not have set sail from Crete and you would have avoided this disastrous loss. [22]I urge you now to keep up your courage; not one of you will be lost, only the ship. [23]For last night an angel of the God to whom (I) belong and whom I serve stood by me [24]and said, 'Do not be afraid, Paul. You are destined to stand before Caesar; and behold, for your sake, God has granted safety to all who are sailing with you.' [25]Therefore, keep up your courage, men; I trust in God that it will turn out as I have been told. [26]We are destined to run aground on some island."

[27]On the fourteenth night, as we were still being driven about on the Adriatic Sea, toward midnight the sailors began to suspect that they were nearing land. [28]They took soundings and found twenty fathoms; a little farther on, they again took soundings and found fifteen fathoms. [29]Fearing that we would run aground on a rocky coast, they dropped four anchors from the stern and prayed for day to come. [30]The sailors then tried to abandon ship; they lowered the dinghy to the sea on the pretext of going to lay out anchors from the bow. [31]But Paul said to the centurion and the soldiers, "Unless these men stay with the ship, you cannot be saved." [32]So the soldiers cut the ropes of the dinghy and set it adrift.

[33]Until the day began to dawn, Paul kept urging all to take some food. He said, "Today is the fourteenth day that you have been waiting, going hungry and eating nothing. [34]I urge you, therefore, to take some food; it will help you survive. Not a hair of the head of anyone of you will be lost." [35]When he said this, he took bread, gave thanks to God in front of them all, broke it, and began to eat. [36]They were all encouraged, and took some food themselves. [37]In all, there were two hundred seventy-six of us on the ship. [38]After they had eaten enough, they lightened the ship by throwing the wheat into the sea.

[39]When day came they did not recognize the land, but made out a bay with a

beach. They planned to run the ship ashore on it, if they could. ⁴⁰So they cast off the anchors and abandoned them to the sea, and at the same time they unfastened the lines of the rudders, and hoisting the foresail into the wind, they made for the beach. ⁴¹But they struck a sandbar and ran the ship aground. The bow was wedged in and could not be moved, but the stern began to break up under the pounding [of the waves]. ⁴²The soldiers planned to kill the prisoners so that none might swim away and escape, ⁴³but the centurion wanted to save Paul and so kept them from carrying out their plan. He ordered those who could swim to jump overboard first and get to the shore, ⁴⁴and then the rest, some on planks, others on debris from the ship. In this way, all reached shore safely.

September 22

St. Thomas of Villanova

If you want God to hear your prayers, hear the voice of the poor. If you want God to anticipate your wants, provide those of the needy without waiting for them to ask you. Especially anticipate the needs of those who are ashamed to beg. To make them ask for alms is to make them buy it.

— St. Thomas of Villanova

☐ ISAIAH 40-41

Promise of Salvation. 40:1 Comfort,
  give comfort to my people,
  says your God.
²Speak to the heart of Jerusalem, and
    proclaim to her
  that her service has ended,
  that her guilt is expiated,
That she has received from the hand of
    the Lord
  double for all her sins.

³A voice proclaims:
In the wilderness prepare the way of
    the Lord!
  Make straight in the wasteland a
    highway for our God!
⁴Every valley shall be lifted up,
  every mountain and hill made low;
The rugged land shall be a plain,
  the rough country, a broad valley.
⁵Then the glory of the Lord shall be
  revealed,

and all flesh shall see it together;
  for the mouth of the Lord has
    spoken.

⁶A voice says, "Proclaim!"
  I answer, "What shall I proclaim?"
"All flesh is grass,
  and all their loyalty like the flower
    of the field.
⁷The grass withers, the flower wilts,
  when the breath of the Lord blows
    upon it."
"Yes, the people is grass!
  ⁸The grass withers, the flower wilts,
  but the word of our God stands
    forever."

⁹Go up onto a high mountain,
  Zion, herald of good news!
Cry out at the top of your voice,
  Jerusalem, herald of good news!
Cry out, do not fear!

Say to the cities of Judah:
Here is your God!
¹⁰Here comes with power
the Lord God,
who rules by his strong arm;
Here is his reward with him,
his recompense before him.
¹¹Like a shepherd he feeds his flock;
in his arms he gathers the lambs,
Carrying them in his bosom,
leading the ewes with care.

Power of God and the Vanity of Idols.

¹²Who has measured with
his palm the waters,
marked off the heavens with a span,
held in his fingers the dust of the
earth,
weighed the mountains in scales
and the hills in a balance?
¹³Who has directed the spirit of the
Lord,
or instructed him as his counselor?
¹⁴Whom did he consult to gain
knowledge?
Who taught him the path of
judgment,
or showed him the way of
understanding?

¹⁵See, the nations count as a drop in
the bucket,
as a wisp of cloud on the scales;
the coastlands weigh no more than
a speck.
¹⁶Lebanon would not suffice for fuel,
nor its animals be enough for burnt
offerings.
¹⁷Before him all the nations are as
nought,
as nothing and void he counts them.

¹⁸To whom can you liken God?
With what likeness can you
confront him?
¹⁹An idol? An artisan casts it,
the smith plates it with gold,
fits it with silver chains.

²⁰Is mulberry wood the offering?
A skilled artisan picks out
a wood that will not rot,
Seeks to set up for himself
an idol that will not totter.
²¹Do you not know? Have you not
heard?
Was it not told you from the
beginning?
Have you not understood from the
founding of the earth?
²²The one who is enthroned above the
vault of the earth,
its inhabitants like grasshoppers,
Who stretches out the heavens like a veil
and spreads them out like a tent to
dwell in,
²³Who brings princes to nought
and makes the rulers of the earth as
nothing.
²⁴Scarcely are they planted, scarcely
sown,
scarcely their stem rooted in the
earth,
When he breathes upon them and they
wither,
and the stormwind carries them
away like straw.
²⁵To whom can you liken me as an
equal?
says the Holy One.
²⁶Lift up your eyes on high
and see who created these:
He leads out their army and numbers
them,
calling them all by name.
By his great might and the strength of
his power
not one of them is missing!
²⁷Why, O Jacob, do you say,
and declare, O Israel,
"My way is hidden from the Lord,
and my right is disregarded by my
God"?
²⁸Do you not know?
Have you not heard?

The LORD is God from of old,
  creator of the ends of the earth.
He does not faint or grow weary,
  and his knowledge is beyond
    scrutiny.
29He gives power to the faint,
  abundant strength to the weak.
30Though young men faint and grow
    weary,
  and youths stagger and fall,
31They that hope in the LORD will
    renew their strength,
  they will soar on eagles' wings;
They will run and not grow weary,
  walk and not grow faint.

The Liberator of Israel. 41:1 Keep
    silence before me,
    O coastlands;
  let the nations renew their strength.
Let them draw near and speak;
  let us come together for judgment.
2Who has stirred up from the East the
    champion of justice,
  and summoned him to be his
    attendant?
To him he delivers nations
  and subdues kings;
With his sword he reduces them to dust,
  with his bow, to driven straw.
3He pursues them, passing on without
    loss,
  by a path his feet scarcely touch.
4Who has performed these deeds?
  Who has called forth the
    generations from the
    beginning?
I, the LORD, am the first,
  and at the last I am he.
5The coastlands see, and fear;
  the ends of the earth tremble:
  they approach, they come on.
6Each one helps his neighbor,
  one says to the other, "Courage!"
7The woodworker encourages the
    goldsmith,

the one who beats with the hammer,
    him who strikes on the anvil,
Saying of the soldering, "It is good!"
  then fastening it with nails so it will
    not totter.

8But you, Israel, my servant,
  Jacob, whom I have chosen,
  offspring of Abraham my friend—
9You whom I have taken from the ends
    of the earth
  and summoned from its far-off
    places,
To whom I have said, You are my
    servant;
  I chose you, I have not rejected
    you—
10Do not fear: I am with you;
  do not be anxious: I am your God.
I will strengthen you, I will help you,
  I will uphold you with my
    victorious right hand.

11Yes, all shall be put to shame and
    disgrace
  who vent their anger against you;
Those shall be as nothing and perish
  who offer resistance.
12You shall seek but not find
  those who strive against you;
They shall be as nothing at all
  who do battle with you.

13For I am the LORD, your God,
  who grasp your right hand;
It is I who say to you, Do not fear,
  I will help you.
14Do not fear, you worm Jacob,
  you maggot Israel;
I will help you—oracle of the LORD;
  the Holy One of Israel is your
    redeemer.
15I will make of you a threshing
    sledge,
  sharp, new, full of teeth,
To thresh the mountains and crush
    them,
  to make the hills like chaff.

[16]When you winnow them, the wind
  shall carry them off,
    the storm shall scatter them.
But you shall rejoice in the LORD;
  in the Holy One of Israel you shall
    glory.
[17]The afflicted and the needy seek water
  in vain,
    their tongues are parched with thirst.
I, the LORD, will answer them;
  I, the God of Israel, will not forsake
    them.
[18]I will open up rivers on the bare
  heights,
    and fountains in the broad valleys;
I will turn the wilderness into a
  marshland,
    and the dry ground into springs of
      water.
[19]In the wilderness I will plant the
  cedar,
    acacia, myrtle, and olive;
In the wasteland I will set the cypress,
  together with the plane tree and the
    pine,
[20]That all may see and know,
  observe and understand,
That the hand of the LORD has done
  this,
    the Holy One of Israel has
      created it.

[21]Present your case, says the LORD;
  bring forward your arguments, says
    the King of Jacob.
[22]Let them draw near and foretell to us
  what it is that shall happen!

What are the things of long ago?
  Tell us, that we may reflect on them
    and know their outcome;
Or declare to us the things to come,
  [23]tell what is to be in the future,
    that we may know that you are gods!
Do something, good or evil,
  that will put us in awe and in fear.
[24]Why, you are nothing
  and your work is nought;
    to choose you is an abomination!

[25]I have stirred up one from the north,
  and he comes;
    from the east I summon him by
      name;
He shall trample the rulers down like
  mud,
    like a potter treading clay.
[26]Who announced this from the
  beginning, that we might know;
    beforehand, that we might say,
      "True"?
Not one of you foretold it, not one
  spoke;
    not one heard you say,
[27]"The first news for Zion: here they
  come,"
    or, "I will give Jerusalem a herald of
      good news."
[28]When I look, there is not one,
  not one of them to give counsel,
    to make an answer when I question
      them.
[29]Ah, all of them are nothing,
  their works are nought,
    their idols, empty wind!

☐ ACTS 28

Winter in Malta. 28:1 Once we had reached safety we learned that the island was called Malta. [2]The natives showed us extraordinary hospitality; they lit a fire and welcomed all of us because it had begun to rain and was cold. [3]Paul had gathered a bundle of brushwood and was putting it on the fire when a viper, escaping from the heat, fastened on his hand. [4]When the natives saw the snake hanging from his hand, they said to one another, "This man must certainly be a murderer; though he escaped the sea, Justice has not let him remain alive." [5]But he shook the snake off into the fire and suffered no harm. [6]They were expecting him to swell up or suddenly to fall down dead but, after waiting a long time and seeing nothing unusual happen to him, they changed their minds and began to say that he was a god. [7]In the vicinity of that place were lands belonging to a man named Publius, the chief of the island. He welcomed us and received us cordially as his guests for three days. [8]It so happened that the father of Publius was sick with a fever and dysentery. Paul visited him and, after praying, laid his hands on him and healed him. [9]After this had taken place, the rest of the sick on the island came to Paul and were cured. [10]They paid us great honor and when we eventually set sail they brought us the provisions we needed.

Arrival in Rome. [11]Three months later we set sail on a ship that had wintered at the island. It was an Alexandrian ship with the Dioscuri as its figurehead. [12]We put in at Syracuse and stayed there three days, [13]and from there we sailed round the coast and arrived at Rhegium. After a day, a south wind came up and in two days we reached Puteoli. [14]There we found some brothers and were urged to stay with them for seven days. And thus we came to Rome. [15]The brothers from there heard about us and came as far as the Forum of Appius and Three Taverns to meet us. On seeing them, Paul gave thanks to God and took courage. [16]When he entered Rome, Paul was allowed to live by himself, with the soldier who was guarding him.

Testimony to Jews in Rome. [17]Three days later he called together the leaders of the Jews. When they had gathered he said to them, "My brothers, although I had done nothing against our people or our ancestral customs, I was handed over to the Romans as a prisoner from Jerusalem. [18]After trying my case the Romans wanted to release me, because they found nothing against me deserving the death penalty. [19]But when the Jews objected, I was obliged to appeal to Caesar, even though I had no accusation to make against my own nation. [20]This is the reason, then, I have requested to see you and to speak with you, for it is on account of the hope of Israel that I wear these chains." [21]They answered him, "We have received no letters from Judea about you, nor has any of the brothers arrived with a damaging report or rumor about you. [22]But we should like to hear you present your views, for we know that this sect is denounced everywhere."

[23]So they arranged a day with him and came to his lodgings in great numbers. From early morning until evening, he expounded his position to them, bearing witness to the kingdom of God and trying to convince them about Jesus from the law of Moses and the prophets. [24]Some were convinced by what he had said, while others did not believe. [25]Without reaching any agreement among themselves they began to leave; then Paul made one final statement. "Well did the holy Spirit speak to your ancestors through the prophet Isaiah, saying:

[26]'Go to this people and say:
You shall indeed hear but not
    understand.
    You shall indeed look but never see.
[27]Gross is the heart of this people;
    they will not hear with their ears;
    they have closed their eyes,
        so they may not see with their eyes
        and hear with their ears
and understand with their heart and be
    converted,
        and I heal them.'

[28]Let it be known to you that this salvation of God has been sent to the Gentiles; they will listen." [29]

[30]He remained for two full years in his lodgings. He received all who came to him, [31]and with complete assurance and without hindrance he proclaimed the kingdom of God and taught about the Lord Jesus Christ.

September 23

St. Pio of Pietrelcina

Do everything for the love of God and His glory without looking at the outcome of the undertaking. Work is judged, not by its result, but by its intention.

— St. Pio of Pietrelcina

☐ ISAIAH 42-43

The Servant of the Lord. 42:1 Here is
my servant whom I uphold,
my chosen one with whom I am
pleased.
Upon him I have put my spirit;
he shall bring forth justice to the
nations.
[2]He will not cry out, nor shout,
nor make his voice heard in the
street.
[3]A bruised reed he will not break,
and a dimly burning wick he will
not quench.
He will faithfully bring forth justice.
[4]He will not grow dim or be bruised
until he establishes justice on the
earth;
the coastlands will wait for his
teaching.

[5]Thus says God, the Lord,
who created the heavens and
stretched them out,
who spread out the earth and its
produce,
Who gives breath to its people
and spirit to those who walk on it:
[6]I, the Lord, have called you for justice,
I have grasped you by the hand;
I formed you, and set you
as a covenant for the people,
a light for the nations,
[7]To open the eyes of the blind,
to bring out prisoners from
confinement,
and from the dungeon, those who
live in darkness.

[8]I am the Lord, Lord is my name;
my glory I give to no other,
nor my praise to idols.
[9]See, the earlier things have come to
pass,
new ones I now declare;
Before they spring forth
I announce them to you.

The Lord's Purpose for Israel. [10]Sing
to the Lord a new song,
his praise from the ends of the
earth:
Let the sea and what fills it resound,
the coastlands, and those who dwell
in them.
[11]Let the wilderness and its cities cry
out,
the villages where Kedar dwells;
Let the inhabitants of Sela exult,
and shout from the top of the
mountains.
[12]Let them give glory to the Lord,
and utter his praise in the coastlands.

[13]The Lord goes forth like a warrior,
like a man of war he stirs up his fury;
He shouts out his battle cry,
against his enemies he shows his
might:
[14]For a long time I have kept silent,
I have said nothing, holding myself
back;
Now I cry out like a woman in labor,
gasping and panting.
[15]I will lay waste mountains and hills,
all their undergrowth I will dry up;
I will turn the rivers into marshes,

and the marshes I will dry up.
¹⁶I will lead the blind on a way they do
not know;
by paths they do not know I will
guide them.
I will turn darkness into light before
them,
and make crooked ways straight.
These are my promises:
I made them, I will not forsake them.

¹⁷They shall be turned back in utter
shame
who trust in idols;
Who say to molten images,
"You are our gods."
¹⁸You deaf ones, listen,
you blind ones, look and see!
¹⁹Who is blind but my servant,
or deaf like the messenger I send?
Who is blind like the one I restore,
blind like the servant of the Lord?
²⁰You see many things but do not
observe;
ears open, but do not hear.
²¹It was the Lord's will for the sake of
his justice
to make his teaching great and
glorious.

²²This is a people plundered and
despoiled,
all of them trapped in holes,
hidden away in prisons.
They are taken as plunder, with no one
to rescue them,
as spoil, with no one to say, "Give
back!"
²³Who among you will give ear to this,
listen and pay attention from
now on?
²⁴Who was it that gave Jacob to be
despoiled,
Israel to the plunderers?
Was it not the Lord, against whom we
have sinned?
In his ways they refused to walk,
his teaching they would not heed.

²⁵So he poured out wrath upon them,
his anger, and the fury of battle;
It blazed all around them, yet they did
not realize,
it burned them, but they did not
take it to heart.

**Promises of Redemption and
Restoration. 43:1** But now, thus
says the Lord,
who created you, Jacob, and formed
you, Israel:
Do not fear, for I have redeemed you;
I have called you by name: you are
mine.
²When you pass through waters, I will
be with you;
through rivers, you shall not be
swept away.
When you walk through fire, you shall
not be burned,
nor will flames consume you.
³For I, the Lord, am your God,
the Holy One of Israel, your savior.
I give Egypt as ransom for you,
Ethiopia and Seba in exchange for
you.
⁴Because you are precious in my eyes
and honored, and I love you,
I give people in return for you
and nations in exchange for your life.
⁵Fear not, for I am with you;
from the east I will bring back your
offspring,
from the west I will gather you.
⁶I will say to the north: Give them up!
and to the south: Do not hold
them!
Bring back my sons from afar,
and my daughters from the ends of
the earth:
⁷All who are called by my name
I created for my glory;
I formed them, made them.
⁸Lead out the people, blind though
they have eyes,
deaf though they have ears.

⁹Let all the nations gather together,
 let the peoples assemble!
Who among them could have declared
 this,
 or announced to us the earlier
 things?
Let them produce witnesses to prove
 themselves right,
 that one may hear and say, "It is
 true!"
¹⁰You are my witnesses—oracle of the
 LORD—
 my servant whom I have chosen
To know and believe in me
 and understand that I am he.
Before me no god was formed,
 and after me there shall be none.
¹¹I, I am the LORD;
 there is no savior but me.
¹²It is I who declared, who saved,
 who announced, not some strange
 god among you;
You are my witnesses—oracle of the
 LORD.
 I am God,
 ¹³yes, from eternity I am he;
There is none who can deliver from my
 hand:
 I act and who can cancel it?

¹⁴Thus says the LORD, your redeemer,
 the Holy One of Israel:
For your sake I send to Babylon;
 I will bring down all her defenses,
 and the Chaldeans shall cry out in
 lamentation.
¹⁵I am the LORD, your Holy One,
 the creator of Israel, your King.
¹⁶Thus says the LORD,
 who opens a way in the sea,
 a path in the mighty waters,
¹⁷Who leads out chariots and
 horsemen,
 a powerful army,

Till they lie prostrate together, never
 to rise,
 snuffed out, quenched like a wick.
¹⁸Remember not the events of the past,
 the things of long ago consider not;
¹⁹See, I am doing something new!
 Now it springs forth, do you not
 perceive it?
In the wilderness I make a way,
 in the wasteland, rivers.
²⁰Wild beasts honor me,
 jackals and ostriches,
For I put water in the wilderness
 and rivers in the wasteland
 for my chosen people to drink,
²¹The people whom I formed for
 myself,
 that they might recount my praise.

²²Yet you did not call upon me, Jacob,
 for you grew weary of me, Israel.
²³You did not bring me sheep for your
 burnt offerings,
 nor honor me with your sacrifices.
I did not exact from you the service of
 offerings,
 nor weary you for frankincense.
²⁴You did not buy me sweet cane,
 nor did you fill me with the fat of
 your sacrifices;
Instead, you burdened me with your
 sins,
 wearied me with your crimes.
²⁵It is I, I, who wipe out,
 for my own sake, your offenses;
 your sins I remember no more.
²⁶Would you have me remember, have
 us come to trial?
 Speak up, prove your innocence!
²⁷Your first father sinned;
 your spokesmen rebelled against me
²⁸Till I repudiated the holy princes,
 put Jacob under the ban,
 exposed Israel to scorn.

☐ GALATIANS 1

Greeting. 1:1 Paul, an apostle not from human beings nor through a human being but through Jesus Christ and God the Father who raised him from the dead, [2]and all the brothers who are with me, to the churches of Galatia: [3]grace to you and peace from God our Father and the Lord Jesus Christ, [4]who gave himself for our sins that he might rescue us from the present evil age in accord with the will of our God and Father, [5]to whom be glory forever and ever. Amen.

[6]I am amazed that you are so quickly forsaking the one who called you by [the] grace [of Christ] for a different gospel [7](not that there is another). But there are some who are disturbing you and wish to pervert the gospel of Christ. [8]But even if we or an angel from heaven should preach [to you] a gospel other than the one that we preached to you, let that one be accursed! [9]As we have said before, and now I say again, if anyone preaches to you a gospel other than the one that you received, let that one be accursed!

[10]Am I now currying favor with human beings or God? Or am I seeking to please people? If I were still trying to please people, I would not be a slave of Christ.

His Call by Christ. [11]Now I want you to know, brothers, that the gospel preached by me is not of human origin. [12]For I did not receive it from a human being, nor was I taught it, but it came through a revelation of Jesus Christ.

[13]For you heard of my former way of life in Judaism, how I persecuted the church of God beyond measure and tried to destroy it, [14]and progressed in Judaism beyond many of my contemporaries among my race, since I was even more a zealot for my ancestral traditions. [15]But when [God], who from my mother's womb had set me apart and called me through his grace, was pleased [16]to reveal his Son to me, so that I might proclaim him to the Gentiles, I did not immediately consult flesh and blood, [17]nor did I go up to Jerusalem to those who were apostles before me; rather, I went into Arabia and then returned to Damascus.

[18]Then after three years I went up to Jerusalem to confer with Cephas and remained with him for fifteen days. [19]But I did not see any other of the apostles, only James the brother of the Lord. [20](As to what I am writing to you, behold, before God, I am not lying.) [21]Then I went into the regions of Syria and Cilicia. [22]And I was unknown personally to the churches of Judea that are in Christ; [23]they only kept hearing that "the one who once was persecuting us is now preaching the faith he once tried to destroy." [24]So they glorified God because of me.

September 24

Our Lady of Mercy

There is no sinner in the world, however much at enmity with God, who cannot recover God's grace by recourse to Mary, and by asking her assistance.

— St. Bridget of Sweden

☐ ISAIAH 44-45

44:1 Hear then, Jacob, my servant,
Israel, whom I have chosen.
²Thus says the LORD who made you,
your help, who formed you from
the womb:
Do not fear, Jacob, my servant,
Jeshurun, whom I have chosen.
³I will pour out water upon the thirsty
ground,
streams upon the dry land;
I will pour out my spirit upon your
offspring,
my blessing upon your descendants.
⁴They shall spring forth amid grass
like poplars beside flowing waters.
⁵One shall say, "I am the LORD's,"
another shall be named after Jacob,
And this one shall write on his hand,
"The LORD's,"
and receive the name Israel.

The True God and False Gods. ⁶Thus
says the LORD, Israel's king,
its redeemer, the LORD of hosts:
I am the first, I am the last;
there is no God but me.
⁷Who is like me? Let him stand up and
declare,
make it evident, and confront me
with it.
Who of old announced future events?
Let them foretell to us the things to
come.
⁸Do not fear or be troubled.
Did I not announce it to you long ago?
I declared it, and you are my
witnesses.

Is there any God but me?
There is no other Rock, I know of
none!
⁹Those who fashion idols are all
nothing;
their precious works are of no avail.
They are their witnesses:
they see nothing, know nothing,
and so they are put to shame.
¹⁰Who would fashion a god or cast an
idol,
that is of no use?
¹¹Look, all its company will be shamed;
they are artisans, mere human beings!
They all assemble and stand there,
only to cower in shame.
¹²The ironsmith fashions a likeness,
he works it over the coals,
Shaping it with hammers,
working it with his strong arm.
With hunger his strength wanes,
without water, he grows faint.
¹³The woodworker stretches a line,
and marks out a shape with a stylus.
He shapes it with scraping tools,
with a compass measures it off,
Making it the copy of a man,
human display, enthroned in a
shrine.
¹⁴He goes out to cut down cedars,
takes a holm tree or an oak.
He picks out for himself trees of the
forest,
plants a fir, and the rain makes it
grow.
¹⁵It is used for fuel:

with some of the wood he warms
    himself,
  makes a fire and bakes bread.
Yet he makes a god and worships it,
    turns it into an idol and adores it!
¹⁶Half of it he burns in the fire,
    on its embers he roasts meat;
  he eats the roast and is full.
He warms himself and says, "Ah!
    I am warm! I see the flames!"
¹⁷The rest of it he makes into a god,
    an image to worship and adore.
He prays to it and says,
    "Help me! You are my god!"
¹⁸They do not know, do not understand;
    their eyes are too clouded to see,
    their minds, to perceive.
¹⁹He does not think clearly;
    he lacks the wit and knowledge to
      say,
"Half the wood I burned in the fire,
    on its embers I baked bread,
  I roasted meat and ate.
Shall I turn the rest into an
    abomination?
    Shall I worship a block of wood?"
²⁰He is chasing ashes!
A deluded mind has led him astray;
    He cannot save himself,
    does not say, "This thing in my right
      hand—is it not a fraud?"

²¹Remember these things, Jacob,
    Israel, for you are my servant!
I formed you, a servant to me;
    Israel, you shall never be forgotten
      by me:
²²I have brushed away your offenses
    like a cloud,
  your sins like a mist;
    return to me, for I have redeemed
      you.
²³Raise a glad cry, you heavens—the
    Lord has acted!
  Shout, you depths of the earth.
Break forth, mountains, into song,
    forest, with all your trees.

For the Lord has redeemed Jacob,
  shows his glory through Israel.

**Cyrus, Anointed of the Lord, Agent
of Israel's Liberation.** ²⁴Thus
    says the Lord, your redeemer,
  who formed you from the womb:
I am the Lord, who made all things,
    who alone stretched out the
      heavens,
    I spread out the earth by myself.
²⁵I bring to nought the omens of
    babblers,
  make fools of diviners,
Turn back the wise
    and make their knowledge foolish.
²⁶I confirm the words of my servant,
    carry out the plan my messengers
      announce.
I say to Jerusalem, Be inhabited!
    To the cities of Judah, Be rebuilt!
    I will raise up their ruins.
²⁷I say to the deep, Be dry!
    I will dry up your rivers.
²⁸I say of Cyrus, My shepherd!
    He carries out my every wish,
Saying of Jerusalem, "Let it be rebuilt,"
    and of the temple, "Lay its
      foundations."

45:1 Thus says the Lord to his
    anointed, Cyrus,
  whose right hand I grasp,
Subduing nations before him,
    stripping kings of their strength,
Opening doors before him,
    leaving the gates unbarred:
²I will go before you
    and level the mountains;
Bronze doors I will shatter,
    iron bars I will snap.
³I will give you treasures of darkness,
    riches hidden away,
That you may know I am the Lord,
    the God of Israel, who calls you by
      name.
⁴For the sake of Jacob, my servant,

of Israel my chosen one,
I have called you by name,
    giving you a title, though you do
        not know me.
⁵I am the LORD, there is no other,
    there is no God besides me.
It is I who arm you, though you do not
        know me,
    ⁶so that all may know, from the
        rising of the sun
    to its setting, that there is none
        besides me.
I am the LORD, there is no other.
    ⁷I form the light, and create the
        darkness,
I make weal and create woe;
    I, the LORD, do all these things.
⁸Let justice descend, you heavens, like
        dew from above,
    like gentle rain let the clouds drop
        it down.
Let the earth open and salvation bud
        forth;
    let righteousness spring up with
        them!
    I, the LORD, have created this.
⁹Woe to anyone who contends with
        their Maker;
    a potsherd among potsherds of the
        earth!
Shall the clay say to the potter, "What
        are you doing?"
    or, "What you are making has no
        handles"?
¹⁰Woe to anyone who asks a father,
        "What are you begetting?"
    or a woman, "What are you giving
        birth to?"
¹¹Thus says the LORD,
    the Holy One of Israel, his maker:
Do you question me about my children,
    tell me how to treat the work of my
        hands?
¹²It was I who made the earth
    and created the people upon it;
It was my hands that stretched out the
        heavens;

I gave the order to all their host.
¹³It was I who stirred him up for justice;
    all his ways I make level.
He shall rebuild my city
    and let my exiles go free
Without price or payment,
    says the LORD of hosts.

¹⁴Thus says the LORD:
The earnings of Egypt, the gain of
        Ethiopia,
    and the Sabeans, tall of stature,
Shall come over to you and belong to
        you;
    they shall follow you, coming in
        chains.
Before you they shall bow down,
    saying in prayer:
"With you alone is God; and there is
        none other,
    no other god!
¹⁵Truly with you God is hidden,
    the God of Israel, the savior!
¹⁶They are put to shame and disgrace,
        all of them;
    they go in disgrace who carve images.
¹⁷Israel has been saved by the LORD,
    saved forever!
You shall never be put to shame or
        disgrace
    in any future age."

¹⁸For thus says the LORD,
The creator of the heavens,
    who is God,
The designer and maker of the earth
    who established it,
Not as an empty waste did he create it,
    but designing it to be lived in:
I am the LORD, and there is no other.
    ¹⁹I have not spoken in secret
    from some place in the land of
        darkness,
I have not said to the descendants of
        Jacob,
    "Look for me in an empty waste."
I, the LORD, promise justice,
    I declare what is right.

²⁰Come and assemble, gather together,
　　you fugitives from among the nations!
They are without knowledge who bear
　　wooden idols
　　and pray to gods that cannot save.
²¹Come close and declare;
　　let them take counsel together:
Who announced this from the
　　beginning,
　　declared it from of old?
Was it not I, the LORD,
　　besides whom there is no other God?
There is no just and saving God
　　but me.

²²Turn to me and be safe,
　　all you ends of the earth,
　　for I am God; there is no other!
²³By myself I swear,
　　uttering my just decree,
　　a word that will not return:
To me every knee shall bend;
　　by me every tongue shall swear,
²⁴Saying, "Only in the LORD
　　are just deeds and power.
Before him in shame shall come
　　all who vent their anger against him.
²⁵In the LORD all the descendants of
　　Israel
　　shall have vindication and glory."

☐ GALATIANS 2

The Council of Jerusalem. 2:1 Then after fourteen years I again went up to Jerusalem with Barnabas, taking Titus along also. ²I went up in accord with a revelation, and I presented to them the gospel that I preach to the Gentiles—but privately to those of repute—so that I might not be running, or have run, in vain. ³Moreover, not even Titus, who was with me, although he was a Greek, was compelled to be circumcised, ⁴but because of the false brothers secretly brought in, who slipped in to spy on our freedom that we have in Christ Jesus, that they might enslave us— ⁵to them we did not submit even for a moment, so that the truth of the gospel might remain intact for you. ⁶But from those who were reputed to be important (what they once were makes no difference to me; God shows no partiality)—those of repute made me add nothing. ⁷On the contrary, when they saw that I had been entrusted with the gospel to the uncircumcised, just as Peter to the circumcised, ⁸for the one who worked in Peter for an apostolate to the circumcised worked also in me for the Gentiles, ⁹and when they recognized the grace bestowed upon me, James and Cephas and John, who were re-

puted to be pillars, gave me and Barnabas their right hands in partnership, that we should go to the Gentiles and they to the circumcised. ¹⁰Only, we were to be mindful of the poor, which is the very thing I was eager to do.

Peter's Inconsistency at Antioch. ¹¹And when Cephas came to Antioch, I opposed him to his face because he clearly was wrong. ¹²For, until some people came from James, he used to eat with the Gentiles; but when they came, he began to draw back and separated himself, because he was afraid of the circumcised. ¹³And the rest of the Jews [also] acted hypocritically along with him, with the result that even Barnabas was carried away by their hypocrisy. ¹⁴But when I saw that they were not on the right road in line with the truth of the gospel, I said to Cephas in front of all, "If you, though a Jew, are living like a Gentile and not like a Jew, how can you compel the Gentiles to live like Jews?"

Faith and Works. ¹⁵We, who are Jews by nature and not sinners from among the Gentiles, ¹⁶[yet] who know that a person is not justified by works of the law but through faith in Jesus Christ, even we have believed in Christ Jesus that we may be justified by faith in Christ and not by works of the law, because by works of the law no one will be justified. [17]But if, in seeking to be justified in Christ, we ourselves are found to be sinners, is Christ then a minister of sin? Of course not! [18]But if I am building up again those things that I tore down, then I show myself to be a transgressor. [19]For through the law I died to the law, that I might live for God. I have been crucified with Christ; [20]yet I live, no longer I, but Christ lives in me; insofar as I now live in the flesh, I live by faith in the Son of God who has loved me and given himself up for me. [21]I do not nullify the grace of God; for if justification comes through the law, then Christ died for nothing.

September 25

St. Herman Contractus

Hail, Holy Queen, Mother of Mercy, our life, our sweetness, and our hope. Turn, most gracious advocate, your eyes of mercy toward us, and after this our exile show unto us the blessed fruit of your womb, Jesus.

— St. Herman Contractus

☐ ISAIAH 46-47

The Gods of Babylon. 46:1 Bel bows
    down, Nebo stoops,
  their idols set upon beasts and cattle;
They must be borne upon shoulders,
  a load for weary animals.
[2]They stoop and bow down together;
  unable to deliver those who bear
      them,
  they too go into captivity.

[3]Hear me, O house of Jacob,
  all the remnant of the house of Israel,
My burden from the womb,
  whom I have carried since birth.
[4]Even to your old age I am he,
  even when your hair is gray I will
      carry you;
I have done this, and I will lift you up,
  I will carry you to safety.

[5]To whom would you liken me as an
    equal,
  compare me, as though we were alike?
[6]There are those who pour out gold
    from a purse
  and weigh out silver on the scales;
They hire a goldsmith to make it into
    a god
  before which they bow down in
      worship.
[7]They lift it to their shoulders to carry;
  when they set it down, it stays,
  and does not move from the place.
They cry out to it, but it cannot answer;
  it delivers no one from distress.

[8]Remember this and be firm,
  take it to heart, you rebels;
[9]remember the former things, those
    long ago:
I am God, there is no other;
  I am God, there is none like me.
[10]At the beginning I declare the outcome;
  from of old, things not yet done.
I say that my plan shall stand,
  I accomplish my every desire.

¹¹I summon from the east a bird of prey,
    from a distant land, one to carry out
      my plan.
Yes, I have spoken, I will accomplish it;
    I have planned it, and I will do it.
¹²Listen to me, you fainthearted,
    far from the victory of justice:
¹³I am bringing on that victory, it is not
    far off,
    my salvation shall not tarry;
I will put salvation within Zion,
    give to Israel my glory.

The Fall of Babylon. 47:1 Come
    down, sit in the dust,
    virgin daughter Babylon;
Sit on the ground, dethroned,
    daughter of the Chaldeans.
No longer shall you be called
    dainty and delicate.
²Take the millstone and grind flour,
    remove your veil;
Strip off your skirt, bare your legs,
    cross through the streams.
³Your nakedness shall be uncovered,
    and your shame be seen;
I will take vengeance,
    I will yield to no entreaty,
    says ⁴our redeemer,
Whose name is the LORD of hosts,
    the Holy One of Israel.

⁵Go into darkness and sit in silence,
    daughter of the Chaldeans,
No longer shall you be called
    sovereign mistress of kingdoms.
⁶Angry at my people,
    I profaned my heritage
And gave them into your power;
    but you showed them no mercy;
Upon the aged
    you laid a very heavy yoke.
⁷You said, "I shall remain always,
    a sovereign mistress forever!"
You did not take these things to heart,
    but disregarded their outcome.
⁸Now hear this, voluptuous one,

enthroned securely,
Saying in your heart,
    "I, and no one else!
I shall never be a widow,
    bereft of my children"—
⁹Both these things shall come to you
    suddenly, in a single day:
Complete bereavement and widowhood
    shall come upon you
Despite your many sorceries
    and the full power of your spells;
¹⁰Secure in your wickedness,
    you said, "No one sees me."
Your wisdom and your knowledge
    led you astray,
And you said in your heart,
    "I, and no one else!"
¹¹But upon you shall come an evil
    you will not be able to charm away;
Upon you shall fall a disaster
    you cannot ward off.
Upon you shall suddenly come
    a ruin you cannot imagine.

¹²Keep on with your spells
    and your many sorceries,
    at which you toiled from your youth.
Perhaps you can prevail,
    perhaps you can strike terror!
¹³You wore yourself out with so many
    consultations!
Let the astrologers stand forth to
    save you,
The stargazers who forecast at each new
    moon
    what would happen to you.
¹⁴See, they are like stubble,
    fire consumes them;
They cannot deliver themselves
    from the spreading flames.
This is no warming ember,
    no fire to sit before!
¹⁵Thus do your wizards serve you
    with whom you have toiled from
      your youth;
They wander their separate ways,
    with none to save you.

☐ GALATIANS 3

Justification by Faith. 3:1 O stupid Galatians! Who has bewitched you, before whose eyes Jesus Christ was publicly portrayed as crucified? [2]I want to learn only this from you: did you receive the Spirit from works of the law, or from faith in what you heard? [3]Are you so stupid? After beginning with the Spirit, are you now ending with the flesh? [4]Did you experience so many things in vain?—if indeed it was in vain. [5]Does, then, the one who supplies the Spirit to you and works mighty deeds among you do so from works of the law or from faith in what you heard? [6]Thus Abraham "believed God, and it was credited to him as righteousness."

[7]Realize then that it is those who have faith who are children of Abraham. [8]Scripture, which saw in advance that God would justify the Gentiles by faith, foretold the good news to Abraham, saying, "Through you shall all the nations be blessed." [9]Consequently, those who have faith are blessed along with Abraham who had faith. [10]For all who depend on works of the law are under a curse; for it is written, "Cursed be everyone who does not persevere in doing all the things written in the book of the law." [11]And that no one is justified before God by the law is clear, for "the one who is righteous by faith will live." [12]But the law does not depend on faith; rather, "the one who does these things will live by them." [13]Christ ransomed us from the curse of the law by becoming a curse for us, for it is written, "Cursed be everyone who hangs on a tree," [14]that the blessing of Abraham might be extended to the Gentiles through Christ Jesus, so that we might receive the promise of the Spirit through faith.

The Law Did Not Nullify the Promise. [15]Brothers, in human terms I say that no one can annul or amend even a human will once ratified. [16]Now the promises were made to Abraham and to his descendant. It does not say, "And to descendants," as referring to many, but as referring to one, "And to your descendant," who is Christ. [17]This is what I mean: the law, which came four hundred and thirty years afterward, does not annul a covenant previously ratified by God, so as to cancel the promise. [18]For if the inheritance comes from the law, it is no longer from a promise; but God bestowed it on Abraham through a promise.

[19]Why, then, the law? It was added for transgressions, until the descendant came to whom the promise had been made; it was promulgated by angels at the hand of a mediator. [20]Now there is no mediator when only one party is involved, and God is one. [21]Is the law then opposed to the promises [of God]? Of course not! For if a law had been given that could bring life, then righteousness would in reality come from the law. [22]But scripture confined all things under the power of sin, that through faith in Jesus Christ the promise might be given to those who believe.

What Faith Has Brought Us. [23]Before faith came, we were held in custody under law, confined for the faith that was to be revealed. [24]Consequently, the law was our disciplinarian for Christ, that we might be justified by faith. [25]But now that faith has come, we are no longer under a disciplinarian. [26]For through faith you are all children of God in Christ Jesus. [27]For all of you who were baptized into Christ have clothed yourselves with Christ. [28]There is neither Jew nor Greek, there is neither slave nor free person, there is not male and female; for you are all one in Christ Jesus. [29]And if you belong to Christ, then you are Abraham's descendant, heirs according to the promise.

September 26

Sts. Cosmas and Damian

You cannot have God for your Father if you don't have the Church for your mother.

— St. Cyprian of Carthage

☐ ISAIAH 48–49

Exhortations to the Exiles. 48:1 Hear
　　this, house of Jacob
　　called by the name Israel,
　　sprung from the stock of Judah,
You who swear by the name of the Lord
　　and invoke the God of Israel
　　without sincerity, without justice,
²Though you are named after the holy
　　city
　　and rely on the God of Israel,
　　whose name is the Lord of hosts.
³Things of the past I declared long ago,
　　they went forth from my mouth, I
　　　　announced them;
　　then suddenly I took action and
　　　　they came to be.
⁴Because I know that you are stubborn
　　and that your neck is an iron sinew
　　and your forehead bronze,
⁵I declared them to you of old;
　　before they took place I informed
　　　　you,
　　That you might not say, "My idol did
　　　　them,
　　my statue, my molten image
　　　　commanded them."
⁶Now that you have heard, look at all
　　this;
　　must you not admit it?
From now on I announce new things
　　to you,
　　hidden events you never knew.
⁷Now, not from of old, they are created,
　　before today you did not hear of
　　　　them,
　　so that you cannot claim, "I have
　　　　known them."
⁸You never heard, you never knew,

　　they never reached your ears
　　　　beforehand.
Yes, I know you are utterly treacherous,
　　a rebel you were named from the
　　　　womb.
⁹For the sake of my name I restrain my
　　anger,
　　for the sake of my renown I hold it
　　　　back from you,
　　lest I destroy you.
¹⁰See, I refined you, but not like silver;
　　I tested you in the furnace of
　　　　affliction.
¹¹For my sake, for my own sake, I do
　　this;
　　why should my name be profaned?
　　My glory I will not give to another.

¹²Listen to me, Jacob,
　　Israel, whom I called!
I, it is I who am the first,
　　and am I the last.
¹³Yes, my hand laid the foundations of
　　the earth;
　　my right hand spread out the
　　　　heavens.
When I summon them,
　　they stand forth at once.

¹⁴All of you assemble and listen:
　　Who among you declared these
　　　　things?
The one the Lord loves shall do his will
　　against Babylon and the offspring of
　　　　Chaldea.
¹⁵I myself have spoken, I have
　　summoned him,
　　I have brought him, and his way
　　　　succeeds!

¹⁶Come near to me and hear this!
From the beginning I did not speak
in secret;
At the time it happens, I am there:
"Now the Lord God has sent me,
and his spirit."

¹⁷Thus says the LORD, your redeemer,
the Holy One of Israel:
I am the LORD, your God,
teaching you how to prevail,
leading you on the way you
should go.
¹⁸If only you would attend to my
commandments,
your peace would be like a river,
your vindication like the waves of
the sea,
¹⁹Your descendants like the sand,
the offspring of your loins like its
grains,
Their name never cut off
or blotted out from my presence.
²⁰Go forth from Babylon, flee from
Chaldea!
With shouts of joy declare this,
announce it;
Make it known to the ends of the earth,
Say: "The LORD has redeemed his
servant Jacob.
²¹They did not thirst
when he led them through dry lands;
Water from the rock he set flowing for
them;
he cleft the rock, and waters welled
forth."
²²There is no peace for the wicked,
says the LORD.

The Servant of the Lord. 49:1 Hear
me, coastlands,
listen, distant peoples.
Before birth the LORD called me,
from my mother's womb he gave
me my name.
²He made my mouth like a sharp-
edged sword,

concealed me, shielded by his hand.
He made me a sharpened arrow,
in his quiver he hid me.
³He said to me, You are my servant,
in you, Israel, I show my glory.

⁴Though I thought I had toiled in vain,
for nothing and for naught spent
my strength,
Yet my right is with the LORD,
my recompense is with my God.
⁵For now the LORD has spoken
who formed me as his servant from
the womb,
That Jacob may be brought back to him
and Israel gathered to him;
I am honored in the sight of the LORD,
and my God is now my strength!
⁶It is too little, he says, for you to be
my servant,
to raise up the tribes of Jacob,
and restore the survivors of Israel;
I will make you a light to the nations,
that my salvation may reach to the
ends of the earth.
⁷Thus says the LORD,
the redeemer, the Holy One of
Israel,
To the one despised, abhorred by the
nations,
the slave of rulers:
When kings see you, they shall stand
up,
and princes shall bow down
Because of the LORD who is faithful,
the Holy One of Israel who has
chosen you.

**The Liberation and Restoration of
Zion.** ⁸Thus says the LORD:
In a time of favor I answer you,
on the day of salvation I help you;
I form you and set you
as a covenant for the people,
To restore the land
and allot the devastated heritages,
⁹To say to the prisoners: Come out!

To those in darkness: Show
yourselves!
Along the roadways they shall find
pasture,
on every barren height shall their
pastures be.
¹⁰They shall not hunger or thirst;
nor shall scorching wind or sun
strike them;
For he who pities them leads them
and guides them beside springs of
water.
¹¹I will turn all my mountains into
roadway,
and make my highways level.
¹²See, these shall come from afar:
some from the north and the west,
others from the land of Syene.

¹³Sing out, heavens, and rejoice, earth,
break forth into song, you
mountains,
For the LORD comforts his people
and shows mercy to his afflicted.

¹⁴But Zion said, "The LORD has
forsaken me;
my Lord has forgotten me."
¹⁵Can a mother forget her infant,
be without tenderness for the child
of her womb?
Even should she forget,
I will never forget you.
¹⁶See, upon the palms of my hands I
have engraved you;
your walls are ever before me.
¹⁷Your children hasten—
your levelers, your destroyers
go forth from you;
¹⁸Look about and see,
they are all gathering and coming
to you.
As I live—oracle of the LORD—
you shall don them as jewels,
bedeck yourself like a bride.

¹⁹Though you were waste and desolate,
a land of ruins,

Now you shall be too narrow for your
inhabitants,
while those who swallowed you up
will be far away.
²⁰The children of whom you were bereft
shall yet say in your hearing,
"This place is too narrow for me,
make room for me to live in."
²¹You shall ask yourself:
"Who has borne me these,
when I was bereft and barren?
Exiled and repudiated,
who has reared them?
I was left all alone;
where then do these come from?"
²²Thus says the Lord GOD:
See, I will lift up my hand to the nations,
and to the peoples raise my signal;
They shall bring your sons in their
arms,
your daughters shall be carried on
their shoulders.
²³Kings shall be your guardians,
their princesses your nursemaids;
Face to the ground, they shall bow
down before you
and lick the dust at your feet.
Then you shall know that I am the
LORD,
none who hope in me shall be
ashamed.
²⁴Can plunder be taken from a warrior,
or captives rescued from a tyrant?
²⁵Thus says the LORD:
Yes, captives can be taken from a warrior,
and plunder rescued from a tyrant;
Those who oppose you I will oppose,
and your sons I will save.
²⁶I will make your oppressors eat their
own flesh,
and they shall be drunk with their
own blood
as though with new wine.
All flesh shall know
that I, the LORD, am your savior,
your redeemer, the Mighty One of
Jacob.

☐ GALATIANS 4

God's Free Children in Christ. 4:1 I mean that as long as the heir is not of age, he is no different from a slave, although he is the owner of everything, [2]but he is under the supervision of guardians and administrators until the date set by his father. [3]In the same way we also, when we were not of age, were enslaved to the elemental powers of the world. [4]But when the fullness of time had come, God sent his Son, born of a woman, born under the law, [5]to ransom those under the law, so that we might receive adoption. [6]As proof that you are children, God sent the spirit of his Son into our hearts, crying out, "Abba, Father!" [7]So you are no longer a slave but a child, and if a child then also an heir, through God.

Do Not Throw This Freedom Away. [8]At a time when you did not know God, you became slaves to things that by nature are not gods; [9]but now that you have come to know God, or rather to be known by God, how can you turn back again to the weak and destitute elemental powers? Do you want to be slaves to them all over again? [10]You are observing days, months, seasons, and years. [11]I am afraid on your account that perhaps I have labored for you in vain.

Appeal to Former Loyalty. [12]I implore you, brothers, be as I am, because I have also become as you are. You did me no wrong; [13]you know that it was because of a physical illness that I originally preached the gospel to you, [14]and you did not show disdain or contempt because of the trial caused you by my physical condition, but rather you received me as an angel of God, as Christ Jesus. [15]Where now is that blessedness of yours? Indeed, I can testify to you that, if it had been possible, you would have torn out your eyes and given them to me. [16]So now have I become your enemy by telling you the truth? [17]They show interest in you, but not in a good way; they want to isolate you, so that you may show interest in them. [18]Now it is good to be shown interest for good reason at all times, and not only when I am with you. [19]My children, for whom I am again in labor until Christ be formed in you! [20]I would like to be with you now and to change my tone, for I am perplexed because of you.

An Allegory on Christian Freedom. [21]Tell me, you who want to be under the law, do you not listen to the law? [22]For it is written that Abraham had two sons, one by the slave woman and the other by the freeborn woman. [23]The son of the slave woman was born naturally, the son of the freeborn through a promise. [24]Now this is an allegory. These women represent two covenants. One was from Mount Sinai, bearing children for slavery; this is Hagar. [25]Hagar represents Sinai, a mountain in Arabia; it corresponds to the present Jerusalem, for she is in slavery along with her children. [26]But the Jerusalem above is freeborn, and she is our mother. [27]For it is written:

> "Rejoice, you barren one who bore no
>   children;
>   break forth and shout, you who
>   were not in labor;
> for more numerous are the children of
>   the deserted one
>   than of her who has a husband."

[28]Now you, brothers, like Isaac, are children of the promise. [29]But just as then the child of the flesh persecuted the child of the spirit, it is the same now. [30]But what does the scripture say?

> "Drive out the slave woman and her son!
>   For the son of the slave woman shall
>   not share the inheritance with
>   the son"

of the freeborn. [31]Therefore, brothers, we are children not of the slave woman but of the freeborn woman.

September 27

St. Vincent de Paul

Religious rituals may be shadows, but they are the shadows of great truths, and it is essential that they should be carried out with the greatest possible attention.

— St. Vincent de Paul

☐ ISAIAH 50–51

Salvation Through the Lord's Servant. 50:1 Thus says the Lord:

Where is the bill of divorce
  with which I dismissed your
    mother?
Or to which of my creditors
  have I sold you?
It was for your sins you were sold,
  for your rebellions your mother was
    dismissed.

²Why was no one there when I came?
  Why did no one answer when I
    called?
Is my hand too short to ransom?
  Have I not the strength to deliver?
See, with my rebuke I dry up the sea,
  I turn rivers into wilderness;
Their fish rot for lack of water,
  and die of thirst.
³I clothe the heavens in black,
  and make sackcloth their covering.

⁴The Lord God has given me
  a well-trained tongue,
That I might know how to answer the
    weary
  a word that will waken them.
Morning after morning
  he wakens my ear to hear as disciples
    do;
⁵The Lord God opened my ear;
  I did not refuse,
  did not turn away.
⁶I gave my back to those who beat me,
  my cheeks to those who tore out my
    beard;

My face I did not hide
  from insults and spitting.

⁷The Lord God is my help,
  therefore I am not disgraced;
Therefore I have set my face like flint,
  knowing that I shall not be put to
    shame.
⁸He who declares my innocence is near.
  Who will oppose me?
  Let us appear together.
Who will dispute my right?
  Let them confront me.
⁹See, the Lord God is my help;
  who will declare me guilty?
See, they will all wear out like a garment,
  consumed by moths.
¹⁰Who among you fears the Lord,
  heeds his servant's voice?
Whoever walk in darkness,
  without any light,
Yet trust in the name of the Lord
  and rely upon their God!
¹¹All you who kindle flames
  and set flares alight,
Walk by the light of your own fire
  and by the flares you have burnt!
This is your fate from my hand:
  you shall lie down in a place of
    torment.

Exhortation To Trust in the Lord.

51:1 Listen to me, you who
  pursue justice,
  who seek the Lord;
Look to the rock from which you were
  hewn,

to the quarry from which you were
taken;
²Look to Abraham, your father,
and to Sarah, who gave you birth;
Though he was but one when I called
him,
I blessed him and made him many.
³Yes, the LORD shall comfort Zion,
shall comfort all her ruins;
Her wilderness he shall make like Eden,
her wasteland like the garden of the
LORD;
Joy and gladness shall be found in her,
thanksgiving and the sound of song.

⁴Be attentive to me, my people;
my nation, give ear to me.
For teaching shall go forth from me,
and my judgment, as light to the
peoples.
⁵I will make my victory come swiftly;
my salvation shall go forth
and my arm shall judge the nations;
In me the coastlands shall hope,
and my arm they shall await.

⁶Raise your eyes to the heavens,
look at the earth below;
Though the heavens vanish like smoke,
the earth wear out like a garment
and its inhabitants die like flies,
My salvation shall remain forever
and my victory shall always be firm.
⁷Hear me, you who know justice,
you people who have my teaching
at heart;
Do not fear the reproach of others;
remain firm at their revilings.
⁸They shall be like a garment eaten by
moths,
like wool consumed by grubs;
But my victory shall remain forever,
my salvation, for all generations.

⁹Awake, awake, put on strength,
arm of the LORD!
Awake as in the days of old,
in ages long ago!

Was it not you who crushed Rahab,
you who pierced the dragon?
¹⁰Was it not you who dried up the sea,
the waters of the great deep,
You who made the depths of the sea
into a way
for the redeemed to pass through?
¹¹Those whom the LORD has ransomed
will return
and enter Zion singing,
crowned with everlasting joy;
They will meet with joy and gladness,
sorrow and mourning will flee.

¹²I, it is I who comfort you.
Can you then fear mortals who die,
human beings who are just grass,
¹³And forget the LORD, your maker,
who stretched out the heavens
and laid the foundations of earth?
All the day you are in constant dread
of the fury of the oppressor
When he prepares himself to destroy;
but where is the oppressor's fury?

¹⁴The captives shall soon be released;
they shall not die and go down into
the pit,
nor shall they want for bread.
¹⁵For I am the LORD, your God,
who stirs up the sea so that its waves
roar;
the LORD of hosts by name.
¹⁶I have put my words into your mouth,
I covered you, shielded by my hand,
Stretching out the heavens,
laying the foundations of the earth,
saying to Zion: You are my people.

The Cup of the Lord. ¹⁷Wake up,
wake up!
Arise, Jerusalem,
You who drank at the LORD's hand
the cup of his wrath;
Who drained to the dregs
the bowl of staggering!
¹⁸She has no one to guide her
of all the children she bore;

She has no one to take her by the hand,
  of all the children she reared!—

[19]Your misfortunes are double;
  who is there to grieve with you?
Desolation and destruction, famine
  and sword!
  Who is there to comfort you?
[20]Your children lie helpless
  at every street corner
  like antelopes in a net.
They are filled with the wrath of the
  LORD,
  the rebuke of your God.

[21]But now, hear this, afflicted one,

drunk, but not with wine,
[22]Thus says the LORD, your Master,
  your God, who defends his people:
See, I am taking from your hand
  the cup of staggering;
The bowl of my wrath
  you shall no longer drink.
[23]I will put it into the hands of your
  tormentors,
  those who said to you,
  "Bow down, that we may walk over
  you."
So you offered your back like the ground,
  like the street for them to walk on.

☐ GALATIANS 5

The Importance of Faith. 5:1 For freedom Christ set us free; so stand firm and do not submit again to the yoke of slavery.

[2]It is I, Paul, who am telling you that if you have yourselves circumcised, Christ will be of no benefit to you. [3]Once again I declare to every man who has himself circumcised that he is bound to observe the entire law. [4]You are separated from Christ, you who are trying to be justified by law; you have fallen from grace. [5]For through the Spirit, by faith, we await the hope of righteousness. [6]For in Christ Jesus, neither circumcision nor uncircumcision counts for anything, but only faith working through love.

Be Not Misled. [7]You were running well; who hindered you from following [the] truth? [8]That enticement does not come from the one who called you. [9]A little yeast leavens the whole batch of dough. [10]I am confident of you in the Lord that you will not take a different view, and that the one who is troubling you will bear the condemnation, whoever he may be. [11]As for me, brothers, if I am still preaching circumcision, why am I still being persecuted? In that case, the stumbling block of the cross has been abolished. [12]Would that those

who are upsetting you might also castrate themselves!

Freedom for Service. [13]For you were called for freedom, brothers. But do not use this freedom as an opportunity for the flesh; rather, serve one another through love. [14]For the whole law is fulfilled in one statement, namely, "You shall love your neighbor as yourself." [15]But if you go on biting and devouring one another, beware that you are not consumed by one another.

[16]I say, then: live by the Spirit and you will certainly not gratify the desire of the flesh. [17]For the flesh has desires against the Spirit, and the Spirit against the flesh; these are opposed to each other, so that you may not do what you want. [18]But if you are guided by the Spirit, you are not under the law. [19]Now the works of the flesh are obvious: immorality, impurity, licentiousness, [20]idolatry, sorcery, hatreds, rivalry, jealousy, outbursts of fury, acts of selfishness, dissensions, factions, [21]occasions of envy, drinking bouts, orgies, and the like. I warn you, as I warned you before, that those who do such things will not inherit the kingdom of God. [22]In contrast, the fruit of the Spirit is love, joy, peace, patience, kindness, generosity, faithfulness, [23]gentleness,

self-control. Against such there is no law. ²⁴Now those who belong to Christ [Jesus] have crucified their flesh with its passions and desires. ²⁵If we live in the Spirit, let us also follow the Spirit. ²⁶Let us not be con-ceited, provoking one another, envious of one another.

September 28

St. Wenceslaus; St. Lawrence Ruiz and Companions

We ought to make some progress, however little, every day, and show some increase of fervor. We ought to act as if we were at war — as, indeed, we are — and never relax until we have won the victory.

— St. Teresa of Ávila

☐ ISAIAH 52–53

Let Zion Rejoice. 52:1 Awake, awake!
Put on your strength, Zion;
Put on your glorious garments,
Jerusalem, holy city.
Never again shall the uncircumcised
or the unclean enter you.
²Arise, shake off the dust,
sit enthroned, Jerusalem;
Loose the bonds from your neck,
captive daughter Zion!
³For thus says the LORD:
For nothing you were sold,
without money you shall be
redeemed.

⁴For thus says the Lord GOD:
To Egypt long ago my people went
down,
to sojourn there;
Assyria, too, oppressed them for
nought.
⁵But now, what am I to do here?
—oracle of the LORD.
My people have been taken away for
nothing;
their rulers mock, oracle of the
LORD;
constantly, every day, my name is
reviled.

⁶Therefore my people shall know my
name
on that day, that it is I who speaks:
Here I am!
⁷How beautiful upon the mountains
are the feet of the one bringing good
news,
Announcing peace, bearing good news,
announcing salvation, saying to
Zion,
"Your God is King!"

⁸Listen! Your sentinels raise a cry,
together they shout for joy,
For they see directly, before their eyes,
the LORD's return to Zion.
⁹Break out together in song,
O ruins of Jerusalem!
For the LORD has comforted his
people,
has redeemed Jerusalem.
¹⁰The LORD has bared his holy arm
in the sight of all the nations;
All the ends of the earth can see
the salvation of our God.

¹¹Depart, depart, go out from there,
touch nothing unclean!
Out from there! Purify yourselves,

you who carry the vessels of the
LORD.

¹²But not in hurried flight will you go
out,
nor leave in headlong haste,
For the LORD goes before you,
and your rear guard is the God of
Israel.

**Suffering and Triumph of the
Servant of the Lord.** ¹³See, my
servant shall prosper,
he shall be raised high and greatly
exalted.
¹⁴Even as many were amazed at him—
so marred were his features,
beyond that of mortals
his appearance, beyond that of
human beings—
¹⁵So shall he startle many nations,
kings shall stand speechless;
For those who have not been told shall
see,
those who have not heard shall
ponder it.

53:1 Who would believe what we have
heard?
To whom has the arm of the LORD
been revealed?
²He grew up like a sapling before him,
like a shoot from the parched earth;
He had no majestic bearing to catch
our eye,
no beauty to draw us to him.
³He was spurned and avoided by men,
a man of suffering, knowing pain,
Like one from whom you turn your
face,
spurned, and we held him in no
esteem.
⁴Yet it was our pain that he bore,
our sufferings he endured.
We thought of him as stricken,
struck down by God and afflicted,
⁵But he was pierced for our sins,
crushed for our iniquity.

He bore the punishment that makes us
whole,
by his wounds we were healed.
⁶We had all gone astray like sheep,
all following our own way;
But the LORD laid upon him
the guilt of us all.
⁷Though harshly treated, he submitted
and did not open his mouth;
Like a lamb led to slaughter
or a sheep silent before shearers,
he did not open his mouth.
⁸Seized and condemned, he was taken
away.
Who would have thought any more
of his destiny?
For he was cut off from the land of the
living,
struck for the sins of his people.
⁹He was given a grave among the wicked,
a burial place with evildoers,
Though he had done no wrong,
nor was deceit found in his mouth.
¹⁰But it was the LORD's will to crush
him with pain.
By making his life as a reparation
offering,
he shall see his offspring, shall
lengthen his days,
and the LORD's will shall be
accomplished through him.
¹¹Because of his anguish he shall see the
light;
because of his knowledge he shall be
content;
My servant, the just one, shall justify
the many,
their iniquity he shall bear.
¹²Therefore I will give him his portion
among the many,
and he shall divide the spoils with
the mighty,
Because he surrendered himself to death,
was counted among the transgressors,
Bore the sins of many,
and interceded for the transgressors.

☐ GALATIANS 6

Life in the Community of Christ. 6:1 Brothers, even if a person is caught in some transgression, you who are spiritual should correct that one in a gentle spirit, looking to yourself, so that you also may not be tempted. ²Bear one another's burdens, and so you will fulfill the law of Christ. ³For if anyone thinks he is something when he is nothing, he is deluding himself. ⁴Each one must examine his own work, and then he will have reason to boast with regard to himself alone, and not with regard to someone else; ⁵for each will bear his own load.

⁶One who is being instructed in the word should share all good things with his instructor. ⁷Make no mistake: God is not mocked, for a person will reap only what he sows, ⁸because the one who sows for his flesh will reap corruption from the flesh, but the one who sows for the spirit will reap eternal life from the spirit. ⁹Let us not grow tired of doing good, for in due time we shall reap our harvest, if we do not give up. ¹⁰So then, while we have the opportunity, let us do good to all, but especially to those who belong to the family of the faith.

Final Appeal. ¹¹See with what large letters I am writing to you in my own hand! ¹²It is those who want to make a good appearance in the flesh who are trying to compel you to have yourselves circumcised, only that they may not be persecuted for the cross of Christ. ¹³Not even those having themselves circumcised observe the law themselves; they only want you to be circumcised so that they may boast of your flesh. ¹⁴But may I never boast except in the cross of our Lord Jesus Christ, through which the world has been crucified to me, and I to the world. ¹⁵For neither does circumcision mean anything, nor does uncircumcision, but only a new creation. ¹⁶Peace and mercy be to all who follow this rule and to the Israel of God.

¹⁷From now on, let no one make troubles for me; for I bear the marks of Jesus on my body.

¹⁸The grace of our Lord Jesus Christ be with your spirit, brothers. Amen.

September 29

Sts. Michael, Gabriel, and Raphael

The angels are the guardians of the divisions of the earth; they are set over nations and regions allotted to them by their Creator. They govern all our affairs and bring us help. Why? Surely, because they are set over us by God's will and command, and they are always near Him.

— St. John of Damascus

☐ ISAIAH 54–55

The New Zion. 54:1 Raise a glad cry,
you barren one who never bore a
child,

break forth in jubilant song, you
who have never been in labor,
For more numerous are the children of
the deserted wife

than the children of her who has a
husband,
   says the LORD.
²Enlarge the space for your tent,
   spread out your tent cloths
      unsparingly;
   lengthen your ropes and make firm
      your pegs.
³For you shall spread abroad to the
      right and left;
   your descendants shall dispossess
      the nations
   and shall people the deserted cities.

⁴Do not fear, you shall not be put to
      shame;
   do not be discouraged, you shall not
      be disgraced.
For the shame of your youth you shall
      forget,
   the reproach of your widowhood no
      longer remember.
⁵For your husband is your Maker;
   the LORD of hosts is his name,
Your redeemer, the Holy One of Israel,
   called God of all the earth.

⁶The LORD calls you back,
   like a wife forsaken and grieved in
      spirit,
A wife married in youth and then cast
      off,
   says your God.
⁷For a brief moment I abandoned you,
   but with great tenderness I will take
      you back.
⁸In an outburst of wrath, for a moment
   I hid my face from you;
But with enduring love I take pity on
      you,
   says the LORD, your redeemer.

⁹This is for me like the days of Noah:
As I swore then that the waters of Noah
   should never again flood the earth,
So I have sworn now not to be angry
      with you,
   or to rebuke you.

¹⁰Though the mountains fall away
   and the hills be shaken,
My love shall never fall away from you
   nor my covenant of peace be
      shaken,
   says the LORD, who has mercy on you.

¹¹O afflicted one, storm-battered and
      unconsoled,
   I lay your pavements in carnelians,
   your foundations in sapphires;
¹²I will make your battlements of rubies,
   your gates of jewels,
   and all your walls of precious stones.
¹³All your children shall be taught by
      the LORD;
   great shall be the peace of your
      children.
¹⁴In justice shall you be established,
   far from oppression, you shall not
      fear,
   from destruction, it cannot come
      near.
¹⁵If there be an attack, it is not my
      doing;
   whoever attacks shall fall before you.

¹⁶See, I have created the smith
   who blows on the burning coals
   and forges weapons as his work;
It is I also who have created
   the destroyer to work havoc.
¹⁷Every weapon fashioned against you
      shall fail;
   every tongue that brings you to trial
   you shall prove false.

This is the lot of the servants of the
      LORD,
   their vindication from me—oracle
      of the LORD.

An Invitation to Grace. 55:1 All you
   who are thirsty,
   come to the water!
You who have no money,
   come, buy grain and eat;
Come, buy grain without money,

wine and milk without cost!
²Why spend your money for what is
  not bread;
  your wages for what does not satisfy?
Only listen to me, and you shall eat well,
  you shall delight in rich fare.
³Pay attention and come to me;
  listen, that you may have life.
I will make with you an everlasting
  covenant,
  the steadfast loyalty promised to
    David.
⁴As I made him a witness to peoples,
  a leader and commander of peoples,
⁵So shall you summon a nation you
  knew not,
  and a nation that knew you not
    shall run to you,
Because of the LORD, your God,
  the Holy One of Israel, who has
    glorified you.

⁶Seek the LORD while he may be found,
  call upon him while he is near.
⁷Let the wicked forsake their way,
  and sinners their thoughts;
Let them turn to the LORD to find
  mercy;
  to our God, who is generous in
    forgiving.
⁸For my thoughts are not your
  thoughts,

nor are your ways my ways—oracle
  of the LORD.
⁹For as the heavens are higher than the
  earth,
  so are my ways higher than your ways,
  my thoughts higher than your
    thoughts.

¹⁰Yet just as from the heavens
  the rain and snow come down
And do not return there
  till they have watered the earth,
  making it fertile and fruitful,
Giving seed to the one who sows
  and bread to the one who eats,
¹¹So shall my word be
  that goes forth from my mouth;
It shall not return to me empty,
  but shall do what pleases me,
  achieving the end for which I sent it.

¹²Yes, in joy you shall go forth,
  in peace you shall be brought home;
Mountains and hills shall break out in
  song before you,
  all trees of the field shall clap their
    hands.
¹³In place of the thornbush, the cypress
  shall grow,
  instead of nettles, the myrtle.
This shall be to the LORD's renown,
  as an everlasting sign that shall not
    fail.

☐ PHILIPPIANS 1

Greeting. 1:1 Paul and Timothy, slaves of Christ Jesus, to all the holy ones in Christ Jesus who are in Philippi, with the overseers and ministers: ²grace to you and peace from God our Father and the Lord Jesus Christ.

Thanksgiving. ³I give thanks to my God at every remembrance of you, ⁴praying always with joy in my every prayer for all of you, ⁵because of your partnership for the gospel from the first day until now. ⁶I am confident of this, that the one who began a good work in you will continue to complete it until the day of Christ Jesus. ⁷It is right that I should think this way about all of you, because I hold you in my heart, you who are all partners with me in grace, both in my imprisonment and in the defense and confirmation of the gospel. ⁸For God is my witness, how I long for all of you with the affection of Christ Jesus. ⁹And this is my prayer: that your love may increase ever more and more in knowledge and every kind of perception, ¹⁰to discern what is of value, so that you may be pure and blameless for the day of Christ, [11]filled with the fruit of righteousness that comes through Jesus Christ for the glory and praise of God.

[12]I want you to know, brothers, that my situation has turned out rather to advance the gospel, [13]so that my imprisonment has become well known in Christ throughout the whole praetorium and to all the rest, [14]and so that the majority of the brothers, having taken encouragement in the Lord from my imprisonment, dare more than ever to proclaim the word fearlessly.

[15]Of course, some preach Christ from envy and rivalry, others from good will. [16]The latter act out of love, aware that I am here for the defense of the gospel; [17]the former proclaim Christ out of selfish ambition, not from pure motives, thinking that they will cause me trouble in my imprisonment. [18]What difference does it make, as long as in every way, whether in pretense or in truth, Christ is being proclaimed? And in that I rejoice.

Indeed I shall continue to rejoice, [19]for I know that this will result in deliverance for me through your prayers and support from the Spirit of Jesus Christ. [20]My eager expectation and hope is that I shall not be put to shame in any way, but that with all boldness, now as always, Christ will be magnified in my body, whether by life or by death. [21]For to me life is Christ, and death is gain. [22]If I go on living in the flesh, that means fruitful labor for me. And I do not know which I shall choose. [23]I am caught between the two. I long to depart this life and be with Christ, [for] that is far better. [24]Yet that I remain [in] the flesh is more necessary for your benefit. [25]And this I know with confidence, that I shall remain and continue in the service of all of you for your progress and joy in the faith, [26]so that your boasting in Christ Jesus may abound on account of me when I come to you again.

Steadfastness in Faith. [27]Only, conduct yourselves in a way worthy of the gospel of Christ, so that, whether I come and see you or am absent, I may hear news of you, that you are standing firm in one spirit, with one mind struggling together for the faith of the gospel, [28]not intimidated in any way by your opponents. This is proof to them of destruction, but of your salvation. And this is God's doing. [29]For to you has been granted, for the sake of Christ, not only to believe in him but also to suffer for him. [30]Yours is the same struggle as you saw in me and now hear about me.

September 30

St. Jerome

True friendship can harbor no suspicion. A friend must speak to a friend as freely as to his second self.

— St. Jerome

☐ ISAIAH 56-57

Salvation for the Just. 56:1 Thus
  says the LORD:
Observe what is right, do what is just,
  for my salvation is about to come,
  my justice, about to be revealed.

[2]Happy is the one who does this,
  whoever holds fast to it:
Keeping the sabbath without
  profaning it,

keeping one's hand from doing any evil.

Obligations and Promises To Share in the Covenant. [3]The foreigner joined to the LORD should not say, "The LORD will surely exclude me from his people"; Nor should the eunuch say, "See, I am a dry tree." [4]For thus says the LORD: To the eunuchs who keep my sabbaths, who choose what pleases me, and who hold fast to my covenant, [5]I will give them, in my house and within my walls, a monument and a name Better than sons and daughters; an eternal name, which shall not be cut off, will I give them. [6]And foreigners who join themselves to the LORD, to minister to him, To love the name of the LORD, to become his servants— All who keep the sabbath without profaning it and hold fast to my covenant, [7]Them I will bring to my holy mountain and make them joyful in my house of prayer; Their burnt offerings and their sacrifices will be acceptable on my altar, For my house shall be called a house of prayer for all peoples. [8]Oracle of the Lord GOD, who gathers the dispersed of Israel— Others will I gather to them besides those already gathered.

Unworthy Shepherds. [9]All you beasts of the field, come to devour, all you beasts in the forest! [10]All the sentinels of Israel are blind, they are without knowledge; They are all mute dogs,

unable to bark; Dreaming, reclining, loving their sleep. [11]Yes, the dogs have a ravenous appetite; they never know satiety, Shepherds who have no understanding; all have turned their own way, each one covetous for gain: [12]"Come, let me bring wine; let us fill ourselves with strong drink, And tomorrow will be like today, or even greater."

57:1 The just have perished, but no one takes it to heart; The steadfast are swept away, while no one understands. Yet the just are taken away from the presence of evil, [2]and enter into peace; They rest upon their couches, the sincere, who walk in integrity.

An Idolatrous People. [3]But you, draw near, you children of a sorceress, offspring of an adulterer and a prostitute! [4]Against whom do you make sport, against whom do you open wide your mouth, and stick out your tongue? Are you not rebellious children, deceitful offspring— [5]You who burn with lust among the oaks, under every green tree; You who immolate children in the wadies, among the clefts of the rocks? [6]Among the smooth stones of the wadi is your portion, they, they are your allotment; Indeed, you poured out a drink offering to them, and brought up grain offerings. With these things, should I be appeased?

⁷Upon a towering and lofty mountain
  you set up your bed,
  and there you went up to offer
    sacrifice.
⁸Behind the door and the doorpost
  you set up your symbol.
Yes, deserting me, you carried up your
    bedding;
  and spread it wide.
You entered an agreement with them,
  you loved their couch, you gazed
    upon nakedness.
⁹You approached the king with oil,
  and multiplied your perfumes;
You sent your ambassadors far away,
  down even to deepest Sheol.
¹⁰Though worn out with the length of
    your journey,
  you never said, "It is hopeless";
You found your strength revived,
  and so you did not weaken.
¹¹Whom did you dread and fear,
  that you told lies,
And me you did not remember
  nor take to heart?
Am I to keep silent and conceal,
  while you show no fear of me?
¹²I will proclaim your justice
  and your works;
  but they shall not help you.
¹³When you cry out,
  let your collection of idols save you.
All these the wind shall carry off,
  a mere breath shall bear them away;
But whoever takes refuge in me shall
    inherit the land,
  and possess my holy mountain.

□ PHILIPPIANS 2

Plea for Unity and Humility. 2:1 If there
is any encouragement in Christ, any solace
in love, any participation in the Spirit, any
compassion and mercy, ²complete my joy
by being of the same mind, with the same
love, united in heart, thinking one thing.

The Way to Peace for God's People.
¹⁴And I say:
Build up, build up, prepare the way,
  remove every obstacle from my
    people's way.
¹⁵For thus says the high and lofty One,
  the One who dwells forever, whose
    name is holy:
I dwell in a high and holy place,
  but also with the contrite and lowly
    of spirit,
To revive the spirit of the lowly,
  to revive the heart of the crushed.
¹⁶For I will not accuse forever,
  nor always be angry;
For without me their spirit fails,
  the life breath that I have given.
¹⁷Because of their wicked avarice I grew
    angry;
  I struck them, hiding myself from
    them in wrath.
But they turned back, following the way
    of their own heart.
¹⁸I saw their ways,
  but I will heal them.
I will lead them and restore full
    comfort to them
  and to those who mourn for them,
¹⁹creating words of comfort.
Peace! Peace to those who are far and
    near,
  says the LORD; and I will heal them.
²⁰But the wicked are like the tossing sea
  which cannot be still,
Its waters cast up mire and mud.
²¹There is no peace for the wicked!
  says my God.

³Do nothing out of selfishness or out of
vainglory; rather, humbly regard others
as more important than yourselves, ⁴each
looking out not for his own interests, but
[also] everyone for those of others.

[5]Have among yourselves the same attitude that is also yours in Christ Jesus,

[6]Who, though he was in the form of
God,
did not regard equality with God
something to be grasped.
[7]Rather, he emptied himself,
taking the form of a slave,
coming in human likeness;
and found human in appearance,
[8]he humbled himself,
becoming obedient to death, even
death on a cross.
[9]Because of this, God greatly exalted
him
and bestowed on him the name
that is above every name,
[10]that at the name of Jesus
every knee should bend,
of those in heaven and on earth and
under the earth,
[11]and every tongue confess that
Jesus Christ is Lord,
to the glory of God the Father.

Obedience and Service in the World.
[12]So then, my beloved, obedient as you have always been, not only when I am present but all the more now when I am absent, work out your salvation with fear and trembling. [13]For God is the one who, for his good purpose, works in you both to desire and to work. [14]Do everything without grumbling or questioning, [15]that you may be blameless and innocent, children of God without blemish in the midst of a crooked and perverse generation, among whom you shine like lights in the world, [16]as you hold on to the word of life, so that

my boast for the day of Christ may be that I did not run in vain or labor in vain. [17]But, even if I am poured out as a libation upon the sacrificial service of your faith, I rejoice and share my joy with all of you. [18]In the same way you also should rejoice and share your joy with me.

Timothy and Paul. [19]I hope, in the Lord Jesus, to send Timothy to you soon, so that I too may be heartened by hearing news of you. [20]For I have no one comparable to him for genuine interest in whatever concerns you. [21]For they all seek their own interests, not those of Jesus Christ. [22]But you know his worth, how as a child with a father he served along with me in the cause of the gospel. [23]He it is, then, whom I hope to send as soon as I see how things go with me, [24]but I am confident in the Lord that I myself will also come soon.

Epaphroditus. [25]With regard to Epaphroditus, my brother and co-worker and fellow soldier, your messenger and minister in my need, I consider it necessary to send him to you. [26]For he has been longing for all of you and was distressed because you heard that he was ill. [27]He was indeed ill, close to death; but God had mercy on him, not just on him but also on me, so that I might not have sorrow upon sorrow. [28]I send him therefore with the greater eagerness, so that, on seeing him, you may rejoice again, and I may have less anxiety. [29]Welcome him then in the Lord with all joy and hold such people in esteem, [30]because for the sake of the work of Christ he came close to death, risking his life to make up for those services to me that you could not perform.

St. Thérèse of Lisieux

Even a little child can scatter flowers, to scent the throne room with their fragrance; even a little child can sing, in its shrill treble, the great canticle of Love. That will be my life: to scatter flowers — to miss no single opportunity of making some small sacrifice, here by a smiling look, there by a kindly word, always doing the tiniest things right, and doing it for love.

— St. Thérèse of Lisieux

☐ ISAIAH 58-59

Reasons for Judgment. 58:1 Cry out
full-throated and unsparingly,
lift up your voice like a trumpet blast;
Proclaim to my people their
transgression,
to the house of Jacob their sins.
²They seek me day after day,
and desire to know my ways,
Like a nation that has done what is just
and not abandoned the judgment of
their God;
They ask of me just judgments,
they desire to draw near to God.
³"Why do we fast, but you do not see it?
afflict ourselves, but you take no
note?"
See, on your fast day you carry out
your own pursuits,
and drive all your laborers.
⁴See, you fast only to quarrel and fight
and to strike with a wicked fist!
Do not fast as you do today
to make your voice heard on high!
⁵Is this the manner of fasting I would
choose,
a day to afflict oneself?
To bow one's head like a reed,
and lie upon sackcloth and ashes?
Is this what you call a fast,
a day acceptable to the Lord?

**Authentic Fasting That Leads to
Blessing.** ⁶Is this not, rather, the
fast that I choose:

releasing those bound unjustly,
untying the thongs of the yoke;
Setting free the oppressed,
breaking off every yoke?
⁷Is it not sharing your bread with the
hungry,
bringing the afflicted and the
homeless into your house;
Clothing the naked when you see them,
and not turning your back on your
own flesh?
⁸Then your light shall break forth like
the dawn,
and your wound shall quickly be
healed;
Your vindication shall go before you,
and the glory of the Lord shall be
your rear guard.
⁹Then you shall call, and the Lord will
answer,
you shall cry for help, and he will
say: "Here I am!"
If you remove the yoke from among you,
the accusing finger, and malicious
speech;
¹⁰If you lavish your food on the hungry
and satisfy the afflicted;
Then your light shall rise in the
darkness,
and your gloom shall become like
midday;
¹¹Then the Lord will guide you always
and satisfy your thirst in parched
places,

will give strength to your bones
And you shall be like a watered garden,
  like a flowing spring whose waters
    never fail.
¹²Your people shall rebuild the ancient
    ruins;
  the foundations from ages past you
    shall raise up;
"Repairer of the breach," they shall call
    you,
  "Restorer of ruined dwellings."

**Authentic Sabbath Observance That
  Leads to Blessing.** ¹³If you refrain
  from trampling the sabbath,
  from following your own pursuits
    on my holy day;
If you call the sabbath a delight,
  the LORD's holy day glorious;
If you glorify it by not following your
    ways,
  seeking your own interests, or
    pursuing your own affairs—
¹⁴Then you shall delight in the LORD,
  and I will make you ride upon the
    heights of the earth;
I will nourish you with the heritage of
    Jacob, your father,
  for the mouth of the LORD has
    spoken.

Salvation Delayed. 59:1 No, the hand
    of the LORD is not too short to
    save,
  nor his ear too dull to hear.
²Rather, it is your crimes
  that separate you from your God,
It is your sins that make him hide his
    face
  so that he does not hear you.
³For your hands are defiled with blood,
  and your fingers with crime;
Your lips speak falsehood,
  and your tongue utters deceit.
⁴No one brings suit justly,
  no one pleads truthfully;
They trust an empty plea and tell lies;

they conceive mischief and bring
    forth malice.
⁵They hatch adders' eggs,
  and weave spiders' webs:
Whoever eats the eggs will die,
  if one of them is crushed, it will
    hatch a viper;
⁶Their webs cannot serve as clothing,
  nor can they cover themselves with
    their works.
Their works are evil works,
  and deeds of violence are in their
    hands.
⁷Their feet run to evil,
  and they hasten to shed innocent
    blood;
Their thoughts are thoughts of
    wickedness,
  violence and destruction are on
    their highways.
⁸The way of peace they know not,
  and there is no justice on their paths;
Their roads they have made crooked,
  no one who walks in them knows
    peace.

Acknowledgment of Transgressions.
⁹That is why judgment is far
    from us
  and justice does not reach us.
We look for light, but there is darkness;
  for brightness, and we walk in
    gloom!
¹⁰Like those who are blind we grope
    along the wall,
  like people without eyes we feel our
    way.
We stumble at midday as if at twilight,
  among the vigorous, we are like the
    dead.
¹¹Like bears we all growl,
  like doves we moan without ceasing.
We cry out for justice, but it is not there;
  for salvation, but it is far from us.
¹²For our transgressions before you are
    many,
  our sins bear witness against us.

Our transgressions are present to us,
 and our crimes we acknowledge:
[13]Transgressing, and denying the LORD,
 turning back from following our God,
Planning fraud and treachery,
 uttering lying words conceived in
 the heart.
[14]Judgment is turned away,
 and justice stands far off;
For truth stumbles in the public square,
 and uprightness cannot enter.
[15]Fidelity is lacking,
 and whoever turns from evil is
 despoiled.

Divine Intervention. The LORD saw
 this, and was aggrieved
 that there was no justice.
[16]He saw that there was no one,
 was appalled that there was none to
 intervene;
Then his own arm brought about the
 victory,
 and his justice sustained him.
[17]He put on justice as his breastplate,
 victory as a helmet on his head;
He clothed himself with garments of
 vengeance,

wrapped himself in a mantle of zeal.
[18]According to their deeds he repays his
 enemies
 and requites his foes with wrath;
 to the coastlands he renders
 recompense.
[19]Those in the west shall fear the name
 of the LORD,
 and those in the east, his glory,
Coming like a pent-up stream
 driven on by the breath of the LORD.
[20]Then for Zion shall come a redeemer,
 to those in Jacob who turn from
 transgression—oracle of the
 LORD.
[21]This is my covenant with them,
 which I myself have made, says the
 LORD:
My spirit which is upon you
 and my words that I have put in
 your mouth
Shall not depart from your mouth,
 nor from the mouths of your children
Nor the mouths of your children's
 children
 from this time forth and forever,
 says the LORD.

☐ PHILIPPIANS 3

Concluding Admonitions. 3:1 Finally,
my brothers, rejoice in the Lord. Writing
the same things to you is no burden for me
but is a safeguard for you.

Against Legalistic Teachers. [2]Beware
of the dogs! Beware of the evil workers!
Beware of the mutilation! [3]For we are the
circumcision, we who worship through the
Spirit of God, who boast in Christ Jesus
and do not put our confidence in flesh,
[4]although I myself have grounds for confidence even in the flesh.

Paul's Autobiography. If anyone else
thinks he can be confident in flesh, all the
more can I. [5]Circumcised on the eighth

day, of the race of Israel, of the tribe of
Benjamin, a Hebrew of Hebrew parentage,
in observance of the law a Pharisee, [6]in zeal
I persecuted the church, in righteousness
based on the law I was blameless.

Righteousness from God. [7][But] whatever gains I had, these I have come to consider a loss because of Christ. [8]More than
that, I even consider everything as a loss
because of the supreme good of knowing
Christ Jesus my Lord. For his sake I have
accepted the loss of all things and I consider them so much rubbish, that I may
gain Christ [9]and be found in him, not having any righteousness of my own based on

the law but that which comes through faith in Christ, the righteousness from God, depending on faith [10]to know him and the power of his resurrection and [the] sharing of his sufferings by being conformed to his death, [11]if somehow I may attain the resurrection from the dead.

Forward in Christ. [12]It is not that I have already taken hold of it or have already attained perfect maturity, but I continue my pursuit in hope that I may possess it, since I have indeed been taken possession of by Christ [Jesus]. [13]Brothers, I for my part do not consider myself to have taken possession. Just one thing: forgetting what lies behind but straining forward to what lies ahead, [14]I continue my pursuit toward the goal, the prize of God's upward calling, in Christ Jesus. [15]Let us, then, who are "perfectly mature" adopt this attitude. And if you have a different attitude, this too God will reveal to you. [16]Only, with regard to what we have attained, continue on the same course.

Wrong Conduct and Our Goal. [17]Join with others in being imitators of me, brothers, and observe those who thus conduct themselves according to the model you have in us. [18]For many, as I have often told you and now tell you even in tears, conduct themselves as enemies of the cross of Christ. [19]Their end is destruction. Their God is their stomach; their glory is in their "shame." Their minds are occupied with earthly things. [20]But our citizenship is in heaven, and from it we also await a savior, the Lord Jesus Christ. [21]He will change our lowly body to conform with his glorified body by the power that enables him also to bring all things into subjection to himself.

October 2

The Guardian Angels

When tempted, invoke your angel. He is more eager to help you than you are to be helped! Ignore the devil and do not be afraid of him: he trembles and flees at the sight of your guardian angel.
— St. John Bosco

☐ ISAIAH 60-61

The Dawning of Divine Glory for Zion. 60:1 Arise! Shine, for your light has come,
the glory of the Lord has dawned upon you.
[2]Though darkness covers the earth,
and thick clouds, the peoples,
Upon you the Lord will dawn,
and over you his glory will be seen.
[3]Nations shall walk by your light,
kings by the radiance of your dawning.

The Nations Come to Zion. [4]Raise your eyes and look about;

they all gather and come to you—
Your sons from afar,
your daughters in the arms of their nurses.
[5]Then you shall see and be radiant,
your heart shall throb and overflow.
For the riches of the sea shall be poured out before you,
the wealth of nations shall come to you.
[6]Caravans of camels shall cover you,
dromedaries of Midian and Ephah;
All from Sheba shall come
bearing gold and frankincense,

and heralding the praises of the
LORD.

7All the flocks of Kedar shall be
gathered for you,
the rams of Nebaioth shall serve
your needs;
They will be acceptable offerings on
my altar,
and I will glorify my glorious house.
8Who are these that fly along like a
cloud,
like doves to their cotes?
9The vessels of the coastlands are
gathering,
with the ships of Tarshish in the lead,
To bring your children from afar,
their silver and gold with them—
For the name of the LORD, your God,
for the Holy One of Israel who has
glorified you.

Honor and Service for Zion.
10Foreigners shall rebuild your
walls,
their kings shall minister to you;
Though in my wrath I struck you,
yet in my good will I have shown
you mercy.
11Your gates shall stand open constantly;
day and night they shall not be
closed
So that they may bring you the wealth
of nations,
with their kings in the vanguard.
12For the nation or kingdom that will
not serve you shall perish;
such nations shall be utterly
destroyed!
13The glory of Lebanon shall come to
you—
the juniper, the fir, and the cypress
all together—
To bring beauty to my sanctuary,
and glory to the place where I stand.
14The children of your oppressors shall
come,
bowing before you;

All those who despised you,
shall bow low at your feet.
They shall call you "City of the LORD,"
"Zion of the Holy One of Israel."
15No longer forsaken and hated,
with no one passing through,
Now I will make you the pride of the ages,
a joy from generation to generation.
16You shall suck the milk of nations,
and be nursed at royal breasts;
And you shall know that I, the LORD,
am your savior,
your redeemer, the Mighty One of
Jacob.
17Instead of bronze I will bring gold,
instead of iron I will bring silver;
Instead of wood, bronze;
instead of stones, iron.
I will appoint peace your governor,
and justice your ruler.
18No longer shall violence be heard of
in your land,
or plunder and ruin within your
borders.
You shall call your walls "Salvation"
and your gates "Praise."

Eternal Light for Zion. 19No longer
shall the sun
be your light by day,
Nor shall the brightness of the moon
give you light by night;
Rather, the LORD will be your light
forever,
your God will be your glory.
20No longer will your sun set,
or your moon wane;
For the LORD will be your light forever,
and the days of your grieving will
be over.
21Your people will all be just;
for all time they will possess the land;
They are the shoot that I planted,
the work of my hands, that I might
be glorified.
22The least one shall become a clan,
the smallest, a mighty nation;

I, the LORD, will swiftly accomplish
    these things when the time comes.

The Anointed Bearer of Glad Tidings. 61:1 The spirit of the
Lord GOD is upon me,
    because the LORD has anointed me;
He has sent me to bring good news to
    the afflicted,
    to bind up the brokenhearted,
To proclaim liberty to the captives,
    release to the prisoners,
2To announce a year of favor from the
    LORD
    and a day of vindication by our God;
To comfort all who mourn;
    3to place on those who mourn in Zion
    a diadem instead of ashes,
To give them oil of gladness instead of
    mourning,
    a glorious mantle instead of a faint
    spirit.

Restoration and Blessing. They will
    be called oaks of justice,
    the planting of the LORD to show
    his glory.
4They shall rebuild the ancient ruins,
    the former wastes they shall raise up
And restore the desolate cities,
    devastations of generation upon
    generation.
5Strangers shall stand ready to pasture
    your flocks,
    foreigners shall be your farmers and
    vinedressers.
6You yourselves shall be called "Priests
    of the LORD,"
    "Ministers of our God" you shall be
    called.

PHILIPPIANS 4

Live in Concord. 4:1 Therefore, my brothers, whom I love and long for, my joy and crown, in this way stand firm in the Lord, beloved.

You shall eat the wealth of the nations
    and in their riches you will boast.
7Because their shame was twofold
    and disgrace was proclaimed their
    portion,
They will possess twofold in their own
    land;
    everlasting joy shall be theirs.

God's Word of Promise. 8For I, the
    LORD, love justice,
    I hate robbery and wrongdoing;
I will faithfully give them their
    recompense,
    an everlasting covenant I will make
    with them.
9Their offspring shall be renowned
    among the nations,
    and their descendants in the midst
    of the peoples;
All who see them shall acknowledge
    them:
    "They are offspring the LORD has
    blessed."

Thanksgiving for God's Deliverance.
    10I will rejoice heartily in the LORD,
    my being exults in my God;
For he has clothed me with garments
    of salvation,
    and wrapped me in a robe of justice,
Like a bridegroom adorned with a
    diadem,
    as a bride adorns herself with her
    jewels.
11As the earth brings forth its shoots,
    and a garden makes its seeds spring up,
So will the Lord GOD make justice
    spring up,
    and praise before all the nations.

2I urge Euodia and I urge Syntyche to come to a mutual understanding in the Lord. 3Yes, and I ask you also, my true yokemate, to help them, for they have struggled at my side in promoting the gospel, along with Clement and my other co-workers, whose names are in the book of life.

Joy and Peace. [4]Rejoice in the Lord always. I shall say it again: rejoice! [5]Your kindness should be known to all. The Lord is near. [6]Have no anxiety at all, but in everything, by prayer and petition, with thanksgiving, make your requests known to God. [7]Then the peace of God that surpasses all understanding will guard your hearts and minds in Christ Jesus.

[8]Finally, brothers, whatever is true, whatever is honorable, whatever is just, whatever is pure, whatever is lovely, whatever is gracious, if there is any excellence and if there is anything worthy of praise, think about these things. [9]Keep on doing what you have learned and received and heard and seen in me. Then the God of peace will be with you.

[10]I rejoice greatly in the Lord that now at last you revived your concern for me. You were, of course, concerned about me but lacked an opportunity. [11]Not that I say this because of need, for I have learned, in whatever situation I find myself, to be self-sufficient. [12]I know indeed how to live in humble circumstances; I know also how to live with abundance. In every circumstance and in all things I have learned the secret of being well fed and of going hungry, of living in abundance and of being in need. [13]I have the strength for everything through him who empowers me. [14]Still, it was kind of you to share in my distress.

[15]You Philippians indeed know that at the beginning of the gospel, when I left Macedonia, not a single church shared with me in an account of giving and receiving, except you alone. [16]For even when I was at Thessalonica you sent me something for my needs, not only once but more than once. [17]It is not that I am eager for the gift; rather, I am eager for the profit that accrues to your account. [18]I have received full payment and I abound. I am very well supplied because of what I received from you through Epaphroditus, "a fragrant aroma," an acceptable sacrifice, pleasing to God. [19]My God will fully supply whatever you need, in accord with his glorious riches in Christ Jesus. [20]To our God and Father, glory forever and ever. Amen.

[21]Give my greetings to every holy one in Christ Jesus. The brothers who are with me send you their greetings; [22]all the holy ones send you their greetings, especially those of Caesar's household. [23]The grace of the Lord Jesus Christ be with your spirit.

October 3

Blessed Columba Marmion

Wouldn't it indeed be a failure of respect to neglect the divine Guest who awaits us in the tabernacle? He dwells there, really present, He who was present in the crib, at Nazareth, upon the mountains of Judea, at the Last Supper, upon the cross. He is there, the same Christ who healed the lepers, stilled the tempest, and promised to the good thief a place in His kingdom. We find there our Savior, our Friend, our elder Brother, in the fullness of His almighty power, in the ever-fruitful virtue of His mysteries, the infinite superabundance of His merits, and the ineffable mercy of His love.

— BLESSED COLUMBA MARMION

☐ ISAIAH 62–63

A New Name for Zion. 62:1 For Zion's
    sake I will not be silent,
  for Jerusalem's sake I will not keep
    still,
Until her vindication shines forth like
    the dawn
  and her salvation like a burning
    torch.
²Nations shall behold your vindication,
  and all kings your glory;
You shall be called by a new name
  bestowed by the mouth of the LORD.
³You shall be a glorious crown in the
    hand of the LORD,
  a royal diadem in the hand of your
    God.
⁴No more shall you be called "Forsaken,"
  nor your land called "Desolate,"
But you shall be called "My Delight is
    in her,"
  and your land "Espoused."
For the LORD delights in you,
  and your land shall be espoused.
⁵For as a young man marries a virgin,
  your Builder shall marry you;
And as a bridegroom rejoices in his
    bride
  so shall your God rejoice in you.
⁶Upon your walls, Jerusalem,

I have stationed sentinels;
By day and by night,
  they shall never be silent.
You who are to remind the LORD,
  take no rest,
⁷And give him no rest,
  until he re-establishes Jerusalem
And makes it the praise of the earth.

**The Blessings of Salvation for God's
People.** ⁸The LORD has sworn by
    his right hand
  and by his mighty arm:
No more will I give your grain
  as food to your enemies;
Nor shall foreigners drink the wine,
  for which you toiled.
⁹But those who harvest shall eat,
  and praise the LORD;
Those who gather shall drink
  in my holy courts.
¹⁰Pass through, pass through the gates,
  prepare a way for the people;
Build up, build up the highway, clear it
    of stones,
  raise up a standard over the nations.
¹¹The LORD has proclaimed
  to the ends of the earth:
Say to daughter Zion,

"See, your savior comes!
See, his reward is with him,
    his recompense before him."
[12]They shall be called "The Holy People,"
    "The Redeemed of the Lord."
And you shall be called "Cared For,"
    "A City Not Forsaken."

The Divine Warrior. 63:1 Who is this
    that comes from Edom,
    in crimsoned garments, from Bozrah?
Who is this, glorious in his apparel,
    striding in the greatness of his
        strength?
"It is I, I who announce vindication,
    mighty to save."
[2]Why is your apparel red,
    and your garments like one who
        treads the wine press?
[3]"The wine press I have trodden alone,
    and from the peoples no one was
        with me.
I trod them in my anger,
    and trampled them down in my
        wrath;
Their blood spurted on my garments,
    all my apparel I stained.
[4]For a day of vindication was in my
        heart,
    my year for redeeming had come.
[5]I looked about, but there was no one
        to help,
    I was appalled that there was no one
        to lend support;
So my own arm brought me victory
    and my own wrath lent me support.
[6]I trampled down the peoples in my
        anger,
    I made them drunk in my wrath,
    and I poured out their blood upon
        the ground."

Prayer for the Return of God's Favor.
    [7]The loving deeds of the Lord I
        will recall,
    the glorious acts of the Lord,
Because of all the Lord has done for us,

the immense goodness to the house
        of Israel,
Which he has granted according to his
        mercy
    and his many loving deeds.
[8]He said: "They are indeed my people,
    children who are not disloyal."
So he became their savior
    [9]in their every affliction.
It was not an envoy or a messenger,
    but his presence that saved them.
Because of his love and pity
    the Lord redeemed them,
Lifting them up and carrying them
    all the days of old.
[10]But they rebelled
    and grieved his holy spirit;
So he turned to become their enemy,
    and warred against them.

[11]Then they remembered the days of old, of
Moses, his servant:

Where is the one who brought up out
        of the sea
    the shepherd of his flock?
Where is the one who placed in their
        midst
    his holy spirit,
[12]Who guided Moses by the hand,
    with his glorious arm?
Where is the one who divided the
        waters before them—
    winning for himself an everlasting
        renown—
[13]Who guided them through the
        depths,
    like horses in open country?
[14]As cattle going down into the valley,
    they did not stumble.
The spirit of the Lord guided them.
Thus you led your people,
    to make for yourself a glorious name.
[15]Look down from heaven and
        regard us
    from your holy and glorious palace!
Where is your zealous care and your
        might,

your surge of pity?
  Your mercy hold not back!
  [16]For you are our father.
  Were Abraham not to know us,
    nor Israel to acknowledge us,
  You, LORD, are our father,
    our redeemer you are named from
      of old.
  [17]Why do you make us wander, LORD,
    from your ways,
    and harden our hearts so that we do
      not fear you?
  Return for the sake of your servants,

☐ JUDE

Address and Greeting. 1 Jude, a slave of Jesus Christ and brother of James, to those who are called, beloved in God the Father and kept safe for Jesus Christ: [2]may mercy, peace, and love be yours in abundance.

Occasion for Writing. [3]Beloved, although I was making every effort to write to you about our common salvation, I now feel a need to write to encourage you to contend for the faith that was once for all handed down to the holy ones. [4]For there have been some intruders, who long ago were designated for this condemnation, godless persons, who pervert the grace of our God into licentiousness and who deny our only Master and Lord, Jesus Christ.

The False Teachers. [5]I wish to remind you, although you know all things, that [the] Lord who once saved a people from the land of Egypt later destroyed those who did not believe. [6]The angels too, who did not keep to their own domain but deserted their proper dwelling, he has kept in eternal chains, in gloom, for the judgment of the great day. [7]Likewise, Sodom, Gomorrah, and the surrounding towns, which, in the same manner as they, indulged in sexual promiscuity and practiced unnatural vice, serve as an example by undergoing a punishment of eternal fire.

the tribes of your heritage.
  [18]Why have the wicked invaded your
    holy place,
    why have our enemies trampled
      your sanctuary?
  [19]Too long have we been like those you
    do not rule,
    on whom your name is not invoked.
  Oh, that you would rend the heavens
    and come down,
    with the mountains quaking before
      you,

[8]Similarly, these dreamers nevertheless also defile the flesh, scorn lordship, and revile glorious beings. [9]Yet the archangel Michael, when he argued with the devil in a dispute over the body of Moses, did not venture to pronounce a reviling judgment upon him but said, "May the Lord rebuke you!" [10]But these people revile what they do not understand and are destroyed by what they know by nature like irrational animals. [11]Woe to them! They followed the way of Cain, abandoned themselves to Balaam's error for the sake of gain, and perished in the rebellion of Korah. [12]These are blemishes on your love feasts, as they carouse fearlessly and look after themselves. They are waterless clouds blown about by winds, fruitless trees in late autumn, twice dead and uprooted. [13]They are like wild waves of the sea, foaming up their shameless deeds, wandering stars for whom the gloom of darkness has been reserved forever.

[14]Enoch, of the seventh generation from Adam, prophesied also about them when he said, "Behold, the Lord has come with his countless holy ones [15]to execute judgment on all and to convict everyone for all the godless deeds that they committed and for all the harsh words godless sinners have uttered against him." [16]These people are

complainers, disgruntled ones who live by their desires; their mouths utter bombast as they fawn over people to gain advantage. **Exhortations.** [17]But you, beloved, remember the words spoken beforehand by the apostles of our Lord Jesus Christ, [18]for they told you, "In [the] last time there will be scoffers who will live according to their own godless desires." [19]These are the ones who cause divisions; they live on the natural plane, devoid of the Spirit. [20]But you, beloved, build yourselves up in your most holy faith; pray in the holy Spirit. [21]Keep yourselves in the love of God and wait for the mercy of our Lord Jesus Christ that leads to eternal life. [22]On those who waver, have mercy; [23]save others by snatching them out of the fire; on others have mercy with fear, abhorring even the outer garment stained by the flesh.

Doxology. [24]To the one who is able to keep you from stumbling and to present you unblemished and exultant, in the presence of his glory, [25]to the only God, our savior, through Jesus Christ our Lord be glory, majesty, power, and authority from ages past, now, and for ages to come. Amen.

October 4

St. Francis of Assisi

Sanctify yourself, and you will sanctify society.

— St. Francis of Assisi

☐ ISAIAH 64-66

64:1 As when brushwood is set ablaze,
  or fire makes the water boil!
Then your name would be made
  known to your enemies
  and the nations would tremble
  before you,
[2]While you worked awesome deeds we
  could not hope for,
[3]such as had not been heard of from
  of old.
No ear has ever heard, no eye ever seen,
  any God but you
  working such deeds for those who
  wait for him.
[4]Would that you might meet us doing
  right,
  that we might be mindful of you in
  our ways!
Indeed, you are angry; we have sinned,
  we have acted wickedly.
[5]We have all become like something
  unclean,

all our just deeds are like polluted
  rags;
We have all withered like leaves,
  and our crimes carry us away like
  the wind.
[6]There are none who call upon your
  name,
  none who rouse themselves to take
  hold of you;
For you have hidden your face from us
  and have delivered us up to our
  crimes.

A Final Plea. [7]Yet, Lord, you are our
  father;
  we are the clay and you our potter:
  we are all the work of your hand.
[8]Do not be so very angry, Lord,
  do not remember our crimes forever;
  look upon us, who are all your people!
[9]Your holy cities have become a
  wilderness;

Zion has become wilderness,
Jerusalem desolation!
¹⁰Our holy and glorious house
in which our ancestors praised you
Has been burned with fire;
all that was dear to us is laid waste.
¹¹Can you hold back, LORD, after all
this?
Can you remain silent, and afflict us
so severely?

65:1 I was ready to respond to those
who did not ask,
to be found by those who did not
seek me.
I said: Here I am! Here I am!
To a nation that did not invoke my
name.
²I have stretched out my hands all day
to a rebellious people,
Who walk in a way that is not good,
following their own designs;
³A people who provoke me
continually to my face,
Offering sacrifices in gardens
and burning incense on bricks,
⁴Sitting in tombs
and spending the night in caves,
Eating the flesh of pigs,
with broth of unclean meat in their
dishes;
⁵Crying out, "Hold back,
do not come near me, lest I render
you holy!"
These things are smoke in my nostrils,
a fire that burns all the day.
⁶See, it stands written before me;
I will not remain quiet until I have
repaid in full
⁷Your crimes and the crimes of your
ancestors as well,
says the LORD.
Since they burned incense on the
mountains,
and insulted me on the hills,
I will at once pour out in full measure
their recompense into their laps.

Fate of the Just and Unjust in Israel. ⁸Thus says the LORD:
As when the juice is pressed from a
cluster,
and someone says, "Do not destroy it,
for there is still good in it,"
So will I do for the sake of my servants:
I will not destroy them all.
⁹From Jacob I will bring forth offspring,
from Judah, those who are to
possess my mountains;
My chosen ones shall possess the land,
my servants shall dwell there.
¹⁰Sharon shall become a pasture for the
flocks,
the Valley of Achor a resting place
for the cattle,
for my people who have sought me.
¹¹But you who forsake the LORD,
who forget my holy mountain,
Who spread a table for Fortune
and fill cups of mixed wine for
Destiny,
¹²You I will destine for the sword;
you shall all bow down for slaughter;
Because I called and you did not answer,
I spoke and you did not listen,
But did what is evil in my sight
and things I do not delight in, you
chose,
¹³therefore thus says the Lord GOD:
My servants shall eat,
but you shall go hungry;
My servants shall drink,
but you shall be thirsty;
My servants shall rejoice,
but you shall be put to shame;
¹⁴My servants shall shout
for joy of heart,
But you shall cry out for grief of heart,
and howl for anguish of spirit.
¹⁵You will leave your name for a curse
to my chosen ones
when the Lord GOD slays you,
and calls his servants by another
name.
¹⁶Whoever invokes a blessing in the land

shall bless by the God of truth;
Whoever takes an oath in the land
    shall swear by the God of truth;
For the hardships of the past shall be
    forgotten
    and hidden from my eyes.

A World Renewed. [17]See, I am creating
    new heavens
    and a new earth;
The former things shall not be
    remembered
    nor come to mind.
[18]Instead, shout for joy and be glad
    forever
    in what I am creating.
Indeed, I am creating Jerusalem to be
    a joy
    and its people to be a delight;
[19]I will rejoice in Jerusalem
    and exult in my people.
No longer shall the sound of weeping
    be heard there,
    or the sound of crying;
[20]No longer shall there be in it
    an infant who lives but a few days,
    nor anyone who does not live a full
        lifetime;
One who dies at a hundred years shall
    be considered a youth,
    and one who falls short of a
        hundred shall be thought
        accursed.
[21]They shall build houses and live in
    them,
    they shall plant vineyards and eat
        their fruit;
[22]They shall not build and others live
    there;
    they shall not plant and others eat.
As the years of a tree, so the years of
    my people;
    and my chosen ones shall long enjoy
    the work of their hands.
[23]They shall not toil in vain,
    nor beget children for sudden
        destruction;

For they shall be a people blessed by
    the LORD
    and their descendants with them.
[24]Before they call, I will answer;
    while they are yet speaking, I will
        hear.
[25]The wolf and the lamb shall pasture
    together,
    and the lion shall eat hay like the
        ox—
    but the serpent's food shall be dust.
None shall harm or destroy
    on all my holy mountain, says the
        LORD.

True and False Worship. 66:1 Thus
    says the LORD:
The heavens are my throne,
    the earth, my footstool.
What house can you build for me?
    Where is the place of my rest?
[2]My hand made all these things
    when all of them came to be—
    oracle of the LORD.
This is the one whom I approve:
    the afflicted one, crushed in spirit,
    who trembles at my word.
[3]The one slaughtering an ox, striking
    a man,
    sacrificing a lamb, breaking a dog's
        neck,
Making an offering of pig's blood,
    burning incense, honoring an
        idol—
These have chosen their own ways,
    and taken pleasure in their own
        abominations.
[4]I in turn will choose affliction for
    them
    and bring upon them what they
        fear.
Because when I called, no one answered,
    when I spoke, no one listened.
Because they did what was evil in my
    sight,
    and things I do not delight in they
        chose,

⁵Hear the word of the Lord,
  you who tremble at his word!
Your kin who hate you
  and cast you out because of my
    name say,
"May the Lord show his glory,
  that we may see your joy";
  but they shall be put to shame.
⁶A voice roaring from the city,
  a voice from the temple;
The voice of the Lord
  rendering recompense to his enemies!

**Blessings of Prosperity and
  Consolation.** ⁷Before she is in
    labor,
  she gives birth;
Before her pangs come upon her,
  she delivers a male child.
⁸Who ever heard of such a thing,
  or who ever saw the like?
Can a land be brought forth in one day,
  or a nation be born in a single
    moment?
Yet Zion was scarcely in labor
  when she bore her children.
⁹Shall I bring a mother to the point of
    birth,
  and yet not let her child be born?
    says the Lord.
Or shall I who bring to birth
  yet close her womb? says your God.
¹⁰Rejoice with Jerusalem and be glad
    because of her,
  all you who love her;
Rejoice with her in her joy,
  all you who mourn over her—
¹¹So that you may nurse and be
    satisfied
  from her consoling breast;
That you may drink with delight
  at her abundant breasts!
¹²For thus says the Lord:
I will spread prosperity over her like a
    river,
  like an overflowing torrent,
  the wealth of nations.

You shall nurse, carried in her arms,
  cradled upon her knees;
¹³As a mother comforts her child,
  so I will comfort you;
  in Jerusalem you shall find your
    comfort.
¹⁴You will see and your heart shall exult,
  and your bodies shall flourish like
    the grass;
The Lord's power shall be revealed to
    his servants,
  but to his enemies, his wrath.
¹⁵For see, the Lord will come in fire,
  his chariots like the stormwind;
To wreak his anger in burning rage
  and his rebuke in fiery flames.
¹⁶For with fire the Lord shall enter
    into judgment,
  and, with his sword, against all
    flesh;
Those slain by the Lord shall be
    many.

¹⁷Those who sanctify and purify themselves to go into the gardens, following one who stands within, eating pig's flesh, abominable things, and mice, shall all together come to an end, with their deeds and purposes—oracle of the Lord.

God Gathers the Nations. ¹⁸I am coming to gather all nations and tongues; they shall come and see my glory. ¹⁹I will place a sign among them; from them I will send survivors to the nations: to Tarshish, Put and Lud, Mosoch, Tubal and Javan, to the distant coastlands which have never heard of my fame, or seen my glory; and they shall proclaim my glory among the nations. ²⁰They shall bring all your kin from all the nations as an offering to the Lord, on horses and in chariots, in carts, upon mules and dromedaries, to Jerusalem, my holy mountain, says the Lord, just as the Israelites bring their grain offering in a clean vessel to the house of the Lord. ²¹Some of these I will take as priests and Levites, says the Lord.

[22]Just as the new heavens and the new
    earth
  which I am making
  Shall endure before me—oracle of the
    LORD—
    so shall your descendants and your
      name endure.
[23]From new moon to new moon,
  and from sabbath to sabbath,
All flesh shall come to worship
  before me, says the LORD.
[24]They shall go out and see the corpses
  of the people who rebelled against
    me;
For their worm shall not die,
  their fire shall not be extinguished;
  and they shall be an abhorrence to
    all flesh.

☐ EPHESIANS 1

Greeting. 1:1 Paul, an apostle of Christ Jesus by the will of God, to the holy ones who are [in Ephesus] faithful in Christ Jesus: [2]grace to you and peace from God our Father and the Lord Jesus Christ.

The Father's Plan of Salvation. [3]Blessed be the God and Father of our Lord Jesus Christ, who has blessed us in Christ with every spiritual blessing in the heavens, [4]as he chose us in him, before the foundation of the world, to be holy and without blemish before him. In love [5]he destined us for adoption to himself through Jesus Christ, in accord with the favor of his will, [6]for the praise of the glory of his grace that he granted us in the beloved.

Fulfillment through Christ. [7]In him we have redemption by his blood, the forgiveness of transgressions, in accord with the riches of his grace [8]that he lavished upon us. In all wisdom and insight, [9]he has made known to us the mystery of his will in accord with his favor that he set forth in him [10]as a plan for the fullness of times, to sum up all things in Christ, in heaven and on earth.

Inheritance through the Spirit. [11]In him we were also chosen, destined in accord with the purpose of the One who accomplishes all things according to the intention of his will, [12]so that we might exist for the praise of his glory, we who first hoped in Christ. [13]In him you also, who have heard the word of truth, the gospel of your salvation, and have believed in him, were sealed with the promised holy Spirit, [14]which is the first installment of our inheritance toward redemption as God's possession, to the praise of his glory.

The Church as Christ's Body. [15]Therefore, I, too, hearing of your faith in the Lord Jesus and of your love for all the holy ones, [16]do not cease giving thanks for you, remembering you in my prayers, [17]that the God of our Lord Jesus Christ, the Father of glory, may give you a spirit of wisdom and revelation resulting in knowledge of him. [18]May the eyes of [your] hearts be enlightened, that you may know what is the hope that belongs to his call, what are the riches of glory in his inheritance among the holy ones, [19]and what is the surpassing greatness of his power for us who believe, in accord with the exercise of his great might, [20]which he worked in Christ, raising him from the dead and seating him at his right hand in the heavens, [21]far above every principality, authority, power, and dominion, and every name that is named not only in this age but also in the one to come. [22]And he put all things beneath his feet and gave him as head over all things to the church, [23]which is his body, the fullness of the one who fills all things in every way.

October 5

St. Faustina Kowalska

I want to be completely transformed into Your mercy and to be Your living reflection, O Lord. May the greatest of all divine attributes, that of Your unfathomable mercy, pass through my heart and soul to my neighbor.

— St. Faustina Kowalska

☐ JEREMIAH 1-2

1:1 The words of Jeremiah, son of Hilkiah, one of the priests from Anathoth, in the land of Benjamin. ²The word of the LORD came to him in the days of Josiah, son of Amon, king of Judah, in the thirteenth year of his reign, ³and again in the days of Jehoiakim, son of Josiah, king of Judah, until the end of the eleventh year of Zedekiah, son of Josiah, king of Judah—down to the exile of Jerusalem, in the fifth month.

Call of Jeremiah. ⁴The word of the
LORD came to me:
⁵Before I formed you in the womb I
knew you,
before you were born I dedicated you,
a prophet to the nations I appointed
you.
⁶"Ah, Lord GOD!" I said,
"I do not know how to speak. I am
too young!"
⁷But the LORD answered me,
Do not say, "I am too young."
To whomever I send you, you
shall go;
whatever I command you, you shall
speak.
⁸Do not be afraid of them,
for I am with you to deliver you—
oracle of the LORD.

⁹Then the LORD extended his hand and touched my mouth, saying to me,

See, I place my words in your mouth!
¹⁰Today I appoint you
over nations and over kingdoms,

To uproot and to tear down,
to destroy and to demolish,
to build and to plant.

¹¹The word of the LORD came to me: What do you see, Jeremiah? "I see a branch of the almond tree," I replied. ¹²Then the LORD said to me: You have seen well, for I am watching over my word to carry it out. ¹³A second time the word of the LORD came to me: What do you see? I replied, "I see a boiling kettle whose mouth is tipped away from the north."

¹⁴The LORD said to me, And from the north evil will pour out over all who dwell in the land.

¹⁵Look, I am summoning
all the kingdoms of the north—
oracle of the LORD—
Each king shall come and set up his
throne
in the gateways of Jerusalem,
Against all its surrounding walls
and against all the cities of Judah.
¹⁶I will pronounce my sentence against
them
for all their wickedness in forsaking
me,
In burning incense to other gods,
in bowing down to the works of
their hands.
¹⁷But you, prepare yourself;
stand up and tell them
all that I command you.
Do not be terrified on account of them,
or I will terrify you before them;

¹⁸For I am the one who today
 makes you a fortified city,
A pillar of iron, a wall of bronze,
 against the whole land:
Against Judah's kings and princes,
 its priests and the people of the
  land.
¹⁹They will fight against you, but not
 prevail over you,
 for I am with you to deliver you—
  oracle of the LORD.

Infidelity of Israel. 2:1 The word of the
LORD came to me: ²Go, cry out this message for Jerusalem to hear!

I remember the devotion of your
 youth,
 how you loved me as a bride,
Following me in the wilderness,
 in a land unsown.
³Israel was dedicated to the LORD,
 the first fruits of his harvest;
All who ate of it were held guilty,
 evil befell them—oracle of the
  LORD.
⁴Listen to the word of the LORD, house
 of Jacob!
 All you clans of the house of Israel,
⁵thus says the LORD:
What fault did your ancestors find in
 me
 that they withdrew from me,
Went after emptiness,
 and became empty themselves?
⁶They did not ask, "Where is the LORD
 who brought us up from the land of
  Egypt,
Who led us through the wilderness,
 through a land of wastes and
  ravines,
A land of drought and darkness,
 a land which no one crosses,
 where no one dwells?"
⁷I brought you into the garden land
 to eat its fine fruits,
But you entered and defiled my land,

you turned my heritage into an
 abomination.
⁸The priests did not ask,
 "Where is the LORD?"
The experts in the law did not
 know me:
 the shepherds rebelled against me.
The prophets prophesied by Baal,
 and went after useless idols.
⁹Therefore I will again accuse you—
 oracle of the LORD—
 even your children's children I will
  accuse.
¹⁰Cross to the coast of Cyprus and see,
 send to Kedar and carefully inquire:
 Where has anything like this been
  done?
¹¹Does any other nation change its
 gods?—
 even though they are not gods at all!
But my people have changed their
 glory
 for useless things.
¹²Be horrified at this, heavens;
 shudder, be appalled—oracle of the
  LORD.
¹³Two evils my people have done:
 they have forsaken me, the source of
  living waters;
They have dug themselves cisterns,
 broken cisterns that cannot hold
  water.
¹⁴Is Israel a slave, a house-born servant?
 Why then has he become plunder?
¹⁵Against him lions roar,
 they raise their voices.
They have turned his land into a waste;
 his cities are charred ruins, without
  an inhabitant.
¹⁶Yes, the people of Memphis and
 Tahpanhes
 shave the crown of your head.
¹⁷Has not forsaking the LORD, your
 God,
 done this to you?
¹⁸And now, why go to Egypt,
 to drink the waters of the Nile?

Why go to Assyria,
    to drink the waters of the River?
¹⁹Your own wickedness chastises you,
    your own infidelities punish you.
Know then, and see, how evil and
        bitter
    is your forsaking the LORD, your
        God,
And your showing no fear of me,
    oracle of the Lord, the GOD of
        hosts.
²⁰Long ago you broke your yoke,
    you tore off your bonds.
    You said, "I will not serve."
On every high hill, under every green
        tree,
    you sprawled and served as a
        prostitute.
²¹But I had planted you as a choice vine,
    all pedigreed stock;
How could you turn out so obnoxious
        to me,
    a spurious vine?
²²Even if you scour it with lye,
    and use much soap,
The stain of your guilt is still before me,
    oracle of the Lord GOD.
²³How can you say, "I am not defiled,
    I have not pursued the Baals"?
Consider your conduct in the Valley,
    recall what you have done:
A skittish young camel,
    running back and forth,
²⁴a wild donkey bred in the
        wilderness,
Sniffing the wind in her desire—
    who can restrain her lust?
None seeking her need tire themselves;
    in her time they will find her.
²⁵Stop wearing out your feet
    and parching your throat!
But you say, "No use! No!
    How I love these strangers,
    after them I must go."
²⁶As the thief is shamed when caught,
    so shall the house of Israel be
        shamed:

They, their kings, their princes,
    their priests and their prophets;
²⁷They say to a piece of wood, "You are
        my father,"
    and to a stone, "You gave me birth."
They turn their backs to me, not their
        faces;
    yet in their time of trouble they cry
        out,
    "Rise up and save us!"
²⁸Where are the gods you made for
        yourselves?
Let them rise up!
Will they save you in your time of
        trouble?
For as numerous as your cities
    are your gods, O Judah!
And as many as the streets of Jerusalem
    are the altars you have set up for
        Baal.
²⁹Why are you arguing with me?
    You have all rebelled against me—
        oracle of the LORD.
³⁰In vain I struck your children;
    correction they did not take.
Your sword devoured your prophets
    like a ravening lion.
³¹You people of this generation,
    consider the word of the Lord:
Have I become a wilderness to Israel,
    a land of gloom?
Why then do my people say, "We have
        moved on,
    we will not come to you any more"?
³²Does a young woman forget her
        jewelry,
    a bride her sash?
Yet my people have forgotten me
    days without number.
³³How well you pick your way
    when seeking love!
In your wickedness,
    you have gone by ways unclean!
³⁴On your clothing is
    the life-blood of the innocent,
    you did not find them committing
        burglary;

[35]Nonetheless you say, "I am innocent;
  at least, his anger is turned away
    from me."
Listen! I will judge you
  on that word of yours, "I have not
    sinned."
[36]How frivolous you have become
  in changing your course!

By Egypt you will be shamed,
  just as you were shamed by
    Assyria.
[37]From there too you will go out,
  your hands upon your head;
For the LORD has rejected those in
  whom you trust,
  with them you will have no success.

☐ EPHESIANS 2

Generosity of God's Plan. 2:1 You were dead in your transgressions and sins [2]in which you once lived following the age of this world, following the ruler of the power of the air, the spirit that is now at work in the disobedient. [3]All of us once lived among them in the desires of our flesh, following the wishes of the flesh and the impulses, and we were by nature children of wrath, like the rest. [4]But God, who is rich in mercy, because of the great love he had for us, [5]even when we were dead in our transgressions, brought us to life with Christ (by grace you have been saved), [6]raised us up with him, and seated us with him in the heavens in Christ Jesus, [7]that in the ages to come he might show the immeasurable riches of his grace in his kindness to us in Christ Jesus. [8]For by grace you have been saved through faith, and this is not from you; it is the gift of God; [9]it is not from works, so no one may boast. [10]For we are his handiwork, created in Christ Jesus for the good works that God has prepared in advance, that we should live in them.

One in Christ. [11]Therefore, remember that at one time you, Gentiles in the flesh, called the uncircumcision by those called the circumcision, which is done in the flesh by human hands, [12]were at that time without Christ, alienated from the community of Israel and strangers to the covenants of promise, without hope and without God in the world. [13]But now in Christ Jesus you who once were far off have become near by the blood of Christ.

[14]For he is our peace, he who made both one and broke down the dividing wall of enmity, through his flesh, [15]abolishing the law with its commandments and legal claims, that he might create in himself one new person in place of the two, thus establishing peace, [16]and might reconcile both with God, in one body, through the cross, putting that enmity to death by it. [17]He came and preached peace to you who were far off and peace to those who were near, [18]for through him we both have access in one Spirit to the Father.

[19]So then you are no longer strangers and sojourners, but you are fellow citizens with the holy ones and members of the household of God, [20]built upon the foundation of the apostles and prophets, with Christ Jesus himself as the capstone. [21]Through him the whole structure is held together and grows into a temple sacred in the Lord; [22]in him you also are being built together into a dwelling place of God in the Spirit.

October 6

St. Bruno; Blessed Marie-Rose Durocher

By your work you show what you love and what you know.
— St. Bruno

☐ **JEREMIAH 3-4**

3:1 If a man divorces his wife
and she leaves him
and then becomes the wife of
another,
Can she return to the first?
Would not this land be wholly
defiled?
But you have played the prostitute
with many lovers,
and yet you would return to me!—
oracle of the Lord.
²Raise your eyes to the heights, and
look,
where have men not lain with you?
Along the roadways you waited for
them
like an Arabian in the wilderness.
You defiled the land
by your wicked prostitution.
³Therefore the showers were withheld,
the spring rain did not fall.
But because you have a prostitute's
brow,
you refused to be ashamed.
⁴Even now do you not call me, "My
father,
you are the bridegroom of my youth?
⁵Will he keep his wrath forever,
will he hold his grudge to the end?"
This is what you say; yet you do
all the evil you can.

Judah and Israel. ⁶The Lord said to
me in the days of King Josiah: Do you see
what rebellious Israel has done? She has
gone up every high mountain, and under
every green tree she has played the prostitute. ⁷And I thought: After she has done
all this, she will return to me. But she did
not return. Then, even though that traitor
her sister Judah, saw ⁸that, in response to
all the adulteries rebel Israel had committed, I sent her away and gave her a bill of
divorce, nevertheless Judah, the traitor, her
sister, was not frightened; she too went off
and played the prostitute. ⁹With her casual
prostitution, she polluted the land, committing adultery with stone and wood. ¹⁰In
spite of all this, Judah, the traitor, her sister,
did not return to me wholeheartedly, but
insincerely—oracle of the Lord.

Restoration of Israel. ¹¹Then the Lord
said to me: Rebel Israel is more just than
traitor Judah. ¹²Go, proclaim these words
toward the north, and say:

Return, rebel Israel—oracle of the
Lord—
I will not remain angry with you;
For I am merciful, oracle of the Lord,
I will not keep my anger forever.
¹³Only admit your guilt:
how you have rebelled against the
Lord, your God,
How you ran here and there to strangers
under every green tree
and would not listen to my voice—
oracle of the Lord.
¹⁴Return, rebellious children—oracle of
the Lord—
for I am your master;
I will take you, one from a city, two
from a clan,
and bring you to Zion.
¹⁵I will appoint for you shepherds after
my own heart,
who will shepherd you wisely and
prudently.

16When you increase in number and
 are fruitful in the land—
 oracle of the LORD—
They will in those days no longer say,
 "The ark of the covenant of the
  LORD!"
They will no longer think of it, or
 remember it,
 or miss it, or make another one.

17At that time they will call Jerusalem "the LORD's throne." All nations will gather together there to honor the name of the LORD at Jerusalem, and they will no longer stubbornly follow their wicked heart. 18In those days the house of Judah will walk alongside the house of Israel; together they will come from the land of the north to the land which I gave your ancestors as a heritage.

Conditions for Forgiveness. 19I
  thought:
 How I would like to make you my
  children!
So I gave you a pleasant land,
 the most beautiful heritage among
  the nations!
You would call me, "My Father," I
  thought,
 and you would never turn away
  from me.
20But like a woman faithless to her
  lover,
 thus have you been faithless to me,
 house of Israel—oracle of the LORD.
21A cry is heard on the heights!
 the plaintive weeping of Israel's
  children,
Because they have perverted their way,
 they have forgotten the LORD, their
  God.
22Return, rebellious children!
 I will heal your rebellions.
"Here we are! We belong to you,
 for you are the LORD, our God.
23Deceptive indeed are the hills,
 the mountains, clamorous;
Only in the LORD our God

is Israel's salvation.
24The shameful thing has devoured
 our ancestors' worth from our
  youth,
Their sheep and cattle,
 their sons and daughters.
25Let us lie down in our shame,
 let our disgrace cover us,
 for we have sinned against the
  LORD, our God,
We and our ancestors, from our youth
  to this day;
 we did not listen to the voice of the
  LORD, our God."

4:1 If you return, Israel—oracle of the
  LORD—
 return to me.
If you put your detestable things out of
  my sight,
 and do not stray,
2And swear, "As the LORD lives,"
 in truth, in judgment, and in
  justice,
Then the nations shall bless themselves
  in him
 and in him glory.

3For to the people of Judah and Jerusalem, thus says the LORD:

Till your untilled ground,
 and do not sow among thorns.
4Be circumcised for the LORD,
 remove the foreskins of your hearts,
 people of Judah and inhabitants of
  Jerusalem;
Or else my anger will break out like
  fire,
 and burn so that no one can quench
  it,
 because of your evil deeds.

The Invasion from the North.
 5Proclaim it in Judah,
 in Jerusalem announce it;
Blow the trumpet throughout the land,
 call out, "Fill the ranks!"

Say, "Assemble, let us march
    to the fortified cities."
[6]Raise the signal—to Zion!
    Seek refuge! Don't stand there!
Disaster I bring from the north,
    and great destruction.
[7]Up comes the lion from its lair,
    the destroyer of nations has set out,
    has left its place,
To turn your land into a desolation,
    your cities into an uninhabited
        waste.
[8]So put on sackcloth,
    mourn and wail:
"The blazing anger of the LORD
    has not turned away from us."
    [9]In that day—oracle of the LORD—
The king will lose heart, and the princes;
    the priests will be horrified,
    and the prophets stunned.
[10]"Ah! Lord GOD," they will say,
    "You really did deceive us
When you said: You shall have peace,
    while the sword was at our very
        throats."
[11]At that time it will be said
    to this people and to Jerusalem,
A scorching wind from the bare heights
    comes
    through the wilderness toward my
        daughter, the people.
Not to winnow, not to cleanse,
    [12]a strong wind from there comes at
        my bidding.
Now I too pronounce
    sentence upon them.
[13]See! like storm clouds he advances,
    like a whirlwind, his chariots;
Swifter than eagles, his horses:
    "Woe to us! we are ruined."
[14]Cleanse your heart of evil, Jerusalem,
    that you may be saved.
How long will you entertain
    wicked schemes?
[15]A voice proclaims it from Dan,
    announces wickedness from Mount
        Ephraim:

[16]"Make this known to the nations,
    announce it against Jerusalem:
Besiegers are coming from the distant
    land,
    shouting their war cry against the
        cities of Judah."
[17]Like watchers in the fields they
    surround her,
    for she has rebelled against me—
        oracle of the LORD.
[18]Your conduct, your deeds, have done
    this to you;
    how bitter is this evil of yours,
    how it reaches to your very heart!
[19]My body! my body! how I writhe!
    The walls of my heart!
My heart beats wildly,
    I cannot be still;
For I myself have heard the blast of the
        horn,
    the battle cry.
[20]Ruin upon ruin is reported;
    the whole land is laid waste.
In an instant my tents are ravaged;
    in a flash, my shelters.
[21]How long must I see the signal,
    hear the blast of the horn!
[22]My people are fools,
    they do not know me;
They are senseless children,
    without understanding;
They are wise at evil,
    but they do not know how to do
        good.
[23]I looked at the earth—it was waste
    and void;
    at the heavens—their light had gone
        out!
[24]I looked at the mountains—they
    were quaking!
All the hills were crumbling!
[25]I looked—there was no one;
    even the birds of the air had flown
        away!
[26]I looked—the garden land was a
    wilderness,
    with all its cities destroyed

before the LORD, before his blazing
 anger.
[27]For thus says the LORD:
The whole earth shall be waste,
 but I will not wholly destroy it.
[28]Because of this the earth shall mourn,
 the heavens above shall darken;
I have spoken, I will not change my
 mind,
 I have decided, I will not turn back.
[29]At the shout of rider and archer
 each city takes to flight;
They shrink into the thickets,
 they scale the rocks:
All the cities are abandoned,
 no one lives in them.

[30]You now who are doomed, what are
 you doing
 dressing in purple,
 bedecking yourself with gold,
Enlarging your eyes with kohl?
 You beautify yourself in vain!
Your lovers reject you,
 they seek your life.
[31]Yes, I hear the cry, like that of a
 woman in labor,
 like the anguish of a mother bearing
 her first child—
The cry of daughter Zion gasping,
 as she stretches out her hands:
"Ah, woe is me! I sink exhausted
 before my killers!"

☐ EPHESIANS 3

Commission to Preach God's Plan. 3:1 Because of this, I, Paul, a prisoner of Christ [Jesus] for you Gentiles— [2]if, as I suppose, you have heard of the stewardship of God's grace that was given to me for your benefit, [3][namely, that] the mystery was made known to me by revelation, as I have written briefly earlier. [4]When you read this you can understand my insight into the mystery of Christ, [5]which was not made known to human beings in other generations as it has now been revealed to his holy apostles and prophets by the Spirit, [6]that the Gentiles are coheirs, members of the same body, and copartners in the promise in Christ Jesus through the gospel.

[7]Of this I became a minister by the gift of God's grace that was granted me in accord with the exercise of his power. [8]To me, the very least of all the holy ones, this grace was given, to preach to the Gentiles the inscrutable riches of Christ, [9]and to bring to light [for all] what is the plan of the mystery hidden from ages past in God who created all things, [10]so that the manifold wisdom of God might now be made known through the church to the principalities and authorities in the heavens. [11]This was according to the eternal purpose that he accomplished in Christ Jesus our Lord, [12]in whom we have boldness of speech and confidence of access through faith in him. [13]So I ask you not to lose heart over my afflictions for you; this is your glory.

Prayer for the Readers. [14]For this reason I kneel before the Father, [15]from whom every family in heaven and on earth is named, [16]that he may grant you in accord with the riches of his glory to be strengthened with power through his Spirit in the inner self, [17]and that Christ may dwell in your hearts through faith; that you, rooted and grounded in love, [18]may have strength to comprehend with all the holy ones what is the breadth and length and height and depth, [19]and to know the love of Christ that surpasses knowledge, so that you may be filled with all the fullness of God.

[20]Now to him who is able to accomplish far more than all we ask or imagine, by the power at work within us, [21]to him be glory in the church and in Christ Jesus to all generations, forever and ever. Amen.

October 7

Our Lady of the Rosary

The Rosary is a crown of roses that we place on the heads of Jesus and Mary.

— St. Louis de Montfort

☐ JEREMIAH 5-6

Universal Corruption. 5:1 Roam the
    streets of Jerusalem,
    look about and observe,
Search through her squares,
    to find even one
Who acts justly
    and seeks honesty,
    and I will pardon her!
²They say, "As the Lord lives,"
    but in fact they swear falsely.
    ³Lord, do your eyes not search for
        honesty?
You struck them, but they did not
        flinch;
    you laid them low, but they refused
        correction;
They set their faces harder than stone,
    and refused to return.
⁴I thought: These are only the lowly,
    they behave foolishly;
For they do not know the way of the
    Lord,
    the justice of their God.
⁵Let me go to the leaders
    and speak with them;
For they must know the way of the
    Lord,
    the justice of their God.
But, one and all, they have broken the
    yoke,
    torn off the harness.
⁶Therefore, lions from the forest slay
    them,
    wolves of the desert ravage them,
Leopards keep watch round their cities:
    all who come out are torn to pieces,
For their crimes are many,
    their rebellions numerous.

⁷Why should I pardon you?
    Your children have forsaken me,
    they swear by gods that are no gods.
I fed them, but they commit adultery;
    to the prostitute's house they throng.
⁸They are lustful stallions,
    each neighs after the other's wife.
⁹Should I not punish them for this?—
    oracle of the Lord;
    on a nation like this should I not
        take vengeance?
¹⁰Climb her terraces, and ravage them,
    destroy them completely.
Tear away her tendrils,
    they do not belong to the Lord.
¹¹For they have openly rebelled
    against me,
    both the house of Israel and the
        house of Judah—
    oracle of the Lord.
¹²They denied the Lord,
    saying, "He is nothing,
No evil shall come to us,
    neither sword nor famine shall we see.
¹³The prophets are wind,
    and the word is not with them.
    Let it be done to them!"
¹⁴Therefore, thus says the Lord, the
    God of hosts,
    because you have said this—
See! I make my words
    a fire in your mouth,
And this people the wood
    that it shall devour!—
¹⁵Beware! I will bring against you
    a nation from far away,
    O House of Israel—oracle of the
        Lord;

A long-lived nation, an ancient nation,
    a people whose language you do not
        know,
    whose speech you cannot
        understand.
¹⁶Their quivers are like open graves;
    all of them are warriors.
¹⁷They will devour your harvest and
        your bread,
    devour your sons and your
        daughters,
Devour your sheep and cattle,
    devour your vines and fig trees;
With their swords they will beat down
    the fortified cities in which you
        trust.

¹⁸Yet even in those days—oracle of the Lord—I will not completely destroy you. ¹⁹And when they ask, "Why has the Lord our God done all these things to us?" say to them, "As you have abandoned me to serve foreign gods in your own land, so shall you serve foreigners in a land not your own."

²⁰Announce this to the house of Jacob,
    proclaim it in Judah:
²¹Pay attention to this,
    you foolish and senseless people,
Who have eyes and do not see,
    who have ears and do not hear.
²²Should you not fear me—oracle of
        the Lord—
    should you not tremble before me?
I made the sandy shore the sea's limit,
    which by eternal decree it may not
        overstep.
Toss though it may, it is to no avail;
    though its billows roar, they cannot
        overstep.
²³But this people's heart is stubborn
        and rebellious;
    they turn and go away,
²⁴And do not say in their hearts,
    "Let us fear the Lord, our God,
Who gives us rain
    early and late, in its time;
Who watches for us

over the appointed weeks of harvest."
²⁵Your crimes have prevented these
        things,
    your sins have turned these blessings
        away from you.
²⁶For criminals lurk among my people;
    like fowlers they set traps,
    but it is human beings they catch.
²⁷Their houses are as full of treachery
    as a bird-cage is of birds;
Therefore they grow powerful and rich,
    ²⁸fat and sleek.
They pass over wicked deeds;
    justice they do not defend
By advancing the claim of the orphan
    or judging the cause of the poor.
²⁹Shall I not punish these things?—
        oracle of the Lord;
    on a nation such as this shall I not
        take vengeance?
³⁰Something shocking and horrible
    has happened in the land:
³¹The prophets prophesy falsely,
    and the priests teach on their own
        authority;
Yet my people like it this way;
    what will you do when the end
        comes?

The Enemy at the Gates. 6:1 Seek
        refuge, Benjaminites,
    from the midst of Jerusalem!
Blow the trumpet in Tekoa,
    raise a signal over Beth-haccherem;
For disaster threatens from the north,
    and mighty destruction.
²Lovely and delicate
    daughter Zion, you are ruined!
³Against her, shepherds come with
        their flocks;
    all around, they pitch their tents
        against her;
    each one grazes his portion.
⁴"Prepare for war against her,
    Up! let us rush upon her at midday!"
"Woe to us! the day is waning,
    evening shadows lengthen!"

⁵"Up! let us rush upon her by night,
　destroy her palaces!"
⁶For thus says the LORD of hosts:
Hew down her trees,
　throw up a siege mound against
　　Jerusalem.
Woe to the city marked for
　punishment;
　there is nothing but oppression
　　within her!
⁷As a well keeps its waters fresh,
　so she keeps fresh her wickedness.
Violence and destruction resound in her;
　ever before me are wounds and blows.
⁸Be warned, Jerusalem,
　or I will be estranged from you,
And I will turn you into a wilderness,
　a land where no one dwells.
⁹Thus says the LORD of hosts:
Glean, glean like a vine
　the remnant of Israel;
Pass your hand, like a vintager,
　repeatedly over the tendrils.
¹⁰To whom shall I speak?
　whom shall I warn, and be heard?
See! their ears are uncircumcised,
　they cannot pay attention;
See, the word of the LORD has become
　for them
　an object of scorn, for which they
　　have no taste.
¹¹But the wrath of the LORD brims up
　within me,
I am weary of holding it in.
I will pour it out upon the child in the
　street,
　upon the young men gathered
　　together.
Yes, husband and wife will be taken,
　elder with ancient.
¹²Their houses will fall to others,
　their fields and their wives as well;
For I will stretch forth my hand
　against those who dwell in the
　　land—oracle of the LORD.
¹³Small and great alike, all are greedy
　for gain;

prophet and priest, all practice
　fraud.
¹⁴They have treated lightly
　the injury to my people:
"Peace, peace!" they say,
　though there is no peace.
¹⁵They have acted shamefully,
　committing abominations,
yet they are not at all ashamed,
　they do not know how to blush.
Therefore they will fall among the
　fallen;
　in the time of their punishment
　　they shall stumble,
　says the LORD.
¹⁶Thus says the LORD:
Stand by the earliest roads,
　ask the pathways of old,
"Which is the way to good?" and
　walk it;
　thus you will find rest for
　　yourselves.
But they said, "We will not walk it."
¹⁷I raised up watchmen for them:
　"Pay attention to the sound of the
　　trumpet!"
But they said, "We will not pay
　attention!"
¹⁸Therefore hear, O nations,
　and know, O earth,
　what I will do with them:
¹⁹See, I bring evil upon this people,
　the fruit of their own schemes,
Because they did not pay attention to
　my words,
　because they rejected my law.
²⁰Of what use to me is incense that
　comes from Sheba,
　or sweet cane from far-off lands?
Your burnt offerings find no favor
　with me,
　your sacrifices do not please me.
²¹Therefore, thus says the LORD:
See, I will place before this people
　obstacles to trip them up;
Parents and children alike,
　neighbors and friends shall perish.

²²Thus says the LORD:
See, a people comes from the land of
    the north,
a great nation, rising from the very
    ends of the earth.
²³Bow and javelin they wield;
    cruel and pitiless are they.
They sound like the roaring sea
    as they ride forth on horses,
Each in his place for battle
    against you, daughter Zion.
²⁴We hear news of them;
    our hands hang helpless,
Anguish takes hold of us,
    pangs like a woman in
    childbirth.
²⁵Do not go out into the field,
    do not step into the street,
For the enemy has a sword;
    terror on every side!

²⁶Daughter of my people, dress in
    sackcloth,
    roll in the ashes.
Mourn as for an only child
    with bitter wailing:
"How suddenly the destroyer
    comes upon us!"
²⁷A tester for my people I have
    appointed you,
    to search and test their way.
²⁸Arch-rebels are they all,
    dealers in slander,
bronze and iron, all of them,
    destroyers they are.
²⁹The bellows are scorched,
    the lead is consumed by the fire;
In vain has the refiner refined,
    the wicked are not drawn off.
³⁰"Silver rejected" they shall be called,
    for the LORD has rejected them.

☐ EPHESIANS 4

Unity in the Body. 4:1 I, then, a prisoner for the Lord, urge you to live in a manner worthy of the call you have received, ²with all humility and gentleness, with patience, bearing with one another through love, ³striving to preserve the unity of the spirit through the bond of peace: ⁴one body and one Spirit, as you were also called to the one hope of your call; ⁵one Lord, one faith, one baptism; ⁶one God and Father of all, who is over all and through all and in all.

Diversity of Gifts. ⁷But grace was given to each of us according to the measure of Christ's gift. ⁸Therefore, it says:

"He ascended on high and took
    prisoners captive;
    he gave gifts to men."

⁹What does "he ascended" mean except that he also descended into the lower [regions] of the earth? ¹⁰The one who descended is also the one who ascended far above all the heavens, that he might fill all things.

¹¹And he gave some as apostles, others as prophets, others as evangelists, others as pastors and teachers, ¹²to equip the holy ones for the work of ministry, for building up the body of Christ, ¹³until we all attain to the unity of faith and knowledge of the Son of God, to mature manhood, to the extent of the full stature of Christ, ¹⁴so that we may no longer be infants, tossed by waves and swept along by every wind of teaching arising from human trickery, from their cunning in the interests of deceitful scheming. ¹⁵Rather, living the truth in love, we should grow in every way into him who is the head, Christ, ¹⁶from whom the whole body, joined and held together by every supporting ligament, with the proper functioning of each part, brings about the body's growth and builds itself up in love.

Renewal in Christ. ¹⁷So I declare and testify in the Lord that you must no longer live as the Gentiles do, in the futility of their minds; ¹⁸darkened in understanding, alienated from the life of God because of their ignorance, because of their hardness of heart, [19]they have become callous and have handed themselves over to licentiousness for the practice of every kind of impurity to excess. [20]That is not how you learned Christ, [21]assuming that you have heard of him and were taught in him, as truth is in Jesus, [22]that you should put away the old self of your former way of life, corrupted through deceitful desires, [23]and be renewed in the spirit of your minds, [24]and put on the new self, created in God's way in righteousness and holiness of truth.

Rules for the New Life. [25]Therefore, putting away falsehood, speak the truth, each one to his neighbor, for we are members one of another. [26]Be angry but do not sin; do not let the sun set on your anger, [27]and do not leave room for the devil. [28]The thief must no longer steal, but rather labor, doing honest work with his [own] hands, so that he may have something to share with one in need. [29]No foul language should come out of your mouths, but only such as is good for needed edification, that it may impart grace to those who hear. [30]And do not grieve the holy Spirit of God, with which you were sealed for the day of redemption. [31]All bitterness, fury, anger, shouting, and reviling must be removed from you, along with all malice. [32][And] be kind to one another, compassionate, forgiving one another as God has forgiven you in Christ.

October 8

Purity prepares the soul for love, and love confirms the soul in purity.

— Blessed John Henry Newman

☐ JEREMIAH 7-8

The Temple Sermon. 7:1 The word came to Jeremiah from the LORD: [2]Stand at the gate of the house of the LORD and proclaim this message there: Hear the word of the LORD, all you of Judah who enter these gates to worship the LORD! [3]Thus says the LORD of hosts, the God of Israel: Reform your ways and your deeds so that I may dwell with you in this place. [4]Do not put your trust in these deceptive words: "The temple of the LORD! The temple of the LORD! The temple of the LORD!" [5]Only if you thoroughly reform your ways and your deeds; if each of you deals justly with your neighbor; [6]if you no longer oppress the alien, the orphan, and the widow; if you no longer shed innocent blood in this place or follow after other gods to your own harm, [7]only then will I let you continue to dwell in this place, in the land I gave your ancestors long ago and forever.

[8]But look at you! You put your trust in deceptive words to your own loss! [9]Do you think you can steal and murder, commit adultery and perjury, sacrifice to Baal, follow other gods that you do not know, [10]and then come and stand in my presence in this house, which bears my name, and say: "We are safe! We can commit all these abominations again!"? [11]Has this house which bears my name become in your eyes a den of thieves? I have seen it for myself!—oracle of the LORD. [12]Go to my place at Shiloh, where I made my name dwell in the beginning. See what I did to it because of the wickedness of my

people Israel. ¹³And now, because you have committed all these deeds—oracle of the LORD—because you did not listen, though I spoke to you untiringly, and because you did not answer, though I called you, ¹⁴I will do to this house, which bears my name, in which you trust, and to the place which I gave you and your ancestors, exactly what I did to Shiloh. ¹⁵I will cast you out of my sight, as I cast away all your kindred, all the offspring of Ephraim.

Abuses in Worship. ¹⁶You, now, must not intercede for this people! Do not raise a cry or prayer in their behalf! Do not press me, for I will not listen to you! ¹⁷Do you not see what they are doing in the cities of Judah, in the streets of Jerusalem? ¹⁸The children gather wood, their fathers light the fire, and the women knead dough to make cakes for the Queen of Heaven, while libations are poured out to other gods—all to offend me! ¹⁹Are they really offending me—oracle of the LORD—or rather themselves, to their own disgrace? ²⁰Therefore, thus says the Lord GOD: my anger and my wrath will pour out upon this place, upon human being and beast, upon the trees of the field and the fruits of the earth; it will burn and not be quenched.

²¹Thus says the LORD of hosts, the God of Israel: Heap your burnt offerings upon your sacrifices; eat up the meat! ²²In speaking to your ancestors on the day I brought them out of the land of Egypt, I gave them no command concerning burnt offering or sacrifice. ²³This rather is what I commanded them: Listen to my voice; then I will be your God and you shall be my people. Walk exactly in the way I command you, so that you may prosper.

²⁴But they did not listen to me, nor did they pay attention. They walked in the stubbornness of their evil hearts and turned their backs, not their faces, to me. ²⁵From the day that your ancestors left the land of Egypt even to this day, I kept on sending all my servants the prophets to you. ²⁶Yet they have not listened to me nor have they paid attention; they have stiffened their necks and done worse than their ancestors. ²⁷When you speak all these words to them, they will not listen to you either. When you call to them, they will not answer you. ²⁸Say to them: This is the nation which does not listen to the voice of the LORD, its God, or take correction. Faithfulness has disappeared; the word itself is banished from their speech.

²⁹Cut off your hair and throw it away!
on the heights raise a lament;
The LORD has indeed rejected and cast off
the generation that draws down his wrath.

³⁰The people of Judah have done what is evil in my eyes—oracle of the LORD. They have set up their detestable things in the house which bears my name, thereby defiling it. ³¹In the Valley of Ben-hinnom they go on building the high places of Topheth to sacrifice their sons and daughters by fire, something I never commanded or considered. ³²Be assured! Days are coming—oracle of the LORD—when they will no longer say "Topheth" or "Valley of Ben-hinnom" but "Valley of Slaughter." For want of space, Topheth will become burial ground. ³³The corpses of this people will be food for the birds of the sky and beasts of the earth, which no one will drive away. ³⁴I will silence the cry of joy, the cry of gladness, the voice of the bridegroom and the voice of the bride, in the cities of Judah and in the streets of Jerusalem; for the land will be turned to rubble.

8:1 At that time—oracle of the LORD—the bones of the kings and princes of Judah, the bones of the priests and the prophets, and the bones of the inhabitants of Jerusalem will be brought out of their graves ²and spread out before the sun, the moon, and the whole host of heaven, which they loved and served, which they followed, consulted, and worshiped. They will not be gathered up for burial, but will lie like dung upon the ground. ³Death will be preferred to life by all the survivors of this wicked people who remain in any of the places to which I banish them—oracle of the LORD of hosts.

Israel's Conduct Incomprehensible.

⁴Tell them: Thus says the LORD:
When someone falls, do they not rise
    again?
    if they turn away, do they not turn
        back?
⁵Why then do these people resist
    with persistent rebellion?
Why do they cling to deception,
    refuse to turn back?
⁶I have listened closely:
    they speak what is not true;
No one regrets wickedness,
    saying, "What have I done?"
Everyone keeps on running their course,
    like a horse dashing into battle.
⁷Even the stork in the sky
    knows its seasons;
Turtledove, swift, and thrush
    observe the time of their return,
But my people do not know
    the order of the LORD.
⁸How can you say, "We are wise,
    we have the law of the LORD"?
See, that has been changed into falsehood
    by the lying pen of the scribes!
⁹The wise are put to shame,
    terrified, and trapped;
Since they have rejected the word of
        the LORD,
    what sort of wisdom do they have?

Shameless in Their Crimes.

¹⁰Therefore,
    I will give their wives to other
        men,
    their fields to new owners.
Small and great alike, all are greedy for
        gain,
    prophet and priest, all practice fraud.

¹¹They have treated lightly
    the injury to the daughter of my
        people:
"Peace, peace!" they say,
    though there is no peace.
¹²They have acted shamefully; they
        have done abominable things,
    yet they are not at all ashamed,
    they do not know how to blush.
Hence they shall be among those who
        fall;
    in their time of punishment they
        shall stumble,
    says the LORD.

Threats of Punishment.

¹³I will gather
        them all in—oracle of the LORD:
    no grapes on the vine,
No figs on the fig trees,
    foliage withered!
Whatever I have given them is gone.
¹⁴Why do we remain here?
    Let us assemble and flee to the
        fortified cities,
    where we will meet our doom;
For the LORD our God has doomed us,
    he has given us poisoned water to
        drink,
    because we have sinned against the
        LORD.
¹⁵We wait for peace to no avail;
    for a time of healing, but terror
        comes instead.
¹⁶From Dan is heard
    the snorting of horses;
The neighing of stallions
    shakes the whole land.
They come to devour the land and
        everything in it,
    the city and its inhabitants.
¹⁷Yes, I will send against you
    poisonous snakes.
Against them no charm will work
    when they bite you—oracle of the
        LORD.

The Prophet's Grief over the People's Suffering.

¹⁸My joy is gone,

grief is upon me,
my heart is sick.
[19]Listen! the cry of the daughter of my
people,
far and wide in the land!
"Is the LORD no longer in Zion,
is her King no longer in her midst?"
Why do they provoke me with their
idols,
with their foreign nonentities?
[20]"The harvest is over, the summer ended,
but we have not yet been saved!"
[21]I am broken by the injury of the
daughter of my people.

I am in mourning; horror has
seized me.
[22]Is there no balm in Gilead,
no healer there?
Why does new flesh not grow
over the wound of the daughter of
my people?
[23]Oh, that my head were a spring of
water,
my eyes a fountain of tears,
That I might weep day and night
over the slain from the daughter of
my people!

☐ EPHESIANS 5

5:1 So be imitators of God, as beloved children, [2]and live in love, as Christ loved us and handed himself over for us as a sacrificial offering to God for a fragrant aroma. [3]Immorality or any impurity or greed must not even be mentioned among you, as is fitting among holy ones, [4]no obscenity or silly or suggestive talk, which is out of place, but instead, thanksgiving. [5]Be sure of this, that no immoral or impure or greedy person, that is, an idolater, has any inheritance in the kingdom of Christ and of God.

Duty to Live in the Light. [6]Let no one deceive you with empty arguments, for because of these things the wrath of God is coming upon the disobedient. [7]So do not be associated with them. [8]For you were once darkness, but now you are light in the Lord. Live as children of light, [9]for light produces every kind of goodness and righteousness and truth. [10]Try to learn what is pleasing to the Lord. [11]Take no part in the fruitless works of darkness; rather expose them, [12]for it is shameful even to mention the things done by them in secret; [13]but everything exposed by the light becomes visible, [14]for everything that becomes visible is light. Therefore, it says:

"Awake, O sleeper,
and arise from the dead,
and Christ will give you light."

[15]Watch carefully then how you live, not as foolish persons but as wise, [16]making the most of the opportunity, because the days are evil. [17]Therefore, do not continue in ignorance, but try to understand what is the will of the Lord. [18]And do not get drunk on wine, in which lies debauchery, but be filled with the Spirit, [19]addressing one another [in] psalms and hymns and spiritual songs, singing and playing to the Lord in your hearts, [20]giving thanks always and for everything in the name of our Lord Jesus Christ to God the Father.

Wives and Husbands. [21]Be subordinate to one another out of reverence for Christ. [22]Wives should be subordinate to their husbands as to the Lord. [23]For the husband is head of his wife just as Christ is head of the church, he himself the savior of the body. [24]As the church is subordinate to Christ, so wives should be subordinate to their husbands in everything. [25]Husbands, love your wives, even as Christ loved the church and handed himself over for her [26]to sanctify her, cleansing her by the bath of water with the word, [27] that he might present to himself the church in splendor, without spot or wrinkle or any such thing, that she might be holy and without blemish. [28] So [also] husbands should love their wives as their own bodies. He who loves his wife loves himself. [29] For no one hates his own flesh but rather nourishes and cherishes it, even as Christ does the church, [30] because we are members of his body.

[31] "For this reason a man shall leave
[his] father and [his] mother
and be joined to his wife,
and the two shall become one flesh."

[32] This is a great mystery, but I speak in reference to Christ and the church. [33] In any case, each one of you should love his wife as himself, and the wife should respect her husband.

October 9

St. Denis and Companions; St. John Leonardi

Let God be the measure of all things.
— St. John Leonardi

☐ JEREMIAH 9-10

The Corruption of the People. 9:1
Oh, that I had in the wilderness
a travelers' lodging!
That I might leave my people
and depart from them.
They are all adulterers,
a band of traitors.
[2] They ready their tongues like a drawn
bow;
with lying, and not with truth,
they are powerful in the land.
They go from evil to evil,
and me they do not know—oracle
of the Lord.
[3] Be on your guard, everyone against his
neighbor;
put no trust in any brother.
Every brother imitates Jacob, the
supplanter,
every neighbor is guilty of slander.
[4] Each one deceives the other,
no one speaks the truth.
They have accustomed their tongues to
lying,
they are perverse and cannot repent.

[5] Violence upon violence,
deceit upon deceit:
They refuse to know me—
oracle of the Lord.
[6] Therefore, thus says the Lord of hosts:
I will refine them and test them;
how else should I deal with the
daughter of my people?
[7] A murderous arrow is their tongue,
their mouths utter deceit;
They speak peaceably with their
neighbors,
but in their hearts they lay an
ambush!
[8] Should I not punish them for these
deeds—oracle of the Lord;
on a nation such as this should I not
take vengeance?

Dirge over the Ravaged Land.
[9] Over
the mountains I shall break out
in cries of lamentation,
over the pastures in the wilderness,
in a dirge:
They are scorched, and no one crosses
them,

no sound of lowing cattle;
Birds of the air as well as beasts,
    all have fled and are gone.
[10]I will turn Jerusalem into a heap of
        ruins,
    a haunt of jackals;
The cities of Judah I will make a waste,
    where no one dwells.

[11]Who is wise enough to understand this? To whom has the mouth of the LORD spoken? Let him declare it!

Why is the land ravaged,
    scorched like a wilderness no one
        crosses?

[12]The LORD said: Because they have abandoned my law, which I set before them, and did not listen to me or follow it, [13]but followed instead their stubborn hearts and the Baals, as their ancestors had taught them, [14]therefore, thus says the LORD of hosts, the God of Israel: See now, I will give this people wormwood to eat and poisoned water to drink. [15]I will scatter them among nations whom neither they nor their ancestors have known; I will send the sword to pursue them until I have completely destroyed them.

[16]Thus says the LORD of hosts:
Inquire, and call the wailing women to
        come;
    summon the most skilled of them.
[17]Let them come quickly
    and raise for us a dirge,
That our eyes may run with tears,
    our pupils flow with water.
[18]The sound of the dirge is heard from
        Zion:
    We are ruined and greatly ashamed;
We have left the land,
    given up our dwellings!
[19]Hear, you women, the word of the
        LORD,
    let your ears receive the word of his
        mouth.
Teach your daughters a dirge,
    and each other a lament:
[20]Death has come up through our
        windows,
    has entered our citadels,
To cut down children in the street,
    young people in the squares.
[21]Corpses shall fall
    like dung in the open field,
Like sheaves behind the harvester,
    with no one to gather them.

True Glory. [22]Thus says the LORD:
Let not the wise boast of his wisdom,
    nor the strong boast of his strength,
    nor the rich man boast of his riches;
[23]But rather, let those who boast, boast
        of this,
    that in their prudence they know me,
Know that I, the LORD, act with fidelity,
    justice, and integrity on earth.
How I take delight in these—oracle of
        the LORD.

False Circumcision. [24]See, days are coming—oracle of the LORD—when I will demand an account of all those circumcised in the foreskin: [25]Egypt and Judah, Edom and the Ammonites, Moab, and those who live in the wilderness and shave their temples. For all the nations are uncircumcised, even the whole house of Israel is uncircumcised at heart.

The Folly of Idolatry. 10:1 Hear the word the LORD speaks to you, house of Israel. [2]Thus says the LORD:

Do not learn the ways of the nations,
    and have no fear of the signs in the
        heavens,
    even though the nations fear them.
[3]For the carvings of the nations are
        nonentities,
    wood cut from the forest,
Fashioned by artisans with the adze,
    [4]adorned with silver and gold.
With nails and hammers they are
        fastened,

so they do not fall.
⁵Like a scarecrow in a cucumber field
   are they,
   they cannot speak;
They must be carried about,
   for they cannot walk.
Do not fear them, they can do no harm,
   neither can they do good.
⁶No one is like you, LORD,
   you are great,
   great and mighty is your name.
⁷Who would not fear you,
   King of the nations,
   for it is your due!
Among all the wisest of the nations,
   and in all their domains,
   there is none like you.
⁸One and all they are stupid and
   senseless,
   the instruction from nonentities—
   only wood!
⁹Silver plates brought from Tarshish,
   and gold from Ophir,
The work of the artisan
   and the handiwork of the smelter,
Clothed with violet and purple—
   all of them the work of skilled
   workers.
¹⁰The LORD is truly God,
   he is the living God, the eternal
   King,
Before whose anger the earth quakes,
   whose wrath the nations cannot
   endure.

¹¹Thus shall you say of them: The gods that did not make heaven and earth—let these perish from earth and from beneath heaven!

¹²The one who made the earth by his
   power,
   established the world by his
   wisdom,
   and by his skill stretched out the
   heavens.
¹³When he thunders, the waters in the
   heavens roar,
and he brings up clouds from the
   end of the earth,
Makes lightning flash in the rain,
   and brings forth the wind from his
   storehouses.
¹⁴Everyone is too stupid to know;
   every artisan is put to shame by his
   idol:
He has molded a fraud,
   without breath of life.
¹⁵They are nothing, objects of ridicule;
   they will perish in their time of
   punishment.
¹⁶Jacob's portion is nothing like them:
   for he is the maker of everything!
Israel is his very own tribe,
   LORD of hosts is his name.

Abandonment of Judah. ¹⁷Gather up
   your bundle from the land,
   City living under siege!
¹⁸For thus says the LORD:
Now, at this time
   I will sling away the inhabitants of
   the land;
I will hem them in,
   that they may be taken.
¹⁹Woe is me! I am undone,
   my wound is beyond healing.
Yet I had thought:
   if I make light of my sickness, I can
   bear it.
²⁰My tent is ruined,
   all its cords are severed.
My children have left me, they are no
   more:
   no one to pitch my tent,
   no one to raise its curtains.
²¹How stupid are the shepherds!
   The LORD they have not sought;
For this reason they have failed,
   and all their flocks scattered.
²²Listen! a rumor! here it comes,
   a great commotion from the land of
   the north:
To make the cities of Judah a desolation,
   the haunt of jackals.

Prayer of Jeremiah. 23I know, Lord,
    that no one chooses their way,
Nor determines their course
    nor directs their own step.
24Correct me, Lord, but with equity,
    not in anger, lest you diminish me.

25Pour out your wrath on the nations
    that do not know you,
    on the tribes that do not call your
    name;
For they have utterly devoured Jacob,
    and laid waste his home.

☐ EPHESIANS 6

Children and Parents. 6:1 Children, obey your parents [in the Lord], for this is right. 2"Honor your father and mother." This is the first commandment with a promise, 3"that it may go well with you and that you may have a long life on earth." 4Fathers, do not provoke your children to anger, but bring them up with the training and instruction of the Lord.

Slaves and Masters. 5Slaves, be obedient to your human masters with fear and trembling, in sincerity of heart, as to Christ, 6not only when being watched, as currying favor, but as slaves of Christ, doing the will of God from the heart, 7willingly serving the Lord and not human beings, 8knowing that each will be requited from the Lord for whatever good he does, whether he is slave or free. 9Masters, act in the same way toward them, and stop bullying, knowing that both they and you have a Master in heaven and that with him there is no partiality.

Battle against Evil. 10Finally, draw your strength from the Lord and from his mighty power. 11Put on the armor of God so that you may be able to stand firm against the tactics of the devil. 12For our struggle is not with flesh and blood but with the principalities, with the powers, with the world rulers of this present darkness, with the evil spirits in the heavens. 13Therefore, put on the armor of God, that you may be able to resist on the evil day and, having done everything, to hold your ground. 14So stand fast with your loins girded in truth, clothed with righteousness as a breastplate, 15and your feet shod in readiness for the gospel of peace. 16In all circumstances, hold faith as a shield, to quench all [the] flaming arrows of the evil one. 17And take the helmet of salvation and the sword of the Spirit, which is the word of God.

Constant Prayer. 18With all prayer and supplication, pray at every opportunity in the Spirit. To that end, be watchful with all perseverance and supplication for all the holy ones 19and also for me, that speech may be given me to open my mouth, to make known with boldness the mystery of the gospel 20for which I am an ambassador in chains, so that I may have the courage to speak as I must.

A Final Message. 21So that you also may have news of me and of what I am doing, Tychicus, my beloved brother and trustworthy minister in the Lord, will tell you everything. 22I am sending him to you for this very purpose, so that you may know about us and that he may encourage your hearts.

23Peace be to the brothers, and love with faith, from God the Father and the Lord Jesus Christ. 24Grace be with all who love our Lord Jesus Christ in immortality.

October 10

St. Daniel Comboni

Missionaries must understand that they are stones hidden under the earth, which will perhaps never come to light, but which will become part of the foundations of a vast, new building.

— St. Daniel Comboni

☐ JEREMIAH 11-12

Plea for Fidelity to the Covenant. 11:1 The word that came to Jeremiah from the LORD: ²Speak to the people of Judah and the inhabitants of Jerusalem, ³and say to them: Thus says the LORD, the God of Israel: Cursed be anyone who does not observe the words of this covenant, ⁴which I commanded your ancestors the day I brought them up out of the land of Egypt, that iron furnace, saying: Listen to my voice and do all that I command you. Then you shall be my people, and I will be your God. ⁵Thus I will fulfill the oath I swore to your ancestors, to give them a land flowing with milk and honey, the one you have today. "Amen, LORD," I answered.

⁶Then the LORD said to me: Proclaim all these words in the cities of Judah and in the streets of Jerusalem: Hear the words of this covenant and obey them. ⁷I warned your ancestors unceasingly from the day I brought them up out of the land of Egypt even to this day: obey my voice. ⁸But they did not listen or obey. They each walked in the stubbornness of their evil hearts, till I brought upon them all the threats of this covenant which they had failed to observe as I commanded them.

⁹A conspiracy has been found, the LORD said to me, among the people of Judah and the inhabitants of Jerusalem: ¹⁰They have returned to the crimes of their ancestors who refused to obey my words. They also have followed and served other gods; the house of Israel and the house of Judah have broken the covenant I made with their ancestors. ¹¹Therefore, thus says the LORD: See, I am bringing upon them a disaster they cannot escape. Though they cry out to me, I will not listen to them. ¹²Then the cities of Judah and the inhabitants of Jerusalem will go and cry out to the gods to whom they have been offering incense. But these gods will give them no help whatever in the time of their disaster.

¹³For as many as your cities
 are your gods, O Judah!
As many as the streets of Jerusalem
 are the altars for sacrifice to Baal.

¹⁴Now, you must not intercede for this people; do not raise on their behalf a cry or prayer! I will not listen when they call to me in the time of their disaster.

Sacrifices of No Avail. ¹⁵What right
 has my beloved in my house,
 while she devises her plots?
Can vows and sacred meat turn away
 your disaster from you?
Will you still be jubilant
 ¹⁶when you hear the great tumult?
The LORD has named you
 "a spreading olive tree, a pleasure to
 behold";
Now he sets fire to it,
 its branches burn.

¹⁷The LORD of hosts who planted you has decreed disaster for you because of the evil done by the house of Israel and by the house of Judah, who provoked me by sacrificing to Baal.

The Plot Against Jeremiah. 18I knew it because the LORD informed me: at that time you showed me their doings.

19Yet I was like a trusting lamb led to slaughter, not knowing that they were hatching plots against me: "Let us destroy the tree in its vigor; let us cut him off from the land of the living, so that his name will no longer be remembered."

20But, you, LORD of hosts, just Judge,
    searcher of mind and heart,
Let me witness the vengeance you take
        on them,
    for to you I have entrusted my
        cause!

21Therefore, thus says the LORD concerning the men of Anathoth who seek your life and say, "Do not prophesy in the name of the LORD; otherwise you shall die by our hand." 22Therefore, thus says the LORD of hosts: I am going to punish them. The young men shall die by the sword; their sons and daughters shall die by famine. 23None shall be spared among them, for I will bring disaster upon the men of Anathoth, the year of their punishment.

12:1 You would be in the right,
        O LORD,
    if I should dispute with you;
    even so, I must lay out the case
        against you.
Why does the way of the wicked
        prosper,
    why do all the treacherous live in
        contentment?
2You planted them; they have taken
        root,
    they flourish and bear fruit as well.
You are upon their lips,
    but far from their thoughts.
3LORD, you know me, you see me,
    you have found that my heart is
        with you.
Pick them out like sheep for the
        butcher,

set them apart for the day of
        slaughter.
4How long must the land mourn,
    the grass of the whole countryside
        wither?
Because of the wickedness of those
    who dwell in it
    beasts and birds disappear,
    for they say, "God does not care
        about our future."

5If running against men has wearied you,
    how will you race against horses?
And if you are safe only on a level
        stretch,
    what will you do in the jungle of the
        Jordan?

6Your kindred and your father's house, even they betray you; they have recruited a force against you. Do not believe them, even when they speak fair words to you.

The Lord's Complaint. 7I have
        abandoned my house,
    cast off my heritage;
The beloved of my soul I have delivered
    into the hand of her foes.
8My heritage has become for me
    like a lion in the thicket;
She has raised her voice against me,
    therefore she has incurred my
        hatred.
9My heritage is a prey for hyenas,
    is surrounded by vultures;
Come, gather together, all you wild
        animals,
    come and eat!
10Many shepherds have ravaged my
        vineyard,
    have trampled down my heritage;
My delightful portion they have turned
    into a desert waste.
11They have made it a mournful waste,
    desolate before me,
Desolate, the whole land,
    because no one takes it to heart.
12Upon every height in the wilderness

marauders have appeared.
The LORD has a sword that consumes
the land from end to end:
    no peace for any living thing.
[13]They have sown wheat and reaped
    thorns,
they have tired themselves out for
    no purpose;
They are shamed by their harvest,
    the burning anger of the LORD.

Judah's Neighbors. [14]Thus says the
LORD, against all my evil neighbors who
plunder the heritage I gave my people Israel
as their own: See, I will uproot them from
their land; the house of Judah I will uproot
in their midst.

[15]But after uprooting them, I will have
compassion on them again and bring
them back, each to their heritage, each to
their land. [16]And if they truly learn my
people's custom of swearing by my name,
"As the LORD lives," just as they taught my
people to swear by Baal, then they shall be
built up in the midst of my people. [17]But
if they do not obey, I will uproot and destroy that nation entirely—oracle of the
LORD.

☐ 1 THESSALONIANS 1

Greeting. 1:1 Paul, Silvanus, and Timothy
to the church of the Thessalonians in God
the Father and the Lord Jesus Christ: grace
to you and peace.

Thanksgiving for Their Faith. [2]We
give thanks to God always for all of you,
remembering you in our prayers, unceasingly [3]calling to mind your work of faith
and labor of love and endurance in hope of
our Lord Jesus Christ, before our God and
Father, [4]knowing, brothers loved by God,
how you were chosen. [5]For our gospel did
not come to you in word alone, but also
in power and in the holy Spirit and [with]
much conviction. You know what sort of
people we were [among] you for your sake.
[6]And you became imitators of us and of
the Lord, receiving the word in great affliction, with joy from the holy Spirit, [7]so that
you became a model for all the believers in
Macedonia and in Achaia. [8]For from you
the word of the Lord has sounded forth not
only in Macedonia and [in] Achaia, but in
every place your faith in God has gone
forth, so that we have no need to say anything. [9]For they themselves openly declare
about us what sort of reception we had
among you, and how you turned to God
from idols to serve the living and true God
[10]and to await his Son from heaven, whom
he raised from [the] dead, Jesus, who delivers us from the coming wrath.

October 11

Blessed Pope John XXIII

To keep me from sin and straying from Him, God has used devotion to the Sacred Heart of Jesus in the Blessed Sacrament. My life vows are destined to be spent in the light irradiating from the tabernacle, and it is to the heart of Jesus that I dare go for the solution of all my problems.

— Blessed Pope John XXIII

☐ JEREMIAH 13-14

Judah's Corruption. 13:1 The Lord said to me: Go buy yourself a linen loincloth; wear it on your loins, but do not put it in water. ²I bought the loincloth, as the Lord commanded, and put it on. ³A second time the word of the Lord came to me thus: ⁴Take the loincloth which you bought and are wearing, and go at once to the Perath; hide it there in a cleft of the rock. ⁵Obedient to the Lord's command, I went to the Perath and buried the loincloth. ⁶After a long time, the Lord said to me: Go now to the Perath and fetch the loincloth which I told you to hide there. ⁷So I went to the Perath, looked for the loincloth and took it from the place I had hidden it. But it was rotted, good for nothing! ⁸Then the word came to me from the Lord: ⁹Thus says the Lord: So also I will allow the pride of Judah to rot, the great pride of Jerusalem. ¹⁰This wicked people who refuse to obey my words, who walk in the stubbornness of their hearts and follow other gods, serving and worshiping them, will be like this loincloth, good for nothing. ¹¹For, as the loincloth clings to a man's loins, so I made the whole house of Israel and the whole house of Judah cling to me—oracle of the Lord—to be my people, my fame, my praise, my glory. But they did not listen.

The Broken Wineflask. ¹²Now speak to them this word: Thus says the Lord, the God of Israel: Every wineflask should be filled with wine. If they reply, "Do we not know that every wineflask should be filled with wine?" ¹³say to them: Thus says the Lord: Beware! I am making all the inhabitants of this land drunk, the kings who sit on David's throne, the priests and prophets, and all the inhabitants of Jerusalem. ¹⁴I will smash them against each other, parents and children together—oracle of the Lord—showing no compassion, I will neither spare nor pity, but I will destroy them.

A Last Warning. ¹⁵Listen and give ear,
do not be arrogant,
for the Lord speaks.
¹⁶Give glory to the Lord, your God,
before he brings darkness;
Before your feet stumble
on mountains at twilight;
Before the light you look for turns to
darkness,
changes into black clouds.
¹⁷If you do not listen to this in your
pride,
I will weep many tears in secret;
My eyes will run with tears
for the Lord's flock, led away to
exile.

Exile. ¹⁸Say to the king and to the
queen mother:
come down from your throne;
From your heads
your splendid crowns will fall.
¹⁹The cities of the Negeb are besieged,
with no one to relieve them;

Judah is taken into exile—all of it—
in total exile.

Jerusalem's Disgrace. ²⁰Lift up your
eyes and see
those coming in from the north.
Where is the flock entrusted to you,
your splendid sheep?
²¹What will you say when rulers are
appointed over you,
those you taught to be allies?
Will not pains seize you
like those of a woman giving birth?
²²If you say to yourself:
"Why have these things happened
to me?"
For your great guilt your skirts are
stripped away
and you are violated.
²³Can Ethiopians change their skin,
leopards their spots?
As easily would you be able to do
good,
accustomed to evil as you are.
²⁴I will scatter them like chaff that flies
on the desert wind.
²⁵This is your lot, the portion I have
measured out to you—
oracle of the LORD.
Because you have forgotten me,
and trusted in deception,
²⁶I now will strip away your skirts,
so that your shame is visible.
²⁷Your adulteries, your neighings,
your shameless prostitutions:
On the hills, in the fields
I see your detestable crimes.
Woe to you, Jerusalem! How long will
it be
before you are clean?

The Great Drought. 14:1 The word of the
LORD that came to Jeremiah concerning
the drought:

²Judah mourns,
her gates are lifeless;
They are bowed to the ground,
and the outcry of Jerusalem goes up.
³The nobles send their servants for water,
but when they come to the cisterns
They find no water
and return with empty jars.
Confounded, despairing, they cover
their heads
⁴because of the ruined soil;
Because there is no rain in the land
the farmers are confounded, they
cover their heads.
⁵Even the doe in the field deserts her
young
because there is no grass.
⁶The wild donkeys stand on the bare
heights,
gasping for breath like jackals;
Their eyes grow dim;
there is no grass.
⁷Even though our crimes bear witness
against us,
act, LORD, for your name's sake—
Even though our rebellions are many,
and we have sinned against you.
⁸Hope of Israel, LORD,
our savior in time of need!
Why should you be a stranger in the
land,
like a traveler stopping only for a
night?
⁹Why are you like someone bewildered,
a champion who cannot save?
You are in our midst, LORD,
your name we bear:
do not forsake us!
¹⁰Thus says the LORD about this
people:
They so love to wander
that they cannot restrain their feet.
The LORD takes no pleasure in them;
now he remembers their guilt,
and will punish their sins.

¹¹Then the LORD said to me: Do not intercede for the well-being of this people.
¹²If they fast, I will not listen to their supplication. If they sacrifice burnt offerings

or grain offerings, I will take no pleasure in them. Rather, I will destroy them with the sword, famine, and plague.

[13]"Ah! Lord God," I replied, "it is the prophets who say to them, 'You shall not see the sword; famine shall not befall you. Indeed, I will give you lasting peace in this place.'"

[14]These prophets utter lies in my name, the LORD said to me: I did not send them; I gave them no command, nor did I speak to them. They prophesy to you lying visions, foolish divination, deceptions from their own imagination. [15]Therefore, thus says the LORD: Concerning the prophets who prophesy in my name, though I did not send them, and who say, "Sword and famine shall not befall this land": by sword and famine shall these prophets meet their end. [16]The people to whom they prophesy shall be thrown out into the streets of Jerusalem because of famine and the sword. No one shall bury them, their wives, their sons, or their daughters, for I will pour out upon them their own wickedness. [17]Speak to them this word:

Let my eyes stream with tears
　　night and day, without rest,
Over the great destruction which
　　overwhelms

the virgin daughter of my people,
　　over her incurable wound.
[18]If I walk out into the field,
　　look! those slain by the sword;
If I enter the city,
　　look! victims of famine.
Both prophet and priest ply their trade
　　in a land they do not know.
[19]Have you really cast Judah off?
　　Is Zion loathsome to you?
Why have you struck us a blow
　　that cannot be healed?
We wait for peace, to no avail;
　　for a time of healing, but terror
　　　　comes instead.
[20]We recognize our wickedness, LORD,
　　the guilt of our ancestors:
　　we have sinned against you.
[21]Do not reject us, for your name's sake,
　　do not disgrace your glorious
　　　　throne.
　　Remember! Do not break your
　　　　covenant with us.
[22]Among the idols of the nations are
　　there any that give rain?
　　Or can the mere heavens send
　　　　showers?
Is it not you, LORD,
　　our God, to whom we look?
　　You alone do all these things.

1 THESSALONIANS 2

Paul's Ministry Among Them. 2:1 For you yourselves know, brothers, that our reception among you was not without effect. [2]Rather, after we had suffered and been insolently treated, as you know, in Philippi, we drew courage through our God to speak to you the gospel of God with much struggle. [3]Our exhortation was not from delusion or impure motives, nor did it work through deception. [4]But as we were judged worthy by God to be entrusted with the gospel, that is how we speak, not as trying to please human beings, but rather God, who judges our hearts. [5]Nor, indeed, did we ever appear with flattering speech, as you know, or with a pretext for greed—God is witness— [6]nor did we seek praise from human beings, either from you or from others, [7]although we were able to impose our weight as apostles of Christ. Rather, we were gentle among you, as a nursing mother cares for her children. [8]With such affection for you, we were determined to share with you not only the gospel of God, but our very selves as well, so dearly beloved had you become to us. [9]You recall, brothers, our toil and drudgery. Working night and day in order not to burden any of you, we proclaimed to you the gospel of God. [10]You are witnesses, and so is God, how devoutly and justly and blamelessly we behaved toward you believers. [11]As you know, we treated each one of you as a father treats his children, [12]exhorting and encouraging you and insisting that you conduct yourselves as worthy of the God who calls you into his kingdom and glory.

Further Thanksgiving. [13]And for this reason we too give thanks to God unceasingly, that, in receiving the word of God from hearing us, you received not a human word but, as it truly is, the word of God, which is now at work in you who believe. [14]For you, brothers, have become imitators of the churches of God that are in Judea in Christ Jesus. For you suffer the same things from your compatriots as they did from the Jews, [15]who killed both the Lord Jesus and the prophets and persecuted us; they do not please God, and are opposed to everyone, [16]trying to prevent us from speaking to the Gentiles that they may be saved, thus constantly filling up the measure of their sins. But the wrath of God has finally begun to come upon them.

Paul's Recent Travel Plans. [17]Brothers, when we were bereft of you for a short time, in person, not in heart, we were all the more eager in our great desire to see you in person. [18]We decided to go to you—I, Paul, not only once but more than once—yet Satan thwarted us. [19]For what is our hope or joy or crown to boast of in the presence of our Lord Jesus at his coming if not you yourselves? [20]For you are our glory and joy.

October 12

At the end of life, we will be judged by love.
— St. John of the Cross

☐ JEREMIAH 15–16

15:1 The Lord said to me: Even if Moses and Samuel stood before me, my heart would not turn toward this people. Send them away from me and let them go. [2]If they ask you, "Where should we go?" tell them, Thus says the Lord: Whoever is marked for death, to death; whoever is marked for the sword, to the sword; whoever is marked for famine, to famine; whoever is marked for captivity, to captivity. [3]Four kinds of scourge I have decreed against them—oracle of the Lord—the sword to kill them; dogs to drag them off; the birds of the sky and the beasts of the earth to devour and destroy them. [4]And I will make them an object of horror to all the kingdoms of the earth because of what Manasseh, son of Hezekiah, king of Judah, did in Jerusalem.

Scene of Tragedy. [5]Who will pity you,
    Jerusalem,
    who will grieve for you?
Who will stop to ask
    about your welfare?
[6]It is you who have disowned me—
    oracle of the Lord—
    turned your back upon me;
I stretched out my hand to destroy you,
    because I was weary of relenting.
[7]I winnowed them with a winnowing
    fork

at the gates of the land;
I have bereaved, destroyed my people;
  they have not turned from their evil
    ways.
⁸Their widows were more numerous
  before me
    than the sands of the sea.
I brought against the mother of youths
  the destroyer at midday;
Suddenly I struck her
  with anguish and terror.
⁹The mother of seven faints away,
  breathing out her life;
Her sun sets in full day,
  she is ashamed, abashed.
Their survivors I will give to the sword
  in the presence of their enemies—
    oracle of the LORD.

Jeremiah's Complaint. ¹⁰Woe to me, my
  mother, that you gave me birth!
  a man of strife and contention to all
    the land!
I neither borrow nor lend,
  yet everyone curses me.
¹¹Tell me, LORD, have I not served you
  for their good?
Have I not interceded with you
  in time of misfortune and anguish?
¹²Can one break iron,
  iron from the north, and bronze?
¹³Your wealth and your treasures
  I give as plunder, demanding no
    payment,
  because of all your sins, throughout
    all your territory.
¹⁴And I shall enslave you to your enemies
  in a land you do not know,
For fire has broken out from my anger,
  it is kindled against you.
¹⁵You know, LORD:
Remember me and take care of me,
  avenge me on my persecutors.
Because you are slow to anger, do not
  banish me;
  know that for you I have borne
    insult.

¹⁶When I found your words, I
  devoured them;
  your words were my joy, the
    happiness of my heart,
Because I bear your name,
  LORD, God of hosts.
¹⁷I did not sit celebrating
  in the circle of merrymakers;
Under the weight of your hand I sat
  alone
  because you filled me with rage.
¹⁸Why is my pain continuous,
  my wound incurable, refusing to be
    healed?
To me you are like a deceptive brook,
  waters that cannot be relied on!
¹⁹Thus the LORD answered me:
If you come back and I take you back,
  in my presence you shall stand;
If you utter what is precious and not
  what is worthless,
  you shall be my mouth.
Then they will be the ones who turn
  to you,
  not you who turn to them.
²⁰And I will make you toward this people
  a fortified wall of bronze.
Though they fight against you,
  they shall not prevail,
For I am with you,
  to save and rescue you—oracle of
    the LORD.
²¹I will rescue you from the hand of the
  wicked,
  and ransom you from the power of
    the violent.

Jeremiah's Life a Warning. 16:1 This
word came to me from the LORD: ²Do
not take a wife and do not have sons and
daughters in this place, ³for thus says the
LORD concerning the sons and daughters
born in this place, the mothers who give
them birth, the fathers who beget them in
this land: ⁴Of deadly disease they shall die.
Unlamented and unburied they will lie like
dung on the ground. Sword and famine

will make an end of them, and their corpses will become food for the birds of the sky and the beasts of the earth.

⁵Thus says the LORD: Do not go into a house of mourning; do not go there to lament or grieve for them. For I have withdrawn my peace from this people—oracle of the LORD—my love and my compassion. ⁶They shall die, the great and the lowly, in this land, unburied and unlamented. No one will gash themselves or shave their heads for them. ⁷They will not break bread with the bereaved to offer consolation for the dead; they will not give them the cup of consolation to drink over the death of father or mother.

⁸Do not enter a house of feasting to sit eating and drinking with them. ⁹For thus says the LORD of hosts, the God of Israel: Before your eyes and in your lifetime, I will silence in this place the song of joy and the song of gladness, the song of the bridegroom and the song of the bride.

¹⁰When you proclaim all these words to this people and they ask you: "Why has the LORD pronounced all this great disaster against us? What is our crime? What sin have we committed against the LORD, our God?"— ¹¹you shall answer them: It is because your ancestors have forsaken me—oracle of the LORD—and followed other gods that they served and worshiped; but me they have forsaken, and my law they did not keep. ¹²And you have done worse than your ancestors. Here you are, every one of you, walking in the stubbornness of your evil heart instead of listening to me. ¹³I will throw you out of this land into a land that neither you nor your ancestors have known; there you can serve other gods day and night because I will not show you mercy.

☐ 1 THESSALONIANS 3

3:1 That is why, when we could bear it no longer, we decided to remain alone in Athens ²and sent Timothy, our brother and

Return from Exile. ¹⁴Therefore, days are coming—oracle of the LORD—when it will no longer be said, "As the LORD lives, who brought the Israelites out of Egypt"; ¹⁵but rather, "As the LORD lives, who brought the Israelites out of the land of the north and out of all the countries to which he had banished them." I will bring them back to the land I gave their ancestors.

Double Punishment. ¹⁶Look!—oracle of the LORD—I will send many fishermen to catch them. After that, I will send many hunters to hunt them out from every mountain and hill and rocky crevice. ¹⁷For my eyes are upon all their ways; they are not hidden from me, nor does their guilt escape my sight. ¹⁸I will at once repay them double for their crime and their sin because they profaned my land with the corpses of their detestable idols, and filled my heritage with their abominations.

Conversion of the Nations. ¹⁹LORD,
   my strength, my fortress,
   my refuge in the day of distress!
To you nations will come
   from the ends of the earth, and say,
"Our ancestors inherited mere frauds,
   empty, worthless."
²⁰Can human beings make for
   themselves gods?
   But these are not gods at all!
²¹Therefore, I will indeed give them
   knowledge;
   this time I will make them
   acknowledge
My strength and my power:
   they shall know that my name is
   LORD.

co-worker for God in the gospel of Christ, to strengthen and encourage you in your faith, ³so that no one be disturbed in these afflictions. For you yourselves know that we are destined for this. [4]For even when we were among you, we used to warn you in advance that we would undergo affliction, just as has happened, as you know. [5]For this reason, when I too could bear it no longer, I sent to learn about your faith, for fear that somehow the tempter had put you to the test and our toil might come to nothing.

[6]But just now Timothy has returned to us from you, bringing us the good news of your faith and love, and that you always think kindly of us and long to see us as we long to see you. [7]Because of this, we have been reassured about you, brothers, in our every distress and affliction, through your faith. [8]For we now live, if you stand firm in the Lord.

Concluding Thanksgiving and Prayer. [9]What thanksgiving, then, can we render to God for you, for all the joy we feel on your account before our God? [10]Night and day we pray beyond measure to see you in person and to remedy the deficiencies of your faith. [11]Now may God himself, our Father, and our Lord Jesus direct our way to you, [12]and may the Lord make you increase and abound in love for one another and for all, just as we have for you, [13]so as to strengthen your hearts, to be blameless in holiness before our God and Father at the coming of our Lord Jesus with all his holy ones. [Amen.]

October 13

The day that is past must not judge the day that is present, nor the present day judge that which is past. It is only the Last Day that judges all.

— St. Francis de Sales

☐ JEREMIAH 17-18

The Sin of Judah and Its Punishment.
17:1 The sin of Judah is written
　with an iron stylus,
Engraved with a diamond point
　upon the tablets of their hearts,

And the horns of their altars, [2]when their children remember their altars and their asherahs, beside the green trees, on the high hills, [3]the peaks in the country.

Your wealth and all your treasures
　I give as plunder,
As payment for all your sins
　throughout your territory,
[4]You will relinquish your hold on your
　heritage
　which I have given you.
I will enslave you to your enemies
　in a land you do not know:
For a fire has broken out from my anger,

burning forever.

True Wisdom. [5]Thus says the Lord:
Cursed is the man who trusts in
　human beings,
　who makes flesh his strength,
　whose heart turns away from the
　　Lord.
[6]He is like a barren bush in the
　wasteland
　that enjoys no change of season,
But stands in lava beds in the wilderness,
　a land, salty and uninhabited.
[7]Blessed are those who trust in the Lord;
　the Lord will be their trust.
[8]They are like a tree planted beside
　the waters
　that stretches out its roots to the
　　stream:
It does not fear heat when it comes,

its leaves stay green;
In the year of drought it shows no
distress,
but still produces fruit.
⁹More tortuous than anything is the
human heart,
beyond remedy; who can
understand it?
¹⁰I, the LORD, explore the mind
and test the heart,
Giving to all according to their ways,
according to the fruit of their deeds.
¹¹A partridge that broods but does not
hatch
are those who acquire wealth unjustly:
In midlife it will desert them;
in the end they are only fools.

The Source of Life. ¹²A throne of glory,
exalted from the beginning,
such is our holy place.
¹³O Hope of Israel, LORD!
all who forsake you shall be put to
shame;
The rebels shall be enrolled in the
netherworld;
they have forsaken the LORD, source
of living waters.

Prayer for Vengeance. ¹⁴Heal me,
LORD, that I may be healed;
save me, that I may be saved,
for you are my praise.
¹⁵See how they say to me,
"Where is the word of the LORD?
Let it come to pass!"
¹⁶Yet I did not press you to send disaster;
the day without remedy I have not
desired.
You know what passed my lips;
it is present before you.
¹⁷Do not become a terror to me,
you are my refuge in the day of
disaster.
¹⁸Let my persecutors be confounded—
not me!
let them be terrified—not me!
Bring upon them the day of disaster,

crush them with double
destruction.

Observance of the Sabbath. ¹⁹Thus said
the LORD to me: Go, stand at the Gate of
Benjamin, where the kings of Judah enter
and leave, and at the other gates of Jerusalem. ²⁰There say to them: Hear the word of
the LORD, you kings of Judah, and all Judah,
and all you inhabitants of Jerusalem who
enter these gates! ²¹Thus says the LORD: As
you love your lives, take care not to carry
burdens on the sabbath, to bring them in
through the gates of Jerusalem. ²²Bring no
burden from your homes on the sabbath.
Do no work whatever, but keep holy the
sabbath day, as I commanded your ancestors, ²³though they did not listen or give
ear, but stiffened their necks so they could
not hear or take correction. ²⁴If you truly
obey me—oracle of the LORD—and carry
no burden through the gates of this city on
the sabbath, keeping the sabbath day holy
and abstaining from all work on it, ²⁵then,
through the gates of this city, kings who sit
upon the throne of David will continue
to enter, riding in their chariots or upon
their horses, along with their princes, and
the people of Judah, and the inhabitants of
Jerusalem. This city will remain inhabited
forever. ²⁶To it people will come from the
cities of Judah and the neighborhood of
Jerusalem, from the land of Benjamin and
from the Shephelah, from the hill country
and the Negeb, to bring burnt offerings and
sacrifices, grain offerings, incense, and thank
offerings to the house of the LORD. ²⁷But if
you do not obey me and keep holy the sabbath day, if you carry burdens and come
through the gates of Jerusalem on the sabbath, I will set fire to its gates—a fire never
to be extinguished—and it will consume the
palaces of Jerusalem.

The Potter's Vessel. 18:1 This word came
to Jeremiah from the LORD: ²Arise and go
down to the potter's house; there you will

hear my word. [3]I went down to the potter's house and there he was, working at the wheel. [4]Whenever the vessel of clay he was making turned out badly in his hand, he tried again, making another vessel of whatever sort he pleased. [5]Then the word of the LORD came to me: [6]Can I not do to you, house of Israel, as this potter has done?—oracle of the LORD. Indeed, like clay in the hand of the potter, so are you in my hand, house of Israel. [7]At one moment I may decree concerning a nation or kingdom that I will uproot and tear down and destroy it; [8]but if that nation against whom I have decreed turns from its evil, then I will have a change of heart regarding the evil which I have decreed. [9]At another moment, I may decree concerning a nation or kingdom that I will build up and plant it; [10]but if that nation does what is evil in my eyes, refusing to obey my voice, then I will have a change of heart regarding the good with which I planned to bless it.

[11]And now, tell this to the people of Judah and the inhabitants of Jerusalem: Thus says the LORD: Look, I am fashioning evil against you and making a plan. Return, all of you, from your evil way; reform your ways and your deeds. [12]But they will say, "No use! We will follow our own devices; each one of us will behave according to the stubbornness of our evil hearts!"

Unnatural Apostasy. [13]Therefore
thus says the LORD:
Ask among the nations—
who has ever heard the like?
Truly horrible things
virgin Israel has done!
[14]Does the snow of Lebanon
desert the rocky heights?
Do the gushing waters dry up
that flow fresh down the mountains?
[15]Yet my people have forgotten me:
they offer incense in vain.
They stumble off their paths,
the ways of old,

Traveling on bypaths,
not the beaten track.
[16]Their land shall be made a waste,
an object of endless hissing:
All passersby will be horrified,
shaking their heads.
[17]Like the east wind, I will scatter them
before their enemies;
I will show them my back, not my face,
in their day of disaster.

Another Prayer for Vengeance. [18]"Come," they said, "let us devise a plot against Jeremiah, for instruction will not perish from the priests, nor counsel from the wise, nor the word from the prophets. Come, let us destroy him by his own tongue. Let us pay careful attention to his every word."

[19]Pay attention to me, O LORD,
and listen to what my adversaries say.
[20]Must good be repaid with evil
that they should dig a pit to take
my life?
Remember that I stood before you
to speak on their behalf,
to turn your wrath away from them.
[21]So now, give their children to famine,
deliver them to the power of the
sword.
Let their wives be childless and widows;
let their husbands die of pestilence,
their youths be struck down by the
sword in battle.
[22]May cries be heard from their homes,
when suddenly you send plunderers
against them.
For they have dug a pit to capture me,
they have hidden snares for my feet;
[23]But you, LORD, know
all their planning for my death.
Do not forgive their crime,
and their sin do not blot out from
your sight!
Let them stumble before you,
in the time of your anger act against
them.

☐ 1 THESSALONIANS 4

General Exhortations. 4:1 Finally, brothers, we earnestly ask and exhort you in the Lord Jesus that, as you received from us how you should conduct yourselves to please God—and as you are conducting yourselves—you do so even more. ²For you know what instructions we gave you through the Lord Jesus.

Holiness in Sexual Contact. ³This is the will of God, your holiness: that you refrain from immorality, ⁴that each of you know how to acquire a wife for himself in holiness and honor, ⁵not in lustful passion as do the Gentiles who do not know God; ⁶not to take advantage of or exploit a brother in this matter, for the Lord is an avenger in all these things, as we told you before and solemnly affirmed. ⁷For God did not call us to impurity but to holiness. ⁸Therefore, whoever disregards this, disregards not a human being but God, who [also] gives his holy Spirit to you.

Mutual Charity. ⁹On the subject of mutual charity you have no need for anyone to write you, for you yourselves have been taught by God to love one another. ¹⁰Indeed, you do this for all the brothers throughout Macedonia. Nevertheless we urge you, brothers, to progress even more, ¹¹and to aspire to live a tranquil life, to mind your own affairs, and to work with your [own] hands, as we instructed you, ¹²that you may conduct yourselves properly toward outsiders and not depend on anyone.

Hope for the Christian Dead. ¹³We do not want you to be unaware, brothers, about those who have fallen asleep, so that you may not grieve like the rest, who have no hope. ¹⁴For if we believe that Jesus died and rose, so too will God, through Jesus, bring with him those who have fallen asleep. ¹⁵Indeed, we tell you this, on the word of the Lord, that we who are alive, who are left until the coming of the Lord, will surely not precede those who have fallen asleep. ¹⁶For the Lord himself, with a word of command, with the voice of an archangel and with the trumpet of God, will come down from heaven, and the dead in Christ will rise first. ¹⁷Then we who are alive, who are left, will be caught up together with them in the clouds to meet the Lord in the air. Thus we shall always be with the Lord. ¹⁸Therefore, console one another with these words.

October 14

Pope St. Callistus I

We must busy ourselves with preparations for our departure from this world. For even if the day when the whole world ends never overtakes us, the end of each of us is right at the door.
— St. John Chrysostom

☐ JEREMIAH 19-20

Symbol of the Potter's Flask. 19:1 Thus said the LORD: Go, buy a potter's earthenware flask. Take along some of the elders of the people and some of the priests, ²and go out toward the Valley of Ben-hinnom, at the entrance of the Potsherd Gate; there proclaim the words which I will speak to you: ³You shall say, Listen to the word of the LORD, kings of Judah and inhabitants of Jerusalem: Thus says the LORD of hosts, the God of Israel: I am going to bring such evil upon this place that the ears of all who hear of it will ring. ⁴All because they have forsaken me and profaned this place by burning incense to other gods which neither they nor their ancestors knew; and because the kings of Judah have filled this place with innocent blood, ⁵building high places for Baal to burn their children in fire as offerings to Baal—something I never considered or said or commanded. ⁶Therefore, days are coming—oracle of the LORD—when this place will no longer be called Topheth, or the Valley of Ben-hinnom, but rather, the Valley of Slaughter. ⁷In this place I will foil the plan of Judah and Jerusalem; I will make them fall by the sword before their enemies, at the hand of those who seek their lives. Their corpses I will give as food to the birds of the sky and the beasts of the earth. ⁸I will make this city a waste and an object of hissing. Because of all its wounds, every passerby will be horrified and hiss. ⁹I will have them eat the flesh of their sons and daughters; they shall eat one another's flesh during the harsh siege under which their enemies and those who seek their lives will confine them.

¹⁰And you shall break the flask in the sight of the men who went with you, ¹¹and say to them: Thus says the LORD of hosts: Thus will I smash this people and this city, as one smashes a clay pot so that it cannot be repaired. And Topheth shall be its burial place, for there will be no other place for burial. ¹²Thus I will do to this place and to its inhabitants—oracle of the LORD; I will make this city like Topheth. ¹³And the houses of Jerusalem and the houses of the kings of Judah shall be defiled like the place of Topheth, all the houses upon whose roofs they burnt incense to the whole host of heaven and poured out libations to other gods.

¹⁴When Jeremiah returned from Topheth, where the LORD had sent him to prophesy, he stood in the court of the house of the LORD and said to all the people: ¹⁵Thus says the LORD of hosts, the God of Israel: I will bring upon this city all the evil I have spoken against it, because they have become stubborn and have not obeyed my words.

20:1 Now the priest Pashhur, son of Immer, chief officer in the house of the LORD, heard Jeremiah prophesying these things. ²So he struck the prophet and put him in the stocks at the upper Gate of Benjamin in the house of the LORD. ³The next morning, after Pashhur had released Jeremiah from the stocks, the prophet said to him: "Instead of Pashhur, the LORD names you 'Terror on every side.' ⁴For thus says the LORD: Indeed, I will hand you over to terror, you and all your friends. Your own eyes shall see them fall by the sword of their enemies. All Judah I will hand over to the power of the king of Babylon, who shall take them captive to Babylon or strike them down with the sword. ⁵All the wealth of this city, all its resources and its valuables, all the treasures of the kings of Judah, I will hand over to their enemies, who will plunder it and carry it away to Babylon. ⁶You, Pashhur, and all the members of your household shall go into exile. To Babylon you shall go; there you shall die and be buried, you and all your friends, because you have prophesied lies to them."

Jeremiah's Interior Crisis. ⁷You

seduced me, LORD, and I let
  myself be seduced;
    you were too strong for me, and you
      prevailed.
All day long I am an object of laughter;
  everyone mocks me.
⁸Whenever I speak, I must cry out,
  violence and outrage I proclaim;
The word of the LORD has brought me
  reproach and derision all day long.
⁹I say I will not mention him,

I will no longer speak in his name.
But then it is as if fire is burning in my
heart,
imprisoned in my bones;
I grow weary holding back,
I cannot!
[10]Yes, I hear the whisperings of many:
"Terror on every side!
Denounce! let us denounce him!"
All those who were my friends
are on the watch for any misstep of
mine.
"Perhaps he can be tricked; then we
will prevail,
and take our revenge on him."
[11]But the LORD is with me, like a
mighty champion:
my persecutors will stumble, they
will not prevail.
In their failure they will be put to utter
shame,
to lasting, unforgettable confusion.
[12]LORD of hosts, you test the just,
you see mind and heart,
Let me see the vengeance you take on
them,
for to you I have entrusted my
cause.

[13]Sing to the LORD,
praise the LORD,
For he has rescued the life of the poor
from the power of the evildoers!

[14]Cursed be the day
on which I was born!
May the day my mother gave me birth
never be blessed!
[15]Cursed be the one who brought the
news
to my father,
"A child, a son, has been born to you!"
filling him with great joy.
[16]Let that man be like the cities
which the LORD relentlessly
overthrew;
Let him hear war cries in the morning,
battle alarms at noonday,
[17]because he did not kill me in the
womb!
Then my mother would have been my
grave,
her womb confining me forever.
[18]Why did I come forth from the
womb,
to see sorrow and pain,
to end my days in shame?

☐ 1 THESSALONIANS 5

Vigilance. 5:1 Concerning times and seasons, brothers, you have no need for anything to be written to you. [2]For you yourselves know very well that the day of the Lord will come like a thief at night. [3]When people are saying, "Peace and security," then sudden disaster comes upon them, like labor pains upon a pregnant woman, and they will not escape.

[4]But you, brothers, are not in darkness, for that day to overtake you like a thief. [5]For all of you are children of the light and children of the day. We are not of the night or of darkness. [6]Therefore, let us not sleep as the rest do, but let us stay alert and sober. [7]Those who sleep go to sleep at night, and those who

are drunk get drunk at night. [8]But since we are of the day, let us be sober, putting on the breastplate of faith and love and the helmet that is hope for salvation. [9]For God did not destine us for wrath, but to gain salvation through our Lord Jesus Christ, [10]who died for us, so that whether we are awake or asleep we may live together with him. [11]Therefore, encourage one another and build one another up, as indeed you do.

Church Order. [12]We ask you, brothers, to respect those who are laboring among you and who are over you in the Lord and who admonish you, [13]and to show esteem for them with special love on account of their work. Be at peace among yourselves.

[14]We urge you, brothers, admonish the idle, cheer the fainthearted, support the weak, be patient with all. [15]See that no one returns evil for evil; rather, always seek what is good [both] for each other and for all. [16]Rejoice always. [17]Pray without ceasing. [18]In all circumstances give thanks, for this is the will of God for you in Christ Jesus. [19]Do not quench the Spirit. [20]Do not despise prophetic utterances. [21]Test everything; retain what is good. [22]Refrain from every kind of evil.

Concluding Prayer. [23]May the God of peace himself make you perfectly holy and may you entirely, spirit, soul, and body, be preserved blameless for the coming of our Lord Jesus Christ. [24]The one who calls you is faithful, and he will also accomplish it. [25]Brothers, pray for us [too].

[26]Greet all the brothers with a holy kiss. [27]I adjure you by the Lord that this letter be read to all the brothers. [28]The grace of our Lord Jesus Christ be with you.

October 15

St. Teresa of Ávila

Christ has no body on earth but yours, no hands but yours, no feet but yours. Yours are the eyes through which Christ's compassion for the world is to look out; yours are the feet with which He is to go about doing good; and yours are the hands with which He is to bless us now.

— ST. TERESA OF ÁVILA

▢ JEREMIAH 21–22

Fate of Zedekiah and Jerusalem. 21:1 The word which came to Jeremiah from the LORD when King Zedekiah sent Pashhur, son of Malchiah, and the priest Zephaniah, son of Maaseiah, to him with this request: [2]Inquire for us of the LORD, because Nebuchadnezzar, king of Babylon, is attacking us. Perhaps the LORD will act for us in accord with his wonderful works by making him withdraw from us. [3]But Jeremiah answered them: This is what you shall report to Zedekiah: [4]Thus says the LORD, the God of Israel: I will turn against you the weapons with which you are fighting the king of Babylon and the Chaldeans who besiege you outside the walls. These weapons I will pile up in the midst of this city, [5]and I myself will fight against you with outstretched hand and mighty arm, in anger, wrath, and great rage! [6]I will strike down the inhabitants of this city, human being and beast; they shall die in a great pestilence. [7]After that—oracle of the LORD—I will hand over Zedekiah, king of Judah, and his ministers and the people in this city who survive pestilence, sword, and famine, to Nebuchadnezzar, king of Babylon, to their enemies and those who seek their lives. He shall strike them down with the edge of the sword, without quarter, without mercy or compassion. [8]And to this people you shall say: Thus says the LORD: See, I am giving you a choice between the way to life and the way to death. [9]Whoever remains in this city shall die by the sword or famine or pestilence. But whoever leaves and surrenders to the Chaldeans who are besieging you shall live and escape with his life. [10]I have set my face against this city, for evil and not for good—oracle of the LORD. It shall be given into the power of the king of Babylon who shall set it on fire.

Oracles Regarding the Kings. [11]To the royal house of Judah:
Hear the word of the LORD,
[12]house of David!
Thus says the LORD:
Each morning dispense justice,
    rescue the oppressed from the hand
        of the oppressor,
Or my fury will break out like fire
    and burn with no one to quench it
    because of your evil deeds.
[13]Beware! I am against you, Ruler of
    the Valley,
Rock of the Plain—oracle of the
    LORD.
You say, "Who will attack us,
    who can storm our defenses?"
[14]I will punish you—oracle of the
    LORD—
as your deeds deserve!
I will kindle a fire in its forest
    that shall devour all its
        surroundings.

22:1 Thus says the LORD: Go down to the palace of the king of Judah and there deliver this word: [2]You shall say: Listen to the word of the LORD, king of Judah, who sit on the throne of David, you, your ministers, and your people who enter by these gates! [3]Thus says the LORD: Do what is right and just. Rescue the victims from the hand of their oppressors. Do not wrong or oppress the resident alien, the orphan, or the widow, and do not shed innocent blood in this place. [4]If you carry out these commands, kings who succeed to the throne of David will continue to enter the gates of this house, riding in chariots or mounted on horses, with their ministers, and their people. [5]But if you do not obey these commands, I swear by myself—oracle of the LORD: this house shall become rubble. [6]For thus says the LORD concerning the house of the king of Judah:

Though you be to me like Gilead,
    like the peak of Lebanon,
I swear I shall turn you into a waste,
    with cities uninhabited.
[7]Against you I will send destroyers,
    each with their tools:
They shall cut down your choice cedars,
    and cast them into the fire.

[8]Many nations will pass by this city and ask one another: "Why has the LORD done this to so great a city?" [9]And they will be told: "Because they have deserted their covenant with the LORD, their God, by worshiping and serving other gods."

Jehoahaz. [10]Do not weep for him who
    is dead,
    nor mourn for him!
Weep rather for him who is going away;
    never again to see
    the land of his birth.

[11]Thus says the LORD concerning Shallum, son of Josiah, king of Judah, his father's successor, who left this place: He shall never return, [12]but in the place where they exiled him, there he shall die; he shall never see this land again.

Jehoiakim. [13]Woe to him who builds
    his house on wrongdoing,
    his roof-chambers on injustice;
Who works his neighbors without pay,
    and gives them no wages.
[14]Who says, "I will build myself a
    spacious house,
    with airy rooms,"
Who cuts out windows for it,
    panels it with cedar,
    and paints it with vermilion.
[15]Must you prove your rank among
    kings
    by competing with them in cedar?
Did not your father eat and drink,

And act justly and righteously?
Then he prospered.
¹⁶Because he dispensed justice to the
weak and the poor,
he prospered.
Is this not to know me?—
oracle of the LORD.
¹⁷But your eyes and heart are set on
nothing
except your own gain,
On shedding innocent blood
and practicing oppression and
extortion.

¹⁸Therefore, thus says the LORD concerning Jehoiakim, son of Josiah, king of Judah:

They shall not lament him,
"Alas! my brother"; "Alas! sister."
They shall not lament him,
"Alas, Lord! alas, Majesty!"
¹⁹The burial of a donkey he shall be
given,
dragged forth and cast out
beyond the gates of Jerusalem.

Jeconiah. ²⁰Climb Lebanon and cry out,
in Bashan lift up your voice;
Cry out from Abarim,
for all your lovers are crushed.
²¹I spoke to you when you were secure,
but you answered, "I will not listen."
This has been your way from your
youth,
not to listen to my voice.
²²The wind shall shepherd all your
shepherds,
your lovers shall go into exile.

Surely then you shall be ashamed and
confounded
because of all your wickedness.
²³You who dwell on Lebanon,
who nest in the cedars,
How you shall groan when pains come
upon you,
like the pangs of a woman in
childbirth!

²⁴As I live—oracle of the LORD—even if you, Coniah, son of Jehoiakim, king of Judah, were a signet ring on my right hand, I would snatch you off. ²⁵I will hand you over to those who seek your life, to those you dread: Nebuchadnezzar, king of Babylon, and the Chaldeans. ²⁶I will cast you out, you and the mother who bore you, into a land different from the land of your birth; and there you will die; ²⁷Neither shall return to the land for which they yearn.

²⁸Is this man Coniah a thing despised,
to be broken,
a vessel that no one wants?
Why are he and his offspring cast out?
why thrown into a land they do not
know?
²⁹O land, land, land,
hear the word of the LORD—
³⁰Thus says the LORD:
Write this man down as childless,
a man who will never prosper in his
life!
Nor shall any of his descendants
prosper,
to sit upon the throne of David,
to rule again over Judah.

☐ COLOSSIANS 1

Greeting. 1:1 Paul, an apostle of Christ Jesus by the will of God, and Timothy our brother, ²to the holy ones and faithful brothers in Christ in Colossae: grace to you and peace from God our Father.

Thanksgiving. ³We always give thanks to God, the Father of our Lord Jesus Christ, when we pray for you, ⁴for we have heard of your faith in Christ Jesus and the love that you have for all the holy ones ⁵because of the hope reserved for you in heaven. Of this you have already heard through the word of truth, the gospel, [6]that has come to you. Just as in the whole world it is bearing fruit and growing, so also among you, from the day you heard it and came to know the grace of God in truth, [7]as you learned it from Epaphras our beloved fellow slave, who is a trustworthy minister of Christ on your behalf [8]and who also told us of your love in the Spirit.

Prayer for Continued Progress. [9]Therefore, from the day we heard this, we do not cease praying for you and asking that you may be filled with the knowledge of his will through all spiritual wisdom and understanding [10]to live in a manner worthy of the Lord, so as to be fully pleasing, in every good work bearing fruit and growing in the knowledge of God, [11]strengthened with every power, in accord with his glorious might, for all endurance and patience, with joy [12]giving thanks to the Father, who has made you fit to share in the inheritance of the holy ones in light. [13]He delivered us from the power of darkness and transferred us to the kingdom of his beloved Son, [14]in whom we have redemption, the forgiveness of sins.

His Person and Work. [15]He is the
image of the invisible God,
the firstborn of all creation.
[16]For in him were created all things in
heaven and on earth,
the visible and the invisible,
whether thrones or dominions or
principalities or powers;
all things were created through him
and for him.
[17]He is before all things,
and in him all things hold together.
[18]He is the head of the body, the
church.

He is the beginning, the firstborn
from the dead,
that in all things he himself might
be preeminent.
[19]For in him all the fullness was pleased
to dwell,
[20]and through him to reconcile all
things for him,
making peace by the blood of his
cross
[through him], whether those on
earth or those in heaven.

[21]And you who once were alienated and hostile in mind because of evil deeds [22]he has now reconciled in his fleshly body through his death, to present you holy, without blemish, and irreproachable before him, [23]provided that you persevere in the faith, firmly grounded, stable, and not shifting from the hope of the gospel that you heard, which has been preached to every creature under heaven, of which I, Paul, am a minister.

Christ in Us. [24]Now I rejoice in my sufferings for your sake, and in my flesh I am filling up what is lacking in the afflictions of Christ on behalf of his body, which is the church, [25]of which I am a minister in accordance with God's stewardship given to me to bring to completion for you the word of God, [26]the mystery hidden from ages and from generations past. But now it has been manifested to his holy ones, [27]to whom God chose to make known the riches of the glory of this mystery among the Gentiles; it is Christ in you, the hope for glory. [28]It is he whom we proclaim, admonishing everyone and teaching everyone with all wisdom, that we may present everyone perfect in Christ. [29]For this I labor and struggle, in accord with the exercise of his power working within me.

October 16

St. Hedwig; St. Margaret Mary Alacoque

One righteous soul can obtain pardon for a thousand sinners.
— St. Margaret Mary Alacoque

☐ JEREMIAH 23-24

A Just Shepherd. 23:1 Woe to the shepherds who destroy and scatter the flock of my pasture—oracle of the Lord. ²Therefore, thus says the Lord, the God of Israel, against the shepherds who shepherd my people: You have scattered my sheep and driven them away. You have not cared for them, but I will take care to punish your evil deeds. ³I myself will gather the remnant of my flock from all the lands to which I have banished them and bring them back to their folds; there they shall be fruitful and multiply. ⁴I will raise up shepherds for them who will shepherd them so that they need no longer fear or be terrified; none shall be missing—oracle of the Lord.

⁵See, days are coming—oracle of the
Lord—
when I will raise up a righteous
branch for David;
As king he shall reign and govern
wisely,
he shall do what is just and right in
the land.
⁶In his days Judah shall be saved,
Israel shall dwell in security.
This is the name to be given him:
"The Lord our justice."

⁷Therefore, the days are coming—oracle of the Lord—when they shall no longer say, "As the Lord lives, who brought the Israelites out of the land of Egypt"; ⁸but rather, "As the Lord lives, who brought the descendants of the house of Israel up from the land of the north"—and from all the lands to which I banished them; they shall again live on their own soil.

The False Prophets. ⁹Concerning the
prophets:
My heart is broken within me,
all my bones tremble;
I am like a drunk,
like one overcome by wine,
Because of the Lord,
because of his holy words.
¹⁰The land is filled with adulterers;
because of the curse the land
mourns,
the pastures of the wilderness are
withered.
Theirs is an evil course,
theirs is unjust power.
¹¹Both prophet and priest are godless!
In my very house I find their
wickedness—
oracle of the Lord.
¹²Hence their way shall become for
them
slippery ground.
Into the darkness they shall be driven,
and fall headlong;
For I will bring disaster upon them,
the year of their punishment—
oracle of the Lord.
¹³Among Samaria's prophets
I saw something unseemly:
They prophesied by Baal
and led my people Israel astray.
¹⁴But among Jerusalem's prophets
I saw something more shocking:
Adultery, walking in deception,
strengthening the power of the
wicked,
so that no one turns from evil;
To me they are all like Sodom,
its inhabitants like Gomorrah.

¹⁵Therefore, thus says the LORD of hosts against the prophets:

Look, I will give them wormwood to eat,
 and poisoned water to drink;
For from Jerusalem's prophets
 ungodliness has gone forth into the
 whole land.
¹⁶Thus says the LORD of hosts:
Do not listen to the words of your
 prophets,
 who fill you with emptiness;
They speak visions from their own fancy,
 not from the mouth of the LORD.
¹⁷They say to those who despise the
 word of the LORD,
 "Peace shall be yours";
And to everyone who walks in hardness
 of heart,
 "No evil shall overtake you."
¹⁸Now, who has stood in the council of
 the LORD,
 to see him and to hear his word?
 Who has heeded his word so as to
 announce it?
¹⁹See, the storm of the LORD!
 His wrath breaks forth
In a whirling storm
 that bursts upon the heads of the
 wicked.
²⁰The anger of the LORD shall not abate
 until he has carried out completely
 the decisions of his heart.
In days to come
 you will understand fully.
²¹I did not send these prophets,
 yet they ran;
I did not speak to them,
 yet they prophesied.
²²Had they stood in my council,
 they would have proclaimed my
 words to my people,
They would have brought them back
 from their evil ways
 and from their wicked deeds.
²³Am I a God near at hand only—
 oracle of the LORD—

and not a God far off?
²⁴Can anyone hide in secret
 without my seeing them?—oracle of
 the LORD.
Do I not fill
 heaven and earth?—oracle of the
 LORD.

²⁵I have heard the prophets who prophesy lies in my name say, "I had a dream! I had a dream!" ²⁶How long? Will the hearts of the prophets who prophesy lies and their own deceitful fancies ever turn back? ²⁷By the dreams they tell each other, they plan to make my people forget my name, just as their ancestors forgot my name for Baal. ²⁸Let the prophets who have dreams tell their dreams; let those who have my word speak my word truthfully!

What has straw to do with wheat?
 —oracle of the LORD.
²⁹Is not my word like fire—oracle of
 the LORD—
 like a hammer shattering rock?

³⁰Therefore I am against the prophets— oracle of the LORD—those who steal my words from each other. ³¹Yes, I am against the prophets—oracle of the LORD—those who compose their own speeches and call them oracles. ³²Yes, I am against the prophets who tell lying dreams—oracle of the LORD—those who lead my people astray by recounting their reckless lies. It was not I who sent them or commanded them; they do this people no good at all—oracle of the LORD.

³³And when this people or a prophet or a priest asks you, "What is the burden of the LORD?" you shall answer, "You are the burden, and I cast you off"—oracle of the LORD. ³⁴If a prophet or a priest or anyone else mentions "the burden of the LORD," I will punish that man and his household. ³⁵Thus you shall ask, when speaking to one another, "What answer did the LORD give?" or "What did the LORD say?" ³⁶But "the burden of the LORD"

you shall mention no more. For each of you, your own word becomes the burden so that you pervert the words of the living God, the LORD of hosts, our God. [37]Thus shall you ask the prophet, "What answer did the LORD give?" or "What did the LORD say?" [38]But if you ask about "the burden of the LORD," then thus says the LORD: Because you use this phrase, "the burden of the LORD," though I forbade you to use it, [39]therefore I will lift you on high and cast you from my presence, you and the city which I gave to you and your ancestors. [40]And I will bring upon you eternal reproach, eternal shame, never to be forgotten.

The Two Baskets of Figs. 24:1 The LORD showed me two baskets of figs placed before the temple of the LORD. This was after Nebuchadnezzar, king of Babylon, had exiled from Jerusalem Jeconiah, son of Jehoiakim, king of Judah, and the princes of Judah, the artisans and smiths, and brought them to Babylon. [2]One basket contained excellent figs, those that ripen early. But the other basket contained very bad figs, so bad they could not be eaten. [3]Then the LORD said to me: What do you see, Jeremiah? "Figs," I replied; "the good ones are very good, but the bad ones very bad, so bad they cannot be eaten." [4]Thereupon this word of the LORD came to me: [5]Thus says the LORD, the God of Israel: Like these good figs, I will also regard with favor Judah's exiles whom I sent away from this place into the land of the Chaldeans. [6]I will look after them for good and bring them back to this land, to build them up, not tear them down; to plant them, not uproot them. [7]I will give them a heart to know me, that I am the LORD. They shall be my people and I will be their God, for they shall return to me with their whole heart. [8]But like the figs that are bad, so bad they cannot be eaten—yes, thus says the LORD—even so will I treat Zedekiah, king of Judah, and his princes, the remnant of Jerusalem remaining in this land and those who have settled in the land of Egypt. [9]I will make them an object of horror to all the kingdoms of the earth, a reproach and a byword, a taunt and a curse, in all the places to which I will drive them. [10]I will send upon them sword, famine, and pestilence, until they have disappeared from the land which I gave them and their ancestors.

☐ COLOSSIANS 2

2:1 For I want you to know how great a struggle I am having for you and for those in Laodicea and all who have not seen me face to face, [2]that their hearts may be encouraged as they are brought together in love, to have all the richness of fully assured understanding, for the knowledge of the mystery of God, Christ, [3]in whom are hidden all the treasures of wisdom and knowledge.

A General Admonition. [4]I say this so that no one may deceive you by specious arguments. [5]For even if I am absent in the flesh, yet I am with you in spirit, rejoicing as I observe your good order and the firmness of your faith in Christ. [6]So, as you received Christ Jesus the Lord, walk in him, [7]rooted in him and built upon him and established in the faith as you were taught, abounding in thanksgiving. [8]See to it that no one captivate you with an empty, seductive philosophy according to human tradition, according to the elemental powers of the world and not according to Christ.

Sovereign Role of Christ. [9]For in him dwells the whole fullness of the deity bodily, [10]and you share in this fullness in him, who is the head of every principality and power. [11]In him you were also circumcised with a circumcision not administered by hand, by stripping off the carnal body, with the circumcision of Christ. [12]You were buried with him in baptism, in which you were also raised with him through faith in the power of God, who raised him from the dead. [13]And even when you were dead [in] transgressions and the uncircumcision of your flesh, he brought you to life along with him, having forgiven us all our transgressions; [14]obliterating the bond against us, with its legal claims, which was opposed to us, he also removed it from our midst, nailing it to the cross; [15]despoiling the principalities and the powers, he made a public spectacle of them, leading them away in triumph by it.

Practices Contrary to Faith. [16]Let no one, then, pass judgment on you in matters of food and drink or with regard to a festival or new moon or sabbath. [17]These

are shadows of things to come; the reality belongs to Christ. [18]Let no one disqualify you, delighting in self-abasement and worship of angels, taking his stand on visions, inflated without reason by his fleshly mind, [19]and not holding closely to the head, from whom the whole body, supported and held together by its ligaments and bonds, achieves the growth that comes from God.

[20]If you died with Christ to the elemental powers of the world, why do you submit to regulations as if you were still living in the world? [21]"Do not handle! Do not taste! Do not touch!" [22]These are all things destined to perish with use; they accord with human precepts and teachings. [23]While they have a semblance of wisdom in rigor of devotion and self-abasement [and] severity to the body, they are of no value against gratification of the flesh.

October 17

St. Ignatius of Antioch

Try to gather more frequently to celebrate God's Eucharist and to praise Him. For when you meet with frequency, Satan's powers are overthrown and his destructiveness is undone by the unanimity of your faith.

— ST. IGNATIUS OF ANTIOCH

☐ JEREMIAH 25-26

Seventy Years of Exile. 25:1 The word that came to Jeremiah concerning all the people of Judah, in the fourth year of Jehoiakim, son of Josiah, king of Judah (the first year of Nebuchadnezzar, king of Babylon). [2]This word the prophet Jeremiah spoke to all the people of Judah and all the inhabitants of Jerusalem: [3]Since the thirteenth year of Josiah, son of Amon, king of Judah, to this day—that is, twenty-three years—the word of the LORD has come to me and I spoke to you untiringly, but you would not listen.

[4]The LORD kept sending you all his servants the prophets, but you refused to listen or pay attention [5]to this message: Turn back, each of you, from your evil way and from your evil deeds; then you shall remain in the land which the LORD gave you and your ancestors, from of old and forever. [6]Do not follow other gods to serve and bow down to them; do not provoke me with the works of your hands, or I will bring evil upon you. [7]But you would not listen to me—oracle of the LORD—and so you

provoked me with the works of your hands to your own harm. [8]Hence, thus says the LORD of hosts: Since you would not listen to my words, [9]I am about to send for and fetch all the tribes from the north—oracle of the LORD—and I will send for Nebuchadnezzar, king of Babylon, my servant; I will bring them against this land, its inhabitants, and all these neighboring nations. I will doom them, making them an object of horror, of hissing, of everlasting reproach. [10]Among them I will put to an end the song of joy and the song of gladness, the voice of the bridegroom and the voice of the bride, the sound of the millstone and the light of the lamp. [11]This whole land shall be a ruin and a waste. Seventy years these nations shall serve the king of Babylon; [12]but when the seventy years have elapsed, I will punish the king of Babylon and that nation and the land of the Chaldeans for their guilt—oracle of the LORD. Their land I will turn into everlasting waste. [13]Against that land I will fulfill all the words I have spoken against it, all that is written in this book, which Jeremiah prophesied against all the nations. [14]They also shall serve many nations and great kings, and thus I will repay them according to their own deeds and according to the works of their hands.

The Cup of Judgment on the Nations.
[15]For thus said the LORD, the God of Israel, to me: Take this cup of the wine of wrath from my hand and have all the nations to whom I will send you drink it. [16]They shall drink, and retch, and go mad, because of the sword I will send among them. [17]I took the cup from the hand of the LORD and gave it as drink to all the nations to whom the LORD sent me: [18]to Jerusalem, the cities of Judah, its kings and princes, to make them a ruin and a waste, an object of hissing and cursing, as they are today; [19]to Pharaoh, king of Egypt, and his servants, princes, all his people [20]and those of mixed ancestry; all the kings of the land of Uz; all the kings of the land of the Philistines:

Ashkelon, Gaza, Ekron, and the remnant of Ashdod; [21]Edom, Moab, and the Ammonites; [22]all the kings of Tyre, of Sidon, and of the shores beyond the sea; [23]Dedan and Tema and Buz, all the desert dwellers who shave their temples; [24]all the kings of Arabia; [25]all the kings of Zimri, of Elam, of the Medes; [26]all the kings of the north, near and far, one after the other; all the kingdoms upon the face of the earth and after them the king of Sheshach shall drink.

[27]Tell them: Thus says the LORD of hosts, the God of Israel: Drink! Get drunk and vomit! Fall, never to rise, before the sword that I will send among you! [28]If they refuse to take the cup from your hand and drink, say to them: Thus says the LORD of hosts: You must drink! [29]Now that I am inflicting evil on this city, called by my name, how can you possibly escape? You shall not escape! I am calling down the sword upon all the inhabitants of the earth—oracle of the LORD of hosts. [30]As for you, prophesy against them all these words and say to them:

The LORD roars from on high,
  from his holy dwelling he raises his
    voice;
Mightily he roars over his sheepfold,
  a shout like that of vintagers echoes
    over all the inhabitants of the earth.
[31]The uproar spreads
  to the end of the earth;
For the LORD has an indictment
  against the nations,
  he enters into judgment against all
    flesh:
The wicked shall be given to the
    sword—
  oracle of the LORD.
[32]Thus says the LORD of hosts:
Look! disaster stalks
  nation after nation;
A violent storm surges
  from the recesses of the earth.

[33]On that day, those whom the LORD has slain will be strewn from one end of

the earth to the other. They will not be mourned, they will not be gathered, they will not be buried; they shall lie like dung upon the ground.

³⁴Howl, you shepherds, and wail!
    roll on the ground, leaders of the
        flock!
The time for your slaughter has come;
    like choice rams you shall fall.
³⁵There is no flight for the shepherds,
    no escape for the leaders of the flock.
³⁶Listen! Wailing from the shepherds,
    howling from the leaders of the
        flock!
For the LORD lays waste their grazing
        place;
³⁷desolate are the peaceful pastures,
    from the burning wrath of the LORD.
³⁸Like a lion he leaves his lair,
    and their land is made desolate
By the sweeping sword,
    and the burning wrath of the LORD.

Jeremiah Threatened with Death. 26:1
In the beginning of the reign of Jehoiakim, son of Josiah, king of Judah, this word came from the LORD: ²Thus says the LORD: Stand in the court of the house of the LORD and speak to the inhabitants of all the cities of Judah who come to worship in the house of the LORD; whatever I command you, tell them, and hold nothing back. ³Perhaps they will listen and turn, all of them from their evil way, so that I may repent of the evil I plan to inflict upon them for their evil deeds. ⁴Say to them: Thus says the LORD: If you do not obey me, by walking according to the law I set before you ⁵and listening to the words of my servants the prophets, whom I kept sending you, even though you do not listen to them, ⁶I will treat this house like Shiloh, and make this city a curse for all the nations of the earth.

⁷Now the priests, the prophets, and all the people heard Jeremiah speaking these words in the house of the LORD. ⁸When Jeremiah finished speaking all that the LORD commanded him to speak to all the people, then the priests, the prophets, and all the people laid hold of him, crying, "You must die! ⁹Why do you prophesy in the name of the LORD: 'This house shall become like Shiloh,' and 'This city shall be desolate, without inhabitant'?" And all the people crowded around Jeremiah in the house of the LORD.

¹⁰When the princes of Judah heard about these things, they came up from the house of the king to the house of the LORD and convened at the New Gate of the house of the LORD. ¹¹The priests and prophets said to the princes and to all the people, "Sentence this man to death! He has prophesied against this city! You heard it with your own ears." ¹²Jeremiah said to the princes and all the people: "It was the LORD who sent me to prophesy against this house and city everything you have heard. ¹³Now, therefore, reform your ways and your deeds; listen to the voice of the LORD your God, so that the LORD will have a change of heart regarding the evil he has spoken against you. ¹⁴As for me, I am in your hands; do with me what is good and right in your eyes. ¹⁵But you should certainly know that by putting me to death, you bring innocent blood on yourselves, on this city and its inhabitants. For in truth it was the LORD who sent me to you, to speak all these words for you to hear."

¹⁶Then the princes and all the people said to the priests and the prophets, "This man does not deserve a death sentence; it is in the name of the LORD, our God, that he speaks to us." ¹⁷At this, some of the elders of the land arose and said to the whole assembly of the people, ¹⁸"Micah of Moresheth used to prophesy in the days of Hezekiah, king of Judah, and he said to all the people of Judah: Thus says the LORD of hosts:

Zion shall be plowed as a field,
    Jerusalem, a heap of ruins,

and the temple mount,
a forest ridge.

¹⁹Did Hezekiah, king of Judah, and all Judah condemn him to death? Did he not fear the LORD and entreat the favor of the LORD, so that the LORD had a change of heart regarding the evil he had spoken against them? We, however, are about to do great evil against ourselves."

The Fate of Uriah. ²⁰There was another man who used to prophesy in the name of the LORD, Uriah, son of Shemaiah, from Kiriath-jearim; he prophesied against this city and this land the same message as Jeremiah. ²¹When King Jehoiakim and all his officers and princes heard his words, the king sought to have him killed. But Uriah heard of it and fled in fear to Egypt. ²²Then King Jehoiakim sent Elnathan, son of Achbor, and others with him into Egypt, ²³and they brought Uriah out of Egypt and took him to Jehoiakim the king, who struck him down with the sword and threw his corpse into the common burial ground. ²⁴But the hand of Ahikam, son of Shaphan, protected Jeremiah, so they did not hand him over to the people to be put to death.

☐ COLOSSIANS 3

Mystical Death and Resurrection. 3:1 If then you were raised with Christ, seek what is above, where Christ is seated at the right hand of God. ²Think of what is above, not of what is on earth. ³For you have died, and your life is hidden with Christ in God. ⁴When Christ your life appears, then you too will appear with him in glory.

Renunciation of Vice. ⁵Put to death, then, the parts of you that are earthly: immorality, impurity, passion, evil desire, and the greed that is idolatry. ⁶Because of these the wrath of God is coming [upon the disobedient]. ⁷By these you too once conducted yourselves, when you lived in that way. ⁸But now you must put them all away: anger, fury, malice, slander, and obscene language out of your mouths. ⁹Stop lying to one another, since you have taken off the old self with its practices ¹⁰and have put on the new self, which is being renewed, for knowledge, in the image of its creator. ¹¹Here there is not Greek and Jew, circumcision and uncircumcision, barbarian, Scythian, slave, free; but Christ is all and in all.

¹²Put on then, as God's chosen ones, holy and beloved, heartfelt compassion, kindness, humility, gentleness, and patience, ¹³bearing with one another and forgiving one another, if one has a grievance against another; as the Lord has forgiven you, so must you also do. ¹⁴And over all these put on love, that is, the bond of perfection. ¹⁵And let the peace of Christ control your hearts, the peace into which you were also called in one body. And be thankful. ¹⁶Let the word of Christ dwell in you richly, as in all wisdom you teach and admonish one another, singing psalms, hymns, and spiritual songs with gratitude in your hearts to God. ¹⁷And whatever you do, in word or in deed, do everything in the name of the Lord Jesus, giving thanks to God the Father through him.

The Christian Family. ¹⁸Wives, be subordinate to your husbands, as is proper in the Lord. ¹⁹Husbands, love your wives, and avoid any bitterness toward them. ²⁰Children, obey your parents in everything, for this is pleasing to the Lord. ²¹Fathers, do not provoke your children, so they may not become discouraged.

Slaves and Masters. ²²Slaves, obey your human masters in everything, not only when being watched, as currying favor, but in simplicity of heart, fearing the Lord. ²³Whatever you do, do from the heart, as for the Lord and not for others, ²⁴knowing that you will receive from the Lord the due payment of the inheritance; be slaves of the Lord Christ. ²⁵For the wrongdoer will receive recompense for the wrong he committed, and there is no partiality.

October 18

St. Luke

Let your speech be brief and savory.
— St. Ephraem the Syrian

☐ JEREMIAH 27-28

Serve Babylon or Perish. 27:1 In the beginning of the reign of Zedekiah, son of Josiah, king of Judah, this word came to Jeremiah from the Lord: ²The Lord said to me: Make for yourself thongs and yoke bars and put them on your shoulders. ³Send them to the kings of Edom, Moab, the Ammonites, Tyre, and Sidon, through the ambassadors who have come to Jerusalem to Zedekiah, king of Judah, ⁴and command them to tell their lords: Thus says the Lord of hosts, the God of Israel, Thus shall you say to your lords: ⁵It was I who made the earth, human being and beast on the face of the earth, by my great power, with my outstretched arm; and I can give them to whomever I think fit. ⁶Now I have given all these lands into the hand of Nebuchadnezzar, king of Babylon, my servant; even the wild animals I have given him to serve him. ⁷All nations shall serve him and his son and his grandson, until the time comes for him and his land; then many nations and great kings will enslave him. ⁸Meanwhile, the nation or the kingdom that will not serve him, Nebuchadnezzar, king of Babylon, or bend its neck under the yoke of the king of Babylon, I will punish that nation with sword, famine, and pestilence—oracle of the Lord—until I finish them by his hand.

⁹You, however, must not listen to your prophets, to your diviners and dreamers, to your soothsayers and sorcerers, who say to you, "Do not serve the king of Babylon." ¹⁰For they prophesy lies to you, so as to drive you far from your land, making me banish you so that you perish. ¹¹The people that bends the neck to the yoke of the king of Babylon to serve him, I will leave in peace on its own land—oracle of the Lord—to cultivate it and dwell on it.

¹²To Zedekiah, king of Judah, I spoke the same words: Bend your necks to the yoke of the king of Babylon; serve him and his people, so that you may live. ¹³Why should you and your people die by sword, famine, and pestilence, in accordance with the word the Lord has spoken to the nation that will not serve the king of Babylon? ¹⁴Do not listen to the words of the prophets who say to you, "Do not serve the king of Babylon." They prophesy lies to you! ¹⁵I did not send them—oracle of the Lord—but they prophesy falsely in my name. As a result I must banish you, and you will perish, you and the prophets who are prophesying to you.

¹⁶To the priests and to all the people I said: Thus says the Lord: Do not listen to the words of your prophets who prophesy to you: "The vessels of the house of the

Lord will soon be brought back from Babylon," for they prophesy lies to you. ¹⁷Do not listen to them! Serve the king of Babylon that you may live. Why should this city become rubble? ¹⁸If they were prophets, if the word of the Lord were with them, then they would intercede with the Lord of hosts, that the vessels remaining in the house of the Lord and in the house of the king of Judah and in Jerusalem should not also go to Babylon. ¹⁹For thus says the Lord of hosts concerning the pillars, the sea, the stands, and the rest of the vessels remaining in this city, ²⁰which Nebuchadnezzar, king of Babylon, did not take when he exiled Jeconiah, son of Jehoiakim, king of Judah, from Jerusalem to Babylon, along with all the nobles of Judah and Jerusalem— ²¹thus says the Lord of hosts, the God of Israel, concerning the vessels remaining in the house of the Lord, in the house of the king of Judah, and in Jerusalem: ²²To Babylon they shall go, and there they shall remain, until the day I look for them—oracle of the Lord; then I will bring them back and restore them to this place.

The Two Yokes. 28:1 That same year, in the beginning of the reign of Zedekiah, king of Judah, in the fifth month of the fourth year, Hananiah the prophet, son of Azzur, from Gibeon, said to me in the house of the Lord in the sight of the priests and all the people: ²"Thus says the Lord of hosts, the God of Israel: I have broken the yoke of the king of Babylon. ³Within two years I will restore to this place all the vessels of the house of the Lord which Nebuchadnezzar, king of Babylon, took from this place and carried away to Babylon. ⁴And Jeconiah, son of Jehoiakim, king of Judah, and all the exiles of Judah who went to Babylon, I will bring back to this place—oracle of the Lord—for I will break the yoke of the king of Babylon."

⁵Jeremiah the prophet answered the prophet Hananiah in the sight of the priests and all the people standing in the house of the Lord, ⁶and said: Amen! thus may the Lord do! May the Lord fulfill your words that you have prophesied, by bringing back the vessels of the house of the Lord and all the exiles from Babylon to this place! ⁷But now, listen to the word I am about to speak in your hearing and the hearing of all the people. ⁸In the past, the prophets who came before you and me prophesied war, disaster, and pestilence against many lands and mighty kingdoms. ⁹But the prophet who prophesies peace is recognized as the prophet whom the Lord has truly sent only when his word comes to pass.

¹⁰Thereupon Hananiah the prophet took the yoke bar from the neck of Jeremiah the prophet and broke it. ¹¹He said in the sight of all the people: "Thus says the Lord: Like this, within two years I will break the yoke of Nebuchadnezzar, king of Babylon, from the neck of all the nations." At that, the prophet Jeremiah went on his way.

¹²After Hananiah the prophet had broken the yoke bar off the neck of the prophet Jeremiah, the word of the Lord came to Jeremiah: ¹³Go tell Hananiah this: Thus says the Lord: By breaking a wooden yoke bar, you make an iron yoke! ¹⁴For thus says the Lord of hosts, the God of Israel: A yoke of iron I have placed on the necks of all these nations serving Nebuchadnezzar, king of Babylon, and they shall serve him; even the wild animals I have given him. ¹⁵And Jeremiah the prophet said to Hananiah the prophet: Listen to this, Hananiah! The Lord has not sent you, and you have led this people to rely on deception. ¹⁶For this, says the Lord, I am sending you from the face of the earth; this very year you shall die, because you have preached rebellion against the Lord. ¹⁷Hananiah the prophet died in that year, in the seventh month.

☐ COLOSSIANS 4

4:1 Masters, treat your slaves justly and fairly, realizing that you too have a Master in heaven.

Prayer and Apostolic Spirit. [2]Persevere in prayer, being watchful in it with thanksgiving; [3]at the same time, pray for us, too, that God may open a door to us for the word, to speak of the mystery of Christ, for which I am in prison, [4]that I may make it clear, as I must speak. [5]Conduct yourselves wisely toward outsiders, making the most of the opportunity. [6]Let your speech always be gracious, seasoned with salt, so that you know how you should respond to each one.

Tychicus and Onesimus. [7]Tychicus, my beloved brother, trustworthy minister, and fellow slave in the Lord, will tell you all the news of me. [8]I am sending him to you for this very purpose, so that you may know about us and that he may encourage your hearts, [9]together with Onesimus, a trustworthy and beloved brother, who is one of you. They will tell you about everything here.

From Paul's Co-Workers. [10]Aristarchus, my fellow prisoner, sends you greetings, as does Mark the cousin of Barnabas (concerning whom you have received instructions; if he comes to you, receive him), [11]and Jesus, who is called Justus, who are of the circumcision; these alone are my co-workers for the kingdom of God, and they have been a comfort to me. [12]Epaphras sends you greetings; he is one of you, a slave of Christ [Jesus], always striving for you in his prayers so that you may be perfect and fully assured in all the will of God. [13]For I can testify that he works very hard for you and for those in Laodicea and those in Hierapolis. [14]Luke the beloved physician sends greetings, as does Demas.

A Message for the Laodiceans. [15]Give greetings to the brothers in Laodicea and to Nympha and to the church in her house. [16]And when this letter is read before you, have it read also in the church of the Laodiceans, and you yourselves read the one from Laodicea. [17]And tell Archippus, "See that you fulfill the ministry that you received in the Lord."

[18]The greeting is in my own hand, Paul's. Remember my chains. Grace be with you.

October 19

Sts. Isaac Jogues, John de Brébeuf, and Companions

My confidence is placed in God, who does not need our help for accomplishing His designs. Our single endeavor should be to give ourselves to the work and to be faithful to Him, and not to spoil His work by our shortcomings.

— St. Isaac Jogues

☐ JEREMIAH 29-30

Letter to the Exiles in Babylon. 29:1 These are the words of the scroll which Jeremiah the prophet sent from Jerusalem to the remaining elders among the exiles, to the priests, the prophets, and all the people whom Nebuchadnezzar exiled from Jerusalem to Babylon. [2]This was after King Jeconiah and the queen mother, the court officials, the princes of Judah and Jerusalem, the artisans and smiths had left Jerusalem. ³Delivered in Babylon by Elasah, son of Shaphan, and by Gemariah, son of Hilkiah, whom Zedekiah, king of Judah, sent to the king of Babylon, the letter read:

⁴Thus says the LORD of hosts, the God of Israel, to all the exiles whom I exiled from Jerusalem to Babylon: ⁵Build houses and live in them; plant gardens and eat their fruits. ⁶Take wives and have sons and daughters; find wives for your sons and give your daughters to husbands, so that they may bear sons and daughters. Increase there; do not decrease. ⁷Seek the welfare of the city to which I have exiled you; pray for it to the LORD, for upon its welfare your own depends. ⁸For thus says the LORD of hosts, the God of Israel: Do not be deceived by the prophets and diviners who are among you; do not listen to those among you who dream dreams, ⁹for they prophesy lies to you in my name; I did not send them—oracle of the LORD.

¹⁰For thus says the LORD: Only after seventy years have elapsed for Babylon will I deal with you and fulfill for you my promise to bring you back to this place. ¹¹For I know well the plans I have in mind for you—oracle of the LORD—plans for your welfare and not for woe, so as to give you a future of hope. ¹²When you call me, and come and pray to me, I will listen to you. ¹³When you look for me, you will find me. Yes, when you seek me with all your heart, ¹⁴I will let you find me—oracle of the LORD—and I will change your lot; I will gather you together from all the nations and all the places to which I have banished you—oracle of the LORD—and bring you back to the place from which I have exiled you. ¹⁵As for your saying, "The LORD has raised up for us prophets here in Babylon"—

¹⁶Thus says the LORD concerning the king sitting on David's throne and all the people living in this city, your kinsmen who did not go with you into exile; ¹⁷thus says the LORD of hosts: I am sending against them sword, famine, and pestilence. I will make them like rotten figs, so spoiled that they cannot be eaten. ¹⁸I will pursue them with sword, famine, and pestilence, and make them an object of horror to all the kingdoms of the earth, a curse, a desolation, a hissing, and a reproach to all the nations among which I have banished them, ¹⁹because they did not listen to my words—oracle of the LORD—even though I kept sending them my servants the prophets, but they would not listen to them—oracle of the LORD.

²⁰As for you, listen to the word of the LORD, all you exiles whom I sent away from Jerusalem to Babylon. ²¹This is what the LORD of hosts, the God of Israel, says about Ahab, son of Kolaiah, and Zedekiah, son of Maaseiah, who prophesy lies to you in my name: I am handing them over to Nebuchadnezzar, king of Babylon, who will kill them before your eyes. ²²And because of them this curse will be used by all the exiles of Judah in Babylon: "May the LORD make you like Zedekiah and Ahab, whom the king of Babylon roasted in fire," ²³because they have committed an outrage in Israel, committing adultery with their neighbors' wives, and alleging in my name things I did not command. I know, I am witness—oracle of the LORD.

The False Prophet Shemaiah. ²⁴To Shemaiah, the Nehelamite, say: ²⁵Thus says the LORD of hosts, the God of Israel: Because you sent documents in your own name to all the people in Jerusalem, to Zephaniah, the priest, son of Maaseiah, and to all the priests saying: ²⁶"It is the LORD who has appointed you priest in place of the priest Jehoiada, to provide officers for the house of the LORD, that you may confine in stocks or pillory any madman who poses as a prophet. ²⁷Why, then, have you not rebuked Jeremiah of Anathoth who poses as a prophet among you? ²⁸For he sent this message to us in Babylon: It will be a long time; build houses to live in; plant gardens and eat their fruit...."

²⁹When the priest Zephaniah read this letter to Jeremiah the prophet, ³⁰the word of the Lord came to Jeremiah: ³¹Send to all the exiles: Thus says the Lord concerning Shemaiah, the Nehelamite: Because Shemaiah prophesies to you, although I did not send him, and has led you to rely on a lie, ³²therefore thus says the Lord, I will punish Shemaiah, the Nehelamite, and his descendants. None of them shall dwell among this people to see the good I will do for this people—oracle of the Lord— because he preached rebellion against the Lord.

The Restoration. 30:1 This word came to Jeremiah from the Lord: ²Thus says the Lord, the God of Israel: Write down on a scroll all the words I have spoken to you. ³For indeed, the days are coming—oracle of the Lord—when I will restore the fortunes of my people Israel and Judah—oracle of the Lord. I will bring them back to the land which I gave to their ancestors, and they shall take possession of it.

⁴These are the words the Lord spoke to Israel and to Judah: ⁵Thus says the Lord:

We hear a cry of fear:
    terror, not peace.
⁶Inquire and see:
    does a male give birth?
Why, then, do I see all these men,
    their hands on their loins
Like women in labor,
    all their faces drained of color?
⁷Ah! How mighty is that day—
    there is none like it!
A time of distress for Jacob,
    though he shall be saved from it.

⁸On that day—oracle of the Lord of hosts—I will break his yoke off your neck and snap your bonds. Strangers shall no longer enslave them; ⁹instead, they shall serve the Lord, their God, and David, their king, whom I will raise up for them.

¹⁰But you, my servant Jacob, do not
        fear!—oracle of the Lord—
    do not be dismayed, Israel!
For I will soon deliver you from places
        far away,
    your offspring from the land of their
        exile;
Jacob shall again find rest,
    secure, with none to frighten him,
¹¹for I am with you—oracle of the
        Lord—to save you.
I will bring to an end all the nations
    among whom I have scattered you;
    but you I will not bring to an end.
I will chastise you as you deserve,
    I will not let you go unpunished.
¹²For thus says the Lord:
Incurable is your wound,
    grievous your injury;
¹³There is none to plead your case,
    no remedy for your running sore,
    no healing for you.
¹⁴All your lovers have forgotten you,
    they do not seek you out.
I struck you as an enemy would strike,
    punishing you cruelly.
¹⁵Why cry out over your wound?
    There is no relief for your pain.
Because of your great guilt,
    your numerous sins,
    I have done this to you.
¹⁶Yet all who devour you shall be
        devoured,
    all your enemies shall go into exile.
All who plunder you shall become
        plunder,
    all who pillage you I will hand over
        to be pillaged.
¹⁷For I will restore your health;
    I will heal your injuries—oracle of
        the Lord.
"The outcast" they have called you,
    "whom no one looks for."
¹⁸Thus says the Lord:

See! I will restore the fortunes of Jacob's
tents,
    on his dwellings I will have
        compassion;
A city shall be rebuilt upon its own
    ruins,
    a citadel restored where it should be.
[19]From them will come praise,
    the sound of people rejoicing.
I will increase them, they will not
    decrease,
    I will glorify them, they will not be
        insignificant.
[20]His children shall be as of old,
    his assembly shall stand firm in my
        presence,
    I will punish all his oppressors.
[21]His leader shall be one of his own,

and his ruler shall emerge from his
    ranks.
He shall approach me when I summon
    him;
    Why else would he dare
    approach me?—oracle of the LORD.
[22]You shall be my people,
    and I will be your God.
[23]Look! The storm of the LORD!
    His wrath breaks out
In a whirling storm
    that bursts upon the heads of the
        wicked.
[24]The anger of the LORD will not abate
    until he has carried out completely
        the decisions of his heart.
In days to come
    you will fully understand it.

☐ 2 PETER 1

Greeting. 1:1 Symeon Peter, a slave and
apostle of Jesus Christ, to those who have
received a faith of equal value to ours
through the righteousness of our God and
savior Jesus Christ: [2]may grace and peace
be yours in abundance through knowledge
of God and of Jesus our Lord.

The Power of God's Promise. [3]His divine power has bestowed on us everything
that makes for life and devotion, through
the knowledge of him who called us by his
own glory and power. [4]Through these, he
has bestowed on us the precious and very
great promises, so that through them you
may come to share in the divine nature, after escaping from the corruption that is in
the world because of evil desire. [5]For this
very reason, make every effort to supple-
ment your faith with virtue, virtue with
knowledge, [6]knowledge with self-control,
self-control with endurance, endurance
with devotion, [7]devotion with mutual affection, mutual affection with love. [8]If
these are yours and increase in abundance,
they will keep you from being idle or un-

fruitful in the knowledge of our Lord Jesus
Christ. [9]Anyone who lacks them is blind
and shortsighted, forgetful of the cleansing
of his past sins. [10]Therefore, brothers, be all
the more eager to make your call and election firm, for, in doing so, you will never
stumble. [11]For, in this way, entry into the
eternal kingdom of our Lord and savior Jesus Christ will be richly provided for you.

Apostolic Witness. [12]Therefore, I will
always remind you of these things, even
though you already know them and are established in the truth you have. [13]I think it
right, as long as I am in this "tent," to stir
you up by a reminder, [14]since I know that
I will soon have to put it aside, as indeed
our Lord Jesus Christ has shown me. [15]I
shall also make every effort to enable you
always to remember these things after my
departure.

[16]We did not follow cleverly devised
myths when we made known to you the
power and coming of our Lord Jesus
Christ, but we had been eyewitnesses of his
majesty. [17]For he received honor and glory

from God the Father when that unique declaration came to him from the majestic glory, "This is my Son, my beloved, with whom I am well pleased." [18]We ourselves heard this voice come from heaven while we were with him on the holy mountain. [19]Moreover, we possess the prophetic message that is altogether reliable. You will do well to be attentive to it, as to a lamp shining in a dark place, until day dawns and the morning star rises in your hearts. [20]Know this first of all, that there is no prophecy of scripture that is a matter of personal interpretation, [21]for no prophecy ever came through human will; but rather human beings moved by the holy Spirit spoke under the influence of God.

October 20

St. Paul of the Cross

It is very good and holy to consider the passion of Our Lord, and to meditate on it, for by this sacred path we reach union with God. In this most holy school we learn true wisdom, for it was there that all the saints learned it.

— ST. PAUL OF THE CROSS

☐ JEREMIAH 31-32

Good News of the Return. 31:1 At that time—oracle of the LORD—
I will be the God of all the families of Israel,
and they shall be my people.
[2]Thus says the LORD:
The people who escaped the sword
find favor in the wilderness.
As Israel comes forward to receive rest,
[3]from afar the LORD appears:
With age-old love I have loved you;
so I have kept my mercy toward you.
[4]Again I will build you, and you shall stay built,
virgin Israel;
Carrying your festive tambourines,
you shall go forth dancing with merrymakers.
[5]You shall again plant vineyards
on the mountains of Samaria;
those who plant them shall enjoy their fruits.

[6]Yes, a day will come when the watchmen
call out on Mount Ephraim:
"Come, let us go up to Zion,
to the LORD, our God."

The Road of Return. [7]For thus says the LORD:
Shout with joy for Jacob,
exult at the head of the nations;
proclaim your praise and say:
The LORD has saved his people,
the remnant of Israel.
[8]Look! I will bring them back
from the land of the north;
I will gather them from the ends of the earth,
the blind and the lame in their midst,
Pregnant women, together with those in labor—
an immense throng—they shall return.
[9]With weeping they shall come,

but with compassion I will guide
    them;
I will lead them to streams of water,
    on a level road, without stumbling.
For I am a father to Israel,
    Ephraim is my firstborn.
¹⁰Hear the word of the LORD, you
    nations,
    proclaim it on distant coasts, and say:
The One who scattered Israel, now
    gathers them;
    he guards them as a shepherd his
        flock.
¹¹The LORD shall ransom Jacob,
    he shall redeem him from a hand
        too strong for him.
¹²Shouting, they shall mount the
    heights of Zion,
    they shall come streaming to the
        LORD's blessings:
The grain, the wine, and the oil,
    flocks of sheep and cattle;
They themselves shall be like watered
    gardens,
    never again neglected.
¹³Then young women shall make merry
    and dance,
    young men and old as well.
I will turn their mourning into joy,
    I will show them compassion and
        have them rejoice after their
        sorrows.
¹⁴I will lavish choice portions on the
    priests,
    and my people shall be filled with
        my blessings—
    oracle of the LORD.

End of Rachel's Mourning. ¹⁵Thus
    says the LORD:
In Ramah is heard the sound of sobbing,
    bitter weeping!
Rachel mourns for her children,
    she refuses to be consoled
    for her children—they are no more!
¹⁶Thus says the LORD:
Cease your cries of weeping,
    hold back your tears!
There is compensation for your
    labor—
    oracle of the LORD—
    they shall return from the enemy's
        land.
¹⁷There is hope for your future—oracle
    of the LORD—
    your children shall return to their
        own territory.
¹⁸Indeed, I heard Ephraim rocking in
    grief:
You chastised me, and I was
    chastised;
    I was like an untamed calf.
Bring me back, let me come back,
    for you are the LORD, my God.
¹⁹For after I turned away, I repented;
    after I came to myself, I struck my
        thigh;
I was ashamed, even humiliated,
    because I bore the disgrace of my
        youth.
²⁰Is Ephraim not my favored son,
    the child in whom I delight?
Even though I threaten him,
    I must still remember him!
My heart stirs for him,
    I must show him compassion!—
        oracle of the LORD.

Summons To Return Home. ²¹Set up
    road markers,
    put up signposts;
Turn your attention to the highway,
    the road you walked.
Turn back, virgin Israel,
    turn back to these your cities.
²²How long will you continue to
    hesitate,
    rebellious daughter?
The LORD has created a new thing
    upon the earth:
    woman encompasses man.

²³Thus says the LORD of hosts, the God
of Israel: When I restore their fortunes in
the land of Judah and in its cities, they shall

again use this greeting: "May the LORD bless you, Tent of Justice, Holy Mountain!" ²⁴Judah and all its cities, the farmers and those who lead the flock shall dwell there together. ²⁵For I will slake the thirst of the faint; the appetite of all the weary I will satisfy. ²⁶At this I awoke and opened my eyes; my sleep was satisfying.

²⁷See, days are coming—oracle of the LORD—when I will sow the house of Israel and the house of Judah with the seed of human beings and the seed of animals. ²⁸As I once watched over them to uproot and tear down, to demolish, to destroy, and to harm, so I will watch over them to build and to plant—oracle of the LORD. ²⁹In those days they shall no longer say,

"The parents ate unripe grapes,
    and the children's teeth are set on
        edge,"

³⁰but all shall die because of their own iniquity: the teeth of anyone who eats unripe grapes shall be set on edge.

The New Covenant. ³¹See, days are coming—oracle of the LORD—when I will make a new covenant with the house of Israel and the house of Judah. ³²It will not be like the covenant I made with their ancestors the day I took them by the hand to lead them out of the land of Egypt. They broke my covenant, though I was their master—oracle of the LORD. ³³But this is the covenant I will make with the house of Israel after those days—oracle of the LORD. I will place my law within them, and write it upon their hearts; I will be their God, and they shall be my people. ³⁴They will no longer teach their friends and relatives, "Know the LORD!" Everyone, from least to greatest, shall know me—oracle of the LORD—for I will forgive their iniquity and no longer remember their sin.

Certainty of God's Promise. ³⁵Thus says the LORD,
Who gives the sun to light the day,

moon and stars to light the night;
Who stirs up the sea so that its waves
        roar,
    whose name is LORD of hosts:
³⁶If ever this fixed order gives way
        before me—oracle of the LORD—
Then would the offspring of Israel cease
    as a people before me forever.
³⁷Thus says the LORD:
If the heavens on high could be
        measured,
    or the foundations below the earth
        be explored,
Then would I reject all the offspring of
        Israel
    because of all they have done—
        oracle of the LORD.

Jerusalem Rebuilt. ³⁸See, days are coming—oracle of the LORD—when the city shall be rebuilt as the LORD's, from the Tower of Hananel to the Corner Gate. ³⁹A measuring line shall be stretched from there straight to the hill Gareb and then turn to Goah. ⁴⁰The whole valley of corpses and ashes, all the terraced slopes toward the Wadi Kidron, as far as the corner of the Horse Gate at the east, shall be holy to the LORD. Never again shall the city be uprooted or demolished.

Pledge of Restoration. 32:1 The word came to Jeremiah from the LORD in the tenth year of Zedekiah, king of Judah, the eighteenth year of Nebuchadnezzar. ²At that time the army of the king of Babylon was besieging Jerusalem, while Jeremiah the prophet was confined to the court of the guard, in the house of the king of Judah. ³Zedekiah, king of Judah, had confined him there, saying: "How dare you prophesy: Thus says the LORD: I am handing this city over to the king of Babylon that he may capture it. ⁴Zedekiah, king of Judah, shall not escape the hands of the Chaldeans: he shall indeed be handed over to the king of Babylon. He shall speak with him face to face and see him eye to eye. ⁵He shall take Zedekiah to Babylon. There he shall remain, until I attend to him—oracle of the LORD. If you fight against the Chaldeans, you cannot win!"

⁶Jeremiah said, This word came to me from the LORD: ⁷Hanamel, son of your uncle Shallum, will come to you with the offer: "Purchase my field in Anathoth, since you, as nearest relative, have the first right of purchase." ⁸And, just as the LORD had said, my cousin Hanamel came to me in the court of the guard and said, "Please purchase my field in Anathoth, in the territory of Benjamin; as nearest relative, you have the first right of possession—purchase it for yourself." Then I knew this was the word of the LORD. ⁹So I bought the field in Anathoth from my cousin Hanamel, weighing out for him the silver, seventeen shekels of silver.

¹⁰When I had written and sealed the deed, called witnesses and weighed out the silver on the scales, ¹¹I accepted the deed of purchase, both the sealed copy, containing title and conditions, and the open copy. ¹²I gave this deed of purchase to Baruch, son of Neriah, son of Mahseiah, in the presence of my cousin Hanamel and the witnesses who had signed the deed of purchase and before all the Judahites sitting around in the court of the guard.

¹³In their presence I gave Baruch this charge: ¹⁴Thus says the LORD of hosts, the God of Israel: Take these deeds of purchase, both the sealed and the open deeds, and put them in an earthenware jar, so they can last a long time. ¹⁵For thus says the LORD of hosts, the God of Israel: They shall again purchase houses and fields and vineyards in this land.

¹⁶After I had given the deed of purchase to Baruch, son of Neriah, I prayed to the LORD: ¹⁷Ah, my Lord GOD! You made the heavens and the earth with your great power and your outstretched arm; nothing is too difficult for you. ¹⁸You continue your kindness through a thousand generations; but you repay the ancestors' guilt upon their children who follow them. Great and mighty God, whose name is LORD of hosts, ¹⁹great in counsel, mighty in deed, whose eyes are fixed on all the ways of mortals, giving to all according to their ways, according to the fruit of their deeds: ²⁰you performed signs and wonders in the land of Egypt and to this day, in Israel and among all peoples, you have made a name for yourself as on this day. ²¹You brought your people Israel out of the land of Egypt with signs and wonders, with a strong hand and an outstretched arm, and great terror. ²²And you gave them this land, as you had sworn to their ancestors to give them, a land flowing with milk and honey. ²³They went in and took possession of it, but they did not listen to your voice. They did not live by your law; they did not do anything you commanded them to do. Then you made all this evil fall upon them. ²⁴See, the siegeworks have arrived at this city to capture it; the city is handed over to the Chaldeans who are attacking it, with sword, starvation, and disease. What you threatened has happened—you can see it for yourself. ²⁵Yet you told me, my Lord GOD: Purchase the field with silver and summon witnesses, when the city has already been handed over to the Chaldeans!

²⁶Then this word of the LORD came to Jeremiah: ²⁷I am the LORD, the God of all the living! Is anything too difficult for me? ²⁸Therefore the LORD says: I am handing over this city to the Chaldeans and to Nebuchadnezzar, king of Babylon, and he shall capture it. ²⁹The Chaldeans who are attacking this city shall go in and set the city on fire, burning it and the houses, on whose roofs incense was burned to Baal and libations were poured out to other gods in order to provoke me. ³⁰From their youth the Israelites and the Judahites have been doing only what is evil in my eyes; the Israelites have been provoking me with

the works of their hands—oracle of the LORD. ³¹This city has so stirred my anger and wrath, from the day it was built to this day, that I must put it out of my sight, ³²for all the evil the Israelites and Judahites have done to provoke me—they, their kings, their princes, their priests, and their prophets, the people of Judah and the inhabitants of Jerusalem. ³³They turned their backs to me, not their faces; though I taught them persistently, they would not listen or accept correction. ³⁴Instead they set up their abominations in the house which bears my name in order to defile it. ³⁵They built high places to Baal in the Valley of Ben-hinnom to sacrifice their sons and daughters to Molech; I never commanded them to do this, nor did it even enter my mind that they would practice this abomination, so as to bring sin upon Judah.

³⁶Now, therefore, thus says the LORD, the God of Israel, concerning this city, which you say is being handed over to the king of Babylon by means of the sword, starvation, and disease: ³⁷See, I am gathering them from all the lands to which I drove them in my rising fury and great anger; I will bring them back to this place and settle them here in safety. ³⁸They shall be my people, and I will be their God. ³⁹I will give them one heart and one way, that they may fear me always, for their own good and the good of their children after them. ⁴⁰With them I will make an everlasting covenant, never to cease doing good to them; I will put fear of me in their hearts so that they never turn away from me. ⁴¹I will take delight in doing good to them: I will plant them firmly in this land, with all my heart and soul.

⁴²For thus says the LORD: Just as I have brought upon this people all this great evil, so I will bring upon them all the good I have promised them. ⁴³Fields shall be purchased in this land, about which you say, "It is a wasteland, without human beings or animals, handed over to the Chaldeans." ⁴⁴They will purchase fields with silver, write up deeds, seal them, and have them witnessed in the land of Benjamin, in the neighborhood of Jerusalem, in the cities of Judah and of the hill country, in the cities of the Shephelah and the Negeb, when I restore their fortunes—oracle of the LORD.

☐ 2 PETER 2

False Teachers. 2:1 There were also false prophets among the people, just as there will be false teachers among you, who will introduce destructive heresies and even deny the Master who ransomed them, bringing swift destruction on themselves. ²Many will follow their licentious ways, and because of them the way of truth will be reviled. ³In their greed they will exploit you with fabrications, but from of old their condemnation has not been idle and their destruction does not sleep.

Lessons from the Past. ⁴For if God did not spare the angels when they sinned, but condemned them to the chains of Tartarus and handed them over to be kept for judgment; ⁵and if he did not spare the ancient world, even though he preserved Noah, a herald of righteousness, together with seven others, when he brought a flood upon the godless world; ⁶and if he condemned the cities of Sodom and Gomorrah [to destruction], reducing them to ashes, making them an example for the godless [people] of what is coming; ⁷and if he rescued Lot, a righteous man oppressed by the licentious conduct of unprincipled people ⁸(for day after day that righteous man living among them was tormented in his righteous soul at the lawless deeds that he saw and heard), ⁹then the Lord knows how to rescue the devout from trial and to keep the unrighteous under punishment for the day of judgment, [10]and especially those who follow the flesh with its depraved desire and show contempt for lordship.

False Teachers Denounced. Bold and arrogant, they are not afraid to revile glorious beings, [11]whereas angels, despite their superior strength and power, do not bring a reviling judgment against them from the Lord. [12]But these people, like irrational animals born by nature for capture and destruction, revile things that they do not understand, and in their destruction they will also be destroyed, [13]suffering wrong as payment for wrongdoing. Thinking daytime revelry a delight, they are stains and defilements as they revel in their deceits while carousing with you. [14]Their eyes are full of adultery and insatiable for sin. They seduce unstable people, and their hearts are trained in greed. Accursed children! [15]Abandoning the straight road, they have gone astray, following the road of Balaam, the son of Bosor, who loved payment for wrongdoing, [16]but he received a rebuke for

his own crime: a mute beast spoke with a human voice and restrained the prophet's madness.

[17]These people are waterless springs and mists driven by a gale; for them the gloom of darkness has been reserved. [18]For, talking empty bombast, they seduce with licentious desires of the flesh those who have barely escaped from people who live in error. [19]They promise them freedom, though they themselves are slaves of corruption, for a person is a slave of whatever overcomes him. [20]For if they, having escaped the defilements of the world through the knowledge of [our] Lord and savior Jesus Christ, again become entangled and overcome by them, their last condition is worse than their first. [21]For it would have been better for them not to have known the way of righteousness than after knowing it to turn back from the holy commandment handed down to them. [22]What is expressed in the true proverb has happened to them, "The dog returns to its own vomit," and "A bathed sow returns to wallowing in the mire."

October 21

St. Margaret Clitherow

I die for love of my Lord Jesu.
— St. Margaret Clitherow (when told to confess her "crimes" at her execution for hiding priests from the Church's persecutors)

☐ JEREMIAH 33-34

Restoration of Jerusalem. 33:1 The word of the LORD came to Jeremiah a second time while he was still confined in the court of the guard: [2]Thus says the LORD who made the earth, giving it shape and stability, LORD is his name: [3]Call to me, and I will answer you; I will tell you great things

beyond the reach of your knowledge. [4]Thus says the LORD, the God of Israel, concerning the houses of this city and the houses of the kings of Judah, which are being torn down because of the siegeworks and the sword: [5]men come to battle the Chaldeans, and to fill these houses with the corpses of those whom I have struck down in my raging anger, when I hid my face from this city because of all their wickedness.

⁶Look! I am bringing the city recovery and healing; I will heal them and reveal to them an abundance of lasting peace. ⁷I will restore the fortunes of Judah and Israel, and rebuild them as they were in the beginning. ⁸I will purify them of all the guilt they incurred by sinning against me; I will forgive all their offenses by which they sinned and rebelled against me. ⁹Then this city shall become joy for me, a name of praise and pride, before all the nations of the earth, as they hear of all the good I am doing for them. They shall fear and tremble because of all the prosperity I give it.

¹⁰Thus says the LORD: In this place, about which you say: "It is a waste without people or animals!" and in the cities of Judah, in the streets of Jerusalem now deserted, without people, without inhabitant, without animal, there shall yet be heard ¹¹the song of joy, the song of gladness, the song of the bridegroom, the song of the bride, the song of those bringing thank offerings to the house of the LORD:
"Give thanks to the LORD of hosts, for the LORD is good; God's love endures forever." For I will restore the fortunes of this land as they were in the beginning, says the LORD.

¹²Thus says the LORD of hosts: In this place, now a waste, without people or animals, and in all its cities there shall again be sheepfolds for the shepherds to rest their flocks. ¹³In the cities of the hill country, of the Shephelah and the Negeb, in the land of Benjamin and the neighborhood of Jerusalem, and in the cities of Judah, flocks will again pass under the hands of the one who counts them, says the LORD.

¹⁴The days are coming—oracle of the LORD—when I will fulfill the promise I made to the house of Israel and the house of Judah. ¹⁵In those days, at that time, I will make a just shoot spring up for David; he shall do what is right and just in the land.

¹⁶In those days Judah shall be saved and Jerusalem shall dwell safely; this is the name they shall call her: "The LORD our justice." ¹⁷For thus says the LORD: David shall never lack a successor on the throne of the house of Israel, ¹⁸nor shall the priests of Levi ever be lacking before me, to sacrifice burnt offerings, to burn cereal offerings, and to make sacrifices.

¹⁹This word of the LORD also came to Jeremiah: ²⁰Thus says the LORD: If you can break my covenant with day and my covenant with night so that day and night no longer appear in their proper time, ²¹only then can my covenant with my servant David be broken, so that he will not have a descendant to act as king upon his throne, and my covenant with the priests of Levi who minister to me. ²²Just as the host of heaven cannot be numbered and the sands of the sea cannot be counted, so I will multiply the descendants of David my servant and the Levites who minister to me.

²³This word of the LORD came to Jeremiah: ²⁴Have you not noticed what these people are saying: "The LORD has rejected the two tribes he had chosen"? They hold my people in contempt as if it were no longer a nation in their eyes. ²⁵Thus says the LORD: If I have no covenant with day and night, if I did not establish statutes for heaven and earth, ²⁶then I will also reject the descendants of Jacob and of David my servant, no longer selecting from his descendants rulers for the offspring of Abraham, Isaac, and Jacob. Yes, I will restore their fortunes and show them mercy.

Fate of Zedekiah. 34:1 The word which came to Jeremiah from the LORD while Nebuchadnezzar, king of Babylon, and all his army and all the earth's kingdoms under his rule, and all the peoples were attacking Jerusalem and all her cities: ²Thus says the LORD, the God of Israel: Go to Zedekiah, king of Judah, and tell him: Thus says the LORD: I am handing this city over to the king of Babylon; he will burn it with fire. [3]You yourself shall not escape his hand; rather you will be captured and fall into his hand. You shall see the king of Babylon eye to eye and speak to him face to face. Then you shall go to Babylon.

[4]Just hear the word of the LORD, Zedekiah, king of Judah! Then, says the LORD concerning you, you shall not die by the sword. [5]You shall die in peace, and they will burn spices for you as they did for your ancestors, the earlier kings who preceded you, and they shall make lament over you, "Alas, Lord." I myself make this promise—oracle of the LORD.

[6]Jeremiah the prophet told all these things to Zedekiah, king of Judah, in Jerusalem, [7]while the army of the king of Babylon was attacking Jerusalem and the remaining cities of Judah, Lachish, and Azekah. Only these fortified cities were left standing out of all the cities of Judah!

The Pact Broken. [8]This is the word that came to Jeremiah from the LORD after King Zedekiah had made a covenant with all the people in Jerusalem to proclaim freedom: [9]Everyone must free their Hebrew slaves, male and female, so that no one should hold another Judahite in servitude. [10]All the princes and the people who entered this covenant agreed to set free their slaves, their male and female servants, so that they should no longer be in servitude. But even though they agreed and freed them, [11]afterward they took back their male and female servants whom they had set free and again forced them into servitude.

[12]Then this word of the LORD came to Jeremiah: [13]Thus says the LORD, the God of Israel: I myself made a covenant with your ancestors the day I brought them out of the land of Egypt, out of the house of slavery: [14]Every seventh year each of you must set free all Hebrews who have sold themselves to you; six years they shall serve you, but then you shall let them go free. Your ancestors, however, did not listen to me or obey me. [15]As for you, today you repented and did what is right in my eyes by proclaiming freedom for your neighbor and making a covenant before me in the house which bears my name. [16]But then you again profaned my name by taking back your male and female slaves whom you had just set free for life; you forced them to become your slaves again. [17]Therefore, thus says the LORD: You for your part did not obey me by proclaiming freedom for your families and neighbors. So I now proclaim freedom for you—oracle of the LORD—for the sword, starvation, and disease. I will make you an object of horror to all the kingdoms of the earth. [18]Those who violated my covenant and did not observe the terms of the covenant they made in my presence—I will make them like the calf which they cut in two so they could pass between its parts— [19]the princes of Judah and of Jerusalem, the court officials, the priests, and all the people of the land, who passed between the parts of the calf. [20]These I will hand over to their enemies, to those who seek their lives: their corpses shall become food for the birds of the air and the beasts of the field.

[21]Zedekiah, king of Judah, and his princes, I will hand also over to their enemies, to those who seek their lives, to the army of the king of Babylon which is now withdrawing from you. [22]I am giving the command—oracle of the LORD—to bring them back to this city. They shall attack and capture it, and burn it with fire; the cities of Judah I will turn into a waste, where no one dwells.

☐ 2 PETER 3

Denial of the Parousia. 3:1 This is now, beloved, the second letter I am writing to you; through them by way of reminder I am trying to stir up your sincere disposition, [2]to recall the words previously spoken by the holy prophets and the commandment of the Lord and savior through your apostles. [3]Know this first of all, that in the last days scoffers will come [to] scoff, living according to their own desires [4]and saying, "Where is the promise of his coming? From the time when our ancestors fell asleep, everything has remained as it was from the beginning of creation." [5]They deliberately ignore the fact that the heavens existed of old and earth was formed out of water and through water by the word of God; [6]through these the world that then existed was destroyed, deluged with water. [7]The present heavens and earth have been reserved by the same word for fire, kept for the day of judgment and of destruction of the godless.

[8]But do not ignore this one fact, beloved, that with the Lord one day is like a thousand years and a thousand years like one day. [9]The Lord does not delay his promise, as some regard "delay," but he is patient with you, not wishing that any should perish but that all should come to repentance. [10]But the day of the Lord will come like a thief, and then the heavens will pass away with a mighty roar and the elements will be dissolved by fire, and the earth and everything done on it will be found out.

Exhortation to Preparedness. [11]Since everything is to be dissolved in this way, what sort of persons ought [you] to be, conducting yourselves in holiness and devotion, [12]waiting for and hastening the coming of the day of God, because of which the heavens will be dissolved in flames and the elements melted by fire. [13]But according to his promise we await new heavens and a new earth in which righteousness dwells.

[14]Therefore, beloved, since you await these things, be eager to be found without spot or blemish before him, at peace. [15]And consider the patience of our Lord as salvation, as our beloved brother Paul, according to the wisdom given to him, also wrote to you, [16]speaking of these things as he does in all his letters. In them there are some things hard to understand that the ignorant and unstable distort to their own destruction, just as they do the other scriptures.

[17]Therefore, beloved, since you are forewarned, be on your guard not to be led into the error of the unprincipled and to fall from your own stability. [18]But grow in grace and in the knowledge of our Lord and savior Jesus Christ. To him be glory now and to the day of eternity. [Amen.]

October 22

☐ JEREMIAH 35-36

The Faithful Rechabites. 35:1 The word that came to Jeremiah from the LORD in the days of Jehoiakim, son of Josiah, king of Judah: ²Go to the house of the Rechabites, speak to them, and bring them to the house of the LORD, to one of the rooms there, and give them wine to drink. ³So I took Jaazaniah, son of Jeremiah, son of Habazziniah, his brothers and all his sons—the whole house of the Rechabites— ⁴and I brought them to the house of the LORD, to the room of the sons of Hanan, son of Igdaliah, the man of God, next to the room of the princes above the room of Maaseiah, son of Shallum, the guard at the entrance. ⁵I set before the Rechabites bowls full of wine, and cups, and said to them, "Drink some wine."

⁶"We do not drink wine," they said to me; "Jonadab, Rechab's son, our father, commanded us, 'Neither you nor your children shall ever drink wine. ⁷Build no house and sow no seed; do not plant vineyards or own any. You must dwell in tents all your lives, so that you may live long on the land where you live as resident aliens.' ⁸We have obeyed Jonadab, Rechab's son, our father, in everything that he commanded us: not drinking wine as long as we live—neither we nor our wives nor our sons nor our daughters; ⁹not building houses to live in; not owning vineyards or fields or crops. ¹⁰We live in tents, doing everything our father Jonadab commanded us. ¹¹But when Nebuchadnezzar, king of Babylon, invaded this land, we said, 'Come, let us go into Jerusalem to escape the army of the Chal-

deans and the army of the Arameans.' That is why we are now living in Jerusalem."

¹²Then the word of the LORD came to Jeremiah: ¹³Thus says the LORD of hosts, the God of Israel: Go, say to the people of Judah and to the inhabitants of Jerusalem: Will you not take correction and obey my words?—oracle of the LORD. ¹⁴The words of Jonadab, Rechab's son, by which he commanded his children not to drink wine, have been upheld: to this day they have not drunk wine; they obeyed their ancestor's command. I, however, have spoken to you time and again. But you did not obey me! ¹⁵Time and again I sent you all my servants the prophets, saying: Turn away, each of you, from your evil way and reform your actions! Do not follow other gods to serve them that you may remain in the land which I gave you and your ancestors. But you did not pay attention. You did not obey me. ¹⁶Yes, the children of Jonadab, Rechab's son, upheld the command which their father laid on them. But this people has not obeyed me! ¹⁷Now, therefore, says the LORD God of hosts, the God of Israel: I will soon bring upon Judah and all the inhabitants of Jerusalem every evil with which I threatened them because I spoke but they did not obey, I called but they did not answer.

¹⁸But to the house of the Rechabites Jeremiah said: Thus says the LORD of hosts, the God of Israel: Since you have obeyed the command of Jonadab, your father, kept all his commands and done everything he commanded you, ¹⁹therefore, thus says the LORD of hosts, the God of Israel: Never shall there fail to be a descendant of Jonadab, Rechab's son, standing in my presence.

Blessed Pope John Paul II

Be not afraid!
— BLESSED POPE JOHN PAUL II

Baruch, the Scribe of Jeremiah. 36:1 In the fourth year of Jehoiakim, son of Josiah, king of Judah, this word came to Jeremiah from the LORD: [2]Take a scroll and write on it all the words I have spoken to you about Israel, Judah, and all the nations, from the day I first spoke to you, from the days of Josiah, until today. [3]Perhaps, if the house of Judah hears all the evil I have in mind to do to them, so that all of them turn from their evil way, then I can forgive their wickedness and their sin. [4]So Jeremiah called Baruch, son of Neriah, and he wrote down on a scroll what Jeremiah said, all the words which the LORD had spoken to him. [5]Then Jeremiah commanded Baruch: "I cannot enter the house of the LORD; I am barred from it. [6]So you yourself must go. On a fast day in the hearing of the people in the LORD's house, read the words of the LORD from the scroll you wrote at my dictation; read them also to all the people of Judah who come up from their cities. [7]Perhaps they will present their supplication before the LORD and will all turn back from their evil way; for great is the anger and wrath with which the LORD has threatened this people."

[8]Baruch, son of Neriah, did everything Jeremiah the prophet commanded; from the scroll he read the LORD's words in the LORD's house. [9]In the ninth month, in the fifth year of Jehoiakim, son of Josiah, king of Judah, all the people of Jerusalem and all those who came from Judah's cities to Jerusalem proclaimed a fast before the LORD. [10]So Baruch read the words of Jeremiah from the scroll in the room of Gemariah, son of the scribe Shaphan, in the upper court of the LORD's house, at the entrance of the New Temple Gate, in the hearing of all the people.

[11]Now Micaiah, son of Gemariah, son of Shaphan, heard all the words of the LORD read from the scroll. [12]So he went down to the house of the king, into the scribe's chamber, where the princes were meeting in session: Elishama, the scribe; Delaiah, son of Shemaiah; Elnathan, son of Achbor; Gemariah, son of Shaphan; Zedekiah, son of Hananiah; and the other princes. [13]Micaiah reported to them all that he had heard Baruch read from his scroll in the hearing of the people. [14]The princes immediately sent Jehudi, son of Nethaniah, son of Shelemiah, son of Cushi, to Baruch with the order: "The scroll you read in the hearing of the people—bring it with you and come." Scroll in hand, Baruch, son of Neriah, went to them. [15]"Sit down," they said to him, "and read it in our hearing." Baruch read it in their hearing, [16]and when they had heard all its words, they turned to each other in alarm and said to Baruch, "We have to tell the king all these things." [17]Then they asked Baruch: "Tell us, please, how did you come to write down all these words? Was it at his dictation?" [18]"Yes, he would dictate all these words to me," Baruch answered them, "while I wrote them down with ink in the scroll." [19]The princes said to Baruch, "Go into hiding, you and Jeremiah; do not let anyone know where you are."

[20]They went in to the king, into the courtyard; they had deposited the scroll in the room of Elishama the scribe. When they told the king everything that had happened, [21]the king sent Jehudi to get the scroll. Jehudi brought it from the room of Elishama the scribe, and read it to the king and to all the princes who were attending the king. [22]Now the king was sitting in his winter house, since it was the ninth month, and a fire was burning in the brazier before him. [23]Each time Jehudi finished reading three or four columns, he would cut off the piece with a scribe's knife and throw it into the fire in the brazier, until the entire scroll was consumed in the fire in the brazier. [24]As they were listening to all these words the king and all his officials did not become alarmed, nor did they tear their garments. [25]And though Elnathan, Delaiah, and Gemariah urged the king not to burn the scroll, he would not listen to them. [26]He commanded Jerahmeel, a royal prince, and

Seraiah, son of Azriel, and Shelemiah, son of Abdeel, to arrest Baruch, the scribe, and Jeremiah the prophet. But the LORD had hidden them away.

²⁷The word of the LORD came to Jeremiah, after the king burned the scroll and the words Jeremiah had dictated to Baruch: ²⁸Take another scroll, and write on it all the words in the first scroll, which Jehoiakim, king of Judah, burned. ²⁹And against Jehoiakim, king of Judah, say this: Thus says the LORD: You are the one who burned that scroll, saying, "Why did you write on it: Babylon's king shall surely come and ravage this land, emptying it of every living thing"? ³⁰The LORD now says of Jehoiakim, king of Judah: No descendant of his shall sit on David's throne; his corpse shall be thrown out, exposed to heat by day, frost by night. ³¹I will punish him and his descendants and his officials for their wickedness; upon them, the inhabitants of Jerusalem, and the people of Judah I will bring all the evil threats to which they did not listen.

³²Then Jeremiah took another scroll and gave it to his scribe, Baruch, son of Neriah, who wrote on it at Jeremiah's dictation all the words contained in the scroll which Jehoiakim, king of Judah, had burned in the fire, adding many words like them.

2 THESSALONIANS 1

Greeting. 1:1 Paul, Silvanus, and Timothy to the church of the Thessalonians in God our Father and the Lord Jesus Christ: ²grace to you and peace from God [our] Father and the Lord Jesus Christ.

Thanksgiving. ³We ought to thank God always for you, brothers, as is fitting, because your faith flourishes ever more, and the love of every one of you for one another grows ever greater. ⁴Accordingly, we ourselves boast of you in the churches of God regarding your endurance and faith in all your persecutions and the afflictions you endure.

⁵This is evidence of the just judgment of God, so that you may be considered worthy of the kingdom of God for which you are suffering. ⁶For it is surely just on God's part to repay with afflictions those who are afflicting you, ⁷and to grant rest along with us to you who are undergoing afflictions, at the revelation of the Lord Jesus from heaven with his mighty angels, ⁸in blazing fire, inflicting punishment on those who do not acknowledge God and on those who do not obey the gospel of our Lord Jesus. ⁹These will pay the penalty of eternal ruin, separated from the presence of the Lord and from the glory of his power, ¹⁰when he comes to be glorified among his holy ones and to be marveled at on that day among all who have believed, for our testimony to you was believed.

Prayer. ¹¹To this end, we always pray for you, that our God may make you worthy of his calling and powerfully bring to fulfillment every good purpose and every effort of faith, ¹²that the name of our Lord Jesus may be glorified in you, and you in him, in accord with the grace of our God and Lord Jesus Christ.

October 23

Jesus said, "You are the light of the world." Now a light does not illumine itself, but instead it diffuses its rays and shines all around upon everything that comes into its view. So it must be with the glowing lives of upright and holy priests. By the brightness of their holiness they must bring light and serenity to all who gaze upon them.

— St. John of Capistrano

☐ JEREMIAH 37-38

Jeremiah in the Dungeon. 37:1 Zedekiah, son of Josiah, became king, succeeding Coniah, son of Jehoiakim; Nebuchadnezzar, king of Babylon, appointed him king over the land of Judah. ²Neither he, nor his officials, nor the people of the land would listen to the words which the LORD spoke through Jeremiah the prophet. ³Yet King Zedekiah sent Jehucal, son of Shelemiah, and Zephaniah, son of Maaseiah the priest, to Jeremiah the prophet with this request: "Please appeal to the LORD, our God, for us." ⁴At this time Jeremiah still came and went freely among the people; he had not yet been put into prison. ⁵Meanwhile, Pharaoh's army had set out from Egypt, and when the Chaldeans who were besieging Jerusalem heard this report, they withdrew from the city.

⁶Then the word of the LORD came to Jeremiah the prophet: ⁷Thus says the LORD, the God of Israel: Thus you must say to the king of Judah who sent you to consult me: Listen! Pharaoh's army, which has set out to help you, will return to Egypt, its own land. ⁸The Chaldeans shall return and attack this city; they shall capture it and destroy it by fire.

⁹Thus says the LORD: Do not deceive yourselves, saying: "The Chaldeans are surely leaving us forever." They are not! ¹⁰Even if you could defeat the whole Chaldean army that is now attacking you, and only the wounded remained, each in his tent, these would rise up and destroy the city with fire.

¹¹Now when the Chaldean army withdrew from Jerusalem because of the army of Pharaoh, ¹²Jeremiah set out from Jerusalem to go to the territory of Benjamin, to receive his share of property among the people. ¹³But at the Gate of Benjamin, the captain of the guard, by the name of Irijah, son of Shelemiah, son of Hananiah, arrested Jeremiah the prophet, saying, "You are deserting to the Chaldeans!" ¹⁴"That is a lie!" Jeremiah answered, "I am not deserting to the Chaldeans." Without listening to him, Irijah kept Jeremiah in custody and brought him to the princes.

¹⁵The princes were enraged at Jeremiah and had Jeremiah beaten and imprisoned in the house of Jonathan the scribe, for they were using it as a jail. ¹⁶And so Jeremiah went into a room in the dungeon, where he remained many days.

¹⁷Then King Zedekiah had him brought to his palace, and he asked him secretly, "Is there any word from the LORD?" "There is!" Jeremiah answered: "You shall be handed over to the king of Babylon." ¹⁸Jeremiah then asked King Zedekiah: "How have I wronged you or your officials or this people, that you should put me in prison? ¹⁹Where are your own prophets who prophesied for you, saying: 'The King of Babylon will not

attack you or this land'? ²⁰Please hear me, my lord king! Grant my petition: do not send me back into the house of Jonathan the scribe, or I shall die there."

²¹So King Zedekiah ordered that Jeremiah be confined in the court of the guard and given a ration of bread every day from the bakers' street until all the bread in the city was eaten up. Thus Jeremiah remained in the court of the guard.

Jeremiah in the Muddy Cistern. 38:1 Shephatiah, son of Mattan, Gedaliah, son of Pashhur, Jucal, son of Shelemiah, and Pashhur, son of Malchiah, heard the words Jeremiah was speaking to all the people: ²Thus says the Lord: Those who remain in this city shall die by means of the sword, starvation, and disease; but those who go out to the Chaldeans shall live. Their lives shall be spared them as spoils of war that they may live. ³Thus says the Lord: This city shall certainly be handed over to the army of the king of Babylon; he shall capture it.

⁴Then the princes said to the king, "This man ought to be put to death. He is weakening the resolve of the soldiers left in this city and of all the people, by saying such things to them; he is not seeking the welfare of our people, but their ruin." ⁵King Zedekiah answered: "He is in your hands," for the king could do nothing with them. ⁶And so they took Jeremiah and threw him into the cistern of Prince Malchiah, in the court of the guard, letting him down by rope. There was no water in the cistern, only mud, and Jeremiah sank down into the mud.

⁷Now Ebed-melech, an Ethiopian, a court official in the king's house, heard that they had put Jeremiah in the cistern. The king happened to be sitting at the Gate of Benjamin, ⁸and Ebed-melech went there from the house of the king and said to him, ⁹"My lord king, these men have done wrong in all their treatment of Jeremiah the prophet, throwing him into the cistern. He will starve to death on the spot, for there is no more bread in the city." ¹⁰Then the king ordered Ebed-melech the Ethiopian: "Take three men with you, and get Jeremiah the prophet out of the cistern before he dies." ¹¹Ebed-melech took the men with him, and went first to the linen closet in the house of the king. He took some old, tattered rags and lowered them by rope to Jeremiah in the cistern. ¹²Then he said to Jeremiah, "Put these old, tattered rags between your armpits and the ropes." Jeremiah did so, ¹³and they pulled him up by rope out of the cistern. But Jeremiah remained in the court of the guard.

¹⁴King Zedekiah summoned Jeremiah the prophet to meet him at the third entrance of the house of the Lord. "I have a question to ask you," the king said to Jeremiah. "Do not hide anything from me." ¹⁵Jeremiah answered Zedekiah: "If I tell you anything, will you not have me put to death? If I counsel you, you will not listen to me!" ¹⁶But King Zedekiah swore to Jeremiah secretly: "As the Lord lives who gave us our lives, I will not kill you, nor will I hand you over to those men who seek your life."

¹⁷Jeremiah then said to Zedekiah: "Thus says the Lord God of hosts, the God of Israel: If you will only surrender to the princes of Babylon's king, you shall save your life; this city shall not be destroyed by fire, and you and your household shall live. ¹⁸But if you do not surrender to the princes of Babylon's king, this city shall fall into the hand of the Chaldeans, who shall destroy it by fire, and you shall not escape their hand."

¹⁹King Zedekiah said to Jeremiah, "I am afraid of the Judahites who have deserted to the Chaldeans; I could be handed over to them, and they will mistreat me." ²⁰"You will not be handed over to them," Jeremiah answered. "I beg you! Please listen to the voice of the Lord regarding what I tell you

so that it may go well with you and your life be spared. [21]But if you refuse to surrender, this is what the LORD has shown: [22]I see all the women who remain in the house of Judah's king being brought out to the princes of Babylon's king, and they are crying:

'They betrayed you, outdid you,
    your good friends!
Now that your feet are sunk in mud,
    they slink away.'

[23]All your wives and children shall be brought out to the Chaldeans, and you shall not escape their hands; you shall be handed over to the king of Babylon, and this city shall be destroyed by fire."

□ 2 THESSALONIANS 2

Christ and the Lawless One. 2:1 We ask you, brothers, with regard to the coming of our Lord Jesus Christ and our assembling with him, [2]not to be shaken out of your minds suddenly, or to be alarmed either by a "spirit," or by an oral statement, or by a letter allegedly from us to the effect that the day of the Lord is at hand. [3]Let no one deceive you in any way. For unless the apostasy comes first and the lawless one is revealed, the one doomed to perdition, [4]who opposes and exalts himself above every so-called god and object of worship, so as to seat himself in the temple of God, claiming that he is a god— [5]do you not recall that while I was still with you I told you these things? [6]And now you know what is restraining, that he may be revealed in his time. [7]For the mystery of lawlessness is already at work. But the one who restrains is to do so only for the present, until he is removed from the scene. [8]And then the lawless one will be revealed, whom the Lord [Jesus] will kill with the breath of his mouth and render powerless by the manifestation of his coming, [9]the

[24]Then Zedekiah said to Jeremiah, "Let no one know about this conversation, or you shall die. [25]If the princes should hear I spoke with you and if they should come and ask you, 'Tell us what you said to the king; do not hide it from us, or we will kill you,' or, 'What did the king say to you?' [26]then give them this answer: 'I petitioned the king not to send me back to Jonathan's house lest I die there.'" [27]When all the princes came to Jeremiah and questioned him, he answered them with the very words the king had commanded. They said no more to him, for nothing had been overheard of the conversation. [28]Thus Jeremiah stayed in the court of the guard until the day Jerusalem was taken.

one whose coming springs from the power of Satan in every mighty deed and in signs and wonders that lie, [10]and in every wicked deceit for those who are perishing because they have not accepted the love of truth so that they may be saved. [11]Therefore, God is sending them a deceiving power so that they may believe the lie, [12]that all who have not believed the truth but have approved wrongdoing may be condemned.

[13]But we ought to give thanks to God for you always, brothers loved by the Lord, because God chose you as the firstfruits for salvation through sanctification by the Spirit and belief in truth. [14]To this end he has [also] called you through our gospel to possess the glory of our Lord Jesus Christ. [15]Therefore, brothers, stand firm and hold fast to the traditions that you were taught, either by an oral statement or by a letter of ours.

[16]May our Lord Jesus Christ himself and God our Father, who has loved us and given us everlasting encouragement and good hope through his grace, [17]encourage your hearts and strengthen them in every good deed and word.

October 24

Christian perfection consists in three things: praying heroically, working heroically, and suffering heroically.

— St. Anthony Mary Claret

☐ JEREMIAH 39-40

The Capture of Jerusalem. When Jerusalem was taken, **39:1** in the ninth year of Zedekiah, king of Judah, in the tenth month, Nebuchadnezzar, king of Babylon, and all his army marched against Jerusalem and placed it under siege. ²In the eleventh year of Zedekiah, on the ninth day of the fourth month, the city wall was breached. ³All the princes of the king of Babylon came and took their seats at the middle gate: Nergal-sharezer of Simmagir, a chief officer; Nebushazban, a high dignitary; and all the rest of the princes of the king of Babylon. ⁴When Zedekiah, king of Judah, and all his warriors saw this, they fled, leaving the city at night by way of the king's garden, through a gate between the two walls. He went in the direction of the Arabah, ⁵but the Chaldean army pursued them; they caught up with Zedekiah in the wilderness near Jericho and took him prisoner. They brought him to Nebuchadnezzar, king of Babylon, in Riblah, in the land of Hamath, and he pronounced sentence upon him. ⁶The king of Babylon executed the sons of Zedekiah at Riblah before his very eyes; the king of Babylon also executed all the nobles of Judah. ⁷He then blinded Zedekiah and bound him in chains to bring him to Babylon.

⁸The Chaldeans set fire to the king's house and the houses of the people and tore down the walls of Jerusalem. ⁹Nebuzaradan, captain of the bodyguard, deported to Babylon the rest of the people left in the city, those who had deserted to him, and the rest of the workers. ¹⁰But Nebuzaradan, captain of the bodyguard, left in the land of Judah some of the poor who had nothing and at the same time gave them vineyards and farms.

Jeremiah Released to Gedaliah's Custody. ¹¹Concerning Jeremiah, Nebuchadnezzar, king of Babylon, gave these orders through Nebuzaradan, captain of the bodyguard: ¹²"Take him and look after him; do not let anything happen to him. Whatever he may ask, you must do for him." ¹³Thereupon Nebuzaradan, captain of the bodyguard, and Nebushazban, a high dignitary, and Nergal-sharezer, a chief officer, and all the nobles of the king of Babylon, ¹⁴had Jeremiah taken out of the courtyard of the guard and entrusted to Gedaliah, son of Ahikam, son of Shaphan, to bring him home. And so he remained among the people.

A Word of Comfort for Ebed-melech. ¹⁵While Jeremiah was still imprisoned in the court of the guard, the word of the Lord came to him: ¹⁶Go, tell this to Ebed-melech the Ethiopian: Thus says the Lord of hosts, the God of Israel: See, I am now carrying out my words against this city, for evil and not for good; this will happen in your presence on that day. ¹⁷But on that day I will deliver you—oracle of the Lord; you shall not be handed over to the men you dread. ¹⁸I will make certain that you escape and do not fall by the sword. Your life will be your spoils of war because you trusted in me—oracle of the Lord.

Jeremiah Still in Judah. 40:1 The word which came to Jeremiah from the Lord, after Nebuzaradan, captain of the bodyguard, had released him in Ramah, where he found him a prisoner in chains among the captives of Jerusalem and Judah being exiled to Babylon. ²The captain of the bodyguard took charge of Jeremiah and said to him, "The LORD, your God, decreed ruin for this place. ³Now he has made it happen, accomplishing what he decreed; because you sinned against the LORD and did not listen to his voice, this decree has been realized against you. ⁴Now, I release you today from the chains upon your hands; if you want to come with me to Babylon, then come: I will look out for you. But if you do not want to come to Babylon, very well. See, the whole land lies before you; go wherever you think good and proper. ⁵Or go to Gedaliah, son of Ahikam, son of Shaphan, whom the king of Babylon has set over the cities of Judah. Stay with him among the people. Or go wherever you want!" The captain of the bodyguard gave him food and gifts and let him go. ⁶So Jeremiah went to Gedaliah, son of Ahikam, in Mizpah, and dwelt with him among the people left in the land.

⁷When the military leaders still in the field with their soldiers heard that the king of Babylon had set Gedaliah, son of Ahikam, over the land and had put him in charge of men, women, and children, from the poor of the land who had not been deported to Babylon, ⁸they and their soldiers came to Gedaliah in Mizpah: Ishmael, son of Nethaniah; Johanan, son of Kareah; Seraiah, son of Tanhumeth; the sons of Ephai of Netophah; and Jezaniah of Beth-maacah.

⁹Gedaliah, son of Ahikam, son of Shaphan, swore an oath to them and their men: "Do not be afraid to serve the Chaldeans. Stay in the land and serve the king of Babylon, so that everything may go well with you. ¹⁰As for me, I will remain in Mizpah, as your representative before the Chaldeans when they come to us. You, for your part, harvest the wine, the fruit, and the oil, store them in jars, and remain in the cities you occupied." ¹¹Then all the Judahites in Moab, in Ammon, in Edom, and those in all other lands heard that the king of Babylon had left a remnant in Judah and had set over them Gedaliah, son of Ahikam, son of Shaphan. ¹²They all returned to the land of Judah from the places to which they had scattered. They went to Gedaliah at Mizpah and had a rich harvest of wine and fruit.

Assassination of Gedaliah. ¹³Now Johanan, son of Kareah, and all the military leaders in the field came to Gedaliah in Mizpah ¹⁴and said to him, "Surely you are aware that Baalis, the Ammonite king, has sent Ishmael, son of Nethaniah, to assassinate you?" But Gedaliah, son of Ahikam, would not believe them. ¹⁵Then Johanan, son of Kareah, said secretly to Gedaliah in Mizpah: "Please let me go and kill Ishmael, son of Nethaniah; no one will know it. What if he assassinates you? All the Judahites who have now rallied behind you would scatter and the remnant of Judah would perish." ¹⁶Gedaliah, son of Ahikam, answered Johanan, son of Kareah, "You must not do that. What you are saying about Ishmael is a lie!"

☐ 2 THESSALONIANS 3

Request for Prayers. 3:1 Finally, brothers, pray for us, so that the word of the Lord may speed forward and be glorified, as it did among you, ²and that we may be delivered from perverse and wicked people, for not all have faith. ³But the Lord is faithful; he will strengthen you and guard you from the evil one. ⁴We are confident of you in the Lord that what we instruct you, you [both] are doing and will continue to do. ⁵May the Lord direct your hearts to the love of God and to the endurance of Christ.

Neglect of Work. [6]We instruct you, brothers, in the name of [our] Lord Jesus Christ, to shun any brother who conducts himself in a disorderly way and not according to the tradition they received from us. [7]For you know how one must imitate us. For we did not act in a disorderly way among you, [8]nor did we eat food received free from anyone. On the contrary, in toil and drudgery, night and day we worked, so as not to burden any of you. [9]Not that we do not have the right. Rather, we wanted to present ourselves as a model for you, so that you might imitate us. [10]In fact, when we were with you, we instructed you that if anyone was unwilling to work, neither should that one eat. [11]We hear that some are conducting themselves among you in a disorderly way, by not keeping busy but minding the business of others. [12]Such people we instruct and urge in the Lord Jesus Christ to work quietly and to eat their own food. [13]But you, brothers, do not be remiss in doing good. [14]If anyone does not obey our word as expressed in this letter, take note of this person not to associate with him, that he may be put to shame. [15]Do not regard him as an enemy but admonish him as a brother. [16]May the Lord of peace himself give you peace at all times and in every way. The Lord be with all of you.

[17]This greeting is in my own hand, Paul's. This is the sign in every letter; this is how I write. [18]The grace of our Lord Jesus Christ be with all of you.

October 25

Of the dogmas and preaching preserved in the Church, some we possess from written teaching and others we receive from the tradition of the apostles, handed on to us in mystery. In respect to piety, both are of the same force.

— St. Basil the Great

☐ JEREMIAH 41-42

41:1 In the seventh month, Ishmael, son of Nethaniah, son of Elishama, of royal descent, one of the king's nobles, came with ten men to Gedaliah, son of Ahikam, at Mizpah. While they were together at table in Mizpah, [2]Ishmael, son of Nethaniah, and the ten with him, stood up and struck down Gedaliah, son of Ahikam, son of Shaphan, with swords. They killed him, since the king of Babylon had set him over the land; [3]Ishmael also killed all the Judahites of military age who were with Gedaliah and the Chaldean soldiers stationed there.

[4]The day after the murder of Gedaliah, before anyone learned about it, [5]eighty men, in ragged clothes, with beards shaved off and gashes on their bodies, came from Shechem, Shiloh, and Samaria, bringing grain offerings and incense for the house of the LORD. [6]Weeping as he went, Ishmael son of Nethaniah, set out from Mizpah to meet them. "Come to Gedaliah, son of Ahikam," he said as he met them. [7]Once they were inside the city, Ishmael, son of Nethaniah, and his men slaughtered them and threw them into the cistern. [8]Ten of them said to Ishmael: "Do not kill us! We have stores of wheat and barley, oil and honey hidden in the field." So he spared them and did not kill them as he had killed

their companions. ⁹The cistern into which Ishmael threw all the bodies of the men he had killed was the large one King Asa made to defend himself against Baasha, king of Israel; Ishmael, son of Nethaniah, filled this cistern with the slain.

¹⁰Ishmael led away the rest of the people left in Mizpah, including the princesses, whom Nebuzaradan, captain of the bodyguard, had consigned to Gedaliah, son of Ahikam. With these captives, Ishmael, son of Nethaniah, set out to cross over to the Ammonites.

Flight to Egypt. ¹¹But when Johanan, son of Kareah, and the other army leaders with him heard about the crimes Ishmael, son of Nethaniah, had committed, ¹²they took all their men and set out to attack Ishmael, son of Nethaniah. They overtook him at the great pool in Gibeon. ¹³At the sight of Johanan, son of Kareah, and the other army leaders, the people with Ishmael rejoiced; ¹⁴all of those whom Ishmael had taken captive from Mizpah went back to Johanan, son of Kareah. ¹⁵But Ishmael, son of Nethaniah, escaped from Johanan with eight men and fled to the Ammonites. ¹⁶Then Johanan, son of Kareah, and all the military leaders took charge of all the rest of the people whom Ishmael, son of Nethaniah, had taken away from Mizpah after he killed Gedaliah, son of Ahikam—the soldiers, the women with children, and court officials, whom he brought back from Gibeon. ¹⁷They set out and stopped at Geruth Chimham near Bethlehem, intending to go into Egypt. ¹⁸They were afraid of the Chaldeans, because Ishmael, son of Nethaniah, had slain Gedaliah, son of Ahikam, whom the king of Babylon had set over the land.

42:1 Then all the military leaders, including Johanan, son of Kareah, Azariah, son of Hoshaiah, and all the people, from the least to the greatest, ²approached Jeremiah the prophet and said, "Please grant our petition; pray for us to the LORD, your God, for all this remnant. As you see, only a few of us remain, but once we were many. ³May the LORD, your God, show us the way we should take and what we should do." ⁴"Very well!" Jeremiah the prophet answered them: "I will pray to the LORD, your God, as you desire; whatever the LORD answers, I will tell you; I will withhold nothing from you." ⁵And they said to Jeremiah, "May the LORD be a true and faithful witness against us if we do not follow all the instructions the LORD, your God, sends us through you. ⁶Whether we like it or not, we will obey the command of the LORD, our God, to whom we are sending you, so that it may go well with us for obeying the command of the LORD, our God."

⁷Ten days passed before the word of the LORD came to Jeremiah. ⁸Then he called Johanan, son of Kareah, his army leaders, and all the people, from the least to the greatest, ⁹and said to them: Thus says the LORD, the God of Israel, to whom you sent me to offer your petition: ¹⁰If indeed you will remain in this land, I will build you up, and not tear you down; I will plant you, not uproot you; for I repent of the evil I have done you. ¹¹Do not fear the king of Babylon, as you do now. Do not fear him—oracle of the LORD—for I am with you to save you, to rescue you from his power. ¹²I will take pity on you, so that he will have pity on you and let you return to your land. ¹³But if you keep saying, "We will not stay in this land," thus disobeying the voice of the LORD, your God, ¹⁴and saying, "No, we will go to the land of Egypt, where we will not see war, nor hear the trumpet alarm, nor hunger for bread. There we will live!" ¹⁵then listen to the word of the LORD, remnant of Judah: Thus says the LORD of hosts, the God of Israel: If you are set on going to Egypt and settling down there once you arrive, ¹⁶the sword you fear shall overtake you in the land of Egypt; the hunger you dread shall pursue you to Egypt and there you shall die. ¹⁷All those determined to go to Egypt to live shall die by the

sword, famine, and disease: not one shall survive or escape the evil that I am bringing upon them. [18]For thus says the Lord of hosts, the God of Israel: Just as my furious wrath was poured out upon the inhabitants of Jerusalem, so shall my anger be poured out on you when you reach Egypt. You shall become a malediction and a horror, a curse and a reproach, and you shall never see this place again.

[19]The Lord has spoken to you, remnant of Judah. Do not go to Egypt! Mark

☐ 2 TIMOTHY 1

Greeting. **1:1** Paul, an apostle of Christ Jesus by the will of God for the promise of life in Christ Jesus, [2]to Timothy, my dear child: grace, mercy, and peace from God the Father and Christ Jesus our Lord.

Thanksgiving. [3]I am grateful to God, whom I worship with a clear conscience as my ancestors did, as I remember you constantly in my prayers, night and day. [4]I yearn to see you again, recalling your tears, so that I may be filled with joy, [5]as I recall your sincere faith that first lived in your grandmother Lois and in your mother Eunice and that I am confident lives also in you.

The Gifts Timothy Has Received. [6]For this reason, I remind you to stir into flame the gift of God that you have through the imposition of my hands. [7]For God did not give us a spirit of cowardice but rather of power and love and self-control. [8]So do not be ashamed of your testimony to our Lord, nor of me, a prisoner for his sake; but bear your share of hardship for the gospel with the strength that comes from God.

[9]He saved us and called us to a holy life, not according to our works but according to his own design and the grace bestowed

well that I am warning you this day. [20]At the cost of your lives you have been deceitful, for you yourselves sent me to the Lord, your God, saying, "Pray for us to the Lord, our God; whatever the Lord, our God, shall say, tell us and we will do it." [21]Today I have told you, but you have not listened to the voice of the Lord your God, in anything that he has sent me to tell you. [22]Have no doubt about this: you shall die by the sword, famine, and disease in the place where you want to go and live.

on us in Christ Jesus before time began, [10]but now made manifest through the appearance of our savior Christ Jesus, who destroyed death and brought life and immortality to light through the gospel, [11]for which I was appointed preacher and apostle and teacher. [12]On this account I am suffering these things; but I am not ashamed, for I know him in whom I have believed and am confident that he is able to guard what has been entrusted to me until that day. [13]Take as your norm the sound words that you heard from me, in the faith and love that are in Christ Jesus. [14]Guard this rich trust with the help of the holy Spirit that dwells within us.

Paul's Suffering. [15]You know that everyone in Asia deserted me, including Phygelus and Hermogenes. [16]May the Lord grant mercy to the family of Onesiphorus because he often gave me new heart and was not ashamed of my chains. [17]But when he came to Rome, he promptly searched for me and found me. [18]May the Lord grant him to find mercy from the Lord on that day. And you know very well the services he rendered in Ephesus.

October 26

What, then, does God watch with pleasure and delight? The Christian who is fighting for Him against riches, against the world, against hell, against himself.

— St. Louis de Montfort

☐ JEREMIAH 43–44

43:1 When Jeremiah finished telling the people all the words the LORD, their God, sent to them, ²Azariah, son of Hoshaiah, Johanan, son of Kareah, and all the others had the insolence to say to Jeremiah: "You lie; the LORD, our God, did not send you to tell us, 'Do not to go to Egypt to live there.' ³Baruch, son of Neriah, is inciting you against us, to hand us over to the Chaldeans to be killed or exiled to Babylon."

⁴So Johanan, son of Kareah, and the rest of the leaders and the people did not listen to the voice of the LORD to stay in the land of Judah. ⁵Instead, Johanan, son of Kareah, and the military leaders took along all the remnant of Judah who had been dispersed among the nations and then had returned to dwell in the land of Judah: ⁶men, women, and children, the princesses and everyone whom Nebuzaradan, captain of the bodyguard, had consigned to Gedaliah, son of Ahikam, son of Shaphan; also Jeremiah, the prophet, and Baruch, son of Neriah. ⁷They went to Egypt—they did not listen to the voice of the LORD—and came to Tahpanhes.

Jeremiah in Egypt. ⁸The word of the LORD came to Jeremiah in Tahpanhes: ⁹Take some large stones in your hand and set them in mortar in the terrace at the entrance to the house of Pharaoh in Tahpanhes, while the Judahites watch. ¹⁰Then say to them: Thus says the LORD of hosts, the God of Israel: I will send for my servant Nebuchadnezzar, king of Babylon. He will place his throne upon these stones which I, Jeremiah, have set up, and stretch his canopy above them. ¹¹He shall come and strike the land of Egypt: with death, those marked for death; with exile, those marked for exile; with the sword, those marked for the sword. ¹²He shall set fire to the temples of Egypt's gods, burn the gods and carry them off. He shall pick the land of Egypt clean, as a shepherd picks lice off his cloak, and then depart victorious. ¹³He shall smash the obelisks at the Temple of the Sun in the land of Egypt and destroy with fire the temples of the Egyptian gods.

44:1 The word that came to Jeremiah for all the Judahites who were living in Egypt, those living in Migdol, Tahpanhes, and Memphis, and in Upper Egypt: ²Thus says the LORD of hosts, the God of Israel: You yourselves have seen all the evil I brought upon Jerusalem and the other cities of Judah. Today they lie in ruins uninhabited, ³because of the evil they did to provoke me, going after other gods, offering incense and serving other gods they did not know, neither they, nor you, nor your ancestors. ⁴Though I repeatedly sent you all my servants the prophets, saying: "You must not commit this abominable deed I hate," ⁵they did not listen or incline their ears in order to turn from their evil, no longer offering incense to other gods. ⁶Therefore the fury of my anger poured forth and kindled fire in the cities of Judah and the streets of Jerusalem, to turn them into the ruined wasteland they are today.

⁷Now thus says the LORD God of hosts, the God of Israel: Why inflict so great an evil upon yourselves, cutting off from Judah man and woman, child and infant, not leav-

ing yourselves even a remnant? ⁸Why do you provoke me with the works of your hands, offering sacrifice to other gods here in the land of Egypt where you have come to live? Will you cut yourselves off and become a curse, a reproach among all the nations of the earth? ⁹Have you forgotten the evil of your ancestors, the evil of the kings of Judah, the evil of their wives, and your own evil and the evil of your wives—all that they did in the land of Judah and in the streets of Jerusalem? ¹⁰To this day they have not been crushed down, nor have they shown fear. They have not followed my law and my statutes that I set before you and your ancestors.

¹¹Therefore, thus says the LORD of hosts, the God of Israel: I have set my face against you for evil, to cut off all Judah. ¹²I will take away the remnant of Judah who insisted on going to the land of Egypt to live there; in the land of Egypt they shall meet their end. They shall fall by the sword or be consumed by hunger. From the least to the greatest, they shall die by sword or hunger; they shall become a malediction, a horror, a curse, a reproach. ¹³Thus I will punish those who live in Egypt, just as I punished Jerusalem, with sword, hunger, and disease, ¹⁴so that none of the remnant of Judah who came to live in the land of Egypt shall escape or survive. No one shall return to the land of Judah. Even though they long to return and live there, they shall not return except as refugees.

¹⁵They answered Jeremiah—all the men who knew that their wives were offering sacrifices to other gods, all the women standing there in the immense crowd, and all the people who lived in Lower and Upper Egypt: ¹⁶"Regarding the word you have spoken to us in the name of the LORD, we are not listening to you. ¹⁷Rather we will go on doing what we proposed; we will offer incense to the Queen of Heaven and pour out libations to her, just as we have done, along with our ancestors, our kings and princes, in the cities of Judah and in the streets of Jerusalem.

Then we had plenty to eat, we prospered, and we suffered no misfortune. ¹⁸But ever since we stopped offering sacrifices to the Queen of Heaven and pouring out libations to her, we lack everything and are being destroyed by sword and hunger." ¹⁹And the women said, "When we offered sacrifices to the Queen of Heaven and poured out libations to her, did we bake cakes in her image and pour out libations to her without our husbands' consent?"

²⁰To all the people, men and women, who gave him this answer, Jeremiah said: ²¹As for the sacrifices you offered in the cities of Judah and in the streets of Jerusalem—you, your ancestors, your kings and princes, and the people of the land—did not the LORD remember them? Did it not enter his mind? ²²The LORD could no longer bear the evil of your deeds, the abominations you were doing; then your land became a waste, a horror, a curse, without even one inhabitant, as it is today. ²³Because you offered sacrifice and sinned against the LORD, not listening to the voice of the LORD, not following his law, his statutes, and his decrees, therefore this evil has overtaken you, as it is today.

²⁴Jeremiah said to all the people and to all the women: Hear the word of the LORD, all you Judahites in the land of Egypt: ²⁵Thus says the LORD of hosts, the God of Israel: You and your wives have carried out with your hands what your mouths have spoken: "We will go on fulfilling the vows we have made to offer sacrifice to the Queen of Heaven and to pour out libations to her." Very well! keep your vows, fulfill your vows! ²⁶And then listen to the word of the LORD, all you Judahites living in Egypt; I swear by my own great name, says the LORD: in the whole land of Egypt, my name shall no longer be pronounced by the lips of any Judahite, saying, "As the Lord GOD lives." ²⁷I am watching over them for evil, not for good. All the Judahites in Egypt shall come to an end by sword or

famine until they are completely destroyed. [28]Those who escape the sword to return from the land of Egypt to the land of Judah shall be few in number. The whole remnant of Judah who came to Egypt to live shall know whose word stands, mine or theirs.

[29]And this shall be a sign to you—oracle of the LORD—I will punish you in this place so that you will know that my words stand solidly against you for evil. [30]Thus says the LORD: See! I will hand over Pharaoh Hophra, king of Egypt, to his enemies, to those seeking his life, just as I handed over Zedekiah, king of Judah, to his enemy Nebuchadrezzar, king of Babylon, to the one seeking his life.

☐ 2 TIMOTHY 2

Timothy's Conduct. 2:1 So you, my child, be strong in the grace that is in Christ Jesus. [2]And what you heard from me through many witnesses entrust to faithful people who will have the ability to teach others as well. [3]Bear your share of hardship along with me like a good soldier of Christ Jesus. [4]To satisfy the one who recruited him, a soldier does not become entangled in the business affairs of life. [5]Similarly, an athlete cannot receive the winner's crown except by competing according to the rules. [6]The hardworking farmer ought to have the first share of the crop. [7]Reflect on what I am saying, for the Lord will give you understanding in everything.

[8]Remember Jesus Christ, raised from the dead, a descendant of David: such is my gospel, [9]for which I am suffering, even to the point of chains, like a criminal. But the word of God is not chained. [10]Therefore, I bear with everything for the sake of those who are chosen, so that they too may obtain the salvation that is in Christ Jesus, together with eternal glory. [11]This saying is trustworthy:

If we have died with him
    we shall also live with him;
[12]if we persevere
    we shall also reign with him.
But if we deny him
    he will deny us.
[13]If we are unfaithful
    he remains faithful,
    for he cannot deny himself.

Warning against Useless Disputes. [14]Remind people of these things and charge them before God to stop disputing about words. This serves no useful purpose since it harms those who listen. [15]Be eager to present yourself as acceptable to God, a workman who causes no disgrace, imparting the word of truth without deviation. [16]Avoid profane, idle talk, for such people will become more and more godless, [17]and their teaching will spread like gangrene. Among them are Hymenaeus and Philetus, [18]who have deviated from the truth by saying that [the] resurrection has already taken place and are upsetting the faith of some. [19]Nevertheless, God's solid foundation stands, bearing this inscription, "The Lord knows those who are his"; and, "Let everyone who calls upon the name of the Lord avoid evil."

[20]In a large household there are vessels not only of gold and silver but also of wood and clay, some for lofty and others for humble use. [21]If anyone cleanses himself of these things, he will be a vessel for lofty use, dedicated, beneficial to the master of the house, ready for every good work. [22]So turn from youthful desires and pursue righteousness, faith, love, and peace, along with those who call on the Lord with purity of heart. [23]Avoid foolish and ignorant debates, for you know that they breed quarrels. [24]A slave of the Lord should not quarrel, but should be gentle with everyone, able to teach, tolerant, [25]correcting

opponents with kindness. It may be that God will grant them repentance that leads to knowledge of the truth, [26]and that they may return to their senses out of the devil's snare, where they are entrapped by him, for his will.

October 27

Nothing is more to be feared than too long a peace. You are deceived if you think that a Christian can live without persecution. He suffers the greatest persecution of all who lives under none. A storm puts a man on his guard and obliges him to exert his utmost efforts to avoid shipwreck.

— St. Jerome

☐ JEREMIAH 45-46

A Message to Baruch. 45:1 The word that Jeremiah the prophet spoke to Baruch, son of Neriah, when he wrote on a scroll words from Jeremiah's own mouth in the fourth year of Jehoiakim, son of Josiah, king of Judah: [2]Thus says the Lord, God of Israel, to you, Baruch. [3]You said, "Woe is me! the Lord has added grief to my pain. I have worn myself out with groaning; rest eludes me." [4]You must say this to him. Thus says the Lord: What I have built, I am tearing down; what I have planted, I am uprooting: all this land. [5]And you, do you seek great things for yourself? Do not seek them! I am bringing evil on all flesh—oracle of the Lord—but I will grant you your life as spoils of war, wherever you may go.

46:1 The word of the Lord that came to Jeremiah the prophet concerning the nations.

Against Egypt. [2]Concerning Egypt. Against the army of Pharaoh Neco, king of Egypt, defeated at Carchemish on the Euphrates by Nebuchadrezzar, king of Babylon, in the fourth year of Jehoiakim, son of Josiah, king of Judah:

[3]Prepare buckler and shield!
    move forward to battle!
[4]Harness the horses,
    charioteers, mount up!
Fall in, with helmets on;
    polish your spears, put on your
        armor.
[5]What do I see?
    Are they panicking, falling apart?
    Their warriors are hammered back,
They flee headlong
    never making a stand.
Terror on every side—
    oracle of the Lord!
[6]The swift cannot flee,
    nor the warrior escape:
There up north, on the banks of the
        Euphrates
    they stumble and fall.
[7]Who is this? Like the Nile, it rears up;
    like rivers, its waters surge.
[8]Egypt rears up like the Nile,
    like rivers, its waters surge.
"I will rear up," it says, "and cover the
        earth,
    destroying the city and its people.
[9]Forward, horses!
    charge, chariots!
March forth, warriors,
    Cush and Put, bearing shields,
    Archers of Lud, stretching bows!"

¹⁰Today belongs to the Lord God of
　hosts,
　　a day of vengeance, vengeance on
　　　his foes!
The sword devours and is sated, drunk
　with their blood:
　　for the Lord God of hosts holds a
　　　sacrifice
　　in the land of the north, on the
　　　River Euphrates.
¹¹Go up to Gilead, procure balm,
　Virgin daughter Egypt!
No use to multiply remedies;
　for you there is no healing.
¹²The nations hear your cries,
　your screaming fills the earth.
Warrior stumbles against warrior,
　both collapse together.

¹³The word that the Lord spoke to Jeremiah the prophet when Nebuchadrezzar, king of Babylon, came to attack the land of Egypt:

¹⁴Proclaim in Egypt, announce in
　Migdol,
　　announce in Memphis and
　　　Tahpanhes!
Say: Fall in, get ready,
　the sword has devoured your
　　neighbors.
¹⁵Why has Apis fled?
　Your champion did not stand,
Because the Lord thrust him down;
　¹⁶he stumbled repeatedly then
　　collapsed.
They said to each other,
　"Get up! We must return to our
　　own people,
To the land of our birth,
　away from the destroying sword."
¹⁷Give Pharaoh, king of Egypt, the
　name
　　"Braggart-missed-his-chance."
¹⁸As I live, says the King
　whose name is Lord of hosts,
Like Tabor above mountains,
　like Carmel above the sea, he comes.

¹⁹Pack your bags for exile,
　enthroned daughter Egypt;
Memphis shall become a wasteland,
　an empty ruin.
²⁰Egypt is a beautiful heifer,
　a horsefly from the north keeps
　　coming.
²¹Even the mercenaries in her ranks
　are like fattened calves;
They too turn and flee together—
　they do not stand their ground,
For their day of ruin comes upon
　them,
　　their time of punishment.
²²Her voice is like a snake!
　Yes, they come in force;
They attack her with axes,
　like those who fell trees.
²³They cut down her forest—oracle of
　the Lord—
　　impenetrable though it be;
More numerous than locusts,
　they cannot be counted.
²⁴Shamed is daughter Egypt,
　handed over to a people from the
　　north.

²⁵The Lord of hosts, the God of Israel, has said: See! I will punish Amon of Thebes and Egypt, gods, kings, Pharaoh, and those who trust in him. ²⁶I will hand them over to those who seek their lives, to Nebuchadrezzar, king of Babylon, and to his officers. But later, Egypt shall be inhabited again, as in days of old—oracle of the Lord.

²⁷But you, my servant Jacob, do not
　fear;
　　do not be dismayed, Israel!
Listen! I will deliver you from far-off
　lands;
　　your offspring, from the land of
　　　their exile.
Jacob shall again find rest,
　secure, with none to frighten him.
²⁸You, Jacob my servant, must not
　fear—oracle of the Lord—

for I am with you;
    I will make an end of all the nations
      to which I have driven you,

But of you I will not make an end:
    I will chastise you as you deserve,
    I cannot let you go unpunished.

☐ 2 TIMOTHY 3

The Dangers of the Last Days. 3:1 But understand this: there will be terrifying times in the last days. ²People will be self-centered and lovers of money, proud, haughty, abusive, disobedient to their parents, ungrateful, irreligious, ³callous, implacable, slanderous, licentious, brutal, hating what is good, ⁴traitors, reckless, conceited, lovers of pleasure rather than lovers of God, ⁵as they make a pretense of religion but deny its power. Reject them. ⁶For some of these slip into homes and make captives of women weighed down by sins, led by various desires, ⁷always trying to learn but never able to reach a knowledge of the truth. ⁸Just as Jannes and Jambres opposed Moses, so they also oppose the truth—people of depraved mind, unqualified in the faith. ⁹But they will not make further progress, for their foolishness will be plain to all, as it was with those two.

Paul's Example and Teaching. ¹⁰You have followed my teaching, way of life, purpose, faith, patience, love, endurance, ¹¹persecutions, and sufferings, such as happened to me in Antioch, Iconium, and Lystra, persecutions that I endured. Yet from all these things the Lord delivered me. ¹²In fact, all who want to live religiously in Christ Jesus will be persecuted. ¹³But wicked people and charlatans will go from bad to worse, deceivers and deceived. ¹⁴But you, remain faithful to what you have learned and believed, because you know from whom you learned it, ¹⁵and that from infancy you have known [the] sacred scriptures, which are capable of giving you wisdom for salvation through faith in Christ Jesus. ¹⁶All scripture is inspired by God and is useful for teaching, for refutation, for correction, and for training in righteousness, ¹⁷so that one who belongs to God may be competent, equipped for every good work.

October 28

Sts. Simon and Jude

The very tradition, teaching, and faith of the Catholic Church from the beginning, which the Lord gave, was preached by the apostles and was preserved by the Fathers. On this was the Church founded, and if anyone departs from this, he neither is, nor any longer ought to be called, a Christian.

— St. Athanasius of Alexandria

☐ JEREMIAH 47-48

Against the Philistines. 47:1 The word of the LORD that came to Jeremiah the prophet concerning the Philistines, before Pharaoh attacked Gaza:

²Thus says the LORD:
See: waters are rising from the
    north,
    to become a torrent in flood;
They shall flood the land and all it
    contains,
    the cities and their inhabitants.
People will howl and wail,
    every inhabitant of the land.
³At the noise of the pounding hooves
    of his steeds,
    the clanking chariots, the rumbling
        wheels,
Parents do not turn back for their
        children;
    their hands hang helpless,
⁴Because of the day that is coming
    to destroy all the Philistines
And cut off from Tyre and Sidon
    the last of their allies.
Yes, the LORD is destroying the
        Philistines,
    the remnant from the coasts of
        Caphtor.
⁵Baldness is visited upon Gaza,
    Ashkelon is reduced to silence;
Ashdod, remnant of their strength,
    how long will you gash yourself?
⁶Ah! Sword of the LORD!
    When will you find rest?

Return to your scabbard;
    stop, be still!
⁷How can it find rest
    when the LORD has commanded it?
Against Ashkelon and the seacoast,
    there he has appointed it.

Against Moab. 48:1 Concerning Moab.
Thus says the LORD of hosts, the God of
Israel:

Ah, Nebo! it is ravaged;
    Kiriathaim is disgraced, captured;
Disgraced and overthrown is the
        stronghold:
    ²Moab's glory is no more.
In Heshbon they plot evil against her:
    "Come! We will put an end to her
        as a nation."
You, too, Madmen, shall be silenced;
    you the sword stalks!
³Listen! an outcry from Horonaim,
    "Ruin and great destruction!"
⁴"Moab is crushed!"
    their outcry is heard in Zoar.
⁵Up the ascent of Luhith
    they go weeping;
At the descent to Horonaim
    they hear cries of anguish:
⁶"Flee, save your lives!
    Be like a wild donkey in the
        wilderness!"
⁷Because you trusted in your works and
        your treasures,
    you also shall be captured.

Chemosh shall go into exile,
    his priests and princes with him.
[8]The destroyer comes upon every city,
    not a city escapes;
Ruined is the valley,
    wasted the plateau—oracle of the
        Lord.
[9]Set up a tombstone for Moab;
    it will soon become a complete
        wasteland,
Its cities turned into ruins
    where no one dwells.
[10]Cursed are they who do the Lord's
        work carelessly,
    cursed those who keep their sword
        from shedding blood.
[11]Moab has been resting from its
        youth,
    suspended above its dregs,
Never poured from flask to flask,
    never driven into exile.
Thus it retained its flavor,
    its bouquet is not lost.

[12]Be assured! The days are coming—oracle of the Lord—when I will send him wine-makers to decant the wine; they shall empty its flasks and smash its jars. [13]Chemosh shall disappoint Moab, just as the house of Israel was disappointed by Bethel, in which they trusted.

[14]How can you say, "We are heroes,
    mighty warriors"?
[15]The one who ravages Moab and its
        cities comes up,
    the best of its youth go down to
        slaughter—
    oracle of the King, whose name is
        Lord of hosts.
[16]Moab's ruin is near at hand,
    its disaster approaches swiftly.
[17]Mourn, all you neighbors,
    all you who know its name!
Say: How the mighty scepter is broken,
    the glorious staff!
[18]Come down from glory, sit on the
        parched ground,
    enthroned daughter Dibon;
Moab's destroyer has fallen upon you,
    has shattered your strongholds.
[19]Stand along the road, keep watch,
    enthroned Aroer;
Ask the fleeing man, the escaping
        woman:
    ask them what has happened.
[20]"Moab is put to shame, destroyed."
    Wail and cry out,
Proclaim it at the Arnon:
    "Moab is destroyed!"

[21]Judgment has come upon the plateau: on Holon, Jahzah, and Mephaath, [22]on Dibon, Nebo, and Beth-diblathaim, [23]on Kiriathaim, Beth-gamul, and Beth-meon, [24]on Kerioth and on Bozrah: on all the cities of the land of Moab, far and near.

[25]The horn of Moab is cut off,
    its arm is broken—oracle of the
        Lord.

[26]Make him drunk because he set himself over against the Lord; let Moab swim in his vomit and become a laughingstock. [27]Has Israel not been a laughingstock to you? Was he caught among thieves that you wag your heads whenever you speak of him?

[28]Abandon the cities, take shelter in the
        crags,
    inhabitants of Moab.
Be like the dove that nests
    in the walls of a gorge.
[29]We have heard of the pride of Moab,
    pride beyond bounds:
His loftiness, his pride, his scorn,
    his insolent heart.
[30]I myself know his arrogance—oracle
    of the Lord—
    liar in word, liar in deed.
[31]And so I wail over Moab,
    over all Moab I cry,
    over the people of Kir-heres I moan.
[32]More than for Jazer I weep for you,
    vine of Sibmah.

Your tendrils trailed down to the sea,
  as far as Jazer they stretched.
Upon your summer harvest and your
  vintage,
  the destroyer has fallen.
³³Joy and gladness are taken away
  from the garden land, the land of
  Moab.
I dry up the wine from the wine vats,
  the treader treads no more,
  the vintage shout is stilled.

³⁴The cry of Heshbon and Elealeh is heard as far as Jahaz; they call from Zoar to Horonaim and to Eglath-shelishiyah; even the waters of Nimrim turn into a wasteland. ³⁵I will leave no one in Moab—oracle of the Lord—to offer burnt offerings on the high place or to make sacrifices to their gods. ³⁶Hence my heart wails like a flute for Moab; my heart wails like a flute for the people of Kir-heres: the wealth they accumulated has perished. ³⁷Every head has been shaved bald, every beard cut off; every hand gashed, and all their loins are draped in sackcloth. ³⁸On all the rooftops of Moab and in all its squares there is mourning. I have shattered Moab like a pot that no one wants—oracle of the Lord. ³⁹How terrified they are, how they wail! How Moab turns its back in shame! Moab has become a laughingstock and a horror to all its neighbors!

⁴⁰For thus says the Lord:
Look there! Like an eagle he swoops,
  spreading his wings over Moab.
⁴¹Cities are captured,
  strongholds seized:

On that day the hearts of Moab's
  warriors
  become like the heart of a woman
  in labor.
⁴²Moab shall be wiped out, a people no
  more,
  because it set itself over against the
  Lord.
⁴³Terror, pit, and trap be upon you,
  enthroned Moab—oracle of the
  Lord.
⁴⁴Those fleeing the terror
  fall into the pit;
Those climbing out of the pit
  are caught in the trap;
Ah, yes! I will bring these things upon
  Moab
  in the year of their punishment—
  oracle of the Lord.
⁴⁵In Heshbon's shadow the fugitives
  stop short, exhausted;
For fire blazes up from Heshbon,
  and flames up from the house of
  Sihon:
It consumes the forehead of Moab,
  the scalp of the noisemakers.
⁴⁶Woe to you, Moab!
  You are finished, people of
  Chemosh!
Your sons are taken into exile,
  your daughters into captivity.
⁴⁷Yet I will restore the fortunes of
  Moab
  in the days to come—oracle of the
  Lord.

Thus far the judgment on Moab.

☐ 2 TIMOTHY 4

Solemn Charge. 4:1 I charge you in the presence of God and of Christ Jesus, who will judge the living and the dead, and by his appearing and his kingly power: ²proclaim the word; be persistent whether it is convenient or inconvenient; convince, reprimand, encourage through all patience and teaching. ³For the time will come when people will not tolerate sound doctrine but, following their own desires and insatiable curiosity, will accumulate teachers ⁴and will stop listening to the truth and will be diverted to myths. ⁵But you, be self-possessed in all circumstances; put up with hardship; perform the work of an evangelist; fulfill your ministry.

Reward for Fidelity. ⁶For I am already being poured out like a libation, and the time of my departure is at hand. ⁷I have competed well; I have finished the race; I have kept the faith. ⁸From now on the crown of righteousness awaits me, which the Lord, the just judge, will award to me on that day, and not only to me, but to all who have longed for his appearance.

Paul's Loneliness. ⁹Try to join me soon, ¹⁰for Demas, enamored of the present world, deserted me and went to Thessalonica, Crescens to Galatia, and Titus to Dalmatia. ¹¹Luke is the only one with me. Get Mark and bring him with you, for he is helpful to me in the ministry. ¹²I have sent Tychicus to Ephesus. ¹³When you come, bring the cloak I left with Carpus in Troas, the papyrus rolls, and especially the parchments.

¹⁴Alexander the coppersmith did me a great deal of harm; the Lord will repay him according to his deeds. ¹⁵You too be on guard against him, for he has strongly resisted our preaching.

¹⁶At my first defense no one appeared on my behalf, but everyone deserted me. May it not be held against them! ¹⁷But the Lord stood by me and gave me strength, so that through me the proclamation might be completed and all the Gentiles might hear it. And I was rescued from the lion's mouth. ¹⁸The Lord will rescue me from every evil threat and will bring me safe to his heavenly kingdom. To him be glory forever and ever. Amen.

Final Greeting. ¹⁹Greet Prisca and Aquila and the family of Onesiphorus. ²⁰Erastus remained in Corinth, while I left Trophimus sick at Miletus. ²¹Try to get here before winter. Eubulus, Pudens, Linus, Claudia, and all the brothers send greetings.

²²The Lord be with your spirit. Grace be with all of you.

October 29

Yoke yourself under the law of God, so that you may be in truth a free man.

— St. Ephraem the Syrian

☐ JEREMIAH 49-50

Against the Ammonites. 49:1 Concerning the Ammonites. Thus says the LORD:

Has Israel no sons?
> none to inherit?
Why has Milcom disinherited Gad,
> why are his people living in its
> > cities?
²Therefore the days are coming—oracle
> of the LORD—
> when I will sound the battle alarm
> against Rabbah of the Ammonites;

It shall become a mound of ruins,
> and its villages destroyed by fire.
Israel shall then inherit those who
> > disinherited it—
> oracle of the LORD.
³Wail, Heshbon, "The ruin is
> > destroyed!"
> shriek, villages of Rabbah!
Put on sackcloth and lament!
> Run back and forth in the
> > sheepfolds.

For Milcom is going into exile,
taking priest and prince with him.
⁴Why boast in your strength,
your ebbing strength, rebellious
daughter?
Why trust in your treasures, saying,
"Who would dare attack me?"
⁵See, I am bringing terror upon you—
oracle of the Lord GOD of hosts—
from all around you;
You shall be scattered, each in headlong
flight,
with no one to gather the fugitives.
⁶But afterward I will restore the
fortunes
of the Ammonites—oracle of the
LORD.

Against Edom. ⁷Concerning Edom.
Thus says the LORD of hosts:

Is there no more wisdom in Teman,
has counsel perished from the
prudent,
is their wisdom gone?
⁸Flee, retreat, hide deep for lodging,
inhabitants of Dedan:
For I bring disaster upon Esau
when I come to punish them.
⁹If vintagers came upon you,
they would leave no gleanings;
If thieves by night,
they would destroy as they pleased.
¹⁰So I myself will strip Esau;
I will uncover his lairs so he cannot
hide.
Offspring and family are destroyed,
neighbors, too; he is no more.
¹¹Leave your orphans behind, I will
keep them alive;
your widows, let them trust in me.

¹²For thus says the LORD: Look, even
those not sentenced to drink the cup must
drink it! Shall you then go unpunished?
You shall not! You shall drink every bit of
it! ¹³By myself I have sworn—oracle of the
LORD—Bozrah shall become an object of

horror, a disgrace, a desolation, and a curse.
Bozrah and all its cities shall become ruins
forever.

¹⁴I have heard a report from the LORD,
a herald has been sent among the
nations:
"Gather together, move against it,
get ready for battle!"
¹⁵I will make you the least among the
nations,
despised by all people!
¹⁶The terror you spread,
the pride of your heart, beguiled you.
You denizens of rocks and crevices,
occupying towering peaks:
Though you build your nest high as the
eagle,
from there I will bring you down—
oracle of the LORD.

¹⁷Edom shall become an object of horror. Passersby recoil in terror, hissing at all
its wounds. ¹⁸As when Sodom, Gomorrah,
and their neighbors were overthrown—oracle of the LORD—no one shall live in it,
nor anyone settle there.

¹⁹As when a lion comes up from a
thicket of the Jordan
to a permanent pasture,
So in an instant, I will chase them off;
I will establish there whomever I
choose.
For who is like me? Who holds me
accountable?
What shepherd can stand against me?
²⁰Therefore, listen to the strategy
the LORD devised for Edom;
The plans he has drawn up
against the inhabitants of Teman:
They shall be dragged away, even the
smallest of the flock;
their pasture shall be aghast because
of them.
²¹With the din of their collapse the
earth quakes,
to the Red Sea the outcry is heard!

²²Look! like an eagle he soars aloft,
  and spreads his wings over Bozrah;
On that day the hearts of Edom's
    warriors become
  like the heart of a woman in labor.

Against Damascus. ²³Concerning Damascus.

  Hamath and Arpad are shamed,
    for they have heard bad news;
  Anxious, they surge like the sea
    which cannot calm down.
²⁴Damascus loses heart, turns to flee;
  panic has seized it.
Distress and pangs take hold,
  like the pain of a woman in labor.
²⁵How can the glorious city be
    abandoned,
  the town of joy!
²⁶But now its young men shall fall in its
    squares,
  all the warriors destroyed on that
    day—
  oracle of the LORD of hosts.
²⁷I will set fire to the wall of Damascus;
  it shall devour the palaces of Ben-
    hadad.

Against Arabia. ²⁸About Kedar and the kingdoms of Hazor, which Nebuchadnezzar, king of Babylon, defeated.

  Thus says the LORD:
  Rise up, attack Kedar,
    destroy the people from the east.
²⁹Their tents and flocks shall be taken
    away,
  their tent curtains and all their goods;
Their camels they carry off,
  they shout over them, "Terror on
    every side!"
³⁰Flee! wander about, hide deep for
    lodging,
  inhabitants of Hazor—oracle of the
    LORD;
For Nebuchadnezzar, king of Babylon,
  has devised a strategy against
    you,

drawn up a plan against you,
³¹Get up! set out against a tranquil
    nation,
  living in security—oracle of the
    LORD—
Without gates or bars,
  dwelling alone.
³²Their camels shall become spoils,
  their hordes of cattle, plunder;
I will scatter to the winds those who
    shave their temples;
  from every side I will bring their
    ruin—
  oracle of the LORD.
³³Hazor shall become a haunt for jackals,
  a wasteland forever,
Where no one lives,
  no mortal stays.

Against Elam. ³⁴The word of the LORD that came to Jeremiah the prophet concerning Elam at the beginning of the reign of Zedekiah, king of Judah:

³⁵Thus says the LORD of hosts:
Look! I will break the bow of Elam,
  the mainstay of their might.
³⁶I will bring upon Elam the four
    winds
  from the four ends of the heavens:
I will scatter them to all these winds,
  until there is no nation
  to which the outcasts of Elam have
    not gone.
³⁷I will terrify Elam before their foes,
  those seeking their life;
I will bring evil upon them,
  my burning wrath—oracle of the
    LORD.
I will send sword after them
  until I have finished them off;
³⁸I will set up my throne in Elam
  and destroy from there king and
    princes—
  oracle of the LORD.
³⁹But at the end of days I will restore
  the fortunes of Elam—oracle of the
    LORD.

The First Oracle Against Babylon. 50:1

The word the LORD spoke against Babylon, against the land of the Chaldeans, through Jeremiah the prophet:

²Proclaim this among the nations,
   announce it!
   Announce it, do not hide it, but say:
Babylon is captured, Bel put to shame,
   Marduk terrified;
   its images are put to shame, its idols
      shattered.
³A nation from the north advances
      against it,
   making the land desolate
So that no one can live there;
   human beings and animals have
      fled.
⁴In those days and at that time—oracle
   of the LORD—
Israelite and Judahite shall come
      together,
Weeping as they come, to seek the
      LORD, their God;
⁵They shall ask for Zion,
   seeking out the way.
"Come, let us join ourselves to the
      LORD
   in an everlasting covenant, never to
      be forgotten."
⁶Lost sheep were my people,
   their shepherds misled them,
   leading them astray on the
      mountains;
From mountain to hill they wandered,
   forgetting their fold.
⁷Whoever happened upon them
      devoured them;
   their enemies said, "We are not
      guilty,
Because they sinned against the LORD,
   the abode of justice, the hope of
      their ancestors."
⁸Flee from the midst of Babylon,
   leave the land of the Chaldeans,
   be like rams at the head of the flock.
⁹See, I am stirring up against Babylon
   a band of great nations from the
      land of the north;
They are arrayed against her,
   from there she shall be taken.
Their arrows are like the arrows of a
      skilled warrior
   who never returns empty-handed.
¹⁰Chaldea shall become plunder;
   all its plunderers shall be enriched—
   oracle of the LORD.
¹¹Yes, rejoice and exult,
   you that plunder my heritage;
Frisk like calves on the grass,
   neigh like stallions!
¹²Your mother will indeed be put to
      shame,
   she that bore you shall be abashed;
See, the last of the nations,
   a wilderness, a dry wasteland.
¹³Because of the LORD's wrath it shall
      be uninhabited,
   become an utter wasteland;
Everyone who passes by Babylon will
      be appalled
   and hiss at all its wounds.
¹⁴Take your posts encircling Babylon,
   you who bend the bow;
Shoot at it, do not spare your arrows,
   ¹⁵raise the war cry against it on every
      side.
It surrenders, its bastions fall,
   its walls are torn down:
This is retribution from the LORD! Take
      retribution on her,
   as she has done, do to her;
   for she sinned against the LORD.
¹⁶Cut off the sower from Babylon
   and those who wield sickles at
      harvest time!
Before the destroying sword,
   all of them turn back to their own
      people,
   all flee to their own land.
¹⁷Israel was a stray sheep
   that lions pursued;
The king of Assyria once devoured
      him;

now Nebuchadnezzar of Babylon
   gnaws his bones.
¹⁸Therefore, thus says the LORD of
   hosts, the God of Israel:
I will punish the king of Babylon and
   his land,
   as I once punished the king of
      Assyria;
¹⁹But I will bring Israel back to its
   pasture,
   to feed on Carmel and Bashan,
And on Mount Ephraim and Gilead,
   until they have their fill.

²⁰In those days, at that time—oracle of
the LORD:

The guilt of Israel may be sought, but
   it no longer exists,
   the sin of Judah, but it can no
      longer be found;
   for I will forgive the remnant I
      preserve.
²¹Attack the land of Merathaim,
   and those who live in Pekod;
Slaughter and put them under the
   ban—oracle of the LORD—
   do all I have commanded you.
²²Battle alarm in the land,
   great destruction!
²³How the hammer of the whole earth
   has been cut off and broken!
What an object of horror
   Babylon has become among the
      nations!
²⁴You ensnared yourself and were
   caught,
   Babylon, before you knew it!
You were discovered and seized,
   because you challenged the LORD.
²⁵The LORD opens his armory,
   brings out the weapons of his wrath;
The Lord GOD of hosts has work to do
   in the land of the Chaldeans.
²⁶Come upon them from every side,
   open their granaries,
Pile them up in heaps and put them
   under the ban;

   do not leave a remnant.
²⁷Slay all the oxen,
   take them down to slaughter;
Woe to them! their day has come,
   the time of their punishment.
²⁸Listen! the fugitives, the refugees
   from the land of Babylon:
They announce in Zion
   the retribution of the LORD, our
      God.
²⁹Call archers out against Babylon,
   all who bend the bow;
Encamp around them;
   let no one escape.
Repay them for their deeds;
   what they have done, do to them,
For they insulted the LORD,
   the Holy One of Israel.
³⁰Therefore their young men shall fall
   in the squares,
   all their warriors shall be stilled on
      that day—
   oracle of the LORD.
³¹I am against you, O Insolence—
   oracle of the Lord GOD of hosts;
For your day has come,
   the time for me to punish you.
³²Insolence stumbles and falls;
   there is no one to raise him up.
I will kindle a fire in his cities
   to devour everything around him.
³³Thus says the LORD of hosts:
Oppressed are the people of Israel,
   together with the people of Judah;
All their captors hold them fast
   and refuse to let them go.
³⁴Strong is their Redeemer,
   whose name is LORD of hosts,
The sure defender of their cause,
   who gives rest to their land,
   but unrest to those who live in
      Babylon.
³⁵A sword upon the Chaldeans—oracle
   of the LORD—
   upon the inhabitants of Babylon,
      her princes and sages!
³⁶A sword upon the soothsayers,

and they become fools!
A sword upon the warriors,
and they tremble;
[37]A sword upon their motley throng,
and they become women!
A sword upon their treasures,
and they are plundered;
[38]A drought upon the waters,
and they dry up!
For it is a land of idols,
soon made frantic by phantoms.
[39]Hence, wildcats shall dwell there with
hyenas,
and ostriches occupy it;
Never again shall it be inhabited or
settled,
from age to age.
[40]As happened when God overturned
Sodom
and Gomorrah and their
neighbors—oracle of the
LORD—
No one shall dwell there,
no mortal shall settle there.
[41]See, a people comes from the north,
a great nation, and mighty kings
rising from the ends of the earth.
[42]Bow and javelin they wield,
cruel and pitiless are they;
They sound like the roaring sea,
as they ride forth on horses,

Each in place for battle
against you, daughter Babylon.
[43]The king of Babylon hears news of
them,
and his hands hang helpless;
Anguish takes hold of him,
like the pangs of a woman giving
birth.
[44]As happens when a lion comes up
from a thicket of the Jordan
to permanent pasture,
So I, in an instant, will chase them off,
and establish there whomever I
choose!
For who is like me? Who can call me to
account?
What shepherd can stand against me?
[45]Therefore, hear the strategy of the
LORD,
which he has devised against
Babylon;
Hear the plans drawn up
against the land of the Chaldeans:
They shall be dragged away, even the
smallest sheep;
their own pasture aghast because of
them.
[46]At the cry "Babylon is captured!" the
earth quakes;
the outcry is heard among the
nations.

☐ PHILEMON

Address and Greeting. 1 Paul, a prisoner for Christ Jesus, and Timothy our brother, to Philemon, our beloved and our co-worker, [2]to Apphia our sister, to Archippus our fellow soldier, and to the church at your house. [3]Grace to you and peace from God our Father and the Lord Jesus Christ.

Thanksgiving. [4]I give thanks to my God always, remembering you in my prayers, [5]as I hear of the love and the faith you have in the Lord Jesus and for all the holy ones, [6]so that your partnership in the faith may become effective in recognizing every good there is in us that leads to Christ.

Plea for Onesimus. [7]For I have experienced much joy and encouragement from your love, because the hearts of the holy ones have been refreshed by you, brother. [8]Therefore, although I have the full right in Christ to order you to do what is proper, [9]I rather urge you out of love, being as I am, Paul, an old man, and now also a prisoner for Christ Jesus. [10]I urge you on behalf of my child Onesimus, whose father I have become in my imprisonment, [11]who was once useless to you but is now useful to [both] you and me. [12]I am sending him, that is, my own heart, back to you. [13]I should have liked to retain him for myself, so that he might serve me on your behalf in my imprisonment for the gospel, [14]but I did not want to do anything without your consent, so that the good you do might not be forced but voluntary. [15]Perhaps this is why he was away from you for a while, that you might have him back forever, [16]no longer as a slave but more than a slave, a brother, beloved especially to me, but even more so to you, as a man and in the Lord. [17]So if you regard me as a partner, welcome him as you would me. [18]And if he has done you any injustice or owes you anything, charge it to me. [19]I, Paul, write this in my own hand: I will pay. May I not tell you that you owe me your very self. [20]Yes, brother, may I profit from you in the Lord. Refresh my heart in Christ.

[21]With trust in your compliance I write to you, knowing that you will do even more than I say. [22]At the same time prepare a guest room for me, for I hope to be granted to you through your prayers.

Final Greetings. [23]Epaphras, my fellow prisoner in Christ Jesus, greets you, [24]as well as Mark, Aristarchus, Demas, and Luke, my co-workers. [25]The grace of the Lord Jesus Christ be with your spirit.

October 30

> *From what does such contrariness arise in habitually angry people, but from a secret cause of too high an opinion of themselves so that it pierces their heart when they see any man esteem them less than they esteem themselves? An inflated estimation of ourselves is more than half the weight of our wrath.*
>
> — St. Thomas More

☐ JEREMIAH 51-52

The Second Oracle Against Babylon. 51:1 Thus says the LORD:

See! I rouse against Babylon,
    and the inhabitants of Chaldea,
    a destroyer wind.
[2]To Babylon I will send winnowers
    to winnow and lay waste the land;
They shall besiege it on every side
    on the day of affliction.
[3]How can the archers draw back their
        bows,
    lift their armor?
Do not spare her young men,
    put the entire army under the ban.
[4]The slain shall fall in the land of
        Chaldea,
    the wounded, in its streets;
[5]For Israel and Judah are not left
        widowed
    by their God, the LORD of hosts,
Even though the land is full of guilt
    against the Holy One of Israel.
[6]Flee from Babylon;
    each of you save your own life,
    do not perish because of her guilt;
This is a time of retribution from the
        LORD,
    [7]who pays out her due.
Babylon was a golden cup in the hand
    of the LORD

making the whole earth drunk;
The nations drank its wine,
thus they have gone mad.
⁸Babylon suddenly falls and is broken:
wail over her!
Bring balm for her wounds,
in case she can be healed.
⁹"We have tried to heal Babylon,
but she cannot be healed.
Leave her, each of us must go to our
own land."
The judgment against her reaches the
heavens,
it touches the clouds.
¹⁰The LORD has brought forth our
vindication;
come, let us tell in Zion
what the LORD, our God, has done.
¹¹Sharpen the arrows,
fill the quivers;
The LORD has stirred up the spirit of
the kings of the Medes,
for his resolve is Babylon's destruction.
Yes, it is retribution from the LORD,
retribution for his temple.
¹²Over the walls of Babylon raise a signal,
reinforce the watch;
Post sentries,
arrange ambushes!
For the LORD has both planned and
carried out
what he spoke against the
inhabitants of Babylon.
¹³You who dwell by mighty waters,
rich in treasure,
Your end has come,
the time at which you shall be cut off!
¹⁴The LORD of hosts has sworn by
himself:
I will fill you with people as
numerous as locusts,
who shall raise over you a joyous
shout!
¹⁵He made the earth by his power,
established the world by wisdom,
and by his skill stretched out the
heavens.

¹⁶When he thunders, the waters in the
heavens roar,
he summons clouds from the ends
of the earth,
Makes lightning flash in the rain,
and brings out winds from their
storehouses.
¹⁷Every man is stupid, ignorant;
every artisan is put to shame by his
idol:
He molds a fraud,
without life-breath.
¹⁸They are nothing, a ridiculous work,
that will perish at the time of
punishment.
¹⁹Jacob's portion is nothing like them:
he is the creator of all things.
Israel is his very own tribe;
LORD of hosts is his name.
²⁰You are my hammer,
a weapon for war;
With you I shatter nations,
with you I destroy kingdoms.
²¹With you I shatter horse and rider,
with you I shatter chariot and
driver.
²²With you I shatter man and woman,
with you I shatter old and young,
with you I shatter the young man
and young woman.
²³With you I shatter shepherd and
flock,
with you I shatter farmer and team,
with you I shatter governors and
officers.
²⁴Thus I will repay Babylon,
all the inhabitants of Chaldea,
For all the evil they committed against
Zion,
before your very eyes—oracle of the
LORD.
²⁵Beware! I am against you,
destroying mountain—oracle of the
LORD—
destroyer of the entire earth,
I will stretch forth my hand against you,
roll you down over the cliffs,

and make you a burnt mountain:
²⁶They will not take from you a
cornerstone,
or a foundation stone;
You shall remain ruins forever—
oracle of the LORD.
²⁷Raise a signal in the land,
sound the trumpet among the
nations;
Dedicate nations for war against her,
summon against her the kingdoms:
Ararat, Minni, and Ashkenaz;
Appoint a recruiting officer against her,
dispatch horses like bristling locusts.
²⁸Dedicate nations for war against her:
the king of the Medes,
Its governors and all its officers,
every land in its domain.
²⁹The earth quakes and writhes,
the LORD's plan against Babylon is
carried out,
Turning the land of Babylon
into a wasteland without
inhabitants.
³⁰Babylon's warriors have ceased to
fight,
they remain in their strongholds;
Dried up is their strength,
they have become women.
Burned down are their homes,
broken their gates.
³¹One runner meets another,
herald meets herald,
Telling the king of Babylon
that his entire city has been taken.
³²The fords have been seized,
marshes set on fire,
warriors panic.

³³For thus says the LORD of hosts, the
God of Israel:

Daughter Babylon is like a threshing
floor
at the time of treading;
Yet a little while,
and the harvest time will come for
her.

³⁴"He consumed me, defeated me,
Nebuchadnezzar, king of Babylon;
he left me like an empty vessel,
Swallowed me like a sea monster,
filled his belly with my delicacies
and cast me out.
³⁵Let my torn flesh be visited upon
Babylon,"
says enthroned Zion;
"My blood upon the inhabitants of
Chaldea,"
says Jerusalem.
³⁶But now, thus says the LORD:
I will certainly defend your cause,
I will certainly avenge you;
I will dry up her sea,
and drain her fountain.
³⁷Babylon shall become a heap of ruins,
a haunt of jackals;
A place of horror and hissing,
without inhabitants.
³⁸They roar like lions,
growl like lion cubs.
³⁹When they are parched, I will set
drink before them
to make them drunk, that they may
be overcome
with everlasting sleep, never to
awaken—
oracle of the LORD.
⁴⁰I will bring them down like lambs to
slaughter,
like rams and goats.
⁴¹How she has been seized, taken
captive,
the glory of the whole world!
What a horror Babylon has become
among the nations:
⁴²against Babylon the sea rises,
she is overwhelmed by roaring waves!
⁴³Her cities have become wasteland,
a parched and arid land
Where no one lives,
no one passes through.
⁴⁴I will punish Bel in Babylon,
and make him vomit up what he
swallowed;

nations shall no longer stream to
him.
Even the wall of Babylon falls!
⁴⁵Leave her, my people; each of you
save your own life
from the burning wrath of the Lord.

⁴⁶Do not be discouraged when rumors spread through the land; this year one rumor comes, next year another: "Violence in the land!" or "Ruler against ruler!" ⁴⁷Realize that the days are coming when I will punish the idols of Babylon; the whole land shall be put to shame, all her slain shall fall in her midst. ⁴⁸Then heaven and earth and everything in them shall shout over Babylon with joy, when the destroyers come against her from the north—oracle of the Lord. ⁴⁹Babylon, too, must fall, you slain of Israel, because by the hand of Babylon the slain of all the earth have fallen.

⁵⁰You who have escaped the sword,
go, do not stand idle;
Remember the Lord from far away,
let Jerusalem come to mind.
⁵¹We are ashamed because we have
heard taunts,
disgrace covers our faces;
strangers have entered sanctuaries in
the Lord's house.
⁵²Therefore see, the days are coming—
oracle of the Lord—
when I will punish her idols,
and throughout the land the
wounded will groan.
⁵³Though Babylon scale the heavens,
and make her strong heights
inaccessible,
my destroyers shall reach her—
oracle of the Lord.
⁵⁴A sound of crying from Babylon,
great destruction from the land of
the Chaldeans;
⁵⁵For the Lord lays Babylon waste,
silences her loud cry,
Waves roaring like mighty waters,
a clamor resounding.

⁵⁶For the destroyer comes upon her,
upon Babylon;
warriors are captured, their bows
broken;
The Lord is a God of recompense,
he will surely repay.

⁵⁷I will make her princes and sages drunk, with her governors, officers, and warriors, so that they sleep an everlasting sleep, never to awaken—oracle of the King, whose name is Lord of hosts.

⁵⁸Thus says the Lord of hosts:
The walls of spacious Babylon shall be
leveled to the ground,
its lofty gates destroyed by fire.
The toil of the peoples is for nothing;
the nations weary themselves for
what the flames consume.

The Prophecy Sent to Babylon. ⁵⁹The mission Jeremiah the prophet gave to Seraiah, son of Neriah, son of Mahseiah, when he went to Babylon with King Zedekiah, king of Judah, in the fourth year of his reign; Seraiah was chief quartermaster. ⁶⁰Jeremiah wrote down on one scroll the disaster that would befall Babylon; all these words were written against Babylon. ⁶¹And Jeremiah said to Seraiah: "When you reach Babylon, see that you read all these words aloud, ⁶²and then say: Lord, you yourself spoke against this place in order to cut it down so that nothing, human being or beast, could live in it, because it is to remain a wasteland forever. ⁶³When you have finished reading this scroll, tie a stone to it and throw it into the Euphrates, ⁶⁴and say: Thus Babylon shall sink. It will never rise, because of the disaster I am bringing upon it." Thus far the words of Jeremiah.

Capture of Jerusalem. 52:1 Zedekiah was twenty-one years old when he became king; he reigned eleven years in Jerusalem. His mother's name was Hamutal, daughter of Jeremiah from Libnah. ²He did what was evil in the sight of the LORD, just as Jehoiakim had done. ³Indeed, the things done in Jerusalem and in Judah so angered the LORD that he cast them out from his presence. Thus Zedekiah rebelled against the king of Babylon. ⁴In the tenth month of the ninth year of his reign, on the tenth day of the month, Nebuchadnezzar, king of Babylon, and his entire army advanced against Jerusalem, encamped around it, and built siege walls on every side. ⁵The siege of the city continued until the eleventh year of King Zedekiah.

⁶On the ninth day of the fourth month, when famine had gripped the city and the people had no more bread, ⁷the city walls were breached. All the soldiers fled and left the city by night through the gate between the two walls which was near the king's garden. With the Chaldeans surrounding the city, they went in the direction of the Arabah. ⁸But the Chaldean army pursued the king and overtook Zedekiah in the wilderness near Jericho; his whole army fled from him. ⁹The king, therefore, was arrested and brought to Riblah, in the land of Hamath, to the king of Babylon, who pronounced judgment on him. ¹⁰As Zedekiah looked on, the king of Babylon slaughtered his sons before his eyes! All the nobles of Judah were slaughtered at Riblah. ¹¹And the eyes of Zedekiah he then blinded, bound him with chains, and the King of Babylon brought him to Babylon and kept him in prison until the day he died.

Destruction of Jerusalem. ¹²On the tenth day of the fifth month, this was in the nineteenth year of Nebuchadnezzar, king of Babylon, Nebuzaradan, captain of the bodyguard, came to Jerusalem as the representative of the king of Babylon. ¹³He burned the house of the LORD, the palace of the king, and all the houses of Jerusalem; every large building he destroyed with fire. ¹⁴Then the Chaldean troops with the captain of the guard tore down all the walls that surrounded Jerusalem.

¹⁵Nebuzaradan, captain of the guard, led into exile the remnant of people left in the city, those who had deserted to the king of Babylon, and the rest of the artisans. ¹⁶But Nebuzaradan, captain of the guard, left behind some of the country's poor as vinedressers and farmers.

¹⁷The bronze pillars that belonged to the house of the LORD, and the wheeled carts and the bronze sea in the house of the LORD, the Chaldeans broke into pieces; they carried away all the bronze to Babylon. ¹⁸They also took the pots, shovels, snuffers, bowls, pans, and all the bronze vessels used for service; ¹⁹the basins, fire holders, bowls, pots, lampstands, pans, the sacrificial bowls made of gold or silver. Along with these furnishings the captain of the guard carried off ²⁰the two pillars, the one sea and its base of twelve oxen cast in bronze, and the wheeled carts King Solomon had commissioned for the house of the LORD. The bronze from all these furnishings was impossible to weigh.

²¹As for the pillars, each of them was eighteen cubits high and twelve cubits in diameter; each was four fingers thick and hollow inside. ²²A bronze capital five cubits high crowned the one pillar, and a network with pomegranates encircled the capital, all of bronze; and so for the other pillar, with pomegranates. ²³There were ninety-six pomegranates on the sides, a hundred pomegranates surrounding the network.

²⁴The captain of the guard also took Seraiah the high priest, Zephaniah the second priest, and the three keepers of the entrance. ²⁵From the city he took one courtier, a commander of soldiers, and seven men in the personal service of the king still in the city, the scribe of the army commander who mustered the people of the land, and sixty of the common people remaining in the city. ²⁶The captain of the guard, Nebuzaradan, arrested them and brought them to the king of Babylon at Riblah, ²⁷who had them struck down and executed in Riblah, in the land of Hamath.

Thus Judah was exiled from the land. [28]This is the number of people Nebuchadnezzar led away captive: in his seventh year, three thousand twenty-three people of Judah; [29]in the eighteenth year of Nebuchadnezzar, eight hundred thirty-two persons from Jerusalem; [30]in the twenty-third year of Nebuchadnezzar, Nebuzaradan, captain of the guard, deported seven hundred forty-five Judahites: four thousand six hundred persons in all.

Favor Shown to Jehoiachin. [31]In the thirty-seventh year of the exile of Jehoiachin, king of Judah, on the twenty-fifth day of the twelfth month, Evil-merodach, king of Babylon, in the inaugural year of his reign, raised up Jehoiachin, king of Judah, and released him from prison. [32]He spoke kindly to him and gave him a throne higher than the thrones of the other kings who were with him in Babylon. [33]Jehoiachin took off his prison garb and ate at the king's table as long as he lived. [34]The allowance given him by the king of Babylon was a perpetual allowance, in fixed daily amounts, all the days of his life until the day of his death.

☐ JAMES 1

1:1 James, a slave of God and of the Lord Jesus Christ, to the twelve tribes in the dispersion, greetings.

Perseverance in Trial. [2]Consider it all joy, my brothers, when you encounter various trials, [3]for you know that the testing of your faith produces perseverance. [4]And let perseverance be perfect, so that you may be perfect and complete, lacking in nothing. [5]But if any of you lacks wisdom, he should ask God who gives to all generously and ungrudgingly, and he will be given it. [6]But he should ask in faith, not doubting, for the one who doubts is like a wave of the sea that is driven and tossed about by the wind. [7]For that person must not suppose that he will receive anything from the Lord, [8]since he is a man of two minds, unstable in all his ways.

[9]The brother in lowly circumstances should take pride in his high standing, [10]and the rich one in his lowliness, for he will pass away "like the flower of the field." [11]For the sun comes up with its scorching heat and dries up the grass, its flower droops, and the beauty of its appearance vanishes. So will the rich person fade away in the midst of his pursuits.

Temptation. [12]Blessed is the man who perseveres in temptation, for when he has been proved he will receive the crown of life that he promised to those who love him. [13]No one experiencing temptation should say, "I am being tempted by God"; for God is not subject to temptation to evil, and he himself tempts no one. [14]Rather, each person is tempted when he is lured and enticed by his own desire. [15]Then desire conceives and brings forth sin, and when sin reaches maturity it gives birth to death.

[16]Do not be deceived, my beloved brothers: [17]all good giving and every perfect gift is from above, coming down from the Father of lights, with whom there is no alteration or shadow caused by change. [18]He willed to give us birth by the word of truth that we may be a kind of firstfruits of his creatures.

Doers of the Word. [19]Know this, my dear brothers: everyone should be quick to hear, slow to speak, slow to wrath, [20]for the wrath of a man does not accomplish the righteousness of God. [21]Therefore, put away all filth and evil excess and humbly welcome the word that has been planted in you and is able to save your souls.

[22]Be doers of the word and not hearers only, deluding yourselves. [23]For if anyone is a hearer of the word and not a doer, he is like a man who looks at his own face in a mirror. [24]He sees himself, then goes off and

promptly forgets what he looked like. ²⁵But the one who peers into the perfect law of freedom and perseveres, and is not a hearer who forgets but a doer who acts, such a one shall be blessed in what he does.

²⁶If anyone thinks he is religious and does not bridle his tongue but deceives his heart, his religion is vain. ²⁷Religion that is pure and undefiled before God and the Father is this: to care for orphans and widows in their affliction and to keep oneself unstained by the world.

October 31

How can a man say he believes in Christ if he doesn't do what Christ commanded him to do?

— St. Cyprian of Carthage

☐ LAMENTATIONS 1-2

The Desolation of Jerusalem. 1:1
How solitary sits the city,
once filled with people.
She who was great among the nations
is now like a widow.
Once a princess among the provinces,
now a toiling slave.

²She weeps incessantly in the night,
her cheeks damp with tears.
She has no one to comfort her
from all her lovers;
Her friends have all betrayed her,
and become her enemies.

³Judah has gone into exile,
after oppression and harsh labor;
She dwells among the nations,
yet finds no rest:
All her pursuers overtake her
in the narrow straits.

⁴The roads to Zion mourn,
empty of pilgrims to her feasts.
All her gateways are desolate,
her priests groan,
Her young women grieve;
her lot is bitter.

⁵Her foes have come out on top,
her enemies are secure;
Because the Lord has afflicted her
for her many rebellions.
Her children have gone away,
captive before the foe.

⁶From daughter Zion has gone
all her glory:
Her princes have become like rams
that find no pasture.
They have gone off exhausted
before their pursuers.

⁷Jerusalem remembers
in days of wretched homelessness,
All the precious things she once had
in days gone by.
But when her people fell into the
hands of the foe,
and she had no help,
Her foes looked on and laughed
at her collapse.

⁸Jerusalem has sinned grievously,
therefore she has become a mockery;
Those who honored her now demean her,
for they saw her nakedness;
She herself groans out loud,
and turns away.

⁹Her uncleanness is on her skirt;
she has no thought of her future.
Her downfall is astonishing,
with no one to comfort her.

"Look, O Lord, at my misery;
how the enemy triumphs!"

¹⁰The foe stretched out his hands
to all her precious things;
She has seen the nations
enter her sanctuary,
Those you forbade to come
into your assembly.

¹¹All her people groan,
searching for bread;
They give their precious things for food,
to retain the breath of life.
"Look, O Lord, and pay attention
to how I have been demeaned!

¹²Come, all who pass by the way,
pay attention and see:
Is there any pain like my pain,
which has been ruthlessly inflicted
upon me,
With which the Lord has tormented me
on the day of his blazing wrath?

¹³From on high he hurled fire down
into my very bones;
He spread out a net for my feet,
and turned me back.
He has left me desolate,
in misery all day long.

¹⁴The yoke of my rebellions is bound
together,
fastened by his hand.
His yoke is upon my neck;
he has made my strength fail.
The Lord has delivered me into the
grip
of those I cannot resist.

¹⁵All my valiant warriors
my Lord has cast away;
He proclaimed a feast against me
to crush my young men;
My Lord has trodden in the wine press
virgin daughter Judah.

¹⁶For these things I weep—My eyes!
My eyes!

They stream with tears!
How far from me is anyone to comfort,
anyone to restore my life.
My children are desolate;
the enemy has prevailed."

¹⁷Zion stretches out her hands,
with no one to comfort her;
The Lord has ordered against Jacob
his foes all around;
Jerusalem has become in their midst
a thing unclean.

¹⁸"The Lord is in the right;
I had defied his command.
Listen, all you peoples,
and see my pain:
My young women and young men
have gone into captivity.

¹⁹I cried out to my lovers,
but they failed me.
My priests and my elders
perished in the city;
How desperately they searched for
food,
to save their lives!

²⁰Look, O Lord, at the anguish I
suffer!
My stomach churns,
And my heart recoils within me:
How bitter I am!
Outside the sword bereaves—
indoors, there is death.

²¹Hear how I am groaning;
there is no one to comfort me.
All my enemies hear of my misery and
rejoice
over what you have done.
Bring on the day you proclaimed,
and let them become like me!

²²Let all their evil come before you
and deal with them
As you have so ruthlessly dealt with me
for all my rebellions.
My groans are many,
my heart is sick."

The Lord's Wrath and Zion's Ruin.

2:1 How the Lord in his wrath
has abhorred daughter Zion,
Casting down from heaven to earth
the glory of Israel,
Not remembering his footstool
on the day of his wrath!

[2] The Lord has devoured without pity
all of Jacob's dwellings;
In his fury he has razed
daughter Judah's defenses,
Has brought to the ground in dishonor
a kingdom and its princes.

[3] In blazing wrath, he cut down entirely
the horn of Israel;
He withdrew the support of his right
hand
when the enemy approached;
He burned against Jacob like a blazing
fire
that consumes everything in its path.

[4] He bent his bow like an enemy;
the arrow in his right hand
Like a foe, he killed
all those held precious;
On the tent of daughter Zion
he poured out his wrath like fire.

[5] The Lord has become the enemy,
he has devoured Israel:
Devoured all its strongholds,
destroyed its defenses,
Multiplied moaning and groaning
throughout daughter Judah.

[6] He laid waste his booth like a garden,
destroyed his shrine;
The Lord has blotted out in Zion
feast day and sabbath,
Has scorned in fierce wrath
king and priest.

[7] The Lord has rejected his altar,
spurned his sanctuary;
He has handed over to the enemy
the walls of its strongholds.
They shout in the house of the Lord
as on a feast day.

[8] The Lord was bent on destroying
the wall of daughter Zion:
He stretched out the measuring line;
did not hesitate to devour,
Brought grief on rampart and wall
till both succumbed.

[9] Her gates sank into the ground;
he smashed her bars to bits.
Her king and her princes are among
the nations;
instruction is wanting,
Even her prophets do not obtain
any vision from the Lord.

[10] The elders of daughter Zion
sit silently on the ground;
They cast dust on their heads
and dress in sackcloth;
The young women of Jerusalem
bow their heads to the ground.

[11] My eyes are spent with tears,
my stomach churns;
My bile is poured out on the ground
at the brokenness of the daughter of
my people,
As children and infants collapse
in the streets of the town.

[12] They cry out to their mothers,
"Where is bread and wine?"
As they faint away like the wounded
in the streets of the city,
As their life is poured out
in their mothers' arms.

[13] To what can I compare you—to what
can I liken you—
O daughter Jerusalem?
What example can I give in order to
comfort you,
virgin daughter Zion?
For your breach is vast as the sea;
who could heal you?

[14] Your prophets provided you visions
of whitewashed illusion;

They did not lay bare your guilt,
    in order to restore your fortunes;
They saw for you only oracles
    of empty deceit.

[15]All who pass by on the road,
    clap their hands at you;
They hiss and wag their heads
    over daughter Jerusalem:
"Is this the city they used to call
    perfect in beauty and joy of all the
       earth?"

[16]They open their mouths against you,
    all your enemies;
They hiss and gnash their teeth,
    saying, "We have devoured her!
How we have waited for this day—
    we have lived to see it!"

[17]The LORD has done what he planned.
    He has fulfilled the threat
Decreed from days of old,
    destroying without pity!
He let the enemy gloat over you
    and exalted the horn of your foes.

[18]Cry out to the Lord from your heart,
    wall of daughter Zion!
Let your tears flow like a torrent
    day and night;
Give yourself no rest,

    no relief for your eyes.

[19]Rise up! Wail in the night,
    at the start of every watch;
Pour out your heart like water
    before the Lord;
Lift up your hands to him
    for the lives of your children,
Who collapse from hunger
    at the corner of every street.

[20]"Look, O LORD, and pay attention:
    to whom have you been so ruthless?
Must women eat their own offspring,
    the very children they have borne?
Are priest and prophet to be slain
    in the sanctuary of the Lord?

[21]They lie on the ground in the streets,
    young and old alike;
Both my young women and young men
    are cut down by the sword;
You killed them on the day of your
      wrath,
    slaughtered without pity.

[22]You summoned as to a feast day
    terrors on every side;
On the day of the LORD's wrath,
    none survived or escaped.
Those I have borne and nurtured,
    my enemy has utterly destroyed."

☐ JAMES 2

Sin of Partiality. 2:1 My brothers, show no partiality as you adhere to the faith in our glorious Lord Jesus Christ. [2]For if a man with gold rings on his fingers and in fine clothes comes into your assembly, and a poor person in shabby clothes also comes in, [3]and you pay attention to the one wearing the fine clothes and say, "Sit here, please," while you say to the poor one, "Stand there," or "Sit at my feet," [4]have you not made distinctions among yourselves and become judges with evil designs?

[5]Listen, my beloved brothers. Did not God choose those who are poor in the world to be rich in faith and heirs of the kingdom that he promised to those who love him? [6]But you dishonored the poor person. Are not the rich oppressing you? And do they themselves not haul you off to court? [7]Is it not they who blaspheme the noble name that was invoked over you? [8]However, if you fulfill the royal law according to the scripture, "You shall love your neighbor as yourself," you are doing well.

⁹But if you show partiality, you commit sin, and are convicted by the law as transgressors. ¹⁰For whoever keeps the whole law, but falls short in one particular, has become guilty in respect to all of it. ¹¹For he who said, "You shall not commit adultery," also said, "You shall not kill." Even if you do not commit adultery but kill, you have become a transgressor of the law. ¹²So speak and so act as people who will be judged by the law of freedom. ¹³For the judgment is merciless to one who has not shown mercy; mercy triumphs over judgment.

Faith and Works. ¹⁴What good is it, my brothers, if someone says he has faith but does not have works? Can that faith save him? ¹⁵If a brother or sister has nothing to wear and has no food for the day, ¹⁶and one of you says to them, "Go in peace, keep warm, and eat well," but you do not give them the necessities of the body, what good is it? ¹⁷So also faith of itself, if it does not have works, is dead.

¹⁸Indeed someone may say, "You have faith and I have works." Demonstrate your faith to me without works, and I will demonstrate my faith to you from my works. ¹⁹You believe that God is one. You do well. Even the demons believe that and tremble. ²⁰Do you want proof, you ignoramus, that faith without works is useless? ²¹Was not Abraham our father justified by works when he offered his son Isaac upon the altar? ²²You see that faith was active along with his works, and faith was completed by the works. ²³Thus the scripture was fulfilled that says, "Abraham believed God, and it was credited to him as righteousness," and he was called "the friend of God." ²⁴See how a person is justified by works and not by faith alone. ²⁵And in the same way, was not Rahab the harlot also justified by works when she welcomed the messengers and sent them out by a different route? ²⁶For just as a body without a spirit is dead, so also faith without works is dead.

November 1

Those in the Catholic Church, whom some rebuke for praying to saints and going on pilgrimages, do not seek any saint as their savior. Instead, they seek saints as those whom their Savior loves, and whose intercession and prayer for the seeker He will be content to hear. For His own sake, He would have those He loves honored. And when they are thus honored for His sake, then the honor that is given them for His sake overflows especially to himself.

— St. Thomas More

☐ LAMENTATIONS 3-5

The Voice of a Suffering Individual. 3:1 I am one who has known affliction
under the rod of God's anger,
²One whom he has driven and forced
to walk
in darkness, not in light;
³Against me alone he turns his hand—
again and again all day long.

⁴He has worn away my flesh and my
skin,
he has broken my bones;
⁵He has besieged me all around
with poverty and hardship;
⁶He has left me to dwell in dark places
like those long dead.

⁷He has hemmed me in with no escape,
weighed me down with chains;
⁸Even when I cry for help,
he stops my prayer;
⁹He has hemmed in my ways with
fitted stones,
and made my paths crooked.

¹⁰He has been a bear lying in wait for me,
a lion in hiding!
¹¹He turned me aside and tore me apart,
leaving me ravaged.
¹²He bent his bow, and set me up
as a target for his arrow.

¹³He pierced my kidneys
with shafts from his quiver.
¹⁴I have become a laughingstock to all
my people,
their taunt all day long;
¹⁵He has sated me with bitterness,
filled me with wormwood.

¹⁶He has made me eat gravel,
trampled me into the dust;
¹⁷My life is deprived of peace,
I have forgotten what happiness is;
¹⁸My enduring hope, I said,
has perished before the Lord.

¹⁹The thought of my wretched
homelessness
is wormwood and poison;
²⁰Remembering it over and over,
my soul is downcast.
²¹But this I will call to mind;
therefore I will hope:

²²The Lord's acts of mercy are not
exhausted,
his compassion is not spent;
²³They are renewed each morning—
great is your faithfulness!
²⁴The Lord is my portion, I tell myself,
therefore I will hope in him.

²⁵The Lord is good to those who trust
in him,
to the one that seeks him;

²⁶It is good to hope in silence
   for the Lord's deliverance.
²⁷It is good for a person, when young,
   to bear the yoke,

²⁸To sit alone and in silence,
   when its weight lies heavy,
²⁹To put one's mouth in the dust—
   there may yet be hope—
³⁰To offer one's cheek to be struck,
   to be filled with disgrace.

³¹For the Lord does not
   reject forever;
³²Though he brings grief, he takes pity,
   according to the abundance of his
     mercy;
³³He does not willingly afflict
   or bring grief to human beings.

³⁴That someone tramples underfoot
   all the prisoners in the land,
³⁵Or denies justice to anyone
   in the very sight of the Most High,
³⁶Or subverts a person's lawsuit—
   does the Lord not see?

³⁷Who speaks so that it comes to pass,
   unless the Lord commands it?
³⁸Is it not at the word of the Most
     High
   that both good and bad take place?
³⁹What should the living complain
     about?
   about their sins!

⁴⁰Let us search and examine our ways,
   and return to the Lord!
⁴¹Let us lift up our hearts as well as our
     hands
   toward God in heaven!
⁴²We have rebelled and been obstinate;
   you have not forgiven us.

⁴³You wrapped yourself in wrath and
     pursued us,
   killing without pity;
⁴⁴You wrapped yourself in a cloud,
   which no prayer could pierce.
⁴⁵You have made us filth and rubbish
   among the peoples.

⁴⁶They have opened their mouths
     against us,
   all our enemies;
⁴⁷Panic and the pit have been our lot,
   desolation and destruction;
⁴⁸My eyes stream with tears over the
     destruction
   of the daughter of my people.

⁴⁹My eyes will flow without ceasing,
   without rest,
⁵⁰Until the Lord from heaven
   looks down and sees.
⁵¹I am tormented by the sight
   of all the daughters of my city.

⁵²Without cause, my enemies snared
     me
   as though I were a bird;
⁵³They tried to end my life in the pit,
   pelting me with stones.
⁵⁴The waters flowed over my head:
   and I said, "I am lost!"

⁵⁵I have called upon your name,
   O Lord,
   from the bottom of the pit;
⁵⁶You heard me call, "Do not let your
     ear be deaf
   to my cry for help."
⁵⁷You drew near on the day I called
     you;
   you said, "Do not fear!"

⁵⁸You pleaded my case, Lord,
   you redeemed my life.
⁵⁹You see, Lord, how I am wronged;
   do me justice!
⁶⁰You see all their vindictiveness,
   all their plots against me.

⁶¹You hear their reproach, Lord,
   all their plots against me,
⁶²The whispered murmurings of my
     adversaries,
   against me all day long;
⁶³Look! Whether they sit or stand,
   I am the butt of their taunt.

⁶⁴Give them what they deserve, LORD,
    according to their deeds;
⁶⁵Give them hardness of heart;
    your curse be upon them;
⁶⁶Pursue them in wrath and destroy
        them
    from under the LORD's heaven!

Miseries of the Besieged City. 4:1
        How the gold has lost its luster,
    the noble metal changed;
Jewels lie scattered
    at the corner of every street.

²And Zion's precious children,
    worth their weight in gold—
How they are treated like clay jugs,
    the work of any potter!

³Even jackals offer their breasts
    to nurse their young;
But the daughter of my people is as
        cruel
    as the ostrich in the wilderness.

⁴The tongue of the infant cleaves
    to the roof of its mouth in thirst;
Children beg for bread,
    but no one gives them a piece.

⁵Those who feasted on delicacies
    are abandoned in the streets;
Those who reclined on crimson
    now embrace dung heaps.

⁶The punishment of the daughter of
        my people
    surpassed the penalty of Sodom,
Which was overthrown in an instant
    with no hand laid on it.

⁷Her princes were brighter than snow,
    whiter than milk,
Their bodies more ruddy than coral,
    their beauty like the sapphire.

⁸Now their appearance is blacker than
        soot,
    they go unrecognized in the streets;
Their skin has shrunk on their bones,
    and become dry as wood.

⁹Better for those pierced by the sword
    than for those pierced by hunger,
Better for those who bleed from
        wounds
    than for those who lack food.

¹⁰The hands of compassionate women
    have boiled their own children!
They became their food
    when the daughter of my people
        was shattered.

¹¹The LORD has exhausted his anger,
    poured out his blazing wrath;
He has kindled a fire in Zion
    that has consumed her foundations.

¹²The kings of the earth did not believe,
    nor any of the world's inhabitants,
That foe or enemy could enter
    the gates of Jerusalem.

¹³Except for the sins of her prophets
    and the crimes of her priests,
Who poured out in her midst
    the blood of the just.

¹⁴They staggered blindly in the streets,
    defiled with blood,
So that people could not touch
    even their garments:

¹⁵"Go away! Unclean!" they cried to
        them,
    "Away, away, do not touch!"
If they went away and wandered,
    it would be said among the nations,
    "They can no longer live here!"

¹⁶The presence of the LORD was their
        portion,
    but he no longer looks upon them.
The priests are shown no regard,
    the elders, no mercy.

¹⁷Even now our eyes are worn out,
    searching in vain for help;
From our watchtower we have watched
    for a nation unable to save.

¹⁸They dogged our every step,
  we could not walk in our squares;
Our end drew near, our time was up;
  yes, our end had come.

¹⁹Our pursuers were swifter
  than eagles in the sky,
In the mountains they were hot on our
    trail,
  they ambushed us in the wilderness.

²⁰The LORD's anointed—our very
    lifebreath!—
  was caught in their snares,
He in whose shade we thought
  to live among the nations.

²¹Rejoice and gloat, daughter Edom,
  dwelling in the land of Uz,
The cup will pass to you as well;
  you shall become drunk and strip
    yourself naked!

²²Your punishment is completed,
    daughter Zion,
  the Lord will not prolong your exile;
The Lord will punish your iniquity,
    daughter Edom,
  will lay bare your sins.

**The Community's Lament to the
    Lord. 5:1** Remember, LORD,
    what has happened to us,
  pay attention, and see our disgrace:
²Our heritage is turned over to strangers,
  our homes, to foreigners.
³We have become orphans, without
    fathers;
  our mothers are like widows.
⁴We pay money to drink our own
    water,
  our own wood comes at a price.
⁵With a yoke on our necks, we are
    driven;
  we are worn out, but allowed no rest.

⁶We extended a hand to Egypt and
    Assyria,
  to satisfy our need of bread.
⁷Our ancestors, who sinned, are no
    more;
  but now we bear their guilt.
⁸Servants rule over us,
  with no one to tear us from their
    hands.
⁹We risk our lives just to get bread,
  exposed to the desert heat;
¹⁰Our skin heats up like an oven,
  from the searing blasts of famine.

¹¹Women are raped in Zion,
  young women in the cities of Judah;
¹²Princes have been hanged by them,
  elders shown no respect.
¹³Young men carry millstones,
  boys stagger under loads of wood;
¹⁴The elders have abandoned the gate,
  the young men their music.

¹⁵The joy of our hearts has ceased,
  dancing has turned into mourning;
¹⁶The crown has fallen from our head:
  woe to us that we sinned!
¹⁷Because of this our hearts grow sick,
  at this our eyes grow dim:
¹⁸Because of Mount Zion, lying
    desolate,
  and the jackals roaming there!

¹⁹But you, LORD, are enthroned
    forever;
  your throne stands from age to age.
²⁰Why have you utterly forgotten us,
  forsaken us for so long?
²¹Bring us back to you, LORD, that we
    may return:
  renew our days as of old.
²²For now you have indeed rejected us
  and utterly turned your wrath
    against us.

☐ JAMES 3

Power of the Tongue. 3:1 Not many of you should become teachers, my brothers, for you realize that we will be judged more strictly, [2]for we all fall short in many respects. If anyone does not fall short in speech, he is a perfect man, able to bridle his whole body also. [3]If we put bits into the mouths of horses to make them obey us, we also guide their whole bodies. [4]It is the same with ships: even though they are so large and driven by fierce winds, they are steered by a very small rudder wherever the pilot's inclination wishes. [5]In the same way the tongue is a small member and yet has great pretensions.

Consider how small a fire can set a huge forest ablaze. [6]The tongue is also a fire. It exists among our members as a world of malice, defiling the whole body and setting the entire course of our lives on fire, itself set on fire by Gehenna. [7]For every kind of beast and bird, of reptile and sea creature, can be tamed and has been tamed by the human species, [8]but no human being can tame the tongue. It is a restless evil, full of deadly poison. [9]With it we bless the Lord and Father, and with it we curse human beings who are made in the likeness of God. [10]From the same mouth come blessing and cursing. This need not be so, my brothers. [11]Does a spring gush forth from the same opening both pure and brackish water? [12]Can a fig tree, my brothers, produce olives, or a grapevine figs? Neither can salt water yield fresh.

True Wisdom. [13]Who among you is wise and understanding? Let him show his works by a good life in the humility that comes from wisdom. [14]But if you have bitter jealousy and selfish ambition in your hearts, do not boast and be false to the truth. [15]Wisdom of this kind does not come down from above but is earthly, unspiritual, demonic. [16]For where jealousy and selfish ambition exist, there is disorder and every foul practice. [17]But the wisdom from above is first of all pure, then peaceable, gentle, compliant, full of mercy and good fruits, without inconstancy or insincerity. [18]And the fruit of righteousness is sown in peace for those who cultivate peace.

November 2

All Souls

We have loved the departed during life; let us not abandon them until we have conducted them by our prayers into the house of the Lord.

— St. Ambrose of Milan

☐ BARUCH 1-2

1:1 Now these are the words of the scroll which Baruch, son of Neriah, son of Mahseiah, son of Zedekiah, son of Hasadiah, son of Hilkiah, wrote in Babylon, [2]in the fifth year, on the seventh day of the month, at the time the Chaldeans took Jerusalem and destroyed it with fire. [3]Baruch read the words of this scroll in the hearing of Jeconiah, son of Jehoiakim, king of Judah, and all the people who came to the reading:

⁴the nobles, kings' sons, elders, and all the people, small and great—all who lived in Babylon by the river Sud.

⁵They wept, fasted, and prayed before the Lord, ⁶and collected such funds as each could afford. ⁷These they sent to Jerusalem, to Jehoiakim the priest, son of Hilkiah, son of Shallum, and to the priests and the whole people who were with him in Jerusalem. ⁸(At the same time he received the vessels of the house of the LORD that had been removed from the temple, to restore them to the land of Judah, on the tenth of Sivan. These silver vessels Zedekiah, son of Josiah, king of Judah, had had made ⁹after Nebuchadnezzar, king of Babylon, carried off as captives Jeconiah and the princes, the skilled workers, the nobles, and the people of the land from Jerusalem, and brought them to Babylon.)

¹⁰The message was: "We send you funds, with which you are to procure burnt offerings, sin offerings, and frankincense, and to prepare grain offerings; offer these on the altar of the LORD our God, ¹¹and pray for the life of Nebuchadnezzar, king of Babylon, and of Belshazzar, his son, that their lifetimes may be as the days of the heavens above the earth. ¹²Pray that the LORD may give us strength, and light to our eyes, that we may live under the protective shadow of Nebuchadnezzar, king of Babylon, and of Belshazzar, his son, to serve them many days, and find favor in their sight. ¹³Pray for us to the LORD, our God, for we have sinned against the LORD, our God. Even to this day the wrath of the LORD and his anger have not turned away from us. ¹⁴On the feast day and during the days of assembly, read aloud in the house of the LORD this scroll that we send you:

¹⁵"To the Lord our God belongs justice; to us, people of Judah and inhabitants of Jerusalem, to be shamefaced, as on this day— ¹⁶to us, our kings, rulers, priests, and prophets, and our ancestors. ¹⁷We have sinned in the LORD's sight ¹⁸and dis-

obeyed him. We have not listened to the voice of the LORD, our God, so as to follow the precepts the LORD set before us. ¹⁹From the day the LORD led our ancestors out of the land of Egypt until the present day, we have been disobedient to the LORD, our God, and neglected to listen to his voice. ²⁰Even today evils cling to us, the curse the LORD pronounced to Moses, his servant, at the time he led our ancestors out of the land of Egypt to give us a land flowing with milk and honey. ²¹For we did not listen to the voice of the LORD, our God, in all the words of the prophets he sent us, ²²but each of us has followed the inclinations of our wicked hearts, served other gods, and done evil in the sight of the LORD, our God.

2:1 "So the LORD carried out the warning he had uttered against us: against our judges, who governed Israel, against our kings and princes, and against the people of Israel and Judah. ²Nowhere under heaven has anything been done like what he did in Jerusalem, as was written in the law of Moses: ³that we would each eat the flesh of our sons, each the flesh of our daughters. ⁴He has made us subject to all the kingdoms around us, an object of reproach and horror among all the peoples around us, where the LORD has scattered us. ⁵We are brought low, not raised high, because we sinned against the LORD, our God, not listening to his voice.

⁶"To the LORD, our God, belongs justice; to us and to our ancestors, to be shamefaced, as on this day. ⁷All the evils of which the LORD had warned us have come upon us. ⁸We did not entreat the favor of the LORD by turning, each one, from the designs of our evil hearts. ⁹The LORD kept watch over the evils, and brought them home to us; for the LORD is just in all the works he commanded us to do, ¹⁰but we did not listen to his voice, or follow the precepts of the LORD which he had set before us.

[11]"And now, LORD, God of Israel, who led your people out of the land of Egypt with a strong hand, with signs and wonders and great might, and with an upraised arm, so that you have made for yourself a name to the present day: [12]we have sinned, we have committed sacrilege, we have violated all your statutes, LORD, our God. [13]Withdraw your anger from us, for we are left few in number among the nations where you have scattered us. [14]Hear, LORD, our prayer of supplication, and deliver us for your own sake: grant us favor in the sight of those who brought us into exile, [15]that the whole earth may know that you are the LORD, our God, and that Israel and his descendants bear your name. [16]LORD, look down from your holy dwelling and take thought of us; LORD, incline your ear to hear us. [17]Open your eyes and see: it is not the dead in Hades, whose breath has been taken from within them, who will declare the glory and vindication to the LORD. [18]The person who is deeply grieved, who walks bowed and feeble, with failing eyes and famished soul, will declare your glory and justice, LORD!

[19]"Not on the just deeds of our ancestors and our kings do we base our plea for mercy in your sight, LORD, our God. [20]You have sent your wrath and anger upon us, as you had warned us through your servants the prophets: [21]Thus says the LORD: Bend your necks and serve the king of Babylon, that you may continue in the land I gave your ancestors; [22]for if you do not listen to the LORD's voice so as to serve the king of Babylon, [23]I will silence from the cities of Judah and from the streets of Jerusalem the cry of joy and the cry of gladness, the voice of the bridegroom and the voice of the bride; and all the land shall be deserted, without inhabitants. [24]But we did not listen to your voice, or serve the king of Babylon, and you carried out the threats you had made through your servants the prophets, that the bones of our kings and the bones of our ancestors would be brought out from their burial places. [25]And indeed, they lie exposed to the heat of day and the frost of night. They died in great suffering, by famine and sword and plague. [26]And you reduced the house which bears your name to what it is today, because of the wickedness of the house of Israel and the house of Judah.

God's Promises Recalled. [27]"But with us, Lord, our God, you have dealt in all your clemency and in all your great mercy. [28]Thus you spoke through your servant Moses, the day you ordered him to write down your law in the presence of the Israelites: [29]If you do not listen to my voice, surely this great and numerous throng will dwindle away among the nations to which I will scatter them. [30]For I know they will not listen to me, because they are a stiff-necked people. But in the land of their exile they shall have a change of heart; [31]they shall know that I, the LORD, am their God. I will give them a heart and ears that listen; [32]and they shall praise me in the land of their exile, and shall remember my name. [33]Then they shall turn back from their stiff-necked stubbornness, and from their evil deeds, because they shall remember the ways of their ancestors, who sinned against the LORD. [34]And I will bring them back to the land I promised on oath to their ancestors, to Abraham, Isaac, and Jacob; and they shall rule it. I will make them increase; they shall not be few. [35]And I will establish for them an eternal covenant: I will be their God, and they shall be my people; and I will never again remove my people Israel from the land I gave them.'"

☐ JAMES 4

Causes of Division. 4:1 Where do the wars and where do the conflicts among you come from? Is it not from your passions that make war within your members? ²You covet but do not possess. You kill and envy but you cannot obtain; you fight and wage war. You do not possess because you do not ask. ³You ask but do not receive, because you ask wrongly, to spend it on your passions. ⁴Adulterers! Do you not know that to be a lover of the world means enmity with God? Therefore, whoever wants to be a lover of the world makes himself an enemy of God. ⁵Or do you suppose that the scripture speaks without meaning when it says, "The spirit that he has made to dwell in us tends toward jealousy"? ⁶But he bestows a greater grace; therefore, it says:

"God resists the proud,
    but gives grace to the humble."

⁷So submit yourselves to God. Resist the devil, and he will flee from you. ⁸Draw near to God, and he will draw near to you. Cleanse your hands, you sinners, and purify your hearts, you of two minds. ⁹Begin to lament, to mourn, to weep. Let your laughter be turned into mourning and your joy into dejection. ¹⁰Humble yourselves before the Lord and he will exalt you.

¹¹Do not speak evil of one another, brothers. Whoever speaks evil of a brother or judges his brother speaks evil of the law and judges the law. If you judge the law, you are not a doer of the law but a judge. ¹²There is one lawgiver and judge who is able to save or to destroy. Who then are you to judge your neighbor?

Warning against Presumption. ¹³Come now, you who say, "Today or tomorrow we shall go into such and such a town, spend a year there doing business, and make a profit"— ¹⁴you have no idea what your life will be like tomorrow. You are a puff of smoke that appears briefly and then disappears. ¹⁵Instead you should say, "If the Lord wills it, we shall live to do this or that." ¹⁶But now you are boasting in your arrogance. All such boasting is evil. ¹⁷So for one who knows the right thing to do and does not do it, it is a sin.

November 3

St. Martin de Porres

When the Lord knows that good health is necessary for our welfare, He sends it to us; and when we need sickness, He sends that too.

— St. Teresa of Ávila

☐ BARUCH 3-4

3:1 "Lord Almighty, God of Israel, the anguished soul, the dismayed spirit cries out to you. ²Hear, Lord, and have mercy, for you are a merciful God; have mercy on us, who have sinned against you: ³for you are enthroned forever, while we are perishing forever. ⁴Lord Almighty, God of Israel, hear the prayer of the dead of Israel, children who sinned against you; they did not listen to the voice of the Lord, their God, and their evils cling to us. ⁵Do not remember the wicked deeds of our ancestors, but remember at this time your power and your name, ⁶for you are the LORD our God; and you, LORD, we will praise! ⁷This is why you put into our hearts the fear of you: that we may call upon your name, and praise you in our exile, when we have removed from our hearts all the wickedness of our ancestors who sinned against you. ⁸See, today we are in exile, where you have scattered us, an object of reproach and cursing and punishment for all the wicked deeds of our ancestors, who withdrew from the LORD, our God."

A. Importance of Wisdom. ⁹Hear,
  Israel, the commandments of life:
  listen, and know prudence!
¹⁰How is it, Israel,
  that you are in the land of your foes,
  grown old in a foreign land,
¹¹Defiled with the dead,
  counted among those destined for
    Hades?
¹²You have forsaken the fountain of
    wisdom!
¹³Had you walked in the way of God,
  you would have dwelt in enduring
    peace.

¹⁴Learn where prudence is,
  where strength, where
    understanding;
That you may know also
  where are length of days, and life,
  where light of the eyes, and peace.
¹⁵Who has found the place of wisdom?
  Who has entered into her treasuries?
¹⁶Where are the rulers of the nations,
  who lorded it over the wild beasts of
    the earth,
¹⁷made sport of the birds in the
    heavens,
Who heaped up the silver,
  the gold in which people trust,
  whose possessions were unlimited,
¹⁸Who schemed anxiously for money,

their doings beyond discovery?
¹⁹They have vanished, gone down to
    Hades,
  and others have risen up in their
    stead.
²⁰Later generations have seen the light
    of day,
  have dwelt on the earth,
But the way to understanding they
  have not known,
²¹they have not perceived her paths
    or reached her;
  their children remain far from the
    way to her.
²²She has not been heard of in Canaan,
  nor seen in Teman.
²³The descendants of Hagar who seek
    knowledge on earth,
  the merchants of Medan and Tema,
  the storytellers and those seeking
    knowledge—
These have not known the way to
    wisdom,
  nor have they kept her paths in
    mind.

B. Inaccessibility of Wisdom. ²⁴O
  Israel, how vast is the dwelling
    of God,
  how broad the scope of his dominion:
²⁵Vast and endless,
  high and immeasurable!
²⁶In it were born the giants,
  renowned at the first,
  huge in stature, skilled in war.
²⁷These God did not choose,
  nor did he give them the way of
    understanding;
²⁸They perished for lack of prudence,
  perished through their own folly.

²⁹Who has gone up to the heavens and
    taken her,
  bringing her down from the clouds?
³⁰Who has crossed the sea and found
    her,
  bearing her away rather than choice
    gold?

³¹None knows the way to her,
    nor has at heart her path.
³²But the one who knows all things
    knows her;
    he has probed her by his knowledge—
The one who established the earth for
    all time,
    and filled it with four-footed
      animals,
³³Who sends out the lightning, and it
    goes,
    calls it, and trembling it obeys him;
³⁴Before whom the stars at their posts
    shine and rejoice.
³⁵When he calls them, they answer,
    "Here we are!"
    shining with joy for their Maker.
³⁶Such is our God;
    no other is to be compared to him:

C. Wisdom Contained in the Law.
    ³⁷He has uncovered the whole
      way of understanding,
    and has given her to Jacob, his
      servant,
    to Israel, his beloved.

³⁸Thus she has appeared on earth,
    is at home with mortals.

4:1 She is the book of the precepts of
    God,
    the law that endures forever;
All who cling to her will live,
    but those will die who forsake her.
²Turn, O Jacob, and receive her:
    walk by her light toward splendor.
³Do not give your glory to another,
    your privileges to an alien nation.
⁴Blessed are we, O Israel;
    for what pleases God is known to us!

A. Baruch Addresses Diaspora. ⁵Take
    courage, my people!
    Remember, O Israel,
⁶You were sold to the nations
    not for destruction;
It was because you angered God

that you were handed over to your
    foes.
⁷For you provoked your Maker
    with sacrifices to demons and not
    to God;
⁸You forgot the eternal God who
    nourished you,
    and you grieved Jerusalem who
    nurtured you.
⁹She indeed saw coming upon you
    the wrath of God; and she said:

B. Jerusalem Addresses Neighbors.
    "Hear, you neighbors of Zion!
    God has brought great mourning
      upon me,
¹⁰For I have seen the captivity
    that the Eternal One has brought
    upon my sons and daughters.
¹¹With joy I nurtured them;
    but with mourning and lament I
      sent them away.
¹²Let no one gloat over me,
    a widow, bereft of many;
For the sins of my children I am left
    desolate,
    because they turned from the law
      of God,
¹³and did not acknowledge his
    statutes;
In the ways of God's commandments
    they did not walk,
    nor did they tread the disciplined
      paths of his justice.

¹⁴"Let Zion's neighbors come—
    Remember the captivity of my sons
      and daughters,
    brought upon them by the Eternal
      One.
¹⁵He has brought against them a nation
    from afar,
    a nation ruthless and of alien speech,
That has neither reverence for old age
    nor pity for the child;
¹⁶They have led away this widow's
    beloved sons,

have left me solitary, without
  daughters.

C. Jerusalem Addresses Diaspora.
¹⁷What can I do to help you?
¹⁸The one who has brought this evil
  upon you
  must himself deliver you from your
    enemies' hands.
¹⁹Farewell, my children, farewell;
  I am left desolate.
²⁰I have taken off the garment of peace,
  have put on sackcloth for my prayer
    of supplication;
  while I live I will cry out to the
    Eternal One.

²¹"Take courage, my children; call
  upon God;
  he will deliver you from oppression,
    from enemy hands.
²²I have put my hope for your
    deliverance in the Eternal One,
  and joy has come to me from the
    Holy One
Because of the mercy that will swiftly
    reach you
  from your eternal Savior.
²³With mourning and lament I sent
  you away,
  but God will give you back to me
  with gladness and joy forever.
²⁴As Zion's neighbors lately saw you
    taken captive,
  so shall they soon see God's
    salvation come to you,
  with great glory and the splendor of
    the Eternal One.

²⁵"My children, bear patiently the
  wrath
  that has come upon you from God;
Your enemies have persecuted you,
  but you will soon see their
    destruction
  and trample upon their necks.
²⁶My pampered children have trodden
  rough roads,

carried off by their enemies like
  sheep in a raid.
²⁷Take courage, my children; call out
  to God!
The one who brought this upon you
  will remember you.
²⁸As your hearts have been disposed to
  stray from God,
  so turn now ten times the more to
    seek him;
²⁹For the one who has brought disaster
  upon you
  will, in saving you, bring you
    eternal joy."

D. Baruch Addresses Jerusalem.
³⁰Take courage, Jerusalem!
The one who gave you your name
  will console you.
³¹Wretched shall be those who harmed
  you,
  who rejoiced at your downfall;
³²Wretched shall be the cities where
    your children were enslaved,
  wretched the city that received your
    children.
³³As that city rejoiced at your collapse,
  and made merry at your downfall,
  so shall she grieve over her own
    desolation.
³⁴I will take from her the rejoicing
  crowds,
  and her exultation shall be turned to
    mourning:
³⁵For fire shall come upon her
  from the Eternal One, for many a
    day,
  to be inhabited by demons for a
    long time.
³⁶Look to the east, Jerusalem;
  see the joy that comes to you from
    God!
³⁷Here come your children whom you
    sent away,
  gathered in from east to west
By the word of the Holy One,
  rejoicing in the glory of God.

☐ JAMES 5

Warning to the Rich. 5:1 Come now, you rich, weep and wail over your impending miseries. [2]Your wealth has rotted away, your clothes have become moth-eaten, [3]your gold and silver have corroded, and that corrosion will be a testimony against you; it will devour your flesh like a fire. You have stored up treasure for the last days. [4]Behold, the wages you withheld from the workers who harvested your fields are crying aloud, and the cries of the harvesters have reached the ears of the Lord of hosts. [5]You have lived on earth in luxury and pleasure; you have fattened your hearts for the day of slaughter. [6]You have condemned; you have murdered the righteous one; he offers you no resistance.

Patience and Oaths. [7]Be patient, therefore, brothers, until the coming of the Lord. See how the farmer waits for the precious fruit of the earth, being patient with it until it receives the early and the late rains. [8]You too must be patient. Make your hearts firm, because the coming of the Lord is at hand. [9]Do not complain, brothers, about one another, that you may not be judged. Behold, the Judge is standing before the gates. [10]Take as an example of hardship and patience, brothers, the prophets who spoke in the name of the Lord. [11]Indeed we call blessed those who have persevered. You have heard of the perseverance of Job, and you have seen the purpose of the Lord, because "the Lord is compassionate and merciful."

[12]But above all, my brothers, do not swear, either by heaven or by earth or with any other oath, but let your "Yes" mean "Yes" and your "No" mean "No," that you may not incur condemnation.

Anointing of the Sick. [13]Is anyone among you suffering? He should pray. Is anyone in good spirits? He should sing praise. [14]Is anyone among you sick? He should summon the presbyters of the church, and they should pray over him and anoint [him] with oil in the name of the Lord, [15]and the prayer of faith will save the sick person, and the Lord will raise him up. If he has committed any sins, he will be forgiven.

Confession and Intercession. [16]Therefore, confess your sins to one another and pray for one another, that you may be healed. The fervent prayer of a righteous person is very powerful. [17]Elijah was a human being like us; yet he prayed earnestly that it might not rain, and for three years and six months it did not rain upon the land. [18]Then he prayed again, and the sky gave rain and the earth produced its fruit.

Conversion of Sinners. [19]My brothers, if anyone among you should stray from the truth and someone bring him back, [20]he should know that whoever brings back a sinner from the error of his way will save his soul from death and will cover a multitude of sins.

November 4

St. Charles Borromeo

Nothing pleases God more than for us to be His Son's helpers and to undertake the charge of saving souls. Nothing brings more joy to the Church than those who restore souls to spiritual life, thus despoiling hell, defeating the devil, casting out sin, opening heaven, making the angels glad, glorifying the Most Holy Trinity, and preparing for themselves a never-fading crown.

— St. Charles Borromeo

☐ BARUCH 5-6

5:1 Jerusalem, take off your robe of
mourning and misery;
put on forever the splendor of glory
from God:
²Wrapped in the mantle of justice from
God,
place on your head the diadem
of the glory of the Eternal One.
³For God will show your splendor to
all under the heavens;
⁴you will be named by God forever:
the peace of justice, the glory of
God's worship.
⁵Rise up, Jerusalem! stand upon the
heights;
look to the east and see your
children
Gathered from east to west
at the word of the Holy One,
rejoicing that they are remembered
by God.
⁶Led away on foot by their enemies
they left you:
but God will bring them back to you
carried high in glory as on royal
thrones.
⁷For God has commanded
that every lofty mountain
and the age-old hills be made low,
That the valleys be filled to make level
ground,
that Israel may advance securely in
the glory of God.

⁸The forests and every kind of fragrant
tree
have overshadowed Israel at God's
command;
⁹For God is leading Israel in joy
by the light of his glory,
with the mercy and justice that are
his.

6:1 A copy of the letter which Jeremiah sent to those led captive to Babylon by the king of the Babylonians, to tell them what God had commanded him:

For the sins you committed before God, you are being led captive to Babylon by Nebuchadnezzar, king of the Babylonians. ²When you reach Babylon you will be there many years, a long time—seven generations; after that I will bring you back from there in peace. ³And now in Babylon you will see gods of silver and gold and wood, carried shoulder high, to cast fear upon the nations. ⁴Take care that you yourselves do not become like these foreigners and let not such fear possess you. ⁵When you see the crowd before them and behind worshiping them, say in your hearts, "You, Lord, are the one to be worshiped!" ⁶For my angel is with you, and he will keep watch on you.

⁷Their tongues are smoothed by woodworkers; they are covered with gold and silver—but they are frauds, and cannot speak. ⁸People bring gold, as though for a girl fond of dressing up, ⁹and prepare

crowns for the heads of their gods. Then sometimes the priests filch the gold and silver from their gods and spend it on themselves, [10]or give part of it to harlots in the brothel. They dress them up in clothes like human beings, these gods of silver and gold and wood. [11]Though they are wrapped in purple clothing, they are not safe from rust and corrosion. [12]Their faces are wiped clean of the cloud of dust which is thick upon them. [13]Each has a scepter, like the human ruler of a district, but none can do away with those that offend against it. [14]Each has in its right hand an ax or dagger, but it cannot save itself from war or pillage. Thus it is known they are not gods; do not fear them.

[15]As useless as a broken pot [16]are their gods, set up in their temples, their eyes full of dust from the feet of those who enter. [17]Their courtyards are walled in like those of someone brought to execution for a crime against the king; the priests reinforce their temples with gates and bars and bolts, so they will not be carried off by robbers. [18]They light more lamps for them than for themselves, yet not one of these can they see. [19]They are like any timber in the temple; their hearts, it is said, are eaten away. Though crawling creatures from the ground consume them and their garments, they do not feel it. [20]Their faces become sooty from the smoke in the temple. [21]Bats and swallows alight on their bodies and heads—any bird, and cats as well. [22]Know, therefore, that they are not gods; do not fear them.

[23]Gold adorns them, but unless someone wipes away the corrosion, they do not shine; they felt nothing when they were molded. [24]They are bought at whatever price, but there is no spirit in them. [25]Since they have no feet, they are carried shoulder high, displaying to all how worthless they are; even those who worship them are put to shame [26]because, if they fall to the ground, the worshipers must pick them up. They neither move of themselves if one sets them upright, nor come upright if they are tipped over; offerings are set out for them as for the dead. [27]Their priests sell their sacrifices for their own advantage. Likewise their wives cure some of the meat, but they do not share it with the poor and the weak; [28]women ritually unclean or at childbirth handle their sacrifices. From such things, know that they are not gods; do not fear them.

[29]How can they be called gods? Women set out the offerings for these gods of silver and gold and wood, [30]and in their temples the priests squat with torn tunic and with shaven hair and beard, and with their heads uncovered. [31]They shout and wail before their gods as others do at a funeral banquet. [32]The priests take some of the clothing from their gods and put it on their wives and children. [33]Whether these gods are treated well or badly by anyone, they cannot repay it. They can neither set up nor remove a king. [34]They cannot give anyone riches or pennies; if one fails to fulfill a vow to them, they will not exact it. [35]They neither save anyone from death, nor deliver the weak from the strong, [36]nor do they restore sight to the blind, or rescue anyone in distress. [37]The widow they do not pity, the orphan they do not help. [38]These gilded and silvered wooden statues are no better than stones from the mountains; their worshipers will be put to shame. [39]How then can it be thought or claimed that they are gods?

[40]Even the Chaldeans themselves have no respect for them; for when they see a deaf mute, unable to speak, they bring forward Bel and expect him to make a sound, as though he could hear. [41]They themselves are unable to reflect and abandon these gods, for they have no sense. [42]And the women, with cords around them, sit by the roads, burning chaff for incense; [43]and whenever one of them is taken aside by some passerby who lies with her, she mocks her neighbor who has not been thought thus worthy, and has not had her

cord broken. [44]All that is done for these gods is a fraud; how then can it be thought or claimed that they are gods?

[45]They are produced by woodworkers and goldsmiths; they are nothing other than what these artisans wish them to be. [46]Even those who produce them are not long-lived; [47]how then can the things they have produced be gods? They have left frauds and disgrace to their successors. [48]For when war or disaster comes upon them, the priests deliberate among themselves where they can hide with them. [49]How then can one not understand that these are not gods, who save themselves neither from war nor from disaster? [50]Beings that are wooden, gilded and silvered, they will later be known for frauds. To all nations and kings it will be clear that they are not gods, but human handiwork; and that God's work is not in them. [51]Is it not obvious that they are not gods?

[52]They set no king over the land, nor do they give rain. [53]They neither vindicate their own rights, nor do they rescue anyone wronged, for they are powerless. [54]They are like crows in midair. For when fire breaks out in the temple of these wooden or gilded or silvered gods, though the priests flee and are safe, they themselves are burned up in the fire like timbers. [55]They cannot resist a king or enemy forces. [56]How then can it be admitted or thought that they are gods?

They are safe from neither thieves nor bandits, these wooden and silvered and gilded gods. [57]Anyone who can will strip off the gold and the silver, and go away with the clothing that was on them; they cannot help themselves. [58]How much better to be a king displaying his valor, or a handy tool in a house, the joy of its owner, than these false gods; better the door of a house, protecting whatever is within, than these false gods; better a wooden post in a palace, than these false gods! [59]The sun and moon and stars are bright, obedient in the task for which they are sent. [60]Likewise the lightning, when it flashes, is a great sight; and the one wind blows over every land. [61]The clouds, too, when commanded by God to proceed across the whole world, fulfill the command; [62]and fire, sent from on high to burn up the mountains and the forests, carries out its command. But these false gods are not their equal, whether in appearance or in power. [63]So it is unthinkable, and cannot be claimed that they are gods. They can neither execute judgment, nor benefit anyone. [64]Know, therefore, that they are not gods; do not fear them.

[65]Kings they can neither curse nor bless. [66]They show the nations no signs in the heavens, nor do they shine like the sun, nor give light like the moon. [67]The beasts are better than they—beasts can help themselves by fleeing to shelter. [68]Thus is it in no way apparent to us that they are gods; so do not fear them.

[69]For like a scarecrow in a cucumber patch, providing no protection, are their wooden, gilded, silvered gods. [70]Just like a thornbush in a garden on which perches every kind of bird, or like a corpse hurled into darkness, are their wooden, gilded, silvered gods. [71]From the rotting of the purple and the linen upon them, you can know that they are not gods; they themselves will in the end be consumed, and be a disgrace in the land. [72]Better the just who has no idols; such shall be far from disgrace!

☐ 1 JOHN 1-2

The Word of Life

1:1 What was from the beginning,
what we have heard,
what we have seen with our eyes,
what we looked upon
and touched with our hands
concerns the Word of life—
²for the life was made visible;
we have seen it and testify to it
and proclaim to you the eternal life
that was with the Father and was
made visible to us—
³what we have seen and heard
we proclaim now to you,
so that you too may have fellowship
with us;
for our fellowship is with the Father
and with his Son, Jesus Christ.
⁴We are writing this so that our joy
may be complete.

God is Light. ⁵Now this is the message that we have heard from him and proclaim to you: God is light, and in him there is no darkness at all. ⁶If we say, "We have fellowship with him," while we continue to walk in darkness, we lie and do not act in truth. ⁷But if we walk in the light as he is in the light, then we have fellowship with one another, and the blood of his Son Jesus cleanses us from all sin. ⁸If we say, "We are without sin," we deceive ourselves, and the truth is not in us. ⁹If we acknowledge our sins, he is faithful and just and will forgive our sins and cleanse us from every wrongdoing. ¹⁰If we say, "We have not sinned," we make him a liar, and his word is not in us.

Christ and His Commandments. 2:1 My children, I am writing this to you so that you may not commit sin. But if anyone does sin, we have an Advocate with the Father, Jesus Christ the righteous one. ²He is expiation for our sins, and not for our sins only but for those of the whole world. ³The way we may be sure that we know him is to keep his commandments. ⁴Whoever says, "I know him," but does not keep his commandments is a liar, and the truth is not in him. ⁵But whoever keeps his word, the love of God is truly perfected in him. This is the way we may know that we are in union with him: ⁶whoever claims to abide in him ought to live [just] as he lived.

The New Commandment. ⁷Beloved, I am writing no new commandment to you but an old commandment that you had from the beginning. The old commandment is the word that you have heard. ⁸And yet I do write a new commandment to you, which holds true in him and among you, for the darkness is passing away, and the true light is already shining. ⁹Whoever says he is in the light, yet hates his brother, is still in the darkness. ¹⁰Whoever loves his brother remains in the light, and there is nothing in him to cause a fall. ¹¹Whoever hates his brother is in darkness; he walks in darkness and does not know where he is going because the darkness has blinded his eyes.

Members of the Community. ¹²I am writing to you, children, because your sins have been forgiven for his name's sake.

¹³I am writing to you, fathers, because you know him who is from the beginning.

I am writing to you, young men, because you have conquered the evil one.

¹⁴I write to you, children, because you know the Father.

I write to you, fathers, because you know him who is from the beginning.

I write to you, young men, because you are strong and the word of God remains in you, and you have conquered the evil one.

¹⁵Do not love the world or the things of the world. If anyone loves the world, the love of the Father is not in him. ¹⁶For all that is in the world, sensual lust, enticement for

the eyes, and a pretentious life, is not from the Father but is from the world. [17]Yet the world and its enticement are passing away. But whoever does the will of God remains forever.

Antichrists. [18]Children, it is the last hour; and just as you heard that the antichrist was coming, so now many antichrists have appeared. Thus we know this is the last hour. [19]They went out from us, but they were not really of our number; if they had been, they would have remained with us. Their desertion shows that none of them was of our number. [20]But you have the anointing that comes from the holy one, and you all have knowledge. [21]I write to you not because you do not know the truth but because you do, and because every lie is alien to the truth. [22]Who is the liar? Whoever denies that Jesus is the Christ. Whoever denies the Father and the Son, this is the antichrist. [23]No one who denies the Son has the Father, but whoever confesses the Son has the Father as well.

Life from God's Anointing. [24]Let what you heard from the beginning remain in you. If what you heard from the beginning remains in you, then you will remain in the Son and in the Father. [25]And this is the promise that he made us: eternal life. [26]I write you these things about those who would deceive you. [27]As for you, the anointing that you received from him remains in you, so that you do not need anyone to teach you. But his anointing teaches you about everything and is true and not false; just as it taught you, remain in him.

Children of God. [28]And now, children, remain in him, so that when he appears we may have confidence and not be put to shame by him at his coming. [29]If you consider that he is righteous, you also know that everyone who acts in righteousness is begotten by him.

November 5

Perfect love means putting up with other people's shortcomings, feeling no surprise at their weaknesses, finding encouragement even in the slightest evidence of good qualities in them.

— St. Thérèse of Lisieux

☐ EZEKIEL 1-3

The Vision: God on the Cherubim. 1:1 In the thirtieth year, on the fifth day of the fourth month, while I was among the exiles by the river Chebar, the heavens opened, and I saw divine visions.— [2]On the fifth day of the month—this was the fifth year of King Jehoiachin's exile— [3]the word of the LORD came to the priest Ezekiel, the son of Buzi, in the land of the Chaldeans by the river Chebar. There the hand of the LORD came upon him.

[4]As I watched, a great stormwind came from the North, a large cloud with flash-ing fire, a bright glow all around it, and something like polished metal gleamed at the center of the fire. [5]From within it figures in the likeness of four living creatures appeared. This is what they looked like: [6]They were in human form, but each had four faces and four wings, [7]and their legs were straight, the soles of their feet like the hooves of a bull, gleaming like polished brass. [8]Human hands were under their wings, and the wings of one touched those of another. [9]Their faces and their wings looked out on all their four sides; they did

not turn when they moved, but each went straight ahead.

¹⁰Their faces were like this: each of the four had a human face, and on the right the face of a lion, and on the left, the face of an ox, and each had the face of an eagle. ¹¹Such were their faces. Their wings were spread out above. On each one, two wings touched one another, and the other two wings covered the body. ¹²Each went straight ahead. Wherever the spirit would go, they went; they did not change direction when they moved. ¹³And the appearance of the living creatures seemed like burning coals of fire. Something indeed like torches moved back and forth among the living creatures. The fire gleamed intensely, and from it lightning flashed. ¹⁴The creatures darting back and forth flashed like lightning.

¹⁵As I looked at the living creatures, I saw wheels on the ground, one alongside each of the four living creatures. ¹⁶The wheels and their construction sparkled like yellow topaz, and all four of them looked the same: their construction seemed as though one wheel was inside the other. ¹⁷When they moved, they went in any of the four directions without veering as they moved. ¹⁸The four of them had rims, high and fearsome—eyes filled the four rims all around. ¹⁹When the living creatures moved, the wheels moved with them; and when the living creatures were raised from the ground, the wheels also were raised. ²⁰Wherever the spirit would go, they went. And they were raised up together with the living creatures, for the spirit of the living creatures was in the wheels. ²¹Wherever the living creatures moved, the wheels moved; when they stood still, the wheels stood still. When they were lifted up from the earth, the wheels were lifted up with them. For the spirit of the living creatures was in the wheels.

²²Above the heads of the living creatures was a likeness of the firmament; it was awesome, stretching upwards like shining crystal over their heads. ²³Beneath the firmament their wings stretched out toward one another; each had two wings covering the body. ²⁴Then I heard the sound of their wings, like the roaring of mighty waters, like the voice of the Almighty. When they moved, the sound of the tumult was like the din of an army. And when they stood still, they lowered their wings. ²⁵While they stood with their wings lowered, a voice came from above the firmament over their heads.

²⁶Above the firmament over their heads was the likeness of a throne that looked like sapphire; and upon this likeness of a throne was seated, up above, a figure that looked like a human being. ²⁷And I saw something like polished metal, like the appearance of fire enclosed on all sides, from what looked like the waist up; and from what looked like the waist down, I saw something like the appearance of fire and brilliant light surrounding him. ²⁸Just like the appearance of the rainbow in the clouds on a rainy day so was the appearance of brilliance that surrounded him. Such was the appearance of the likeness of the glory of the LORD. And when I saw it, I fell on my face and heard a voice speak.

Eating of the Scroll. 2:1 The voice said to me: Son of man, stand up! I wish to speak to you. ²As he spoke to me, the spirit entered into me and set me on my feet, and I heard the one who was speaking ³say to me: Son of man, I am sending you to the Israelites, a nation of rebels who have rebelled against me; they and their ancestors have been in revolt against me to this very day. ⁴Their children are bold of face and stubborn of heart—to them I am sending you. You shall say to them: Thus says the Lord GOD. ⁵And whether they hear or resist—they are a rebellious house—they shall know that a prophet has been among them. ⁶But as for you, son of man, do not fear them or their words. Do not fear, even though there are briers or thorns and you sit among scorpions. Do not be afraid of their words or be terrified by their looks for they are a rebellious house. ⁷You must speak my words to them, whether they hear or resist, because they are rebellious. ⁸But you, son of man, hear me when I speak to you and do not rebel like this rebellious house. Open your mouth and eat what I am giving you.

⁹It was then I saw a hand stretched out to me; in it was a written scroll. ¹⁰He unrolled it before me; it was covered with writing front and back. Written on it was: Lamentation, wailing, woe!

3:1 He said to me: Son of man, eat what you find here: eat this scroll, then go, speak to the house of Israel. ²So I opened my mouth, and he gave me the scroll to eat. ³Son of man, he said to me, feed your stomach and fill your belly with this scroll I am giving you. I ate it, and it was as sweet as honey in my mouth. ⁴Then he said to me, Son of man, go now to the house of Israel, and speak my words to them. ⁵Not to a people with obscure speech and difficult language am I sending you, but to the house of Israel. ⁶Nor to many nations of obscure speech and difficult language whose words you cannot understand. For if I were to send you to these, they would listen to you. ⁷But the house of Israel will refuse to listen to you, since they refuse to listen to me. For the whole house of Israel is stubborn of brow and hard of heart. ⁸Look! I make your face as hard as theirs, and your brow as stubborn as theirs. ⁹Like diamond, harder than flint, I make your brow. Do not be afraid of them, or be terrified by their looks, for they are a rebellious house.

¹⁰Then he said to me, Son of man, take into your heart all my words that I speak to you; hear them well. ¹¹Now go to the exiles, to your own people, and speak to them.

Say to them, whether they hear or refuse to hear: Thus says the LORD God!

¹²Then the spirit lifted me up, and I heard behind me a loud rumbling noise as the glory of the LORD rose from its place: ¹³the noise of the wings of the living creatures beating against one another, and the noise of the wheels alongside them, a loud rumbling. ¹⁴And the spirit lifted me up and took me away, and I went off, my spirit angry and bitter, for the hand of the LORD pressed hard on me. ¹⁵Thus I came to the exiles who lived at Tel-abib by the river Chebar; and there where they dwelt, I stayed among them distraught for seven days. ¹⁶At the end of the seven days, the word of the LORD came to me:

The Prophet as Sentinel. ¹⁷Son of man, I have appointed you a sentinel for the house of Israel. When you hear a word from my mouth, you shall warn them for me.

¹⁸If I say to the wicked, You shall surely die—and you do not warn them or speak out to dissuade the wicked from their evil conduct in order to save their lives—then they shall die for their sin, but I will hold you responsible for their blood. ¹⁹If, however, you warn the wicked and they still do not turn from their wickedness and evil conduct, they shall die for their sin, but you shall save your life.

²⁰But if the just turn away from their right conduct and do evil when I place a stumbling block before them, then they shall die. Even if you warned them about their sin, they shall still die, and the just deeds that they performed will not be remembered on their behalf. I will, however, hold you responsible for their blood. ²¹If, on the other hand, you warn the just to avoid sin, and they do not sin, they will surely live because of the warning, and you in turn shall save your own life.

Ezekiel Mute. ²²The hand of the LORD came upon me there and he said to me: Get up and go out into the plain, where I will speak with you. ²³So I got up and went out into the plain. There it was! The glory of the LORD was standing there like the glory I had seen by the river Chebar. Then I fell on my face, [24]but the spirit entered into me, set me on my feet; he spoke to me, and said: Go, shut yourself in your house. [25]As for you, son of man, know that they will put ropes on you and bind you with them, so that you cannot go out among them. [26]And I will make your tongue stick to the roof of your mouth so that you will be mute, no longer one who rebukes them for being a rebellious house. [27]Only when I speak to you and open your mouth, shall you say to them: Thus says the LORD God: Let those who hear, hear! Let those who resist, resist! They are truly a rebellious house.

☐ 1 JOHN 3

3:1 See what love the Father has bestowed on us that we may be called the children of God. Yet so we are. The reason the world does not know us is that it did not know him. [2]Beloved, we are God's children now; what we shall be has not yet been revealed. We do know that when it is revealed we shall be like him, for we shall see him as he is. [3]Everyone who has this hope based on him makes himself pure, as he is pure.

Avoiding Sin. [4]Everyone who commits sin commits lawlessness, for sin is lawlessness. [5]You know that he was revealed to take away sins, and in him there is no sin. [6]No one who remains in him sins; no one who sins has seen him or known him. [7]Children, let no one deceive you. The person who acts in righteousness is righteous, just as he is righteous. [8]Whoever sins belongs to the devil, because the devil has sinned from the beginning. Indeed, the Son of God was revealed to destroy the works of the devil. [9]No one who is begotten by God commits sin, because God's seed remains in him; he cannot sin because he is begotten by God. [10]In this way, the children of God and the children of the devil are made plain; no one who fails to act in righteousness belongs to God, nor anyone who does not love his brother.

[11]For this is the message you have heard from the beginning: we should love one another, [12]unlike Cain who belonged to the evil one and slaughtered his brother. Why did he slaughter him? Because his own works were evil, and those of his brother righteous. [13]Do not be amazed, [then,] brothers, if the world hates you. [14]We know that we have passed from death to life because we love our brothers. Whoever does not love remains in death. [15]Everyone who hates his brother is a murderer, and you know that no murderer has eternal life remaining in him. [16]The way we came to know love was that he laid down his life for us; so we ought to lay down our lives for our brothers. [17]If someone who has worldly means sees a brother in need and refuses him compassion, how can the love of God remain in him? [18]Children, let us love not in word or speech but in deed and truth.

Confidence before God. [19][Now] this is how we shall know that we belong to the truth and reassure our hearts before him [20]in whatever our hearts condemn, for God is greater than our hearts and knows everything. [21]Beloved, if [our] hearts do not condemn us, we have confidence in God [22]and receive from him whatever we ask, because we keep his commandments and do what pleases him. [23]And his commandment is this: we should believe in the name of his Son, Jesus Christ, and love one another just as he commanded us. [24]Those who keep his commandments remain in him, and he in them, and the way we know that he remains in us is from the Spirit that he gave us.

November 6

The fear of God prepares a place for love. But once love has begun to dwell in our hearts, the fear that prepared the place for it is driven out. In sewing, the needle introduces the thread into the cloth. The needle goes in, but the thread cannot follow unless the needle comes out first. In the same way, the fear of God first occupies our minds, but it does not remain there, because it enters only in order to introduce love.

— St. Augustine of Hippo

☐ EZEKIEL 4–5

Acts Symbolic of Siege and Exile. 4:1 You, son of man, take a clay tablet; place it in front of you, and draw on it a city, Jerusalem. ²Lay siege to it: build up siege works, raise a ramp against it, pitch camps and set up battering rams all around it. ³Then take an iron pan and set it up as an iron wall between you and the city. Set your face toward it and put it under siege. So you must lay siege to it as a sign for the house of Israel. ⁴Then lie down on your left side, while I place the guilt of the house of Israel upon you. As many days as you lie like this, you shall bear their guilt. ⁵I allot you three hundred and ninety days during which you must bear the guilt of the house of Israel, the same number of years they sinned. ⁶When you have completed this, you shall lie down a second time, on your right side to bear the guilt of the house of Judah forty days; I allot you one day for each year. ⁷Turning your face toward the siege of Jerusalem, with bared arm you shall prophesy against it. ⁸See, I bind you with ropes so that you cannot turn from one side to the other until you have completed the days of your siege.

⁹Then take wheat and barley, beans and lentils, millet and spelt; put them into a single pot and make them into bread. Eat it for as many days as you lie upon your side, three hundred and ninety days. ¹⁰The food you eat shall be twenty shekels a day by weight; each day you shall eat it. ¹¹And the water you drink shall be the sixth of a hin by measure; each day you shall drink it. ¹²And the barley cake you eat you must bake on human excrement in the sight of all. ¹³The LORD said: Thus the Israelites shall eat their food, unclean, among the nations where I drive them. ¹⁴"Oh no, Lord GOD," I protested. "Never have I defiled myself nor have I eaten carrion flesh or flesh torn by wild beasts, nor from my youth till now has any unclean meat entered my mouth." ¹⁵Very well, he replied, I will let you use cow manure in place of human dung. You can bake your bread on that. ¹⁶Then he said to me: Son of man, I am about to break the staff of bread in Jerusalem so they shall eat bread which they have weighed out anxiously and drink water which they have measured out fearfully. ¹⁷Because they lack bread and water they shall be devastated; each and every one will waste away because of their guilt.

5:1 Now you, son of man, take a sharp sword and use it like a barber's razor, to shave your head and your beard. Then take a balance scale for weighing and divide the hair. ²Set a third on fire within the city, when the days of your siege are completed; place another third around the city and strike it with the sword; the final third scatter to the wind and then unsheathe the sword after it. ³But take a few of the hairs and tie them in the hem of your garment. ⁴Take some of these and throw them into the fire and burn them in the fire. Because of this, fire will flash out against the whole house of Israel.

⁵Thus says the Lord GOD: This is Jerusalem! I placed it in the midst of the nations, surrounded by foreign lands. ⁶But it rebelled against my ordinances more wickedly than the nations, and against my statutes more than the foreign lands around it; they rejected my ordinances and did not walk in my statutes. ⁷Therefore, thus says the Lord GOD: Because you have caused more uproar than the nations surrounding you, not living by my statutes nor carrying out my judgments, nor even living by the ordinances of the surrounding nations; ⁸therefore, thus says the Lord GOD: See, I am coming against you! I will carry out judgments among you while the nations look on. ⁹Because of all your abominations I will do to you what I have never done before, the like of which I will never do again. ¹⁰Therefore, parents will eat their children in your midst, and children will eat their parents. I will inflict punishments upon you and scatter all who remain to the winds.

¹¹Therefore, as I live, says the Lord GOD, because you have defiled my sanctuary with all your atrocities and all your abominations, I will surely withdraw and not look upon you with pity nor spare you. ¹²A third of your people shall die of disease or starve to death within you; another third shall fall by the sword all around you; a third I will scatter to the winds and pursue them with the sword.

¹³Thus my anger will spend itself; I will vent my wrath against them until I am satisfied. Then they will know that I the LORD spoke in my passion when I spend my wrath upon them. ¹⁴I will make you a desolation and a reproach among the nations around you, in the sight of every passerby. ¹⁵And you will be a reproach and a taunt, a warning and a horror to the nations around you when I execute judgments against you in angry wrath, with furious chastisements. I, the LORD, have spoken! ¹⁶When I loose against you the deadly arrows of starvation that I am sending to destroy you, I will increase starvation and will break your staff of bread. ¹⁷I will send against you starvation and wild beasts who will leave you childless, while disease and bloodshed sweep through you. I will bring the sword against you. I, the LORD, have spoken.

☐ 1 JOHN 4

Testing the Spirits. 4:1 Beloved, do not trust every spirit but test the spirits to see whether they belong to God, because many false prophets have gone out into the world. ²This is how you can know the Spirit of God: every spirit that acknowledges Jesus Christ come in the flesh belongs to God, ³and every spirit that does not acknowledge Jesus does not belong to God. This is the spirit of the antichrist that, as you heard, is to come, but in fact is already in the world. ⁴You belong to God, children, and you have conquered them, for the one who is in you is greater than the one who is in the world. ⁵They belong to the world; accordingly, their teaching belongs to the world, and the world listens to them. ⁶We belong to God, and anyone who knows God listens to us, while anyone who does not belong to God refuses to hear us. This is how we know the spirit of truth and the spirit of deceit.

God's Love and Christian Life. ⁷Beloved, let us love one another, because love is of God; everyone who loves is begotten by God and knows God. ⁸Whoever is without love does not know God, for God is love. [9]In this way the love of God was revealed to us: God sent his only Son into the world so that we might have life through him. [10]In this is love: not that we have loved God, but that he loved us and sent his Son as expiation for our sins. [11]Beloved, if God so loved us, we also must love one another. [12]No one has ever seen God. Yet, if we love one another, God remains in us, and his love is brought to perfection in us.

[13]This is how we know that we remain in him and he in us, that he has given us of his Spirit. [14]Moreover, we have seen and testify that the Father sent his Son as savior of the world. [15]Whoever acknowledges that Jesus is the Son of God, God remains in him and he in God. [16]We have come to know and to believe in the love God has for us.

God is love, and whoever remains in love remains in God and God in him. [17]In this is love brought to perfection among us, that we have confidence on the day of judgment because as he is, so are we in this world. [18]There is no fear in love, but perfect love drives out fear because fear has to do with punishment, and so one who fears is not yet perfect in love. [19]We love because he first loved us. [20]If anyone says, "I love God," but hates his brother, he is a liar; for whoever does not love a brother whom he has seen cannot love God whom he has not seen. [21]This is the commandment we have from him: whoever loves God must also love his brother.

November 7

God did not tell us to follow Him because He needed our help, but because He knew that loving Him would make us whole.

— St. Irenaeus of Lyons

☐ EZEKIEL 6–7

Against the Mountains of Israel. 6:1 The word of the LORD came to me: [2]Son of man, set your face toward the mountains of Israel and prophesy against them: [3]You shall say: Mountains of Israel, hear the word of the Lord GOD. Thus says the Lord GOD to the mountains and hills, to the ravines and valleys: Pay attention! I am bringing a sword against you, and I will destroy your high places. [4]Your altars shall be laid waste, your incense stands smashed, and I will throw your slain down in front of your idols. [5]Yes, I will lay the corpses of the Israelites in front of their idols, and scatter your bones around your altars. [6]Wherever you live, cities shall be ruined and high places laid waste, in order that your altars be laid waste and devastated, your idols broken and smashed, your incense altars hacked to pieces, and whatever you have made wiped out. [7]The slain shall fall in your midst, and you shall know that I am the LORD. [8]But I will spare some of you from the sword to live as refugees among the nations when you are scattered to foreign lands. [9]Then your refugees will remember me among the nations to which they have been exiled, after I have broken their lusting hearts that turned away from me and their eyes that lusted after idols. They will loathe themselves for all the evil they have done, for all their abominations. [10]Then they shall know that I the LORD did not threaten in vain to inflict this evil on them.

[11]Thus says the Lord GOD: Clap your hands, stamp your feet, and cry "Alas!" for

all the evil abominations of the house of Israel! They shall fall by the sword, starvation, and disease. ¹²Those far off shall die of disease, those nearby shall fall by the sword, and those who survive and are spared shall perish by starvation; thus will I spend my fury upon them. ¹³They shall know that I am the LORD, when their slain lie among their idols, all around their altars, on every high hill and mountaintop, beneath every green tree and leafy oak—any place they offer sweet-smelling oblations to all their idols. ¹⁴I will stretch out my hand against them; I will make the land a desolate waste, from the wilderness to Riblah, wherever they live. Thus they shall know that I am the LORD.

The End Has Come. 7:1 The word of the LORD came to me: ²Son of man, now say: Thus says the Lord GOD to the land of Israel: An end! The end comes upon the four corners of the land! ³Now the end is upon you; I will unleash my anger against you, judge you according to your ways, and hold against you all your abominations. ⁴My eye will not spare you, nor will I have pity; but I will hold your conduct against you, since your abominations remain within you; then shall you know that I am the LORD.

⁵Thus says the Lord GOD: Evil upon evil! See it coming! ⁶An end is coming, the end is coming; it is ripe for you! See it coming! ⁷The crisis has come for you who dwell in the land! The time has come, near is the day: panic, no rejoicing on the mountains. ⁸Soon now I will pour out my fury upon you and spend my anger against you; I will judge you according to your ways and hold against you all your abominations. ⁹My eye will not spare, nor will I take pity; I will hold your conduct against you since your abominations remain within you, then you shall know that it is I, the LORD, who strikes.

¹⁰The day is here! Look! it is coming! The crisis has come! Lawlessness is blooming, in-

solence budding; ¹¹the violent have risen up to wield a scepter of wickedness. But none of them shall remain; none of their crowd, none of their wealth, for none of them are innocent. ¹²The time has come, the day dawns. The buyer must not rejoice, nor the seller mourn, for wrath is coming upon all the throng. ¹³Assuredly, the seller shall not regain what was sold, as long as they all live; for the vision is for the whole crowd: it shall not be revoked! Yes, because of their guilt, they shall not hold on to life. ¹⁴They will sound the trumpet and get everything ready, but no one will go out to battle, for my wrath weighs upon all the crowd.

¹⁵The sword is outside; disease and hunger are within. Whoever is in the fields will die by the sword; whoever is in the city disease and hunger will devour. ¹⁶If their survivors flee, they will die on the mountains, moaning like doves of the valley on account of their guilt. ¹⁷All their hands will hang limp, and all their knees turn to water. ¹⁸They put on sackcloth, horror clothes them; shame is on all their faces, all their heads are shaved bald. ¹⁹They fling their silver into the streets, and their gold is considered unclean. Their silver and gold cannot save them on the day of the LORD's wrath. They cannot satisfy their hunger or fill their bellies, for it has been the occasion of their sin. ²⁰In their beautiful ornaments they took pride; out of them they made their abominable images, their detestable things. For this reason I will make them unclean. ²¹I will hand them over as spoils to foreigners, as plunder to the wicked of the earth, so that they may defile them. ²²I will turn my face away from them. My treasure will be defiled; the violent will enter and defile it. ²³They will wreak slaughter, for the land is filled with bloodshed and the city with violence. ²⁴I will bring in the worst of the nations to take possession of their houses. I will put an end to their proud strength, and their sanctuaries will be defiled. ²⁵When anguish comes, they will

seek peace, but there is none. [26]Disaster after disaster, rumor upon rumor. They keep seeking a vision from the prophet; instruction from the priest is missing, and counsel from the elders. [27]The king mourns, the

☐ 1 JOHN 5

Faith is Victory over the World. 5:1 Everyone who believes that Jesus is the Christ is begotten by God, and everyone who loves the father loves [also] the one begotten by him. [2]In this way we know that we love the children of God when we love God and obey his commandments. [3]For the love of God is this, that we keep his commandments. And his commandments are not burdensome, [4]for whoever is begotten by God conquers the world. And the victory that conquers the world is our faith. [5]Who [indeed] is the victor over the world but the one who believes that Jesus is the Son of God?

[6]This is the one who came through water and blood, Jesus Christ, not by water alone, but by water and blood. The Spirit is the one that testifies, and the Spirit is truth. [7]So there are three that testify, [8]the Spirit, the water, and the blood, and the three are of one accord. [9]If we accept human testimony, the testimony of God is surely greater. Now the testimony of God is this, that he has testified on behalf of his Son. [10]Whoever believes in the Son of God has this testimony within himself. Whoever does not believe God has made him a liar by not believing the testimony God has given about his Son. [11]And this is the testimony: God gave us eternal life, and this life

prince is terror-stricken, the hands of the common people tremble. I will deal with them according to their ways, and according to their judgments I will judge them. They shall know that I am the LORD.

is in his Son. [12]Whoever possesses the Son has life; whoever does not possess the Son of God does not have life.

Prayer for Sinners. [13]I write these things to you so that you may know that you have eternal life, you who believe in the name of the Son of God. [14]And we have this confidence in him, that if we ask anything according to his will, he hears us. [15]And if we know that he hears us in regard to whatever we ask, we know that what we have asked him for is ours. [16]If anyone sees his brother sinning, if the sin is not deadly, he should pray to God and he will give him life. This is only for those whose sin is not deadly. There is such a thing as deadly sin, about which I do not say that you should pray. [17]All wrongdoing is sin, but there is sin that is not deadly.

[18]We know that no one begotten by God sins; but the one begotten by God he protects, and the evil one cannot touch him. [19]We know that we belong to God, and the whole world is under the power of the evil one. [20]We also know that the Son of God has come and has given us discernment to know the one who is true. And we are in the one who is true, in his Son Jesus Christ. He is the true God and eternal life. [21]Children, be on your guard against idols.

November 8

When you hear Jesus outraged by men, try to make reparation.
You, at least, love Him, so keep your heart quite pure for Him.
— St. Elizabeth of the Trinity

☐ EZEKIEL 8-9

8:1 In the sixth year, on the fifth day of the sixth month, as I was sitting in my house, with the elders of Judah sitting before me, the hand of the Lord God fell upon me there. ²I looked up and there was a figure that looked like a man. Downward from what looked like his waist, there was fire; from his waist upward, like the brilliance of polished bronze.

Vision of Abominations in the Temple. ³He stretched out the form of a hand and seized me by the hair of my head. The spirit lifted me up between earth and heaven and brought me in divine vision to Jerusalem to the entrance of the inner gate facing north where the statue of jealousy that provokes jealousy stood. ⁴There I saw the glory of the God of Israel, like the vision I had seen in the plain. ⁵He said to me: Son of man, lift your eyes to the north! I looked to the north and there in the entry north of the altar gate was this statue of jealousy. ⁶He asked, Son of man, do you see what they are doing? Do you see the great abominations that the house of Israel is practicing here, so that I must depart from my sanctuary? You shall see even greater abominations!

⁷Then he brought me to the entrance of the courtyard, and there I saw a hole in the wall. ⁸Son of man, he ordered, dig through the wall. I dug through the wall—there was a doorway. ⁹Go in, he said to me, and see the evil abominations they are doing here. ¹⁰I went in and looked—figures of all kinds of creeping things and loathsome beasts, all the idols of the house of Israel, pictured around the wall. ¹¹Before them

stood seventy of the elders of the house of Israel. Among them stood Jaazaniah, son of Shaphan, each with censer in hand; a cloud of incense drifted upward. ¹²Then he said to me: Do you see, son of man, what the elders of the house of Israel are doing in the dark, each in his idol chamber? They think: "The Lord cannot see us; the Lord has forsaken the land." ¹³He said: You will see them practicing even greater abominations.

¹⁴Then he brought me to the entrance of the north gate of the house of the Lord. There women sat and wept for Tammuz. ¹⁵He said to me: Do you see this, son of man? You will see other abominations, greater than these! ¹⁶Then he brought me into the inner court of the house of the Lord. There at the door of the Lord's temple, between the porch and the altar, were about twenty-five men with their backs to the Lord's temple and their faces toward the east; they were bowing eastward to the sun. ¹⁷He said: Do you see, son of man? Are the abominable things the house of Judah has done here so slight that they should also fill the land with violence, provoking me again and again? Now they are putting the branch to my nose! ¹⁸Therefore I in turn will act furiously: my eye will not spare, nor will I take pity. Even if they cry out in a loud voice for me to hear, I shall not listen to them.

Slaughter of the Idolaters. 9:1 Then he cried aloud for me to hear: Come, you scourges of the city! ²And there were six men coming from the direction of the upper gate which faces north, each with a weapon of destruction in his hand. In their midst was a man dressed in linen, with a scribe's case at his waist. They entered and stood beside the bronze altar. ³Then the glory of the God of Israel moved off the cherub and went up to the threshold of the temple. He called to the man dressed in linen with the scribe's case at his waist, ⁴and the LORD said to him: Pass through the city, through the midst of Jerusalem, and mark an X on the foreheads of those who grieve and lament over all the abominations practiced within it. ⁵To the others he said in my hearing: Pass through the city after him and strike! Do not let your eyes spare; do not take pity. ⁶Old and young, male and female, women and children— wipe them out! But do not touch anyone marked with the X. Begin at my sanctuary.

So they began with the elders who were in front of the temple. ⁷Defile the temple, he said to them, fill its courts with the slain. Then go out and strike in the city.

⁸As they were striking, I was left alone. I fell on my face, crying out, "Alas, Lord GOD! Will you destroy all that is left of Israel when you pour out your fury on Jerusalem?" ⁹He answered me: The guilt of the house of Israel and the house of Judah is too great to measure; the land is filled with bloodshed, the city with lawlessness. They think that the LORD has abandoned the land, that he does not see them. ¹⁰My eye, however, will not spare, nor shall I take pity, but I will bring their conduct down upon their heads.

¹¹Just then the man dressed in linen with the scribe's case at his waist made his report: "I have done as you commanded!"

☐ 2 JOHN

1 The Presbyter to the chosen Lady and to her children whom I love in truth— and not only I but also all who know the truth— ²because of the truth that dwells in us and will be with us forever. ³Grace, mercy, and peace will be with us from God the Father and from Jesus Christ the Father's Son in truth and love.

⁴I rejoiced greatly to find some of your children walking in the truth just as we were commanded by the Father. ⁵But now, Lady, I ask you, not as though I were writing a new commandment but the one we have had from the beginning: let us love one another. ⁶For this is love, that we walk according to his commandments; this is the commandment, as you heard from the beginning, in which you should walk.

⁷Many deceivers have gone out into the world, those who do not acknowledge Jesus Christ as coming in the flesh; such is the deceitful one and the antichrist. ⁸Look to yourselves that you do not lose what we worked for but may receive a full recompense. ⁹Anyone who is so "progressive" as not to remain in the teaching of the Christ does not have God; whoever remains in the teaching has the Father and the Son. ¹⁰If anyone comes to you and does not bring this doctrine, do not receive him in your house or even greet him; ¹¹for whoever greets him shares in his evil works.

¹²Although I have much to write to you, I do not intend to use paper and ink. Instead, I hope to visit you and to speak face to face so that our joy may be complete. ¹³The children of your chosen sister send you greetings.

November 9

The Dedication of the Basilica of St. John Lateran

It is on Peter that He builds the Church, and to him that He entrusts the sheep to feed. And although He assigns a like power to all the apostles, yet He founded a single chair, thus establishing by His own authority the source and hallmark of the Church's unity.

— St. Cyprian of Carthage

☐ EZEKIEL 10-11

10:1 Then I looked and there above the firmament over the heads of the cherubim was something like a sapphire, something that looked like a throne. ²And he said to the man dressed in linen: Go within the wheelwork under the cherubim; fill both your hands with burning coals from the place among the cherubim, then scatter them over the city. As I watched, he entered. ³Now the cherubim were standing to the south of the temple when the man went in and a cloud filled the inner court. ⁴The glory of the LORD had moved off the cherubim to the threshold of the temple; the temple was filled with the cloud, the whole court brilliant with the glory of the LORD. ⁵The sound of the wings of the cherubim could be heard as far as the outer court; it was like the voice of God Almighty speaking. ⁶He commanded the man dressed in linen: Take fire from within the wheelwork among the cherubim. The man entered and stood by one of the wheels. ⁷Thereupon a cherub stretched out a hand from among the cherubim toward the fire in the midst of the cherubim, took some, and put it in the hands of the one dressed in linen. He took it and came out. ⁸Something like a human hand was visible under the wings of the cherubim. ⁹I also saw four wheels beside the cherubim, one wheel beside each cherub, and the wheels appeared to have the sparkle of yellow topaz. ¹⁰And the appearance of the four all seemed alike, as though one wheel were inside the other.

¹¹When they moved, they went in any of the four directions without veering as they moved; in whatever direction the first cherub faced, the others followed without veering as they went. ¹²Their entire bodies—backs, hands, and wings—and wheels were covered with eyes all around like the four wheels. ¹³I heard the wheels called "wheelwork." ¹⁴Each living creature had four faces: the first a cherub, the second a human being, the third a lion, the fourth an eagle. ¹⁵When the cherubim rose up, they were indeed the living creatures I had seen by the river Chebar. ¹⁶When the cherubim moved, the wheels went beside them; when the cherubim lifted up their wings to rise from the earth, even then the wheels did not leave their sides. ¹⁷When they stood still, the wheels stood still; when they rose up, the wheels rose up with them, for the spirit of the living creatures was in them. ¹⁸Then the glory of the LORD left the threshold of the temple and took its place upon the cherubim. ¹⁹The cherubim lifted their wings and rose up from the earth before my eyes as they departed with the wheels beside them. They stopped at the entrance of the eastern gate of the LORD's house, and the glory of the God of Israel was up above them. ²⁰These were the living creatures I had seen beneath the God of Israel by the river Chebar. Now I knew they were cherubim. ²¹Each of them had four faces and four wings, and something like human hands under their wings. ²²Their faces looked just

like the faces I had seen by the river Chebar; and each one went straight ahead.

Death for the Remnant in Jerusalem.

11:1 The spirit lifted me up and brought me to the east gate of the house of the Lord facing east. There at the entrance of the gate were twenty-five men; among them I saw the public officials Jaazaniah, son of Azzur, and Pelatiah, son of Benaiah. ²The Lord said to me: Son of man, these are the men who are planning evil and giving wicked counsel in this city. ³They are saying, "No need to build houses! The city is the pot, and we are the meat." ⁴Therefore prophesy against them, son of man, prophesy! ⁵Then the spirit of the Lord fell upon me and told me to say: Thus says the Lord: This is how you talk, house of Israel. I know the things that come into your mind! ⁶You have slain many in this city, filled its streets with the slain. ⁷Therefore thus says the Lord God: The slain whom you piled up in it, that is the meat; the pot is the city. But you I will bring out of it. ⁸You fear the sword—that sword I will bring upon you—oracle of the Lord God. ⁹I will bring you out of the city, hand you over to foreigners, and execute judgments against you. ¹⁰By the sword you shall fall. At the borders of Israel I will judge you so that you will know that I am the Lord. ¹¹The city shall not be a pot for you, nor shall you be meat within it. At the borders of Israel I will judge you, ¹²so you shall know that I am the Lord, whose statutes you did not follow, whose ordinances you did not keep. Instead, you acted according to the ordinances of the nations around you.

¹³While I was prophesying, Pelatiah, the son of Benaiah, dropped dead. I fell down on my face and cried out in a loud voice: "Alas, Lord God! You are finishing off what remains of Israel!"

Restoration for the Exiles.

¹⁴The word of the Lord came to me: ¹⁵Son of man, the inhabitants of Jerusalem are saying about all your relatives, the other exiles, and all the house of Israel, "They are far away from the Lord. The land is given to us as a possession." ¹⁶Therefore say: Thus says the Lord God: I have indeed sent them far away among the nations, scattered them over the lands, and have been but little sanctuary for them in the lands to which they have gone. ¹⁷Therefore, thus says the Lord God, I will gather you from the nations and collect you from the lands through which you were scattered, so I can give you the land of Israel. ¹⁸They will enter it and remove all its atrocities and abominations. ¹⁹And I will give them another heart and a new spirit I will put within them. From their bodies I will remove the hearts of stone, and give them hearts of flesh, ²⁰so that they walk according to my statutes, taking care to keep my ordinances. Thus they will be my people, and I will be their God. ²¹But as for those whose hearts are devoted to their atrocities and abominations, I will bring their conduct down upon their heads—oracle of the Lord God.

²²Then the cherubim lifted their wings and the wheels alongside them, with the glory of the God of Israel above them. ²³The glory of the Lord rose up from the middle of the city and came to rest on the mountain east of the city. ²⁴In a vision, the spirit lifted me up and brought me back to the exiles in Chaldea, by the spirit of God. The vision I had seen left me, ²⁵and I told the exiles everything the Lord had shown me.

☐ 3 JOHN

1 The Presbyter to the beloved Gaius whom I love in truth.

²Beloved, I hope you are prospering in every respect and are in good health, just as your soul is prospering. ³I rejoiced greatly when some of the brothers came and testified to how truly you walk in the truth. ⁴Nothing gives me greater joy than to hear that my children are walking in the truth.

⁵Beloved, you are faithful in all you do for the brothers, especially for strangers; ⁶they have testified to your love before the church. Please help them in a way worthy of God to continue their journey. ⁷For they have set out for the sake of the Name and are accepting nothing from the pagans. ⁸Therefore, we ought to support such persons, so that we may be co-workers in the truth.

⁹I wrote to the church, but Diotrephes, who loves to dominate, does not acknowledge us. ¹⁰Therefore, if I come, I will draw attention to what he is doing, spreading evil nonsense about us. And not content with that, he will not receive the brothers, hindering those who wish to do so and expelling them from the church.

¹¹Beloved, do not imitate evil but imitate good. Whoever does what is good is of God; whoever does what is evil has never seen God. ¹²Demetrius receives a good report from all, even from the truth itself. We give our testimonial as well, and you know our testimony is true.

¹³I have much to write to you, but I do not wish to write with pen and ink. ¹⁴Instead, I hope to see you soon, when we can talk face to face. ¹⁵Peace be with you. The friends greet you; greet the friends there each by name.

November 10

Pope St. Leo the Great

The tempter, ever on the lookout, wages war most violently against those whom he sees most careful to avoid sin.

— POPE ST. LEO THE GREAT

☐ EZEKIEL 12-13

Acts Symbolic of the Exile. 12:1 The word of the LORD came to me: ²Son of man, you live in the midst of a rebellious house; they have eyes to see, but do not see, and ears to hear but do not hear. They are such a rebellious house! ³Now, son of man, during the day while they watch, pack a bag for exile, and again while they watch, go into exile from your place to another place; perhaps they will see that they are a rebellious house. ⁴During the day, while they watch, bring out your bag, an exile's bag. In the evening, again while they watch, go out as if into exile. ⁵While they watch, dig a hole through the wall and go out through it. ⁶While they watch, shoulder your load and go out in darkness. Cover your face so you cannot see the land, for I am making you a sign for the house of Israel!

⁷I did just as I was commanded. During the day I brought out my bag, an exile's bag. In the evening while they watched, I dug a hole through the wall with my hands and set out in darkness, shouldering my load.

⁸In the morning, the word of the LORD came to me: ⁹Son of man, did not the house of Israel, that house of rebels, say, "What are you doing?" ¹⁰Tell them: Thus says the Lord GOD: This load is the prince in Jerusalem and the whole house of Israel within it. ¹¹Say, I am a sign for you: just as I have done, so it shall be done to them; into exile, as captives they shall go. ¹²The prince among them shall shoulder his load in darkness and go out through the hole they dug in the wall to bring him out. His face shall be covered so that he cannot even see the ground. ¹³I will spread my net over him and he shall be caught in my snare. I will bring him into Babylon, to the land of the Chaldeans, though he shall not see it, and there he shall die. ¹⁴All his retinue, his aides and all his troops, I will scatter to the winds and pursue them with the sword. ¹⁵Then they shall know that I am the LORD, when I disperse them among the nations and scatter them throughout the lands. ¹⁶But I will let a few of them escape the sword, starvation, and plague, so that they may recount all their abominations among the nations to which they go. Thus they may know that I am the LORD.

¹⁷The word of the LORD came to me: ¹⁸Son of man, eat your bread trembling and drink your water shaking with fear. ¹⁹And say to the people of the land: Thus says the Lord GOD about the inhabitants of Jerusalem in the land of Israel: they shall eat their bread in fear and drink their water in horror, because the land will be emptied of what fills it—the lawlessness of all its inhabitants. ²⁰Inhabited cities shall be in ruins, the land a desolate place. Then you shall know that I am the LORD.

Prophecy Ridiculed. ²¹The word of the LORD came to me: ²²Son of man, what is this proverb you have in the land of Israel: "The days drag on, and every vision fails"? ²³Say to them therefore: Thus says the Lord GOD: I will put an end to that proverb; they shall never use it again in Israel. Say to them instead: "The days are at hand and every vision fulfilled." ²⁴No longer shall there be any false visions or deceitful divinations within the house of Israel, ²⁵for whatever word I speak shall happen without delay. In your days, rebellious house, whatever I speak I will bring about—oracle of the Lord GOD.

²⁶The word of the LORD came to me: ²⁷Son of man, listen! The house of Israel is saying, "The vision he sees is a long time off; he prophesies for distant times!" ²⁸Say to them therefore: Thus says the Lord GOD: None of my words shall be delayed any longer. Whatever I say is final; it shall be done—oracle of the Lord GOD.

Against the Prophets of Peace. 13:1 The word of the LORD came to me: ²Son of man, prophesy against the prophets of Israel, prophesy! Say to those who prophesy their own thoughts: Hear the word of the LORD! ³Thus says the Lord GOD: Woe to those prophets, the fools who follow their own spirit and see nothing. ⁴Like foxes among ruins are your prophets, Israel! ⁵You did not step into the breach, nor repair the wall around the house of Israel so it would stand firm against attack on the day of the LORD. ⁶False visions! Lying divinations! They say, "The oracle of the LORD," even though the LORD did not send them. Then they expect their word to be confirmed! ⁷Was not the vision you saw false? Did you not report a lying divination when you said, "Oracle of the LORD," even though I never spoke? ⁸Therefore thus says the Lord GOD: Because you have spoken falsehood and seen lying visions, therefore, for certain I am coming at you—oracle of the Lord GOD. ⁹My hand is against the prophets who see false visions and who make lying divinations. They shall not belong to the community of my people. They shall not be written in the register of the house of Israel, nor shall they enter the land of Israel. Thus you shall know that I am the LORD.

[10]Because they led my people astray, saying, "Peace!" when there is no peace, and when a wall is built, they cover it with whitewash, [11]say then to the whitewashers: I will bring down a flooding rain; hailstones shall fall, and a stormwind shall break forth. [12]When the wall has fallen, will you not be asked: "Where is the whitewash you spread on it?"

[13]Therefore thus says the Lord GOD: In my fury I will let loose stormwinds; because of my anger there will be flooding rain, and hailstones will fall with destructive wrath. [14]I will tear down the wall you whitewashed and level it to the ground, laying bare its foundations. When it falls, you shall be crushed beneath it. Thus you shall know that I am the LORD. [15]When I have poured out my fury on the wall and its whitewashers, it will fall. Then I will say to you: No wall! No whitewashers— [16]the prophets of Israel who prophesy to Jerusalem and see visions of peace for it when there is no peace—oracle of the Lord GOD.

Against Witches. [17]As for you, son of man, now set your face against the daughters of your people who play the prophet from their own thoughts, and prophesy against them. [18]You shall say, Thus says the Lord GOD: Woe to those who sew amulets for the wrists of every arm and make veils for every head size to snare lives! You ensnare the lives of my people, even as you preserve your own lives! [19]You have profaned me among my people for handfuls of barley and crumbs of bread, slaying those who should not be slain, and keeping alive those who should not live, lying to my people, who listen to lies. [20]Therefore thus says the Lord GOD: See! I am coming after your amulets by which you ensnare lives like prey. I will tear them from your arms and set free the lives of those you have ensnared like prey. [21]I will tear off your veils and deliver my people from your power, so that they shall never again be ensnared by your hands. Thus you shall know that I am the LORD. [22]Because you discourage the righteous with lies when I did not want them to be distressed, and encourage the wicked so they do not turn from their evil ways and save their lives, [23]therefore you shall no longer see false visions or practice divination again. I will deliver my people from your hand. Thus you shall know that I am the LORD.

☐ LUKE 1

1:1 Since many have undertaken to compile a narrative of the events that have been fulfilled among us, [2]just as those who were eyewitnesses from the beginning and ministers of the word have handed them down to us, [3]I too have decided, after investigating everything accurately anew, to write it down in an orderly sequence for you, most excellent Theophilus, [4]so that you may realize the certainty of the teachings you have received.

Announcement of the Birth of John. [5]In the days of Herod, King of Judea, there was a priest named Zechariah of the priestly division of Abijah; his wife was from the daughters of Aaron, and her name was Elizabeth. [6]Both were righteous in the eyes of God, observing all the commandments and ordinances of the Lord blamelessly. [7]But they had no child, because Elizabeth was barren and both were advanced in years. [8]Once when he was serving as priest in his division's turn before God, [9]according to the practice of the priestly service, he was chosen by lot to enter the sanctuary of the Lord to burn incense. [10]Then, when the whole assembly of the people was praying outside at the hour of the incense offering, [11]the angel of the Lord appeared to him, standing at the right of the altar of incense. [12]Zechariah was troubled by what he saw, and fear came upon him. [13]But the angel said to him, "Do not be afraid, Zechariah, because your prayer has been heard. Your wife Elizabeth will bear you a son, and you shall name him John. [14]And you will have joy and gladness, and many will rejoice at his birth, [15]for he will be great in the sight of [the] Lord. He will drink neither wine nor strong drink. He will be filled with the holy Spirit even from his mother's womb, [16]and he will turn many of the children of Israel to the Lord their God. [17]He will go before him in the spirit and power of Elijah to turn the hearts of fathers toward children and the disobedient to the understanding of the righteous, to prepare a people fit for the Lord." [18]Then Zechariah said to the angel, "How shall I know this? For I am an old man, and my wife is advanced in years." [19]And the angel said to him in reply, "I am Gabriel, who stand before God. I was sent to speak to you and to announce to you this good news. [20]But now you will be speechless and unable to talk until the day these things take place, because you did not believe my words, which will be fulfilled at their proper time."

[21]Meanwhile the people were waiting for Zechariah and were amazed that he stayed so long in the sanctuary. [22]But when he came out, he was unable to speak to them, and they realized that he had seen a vision in the sanctuary. He was gesturing to them but remained mute. [23]Then, when his days of ministry were completed, he went home. [24]After this time his wife Elizabeth conceived, and she went into seclusion for five months, saying, [25]"So has the Lord done for me at a time when he has seen fit to take away my disgrace before others."

Announcement of the Birth of Jesus. [26]In the sixth month, the angel Gabriel was sent from God to a town of Galilee called Nazareth, [27]to a virgin betrothed to a man named Joseph, of the house of David, and the virgin's name was Mary. [28]And coming to her, he said, "Hail, favored one! The Lord is with you." [29]But she was greatly troubled at what was said and pondered what sort of greeting this might be. [30]Then the angel said to her, "Do not be afraid, Mary, for you have found favor with God. [31]Behold, you will conceive in your womb and bear a son, and you shall name him Jesus. [32]He will be great and will be called Son of the Most High, and the Lord God will give him the throne of David his father, [33]and he will rule over the house of Jacob forever, and of his kingdom there will be no end." [34]But Mary said to the angel, "How can this be, since I have no relations with a man?" [35]And the angel said to her in reply, "The holy Spirit will come upon you, and the power of the Most High will overshadow you. Therefore the child to be born will be called holy, the Son of God. [36]And behold, Elizabeth, your relative, has also conceived a son in her old age, and this is the sixth month for her who was called barren; [37]for nothing will be impossible for God." [38]Mary said, "Behold, I am the handmaid of the Lord. May it be done to me according to your word." Then the angel departed from her.

Mary Visits Elizabeth. [39]During those days Mary set out and traveled to the hill country in haste to a town of Judah, [40]where she entered the house of Zechariah and greeted Elizabeth. [41]When Elizabeth heard Mary's greeting, the infant leaped in her womb, and Elizabeth, filled with the holy Spirit, [42]cried out in a loud voice and said, "Most blessed are you among women, and blessed is the fruit of your womb. [43]And how does this happen to me, that the mother of my Lord should come to me? [44]For at the moment the sound of your greeting reached my ears, the infant in my womb leaped for joy. [45]Blessed are you who believed that what was spoken to you by the Lord would be fulfilled."

The Canticle of Mary. [46]And Mary said:

"My soul proclaims the greatness of the
    Lord;
   [47]my spirit rejoices in God my savior.

⁴⁸For he has looked upon his
handmaid's lowliness;
behold, from now on will all ages
call me blessed.
⁴⁹The Mighty One has done great
things for me,
and holy is his name.
⁵⁰His mercy is from age to age
to those who fear him.
⁵¹He has shown might with his arm,
dispersed the arrogant of mind and
heart.
⁵²He has thrown down the rulers from
their thrones
but lifted up the lowly.
⁵³The hungry he has filled with good
things;
the rich he has sent away empty.
⁵⁴He has helped Israel his servant,
remembering his mercy,
⁵⁵according to his promise to our fathers,
to Abraham and to his descendants
forever."

⁵⁶Mary remained with her about three months and then returned to her home.

The Birth of John. ⁵⁷When the time arrived for Elizabeth to have her child she gave birth to a son. ⁵⁸Her neighbors and relatives heard that the Lord had shown his great mercy toward her, and they rejoiced with her. ⁵⁹When they came on the eighth day to circumcise the child, they were going to call him Zechariah after his father, ⁶⁰but his mother said in reply, "No. He will be called John." ⁶¹But they answered her, "There is no one among your relatives who has this name." ⁶²So they made signs, asking his father what he wished him to be called. ⁶³He asked for a tablet and wrote, "John is his name," and all were amazed. ⁶⁴Immediately his mouth was opened, his tongue freed, and he spoke blessing God. ⁶⁵Then fear came upon all their neighbors, and all these matters were discussed throughout the hill country of Judea. ⁶⁶All who heard these things took them to heart, saying,

"What, then, will this child be?" For surely the hand of the Lord was with him.

The Canticle of Zechariah. ⁶⁷Then Zechariah his father, filled with the holy Spirit, prophesied, saying:

⁶⁸"Blessed be the Lord, the God of
Israel,
for he has visited and brought
redemption to his people.
⁶⁹He has raised up a horn for our
salvation
within the house of David his
servant,
⁷⁰even as he promised through the
mouth of his holy prophets from
of old:
⁷¹salvation from our enemies and from
the hand of all who hate us,
⁷²to show mercy to our fathers
and to be mindful of his holy
covenant
⁷³and of the oath he swore to Abraham
our father,
and to grant us that,
⁷⁴rescued from the hand of enemies,
without fear we might worship him
⁷⁵in holiness and righteousness
before him all our days.
⁷⁶And you, child, will be called prophet
of the Most High,
for you will go before the Lord to
prepare his ways,
⁷⁷to give his people knowledge of
salvation
through the forgiveness of their sins,
⁷⁸because of the tender mercy of our
God
by which the daybreak from on high
will visit us
⁷⁹to shine on those who sit in darkness
and death's shadow,
to guide our feet into the path of
peace."

⁸⁰The child grew and became strong in spirit, and he was in the desert until the day of his manifestation to Israel.

November 11

St. Martin of Tours

Neither is there any other cause of the Incarnation except this alone: He saw us bowed down to the ground, perishing, tyrannized by death; and He had mercy.

— St. John Chrysostom

☐ EZEKIEL 14-15

Idolatry and Unfaithfulness. 14:1 Some elders of Israel came and sat down before me. ²Then the word of the LORD came to me: ³Son of man, these men keep the memory of their idols alive in their hearts, setting the stumbling block of their sin before them. Should I allow myself to be consulted by them? ⁴Therefore say to them: Thus says the Lord GOD: If any of the house of Israel who keep the memory of their idols in their hearts, setting the stumbling block of their sin before them, come to a prophet, I the LORD will answer in person because of their many idols, ⁵in order to catch the hearts of the house of Israel, estranged from me because of all their idols.

⁶Therefore say to the house of Israel: Thus says the Lord GOD: Return, turn away from your idols; from all your abominations, turn your faces. ⁷For if anyone of the house of Israel or any alien residing in Israel who are estranged from me and who keep their idols in their hearts, setting the stumbling block of their sin before them, come to ask a prophet to consult me on their behalf, I the LORD will answer them in person. ⁸I will set my face against them and make them a sign and a byword, and cut them off from the midst of my people. Thus you shall know that I am the LORD.

⁹As for the prophet, if he speaks a deceiving word, I the LORD am the one who deceives that prophet. I will stretch out my hand against him and destroy him from the midst of my people Israel. ¹⁰They will be punished for their own sins, the inquirer and the prophet alike, ¹¹so that the house

of Israel may no longer stray from me, no longer defile themselves by all their sins. Then they shall be my people, and I shall be their God—oracle of the Lord GOD.

Just Cause. ¹²The word of the LORD came to me: ¹³Son of man, if a land sins against me by breaking faith, and I stretch out my hand against it, breaking its staff of bread and setting famine loose upon it, cutting off from it human being and beast alike— ¹⁴even if these three were in it, Noah, Daniel, and Job, they could only save themselves by their righteousness— oracle of the Lord GOD. ¹⁵If I summoned wild beasts to prowl the land, depopulating it so that it became a wasteland which no one would cross because of the wild beasts, ¹⁶and these three were in it, as I live—oracle of the Lord GOD—I swear they could save neither sons nor daughters; they alone would be saved, but the land would become a wasteland. ¹⁷Or if I bring the sword upon this land, commanding the sword to pass through the land cutting off from it human being and beast alike, ¹⁸and these three were in it, as I live—oracle of the Lord GOD— they could save neither sons nor daughters; they alone would be saved. ¹⁹Or if I send plague into this land, pouring out upon it my bloody wrath, cutting off from it human being and beast alike, ²⁰even if Noah, Daniel, and Job were in it, as I live—oracle of the Lord GOD—they could save neither son nor daughter; they would save only themselves by their righteousness.

²¹Thus says the Lord GOD: Even though I send against Jerusalem my four evil pun-

ishments—sword, famine, wild beasts, and plague—to cut off from it human being and beast alike, ²²there will still be some survivors in it who will bring out sons and daughters. When they come out to you and you see their ways and their deeds, you shall be consoled regarding the evil I brought on Jerusalem, everything I brought upon it. ²³They shall console you when you see their ways and their deeds, and you shall know that not without reason did I do to it everything I did—oracle of the Lord GOD.

Parable of the Vine. 15:1 The word of the LORD came to me:

²Son of man,
    what makes the wood of the vine
Better than the wood of branches
    found on the trees in the forest?
³Can wood be taken from it
    to make something useful?
Can someone make even a peg out
    of it
    on which to hang a vessel?

⁴Of course not! If it is fed to the fire for
    fuel,
    and the fire devours both ends of it,
Leaving the middle charred,
    is it useful for anything then?
⁵Even when it is whole
    it cannot be used for anything;
So when fire has devoured and
    charred it,
    how useful can it be?
⁶Therefore, thus says the Lord GOD:
Like vine wood among forest trees,
    which I have given as fuel for fire,
So I will give the inhabitants of
    Jerusalem.
⁷I will set my face against them:
Although they have escaped the fire,
    the fire will still devour them;
You shall know that I am the LORD,
    when I set my face against them.
⁸Yes, I will make the land desolate,
    because they are so unfaithful—
    oracle of the Lord GOD.

☐ LUKE 2

The Birth of Jesus. 2:1 In those days a decree went out from Caesar Augustus that the whole world should be enrolled. ²This was the first enrollment, when Quirinius was governor of Syria. ³So all went to be enrolled, each to his own town. ⁴And Joseph too went up from Galilee from the town of Nazareth to Judea, to the city of David that is called Bethlehem, because he was of the house and family of David, ⁵to be enrolled with Mary, his betrothed, who was with child. ⁶While they were there, the time came for her to have her child, ⁷and she gave birth to her firstborn son. She wrapped him in swaddling clothes and laid him in a manger, because there was no room for them in the inn.

⁸Now there were shepherds in that region living in the fields and keeping the night watch over their flock. ⁹The angel of the Lord appeared to them and the glory of the Lord shone around them, and they were struck with great fear. ¹⁰The angel said to them, "Do not be afraid; for behold, I proclaim to you good news of great joy that will be for all the people. ¹¹For today in the city of David a savior has been born for you who is Messiah and Lord. ¹²And this will be a sign for you: you will find an infant wrapped in swaddling clothes and lying in a manger." ¹³And suddenly there was a multitude of the heavenly host with the angel, praising God and saying:

¹⁴"Glory to God in the highest
    and on earth peace to those on
        whom his favor rests."

The Visit of the Shepherds. ¹⁵When the angels went away from them to heaven, the shepherds said to one another, "Let us go, then, to Bethlehem to see this thing that has taken place, which the Lord has made known to us." ¹⁶So they went in haste and found Mary and Joseph, and the infant lying in the manger. ¹⁷When they saw this, they made known the message that had been told them about this child. ¹⁸All who heard it were amazed by what had been told them by the shepherds. ¹⁹And Mary kept all these things, reflecting on them in her heart. ²⁰Then the shepherds returned, glorifying and praising God for all they had heard and seen, just as it had been told to them.

The Circumcision and Naming of Jesus. ²¹When eight days were completed for his circumcision, he was named Jesus, the name given him by the angel before he was conceived in the womb.

The Presentation in the Temple. ²²When the days were completed for their purification according to the law of Moses, they took him up to Jerusalem to present him to the Lord, ²³just as it is written in the law of the Lord, "Every male that opens the womb shall be consecrated to the Lord," ²⁴and to offer the sacrifice of "a pair of turtledoves or two young pigeons," in accordance with the dictate in the law of the Lord.

²⁵Now there was a man in Jerusalem whose name was Simeon. This man was righteous and devout, awaiting the consolation of Israel, and the holy Spirit was upon him. ²⁶It had been revealed to him by the holy Spirit that he should not see death before he had seen the Messiah of the Lord. ²⁷He came in the Spirit into the temple; and when the parents brought in the child Jesus to perform the custom of the law in regard to him, ²⁸he took him into his arms and blessed God, saying:

²⁹"Now, Master, you may let your servant go
in peace, according to your word,
³⁰for my eyes have seen your salvation,

³¹which you prepared in sight of all the peoples,
³²a light for revelation to the Gentiles, and glory for your people Israel."

³³The child's father and mother were amazed at what was said about him; ³⁴and Simeon blessed them and said to Mary his mother, "Behold, this child is destined for the fall and rise of many in Israel, and to be a sign that will be contradicted ³⁵(and you yourself a sword will pierce) so that the thoughts of many hearts may be revealed." ³⁶There was also a prophetess, Anna, the daughter of Phanuel, of the tribe of Asher. She was advanced in years, having lived seven years with her husband after her marriage, ³⁷and then as a widow until she was eighty-four. She never left the temple, but worshiped night and day with fasting and prayer. ³⁸And coming forward at that very time, she gave thanks to God and spoke about the child to all who were awaiting the redemption of Jerusalem.

The Return to Nazareth. ³⁹When they had fulfilled all the prescriptions of the law of the Lord, they returned to Galilee, to their own town of Nazareth. ⁴⁰The child grew and became strong, filled with wisdom; and the favor of God was upon him.

The Boy Jesus in the Temple. ⁴¹Each year his parents went to Jerusalem for the feast of Passover, ⁴²and when he was twelve years old, they went up according to festival custom. ⁴³After they had completed its days, as they were returning, the boy Jesus remained behind in Jerusalem, but his parents did not know it. ⁴⁴Thinking that he was in the caravan, they journeyed for a day and looked for him among their relatives and acquaintances, ⁴⁵but not finding him, they returned to Jerusalem to look for him. ⁴⁶After three days they found him in the temple, sitting in the midst of the teachers, listening to them and asking them questions, ⁴⁷and all who heard him were astounded at his understanding and his answers. [48]When his parents saw him, they were astonished, and his mother said to him, "Son, why have you done this to us? Your father and I have been looking for you with great anxiety." [49]And he said to them, "Why were you looking for me? Did you not know that I must be in my Father's house?" [50]But they did not understand what he said to them. [51]He went down with them and came to Nazareth, and was obedient to them; and his mother kept all these things in her heart. [52]And Jesus advanced [in] wisdom and age and favor before God and man.

November 12

St. Josaphat

Where sin was hatched, let tears now wash the nest.
— St. Robert Southwell

☐ **EZEKIEL 16-17**

A Parable of Infidelity. 16:1 The word of the LORD came to me: [2]Son of man, make known to Jerusalem her abominations. [3]You shall say, Thus says the Lord GOD to Jerusalem: By origin and birth you belong to the land of the Canaanites; your father was an Amorite, your mother a Hittite. [4]As for your birth, on the day you were born your navel cord was not cut; you were not washed with water or anointed; you were not rubbed with salt or wrapped in swaddling clothes. [5]No eye looked on you with pity or compassion to do any of these things for you. Rather, on the day you were born you were left out in the field, rejected.

[6]Then I passed by and saw you struggling in your blood, and I said to you in your blood, "Live!" [7]I helped you grow up like a field plant, so that you grew, maturing into a woman with breasts developed and hair grown; but still you were stark naked. [8]I passed by you again and saw that you were now old enough for love. So I spread the corner of my cloak over you to cover your nakedness; I swore an oath to you and entered into covenant with you— oracle of the Lord GOD—and you became mine. [9]Then I bathed you with water, washed away your blood, and anointed you with oil. [10]I clothed you with an embroidered gown, put leather sandals on your feet; I gave you a fine linen sash and silk robes to wear. [11]I adorned you with jewelry, putting bracelets on your arms, a necklace about your neck, [12]a ring in your nose, earrings in your ears, and a beautiful crown on your head. [13]Thus you were adorned with gold and silver; your garments made of fine linen, silk, and embroidered cloth. Fine flour, honey, and olive oil were your food. You were very, very beautiful, fit for royalty. [14]You were renowned among the nations for your beauty, perfected by the splendor I showered on you—oracle of the Lord GOD.

[15]But you trusted in your own beauty and used your renown to serve as a prostitute. You poured out your prostitution on every passerby—let it be his. [16]You took some of your garments and made for yourself gaudy high places, where you served as a prostitute. It has never happened before, nor will it happen again! [17]You took the splendid gold and silver ornaments that I had given you and made for yourself male images and served as a prostitute

with them. ¹⁸You took your embroidered garments to cover them; my oil and my incense you set before them; ¹⁹the food I had given you, the fine flour, the oil, and the honey with which I fed you, you set before them as a pleasant odor, says the Lord GOD. ²⁰The sons and daughters you bore for me you took and offered as sacrifices for them to devour! Was it not enough that you had become a prostitute? ²¹You slaughtered and immolated my children to them, making them pass through fire. ²²In all your abominations and prostitutions you did not remember the days of your youth when you were stark naked, struggling in your blood.

²³Then after all your evildoing—woe, woe to you! oracle of the Lord GOD— ²⁴you built yourself a platform and raised up a dais in every public place. ²⁵At every intersection you built yourself a dais so that you could degrade your beauty by spreading your legs for every passerby, multiplying your prostitutions. ²⁶You served as a prostitute with the Egyptians, your big-membered neighbors, and multiplied your prostitutions to provoke me. ²⁷Therefore I stretched out my hand against you and reduced your allotment, and delivered you over to the whim of your enemies, the Philistines, who were revolted by your depraved conduct. ²⁸You also served as a prostitute for the Assyrians, because you were not satisfied. Even after serving as a prostitute for them, you were still not satisfied. ²⁹You increased your prostitutions again, now going to Chaldea, the land of traders; but despite this, you were still not satisfied.

³⁰How wild your lust!—oracle of the Lord GOD—that you did all these works of a shameless prostitute, ³¹when you built your platform at every intersection and set up your high place in every public square. But unlike a prostitute, you disdained payment. ³²Adulterous wife, taking strangers in place of her husband! ³³Prostitutes usually receive gifts. But you bestowed gifts on all your lovers, bribing them to come to you for prostitution from every side. ³⁴Thus in your prostitution you were different from any other woman. No one solicited you for prostitution. Instead, you yourself offered payment; what a reversal!

³⁵Therefore, prostitute, hear the word of the LORD! ³⁶Thus says the Lord GOD: Because you poured out your lust and exposed your nakedness in your prostitution with your lovers and your abominable idols, because you gave the life-blood of your children to them, ³⁷therefore, I will now gather together all your lovers with whom you found pleasure, both those you loved and those you hated; I will gather them against you from all sides and expose you naked for them to see. ³⁸I will inflict on you the sentence of adultery and murder; I will bring on you bloody wrath and jealous anger. ³⁹I will hand you over to them to tear down your platform and demolish your high place, to strip you of your garments and take away your splendid ornaments, leaving you stark naked. ⁴⁰They shall lead an assembly against you to stone you and hack you to pieces with their swords. ⁴¹They shall set fire to your homes and inflict punishments on you while many women watch. Thus I will put an end to your prostitution, and you shall never again offer payment. ⁴²When I have spent my fury upon you I will stop being jealous about you, and calm down, no longer angry. ⁴³Because you did not remember the days of your youth but enraged me with all these things, see, I am bringing down your ways upon your head—oracle of the Lord GOD. Have you not added depravity to your other abominations?

⁴⁴See, everyone who makes proverbs will make this proverb about you, "Like mother, like daughter." ⁴⁵Yes, you are truly the daughter of your mother who rejected her husband and children: you are truly a sister to your sisters who rejected their husbands and children—your mother was a

Hittite and your father an Amorite. ⁴⁶Your elder sister was Samaria with her daughters to the north of you; and your younger sister was Sodom and her daughters, south of you. ⁴⁷Not only did you walk in their ways and act as abominably as they did, but in a very short time you became more corrupt in all your ways than they were. ⁴⁸As I live—oracle of the Lord God—I swear that your sister Sodom with her daughters have not done the things you and your daughters have done! ⁴⁹Now look at the guilt of your sister Sodom: she and her daughters were proud, sated with food, complacent in prosperity. They did not give any help to the poor and needy. ⁵⁰Instead, they became arrogant and committed abominations before me; then, as you have seen, I removed them. ⁵¹Samaria did not commit half the sins you did. You have done more abominable things than they did. You even made your sisters look righteous, with all the abominations you have done. ⁵²You, then, must bear your disgrace, for you have made a case for your sisters! Because your sins are more abominable than theirs, they seem righteous compared to you. Blush for shame, and bear the disgrace of having made your sisters appear righteous.

⁵³I will restore their fortunes, the fortunes of Sodom and her daughters, the fortunes of Samaria and her daughters—and your fortunes along with them. ⁵⁴Thus you must bear your disgrace and be ashamed of all you have done to bring them comfort. ⁵⁵Yes, your sisters, Sodom and her daughters, Samaria and her daughters, shall return to the way they were, and you and your daughters shall return to the way you were. ⁵⁶Did you not hold your sister Sodom in bad repute while you felt proud of yourself, ⁵⁷before your evil was exposed? Now you are like her, reproached by the Arameans and all their neighbors, despised on all sides by the Philistines. ⁵⁸The penalty of your depravity and your abominations—you must bear it all—oracle of the Lord.

⁵⁹For thus says the Lord God: I will deal with you for what you did; you despised an oath by breaking a covenant. ⁶⁰But I will remember the covenant I made with you when you were young; I will set up an everlasting covenant with you. ⁶¹Then you shall remember your ways and be ashamed when you receive your sisters, those older and younger than you; I give them to you as daughters, but not by reason of your covenant. ⁶²For I will re-establish my covenant with you, that you may know that I am the Lord, ⁶³that you may remember and be ashamed, and never again open your mouth because of your disgrace, when I pardon you for all you have done—oracle of the Lord God.

The Eagles and the Vine. 17:1 The word of the Lord came to me: ²Son of man, propose a riddle, and tell this proverb to the house of Israel: ³Thus says the Lord God:

The great eagle, with wide wingspan
   and long feathers, with thick
      plumage,
   many-hued, came to Lebanon.
He plucked the crest of the cedar,
   ⁴broke off its topmost branch,
And brought it to a land of merchants,
   set it in a city of traders.
⁵Then he took some native seed
   and planted it in fertile soil;
A shoot beside plentiful waters,
   like a willow he planted it,
⁶That it might sprout and become a
     vine,
   dense and low-lying,
With its branches turned toward him,
   its roots beneath it.
Thus it became a vine, produced
     branches,
   and put forth shoots.
⁷Then another great eagle appeared,
   with wide wingspan, rich in plumage,
And see! This vine bent its roots to
     him,

sent out branches for him to water.
From the bed where it was planted,
⁸it was transplanted to a fertile field
By abundant waters, to produce
branches,
to bear fruit, to become a majestic
vine.
⁹Say: Thus says the Lord GOD: Can it
thrive?
Will he not tear up its roots
and strip its fruit?
Then all its green leaves will wither—
neither strong arm nor mighty
nation
is needed to uproot it.
¹⁰True, it is planted; but will it thrive?
Will it not wither up
When the east wind strikes it,
wither in the very bed where it
sprouted?

¹¹The word of the LORD came to me:
¹²Now say to the rebellious house:
Do you not understand this? Tell
them!
The king of Babylon came to Jerusalem
and took away its king and officials
and brought them to him in
Babylon.
¹³After removing the nobles from the
land,
he then took one of the royal line
And made a covenant with him,
binding him under oath,
¹⁴To be a humble kingdom,
without high aspirations,
to keep his covenant and so survive.
¹⁵But this one rebelled against him
by sending envoys to Egypt
To obtain horses and a mighty army.
Can he thrive?
Can he escape if he does this?
Can he break a covenant and go
free?
¹⁶As I live—oracle of the Lord GOD—
in the house of the king who set
him up to rule,

Whose oath he ignored and whose
covenant he broke,
there in Babylon I swear he shall
die!
¹⁷Pharaoh shall not help him on the
day of battle,
with a great force and mighty
horde,
When ramps are thrown up and siege
works built
for the cutting down of many lives.
¹⁸He ignored his oath, breaking his
covenant;
even though he gave his hand, he
did all these things—
he shall not escape!
¹⁹Therefore, thus says the Lord GOD:
As I live, my oath which he
spurned,
And my covenant which he broke,
I will bring down on his head.
²⁰I will spread my net over him,
and he will be caught in my snare.
I will bring him to Babylon
to judge him there
because he broke faith with me.
²¹Any among his forces who escape
will fall by the sword,
And whoever might survive
will be scattered to the winds.
Thus you will know that I the LORD
have spoken.
²²Thus says the Lord GOD:
I, too, will pluck from the crest of the
cedar
the highest branch.
From the top a tender shoot
I will break off and transplant
on a high, lofty mountain.
²³On the mountain height of Israel
I will plant it.
It shall put forth branches and bear
fruit,
and become a majestic cedar.
Every small bird will nest under it,
all kinds of winged birds will dwell
in the shade of its branches.

²⁴Every tree of the field will know
  that I am the LORD.
I bring low the high tree,
  lift high the lowly tree,
Wither up the green tree,
  and make the dry tree bloom.
As I, the LORD, have spoken, so will
  I do!

☐ LUKE 3

The Preaching of John the Baptist. 3:1 In the fifteenth year of the reign of Tiberius Caesar, when Pontius Pilate was governor of Judea, and Herod was tetrarch of Galilee, and his brother Philip tetrarch of the region of Ituraea and Trachonitis, and Lysanias was tetrarch of Abilene, ²during the high priesthood of Annas and Caiaphas, the word of God came to John the son of Zechariah in the desert. ³He went throughout [the] whole region of the Jordan, proclaiming a baptism of repentance for the forgiveness of sins, ⁴as it is written in the book of the words of the prophet Isaiah:

"A voice of one crying out in the
    desert:
'Prepare the way of the Lord,
    make straight his paths.
⁵Every valley shall be filled
    and every mountain and hill shall be
      made low.
The winding roads shall be made
      straight,
    and the rough ways made smooth,
⁶and all flesh shall see the salvation of
    God.'"

⁷He said to the crowds who came out to be baptized by him, "You brood of vipers! Who warned you to flee from the coming wrath? ⁸Produce good fruits as evidence of your repentance; and do not begin to say to yourselves, 'We have Abraham as our father,' for I tell you, God can raise up children to Abraham from these stones. ⁹Even now the ax lies at the root of the trees. Therefore every tree that does not produce good fruit will be cut down and thrown into the fire."

¹⁰And the crowds asked him, "What then should we do?" ¹¹He said to them in reply, "Whoever has two tunics should share with the person who has none. And whoever has food should do likewise." ¹²Even tax collectors came to be baptized and they said to him, "Teacher, what should we do?" ¹³He answered them, "Stop collecting more than what is prescribed." ¹⁴Soldiers also asked him, "And what is it that we should do?" He told them, "Do not practice extortion, do not falsely accuse anyone, and be satisfied with your wages."

¹⁵Now the people were filled with expectation, and all were asking in their hearts whether John might be the Messiah. ¹⁶John answered them all, saying, "I am baptizing you with water, but one mightier than I is coming. I am not worthy to loosen the thongs of his sandals. He will baptize you with the holy Spirit and fire. ¹⁷His winnowing fan is in his hand to clear his threshing floor and to gather the wheat into his barn, but the chaff he will burn with unquenchable fire." ¹⁸Exhorting them in many other ways, he preached good news to the people. ¹⁹Now Herod the tetrarch, who had been censured by him because of Herodias, his brother's wife, and because of all the evil deeds Herod had committed, ²⁰added still another to these by [also] putting John in prison.

The Baptism of Jesus. ²¹After all the people had been baptized and Jesus also had been baptized and was praying, heaven was opened ²²and the holy Spirit descended upon him in bodily form like a dove. And a voice came from heaven, "You are my beloved Son; with you I am well pleased."

The Genealogy of Jesus. ²³When Jesus began his ministry he was about thirty years of age. He was the son, as was thought, of Joseph, the son of Heli, ²⁴the son of Matthat, the son of Levi, the son of Melchi, the son of Jannai, the son of Joseph, ²⁵the son of Mattathias, the son of Amos, the son of Nahum, the son of Esli, the son of Naggai, ²⁶the son of Maath, the son of Mattathias, the son of Semein, the son of Josech, the son of Joda, ²⁷the son of Joanan, the son of Rhesa, the son of Zerubbabel, the son of Shealtiel, the son of Neri, ²⁸the son of Melchi, the son of Addi, the son of Cosam, the son of Elmadam, the son of Er, ²⁹the son of Joshua, the son of Eliezer, the son of Jorim, the son of Matthat, the son of Levi, ³⁰the son of Simeon, the son of Judah, the son of Joseph, the son of Jonam, the son of Eliakim, ³¹the son of Melea, the son of Menna, the son of Mattatha, the son of Nathan, the son of David, ³²the son of Jesse, the son of Obed, the son of Boaz, the son of Sala, the son of Nahshon, ³³the son of Amminadab, the son of Admin, the son of Arni, the son of Hezron, the son of Perez, the son of Judah, ³⁴the son of Jacob, the son of Isaac, the son of Abraham, the son of Terah, the son of Nahor, ³⁵the son of Serug, the son of Reu, the son of Peleg, the son of Eber, the son of Shelah, ³⁶the son of Cainan, the son of Arphaxad, the son of Shem, the son of Noah, the son of Lamech, ³⁷the son of Methuselah, the son of Enoch, the son of Jared, the son of Mahalaleel, the son of Cainan, ³⁸the son of Enos, the son of Seth, the son of Adam, the son of God.

November 13

St. Frances Xavier Cabrini

I have started houses with no more than the price of a loaf of bread and prayers, for with Him who comforts me, I can do anything.

— St. Frances Xavier Cabrini

☐ **EZEKIEL 18-19**

Personal Responsibility. 18:1 The word of the LORD came to me: Son of man, ²what is the meaning of this proverb you recite in the land of Israel:

> "Parents eat sour grapes,
>   but the children's teeth are set on
>   edge"?

³As I live—oracle of the Lord GOD: I swear that none of you will ever repeat this proverb in Israel. ⁴For all life is mine: the life of the parent is like the life of the child, both are mine. Only the one who sins shall die!

⁵If a man is just—if he does what is right, ⁶if he does not eat on the mountains, or raise his eyes to the idols of the house of Israel; if he does not defile a neighbor's wife, or have relations with a woman during her period; ⁷if he oppresses no one, gives back the pledge received for a debt, commits no robbery; gives food to the hungry and clothes the naked; ⁸if he does not lend at interest or exact usury; if he refrains from evildoing and makes a fair judgment between two opponents; ⁹if he walks by my statutes and is careful to observe my ordinances, that man is just—he shall surely live—oracle of the Lord GOD.

¹⁰But if he begets a son who is violent and commits murder, or does any of these things, ¹¹even though the father does none of them—a son who eats on the mountains,

defiles the wife of his neighbor, [12]oppresses the poor and needy, commits robbery, does not give back a pledge, raises his eyes to idols, does abominable things, [13]lends at interest and exacts usury—this son certainly shall not live. Because he practiced all these abominations, he shall surely be put to death; his own blood shall be on him.

[14]But, in turn, if he begets a son who sees all the sins his father commits, yet fears and does not imitate him— [15]a son who does not eat on the mountains, or raise his eyes to the idols of the house of Israel, or defile a neighbor's wife; [16]who does not oppress anyone, or exact a pledge, or commit robbery; who gives his food to the hungry and clothes the naked; [17]who refrains from evildoing, accepts no interest or usury, but keeps my ordinances and walks in my statutes—this one shall not die for the sins of his father. He shall surely live! [18]Only the father, since he committed extortion and robbed his brother, and did what was not good among his people—he will die because of his sin! [19]You ask: "Why is not the son charged with the guilt of his father?" Because the son has done what is just and right and has been careful to observe all my statutes—he shall surely live! [20]Only the one who sins shall die. The son shall not be charged with the guilt of his father, nor shall the father be charged with the guilt of his son. Justice belongs to the just, and wickedness to the wicked.

[21]But if the wicked man turns away from all the sins he has committed, if he keeps all my statutes and does what is just and right, he shall surely live. He shall not die! [22]None of the crimes he has committed shall be remembered against him; he shall live because of the justice he has shown. [23]Do I find pleasure in the death of the wicked—oracle of the Lord GOD? Do I not rejoice when they turn from their evil way and live?

[24]And if the just turn from justice and do evil, like all the abominations the wicked do, can they do this evil and still live? None of the justice they did shall be remembered, because they acted treacherously and committed these sins; because of this, they shall die. [25]You say, "The LORD's way is not fair!" Hear now, house of Israel: Is it my way that is unfair? Are not your ways unfair? [26]When the just turn away from justice to do evil and die, on account of the evil they did they must die. [27]But if the wicked turn from the wickedness they did and do what is right and just, they save their lives; [28]since they turned away from all the sins they committed, they shall live; they shall not die. [29]But the house of Israel says, "The Lord's way is not fair!" Is it my way that is not fair, house of Israel? Is it not your ways that are not fair?

[30]Therefore I will judge you, house of Israel, all of you according to your ways— oracle of the Lord GOD. Turn, turn back from all your crimes, that they may not be a cause of sin for you ever again. [31]Cast away from you all the crimes you have committed, and make for yourselves a new heart and a new spirit. Why should you die, house of Israel? [32]For I find no pleasure in the death of anyone who dies—oracle of the Lord GOD. Turn back and live!

Allegory of the Lions. 19:1 As for you, raise a lamentation over the princes of Israel, [2]and say:

What a lioness was your mother,
    a lion among lions!
She made her lair among young lions,
    to raise her cubs;
[3]One cub she raised up,
    a young lion he became;
He learned to tear apart prey,
    he devoured people.
[4]Nations heard about him;
    in their pit he was caught;
They took him away with hooks
    to the land of Egypt.

5When she realized she had waited in
 vain,
 she lost hope.
She took another of her cubs,
 and made him a young lion.
6He prowled among the lions,
 became a young lion;
He learned to tear apart prey,
 he devoured people.
7He ravaged their strongholds,
 laid waste their cities.
The earth and everything in it were
 terrified
 at the sound of his roar.
8Nations laid out against him
 snares all around;
They spread their net for him,
 in their pit he was caught.
9They put him in fetters and took him
 away
  to the king of Babylon,
So his roar would no longer be heard
 on the mountains of Israel.

☐ LUKE 4

The Temptation of Jesus. 4:1 Filled with
the holy Spirit, Jesus returned from the Jordan and was led by the Spirit into the desert
2for forty days, to be tempted by the devil.
He ate nothing during those days, and when
they were over he was hungry. 3The devil
said to him, "If you are the Son of God,
command this stone to become bread." 4Je-
sus answered him, "It is written, 'One does
not live by bread alone.'" 5Then he took him
up and showed him all the kingdoms of the
world in a single instant. 6The devil said to
him, "I shall give to you all this power and
their glory; for it has been handed over to
me, and I may give it to whomever I wish.
7All this will be yours, if you worship me."
8Jesus said to him in reply, "It is written:

'You shall worship the Lord, your God,

Allegory of the Vine Branch. 10Your
 mother was like a leafy vine
 planted by water,
Fruitful and full of branches
 because of abundant water.
11One strong branch grew
 into a royal scepter.
So tall it towered among the clouds,
 conspicuous in height,
 with dense foliage.
12But she was torn out in fury
 and flung to the ground;
The east wind withered her up,
 her fruit was plucked away;
Her strongest branch dried up,
 fire devoured it.
13Now she is planted in a wilderness,
 in a dry, parched land.
14Fire flashed from her branch,
 and devoured her shoots;
Now she does not have a strong branch,
 a royal scepter!

This is a lamentation and serves as a
lamentation.

and him alone shall you serve.'"
9Then he led him to Jerusalem, made him
stand on the parapet of the temple, and
said to him, "If you are the Son of God,
throw yourself down from here, 10for it is
written:

'He will command his angels
 concerning you,
 to guard you,'

11and:

'With their hands they will support
 you,
 lest you dash your foot against a
  stone.'"

12Jesus said to him in reply, "It also says,
'You shall not put the Lord, your God, to

the test.'" [13]When the devil had finished every temptation, he departed from him for a time.

The Beginning of the Galilean Ministry. [14]Jesus returned to Galilee in the power of the Spirit, and news of him spread throughout the whole region. [15]He taught in their synagogues and was praised by all.

The Rejection at Nazareth. [16]He came to Nazareth, where he had grown up, and went according to his custom into the synagogue on the sabbath day. He stood up to read [17]and was handed a scroll of the prophet Isaiah. He unrolled the scroll and found the passage where it was written:

[18]"The Spirit of the Lord is upon me,
    because he has anointed me
        to bring glad tidings to the poor.
He has sent me to proclaim liberty to
    captives
    and recovery of sight to the blind,
        to let the oppressed go free,
[19]and to proclaim a year acceptable to
    the Lord."

[20]Rolling up the scroll, he handed it back to the attendant and sat down, and the eyes of all in the synagogue looked intently at him. [21]He said to them, "Today this scripture passage is fulfilled in your hearing." [22]And all spoke highly of him and were amazed at the gracious words that came from his mouth. They also asked, "Isn't this the son of Joseph?" [23]He said to them, "Surely you will quote me this proverb, 'Physician, cure yourself,' and say, 'Do here in your native place the things that we heard were done in Capernaum.'" [24]And he said, "Amen, I say to you, no prophet is accepted in his own native place. [25]Indeed, I tell you, there were many widows in Israel in the days of Elijah when the sky was closed for three and a half years and a severe famine spread over the entire land. [26]It was to none of these that Elijah was sent, but only to a widow in Zarephath in the land of Sidon. [27]Again, there were many lepers in Israel during the time of Elisha the prophet; yet not one of them was cleansed, but only Naaman the Syrian." [28]When the people in the synagogue heard this, they were all filled with fury. [29]They rose up, drove him out of the town, and led him to the brow of the hill on which their town had been built, to hurl him down headlong. [30]But he passed through the midst of them and went away.

The Cure of a Demoniac. [31]Jesus then went down to Capernaum, a town of Galilee. He taught them on the sabbath, [32]and they were astonished at his teaching because he spoke with authority. [33]In the synagogue there was a man with the spirit of an unclean demon, and he cried out in a loud voice, [34]"Ha! What have you to do with us, Jesus of Nazareth? Have you come to destroy us? I know who you are—the Holy One of God!" [35]Jesus rebuked him and said, "Be quiet! Come out of him!" Then the demon threw the man down in front of them and came out of him without doing him any harm. [36]They were all amazed and said to one another, "What is there about his word? For with authority and power he commands the unclean spirits, and they come out." [37]And news of him spread everywhere in the surrounding region.

The Cure of Simon's Mother-in-Law. [38]After he left the synagogue, he entered the house of Simon. Simon's mother-in-law was afflicted with a severe fever, and they interceded with him about her. [39]He stood over her, rebuked the fever, and it left her. She got up immediately and waited on them.

Other Healings. [40]At sunset, all who had people sick with various diseases brought them to him. He laid his hands on each of them and cured them. [41]And demons also came out from many, shouting, "You are the Son of God." But he rebuked them and did not allow them to speak because they knew that he was the Messiah.

Jesus Leaves Capernaum. [42]At daybreak, Jesus left and went to a deserted place. The crowds went looking for him, and when they came to him, they tried to prevent him from leaving them. ⁴³But he said to them, "To the other towns also I must proclaim the good news of the kingdom of God, because for this purpose I have been sent." ⁴⁴And he was preaching in the synagogues of Judea.

November 14

We will lie down for such a long time after death that it is worthwhile to keep standing while we are alive. Let us work now; one day we will rest.

— St. Agostina Pietrantoni

☐ EZEKIEL 20-21

Israel's History of Infidelity. 20:1 In the seventh year, on the tenth day of the fifth month, some of the elders of Israel came to consult the LORD and sat down before me. ²Then the word of the LORD came to me: ³Son of man, speak to the elders of Israel and say to them: Thus says the Lord GOD: Have you come to consult me? As I live, I will not allow myself to be consulted by you!—oracle of the Lord GOD.

⁴Will you judge them? Will you judge, son of man? Tell them about the abominations of their ancestors, ⁵and say to them: Thus says the Lord GOD: The day I chose Israel, I swore to the descendants of the house of Jacob; I revealed myself to them in the land of Egypt and swore to them, saying: I am the LORD, your God. ⁶That day I swore to bring them out of the land of Egypt to the land I had searched out for them, a land flowing with milk and honey, a jewel among all lands. ⁷Then I said to them: Throw away, each of you, the detestable things that held your eyes; do not defile yourselves with the idols of Egypt: I am the LORD, your God.

⁸But they rebelled and refused to listen to me; none of them threw away the detestable things that held their eyes, nor did they abandon the idols of Egypt. Then I considered pouring out my fury and spending my anger against them there in the land of Egypt. ⁹I acted for the sake of my name, that it should not be desecrated in the eyes of the nations among whom they were: in the eyes of the nations I had made myself known to them, to bring them out of the land of Egypt. ¹⁰Therefore I led them out of the land of Egypt and brought them into the wilderness. ¹¹Then I gave them my statutes and made known to them my ordinances, so that everyone who keeps them has life through them. ¹²I also gave them my sabbaths to be a sign between me and them, to show that it is I, the LORD, who makes them holy.

¹³But the house of Israel rebelled against me in the wilderness. They did not observe my statutes, and they rejected my ordinances that bring life to those who keep them. My sabbaths, too, they desecrated grievously. Then I considered pouring out my fury on them in the wilderness to put an end to them, ¹⁴but I acted for the sake of my name, so it would not be desecrated in the eyes of the nations in whose sight I had brought them out. ¹⁵Nevertheless in the wilderness I swore to them that I would not bring them into the land I had given them—a land flowing with milk and honey, a jewel among all the lands. ¹⁶Their hearts followed after their idols so closely

that they did not live by my statutes, but rejected my ordinances and desecrated my sabbaths. ¹⁷But I looked on them with pity, not wanting to destroy them, so I did not put an end to them in the wilderness.

¹⁸Then I said to their children in the wilderness: Do not follow the statutes of your parents. Do not keep their ordinances. Do not defile yourselves with their idols. ¹⁹I am the LORD, your God: follow my statutes and be careful to observe my ordinances; ²⁰keep holy my sabbaths as a sign between me and you so that you may know that I am the LORD, your God. ²¹But their children rebelled against me: they did not follow my statutes or keep my ordinances that bring life to those who observe them; my sabbaths they desecrated. Then I considered pouring out my fury on them, spending my anger against them in the wilderness; ²²but I stayed my hand, acting for the sake of my name, lest it be desecrated in the eyes of the nations, in whose sight I had brought them out. ²³Nevertheless I swore to them in the wilderness that I would disperse them among the nations and scatter them in other lands, ²⁴because they did not carry out my ordinances, but rejected my statutes and desecrated my sabbaths, having eyes only for the idols of their ancestors. ²⁵Therefore I gave them statutes that were not good, and ordinances through which they could not have life. ²⁶I let them become defiled by their offerings, by having them make a fiery offering of every womb's firstborn, in order to ruin them so they might know that I am the LORD.

²⁷Therefore speak to the house of Israel, son of man, and tell them: Thus says the Lord GOD: In this way also your ancestors blasphemed me, breaking faith with me. ²⁸When I brought them to the land I had sworn to give them, and they saw all its high hills and leafy trees, there they offered sacrifices, there they made offerings to provoke me, there they sent up sweet-smelling oblations, there they poured out their libations. ²⁹So I said to them, "What is this high place to which you go?" Thus its name became "high place" even to this day. ³⁰Therefore say to the house of Israel: Thus says the Lord GOD: Will you defile yourselves in the way your ancestors did? Will you lust after their detestable idols? ³¹By offering your gifts, by making your children pass through the fire, you defile yourselves with all your idols even to this day. Shall I let myself be consulted by you, house of Israel? As I live—oracle of the Lord GOD—I swear I will not let myself be consulted by you!

³²What has entered your mind shall never happen: You are thinking, "We shall be like the nations, like the peoples of foreign lands, serving wood and stone." ³³As I live—oracle of the Lord GOD—with mighty hand and outstretched arm, with wrath poured out, I swear I will be king over you! ³⁴With mighty hand and outstretched arm, with wrath poured out, I will bring you out from the nations and gather you from the countries over which you are scattered; ³⁵I will lead you to the wilderness of the peoples and enter into judgment with you face to face. ³⁶Just as I entered into judgment with your ancestors in the wilderness of the land of Egypt, so will I enter into judgment with you—oracle of the Lord GOD. ³⁷Thus I will make you pass under the staff and will impose on you the terms of the covenant. ³⁸I will sort out from you those who defied me and rebelled against me; from the land where they resided as aliens I will bring them out, but they shall not return to the land of Israel. Thus you shall know that I am the LORD.

³⁹As for you, house of Israel, thus says the Lord GOD: Go! each of you, and worship your idols. Listen to me! You shall never again desecrate my holy name with your offerings and your idols! ⁴⁰For on my holy mountain, on the highest mountain in Israel—oracle of the Lord GOD—there

the whole house of Israel shall worship me; there in the land I will accept them all, there I will claim your tributes, the best of your offerings, from all your holy things. ⁴¹As a sweet-smelling oblation I will accept you, when I bring you from among the nations and gather you out of the lands over which you were scattered; and through you I will manifest my holiness in the sight of the nations. ⁴²Thus you shall know that I am the LORD, when I bring you back to the soil of Israel, the land I swore to give your ancestors. ⁴³There you shall remember your ways, all the deeds by which you defiled yourselves; and you shall loathe yourselves because of all the evil you did. ⁴⁴And you shall know that I am the LORD when I deal with you thus, for the sake of my name, not according to your evil ways and wanton deeds, house of Israel—oracle of the Lord GOD.

The Sword of the Lord. 21:1 The word of the LORD came to me: ²Son of man, turn your face to the south: preach against the south, prophesy against the forest land in the south. ³Say to the forest in the south: Hear the word of the LORD! Thus says the Lord GOD: See! I am kindling a fire in you that shall devour every green tree as well as every dry tree. The blazing flame shall not be quenched so that from south to north every face shall be scorched by it. ⁴All flesh shall see that I, the LORD, have kindled it; it shall not be quenched.

⁵But I said, "Ah! Lord GOD, they are saying about me, 'Is not this the one who is forever spinning parables?'" ⁶Then the word of the LORD came to me: ⁷Son of man, turn your face toward Jerusalem: preach against its sanctuary, prophesy against the land of Israel. ⁸Say to the land of Israel: Thus says the LORD: See! I am coming against you; I will draw my sword from its scabbard and cut off from you the righteous and the wicked. ⁹Thus my sword shall come out from its scabbard against

all flesh from south to north ¹⁰and all flesh shall know that I, the LORD, have drawn my sword from its scabbard. It cannot return again.

Act Symbolic of the City's Fall. ¹¹As for you, son of man, groan! with shattered loins and bitter grief, groan in their sight. ¹²When they ask you, "Why are you groaning?" you shall say: Because of what I heard! When it comes every heart shall melt, every hand fall helpless; every spirit will grow faint, and every knee run with water. See, it is coming, it is here!—oracle of the Lord GOD.

Song of the Sword. ¹³The word of the LORD came to me: ¹⁴Son of man, prophesy! say: Thus says the LORD:

A sword, a sword has been sharpened,
    a sword, a sword has been
        burnished:
¹⁵Sharpened to make a slaughter,
    burnished to flash lightning!
Why should I stop now?
    You have rejected the rod and every
        judgment!
¹⁶I have given it over to the burnisher
    that he might hold it in his hand,
A sword sharpened and burnished
    to be put in the hands of an
        executioner.
¹⁷Cry out and howl, son of man,
    for it is destined for my people,
For all the princes of Israel,
    victims of the sword with my
        people.
Therefore, slap your thigh,
    ¹⁸for it is tested, and why not?
Since you rejected my staff,
    should it not happen?—
        oracle of the Lord GOD.
¹⁹As for you, son of man, prophesy,
    and clap your hands!
Let the sword strike twice, a third time.
    It is a sword of slaughter,
A sword for slaughtering,
    whirling around them all,

20That every heart may tremble;
  for many will be made to stumble.
At all their gates
  I have stationed the sword for
    slaughter,
Made it flash lightning,
  drawn for slaughter.
21Slash to the right!
  turn to the left,
Wherever your edge is directed!
22Then I, too, shall clap my hands,
  and spend my fury.
I, the LORD, have spoken.

Nebuchadnezzar at the Crossroads.
23The word of the LORD came to me: 24Son of man, make for yourself two roads over which the sword of the king of Babylon can come. Both roads shall start out from the same land. Then put a signpost at the head of each road 25so the sword can come to Rabbah of the Ammonites or to Judah and its fortress, Jerusalem. 26For the king of Babylon is standing at the fork of the two roads to read the omens: he shakes out the arrows, inquires of the teraphim, inspects the liver. 27Into his right hand has fallen the lot marked "Jerusalem": to order the slaughter, to raise the battle cry, to set the battering rams against the gates, to throw up a ramp, to build siege works. 28In the eyes of those bound by oath this seems like a false omen; yet the lot taken in hand exposes the wickedness for which they, still bound by oath, will be taken in hand. 29Therefore thus says the Lord GOD: Because your guilt has been exposed, your crimes laid bare, your sinfulness revealed in all your deeds—because you have been exposed, you shall be taken in hand. 30And as for you, depraved and wicked prince of Israel, a day is coming to end your life of crime. 31Thus says the Lord GOD: Off with the turban and away with the crown! Nothing shall be as it was! Exalt the lowly and bring the exalted low! 32A ruin, a ruin, a ruin, I shall make it! Nothing will be the same until the one comes to whom I have given it for judgment.

To the Ammonites. 33As for you, son of man, prophesy: Thus says the Lord GOD to the Ammonites and their insults:

O sword, sword drawn for slaughter,
  burnished to consume, to flash
    lightning!
34Your false visions and lying omens,
Set you over the necks of the slain,
  the wicked whose day had come—
  an end to their life of crime.
35Return to your scabbard!
  In the place you were created,
In the land of your origin,
  I will judge you.
36I will pour out my anger upon you,
  breathing my fiery wrath against
    you;
I will hand you over to ravagers,
  artisans of destruction!
37You shall be fuel for the fire,
  your blood shall flow throughout
    the land;
You shall not be remembered,
  for I, the LORD, have spoken.

□ LUKE 5

The Call of Simon the Fisherman. 5:1
While the crowd was pressing in on Jesus and listening to the word of God, he was standing by the Lake of Gennesaret. 2He saw two boats there alongside the lake; the fishermen had disembarked and were washing their nets. 3Getting into one of the boats, the one belonging to Simon, he asked him to put out a short distance from the shore. Then he sat down and taught the crowds from the boat. 4After he had finished speaking, he said to Simon, "Put out into deep water and lower your nets for a catch." 5Simon said in reply, "Master, we have worked

hard all night and have caught nothing, but at your command I will lower the nets." ⁶When they had done this, they caught a great number of fish and their nets were tearing. ⁷They signaled to their partners in the other boat to come to help them. They came and filled both boats so that they were in danger of sinking. ⁸When Simon Peter saw this, he fell at the knees of Jesus and said, "Depart from me, Lord, for I am a sinful man." ⁹For astonishment at the catch of fish they had made seized him and all those with him, ¹⁰and likewise James and John, the sons of Zebedee, who were partners of Simon. Jesus said to Simon, "Do not be afraid; from now on you will be catching men." ¹¹When they brought their boats to the shore, they left everything and followed him.

The Cleansing of a Leper. ¹²Now there was a man full of leprosy in one of the towns where he was; and when he saw Jesus, he fell prostrate, pleaded with him, and said, "Lord, if you wish, you can make me clean." ¹³Jesus stretched out his hand, touched him, and said, "I do will it. Be made clean." And the leprosy left him immediately. ¹⁴Then he ordered him not to tell anyone, but "Go, show yourself to the priest and offer for your cleansing what Moses prescribed; that will be proof for them." ¹⁵The report about him spread all the more, and great crowds assembled to listen to him and to be cured of their ailments, ¹⁶but he would withdraw to deserted places to pray.

The Healing of a Paralytic. ¹⁷One day as Jesus was teaching, Pharisees and teachers of the law were sitting there who had come from every village of Galilee and Judea and Jerusalem, and the power of the Lord was with him for healing. ¹⁸And some men brought on a stretcher a man who was paralyzed; they were trying to bring him in and set [him] in his presence. ¹⁹But not finding a way to bring him in because of the crowd, they went up on the roof and lowered him on the stretcher through the tiles into the middle in front of Jesus. ²⁰When

he saw their faith, he said, "As for you, your sins are forgiven." ²¹Then the scribes and Pharisees began to ask themselves, "Who is this who speaks blasphemies? Who but God alone can forgive sins?" ²²Jesus knew their thoughts and said to them in reply, "What are you thinking in your hearts? ²³Which is easier, to say, 'Your sins are forgiven,' or to say, 'Rise and walk'? ²⁴But that you may know that the Son of Man has authority on earth to forgive sins"—he said to the man who was paralyzed, "I say to you, rise, pick up your stretcher, and go home." ²⁵He stood up immediately before them, picked up what he had been lying on, and went home, glorifying God. ²⁶Then astonishment seized them all and they glorified God, and, struck with awe, they said, "We have seen incredible things today."

The Call of Levi. ²⁷After this he went out and saw a tax collector named Levi sitting at the customs post. He said to him, "Follow me." ²⁸And leaving everything behind, he got up and followed him. ²⁹Then Levi gave a great banquet for him in his house, and a large crowd of tax collectors and others were at table with them. ³⁰The Pharisees and their scribes complained to his disciples, saying, "Why do you eat and drink with tax collectors and sinners?" ³¹Jesus said to them in reply, "Those who are healthy do not need a physician, but the sick do. ³²I have not come to call the righteous to repentance but sinners."

The Question about Fasting. ³³And they said to him, "The disciples of John fast often and offer prayers, and the disciples of the Pharisees do the same; but yours eat and drink." ³⁴Jesus answered them, "Can you make the wedding guests fast while the bridegroom is with them? ³⁵But the days will come, and when the bridegroom is taken away from them, then they will fast in those days." ³⁶And he also told them a parable. "No one tears a piece from a new cloak to patch an old one. Otherwise, he will tear the new and the piece from it will not match the old cloak. ³⁷Likewise, no one pours new wine into old wineskins. Otherwise, the new wine will burst the skins, and it will be spilled, and the skins will be ruined. ³⁸Rather, new wine must be poured into fresh wineskins. ³⁹[And] no one who has been drinking old wine desires new, for he says, 'The old is good.'"

November 15

St. Albert the Great

To forgive those who have injured us in our body, our reputation, our goods, is more advantageous to us than to cross the seas to venerate the sepulchre of the Lord.

— St. Albert the Great

☐ EZEKIEL 22–23

Crimes of Jerusalem. 22:1 The word of the Lord came to me: ²You, son of man, will you judge? will you judge the city of bloodshed? Then make known all its abominations, ³and say: Thus says the Lord God: O city that sheds blood within itself so that its time has come, that has made idols for its own defilement: ⁴By the blood you shed you have become guilty, and by the idols you made you have become defiled. You have brought on your day, you have come to the end of your years. Therefore I make you an object of scorn for the nations and a laughingstock for all lands. ⁵Those near and those far off will mock you: "Defiled of Name! Queen of Tumult!" ⁶See! the princes of Israel within you use their power to shed blood. ⁷Within you, father and mother are dishonored; they extort the resident alien in your midst; within you, they oppress orphans and widows. ⁸What I consider holy you have rejected, and my sabbaths you have desecrated. ⁹In you are those who slander to cause bloodshed; within you are those who feast on the mountains; in your midst are those whose actions are depraved. ¹⁰In you are those who uncover the nakedness of their fathers; in you those who coerce women to intercourse during their period. ¹¹There are those in you who do abominable things with their neighbors' wives, men who defile their daughters-in-law by incest, men who coerce their sisters to intercourse, the daughters of their own fathers. ¹²There are those in you who take bribes to shed blood. You exact interest and usury; you extort profit from your neighbor by violence. But me you have forgotten—oracle of the Lord God.

¹³See, I am clapping my hands because of the profits you extorted and the blood shed in your midst. ¹⁴Will your heart remain firm, will your hands be strong, in the days when I deal with you? I am the Lord; I have spoken, and I will act! ¹⁵I will disperse you among the nations and scatter you over other lands, so that I may purge your filth. ¹⁶In you I will allow myself to be desecrated in the eyes of the nations; thus you shall know that I am the Lord.

¹⁷The word of the Lord came to me: ¹⁸Son of man, the house of Israel has become dross to me. All of them are copper, tin, iron, and lead within a furnace; they have become the dross from silver. ¹⁹Therefore thus says the Lord God: Because all of you have become dross, See! I am gathering you within Jerusalem. ²⁰Just as silver,

copper, iron, lead, and tin are gathered within a furnace to be blasted with fire to smelt it, so I will gather you together in my furious wrath, put you in, and smelt you. ²¹When I have assembled you, I will blast you with the fire of my anger and smelt you with it. ²²Just as silver is smelted in a furnace, so you shall be smelted in it. Thus you shall know that I, the LORD, have poured out my fury on you.

²³The word of the LORD came to me: ²⁴Son of man, say to her: You are an unclean land receiving no rain at the time of my fury. ²⁵A conspiracy of its princes is like a roaring lion tearing prey; they devour people, seizing their wealth and precious things, making many widows within her. ²⁶Her priests violate my law and desecrate what I consider holy; they do not distinguish between holy and common, nor teach the difference between unclean and clean; they pay no attention to my sabbaths, so that I have been desecrated in their midst. ²⁷Within her, her officials are like wolves tearing prey, shedding blood and destroying lives to extort profit. ²⁸And her prophets cover them with whitewash, seeing false visions and performing lying divinations, saying, "Thus says the Lord GOD," although the LORD has not spoken. ²⁹The people of the land practice extortion and commit robbery; they wrong the poor and the needy, and oppress the resident alien without justice. ³⁰Thus I have searched among them for someone who would build a wall or stand in the breach before me to keep me from destroying the land; but I found no one. ³¹Therefore I have poured out my fury upon them; with my fiery wrath I have consumed them, bringing down their ways upon their heads—oracle of the Lord GOD.

The Two Sisters. 23:1 The word of the LORD came to me: ²Son of man, there were two women, daughters of the same mother. ³Even as young girls, they were prostitutes, serving as prostitutes in Egypt. There the Egyptians fondled their breasts and caressed their virgin nipples. ⁴Oholah was the name of the elder, and the name of her sister was Oholibah. They became mine and gave birth to sons and daughters. As for their names: Samaria was Oholah and Jerusalem, Oholibah. ⁵Oholah became a prostitute while married to me and lusted after her lovers, the Assyrians: warriors ⁶dressed in purple, governors and officers, all of them handsome young soldiers, mounted on horses. ⁷She gave herself as a prostitute to them, to all the Assyrian elite; with all those for whom she lusted, she also defiled herself with their idols. ⁸She did not abandon the prostitution she had begun with the Egyptians, who had lain with her when she was young, fondling her virgin breasts and pouring out their lust upon her. ⁹Therefore I handed her over to her lovers, to the Assyrians for whom she lusted. ¹⁰They exposed her nakedness; her sons and daughters they took away, and her they killed with the sword. She became a byword for women because of the sentence carried out against her.

¹¹Although her sister Oholibah saw all this, her lust was more depraved than her sister's; she outdid her in prostitution. ¹²She too lusted after the Assyrians, governors and officers, warriors impeccably clothed, mounted on horses, all of them handsome young soldiers. ¹³I saw that she had defiled herself—now both had gone down the same path. ¹⁴She went further in her prostitution: She saw male figures drawn on the wall, images of Chaldeans drawn with vermilion, ¹⁵with sashes tied about their waists, flowing turbans on their heads, all looking like chariot warriors, images of Babylonians, natives of Chaldea. ¹⁶As soon as she set eyes on them she lusted for them, and she sent messengers to them in Chaldea. ¹⁷The Babylonians came to her, to her love couch; they defiled her with their impurities. But as soon as they had defiled

her, she recoiled from them. ¹⁸When her prostitution was discovered and her shame revealed, I recoiled from her as I had recoiled from her sister. ¹⁹But she increased her prostitution, recalling the days of her youth when she had served as a prostitute in the land of Egypt. ²⁰She lusted for the lechers of Egypt, whose members are like those of donkeys, whose thrusts are like those of stallions.

²¹You reverted to the depravity of your youth, when Egyptians fondled your breasts, caressing your young nipples. ²²Therefore, Oholibah, thus says the Lord GOD: I will now stir up your lovers against you, those from whom you recoiled, and I will bring them against you from every side: ²³the men of Babylon and all of Chaldea, Pekod, Shoa and Koa, along with all the Assyrians, handsome young soldiers, all of them governors and officers, charioteers and warriors, all of them horsemen. ²⁴They shall invade you with armor, chariots and wagons, a horde of peoples; they will array against you on every side bucklers and shields and helmets. I will give them the right of judgment, and they will judge you according to their standards. ²⁵I will direct my jealousy against you, so that they deal with you in fury, cutting off your nose and ears; what is left of you shall fall by the sword. They shall take away your sons and daughters, and what is left of you shall be devoured by fire. ²⁶They shall strip off your clothes and seize your splendid jewelry. ²⁷I will put an end to your depravity and to your prostitution from the land of Egypt; you shall no longer look to them, nor even remember Egypt again.

²⁸For thus says the Lord GOD: I am now handing you over to those whom you hate, to those from whom you recoil. ²⁹They shall treat you with hatred, seizing all that you worked for and leaving you stark naked, so that your indecent nakedness is exposed. Your depravity and prostitution ³⁰brought these things upon you because

you served as a prostitute for the nations, defiling yourself with their idols. ³¹Because you followed your sister's path, I will put her cup into your hand.

³²Thus says the Lord GOD:

The cup of your sister you shall drink,
  deep and wide;
It brings ridicule and mockery,
  it holds so much;
³³You will be filled with drunkenness
  and grief—
  A cup of horror and devastation,
  the cup of your sister Samaria;
³⁴You shall drink it dry,
  its very sherds you will gnaw;
And you shall tear out your breasts;
  for I have spoken—oracle of the
  Lord GOD.

³⁵Therefore thus says the Lord GOD: You have forgotten me and cast me behind your back; now suffer for your depravity and prostitution.

³⁶Then the LORD said to me: Son of man, would you judge Oholah and Oholibah? Then make known to them their abominations. ³⁷For they committed adultery, and blood covers their hands. They committed adultery with their idols; even the children they bore for me they burnt as food for them. ³⁸And they also did this to me: on that day, they defiled my sanctuary and desecrated my sabbaths. ³⁹On the very day they slaughtered their children for their idols, they entered my sanctuary to desecrate it. Thus they acted within my house! ⁴⁰Moreover, they sent for men who had to come from afar; when a messenger was sent to them, they came. On their account you bathed, painted your eyes, and put on jewelry. ⁴¹You sat on a magnificent couch, set before it a table, on which to lay my incense and oil. ⁴²The cries of a mob! The shouts of men coming in from the wilderness! They put bracelets on the women's arms and splendid crowns on their heads. ⁴³I said: "That worn-out one still has adulteries

in her! Now they engage her as a prostitute and she…" ⁴⁴And indeed they did come in to her as men come in to a prostitute. Thus they came to Oholah and Oholibah, the depraved women. ⁴⁵The righteous shall certainly punish them with sentences given to adulterers and murderers, for they committed adultery, and blood is on their hands.

⁴⁶Indeed, thus says the Lord GOD: Raise up an army against them and hand them over to terror and plunder. ⁴⁷The army will stone them and hack them to pieces with their swords. They will kill their sons and daughters and set fire to their houses. ⁴⁸Thus I will put an end to depravity in the land, and all women will be warned not to imitate your depravity. ⁴⁹They shall inflict on you the penalty of your depravity, and you shall pay for your sins of idolatry. Then you shall know that I am the Lord GOD.

☐ LUKE 6

Debates about the Sabbath. 6:1 While he was going through a field of grain on a sabbath, his disciples were picking the heads of grain, rubbing them in their hands, and eating them. ²Some Pharisees said, "Why are you doing what is unlawful on the sabbath?" ³Jesus said to them in reply, "Have you not read what David did when he and those [who were] with him were hungry? ⁴[How] he went into the house of God, took the bread of offering, which only the priests could lawfully eat, ate of it, and shared it with his companions." ⁵Then he said to them, "The Son of Man is lord of the sabbath."

⁶On another sabbath he went into the synagogue and taught, and there was a man there whose right hand was withered. ⁷The scribes and the Pharisees watched him closely to see if he would cure on the sabbath so that they might discover a reason to accuse him. ⁸But he realized their intentions and said to the man with the withered hand, "Come up and stand before us." And he rose and stood there. ⁹Then Jesus said to them, "I ask you, is it lawful to do good on the sabbath rather than to do evil, to save life rather than to destroy it?" ¹⁰Looking around at them all, he then said to him, "Stretch out your hand." He did so and his hand was restored. ¹¹But they became enraged and discussed together what they might do to Jesus.

The Mission of the Twelve. ¹²In those days he departed to the mountain to pray, and he spent the night in prayer to God. ¹³When day came, he called his disciples to himself, and from them he chose Twelve, whom he also named apostles: ¹⁴Simon, whom he named Peter, and his brother Andrew, James, John, Philip, Bartholomew, ¹⁵Matthew, Thomas, James the son of Alphaeus, Simon who was called a Zealot, ¹⁶and Judas the son of James, and Judas Iscariot, who became a traitor.

Ministering to a Great Multitude. ¹⁷And he came down with them and stood on a stretch of level ground. A great crowd of his disciples and a large number of the people from all Judea and Jerusalem and the coastal region of Tyre and Sidon ¹⁸came to hear him and to be healed of their diseases; and even those who were tormented by unclean spirits were cured. ¹⁹Everyone in the crowd sought to touch him because power came forth from him and healed them all.

Sermon on the Plain. ²⁰And raising his eyes toward his disciples he said:

"Blessed are you who are poor,
  for the kingdom of God is yours.
²¹Blessed are you who are now hungry,
  for you will be satisfied.
Blessed are you who are now weeping,
  for you will laugh.

²²Blessed are you when people hate you,
and when they exclude and insult
you,
and denounce your name as evil
on account of the Son of Man.

²³Rejoice and leap for joy on that day! Behold, your reward will be great in heaven. For their ancestors treated the prophets in the same way.

²⁴But woe to you who are rich,
for you have received your
consolation.
²⁵But woe to you who are filled now,
for you will be hungry.
Woe to you who laugh now,
for you will grieve and weep.
²⁶Woe to you when all speak well of you,
for their ancestors treated the false
prophets in this way.

Love of Enemies. ²⁷"But to you who hear I say, love your enemies, do good to those who hate you, ²⁸bless those who curse you, pray for those who mistreat you. ²⁹To the person who strikes you on one cheek, offer the other one as well, and from the person who takes your cloak, do not withhold even your tunic. ³⁰Give to everyone who asks of you, and from the one who takes what is yours do not demand it back. ³¹Do to others as you would have them do to you. ³²For if you love those who love you, what credit is that to you? Even sinners love those who love them. ³³And if you do good to those who do good to you, what credit is that to you? Even sinners do the same. ³⁴If you lend money to those from whom you expect repayment, what credit [is] that to you? Even sinners lend to sinners, and get back the same amount. ³⁵But rather, love your enemies and do good to them, and lend expecting nothing back; then your reward will be great and you will be children of the Most High, for he himself is kind to the ungrateful and the wicked. ³⁶Be merciful, just as [also] your Father is merciful.

Judging Others. ³⁷"Stop judging and you will not be judged. Stop condemning and you will not be condemned. Forgive and you will be forgiven. ³⁸Give and gifts will be given to you; a good measure, packed together, shaken down, and overflowing, will be poured into your lap. For the measure with which you measure will in return be measured out to you." ³⁹And he told them a parable, "Can a blind person guide a blind person? Will not both fall into a pit? ⁴⁰No disciple is superior to the teacher; but when fully trained, every disciple will be like his teacher. ⁴¹Why do you notice the splinter in your brother's eye, but do not perceive the wooden beam in your own? ⁴²How can you say to your brother, 'Brother, let me remove that splinter in your eye,' when you do not even notice the wooden beam in your own eye? You hypocrite! Remove the wooden beam from your eye first; then you will see clearly to remove the splinter in your brother's eye.

A Tree Known by Its Fruit. ⁴³"A good tree does not bear rotten fruit, nor does a rotten tree bear good fruit. ⁴⁴For every tree is known by its own fruit. For people do not pick figs from thornbushes, nor do they gather grapes from brambles. ⁴⁵A good person out of the store of goodness in his heart produces good, but an evil person out of a store of evil produces evil; for from the fullness of the heart the mouth speaks.

The Two Foundations. ⁴⁶"Why do you call me, 'Lord, Lord,' but not do what I command? ⁴⁷I will show you what someone is like who comes to me, listens to my words, and acts on them. ⁴⁸That one is like a person building a house, who dug deeply and laid the foundation on rock; when the flood came, the river burst against that house but could not shake it because it had been well built. ⁴⁹But the one who listens and does not act is like a person who built a house on the ground without a foundation. When the river burst against it, it collapsed at once and was completely destroyed."

November 16

St. Margaret of Scotland; St. Gertrude the Great

Jesus told me, "My heaven would not be complete without you."
— St. Gertrude the Great

☐ **EZEKIEL 24-25**

Allegory of the Pot. 24:1 On the tenth day of the tenth month, in the ninth year, the word of the Lord came to me: [2]Son of man, write down today's date this very day, for on this very day the king of Babylon lays siege to Jerusalem. [3]Propose this parable to the rebellious house and say to them: Thus says the Lord God:

Put the pot on, put it on!
 Pour in some water;
[4]Add to it pieces of meat,
 all choice pieces;
With thigh and shoulder,
 with choice cuts fill it.
[5]Choose the pick of the flock,
 then pile logs beneath it;
Bring it to a boil,
 cook all the pieces in it.
[6]Therefore thus says the Lord God:
 Woe to the city full of blood!
A pot containing filth,
 whose filth cannot be removed!
Take out its pieces one by one,
 for no lot has fallen on their behalf.
[7]For her blood is still in her midst;
 on a bare rock she left it;
She did not pour it on the ground
 to be covered with dirt.
[8]To arouse wrath, to exact vengeance,
 I have left her blood on bare rock
 not to be covered.
[9]Therefore, thus says the Lord God:
 Woe to the city full of blood!
 I will make the pyre great!
[10]Pile on the wood, kindle the fire.
 Cook the meat, stir the spicy mixture,
 char the bones!
[11]Then set it empty on the coals,

to heat up until its copper glows,
So its impurities melt,
 its filth disappears.
[12]The toil is exhausting,
 but the great filth will not come
 out—
Filth, even with fire.
[13]Even in defiling yourself with
 depravity
 I would still have cleansed you,
 but you would not have your
 impurity cleansed.
You will not be cleansed now
 until I wreak my fury on you.
[14]I, the Lord, have spoken;
 it will happen!
 I will do it and not hold back!
 I will not have pity or relent.
By your conduct and deeds you shall
 be judged—
 oracle of the Lord God.

Ezekiel as a Sign for the Exiles. [15]The word of the Lord came to me: [16]Son of man, with a sudden blow I am taking away from you the delight of your eyes, but do not mourn or weep or shed any tears. [17]Groan, moan for the dead, but make no public lament; bind on your turban, put your sandals on your feet, but do not cover your beard or eat the bread of mourners. [18]I spoke to the people in the morning. In the evening my wife died. The next morning I did as I had been commanded. [19]Then the people asked me, "Will you not tell us what all these things you are doing mean for us?" [20]I said to them, The word of the Lord came to me: [21]Say to the house of Israel: Thus says the Lord God: I will now desecrate my sanctuary, the pride of your strength, the delight of your eyes, the concern of your soul. The sons and daughters you left behind shall fall by the sword. [22]Then you shall do as I have done, not covering your beards nor eating the bread of mourning. [23]Your turbans shall remain on your heads, your sandals on your feet. You shall not mourn or weep, but you shall waste away because of your sins and groan to one another. [24]Ezekiel shall be a sign for you: everything he did, you shall do. When it happens, you shall know that I am the Lord God.

End of Ezekiel's Muteness. [25]As for you, son of man, truly, on the very day I take away from them their strength, their glorious joy, the delight of their eyes, the desire of their soul, the pride of their hearts, their sons and daughters, [26]on that day a survivor will come to you so that you may hear it with your own ears. [27]On that day, with the survivor, your mouth shall be opened; you shall speak and be mute no longer. You shall be a sign to them, and they shall know that I am the Lord.

Against Ammon. 25:1 The word of the Lord came to me: [2]Son of man, turn toward the Ammonites and prophesy against them. [3]Say to the Ammonites: Hear the word of the Lord! Thus says the Lord God: Because you jeered at my sanctuary when it was desecrated, at the land of Israel when it was destroyed, and at the house of Judah when they went into exile, [4]therefore I am giving you to people from the east as a possession. They shall set up their encampments among you and pitch their tents in your midst; they shall eat your produce and drink your milk. [5]And I will turn Rabbah into a pasture for camels and all of Ammon into a grazing place for flocks. Then you shall know that I am the Lord.

[6]For thus says the Lord God: Because you rejoiced over the land of Israel with scorn in your heart, clapping your hands and stamping your feet, [7]therefore, see, I am stretching out my hand against you and giving you up as plunder to the nations. I will cut you off from the peoples and wipe you out of the lands. I will destroy you, and you shall know that I am the Lord.

Against Moab. [8]Thus says the Lord God: Because Moab said, "See! the house of Judah is like all the other nations," [9]therefore, I am exposing the whole flank of Moab with its cities, the jewels of its land: Beth-jesimoth, Baalmeon, and Kiriathaim. [10]I will hand it over, along with the Ammonites, to the people from the east that it may not be remembered among the nations. [11]I will execute judgment upon Moab that they may know that I am the Lord.

Against Edom. [12]Thus says the Lord God: Because Edom took vengeance on the house of Judah and incurred terrible guilt by taking vengeance on them, [13]therefore thus says the Lord God: I will stretch out my hand against Edom and cut off from it human being and beast alike. I will turn it into ruins from Teman to Dedan; they shall fall by the sword. [14]I will put my vengeance against Edom into the hands of my people Israel; they will deal with Edom in accord with my furious anger. Thus they shall know my vengeance!—oracle of the Lord God.

Against the Philistines. [15]Thus says the Lord God: Because the Philistines acted vengefully and exacted vengeance with intentional malice, destroying with undying hostility, [16]therefore thus says the Lord God: See! I am stretching out my hand against the Philistines, and I will cut off the Cherethites and wipe out the remnant on the seacoast. [17]Thus I will execute great acts of vengeance on them, punishing them furiously. Then they shall know that I am the Lord, when I wreak my vengeance on them.

☐ LUKE 7

The Healing of a Centurion's Slave. 7:1
When he had finished all his words to the people, he entered Capernaum. ²A centurion there had a slave who was ill and about to die, and he was valuable to him. ³When he heard about Jesus, he sent elders of the Jews to him, asking him to come and save the life of his slave. ⁴They approached Jesus and strongly urged him to come, saying, "He deserves to have you do this for him, ⁵for he loves our nation and he built the synagogue for us." ⁶And Jesus went with them, but when he was only a short distance from the house, the centurion sent friends to tell him, "Lord, do not trouble yourself, for I am not worthy to have you enter under my roof. ⁷Therefore, I did not consider myself worthy to come to you; but say the word and let my servant be healed. ⁸For I too am a person subject to authority, with soldiers subject to me. And I say to one, 'Go,' and he goes; and to another, 'Come here,' and he comes; and to my slave, 'Do this,' and he does it." ⁹When Jesus heard this he was amazed at him and, turning, said to the crowd following him, "I tell you, not even in Israel have I found such faith." ¹⁰When the messengers returned to the house, they found the slave in good health.

Raising of the Widow's Son. ¹¹Soon afterward he journeyed to a city called Nain, and his disciples and a large crowd accompanied him. ¹²As he drew near to the gate of the city, a man who had died was being carried out, the only son of his mother, and she was a widow. A large crowd from the city was with her. ¹³When the Lord saw her, he was moved with pity for her and said to her, "Do not weep." ¹⁴He stepped forward and touched the coffin; at this the bearers halted, and he said, "Young man, I tell you, arise!" ¹⁵The dead man sat up and began to speak, and Jesus gave him to his mother. ¹⁶Fear seized them all, and they glorified God, exclaiming, "A great prophet has arisen in our midst," and "God has visited his people." ¹⁷This report about him spread through the whole of Judea and in all the surrounding region.

The Messengers from John the Baptist. ¹⁸The disciples of John told him about all these things. John summoned two of his disciples ¹⁹and sent them to the Lord to ask, "Are you the one who is to come, or should we look for another?" ²⁰When the men came to him, they said, "John the Baptist has sent us to you to ask, 'Are you the one who is to come, or should we look for another?'" ²¹At that time he cured many of their diseases, sufferings, and evil spirits; he also granted sight to many who were blind. ²²And he said to them in reply, "Go and tell John what you have seen and heard: the blind regain their sight, the lame walk, lepers are cleansed, the deaf hear, the dead are raised, the poor have the good news proclaimed to them. ²³And blessed is the one who takes no offense at me."

Jesus' Testimony to John. ²⁴When the messengers of John had left, Jesus began to speak to the crowds about John. "What did you go out to the desert to see—a reed swayed by the wind? ²⁵Then what did you go out to see? Someone dressed in fine garments? Those who dress luxuriously and live sumptuously are found in royal palaces. ²⁶Then what did you go out to see? A prophet? Yes, I tell you, and more than a prophet. ²⁷This is the one about whom scripture says:

'Behold, I am sending my messenger
    ahead of you,
  he will prepare your way before
    you.'

²⁸I tell you, among those born of women, no one is greater than John; yet the least in the kingdom of God is greater than he." ²⁹(All the people who listened, including

the tax collectors, and who were baptized with the baptism of John, acknowledged the righteousness of God; [30]but the Pharisees and scholars of the law, who were not baptized by him, rejected the plan of God for themselves.)

[31]"Then to what shall I compare the people of this generation? What are they like? [32]They are like children who sit in the marketplace and call to one another,

'We played the flute for you, but you
did not dance.
We sang a dirge, but you did not
weep.'

[33]For John the Baptist came neither eating food nor drinking wine, and you said, 'He is possessed by a demon.' [34]The Son of Man came eating and drinking and you said, 'Look, he is a glutton and a drunkard, a friend of tax collectors and sinners.' [35]But wisdom is vindicated by all her children."

The Pardon of the Sinful Woman. [36]A Pharisee invited him to dine with him, and he entered the Pharisee's house and reclined at table. [37]Now there was a sinful woman in the city who learned that he was at table in the house of the Pharisee. Bringing an alabaster flask of ointment, [38]she stood behind him at his feet weeping and began to bathe his feet with her tears. Then she wiped them with her hair, kissed them, and anointed them with the ointment. [39]When the Pharisee who had invited him saw this he said to himself, "If this man were a prophet, he would know who and what sort of woman this is who is touching him, that she is a sinner." [40]Jesus said to him in reply, "Simon, I have something to say to you." "Tell me, teacher," he said. [41]"Two people were in debt to a certain creditor; one owed five hundred days' wages and the other owed fifty. [42]Since they were unable to repay the debt, he forgave it for both. Which of them will love him more?" [43]Simon said in reply, "The one, I suppose, whose larger debt was forgiven." He said to him, "You have judged rightly." [44]Then he turned to the woman and said to Simon, "Do you see this woman? When I entered your house, you did not give me water for my feet, but she has bathed them with her tears and wiped them with her hair. [45]You did not give me a kiss, but she has not ceased kissing my feet since the time I entered. [46]You did not anoint my head with oil, but she anointed my feet with ointment. [47]So I tell you, her many sins have been forgiven; hence, she has shown great love. But the one to whom little is forgiven, loves little." [48]He said to her, "Your sins are forgiven." [49]The others at table said to themselves, "Who is this who even forgives sins?" [50]But he said to the woman, "Your faith has saved you; go in peace."

November 17

St. Elizabeth of Hungary

As in heaven Your will, Father, is punctually performed, so may it be done on earth by all creatures, particularly in me and by me.

— St. Elizabeth of Hungary

☐ EZEKIEL 26-27

Against the City of Tyre. 26:1 On the first day of the eleventh month of the eleventh year, the word of the LORD came to me:

²Son of man, because Tyre said of Jerusalem:
"Aha! The gateway of the peoples is smashed!
    It has been turned over to me;
    I will be enriched by its ruin!"
³therefore thus says the Lord GOD:
See! I am coming against you, Tyre;
    I will churn up against you many nations,
    just as the sea churns up its waves.
⁴They will destroy the walls of Tyre
    and tear down its towers;
I will scrape off its debris
    and leave it a bare rock.
⁵It will become a place for drying nets
    in the midst of the sea.
For I have spoken—oracle of the Lord GOD:
    she will become plunder for the nations.
⁶Her daughter cities on the mainland
    will be slaughtered by the sword;
    then they shall know that I am the LORD.
⁷Indeed thus says the Lord GOD:
I am bringing up against Tyre
    from the north, Nebuchadnezzar,
King of Babylon, king of kings,
    with horses and chariots, with cavalry,
    and a mighty horde of troops.

⁸Your daughter cities on the mainland
    he shall slay with the sword.
He shall build a siege wall around you,
    throw up a ramp against you,
    and raise his shields about you.
⁹He shall pound your walls with battering-rams
    and break down your towers with his axes.
¹⁰From the surging of his horses
    he will cover you with dust;
    from the noise of warhorses,
    wheels and chariots.
Your walls will shake
    when he enters your gates,
    even as one enters a city that is breached.
¹¹With the hooves of his horses
    he will trample all your streets;
Your people he will slay by the sword;
    your mighty pillars will collapse.
¹²They shall plunder your wealth
    and pillage your goods;
They will tear down your walls
    and demolish your splendid houses.
Your stones, timbers, and debris
    they will cast into the sea.
¹³I will bring an end to the noise of your songs;
    the music of your lyres will be heard no more.
¹⁴I will turn you into bare rock,
    you will become a place for drying nets.
You shall never be rebuilt,
    for I the LORD have spoken—
    oracle of the Lord GOD.

¹⁵Thus says the Lord God to Tyre:
At the sound of your downfall,
     at the groaning of the wounded,
When victims are slain within you,
     will the islands not quake?
¹⁶All the princes of the sea
     will step down from their thrones,
Lay aside their robes,
     and strip off their embroidered
          garments.
Clothed in mourning,
     they will sit on the ground
And tremble, horror-struck
     and appalled at you.
¹⁷They will raise lament over you
     and say to you:
How you have perished,
     gone from the seas,
     Renowned City!
Once she was mighty on the sea,
     she and her inhabitants,
Those who spread their terror
     to all who dwelt nearby.
¹⁸On this, the day of your fall,
     the islands quake!
The islands in the sea
     are terrified at your passing.
¹⁹Indeed thus says the Lord God:
When I make you a ruined city
     like cities no longer inhabited,
When I churn up the deep
     and its mighty waters cover you,
²⁰Then I will thrust you down
     with those who go down to
          the pit,
     to those of the bygone age;
I will make you dwell in the
     netherworld,
     in the everlasting ruins,
     with those who have gone down to
          the pit,
So you will never return
     or have a place in the land of the
          living.
²¹I will make you a horror,
     and you shall be no more;
You shall be sought for,

but never found again—
     oracle of the Lord God.

The Ship Tyre. 27:1 The word of the Lord came to me: ²You, son of man, raise a lament over Tyre, ³and say to Tyre, who sits at the entrance to the sea, trader to peoples on many coastlands, Thus says the Lord God:

Tyre, you said, "I am a ship,
     perfect in beauty;
⁴In the heart of the sea was your
          territory;
     your builders perfected your beauty.
⁵With juniper wood from Senir
     they built all your decks;
A cedar from Lebanon they took
     to make you a mast.
⁶With oaks of Bashan
     they fashioned your oars,
Your bridge, of ivory-inlaid cypress
          wood
     from the coasts of Kittim.
⁷Fine embroidered linen from Egypt
     became your sail;
Your awnings were made of purple and
          scarlet
     from the coasts of Elishah.
⁸Inhabitants of Sidon and Arvad
     were your oarsmen;
Your own sages, Tyre, were on board,
     serving as your sailors.
⁹The elders and sages of Gebal
     were with you to caulk your seams.
Every ship and sailor on the sea
     came to you to carry on trade.
¹⁰Persia and Lud and Put
     were warriors in your army;
Shield and helmet they hung on you
     to enhance your splendor.
¹¹The men of Arvad and Helech
     were on your walls all around
And Gamadites on your towers;
     they hung their shields around your
          walls,
     they made your beauty perfect.

¹²Tarshish traded with you,
 so great was your wealth,
Exchanging for your wares
 silver, iron, tin, and lead.
¹³Javan, Tubal, and Meshech
 also traded with you,
Exchanging slaves and bronze vessels
 for your merchandise.
¹⁴Horses, steeds, and mules from Beth-
 togarmah
 were exchanged for your wares.
¹⁵Men of Rhodes trafficked with you;
 many coastlands were your agents;
Ivory tusks and ebony wood
 they brought back as your payment.
¹⁶Edom traded with you for your many
 wares:
 garnets, purple dye, embroidered
 cloth,
Fine linen, coral, and rubies
 they gave you as merchandise.
¹⁷Judah and the land of Israel
 trafficked with you:
Minnith wheat, grain, honey, oil, and
 balm
 they gave you as merchandise.
¹⁸Damascus traded with you for your
 many wares,
 so great was your wealth,
 exchanging Helbon wine and Zahar
 wool.
¹⁹Javan exchanged wrought iron, cassia,
 and aromatic cane
 from Uzal for your wares.
²⁰Dedan traded with you for riding gear.
²¹Arabia and the sheikhs of Kedar were
 your agents,
 dealing in lambs, rams, and goats.
²²The merchants of Sheba and Raamah
 also traded with you,
 exchanging for your wares the very
 best spices,
 all kinds of precious stones, and
 gold.
²³Haran, Canneh, and Eden,
 the merchants of Sheba, Asshur, and
 Chilmad,

²⁴Traded with you, marketing rich
 garments,
 purple cloth, embroidered fabric,
 varicolored carpets, and braided
 cords.
²⁵The ships of Tarshish sailed for you
 with your goods;
You were full and heavily laden
 in the heart of the sea.
²⁶Out into deep waters
 your oarsmen brought you;
The east wind shattered you
 in the heart of the sea.
²⁷Your wealth, your goods, your wares,
 your sailors, your crew,
The caulkers of your seams,
 those who traded for your goods,
All the warriors with you,
 the whole crowd with you
Sank into the heart of the sea
 on the day of your downfall.
²⁸At the sound of your sailors' shouts
 the waves shudder,
²⁹Down from their ships
 come all who ply the oars;
Sailors, all the seafaring crew,
 stand on the shore.
³⁰They raise their voices over you
 and shout their bitter cries;
They pour dust on their heads
 and cover themselves with ashes.
³¹For you they shave their heads bald
 and put on sackcloth;
For you they weep bitterly,
 in anguished lament.
³²They raise a lament for you;
 they wail over you:
"Who was ever destroyed like Tyre
 in the midst of the sea?"
³³By exporting your goods by sea
 you satisfied many peoples,
With your great wealth and merchandise
 you enriched the kings of the earth.
³⁴Now you are wrecked in the sea,
 in the watery depths;
Your wares and all your crew
 have fallen down with you.

³⁵All who dwell on the coastlands
  are aghast over you;
Their kings are terrified,
  their faces distorted.

³⁶The traders among the peoples
  now hiss at you;
You have become a horror,
  you shall be no more.

☐ LUKE 8

Galilean Women Follow Jesus. 8:1 Afterward he journeyed from one town and village to another, preaching and proclaiming the good news of the kingdom of God. Accompanying him were the Twelve ²and some women who had been cured of evil spirits and infirmities, Mary, called Magdalene, from whom seven demons had gone out, ³Joanna, the wife of Herod's steward Chuza, Susanna, and many others who provided for them out of their resources.

The Parable of the Sower. ⁴When a large crowd gathered, with people from one town after another journeying to him, he spoke in a parable. ⁵"A sower went out to sow his seed. And as he sowed, some seed fell on the path and was trampled, and the birds of the sky ate it up. ⁶Some seed fell on rocky ground, and when it grew, it withered for lack of moisture. ⁷Some seed fell among thorns, and the thorns grew with it and choked it. ⁸And some seed fell on good soil, and when it grew, it produced fruit a hundredfold." After saying this, he called out, "Whoever has ears to hear ought to hear."

The Purpose of the Parables. ⁹Then his disciples asked him what the meaning of this parable might be. ¹⁰He answered, "Knowledge of the mysteries of the kingdom of God has been granted to you; but to the rest, they are made known through parables so that 'they may look but not see, and hear but not understand.'

The Parable of the Sower Explained. ¹¹"This is the meaning of the parable. The seed is the word of God. ¹²Those on the path are the ones who have heard, but the devil comes and takes away the word from their hearts that they may not believe and be saved. ¹³Those on rocky ground are the ones who, when they hear, receive the word with joy, but they have no root; they believe only for a time and fall away in time of trial. ¹⁴As for the seed that fell among thorns, they are the ones who have heard, but as they go along, they are choked by the anxieties and riches and pleasures of life, and they fail to produce mature fruit. ¹⁵But as for the seed that fell on rich soil, they are the ones who, when they have heard the word, embrace it with a generous and good heart, and bear fruit through perseverance.

The Parable of the Lamp. ¹⁶"No one who lights a lamp conceals it with a vessel or sets it under a bed; rather, he places it on a lampstand so that those who enter may see the light. ¹⁷For there is nothing hidden that will not become visible, and nothing secret that will not be known and come to light. ¹⁸Take care, then, how you hear. To anyone who has, more will be given, and from the one who has not, even what he seems to have will be taken away."

Jesus and His Family. ¹⁹Then his mother and his brothers came to him but were unable to join him because of the crowd. ²⁰He was told, "Your mother and your brothers are standing outside and they wish to see you." ²¹He said to them in reply, "My mother and my brothers are those who hear the word of God and act on it."

The Calming of a Storm at Sea. ²²One day he got into a boat with his disciples and said to them, "Let us cross to the other side of the lake." So they set sail, ²³and while they were sailing he fell asleep. A squall blew over the lake, and they were taking in water and were in danger. ²⁴They came and woke him saying, "Master, master, we are perishing!" He awakened, rebuked the wind and the waves, and they subsided and there was a calm. ²⁵Then he asked them, "Where is your faith?" But they were filled with awe and amazed and said to one another, "Who then is this, who commands even the winds and the sea, and they obey him?"

The Healing of the Gerasene Demoniac. ²⁶Then they sailed to the territory of the Gerasenes, which is opposite Galilee. ²⁷When he came ashore a man from the town who was possessed by demons met him. For a long time he had not worn clothes; he did not live in a house, but lived among the tombs. ²⁸When he saw Jesus, he cried out and fell down before him; in a loud voice he shouted, "What have you to do with me, Jesus, son of the Most High God? I beg you, do not torment me!" ²⁹For he had ordered the unclean spirit to come out of the man. (It had taken hold of him many times, and he used to be bound with chains and shackles as a restraint, but he would break his bonds and be driven by the demon into deserted places.) ³⁰Then Jesus asked him, "What is your name?" He replied, "Legion," because many demons had entered him. ³¹And they pleaded with him not to order them to depart to the abyss.

³²A herd of many swine was feeding there on the hillside, and they pleaded with him to allow them to enter those swine; and he let them. ³³The demons came out of the man and entered the swine, and the herd rushed down the steep bank into the lake and was drowned. ³⁴When the swineherds saw what had happened, they ran away and reported the incident in the town and throughout the countryside. ³⁵People came out to see what had happened and, when they approached Jesus, they discovered the man from whom the demons had come out sitting at his feet. He was clothed and in his right mind, and they were seized with fear. ³⁶Those who witnessed it told them how the possessed man had been saved. ³⁷The entire population of the region of the Gerasenes asked Jesus to leave them because they were seized with great fear. So he got into a boat and returned. ³⁸The man from whom the demons had come out begged to remain with him, but he sent him away, saying, ³⁹"Return home and recount what God has done for you." The man went off and proclaimed throughout the whole town what Jesus had done for him.

Jairus's Daughter and the Woman with a Hemorrhage. ⁴⁰When Jesus returned, the crowd welcomed him, for they were all waiting for him. ⁴¹And a man named Jairus, an official of the synagogue, came forward. He fell at the feet of Jesus and begged him to come to his house, ⁴²because he had an only daughter, about twelve years old, and she was dying. As he went, the crowds almost crushed him. ⁴³And a woman afflicted with hemorrhages for twelve years, who [had spent her whole livelihood on doctors and] was unable to be cured by anyone, ⁴⁴came up behind him and touched the tassel on his cloak. Immediately her bleeding stopped. ⁴⁵Jesus then asked, "Who touched me?" While all were denying it, Peter said, "Master, the crowds are pushing and pressing in upon you." ⁴⁶But Jesus said, "Someone has touched me; for I know that power has gone out from me." ⁴⁷When the woman realized that she had not escaped notice, she came forward trembling. Falling down before him, she explained in the presence of all the people why she had touched him and how she had been healed immediately. ⁴⁸He said to her, "Daughter, your faith has saved you; go in peace."

⁴⁹While he was still speaking, someone from the synagogue official's house arrived and said, "Your daughter is dead; do not trouble the teacher any longer." ⁵⁰On hear-

ing this, Jesus answered him, "Do not be afraid; just have faith and she will be saved." [51]When he arrived at the house he allowed no one to enter with him except Peter and John and James, and the child's father and mother. [52]All were weeping and mourning for her, when he said, "Do not weep any longer, for she is not dead, but sleeping."

[53]And they ridiculed him, because they knew that she was dead. [54]But he took her by the hand and called to her, "Child, arise!" [55]Her breath returned and she immediately arose. He then directed that she should be given something to eat. [56]Her parents were astounded, and he instructed them to tell no one what had happened.

November 18

The Dedication of the Basilicas of Sts. Peter and Paul; St. Rose Philippine Duchesne

We cultivate a very small field for Christ, but we love it, knowing that God does not require great achievements but a heart that holds back nothing for self.

— St. Rose Philippine Duchesne

☐ EZEKIEL 28-29

The Prince of Tyre. 28:1 The word of the Lord came to me: [2]Son of man, say to the prince of Tyre: Thus says the Lord God:

Because you are haughty of heart,
     you say, "I am a god!
I sit on a god's throne
     in the heart of the sea!"
But you are a man, not a god;
     yet you pretend
     you are a god at heart!
[3]Oh yes, you are wiser than Daniel,
     nothing secret is too obscure for you!
[4]By your wisdom and intelligence
     you made yourself rich,
     filling your treasuries with gold and
          silver.
[5]Through your great wisdom in trading
     you heaped up riches for yourself—
     your heart is haughty because of
          your riches.
[6]Therefore thus says the Lord God:
Because you pretend you are a god at
     heart,

[7]Therefore, I will bring against you
     strangers, the most bloodthirsty of
          nations.
They shall draw their swords
     against your splendid wisdom,
     and violate your radiance.
[8]They shall thrust you down into the
          pit:
     you shall die a violent death
     in the heart of the sea.
[9]Then, face to face with your killers,
     will you still say, "I am a god"?
No, you are a man, not a god,
     handed over to those who slay you.
[10]You shall die the death of the
          uncircumcised
     handed over to strangers,
     for I have spoken—oracle of the
          Lord God.

[11]The word of the Lord came to me: [12]Son of man, raise a lament over the king of Tyre, and say to him: Thus says the Lord God:

You were a seal of perfection,
  full of wisdom, perfect in beauty.
¹³In Eden, the garden of God, you
    lived;
  precious stones of every kind were
    your covering:
Carnelian, topaz, and beryl,
  chrysolite, onyx, and jasper,
  sapphire, garnet, and emerald.
Their mounts and settings
  were wrought in gold,
  fashioned for you the day you were
    created.
¹⁴With a cherub I placed you;
  I put you on the holy mountain of
    God,
  where you walked among fiery stones.
¹⁵Blameless were you in your ways
  from the day you were created,
Until evil was found in you.
  ¹⁶Your commerce was full of
    lawlessness, and you sinned.
Therefore I banished you from the
    mountain of God;
  the cherub drove you out
  from among the fiery stones.
¹⁷Your heart had grown haughty
  because of your beauty;
You corrupted your wisdom
  because of your splendor.
I cast you to the ground,
  I made you a spectacle
  in the sight of kings.
¹⁸Because of the enormity of your guilt,
  and the perversity of your trade,
  you defiled your sanctuary.
I brought fire out of you;
  it devoured you;
I made you ashes on the ground
  in the eyes of all who see you.
¹⁹All the nations who knew you
  are appalled on account of you;
You have become a horror,
  never to be again.

Against Sidon. ²⁰The word of the LORD
came to me: ²¹Son of man, turn your face
toward Sidon and prophesy against it.
²²Thus says the Lord GOD:

Watch out! I am against you, Sidon;
  I will win glory for myself in your
    midst.
They shall know that I am the LORD,
  when I deliver judgment upon it
  and manifest my holiness in it.
²³I will send disease into it;
  blood will fill its streets,
Within it shall fall
  those slain by the sword
  raised against it on every side.
Then they shall know that I am the
    LORD.
²⁴No longer will there be a thorn that
    tears
  or a brier that scratches for the
    house of Israel
From the surrounding neighbors
  who despise them;
  thus they shall know that I am the
    LORD.

²⁵Thus says the Lord GOD: When I
gather the house of Israel from the peoples
among whom they are scattered, and I
manifest my holiness through them in the
sight of the nations, then they shall live on
the land I gave my servant Jacob. ²⁶They
shall dwell on it securely, building houses
and planting vineyards. They shall dwell
securely while I execute judgment on all
their neighbors who treated them with
contempt; then they shall know that I, the
LORD, am their God.

Egypt the Crocodile. 29:1 In the tenth
year, on the twelfth day of the tenth month,
the word of the LORD came to me: ²Son of
man, turn your face toward Pharaoh, king
of Egypt, and prophesy against him and
against all Egypt. ³Say to him: Thus says
the Lord GOD:

Pay attention! I am against you,
  Pharaoh, king of Egypt,

Great dragon crouching
    in the midst of the Nile,
Who says, "The Nile belongs to me;
    I made it myself!"
⁴I will put hooks in your jaws
    and make all the fish of your Nile
Cling to your scales;
    I will drag you up from your Nile,
With all the fish of your Nile
    clinging to your scales.
⁵I will hurl you into the wilderness,
    you and all the fish of your Nile.
You will fall into an open field,
    you will not be picked up or
        gathered together.
To the beasts of the earth
    and the birds of the sky
    I give you as food.
⁶Then all the inhabitants of Egypt
    will know that I am the LORD.
Because you were a staff of reeds
    for the house of Israel:
⁷When they took hold of you, you
        would splinter,
    throwing shoulders out of joint.
When they leaned on you, you would
        break,
    pitching them down headlong.
⁸Therefore thus says the Lord GOD:
Look! I am bringing the sword against
        you
    to cut off from you people and
        animals.
⁹The land of Egypt shall become a
        desolate waste;
    then they shall know that I am the
        LORD.
Because you said, "The Nile belongs
        to me;
    I made it!"
¹⁰Beware! I am against you
    and against your Nile.
I will turn the land of Egypt into ruins,
    into a dry, desolate waste,
From Migdol to Syene,
    up to the border of Ethiopia.
¹¹No foot shall pass through it,

no human being or beast cross it;
    it will remain uninhabited for forty
        years.
¹²I will make the land of Egypt the
        most desolate
    among desolate lands;
Its cities, the most deserted
    among deserted cities for forty years;
I will scatter the Egyptians among the
        nations
    and disperse them throughout other
        lands.
¹³But thus says the Lord GOD:
    At the end of forty years
I will gather the Egyptians
    from among the peoples
    where they are scattered;
¹⁴I will restore Egypt's fortunes,
    bringing them back to the land of
        Pathros,
    the land of their origin.
But there it will be a lowly kingdom,
    ¹⁵lower than any other kingdom,
    no longer able to set itself above the
        nations.
I will make them few in number,
    so they cannot rule other nations.
¹⁶No longer shall they be security
    for the house of Israel,
But a reminder of its iniquity
    in turning away to follow them.
Then they shall know that I am the
    Lord GOD.

Wages for Nebuchadnezzar. ¹⁷In the twenty-seventh year on the first day of the first month, the word of the LORD came to me: ¹⁸Son of man, Nebuchadnezzar, the king of Babylon, has made his army wage a hard campaign against Tyre; their heads grew bald, their shoulders rubbed raw, yet neither he nor his army received compensation from Tyre for all the effort they expended against it. ¹⁹Therefore thus says the Lord GOD: See! I am giving to Nebuchadnezzar, king of Babylon, the land of Egypt! He will carry off its wealth, plundering and pillaging whatever he can find to provide pay for his army. [20]As payment for his toil I give him the land of Egypt—oracle of the Lord GOD.

LUKE 9

The Mission of the Twelve. 9:1 He summoned the Twelve and gave them power and authority over all demons and to cure diseases, [2]and he sent them to proclaim the kingdom of God and to heal [the sick]. [3]He said to them, "Take nothing for the journey, neither walking stick, nor sack, nor food, nor money, and let no one take a second tunic. [4]Whatever house you enter, stay there and leave from there. [5]And as for those who do not welcome you, when you leave that town, shake the dust from your feet in testimony against them." [6]Then they set out and went from village to village proclaiming the good news and curing diseases everywhere.

Herod's Opinion of Jesus. [7]Herod the tetrarch heard about all that was happening, and he was greatly perplexed because some were saying, "John has been raised from the dead"; [8]others were saying, "Elijah has appeared"; still others, "One of the ancient prophets has arisen." [9]But Herod said, "John I beheaded. Who then is this about whom I hear such things?" And he kept trying to see him.

The Return of the Twelve and the Feeding of the Five Thousand. [10]When the apostles returned, they explained to him what they had done. He took them and withdrew in private to a town called Bethsaida. [11]The crowds, meanwhile, learned of this and followed him. He received them and spoke to them about the kingdom of God, and he healed those who needed to be cured. [12]As the day was drawing to a close, the Twelve approached him and said, "Dismiss the crowd so that they can go to the surrounding villages and farms

[21]On that day I will make a horn sprout for the house of Israel, and I will let you again open your mouth in their midst; then they shall know that I am the LORD.

and find lodging and provisions; for we are in a deserted place here." [13]He said to them, "Give them some food yourselves." They replied, "Five loaves and two fish are all we have, unless we ourselves go and buy food for all these people." [14]Now the men there numbered about five thousand. Then he said to his disciples, "Have them sit down in groups of [about] fifty." [15]They did so and made them all sit down. [16]Then taking the five loaves and the two fish, and looking up to heaven, he said the blessing over them, broke them, and gave them to the disciples to set before the crowd. [17]They all ate and were satisfied. And when the leftover fragments were picked up, they filled twelve wicker baskets.

Peter's Confession about Jesus. [18]Once when Jesus was praying in solitude, and the disciples were with him, he asked them, "Who do the crowds say that I am?" [19]They said in reply, "John the Baptist; others, Elijah; still others, 'One of the ancient prophets has arisen.'" [20]Then he said to them, "But who do you say that I am?" Peter said in reply, "The Messiah of God." [21]He rebuked them and directed them not to tell this to anyone.

The First Prediction of the Passion. [22]He said, "The Son of Man must suffer greatly and be rejected by the elders, the chief priests, and the scribes, and be killed and on the third day be raised."

The Conditions of Discipleship. [23]Then he said to all, "If anyone wishes to come after me, he must deny himself and take up his cross daily and follow me. [24]For whoever wishes to save his life will lose it, but whoever loses his life for my sake will save it. ²⁵What profit is there for one to gain the whole world yet lose or forfeit himself? ²⁶Whoever is ashamed of me and of my words, the Son of Man will be ashamed of when he comes in his glory and in the glory of the Father and of the holy angels. ²⁷Truly I say to you, there are some standing here who will not taste death until they see the kingdom of God."

The Transfiguration of Jesus. ²⁸About eight days after he said this, he took Peter, John, and James and went up the mountain to pray. ²⁹While he was praying his face changed in appearance and his clothing became dazzling white. ³⁰And behold, two men were conversing with him, Moses and Elijah, ³¹who appeared in glory and spoke of his exodus that he was going to accomplish in Jerusalem. ³²Peter and his companions had been overcome by sleep, but becoming fully awake, they saw his glory and the two men standing with him. ³³As they were about to part from him, Peter said to Jesus, "Master, it is good that we are here; let us make three tents, one for you, one for Moses, and one for Elijah." But he did not know what he was saying. ³⁴While he was still speaking, a cloud came and cast a shadow over them, and they became frightened when they entered the cloud. ³⁵Then from the cloud came a voice that said, "This is my chosen Son; listen to him." ³⁶After the voice had spoken, Jesus was found alone. They fell silent and did not at that time tell anyone what they had seen.

The Healing of a Boy with a Demon. ³⁷On the next day, when they came down from the mountain, a large crowd met him. ³⁸There was a man in the crowd who cried out, "Teacher, I beg you, look at my son; he is my only child. ³⁹For a spirit seizes him and he suddenly screams and it convulses him until he foams at the mouth; it releases him only with difficulty, wearing him out. ⁴⁰I begged your disciples to cast it out but they could not." ⁴¹Jesus said in reply, "O faithless and perverse generation, how long

will I be with you and endure you? Bring your son here." ⁴²As he was coming forward, the demon threw him to the ground in a convulsion; but Jesus rebuked the unclean spirit, healed the boy, and returned him to his father. ⁴³And all were astonished by the majesty of God.

The Second Prediction of the Passion. While they were all amazed at his every deed, he said to his disciples, ⁴⁴"Pay attention to what I am telling you. The Son of Man is to be handed over to men." ⁴⁵But they did not understand this saying; its meaning was hidden from them so that they should not understand it, and they were afraid to ask him about this saying.

The Greatest in the Kingdom. ⁴⁶An argument arose among the disciples about which of them was the greatest. ⁴⁷Jesus realized the intention of their hearts and took a child and placed it by his side ⁴⁸and said to them, "Whoever receives this child in my name receives me, and whoever receives me receives the one who sent me. For the one who is least among all of you is the one who is the greatest."

Another Exorcist. ⁴⁹Then John said in reply, "Master, we saw someone casting out demons in your name and we tried to prevent him because he does not follow in our company." ⁵⁰Jesus said to him, "Do not prevent him, for whoever is not against you is for you."

Departure for Jerusalem; Samaritan Inhospitality. ⁵¹When the days for his being taken up were fulfilled, he resolutely determined to journey to Jerusalem, ⁵²and he sent messengers ahead of him. On the way they entered a Samaritan village to prepare for his reception there, ⁵³but they would not welcome him because the destination of his journey was Jerusalem. ⁵⁴When the disciples James and John saw this they asked, "Lord, do you want us to call down fire from heaven to consume them?" ⁵⁵Jesus turned and rebuked them, ⁵⁶and they journeyed to another village.

The Would-be Followers of Jesus. [57]As they were proceeding on their journey someone said to him, "I will follow you wherever you go." [58]Jesus answered him, "Foxes have dens and birds of the sky have nests, but the Son of Man has nowhere to rest his head." [59]And to another he said, "Follow me." But he replied, "[Lord,] let me go first and bury my father." [60]But he answered him, "Let the dead bury their dead. But you, go and proclaim the kingdom of God." [61]And another said, "I will follow you, Lord, but first let me say farewell to my family at home." [62][To him] Jesus said, "No one who sets a hand to the plow and looks to what was left behind is fit for the kingdom of God."

November 19

St. Mechtild of Magdeburg

God says to the soul: "I come to my love as dew on the flowers."
— St. Mechtild of Magdeburg

☐ **EZEKIEL 30-31**

The Day of the Lord Against Egypt. 30:1 The word of the LORD came to me: [2]Son of man, prophesy and say: Thus says the Lord GOD:

Wail: "Alas the day!"
[3]Yes, a day approaches,
a day of the Lord approaches:
A day of dark cloud,
a time appointed for the nations.
[4]A sword will come against Egypt,
there will be anguish in Ethiopia,
When the slain fall in Egypt
when its hordes are seized,
its foundations razed.
[5]Ethiopia, Put, and Lud,
all the mixed rabble and Kub,
and the people of allied lands
shall fall by the sword with them.
[6]Thus says the LORD:
The pillars of Egypt shall fall,
and its proud strength sink;
From Migdol to Syene,
its people will fall by the sword—
oracle of the Lord GOD.
[7]It shall be the most desolate
among desolate lands,
Its cities the most ruined
among ruined cities.
[8]They shall know that I am the LORD,
when I set fire to Egypt,
and all its allies are shattered.
[9]On that day, messengers from me
will go forth in ships
to terrorize confident Ethiopia.
Anguish will be among them
on Egypt's day—it is certainly
coming!
[10]Thus says the Lord GOD:
I will put an end to Egypt's hordes
by the hand of Nebuchadnezzar,
king of Babylon:
[11]He and his army with him,
the most ruthless of nations,
will be brought in to devastate the
land.
They will draw their swords against
Egypt
and fill the land with the slain.
[12]Then I will dry up the streams of the
Nile,
and sell the land into evil hands;
By the hand of foreigners I will devastate

the land and everything in it.
I, the Lord, have spoken.
¹³Thus says the Lord God:
I will destroy idols,
and put an end to images in
Memphis.
There will never again be a prince
over the land of Egypt.
Instead, I will spread fear
throughout the land of Egypt.
¹⁴I will devastate Pathros,
set fire to Zoan,
and execute judgment against
Thebes.
¹⁵I will pour out my wrath on
Pelusium,
the fortress of Egypt,
and cut off the troops of Thebes.
¹⁶I will set fire to Egypt;
Pelusium will writhe in anguish,
Thebes will be breached,
and Memphis besieged in daylight.
¹⁷The warriors of On and Pi-beseth
will fall by the sword,
the cities taken captive.
¹⁸In Tahpanhes, the day will turn dark
when I break the scepter of Egypt
there
and put an end to its proud
strength.
Dark clouds will cover it,
and its women will go into captivity.
¹⁹I will execute judgment against Egypt
that they may know that I am the
Lord.

Pharaoh's Broken Arm. ²⁰On the seventh day of the first month in the eleventh year, the word of the Lord came to me: ²¹Son of man, I have broken the arm of Pharaoh, king of Egypt. See! It has not been immobilized for healing, nor set with a splint to make it strong enough to grasp a sword. ²²Therefore thus says the Lord God: See! I am coming against Pharaoh, king of Egypt. I will break both his arms, the strong one and the broken one, making

the sword fall from his hand. ²³I will scatter the Egyptians among the nations and disperse them throughout other lands. ²⁴I will, however, strengthen the arms of the king of Babylon and put my sword in his hand so he can bring it against Egypt for plunder and pillage. ²⁵When I strengthen the arms of the king of Babylon, and the arms of Pharaoh collapse, they shall know that I am the Lord, because I put my sword into the hand of the king of Babylon to wield against the land of Egypt. ²⁶When I scatter the Egyptians among the nations and disperse them throughout other lands, they shall know that I am the Lord.

Allegory of the Cedar. 31:1 On the first day of the third month in the eleventh year, the word of the Lord came to me: ²Son of man, say to Pharaoh, the king of Egypt, and to his hordes: In your greatness, whom do you resemble?

³Assyria! It is Assyria!
A cedar of Lebanon—
Beautiful branches,
thick shade,
Towering heights,
its crown in the clouds!
⁴The waters made it grow,
the deep made it tall,
Letting its currents flow
around the place it was planted,
Then sending its channels
to all the other trees of the field.
⁵Thereupon it towered in height
above all the trees in the field;
Its branches were numerous
and its boughs long,
Because of the many waters
sent to its shoots.
⁶In its branches nested
all the birds of the sky;
Under its boughs all the wild animals
gave birth,
And in its shade dwelt
all the mighty nations.

7It was magnificent in size
and in the length of its branches,
For its roots reached down
to the many waters.
8In the garden of God,
no cedars could rival it,
No juniper could equal its branches,
no plane tree match its boughs.
No tree in the garden of God
could match its beauty.
9I made it beautiful
with abundant foliage,
So that all the trees in Eden
were envious of it.
10Therefore, thus says the Lord GOD:
Because it was arrogant about its
height,
lifting its crown among the clouds
and exalting itself because of its size,
11I handed it over to a ruler of nations
to deal with it according to its evil.
I have cast it off,
12and foreigners have cut it down,
The most ruthless nations,
have hurled it on the mountains.
Its boughs fell into every valley
and its branches lay broken
in every ravine in the land.
All the peoples of the earth
departed from its shade
when it was hurled down.
13On its fallen trunk
sit all the birds of the sky;
Beside its fallen branches,
are found all the beasts of the field.
14This has happened so no well-watered
tree
will gain such lofty height,

or lift its crown to the clouds.
Not one of those fed by water
will tower in height over the rest.
For all of them are destined for death,
for the underworld, among mere
mortals,
with those who go down to the pit.
15Thus says the Lord GOD:
On the day it went down to Sheol,
I made the deep close up
in mourning for it.
I restrained the currents of the deep,
and held back the many waters.
I darkened Lebanon because of it,
and all the trees of the field
languished because of it.
16At the sound of its fall,
I made nations shudder,
When I cast it down to Sheol
with those who go down to the pit.
In the underworld
all the trees of Eden took comfort:
Lebanon's choicest and best,
all that were fed by the waters.
17They too will go down to Sheol,
to those slain by the sword,
Its allies who dwelt
in its shade among the nations.
18To whom among the trees of Eden
do you compare in glory and
greatness?
You will be brought down
with the trees of Eden to the
underworld,
And lie among the uncircumcised,
with those slain by the sword.
Such is Pharaoh and all his hordes—
oracle of the Lord GOD.

☐ LUKE 10

The Mission of the Seventy-two. 10:1 After this the Lord appointed seventy [-two] others whom he sent ahead of him in pairs to every town and place he intended to visit. 2He said to them, "The harvest is abundant but the laborers are few; so ask the master of the harvest to send out laborers for his harvest. 3Go on your way; behold, I am sending you like lambs among wolves. 4Carry no money bag, no sack, no sandals; and greet no one along the way. ⁵Into whatever house you enter, first say, 'Peace to this household.' ⁶If a peaceful person lives there, your peace will rest on him; but if not, it will return to you. ⁷Stay in the same house and eat and drink what is offered to you, for the laborer deserves his payment. Do not move about from one house to another. ⁸Whatever town you enter and they welcome you, eat what is set before you, ⁹cure the sick in it and say to them, 'The kingdom of God is at hand for you.' ¹⁰Whatever town you enter and they do not receive you, go out into the streets and say, ¹¹'The dust of your town that clings to our feet, even that we shake off against you.' Yet know this: the kingdom of God is at hand. ¹²I tell you, it will be more tolerable for Sodom on that day than for that town.

Reproaches to Unrepentant Towns. ¹³"Woe to you, Chorazin! Woe to you, Bethsaida! For if the mighty deeds done in your midst had been done in Tyre and Sidon, they would long ago have repented, sitting in sackcloth and ashes. ¹⁴But it will be more tolerable for Tyre and Sidon at the judgment than for you. ¹⁵And as for you, Capernaum, 'Will you be exalted to heaven? You will go down to the netherworld.'" ¹⁶Whoever listens to you listens to me. Whoever rejects you rejects me. And whoever rejects me rejects the one who sent me."

Return of the Seventy-two. ¹⁷The seventy [-two] returned rejoicing, and said, "Lord, even the demons are subject to us because of your name." ¹⁸Jesus said, "I have observed Satan fall like lightning from the sky. ¹⁹Behold, I have given you the power 'to tread upon serpents' and scorpions and upon the full force of the enemy and nothing will harm you. ²⁰Nevertheless, do not rejoice because the spirits are subject to you, but rejoice because your names are written in heaven."

Praise of the Father. ²¹At that very moment he rejoiced [in] the holy Spirit and said, "I give you praise, Father, Lord of heaven and earth, for although you have hidden these things from the wise and the learned you have revealed them to the childlike. Yes, Father, such has been your gracious will. ²²All things have been handed over to me by my Father. No one knows who the Son is except the Father, and who the Father is except the Son and anyone to whom the Son wishes to reveal him."

The Privileges of Discipleship. ²³Turning to the disciples in private he said, "Blessed are the eyes that see what you see. ²⁴For I say to you, many prophets and kings desired to see what you see, but did not see it, and to hear what you hear, but did not hear it."

The Greatest Commandment. ²⁵There was a scholar of the law who stood up to test him and said, "Teacher, what must I do to inherit eternal life?" ²⁶Jesus said to him, "What is written in the law? How do you read it?" ²⁷He said in reply, "You shall love the Lord, your God, with all your heart, with all your being, with all your strength, and with all your mind, and your neighbor as yourself." ²⁸He replied to him, "You have answered correctly; do this and you will live."

The Parable of the Good Samaritan. ²⁹But because he wished to justify himself, he said to Jesus, "And who is my neighbor?" ³⁰Jesus replied, "A man fell victim to robbers as he went down from Jerusalem to Jericho. They stripped and beat him and went off leaving him half-dead. ³¹A priest happened to be going down that road, but when he saw him, he passed by on the opposite side. ³²Likewise a Levite came to the place, and when he saw him, he passed by on the opposite side. ³³But a Samaritan traveler who came upon him was moved with compassion at the sight. ³⁴He approached the victim, poured oil and wine over his wounds and bandaged them. Then he lifted him up on his own animal, took him to an inn and cared for him. ³⁵The next day he took out two silver coins and gave them to the innkeeper with the instruction, 'Take care of him. If you spend more than what I have given you, I shall repay you on my way back.' ³⁶Which of these three, in your opinion, was neighbor to the robbers' victim?" ³⁷He answered, "The one who treated him with mercy." Jesus said to him, "Go and do likewise."

Martha and Mary. ³⁸As they continued their journey he entered a village where a woman whose name was Martha welcomed

him. ³⁹She had a sister named Mary [who] sat beside the Lord at his feet listening to him speak. ⁴⁰Martha, burdened with much serving, came to him and said, "Lord, do you not care that my sister has left me by myself to do the serving? Tell her to help me." ⁴¹The Lord said to her in reply, "Martha, Martha, you are anxious and worried about many things. ⁴²There is need of only one thing. Mary has chosen the better part and it will not be taken from her."

November 20

What mysteries are contained in the Our Father! How many and how great are they, collected briefly in words, but spiritually abundant in virtue! There is absolutely nothing passed over that is not comprehended in these our prayers and petitions — a summary of heavenly doctrine.

— ST. CYPRIAN OF CARTHAGE

☐ EZEKIEL 32–33

Lament over Pharaoh. 32:1 On the first day of the twelfth month in the twelfth year, the word of the LORD came to me: ²Son of man, utter a lament over Pharaoh, the king of Egypt, and say to him:

You liken yourself to a lion among
  nations,
 but you are like the monster in the
   sea!
Thrashing about in your streams,
 churning the water with your feet,
 polluting the streams.
³Thus says the Lord GOD:
I will cast my net over you
 by assembling many armies,
 and I will hoist you up in my mesh.
⁴I will hurl you onto the land,
 cast you into an open field.
I will make all the birds of the sky
 roost upon you,

The beasts of the whole earth
 gorge themselves on you.
⁵I will strew your flesh on the mountains,
 and fill the valleys with your corpse.
⁶I will drench the land,
 pouring out your blood on the
  mountain;
 filling up the ravines with you.
⁷When I extinguish you,
 I will cover the heavens
 and darken all its stars.
The sun I will cover with clouds;
 the moon will not give light.
⁸All the shining lights in the heavens
 I will darken over you;
I will spread darkness over your land—
 oracle of the Lord GOD.
⁹I will trouble the hearts
 of many peoples,
When I bring you captive
 among the nations,

to lands you do not know.
¹⁰I will fill many nations with horror;
 their kings will shudder at you,
 when I brandish my sword in their
 faces.
They will tremble violently
 fearing for their lives on the day of
 your fall.
¹¹For thus says the Lord God:
The sword of the king of Babylon
 will come against you.
¹²I will cut down your hordes
 with the swords of warriors,
 all of them, ruthless nations;
They will lay waste the glory of Egypt,
 and all its hordes will be destroyed.
¹³I will wipe out all the livestock
 from the banks of its many waters;
No human foot will disturb them
 again,
 no animal hoof stir them up.
¹⁴Then I will make their waters clear
 and their streams flow like oil—
 oracle of the Lord God.
¹⁵When I make Egypt a wasteland
 and the land destitute of everything,
When I strike down all its inhabitants
 they shall know that I am the Lord.
¹⁶This is the lamentation
 women of all nations will chant;
They will raise it over Egypt;
 over all its hordes they will chant
 it—
 oracle of the Lord God.

Another Lament over Egypt. ¹⁷On the fifteenth day of that month in the twelfth year, the word of the Lord came to me: ¹⁸Son of man, wail over the hordes of Egypt—
 you and the women of mighty
 nations—
Send them down to the underworld,
 with those who go down into the
 pit.
¹⁹Whom do you excel in beauty? Go
 down!

Be laid to rest with the
 uncircumcised!
²⁰Among those slain by the sword they
 will fall,
 for the sword has been appointed!
Seize Egypt and all its hordes.
²¹Out of Sheol the mighty warriors
 will speak to him and his allies:
Let them descend and lie down among
 the uncircumcised,
 those slain by the sword!
²²There is Assyria and all its company,
 around it are its graves,
 all of them slain, fallen by the
 sword.
²³The graves are set
 in the recesses of the pit;
Its company is assembled
 around its grave,
All of them slain, fallen by the sword,
 those who spread terror in the land
 of the living.
²⁴There is Elam and all its horde
 around its grave,
All of them slain, fallen by the sword;
 they descended uncircumcised
 into the underworld,
Those who spread their terror
 in the land of the living.
They bear their disgrace
 with those who go down into the
 pit.
²⁵Among the slain is set its bed,
 with all its horde around its grave;
All of them uncircumcised,
 slain by the sword
Because of the terror they spread
 in the land of the living.
They bear their disgrace
 with those who go down into the
 pit.
 Among the slain it is set!
²⁶There is Meshech and Tubal and all
 the hordes
 surrounding it with their graves.
All of them uncircumcised,
 slain by the sword

Because they spread their terror
    in the land of the living.
²⁷They do not rest with the warriors
    who fell in ancient times,
  who went down to Sheol fully armed.
Their swords were placed under their
    heads
    and their shields laid over their bones;
For there was terror of these warriors
    in the land of the living.
²⁸But as for you, among the
    uncircumcised
  you will be broken and laid to rest
    with those slain by the sword.
²⁹There is Edom, all its kings and
    princes,
  who, despite their might,
  are put with those slain by the
    sword.
They lie among the uncircumcised,
  with those who go down into the
    pit.
³⁰There are the generals of the north
    and all the Sidonians
Who have gone down with the slain,
  because of the terror their might
    inspired.
They lie uncircumcised
  with those slain by the sword,
And bear their shame with those
  who have gone down into the pit.
³¹When Pharaoh sees them,
  he will be consoled on behalf of all
    his hordes,
  slain by the sword—
Pharaoh and all his army—
  oracle of the Lord GOD.
³²I spread terror of him
  in the land of the living;
Now he is laid among the
    uncircumcised,
  with those slain by the sword—
Pharaoh and all his horde—
  oracle of the Lord GOD.

The Prophet as Sentinel. 33:1 The word of the LORD came to me: ²Son of man, speak to your people and tell them: When I bring the sword against a land, if the people of that land select one of their number as a sentinel for them, ³and the sentinel sees the sword coming against the land, he should blow the trumpet to warn the people. ⁴If they hear the trumpet but do not take the warning and a sword attacks and kills them, their blood will be on their own heads. ⁵They heard the trumpet blast but ignored the warning; their blood is on them. If they had heeded the warning, they could have escaped with their lives. ⁶If, however, the sentinel sees the sword coming and does not blow the trumpet, so that the sword attacks and takes someone's life, his life will be taken for his own sin, but I will hold the sentinel responsible for his blood.

⁷You, son of man—I have appointed you as a sentinel for the house of Israel; when you hear a word from my mouth, you must warn them for me. ⁸When I say to the wicked, "You wicked, you must die," and you do not speak up to warn the wicked about their ways, they shall die in their sins, but I will hold you responsible for their blood. ⁹If, however, you warn the wicked to turn from their ways, but they do not, then they shall die in their sins, but you shall save your life.

Individual Retribution. ¹⁰As for you, son of man, speak to the house of Israel: You people say, "Our crimes and our sins weigh us down; we are rotting away because of them. How can we survive?" ¹¹Answer them: As I live—oracle of the Lord GOD—I swear I take no pleasure in the death of the wicked, but rather that they turn from their ways and live. Turn, turn from your evil ways! Why should you die, house of Israel?

¹²As for you, son of man, say to your people: The justice of the just will not save them on the day they sin; the wickedness of the wicked will not bring about their downfall on the day they turn from their

wickedness. No, the just cannot save their lives on the day they sin. ¹³Even though I say to the just that they shall surely live, if they, relying on their justice, do wrong, none of their just deeds shall be remembered; because of the wrong they have done, they shall die. ¹⁴And though I say to the wicked that they shall die, if they turn away from sin and do what is just and right— ¹⁵returning pledges, restoring stolen goods, walking by statutes that bring life, doing nothing wrong—they shall surely live; they shall not die. ¹⁶None of the sins they committed shall be remembered against them. If they do what is right and just, they shall surely live.

¹⁷Your people say, "The way of the Lord is not fair!" But it is their way that is not fair. ¹⁸When the just turn away from justice and do wrong, they shall die for it. ¹⁹When the wicked turn away from wickedness and do what is right and just, because of this they shall live. ²⁰But still you say, "The way of the Lord is not fair!" I will judge each of you according to your ways, house of Israel.

The Survivor from Jerusalem. ²¹On the fifth day of the tenth month, in the twelfth year of our exile, the survivor came to me from Jerusalem and said, "The city is taken!" ²²The hand of the Lord had come upon me the evening before the survivor arrived and opened my mouth when he reached me in the morning. My mouth was opened, and I was mute no longer.

Those Left in Judah. ²³The word of the Lord came to me: ²⁴Son of man, these who live among the ruins in the land of Israel are saying: "Abraham was only one person, yet he was given possession of the land. Since we are many, the land must be given to us as our possession." ²⁵Therefore say to them: Thus says the Lord God: You eat on the mountains, you raise your eyes to your idols, you shed blood—yet you would keep possession of the land? ²⁶You rely on your swords, you commit abominations, each defiles his neighbor's wife—yet you would keep possession of the land? ²⁷Say this to them: Thus says the Lord God: As I live, those among the ruins shall fall by the sword; those in the open field I have made food for the wild beasts; and those in rocky hideouts and caves shall die by the plague. ²⁸I will make the land a desolate waste, so that its proud strength will come to an end, and the mountains of Israel shall be so desolate that no one will cross them. ²⁹Thus they shall know that I am the Lord, when I make the land a desolate waste because of all the abominations they committed.

Popular Misunderstanding. ³⁰As for you, son of man, your people are talking about you beside the walls and in the doorways of houses. They say to one another, "Let's go hear the latest word that comes from the Lord." ³¹My people come to you, gathering as a crowd and sitting in front of you to hear your words, but they will not act on them. Love songs are on their lips, but in their hearts they pursue dishonest gain. ³²For them you are only a singer of love songs, with a pleasant voice and a clever touch. They listen to your words, but they do not obey them. ³³But when it comes—and it is surely coming!—they shall know that there was a prophet among them.

☐ LUKE 11

The Lord's Prayer. 11:1 He was praying in a certain place, and when he had finished, one of his disciples said to him, "Lord, teach us to pray just as John taught his disciples." ²He said to them, "When you pray, say:

> Father, hallowed be your name,
>   your kingdom come.
>   ³Give us each day our daily bread
>   ⁴and forgive us our sins
>   for we ourselves forgive everyone in
>   debt to us,
>   and do not subject us to the final
>   test."

Further Teachings on Prayer. ⁵And he said to them, "Suppose one of you has a friend to whom he goes at midnight and says, 'Friend, lend me three loaves of bread, ⁶for a friend of mine has arrived at my house from a journey and I have nothing to offer him,' ⁷and he says in reply from within, 'Do not bother me; the door has already been locked and my children and I are already in bed. I cannot get up to give you anything.' ⁸I tell you, if he does not get up to give him the loaves because of their friendship, he will get up to give him whatever he needs because of his persistence.

The Answer to Prayer. ⁹"And I tell you, ask and you will receive; seek and you will find; knock and the door will be opened to you. ¹⁰For everyone who asks, receives; and the one who seeks, finds; and to the one who knocks, the door will be opened. ¹¹What father among you would hand his son a snake when he asks for a fish? ¹²Or hand him a scorpion when he asks for an egg? ¹³If you then, who are wicked, know how to give good gifts to your children, how much more will the Father in heaven give the holy Spirit to those who ask him?"

Jesus and Beelzebul. ¹⁴He was driving out a demon [that was] mute, and when the demon had gone out, the mute person spoke and the crowds were amazed. ¹⁵Some of them said, "By the power of Beelzebul, the prince of demons, he drives out demons." ¹⁶Others, to test him, asked him for a sign from heaven. ¹⁷But he knew their thoughts and said to them, "Every kingdom divided against itself will be laid waste and house will fall against house. ¹⁸And if Satan is divided against himself, how will his kingdom stand? For you say that it is by Beelzebul that I drive out demons. ¹⁹If I, then, drive out demons by Beelzebul, by whom do your own people drive them out? Therefore they will be your judges. ²⁰But if it is by the finger of God that [I] drive out demons, then the kingdom of God has come upon you. ²¹When a strong man fully armed guards his palace, his possessions are safe. ²²But when one stronger than he attacks and overcomes him, he takes away the armor on which he relied and distributes the spoils. ²³Whoever is not with me is against me, and whoever does not gather with me scatters.

The Return of the Unclean Spirit. ²⁴"When an unclean spirit goes out of someone, it roams through arid regions searching for rest but, finding none, it says, 'I shall return to my home from which I came.' ²⁵But upon returning, it finds it swept clean and put in order. ²⁶Then it goes and brings back seven other spirits more wicked than itself who move in and dwell there, and the last condition of that person is worse than the first."

True Blessedness. ²⁷While he was speaking, a woman from the crowd called out and said to him, "Blessed is the womb that carried you and the breasts at which you nursed." ²⁸He replied, "Rather, blessed are those who hear the word of God and observe it."

The Demand for a Sign. ²⁹While still more people gathered in the crowd, he said to them, "This generation is an evil generation; it seeks a sign, but no sign will be given it, except the sign of Jonah. [30]Just as Jonah became a sign to the Ninevites, so will the Son of Man be to this generation. [31]At the judgment the queen of the south will rise with the men of this generation and she will condemn them, because she came from the ends of the earth to hear the wisdom of Solomon, and there is something greater than Solomon here. [32]At the judgment the men of Nineveh will arise with this generation and condemn it, because at the preaching of Jonah they repented, and there is something greater than Jonah here.

The Simile of Light. [33]"No one who lights a lamp hides it away or places it [under a bushel basket], but on a lampstand so that those who enter might see the light. [34]The lamp of the body is your eye. When your eye is sound, then your whole body is filled with light, but when it is bad, then your body is in darkness. [35]Take care, then, that the light in you not become darkness. [36]If your whole body is full of light, and no part of it is in darkness, then it will be as full of light as a lamp illuminating you with its brightness."

Denunciation of the Pharisees and Scholars of the Law. [37]After he had spoken, a Pharisee invited him to dine at his home. He entered and reclined at table to eat. [38]The Pharisee was amazed to see that he did not observe the prescribed washing before the meal. [39]The Lord said to him, "Oh you Pharisees! Although you cleanse the outside of the cup and the dish, inside you are filled with plunder and evil. [40]You fools! Did not the maker of the outside also make the inside? [41]But as to what is within, give alms, and behold, everything will be clean for you. [42]Woe to you Pharisees! You pay tithes of mint and of rue and of every garden herb, but you pay no attention to judgment and to love for God. These you should have done, without overlooking the others. [43]Woe to you Pharisees! You love the seat of honor in synagogues and greetings in marketplaces. [44]Woe to you! You are like unseen graves over which people unknowingly walk."

[45]Then one of the scholars of the law said to him in reply, "Teacher, by saying this you are insulting us too." [46]And he said, "Woe also to you scholars of the law! You impose on people burdens hard to carry, but you yourselves do not lift one finger to touch them. [47]Woe to you! You build the memorials of the prophets whom your ancestors killed. [48]Consequently, you bear witness and give consent to the deeds of your ancestors, for they killed them and you do the building. [49]Therefore, the wisdom of God said, 'I will send to them prophets and apostles; some of them they will kill and persecute' [50]in order that this generation might be charged with the blood of all the prophets shed since the foundation of the world, [51]from the blood of Abel to the blood of Zechariah who died between the altar and the temple building. Yes, I tell you, this generation will be charged with their blood! [52]Woe to you, scholars of the law! You have taken away the key of knowledge. You yourselves did not enter and you stopped those trying to enter." [53]When he left, the scribes and Pharisees began to act with hostility toward him and to interrogate him about many things, [54]for they were plotting to catch him at something he might say.

November 21

The Presentation of Mary

It was fitting for the Queen of virgins, by a singular privilege of sanctity, to lead a life entirely free from sin, so that while she ministered to the Destroyer of death and sin, she should obtain the gift of life and righteousness for all.

— St. Bernard of Clairvaux

☐ EZEKIEL 34-35

Parable of the Shepherds. 34:1 The word of the Lord came to me: ²Son of man, prophesy against the shepherds of Israel. Prophesy and say to them: To the shepherds, thus says the Lord God: Woe to the shepherds of Israel who have been pasturing themselves! Should not shepherds pasture the flock? ³You consumed milk, wore wool, and slaughtered fatlings, but the flock you did not pasture. ⁴You did not strengthen the weak nor heal the sick nor bind up the injured. You did not bring back the stray or seek the lost but ruled them harshly and brutally. ⁵So they were scattered for lack of a shepherd, and became food for all the wild beasts. They were scattered ⁶and wandered over all the mountains and high hills; over the entire surface of the earth my sheep were scattered. No one looked after them or searched for them.

⁷Therefore, shepherds, hear the word of the Lord: ⁸As I live—oracle of the Lord God—because my sheep became plunder, because my sheep became food for wild beasts, for lack of a shepherd, because my shepherds did not look after my sheep, but pastured themselves and did not pasture my sheep, ⁹therefore, shepherds, hear the word of the Lord: ¹⁰Thus says the Lord God: Look! I am coming against these shepherds. I will take my sheep out of their hand and put a stop to their shepherding my flock, so that these shepherds will no longer pasture them. I will deliver my flock from their mouths so it will not become their food.

¹¹For thus says the Lord God: Look! I myself will search for my sheep and examine them. ¹²As a shepherd examines his flock while he himself is among his scattered sheep, so will I examine my sheep. I will deliver them from every place where they were scattered on the day of dark clouds. ¹³I will lead them out from among the peoples and gather them from the lands; I will bring them back to their own country and pasture them upon the mountains of Israel, in the ravines and every inhabited place in the land. ¹⁴In good pastures I will pasture them; on the mountain heights of Israel will be their grazing land. There they will lie down on good grazing ground; in rich pastures they will be pastured on the mountains of Israel. ¹⁵I myself will pasture my sheep; I myself will give them rest—oracle of the Lord God. ¹⁶The lost I will search out, the strays I will bring back, the injured I will bind up, and the sick I will heal; but the sleek and the strong I will destroy. I will shepherd them in judgment.

Separation of the Sheep. ¹⁷As for you, my flock, thus says the Lord God: I will judge between one sheep and another, between rams and goats. ¹⁸Was it not enough for you to graze on the best pasture, that you had to trample the rest of your pastures with your hooves? Or to drink the clearest water, that you had to pollute the rest with your hooves? ¹⁹Thus my flock had to graze on what your hooves had trampled and drink what your hooves had polluted.

²⁰Therefore thus says the Lord GOD: Now I will judge between the fat and the lean. ²¹Because you push with flank and shoulder, and butt all the weak sheep with your horns until you drive them off, ²²I will save my flock so they can no longer be plundered; I will judge between one sheep and another. ²³I will appoint one shepherd over them to pasture them, my servant David; he shall pasture them and be their shepherd. ²⁴I, the LORD, will be their God, and my servant David will be prince in their midst. I, the LORD, have spoken.

²⁵I will make a covenant of peace with them and rid the country of wild beasts so they will dwell securely in the wilderness and sleep in the forests. ²⁶I will settle them around my hill and send rain in its season, the blessing of abundant rain. ²⁷The trees of the field shall bear their fruits, and the land its crops, and they shall dwell securely on their own soil. They shall know that I am the LORD when I break the bars of their yoke and deliver them from the power of those who enslaved them. ²⁸They shall no longer be plundered by the nations nor will wild beasts devour them, but they shall dwell securely, with no one to frighten them. ²⁹I will prepare for them peaceful fields for planting so they are never again swept away by famine in the land or bear taunts from the nations. ³⁰Thus they shall know that I, the LORD, their God, am with them, and that they are my people, the house of Israel—oracle of the Lord GOD. ³¹Yes, you are my flock: you people are the flock of my pasture, and I am your God—oracle of the Lord GOD.

Against Edom. 35:1 The word of the LORD came to me: ²Son of man, set your face against Mount Seir and prophesy against it. ³Say to it: Thus says the Lord GOD: Watch out! I am against you, Mount Seir. I will stretch out my hand against you and turn you into a desolate waste. ⁴Your cities I will turn into ruins, and you shall be a desolation; then you shall know that I am the LORD.

⁵Because you nursed a long-standing hatred and handed the Israelites over to the sword at the time of their collapse, at the time of their final punishment, ⁶therefore, as I live—oracle of the Lord GOD—you are guilty of blood, and blood, I swear, shall pursue you. ⁷I will make Mount Seir a desolate waste and cut off from it anyone who travels across it and back. ⁸I will fill its mountains with the slain; those slain by the sword shall fall on your hills, into your valleys and all your ravines.

⁹I will make you a desolation forever,
   your cities will not be inhabited,
   and you shall know that I am the
      LORD.

¹⁰Because you said: The two nations and the two lands belong to me; let us take possession of them—although the LORD was there—¹¹therefore, as I live—oracle of the Lord GOD—I will deal with you according to the anger and envy you dealt out to them in your hatred, and I will make myself known to them when I execute judgment on you, ¹²then you shall know that I am the LORD.

I have heard all the insults you spoke against the mountains of Israel, saying: They are desolate; they have been given to us to devour. ¹³You boasted against me with your mouths and used insolent words against me. I heard everything! ¹⁴Thus says the Lord GOD: Because you rejoiced that the whole land was desolate, so I will do to you. ¹⁵As you rejoiced over the devastation of the heritage of the house of Israel, the same I will do to you: you will become a ruin, Mount Seir, and the whole of Edom, all of it! Then they shall know that I am the LORD.

☐ LUKE 12

The Leaven of the Pharisees. 12:1 Meanwhile, so many people were crowding together that they were trampling one another underfoot. He began to speak, first to his disciples, "Beware of the leaven—that is, the hypocrisy—of the Pharisees.

Courage under Persecution. 2"There is nothing concealed that will not be revealed, nor secret that will not be known. 3Therefore whatever you have said in the darkness will be heard in the light, and what you have whispered behind closed doors will be proclaimed on the housetops. 4I tell you, my friends, do not be afraid of those who kill the body but after that can do no more. 5I shall show you whom to fear. Be afraid of the one who after killing has the power to cast into Gehenna; yes, I tell you, be afraid of that one. 6Are not five sparrows sold for two small coins? Yet not one of them has escaped the notice of God. 7Even the hairs of your head have all been counted. Do not be afraid. You are worth more than many sparrows. 8I tell you, everyone who acknowledges me before others the Son of Man will acknowledge before the angels of God. 9But whoever denies me before others will be denied before the angels of God.

Sayings about the Holy Spirit. 10"Everyone who speaks a word against the Son of Man will be forgiven, but the one who blasphemes against the holy Spirit will not be forgiven. 11When they take you before synagogues and before rulers and authorities, do not worry about how or what your defense will be or about what you are to say. 12For the holy Spirit will teach you at that moment what you should say."

Saying against Greed. 13Someone in the crowd said to him, "Teacher, tell my brother to share the inheritance with me." 14He replied to him, "Friend, who appointed me as your judge and arbitrator?" 15Then he said to the crowd, "Take care to guard against all greed, for though one may be rich, one's life does not consist of possessions."

Parable of the Rich Fool. 16Then he told them a parable. "There was a rich man whose land produced a bountiful harvest. 17He asked himself, 'What shall I do, for I do not have space to store my harvest?' 18And he said, 'This is what I shall do: I shall tear down my barns and build larger ones. There I shall store all my grain and other goods 19and I shall say to myself, "Now as for you, you have so many good things stored up for many years, rest, eat, drink, be merry!" ' 20But God said to him, 'You fool, this night your life will be demanded of you; and the things you have prepared, to whom will they belong?' 21Thus will it be for the one who stores up treasure for himself but is not rich in what matters to God."

Dependence on God. 22He said to [his] disciples, "Therefore I tell you, do not worry about your life and what you will eat, or about your body and what you will wear. 23For life is more than food and the body more than clothing. 24Notice the ravens: they do not sow or reap; they have neither storehouse nor barn, yet God feeds them. How much more important are you than birds! 25Can any of you by worrying add a moment to your lifespan? 26If even the smallest things are beyond your control, why are you anxious about the rest? 27Notice how the flowers grow. They do not toil or spin. But I tell you, not even Solomon in all his splendor was dressed like one of them. 28If God so clothes the grass in the field that grows today and is thrown into the oven tomorrow, will he not much more provide for you, O you of little faith? 29As for you, do not seek what you are to eat and what you are to drink, and do not worry anymore. 30All the nations of the world seek for these things, and your Father knows that you need them. 31Instead, seek his kingdom, and these other things will be given you besides. ³²Do not be afraid any longer, little flock, for your Father is pleased to give you the kingdom. ³³Sell your belongings and give alms. Provide money bags for yourselves that do not wear out, an inexhaustible treasure in heaven that no thief can reach nor moth destroy. ³⁴For where your treasure is, there also will your heart be.

Vigilant and Faithful Servants. ³⁵"Gird your loins and light your lamps ³⁶and be like servants who await their master's return from a wedding, ready to open immediately when he comes and knocks. ³⁷Blessed are those servants whom the master finds vigilant on his arrival. Amen, I say to you, he will gird himself, have them recline at table, and proceed to wait on them. ³⁸And should he come in the second or third watch and find them prepared in this way, blessed are those servants. ³⁹Be sure of this: if the master of the house had known the hour when the thief was coming, he would not have let his house be broken into. ⁴⁰You also must be prepared, for at an hour you do not expect, the Son of Man will come."

⁴¹Then Peter said, "Lord, is this parable meant for us or for everyone?" ⁴²And the Lord replied, "Who, then, is the faithful and prudent steward whom the master will put in charge of his servants to distribute [the] food allowance at the proper time? ⁴³Blessed is that servant whom his master on arrival finds doing so. ⁴⁴Truly, I say to you, he will put him in charge of all his property. ⁴⁵But if that servant says to himself, 'My master is delayed in coming,' and begins to beat the menservants and the maidservants, to eat and drink and get drunk, ⁴⁶then that servant's master will come on an unexpected day and at an unknown hour and will punish him severely and assign him a place with the unfaithful. ⁴⁷That servant who knew his master's

will but did not make preparations nor act in accord with his will shall be beaten severely; ⁴⁸and the servant who was ignorant of his master's will but acted in a way deserving of a severe beating shall be beaten only lightly. Much will be required of the person entrusted with much, and still more will be demanded of the person entrusted with more.

Jesus: A Cause of Division. ⁴⁹"I have come to set the earth on fire, and how I wish it were already blazing! ⁵⁰There is a baptism with which I must be baptized, and how great is my anguish until it is accomplished! ⁵¹Do you think that I have come to establish peace on the earth? No, I tell you, but rather division. ⁵²From now on a household of five will be divided, three against two and two against three; ⁵³a father will be divided against his son and a son against his father, a mother against her daughter and a daughter against her mother, a mother-in-law against her daughter-in-law and a daughter-in-law against her mother-in-law."

Signs of the Times. ⁵⁴He also said to the crowds, "When you see [a] cloud rising in the west you say immediately that it is going to rain—and so it does; ⁵⁵and when you notice that the wind is blowing from the south you say that it is going to be hot—and so it is. ⁵⁶You hypocrites! You know how to interpret the appearance of the earth and the sky; why do you not know how to interpret the present time?

Settlement with an Opponent. ⁵⁷"Why do you not judge for yourselves what is right? ⁵⁸If you are to go with your opponent before a magistrate, make an effort to settle the matter on the way; otherwise your opponent will turn you over to the judge, and the judge hand you over to the constable, and the constable throw you into prison. ⁵⁹I say to you, you will not be released until you have paid the last penny."

November 22

St. Cecilia

The mere renunciation of sins is not sufficient for the salvation of penitents, but fruits worthy of repentance are also required of them.

— St. Basil the Great

☐ EZEKIEL 36–37

Regeneration of the Land. 36:1 As for you, son of man, prophesy to the mountains of Israel and say: Mountains of Israel, hear the word of the LORD! [2]Thus says the Lord GOD: Because the enemy said about you, "Ha! the ancient heights have become our possession," [3]therefore prophesy and say: Thus says the Lord GOD: because you have been ridiculed and hounded on all sides for becoming a possession for the remaining nations and have become a byword and a popular jeer, [4]therefore, mountains of Israel, hear the word of the Lord GOD: Thus says the Lord GOD to the mountains and hills, to the ravines and valleys, to the desolate ruins and abandoned cities, plundered and mocked by the nations remaining around you: [5]therefore thus says the Lord GOD: Truly, with burning jealousy I speak against the remaining nations and against Edom; they all took possession of my land for plunder with wholehearted joy and utter contempt. [6]Therefore, prophesy concerning the land of Israel and say to the mountains and hills, to the ravines and valleys: Thus says the Lord GOD: See! in my jealous fury I speak, because you endured the reproach of the nations. [7]Therefore, thus says the Lord GOD: I raise my hand and swear: the nations around you shall bear their own reproach.

[8]But you, mountains of Israel, you will sprout branches and bear fruit for my people Israel, for they are coming soon. [9]Look! I am for you! I will turn my face toward you; you will be plowed and planted. [10]Upon you I will multiply the whole house of Israel; cities shall be resettled and ruins rebuilt. [11]Upon you I will multiply people and animals so they can multiply and be fruitful. I will resettle you as in the past, and make you more prosperous than at your beginning; then you shall know that I am the LORD.

[12]Upon you I will have them walk, my people Israel. They shall possess you, and you shall be their heritage. Never again shall you rob them of their children.

[13]Thus says the Lord GOD: Because they say of you, "You devour your own people, you rob your nation of its children," [14]therefore, you shall never again devour your people or rob your nation of its children—oracle of the Lord GOD. [15]I will no longer make you listen to the reproach of nations. You will never again endure insults from the peoples. Never again shall you rob your nation of its children—oracle of the Lord GOD.

Regeneration of the People. [16]The word of the LORD came to me: [17]Son of man, when the house of Israel lived in its land, they defiled it with their behavior and their deeds. In my sight their behavior was like the impurity of a woman in menstruation. [18]So I poured out my fury upon them for the blood they poured out on the ground and for the idols with which they defiled it. [19]I scattered them among the nations, and they were dispersed through other lands; according to their behavior and their deeds I carried out judgment against them. [20]But when they came to the nations, where they went, they desecrated my holy name, for people said of them: "These are the people of the LORD, yet they had to leave their land." ²¹So I relented because of my holy name which the house of Israel desecrated among the nations to which they came. ²²Therefore say to the house of Israel: Thus says the Lord GOD: Not for your sake do I act, house of Israel, but for the sake of my holy name, which you desecrated among the nations to which you came. ²³But I will show the holiness of my great name, desecrated among the nations, in whose midst you desecrated it. Then the nations shall know that I am the LORD—oracle of the Lord GOD—when through you I show my holiness before their very eyes. ²⁴I will take you away from among the nations, gather you from all the lands, and bring you back to your own soil. ²⁵I will sprinkle clean water over you to make you clean; from all your impurities and from all your idols I will cleanse you. ²⁶I will give you a new heart, and a new spirit I will put within you. I will remove the heart of stone from your flesh and give you a heart of flesh. ²⁷I will put my spirit within you so that you walk in my statutes, observe my ordinances, and keep them. ²⁸You will live in the land I gave to your ancestors; you will be my people, and I will be your God. ²⁹I will deliver you from all your impurities. I will summon the grain and make it plentiful; I will not send famine against you. ³⁰I will increase the fruit on your trees and the crops in your fields so that you no longer endure reproach from the nations because of famine. ³¹Then you will remember your evil behavior and your deeds that were not good; you will loathe yourselves for your sins and your abominations. ³²Not for your sake do I act—oracle of the Lord GOD. Let this be known to you! Be ashamed and humbled because of your behavior, house of Israel.

³³Thus says the Lord GOD: When I cleanse you of all your guilt, I will resettle the cities and the ruins will be rebuilt. ³⁴The desolate land will be tilled—once a wasteland in the eyes of every passerby. ³⁵They will say,

"This once-desolate land has become like the garden of Eden. The cities once ruined, laid waste and destroyed, are now resettled and fortified." ³⁶Then the surrounding nations that remain shall know that I, the LORD, have rebuilt what was destroyed and replanted what was desolate. I, the LORD, have spoken: I will do it. ³⁷Thus says the Lord GOD: This also I will be persuaded to do for the house of Israel: to multiply them like sheep. ³⁸Like sheep for sacrifice, like the sheep of Jerusalem on its feast days, the ruined cities shall be filled with flocks of people; then they shall know that I am the LORD.

Vision of the Dry Bones. 37:1 The hand of the LORD came upon me, and he led me out in the spirit of the LORD and set me in the center of the broad valley. It was filled with bones. ²He made me walk among them in every direction. So many lay on the surface of the valley! How dry they were! ³He asked me: Son of man, can these bones come back to life? "Lord GOD," I answered, "you alone know that." ⁴Then he said to me: Prophesy over these bones, and say to them: Dry bones, hear the word of the LORD! ⁵Thus says the Lord GOD to these bones: Listen! I will make breath enter you so you may come to life. ⁶I will put sinews on you, make flesh grow over you, cover you with skin, and put breath into you so you may come to life. Then you shall know that I am the LORD. ⁷I prophesied as I had been commanded. A sound started up, as I was prophesying, rattling like thunder. The bones came together, bone joining to bone. ⁸As I watched, sinews appeared on them, flesh grew over them, skin covered them on top, but there was no breath in them. ⁹Then he said to me: Prophesy to the breath, prophesy, son of man! Say to the breath: Thus says the Lord GOD: From the four winds come, O breath, and breathe into these slain that they may come to life. ¹⁰I prophesied as he commanded me, and the breath entered them; they came to life and stood on their feet, a vast army. [11]He said to me: Son of man, these bones are the whole house of Israel! They are saying, "Our bones are dried up, our hope is lost, and we are cut off." [12]Therefore, prophesy and say to them: Thus says the Lord GOD: Look! I am going to open your graves; I will make you come up out of your graves, my people, and bring you back to the land of Israel. [13]You shall know that I am the LORD, when I open your graves and make you come up out of them, my people! [14]I will put my spirit in you that you may come to life, and I will settle you in your land. Then you shall know that I am the LORD. I have spoken; I will do it—oracle of the LORD.

The Two Sticks. [15]Thus the word of the LORD came to me: [16]As for you, son of man, take one stick and write on it, "Judah and those Israelites associated with it." Then take another stick and write on it: "Joseph, Ephraim's stick, and the whole house of Israel associated with it." [17]Join the two sticks together so they become one stick in your hand. [18]When your people ask you, "Will you not tell us what you mean by all this?" [19]answer them: Thus says the Lord GOD: I will take the stick of Joseph, now in Ephraim's hand, and the tribes of Israel associated with it, and join to it the stick of Judah, making them one stick; they shall become one in my hand. [20]The sticks on which you write, you must hold in your hand in their sight. [21]Say to them: Thus says the Lord GOD: I will soon take the Israelites from among the nations to which they have gone and gather them from all around to bring them back to their land. [22]I will make them one nation in the land, upon the mountains of Israel, and there shall be one king for them all. They shall never again be two nations, never again be divided into two kingdoms.

[23]No longer shall they defile themselves with their idols, their abominations, and all their transgressions. I will deliver them from all their apostasy through which they sinned. I will cleanse them so that they will be my people, and I will be their God. [24]David my servant shall be king over them; they shall all have one shepherd. They shall walk in my ordinances, observe my statutes, and keep them. [25]They shall live on the land I gave to Jacob my servant, the land where their ancestors lived; they shall live on it always, they, their children, and their children's children, with David my servant as their prince forever. [26]I will make a covenant of peace with them; it shall be an everlasting covenant with them. I will multiply them and put my sanctuary among them forever. [27]My dwelling shall be with them; I will be their God, and they will be my people. [28]Then the nations shall know that I, the LORD, make Israel holy, by putting my sanctuary among them forever.

☐ LUKE 13

A Call to Repentance. 13:1 At that time some people who were present there told him about the Galileans whose blood Pilate had mingled with the blood of their sacrifices. [2]He said to them in reply, "Do you think that because these Galileans suffered in this way they were greater sinners than all other Galileans? [3]By no means! But I tell you, if you do not repent, you will all perish as they did! [4]Or those eighteen people who were killed when the tower at Siloam fell on them—do you think they were more guilty than everyone else who lived in Jerusalem? [5]By no means! But I tell you, if you do not repent, you will all perish as they did!"

The Parable of the Barren Fig Tree. [6]And he told them this parable: "There once was a person who had a fig tree planted in his orchard, and when he came in search of fruit on it but found none, [7]he said to the gardener, 'For three years now I have come in search of fruit on this fig tree but have found none. [So] cut it down. Why should it exhaust the soil?' [8]He said to him in reply, 'Sir, leave it for this year also, and I shall cultivate the ground around it and fertilize it; [9]it may bear fruit in the future. If not you can cut it down.'"

Cure of a Crippled Woman on the Sabbath. [10]He was teaching in a synagogue on the sabbath. [11]And a woman was there who for eighteen years had been crippled by a spirit; she was bent over, completely incapable of standing erect. [12]When Jesus saw her, he called to her and said, "Woman, you are set free of your infirmity." [13]He laid his hands on her, and she at once stood up straight and glorified God. [14]But the leader of the synagogue, indignant that Jesus had cured on the sabbath, said to the crowd in reply, "There are six days when work should be done. Come on those days to be cured, not on the sabbath day." [15]The Lord said to him in reply, "Hypocrites! Does not each one of you on the sabbath untie his ox or his ass from the manger and lead it out for watering? [16]This daughter of Abraham, whom Satan has bound for eighteen years now, ought she not to have been set free on the sabbath day from this bondage?" [17]When he said this, all his adversaries were humiliated; and the whole crowd rejoiced at all the splendid deeds done by him.

The Parable of the Mustard Seed. [18]Then he said, "What is the kingdom of God like? To what can I compare it? [19]It is like a mustard seed that a person took and planted in the garden. When it was fully grown, it became a large bush and 'the birds of the sky dwelt in its branches.'"

The Parable of the Yeast. [20]Again he said, "To what shall I compare the kingdom of God? [21]It is like yeast that a woman took and mixed [in] with three measures of wheat flour until the whole batch of dough was leavened."

The Narrow Door; Salvation and Rejection. [22]He passed through towns and villages, teaching as he went and making his way to Jerusalem. [23]Someone asked him, "Lord, will only a few people be saved?" He answered them, [24]"Strive to enter through the narrow door, for many, I tell you, will attempt to enter but will not be strong enough. [25]After the master of the house has arisen and locked the door, then will you stand outside knocking and saying, 'Lord, open the door for us.' He will say to you in reply, 'I do not know where you are from.' [26]And you will say, 'We ate and drank in your company and you taught in our streets.' [27]Then he will say to you, 'I do not know where [you] are from. Depart from me, all you evildoers!' [28]And there will be wailing and grinding of teeth when you see Abraham, Isaac, and Jacob and all the prophets in the kingdom of God and you yourselves cast out. [29]And people will come from the east and the west and from the north and the south and will recline at table in the kingdom of God. [30]For behold, some are last who will be first, and some are first who will be last."

Herod's Desire to Kill Jesus. [31]At that time some Pharisees came to him and said, "Go away, leave this area because Herod wants to kill you." [32]He replied, "Go and tell that fox, 'Behold, I cast out demons and I perform healings today and tomorrow, and on the third day I accomplish my purpose. [33]Yet I must continue on my way today, tomorrow, and the following day, for it is impossible that a prophet should die outside of Jerusalem.'

The Lament over Jerusalem. [34]"Jerusalem, Jerusalem, you who kill the prophets and stone those sent to you, how many times I yearned to gather your children together as a hen gathers her brood under her wings, but you were unwilling! [35]Behold, your house will be abandoned. [But] I tell you, you will not see me until [the time comes when] you say, 'Blessed is he who comes in the name of the Lord.'"

November 23

Pope St. Clement I; St. Columban; Blessed Miguel Augustin Pro

We ought to speak, shout out against injustices, with confidence and without fear. We proclaim the principles of the Church, the reign of love, without forgetting that it is also a reign of justice.

— BLESSED MIGUEL AUGUSTIN PRO

☐ EZEKIEL 38-39

First Prophecy Against Gog. 38:1 The word of the LORD came to me: ²Son of man, turn your face against Gog of the land of Magog, the chief prince of Meshech and Tubal, and prophesy against him. ³Say: Thus says the Lord GOD: See! I am coming against you, Gog, chief prince of Meshech and Tubal. ⁴I will turn you around and put hooks in your jaws to lead you out with all your army, horses and riders, all well armed, a great company, all of them with bucklers and shields, carrying swords: ⁵Persia, Cush, and Put with them, all with shields and helmets; ⁶Gomer and all its troops, Beth-togarmah from the recesses of Zaphon and all its troops—many nations will accompany you. ⁷Prepare and get ready, you and the company mobilized for you, but in my service. ⁸After many days you will be called to battle; in the last years you will invade a land that has survived the sword—a people gathered from many nations back to the long-deserted mountains of Israel, brought forth from the nations to dwell securely. ⁹You shall come up like a sudden storm, covering the land like a cloud, you and all your troops and the many nations with you.

¹⁰Thus says the Lord GOD: On that day thoughts shall cross your mind, and you shall devise an evil plan. ¹¹You will say, "I will invade a land of open villages and attack a peaceful people who live in security—all of them living without city walls, bars, or gates"— ¹²in order to plunder and pillage, turning your hand against resettled ruins, against a people gathered from the nations, a people whose concern is cattle and goods, dwelling at the center of the earth. ¹³Sheba and Dedan, the merchants of Tarshish and all its "young lions" shall ask you: "Have you come here to plunder? Have you summoned your army for pillage, to carry off silver and gold, to take away cattle and goods, to seize much plunder?"

Second Prophecy Against Gog. ¹⁴Therefore, prophesy, son of man, and say to Gog: Thus says the Lord GOD: On that day, when my people Israel dwell securely, will you not take action, ¹⁵leaving your base in the recesses of Zaphon, you and many nations with you, all mounted on horses, a great company, a mighty army? ¹⁶You shall rise up over my people Israel like a cloud covering the land. In those last days, I will let you invade my land so that the nations acknowledge me, when in their sight I show my holiness through you, Gog.

¹⁷Thus says the Lord GOD: About you I spoke in earlier times through my servants, the prophets of Israel, who prophesied at that time that I would let you invade them. ¹⁸But on that day, the day Gog invades the land of Israel—oracle of the Lord GOD— my fury will flare up in my anger, ¹⁹and in my jealousy, with fiery wrath, I swear on that day there will be a great earthquake in the land of Israel. ²⁰Before me will tremble the fish of the sea and the birds of the air, the beasts of the field and everything that crawls on the ground, and everyone on the face of the earth. Mountains will be

overturned, terraces will collapse, and every wall will fall to the ground. ²¹Against him I will summon every terror—oracle of the Lord GOD; every man's sword will be raised against his brother. ²²I will execute judgment on him: disease and bloodshed; flooding rain and hailstones, fire and brimstone, I will rain down on him, on his troops and on the many nations with him. ²³And so I will show my greatness and holiness and make myself known in the sight of many nations. Then they shall know that I am the LORD.

Third Prophecy Against Gog. 39:1 You, son of man, prophesy against Gog, saying: Thus says the Lord GOD: Here I am, Gog, coming at you, chief prince of Meshech and Tubal. ²I will turn you around, even though I urged you on and brought you up from the recesses of Zaphon and let you attack the mountains of Israel. ³Then I will strike the bow from your left hand and make the arrows drop from your right. ⁴Upon the mountains of Israel you shall fall, you and all your troops and the peoples with you. I will give you as food to birds of prey of every kind and to wild beasts to be eaten. ⁵In the open field you shall fall, for I have spoken—oracle of the Lord GOD.

⁶I will send fire against Magog and against those who live securely on the seacoast, and they will know that I am the LORD. ⁷I will reveal my holy name among my people Israel, and I will never again allow my holy name to be defiled. Then the nations shall know that I am the LORD, the Holy One of Israel. ⁸Yes, it is coming! It shall happen—oracle of the Lord GOD. This is the day I decreed.

⁹Everyone living in the cities of Israel shall go out and set fire to the weapons, buckler and shield, bows and arrows, clubs and spears; for seven years they shall make fires with them. ¹⁰They will not need to bring in wood from the fields or cut down trees in the forests, for they will make fires with the weapons, plundering those who plundered them, pillaging those who pillaged them—oracle of the Lord GOD.

¹¹On that day I will give Gog a place for his tomb in Israel, the Valley of Abarim, east of the sea. It will block the way of travelers. There Gog shall be buried with all his horde; it shall be called "Valley of Hamon-Gog." ¹²For seven months the house of Israel shall bury them in order to cleanse the land. ¹³All the people of the land shall take part in the burials, making a name for themselves on the day I am glorified—oracle of the Lord GOD. ¹⁴Men shall be permanently assigned to pass through the land, burying those who lie unburied in order to cleanse the land. For seven months they shall keep searching. ¹⁵When these pass through the land and see a human bone, they must set up a marker beside it, until the gravediggers bury it in the Valley of Hamon-Gog. ¹⁶Also the name of the city is Hamonah. Thus the land will be cleansed.

¹⁷As for you, son of man, thus says the Lord GOD: Say to birds of every kind and to every wild beast: "Assemble! Come from all sides for the sacrifice I am making for you, a great slaughter on the mountains of Israel. You shall eat flesh and drink blood! ¹⁸You shall eat the flesh of warriors and drink the blood of the princes of the earth: rams, lambs, and goats, bulls and fatlings from Bashan, all of them. ¹⁹From the sacrifice I slaughtered for you, you shall eat fat until you are sated and drink blood until you are drunk. ²⁰At my table you shall be sated with horse and rider, with warrior and soldier of every kind—oracle of the Lord GOD.

Israel's Return. ²¹Then I will display my glory among the nations, and all the nations will see the judgment I executed, the hand I laid upon them. ²²From that day forward the house of Israel shall know that I am the LORD, their God. ²³The nations shall know that the house of Israel went into exile because of its sins. Because they betrayed me, I hid my face from them, handing them over to their foes, so they all fell by the sword. ²⁴According to their defilement and their crimes I dealt with them, hiding my face from them.

²⁵Therefore, thus says the Lord GOD: Now I will restore the fortunes of Jacob and take pity on the whole house of Israel; I am zealous for my holy name. ²⁶They will forget their shame and all the infidelities they committed against me when they live securely on their own land with no one to frighten them. ²⁷When I bring them back from the nations and gather them from the lands of their enemies, I will show my holiness through them in the sight of many nations. ²⁸Thus they shall know that I, the LORD, am their God, since I who exiled them among the nations will gather them back to their land, not leaving any of them behind. ²⁹I will no longer hide my face from them once I pour out my spirit upon the house of Israel—oracle of the Lord GOD.

☐ LUKE 14

Healing of the Man with Dropsy on the Sabbath. 14:1 On a sabbath he went to dine at the home of one of the leading Pharisees, and the people there were observing him carefully. ²In front of him there was a man suffering from dropsy. ³Jesus spoke to the scholars of the law and Pharisees in reply, asking, "Is it lawful to cure on the sabbath or not?" ⁴But they kept silent; so he took the man and, after he had healed him, dismissed him. ⁵Then he said to them, "Who among you, if your son or ox falls into a cistern, would not immediately pull him out on the sabbath day?" ⁶But they were unable to answer his question.

Conduct of Invited Guests and Hosts. ⁷He told a parable to those who had been invited, noticing how they were choosing the places of honor at the table. ⁸"When you are invited by someone to a wedding banquet, do not recline at table in the place of honor. A more distinguished guest than you may have been invited by him, ⁹and the host who invited both of you may approach you and say, 'Give your place to this man,' and then you would proceed with embarrassment to take the lowest place. ¹⁰Rather, when you are invited, go and take the lowest place so that when the host comes to you he may say, 'My friend, move up to a higher position.' Then you will enjoy the esteem of your companions at the table. ¹¹For everyone who exalts himself will be humbled, but the one who humbles himself will be exalted." ¹²Then he said to the host who invited him, "When you hold a lunch or a dinner, do not invite your friends or your brothers or your relatives or your wealthy neighbors, in case they may invite you back and you have repayment. ¹³Rather, when you hold a banquet, invite the poor, the crippled, the lame, the blind; ¹⁴blessed indeed will you be because of their inability to repay you. For you will be repaid at the resurrection of the righteous."

The Parable of the Great Feast. ¹⁵One of his fellow guests on hearing this said to him, "Blessed is the one who will dine in the kingdom of God." ¹⁶He replied to him, "A man gave a great dinner to which he invited many. ¹⁷When the time for the dinner came, he dispatched his servant to say to those invited, 'Come, everything is now ready.' ¹⁸But one by one, they all began to excuse themselves. The first said to him, 'I have purchased a field and must go to examine it; I ask you, consider me excused.' ¹⁹And another said, 'I have purchased five yoke of oxen and am on my way to evaluate them; I ask you, consider me excused.' ²⁰And another said, 'I have just married a woman, and therefore I cannot come.'

[21]The servant went and reported this to his master. Then the master of the house in a rage commanded his servant, 'Go out quickly into the streets and alleys of the town and bring in here the poor and the crippled, the blind and the lame.' [22]The servant reported, 'Sir, your orders have been carried out and still there is room.' [23]The master then ordered the servant, 'Go out to the highways and hedgerows and make people come in that my home may be filled. [24]For, I tell you, none of those men who were invited will taste my dinner.'"

Sayings on Discipleship. [25]Great crowds were traveling with him, and he turned and addressed them, [26]"If any one comes to me without hating his father and mother, wife and children, brothers and sisters, and even his own life, he cannot be my disciple. [27]Whoever does not carry his own cross and come after me cannot be my disciple. [28]Which of you wishing to construct a tower does not first sit down and calculate the cost to see if there is enough for its completion? [29]Otherwise, after laying the foundation and finding himself unable to finish the work the onlookers should laugh at him [30]and say, 'This one began to build but did not have the resources to finish.' [31]Or what king marching into battle would not first sit down and decide whether with ten thousand troops he can successfully oppose another king advancing upon him with twenty thousand troops? [32]But if not, while he is still far away, he will send a delegation to ask for peace terms. [33]In the same way, everyone of you who does not renounce all his possessions cannot be my disciple.

The Simile of Salt. [34]"Salt is good, but if salt itself loses its taste, with what can its flavor be restored? [35]It is fit neither for the soil nor for the manure pile; it is thrown out. Whoever has ears to hear ought to hear."

November 24

Sts. Andrew Dung-Lac and Companions

I'm certain of this: If my conscience were burdened with all the sins it's possible to commit, I would still go and throw myself into Our Lord's arms, my heart all broken up with contrition. I know what tenderness He has for any prodigal son of His who comes back to Him.

— St. Thérèse of Lisieux

☐ EZEKIEL 40–41

The Man with a Measure. 40:1 In the twenty-fifth year of our exile, at the beginning of the year, on the tenth day of the month, fourteen years after the city had been captured, on that very day the hand of the LORD came upon me and brought me back there. [2]In a divine vision he brought me to the land of Israel, where he set me down on a very high mountain. In front of me, there was something like a city built on it. [3]He brought me there, and there standing in the gateway was a man whose appearance was like bronze! He held in his hand a linen cord and a measuring rod. [4]The man said to me, "Son of man, look carefully and listen intently. Pay strict attention to everything I show you, for you have been brought here so that I might show it to you. Then you must tell the house of Israel everything you see." ⁵There an outer wall completely surrounded the temple. The measuring rod in the man's hand was six cubits long, each cubit being a cubit plus a handbreadth; he measured the width of the structure, one rod, and its height, one rod.

The East Gate. ⁶Going to the gate facing east, he climbed its steps and measured the threshold of the outer gateway as one rod wide. ⁷Each cell was one rod long and one rod wide, and there were five cubits between the cells; the threshold of the inner gateway adjoining the vestibule of the gate facing the temple was one rod wide. ⁸He also measured the vestibule of the inner gate, ⁹eight cubits, and its posts, two cubits each. The vestibule faced the inside. ¹⁰On each side of the east gatehouse were three cells, all the same size; their posts were all the same size. ¹¹He measured the width of the gate's entryway, ten cubits, and the length of the gate itself, thirteen cubits. ¹²The borders in front of the cells on both sides were one cubit, while the cells themselves measured six cubits by six cubits from one opening to the next. ¹³Next he measured the gatehouse from the back wall of one cell to the back wall of the cell on the opposite side through the openings facing each other, a width of twenty-five cubits. ¹⁴All around the courtyard of the gatehouse were posts six cubits high. ¹⁵From the front of the gatehouse at its outer entry to the gateway of the porch facing inward, the length was fifty cubits. ¹⁶There were recessed windows in the cells on all sides and in the posts on the inner side of the gate. Posts and windows were all around the inside, with palm trees decorating the posts.

The Outer Court. ¹⁷Then he brought me to the outer court, where there were chambers and pavement laid all around the courtyard: thirty chambers facing the pavement. ¹⁸The pavement lay alongside the gatehouses, the same length as the gates; this was the lower pavement. ¹⁹He measured the length of the pavement from the front of the lower gate to the outside of the inner gate, one hundred cubits. He then moved from the east to the north side.

The North Gate. ²⁰He measured the length and width of the north gate of the outer courtyard. ²¹Its cells, three on each side, its posts, and its vestibule had the same measurements as those of the first gate, fifty cubits long and twenty-five cubits wide. ²²Its windows, its vestibule, and its palm decorations had the same proportions as those of the gate facing east. Seven steps led up to it, and its vestibule faced the inside. ²³The inner court had a gate opposite the north gate, just as at the east gate; he measured one hundred cubits from one gate to the other.

The South Gate. ²⁴Then he led me to the south. There, too, facing south, was a gate! He measured its posts and vestibule; they were the same size as the others. ²⁵The gate and its vestibule had windows on both sides, like the other windows, fifty cubits long and twenty-five cubits wide. ²⁶Seven steps led up to it, its vestibule faced inside; and palms decorated each of the posts opposite one another. ²⁷The inner court also had a gate facing south. He measured it from gate to gate, facing south, one hundred cubits.

Gates of the Inner Court. ²⁸Then he brought me to the inner courtyard by the south gate, where he measured the south gateway; its measurements were the same as the others. ²⁹Its cells, posts, and vestibule were the same size as the others, fifty cubits long and twenty-five cubits wide. ³⁰The vestibules all around were twenty-five cubits long and five cubits wide. ³¹Its vestibule faced the outer court; palms decorated its posts, and its stairway had eight steps. ³²Then he brought me to the inner courtyard on the east and measured the gate there; its dimensions were the same as the others. [33]Its cells, posts, and vestibule were the same size as the others. The gate and its vestibule had windows on both sides, fifty cubits long and twenty-five cubits wide. [34]Its vestibule faced the outer court, palms decorated the posts opposite each other, and it had a stairway of eight steps. [35]Then he brought me to the north gate, where he measured the dimensions [36]of its cells, posts, and vestibule; they were the same. The gate and its vestibule had windows on both sides, fifty cubits long and twenty-five cubits wide. [37]Its vestibule faced the outer court; palm trees decorated its posts opposite each other, and it had a stairway of eight steps.

Side Rooms. [38]There was a chamber opening off the vestibule of the gate where burnt offerings were washed. [39]In the vestibule of the gate there were two tables on either side for slaughtering the burnt offerings, purification offerings, and reparation offerings. [40]Two more tables stood along the wall of the vestibule by the entrance of the north gate, and two tables on the other side of the vestibule of the gate. [41]There were thus four tables on one side of the gate and four tables on the other side, eight tables in all, for slaughtering. [42]The four tables for burnt offerings were made of cut stone, one and a half cubits long, one and a half cubits wide, and one cubit high; the instruments used for slaughtering burnt offerings and other sacrifices were kept [43]on shelves the width of one hand, fixed all around the room; but on the tables themselves was the meat for the sacrifices. [44]Outside the inner gatehouse there were two rooms on the inner courtyard, one beside the north gate, facing south, and the other beside the south gate, facing north. [45]He said to me, "This chamber facing south is reserved for the priests who have charge of the temple area, [46]while this chamber facing north is reserved for the priests who have charge of the altar; they are the sons of Zadok, the only Levites who may come near to minister to the LORD." [47]He measured the courtyard, a square one hundred cubits long and a hundred cubits wide, with the altar standing in front of the temple.

The Temple Building. [48]Then he brought me into the vestibule of the temple and measured the posts, five cubits on each side. The gateway was fourteen cubits wide, its side walls three cubits. [49]The vestibule was twenty cubits long and twelve cubits wide; ten steps led up to it, and there were columns by the posts, one on each side.

41:1 Then he brought me to the nave and measured the posts; each was six cubits wide. [2]The width of the entrance was ten cubits, and the walls on either side measured five cubits. He measured the nave, forty cubits long and twenty cubits wide.

[3]Then he went inside and measured the posts at the other entrance, two cubits wide. The entrance was six cubits wide, with walls seven cubits long on each side. [4]Next he measured the length and width of the room beyond the nave, twenty cubits long and twenty cubits wide. He said to me, "This is the holy of holies."

[5]Then he measured the wall of the temple, six cubits wide, and the width of the side chambers stretching all around the temple, four cubits each. [6]There were thirty side chambers, chamber upon chamber in three stories; terraces on the outside wall of the temple enclosing the side chambers provided support, but there were no supports for the temple wall itself. [7]A broad passageway led up the side chambers, for the house was enclosed all the way up and all the way around. Thus the temple was widened by the ascent that went from the lowest story through the middle one to the highest story. [8]I saw a raised platform all around the temple, the foundation for the side chambers; the width of this terrace was a full rod, six cubits. [9]The width of the outside wall enclosing the side chambers

was five cubits. There was an open space between the side chambers of the temple [10]and the other chambers that measured twenty cubits around the temple on all sides. [11]The side chambers had entrances to the open space, one entrance on the north and the other on the south. The width of the wall surrounding the open space was five cubits. [12]The building opposite the restricted area on the west side was seventy cubits long and ninety cubits wide, with walls five cubits thick all around it. [13]Thus he measured the temple, one hundred cubits long. The restricted area, its building and walls, measured a hundred cubits in length. [14]The temple facade, along with the restricted area to the east, was also one hundred cubits wide. [15]He then measured the building opposite the restricted area which was behind it, together with its terraces on both sides, one hundred cubits.

Interior of the Temple. The inner nave and the outer vestibule [16]were paneled; the windows had recesses and precious wood trim around all three sides except the sill. Paneling covered the walls from the floor up to the windows and even the window sections. [17]Even above the doorway and in the inner part of the temple and outside as well, around all the walls inside and out, [18]were figures of cherubim and palm trees: a palm tree between each pair of cherubim. Each cherub had two faces: [19]the face of a human being looked toward one palm tree and the face of a lion looked toward the other palm tree. Thus the figures covered all the walls around the temple. [20]From the floor to the lintel of the door, cherubim and palm trees decorated the walls. [21]The nave had a square door frame, and inside facing the holy place was something that looked like [22]a wooden altar, three cubits high, two cubits long, and two cubits wide. It had corners and a wooden base and sides. He said to me, "This is the table that stands before the LORD." [23]The nave had a double door, and the holy place [24]also had a double door; each door had two sections that could move; two sections on one door, and two on the other. [25]Cherubim and palm trees decorated the doors of the nave like the decoration on the walls. Outside a wooden lattice faced the vestibule. [26]There were recessed windows and palm trees on the side walls of the vestibule. The side chambers of the temple also had latticework.

☐ LUKE 15

The Parable of the Lost Sheep. 15:1 The tax collectors and sinners were all drawing near to listen to him, [2]but the Pharisees and scribes began to complain, saying, "This man welcomes sinners and eats with them." [3]So to them he addressed this parable. [4]"What man among you having a hundred sheep and losing one of them would not leave the ninety-nine in the desert and go after the lost one until he finds it? [5]And when he does find it, he sets it on his shoulders with great joy [6]and, upon his arrival home, he calls together his friends and neighbors and says to them, 'Rejoice with me because I have found my lost sheep.' [7]I tell you, in just the same way there will be more joy in heaven over one sinner who repents than over ninety-nine righteous people who have no need of repentance.

The Parable of the Lost Coin. [8]"Or what woman having ten coins and losing one would not light a lamp and sweep the house, searching carefully until she finds it? [9]And when she does find it, she calls together her friends and neighbors and says to them, 'Rejoice with me because I have found the coin that I lost.' [10]In just the same way, I tell you, there will be rejoicing among the angels of God over one sinner who repents."

The Parable of the Lost Son. [11]Then he said, "A man had two sons, [12]and the younger son said to his father, 'Father, give me the share of your estate that should come to me.' So the father divided the property between them. [13]After a few days, the younger son collected all his belongings and set off to a distant country where he squandered his inheritance on a life of dissipation. [14]When he had freely spent everything, a severe famine struck that country, and he found himself in dire need. [15]So he hired himself out to one of the local citizens who sent him to his farm to tend the swine. [16]And he longed to eat his fill of the pods on which the swine fed, but nobody gave him any. [17]Coming to his senses he thought, 'How many of my father's hired workers have more than enough food to eat, but here am I, dying from hunger. [18]I shall get up and go to my father and I shall say to him, "Father, I have sinned against heaven and against you. [19]I no longer deserve to be called your son; treat me as you would treat one of your hired workers."' [20]So he got up and went back to his father. While he was still a long way off, his father caught sight of him, and was filled with compassion. He ran to his son, embraced him and kissed him. [21]His son said to him, 'Father, I have sinned against heaven and against you; I no longer deserve to be called your son.' [22]But his father ordered his servants, 'Quickly bring the finest robe and put it on him; put a ring on his finger and sandals on his feet. [23]Take the fattened calf and slaughter it. Then let us celebrate with a feast, [24]because this son of mine was dead, and has come to life again; he was lost, and has been found.' Then the celebration began. [25]Now the older son had been out in the field and, on his way back, as he neared the house, he heard the sound of music and dancing. [26]He called one of the servants and asked what this might mean. [27]The servant said to him, 'Your brother has returned and your father has slaughtered the fattened calf because he has him back safe and sound.' [28]He became angry, and when he refused to enter the house, his father came out and pleaded with him. [29]He said to his father in reply, 'Look, all these years I served you and not once did I disobey your orders; yet you never gave me even a young goat to feast on with my friends. [30]But when your son returns who swallowed up your property with prostitutes, for him you slaughter the fattened calf.' [31]He said to him, 'My son, you are here with me always; everything I have is yours. [32]But now we must celebrate and rejoice, because your brother was dead and has come to life again; he was lost and has been found.'"

November 25

This covetous gathering and miserly keeping of wealth, with all the delight that we take in beholding it, is only a very gay and golden dream, in which we imagine we have great riches; and in the sleep of this life we are glad and proud of it. But when death has once awakened us, our dream shall vanish, and of all the treasure that we only dreamed about, we shall not find one penny left in our hand.

— St. Thomas More

☐ EZEKIEL 42-43

Other Structures. 42:1 Then he led me north to the outer court, bringing me to some chambers on the north side opposite the restricted area and the north building. ²They were a hundred cubits long on the north side and fifty cubits wide. ³Built in rows at three different levels, they stood between the twenty cubits of the inner court and the pavement of the outer court. ⁴In front of the chambers was a walkway ten cubits wide on the inside of a wall one cubit wide. The doorways faced north. ⁵The upper chambers were shorter because they lost space to the lower and middle tiers of the building. ⁶Because they were in three tiers, they did not have foundations like the court, but were set back from the lower and middle levels from the ground up. ⁷The outside walls ran parallel to the chambers along the outer court, a length of fifty cubits. ⁸The chambers facing the outer court were fifty cubits long; thus the wall along the nave was a hundred cubits. ⁹At the base of these chambers, there was an entryway from the east so that one could enter from the outer court ¹⁰where the wall of the court began.

To the south along the side of the restricted area and the building there were also chambers ¹¹with a walkway in front of them. They looked like the chambers on the north side in length and width, in their exits, their design, and their doorways. ¹²At the base of the chambers on the south side there was an entry at the end of a walkway in front of the protective wall by which one could enter from the east. ¹³He said to me, "The north and south chambers facing the restricted area are the chambers of the holy place where the priests who approach the Lord shall eat the most holy meals. Here they shall place the most holy offerings: the grain offerings, the purification offerings, and the reparation offerings; for the place is holy. ¹⁴When the priests have entered, they must not go out again from the holy place into the outer court without leaving the garments in which they ministered because they are holy. They shall put on other garments before approaching the area for the people."

Measuring the Outer Court. ¹⁵When he finished measuring the interior of the temple area, he brought me out by way of the gate facing east and measured all around it. ¹⁶He measured the east side, five hundred cubits by his measuring rod. Then he turned ¹⁷and measured the north side: five hundred cubits by his measuring rod. He turned ¹⁸and measured the south side, five hundred cubits by his measuring rod. ¹⁹He turned and measured the west side, also five hundred cubits by his measuring rod. ²⁰Thus he measured it on the four sides. It was surrounded by a wall five hundred cubits long and five hundred cubits wide, to separate the sacred from the profane.

The Glory of the Lord Returns. 43:1 Then he led me to the gate facing east, ²and there was the glory of the God of Israel coming from the east! His voice was like the roar of many waters, and the earth shone with his glory. ³The vision I saw was like the vision I had seen when he came to destroy the city and like the vision I had seen by the river Chebar—I fell on my face. ⁴The glory of the Lord entered the temple by way of the gate facing east. ⁵Then the spirit lifted me up and brought me to the inner court. And there the glory of the Lord filled the temple! ⁶I heard someone speaking to me from the temple, but the man was standing beside me. ⁷The voice said to me: Son of man, do you see the place for my throne, and the place for the soles of my feet? Here I will dwell among the Israelites forever. The house of Israel, neither they nor their kings, will never again defile my holy name, with their prostitutions and the corpses of their kings at their death. ⁸When they placed their threshold against my threshold and their doorpost next to mine, with only a wall between me and them, they defiled my holy name by the abominations they committed, and I devoured them in my wrath. ⁹From now on, let them put their prostitution and the corpses of their kings far from me, and I will dwell in their midst forever.

The Law of the Temple. ¹⁰As for you, son of man, describe the temple to the house of Israel so they are ashamed for their sins. Let them measure its layout. ¹¹If they are ashamed for all they have done, tell them about the layout and design of the temple, its exits and entrances, with all its regulations and instructions; write it down for them to see, that they may carefully observe all its laws and statutes. ¹²This is the law for the temple: the entire area on top of the mountain all around will be a most holy place. This is the law for the temple.

The Altar. ¹³These were the dimensions of the altar in cubits, a cubit being one cubit plus a handbreadth. The channel was one cubit deep by one cubit wide, and its rim had a lip one span wide all around it. The height of the altar itself was as follows: ¹⁴from the channel at floor level up to the lower ledge was two cubits, with the ledge one cubit wide; from the lower ledge to the upper ledge, four cubits, with the ledge one cubit wide. ¹⁵The altar hearth was four cubits high, and extending up from the top of the hearth were four horns. ¹⁶The hearth was twelve cubits long and twelve cubits wide, a square with four equal sides. ¹⁷The upper ledge was fourteen cubits long and fourteen cubits wide on all four sides. The rim around it was half a cubit, with a channel one cubit all around. The steps faced east.

¹⁸Then he said to me: Son of man, thus says the Lord God: These are the statutes for the altar when it is set up for sacrificing burnt offerings and splashing blood on it. ¹⁹A young bull must be brought as a purification offering to the priests, the Levites descended from Zadok, who come near to serve me—oracle of the Lord God. ²⁰You shall take some of its blood and smear it on the four horns of the altar, and on the four corners of the ledge, and all around its rim. Thus you shall purify and purge it. ²¹Then take the bull as purification offering and burn it in the appointed place outside the sanctuary. ²²On the second day present an unblemished male goat as a purification offering, to purify the altar as you did with the bull. ²³When you have completed the purification, you must bring an unblemished young bull and an unblemished ram from the flock ²⁴and present them before the Lord. The priests shall throw salt on them and sacrifice them as burnt offerings to the Lord. ²⁵Daily for seven days you shall give a male goat as a purification offering; and a young bull and a ram from the flock, all unblemished, shall be offered ²⁶for seven days. Thus they shall purge the

altar, in order to cleanse and dedicate it. [27]And when these days are over, from the eighth day on, the priests shall sacrifice your burnt offerings and communion offerings on the altar. Then I will be pleased with you—oracle of the Lord God.

☐ LUKE 16

The Parable of the Dishonest Steward.
16:1 Then he also said to his disciples, "A rich man had a steward who was reported to him for squandering his property. [2]He summoned him and said, 'What is this I hear about you? Prepare a full account of your stewardship, because you can no longer be my steward.' [3]The steward said to himself, 'What shall I do, now that my master is taking the position of steward away from me? I am not strong enough to dig and I am ashamed to beg. [4]I know what I shall do so that, when I am removed from the stewardship, they may welcome me into their homes.' [5]He called in his master's debtors one by one. To the first he said, 'How much do you owe my master?' [6]He replied, 'One hundred measures of olive oil.' He said to him, 'Here is your promissory note. Sit down and quickly write one for fifty.' [7]Then to another he said, 'And you, how much do you owe?' He replied, 'One hundred kors of wheat.' He said to him, 'Here is your promissory note; write one for eighty.' [8]And the master commended that dishonest steward for acting prudently.

Application of the Parable. "For the children of this world are more prudent in dealing with their own generation than are the children of light. [9]I tell you, make friends for yourselves with dishonest wealth, so that when it fails, you will be welcomed into eternal dwellings. [10]The person who is trustworthy in very small matters is also trustworthy in great ones; and the person who is dishonest in very small matters is also dishonest in great ones. [11]If, therefore, you are not trustworthy with dishonest wealth, who will trust you with true wealth? [12]If you are not trustworthy with what belongs to another, who will give you what is yours? [13]No servant can serve two masters. He will either hate one and love the other, or be devoted to one and despise the other. You cannot serve God and mammon."

A Saying against the Pharisees. [14]The Pharisees, who loved money, heard all these things and sneered at him. [15]And he said to them, "You justify yourselves in the sight of others, but God knows your hearts; for what is of human esteem is an abomination in the sight of God.

Sayings about the Law. [16]"The law and the prophets lasted until John; but from then on the kingdom of God is proclaimed, and everyone who enters does so with violence. [17]It is easier for heaven and earth to pass away than for the smallest part of a letter of the law to become invalid.

Sayings about Divorce. [18]"Everyone who divorces his wife and marries another commits adultery, and the one who marries a woman divorced from her husband commits adultery.

The Parable of the Rich Man and Lazarus. [19]"There was a rich man who dressed in purple garments and fine linen and dined sumptuously each day. [20]And lying at his door was a poor man named Lazarus, covered with sores, [21]who would gladly have eaten his fill of the scraps that fell from the rich man's table. Dogs even used to come and lick his sores. [22]When the poor man died, he was carried away by angels to the bosom of Abraham. The rich man also died and was buried, [23]and from the netherworld, where he was in torment, he raised his eyes and saw Abraham far off and Lazarus at his side. [24]And he cried out,

'Father Abraham, have pity on me. Send Lazarus to dip the tip of his finger in water and cool my tongue, for I am suffering torment in these flames.' ²⁵Abraham replied, 'My child, remember that you received what was good during your lifetime while Lazarus likewise received what was bad; but now he is comforted here, whereas you are tormented. ²⁶Moreover, between us and you a great chasm is established to prevent anyone from crossing who might wish to go from our side to yours or from your side to ours.' ²⁷He said, 'Then I beg you, father, send him to my father's house, ²⁸for I have five brothers, so that he may warn them, lest they too come to this place of torment.' ²⁹But Abraham replied, 'They have Moses and the prophets. Let them listen to them.' ³⁰He said, 'Oh no, father Abraham, but if someone from the dead goes to them, they will repent.' ³¹Then Abraham said, 'If they will not listen to Moses and the prophets, neither will they be persuaded if someone should rise from the dead.'"

November 26

St. Leonard of Port Maurice

Impress on yourself this great truth: Even if all hell's devils come after you to tempt you, you won't sin unless you want to — provided that you don't trust in your own powers, but in the assistance of God. He doesn't refuse help to those who ask it with a lively faith.

— St. Leonard of Port Maurice

☐ EZEKIEL 44-45

The Closed Gate. 44:1 Then he brought me back to the outer gate of the sanctuary facing east, but it was closed. ²The Lord said to me: This gate must remain closed; it must not be opened, and no one should come through it. Because the Lord, the God of Israel, came through it, it must remain closed. ³Only the prince may sit in it to eat a meal in the presence of the Lord; he must enter through the vestibule of the gate and leave the same way.

Admission to the Temple. ⁴Then he brought me by way of the north gate to the facade of the temple. I looked—and the glory of the Lord filled the Lord's house! I fell on my face. ⁵The Lord said to me: Son of man, pay close attention, look carefully, and listen intently to everything I tell you about all the statutes and laws of the Lord's house. Pay close attention to the entrance into the temple and all the exits of the sanctuary. ⁶Say to that rebellious house, the house of Israel: Thus says the Lord God: Enough of all your abominations, house of Israel! ⁷You have admitted foreigners, uncircumcised in heart and flesh, into my sanctuary to profane it when you offered me food, the fat and blood. Thus you have broken my covenant by all your abominations. ⁸Instead of caring for the service of my sanctuary, you appointed these foreigners to care for the service of my sanctuary. ⁹Thus says the Lord God: No foreigners, uncircumcised in heart and flesh, shall ever enter my sanctuary: not even any of the foreigners who live among the Israelites.

Levites. ¹⁰As for the Levites who went far away from me when Israel strayed from me after their idols, they will bear the consequences of their sin. ¹¹They will serve in my sanctuary only as gatekeepers and temple servants; they will slaughter burnt offerings and sacrifices for the people. They will stand before the people to serve them. ¹²Because they used to serve them before their idols, thus becoming a stumbling block to the house of Israel, therefore I have sworn an oath against them, says the Lord GOD, and they will bear the consequences of their sin. ¹³They shall no longer come near to serve as my priests, nor shall they touch any of my sacred things or my most sacred offerings, for they must bear their shame, the abominations they committed. ¹⁴Instead I will make them responsible for the service of the temple and all its work, for everything that must be done in it.

Priests. ¹⁵As for the levitical priests, sons of Zadok, who took charge of my sanctuary when the Israelites strayed from me, they may approach me to serve me and stand before me to offer the fat and the blood—oracle of the Lord GOD. ¹⁶They may enter my sanctuary; they may approach my table to serve me and carry out my service. ¹⁷Whenever they enter the gates of the inner court, they shall wear linen garments; they shall not put on anything woolen when they serve at the gates of the inner court or within the temple. ¹⁸They shall have linen turbans on their heads and linen undergarments on their loins; they shall not gird themselves with anything that causes sweat. ¹⁹And when they go out to the people in the outer court, they shall take off the garments in which they served and leave them in the rooms of the sanctuary, and put on other garments so they do not transmit holiness to the people by their garments.

²⁰They shall not shave their heads nor let their hair hang loose, but they shall keep their hair carefully trimmed. ²¹No priest shall drink wine before he enters the inner court. ²²They shall not take as wives either widows or divorced women, but only unmarried women from the line of Israel; however, they may take as wives widows who are widows of priests. ²³They shall teach my people to distinguish between sacred and profane and make known to them the difference between clean and unclean. ²⁴In legal cases they shall stand as judges, judging according to my ordinances. They shall observe all my laws and statutes regarding all my appointed feasts, and they shall keep my sabbaths holy.

²⁵They shall not make themselves unclean by going near a dead body; only for their father, mother, son, daughter, brother, or unmarried sister may they make themselves unclean. ²⁶After he is again clean, he must wait an additional seven days; ²⁷on the day he enters the inner court to serve in the sanctuary, he shall present a purification offering for himself—oracle of the Lord GOD. ²⁸I will be their heritage: I am their heritage! You shall not give them any property in Israel, for I am their property! ²⁹They shall eat grain offerings, purification offerings, and reparation offerings; anything under the ban in Israel belongs to them; ³⁰all the choicest first fruits of every kind and all the best of your offerings of every kind shall belong to the priests; the best of your dough you shall also give to the priests to bring a blessing upon your house. ³¹The priests shall not eat anything, whether bird or animal, that died naturally or was killed by wild beasts.

The Holy Portion. 45:1 When you apportion the land heritage by heritage, you shall set apart a holy portion for the LORD, holier than the rest of the land—twenty-five thousand cubits long and twenty thousand cubits wide; the entire area shall be holy. ²Of this land a square plot, five hundred by five hundred cubits, shall be assigned to the sanctuary, with fifty cubits of free space around it. ³From this tract also measure off a length of twenty-five thousand cubits and a width of ten thousand cubits; on it the sanctuary, the holy of holies, shall stand. [4]This shall be the sacred part of the land belonging to the priests, the ministers of the sanctuary, who draw near to minister to the LORD; it shall be a place for their homes and an area set apart for the sanctuary. [5]There shall also be a strip twenty-five thousand cubits long and ten thousand wide for the Levites, the ministers of the temple, so they have cities to live in. [6]You shall assign a strip five thousand cubits wide and twenty-five thousand long as the property of the city parallel to the sacred tract; this shall belong to the whole house of Israel. [7]A section shall belong to the prince, bordering both sides of the sacred tract and city combined, extending westward on the west side and eastward on the east side, corresponding in length to one of the tribal portions from the west boundary to the east boundary [8]of the land. This shall be his property in Israel so that my princes will no longer oppress my people, but will leave the land to the house of Israel according to its tribes. [9]Thus says the Lord GOD: Enough, you princes of Israel! Put away violence and oppression, and do what is just and right! Stop evicting my people!—oracle of the Lord GOD.

Weights and Measures. [10]You shall have honest scales, an honest ephah, and an honest bath. [11]The ephah and the bath shall be the same size: the bath equal to one tenth of a homer, and the ephah equal to one tenth of a homer; their capacity is based on the homer. [12]The shekel shall be twenty gerahs. Twenty shekels plus twenty-five shekels plus fifteen shekels make up a mina for you.

Offerings. [13]This is the offering you must make: one sixth of an ephah from each homer of wheat and one sixth of an ephah from each homer of barley. [14]This is the regulation for oil: for every bath of oil, one tenth of a bath, computed by the kor, made up of ten baths, that is, a homer, for ten baths make a homer. [15]Also, one sheep from the flock for every two hundred from the pasture land of Israel, for the grain offering, the burnt offering, and communion offerings, to make atonement on their behalf—oracle of the Lord GOD. [16]All the people of the land shall be responsible for these offerings to the prince in Israel. [17]It shall be the duty of the prince to provide burnt offerings, grain offerings, and libations on feast days, new moons, and sabbaths, on all the festivals of the house of Israel. He shall provide the purification offering, grain offering, burnt offering, and communion offerings, to make atonement on behalf of the house of Israel.

The Passover. [18]Thus says the Lord GOD: On the first day of the first month you shall take an unblemished young bull to purify the sanctuary. [19]The priest shall take some of the blood from the purification offering and smear it on the doorposts of the house, on the four corners of the ledge of the altar, and on the doorposts of the gates of the inner courtyard. [20]You shall repeat this on the seventh day of the month for those who have sinned inadvertently or out of ignorance; thus you shall purge the temple. [21]On the fourteenth day of the first month you shall observe the feast of Passover; for seven days unleavened bread must be eaten. [22]On that day the prince shall sacrifice, on his own behalf and on behalf of all the people of the land, a bull as a purification offering. [23]On each of the seven days of the feast he shall sacrifice, as a burnt offering to the LORD, seven bulls and seven rams without blemish, and as a purification offering he shall sacrifice one male goat each day. [24]As a grain offering he shall offer one ephah for each bull and one ephah for each ram and one hin of oil for each ephah.

The Feast of Booths. [25]In the seventh month, on the fifteenth day of the seventh month, on the feast day and for the next seven days, he shall make the same offerings: the same purification offerings, burnt offerings, grain offerings, and offerings of oil.

☐ LUKE 17

Temptations to Sin. 17:1 He said to his disciples, "Things that cause sin will inevitably occur, but woe to the person through whom they occur. ²It would be better for him if a millstone were put around his neck and he be thrown into the sea than for him to cause one of these little ones to sin. ³Be on your guard! If your brother sins, rebuke him; and if he repents, forgive him. ⁴And if he wrongs you seven times in one day and returns to you seven times saying, 'I am sorry,' you should forgive him."

Saying of Faith. ⁵And the apostles said to the Lord, "Increase our faith." ⁶The Lord replied, "If you have faith the size of a mustard seed, you would say to [this] mulberry tree, 'Be uprooted and planted in the sea,' and it would obey you.

Attitude of a Servant. ⁷"Who among you would say to your servant who has just come in from plowing or tending sheep in the field, 'Come here immediately and take your place at table'? ⁸Would he not rather say to him, 'Prepare something for me to eat. Put on your apron and wait on me while I eat and drink. You may eat and drink when I am finished'? ⁹Is he grateful to that servant because he did what was commanded? ¹⁰So should it be with you. When you have done all you have been commanded, say, 'We are unprofitable servants; we have done what we were obliged to do.'"

The Cleansing of Ten Lepers. ¹¹As he continued his journey to Jerusalem, he traveled through Samaria and Galilee. ¹²As he was entering a village, ten lepers met [him]. They stood at a distance from him ¹³and raised their voice, saying, "Jesus, Master! Have pity on us!" ¹⁴And when he saw them, he said, "Go show yourselves to the priests." As they were going they were cleansed. ¹⁵And one of them, realizing he had been healed, returned, glorifying God in a loud voice; ¹⁶and he fell at the feet of Jesus and thanked him. He was a Samaritan. ¹⁷Jesus said in reply, "Ten were cleansed, were they not? Where are the other nine? ¹⁸Has none but this foreigner returned to give thanks to God?" ¹⁹Then he said to him, "Stand up and go; your faith has saved you."

The Coming of the Kingdom of God. ²⁰Asked by the Pharisees when the kingdom of God would come, he said in reply, "The coming of the kingdom of God cannot be observed, ²¹and no one will announce, 'Look, here it is,' or, 'There it is.' For behold, the kingdom of God is among you."

The Day of the Son of Man. ²²Then he said to his disciples, "The days will come when you will long to see one of the days of the Son of Man, but you will not see it. ²³There will be those who will say to you, 'Look, there he is,' [or] 'Look, here he is.' Do not go off, do not run in pursuit. ²⁴For just as lightning flashes and lights up the sky from one side to the other, so will the Son of Man be [in his day]. ²⁵But first he must suffer greatly and be rejected by this generation. ²⁶As it was in the days of Noah, so it will be in the days of the Son of Man; ²⁷they were eating and drinking, marrying and giving in marriage up to the day that Noah entered the ark, and the flood came and destroyed them all. ²⁸Similarly, as it was in the days of Lot: they were eating, drinking, buying, selling, planting, building; ²⁹on the day when Lot left Sodom, fire and brimstone rained from the sky to destroy them all. ³⁰So it will be on the day the Son of Man is revealed. ³¹On that day, a person who is on the housetop and whose belongings are in the house must not go down to get them, and likewise a person in the field must not return to what was left behind. ³²Remember the wife of Lot. ³³Whoever seeks to preserve his life will lose it, but whoever loses it will save it. ³⁴I tell you, on that night there will be two people in one bed; one will be taken, the other left. [35]And there will be two women grinding meal together; one will be taken, the other left." [36] [37]They said to him in reply, "Where, Lord?" He said to them, "Where the body is, there also the vultures will gather."

November 27

A child is a pledge of immortality, for he bears upon him in figure those high and eternal excellences in which the joy of heaven consists, and which would not thus be shadowed forth by the all-gracious Creator, were they not one day to be realized.

— Blessed John Henry Newman

☐ EZEKIEL 46–48

Sabbaths. 46:1 Thus says the Lord God: The gate of the inner court facing east shall remain closed throughout the six working days, but on the sabbath and on the day of the new moon it shall be open. [2]Then the prince shall enter from outside by way of the vestibule of the gate and remain standing at the doorpost of the gateway while the priests sacrifice his burnt offerings and communion offerings; then he shall bow down in worship at the opening of the gate and leave. But the gate shall not be closed until evening. [3]The people of the land also shall bow down in worship before the Lord at the opening of this gate on the sabbaths and new moons. [4]The burnt offerings which the prince sacrifices to the Lord on the sabbath shall consist of six unblemished lambs and an unblemished ram, [5]together with a grain offering of one ephah for the ram and whatever he pleases for the lambs, and a hin of oil for each ephah. [6]On the day of the new moon, he shall provide an unblemished young bull, six lambs, and a ram without blemish, [7]with a grain offering of one ephah for the bull and an ephah for the ram, and for the lambs whatever he can, and for each ephah a hin of oil.

Ritual Laws. [8]When the prince enters, he shall always enter and depart by the vestibule of the gate. [9]When the people of the land come before the Lord to bow down on the festivals, if they enter by the north gate they shall leave by the south gate, and if they enter by the south gate they shall leave by the north gate. They shall not go back by the gate through which they entered; everyone shall leave by the opposite gate. [10]When they come in, the prince shall be with them; he shall also leave with them. [11]On feasts and festivals, the grain offering shall be an ephah for a bull, an ephah for a ram, but for the lambs whatever they please, and a hin of oil with each ephah. [12]When the prince makes a freewill offering to the Lord, whether a burnt offering or communion offering, the gate facing east shall be opened for him, and he shall bring his burnt offering or peace offering as he does on the sabbath. Then he shall leave, and the gate shall be closed after his departure. [13]Every day you shall bring as a burnt offering to the Lord an unblemished year-old lamb; you shall offer it every morning, [14]and with it every morning a grain offering of one sixth of an ephah, with a third of a hin of oil to moisten the fine flour. This grain offering for the Lord is a perpetual statute. [15]The lamb, the grain offering, and the oil you must bring every morning as a perpetual burnt offering.

The Prince and the Land. [16]Thus says the Lord God: If the prince makes a gift of part of his heritage to any of his sons, it belongs to his sons; that property is their heritage. [17]But if he makes a gift of part of his heritage to one of his servants, it belongs to him until the year of release; then it reverts to the prince. Only the heritage given to his sons belongs to him. [18]The prince shall not seize any part of the heritage of the people by forcing them off their property. From his own property he shall provide heritage for his sons, so that none of my people will be driven off their property.

The Temple Kitchens. [19]Then he brought me through the entrance at the side of the gateway to the chambers reserved for the priests, which faced north. There I saw a place at the far west end, [20]about which he said to me, "This is the place where the priests cook the reparation offerings and the purification offerings and bake the grain offerings, so they do not have to bring them into the outer court and so transmit holiness to the people." [21]Then he led me into the outer court and had me cross to the four corners of the court, and there, in each corner, was another court! [22]In all four corners of the courtyard there were courts set off, each forty cubits long by thirty cubits wide, all four of them the same size. [23]A stone wall surrounded them on four sides, and ovens were built along the bottom of the walls all the way around. [24]He said to me, "These are the kitchens where the temple ministers cook the sacrifices of the people."

The Wonderful Stream. 47:1 Then he brought me back to the entrance of the temple, and there! I saw water flowing out from under the threshold of the temple toward the east, for the front of the temple faced east. The water flowed out toward the right side of the temple to the south of the altar. [2]He brought me by way of the north gate and around the outside to the outer gate facing east; there I saw water trickling from the southern side. [3]When he continued eastward with a measuring cord in his hand, he measured off a thousand cubits and had me wade through the water; it was ankle-deep. [4]He measured off another thousand cubits and once more had me wade through the water; it was up to the knees. He measured another thousand cubits and had me wade through the water; it was up to my waist. [5]Once more he measured off a thousand cubits. Now it was a river I could not wade across. The water had risen so high, I would have to swim—a river that was impassable. [6]Then he asked me, "Do you see this, son of man?" He brought me to the bank of the river and had me sit down. [7]As I was returning, I saw along the bank of the river a great many trees on each side. [8]He said to me, "This water flows out into the eastern district, runs down into the Arabah and empties into the polluted waters of the sea to freshen them. [9]Wherever it flows, the river teems with every kind of living creature; fish will abound. Where these waters flow they refresh; everything lives where the river goes. [10]Fishermen will stand along its shore from En-gedi to En-eglaim; it will become a place for drying nets, and it will abound with as many kinds of fish as the Great Sea. [11]Its marshes and swamps shall not be made fresh, but will be left for salt. [12]Along each bank of the river every kind of fruit tree will grow; their leaves will not wither, nor will their fruit fail. Every month they will bear fresh fruit because the waters of the river flow out from the sanctuary. Their fruit is used for food, and their leaves for healing."

Boundaries of the Land. [13]Thus says the Lord God: These are the boundaries of the land which you shall apportion among the twelve tribes of Israel, with Joseph having two portions. [14]You shall apportion it equally because I swore to give it to your ancestors as a heritage; this land, then, is your heritage. [15]These are the borders of the land: on the northern side, from the Great Sea in the direction of Hethlon, Lebo-hamath to Zedad, [16]Berothah, and Sibraim, along the frontiers of Damascus and Hamath, to Hazar-enon, on the border of Hauran. [17]Thus the border extends from the sea to Hazar-enon, north of the border of Damascus, the frontier of Hamath to the north. This is the northern boundary. [18]The eastern border shall be between Damascus and Hauran; while the Jordan will form the border between Gilead and the land of Israel down to the eastern sea as far as Tamar. This is the eastern boundary. [19]The southern border shall go southward from Tamar to the waters of Meribath-kadesh, on to the Wadi of Egypt, and into the Great Sea. This is the southern boundary. [20]The western border shall have the Great Sea as a boundary as far as a point opposite Lebo-hamath. This is the western boundary.

The Northern Portions. [21]You shall divide this land according to the tribes of Israel. [22]You shall allot it as heritage for yourselves and for the resident aliens in your midst who have fathered children among you. You shall treat them like native Israelites; along with you they shall receive a heritage among the tribes of Israel. [23]In whatever tribe the resident alien lives, there you shall assign his heritage—oracle of the Lord God.

48:1 These are the names of the tribes:

At the northern end, along the side of the way to Hethlon, Lebo-hamath, and Hazar-enon, the border of Damascus, and northward up to the frontier with Hamath, from the eastern border to the western: Dan, one portion. [2]Along the territory of Dan from the eastern border to the western border: Asher, one portion. [3]Along the territory of Asher from the eastern border to the western border: Naphtali, one portion. [4]Along the territory of Naphtali from the eastern border to the western border: Manasseh, one portion. [5]Along the territory of Manasseh from the eastern border to the western border: Ephraim, one portion. [6]Along the territory of Ephraim from the eastern border to the western border: Reuben, one portion. [7]Along the territory of Reuben from the eastern border to the western border: Judah, one portion.

The Sacred Tract. [8]Along the territory of Judah from the eastern border to the western border is the tract you shall set apart, twenty-five thousand cubits wide and as long as one of the portions from the eastern border to the western border. The sanctuary shall stand in the center of the tract. [9]The tract you set apart for the Lord shall be twenty-five thousand cubits long by twenty thousand wide. [10]The sacred tract will be given to the following: the priests shall have twenty-five thousand cubits on the north, ten thousand on the west, ten thousand on the east, and twenty-five thousand on the south. The sanctuary of the Lord shall be in its center. [11]The consecrated priests, the Zadokites, who fulfilled my service and did not stray with the Israelites as the Levites did, [12]shall have their own tract set apart, next to the territory of the Levites, separate from the most holy tract. [13]The Levites shall have territory corresponding to that of the priests, twenty-five thousand cubits long and ten thousand cubits wide. The whole tract shall be twenty-five thousand cubits long and twenty thousand wide. [14]They may not sell or exchange or transfer any of it, the best part of the land, for it is sacred to the Lord. [15]The remaining section, five thousand cubits long and twenty-five thousand cubits wide, is profane land, assigned to the city for dwellings and pasture. The city is at its center. [16]These are the dimensions of the city: the north side, forty-five hundred cubits; the south side, forty-five hundred cubits; the east side, forty-five hundred cubits; and the west side, forty-five hundred cubits. ¹⁷The pasture land for the city extends north two hundred fifty cubits, south two hundred fifty cubits, east two hundred fifty cubits, and west two hundred fifty cubits. ¹⁸The remaining section runs eastward along the sacred tract for ten thousand cubits and westward ten thousand cubits. Its produce shall provide food for the workers of the city. ¹⁹The workers of the city, from all the tribes of Israel, shall cultivate it. ²⁰The entire sacred tract measures twenty-five thousand by twenty-five thousand cubits; as a square you shall set apart the sacred tract together with the city property.

²¹The remaining land on both sides of the sacred tract and the property of the city shall belong to the prince, extending eastward twenty-five thousand cubits up to the eastern boundary, and westward twenty-five thousand cubits to the western boundary. This portion belongs to the prince and corresponds to the tribal portions. The sacred tract and the sanctuary of the temple shall be in the middle. ²²Except for the Levites' property and the city's property, which are in the middle of the prince's property, the territory between the portion of Judah and the portion of Benjamin shall belong to the prince.

The Southern Portions. ²³These are the remaining tribes:

From the eastern border to the western border: Benjamin, one portion. ²⁴Along the territory of Benjamin from the eastern border to the western border: Simeon, one portion. ²⁵Along the territory of Simeon from the eastern border to the western border: Issachar, one portion. ²⁶Along the territory of Issachar from the eastern border to the western border: Zebulun, one portion. ²⁷Along the territory of Zebulun from the eastern border to the western border: Gad, one portion. ²⁸Along the territory of Gad shall be the southern border. This boundary shall extend from Tamar to the waters of Meribath-kadesh, and along the Wadi of Egypt to the Great Sea. ²⁹This is the land you shall apportion as a heritage among the tribes of Israel, and these are their portions—oracle of the Lord GOD.

The Gates of the City. ³⁰These are the exits from the city: On the north side, measuring forty-five hundred cubits— ³¹the gates are named after the tribes of Israel—on the north, three gates: the gate of Reuben, one; the gate of Judah, one; and the gate of Levi, one. ³²On the east side, measuring forty-five hundred cubits, three gates: the gate of Joseph, one; the gate of Benjamin, one; and the gate of Dan, one. ³³On the south side, measuring forty-five hundred cubits, three gates: the gate of Simeon, one; the gate of Issachar, one; and the gate of Zebulun, one. ³⁴On the west side, measuring forty-five hundred cubits, three gates: the gate of Gad, one; the gate of Asher, one; and the gate of Naphtali, one. ³⁵The circuit of the city shall be eighteen thousand cubits. From now on the name of the city is "The LORD is there."

□ LUKE 18

The Parable of the Persistent Widow.
18:1 Then he told them a parable about the necessity for them to pray always without becoming weary. He said, ²"There was a judge in a certain town who neither feared God nor respected any human being. ³And a widow in that town used to come to him and say, 'Render a just decision for me against my adversary.' ⁴For a long time the judge was unwilling, but eventually he thought, 'While it is true that I neither fear God nor respect any human being, ⁵because this widow keeps bothering me I shall deliver a just decision for her lest she finally come and strike me.'" ⁶The Lord said, "Pay attention to what the dishonest

judge says. [7]Will not God then secure the rights of his chosen ones who call out to him day and night? Will he be slow to answer them? [8]I tell you, he will see to it that justice is done for them speedily. But when the Son of Man comes, will he find faith on earth?"

The Parable of the Pharisee and the Tax Collector. [9]He then addressed this parable to those who were convinced of their own righteousness and despised everyone else. [10]"Two people went up to the temple area to pray; one was a Pharisee and the other was a tax collector. [11]The Pharisee took up his position and spoke this prayer to himself, 'O God, I thank you that I am not like the rest of humanity—greedy, dishonest, adulterous—or even like this tax collector. [12]I fast twice a week, and I pay tithes on my whole income.' [13]But the tax collector stood off at a distance and would not even raise his eyes to heaven but beat his breast and prayed, 'O God, be merciful to me a sinner.' [14]I tell you, the latter went home justified, not the former; for everyone who exalts himself will be humbled, and the one who humbles himself will be exalted."

Saying on Children and the Kingdom. [15]People were bringing even infants to him that he might touch them, and when the disciples saw this, they rebuked them. [16]Jesus, however, called the children to himself and said, "Let the children come to me and do not prevent them; for the kingdom of God belongs to such as these. [17]Amen, I say to you, whoever does not accept the kingdom of God like a child will not enter it."

The Rich Official. [18]An official asked him this question, "Good teacher, what must I do to inherit eternal life?" [19]Jesus answered him, "Why do you call me good? No one is good but God alone. [20]You know the commandments, 'You shall not commit adultery; you shall not kill; you shall not steal; you shall not bear false witness; honor your father and your mother.'"

[21]And he replied, "All of these I have observed from my youth." [22]When Jesus heard this he said to him, "There is still one thing left for you: sell all that you have and distribute it to the poor, and you will have a treasure in heaven. Then come, follow me." [23]But when he heard this he became quite sad, for he was very rich.

On Riches and Renunciation. [24]Jesus looked at him [now sad] and said, "How hard it is for those who have wealth to enter the kingdom of God! [25]For it is easier for a camel to pass through the eye of a needle than for a rich person to enter the kingdom of God." [26]Those who heard this said, "Then who can be saved?" [27]And he said, "What is impossible for human beings is possible for God." [28]Then Peter said, "We have given up our possessions and followed you." [29]He said to them, "Amen, I say to you, there is no one who has given up house or wife or brothers or parents or children for the sake of the kingdom of God [30]who will not receive [back] an overabundant return in this present age and eternal life in the age to come."

The Third Prediction of the Passion. [31]Then he took the Twelve aside and said to them, "Behold, we are going up to Jerusalem and everything written by the prophets about the Son of Man will be fulfilled. [32]He will be handed over to the Gentiles and he will be mocked and insulted and spat upon; [33]and after they have scourged him they will kill him, but on the third day he will rise." [34]But they understood nothing of this; the word remained hidden from them and they failed to comprehend what he said.

The Healing of the Blind Beggar. [35]Now as he approached Jericho a blind man was sitting by the roadside begging, [36]and hearing a crowd going by, he inquired what was happening. [37]They told him, "Jesus of Nazareth is passing by." [38]He shouted, "Jesus, Son of David, have pity on me!" [39]The people walking in front rebuked him, telling him to be silent, but he kept calling out all the more, "Son of David, have pity on me!" ⁴⁰Then Jesus stopped and ordered that he be brought to him; and when he came near, Jesus asked him, ⁴¹"What do you want me to do for me? you?" He replied, "Lord, please let me see." ⁴²Jesus told him, "Have sight; your faith has saved you." ⁴³He immediately received his sight and followed him, giving glory to God. When they saw this, all the people gave praise to God.

November 28

St. Catherine Labouré

I knew nothing; I was nothing. For this reason God picked me out.

— St. Catherine Labouré

☐ DANIEL 1–2

The Food Test. 1:1 In the third year of the reign of Jehoiakim, king of Judah, King Nebuchadnezzar of Babylon came and laid siege to Jerusalem. ²The Lord handed over to him Jehoiakim, king of Judah, and some of the vessels of the temple of God, which he carried off to the land of Shinar and placed in the temple treasury of his god.

³The king told Ashpenaz, his chief chamberlain, to bring in some of the Israelites, some of the royal line and of the nobility. ⁴They should be young men without any defect, handsome, proficient in wisdom, well informed, and insightful, such as could take their place in the king's palace; he was to teach them the language and literature of the Chaldeans. ⁵The king allotted them a daily portion of food and wine from the royal table. After three years' training they were to enter the king's service. ⁶Among these were Judeans, Daniel, Hananiah, Mishael, and Azariah. ⁷The chief chamberlain changed their names: Daniel to Belteshazzar, Hananiah to Shadrach, Mishael to Meshach, and Azariah to Abednego.

⁸But Daniel was resolved not to defile himself with the king's food or wine; so he begged the chief chamberlain to spare him this defilement. ⁹Though God had given Daniel the favor and sympathy of the chief chamberlain, ¹⁰he said to Daniel, "I am afraid of my lord the king, who allotted your food and drink. If he sees that you look thinner in comparison to the other young men of your age, you will endanger my life with the king." ¹¹Then Daniel said to the guardian whom the chief chamberlain had put in charge of Daniel, Hananiah, Mishael, and Azariah, ¹²"Please test your servants for ten days. Let us be given vegetables to eat and water to drink. ¹³Then see how we look in comparison with the other young men who eat from the royal table, and treat your servants according to what you see." ¹⁴He agreed to this request, and tested them for ten days; ¹⁵after ten days they looked healthier and better fed than any of the young men who ate from the royal table. ¹⁶So the steward continued to take away the food and wine they were to receive, and gave them vegetables.

¹⁷To these four young men God gave knowledge and proficiency in all literature and wisdom, and to Daniel the understanding of all visions and dreams. ¹⁸At the end

of the time the king had specified for their preparation, the chief chamberlain brought them before Nebuchadnezzar. ¹⁹When the king had spoken with all of them, none was found equal to Daniel, Hananiah, Mishael, and Azariah; and so they entered the king's service. ²⁰In any question of wisdom or understanding which the king put to them, he found them ten times better than any of the magicians and enchanters in his kingdom. ²¹Daniel remained there until the first year of King Cyrus.

Nebuchadnezzar's Dream. 2:1 In the second year of his reign, King Nebuchadnezzar had a dream which left his spirit no rest and robbed him of his sleep. ²So he ordered that the magicians, enchanters, sorcerers, and Chaldeans be summoned to interpret the dream for him. When they came and presented themselves to the king, ³he said to them, "I had a dream which will allow my spirit no rest until I know what it means." ⁴The Chaldeans answered the king in Aramaic: "O king, live forever! Tell your servants the dream and we will give its meaning." ⁵The king answered the Chaldeans, "This is what I have decided: unless you tell me the dream and its meaning, you shall be cut to pieces and your houses made into a refuse heap. ⁶But if you tell me the dream and its meaning, you shall receive from me gifts and presents and great honors. Therefore tell me the dream and its meaning."

⁷Again they answered, "Let the king tell his servants the dream and we will give its meaning." ⁸But the king replied: "I know for certain that you are bargaining for time, since you know what I have decided. ⁹If you do not tell me the dream, there can be but one decree for you. You have conspired to present a false and deceitful interpretation to me until the crisis is past. Tell me the dream, therefore, that I may be sure that you can also give its correct interpretation."

¹⁰The Chaldeans answered the king: "There is not a man on earth who can do what you ask, O king; never has any king, however great and mighty, asked such a thing of any magician, enchanter, or Chaldean. ¹¹What you demand, O king, is too difficult; there is no one who can tell it to the king except the gods, who do not dwell among people of flesh." ¹²At this the king became violently angry and ordered all the wise men of Babylon to be put to death. ¹³When the decree was issued that the wise men should be slain, Daniel and his companions were also sought out.

¹⁴Then Daniel prudently took counsel with Arioch, the chief of the king's guard, who had set out to kill the wise men of Babylon. ¹⁵He asked Arioch, the officer of the king, "What is the reason for this harsh order from the king?" When Arioch told him, ¹⁶Daniel went and asked for time from the king, that he might give him the interpretation.

¹⁷Daniel went home and informed his companions Hananiah, Mishael, and Azariah, ¹⁸that they might implore the mercy of the God of heaven in regard to this mystery, so that Daniel and his companions might not perish with the rest of the wise men of Babylon. ¹⁹During the night the mystery was revealed to Daniel in a vision, and he blessed the God of heaven:

²⁰"Blessed be the name of God forever
     and ever,
        for wisdom and power are his.
²¹He causes the changes of the times
     and seasons,
        establishes kings and deposes them.
He gives wisdom to the wise
     and knowledge to those who
        understand.
²²He reveals deep and hidden things
     and knows what is in the darkness,
        for the light dwells with him.
²³To you, God of my ancestors,
     I give thanks and praise,
        because you have given me wisdom
           and power.

Now you have shown me what we
asked of you,
you have made known to us the
king's dream."

²⁴So Daniel went to Arioch, whom the
king had appointed to destroy the wise men
of Babylon, and said to him, "Do not put
the wise men of Babylon to death. Bring me
before the king, and I will tell him the interpretation of the dream." Arioch quickly
brought Daniel to the king and said, ²⁵"I
have found a man among the Judean exiles
who can give the interpretation to the king."
²⁶The king asked Daniel, whose name was
Belteshazzar, "Can you tell me the dream
that I had and its meaning?" ²⁷In the king's
presence Daniel made this reply:

"The mystery about which the king has
inquired, the wise men, enchanters, magicians, and diviners could not explain to the
king. ²⁸But there is a God in heaven who
reveals mysteries, and he has shown King
Nebuchadnezzar what is to happen in the
last days; this was your dream, the visions
you saw as you lay in bed. ²⁹To you in your
bed there came thoughts about what should
happen in the future, and he who reveals
mysteries showed you what is to be. ³⁰To
me also this mystery has been revealed; not
that I am wiser than any other living person,
but in order that its meaning may be made
known to the king, that you may understand the thoughts of your own mind.

³¹"In your vision, O king, you saw a
statue, very large and exceedingly bright,
terrifying in appearance as it stood before
you. ³²Its head was pure gold, its chest and
arms were silver, its belly and thighs bronze,
³³its legs iron, its feet partly iron and partly
clay. ³⁴While you watched, a stone was
hewn from a mountain without a hand being put to it, and it struck its iron and clay
feet, breaking them in pieces. ³⁵The iron,
clay, bronze, silver, and gold all crumbled
at once, fine as the chaff on the threshing floor in summer, and the wind blew

them away without leaving a trace. But the
stone that struck the statue became a great
mountain and filled the whole earth.

³⁶"This was the dream; the interpretation we shall also give in the king's presence. ³⁷You, O king, are the king of kings;
to you the God of heaven has given dominion and strength, power and glory;
³⁸human beings, wild beasts, and birds of
the air, wherever they may dwell, he has
handed over to you, making you ruler
over them all; you are the head of gold.
³⁹Another kingdom shall take your place,
inferior to yours, then a third kingdom,
of bronze, which shall rule over the whole
earth. ⁴⁰There shall be a fourth kingdom,
strong as iron; it shall break in pieces and
subdue all these others, just as iron breaks
in pieces and crushes everything else.
⁴¹The feet and toes you saw, partly of clay
and partly of iron, mean that it shall be
a divided kingdom, but yet have some of
the hardness of iron. As you saw the iron
mixed with clay tile, ⁴²and the toes partly
iron and partly clay, the kingdom shall be
partly strong and partly fragile. ⁴³The iron
mixed with clay means that they shall seal
their alliances by intermarriage, but they
shall not stay united, any more than iron
mixes with clay. ⁴⁴In the lifetime of those
kings the God of heaven will set up a kingdom that shall never be destroyed or delivered up to another people; rather, it shall
break in pieces all these kingdoms and put
an end to them, and it shall stand forever.
⁴⁵That is the meaning of the stone you saw
hewn from the mountain without a hand
being put to it, which broke in pieces the
iron, bronze, clay, silver, and gold. The
great God has revealed to the king what
shall be in the future; this is exactly what
you dreamed, and its meaning is sure."

⁴⁶Then King Nebuchadnezzar fell down
and worshiped Daniel and ordered sacrifice and incense offered to him. ⁴⁷To Daniel
the king said, "Truly your God is the God
of gods and Lord of kings and a revealer

of mysteries; that is why you were able to reveal this mystery." [48]He advanced Daniel to a high post, gave him many generous presents, made him ruler of the whole province of Babylon and chief prefect over all the wise men of Babylon. [49]At Daniel's request the king made Shadrach, Meshach, and Abednego administrators of the province of Babylon, while Daniel himself remained at the king's court.

☐ LUKE 19

Zacchaeus the Tax Collector. 19:1 He came to Jericho and intended to pass through the town. [2]Now a man there named Zacchaeus, who was a chief tax collector and also a wealthy man, [3]was seeking to see who Jesus was; but he could not see him because of the crowd, for he was short in stature. [4]So he ran ahead and climbed a sycamore tree in order to see Jesus, who was about to pass that way. [5]When he reached the place, Jesus looked up and said to him, "Zacchaeus, come down quickly, for today I must stay at your house." [6]And he came down quickly and received him with joy. [7]When they all saw this, they began to grumble, saying, "He has gone to stay at the house of a sinner." [8]But Zacchaeus stood there and said to the Lord, "Behold, half of my possessions, Lord, I shall give to the poor, and if I have extorted anything from anyone I shall repay it four times over." [9]And Jesus said to him, "Today salvation has come to this house because this man too is a descendant of Abraham. [10]For the Son of Man has come to seek and to save what was lost."

The Parable of the Ten Gold Coins. [11]While they were listening to him speak, he proceeded to tell a parable because he was near Jerusalem and they thought that the kingdom of God would appear there immediately. [12]So he said, "A nobleman went off to a distant country to obtain the kingship for himself and then to return. [13]He called ten of his servants and gave them ten gold coins and told them, 'Engage in trade with these until I return.' [14]His fellow citizens, however, despised him and sent a delegation after him to announce, 'We do not want this man to be our king.' [15]But when he returned after obtaining the kingship, he had the servants called, to whom he had given the money, to learn what they had gained by trading. [16]The first came forward and said, 'Sir, your gold coin has earned ten additional ones.' [17]He replied, 'Well done, good servant! You have been faithful in this very small matter; take charge of ten cities.' [18]Then the second came and reported, 'Your gold coin, sir, has earned five more.' [19]And to this servant too he said, 'You, take charge of five cities.' [20]Then the other servant came and said, 'Sir, here is your gold coin; I kept it stored away in a handkerchief, [21]for I was afraid of you, because you are a demanding person; you take up what you did not lay down and you harvest what you did not plant.' [22]He said to him, 'With your own words I shall condemn you, you wicked servant. You knew I was a demanding person, taking up what I did not lay down and harvesting what I did not plant; [23]why did you not put my money in a bank? Then on my return I would have collected it with interest.' [24]And to those standing by he said, 'Take the gold coin from him and give it to the servant who has ten.' [25]But they said to him, 'Sir, he has ten gold coins.' [26]'I tell you, to everyone who has, more will be given, but from the one who has not, even what he has will be taken away. [27]Now as for those enemies of mine who did not want me as their king, bring them here and slay them before me.'"

The Entry into Jerusalem. [28]After he had said this, he proceeded on his journey up to Jerusalem. ²⁹As he drew near to Bethphage and Bethany at the place called the Mount of Olives, he sent two of his disciples. ³⁰He said, "Go into the village opposite you, and as you enter it you will find a colt tethered on which no one has ever sat. Untie it and bring it here. ³¹And if anyone should ask you, 'Why are you untying it?' you will answer, 'The Master has need of it.'" ³²So those who had been sent went off and found everything just as he had told them. ³³And as they were untying the colt, its owners said to them, "Why are you untying this colt?" ³⁴They answered, "The Master has need of it." ³⁵So they brought it to Jesus, threw their cloaks over the colt, and helped Jesus to mount. ³⁶As he rode along, the people were spreading their cloaks on the road; ³⁷and now as he was approaching the slope of the Mount of Olives, the whole multitude of his disciples began to praise God aloud with joy for all the mighty deeds they had seen. ³⁸They proclaimed:

"Blessed is the king who comes in the
    name of the Lord.
Peace in heaven and glory in the
    highest."

³⁹Some of the Pharisees in the crowd said to him, "Teacher, rebuke your disciples." ⁴⁰He said in reply, "I tell you, if they keep silent, the stones will cry out!"

The Lament for Jerusalem. ⁴¹As he drew near, he saw the city and wept over it, ⁴²saying, "If this day you only knew what makes for peace—but now it is hidden from your eyes. ⁴³For the days are coming upon you when your enemies will raise a palisade against you; they will encircle you and hem you in on all sides. ⁴⁴They will smash you to the ground and your children within you, and they will not leave one stone upon another within you because you did not recognize the time of your visitation."

The Cleansing of the Temple. ⁴⁵Then Jesus entered the temple area and proceeded to drive out those who were selling things, ⁴⁶saying to them, "It is written, 'My house shall be a house of prayer, but you have made it a den of thieves.'" ⁴⁷And every day he was teaching in the temple area. The chief priests, the scribes, and the leaders of the people, meanwhile, were seeking to put him to death, ⁴⁸but they could find no way to accomplish their purpose because all the people were hanging on his words.

November 29

The virtue of innocence is held as foolishness by the wise of this world. Anything that is done out of innocence, they doubtless consider to be stupidity, and whatever truth approves of, in practice is called folly by men of worldly wisdom.

— POPE ST. GREGORY THE GREAT

☐ DANIEL 3

The Fiery Furnace. 3:1 King Nebuchadnezzar had a golden statue made, sixty cubits high and six cubits wide, which he set up in the plain of Dura in the province of Babylon. ²He then ordered the satraps, prefects, and governors, the counselors, treasurers, judges, magistrates and all the officials of the provinces to be summoned to the dedication of the statue which he had set up. ³The satraps, prefects, and governors, the counselors, treasurers, judges, magistrates and all the officials of the provinces came together for the dedication and stood before the statue which King Nebuchadnezzar had set up. ⁴A herald cried out: "Nations and peoples of every language, ⁵when you hear the sound of the horn, pipe, zither, dulcimer, harp, double-flute, and all the other musical instruments, you must fall down and worship the golden statue which King Nebuchadnezzar has set up. ⁶Whoever does not fall down and worship shall be instantly cast into a white-hot furnace." ⁷Therefore, as soon as they heard the sound of the horn, pipe, zither, dulcimer, harp, double-flute, and all the other musical instruments, the nations and peoples of every language all fell down and worshiped the golden statue which King Nebuchadnezzar had set up.

⁸At that point, some of the Chaldeans came and accused the Jews ⁹to King Nebuchadnezzar: "O king, live forever! ¹⁰O king, you issued a decree that everyone who heard the sound of the horn, pipe, zither, dulcimer, harp, and double-flute, and all the other musical instruments should fall down and worship the golden statue; ¹¹whoever did not was to be cast into a white-hot furnace. ¹²There are certain Jews whom you have made administrators of the province of Babylon: Shadrach, Meshach, and Abednego; these men, O king, have paid no attention to you; they will not serve your god or worship the golden statue which you set up."

¹³Nebuchadnezzar flew into a rage and sent for Shadrach, Meshach, and Abednego, who were promptly brought before the king. ¹⁴King Nebuchadnezzar questioned them: "Is it true, Shadrach, Meshach, and Abednego, that you will not serve my god, or worship the golden statue that I set up? ¹⁵Now, if you are ready to fall down and worship the statue I made, whenever you hear the sound of the horn, pipe, zither, dulcimer, harp, double-flute, and all the other musical instruments,

then all will be well; if not, you shall be instantly cast into the white-hot furnace; and who is the God who can deliver you out of my hands?" ¹⁶Shadrach, Meshach, and Abednego answered King Nebuchadnezzar, "There is no need for us to defend ourselves before you in this matter. ¹⁷If our God, whom we serve, can save us from the white-hot furnace and from your hands, O king, may he save us! ¹⁸But even if he will not, you should know, O king, that we will not serve your god or worship the golden statue which you set up."

¹⁹Nebuchadnezzar's face became livid with utter rage against Shadrach, Meshach, and Abednego. He ordered the furnace to be heated seven times more than usual ²⁰and had some of the strongest men in his army bind Shadrach, Meshach, and Abednego and cast them into the white-hot furnace. ²¹They were bound and cast into the white-hot furnace with their trousers, shirts, hats and other garments, ²²for the king's order was urgent. So huge a fire was kindled in the furnace that the flames devoured the men who threw Shadrach, Meshach, and Abednego into it. ²³But these three fell, bound, into the midst of the white-hot furnace.

Prayer of Azariah. ²⁴They walked about in the flames, singing to God and blessing the Lord. ²⁵Azariah stood up in the midst of the fire and prayed aloud:

²⁶"Blessed are you, and praiseworthy,
  O Lord, the God of our ancestors,
  and glorious forever is your name.
²⁷For you are just in all you have done;
  all your deeds are faultless, all your
    ways right,
  and all your judgments proper.
²⁸You have executed proper judgments
  in all that you have brought upon us
  and upon Jerusalem, the holy city of
    our ancestors.
By a proper judgment you have done
  all this

because of our sins;

²⁹For we have sinned and transgressed
by departing from you,
and we have done every kind of evil.
³⁰Your commandments we have not
heeded or observed,
nor have we done as you ordered us
for our good.
³¹Therefore all you have brought
upon us,
all you have done to us,
you have done by a proper
judgment.
³²You have handed us over to our
enemies,
lawless and hateful rebels;
to an unjust king, the worst in all
the world.
³³Now we cannot open our mouths;
shame and reproach have come
upon us,
your servants, who revere you.
³⁴For your name's sake, do not deliver
us up forever,
or make void your covenant.
³⁵Do not take away your mercy from us,
for the sake of Abraham, your
beloved,
Isaac your servant, and Israel your
holy one,
³⁶To whom you promised to multiply
their offspring
like the stars of heaven,
or the sand on the shore of the sea.
³⁷For we are reduced, O Lord, beyond
any other nation,
brought low everywhere in the
world this day
because of our sins.
³⁸We have in our day no prince,
prophet, or leader,
no burnt offering, sacrifice,
oblation, or incense,
no place to offer first fruits, to find
favor with you.
³⁹But with contrite heart and humble
spirit

let us be received;
As though it were burnt offerings of
rams and bulls,
or tens of thousands of fat lambs,
⁴⁰So let our sacrifice be in your
presence today
and find favor before you;
for those who trust in you cannot be
put to shame.
⁴¹And now we follow you with our
whole heart,
we fear you and we seek your face.
Do not put us to shame,
⁴²but deal with us in your kindness
and great mercy.
⁴³Deliver us in accord with your wonders,
and bring glory to your name,
O Lord:
⁴⁴Let all those be put to shame
who inflict evils on your servants;
Let them be shamed and powerless,
and their strength broken;
⁴⁵Let them know that you alone are the
Lord God,
glorious over the whole world."

⁴⁶Now the king's servants who had
thrown them in continued to stoke the furnace with naptha, pitch, tow, and brush.
⁴⁷The flames rose forty-nine cubits above the
furnace, ⁴⁸and spread out, burning the Chaldeans that it caught around the furnace.
⁴⁹But the angel of the Lord went down into
the furnace with Azariah and his companions, drove the fiery flames out of the furnace, ⁵⁰and made the inside of the furnace
as though a dew-laden breeze were blowing
through it. The fire in no way touched them
or caused them pain or harm. ⁵¹Then these
three in the furnace with one voice sang,
glorifying and blessing God:

⁵²"Blessed are you, O Lord, the God of
our ancestors,
praiseworthy and exalted above all
forever;
And blessed is your holy and glorious
name,

praiseworthy and exalted above all
for all ages.

[53]Blessed are you in the temple of your
holy glory,
praiseworthy and glorious above all
forever.

[54]Blessed are you on the throne of your
kingdom,
praiseworthy and exalted above all
forever.

[55]Blessed are you who look into the
depths
from your throne upon the
cherubim,
praiseworthy and exalted above all
forever.

[56]Blessed are you in the firmament of
heaven,
praiseworthy and glorious forever.

[57]Bless the Lord, all you works of the
Lord,
praise and exalt him above all
forever.

[58]Angels of the Lord, bless the Lord,
praise and exalt him above all
forever.

[59]You heavens, bless the Lord,
praise and exalt him above all
forever.

[60]All you waters above the heavens,
bless the Lord,
praise and exalt him above all
forever.

[61]All you powers, bless the Lord;
praise and exalt him above all
forever.

[62]Sun and moon, bless the Lord;
praise and exalt him above all
forever.

[63]Stars of heaven, bless the Lord;
praise and exalt him above all
forever.

[64]Every shower and dew, bless the
Lord;
praise and exalt him above all
forever.

[65]All you winds, bless the Lord;

praise and exalt him above all
forever.

[66]Fire and heat, bless the Lord;
praise and exalt him above all
forever.

[67]Cold and chill, bless the Lord;
praise and exalt him above all
forever.

[68]Dew and rain, bless the Lord;
praise and exalt him above all
forever.

[69]Frost and chill, bless the Lord;
praise and exalt him above all
forever.

[70]Hoarfrost and snow, bless the Lord;
praise and exalt him above all
forever.

[71]Nights and days, bless the Lord;
praise and exalt him above all
forever.

[72]Light and darkness, bless the Lord;
praise and exalt him above all
forever.

[73]Lightnings and clouds, bless the
Lord;
praise and exalt him above all
forever.

[74]Let the earth bless the Lord,
praise and exalt him above all
forever.

[75]Mountains and hills, bless the Lord;
praise and exalt him above all
forever.

[76]Everything growing on earth, bless
the Lord;
praise and exalt him above all
forever.

[77]You springs, bless the Lord;
praise and exalt him above all
forever.

[78]Seas and rivers, bless the Lord;
praise and exalt him above all
forever.

[79]You sea monsters and all water
creatures, bless the Lord;
praise and exalt him above all
forever.

[80]All you birds of the air, bless the
Lord;
praise and exalt him above all
forever.
[81]All you beasts, wild and tame, bless
the Lord;
praise and exalt him above all
forever.
[82]All you mortals, bless the Lord;
praise and exalt him above all
forever.
[83]O Israel, bless the Lord;
praise and exalt him above all
forever.
[84]Priests of the Lord, bless the Lord;
praise and exalt him above all
forever.
[85]Servants of the Lord, bless the Lord;
praise and exalt him above all
forever.
[86]Spirits and souls of the just, bless the
Lord;
praise and exalt him above all
forever.
[87]Holy and humble of heart, bless the
Lord;
praise and exalt him above all
forever.
[88]Hananiah, Azariah, Mishael, bless the
Lord;
praise and exalt him above all
forever.
For he has delivered us from Sheol,
and saved us from the power of
death;
He has freed us from the raging flame
and delivered us from the fire.
[89]Give thanks to the Lord, who is
good,
whose mercy endures forever.
[90]Bless the God of gods, all you who
fear the Lord;
praise and give thanks,
for his mercy endures forever."

Deliverance from the Furnace. [91]Then
King Nebuchadnezzar was startled and
rose in haste, asking his counselors, "Did
we not cast three men bound into the
fire?" "Certainly, O king," they answered.
[92]"But," he replied, "I see four men un-
bound and unhurt, walking in the fire,
and the fourth looks like a son of God."
[93]Then Nebuchadnezzar came to the opening of the white-hot furnace and called:
"Shadrach, Meshach, and Abednego, servants of the Most High God, come out."
Thereupon Shadrach, Meshach, and Abednego came out of the fire. [94]When the satraps, prefects, governors, and counselors
of the king came together, they saw that
the fire had had no power over the bodies of these men; not a hair of their heads
had been singed, nor were their garments
altered; there was not even a smell of fire
about them. [95]Nebuchadnezzar exclaimed,
"Blessed be the God of Shadrach, Meshach,
and Abednego, who sent his angel to deliver the servants that trusted in him; they
disobeyed the royal command and yielded
their bodies rather than serve or worship
any god except their own God. [96]Therefore
I decree for nations and peoples of every
language that whoever blasphemes the God
of Shadrach, Meshach, and Abednego shall
be cut to pieces and his house made into a
refuse heap. For there is no other God who
can rescue like this." [97]Then the king promoted Shadrach, Meshach, and Abednego
in the province of Babylon.

[98]King Nebuchadnezzar to the nations
and peoples of every language, wherever they dwell on earth: May your peace
abound! [99]It has seemed good to me to
publish the signs and wonders which the
Most High God has accomplished in my
regard.

[100]How great are his signs, how mighty
his wonders;
his kingship is an everlasting
kingship,
and his dominion endures through
all generations.

☐ LUKE 20

The Authority of Jesus Questioned. 20:1 One day as he was teaching the people in the temple area and proclaiming the good news, the chief priests and scribes, together with the elders, approached him ²and said to him, "Tell us, by what authority are you doing these things? Or who is the one who gave you this authority?" ³He said to them in reply, "I shall ask you a question. Tell me, ⁴was John's baptism of heavenly or of human origin?" ⁵They discussed this among themselves, and said, "If we say, 'Of heavenly origin,' he will say, 'Why did you not believe him?' ⁶But if we say, 'Of human origin,' then all the people will stone us, for they are convinced that John was a prophet." ⁷So they answered that they did not know from where it came. ⁸Then Jesus said to them, "Neither shall I tell you by what authority I do these things."

The Parable of the Tenant Farmers. ⁹Then he proceeded to tell the people this parable. "[A] man planted a vineyard, leased it to tenant farmers, and then went on a journey for a long time. ¹⁰At harvest time he sent a servant to the tenant farmers to receive some of the produce of the vineyard. But they beat the servant and sent him away empty-handed. ¹¹So he proceeded to send another servant, but him also they beat and insulted and sent away empty-handed. ¹²Then he proceeded to send a third, but this one too they wounded and threw out. ¹³The owner of the vineyard said, 'What shall I do? I shall send my beloved son; maybe they will respect him.' ¹⁴But when the tenant farmers saw him they said to one another, 'This is the heir. Let us kill him that the inheritance may become ours.' ¹⁵So they threw him out of the vineyard and killed him. What will the owner of the vineyard do to them? ¹⁶He will come and put those tenant farmers to death and turn over the vineyard to others." When the people heard this, they exclaimed, "Let it not be so!" ¹⁷But he looked at them and asked, "What then does this scripture passage mean:

'The stone which the builders rejected has become the cornerstone'?

¹⁸Everyone who falls on that stone will be dashed to pieces; and it will crush anyone on whom it falls." ¹⁹The scribes and chief priests sought to lay their hands on him at that very hour, but they feared the people, for they knew that he had addressed this parable to them.

Paying Taxes to the Emperor. ²⁰They watched him closely and sent agents pretending to be righteous who were to trap him in speech, in order to hand him over to the authority and power of the governor. ²¹They posed this question to him, "Teacher, we know that what you say and teach is correct, and you show no partiality, but teach the way of God in accordance with the truth. ²²Is it lawful for us to pay tribute to Caesar or not?" ²³Recognizing their craftiness he said to them, ²⁴"Show me a denarius; whose image and name does it bear?" They replied, "Caesar's." ²⁵So he said to them, "Then repay to Caesar what belongs to Caesar and to God what belongs to God." ²⁶They were unable to trap him by something he might say before the people, and so amazed were they at his reply that they fell silent.

The Question about the Resurrection. ²⁷Some Sadducees, those who deny that there is a resurrection, came forward and put this question to him, ²⁸saying, "Teacher, Moses wrote for us, 'If someone's brother dies leaving a wife but no child, his brother must take the wife and raise up descendants for his brother.' ²⁹Now there were seven brothers; the first married a woman but died childless. ³⁰Then the second ³¹and the third married her, and likewise all the seven died childless. ³²Finally the woman also died. ³³Now at the resurrection whose wife will that woman be? For all seven had been married to her." ³⁴Jesus said to them, "The children of this age marry and are given in marriage; ³⁵but those who are deemed worthy to attain to the coming age and to the resurrection of the dead neither marry nor are given in marriage. ³⁶They can no longer die, for they are like angels; and they are the children of God because they are the ones who will rise. ³⁷That the dead will rise even Moses made known in the passage about the bush, when he called 'Lord' the God of Abraham, the God of Isaac, and the God of Jacob; ³⁸and he is not God of the dead, but of the living, for to him all are alive." ³⁹Some of the scribes said in reply, "Teacher, you have answered well." ⁴⁰And they no longer dared to ask him anything.

The Question about David's Son. ⁴¹Then he said to them, "How do they claim that the Messiah is the Son of David? ⁴²For David himself in the Book of Psalms says:

'The Lord said to my lord,
"Sit at my right hand
⁴³till I make your enemies your
footstool."'

⁴⁴Now if David calls him 'lord,' how can he be his son?"

Denunciation of the Scribes. ⁴⁵Then, within the hearing of all the people, he said to [his] disciples, ⁴⁶"Be on guard against the scribes, who like to go around in long robes and love greetings in marketplaces, seats of honor in synagogues, and places of honor at banquets. ⁴⁷They devour the houses of widows and, as a pretext, recite lengthy prayers. They will receive a very severe condemnation."

November 30

St. Andrew

In vain, then, do we attempt to compute definitely the years that may remain to this world, when we may hear from the mouth of the Truth himself that it is not for us to know this.

— St. Augustine of Hippo

☐ DANIEL 4

Nebuchadnezzar's Madness. 4:1 I, Nebuchadnezzar, was at home in my palace, content and prosperous. ²I had a terrifying dream as I lay in bed, and the images and my visions frightened me. ³So I issued a decree that all the wise men of Babylon should be brought before me to give the interpretation of the dream. ⁴When the magicians, enchanters, Chaldeans, and diviners had come in, I related the dream before them; but none of them could tell me its meaning. ⁵Finally there came before me Daniel, whose name is Belteshazzar after the name of my god, and in whom is a spirit of the holy gods. I repeated the dream to him: ⁶"Belteshazzar, chief of the magicians, I know that a spirit of the holy gods is in you and no mystery is too difficult for you; this is the dream that I saw, tell me its meaning.

⁷"These were the visions I saw while in bed: I saw a tree of great height at the center of the earth. ⁸It was large and strong, with its top touching the heavens, and it could be seen to the ends of the earth. ⁹Its leaves were beautiful, its fruit abundant,

providing food for all. Under it the wild beasts found shade, in its branches the birds of the air nested; all flesh ate of it. ¹⁰In the vision I saw while in bed, a holy watcher came down from heaven ¹¹and cried aloud in these words:

'Cut down the tree and lop off its
    branches,
    strip off its leaves and scatter its
        fruit;
Let the beasts flee from beneath it, and
    the birds from its branches,
    ¹²but leave its stump in the earth.
Bound with iron and bronze,
    let him be fed with the grass of the
        field
    and bathed with the dew of heaven;
    let his lot be with the beasts in the
        grass of the earth.
¹³Let his mind be changed from a
    human one;
    let the mind of a beast be given him,
    till seven years pass over him.
¹⁴By decree of the watchers is this
    proclamation,
    by order of the holy ones, this
        sentence;
That all who live may know
    that the Most High is sovereign over
        human kingship,
    Giving it to whom he wills,
    and setting it over the lowliest of
        mortals.'

¹⁵"This is the dream that I, King Nebuchadnezzar, had. Now, Belteshazzar, tell me its meaning. None of the wise men in my kingdom can tell me the meaning, but you can, because the spirit of the holy gods is in you."

¹⁶Then Daniel, whose name was Belteshazzar, was appalled for a time, dismayed by his thoughts. "Belteshazzar," the king said to him, "do not let the dream or its meaning dismay you." "My lord," Belteshazzar replied, "may this dream be for your enemies, and its meaning for your foes.

¹⁷The tree that you saw, large and strong, its top touching the heavens, that could be seen by the whole earth, ¹⁸its leaves beautiful, its fruit abundant, providing food for all, under which the wild beasts lived, and in whose branches the birds of the air dwelt— ¹⁹you are that tree, O king, large and strong! Your majesty has become so great as to touch the heavens, and your rule reaches to the ends of the earth. ²⁰As for the king's vision of a holy watcher, who came down from heaven and proclaimed: 'Cut down the tree and destroy it, but leave its stump in the earth. Bound with iron and bronze, let him be fed with the grass of the field, and bathed with the dew of heaven; let his lot be with wild beasts till seven years pass over him'— ²¹here is its meaning, O king, here is the sentence that the Most High has passed upon my lord king: ²²You shall be cast out from human society and dwell with wild beasts; you shall be given grass to eat like an ox and be bathed with the dew of heaven; seven years shall pass over you, until you know that the Most High is sovereign over human kingship and gives it to whom he will. ²³The command that the stump of the tree is to be left means that your kingdom shall be preserved for you, once you have learned that heaven is sovereign. ²⁴Therefore, O king, may my advice be acceptable to you; atone for your sins by good deeds, and for your misdeeds by kindness to the poor; then your contentment will be long lasting."

²⁵All this happened to King Nebuchadnezzar. ²⁶Twelve months later, as he was walking on the roof of the royal palace in Babylon, ²⁷the king said, "Babylon the great! Was it not I, with my great strength, who built it as a royal residence for my splendor and majesty?" ²⁸While these words were still on the king's lips, a voice spoke from heaven, "It has been decreed for you, King Nebuchadnezzar, that your kingship is taken from you! ²⁹You shall be cast out from human society, and shall dwell with wild

beasts; you shall be given grass to eat like an ox, and seven years shall pass over you, until you learn that the Most High is sovereign over human kingship and gives it to whom he will." [30]At once this was fulfilled. Nebuchadnezzar was cast out from human society, he ate grass like an ox, and his body was bathed with the dew of heaven, until his hair grew like the feathers of an eagle, and his nails like the claws of a bird.

[31]When this period was over, I, Nebuchadnezzar, raised my eyes to heaven; my reason was restored to me, and I blessed the Most High, I praised and glorified the One who lives forever,

Whose dominion is an everlasting dominion,
and whose kingdom endures through all generations.

[32]All who live on the earth are counted as nothing;
he does as he wills with the powers of heaven
and with those who live on the earth.
There is no one who can stay his hand or say to him, "What have you done?"

[33]At the same time my reason returned to me, and for the glory of my kingdom, my majesty and my splendor returned to me. My counselors and nobles sought me out; I was restored to my kingdom and became much greater than before. [34]Now, I, Nebuchadnezzar, praise and exalt and glorify the King of heaven, all of whose works are right and ways just; and who is able to humble those who walk in pride.

☐ LUKE 21

The Poor Widow's Contribution. 21:1 When he looked up he saw some wealthy people putting their offerings into the treasury [2]and he noticed a poor widow putting in two small coins. [3]He said, "I tell you truly, this poor widow put in more than all the rest; [4]for those others have all made offerings from their surplus wealth, but she, from her poverty, has offered her whole livelihood."

The Destruction of the Temple Foretold. [5]While some people were speaking about how the temple was adorned with costly stones and votive offerings, he said, [6]"All that you see here—the days will come when there will not be left a stone upon another stone that will not be thrown down."

The Sign of the End. [7]Then they asked him, "Teacher, when will this happen? And what sign will there be when all these things are about to happen?" [8]He answered, "See that you not be deceived, for many will come in my name, saying, 'I am he,' and 'The time has come.' Do not follow them!

[9]When you hear of wars and insurrections, do not be terrified; for such things must happen first, but it will not immediately be the end." [10]Then he said to them, "Nation will rise against nation, and kingdom against kingdom. [11]There will be powerful earthquakes, famines, and plagues from place to place; and awesome sights and mighty signs will come from the sky.

The Coming Persecution. [12]"Before all this happens, however, they will seize and persecute you, they will hand you over to the synagogues and to prisons, and they will have you led before kings and governors because of my name. [13]It will lead to your giving testimony. [14]Remember, you are not to prepare your defense beforehand, [15]for I myself shall give you a wisdom in speaking that all your adversaries will be powerless to resist or refute. [16]You will even be handed over by parents, brothers, relatives, and friends, and they will put some of you to death. [17]You will be hated by all because of my name, [18]but not a hair on your head will be destroyed. [19]By your perseverance you will secure your lives.

The Great Tribulation. [20]"When you see Jerusalem surrounded by armies, know that its desolation is at hand. [21]Then those in Judea must flee to the mountains. Let those within the city escape from it, and let those in the countryside not enter the city, [22]for these days are the time of punishment when all the scriptures are fulfilled. [23]Woe to pregnant women and nursing mothers in those days, for a terrible calamity will come upon the earth and a wrathful judgment upon this people. [24]They will fall by the edge of the sword and be taken as captives to all the Gentiles; and Jerusalem will be trampled underfoot by the Gentiles until the times of the Gentiles are fulfilled.

The Coming of the Son of Man. [25]"There will be signs in the sun, the moon, and the stars, and on earth nations will be in dismay, perplexed by the roaring of the sea and the waves. [26]People will die of fright in anticipation of what is coming upon the world, for the powers of the heavens will be shaken. [27]And then they will see the Son of Man coming in a cloud with power and great glory. [28]But when these signs begin to happen, stand erect and raise your heads because your redemption is at hand."

The Lesson of the Fig Tree. [29]He taught them a lesson. "Consider the fig tree and all the other trees. [30]When their buds burst open, you see for yourselves and know that summer is now near; [31]in the same way, when you see these things happening, know that the kingdom of God is near. [32]Amen, I say to you, this generation will not pass away until all these things have taken place. [33]Heaven and earth will pass away, but my words will not pass away.

Exhortation to be Vigilant. [34]"Beware that your hearts do not become drowsy from carousing and drunkenness and the anxieties of daily life, and that day catch you by surprise [35]like a trap. For that day will assault everyone who lives on the face of the earth. [36]Be vigilant at all times and pray that you have the strength to escape the tribulations that are imminent and to stand before the Son of Man."

Ministry in Jerusalem. [37]During the day, Jesus was teaching in the temple area, but at night he would leave and stay at the place called the Mount of Olives. [38]And all the people would get up early each morning to listen to him in the temple area.

December 1

The more we lack in this world, the more surely we discover the best thing the world has to offer us: the cross.

— BLESSED CHARLES DE FOUCAULD

☐ DANIEL 5–6

The Writing on the Wall. 5:1 King Belshazzar gave a great banquet for a thousand of his nobles, with whom he drank. ²Under the influence of the wine, he ordered the gold and silver vessels which Nebuchadnezzar, his father, had taken from the temple in Jerusalem, to be brought in so that the king, his nobles, his consorts, and his concubines might drink from them. ³When the gold vessels taken from the temple, the house of God in Jerusalem, had been brought in, and while the king, his nobles, his consorts, and his concubines were drinking ⁴wine from them, they praised their gods of gold and silver, bronze and iron, wood and stone.

⁵Suddenly, opposite the lampstand, the fingers of a human hand appeared, writing on the plaster of the wall in the king's palace. When the king saw the hand that wrote, ⁶his face became pale; his thoughts terrified him, his hip joints shook, and his knees knocked. ⁷The king shouted for the enchanters, Chaldeans, and diviners to be brought in. "Whoever reads this writing and tells me what it means," he said to the wise men of Babylon, "shall be clothed in purple, wear a chain of gold around his neck, and be third in governing the kingdom." ⁸But though all the king's wise men came in, none of them could either read the writing or tell the king what it meant. ⁹Then King Belshazzar was greatly terrified; his face became pale, and his nobles were thrown into confusion.

¹⁰When the queen heard of the discussion between the king and his nobles, she entered the banquet hall and said, "O king, live forever! Do not let your thoughts terrify you, or your face become so pale! ¹¹There is a man in your kingdom in whom is a spirit of the holy gods; during the lifetime of your father he showed brilliant insight and god-like wisdom. King Nebuchadnezzar, your father, made him chief of the magicians, enchanters, Chaldeans, and diviners. ¹²Because this Daniel, whom the king named Belteshazzar, has shown an extraordinary spirit, knowledge, and insight in interpreting dreams, explaining riddles and solving problems, let him now be summoned to tell you what this means."

¹³Then Daniel was brought into the presence of the king. The king asked him, "Are you the Daniel, one of the Jewish exiles, whom my father, the king, brought from Judah? ¹⁴I have heard that the spirit of the gods is in you, that you have shown brilliant insight and extraordinary wisdom. ¹⁵The wise men and enchanters were brought in to me to read this writing and tell me its meaning, but they could not say what the words meant. ¹⁶But I have heard that you can give interpretations and solve problems; now, if you are able to read the writing and tell me what it means, you shall be clothed in purple, wear a chain of gold around your neck, and be third in governing the kingdom."

¹⁷Daniel answered the king: "You may keep your gifts, or give your presents to someone else; but the writing I will read for the king, and tell what it means. ¹⁸The Most High God gave your father Nebu-

chadnezzar kingship, greatness, splendor, and majesty. ¹⁹Because he made him so great, the nations and peoples of every language dreaded and feared him. Whomever he willed, he would kill or let live; whomever he willed, he would exalt or humble. ²⁰But when his heart became proud and his spirit hardened by insolence, he was put down from his royal throne and deprived of his glory; ²¹he was cast out from human society and his heart was made like that of a beast; he lived with wild asses, and ate grass like an ox; his body was bathed with the dew of heaven, until he learned that the Most High God is sovereign over human kingship and sets over it whom he will. ²²You, his son, Belshazzar, have not humbled your heart, though you knew all this; ²³you have rebelled against the Lord of heaven. You had the vessels of his temple brought before you, so that you and your nobles, your consorts and your concubines, might drink wine from them; and you praised the gods of silver and gold, bronze and iron, wood and stone, that neither see nor hear nor have intelligence. But the God in whose hand is your very breath and the whole course of your life, you did not glorify. ²⁴By him was the hand sent, and the writing set down.

²⁵"This is the writing that was inscribed: Mene, Tekel, and Peres. These words mean: ²⁶Mene, God has numbered your kingdom and put an end to it; ²⁷Tekel, you have been weighed on the scales and found wanting; ²⁸Peres, your kingdom has been divided and given to the Medes and Persians."

²⁹Then by order of Belshazzar they clothed Daniel in purple, with a chain of gold around his neck, and proclaimed him third in governing the kingdom. ³⁰That very night Belshazzar, the Chaldean king, was slain:

6:1 And Darius the Mede succeeded to the kingdom at the age of sixty-two.

The Lions' Den. ²Darius decided to appoint over his entire kingdom one hundred and twenty satraps. ³These were accountable to three ministers, one of whom was Daniel; the satraps reported to them, so that the king should suffer no loss. ⁴Daniel outshone all the ministers and satraps because an extraordinary spirit was in him, and the king considered setting him over the entire kingdom. ⁵Then the ministers and satraps tried to find grounds for accusation against Daniel regarding the kingdom. But they could not accuse him of any corruption. Because he was trustworthy, no fault or corruption was to be found in him. ⁶Then these men said to themselves, "We shall find no grounds for accusation against this Daniel except in connection with the law of his God." ⁷So these ministers and satraps stormed in to the king and said to him, "King Darius, live forever! ⁸All the ministers of the kingdom, the prefects, satraps, counselors, and governors agree that the following prohibition ought to be put in force by royal decree: for thirty days, whoever makes a petition to anyone, divine or human, except to you, O king, shall be thrown into a den of lions. ⁹Now, O king, let the prohibition be issued over your signature, immutable and irrevocable according to the law of the Medes and Persians." ¹⁰So King Darius signed the prohibition into law.

¹¹Even after Daniel heard that this law had been signed, he continued his custom of going home to kneel in prayer and give thanks to his God in the upper chamber three times a day, with the windows open toward Jerusalem. ¹²So these men stormed in and found Daniel praying and pleading before his God. ¹³Then they went to remind the king about the prohibition: "Did you not sign a decree, O king, that for thirty days, whoever makes a petition to anyone, divine or human, except to you, O king, shall be cast into a den of lions?" The king answered them, "The decree is absolute,

irrevocable under the law of the Medes and Persians." [14]To this they replied, "Daniel, one of the Jewish exiles, has paid no attention to you, O king, or to the prohibition you signed; three times a day he offers his prayer." [15]The king was deeply grieved at this news and he made up his mind to save Daniel; he worked till sunset to rescue him. [16]But these men pressed the king. "Keep in mind, O king," they said, "that under the law of the Medes and Persians every royal prohibition or decree is irrevocable." [17]So the king ordered Daniel to be brought and cast into the lions' den. To Daniel he said, "Your God, whom you serve so constantly, must save you." [18]To forestall any tampering, the king sealed with his own ring and the rings of the lords the stone that had been brought to block the opening of the den.

[19]Then the king returned to his palace for the night; he refused to eat and he dismissed the entertainers. Since sleep was impossible for him, [20]the king rose very early the next morning and hastened to the lions' den. [21]As he drew near, he cried out to Daniel sorrowfully, "Daniel, servant of the living God, has your God whom you serve so constantly been able to save you from the lions?" [22]Daniel answered the king: "O king, live forever! [23]My God sent his angel and closed the lions' mouths so that they have not hurt me.

For I have been found innocent before him; neither have I done you any harm, O king!" [24]This gave the king great joy. At his order Daniel was brought up from the den; he was found to be unharmed because he trusted in his God. [25]The king then ordered the men who had accused Daniel, along with their children and their wives, to be cast into the lions' den. Before they reached the bottom of the den, the lions overpowered them and crushed all their bones.

[26]Then King Darius wrote to the nations and peoples of every language, wherever they dwell on the earth: "May your peace abound! [27]I decree that throughout my royal domain the God of Daniel is to be reverenced and feared:

"For he is the living God, enduring
    forever,
  whose kingdom shall not be
    destroyed,
  whose dominion shall be without
    end,
[28]A savior and deliverer,
  working signs and wonders in
    heaven and on earth,
  who saved Daniel from the lions'
    power."

[29]So Daniel fared well during the reign of Darius and the reign of Cyrus the Persian.

☐ LUKE 22

The Conspiracy against Jesus. 22:1 Now the feast of Unleavened Bread, called the Passover, was drawing near, [2]and the chief priests and the scribes were seeking a way to put him to death, for they were afraid of the people. [3]Then Satan entered into Judas, the one surnamed Iscariot, who was counted among the Twelve, [4]and he went to the chief priests and temple guards to discuss a plan for handing him over to them. [5]They were pleased and agreed to pay him money. [6]He accepted their offer and sought a favorable opportunity to hand him over to them in the absence of a crowd.

Preparations for the Passover. [7]When the day of the feast of Unleavened Bread arrived, the day for sacrificing the Passover lamb, [8]he sent out Peter and John, instructing them, "Go and make preparations for us to eat the Passover." [9]They asked him, "Where do you want us to make the preparations?" [10]And he answered them, "When you go into the city, a man will meet you carrying a jar of water. Follow him into the house that he enters [11]and say to the master of the house, 'The teacher says to you, "Where is the guest room where I may eat the Passover with my disciples?"' [12]He will show you a large upper room that is furnished. Make the preparations there." [13]Then they went off and found everything exactly as he had told them, and there they prepared the Passover.

The Last Supper. [14]When the hour came, he took his place at table with the apostles. [15]He said to them, "I have eagerly desired to eat this Passover with you before I suffer, [16]for, I tell you, I shall not eat it [again] until there is fulfillment in the kingdom of God." [17]Then he took a cup, gave thanks, and said, "Take this and share it among yourselves; [18]for I tell you [that] from this time on I shall not drink of the fruit of the vine until the kingdom of God comes." [19]Then he took the bread, said the blessing, broke it, and gave it to them, saying, "This is my body, which will be given for you; do this in memory of me." [20]And likewise the cup after they had eaten, saying, "This cup is the new covenant in my blood, which will be shed for you.

The Betrayal Foretold. [21]"And yet behold, the hand of the one who is to betray me is with me on the table; [22]for the Son of Man indeed goes as it has been determined; but woe to that man by whom he is betrayed." [23]And they began to debate among themselves who among them would do such a deed.

The Role of the Disciples. [24]Then an argument broke out among them about which of them should be regarded as the greatest. [25]He said to them, "The kings of the Gentiles lord it over them and those in authority over them are addressed as 'Benefactors'; [26]but among you it shall not be so. Rather, let the greatest among you be as the youngest, and the leader as the servant. [27]For who is greater: the one seated at table or the one who serves? Is it not the one seated at table? I am among you as the one who serves. [28]It is you who have stood by me in my trials; [29]and I confer a kingdom on you, just as my Father has conferred one on me, [30]that you may eat and drink at my table in my kingdom; and you will sit on thrones judging the twelve tribes of Israel.

Peter's Denial Foretold. [31]"Simon, Simon, behold Satan has demanded to sift all of you like wheat, [32]but I have prayed that your own faith may not fail; and once you have turned back, you must strengthen your brothers." [33]He said to him, "Lord, I am prepared to go to prison and to die with you." [34]But he replied, "I tell you, Peter, before the cock crows this day, you will deny three times that you know me."

Instructions for the Time of Crisis. [35]He said to them, "When I sent you forth without a money bag or a sack or sandals, were you in need of anything?" "No, nothing," they replied. [36]He said to them, "But now one who has a money bag should take it, and likewise a sack, and one who does not have a sword should sell his cloak and buy one. [37]For I tell you that this scripture must be fulfilled in me, namely, 'He was counted among the wicked'; and indeed what is written about me is coming to fulfillment." [38]Then they said, "Lord, look, there are two swords here." But he replied, "It is enough!"

The Agony in the Garden. [39]Then going out he went, as was his custom, to the Mount of Olives, and the disciples followed him. [40]When he arrived at the place he said to them, "Pray that you may not undergo the test." [41]After withdrawing about a stone's throw from them and kneeling, he prayed, [42]saying, "Father, if you are willing, take this cup away from me; still, not my will but yours be done." [[43]And to strengthen him an angel from heaven appeared to him. [44]He was in such agony and he prayed so fervently that his sweat became like drops of blood falling on the ground.] [45]When he rose from prayer and returned to his disciples, he found them sleeping from grief. [46]He said to them,

"Why are you sleeping? Get up and pray that you may not undergo the test."

The Betrayal and Arrest of Jesus. [47]While he was still speaking, a crowd approached and in front was one of the Twelve, a man named Judas. He went up to Jesus to kiss him. [48]Jesus said to him, "Judas, are you betraying the Son of Man with a kiss?" [49]His disciples realized what was about to happen, and they asked, "Lord, shall we strike with a sword?" [50]And one of them struck the high priest's servant and cut off his right ear. [51]But Jesus said in reply, "Stop, no more of this!" Then he touched the servant's ear and healed him. [52]And Jesus said to the chief priests and temple guards and elders who had come for him, "Have you come out as against a robber, with swords and clubs? [53]Day after day I was with you in the temple area, and you did not seize me; but this is your hour, the time for the power of darkness."

Peter's Denial of Jesus. [54]After arresting him they led him away and took him into the house of the high priest; Peter was following at a distance. [55]They lit a fire in the middle of the courtyard and sat around it, and Peter sat down with them. [56]When a maid saw him seated in the light, she looked intently at him and said, "This man too was with him." [57]But he denied it saying, "Woman, I do not know him." [58]A short while later someone else saw him and said, "You too are one of them"; but Peter answered, "My friend, I am not." [59]About an hour later, still another insisted, "Assuredly, this man too was with him, for he also is a Galilean." [60]But Peter said, "My friend, I do not know what you are talking about." Just as he was saying this, the cock crowed, [61]and the Lord turned and looked at Peter; and Peter remembered the word of the Lord, how he had said to him, "Before the cock crows today, you will deny me three times." [62]He went out and began to weep bitterly. [63]The men who held Jesus in custody were ridiculing and beating him. [64]They blindfolded him and questioned him, saying, "Prophesy! Who is it that struck you?" [65]And they reviled him in saying many other things against him.

Jesus before the Sanhedrin. [66]When day came the council of elders of the people met, both chief priests and scribes, and they brought him before their Sanhedrin. [67]They said, "If you are the Messiah, tell us," but he replied to them, "If I tell you, you will not believe, [68]and if I question, you will not respond. [69]But from this time on the Son of Man will be seated at the right hand of the power of God." [70]They all asked, "Are you then the Son of God?" He replied to them, "You say that I am." [71]Then they said, "What further need have we for testimony? We have heard it from his own mouth."

December 2

It is the nature of love ever to give and to take, to love and to be loved, and these two things meet in anyone who loves. Thus the love of Christ is both avid and generous. If He absorbs us utterly into himself, in return He gives us His very Self again.

— BLESSED JOHN VAN RUYSBROECK

☐ DANIEL 7-8

The Beasts and the Judgment. 7:1 In the first year of King Belshazzar of Babylon, as Daniel lay in bed he had a dream, visions in his head. Then he wrote down the dream; the account began: ²In the vision I saw during the night, suddenly the four winds of heaven stirred up the great sea, ³from which emerged four immense beasts, each different from the others. ⁴The first was like a lion, but with eagle's wings. While I watched, the wings were plucked; it was raised from the ground to stand on two feet like a human being, and given a human mind. ⁵The second beast was like a bear; it was raised up on one side, and among the teeth in its mouth were three tusks. It was given the order, "Arise, devour much flesh." ⁶After this I looked and saw another beast, like a leopard; on its back were four wings like those of a bird, and it had four heads. To this beast dominion was given. ⁷After this, in the visions of the night I saw a fourth beast, terrifying, horrible, and of extraordinary strength; it had great iron teeth with which it devoured and crushed, and it trampled with its feet what was left. It differed from the beasts that preceded it. It had ten horns. ⁸I was considering the ten horns it had, when suddenly another, a little horn, sprang out of their midst, and three of the previous horns were torn away to make room for it. This horn had eyes like human eyes, and a mouth that spoke arrogantly. ⁹As I watched,

Thrones were set up
    and the Ancient of Days took his
        throne.

His clothing was white as snow,
    the hair on his head like pure wool;
His throne was flames of fire,
    with wheels of burning fire.
¹⁰A river of fire surged forth,
    flowing from where he sat;
Thousands upon thousands were
        ministering to him,
    and myriads upon myriads stood
        before him.

The court was convened, and the books were opened. ¹¹I watched, then, from the first of the arrogant words which the horn spoke, until the beast was slain and its body destroyed and thrown into the burning fire. ¹²As for the other beasts, their dominion was taken away, but they were granted a prolongation of life for a time and a season. ¹³As the visions during the night continued, I saw coming with the clouds of heaven

One like a son of man.
When he reached the Ancient of Days
    and was presented before him,
¹⁴He received dominion, splendor, and
        kingship;
    all nations, peoples and tongues will
        serve him.
His dominion is an everlasting
        dominion
    that shall not pass away,
    his kingship, one that shall not be
        destroyed.

¹⁵Because of this, my spirit was anguished and I, Daniel, was terrified by my visions.

¹⁶I approached one of those present and asked him the truth of all this; in answer, he made known to me its meaning: ¹⁷"These four great beasts stand for four kings which shall arise on the earth. ¹⁸But the holy ones of the Most High shall receive the kingship, to possess it forever and ever."

¹⁹Then I wished to make certain about the fourth beast, so very terrible and different from the others, devouring and crushing with its iron teeth and bronze claws, and trampling with its feet what was left; ²⁰and about the ten horns on its head, and the other one that sprang up, before which three horns fell; and about the horn with the eyes and the mouth that spoke arrogantly, which appeared greater than its fellows. ²¹For, as I watched, that horn made war against the holy ones and was victorious ²²until the Ancient of Days came, and judgment was pronounced in favor of the holy ones of the Most High, and the time arrived for the holy ones to possess the kingship. ²³He answered me thus:

"The fourth beast shall be a fourth
    kingdom on earth,
    different from all the others;
The whole earth it shall devour,
    trample down and crush.
²⁴The ten horns shall be ten kings
    rising out of that kingdom;
another shall rise up after them,
Different from those before him,
    who shall lay low three kings.
²⁵He shall speak against the Most High
    and wear down the holy ones of the
    Most High,
intending to change the feast days
    and the law.
They shall be handed over to him
    for a time, two times, and half a
    time.
²⁶But when the court is convened,
    and his dominion is taken away
to be abolished and completely
    destroyed,

²⁷Then the kingship and dominion and
    majesty
    of all the kingdoms under the
        heavens
    shall be given to the people of the
        holy ones of the Most High,
Whose kingship shall be an everlasting
    kingship,
    whom all dominions shall serve and
        obey."

²⁸This is the end of the report. I, Daniel, was greatly terrified by my thoughts, and my face became pale, but I kept the matter to myself.

The Ram and the He-goat. 8:1 After this first vision, I, Daniel, had another, in the third year of the reign of King Belshazzar. ²In my vision I saw myself in the fortress of Susa in the province of Elam; I was beside the river Ulai. ³I looked up and saw standing by the river a ram with two great horns, the one larger and newer than the other. ⁴I saw the ram butting toward the west, north, and south. No beast could withstand it or be rescued from its power; it did what it pleased and grew powerful.

⁵As I was reflecting, a he-goat with a prominent horn on its forehead suddenly came from the west across the whole earth without touching the ground. ⁶It came to the two-horned ram I had seen standing by the river, and rushed toward it with savage force. ⁷I saw it reach the ram; enraged, the he-goat attacked and shattered both its horns. The ram did not have the strength to withstand it; the he-goat threw the ram to the ground and trampled upon it. No one could rescue the ram from its power.

⁸The he-goat grew very powerful, but at the height of its strength the great horn was shattered, and in its place came up four others, facing the four winds of heaven. ⁹Out of one of them came a little horn which grew and grew toward the south, the east, and the glorious land. ¹⁰It grew even

to the host of heaven, so that it cast down to earth some of the host and some of the stars and trampled on them. [11]It grew even to the Prince of the host, from whom the daily sacrifice was removed, and whose sanctuary was cast down. [12]The host was given over together with the daily sacrifice in the course of transgression. It cast truth to the ground, and was succeeding in its undertaking.

[13]I heard a holy one speaking, and another said to whichever one it was that spoke, "How long shall the events of this vision last concerning the daily sacrifice, the desolating sin, the giving over of the sanctuary and the host for trampling?" [14]He answered him, "For two thousand three hundred evenings and mornings; then the sanctuary shall be set right."

[15]While I, Daniel, sought the meaning of the vision I had seen, one who looked like a man stood before me, [16]and on the Ulai I heard a human voice that cried out, "Gabriel, explain the vision to this man." [17]When he came near where I was standing, I fell prostrate in terror. But he said to me, "Understand, O son of man, that the vision refers to the end time." [18]As he spoke to me, I fell forward unconscious; he touched me and made me stand up. [19]"I will show you," he said, "what is to happen in the last days of wrath; for it is for the appointed time of the end.

[20]"The two-horned ram you saw represents the kings of the Medes and Persians.

[21]The he-goat is the king of the Greeks, and the great horn on its forehead is the first king. [22]The four that rose in its place when it was shattered are four kingdoms that will issue from his nation, but without his strength.

[23]"At the end of their reign,
when sinners have reached their
measure,
There shall arise a king,
impudent, and skilled in intrigue.
[24]He shall be strong and powerful,
bring about fearful ruin,
and succeed in his undertaking.
He shall destroy powerful peoples;
[25]his cunning shall be against the
holy ones,
his treacherous conduct shall
succeed.
He shall be proud of heart
and destroy many by stealth.
But when he rises against the Prince of
princes,
he shall be broken without a hand
being raised.
[26]As for the vision of the evenings and
the mornings,
what was spoken is true.
But you, keep this vision secret:
it is for the distant future."

[27]I, Daniel, was weak and ill for some days; then I arose and took care of the king's affairs. But the vision left me desolate, without understanding.

☐ LUKE 23

Jesus before Pilate. 23:1 Then the whole assembly of them arose and brought him before Pilate. [2]They brought charges against him, saying, "We found this man misleading our people; he opposes the payment of taxes to Caesar and maintains that he is the Messiah, a king." [3]Pilate asked him, "Are you the king of the Jews?" He said to him in reply, "You say so." [4]Pilate then addressed the chief priests and the crowds, "I find this man not guilty." [5]But they were adamant and said, "He is inciting the people with his teaching throughout all Judea, from Galilee where he began even to here."

Jesus before Herod. [6]On hearing this Pilate asked if the man was a Galilean; [7]and upon learning that he was under Herod's jurisdiction, he sent him to Herod who was in Jerusalem at that time. [8]Herod was very glad to see Jesus; he had been wanting to see him for a long time, for he had heard about him and had been hoping to see him perform some sign. [9]He questioned him at length, but he gave him no answer. [10]The chief priests and scribes, meanwhile, stood by accusing him harshly. [11][Even] Herod and his soldiers treated him contemptuously and mocked him, and after clothing him in resplendent garb, he sent him back to Pilate. [12]Herod and Pilate became friends that very day, even though they had been enemies formerly. [13]Pilate then summoned the chief priests, the rulers, and the people [14]and said to them, "You brought this man to me and accused him of inciting the people to revolt. I have conducted my investigation in your presence and have not found this man guilty of the charges you have brought against him, [15]nor did Herod, for he sent him back to us. So no capital crime has been committed by him. [16]Therefore I shall have him flogged and then release him." [17]

The Sentence of Death. [18]But all together they shouted out, "Away with this man! Release Barabbas to us." [19](Now Barabbas had been imprisoned for a rebellion that had taken place in the city and for murder.) [20]Again Pilate addressed them, still wishing to release Jesus, [21]but they continued their shouting, "Crucify him! Crucify him!" [22]Pilate addressed them a third time, "What evil has this man done? I found him guilty of no capital crime. Therefore I shall have him flogged and then release him." [23]With loud shouts, however, they persisted in calling for his crucifixion, and their voices prevailed. [24]The verdict of Pilate was that their demand should be granted. [25]So he released the man who had been imprisoned for rebellion and murder, for whom they asked, and he handed Jesus over to them to deal with as they wished.

The Way of the Cross. [26]As they led him away they took hold of a certain Simon, a Cyrenian, who was coming in from the country; and after laying the cross on him, they made him carry it behind Jesus. [27]A large crowd of people followed Jesus, including many women who mourned and lamented him. [28]Jesus turned to them and said, "Daughters of Jerusalem, do not weep for me; weep instead for yourselves and for your children, [29]for indeed, the days are coming when people will say, 'Blessed are the barren, the wombs that never bore and the breasts that never nursed.' [30]At that time people will say to the mountains, 'Fall upon us!' and to the hills, 'Cover us!' [31]for if these things are done when the wood is green what will happen when it is dry?" [32]Now two others, both criminals, were led away with him to be executed.

The Crucifixion. [33]When they came to the place called the Skull, they crucified him and the criminals there, one on his right, the other on his left. [34][Then Jesus said, "Father, forgive them, they know not what they do."] They divided his garments by casting lots. [35]The people stood by and watched; the rulers, meanwhile, sneered at him and said, "He saved others, let him save himself if he is the chosen one, the Messiah of God." [36]Even the soldiers jeered at him. As they approached to offer him wine [37]they called out, "If you are King of the Jews, save yourself." [38]Above him there was an inscription that read, "This is the King of the Jews." [39]Now one of the criminals hanging there reviled Jesus, saying, "Are you not the Messiah? Save yourself and us." [40]The other, however, rebuking him, said in reply, "Have you no fear of God, for you are subject to the same condemnation? [41]And indeed, we have been condemned justly, for the sentence we received corresponds to our crimes, but this man has done nothing criminal." [42]Then he said, "Jesus, remember me when you come into your kingdom." [43]He replied to him,

"Amen, I say to you, today you will be with me in Paradise."

The Death of Jesus. [44]It was now about noon and darkness came over the whole land until three in the afternoon [45]because of an eclipse of the sun. Then the veil of the temple was torn down the middle. [46]Jesus cried out in a loud voice, "Father, into your hands I commend my spirit"; and when he had said this he breathed his last. [47]The centurion who witnessed what had happened glorified God and said, "This man was innocent beyond doubt." [48]When all the people who had gathered for this spectacle saw what had happened, they returned home beating their breasts; [49]but all his acquaintances stood at a distance, including the women who had followed him from Galilee and saw these events.

The Burial of Jesus. [50]Now there was a virtuous and righteous man named Joseph who, though he was a member of the council, [51]had not consented to their plan of action. He came from the Jewish town of Arimathea and was awaiting the kingdom of God. [52]He went to Pilate and asked for the body of Jesus. [53]After he had taken the body down, he wrapped it in a linen cloth and laid him in a rock-hewn tomb in which no one had yet been buried. [54]It was the day of preparation, and the sabbath was about to begin. [55]The women who had come from Galilee with him followed behind, and when they had seen the tomb and the way in which his body was laid in it, [56]they returned and prepared spices and perfumed oils. Then they rested on the sabbath according to the commandment.

December 3

St. Francis Xavier

The better friends you are, the more you can talk straight. But while you are only on nodding terms, be slow to scold.

— St. Francis Xavier

☐ DANIEL 9-12

The Seventy Weeks of Years. 9:1 It was the first year that Darius, son of Ahasuerus, of the race of the Medes, reigned over the kingdom of the Chaldeans; [2]in the first year of his reign, I, Daniel, perceived in the books the number of years the LORD had decreed to the prophet Jeremiah: Jerusalem was to lie in ruins for seventy years.

[3]I turned to the Lord God, to seek help, in prayer and petition, with fasting, sackcloth, and ashes. [4]I prayed to the LORD, my God, and confessed, "Ah, Lord, great and awesome God, you who keep your covenant and show mercy toward those who love you and keep your commandments and your precepts! [5]We have sinned, been wicked and done evil; we have rebelled and turned from your commandments and your laws. [6]We have not obeyed your servants the prophets, who spoke in your name to our kings, our princes, our ancestors, and all the people of the land. [7]Justice, O Lord, is on your side; we are shamefaced even to this day: the men of Judah, the residents of Jerusalem, and all Israel, near and far, in all the lands to which you have scattered them because of their treachery toward you. [8]O LORD, we are ashamed, like our kings, our princes, and our ancestors, for having sinned against you. [9]But

to the Lord, our God, belong compassion and forgiveness, though we rebelled against him [10]and did not hear the voice of the LORD, our God, by walking in his laws given through his servants the prophets. [11]The curse and the oath written in the law of Moses, the servant of God, were poured out over us for our sins, because all Israel transgressed your law and turned aside, refusing to hear your voice. [12]He fulfilled the words he spoke against us and against those who ruled us, by bringing upon us an evil—no evil so great has happened under heaven as happened in Jerusalem. [13]As it is written in the law of Moses, this evil has come upon us. We did not appease the LORD, our God, by turning back from our wickedness and acting according to your truth, [14]so the LORD kept watch over the evil and brought it upon us. The LORD, our God, is just in all that he has done: we did not listen to his voice.

[15]"Now, Lord, our God, who led your people out of the land of Egypt with a strong hand, and made a name for yourself even to this day, we have sinned, we are guilty. [16]Lord, in keeping with all your just deeds, let your anger and your wrath be turned away from your city Jerusalem, your holy mountain. On account of our sins and the crimes of our ancestors, Jerusalem and your people have become the reproach of all our neighbors. [17]Now, our God, hear the prayer and petition of your servant; and for your own sake, Lord, let your face shine upon your desolate sanctuary. [18]Give ear, my God, and listen; open your eyes and look upon our desolate city upon which your name is invoked. When we present our petition before you, we rely not on our just deeds, but on your great mercy. [19]Lord, hear! Lord, pardon! Lord, be attentive and act without delay, for your own sake, my God, because your name is invoked upon your city and your people!"

[20]I was still praying to the LORD, my God, confessing my sin and the sin of my people Israel, presenting my petition concerning the holy mountain of my God— [21]I was still praying, when the man, Gabriel, whom I had seen in vision before, came to me in flight at the time of the evening offering. [22]He instructed me in these words: "Daniel, I have now come to give you understanding. [23]When you began your petition, an answer was given which I have come to announce, because you are beloved. Therefore, mark the answer and understand the vision.

[24]"Seventy weeks are decreed
for your people and for your holy
city:
Then transgression will stop and sin
will end,
guilt will be expiated,
Everlasting justice will be introduced,
vision and prophecy ratified,
and a holy of holies will be anointed.
[25]Know and understand:
From the utterance of the word
that Jerusalem was to be rebuilt
Until there is an anointed ruler,
there shall be seven weeks.
In the course of sixty-two weeks
it shall be rebuilt,
With squares and trenches,
in time of affliction.
[26]After the sixty-two weeks
an anointed one shall be cut down
with no one to help him.
And the people of a leader who will
come
shall destroy the city and the
sanctuary.
His end shall come in a flood;
until the end of the war, which is
decreed,
there will be desolation.
[27]For one week he shall make
a firm covenant with the many;
Half the week
he shall abolish sacrifice and
offering;

In their place shall be the desolating
abomination
until the ruin that is decreed
is poured out upon the desolator.""

An Angelic Vision. 10:1 In the third year of Cyrus, king of Persia, a revelation was given to Daniel, who had been named Belteshazzar. The revelation was certain: a great war; he understood this from the vision. ²In those days, I, Daniel, mourned three full weeks. ³I ate no savory food, took no meat or wine, and did not anoint myself at all until the end of the three weeks.

⁴On the twenty-fourth day of the first month I was on the bank of the great river, the Tigris. ⁵As I looked up, I saw a man dressed in linen with a belt of fine gold around his waist. ⁶His body was like chrysolite, his face shone like lightning, his eyes were like fiery torches, his arms and feet looked like burnished bronze, and the sound of his voice was like the roar of a multitude. ⁷I alone, Daniel, saw the vision; but great fear seized those who were with me; they fled and hid themselves, although they did not see the vision. ⁸So I was left alone to see this great vision. No strength remained in me; I turned the color of death and was powerless. ⁹When I heard the sound of his voice, I fell face forward unconscious.

¹⁰But then a hand touched me, raising me to my hands and knees. ¹¹"Daniel, beloved," he said to me, "understand the words which I am speaking to you; stand up, for my mission now is to you." When he said this to me, I stood up trembling. ¹²"Do not fear, Daniel," he continued; "from the first day you made up your mind to acquire understanding and humble yourself before God, your prayer was heard. Because of it I started out, ¹³but the prince of the kingdom of Persia stood in my way for twenty-one days, until finally Michael, one of the chief princes, came to help me. I left him there with the prince of the kingdom of Persia, ¹⁴and came to make

you understand what shall happen to your people in the last days; for there is yet a vision concerning those days."

¹⁵While he was speaking thus to me, I fell forward and kept silent. ¹⁶Then something like a hand touched my lips; I opened my mouth and said to the one standing before me, "My lord, I was seized with pangs at the vision and I was powerless. ¹⁷How can my lord's servant speak with you, my lord? For now no strength or even breath is left in me." ¹⁸The one who looked like a man touched me again and strengthened me, saying, ¹⁹"Do not fear, beloved. Peace! Take courage and be strong." When he spoke to me, I grew strong and said, "Speak, my lord, for you have strengthened me." ²⁰"Do you know," he asked, "why I have come to you? Soon I must fight the prince of Persia again. When I leave, the prince of Greece will come; ²¹but I shall tell you what is written in the book of truth. No one supports me against these except Michael, your prince, **11:1** and in the first year of Darius the Mede I stood to strengthen him and be his refuge.

The Hellenistic Age. 11:2 "Now I shall tell you the truth.

"Three kings of Persia are yet to appear; and a fourth shall acquire the greatest riches of all. Strengthened by his riches, he shall stir up all kingdoms, even that of Greece. ³But a powerful king shall appear and rule with great might, doing as he wills. ⁴No sooner shall he appear than his kingdom shall be broken and divided in four directions under heaven; but not among his descendants or in keeping with his mighty rule, for his kingdom shall be torn to pieces and belong to others.

⁵"The king of the south shall grow strong, but one of his princes shall grow stronger still and govern a domain greater than his. ⁶After some years they shall become allies: the daughter of the king of the south shall come to the king of the north to carry out

the alliance. But she shall not retain power: and his offspring shall not survive, and she shall be given up, together with those who brought her, her son, and her supporter in due time. [7]A descendant of her line shall succeed to his place, and shall come against the army, enter the stronghold of the king of the north, attack and conquer them. [8]Even their gods, with their molten images and their precious vessels of silver and gold, he shall carry away as spoils of war into Egypt. For years he shall have nothing to do with the king of the north. [9]Then the latter shall invade the land of the king of the south, and return to his own country.

[10]"But his sons shall be aroused and assemble a great armed host, which shall pass through like a flood and again surge around the stronghold. [11]The king of the south, enraged, shall go out to fight against the king of the north, who shall field a great host, but the host shall be given into his hand. [12]When the host is carried off, in the pride of his heart he shall bring down tens of thousands, but he shall not triumph. [13]For the king of the north shall raise another army, greater than before; after some years he shall attack with this large army and great resources. [14]In those times many shall resist the king of the south, and violent ones among your people shall rise up in fulfillment of vision, but they shall stumble. [15]When the king of the north comes, he shall set up siegeworks and take the fortified city by storm. The forces of the south shall not withstand him, and not even his picked troops shall have the strength to withstand. [16]The invader shall do as he wills, with no one to withstand him. He shall stop in the glorious land, and it shall all be in his power. [17]He shall resolve to come with the entire strength of his kingdom. He shall make an alliance with him and give him a daughter in marriage in order to destroy him, but this shall not stand. [18]He shall turn to the coastland and take many prisoners, but a commander shall put an end to his shameful conduct, so that he cannot retaliate. [19]He shall turn to the strongholds of his own land, but shall stumble and fall, to be found no more. [20]In his stead one shall arise who will send a collector of tribute through the glorious kingdom, but he shall soon be destroyed, though not in conflict or in battle.

[21]"There shall arise in his place a despicable person, to whom the royal insignia shall not be given. He shall enter by stealth and seize the kingdom by fraud. [22]Armed forces shall be completely overwhelmed by him and crushed, even the prince of the covenant. [23]After making alliances, he shall treacherously rise to power with only a few supporters. [24]By stealth he shall enter prosperous provinces and do that which his fathers or grandfathers never did; he shall distribute spoil, plunder, and riches among them and devise plots against their strongholds. [25]He shall rouse his strength and courage to meet the king of the south with a great army; the king of the south shall go into battle with a very large and strong army, but he shall not stand because of the plots devised against him. [26]Even his table companions shall seek to destroy him, his army shall be overwhelmed, and many shall be struck down. [27]The two kings, resolved on evil, shall sit at table together and exchange lies, but they shall have no success, because the appointed end is not yet.

[28]"He shall turn back toward his land with great riches, his mind set against the holy covenant; he shall take action and return to his land. [29]At the time appointed he shall come again to the south, but this time it shall not be as before. [30]When ships of the Kittim confront him, he shall lose heart and retreat. Then he shall rage against the holy covenant and take action; he shall again favor those who forsake the holy covenant. [31]Armed forces shall rise at his command and defile the sanctuary stronghold, abolishing the daily sacrifice and setting up the desolating abomination. [32]By his deceit

he shall make some who were disloyal forsake the covenant; but those who remain loyal to their God shall take strong action. ³³Those with insight among the people shall instruct the many; though for a time the sword, flames, exile, and plunder will cause them to stumble. ³⁴When they stumble, they will be helped, but only a little; many shall join them, but out of treachery. ³⁵Some of those with insight shall stumble so that they may be tested, refined, and purified, until the end time which is still appointed to come.

³⁶"The king shall do as he wills, exalting himself and making himself greater than any god; he shall utter dreadful blasphemies against the God of gods. He shall prosper only till the wrath is finished, for what is determined must take place. ³⁷He shall have no regard for the gods of his ancestors or for the one in whom women delight; for no god shall he have regard, because he shall make himself greater than all. ³⁸Instead, he shall give glory to the god of strongholds; a god unknown to his ancestors he shall glorify with gold, silver, precious stones, and other treasures. ³⁹He shall act for those who fortify strongholds, a people of a foreign god, whom he has recognized. He shall greatly honor them; he shall make them rule over the many and distribute the land as a reward.

⁴⁰"At the end time the king of the south shall engage him in battle but the king of the north shall overwhelm him with chariots and horsemen and a great fleet, passing through the lands like a flood. ⁴¹He shall enter the glorious land and many shall fall, except Edom, Moab, and the chief part of Ammon, which shall escape his power. ⁴²He shall extend his power over the land, and not even Egypt shall escape. ⁴³He shall control the riches of gold and silver and all the treasures of Egypt; Libya and Ethiopia shall be in his entourage. ⁴⁴When reports from the east and the north disturb him, he shall set out with great fury to destroy many, putting them under the ban. ⁴⁵He shall pitch the tents of his royal pavilion between the sea and the glorious holy mountain, but he shall come to his end with none to help him.

The Resurrection. 12:1 "At that time
    there shall arise Michael,
      the great prince,
      guardian of your people;
It shall be a time unsurpassed in
    distress
    since the nation began until that
      time.
At that time your people shall escape,
    everyone who is found written in
      the book.
²Many of those who sleep
    in the dust of the earth shall awake;
Some to everlasting life,
    others to reproach and everlasting
      disgrace.
³But those with insight shall shine
    brightly
    like the splendor of the firmament,
And those who lead the many to
    justice
    shall be like the stars forever.

⁴"As for you, Daniel, keep secret the message and seal the book until the end time; many shall wander aimlessly and evil shall increase."

⁵I, Daniel, looked and saw two others, one standing on either bank of the river. ⁶One of them said to the man clothed in linen, who was upstream, "How long shall it be to the end of these appalling things?" ⁷The man clothed in linen, who was upstream, lifted his hands to heaven; and I heard him swear by him who lives forever that it should be for a time, two times, and half a time; and that, when the power of the destroyer of the holy people was brought to an end, all these things should end. ⁸I heard, but I did not understand; so I asked, "My lord, what follows this?" ⁹"Go,

Daniel," he said, "because the words are to be kept secret and sealed until the end time. ¹⁰Many shall be refined, purified, and tested, but the wicked shall prove wicked; the wicked shall have no understanding, but those with insight shall. ¹¹From the time that the daily sacrifice is abolished and the desolating abomination is set up, there shall be one thousand two hundred and ninety days. ¹²Blessed are they who have patience and persevere for the one thousand three hundred and thirty-five days. ¹³Go, take your rest, you shall rise for your reward at the end of days."

☐ LUKE 24

The Resurrection of Jesus. 24:1 But at daybreak on the first day of the week they took the spices they had prepared and went to the tomb. ²They found the stone rolled away from the tomb; ³but when they entered, they did not find the body of the Lord Jesus. ⁴While they were puzzling over this, behold, two men in dazzling garments appeared to them. ⁵They were terrified and bowed their faces to the ground. They said to them, "Why do you seek the living one among the dead? ⁶He is not here, but he has been raised. Remember what he said to you while he was still in Galilee, ⁷that the Son of Man must be handed over to sinners and be crucified, and rise on the third day." ⁸And they remembered his words. ⁹Then they returned from the tomb and announced all these things to the eleven and to all the others. ¹⁰The women were Mary Magdalene, Joanna, and Mary the mother of James; the others who accompanied them also told this to the apostles, ¹¹but their story seemed like nonsense and they did not believe them. ¹²But Peter got up and ran to the tomb, bent down, and saw the burial cloths alone; then he went home amazed at what had happened.

The Appearance on the Road to Emmaus. ¹³Now that very day two of them were going to a village seven miles from Jerusalem called Emmaus, ¹⁴and they were conversing about all the things that had occurred. ¹⁵And it happened that while they were conversing and debating, Jesus himself drew near and walked with them, ¹⁶but their eyes were prevented from recognizing him. ¹⁷He asked them, "What are you discussing as you walk along?" They stopped, looking downcast. ¹⁸One of them, named Cleopas, said to him in reply, "Are you the only visitor to Jerusalem who does not know of the things that have taken place there in these days?" ¹⁹And he replied to them, "What sort of things?" They said to him, "The things that happened to Jesus the Nazarene, who was a prophet mighty in deed and word before God and all the people, ²⁰how our chief priests and rulers both handed him over to a sentence of death and crucified him. ²¹But we were hoping that he would be the one to redeem Israel; and besides all this, it is now the third day since this took place. ²²Some women from our group, however, have astounded us: they were at the tomb early in the morning ²³and did not find his body; they came back and reported that they had indeed seen a vision of angels who announced that he was alive. ²⁴Then some of those with us went to the tomb and found things just as the women had described, but him they did not see." ²⁵And he said to them, "Oh, how foolish you are! How slow of heart to believe all that the prophets spoke! ²⁶Was it not necessary that the Messiah should suffer these things and enter into his glory?" ²⁷Then beginning with Moses and all the prophets, he interpreted to them what referred to him in all the scriptures. ²⁸As they approached the village to which they were going, he gave the impression that he was going on farther. ²⁹But they urged him, "Stay with us, for it is nearly evening and the day is almost over." So he went in to stay with them. ³⁰And it happened that, while he was with them at table, he took bread, said the blessing, broke it, and gave it to them. ³¹With that their eyes were opened and they recognized him, but he vanished from their sight. ³²Then they said to each other, "Were not our hearts burning [within us] while he spoke to us on the way and opened the scriptures to us?" ³³So they set out at once and returned to Jerusalem where they found gathered together the eleven and those with them ³⁴who were saying, "The Lord has truly been raised and has appeared to Simon!" ³⁵Then the two recounted what had taken place on the way and how he was made known to them in the breaking of the bread.

The Appearance to the Disciples in Jerusalem. ³⁶While they were still speaking about this, he stood in their midst and said to them, "Peace be with you." ³⁷But they were startled and terrified and thought that they were seeing a ghost. ³⁸Then he said to them, "Why are you troubled? And why do questions arise in your hearts? ³⁹Look at my hands and my feet, that it is I myself. Touch me and see, because a ghost does not have flesh and bones as you can see I have."

⁴⁰And as he said this, he showed them his hands and his feet. ⁴¹While they were still incredulous for joy and were amazed, he asked them, "Have you anything here to eat?" ⁴²They gave him a piece of baked fish; ⁴³he took it and ate it in front of them. ⁴⁴He said to them, "These are my words that I spoke to you while I was still with you, that everything written about me in the law of Moses and in the prophets and psalms must be fulfilled." ⁴⁵Then he opened their minds to understand the scriptures. ⁴⁶And he said to them, "Thus it is written that the Messiah would suffer and rise from the dead on the third day ⁴⁷and that repentance, for the forgiveness of sins, would be preached in his name to all the nations, beginning from Jerusalem. ⁴⁸You are witnesses of these things. ⁴⁹And [behold] I am sending the promise of my Father upon you; but stay in the city until you are clothed with power from on high."

The Ascension. ⁵⁰Then he led them [out] as far as Bethany, raised his hands, and blessed them. ⁵¹As he blessed them he parted from them and was taken up to heaven. ⁵²They did him homage and then returned to Jerusalem with great joy, ⁵³and they were continually in the temple praising God.

December 4

St. John of Damascus

A single opinion cannot overturn the unanimous tradition of the whole Church, which has spread to the ends of the earth.

— St. John of Damascus

☐ DANIEL 13-14

Susanna. 13:1 In Babylon there lived a man named Joakim, ²who married a very beautiful and God-fearing woman, Susanna, the daughter of Hilkiah; ³her par-ents were righteous and had trained their daughter according to the law of Moses. ⁴Joakim was very rich and he had a garden near his house. The Jews had recourse to him often because he was the most respected of them all.

⁵That year, two elders of the people were appointed judges, of whom the Lord said, "Lawlessness has come out of Babylon, that is, from the elders who were to govern the people as judges." ⁶These men, to whom all brought their cases, frequented the house of Joakim. ⁷When the people left at noon, Susanna used to enter her husband's garden for a walk. ⁸When the elders saw her enter every day for her walk, they began to lust for her. ⁹They perverted their thinking; they would not allow their eyes to look to heaven, and did not keep in mind just judgments. ¹⁰Though both were enamored of her, they did not tell each other their trouble, ¹¹for they were ashamed to reveal their lustful desire to have her. ¹²Day by day they watched eagerly for her. ¹³One day they said to each other, "Let us be off for home, it is time for the noon meal." So they went their separate ways. ¹⁴But both turned back and arrived at the same spot. When they asked each other the reason, they admitted their lust, and then they agreed to look for an occasion when they could find her alone.

¹⁵One day, while they were waiting for the right moment, she entered as usual, with two maids only, wanting to bathe in the garden, for the weather was warm. ¹⁶Nobody else was there except the two elders, who had hidden themselves and were watching her. ¹⁷"Bring me oil and soap," she said to the maids, "and shut the garden gates while I bathe." ¹⁸They did as she said; they shut the garden gates and left by the side gate to fetch what she had ordered, unaware that the elders were hidden inside.

¹⁹As soon as the maids had left, the two old men got up and ran to her. ²⁰"Look," they said, "the garden doors are shut, no one can see us, and we want you. So give in to our desire, and lie with us. ²¹If you refuse, we will testify against you that a young man was here with you and that is why you sent your maids away."

²²"I am completely trapped," Susanna groaned. "If I yield, it will be my death; if I refuse, I cannot escape your power. ²³Yet it is better for me not to do it and to fall into your power than to sin before the Lord." ²⁴Then Susanna screamed, and the two old men also shouted at her, ²⁵as one of them ran to open the garden gates. ²⁶When the people in the house heard the cries from the garden, they rushed in by the side gate to see what had happened to her. ²⁷At the accusations of the old men, the servants felt very much ashamed, for never had any such thing been said about Susanna.

²⁸When the people came to her husband Joakim the next day, the two wicked old men also came, full of lawless intent to put Susanna to death. ²⁹Before the people they ordered: "Send for Susanna, the daughter of Hilkiah, the wife of Joakim." When she was sent for, ³⁰she came with her parents, children and all her relatives. ³¹Susanna, very delicate and beautiful, ³²was veiled; but those transgressors of the law ordered that she be exposed so as to sate themselves with her beauty. ³³All her companions and the onlookers were weeping.

³⁴In the midst of the people the two old men rose up and laid their hands on her head. ³⁵As she wept she looked up to heaven, for she trusted in the Lord wholeheartedly. ³⁶The old men said, "As we were walking in the garden alone, this woman entered with two servant girls, shut the garden gates and sent the servant girls away. ³⁷A young man, who was hidden there, came and lay with her. ³⁸When we, in a corner of the garden, saw this lawlessness, we ran toward them. ³⁹We saw them lying together, but the man we could not hold, because he was stronger than we; he opened the gates and ran off. ⁴⁰Then we seized this one and asked who the young man was, ⁴¹but she refused to tell us. We testify to this." The assembly believed them, since they were elders and judges of the people, and they condemned her to death.

⁴²But Susanna cried aloud: "Eternal God, you know what is hidden and are aware of all things before they come to be: ⁴³you know that they have testified falsely against me. Here I am about to die, though I have done none of the things for which these men have condemned me."

⁴⁴The Lord heard her prayer. ⁴⁵As she was being led to execution, God stirred up the holy spirit of a young boy named Daniel, ⁴⁶and he cried aloud: "I am innocent of this woman's blood." ⁴⁷All the people turned and asked him, "What are you saying?" ⁴⁸He stood in their midst and said, "Are you such fools, you Israelites, to condemn a daughter of Israel without investigation and without clear evidence? ⁴⁹Return to court, for they have testified falsely against her."

⁵⁰Then all the people returned in haste. To Daniel the elders said, "Come, sit with us and inform us, since God has given you the prestige of old age." ⁵¹But he replied, "Separate these two far from one another, and I will examine them."

⁵²After they were separated from each other, he called one of them and said: "How you have grown evil with age! Now have your past sins come to term: ⁵³passing unjust sentences, condemning the innocent, and freeing the guilty, although the Lord says, 'The innocent and the just you shall not put to death.' ⁵⁴Now, then, if you were a witness, tell me under what tree you saw them together." ⁵⁵"Under a mastic tree," he answered. "Your fine lie has cost you your head," said Daniel; "for the angel of God has already received the sentence from God and shall split you in two." ⁵⁶Putting him to one side, he ordered the other one to be brought. "Offspring of Canaan, not of Judah," Daniel said to him, "beauty has seduced you, lust has perverted your heart. ⁵⁷This is how you acted with the daughters of Israel, and in their fear they yielded to you; but a daughter of Judah did not tolerate your lawlessness. ⁵⁸Now, then, tell me under what tree you surprised them together." ⁵⁹"Under an oak," he said. "Your fine lie has cost you also your head," said Daniel; "for the angel of God waits with a sword to cut you in two so as to destroy you both."

⁶⁰The whole assembly cried aloud, blessing God who saves those who hope in him. ⁶¹They rose up against the two old men, for by their own words Daniel had convicted them of bearing false witness. They condemned them to the fate they had planned for their neighbor: ⁶²in accordance with the law of Moses they put them to death. Thus was innocent blood spared that day.

⁶³Hilkiah and his wife praised God for their daughter Susanna, with Joakim her husband and all her relatives, because she was found innocent of any shameful deed. ⁶⁴And from that day onward Daniel was greatly esteemed by the people.

Bel and the Dragon. 14:1 After King Astyages was gathered to his ancestors, Cyrus the Persian succeeded to his kingdom. ²Daniel was a companion of the king and was held in higher honor than any of the Friends of the King. ³The Babylonians had an idol called Bel, and every day they provided for it six bushels of fine flour, forty sheep, and six measures of wine. ⁴The king revered it and went every day to worship it; but Daniel worshiped only his God. ⁵When the king asked him, "Why do you not worship Bel?" Daniel replied, "Because I do not revere idols made with hands, but only the living God who made heaven and earth and has dominion over all flesh." ⁶Then the king continued, "You do not think Bel is a living god? Do you not see how much he eats and drinks every day?" ⁷Daniel began to laugh. "Do not be deceived, O king," he said; "it is only clay inside and bronze outside; it has never eaten or drunk anything." ⁸Enraged, the king called his priests and said to them, "Unless you tell me who it is that consumes these provisions, you shall die. But if you can show that Bel consumes them, Daniel shall die for blaspheming Bel." ⁹Daniel said to the king, "Let it be as you say!"

There were seventy priests of Bel, besides their wives and children. ¹⁰When the king went with Daniel into the temple of Bel, ¹¹the priests of Bel said, "See, we are going to leave. You, O king, set out the food and prepare the wine; then shut the door and seal it with your ring. ¹²If you do not find that Bel has eaten it all when you return in the morning, we are to die; otherwise Daniel shall die for his lies against us." ¹³They were not perturbed, because under the table they had made a secret entrance through which they always came in to consume the food. ¹⁴After they departed the king set the food before Bel, while Daniel ordered his servants to bring some ashes, which they scattered through the whole temple; the king alone was present. Then they went outside, sealed the closed door with the king's ring, and departed. ¹⁵The priests entered that night as usual, with their wives and children, and they ate and drank everything.

¹⁶Early the next morning, the king came with Daniel. ¹⁷"Are the seals unbroken, Daniel?" he asked. And Daniel answered, "They are unbroken, O king." ¹⁸As soon as he had opened the door, the king looked at the table and cried aloud, "You are great, O Bel; there is no deceit in you." ¹⁹But Daniel laughed and kept the king from entering. He said, "Look at the floor and consider whose footprints these are." ²⁰"I see the footprints of men, women, and children!" said the king. ²¹In his wrath the king arrested the priests, their wives, and their children. They showed him the secret door by which they used to enter to consume what was on the table. ²²The king put them to death, and handed Bel over to Daniel, who destroyed it and its temple.

²³There was a great dragon which the Babylonians revered. ²⁴The king said to Daniel, "You cannot deny that this is a living god, so worship it." ²⁵But Daniel answered, "I worship the Lord, my God, for he is the living God. ²⁶Give me permission, O king, and I will kill this dragon without sword or club." "I give you permission," the king said. ²⁷Then Daniel took some pitch, fat, and hair; these he boiled together and made into cakes. He put them into the mouth of the dragon, and when the dragon ate them, he burst. "This," he said, "is what you revered."

²⁸When the Babylonians heard this, they were angry and turned against the king. "The king has become a Jew," they said; "he has destroyed Bel, killed the dragon, and put the priests to death." ²⁹They went to the king and demanded: "Hand Daniel over to us, or we will kill you and your family." ³⁰When he saw himself threatened with violence, the king was forced to hand Daniel over to them. ³¹They threw Daniel into a lions' den, where he remained six days. ³²In the den were seven lions. Two carcasses and two sheep had been given to them daily, but now they were given nothing, so that they would devour Daniel.

³³The prophet Habakkuk was in Judea. He mixed some bread in a bowl with the stew he had boiled, and was going to bring it to the reapers in the field, ³⁴when an angel of the Lord told him, "Take the meal you have to Daniel in the lions' den at Babylon." ³⁵But Habakkuk answered, "Sir, I have never seen Babylon, and I do not know the den!" ³⁶The angel of the Lord seized him by the crown of his head and carried him by the hair; with the speed of the wind, he set him down in Babylon above the den. ³⁷"Daniel, Daniel," cried Habakkuk, "take the meal God has sent you." ³⁸"You have remembered me, O God," said Daniel; "you have not forsaken those who love you." ³⁹So Daniel ate, but the angel of God at once brought Habakkuk back to his own place.

⁴⁰On the seventh day the king came to mourn for Daniel. As he came to the den and looked in, there was Daniel, sit-

ting there. [41]The king cried aloud, "You are great, O Lord, the God of Daniel, and there is no other besides you!" [42]He brought Daniel out, but those who had tried to destroy him he threw into the den, and they were devoured in a moment before his eyes.

☐ REVELATION 1

1:1 The revelation of Jesus Christ, which God gave to him, to show his servants what must happen soon. He made it known by sending his angel to his servant John, [2]who gives witness to the word of God and to the testimony of Jesus Christ by reporting what he saw. [3]Blessed is the one who reads aloud and blessed are those who listen to this prophetic message and heed what is written in it, for the appointed time is near.

Greeting. [4]John, to the seven churches in Asia: grace to you and peace from him who is and who was and who is to come, and from the seven spirits before his throne, [5]and from Jesus Christ, the faithful witness, the firstborn of the dead and ruler of the kings of the earth. To him who loves us and has freed us from our sins by his blood, [6]who has made us into a kingdom, priests for his God and Father, to him be glory and power forever [and ever]. Amen.

[7]Behold, he is coming amid the clouds,
　　and every eye will see him,
　　even those who pierced him.
All the peoples of the earth will lament
　　him.
　　Yes. Amen.

[8]"I am the Alpha and the Omega," says the Lord God, "the one who is and who was and who is to come, the almighty."

The First Vision. [9]I, John, your brother, who share with you the distress, the kingdom, and the endurance we have in Jesus, found myself on the island called Patmos because I proclaimed God's word and gave testimony to Jesus. [10]I was caught up in spirit on the Lord's day and heard behind me a voice as loud as a trumpet, [11]which said, "Write on a scroll what you see and send it to the seven churches: to Ephesus, Smyrna, Pergamum, Thyatira, Sardis, Philadelphia, and Laodicea." [12]Then I turned to see whose voice it was that spoke to me, and when I turned, I saw seven gold lampstands [13]and in the midst of the lampstands one like a son of man, wearing an ankle-length robe, with a gold sash around his chest. [14]The hair of his head was as white as white wool or as snow, and his eyes were like a fiery flame. [15]His feet were like polished brass refined in a furnace, and his voice was like the sound of rushing water. [16]In his right hand he held seven stars. A sharp two-edged sword came out of his mouth, and his face shone like the sun at its brightest.

[17]When I caught sight of him, I fell down at his feet as though dead. He touched me with his right hand and said, "Do not be afraid. I am the first and the last, [18]the one who lives. Once I was dead, but now I am alive forever and ever. I hold the keys to death and the netherworld. [19]Write down, therefore, what you have seen, and what is happening, and what will happen afterwards. [20]This is the secret meaning of the seven stars you saw in my right hand, and of the seven gold lampstands: the seven stars are the angels of the seven churches, and the seven lampstands are the seven churches.

December 5

☐ HOSEA 1-2

1:1 The word of the LORD that came to Hosea son of Beeri, in the days of Uzziah, Jotham, Ahaz, Hezekiah, kings of Judah, and in the days of Jeroboam, son of Joash, king of Israel.

Marriage of Hosea and Gomer. ²When the LORD began to speak with Hosea, the LORD said to Hosea: Go, get for yourself a woman of prostitution and children of prostitution, for the land prostitutes itself, turning away from the LORD.

³So he went and took Gomer, daughter of Diblaim; and she conceived and bore him a son. ⁴Then the LORD said to him: Give him the name "Jezreel," for in a little while I will punish the house of Jehu for the bloodshed at Jezreel and bring to an end the kingdom of the house of Israel; ⁵on that day I will break the bow of Israel in the valley of Jezreel.

⁶She conceived again and bore a daughter. The LORD said to him: Give her the name "Not-Pitied," for I will no longer feel pity for the house of Israel: rather, I will utterly abhor them. ⁷Yet for the house of Judah I will feel pity; I will save them by the LORD, their God; but I will not save them by bow or sword, by warfare, by horses or horsemen.

⁸After she weaned Not-Pitied, she conceived and bore a son. ⁹Then the LORD said: Give him the name "Not-My-People," for you are not my people, and I am not "I am" for you.

2:1 The number of the Israelites
will be like the sand of the sea,
  which can be neither measured nor
    counted.
Instead of being told,
  "You are Not-My-People,"

They will be called,
  "Children of the living God."
²Then the people of Judah and of Israel
  will gather together;
They will appoint for themselves one
    head
  and rise up from the land;
  great indeed shall be the day of
    Jezreel!
³Say to your brothers, "My People,"
  and to your sisters, "Pitied."

The Lord and Israel His Spouse.
⁴Accuse your mother, accuse!
  for she is not my wife,
    and I am not her husband.
Let her remove her prostitution from
    her face,
  her adultery from between her
    breasts,
⁵Or I will strip her naked,
  leaving her as on the day of her
    birth;
I will make her like the wilderness,
  make her like an arid land,
    and let her die of thirst.
⁶I will have no pity on her children,
  for they are children of prostitution.
⁷Yes, their mother has prostituted
    herself;
  she who conceived them has acted
    shamefully.
For she said, "I will go after my lovers,
  who give me my bread and my water,
  my wool and my flax, my oil and
    my drink."
⁸Therefore, I will hedge in her way with
    thorns
  and erect a wall against her,
  so that she cannot find her paths.

⁹If she runs after her lovers, she will not
    overtake them;
  if she seeks them she will not find
    them.
Then she will say,
  "I will go back to my first husband,
    for I was better off then than now."

¹⁰She did not know
  that it was I who gave her
  the grain, the wine, and the oil,
I who lavished upon her silver,
  and gold, which they used for Baal,
¹¹Therefore I will take back my grain in
    its time,
  and my wine in its season;
I will snatch away my wool and my flax,
  which were to cover her nakedness.
¹²Now I will lay bare her shame
  in full view of her lovers,
  and no one can deliver her out of
    my hand.
¹³I will put an end to all her joy,
  her festivals, her new moons, her
    sabbaths—
  all her seasonal feasts.
¹⁴I will lay waste her vines and fig trees,
  of which she said, "These are the fees
  my lovers have given me";
I will turn them into rank growth
  and wild animals shall devour them.
¹⁵I will punish her for the days of the
    Baals,
  for whom she burnt incense,
When she decked herself out with her
    rings and her jewelry,
  and went after her lovers—
  but me she forgot—oracle of the
    LORD.
¹⁶Therefore, I will allure her now;
  I will lead her into the wilderness
  and speak persuasively to her.
¹⁷Then I will give her the vineyards she
    had,

and the valley of Achor as a door of
    hope.
There she will respond as in the days of
    her youth,
  as on the day when she came up
    from the land of Egypt.

¹⁸On that day—oracle of the LORD—
You shall call me "My husband,"
  and you shall never again call me
    "My baal."
¹⁹I will remove from her mouth the
    names of the Baals;
  they shall no longer be mentioned
    by their name.
²⁰I will make a covenant for them on
    that day,
  with the wild animals,
With the birds of the air,
  and with the things that crawl on
    the ground.
Bow and sword and warfare
  I will destroy from the land,
  and I will give them rest in safety.

²¹I will betroth you to me forever:
  I will betroth you to me with justice
    and with judgment,
  with loyalty and with compassion;
²²I will betroth you to me with
    fidelity,
  and you shall know the LORD.
²³On that day I will respond—oracle of
    the LORD—
  I will respond to the heavens,
  and they will respond to the earth;
²⁴The earth will respond to the grain,
  and wine, and oil,
  and these will respond to Jezreel.
²⁵I will sow her for myself in the land,
  and I will have pity on Not-Pitied.
I will say to Not-My-People, "You are
    my people,"
  and he will say, "My God!"

☐ REVELATION 2:1-11

To Ephesus. 2:1 "To the angel of the church in Ephesus, write this:

"'The one who holds the seven stars in his right hand and walks in the midst of the seven gold lampstands says this: ²"I know your works, your labor, and your endurance, and that you cannot tolerate the wicked; you have tested those who call themselves apostles but are not, and discovered that they are impostors. ³Moreover, you have endurance and have suffered for my name, and you have not grown weary. ⁴Yet I hold this against you: you have lost the love you had at first. ⁵Realize how far you have fallen. Repent, and do the works you did at first. Otherwise, I will come to you and remove your lampstand from its place, unless you repent. ⁶But you have this in your favor: you hate the works of the Nicolaitans, which I also hate.

⁷""Whoever has ears ought to hear what the Spirit says to the churches. To the victor I will give the right to eat from the tree of life that is in the garden of God.'"

To Smyrna. ⁸"To the angel of the church in Smyrna, write this:

"'The first and the last, who once died but came to life, says this: ⁹"I know your tribulation and poverty, but you are rich. I know the slander of those who claim to be Jews and are not, but rather are members of the assembly of Satan. ¹⁰Do not be afraid of anything that you are going to suffer. Indeed, the devil will throw some of you into prison, that you may be tested, and you will face an ordeal for ten days. Remain faithful until death, and I will give you the crown of life.

¹¹""Whoever has ears ought to hear what the Spirit says to the churches. The victor shall not be harmed by the second death."'"

December 6 ———————————

St. Nicholas

Some have a wicked and deceitful way of flaunting the Name about, while acting in a way unworthy of God. They are mad dogs that bite secretly. You must be on your guard against them, for it is hard to heal their bite.

— ST. IGNATIUS OF ANTIOCH

☐ HOSEA 3-4

Hosea and His Wife Reunited. 3:1 Again the LORD said to me:

Go, love a woman
　　who is loved by her spouse but
　　　　commits adultery;
Just as the LORD loves the Israelites,
　　though they turn to other gods
　　and love raisin cakes.

²So I acquired her for myself for fifteen pieces of silver and a homer and a lethech of barley. ³Then I said to her:

"You will wait for me for many days;
　　you will not prostitute yourself
Or belong to any man;
　　I in turn will wait for you."

⁴For the Israelites will remain many days

without king or prince,
Without sacrifice or sacred pillar,
  without ephod or household gods.
⁵Afterward the Israelites will turn back
  and seek the LORD, their God,
  and David, their king;
They will come trembling to the LORD
  and to his bounty, in the last days.

Indictment of Israel. 4:1 Hear the
  word of the LORD, Israelites,
  for the LORD has a dispute
  with the inhabitants of the land:
There is no fidelity, no loyalty,
  no knowledge of God in the land.
²Swearing, lying, murder,
  stealing and adultery break out;
  bloodshed follows bloodshed.
³Therefore the land dries up,
  and everything that dwells in it
    languishes:
The beasts of the field,
  the birds of the air,
  and even the fish of the sea perish.

Guilt of Priest and of People. ⁴But let
  no one accuse, let no one rebuke;
  with you is my dispute, priest!
⁵You will stumble in the day,
  and the prophet will stumble with
    you at night;
  I will make an end of your mother.
⁶My people are ruined for lack of
    knowledge!
  Since you have rejected knowledge,
  I will reject you from serving as my
    priest;
  Since you have forgotten the law of
    your God,
  I will also forget your children.

⁷The more they multiplied, the more
    they sinned against me,
  I will change their glory into shame.
⁸They feed on the sin of my people,
  and are greedy for their iniquity.
⁹Like people, like priest:
  I will punish them for their ways,

and repay them for their deeds.
¹⁰They will eat but not be satisfied,
  they will promote prostitution but
    not increase,
Because they have abandoned the
    LORD,
  devoting themselves
  ¹¹to prostitution.
Aged wine and new wine
  take away understanding.
¹²My people consult their piece of
    wood,
  and their wand makes
    pronouncements for them,
For the spirit of prostitution has led
    them astray;
  they prostitute themselves, forsaking
    their God.
¹³On the mountaintops they offer
    sacrifice
  and on the hills they burn incense,
Beneath oak and poplar and terebinth,
  because of their pleasant shade.
Therefore your daughters prostitute
    themselves,
  and your daughters-in-law commit
    adultery.
¹⁴I will not punish your daughters for
    their prostitution,
  nor your daughters-in-law for their
    adultery,
Because the men themselves consort
    with prostitutes,
  and with temple women they offer
    sacrifice!
Thus a people without understanding
    comes to ruin.

¹⁵Though you prostitute yourself,
    Israel,
  do not let Judah become guilty!
Do not come to Gilgal,
  do not go up to Beth-aven,
  do not swear, "As the Lord lives!"
¹⁶For like a stubborn cow,
  Israel is stubborn;
Will the LORD now pasture them,

like lambs in a broad meadow?
¹⁷Ephraim is bound to idols,
let him alone!
¹⁸When their drinking is over,
they give themselves to
prostitution;

they love shame more than their
honor.
¹⁹A wind has bound them up in its
wings;
they shall be ashamed because of
their altars.

☐ REVELATION 2:12-29

To Pergamum. 2:12 "To the angel of the church in Pergamum, write this:

"'The one with the sharp two-edged sword says this: ¹³I know that you live where Satan's throne is, and yet you hold fast to my name and have not denied your faith in me, not even in the days of Antipas, my faithful witness, who was martyred among you, where Satan lives. ¹⁴Yet I have a few things against you. You have some people there who hold to the teaching of Balaam, who instructed Balak to put a stumbling block before the Israelites: to eat food sacrificed to idols and to play the harlot. ¹⁵Likewise, you also have some people who hold to the teaching of [the] Nicolaitans. ¹⁶Therefore, repent. Otherwise, I will come to you quickly and wage war against them with the sword of my mouth.

¹⁷"'Whoever has ears ought to hear what the Spirit says to the churches. To the victor I shall give some of the hidden manna; I shall also give a white amulet upon which is inscribed a new name, which no one knows except the one who receives it.'"

To Thyatira. ¹⁸"To the angel of the church in Thyatira, write this:

"'The Son of God, whose eyes are like a fiery flame and whose feet are like polished brass, says this: ¹⁹I know your works, your love, faith, service, and endurance, and that your last works are greater than

the first. ²⁰Yet I hold this against you, that you tolerate the woman Jezebel, who calls herself a prophetess, who teaches and misleads my servants to play the harlot and to eat food sacrificed to idols. ²¹I have given her time to repent, but she refuses to repent of her harlotry. ²²So I will cast her on a sickbed and plunge those who commit adultery with her into intense suffering unless they repent of her works. ²³I will also put her children to death. Thus shall all the churches come to know that I am the searcher of hearts and minds and that I will give each of you what your works deserve. ²⁴But I say to the rest of you in Thyatira, who do not uphold this teaching and know nothing of the so-called deep secrets of Satan: on you I will place no further burden, ²⁵except that you must hold fast to what you have until I come.

²⁶"'To the victor, who keeps to my
ways until the end,
I will give authority over the
nations.
²⁷He will rule them with an iron rod.
Like clay vessels will they be
smashed,

²⁸just as I received authority from my Father. And to him I will give the morning star.

²⁹"'Whoever has ears ought to hear what the Spirit says to the churches.'"

December 7

St. Ambrose of Milan

The devil's snare doesn't catch you unless you're already nibbling on the devil's bait.

— St. Ambrose of Milan

☐ HOSEA 5:1–6:11A

Guilt of the Religious and Political Leaders. 5:1 Hear this, priests,
Pay attention, house of Israel,
Household of the king, give ear!
    For you are responsible for judgment.
But you have been a snare at Mizpah,
    a net spread upon Tabor,
²a pit dug deep in Shittim.
    Now I will discipline them all.

³I know Ephraim,
    and Israel is not hidden from me:
Now, Ephraim, you have practiced prostitution,
    Israel is defiled.
⁴Their deeds do not allow them
    to return to their God;
For the spirit of prostitution is in them,
    and they do not know the LORD.

⁵The arrogance of Israel bears witness
    against him;
    Israel and Ephraim stumble because
        of their iniquity,
    and Judah stumbles with them.
⁶With their flocks and herds they will go
    to seek the LORD, but will not find
        him;
    he has withdrawn from them.
⁷They have betrayed the LORD,
    for they have borne illegitimate
        children;
Now the new moon will devour them
    together with their fields.

Political Upheavals. ⁸Blow the ram's
    horn in Gibeah,
    the trumpet in Ramah!

Sound the alarm in Beth-aven:
    "Look behind you, Benjamin!"
⁹Ephraim shall become a wasteland
    on the day of punishment:
Among the tribes of Israel
    I announce what is sure to be.
¹⁰The princes of Judah have become
    like those who move a boundary
        line;
Upon them I will pour out
    my wrath like water.
¹¹Ephraim is oppressed, crushed by
        judgment,
    for he has willingly gone after filth!
¹²I am like a moth for Ephraim,
    like rot for the house of Judah.
¹³When Ephraim saw his infirmity,
    and Judah his sore,
Ephraim went to Assyria,
    and sent to the great king.
But he cannot heal you,
    nor take away your sore.
¹⁴For I am like a lion to Ephraim,
    like a young lion to the house of
        Judah;
It is I who tear the prey and depart,
    I carry it away and no one can save it.

Insincere Conversion. ¹⁵I will go back
    to my place
    until they make reparation
    and seek my presence.
In their affliction, they shall look for me.

6:1 "Come, let us return to the
        LORD,
For it is he who has torn, but he will
    heal us;

he has struck down, but he will
    bind our wounds.
[2]He will revive us after two days;
    on the third day he will raise us up,
    to live in his presence.
[3]Let us know, let us strive to know the
    LORD;
    as certain as the dawn is his coming.
He will come to us like the rain,
    like spring rain that waters the earth."

[4]What can I do with you, Ephraim?
    What can I do with you, Judah?
Your loyalty is like morning mist,
    like the dew that disappears early.
[5]For this reason I struck them down
    through the prophets,
    I killed them by the words of my
        mouth;
    my judgment shines forth like the
        light.

[6]For it is loyalty that I desire, not
    sacrifice,
    and knowledge of God rather than
        burnt offerings.

Further Crimes of Israel. [7]But they, at
    Adam, violated the covenant;
    there they betrayed me.

[8]Gilead is a city of evildoers,
    tracked with blood.
[9]Like brigands lying in wait
    is the band of priests.
They murder on the road to Shechem,
    indeed they commit a monstrous
        crime.
[10]In the house of Israel I have seen a
    horrible thing:
    there is found Ephraim's prostitution,
    Israel is defiled.
[11]For you also, Judah,
    a harvest has been appointed!

☐ REVELATION 3:1-13

To Sardis. 3:1 "To the angel of the church
in Sardis, write this:

""The one who has the seven spirits of
God and the seven stars says this: "I know
your works, that you have the reputation of
being alive, but you are dead. [2]Be watchful
and strengthen what is left, which is going to die, for I have not found your works
complete in the sight of my God. [3]Remem-
ber then how you accepted and heard; keep
it, and repent. If you are not watchful, I
will come like a thief, and you will never
know at what hour I will come upon you.
[4]However, you have a few people in Sardis
who have not soiled their garments; they
will walk with me dressed in white, because
they are worthy.

[5]""The victor will thus be dressed in
white, and I will never erase his name from
the book of life but will acknowledge his
name in the presence of my Father and of
his angels.

[6]""Whoever has ears ought to hear
what the Spirit says to the churches."
To Philadelphia. [7]"To the angel of the
church in Philadelphia, write this:

""The holy one, the true,
    who holds the key of David,
    who opens and no one shall close,
    who closes and no one shall open,
says this:
[8]""I know your works (behold, I have
left an open door before you, which no
one can close). You have limited strength,
and yet you have kept my word and have
not denied my name. [9]Behold, I will make
those of the assembly of Satan who claim to
be Jews and are not, but are lying, behold I
will make them come and fall prostrate at
your feet, and they will realize that I love
you. [10]Because you have kept my message of
endurance, I will keep you safe in the time
of trial that is going to come to the whole

world to test the inhabitants of the earth. [11]I am coming quickly. Hold fast to what you have, so that no one may take your crown.

[12]"""The victor I will make into a pillar in the temple of my God, and he will never leave it again. On him I will inscribe the name of my God and the name of the city of my God, the new Jerusalem, which comes down out of heaven from my God, as well as my new name.

[13]"""Whoever has ears ought to hear what the Spirit says to the churches."""

December 8

The Immaculate Conception of Our Lady

We consecrate ourselves at one and the same time to the most holy Virgin and to Jesus Christ: to the most holy Virgin as to the perfect means that Jesus Christ himself has chosen by which to unite himself to us, and us to Him; and to Our Lord as to our Final End, to whom as our Redeemer and our God, we owe all we are.

— St. Louis de Montfort

☐ HOSEA 6:11B-8:14

6:11B When I would have restored the
 fortunes of my people,
  7:1when I would have healed Israel,
The guilt of Ephraim was revealed,
 the wickedness of Samaria:
  They practiced falsehood.
Thieves break in,
 bandits roam outside.
[2]Yet they do not call to mind
 that I remember all their wickedness.
Now their crimes surround them,
 present to my sight.

Israel's Domestic Politics. [3]With their
 wickedness they make the king
  rejoice,
 the princes too, with their
  treacherous deeds.
[4]They are all adulterers,
 like a blazing oven,
Which the baker quits stoking,
 after the dough's kneading until its
  rising.
[5]On the day of our king,
they made the princes sick with
 poisoned wine;
he extended his hand to the scoffers.
[6]For they draw near in ambush
 with their hearts like an oven.
All the night their anger sleeps;
 in the morning it flares like a
  blazing fire.
[7]They are all heated like ovens,
 and consume their rulers.
All their kings have fallen;
 none of them calls upon me.

Israel's Foreign Politics. [8]Ephraim is
 mixed with the nations,
 Ephraim is an unturned cake.
[9]Strangers have consumed his strength,
 but he does not know it;
Gray hairs are strewn on his head,
 but he takes no notice of it.
[10]The arrogance of Israel bears witness
 against him;
 yet they do not return to the Lord,
  their God,
 nor seek him, despite all this.

¹¹Ephraim is like a dove,
   silly and senseless;
They call upon Egypt,
   they go to Assyria.
¹²When they go I will spread my net
      around them,
   like birds in the air I will bring them
      down.
   I will chastise them when I hear of
      their assembly.
¹³Woe to them, for they have strayed
      from me!
   Ruin to them, for they have rebelled
      against me!
Though I wished to redeem them,
   they spoke lies against me.
¹⁴They have not cried to me from their
      hearts
   when they wailed upon their beds;
For wheat and wine they lacerated
      themselves;
   they rebelled against me.
¹⁵Though I trained and strengthened
      their arms,
   yet they devised evil against me.
¹⁶They have again become useless,
   they have been like a treacherous
      bow.
Their princes shall fall by the sword
   because of the insolence of their
      tongues;
   thus they shall be mocked in the
      land of Egypt.

**Corruption of Cult, Domestic and
Foreign Politics. 8:1** Put the
   trumpet to your lips!
   One like an eagle is over the house
      of the LORD!
Because they have violated my
      covenant,
   and rebelled against my law,
²They cry out to me,
   "My God! We know you!"
³But Israel has rejected what is good;
   the enemy shall pursue him.

⁴They made kings, but not by my
      authority;
   they established princes, but
      without my knowledge.
With their silver and gold
   they made idols for themselves,
   to their own destruction.
⁵He has rejected your calf, Samaria!
   My wrath is kindled against them;
How long will they be incapable of
      innocence
   in Israel?
⁶An artisan made it,
   it is no god at all.
The calf of Samaria
   will be dashed to pieces.

⁷When they sow the wind,
   they will reap the whirlwind;
The stalk of grain that forms no head
   can yield no flour;
Even if it could,
   strangers would swallow it.
⁸Israel is swallowed up;
   now they are among the nations,
   like a useless vessel.
⁹For they went up to Assyria—
   a wild ass off on its own—
   Ephraim bargained for lovers.
¹⁰Even though they bargain with the
      nations,
   I will now gather them together;
They will soon succumb
   under the burden of king and princes.

¹¹When Ephraim made many altars to
      expiate sin,
   they became altars for sinning.
¹²Though I write for him my many
      instructions,
   they are considered like a stranger's.
¹³They love sacrifice,
   they sacrifice meat and eat it,
   but the LORD is not pleased with
      them.
Now he will remember their guilt
   and punish their sins;
   they shall return to Egypt.

[14]Israel has forgotten his maker
  and has built palaces.
Judah, too, has fortified many cities,

☐ REVELATION 3:14-22

To Laodicea. 3:14 "To the angel of the church in Laodicea, write this:

""The Amen, the faithful and true witness, the source of God's creation, says this: [15]"I know your works; I know that you are neither cold nor hot. I wish you were either cold or hot. [16]So, because you are lukewarm, neither hot nor cold, I will spit you out of my mouth. [17]For you say, 'I am rich and affluent and have no need of anything,' and yet do not realize that you are wretched, pitiable, poor, blind, and naked. [18]I advise you to buy from me gold refined by fire so that you may be rich, and white garments to

but I will send fire upon his cities,
  to devour their strongholds.

put on so that your shameful nakedness may not be exposed, and buy ointment to smear on your eyes so that you may see. [19]Those whom I love, I reprove and chastise. Be earnest, therefore, and repent.

[20]""Behold, I stand at the door and knock. If anyone hears my voice and opens the door, [then] I will enter his house and dine with him, and he with me. [21]I will give the victor the right to sit with me on my throne, as I myself first won the victory and sit with my Father on his throne.

[22]""Whoever has ears ought to hear what the Spirit says to the churches.""

December 9

St. Juan Diego

God is not dependent on anything for His beauty; His beauty is not limited to certain times or aspects; but He is beautiful by himself, through himself, and in himself. He is eternal beauty — not changing from one moment to the next — constantly the same beyond all change or alteration, increase or addition.

— St. Gregory of Nyssa

☐ HOSEA 9-10

From Days of Celebration to Days of Punishment. 9:1 Do not rejoice, Israel,
  do not exult like the nations!
For you have prostituted yourself,
    abandoning your God,
  loving a prostitute's fee
  upon every threshing floor.
[2]Threshing floor and wine press will
    not nourish them,
  the new wine will fail them.

[3]They will not dwell in the Lord's land;
  Ephraim will return to Egypt,

and in Assyria they will eat unclean
    food.
[4]They will not pour libations of wine to
    the Lord,
  and their sacrifices will not please
    him.
Their bread will be like mourners' bread,
  that makes unclean all who eat of it;
Their food will be for their own
    appetites;
  it cannot enter the house of the Lord.

[5]What will you do on the festival day,
  the day of the Lord's feast?

⁶When they flee from the devastation,
Egypt will gather them, Memphis
will bury them.
Weeds will overgrow their silver treasures,
and thorns, their tents.

⁷They have come, the days of
punishment!
they have come, the days of
recompense!
Let Israel know it!
"The prophet is a fool,
the man of the spirit is mad!"
Because your iniquity is great,
great, too, is your hostility.
⁸The watchman of Ephraim, the people
of my God, is the prophet;
yet a fowler's snare is on all his ways,
hostility in the house of his God.
⁹They have sunk to the depths of
corruption,
as in the days of Gibeah;
God will remember their iniquity
and punish their sins.

**From Former Glory to a History of
Corruption.** ¹⁰Like grapes in the
desert,
I found Israel;
Like the first fruits of the fig tree, its
first to ripen,
I looked on your ancestors.
But when they came to Baal-peor
and consecrated themselves to the
Shameful One,
they became as abhorrent as the
thing they loved.
¹¹Ephraim is like a bird:
their glory flies away—
no birth, no pregnancy, no
conception.
¹²Even though they bring up their
children,
I will make them childless, until no
one is left.
Indeed, woe to them
when I turn away from them!
¹³Ephraim, as I saw, was a tree

planted in a meadow;
But now Ephraim will bring out
his children to the slaughterer!
¹⁴Give them, Lord!
give them what?
Give them a miscarrying womb,
and dry breasts!
¹⁵All their misfortune began in Gilgal;
yes, there I rejected them.
Because of their wicked deeds
I will drive them out of my house.
I will love them no longer;
all their princes are rebels.
¹⁶Ephraim is stricken,
their root is dried up;
they will bear no fruit.
Were they to bear children,
I would slay the beloved of their
womb.
¹⁷My God will disown them
because they have not listened to him;
they will be wanderers among the
nations.

**Destruction of Idolatrous Cultic
Objects.** 10:1 Israel is a
luxuriant vine
whose fruit matches its growth.
The more abundant his fruit,
the more altars he built;
The more productive his land,
the more sacred pillars he set up.
²Their heart is false!
Now they will pay for their guilt:
God will break down their altars
and destroy their sacred pillars.
³For now they will say,
"We have no king!
Since we do not fear the Lord,
the king—what could he do for us?"
⁴They make promises,
swear false oaths, and make covenants,
While lawsuits sprout
like poisonous weeds in the furrows
of a field!

⁵The inhabitants of Samaria are afraid

for the calf of Beth-aven;
Its people mourn for it
and its idolatrous priests wail over it,
—over its glory which has departed
from it.
⁶It too will be carried to Assyria,
as an offering to the great king.
Ephraim will be put to shame,
Israel will be shamed by his
schemes.

⁷Samaria and her king will disappear,
like a twig upon the waters.
⁸The high places of Aven will be
destroyed,
the sin of Israel;
thorns and thistles will overgrow
their altars.
Then they will cry out to the
mountains, "Cover us!"
and to the hills, "Fall upon us!"

War Because of Israel's Wickedness.
⁹Since the days of Gibeah
you have sinned, Israel.
There they took their stand;
will war not reach them in Gibeah?
Against a perverse people
¹⁰I came and I chastised them;
Peoples will be gathered against them
when I bind them to their two crimes.

¹¹Ephraim was a trained heifer,
that loved to thresh;
I myself laid a yoke
upon her beautiful neck;
I will make Ephraim break ground,
Judah must plow,
Jacob must harrow for himself:
¹²"Sow for yourselves justice,
reap the reward of loyalty;
Break up for yourselves a new field,
for it is time to seek the LORD,
till he comes and rains justice upon
you."
¹³But you have plowed wickedness,
reaped perversity,
and eaten the fruit of falsehood.
Because you have trusted in your own
power,
and in your many warriors,
¹⁴The clamor of war shall break out
among your people
and all your fortresses shall be ravaged
As Salman ravaged Beth-arbel on the
day of war,
smashing mothers along with their
children.
¹⁵So it will be done to you, Bethel,
because of your utter wickedness:
At dawn the king of Israel
will utterly disappear.

☐ REVELATION 4

Vision of Heavenly Worship. 4:1 After this I had a vision of an open door to heaven, and I heard the trumpetlike voice that had spoken to me before, saying, "Come up here and I will show you what must happen afterwards." ²At once I was caught up in spirit. A throne was there in heaven, and on the throne sat ³one whose appearance sparkled like jasper and carnelian. Around the throne was a halo as brilliant as an emerald. ⁴Surrounding the throne I saw twenty-four other thrones on which twenty-four elders sat, dressed in white garments and with gold crowns on their heads. ⁵From the throne came flashes of lightning, rumblings, and peals of thunder. Seven flaming torches burned in front of the throne, which are the seven spirits of God. ⁶In front of the throne was something that resembled a sea of glass like crystal.

In the center and around the throne, there were four living creatures covered with eyes in front and in back. ⁷The first creature resembled a lion, the second was like a calf, the third had a face like that of a human being, and the fourth looked like an eagle in flight. ⁸The four living creatures, each of them with six wings, were covered with eyes inside and out. Day and night they do not stop exclaiming:

"Holy, holy, holy is the Lord God
    almighty,
      who was, and who is, and who is to
        come."

9Whenever the living creatures give glory and honor and thanks to the one who sits on the throne, who lives forever and ever,

10the twenty-four elders fall down before the one who sits on the throne and worship him, who lives forever and ever. They throw down their crowns before the throne, exclaiming:

11"Worthy are you, Lord our God,
    to receive glory and honor and
      power,
for you created all things;
    because of your will they came to be
      and were created."

December 10

Blessed be He whom our mouth cannot adequately praise, because His Gift is too great for the skill of orators to tell; neither can human abilities adequately praise His goodness. For, praise Him as we may, it is too little. Yet since it is useless to be silent and constrain ourselves, may our feebleness excuse such praise as we can sing!

— St. Ephraem the Syrian

☐ HOSEA 11–12

The Disappointment of a Parent.
    11:1 When Israel was a child I
    loved him,
  out of Egypt I called my son.
2The more I called them,
  the farther they went from me,
Sacrificing to the Baals
  and burning incense to idols.
3Yet it was I who taught Ephraim to
  walk,
  who took them in my arms;
  but they did not know that I cared
    for them.
4I drew them with human cords,
  with bands of love;
I fostered them like those
  who raise an infant to their cheeks;
  I bent down to feed them.

5He shall return to the land of Egypt,

Assyria shall be his king,
  because they have refused to repent.
6The sword shall rage in his cities:
  it shall destroy his diviners,
  and devour them because of their
    schemings.
7My people have their mind set on
  apostasy;
  though they call on God in unison,
  he shall not raise them up.

But Love Is Stronger and Restores.
    8How could I give you up,
    Ephraim,
  or deliver you up, Israel?
How could I treat you as Admah,
  or make you like Zeboiim?
My heart is overwhelmed,
  my pity is stirred.
9I will not give vent to my blazing anger,

I will not destroy Ephraim again;
For I am God and not a man,
  the Holy One present among you;
  I will not come in wrath.
¹⁰They shall follow the LORD,
  who roars like a lion;
When he roars,
  his children shall come frightened
    from the west,
¹¹Out of Egypt they shall come
    trembling, like birds,
  like doves, from the land of Assyria;
And I will resettle them in their homes,
  oracle of the LORD.

Infidelity of Israel. 12:1 Ephraim has
    surrounded me with lies,
  the house of Israel, with deceit;
Judah still wanders about with gods,
  and is faithful to holy ones.
²Ephraim shepherds the wind,
  and pursues the east wind all day
    long.
He multiplies lies and violence:
  They make a covenant with Assyria,
  and oil is carried to Egypt.

³The LORD has a dispute with Judah,
  and will punish Jacob for his conduct,
  and repay him for his deeds.
⁴In the womb he supplanted his brother,
  and in his vigor he contended with
    a divine being;
⁵He contended with an angel and
    prevailed,
  he wept and entreated him.
At Bethel he met with him,

and there he spoke with him.
⁶The LORD is the God of hosts,
  the LORD is his name!
⁷You must return to your God.
  Maintain loyalty and justice
  and always hope in your God.

⁸A merchant who holds a false balance,
  he loves to extort!
⁹Ephraim has said,
  "How rich I have become;
  I have made a fortune!"
All his gain will not suffice
  for the guilt of his sin.
¹⁰I the LORD have been your God,
  since the land of Egypt;
I will again have you live in tents,
  as on feast days.
¹¹I spoke to the prophets,
  I granted many visions,
  and through the prophets I told
    parables.
¹²In Gilead is falsehood, they have
    come to nothing;
  in Gilgal they sacrifice bulls,
But their altars are like heaps of stones
  in the furrows of the field.

¹³Jacob fled to the land of Aram,
  and Israel served for a wife;
  for a wife he tended sheep.
¹⁴But by a prophet the LORD brought
    Israel out of Egypt,
  and by a prophet Israel was tended.
¹⁵Ephraim has aroused bitter anger,
  so his Lord shall cast his bloodguilt
    upon him
  and repay him for his scorn.

☐ REVELATION 5:1-10

The Scroll and the Lamb. 5:1 I saw a scroll in the right hand of the one who sat on the throne. It had writing on both sides and was sealed with seven seals. ²Then I saw a mighty angel who proclaimed in a loud voice, "Who is worthy to open the scroll and break its seals?" ³But no one in heaven or on earth or under the earth was able to open the scroll or to examine it. ⁴I shed many tears because no one was found worthy to open the scroll or to examine it. ⁵One of the elders said to me, "Do not weep. The lion of the tribe of Judah, the root of David, has triumphed, enabling him to open the scroll with its seven seals."

⁶Then I saw standing in the midst of the throne and the four living creatures and the elders, a Lamb that seemed to have been slain. He had seven horns and seven eyes; these are the [seven] spirits of God sent out into the whole world. ⁷He came and received the scroll from the right hand of the one who sat on the throne. ⁸When he took it, the four living creatures and the twenty-four elders fell down before the Lamb. Each of the elders held a harp and gold bowls filled with incense, which are the prayers of the holy ones. ⁹They sang a new hymn:

> "Worthy are you to receive the scroll
>   and to break open its seals,
>   for you were slain and with your
>   blood you purchased for
>   God
>   those from every tribe and tongue,
>   people and nation.
> ¹⁰You made them a kingdom and
>   priests for our God,
>   and they will reign on earth."

December 11

Pope St. Damasus I

He who walking on the sea could calm the bitter waves, who gives life to the dying seeds of the earth; He who was able to loose the mortal chains of death, and after three days' darkness could bring Lazarus to the upper world again for his sister Martha: He, I believe, will make me rise again from the dust.

— POPE ST. DAMASUS I

☐ HOSEA 13-14

The Death of Ephraim. 13:1 When
    Ephraim spoke there was terror;
    he was exalted in Israel;
  but he became guilty through Baal
    and died.

²Now they continue to sin,
    making for themselves molten images,
Silver idols according to their skill,
    all of them the work of artisans.
"To these, offer sacrifice," they say.
    People kiss calves!
³Therefore, they will be like a morning
    cloud
  or like the dew that vanishes with
    the dawn,
Like chaff storm-driven from the
    threshing floor
  or like smoke out of the window.

⁴I, the LORD, am your God,
    since the land of Egypt;
Gods apart from me you do not know;
    there is no savior but me.
⁵I fed you in the wilderness,
    in the parched land.
⁶When I fed them, they were satisfied;
    when satisfied, they became proud,
    therefore they forgot me.
⁷So, I will be like a lion to them,
    like a leopard by the road I will keep
        watch.
⁸I will attack them like a bear robbed
        of its young,
    and tear their hearts from their
        breasts;

I will devour them on the spot like a
lion,
as a wild animal would rip them
open.

⁹I destroy you, Israel!
who is there to help you?
¹⁰Where now is your king,
that he may rescue you?
And all your princes,
that they may defend you?
Of whom you said,
"Give me a king and princes"?
¹¹I give you a king in my anger,
and I take him away in my wrath.

¹²The guilt of Ephraim is wrapped up,
his sin is stored away.
¹³The birth pangs will come for him,
but this is an unwise child,
Who, when it is time, does not present
himself
at the mouth of the womb.
¹⁴Shall I deliver them from the power
of Sheol?
shall I redeem them from death?
Where are your plagues, O death!
where is your sting, Sheol!
Compassion is hidden from my
eyes.

¹⁵Though Ephraim may flourish among
his brothers,
an east wind will come, a wind from
the LORD,
rising from the wilderness,
That will dry up his spring,
and leave his fountain dry.
It will loot his treasury
of every precious thing.

14:1 Samaria has become guilty,
for she has rebelled against her God.
They shall fall by the sword,
their infants shall be dashed to
pieces,
their pregnant women shall be
ripped open.

Sincere Conversion and New Life.
²Return, Israel, to the LORD,
your God;
you have stumbled because of your
iniquity.
³Take with you words,
and return to the LORD;
Say to him, "Forgive all iniquity,
and take what is good.
Let us offer the fruit of our lips.
⁴Assyria will not save us,
nor will we mount horses;
We will never again say, 'Our god,'
to the work of our hands;
for in you the orphan finds
compassion."
⁵I will heal their apostasy,
I will love them freely;
for my anger is turned away from
them.
⁶I will be like the dew for Israel:
he will blossom like the lily;
He will strike root like the Lebanon
cedar,
⁷and his shoots will go forth.
His splendor will be like the olive tree
and his fragrance like Lebanon
cedar.
⁸Again they will live in his shade;
they will raise grain,
They will blossom like the vine,
and his renown will be like the wine
of Lebanon.

⁹Ephraim! What more have I to do
with idols?
I have humbled him, but I will take
note of him.
I am like a verdant cypress tree.
From me fruit will be found for you!

Epilogue. ¹⁰Who is wise enough to
understand these things?
Who is intelligent enough to know
them?
Straight are the paths of the LORD,
the just walk in them,
but sinners stumble in them.

☐ REVELATION 5:11-14

5:11 I looked again and heard the voices of many angels who surrounded the throne and the living creatures and the elders. They were countless in number, [12]and they cried out in a loud voice:

"Worthy is the Lamb that was slain
to receive power and riches, wisdom and strength,
honor and glory and blessing."

[13]Then I heard every creature in heaven and on earth and under the earth and in the sea, everything in the universe, cry out:

"To the one who sits on the throne and to the Lamb
be blessing and honor, glory and might,
forever and ever."

[14]The four living creatures answered, "Amen," and the elders fell down and worshiped.

December 12

Our Lady of Guadalupe

The weapon of the second Eve, the Mother of God, is prayer.
— BLESSED JOHN HENRY NEWMAN

☐ JOEL 1-2

1:1 The word of the LORD which came to Joel, the son of Pethuel.

[2]Listen to this, you elders!
Pay attention, all who dwell in the land!
Has anything like this ever happened in your lifetime,
or in the lifetime of your ancestors?
[3]Report it to your children.
Have your children report it to their children,
and their children to the next generation.
[4]What the cutter left,
the swarming locust has devoured;
What the swarming locust left,
the hopper has devoured;
What the hopper left,
the consuming locust has devoured.
[5]Wake up, you drunkards, and weep;
wail, all you wine drinkers,
Over the new wine,
taken away from your mouths.
[6]For a nation invaded my land,
powerful and past counting,
With teeth like a lion's,
fangs like those of a lioness.
[7]It has stripped bare my vines,
splintered my fig tree,
Shearing off its bark and throwing it away,
until its branches turn white.
[8]Wail like a young woman dressed in sackcloth
for the husband of her youth.
[9]Grain offering and libation are cut off
from the house of the LORD;
In mourning are the priests,
the ministers of the LORD.
[10]The field is devastated;
the farmland mourns,
Because the grain is devastated,

the wine has dried up,
the oil has failed.
¹¹Be appalled, you farmers!
wail, you vinedressers,
Over the wheat and the barley,
because the harvest in the field is
ruined.
¹²The vine has dried up,
the fig tree has withered;
The pomegranate, even the date palm
and the apple—
every tree in the field has dried up.
Joy itself has dried up
among the people.

Cry Out to the Lord. ¹³Gird
yourselves and lament, you
priests!
wail, ministers of the altar!
Come, spend the night in sackcloth,
ministers of my God!
For the grain offering and the libation
are withheld from the house of your
God.
¹⁴Proclaim a holy fast!
Call an assembly!
Gather the elders,
all who dwell in the land,
To the house of the LORD, your God,
and cry out to the LORD!
¹⁵O! The day!
For near is the day of the LORD,
like destruction from the Almighty
it is coming!
¹⁶Before our very eyes
has not food been cut off?
And from the house of our God,
joy and gladness?
¹⁷The seed lies shriveled beneath clods
of dirt;
the storehouses are emptied.
The granaries are broken down,
for the grain is dried up.
¹⁸How the animals groan!
The herds of cattle are bewildered!
Because they have no pasture,
even the flocks of sheep are starving.

¹⁹To you, LORD, I cry!
for fire has devoured the wilderness
pastures,
flame has scorched all the trees in
the field.
²⁰Even the animals in the wild
cry out to you;
For the streams of water have run dry,
and fire has devoured the wilderness
pastures.

The Day Approaches. 2:1 Blow the
horn in Zion,
sound the alarm on my holy
mountain!
Let all the inhabitants of the land
tremble,
for the day of the LORD is coming!
Yes, it approaches,
²a day of darkness and gloom,
a day of thick clouds!
Like dawn spreading over the
mountains,
a vast and mighty army!
Nothing like it has ever happened in
ages past,
nor will the future hold anything
like it,
even to the most distant
generations.
³Before it, fire devours,
behind it flame scorches.
The land before it is like the garden of
Eden,
and behind it, a desolate
wilderness;
from it nothing escapes.
⁴Their appearance is that of horses;
like war horses they run.
⁵Like the rumble of chariots
they hurtle across mountaintops;
Like the crackling of fiery flames
devouring stubble;
Like a massive army
in battle formation.
⁶Before them peoples tremble,
every face turns pale.

[7]Like warriors they run,
   like soldiers they scale walls,
Each advancing in line,
   without swerving from the course.
[8]No one crowds the other;
   each advances in its own track;
They plunge through the weapons;
   they are not checked.
[9]They charge the city,
   they run upon the wall,
   they climb into the houses;
Through the windows
   they enter like thieves.

[10]Before them the earth trembles;
   the heavens shake;
Sun and moon are darkened,
   and the stars withhold their
      brightness.
[11]The LORD raises his voice
   at the head of his army;
How immense is his host!
   How numerous those who carry out
      his command!
How great is the day of the LORD!
   Utterly terrifying! Who can
      survive it?

Return to the Lord. [12]Yet even now—
   oracle of the LORD—
   return to me with your whole heart,
   with fasting, weeping, and mourning.
[13]Rend your hearts, not your garments,
   and return to the LORD, your God,
For he is gracious and merciful,
   slow to anger, abounding in
      steadfast love,
   and relenting in punishment.
[14]Perhaps he will again relent
   and leave behind a blessing,
Grain offering and libation
   for the LORD, your God.
[15]Blow the horn in Zion!
   Proclaim a fast,
   call an assembly!
[16]Gather the people,
   sanctify the congregation;
Assemble the elderly;

gather the children,
   even infants nursing at the breast;
Let the bridegroom leave his room,
   and the bride her bridal tent.
[17]Between the porch and the altar
   let the priests weep,
   let the ministers of the LORD weep
      and say:
"Spare your people, LORD!
   do not let your heritage become a
      disgrace,
   a byword among the nations!
Why should they say among the peoples,
   'Where is their God?'"

The Lord Relents. [18]Then the LORD grew jealous for his land and took pity on his people. [19]In response the LORD said to his people:

I am sending you
   grain, new wine, and oil,
   and you will be satisfied by them;
Never again will I make you
   a disgrace among the nations.
[20]The northerner I will remove far
      from you,
   driving them out into a dry and
      desolate land,
Their vanguard to the eastern sea,
   their rearguard to the western sea,
And their stench will rise,
   their stink will ascend,
What great deeds the Lord has done!
[21]Do not fear, O land!
   delight and rejoice,
   for the LORD has done great things!
[22]Do not fear, you animals in the wild,
   for the wilderness pastures sprout
      green grass.
The trees bear fruit,
   the fig tree and the vine produce
      their harvest.
[23]Children of Zion, delight
   and rejoice in the LORD, your God!
For he has faithfully given you the
      early rain,
   sending rain down on you,

the early and the late rains as before.
²⁴The threshing floors will be full of
　grain,
　the vats spilling over with new wine
　　and oil.
²⁵I will repay you double
　what the swarming locust has eaten,
The hopper, the consuming locust, and
　the cutter,
　my great army I sent against you.
²⁶You will eat until you are fully satisfied,

then you will praise the name of the
　Lord, your God,
Who acts so wondrously on your behalf!
My people will never again be put
　　to shame.
²⁷Then you will know that I am in the
　midst of Israel:
I, the Lord, am your God, and
　　there is no other;
my people will never again be put to
　shame.

□ REVELATION 6

The First Six Seals. 6:1 Then I watched while the Lamb broke open the first of the seven seals, and I heard one of the four living creatures cry out in a voice like thunder, "Come forward." ²I looked, and there was a white horse, and its rider had a bow. He was given a crown, and he rode forth victorious to further his victories.

³When he broke open the second seal, I heard the second living creature cry out, "Come forward." ⁴Another horse came out, a red one. Its rider was given power to take peace away from the earth, so that people would slaughter one another. And he was given a huge sword.

⁵When he broke open the third seal, I heard the third living creature cry out, "Come forward." I looked, and there was a black horse, and its rider held a scale in his hand. ⁶I heard what seemed to be a voice in the midst of the four living creatures. It said, "A ration of wheat costs a day's pay, and three rations of barley cost a day's pay. But do not damage the olive oil or the wine."

⁷When he broke open the fourth seal, I heard the voice of the fourth living creature cry out, "Come forward." ⁸I looked, and there was a pale green horse. Its rider was named Death, and Hades accompanied him. They were given authority over a quarter of the earth, to kill with sword, famine, and plague, and by means of the beasts of the earth.

⁹When he broke open the fifth seal, I saw underneath the altar the souls of those who had been slaughtered because of the witness they bore to the word of God. ¹⁰They cried out in a loud voice, "How long will it be, holy and true master, before you sit in judgment and avenge our blood on the inhabitants of the earth?" ¹¹Each of them was given a white robe, and they were told to be patient a little while longer until the number was filled of their fellow servants and brothers who were going to be killed as they had been.

¹²Then I watched while he broke open the sixth seal, and there was a great earthquake; the sun turned as black as dark sackcloth and the whole moon became like blood. ¹³The stars in the sky fell to the earth like unripe figs shaken loose from the tree in a strong wind. ¹⁴Then the sky was divided like a torn scroll curling up, and every mountain and island was moved from its place. ¹⁵The kings of the earth, the nobles, the military officers, the rich, the powerful, and every slave and free person hid themselves in caves and among mountain crags. ¹⁶They cried out to the mountains and the rocks, "Fall on us and hide us from the face of the one who sits on the throne and from the wrath of the Lamb, ¹⁷because the great day of their wrath has come and who can withstand it?"

December 13

St. Lucy

Those whose hearts are pure are the temples of the Holy Spirit.
— St. Lucy

☐ JOEL 3-4

The Day of the Lord. 3:1 It shall
come to pass
I will pour out my spirit upon all
flesh.
Your sons and daughters will prophesy,
your old men will dream dreams,
your young men will see visions.
²Even upon your male and female
servants,
in those days, I will pour out my
spirit.
³I will set signs in the heavens and on
the earth,
blood, fire, and columns of smoke;
⁴The sun will darken,
the moon turn blood-red,
Before the day of the LORD arrives,
that great and terrible day.
⁵Then everyone who calls upon the
name of the LORD
will escape harm.
For on Mount Zion there will be a
remnant,
as the LORD has said,
And in Jerusalem survivors
whom the LORD will summon.

The Lord's Case Against the Nations.
4:1 For see, in those days and at
that time,
when I restore the fortunes
of Judah and Jerusalem,
²I will gather all the nations
and bring them down to the Valley
of Jehoshaphat.
There I will enter into judgment with
them
on behalf of my people, my
heritage, Israel;

Because they scattered them among the
nations,
they divided up my land.
³For my people they cast lots,
trading a young boy for the price of
a prostitute,
exchanging a young girl for the wine
they drank.

⁴Moreover, what are you doing to me,
Tyre and Sidon, and all the regions of Philistia? Are you paying me back for something? If you are, I will very quickly turn
your deeds back upon your own head. ⁵You
took my silver and my gold and brought my
priceless treasures into your temples! ⁶You
sold the people of Judah and Jerusalem to
the Greeks, taking them far from their own
country! ⁷Look! I am rousing them from
the place to which you sold them, and I will
turn your deeds back upon your own head.
⁸I will sell your sons and daughters to the
Judahites who will sell them to the Sabeans,
a distant nation. The LORD has spoken!

The Nations Destroyed. ⁹Announce
this to the nations:
Proclaim a holy war!
Alert the warriors!
Let all the soldiers
report and march!
¹⁰Beat your plowshares into swords,
and your pruning knives into spears;
let the weakling boast, "I am a
warrior!"

¹¹Hurry and come, all you neighboring
peoples,
assemble there!
Bring down, LORD, your warriors!

¹²Let the nations rouse themselves and come up
to the Valley of Jehoshaphat;
For there I will sit in judgment
upon all the neighboring nations.

¹³Wield the sickle,
for the harvest is ripe;
Come and tread,
for the wine press is full;
The vats overflow,
for their crimes are numerous.
¹⁴Crowds upon crowds
in the Valley of Decision;
For near is the day of the LORD
in the Valley of Decision.
¹⁵Sun and moon are darkened,
and the stars withhold their
brightness,
¹⁶The LORD roars from Zion,
and from Jerusalem raises his voice,
The heavens and the earth quake,
but the LORD will be a shelter for
his people,
a fortress for the people of Israel.

A Secure Future for Judah. ¹⁷Then
you will know that I the LORD
am your God,
dwelling on Zion, my holy mountain;
Jerusalem will be holy,
and strangers will never again travel
through her.
¹⁸On that day
the mountains will drip new wine,
and the hills flow with milk,
All the streams of Judah
will flow with water.
A spring will rise from the house of the
LORD,
watering the Valley of Shittim.
¹⁹Egypt will be a waste,
Edom a desolate wilderness,
Because of violence done to the
Judahites,
because they shed innocent blood in
their land.
²⁰But Judah will be inhabited forever,
and Jerusalem for all generations.
²¹I will avenge their blood,
and I will not acquit the guilt.
The LORD dwells in Zion.

☐ REVELATION 7:1-8

The 144,000 Sealed. 7:1 After this I saw four angels standing at the four corners of the earth, holding back the four winds of the earth so that no wind could blow on land or sea or against any tree. ²Then I saw another angel come up from the East, holding the seal of the living God. He cried out in a loud voice to the four angels who were given power to damage the land and the sea, ³"Do not damage the land or the sea or the trees until we put the seal on the foreheads of the servants of our God." ⁴I heard the number of those who had been marked with the seal, one hundred and forty-four thousand marked from every tribe of the Israelites: ⁵twelve thousand were marked from the tribe of Judah, twelve thousand from the tribe of Reuben, twelve thousand from the tribe of Gad, ⁶twelve thousand from the tribe of Asher, twelve thousand from the tribe of Naphtali, twelve thousand from the tribe of Manasseh, ⁷twelve thousand from the tribe of Simeon, twelve thousand from the tribe of Levi, twelve thousand from the tribe of Issachar, ⁸twelve thousand from the tribe of Zebulun, twelve thousand from the tribe of Joseph, and twelve thousand were marked from the tribe of Benjamin.

December 14

St. John of the Cross

God is more pleased by one work, however small, done secretly, without desire that it be known, than a thousand done with desire that men know of them.

— St. John of the Cross

☐ AMOS 1-2

1:1 The words of Amos, who was one of the sheepbreeders from Tekoa, which he received in a vision concerning Israel in the days of Uzziah, king of Judah, and in the days of Jeroboam, son of Joash, king of Israel, two years before the earthquake. [2] He said:

The Lord roars from Zion,
    and raises his voice from Jerusalem;
The pastures of the shepherds languish,
    and the summit of Carmel withers.

Aram. [3] Thus says the Lord:

For three crimes of Damascus, and
        now four—
    I will not take it back—
Because they threshed Gilead
    with sledges of iron,
[4] I will send fire upon the house of
        Hazael,
    and it will devour the strongholds of
        Ben-hadad.
[5] I will break the barred gate of
        Damascus;
    From the Valley of Aven I will cut
        off the one enthroned,
And the sceptered ruler from Beth-eden;
    the people of Aram shall be exiled to
        Kir, says the Lord.

Philistia. [6] Thus says the Lord:

For three crimes of Gaza, and now
        four—
    I will not take it back—
Because they exiled an entire
        population,

handing them over to Edom,
[7] I will send fire upon the wall of Gaza,
    and it will devour its strongholds;
[8] From Ashdod I will cut off the one
        enthroned
    and the sceptered ruler from
        Ashkelon;
I will turn my hand against Ekron,
    and the last of the Philistines shall
        perish,
    says the Lord God.

Tyre. [9] Thus says the Lord:

For three crimes of Tyre, and now
        four—
    I will not take it back—
Because they handed over an entire
        population to Edom,
    and did not remember their
        covenant of brotherhood,
[10] I will send fire upon the wall of Tyre,
    and it will devour its strongholds.

Edom. [11] Thus says the Lord:

For three crimes of Edom, and now
        four—
    I will not take it back—
Because he pursued his brother with
        the sword,
    suppressing all pity,
Persisting in his anger,
    his wrath raging without end,
[12] I will send fire upon Teman,
    and it will devour the strongholds of
        Bozrah.

Ammon. [13] Thus says the Lord:

For three crimes of the Ammonites,
  and now four—
 I will not take it back—
Because they ripped open pregnant
  women in Gilead,
 in order to extend their territory,
¹⁴I will kindle a fire upon the wall of
  Rabbah,
 and it will devour its strongholds
Amid war cries on the day of battle,
 amid stormwind on the day of
  tempest.
¹⁵Their king shall go into exile,
 he and his princes with him, says
  the LORD.

Moab. 2:1 Thus says the LORD:

For three crimes of Moab, and now
  four—
 I will not take it back—
Because he burned to ashes
 the bones of Edom's king,
²I will send fire upon Moab,
 and it will devour the strongholds
  of Kerioth;
Moab shall meet death amid uproar,
 battle cries and blasts of the ram's
  horn.
³I will cut off the ruler from its midst,
 and all the princes I will slay with
  him, says the LORD.

Judah. ⁴Thus says the LORD:

For three crimes of Judah, and now
  four—
 I will not take it back—
Because they spurned the instruction
  of the LORD,
 and did not keep his statutes;
Because the lies which their ancestors
  followed
 have led them astray,
⁵I will send fire upon Judah,
 and it will devour the strongholds
  of Jerusalem.

Israel. ⁶Thus says the LORD:

For three crimes of Israel, and now
  four—
 I will not take it back—
Because they hand over the just for
  silver,
 and the poor for a pair of sandals;
⁷They trample the heads of the
  destitute
 into the dust of the earth,
 and force the lowly out of
  the way.
Son and father sleep with the
  same girl,
 profaning my holy name.
⁸Upon garments taken in pledge
 they recline beside any altar.
Wine at treasury expense
 they drink in their temples.
⁹Yet it was I who destroyed the
  Amorites before them,
 who were as tall as cedars,
 and as strong as oak trees.
I destroyed their fruit above
 and their roots beneath.
¹⁰It was I who brought you up from
  the land of Egypt,
 and who led you through the desert
  for forty years,
 to occupy the land of the
  Amorites;
¹¹I who raised up prophets among
  your children,
 and nazirites among your young
  men.
Is this not so, Israelites?—
 oracle of the LORD.
¹²But you made the nazirites drink
  wine,
 and commanded the prophets,
  "Do not prophesy!"
¹³Look, I am groaning beneath you,
 as a wagon groans when laden with
  sheaves.
¹⁴Flight shall elude the swift,
 and the strong shall not retain
  strength;
The warrior shall not save his life,

¹⁵nor shall the archer stand his ground;
The swift of foot shall not escape,
    nor shall the horseman save his life.

¹⁶And the most stouthearted of warriors
    shall flee naked on that day—
    oracle of the LORD.

☐ REVELATION 7:9-17

Triumph of the Elect. 7:9 After this I had a vision of a great multitude, which no one could count, from every nation, race, people, and tongue. They stood before the throne and before the Lamb, wearing white robes and holding palm branches in their hands. ¹⁰They cried out in a loud voice:

"Salvation comes from our God, who
    is seated on the throne,
    and from the Lamb."

¹¹All the angels stood around the throne and around the elders and the four living creatures. They prostrated themselves before the throne, worshiped God, ¹²and exclaimed:

"Amen. Blessing and glory, wisdom
    and thanksgiving,
    honor, power, and might
    be to our God forever and ever. Amen."

¹³Then one of the elders spoke up and said to me, "Who are these wearing white robes, and where did they come from?" ¹⁴I said to him, "My lord, you are the one who knows." He said to me, "These are the ones who have survived the time of great distress; they have washed their robes and made them white in the blood of the Lamb.

¹⁵"For this reason they stand before
        God's throne
    and worship him day and night in
        his temple.
    The one who sits on the throne will
        shelter them.
¹⁶They will not hunger or thirst
        anymore,
    nor will the sun or any heat strike
        them.
¹⁷For the Lamb who is in the center of
        the throne will shepherd them
    and lead them to springs of life-
        giving water,
    and God will wipe away every tear
        from their eyes."

December 15

Do you think that God comes to you all by himself? You may be sure that such a King is not left alone by the attendants of His court; but they attend Him, praying to Him for us, and for our welfare, because they are full of love.

— St. Teresa of Ávila

☐ AMOS 3-4

First Summons. 3:1 Hear this word,
  Israelites, that the LORD speaks
  concerning you,
  concerning the whole family I
    brought up from the land of
    Egypt:
²You alone I have known,
  among all the families of the earth;
Therefore I will punish you
  for all your iniquities.

³Do two journey together
  unless they have agreed?
⁴Does a lion roar in the forest
  when it has no prey?
Does a young lion cry out from its den
  unless it has seized something?
⁵Does a bird swoop down on a trap on
    the ground
  when there is no lure for it?
Does a snare spring up from the ground
  without catching anything?
⁶Does the ram's horn sound in a city
  without the people becoming
    frightened?
Does disaster befall a city
  unless the LORD has caused it?

⁷(Indeed, the Lord GOD does nothing
without revealing his plan to his servants
the prophets.)

⁸The lion has roared,
  who would not fear?
The Lord GOD has spoken,
  who would not prophesy?

⁹Proclaim this in the strongholds of
  Assyria,
in the strongholds of the land of
  Egypt:
"Gather on the mount of Samaria,
  and see the great disorders within it,
  the oppressions within its midst."
¹⁰They do not know how to do what is
    right—
  oracle of the LORD—
Storing up in their strongholds
  violence and destruction.
¹¹Therefore thus says the Lord GOD:
An enemy shall surround the land,
  tear down your fortresses,
  and pillage your strongholds.
¹²Thus says the LORD:
As the shepherd rescues from the
    mouth of the lion
  a pair of sheep's legs or the tip of an
    ear,
So shall the Israelites escape,
  those who dwell in Samaria,
With the corner of a couch
  or a piece of a cot.

¹³Hear and bear witness against the
    house of Jacob—
  an oracle of the Lord GOD, the God
    of hosts:
¹⁴On the day when I punish Israel for
    its crimes,
  I will also punish the altars of
    Bethel;
The horns of the altar shall be broken
    off
  and fall to the ground.
¹⁵I will strike the winter house
  and the summer house;

The houses of ivory shall lie in ruin,
and their many rooms shall be no
more—
oracle of the LORD.

Second Summons. 4:1 Hear this
word, you cows of Bashan,
who live on the mount of Samaria:
Who oppress the destitute
and abuse the needy;
Who say to your husbands,
"Bring us a drink!"
2The Lord GOD has sworn by his
holiness:
Truly days are coming upon you
when they shall drag you away with
ropes,
your children with fishhooks;
3You shall go out through the breached
walls
one in front of the other,
And you shall be exiled to Harmon—
oracle of the LORD.

4Come to Bethel and sin,
to Gilgal and sin all the more!
Each morning bring your sacrifices,
every third day your tithes;
5Burn leavened bread as a thanksgiving
sacrifice,
proclaim publicly your voluntary
offerings,
For so you love to do, Israelites—
oracle of the Lord GOD.

6Though I made your teeth
clean of food in all your cities,
and made bread scarce in all your
dwellings,
Yet you did not return to me—
oracle of the LORD.
7And I withheld the rain from you
when the harvest was still three
months away;

I sent rain upon one city
but not upon another;
One field was watered by rain,
but the one I did not water dried up;
8Two or three cities staggered to
another to drink water
but were not satisfied;
Yet you did not return to me—
oracle of the LORD.
9I struck you with blight and mildew;
locusts devoured your gardens and
vineyards,
the caterpillar consumed your fig
trees and olive trees;
Yet you did not return to me—
oracle of the LORD.
10I sent upon you pestilence like that of
Egypt;
with the sword I killed your young
men and your captured horses,
and to your nostrils I brought the
stench of your camps;
Yet you did not return to me—
oracle of the LORD.
11I overthrew you
as when God overthrew Sodom and
Gomorrah;
you were like a brand plucked from
the fire,
Yet you did not return to me—
oracle of the LORD.
12Therefore thus I will do to you, Israel:
and since I will deal thus with you,
prepare to meet your God, O Israel!
13The one who forms mountains and
creates winds,
and declares to mortals their
thoughts;
Who makes dawn into darkness
and strides upon the heights of the
earth,
the LORD, the God of hosts, is his
name!

☐ REVELATION 8:1-5

The Seven Trumpets. 8:1 When he broke open the seventh seal, there was silence in heaven for about half an hour. [2]And I saw that the seven angels who stood before God were given seven trumpets.

The Gold Censer. [3]Another angel came and stood at the altar, holding a gold censer. He was given a great quantity of incense to offer, along with the prayers of all the holy ones, on the gold altar that was before the throne. [4]The smoke of the incense along with the prayers of the holy ones went up before God from the hand of the angel. [5]Then the angel took the censer, filled it with burning coals from the altar, and hurled it down to the earth. There were peals of thunder, rumblings, flashes of lightning, and an earthquake.

December 16 ————————————————

Blessed Mary of the Angels

O Lamb of God! Imprint on my heart such repentance that I may prefer to die rather than ever to offend You again.

— BLESSED MARY OF THE ANGELS

☐ AMOS 5-6

Third Summons. 5:1 Hear this word
which I utter concerning you,
this dirge, house of Israel:
[2]She is fallen, to rise no more,
virgin Israel;
She lies abandoned on her land,
with no one to raise her up.
[3]For thus says the Lord GOD
to the house of Israel:
The city that marched out with a
thousand
shall be left with a hundred,
Another that marched out with a
hundred
shall be left with ten.
[4]For thus says the LORD
to the house of Israel:
Seek me, that you may live,
[5]but do not seek Bethel;
Do not come to Gilgal,
and do not cross over to Beer-sheba;
For Gilgal shall be led into exile
and Bethel shall be no more.

[6]Seek the LORD, that you may live,
lest he flare up against the house of
Joseph like a fire
that shall consume the house of Israel,
with no one to quench it.

[8]The one who made the Pleiades and
Orion,
who turns darkness into dawn,
and darkens day into night;
Who summons the waters of the sea,
and pours them out on the surface
of the earth;
[9]Who makes destruction fall suddenly
upon the stronghold
and brings ruin upon the fortress,
the LORD is his name.

First Woe. [7]Woe to those who turn
justice into wormwood
and cast righteousness to the
ground,
[10]They hate those who reprove at the
gate

and abhor those who speak with
     integrity;
¹¹Therefore, because you tax the destitute
     and exact from them levies of grain,
Though you have built houses of hewn
     stone,
     you shall not live in them;
Though you have planted choice
     vineyards,
     you shall not drink their wine.
¹²Yes, I know how many are your crimes,
     how grievous your sins:
Oppressing the just, accepting bribes,
     turning away the needy at the gate.
¹³(Therefore at this time the wise are
     struck dumb
     for it is an evil time.)

¹⁴Seek good and not evil,
     that you may live;
Then truly the LORD, the God of hosts,
     will be with you as you claim.
¹⁵Hate evil and love good,
     and let justice prevail at the gate;
Then it may be that the LORD, the God
     of hosts,
     will have pity on the remnant of
          Joseph.

¹⁶Therefore, thus says the LORD,
     the God of hosts, the Lord:
In every square there shall be
     lamentation,
     and in every street they shall cry,
          "Oh, no!"
They shall summon the farmers to wail
     and the professional mourners to
          lament.
¹⁷And in every vineyard there shall be
     lamentation
     when I pass through your midst,
          says the LORD.

Second Woe. ¹⁸Woe to those who
     yearn
     for the day of the LORD!
What will the day of the LORD mean
     for you?

It will be darkness, not light!
¹⁹As if someone fled from a lion
     and a bear met him;
Or as if on entering the house
     he rested his hand against the wall,
     and a snake bit it.
²⁰Truly, the day of the LORD will be
     darkness, not light,
     gloom without any brightness!

²¹I hate, I despise your feasts,
     I take no pleasure in your
          solemnities.
²²Even though you bring me your
          burnt offerings and grain
          offerings
     I will not accept them;
Your stall-fed communion offerings,
     I will not look upon them.
²³Take away from me
     your noisy songs;
The melodies of your harps,
     I will not listen to them.
²⁴Rather let justice surge like waters,
     and righteousness like an unfailing
          stream.
²⁵Did you bring me sacrifices and grain
          offerings
     for forty years in the desert,
          O house of Israel?
²⁶Yet you will carry away Sukuth, your
          king,
     and Kaiwan, your star-image,
     your gods that you have made for
          yourselves,
²⁷As I exile you beyond Damascus,
     says the LORD,
     whose name is the God of hosts.

Third Woe. 6:1 Woe to those who are
     complacent in Zion,
     secure on the mount of Samaria,
Leaders of the first among nations,
     to whom the people of Israel turn.
²Pass over to Calneh and see,
     go from there to Hamath the great,
     and down to Gath of the Philistines.

Are you better than these kingdoms,
or is your territory greater than
theirs?
³You who would put off the day of
disaster,
yet hasten the time of violence!
⁴Those who lie on beds of ivory,
and lounge upon their couches;
Eating lambs taken from the flock,
and calves from the stall;
⁵Who improvise to the music of the
harp,
composing on musical instruments
like David,
⁶Who drink wine from bowls,
and anoint themselves with the best
oils,
but are not made ill by the collapse
of Joseph;
⁷Therefore, now they shall be the first
to go into exile,
and the carousing of those who
lounged shall cease.
⁸The Lord GOD has sworn by his very
self—
an oracle of the LORD, the God of
hosts:
I abhor the pride of Jacob,
I hate his strongholds,
and I will hand over the city with
everything in it;
⁹Should there remain ten people
in a single house, these shall die.
¹⁰When a relative or one who prepares
the body picks up the remains
to carry them out of the house,
If he says to someone in the recesses of
the house,
"Is anyone with you?" and the
answer is, "No one,"
Then he shall say, "Silence!"
for no one must mention the name
of the LORD.
¹¹Indeed, the LORD has given the
command
to shatter the great house to bits,
and reduce the small house to
rubble.
¹²Can horses run over rock,
or can one plow the sea with oxen?
Yet you have turned justice into gall,
and the fruit of righteousness into
wormwood,
¹³You who rejoice in Lodebar,
and say, "Have we not, by our own
strength,
seized Karnaim for ourselves?"
¹⁴Look, I am raising up against you,
house of Israel—
oracle of the LORD, the God of
hosts—
A nation that shall oppress you
from Lebo-hamath even to the
Wadi Arabah.

☐ REVELATION 8:6-13

The First Four Trumpets. 8:6 The seven angels who were holding the seven trumpets prepared to blow them.

⁷When the first one blew his trumpet, there came hail and fire mixed with blood, which was hurled down to the earth. A third of the land was burned up, along with a third of the trees and all green grass.

⁸When the second angel blew his trumpet, something like a large burning mountain was hurled into the sea. A third of the sea turned to blood, ⁹a third of the creatures living in the sea died, and a third of the ships were wrecked.

¹⁰When the third angel blew his trumpet, a large star burning like a torch fell from the sky. It fell on a third of the rivers and on the springs of water. ¹¹The star was called "Wormwood," and a third of all the water turned to wormwood. Many people

died from this water, because it was made bitter.

[12]When the fourth angel blew his trumpet, a third of the sun, a third of the moon, and a third of the stars were struck, so that a third of them became dark. The day lost its light for a third of the time, as did the night.

[13]Then I looked again and heard an eagle flying high overhead cry out in a loud voice, "Woe! Woe! Woe to the inhabitants of the earth from the rest of the trumpet blasts that the three angels are about to blow!"

December 17

There are four remedies against the fear of divine judgment. The first is good deeds. The second is confession and repentance of the evil done. The third is almsgiving, which cleanses us from all stains. The fourth is charity, namely, the love of God and our neighbor.

— ST. THOMAS AQUINAS

☐ AMOS 7-9

First Vision: The Locust Swarm. 7:1 This is what the Lord GOD showed me: He was forming a locust swarm when the late growth began to come up (the late growth after the king's mowing). [2]When they had finished eating the grass in the land, I said:

Forgive, O Lord GOD!
    Who will raise up Jacob?
    He is so small!

[3]The LORD relented concerning this. "This shall not be," said the Lord GOD.

Second Vision: The Rain of Fire. [4]This is what the Lord GOD showed me: He was summoning a rain of fire. It had devoured the great abyss and was consuming the fields. [5]Then I said:

Cease, O Lord GOD!
    Who will raise up Jacob?
    He is so small!

[6]The LORD relented concerning this. "This also shall not be," said the Lord GOD.

Third Vision: The Plummet. [7]This is what the Lord GOD showed me: He was

standing, plummet in hand, by a wall built with a plummet. [8]The Lord GOD asked me, "What do you see, Amos?" And I answered, "A plummet." Then the LORD said:

See, I am laying the plummet
    in the midst of my people Israel;
    I will forgive them no longer.
[9]The high places of Isaac shall be laid
        waste,
    and the sanctuaries of Israel made
        desolate;
    and I will attack the house of
        Jeroboam with the sword.

Biographical Interlude: Amos and Amaziah. [10]Amaziah, the priest of Bethel, sent word to Jeroboam, king of Israel: "Amos has conspired against you within the house of Israel; the country cannot endure all his words. [11]For this is what Amos says:

'Jeroboam shall die by the sword,
    and Israel shall surely be exiled from
        its land.'"

¹²To Amos, Amaziah said: "Off with you, seer, flee to the land of Judah and there earn your bread by prophesying! ¹³But never again prophesy in Bethel; for it is the king's sanctuary and a royal temple." ¹⁴Amos answered Amaziah, "I am not a prophet, nor do I belong to a company of prophets. I am a herdsman and a dresser of sycamores, ¹⁵but the LORD took me from following the flock, and the LORD said to me, 'Go, prophesy to my people Israel.' ¹⁶Now hear the word of the LORD:

You say: 'Do not prophesy against
　　Israel,
　　do not preach against the house of
　　　Isaac.'
¹⁷Therefore thus says the LORD:
Your wife shall become a prostitute in
　　the city,
　　and your sons and daughters shall
　　　fall by the sword.
Your land shall be parcelled out by
　　measuring line,
　　and you yourself shall die in an
　　　unclean land;
　　and Israel shall be exiled from its
　　　land."

Fourth Vision: The Summer Fruit. 8:1
This is what the Lord GOD showed me: a basket of end-of-summer fruit. ²He asked, "What do you see, Amos?" And I answered, "A basket of end-of-summer fruit." And the LORD said to me:

The end has come for my people Israel;
　　I will forgive them no longer.
³The temple singers will wail on that
　　day—
　　oracle of the Lord GOD.
Many shall be the corpses,
　　strewn everywhere—Silence!

⁴Hear this, you who trample upon the
　　needy
　　and destroy the poor of the land:
⁵"When will the new moon be over,"
　　you ask,
　　"that we may sell our grain,
And the sabbath,
　　that we may open the grain-bins?
We will diminish the ephah,
　　add to the shekel,
　　and fix our scales for cheating!
⁶We will buy the destitute for silver,
　　and the poor for a pair of sandals;
　　even the worthless grain we will
　　　sell!"
⁷The LORD has sworn by the pride of
　　Jacob:
　　Never will I forget a thing they have
　　　done!
⁸Shall not the land tremble because of
　　this,
　　and all who dwell in it mourn?
It will all rise up and toss like the Nile,
　　and subside like the river of Egypt.
⁹On that day—oracle of the Lord
　　GOD—
　　I will make the sun set at midday
　　and in broad daylight cover the land
　　　with darkness.
¹⁰I will turn your feasts into mourning
　　and all your songs into dirges.
I will cover the loins of all with
　　sackcloth
　　and make every head bald.
I will make it like the time of
　　mourning for an only child,
　　and its outcome like a day of bitter
　　　weeping.
¹¹See, days are coming—oracle of the
　　Lord GOD—
　　when I will send a famine upon the
　　　land:
Not a hunger for bread, or a thirst for
　　water,
　　but for hearing the word of the
　　　LORD.
¹²They shall stagger from sea to sea
　　and wander from north to east
In search of the word of the LORD,

but they shall not find it.

¹³On that day, beautiful young women
and young men
shall faint from thirst,
¹⁴Those who swear by Ashima of
Samaria,
and who say, "By the life of your
god, O Dan,"
"By the life of the Power of Beer-
sheba!"
They shall fall, never to rise again.

Fifth Vision: The Destruction of the Sanctuary. 9:1 I saw the Lord standing beside the altar. And he said:

Strike the capitals
so that the threshold shakes!
Break them off on the heads of
them all!
Those who are left I will slay with the
sword.
Not one shall get away,
no survivor shall escape.
²Though they dig down to Sheol,
even from there my hand shall take
them;
Though they climb to the heavens,
even from there I shall bring them
down.
³Though they hide on the summit of
Carmel,
there too I will hunt them down
and take them;
Though they hide from my gaze at the
bottom of the sea,
there I will command the serpent to
bite them.
⁴Though they go into captivity before
their enemies,
there I will command the sword to
slay them.
I will fix my gaze upon them
for evil and not for good.
⁵The Lord God of hosts,
Who melts the earth with his touch,

so that all who dwell on it mourn,
So that it will all rise up like the Nile,
and subside like the river of Egypt;
⁶Who has built his upper chamber in
heaven,
and established his vault over the
earth;
Who summons the waters of the sea
and pours them upon the surface of
the earth—
the LORD is his name.

⁷Are you not like the Ethiopians to me,
O Israelites?—oracle of the LORD—
Did I not bring the Israelites from the
land of Egypt
as I brought the Philistines from
Caphtor
and the Arameans from Kir?
⁸See, the eyes of the Lord GOD are on
this sinful kingdom,
and I will destroy it from the face of
the earth—
But I will not destroy the house of
Jacob completely—
oracle of the LORD.
⁹For see, I have given the command
to sift the house of Israel among all
the nations,
As one sifts with a sieve,
letting no pebble fall to the ground.
¹⁰All sinners among my people shall die
by the sword,
those who say, "Disaster will not
reach or overtake us."

¹¹On that day I will raise up
the fallen hut of David;
I will wall up its breaches,
raise up its ruins,
and rebuild it as in the days of old,
¹²That they may possess the remnant of
Edom,
and all nations claimed in my
name—
oracle of the LORD, the one who
does this.
¹³Yes, days are coming—

oracle of the LORD—
When the one who plows shall
    overtake the one who reaps
and the vintager, the sower of the
    seed;
The mountains shall drip with the juice
    of grapes,
and all the hills shall run with it.
[14]I will restore my people Israel,

they shall rebuild and inhabit their
    ruined cities,
Plant vineyards and drink the wine,
    set out gardens and eat the fruits.
[15]I will plant them upon their own
    ground;
never again shall they be plucked
From the land I have given them—
    the LORD, your God, has spoken.

☐ REVELATION 9:1-11

The Fifth Trumpet. 9:1 Then the fifth angel blew his trumpet, and I saw a star that had fallen from the sky to the earth. It was given the key for the passage to the abyss. [2]It opened the passage to the abyss, and smoke came up out of the passage like smoke from a huge furnace. The sun and the air were darkened by the smoke from the passage. [3]Locusts came out of the smoke onto the land, and they were given the same power as scorpions of the earth. [4]They were told not to harm the grass of the earth or any plant or any tree, but only those people who did not have the seal of God on their foreheads. [5]They were not allowed to kill them but only to torment them for five months; the torment they inflicted was like that of a scorpion when it stings a person. [6]During that time these people will seek death but will not find it, and they will long to die but death will escape them.

[7]The appearance of the locusts was like that of horses ready for battle. On their heads they wore what looked like crowns of gold; their faces were like human faces, [8]and they had hair like women's hair. Their teeth were like lions' teeth, [9]and they had chests like iron breastplates. The sound of their wings was like the sound of many horse-drawn chariots racing into battle. [10]They had tails like scorpions, with stingers; with their tails they had power to harm people for five months. [11]They had as their king the angel of the abyss, whose name in Hebrew is Abaddon and in Greek Apollyon.

December 18

If God turns nations' poisonous joys into bitterness, if He corrupts their pleasures, and if He scatters thorns along the path of their riot, the reason is that He loves them still. And this is the holy cruelty of the Physician, who, in extreme cases of sickness, makes us take most bitter and most horrible medicines. The greatest mercy of God is not to let those nations remain in peace with each other who are not at peace with Him.

— St. Pio of Pietrelcina

☐ OBADIAH

Edom's Fall Decreed.1 The vision of
Obadiah.
Thus says the Lord God concerning
Edom:
We have heard a message from the Lord,
and a herald has been sent among
the nations:
"Rise up, so we may go to war
against it!"
²Now I make you least among the
nations;
you are utterly contemptible.
³The pride of your heart has deceived
you—
you who dwell in mountain crevices,
in your lofty home,
Who say in your heart,
"Who will bring me down to earth?"
⁴Though you soar like the eagle,
and your nest is set among the stars,
From there I will bring you down—
oracle of the Lord.
⁵If thieves came to you, robbers by
night
—how you have been destroyed!—
would they not steal merely till they
had enough?
If grape pickers came to you,
would they not leave some
gleanings?
⁶How Esau has been searched out,
his treasures hunted down!
⁷To the border they have driven you—

all your allies;
Your partners have deceived you,
they have overpowered you;
Those who eat your bread
will replace you with foreigners,
who have no understanding.

Edom's Betrayal of Judah. ⁸On that
day—oracle of the Lord—will
I not
make the wise disappear from
Edom,
and understanding from Mount
Esau?
⁹Teman, your warriors will be terror-
stricken,
so that everyone on Mount Esau
will be cut down.
¹⁰Because of violence to your brother
Jacob,
disgrace will cover you,
you will be done away with forever!
¹¹On the day you stood by,
the day strangers carried off his
possessions,
And foreigners entered his gates
and cast lots for Jerusalem,
you too were like one of them.
¹²Do not gloat over the day of your
brother,
the day of his disaster;
Do not exult over the people of Judah
on the day of their ruin;

Do not speak haughtily
    on the day of distress!
¹³Do not enter the gate of my people
    on the day of their calamity;
Do not gloat—especially you—over
      his misfortune
    on the day of his calamity;
Do not lay hands upon his
      possessions
    on the day of his calamity!
¹⁴Do not stand at the crossroads
    to cut down his survivors;
Do not hand over his fugitives
    on the day of distress!

Edom's Fall and Judah's Restoration.
    ¹⁵Near is the day of the Lord
    against all the nations!
As you have done, so will it be done
      to you,
    your conduct will come back upon
      your own head;
¹⁶As you drank upon my holy
      mountain,
    so will all the nations drink
      continually.
Yes, they will drink and swallow,

and will become as though they had
      not been.
¹⁷But on Mount Zion there will be
    some who escape;
    the mountain will be holy,
And the house of Jacob will take
      possession
    of those who dispossessed them.
¹⁸The house of Jacob will be a fire,
    the house of Joseph a flame,
    and the house of Esau stubble.
They will set it ablaze and devour it;
    none will survive of the house of
      Esau,
    for the Lord has spoken.

¹⁹They will take possession of the Negeb, Mount Esau, the Shephelah, and Philistia, possess the countryside of Ephraim, the countryside of Samaria, Benjamin, and Gilead. ²⁰The exiles of this Israelite army will possess the Canaanite land as far as Zarephath, and the exiles of Jerusalem who are in Sepharad will possess the cities of the Negeb. ²¹And deliverers will ascend Mount Zion to rule Mount Esau, and the kingship shall be the Lord's.

☐ REVELATION 9:12-21

9:12 The first woe has passed, but there are two more to come.

The Sixth Trumpet. ¹³Then the sixth angel blew his trumpet, and I heard a voice coming from the [four] horns of the gold altar before God, ¹⁴telling the sixth angel who held the trumpet, "Release the four angels who are bound at the banks of the great river Euphrates." ¹⁵So the four angels were released, who were prepared for this hour, day, month, and year to kill a third of the human race. ¹⁶The number of cavalry troops was two hundred million; I heard their number. ¹⁷Now in my vision this is how I saw the horses and their riders. They wore red, blue, and yellow breastplates, and the horses' heads were like heads of lions, and out of their mouths came fire, smoke, and sulfur. ¹⁸By these three plagues of fire, smoke, and sulfur that came out of their mouths a third of the human race was killed. ¹⁹For the power of the horses is in their mouths and in their tails; for their tails are like snakes, with heads that inflict harm.

²⁰The rest of the human race, who were not killed by these plagues, did not repent of the works of their hands, to give up the worship of demons and idols made from gold, silver, bronze, stone, and wood, which cannot see or hear or walk. ²¹Nor did they repent of their murders, their magic potions, their unchastity, or their robberies.

December 19

Only after the Last Judgment will Mary get any rest; from now until then, she is much too busy with her children.

— St. John Vianney

☐ JONAH

Jonah's Disobedience and Flight. 1:1 The word of the LORD came to Jonah, son of Amittai: ²Set out for the great city of Nineveh, and preach against it; for their wickedness has come before me. ³But Jonah made ready to flee to Tarshish, away from the LORD. He went down to Joppa, found a ship going to Tarshish, paid the fare, and went down in it to go with them to Tarshish, away from the LORD.

⁴The LORD, however, hurled a great wind upon the sea, and the storm was so great that the ship was about to break up. ⁵Then the sailors were afraid and each one cried to his god. To lighten the ship for themselves, they threw its cargo into the sea. Meanwhile, Jonah had gone down into the hold of the ship, and lay there fast asleep. ⁶The captain approached him and said, "What are you doing asleep? Get up, call on your god! Perhaps this god will be mindful of us so that we will not perish."

⁷Then they said to one another, "Come, let us cast lots to discover on whose account this evil has come to us." So they cast lots, and the lot fell on Jonah. ⁸They said to him, "Tell us why this evil has come to us! What is your business? Where do you come from? What is your country, and to what people do you belong?" ⁹"I am a Hebrew," he replied; "I fear the LORD, the God of heaven, who made the sea and the dry land."

¹⁰Now the men were seized with great fear and said to him, "How could you do such a thing!"—They knew that he was fleeing from the LORD, because he had told them. ¹¹They asked, "What shall we do with you, that the sea may calm down for us?" For the sea was growing more and more stormy.

¹²Jonah responded, "Pick me up and hurl me into the sea and then the sea will calm down for you. For I know that this great storm has come upon you because of me." ¹³Still the men rowed hard to return to dry land, but they could not, for the sea grew more and more stormy. ¹⁴Then they cried to the LORD: "Please, O LORD, do not let us perish for taking this man's life; do not charge us with shedding innocent blood, for you, LORD, have accomplished what you desired." ¹⁵Then they picked up Jonah and hurled him into the sea, and the sea stopped raging. ¹⁶Seized with great fear of the LORD, the men offered sacrifice to the LORD and made vows.

Jonah's Prayer. 2:1 But the LORD sent a great fish to swallow Jonah, and he remained in the belly of the fish three days and three nights. ²Jonah prayed to the LORD, his God, from the belly of the fish:

³Out of my distress I called to the LORD,
  and he answered me;
From the womb of Sheol I cried for help,
  and you heard my voice.
⁴You cast me into the deep, into the
    heart of the sea,
  and the flood enveloped me;
All your breakers and your billows
  passed over me.
⁵Then I said, "I am banished from your
    sight!
  How will I again look upon your
    holy temple?"
⁶The waters surged around me up to
    my neck;
  the deep enveloped me;

seaweed wrapped around my head.
⁷I went down to the roots of the
mountains;
to the land whose bars closed
behind me forever,
But you brought my life up from the pit,
O Lord, my God.

⁸When I became faint,
I remembered the Lord;
My prayer came to you
in your holy temple.
⁹Those who worship worthless idols
abandon their hope for mercy.
¹⁰But I, with thankful voice,
will sacrifice to you;
What I have vowed I will pay:
deliverance is from the Lord.

¹¹Then the Lord commanded the fish to vomit Jonah upon dry land.

Jonah's Obedience and the Ninevites' Repentance. 3:1 The word of the Lord came to Jonah a second time: ²Set out for the great city of Nineveh, and announce to it the message that I will tell you. ³So Jonah set out for Nineveh, in accord with the word of the Lord. Now Nineveh was an awesomely great city; it took three days to walk through it. ⁴Jonah began his journey through the city, and when he had gone only a single day's walk announcing, "Forty days more and Nineveh shall be overthrown," ⁵the people of Nineveh believed God; they proclaimed a fast and all of them, great and small, put on sackcloth.

⁶When the news reached the king of Nineveh, he rose from his throne, laid aside his robe, covered himself with sackcloth, and sat in ashes. ⁷Then he had this proclaimed throughout Nineveh: "By decree of the king and his nobles, no man or beast, no cattle or sheep, shall taste anything; they shall not eat, nor shall they drink water. ⁸Man and beast alike must be covered with sackcloth and call loudly to God; they all must turn from their evil way and from the violence of their hands. ⁹Who knows? God may again repent and turn from his blazing wrath, so that we will not perish." ¹⁰When God saw by their actions how they turned from their evil way, he repented of the evil he had threatened to do to them; he did not carry it out.

Jonah's Anger and God's Reproof. 4:1 But this greatly displeased Jonah, and he became angry. ²He prayed to the Lord, "O Lord, is this not what I said while I was still in my own country? This is why I fled at first toward Tarshish. I knew that you are a gracious and merciful God, slow to anger, abounding in kindness, repenting of punishment. ³So now, Lord, please take my life from me; for it is better for me to die than to live." ⁴But the Lord asked, "Are you right to be angry?"

⁵Jonah then left the city for a place to the east of it, where he built himself a hut and waited under it in the shade, to see what would happen to the city. ⁶Then the Lord God provided a gourd plant. And when it grew up over Jonah's head, giving shade that relieved him of any discomfort, Jonah was greatly delighted with the plant. ⁷But the next morning at dawn God provided a worm that attacked the plant, so that it withered. ⁸And when the sun arose, God provided a scorching east wind; and the sun beat upon Jonah's head till he became faint. Then he wished for death, saying, "It is better for me to die than to live."

⁹But God said to Jonah, "Do you have a right to be angry over the gourd plant?" Jonah answered, "I have a right to be angry—angry enough to die." ¹⁰Then the Lord said, "You are concerned over the gourd plant which cost you no effort and which you did not grow; it came up in one night and in one night it perished. ¹¹And should I not be concerned over the great city of Nineveh, in which there are more than a hundred and twenty thousand persons who cannot know their right hand from their left, not to mention all the animals?"

☐ REVELATION 10

The Angel with the Small Scroll. 10:1 Then I saw another mighty angel come down from heaven wrapped in a cloud, with a halo around his head; his face was like the sun and his feet were like pillars of fire. ²In his hand he held a small scroll that had been opened. He placed his right foot on the sea and his left foot on the land, ³and then he cried out in a loud voice as a lion roars. When he cried out, the seven thunders raised their voices, too. ⁴When the seven thunders had spoken, I was about to write it down; but I heard a voice from heaven say, "Seal up what the seven thunders have spoken, but do not write it down." ⁵Then the angel I saw standing on the sea and on the land raised his right hand to heaven ⁶and swore by the one who lives forever and ever, who created heaven and earth and sea and all that is in them,

"There shall be no more delay. ⁷At the time when you hear the seventh angel blow his trumpet, the mysterious plan of God shall be fulfilled, as he promised to his servants the prophets."

⁸Then the voice that I had heard from heaven spoke to me again and said, "Go, take the scroll that lies open in the hand of the angel who is standing on the sea and on the land." ⁹So I went up to the angel and told him to give me the small scroll. He said to me, "Take and swallow it. It will turn your stomach sour, but in your mouth it will taste as sweet as honey." ¹⁰I took the small scroll from the angel's hand and swallowed it. In my mouth it was like sweet honey, but when I had eaten it, my stomach turned sour. ¹¹Then someone said to me, "You must prophesy again about many peoples, nations, tongues, and kings."

December 20

> *It is frequently in pain of the body, amid the very hands of persecutors, that Christ is really found. In a little while, in a brief moment, when you have escaped the hands of your persecutors, and have not given in to the ways of the world, Christ will meet you and will not allow you to be tempted further.*
>
> — St. Ambrose of Milan

☐ MICAH 1-3

1:1 The word of the LORD which came to Micah of Moresheth in the days of Jotham, Ahaz, and Hezekiah, kings of Judah, which he saw concerning Samaria and Jerusalem.

²Hear, O peoples, all of you,
  give heed, O earth, and all that is
    in it!
Let the Lord GOD be witness against you,
  the Lord from his holy temple!

³For see, the LORD goes out from his
    place
  and descending, treads upon the
    heights of the earth.
⁴The mountains melt under him
  and the valleys split open,
Like wax before the fire,
  like water poured down a slope.
⁵All this is for the crime of Jacob,
  for the sins of the house of Israel.

What is the crime of Jacob? Is it not
　　　Samaria?
And what is the sin of the house of
　　　Judah?
　　　Is it not Jerusalem?
⁶So I will make Samaria a ruin in the
　　　field,
　　a place to plant vineyards;
I will throw its stones into the valley,
　　and lay bare its foundations.
⁷All its carved figures shall be broken
　　　to pieces,
　　all its wages shall be burned in the
　　　fire,
　　and all its idols I will destroy.
As the wages of a prostitute it gathered
　　　them,
　　and to the wages of a prostitute they
　　　shall return.

⁸For this I will lament and wail,
　　go barefoot and naked;
I will utter lamentation like the jackals,
　　mourning like the ostriches,
⁹For her wound is incurable;
　　it has come even to Judah.
It has reached to the gate of my people,
　　even to Jerusalem.

¹⁰Do not announce it in Gath,
　　do not weep at all;
In Beth-leaphrah
　　roll in the dust.
¹¹Pass by,
　　you who dwell in Shaphir!
The inhabitants of Zaanan
　　do not come forth from their city.
There is lamentation in Beth-ezel.
　　It will withdraw its support from
　　　you.
¹²The inhabitants of Maroth
　　hope for good,
But evil has come down from the LORD
　　to the gate of Jerusalem.
¹³Harness steeds to the chariots,
　　inhabitants of Lachish;
You are the beginning of sin
　　for daughter Zion,

For in you were found
　　the crimes of Israel.
¹⁴Therefore you must give back the
　　　dowry
　　to Moresheth-gath;
The houses of Achzib are a dry stream
　　　bed
　　to the kings of Israel.
¹⁵Again I will bring the conqueror to
　　　you,
　　inhabitants of Mareshah;
The glory of Israel shall come
　　even to Adullam.
¹⁶Make yourself bald, cut off your hair,
　　for the children whom you cherish;
Make yourself bald as a vulture,
　　for they are taken from you into
　　　exile.

2:1 Ah! you plotters of iniquity,
　　who work out evil on your beds!
In the morning light you carry it out
　　for it lies within your power.
²You covet fields, and seize them;
　　houses, and take them;
You cheat owners of their houses,
　　people of their inheritance.

³Therefore thus says the LORD:
Look, I am planning against this family
　　　an evil
　　from which you cannot free your
　　　necks;
Nor shall you walk with head held
　　　high,
　　for it will be an evil time.
⁴On that day you shall be mocked,
　　and there will be bitter lament:
"Our ruin is complete,
　　our fields are divided among our
　　　captors,
The fields of my people are measured
　　　out,
　　and no one can get them back!"
⁵Thus you shall have no one
　　in the assembly of the LORD
　　to allot to you a share of land.

⁶"Do not preach," they preach,
    "no one should preach of these
        things!
    Shame will not overtake us."
⁷How can it be said, house of Jacob,
    "Is the LORD short of patience;
    are these the Lord's deeds?"
Do not my words promise good
    to the one who walks in justice?
⁸But you rise up against my people as
        an enemy:
    you have stripped off the garment
        from the peaceful,
From those who go their way in
        confidence,
    as though it were spoils of war.
⁹The women of my people you drive out
    from their pleasant houses;
From their children you take away
    forever the honor I gave them.

¹⁰"Get up! Leave,
    this is no place to rest";
Because of uncleanness that destroys
    with terrible destruction.
¹¹If one possessed of a lying spirit
    speaks deceitfully, saying,
"I will preach to you wine and strong
        drink,"
    that one would be the preacher for
        this people.

¹²I will gather you, Jacob, each and
        every one,
    I will assemble all the remnant of
        Israel;
I will group them like a flock in the
        fold,
    like a herd in its pasture;
    the noise of the people will resound.

¹³The one who makes a breach goes up
        before them;
    they make a breach and pass
        through the gate;
Their king shall go through before
        them,
    the LORD at their head.

3:1 And I said:
Hear, you leaders of Jacob,
    rulers of the house of Israel!
Is it not your duty to know what is
        right,
    ²you who hate what is good, and
        love evil?
You who tear their skin from them,
    and their flesh from their bones;
³Who eat the flesh of my people,
    flay their skin from them,
    and break their bones;
Who chop them in pieces like flesh in
        a kettle,
    like meat in a pot.
⁴When they cry to the LORD,
    he will not answer them;
He will hide his face from them at that
        time,
    because of the evil they have done.

⁵Thus says the LORD regarding the
        prophets:
    O you who lead my people astray,
When your teeth have something to
        bite
    you announce peace,
But proclaim war against the one
    who fails to put something in your
        mouth.
⁶Therefore you shall have night, not
        vision,
    darkness, not divination;
The sun shall go down upon the
        prophets,
    and the day shall be dark for them.
⁷Then the seers shall be put to shame,
    and the diviners confounded;
They shall all cover their lips,
    because there is no answer from God.
⁸But as for me, I am filled with power,
    with the spirit of the LORD,
    with justice and with might;
To declare to Jacob his crimes
    and to Israel his sins.

⁹Hear this, you leaders of the house of
        Jacob,

you rulers of the house of Israel!
You who abhor justice,
    and pervert all that is right;
[10]Who build up Zion with bloodshed,
    and Jerusalem with wickedness!
[11]Its leaders render judgment for a bribe,
    the priests teach for pay,
    the prophets divine for money,

While they rely on the LORD, saying,
    "Is not the LORD in the midst of us?
    No evil can come upon us!"
[12]Therefore, because of you,
    Zion shall be plowed like a field,
    and Jerusalem reduced to rubble,
And the mount of the temple
    to a forest ridge.

☐ REVELATION 11

The Two Witnesses. 11:1 Then I was given a measuring rod like a staff and I was told, "Come and measure the temple of God and the altar, and count those who are worshiping in it. [2]But exclude the outer court of the temple; do not measure it, for it has been handed over to the Gentiles, who will trample the holy city for forty-two months. [3]I will commission my two witnesses to prophesy for those twelve hundred and sixty days, wearing sackcloth." [4]These are the two olive trees and the two lampstands that stand before the Lord of the earth. [5]If anyone wants to harm them, fire comes out of their mouths and devours their enemies. In this way, anyone wanting to harm them is sure to be slain. [6]They have the power to close up the sky so that no rain can fall during the time of their prophesying. They also have power to turn water into blood and to afflict the earth with any plague as often as they wish.

[7]When they have finished their testimony, the beast that comes up from the abyss will wage war against them and conquer them and kill them. [8]Their corpses will lie in the main street of the great city, which has the symbolic names "Sodom" and "Egypt," where indeed their Lord was crucified. [9]Those from every people, tribe, tongue, and nation will gaze on their corpses for three and a half days, and they will not allow their corpses to be buried. [10]The inhabitants of the earth will gloat over them and be glad and exchange gifts because these two prophets tormented the inhabitants of the earth. [11]But after the three and a half days, a breath of life from God entered them. When they stood on their feet, great fear fell on those who saw them. [12]Then they heard a loud voice from heaven say to them, "Come up here." So they went up to heaven in a cloud as their enemies looked on. [13]At that moment there was a great earthquake, and a tenth of the city fell in ruins. Seven thousand people were killed during the earthquake; the rest were terrified and gave glory to the God of heaven.

[14]The second woe has passed, but the third is coming soon.

The Seventh Trumpet. [15]Then the seventh angel blew his trumpet. There were loud voices in heaven, saying, "The kingdom of the world now belongs to our Lord and to his Anointed, and he will reign forever and ever." [16]The twenty-four elders who sat on their thrones before God prostrated themselves and worshiped God [17]and said:

"We give thanks to you, Lord God almighty,
    who are and who were.
For you have assumed your great power
    and have established your reign.
[18]The nations raged,
    but your wrath has come,
    and the time for the dead to be judged,
and to recompense your servants,
    the prophets,

and the holy ones and those who
fear your name,
the small and the great alike,
and to destroy those who destroy the
earth."

¹⁹Then God's temple in heaven was opened, and the ark of his covenant could be seen in the temple. There were flashes of lightning, rumblings, and peals of thunder, an earthquake, and a violent hailstorm.

December 21

St. Peter Canisius

Let the world indulge its madness, for it cannot endure and passes like a shadow. It is growing old and is, I think, in its last decrepit stage. But we, buried deeply in the wounds of Christ, why should we be dismayed?

— ST. PETER CANISIUS

☐ MICAH 4-7

4:1 In days to come
the mount of the LORD's house
Shall be established as the highest
mountain;
it shall be raised above the hills,
And peoples shall stream to it:
²Many nations shall come, and say,
"Come, let us climb the LORD's
mountain,
to the house of the God of Jacob,
That he may instruct us in his ways,
that we may walk in his paths."
For from Zion shall go forth
instruction,
and the word of the LORD from
Jerusalem.
³He shall judge between many peoples
and set terms for strong and distant
nations;
They shall beat their swords into
plowshares,
and their spears into pruning hooks;
One nation shall not raise the sword
against another,
nor shall they train for war again.
⁴They shall all sit under their own
vines,

under their own fig trees,
undisturbed;
for the LORD of hosts has spoken.
⁵Though all the peoples walk,
each in the name of its god,
We will walk in the name of the LORD,
our God, forever and ever.

⁶On that day—oracle of the LORD—
I will gather the lame,
And I will assemble the outcasts,
and those whom I have afflicted.
⁷I will make of the lame a remnant,
and of the weak a strong nation;
The LORD shall be king over them on
Mount Zion,
from now on and forever.

⁸And you, O tower of the flock,
hill of daughter Zion!
To you it shall come:
the former dominion shall be
restored,
the reign of daughter Jerusalem.

⁹Now why do you cry out so?
Are you without a king?
Or has your adviser perished,

That you are seized with pains
 like a woman in labor?
¹⁰Writhe, go into labor,
 O daughter Zion,
 like a woman giving birth;
For now you shall leave the city
 and camp in the fields;
To Babylon you shall go,
 there you shall be rescued.
There the LORD shall redeem you
 from the hand of your enemies.

¹¹And now many nations are gathered
 against you!
 They say, "Let her be profaned,
 let our eyes see Zion's downfall!"
¹²But they do not know the thoughts
 of the LORD,
 nor understand his plan:
He has gathered them
 like sheaves to the threshing floor.
¹³Arise and thresh, O daughter Zion;
 your horn I will make iron
And your hoofs I will make bronze,
 that you may crush many peoples;
You shall devote their spoils to the
 LORD,
 their riches to the Lord of the whole
 earth.

¹⁴Now grieve, O grieving daughter!
 "They have laid siege against us!"
With the rod they strike on the cheek
 the ruler of Israel.

5:1 But you, Bethlehem-Ephrathah
 least among the clans of Judah,
From you shall come forth for me
 one who is to be ruler in Israel;
Whose origin is from of old,
 from ancient times.
²Therefore the Lord will give them up,
 until the time
 when she who is to give birth has
 borne,
Then the rest of his kindred shall return
 to the children of Israel.
³He shall take his place as shepherd

by the strength of the LORD,
 by the majestic name of the LORD,
 his God;
And they shall dwell securely, for now
 his greatness
 shall reach to the ends of the earth:
⁴he shall be peace.
If Assyria invades our country
 and treads upon our land,
We shall raise against it seven
 shepherds,
 eight of royal standing;
⁵They shall tend the land of Assyria
 with the sword,
 and the land of Nimrod with the
 drawn sword;
They will deliver us from Assyria,
 when it invades our land,
 when it treads upon our borders.

⁶The remnant of Jacob shall be
 in the midst of many peoples,
Like dew coming from the LORD,
 like showers on the grass,
Which wait for no one,
 delay for no human being.
⁷And the remnant of Jacob shall be
 among the nations,
 in the midst of many peoples,
Like a lion among beasts of the forest,
 like a young lion among flocks of
 sheep;
When it passes through it tramples;
 it tears and no one can rescue.
⁸Your hand shall be lifted above your
 foes,
 and all your enemies shall be cut
 down.

⁹On that day—oracle of the
 LORD—
I will destroy the horses from your midst
 and ruin your chariots;
¹⁰I will destroy the cities of your land
 and tear down all your fortresses.
¹¹I will destroy the sorcery you practice,
 and there shall no longer be
 soothsayers among you.

¹²I will destroy your carved figures
    and the sacred stones from your
        midst;
And you shall no longer worship
    the works of your hands.
¹³I will tear out the asherahs from your
        midst,
    and destroy your cities.
¹⁴I will wreak vengeance in anger and
        wrath
    upon the nations that have not
        listened.

6:1 Hear, then, what the LORD says:
Arise, plead your case before the
        mountains,
    and let the hills hear your voice!
²Hear, O mountains, the LORD's case,
    pay attention, O foundations of the
        earth!
For the LORD has a case against his
        people;
    he enters into trial with Israel.
³My people, what have I done to you?
    how have I wearied you? Answer me!
⁴I brought you up from the land of
        Egypt,
    from the place of slavery I ransomed
        you;
And I sent before you Moses,
    Aaron, and Miriam.
⁵My people, remember what Moab's
        King Balak planned,
    and how Balaam, the son of Beor,
        answered him.
Recall the passage from Shittim to
        Gilgal,
    that you may know the just deeds of
        the LORD.
⁶With what shall I come before the
        LORD,
    and bow before God most high?
Shall I come before him with burnt
        offerings,
    with calves a year old?
⁷Will the LORD be pleased with
    thousands of rams,

with myriad streams of oil?
Shall I give my firstborn for my crime,
    the fruit of my body for the sin of
        my soul?
⁸You have been told, O mortal, what
        is good,
    and what the LORD requires of you:
Only to do justice and to love
        goodness,
    and to walk humbly with your God.
⁹The LORD cries aloud to the city
    (It is prudent to fear your name!):
    Hear, O tribe and city assembly,
¹⁰Am I to bear criminal hoarding
    and the accursed short ephah?
¹¹Shall I acquit crooked scales,
    bags of false weights?
¹²You whose wealthy are full of
        violence,
    whose inhabitants speak falsehood
    with deceitful tongues in their
        mouths!
¹³I have begun to strike you
    with devastation because of your sins.
¹⁴You shall eat, without being satisfied,
    food that will leave you empty;
What you acquire, you cannot save;
    what you do save, I will deliver up
        to the sword.
¹⁵You shall sow, yet not reap,
    tread out the olive, yet pour no oil,
    crush the grapes, yet drink no wine.
¹⁶You have kept the decrees of Omri,
    and all the works of the house of
        Ahab,
    and you have walked in their
        counsels;
Therefore I will deliver you up to ruin,
    and your citizens to derision;
    and you shall bear the reproach of
        the nations.

7:1 Woe is me! I am like the one who
        gathers summer fruit,
    when the vines have been gleaned;
There is no cluster to eat,
    no early fig that I crave.

²The faithful have vanished from the
   earth,
   no mortal is just!
They all lie in wait to shed blood,
   each one ensnares the other.
³Their hands succeed at evil;
   the prince makes demands,
The judge is bought for a price,
   the powerful speak as they please.
⁴The best of them is like a brier,
   the most honest like a thorn hedge.
The day announced by your sentinels!
   Your punishment has come;
   now is the time of your confusion.
⁵Put no faith in a friend,
   do not trust a companion;
With her who lies in your embrace
   watch what you say.
⁶For the son belittles his father,
   the daughter rises up against her
      mother,
The daughter-in-law against her
      mother-in-law,
   and your enemies are members of
      your household.

⁷But as for me, I will look to the LORD,
   I will wait for God my savior;
   my God will hear me!
⁸Do not rejoice over me, my enemy!
   though I have fallen, I will arise;
   though I sit in darkness, the LORD is
      my light.
⁹I will endure the wrath of the LORD
   because I have sinned against him,
Until he pleads my case,
   and establishes my right.
He will bring me forth to the light;
   I will see his righteousness.
¹⁰When my enemy sees this,
   shame shall cover her:
She who said to me,
   "Where is the LORD, your God?"
My eyes shall see her downfall;
   now she will be trampled underfoot,
   like mud in the streets.
¹¹It is the day for building your walls;

on that day your boundaries shall be
   enlarged.
¹²It is the day when those from Assyria
   to Egypt
   shall come to you,
And from Tyre even to the River,
   from sea to sea, and from mountain
      to mountain;
¹³And the earth shall be a waste
   because of its inhabitants,
   as a result of their deeds.

¹⁴Shepherd your people with your staff,
   the flock of your heritage,
That lives apart in a woodland,
   in the midst of an orchard.
Let them feed in Bashan and Gilead,
   as in the days of old;
¹⁵As in the days when you came from
      the land of Egypt,
   show us wonderful signs.
¹⁶The nations will see and will be put
      to shame,
   in spite of all their strength;
They will put their hands over their
      mouths;
   their ears will become deaf.
¹⁷They will lick the dust like a snake,
   like crawling things on the ground;
They will come quaking from their
      strongholds;
   they will tremble in fear of you, the
      LORD, our God.
¹⁸Who is a God like you, who removes
      guilt
   and pardons sin for the remnant of
      his inheritance;
Who does not persist in anger forever,
   but instead delights in mercy,
¹⁹And will again have compassion on us,
   treading underfoot our iniquities?
You will cast into the depths of the sea
   all our sins;
²⁰You will show faithfulness to Jacob,
   and loyalty to Abraham,
As you have sworn to our ancestors
   from days of old.

☐ REVELATION 12

The Woman and the Dragon. 12:1 A great sign appeared in the sky, a woman clothed with the sun, with the moon under her feet, and on her head a crown of twelve stars. ²She was with child and wailed aloud in pain as she labored to give birth. ³Then another sign appeared in the sky; it was a huge red dragon, with seven heads and ten horns, and on its heads were seven diadems. ⁴Its tail swept away a third of the stars in the sky and hurled them down to the earth. Then the dragon stood before the woman about to give birth, to devour her child when she gave birth. ⁵She gave birth to a son, a male child, destined to rule all the nations with an iron rod. Her child was caught up to God and his throne. ⁶The woman herself fled into the desert where she had a place prepared by God, that there she might be taken care of for twelve hundred and sixty days.

⁷Then war broke out in heaven; Michael and his angels battled against the dragon. The dragon and its angels fought back, ⁸but they did not prevail and there was no longer any place for them in heaven. ⁹The huge dragon, the ancient serpent, who is called the Devil and Satan, who deceived the whole world, was thrown down to earth, and its angels were thrown down with it. ¹⁰Then I heard a loud voice in heaven say:

"Now have salvation and power come,
    and the kingdom of our God
    and the authority of his Anointed.

For the accuser of our brothers is cast
    out,
    who accuses them before our God
        day and night.
¹¹They conquered him by the blood of
        the Lamb
    and by the word of their testimony;
    love for life did not deter them from
        death.
¹²Therefore, rejoice, you heavens,
    and you who dwell in them.
But woe to you, earth and sea,
    for the Devil has come down to you
        in great fury,
    for he knows he has but a short time."

¹³When the dragon saw that it had been thrown down to the earth, it pursued the woman who had given birth to the male child. ¹⁴But the woman was given the two wings of the great eagle, so that she could fly to her place in the desert, where, far from the serpent, she was taken care of for a year, two years, and a half-year. ¹⁵The serpent, however, spewed a torrent of water out of his mouth after the woman to sweep her away with the current. ¹⁶But the earth helped the woman and opened its mouth and swallowed the flood that the dragon spewed out of its mouth. ¹⁷Then the dragon became angry with the woman and went off to wage war against the rest of her offspring, those who keep God's commandments and bear witness to Jesus. ¹⁸It took its position on the sand of the sea.

December 22

The instance cannot be found in the history of mankind in which an anti-Christian power could long abstain from persecution.

— BLESSED JOHN HENRY NEWMAN

☐ NAHUM

1:1 Oracle concerning Nineveh. The book of the vision of Nahum of Elkosh.

God's Terrifying Appearance. [2]A
jealous and avenging God is the LORD,
an avenger is the LORD, full of wrath;
The LORD takes vengeance on his adversaries,
and rages against his enemies;
[3]The LORD is slow to anger, yet great in power;
the LORD will not leave the guilty unpunished.
In stormwind and tempest he comes,
and clouds are the dust at his feet;
[4]He roars at the sea and leaves it dry,
and all the rivers he dries up.
Laid low are Bashan and Carmel,
and the bloom of Lebanon withers;
[5]The mountains quake before him,
and the hills dissolve;
The earth is laid waste before him,
the world and all who dwell in it.
[6]Before his wrath, who can stand firm,
and who can face his blazing anger?
His fury is poured out like fire,
and boulders break apart before him.
[7]The LORD is good to those who wait for him,
a refuge on the day of distress,
Taking care of those who look to him for protection,
[8]when the flood rages;
He makes an end of his opponents,
and pursues his enemies into darkness.

Nineveh's Judgment and Judah's Restoration. [9]What do you plot against the LORD,
the one about to bring total destruction?
No opponent rises a second time!
[10]Like a thorny thicket, they are tangled,
and like drunkards, they are drunk;
like dry stubble, they are utterly consumed.
[11]From you has come
one plotting evil against the LORD,
one giving sinister counsel.
[12]Thus says the LORD:
though fully intact and so numerous,
they shall be mown down and disappear.
Though I have humbled you,
I will humble you no more.
[13]Now I will break his yoke off of you,
and tear off your bonds.
[14]The LORD has commanded regarding you:
no descendant will again bear your name;
From the house of your gods I will abolish
the carved and the molten image;
I will make your grave a dung heap.

2:1 At this moment on the mountains
the footsteps of one bearing good news,
of one announcing peace!
Celebrate your feasts, Judah,
fulfill your vows!

For never again will destroyers invade you;
  they are completely cut off.

The Attack on Nineveh. ²One who
    scatters has come up against you;
    guard the rampart,
Watch the road, brace yourselves,
  marshal all your strength!
³The LORD will restore the vine of Jacob,
  the honor of Israel,
Because ravagers have ravaged them
  and ruined their branches.
⁴The shields of his warriors are
    crimsoned,
  the soldiers clad in scarlet;
Like fire are the trappings of the chariots
  on the day he prepares for war;
  the cavalry is agitated!
⁵The chariots dash madly through the
    streets
  and wheel in the squares,
Looking like torches,
  bolting like lightning.
⁶His picked troops are called,
  ranks break at their charge;
To the wall they rush,
  their screen is set up.
⁷The river gates are opened,
  the palace is washed away.
⁸The mistress is led forth captive,
  and her maidservants led away,
Moaning like doves,
  beating their breasts.
⁹Nineveh is like a pool
  whose waters escape;
"Stop! Stop!"
  but none turns back.
¹⁰"Plunder the silver, plunder the gold!"
  There is no end to the treasure,
  to wealth in every precious thing!

¹¹Emptiness, desolation, waste;
  melting hearts and trembling knees,
Churning in every stomach,
  every face turning pale!
¹²Where is the lionesses' den,
  the young lions' cave,

Where the lion went in and out,
  and the cub, with no one to disturb
    them?
¹³The lion tore apart enough for his
    cubs,
  and strangled for his lionesses;
He filled his lairs with prey,
  and his dens with torn flesh.
¹⁴I now come against you—
  oracle of the LORD of hosts—
I will consume your chariots in smoke,
  and the sword will devour your
    young lions;
Your preying on the land I will bring to
    an end,
  the cry of your lionesses will be
    heard no more.

3:1 Ah! The bloody city,
  all lies,
Full of plunder,
  whose looting never stops!
²The crack of the whip,
  the rumbling of wheels;
Horses galloping,
  chariots bounding,
³Cavalry charging,
  the flash of the sword,
  the gleam of the spear;
A multitude of slain,
  a mass of corpses,
Endless bodies
  to stumble upon!
⁴For the many debaucheries of the
    prostitute,
  a charming mistress of witchcraft,
Who enslaved nations with her
    prostitution,
  and peoples by her witchcraft:
⁵I now come against you—
  oracle of the LORD of hosts—
  and I will lift your skirt above your
    face;
I will show your nakedness to the
    nations,
  to the kingdoms your shame!

⁶I will cast filth upon you,
  disgrace you and make you a
    spectacle;
⁷Until everyone who sees you
  runs from you saying,
"Nineveh is destroyed;
  who can pity her?
Where can I find
  any to console you?"

Nineveh's Inescapable Fate. ⁸Are you
    better than No-amon
  that was set among the Nile's canals,
Surrounded by waters,
  with the river for her rampart
  and water for her wall?
⁹Ethiopia was her strength,
  and Egypt without end;
Put and the Libyans
  were her allies.
¹⁰Yet even she became an exile,
  and went into captivity;
Even her little ones were dashed to pieces
  at the corner of every street;
For her nobles they cast lots,
  and all her great ones were put into
    chains.
¹¹You, too, will drink of this;
  you will be overcome;
You, too, will seek
  a refuge from the foe.
¹²But all your fortresses are fig trees,
  bearing early figs;
When shaken, they fall
  into the devourer's mouth.
¹³Indeed your troops
  are women in your midst;
To your foes are open wide
  the gates of your land,

fire has consumed their bars.
¹⁴Draw water for the siege,
  strengthen your fortresses;
Go down into the mud
  and tread the clay,
  take hold of the brick mold!
¹⁵There the fire will consume you,
  the sword will cut you down;
  it will consume you like the
    grasshoppers.

Multiply like the grasshoppers,
  multiply like the locusts!
¹⁶You have made your traders more
    numerous
  than the stars of the heavens;
  like grasshoppers that shed their
    skins and fly away.
¹⁷Your sentries are like locusts,
  and your scribes like locust swarms
Gathered on the rubble fences
  on a cold day!
Yet when the sun rises, they vanish,
  and no one knows where they have
    gone.

¹⁸Your shepherds slumber,
  O king of Assyria,
  your nobles have gone to rest;
Your people are scattered upon the
    mountains,
  with none to gather them.
¹⁹There is no healing for your hurt,
  your wound is fatal.
All who hear this news of you
  clap their hands over you;
For who has not suffered
  under your endless malice?

☐ REVELATION 13

The First Beast. 13:1 Then I saw a beast come out of the sea with ten horns and seven heads; on its horns were ten diadems, and on its heads blasphemous name[s]. ²The beast I saw was like a leopard, but it had feet like a bear's, and its mouth was like the mouth of a lion. To it the dragon gave its own power and throne, along with great authority. ³I saw that one of its heads seemed to have been mortally wounded, but this mortal wound was healed. Fascinated, the whole world followed after the beast. [4]They worshiped the dragon because it gave its authority to the beast; they also worshiped the beast and said, "Who can compare with the beast or who can fight against it?"

[5]The beast was given a mouth uttering proud boasts and blasphemies, and it was given authority to act for forty-two months. [6]It opened its mouth to utter blasphemies against God, blaspheming his name and his dwelling and those who dwell in heaven. [7]It was also allowed to wage war against the holy ones and conquer them, and it was granted authority over every tribe, people, tongue, and nation. [8]All the inhabitants of the earth will worship it, all whose names were not written from the foundation of the world in the book of life, which belongs to the Lamb who was slain.

[9]Whoever has ears ought to hear these words.

[10]Anyone destined for captivity goes into captivity.

Anyone destined to be slain by the sword shall be slain by the sword.

Such is the faithful endurance of the holy ones.

The Second Beast. [11]Then I saw another beast come up out of the earth; it had two horns like a lamb's but spoke like a dragon. [12]It wielded all the authority of the first beast in its sight and made the earth and its inhabitants worship the first beast, whose mortal wound had been healed. [13]It performed great signs, even making fire come down from heaven to earth in the sight of everyone. [14]It deceived the inhabitants of the earth with the signs it was allowed to perform in the sight of the first beast, telling them to make an image for the beast who had been wounded by the sword and revived. [15]It was then permitted to breathe life into the beast's image, so that the beast's image could speak and [could] have anyone who did not worship it put to death. [16]It forced all the people, small and great, rich and poor, free and slave, to be given a stamped image on their right hands or their foreheads, [17]so that no one could buy or sell except one who had the stamped image of the beast's name or the number that stood for its name.

[18]Wisdom is needed here; one who understands can calculate the number of the beast, for it is a number that stands for a person. His number is six hundred and sixty-six.

December 23

St. John of Kanty

All the wealth of the world cannot be compared with the happiness of living together happily united.

— ST. MARGUERITE D'YOUVILLE

☐ HABAKKUK

1:1 The oracle which Habakkuk the prophet received in a vision.

Habakkuk's First Complaint. [2]How long, O LORD, must I cry for help
and you do not listen?
Or cry out to you, "Violence!"
and you do not intervene?
[3]Why do you let me see iniquity?
why do you simply gaze at evil?
Destruction and violence are before me;
there is strife and discord.
[4]This is why the law is numb
and justice never comes,
For the wicked surround the just;
this is why justice comes forth
perverted.

God's Response. [5]Look over the nations and see!
Be utterly amazed!
For a work is being done in your days
that you would not believe, were it
told.
[6]For now I am raising up the
Chaldeans,
that bitter and impulsive people,
Who march the breadth of the land
to take dwellings not their own.
[7]They are terrifying and dreadful;
their right and their exalted position
are of their own making.
[8]Swifter than leopards are their horses,
and faster than desert wolves.
Their horses spring forward;
they come from far away;
they fly like an eagle hastening to
devour.
[9]All of them come for violence,
their combined onslaught, a
stormwind
to gather up captives like sand.
[10]They scoff at kings,
ridicule princes;
They laugh at any fortress,
heap up an earthen ramp, and
conquer it.
[11]Then they sweep through like the
wind and vanish—
they make their own strength their
god!

Habakkuk's Second Complaint. [12]Are
you not from of old, O LORD,
my holy God, immortal?
LORD, you have appointed them for
judgment,
O Rock, you have set them in place
to punish!
[13]Your eyes are too pure to look upon
wickedness,
and the sight of evil you cannot
endure.
Why, then, do you gaze on the faithless
in silence
while the wicked devour those more
just than themselves?
[14]You have made mortals like the fish
in the sea,
like creeping things without a
leader.
[15]He brings them all up with a hook,
and hauls them away with his net;
He gathers them in his fishing net,
and then rejoices and exults.
[16]Therefore he makes sacrifices to his
net,

and burns incense to his fishing net;
For thanks to them his portion is rich,
and his meal lavish.
¹⁷Shall they, then, keep on drawing his
sword
to slaughter nations without mercy?

2:1 I will stand at my guard post,
and station myself upon the rampart;
I will keep watch to see what he will
say to me,
and what answer he will give to my
complaint.

God's Response. ²Then the LORD
answered me and said:
Write down the vision;
Make it plain upon tablets,
so that the one who reads it may run.
³For the vision is a witness for the
appointed time,
a testimony to the end; it will not
disappoint.
If it delays, wait for it,
it will surely come, it will not be late.
⁴See, the rash have no integrity;
but the just one who is righteous
because of faith shall live.

Sayings Against Tyrants. ⁵Indeed
wealth is treacherous;
a proud man does not succeed.
He who opens wide his throat like Sheol,
and is insatiable as death,
Who gathers to himself all the nations,
and collects for himself all the
peoples—
⁶Shall not all these take up a taunt
against him,
and make a riddle about him, saying:

Ah! you who store up what is not yours
—how long can it last!—
you who load yourself down with
collateral.
⁷Will your debtors not rise suddenly?
Will they not awake, those who
make you tremble?

You will become their spoil!
⁸Because you plundered many nations,
the remaining peoples shall plunder
you;
Because of the shedding of human
blood,
and violence done to the land,
to the city and to all who live in it.

⁹Ah! you who pursue evil gain for your
household,
setting your nest on high
to escape the reach of misfortune!
¹⁰You have devised shame for your
household,
cutting off many peoples, forfeiting
your own life;
¹¹For the stone in the wall shall cry out,
and the beam in the frame shall
answer it!

¹²Ah! you who build a city by bloodshed,
and who establish a town with
injustice!
¹³Is this not from the LORD of hosts:
peoples toil for what the flames
consume,
and nations grow weary for nothing!
¹⁴But the earth shall be filled
with the knowledge of the LORD's
glory,
just as the water covers the sea.

¹⁵Ah! you who give your neighbors
the cup of your wrath to drink, and
make them drunk,
until their nakedness is seen!
¹⁶You are filled with shame instead of
glory;
drink, you too, and stagger!
The cup from the LORD's right hand
shall come around to you,
and utter shame shall cover your
glory.
¹⁷For the violence done to Lebanon
shall cover you,
and the destruction of the animals
shall terrify you;

Because of the shedding of human
blood,
and violence done to the land,
to the city and to all who live in it.

¹⁸Of what use is the carved image,
that its maker should carve it?
Or the molten image, the lying oracle,
that its very maker should trust in it,
and make mute idols?
¹⁹Ah! you who say to wood, "Awake!"
to silent stone, "Arise!"
Can any such thing give oracles?
It is only overlaid with gold and silver,
there is no breath in it at all.
²⁰But the LORD is in his holy temple;
silence before him, all the earth!

Hymn About God's Reign. 3:1 Prayer
of Habakkuk, the prophet. According to
Shigyonot.

²O LORD, I have heard your renown,
and am in awe, O LORD, of your
work.
In the course of years revive it,
in the course of years make yourself
known;
in your wrath remember compassion!

³God came from Teman,
the Holy One from Mount Paran.
His glory covered the heavens,
and his praise filled the earth;
⁴his splendor spread like the light.
He raised his horns high,
he rejoiced on the day of his
strength.
⁵Before him went pestilence,
and plague followed in his steps.
⁶He stood and shook the earth;
he looked and made the nations
tremble.
Ancient mountains were shattered,
the age-old hills bowed low,
age-old orbits collapsed.
⁷The tents of Cushan trembled,

the pavilions of the land of Midian.
⁸Was your anger against the rivers,
O LORD?
your wrath against the rivers,
your rage against the sea,
That you mounted your steeds,
your victorious chariot?
⁹You readied your bow,
you filled your bowstring with
arrows.
You split the earth with rivers;
¹⁰at the sight of you the mountains
writhed.
The clouds poured down water;
the deep roared loudly.
The sun forgot to rise,
¹¹the moon left its lofty station,
At the light of your flying arrows,
at the gleam of your flashing spear.
¹²In wrath you marched on the earth,
in fury you trampled the nations.
¹³You came forth to save your people,
to save your anointed one.
You crushed the back of the wicked,
you laid him bare, bottom to neck.

¹⁴You pierced his head with your shafts;
his princes you scattered with your
stormwind,
as food for the poor in unknown
places.
¹⁵You trampled the sea with your horses
amid the churning of the deep
waters.

¹⁶I hear, and my body trembles;
at the sound, my lips quiver.
Decay invades my bones,
my legs tremble beneath me.
I await the day of distress
that will come upon the people who
attack us.

¹⁷For though the fig tree does not
blossom,
and no fruit appears on the vine,
Though the yield of the olive fails

and the terraces produce no
    nourishment,
Though the flocks disappear from
    the fold
    and there is no herd in the stalls,
[18]Yet I will rejoice in the LORD
    and exult in my saving God.

☐ REVELATION 14

The Lamb's Companions. 14:1 Then I looked and there was the Lamb standing on Mount Zion, and with him a hundred and forty-four thousand who had his name and his Father's name written on their foreheads. [2]I heard a sound from heaven like the sound of rushing water or a loud peal of thunder. The sound I heard was like that of harpists playing their harps. [3]They were singing [what seemed to be] a new hymn before the throne, before the four living creatures and the elders. No one could learn this hymn except the hundred and forty-four thousand who had been ransomed from the earth. [4]These are they who were not defiled with women; they are virgins and these are the ones who follow the Lamb wherever he goes. They have been ransomed as the firstfruits of the human race for God and the Lamb. [5]On their lips no deceit has been found; they are unblemished.

The Three Angels. [6]Then I saw another angel flying high overhead, with everlasting good news to announce to those who dwell on earth, to every nation, tribe, tongue, and people. [7]He said in a loud voice, "Fear God and give him glory, for his time has come to sit in judgment. Worship him who made heaven and earth and sea and springs of water." [8]A second angel followed, saying:

"Fallen, fallen is Babylon the great,
    that made all the nations drink
    the wine of her licentious passion."

[9]A third angel followed them and said in a loud voice, "Anyone who worships the beast or its image, or accepts its mark on forehead or hand, [10]will also drink the wine of God's fury, poured full strength into the cup of his wrath, and will be tormented in burning sulfur before the holy angels and before the Lamb. [11]The smoke of the fire that torments them will rise forever and ever, and there will be no relief day or night for those who worship the beast or its image or accept the mark of its name." [12]Here is what sustains the holy ones who keep God's commandments and their faith in Jesus.

[13]I heard a voice from heaven say, "Write this: Blessed are the dead who die in the Lord from now on." "Yes," said the Spirit, "let them find rest from their labors, for their works accompany them."

The Harvest of the Earth. [14]Then I looked and there was a white cloud, and sitting on the cloud one who looked like a son of man, with a gold crown on his head and a sharp sickle in his hand. [15]Another angel came out of the temple, crying out in a loud voice to the one sitting on the cloud, "Use your sickle and reap the harvest, for the time to reap has come, because the earth's harvest is fully ripe." [16]So the one who was sitting on the cloud swung his sickle over the earth, and the earth was harvested.

[17]Then another angel came out of the temple in heaven who also had a sharp sickle. [18]Then another angel [came] from the altar, [who] was in charge of the fire, and cried out in a loud voice to the one who had the sharp sickle, "Use your sharp

[19]GOD, my Lord, is my strength;
    he makes my feet swift as those of
    deer
    and enables me to tread upon the
    heights.

For the leader; with stringed instruments.

sickle and cut the clusters from the earth's vines, for its grapes are ripe." [19]So the angel swung his sickle over the earth and cut the earth's vintage. He threw it into the great wine press of God's fury. [20]The wine press was trodden outside the city and blood poured out of the wine press to the height of a horse's bridle for two hundred miles.

December 24

Christmas Eve

In this night of reconciliation, let none be angry or gloomy. In this night that stills everything, let nothing threaten or disturb. This night belongs to the sweet One; let nothing bitter or harsh be in it. In this night that belongs to the meek One, let there be nothing high or haughty. In this day of pardoning, let us not exact punishments for trespasses.

— St. Ephraem the Syrian

☐ ZEPHANIAH

1:1 The word of the LORD which came to Zephaniah, the son of Cushi, the son of Gedaliah, the son of Amariah, the son of Hezekiah, in the days of Josiah, the son of Amon, king of Judah.

The Day of the Lord: Judgment on Judah. [2]I will completely sweep away all things
from the face of the land—oracle of the LORD.
[3]I will sweep away human being and beast alike,
I will sweep away the birds of the sky, and the fish of the sea.
I will make the wicked stumble;
I will eliminate the people
from the face of the land—oracle of the LORD.
[4]I will stretch out my hand against Judah,
and against all the inhabitants of Jerusalem;
I will eliminate from this place
the last vestige of Baal,
the name of the idolatrous priests.

[5]And those who bow down on the roofs to the host of heaven,
And those who bow down to the LORD but swear by Milcom;
[6]And those who have turned away from the LORD,
and those who have not sought the LORD,
who have not inquired of him.

[7]Silence in the presence of the Lord GOD!
for near is the day of the LORD,
Yes, the LORD has prepared a sacrifice,
he has consecrated his guests.
[8]On the day of the LORD's sacrifice
I will punish the officials and the king's sons,
and all who dress in foreign apparel.
[9]I will punish, on that day,
all who leap over the threshold,
Who fill the house of their master
with violence and deceit.
[10]On that day—oracle of the LORD—
A cry will be heard from the Fish Gate,
a wail from the Second Quarter,

loud crashing from the hills.
[11]Wail, O inhabitants of Maktesh!
  for all the merchants are destroyed,
  all who weigh out silver, done away
    with.

[12]At that time,
I will search Jerusalem with lamps,
  I will punish the people
  who settle like dregs in wine,
Who say in their hearts,
  "The Lord will not do good,
  nor will he do harm."
[13]Their wealth shall be given to plunder
  and their houses to devastation;
They will build houses,
  but not dwell in them;
They will plant vineyards,
  but not drink their wine.
[14]Near is the great day of the LORD,
  near and very swiftly coming.
The sound of the day of the LORD!
    Piercing—
  there a warrior shrieks!
[15]A day of wrath is that day,
  a day of distress and anguish,
  a day of ruin and desolation,
A day of darkness and gloom,
  a day of thick black clouds,
[16]A day of trumpet blasts and battle cries
  against fortified cities,
  against lofty battlements.
[17]I will hem the people in
  till they walk like the blind,
  because they have sinned against the
    LORD;
And their blood shall be poured out
    like dust,
  and their bowels like dung.
[18]Neither their silver nor their gold
  will be able to save them.
On the day of the LORD's wrath,
  in the fire of his passion,
  all the earth will be consumed.
For he will make an end, yes, a sudden
    end,
  of all who live on the earth.

[2:1] Gather, gather yourselves together,
  O nation without shame!
[2]Before you are driven away,
  like chaff that disappears;
Before there comes upon you
  the blazing anger of the LORD;
Before there comes upon you
  the day of the LORD's anger.
[3]Seek the LORD,
  all you humble of the land,
  who have observed his law;
Seek justice,
  seek humility;
Perhaps you will be sheltered
  on the day of the LORD's anger.

Judgment on the Nations. [4]For Gaza
    shall be forsaken,
  and Ashkelon shall be a waste,
Ashdod they shall drive out at midday,
  and Ekron shall be uprooted.
[5]Ah! You who dwell by the seacoast,
  the nation of Cherethites,
  the word of the LORD is against you!
O Canaan, land of the Philistines,
  I will leave you to perish without an
    inhabitant!
[6]You shall become fields for shepherds,
  and folds for flocks.
[7]The seacoast shall belong
  to the remnant of the house of Judah;
  by the sea they shall pasture.
In the houses of Ashkelon
  they shall lie down in the evening.
For the LORD their God will take care
    of them,
  and bring about their restoration.

[8]I have heard the taunts uttered by
    Moab,
  and the insults of the Ammonites,
When they taunted my people
  and made boasts against their
    territory.
[9]Therefore, as I live—
  oracle of the LORD of hosts—
  the God of Israel,
Moab shall become like Sodom,

the Ammonites like Gomorrah:
A field of weeds,
   a salt pit,
   a waste forever.
The remnant of my people shall
      plunder them,
   the survivors of my nation
         dispossess them.
¹⁰This will be the recompense for their
      pride,
   because they taunted and boasted
      against
   the people of the LORD of hosts.
¹¹The LORD shall inspire them with
      terror
   when he makes all the gods of earth
      waste away;
Then the distant shores of the nations,
   each from its own place,
   shall bow down to him.

¹²You too, O Cushites,
   shall be slain by the sword of the
      LORD.
¹³He will stretch out his hand against
      the north,
   to destroy Assyria;
He will make Nineveh a waste,
   dry as the desert.
¹⁴In her midst flocks shall lie down,
   all the wild life of the hollows;
The screech owl and the desert owl
   shall roost in her columns;
The owl shall hoot from the window,
   the raven croak from the doorway.
¹⁵Is this the exultant city
   that dwelt secure,
That told itself,
   "I and there is no one else"?
How it has become a waste,
   a lair for wild animals!
Those who pass by it
   hiss, and shake their fists!

Jerusalem Reproached. 3:1 Ah!
      Rebellious and polluted,
   the tyrannical city!

²It listens to no voice,
   accepts no correction;
In the LORD it has not trusted,
   nor drawn near to its God.
³Its officials within it
   are roaring lions;
Its judges are desert wolves
   that have no bones to gnaw by
      morning.
⁴Its prophets are reckless,
   treacherous people;
Its priests profane what is holy,
   and do violence to the law.
⁵But the LORD in its midst is just,
   doing no wrong;
Morning after morning rendering
      judgment
   unfailingly, at dawn;
   the wicked, however, know no
      shame.

⁶I have cut down nations,
   their battlements are laid waste;
I have made their streets deserted,
   with no one passing through;
Their cities are devastated,
   with no one dwelling in them.
⁷I said, "Surely now you will fear me,
   you will accept correction;
They cannot fail to see
   all I have brought upon them."
Yet the more eagerly they have done
   all their corrupt deeds.

**The Nations Punished and Jerusalem
   Restored.** ⁸Therefore, wait for
      me—oracle of the LORD—
   until the day when I arise as accuser;
For it is my decision to gather nations,
   to assemble kingdoms,
In order to pour out upon them my
      wrath,
   all my blazing anger;
For in the fire of my passion
   all the earth will be consumed.

⁹For then I will make pure
   the speech of the peoples,

That they all may call upon the name
    of the Lord,
  to serve him with one accord;
[10]From beyond the rivers of Ethiopia
    and as far as the recesses of the North,
    they shall bring me offerings.

  [11]On that day
You will not be ashamed
  of all your deeds,
    when you rebelled against me;
For then I will remove from your midst
    the proud braggarts,
And you shall no longer exalt yourself
    on my holy mountain.
[12]But I will leave as a remnant in your
    midst
  a people humble and lowly,
Who shall take refuge in the name of
    the Lord—
  [13]the remnant of Israel.
They shall do no wrong
  and speak no lies;
Nor shall there be found in their mouths
  a deceitful tongue;
They shall pasture and lie down
  with none to disturb them.
[14]Shout for joy, daughter Zion!
  sing joyfully, Israel!
Be glad and exult with all your heart,
  daughter Jerusalem!
[15]The Lord has removed the judgment
  against you,

he has turned away your enemies;
The King of Israel, the Lord, is in your
  midst,
  you have no further misfortune to
    fear.
  [16]On that day, it shall be said to
    Jerusalem:
Do not fear, Zion,
  do not be discouraged!
[17]The Lord, your God, is in your midst,
  a mighty savior,
Who will rejoice over you with
    gladness,
  and renew you in his love,
Who will sing joyfully because of you,
  [18]as on festival days.

I will remove disaster from among you,
  so that no one may recount your
    disgrace.
[19]At that time I will deal
  with all who oppress you;
I will save the lame,
  and assemble the outcasts;
I will give them praise and renown
  in every land where they were
    shamed.
[20]At that time I will bring you home,
  and at that time I will gather you;
For I will give you renown and praise,
  among all the peoples of the earth,
When I bring about your restoration
  before your very eyes, says the Lord.

☐ REVELATION 15

The Seven Last Plagues. 15:1 Then I saw in heaven another sign, great and awe-inspiring: seven angels with the seven last plagues, for through them God's fury is accomplished.

[2]Then I saw something like a sea of glass mingled with fire. On the sea of glass were standing those who had won the victory over the beast and its image and the number that signified its name. They were hold-ing God's harps, [3]and they sang the song of Moses, the servant of God, and the song of the Lamb:

  "Great and wonderful are your works,
    Lord God almighty.
  Just and true are your ways,
    O king of the nations.
  [4]Who will not fear you, Lord,
    or glorify your name?

For you alone are holy.
All the nations will come
and worship before you,
for your righteous acts have been
revealed."

⁵After this I had another vision. The temple that is the heavenly tent of testimony opened, ⁶and the seven angels with the seven plagues came out of the temple.

They were dressed in clean white linen, with a gold sash around their chests. ⁷One of the four living creatures gave the seven angels seven gold bowls filled with the fury of God, who lives forever and ever. ⁸Then the temple became so filled with the smoke from God's glory and might that no one could enter it until the seven plagues of the seven angels had been accomplished.

December 25

The Nativity of Our Lord

Celebrate the feast of Christmas every day, even every moment in the interior temple of your spirit, remaining like a baby in the bosom of the heavenly Father, where you will be reborn each moment in the Divine Word, Jesus Christ.

— St. Paul of the Cross

☐ HAGGAI

Prophetic Call to Work on the Temple. 1:1 On the first day of the sixth month in the second year of Darius the king, the word of the Lord came through Haggai the prophet to the governor of Judah, Zerubbabel, son of Shealtiel, and to the high priest Joshua, son of Jehozadak: ²Thus says the Lord of hosts: This people has said: "Now is not the time to rebuild the house of the Lord."

³Then the word of the Lord came through Haggai the prophet: ⁴Is it time for you to dwell in your paneled houses while this house lies in ruins?

⁵Now thus says the Lord of hosts:
Reflect on your experience!
⁶You have sown much, but have
brought in little;
you have eaten, but have not been
satisfied;
You have drunk, but have not become
intoxicated;

you have clothed yourselves, but
have not been warmed;
And the hired worker labors for a bag
full of holes.

⁷Thus says the Lord of hosts:

Reflect on your experience!
⁸Go up into the hill country;
bring timber, and build the house
that I may be pleased with it,
and that I may be glorified, says the
Lord.
⁹You expected much, but it came to
little;
and what you brought home, I blew
away.
Why is this?—oracle of the Lord of
hosts—
Because my house is the one which
lies in ruins,
while each of you runs to your own
house.

¹⁰Therefore, the heavens withheld the
dew,
and the earth its yield.
¹¹And I have proclaimed a devastating
heat
upon the land and upon the
mountains,
Upon the grain, the new wine, and the
olive oil,
upon all that the ground brings forth;
Upon human being and beast alike,
and upon all they produce.

Response of Leaders and People.
¹²Then Zerubbabel, son of Shealtiel, and
the high priest Joshua, son of Jehozadak,
and all the remnant of the people obeyed
the LORD their God, and the words of Haggai the prophet, since the LORD their God
had sent him; thus the people feared the
LORD. ¹³Then Haggai, the messenger of the
LORD, proclaimed to the people as the message of the LORD: I am with you!—oracle
of the LORD.

¹⁴And so the LORD stirred up the spirit
of the governor of Judah, Zerubbabel, son
of Shealtiel, and the spirit of the high priest
Joshua, son of Jehozadak, and the spirit of
all the remnant of the people, so that they
came to do the work in the house of the
LORD of hosts, their God, ¹⁵on the twenty-
fourth day of the sixth month in the second year of Darius the king.

Assurance of God's Presence. 2:1 On the
twenty-first day of the seventh month, the
word of the LORD came through Haggai
the prophet: ²Speak to the governor of Judah, Zerubbabel, son of Shealtiel, and to
the high priest Joshua, son of Jehozadak,
and to the remnant of the people:

³Who is left among you
who saw this house in its former
glory?
And how do you see it now?
Does it not seem like nothing in
your eyes?

⁴Now be strong, Zerubbabel—oracle
of the LORD—
be strong, Joshua, son of Jehozadak,
high priest,
Be strong, all you people of the land—
oracle of the LORD—
and work! For I am with you—
oracle of the LORD of hosts.
⁵This is the commitment I made to you
when you came out of Egypt.
My spirit remains in your midst;
do not fear!

⁶For thus says the LORD of hosts:

In just a little while,
I will shake the heavens and the earth,
the sea and the dry land.
⁷I will shake all the nations,
so that the treasures of all the
nations will come in.
And I will fill this house with glory—
says the LORD of hosts.

⁸Mine is the silver and mine the gold—
oracle of the LORD of hosts.

⁹Greater will be the glory of this house
the latter more than the former—
says the LORD of hosts;
And in this place I will give you
peace—
oracle of the LORD of hosts.

**Priestly Ruling with Prophetic In-
terpretation.** ¹⁰On the twenty-fourth day
of the ninth month in the second year of
Darius, the word of the LORD came to
Haggai the prophet: ¹¹Thus says the LORD
of hosts: Ask the priests for a ruling: ¹²If
someone carries sanctified meat in the fold
of a garment and the fold touches bread,
soup, wine, oil, or any other food, do they
become sanctified? "No," the priests answered. ¹³Then Haggai asked: "If a person
defiled from contact with a corpse touches
any of these, do they become defiled?" The
priests answered, "They become defiled."
¹⁴Then Haggai replied:

So is this people, and so is this nation
   in my sight—oracle of the LORD—
And so is all the work of their hands;
   what they offer there is defiled.

¹⁵Now reflect, from this day forward—before you set stone to stone in the temple of the LORD, ¹⁶what was your experience?

When one went to a heap of grain for
   twenty ephahs,
   there were only ten;
When one went to a vat to draw fifty
   ephahs,
   there were only twenty.
¹⁷I struck you, and all the work of your
   hands,
   with searing wind, blight, and hail,
   yet you did not return to me—
   oracle of the LORD.

¹⁸Reflect from this day forward, from the twenty-fourth day of the ninth month. From the day on which the temple of the LORD was founded, reflect!

¹⁹Is there still seed in the storehouse?

Have the vine, the fig, the
   pomegranate,
   and the olive tree still not borne fruit?
From this day, I will bless you.

Future Hope. ²⁰The word of the LORD came a second time to Haggai on the twenty-fourth day of the month: ²¹Speak to Zerubbabel, the governor of Judah:

I will shake the heavens and the earth;
²²I will overthrow the thrones of
   kingdoms,
   and destroy the power of the
      kingdoms of the nations.
I will overthrow the chariots and their
   riders,
   and the riders with their horses
   will fall by each other's swords.

²³On that day—oracle of the LORD of hosts—I will take you, my servant, Zerubbabel, son of Shealtiel—oracle of the LORD—and I will make you like a signet ring, for I have chosen you—oracle of the LORD of hosts.

☐ REVELATION 16

The Seven Bowls. 16:1 I heard a loud voice speaking from the temple to the seven angels, "Go and pour out the seven bowls of God's fury upon the earth."

[2]The first angel went and poured out his bowl on the earth. Festering and ugly sores broke out on those who had the mark of the beast or worshiped its image.

[3]The second angel poured out his bowl on the sea. The sea turned to blood like that from a corpse; every creature living in the sea died.

[4]The third angel poured out his bowl on the rivers and springs of water. These also turned to blood. [5]Then I heard the angel in charge of the waters say:

"You are just, O Holy One,
who are and who were,
in passing this sentence.
[6]For they have shed the blood of the
holy ones and the prophets,
and you [have] given them blood to
drink;
it is what they deserve."

[7]Then I heard the altar cry out,

"Yes, Lord God almighty,
your judgments are true and just."

[8]The fourth angel poured out his bowl on the sun. It was given the power to burn people with fire. [9]People were burned by the scorching heat and blasphemed the name of God who had power over these plagues, but they did not repent or give him glory.

[10]The fifth angel poured out his bowl on the throne of the beast. Its kingdom was plunged into darkness, and people bit their tongues in pain [11]and blasphemed the God of heaven because of their pains and sores. But they did not repent of their works.

[12]The sixth angel emptied his bowl on the great river Euphrates. Its water was dried up to prepare the way for the kings of the East. [13]I saw three unclean spirits like frogs come from the mouth of the dragon, from the mouth of the beast, and from the mouth of the false prophet. [14]These were demonic spirits who performed signs. They went out to the kings of the whole world to assemble them for the battle on the great day of God the almighty. [15]("Behold, I am coming like a thief." Blessed is the one who watches and keeps his clothes ready, so that he may not go naked and people see him exposed.) [16]They then assembled the kings in the place that is named Armageddon in Hebrew.

[17]The seventh angel poured out his bowl into the air. A loud voice came out of the temple from the throne, saying, "It is done." [18]Then there were lightning flashes, rumblings, and peals of thunder, and a great earthquake. It was such a violent earthquake that there has never been one like it since the human race began on earth. [19]The great city was split into three parts, and the gentile cities fell. But God remembered great Babylon, giving it the cup filled with the wine of his fury and wrath. [20]Every island fled, and mountains disappeared. [21]Large hailstones like huge weights came down from the sky on people, and they blasphemed God for the plague of hail because this plague was so severe.

December 26

St. Stephen

The death of the martyrs blossoms in the faith of the living.
— POPE ST. GREGORY THE GREAT

☐ ZECHARIAH 1-3

Call for Obedience. 1:1 In the second year of Darius, in the eighth month, the word of the LORD came to the prophet Zechariah, son of Berechiah, son of Iddo: ²The LORD was very angry with your ancestors. ³Say to them: Thus says the LORD of hosts, Return to me—oracle of the LORD of hosts—and I will return to you, says the LORD of hosts. ⁴Do not be like your ancestors to whom the earlier prophets proclaimed: Thus says the LORD of hosts: Turn from your evil ways and from your wicked deeds. But they did not listen or pay attention to me—oracle of the LORD.—⁵Your ancestors, where are they? And the prophets, can they live forever? ⁶But my words and my statutes, with which I charged my servants the prophets, did these not overtake your ancestors? Then they repented and admitted: "Just as the LORD of hosts intended to treat us according to our ways and deeds, so the LORD has done."

First Vision: Horses Patrolling the Earth. ⁷In the second year of Darius, on the twenty-fourth day of Shebat, the eleventh month, the word of the LORD came to the prophet Zechariah, son of Berechiah, son of Iddo:

⁸I looked out in the night, and there was a man mounted on a red horse standing in the shadows among myrtle trees; and behind him were red, sorrel, and white horses. ⁹I asked, "What are these, my lord?" Then the angel who spoke with me answered, "I will show you what these are." ¹⁰Then the man who was standing among the myrtle trees spoke up and said, "These are the ones whom the LORD has sent to patrol the earth." ¹¹And they answered the angel of the LORD, who was standing among the myrtle trees: "We have been patrolling the earth, and now the whole earth rests quietly." ¹²Then the angel of the LORD replied, "LORD of hosts, how long will you be without mercy for Jerusalem and the cities of Judah that have felt your anger these seventy years?" ¹³To the angel who spoke with me, the LORD replied favorably, with comforting words.

Oracular Response. ¹⁴The angel who spoke with me then said to me, Proclaim: Thus says the LORD of hosts:

I am jealous for Jerusalem
    and for Zion intensely jealous.
¹⁵I am consumed with anger
    toward the complacent nations;
When I was only a little angry,
    they compounded the disaster.
¹⁶Therefore, thus says the LORD:
I return to Jerusalem in mercy;
    my house will be rebuilt there—
        oracle of the LORD of hosts—
and a measuring line will be
        stretched over Jerusalem.
¹⁷Proclaim further: Thus says the LORD
    of hosts:
My cities will again overflow with
    prosperity;
        the LORD will again comfort Zion,
    and will again choose Jerusalem.

Second Vision: The Four Horns and the Four Smiths. 2:1 I raised my eyes and looked and there were four horns. ²Then I asked the angel who spoke with me, "What are those?" He answered, "Those are the horns that scattered Judah, Israel, and Jerusalem."

³Then the LORD showed me four workmen. ⁴And I said, "What are these coming to do?" And the LORD said, "Those are the horns that scattered Judah, so that none could raise their heads any more; and these have come to terrify them—to cut down the horns of the nations that raised their horns to scatter the land of Judah."

Third Vision: The Man with the Measuring Cord. ⁵I raised my eyes and looked, and there was a man with a measuring cord in his hand. ⁶I asked, "Where are you going?" And he said, "To measure Jerusalem—to see how great its width is and how great its length." ⁷Then the angel who spoke with me advanced as another angel came out to meet him ⁸and he said to the latter, "Run, speak to that official: Jerusalem will be unwalled, because of the abundance of people and beasts in its midst. ⁹I will be an encircling wall of fire for it—oracle of the LORD—and I will be the glory in its midst."

Expansion on the Themes of the First Three Visions. ¹⁰Up! Up! Flee from the land of the north—oracle of the LORD;—For like the four winds of heaven I have dispersed you—oracle of the LORD. ¹¹Up, Zion! Escape, you who dwell in daughter Babylon! ¹²For thus says the LORD of hosts after the LORD's glory had sent me, concerning the nations that have plundered you: Whoever strikes you strikes me directly in the eye. ¹³Now I wave my hand over them, and they become plunder for their own servants. Thus you shall know that the LORD of hosts has sent me. ¹⁴Sing and rejoice, daughter Zion! Now, I am coming to dwell in your midst—oracle of the LORD. ¹⁵Many nations will bind themselves to the LORD on that day. They will be my people, and I will dwell in your midst. Then you shall know that the LORD of hosts has sent me to you. ¹⁶The LORD will inherit Judah as his portion of the holy land, and the LORD will again choose Jerusalem. ¹⁷Silence, all people, in the presence of the LORD, who stirs forth from his holy dwelling.

Prophetic Vision: Joshua the High Priest. 3:1 Then he showed me Joshua the high priest standing before the angel of the LORD, while the adversary stood at his right side to accuse him. ²And the angel of the LORD said to the adversary, "May the LORD rebuke you, O adversary; may the LORD who has chosen Jerusalem rebuke you! Is this not a brand plucked from the fire?"

³Now Joshua was standing before the angel, clad in filthy garments. ⁴Then the angel said to those standing before him, "Remove his filthy garments." And to him he said, "Look, I have taken your guilt from you, and I am clothing you in stately robes." ⁵Then he said, "Let them put a clean turban on his head." And they put a clean turban on his head and clothed him with the garments while the angel of the LORD was standing by. ⁶Then the angel of the LORD charged Joshua: ⁷"Thus says the LORD of hosts: If you walk in my ways and carry out my charge, you will administer my house and watch over my courts; and I will give you access to those standing here."

Supplementary Oracle. ⁸"Hear, O Joshua, high priest! You and your associates who sit before you! For they are signs of things to come! I will surely bring my servant the Branch. ⁹Look at the stone that I have placed before Joshua. On this one stone with seven facets I will engrave its inscription—oracle of the LORD of hosts—and I will take away the guilt of that land in one day. ¹⁰On that day—oracle of the LORD of hosts—you will invite one another under your vines and fig trees."

☐ REVELATION 17

Babylon the Great. 17:1 Then one of the seven angels who were holding the seven bowls came and said to me, "Come here. I will show you the judgment on the great harlot who lives near the many waters. [2]The kings of the earth have had intercourse with her, and the inhabitants of the earth became drunk on the wine of her harlotry." [3]Then he carried me away in spirit to a deserted place where I saw a woman seated on a scarlet beast that was covered with blasphemous names, with seven heads and ten horns. [4]The woman was wearing purple and scarlet and adorned with gold, precious stones, and pearls. She held in her hand a gold cup that was filled with the abominable and sordid deeds of her harlotry. [5]On her forehead was written a name, which is a mystery, "Babylon the great, the mother of harlots and of the abominations of the earth." [6]I saw that the woman was drunk on the blood of the holy ones and on the blood of the witnesses to Jesus.

Meaning of the Beast and Harlot. When I saw her I was greatly amazed. [7]The angel said to me, "Why are you amazed? I will explain to you the mystery of the woman and of the beast that carries her, the beast with the seven heads and the ten horns. [8]The beast that you saw existed once but now exists no longer. It will come up from the abyss and is headed for destruction. The inhabitants of the earth whose names have not been written in the book of life from the foundation of the world shall be amazed when they see the beast, because it existed once but exists no longer, and yet it will come again. [9]Here is a clue for one who has wisdom. The seven heads represent seven hills upon which the woman sits. They also represent seven kings: [10]five have already fallen, one still lives, and the last has not yet come, and when he comes he must remain only a short while. [11]The beast that existed once but exists no longer is an eighth king, but really belongs to the seven and is headed for destruction. [12]The ten horns that you saw represent ten kings who have not yet been crowned; they will receive royal authority along with the beast for one hour. [13]They are of one mind and will give their power and authority to the beast. [14]They will fight with the Lamb, but the Lamb will conquer them, for he is Lord of lords and king of kings, and those with him are called, chosen, and faithful."

[15]Then he said to me, "The waters that you saw where the harlot lives represent large numbers of peoples, nations, and tongues. [16]The ten horns that you saw and the beast will hate the harlot; they will leave her desolate and naked; they will eat her flesh and consume her with fire. [17]For God has put it into their minds to carry out his purpose and to make them come to an agreement to give their kingdom to the beast until the words of God are accomplished. [18]The woman whom you saw represents the great city that has sovereignty over the kings of the earth."

December 27 ———————————————

St. John

God overthrows the thrones of those who are disobedient to His law.

— St. Avitus of Vienne

☐ ZECHARIAH 4-6

Fourth Vision: The Lampstand and the Two Olive Trees. 4:1 Then the angel who spoke with me returned and aroused me, like one awakened from sleep. ²He said to me, "What do you see?" I replied, "I see a lampstand all of gold, with a bowl on top of it. There are seven lamps on it, with seven spouts on each of the lamps that are on top of it. ³And beside it are two olive trees, one on the right of the bowl and one to its left." ⁴Then I said to the angel who spoke with me, "What are these things, my lord?" ⁵And the angel who spoke with me replied, "Do you not know what these things are?" I said, "No, my lord."

An Oracle. ⁶Then he said to me: "This is the word of the LORD to Zerubbabel: Not by might, and not by power, but by my spirit, says the LORD of hosts. ⁷Who are you, O great mountain? Before Zerubbabel you become a plain. He will bring forth the first stone amid shouts of 'Favor, favor be upon it!'"

⁸Then the word of the LORD came to me: ⁹The hands of Zerubbabel have laid the foundations of this house, and his hands will finish it. Thus you shall know that the LORD of hosts has sent me to you. ¹⁰For whoever has scorned such a day of small things will rejoice to see the capstone in the hand of Zerubbabel.

Resumption of the Vision: Explanation of Lamps and Trees. "These seven are the eyes of the LORD that range over the whole earth." ¹¹I then asked him, "What are these two olive trees, on the right of the lampstand and on its left?" ¹²A second time I asked, "What are the two streams from the olive trees that pour out golden oil through two taps of gold?" ¹³He said to me, "Do you not know what these are?" I answered, "No, my lord." ¹⁴Then he said, "These are the two anointed ones who stand by the Lord of the whole earth."

Fifth Vision: The Flying Scroll. 5:1 Then I raised my eyes again and saw a flying scroll. ²He asked me, "What do you see?" I answered, "I see a flying scroll, twenty cubits long and ten cubits wide." ³Then he said to me: "This is the curse which is to go forth over the whole land. According to it, every thief and every perjurer will be expelled. ⁴I will send it forth—oracle of the LORD of hosts—so that it will come to the house of the thief, and into the house of the one who swears falsely by my name. It shall lodge within each house, consuming it, timber and stones."

Sixth Vision: The Basket of Wickedness. ⁵Then the angel who spoke with me came forward and said to me, "Raise your eyes and look. What is this that comes forth?" ⁶I said, "What is it?" And he answered, "This is the basket that is coming." And he said, "This is their guilt in all the land." ⁷Then a leaden cover was lifted, and there was a woman sitting inside the basket. ⁸He said, "This is Wickedness," and he thrust her inside the basket, pushing the leaden weight into the opening.

⁹Then I raised my eyes and saw two women coming forth with wind under their wings—they had wings like the wings of a stork—and they lifted the basket into the air. ¹⁰I said to the angel who spoke with me,

"Where are they taking the basket?" ¹¹He replied, "To build a temple for it in the land of Shinar. When the temple is constructed, they will set it there on its base."

Seventh Vision: Four Chariots. 6:1 Again I raised my eyes and saw four chariots coming out from between two mountains; and the mountains were of bronze. ²The first chariot had red horses, the second chariot black horses, ³the third chariot white horses, and the fourth chariot dappled horses—all of them strong horses. ⁴I asked the angel who spoke with me, "What are these, my lord?" ⁵The angel answered me, "These are the four winds of the heavens, which are coming forth after presenting themselves before the LORD of all the earth. ⁶The one with the black horses is going toward the land of the north, and the white horses go toward the west, and the dappled ones go toward the land of the south." ⁷These strong horses went out, eager to set about patrolling the earth, for he said, "Go, patrol the earth!" So they patrolled the earth. ⁸Then he cried out to me and said, "See, those who go forth to the land of the north provide rest for my spirit in the land of the north."

The Crowning. ⁹Then the word of the LORD came to me: ¹⁰Take from the exiles—Heldai, Tobijah, Jedaiah—and go the same day to the house of Josiah, son of Zephaniah. (These had come from Babylon.) ¹¹You will take silver and gold, and make crowns; place one on the head of Joshua, son of Jehozadak, the high priest. ¹²And say to him: Thus says the LORD of hosts: There is a man whose name is Branch — and from his place he will branch out and he will build the temple of the LORD. ¹³He will build the temple of the LORD, and taking up the royal insignia, he will sit as ruler upon his throne. The priest will be at his right hand, and between the two of them there will be peaceful understanding. ¹⁴The other crown will be in the temple of the LORD as a gracious reminder to Heldai, Tobijah, Jedaiah, and the son of Zephaniah. ¹⁵And they who are from afar will come and build the temple of the LORD, and you will know that the LORD of hosts has sent me to you. This will happen if you truly obey the LORD your God.

☐ REVELATION 18

The Fall of Babylon. 18:1 After this I saw another angel coming down from heaven, having great authority, and the earth became illumined by his splendor. ²He cried out in a mighty voice:

"Fallen, fallen is Babylon the great.
　She has become a haunt for demons.
She is a cage for every unclean spirit,
　a cage for every unclean bird,
　[a cage for every unclean] and
　　disgusting [beast].
³For all the nations have drunk
　the wine of her licentious passion.
The kings of the earth had intercourse
　with her,
　　and the merchants of the earth
　　grew rich from her drive for
　　luxury."

⁴Then I heard another voice from heaven say:

"Depart from her, my people,
　so as not to take part in her sins
　and receive a share in her plagues,
⁵for her sins are piled up to the sky,
　and God remembers her crimes.
⁶Pay her back as she has paid others.
　Pay her back double for her deeds.
　Into her cup pour double what she
　　poured.

⁷To the measure of her boasting and
wantonness
repay her in torment and grief;
for she said to herself,
'I sit enthroned as queen;
I am no widow,
and I will never know grief.'
⁸Therefore, her plagues will come in
one day,
pestilence, grief, and famine;
she will be consumed by fire.
For mighty is the Lord God who
judges her."

⁹The kings of the earth who had intercourse with her in their wantonness will weep and mourn over her when they see the smoke of her pyre. ¹⁰They will keep their distance for fear of the torment inflicted on her, and they will say:

"Alas, alas, great city,
Babylon, mighty city.
In one hour your judgment has
come."

¹¹The merchants of the earth will weep and mourn for her, because there will be no more markets for their cargo: ¹²their cargo of gold, silver, precious stones, and pearls; fine linen, purple silk, and scarlet cloth; fragrant wood of every kind, all articles of ivory and all articles of the most expensive wood, bronze, iron, and marble; ¹³cinnamon, spice, incense, myrrh, and frankincense; wine, olive oil, fine flour, and wheat; cattle and sheep, horses and chariots, and slaves, that is, human beings.

¹⁴"The fruit you craved
has left you.
All your luxury and splendor are
gone,
never again will one find them."

¹⁵The merchants who deal in these goods, who grew rich from her, will keep their distance for fear of the torment inflicted

on her. Weeping and mourning, ¹⁶they cry out:

"Alas, alas, great city,
wearing fine linen, purple and
scarlet,
adorned [in] gold, precious stones,
and pearls.
¹⁷In one hour this great wealth has
been ruined." Every captain of a
ship, every traveler at sea, sailors,
and seafaring merchants stood at
a distance

¹⁸and cried out when they saw the smoke of her pyre, "What city could compare with the great city?" ¹⁹They threw dust on their heads and cried out, weeping and mourning:

"Alas, alas, great city,
in which all who had ships at sea
grew rich from her wealth.
In one hour she has been ruined.
²⁰Rejoice over her, heaven,
you holy ones, apostles, and
prophets.
For God has judged your case against
her."

²¹A mighty angel picked up a stone like a huge millstone and threw it into the sea and said:

"With such force will Babylon the
great city be thrown down,
and will never be found again.
²²No melodies of harpists and
musicians,
flutists and trumpeters,
will ever be heard in you again.
No craftsmen in any trade
will ever be found in you again.
No sound of the millstone
will ever be heard in you again.
²³No light from a lamp
will ever be seen in you again.
No voices of bride and groom

will ever be heard in you again.
Because your merchants were the great
ones of the world,
all nations were led astray by your
magic potion.

[24]In her was found the blood of
prophets and holy ones
and all who have been slain on the
earth."

December 28

The Holy Innocents

I give thanks to Almighty God that He has not considered me unworthy to be the mother of a child admitted into the heavenly kingdom. Having left the world in the white robe of his innocence, he will rejoice in the presence of God through all eternity.
— St. Clotilda

☐ ZECHARIAH 7–9

A Question About Fasting. 7:1 In the fourth year of Darius the king, the word of the Lord came to Zechariah, on the fourth day of the ninth month, Kislev. [2]Bethel-sarezer sent Regem-melech and his men to implore the favor of the Lord [3]and to ask the priests of the house of the Lord of hosts, and the prophets, "Must I weep and abstain in the fifth month as I have been doing these many years?" [4]Then the word of the Lord of hosts came to me: [5]Say to all the people of the land and to the priests: When you fasted and lamented in the fifth and in the seventh month these seventy years, was it really for me that you fasted? [6]When you were eating and drinking, was it not for yourselves that you ate and for yourselves that you drank?

[7]Are these not the words which the Lord proclaimed through the earlier prophets, when Jerusalem and its surrounding cities were inhabited and secure, when the Negeb and the Shephelah were inhabited? [8]The word of the Lord came to Zechariah: [9]Thus says the Lord of hosts: Judge with true justice, and show kindness and compassion toward each other. [10]Do not oppress the widow or the orphan, the resident alien or the poor; do not plot evil against one another in your hearts. [11]But they refused to listen; they stubbornly turned their backs and stopped their ears so as not to hear. [12]And they made their hearts as hard as diamond so as not to hear the instruction and the words that the Lord of hosts had sent by his spirit through the earlier prophets. So great anger came from the Lord of hosts: [13]Just as when I called out and they did not listen, so they will call out and I will not listen, says the Lord of hosts. [14]And I will scatter them among all the nations that they do not know. So the land was left desolate behind them with no one moving about, and they made a pleasant land into a wasteland.

Seven Oracles: Judah and Zion Restored. 8:1 Then the word of the Lord of hosts came: [2]Thus says the Lord of hosts:

I am intensely jealous for Zion,
stirred to jealous wrath for her.

[3]Thus says the Lord:

I have returned to Zion,
and I will dwell within Jerusalem;
Jerusalem will be called the faithful
city,
and the mountain of the LORD of
hosts, the holy mountain.

[4]Thus says the LORD of hosts:

Old men and old women will again sit in the streets of Jerusalem, each with staff in hand because of old age. [5]The city will be filled with boys and girls playing in its streets.

[6]Thus says the LORD of hosts:

Even if this should seem impossible in the eyes of the remnant of this people in those days, should it seem impossible in my eyes also?—oracle of the LORD of hosts.

[7]Thus says the LORD of hosts:

I am going to rescue my people from the land of the rising sun, and from the land of the setting sun. [8]I will bring them back to dwell within Jerusalem. They will be my people, and I will be their God, in faithfulness and justice.

[9]Thus says the LORD of hosts:

Let your hands be strong, you who now hear these words which were spoken by the prophets when the foundation of the house of the LORD of hosts was laid for the building of the temple. [10]For before those days, there were no wages for people, nor hire for animals. Those who came and went were not safe from the enemy, for I set neighbor against neighbor. [11]But now I will not deal with the remnant of this people as in former days—oracle of the LORD of hosts.

[12]For there will be a sowing of peace:
the vine will yield its fruit,
the land will yield its crops,
and the heavens will yield their dew.

I will give all these things to the remnant of this people to possess. [13]Just as you became a curse among the nations, O house of Judah and house of Israel, so will I save you that you may be a blessing. Do not fear; let your hands be strong.

[14]Thus says the LORD of hosts:

Just as I intended to harm you when your ancestors angered me—says the LORD of hosts—and I did not relent, [15]so again in these days I intend to favor Jerusalem and the house of Judah; do not fear! [16]These then are the things you must do: Speak the truth to one another; judge with honesty and complete justice in your gates. [17]Let none of you plot evil against another in your heart, nor love a false oath. For all these things I hate—oracle of the LORD.

Three Oracles: Judah and the Nations.
[18]The word of the LORD of hosts came to me:

[19]Thus says the LORD of hosts:

The fast days of the fourth, the fifth, the seventh, and the tenth months will become occasions of joy and gladness, and happy festivals for the house of Judah. So love faithfulness and peace!

[20]Thus says the LORD of hosts:

There will yet come peoples and inhabitants of many cities; [21]and the inhabitants of one city will approach those of another, and say, "Come! let us go to implore the favor of the LORD and to seek the LORD of hosts. I too am going." [22]Many peoples and strong nations will come to seek the LORD of hosts in Jerusalem and to implore the favor of the LORD.

[23]Thus says the LORD of hosts:

In those days ten people from nations of every language will take hold, yes, will take hold of the cloak of every Judahite and say, "Let us go with you, for we have heard that God is with you."

Restoration of the Land of Israel. 9:1
An oracle: the word of the LORD
is against the land of Hadrach,
and Damascus is its destination,
For the cities of Aram are the LORD's,
as are all the tribes of Israel.
[2]Hamath also on its border,
Tyre too, and Sidon, no matter how
clever they be.

³Tyre built itself a stronghold,
  and heaped up silver like dust,
  and gold like the mud of the streets.
⁴But now the Lord will dispossess it,
  and cast its wealth into the sea,
  and it will be devoured by fire.
⁵Ashkelon will see it and be afraid;
  Gaza too will be in great anguish;
  Ekron also, for its hope will wither.
The king will disappear from Gaza,
  Ashkelon will not be inhabited,
  ⁶and the illegitimate will rule in
    Ashdod.
I will destroy the pride of the
    Philistines
  ⁷and take from their mouths their
    bloody prey,
  their disgusting meat from between
    their teeth.
They will become merely a remnant for
    our God,
  and will be like a clan in Judah;
  Ekron will be like the Jebusites.
⁸I will encamp at my house,
  a garrison against invaders;
No oppressor will overrun them again,
  for now I have seen their affliction.

The King's Entry into Jerusalem.
  ⁹Exult greatly, O daughter Zion!
  Shout for joy, O daughter
    Jerusalem!
Behold: your king is coming to you,
  a just savior is he,
Humble, and riding on a donkey,
  on a colt, the foal of a donkey.
¹⁰He shall banish the chariot from
    Ephraim,
  and the horse from Jerusalem;
The warrior's bow will be banished,
  and he will proclaim peace to the
    nations.

His dominion will be from sea to sea,
  and from the River to the ends of
    the earth.

Restoration of the People.
¹¹As for you, by the blood of your
    covenant,
  I have freed your prisoners from a
    waterless pit.
¹²Return to a fortress,
  O prisoners of hope;
This very day, I announce
  I am restoring double to you.
¹³For I have bent Judah as my bow,
  I have set Ephraim as its arrow;
I will arouse your sons, O Zion,
  against your sons, O Yavan,
  and I will use you as a warrior's
    sword.
¹⁴The LORD will appear over them,
  God's arrow will shoot forth as
    lightning;
The Lord GOD will sound the ram's
    horn,
  and come in a storm from the
    south.
¹⁵The LORD of hosts will protect them;
  they will devour and conquer with
    sling stones,
  they will drink and become heated
    as with wine;
  they will be full like bowls—like the
    corners of the altar.
¹⁶And the LORD their God will save
    them:
  the people, like a flock on that day;
For like gemstones of a crown
  they will shine on the land.
¹⁷Then how good and how lovely!
  Grain will make the young men
    flourish,
  and new wine the young women.

☐ REVELATION 19

19:1 After this I heard what sounded like the loud voice of a great multitude in heaven, saying:

"Alleluia!
Salvation, glory, and might belong to
    our God,
    [2]for true and just are his judgments.
He has condemned the great harlot
    who corrupted the earth with her
        harlotry.
He has avenged on her the blood of
    his servants."

[3]They said a second time:

"Alleluia! Smoke will rise from her
    forever and ever."

[4]The twenty-four elders and the four living creatures fell down and worshiped God who sat on the throne, saying, "Amen. Alleluia."

The Victory Song. [5]A voice coming from the throne said:

"Praise our God, all you his servants,
    [and] you who revere him, small
        and great."

[6]Then I heard something like the sound of a great multitude or the sound of rushing water or mighty peals of thunder, as they said:

"Alleluia!
The Lord has established his reign,
    [our] God, the almighty.
[7]Let us rejoice and be glad
    and give him glory.
For the wedding day of the Lamb has
    come,
    his bride has made herself ready.
[8]She was allowed to wear
    a bright, clean linen garment."

(The linen represents the righteous deeds of the holy ones.)

[9]Then the angel said to me, "Write this: Blessed are those who have been called to the wedding feast of the Lamb." And he said to me, "These words are true; they come from God." [10]I fell at his feet to worship him. But he said to me, "Don't! I am a fellow servant of yours and of your brothers who bear witness to Jesus. Worship God. Witness to Jesus is the spirit of prophecy."

The King of Kings. [11]Then I saw the heavens opened, and there was a white horse; its rider was [called] "Faithful and True." He judges and wages war in righteousness. [12]His eyes were [like] a fiery flame, and on his head were many diadems. He had a name inscribed that no one knows except himself. [13]He wore a cloak that had been dipped in blood, and his name was called the Word of God. [14]The armies of heaven followed him, mounted on white horses and wearing clean white linen. [15]Out of his mouth came a sharp sword to strike the nations. He will rule them with an iron rod, and he himself will tread out in the wine press the wine of the fury and wrath of God the almighty. [16]He has a name written on his cloak and on his thigh, "King of kings and Lord of lords."

[17]Then I saw an angel standing on the sun. He cried out [in] a loud voice to all the birds flying high overhead, "Come here. Gather for God's great feast, [18]to eat the flesh of kings, the flesh of military officers, and the flesh of warriors, the flesh of horses and of their riders, and the flesh of all, free and slave, small and great." [19]Then I saw the beast and the kings of the earth and their armies gathered to fight against the one riding the horse and against his army. [20]The beast was caught and with it the false prophet who had performed in its sight the signs by which he led astray those who had accepted the mark of the beast and those who had worshiped its image. The two were thrown alive into the fiery pool burning with sulfur. [21]The rest were killed by the sword that came out of the mouth of the one riding the horse, and all the birds gorged themselves on their flesh.

December 29

St. Thomas Becket

In this world sow seeds of righteousness, and in the resurrection gather them in.

— St. Ephraem the Syrian

☐ ZECHARIAH 10-12

The Lord Strengthens Judah and Rescues Ephraim. 10:1 Ask
the Lord for rain in the spring
season,
the Lord who brings storm clouds,
and heavy rains,
who gives to everyone grain in the
fields.
²For the teraphim have spoken nonsense,
the diviners have seen false visions;
Deceitful dreams they have told,
empty comfort they have offered.
This is why they wandered like sheep,
wretched, for they have no shepherd.
³My wrath is kindled against the
shepherds,
and I will punish the leaders.
For the Lord of hosts attends to the
flock, the house of Judah,
and will make them like a splendid
horse in battle.
⁴From them will come the tower,
from them the tent peg,
from them the bow of war,
from them every officer.
⁵Together they will be like warriors,
trampling the mud of the streets in
battle.
They will wage war because the Lord
is with them,
and will put the horsemen to
shame.
⁶I will strengthen the house of Judah,
the house of Joseph I will save;
I will bring them back, because I have
mercy on them;
they will be as if I had never cast
them off,

for I am the Lord their God, and I
will answer them.
⁷Then Ephraim will be like a hero,
and their hearts will be cheered as
by wine.
Their children will see and rejoice—
their hearts will exult in the Lord.
⁸I will whistle for them and gather
them in;
for I will redeem them
and they will be as numerous as
before.
⁹I sowed them among the nations,
yet in distant lands they will
remember me;
they will bear their children and
return.
¹⁰I will bring them back from the land
of Egypt,
and gather them from Assyria.
To the land of Gilead and to Lebanon I
will bring them,
until no room is found for them.
¹¹I will cross over to Egypt
and smite the waves of the sea,
and all the depths of the Nile will
dry up.
The pride of Assyria will be cast down,
and the scepter of Egypt disappear.
¹²I will strengthen them in the Lord,
in whose name they will walk—
oracle of the Lord.

The Cry of Trees, Shepherds, and Lions. 11:1 Open your doors,
Lebanon,
that fire may devour your cedars!
²Wail, cypress trees,

for the cedars are fallen,
the mighty are destroyed!
Wail, oaks of Bashan,
for the dense forest is cut down!
³Listen! the wailing of shepherds,
their glory has been destroyed.
Listen! the roaring of young lions,
the thickets of the Jordan are
destroyed.

The Shepherd Narrative. ⁴Thus says the Lord, my God: Shepherd the flock to be slaughtered. ⁵For they who buy them slay them and are not held accountable; while those who sell them say, "Blessed be the Lord, I have become rich!" Even their own shepherds will not pity them. ⁶For I will no longer pity the inhabitants of the earth—oracle of the Lord.—Yes, I will deliver them into each other's power, or into the power of their kings; they will crush the earth, and I will not deliver it out of their power.

⁷So I shepherded the flock to be slaughtered for the merchants of the flock. I took two staffs: one I called Delight, and the other Union. Thus I shepherded the flock. ⁸In a single month, I did away with the three shepherds, for I wearied of them, and they disdained me. ⁹"I will not shepherd you," I said. "Whoever is to die shall die; whoever is to be done away with shall be done away with; and those who are left shall devour one another's flesh."

¹⁰Then I took my staff Delight and snapped it in two, breaking my covenant which I had made with all peoples. ¹¹So it was broken on that day. The merchants of the flock, who were watching me, understood that this was the word of the Lord. ¹²Then I said to them, "If it seems good to you, give me my wages; but if not, withhold them." And they counted out my wages, thirty pieces of silver. ¹³Then the Lord said to me, Throw it in the treasury—the handsome price at which they valued me. So I took the thirty pieces of silver and threw them into the treasury in the house of the Lord. ¹⁴Then I snapped in two my second staff, Union, breaking the kinship between Judah and Israel.

¹⁵The Lord said to me: This time take the gear of a foolish shepherd. ¹⁶For I am raising up a shepherd in the land who will take no note of those that disappear, nor seek the strays, nor heal the injured, nor feed the exhausted; but he will eat the flesh of the fat ones and tear off their hoofs!

Oracle to the Worthless Shepherd.
¹⁷Ah! my worthless shepherd
who forsakes the flock!
May the sword fall upon his arm
and upon his right eye;
His arm will surely wither,
and his right eye surely go blind!

Oracles Concerning the Nations and Judah. 12:1 An oracle: The word of the Lord concerning Israel—oracle of the Lord, who spreads out the heavens, lays the foundations of the earth, and fashions the human spirit within: ²See, I will make Jerusalem a cup of reeling for all peoples round about. Judah will be besieged, even Jerusalem. ³On that day I will make Jerusalem a heavy stone for all peoples. All who attempt to lift it will injure themselves badly, though all the nations of the earth will gather against it. ⁴On that day—oracle of the Lord—I will strike every horse with fright, and its rider with madness. But over the house of Judah I will keep watch, while I strike blind all the horses of the peoples. ⁵Then the clans of Judah will say to themselves, "The inhabitants of Jerusalem have their strength in the Lord of hosts, their God." ⁶On that day I will make the clans of Judah like a brazier of fire in the woodland and like a burning torch among sheaves, and they will devour right and left all the surrounding peoples; but Jerusalem will again inhabit its own place.

⁷The Lord will save the tents of Judah first, that the glory of the house of David

and the glory of the inhabitants of Jerusalem may not be exalted over Judah. [8]On that day the LORD will shield the inhabitants of Jerusalem, so that the weakest among them will be like David on that day; and the house of David will be like God, like the angel of the LORD before them.

[9]On that day I will seek the destruction of all nations that come against Jerusalem. [10]I will pour out on the house of David and on the inhabitants of Jerusalem a spirit of mercy and supplication, so that when they look on him whom they have thrust through, they will mourn for him as one mourns for an only child, and they will grieve for him as one grieves over a firstborn.

Catalogue of Mourners. [11]On that day the mourning in Jerusalem will be as great as the mourning for Hadadrimmon in the plain of Megiddo. [12]And the land shall mourn, each family apart: the family of the house of David, and their women; the family of the house of Nathan, and their women; [13]the family of the house of Levi, and their women; the family of Shimei, and their women; [14]and all the rest of the families, each family apart, and the women apart.

☐ REVELATION 20

The Thousand-year Reign. 20:1 Then I saw an angel come down from heaven, holding in his hand the key to the abyss and a heavy chain. [2]He seized the dragon, the ancient serpent, which is the Devil or Satan, and tied it up for a thousand years [3]and threw it into the abyss, which he locked over it and sealed, so that it could no longer lead the nations astray until the thousand years are completed. After this, it is to be released for a short time.

[4]Then I saw thrones; those who sat on them were entrusted with judgment. I also saw the souls of those who had been beheaded for their witness to Jesus and for the word of God, and who had not worshiped the beast or its image nor had accepted its mark on their foreheads or hands. They came to life and they reigned with Christ for a thousand years. [5]The rest of the dead did not come to life until the thousand years were over. This is the first resurrection. [6]Blessed and holy is the one who shares in the first resurrection. The second death has no power over these; they will be priests of God and of Christ, and they will reign with him for [the] thousand years.

[7]When the thousand years are completed, Satan will be released from his prison. [8]He will go out to deceive the nations at the four corners of the earth, Gog and Magog, to gather them for battle; their number is like the sand of the sea. [9]They invaded the breadth of the earth and surrounded the camp of the holy ones and the beloved city. But fire came down from heaven and consumed them. [10]The Devil who had led them astray was thrown into the pool of fire and sulfur, where the beast and the false prophet were. There they will be tormented day and night forever and ever.

The Large White Throne. [11]Next I saw a large white throne and the one who was sitting on it. The earth and the sky fled from his presence and there was no place for them. [12]I saw the dead, the great and the lowly, standing before the throne, and scrolls were opened. Then another scroll was opened, the book of life. The dead were judged according to their deeds, by what was written in the scrolls. [13]The sea gave up its dead; then Death and Hades gave up their dead. All the dead were judged according to their deeds. [14]Then Death and Hades were thrown into the pool of fire. (This pool of fire is the second death.) [15]Anyone whose name was not found written in the book of life was thrown into the pool of fire.

December 30

God always was, and is, and will be; or better, He always is: "Was" and "will be" are portions of time as we reckon it, and are of a changing nature. He, however, is ever existing. He gathers in himself the whole of being, because He neither has beginning nor will He have an end. He is like some great Sea of Being, limitless and unbounded, transcending every conception of time and nature.

— St. Gregory Nazianzus

☐ ZECHARIAH 13-14

Oracles Concerning the End of False Prophecy. 13:1 On that day a fountain will be opened for the house of David and the inhabitants of Jerusalem, to purify from sin and uncleanness.

²On that day—oracle of the LORD of hosts—I will destroy the names of the idols from the land, so that they will be mentioned no more; I will also remove the prophets and the spirit of uncleanness from the land. ³If any still prophesy, their father and mother who bore them will say, "You will not live, because you have spoken a lie in the name of the LORD." Their father and mother who bore them will thrust them through when they prophesy.

⁴On that day, all prophets will be ashamed of the visions they prophesy; and they will not put on the hairy mantle to mislead, ⁵but each will say, "I am not a prophet. I am a tiller of the soil, for I have owned land since my youth." ⁶And if anyone asks, "What are these wounds on your chest?" each will answer, "I received these wounds in the house of my friends."

The Song of the Sword. ⁷Awake, O
  sword, against my shepherd,
   against the one who is my associate
   —oracle of the LORD of hosts.
 Strike the shepherd
   that the sheep may be scattered;
 I will turn my hand against the little
   ones.

⁸In all the land—oracle of the LORD—
   two thirds of them will be cut off
     and perish,
   and one third will be left.
⁹I will bring the one third through the
     fire;
   I will refine them as one refines
     silver,
   and I will test them as one tests
     gold.
 They will call upon my name, and I
     will answer them;
 I will say, "They are my people,"
   and they will say, "The LORD is my
     God."

Devastation and Rescue of Jerusalem. 14:1 A day is coming for the LORD when the spoils taken from you will be divided in your midst. ²And I will gather all the nations against Jerusalem for battle: The city will be taken, houses will be plundered, women raped; half the city will go into exile, but the rest of the people will not be removed from the city. ³Then the LORD will go forth and fight against those nations, fighting as on a day of battle. ⁴On that day God's feet will stand on the Mount of Olives, which is opposite Jerusalem to the east. The Mount of Olives will be split in two from east to west by a very deep valley, and half of the mountain will move to the north and half of it to the south. ⁵You will flee by the valley between the mountains, for the valley between the mountains will reach to Azal. Thus you will flee as you fled because of the earthquake in the days of Uzziah king of Judah. Then the LORD, my God, will come, and all his holy ones with him.

Jerusalem Restored. ⁶On that day there will no longer be cold or frost. ⁷There will be one continuous day—it is known to the LORD—not day and night, for in the evening there will be light. ⁸On that day, fresh water will flow from Jerusalem, half to the eastern sea, and half to the western sea. This will be so in summer and in winter. ⁹The LORD will be king over the whole earth; on that day the LORD will be the only one, and the LORD's name the only one. ¹⁰All the land will turn into a plain, from Geba to Rimmon, south of Jerusalem, which will stand exalted in its place—from the Gate of Benjamin to the place of the first gate, to the Corner Gate and from the Tower of Hananel to the king's wine presses. ¹¹The city will be inhabited; never again will it be doomed. Jerusalem will dwell securely.

The Fate of Jerusalem's Foes. ¹²And this will be the plague with which the LORD will strike all the peoples that have fought against Jerusalem: their flesh will rot while they stand on their feet, and their eyes will rot in their sockets, and their tongues will rot in their mouths. ¹³On that day a great panic from the LORD will be upon them. They will seize each other's hands, and their hands will be raised against each other. ¹⁴Even Judah will fight against Jerusalem. The riches of all the surrounding nations will be gathered together—gold, silver, and garments—in great abundance. ¹⁵Like the plague on human beings will be the plague upon the horses, mules, camels, donkeys, and upon all the beasts that are in those camps.

The Future: Jerusalem, Judah, and the Nations. ¹⁶Everyone who is left of all the nations that came against Jerusalem will go up year after year to bow down to the King, the LORD of hosts, and to celebrate the feast of Booths. ¹⁷Should any of the families of the earth not go up to Jerusalem to bow down to the King, the LORD of hosts, then there will be no rain for them. ¹⁸And if the family of Egypt does not go up or enter, upon them will fall the plague, with which the LORD strikes the nations that do not go up to celebrate the feast of Booths. ¹⁹This will be the punishment of Egypt and the punishment of all the nations that do not go up to celebrate the feast of Booths.

²⁰On that day, "Holy to the LORD" will be written on the horses' bells. The pots in the house of the LORD will be as the basins before the altar. ²¹Every pot in Jerusalem and in Judah will be holy to the LORD of hosts. All who come to sacrifice will take them and cook in them. No longer will there be merchants in the house of the LORD of hosts on that day.

☐ REVELATION 21

The New Heaven and the New Earth. 21:1 Then I saw a new heaven and a new earth. The former heaven and the former earth had passed away, and the sea was no more. ²I also saw the holy city, a new Jerusalem, coming down out of heaven from God, prepared as a bride adorned for her husband. ³I heard a loud voice from the throne saying, "Behold, God's dwelling is with the human race. He will dwell with them and they will be his people and God himself will always be with them [as their God]. ⁴He will wipe every tear from their eyes, and there shall be no more death or mourning, wailing or pain, [for] the old order has passed away."

⁵The one who sat on the throne said, "Behold, I make all things new." Then he said, "Write these words down, for they

are trustworthy and true." ⁶He said to me, "They are accomplished. I [am] the Alpha and the Omega, the beginning and the end. To the thirsty I will give a gift from the spring of life-giving water. ⁷The victor will inherit these gifts, and I shall be his God, and he will be my son. ⁸But as for cowards, the unfaithful, the depraved, murderers, the unchaste, sorcerers, idol-worshipers, and deceivers of every sort, their lot is in the burning pool of fire and sulfur, which is the second death."

The New Jerusalem. ⁹One of the seven angels who held the seven bowls filled with the seven last plagues came and said to me, "Come here. I will show you the bride, the wife of the Lamb." ¹⁰He took me in spirit to a great, high mountain and showed me the holy city Jerusalem coming down out of heaven from God. ¹¹It gleamed with the splendor of God. Its radiance was like that of a precious stone, like jasper, clear as crystal. ¹²It had a massive, high wall, with twelve gates where twelve angels were stationed and on which names were inscribed, [the names] of the twelve tribes of the Israelites. ¹³There were three gates facing east, three north, three south, and three west. ¹⁴The wall of the city had twelve courses of stones as its foundation, on which were inscribed the twelve names of the twelve apostles of the Lamb.

¹⁵The one who spoke to me held a gold measuring rod to measure the city, its gates, and its wall. ¹⁶The city was square,

its length the same as [also] its width. He measured the city with the rod and found it fifteen hundred miles in length and width and height. ¹⁷He also measured its wall: one hundred and forty-four cubits according to the standard unit of measurement the angel used. ¹⁸The wall was constructed of jasper, while the city was pure gold, clear as glass. ¹⁹The foundations of the city wall were decorated with every precious stone; the first course of stones was jasper, the second sapphire, the third chalcedony, the fourth emerald, ²⁰the fifth sardonyx, the sixth carnelian, the seventh chrysolite, the eighth beryl, the ninth topaz, the tenth chrysoprase, the eleventh hyacinth, and the twelfth amethyst. ²¹The twelve gates were twelve pearls, each of the gates made from a single pearl; and the street of the city was of pure gold, transparent as glass.

²²I saw no temple in the city, for its temple is the Lord God almighty and the Lamb. ²³The city had no need of sun or moon to shine on it, for the glory of God gave it light, and its lamp was the Lamb. ²⁴The nations will walk by its light, and to it the kings of the earth will bring their treasure. ²⁵During the day its gates will never be shut, and there will be no night there. ²⁶The treasure and wealth of the nations will be brought there, ²⁷but nothing unclean will enter it, nor any[one] who does abominable things or tells lies. Only those will enter whose names are written in the Lamb's book of life.

December 31

You will no sooner have resolved to give yourself to God than hell will send out its forces against you. Don't be discouraged. Remember that the prize for which you are striving is worth more than all you can ever give to purchase it.

— St. Louis of Granada

☐ MALACHI

1:1 An oracle. The word of the Lord to Israel through Malachi.

Israel Preferred to Edom. ²I love you,
   says the Lord;
but you say, "How do you love us?"
³Was not Esau Jacob's brother?—oracle
   of the Lord.
   I loved Jacob, but rejected Esau;
I made his mountains a waste,
   his heritage a desert for jackals.
⁴If Edom says, "We have been crushed,
   but we will rebuild the ruins,"
Thus says the Lord of hosts:
   They indeed may build, but I will
      tear down,
And they shall be called "territory of
   wickedness,"
   the people with whom the Lord
      is angry forever.
⁵Your own eyes will see it, and you
   will say,
   "Great is the Lord, even beyond the
      territory of Israel."

**Offense in Sacrifice and Priestly
   Duty.** ⁶A son honors his father,
   and a servant fears his master;
If, then, I am a father,
   where is the honor due to me?
And if I am a master,
   where is the fear due to me?
So says the Lord of hosts to you,
   O priests,
   who disdain my name.

But you ask, "How have we disdained
   your name?"
⁷By offering defiled food on my altar!
You ask, "How have we defiled it?"
   By saying that the table of the Lord
      may be disdained!
⁸When you offer a blind animal for
   sacrifice,
   is there no wrong in that?
When you offer a lame or sick animal,
   is there no wrong in that?
Present it to your governor!
   Will he be pleased with you—or
      show you favor?
   says the Lord of hosts.
⁹So now implore God's favor, that he
   may have mercy on us!
   You are the ones who have done this;
Will he show favor to any of you?
   says the Lord of hosts.
¹⁰Oh, that one of you would just shut
   the temple gates
   to keep you from kindling fire on
      my altar in vain!
I take no pleasure in you, says the
   Lord of hosts;
   and I will not accept any offering
      from your hands!
¹¹From the rising of the sun to its
   setting,
   my name is great among the nations;
Incense offerings are made to my name
   everywhere,
   and a pure offering;

For my name is great among the
nations,
says the LORD of hosts.
[12]But you profane it by saying
that the LORD's table is defiled,
and its food may be disdained.
[13]You say, "See what a burden this is!"
and you exasperate me, says the
LORD of hosts;
You bring in what is mutilated, or
lame, or sick;
you bring it as an offering!
Will I accept it from your hands?
says the LORD.
[14]Cursed is the cheat who has in his
flock an intact male,
and vows it, but sacrifices to the
LORD a defective one instead;
For a great king am I, says the LORD of
hosts,
and my name is feared among the
nations.

2:1 And now, priests, this commandment
is for you:
If you do not listen,
[2]And if you do not take to heart
giving honor to my name, says the
LORD of hosts,
I will send a curse upon you
and your blessing I will curse.
In fact, I have already cursed it,
because you do not take it to heart.
[3]I will rebuke your offspring;
I will spread dung on your faces,
Dung from your feasts,
and will carry you to it.
[4]You should know that I sent you this
commandment
so that my covenant with Levi
might endure,
says the LORD of hosts.
[5]My covenant with him was the life
and peace which I gave him,
and the fear he had for me,
standing in awe of my name.
[6]Reliable instruction was in his mouth,

no perversity was found upon his
lips;
He walked with me in integrity and
uprightness,
and turned many away from evil.
[7]For a priest's lips preserve knowledge,
and instruction is to be sought from
his mouth,
because he is the messenger of the
LORD of hosts.
[8]But you have turned aside from the
way,
and have caused many to stumble
by your instruction;
You have corrupted the covenant of
Levi,
says the LORD of hosts.
[9]I, therefore, have made you
contemptible
and base before all the people,
For you do not keep my ways,
but show partiality in your
instruction.

Marriage and Divorce. [10]Have we not
all one father?
Has not one God created us?
Why, then, do we break faith with each
other,
profaning the covenant of our
ancestors?
[11]Judah has broken faith; an
abominable thing
has been done in Israel and in
Jerusalem.
Judah has profaned the LORD's holy
place, which he loves,
and has married a daughter of a
foreign god.
[12]May the LORD cut off from the man
who does this
both witness and advocate from the
tents of Jacob,
and anyone to bring an offering to
the LORD of hosts!
[13]This also you do: the altar of the
LORD you cover

with tears, weeping, and groaning,
Because the Lord no longer takes note
of your offering
or accepts it favorably from your
hand.
[14]And you say, "Why?"—
Because the LORD is witness
between you and the wife of your
youth
With whom you have broken faith,
though she is your companion, your
covenanted wife.
[15]Did he not make them one, with
flesh and spirit?
And what does the One require?
Godly offspring!
You should be on guard, then, for your
life,
and do not break faith with the wife
of your youth.
[16]For I hate divorce,
says the LORD, the God of Israel,
And the one who covers his garment
with violence,
says the LORD of hosts.
You should be on guard, then, for your
life,
and you must not break faith.

Purification and Just Judgment.
[17]You have wearied the LORD
with your words,
yet you say, "How have we wearied
him?"
By saying, "All evildoers
are good in the sight of the LORD,
And he is pleased with them,"
or "Where is the just God?"

The Messenger of the Covenant.
3:1 Now I am sending my
messenger—
he will prepare the way before me;
And the lord whom you seek will come
suddenly to his temple;
The messenger of the covenant whom
you desire—

see, he is coming! says the LORD of
hosts.
[2]But who can endure the day of his
coming?
Who can stand firm when he
appears?
For he will be like a refiner's fire,
like fullers' lye.
[3]He will sit refining and purifying
silver,
and he will purify the Levites,
Refining them like gold or silver,
that they may bring offerings to the
LORD in righteousness.
[4]Then the offering of Judah and
Jerusalem
will please the LORD,
as in ancient days, as in years gone
by.
[5]I will draw near to you for judgment,
and I will be swift to bear witness
Against sorcerers, adulterers, and
perjurers,
those who deprive a laborer of
wages,
Oppress a widow or an orphan,
or turn aside a resident alien,
without fearing me, says the LORD
of hosts.

**Gifts for God, Blessings for the
People.** [6]For I, the LORD, do not
change,
and you, sons of Jacob, do not cease
to be.
[7]Since the days of your ancestors you
have turned aside
from my statutes and have not kept
them.
Return to me, that I may return to
you,
says the LORD of hosts.
But you say, "Why should we return?"
[8]Can anyone rob God? But you are
robbing me!
And you say, "How have we robbed
you?"

Of tithes and contributions!
[9]You are indeed accursed,
    for you, the whole nation, rob me.
[10]Bring the whole tithe
    into the storehouse,
That there may be food in my house.
    Put me to the test, says the LORD of
        hosts,
And see if I do not open the floodgates
    of heaven for you,
    and pour down upon you blessing
        without measure!
[11]I will rebuke the locust for you
    so that it will not destroy your crops,
And the vine in the field will not be
        barren,
    says the LORD of hosts.
[12]All the nations will call you blessed,
    for you will be a delightful land,
    says the LORD of hosts.

The Need To Serve God. [13]Your words
    are too much for me, says the
    LORD.
    You ask, "What have we spoken
        against you?"
[14]You have said, "It is useless to serve
        God;
    what do we gain by observing God's
        requirements,
And by going about as mourners
    before the LORD of hosts?
[15]But we call the arrogant blessed;
    for evildoers not only prosper
    but even test God and escape."
[16]Then those who fear the LORD spoke
    with one another,
    and the LORD listened attentively;
A record book was written before him
    of those who fear the LORD and
        esteem his name.
[17]They shall be mine, says the LORD of
        hosts,

my own special possession, on the
    day when I take action.
And I will have compassion on them,
    as a man has compassion on his son
    who serves him.
[18]Then you will again distinguish
    between the just and the wicked,
Between the person who serves God,
    and the one who does not.
[19]For the day is coming, blazing like an
    oven,
    when all the arrogant and all
        evildoers will be stubble,
And the day that is coming will set
    them on fire,
    leaving them neither root nor
        branch,
    says the LORD of hosts.
[20]But for you who fear my name, the
    sun of justice
    will arise with healing in its wings;
And you will go out leaping like calves
    from the stall
    [21]and tread down the wicked;
They will become dust under the soles
    of your feet,
    on the day when I take action, says
        the LORD of hosts.

Moses and Elijah. [22]Remember the
    law of Moses my servant,
    whom I charged at Horeb
With statutes and ordinances
    for all Israel.
[23]Now I am sending to you
    Elijah the prophet,
Before the day of the LORD comes,
    the great and terrible day;
[24]He will turn the heart of fathers to
    their sons,
    and the heart of sons to their
        fathers,
Lest I come and strike
    the land with utter destruction.

☐ REVELATION 22

22:1 Then the angel showed me the river of life-giving water, sparkling like crystal, flowing from the throne of God and of the Lamb ²down the middle of its street. On either side of the river grew the tree of life that produces fruit twelve times a year, once each month; the leaves of the trees serve as medicine for the nations. ³Nothing accursed will be found there anymore. The throne of God and of the Lamb will be in it, and his servants will worship him. ⁴They will look upon his face, and his name will be on their foreheads. ⁵Night will be no more, nor will they need light from lamp or sun, for the Lord God shall give them light, and they shall reign forever and ever.

⁶And he said to me, "These words are trustworthy and true, and the Lord, the God of prophetic spirits, sent his angel to show his servants what must happen soon." ⁷"Behold, I am coming soon." Blessed is the one who keeps the prophetic message of this book.

⁸It is I, John, who heard and saw these things, and when I heard and saw them I fell down to worship at the feet of the angel who showed them to me. ⁹But he said to me, "Don't! I am a fellow servant of yours and of your brothers the prophets and of those who keep the message of this book. Worship God."

¹⁰Then he said to me, "Do not seal up the prophetic words of this book, for the appointed time is near. ¹¹Let the wicked still act wickedly, and the filthy still be filthy. The righteous must still do right, and the holy still be holy."

¹²"Behold, I am coming soon. I bring with me the recompense I will give to each according to his deeds. ¹³I am the Alpha and the Omega, the first and the last, the beginning and the end."

¹⁴Blessed are they who wash their robes so as to have the right to the tree of life and enter the city through its gates. ¹⁵Outside are the dogs, the sorcerers, the unchaste, the murderers, the idol-worshipers, and all who love and practice deceit.

¹⁶"I, Jesus, sent my angel to give you this testimony for the churches. I am the root and offspring of David, the bright morning star."

¹⁷The Spirit and the bride say, "Come." Let the hearer say, "Come." Let the one who thirsts come forward, and the one who wants it receive the gift of life-giving water.

¹⁸I warn everyone who hears the prophetic words in this book: if anyone adds to them, God will add to him the plagues described in this book, ¹⁹and if anyone takes away from the words in this prophetic book, God will take away his share in the tree of life and in the holy city described in this book.

²⁰The one who gives this testimony says, "Yes, I am coming soon." Amen! Come, Lord Jesus!

²¹The grace of the Lord Jesus be with all.